THE CULTURE OF
THE EUROPEANS

THE CULTURE OF THE EUROPEANS

FROM 1800 TO THE PRESENT

DONALD SASSOON

Harper*Press*
An Imprint of HarperCollinsPublishers

HarperCollins*Publishers*
77–85 Fulham Palace Road,
Hammersmith, London w6 8jb
www.harpercollins.co.uk

Published by HarperCollins*Publishers* 2006

1 3 5 7 9 8 6 4 2

The author asserts the moral right to
be identified as the author of this work

A catalogue record for this book is
available from the British Library

ISBN 13 978-0-00-255879-2
ISBN 10 0-00-255879-3

Set in PostScript Linotype Minion with
Galliard and Castellar display by
Rowland Phototypesetting Ltd,
Bury St Edmunds, Suffolk

Printed and bound by Bercker, Germany

To Eric Hobsbawm,
il miglior maestro

CONTENTS

PART III   1880–1920: The Revolution

INTRODUCTION

An Abundance of Culture

At nine o'clock on a weekday morning in December 2000, South Clapham underground station in South London is still crowded with people trying to board 'the tube'. The line splits at Kennington station, with some trains proceeding towards the City and others towards the West End. There the trains will disgorge the majority of passengers who will spend the rest of the day in offices and shops. Inside the train, some have the vacant, bored look of those with nothing to do, but some glance at the advertising or read the 'Poem on the Underground' – a scheme launched in 1986 by an American writer living in London to bring poetry to passengers. They read – maybe for the first time – Shelley's 'Ozymandias' ('I met a traveller from an antique land . . .'). Others, the majority, busy themselves in various ways. Some of the women read magazines. Others, particularly the lucky ones able to secure a seat, read a daily paper. There, a young man looks, distractedly, at the *Sun*, the largest-selling tabloid; a young woman reads the *Daily Mail*, another high-selling daily; but almost the whole of the British daily press is represented in this one carriage – including the liberal *Guardian*, read by another woman, and the *Financial Times*, in the hands of a man who does not look like a banker (no tie, no grey suit). The 'best-selling' daily, however, is one which is not sold but given away free and called, appropriately, *Metro* – and also available in Stockholm, Prague, Budapest, Amsterdam, Rome, Toronto, Athens, Warsaw, and Helsinki.

Some read books. The titles are not easy to fathom. Perhaps they are the current best-sellers. Well-trained eyes can identify the distinctive black cover of a Penguin classic read by a young woman, perhaps a student, oblivious to the world around her. Could it be *Madame Bovary*, or a Jane Austen, or one of the shorter Tolstoys? High-culture vultures can only speculate, rejoicing: civilisation has not yet ended; high culture lives on. One (older) person is rapidly completing a crossword puzzle; another (younger, male) is nervously playing with his Nintendo GameBoy machine, developing, no doubt, his reflexes. Other passengers have tiny earphones stuck into their ears, the wire disappearing into their bags or jackets and connected to an unseen disc or cassette player – the iPod is yet to come.

The tube is heaving with the consumption of culture.

Most of the passengers would have started their day listening to the radio, or eating their hurried breakfast watching some of the morning shows on television, perhaps with their children, or reading yesterday's newspaper or even today's, delivered by a newsboy on his rounds. Some of the passengers, those who work in shops or restaurants, will spend the rest of the day listening, whether they like it or not, to music. Some – many – work in the culture-producing business themselves, selling books and records, working for publishers, making their way to recording and film and video studios, working for one of the television networks or radio stations, or one of the magazines and newspapers which have offices in London, or in the growing software and computing service sector. They are among the 900,000 people employed in what the Department of Culture calls 'the creative industries', that is, 'Those industries which have their origin in individual creativity, skill and talent and which have a potential for wealth and job creation through the generation and exploitation of intellectual property.'[1]

After a day's work some of these Londoners will linger on in the centre of town, meeting friends or loved ones or, on their own or with others, will go to a cinema, a theatre, a concert, the opera, a club, or a wine bar or pub where more music will be provided while they drink and talk. The majority, however, will go home, and there they will sit in front of the television. The set might have been switched on earlier by the children – who spent the day at school, imbibing, one hopes, culture – or other members of the household. Some may sit before a computer, playing games or surfing the net. If there is nothing of interest on television they can watch a programme they have previously recorded or a video rented from a shop, or they can listen to the radio, or read a book, for these are still written, published and sold in numbers far greater than in previous centuries – despite the 'death of the book' predicted in a spate of books. There are, of course, those who do not work or go to school. Some are unemployed, but they still have a television and a radio. The majority, however, are retired, their working days behind. They spend the day watching television, listening to the radio, reading, attending to their hobbies, working part-time in voluntary organisations, or even going to classes, learning new skills.

In the other cities of Europe similar scenes are being played out. The choice may not be quite as considerable as it is in London, one of the great cultural centres of the world, but it is still vast.

The road to this bountiful supply of cultural artefacts, a situation so many take for granted, was long. Two centuries before, in 1800, most of the counterparts of our Clapham passengers could neither read nor write. School was not compulsory. Universities were attended by a tiny élite. There were no paid holidays. People did not retire, and in any case died young. Most would not have been able to afford books or even to borrow them from a lending library. Those who went to work, in the fields or the factories, seldom read anything. Their only experience of music, if any, might have been in the local church on Sundays, or during one of the rare festivals and fairs held during the year. There was the odd folk song and the odd penny novel or ballad, but on the whole the pleasures of reading were largely confined to the middle classes, still a narrow stratum even in Great Britain, then the richest country in the world, and perhaps their servants. The aristocracy was, of course, more privileged. Books were available to them, as were concerts and shows; but even they, in 1800, were culturally deprived compared to an ordinary shop assistant in 2000.

The history of the extraordinary expansion of cultural consumption over the last two hundred years constitutes the subject-matter of this work.

Culture and Cultural Production

Culture is a strange and loaded word. Today, in common parlance, it is used mainly in an anthropological sense as suggested in 1871 by Edward Burnett Tylor in his *Primitive Culture*: 'Culture or civilization, taken in its wide ethnographic sense, is that complex whole which includes knowledge, belief, art, morals, law, custom, and any other capabilities and habits acquired by man as a member of society.'[2] Tylor, of course, a good Victorian like Karl Marx, distinguished between the civilisation of the 'lower tribes' and that of the 'higher nations'. 'Culture', in the singular, has quite a different meaning, as Fernand Braudel pointed out, than 'cultures' in the plural.[3] The singular is absolutist; the plural is relativist. Cultures denote a set of values as well as a set of practices: the food we eat, the clothes we wear, the kind of leisure we pursue, the rituals we abide by, the traditions we embrace or invent, and the ideas we follow. Here culture is – to use a contemporary expression – life-style.

In its modern genesis, which can be traced to the Enlightenment, culture also suggests civilisation and excellence. The optimistic version of this – some would call it, with hindsight, downright naïve – was propounded by Condorcet in 1787: 'The more civilisation spreads across the planet, the more we will witness the disappearance of wars and conquests, slavery and misery.'[4] The pessimistic view, a reactionary counter-Enlightenment position which endures to this day, argued that as culture spread it would inevitably deteriorate before the vulgar taste of the new public. The meaning of culture as civilised excellence (to be spread to all or withheld for the few) was embodied in the way the Germans used the word *Kultur* in the nineteenth century. This was also the sense in which Matthew Arnold, in *Culture and Anarchy* (1869), defined culture: 'having its origin in the love of perfection; it is a study of perfection. It moves by the force, not merely or primarily of the scientific passion for pure knowledge, but also of the moral and social passion for doing good.'[5] This has, inevitably, a political subtext: it suggests a clash between different cultures, between dominant and subordinate social groups.

The proliferation of the word 'culture' has been particularly marked in the last decades, usually in the sense of 'identities'. The presence of various 'cultures' within a particular country has produced the label of 'multi-cultural' society, as if the nineteenth century was 'mono-cultural' (whereas, in fact, class and regional divisions were deeper). A cursory look at the Library of Congress catalogue reveals hundreds of publications purporting to throw light on various kinds of cultures: the culture of government, of opposition, of decentralisation, the 'excuse culture', the 'risk culture', the 'blame culture', the 'caring culture', the 'culture of contentment', the 'culture of classroom silence', the culture of noise, the culture of terror, of citizenship, of collusion, of censorship . . . The word is used to mean little more than a set of beliefs, a trend, or a state of affairs.

The concept of culture is also used to suggest specific artefacts: literature, music, films and performances. Here an old battle continues, familiar to us all, since considerable energies are spent to establish the distinction between 'high' or 'good' culture and 'low' or 'mass' culture – in other words, the difference between the Good and the Bad. The entire argument is often encapsulated by the question of whether Jane Austen is better than Barbara Cartland. Since it may well be the case that those who have read Jane Austen have not read Barbara Cartland, and vice-versa, the question, in reality, disguises a more political interrogation: namely, who decides the answer. It is a question of power. The common-sense riposte, of course, is quite simple.

Since this seems to be a matter of aesthetic judgment, relativism seems the obvious course. Some prefer Barbara Cartland, others prefer Jane Austen. Perhaps some prefer Barbara Cartland at some particular time and Jane Austen at others. Books, after all, do not have the same impact whenever we read them. *Anna Karenina* may not mean the same to a young woman of eighteen and to the same woman twenty years later, lumbered with a now boring husband and meeting a charming man.

Librarians, whose job is to classify and not to express value-judgments, cannot tell the difference between Austen and Cartland. As both are British novelists, they are both classified, with equanimity, under sub-section '823' of the Dewey Classification system, highlighting what these authors have in common. The tax authorities have an equally balanced view: books by Jane Austen and Barbara Cartland share the same rate of Value Added Tax (zero in Great Britain), along with all other books, newspapers and magazines (none excluded). That way the sanctity of the printed text (unlike plays and films) is established in law.

Yet Austen and Cartland have in common more than being British novelists. They are both very popular, and though both are dead, they still make money for their publishers. They write within a recognisable genre loosely described as women's romance – the story of how the heroine will get her man. Jane Austen has been read for two hundred years, while in so far as Cartland is concerned, it is too early to tell. But their works are both part of an industrial and commercial network of printers, proofreaders, booksellers, readers, and they both (here Jane Austen has the edge) offer material to critics, film-makers, essay-writers, university teachers and academic researchers. Writers like them, as well as composers, musicians, actors, producers, film-makers, never produce their wares in isolation. They write (or compose, make films, etc.) for a public. Their artefacts are distributed in a variety of ways: books through lending libraries, serialisation in newspapers, and booksellers; films through cinemas and television; music live in concert performances, then as records and radio programmes, and more recently downloaded from the internet. The way in which the stuff is distributed shapes its content, as does the public towards whom it is directed. Cultural production has a context, a network, a set of relationships. And what is 'high' culture in one epoch can be 'pop' in another. The *Mona Lisa*, a Renaissance masterpiece, and hence, as convention would have it, 'high culture', is today one of the most popular images in the world. *The Pilgrim's Progress* was long regarded as an exemplar of popular Christianity – today it can hardly be regarded as 'commercial'. Matters can proceed in reverse order: from the 'people' to the 'élites'. Folk tunes are revered in some populist middle-class circles, as they were by the Romantics. Fairy tales, once rewritten by writers such as Perrault or the Grimm brothers, became part of the education of the nobility. Jazz has become an élite genre of the intellectual middle classes.

Culture, all culture, feeds on itself and moves on. The producers of culture, the writers and artists, are consumers themselves. Some biographers often trace the influences on their subjects to their families and *milieu*, but perhaps the most important influence is not what their siblings did, or how their mothers treated them, or what kind of real-life 'role model' they had, but the culture they imbibed. Those who have the talent for writing novels and songs were, at first, readers and listeners. Before becoming writers, writers were readers who wanted to be like the writers they loved – so begins the work of imitation and innovation.[6]

Culture proceeds incrementally, building on whatever was available before, sometimes using a well-tried and established formula, other times innovating radically. No one is sure what is going to 'work'. As the failure rate is high, it is prudent to be conservative. One produces what the public already likes, but since this is a competitive market, it also pays to be innovative. Continuity is built-in in the history of culture, as is innovation. The revolutionary technological advances of the last two hundred years – recording, cinema, radio and television – have spread culture to an unprecedented extent, but have not altered the constant struggle between conservatism and innovation.

Culture creates its own markets. The consumption of culture enhances the desire for more culture (some even say that they are 'addicted' to particular genres). The cultural industry is an industry of pleasure which feeds on itself and is limitless. One could argue that, in this sense, all consumption is hedonistic: food, clothes, cars, furniture, gadgets. Cultural producers are aware of this. But the pleasure of consumption is also a pleasure of possession, because the consumer never faces the object of consumption as an isolated individual. We want some things few people have, but we also want things everyone has. Being in a market is a social activity.

The act of purchase often indicates identity: I bought a Bible because I am a Christian, I bought Proust because I am an intellectual, I bought *Playboy* magazine because I am a young man-about-town and like girls (though others may regard me as a pathetic masturbator without the imagination to conjure up my own fantasies).

The incentive to imitate and adapt culture is ancient and, as has been noted in the past, is a great force for conservatism and continuity. Sismondi, one of the founders of Romanticism, at the beginning of his *De la littérature du Midi de l'Europe* (1813), rejected the 'servile imitation' of classicism thus:

> New nations have often adopted a foreign literature with fanatical admiration. The genius of another has been offered as a perfect model of greatness and beauty. Spontaneity has been repressed to make room for servile imitation. The development of a national novel spirit has been sacrificed to the desire of reproducing something which totally conforms to the model one had under one's eyes.[7]

The Romans, he explained, followed the Greeks; the Arabs devoted themselves to the cult of Aristotle; the Italians and the French imitated the classics, and the Germans, Poles and Russians accepted the literary rule of the French. But this, he claimed, was all in the past. Modernity had arrived accompanied by an unprecedented respect for the past (classical novels, buildings, etc.), and at the same time an unprecedented urge to say something new in a new way. In the past, the pressures were to do the same thing repeatedly.

Fortunately for progress, the continuity spirit was counterbalanced by the spirit of innovation: 'Let's give the customers what they know' brings forth the cry 'Let's give the customers something new.' The avant-garde can be seen as risk-takers breaking a path for those behind. If they fail – as they often do – they fail in solitude, aggrieved at the incomprehension of their contemporaries and consoling themselves that a future age will understand them. But when they don't fail, they open the gates to less brave though shrewder followers who will be recompensed in cash for what they never gained in cultural prestige. Innovative or experimental or avant-garde culture is a self-conscious desire to break with the past. Culture and art have evolved more or less gradually, and there have always been novelties punctuating its course, but only recently have the innovations been so deliberate. Schoenberg tried to change the way we listen to music, Joyce the way we write and read novels, and Kandinsky or Jackson Pollock we way we paint. The incomprehension which much of this attracts is a function of the deliberate nature of such cultural provocations.[8]

In stories, plots are of limited importance. It may well be, as Vladimir Propp claimed, that there are a limited number of them.[9] And it may also be the case that there are a limited number of characters; but this is like saying that – in most Western music – there are only seven notes. What matters is how the story is told. Is the author the hero, or is he/she an intrusive narrator who guides the reader along? Does the story start in the middle? How much freedom of interpretation does it allow the reader to have?[10] There are infinite ways of capturing the emotions of readers.

Readers and listeners have a role to play. They bring their own circumstances and experiences to an understanding of what they consume. When Roland Barthes announced the 'death of the author', he meant that once a 'text' (which can be a painting or a piece of music) is out in the public domain, the author is no longer in charge of his or her creation; the audience is. Much literary criticism has been confined to an examination of the author and his/her text. But a text, since it can be deciphered in a variety of ways, seldom discloses a single meaning. The text is a tissue of quotations 'drawn from the innumerable centres of culture'.[11] There is no original meaning. Consumers bring to the text their own *Erwartungshorizont* or horizon of expectation – as suggested by the 'theorist of reception' Hans Robert Jauss.[12] No two readers are likely to have, consistently, the same cultural associations.[13] It is quite a different experience, for instance, to read a detective novel without knowing that it belongs to a literary genre, and reading it in the full knowledge of the conventions of that genre.

Genres are always constructed *a posteriori*. For instance, twelfth- and thirteenth-century epic texts, such as the *Nibelungenlied*, were classified in the nineteenth century as *das Deutsche Heldenepos*, that is the Heroic German Epic, in a desire to find a *Germanische Weltanschauung* (a German world-view).[14] What matters to us here is how a cultural form or a genre – for instance the epistolary novel – travels and is adapted in a new *milieu*. Many narrative genres, such as the crime story or the epic, seem to have a general appeal, cutting across religious, cultural and national boundaries with little change. The same occurs, for instance, with food. This is deemed to possess uniquely 'local' qualities, since we talk of 'Italian', 'French' and 'Chinese' food. In a global age, local food becomes global either by being imported by immigrants (Italian and Chinese) or adopted by élites, or, more recently, marketed by international corporations. Thus America's fast food, the spread of which seems to bring about an anxiety similar to that surrounding the advance of its culture, is based on food originally developed in various parts of the world, modifying it to suit the taste of a broad inter-ethnic community, experimenting freely without being bound by a tradition rigidly inherited from a specific group (thus producing pasta with curry, ice creams with an infinite range of flavours, and what we now call fusion food). The results usually bear the mark of their specific 'national' origin, either by keeping the original name (pizza, tacos, kebabs) or by indicating an assumed origin (*hamburgers*, *French* fries, *frankfurt*ers). What is American is the global reach of the enterprise which marketed them. Italians may have invented espresso coffee and pizzas, and may be renowned for their ice cream, but the world-wide chains selling these products are American companies trading under names such as Starbucks, Pizza Hut and Häagen-Dazs.

Culture proceeds analogously. This is not to say that a book is like a pizza, or a film like an ice cream, for cultural goods are bearers of symbols of quality, class, distinction (so, of course, are some foods: some cheeses are 'nobler' than others, some wines are 'finer' than others). But the main point stands: capitalist production is about standardisation. Cultural production, even at its most formulaic, even at its most 'capitalist', is far more differentiated – each book, each song, each play is a risky investment.

Repetition and innovation, reproduction and adaptation are the names of the game. The premise of *The Iliad*, the elopement of a queen and the expedition launched to rescue her, can be found elsewhere – as is the story of the return home of a soldier after a long war (the premise of *The Odyssey*). Tales such as what Europeans call Cinderella, Cendrillon, Cenerentola or Aschenputtel may have originated in one particular region or – what is more likely – in several regions, but the basic elements of the plot (a rotten childhood redeemed by marrying a person of higher status) are adapted, embellished or meshed with others. This is why narrative genres have flexible boundaries which cannot be established once and for all.[15] Moreover, successful genres and texts, precisely because they are imitated and adapted, lose their localised and provincial traits and acquire elements which permit them to venture into a wider world. Genres must evolve to survive.[16]

Culture and Money

In this context, the celebrated debate on the respective merits of high and low culture should be seen as an exercise in marketing. The distinctiveness of high culture is that it addresses itself to determinate sections of society, promising not just a way to while away the hours, but also the acquisition of symbolic values – what Bourdieu calls 'cultural capital'.[17] By reading Jane Austen (or Tolstoy, or Proust, etc.) not only do I have fun, but I identify myself with that distinctive class of people who are members of the high culture club.

Experts, academics and similar specialists are in charge of deciding who is to be included in the club, ensuring that their works will have a far longer lease of life than the rest. The process is sometimes slow: Baudelaire, 'out' until the First World War, was gradually upgraded in the 1920s. The definition of a canon is part of a struggle among the 'intellectuals' and other élites for the definition of a hierarchy of cultural values.

The word popular, in many languages, denotes not just what is successful but also (often because it is successful) what belongs to the 'people' and not the élite. 'Popular' culture is counterposed to culture *tout court*, popular religion to religion, popular art to art, popular medicine to medicine.[18] Yet there was never in European history a time in which popular culture was not somehow under the influence of the culturally powerful. Popular religious festivals might have had some subversive effects, but Christianity cannot be simply characterised as a force emanating 'from below'. Some manifestations of contemporary mass culture may have had a 'subversive' origin, but to the extent that they are successful they become part of a wider commercial system.

Some cultural theorists define 'popular' culture as consumer culture.[19] But this is imprecise, since all culture is consumed. Flaubert and Tolstoy, by now, have probably sold more books than their more popular contemporaries. Others seek to underline the 'formulaic' aspect of popular culture. Robert Scholes, for instance, makes a distinction between the formula writer, who simply reproduces the convention of an established genre, and 'writers of genius', who enrich the genre of the novel because they are aware of new possibilities or are able to adapt the tradition to a new real situation.[20] That may be so, but all culture is 'formulaic' if, by this expression, we mean simply some kind of template from which a variety of products can be derived. Seriality and repetition are hardly new: much Renaissance art is based on a limited number of subjects.

So while I will frequently use the distinction between high and low, I will regard it largely as a question of audiences and markets. What is of some interest are the differences between the community of all those who partake of 'high' culture and the community of all those who partake of 'popular' culture. These 'communities' are not monolithic blocs. Their boundaries are porous. The access to the kind of cultural baggage necessary for an understanding and appreciation of a wider array of cultural goods is constantly modified. Those who are unable to read, have no money to buy books, grow up in bookless homes, or have no time to read books, are deprived of the kind of education that may allow them to decide whether or not they like Jane Austen (for no one *has* to like Jane Austen). A considerable part of humanity suffers this predicament, since – according to UNESCO – there were about 860 million illiterate adults in the world in 2000 (two out of three of them women).[21]

Since people are better off now than two hundred years ago, at least in the West, and have more money, more time and more education, the consumption of both high and low culture has increased enormously – unsurprisingly. Audiences have increased well beyond the imagination of the cultural producers of two centuries ago. Bach wrote almost three hundred cantatas specifically for the congregation of St Thomas's church in Leipzig – as well as the St John Passion, the St Matthew Passion, the Mass in B Minor and The Art of the Fugue. Today, Bach may not be on the charts, but his works have an audience which surpasses his wildest dreams and expectations.

Humanity may have got better at the business of war, killing more people at a faster rate than ever before, but it also consumes far more culture. It does so in a variety of ways, but above all through markets – the production, distribution and sale of cultural artefacts and, more recently, through the public ownership of the means of diffusing culture – the education system and, above all, public broadcasting. Cultural markets, and the division of labour which sustains them, are the subject-matter of this book. I have tried to avoid just combining conventional histories of various cultural forms – a history of literature, a history of the cinema, a history of music and so on – in favour of a broad survey of the markets of cultural production.

Of course, much culture is exchanged outside the cash nexus. We have conversations, we play music to each other, we tell jokes. Traditional forms of 'community' cultures are still around us – singing in church, for instance. Some 'performances' are still quite free, if one can endure them: a politician kissing babies, glad-handing, flesh-pressing; an evangelical preacher Bible-thumping, sin-hounding, devil-dodging; a princess being buried amidst crowds thrilled to be mourning. Much of the culture which went on in the private sphere has been annexed by the market, by capitalism, as many lament. But much other production which went on in the private sphere – growing one's own food, cooking one's meals, making one's clothes and furniture – has equally been taken over by the market.

The focus of this book is, quite unashamedly, on culture as a business, a profession; culture as a set of relationships. The story of culture, as it is narrated here, is the story of production for a market. It is the story of what the passengers on the London underground and their counterparts in the rest of Europe and in the preceding two centuries have been doing to while away the hours during the course of their life – limiting the scope to what they read, they hear, they see.

Culture is about money, but not only about money. Culture can bring pleasure and prestige. This is why some people would rather be writers than accountants, and some publishers would rather publish books than manufacture screwdrivers, though there might be, for many of them, more money in accountancy or in making screwdrivers.

A considerable amount of risk surrounds the world of cultural production. Films, so costly, are a high-risk exercise, but so is novel-writing. Film producers start with an idea, while publishers intervene at a late stage by selecting from a mass of as yet unpublished but often already written novels. Will they sell a sufficient number of copies to make a profit? This is their gamble. There are considerable expenses to produce a single copy: editing, setting and printing the book, marketing and distribution. Out of all the novels published, only some make a profit, and out of these, only a very few make huge profits. Some make a profit only in the short term, others in the long term, when immortality beckons to the now dead author, and some cash for generations of publishers.

Behind all this, though, there is the universe of those who suffered alone and unrecognised, like so many spermatozoa destined never to reach the ovum and yet indispensable to the creative process.

Time and Space

The story begins in 1800, for it is on the cusp between the eighteenth and the nineteenth centuries that the business of culture leaves behind its pre-industrial phase, at least in the countries and areas which constitute the economic and social core of Europe (Great Britain, France, the Italian peninsula and the German-speaking lands). A book-reading public of some consistency begins to appear, and along with it a large number of printers and publishers, a network of lending libraries, and a proper book market. Concert performances, a rarity in Europe before 1800, begin to develop. Musical instruments, the piano in particular, become ubiquitous in the homes of the new middle classes, as they had been in those of the aristocracy. Advances in print technology facilitate the diffusion of musical scores. Virtuoso musicians travel across Europe, as do opera singers. The opera, previously under courtly patronage, is increasingly performed before a paying bourgeois audience. The state control over theatres is reduced, censorship relaxed; as a result there are more theatres and larger audiences. There is an unremitting expansion of cultural producers such as writers, playwrights, composers, singers, actors. The daily and periodical press, already thriving in some countries, such as Great Britain, grows in importance. Here too deregulation, in the sense of a lowering of taxation and a lessening of censorship, has a marked effect on sales, as do technological advances.

These processes are accompanied, of course, by the development of the middle classes, the main consumers of the new commercial culture. Such consumption is not, however, confined to them, since the expanding armies of domestic servants as well as the factory proletariat consume penny pamphlets and magazines. None of this happens *ab novo*, for the foundations had been erected in previous decades and centuries, but the pace of change is rapid and constantly accelerates throughout the nineteenth century. The growth of education helps the process along, creating a subsidiary market for textbooks, increasing the number of teachers, and laying down the basis for new generations of readers and writers.

Parts One (1800–1830) and Two (1830–1880) of this work – some twenty-nine chapters – deal essentially with a culture whose consumption takes two forms: as a printed text (books, newspapers, images and musical scores) and as live performance.

Part Three (1880–1920) focuses on developments that completely revolutionise the diffusion of culture. A mass market for newspapers and periodicals comes into being, prevalently in Great Britain and France. New literary genres become popular – such as the comic strip and the crime novel. The invention of the gramophone utterly changes the way in which music is consumed and produced. Until then, to hear music, one had to be present at someone else's performance or able to perform oneself. Now one could bring home the music of great specialists and listen to it repeatedly. Music production followed the various formats into which music could be recorded and sold. With the invention of the cinema and its popularisation, a new cultural form, which addressed itself to all social classes, heralded the 'democratic' culture of a democratic age. It is the beginning of genuine mass entertainment. The cinema also marks the end of European near-self-sufficiency in cultural matters, the situation prevailing throughout the nineteenth century. Europeans began to consume, increasingly, cultural products originating in the USA, particularly films and music.

This American advance – particularly pronounced in the new mass art, the cinema and popular music (both recorded and broadcast) – constitutes one of the main themes of Part Four (1920–1960), since I take 'European culture' to mean what Europeans consume, and not just what they produce. The other major theme of this section is the intervention of the state in cultural matters. This exceeded, by far, the kind of political and moral censorship exercised in the nineteenth century. Authoritarian regimes of a new type – the USSR, above all, but also fascist Italy and Nazi Germany – sought, not always successfully, to bolster particular cultural tendencies and prevent others. The most important form of state intervention, however, was that over broadcasting, which was placed under direct or indirect state control even in those countries, such as Great Britain and France, where political and economic liberalism prevailed.

The concluding part, Part Five, examines a world which is still around us – a world in which consuming or producing culture has become the principal activity of Europeans. It opens with the rise of television, mapping, in three chapters, the progress of broadcasting, its diversification into genres, the impact and significance of American export of television programmes and ideas, the gradual decrease in the importance of 'public service' broadcasting, and the contemporary fragmentation of television. The chapters that follow provide an examination of the development of mass paperbacks and periodicals, the impact of television on the cinema, the explosion of popular music, and the survival of the theatre. The much-disputed matter of American cultural hegemony is at the centre of every chapter in this section.

The geographical compass of the study is Europe – the ill-defined area that spreads from western Russia and the Bosphorus to Portugal and Ireland, from Scandinavia to Sicily. Some core countries, Great Britain, Germany, France, but also Italy and Russia, are dealt with far more than others. This treatment is a direct consequence of their greater role in exporting specific cultural artefacts and genres to the rest of Europe. In the nineteenth century, for instance, in literature, particularly in popular novels, France and Great Britain predominated; in instrumental music it was the Germans, but also the Russians; in opera the Italians ruled; the melodrama belonged to the French; the operetta was first French and then Austrian. I have tried, of course, to deal with the latecomers as well as with the path-breakers, and with the numerous exceptions that broke the barriers of language and obtained international successes – authors such as Collodi, the Italian creator of Pinocchio; Henryk Sienkiewicz, the Polish author of an international best-seller of 1896, *Quo Vadis?*; and Hans Christian Andersen, who from peripheral Denmark became one of the best-known children's writers of all times.

I have tried to examine the vicissitudes of cultural processes. How artefacts travel from one country to another, how they are adapted to local circumstances or transformed into another medium, and how assorted nationalisms and prejudices have tried to protect particular cultures, not always with deleterious effects. The long-term trend has been towards greater homogeneity and standardisation, following the general pattern of the growth in consumption, communications and global trade. Technological improvements and innovations have enabled the expansion of markets, but have also made cultural operators more cautious. Technological revolutions have been accompanied by a conservative attitude in the production of genres. Consider the melodrama: popular among the theatre-going middle classes in the early nineteenth century and the readers of serialised novels, it successfully survives in numerous television serials; the farce is reincarnated as a sit-com; the crime story is as popular as ever on television screens throughout the world; the medieval epic found new life in science fiction and comic strips; the glamour surrounding opera singers is found again with film stars and pop idols.

The search for ever larger audiences compels cultural products to travel the globe, and though the trend never proceeds uniformly, it is a force towards standardisation. This is hardly a new phenomenon: the formation of world religions based on sacred texts is the most obvious instance of the formation of what many have called 'the global village'. There are other instances of standardisation. Almost everywhere in the world, for instance, the beginning of the legal year is now 1 January – even in countries where Christianity is a minority religion and where a religious calendar exists alongside the Western year. Such conventions are recent. In the Middle Ages, the year began on Christmas Day in Germany, Switzerland, Portugal and Spain; in Venice it was 1 March; in England 25 March. In France it started on Easter Day (which, of course, changed every year); 1 January was adopted as the start of the legal year only in 1564, under Charles IX. Russia, under Peter the Great, followed in 1725, England in 1752, before Napoleon imposed it on much of Europe.[22]

Today, throughout the world, significant minorities watch the same films, the same television programmes, listen to the same music, and read the same international best-sellers. Culture wars are fought, sometimes not metaphorically, but they are fought transnationally, across borders, using common means of communication. They are the inevitable result of the movement of cultural artefacts.

I have tried to include in the narrative the production, distribution and consumption of the kind of cultural artefacts available to Europeans over the last two hundred years: novels, non-fiction, textbooks, self-help books, newspapers and periodicals; concert music, musical instruments and musical scores. I have dealt with singers, composers and virtuosi; the various theatrical genres including the opera; the recording of music and how this has changed the production of music; the birth of the cinema and its evolution throughout the twentieth century; the organisation and growth of broadcasting; the spread of music in its various forms including popular music; the connection between some narrative genres, such as the serialised novel and the comic strip, and the expansion of the press; the role played by illustrations in books and periodicals. In the conclusion I look at the renewal of older forms of cultural consumption, such as museums, and the development of the internet.

The fine arts have been left out, and perhaps a word of explanation is in order. Including them would, of course, have made a long book even longer, but the reasons for the exclusion are more weighty. The market for fine art (paintings and three-dimensional objects) is essentially a speculative market of objects which are defined as art by a relatively restricted élite (collectors, gallery-owners, museum directors, art critics). In fact the art market correlates approximately with the stock market.[23] This was not always the case: patrons commissioned paintings for their own use; resale value was irrelevant. In the period which concerns us, this activity has passed largely into the hands of public bodies which exercise, on behalf of a wider community, the functions once exercised by the aristocracy.

Most people have an idea of what a novel or a play might look like, or a piece of music might sound like – bar a tiny proportion of highly experimental manifestations – without consulting experts. This is not so with contemporary art. Art specialists may be annoyed and bored by the constant jokes made at the expense of rotting fish or piles of bricks which are exhibited in art galleries and win prizes, but similar outcries seldom occur with a literary prize. Every Goncourt or Booker Prize-winning novel has its opponents, but no one disputes its status as a novel, only its claim to excellence. Actors may be forced to act while being almost completely buried in sand, but Beckett's *Happy Days* is still a play. Occasionally status is disputed, as with James Joyce's *Finnegans Wake* or, in music, the deliberate cacophony aimed at subverting melody, or even total silence (as in John Cage's most notorious 'composition', '4'33'). Most music, however, is recognisable as such. New architecture may be daringly modern, but in the end the buildings must stand up. In fine art, not only is it easier to innovate, but it would be impossible to survive as an artist simply by slightly modifying what has gone on before.[24] One can imagine Jane Austen returning to earth and being given a book by Barbara Cartland. She might mock it, or be surprised by its 'daring' effrontery, but she would have no doubt that it was indeed a novel written by a fellow novelist. Mozart might approve or disapprove of the Beatles, but he would recognise 'Lucy in the Sky with Diamonds' as a piece of music. It is, however, highly unlikely that Michelangelo, faced by a Jackson Pollock, could fathom that this was the work of a revered modern master.

Compared with the market for music, print, moving images, performances, etc., the market for fine art (regardless of the enormous amounts of money involved) is exceptionally narrow. This is a market for unique objects. The value of each artistic product is determined by the market, that is by how much someone is prepared to pay for it. This value is in turn determined by two sets of expectations: the future value of the work, and its aesthetic value as ratified by experts. The speculative nature of the product is evident to all. This is not the case with reproducible commodities. A book by Tolstoy does not cost more than one by Barbara Cartland just because Tolstoy is regarded by experts as the better writer. An expensive academic book is not 'better' than a cheap one – the high price merely suggests that the publishers do not think it will sell many copies. One pays the same amount to see a film that cost $250 million as one made on a shoestring.[25]

The monetary value of fine art is determined by its resale value. This is not the case for all other cultural artefacts. No one buys *War and Peace* because it will go up in price (unless, of course, it is a rare edition, and in this case it is not the text that matters but the rarity of the object, its approximation to a unique object). Auction prices would slump dramatically if the general expectation was that prices would constantly fall. Of course, many buyers actually derive pleasure and satisfaction from hanging a Monet on their walls, just as they would with a piece of furniture, but not many would be prepared to pay millions for a painting if they thought it would be worth half that in a few years' time. Such calculations are quite alien to the cultural markets examined in this work. Today's newspaper is worth fifty pence or so. Tomorrow it is worth nothing.

Since there is no definition of 'art' (except the tautological one that art is what those responsible for defining it say it is), it can often straddle into other domains. Thus performance art, even though it takes place in a museum or exhibition setting, belongs properly to the general class of theatrical performance. For instance, in 1975 the Stedelijk Museum of Amsterdam bought the behaviour of the German artist Henk Jurriaans for one month between 1 and 2 p.m. each day. The artist was said to behave 'normally' during this period because 'he was not performing'. So during that period of time Mr Jurriaans had become a work of art.[26] In reality he was performing and behaving like an actor.

Excluded from the art market, and therefore included in this book, are all reproducible art objects: posters, reproductions, art in books, prints (except for rare prints). Our world, a world where the mastery of written text is available to the majority and not to a small élite, is nevertheless a world overwhelmingly dominated by images, by the visual. The legal possession of images is somewhat tangential to this world. From the point of view of public consumption, what matters is whether they are publicly exhibited. Fine art, once it is reproduced in art books, posters and postcards, that is once it is transformed into a mass-produced commodity, can reach a very large audience. This high visibility – together with the ever increasing spread of education in the arts thanks to television, newspapers, periodicals, films and schooling – contributes decisively to the success of art exhibitions, which since the 1960s have attracted millions of visitors.

The cultural artefacts surveyed here, their coming into being, their sale, their consumption, their trade, serve a multiplicity of purposes. They have symbolic value; they define identities; they bring prestige and fame; they provide employment; they inform; and they entertain. Above all, they help us to while away the time. That so much effort should be expended in the pursuit of something apparently so trivial – trivial, that is, compared to weighty matters such as war and peace, the struggle against disease, and the procuring of food and shelter – is the hallmark of civilisation.

I

1800–1830

THE PRE-CONDITIONS

1

Sources of Cultural Expansion

Population

WHO WERE THE EUROPEANS WHO, in 1800, were willing and able to buy books, borrow them from lending libraries, subscribe to newspapers and magazines, attend concerts, go to the theatre and play music at home having purchased musical instruments and scores?

What was the potential of these rapidly developing cultural markets? Assessing their growth potential is pure guesswork. It is reasonable, however, to assume that cultural markets will grow more in rich countries than in poor ones, and in large ones than small ones. It is, after all, a 'universally held truth' that the rich spend more than the poor. Countries that are both large and wealthy consume more than those with a tiny and destitute population.

Today, the European Union – neither a country nor a linguistic entity – is the largest cultural market in the world. With over 450 million inhabitants, the EU cannot match China or India in population, or the USA and Japan in wealth, but it is richer than the former and bigger than the latter. Almost all Europeans can afford to buy a book, a radio, a record, a newspaper, and practically all of them have a television – by contrast 'only' eighty-two million households in India had their own television in 2003.[1]

The Europe of 1800 was quite a different matter. It was poor and relatively underpopulated. There are no reliable data, but a total population of 195 million people is a plausible estimate.

Russia had fewer than forty million people. Next came France with 29.3 million. German-speakers, excluding those in Austria, were 24.5 million. The Austrian Empire comprised 23.3 million inhabitants – a little more than the population of modern Romania. Next came the Italian states with 18.3 million, then Spain with 10.6 million. The recently established United Kingdom of Great Britain had only 8.6 million.[2]

By 1850 the number of Europeans had increased by almost 50 per cent, to 288 million. By 1900 there were 422 million Europeans. This unprecedented growth had affected all the Continent's countries, especially the richest, Great Britain, whose population more than trebled in the course of the nineteenth century. Even Ireland, in spite of the high mortality rate following the disastrous famine of 1845, saw an increase of population between 1800 and 1850: from five million to 6.6 million. Its population did drop by 1900 to 4.5 million, but this was due to emigration rather than starvation (though, of course, the emigration was caused largely by hunger and poverty).

Though health and longevity continued to improve, Europe did not grow as fast in 1850–1900. There were fewer epidemics than before and virtually no wars, but birth control led to smaller families and Europeans emigrated in massive numbers. This emigration had considerable consequence for the developments of cultural markets in Europe, North America and the rest of the world.

Today we think of migrant workers as coming from the so-called 'Third World'. In the nineteenth century, most migrants were Europeans. In the eighteenth century the most massive 'emigration' had been an enforced one: the slave trade. Taken in its entirety (between 1500 and the middle of the nineteenth century) this was the largest forcible migration in world history, involving the transportation of between eleven and twelve million Africans as slaves to the Americas – from Canada to Brazil. Although the slave trade was abolished in the first decade of the nineteenth century, considerable internal movement continued within Africa throughout the century, largely because of African wars. In China the opening of the Treaty Ports in 1842 led to millions of Chinese moving to South-East Asia, Australia and California.[3] The number of Chinese, Indian and Japanese emigrants was considerable, most of it directed towards the rest of Asia, the Caribbean and, to a lesser extent, to the USA and Latin America. However, their numbers did not match that of European migrants.

Between 1851 and 1915 forty-one million Europeans went to the Americas and Australia. At first (1846–65) most (70 per cent) came from the United Kingdom, followed by Germany with 20 per cent. But in the 1891–1915 period Italians topped the emigration league (26 per cent), just preceding the UK (25 per cent). The Europeans who emigrated in the course of the nineteenth century settled in areas dominated by the English language: the USA (70 per cent), Canada (6 per cent) and Australia (6 per cent). Ten per cent went to Argentina and 6 per cent to Brazil.[4] Between 1860 and 1913 an annual average of 125,000 British took passage to an extra-European country. In 1887 alone (a peak year), 202,000 went to the USA. They were not escaping persecution or starvation. They were attracted by the prospect of improving their lives.[5] The spread of colonies offered further space to European settlers. In comparison to the economic migrants of the late twentieth century these settlers had considerable advantages. The possession of advanced weaponry and the backing of strong states meant they could thrust their way in instead of begging to be accepted.

This emigration impacted on cultural markets by establishing or reinforcing a great degree of linguistic homogeneity. The children of the Poles, the Germans, the Italians, the Jews, the Swedes who went to Latin America and the USA became Spanish-, Portuguese- or English-speakers. According to the first census, in 1790, the number of English-speakers in the USA (excluding the Native Americans and the African slaves) amounted to little over four million. By the end of the nineteenth century this had grown to fifty million.

Emigration to the United States and the British colonies and dominions represented – in the long run – a net linguistic loss for all European languages other than English. The relatively high literacy rate of immigrants contributed further to the expansion of cultural markets in the USA. The 'wretched refuse' of Europe's 'teeming shore', to quote Emma Lazarus's famous sonnet engraved on the pedestal of the Statue of Liberty, were not as ignorant as those who had stayed behind. Three-quarters of those entering the USA in 1900–10 were literate. Among Turks the literacy rate was 56 per cent (the same as in Egypt in 1995), among Italians it was almost 70 per cent for southerners and 85 per cent for northerners, and it was well over 90 per cent among Bohemians (96.8 per cent), Irish (96 per cent), Armenians (92.1 per cent) and Jews (93.3 per cent).[6]

Immigration led to new forms of cultural preservations. The culture of the 'old country', much of it oral, continued to evolve and was more carefully preserved by the emigrants in their new adoptive country.[7] They selected specific features of their home culture, often the popular elements such as the food and the music, and turned them into a badge of identity. In their new country the immigrants often tenderly preserved and cherished the memory of a lost world which in their native land was rapidly disappearing under the weight of modernity. Thus Italian songs composed at the end of the nineteenth century, such as the renowned 'O Sole Mio' (1898), were still being played in jukeboxes in New York's Little Italy in the late 1960s while they were no longer heard in Milan's bars and cafés – unlike Elvis Presley and his Italian imitators.

Immigrants who found themselves part of one group among many in a multicultural society absorbed 'alien' cultural baggage far more rapidly than they would have otherwise, however ghettoised their conditions. Thus emigration created a population particularly receptive to cultural innovations. Cultural entrepreneurs, if they wanted to reach more than a single group, had to produce for a culturally diverse society – hence the remarkable successes of the American cultural industry in the twentieth century.

The urban concentration of immigrants further contributed to the growth of the cultural industry because emigration was a form of international urbanisation by which many left 'their' countryside for foreign cities. To put it brutally: migrants abandoned cultural rural backwaters and went to thrusting and thriving cities, the seats of modernity, where the considerable presence of the urban middle classes ensured the constant development of cultural markets. Cultural production tended to be located in the larger centres. Cities and not the countryside, urban life and not rural life, had been the hub of culture in Europe since the Middle Ages. In the great Italian cities, Milan, Genoa, Venice and Florence, but also in London, Paris, Cologne, Bruges, Toulouse and Seville, the pulsating life of commerce and culture stood in sharp contrast to the lethargy of the countryside as early as the twelfth century.[8] There is more than a grain of truth in Karl Marx's abusive remark about 'the idiocy of rural life'.

The thriving theatrical life of nineteenth-century Britain, and its considerable press and publishing industry, were results of its urban dimension. By 1851 Great Britain had become the first major country in which the urban population outstripped the rural. In Germany – land of many cities – this occurred only in 1891. France had to wait until 1931. And in England, people were disproportionately concentrated in just one city, that had become the home of the most developed cultural market of its time. This city, London, was in 1800 the largest in the world, with one million inhabitants. It was home to 10 per cent of the British population, while Paris was half the size and the home of only one in forty of the French.[9] Other cities trailed far behind. Vienna, the capital of a large multinational empire, had only 250,000 inhabitants, Berlin only 172,000. In Italy, whose urban civilisation was the oldest in Europe, cities were smaller, and only Naples, with 350,000 inhabitants, could compete with the larger European countries. Rome, Milan and Venice had fewer than 200,000 inhabitants.

In an age without rapid transport and a pre-industrial communication system, networking was even more important than it is now. Authors went where other producers (publishers, printers, etc.) operated. In France a writer's fame was usually made in Paris (hence the profusion of novels about young provincials going to the capital to make a name for themselves). This was true in London too, though novelists of great fame could live where they wanted: Walter Scott in Scotland, Maria Edgeworth in Ireland, and Jane Austen (unknown in her lifetime) in Hampshire. Thomas de Quincey spent twelve years in Edinburgh, the other great literary centre of early-nineteenth-century Britain, where some of the leading literary magazines of the time were published (*Blackwood's Edinburgh Magazine* and the *Edinburgh Review*).

It is an inescapable fact that wealth provides the leisure time required for cultural pursuits, however many peasant communities were able to enjoy some enforced leisure in the long winter months – certainly more than the overworked industrial proletariat of the eighteenth and nineteenth centuries. What did people do in late-medieval Europe in their 'spare' time? Some played cards, talked, gossiped. The church provided, on Sunday, a form of entertainment: some singing, some preaching. In pre-industrial societies, much of what we would call leisure was adequately provided for in the form of non-literary pursuits such as religious festivals and irregular breaks from work.[10] Most of this occurred outside the market. Culture may have been limited, but it was 'free'.

The nineteenth-century revolution in communication and transport contributed decisively to the growing unification of cultural markets. As books, newspapers, periodicals, musical scores as well as musicians, actors, storytellers and singers could move around more rapidly, local markets turned into national and international ones. There were better and faster ships, a wider network of canals and better roads.

Transatlantic shipping routes linking Great Britain (Liverpool) and the USA developed rapidly. From 1869 the Suez Canal made European commerce with Asia more rapid and safe. In 1830 a letter from London to Bombay had to go by ship round the Cape of Good Hope, and took five to eight months to reach its destination. The reply, allowing for monsoon, would mean that a simple exchange could take two years. Following the opening of the canal the message would proceed by steam train, steam boat and camel via Alexandria to Suez, and reached its destination after thirty-five days.[11] One result was that between 1840 and 1880 the cost of sending books dropped by 75 per cent.[12]

These developments had a powerful effect on cultural integration within each nation and throughout the Continent. Everything became increasingly homogeneous and standardised. The metre, established by the French in the 1790s, became widely adopted as a unit of measurement – except in the Anglo-Saxon world. The Greenwich meridian, from which the longitude of all points on the earth is measured, was internationally recognised in 1885. Before the railways, time varied slightly from town to town, but by the end of the century uniform time zones were established.[13]

A national rail network was pivotal for the formation of a national press, while the British distribution of journals and books was facilitated by the excellence of its postal system.[14] By 1850 almost all European countries had a railway line – the exceptions being Finland, Sweden, Greece, Romania, Bulgaria and Portugal, but these caught up in the following two decades.

Wealth

In today's highly developed societies, though most people can read, much entertainment – television, radio, recorded sound and the cinema – does not require literacy. In the nineteenth century reading was the essential cultural pursuit. Initially it was restricted largely to the middle and upper classes. It is often assumed that prosperity, industrialisation and urbanisation increase literacy and hence lead to a multiplication of potential readers. However, the fit between a nation's wealth and its literacy rates is far from perfect – nor is there a firm connection between literacy (the ability to read) and reading (the actual reading).

Although literacy was much lower in eastern than in western Europe, the economic gap between the two in 1800 was not remarkable: the western part was only 7 per cent higher (in GNP per capita) than the European average. The wealth gap increased throughout the nineteenth century, to the detriment of the easterners. The literacy gap did not substantially change.[15] In 1859 Scotland was more literate but poorer than England – England caught up with the Scottish level of 1859 only in 1886. Studies conducted on convicted criminals (a captive audience in every sense) revealed that in the 1830s Scottish offenders were better educated than their English counterparts.[16] At the beginning of the nineteenth century 70 per cent of the population of

Switzerland was literate. The country was then poor, but it had established one of the first systems of free and compulsory primary schools.[17] In Finland in 1880 the completely illiterate were less than 2 per cent, fewer than in France, which was much richer than Finland. Iceland had a highly literate population even in the eighteenth century when the country was in misery.[18]

What remains unquestionable is that whenever literacy is less than universal, the ability to read is a class and often also a gender issue. This was as true in medieval Europe as in medieval India, where literacy was common among men of the Brahman (priests and law-givers) and Kashttriya (rulers and military) classes.[19]

It is also likely that, in comparison to medieval cities, a greater proportion of the inhabitants of the great cities of antiquity were literate or at least educated, particularly in Byzantium, though, as William Harris points out, 'We shall obviously never know in a clear-cut numerical way how many people were literate, semi-literate, or illiterate in the Graeco-Roman world.'[20]

The 'West' was certainly culturally backward in comparison with China and the Arab world. Arab universities were thriving well before Bologna, Oxford and Cambridge appeared. The royal library of Cordoba in Andalusia under al-Hakam II possessed some 400,000 books in the tenth century, while the library of the famous monastery of St Gall in Switzerland had around four hundred books.[21] As for philosophical awareness among the common people, it is likely that there was more of it in Byzantium than in medieval Rome or London. At least this is the impression one obtains from testimonies such as those of St Gregory of Nyssa, one of the Cappadocian Fathers, who was struck and somewhat alarmed by the passion for theological arguments in fourth-century Constantinople.

> Everywhere in the city . . . in the alleys, the streets, the squares if you ask about the rate of exchange, you get a philosophical lecture on that which is created and that which is not. You ask the price and value of bread, they reply that the Father is superior and the Son subordinate. You inquire whether the public bath is adequate, and the response is that the Son was made out of nothing.[22]

On average women were less literate than men, even in high society, until the eighteenth century when middle- and upper-class women began to consume more fiction than men, wrote more letters and kept more diaries. It is often assumed that they had more leisure time than their husbands, but one should not take too literally the term 'lady of leisure'. Many of these ladies had five to ten servants to organise – more personnel than the majority of today's small enterprises.[23] Only aristocrats and the really rich could afford to employ supervisory servants (such as butlers) charged with managing the household. At this level of wealth both sexes had considerable leisure time, though men had a wider range of activities than women: fox-hunting, net-working, travelling, theatre-going, joining clubs, whoring, drinking in public places, and so on.

The evidence that novel-reading was a major occupation of middle- and upper-class women is not compelling. It was less true of, say, eighteenth-century Russia and Italy than of England and France, where women were not barred from lending libraries and places where books were available, where there were many female writers and magazines specifically targeted at the female middle- and upper-class market. Madame de Staël, writing in 1810, pointed out that women and men mixed together more often in literary salons in France than in Berlin. Some might argue that men-only clubs in London would have kept women apart too, and not to the detriment of the intellectual life of English women (the reverse might have been true).[24]

The *Ladies' Mercury*, published in London since 1693, sought to provide answers to questions regarding love, marriage, sex and dress. Its success was such that a few years later, in 1704, the rival *Ladies' Diary* was launched. Women did not just read the feminine press: Richard Steele's *Tatler* (1709) – a literary and political review – had a considerable readership among women. Nor did women just read about 'feminine' matters: in 1749 the *Ladies' Maga-zine*, a monthly priced at one shilling, provided detailed accounts of murders and other crimes, allegedly narrated by eye-witnesses. In 1770 another publi-cation, the *Lady's Magazine*, gave embroidery patterns and sheet music away with each number, and also serialised novels and published literary contri-butions from readers. Many of the women's magazines were meant to provide guidance to the lady of the house in the art of household management: how to prepare and preserve food, how to avoid waste, how to keep accounts. Later, the magazines carried more useful advice, such as how to catch men of fortune and what fashionable women were supposed to wear.[25]

This kind of culture was a harbinger of later bourgeois consumerism. Its full blossoming required a more decisive move towards the manufacturing of an unprecedented range of goods. At the beginning of the nineteenth century production was not yet industrial and the model of consumption was still aristocratic.[26] Proper bourgeois consumerism had still to find its own ethos, for consumerism, like sex, requires a set of beliefs: what to buy, when to buy, where to buy. As the century marched on, aspects of the consumer society with which we are now familiar began to appear in the more advanced countries: greetings cards, the commercialisation of Christmas, window shopping and advertising. In 1800 few parents would have had the idea of buying toys for their children; by 1900 it had become normal.[27]

A key factor in the development of cultural consumption was fashion. Fashion entails communication, a desire to conform, and a concept of group belonging. Buying certain cultural items, like a particular kind of clothes, or behaving in a particular way, are among the many ways in which we signal who we are or what we would like to be. This, of course, long precedes capitalist societies. Renaissance princes were in the business of conspicuous consumption, following fashion and demarcating themselves from others as much as the *nouveaux riches* of later years.[28]

In painting and to a far lesser extent in music, a market of some significance existed as early as the seventeenth century. Italian artists, for instance, operated in a Europe-wide market, selling a considerable proportion of their output to foreigners.[29]

What gives capitalist consumption its particular dimension is that it is the mechanism for its own subsequent growth. The growth of cultural markets was part of the general expansion of market economies. It reduced and eventually eliminated the patronage relationship between cultural producers and their patrons, in favour of a commercial nexus. It provided the conditions for the emergence of the professional: people who write, compose and paint for a market of paying customers.

But cultural markets are diverse. To make a living over a lifetime a painter requires only a relatively small number of prosperous customers. Independent professional writers need a significant mass – which is why they appeared only towards the eighteenth century and in countries with relatively advanced market economies. Unsurprisingly, this development was welcomed with glee by the more successful writers. Thus Oliver Goldsmith in 1762: 'At present the few poets of England no longer depend on the Great for subsistence, they have now no other patrons but the public, and the public, collectively considered, is a good and generous master.'[30] Not all were as enthusiastic: 'The writer has not always the choice of his subject,' commented Samuel Johnson, 'but is compelled to accept any task that is thrown before him.'[31] It might be easier to satisfy a patron one knows than an unfamiliar multitude. Besides, Goldsmith himself, who sold his novel *The Vicar of Wakefield* for £60 to keep his creditors at bay, was not as free as he liked to think. He was forced by his extravagant lifestyle to accept any commission thrown at him:

translations, abridgements of classics, potted histories of England, Greece and Rome.[32]

Writing remains to this day a peculiar trade. Like acting and other artistic pursuits it provides a strong non-monetary incentive, which takes the form of prestige, fame, a sense of mission or calling. Eventually some writers realise that what they do for pleasure and fame can be remunerative, as was the case with Jane Austen. She published *Sense and Sensibility* at her own expense, and was grateful for the few hundred pounds she got for *Pride and Prejudice*, *Emma* and *Mansfield Park*. Yet for such relatively small sums to be paid to almost unknown writers an entire structure is indispensable: readers, printers, publishers, lending libraries, magazines and reviewers. Even if all writers were content to write in a garret for no money at all, all these other elements would still be required. While the starving creative writer is a fixture of romantic writing, the penniless publisher and the impecunious printer – should they exist – inspire no poetry. Yet they all need a prosperous public keen to spend money on culture.

Politics

So wealth matters, as does population. Does politics matter? Is there a connection between the growth of cultural markets and political institutions? Are more books and newspapers sold, more plays performed, and more music available under liberal than under authoritarian regimes? In the nineteenth century Great Britain and France had huge cultural markets, were major exporters of cultural products and were among the most liberal countries of nineteenth-century Europe. They were also the richest. Which factor was more important, money or freedom? Some, today, argue that the two go together. This was certainly the assumption of progressive spirits in the early nineteenth century such as Madame de Staël: 'The examples of England and America show that free institutions enrich the knowledge and the wisdom of the people.'[33]

By the twentieth century this hypothesis, so comfortable to liberals, was less well-founded. Authoritarian regimes, particularly communist ones, turned out to be major consumers and producers of culture.

In terms of the volume of its cultural production and, more arguably, in terms of its quality (an elusive concept), the USSR held its own with most other countries, as did the communist states of eastern and central Europe.

Under communism Russians read more than Americans, Poles more than Italians. The central Asian populations of the old USSR did better, in terms of literacy and cultural variety, than their counterparts in much of the rest of Central Asia or in the Middle East. While not having access to the full panoply of Western cultural products might be regarded as a major disadvantage, others might argue that, deprived of airport novels, the Russians were forced to read Tolstoy. The fall of communism opened the doors to the delights of reading Tom Clancy, to the detriment of Anton Chekhov. Censorship is certainly a major constraint, but 'free' markets too constrain production and consumption: that which is not commercial is less likely to be produced.

In the eighteenth and nineteenth centuries one of the main effects of censorship was to increase the cost of forbidden books. Dealing in prohibited books could be profitable, though dangerous, for large and well-established booksellers, but the evidence suggests that, in eighteenth-century France, it was relatively easy to obtain them if one was prepared to pay the price.[34] Much of the book trade was in the hands of itinerant hawkers, constantly on the move and often carrying forbidden books and pirated editions. The network of clandestine traders was part of a wider network of sellers that prospered *because* of the restrictions of censorship.[35]

The main effect of censorship was to act as a deterrent, because it is difficult to draw clear guidelines to orient writers eager to write acceptably salacious or politically daring material. The censors themselves were aware of the problem. Chrétien-Guillaume de Malesherbes, in charge of censorship of books in France in the 1750s, wrote in his *Mémoires sur la librairie* (1759) that a distinction should be made between 'obscene' books and 'merely licentious' ones. The former were to be confiscated, but one should turn a blind eye to the latter lest one ended up impounding the whole of Rabelais or the tales of la Fontaine.[36]

Censorship could ruin a publisher. The French publisher Mame went bankrupt because the police seized their stock of Madame de Staël's *De l'Allemagne* in 1810.[37] Even more inhibiting than state censorship was the self-censorship of the publishers, forever poised between the commercial need to publish something which would be bought and talked about and the fear of offending the authorities. Established writers, whose advice is often sought by publishers, may constitute a further obstacle. An unconscious defence of their own turf or of their own positions makes some of them as strict as any state censor. Thus, the well-established poet Thomas Moore, asked by the publishers John Murray to advise on whether to publish Byron's *Don Juan*, ruled against it on grounds of immorality.[38] Murray went ahead nevertheless, and *Don Juan* was, of course, a best-seller (partly because of its immorality).

However, in Europe throughout the nineteenth century the political regulation of culture was considerably loosened. The process was far from uniform, and a relapse into repression occasionally followed liberalisation, but the trend was with liberalism. By the middle of the century the press, publishing and the theatre were less taxed and freer than ever before. In England stamp duty on newspapers was reduced in 1836 and abolished in 1855, while the restriction on theatrical life to a few venues was ended in 1843.

Censorship affected the theatre and other public performances far more than it did the written text, a double standard that has remained in force to this day. On the whole censorship has always been far more stringent for the more popular cultural products. Variety shows have been more censored than operas, serialised novels more than bound volumes, paperbacks more than luxury editions, television more than the cinema and the cinema more than the theatre.

Education

The state role, though, was far from being purely negative in the expansion of cultural markets. A consolidated and centralised political system committed to economic development facilitated the unification of markets. The state education system provided a market for textbooks, taught people a national language, and created future readers. Schools removed children from their local and familial culture and compelled them to face those of others. Separation from the family *milieu*, whether for only a few hours a day or for whole parts of the year, is another factor contributing to cultural dynamism, particularly if the contrast between family values and those of the education system is considerable.

The state has played a dominant role in education only since the nineteenth century. At other times it intervened, if at all, with a political purpose: in seventeenth-century Scotland in order to achieve religious conformity; in eighteenth-century Russia in order achieve political centralisation. In Britain the state made primary education compulsory only in 1881, having overcome the resistance of the Anglican and non-conformist clergy, who had a virtual monopoly on voluntary education, catering for the wealthier classes who paid for educating their own children and did not see why they should pay for other people's.[39] In fact over 50 per cent of children already attended school in 1816, and 80 per cent by 1835.[40] In France, when compulsory education was introduced in 1882 (the Ferry Laws) a significant number of children were already going to school.[41] In the USA, only in 1918 did all states make primary education compulsory for all, but Massachusetts had done so as early as 1852 and New York in 1853.

Universal literacy does not create a market for books, let alone a universal readership. It is true that illiterates don't read, but to read a book it is not sufficient to know how to read. One needs the money to buy it or to borrow it; one needs time free from work; one needs the social incentive to read; and one needs the education to understand it. Not many of these conditions existed for most people in the nineteenth century. And in the twentieth century, when finally the eight-hour day became a reality for most workers, new cheap leisure activities competing with books emerged: the cinema, radio, and above all television – and no skills were required for any of these. The road to reading books was always full of obstacles.

Moreover, the expansion of literacy is not fuelled by the desire to read books. This is not why parents send their children to schools or why states made school compulsory. As the nineteenth century moved on, it became increasingly necessary to have a literate working class and a larger middle class. Before that time literacy was not relevant to most occupations. Then it became apparent that learning how to read would improve one's children's chances in life. For the lower orders, social advancement was a strong inducement for learning how to read. For those who were born in a higher social group, literacy was part of one's world, a necessary social skill. This was not always the case. Neither the Emperor Charlemagne nor King Alfred was taught to read and write.[42] That does not mean they were ignorant or that they were lazy. Einhard in his famous Life of Charlemagne (AD 830) tells us that the emperor could speak Latin, understand Greek, took lessons in grammar, rhetoric, astronomy and mathematics, and 'he also tried to write and used to keep tablets and blanks in bed under his pillow, that at leisure hours he might accustom his hand to form the letters; however, as he did not begin his efforts in due season, but late in life, they met with ill success'.[43]

It is tempting to assume that the history of literacy is one of constant if irregular growth until the arrival of compulsory state education, but the evidence for this is rather slim. A higher percentage of children went to school in Florence in 1338 than in 1911. In the Middle Ages literacy in northern Italy was among the highest in Europe, then Italy lost ground.[44] In Spain around 1625, literacy was probably about the same as in France or Britain, but by 1860 Spain had one of the lowest literacy rates in Europe. Even in the 1920s the majority of the country's population was still unable to read.[45]

After the invention of movable type in the fifteenth century the growth of literacy was faster in Protestant than in Catholic Europe, except for the (Catholic) southern German states. By the middle of the nineteenth century the most literate areas in Europe were Germany, Holland, Switzerland and the Scandinavian countries.[46]

Where was Europe's literacy line? French geographers believed that it bisected France in the middle. The Maggiolo line – named after Louis Maggiolo, author of an 1877 study of French literacy in the seventeenth and eighteenth centuries – started in the west at Saint-Malo and went all the way to Geneva. North of the line the level of schooling and literacy (as defined by the ability to sign one's name) was high, while southern France wallowed in the Mediterranean sun and in backwardness.

The division had come to the surface in the 1820s, and was exploited by anticlerical republicans, for whom ignorance equated with the power of the Church and the strength of Catholicism. They pointed to high illiteracy in reactionary Vendée, but not to the fact that it was low in staunchly Catholic Alsace.[47] A north–south literacy divide was also found in other countries such as Holland, Italy and England.[48]

The anti-Catholics had a point: until the eighteenth century the Roman Catholic Church thought that literacy facilitated the spread of Lutheran ideas into the countryside, which is why the Bishop of Graz-Seckau suggested in the late eighteenth century that rural schools should be abolished 'to dry up the source of poisonous heresy'. The good bishop lost his battle with the secular authorities, but he was symptomatic of Catholicism's fear of popular literacy.[49] The result was that the Austrian territories of Italy had some form of elementary schooling in the early nineteenth century, while in the Papal States the Church remained firmly opposed to the spread of education.[50] In Spain as late as the middle of the eighteenth century the Holy Inquisition even prohibited the publication of popular histories such as *Historia de Carlo Magno* and a *La Historia de la Pasión de Jesu Cristo*.[51] In Russia modernising rulers such as Peter the Great (1672–1725) and Catherine the Great (1729–96) launched literacy campaigns, but with little success: even in 1850 most of the Russian population was illiterate.[52] This is not surprising, as Russia, along with many countries in eastern and central Europe, lacked the literary institutions, the professional writers, the commercially successful publishers and booksellers which had existed in France and England since the early eighteenth century. Above all, Russia lacked the social mobility that could have provided an incentive to have one's children educated.

Educating the poor was regarded as unnecessary or dangerous even in England. In 1723 Bernard Mandeville, in a new edition of his *Fable of the Bees*, argued that: 'To make the Society Happy ... it is requisite that great numbers of them should be Ignorant as well as Poor ... Going to School in comparison to Working is Idleness.' A hundred years later such ideas were still common. A Bill aimed at providing elementary schools was defeated in the House of Lords in 1807. Among those opposed were the Archbishop of Canterbury and the President of the Royal Society, who argued that the project of giving education to the labouring classes would be

> ... prejudicial to their morals and happiness; it would teach them to despise their lot in life, instead of making them good servants in agriculture, and other laborious employment to which their rank in society had destined them; instead of teaching them subordination, it would render them factious and refractory, as was evident in the manufacturing counties; it would enable them to read seditious pamphlets, vicious books, and publications against Christianity; it would render them insolent to their superiors. . .[53]

Perhaps they were not entirely wrong. The people behind the major revolutions in European history (England in 1640, France in 1789 and Russia in 1917) were far from illiterate. Contemporary terrorists are seldom ignorant peasants. One of the benefits of education is a disposition to challenge authority. In 1829 a French journalist wrote that workers might drink less if they used the lending libraries, but what if what their reading turned out to be more damaging to the well-being of society than their drinking?[54] In Vienna all the lending libraries were closed in 1798 out of fear of French revolutionary influence. The ban was lifted in 1811. But the Viennese need not have worried: there were then only four libraries in the city, while Berlin had sixty.[55]

An increase in literacy does not necessarily require an expansion in formal schooling. In Sweden King Charles XI and the Lutheran Church launched a literacy campaign in 1686. Its success was remarkable: by 1740 over 90 per cent of the population could pass a reading test. Children were taught by parents and neighbours, who had been taught by priests. Everyone in the household and in the village was tested once a year. Those who failed could not take communion or marry. The rationale of this campaign, which placed a special priority on the education of women, was essentially conservative: extensive literacy would enable the wider diffusion of religious texts. The result, however, was that the Swedes became the most literate people in eighteenth-century Europe. As a Scottish evangelist wrote during a trip to Sweden, 'You seldom meet anyone above ten or twelve who cannot read.'[56] Many areas which achieved near-universal levels of literacy before the end of the eighteenth century were strongly Protestant: lowland Scotland, the French Huguenots, strongholds of Lutheranism in Germany and of Calvinism in Switzerland.[57] Though Britain was one of the last European countries to adopt the principle of compulsory primary education, most parishes would have had a school even in the sixteenth century, possibly earlier: in the 1470s between 40 and 50 per cent of the population could sign their names.[58]

Measuring literacy is not easy and its significance not obvious. Even today we are not sure what is meant by literacy. Changing definitions may have a significant impact on statistics. For instance, in 1992 the US government report *Adult Literacy in America*, published by the National Center for Education Statistics, sounded the alarm: 47 per cent of Americans scored in the lowest two of five literacy categories. This meant that they could not read a simple news article, or even understand a bus schedule. A new report published ten years later admitted that the statisticians had initially misread the data, and triumphantly announced that illiteracy was really only 5 per cent rather than the initial 'almost 50 per cent'.[59]

The traditional test of literacy consisted of finding out how many people could perform simple operations such as signing their name in the marriage register. This 'signature literacy' does not give an adequate indication of the number of people actually willing and able to read even a simple prose passage.[60]

The development of a market for printed texts requires individuals who are not just able to sign their names, but who are literate enough to read a relatively complex text such as a simple story a few pages long, or an article in a newspaper, or a succession of captions at the bottom of illustrations. There are no satisfactory statistics to measure this kind of literacy. Even the figures of those who completed elementary school are not adequate, because literacy involves not only the acquisition of the skill but its constant use. Those who live in an environment in which reading is unnecessary for everyday purposes will forget how to read. The consequence of all this is that it is likely that in the mid-nineteenth century half the European population (more, if we include Russia) was totally illiterate, and a further 25 per cent would have been unable to understand even a simple written text.[61]

Data on the ability to sign one's name may, however, provide adequate comparative data: the pool of potential readers may be proportionate to the wider population of 'signature-literates'. For instance, in the late 1860s the market for books was far more developed in England and France (where the percentage of those who could not sign their names was 'only' 25–30 per cent) than in Italy, where the 'signature-illiterate' made up 70 per cent of the population.[62]

But how reliable are these statistics? Even for nineteenth-century Italy we rely on contemporary estimates based on extremely dubious statistical knowledge. There was no bishops' investigation as in Sweden, no tradition of signing a marriage registry, and, until 1860, not even a unified country.[63] In any case, most Italians in the nineteenth century could not speak Italian. Even if they could read fluently they would have been able to understand only their local dialect, and not much literature was available in that.

By the end of the nineteenth century we have better data for France, thanks to military service. Of the six million conscripted soldiers investigated in 1881–1900, 8 per cent could neither read nor write, 2 per cent could only read, and 87 per cent could do both but had not reached the end of elementary school. How many of these were likely to read a simple book or a newspaper? If we assume that a potential reader needed to have at least finished primary school – a generous assumption – then the pool of potential readers in France could not have been much higher than 3 per cent. Even in Germany it has been estimated that in 1800, though a quarter of the population of twenty-two million could read, the actual reading public was around 300,000.[64]

From the point of view of the publishing trade (books and newspapers), the expansion of higher education (which was significant in 1790–1810) was of greater importance than that of primary schooling. Higher education – defined as all education into early adulthood – created a demand for books, journals, reviews and textbooks. It enabled a larger and larger proportion of the middle classes to have access to the world of books. The proliferation of the professions (medicine, the law and teaching) widened the importance of possessing intellectual capital, of being informed, and of achieving a certain cultural status.[65]

The trend was towards greater units. The myriad of small states that prevailed in pre-revolutionary Europe disappeared. Literary languages turned into national languages, while dialects began their long decline. Economic unification proceeded apace with the gradual lowering, in the course of the century, of customs barriers. Population grew, as did education. The foundations for the prodigious expansion of cultural markets were laid.

2

Triumphant Languages

The Appeal of Literary Languages

THROUGHOUT THE NINETEENTH CENTURY national languages emerged, demoting regional languages to the rank of dialects. But dialects – languages without armies – do not die without a struggle. The national language, as if conscious of its eventual victory, can be magnanimous. The dialect is allowed to survive in the private sphere, at home, or among old men chattering in pubs and cafés, and women gossiping on the doorstep. The 'real' language is the written language, the language of the future, the language of law and order, the language of education. It rules in the schools and universities, where the cleverer children of those who still speak dialect are sent to find better prospects. The national language rules in the armed forces, where dialect-speakers are conscripted and transformed into citizens and patriots. It reigns supreme in the public administration, where the rules of bureaucracy, the forms to fill in, the letters to write are all in one language. It commands where power and wealth and work can be found. It commands in the cities, in the great centres of learning. This is where, eventually, Breton lost to French, Gaelic to English. This is where Italian, standard German and 'proper' English emerged. It is rare in Europe to find a non-dominant language which is able to produce a literature unless the language dominates elsewhere.

Languages not backed by authoritative literary texts survive with difficulty. However, thanks to a literature and the apparatus of vested interests which accompanies it (teachers, administrators, etc.), written languages such as Sanskrit, Ancient Greek and Latin, though 'dead', have outlasted dialects. As late as 1814 there were more translations into French from Latin than from any other language.[1] Above all, national languages have the singular advantage of being backed by the modern state. Without it, Portuguese, originally the dialect of Lisbon and the literary language used by Luis de Camões (c.1524–80) in the 'national' epic *Os Lusíadas*, would have suffered the fate of Catalan and Andalusian: subjugation by Castilian. Instead, on the back of an empire which included Brazil and large parts of Africa, Portuguese became one of the most spoken languages in the world.

Some of the numerous Italian dialects, such as Sicilian and Venetian, produced a written literature. But it was Tuscan that towered above all the others, thanks to outstanding writers of the calibre of Dante, Francesco Petrarca, and Giovanni Boccaccio, revered throughout Europe. This helped Tuscan to become the literary language of educated Italians, and eventually the language of all Italians after the country became an independent state in 1861. At that time Italian was habitually spoken by only 400,000 people in Tuscany, 70,000 in Rome, and perhaps 160,000 people in the rest of the country, almost all members of the educated classes – in all, 630,000 out of twenty million.[2]

A literary language has further advantages over dialects: because it can be recorded, it is easier to preserve, transport, and diffuse it, and hence to teach it. The recorded text is the currency of the expansion of cultural markets. Texts can be sold at any time, while oral culture can only be sold at the moment of performance – as music was before the invention of notation.

Writing, of course, existed long before the development of cultural markets. Leaving aside the problem of how to distinguish between signs and writing (a drawing of an owl is as much a way of representing the idea of an owl as is the word or the ideogram 'owl'), current historical convention attributes the discovery of alphabetical writing – where signs represent sounds and not things – to the populations of the eastern Mediterranean some 3,500 years ago. But a method for recording information could well have been discovered independently in different environments.[3] Alphabets became the most widespread form of recording words, used throughout the Mediterranean, Europe, North Africa, Central Asia and India, and were eventually adopted as far as Korea (replacing, in the fifteenth century, the Chinese characters hitherto used).

Writing, however, was not used in South America until the arrival of the Spaniards, while south of the Sahara it was established by Arab traders. The major religions of the Eurasian landmass – Judaism, Hinduism, Buddhism, Christianity and Islam – were all book-based, unlike those of the Asante or the Kikuyu in Africa, or the Inca in South America or even the Maya (who, unlike the Inca, used writing).[4]

Writing introduced or strengthened a kind of diglossia (the co-existence of two languages in the same community) between a 'high' or literary form – such as classical Mandarin, Mishnaic or rabbinical Hebrew, classical Arabic (*al-fushā*), Sanskrit and Latin – and a 'low' demotic language.[5] The learned and highly codified language tended to be used almost exclusively by intellectuals, almost all of them male. Unlike the vernacular, that is the *mother* tongue learned from one's mother, the high form was learned by men from men, largely through formal education, and was seldom used in ordinary conversation.[6] Of the tens of thousands of books written in Latin before the eighteenth century, virtually none were written by women.[7] And in sixteenth-century century Europe most printed 'high' literature was in Latin or, in Russia, in Church Slavonic. Of the 6,000 books at the Bodleian library in c.1600, only thirty-six were in English.[8]

Until the eighteenth century Church Slavonic was the written language in Russia. Its use entailed the adoption of the Cyrillic alphabet – as was the case for Belorussian, Serbian, Macedonian and Bulgarian and, until the nineteenth century, even Romanian, a Latin language. Russian as a literary language is therefore fairly recent. It owed its origins to Mikhail Lomonosov (1711–65) – scientist, unsung genius (outside his country), founder of Moscow University and author of a grammar that combined Old Church Slavonic with the vernacular.[9]

The establishment of national languages opened possibilities. It was achieved by fighting on two fronts: against Latin, the 'universal' language, and against possible competitors, the dialects. The elimination of Latin was an act of democratisation because it widened access to cultural markets to new social groups and enabled the diffusion of new genres of writing (narrative and popular non-fiction). The establishment of a text-based culture provides a considerable incentive towards linguistic homogenisation. The official language, in reality the dominant 'dialect', becomes a 'language'.

The case for the use of a 'national' vernacular had been made well before the modern era. Dante's *De Vulgari eloquentia* (On the Common Speech, 1304–05) was a pamphlet (in Latin) in favour of the adoption of Italian. Joachim du Bellay's *La Deffence et illustration de la langue françoyse* (1549) made a similar case on behalf of French.

The language raised to the level of 'national' or official' language was usually that commonly spoken by the political élites. English was what was spoken in London. French was the language spoken in and around Paris. But there were exceptions. Italian was not the language of Piedmont and the House of Savoy, who led the unification of Italy and became the country's first rulers. Their patois was closer to French than to Italian. Sardinia, also ruled by Savoy, was regarded by the Piedmontese as a barbaric land where people spoke an incomprehensible dialect.[10] Yet not even the Piedmontese considered imposing their patois on the rest of the country. The Italian cultural establishment was unanimous: the language of the new state had to be Italian. And so it was, even though most Italians did not speak it and the first king of Italy, Victor Emmanuel II, continued to address his ministers in his local dialect and not in Italian – a language he did not speak well.[11]

Self-advancement was a powerful motive for adopting the ruling language. In Ireland, Gaelic, in decline since the 1690s, was surviving well into the nineteenth century in spite of English rule. Yet in the twenty-five years that followed the famine – the 'Great Hunger' of 1845–50 – the Irish switched to English. This was due more to parental choice than to British oppression. Knowing English, ambitious parents believed, would improve their children's prospects. The Irish used English to promote Irish nationalism, and Gaelic remained confined to rural backwardness.[12] The prominence of Dublin in British cultural life further contributed to the victory of English; Dublin was the seat of a major university and an important publishing centre (its printers were cheaper and more efficient than London's).[13] Most authors published in London were thus also published in Dublin – sometimes in Dublin first. Thus Ireland was never a backward colony, but a major centre of intellectual production.

So prevalent was the idea that a nation required a written literature in its 'own' language that nationalist intellectuals proceeded to write down what they, somewhat arbitrarily, defined as the national culture. Literature, explained the German scholar Friedrich Schlegel (1772–1829) in his 1815 Vienna lectures, was the means 'by which the spirit of an age and the character of a nation express themselves ... An artistic and highly finished literature is undoubtedly one of the greatest advantages any nation can possess.'[14]

What patriotic intellectuals wanted was to ennoble 'their' language by giving it a literature. And they were right: written-down words mattered more than words flying into the air. The first printed Bibles in translation were all in literary languages that have handsomely survived into the twenty-first century: German (1466), Italian (1471), French (1487), Dutch (1526),

English (1535), Swedish (1541) and Danish (1550). Throughout Europe, especially among submerged, repressed or weak nationalities, intellectuals produced textbooks and dictionaries, and collected folk stories using a suitable spoken language.

Major dictionaries had started appearing in the seventeenth century, but the great century for dictionaries was the nineteenth. In 1854 the Grimm brothers published the first volume of *Deutsches Wörterbuch*, the standard German dictionary (completed only in 1954). This provided the impetus for Émile Littré's *Dictionnaire de la langue française*, the Dutch *Woordenboek der Nederlandsche Taal* and the *New English Dictionary* (NED), later known as the *Oxford English Dictionary* (1857–1928).

The nineteenth century was also a great century for grammars, a science at which German scholars excelled. As a consequence the standardisation of the written form of many Slav languages was based on the scientific criteria established by German scholars, and several Slav grammars were actually written by Germans, such as G.S. Bandke (Polish), Jernej Kopitar (Slovenian) and Josef Dobrovslky (Czech), all published around 1808.[15] In Hungary the language reform movement, led by Ferenc Kazinczy (1759–1831), created new words by translating terms from foreign languages, standardised grammatical rules and enriched the vocabulary with thousands of new words.[16] The Hungarian language was seen by the Hungarian nobility as integral to the Magyar identity. The modernisation of the language was accompanied by the development of literature in Hungarian, mainly poetry: Mihály Csokonai Vitéz, Sándor Petöfi and Mihály Vörösmarty.[17]

In Bulgaria and Serbia, where Slaveno-Serbian was the language of Orthodox liturgy, not that spoken by the common people, Vuk Stefanović Karadžić (1787–1864) produced a grammar (1814) and a dictionary (1818) in order to establish a literary language. This was based on the peasant dialect spoken in Herzegovina but understood in most of Serbia and Croatia. In Croatia the nationalist intelligentsia opted for the Štovakian dialect – once used by Dubrovnik Renaissance writers – as the basis for the development of modern Serbo-Croat.[18] In parts of south-eastern Europe, the attempt to establish linguistic uniformity continued well into the twentieth century.

In Albania – unbeknown to the rest of the world – four main dialects fought it out for centuries with varying results. Finally, between 1909 and the Second World War the official language was declared to be the Gheg dialect – still spoken in Kosovo. After the war, however, the quite different Tosk dialect was declared to be 'Albanian', but its victory as the language 'spoken by the entire nation' was achieved only in the middle of the 1980s, more than seventy years after Albania had become independent.[19]

It was particularly difficult to construct a national literature in the Balkans, because during the centuries of Turkish rule there was no substantial local aristocratic élite or even a middle class, the class which generated writers and readers.[20] When the Turks were driven out in the later half of the nineteenth century, the local populations were overwhelmingly rural with no significant national bourgeoisie – Hegel and Marx called them 'non-historic nations'. When they finally acquired some vestiges of nationhood, they were ruled by largely military-political élites with little cultural identity (a state of affairs common in many post-colonial societies). To achieve a written culture in a small and poor country under foreign domination is an uphill task. The members of local élites had usually studied abroad or in foreign schools, and had little in common with the local population.

Albania, for instance, did not have a single secular school in any of the four versions of Albanian until 1887, when finally one was established in Korça. And it was for boys only; girls had to wait another four years. Previously, middle-class Albanians had been educated in foreign schools funded by their wealthy countrymen who had emigrated to Romania, Bulgaria, Italy and Egypt. Until 1912, when the country became independent, the languages used in education were Turkish, Greek or Serbian, and occasionally Italian, not Albanian.[21] The first 'Albanian' newspapers were in Greek and Italian (*L'Albanese d'Italia*, 1848). How to write Albanian was also a problem. At the Alphabet Congress of 1908 no agreement was reached over whether to use Latin or Arabic characters – though subsequently the Latin form was adopted.[22] Changing characters occurs more frequently than is thought, especially in weak countries dominated by others. Most Western countries have had the same Roman alphabet for centuries, but in 1928 Turkey, under the dictatorship of its modernising ruler Kemal Atatürk, changed the alphabet from the Arabic to the Roman. In Azerbaijan, in the Azeri language (similar to Turkish) the Arabic script was abandoned in 1940 in favour of the Cyrillic script. After the fall of communism a ten-year transition to the Roman script was begun, and was completed in 2001.

From the end of the fifteenth century Polish gained in importance, displacing Latin as the administrative language of the multi-ethnic Polish-Lithuanian commonwealth. This was partly due to the development of a Polish literary language under the influence of the Reformation. By the seventeenth century Polish had become the cultural language of the Lithuanian and Ruthenian nobility. But even in Poland language could not be used to establish the identity of the nation, since its boundaries, such as they were, included peasants who did not speak Polish but Ukrainian, Belorussian and Lithuanian. The great unifying factor was Catholicism, including national-cum-religious symbols such the Black Madonna of Częstochowa.[23]

Poland had ceased to be a state, but at least it had been one. Without statehood it is not easy to produce a literature. Macedonia, which gained its independence only in 1991, had never been a state and had no written literature until the nineteenth century.[24] Though a written form of Finnish had existed since the fourteenth century, Finnish literature is also relatively recent. This is hardly surprising, considering that the Finnish language emerged out of several dialects only between 1820 and 1860, that Finland's small population was long trapped between two major linguistic groups (Slavonic and Germanic), that the country was attached to Sweden for six centuries until 1809 and then became subordinated to the Russian tsar, and that its upper classes spoke Swedish.[25]

Norwegian too became a literary language rather late. The country itself was dominated by Denmark from 1523 until 1814, when the Treaty of Kiel transferred it to Sweden. Norway became independent only in 1905. It had no agreed language. The dominant classes spoke a language close to Danish known as *rigsmål* in the nineteenth century and *bokmål* (the 'book language' or literary language) after 1929. The common people spoke *landsmål* (the 'language of the countryside'), today known as *nynorsk* (new Norwegian). The 'book language' triumphed over the popular language, which is today used by less than 15 per cent of the population.[26]

One can wax sentimental about languages disappearing, but the fact is that a uniform language facilitates the expansion of cultural markets. And larger markets elbow out weaker ones. In eighteenth-century Scotland, as the reading public turned to English, so did Scottish writers. Gaelic – occasionally used in poetry (by Robert Burns, for example) – disappeared in the course of the nineteenth century even as a spoken form, except in peripheral areas such as the Western Isles. The process was accelerated by the emigration of one and half million Scots between 1861 and 1913, the equivalent of 30 per cent of the 1911 population.[27] The loss of the language, however, constitutes an overall cultural gain, since – thanks to English – elements of Scottish (or Irish) culture could become widely diffused and adapted to an extent unimaginable for other small nations.

Language and Markets

When, in 1848, Jacob Grimm declared at the Frankfurt Assembly: 'It is not rivers or mountains that form the womb of a people; rather, their language alone establishes the borders of a people, dispersed over mountain and stream,' he was upholding an idea that had been common currency among nationalists for over half a century – that a people is the essence of all those who speak the same language.[28] But though all Germans spoke 'German', it was not yet the (standard) German that eventually prevailed, the successor to the High German used in the Lutheran Bible. The 'German' Germans spoke was so diverse that communication between speakers of non-contiguous regions was almost impossible. There was no uniformity, and hence, if Grimm was right, there was no national essence. 'Being German' had to be constructed along with nationhood.

This was true even in France. At the beginning of the nineteenth century only a minority of those residing within French territory spoke French. The rest spoke a multitude of dialects. One million spoke Breton, another million spoke German, one hundred thousand spoke Basque, others spoke Flemish or Italian. The south-west of France was linguistically fragmented into numerous patois. Even at the end of the nineteenth century, in Picardie, a few miles from Paris, many spoke a dialect few Parisians could understand. In Marseilles, a great linguist declared, 'one needs an interpreter'.[29] In Brittany, Limousin and Provence interpreters were needed in law courts until the end of the nineteenth century.[30]

The strength of dialects dismayed French revolutionaries such as the abbot Henri Grégoire (1750–1831), a brave man who led the battle for the abolition of slavery and for the emancipation of the Jews (1788) before turning against the dialects. In 1794 ('Year Two of the République, *une et indivisible*') he published his uncompromisingly entitled *Sur la necessité et les moyens d'anéantir les patois et d'universaliser l'usage de la langue française* (Why and How the Patois Must be Destroyed and French Made Universal).[31] Its implementation turned out to be far less repressive than the title suggests. If the revolutionaries wanted to be understood, it was necessary to use the local language, which is why the Abbé Chambon, a correspondent of Grégoire, had to use Catalan in Perpignan to explain the decrees of the National Assembly.[32] The Abbé Grégoire lamented that French, though loved and used throughout Europe, was barely spoken in France. French citizens spoke Breton, Normand, Picard, Walloon, Flemish, Champenois, Franc-comtois, Catalan, Gascon, Languedocien, etc.

An Italianate dialect was spoken in Corsica. German, lamentably, was spoken on the 'French' Rhine, and a 'poor Negro idiom' (Creole) in some of the colonies. The result, added Grégoire, was that six million Frenchmen could not speak a word of French, and another six could not sustain a normal conversation in it. Unless French became universal, public administration would continue to be the preserve of the 'respectable classes'.

Strictly speaking, French had been compulsory for state transactions since the sixteenth century, but private transactions had been left to their own devices. On the basis of Grégoire's report, the Republican Decree of 20 July 1794 established that all contracts had to be written in French.[33] This was a start. Education, social and geographical mobility, favouritism, repression, the expansion of public administration, the press, books and conscription did the rest. Linguistic harmonisation proceeded, and though the resistance of the patois was formidable, French eventually won the day. Patois was confined to family and village.

There were, of course, many speakers of French outside France, particularly in Wallonia (a province of Belgium, a state created in 1830 by the union of French-speaking Wallonia with Dutch-speaking areas), where the *langue d'oïl* (from which modern French originates) prevailed, while most of southeastern France still spoke variations of the *langue d'oc*. French was also spoken in Switzerland, where in 1815 the French cantons of Neuchâtel, Valais and Geneva were integrated into the new multi-language Helvetic Confederation. And there were also French-speakers in Canada and in the colonies. These French-speaking communities survived – at least in part – because what was a minority language in their country was, in the wider world, a major international language. The benefit accruing to the cultural industry was considerable. It has been estimated that in the 1760s, 60 per cent of books not allowed by the French state were published outside its borders, mainly in Flanders and Switzerland.[34]

The francophone Belgian bourgeoisie developed its identity first by imposing, until relatively recently, French as the official language, and then by regarding French literature as their literature.[35] While the Walloons were able to connect with a wider and internationally influential linguistic community, Flemish writers produced a literature barely known in the rest of the world, unlike their painters. Pictures reach where words cannot. It helps to write in an international language. Would Hergé and Georges Simenon (the best-known Belgian writers) have achieved international fame had their Tintin and Maigret spoken Flemish?

Flemish culture, if it wanted to travel, had to be turned into French. Thus the Belgian writer Charles de Coster wrote the popular *Les Aventures d'Ulenspiegel* in French (1867), adapting a picaresque medieval German story about the Flemish hero of the resistance against Spain and clerical obscurantism. This made Ulenspiegel famous.

The pull of France was such that 'Belgian literature' was never regarded, outside Belgium, as having any autonomy.[36] The price paid by Belgian national pride was considerable. Well-known twentieth-century Belgian writers such as Maurice Maeterlinck (Nobel Prize 1911), Georges Simenon and Marguerite Yourcenar, moved to Paris and were regarded by all and sundry as French writers. They were simply following in the footsteps of pillars of 'French' literature such as the Swiss-born Jean-Jacques Rousseau and Benjamin Constant.

In 1800, the linguistic boundaries of German, English and French were wider than those of Germany, England and France. This was also true of Greece, then under Turkish occupation. The country was small in size and population. Athens, even in 1834 when it became the capital, was a poor village of ten thousand inhabitants. The population of the entire country was around 650,000. They were mostly illiterate. The obstacles to the development of cultural markets appeared formidable. Nevertheless, book production was of some significance, not because of the Greeks of Greece but because of Greeks abroad, notably in Alexandria (Egypt), then the first Greek city in the world, where a considerable intellectual community looked towards Europe and European literature to provide the cultural basis for an anti-Turkish nationalism.

In Italy – as we have seen – the situation was different. Italian was barely spoken abroad, or indeed inside the country. The language problem could only be tackled after political unification. In 1862 Emilio Broglio, then minister of education, appointed a commission presided over by Alessandro Manzoni, the country's most illustrious writer, to determine how to 'universalise' *la buona lingua* (the proper language) – seventy years after Grégoire had tried to do the same in France. No consensus was reached and Manzoni resigned. Much of the disagreement concerned the kind of Tuscan to be used. Should it be that of literature, that of educated Florentines, or that of the common Florentine people?[37]

In fact dialects continued to prevail for everyday usage among most Italians until the 1950s. Their likely extinction in the near future – the new generations are growing up in almost complete ignorance of the local dialect

– will have been the outcome of mass education, internal immigration and, above all, television, rather than a deliberate political act.

This long-lasting diglossia partly explains a phenomenon examined at greater length later on: the almost complete lack of a popular literature in Italy. Italian had been, after Latin, the dominant European language in the sixteenth and seventeenth centuries. Then it lost ground to French. For six hundred years Italian literature 'floated' – as the Italian literary critic Alberto Asor Rosa wrote – 'in an immense ocean of non-Italian-speakers'.[38] The majority of those who spoke only the local dialect were illiterate. So any writer who wished to be widely read had to use the language of the élite minority. Inevitably, this made the construction of a text-based wider popular culture somewhat difficult. In nineteenth-century Italy, popular narrative was unable to match that of either France or Britain: the narrow linguistic base of Italian prevented it.

Some dialects, however, could be used in a literary market, as long as they found favour with the upper classes. The contrasting fortunes of the Milanese poet Carlo Porta and his great Roman counterpart Giuseppe Gioachino Belli is an interesting case. Porta, writing during the Napoleonic period, was, unlike Belli, very popular in his lifetime.[39] Milanese dialect was spoken by everyone regardless of social status. The educated classes also spoke French but not Italian. As a result Porta's poems were published and circulated among an educated public. He even tried to translate Dante's *Divine Comedy* into Milanese.

Belli's satirical sonnets, written in Roman dialect (and inspired by Porta's Milanese poetry), built on the tradition of anonymous flyers or *pasquinate* (so-called because the flyers were attached to the statue of Pasquino), irreverent rhymes dating from the sixteenth century. But – unlike Milan, Venice or Naples – the Roman élites did not speak this dialect, and those who did, the common people, were illiterate. Porta's market was limited to Milan and its province, but Belli's was non-existent. Belli was no fool. He knew his works would not sell. He wrote in order to describe what he believed the people thought, in order to produce a kind of literary anthropology: 'Here I depict,' he wrote in the introduction to his sonnets, 'the ideas of an ignorant pleb.'[40] Belli never acknowledged authorship, and tried to burn his impertinent poems when stricken by the remorseful pangs of Catholicism. He became known after his death, when Luigi Morandi in 1886–89 edited an anthology of his writings.[41]

In wealthy cities dialects could be used successfully in theatrical performances. In eighteenth-century Venice Goldoni had written plays in Venetian dialects for sophisticated and learned audiences. But this restricted the market. Venice was too small, Goldoni's enemies too numerous, and greater glory and more money could be obtained elsewhere – or so he thought, mistakenly. In 1762 Goldoni went to Paris to manage the Théâtre-Italien, but Parisians expected clownish Italian improvisations. Eventually the success of the *Bourreau bienfaisant*, a comedy he wrote in French for the marriage of the future Louis XVI, got him a royal pension, but it was revoked after the French Revolution and he died in poverty.

Using local dialects remained acceptable in the theatre for the whole of the nineteenth century and beyond because the local bourgeoisie was more comfortable with them. The playwright Luigi Capuana even translated some of his Italian plays (*Giacinta*) into his native Sicilian dialect to achieve a greater success.[42] In Vienna the major popular theatres specialised in comic dialect plays.[43]

It was different for books, as Alessandro Manzoni realised. In 1827 he published the first edition of his celebrated novel *I Promessi sposi* (The Betrothed), written in an Italian reverberating with French words and archaic expressions. After all, Italian was not Manzoni's first language, which was the Milanese dialect, nor his second, which was French, but his third. Following a stay in Florence he rewrote the novel using the kind of Florentine spoken by the educated classes. This second version, which has circulated ever since, was published in serialised form in 1840–42 to great acclaim. It was soon consecrated as the model for modern Italian literature. Writing in Italian meant prestige as well as a wider market – an irresistible combination.

'Italian' had long been a literary tradition, but was not yet a national language. It suffered from severe handicaps: poverty, the absence of a central authority (until 1861), and the resistance of the Catholic Church to education in the countryside. There were, however, counterbalancing factors: the strong network of urban life and the inheritance of the extraordinary and unparalleled contribution made by Italy in the fourteenth and fifteenth centuries to Western culture. Supreme in all forms of art and science, Italy had the best engineers, architects, mathematicians, scientists, bankers, accountants, explorers, musicians, painters, sculptors, poets, political scientists and historians. While printing was invented in northern Europe, by the end of the fifteenth century the centre of European book production was Venice, the richest city in Europe. Its printers even used Greek and Cyrillic characters to export their production to south-eastern Europe.[44]

By the nineteenth century, such splendour mattered little. Italy had become a laggard country, in awe of foreign achievements and trailing behind France and Great Britain in most cultural fields, with one notable exception: opera.

The Hegemony of French

In the early years of the nineteenth century, Madame de Staël, travelling in Germany, remarked that 'the Poles and the Russians' – meaning, of course, those she met – spoke only French and did not deign to speak German.[45] For much of the century French remained the hegemonic language among the European élites. It left its mark in the language of diplomacy: *chargé d'affaires, attaché*; dance: *minuet, gavotte, chaconne* and *sarabande*; ballet: *entrechat, rond de jambe, jeté, arabesque*; in the new economic science: *laissez-faire, entrepreneur*. A considerable part of military vocabulary is of French origin: *cavallerie, dragon, cuirassier* and *artillerie*. Of course all European languages borrow heavily from non-European ones. The words admiral and magazine come from Arabic (*al-amir*: commandant, and *makzin*), tomato and chocolate are Aztec, puma is in Quechua, maize is in Arawak (a Native American language), jungle and veranda are Hindi, divan Persian. But many of such extra-European words were first adopted by a dominant European language, usually French or English (or Spanish for many Arab words), and then made their way into other European languages.

By the end of the eighteenth century translations from French dominated book production, and many translations from other languages such as English, Spanish, and Portuguese were re-translations from French.[46] The habit of re-translating still endures in popular literature. A romantic novel published in Italy in 1981 as *Eva e il mercenario* was a translation of the 1978 French *Ève et le mercenaire* – itself a translation from the original *Time of the Temptress* (1977) by Violet Winspear.[47]

French hegemony was facilitated by the demographic factor: in 1801 the French outnumbered the English by three to one. France was at the centre of the Continent at a time when Great Britain was really an offshore island.[48]

Leipzig – the centre of the eighteenth-century European book trade – had more booksellers trading with their Parisian counterparts than with booksellers in any other German city. Madame de Staël was astonished by the number of French books sold in Leipzig. She claimed that she had met innkeepers and travelling salesmen who were familiar with French literature and the ideas of the Enlightenment.[49] In the early 1780s, out of the 1,582 foreign-language titles in the category 'art and letters' available in Leipzig bookshops, 41 per cent were French, 21 per cent English, 19 per cent Italian, and 8 per cent Dutch. Of the 310 translations into German, 160 – more than half – were from French, 102 from English, thirteen from Italian, and eleven from Dutch. Until the late eighteenth century most Dutch literary journals were written in French.[50]

At the court of Frederick II of Prussia – who despised German – the only language allowed was French. In 1784 the winner of the 1784 prize of the Berlin Academy of Sciences was Antoine de Rivarol, a Frenchman who had championed the superiority of French (*Discours sur l'universalité de la langue française*).[51] His argument was based on the evident superiority of French literature (English literature, from Chaucer to Milton via Shakespeare, was not highly regarded), on the greatness of Louis XIV and, above all, on the greater logic of French: 'What is not clear is not French; what is not clear is English, Italian, Greek, or Latin' – all languages based on mere instinct and passion.[52]

These views prevailed for decades, until such times when, with equal assurance, people claimed that German was a language suited to philosophy, or that English was clearer. But at the time, Rivarol's opinions were shared by most as a matter of course, and by the French intelligentsia from Montesquieu to Voltaire. Foreigners agreed, from the King of Prussia to Carlo Goldoni, who in his *Mémoires* – written in French (as were those of his fellow Venetian Giacomo Casanova) – wrote that the French set the intellectual and civil standards for the whole of Europe.[53] Even in the eighteenth century intellectuals were celebrated in France. One could buy a pipe carved in Voltaire's likeness or play with cards bearing the faces of the *philosophes*.[54]

The British were more attentive to French culture than to that of other countries. British aristocrats were eager to follow the French in fashion, in luxury products and in food, though they also regarded the French as effeminate and/or immoral.

In eighteenth-century Russia 'France' was coterminous with 'Europe', and hence with civilisation. This francophilia, deliberately built up by Peter the Great and Catherine the Great – another who wrote her *Mémoires* in French – withstood German influence and survived even the Napoleonic wars. Since Louis XIV most of the Continent, claimed Madame de Staël, had devoted their *amour-propre* to imitating the French.[55]

The only possible rival to French was English. Eighteenth-century British novels were translated on the Continent almost immediately. British periodicals such as the *Edinburgh Review* and the *Quarterly Review* were avidly read, imitated and plagiarised. British thinkers were translated, commented upon and discussed. In Italy anglophilia became a distinctive trait of the progressive élites in the eighteenth century.[56]

Even in France admiration for British liberties was common among the progressive intelligentsia before the Revolution. British thinkers were revered. Adam Smith's *The Theory of Moral Sentiments* (1759) was translated into French in 1764, ahead of Germany (1770) and Russia (1868). His *Wealth of Nations* (1776) was translated into French only two years after its publication in English.[57] British 'Gothic' novels became fashionable, as did British travel books.

For obvious reasons French anglophilia subsided during the Napoleonic Wars, but it returned with a vengeance during the Restoration. The image of the stylish dandy became popular, as were British-style clubs. In 1834 the most exclusive club for *le tout Paris* was the Jockey Club – named after the English horse-racing club created in 1750. Jockey Clubs were established wherever there was a strong British influence, as in Buenos Aires. Byron (or 'Biron' as the French occasionally spelt it) became an irresistible iconic figure: a great poet dying on the battlefield fighting for Greek independence.

Continental authors peopled their stories with noble lords. Balzac's first novels were signed Lord R'Hoone (an anagram of his first name, Honoré).[58]

The French belief in their superiority over all other Europeans was held with less conviction when it came to Great Britain, because British economic advances had been too impressive to be ignored, and its liberties were more extensive than those of France.

Yet French cultural hegemony increased throughout the nineteenth century, helped by the success of romantic and realist literature. Its authors, from Balzac to George Sand, from Dumas to Hugo, were known throughout Europe. In 1870 the prestigious journal the *Revue des deux mondes* claimed to have 28,000 subscribers *outside* France.[59]

The French remained quite sure that theirs was 'the best' language, and did not bother to use powerful arguments to demonstrate it. Here is Edmond Arnould's, in his treatise on literary theory published in 1858:

> Italian is too sweet, Spanish too resonant; besides, these two languages
> are entirely southern and as such not congenial to the anatomy of northern
> people. Moreover, the nations they represent, far from being able to
> extend their influence, are inspired by that of foreigners. I would exclude

German for similar reasons: it is too northern. Its harshness and lack of precision is unacceptable to the peoples of the south. English, also too Germanic, has spread, thanks to the adventurous nature of the nation that speaks it, to the corners of the world, but it has taken root exclusively among the Anglo-Saxon race – in any case it has a fine future in the new world where it is called upon to civilise a continent. As for the Slavonic languages I shall say nothing of them as they are unknown to me. There remains, then, French . . .'[60]

And English?

Thanks to immigration and the rapidly expanding British Empire, English gained ground over French and Spanish throughout the nineteenth century. Firmly implanted in the USA, English became the language of forcibly deported Africans and waves of immigrants speaking Italian, Yiddish, Polish, Chinese, German and Swedish. But what was this English? The origin of contemporary standard English was the London dialect of c.1400 (itself a hybrid of various Essex patois). This is hardly surprising given the centrality of London in the mercantile and political life of the country. Even before becoming the home of the printing industry, London English was used in a vast number of manuscripts copied by Chancery scribes who set the standard for all copyists.[61] William Tyndale's translation of the Bible, the first English text to be printed (from 1525, albeit in Cologne), virtually established what we regard as standard sixteenth-century vernacular English, and formed the basis for the Authorised Version. Yet until c.1700 the varieties of 'English' were so many that there was no national language.[62] In the late eighteenth century a progressive codification of the language resulted in what was later known as Queen's or King's English, received pronunciation, standard English, Oxford English and, in the twentieth century, BBC English. Yet dialects were still alive at the end of the nineteenth century. In 1877 there were still forty almanacs published in dialect – all but four of them in the West Riding of Yorkshire. In Lancashire there were at least twenty different forms of dialects.[63]

English was relatively more widespread in England than French was in France, not to speak of Italian in Italy. However, unlike the various Continental countries, the class element prevailed over the regional one. A regional accent or a regional dialect denoted a lower-class origin. Genteel Jane Eyre, the eponymous heroine of Charlotte Brontë's novel (1847), can barely understand the language of the children she teaches in the rural locality she gets to after leaving Mr Rochester.[64] They do not belong to her world. In Elizabeth Gaskell's *North and South* (1854–55) the author deliberately uses some dialect words to stress not the regional diversity between north and south, but the fact that northerners could not speak proper English. In music halls and later in films and radio and television plays, a regional accent would be used to represent, often pejoratively, ordinary working-class characters.[65]

The contempt for popular manners and language was given official form by the 1861 Parliamentary Report on the State of National Education. Its hostility to regional speech was shared by educated classes throughout the country, who regarded its use, justifiably, as an obstacle to social advancement.[66]

English would become an international language only in the second half of the twentieth century, largely because it was also the language of the USA. Nevertheless its global reach was already obvious in the middle of the nineteenth century, when Jacob Grimm announced that 'English may be called justly a language of the world and seems, like the English nation, to be destined to reign in future with still more extensive sway over all parts of the globe.'[67] The country combined great wealth, a thriving culture, major scientific achievements and political freedom. There could be no greater contrast, for intellectuals throughout Europe, than that between the thriving and apparently free British press and its heavily controlled counterparts in Russia, Austria, the various Italian states and Prussia. The political calm prevailing in Great Britain contrasted with the turmoil of France. Goethe was conscious of this, and gave in 1828 a rather sunny description of what it must have felt like to be an arrogant Englishman:

> ... the English in general appear to have certain advantages over many others. Here in Weimar, we see only a few of them, and probably by no means the best; but what fine handsome people they are! And however young they come here, they feel no embarrassment in this foreign atmosphere; their deportment in society is as easy as if they were lords of everywhere and the whole world belonged to them ... The happiness of personal freedom, the consciousness of an English name and of the importance attached to it by other nations, is an advantage even to the children; for in their own family, as well as in school, they are treated with far more respect, and enjoy a far freer development, than is the case with us Germans.[68]

Though English was not (yet) a fashionable language, its literature had been a major presence on the Continent since the early eighteenth century. Daniel

Defoe's *Robinson Crusoe* was translated into French, German and Dutch within a year of its publication in 1719, and was soon abridged to make it more popular. It has remained one of the great novels of all times, endlessly adapted. Jean-Jacques Rousseau recommended it as the first book 'my Émile will read; it will be, for a long while, his entire library'.[69] In 1832 it was the most used non-religious fiction book in primary French schools, adapted as *Robinson dans son île*.[70]

Jonathan Swift's *Gulliver's Travels* – published anonymously in 1726 – was almost as successful. It was immediately translated into French, and from French into German and other languages. The novel's satirical intentions were lost in the translation, though, and it was regarded as an adventure book suitable for children.

At the time translators would take considerable liberties with texts, adapting them to the requirements of the domestic market. Thus part of the success of Laurence Sterne's novels in Germany was due to Johann-Joachim Christoph Bode's translations, which were even more jocular and idiosyncratic than the originals.[71]

In eighteenth-century France, England was admired by Enlightenment philosophers as the seat of liberties, but the English were often regarded as uncouth, and occasionally described as savages, even *Europe's* savages (well before the arrival of football hooligans) by the likes of Robert-Martin Lesuire, author of the satirical *Les Sauvages de l'Europe* (1760). Here an unfortunate couple of French anglophiles, admirers of Richardson and Fielding, are taken from the boat to London in a shabby carriage driven by an inebriated coachman. Arrived at an inn, they are made to sit at a dirty table and served barely cooked beef; they are horrified by the public executions at Tyburn, by the coarseness of the people, by the easily arranged marriages of which one of the travellers falls victim. It is with great relief that they return to Paris. Twenty years later Lesuire returned to his target and published *Les Amants François à Londres ou Les Délices de l'Angleterre* (1780), a novel about another unfortunate couple visiting an England where the people drink only beer and do not know how to use forks.[72]

The defeat of Napoleon and the Restoration brought about a wave of anglophilia in France too, especially in royalist circles, where it was fashionable to affect an English accent. Between 1825 and 1901 the *Revue Britannique* consisted entirely of articles translated from British periodicals such as the *Edinburgh Review*. In 1829 a new journal, inspired in tone and content by the *Edinburgh Review*, was launched; it was *La Revue des deux mondes*, which soon became the most prestigious French journal of the nineteenth century, and is still published in the twenty-first.[73]

After the Napoleonic wars some Russian newspapers and periodicals extolled British culture against that of the French, helped by the considerable interest in *Robinson Crusoe* (translated into Russian in 1764, with four editions by 1797), Byron's love life and poetry, Walter Scott's historical novels, and admiration for British press freedom.[74] By the 1830s articles from the *Edinburgh Review*, the *Quarterly Review*, *Blackwood's Edinburgh Magazine* and the *Westminster Review* (founded by Jeremy Bentham and James Mill in 1824) were regularly translated. The 'Lake' poets William Wordsworth and Samuel Taylor Coleridge were so admired in Russia that British press criticisms of Coleridge puzzled the Russians.

This cultural flow was almost entirely one-way. Early-nineteenth-century Russian literature – including Pushkin and Lermontov – was virtually unknown in Britain.[75]

Translations could, of course, enable texts to penetrate foreign markets, though they increased the costs of production – as if they were tariffs levied against imported books. A text written in a language known by local intellectual élites (i.e. a language like French) would have had a head start. Its chances of being translated for the rest of the reading public were high. Countries with a large cultural production, such as France and Britain, remained modest importers. The percentage of translation into English was, in 1800, 3.78 per cent of total production; in 1870 it was even lower: 2.88 per cent.[76]

A corpus of international literature was being formed. In c.1800 the educated élites – still the majority of the book-reading public – were expected to have read the main Greek and Latin classics, some of the works of the Renaissance (especially the Italians), and some of the French classics. When it came to recent literature, all they were expected to know, apart from that of their own country, was that of France and Great Britain. Outside these two countries, for most of the nineteenth century very few writers managed to break into the European markets. Patriotism and resentment against dominant languages such as English, French, Russian, Ottoman and High German led writers to write in 'their' language: Czech, Hungarian, Ukrainian, Serbian, Polish, Norwegian, etc.[77] In so doing they inevitably confined themselves to a much smaller market – a situation faced today by many African writers, who by writing in English or French open themselves to a far wider market than if they use 'their' language.

To write in a language which has limited appeal is a major handicap even for great writers. This was true in the nineteenth century even for writers in German, a language which was almost as widely spoken as French and English, and which produced writers of the fame of Goethe, Schiller, Herder and the Grimm brothers – all known and read throughout Europe. In much of Slavic-speaking Europe German was becoming an influential language. Indeed, it was the main means of communication at the first Congress of Slavic intellectuals in 1837.[78] German influence grew after 1850 thanks to the formation of a powerful German state centred around Prussia in the 1860s and the existence of a multinational empire, dominated by Austria. The Germans, however, produced relatively no internatinally popular literature in the course of the nineteenth century, no novelists of the fame of Dumas or Dickens or Balzac or Verne. The German language travelled mainly because of the excellence of its universities and the diffusion of its social sciences and philosophy. It never seriously endangered the dominance of French or the growing power of English.

3

Publishing

Books and Money

AS PUBLISHERS OFTEN TELL THEIR AUTHORS, publishing is not a hugely profitable business. In the nineteenth century – though fortunes could be made in publishing – they were probably right. The great tycoons were making steel, digging coal, running railways. The bankers financing them got even richer. And richer still was parasitic Old Wealth living off landed estates.[1] The book trade was small and risky. Instead of producing large quantities of the same commodity – such as timber or steel – a publisher had to produce a large number of titles competing against each other. The success of each title was (and is) often based on guesswork. It was rare for every book published to cover its costs. Originally authors were paid – when they were paid – an agreed sum on publication and had no share in any profit the book made. Publishers bore the main risks, but if a book made a profit they were not required to share it with the author, as is the case now. The author's enhanced fame, however, would increase his bargaining power and he was free to go to other publishers who had incurred none of the risks inherent in a first book.

The process of publication consisted in a writer writing a text, a publisher preparing it for the printer, a printer to print it and a bookseller to sell it to a reader.[2] Until the end of the eighteenth century it was a common practice for publishers to sell the uncut and unbound sheets to booksellers who then bound the book.[3] Often the roles of printers, publishers and booksellers were combined. Some writers were printers (Samuel Richardson, author of *Clarissa*), some were publishers (Horace Walpole, author of *The Castle of Otranto*), but their functions remained distinct.[4]

Towards the end of the eighteenth century the most usual combination was for printers to be publishers too, as was Joseph Johnson, one of half a dozen printers located in the City of London. He was rather successful, publishing and printing over one hundred books a year – a remarkably distinguished list which included Samuel Taylor Coleridge, William Blake, William Godwin, Tom Paine, Mary Wollstonecraft, William Wordsworth, Joseph Priestley (the scientist), Benjamin Franklin and Thomas Malthus.[5]

The economics of publishing are not easy to calculate. Martin Lyons tried to do so for Balzac's first important book, *Les Chouans* (1830). The initial print run of 1,000 copies cost 4,500 livres. Balzac was paid 1,000 livres; the paper cost another 1,000. To this should be added 1,200 livres for printing and 1,300 livres for binding, advertising, interest payments, etc. The publishers sold the printed copies to booksellers and lending libraries for five livres each – obtaining 5,000 livres. After deducting the costs, they were left with a profit of 500 livres, half Balzac's earnings. The booksellers, having bought the books for five livres, sold them at twelve – making, if all books were sold, a total of 12,000 livres. Thus the booksellers' income amounted to 7,000 livres from which one should subtract the cost of running the bookshops. Significant profits for the publisher depended on subsequent printings, at decreasing costs.[6] David Bellos has calculated that in France, in the years following the Restoration of 1815, the cost of a book printed in a 1,000-copy print run was nearly one franc per copy. It could be sold for 3.3 francs, a gross profit of 2.3.[7]

Most of what was published consisted not of books, and least of all novels, but pamphlets, circulars and billboards, as well as scholarly and scientific publications. These were seldom sold with any hope or intent of profit; indeed, many were subsidised and/or given away. They were a way of disseminating information: authors, patrons and institutions simply wanted a work to be published, and contacted publishers/printers for this specific purpose. The relation was thus not a capitalist one, involving production for exchange, but a direct relationship between authors and printers, not unlike that between the contractor of a work and the artisan executing it. This side of the business still survives today, but it was of far greater incidence in the early nineteenth century. It provided printers and publishers with a stable and low-risk source of revenue to offset against risks incurred in the jungle of 'real' publishing.

Admittedly, in the first half of the nineteenth century this jungle was very small. Books were expensive and few could afford them. It was often far more profitable to bring out an expensive edition of a book rather than a cheap one. Selling two hundred copies of a three-volume novel at one and half guineas each would bring in just over £316; selling 20,000 copies of a 'penny dreadful' (when there were 240 pennies in a pound) would bring in only just over £83.[8]

Only at the end of the nineteenth century did books become cheap and a popular literature begin to develop. Previously, printing and selling a few hundred copies was the norm, one thousand was considerable, ten thousand – in the short term (the term that matters) – almost impossible.

Printing was invented in the fifteenth century, but for three centuries the market for books was limited. The print revolution, as is the case with many revolutions, turns out to have been less dramatic at first than it may appear in retrospect.

The History of the Book

Innovations often replicate or include aspects of what they replace, ensuring a continuity at the level of symbols and language. Thus aeroplanes have captains like ships; cars have horsepower; computers still have the 'qwerty' keyboards developed for typewriters; and computer programmes are arranged in 'folders' and 'files'. The printed book was similarly indebted to the 'codex', as bound manuscript books were called. It imitated its pagination and used folios (i.e. pages folded in notebooks). It was finished by hand, had ornate illustrations, and was very expensive.[9]

By the time printing was invented in the fifteenth century, scripts had become increasingly uniform (though not by today's standards). During the Middle Ages there had been a multiplicity of writing styles in Europe, as practised by different schools of copyists. In southern Italy the monastery of Monte Cassino had developed the Beneventan script, in English and Irish monasteries the 'Insular' style was employed. France used first the Meroving-ian, then the Carolingian. In the twelfth century the Gothic emerged and remained popular for a very long time, especially in Germany. Eventually there emerged the modern Roman type, widely used today

Different styles were inevitable as long as the production of books was in the hands of copyists and the market narrow. Once expansion set in, a uniformity of format was required. A larger production of books demands common standards – a process characteristic of all forms of industrialisation.

Printing was part of the wider revolution which led to the modern book.

The bound manuscript book, the 'codex', constituted a significant advance over the scroll. To read a scroll it is necessary (or at any rate easier) to proceed chronologically, from the beginning to the end. To use a modern analogy: the scroll is like a videotape or an audiocassette, while the book is like a CD or a vinyl record. The book, unlike the scroll, has pages, and consequently it is possible to go straight to the middle, read certain passages, then skip a few pages, then return to a previous section – as one can with a record or a CD. It makes studying two books at the same time relatively easy. Both can be open on one's desk as one leafs through them alternately. Imagine doing this with two scrolls. One needs both hands to unroll a scroll, then one must set paperweights at either end, then open another scroll, and all this needs much space. Scrolls make copying difficult – and in fact many copyists were not, strictly speaking, copying, but taking down dictation (that way many copies could be produced at once, by several copyists working at the same time).[10] The transition from scroll to codex was thus almost as 'revolutionary' as printing.

The ways in which books are read had also changed over time. In an age when paper (itself a cost-lowering novelty) was still prohibitively expensive, it paid to minimise the space between words – or not to have them at all. Reading a text without blanks indicating the pause between words is not easy, unless one reads it aloud – though the Koreans seemed to have coped perfectly well at least until the end of the nineteenth century, when they still wrote sentences (vertically) without spaces between words. In the seventh and eighth centuries silent reading was confined to some monastic orders. The introduction of a separation between words by Irish and Anglo-Saxon scribes of the High Middle Ages made silent reading easier. By the twelfth century silent reading had reached the universities. Two centuries later even the aristocracy could cope with it. People could now read faster, read more and read more difficult texts (where the text is simple, i.e. similar to the spoken word, the lack of spaces between words is a relatively minor obstacle to silent reading).[11] Complex punctuation marks, including the semicolon, were used in manuscripts of the fifteenth century, such as those of 'the Master of Jean Chevrot', an anonymous illustrator of Bruges in the 1450s. The full panoply of punctuation marks – including full stop, colon, semicolon and comma – was introduced in typeface by printers such as the Venetian Aldus Manutius at the end of the fifteenth century. Between 1750 and 1850, throughout Europe and North America the silent and individual reading of increasingly secular texts came to be dominant.[12]

As long as books, whether in manuscript form or as printed texts, were expensive commodities, their use was confined to essential and important matters controlled by the Church and government, hence religion, commerce, laws, chronicles (the official truth), inventories and accounts. Until the mid-seventeenth century religious works accounted for nearly half the print output. There was no need to waste precious paper, expensive time and a great deal of effort on mere stories and poems, i.e. on pleasurable and hence 'useless' literature. And the little entertainment that was written down was to be cherished, read and reread, memorised and recited. It was not to be read rapidly and then discarded or given away.

Printing was originally regarded as no more than a technologically superior way of preserving a record of the present and the works of the past, and disseminating them. By itself printing did not lead to a pronounced increase in new literary genres.[13] It did not involve a total break with the past. There was no sudden print revolution. Even in commercially-minded Elizabethan England, the older technology of copying manuscripts had more prestige than the printed text.[14] Not so different from today, when the printed academic article still has greater prestige than the electronic text.

All innovation inevitably generates alarm and complaints about the end of civilisation. Printing, an invention of the fifteenth century, was still attracting grumbles in the nineteenth from writers, who after all were among its beneficiaries. As late as 1804 Friedrich Schlegel in his essay 'Vom Wesen der Kritik' would write disapprovingly that 'the invention of the printing press and the expansion of the book trade have generated a huge mass of totally worthless and silly writings'.[15] And in 1833 Thomas Carlyle, the most perceptive reactionary of his age, had a premonition of the consequences which he put in the mouth of his Professor Teufelsdröckh:

> He who first shortened the labour of Copyists by device of Movable Types was disbanding hired Armies, and cashiering most Kings and Senators, and creating a whole new Democratic world; he had invented the Art of Printing.[16]

A market does not expand just because technology improves. Other conditions are required: costs must be lowered, prices brought down, and people must have more money. By itself the Bible printed with hand-set movable type cast in 1456 by Johannes Gutenberg (the first European to do so) would not have brought about a revolution in the book industry – a revolution which, in any case, could not have occurred without another great technological innovation widely available in Europe in the late fourteenth century: paper, an invention taught to the West by the Arabs, who in turn had acquired it from China.[17] Paper was part of daily life in China in the fourth century; it spread westwards thanks to Buddhist monks and Silk Road merchants reaching Samarkand and Baghdad in the eighth century and Muslim Europe in the twelfth.[18] The Chinese, as everyone knows, had invented printing centuries before the Europeans, and had started printing books in the ninth century, but they did not develop the movable-type press, largely because printing with Chinese characters was excessively laborious. Even here the Europeans were beaten by the Koreans, who invented the first movable metal-type printing press.[19] Paper and printing linked the Far East, the Near East and the West. Globalisation has existed for longer than one assumes. European printing presses became faster than those of China only in the nineteenth century.

The introduction of printing in the West certainly simplified dramatically the process of book production. Before the invention of printing, those wishing to buy a new book would have to address themselves to a stationer who would arrange to have the text copied and bound. In the fifty years following Gutenberg's innovation 6,000 titles were printed, with an average print run of 1,000 copies. In England alone during the sixteenth century some 5,100 titles were published.[20]

Printing also presented a commercial problem. The advantage of a book trade based on copied manuscripts was that it was analogous to the now fashionable 'just-in-time' production, which makes holding stocks unnecessary. If you wanted a book copied, someone would copy it for you, just as if one wanted a table made, a craftsman would make it. Printing, however, could be made more competitive than copied texts only if at least a few hundred copies were produced. Printing on demand made no sense then (and is beginning to make sense only now). It was thus necessary to hold stocks, make assumptions about future sales, and take risks, In other words it required an entrepreneurial system and the attitude which went with it.[21] With a restricted market, the idea of a stationary shop waiting for customers to materialise was impractical. It was necessary to devise a new distribution system to take books to scattered customers – hence the development of specialist book fairs and the growth of a network of itinerant booksellers or peddlers.

Printing spread quickly from Gutenberg's Mainz to the main European commercial centres, reaching Cologne in 1464, Rome in 1467, Venice in 1469 and Paris in 1470.[22] It reached London only in 1476, and finally the New World, when in 1539 a printing press was installed in Mexico. Muscovite Russia got its first printing press only in the 1560s. The first printing office in what is now the United States was opened in 1638 in Massachusetts.[23]

Throughout the sixteenth and seventeenth centuries the book trade remained very limited. Printers did not dare to publish too many copies. It was better to publish fewer and sell the entire stock. Luther's German Bible was first printed in an edition of 4,000 copies,[24] but this was exceptional: the average print run was about 1,000–1,500 – the same as now for most academic books. The growth in the number of titles, however, was remarkable everywhere. In Muscovy in the early 1600s fewer than thirty titles a year were produced by 1612; by 1700 this had gone up to five hundred a year. In England forty-six new titles were printed in 1500, 259 in 1600 and 577 in 1640. Assuming an average print run of 1,000 copies, it follows that between 300,000 and 500,000 volumes were printed every year in England between 1600 and 1640.[25]

Such figures look impressive, and they certainly show that Europeans had succeeded in establishing a thriving commerce in printed matter before 1700. Nevertheless, this was still a limited market – as most markets were. As Lisa Jardine explains, books were still luxury objects, 'associated with exclusivity and ostentatious expenditure'.[26] Hence their remarkable hand-made illustrations, their expensive binding, their weight. Paper remained formidably expensive until the first half of the nineteenth century. In the sixteenth century a copy of the New Testament cost the equivalent of a week's wages of an artisan.[27] In the nineteenth century books were still dear. The price for the standard three-volume novel, such as those of Walter Scott, was for most of the nineteenth century one and half guineas (£1.11s.6d), at a time when it would take an artisan, such as a carriage-maker, about a week to earn that amount.[28] The seven volumes of Richardson's *Clarissa* (1747–48), at three shillings each, cost one guinea (one pound and one shilling). There existed, of course, shorter and cheaper works. Penelope Aubin's slim books – some as short as twenty pages – could be had for one shilling and sixpence.[29] In proportion, however, *Clarissa* was cheaper – its 2,474 pages worked out at 9.8 pages per penny, while one penny would buy only 2.5 pages of Aubin's *The Strange Adventures of the Count de Vinevil*, which was forty-five pages long. Printing eventually did make books cheaper, but it took a long time. Thomas Hobbes was one of the many who was unimpressed by printing; the fourth chapter of his *Leviathan* (1651) opened with the affirmation that:

'. . . the invention of printing, though ingenious, compared with the invention of letters, is no great matter'.[30]

Expansion

A succession of technological innovations originally devised for newspapers helped to lower costs and expand book publishing. First, in 1812, the cylinder press was invented: the paper was pressed by a revolving cylinder against a flat printing surface. Then there was the rotary press: both the papers and the printing plate were carried by cylinders. In the 1830s costs dropped further thanks to the steam-powered mechanical press and better paper-making and binding machines. Meanwhile the railway reduced distribution costs. Then there was, towards the last quarter of the century, the introduction of rotary printing machines fed by paper from a huge roll through a set of revolving cylinders. In 1885 Ottmar Mergenthaler paved the way for the highly success-ful linotype machine (a hot-metal typesetting device able to cast whole lines of type at one time) which was soon installed at the *New York Tribune*. The monotype, more versatile than the linotype, and photo engraving led to further cost reductions, as did the introduction of electricity.

The expansion of the printed word (books, magazines, journals and newspapers) was the backbone of the expansion of the cultural industry as a whole. This growth led to a wide diversification of products. When a mass of similar but not identical commodities are produced it is necessary to find ways of classifying and distinguishing them. There was thus an ever-increasing proliferation of genres. Almost all the literary genres which became common in the twentieth century were already popular in the nineteenth: the historical novel, the romance, the erotic novel, the detective story, the biography, the popular history book, the popular science book, cookery books, diet books, health books, the western, travelogues, the illustrated book, memoirs, diaries, self-improvement books, children's books – and, towards the end of the nineteenth century, the science fiction story, the comic strip, and the popular daily. As early as 1821 the Paris bookseller Alexandre Pigoreau, in his *Petite bibliographie biographico-romancière*, provided a lengthy list of genres, including *romans historiques, romans sentimentaux, romans pathétiques et larmoyants, romans et histoires de convents de moines* (monastery novels) and *romans de brigands*.[31] These were all 'entertainment books'. And this was the beginning of real change. Books were no longer just for weighty matter. One could bring home a story to read on one's own or with others for pleasure – and reread it as often as one wished.

It is only in the nineteenth century that the printed word, newspapers and books, became the only cultural commodity one could bring home and consume without any special skills, save literacy, or special equipment – unlike music sheets.

The expansion was considerable. In France, prior to 1810, some 1,000 titles were published each year. By 1815 (at the end of the Napoleonic wars and the ensuing economic crisis) 3,357 titles (including reprints) were published. Fifteen years later French production had doubled to 6,739. By 1860 it had almost doubled again to 11,905, and it expanded to 14,195 in 1875.[32] These figures should not be taken too literally, for there are no agreed data. Roger Chartier sets the figure for 1800 at 2,000 titles.[33] Frédéric Barbier and Catherine Bertho Lavenir think that 6,000 titles were sold in France in 1770.[35] Mollier has slightly different and not quite comparable data: 1,000 published (as opposed to 'sold') in 1788, and 8,000 in 1825.[35]

Be that as it may, all agree that the book trade expanded rapidly. Such growth was generalised, though highly uneven. In Italy book consumption grew between 1820 and 1900 by 82 per cent in the number of titles, but most of it was concentrated in the northern urban centres.[36] In 1816, 653 titles were published in the north-eastern regions of Lombardy and Venetia (under Austrian sovereignty), while the whole Kingdom of Naples (the entire south including Sicily) published only 114 titles.[37] By the early part of the nineteenth century Milan had emerged as the true publishing centre of Italy – as it still is – and the city with the largest number of booksellers.

Research in book production is a difficult business. The statistics reported above are for *titles* – far easier to establish than the figures for the number of copies produced. In the early part of the nineteenth century most books were borrowed from lending libraries, so the number of readers exceeded the number of copies sold. To estimate the number of borrowers would require lengthy research in the archives of each lending library. It is also impossible to estimate the size of the market for second-hand books, a thriving market given the cost of the books. Even if we knew the quantity of copies printed we would still need to find out the number of copies sold. Furthermore, there were pirated editions – of French books in Belgium, of British books in the USA – almost certainly of the most successful novels.[38]

In 1982 the editor of the *Canadian Review of Comparative Literature*, in preparing a special issue on the popular novel in the nineteenth century, explained that he had asked the contributors to provide best-seller lists to be collated at the end of the volume, but most had refused on the grounds that it would be impossible to obtain precise figures.[39] Specialist bibliometricians regularly warn that nineteenth-century book statistics are unreliable, and that it is necessary to comb the archives of publishers and booksellers, a laborious task.[40]

The more reliable statistics are those based on the registration of book titles in the great national libraries following the introduction of legislation compelling publishers to deposit a copy of each book published. Thus in France the main source available is the *Bibliographie de la France*, established by Napoleon in 1811 to regulate and control literary production. Of course, the figures rely on the extent to which publishers complied with the legislation. This, at least in England, can be assumed to be reliable – if at all – only after the introduction of copyright registration in the late 1850s. It would still under-represent cheap publications for the working classes and anything regarded as trivial, ephemeral, vulgar or obscene.[41] With these caveats in mind the figures for new titles in Great Britain for the years 1801–1870 look like this:[42]

1801–10	4,585
1811–20	6,821
1821–30	9,179
1831–40	11,074
1841–50	13,785
1851–60	17,418
1861–70	18,015

The grand total for the seventy years following 1800 is almost three times that for the whole of the eighteenth century.

By comparison, Russia had published less than 10,000 works in the last three-quarters of the eighteenth century, in spite of the modernising efforts of Peter the Great and Catherine II.[43] Printing expanded very slowly. The country was enormous. Paper was expensive. There were few functions requiring literacy, there was no legal profession, no guilds, and the Orthodox Church did not actively encourage primary education. The Bible circulated little. In the last decades of the seventeenth century only six or seven titles a year were printed, in 1700–25 forty-five a year, and in 1788 five hundred titles. The main cause for such expansion was the reforms of Peter the Great: the state took over the business of printing, and the state élite was transformed into European cosmopolitan gentry.[44] Excluding newspapers, journals, calendars and booksellers' catalogues, some 9,700 works were published in Russia during the last three-quarters of the eighteenth century. Writing in 1802, the historian Nikolai Karamzin noted with elation that in the past twenty-five years the turnover of the Moscow book trade had increased twenty-fold.[45]

By 1830 Spain was publishing some 300–350 titles a year. Production and distribution tended to be particularly concentrated in Barcelona and Madrid. A centralised, i.e. national, market for books did not emerge until the end of the century.[46]

In Germany too, book production increased rapidly in the first half of the nineteenth century, from 3,772 titles in 1820 to 13,008 in 1845 – far more than France, less than England. Novels accounted for only 5 to 7 per cent of the total. Of these, translations, mainly from English and French, amounted to 11 per cent in 1820, 20 per cent in 1830 and 48 per cent in 1845.[47]

There was an expansion of the reading public and of books, pamphlets and periodicals, and a corresponding expansion of places where books could be read, such as literary cafés and salons. By the 1830s Bavaria had one hundred bookshops, Prussia three hundred. Of course the size of the book-reading public was still tiny by later standards. Well-known weeklies such as Nicolai's *Allgemeine Deutsche Bibliothek* and Wieland's *Der Teutsche Merkur* sold no more than 2,000 copies. The educated public in Prussia at the end of the eighteenth century was around 5 per cent of the adult population. But between 1821 and 1840 the number of books published in Prussia increased by 150 per cent. Institutions such as reading libraries and lending libraries expanded very fast in the 1840s. So did the press: the *Vossische Zeitung* doubled its circulation to 20,000 during the 1840s.[48]

All the data reported above should be treated with caution. Copyright legislation encouraged publishers to register all material they sought to protect: music sheets, fliers, circulars and all sorts of printed material which would not be regarded as 'books'. Conversely, not counted as 'books' were the vast amounts of newsprint and periodicals which, as the century wore on, flooded western Europe. Marc Angenot, faced with the scarcely believable figure of 21,719 'books' published in France in 1890 alone, pruned the list of all works not reaching thirty pages or so, and found that the figure was reduced to 5,500.[49] It is reasonable to assume that similar operations, if performed for other years, would also result in substantial reductions.

National Culture

There is no necessary connection between the development of the book trade and the expansion of a national culture. An efficient book distribution system may simply efficiently distribute 'foreign' cultural products, while an inefficient one acts as a form of protectionism against outside culture. The Germans by the eighteenth century had developed the most efficient system of distribution of books in Europe, but they imported many more French and British texts than they exported.

Paris and London were the centres of French and British cultural life. Everything, including the book trade, was organised around them. Provincial printers catered for their own limited regional market. But in Germany there was no centralised state. Indeed there was no state at all. Booksellers were scattered across dozens of small states. They decided to coordinate their trade at Leipzig, which had a major commercial fair. They were probably inspired by the old Frankfurt fair of the sixteenth century, where the first official catalogue of books to be sold had been printed in 1590 (and where, since 1950, the most important book fair in the world has been held). From Leipzig booksellers could obtain catalogues and order books from a central source, instead of writing to all the booksellers spread everywhere.

Leipzig – in keen competition with Flemish booksellers – became the centre of the book trade for the whole of northern Europe. The trade was conducted in German. The most important booksellers to settle in St. Petersburg were German – such as Weitbrecht.[50] As Jews were significant players in the commercial life of Leipzig, many of them became printers, publishers and booksellers, a possible explanation for the numerous Jewish publishers of German origins in nineteenth-century Europe and North America.

Vienna was the other pole of German publishing in the late eighteenth and early nineteenth century. Austrian publishers were allowed (and even encouraged) to pirate books from other countries. These were reprinted and often translated into Serbo-Croat and modern Greek, turning Vienna into a publishing centre for the whole of the Balkans.[51]

German presence in Poland was equally significant. In 1795 Poland ceased to exist as an independent state and was partitioned between Russia, Prussia and Austria. In the Polish provinces of Prussia (which included Pomerania) and in Greater Poland (Wielkopolska) there was constant interchange with the highly professional German book trade, massive pressures towards Germanisation, and the establishment of major publishing centres in Poznan and Gdansk (Danzig). It was in this Prussian zone that in the first half of the nineteenth century, before the repression of 1848, the main Polish classics were published, including, in 1828–29, the selected works of Adam Mickiewicz.[52]

These German distribution networks were the backbone of Europe's largest book-reading market. They enabled a high number of professional writers to make a living. An estimate puts their numbers at 2,000 to 3,000 strong.[53] Many of them specialised in *Trivialliteratur* (trivial novels), sometimes condescendingly referred to as *Volksliteratur* (popular literature) or denounced as *Schmutz und Schund* (smut and trash). This genre dealt mainly with tales of knights, robbers and terrible happenings (*Ritter-Räuber-und Schauerromane*). The majority of German readers read books such as *Rinaldo Rinaldini, der Räuberhauptmann* (Rinaldo Rinaldini, Robber Captain, 1799–1800) by Christian August Vulpius (1762–1827). This was perhaps the best-selling German novel of the day, and was even translated into several languages.[54] It is the largely derivative story of a Corsican shepherd who aspires to higher things, turns into a Robin Hood-type robber, seduces women, and leads a rebellion against French occupation.[55] But, notwithstanding Vulpius (and, at the upper end of the market, his brother-in-law Goethe), the Germans never became the masters of European narrative fictions. Very few German authors could compete with Walter Scott (and before him with Richardson or Defoe) or, later, with Charles Dickens, W.M. Thackeray, Alexandre Dumas, George Sand or Eugène Sue. Popular German authors were popular only in Germany, while those who were celebrated, like Schiller and Goethe, had relatively limited markets – the notable exceptions being Goethe's *The Sorrows of Young Werther* (1774) – a real European best-seller, and still regarded by Madame de Staël in 1810 as the one novel with no competitors,[56] and the fairy tales of Jacob and Wilhelm Grimm, which became popular outside Germany in the latter part of the nineteenth century.

4

Peddling Stories

Cheap Books

BOOKS WERE PRODUCED AND READ in cities while the rural classes, rich
and poor, remained culturally deprived until the advent of radio and television, with few bookshops, few theatres, few concerts, and few scholars and
intellectuals in their midst. Each urban market, however, was too small to
absorb the entire output of publishers. Bookshops existed even in the sixteenth century, but they were in the business of diffusing learned culture,
not entertainment. The few universities that existed were blessed with an
exuberance of sellers. As early as the 1550s, for instance, Poitiers, a major
university centre, had twenty-three bookshops for a population of 2,000
students – more than one bookshop for each hundred students – while the
entire administration of the university consisted of three people: a secretary,
a treasurer and the porter.[1]

A network of itinerant booksellers had developed alongside permanent
bookshops since the sixteenth century. Europe was criss-crossed by an international trade carried out by peddlers who would travel by cart, stop in a
city, set up their stall for a few weeks and hire people to scour the countryside
for possible customers. By the 1780s and 1790s their stock had a considerable
range: not only the usual lives of saints but also leather-bound classics by
Montaigne and pirated novelties such as Beaumarchais's plays.[2] These peddlers moved from fair to fair, and occasionally from country to country. They
sold simple, short books, seldom longer than eight pages, illustrated with
woodblock images. In Germany such booklets were called *Volksbücher* (popular books) or *Flugschriften* (primitive works), or when illustrated, *Bilderbogen*
or 'image-pages' that told stories through a succession of images – the
ancestors of our comic strips. In Sweden the booklets were known as *Skilling-*

tryck, in Russia as *lubok*, in Spain as *pliegos*. In England they were called chapbooks ('cheap books'), and the peddlers 'chapmen' (the origin of the colloquialism 'chap').

This distribution system increased the size of the market and contributed to its further expansion. In 1664, a stock of thousands of chapbooks and ballad sheets was held by printers such as Charles Tias in their London warehouses, where peddlers came from all over the country to replenish their supplies.[3]

The largest centre of the production of chapbooks, however, was neither London nor Paris but Troyes, in Champagne. The covers of the booklets published here were a shade of blue, hence the name adopted since the eighteenth century, La Bibliothèque Bleue.[4] This was not bold and innovative publishing. The largest Troyes printers, the Oudots and their rivals the Garniers, in the absence of any copyright legislation, simply reprinted existing literature which had been published in other formats or had circulated orally.[5] The business of popularisation was so profitable that the Troyes printers were able to convince the authorities to increase the number of licensed peddlers throughout the seventeenth century.[6] The inventory of the printer Étienne Garnier, drawn up in 1789 at the request of his widow, listed a stock of 443,069 books in his warehouse. Of these 42.7 per cent were religious books, 28.8 per cent were classified as fiction, including Charles Perrault's famous *Histoires ou contes du temps passé* (1697), and 26.8 per cent were practical manuals.[7]

These texts – like all culture destined for ordinary people – were often disparaged. In reality, the actual consumers were not the poor, or the unskilled artisans or the peasants, most of whom were illiterate, but the lower and not-so-lower middle classes who did not have the education and/or the patience to read 'erudite' texts – those Coleridge called 'the lower classes of the reading public' (1817).[8]

As both the cost of producing books and the market increased, peddlers gave way to permanent bookshops and the cheap book gave way to the cheap newspapers. Prices dropped. Baudot, the successor of the famous publisher Oudot de Troyes, had to close in 1863 – the same year *Le Petit journal* first saw the light.[9]

Was there a tradition of reading among the popular classes prior to 1800? If so, it could not have been strong: the obstacles to literacy and high prices would have prevented them. The peddlers found their market among the better-off. The material they sold was simple and often naïve, but this would not have prevented the middle and upper classes from enjoying it, just as today's business classes are formidable consumers of so-called airport novels and popular films. Seventeenth-century readers, much as later consumers of the *Reader's Digest*, liked simplified and reduced versions of picaresque novels such *La Vida de Lazarillo de Tormes*, translated into French soon after its publication in Spain in 1554.[10] In England they bought *Robinson Crusoe* in a drastically condensed form – eight pages – with a long title (*Voyages and Travels: being the Life and Adventures of Robinson Crusoe of York, Mariner*) and an abrupt ending – the shipwreck – as the main 'action' was about to start.[11] Nineteenth-century French chapbooks provided adaptations, summaries and digested accounts of longer and more established books such as the novels of Alexandre Dumas, Paul de Kock, Eugène Sue, Sophie Cottin and Jean-Jacques Rousseau.[12]

Chapbooks also recycled medieval romances, such as the poems of the celebrated *trouvère* Chrétien de Troyes – his *Perceval ou Li conte dou Graal* (c.1181) – or the various versions of *Tristan et Iseut*.[13] This blend of Celtic and French mythology had been an enormous success in the twelfth century. In Ireland too, chapbooks printed in Dublin in the eighteenth and nineteenth centuries and sold throughout the countryside (some in Gaelic) consisted largely of popularised aristocratic culture, hence chivalric romances, ancient myths and picaresque stories of noblemen turned bandits.[14]

In Russia chapbooks known as *lubki*, in production since the seventeenth century, were still being peddled in the nineteenth.[15] Like most popular literature this *lubochnaia literatura* consisted mainly of religious works originally produced for a largely upper-class audience. By the eighteenth century they could be found in the homes of some of the humbler inhabitants of the cities as well – evidence that the *lubok* had contributed to the expansion of the Russian reading public. Prior to the 1760s Russian literature amounted to little more than folk tales and translated chivalric romances. The readers were the newly literate groups, merchants and military men, scribes and low-ranking service nobility. The themes of many of the stories met the upwardly mobile aspirations of the readers: tales in which the hero is forced to leave home, rights a wrong and/or finds a bride, travels to make his fortune.[16]

The European book market of the seventeenth and eighteenth centuries was flooded with such popular themes. Plagiarism and imitation were rife. In Spain one could find books called *El Arte de explicar los sueños* (The Art of Explaining Dreams), *La Cocinera moderna* (Modern Cookery), *El*

Escribiende de los enamoratos (Lovers' Stratagems), which were local versions of similar books peddled in Germany or France.

Readers and listeners liked fairy tales, tales of chivalry, of magic and – above all – lives of saints. The evidence that the latter were the favourite books of the times is compelling, but it may not be a reflection of popular preferences, which we have no way of establishing, but of the fact that such books were approved by the political and religious authorities while providing the kind of pleasure associated with the novel-like story of an exemplary person who, after various adventures, achieves his or her goal. The basic plot outline of such hagiographic texts would have been entirely familiar to readers and their audiences (since the literate would occasionally read to the illiterate) – familiarity being an essential element of popular genres. The enhancement of pleasure was in the added details and new twists in the story – much as the general plot of detective stories is completely predictable (the murderer will be identified), while the mystery of its solution provides the necessary incentive for reading on.[17] But religious stories were only one of the great genres of the time. There were also practical manuals full of sound advice for rural folks, such as *Noth-und-Hülfsbüchlein für Bauerleute* (Help manual for farmers), published in Germany in 1788 by Rudolf Zacharias Becker. The content was geared to the right market and the price was low; as a result Becker sold thousands of copies and reprinted it eleven times in 1791.[18] The poem *Flos medicinae* – filled with advice on how to look after one's health and behave at dinner – was in print for four centuries, accumulating three hundred editions in France between 1474 and 1846.

Almanacs too (the word is Arabic in origin: *al mankh*) contained useful advice. Easy to read, these ancestors of modern magazines were, before 1800, the most widely disseminated printed texts. They contained woodcut illustrations with astrological symbols, information about local fairs, practical agricultural advice, some short stories usually of a morally edifying kind, proverbs, etc. In England by the middle of the eighteenth century they were among the few publications catering for a national market.[19] Spanish versions, known as the *Lunário perpetuo*, became common in Latin America. In France they were still selling by the millions in the middle of the nineteenth century.[20]

Almanacs were also very popular in Russia, and for far longer than in the West. At first there were more or less elaborate calendars containing the usual anecdotes, light verses and seasonal information. Then a kind of 'literary' almanac evolved. This more sophisticated version was aimed at the middle classes with literary pretensions. Eventually they included selections from longer works. Their elegant appearance and their use as Christmas and New Year presents shows that, unlike in France, Germany and Great Britain, in Russia almanacs emancipated themselves from the 'low' culture of the *lubok* to become, as Pushkin declared in 1827, 'the representatives of our literature'.[21] They were, in fact, the forerunners of the 'thick' journals (so-called because they were published in thick – *tolstyi* – monthly issues) around which much of Russian literary life in the nineteenth and twentieth centuries was organised.[22]

Peddlers and Booksellers

The backbone of the itinerant trade were the chapmen, called *colporteurs* in France, *gårdfarihandlarar* or 'tradesmen travelling to farms' in Sweden, *leggendai* in Italy (because they specialised in selling the lives of the saints or legends), *Jahrmarktströdler* or *Colporteur* in Germany, *repartitor* in Spain, and *ofeni* in Russia.

An anonymous French painting of 1623 portrays a *colporteur* holding a copy of the *Almanach pour l'an 1622* by the astrologer Delarivey of Troyes and carrying his books tied to his hat or in a basket rucksack tied around his waist and shoulders.[23]

The narrowness of the market meant that, almost from its inception, the book trade was a global trade (if by 'global' we mean Europe-wide). *Colporteurs* such as these would replenish their stocks at Troyes and then proceed on a grand business tour of France. Some would go on to northern Italy or Spain and Portugal.[24] Other peddlers started out in Venice – another book-making centre – and went east towards Dubrovnik, Belgrade and Buda and into Transylvania, where they would often sell their remaining stock on to local peddlers who took them further.[25] The Venice network was dominated by the printer-booksellers such as the Remondini, originally from Bassano del Grappa, who specialised in illustrated religious books. These were carried by up to 2,000 peddlers as far as Germany, Poland, Hungary, Holland, Spain, Flanders and even into Russia.

In Poland too, in the eighteenth century, travelling salesmen and peddlers often carried books printed by printer-booksellers such as Michal Gröll in Warsaw, who was part of a wider European network with dealers in Paris, Amsterdam, Leipzig, Berlin and Dresden.

Italy, urbanised before the rest of Europe but with a very limited reading public, relied overwhelmingly on bookshops for the sale of books.[26] Even there, however, there were itinerant booksellers, mainly from Montereggio in the Val di Magra in Tuscany who traded in the north, but there was little trace of them during the Napoleonic occupation, and the Austrians banned a trade which was so difficult to control.[27]

In Spain, the peddlers or *repartitores* sold new and used books door to door, avoiding the tax on books, and surreptitiously selling 'immoral' books known as *libros insanos* ('unhealthy' books). They were almost excluded from the thriving school and religious book markets which were in the hands of the *matuteros* – schoolteachers, priests and school concierges making a little money on the side.[28] Because many *repartitores* in both Spain and Portugal were blind, the novels they sold came to be known as *romance de ciegos* (novels of the blind). Since 1739 they had been organised into a guild (formally abolished only in 1836). Each member was entitled to sell *pliegos* (chapbooks), *romance* (ballads), *coplas* (songs in couplets), *aleluyas* (an illustration accompanied by a story told in rhymes or in prose printed underneath) and *historias* (usually the life of some historical character). Some or most of these were known as literature of *cordel* (cord), so-called because the books and pamphlets hung on cords across arcades.[29]

In Spain too, along with cheap romances, the chapbooks helped disseminate, in a simplified form, some of the masterpieces of the high literature of the Spanish Golden Age as well as works by renowned French writers such as Madame de Staël, Alexandre Dumas and Eugène Sue.[30]

As Spain entered modernity rather late, the peddlers lasted longer there than elsewhere. They survived by selling luxury books or delivering magazines to subscribers.[31] By the 1930s they were driving vans containing as many as 2,000 books on behalf of a consortium of editors (Agrupación de editores españoles). Even in the early nineteenth century, however, they had developed relatively sophisticated marketing techniques such as having a leaflet with the contents of the next series of books they would sell to prospective customers.[32]

The peddlers' book trade represented a possible threat to the careful control exercised by the authorities on what people read. The peddlers were taxed, their wares censored or confiscated. In France in the mid-eighteenth century royal decrees subjected them to the death penalty if they were caught dealing in forbidden books. Formally the peddlers were restricted to selling almanacs, short prayer books and alphabet primers, but the trade continued unabated into the nineteenth century.

In the 1770s Noël Gille, known as 'Pistole', a near-illiterate peddler who travelled in and around Paris and in the Loire valley, carried his stock in a cart pulled by two horses – a sign of prosperity making him a *colporteur voiturier* rather than a mere *porte-balle* who carried books in a box on his back. His wide range included the collected works of Voltaire in fifty-two volumes, religious books, law books, history books – including a history of England – classics of literature (*Don Quixote, Robinson Crusoe, Clarissa, Paradise Lost*), cookery books such as *La Cuisinière bourgeoise*, grammar books, Buffon's *Histoire naturelle*, and dictionaries. His customers were not the poor or the lower classes (who seldom bought any reading material) but, in order of importance, clergymen, scholars, lawyers, doctors and civil servants, as well as provincial bookshops. Eventually the authorities caught up with this remarkable and unsung purveyor of culture. He had in his possession two forbidden books: Diderot's daring *Les Bijoux indiscrets* and Jean-Jacques Rousseau's *Pensées*. He was jailed for two months and declared bankrupt. Perhaps his fortunes revived, because when he died in 1824 at the age of eighty he was still being described as a *marchand libraire*, a bookseller.[33]

Stories, Canards and Ballads

Imagine a peddler arriving in a village during a fair. To attract customers, he starts telling or singing the story contained in the books he wants to sell. People gather round him. Some will drop a coin. Others, enticed by the story, will buy one of his chapbooks. The peddler is thus also a performer who sells 'the book of the show' – his show. Some of the purchasers might be storytellers themselves, buying the text of their future performance. Others will acquire some local prestige because in the winter evenings they will read aloud, again and again, the story they purchased.

Some of the stories, printed on a broadsheet with one or more pictures, became ballads to be sung ('broadsheet ballads' or 'broadsides'). The performer would sing and read the text, illustrating it by pointing to the picture, and later selling a few sheets. The ballads would often tell the story of some crime among lower-class folk, a domestic killing, embellished out of all recognition to make it even more alluring. It is estimated that between three and four million broadsides were printed in England in the second half of the sixteenth century.[34] In France chapbooks offering these sensational news stories would be called *canards* – the title cried in the streets in a duck-like sound (hence the name). The *canard*, the ancestor of the modern tabloid, was often little more than a woodcut illustration with a short text describing prodigies, monsters, miracles, satanic manifestations, dragons, large snakes, earthquakes, and offered detailed accounts of murders, trials of criminals, horrific descriptions of tortures – such as flesh removed by pincers, molten lead poured in the wounds – and executions.[35] Some provided 'strange but true stories' like that of the woman who gave birth to female quintuplets all of whom survived (in the mid-eighteenth century). Others supplied coarse humour, such as a French treatise on the art of farting – *L'Art de péter* – with its taxonomy of farts: the 'gunshot', the 'dulcet', the 'no strength', the 'flute', etc.[36] Or worse: *Le Trou du cul du père du Chêne*.

There was, as there is today, a great interest in serial killers and family murders. In 1610 a *canard* tells the *New and Extraordinary Story, of a young woman (the daughter of Monsieur de Mont-Croisié) who hanged her father for having forced her to marry – against her will and in spite of her tears – an elderly man who was impotent, obsessively jealous and who tormented her unceasingly.* She was executed in Nice on 14 March 1609.[37]

The British had their own equivalent. Books and pamphlets narrated the deeds of Joan Bracey, the highwaywoman, of Gilder-Roy, a Scottish robber and breaker of hearts, of Moll Cutpurse, the masculine mistress of the underworld, and of Colonel Blood, the man who stole the crown from the Tower of London. Many of these tales appeared in the 1730s in Captain Charles Johnson's *A General History of the Lives and Adventures of the Most Famous Highwaymen, Murderers, Street-Robbers*, to which was added *A Genuine Account of the Voyages and Plunders of the Most Notorius Pyrates*.

There was also Captain Alexander Smith's *A Compleat HISTORY of the LIVES and ROBBERIES of the Most Notorious Highway-men, Foot-Pads, Shop-Lifts, and Cheats of both Sexes, in and about London and Westminster, and all Parts of Great Britain, for above an Hundred Years past, continued to the present time. Wherein their most Secret and Barbarous Murders, Unparallel'd Robberies, Notorious Thefts, and Unheard-of Cheats, are set in a true Light, and expos'd to publick View, for the common Benefit of Mankind.* The fifth edition (1719) included also 'Two Hundred Robberies lately committed'. Many readers were also delighted by George Borrow's *CELEBRATED TRIALS, and Remarkable Cases of CRIMINAL JURISPRUDENCE FROM THE EARLIEST RECORDS to THE YEAR 1825*. Even more downmarket was the *Malefactor's Register or Newgate Calendar* with its stories of crimes and criminals. This was purportedly an 'accurate' biographical record of the more notorious criminals confined at Newgate. It was started in 1773 and continued at intervals for many years, reaching five volumes. As the execution of criminals was a much-loved spectacle, it is not surprising that some members of the public would have been keen to find out more about the lives of those they had seen executed – the celebrities of the day. The plots of the *Newgate Calendar* were ransacked by novelists throughout the nineteenth century.

The sale of some of these broadsheets could be formidable. It has been claimed that over one million copies were sold of the *Last Dying Speech and Confession of the Murderer of Maria Marten* (1828), published by James Cat-nach, owner of the Catnach Press, specialising in crime stories.[38] This is the salient part of the confession of William Corder, Maria Marten's murderer:

> I then went home and fetched my gun, my pickaxe and my spade,
> I went into the Red Barn, and there I dug her grave.
> With heart so light, she thought no harm to meet me she did go,
> I murdered her all in the Barn and laid her body low;
> After the horrid deed was done, she lay weltering in her gore,
> Her bleeding, mangled body I buried under the Red Barn floor.[39]

Chapbooks published in Great Britain and France in the late eighteenth and early nineteenth centuries dealt with subjects as diverse as the Biblical *Joseph and His Brethren*, the medieval legend of *The Wandering Jew* and *The History of Dr. John Faustus*, the useful *A Timely Warning to Rash and Disobedient Children*, ghost-story serials such as *The Portsmouth Ghost*, *The Guildford Ghost*, etc., bandit stories – usually about Wat Tyler and Jack Straw in England, and Cartouche and Mandrin in France – often ending up with horrific descriptions of executions and mangled corpses. There were also stories of female bandits, such as the enticingly titled *The Whole Life and Adventures of Miss Davis commonly called The Beauty in Disguise. With a full, true and particular Account of her robbing Mr. W. of Gosfield in Essex of Eleven Hundred Pounds in Cash and Bank Notes for which she now lays to take her trial at Chelmsford Assizes* (1785) – and all in eight pages. Other novels had women as main protagonists pursued by libidinous old men, then ravished by brigands who fall in love with them. There were also stories of famous sovereigns and their favourites, such as *The History of the Most Renowned Queen Elizabeth and her Great Favourite the Earl of Essex*, and adaptations of risqué novels such as Defoe's *Moll Flanders*.[40]

The old broadsheet, often little more than an illustration with a caption, survived well into the nineteenth century (and beyond, in the form of the comic strip). The combination of text and visual was appealing. It could be used as a satirical, religious or patriotic print – like the highly popular *Image d'Épinal*, which started in France in 1825. The genre was international. In Japan, the broadsheets or *kawaraban* were still commonly sold in the middle of the nineteenth century. In Latin America, and particularly in Brazil, there was a thriving market for these *folhetos* until the 1960s. When the populist dictator Getúlio Vargas died in 1954, 70,000 copies of a *folheto* narrating the circumstances of his suicide were sold.[41]

At the beginning of the nineteenth century, though the development of a significant publishing market was still some way off, men of letters began to fear that cheap literature in the wrong hands would become a threat to civilised living. They feared that 'bad' books would feed the reveries of new, unsophisticated readers who could be easily corrupted. There was also some resentment that well-established classics, the knowledge of which had hitherto been the prerogative of the educated classes, were now available, in a simplified form, to the less educated. The religious and political authorities had long been worried about this kind of literature. The peddler was so obviously an outsider, often from the city, and inevitably the carrier of irreligious, dangerous and obscene literature. What was even more threatening was that the peddlers were difficult to control and might subvert the countryside. Thus in France a Commission de Surveillance set up in 1852 by Napoleon III required each separate booklet and chapbook to have a stamp of approval. By the time the Commission was abolished in 1880 the number of regular bookshops had vastly expanded and the *colportage* or peddling of books had started to decline anyway.

Not all regarded the expansion of the book trade as a threat to civilisation. Authentic liberals like Giuseppe Pecchio, an Italian admirer of Adam Smith, saw it as a harbinger of modernity, part of the approaching industrial society. In his *Sino a qual punto le Produzioni Scientifiche e Letterarie seguano le leggi economiche della produzione in generale* (To What Extent Scientific and Literary Production Follows the Economic Laws of Production in General, 1832) he claimed that there was no difference between literary products and any other goods, noting that, traditionally, writers were content to receive in fame and honours a kind of payment which partly compensated them for their small emoluments.[42] He realised, however, that cultural production for profit

> would bring to light a very large number of second-rate works, frivolous
> stuff, especially novels, novellas, memoirs, travel books and other gossips.
> But what does it matter? . . . it is always better to read than not to read.
> In the midst of quantity some works will arise which will defeat the

passage of time and will enrich the libraries of the future. Let us understand that the repetition and the quantity of labour lead to perfection.[43]

This eminently modern and 'democratic' position accepted that, in cultural production, quality is not necessarily the enemy of quantity. In the past, Pecchio explained, authors had to pander to the whims of the princes who protected them, or die in poverty. Now they would have to pander to the whims of their readers. This would make authors rich and committed to free government.[44] In so far as predictions go, for one written in 1832, this is far from inaccurate.

Most writers, however, were poor. Few best-selling authors became rich. Balzac's fame was remarkable, but so were his financial difficulties. Eliza Parsons, the author of the horrific *The Castle of Wolfenbach* (1793) 'plugged' in Jane Austen's *Northanger Abbey*,[45] could barely make ends meet. Parsons had started writing because the death of her husband, a turpentine manufacturer, had left her ruined with eight children to support. As she wrote in 1792: 'Born and accustomed to affluence I had no recourse but my Needle and Pen, poor and Insufficient supports for so large a Family. Yet I was compelled to Avail myself of the Fashion of the times and write Novels . . . Necessity not inclination, nor any Opinion of my Talents induced me to turn Author.' William Lane, the Minerva publishers, paid her £30 per novel, better than most, but she still needed to supplement her earnings by doing needlework for the Royal Household. Even so she could only make £100 a year. Coleridge thought one needed £250 to live comfortably (and not with eight children). Eliza Parsons had to apply to the newly established Literary Fund for impecunious writers because she was incapacitated for six months due to a broken leg. Later she was imprisoned for debt she had incurred because the Royal Household had been late in paying her for her needlework.[46]

Making a living writing novels was difficult. It is thus not surprising if, of the five female novelists active in England between 1780 and 1815 still known today (Elizabeth Inchbald, Jane Austen, Fanny Burney, Ann Radcliffe and Maria Edgeworth), only Mrs Inchbald (now the least well-known) lacked private means. However, she was also a playwright and beautiful, and had a relatively well-remunerated stage career.[47] As writing required some kind of education it is not surprising that a disproportionate number of authors came from the middle classes and the aristocracy. The annals of literature are replete with instances of writers able to exercise their craft without the worry of bills to pay because of their private wealth. Horace Walpole, the son of Britain's longest-serving (and first) Prime Minister, simply printed copies of the first edition of *The Castle of Otranto* (1765) and distributed them to his friends. Matthew 'Monk' Lewis, the author of the horror novel *The Monk* (1796), was the son of a wealthy senior civil servant and a Member of Parliament. His predecessor in his parliamentary seat was William Beckford, the famous author of the Orientalist novel *The History of the Caliph Vathek* (1786), whose family owned a sugar plantation in Jamaica and a big house in Soho.

It is difficult to estimate the average revenue of professional writers. The data we have usually concern famous writers who are, by definition, in a special category. But there were many who made a considerable amount of money – more, in fact, than most other cultural producers except for opera singers. By the 1850s the market had changed for the better from the point of view of authors. Expansion worked to their advantage. In the middle of the century the French Romantic writer Alphonse de Lamartine signed a contract for the publication of his collected works which included a considerable amount of poetry and essays still to be written. For this he was going to get 710,000 francs – more than Balzac had earned in his entire life as a writer,[48] and much more than the estimated value of the Mona Lisa: a paltry 90,000 francs.[49] The commercially astute Victor Hugo amassed considerable wealth. Some publishers – always in fear of letting a successful author escape – lost money because they paid their authors excessive amounts. Major poets managed to sell as well as popular fiction writers.[50]

A few lucky authors were overwhelmed by the mass of impecunious colleagues and bankrupt publishers. A large print run was very risky and hence very rare. In France, even relatively successful authors such as Balzac did not earn that much, and his publishers lost money: by 1846 their costs were 120,000 francs against revenues of 114,000 francs, including the stocks of still unsold books.[51] For most writers earning a living was a struggle. They were hampered by the low print run of most publications (1,000 per edition on the whole), and hence by the size of the market. Lending libraries increased the number of readers but not the revenue. The case of Balzac is emblematic. He belonged to this first generation of professional writers. He had worked hard, written much, published much. Commercially he was a failure, lived in debt, died in debt. One might add that his misfortune was to die at a relatively early age. Had he survived long enough he would made a considerable amount of money when Louis Hachette published *Eugénie Grandet* and *Pierrette* for his Bibliothèque des Chemins de Fer (1855).[52] Balzac was now available at train stations. During his lifetime his sales went up and down eight times in twenty-one years, not an unusual experience for a writer.[53]

And what did the readers read? In Alessandro Manzoni's *I Promessi sposi*, set in 1628–30, among the countless characters there is a village tailor – 'the salt of the earth' (the Italian rendition is, appropriately, *la migliore pasta del mondo*), says Manzoni with characteristic condescension. The tailor is literate and has read 'more than once' the *leggendari* (a collection of saints' lives), as well as *Guerrin Meschino*, a French chivalric story adapted into Italian by Andrea da Barberino in the fourteenth century.[54] These stories, explains the editor in a footnote, were until 'extremely recently' very popular in the Italian countryside.[55]

Of that claim we cannot be sure, but the tailor's list would have been amply confirmed by an earlier survey conducted by the Abbé Grégoire, Deputy to the National Assembly in revolutionary France. On 13 August 1790, four years before calling for the eradication of dialects (see page 28), Grégoire had sent a circular letter to hundreds of parish priests asking them to investigate the use of the local patois and their parishioners' reading habits. This was one of the earliest sociological investigations in the matter. It was, by modern standards, rather unscientific (there were only forty-three respondents), but, in history, this is better than nothing. Many of the respondents pointed out that rural people had no reading habits at all, indeed most could not read. Some, perhaps ingratiatingly, declared that the Revolution had awakened in the peasants an appetite for books and a desire to become literate. Some remarked that very few books circulated in the countryside, others that there were not enough schoolteachers available. Though the Catholic Church in France was not against literacy, some of the parish priests were not very keen: wouldn't literate boys feel superior to the others? Wouldn't literate girls start behaving mischievously?[56] Many priests did not read much themselves and would not have considered following the example of Grégoire, who before the Revolution had founded a lending library in his parish.

The survey, as expected, revealed that the most widely read books had a religious theme: catechisms, collections of hymns, Christmas carols, psalms, books of hours (prayer books, often lavishly illustrated) and lives of saints. This was a reflection of Church policy on the distribution of books to country parishes rather than consumer preferences. Legislation passed in 1777 allowed the untaxed reprinting of these 'good' texts, bringing the total number of books in circulation in France in the ten years leading up to the Revolution to 1,363,700.[57] The next group of 'rural best-sellers' were the Bibliothèque Bleue books. The preferred genres were chivalric romance, tales of magic, tales of noble bandits – these books would be read and re-read 'up to twenty times' and often they would be read aloud.[58]

Enlightenment intellectuals would have found here plenty to confirm their negative view of rural culture: an assemblage of illiterate semi-savages held together by primitive religious beliefs, superstitions and trivial fables. Given the paltry evidence, of course, a diametrically different conclusion could be reached: in a community where only a few could read, the current habit of individual and silent reading (curled up in bed, on a sofa, on a train, in a plane criss-crossing the ocean, etc.) was unlikely. Instead there was an extensive practice of 'public' reading, with the children themselves reading to their parents. Imagine the scene of an eighteenth-century *veillée paysanne* (peasant vigil): in the long winter evenings the rural household gathers around the fire, mending, darning, cooking, salting, making preserves, repairing tools, making clothes. In the background an older child, recently literate thanks to the new village school, reads aloud the story of the life of San Francis of Assisi: peasant culture at its purest and best. Perhaps, given the paucity of the accounts, humble reading in peasant huts is just a myth cultivated by Romantic intellectuals to celebrate the innocence of the countryside. However, more recently Jean-Claude Farci has suggested that as late as the nineteenth century in rural Brittany there was a practice of family reading where the young child, often the first to be sent to school, would be asked to read from *La Vie des saints*.[59]

Roger Chartier disagrees. These *veillées*, he claims, did take place but were often occasions for secular amusements, usually of an 'improper' kind such as dancing, playing cards and singing. Chartier concludes: 'Although it is certain that the *veillée* was in fact a practice of village sociability (perhaps less universal in France than was thought, however), it seems most doubtful that it was customarily a place for reading.'[60] As usual we know little about peasants' habits and attitudes except through the eyes of others, the literate observers. And it is these and not the peasants who, in the field of culture, make history, or at the very least write it.

As is to be expected, a considerable proportion of sixteenth- and seven-teenth-century readers of books belonged to the intellectual classes (holders of office, the clergy, lawyers, doctors and men of letters) as well as to the nobility. But craftsmen and traders read too. A study of estate inventories in sixteenth-century Amiens, a town with 20,000 inhabitants, showed that of 4,442 inventories only 887 (20 per cent) mentioned books. Of these 259 were the estates of merchants, and ninety-eight of craftsmen. Thus almost half of book-owners belonged to what were then called the 'popular classes' (the peasantry and the poor were not included in this category). However, only 11.6 per cent of merchants and artisans taken together owned books, while almost all doctors and 72 per cent of priests had at least one book among their possessions.[61]

By the beginning of the nineteenth century the reading public of a much expanded book market was overwhelmingly constituted of members of the professions and the rest of the bourgeoisie.[62] It gradually expanded to include the lower middle classes and the skilled workers. To do so a mechanism for distributing books other than by selling them had to be found.

Borrowing

Writers write books, publishers publish them, and readers read them. But somehow a mechanism must be devised to link the reader to the book. As we have seen, peddling them was a solution. Taking the book directly to the customers has remained one of the most important ways of distributing books. Door-to-door marketing is now regarded as expensive, but using the postal system has proved very effective. One can buy a book by joining a book club, and more recently and successfully, via the internet. Books have been positioned where potential customers might be: at a kiosk selling news-papers, in supermarkets (where many of today's best-sellers are sold – at least in Great Britain and the USA) or as an optional extra with one's daily paper – as is often done, for instance, in Italy, resulting in extremely large sales.

At the beginning of the eighteenth century these were not available options. The books peddled in fairs and markets belonged to a specific genre: short, coarse and badly printed. It was cheap literature. 'Good' literature was expensive. This was the greatest obstacle to the expansion of the market. Pope's translation of *The Iliad* sold at over £6. *Tom Jones* could be had for eighteen shillings. George Lyttelton's *History of the Life of Henry II*, a substan-tial but popular history in six volumes, cost over £9. *Robinson Crusoe* may have been a very popular novel, but when it came out in 1719 it cost five shillings, the weekly earnings of an unskilled labourer (the equivalent of £200 today).[63] Ann Radcliffe's *Udolpho* (1794) cost £1.5s., more than an English *skilled* worker would have earned in a week.[64] The same book, still in print two hundred years later, can be had for the same amount – but that now represents the equivalent of fifteen minutes' work for someone on the statutory minimum wage, and less than a one-stop journey on the London Underground. Owning books outright was a mark of intellect and civilisation, and there were of course some very wealthy aristocrats for whom collecting books was like collecting paintings: for instance Count Waldstein, who owned a library of well over 10,000 volumes in his Bohemian castle, and who in the 1780s and 1790s entrusted it to Giacomo Casanova to sort out.

However, it was not necessary to buy a book in order to read it. One could borrow it. In fact there was a practice of informal lending within a circle of friends or a family, and there were, at the end of the eighteenth century, a few public libraries. In 1784 in Paris there were eighteen libraries open to the public (including university libraries), but many were opened for only a few hours a day or loaned books only to scholars.[65]

The lending library emerged to provide books on loan to paying subscribers. Its origins were varied. Most commonly, a bookseller would add to his normal business a stock of books which he would lend at a price. Not everyone could afford the yearly fee, but it was cheaper than buying books. In Bath at the end of the eighteenth century the subscription was set at £1 a year, at a time when a domestic servant would only earn £7 or £8 a year.[66] Joseph Barber in Newcastle and Francis Noble in London, less fancy than Bath, were cheaper: twelve shillings a year.[67] A loaf of bread cost under two and a half pence. There were many options. You could pay-as-you-borrowed (a set sum per book), or pay a yearly fee and borrow as much as you wanted, or a combination of the two.

In the first decades of the nineteenth century lending libraries developed everywhere in Europe. Some grew out of bookshops, others from reading associations and clubs. The first real lending library in Great Britain was attached to an Edinburgh bookseller, Andrew Ramsay, in 1725.[68] In England in 1770 the publisher William Lane set up a circulating library which claimed to include among its 10,000 volumes every novel in English.[69] By 1800 there were 122 lending libraries in London and 268 in the rest of England.[70] In Spain lending libraries started later, but by the 1830s a new one was opening every year.[71] In Germany by 1800 there was at least one *Lesegesellschaft* or reading club in every town. By 1811 there were twenty-seven in Berlin (a much smaller city than London) and sixteen in Dresden. Alongside these were also the commercial lending libraries or *Leihbibliotek* whose main staples were not the works of Goethe, Schiller or Wieland (some libraries did not even hold them), but the eighteenth-century equivalent of pulp books: the Enlightenment Gothic novel such as Karl Grosse's *Der Genius* or Christian

August Vulpius's *Rinaldo Rinaldini*, and the works of authors such as Carl Gottlob Cramer (1758–1817) and Christian Heinrich Spiess (1755–99). These libraries were the main source of literature for women and servants.[72]

About three-quarters of the 5,000 novels produced in Germany between 1750 and 1800 went to lending libraries. Research has established that the borrowers were mainly men.[73] However, borrowers and readers are not necessarily the same thing. Readers would often send their servants to borrow books, and husbands would borrow them on behalf of their wives, so the borrowing record does not necessarily reveal the principal reader. If diarists are to be believed, women were the main consumers of novels, but then they were probably also the main keepers of diaries. One can safely surmise that, in a society where most occupations were prohibited to middle- and upper-class women, and where the segregation between the sexes was marked, reading books was probably one of the activities where gender distinction was less pronounced.

In Italy there were relatively few lending libraries. Poor literacy and linguistic fragmentation restricted the market. One way for Italian publishers to lower the risks was to pre-sell a series of books (a collection) by finding a common theme. Marketed as a *biblioteca* (i.e. a library), they were intended to attract the relatively few book-buying customers to purchasing up front an entire collection, usually of the classics. The pioneer of this was Giovanni Silvestri, whose *Biblioteca scelta di opere italiane antiche e moderne* (1813) had published hundreds of volumes by 1848.[74] Italian printers and publishers could not even rely on the growing market for school and university books, because in the Lombardo-Veneto this trade was a state monopoly.[75] The sale of opera librettos, which could have been profitable (54,700 were sold in one year alone), did not favour booksellers because the theatres sold them directly to the public.[76]

In France the golden period of the *cabinets de lecture* was 1815–48 (some survived into the twentieth century).[77] Their expansion at the time was facilitated by the financial crisis of 1826 which led to the bankruptcy of many publishers and printers. Their unsold stocks were used to set up lending libraries.[78] The numbers are difficult to establish. According to Françoise Parent-Lardeur, by 1830 in Paris alone there were some 520 *boutiques à lire* or *cabinets de lecture*. Some of these *cabinets* had only a few journals, others nearly 20,000 volumes.[79] According to David Bellos, the number was not as high: sixty-one in 1826, 126 in 1829 and 150 in 1833.[80] Claude Pichois's figures are different still: eighty-six in 1835, rising to a peak of 177 in 1844.[81] The variations are caused, at least in part, by the somewhat arbitrary definition of a lending library, since many bookshops gave their customers the option of 'renting' books instead of buying them outright. But all agree that the numbers increased until the late 1830s, then cheaper books and serialisation put a stop to the expansion.

Parisian students, concentrated in the Latin Quarter, preferred the *cabinets de lecture* to the much colder university libraries. Many *cabinets* in fact doubled up as bookshops; one could either buy or borrow. The bourgeois classes too would regularly borrow books, sometimes as many as a hundred at a time, taking them for the summer to their country homes. Sometimes the servants would borrow books for themselves, hence the pejorative expression – still used in culturally condescending circles – of *romans pour femmes de chambre*, denoting a low genre of literature appreciated by working-class women. Finally, in the more aristocratic districts lending libraries were *de facto* comfortable clubs for reading, and acquired the status of real literary salons.

In France, Great Britain and Germany, and certainly in Italy, the new bourgeoisie were the main customers of the *cabinets de lecture*. The members of the lower classes who made use of them were those in contact with the higher classes: servants, concierges, artisans, shopkeepers.[82] In all cases the urban classes, and particularly the professional middle classes, were overwhelmingly the main users of lending libraries. Bookshops and lending libraries were heavily concentrated in the intellectual centres rather than in the aristocratic areas. For instance, in Paris bookshops and *cabinets de lecture* were along the left bank of the Seine, not far from the Sorbonne and not in the wealthy areas.[83] Books in the eighteenth and nineteenth centuries were not goods one bought locally on the spur of the moment. They were worth a special trip.

Lending libraries dominated the distribution of books throughout the nineteenth century, particularly in the countries with the largest reading public, i.e. France, Britain and Germany. Their success depended on a number of conditions. In the first place it was necessary that there should be a public willing to read books, especially novels, but deterred by their cost. Secondly there should be no source of free borrowing, such as public libraries. In early-nineteenth-century France and Britain some schemes were mooted to establish free 'public' libraries for the people, but these would only come to fruition later in the century. During the Restoration in France the idea of literature for the people was floated by the champions of the *bibliothèques populaires*, while the Church set up its own Société Catholique des Bons Livres in 1827.[84]

Lending libraries provided a regular market for publishers (as university libraries do now), but they also represented an obstacle to the wider diffusion of books, because it was in their interest for books to remain expensive. However, until about 1800 many lending libraries were owned by booksellers – hedging their bets by operating in two potentially conflicting businesses. A clearer separation of the roles emerged around that time, but the Napoleonic wars, by pushing up the cost of paper, ensured that books stayed expensive. After 1815 the expansion of the book-reading public and the corresponding increase in the number of novels published led to a clearer separation between 'high' and 'low' genres. The lending libraries remained firmly in control of the more expensive 'literary' end of the market, but continued to eschew cheap novels. Some of the expensive novels, however, were serialised in journals before being published. Their success determined how many copies would be bought by the lending libraries.

Reading Aloud

The same copy of a book could thus be read by a large number of people. By dividing each book into three volumes, each part could be lent separately, making it possible for three readers to read the same book at the same time. Soon publishers, for whom lending libraries became an important market, printed books already divided into separate volumes even when, like Jane Austen's *Northanger Abbey*, they were already short. Alexandre Dumas' massive *Le Comte de Monte-Cristo* was at one stage divided into eighteen volumes.[85] By the second half of the nineteenth century, when the largest lending library, Mudie's, had established its dominance, the three-decker novel had become the standard length in Victorian Britain.

Readers themselves were able to multiply the number of consumers of books by the simple expedient of reading aloud. This was not always the literate reading to the illiterate. It was family reading, almost the late-eighteenth- and nineteenth-century equivalent of watching television together.

Nowadays reading is a private activity. Readers carve out for themselves a world of their own even against a background of noise and crowds. People read in solitude, whether in their own homes or on trains, planes, beaches and in libraries. Yet there are still situations where reading aloud prevails: one may read to one's children even when they can already read themselves, to encourage that love of books allegedly imperilled by television. Reading aloud is common in schools and when it is necessary to promote an atmosphere of community in a religious setting, where well-known passages are read from holy texts. In some cultural festivals authors read from their own works, and the reading becomes almost a piece of theatre, enabling an audience to reach some kind of intimacy with a writer they admire.

A society in which people frequently read aloud may well have an effect on the kind of novel written. Much early Roman literature was intended for reading aloud. There were then no aids such as spectacles to enable the older Roman gentleman to read in solitude by the weak light of an oil lamp, and the cost of scrolls and copyists was considerable. Better to keep one or more trained readers, often Greek slaves, to read to his master and his friends. Thus the cultured book-lover in antiquity listened more often than he read.[86] It is also likely, for instance, that Cervantes wrote *Don Quixote* on the assumption that it would have listeners as well as readers.[87] Even in the nineteenth century, reading aloud was still common. George Eliot read Goethe, Heine and Shakespeare aloud to George Lewes and friends 'for about three hours every evening'.[88] In Evelyn Waugh's *Brideshead Revisited* (1945), largely set before the Second World War, Lady Marchmain reads from George and Weedon Grossmith's *The Diary of a Nobody* in the drawing room 'with great spirit until ten o'clock'.[89] The invention of cassettes later facilitated the marketing of 'audio books', particularly useful for the blind or for drivers on long car journeys.

Books, still an expensive commodity, could be borrowed from a lending library for a limited period of time. By reading a book aloud it was possible to achieve an efficient use of time and ensure a rapid turnover. The equally scarce house lights could be concentrated around the reader while the rest of the family, or at least those not working, could remain in semi-darkness. A typical image, transmitted in many books, letters and contemporary accounts, was that of the paterfamilias reading a book, his wife busy with needlework, and his children and perhaps his servants listening dutifully. Thomas Bowdler (1754–1825), the expurgator of Shakespeare, mused: 'I can hardly imagine a more pleasing occupation for a winter's evening in the country, than for a father to read one of Shakespeare's plays to his family circle.'[90] A good reader, like a good actor, could electrify his tiny audience. In a letter of 1814 the novelist Maria Edgeworth wrote: 'We have this moment finished Waverley. It was read aloud to this large family, and I wish the author could have witnessed the impression it made – the strong hold it seized of the feelings both of young and old . . . We were so possessed with the belief that the whole story and every character in it was real, that we could not endure the occasional addresses from the author to the reader.'[91] George Eliot recollected reading Walter Scott aloud to her father during the last five or six years of his life.[92] On 4 January 1819, the Irish poet Thomas Moore recorded in his diary that he had just finished reading Scott's *The Heart of Midlothian* to his wife Bessy: 'A most extravagant and incredible story, but full of striking situations, & picturesque sketches.'[93]

Packaging

A book could be published in parts, as a serial appearing at regular intervals, numbered consecutively, monthly or weekly. An alternative was to include the parts in a periodical or a daily paper. In effect the reader was buying the book in instalments. However, there were considerable risks for the publishers: it was necessary to keep readers in thrall to the book, otherwise they would not buy the next instalment, while the publisher would have paid its advance to the author up front. Only a small proportion of the literary output of the nineteenth century was serialised, but since this turned out to include almost all the authors still read today (such as Dickens), there is a general assumption that it was the standard form of publication.[94]

The real boom of the serialised novel occurred after 1830. Here it will suffice to note that serialisation prevailed in the lead countries (Great Britain, France and Germany) not just because they had more readers, but because they had a wider press. Newspapers thought they would increase their sales by carrying a novel (or several novels) as well as the news and feature stories. The idea percolated into other countries. In Italy, so strong was the idea that novels were a quintessentially British product that the first magazines dedicated to their serialisation advertised their provenance overtly. Thus in 1815 the Milan publishing house Benincasa started a journal called *Il Romanzi-ere inglese*, exclusively dedicated to the serialisation of British novels. Benincasa's main competitor Bertolotti (also of Milan) responded with *Il Novelliere britannico*.[95]

How a book is sold often determines the cultural value attributed to it. Cheap paperbacks with garish covers sold in supermarkets are 'lower' in prestige than tomes to be found only in refined bookshops, though the authors of the former may simply shrug their shoulders and smile as they peruse their bank statement. In the early nineteenth century, however, the identifying characteristics of the serious novel were not clear, though it was generally accepted that books sold by peddlers were 'low', even lower than books serialised in women's magazines. But, on the whole, the intellectual and cultural élites who make these decisions were still unfamiliar with the genre. Even later in the nineteenth century the boundaries between high and low were not clear. The term *feuilleton* (serialised novel) became a general French term of abuse for the cheap and trivial. But one of the first *feuilletons* in a daily paper was Balzac's *La Vieille fille*, which came out in twelve daily episodes starting on 23 October 1836. Flaubert's *Madame Bovary* (1856) was serialised, as were Zola's novels. Dickens's novels were sold at railway stations. On the basis of plots alone it would be difficult to make distinctions between 'high' and low' genres. It is possible to describe *Oedipus Rex* as a detective story, *The Odyssey* as an adventure yarn, Jane Austen's novels as Mills & Boon-type romances (how to get Mr Right to marry me) and *Madame Bovary* as a sex-and-shopping novel (bored housewife has lovers, gets into debt to buy pretty frocks, finally kills herself). George Eliot, regarded in her lifetime as a philosophical and difficult writer, very different from Dickens or Wilkie Collins, uses in *Felix Holt* (1866) similar plot devices to theirs: mistaken identity, inheritance and blackmail.[96]

Vladimir Nabokov regarded Balzac as a purveyor of 'cheap platitudes'.[97] When Balzac was living many would have agreed. Here was someone who tried his hand at the popular genres: the historical novel (*Les Chouans*, 1829), the Gothic (*La Peau de chagrin*, 1831), the erotic short story (*Contes drolatiques*, 1832), before moving on to the realist novel, using, on the way, many of the most conventional themes from popular literature: the devoted prostitute, the secret society, the Faustian pact with the supreme (and fascinating) incarnation of evil, the heartless miser, the selfish woman, the utterly devoted father, the rich man in love. These themes and characters ensured his popularity in his lifetime, the waning of his fame until the 1870s and his subsequent canonisation.

The texts written by the author did not always reach the public in their pristine form. If a novel was regarded by the publishers as too long it could be drastically cut, often without informing the author. There was no hesitation in ridding novels of the unnecessary and pretentious embellishments with which authors lengthened them. The digest was born. This too lasted well into the twentieth century thanks to the world-known *Reader's Digest* abridged books, which could cut down a blockbuster into a slim volume by eliminating 'redundant' dialogue, descriptions, subsidiary plots and digressions. Abridgement could also be used to eliminate unsuitable and immoral passages. The famous Thomas Bowdler, whose surname is commonly used in English to indicate expurgation, produced in 1818 *The Family Shakespeare*, 'in which', he claimed, 'nothing is added to the original text; but those words and expressions are omitted which cannot with propriety be read aloud in a family'.[98] Thus the scene in *Henry V* where Princess Catherine of France is given an English-language lesson before meeting the King is completely excised – even though the obscene puns would be detected only by the cognoscenti.[99] Bowdler has been universally reviled ever since as a narrow-minded representative of Victorian prudery (though his work was published well before Queen Victoria ascended the throne). There is much that is true in this, but one must note that even today Shakespeare's plays (especially the big tragedies such as *Hamlet* and *King Lear*) are hardly ever performed in their entirety, but are cut to fit the attention span of the modern audience – an audience which, unlike the one Shakespeare wrote for, is silent throughout.

Authors often willingly cooperated. Samuel Richardson facilitated the process of the abridging of *Clarissa* by providing an index to the second edition, on the assumption that his readers, by the time they approached the end, would have forgotten the beginning and 'would not chuse to read seven Tedious Volumes over again'. Indeed the lengthy table of contents of the gigantic novel was republished as a separate pamphlet in 1749, and sold briskly to those who wanted to read only the plot outline.[100]

Henry Colburn, the publisher of the so-called 'silver-fork' novels (the mocking term is William Hazlitt's) set in fashionable London society, employed an entire editorial staff to rewrite the novels of the less talented among his authors. He was a true pioneer in marketing books, a promotional genius, a real publisher rather than a mere printer, the kind of patron authors would love or hate to have. He conceived the books, produced them, edited them, promoted them. It was said that 'to his novelists he was both midwife and wet-nurse'. Colburn advertised widely and used his journals to puff his authors. He even paid newspapers and bribed journalists to insert in their gossip and society columns suggestions such as, 'We hear that anyone who is anyone is reading Mrs. X's last novel.' In 1817, realising that a literary magazine would help promote his books, he launched the *Literary Gazette*, and in 1818 the *Athenaeum*. Knowing full well that one could make money out of snobs (he was the first publisher of *Burke's Peerage*), Colburn commissioned lengthy reviews by writers he chose, wrote editorials about novels he was going to publish hinting that the authors were, in real life, members of the aristocracy, and that the characters were based on real people discussed in fashionable circles. He was not regarded as a gentleman publisher like John Murray, William Blackwood and Archibald Constable, but he became a rich man.[101]

There was more than one way of cutting up a book. Novels, it was realised, though an inferior genre, might contain pearls of wisdom which the discerning reader would underline or copy into a book. Instead of getting rid of the digressions and asides and leaving the plot, as in the digest, one could do the reverse: remove the plot and keep the asides. Readers would not have to select for themselves the choicest passages – or even read the book – publishers would do it for them. This eighteenth-century habit, which endured into the nineteenth, resulted in the production of anthologies and collections. Some writers even introduced into their narrative 'quotable quotes' and aphorisms in the hope of being anthologised. The fashion – pioneered in England by Vicesimus Knox, the compiler of *Elegant Extracts* (1784) – lasted well into the nineteenth century. Thus, in 1871, the year in which *Middlemarch* was serialised, Alexander Main, a devotee of George Eliot's, brought out *Wise, Witty and Tender Sayings in Prose and Verse Selected from the Works of George Eliot*. This was followed in 1878 by *The George Eliot Birthday Book*, a diary containing a 'George Eliot Thought' for every day of the year.[102]

5

Foundation Stories

Nation-Building

THE ENCHANTMENT with pre-industrial popular culture, and with peasant culture in particular, has continued to this day. To romanticise rural civilisation is a characteristic of modernity and of urban life; it accompanies the rise of industry and of the modern bourgeoisie.

Such fascination for the old ways, however, is not just an attitude, but also part of the lucid project of nation-building. This may appear as a paradox, since to build a nation one must eliminate all kinds of fragmentation, localism and regionalism – everything that smacks of pastoral life. The paradox was (partially) resolved by trying to build the new 'national' culture on the basis of the 'authentic' culture of the people.

The aim was one state, one nation, one people, one language and one culture. It was thus necessary not only to unify the country linguistically (see pages 21–33), but also to 'rediscover' the 'real' culture of the people. The way to do this was to legitimise the vernacular by writing grammars and dictionaries and collecting folk poems, fairy tales and songs.

This Romantic nationalism aimed to replace oral traditions and orally transmitted stories with written texts, and to establish proper language rules where there was uncertainty. This is the central characteristic of what we now call 'the modern': the complete subversion of the traditional (what was oral) into its opposite (what is recorded and fixed) in order to save it.

Inevitably, the early Romantic movement clashed with previously established neo-classical high culture which traced all 'real' culture to antiquity, that is to Rome and Greece. Such cultural revolution against neo-classicism was not as grandiose as it may appear. Neo-classicism itself had been established only since the first half of the eighteenth century, and was far more concerned with the figurative arts than with literature. In Britain it consisted essentially of artists visiting Rome in the mid-1750s and turning themselves into agents for British collectors.[1] At the same time, like the French and German artists, they followed the advice of Johann Winckelmann, the leading art historian of his age, and imitated the ideal forms of Graeco-Roman art.[2] Thanks to Winckelmann and others like him, intellectuals began to occupy a strategic position in determining what is and is not culture and in reducing the significance of popes, princes and patrons as arbiters of taste. Thus neo-classicism too was 'modern'.

However, the new Romantic intelligentsia wanted to celebrate non-classical culture. Its leading lights were Germans, members of an invented nation with no state and no boundaries, united only by the language and education of its élite. The unity of the German people, they thought, could only be found in the people themselves, in their language, their art, their culture, their history. And this was true not only of the Germans, but of all people. Thus the leading theorist of the Romantic movement, Friedrich Schlegel, in his 1815 Vienna lectures *Geschichte der Alten und Neuen Literatur* (History of Ancient and Modern Literature), dealt at length with Indian, Hebrew and Anglo-Saxon cultures, which, he insisted, were just as great as classical Greek and Roman cultures, and said Homer's work was comparable 'with Indian, Persian, or northern, old-German heroic and mythological songs'.[3] Schlegel's brother August was responsible for the translation into German not only of Shakespeare and Pedro Calderón de la Barca but of the main Indian and Persian literary texts, including the Sanskrit *Bhagavad Gita* and the *Ramayana*. This nationalism, far from being narrow-minded or provincial, produced something akin to a 'national cosmopolitanism', a belief in the ability of any people to produce beauty and greatness.

The Romantic intellectuals remained firmly committed to the superiority of written culture, the defining mark of the civilisations of Greece and Rome. These had produced written codes and Homer and Virgil, while the tribes of Europe had only unwritten conventions and sagas held together by unstable memories and dubious texts. The aim of the Romantic revolution was to make the 'national' past available to the members of the new community, the citizens, by writing down a knowledge which had been transmitted orally. They promoted the idea of the worth of popular culture and drafted onto their side everything which was not an expression of classical Greece and Rome. This included Dante, Ariosto, Boccaccio, Shakespeare, as well as Cervantes – all suitably reinterpreted as pioneers leading up to the modern era.[4]

'This is where I look for and find the Romantic,' wrote Schlegel in 1799, '– in the older moderns, in Shakespeare, Cervantes, in Italian poetry, in that age of knights, love, and fairytales in which the thing itself and the word for it originated.'[5]

The political objective was the establishment of the cultural hegemony of the national bourgeoisie, the class that would represent the nation and its people. The era of the aloof thinker was over, claimed Schlegel: 'The isolation of the learned, as a distinctive body, from the great mass of the people, is the most formidable obstacle in the way of national civilisation.'[6]

The 'popular' culture Schlegel and his followers promoted, and occasionally invented, was assumed to have remained unaltered by time, immemorial and authentic. In the real world, however, there is no natural progression from oral to written literature. Much oral literature probably started out as written culture disseminated orally. To attribute to this literature a 'nationality' was quite anachronistic. For instance, in eighteenth-century Iceland there were no fewer than three oral versions of the story of Griselda, which probably arrived from Holland and was based on Chaucer's *The Clerk's Tale*, in turn based on a French version of a story told by Petrarch which is a version of the last tale in Boccaccio's *Decameron*.[7]

The priority for the early Romantics was the rediscovery of the poetry of the people, not its prose – all the better to compete with the great classics of antiquity. Each nation had to find its own Homer – a hunt which had started in earnest well before the Romantic revolution.

Hunting for Homer

In 1760 the Scottish poet James MacPherson published in English *Fragments of Ancient Poetry Collected in the Highlands of Scotland*, largely written by himself. Two years later it was the turn of *Fingal, an Ancient Epic Poem in Six Books*, which he attributed to a Gaelic bard, Ossian, son of a legendary Irish chieftain, Fingal or Finn Mac Cumhail, or Finn MacCool ('the fair son of Cool'). By then Scottish independence was dead, its corpse decomposing on the battlefield of Culloden, but its memory surviving in tuneful songs about the heroic Bonnie Prince Charlie – in real life a dim-witted drunkard. From then on Scotland's fate was subsumed to that of England. As the Union with England became consolidated, cultural pride became increasingly permissible, even encouraged. It posed no threat to anyone, and would provide cohesion as well as consolation to the Scottish intelligentsia. It was thus desirable to have an epic that was both national and the product of a single genius – a Scottish Homer or Virgil. Ossian, son of Fingal, would do.

The book was immensely successful. The cult of Ossian swept throughout Europe, in Germany above all, and reaching even Italy, otherwise more reluctant to join the fashion for folk culture.[8] Ossian (i.e. Macpherson) was translated into German in the 1770s by none other than Goethe for the Leipzig publisher Fleischer. It soon appeared in Italian, French, Spanish, Dutch, Danish, Swedish, Polish and Russian – in other words, in more languages than any other eighteenth-century English work except for *Robinson Crusoe*.[9]

The authenticity of Ossian was quickly challenged. In 1775 Samuel Johnson declared that 'as there is no reason to suppose that the inhabitants of the Highlands and Hebrides ever wrote their native language, it is not to be credited that a long poem was preserved among them'.[10] In 1805 an investigation established that Macpherson had written the poems himself, inserting various fragments of authentic Gaelic poems. Clearly the Ossian debate disturbed the English perception of their own cultural superiority.[11] Nevertheless, the poems were regarded as genuine by German writers such as Johann Gottfried Herder, Goethe and Friedrich Gottlieb Klopstock, and all those who wanted to believe in Ossian. The success of such largely unconscious marketing requires some form of literary fanfare: the texts to be promoted should be consistently mentioned in other texts. Thus Ossian soon obtained the imprimatur of modernity by being mentioned in Goethe's European best-seller *Die Leiden des jungen Werthers* (The Sorrows of Young Werther, 1774), in the scene where Charlotte and Werther are moved to tears over Ossian's 'Songs of Selma'. In this way novels themselves acted as advertisements for other works, establishing, as in this case, what a person of taste and sensibility read.

Ossian was regularly 'advertised' by nationalist writers. Vittorio Alfieri (1749–1803), the major Italian playwright and poet of his time, whose tragic dramas were regarded after his death as seeking to revive the national spirit of Italy, was enamoured of Ossian, whose verses he says he tried to reproduce in his plays.[12] Enthusiasm for Ossian was not at all confined to the Romantic movement, or to writers. The American President Thomas Jefferson regarded Ossian as 'the greatest Poet that had ever existed', and filled his 'commonplace book' with quotes from him.[13] Napoleon, a great admirer of Ossian, commissioned neo-classical paintings to celebrate the Gaelic bard: François

Gérard's *Ossian évoque les fantômes au son de la harpe* (1800–1810) and Anne-Louis Girodet's *Les ombres des héros français reçues par Ossian dans l'Elysée aérien* (1801). In 1812 Ingres painted the better-known *Le Rêve d'Ossian* influenced by Gérard. Two operas with Ossian themes were produced, to great acclaim, at the beginning of the nineteenth century: Jean-François Lesueur's *Ossian, ou Les bardes* (1804) and Etienne-Nicolas Méhul's *Uthal* (1806). Ossian was often mentioned, always respectfully, by popular writers of the period, such as Sophie Cottin in her novel *Malvina* (1800).[14]

There was a vogue for Scottish and Irish folk songs. George Thomson, a member of the Edinburgh Musical Society, published a collection of texts (*Select Collection of Original Scottish Airs*, 1793) and tried, successfully, to interest leading Continental composers, including Beethoven, in writing the music for them.[15]

The 'discovery' of Ossian proved that Scotland had an ancient literature as worthy of celebration as Virgil and Homer. 'Ossian has ousted Homer in my heart,' wrote Goethe's young Werther.[16] To drive the point home it was said that Ossian was blind, like Homer. Inevitably, the poems drew criticisms and parody, but were still regarded by some Scots as authentic nearly 150 years after their publication.[17]

A major literary trend had been launched. Bishop Thomas Percy edited in 1765 *The Reliques of Ancient English Poetry*, consisting of old heroic ballads and songs. He had previously edited and translated Icelandic runic poetry (1763) and, in 1770, translated *Northern Antiquities*, which contained literary fragments from ancient Danish, Saxon and Icelandic. In 1810 in Germany, Ludwig Achim Arnim and Clemens Maria Brentano, influenced by the success of the *Reliques*, compiled their folk collection *Des Knaben Wunderhorn*, whose texts were widely set as songs by Mendelssohn, Schumann, Brahms, Mahler and Schoenberg and many others.

Folk Culture

Though there had been some interest earlier in the eighteenth century in old English ballads – that of 'Chevy Chase' had been published by Addison in the *Spectator* in May 1711 – popular culture, in the sense of the culture of the people, long believed by the old élites to be either non-existent or worthless, was now staging a rebirth. The construction of national literature had become an international trend.[18] Cultural nationalists like Johann Gottfried Herder

(1744–1803) lamented the fact that Germany was linguistically fragmented, that its aristocracy regarded foreign languages (whether Latin or French) as superior, and that artists were in awe of foreign models. Against the background of a veritable explosion in book production and readership, he argued that writers should adopt cultural models from the past.

In a letter addressed to an imaginary friend sceptical of the discovery of Ossian, Herder insisted that Ossian was 'a poet full of the grandeur, innocence, simplicity, activity and bliss of human life'.[19] He added that 'Ossian's poems are songs, songs of the people, folk songs, the songs of an unsophisticated people living close to the senses, songs which have been long handed down by oral tradition.'[20] 'We Germans too', he added, had poems like these Scottish ballads. 'But who is there to collect them? To care about them? To care about the songs of the people, from the streets and alleys and fish markets?'

Herder followed his own advice, and in 1778–79 published anthologies of folk tales from other countries, *Volkslieder* and *Volkspoesie*, containing verse by Homer, Shakespeare (rebranded respectively as illustrious Greek and English folk poets), Ossian and many others. He collected Biblical poems under the telling title *Vom Geist der ebräischen Poesie* (The Spirit of Hebrew Poetry) – suggesting they were the words of a people, not the Word of God. He contrasted *Volkspoesie* to the poetry and art of the educated *Kunstdichtung*, the former innocent and natural, the latter civilised and refined; the former real, the latter artificial: '. . . the more barbarous a people is . . . the more alive, the freer, the closer to the senses, the more lyrically dynamic its songs will be, if songs it has'.[21]

With Herder the patronising or disdainful attitude towards popular culture began to change. He persuaded intellectuals, including Goethe, that folklore and popular myths were the creative product of the *Volk*, the people, of which they were the true expression. Herder was not shouting in the wilderness. An important step in Goethe's cultural development was his encounter with Herder in September 1770. Another was writing the poem 'Erlkönig' as if it were an expression of German folk poetry. Herder imparted to Goethe an enthusiasm for popular poetry, primitivism and the poems of Ossian, and was of decisive importance for Goethe's drama of German chivalry, *Götz von Berlichingen* (1773).[22]

Herder had caught the mood of a new generation of Romantics desirous to connect to a lost popular culture. Almost every well-known German writer of the period was influenced by his programme of national literary renewal:

Novalis, Johann Hölderlin, August and Friedrich Schlegel, Friedrich Schelling and Karl Ottfried Muller.

In France, Madame Germaine de Staël was the leading admirer of Herder. She got Schlegel to tutor her children, and her cousin Madame Necker de Saussure translated Schlegel's lectures on literature into French. De Staël's high station in life – a sophisticated intellectual and the daughter of the great banker Jacques Necker – was no impediment to her celebration of rustic simplicity.[23] She thought that a 'truly national literature' could be built on the basis of the songs of the troubadours.[24] Like Herder she held such views within a new cosmopolitan framework, though remaining utterly convinced of the superiority of French culture. In her best-selling novel *Corinne ou l'Italie* (1807) – an 'immortal book' to be read once a year, according to Elizabeth Barrett (later Browning) – de Staël made fun of the narrow cultural nationalism of the Comte d'Erfeuil, who defends French taste and elegance against the 'incongruities' of the Greeks and the 'monstrosities' of Shakespeare: 'our theatre is the best in Europe, I think not even the English would presume to set Shakespeare against it'.[25] To the parochial Count, Madame de Staël opposes the heroine Corinne – inspired by the famous improviser Corilla Olimpica – a beautiful, fiercely independent and highly educated foreign lady, English by birth, Italian by adoption, thus combining north and south, and a new aesthetic principle of cultural cosmopolitanism: the union of differences.[26] It is on the basis of this principle that Oswal, the Scottish lord in love with Corinne, tells her admiringly that 'a source of your incomparable grace is that you combine all the charms of different nations'.[27]

Madame de Staël, in her influential *De l'Allemagne*, sought to make German literature known in France. In fact, almost all the German writers mentioned by her had been translated into French (in any case, she did not know German). Far from revealing unknown writers, she was championing her own selection. There was actually considerable cultural interchange between Germany and France, thanks to the presence in Paris of German publishers such as Cramers, Henrichs and Schoell.[28] What Madame de Staël did was to use her considerable intellectual patronage to construct an image of Germany which, in France at least, would last until the Franco–Prussian war of 1870: a country of idealists and dreamers.[29] After 1870 Germany's image deteriorated; it turned into a nation of bloodthirsty, technologically superior militarists – an image abundantly reinforced by Nazism.

Little attention was paid to authentic popular culture, i.e. what the 'people', the peasants, actually read and heard: the naïve religious pamphlets, the simple fairy tales, and the crime stories sold by the peddlers all over Europe. Ethnographic societies stylised and romanticised peasant folk dress, showing a pleasant array of bright colours and pretty frocks, while in reality authentic peasant clothes were drab – colour being expensive. Peasant voices and stories were transcribed and modified to make them sound literary so that they could be enjoyed by the educated public of readers.[30]

Folklore obviously fulfilled a modern longing, because interest in it has lasted to this day and is now part of a thriving heritage industry. How recent an invention it is can be determined by the origin of the word itself: 'folklore' was coined in the 1840s by the English antiquary William John Thoms, an admirer of the Grimm brothers, and was widely adopted in other languages, including French, Italian and Spanish. The Germans eventually used a term proposed by H.W. Riehl in 1858: *Volkskunde* – an ambiguous word which means both the science of the people, in the sense of emanating from them, and the scientific study of the people, with the people now an object of observation.

By the middle of the nineteenth century the construction of 'the people' as an object of sentimental interest was in full swing in most European countries, but nowhere more so than in Russia. At the beginning of the century the Russian nobility had a very rudimentary idea of what 'the people' were. Its literary construction thus followed Western models. When 'the people' speak in Nikolai Karamzin's *Poor Lisa* (1792), they bear the unmistakable accents of characters from Jean-Jacques Rousseau's *Nouvelle Héloïse* with a dash of Voltaire and, above all, of Richardson's *Clarissa*.[31] The new generation of Russian intellectuals, attracted by the German myth of the *Volk*, by the poetry of Ossian and the novels of Walter Scott, and longing to be 'civilised' like the French or the English, tried to follow Herder and Schelling in the discovery of the Russian people and its culture. Upon finding out that even in the business of discovering the people they were lagging behind Germany by some thirty years, they reacted by seeking refuge in a celebration of Russian 'peculiarity'. As Pushkin wrote: 'Russia never had anything in common with the rest of Europe. Her history demands a different thought and a different formula.'[32] Here too, however, the Russians were unoriginal. The idea of being exceptional, unique, having a special destiny, etc., was a common European trope, with each country believing itself to be pursuing a departure from the normal road – i.e. that of the British or the French.

Unable to join England and France, some Russian intellectuals at first sought comfort in the discovery that the Russian people had been spared the disasters which had befallen 'Europe': godless revolutions in France, the worship of money and industry in England.[33] The Russian people had remained immune from such misfortunes. Many foreigners disagreed. The Marquis Astolphe de Custine, in a popular book first published in 1843, *La Russie en 1839*, one of the earliest west European indictments of Russian barbarism, wrote that Russia was 'a strange land ... which gives birth to slaves who believe whatever they are told on bended knees; spies who have no convictions at all, the better to pin down those held by others; and ironists who exaggerate its ills ... The profession of misleading foreigners is one known only in Russia.'[34] But Russians could find supporters in less critical admirers such as Baron Franz August Maria Haxthausen, a German aristocrat who in a book published at the same time as Custine's extolled the distinctive virtues of the organisation of the Russian village, the *mir*, as a bulwark against excessive industrialisation and its inevitable evils: pauperisation and the formation of a proletarian mob.[35]

This slavophile position permeated all strands of Russian high culture and politics and gave rise to left-wing as well as conservative variants. The importance and idealisation of 'the people' in Russian cultural production remained one of its central characteristics, without close parallel in western Europe. In Russian novels, plays and later in films, the presence of the people is often conspicuous: wise *mujiks* with long white beards mumbling deep thoughts, jolly Volga boatmen with wonderful bass voices, free and irrepressible Cossacks riding across the steppes while getting drunk – the staple of later cinematic stereotypes. In Russian operas the people often erupt on the stage, seldom as protagonists but frequently as the chorus, symbols of wise, pre-modern innocence, fulfilling the role that noble savages and ancient wisdom have in Western culture. Yet the populism of the Russian intelligentsia never really celebrated 'Old Russia', which was regarded as primitive, slave to the religious heritage of the Byzantine period and to localism (ancient Kiev, Novgorod, Moscow).[36]

The Saga

The search for the popular roots of culture was particularly intense in smaller countries dominated by others. There the Romantic intelligentsia was unsure of itself and of its past, as was often the case in areas under Austrian or Russian or Turkish rule. Their efforts led to the formation of patriotic societies aimed at fostering the use of a 'national' language. This was no easy task. In Latvia all education other than primary was in German until the 1890s. Educated people were regarded as German. Latvian had no written form. The few 'Latvian' songs that existed had first been published in a Latin version – such as Fredericus Menius's *De Origine Livonorum* (1632). In the early nineteenth century Latvian nationalists, following the lead of Herder, became interested in Latvian oral culture. Unable to find suitable epic poetry, they made it up using available material, including some in German. Oral folk culture, though it obviously lacked any 'national' dimension, was drafted into the service of the Latvian nation by patriots like Ansis Lerchis-Puskaitis and Krishjânis Barons, who supervised a massive collection of folk songs, the *Latvju Dainas*, in the 1890s.[37] These are regarded today as an essential part of Latvian identity and are taught in all schools as part of the curriculum.

Such systematic invention and reinvention of the past, such thorough-going exploitation of history in the service of a political project, was the norm across Europe, and remained so throughout much of the twentieth century, when it became a global phenomenon.

Before the middle of the nineteenth century 'national' poets were springing up everywhere, like Vasile Alecsandri, whose collected popular poetry *Doine* (1855) became very influential in his native Romania. The Swedes had started earlier: between 1814 and 1818 Erik Gustaf Geijer and Arvid August Afzelius published the *Svenska Folk-visor*, a collection of folk tales, hoping it would become the foundation of national Swedish poetry. In Denmark Adam Oehlenschläger, the country's 'national poet', produced in 1802 the epic poem *Guldhornene* (Golden Horn), about the mythic Viking horns which are now a standby of any films about the Viking era.[38] In Serbia, Vuk Stefanović Karadžić, the author of the first Serbian grammar (see page 25), published his influential *Srpske Narodne Pjesne*, a collection of Serbian popular poetry, called *guslari* in Serbian after the one-stringed instrument *gusle*. Karadžić's songs, in the words of the historian Andrew Wachtel, 'brought Serbia onto the world cultural scene for the first time and spurred translations by . . . Goethe, Walter Scott, Mérimée and Pushkin'.[39]

Ethnographers busied themselves collecting folk songs and poetry. The purpose of all this was more political and ideological than scientific. The texts found were polished, redesigned and rewritten for a literary audience. Inevitably their authenticity was challenged as some became suspicious of the number of ancient manuscripts miraculously found in the depths of monasteries.[40] In Spain some scholars wrote epic Basque songs in old Castilian, not realising that the Basque language had not the slightest connection with Castilian, a discovery made in 1821 by the great German philologist Wilhelm von Humboldt.[41]

Lithuania's rural epic *Metai* (The Seasons) had been written in 1765–75 by the country's first major poet, Kristijonas Donelaitis. It was the first extensive poetic text in Lithuanian and dealt with the heroic figure of a plain country pastor who spoke for his people in their own language. It attracted so little attention that it was published only fifty years later, in 1818. Even then it attracted no great interest in Lithuania itself, and came to general attention only when it was praised by Soviet scholars for being on the side of the toiling masses, at a time when Lithuania was under Soviet domination.[42]

Finnish cultural patriotism had started as early as 1770, when the Aurora Society was founded in the then capital of Turku, but the Finns discovered their own national epic only in 1835 with the publication of *Kalevala*. This purported to be a collection of epic poems recorded by – among others – the folklorist Elias Lönnrot (1802–84) from the oral poetry of the rural inhabitants of north-eastern Finland where Karelian was spoken. At that time there was no written Finnish literature at all, and major Finnish writers such as Johan Ludvig Runeberg (the Finnish 'national poet') and Zacharias Topelius (author of fairy tales) wrote in Swedish and could read the *Kalevala* only in translation. Lönnrot wanted to provide the Finns with their *Iliad*, or their *Nibelungenlied*, or, at the very least, with their Ossian. But the *Kalevala*, far from being an ancient epic, was Lönnrot's own creation, based on orally transmitted material he had gathered.[43] He wished to show that Finland too had a literature to be proud of, and that *consequently* it was a real nation. Using classical and foreign literary models of what an epic should look like, he moulded his Finnish-Karelian material to the taste of his educated readers and made it coherent.

By the beginning of the twentieth century it had become the duty of every young Finn to study the *Kalevala*. Children were named after *Kalevala* characters, as were streets, newspapers and theatres. It became the most translated work of Finnish literature. Its German version inspired Longfellow, who wrote in 1855 *The Song of Hiawatha* in imitation of the *Kalevala* meter.

Icelandic sagas appear to rest on more solid foundations, having been written down as early as the twelfth and thirteenth centuries. These texts (the word *saga* in Old Norse means 'that which is told') presume to have identifiable authors such as the *skaldic* (court) poet Egill Skallagrimsson (910–90). Most deal with the lives of Scandinavian kings and ruling families.

The sagas were aristocratic, not 'popular', literature, and they were not 'pure', but influenced by French chivalric texts. They turned out to be particularly popular in England when translated by Samuel Laing in 1844 (their affinity with *Beowulf* was regarded as a link with 'England' before the Norman Conquest). Many were tales of martyrs, trolls and ghosts.[44]

Epics provided the best foundation story for nation-building. Appropriate texts, selected by nationalist élites and eventually adopted in schools, provided the new national community with a shared knowledge of its past. The intention was to establish an alternative to hitherto prevailing narratives such as the Bible or classical culture. Of course, in the real world a multiplicity of narratives co-existed with a multiplicity of identities. The Bible itself is a blend of alleged history, practical advice, rules and laws, poetry, fairy tales and much else besides. And it was difficult, if not impossible, to dislodge the Bible and Homer: they were protected by too many vested interests, too many priests and too many teachers. What really mattered for the formation of a national community was a common education, a common history and common books, regardless of where these came from.

Besides, not all countries required an epic. The French used a particular version of the history of France as the foundation myth of the French nation, and the English did likewise. In both countries historians who offered a suitably upbeat version of history gained considerable prestige. It was the kind of history in which the people appeared to be always protagonists as long as they followed wise rulers, and where each wise ruler was depicted by a telling anecdote of dubious authenticity – the kind of history satirised in England in the wonderful *1066 and All That* by W.C. Sellar and R.J. Yeatman (1930).

In later years, perhaps regretting the lack of a national epic, the French found a suitable one by adopting the most famous of the *chansons de geste*: the *Chanson de Roland*. Henri Monin, a young scholar, had the good luck to discover the manuscript of the epic poem, long regarded as lost, in the Royal Library in 1832. Then, as if by enchantment, other lost manuscripts of the *Chanson* were found, including one at the Bodleian Library in Oxford, since then regarded as the most authoritative (and, along with the Magna Carta, one of the Bodleian's main treasures). Attributed to the Norman poet Turold, the *Chanson* recounts the battle of Roncesvalles between the Francs and the Saracens in 778 and the heroic deeds of Roland, one of Charlemagne's knights, who dies on the battlefield. Charlemagne did fight in 778, but against Basque Christian tribes, not the Saracens. And Roland gets only one line in Einhard's contemporary life of Charlemagne.[45] But the legend had been going round Europe for centuries, had been reported in booklets of the Bibliothèque Bleue, and Roland, as Orlando, was the hero of Ariosto's famous epic poem *Orlando Furioso* (1516).

The poem was criticised by some (the language is barbaric, the verse is monotonous, etc.). But the more *engagé* nineteenth-century historians and critics praised it to the sky. Jules Michelet wrote that in the sublime *Chanson* 'we can hear the voice of the people and its heroes'; for Ludovic Vitet, in the *Revue des deux mondes* (1852), 'the poem is full of love of country, love of France, of sweet France'; Pierre de Saint-Victor intoned in 1872: 'What a rough masterpiece emerges out of this primitive idiom . . . It is the infancy of art, yet a Herculean infancy which, in one leap, attains the sublime.'[46]

The *Chanson* never functioned as a founding myth of French nationalism to the same extent as the *Nibelungenlied* did for the Germans.[47] France, like England, required no founding myth to be recovered from the debris of its history. France already had an identity, and had been an independent nation for centuries. The problem for French republicans was to find an appropriate national rallying point quite distinct from that of the monarchist and Catholic supporters of the *ancien régime.*

Folklore was always a double-edged cultural weapon. By promoting local consciousness it worked in favour of conservatives against nationalists, yet it was sometimes too 'democratic' for the former, while remaining too feudal for the progressives.

Thus Scottish folklore became tolerable only when it had become quaint and harmless. Tartan colours could be worn again in 1782, once the Highlands had been thoroughly pacified. Similarly in France the revival of Breton, promoted after 1807 by the Académie Celtique, a reaction against the dominance of French, led to nothing grander than translations into Breton, such as of lives of saints, still selling thousands of copies in the middle of the nineteenth century, and a translation of the Bible in 1827.[48] In 1839 a collection of purported 'old' popular songs, *Barzaz Breiz* (The Poetry of Brittany), was 'discovered', having been 'improved' – or entirely made up – by the editor, Hersart de Villemarqué.

Such resurrections of folk literature occurred all over Europe. Even in Italy, where the intelligentsia was the least affected by populism, there was a renewed interest in folklore, though it was extremely condescending, a kind of home-grown Orientalism. In Naples 'books, lithograph, operas and ballet chronicled the salty doings among the *basso popolo*'.[49] In Catalonia, the nineteenth-century revival of the language, the *Renaixença*, took its inspiration from French revolutionary ideas as well as local nationalist poets such as Benaventura Aribau, the author of the famous *Oda a la pàtria* (1833).[50]

In Ireland there was considerable delay in the collecting of folk tales and their 'improvement'. The golden age of this revival occurred towards the end of the nineteenth century, when a national literature celebrating Irish folklore in English was developed by W.B. Yeats (*Fairy and Folk Tales of the Irish Peasantry*, 1888, and his *Irish Fairy Tales*, 1889), Lady Gregory (*Cuchulain of Muirthemme*, 1902) and George Moore (the play *Diarmuid and Grania*, written with Yeats in 1901). This was, of course, part of a wider literary revival, one of the components of the new Irish nationalism.[51]

Neither the French nor the English needed to create a national literature. Nor did the authorities need folklore to support a national identity. Anyway, there was not such a thing as *French* or *English* folklore. Folklore was a regional question – of relevance only in places such as Cornwall, Wales, or Scotland or Alsace, Brittany and Occitanie.[52] The cult of the French as an indivisible people – just like the invention of the 'British' – was promoted by mainstream intellectuals: Lamennais (*Le Livre du peuple*), Michelet (*Le Peuple*, 1846), Victor Hugo (*Claude Geux*, *Les Misérables* and much else), Sainte-Beuve, Nodier and Lamartine.[53]

Inventing the French and the English was not as complex a task as 'making' the Hungarians, the Italians, the Russians or the Germans. In the new cultural markets of literature emerging in the nineteenth century the British and the French already had a significant lead. The problem with hegemonic countries, however, is that they are incurably provincial. They export their culture, their books and their plays; their institutions are copied and their ideas are adapted; they bask in the veneration of others, and take it all for granted. And they draw the obvious conclusion: being the object of universal admiration means there is little that matters elsewhere, little needs to be imported or adapted into their culture.

As the nineteenth century unfolded, the French knew nothing of German philosophy, very little of which was translated. Even Herder was not available in French until 1825. Tissot, the first great translator of Immanuel Kant, learned German 'on the job', *while* translating Kant. Most of Hegel was translated into French only in the twentieth century (by then modern philosophy had moved on somewhat).[54] The French and English élites were, of course, curious about other countries. They avidly read travellers' accounts (written by their countrymen), bought guidebooks written by English writers, and explored the rest of Europe with the curiosity of anthropologists. They did not think they had much to learn. The Continentals themselves agreed: they had much to learn from the British and the French, and little to teach them. France and England led where others followed. The others tried to catch up.

6

※

Fairy Tales

Once Upon a Time

FAIRY-TALE BOOKS have been best-sellers since the nineteenth century.
Once upon a time, however, there was little money to be made out of them.
There were professional storytellers, but the typical teller of tales was a
member of the family or of a circle of friends, who derived non-monetary
compensation from telling a story: admiration, pleasure, prestige, perhaps
some food and drink.

Today, the nearest thing to this kind of storytelling is joke-telling – the
most important surviving form of oral culture transmitted outside the
market. Though there are jokebooks, and professional comedians tell jokes
on television and in the music hall and cabaret, the vast majority of jokes are
told by friends to friends. The system is amazingly efficient. The speed of the
circulation of jokes, even in the pre-internet age, never ceased to surprise.
There are further similarities between jokes and fairy tales: both rely significantly on the ability of the narrator to 'act' the parts, mimic accents and
voices, embroider their act, and know when and how to bring it to its closing
punch-line with just the right timing. In both jokes and tales, few care to
trace the 'original' or authentic source.

Most collecting and writing down of fairy tales took place in the nineteenth century, but it was hardly a novel endeavour. The oldest known
collection, India's *Panchatantra*, attributed to Vishnusharman, was written
down between the fourth and third centuries BC. During the Middle Ages,
in what were then the major cultural centres of the world, Islam and China,
fairy tales were codified earlier than in Europe, as was the case with *The
Thousand and One Nights*, written down in its final Arabic version in the
fourteenth century.

In sixteenth- and seventeenth-century Europe, fairy tales or fantasy stories were among the most popular secular books. Many had been diffused through chapbooks like those of the Bibliothèque Bleue. The great best-sellers of nineteenth-century France were collections written by seventeenth-century authors such as Charles Perrault (whose 1697 collection *Histoires ou contes du temps passé* included 'Little Red Riding Hood', 'Bluebeard', 'Sleeping Beauty' and 'Puss in Boots') and Jean de la Fontaine, whose over two hundred fables, published between 1668 and 1694, were in turn adaptations of other fables. In seventeenth- and eighteenth-century France a significant number of women were writing up fairy stories: Perrault's niece Marie-Jeanne Lhéritier de Villandon (1664–1734), Marie Catherine le Jumel, Baronne d'Aulnoy, author of three volumes of *Contes des Fées*, Charlotte-Rose de la Force (1670–1716) and Jeanne-Marie Leprince de Beaumont (1711–80).

Though it was generally assumed, following the Romantics, that fairy tales were 'the voice of the people', charming leftovers from the infancy of humankind, suitable for children and women, the earliest literary fairy tales were an adult genre written by aristocrats and intellectuals for aristocratic and educated audiences. The *Panchatantra* – at least in its written version – presented itself as a manual for the education of a young prince in the ways of the world. Its international success was largely due to its appeal to the educated classes, hence its translation from the original Sanskrit (now lost) to Pahlavi (a Persian language), Arabic, Greek and Turkish, as well as German – and from German to further translations into other European languages.

The 'voice of the people' theory requires that each fairy tale has an original authentic version, a starting point. This is a specifically nineteenth-century Western view (still surviving today), prizing the unique product and the clear identity of a single author. Yet this is a position difficult to sustain, since it is impossible to conceive of an utterly original work of culture, one with no history and no source of inspiration outside itself. Most cultural artefacts are variations of what went before. As Claude Lévi-Strauss explained in 1958, a myth or story is not a single construct, but is made up of all its known variants.[1] In his memoirs, *Tristes Tropiques*, he emphasises that 'human societies as individuals – in their games, their dreams, their visions – never create absolutely, but simply choose certain combinations for a repertory of ideas'.[2] There is no authentic or original myth or tale, just as there is no 'original' recipe in the art of cookery, no 'original' meatballs, as Angela Carter observed, but the constant adaptation, reinterpretation and recreation of what went before.[3] Even if there had been an original author, the story would not come to us in a straight line but as a body of different versions. It is not surprising that the triumphant variants, and the variants of these variants, filtered by audiences and cultures and tested by time and repetition, secured wide favour and popularity. They would be the 'best' versions, the most appealing, perhaps the most embellished, but not necessarily the most authentic. Fairy tales survive Darwinistically, adapting themselves to the cultural environment, the mentality and taste of those who tell them and those who listen to them.

This is a field where generalisations are more dangerous than usual. One can imagine the 'original' of a well-known fairy tale – had it existed – as simply the primitive first draft of a work in progress. This is then enriched by constant retelling, acquiring complexity and refinement, and finally emerges from this lengthy process sturdy yet malleable and open to further adaptations.

But one can imagine the opposite case. 'In the beginning' there is a refined and aristocratic original story (or piece of music, or image), crafted for the exquisite taste of a small élite by a now unknown genius. Eventually this story is handed down to the common people, vulgar and uncouth. As they possess neither the education nor the inclination to appreciate such a cultural gift, the gift itself must shed its original patrician delicacy and turn itself into a crude and loutish product – yet another example of the decadence from a Golden Age.

Both these theories suffer from excessive determinism, the assumption that history proceeds in a straight line, either from primitive society to civilisation, or from splendour to decadence, and that indeed there are entities which can be demarcated and labelled as 'civilisation' and 'barbarism'.

But what if fairy tales are simply the expression of a finite number of plots or frameworks? What if all stories had a similar deep structure? Vladimir Propp, a twentieth-century Russian ethnographer, tried to show that all tales – or at least the Russian tales he analysed – have a similar structure or morphology.[4] His scheme consists of thirty-one narrative functions, the basic units which make the story progress (not all of which need to be present in every tale): these include 'departure' or 'absentation', encounter with the villain, test, hero's reaction, receipt of magical agent, pursuit, rescue, unrecognised arrival, unfounded claims, recognition, exposure, punishment, wedding, etc. An initially good situation – one where nothing is missing and everyone is content – is disrupted: someone dies, or a lack of something is noticed, or something is stolen. The point is that the hero has a motivation and a mission: to find a way of re-establishing the original situation. Alternatively, the initial situation lacks something: money, or a husband or a wife, or health. The hero's task is to find what is missing. His will is tested; he (occasionally she) acquires magic powers or helpers endowed with magic powers; encounters a villain; has to choose between (usually) three different gifts, and so on. Eventually the hero is rewarded by wealth and/or a good marriage.[5] The action is situated in an unspecified past ('Once upon a time'). In fact many fairy tales have the same structure as the epic: in its simplest form, it is the story of the struggle of an individual against the world: *ego contra mundum*. Even the less experienced reader or listener becomes rapidly acquainted with the formulaic aspects of the tales. Far from diminishing the pleasure, this heightens it, especially in children.

The deep structure of the story can be unearthed by removing all aspects not functional to it. For instance, 'Little Red Riding Hood' 'works' equally if we change the colour of the mantle from red to green, or the wolf into a bear. The hero could be a boy as well as a girl, or indeed an adult. The villain does not have to be an animal. It could be a brigand. However, if we change the wolf into a dove, the story would have to alter fundamentally.[6] James Thurber's 1940 'updating' of it, for instance, changes only the ending:

> ... she saw it was not her grandmother but the wolf, for even in a nightcap a wolf does not look any more like your grandmother than the Metro-Goldwyn lion looks like Calvin Coolidge. So the little girl took an automatic out of her basket and shot the wolf dead. Moral: it is not so easy to fool little girls nowadays as it used to be.[7]

Which, presumably, inspired Roald Dahl's 1982 retelling:

> The small girl smiles. One eyelid flickers.
> She whips a pistol from her knickers.
> She aims it at the creature's head
> And bang bang bang, she shoots him dead.
> A few weeks later, in the wood,
> I came across Miss Riding Hood.
> But what a change! No cloak of red,
> No silly hood upon her head.
> She said 'Hello, and please note
> My lovely furry wolfskin coat.'[8]

Oral transmission of fairy tales accelerates their diversity, but it also adds an element of conservatism, since every retelling modifies the previous version. Writing down the story, however, could turn out to be an even more conservative measure – the equivalent of embalming a recorded text. This ensures its wider diffusion, while at the same time encouraging more radical departures from that handed down. 'Cinderella' may inspire not a fairy tale, but a romantic story about an orphan: abused at home by aunt and cousins and bullied at school, she becomes a governess and eventually finds a Mr Right or Prince Charming who is expected to rescue her from her 'bad situation' and turn her into a princess, or, at the very least, a happily married, prosperous woman. By cunningly amalgamating this story with 'Bluebeard' Mr Right becomes a mysterious man with a secret (a mad wife in the attic). Further tinkering with additional bits from 'Beauty and the Beast' and Mr Right could become a certain Mr Rochester who, blind and badly burnt, marries Charlotte Brontë's Jane Eyre.

Recording Tales

In Europe literary versions of fairy tales began to appear in the sixteenth and seventeenth centuries. The Italians were in the forefront (as in so much else in European commerce and culture). Boccaccio had pioneered the art of the short story, but Giovan Francesco Straparola's Le Piacevoli notti (Venice, 1550–53) was one of the first collections to include fairy tales. He also used a 'framing procedure' – the story within a story – imagining a group of aristocrats in exile telling each other stories, as did Gianbattista Basile in his Lo Cunto de li cunti (The Tale of Tales), written in Neapolitan and published posthumously in the 1630s.[9]

The framing mechanism had been used before in 'high' literature. Boccaccio's Decameron and Chaucer's Canterbury Tales are held together by the tale of a group of people telling stories to each other to while away the hours. Scheherazade or Shahrāzād, the imagined author of The Thousand and One Nights, is herself the heroine in the story of a young woman who constantly delays her execution by sustaining the interest of the Sultan in her stories. Significantly the storyteller here is a woman, as is Murasaki Shikibu, the author of Genji Monogatari, the long romance describing the court life of Heian Japan in the tenth century. Women were, in all probability, the main transmitters and adapters of fairy tales (and the main source for collectors like the Grimm brothers), as governesses, mothers and grandmothers. Straparola himself claimed to have heard some of his stories from a woman, as did Basile and Perrault.[10] Fairy tales constituted one of the rare points of contact between aristocratic culture and popular culture in the eighteenth century. The connection, at times, was direct: the tale would be told to the children of the better-off by their nannies.[11] Thus Pushkin first heard Russian folk tales from his nurse Arina Rodionovna, and later used some of them in his own works, such as *Ruslan and Ludmila*; for others, such as *The Golden Cockerel*, he used the French translation of one of Washington Irving's Arabian tales ('The Alhambra').[12]

The frequent characterisation of the putative author as a woman sufficed to characterise fairy tales as a low – if charming – genre: stories told by a nurse, perhaps illiterate, to a still illiterate child. In all likelihood most itinerant narrators were men, while female narrators prevailed in the home. For men fairy tales were a market activity, a performance in the public sphere for which one got paid, unlike women, for whom telling stories was one of the many unpaid activities undertaken in the private domain.

Fairy tales travelled freely across age groups, between high and low classes, and across cultures, though the flow was seldom evenly balanced. Originally, stories coming from the East prevailed (we are, of course, talking about the stories that have survived). Take, for instance, the epic story of Gilgamesh, ruler of Uruk in Babylon (present-day Warka in Iraq), and his friendship with Enkidu. This was written some two thousand years before Christ and contains accounts which surfaced later in the Bible (the Flood) and *The Iliad* (the friendship between Patroclus and Achilles). Eventually episodes from the Gilgamesh epic were reproduced in Oriental carpets, some of which were bought by Venetians. In AD 978 the Doge of Venice Pietro Orseolo became a monk and travelled all the way to the abbey of St Michel de Cuixa in the Pyrenees. The motifs of the Oriental carpets he had brought with him were then used to decorate the capitals of the columns of the cloister. Thus Gilgamesh's truly epic journey reached the Pyrenees, having begun, three thousand years earlier, in Babylon.

Until the sixteenth and seventeenth centuries, Islam knew more about Christianity than Christianity knew about Islam, but the situation began to reverse as the great European fear of the Turks escalated, and with it an intense and growing interest in the Orient. In 1543 the Latin translation of the Koran was printed in Basel.[13] Secular stories prepared the ground for the reception of *The Thousand and One Nights* (*Alf layla wa-layla*), translated in 1704 by Antoine Galland (1646–1715), a French diplomat posted in Constantinople. This milestone in the Western view of the Orient was retranslated from French into other European languages, including English in 1705 and

German in 1712. Direct translation from Arabic followed later in the nine-teenth century. Most of the famous tales originated from further afield than the Arab world. The legendary storyteller's name, Scheherazade, is of Persian origin, but many of the stories, including the overall framing story, are Indian, and appear in the book of tales *Kathasaritsagara*, composed by the Kashmīri poet Somadeva in about 1070.

In Europe the most successful fairy tales, after those of Perrault, were those collected by the German philologists and ethnographers Jacob and Wilhelm Grimm. Jacob Grimm may have regarded his most important work to have been his famous *Deutsche Grammatik* (German Grammar, 1819) but the two brothers gained immortality thanks to the collection of folk tales published in 1812–15 (*Kinder- und Hausmärchen*) and expanded in 1857 as *Grimm's Fairy Tales*. At first Ludwig Bechstein's rival *Deutsches Märchenbuch* (The German Book of Fairy Tales, 1845) was more successful, but by the 1870s the Grimms' tales had become part of the school curriculum in Germany and elsewhere. By the beginning of the twentieth century they were outselling every book in Germany except for the Bible.[14]

The Grimms' starting point was Herder's assumption that folklore was the origin of a national literature. Like Herder's, the Grimms' nationalism was neither exclusive nor aimed at demonstrating the superiority of Germany. They were more than willing to find the source of Germanness in other national traditions and, reciprocally, traces of other national traditions in that of Germany. This 'universalist nationalism' made Jacob Grimm much appreciated in France, where he was made Chevalier de la Légion d'honneur in 1841.[15]

An important reason for the success of the stories the Grimms wrote up was that, though the brothers' intention was to find the source of authentic German culture, the tales themselves were not particularly German. Some of them came from prosperous Huguenot families. Dortchen Wild, the source for 'Hansel and Gretel', was of French origin. Some stories, by the time they had reached the brothers, had been thoroughly Germanised. Indeed the Grimms, in the second edition of their collection, excluded some which had reached them via Jeanette Hassenpflug because they had realised these were too close to their literary French origins – the famous stories of Charles Perrault.[16] Far from being old peasant women who had kept an oral tradition alive, the Grimms' informants were educated middle-class women – Dortchen Wild was a pharmacist's daughter – who had heard them from their governesses and servants.[17]

A significant explanation for the success of the Grimms was that their basic assumption was wrong. They had assumed that if one went back in time one could find the essence of the German nation (or of the French, the Scottish, etc.). In reality, folk tales could not possibly express nationality. The same tale cropped up in various countries, just as Biblical stories – such as the Flood – appear in other sacred texts. Some stories were truly 'global'. For instance, some versions of the Cinderella tale were popular in China and India before turning up in Europe in the collections of Basile, Perrault and the Grimms. Viktor Shklovsky cites an 1894 study which traced the legend of Dido, who seized control of vast tracts of land through cunning (covering it with a cowhide cut into strips), to almost twenty cultures, including Indian, Indo-Chinese, Serbian, Turkish, Jewish, Russian and Native North American.[18]

Everyone liked the stories of the Grimm brothers precisely because they were *not* culture-bound (just as so many non-Americans like American films). There is nothing particularly French or Italian or German in 'French', or 'Italian', or 'German' fairy stories. The story of Bluebeard may well have originated in the criminal activities of Gilles de Rais, who was executed in France in the fifteenth century for murdering over 140 children, but serial killers and wife-murderers are universal types.

The Grimms had noble intentions in collecting the tales 'of the people', but they also understood their largely middle-class market, and knew what would be regarded as offensive. So they systematically expurgated and censored their tales.[19] A version where Sleeping Beauty awakes from her slumber to find Prince Charming having sex with her is suitably modified. Cruel and abusive mothers become, more acceptably, cruel and abusive stepmothers. In the Perrault version 'Little Red Riding Hood' ends with the tragic death of the little girl and her grandmother – a reminder never to trust strangers – but in that of the Grimm brothers there is a happy ending – they emerge from the entrails of the wolf killed by a hunter.[20] An earlier version is quite gory: the wolf, having killed the grandmother, puts her flesh on a plate and her blood in a bottle. Anecdotal evidence suggests that children's favourite passages are always the goriest. Charles Lamb was well aware of this. In 1808, against his publishers' pressure to modify his retelling of the story of Cyclops in his *The Adventures of Ulysses*, he left intact the words 'he dashed their brains against the earth, and (shocking to relate) tore in pieces their limbs, and devoured them, yet warm and trembling, making a lion's meal of them, lapping the blood; for the Cyclops are *man-eaters*, and esteem human flesh to be a delicacy far above goats' or kids''.[21]

Folk tales became a literary genre deemed suitable for children because they were adapted to fit parents' view of what was fit for their offspring. The toning down of the sexual and gory elements met the demands of the relatively homogeneous taste of the European middle classes. The 'horrific' component of the fairy tale was reinforced by the popularity of crime reporting in chapbooks and broadsheets. The renown of 'Little Red Riding Hood' as a chapbook story coincided with reports of real beasts devouring real travellers, a not uncommon event even in the second half of the eighteenth century.

New 'fairy tales' continued to be produced, including the great success stories of Carlo Collodi's *Pinocchio* (1880), Hans Christian Andersen's tales and Lewis Carroll's *Alice's Adventures in Wonderland* (1865) and *Through the Looking Glass* (1872). Stories which became globally successful were subsequently turned into films by Walt Disney, thus acquiring a new lease of life. Disney's versions treated royalty in a mildly disrespectful way, while celebrating the hero or heroine's sense of individual initiative. By 'Americanising' the fairy tale in this way the Disney Corporation, far from betraying Perrault or the Grimms, was following in their footsteps, adapting an endlessly adapted story with no fixed version to suit their markets.[22]

Out of adapted folk tales and novels a distinctive children's literature emerged in the nineteenth century.[23] There were some precedents in the eighteenth century, mainly in England, which has remained in the forefront of children's literature to this day. In London near St Paul's Cathedral, John Newberry opened the first bookshop for children in the world as early as 1750. He sold not just fairy tales but also abridged versions of *Robinson Crusoe* and *Gulliver's Travels*.[24] The genre turned out to be an immensely profitable growth area. In France in 1811, 'children's literature' consisted of eighty titles; by 1890 there were over a thousand.[25]

Because folk tales were assumed to reveal something about the culture of the nation, and because they turned out to be an extremely popular genre, ethnographers all over Europe, in the footsteps of the Grimm brothers, were busy collecting their own 'national' folk tales. Some countries had to wait for years: the first collections of Portuguese folk tales appeared only in the late nineteenth century: Adolfo Coelho's *Contos nacionais* (1879) and Teófilo Braga's *Contos tradicionais do povo Português* (1883).[26]

The printed version of fairy tales acquired a permanency that the oral rendition could not have, much as recorded music tends to displace orally transmitted musical traditions. Fairly tales and novel-writing fertilised each other with ideas of how to tell a story. Many fairy tales were written at a time when novel-writing was developing. Narrative techniques of suspense were common to both. A pattern of repetitive plots and narrative structures emerged. This included conventions as to what readers might expect. The number three, for instance, has a special importance in a variety of stories: fairy-tale kings often have three sons or three daughters, there are usually three items to choose from (as with the rings and caskets in Shakespeare's *Merchant of Venice*). Shklovsky points out that in the *Chanson de Roland* the hero is asked three times to blow his horn to attract the attention of Charlemagne's army, and does so only at the third request. It is only after the horn is blown for the third time that Charlemagne is convinced to return in an unsuccessful attempt to save the Frankish troops attacked by the Moors. Bluebeard's wife, in Perrault's tale, has to ask her sister Anna three times whether she sees help coming. There are obvious antecedents in religious mythology: three kings or magi turn up at the birth of Jesus, three men are crucified on Mount Golgotha, Jesus announces that Peter will betray him three times, his resurrection occurs three days after the crucifixion. The Holy Trinity is at the centre of most versions of Christianity. Other religions too privilege the number three. Buddhism has three fundamental objects of worship, or Triratna ('three jewels' in Sanskrit): the Buddha, his doctrine (*dharma*) and his clergy (the *sangha*).

Numbers such as three or seven or twelve are simple narrative devices, but readers and listeners quickly become familiar with more complex mechanisms, such as slowing down the story to accentuate suspense by generating a digression precisely when the reader wants the writer to go faster.[27] A narrative convention arises between tellers and listeners, what Coleridge called in 1817 the 'willing suspension of disbelief for the moment, which constitutes poetic faith'. This enables us to accept readily the world of fairy stories and supernatural tales on their own terms, as well as the construction of so-called realist novels (for these too require scarcely believable coincidences and plot devices).[28] Thus we can be involved in the story yet 'estranged' from it, as Shklovsky has pointed out, because it deals with a world with which we are not familiar.[29] A rationalist reader of Mary Shelley's *Frankenstein* might point out that it would surely have been easier for Viktor Frankenstein to revive a recently deceased corpse than to trudge in morgues and abattoirs, gather decaying flesh, rotting skins and old bones, stick them together and *then* perform what surely must be the really difficult feat of giving it the spark of life. But the story 'works' better the way Shelley tells it: it heightens

Man's pretension to do the work of Nature. It makes Frankenstein the real creator of 'the Creature'. Similarly, take the popular twentieth-century comic strip *Superman*, in which the hero has extraordinary powers, but instead of resolving all the problems of the world in one go, or, at the very least, eliminating poverty and wiping out communism, he is busy putting out fires, arresting muggers and rescuing cats, and spends an amazing amount of time foiling the plans of the arch-villain Lex Luthor, instead of finishing him off once and for all. But every reader knows that in serial stories arch-villains cannot be definitively defeated. Like Satan, they must be immortal if we want the story to go on.

Just as fairy tales had to adapt to their ever-changing audiences, so the authors of novels, if they were to be popular, had to adapt themselves to their assumed audience. Writers of fiction are never entirely free. As soon as they choose an established genre they must accept its conventions. Variations are necessary in order to distinguish one's own work from that preceding it, but one has to respect one's market, and one's readers' expectations. For instance, in the eighteenth century it was widely assumed that a woman could not be raped unless she eventually consented. To make it absolutely clear that Clarissa had not consented to be raped by Lovelace, Samuel Richardson has her drugged first. Had she been conscious, as Margaret Doody has pointed out, 'Lovelace and many readers would have agreed that she had really consented, and that any bodily and vocal resistance was just play.'[30] The sleeping-potion device was regularly used by many Gothic writers when they needed to engineer a rape or an attempted rape while maintaining intact the heroine's purity of soul.

That fairy tales were testing grounds for subsequent genres is fairly evident when we consider the kind of stories they provide: the horrific, the magic, the hopeful. A woman marries an authoritarian older man who turns out to be a serial killer ('Bluebeard'). A girl walks in the woods and is ravished by a monster pretending to be her grandmother. People are not what they seem. The family is a nest of persecutors ('Snow White', 'Hansel and Gretel', 'Cinderella', 'Sleeping Beauty'). One is unfairly accused, but truth will out. One of the most common narrative themes is that the apparent parents of the protagonist are not the real ones. The real ones are far more interesting. This can lead to dramatic plot developments – as Oedipus found out to his cost. This powerful and irresistible fantasy is used in almost all literary forms, from the Bible (Jesus is not the son of a carpenter, but the Son of God, a feat difficult to top; and Moses is an Egyptian prince), mythology (Dionysus), the adventure story (Tarzan is in reality Lord Greystoke), the comic strip (Superman hails from Krypton, not from boring Middle America), eighteenth-century novels such as Fielding's *Tom Jones* and Pigault-Lebrun's equally successful *L'Enfant du carnaval* (1796). The fantasy was used in an endless stream of Victorian novels, having previously been gently mocked by Beaumarchais in *The Marriage of Figaro* and later by Oscar Wilde in *The Importance of Being Earnest* (the famous 'To lose one parent may be regarded as a misfortune; to lose both looks like carelessness'). Narrative ploys are constantly reinforced by being taken up again and again. The imitation is hardly ever from the 'original' which is lost in time, but from the most recent replica.

At the source of much so-called high literature there is often an ocean of popular plots. Throughout the nineteenth century there was a systematic incorporation of fairy-tale motifs into refined novels and poems produced for the consumption of the literate classes, from Victor Hugo's *La Légende des siècles* to Shelley's *Prometheus Unbound* and Goethe's *Faust* – as there was for so much visual art before the nineteenth century.[31] Tirso de Molina's *El Burlador de Sevilla y convidado de piedra* (The Trickster of Seville and the Guest of Stone, 1630) – on which subsequent versions of the story of Don Juan were based – rests on folk tales in which a young man insults the ghost of a dead man and then invites him for dinner. The dead man turns up, dines and then returns the invitation. At the second meal the young man is punished or terrified into repentance. Dorothy Epplen MacKay has collected eighty-one adaptations of this tale – including fifteen in Germany, fifteen in Spain and seven in Italy.[32] The story was used by – among others – Molière, Goldoni, Purcell, Gluck, Mozart and da Ponte, Byron, Pushkin, Alexandre Dumas and George Bernard Shaw.

A major reason why certain plots are constantly recycled is that they can be interpreted in different ways. Don Juan was seen by the Romantics as a positive hero, a successful seducer haughtily scorning the conventional attitudes of the masses and mocking ordinary, happily married couples, until he is dragged to hell by the forces of reaction.[33] But he can also be regarded as an enemy of decency and morality; or a pathetic and vainglorious misogynist who, in the end, gets his comeuppance. Many readers like their villains clearly defined. If one is going to depict evil, one might as well make it absolute and easily identifiable. In the first chapter the villain should slap the child, abuse the young maid and kick the dog. However a more complex villain, i.e. one who might not be a villain after all, may be more likely to survive across time and culture. Complex characters, not just complex baddies, will be seen differently by different audiences. Novelists, especially novelists of some power and sophistication, are therefore even less in control of how their characters will be viewed. Goethe, when writing *Die Leiden des jungen Werthers*, probably meant to make gentle fun of the fashionable melancholia of the young sentimental lover. Yet most of his readers believed he meant to glorify it. Such problems do not occur in fairy tales. The Big Bad Wolf and the Ugly Sisters are, unmistakably, bad and ugly, and no amount of liberal rationalisation (wolves too must eat, ugliness is not a sin) will modify their image.

7

Novels

National Poets

NATIONAL POETS ARE USEFUL. Most nations have one – an optional extra in the process of nation-building. National poets unite the élites and instil reverence for the intellect in the minds of the lower orders, providing a source of pride to all and sundry. Some are even very good. National poets don't have to be poets – they could be novelists, essayists or playwrights – but mostly they are. Poetry is noblest, though plays are better, for they can travel the world and entertain the middle classes. Poetry can be difficult. It is often read in solitude. Even public poetry reading is, except in twentieth-century Russia, a matter for the drawing room and the literary salon. Plays, on the other hand, are consumed collectively, can give rise to a feeling of community and participation, are easier to teach, can have an exciting story line, and can be constantly adapted and updated to suit the mood of the times. England is lucky to have Shakespeare. The film *Henry V* made in 1944 with Laurence Olivier directing and playing the title role is suitably patriotic, while the 1989 version (directed by and starring Kenneth Branagh) is appropriately multi-culturalist. The fate of the poet Dante Alighieri, justly revered in Italy but hardly read anywhere else, contrasts with that of Shakespeare, performed and adapted throughout the world.

Shakespeare was already consecrated as England's national poet in the middle of the eighteenth century when his memorial statue was placed in Westminster Abbey (1741), and a festival celebrating the bicentenary of his birth was held in 1764. Other countries' national poets emerged only in the nineteenth century along with nationalism. It was not always obvious who was to be the national poet. The English, after all, could have gone for the radical John Milton rather than the more consensual Shakespeare. The

Germans settled on Goethe rather than Schiller; the Spanish on Cervantes, a novelist, rather than his Golden Age contemporary Lope de Vega, a playwright; the Portuguese for Camões (there was no one else); the Italians adopted Dante over Ariosto, Petrarch and Boccaccio. The Russians eventually agreed that Pushkin was their man – though he reached his iconic status only in 1880 when a monument to this grandson of a black general was hailed by the élite of Russian intellectual life gathered in Moscow. The crowd included Turgenev, Dostoevsky and Ostrovsky, but not Tolstoy, to whom such celebrations seemed 'unnatural', and who wanted to discourage any celebration for his own eightieth birthday. Ivan Turgenev declared that Pushkin had created both the Russian language and its literature. Dostoevsky thought he embodied the Russian spirit, and turned him almost into a messiah.[1] The Scots tried Ossian (see pages 80–2), but settled for Robert Burns. The republic of Georgia – to stress its ancient culture – embraced Shota Rustaveli, a twelfth-century poet, author of the national epic *Vekhist-qaosani* (The Knight in the Panther's Skin).

Countries struggling for national independence adopted patriotic poets like Sándor Petöfi (1822–49) in Hungary and Henrik Arnold Wergeland (1808–45) in Norway. It did not always matter that occasionally the national poets had only a loose connection with the alleged fatherland. Thus the Poles beatified Adam Mickiewicz (1798–1855) as their leading poet. He had struggled for Polish independence, but he hardly knew Poland, was born in Zaosie (a Lithuanian town, now, after various name changes, in Belarus), studied at the University of Vilna in Lithuania, lived in exile in Paris and died in Constantinople, now Istanbul.

Other national poets had even shakier national credentials. The national poet of Finland, Johan Ludvig Runeberg (1804–77), author of 'Vårt Land' (Our Country), which became the Finnish national anthem 'Maamme', wrote in Swedish. The Greek national poet Dionysos Solomos (1798–1857) had his 'Hymn to Liberty' turned into the national anthem in 1864, but he had first published it in Paris in 1823. Solomos, a native of Xantos, spoke Italian, the language of the local aristocracy, was educated in Cremona (Italy), was a British subject for most of his life, and never set foot on mainland Greece.

Other national poets are more recent, and their titles not uncontested : Nicolás Guillén (1902–87) for Cuba, Pablo Neruda (1904–73) for Chile, Gaspar Octavio Hernández (1893–1918) (or Ricardo Miró, 1883–1940) for Panama, Muhammad Iqbal (1873–1938) for Pakistan, Jorge Artel (1909–94) for Colombia, Rabindranath Tagore (1861–1941) for India.

France always lacked a national poet. Rabelais was too coarse and scatological, Racine too ponderous, and Molière 'just' a comedian. Victor Hugo spent much of his life working hard for the job, and got as near to it as humanly possible. He was so genuinely and popularly admired that he had a main Parisian avenue named after him while he was living on it. His funeral was the grandest in French history. But somehow the literary establishment never gave him its blessing, probably because he was too easy and popular – typical was the *mot* of André Gide who, when asked who was the greatest French writer, replied, '*Victor Hugo, hélas!*'

National poets were taught in schools in order to provide generations of children with a shared experience, and to create the consciousness of a national community. Poetry was regarded as a noble genre, fit for the nation. Poetry was divine, prose was common. After all, Homer had written poetry, not prose. The popularity of *The Iliad* and *The Odyssey* probably owed something to the beauty of the verse, much of which was obviously lost in translation, and to the unwavering support of successive intellectual élites. But what ensured their enduring success was the exciting nature of the stories they told. The eponymous hero of *The Odyssey* has a task: to return home to his family after a long war, but he is constantly distracted by events, some of his own making. In the course of his travels Odysseus encounters obstacles and surmounts them, meets interesting people, kills some (the Cyclops Polyphemus) and loves others (the nymph Calypso), and then moves on, well before boredom sets in, either for himself or for the reader. The story ends with a climax of extraordinary violence: back at Ithaca Odysseus kills all his wife's suitors. The other great classic, *The Iliad*, offers the template for another genre, the examination of a fragment from a wider story. We 'zoom' into micro-history during the last year of the ten-year-long siege of Troy. While *The Odyssey* has a central actor, no single character prevails in *TheIliad*. A crowd of major protagonists – Achilles, Hector, Patroclus, Agamemnon, the god Apollo – co-exist alongside others who are almost as significant.

These epics are in fact 'novels in verse'. Ancient literature abounds with such 'quasi-novels' and stories which can be characterised as novels.[2] There is a surviving Latin prose narrative, based on a Greek model, Apuleius' *The Golden Ass* (c. AD 200). Is it a novel, or a collection of short stories held together by a frame mechanism? Longus' *Daphnis and Chloe*, a story of sexual initiation between two young lovers, their subsequent separation and reuniting, was written in AD 200. It re-emerged in Renaissance Europe, and circulated widely in the original for the international community of scholars, and in various translations and adaptations for the others.[3]

In Italy during the sixteenth century there was a flowering of short stories in prose, such as Boccaccio's *Decameron* and Matteo Bandello's *Novelle* (214 tales published in four volumes between 1554 and 1573). These were included in collections like William Painter's *Palace of Pleasure* (1566–67), which provided the themes for several important Elizabethan plays, notably Shakespeare's *Romeo and Juliet* (1594–95), *Much Ado About Nothing* (1598–99) and *Twelfth Night* (1601–02), and John Webster's *The Duchess of Malfi* (1613–14). In France in the 1530s François Rabelais wrote in a comic key the stories of Gargantua and Pantagruel, a genre which saw its foremost Italian representative in the series of books on *Bertoldo e Bertoldino* (1618) by Giulio Cesare Croce (1550–1609). The romances of Gautier de Costes de la Calprenède (*Cassandre*, 1642–60) and of Madeleine de Scudéry (*Artamène ou le grand Cyrus*, 1649–53) were very popular in seventeenth-century France, while in Spain appeared Cervantes's *Don Quixote* (1605 and 1614), and in Germany Grimmelshausen's *Simplicissimus* (1669–72) became recognised as one of the earliest examples of the German 'novel'. In Spain Jorge de Montemayor's *Diana* (1559), provided Shakespeare with the plot of *Two Gentlemen of Verona* (1594), as well as some ideas for *A Midsummer Night's Dream* (1595). The cross-fertilisation at this early stage is such that it is pointless to try to trace the primacy of any strand.

New fiction in verse was still very popular at the beginning of the nineteenth century. Walter Scott's *Lady of the Lake* (1810) sold over 20,000 copies in six months. Byron's *Corsair* sold 13,000 copies on the day of publication in 1814, and 20,000 in its first fortnight – though the claim, a little far-fetched, was made nine years after the event by Byron himself in a letter.[4] Victor Hugo's *Odes et poésies diverses*, published in 1822 when the author was only twenty, sold 1,500 copies in four months and earned the author 750 francs – well over a year's rent.[5] Lamartine's complete poetical works achieved a print run of 6,000 in 1845.[6] All of this pales into insignificance before the achievement of Thomas Moore, for a while Ireland's national poet, one of the leading poets of his time, on a par with Byron, now almost forgotten. His *Lalla Rookh*, Orientalist tales in verse, first published in 1817, reached twenty editions by 1840, earning its author the considerable sum of £3,000.[7] This was thirty times what a London skilled artisan would have earned in a year. Today not many poets can claim that much.

Poetry, nevertheless, could never have become the driving force opening up a new mass market for books. By the beginning of the nineteenth century it was becoming clear that the future (meaning fame and money) belonged to novels, and not to poetry or short stories. The novel may have been a low genre, but in the long run that's the genre that counts. When victory arrives, the low genre, by a kind of parthenogenesis, will have generated its own set of gradations, from the refined and difficult loved by the intelligentsia and the avant-garde, to the middlebrow read passionately by the average educated reader, to the low genre for the growing mass of readers, to the trashy and vulgar for discerning minorities.

A Low Genre

For Aristotle, fiction (i.e. poetry) was a superior genre because it dealt with the universal – unlike historians, always pedestrian, who tell the story of particular beings:

> The difference between the historian and the poet is not that between using verse or prose; Herodotus' work could be versified and would be just as much a kind of history in verse as in prose. No, the difference is this: that the one relates actual events, the other the kind of things that might occur. Consequently poetry is more philosophical and more elevated than history, since poetry relates more of the universal, while history relates to particulars.[8]

Then fiction turned into a low genre. This term must be interpreted strictly, for everything about the novel was low. The writers were not scholars but ordinary people or scholars slumming it. The heroes, unlike classical heroes, were not kings and princes and sons and daughters of gods and goddesses, but common people: Tom Jones, Moll Flanders, Robinson Crusoe, Eugénie Grandet, Julien Sorel. The readers were equally common. Such distinction, for narratives, takes some time to become established, partly because the distinction between high and low genres presupposes the existence of a mass market, partly because the traditional distinction (pre-1800) was between 'high' genres (such as poetry) and low ones (such as fiction). Even after having had eight novels published, Balzac regarded verse as superior.[9] Trollope, having become rich thanks to his novels, could still write: 'there still exists among us Englishmen a prejudice in respect to novels ... By the common consent of all mankind who have read, poetry takes the highest place in literature.' Yet he also enthused about the universal pleasure of novels, which are read 'right and left, above stairs and below, in town houses and in country parsonages, by young countesses and by farmers' daughters, by old lawyers and by young students'.[10]

Soon distinctions between authors within the field of fictional narrative started to be made. Some writers, now regarded unequivocally as part of the high canon of literature, such as Balzac, were often seen as belonging to the low genre, but popularity came too late: for the first quarter-century after his death in 1850 he was less popular than Sue, Dumas and Sand. Then his sales increased. In English-speaking countries he was regarded as a typically revolting French novelist (Elizabeth Barrett Browning's enthusiasm was exceptional).[11] Nabokov concurred, though he disparaged equally Thomas Mann and Dostoevsky.[12]

Countries with a relatively large readership – Germany, Britain and France – had more than their fair share of popular writers who provided cheap fiction to the middle classes and their servants. Other countries had a better class of books, but this was not because their middle or working classes had better taste in literature, but because their middle class was smaller and read imported fiction, while their working classes read nothing at all.

In 1800 the novel's hour of triumph had not yet arrived, though perceptive observers were already ringing the alarm bells. And not just in London or Paris, where a steady stream of novels were published throughout the eighteenth century, but also in Russia, where they had just arrived. Here is the Russian historian and poet Nikolai Karamzin, in 1802, reporting that whenever he asked booksellers which books were selling well,

> all, without even thinking, answered 'novels!' No wonder, for this genre
> is undoubtedly captivating to the larger part of the public; it takes pos-
> session of the heart and the imagination, shows pictures of 'Society' and
> of people like ourselves in interesting situations, represents the strongest
> and at the same time the most ordinary passion in its various effects.[13]

In 1795 only five novels had been issued by the Russian presses, but by 1800 well over eight hundred published works were classified as novels (*romany*) or novellas (*povesti*) or tales (*skazki*).[14] Of the 211 novels published between 1801 and 1805, however, the vast majority (176) were translations. The transfer from abroad was even more considerable than these figures suggest, for among the 'Russian' novels there were many imitations and adaptations such as *The Russian Werther*.[15] These novels were bought not just by the upper classes but by the merchants, clerks, petty bureaucrats and tradesmen of Moscow and St Petersburg.[16]

In Italy it was much the same. Pietro Chiari, one of the few eighteenth-century Italian novelists (and one of the very few translated into English), author of some forty novels as well as plays and opera librettos, wrote in his novel *La Francese in Italia* (1759): 'To live one needs money rather than praise . . . These days booksellers want nothing but novels, and I must comply and give them novels, if I want to write books that sell.'[17]

Though some non-fiction can entertain and appeal to the emotions, nothing beats novels. Goethe's *The Sorrows of Young Werther*, Jean-Jacques Rousseau's *La Nouvelle Héloïse* and Samuel Richardson's *Clarissa* made eighteenth-century Europe cry. Their success and the fame gained by these authors encouraged others to such an extent that the nineteenth century saw an avalanche of novels. Franco Moretti tells us that in nineteenth-century Britain alone some 30,000 novels were published, perhaps more, 'no one really knows'.[18] John Sutherland, examining the annual reports of the *Publisher's Circular*, calculated that 60,000 novels were produced during the reign of Queen Victoria, and that there were as many as 7,000 novelists.[19] Of these, the canon selected some two hundred or so novels. The rest is a 'lost continent'.

This avalanche of novels upset the intelligentsia – busy writing and reading non-fiction. It was not just that novels were an inferior genre, but they also attracted the wrong audience. Instead of elevating the people, they provided them with mindless entertainment. Such alarmed reaction to the expansion of cultural markets is a constant refrain in the history of culture. At every expansion of the markets for culture, at every new technological breakthrough, at every innovation, we encounter cries of panic about the end of civilisation. Today a child engrossed in a novel, rather than in a television programme or a video game, brings tears of joy to educators and parents. Yet at the beginning of the nineteenth century many literati were shaking their heads at the prospect of more and more novels being read by the middle classes. Novels could fall into the hands of children and impressionable adults – such as women. Novels had 'feminine' characteristics: they were subjective, emotional and passive, while high culture was 'masculine', that is objective, ironic and 'in control'.[20] To indulge in fantasies and stories can cause harm. The habit of reading novels was a sure sign that a young man or woman was on the way down.[21] Writing in 1847 Charles Louandre complained that this 'huge' literary production aimed to satisfy the curiosity of book borrowers who 'read with the intention of learning nothing and are strongly resolved not to tire themselves by thinking. Maybe one should sympathise with those writers who have condemned themselves to the task of entertaining the idle, a not small group in France, especially in Paris, people who are well off enough not to have to work, and not rich enough to entertain themselves in an expensive manner.'[22]

Men of refinement read history books, treatises on morals, political pamphlets, perhaps satirical poems. When they turned to the daring and the bawdy, they did not allow their senses to be touched. Women, on the other hand, would indulge in impulsive and temperamental reading; they would be impatient with the plot, anxiously turning the pages. Women were expected to confine their interest to the 'family', to the realm of the private, to gossip – but this was exactly the kind of material which was the basis for most novels.[23] And as the story of an exemplary existence with no temptation is exceedingly boring or difficult to tell, it was inevitable that writers would deal with sex, desires, cross dressing, disobeying one's parents, murder, jealousy, and falling in love. This had been the stuff of fairy tales, of epic stories. It could hardly be kept out of novels.

That women could become dangerous if educated had been a received truth for a long time. Mariken van Nieumeghen, the protagonist of the eponymous medieval Dutch miracle play, makes a Faustian pact with the devil: he can possess her in exchange for supreme knowledge. The idea that books and romantic stories can lead people astray is encouraged by writers themselves, who are happy to believe that stories can make a difference. Cervantes attributed Don Quixote's folly to the books he had read. Mary Wollstonecraft in her *Vindication of the Rights of Women* (1792) criticised 'the reveries of the stupid novelists, who, knowing little of human nature, work up stale tales, and describe meretricious scenes, all retailed in sentimental jargon, which equally tend to corrupt the taste, and draw the heart aside from its daily duties'.[24] If Emma Bovary had not been addicted to cheap romances she might have been satisfied with her husband and her life. Flaubert himself implicitly warned against generalising from Emma's experience when he included the proposition 'Novels corrupt the masses' (*Les romans pervertissent les masses*) in his catalogue of clichés (*Dictionnaire des idées reçues*). Indeed, Flaubert himself, usually regarded as the aristocrat of French prose, had read and enjoyed popular literature, such as the yellow-covered paperbacks of the series called '*physiologie*' detailing, often humorously, the traits of various professions and published in the early 1840s, and used them in his works.[25] Paolo Malatesta da Rimini and Francesca dei da Polenta di Ravenna fell in adulterous love while reading the story of the illicit liaison between Lancelot and Guinevere. They end up, still in love, among the lustful souls of Dante's second circle of the *Inferno*. Bertha, the young heroine of Tieck's *Der Blonde Eckbert* (1797), reads fairy tales and has fantasies which make her impatient 'to seek the great wide world I had read so much about'.[26] Tatyana has little knowledge of the world and can judge Eugene Onegin only from the romantic novels she reads.

> Now she devours, with what attention,
> delicious novels, laps them up;
> and all their ravishing invention
> with sheer enchantment fills her cup.[27]

And what were Tatyana's deliciously dangerous books? Richardson's *Clarissa*, Rousseau's *La Nouvelle Héloïse* and *Delphine* by Madame de Staël. But, more often than not, empty-headed characters read trivial novels – that is, those the author regards as trivial. Thus in Thomas Mann's *Buddenbrooks: The Decline of a Family* (1901), the fifteen-year-old Antonie is sent to a boarding school after being caught reading Heinrich Clauren's *Mimili* (1816), a popular sentimental novel. The appeal of this theme is long-lasting: in Ian McEwan's *Atonement* (2001), Briony Tallis, her thirteen-year-old mind weaned on fables and stories, 'sees' an event which did not take place, with tragic consequences.

Early practitioners were quite aware that they were dealing with a low status form for low status people. Fanny Burney, in her preface to her anonymously published *Evelina or the History of a Young Lady's Entrance into the World* (1778), wrote: 'In the republic of letters, there is no member of such inferior rank, or who is so much disdained by his brethren of the quill as the humble Novelist.'[28] All the more reason, she added, for novelists to be particularly grateful to those writers who, by their excellence, have rescued the genre from depravity: Rousseau, Samuel Johnson, Marivaux, Fielding, Richardson and Smollett. Henry Mackenzie (1745–1831), after Laurence Sterne the chief representative in English fiction of the 'sentimental' genre – a term denoting, at the time, a 'moral' novel dealing with feelings and sentiments – wrote that 'No species of composition is more generally read by one class of readers, or more undervalued by another, than that of the novel.'[29] In Russia Mikhail V. Lomonosov excluded novels from his treatise on the Russian language and declared that 'fairy tales (*skazki*) which the French call novels . . . only serve to corrupt human morals and imprison mankind in luxury and carnal passion'.[30]

One of the first German treatises on literature, Eschenburg's *Entwurf einer Theorie und Literatur der schönen Wissenschaften* (1783), dedicated only nine pages to novels, short stories and fairy tales.[31] Schlegel, in his lectures on literature, barely mentions novels, though he discussed Arabic songs, poetry, philosophy and chivalric epics.[32] The great Russian critic Vissarion G. Belinsky (1811–48) lamented in 1835 that literature had become dominated by the novel, and poetry and philosophy were becoming unfashionable.[33]

In Louis-Sébastien Mercier's utopian novel set in 2440 (*L'An 2440*, published in 1771), only the good books have been preserved (they fill up only four cupboards), the others – the frivolous, the useless and the dangerous – have been burnt, including 100,000 poems, 1,600,000 travel memoirs and *a thousand million* novels.[34]

Novels, clearly, needed defending, and champions appeared as early as the eighteenth century. Clara Reeve, the celebrated author of *The Old English Baron*, wrote what amounted to a treatise in defence of 'good' novels: *The progress of romance, through times, countries, and manners: with remarks on the good and bad effects of it, on them respectively, in a course of evening conversations* (1785). Novels, she explained, are the outcome of history, and epic stories and fables that have been 'the favourite entertainment of the most savage, as well as the most civilised people'. Her survey is aimed at establishing a canon of 'good' novels: Boccaccio, for 'the Italians were the first that excelled in novel-writing'; Aphra Behn, of whom she says that there are 'strong marks of genius in all her works . . . she wrote in an age, and to a court of licentious manners and perhaps we ought to ascribe to these . . . the loose turn of her stories'; Madame de Lafayette's *La Princesse de Clèves* (1678) she does not like much, for 'it influences young minds in favour of a certain fatality in love matters'; while *Robinson Crusoe* is most suitable for children. Richardson's *Pamela* is better than his *Clarissa*. John James (sic) Rousseau's *Nouvelle Héloïse* is 'a dangerous book to put into the hands of youth, it awakens and nourishes those passions, which is the exercise of reason'. As for Laurence Sterne, she admits to not having read *Tristram Shandy* half through.[35]

By 1833 the *Journal des Demoiselles* (15 February) was praising the positive effects of reading on women.[36] Vigny decreed that books brought freedom and that tyrants were afraid of them. In his poem 'Wanda Histoire Russe', he has the Tsar deny the request that the children of an exile be taught to read, saying: '*Un esclave a besoin d'un marteau, non d'un livre*' ('A slave needs a hammer, not a book').[37]

The *bien pensants* who disparaged early novels were not entirely wrong. It really was a low genre, rescued much later by writers who entered the respectable canon. James Arbuckle in 1725 in the *Dublin Journal* lampooned the 'fabulous adventures and memoirs of pirates, whores and pickpockets wherewith for sometime past the press has so prodigiously swarmed'.[38] As the middle classes grew in size and liked reading novels, a new breed of novelists – mostly second-rate, but some of the calibre of Fielding and Defoe – arose to meet the demand. They made the genre more respectable, exercised more care. Competition between writers and market expansion led to improvements in the representation of characters and greater sophistication in narrative technique. Novelists became more skilled at marketing their stories, deploying a familiar hypocritical trick: juicy descriptions of criminal activities and depraved behaviour presented as a warning to others. In the end, but not before, the criminal repented or was hanged. Even in the 1770s it was still widely held that the function of the novel should be educational and that it should inculcate morality. Writers wrote for entertainment and inserted sermon-like digressions on the virtues of domestic felicity.[39] Bawdy or sexy novels, like *Fanny Hill*, were often marketed as exemplary: 'Let me tell you in great detail,' they appeared to say, 'what a terrible sinner I have been and the many men I have slept with and all the terrible things I have done with them and how I paid a heavy price and how, once I repented, everything has turned out for the better.' So strong has been this defence, so difficult to disprove, though so patently self-serving, that it is even now built into many works of fiction which may incur the wrath of respectable society, and used abundantly in the salacious press.

Erotic stories can gain considerable appeal if they are suitably packaged as *livres philosophiques*. Thus the Marquis Donatien de Sade's *La Philosophie dans le boudoir* (1795) has found a place on the bookshelves of many intellectuals because its lengthy pornographic descriptions of group sex (mainly homosexual and heterosexual buggery and oral sex) are intersected with philosophical discussions of a libertarian nature.[40] In Germany love stories with an erotic flavour often masqueraded as social novels. In his notorious *Mimili*, Heinrich Clauren (1771–1854) tells the story of a man of the world's experiences before and after meeting the innocent Swiss maid Mimili.[41] Even now sexy books for intellectuals or for those with intellectual pretensions can sell well if stylishly written and padded with 'high' culture suggestions, as is evidenced by the success of Pauline Réage's sado-masochistic *Histoire d'O* (1954), which sports a preface by a member of the Académie Française and, more recently, of *La Vie sexuelle de Catherine M* (2001) by Catherine Millet, a distinguished art critic.

Realism

Novelists themselves knew the place of their genre – one of the reasons why Madame de Lafayette did not sign the first editions of *La Princesse de Clèves*, a novel which has been continuously in print since then.[42] Most novels were published anonymously, and not just those by women. Successful writers such as Walter Scott revealed their names only when the secret could no longer be kept. Authors conspired to pretend that they were not novelists, or that the novel was not a novel but a true story. The allure of authenticity was strong, and still is. A true story has more appeal than a fabricated one. Cervantes claimed that the story of Don Quixote had been narrated by an Arab historian. Karamzin 'found' a manuscript containing the story of Martha the Posadnik. Many of Walter Scott's novels were based on 'true' stories told to others who transcribed them. Manzoni pretended to have used the material from an anonymous author of the seventeenth century, indeed he starts *I Promessi sposi* with the high-flying baroque language of seventeenth-century Italian, a virtual parody, before explaining that he will translate the text into proper Italian. Marivaux (1688–1763) 'found' the text of *La Vie de Marianne* (1731–42) in a country house he had just bought. Even an early novel such as Aphra Behn's *Oroonoko* (1688) claimed to be the accurate depiction of true events, including Oroonoko's final execution, during which he is castrated, his nose and ears are cut off and his limbs removed while he continues to smoke his pipe rather calmly.[43] Such claims, presumably, fooled no one, yet this strategy could backfire: Richardson presented himself as the mere editor of Pamela's letters, but when *Pamela* turned out to be a success, other writers wrote sequels claiming that they had found more letters of the famous Pamela, and even a *Memoir of the Life of Lady H., the Celebrated Pamela* (1740).[44] Authenticity devices were abundantly used in Russia, especially in the novels of the 1820s.[45] By the early nineteenth century the claim that a novel was a true story was intended to signal that its story was realistic, that it could have happened. This was the meaning Balzac gave to the declaration 'All is true' (in English in the original) in his preface to *Le Père Goriot*.

When, however, Defoe insisted that the story of Robinson Crusoe was true, he was making a legitimate claim. *The Surprising Adventures of Robinson Crusoe* (1719) was inspired by the true story of Alexander Selkirk, who was marooned on an uninhabited island (Más a Tierra in the Juan Fernández off the coast of Chile) for five years – though there were previous semi-fictional accounts of castaways available (such as Henry Neville's *Isle of Pine*, 1668). By insisting on the truthful basis of fiction, the genre was ennobled.

For many of the writers still valued today, writing novels was not their main job. Voltaire regarded himself principally as a philosopher, and his ambition was to be recognised as a great playwright. Novels such as *Candide*, for which he is now best known, were enjoyable digressions. Tragedies were the real thing. His contemporaries agreed. Voltaire's apotheosis followed the opening of his last tragedy *Irène* at the Comédie-Française on 16 March 1778 – and for weeks after that he received a stream of well-wishers and pilgrims.[46] We remember Henry Fielding as a novelist, but in his time he was a magistrate, a good and honest one by all accounts, a political journalist and a successful playwright. Defoe is remembered for *Robinson Crusoe*, *Moll Flanders* (1722) and *Roxana* (1724). But his collected bibliography amounts to 548 items. *Robinson Crusoe* was number 412. It was his first novel, and he was nearly sixty when it was published. And the year he wrote it, he wrote sixteen other books, all non-fiction, including: *The History of the Reign of King George*; *From the Death of her late Majesty Queen Anne, to the First of August*; *A Letter to the Dissenters*; *The Anatomy of Exchange-Alley: or, A System of Stock-Jobbing*; and *Some Account of the Life, and most Remarkable Actions, of George Henry Baron de Goertz, Privy-Counsellor and Chief Minister of State, to the Late King of Sweden*.

For a first novel, *Robinson* was an astounding success. In Defoe's lifetime it went into eight editions plus five pirated ones, and a serialised version was published in the *Original London Post*.[47] *Robinson*'s structure sounds unappealing, since there is only one character for most of the book, the second character speaks very little, and there are no women or 'romantic interest'. But the hero is an utterly conventional man in an utterly unconventional situation: the reader can readily identify with him and his struggle against difficulties and odds – the stuff of all epics.

Crusoe was translated into German only a year after it was first published; it spawned imitations and adaptations such as Gottfried Schnabel's *Insel Felsenburg* (Felsenburg Island, 1731) and *Robinson der Jüngere* (The New Robinson, 1779), by Joachim Heinrich Campe – one of the first German writers to write specifically for children.[48] By 1898 *Crusoe* had been translated into 110 languages including Coptic, Armenian and Bengali.[49]

One of the most successful adaptations was *The Swiss Family Robinson* (*Der Schweizerische Robinson*, 1812), written by Johann Rudolf Wyss on the basis of a story devised by his father, a Swiss clergyman. Here it is not a lone man who is stranded on a desert island, but an entire family: mother, father and no fewer than four children of varying ages and sex: enough for a large number of readers to identify with. This book, one of the earliest specifically aimed at children, was highly successful even though the author was unknown and the book was not particularly well written.

Variants of the story have continued to be published in the twentieth century, from Michel Tournier's *Vendredi; ou Les Limbes du pacifique* (1967, English trans.: *The Other Island*), Muriel Spark's *Robinson* (1958) and J.M. Coetzee's *Foe* (1986).[50] The theme has remained a fascinating one: three hundred years after the appearance of the book, a Hollywood film inspired by it (*Cast Away*, 2000, with Tom Hanks) was showered with prizes. The biography of the 'true' Crusoe, Alexander Selkirk, Diana Souhami's *Selkirk's Island*, won a major British literary prize, the Whitbread, in 2001.

What is a Novel?

Definitions are always problematic. The rather vague 'prose narrative' would send us back to a futile attempt to establish the precise borderline between prose and poetry. What is significant is that from the eighteenth century onward there was a growing demand for some kind of fictional or invented narrative, which people called novels or 'romances' – the term used in many European languages such as French (*roman*), German (*Roman*) and Italian (*romanzo*). The word '*roman*' makes clear the low origin of the genre, for it derives from the Old French *romanz*, meaning the Roman language of popular speech as opposed to classical Latin.

Is the 'novel' a uniquely Western genre? Stories are universal, but it is perfectly possible to define the novel in such a way as to eliminate most non-Western narratives, including *One Thousand and One Nights* and *Tales of Genji*.[51] What we know is that the longish prose fiction – that which cannot quite be read in a single sitting – which became increasingly popular in Europe in the nineteenth century continued to be regarded as an inferior genre in most of Asia until the middle of the twentieth century; in Korea the refined genres are still the essay and the short story. Of course, length is hardly a useful criterion. The epic story is really often little more than a series of short stories linked together by a hero who travels between two points. We know that a genre is established whenever parodies of it are produced, for a parody succeeds to the extent that what it mocks is widely recognised. Early novels parodied established genres. Miguel de Cervantes's *El ingenioso hidalgo Don Quijote de la Mancha* (1605 and 1615) parodied the chivalric genre, Swift's *Gulliver's Travels* (1726) could be read as a satire on travel writing, Diderot's *Jacques le fataliste* (1773) and Sterne's *Tristram Shandy* (1759–67) parodied the realistic novel almost at the same time as it was invented.

But was there, by the end of the eighteenth century, a common understanding among the reading public of what constituted a novel? There had to be length, to distinguish it from the short story. There had to be prose, to distinguish it from poetry. There had to be a plot (what the Russian formalists called the *fabula*) as well as a sequence of events (the *siuzhet*). This barely adds up to a useful definition. And what would be the point of a definition if not to establish the 'origin of the novel', yet another pointless pursuit for the original starting point? The fact that a much-touted candidate for such a position is Cervantes's *Don Quixote* suggests that the 'first' novel had to be 'great'. Yet Cervantes had written a pastoral novel, *La Galatea*, twenty years earlier. Was this the first not-so-great novel? Greatness is a question of aesthetics, not of history. Ranking novels, like ranking painters and composers, can be fun. Some specialists, like Harold Bloom, invest considerable time in this parlour game: Cervantes, Bloom authoritatively tells us, 'has in common with Shakespeare the universality of his genius, and he is the only possible peer of Dante and Shakespeare in the Western Canon', and, what's more, 'No writer since has matched them, not Tolstoy or Goethe, Dickens, Proust, Joyce.'[52] In the final analysis, this tells us little about the rise of the novel, much about current taste.

The really interesting question in this debate is not who are the great writers, but who decides who they are, and how. When did the literary canon emerge? When did the first 'great' novels appear? The circle of pre-1800 candidates was rather narrow: England deployed five men: Daniel Defoe, Samuel Richardson, Henry Fielding, Tobias Smollett and Laurence Sterne; Ireland: Jonathan Swift; Spain: Miguel Cervantes; France produced Madame de Lafayette, Rousseau and Diderot; and Germany had Goethe.

In reality the development of the novel is not just connected to the novelists, i.e. people who have a story to tell, but to the rise of a set of economic and social relations within which those who have a story to tell can have it printed and make a living out of it. In other words, novelists exist because there is a market for novels, because there are writers, printers and booksellers and publishers, and above all, because there are readers. Daniel Defoe, one of the 'fathers' of the English novel, was quite aware of this, and regarded writing as a manufacture which, under certain conditions, 'wou'd necessarily employ as many hands as the Woollen Manufacture, and would as much have deserv'd the Name of Manufacture'.[53]

The traditional debate about the rise of the novel left out English writers earlier than Defoe and company, usually on the ground of quality. As many of these pioneers were women, they were rescued by feminist critics: Aphra Behn, author of the best-selling *Love Letters Between a Nobleman and his Sister* (1684–87) and *Oroonoko* (c.1688), Mary Delarivier Manley, known for her anti-Whig political satires: *The Secret History of Queen Zarah and the Zaraians* (1705) and *The New Atalantis* (1709), and Eliza Haywood (*Love in Excess*, 1719). The conditions which made these works successful were only partly to do with their quality. One was that the decline of the British theatre at the time had made the print market the best alternative for those who, like Aphra Behn, wanted to earn a living by writing. Another was the existence of a narrative genre dealing with love and sex scandals, as well as a great deal of prurient interest in the 'disreputable' or intimate lives of members of the upper classes. This had prepared the terrain for Behn and her colleagues who understood that there was a strong demand for such stories. They also built on the English success of French novels such as Madame de Lafayette's *La Princesse de Clèves* (1678), quickly translated into English (1679). William Warner points out that the spectacular success of Defoe's *Roxana* was part of the same fashion which had consecrated that of Behn. They were both in the business of giving the public what they wanted: erotic, bawdy and coarse stories.[54] The works of Aphra Behn, Delarivier Manley and Eliza Haywood never became part of the literary canon, unlike those of Defoe and Fielding. But *at the time* novelists were not part of the English literary establishment, which was then dominated by poets like Alexander Pope. And it was Pope who, in his satire *The Dunciad*, offered Eliza Haywood as the prize in a urinating competition:

> . . . Who best can send on high
> The salient spout, far-streaming to the sky,

describing her in a note as one of 'those shameless scribblers' of the female sex who 'in libellous memoirs and novels, reveal the faults and misfortunes of both sexes'.[55] Pope's attack was not entirely undeserved: Eliza Haywood in her *Memoirs of a certain Island adjacent to the Kingdom of Utopia* (1724) had attacked the character of Martha Blount, Pope's friend. In the middle of the nineteenth century even Defoe had not quite made it into the canon: an early edition of Chambers's *Cyclopaedia of English Literature* (1843) lambasted him for 'wandering so frequently into the low and disgusting purlieus of vice'.[56]

Novels and the Bourgeoisie

The 'faults and misfortunes of both sexes' were exactly what the new bourgeoisie and much of the old aristocracy liked to read about. Readers taught writers, especially professional writers, what they liked. Writers, if they wanted to sell, conformed to such requests while trying to provide a little variation.

As readers became familiar with the form, they assumed the next novel would conform to their expectations. A set of unwritten conventions between readers and writers emerged. However realistic the novel was meant to be, the characters had to be strongly delineated, and hence be relatively simple with few traits. Conversations would not replicate real speech just as speech in plays has little connection with authentic live conversation, which is full of hesitations, unfinished sentences, overlapping dialogue and reciprocal interruptions, and enriched by a complex body language which, if described in detail by the author, would make the plot development impossible to follow. Similarly, conversations between more than two or three characters should be exceedingly rare.[57] Details had to be functional to the narrative: if a character is crippled there must be a reason. If a character meets a childhood friend by chance, this encounter must, before the end of the novel, be of some significance to the story. In real life, much of what occurs to us is of no consequence.

Successful books provide easily recyclable characters and situations. There are themes and plots which have a particularly modern appeal: Don Juan, who seduces women and challenges conventions; Faust, who makes a pact with the devil in order to experience power and sensations; Robinson Crusoe, who rebuilds his own world against a hostile environmen; and Don Quixote, who pursues impossible dreams because he is not at home in the real world.[58]

In many fairy tales, heroes follow rules they have received from others – you shall cross a river, find a horse, meet an old man, give him a ring, etc. They will succeed if they adhere strictly to the rules. The religious undertones are obvious. The hero is an ethical being. In modern novels heroes are individuals who must decide for themselves what to do and when to break the rules. These are 'bourgeois' heroes, and the novel has been generally regarded as a bourgeois genre celebrating individualism. Thus Adorno: 'The novel was the literary form specific to the bourgeoisie. At its origins stands the experience of the disenchanted world in *Don Quixote* . . .'[59]

Many nineteenth-century novels attacked rank and nobility: what mattered was the true nobility of spirit. This pleased their bourgeois readers, though the resort to an older fairy tale convention, namely that the commoner was really an aristocrat, removed even the appearance of subversion. There was a vague anti-bourgeois populism which has persisted to this day in films: the rich are often mean and/or unhappy, money is not everything and is renounced by noble souls, and the single-minded pursuit of greed leads nowhere.

Is individualism indissolubly linked to the 'bourgeois' novel? I am not sure. Bourgeois heroes are often also selfless, follow an ethical code, and are kind and considerate towards the poor and the oppressed, while individualism can easily be found in ancient literature. Is not individualism a signal trait of Achilles, who sulks in his tent while around him the Greek army is decimated by illness, and all because he did not get his girl?

Nor is it obvious at all why popular novels celebrating individualism should be particularly functional to capitalism. Capitalist corporations do not necessarily promote individualism; they require their employees to obey rules and do as they are told. And when bourgeois novels promote individualism, it is more often than not the man's, just as in novels of the past. The imaginative and restless man who breaks the rule is often, in novels, a good, thrusting individualist, but the women who do so end miserably – especially in nineteenth-century 'bourgeois' novels, as Emma Bovary and Anna Karenina know to their cost. A high-class prostitute who defies conventions and is 'free', like the eponymous protagonist of Zola's *Nana*, ends up killed by smallpox, her legendary looks ravaged. The positive heroine is allowed to be unconventional as long as she does so in a 'feminine' way, by refusing to marry the wrong man, one chosen by her parents, in favour of the right man – but marry she must.

In the not entirely bourgeois eighteenth century things could be quite different: Moll Flanders and Roxana repent and live happily ever after, having had plenty of sex and fun. Fanny Hill, the heroine of John Cleland's *Memoirs of a Woman of Pleasure* (1748), has a happy end after a stimulating career in various brothels and is none the worse for it. Not so the author, who was imprisoned for pornography. As for his novel, it became legally available in England only in 1970 – long after the arrival of the bourgeoisie.

What makes a novel popular is unclear even after it has become popular, though hindsight facilitates the production of endless theories. There may be a link between certain social changes and the development of some genres. Lawrence Stone, for instance, suggested that there is a connection between the growth of romantic love as a reason for marriage and the growth of novels dealing with romantic love.[60]

Among the most successful novels of the period of the French Restoration were the now forgotten, somewhat Gothic *Le Solitaire* (1821) and *L'Étrangère* (1825) by Charles-Victor d'Arlincourt (1788–1856). They were translated into at least ten languages, and adapted many times for the theatre; Bellini based his opera *La Straniera* on *L'Étrangère* and had also considered adapting *Le Solitaire*.[61] D'Arlincourt's fame in France was said to match that of Walter Scott in England. D'Arlincourt himself, surprised by its success, tried, unsuccessfully, to discover the secret of its popularity by becoming the literary critic of his own work, stripping it to its essential elements in order to write a new novel which is similar to the previous one yet different.[62]

When a genre becomes popular it leads to others entering the same market. The success of novels like *Clarissa* and *Tom Jones* led writers who had intended to produce plays or poetry to turn to novels: Sarah Fielding, Charlotte Lennox, Laurence Sterne, Horace Walpole, Richard Graves and Oliver Goldsmith.[63] Strictly speaking every novel is unique, but once a formula has proved to be successful it facilitates the writing of a number of novels with similar plots and characters.

There is a link between the novel and capitalist society, but this is not necessarily ideological. It is, rather, that the mass production of novels is part and parcel of industrialisation. The contents *per se* are not particularly 'capitalist', and readers often find in a book the ideology they want. In any case the expansion of the book market in the nineteenth century was not primarily based on new novels, or even on new books. The new reading public read books which, in a previous epoch, had been the preserve of a smaller élite. Religious books like Fleury's *Catéchisme historique* (1679) were as popular as ever. Torquato Tasso's *Gerusalemme liberata* (1575) was reprinted continuously and sold, in France alone, 45,000 copies between 1812 and 1830 at a time when very few novels managed to sell more than 1,000 copies. As we have seen (pages 99–101), the old folk tales of pre-capitalist days were lapped up in earnest by the new bourgeoisie. The main French best-seller of the nineteenth century was the *Contes et nouvelles en vers* of Jean de la Fontaine, written in the seventeenth, which sold between 500,000 and 750,000 copies.[64] It was regarded as an ideal children's book, with the kind of morals anyone could approve – even though Rousseau regarded such tales as beyond the comprehension of a child.[65]

8

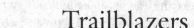

Trailblazers

Adapting Success

THE NOVELS that launched new genres were often internationally successful. Though many used old plots, they did so in new and exciting ways, in
turn generating imitations and adaptations. Culture progresses on the back
of triumphs.

El ingenioso hidalgo Don Quijote de la Mancha was successful at the outset.
It had taken four centuries for Dante's *Divine Comedy* – started in 1307,
printed in 1481 – to become known throughout Europe (it was translated in
America only in 1865–67 by Longfellow).[1] Within a year of the publication
of *Don Quixote* there were already three pirated editions. To exploit its
popularity, Cervantes started writing a sequel. In 1615, as he was about to
finish it, he found out that a certain Alfonso Fernández de Avellaneda (a
pseudonym) had published in Tarragona *The Second Volume of the Ingenious
Knight Don Quixote de la Mancha.* Cervantes retaliated immediately by
'changing' Don Quixote's plan: instead of continuing towards Saragossa he
had him ride into Barcelona to denounce the impostor.[2]

Franco Moretti has mapped out the wave of translations of this first international best-seller: the Don was first translated into English in 1612 (Part Two,
published in 1615, was in English in 1620), then, in quick succession, into French
and Dutch. By 1622 it had reached Venice. By 1648 it was in German. By the end
of the eighteenth century the 'knight of the sorrowful countenance' had arrived
in Denmark, Russia, Poland, Portugal and Sweden. In 1848 there was a Yiddish
translation, in 1872 one in Chinese, in 1880 in Gujarati, and in 1896 in Japanese.[3]
But it was in England that the triumph of the Don was particularly marked.
Not only was it the seat of the first translation, but also of the first critical
edition, of the first published commentary, of the first biography.[4]

In the eighteenth century there were nearly twenty English editions of *Don Quixote*. Henry Fielding wrote in the preface of his novel *Joseph Andrews* that it was written 'in imitation' of Cervantes. Tobias Smollett (who had translated *Don Quixote*) openly based his *The Life and Adventures of Sir Lancelot Greaves* (1760–61) on it. Charlotte Lennox wrote *The Female Quixote*, one of the most popular novels of the second half of the eighteenth century, about an impressionable young woman headily under the influence of novels (1752). Years later, the Mexican novelist José Fernandez de Lizardi followed with *La Quijotita y su prima* (The Female Quixote and her Cousin, 1819). In 1773 Richard Graves wrote *The Spiritual Quixote*. Don Quixote may have inspired Pushkin for the characterisation of Tatyana, the heroine of *Eugene Onegin*, Gogol for Chichikov, the protagonist of *Dead Souls* (1842), and Dostoevsky for his Prince Myshkin, the Christ-like hero of *The Idiot*.[5] William Hazlitt (1815), Samuel Coleridge (1818), John Lockhart (1822) and Charles Lamb (1833) all wrote important essays on *Don Quixote*.

The *Grove Dictionary of Music* lists well over fifty musical compositions inspired by the story of Don Quixote, including those by Purcell, Telemann, Richard Strauss, Ravel, Mendelssohn, Massenet and Manuel de Falla. There have been numerous film versions, including one in 1909 (France), in 1916 (US), a British one in 1923, one by Georg Pabst in 1933, and Grigori Kozintsev's film in 1957, with Cherkasov in the title role. In 1869 it was the subject of a famous ballet by Petipa, to music by Ludwig Minkus. In 1965 it was the turn of the musical *Man of la Mancha*, followed in 1972 by a film version of it with Peter O'Toole as Don Quixote and Sophia Loren as Dulcinea. And finally, in 2002, there was a film, *Lost in La Mancha*, about Terry Gilliam's failure to make the film *The Man Who Killed Don Quixote*.

Part of the reason for the success of the book was that it was a work open to a variety of interpretations. *Don Quixote*'s first readers, unlike today's, were familiar with the romances and chivalric stories which stimulate the hero's fantasies. This may account for some of its original success, as it does for the author's lack of sympathy for Don Quixote during all his travails and tribulations. Cervantes must have felt that someone stupid enough to believe silly stories deserves everything he gets. In comic literature, it is essential for the reader to feel superior to the hero. Later readers, however, identified with Don Quixote, as Samuel Johnson said he did. The Romantics – Victor Hugo, Chateaubriand, Théophile Gautier – took *Don Quixote* seriously, idealising the hero as an ethical spirit in a coarse world devoid of values, thus denying the author's satirical purpose.[6] Nietzsche said that 'Today, we read the whole

Don Quixote with a bitter taste in our months, almost with a sense of torture,' while Cervantes' contemporaries read it 'as the most cheerful of books ... they almost laughed themselves to death over it'.[7] Don Quixote eventually became a loveable anti-modernist reactionary, someone who looked back to the manners and gentility of the past with fondness.

This novel has a structure, widely imitated in subsequent popular narrative, which consists in having two protagonists, a hero and his helper. The helper, in folk tales, is usually an occasional presence. Here, he is continuously in the story, providing a sharp contrast. Don Quixote is tall and thin, his helper Sancho Panza is short and fat. Don Quixote is larger than life, virtually insane; Panza is a recognisable human being, the prototype for subsequent loyal servants of difficult-to-follow heroes. Readers can choose to identify with either the hero or his down-to-earth acolyte, or alternate between them. The device also enables a conversation to take place between the two protagonists in order to make the reader aware of what is going on – almost eavesdropping without the intervention of the narrator. Such structure turned out to be particularly helpful in later genres, such as crime stories, where the much-too-clever detective explains what is going on to his less-than-shrewd companion, thus indirectly informing the reader of the state of play. The master-and-servant ploy, however, has been abundantly used in all kinds of narrative, from Catalinón in Tirso de Molina's *El Burlador de Sevilla* (1630, later Leporello in *Don Giovanni*), to Friday in *Robinson Crusoe*, Hugh Strap in Smollett's *Roderick Random* (1748), Benjamin Partridge in *Tom Jones*, Paolo, Vivaldi's servant, in Radcliffe's *The Italian* (1797). The comic role of the servant/helper became a fixture of eighteenth-century comedies such as those of Goldoni, down to Phileas Fogg's Passepartout in Jules Verne's *Round the World in Eighty Days*, the Lone Ranger's Tonto, Tintin's Captain Haddock, Astérix's Obélix and in dozens of novels and films where leading characters, thanks to their aura and charisma, acquire loyal and devoted servants, willing to sacrifice their lives – a classic fantasy.

The overall structure of *Don Quixote*, however, still resembles that of the epic it seeks to mock: a series of adventurous episodes linked together by a hero on a quest – that is, a series of short stories held together by a frame. New mechanisms had to be devised in order to tell modern stories dealing with intimacy, family life, and sex.

Writing Letters

In 1739 Samuel Richardson, a London printer, began to write a volume of model letters (*Letters Written to and for Particular Friends on the Important Occasions*), to be used by 'Country Readers' uncertain of their letter-writing skills. At the same time he wrote *Pamela; or Virtue Rewarded* (1740), in the epistolary form, the story of how a young maid successfully resists the advances of her master. She is not insensitive to his charms, but her virginity is her only possession and she must sell it dearly. In the end, victory is hers: her master redeems himself by proposing, Pamela accepts and, Cinderella-like, turns into a Lady.

This, it seems, was the first time that letter-writing was used as a device to write a fully-fledged novel, though Montesquieu, in his *Lettres Persanes* (1721), had used fictional letters written by a Persian ambassador in Paris to produce a critical social commentary of his society, and, of course, St Paul's thoughts were written in the form of Epistles.

Pamela was translated into French shortly after it was first published. Almost immediately numerous anonymous derivations, imitations and fake translations appeared, including *Anti-Paméla ou mémoires de M.D.* (1742) and *L'Anti-Paméla ou la fausse innocence découverte* (1743).[8] Robert-Martin Lesuire contributed his *La Paméla française ou lettres d'une jeune paysanne* as late as 1803. *Pamela* became a great European success. It was translated into German soon after its publication, once in 1742 and then again in 1743. It inspired Voltaire's play *Nanine* (1749). In Russia, P.I. Lvov wrote, in 1789, *A Russian Pamela*. In Italy in the 1750s there were three plays called *Pamela Maritata*, one by Pietro Chiari, one by Francesco Cerlone, and another by Carlo Goldoni, who also wrote *La Pamela nubile* (The Unmarried Pamela). Goldoni, in his memoirs, illustrated a familiar attitude towards the uninhibited use of other people's work:

> For some time, the novel of Pamela had been the delight of the Italians, and my friends urged me strongly to turn it into a comedy. I was acquainted with the work; and felt no difficulty in seizing the spirit of it, and approximating the objects; but the moral aim of the English author was not reconcilable with the manners and laws of my country. A nobleman in London does not derogate from his nobility in marrying a peasant; but at Venice, a patrician who should marry a plebeian, would deprive his children of the patrician nobility, and they would lose their right . . . I did not however begin the work till I had invented a denouement which, instead of being dangerous, might serve as a model to virtuous lovers, and render the catastrophe both more agreeable and more interesting.[9]

The Goldoni plays inspired operas by Pietro Generali (1804) and Giuseppe Farinelli for the carnival of 1806. Henry Fielding mercilessly parodied it in his *An Apology for the Life of Mrs. Shamela Andrews* – where Pamela is portrayed as a manipulative gold-digger – and Henry Giffard adapted it for the London stage.[10]

Most of the letters in *Pamela* were written by 'Pamela' herself. Hers was by far the main voice. The success of *Pamela* induced Richardson to try a more complex operation. *Clarissa; or the History of a Young Lady* (1747–48) is told from the point of view of four characters exchanging letters: Clarissa, her would-be seducer Lovelace and their respective best friends, Anna Howe and Jack Belford. Such multi-voiced and shifting-point-of-view narrative is, 250 years later, still regarded as a remarkable feat – as shown by the success of popular books such as Iain Pears's *An Instance of the Fingerpost* (1997) and the prize-winning *English Passengers* by Matthew Kneale (2000). *Clarissa* was a great success. Richardson had been a prosperous printer; he died a rich novelist, leaving a fortune of £14,000.[11]

Clarissa was a path-breaker in the 'sentimental' genre. The plots of such novels usually turned around the tension between equally valuable moral imperatives, often a particularly female dilemma: such as duty to the family (children, husband, parents) and duty to individual happiness. Such clashes had occasionally found a manly version, for instance in Corneille's *Le Cid* (1637), while conflicts between duty to the *polis* and duties to the family are often found in Greek drama (from Sophocles' *Antigone* to Euripides' *Iphigenia in Aulis*). In *Clarissa*, however, the conflict is between two views of the world, that of Clarissa and that of Lovelace. The seduction theme, which dominates the novel, enables the narrator to discuss illegal sex in a moral way.

The outline of the novel, one of the longest in English, is relatively simple. Lovelace, a young aristocrat, attempts to seduce Clarissa Harlowe, an heiress. At first she finds him charming, but resists him, assuming that he will eventually ask to marry her. Instead, he abducts her, drugs her and rapes her. She receives no support from her family, who are angered because she wishes to decide for herself what to do with the money she has inherited. Abandoned by all, aggrieved by the loss of her honour, Clarissa dies, after forgiving everyone. Later Lovelace is killed in a duel.

There is not the slightest doubt that Richardson sided with the heroine – this is not a work where one can remain neutral. Today, too, everyone – feminists, progressives, as well as traditional conservatives – would side with Clarissa. She may appear to be a feeble and weak woman, but she resists everyone: her greedy and unfeeling family as well as her boorish and violent suitor. She proclaims her right to choose what to do with her wealth and her body. She would rather die than abandon her principles. At the time, however, a considerable proportion of the reading public, particularly on the Continent, sided with the 'villain'. In the eighteenth century, the libertine Lovelace could be regarded as a free spirit, a true child of the Enlightenment, Clarissa as a deeply traditional woman with inflexible views of what her duties are. This could co-exist with another view of Clarissa: she is utterly modern because she wants the same rights as men, while Lovelace is utterly reactionary because he believes in aristocratic privilege. Clarissa Harlowe is a Puritan, frugal, strict with herself – in other words, the backbone of the bourgeoisie. Lovelace looks down on the Harlowes because of his higher birth, yet his freedom is not the result of his character but of his wealth and connection.[12] He thinks he can obtain with force what his charms fail to bring him, that once he has penetrated Clarissa she will be his.[13] Clarissa is a paragon of virtue, a secular saint. Lovelace is Lucifer – all the more excited by the apparent impregnability of his prey. The structure of the novel, which enables the principal characters to explain their reasons, grants the readers a great freedom to see in it what they want: morality, Christianity, a plea for equality, a new attitude towards women, individualism. The author himself embodied such contradictions. He was a deeply Christian man who wrote revolutionary novels. Novels such as these can encompass the entire political spectrum of the book-buying public – no mean feat. They may well be literary masterpieces, but they also address themselves to a very wide market.

Any consideration of the European fortune of this lengthy novel must include how it was translated. The liberties taken by translators at the time meant that the foreign-language text was often more an adaptation than a translation, and this may account for Clarissa's reception. Initially there were two Continental translations, one into French by Antoine François de Prévost (1751) – who also translated Richardson's other novels – the other into German by Johann David Michaelis (1749–53). Michaelis was an academic who had never written any fiction, only a few poems, including one significantly called 'Petition to His Royal Majesty in Prussia to found a University for the Fair Sex'. He shared Richardson's veneration for the virtues and duties attributed to women, regarded Clarissa as a treatise written in the form of a novel, and produced a faithful though ponderous translation.[14]

The French translator, the Abbé Prévost, was of a different temper. He was, above all, a novelist in his own right, author of the famous Histoire du *chevalier des Grieux et de Manon Lescaut* (1731), the story of a woman irresistibly attracted to wealth and pleasure, a novel which inspired two major operas, Jules Massenet's *Manon* (1884) and Giacomo Puccini's *Manon Lescaut* (1893). Prévost reshaped Clarissa to suit his reading public. Faced with the original 2,474 pages, he drastically cut it down, excising in particular all the long passages where Clarissa explained her inner turmoil and her commitment to duty. He called it *Lettres anglaises* to cash in on the novelty of the epistolary novel. Lovelace was made to appear less despicable, Clarissa more priggish. 'This Gentleman has left out a great deal of the Book,' lamented Richardson. Yet it was Prévost's version, and not Michaelis's, which was primarily responsible for Richardson's popularity in Europe, and not only because of the wider diffusion of French.[15] The German version was quickly forgotten, and the British original was more quoted than read. Richardson-Prévost sailed on. Prévost, emboldened or fed up with his author, entirely rewrote Richardson's third and last novel, the even longer and slumbering *The History of Sir Charles Grandison* (1753–54). Eventually, in 1786, in France too there appeared a full translation of *Clarissa*, but Prévost's version remained popular for a long time.

The Continental success of *Clarissa* surpassed that of *Pamela*. Diderot wrote an *Éloge de Richardson* (1766) praising his psychological depth, and credited him and Fielding with having rescued the novel from debased genres such as sentimentality and Gothic horror, the novel of manners, the picaresque novel. The Marquis de Sade and Choderlos de Laclos were fascinated by *Clarissa*. The epistolary novel appeared as an alluring novelty. This was reinforced by the recent fashion, particularly among high society women, for writing letters. A novel built around private correspondence had a great appeal – like reading other people's letters and discovering their intimate thoughts, something to entice the voyeur in us. The formulaic situations could be easily woven endlessly inside the narrative: virtue rewarded, chastity upheld, seductions, attempted seductions, deaths *à la* Clarissa.

Novels like *Clarissa* also contributed to the rescue of the novel from a low genre by building up the image of an exemplary protagonist, in sharp contrast with good-time girls like Moll Flanders. Young women, reading *Clarissa*, would take her as a role model and admire her determination to preserve her purity – or so it was hoped.

On the back of *Pamela* and *Clarissa*, epistolary novels became all the rage in the eighteenth century and beyond. Some have remained celebrated as great classics: Goethe's *Werther* (1744), Jean-Jacques Rousseau's *La Nouvelle*

Héloise (1761), Fanny Burney's *Evelina: or the History of a Young Lady's Entrance into the World* (1778), Pierre Choderlos de Laclos's *Les Liaisons dangereuses* (1782), Ugo Foscolo's *Le Ultime lettere di Jacopo Ortis* (1798–1802, the alleged 'first' literary Italian novel), Frances Moore Brooke's *The History of Emily Montague* (1769, the alleged 'first' Canadian novel), Madame de Staël's *Delphine* (1802). The Parisian bookseller Alexandre Pigoreau listed in his catalogue of 1,505 books (*Petite bibliographie biographico-romancière*, 1821) two hundred epistolary novels, adding, however, that they all belonged to the previous century: '*On n'en veut point aujourd'hui; telle est la volonté générale*' ('Nowadays we don't want any. Such is the general will').[16]

The genre enabled the author to adopt a kind of narrative transvestism.[17] Richardson, by writing Pamela's and Clarissa's letters, accomplished a remarkable feat: a man of fifty turning himself into a young woman confronting a leery seducer. One could achieve the same results with first-person narrative. Thus Defoe turned himself into Roxana and Moll Flanders.[18] Marivaux turned himself into Marianne, the Abbé Prevost into Manon Lescaut. Choderlos de Laclos, in his epistolary novel *Les Liaisons dangereuses*, was able to become not only the cynical and self-deluded Valmont but also the scheming and free-thinking Marquise de Merteuil, the austere Madame de Tourvel and the young not-so-ingénue convent girl Cécile. Flaubert famously declared that he *was* Emma Bovary, and Theodor Fontane identified with Effi Briest. It soon became clear that one of the gifts of the talented writer was that of assuming diverse personae, thus appealing to a wider range of possible readers.

The epistolary genre was also abundantly used by popular writers, from John Cleland (*Fanny Hill*, 1748) and Sophie von la Roche (*Geschichte des Fräuleins von Sternheim*, History of Lady Sternheim, 1771) to the eighteen-year-old Jane Austen in her *Lady Susan* (1793). The *Clarissa* model spread throughout Europe and beyond: it was, it is said, the first novel printed on American soil (by Benjamin Franklin in 1744). Bizet started writing an opera based on *Clarissa*, a project never completed – it would have made an interesting complement to *Carmen*.

Getting Scared

Structures are useful to writers. The hero proceeds from A to B and 'things happen' – and one gets the epic and a wonderful framework for storytelling. It has proved endlessly adaptable, from the *Odyssey* and the *Aeneid* to 'road movies' such as Dennis Hopper's hippie *Easy Rider* (1969), Ridley Scott's feminist *Thelma and Louise* (1991) and the Australian transvestite film *The Adventures of Priscilla, Queen of the Desert* (1994).

Epistolary novels remove the authorial voice and provide a framework of complex subjectivity: each character is allowed to explain the world as she or he sees it. A variant of this is the diary or the autobiographical form, where the author becomes the 'I' through whom everything is seen. What is required is that readers should identify with characters, and care for them. It helps if the character is like the reader: thrown into a story he does not understand yet. One must persevere (the reader in reading, the hero in his struggles), and in the end . . . all will be well. Mysteries and lurking dangers add to the excitement. A romantic element is highly desirable because it enables a double identification: with the hero (male or female) as well as with the person loved by the hero. Finally, a villain is required. In simple stories there is little or no identification with the villain. He may, initially, appear as a friend, but his devious and treacherous intentions must emerge in the end. Otherwise the villain should be an absolute 'other' belonging to a different country, class, religion, with different looks or colour. He (or she) must not belong to the same universe as the reader.

This is the plot basis for the so-called Gothic (because it was often set in a decaying abbey) or horror story. The horror tale has turned out to be one of the most successful and long-lasting genres ever, infinitely malleable as short story, novel, comic strip, film, radio play, television series and musical.

An obvious antecedent was the popular folk tale, peopled with dragons, demons and monsters. In eighteenth-century Europe the interest in and popularity of 'monsters', whether 'natural' (people with deformities) or 'supernatural' (miracles and prodigies), was so well established that the development of a rationalist and scientific outlook among the educated classes in the middle of the eighteenth century reinforced rather than displaced the fascination with them.[19] The display of strange or deformed animals was a common sight in London – a major attraction for both the educated and the uneducated.[20] Freak shows ('freaks' included people from non-white races) remained popular through to the middle of the nineteenth century and well into the twentieth: giants, bearded women and dwarves such as 'General Tom Thumb' made famous by Barnum.[21]

Monsters, however, were relatively rare in the eighteenth-century horror story, though they appear with greater frequency in the nineteenth when Dr Frankenstein creates one, Dr Jekyll turns into one (Mr Hyde is an uninhibited man, hence a monster), and Dracula comes in from Transylvania. In the twentieth century, monsters will come in from outer space, from the past, and from the future. The cinema will recycle all the monsters of the past and add new ones. All such stories, however, have antecedents. There are various medieval Jewish legends about the Golem, a kind of automaton infused with life by the magic of rabbis, such as the creature created by Rabbi Löw in sixteenth-century Prague which he was forced to destroy when it proved to be uncontrollable. There is an even earlier legend about an automaton built by Albert of Köln, the teacher of St Thomas, thanks to a magic formula learned from the Arabs.[22]

In the eighteenth century monsters were usually priests or foreigners or both, not 'blobs' from outer space. Plot variations included the nun story: a young woman is forced to take her vows by dastardly people, or by her parents or her guardian. Like her readers, she has no strong religious conviction and would much rather be reunited with her lover. She is the classic damsel in distress whose cry for help cannot go unanswered. The plot was so appealing that, in spite of its obvious anti-clerical implications, it was used by Catholic writers like Manzoni for the most exciting subplot of his *I Promessi sposi*, the episode of the Nun of Monza.

Then we have the pact with the devil (*Faust*, *Frankenstein*, etc.) by scientists and intellectuals who want to rival God or become God-like (by obtaining eternal youth) instead of sitting at home quietly reading novels. The anti-scientific element will become more pronounced in twentieth-century science fiction, with the theme of the experiment gone wrong generating mutations and monsters no one can control.

And then there is the conspiracy; in the nineteenth century this is usually by Jesuits, to take over the world (as in Eugène Sue's *Le Juif errant*, 1844–45). This is later easily adapted by replacing the Jesuits with Communists or Jews or the CIA or the Black Hand, Islamic fundamentalists or invaders from outer space. Gothic novels of the period 1770–1840 were hardly ever set in Great Britain. Only one of the sixty Franco Moretti sampled was set in London (and that was in the Renaissance); the others are all in Germany, France or Italy, or further afield.[23]

The Castle of Otranto by Horace Walpole (1764), one of the most successful early Gothic novels, had all the right ingredients: the mysterious manuscript, the ancestral portrait, the usurper, the persecuted heroine, the noble
peasant, the hermit, the monk, feudalism, the castle in ruins, etc. The setting
is usually Italian, Mediterranean, occasionally Bavarian (the Black Forest) or
Scottish. As Italy became familiar, the genre would move on, to places like
Transylvania with Bram Stoker's *Dracula* (1897), or to ancient Egypt or
ancient Rome as in Théophile Gautier's *La Morte amoureuse* (1836) or *Une
Nuit de Cléopatre* (1838).

Each author built on the success of his or her immediate predecessors –
the surest sign of the birth of a genre. Clara Reeve's famous *The Old English
Baron* (originally *The Champion of Virtue*, 1777) was explicitly written – as
the author acknowledged in the Preface – 'upon the same plan' as Walpole's
The Castle of Otranto. Matthew Gregory Lewis wrote *The Monk* in 1796 (at
the age of nineteen), 'induced', as he explained, 'to go on with it by reading
[Ann Radcliffe's] *The Mysteries of Udolpho*; which is in my opinion one of
the most interesting Books that ever have been published'.[24] The literary
references to *Udolpho* as a popular read for young women are endless. Here
is the young Becky Sharp, the heroine of Thackeray's *Vanity Fair* (1847–48),
to her friend Miss Amelia Sedley: 'And, oh, my dear, the great hall I am sure
is as big and as glum as the great hall in the dear castle of Udolpho.'[25] In
Jane Austen's *Northanger Abbey* (1818) the heroine, Catherine Morland, is
introduced to the Gothic novel by Isabella Thorpe at the fashionable resort
of Bath:

> 'But, my dearest Catherine, what have you been doing with yourself all
> this morning? Have you gone on with Udolpho?'
>
> 'Yes, I have been reading it ever since I woke; and I am got to the
> black veil.'
>
> 'Are you, indeed? How delightful! Oh! I would not tell you what is
> behind the black veil for the world! Are not you wild to know?'
>
> 'Oh! yes, quite; what can it be? But do not tell me: I would not be
> told upon any account. I know it must be a skeleton; I am sure it is
> Laurentina's skeleton. Oh! I am delighted with the book! I should like to
> spend my whole life in reading it, I assure you; if it had not been to meet
> you, I would not have come away from it for all the world.'
>
> 'Dear creature, how much I am obliged to you; and when you have
> finished Udolpho, we will read The Italian together; and I have made out
> a list of ten or twelve more of the same kind for you.'
>
> 'Have you, indeed? How glad I am! What are they all?'
>
> 'I will read you their names directly; here they are in my pocket-book.

Castle of Wolfenbach, Clermont, Mysterious Warnings, Necromancer of the Black Forest, Midnight Bell, Orphan of the Rhine, and Horrid Mysteries. Those will last us some time.'

'Yes; pretty well; but are they all horrid? Are you sure they are all horrid?'

'Yes, quite sure; for a particular friend of mine, a Miss Andrews, a sweet girl, one of the sweetest creatures in the world, has read every one of them.'[26]

And horrid was the right word: in Eliza Parsons's *The Castle of Wolfenbach* (1793) the wicked Count compels young Victoria to watch her beloved being tortured to death before being locked up into a dark windowless chamber with the headless body. Horror did not make writers rich – Eliza Parsons died in poverty – but novels like *Udolpho* (1794) and *The Italian* (1797) made Ann Radcliffe the most celebrated Gothic writer of her time (and her books are still profitably in print in cheap popular editions). The authors themselves were not always conscious of writing in the Gothic or horror genre. Radcliffe uses the term 'a romance', meaning a work of fantasy, as the subtitle for *The Mysteries of Udolpho*.

The Italian was a clever piece of literary marketing, beginning with the title and setting. Italy was well-known to eighteenth-century British readers. They were familiar with Italian history from classical literature and the great number of travel books available at the time. The country was the highlight of the European tour. British aristocrats and high bourgeois alike filled their mansions and country homes, built in accordance with the principles of the architect Palladio, with Old Masters shipped from Italy. Yet Italy was also a country of mystery, allegedly in thrall to what Protestant England regarded as the epicentre of spiritual corruption: the Pope and the Roman Catholic Church.[27] *The Italian* is a classic story in which a variety of familiar narrative elements are cleverly blended: two people of high social rank, Ellena di Rosalba and Vivaldi, are in love and have to surmount obstacles before being able to marry. The obstacles, just as in Manzoni's classic *I Promessi sposi*, are powerful people: Vivaldi's own mother and the cunning and cruel monk Schedoni (a former aristocrat). There is a kidnap, evil priests, some good ones, and the dreaded Holy Inquisition.

Ann Radcliffe did reasonably well out of her trade. She was paid £500 for *The Mysteries of Udolpho* and £800 for *The Italian* (approximately £60,000 at today's values). Jane Austen had been offered only £10 for *Northanger Abbey* (then entitled *Susan*) in 1803, though she got £300 for *Emma*. Radcliffe, who chose to retire at thirty-two, was very famous in her lifetime, unlike Austen. Her novels went into many editions, were condensed as chapbooks, were adapted for the stage, and were widely imitated: a spate of novels bearing similar titles – *The Mysteries of the Forest*, *The Monk of Udolpho*, *Italian Mysteries* – sometimes even bearing her name, barely disguised ('Mary Anne Radcliffe') were sold throughout Europe, or at least in novel-reading Europe, which was not that large a continent. In Spain, for instance, the first translation of a Radcliffe novel came out only in 1819: this was *A Sicilian Romance*, originally published in 1790 and now retranslated from the French. *The Mysteries of Udolpho* only came out in 1832.[28] Radcliffe's writing career may have been facilitated by her being childless and by the encouragement she received from her husband, the owner and editor of the newspaper *English Chronicle*.[29] In terms of sales it is highly probable that Lewis's *Ambrosio, or the Monk* (1795) (which resorted to a supernatural explanation) surpassed Radcliffe, perhaps because Ambrosio's lust for the seductress Matilda (a demon) and the chaste Antonia was described in bold details, along with tantalising glimpses of murders, transvestism, torture, rape, incest, profanation and necrophilia as well as the Holy Inquisition – an irresistible mixture.

Walpole, Radcliffe and Lewis established the Gothic novel as a quintessentially English genre – though its origins could be traced to Germany. As usual, British critics of the genre lamented its foreign origins. Such horrid novels embodied – they thought – the worst tendencies of the German character: uncontrolled emotions, revolutionary sentiments, and sexual deviancies of all types. Of the seven 'horrid' novels mentioned by Jane Austen in *Northanger Abbey*, two were German: Karl Grosse's *Horrid Mysteries* (1796; the original title was the less marketable *Der Genius*) and Karl Friedrich Kahlert's *The Necromancer* (1794). Walter Scott, introducing *Waverley* in 1814, remarked that had he called it *Waverley. A Romance from the German*, readers would have expected 'a profligate abbot, an oppressive duke, a secret and mysterious association of Rosycrucians and illuminati, with all their properties of black cowls, caverns, daggers, electrical machines, trap-doors, and dark lanterns'.[30] His article on supernatural fiction published in the *Foreign Quarterly Review* (July 1827) assumed that the Germans were particularly good at fantastic tales. There was, in any case, a considerable amount of literary trade between England and Germany in the 1790s. Lewis and Radcliffe were translated into German, and Lewis in turn was the translator of *Abaellino, der grosse Bandit* by the Swiss Heinrich Zschokke (1771–1848), written in the older genre of stories about bandits who are really gentlemen.[31]

Whatever its origins, the genre was clearly British. It is estimated that between 1764 and 1820, that is between the publication of Horace Walpole's *The Castle of Otranto* and that of Charles Maturin's *Melmoth the Wanderer*, some 4,500 to 5,000 Gothic novels were published in Britain alone, the majority written by women.[32] Some of the more outstanding practitioners of the genre were Irish, like Maturin and Sheridan le Fanu, the author of *Uncle Silas* (1864), and Bram Stoker, the author of the famous *Dracula* (1897). Some publishers, such as William Lane's Minerva Press, specialised in the genre – they had published six out of the seven novels 'recommended' by Jane Austen's Isabella Thorpe in *Northanger Abbey*. Founded in 1790, the Minerva Press quickly became the largest employer of hack writers in the country, mostly women. In 1798 William Lane issued a list of his top ten best-sellers: they were all by women. The readership of even such a 'low' genre as Lane's Minerva novels was overwhelmingly middle class, even though the books were regarded as trash by most critics.

Some Gothic novels, such as those of the prolific Sarah Wilkinson, were little more than chapbooks some twenty-four pages long, recycling standard themes. Their distribution by peddlers ensured an even wider diffusion of the genre. Lewis's *The Monk* was abridged as a chapbook almost as soon as it was published (and it inspired Charles Gounod's second opera, *La Nonne sanglante* in 1854). The late-eighteenth-century novel *Zofloya; or, The Moor*, by Charlotte Dacre, was available in a modified version as a chapbook with the title *The Demon of Venice* (1810). Its mix of sex and violence may have contributed to its reissue by the respectable Oxford University Press in 1997.[33]

A new genre may require some time to be accepted. In the 1780s most critics still objected to books that subverted 'nature' and dealt in 'the strange luxury of artificial terror'.[34] The highbrow *Edinburgh Review* thought Walpole's *The Castle of Otranto* puerile, though Clara Reeve's less extravagant *Old English Baron* was favourably received.[35] By the 1790s the critics had become used to the new genre. Ann Radcliffe's *The Mysteries of Udolpho* was enthusiastically received, while Coleridge reviewed Lewis's *The Monk* seriously, though he regarded it as obscene.[36]

At first the British Gothic novel – variously classified as *gotique*, *romantique*, *sépulcral* or *noir* – was not taken seriously in France. The *Mercure de France* (April 1767), commenting on the first French translation of Walpole's *Castle of Otranto* (published in Amsterdam), declared it only 'suitable for enabling one to spend a few pleasant hours'. A similar cool reception faced Clara Reeve's *The Old English Baron* (1778), which came out in French in 1787. Neither was read widely. But in 1782 Madame de Genlis, one of the most popular writers of her day, had used Gothic themes in her *Adèle et Théodore*, the story of an unhappy woman kept imprisoned by her jealous husband for nine years. In *Alphonsine* (1806) she returned to the same motif with the story of how the Comte de Moncalde keeps his wife in a cave for three years, vainly trying to poison her. She is found only after the death of her husband ... by his second wife.[37] While the influence of Radcliffe is evident, it also shows the enduring nature of the Bluebeard story.

Thus encouraged, François-Guillaume Ducray-Duminil (1761–1819) started churning out 'horrid' novels ('*romans terrifiants*') such as *Coelina, ou l'enfant du mystère* (1798), the story of the unlucky Coelina (yet another reincarnation of Cinderella) who is persecuted by her (male) relatives.[38] This was one of the great literary successes of the eighteenth century, running into eleven editions, though it is unlikely to have sold the 1.2 million copies some claim.[39]

By 1800 now-forgotten French imitations – such as *Château noir, ou les souffrances de la jeune Ophelle* by Mme Mérard de Saint-Juste (1799) – had flooded the market, helped by the fact that the demand for the Gothic was much greater than the supply of novels by Radcliffe and Lewis. Of course, one could always supply more 'authentic' English Gothic thanks to alleged 'translations' produced by writers like the prolific Étienne Léon de Lamothe-Houdancourt, who 'enriched' the corpus of the works of Ann Radcliffe with *L'Ermite de la tombe mystérieuse* (1817), 'translated from Anne [sic] Radcliffe'.[40] George Sand recalls, with nostalgia, that when young in Nohant she had read with 'delight and terror' the *Château des Pyrénées* by 'Madame Radcliffe', and that she and her friends had their heads so full of Scottish and Irish legends as 'to make one's hair stand on end'. In fact, the book she mentioned, *Les Visions du Château des Pyrénées* – to give it its correct title – was not a genuine Radcliffe novel at all, but had been penned in 1809 by one of her many French imitators, a certain Cantiran de Boirie. Still, it seemed to have fulfilled its purpose: to delight and scare the young George Sand and many like her.[41] Gautier, having reached Venice in 1850, wrote back: 'We felt we were travelling in a novel by ... Anne Radcliff [sic] ... The old histories of the Three Inquisitors, the Council of Ten ... masked spies. A cold terror, damp and black all around us, had taken possession of us.'[42]

The real take-off of the British Gothic in France occurred after the Revolution. Radcliffe was praised by the periodical *Décade philosophique* because, unlike other Gothic novelists, she always gave a rational explanation for apparently supernatural phenomena. In Britain this was not regarded as particularly praiseworthy, but in France rationalism mattered – even in horror stories. The *Mercure* also praised her anticlericalism – in reality Protestant anti-Catholicism.[43] In a letter to his younger sister Pauline Beyle in July 1804, Stendhal tells her to make sure her son Gaétan reads not only the usual classics as well as Cervantes, but also *The Mysteries of Udolpho* and *The Italian* – the only novels by a living writer he lists.[44] In Russia novels dealing with the apparently supernatural had a self-conceived mission: to demonstrate that the supernatural was a superstition. In the West, especially in England, it was not necessary to demonstrate that Frankenstein could not create a monster or that ghosts did not exist – British or French readers did not believe in these things. Superstition was no longer an issue – unlike in Russia.[45]

By the time Mary Shelley's *Frankenstein* was published in 1818, the superiority of British women in the art of generating horror was recognised by many, including Balzac, who has one of his characters declare that 'When it comes to bizarre conceptions, women's imagination reaches further than that of men, as witnessed by Mistress Shelley's Frankenstein . . . and the works of Ann Radcliffe.'[46] He then lifted the plot for his novel *The Centenarian or the Two Béringhenns* from Maturin's *Melmoth* (1822).[47]

The genre turned out to be particularly adaptable to the theatre. In London, in 1797, Henry William Grosette used various subplots from Lewis's *The Monk* for his melodrama *Raymond and Agnes; or the Bleeding Nun of Lindenberg.*[48] In Paris Charles Guilbert de Pixérécourt's *Château des Apennins, ou le fantôme vivant* (1799) was a huge success.[49] After 1815, with the Restoration, and in particular with the development of the Romantic movement and the surge in melodrama, the Gothic had become firmly established in France. By the 1820s and 1830s the typical lending library novel was a British Gothic.[50] Étienne Delécluze in his *Souvenir de soixante ans* attributed to the reading of Gothic novels the melancholia which seemed to afflict so many young men.[51] The formula behind the genre was so obvious that in 1798 the periodical *Spectateur du nord* provided prospective writers with the recipe for writing a good Gothic: take a castle in ruins, have long corridors with lots of doors, no fewer than three corpses still dripping with blood, including an old lady stabbed and hanged, add a few bandits, some muffled sounds and horrific noise.[52] As has been noted, parodies are the surest indication of a popular genre. In 1799 appeared the appropriately titled *Nuit anglaise*, the story of a practical joke played on a voracious reader of Gothic novels. His friends, in disguise, take him while asleep to a horrific ruined castle full of secret closets. To escape he has to sign a pact with the devil whereby he undertakes never to read again an English novel except those of Richardson, Fielding, and other similarly respectable writers.

The British Gothic swept throughout Europe. In Poland, though the most fashionable foreign novels were by French Romantics such as Chateaubriand, the Gothic à la Radcliffe inspired novelists like Anna Mostowska.[53] Carl Jonas Love Almqvist's romantic classic Drottningens juvelsmycke (The Queen's Jewels, 1834) could be classified as a Swedish Gothic.[54]

The genre was very successful in Germany too, where it was known as Schauerromane ('terror fiction'), though it was not exported elsewhere and never achieved the international fame of the British Gothic. According to Madame de Staël, writing in 1808–10 on her travels in Germany, everyone was fascinated by stories of ghosts and witches.[55]

Some themes, such as that of the vampire, had been pioneered in Germany well before the advent of Bram Stoker's Dracula in 1897. An examination of 126 out of nearly four hundred novels published in 1800 in Germany revealed that thirty-seven could be classified as 'Gothic'.[56] E.T.A. Hoffmann has remained the best-known of the 'Gothic' German writers because some of his fantastic tales were used by Jacques Offenbach for his opera Les Contes d'Hoffmann (1880) and by Léo Delibes in the ballet Coppélia (1870). He had made use, well before Robert Louis Stevenson's The Strange Case of Dr Jekyll and Mr Hyde (1886), of the split personality or doppelgänger character in his novel Die Elixiere des Teufels (The Devil's Elixir, 1815–16).

One of the main reasons behind the popularity of the Gothic was that it could be enjoyed by people of different educational levels (like, in the twentieth century, the detective story and science fiction). It did not have any obvious class connotation. It could be found as easily in the library of educated families such as that of Jane Austen or, as a simplified chapbook, in the modest room of a Victorian maid.

Were Gothic books best-sellers? We do not have accurate figures, and in any case, some popular writers achieved significant sales not with one or two successful books but, quite simply, because they were very prolific and flooded the market. Besides, 'horror' is only one possible classification. As most Gothic stories deal with romance, one might as well include them in the love-and-sex novels which were then as popular as they are now.

The big sellers of the late eighteenth and early nineteenth centuries are now virtually forgotten. Even in their days Pigault-Lebrun (1753–1835) and

Paul de Kock (1793–1871) probably sold only a few thousand copies of each of their books, but they wrote much and were extremely well-known by the book-reading public in France and elsewhere in Europe. De Kock was the author of one hundred books and two hundred plays, mainly bawdy stories of amiable bourgeois in hot pursuit of accommodating 'grisettes'. He was later regarded, snobbishly, as a writer for concierges, but at the time he appealed to a wide range of tastes.[57] A typical de Kock character is Georgette, the heroine of the eponymous novel, who sleeps around with aristocrats and suffers the consequences. De Kock was building on the earlier literary (and financially unsuccessful) works of Rétif de la Bretonne (1734–1806). Known pejoratively as the Voltaire of the *femme de chambre* (the chambermaid's Voltaire) or the Rousseau *du ruisseau* (the Rousseau of the gutter), Rétif (or Restif), who was also a printer, wrote dozens of books – and a sixty-thousand-page autobiography – mixing, as was often the case in the eighteenth century, libertine and philosophical reflections with erotic descriptions and violence.[58] The dividing line between low and high genre being unclear, he was translated into German, where he was regarded as a major French writer – as evidenced in a letter from Schiller to Goethe.[59] In his *Le Paysan perverti* (1775), an epistolary novel with daring illustrations by Louis Binet, he introduced in the plot an eye-gouging, an arm-chopping, a fratricide and an incest.[60]

Pigault-Lebrun's books were often the life story of *un enfant du peuple* (such as *L'Enfant du carnaval*, his greatest success) who in the course of his adventures learns to despise authorities and priests.[61] Also popular were his more *risqué* novels: in *Monsieur de Roberville* (1809) a newly married couple decide to spend months in bed, the neighbours complain, and eventually, when the pair are bored with each other, the hero, who is dim, ends up cuckolded. The book was banned between 1825 and 1852 (a period in which censorship was particularly strong). Also popular were erotic novels with titles like *Clémentine, orpheline androgyne* and *Les Nymphes du Palais-Royal* – some were written by women, such as the Comtesse de Choiseul-Meuse (*Julie ou j'ai sauvé ma rose*).[62]

9

Walter Scott
'in Unclouded Splendour'[1]

Scott's Star

THE SUCCESSES OF British novels on the Continent, and particularly in France – their launching pad towards the rest of Europe – laid the foundations for further successes. The national origin of cultural goods often functions like a brand name: Hollywood films, French food, Italian design. Thanks to Fielding, Defoe and Richardson, the novel was seen as a quintessentially 'English' product – Continental Europe, particularly in the early nineteenth century, had no conception of the term 'British'. There were further reasons for English dominance: British technological-industrial advances, growing wealth, and relatively liberal institutions. The country was vaguely filling the role that the United States would assume some two hundred years later. 'Vaguely', because Great Britain, even at its height, was never as globally dominant as the USA after the collapse of the Soviet Union.

The great rival, France, had been temporarily restrained. Waterloo had wiped out France's global military ambitions. The great season of the French novel was yet to come: in 1815 Balzac (born in 1799), Hugo (1802), Alexandre Dumas (1802), Eugène Sue (1804) and George Sand (1804) were still at school, learning the trade. Europe was busy digesting and enjoying the constant influx of British novels high and low, the steady stream of Romantic poetry, the regular arrival of English and Scottish journals, the discovery of Shakespeare.

The Romantic revolution had prepared the literary classes to become receptive to national cultures, to national history, to local culture, to the primitive and the strange, and to tales of mystery and folklore. There was a growing internationalisation of culture: the French did not merely export their writers, they also read those of other countries, mainly British poets such as Byron, Thomas Moore, Southey and Shelley, but also Goethe and

Schiller from Germany and the Spanish *romancero* and drama. There were even extra-European imports: classics from the Near East, Persia and India, and new writing from China. The anonymous Chinese novel *Iu kiao li, ou les deux cousines* (the story of a wealthy man who needs to find a husband for his desirable daughter and the severe tests to which he subjects the suitors) translated in 1826 by Abel Rémusat, a distinguished French sinologist, became quite popular in French salons and was translated into English in the following year.

Mythological, religious and pastoral subjects had prevailed in the eighteenth century, but in the 1770s and 1780s the idea of adventuring into the past came to the fore. Historical paintings came to be regarded as the summit of the fine arts. In France only six historical paintings were exhibited at the Salon of 1804, then eighteen in 1806, twenty-five in 1810, and eighty-six in 1814.[2] Everywhere, especially in England, collecting historical portraits had become very fashionable.[3]

History teaching, even in the middle of the nineteenth century, was still of little importance in English universities and public schools, but interest in history was widespread in Britain and throughout the Continent. It was widely used as a polemical weapon in political debates, where historical facts and citations were commonly used to score points.[4]

This was the context of the rise of the historical novel.

The global success of Walter Scott's novels was far in excess of that of any previous living novelist. He was widely borrowed from lending libraries as his reputation as a great 'page-turner' grew. In the late 1820s his entire *oeuvre* – some thirty volumes – was reprinted and sold in monthly instalments to 30,000 subscribers in Britain.[5]

Scott's influence in Europe and North America was enormous. The novelist Maria Edgeworth wrote that an American guest informed her that the last Scott novel was out in the United States only a month after its London publication, and at a cheaper price.[6] His novels were adapted into plays and operas, and, in the twentieth century, into films and television series. Themes from his novels provided the impetus for what we now call 'merchandising' (tartans, plaids, ballads, etc.). He almost invented the popular image of Scotland – one which has endured to this day: 'Hollywood Scotland' and 'Heritage Scotland' must be credited to, or blamed on, Walter Scott.

Thanks to this frenetic and tireless writer, others realised the potential appeal of 'historical novels': a kind of time machine enabling the reader to be transported to yesteryear. One could obtain a similar effect with classics, too, but a living author could tailor the story to contemporary taste, emphasising what was different, what was similar and, above all, providing a reassuring picture of the past. One could learn about history surreptitiously while having fun, instead of ploughing through lengthy and tedious tomes written by professional historians and packed with burdensome facts. From a popular perspective, Alexandre Dumas was, in his time, France's leading historian. As Gramsci remarked, the popularity of French historical novels resulted in Italians knowing more about the French monarchical and revolutionary tradition than their own.[7]

The historical novel turned out to be one of the key genres throughout the successive two centuries, easily adaptable to other media. The persistent popularity of historical novels, from Walter Scott onward, has involved 'a mobilisation of previous historical knowledge generally acquired through the schoolbook history manuals devised for whatever legitimising purpose by this or that national tradition'.[8]

The popularity of the historical drama – Shakespeare, Racine and Schiller are names who stand above so many – showed that there was a keen audience for fictionalised history. Myths and epics too dealt with the past. Much of the Bible purports to be 'history'. More generally, the structure of most narratives implies that what is being told is an event that has taken place at some time other than the present. History – loosely defined – was always of interest. Moreover, history was a serious matter, unlike the frivolous novel. By combining the two, as Anthony Trollope gratefully acknowledged, novel-reading was made respectable.[9]

In Walter Scott's days novel-reading was not so respectable. Scott, who had built up a reputation as a poet, a scholar and a lawyer, thought it prudent to remain anonymous when he published *Waverley* in 1814. His subsequent books were signed 'the author of *Waverley*' – as if to say: 'Those who liked *Waverley* will also like . . .' The mystery of the authorship seems to have worked as an unconscious marketing ploy. It had become part of the gossip of the literate classes.[10] Maria Edgeworth wrote excitedly to Sophy Ruxton on 17 January 1822: 'I have heard an anecdote of Walter Scott which proves beyond a doubt – if a doubt remained – that he is the author of the novels attributed to him.'[11] Eventually, on 23 February 1827 at an official dinner, Scott publicly confessed that he was the author of the most successful novels of his day: '. . . the joke had lasted long enough', he wrote, 'and I was tired of it'.[12] Jane Austen had no doubt as early as September 1814 (*Waverley* had been out only since July): 'Walter Scott has no business to write novels, especially good ones. It is not fair. He has Fame and Profit enough as a Poet, and should not be taking the bread out of people's mouths.'[13]

The historical novel could straddle several genres. It could contain a strong love story and the thrill of the Gothic genre. Scott's Scotland was often a barbaric and primitive land, whose people were imbued with a tribal sense of themselves. If Italy and Greece appeared remote to British readers, Scotland was equally dark and mysterious. Of this Scott was supremely conscious. In his preface to *Rob Roy* (1818) he wrote that 'within forty miles of Glasgow' characters like Rob Roy 'blending the wild virtues, the subtle policy, and unrestrained license of an American Indian, [were] flourishing ... during the Augustan age of Queen Anne and George I'. One should draw a 'strong contrast', he wrote, between the 'civilised and cultivated mode of life on the one side of the Highland line, and the wild and lawless adventures undertaken by those on the other side'.[14]

Scott had the literary background ideally suited to the development of the genre. He was familiar with Scottish folklore – in 1802 he had published his collection of Scottish ballads and myths, *Minstrelsy of the Scottish Border* – tragic slayings, escapes and rescues. He was also familiar with a wide range of European literature: he had translated Goethe's play *Goetz von Berlichingen* as well as Gottfried Bürger's ballads (such as the celebrated *Lenora*, written in 1774). From Defoe, Fielding and Richardson, he had learnt the value of realistic descriptions and characters.[15] He knew his market, his audience, his critics; he knew what was wanted and he was ready to deliver.

Scott combined two powerful trends, a cultural nationalism *à la* Herder, but totally disconnected from political nationalism (which made it unthreatening to the political establishment), and the ability to make Europeans interested in his 'regional' history.[16] Scott was a variant of the classic case of the insider/outsider. He was a fully-fledged member of the establishment, who was even offered the post of Poet Laureate (he declined). He possessed all the cultural capital required: education, self-confidence, audience and language. At the same time, as a Scot, he was an outsider, not quite at home in the London-centred cultural and literary establishment. His role as cultural mediator was thus considerably enhanced. He could tell the world about the primitive Scots, because he was 'one of them'; but he was also civilised, hence 'one of us'. This ambivalent position confers on the insider/outsider a unique advantage which Walter Scott used, almost unconsciously. It conferred upon him a kind of objectivity, celebrated by the Hungarian Marxist critic Georg Lukács with these words:

> Scott, the great realist, recognises that no civil war in history has been so violent as to turn the entire population without exception into fanatical partisans of one or other of the contending camps with fluctuating sympathies now for this side now for the other.[17]

As an outsider/insider, Scott was in good company: some of the greatest minds of eighteenth-century Britain were Scottish (David Hume, Adam Smith and Adam Ferguson); and he was joined by subsequent generations of insiders/outsiders who knew the dominant culture without being entirely part of it: the various provincials who launched themselves at the conquest of Paris (Balzac, Zola, Flaubert); the southern Italians who made their mark in philosophy, political theory, and literature (Giordano Bruno, Giambattista Vico, Francesco de Sanctis, Giovanni Verga, Luigi Pirandello, Benedetto Croce, Antonio Gramsci); the women writers who forced their way into the literary canon (George Eliot, Emily Dickinson, George Sand, Grazia Deledda); the Irish without whom the very canon of 'English' literature would be dramatically different and poorer (Swift, Oscar Wilde, James Joyce, Yeats, etc.), and the numerous Jews, Anglo-Indians and African-Americans who came to dominate the high peaks of European and North American literature in the twentieth century, from Marcel Proust to Albert Cohen, from Saul Bellow to Philip Roth, from R.K. Narayan to Salman Rushdie, from Elias Canetti to V.S. Naipaul, from Franz Kafka to Primo Levi, from Maya Angelou to Toni Morrison.

Scott influenced an entire generation of novelists. His Continental popularity began with a genre which combined high culture with the new fashion for the epic. Scott could be regarded as the expression of an 'oppressed' nation, and one could be fascinated by the Scottish past without in any way supporting the idea of secession – much as in the twentieth century one could love jazz or admire black musicians without the slightest commitment to civil rights and racial emancipation. Scott demonstrated that local 'national' history could be just as fascinating to outsiders as to the indigenous readers. His main characters were entirely fictional, but they operated within verifiable historical events and met real historical characters.

His poems, above all 'The Lady of the Lake' (1810), enhanced the curiosity of the reading public about the Scottish Highlands. His first major novel, *Waverley* (1814), about the Jacobite rebellion of 1745, made Scott world famous. Then he produced a steady stream of novels, including *Guy Mannering* (1815), *Old Mortality* (1816), *Rob Roy* (1818) and *The Heart of Midlothian* (1818).

As a Romantic defender of the *ancien régime*, Scott knew how to describe the anxiety and nostalgia brought about by rapid social change, and the psychological tension and personal tragedy of those who appear to be on the 'wrong' side of history. And change, in the aftermath of the French Revolution and the Napoleonic Wars, was sweeping through much of Europe. Yet Scott and his novels were no threat to anyone at all.

On the whole, the historical novel was a reassuring genre. What happened had to happen. Most of the historical novels of the first half of the nineteenth century, though sympathetic to rebels, end with an account of how they are crushed by a central authority – whether Balzac's Chouans or Gogol's Cossacks in *Taras Bulba*.[18]

As with most genres, the attempt to arrive at a strict definition of the historical novel is a waste of time; it all comes down to an invisible contract between readers and writers: some material is regarded as fictional, and some as historically accurate. A historical work is one where, in the words of a critic, 'historical probability reaches a certain level of structural prominence' – an 'impotent and lame conclusion, objectionable on several counts', he admits.[19]

In Scott's novels the identification of the reader with the hero is achieved through a simple device. The hero, like the reader, is an outsider to whom local customs and history must be explained as the action proceeds. At the same time the author avoids taking sides. That way the outcome appears to be open, the result of objective circumstances and not the whim of the author. The Russian novelist Nikolai Karamzin had used this device some ten years before Scott in his historical stories such as *Martha the Posadnik*, set in the fifteenth century, but he was writing in Russian, and thus remained unknown (as he still is) to the vast majority of non-Russian readers.[20] Scott used a fast-paced narrative, enthralling readers on the first page of the novel and not allowing them any respite until they reach the end. This required the transformation of history into a story where the behaviour of human beings, their feelings and actions, were far more important than the forces which shaped them. As Thomas Carlyle put it, Scott's work 'was like a new discovered continent in literature'. He had arrived in time to rescue British literature, which 'lay all puking and sprawling in Werterism [sic], Byronism, and other Sentimentalism tearful or spasmodic (fruit of internal *wind*)';

> ... these Historical Novels have taught all men this truth ... that the bygone ages of the world were actually filled by living men, not by protocols, state-papers, controversies and abstractions were they, not dia-

grams and theorems; but men, in buff or other coats and breeches, with colour in the cheeks, with passions in their stomach, and the idioms, features and vitalities of very men.[21]

Scott proved with his most popular novels, such as *Ivanhoe*, that one could be loved by the general reading public as well as by the cultural élites. Major nineteenth-century German literary critics such as Julian Schmidt agreed that Scott exercised more influence than any other author.[22] The diffusion of his novels demonstrated that the creation of a common European culture could proceed through the export of the cultural products of dominant countries and their purchase by a new reading public, keen to read novels. Scott arrived to tap this new market: the right man at the right place with the right product. Like all great popular writers after him (Balzac, Dumas, Verne, Tolkien and Hergé, the author of Tintin), Scott created a fantasy world out of a real world in a steady stream of novels. Scott had the ability – essential for a popular writer – to write fast, thus guaranteeing a constant supply of works for his market. 'It is no wonder that the public repay with lengthened applause and gratitude the pleasure they receive. He writes as fast as they can read, and he does not write himself down. He is always in the public eye, and we do not tire of him,' wrote William Hazlitt.[23]

This is important, because any novelty immediately generates a multitude of imitators. It is thus essential to keep ahead. In 1819 alone – Scott's best year financially, during which he is said to have earned £14,000 – he published three novels, including two of his most famous, *The Bride of Lamermoor* and *Ivanhoe* (his first novel set neither in Scotland nor in the recent past), as well as literary criticism, essays and journalism.[24] Adaptations for the London stage took place within weeks of publication – sometimes several plays based on one novel, such as *Ivanhoe* at Covent Garden and *The Hebrew* (a development of the Rebecca and Isaac subplot) at the Drury Lane. Hazlitt wrote in 1820 that as soon as Scott published a novel, Messrs Harris and Ellston set their painters to paint backdrops, musicians to write a score and script writers to turn it into a play.[25] There were numerous spin-offs, such as one brought out in 1818 by Constable, Scott's publishers, called *Criminal Trials, Illustrative of the Tale Entitled 'The Heart of Mid-Lothian'*.[26]

Scott's acquisition of his printer, James Ballantyne & Co., and of his publisher, Archibald Constable & Co., could be seen as an attempt to control the entire production cycle of his output. The economic crisis of 1826 ruined his printing business, and Scott lost a considerable fortune (£46,000) and became responsible for the entire debt – nearly £100,000.[27] Thereafter Scott was, in practice, writing to pay off his debt and maintain his expensive lifestyle. The result was that between 1826 and his death in 1832 he wrote five novels, one collection of short stories, the nine-volume *Life of Napoleon*, a history of Scotland, two volumes of essays and a journal over eight hundred pages long.[28] It is remarkable that he should have been able to repay all his debts by the time he died. But then Scott was exceedingly well remunerated, especially by today's standards. In 1818 he received from the *Quarterly Review* the sum of ninety guineas just for a review of Byron's *Childe Harold*.[29]

Scott and the Continent

Scott was lucky to be writing in an idiom that was already 'global', as it was spoken in America and in the colonies, and was second in Europe only to French. Had he been writing in Gaelic (or any other peripheral language) he would have remained unknown.

The export of a written text could not have occurred without the existence of a considerable corpus of translators. As most translators in Europe could translate only from French, the French market was the necessary springboard for success elsewhere. Had Scott not been extremely popular in France he would not have been as successful in the rest of Europe. The importance of obtaining a French translation in order to be re-translated elsewhere can be gauged by the large number of English novels translated into Russian from French in the course of the eighteenth century.[30] Of the 245 English-language books translated into Russian between 1741 and 1800, only forty-eight were translated directly from English, while 132 were re-translations of French versions, the remainder reaching Russian readers from German (forty-six), Polish (two) and one from Italian.[31] In Spain and Italy too it was common to translate Scott (and Fenimore Cooper) from French. To make matters more difficult for readers, in Spain Scott's works were regularly cut and censored.[32]

Seldom has a foreign writer had so much influence in France. There are claims that a single bookseller-printer – Gosselin of Paris – sold over one million copies of Scott's novels.[33] The claim is unsustainable, but the fact that it could be made in a book published at the end of the nineteenth century is remarkable. The truth is that between 1820 and 1851 twenty editions of the complete works of Scott were published in France alone, selling all in all some 45,000 copies.[34] This is a remarkable achievement.

Translators competed to render Scott into French.[35] A book about him –
Paul Lacroix's *Les Soirées de Walter Scott à Paris* (1829) – sold over 100,000
copies.[36] The journal *Les Débats* of 8 May 1820 declared Scott to be the
fashionable novelist of the hour: his last novel, *Ivanhoe,* had been almost
completely sold out.[37] The *Revue encyclopédique* (1823) pronounced Walter
Scott novels to be, from 'any point of view', the best in the whole of Europe.[38]
The journal *L'Abeille* of 1821 – in what sounds like a paid advertisement (and
probably was) – commented:

> Hâtez-vous, Messieurs et vous surtout Mesdames; c'est du merveilleux,
> c'est du nouveau! La première edition est épuisée, la seconde est retenue
> d'avance, la troisième disparaîtra, à peine sortie de la presse. Accourez,
> achetez; mauvais, ou bon, qu'importe! Sir Walter Scott y a mis son nom,
> cela suffit et vive l'Angleterre et les Anglais.
>
> (Make haste, gentlemen and, in particular, you, ladies. It's wonderful!
> It's new! The first edition has sold out, the second is pre-sold, the third
> will vanish as soon as it is published. Hurry, buy it, never mind whether
> it's good or bad! It's by Sir Walter Scott. This is enough and long live
> England and the English.)[39]

The Paris stage had plays featuring characters from the Waverley novels, such
as *Têtes Rondes et Cavaliers* by François Ancelot and Xavier-Boniface Santine,
first performed at the Vaudeville in September 1833.[40]

The catalogues of the French lending libraries confirm Scott's enormous
popularity.[41] Delacroix was only one of dozens of painters who used Scottish
themes based on Scott's works.[42] In Paris *walterscottomanie* was such that the
Duchess of Berry had masked balls with a Waverley novels theme. People
sported '*cravattes à la Walter Scott*'. Tartan became fashionable for women.[43]
In 1822 King George IV dressed up in tartan for his official visit to Scotland,
and a stage adaptation of *Rob Roy* was chosen to celebrate the first night of
his stay.[44] In Italy, according to a report of the *Giornale del Regno delle due
Sicilie*, in February 1829 there was a ball organised by Queen Maria Teresa
where the most fashionable dresses were inspired by *Ivanhoe*.[45] Illustrators
were constantly representing scenes from the famous novels. Waverley balls
were held in London under the patronage of Prince Albert to raise funds for
a memorial to Scott (inaugurated in 1846). In 1824 Schubert wrote songs
based on *The Lady of the Lake* and *Ivanhoe*.

Over eighty operas were composed on the basis of Scott's stories.[46] They
included two which are still very famous: Donizetti's *Lucia di Lammermoor*
(1835), based on *The Bride of Lammermoor*, and Bizet's *La Jolie fille de Perth*

(1867). Others included the then much celebrated composer, Daniel Auber (whose *Leicester* was adapted by Scribe from *Kenilworth*), Berlioz's early overture *Rob-Roy* (1832) and Friedrich von Flotow's own *Rob Roy* (1836), Otto Nicolai (*Il Templaro*, based on *Ivanhoe*), Heinrich Marschner (*Der Templer und die Jüdin*, also based on *Ivanhoe*), Rossini (first *La Donna del lago*, 1819, based on *The Lady of the Lake* and then *Ivanhoë* in 1826 – in reality a work by Antonio Pacini using, with Rossini's blessing, music adapted from several of Rossini's operas), and Sullivan's grand opera *Ivanhoe* in 1891. Three of Scott's novels (*Guy Mannering*, *The Monastery* and *The Abbot*) were pillaged by Eugène Scribe to produce the text for François-Adrien Boieldieu's *opera buffa La Dame blanche*, now almost forgotten, but when it opened in 1825 it had 129 Parisian performances in its first twelve months, and was still being performed regularly in the 1880s.[47]

On the back of Scott a spate of historical novels inundated Europe. Most left no trace, but some became classics in their own right: Manzoni's *I Promessi sposi*, Victor Hugo's *Notre-Dame de Paris*, Mérimée's *Chronique du temps de Charles IX* (1829) and Vigny's *Cinq-Mars* (1826) – for which Vigny was hailed as the French Walter Scott, to Balzac's annoyance, for he coveted the title for himself.[48] Publishers asked their authors for 'Scott novels'. Budding authors like George Eliot tried out their skills, at least initially, by writing in the manner of Scott.[49] Later she recollected reading Scott aloud to her father during the last five or six years of his life: 'No other writer would serve as a substitute for Scott, and my life at that time would have been much more difficult without him.'[50]

Balzac revered Scott and regarded him as a genius. Byron pales into insignificance beside him, he wrote to Madame Hanska in January 1838. The plot of *Kenilworth* is 'the grandest, most complete, most extraordinary of all'.[51] Balzac's first major novel, *Les Chouans*, started out as a historical love story *à la* Scott narrating the royalist revolt in western France against the French revolutionary government of 1799. Allusions to Scott are frequent in Balzac's novels. In *Le Curé de village*, Véronique Graslin, disappointed with marital sex, reads the novels of Walter Scott (as well as Byron, Goethe and Schiller).[52] In *Illusions perdues* (1837), the protagonist, Lucien de Rubempré, attempts to write a historical novel in the style of Scott (*L'Archer de Charles IX*). He is under the misapprehension that publishers, having glanced at the opening pages, would open their wallets and ask 'How much do you want?'[53] The lesson of Scott, Balzac knew, because he too had tried his hand at imitation, is not to try to be quite like him. Lucien's friend Daniel d'Arthez

(Balzac's mature alter ego) proffers some wise advice: 'If you don't want to ape Walter Scott you must adopt a different style and, in so doing, you would be doing like him.'[54] Frédéric Moreau, the ambitious but shallow hero of Flaubert's *L'Éducation sentimentale* (1869), aspired to be one day the Walter Scott of France.[55] Jeanne's mother in Guy de Maupassant's *Une Vie* finds peace in the works of Walter Scott.[56]

Stendhal is reputed to have declared that Scott was 'our father'.[57] The Russian critic Vissarion Belinsky said, in 1844, that Scott had 'written one very bad history and a multitude of excellent novels'. Heine called him the heir of Cervantes.[58] In 1832, as the news of Scott's impending death spread round Europe, Lamartine wrote a mushy poem in his honour. Scott's books were described as ideal family reading matter. Young virginal women, wrote Lamartine, instead of hiding his books from their mothers, read and reread openly the most loved passages; they then fell asleep as pure as before, their heart enriched by love and grace:[59]

> La vierge, en te lisant, qui ralentit son pas,
> Si sa mère survient, ne te dérobe pas,
> Mais relit au grand jour le passage qu'elle aime,
> Comme en face du ciel tu l'écrivis toi-même,
> Et s'endort aussi pure après l'avoir fermé,
> Mais de grâce et d'amour le coeur plus parfumé.

The most influential French critic of his day, Sainte-Beuve, in his obituary for Scott (*Le Globe*, 27 September 1832), wrote: 'It is not a grief for England only; it is a sorrow for France and the whole civilised world ... *Waverley* ... was the first of the series of masterpieces which have been the delight and joy of Europe.'[60] Scott had achieved the dream of all novelists: to be popular *and* to be accepted by the literary fraternity, to achieve fame and acquire cultural prestige. Literature was still at the stage where serious writers did not think that their legitimacy required them to be regarded as 'difficult' by the wider public – which, admittedly, was still rather restricted. Goethe's popular success with *Werther* marked him for life: for once he had been at one with his public. He had been delighted to have discovered the *Zeitgeist* and to have written it.[61] Schiller too could declare that he wrote only for the public: 'The public is now everything for me, my study, my sovereign, my trusted friend. To it alone do I now belong.'[62]

Charles Louandre, surveying literary production from the vantage point of 1847, noted the continuing popularity of the historical novel, 'invented by Walter Scott', but he accused 'Scott's imitators' of not knowing history, of empathising with 'the dangerous classes' and of having produced few durable works.[63]

Dumas said when he read *Ivanhoe* it was 'the *coup de foudre*', and promptly translated it. Goethe declared in 1828 that one could not find in *The Fair Maid of Perth* a single weak passage, while *Waverley* 'may without hesitation be set beside the best work that has ever been written in this world'.[64] Three years later, his enthusiasm was even greater. After reading *Ivanhoe* he declared that Walter Scott had no equal, 'and we need not wonder at the effect he produces on the whole reading world. He gives me much to think of; and I discover in him a wholly new art with laws of its own.'[65]

The revival of the Spanish novel began with the translation of Walter Scott's.[66] In the earlier part of the nineteenth century Scott was one of the most important English writers in Portugal. The vogue for Scott was enhanced by the publication of many of his writings in magazines like *O Panorama* and *Cosmorama litterário*; his influence on Portuguese writers like Alexandre Herculano and Almeida Garrett has been remarkable. Most of the translations into Portuguese took place some twenty to thirty years after their original appearance in English and French – *The Bride of Lammermoor* (1819) in 1836, *Heart of Midlothian* (1818) in 1838, *Ivanhoe* (1820) in 1837. The effect was dramatic: the take-off of Portuguese historical novels occurred in the years after the 1830s, that is after the publication of Scott's works in Portuguese.[67] Such developments, however, would not have happened without the return of intellectuals who had been in exile (mainly in Paris) during the Peninsular and civil wars of the first quarter of the century.

Miklós Jósika (1794–1865), the prolific creator of the Hungarian historical novel, used Scott and Scotland as a model for his representation of Transylvania.[68] In Holland, though Adriaan Loosjes had written one of the country's first historical novels, *Het leven van Maurits Lijnlager* (The Life of Maurits Lijnlager, 1808), it was only in the 1830s, after Scott had become popular, that a spate of historical novels appeared – as evidenced by the works of Geertruida Bosboom-Toussain (1812–86) and Jacob Van Lennep (1802–68). Scott was one of the first novelists to be translated into Romanian.[69]

In Russia the taste for the historical novel had been prepared by Karamzin, author of the multi-volume *History of the Russian State*. But for a genre to be successful in Russia, it had to be imported from the West, and hence Karamzin never stood a chance against Scott. Scott was praised by major writers like Lermontov and Gogol; Pushkin called him 'the Scottish sorcerer', and a stream of popular novels were directly or indirectly inspired by him.[70]

Aleksandra Kobiakova (1823–92) wrote in her autobiography *Russkoe slovo* that the first book that sparked her imagination was *Yuri Miloslavski, or the Russians in 1612* by Mikhail Zagoskin (1789–1852), a historical novel *à la* Scott which in turn encouraged a flood of similar novels after its publication in 1829. Kobiakova wrote: 'it shaped my taste once and for all, and the string of historical novels that followed compelled me to turn my attention to my nation's history. A new world rose before me . . .'[71] Even Hans Christian Andersen, influenced by Walter Scott, tried writing historical fiction before turning, more profitably, to children's stories.[72]

In Italy, the fashion for the novels of 'Gualtiero' Scott reached the country on the back of his French fame. There was wide coverage – almost unanimously favourable – of Scott in the periodical press. Many Italian readers had been reading Scott in French, but in August 1821 Vincenzo Ferrario, a publisher, started the publication of the historical novels of Scott (*Romanzi storici di Walter Scott*), starting with *Kenilworth*. In 1828 two other publishers entered the field. By 1830 two more followed, so that by then some five publishers – all in Milan – were producing collections of Walter Scott's works (without paying him a penny).[73] New words – directly borrowed from Scott – were introduced into the Italian language – words such as *plaid* and *clan*.[74] Rovani in his book *Cento anni* (1857) celebrated Walter Scott as having been, forty years previously, the most avidly read writer in Europe and the most imitated in France and Italy.[75]

The publication of Scott's novels enhanced the development of the Italian historical novel. Manzoni read many of Scott's novels as he was writing the first draft of *I Promessi sposi*. Also inspired by Scott were Giovan Battista Bazzoni's *Il Castello di Trezzo*, Domenico Guerrazzi's *La Battaglia di Benevento*, Vincenzo Lancetti's *Cabrino Fondulo* and Carlo Varese's *Sibilla Odaleta* – all in 1827. They were followed by Cesare Cantù's *Margherita Pusterla* (1838), Tommaso Grossi's *Marco Visconti* (1834) and Massimo d'Azeglio's *Ettore Fieramosca* (1833).[76] In Italian hands, however, the historical novel became bound up with the struggle for Italian unity, and hence acquired a political intent that was entirely absent in Scott.[77] German readers preferred Scott to their own romantic historical novelists, probably because Scott wrote about the past from the point of view of the present, while the German novelists tried to adopt a medieval perspective, thus mystifying their readers. The trick of the genre, much disapproved of by historians but wholeheartedly adopted by the film industry, lies precisely in adopting the contemporary point of view – that of the customers. To sell their works German writers had to openly avow that they were imitating Scott, as did F.P. Richter, author of *Jacobine oder der Ritter des Geheimnisses – Ein historischer Roman nach dem Englischen des Walter Scott* (Jacobine and the Knight of the Secret – A Historical Novel after the English of Walter Scott).

Scott had become a brand name – even though he was still pretending to remain anonymous. Like all brand names, he generated counterfeits. In 1823 an enterprising German publisher commissioned Willibald Alexis (pseudonym of Wilhelm Häring, 1798–1871), a nationalist writer, to 'translate' a Walter Scott novel, *Walladmor* (1824), which in reality Alexis would write himself.[78] The choice was not haphazard: Alexis was the main German follower of Scott. The novel was moderately successful in Germany. Scott, his curiosity aroused, ordered a copy through Bohn, a London bookseller of German books. Thomas de Quincey (author of *Confessions of an English Opium Eater*, 1821) happened to be at Bohn's and was allowed to peer inside the folds of *Walladmor* as long as he did not cut the pages. He gleaned enough information to review it for the *London Magazine* (1824) under the title of 'Walladmor: Sir Walter Scott's German Novel', denouncing it as 'the boldest hoax of our time'. This piqued the interest of readers. Couldn't this hoax be made available in English? A market appeared to have been created. De Quincey agreed to undertake the translation of 'Scott's German novel' into English. When he read the book with due attention, he realised that it was 'almighty nonsense'. As he was short of money he could not afford to turn down the commission, but instead of translating Alexis's three ponderous volumes, he slimmed them down into one, changing the plot, the climax and some of the characters.[79] The English rendition of *Walladmor* is thus an example of the difficulties that can be involved in identifying the 'real' author, since at least in this case there are three candidates: Scott, who inspired it and without whom it would not have been written; Alexis, who wrote the 'original' German version; and de Quincey, who rewrote it for the British.

This was a time in which intellectual property was even less respected than it is now. Authors, especially if foreign and unknown, mattered little. In the eighteenth century Russian booksellers, in the hope of boosting sales, would attribute new novels to well-known authors. Thus in 1788 when *Roderick Random* was translated into Russian (from German), they simply removed any reference to the real author, Tobias Smollett, who was not known in Russia, and attributed the book to Henry Fielding, who was. Another ploy was for a Russian novel to pretend that it was a translation; thus Fedor Emin, in his preface to his own novel *The Garden of Love*, claimed that it was translated from the Portuguese: in eighteenth-century Russia, to come from abroad was the highest form of literary legitimacy.[80]

So it is not surprising that Scott imitations continued well into the late nineteenth century. Theodor Fontane, one of the major German novelists of the time, borrowed from *Waverley* the plot for his *Vor dem Sturm* (Before the Storm, 1878): the hero falls in love with a clever and spirited young woman, the match is encouraged by ambitious relatives. The hero, however, is rejected, and after maturing through war, finds true love with the local and simpler girl who had loved him secretly all along.[81] Fontane followed Scott's principle that a historical novel should not deal with a period more than sixty years removed.

There were, inevitably, dissenting voices to the Scott cult. Stendhal, though an admirer of Scott, preferred Madame de Lafayette, for being able to represent 'the passions and feelings that inhabit the souls', while Scott could only represent characters and situations.[82] Later he wondered whether posterity would confirm the contemporary view which ranked Scott just after Shakespeare.[83] Stendhal's query was legitimate. Later in the century, and even more so in the twentieth century, Scott suffered the fate of many popular writers: after much fame, much oblivion; high name recognition, but few readers.

Flaubert, in his cruelly comic unfinished masterpiece *Bouvard et Pécuchet*, has the eponymous heroes, realising that 'history without imagination' is but a poor thing, launch into an accelerated reading of historical novels. They start, of course, with Walter Scott: '*ce fut comme la surprise d'un monde nouveau*' – the discovery of a new world. Alas, surprise turns to boredom as soon as they crack the formula: the heroine always lives in the country, usually with her father. Her lover has been abandoned as a child but later regains his position and defeats his rivals; philosophically-inclined beggars often crop up with 'deep' thoughts. The girls are pure, the valets comic and the dialogues endless.[84] One of the characters in Balzac's *Illusions perdues* proffers similar criticisms, adding that Scott's heroines never change and are all like Clarissa Harlowe.[85]

Critical interest in Scott's works is still thriving: 792 essays and books on him were published throughout the world between 1970 and 1985.[86] But his standing in the marketplace is not what it was: 'the Waverley Novels remain the least appreciated and least-read body of major fiction in English'.[87] By 1898, at least in France, Scott's star had waned.[88] But when he died, the tributes were glowing. The obituary in *The Times* (25 September 1832) called him 'one of the greatest of the great', ranking him along with Goethe, who had died a few months before. Edinburgh's main train station was called after his novel: it still is Waverley Station – an unusual move in Britain, where places are seldom given literary names. Not even the French, who like to celebrate their writers, have thought, understandably, to call the Gare du Nord in Paris *Les Misérables* or, worse, *À la Recherche du temps perdu.*

In Italy, where prevailing literary criticism was mainly concerned with establishing a ranking order, Scott was regarded as escapist literature, a writer for young people, or for women.[89] Father Antonio Bresciani in the 1861 preface to his *L'Ebreo di Verona* (1850) claimed that his own novels contained only facts, and not fantasies as in 'Walterscott' (sic).[90] The historical novel was considered particularly harmful because it confused people with its mixture of truth and falsehood.[91]

This view was put forward even in 'modernising' journals such *Antologia*, where Sansoni Uzielli in December 1823 explained that the success of Scott's *Waverley* in France was due to the importance and influence which women had acquired in politics and customs. Niccolo Tommaseo (1802–74), who signed his reviews 'K.X.Y.' (letters which do not exist in the Italian alphabet), had declared the historical novel to be a mere passing phase ('Del romanzo storico', in *Antologia*, September 1830). This did not prevent him from writing his own historical novella, *Il Duca di Atene* (1837).[92] Manzoni, author of Italy's major historical novel, *I Promessi sposi*, expressed the same view in his *Del Romanzo storico e, in genere, dei componimenti misti di storia e d'invenzione* (1840).[93] However, the young Francesco de Sanctis told his students at the University of Naples in the 1840s that Scott was the equal of Manzoni, and rescued both from what he called the censorious critics.[94] None of these critics, of course, had impinged in the slightest on Scott's wide success in Italy.

In France the critic Jean-Marie Nisard, usually associated with upholding the classics against the Romantics, grudgingly accepted, in *Le Journal des débats* in 1830, that Scott owed his success to the fact that he managed to please two distinct classes of readers, 'the mass of the public and the educated people'. Heine wrote in 1822 that 'everyone is reading Walter Scott', from the seamstress to the Earl, and 'ladies, in particular, like his works'.[95] In the 1860s, in his *Histoire de la littérature anglaise*, Hippolyte Taine wrote that Scott was read by duchesses and milliners alike.[96] In 1883 the Commission des Bibliothèques Populaires deemed Scott to be particularly suitable for 'popular libraries'. The archives of lending libraries show that in the 1860s Scott was read by a variety of people: lawyers, students, artisans – in other words the reading public of nineteenth-century Europe. Scott thus played a leading role in the formation of a mass literary public in France, and broke class boundaries.

His heroes are more or less mediocre gentlemen, equipped with decency and moral fortitude, but, as Lukács wrote, quite incapable of sweeping human passion. His women are 'philistinely correct . . . There is no room in these novels for the interesting and complex tragedies and comedies of love and marriage.'[97] Undemanding and undisturbing, Scott's heroes are the ideal substance for bourgeois self-identification. Each new reader, enchanted by this world, would find it again in all subsequent novels. Thus the voyage of exploration, and the delights engendered, could be repeated again and again. Scott was also a 'masculine' author, more at home in descriptions of battle-fields and action than of domestic life, and he thus secured for the novels a male readership not adequately catered for by many of the romances available – though studies of libraries' lending records suggest that women were probably a majority of his readership.[98] The hero as an average person, unexceptional and unheroic, could be found in the literature of eighteenth-century Britain and France. Scott made him into the standard hero.

Writers followed in Scott's footsteps, not in the themes chosen or the genre, but in the market he had discovered: the 'average educated reader'. And this 'average reader' could even be highly educated, one who wished, at the end of a tiring day, to curl up in bed with a good novel. It could be someone like Goethe, who said of Scott: 'I know what he is after and what he can do. He would always entertain me.'[99] Geniuses too need to relax.

10

Cultural Hegemony

The Losers

IN HIS LATER YEARS Goethe was fond of declaring that the era of world literature, *Weltliteratur*, had dawned. Marx, in *The Communist Manifesto*, concurred:

> The intellectual creations of individual nations become common property. National one-sidedness and narrow-mindedness become more and more impossible, and from the numerous national and local literatures, there arises a world literature.[1]

In reality this 'world literature' – to the extent that it existed at all – consisted largely of the classical canon: what educated people were supposed to have been taught and to have read. To this were added modern works, whether poetry, fiction or non-fiction, which though largely 'national', that is written in the various vernaculars, were read by cosmopolitan élites, thus transcending national boundaries. These international works were mainly French and British, particularly in the more popular genres such as the novel. This is the conclusion reached by Franco Moretti in his remarkable *Atlas of the European Novel 1800–1900*, in which he followed the fortunes of a sample of British and French popular novels in different countries including Denmark, Hungary, Italy and Poland.[2]

Even the Germans were unable to reach a wider audience, as Goethe was painfully aware:

> ... what a pitiful figure is made by us Germans! Of our old songs – no less important than those of Scotland – how many have lived among the people in the days of my youth? ... Of my own songs, how many live? Perhaps one or another of them may be sung by a pretty girl to the piano; but among the people they have no sound.[3]

One should beware, however, of such rosy views of other countries' cultural standards. Goethe, in the passage just quoted, exclaimed: 'With what sensations I remember when passages from Tasso were sung to me by Italian fishermen!' Madame de Staël makes a similar claim for Tasso's popularity, though in her case she had heard it declaimed by 'the gondoliers of Venice'. She lamented that French poetry was not diffused among the French people while Spaniards of all classes knew Calderon, the Portuguese were familiar with Camões, and that in England Shakespeare was admired by 'the common people' as much as by the superior classes. Goethe must have found some consolation in Madame de Staël's comment that in Germany 'Goethe's poetry is used in songs from the Rhine to the Baltic sea'.[4]

Nevertheless, it was perfectly true that when it came to the most popular of literary genres, the novel, Germany, like Italy and unlike England and France, had produced hardly any of any great renown before the end of the eighteenth century. One exception was Hans Jakob Christoffel von Grimmelshausen's *Der abentheuerliche Simplicius Simplicissimus* (The Adventurous Simplicius Simplicissimus, 1668), written in the manner of the Spanish picaresque novel. Two years later Grimmelshausen published the other great popular book of seventeenth-century Germany, *Lebensbeschreibung der Erzbetrügerin Courasche* (Life of Courasche the Trickster), the racy, picaresque first-person narrative of a woman, Courasche, the name she gives to her sexual organ, who survives the Thirty Years War by marrying often and sleeping around.[5] This was not translated into English until 1912. The story is now best known thanks to Bertolt Brecht's use of the plot for his famous play *Mother Courage*.

In nineteenth-century German-language literature we encounter brilliant short-story writers, such as Ludwig Tieck, E.T.A. Hoffmann, Theodor Storm and Heinrich von Kleist, who also wrote plays; poets such as Heinrich Heine and Novalis; playwrights such as Georg Büchner and Christian Dietrich Grabbe; historians of the calibre of Leopold von Ranke, the Swiss Jakob Burckhardt and Theodor Mommsen; but no novelist of particular international repute until, perhaps, Theodor Fontane, the author of *Effi Briest* (1895) – hardly a household name outside Germany. Heine was also a major prose writer, but as Adorno put it, his stature 'in the utterly dismal level of the era between Goethe and Nietzsche is immediately self-evident'.[6] There were, of course, some nineteenth-century German popular novelists such as Karl May and Friedrich Gerstäcker, but their popularity stopped at the borders of the German-speaking world. The twentieth century changed all that: Thomas Mann, Robert Musil, Franz Kafka, Alfred Döblin and popular writers such as Vicky Baum put the novel in German on the map.

But in the early nineteenth century the Germans did not do very well. If we examine a study of translations into French between 1810 and 1840, we find, as expected, that the most translated author was Walter Scott, with 356 works. The second was a German author, but it was Christoph Schmidt (1768–1854), who wrote children's books used in schools, with 298. The third was Alfonso Maria de' Liguori (1696–1787), an Italian churchman, founder of the Congregation of the Redemptorists, author of numerous Latin theological texts, who was made a saint by Pope Gregory XVI in 1839. Four classics followed: Horace, Shakespeare, Homer and Cicero; then a poet, Byron, and a novelist, Maria Edgeworth. They were followed by the Italian Silvio Pellico, whose prison memoirs did better than Schiller and Goethe.[7]

Yet Goethe's *The Sorrows of Young Werther* (1774) had been the great success of the last quarter of the eighteenth century. It established Goethe as a European celebrity overnight. Within a year of publication the book was condemned by the theological faculty of Leipzig University – an action which increased its sales and fame. 'The effect of this little book,' wrote Goethe, who knew a thing or two about the *Zeitgeist*, 'was great, indeed immense, and principally because it hit exactly the right moment.'[8] The patriotic journalist C.F.D. Schubart told Goethe that thanks to him his German heart could swell with 'noble pride', adding, 'we can oppose to foreign nations a man whom they do not have and to judge by their yearning for fossilisation will never have'.[9] But even Goethe, to become global, needed some help from the British and the French. It was Thomas Carlyle who did most to establish his reputation in Britain, and who translated *Wilhelm Meister's Apprenticeship* in 1824. Matthew Arnold and George Eliot and G.H. Lewes all admired Goethe, and Lewes wrote the first full biography of him in any language (1855).

Werther was translated into French and adapted into a play a year after its publication. In 1779 it was available in English, and there were seven more English editions in the ensuing twenty years. By 1800 Werther's sorrows were available in most European languages, as well as in Chinese. When Goethe met Napoleon in 1808 *Werther* was the main topic of conversation, the Emperor claiming to have read it seven times. Even Mary Shelley's monster ('the Creature' in *Frankenstein*) read *Werther*. It was widely pirated within Germany itself (eleven editions within a year of publication). There were, of course, parodies and criticisms. One could even buy a service of Chinese porcelain decorated with scenes from it. Did reading *Werther* encourage suicides? In January 1778 a young aristocrat, Christel von Lassberg, drowned herself out of unrequited love; a copy of *Werther* was found on her body – or so it was said.[10]

Werther fell squarely into the sentimental genre, using the epistolary technique pioneered by Richardson and imported into Germany by popular writers such as Sophie von la Roche. The novel's brief domination of the British scene was helped by favourable circumstances: when it came out in Britain the major English writers of the century (Fielding and co.) were dead.[11] *Werther* had a great advantage over Richardson's *Clarissa*: it was a dramatically shorter and much tighter novel. Written in just over two months, it could be read in one sitting. Unlike most previous epistolary novels there was only one letter-writer, young Werther himself, who traces the course of his love for Charlotte (who is already engaged to the unremarkable Albert). The relationship (and the novel's success with the public) is strengthened by frequent literary allusions: when Charlotte and Werther realise they love each other, she looks into his eyes and says 'Klopstock,' referring to Friedrich Gottlieb Klopstock, the most revered poet of the day, whose ode 'Die Frühlingsfeier' (Celebration of Spring, 1759) could be recited instantly by all well-bred young men and women.[12] There are various references to Ossian, and when Werther is found dead, the text of Gotthold Lessing's famous play *Emilia Galotti* 'lay open on his desk'.[13]

The absence of major prose writers in German had been often remarked by the Germans themselves. Even towards the end of the nineteenth century, critics such as Robert Prutz in his *Schriften zur Literatur und Politik* complained that Germany had not produced novelists like those of Britain: no Richardson, no Smollett and Fielding, no Sterne and Scott.[14]

Similar anxious complaints were incessantly aired in other countries, and not just about literature. It was the beginning of the modern fear of backwardness, of being left behind, after France or Britain or both, of having missed out on everything: modernity, culture, civilisation, wealth and national dignity. This fear was all-pervasive, especially among the intelligentsia. The expansion of cultural markets, by disseminating knowledge in general, had disseminated the awareness of one's inferiority. To catch up, one could imitate what others did; but in so doing, wasn't one simply confirming one's backwardness? Decades later it was the turn of the French, and then the British, to fear the advance of the Germans in military prowess, education, technology, social sciences. For a while, in the 1950s, there was even a fear

that the superior organisation of the USSR, as evidenced by its space programme, would spell the end of the West. Eventually, everyone was overtaken
by the Americans, with no apparent hope of catching up.

Hegemonic countries such as France were worried, even in 1847, about
being left behind. Charles Louandre complained that the French did not
appreciate home-grown talent, often preferring Walter Scott, Bulwer-Lytton
and Dickens, whose success in France had been 'prodigious'. 'We import
more than we export and when we export it is not the best. Foreigners want
stuff like the *Mystères de Paris* and the novels of Paul de Kock. Writing has
become a matter of profit and pleasure, speculation and greed.[15]

The reality of backwardness was particularly infuriating to countries with
a resplendent past. None more so than Italy, which could boast of two golden
ages: the glory that was Rome and the splendours of the Renaissance. Italian
intellectuals were reduced to looking disconsolately at other peoples' glories
and splendours. The rising nationalism of Italy's middle classes, the impact
of the Napoleonic conquest, the widespread knowledge of a time when Italy
led Europe in all cultural matters, exacerbated these sentiments. To catch up
it became necessary to learn from others, unwittingly reinforcing the dominance of the foreign model. A spate of journals, such as Giacinto Battaglia's
L'Indicatore Lombardo (1829), contained mainly translations from the foreign
press.[16] Antonio Fortunato Stella's *Lo Spettatore* (1824) carried only translations from *Le Spectateur français*, edited in France by Conrad Malte-Brun.[17]
As Madame de Staël explained, writing in January 1816 in the first issue of
the Milan journal *La Biblioteca italiana*, frequent translations from French,
German and English could wean away Italian intellectuals from their pedestrian imitation of the classics.[18]

The most important Italian intellectual network of the time was created
not by an Italian but by a Swiss, a native of Geneva, Gian Pietro Vieusseux,
who in 1819 started in Florence a *cabinet de lecture*.[19] The Gabinetto Vieusseux
still thrives, a stone's throw from the Duomo. Vieusseux's journal, *Antologia*,
was the most evident expression of the fear of backwardness which pervaded
Italian intellectuals: it declared that France, Great Britain and Germany were
the most advanced nations in Europe, and accordingly promised that only
translations from the British *Edinburgh Review* and *Quarterly Review*, the
French *Revue encyclopédique* and the German *Hermes* would appear in its
pages. Italian writers were excluded, though this policy was soon rescinded.[20]
Antologia was regarded at the time as Italy's most important and influential
literary journal. Its meagre readership puts such claims into perspective.

When it started in 1820 it had one hundred subscribers, in 1829 it had 530, and by the time it was closed by the authorities in 1833 it had 629, more than half of these in Tuscany. Its readership was certainly greater than the figures suggest, but quite clearly Italy had a long way to go: in 1828 France had 490 periodicals (Paris alone had 176), Britain had 483, even Russia had eighty-four, while an 'advanced' Italian state such as Piedmont had only eight, and Tuscany six.[21]

One of the consequences of such a restricted cultural market was that it provided very little ready cash. In 1809 the celebrated poet Ugo Foscolo, in his *Della morale letteraria*, expressed his envy of Britain, of its numerous readers and thriving book trade, and of its strong laws which enabled writers to grow rich and independent. In Great Britain, but not in Italy, grumbled Foscolo, a man of letters who gave pleasure to his fellow citizens could become rich through his art while maintaining his integrity.[22]

Educated Italian households felt that they needed to decorate their book-shelves with leather-bound hallowed texts. This meant that Virgil, Horace, Cicero and Homer always sold well, as did Dante and Petrarca: they were required reading for the gentlemen of the time. Théophile Gautier reported that in 1850–51 in Milan, then under Austrian rule, there were more non-fiction books than literature in the bookshops, though one could always find books by Dumas and Sue.[23] In the middle of the nineteenth century an Italian best-selling writer was more likely to be the author of the texts of famous operas, such as Felice Romani, the lucky librettist of operas such as *Norma* and *La Sonnambula*, than a novelist.

Italy's literary scene remained essentially imitative and dependent on France. In Milan, even after the collapse of Napoleon and the establishment of Austrian sovereignty, the diffusion of French books remained unabated; indeed, it increased, because the children of the well-to-do were taught in French, and books in French were printed in Italy.[24]

Importing books and translating them was a more profitable and a less risky business for publishers. The original authors and publishers were hardly ever paid. The translators were poorly remunerated: a two-hundred-page book a month would bring the translator one hundred lire in Milan, more or less the income of a primary schoolteacher, while a university professor could earn no less than 225 lire a month, and most would earn up to 500 lire – which was still half what a senior civil servant would earn (a dismal differential which seems to have remained unaltered).[25]

The main obstacles facing the book trade – apart from the low level of

literacy and the poverty – were the risks facing the publishers in a situation in which there was no intellectual property agreement among the various Italian states. Milan booksellers knew that their books were often reprinted elsewhere with impunity. Best-selling books, like Manzoni's *I Promessi sposi*, were regularly pirated. Moreover, each Italian state set up its own customs duties. Thus a book printed by Silvestri in Milan with a price tag of four lire would cost a further 1.5 lire when imported into the Kingdom of Naples.[26] By 1848 the situation had improved a little, because the Italian states (except for the Kingdom of Naples) had joined into a tariff convention. But fragmentation continued, because it proved impossible to follow the example of the Leipzig Book Fair which had organised the book trade in Germany.[27] The inefficiency of booksellers and obsolete technology compounded the difficulties: in 1847 in Naples alone there were some 114 printers (against sixty in Paris), but most of them used old-fashioned technology.[28]

British and French hegemony was not due to an uneven distribution of talents which had miraculously awarded France and Britain a higher proportion of novelists. It was due, *inter alia*, to a more developed and better-organised market which created a demand and attracted more writers. By 1814 there were *six hundred* booksellers in London alone, and the city had become the centre of European publishing.[29]

Novel-writing was still regarded as a low genre, but one could make money from it, and the more money could be made, the more bourgeois society responded by conferring prestige to authors. Disdain rapidly turned to admiration.

In Italy, however, men of letters never lost an opportunity to disparage the novel. All that was necessary, commented Niccolò Tommaseo in March 1830 in *Antologia*, was to know the plot, and for this a good summary in a literary journal was sufficient and would save the discerning reader time and expense.[30]

Italy also had fewer readers, and not just because literacy was lower than in Britain or France, but because there were fewer educated women – the main consumers of novels – than in France, Germany or Britain. Consequently there were no women writers of significance. There was no Italian (or Spanish) Jane Austen and George Sand, no Sophie Cottin or Fanny Burney. Significantly, in the absence of women writers, there were Italian novels written for women by men pretending to be women. The most successful in the eighteenth century were those by the abbot Pietro Chiari (1711–85), author of a string of novels with women protagonists writing in the first

person: *La Cantatrice in disgrazia* (1754), *La Filosofessa italiana* (1765), *La Francese in Italia* (1759), *La Ballerina onorata, ossia memorie d'una figlia naturale del duca N. V. scritte da lei medesima* (1754), *Le Pazzie fortunate in amore. Memorie di Miledi Dorvei scritte da lei medesima l'anno passato* (1783) and many others. The heroines often confronted accusingly the injustices women had to suffer, their lack of rights and the privileges of men. The protagonist of *La Cantatrice in disgrazia* (The Disgraced Singer) declares: 'I write prevalently for people of my sex for I consider them better able to experience pity and tenderness than men. To understand the burden of certain calamities it is necessary to be a woman, to share their feelings and to have felt what I have felt.'[31]

One would have thought that Chiari (who was also a successful playwright and Goldoni's main rival) would have been regarded not just as a clever abbot, but as a trailblazer. Here was someone who had drawn the lesson from Samuel Richardson's feminine novel of sensitivity and was trying to become its Italian emulator.[32] He was the pioneer of a particular Italian sub-genre which consisted in adapting foreign products for the benefit of Italian consumers, thus meeting the demand for popular culture not met by native writers. Chiari gained money but not lasting fame in his native country. None of his novels can be found in the Biblioteca Nazionale in Rome; none are reprinted. The great nineteenth-century literary critic Francesco de Sanctis recognised Chiari's achievements – in a backhanded sort of way. Chiari's chief merit was to give the public what it wanted: 'It would be interesting to analyse Chiari's numerous works, today all but forgotten, because it would show the spirit of his time.' Chiari's stories of uncommon women (philosophers, giantesses, courtesans) and abducted nuns, midnight struggles and balconies being climbed were, de Sanctis added, a mixture of the old and the new, 'what was most extravagant in the new and most coarse in what was old'.[33]

In his day Chiari was mocked and denounced as a mere imitator by critics who were well acquainted with those he imitated. One such critic was Giuseppe Marc'Antonio Baretti, a writer and lexicographer. He had lived in London in the 1750s, where he discovered the great British novelists and compiled an Anglo–Italian dictionary. Upon his return he started a bi-monthly review of books, *La Frusta letteraria* (The Literary Whip), inspired by British literary journals. In one of his essays, purporting to advise a young Milanese lady on what to read (1764), he warned her against the novels of Abbate Chiari, which he regarded as the worst in Europe.[34] As a true *esterofilo* (lover of all things foreign), Baretti was an enemy of anything new and anything Italian.

In spite, or because, of Chiari's efforts, the main fictional literature in Italy was French. Vittori Alfieri, in his autobiography *Vita* (1951), explains that the novels he read when he was young were all French because there were no readable Italian ones.[35] Madame de Lafayette's *La Princesse de Clèves*, Fénelon's *Aventures de Télémaque*, and Marivaux's and Voltaire's novels were what the educated Italian read.[36] They also read the novels of writers who are today less famous, such as Sophie Cottin, whose novella *Elisabeth, ou les exilés de Sibérie* had been published by three different publishers in Milan alone. English-language novels too were fashionable in Italy, not only the omnipresent Scott, but also Maria Edgeworth, published by Picotti in Venice, Ann Radcliffe and Fenimore Cooper, whose *Last of the Mohicans* was published in Milan in 1828, only two years after its publication in English.[37]

By the early eighteenth century even the theatre had followed the rest of Italian culture into a historic decline, and French plays were regularly patronised by the aristocratic classes.[38] Much as a second division football team loses its best players to the first division, Italy lost to the French its most successful writers: Goldoni went to Paris to run the Italian Theatre, and Pietro Metastasio (whose operatic librettos dominated the eighteenth century) became the court poet in Vienna. The French also 'imported' Cesare Beccaria (1738–94), the author of the first major sustained critique of capital punishment, *Dei Delitti e delle pene* (On Crimes and Punishments, 1764) – a book that owed its European fame to André Morellet's French translation (1765) and his drastic editing.

This is not to say that there were no successful Italian novels. Many of the ones written in the eighteenth century were simple adaptations of successful foreign novels, such as Zaccaria Serimàn's *Viaggi di Enrico Warton* (1749), patently inspired by Swift. In the nineteenth century they were more original and more successful. Francesco Domenico Guerrazzi's *L'Assedio di Firenze* (The Siege of Florence, 1836) was reprinted fifty times by 1916, and his *Battaglia di Benevento* was equally successful.[39] In the 1830s Massimo d'Azeglio's *Ettore Fieramosca* (1833) was a great success.[40] But such fame was limited to Italy, where d'Azeglio was made even more famous by becoming Piedmont's prime minister in 1849 and marrying Manzoni's daughter. While Balzac and Scott were read everywhere and are now widely available in cheap paperback editions in many languages, then no one outside Italy read d'Azeglio's *Ettore Fieramosca*, and no one reads it today even in Italy.

And what about the most celebrated nineteenth-century Italian novelist, Alessandro Manzoni? By 1839 he had produced what he regarded as the final version of *I Promessi sposi*. Its basic structure was that of the conventional melodrama: an innocent man and a virtuous woman of humble background face numerous obstacles to their happiness; when everything seems lost their enemies are routed and they are united at last. The art of *I Promessi sposi* – as is the case in most good books – lies not in the plot.

A large number of illustrations had been used to attract buyers to *I Promessi sposi*, but this increased costs and required the publishers to sell at least 10,000 copies to turn a profit. This was far too many for the Italian market: only 4,600 were sold – a respectable figure, but not enough to prevent a serious loss.[41] *I Promessi sposi* eventually came to be regarded as *the* great Italian novel (perhaps for lack of serious competition), and was taught in all schools, but in the rest of Europe Manzoni was regarded at best as a local variant of Walter Scott. The real Italian best-seller of the first half of the century was not a novel but a memoir: Silvio Pellico's *Le Mie prigioni* (1832), a harrowing account of ten years spent as a political prisoner in various Austrian jails (where the author discovered Jesus), rapidly translated into French by Antoine de Latour (twenty-three impressions in France alone in the 1830s), and from there into other European languages. Otherwise Italy was present in the international book market with its ancient glories: Boccaccio, Petrarca, Tasso, Ariosto and, of course, Dante.[42]

In Spain, as in Italy, the obsession with cultural backwardness anguished the intelligentsia. The days of Cervantes and of the Spanish Golden Age had long gone. By the eighteenth century the few novels read in Spain were foreign and overwhelmingly French, which the censors had emasculated into 'moral' stories 'suitable for young ladies'.[43] Until the 1860s the Spanish reading public read and reread its own classics, short popular novels sold by blind peddlers (see Chapter Four), and translations of the usual favourites: Walter Scott, Sophie Cottin, Chateaubriand, Fenimore Cooper and Victor Hugo. The few literary novels of the time were written by nobles and *hidalgos* and read by members of the same group.[44] The denunciation of backwardness became a literary genre in its own right. The best-known Spanish writer of the immediate post-Napoleonic era was not a novelist but a satirical journalist, Mariano José de Larra (1809–37). His exasperation with Spanish provincialism and conventionality was the main theme of his articles in his *El Pobrecito hablador* (1832–33) and of his *Articulos de costumbres*, sketches where he denounced the backwardness of Spanish society.[45] However, the success of foreign novelists helped to expand the market for fiction, especially after the liberalisation that followed the death of King Fernando VII in 1833.[46] Only towards the end of the nineteenth century, with writers of the importance of Benito Pérez Galdós, did the Spanish novel acquire some renown.

Russia, unlike Italy or Spain, could offer a potentially wider market, though literacy was very low. At the beginning of the nineteenth century, while the novel was the most popular genre, the petty nobility had access to light comedies, comic operas and melodrama, and the lower classes saw Polish farces and read *lubki* sold by peddlers, the Life of the Fathers of the Church, and morally edifying tales.[47] The average Russian intellectuals, like their counterparts elsewhere, read the usual major French and English books.[48] But they also read lesser-known English novels in Russian translation (all aristocrats could read French, few could read English), such as Frances Sheridan's *The History of Nourjahad* (1767), Aphra Behn's *Oroonoko* (1688) and William Beckford's *The History of Caliph Vathek* (1782), written in French. These were all classified as Orientalist novels (including *Oroonoko*, which is not about the 'Orient' but about an African prince sold into slavery in Surinam), the setting of which seemed particularly appealing to the Russian reading public. It is thus hardly surprising if the main literary influences on Nikolai Mikhailovich Karamzin, the most important Russian prose writer of his time, were French and British. His sentimental novel *Poor Lisa* (1792) is reminiscent of Richardson's *Pamela*, being about the seduction of an innocent peasant girl by an unworthy and wealthy man, and her subsequent suicide by drowning in a lake, later to become the object of pilgrimages and tourist visits.[49] The other great success of the time was *A Russian Gil Blas* by Vasily T. Narezhny, directly inspired by Alain-René le Sage's picaresque eighteenth-century novel *Histoire de Gil Blas*. The first half of Narezhny's work appeared in 1814, but the rest was banned, usually for alleged immorality; the entire work was published only in 1938, at the height of Stalinist terror.[50] The conventions of English and French literature were used *en masse*, but they were also parodied – a sign that the originals were known to readers either in translation or in the original.[51]

In the first quarter of the nineteenth century the best-known Russian writer abroad was Ivan Andreevich Krylov (1768–1844), whose tales (largely adaptations of those of la Fontaine) were translated into English, French and German. Such was the prestige gained that in 1823 the Russian academy awarded him a gold medal.[52] His fame was not short-lived: in 1877 Charles Edward Turner, an English lecturer at the University of St Petersburg, wrote that Krylov was still the best-known Russian writer abroad.[53] If true, this was a remarkable feat, because by then Russia had produced Pushkin and Lermontov, Gogol's *Dead Souls* (1842), Dostoevsky's *Crime and Punishment* (1866), Tolstoy's *War and Peace* (1869) and Turgenev's *Fathers and Sons* (1862), and all had been translated into English and French. Yet Krylov came tops, at least for some.

In Russia in this period several tendencies converged. One was the collection of local folklore – such as the short stories of Mikhail Chulkov (1743–92) (*The Mocker*). Another was the imitation of foreign works, such as *The Letters of Ernest and Doravra* by Fedor Emin (1735–70), modelled after Rousseau's *La Nouvelle Héloïse*. Chulkov's most famous work, *Prigozhaia povarikha* (The Comely Cook, 1770), was inspired by Defoe's *Moll Flanders*. Adventure stories, sometimes even with English characters, such as *The English Milord Georg* by Matvei Komarov, were also popular.

The Comely Cook was a novelty. It was set in Russia, and not in some far-flung place. Its characters span most of the social structure. Stereotypes were avoided: the 'high class' characters were not all good, and the 'low' ones were not all stupid or wicked. The dialogue was realistic. However, the success of *The Comely Cook* did not last. It was not reprinted until 1904.[54]

Three of the most widely read Russian novels (*povest'*, or tale) of the nineteenth century were written in the eighteenth. The first, *Bova Korolevich* (Bova the King's Son), was a version of a French chivalric romance popular in the Middle Ages, which reached Russia from a Serbian translation of the sixteenth century. There were many versions of *Bova Korolevich*. The one aimed at the nobility was written as if it were a foreign novel; the one for the lower classes resembled a heroic fairy tale. The other two successes were both by Komarov: *Van'ka Kain* (1779), the story of a brigand, and *The English Milord Georg* (1782).[55] All these novels remained widely available and popular throughout the Soviet period.

The Italians and Spaniards could take comfort from ancient glories. The Russians eventually capitalised on the size of the country, its cultured aristocracy and its large intelligentsia to produce unparalleled novelists. Bulgarians were not so lucky. They had no renowned literary past. Bulgaria had been under Turkish domination for almost five centuries (1396–1878). It was linguistically divided. Its upper class was totally isolated from the rest of the people. It is true that, as in much of central and eastern Europe (Prussia, Bohemia, Hungary and Poland) the aristocracy was larger than its equivalent in the west (10 per cent of Poles and 5 per cent of Hungarians were 'aristocrats', against 1 per cent of French). Nevertheless, it much preferred rural or military pursuits to literary ones. In other words, untrammelled philistine attitudes prevailed. The peasantry was unable to move out into the middle classes.[56] Those who did, and who could have provided a market for books, were Germans or Jews living in Bulgaria. Neither were interested in reading anything in Bulgarian, or would have been able to read it had there been anything worth reading. The Germans stuck to their language, while the Jews read German and spoke Yiddish – a Middle German dialect containing less than 5 per cent of Slavonic words.

It is thus not surprising if a literary Bulgarian language based on the vernacular of its eastern dialects, Novobulgarski (New Bulgarian), was established only in the nineteenth century. Previously Bulgarian literature – such as it was – was written in Old Church Slavonic. As a result the first book in Bulgarian was printed as late as 1806: *Nedelki*, by Bishop Sofronii Vrachanski. In 1826 there were just sixteen modern printed books in Bulgarian. Even in 1842 there were only seventy-seven. The first journal appeared in 1844.[57] In 1846 the first major celebration of the Bulgarian past, *Mati Bulgaria* (Mother Bulgaria) by Neofir Bozveli (1785–1848), appeared. In the nineteenth century the chances of becoming an internationally well-known Bulgarian writer were nil.

Poland was different. Its aristocracy insisted it belonged to the West. Poles, after all, were Catholics, and not Orthodox as in the 'barbaric East'. Poland had its own Renaissance in the sixteenth century, and its own Enlightenment in the second half of the eighteenth century. What the country lacked was national independence, the Kingdom of Poland having disappeared in 1772. Poles had become a nation without a state, the norm in most of eastern Europe. Until the last quarter of the nineteenth century the majority of readers of novels were landed gentry, often patriotic, usually idealising the past, the Poland of the Golden Age. Middle-class life found little space in novels of this period.[58] Without a state and under the Russian yoke, the Polish middle classes followed their aristocracy in developing a 'pathology of martyrdom', crying while reading Mickiewicz's works (but not necessarily agreeing with him), producing plenty of poetry and drama, none of which was known anywhere else.[59] Until the 1870s the country produced virtually no novels except the historical fiction of Józef Ignacy Kraszewski. Then a remarkable season of novel-writing opened, crowned by an international best-seller: Henryk Sienkiewicz's *Quo Vadis?* (1896), a novel set in Ancient Rome, among persecuted Christians. Poles read into it a subtext of victimhood and oppression. Foreigners just enjoyed the tale.

Scandinavians did not fare well either. Among the first major Swedish writers were poets and playwrights – Per Atterbom (1790–1855), Johan Erik Stagnelius (1793–1823), Erik Gustaf Geijer (1783–1847) and Esaias Tegnér (1782–1846), who wrote about Viking mythology – but no novelists. The nearest thing to an exception was Carl Jonas Love Almqvist (1793–1866), author of a novel of such sexual daring – *Hvad är kärleken?* (What is Love?, 1816) – that it was published in an unexpurgated version only in the twentieth century, as was his proto-feminist novel *Det går an* (It Can Be Done, 1839).[60]

And what of France, one of the two culturally hegemonic countries in Europe? What did the French translate? What did they read? Between 1810 and 1840 there were 11,688 translations into French – 6.7 per cent of total book production (with a high of 8.5 per cent in 1838 and a low of 3.9 per cent in 1831). More than half were from Latin (3,953) and English (3,082).[61] German followed with 1,817, and then Italian with 1,210. There were 845 translations from Ancient Greek, and 339 from Spanish. There were more translations from Hebrew (ninety) and Arabic (eighty-six) than from Russian (sixty-eight), and more from Portuguese (fifty-six) than from Polish (fifty). Once we eliminate the 'dead' languages, in so far as the French were concerned, there was access to only three literary traditions: English, German and Italian.

Nationality and Gender

Do novels have a 'nationality' beyond the nationality of the author, or the language they are written in? Do novels carry a 'national' point of view? Nationalities, after all, are not stable concepts. Some come and go. At the end of the nineteenth century no one called himself a Yugoslav. By the end of the 1960s most of the country's inhabitants did. By the year 2000 only a few described themselves so.[62]

Jane Austen's novels are 'English' not because they advertise their Englishness – they don't – but because they assume Englishness as the natural setting for that genre of novels. English readers do not read an 'English' novel. They read a Jane Austen novel, or a romance, or a classic, or a novel of sensibility, or whatever. It is foreigners who find *Pride and Prejudice* quintessentially English, set in a quintessential England among quintessentially English people.

Englishness does not require an English setting, or even English characters. Ann Radcliffe's *The Italian* remains English, even though it is entirely set in Italy and none of the characters is English. But the hero and heroine behave like English characters, and the Italy that is portrayed is invented by an Englishwoman. Of course, none of this is apparent to every reader. An innocent reader who picked up *The Italian* for the first time in a pirated translation signed with an Italian-sounding name such as 'Anna La Cliffa' might well regard it as the work of an Italian.

But such innocence is rare. Most novels are defined by a context. They are packaged, labelled, marketed, reviewed, talked about. Readers approach them with some expectations. They know, or think they know, something about the novel before they even begin to read the first page. And, however often they are wrong, every time they start a new novel, they start with a hunch, a conjecture, an assumption about the kind of novel it is.

Those who wanted to find something particularly English in Jane Austen or Fanny Burney, something English or Irish in Maria Edgeworth, something Scottish in Walter Scott or French in Balzac, found it easily. The Europeans who came into the possession of British and French fiction assumed they were acquiring some knowledge of what life was like in France or Great Britain. They were under the impression that, while being entertained, they were learning about a society which, though not wildly dissimilar from their own, was clearly distinct – much as many of those who in the 1980s watched the top-rated television serial *Dallas* thought that they were gaining some insights into how the Texan rich lived.

The result was asymmetric knowledge. For English readers, Italy was the country described by British travellers and depicted in Gothic novels. For Italians, Britain was the country represented by English writers like Defoe, Fielding and Richardson. Britain and France presented themselves through their own writers. Other countries depended on the British and the French, and to a lesser extent the Germans.

The international image of nineteenth-century Spain, for instance, was largely constructed by the French. In the sixteenth century, however, that image was solidly in Spanish hands – one can think of the influential picaresque *Lazarillo de Tormes*, which had already been translated ten times before the end of the sixteenth century.[63] But by the nineteenth century, Spanish decadence and France's literary splendour had done their work. Spain became a French invention. To mention only the best-known of such building blocks: Beaumarchais's two famous comedies, *Le Barbier de Seville* (1775) and *Le Mariage de Figaro* (1784), turned into great operatic 'hits' by Rossini and

Mozart. Then there is Victor Hugo with *Hernani* (1830), adapted by Verdi into the opera *Ernani* (1844), and *Ruy Blas* (1835); then the fashionable playwright (fashionable then) Casimir Delavigne, with *La Fille du Cid* (1839); then Théophile Gautier with *Voyage en Espagne* (1845) and many of his poems; then Prosper Mérimée with *Carmen* in 1846, which was turned by Bizet into one of the most famous of all operas.[64] By the middle of the nineteenth century flamenco music and dance had entered French café life, as had the Spanish guitar. By the end of the century Spain had irremediably become the land of bullfights, sun, passion, haughty women, proud *hidalgos* and sexually suggestive Gypsy tunes.

There is thus an imperialist dimension in cultural hegemony. What is at stake is not land or economic resources, but images and identities. There is a world of difference between deciding one's image and having others decide it for you – particularly when the operation is so thorough that everyone, including the culturally colonised, accept it. The 'West' lambasted by Edward Said in *Orientalism* and *Culture and Imperialism* as the definer of 'the Orient' is in reality a narrower West, at least in the nineteenth century, one largely encompassed by the Great Powers, in particular by France and Great Britain. And they didn't just define the Orient, they defined most of Europe too.

And the Americans? At first even the 'western' genre was in the hands of Europeans. Chateaubriand had inaugurated the Romantic view of the American Indian as a noble and brave savage in his novels *Atala* (1801) and *René* (1802). His success was remarkable. In France, until the arrival of Victor Hugo, he was regarded as the greatest living novelist. His complete works were translated into several languages, including Hungarian.[65] Chateaubriand is now barely read, but in the 1800s American writers were scarcely known in Europe. Matters changed with James Fenimore Cooper (1789–1851). His *The Last of the Mohicans*, first published in 1826, had four reprints by 1830, and a further five by 1850. The critical comments were not always positive. The *London Magazine* of May 1826, under the heading 'The Last American Novel', wrote that '*The Last of the Mohicans* is clearly by much the worst of Mr. Cooper's performances.' The reviewer, the American novelist John Neal, had been the author of unpopular novels before sailing to Britain to take the post of chief critic at *Blackwood's Edinburgh Magazine*. Oozing envy from every paragraph, Neal declared that the problem with Cooper was that he wrote too much: 'No writer, be he great or little, known or unknown, can be trusted long with the duty of manufacturing fictions for the public.' Cooper was declared to be a failed follower of Walter Scott.[66] Not so for

George Sand, writing in 1856: 'Cooper has often been compared to Walter Scott. It is a great honour to which Cooper is not unworthy; but it has also been claimed that Cooper was merely an accomplished and felicitous imitator of the great master: such is not my own feeling.'[67] The only other American writer enjoying a degree of European popularity in the first quarter of the nineteenth century was Washington Irving (1783–1859). In 1819 Irving published his successful collection of short stories and essays *The Sketch-Book of Geoffrey Crayon, Esq.*, which included the 'legends' of Rip van Winkle (who slept for twenty years to find himself in the post-revolutionary United States) and that of Sleepy Hollow – another of those 'found' manuscripts, this time discovered 'among the papers of the late Diedrich Knickerbocker' (Irving's favourite pen name). These stories were staple reading of the middle classes, especially in England, but were often regarded as part of a low genre. Elizabeth Gaskell, in her novel *North and South* (1855), has John Thornton's not very clever sister Fanny absorbed in Washington Irving's *Legends of the Alhambra* (1832), while the heroine, Margaret Hale, is loftily reading Dante.

There were also American women writing westerns, above all Catharine Maria Sedgwick (1789–1867), one of the most popular mid-nineteenth-century female American authors before Harriet Beecher Stowe, and like her generally sympathetic to oppressed people, notably in her novel *Hope Leslie* (1827), an account of the seventeenth-century Pequot War in which the Puritans are represented, not unjustifiably, as genocidal bigots, and the Indians as noble and wonderful.

Nationality is only one perspective. There is a gender perspective which is present in fiction (novels, plays, films) to a far greater extent than in any other cultural genre. Masculine power may prevail everywhere – in music, painting, drama, philosophy and history – but in novel-writing it encounters, from the start, a significant resistance. Of course, patriarchal ideas structure women's thoughts as well as men's, but the presence of women among novelists was far greater than in other arts and crafts. Until the end of the nineteenth century, writing novels was one of the few professions open to a genteel woman (being an actress was not respectable). Whether some regarded novel-writing as a 'feminine' occupation because it was a low genre, or because there were already so many women writers, is a debatable point, but there is no doubt about the importance of women writers. Schiller was 'really astonished how our womenfolk are now able to acquire, merely as amateurs, a certain skill in writing which comes close to art'.[68] Of the fifty British novelists of the years 1660–1800 listed in the *Dictionary of Literary*

Bibliography, twenty are women.[69] One hundred and fifty of the authors listed by the bookseller Alexandre Pigoreau in his catalogue of 1,505 books *Petite bibliographie biographico-romancière* (1821) are women.[70]

Many, of course, wrote romances – novels whose main theme was the relations between men and women. Some of the very early exemplars of the genre exhibited extraordinary psychological insight. Take, for instance Madame de Lafayette's *La Princesse de Clèves* (1678). Everything in the story is presented as if it were true. The style is utterly dispassionate; the narrator is aloof. The plot starts in a conventional manner: the heroine, the Princesse de Clèves, loves a man who is not her husband. But what makes the story unusual is that the Princess explains the situation to her husband – 'I love another,' she says. She does not seek forgiveness, for there is nothing to forgive, as she has done nothing. She does not seek his consent to an illicit affair, for she would not dream of having one. She tells him what she feels for no other reason than to let him, the companion of her life, understand her predicament and to reassure him that she will never sleep with the man she loves. Then she also lets her suitor know that his love is requited, but that she will avoid seeing him and that she will never be his. In the meantime her husband is devoured by jealousy – but he cannot complain, his wife has told him everything and has promised to remain faithful out of duty and respect, though not out of love. Knowing he is not loved, he dies of heartache. Still the heroine remains faithful to her husband, even after his death. An honest woman may be more dangerous than a *femme fatale*.

Madame de Lafayette's book is now a justly revered classic. Other women writers of the eighteenth century are today quite forgotten, but in their days they were widely admired. Among them was the French writer Marie-Jeanne Riccoboni (1714–92), who had married an Italian actor, and was an actress herself. She lived for a while in London, where she became acquainted with English novels, particularly Fielding's *Amelia*, which she translated into French. She then completed Marivaux's *La Vie de Marianne*, which was regarded by several of her contemporaries as far superior to the unfinished original.[71] Her own *Histoire de Miss Jenny* (1764) was translated by Goldoni, who prefaced it with the declaration that the famous author – the *célèbre autrice* – was admired throughout Europe. In her *Essai sur les fictions*, Madame de Staël ranked Madame Riccoboni just below Richardson and on a par with Madame de Lafayette, Bernardin de Saint-Pierre and Fanny Burney.[72] She was republished (often in collections with works by other authors) throughout the nineteenth century, then disappeared completely until she was rescued from oblivion by late-twentieth-century feminist literary critics.

Madame de Genlis (Stephanie-Félicité de Saint-Aubin, Comtesse de Genlis) has remained better known. She was the author of numerous plays and some one hundred historical romances, including *Alphonsine, ou la tendresse maternelle* and the best-seller *La Duchesse de la Vallière* (eleven editions in 1823 alone). Madame de Genlis dominated the literary marketplace during a long writing career which spanned forty years, from 1780 to 1820. Jane Austen was reading her *Les Veillées du Château* (1784) sixteen years after its publication.[73] George Sand was read Genlis by her mother, but by then Genlis had been almost forgotten.[74] Then there was Sophie Cottin, the famous author of *Claire d'Albe* (1799), an epistolary novel. This story, though supposed to encourage marital fidelity, dealt with a daring topic (the plot is similar to Racine's *Phèdre*): the young Claire is married to an older man (as was Madame Cottin herself). They live quietly in the countryside until she discovers that Frédéric, her husband's adopted son, is passionately in love with her. She finds herself attracted to him. Claire and Frédéric try to resist the lure of love and sex. They finally succumb, but only once. Once is enough, however, to make Claire die of remorse – death being routinely the destiny of adulteresses in literature. Frédéric, of course, lives to love another day. 'Sentimental' novelists like Sophie Cottin, Madame de Genlis and Madame de Staël remained among the most popular writers throughout the French Restoration.[75] They inspired storylines in women writers in other countries, sometimes even the titles; for instance, *Malvina, or the heart's intuition* (1816), by the Polish writer Maria Wirtemberska, shares with Madame Cottin's novel *Malvina* the main outlines of the plot: a young woman is unhappily married, and after her husband's death falls in love with a stranger who turns out to be an aristocrat.[76]

The temptation of love is one of the great themes of literature. Another consisted in the depiction of the strategy to be employed by a young woman to secure a suitable husband. This was obviously a matter of greater significance in the eighteenth and nineteenth centuries than it is now. Given the relative ease of divorce, today one can try and try again. If Mr Right turns out to be Mr Wrong, there may be a better prospect around the corner. Nevertheless, the persistence of this theme over the last two centuries suggests a formidable continuity of circumstances. To get the right man and, once one has married him, to discover that there are better ones around, was a theme of great interest to the growing female reading public.

Women writers took advantage of such a strong market. It provided them with a profession, respect, fame and financial rewards. Madame de Staël received 7,200 francs – a huge sum – from her publishers for the manuscript of *Corinne* on the strength of the 1802 success *Delphine*.[77] Sophie Cottin achieved fame and money with *Claire d'Albe* (1799), *Amélie Mansfield* (1802) and *Mathilde* (1805), as did the Duchesse (Claire) de Duras, author of *Édouard* (1825) and *Ourika*. Many British female writers enjoyed the same rewards. But the significant esteem in which women writers were held at the time was a phenomenon limited to France and Britain, the big producers of novels. There are exceptions, such as Germany's Sophie von la Roche, but otherwise the prospects for women writers in Germany were not very good: of the ninety-seven authors reviewed in 1800 in the *Neue Allgemeine Deutsche Bibliothek* and the *Allgemeine Litteratur-Zeitung*, only four were women.[78] The roll-call in England was substantially greater. It included Aphra Behn and Delarivier Manley, Eliza Haywood and Charlotte Lennox, Sarah Fielding and Frances Sheridan, Ann Radcliffe and Fanny Burney, and many others – all paving the way for the more famous nineteenth-century writers including Jane Austen, the Brontë sisters and George Eliot, as well as their counterparts in the USA (Harriet Beecher Stowe, author of *Uncle Tom's Cabin*, 1852; Louisa May Alcott, author of *Little Women*, 1868–69). Outside the Anglo–French hegemonic condominium, most women writers, with some exceptions, had to wait for recognition until the last quarter of the nineteenth century.

11

This is Not a Fiction

History and Religion

IN ENGLISH, if it is not a fiction, if it is not poetry, if it is not drama, it is non-fiction. In French there is no equivalent literal rendition. We are reduced to the inelegant *ouvrages autres que les romans* or *ouvrages non romanesques* – 'works other than novels'. In French bookshops the 'non-fiction' section is the *rayon des ouvrages généraux*. Italian is equally circumlocutory: *opere non di narrativa*. In German, non-fiction books are *Sachbücher*, or factual books.

As usual, the problem is not with the language but with the world. The vast majority of books are 'non-fiction', but non-fiction is not a genre. It is a container term, a galaxy of types and genres of prose works, lumped together in the vast category of all that which 'is not made up'. In the nineteenth century in Britain, the term 'fiction' was used depreciatingly. Fiction is deceit, dissimulation, invention. Non-fiction is reality. It is the truth. It is philosophy, history, theology, biography, autobiography, political pamphlets, scientific and technical manuals, law books, atlases, telephone directories, travel writing, advice and counselling books, cookery books, government reports, reference books, school books, the Bible and the Koran, music books, art books, grammars, medical texts, bibliographies, books about books – in other words, over 90 per cent of books published. This was so in 1800, and it is so today.

Of course, novels, taken together, sell more than other genres, today as well as fifty years ago, but we have no reliable overall sales figures for the nineteenth century. In 2003, in the top one hundred best-selling paperbacks sold in the UK (the majority of books sold) there were eighty-seven novels. 'Non-fiction' consisted of three autobiographies and four biographies – non-fiction made to look like fiction, or occasionally the other way round – plus one travel book, one reportage and four diet books (all by Dr Atkins).[1] There are no similar statistics for 1803, because most books were not bought but borrowed from libraries, read in coffee houses, clubs or *cabinets de lecture*, or in instalments, in journals and newspapers.

The majority of titles – and here we are on firmer ground – were 'non-fiction'. David Bellos has estimated that of the 3,727 *new* titles printed in France in 1828, only 267 were novels (7.1 per cent), while there were 708 books classified under the rubric of religion and, in those civilised days, 736 (19.7 per cent) under that of history.[2] Maurice Crubellier estimated that the total number of new titles in France in 1830 was 4,380 – an increase of 653 over the 3,727 estimated by Bellos for 1828.[3] Roger Chartier claims that in 1780, 10 per cent of the books published in France were 'religious'.[4] Martin Lyons thinks that this was still the annual share of theology books in the 1820s, but Bellos's figures suggest that religious books were nearer to 20 per cent.[5] John Brewer notes that the eighteenth-century holdings of the British Library and the university libraries of Oxford and Cambridge list 50,000 religious titles, out of less than 200,000 titles.[6]

Simon Eliot, on the basis of yet another set of statistics, plausibly more reliable than those used previously, has established that in the years 1800–70, 20 per cent of titles could be classified as 'religion', and 20–24 per cent as 'literature' (Dewey classification 800–899); within this last category, those which could be described as stories, tales, novels or romances made up 7.45 per cent of the total, increasing to 11.15 per cent in 1870.[7] In Britain between 1816 and 1851, out of a total of 45,000 books published – as estimated in the 1950s by R.K. Webb – just over 10 per cent were classified as 'religion, history and geography', while fiction accounted for only 3,500.[8] This confirms the view that novels made up about 7–8 per cent of the total.

Overlapping categories make many such classifications not very useful. The category of 'religious' texts is rather amorphous. It encompasses complex theological treatises, stories from the Bible, and lives of saints. There is quite a difference between the reader of the influential devotional treatise *De Imitatione Christi* (Imitation of Christ) by Thomas à Kempis (c.1379–1471) and the reader of the illustrated life of a saint. The enduring popularity of 'religious' texts can in part be explained by the support they received from religious establishments and influential people such as parish priests. But when all is said and done, the main cause behind the public appetite for religious texts is, quite simply, that people were very religious. If religion was packaged in an exciting manner, it could sell remarkably. John Bunyan's

Pilgrim's Progress (1678–84), translated into a hundred languages and a best-seller until the beginning of the twentieth history, succeeded because it conflated the epic genre with religious allegory and described in a compelling and colloquial style the vicissitudes of the heroes, Christian and his wife Christiana, on their epic journey from the City of Destruction to the Celestial City. Even a less exciting religious book such as Lamennais's *Paroles d'un croyant* (1833) could become a best-seller in France in the 1830s.

Religious books, however classified, began to decline as a proportion of the total as early as the eighteenth century, but they remained a popular genre throughout the nineteenth century. Secularisation was gaining ground, but religion was defended by institutions and an ideology tested in the course of centuries. It remained a dominant force in culture. It dominated music: most of the music Europeans heard in the nineteenth century was church music.

A considerable amount of non-fiction, however, consisted of stories: true stories, or at the very least stories purporting to be true, and much of this could be classified as 'history'. The historical novel was regarded as a higher genre precisely because it was connected to the 'noble' activity of writing history. It was fiction, but a fiction closer to the truth than romances and fairy tales. The context was ideal: national history had become popular, nationalism was rapidly developing, and the search for historical roots was all the rage among the liberal intelligentsia.

Even the non-historical novel provided the author with the possibility of introducing into the main body of the story some historical events, the way Fielding integrated the Jacobite Rising of 1745 into *Tom Jones*.[9] There has always been a considerable number of people curious about the past, whether that of their family, community or village. This liking for history has encouraged not only historical novels, but even the introduction of much 'straight' history into them, such as Manzoni's historical reconstruction of the plague in Milan (*I Promessi sposi*) and Victor Hugo's rather lengthy digressions on the Battle of Waterloo and the sewers of Paris in *Les Misérables*. It can be argued that the scholarly study and writing of history started only in the nineteenth century with Leopold von Ranke (1795–1886), who advocated basing history on the record of contemporaries rather than relying on tradition. Ranke's may have been better history than his predecessors, but history books had been around for at least two and a half thousand years, since Herodotus wrote his account of the Persian Wars.

Historical novels contributed to encourage historians to write for a wider, non-specialist market. As Macaulay wrote in the *Edinburgh Review* in May

1828: 'by judicious selection, rejection, and arrangement, he gives to truth those attractions which have been usurped by fiction'. 'He' being the 'perfect historian'.[10] Just as many novelists gave a serious tone to their fiction by incorporating 'real' history, so many historians did not resist incorporating into their narrative entertaining anecdotes which enlivened the story, but for which there is no evidence. These were incorporated into school texts and were remembered when all else (dates, names, causes and consequences) was forgotten. Hence the enduring strength of the image of King Canute sitting on the beach commanding the waves to go back; of George Washington telling his father he cannot tell a lie; of Newton discovering the law of gravity thanks to a falling apple; of Marie Antoinette saying 'Let them eat cake,' thus causing the French Revolution; of Julius Caesar exclaiming 'Et tu Brute' as he dies (one of an endless stream of famous last words); and an endless supply of historical clichés, from the eternally dark and unhealthy Middle Ages, to savages being proud and noble, to the Gauls being 'the ancestors' of the French and ancient Greeks being the ancestors of modern Greeks.

Travelling

Travel books began to become popular at the beginning of the nineteenth century, though the real expansion in this genre occurred towards the middle of the century with the spread of actual travelling, thanks to better transport, greater mobility and increased prosperity. Describing one's travels, however, is an ancient genre. Marco Polo's memoirs, written up by a novelist called Rustichello, first published at the beginning of the fourteenth century in French, have remained one of the most famous examples of travel writing. Another Venetian, Niccolò dei Conti, travelled in the 1420s and 1430s throughout the Middle East, going all the way to India. To save his life he was forced to abjure Christianity, and on his return in 1447 he was instructed by the Pope as a penance to dictate his travel memoirs to the papal secretary, Giovanni Poggio Bracciolini. They were not published until 1723. There were also Arab travellers and Berbers such as Ibn Battūtah (1304–69), who wrote about his travels in *Rihlah* (Journeys), but he was not translated into French until the middle of the nineteenth century and into English until the 1920s.

In the eighteenth century the typical traveller was a gentleman who wrote to inform other gentlemen (and ladies) of what he had seen. Soon travelogues were an accepted literary genre, sought by the ever larger number of those who, in the footsteps of the aristocracy, went on their own not quite so grand Grand Tours. Some of these 'tourists' (the word came into use only c.1800) used books containing handy phrases in foreign languages. *The Gentleman's Pocket Companion for Travelling into Foreign Parts*, published in 1722, even provided helpful hints on how to propose sex to the hotel's chambermaid (in French, German and Italian).[11]

Three out of the four most borrowed books from the Bristol Library between 1773 and 1784 were travelogues.[12]

In England, the most successful general tourist guide of the early part of the nineteenth century was Mariana Starke's *Information and Directions for Travellers on the Continent* (1820) – mainly about Italy – which even provided a classification of works of art (this cannot be missed, this can be skipped, etc.), inns and hotels and even the cost of laundry services in Naples.[13]

A favourite reason for travel was the discovery of the 'origins of civilisation' which meant Italy, Greece and, later on, Egypt. The more daring went to the 'confines' of civilisation, i.e. the Balkans, Turkish Europe and the Slavic countries – all regarded as almost barbarian. Here one would find useful William Coxe's *Travels into Poland* (1785), Edmund Spencer's *Travels in Circassia, Krim, Tartary* (1837), Francis Hervé's *A Residence in Greece and Turkey* (1837) and Elizabeth Craven's *A Journey Through the Crimea to Constantinople* (Dublin, 1789).[14]

Most travel writing was by French, British, and German authors, largely because they did most of the travelling. But there were also Italians such as Alberto Fortis, who wrote *Viaggio in Dalmazia* (Venice, 1774), and Spaniards like Domingo Badía y Leblich (1766–1818), who travelled throughout the Middle East disguised as 'Ali Bey' and was the first (non-Muslim) European to visit Mecca, recording his travels in a book written in French, *Ali Bey en Asie et en Afrique* (1814).

Many important writers contributed to the genre: Goethe (Italy), Théophile Gautier (Spain and Italy), Stendhal (Italy), Dickens (Italy and America), Flaubert (Egypt). The boundaries of the genre were never clear. Madame de Staël's novels *Delphine* and *Corinne ou l'Italie* were classed among travelogues at the Bibliothèque Nationale for much of the nineteenth century.[15] Byron's *Childe Harold's Pilgrimage* was sometimes read as a poetic travelogue.

The genre grew in popularity and became a great favourite among the Victorians. In Britain, home of the highest proportion of nineteenth-century tourists (closely followed by Germany), travel books turned into money-spinners. The story of Fanny Trollope (1780–1863), mother of the novelist Anthony, is exemplary. She set sail for America in 1827, with three of her children in tow (her son Anthony and her seriously ill husband were left behind). She had hoped to join a utopian community, but a series of misadventures left her penniless. The book she wrote, *The Domestic Manners of the Americans*, however, was a sensation in Europe (and, in a different way, in the United States).[16] The tone was forthright, the sentiments high-minded. Above all, the book confirmed its British readers in their feelings of superiority: 'The total want of all the usual courtesies of the table, the voracious rapidity with which the viands were seized and devoured, the strange uncouth phrases and pronunciation; the loathsome spitting from the contamination of which it was absolutely impossible to protect our dresses.'[17] Of Cincinnati she concluded: 'I do not quite sympathise with those who consider Cincinnati as one of the wonders of the earth.'[18] In fact she found it terribly dull, everyone too busy making money to have fun. Of Americans in general she found: 'I very seldom during my whole stay in the country heard a sentence elegantly turned, and correctly pronounced from the lips of an American. There is always something either in the expression or the accent that jars the feelings and shocks the taste.'[19] She was equally shocked by the hold religion had on Americans, and constantly contrasted America's claim to be the world's leading democracy with the dispossession of the Indians, the widespread poverty of the immigrants, and the institution of slavery. She concluded with a peremptory: 'I do not like them. I do not like their principles, I do not like their manners, I do not like their opinions.'[20]

The book was a runaway success, and made Mrs Trollope rich. This led her to produce more travel books, indicting, one after the other, *Paris and the Parisians* (1836), *Vienna and the Austrians* (1838), and *A Visit to Italy* (1842). Her acerbic description of the French contained enough material to infuriate them: from her declaration that the Napoleonic hat, the tricorn, was the most grotesque headwear in Europe to her reference to the peculiar smell of the Continent (upon landing at Calais) and the lax French attitude towards cleaning.[21] She approved of Italy in the way nineteenth-century English people did. Italy meant Tuscany: Florence in spring, and then Bagni di Lucca to avoid the mosquitoes of the summer. To many, it still does. Rome she found filthy.[22] Eventually she settled in Florence, where she died and was buried. Having started writing at the age of fifty-two for economic reasons, she went on writing for almost a quarter of a century, producing thirty-five novels and six travel books.[23]

Though clearly in the non-fiction category, the travelogue resembled the epic story. The author, with whom the reader inevitably identified, recounted a few episodes of his or her stay, proffered a view about how strange or wise or stupid foreigners were, and then moved on. Travel books owed their success to the literary interest in distant places, but they also provided descriptions of places which novelists could use without moving from home. Thus a vicious circle was established: novelists reinforced travel books, while the authors of travel books went abroad with ready-made images of what they were supposed to encounter. But such a circuit is inherently unstable, and stereotypes were never permanent. Until about the end of the eighteenth century the description of the Orient by Europeans was often marked by an attitude of unproblematic moral and cultural superiority. Orientals (mainly Arabs, Turks and Chinese), though generally regarded as urban and 'civilised', unlike black Africans or American Indians, were usually depicted either as amazingly cruel or stupid, or both. Hence the abundance of comically fierce Muslims in plays and books, such as Mozart's Osmin, the overseer of the harem in *The Abduction from the Seraglio* (*Die Entführung aus dem Serail*, 1782), and also in Rossini's *L'Italiana in Algeri* and *Il Turco in Italia*. There was, however, thanks to Spanish chivalric romances, a psychological and aesthetic admiration for the Moors which became one of the components of exoticism and romanticism. The Turk, Infidel or Saracen were becoming established roles in courtly and popular entertainment in Renaissance Europe, and were thus entering folklore.[24] A different image, however, was constructed by Enlightenment thinkers such as Voltaire and Montesquieu (*Lettres Persanes*), who described Orientals as possessing a special kind of wisdom – not having gone through a Catholic education was regarded as particularly advantageous.

Napoleon's Egyptian expedition (1798) was explicitly and ideologically justified as a scientific venture (after the event) on the basis of the renown of travelogues such as *Voyage en Égypte et en Syrie* by the Comte de Volney (1787), and it gave further impetus to the modern, still extant, interest and vogue for all things Oriental.[25] A steady stream of Europeans voyaged towards the Orient, attracted by the classical past, exoticism, imagined sensual charms and Biblical stories. Among them was Chateaubriand, who had been there (*Itinéraire de Paris à Jerusalem*, 1811), and Alexandre Dumas, who hadn't, but whose *Quinze jours au Sinaï*, published in Paris in 1839, went through twenty-five editions in France and was widely translated. It provided many people with an image of the Orient, just as Dumas's novels had familiarised them with French history.[26] Much of this, however, had been preceded by a flow of popular novels set in the Orient. Typical of these was Penelope Aubin's *The Strange Adventures of the Count de Vinevil*, a formulaic short novel of the 1720s: the Muslims are treacherous and lusty, and the Christians innocent and pure.[27] The Russian popular novelist Fedor Emin set his stories in the Near East, where heroes are shipwrecked, enslaved, raised as Oriental princes or fall in love with the beautiful daughter of an Arab caliph or a Turkish pasha. Komarov's famous *Milord George* has the eponymous hero abducted by pirates and kept captive by the Moorish Queen, the beautiful Musalmina.[28] Being captured by cruel pirates provided an ideal means for a character to be ejected from his or her normal environment into a new, exciting, adventurous life in which he or she would find true love – a common fantasy, shared no doubt by many readers. This kind of Orient captured the imagination of the very young Charles Dickens, brought up on the *Arabian Nights* and the *Tales of the Genii*, who penned, at the age of nine or ten, the seldom performed tragedy *Mismar, the Sultan of India*.[29] Major Dobbin in Thackeray's *Vanity Fair* is found absorbed in the *Arabian Nights*, as is David Copperfield.[30] So diffuse was the Orientalist motif in novels that studies examining this phenomenon began to appear at the beginning of the nineteenth century.[31] Behind tales of being taken in captivity there was a historical reality: throughout the seventeenth century and for much of the eighteenth Muslim corsairs enslaved tens of thousands of Europeans from Italy, France, Spain, Portugal and even England by capturing ships or raiding coastlines. These were not traded as African plantation slaves were, but were often returned to their country after the payment of a ransom.[32]

Travel literature was eagerly imported. Gian Pietro Vieusseux thought it could contribute to the modernisation of the Italians, expand their horizons and help them find out about the world. By 1863, when he died, 10 per cent of the holding of his lending library (the 'Gabinetto Vieusseux') was made up of such books, many in their original language. In 1815 the enterprising Milan publisher Giambattista Sonzogno started a travel book series called *Raccolta de' viaggi più interessanti eseguiti nelle varie parti del mondo dopo quelli del celebre Cook* – 'most interesting travels since those of the famous Captain Cook' – starting with *Voyage Around the World* by the French explorer Jean-François de la Pérouse, originally and posthumously published in 1797. By 1832 Sonzogno had published a further forty-seven works, including the accounts of explorers such as the Scot Mungo Park and the German Alexander von Humboldt. Realising that he was as much in the entertainment as the educational business, he pruned the more burdensome scientific sections from much of this literature.[33]

'How-To' Books

Travel books guided readers through strange, mysterious and exotic places where they were unlikely to go in real life. Other books set themselves up as guides to an equally mysterious world: the surrounding social order. Such guides were all the more useful as social mobility was increasing all the time. Untrained by one's parents, who might have belonged to a different class and a different era, one needed to be guided in the art of behaving under new circumstances, hence the need for books of manners.

From a certain point of view, religious books are the archetypes of the genre. They instruct on how to be a good Christian, Muslim or Jew. They explain that if one wants to please God, avoid persecution, gain a place in Paradise and be spared burning in everlasting damnation, one must be good, not covet one's neighbour's possessions (wife, donkey, Porsche), not eat certain foods or not eat at certain times, and control one's sexual instinct.

There were books intended even for those who had decided to become a recluse from the world. *Ancrene Riwle*, a classic written in Middle English in around 1230, was a guide for the young woman who had decided to become an anchoress or hermit. It offered helpful tips on how to resist sin and temptation, and how to run the anchorage. More secular 'how-to' books appeared during the Renaissance. The most famous was Machiavelli's *The Prince* (1513), a manual explaining how to make friends, divide enemies, take over states and run them. Equally famous were books explaining how to be a gentleman: Baldissare Castiglione's *Il Cortigiano* (The Courtier, 1528) – translated into English in 1561 – and the *Galateo* by the priest Giovanni della Casa (1558), translated into English in 1576 and still in use in the nineteenth century, having spawned a large number of imitators. The appeal of such books resided in the fact that one could read them without necessarily intending to use them. They functioned equally well as descriptions of how the higher classes are supposed to behave, just as one might read a cookery book out of curiosity about the preparation of food.

Castiglione had started the trend of advice on how to behave in conversation. He had illustrious followers, including Montaigne, whose essay *De l'Art de conférer* (1580) contained the conversational rules to be followed, what to say and how to say it. The vogue for such manuals reached its height towards the second half of the eighteenth century when major authors, such as Swift with his *Hints Towards an Essay on Conversation*, joined in what was clearly a lucrative market.[34]

The possibility of multiple use of such texts was what made Puget de la Serre's widely pirated *Secrétaire à la Mode ou Méthode facile d'escrire selon le temps diverses Lettres de Compliment, Amoureuses ou Morales* (1640) so successful. Étienne Garnier, a Troyes publisher, held in stock 1,848 copies of this book as late as 1789 – 150 years after it was first published. The *Secrétaire à la Mode* offered samples of letters meant originally to help the *nouvelle bourgeoisie* in the arcane art of correspondence, but what probably also fascinated people was to know how others lived and thought, and to fantasise about the kind of love letters one might like to send or receive.[35]

There were books teaching magical tricks, how to play games, and the inevitable 'how-to-get-your-man' books, such as the short (sixteen pages) *Catéchisme à l'usage des grandes filles pour être mariées, augmenté de la manière d'attirer les amants*, of which there were many editions in the course of the eighteenth and nineteenth centuries.[36]

'How-to' books could be divided into three broad categories: those that purported to give practical instruction of a technical nature to social groups eager to use 'scientific' methods in order to improve their prospects; those that appealed to a rising class eager to learn the manners and behaviour of a higher and better-established class with which they hoped to mix; those that instructed the élites in 'peripheral' countries (i.e. all European countries except for France and Great Britain) how the élites in France and England behaved. The Russian aristocracy, eager for enlightenment from the west, were avid consumers of this latter genre from the middle of the eighteenth century, including translations of books like Hester Chapone's *Letters on the Improvement of the Mind Addressed to a Young lady* (1773) and Sarah Pennington's *An Unfortunate Mother's Advice to her Absent Daughters* (1761).[37]

Cookery books would fall under the rubric of texts of 'practical instruction'. These would be equally useful to the hostess preparing a dinner party, enabling her to give sound advice to her cook, as to the aspirant chef seeking employment among the *nouveaux riches*. In France, Nicolas Oudot, the publishers of the Bibliothèque Bleue at Troyes, produced books of cooking instruction and apprenticeship, such as *Le Cuisinier français enseignant la manière de bien apprêter et d'assaisonner toutes sortes de viandes grasses et maigres* by the famous la Varenne (1668).[38] *La Cuisinière bourgeoise*, addressed to women with the advice to encourage the servants to read it, so as not to waste time explaining things over and over, was reprinted thirty-two times between 1815 and 1840.[39] In the same category were books about health, whose success was directly related to the general distrust of the medical profession. Thus the aptly named *La Médecine sans médecin* by Rouvière was a great success in the 1820s, with thirteen reprints between 1823 and 1830.[40] But 'how-to-stay-healthy' books have been popular since the dawn of the printing presses. Among the earliest examples were *How Venetians can Always Stay Healthy* (1565) and the optimistic *How a Man can Live More than 120 Years* (1556) by Tommaso Rangone (1493–1577), a physician to the Venetian fleet and public health consultant to the Republic. Nicolas Oudot, before producing his best-selling book on how to cook fatty meat, had published Philbert Guilbert's medical self-help book *Le Médecin charitable* (1645). The popularity of health books increased constantly, especially in countries prone to hypochondria such as France: *La Médecine de la famille* (1849) by H. Crosilhes was popular in Paris in the 1850s, as were *La Médecine domestique et la pharmacie usuelle* (1874) and *La Science mise à la portée de tous: hygiène et médecine des deux sexes* (1885). The vogue increased exponentially over the following century. In the late twentieth century the vogue for health books spread to periodicals: in 1970 in France there were two magazines entirely devoted to health matters; by the year 2000 there were twenty. The best-selling one, *Top Santé* (monthly), claimed five million readers.[41]

Often it was possible (for the French) to achieve the feat of combining gastronomy and health: in 1750 the *Dictionnaire des alimens* claimed that '*la plus nouvelle*' and most interesting cookery was based on healthy eating. In the same period the celebrated chef Menon, known as the author of cookery books aimed at specific classes – from *Les Soupers de la cour 'pour les grandes tables*' to *La Cuisinière bourgeoise* for the middle classes – published *La Cuisine et l'office de la santé* (1758), for the 'common urban dweller concerned about his health'.[42] These are the antecedents to contemporary best-sellers such as *Dr Atkins' New Diet Revolution*, which sold well over a million copies in Britain in 2003 alone.

The most popular genre, however, was the book of manners. As the middle classes expanded and some of their numbers were ennobled thanks to their newly acquired wealth, they had to acquire manners befitting their new position. The book of manners could, of course, take the form of a novel. Many novels came to be treated as handbooks on language and etiquette – such as the so-called 'silver-fork' novels. A really successful silver-fork novel must be written in such a way that it can be understood by those who, though they do not belong to the 'in' circle, may fool themselves into the belief that they do, or are about to join it. The leading practitioners of the genre, Theodore Hook, Thomas H. Lister and Catherine Grace Gore, and the better-known Edward Bulwer-Lytton (*Pelham*, 1828) provided invaluable learning material for the *nouveaux riches*.[43] These novels were invariably set west of Regent Street, where all civilised life was conducted (it is said that 'Beau' Brummel was embarrassed to have been seen one night as far east as the Strand; he explained that he had got lost).[44]

The how-to books enabled women to enter the non-fiction market, from which they had remained hitherto marginalised. Books of manners eventually became one of their dominions. Until well into the nineteenth century few women tried their hand at history; one of the rare exceptions in Britain was Charlotte Cowley's *The Ladies' History of England: From the Descent of Julius Caesar, to the Summer of 1780, Calculated for the Use of the Ladies of Great Britain and Ireland; and Likewise adapted to General Use, Entertainment, and Instruction* (1780).[45] In France, one of the most successful popular history books was Madame de Saint-Ouen's short *Histoire de France*: forty-six impressions between 1827 and 1860. In the 1830s Hachette reprinted it in massive print runs: 20,000 (and 40,000 in the 1840s). Its success, like that of history books throughout the nineteenth and for most of the twentieth century, was due to its political correctness. This ensured that it would be adopted in schools – the royal road to best-sellerdom.[46]

But the non-fiction genre at which women excelled was biography and autobiography – a genre which shares with fiction a similar structure, as it deals with the growth and development of a person. The increase in literacy in the eighteenth century among women enhanced letter-writing and diary-keeping (making the fortune, in the early nineteenth century, of London bookbinder John Letts, who started producing the Letts diaries in 1812).[47] Many well-known writers opened their hearts to meet people's desire to know the real person behind the writer they loved, or to find out, vicariously, the intimate secrets of others; hence Thomas de Quincey's *Confessions of an English Opium-Eater*, George Sand's *Histoire de ma vie*, Goethe's *Aus meinem Leben. Dichtung und Wahrheit*, John Stuart Mill's *Autobiography*, Stendhal's *Vie de Henry Brulard*, Anthony Trollope's *An Autobiography*, Kropotkin's *Memoirs of a Revolutionist*, Ernest Renan's *Souvenirs d'enfance et de jeunesse*, Napoleon's *Le Mémorial de Sainte Hélène*, etc.[48] But the genre had been popular throughout the eighteenth century. And the author did not need to be a literary celebrity. Laetitia Pilkington's *Memoirs* were a great success when they came out in 1748, because they were the story of a woman and her unhappy marriage 'told aloud in an age when women were supposed to keep quiet'.[49] Laetitia, however, far from suffering in silence, took her revenge on her husband's infidelity by having plenty of lovers too, making her *Memoirs* as titillating as Defoe's *Moll Flanders*.[50]

Laetitia Pilkington's own model may have been fiction, but in turn she provided a model for similar stories, such as the *Memoirs Written by Herself* (1825) by Harriette Wilson, a famous courtesan, who assured her various lovers that in exchange for some payment they would not be included, or would be given a favourable report. The parallels with the successful contemporary autobiographical genre known as the 'kiss-and-tell' book are obvious, but few of today's exemplars have such a titillating beginning as Harriette Wilson's 'I shall not say why or how I became, at the age of fifteen, the mistress of the Earl of Craven.'

Thanks to such developments the quality gap between non-fiction and novels began to narrow. Novels became increasingly diverse, spanning a range from the simple to the complex, from the penny dreadful to the literary, whilst non-fiction could no longer be regarded as high-minded accounts of 'the truth'.

12

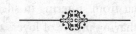

News and Pictures

Advertising

SAGAS, EPIC POEMS AND PEDDLERS' LITERATURE contributed to the formation of communities of readers throughout Europe; the press, however, was the crucial factor in such expansion. Newspapers and journals were cheaper than books, reported on new novels and serialised some of them; they made some people famous and turned others into public villains. They gossiped about the private lives of the rich and powerful, to the delight and curiosity of the 'middling sort'. They provided people with common topics of conversation and new avenues of sociability. They ensured that communities separated by distance shared knowledge about 'their' country, 'their' sovereign, and 'their' government. Readers, through newspapers, discovered common identities with people 'like them'.

Hegel, who had been the editor of a newspaper, the *Bamberger Zeitung*, commented in his diary that 'Reading the morning paper is the realist's morning prayer,' a way of orienting one's attitude to the world 'as it really is'.[1]

Newspapers deployed a kind of power which was exquisitely modern and 'democratic'. The power of the press derived from markets, from consumers, from money. Those who published newspapers had to please neither God nor sovereign, but only their readers, their owners and their sponsors. They had to transmute ideas, principles, news, information, anything and everything into a merchandise, a commodity. They were the first software merchants. Perceptive minds promptly baptised this new power the 'fourth estate' of the realm. In his essay 'The Hero as Man of Letters' Carlyle wrote:

> Burke said that there were Three Estates in Parliament; but, in the Reporters' Gallery yonder, there sat a Fourth Estate more important far

than they all. It is not a figure of speech, or witty saying; it is a literal fact, – very momentous to us in these times.[2]

And, in his *The French Revolution*, he added:

> Alas, yes: Speculation, Philosophism, once the ornament and wealth of the saloon, will now coin itself into mere Practical Propositions, and circulate on street and highway, universally; with results! A Fourth Estate, of Able Editors, springs up; increases and multiplies; irrepressible, incalculable.[3]

In France the press was even more powerful, or so it was thought. Bagehot wrote that in England a young man with political ambitions would 'look to the bar', in France he becomes a journalist.[4] Charles de Rémusat recalled that the press was the main resource of the dissident intellectuals during the Restoration: 'All of us who thought in those wars . . . whatever we are we were made by the press.'[5]

By providing endless accounts of what happened to other people, newspapers supplied nineteenth-century novelists with priceless material. Balzac, Zola, and Dickens were among the many who were constantly inspired by the sections of newspapers dealing with day-to-day life. Stendhal urged his correspondent Louis Chaudru de Raynal to send him more stories '*de suicides ou de crimes par amour*'. With relish he recounted, in the same letter, the recent case of a lady, a neighbour of Stendhal's as it happened, who poisoned her children and husband hoping to join her lover, a Mr. Ribera, in Brazil. '*Elle avait des yeux noirs d'une douceur et d'une beauté frappantes, elle faisait révolution en entrant dans un salon*' (Her eyes were black, strikingly sweet and beautiful; as she entered a salon, revolutions would break out).[6] Thomas Hardy picked up possible stories in the press (mainly back issues of the *Dorset County Chronicle*) and copied them into a notebook labelled 'Facts from Newspapers'. It was there that he found the story of the selling of wives he used in *The Mayor of Casterbridge*.[7] The reporting of crimes, murderers, investigators and unaccounted mysteries provided the impetus for the diffusion of one of the most successful fictional genres: the crime novel.

The press imparted training to aspiring writers, as well as some ready cash. Balzac, for instance, earned some 5,000 francs between the end of 1829 and the middle of 1831 from journalism, and almost nothing from his novels.[8] In eighteenth-century Russia, where writing was still regarded as a hobby of the nobility, the emergence of the new literary periodicals provided writers such as Nikolai Karamzin with a regular income.[9] Everywhere journalism, from its inception, provided writers with the apprenticeship, the income and the renown which helped them in their profession as writers: from Aphra Behn to Defoe, from Fielding to Dickens and Zola, from Hemingway to Ken Follett.

The press favoured the consolidation of dominant languages, that is those spoken by the dominant classes. In the eighteenth century, 90 per cent of Brussels's population spoke Flemish, but all the fifteen major periodicals available at the time were in French.[10] Where there was no settled literary language, newspapers facilitated its establishment, as was the case in Croatia with Pan-Slavic newspapers such as the *Novine horvatzke* (Croatian News, 1835–36).[11]

Above all, the press *sold* news. But news was often little more than gossip written by 'paragraph writers' who picked up stories in coffee houses and clubs. Information was mainly obtained from church sermons, personal contacts, private correspondence and a network of travellers and informers. Modern newspapers developed gradually. In the early sixteenth century there were occasional sheets describing single events, such as the Spanish *Relación de lo que pasó al Emperador en Bornes con Lutero en 1521* – an account of the historic Diet of Worms of April 1521, when Martin Luther was asked, in vain, to recant in the presence of the Emperor Charles V. Then there was the publication of chronicles of current affairs – the *coranto* in Spain and *courants* in France. Later still there were the 'diurnals', or dailies, which provided regular news about an institution, such as the 1640s *Perfect Diurnall of the Passages in Parliament*.

In Holland, a great newspaper centre, there was a regular paper, a fortnightly, as early as 1605, published by the printer Abraham Verhoeve, called *Nieuwe Tijdinghen*. Strasbourg had a weekly in 1609, Cologne and Amsterdam in 1620, Paris in 1631, Florence in 1636, Madrid in 1661. Germany had over two hundred newspapers before 1700. The first regular daily was produced in Leipzig in 1660 (the *Einkommende Zeitung*). London's first daily newspaper, the *Daily Courant*, saw the light of day in 1702. Spain's first daily (*Diario noticioso*) was started in 1758. By 1782 there were fifty papers circulating in provincial England, printing a total of 400,000 copies a year.[12]

Such proliferation of newspapers and magazines in England was facilitated by the Licensing Act of 1695, which discontinued the practice established by Henry VIII requiring printers to submit manuscripts to Church authorities. At a stroke England acquired the freest press in Europe. By the end of the eighteenth century there were already national papers – defined as newspapers with the *ambition* to reach all the main cities, evidence that a distribution system was being developed. Other countries, including France, which did not have a daily until the *Journal de Paris* in 1777 (seventy-five years after London), lagged far behind. Newspapers in Germany, especially in Prussia under Frederick II, were severely controlled, hampering expansion.

Article 11 of the Declaration of the Rights of Man of 26 August 1789 proclaimed the freedom of communicating one's thoughts and opinions as one of the most precious rights of French citizens. The consequences were astonishing: between 1789 and 1800 some 1,500 new papers appeared. The expansion was, of course, more marked in the years of virtually unlimited press freedom (1789–92) than during the Terror, but even in the years following the defeat of the Jacobins, the press continued to prosper until the Napoleonic coup of 1799.

In America too there was a rapid development of newspapers and periodicals after the War of Independence. Previously there had been only sixteen. By 1825 there were one hundred periodicals, by 1850 six hundred.

The press was substantially an urban affair. Transport, market size and cultural limitations made it difficult to distribute newspapers in the countryside. Even in cities there was a problem of distribution. In England the linchpin of the system was the network of coffee houses, which regularly subscribed to newspapers for the use of their clients and in order to attract them. By 1714 there were more than five hundred coffee houses in London alone, as well as 8,659 brandy shops, 5,875 beer houses, and 447 taverns.[13] The London press of the eighteenth century was relatively cheap: the *Daily Universal Register* cost two and half pennies (a little cheaper than its competitors). Regular purchase of a London paper was within the reach of all who could read.[14] London had become Europe's major media centre. The *Daily Courant* was followed by the *Evening Post* (1706), the *London Journal* (1723) and, later in the century, the *Daily Advertiser*, the *Westminster Journal*, *Lloyd's Evening Post*, the *Morning Chronicle* and many others.[15]

The papers were cheap because, though ostensibly selling news, they were in the business of selling advertising – the real commercial backbone of the enterprise. There were no headlines, no artwork, the articles were short and usually unsigned. The front page of the first issue of the *Daily Universal Register*, on 1 January 1785 – it became *The Times* in 1788 – carried in its left-hand column announcements for the two licensed theatres, while the whole of the second column was devoted to personal announcements. The remaining two columns contained an editorial setting out the purpose of the new paper. The order of this agenda is revealing: 'to facilitate the *commercial* intercourse between the different parts of the community through the channel of advertisements; to record occurrences and to abridge parliamentary debates'.[16]

The Times claimed – as it still does – not to have any political affiliation at all. Presumably it did not wish to lose custom by offending anyone, as it had to compete with eight other London dailies. In reality its political affiliation was for sale: its editor had agreed to publish material favourable to the government for £300 a year. The theatre review section was similarly open to bribes, and was really just an extension of advertising.[17] The constant self-congratulatory celebration of the sharp demarcation between reporting and comment ('Comment is free but facts are sacred,' attributed to editor of the *Manchester Guardian* C.P. Scott in 1921) became part of self-serving press propaganda much later. From its inception *The Times* was an avowedly commercial enterprise whose survival depended on advertising. This dependency, however, decreased steadily, from 65 per cent reliance in 1812 to 33 per cent in 1827.[18]

Advertising had been made indispensable by the huge increase in the tax on newspapers between 1789 and 1815, which made British papers more expensive than their French counterparts. Advertising would help contain the price. A side effect of the tax or stamp duty, quite apart from raising government income, was that it contained the rapid growth of the radical press, which found it difficult to obtain advertising revenue in spite of its high sales.[19] In France very few dailies managed to sell more than 10,000 copies – the print run of the *Journal des débats* and *Le Constitutionnel*.[20] Advertising was less developed than in Britain, and the tax levied by the state accounted for a significant proportion of the costs.

It soon became clear that no daily newspaper would ever be able to be financed entirely by its sales. Advertising, which at the time consisted largely of personal announcements – introduced into cultural markets an economic concept of enormous magnitude: the idea that the size and quality of a newspaper's readership was a commodity that could be sold to advertisers. Advertisers took the place of patrons. They would pay to make their products known, subsidising the newspapers, thus containing the selling price, which in turn would contribute to the expansion of the readership, which, in a kind of virtuous circle, made further advertising more likely. This principle, eventually adopted again in the age of broadcasting and the internet, established a dual market: news would be sold to paying customers, space to advertisers.

At the beginning of the nineteenth century, however, there were relatively few goods that could be advertised. Distinctive consumer goods – brands – selling over a relatively wide territory were scarce. The almost complete lack of cheap consumer products with a large potential market delayed the formation of a popular press, since this could only have been funded by carrying advertising addressed to its readers.[21] Most advertising consisted of property for sale and jobs; the rest was mainly for cloth and medicine. Thus there was a structural limit to the extension of the press in the first half of the nineteenth century. A comparison of advertising carried between 1812 and 1827 in a British national daily, *The Times*, and a provincial weekly, the *Windsor and Eton Express*, shows that around half of the advertising was for property, while offers of employment were far more prominent in *The Times* than in the *Windsor and Eton Express*, because in and around Windsor jobs could be found by word of mouth.

By 1779 there were five dailies and eight weeklies in London alone, and about forty dailies in the provinces. By the early 1800s Britain was the country with the strongest readership per capita, as well as a well-differentiated national press. Henry Richard Fox Bourne, writing in 1887, had a clear view of audiences and niche markets in his review of the morning press of 1811: aligned against *The Times* was the energetic *Morning Chronicle*, the organ of the Whigs, while the *Morning Post* and the *Morning Herald* satisfied Tory readers, the first giving prominence to government matters, the second to 'aristocratic gossip'. Then there was the *Public Ledger* for the 'commercial class'; the *Morning Advertiser*, aimed at 'licensed victuallers'; the *British Press* for booksellers; and the *Day* for auctioneers. The prominent position held by *The Times* was attributed to lively journalists such as leader writer Edward Sterling, who 'by his forcible style of writing, only too cautious to the extent of always keeping on the popular side, or rather the side taken by the more comfortable and prosperous portion of the community, secured for *the Times* its nickname of "the Thunderer"'.[22] Note the equation of the popular side with the prosperous section of the community – quite right in the context of newspaper readers in 1811.

Periodicals

Sitting uneasily between the dailies and weeklies and the 'book' were the periodical journals. Any distinction between these forms of printed texts is purely conventional. What is of significance is that towards the beginning of the eighteenth century in England, the pioneer in this field, new literary and political magazines appeared such as *The Political State of Great Britain* (1711), a register of parliamentary debates and of important articles and books published. This genre helped the formation of the reading public's sense of history.

While the press was still essentially an advertising service, journals such as the *Tatler*, founded by Joseph Addison and Richard Steele in 1709, and its illustrious successor the *Spectator* (1711), thought of themselves as being at the centre of a network of readers. The idea of 'interactivity', where the readers were not supposed to be passive recipients of texts, was pioneered with the institutionalisation of letters to the editors. From the first issue of the *Tatler* Addison and Steele invited readers to write, and in the second issue they published twenty-one letters – some of these probably drafted by the editors themselves.[23] Addison and Steele, a 'new breed of media-men', aspired to turn coarse and argumentative fellows into 'coffee-house conversationalists'.[24] In accounting for the success of the *Tatler* among those it criticised, John Gay wrote that Steele 'ventur'd to tell the Town, that they were a parcel of Fops, Fools, and vain Cocquets; but in such a manner, as even pleased them'.[25] The *Spectator*, the *Tatler* and other English magazines (as well as French) were regularly plundered by others such as the Italian *Gazzetta Veneta* (1760), the *Osservatore Veneto* (1761) of Gaspare Gozzi and *La Frusta letteraria* (1763–65) of Giuseppe Marc'Antonio Baretti.[26] Imported into Russia, Addison and Steele's *Spectator* gave the Russian reading public their first taste of British literature.[27] The British continued to lead in this sector. Between 1790 and 1832 over 4,000 journals were published in Britain.[28]

In Germany the English influence was crucial. The early periodicals were based on the *Tatler* and the *Spectator*. In spite of their high cost they were widely read through a growing number of reading societies. By the end of the eighteenth century there were hundreds of journals in Germany. There were also *moralische Wochenschriften* (moralising weeklies) aimed at middle-class women. A successful novelist like Sophie von la Roche started to edit her own periodical in 1783–84: *Ponoma für Teutschlands Töchter* (Ponoma for Germany's Daughters).[29] British journals could be seen everywhere in

Europe's better salons. The Irish journalist and traveller Michael J. Quin, when staying at the home of a Magyar aristocrat, Count Szechnyi, reported noticing in the Count's library the *Edinburgh* and *Quarterly* reviews, as well as 'several of our "Annuals" and other English and French periodical publications'.[30]

Booksellers were quick to understand that journals were ideally suited for advertising books. All those who read them were potential or actual book-readers. Booksellers were already in the habit of using print to sell print by publishing their catalogues. In 1785 John Pendrel published his *The London and Country Printers, Booksellers and Stationers Vade Mecum*, which provided a list of forty-nine provincial newspapers, their towns, their owners and the addresses of their London agents through whom one could place advertising.[31]

Browsing in bookshops was very rare. People depended on word of mouth, the booksellers' advice and, far more than today, on the reviews which appeared regularly in literary journals. Many reviewers, of course, wrote books themselves, as did many journalists. Daniel Defoe, for instance, now best remembered as the author of *Robinson Crusoe*, one of the most successful novels of all time, was a remarkable journalist who pioneered many features still widely used: the leading article, investigative reporting, the foreign news analysis, the agony aunt, the gossip column, the candid obituary, and even the soul-searching piece. At the same time periodicals which had hitherto confined themselves to reviewing scholarly and scientific works decided to expand their audience by publishing reviews of poetry and even of novels, then a 'low' genre. The pioneer was a bookseller, Ralph Griffiths, who realised that the main problem facing the trade was how to reach potential readers. His *Monthly Review*, launched in May 1749, was dedicated to reviewing *all* books published. His success attracted others, such as Tobias Smollett's *Critical Review* (1756). Finally, in 1802 the quarterly *Edinburgh Review* appeared, followed in 1809 by the *Quarterly Review*.[32] These publications were read by the 'intellectual' upper and middle classes, that is by the clergy and professional men, often in lending libraries and clubs, for they were not cheap: a yearly subscription would cost £1.10s. – the price of a book. The reviews became a major factor in the marketing of new books, attracting advertising from booksellers and publishers.[33]

Between 1815 and 1832 twenty new journals appeared, including *Blackwood's Magazine*, the *London Magazine* and *Fraser's Magazine*, less intellectual than the *Edinburgh* and *Quarterly Review*, and offering a variety of short stories, essays, reviews and poetry.[34]

Entry costs for publishing magazines were relatively low, so as soon as magazines became profitable, new entrants lowered profits. High profits were thus dependent on a constant expansion of the reading public. As this occurred, this public became more diversified, making the publication of a magazine of interest to all readers increasingly difficult. The way forward was to accept the segmentation of the market. These ceaseless changes meant that publishers, if they wanted to survive, had to be constantly in contact with an ever-changing audience. Thus, in England, cheaper monthlies and weeklies began to appear, such as the *Athenaeum*, which succeeded in achieving a circulation of 18,000 copies a week in 1830 by reducing its price from eight to four pence.[35]

But profit – as is often the case in the cultural industries – was far from being the only reason for publishing a magazine. There was also the enjoyment of being an editor and publisher, the prestige gained in literary and political circles, and the influence that went with it. These non-monetary rewards meant that prestige periodicals never needed to be particularly profitable.

Journals required not only readers, but writers as well. The *Edinburgh Review* attracted good-quality writers by paying them better than their competitors. This was more easily achieved because it was a quarterly, at a time when most periodicals were monthly. Four issues cost less to deliver than twelve. The huge increase in the cost of paper and printing associated with the Napoleonic wars forced many of the monthlies out of business, leaving the field clear for the Whig *Edinburgh Review* and its Tory competitor the *Quarterly Review*.[36] The quarterlies reviewed only a selection of books and not the entire production, thus growing in authority and prestige, making decisions for their readers and becoming literary arbiters. By 1805 the *Edinburgh Review*'s print run had reached 4,000 copies, increasing to a peak of 13,500 copies in 1818, while the *Quarterly Review* was selling 14,000 in 1817.[37] Writing for the literary magazines soon became an author's quickest way of earning money.

At a time when books would sell some 1,000 copies, the print runs of the more successful magazines made them highly profitable. Each issue represented the same amount of print and paper as a book, but it sold ten times more. As the magazines were sold on subscription, publishers had an estimate of how many copies would sell, and they were getting the money in advance. On the negative side was the fact that while a book cost a publisher nothing until the manuscript was accepted, magazines required editors, sub-editors, staff writers – all of whom who needed to be paid regularly.[38]

There were also hidden benefits. Publishers of magazines published books as well, and it was a common practice to review favourably 'in house' books. Reviewers acquired considerable power. Previously authors hoped that their patrons would talk favourably about their works in elegant salons and literary circles, thus ensuring sales and renown. Now the age of the private patron was coming to a close; being well reviewed, and patronised by editors, were what mattered.

A new kind of uncertainty appeared in cultural production. Guessing what patrons might like was difficult enough, but patrons, at least, tended to belong to a narrow class of people with relatively similar tastes. This was less and less true even in the seventeenth century. In 1664 the painter Salvatore Rosa complained that 'As for commissions, for the last year there's been absolutely nothing – even from a dog.' Five years later he was so popular that he was turning down important commissions from all over Europe.[39] Markets started tending towards standardisation even in the arts. The English upper classes, having discovered Rome and Italian art, wanted to have their portraits painted in Italy and to bring back Italian landscapes. Canaletto painted more than three-quarters of his pictures for Englishmen – much of this production offered slightly different views of the same Venetian canals and buildings.[40]

The new 'democratic' mass market was quite different. It is not easy to estimate future demand for a new product. Cultural producers – composers, writers, painters – had to learn to live in a climate of insecurity. They were compelled to offer something new: rewriting the same book or producing the same piece of music again and again brings no reward and finds no customers. In the visual arts exact repetition might be a plausible strategy, and is adopted in prints and in cast sculptures, but not frequently in painting. One can and one does, of course, milk a new genre for all that it is worth, and while rewriting the same book does not pay, writing a similar one may pay handsomely. Indeed, this is what many consumers expect: the recreation of the pleasure derived from the original consumption.

It did not take long to discover that magazines dealing with gossip and scandal could be rather successful in Britain. The scandal press was not politically subversive, which is why it was somewhat tolerated. In fact it was, as it is now, overwhelmingly conservative – for instance the arch-Tory *John Bull* (1820) and the *Age* (1825). The *Satirist* was liberal, but hostile to Chartists and the anti-slavery movement. All three were clearly aimed at the middle classes, all published gossip and abusive remarks about famous people. Such stories fulfilled a deep-seated desire to mock authority while reassuring readers that they were part of a privileged group, privy to what others didn't know. Many of these scandal-mongering sheets sold 2,500 to 3,000 copies a week. Some did far better. For instance, the *Town*, founded by Renton Nicholson in 1837, probably sold as many as 10,000. Because it refused to pay stamp duty it was not allowed to publish the political, legal and other news that made up most of the contents of its rivals.[41] Released from such obligation, the *Town* 'proposed a world in which everyone, from grocery porters to the royal couple, was mostly engaged in thinking about sex' – even reporting, on 30 May 1840, an alleged quarrel between Prince Albert and Queen Victoria during which Albert deprived the Queen of sex, after which 'his sulky Highness locked his German self and his German sausage in the *cabinet* all night'.[42]

This genre was not new. The French *chroniques scandaleuses* devoted to the 'inside' story of life and sex at Versailles had been popular since the eighteenth century.[43] The private lives of members of royal households fascinated Europeans in the eighteenth and nineteenth centuries as much as the goings-on on Olympus among the gods appear to have fascinated the ancient Greeks, or those in the British royal family still appear to fascinate readers in the twenty-first century.

The difference between then and now was that in the past the powers-that-be could retaliate. The *Town* had tried to protect itself from accusations of subversion by consistently attacking working-class organisations, but it went too far in its scandal-mongering too often, and was regularly sued, and eventually driven out of business. Then the Obscene Publication Act of 1857 which enormously strengthened the censorship powers of the state sealed the fate of such press for the rest of the Victorian era.[44]

After several false starts and short-lived publications such as George Miller's *Cheap Magazine* (1813–14), the development of the respectable popular press in Britain began in earnest with the launch of Charles Knight's *Penny Magazine* (1832), soon imitated abroad by many – including the German *Pfennig Magazin*.

Two distinct markets developed in France, too. Alongside respectable and responsible newspapers such as *Le Journal des débats*, *Le Conservateur*, *Le Constitutionnel* and *Le Globe* (1824), there was an array of often short-lived *petits journaux* whose appeal relied on satire, scandal and gossip: *Le Figaro*, *Le Diable boiteux*, *Le Charivari*. Unlike their British counterparts, however, the French magazines were almost all opposed to the government.

Printing the Image

Alongside newspapers and periodicals, the eighteenth century saw a huge development in the market for engraved prints. The aristocracy and the richer members of the middle classes could continue collecting unique works of art, but thanks to prints it was possible to see and own the works of famous painters such as François Boucher and Jean-Honoré Fragonard. In England a great tradition of engravers – William Hogarth, James Gillray and Thomas Rowlandson are the best-known – depicted, often in a satirical way, eighteenth-century British social life. The key figure was Hogarth (1697–1764), who dominated art in England in the first half of the eighteenth century – the only country in Europe where this role was in the hands of a 'humble' engraver rather than a painter in the classical mould. Hogarth produced primarily for the aristocracy, but he created a market for other engravers who could sell to the expanding middle classes keen to ape the aristocracy and hang artwork in their homes. One of the reasons behind Hogarth's popularity is that he connected narrative to the image (as the cheap engravers of chapbooks had done before him), producing a series of prints which told a story – at the same time as Richardson was writing *Pamela* and *Clarissa*. The engravings known as *The Harlot's Progress* (c.1731) are in fact a picture-book story of a how young country girl who arrives in London is lured into prostitution, ends up in jail, falls ill and dies – a kind of unlucky Moll Flanders. Hogarth's prints often used captions to tell a story. He not only used a clear narrative title (e.g. *Strolling Actresses Dressing in a Barn*, 1738), but also words skilfully inserted on the print itself: newspapers, titles of books, emblems. Such a legacy would be exploited and developed in the illustrations used in books throughout the nineteenth century. By 1780 the quality of English prints, especially landscape prints (English gardens had become fashionable), 'began to catch the eye of continental connoisseurs and to take their place in an international effort to record works of art that was proceeding all over Europe. Indeed, certain British artists now took a leading role by recording outstanding paintings and antique sculptures in Italy and France as well as in Britain.'[45] The numerous print shops in London, especially in Pall Mall, Piccadilly and Bond Street, made it the world's leading centre. The position of John Boydell (whose shop had opened in Cheapside in the 1760s) as the leading print-seller was secured because of his near-monopoly of Old Master paintings in English collections.[46] There was also a close connection between the theatres and eighteenth-century prints. Actors and scenes from fashionable plays were among the favourite subjects for popular prints.[47]

For prints to be used in books it was necessary to develop a system of cheap reproduction of high quality. Lithography was just such a technique. It enabled the expansion of the market for prints which previously could be obtained only with woodcutting or engraving. The new process employed wax crayon to write on stone, the stone surface was made wet, and the written or drawn areas were left free of water: as the grease-based ink stuck only to the water-free area it left an image on the paper as it passed through a press. The invention, credited to Aloysius Senefelder, was patented in Bavaria in 1799 – though it came to be called 'lithography' later, probably in France. It reached England in 1800, when Senefelder took a patent there, and was fairly generally adopted after 1813. By 1820 the invention had spread throughout Germany.[48] Lithography stands between the invention of movable type and the recent electronic revolution. It did not supply simple reproduction, but allowed the creation of multiple 'originals' of high quality and at low cost. Its initial impact was in the mass production of maps and other topographic material, and in music printing. It enabled an image to be sold directly. Artists, including distinguished painters such as Ingres and Géricault, took advantage of the procedure.[49] Lithography could also be used to enhance the value of printed works by adding illustrations. It is in this indirect mode (attracting attention, enhancing value, or as an artefact where the text and the visual element are inextricably fused – such as the glossy magazine and the comic strip) that the visual image (either designed by an artist or as a photograph) found its commercial use and unprecedented development.

Though it was introduced in France at the same time as in Britain, lithography became successful there only after 1815, that is with the peace following the defeat of Napoleon.[50] By 1828 there were 223 lithographic firms in and around Paris, and in 1839, ninety in Paris alone. By then lithography was part of an industry rated eleventh in economic importance in France.[51]

Lithography could be used in all the ways made known by the preceding dominant art form, such as painting and engraving: the portrait, the landscape, the religious motif, as well as erotic and pornographic representations of women. It generated new forms or vastly enhanced older ones: for instance the political cartoon, of which Honoré Daumier (1808–79) was the great pioneer in France. His cartoons of King Louis Philippe made him famous and cost him a spell in prison. The law of 1835 banned political satire and forced Daumier to turn towards a less overtly political genre. He denounced judges and lawyers, the excessive length of Eugène Sue's novel *Les Mystères de Paris*, and educated women by representing them as ridiculous and unspeakably ugly – see his series *Les Bas-bleus* (The Bluestockings, published in *Le Charivari*, January–August 1844).[52]

Lithography was also used in 1829 by J.J. Granville for a series called *Les Métamorphoses du jour*, with fully dressed human beings represented with the heads of animals. The theme of human and animal resemblance was important in French popular and aristocratic culture: speaking animals were a regular feature of the fables of la Fontaine, still one of the best-selling texts in the nineteenth century, and are one of Walt Disney's most successful formulas. In or around 1771 an unknown artist represented, in *The Harmoniac Meeting*, Teresa Cornelys's opera being played and performed by people with animal heads.[53] Lithographs were also used to represent elegant and charming women – the *lorettes* and *grisettes* made famous by risqué literature. Here the most famous practitioner was Gavarni (1804–66), who became famous when he was appointed as fashion illustrator for *La Mode* in 1830 (note his series *Les Lorettes*, 1841).[54] He also illustrated collections of fairy stories, Hoffmann's *Fantastic Tales* and famous novels such as *Robinson Crusoe* (in 1861) and Swift's *Gulliver's Travels* (in 1862), and produced lithographic prints drawing attention to the conditions of the working class in Britain, where he had been in 1847. In Russia, lithography appeared in the 1820s, and was rapidly applied with great success to the printing of the *lubki* (chapbooks).[55]

Illustrations were used as a support for the text in a newspaper or book, or were bought separately. The sale of religious images and of religious books, particularly the lives of saints, constituted an early example of merchandising. Characters made famous in popular books would often appear in prints that were sold separately. For instance, the heroes and heroines of Chateaubriand's *Atala* (1801, twelve editions in five years) were represented and sold as prints, and regularly used to decorate the walls of restaurants and inns.[56]

Book illustrations were usually decisive in providing the reader with a firmly fixed image of the characters in the text. In so doing the illustrator added his voice to that of the author in conditioning the reader. Some images were so successful that they shaped all further representation of the characters. Thus the first edition of Robinson Crusoe contained a representation of the hero which remained almost unchanged in all subsequent iconography, down to the head-cover made with twigs and grass.[57] Almost all nineteenth-century novels had at least one illustration representing the main character.

A far more extensive visual culture was coming into being. In combination with aural culture, listening and seeing, particularly 'seeing while listening' (opera, theatre, cinema, television, music videos), it would eventually overwhelm printed culture. Private reading was never the dominant form of leisure, though until the end of the nineteenth century it was probably the dominant form of marketable culture. As a leisure activity, however, the consumption of newspapers and books remained a minority pursuit. Reading had always had powerful competitors: theatres, shows, concerts, choral societies, gardening, clubs and associations, craft and sewing.[58]

13

The Music Market

Music Recorded

TODAY, MUSIC IS OFTEN REGARDED as the indispensable accompaniment to restaurant meals and to drinking in public places. 'It creates an atmosphere,' say those who enjoy or provide it. It also creates one at funerals, military parades, rallies, religious ceremonies and coronations – all events at which music is also burdened with the task of evoking feelings of community and solidarity. Music is proffered when we are put 'on hold' by telephone receptionists or answering systems, in lifts, in taxis, waiting for a plane to take off, and just sitting in a public lounge. Such 'free' delights were unavailable at the beginning of the nineteenth century. It was a world without recorded or broadcast sound, full of silence and natural noise. If one wanted to hear music, one had to play it in one's own home, or go somewhere, usually a church. Some singing was done while working and some while drinking in taverns. Much secular music was developed for social occasions such as dancing (sarabande, gavotte, polonaise, etc.). The better-off would go to the opera or to a concert. The rich paid people to make music in their homes. Itinerant singers and musicians performed in fairs and marketplaces. In the Middle Ages the more refined homes and mansions were visited by poet-composers – *Minnesänger* (singers of love songs) in Germany and troubadours in France. Many poets were aristocrats themselves – the separation between producers and consumers was not as clear-cut as it is now. There were also merchants of 'popular' songs – in effect, peddlers of texts. They would sing their song, accompanying themselves with a fiddle while pointing to pictures painted on a scrolling canvas. Later booklets with the texts of the songs would be sold to the audience.[1]

One thing is clear: text-based music has always been far more popular than purely instrumental music. The mood and feelings generated by music are enhanced once text provides meaning to the sound. Various textual inclusions in music, not only texts set to music, but the notes to the score, help the interpreter to provide a meaning which makes the music easier to appreciate.[2] By giving a title to instrumental music it is possible to condition listeners to conjure up a meaning for it. One may be told that the music speaks for itself, but it is one thing to listen to Beethoven's piano sonata no. 14 in C sharp minor, op. 27 no. 2, and another to listen to Beethoven's 'Moonlight' sonata (the same work), with its suggestion of quivering lunar rays on a glittering lake. If one listens to concertos called 'The Four Seasons' by Vivaldi it is difficult to resist imagining an appropriate landscape with particular weather conditions as the music unfolds. Composers understood this, hence the proliferation of titles, though some were added much later, when the composer was dead, as was the case with the 'Moonlight' sonata. Haydn called his sixth, seventh and eighth symphonies 'Le Matin', 'Le Midi' and 'Le Soir', but it was the audience that called his 83rd 'La Poule' (The Hen), probably because of the oboe sounds in the first movement.[3]

Until the eighteenth century music consumption usually occurred outside the market. Music was not 'sold', and it could not be easily 'bought'. The place where most music was performed and heard was in church. Though church music generated a market in hymn books and music sheets, it was 'free' music. The music performed in aristocratic homes was largely based on a private transaction between patron and composer, as in a craft economy: from the producer directly to the consumer. The more humble kind of music had an equally limited market: a few travellers singing on market days, others in a pub or on a festival day, travelling troupes performing songs and texts. To the extent that it was a market, it was one dominated by performers (as it is now), for composers were either unknown or were themselves the performers. That kind of music had no fixed texts, scores or notations, and was subject to endless variations and improvisations around a theme – as is still the case with much non-Western music.

To become commercial, music had to be emancipated from the Church and from aristocratic patronage. What was required was a new class rich enough to finance the commercial development of appropriate venues (opera houses and concert halls) and purchase musical instruments for the home, and willing to ensure that they or their offspring would possess the necessary skills to be able to perform at home. This class should also have the 'right' mentality: the desire to follow in the footsteps of the aristocracy by developing a taste for a particular music.

The commercialisation of music led to the great nineteenth-century musical tradition, but as is often the case, to what the older aristocratic courtiers regarded as a deterioration in standards. Thus in Vienna, the death of Emperor Joseph II (1790), a major patron of the opera, and the accession of Leopold II coincided with a vogue for Neapolitan comic operas which debunked social pretensions. The main beneficiary was Domenico Cimarosa, particularly his *Il Matrimonio segreto* (the libretto was based on George Colman's play), which was performed fifty-five times between 1792 and 1800, while none of Mozart's da Ponte operas was performed in Vienna between 1792 and 1797.[4] Resident composers were frustrated by the systematic importation of Neapolitan *opera buffa* – 'Farces from Tyrol,' sneered Madame de Staël (writing in 1810), adding, however, that these entertained the aristocrats as much as the people.[5]

The right class with the right attitude was not enough to create a commercial musical market. A market economy was required, and with it incentives for innovations and adaptations which favoured, for instance, the diffusion and production of certain musical instruments, the commercialisation of performance, the production of music sheets, contractual agreements between performers and impresarios, and so on. The commercialisation of music in the West was further facilitated by the homogeneity of its musical tradition. All Western music, by the seventeenth century – whether secular of religious – was organised around a focal point, that is a given note, hence 'tonal music' and the harmonic system.

The Western musical tradition is recent. We have no idea what Greek and Roman music sounded like. We are not even sure how notes were sung in the fifteenth century, or how fast or at what pitch. We assume, but are not certain, that early unaccompanied Christian chants were related to those of Jewish synagogues. What we do know is that for most of the Middle Ages, almost ten centuries, Western music – like much Western art and architecture – was overwhelmingly Christian. Its evolution was slow. By the tenth century, unaccompanied chants were made more complex by introducing more voice parts, a development known as polyphony. We also know very little of what secular music sounded like before the fifteenth century, except for the courtly songs of the *Minnesänger* and the troubadours of the thirteenth century and their fourteenth-century successors, the authors of French *chansons*, Italian *lai*, ballads and madrigals.

The invention of notation added to the homogeneity of Western music. It enabled it to be recorded far more precisely than non-European music. Notation is a way of representing sounds on paper to enable skilled performers to deduce from them the kind of sounds they are expected to produce. Without notation, the only way to learn a piece of music is directly from another musician. Inventing notation was like inventing writing. Music without notation was like a purely oral literature.

Written notation of music as a mnemonic aid – in the sense of some signs indicating pitch – had appeared in various cultures where there was already a well-established form of writing: China, Korea, India and Japan. Writing signs could mean simply noting when music rises and falls. In the East this is all that notation provided for. With no detailed record of how music is to be performed, there is, strictly speaking, no concept of the 'real' or first composer. This reinforced the supremacy of musicians, who are judged on their performance – as is the case with jazz.

The Western way was quite different. The construction of a relatively complex system of notation was initiated by Guido d'Arezzo in the eleventh century. By the fourteenth century the five-line staff had become accepted. Further developments and innovations were introduced throughout Europe. An international repertory was gradually formed. As music notation became widespread, roughly coincidentally with the invention of printing, it developed to sophisticated heights, enabling a composer to write very complex music for a very large number of different instruments. Without notation as it had developed in the seventeenth century, it is unlikely that there could have been anything resembling the modern symphonic orchestra, or the works of Beethoven and Wagner.[6]

The notation of music opened new possibilities for the commercialisation of music, since notation, being a form of record, permits duplication. This made it possible, in the long run, for courtly music to be adapted so as to obtain a wider popular appeal, unlike Indian classical music (in so far as one can generalise about 'Indian' music), whether Hindustani (in northern India) or Carnatic (in the south). These remained the preserve of master performers, who were more 'refined' and 'élitist' than their Western counterparts, since they performed exclusively before the aristocracy or at rare music festivals.[7] Only towards the end of the nineteenth century did the patronage of Indian music begin to shift from the aristocracy and the temples towards the new upper-middle classes.

Until the arrival of a sophisticated system of notation, all Western music

– like all other music – was ephemeral. We can read the philosophical and poetic texts of the ancient Greeks, see reconstructions of their plays, and admire their architecture and sculptures. But we do not know what music they played – though music archaeologists have been able to reconstruct some notation from fragments which have reached us from the third century, 'ostensibly preserving music from Euripides' *Orestes* and *Iphigenia in Aulis*'.[8]

The absence of a classical tradition commensurate to that of written culture meant that, at least until the eighteenth century, music was regarded as a low cultural form. It was a 'learned' culture, in the sense that training was required, but it was devoid of a corpus of classical work. There was no musical equivalent of Homer or Virgil. Most of the music one heard in the seventeenth and eighteenth centuries was either anonymous (ballads, folk songs) or by living composers who could not have the canonical aura that is acquired through the passage of time.[9] The best musicians and composers were regarded as excellent craftsmen, not great artists. Philosophers and thinkers had Plato and Aristotle as antecedents. Writers had Homer and Virgil. Visual artists had ancient sculptures and the paintings of the Renaissance. But the Western musical canon could be made to stretch back, at most, to the twelfth century and the German nun Hildegard of Bingen (1098–1179), and then to include the French Guillaume de Machaut (c.1300–77), the Flemish Orlando di Lasso (1532–94) and the English William Byrd (c.1543–1623) – names hardly familiar outside musicological circles. It is only since Giovanni Palestrina (1525–94) and Claudio Monteverdi (1567–1643) that a canon of classical music has developed – Italian supremacy being enshrined in its terminology (tempo, andante, allegro, etc.) The actual repertory, as performed in the main concert halls of Europe and North America, is dominated by work written between c.1700 (Vivaldi and Bach) and 1911 (Mahler's death).

The low ranking of music was reinforced by the lowly social origins of the musicians themselves. Not only did they almost never come from the ranks of the aristocracy, but unlike writers they seldom originated from the learned classes – the lawyers, scholars and clergymen. The majority of court orchestral musicians were often the sons or relatives of court retainers.[10] In eighteenth-century Russia many wealthy nobles had established their own domestic orchestra and choir on their estates, and many of the leading performers were serfs trained by west European teachers.[11]

Music-playing and music-making was, like acting, a family occupation, not a move towards a higher social position. Johann Sebastian Bach was born into a family that over seven generations produced dozens of important musicians, including several of his sons. He received his musical instruction from his father and then from his elder brother, the organist Johann Christoph Bach. His second wife, Anna Magdalena Wilcken, the daughter of a court musician, was herself a singer and eventually his copyist (as well as bearing him thirteen children, and raising the seven he had from his first wife).

Unlike literacy, the ability to write music was never regarded as among the skills of educated people, nor as one to be taught to all in primary or secondary education. In much of the West, music has usually been left to the private initiative of parents or of the children themselves, as was reading before the expansion of state-sponsored education. In Italy, the land of the *bel canto*, until the 1960s it was impossible to enter any faculty of any university without having been taught Latin in secondary school; for the humanities ancient Greek was regarded as necessary; yet even the barest rudiments of musical culture were dispensed with. Playing an instrument was regarded as part of the education of refined young women, but not of their male counterparts, another sign that music was held in lower esteem than other arts. In Victorian Britain writing ballads turned out to be a financially rewarding niche for female composers, but otherwise few women were in the music business other than as singers. Amateur musicians were women, the professionals were men. The divide is significant, similar to that still extant in cooking, a field where prestigious chefs are almost all men while everyday, unpaid family cooking remains solidly in the hands of women.

Because they regarded themselves as craftsmen, composers and musicians behaved liked any other craft guild by protecting their employment, and seeking to control entry into the profession. In France in the late seventeenth and early eighteenth centuries, musicians sought to exclude Italian composers and performers, who were popular throughout Europe – an early example of cultural nationalism and quotas, whose inevitable result was to make a knowledge of Italian music the mark of the real connoisseur in France.[12] At German courts there were often foreign singers, particularly Italians, but orchestra personnel were usually German.[13]

In the eighteenth century the professionalism of the author was still in its infancy. Proper copyright legislation was rudimentary. A Queen Anne statute of 1710 limited copyright to a fourteen-year term, renewable once for another fourteen years. Enforcement was always problematic. In the performing arts the author was not regarded as the owner of his work. The attitude towards the integrity of the work closely resembled that of present-day Hollywood towards the adaptation of literary works. Librettos were tampered with, cut, edited and altered. Thus in France in 1801, as the Paris Opéra was not allowed to present an opera set to a foreign librettist's text, Mozart's *The Magic Flute* was transformed with drastic changes to the plot, the elimination of some characters, the addition or renaming of others, the insertion of music from other Mozart operas (*Don Giovanni*, *The Marriage of Figaro* and *La Clemenza di Tito*), and even snatches from some of Haydn's symphonies. Berlioz was outraged:

> Then, when this horrid mixture was manufactured, it was given the title of *Les Mystères d'Isis* . . . It was then published in this state . . . and the man who had arranged it, engraved, next to the name of Mozart, his own name, the name of a cretin, the name of a desecrator, his name of Lachnicht.[14]

This 'horrid mixture' was very popular, and became one of the most frequently performed operas between 1799 and 1809.[15] Paris had to wait until 1863 to enjoy the original version.

There were specialist adapters, like François Castil-Blaze, one of Berlioz's numerous *bêtes noires*, who turned Carl Maria von Weber's *Der Freischütz* (1821) into *Robin des Bois*. Much the same was happening in the 1810s and 1820s in London, where the new musical director of Covent Garden, the composer Henry Bishop, did not hesitate to insert some of his own music into Mozart's *The Marriage of Figaro* and Rossini's *La Cenerentola*. Bishop, the first musician ever to be knighted, proceeded to introduce his own songs into dozens of operas – now, however, he is remembered, if at all, as the author of the tune of 'Home, Sweet Home'.

It was not unusual for particularly renowned singers to sing their favourite arias, regardless of the actual work they were supposed to be performing. These singers were quite conscious that, to all intent and purposes, they were the most important element of the show – in so far as anyone actually paid attention to it. The predominance of actors and particularly of singers, in determining the character of the performance made them, *de facto*, the authors of the work. This is a practice that has continued to dominate performance arts, particularly in the cinema, where actors are often regarded as the main box-office pull.

In the eighteenth century, composers earned their living not by composing, but by performing or teaching music to the children of the aristocracy. They wrote music for specific occasions, as if it were ephemeral. Bach, for instance, during his time as choirmaster of St Thomas's church in Leipzig from 1723 to his death in 1750, wrote 295 cantatas to be performed on Sundays. Of these 202 have survived, and many are still performed today. But his contemporaries revered him mainly as a great organist, while regarding his compositions as just old-fashioned contrapuntal music – the kind of routine compositions one would write for a church choir. Bach's *Well-Tempered Clavier* and *The Art of Fugue* – now regarded as monuments of Western music – were originally composed to teach keyboard technique and musicianship to his relatives and pupils. As it turned out, they provided the foundation of music education for two centuries, and have been played on the harpsichord, the organ, the clavichord, the piano, and by a string quartet, a full orchestra, a jazz band and the Swingle Singers.[16] Had notation not been invented, Bach's music might have disappeared forever, because he began to be highly regarded only in the middle of the nineteenth century.

The musicians themselves 'sold' directly to the consumers, such as the courts, the patrons or the churches, or audiences gathered during festivals and markets. There was little money in composing. One did not get extra money if one's composition was played over and over again. Gluck could afford not to care about the fate of his music, precisely because he received a good salary as a court composer.[17] Mozart, to earn a living, had to perform his music to subscribers, or teach, or find a patron to whom he would dedicate his music. He would not have made more money if others performed his music, so he had no pecuniary interest in providing anyone with his compositions, and hence no interest in publishing them. Composers were reluctant to part from their work, and in any case many of them were employed by patrons, and permission from these had to be obtained.

Haydn, the choirmaster with the aristocratic Hungarian Esterházy family, was not expected to publish his music without the Prince's permission. After 1779 he was given the freedom to sell his compositions to music publishers, as long as he remained in the Prince's employment. Haydn developed his entrepreneurial skills selling his work in various countries, though sometimes this led to legal complications, since his Austrian publishers assumed they could sell abroad as well. This made Haydn known well beyond the circle of the Esterházy family and their guests. Until then he had been an important servant, an 'officer of the household', the third highest paid, but nevertheless an employee of the four Esterházy princes he served. The new 1779 contract he entered into with his most musically aware patron, Prince Miklós Esterházy, made it clear what he was supposed to do: 'to produce at any time and in any place and for any occasion, following the good wishes of His Highness any music commanded by His Highness'. This implied, literally, that he was responsible for any musical activity: composing symphonies, operas, masses, dance and chamber music for entertainment, conducting his small orchestra in performing his own works as well as that of other composers, and supervising the upkeep of the instruments and the music library.[18]

Notation

It was only when concert orchestras started performing the music of composers who were not present, or who were dead, that the musical score became important. Until then it was useful for amateur practitioners who performed for their own pleasure and that of their relatives and friends. Thus there were two sharply distinct markets for music: one for live performance and one for music sheets. When composers composed for others (as was the case in operas and choral music), they usually had particular performers in mind. Bach indicated in his arias all the graces and trills and other ornamental details with great precision, because he was composing his music for a church with a small choir. In London, Handel had singers of international reputation who did not require, and would have resented, such elaborate descriptions.[19] Composers did not write, as they would now, for performers in general. Their work was determined by the skills of particular performers, the instruments at their disposal, and the conditions in which the music would be consumed.

Like the invention of writing, with which it is obviously associated, the invention of notation 'fixed' the text. Notation enabled the separation of the composer from the performer. The musical score was a code whereby the composer provided all subsequent performers with precise instructions: what notes to play, whether to keep the finger on the piano key or the violin string before moving on to the next (*legato*) or to remove it immediately (*staccato*) and so on.[20] In the final analysis, however, even notated music, like a play in the theatre, was in the hands of performers. The 'text', i.e. the score, could not provide sufficiently detailed explanation of how a particular piece of music should be played. In literature (as in painting), though the author has no control over how the work is received, once the 'text' is finished, it goes, relatively unchanged, to the consumer. This is not so with performance. In theory a theatrical performer might require only the bare outline of a plot, as in the Indonesian shadow plays analysed by Clifford Geerz, where *dalang* (the puppeteer) makes up much of the performance as he goes along.[21] The text of a play or a musical score inevitably concedes some latitude to the performers. Playwrights can encode emotions or emphasis in the text, but cannot dictate intensity, pitch of voice, or gestures.

With music, the composer has even less power. The score can establish fairly accurately how each note stands relative to the others, but it cannot establish the dynamics, the timbre, the *vibrato*, the *rubato*.[22] The tempo of the music is vaguely, if at all, indicated in words: *allegro*, *andante*; and the volume with *piano*, *forte*, *fortissimo*, etc. Notation preserves only limited aspects of the music.

Thus, even with notation, there is some element of improvisation in all music performances. In what is today called 'early music' this was considerable, with players dressing up their parts with ornaments. Gradually composers established greater authority for the score, and were more able – in theory at least – to constrain the singers and the musicians.

Music Publishing

Printing scores – as opposed to copying them – began to take off only in the eighteenth century. The business spread from London (1700) to Paris (1740) and Amsterdam. By the end of the eighteenth century Vienna became a major centre of music publishing, though France remained a net exporter of both musical instruments and music sheets for much of the nineteenth century.[23] This was a highly specialised market, dominated by a few family firms (often managed by women who had inherited the business from their husbands) relying on the authorisation (the 'privilege') granted by rulers. Thus the Ballard family, one of the most important Paris music publishers, enjoyed a virtual monopoly from the sixteenth century, when it was granted the original concession of the privilege, which lapsed only in 1766.[24] The composer Anton Diabelli was one of the new generation of entrepreneurial music publishers in Austria. He set up a company in 1817, which he used at first to publish his own works as well as popular songs and dance music. By 1821 he started publishing Schubert's music. In 1823 he composed a waltz theme and asked fifty composers to write variations, intending to publish the results – a marketing ruse which led to Beethoven's famous *Diabelli Variations*.

By the early nineteenth century the German-speaking world dominated European music publishing, the result of the excellence and popularity of German music production, which had supplanted the Italians in all forms except opera. The centre of this hegemony was Leipzig, also the centre of the German book trade. It was there that moveable type (*Notentypendruck*) replaced the more expensive copper plate method of printing music. Music publishing involved 'serious' music as well as 'trivial' music. *Trivialmusik* consisted of salon orchestrations, arrangements of opera favourites, sentimental songs, children's songs and music sheets for learning how to play. Visitors to Germany, such as Madame de Staël, were struck by the high level of musical culture. She claimed that, while visiting 'a very poor home' she was welcomed by the master and mistress of the house improvising music on the harpsichord.[25]

It is at this time that we can begin to use the expression 'the music industry.' The expansion of private consumption of music favoured music-sheet publishers, often booksellers or engravers, as well as instrument manufacturers.[26] Still, in the second half of the eighteenth century the cost of printed music remained very high – the home visited by Madame de Staël could not have been as poor as she thought. In the eighteenth century music-sheet printing was (and still is) more complex and expensive than printing a text. The engraving was a labour-intensive process, difficult to mechanise. While the printer does not need to know about literature, or even to understand his text, the engraver must know about music. Composers sold printed music one sheet at a time. During the 1770s and 1780s most publishers' catalogues had between one hundred and 1,500 items. Large ones, like Boosey of London, had 10,000 *foreign* publications in 1824, while Whistler & Hoffmeister (of Leipzig) had 44,000 items.[27] Franz Anton Hoffmeister was a composer/conductor who had become a church music master in Vienna in the 1780s. He opened a music shop, and then a music publishing house, then two more shops, all the while composing eight operas, 156 quartets, thirty concertos – and finding time to teach.[28] We can only surmise that his teaching duties were not too onerous. In October 1799 he played some of his works in Leipzig, where he met Ambrosius Kühnel, a book and art dealer as well as an organist. They joined forces to found Hoffmeister & Kühnel Bureau de Musique, which became a major music publishing house. They republished some of Bach's works, paying a monthly allowance to one of his daughters who was living in reduced circumstances, and complete editions of Haydn's string quartets. They contacted Beethoven, who wrote back (on 15 January

1801) offering his just-composed septet for twenty ducats. In the same letter he detailed his pricing policy: twenty ducats for a symphony (op. 21 no. 1), ten ducats for his piano concerto in B flat (no. 2), and twenty for a piano sonata he described as 'first rate' (the sonata in B, no. 11). The reason why the sonata cost as much as the septet and the symphony was quite simple: 'I find that a septet or a symphony does not sell as well as a sonata'. The piano concerto he was prepared to sell for only ten ducats because 'I do not consider it to be one of my best'.[29] Hoffmeister bought the lot.

The relationship between Beethoven and the firm (which became C.F. Peters, Leipzig, Bureau de Musique in 1814 when the book dealer Carl Friedrich Peters bought it), interrupted in 1801, was revived in 1822, but the unreliability of Beethoven, and Peters's depression, put paid to it once again. Peters would complain to Beethoven that he had been sent only one March instead of the agreed four, and that the missing three had been substituted by three *Zapfenstreiche* (Tattoos), adding tartly, '*Zapfenstreiche* are perhaps popular in Vienna, I, however, cannot use them.'[30]

Beethoven's fame, as we know, survived his temper and his unreliability. But Peters prospered too, and became the most prestigious music publishing house in Germany, particularly after 1831 when it was bought by Max Abraham. The development of such firms was closely connected to new technological improvements following the introduction of lithography in the printing of music at the end of the eighteenth century. Printing music, however, remained difficult: until relatively recently there was no adequate typewriter able to 'write' music.[31] Even the music examples in the 1980 *New Grove Dictionary* were still based on a graphic lithographic process.

Such was the domination of German music publishing that Italians, hitherto hegemonic in music composition and in the manufacturing of string instruments, learned the new business at the feet of the Germans. Thus Giovanni Ricordi (1785–1853) first studied the skill of printing music in Leipzig as an apprentice with the publisher Breitkopf & Härtel – one of the first to publish, at the beginning of the nineteenth century, the collected works of masters such as Haydn and Mozart. By the end of the century much of the firm's catalogue was devoted to the great classical masters. At the end of his apprenticeship, in 1808, Ricordi returned to Milan, where he had previously been a music copyist and a prompter at La Scala. In a relatively short period of time he founded what became the largest music publisher in Italy, publishers of Gioacchino Rossini and, later, of Paganini, Bellini, Donizetti, Verdi and Puccini.

Musical Instruments

Notation enabled anyone with moderate skills to perform musical compositions they had never heard before. And they could do so in their own homes or surrounded by a public of their peers, their friends and relatives. Such non-market consumption of music generated a kind of industry: the manufacture of musical instruments and the production of music sheets and hymn books. The twelve shops which sold music sheets in London in 1750 had expanded to 124 in 1824.[32]

By the first decades of the nineteenth century, fuelled by the economic boom after the end of the Napoleonic wars, the piano was replacing the dining table as the most expensive item of furniture in middle-class homes.[33] The piano was *the* modern instrument. It had been invented around 1709 by Bartolomeo Cristofori of Padua. Unlike its predecessor the harpsichord, it had a hammer-and-lever action whereby the player could make the sound louder (*forte*) or softer (*piano*) – hence 'fortepiano'. Though the Italians soon lost interest in the piano, the instrument was constantly improved over the next century, mainly by German and Austrian craftsmen such as Johann Christoph Zumpe, who invented the so-called 'square' piano in 1760.

Wars and political turmoil forced many German craftsmen to find refuge in England, where there was both a market for their products and a favourable commercial environment. Thus Sebastian Érard, born in Strasbourg in 1752, left Paris after the Revolution and opened a factory in Great Marlborough Street in London in 1792 manufacturing square pianos.[34] By 1821 he had patented the double escapement action, one of the many technological innovations of the period.[35] The Érard piano gained ground on the Continent: at one time or another virtuosi and composers such as Johann Hummel, Sigismond Thalberg, Ignaz Moscheles, Verdi and Mendelssohn possessed one.[36] London was then (as now) a major centre of musical life. Sophisticated and wealthy élites patronised concerts and musicians. Music entrepreneurs surfaced earlier than elsewhere, using advertising. As a result London's musical life was more vibrant that that of Vienna or Paris, in spite of the lack of outstanding home-grown music. England was, as the Germans had it, *das Land ohne Musik* (the land without music), but great commercial nations import what they don't produce themselves. As a result England attracted the most famous performers and composers of Europe, and was also the home of Broadwood, the most important piano manufacturer of the nineteenth century until it was supplanted by the German-American Steinway.

By the end of the century, though it had not produced great composers, Britain – as an Italian government official visiting the country in 1897 reported – was one of the few countries in the world 'where music is made the object of such enthusiastic worship'.[37]

By the end of the eighteenth century the market for musical instruments had expanded substantially. Given its size and cost, once acquired, the piano inevitably became the focus of domestic musical life. Soon printed collections of songs began to appear with titles such as *Songs for the Family Circle*, *Little Songs for Little Girls*, *Melodious Songs for the Fair Sex* and *Lullabies for German Wet Nurses*.[38] Having bought the piano, one could buy a manual such as the influential *The Right Way to Play the Pianoforte* (1797) by Johann Peter Milchmayer, court musician to the Elector of Bavaria.[39]

In the new era of 'sensibility' heralded by lachrymose novels such as Richardson's *Clarissa*, Goethe's *Werther* and Rousseau's *Nouvelle Héloïse*, the piano was particularly suited to produce similar musical effects. A *vibrato* effect could be easily achieved by rocking the finger without releasing the key, producing a pulsating prolongation of the tone, thus imitating, in the music historian Arthur Loesser's words, 'the throbbing heart, the panting breast, the trembling lip, the quivering voice'.[40] The piano, like its forerunners the harpsichord and the clavichord, allowed a young woman to maintain a demure position, her feet held together, her face arranged in a polite smile of concentration. The flute, a man's instrument, would have compelled her to puff her cheeks, altering her looks in a ridiculous manner. The demonic violin would have forced her into most unbecoming jerking movements. In Thomas Mann's *Buddenbrooks* (1901), the opening chapters of which are set before the middle of the nineteenth century, Gerda Arnolden is regarded as strange because she opts for the violin over the piano. Playing the cello was unthinkable, since it would force her into an unmistakably obscene posture – her body would have been compelled to embrace the instrument with her legs widely parted.[41] There were, however, always exceptions, especially in less inhibited circles: one of Casanova's lovers, Henriette, learned to play the cello, but it had required a bishop's intervention to convince the Mother Superior of her boarding school to let her play it.[42] Louis XV's daughter, also a Henriette, was portrayed playing a viola da gamba held between her parted legs in 1752.[43]

Views on the suitability or otherwise of certain instruments for women had a long history. Baldissare Castiglione, in *The Courtier* (1528), wrote that when a woman was dancing 'I should not wish to see her use movements that are too forceful or energetic, nor, when she is singing or playing a musical instrument, to use those abrupt and frequent *diminuendos* that are ingenious but not beautiful. And I suggest she should choose instruments suited to her purpose. Imagine what an ungainly sight it would be to have a woman playing drums, fifes, trumpets or other instruments of that sort.'[44] One cannot imagine Schiller writing the poem '*Laura am Clavier*' (Laura at the Piano, 1781) had Laura been a trumpet player:

> When the strings thy fingers sweep,
> Laura, all my spirits fail,
> Marble-cold my forces sleep,
> Life and Death before thee quail.[45]

The piano is easy to learn – it is perfectly possible to strike a recognisable tune after less than one hour's tuition; not so with the violin. It is also very conspicuous. It was immediately noticed by visitors, signalling that the household was refined and genteel. Along with the violin, the piano or harpsichord was at the centre of the eighteenth-century orchestra. With the growth of secular music the organ lost its dominant role in musical life, although it remained central to Christian liturgy. After Bach no major organ composer emerged until Olivier Messiaen (1908–92), and his organ masterpiece *Quatuor pour la fin du temps* (Quartet for the End of Time, 1941).

The remarkable versatility of the piano meant that it could be used both in the privacy of the home, played by a solitary performer or as an accompaniment to singing, or in a full-sized orchestra. It could also be used, even on its own, to play dance music. In aristocratic and, in the nineteenth century, bourgeois homes, there was often an after-dinner performance in the presence of guests, when young women could show off their skills before prospective husbands, and, occasionally, a little dance – an image made familiar by many novels of the period, such as Jane Austen's *Emma*. A good piano, however, was an extremely expensive item. In Vienna in 1773 a piano cost between three and seven hundred florins, at a time when a court councillor, a senior position, would earn 4,000 florins a year.[46] In 1840 it would have taken a working man some 1,200 working days to buy a Pleyel grand piano – rather like buying a brand-new Porsche today.[47] Transportation was also a major cost. When the British firm of Broadwood sent Beethoven (by then virtually deaf) a grand piano in 1817, it had to be shipped from London to Trieste via Gibraltar, then transported by horse-drawn carriage over rough mountain roads, uphill and downhill for 360 miles across the Alps until it reached Beethoven in Vienna.[48]

The great piano manufacturers of the time amassed considerable fortunes. When John Broadwood died in 1812 at the age of eighty, he left an estate of £100,000 and one of the largest piano-making businesses in the world. The origin of the house of Broadwood is itself an interesting example of the international nature of the business and of the fruitful effects of migration. In 1718 a sixteen-year-old apprentice, Burkat Shudi, left Switzerland for London, where he found employment at the harpsichord workshop of Hermann Tabel in Soho. Tabel, in turn, had learned his craft in Antwerp, at the Ruckers workshop, one of the most famous harpsichord-makers of the seventeenth century. In 1728 Shudi started his own workshop and established himself as one of the great harpsichord-makers of the country. Having succeeded in obtaining the custom of Handel (himself an 'immigrant' from Germany), he then obtained that of various members of the royal family, including the King (another German 'immigrant'). In 1861 the cabinet-maker John Broadwood came to London from his native village of Oldhamstocks, in the Lothian hills of Scotland. He started working in Shudi's workshop, and in 1769 married the boss's daughter, Barbara. At Shudi's death in 1773 he inherited the firm (in partnership with Shudi's son), becoming the effective head of Shudi & Broadwood (it became John Broadwood & Sons in 1808). He joined forces with another Scot, Robert Stodart, and a Dutchman, Americus Backers, and designed a piano to fit in a harpsichord case – the origin of the 'grand' (1777). He continued to develop the piano, and built up the business by hiring the best foreign craftsmen and by being in constant touch with all innovations.

By 1800 Broadwood was manufacturing almost five hundred pianos a year, reaching a peak of one thousand square pianos and four hundred grand pianos in the 1820s. Business acumen played a part, but the times were favourable – and not just for the British. In Augsburg (Bavaria), Johann Andreas Stein left a thriving business when he died in 1792. His daughter Nanette – one of Johann's fifteen children – transformed her father's business. While he had been producing seventeen or eighteen pianos a year, by 1809 Nanette had manufactured eight hundred, mainly by expanding the business in response to the increase in demand.[49] Ignace Joseph Pleyel, a pupil of Haydn's from Rumperstal in Lower Austria, opened a piano factory in Paris in 1807 that became celebrated for its grand pianos. But he also realised that there was a market in the new, smaller 'cottage pianos' devised by Robert Wornum in 1809. In 1828 Ignaz Bösendorfer set up his own business in Vienna. These names continued to dominate the piano business for over a hundred years, constantly improving the instrument, which eventually consisted of over 5,000 interconnecting parts. The advances tailed off towards the end of the nineteenth century, after which subsequent improvements were largely cosmetic.

Most early-nineteenth-century pianos were 'square' pianos. These were cheaper and more compact than the horizontal or 'grand' piano, and could therefore be fitted more easily into the relatively modest homes of the *nouvelle bourgeoisie*. By the middle of the century, further space-saving was achieved thanks to the upright.

In spite of the growth in demand, the only way a piano manufacturer could expand was to trade internationally. By 1845 Vienna had 108 piano-makers, far too many for Austria alone (for there were other piano centres in the Empire). Already in 1783 Broadwood supplied harpsichords to Josef Haydn in Vienna, and was also exporting to Russia, Denmark, Portugal, Italy, France, the West Indies and America. The role of famous practitioners and of their works contributed to shape the market: Haydn's piano sonatas, then Mozart's and Beethoven's piano concertos, and the great virtuosi who came after them, such as Liszt and Chopin. The stars of the European musical circuit were given pianos by manufacturers so that they could benefit from the association. This was the reason why, in 1817, John Broadwood's son Thomas decided to send Beethoven the grand, triple-stringed piano that had to undertake such a laborious journey to reach Vienna. The composer, already the object of a great cult throughout Europe, was appropriately grateful, and before even receiving the instrument provided the firm with the expected quotable quote in a letter of 7 February 1818: 'My very dear friend Broadwood, I have never felt a greater pleasure at the intimation of the arrival of this piano with which you are honouring me as a present. I shall look upon it as an altar upon which I shall place the most beautiful offerings of my spirit to the divine Apollo. As soon as I receive your excellent instrument, I shall immediately send you the fruits of the first moments of inspiration I spend at it, as a souvenir to you from me.' This letter was widely used in the firm's advertising, and Broadwood still boasts about it on its website.[50]

Singing Texts

The boom of the piano generated an increased demand for related commodities such as sheet music. It was the dawn of the drawing-room song, the literary ballad and an entirely new body of secular songs (roughly and imprecisely defined as a text to be inflected by means of musical notes). Such developments were enhanced by the invention of national consciousness, the Romantics' discovery of folklore, and – around the middle of the nineteenth century – the establishment of specifically children's songs. In fact the English term 'popular songs' was translated by Johann Gottfried Herder as *Nationalgesänge*: 'national songs'. Secular songs were common in medieval times. Those that have survived are usually student songs about women and wine. Later in the century songs were sold mainly as part of a wider entertainment in cabarets, variety shows, café concerts and vaudeville. The words circulated orally, but also through publications such as *La Clé du Caveau* (by the publisher Pierre Capelle), reprinted seven times between 1811 and 1872. This was the result of the creation of the Caveaux in Paris, a drinking club where the guests would sing original texts on well-known tunes.[51]

The French Revolution had brought about a massive musical production, more than 2,500 hymns and songs, usually new words on old tunes, sung by street singers, peddlers, etc.[52] The Revolution also saw the emergence of 'national' songs, often patriotic, which were meant to appeal to a nationwide audience.[53] Pierre Béranger (1780–1857), a prolific author of revolutionary songs, was the best-known practitioner of this new kind of sung poetry, which evolved into a distinctive French genre, as did the venues where they were performed: the cabarets. The aura of subversiveness of such urban songs was enhanced by the requirement, in 1844, that all members of the audience provide the sergeant at the entrance of the cabaret with their names and addresses. Béranger's own *Chansons inédites* (1828) led to a trial for anti-monarchism, the inevitable rallying around him of much of the French intelligentsia (Hugo, Dumas, Vigny, etc.), and his equally inevitable international fame. He was praised by Goethe, the Hungarian national poet Petöfi, Heinrich Heine, Karl Marx, Garibaldi and Pushkin.[54]

There had been satirical songs and ditties before (particularly in the eighteenth century), but a strong connection between politics and songs really came about in the nineteenth century, when democratic politics begins to appear. This development is symbolised by the invention of national anthems, beginning with 'La Marseillaise', written in 1792 by Rouget de Lisle and adopted by France in 1795. At first national anthems were essentially a 'republican' innovation, and hence adopted in Latin American countries, such as Argentina as early as 1813. They then became fashionable all over Europe: Finland's 'Maamme' (Our Land) was adopted in 1848, Denmark's

'Der er et Yndigt Land' (There is a Lovely Land) in 1844, Hungary's 'Himnusz' in 1844. 'God Save the King' (1745) was used as national anthem in the early nineteenth century. The Greek 'Imnos eis tin Eleftherian' (Hymn to Freedom) was adopted in 1864, Japan's 'Kimigayo' in 1893, Norway's 'Ja, Vi Elsker Dette Landet' (Yes, We Love this Land) in 1864. 'The Star-Spangled Banner', composed in the early nineteenth century, was adopted in 1931.

Another musical genre born around the time of the French Revolution was a new kind of funeral music, such as the *Marche lugubre* by François-Joseph Gossec (1734–1829, and author in 1760 of a famous *Messe des morts*), used in all funerals of the Revolution and re-emerging fifteen years later in Beethoven's piano sonata opus 26 – it remains the conventional view of what funeral music is. Yet another is the 'civic hymn', performed by a powerful choir for patriotic purposes. Throughout the nineteenth century the musical expression of patriotic ardour would be expressed by the choir, previously the prerogative of church worship. The state encouraged other 'patriotic songs' and their use in schools as a useful way of instilling an *esprit de corps* among the pupils. The emergent working-class movement followed suit. Both borrowed, in this as in much else, the idea from religion, which had established the connection between singing and praising God since the dawn of time.

Singing in schools and churches, and standing to attention for the anthem hardly constitute a market. Songs entered the commercial world gradually and with difficulty. Even the more refined songs, poetry set to music (*lieder*, *chansons*, etc.) or folk songs arranged with a proper accompaniment, were long excluded from the fee-paying concert circuit. Schubert's *lieder* were really written for his friends, like most of his chamber music. There were, of course, songs performed in cafés and pubs. Here payment was either directly from the customers to the performer – as at a fair when a hat is passed round – or indirectly: the provider of drinks and food would pay the performer, whose job it was to attract customers to drink and eat.

The 'hunt' for folk tales, accelerated by the Romantic revolution, also brought about a hunt for folk songs. These were adapted to the prevailing Western musical styles so as to make them acceptable to middle- and upper-class audiences. Most major composers (such as Beethoven and Haydn) arranged folk songs and children's songs – Mozart arranged 'Twinkle Twinkle, Little Star'. In Russia the first *Collection of Russian Folk Songs*, put together by Nikolai Lvov and Ivan Prach in 1790, became the main source for 'authentic' folk tunes for the nineteenth century, and was regularly used by Russian composers or by Western composers in need of Russian colour.[55]

In the early nineteenth century the differentiation in genres was in its infancy. A popular tune would be adapted to a changing text and would move across genres, as the origins of some well-known French songs 'for children' demonstrate. The song 'Au Clair de la lune (mon ami Pierrot)' originated around 1790 at the Théâtre de la Foire, when an unknown author placed the rhymes of a vaudeville on a well-known tune (once, wrongly, attributed to Jean-Baptiste Lully). In 1820 the song had become popular, but the character Pierrot (Pedrolino) had been known to Parisian theatre-goers since the sixteenth century, when the commedia dell'arte was performed at the Théâtre des Italiens. Then 'Au Clair de la lune' was turned into a song for children, even though the words contained sexual innuendoes:

> Prête-moi ta plume
> Pour écrire un mot.
> Ma chandelle est morte,
> Je n'ai plus de feu.

(Lend me your pen/To write a word./My candle is burnt out/and my fire is cold)

The '*plume*' to be borrowed had a phallic connotation, '*je n'ai plus de feu*' was suggestive of sexual impotence, and there are further innuendoes. If these are not pointed out, the rhymes are harmless enough, and suitable for children. The song was widely taught in French schools from the late 1870s, and is still very popular even outside France, its melodic construction being regarded as particularly useful by those teaching musical skills.[56] Another song which became a 'classic' thanks to the educational system was the seventeenth-century 'Frère Jacques', used in schools from the end of the nineteenth century.[57]

Popular songs could become long-lasting if they found an audience among the upper classes. Thus the French eighteenth-century nursery song 'Malbrough s'en va-t-en guerre'– a possible reference to the Duke of Marlborough's campaigns – was so liked by Marie Antoinette that the whole Court adopted it in 1781. Such consecration suggests the gradual establishment of a national and international repertory originating from old songs which have been transformed over a long period of time. For instance, the first written version of 'Sur le pont d'Avignon' has been traced to 1846, though its origin may be much older. It then became fixed in this version when it was used in schools as part of the curriculum.[58] 'Il était un petit navire' originated in August 1858 in the vaudeville play *Méridien* by Clairville. The words were often used with different tunes, until it became established in the present version in the course of the twentieth century. Popular music at the beginning of the nineteenth century was used purely for common entertainment or to accompany work. There was no copyright, no intellectual property, no defence of the 'integrity' of the song – the concept would have been considered ridiculous. It was not an object of commerce except in the sense that common street singers sang, literally, for their supper. The era of the millionaire superstars of contemporary pop was a long way off.

Dancing Music

Where did one dance? Obviously in the streets and squares on special days, on festivals or at carnivals, or, if one was grand, in manor homes and *châteaux*. Ballrooms, nightclubs and dance halls developed only in the nineteenth century, but their antecedents can be traced to eighteenth-century London – home of the largest bourgeoisie in Europe, and of an aristocracy that was more self-confident and freer than that of France, where it was still closely controlled by the King. The initiative came from a shrewd Italian singer, Teresa Cornelys. Born into a theatrical family, Madame Cornelys was familiar with the entertainment industry provided by her native city, Venice. Trained as a soprano, she travelled extensively in Europe before arriving in Soho in 1759. Only seven months after her arrival she had rented Carlisle House, one of the largest houses in Soho Square. At vast expense she turned it into a semi-private club, charging an appropriately expensive membership fee (to give it a tone of exclusivity) while advertising its events on the front page of the *Public Advertiser* to create interest among potential customers. Teresa Cornelys's friends in high places, such as Elizabeth Chudleigh, mistress of the Duke of Kingston, used their influence to promote Carlisle House, which was in effect a kind of nightclub, frequented by up to a thousand guests at a time. They drank mixed drinks (the word 'cocktail' had not yet been invented) such as champagne and orange-flavoured barley water, dined, listened to a chamber orchestra, talked, danced and gambled.[59]

Most entertainment of this kind, however, remained in the private domain until the nineteenth century. Dancing at home had become a pastime not just among the élites but also among the petty aristocracy and the provincial bourgeoisie. New dances developed to replace not only the sarabande, chaconne and gavotte, which in spite of their popular origins had become highly formalised, but the aristocratic and hierarchical minuet, the mastery of which required formal instruction. This is where the waltz came in. At the end of the eighteenth century it became a favourite in Vienna, though in the provinces it was regarded as a form of lower-class lewdness, because the couples had to touch each other.[60] Waltzing at home became respectable, yet daring. Goethe's young Werther is overwhelmed with happiness and passion while waltzing with Charlotte:

> Never in all my life have I danced so well. I was no longer a mere mortal. Holding the most adorable of creatures in my arms, flying about with her like lightning, so that I forgot everything about me ... I swore that a girl I loved ... should never waltz with anyone but me, not even if it cost me my life.[61]

In Jane Austen's *Emma* Frank Churchill sings several songs with Jane Fairfax (who plays on a 'square' Broadwood piano) at a party at the 'worthy Coles'. But within five minutes of the end of 'the concert part of the evening', the suggestion that the guests should dance is found so exciting that everything is rapidly cleared away to make room. Then 'Frank Churchill, coming up with most becoming gallantry to Emma, had secured her hand, and led her up to the top'.[62] This is a further sign confirming Emma in her false belief that she is the object of Frank's attention.

By 1816 waltz mania was in full swing in London. At the Almack in London as well as in Bath, it became *de rigueur* to know how to waltz. Responding to widespread demand, Thomas Wilson included 'A description of the correct method of waltzing' in his *A Companion to the Ball Room, containing a Choice Collection of the most Original and Admired Country Dance* [...] *and Waltz Tunes* [...] (1816).[63] In Vienna large dance halls were opened, including the Sperl and the Apollosaal (1808), which could accommodate 6,000 dancers. The waltz was given legitimacy by serious composers, from Beethoven, who introduced it in his *Diabelli Variations*, to Carl Maria von Weber, who had used the waltz in his famous piano composition *Aufforderung zum Tanz* (Invitation to the Dance, 1819). Liszt and Chopin further exploited the waltz craze, and dance bands flourished, making the waltz the most important dance of the nineteenth century. The aristocratic minuet, as least as danced at court, reflected a complex social order. One couple at a time performed the steps while everyone else watched them, their turn dictated by a strict hierarchical pattern. By comparison, the waltz was relatively easy to learn, vertiginously free in its practice, yet bound by rules. The waltz was, as Rémi Hess, its leading historian, explained, both romantic and bourgeois, and became the expression of a new social identity underpinning the new social order: the couple.[64] Madame de Genlis, in her *Dictionnaire critique et raisonné des etiquettes de la cour* (1818), warned of its dangers:

> The young lady, lightly clothed, throws herself into the arms of the young man, who clasps her to his breast and who sweeps her off her feet so precipitously that her heart can't help starting to pound, and her head begins to spin! That is what the waltz does! . . . Today's young people are so natural that they care not a fig for refinement, and they dance the waltz with notorious simplicity and passion.[65]

14

Audiences and Performers

The Problem with the Audience

READING QUIETLY, ON ONE'S OWN, is, we have seen, a relatively recent practice. Listening quietly, respectfully, *attentively* to actors, singers or musicians is even more recent. Until the early part of the nineteenth century audiences paid little attention to what was being performed in public. Later they grew more disciplined, and finally the listening angel of silence descended upon concert halls and opera houses, theatres and darkened cinemas.

There are, however, significant and numerous exceptions. Cinema audiences in some parts of the world are not quiet. They make loud comments, interject, whistle. When the actors kiss they manifest approval or objections. Elsewhere they munch popcorn with joyless greed, or suck sweets extracted excruciatingly slowly from noisy plastic wrappers. In restaurants, nightclubs, some jazz venues, the audience may treat the music merely as background to other activities, such as conversation – just as some eighteenth-century opera audiences did. Even at some concerts and plays, the wheezing and coughing from the weaker or more elderly members of the audience encounters its natural counterpart in the distracted turning of programme pages from bored executives who are there only because their company has sponsored the event. More recently, in spite of profuse warnings, ringing mobile telephones compete, infuriatingly, with the performance.

Audience participation is a different matter. Far from signalling a lack of attention, it can signify deep involvement. In some settings, such as jazz clubs, the audience accompanies the music and its rhythm by stamping their feet, moving their bodies and shaking their heads. In pop concerts the audience vies with the performers for the role of protagonist, shouting and screaming in mock hysterics, delighted to share the event with a community of like-minded people. The actual performers are almost disembodied, their tiny figures dwarfed by their images projected on a gigantic screen; the volume of their music vastly amplified by potent loudspeakers. They almost act as if their presence is a symbol of their existence, while their real existence is projected electronically. But even the loudest of pop concert audiences, far from being indifferent to the performance, symbolise by their presence their approbation of music they have become acquainted with from radio and recordings.

The same cannot be said for the more aristocratic audiences in the eighteenth century. Their behaviour reflected the absence of any profound interest in the performance. To have an idea of the degree of attention pre-1800 audiences paid to what they were watching or listening to, we should consider not modern audiences, but the relatively relaxed and distracted way in which people watch television: they speak on the telephone, they go to the toilet whenever they feel like it, they make themselves a drink, they eat, they talk loudly, they 'zap' from channel to channel, and then abruptly switch the set off when they are tired or bored.

Before 1800, in popular theatres and in taverns some attention was paid to the action on the stage, but in the opera houses patronised by the upper classes bedlam reigned. At the Paris Opéra, the system made the subscribers, in fact, tenants of the theatre box, where they could do as they saw fit. Punctuality and silence were not thought to be necessary, or even desirable. In upper-class circles it was regarded as unfashionable to arrive on time. Listening to the music or staying until the end was deemed bourgeois, typical of street merchants. Attentiveness was a social *faux pas*. Conversations would take place in each box and across boxes. People greeted each other loudly, got drunk, sang.[1] The opera house was like a twentieth-century nightclub: people dropped in when it suited them, and would come and go during the performance.[2]

At the French Opéra, then called the Académie de Musique, oil lamps and candles filled the front of the theatre with thick clouds of smoke, though at least they enabled the spectators to identify their acquaintances.[3] English playhouses in the early nineteenth century were full of uneducated, rowdy elements of the lower classes, more attracted by famous actors and special effects than the texts of plays.[4]

At the Opéra (then at the Palais Royal), the most sought-after seats were the six boxes *on* the stage (three on each side). Not because visibility was better – it was worse: these side spectators could barely see the action on stage because they were blinded by the oil lamps. But – and this was the essential thing – everyone could see *them*. Visibility to others was crucial.[5] The audience was the show. One should regard the eighteenth-century opera as a social event, in which the audience was part of the performance, and the opera house as one of the public spaces where the Parisian nobility could gather. Some of this continued well into the nineteenth century, though such behaviour was seen as less and less acceptable. In Balzac's novel *La Peau de chagrin* (1831), the beautiful and heartless Foedora knows *she* is the show, not what is on stage:

> She did not listen to the music. The divine notes of Rossini and Cimarosa did not move her, brought no poetry in her life. Her soul was barren. Foedora offered herself as a spectacle within a spectacle. Her opera glasses travelled incessantly from box to box . . . she was a victim of fashion; her box, her hat, her carriage, her person – this was her world.[6]

Such a narcissistic tendency has not entirely disappeared to this day, as demonstrated by the habit of 'dressing up' for a performance, as if to act as a counterpart to the actors: both actors and audience impersonate someone else – the actors their characters, while the members of the audience play the role of people who go to the theatre.

In the eighteenth century the protagonists were the aristocrats, regarded as the arbiters of taste. The more common spectators were like extras in someone else's show. They looked at the aristocrats in the boxes to gauge whether the show was satisfactory, applauding when the aristocrats applauded. The books of etiquette they had consulted instructed them that it was impolite to express pleasure or disgust before a 'person of quality' had done so.[7] It was forbidden to show approval until the monarch or prince, if present, had started the applause. Otherwise one could express one's critical feelings by shouting 'boo' (in Latin countries) or by hissing (in England), or shouting '*Bravo, bravissima*' and '*Da capo*' ('Again' – the Italian was *de rigueur*) or demanding an '*encore*' (in France and England) or a '*bis*' (in Italy and Spain).

Politics, in the shape of the French Revolution, as well as economics, in the shape of the rise of the entrepreneurial classes, contributed towards encouraging the further rise of the audience to a position of dominance. The Jacobins introduced seats in the *parterre* (today's stalls), boxes alongside the stage were eliminated and the audience became more representative.[8]

The entrenched subscription system was obviously an obstacle to new entrants. In 1788 the least expensive box at the Opéra in Paris cost, annually, three times what a Parisian worker would earn in a year. At the Comédie-Française, two-thirds of the audience was standing, paying for the privilege what was the equivalent of a worker's daily wages.[9] One should avoid the temptation to compare purchasing power across two centuries too schematically, but in this case at least the contrast is not as pronounced as might appear. The most expensive seats in a West End theatre (not the opera or a musical) in London in 2004 were approximately £40 – around eight times the minimum hourly wage – but the cheapest were approximately four times the minimum hourly wage. Top prices for cinema seats were £10.

Modern cinema venues and commercial theatres are not subsidised, while in late-eighteenth-century France none of the state theatres was run on anything remotely resembling commercial criteria – here the situation has not changed. The boxes at the Opéra were controlled by the aristocracy. Almost one in ten were reserved for members of the royal family, dukes and peers of the realm. The others were set aside for the political nobility, senior civil servants, senior army ranks, King's counsellors and other senior state employees. In the section of the stalls where one could sit, a considerable number of places were given *gratis* under the patronage of the aristocracy to army officers, some of the King's servants, secretaries of ministers. There was a rigorous enforcement of rules concerning who could sit where.[10] Up to the eve of the Revolution, the King would send a list to the management of the Opéra with the names of those to be admitted by royal favour. Until 1787 he would even specify where they should sit. Thus, up to three hundred spectators attending a performance occupied the best seats without paying a penny.[11]

Towards the end of the eighteenth century, matters slowly began to change. Evelina, the heroine of Fanny Burney's eponymous novel, declares: 'I am quite astonished to find how little music is attended to in silence; for though everybody seems to admire, hardly anybody listens.'[12] The more attentive behaviour which was characteristic of audiences at private performances of chamber music began to be adopted in the public arena. Why this should be the case is not immediately obvious. Perhaps the new opera houses pioneered in Italy had better acoustics, thanks to the heavily draped tiers of boxes, which ensured that the reverberation of sound would be short, and flat ceilings with baroque décor which prevented echoes and diffused the sound. This was not the case elsewhere. For instance, the King's Theatre in the Haymarket, built by Vanbrugh in 1704–05 with an exaggerated vaulted roof, made it difficult to hear the actors and the music, though one could always contemplate the beautiful ceiling.

Perhaps the performances began genuinely to interest the audiences. In the case of music, audiences' attention was more difficult to obtain at a time when most music was being heard for the first time. Music is often appreciated and loved only after repeated listening. This, however, did not become widely available until the twentieth century, thanks to broadcast and recorded music. In the nineteenth century the opportunities to watch or listen for a second time to a particular opera, symphony or play in later years would be rare. The better-heeled opera audiences tended to go to the same opera throughout the season. In this instance, a certain lack of attention was, if not justified, at least understandable: those who had heard the same opera twenty times in a row – as could happen in some Italian cities or at the Paris Opéra – would simply want to skip the bits they regarded as boring while paying attention to the highlights.[13] By the nineteenth century, groups of genuine music lovers, known in Paris as the *dilettanti* (in the original Italian sense, people who find delight (*diletto*) in the works performed) began to dictate taste, idolising certain singers and composers.[14]

Some composers or performers, better able to cater to the taste of the public, did seem to make a difference. The arrival of Christoph Gluck on the Paris musical scene in 1774 and his great success – the Opéra doubled its receipts – is a clear illustration of the audience responding favourably to quality and novelty.[15] The audience itself was, of course, beginning to change. It is not always clear, in real life, what comes first: a demanding audience or a new generation of good composers and playwrights eager to please them. The fact is that in the 1770s there were reports of the birth of a more attentive audience. And in some instances quality manifested itself and silence descended, as in Venice on 24 November 1734 when Goldoni's first play, *Belisario*, was staged, and the audience, usually very noisy, listened in unprecedented silence – or so he claimed.[16]

Some spectators, including Jean-Jacques Rousseau, wept during Gluck's *Orphée et Eurydice*, appropriately reworked with a French libretto.[17] This was Gluck's second triumph, for he had already delighted Parisian audiences with his *Iphigénie en Aulide* in 1774. Along with Gluck a new generation of Italian opera composers, now largely forgotten, came to the fore: Niccolò Piccinni, Antonio Sacchini and Niccolò Jomelli. The rivalry among them attracted considerable attention and divided opera-goers.[18] Between 1774 and 1781 a veritable war was waged between the champions of Gluck and those of Piccinni. All of this considerably boosted the parlous finances of the Paris Opéra.

The audience was becoming more socially diversified, more bourgeois, less aristocratic and more intellectual. In Paris and Vienna they listened to Gluck, and later to his successor and former pupil Antonio Salieri. Salieri's *Les Danaïdes* (1781) was given 127 times at the Paris Opéra. His *Tarare* survived the Revolution and was performed 131 times at the Opéra as late as 1826.

If Gluck had opened the way to the listening audience, Rossini secured it. But even Rossini did not always get the degree of attention he wanted. In 1812 he inserted in his opera *Ciro in Babilonia* an aria ('Chi disprezza gli infelici') based on a single repeated B flat. This quickly became known as the *aria del sorbetto*, to be sung by a minor singer – the *seconda donna*, not the *prima* – while the audience were eating their ice cream.[19] The singer Anna Savinelli was, according to Rossini, 'unspeakably ugly', and equipped with a single good note (the B flat, evidently).[20] Palming off an aria in the middle of the second act to a minor character when everyone would be eating their sherbet, with much consequent clinking of spoons and glasses, was a well-established practice even before Rossini, but it must have been a useful trick, since he used it again in old Berta's aria in the solo scene (the sixth) in the second act of *Il Barbiere di Siviglia* ('Che vecchio sospettoso!'). Stendhal thought it was delightful.[21]

Such precautions were necessary even in Milan's La Scala, then the most beautiful opera house in Europe, completed in 1778 and able to accommodate 2,300 people. La Scala's acoustics were superior to anything in France, but the audience was even less attentive than in Paris. The boxes of La Scala belonged outright to leading Milanese families such as the Visconti, the Serbelloni and the Barbò di Soresina. They even had boxes for their servants. These boxes were provided with thick silk curtains which could shut out the stage and muffle the 'noise' (i.e. the operatic arias) coming from the stage, thus enabling the box owners to play cards, drink, eat *risotti*, chicken, *cotolette alla milanese* (breaded veal cutlet known everywhere else as *Wiener schnitzel*) and ice creams, and to gossip undisturbed. On the stage the prompter would make himself useful by ringing a bell when a particularly good aria was about to come up. The silk curtains would all open at once, everyone would listen carefully, burst into applause, shout *bravo* and *brava* and then return to their games and chats.[22] Such behaviour so outraged Berlioz that he wrote: 'I would rather be forced to sell pepper and cinnamon in the rue Saint-Denis than write an opera for the Italians.'[23]

The director of the Paris Opéra, a heavily subsidised theatre, complained in 1804 that the 1,700 spectators had to 'struggle against the accumulation of breaths, odours, and candle smoke . . . We suffocate, can see little, and hear even less.'[24] A loud whistle by the stage director would signal a change of scene. In an attempt to get the audience to pay attention, special effects and machines were introduced: chariots were lowered from the ceilings, while creaking multi-hinged floors were rolled out for nautical scenes.[25]

At La Scala in 1817, for the first night of Rossini's *La Gazza ladra* the great Milanese families occupied the first two rows of boxes. Of the original 144 boxes, forty or so – mostly in the less prestigious fourth level – had changed hands, and were now owned by other nobles. Three of the new owners were not even aristocrats, but professional bourgeois. Down in the stalls one could see officers in their Austrian uniforms, young aristocrats and the new bourgeoisie, mainly shop-owners and professionals.[26] There were practically no women in the stalls, save for the odd *cocotte*.

In the 1750s, at the Opéra, the most luxurious theatre in France, there were 135 annual subscribers to the first-level boxes (the best); they were all aristocrats, except for seven rich commoners. On the second and third levels the boxes were cheaper. This was the territory of the lesser nobles, the better-off clergy, lawyers and the prosperous bourgeoisie. Where today are the stalls, the *parterre*, stood (literally, for there were no seats) a large crowd (up to 1,000 people) of servants, often drunk, officers, dandies, the lower bourgeoisie, and all those who aspired to join the Parisian élites. The conditions for listening from the *parterre* were even worse than from the boxes: the crowd was always on the verge of pandemonium, their singing frequently drowned out the performers, pets were allowed to run amok, defecating uninhibitedly, while armed guards tried to stop excesses.[27] At the very top, in the *paradis* ('the gods'), it was even worse. Though the spectators could sit on long benches nailed to the floor, they were surrounded by tiny closets, each containing a wooden bucket. These were the toilets. The smell was often unbearable. And this was the case in all civilised theatres, such as La Scala, where internal sanitary regulations (1789) required a number of large buckets for urine only. These rapidly overfilled. Elsewhere the fastidious had to leave the theatre and search for an inn, or the street. The rich, of course, could get their valet to bring them a pot in their box.[28]

Noisy behaviour was common everywhere. Mozart, writing to his father in 1778, described a performance in Munich in which two actresses were hissed off the stage; when the officers responsible were asked to be less noisy, they replied that as they had paid for their seats they could do what they wanted.[29]

At the peak of his fame Rossini was able – finally – to obtain the undivided attention of the audience. At the Paris première of his last work, *Guillaume Tell* (1829), three knocks announced the beginning of the performance. The audience went quiet. When the conductor, François-Antoine Habeneck, raised his arm, there was a religious silence.[30] Lesser names than Rossini still found it difficult to make themselves heard. And audience behaviour was not the same everywhere. Around 1820 many Parisian venues were still platforms for the rich to parade themselves while the less rich gaped in wonder. But the atmosphere at the Comédie-Française was quite different. Hazlitt commented in 1825 that it would shame a London audience: 'Not only was the strictest silence observed, as soon as the curtain drew up, but no one moved or attempted to move.'[31] Occasionally, people would fall asleep, even during Haydn's London concerts, though perhaps not during his 'Surprise' symphony, the sudden *fortissimi* of which were intended to waken slumbering members of the audience. Somnolence was hardly surprising, as concerts often lasted well past midnight.[32] Besides, falling asleep at concerts still occurs in the twenty-first century.

As the theatre became more market-dependent, the role of the aristocracy as dictators of taste began to falter. Watching the aristocracy provided only limited entertainment for the middle classes. When all was said and done, the bourgeois ethos consisted in getting value for money. Those bourgeois who liked high culture wanted to absorb it in peace. And theatres needed wider, paying audiences. The monopoly of classical styles in élite theatres – those performing Racine, Molière and Corneille at the Comédie-Française in Paris – was being challenged. Popular folk forms, such as the fairy tale, were being revived in both literature and the theatre. The vulgar, the ribald and the hyperbolic, characteristic of high culture at the time of Rabelais, became an aspect of the French radical romantic movement of the 1830s.[33]

By the standards of refined society, entertainment for the lower orders was and still is (almost by definition) coarse. At the end of the eighteenth century the typical Parisian market-fair theatre had taken on board the Italian commedia dell'arte and driven it more downmarket. Scatological humour abounded: in *Le Marchand de merde* (The Shit Merchant), Arlequin convinces an apothecary to buy a barrel of excrement. There was also comic entertainment, acrobats, freaks, Chinese shadows, lions, tigers, elephants and rhinoceroses. Circus acts with strange animals were introduced. To please European powers Muhammad Ali, Ottoman Viceroy of Egypt, sent two animals with unusually extended necks, one to Paris, the other to London. The London one died immediately. The French one arrived in Paris in July 1827. In two months 100,000 Parisians went to see the creature known in Arabic as *zarafa*, whence giraffe.[34]

London vied with Paris in popular spectacles. The vogue for pleasure gardens had started in the eighteenth century, and continued in the nineteenth. In 1832 the Cremorne Gardens were opened in Chelsea first as a sports club, then as a venue for evening dances, pony races and ballooning. The Georgian gardens disappeared to make way for more profitable houses. Fairs were held in larger open areas such as Hampstead Heath and Blackheath, where there were sports, slides and donkey rides.[35]

London Zoo was established in 1828, and boasted the largest animal collection in the world. There were puppet shows in the Little Piazza in Covent Garden, there was 'the tall woman of Essex' and 'the Ethiopian Savage' in Fleet Street, and a magic lantern show near Leicester Square.[36] Sports too offered entertainment to the public, either as participants or as spectators. In eighteenth-century London these included shooting competitions, sculling on the Thames, ball games (including football) and bowling. Public hangings were still a popular show until their abolition in 1868 (hanging continued for another hundred years, but out of sight of the public). By the Thames there was bull- and bear-baiting as well as bare-knuckle boxing. Cock fighting and dog fights survived legally into the nineteenth century (cock fighting was banned in 1849).[37] Before the end of the nineteenth century all working-class cruel sports involving animals had been banned. By contrast, hunting foxes with dogs – a middle- and upper-class passion – survived into the twenty-first century.

Concert Halls

Until the invention of a procedure whereby sound could be recorded, the market was not a major form of distribution of music until the nineteenth century. But there were ways of making money with music. At the end of the eighteenth century, piano concertos were the most effective ways for composers to establish themselves in instrumental music. They would be the ones playing the piano in a setting where their virtuosity – backed by an orchestra – could be appreciated. This is what Beethoven did as a young virtuoso pianist and composer. By the time he wrote his fifth and last piano concerto (the 'Emperor') in 1809, he had become almost deaf, and as he could no longer perform in public he never wrote another concerto, though he did compose piano sonatas.[38]

The era of patronage, however, was far from ended. Without patrons, even Beethoven would not have been able to survive. Even with them he existed in a state of shabby poverty. Yet he was widely revered while alive, a necessary precondition not only for his subsequent apotheosis but also for his prestige and standing in Vienna in the 1790s.[39] Beethoven could not have used, when in Vienna, the old structures of patronage (paid employment as a *Kapellmeister*), nor could he yet become a truly independent professional virtuoso. A new system of payment was devised for composers/performers: sponsorship by wealthy patrons for public or private salon performances. Thus the need for patrons remained paramount, especially among composers, until the end of the nineteenth century. In fact, in the field of serious music, patronage still exists, since no large concert hall or opera house can operate without some form of public or private subsidy. Composers have always been far less well paid than performers. Beethoven himself restricted himself to composition only when his deafness made it impossible for him to earn a living as a virtuoso – which is why the last years of his life were spent in penury.

When Beethoven arrived in Vienna in 1792, the competition among performers was considerable, as was that between different groups of patrons. The old aristocracy, the new aristocracy and the new bourgeoisie were involved in a struggle for cultural supremacy. One way in which this could be resolved was by distinguishing between different levels of musical expression: attributing to some a higher social value than to others. And this is the background behind the construction of 'the genius' of Beethoven, according to the interesting thesis advanced by the music historian Tia DeNora. Her view is that Beethoven's rise to fame was helped by his exceptional aristocratic connections in Vienna and the kind of sponsors he had.[40] DeNora suggests that the Czech composer Jan Ladislav Dussek, like Beethoven a pupil of Haydn, might have enjoyed the fame of Beethoven, instead of sinking into obscurity, had he had the right kind of patrons. Much of Dussek's subsequent activities took place in London, where a less personal 'market' relationship prevailed in the music world than in Vienna.[41] Perhaps Beethoven was lucky in having aristocratic patrons like Count Waldstein (to whom he dedicated the famous sonata in C major, op. 53, 'Waldstein'), who had a greater claim to taste than the *nouveaux riches*, and was thus able to confer on him a symbolic value which the others could not. This, of course, leaves entirely open and unanswered (some would say unanswerable) the question of whether Beethoven 'deserves' to be regarded as a genius. And in any case, the relationship did not have to be one-way, from patron to composer. One could argue that, having obtained an initial push, Beethoven was later able to capitalise on his prestige as a genius to the advantage of the higher-ranking patrons.

The growth of new bourgeois élites led to an expansion in the demand for concert music. This required a public of music lovers, or at least a public keen to participate in the kind of entertainment which most resembled that which had hitherto been available to the aristocracy, and a municipal authority prepared to support music as a civic amenity. In other words, it required bourgeois self-consciousness. One of the first organisations which entered this market was the Collegium Musicum of Frankfurt in 1712, followed, in 1721, by that of Hamburg.[42] In 1743 sixteen Leipzig businessmen formed what they called the Grosse Concert. Bach, who was Thomaskantor (choirmaster of St Thomas's church) in Leipzig at the time, was not even consulted, because he was not sufficiently up to date with the then fashionable Italian style. Hamburg, Frankfurt and Leipzig were in the forefront of the concert movement because they were the leading bourgeois towns of Germany, unencumbered by a powerful court – for where an important court existed, as in Berlin, Stuttgart and Munich, it could provide employment to the best performers and delay the formation of concert halls. Vienna, as an imperial capital, trailed behind London and Paris in public concerts because its aristocracy did not sponsor them, and the middle classes were less wealthy and sophisticated than those in France and England.[43] Technological advances had made instruments and sheet music cheaper. This enabled the middle classes to provide themselves with the musical education and taste which had hitherto been the property of the aristocracy.

Only in 1810 were the good burghers of Munich granted the use of the court orchestra for public performances.[44] Gradually more court theatres were turned over to a commercial management on behalf of the courts and began to admit a paying audience.[45] In Paris, just as audiences were rediscovering opera in the 1770s, they were also becoming interested in public concerts (a competitor which the Opéra was trying to prevent). Previously the only public places where one could hear instrumental and chamber music – but only sacred music – were the *concerts spirituels*, started in 1725, and held in various theatres.[46]

The development of larger halls where concerts could be performed increased the size of both the audience and the orchestra. Early symphonies could be performed by a relatively small group of musicians. By the end of the seventeenth century the string group had become the core of the orchestra, and within it emerged in its leading role the violin – previously regarded as a peasant fiddle. By the end of the eighteenth century performances of a score become more standardised, partly because notation improved, and partly because the composers themselves began to travel a great deal more. The conductor began his historical ascent: from a humble 'time marker', a *batteur de mésure* marking time by striking a stick, the role passed to the leading violinist, who conducted by waving his bow.[47] Until the middle of the 1840s most orchestras took their conductors by rotation from among their own members, and had only one rehearsal for each concert.[48] Eventually the conductor reached his present dizzy status as the venerated and feared ruler of the orchestra. As early as November 1807 an article by Gottfried Weber in the *Allgemeine Musikalische Zeitung* explained that it was necessary for the conductor to behave like a Napoleon (the real Napoleon was then ruling most of Continental Europe) for 'the greater good of the whole'. He added that conductors should use the short baton, which is visible and not audible.[49] Soon the baton became *de rigueur*: it was used by Carl Maria von Weber in Germany; Louis Spohr introduced it in England, and Gaspare Spontini adopted it with relish in Berlin, collecting busts of himself in Napoleonic posture.[50]

Eventually concert halls became an international business, although there were few in France or Italy. Charles Burney, the father of the famous novelist Fanny Burney, barely mentions concert life in his *The Present State of Music in France and Italy* (1771), the result of a six-month Continental tour.[51] By 1800, however, matters had changed. In England a thriving concert life had come into existence as early as the 1730s. In 1740, the German critic Johann Mattheson reported with some astonishment that many concerts were offered to a *paying* audience in England.[52] In 1764 Teresa Cornelys started, with Johann Christian Bach (the son of Johann Sebastian) and another London-based German composer, Carl Friedrich Abel, a series of subscription concerts that became famous.[53]

In 1783 various European musicians, including Johann Peter Salomon, a

German-born violinist, established in London the 'Professional Concerts' as a business enterprise. Then Salomon went his own way and started his own organisation. In 1791, taking advantage of Prince Nicolaus Esterházy's death, he brought Haydn to London to great acclaim.[54] 'Giuseppe Hayden' as the composer was sometimes labelled in London, was paid handsomely: £50 for each performance. He gave twenty recitals, which earned him £1,000, to which a bonus of £200 was added.[55] He was also paid £300 to compose an opera, £300 for his twelve 'Salomon' or 'London' symphonies, plus £200 for the copyright.[56] On 16 May 1791 he gave a benefit concert (i.e. a concert entirely for his own profit) which brought him £350 – tickets cost half a guinea, a considerable sum, but roughly in line with the one-off five-guinea subscription fee charged by Mrs Cornelys for her concert series.[57]

Haydn gave music lessons to aristocrats, was invited to parties, and even found a girlfriend, Rebecca Schroeter, the attractive widow of a musician. He heard Handel's *Messiah*. In two seasons in London (1791–92 and 1794–95), Haydn had made more money, and unquestionably had more fun, than in twenty years at the Esterházy court. Economically advanced London, with its rising middle class, could offer him more money, more admiration and respect, and larger audiences and concert halls than could his aristocratic patron, the Prince Esterházy. This led Haydn to produce a different kind of music, and, particularly, more complex symphonies than the relatively short pieces of work which could be performed by the small orchestra suited to the salon of an aristocrat. The new concert halls enabled composers to think of larger-scale works. Haydn's late (London) symphonies and all of Beethoven's were clearly intended for the new type of large concert hall, and not for after-dinner relaxation.[58] In France too, Haydn had great success. Between 1800 and 1815 his symphonies were played, in Paris alone, 119 times.[59]

Though Mozart was well-known and was regularly performed after 1815, he never did gain, during the nineteenth century, the status Haydn had before 1815 or Beethoven in the 1830s. In 1784 Mozart launched his own series of subscription concerts in the hall of the Trattnerhof in Vienna, gaining 176 subscribers who paid six gulden each for three concerts, generating a gross income of just over 1,000 gulden, but we don't know what his expenses were.[60] His subscribers included nobles, officers but very few bourgeois (though these had flocked to hear his German opera *Die Entführung aus dem Serail* two years previously).[61] Mozart's concerts, like those of all his contemporaries, were written with an audience in mind, not for music publishers. The presence of an audience determined certain conventions, such as that of starting a concerto or symphony with a burst of violins to silence them. This is indeed how Mozart's 'Paris' Symphony (no. 31 in D) begins, gradually building a dialogue and, in the last movement, bursting into a *forte* to solicit applause. He wrote to his father: '. . . there was a tremendous burst of applause. But as I knew, when I wrote it, what effect it would surely produce, I had introduced the passage again at the close – when there were shouts of "Da capo".'[62]

London was a great centre of musical consumption. But while it imported Continental talents and music, it produced very little, and exported nothing of significance. The main advantage of such a situation was that London audiences could see and listen to what was best from the Continent. The disadvantage was that it would prove almost impossible for English composers or musicians to succeed in the face of such formidable competition. As a result England remained a laggard country in music for almost the whole of the nineteenth century. But it welcomed foreigners. Muzio Clementi, an Italian-born composer and piano virtuoso, settled in London in the 1770s and opened his own publishing house and piano factory in 1798. In 1811 the house of Novello opened in London, specialising in cheap editions of musical scores. The main market for these early publishers was the kind of *Hausmusik* (home music) which could be performed by amateur soloists and small ensemble players, and by piano-accompanied singers for their own entertainment and that of their friends and relatives. Finally there was the London Philharmonic Society (1813), which declared that its aim was to promote the performance of 'the best and most approved instrumental music'.[63] This entailed importing Continental music.

The better-off groups competed directly with the old aristocracy for places in the more famous concert halls. This led to the building of new venues, and encouraged more people to enter the musical profession. Musical activities which took non-market forms, such as informal secular singing clubs (in France) and church-based choral societies (in Great Britain and Germany) expanded, providing both the personnel for the expansion of the music industry and a larger public which included, at least in London, Paris and the main German cities, many artisans, clerical workers and shop-keepers.[64] More music teachers and musicians provided singing classes and choral instruction to meet the increased demand for music. In 1819 a new charity in Paris, the Société pour l'Instruction Elémentaire, decided to promote the teaching of music and to entrust it to Guillaume Wilhelm (1781–1842), who devised a system for teaching music to children. The result was the Orphéon, a private society for the teaching of singing in schools. Further subsidies enabled him to enrol some 5,000 children and adults. In 1836 *le tout Paris* was invited to a concert of choral music by 'ordinary workers' and the children of local schools. It was a triumph. The idea of popular musical culture had arrived (the intention behind much of this was to keep the working classes away from drink, immorality and revolutions). Most of what they sang came from the established high culture repertory. Delphine Gay, the celebrated columnist of *La Presse*, wrote in June 1836: 'The singing of these workers induced in me a profound emotion. It was like listening to heavenly symphonies, the brotherly chorus of angels and cherubs. But the angels were carpenters, printers and artisans, and among the cherubs we could see a puffy Negro keeping time with ebony fingers.'[65]

Such publicly subsidised systems further increased the size of the market for sheet-music publishers. Artisans who had learned to sing and play musical instruments used these skills in a semi-professional way in the theatres, cafés and dance halls.

The singing-school movement spread to Great Britain via Joseph Mainzer, who left Paris for political reasons in 1841. One of Mainzer's British pupils, John Hullah, who had also studied in Paris under Guillaume Wilhem, obtained private support and direct government funding with the 1870 Education Act.[66] Thus a mixture of public help and private initiative enlarged the audiences for music. The great classical music repertory formed between 1780 and 1900, which became the backbone of consecrated Western music in the twentieth century, was buttressed by formidable institutional developments. Music was no longer purely the prerogative of the salon, the street or the church. This is also the period when 'classical' music was born. The actual term was not used in English in its present sense of 'consecrated' before 1836 (according to the *Oxford English Dictionary*), and was probably an imitation of the German and French usage (*classique* and *klassisch*).

In Paris in the first years of the 1800s there were already three major concert societies offering regular performances. One of them, the Concerts des Amateurs (founded in 1769), had six hundred subscribers. With eighty players (all non-professional), it was the largest orchestra in France, and one of the best in Europe. Haydn was the absolute favourite composer. During the first two decades of the nineteenth century few concert programmes failed to include at least one piece by him. Among the most frequently played were his London symphonies, particularly no. 103 ('The Drum Roll') and no. 100 ('The Military'). These are still among the most popular of his works.[67] The orchestra of the Concerts de la rue de Grenelle was a smaller, all-professional group – though two days a week were reserved for performances by an all-women amateur orchestra with the audience restricted to their relatives, 'to avoid embarrassment'. Both the Amateurs and the rue de Grenelle folded because of the success of the third performing orchestra: the Exercises, made up of students of the recently formed Conservatoire and their teachers, and sanctioned by the government. This started in November 1801. The quality of its music, reports say, was superior to that of either of its rivals.[68]

Performers

Performers always prevailed over authors. They became more famous; they made more money. They still do. Singers and virtuosi do better than composers; actors better than playwrights, scriptwriters and directors. The front of the stage is always more rewarding than the backroom, at least for those who have made it to the top.

Even in the eighteenth century, opera was dominated by the singers, in particular by the female voice, and before that by the castrato (so-called male sopranos or 'sopranisti'). Most of the great castrati and female singers accumulated vast fortunes. The accounts of Naples's San Carlo Theatre for the 1739 season show that the soprano Vittoria Tesi topped the earning table with 3,396 ducats; she was followed by another soprano, Anna Maria Peruzzi, with 2,768 ducats; third was the castrato Mariano Nicolino, with 1,838 ducats. Nicola Porpora, the composer of *Semiramide*, one of the four operas per-formed during that season, famous throughout Italy, got only two hundred ducats. The following season a castrato was the biggest earner, with 3,693 ducats, while a humble copyist would earn only eight ducats for the entire season. For the 1816 opening of *Il Barbiere di Siviglia* in Rome (savagely booed by a loud *claque* of supporters of Paisiello, author of a previous *Barbiere*), the young Rossini was paid four hundred scudi, the alto Geltrude Righetti-Giorgi in the role of Rosina got five hundred scudi, and the famous Spanish tenor Manuel García, in the role of Count Almaviva received 1,200 scudi.[69]

Dancers too were much praised. In the 1770s most performances at the Paris Opéra consisted of works in which there was as much dancing as singing, and often more. Even in the *tragédie lyrique*, the genre associated with Jean-Baptiste Lully (1633–87), who was still the most performed composer, dancing accounted for almost half the action.[70] Gluck tried to reduce the importance of ballet in the opera. He encountered predictable resistance from the dancers, but also from the public, who enjoyed the dance scenes as much as, perhaps more than, the singing. He conformed, inserting suitable ballet scenes in his *Alceste* and desisting from demanding the elimination of special effects.[71] The ballet was so important that advertisements for an opera in 1804 did not mention the name of the composer or the librettist, went quickly through the names of the singers, and then listed the main dancers, which act they would appear in and what steps they would perform (e.g.: 'M. Saint-Amand will reappear in Act 2 and dance a *pas russe* with Mme Gardel . . .').[72]

The composers' strategy was understandable: they sought to eliminate anything which stood in the way of their music. They failed: throughout the nineteenth century, especially in Paris, a ballet scene was mandatory in all operas; even Verdi had to acquiesce. Choruses were valued for their power, rather than their musicality. Special effects became ever more complex, sustained by constantly improving technology. Stage managers did not refrain from using animals to enhance public attention, as when, in 1829, dogs, goats, donkeys and sheep were used to suggest a pastoral atmosphere in Rossini's *Guillaume Tell*.[73] The individual score each member of the orchestra had to play from often contained mistakes, because the copyist had to make a copy for each instrument using the composer's text.[74] Ballets, the most eagerly awaited moment of the evening, were little more than a series of jumps, pirouettes and acrobatics; it was the feat, not the grace, that mattered. Only towards the 1830s and 1840s, and only thanks to a new generation of ballerinas – notably Marie Taglioni, Lise Noblet and Carlotta Grisi – did something resembling the modern ballet come into being.[75]

The best opera market in late-eighteenth-century Europe, from the point of view of singers, was London. No opera, and certainly no Italian opera, could have a hope of success on the London stage without a fashionable foreign singer, preferably Italian. Hogarth, in his *Masquerades and Operas* (1724), satirised the love for foreign art, and Italian opera in particular. Understandably enough, this was resented by local talents. Such animosity manifested itself in the famous duet between Polly Peachum and Lucy Lockit, rivals for the favours of the highwayman Macheath in John Gay's *The Beggar's Opera* (1728). Its high coloratura style was an obvious barb aimed at the pretensions of Italian opera in one of the rare English works – in this case a 'ballad opera' – able to challenge Italian supremacy.

In London, great castrati could command large sums. Farinelli (Carlo Broschi, 1705–82) earned £1,500 and Caffarelli £1,000 in a single season. Giovanni Battista Velluti, the last great castrato, could earn, at the beginning of the nineteenth century, £2,500 in a season. In general, if one was Italian one was paid twice as much as a British performer.[76] Farinelli, the most renowned of the castrati, earned vast sums in Italy, London, Paris and Madrid. In London, performers also received all sort of presents and perks. The London papers were full of lists of presents, such as 'a pair of diamond earrings given by . . .', so one should think of the fees in terms of a package.

Women earned even more – singing was the only profession, along with prostitution, in which men could not match them. The great diva Francesca Cuzzoni was paid £2,000 for the season in 1723, a yearly salary which came within the reach of a junior teacher in a British university only in 1973, 250 years later. La Cuzzoni could add to her earnings, and did, with private and provincial appearances. Her high fees were reported with awe by the press. She should have asked for more, or invested what she got better. By 1850 her voice was gone. She wound up in prison for her debts, and ended her days in Bologna as a button-maker.[77]

In England, singers were paid more than in Paris.[78] The finest English soprano of her time, Elizabeth Billington (born 1765–68?, died 1818) was known for the very high fees she was able to extract as well as for the excellence of her voice. The great diva Angelica Catalani built up a fortune of £50,000 (a fabulous £16,700 in 1807 alone) during her London stay, singing at the Drury Lane, the King's Theatre and Covent Garden – but she also got into trouble. In 1809 the Covent Garden management attempted to raise admission prices to a top of seven shillings (partly to cover major rebuilding costs). It was forced to back down after what became known as the 'Old Price' riots: the infuriated opera-goers, who carried on their protest for over two months, attributed the increase to the enormous fee paid to Catalani (whom they worshipped). This is the classic conundrum for theatres (and for sporting events) the world over: a famous star can fill a theatre, but can also impose exorbitant costs. London's loss was Paris's gain. La Catalani moved to Paris in 1814, and became the director of the Théâtre-Italien.[79]

Large fees were built into the opera genre. In 1827 Giuditta Pasta obtained a fee of £2,365 for the summer season, while soloists earned as little as £75.[80] If we are to believe William Hazlitt, in Paris at the time, she deserved every penny:

She does not act the character – she is it, looks it, breathes it. She does not study for an effect, but strives to possess herself of the feeling which should dictate what she is to do, and which gives birth to the proper degree of grace, dignity, ease, or force . . . her whole style and manner is in perfect keeping, as if she were really a love-sick, care-crazed maiden, occupied with one deep sorrow . . . This alone is true nature and true art.[81]

Le Courier du théâtre complained in 1829 that Maria Malibran had received 14,000 francs for a single benefit concert, bringing her earnings for that year to 94,000 francs.[82] To give an idea of the size of that sum, it may be sufficient to note that a cheap meal in a Paris restaurant at the time could be had for less than a franc, and that when Victor Hugo's family moved into the rue Vaugirard in 1824, he paid for his six small rooms, the maid's room and the luxury of a water closet on the landing for the family's exclusive use, 625 francs a year.[83] Another way of looking at it is to point out that with her earnings for that one year Malibran, the greatest mezzo-soprano of her age, could have bought the Louvre's painting number 300 – *Le Portrait de Mona Lisa connue sous le nom de la Joconde*, which had been valued at 80,000 francs in 1821.[84] Performers' earnings continued to increase. Around 1830 Laure Cinti and Julie Dorus-Gras received 30,000 francs a year, Giuditta Pasta 30–35,000.[85] In 1855 at the Opéra the German-born soprano Sophie Cruvelli received 100,000 francs, twice what the entire administrative personnel received.[86]

And the men? There were exceptions, such as Gilbert Duprez, who made 70,000 francs in 1848, but it was not until the twentieth century that male performers (one can think of the bass Feodor Chaliapin and the tenor Enrico Caruso) became box-office draws on a par with women singers. It is not clear what the explanation is for this only too rare case of pay discrimination in favour of women (it also exists in ballet). The only way for a male performer to match female earnings was to subject himself to castration before puberty, to ensure that the vocal chords would not thicken. The consequences of this irreversible demasculinisation were a very hairy head, an absence of hair on the rest of the body, a greater likelihood of obesity in later age, and infertility (though, contrary to popular belief, sexual performance was not unduly impaired).[87]

Yet not even the unkindest cut would enable a male singer to match the prestige of great singers such as Malibran, who conquered London audiences singing Rosina in the first British performance of Rossini's *Barbiere*. We have no idea how well she sang, but Rossini thought she was a musical genius, while the critic Étienne-Jean Delécluze wrote in his journal that she was also a wonderful actress.[88] Malibran was probably the first modern 'diva'. She became a cult figure, whose image was enhanced by endless anecdotes about her kindness and saintliness.[89] By contrast, and following a well-established narrative, her rival Giuditta Pasta, it was decreed, would conform to the other stereotype, that of the fiery and temperamental soprano.

Stories of the caprices of leading female opera singers, particularly the sopranos, gave rise to the notorious image of the demanding and tempera-mental *prima donna* (there was a *primo uomo*, but the term never stuck) – a kind of precursor of Hollywood stars. Though such tales have some founda-tion in reality, we should remind ourselves that in the eighteenth and nine-teenth centuries, performing in the opera was virtually the only profession open to women of relatively modest origins. It was the only way they could become rich and famous in their own right, and by their own effort (other than marrying someone rich). Their so often reviled tantrums might compare favourably to the difficulties many men of humble origins have had in coping with the sudden wealth and fame which excellence in music or sport can bring – recent examples being Elvis Presley and Michael Jackson or Mike Tyson and Maradona. In any case, one never knew how long one's renown would last. In other professions, such as medicine or the law, one's reputation usually increases and then levels off; it seldom collapses.

The best-known singers behaved like ordinary profit-maximising entre-preneurs: Adelina Patti, in the early stages of her career in London, after successes in New York, could take advantage of the growing rivalry between Her Majesty's Theatre and Covent Garden to sign extremely favourable con-tracts – as detailed in the memoirs of her manager and brother-in-law Maurice Strakosch.[90] By 1890 Patti could demand and obtain 20,000 lire for an evening, while a lead tenor in a provincial opera house could get as little as six lire.[91] The other side effect of high-earning singers was the under-employment of minor singers, but this meant that the numerous opera houses in smaller provincial towns could hire them on the cheap.[92]

If one wanted quality, one had to pay over the odds. Carl Maria von Weber's yearly salary at the Dresden opera house (1817–21) was 1,500 thalers. His task was to set up a German-language opera company, write operas and conduct them. The orchestra was very good, but he needed to recruit good singers. Though initially he tried to perform a repertory which could do without top sopranos, he soon realised that he needed stars like the coloratura soprano Caroline Willmann and the dramatic soprano Wilhelmine Shroeder-Devrient. The going rate for a first soprano was 5,000 thalers; the second soprano and first two tenors would get 2,000 thalers each. Only the third-ranking sopranos would be content with the same salary as Weber.[93] At least he was earning more than the first violin.

The phenomenon of highly paid superstars is thus not new. Some professions and activities provide very large rewards for a small number of people, particularly for performances seen on the stage or television, at the cinema and in sport. This does not happen among schoolteachers or bakers. The earnings of performers increase in some proportion with the number of people they can reach. Footballers do not play any less hard before a full stadium of 20,000 spectators than when they are watched by a hundred million people on television. But the revenue generated is immensely greater, and a share of it will find its way to these talented individuals. These high rewards attract more entrants into the profession, resulting in even fiercer competition among them. The result is that the more talented ones (or those with the better public relations system) will get more money, since to listen to or see a superstar does not cost much more than to see a second-rate talent.[94] Thus it may seem that a leading soprano in the 1800s was well paid, but in fact she earned much less than she would have had she been able to use modern means of communication such as television and radio broadcasting, and recordings of her performances.

It was not easy, even in the nineteenth century, to be a superstar. In opera singing the discipline required is nothing short of extraordinary. It is a complex and demanding form, requiring not only the ability to sing, but to make one's voice 'act'. No moment of relaxation is permissible. Every single performance is of paramount importance. The public, having paid much, expects even more. The fatigue of constant travelling before the era of the railways, the need to maintain one's physical condition at its peak, the incessant competition from younger and fitter rivals, the judgement of critics who, having celebrated the rise, cannot wait to write the story of the fall – all and more of this would cause serious anxiety in even the most balanced human being.

In any case, the very large fees extracted by famous singers account for only a proportion of the expenses of producing an opera. There were the other singers, the composer, the librettist, the conductor, the members of the orchestra, the stage-hands and other craftsmen who painted the backdrop and made the clothes; then there was the prompter, the management and the other personnel of the opera house.[95] There is seldom an audience large enough to cover such costs, which is why a subsidy of some sort has always been necessary, or other sources of revenuehad to be found.

Composers and musical stars were faced with a 'global' (i.e. European) market as early as the eighteenth century. While actors were limited by the territoriality of language, opera stars operated on a vast international stage. By the time she was twenty-one, Angelica Catalani had already sung throughout Italy, in Venice, Livorno, Rome, Florence, Trieste and Milan. Then she sang in Lisbon, Madrid, Paris, London (1806–13), throughout Germany, Denmark, Stockholm, Brussels, Amsterdam, Warsaw, St. Petersburg, Brussels and Dublin, before concluding her extraordinary career at La Scala in Milan in November 1832.[96]

Sopranos not only attracted the crowds, but also had an impact on composers, who wrote a part for a particular singer, much as a film-maker might have in mind a particular actress. Thus Bellini wrote *La Sonnambula* and *Norma* for Giuditta Pasta; Donizetti too had Giuditta Pasta in mind for his *Anna Bolena*, and Fanny Persiani for *Lucia di Lammermoor*.[97] Ten of the eighteen operas composed by Rossini between 1815 and 1823 were written for Isabella Colbran (whom he married).[98]

Many singers were aware of their bargaining power and used it to the full, to demand not only large sums but a considerable say in how the work should be performed. Caroline Jagemann (1777–1848), a German soprano much admired by Goethe in spite of the exasperation she provoked in him, was the star of the Weimar court theatre. In 1802 she quarrelled with the conductor, who claimed that he and not she should decide the tempi of her arias as Donna Anna in Mozart's *Don Giovanni*. She ignored him, and outpaced the orchestra amidst the applause and encouragement of the audience.[99]

Where a man could make an impact was as a virtuoso. Here the piano and the violin dominated completely. A new breed of itinerant music players appeared, quite unlike lowly marketplace performers. Paganini, Liszt and Chopin brought the virtuoso into the salon and the concert hall. Later, men would place themselves centre stage in music performances, challenging the supremacy of the *prima donna* by establishing the conductor as a *primo uomo*.

15

❦

Opera

An Italian Genre

SINCE ANCIENT TIMES, spectacles, shows, dramas, plays and theatrical representations have used songs and music along with the spoken word. The specific musical theatre we now call *opera* (Italian for 'work' in general) had its origin in late Renaissance Italy. The performance was usually in Italian, whether in Florence, Mantua, Rome or Venice. The audiences of the first operas were, by the standard of the time, relatively socially mixed – i.e. bourgeois and nobility. Europe's first opera house, the Teatro San Cassiano, was built in 1637 in Venice, the major commercial centre on the Continent. Even in such a mercantile city the opera was not regarded as a commercial enterprise. It was a loss-making business undertaken for prestige and entertainment during 'the season', the period which lasted from the day after Christmas to Shrove Tuesday, and which attracted visitors from all over Europe. By 1641 Venice (a city of 150,000 inhabitants) already had four opera houses; nine by 1670. It has been calculated that between 1637 and 1678 some 150 operas were composed.[1] As the commercial and economic power of Venice declined, the splendour of its opera increased. Since the city was Italy's main 'tourist' centre, its opera became known in every court in Europe. The operatic season was short, giving singers time to tour, and the closure of the Venetian opera houses during the War of Candia (now Iraklion in Crete) with Turkey in 1697–99 further encouraged touring.[2]

Until c.1820 the Italian opera consisted of highly successful *opera buffa*, or comic opera, and works based on classical and neoclassical stories (*opera seria*). Both relied on the virtuosity of the singers rather than the originality of the music. The text, or libretto – long regarded as far more important than the music, and the librettist as more gifted than the composer – consisted of similar plots, all well known to the audience, and constantly repeated.[3] Opera texts in the eighteenth century were totally dominated by Pietro Metastasio (1698–1782), who in the course of his long life wrote only twenty-seven librettos, but these were set to music some eight hundred times by composers including Handel, Mozart, Gluck, Pergolesi and Niccoló Jommelli. Metastasio's *La Clemenza di Tito*, for instance, was set by both Gluck and Mozart. Part of the international success of the Italian opera was that its stories originated from mainstream European literature: Greek myths, Roman history, the Bible and folk tales. Later, successful novels and plays were adapted into operas. It was not necessary to know Italian perfectly to follow an Italian opera, provided one was familiar with the classics, the Bible, some literary texts (Schiller, Shakespeare) and recent popular literature (such as Walter Scott). Plots would be restructured with the nonchalance of a Hollywood producer.

Italian operas, even abroad, were usually performed in Italian by Italian singers and musicians, in what became known as a specifically Italianate way of singing. Language was no barrier to enjoyment, since the plots were roughly the same, the better-educated aristocrats knew the language, and much of the audience scarcely paid attention to the words or even to the music. However, even in the larger cities, the potential opera public was small. This compelled singers and musicians to tour constantly in order to reach a larger audience. In so doing the genre was internationalised. The dominance of Italian opera was enhanced by the frenetic activities of troupes such as the Mingotti Travelling Italian Opera Company, which exported opera from Italy to the courts of Europe. The company (three male and five female singers) was active in the 1730s and 1740s in Germany, Denmark and the Austrian empire, including Prague, Graz, Frankfurt, Dresden, Copenhagen and Brno – where it inaugurated a new opera house, the Theater in der Tafern.[4]

Considering the technology – or lack of it – available at the time, the genre seems to have expanded very rapidly. The 'first' opera is supposed to have been Claudio Monteverdi's *Orfeo* in 1607 – a purely conventional landmark, there having been '*dramma per musica*' before, though none had the musical complexity of *Orfeo*. A mere twenty years later opera had spread throughout most of the Habsburg empire, and reached the court of Sigismund III in Warsaw in 1627. Only two politically dominant countries, declining Spain and ascendant France, were reluctant to adopt the new foreign genre. Concessions had to be made to French and Spanish provincialism.

The first opera performed in Madrid seems to have been a now lost Italian work set to *La Selva sin amor* by the prolific Golden Age playwright Lope de Vega. For its French première in 1645, Francesco Sacrati's *La Finta pazza* – also now lost – championed by the most powerful statesman of France, Cardinal Jules Mazarin (an Italian), had to be translated into French and performed by French dancers and singers, though the instrumentalists, the choreographer and the stage designer were Italian.[5] Its success, however, was due more to the spectacular stage effects than the singing.

A Florentine, Giambattista Lulli, who had arrived in France in 1646 at the age of fourteen, adapted Italian music to French taste, introducing spoken *récitatifs* (in Alexandrine verses just like Racine).[6] He also transformed himself into Monsieur Jean-Baptiste de Lully and, thus Frenchified, became Music Master to the Royal Family, obtained from the King the exclusive right to stage opera performance in Paris, and made opera popular in France.

In Germany, opera developed first in Hamburg, the most bourgeois of German cities. Though the commercial prosperity of Hamburg declined drastically during the Thirty Years' War (1618–48), the city was still rich enough to build the first German opera house in 1678. The main composers were usually German, though they more often than not adapted, plagiarised and imitated Italian operas. For twenty-five years (c.1695–1720), Hamburg opera was dominated by Reinhard Keiser, who composed dozens of operas, some with arias in Italian. Keiser was surrounded by able musicians. One of them, a violinist turned harpsichordist, became exceptionally famous: Georg Friedrich Handel. Handel's earliest operas, *Almira* and *Nero* (now lost), with Italian texts, were performed first in Hamburg.[7] But no ambitious German composer could avoid spending some time in Italy in order to become familiar with the Italianate style. During his stay in Italy (1705–10) Handel mastered Italian opera so effectively that his *Agrippina* was first performed in Venice (1709), and achieved a remarkable success. His Italian fame led to his appointment as Kapellmeister in Hanover in 1710.

In 1711 Handel went to England, where opera was becoming popular thanks to 'native' products such as *Venus and Adonis* by John Blow (a work then called a 'masque') and *Dido and Aeneas* (1689) by Henry Purcell. These works were in part based on a domestic tradition of English courtly spectacle, but also incorporated French and Italian elements. They were quickly over-shadowed, however, by the success of Handel's *Rinaldo*. Handel decided to remain in London, where a musician could become richer than in Germany, even though he was contractually expected to return to Hanover. There was some embarrassment in 1714 when his former employer, the Elector of Hanover, turned up in London, having become King of Britain as George I. The two, however, were quickly reconciled. King George, a native of Osnabrück, was thoroughly German, and never mastered English. He was pleased to have another German-speaker at court, particularly one of such distinction. Soon Handel had become a personal protégé of the court as Music Master to the King's children. Opera became part of London's cultural life largely thanks to Handel, rather than to Purcell's pioneering efforts. By 1720 Handel had become the artistic director of the Royal Academy of Music at the King's Theatre in the Haymarket. By 1730 he had written his best operas – all in Italian (*Giulio Cesare, Tamerlano* and *Rodelinda*) – and had attracted to London the greatest Continental singers: the castrato Senesino and the *prime donne* Francesca Cuzzoni and Bordoni.[8]

From its origins in the seventeenth century to the end of the eighteenth century, opera remained fundamentally Italian, not just in the sense that most composers and singers were Italian, though a majority were, but that the language of the librettos and the style of the music were Italian. The great German opera composers – Handel, Gluck, Haydn, Mozart – all wrote operas that were substantially in the Italian mode. However, they – especially Gluck – did grow impatient with the conventions of Italian opera, and sought to reform it by eliminating florid descriptions, superfluous ornaments and returning to a simpler form. Gluck had obviously caught the mood of the public. Audiences' previous lack of attention suggests that Italian domination had been achieved mainly because of an absence of serious competitors. In fact, between Monteverdi's *L'Incoronazione di Poppea* (The Coronation of Poppaea, 1642) and Cimarosa's *Il Matrimonio segreto* (The Secret Marriage, 1792 – after an English play by George Colman), there are hardly any Italian operas which remain part of the current repertory – Pergolesi's *La Serva padrona* (The Maid Turned Mistress, 1733) being the main exception. The best-known composer, Vivaldi, wrote over forty operas, none of which has been regularly performed anywhere in the world in the past century or so – unlike his 'Four Seasons' concerti, whose invasive presence grows by the year.

It would be quite wrong, however, to see in Gluck's popularity the end of Italian dominance. His greatest and most enduring success, *Orfeo ed Euridice* (1762), is, musically speaking, an Italian opera influenced by the French style. Apart from distinct genres such as the English ballad opera or the German *Singspiel* (song-play), there was no operatic idiom available outside that of Italy. Gluck used an Italian libretto for his *Orfeo*, but not

Metastasio's, preferring instead a text by his friend the Italian poet Ranieri Calzabigi, who produced a lucid plot without the usual ludicrous complexities.

Nevertheless, in the context of the time, Gluck rapidly became the representative of the 'anti-Italian' trend in opera, and the arch-rival of the leading Italian opera composer of the day, Niccolò Piccinni. It was said that *le tout Paris* was divided between *les Piccinistes* and *les Gluckistes*. The Paris Opéra, with considerable marketing skills, asked each of the two rivals to compose an opera on the same text, *Iphigénie en Tauride*. Gluck made it sound as French as possible. His version, an Italian opera 'adapted' to French musical taste,[9] was a sensational success. Gluck's victory demonstrated that it was not necessary to be Italian to write Italian operas – just as, if the comparison is not too daring, the Italian 'spaghetti westerns' of the 1970s proved that it was not necessary to be an American to make a good western. Mozart continued the tradition of Italianised opera, particularly in his three masterpieces – *La Nozze di Figaro*, *Così fan Tutte* and *Don Giovanni* – all with librettos by an Italian, Lorenzo da Ponte.

Seldom has a cultural genre been so closely associated with a single country. In the nineteenth century, when Italian domination was being undermined by the advance of German, Russian and French composers, opera still conjured up in the public mind the word 'Italy', just as the cinema, in the twentieth century, became an essentially American genre. The restriction of much of the opera repertory to works composed between Gluck's *Orfeo* (1762) and Puccini's *Turandot* (1926) has enshrined Italian domination. The standard English-language guide to the opera repertoire, Gustave Kobbé's *Complete Opera Book*, listed in its ninth edition (1976) some sixty-one nineteenth-century Italian operas (twenty-one by Verdi) against thirty-six French and thirty-one German (twelve by Wagner). Of course, the renown of individual operas changes constantly with the passing of time. Mozart's *Così fan tutte* was seldom performed before 1939. Kobbé's plans for the first edition of his famous reference book (1922) left out Verdi's *Don Carlos* and barely mentioned *La Forza del destino*.

Italian operatic domination had been repeatedly challenged, above all by the French, as early as the eighteenth century. This was a political challenge as much as an artistic one, a bitter struggle for patronage and funds in which every argument that could be mustered was used – not an uncommon situation. The pro-Italian lobby, though, was strong, and French composers must not have relished reading François Raguenet's *Parallèle des Italiens et des Français en ce qui regarde la musique et les opéras* (1702), in which Italian opera and music are contrasted favourably in every possible way to their French counterparts. The language is more musical, the arias are better, the music more exciting, while French music is flat and boring. Italian castrati sing better than French women, and can act as well. We had Lully, concedes Raguenet, but he was originally Italian, and now that he is dead there is nothing left.[10] Fifty years later, Jean-Jacques Rousseau was still denigrating French opera. In his *Lettre sur la musique française* (1753) he declared that the French language was quite unsuitable to be set to music, and that French singing was unbearable. The success of Italian opera in mid-eighteenth-century Paris revived the *querelle*. But why were the Italians more successful? Romantic theories of national character, or *Volksgeist*, would simply attribute their success to 'the Italian musical genius' – one of the many nineteenth-century concepts which survived into the twentieth, duly transformed into dull clichés (along with American ingenuity, French *savoir-faire*, British fair play, German technological excellence and – with less complimentary under-tones – 'the natural sense of rhythm of the Negro' and 'the business acumen of the Jew').

The real cause of Italian operatic success must be found in the contrasting environments facing French and Italian composers. The French were composing for a narrow élite, a national market entirely centred on Paris, and were entirely dependent on it. The Italians, even if they had no other ambition than to triumph in Italy alone, were composing for several great operatic centres – Venice, Florence, Naples, Milan and Rome – and a multi-tude of minor ones. A ferocious selection process was at work, weeding out the less innovative and dazzling, the provincial and the boring. The winners could roam throughout Europe enjoying the enormous 'brand' advantage of 'made in Italy' created by their predecessors. French composers looked only to Paris. The Italians – at least where opera was concerned – thought in 'global' terms.

It would be wrong to reduce Italian success to the excellence of its composers and performers. These were merely the visible and audible part of the complex organisational business of setting up a season for a leading opera house. This was the task of the impresario, hired by a theatre to manage its affairs. Soon the impresario turned into a businessman, able to attract performers and composers, and producing a 'season'. In the first quarter of the nineteenth century, the most important Italian impresario was Domenico Barbaia (1778–1841).[11] He had started his working life as a waiter, and later made money by marketing a concoction of chocolate, coffee and whipped cream which delighted gourmands throughout Italy. In 1809 Barbaia obtained the gaming concession at the San Carlo opera house in Naples, where he introduced roulette. The funds generated from the gambling business enabled him to expand into the organisation of the operatic side of the business.

Barbaia was instrumental in commissioning work from the up-and-coming generation, signing up, in 1815, the rising star Gioachino Rossini as composer and artistic director of the San Carlo, with a six-year contract. Rossini undertook to compose two operas a year, and to direct revivals of older works. He would receive an annual salary and a share in the proceeds of the gaming tables. In 1825 Barbaia, by then also impresario of La Scala in Milan, signed up Bellini to compose for both the San Carlo and La Scala; in 1827 he signed up Donizetti on a three-year contract. Barbaia remained the chief organiser of Naples's operatic life until 1840. Having been one of the first to recognise Rossini's genius, he was equally pivotal in the careers of Bellini, Donizetti and Carl Maria von Weber, often commissioning their works and assembling exceptionally strong casts. These included the greatest singers of the time: tenors such as the Italian Giovanni Davide, the French Adolphe Nourrit and Gilbert Duprez, the first 'King of the High Cs'; then there was the great Maria Malibran, the celebrated Giuditta Pasta, and the famous soprano Isabella Colbran, who was Barbaia's mistress before becoming Rossini's wife. Barbaia also operated outside Italy, leasing, in 1822, the Kärntnertortheater in Vienna, where he had six of Rossini's operas staged.[12]

Barbaia operated in a favourable political environment. The Bourbon rulers of Naples had been forced into exile in 1799 by Napoleon, who made his brother Joseph Bonaparte King of Naples in 1806. Joseph was succeeded (as King) by Joachim Murat, one of Napoleon's generals, in August 1808. Thanks to Murat the theatrical life of Naples was entirely reorganised. He appointed Barbaia to modernise the San Carlo, which had been built in 1737. Naples was then regarded as the operatic capital of Italy. It had famous composers like Domenico Cimarosa and Giovanni Paisiello. The lavish San Carlo was beautifully decorated: each box was like a miniature drawing room.[13] Patronage was required to fund such splendour, but it was not enough. Most opera houses, including La Scala, had to double up as gambling houses. It was often the case that one paid simply to enter the foyer to drink and gamble. Those who wanted to enter the auditorium and hear the opera had to pay extra. When the Bourbon kings returned in 1815 they abolished the gambling concession at the San Carlo, in deference to newly prevailing morals. However, they kept Barbaia, whose prestige made him unassailable, and provided plenty of funds to enhance even further Naples's theatrical life. When the San Carlo was gutted by fire in 1816 it was rebuilt in just over a year and just as lavishly – 180 years later it took over eight years to rebuild Venice's La Fenice after it was destroyed by fire in 1996.

Directly and indirectly, Italian opera triumphed all over Europe: at the Imperial Court in Vienna, at that of Louis XIV at Versailles, in Spain where the italophile Philip V had the Teatro de los Caños built specifically for Italian opera, in Hamburg, Bayreuth and Dresden, in London and Berlin.[14] Everywhere the Italians were celebrated, imitated and plagiarised. Lesser Italian composers could promote themselves on the backs of the more famous. Italians also dominated the entire field of secular vocal music: the aria, the cantata, the canzone, the canzonetta, the serenata, the chamber duet. Their production was gigantic, and only a fraction of it was published. Much of it was written primarily for private performances by professional singers or gifted amateurs. Opera was for a wider public.

As soon as a composer had established himself, it was in his interest to flood the market. Cavalli composed some forty operas; Alessandro Scarlatti more than seventy; Albinoni nearly fifty, though he is now known mainly for an adagio he never composed. Opera was an expensive genre – the most expensive of all performance arts. In eighteenth-century London, opera seats were four times more expensive than those of the playhouse. Costs of production rose steadily, particularly for grand opera. The scenery of Halévy's *La Juive* (1831) at the Paris Opéra cost 44,999 francs, that of Meyerbeer's *Robert le Diable* (1835) 43,545 francs. The production of Verdi's *Don Carlos* in 1867 cost 124,288 francs, not including the payment of performers. Small details, recurring every day, could increase the cost: to blacken the chorus and extras of Meyerbeer's *L'Africaine* cost 128 francs per evening (the opera was performed a hundred times).[15]

In 1721, subscribers to the King's Theatre in Haymarket, London (after 1837 it became Her Majesty's Theatre – or His, depending on the gender of the monarch), were charged twenty guineas for fifty operatic performances. The subscribers were given an engraved ivory or silver ticket that was transferable, thus generating a secondary market. By the beginning of the nineteenth century the subscription to a box at His Majesty's Theatre had escalated to between 180 and 300 guineas. The ranks of the aristocracy, who had long resorted to renting out their boxes, were not large enough to fill the two hundred boxes available for the entire season; the consequence was that the doors were opened to the new bourgeoisie. By the middle of the nineteenth century the bourgeoisie began to occupy even the boxes which had hitherto been the preserve of the nobility. Booksellers started buying tickets in bulk at special discount and selling them to out-of-town people, who now had easy access to London thanks to the railways.[16] The 'masses' (i.e. the upper middle classes) were taking over the former preserves of the aristocracy and transforming them into proper cultural venues. Dozens of English composers delighted the crowds at Covent Garden in this period – people like William Shield, J.A. Fisher, Charles Dibdin and Thomas Linley – none of whom is remembered today.

The *embourgeoisement* of the theatre proceeded apace everywhere. In 1792 in Venice, La Fenice was opened for ballet and *opera seria*. The economic decline and crisis of the eighteenth century had reduced the number of Venetian theatres, but this provided a business opportunity for a new breed of entrepreneurs. Giovanni Gallo bought the San Benedetto (1810) and the San Giovanni Grisostomo (1819), while another local entrepreneur, Giuseppe Camploy (1794–1889), bought the San Samuele theatre in 1852 and restored it. By then Venice had become of secondary importance as a theatrical centre; other Italian cities, above all Naples and Milan, held sway. In Venice, the city of Goldoni, plays were imported from France – only the opera was Italian.[17]

Between the end of the eighteenth century and the middle of the nineteenth, the capital cities of the various Italian states built ample theatres with balconies and stalls in which it was possible to perform both opera and drama. New or enlarged opera theatres were opened throughout the country. In Milan, after the fire in the Regio Ducal Teatro (1776), the new La Scala was opened in 1778 with a performance of *L'Europa riconosciuta* by Antonio Salieri. In 1801 the Teatro Grande opened in Trieste, the Teatro Nuovo in Piacenza in 1804, the Concordi in Cremona in 1808, and in Catania, the Teatro Bellini in 1812. The spread of these opera houses was facilitated by Italy's division into separate states, each with its own court and aristocracy. Each court wanted its own opera house. Soon every town wanted to do the same, and local notables tried to find the necessary funds. While in France and Great Britain everything was concentrated in the capital, in Italy by 1868, according to a government survey, there were 775 theatres (performing both drama and opera). There was not just Naples and Milan, but also Venice, Padua, Verona, Parma, Mantua, Ferrara, Modena, Ravenna, Lucca, Florence (La Pergola), Genoa (Carlo Felice), Rome (Argentina and the Costanzi), Turin (Regio), Bologna (Comunale). In the Po valley there were quite a number of reasonably sized towns able to stage operas on market days. In the Emilia-Romagna between 1830 and 1895, forty-three towns had at least ,one opera performed.[18] Most of these theatres had been built following the traditional eighteenth-century 'beehive' layout (*sala all'italiana*). This architecture, imitated throughout Europe, reflected a social hierarchy (boxes, stalls and, way up, the 'gods', with its own entrance).[19]

Opera theatres also spread throughout Germany – as fragmented as Italy – with the construction of a gigantic 2,000-seat opera house in Dresden (1719), and in 1742 the Lindenoper on Unter den Linden in Berlin[20] and the rococo Markgräfliches Opernhaus in Bayreuth. In 1825 the Russians opened the Bolshoi ('Big') Theatre in Moscow, on the site of the Petrovsky Theatre. New blood and new money had to fill these spaces.

At the Paris Opéra in 1788 there were still 369 subscribers to boxes. By 1819 there were only sixty-six. There was also a change in class. In 1788 the subscribers were mainly aristocrats. By the 1820s, in spite of the restoration of the monarchy, many ordinary names could be found among the sub-scribers. The French Revolution had enormously accelerated the process of making the opera more business-oriented. In 1791 the Constituent Assembly had abolished the system of 'privileges', whereby all the Paris theatres had to pay a due to the Opéra. Now anyone could open a theatre and stage any opera or play. This of course inflicted a serious loss to the Opéra. Opera-goers were still an élite, but a new one. The majority of the audiences were made up of single-ticket buyers, a transient public which according to reports included many people from out of Paris. The Opéra was becoming a tourist attraction.[21]

The domination of religious ideas and aristocratic habits had constrained opera performances. All stage representations were banned during Lent, as well as on Sundays (they still are in many countries) and religious festivals. The season was further restricted by the habit of aristocratic patrons of spending the summer months at their country estates.[22] The main operatic season, especially in Catholic countries, was very short: from Christmas to Shrove Tuesday. In Protestant countries, such as Prussia, it was a little longer: from November to March, with performances twice a week. Provincial theatres had to adapt their season to that of the bigger cities in the hope of attracting singers.

The new concern for a wider audience was a reflection of the transforma-tion of the theatre, and in particular of the opera. The architecture of new theatres showed signs of independence from the customs and hierarchies of the court. At the Théâtre de la Porte de Saint-Martin in Paris the interiors of all the boxes were decorated, democratically, in the same way.[23] In some places the *embourgeoisement* of the opera proceeded more gradually. As late, as 1884 almost all the thirty-six privately-owned boxes at the Teatro Comunale of Bologna were still held by aristocrats.[24] One should bear in mind, however, that the Italian aristocracy – like that of Germany – was rather 'bourgeois' and entrepreneurial, and that the multiplicity of courts before unification had multiplied titles of nobility, which were further expanded after unification.

In Germany there was already a distinctive opera genre favoured by the bourgeoisie and generally regarded as 'low'. This was the *Singspiel*, mainly comic operas in which arias would be followed by spoken dialogue – not unlike the English ballad opera (John Gay's famous *Beggar's Opera* being the best-known example). Most of the early *Singspiels* were produced in Leipzig, before gradually expanding into other German-speaking cities. It was a particularly successful genre, evolving into the operetta in the nineteenth century and, in the twentieth, into the most successful and profitable form of theatre: the musical.

The *Singspiel* sharply demarcated the songs from the rest of the plot. Thus freed from the constraints of the narrative, they could be simply an illustration of the play. It reached its zenith in the eighteenth century. Mozart's *Die Entführung aus dem Serail* (The Abduction from the Seraglio, 1782) and *Die Zauberflöte* (The Magic Flute, 1791) are perhaps the best-known instances of the genre, though hardly typical. *The Magic Flute* was composed at a time when Mozart was out of favour at court under the new Emperor, Leopold II. In need of money, he agreed to write a *Singspiel* for Emanuel Schikaneder, a theatrical impresario, actor and singer, and manager of a touring company. Schikaneder was a specialist in 'low' genres and in Shakespeare (then often performed as a low genre).

Mozart interrupted composing *The Magic Flute* twice for financial reasons. One time was to write his famous Requiem, the other because he had received a commission to write an opera to celebrate the coronation of Leopold as King of Bohemia. The result was *La Clemenza di Tito*, for which he got 200 gulden, good press reviews, and the displeasure of the new Empress, who regarded it as '*una porcheria tedesca*' – German rubbish.[25] *The Magic Flute*, however, was a great success with its audience and throughout the German-speaking world, as had been *Die Entführung aus dem Serail* and all Mozart's Italian operas – except in Vienna. If Mozart had not died in December 1791 he would have made more money from his 'downmarket'

Magic Flute than he received from the patron of the Requiem or from the King of Bohemia. Frenchified as *Les Mystères d'Isis* (see page 215), it was one of the most frequently performed operas between 1799 and 1809.[26] It was the first opera of international fame to be staged at Stockholm's Opera House (on 30 May 1812), and was performed a further 179 times over the next fifty years.[27]

German composers who remained faithful to a distinctive German style, such as Heinrich Marschner (1795–1861) and Albert Lortzing (1801–51), who was still widely performed in Germany a hundred years later, were relatively little performed outside Germany.[28] After Mozart and until Wagner, with a few exceptions such as Carl Maria von Weber, the most celebrated German composers, such as Schubert, Schumann, Mendelssohn and Brahms, either stayed well away from or never had any success with operas; Schubert's were never performed to a paying public during his lifetime. Beethoven wrote only one, albeit a masterpiece (*Fidelio*). With the opera houses under the sway of dead composers (such as Mozart) or living Italian ones (particularly the big four: Rossini, Bellini, Donizetti and Verdi), German composers, when they composed for the human voice, concentrated on a distinctive genre: the song or *lied*. Commercially this was the poor end of the market, yet one could become successful without having to convince anyone to stage a major opera production. A song would be printed on a music sheet, and purchased and widely performed in the drawing rooms of the rapidly expanding middle classes. All it required was a young man (more rarely a young woman) with a good voice, accompanied on the piano, usually by a young woman.

In Russia, opera was more rooted in national literature and folklore. Pushkin inspired Glinka's *Ruslan and Ludmila*, Tchaikovsky's *Eugene Onegin*, *Mazepa* and *The Queen of Spades*, Mussorgsky's *Boris Godunov*, Dargomyzhsky's *The Stone Guest* (in turn an adaptation of the Don Juan story) and Rimsky-Korsakov's *The Golden Cockerel* and *The Tale of Tsar Saltan*. In Germany the record is more mixed. Beethoven's *Fidelio* was based on a French play; Carl Maria von Weber's *Der Freischütz* (The Free-Shooter, 1821) on a German tale, but his *Euryanthe* (1823) and *Oberon* (1826) were adaptations from French stories (*Oberon* had an English libretto based on a French peddler's booklet published in the Bibliothèque Bleue). Albert Lortzing's *Zar und Zimmermann*, popular in Germany but nowhere else, originated from a French play. With Wagner there is a clear turn towards ancient Germanic myths. Dvořák adapted Czech and not-so-Czech folk tales (*Kate and the Devil* and *Rusalka*).

Themes and opera plots could be locally based, and some folk tunes and church music incorporated, but music composition remained international, subjected to standards established by those regarded as the best practitioners of the genre. When writing a symphony in 1840 it was impossible to ignore Mozart, Haydn and, above all, Beethoven. There was an international style. Even a nationalist composer such as Mikhail Glinka was forced, like other Russians, to acquire it by studying in Italy and Germany. The German-born Giacomo Meyerbeer (*né* Jakob Liebmann Beer), who became the major representative of the French grand opera, trained in Venice in 1815, adopted Rossini's style and wrote six Italian-style operas before developing his own.

Rossini's Star

The great nineteenth-century Italian opera composers hardly ever used major Italian literary works. They preferred Schiller, or Victor Hugo, or Scott, or Goethe, or Spanish drama, or Shakespeare. Of Rossini's thirty-nine operas, thirteen were adapted from French stories, three from Great Britain and one from Germany. His Paris opera *Il Viaggio a Reims*, written for the inauguration of King Charles X, was inspired by a famous French novel set in Italy (*Corinne* by Madame de Staël). The French too eschewed their major writers, though not as systematically as did the Italians: Berlioz and Gounod adapted Goethe and Shakespeare, Bizet adapted Walter Scott and Mérimée.

In 1801 Napoleon created a new theatre, the Théâtre-Italien (at first called the Opéra Buffa), dedicated to the Italian style of singing. Cimarosa was then the most popular composer in Paris. His great *opera buffa* success, *Il Matrimonio segreto*, first performed in Vienna in 1792, then at La Scala in 1793 and in London in 1794, was still popular in Paris ten years later, as was Giovanni Paisiello (*Il Barbiere di Siviglia*, 1782) twenty years later. The success of the Italians was underscored by the wide number of Italian singers who performed on the Paris stage in new Italian works.

The main non-Italian singers performing in France at the time, Laure Cinti, Julie Dorus and Cornélie Falcon, were all firmly in the Italian camp. The most popular male singer, Adolphe Nourrit, had been trained by Rossini. Italian terminology was systematically introduced. The *chanteuse* became a *cantatrice*. The term *prima donna* became widely established, as was the (Italian) use of the article 'la' before the *prima donna*'s surname – as in 'la' Malibran.[29]

By the 1820s the Théâtre-Italien had become the leading theatre in Paris. Until the revolution of 1848, explained the nineteenth-century impresario Maurice Starkosch in his memoirs, to be a subscriber at the Théâtre-Italien was almost like having a title of nobility.[30] It had more subscribers than any other theatre in Paris. It was the first to present Mozart's three Italian operas in the original Italian versions by da Ponte. The repercussions for the other main opera houses were considerable: the Opéra and the Opéra-Comique adopted the Italian vogue, either directly, by performing Rossini's works, or by championing composers who had adopted the Italian style.[31] The greatest *coup* pulled off by the Théâtre-Italien was to lure Rossini to become its director. Rossini was not a good administrator, but he turned the Théâtre-Italien into the crown jewel of Restoration society. When he arrived in Paris in 1823, audiences were already mad for his music. By the time the curtain rose on his works the theatre was already full, few members of the audience were late and everyone was ready to listen. It seemed that the flow of his Parisian productions would never stop: *L'Italiana in Algeri* (1817), *L'Inganno felice* and *Il Barbiere di Siviglia* in 1819, *Il Turco in Italia* and *Torvaldo e Dorliska* (1820); three more including *La Gazza ladra* in 1821, then *Tancredi*, *Mosé in Egitto* and *Cenerentola* in 1822, *Il Viaggio a Reims* and *Semiramide* in 1825 and *Zelmira* in 1826. In 1822, 119 of the 154 performances at the theatre were of Rossini's works, and in 1825, 129 out of 174. In Paris Rossini wrote and staged five new operas in as many years, beginning with *Il Viaggio a Reims* in 1825 and concluding with *Guillaume Tell* in 1829. His earnings were considerable. He was granted 10,000 francs over and above what a decree of 1816 had established a composer should earn for a major opera, which was 250 francs per performance.[32]

Rossini was a major cult figure. In November 1823 in Paris a gigantic party assembled for a banquet in his honour. This was satirised a fortnight later in a vaudeville act written by Eugène Scribe and Edmond Mazères (*Rossini à Paris ou Le grand dîner*). In London he also earned vast sums, not only from the fees for performances of his works at the King's Theatre but from his numerous private and public appearances. His fee for just 'appearing' at an event was fifty guineas. He was further merchandising himself by organising recitals of his best-known arias by the best singers of the time: Giuditta Pasta, Angelica Catalani, Manuel García and Isabella Colbran.[33]

To attend one of Rossini's operas was an event. Byron, who was in Venice in 1819, wrote: 'There has been a splendid Opera lately at San Benedetto – by Rossini – who came in person to play the Harpsichord – the People followed him about – crowned him – cut off his hair "for memory"; he was Shouted and Sonneted and feasted – and immortalised much more than either of the Emperors.' An English traveller noted that Rossini's tunes could frequently be heard being whistled by artisans.'[34] On 20 September 1824 at six in the evening Hegel arrived in Vienna from Prague. By seven he had found a suitable inn. By 7.30 he was already at the opera for Rossini's *Barbiere di Siviglia*. Later he wrote to his wife Marie: 'As long as there is enough money to pay for the Italian opera and the trip back home – I'm staying in Vienna.' In Berlin, critics and connoisseurs were still dubious about Rossini, but the audiences loved his work. Hegel thought that the Berlin critics were simply unable to appreciate the skills of Rossini and of the Italian singers: 'Just as satin is for grand ladies, *pâté de foie gras* for educated palates, so Rossini's music is only created for Italian voices.'[35]

Rossini's fame was enhanced by his reputation as a brilliant conversationalist and a famous gourmand. A particularly succulent and cholesterol-rich dish, *tournedos Rossini* – beef fillet topped with *pâté de foie gras* – was named after him by the great chef of the restaurant La Maison dorée, Casimir Moisson. When Rossini, after a stay in Italy, came back to Paris in 1843, 2,000 people signed a two-month waiting list to visit him.[36] By the time he was thirty-seven, in 1829, Rossini had exhausted himself. He went into semi-retirement, and though he continued to be the centre of attention, he wrote no new operas. He may have been affected by severe depression, but he went on living the good life until his dying day, rich, courted, and sought after for his wit and amiability.

Writers celebrated Rossini. Stendhal wrote a *Vie de Rossini* (1823), though, as usual, this was more about Stendhal than Rossini. He declared that, 'since the death of Napoleon, there is only one man who is talked about every day in Moscow as in Naples, in London as in Vienna, in Paris as in Calcutta'.[37] Balzac missed no opportunities to puff him: he dedicated his *Le Contrat de mariage* to him, called him 'the new musical star' in *Les Illusions perdues* and described his work as 'sacred music expressed to the highest degree' in *La Duchesse de Langeais*.[38] In *Massimila Doni* there is discussion of Rossini's *Mosé* which lasts several pages, in the course of which the protagonist exclaims that only an Italian could feel the complaints of a wronged people: 'You old German masters, Handel, Sebastian Bach, and even you, Beethoven, on your knees, here is the Queen of the Arts, here is triumphant Italy!'[39] Inevitably there were dissidents, such as the critic of the review *Le Pandore*: 'Who will deliver us from M. Rossini ... this petty musician who rebels against the wise laws of counterpoint?'[40] When Rossini died in 1868 *The Times* wrote that 'several of his operas will only perish with the art of music itself', and that with Rossini 'has departed one of the most remarkable geniuses and one of the kindliest spirits of the nineteenth century'.[41] Berlioz, by contrast, wrote in his *Mémoires* that 'the fanaticism that he sparked in the fashionable Paris world caused in me a violent anger'.[42]

The advent of Rossini put an end to the great debate of the mid-eighteenth century between the champions of French music and those of Italian opera. The Italians had won.[43] However, the nineteenth-century capital of opera was Paris, whose pull was so remarkable that no Italian city, not even Naples with its San Carlo or Milan with La Scala, could rival it. The major Italian composers, from Rossini and Verdi, once they had achieved fame in Italy sought the ultimate consecration: a Parisian triumph. Paris functioned as a kind of global legitimation of one's success. London, with no major musical tradition of its own, came second; Berlin third, having supplanted Vienna in the last decades of the nineteenth century. The hour of New York (or Hollywood) had yet to come.

Just as the success of French and British popular writers inhibited the development of commercial mass culture in other European countries, so the success of the Italians and to a lesser extent of the Germans and French in the field of opera virtually blocked the rise of opera in the rest of Europe. Spain produced great singers, such as Manuel García (the first interpreter of the Count in Rossini's *Barbiere*) and his even more famous daughter Maria Malibran (then still Miss García, the first interpreter of Rosina in the same opera), but virtually no opera throughout the nineteenth century. Its main achievement in the field of theatrical music was the *zarzuela*, the distinctive Spanish operetta, exportable only to Latin America. Similarly, Britain remained until the end of the nineteenth century essentially a consumer of music, particularly opera, rather than a producer. Only in the second half of the twentieth century, when the terrain was clear of much competition, did the country score a remarkable success with Benjamin Britten, virtually the only British composer of global significance. Otherwise, like Spain, Britain produced its own kind of light opera, monopolised by Gilbert and Sullivan, which delighted London audiences but remained almost unperformed abroad except in the USA and the 'white' colonies.

Elsewhere the development of opera, and of music more generally, was related to the development of national consciousness. The huge expense associated with its production meant that opera could seldom be staged on

a practical commercial basis. It thus depended either on aristocratic patronage, or on the financial support of the middle classes. The latter wanted
opera in the vernacular, partly for nationalist reasons, partly because, unlike
the upper classes, they knew no Italian. This worked somewhat to the advantage of native composers. Thus Russia produced a major operatic tradition,
largely state-supported, as did Bohemia and Hungary, but these developments
came well after the middle of the nineteenth century, although misleading
claims are often made as to the dates of the 'first' opera in Czech, Russian
or Polish.[44] Poland had an early start, but the partition of the country in 1795
eliminated royal patronage and damaged the development of an autarchic
Polish opera. Clearly the support of the state (or the court) was essential.
Nevertheless, the spirit of cultural nationalism was strong enough to enable
the production in Poland, by 1830, of some 130 operas, though most were
imitative of foreign models.[45] It was much simpler to translate the librettos
into Polish. Thus Rossini's operas were usually performed in Polish at the
National Theatre of Warsaw. The press coverage did not deal with their
intrinsic worth, for no one doubted that Rossini was a genius, but on the
performances of the singers, lamenting the fact that it was difficult for a
country with a limited operatic tradition to produce performers adequate to
the music.[46] Subsequent developments would show that good voices could
come from anywhere. In the second half of the twentieth century great
sopranos came from New Zealand (Kiri te Kanawa), Australia (Joan Sutherland, but there was already Nellie Melba early in the century), Greece (Maria
Callas), Norway (Kirsten Flagstad) and Sweden (Birgit Nilsson, preceded by
Jenny Lind in the nineteenth century). Such internationalisation reflected the
global reach of Italian opera.

16

Theatre

Transience

MUSIC WAS EVENTUALLY RECORDED: first, in the 1870s, on foil-covered rotating cylinders, then wax cylinders, then flat discs, then magnetic tapes, shellac, vinyl, audio cassettes, and digitally on compact discs. The theatre, however is essentially unrecordable. Even though it may be preserved on film or audio tape, each separate performance is transient. It lives only in the memory. At the end of the last performance the set is broken up, the costumes and props are recycled for other shows. There is rarely an accurate archival record of how the production was rehearsed and staged. Everything melts away.[1] The text alone remains.

Plays usually start in the middle of a situation of which the audience knows nothing. Gradually, light descends as characters behave in ways people never or seldom behave in real life: they reveal much of themselves and their pasts in conversations with other characters whom, in the play, they have known for years. This unrealistic dialogue is pronounced both in so-called realistic or naturalistic plays, such as those of Ibsen, or in the modernist plays of Harold Pinter or Samuel Beckett. No everyday conversation remotely resembles the way characters speak to each other in drama.

The play is a story which is 'acted out'. This is true even of the most didactic or propagandistic theatre – from medieval morality plays to socialist agitprop. A 'non-fiction' theatre would amount to a lecture. The printed text, inevitably, can encompass a far wider range than the theatre. But the theatre is older than the book, and more universal. It can be found in almost every society, including those which do not have writing. Writing is about record-keeping, accounts, chronicles and, occasionally, entertainment. The theatre, even when it contains a prevalently religious or political message, is always a form of entertainment.

A precise definition of the theatre is problematic. Can one distinguish clearly between the tale that is told and the tale that is acted? An itinerant traveller stops in a village, in the marketplace. He tells a story to those willing to listen and pay. He does not impersonate characters. He is not 'acting'. Or is he? In the course of his storytelling, he pauses, slightly altering his voice and his demeanour to make the audience aware that it is not he but a character who is speaking 'through him'. Such acts of interpretation are achieved almost unconsciously. When we tell the story of Little Red Riding Hood to a child, do we not change our voice when we 'impersonate', i.e. act out, the character of the Big Bad Wolf? There are storytellers so talented that they can make the most dispiriting narrative acquire a life of its own, just as terrible acting can easily ruin a play by the most revered of writers.

The theatre needs more than a text and a voice. It needs an audience. The theatre is a set of relations between a collectivity, the audience, which assembles in a public space to observe 'in real time' another collectivity (a cast of actors, even a single actor). Each collectivity must use its imagination, its fantasy. The actors pretend to be other than themselves. They are Greek gods, *femmes fatales*, scorned lovers, forlorn tramps, uncomprehending husbands, bloodthirsty tyrants. The audience pretend that the actors *are* the characters they represent. They hate the fictional villains and admire the fictional heroes. Actors and audiences, when they encounter each other in the theatre, satisfy, however fleetingly, a deeply felt human wish, the desire to create another world and another self.

We know as little about the origins of the theatre as we know about the origins of storytelling. We have a reasonably good idea of how Greek drama was performed in antiquity, but we know little about its audience. In ancient Athens, a playwright would present four works once a year at the theatre of Dionysus on the slope of the hill below the Acropolis: three tragedies and a short, comic 'satyr' play. The performance would take place throughout the day (with no interruptions within each play), terminating before sunset. We also know little about Greek playwrights, for only four of them have left us some of their completed plays: Aeschylus, Sophocles, Euripides and Aristophanes. Roman theatre fared scarcely better: Plautus, Terence and Seneca are all we have. Time is a great destroyer of everything that is not recorded. And many works that are not destroyed are forgotten by posterity. Few plays from the many thousands written between the sixteenth century and the middle of the nineteenth century are regularly performed today.

A modern performance of Aeschylus' trilogy *Oresteia* (458 BC) would last five hours, at a brisk pace. The first play (*Agamemnon*) tells how Agamemnon, returning victorious from Troy, is murdered by his adulterous wife Clytemnestra, to avenge their daughter whom Agamemnon had sacrificed to the gods. The second play (*Choephori*) tells of Orestes, the son of Agamemnon and Clytemnestra, who avenges his father by killing both his mother and her lover. In the third (*Eumenides*), Orestes is tried and is acquitted thanks to the intervention of the god Apollo and the goddess Athena. It is tempting to underline how the plot elements of the *Oresteia* – a child sacrifice, adultery, a wife who kills her husband, a son who kills his mother, the whole thing climaxing in a court of law – have remained popular with the public these last 2,500 years. Audiences, however, do not simply absorb a plot in isolation from the cultural context. We know that most modern audiences in the West would sympathise with Sophocles' Antigone, who buries her dead brothers in opposition to her uncle the King's prohibition. She would be regarded as a feisty heroine who resists state power and follows her conscience. But in ancient Greece the concept of 'following one's conscience' would be out of place: Antigone was upholding traditional religious values. In Sophocles' *Oedipus*, Oedipus, having discovered that he has killed his father and married his mother Jocasta, is so consumed by guilt that he blinds himself, while Jocasta kills herself. An unprepared modern audience would understand the grief felt, but not the guilt manifested by Oedipus and his mother. Their 'sin' was unintentional, and hence eminently forgivable.

The text, of course, represents only one aspect of the play. The meaning of the play is determined by the staged performance. Most modern audiences of classical Greek drama would be averse to the use of the chorus, the mythical allusions and a literal translation of the original language. As a critic explained, 'to reproduce a Greek tragedy today would be a theatrical exercise in theatrical embalming', and 'it would be quite impossible to replicate the shared civic experience that was Athenian theatre'.[2] The Greek theatre seems to many of us 'modern' not because it *is* modern, which it plainly is not, but because it is sufficiently open-ended to enable us (audience and actors) to determine new meanings. One of the conditions enabling a work of art to survive beyond the immediate present is that it should be 'polysemic', i.e. allow different readings. For much of the intervening period between antiquity and the modern age, mythology (including religious mythology) itself provided many of the plots required for theatrical representations. St Gregory of Nyssa, writing in the fourth century to the Sophist Stagirios, described how the 'actors' (the Greek term suggests 'maker of marvels') would choose as a topic for their performance a historical myth or some ancient tales, which they would narrate to their audience. They would wear masks and costumes, and use painted panels as a backdrop.[3]

Biblical stories and Greco-Roman mythology were endlessly adapted to produce the religious and secular theatre of the Middle Ages: the English miracle plays, the German *Mysterienspiel*, the *rappresentazioni sacre* in Italy and *auto sacramental* in Spain, the French *mystères*, the 'Jesuit' plays, etc. These were often performed out of doors, in marketplaces, occasionally in churches (liturgical drama). The more popular the setting, the more unavoidable was the use of the vernacular, though there was great reliance on gestures, effects and costumes. The Church, having dominated medieval theatre and fearing it was about to lose its monopoly, sought to limit theatrical performances outright, to have them heavily censored, or to allow only representations of scenes from the Bible in decorous settings.

The Romans had built permanent arenas which could also be used for sporting events and gladiatorial contests, but most theatrical representations until the sixteenth century took place in the open, on temporary structures. Only in 1576 did London acquire, thanks to the actor James Burbage, its first public theatre. The Globe, used by Shakespeare's company, was built in 1599. It was an open-air building with standing room for the majority of the audience. Scenery was rudimentary or non-existent in the 'respectable' permanently fixed theatres, but was used not infrequently in the outdoor pantomime and mystery plays. Contemporary clothes were worn by actors even in plays set in the past, such as Shakespeare's Roman plays. The conventions of theatre architecture that prevailed were not those of England, but of Renaissance Italy, such as the Teatro Olimpico in Vicenza (1580), designed following the principles of Andrea Palladio.

The Italians used the techniques of perspective painting developed during the Renaissance to make enclosed spaces look larger and deeper. Complex machinery was used to produce special effects. By the beginning of the seventeenth century, revolving painted screens (*telari*) were used to provide changes of scenery. Soon these innovations spread throughout Europe, and were introduced into England by Inigo Jones (1573–1652), who had studied in Italy. Italian advances in stage design, however, were not matched by the development of a tradition of playwriting. The Italian theatre was dominated by actor-centred improvisations such as those of the commedia dell'arte, which made playwrights unnecessary. Actors embroidered on simple plots and standard characters. Those who could write a play found it more profitable and easier to write opera librettos. This may explain why, apart from Goldoni and Carlo Gozzi, there were hardly any playwrights of note in Italy until the nineteenth century.

The Commedia dell'Arte dominated the commercial European theatre from the middle of the sixteenth century to the middle of the eighteenth. It relied on a constant repetition of plots and situations – generally older men (guardians, parents) trying to prevent the marriage of two likeable young people in love with each other. It was performed by itinerant professionals (hence 'dell'arte', i.e. belonging to the artistic profession) who used, precisely because there were no shared languages among its varying audiences, music, dance and, above all, mimicry. Masks were often worn. The absence of texts enabled actors to respond promptly to the mood of their different audiences, trying all the time to engage with them.

The pantomime was an adaptation of the Commedia dell'Arte. Here there was little or no spoken dialogue. It used the standard Italian characters such as Arlecchino, usually the greedy servant (possibly a descendant of 'Herlequin', in turn perhaps derived from the German Erlenkönig, one of the names of the Anglo-Saxon god Woden and the Scandinavian Odin), Colombina, her mistress's confidante, the truculent but clownesque Capitano Scaramuccia (occasionally Captain Matamoros or 'killer of Moors'), the lecherous miser Pantalone (Pantaloon, based on the sixteenth-century Venetian character dressed in loose trousers) and the long-nosed Pulcinella. In Great Britain, puppet shows using stringed marionettes were imported from Italy shortly after the Restoration of 1660. By the early eighteenth century this had become a low, if popular, genre performed mainly at country fairs. The chief character, Punch – the Italian Pulcinella – became in Britain the inveterate beater of his long-suffering wife Joan or Judy. The result was the allegedly amusing Punch and Judy show. In the early nineteenth century it was performed regularly thanks to Joseph Grimaldi (the son of an Italian actor), who – amalgamating various Italian characters with that of the Elizabethan fool – invented the character of Joey the Clown, and perhaps its characteristic costume.[4] Pantomime still endures in our own day, though mainly at Christmas when parents drag their television-raised progeny to it as a kind of pilgrimage into one's 'heritage'.

Originally the pantomime was regarded as popular and not 'erudite', simply because it was not written down. However, in the eighteenth century the divide between popular entertainment and the 'real' theatre was somewhat loose. For instance, in Sweden in 1785 near the castle of Drottningholm the entertainment on offer was eclectic: short plays illustrating well-known French proverbs, a puppet show, an Italian *opera buffa*, the tightrope walker Spinacuta, performing animals, and Dr Barri from Paris, who practised tooth extraction – in those days a public spectacle. There was also Mademoiselle Alexandra Calipoliti, who pretended to be a Greek dancer from the Turkish Sultan's theatre in Constantinople, though she was in fact German and called Augusta Deyss.[5]

The English theatre began to acquire influence in Europe only after the mid-eighteenth century, thanks to the growing reputation of Shakespeare. Already recognised since the middle of the seventeenth century by the English as *the* English writer, he had to wait another century to become acknowledged as one of the greatest European writers.[6] There were translations before then, but twenty-two of his plays were translated into German by Christoph Martin Wieland between 1762 and 1766.[7] A few years later, in 1775–77, the complete works, suitably adapted to fit native taste, were translated into German again by J.J. Eschenburg, and into French by Pierre le Tourneur in 1776–83.[8]

Shakespeare owed his growing reputation in England not to scholarly efforts but to those of actors and theatre managers such as David Garrick (1717–79), who produced twenty-four of the plays and promoted the celebration, in 1769 at Stratford-upon-Avon, of the two hundredth anniversary of Shakespeare's birth (though he was actually born in 1564). Such was French cultural prestige that Shakespeare's acceptance in Europe required some kind of French legitimisation. Voltaire was partly responsible for his fame in Germany. Catherine of Russia corresponded extensively with him about Shakespeare, and translated *The Merry Wives of Windsor* (from French) into Russian. Yet Voltaire had mixed feelings about Shakespeare, 'whom the English take for a Sophocles . . . a genius full of strength and power, artlessness and magnificence, without the slightest spark of good taste or knowledge of the rules'.[9] The 'rules', of course, were those of Aristotle's *Poetics*: tragedy must show a conflict unfolding in a single day, at the end of which a cathartic release must be achieved. Other rules were added later: the events had to take place in the same location, heroes had to be high-born, the drama had to have a beginning, a middle and an end. The great seventeenth-century French playwrights, Pierre Corneille, Jean Racine and Molière, followed the rules strictly. English playwrights seldom observed them. Roman playwrights did not do so either. And the dominant classical influence in Elizabethan drama was the Roman Seneca, a playwright, rather than the Greek Aristotle, who only wrote about the theatre. The Elizabethans liked Seneca's penchant for mixing the gory and the comic, for blending different plots in the same play and ignoring all the sacred unities of time and space – techniques which Shakespeare adopted.

As the nineteenth century approached, such rules began to be questioned on the Continent as well, meeting strong resistance: in 1780 the King of Prussia, Frederick II ('the Great'), wrote and published, in French naturally, a treatise called *De la Littérature Allemande* in which he condemned the tendencies of the German theatre to follow the non-classical model of Shakespeare and its 'detestable and disgusting' platitudes. The target was Goethe's tragedy *Götz von Berlichingen* (1773), written under the inspiration of the pro-Shakespearian father of German Romanticism Johann Gottfried Herder.[10]

Eventually the 'rules' were abandoned by all and sundry, and matters improved for Shakespeare's supporters. By 1839 the vogue for his plays in Germany was such that Heine claimed in his *Shakespeares Mädchen und Frauen* that the Germans understood Shakespeare better than the English. In the 1830s and 1840s Shakespeare had become the idol of the Russian intelligentsia; the young Mikhail Lermontov and the young Fyodor Dostoevsky were among those enthralled by *Hamlet*.[11] The fame of Shakespearian drama also grew in Germany – and to a lesser extent in France – throughout the nineteenth century. Quotations from his works were collected, his plays carefully staged. Drama directors went to London to observe Edmund Kean performing *Hamlet* before staging it in Germany using similar techniques and principles.[12]

Thus, in spite of the still rudimentary communication network, something approaching a European stage culture was being formed. This was not an amalgam of local cultures, but was characterised by a system similar to the exchange of material goods: some countries specialised in or dominated certain fields, their cultural wares often adapted to local taste. Successful genres were then imitated and developed further. For example, George Lillo's famous play *The London Merchant or the History of George Barnwell* (1731) was very successful in Germany and France. It was the story of a young man, infatuated by a harlot, who murders his uncle for money before dying repentant on the gallows – a combination of the universally loved themes of sex, money and violence.

An international genre emerged, called by the French the *comédie larmoyante* (we would call it 'a weepy'), usually the story of a pathetic heroine unjustly accused while trying to defend her virtue. Normally the story had a happy conclusion. The genre was used by most eighteenth-century play-wrights, high and low, the unremembered and the canonised; hundreds of plays were produced in a frenetic bout of self-reference, plagiarism, inspiration, adaptation. One of the leading practitioners of the genre was the now entirely forgotten but then immensely popular Pierre Claude Nivelle de la Chaussé (1692–1754), author of a *Paméla* (after Richardson). The same source was used by Voltaire for his own *comédie larmoyante, Nanine*. In fact, as soon as some-thing 'worked', in the sense that it was successful, it was immediately rejigged and re-adapted. No sooner had Jean-Marie-Théodore Baudouin d'Aubigny and Louis-Charles Caigniez obtained a modicum of success with their 'maid and the thieving magpie' plot in the melodrama *La Pie voleuse; ou la servante du Palaiseau* (1815), than S.J. Arnold had stolen it (*The Maid and the Magpie, or Which is the Thief*, 1815) and Rossini adapted it in his *La Gazza ladra* (1817). Thirty years later the plot was still being used on the London stage, by the likes of C. Stansfield Jones with his *The Maid and the Magpie* (1848).

Recycling French, British and German farces and melodramas was much easier to do, and just as remunerative, as writing original work. In Sweden, the first original play written in Swedish to be performed at a royal theatre was Count Carl Gyllenborg's 1737 comedy *Den svenska sprätthöken* (The Swedish Fop). But this was an exception. Sweden lacked playwrights, and was forced to import massively. Towards the end of 1760 Carl August Ehrensvärd complained that 'The taste for the French theatre is so common and so captivating that the Swedish theatre is in banishment in its own country,' adding, perhaps with some exaggeration, that

> In the centre of the city, where some old and shambling hovels form a narrow alley, high up in an attic, where the daylight can penetrate with difficulty, where Art has been denied stairs, where one must scramble on a rickety and steep ladder – that is where the Swedish theatre has found its miserable abode . . . There was fighting like at an inn. The actors were acquired from the debtors' prison or were a rabble of soldiers . . . The actresses had been picked up from workhouses and the musicians came from houses of low repute. One went to the theatre to laugh at the worst one could imagine. The various acts of the tragedies were played in reverse order – one hung the unfortunate naked in the gallows, one booed out the actor who was not funny enough and laughed at the tragedies. The spectators participated in the performance as much as the actors them-selves.[13]

Gyllenborg himself translated plays such as Richard Steele's *The Lying Lover; or, the Ladies' Friendship* (1703), an unsuccessful early work. Steele's play was also used by Samuel Foote for 'his' comedy *The Liar* in 1762. Steele himself had taken it from *Le Menteur* (1643) by Corneille, who in turn had adapted it from Ruiz de Alarcón's *La Verdad sospechosa* (Truth is Suspect, 1634) – also the source for Goldoni's *Il Bugiardo* (The Liar, 1750). Enough to make a modern intellectual property lawyer relish the legal battles ahead, though even today one can get away with adaptations of works whose authors have long been dead.

Actors

The melodramas, farces and comedies favoured by most eighteenth-century audiences were usually performed by touring companies directed by actor-managers. Such plays were more exciting than the standard fare of old and small court theatres, where acting consisted of little more than the French style of declaiming prose with a limited range of codified movements to indicate emotions. An influential treatise by Francis Lang, the abbot of the church of Saint-Michel in Paris, the *Traité sur les règles du jeu d'acteur* (1727), taught how to show surprise, or to warn (bend three fingers and point with the index). A similar manual, *Ideen zu einer Mimik*, by I. Engel, appeared in Berlin in 1788, and was adopted even by Russian actors.[14] The idea of someone being in charge of 'directing' an opera or a play had not yet come about. In the theatre the head of the company, usually the leading actor, would allocate parts and oversee the rehearsals. Well into the nineteenth century, opera and theatre production consisted of little more than directing the actors' or the singers' entries and exits. The design was confined to decisions over whether or not to have a chair or a table. Lighting was expensive and inadequate. Actors often performed in a dim light, so even though they were near the audience, it was possible for an elderly actress to pretend to be a young maid.[15] Only towards the 1820s was gas lighting used along with the more traditional candles and oil lamps – and they stayed up during the entire performance.

Just as in the eighteenth century composers performed their own works, so in the theatre many playwrights were also actors – as had been the case with Sophocles and Aeschylus, Shakespeare and Molière. There was a particular preponderance of actor-writers in the comic genres, where the written text provides only a general indication of how a part should be played. Thus, for instance, in Vienna in the 1810s and 1820s, where this genre was thriving, the comic actor Ferdinand Raimund (real name Jakob Raimann, 1790–1836), unable to find sufficient texts commensurate with his skills, began to write his own farces to great acclaim.[16] During the early phase of the cinema, comic actors were often also the authors of their own films (Charlie Chaplin and Buster Keaton being the best-known exponents of a tradition continued by Woody Allen).

Travelling players ensured that the English theatre became known on the Continent (particularly in Holland and Germany) during the sixteenth and seventeenth centuries. At first their repertory consisted essentially of short comic sketches, where the slapstick effects were of far greater importance than a text declaimed in English mixed with Dutch or German. In the seventeenth century, particularly during the Puritan Interregnum, when the Parliament Ordinance of 1642 led to the closing of theatres and the disbanding of acting companies, the English repertory abroad was expanded to include longer plays. In Germany and Austria, such was the prestige of the *Englische Komödianten* (The English Comedians) that the name was used by visiting companies as late as the middle of the eighteenth century. During 1767–77 almost fifty English comedies were translated into German. By the nineteenth century, English actors and theatre managers were the most innovative in Europe in acting techniques and stage effects. A book on theatrical special effects published in France in 1873 acknowledged that it was the English who first perfected the art of making traps (hence *trappe anglaise*) to enable actors to erupt from below the stage or disappear suddenly.[17] The English made such abundant use of movement on stage that in France, at least at the beginning of the nineteenth century, audiences were shocked by such disregard for the staid principles of French acting. Stendhal had gone to London in 1821, and had seen a performance of *Othello*. He wrote, slightly perplexed, that the English, an 'angry people', had gestures different from the French to express the same feelings.[18] Heine wrote that the first time he was present at the representation of an English tragedy he was 'struck with a gesticulation that bore a great resemblance to that of a pantomime'.[19] Gestures were important on the London stage. The illustrations of books such as Henry Siddons's *Practical Illustrations of Rhetorical Gesture and Action* (1822) and Gilbert Austin's *Chironomia, or A Treatise on Rhetorical Delivery* (1806) suggest a common field of shared gestures to be used by actors.[20]

The actor who had intrigued Stendhal was the great Edmund Kean, who dominated the London stage from the Drury Lane Theatre. William Hazlitt had commented regularly on Kean's acting since his 1814 debut as Shylock –

when he thought that 'in giving effect to the conflict of passion ... in keenness of sarcasm ... in giving perpetually fresh shocks of delight and surprise, it would be difficult to single out a competitor'. In May 1814, having seen Kean's Iago, Hazlitt wrote:

> We have already stated it as our opinion, that Mr. Kean is not a literal transcriber of his author's text; he translates his characters with great freedom and ingenuity into a language of his own; but at the same time we cannot help preferring his liberal and spirited dramatic versions, to the dull, literal commonplace monotony of his competitors.[21]

Heine was equally impressed with Kean's Shylock: 'his voice becomes servile ... only the slightest touch of concentrated anger can be discerned; round his complacent lips little serpents writhe rapidly ... But words are useless. The best description cannot give an idea of Edmund Kean's manner.' This was much imitated, continued Heine, 'but the eagle's glance, that piercing fire which can look into the kindred light of the sun, Kean's eye, that magic lightning, that wizard flame, no ordinary theatre-bird can simulate it'.[22]

In September 1827 Kean, Charles Kemble and Harriet Smithson went to Paris and spent the entire theatrical season at the Odéon performing Shakespeare in English. Instead of advancing towards the middle of the stage as at the Comédie Française, declaiming beautiful verse and then retiring gracefully, the English actors actually ... acted. Étienne-Jean Delécluze, having seen them perform *Richard III*, reported in his *Journal* (26 May 1828) that as Richard, Kean's pangs of death were highly realistic, and thought it odd that the English tried so hard to represent agony with 'minute exactitude ... Richard fights against Richmond, he is hit, his sword falls, he tries to fight without it, falls again, wriggles on the floor while speaking his lines'. Delécluze was somewhat disapproving (such 'pantomime' is not in the play, he complained), but the French public liked the acting, and Kean's fame was such that the performance was sold out ten days before its first night on 12 May 1828.[23]

The French public still regarded Shakespeare as unconventional and daring, but a few years later, suitably adapted to French taste, and in French, he began to be regularly performed. For a few years Harriet Smithson kept English-language Shakespeare going in Paris, but to no avail. She gave up and married Berlioz, a great lover of Shakespeare. Frédéric Soulié wrote 'his' Shakespeare's *Roméo et Juliette* for the Odéon in 1828, and Victor Ducange adapted *Macbeth* in 1829 at the theatre of Saint-Martin.

This was a period of great expansion of the theatre in Paris. More theatres were built, more plays were written, and more money was made out of it than anywhere else in Europe. Great stars were born. There was François-Joseph Talma (1763–1826), reputedly the first actor to insist on using costumes appropriate to the time and place depicted in the play. There was the flamboyant Frédéric Lemaître (1800–76), a romantic actor for whom Victor Hugo wrote *Ruy Blas* (1838). And there was Mademoiselle Mars (Anne Boutet, 1779–1847), who specialised in roles of *coquettes* and *ingénues* in plays by Molière and Marivaux at the Comédie-Française, and was the first Doña Sol in Hugo's *Hernani*. The Théâtre des Funambules, built in 1813, was strictly for popular and escapist genres: tightrope dancing, farces and commedia dell'arte plays, where the mime Jean-Gaspard Deburau became famous for his pale-faced clown Pierrot – one of the subjects of Marcel Carné's classic film *Les Enfants du paradis* (1945), in which Lemaître too is represented.

Pleasing the Audience

The move towards a more professional theatre, with a more attentive audience and showing works of better quality, coincided with the growing prosperity of the middle classes. Though many of them wished to ape the aristocrats, they also developed habits peculiar to the bourgeoisie. Being at the theatre was certainly a symbol of their new, exalted status – as it is now – but it was not sufficient to please them. They were paying to stand or to sit in uncomfortable seats. They needed entertaining, too. The show began to matter. This is one of the reasons why on the English stage, the most commercially oriented in Europe, actors and impresarios had to introduce innovations in order to get the audience to pay attention to what was going on. In 1762 David Garrick expanded the seating and removed the spectators from the stage, improved the lighting of the stage and dimmed that in the auditorium. He introduced 'after-pieces' which would follow the main performance, crammed with popular bits of entertainment: songs, *tableaux vivants*, pageantry.[24] The typical London show in the Garrick era would start with some music, then some kind of prologue, and then the three-act play. Between acts there would be some singing and dancing, magic tricks and circus acts. The evening would be concluded with something 'light', a pantomime or a short farce.

In France, interest in the theatre expanded considerably at the time of the Revolution, particularly in the new styles of republican tragedies and patriotic vaudeville. As subsidies were still necessary, the favoured writers were those who were revolutionary, or able to pretend to be so. The managements had to please both the public and the new rulers, just as before they had tried to please the court and the new moneyed customers. With the defeat of the Jacobins, while a few patriotic plays had entered the repertory, notably Chenier's anti-monarchist *Charles IX, ou la Saint-Barthélémy*, the repertory had not much changed from pre-revolutionary days. By 1796–97, as long as one played the 'Marseillaise' and the 'Ça ira' at the beginning or at the end theatres could go on producing Molière, Racine and other favourites.[25]

Some form of liberalisation of theatre life had preceded the Revolution. The most prestigious theatre, the Opéra, once a court theatre, had been opened to the public. The conjunction of new wealth and liberalisation (one could open a theatre without a permit, and there was no overt censorship in the years following the Revolution) increased the size of theatre audiences. The Napoleonic decree of 1806 tried to return to some form of control. No new theatres could be built without permission. No venue could stage a work from the repertoire of the Opéra, the Comédie-Française or the Opéra-Comique without paying them a fee. Ballets with historic or mythological themes could only be staged at the Opéra (to the detriment of the Théâtre de la Porte Saint-Martin). In 1807 Napoleon closed all theatres, including the Porte Saint-Martin (used for great spectacles and melodrama), which was, with 2,000 seats, the largest in Paris. He kept open the four (subsidised) official theatres: the Théâtre-Français, the Opéra, the Opéra-Comique and the Opéra Bouffe, as well as four secondary theatres: the Théâtre des Vaudevilles (for short plays mixing songs and satire), the Théâtre des Variétés (for 'vulgar, licentious or rustic' entertainment, i.e. vaudeville), the Ambigu-Comique and the Théâtre de la Gaieté (pantomimes, farces and harlequin-ades, and the occasional melodrama).[26]

The Napoleonic decree established rigid rules: the repertory of the Opéra-Comique could include 'any comedy or drama containing songs, light melodies, and ensemble pieces', as long as the dialogue was spoken – the contents did not have to be comic. Thus Cherubini's *Médée*, which ends tragically, was performed at the Opéra-Comique because of its spoken dialogues. Spontini's *Vestale* (1807), which ends happily but had no spoken parts, was performed at the Opéra.[27] The theatre, though not open all year round, was more available than many of the alternative live entertainments, even if one includes the circus, balls and *cafés chantants*. Dominique Leroy has calculated that in Paris in 1817–18 some two million theatre seats were sold. By 1850, five million seats were sold annually.[28]

The English theatre followed a pattern not dissimilar to that of the French – a process of increasing liberalisation followed by unparalleled expansion. London's theatres had remained closed from 1642 for the entire period of the republican Commonwealth. In 1662, one of the first acts of Charles II was to grant a royal patent (i.e. authorisation by the Crown) to only two theatres – the Drury Lane and Covent Garden (at first called the Lincoln's Inn Fields). These were the only ones allowed to perform 'serious' plays. By the mid-eighteenth century five more theatres were opened, as well as an opera house – the Queen's Theatre (later Her/His Majesty's) in the Haymarket (1705), which specialised in Italian operas. In 1794 the Drury Lane was rebuilt and expanded so that it could sit 3,611 people. Because of its enormous size it had to present relatively 'popular' fare: light operas and farces, in reality not much different from what was shown at Covent Garden. Even in the middle of the eighteenth century it tried to appeal to three distinct classes, each of which knew their place: the aristocracy sat in the boxes, the middle classes and their hangers-on sat in the 'pit', and the so-called 'middle gallery' was reserved for the lower orders: artisans, journeymen and servants.[29] It was only in 1843 that the Theatres Act de-licensed the theatre, though the Lord Chamberlain could withhold permission to stage a play in the interest of public morality. De-licensing led to a surge in theatres in Victorian England, with some 300,000 seats being created. Theatre-building continued alongside the development of the cinema well into the 1920s.[30]

This expansion in theatres and seats was paralleled by an expansion in productions. Twice as many plays were written between 1750 and 1800 as in the preceding fifty years – though few of these have become 'canonised': Goldsmith's *She Stoops to Conquer* (1773), Sheridan's *The Rivals* (1775) and *The School for Scandal* (1777) – all comedies.[31] Raymond Williams described the period as 'the most barren in our dramatic history'.[32] It may have been barren in long-lasting works, but theatrically speaking, it was a period of unprecedented growth, helped by the expansion of the urban population. By the middle of the nineteenth century there were twenty-one theatres in London and seventy-five in the provinces. By 1900 there were sixty-three theatres in London and three hundred in the provinces.

All over Europe, hack writers were busy turning successful novels into plays. Walter Scott – as we saw on pages 152–3 – was endlessly adapted both for the stage and the opera. This was true of every successful writer. Alessandro Manzoni's *I Promessi sposi* may have sold less than he had hoped, but its first version was turned into a play by Giambattista Nasi in 1827, almost as soon as it was published. A year later there was another musical adaptation of it in Florence. In 1830, while Manzoni was still working at refining his Italian-language version, Giuseppe Checcherini was busy turning it into a melodrama in Neapolitan dialect, giving it a local tone, for instance by having Don Abbondio's servant ask whether he would like a good cup of coffee – a beverage then unknown in the rural north.[33]

High-culture dramas, attended by the bourgeoisie and the aristocracy, were subsidised. The reasons given by those who had power in deciding the level of subsidies were moral, educational or political. The 'low' theatrical genres, including farce, comic plays, and vaudeville, could look after themselves, since they were by definition popular and commercial. Then as now, high art was dramatic, the comic was low though popular. The labouring classes were excluded from the theatre by education, cost and distance (the theatres were usually in the more elegant districts). Before the French Revolution, what the higher classes called *le peuple*, meaning traders and artisans, could attend live performances at fairs, where actors and mimes would play farces and comic scenes, often adapted from the 'respectable' repertory. Just as excluded from theatrical life were those who lived outside the main cities. Going to the theatre, before the railways, was an enterprise beyond most people. In her surviving letters, Jane Austen mentions visiting people a great deal, and talks about a grand gala, a concert with illuminations and fireworks, but she hardly ever mentions the theatre. Occasionally there is an allusion to a play (Kotzebue's *The Birthday Party*) or a reference to seeing a Shakespeare play at Covent Garden (but which?). On 23 April 1805 she mentions going to a concert. We know what she wore ('I wore my crape sleeves'), but not whether the concert was any good or what was performed.[34]

In Paris at the beginning of the nineteenth century the *nouveaux riches* and the petty or recently ennobled aristocrats would go to the Théâtre-Français (in the footsteps of the aristocracy), but they also went to the *théâtres des boulevards*, where they mingled with the middle and lower middle classes. There they enjoyed, almost exclusively, the melodrama (so called because originally it made considerable use of music). The Gaieté, the Ambigu and the Porte Saint-Martin showed a steady fare of melodramas with prestigious actors like Frédérick Lemaître. Though it stood at the lowest level of the respectable theatre, just above the comic performance, the melodrama was popular with the bourgeoisie. The taste of the aristocracy was not any 'higher'. Outside the main cities, where aristocrats still believed that they should keep up appearances and patronise high culture, local theatres, once court theatres, merely replicated the taste of the boulevard theatre. Thus at Count Wallenstein's castle theatre in Litomyšl in Bohemia, the first play to be performed on the new stage (1798) was Friedrich Wilhem Zigler's farce *Liebhaber und Nebenbuhler in einer Person* (The Lover and the Rival in One Person) – with all the parts played by the Count and his family.

The most frequently performed author, however, in Germany and elsewhere, was August Kotzebue (1761–1819), the now entirely forgotten, but then unforgettable, master of the German melodrama.[35] His European renown was far greater than that of Schiller. To obtain it he had to work hard, producing over two hundred plays. He managed the Hoftheater of Vienna, then went to Russia where he directed the theatre in St. Petersburg. His *Menschenhass und Reue* (1789) was very successful in England as *The Stranger* (1798), and he was imitated by Richard Brinsley Sheridan in the play *Pizarro* (1799). His play *Das Kind der Liebe*, adapted by Elizabeth Inchbald as *Lover's Vow* (1798), features in Jane Austen's *Mansfield Park*.[36] The end of this 'most successful purveyor . . . of opiates to the bourgeoisie, the representative of all that was unreal and ephemeral in contemporary literature', to use Nicholas Boyle's words,[37] was, to say the least, dramatic: he was murdered by a revolutionary student, Karl Sand, who suspected him, not without cause, of being a Russian spy. Kotzebue was performed, on and off, throughout the nineteenth century, mainly in German-speaking lands and where the German theatre was influential – such as Hungary, Serbia and throughout the Balkans – but also in Britain and the USA (where there was a large German-speaking community). In France he was still, at the beginning of the nineteenth century, the most famous German writer – of Goethe only *Werther* had survived outside scholarly circles.[38]

The French melodrama, as one would expect, was largely home-grown, though often it adapted foreign plays and novels. In the early nineteenth century it was almost synonymous with Guilbert de Pixérécourt (1773–1844), who had once declared, 'I write for those who cannot read.'[39] Pixérécourt's plays – he wrote 111, directing almost all of them – were performed in the *théâtres des boulevards*, which were patronised by a far less exclusive audience than those of the official theatres, and were less bound by convention. His plays are supposed to have been performed 30,000 times in his lifetime, and enormous queues formed to obtain seats for major successes such as his version of *Robinson Crusoe* (described as a '*grand spectacle*') at the Théâtre de la Porte Saint-Martin in 1805. Many of his plots were borrowed from English and German novels and plays. *Le Château des Apennins, ou le fantasme vivant* was an adaptation of Ann Radcliffe's *The Mysteries of Udolpho*. From Schiller he took *Wilhelm Tell* for his *Guillaume Tell* and turned *Die Räuber* into *Robert le Diable*. His *Le Château de Loch-Leven* was an imitation of Walter Scott. In turn, he himself was widely imitated and adapted, particularly in England and Italy. His most famous play, *Coelina ou l'enfant du mystère* (1800) – performed 387 times in Paris and 1,089 times in the provinces – was promptly rendered into English as *A Tale of Mystery* in 1802 before being translated into all the main European languages.[40]

Pixérécourt was quite conscious that the melodrama had to be kept simple: nothing in it should be beyond the reach and the understanding of the industrious and manufacturing classes ... in order to keep this class on a path of moral rectitude so necessary for the peace of every family and of the whole of society.'[41] The melodrama was becoming the popular choice of the new European middle classes – many of whom were unfamiliar with the classics, and hence 'uneducated' as the term was understood under the *ancien régime*. But the bourgeoisie is no monolith. The growth of the professional classes was such that their weight became increasingly manifest in the competition for the definition of high art. A battle for cultural hegemony was being fought between classes and groups within classes. Nowhere was this more marked than in France, where momentous political changes were taking place. In this highly charged context it was unavoidable that the more prestigious setting of cultural life, above all the theatre, would become highly politicised. This was barely the case in England. In France, clashes between the supporters of the classical theatre and the new Romantic theatre, whose dominant figure was Victor Hugo, replicated the political battles going on elsewhere. The pre-nineteenth-century classical French theatre survived, but in the 1820s and 1830s tragedy – regarded by Aristotle as the highest genre – was the least successful. At the Théâtre-Français, all the hits were comedies. In 1835 in Paris 159 out of 221 new plays were vaudeville, in 1836 218 out of 295, and in 1837 201 out of 296. There were hardly any new tragedies.[42]

There was, however, one successful writer of tragedies in the years 1815–30: Casimir Delavigne (1793–1843), whose plays survive only in their operatic adaptations: *Les Vêpres Siciliennes* (Verdi) and *Martin Faliero* (Donizetti). In his day Goethe ranked him on a par with Hugo, and in saying so intended to praise Hugo (who was young at the time).[43] In France itself Delavigne was more popular than Musset or Hugo. Now he is not even mentioned in the 1992 edition of the *Concise Oxford Companion to the Theatre*.

Pixérécourt's melodramas too are no longer performed, but at least one can read his collected works. This is not the case for his main rival, Victor Ducange, who between 1813 and 1833 produced forty-six plays (some with a co-author), and whose reputation extended to all countries influenced by French culture.[44] By the end of the century, *La Grande encyclopédie* noted that his novels, once '*très lus*' (much read), were 'today' '*profondément ignorés*' (totally unknown). He was still mentioned in the *Encyclopaedia Britannica* of 1910, and was given nine lines in the twenty-volume 1982 *La Grande encyclopédie Larousse*, but he is otherwise quite forgotten. There is no complete edition of his work, nor a biography. Only twenty-four of his plays survive.[45]

The victory of the melodrama was not undeserved. It overtly refused to imitate the classical theatre. It was more innovatory than the Romantic theatre (much of which was still written in verse). It privileged the visual element over the poetic one – in other words, it could exist only in performance. In the French classical theatre (as in the Greek one, and unlike the English) all the exciting action (murders, rapes, etc.) takes place offstage. People endlessly talk about what happened and what might happen, but in front of the audience they never do anything. In the melodrama you actually get to see them do things – as in Shakespeare.[46]

Each melodrama, of course, was highly ephemeral. The genre's formulaic plots and stereotypical characters could be endlessly replicated, thus forcing previous efforts into oblivion. But the genre was not ephemeral, and it carries on, as young as ever, in television sagas. It is also an easy genre. The audience is not required to work out for themselves the moral dimension of the characters: the young hero, the persecuted heroine, the noble or tyrannical father, an easily identifiable villain, and a light comic role. The distinctive advantage of the melodrama was that it tried to be realistic, had a coherent plot, modern clothes, and characters the public might conceivably encounter in real life. In this sense the melodrama was the true pioneer of the modern film and, later, of the television 'soap'. Some of the plots managed to convey a denunciation of injustice, without ever blaming society. The hero is a victim, but the cause of his or her misfortunes is usually the misdeeds of a wicked person or sheer bad luck. In the end, the situation is satisfactorily resolved and the proper order of things restored. Secondary characters, usually more fallible than the hero, enable the audience to identify more readily. The villain must, by his looks or action, reveal his true nature early in the play – unlike another successful genre, the detective story, where the excitement often consists precisely in not being able to identify the villain for virtually the entire narrative. The similarities between the theatrical melodrama and the film (particularly the silent film) are striking. Music would accompany the stage performance to indicate mood, emotions and expectations. Melodramas were full of violence. A French newspaper article in 1826 (*Le Pandore*) ironically pointed out that in the preceding year at the Opéra and the Italiens there had been 107 suicides, three poisonings and nine attempted arsons.[47]

Once Pixérécourt's star began to wane, his place as the leading French playwright of the day was taken by Eugène Scribe. Scribe had the singular ability to use risqué topics without ever offending the conventions of his time. For instance, in his play *Oscar ou le mari qui trompe sa femme*, we have a husband who arranges an assignation with a young woman in a dark cave; the message is intercepted by his wife, who turns up instead, disguised. He thus becomes the lover of his wife. So, strictly speaking, there is no adultery. The idea, of course, is straight out of Beaumarchais's (and Mozart's) *Marriage of Figaro*, with an ordinary bourgeois instead of a count and a countess. By the 1820s Scribe was probably the richest playwright in Europe: if we are to believe the *Dictionnaire théâtral*, in 1825 he earned 50,000–60,000 francs – enough to buy a prestigious home in one of Paris's more elegant districts. Envious critics estimated his fortune to be in the region of 2–3 million francs.[48]

While operas and music in general travelled relatively rapidly across state boundaries, and famous books were swiftly translated, the theatre remained a highly national genre. The French liked British novelists and Italian opera, but in the nineteenth century they staged a little Shakespeare, and not much Goethe or Schiller.[49] The situation has barely changed. In the temple of French theatre, the Comédie-Française, the thirty most-performed playwrights in the years from its foundation in 1680 to 1996 were all French except for Shakespeare, who ranks twenty-second, with 1,853 performances. This is totally outdistanced by Molière in top place, with 31,844 performances. The most-performed play in those three hundred years was Molière's *Tartuffe* – in fact the top six are all by Molière – and there are no foreign plays in the top fifty, not even Schiller and Goethe.[50] Scribe was tenth, thanks to the nineteenth century. French provincialism was matched by that of Britain, where few foreign playwrights were performed in the nineteenth century.

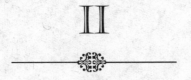

II

1830–1880

THE TRIUMPH OF
BOURGEOIS CULTURE

17

Books for the People

A Bourgeois World

DURING THE MIDDLE DECADES of the nineteenth century the old aristocratic order saw its power gradually slipping away. The world – 'its' world – was becoming bourgeois. In most of Europe the landed gentry held on to the trappings of power and still dominated the armed forces and politics, but their ranks were enormously swelled by recently ennobled industrialists and bankers. Aristocratic titles were increasingly devalued. Aristocratic values were contested, absorbed and transformed by an ever growing middle class. Perceptive minds understood it at once: the bourgeoisie had 'pushed into the background every class handed down from the Middle Ages'.[1]

Underpinning the triumph of the bourgeois order was a manufacturing, commercial and transport revolution which first swept throughout Europe and North America, and then throughout the world. Political changes accompanied this revolution. No country was spared. It was as if history had speeded up; what had previously taken decades or centuries was squeezed into a few years.

One country was not new to such turmoil: France. Between 1789 and 1815 the country had undergone a revolution against absolutist rule, then a republican transformation; this turned into the Napoleonic empire. Its collapse led to the return of the Bourbon monarchy. But matters did not settle down. In July 1830, the Bourbons were discarded in favour of the seemingly more modern Orléans, and Louis Philippe, the son of Philippe Égalité, the cousin of Louis XVI who had supported the Revolution, became King. Then, in quick succession, France experienced a republic (1848), a *coup d'état* (1851), twenty-year rule by the Emperor Napoleon III, a military defeat by the Prussians in 1870, and a civil war (the Paris Commune of 1871). After a bloodbath far greater than that of the Terror, it returned to being a republic – for good.

Great changes pervaded other parts of Europe too. In 1830 Italy and Germany were not nations but mere geographical expressions reflecting a fragmented political reality. 'Italy' and 'Germany' were the names given by nationalist intellectuals to their fantasies. A few decades, and a few wars, later, Italy and Germany had become nation states. The fantasy had become reality.

In 1830 Russia was the paragon of absolutism and backwardness; by 1880 it was home to a strong middle class and a remarkable intelligentsia, serfdom had been abolished and industrialisation was proceeding at great speed. In 1830 Austria was an absolutist multinational empire. In 1867, after the *Ausgleich* (compromise) with Hungary, it turned itself into the Austro-Hungarian Empire. By 1880 it was a haven of constitutional liberalism.

In 1830 Britain was ruled by an oligarchy whose power rested on a narrow suffrage and a rigged electoral system. By 1880 the sovereign was little more than a figurehead surrounded by an elaborate ceremonial system (itself a reflection of the increasingly democratic and popular nature of British institutions). The electorate became one of the largest in the world, thanks to the Reform Bills of 1832 and 1867. Catholics were allowed to sit in Parliament in 1828. Jews had to wait another thirty years, women a further sixty after them. Britain was almost a democracy.

In the USA the westward expansion of the white settlers continued throughout this period. In the 1840s, the line of settlement was just west of the Mississippi. By 1850 California had become a state and the west had been conquered. The Indian wars led to the virtual extermination of the native population and the herding of its survivors into separate settlements. The Civil War (1861–65) led to the abolition of slavery. America was now a nation ready to receive a new wave of European immigrants and to start a period of staggering economic growth.

Throughout Europe, socialist parties, non-existent in 1830, were by 1880 powerful organisations fighting for reforms. At the time their aims were deemed unrealistic, yet they were all implemented well before the end of the twentieth century. Before 1830 only a small platoon of women defied traditional conceptions of femininity and of women's role in the world. By 1880, though still disenfranchised, British women had achieved significant access to education, including higher education, improved legal rights within marriage, and better employment opportunities. In the 1860s a suffragette movement had started its long voyage towards full political rights. By the 1920s this was a reality in most of western Europe. In Europe, Christianity, and above all the Roman Catholic Church, began its long decline, each faltering step matching the forward march of individual rights.

By 1880 the European powers were poised to complete the global imperial expansion they had started a century earlier. The most powerful of them all, Great Britain, having wound down the East India Company, became master of India, eliminated impediment to its trade with China through the Opium Wars (1856–60), and established an informal empire in most of Latin America. Africa was soon carved up between France and Great Britain – the rest of Europe grabbing the left-overs of the feast and exhibiting varying degrees of cruelty and savagery. In Japan the Meiji restoration of 1868 signalled a momentous change in the nation's history. To keep the West at bay, Japan began its systematic modernisation in imitation of it.

These changes were accompanied by an unprecedented expansion in the commerce of written texts: books, newspapers, magazines, pamphlets and manuals. Much of this growth was due to the expansion of education itself, and was in turn caused by greater access to cultural goods. But there was also a considerable extension in leisure time, and an increasingly vocal and organised demand for more. The key demand of the newly formed trade unions in all countries was for the eight-hour day. They achieved their goal by the 1920s through a mix of collective bargaining (mainly in Anglo-Saxon countries) and legislation (in most of Europe).

The middle classes, the backbone of the reading classes, expanded constantly. Wages and salaries increased too, while the cost of books and newspapers decreased. The young stayed at school longer, fewer women went to work, and people lived longer. One of the consequences was greater leisure time. For most people, attending shows, cabarets, theatres and circus acts was still an occasional affair. This left the written text as the main cultural commodity, that could be privately and individually bought and privately and individually consumed. The decades after 1880 saw the rise of rivals to the written text: the gramophone and the record, the radio and the cinema. In the decades 1830–1880, however, the book ruled supreme, and the written word was getting cheaper.

Sell Them Cheap

Since paper for publishing was made of cotton and linen rags, its cost was closely related to the availability of discarded clothes, and these would only be discarded if they were cheap. Consequently, cheap paper could only have occurred with the industrialisation of textiles.[2] While few major technological innovations in printing had occurred since Gutenberg, the decades after 1830 saw a flurry of innovations which all tended to lower costs while improving quality: technological innovations in the production of paper, improved steam presses, better lithography, stereotype, monotype and linotype.[3] One of the consequences was a publishing boom. In Germany production more than trebled between 1840 – when 6,200 titles were published – and 1894.[4] In France the increase was equally impressive, though total numbers were lower: 4,630 titles in 1840 and 14,195 in 1875.[5] Novels, poetry and plays constituted around 10 per cent of total production. In France some 630 novels on average, more than ten a week, were published each year in the 1880s.[6]

There were some large publishing enterprises with more than a thousand employees, such as those, in France, of Napoléon Chaix, Hachette and Alfred Mame. But the key to wealth in publishing was not in convincing thousands of readers to buy books, but in getting state backing or establishing a monopoly. Napoléon Chaix made his money because he had been granted the monopoly of printing railway timetables. Mame and Hachette, both educational publishers, owed their fortunes to their ability to cultivate political, religious and educational élites. A Ministry of Education decision to put one's grammar on the school curriculum was worth tens of thousands of readers a year.

In the mid-nineteenth century, ordinary readers did not buy books. They borrowed them. Publishers did not sell to readers but to lenders, who made money lending to readers – as video shops do today. The business resembled today's academic market, where scholarly monographs in print runs between 500 and 1,500 copies are sold to university libraries, where it is hoped someone will read them. Lending libraries would purchase up to a thousand copies of a novel, thus guaranteeing a reasonable rate of return to publishers.

It was difficult to expand this kind of market. One could take advantage of the lowering of costs, manufacture cheap books, and sell more copies directly to readers. But lending libraries objected. They wanted expensive leather-bound editions that would withstand the wear and tear of borrowing and whose price would deter purchasers. They insisted that no cheap edition of a book could be produced while they were trying to lend it. Publishers could ignore them, but this was risky. The most powerful British lending library, that of Charles Edward Mudie, had such a large market share that it could influence what was to be published. It insisted that novels should be printed in three volumes – the famous three-decker – so that each could be divided among three subscribers. Publishers ended up favouring long novels in order to placate Mudie. This kept the price of British novels artificially high for decades, at one and a half guineas; but Mudie's obtained a 50 per cent discount for bulk buying. Some publishers, such as Bentley, resisted, but most caved in.[7] Publishers grew so dependent on selling to lenders that in 1863 a group of them formed a cartel to rescue Mudie's from bankruptcy, which would have deprived them of a secure market. Mudie's was turned into a public limited company, virtually controlled by the publishers. No longer pre-eminent, it survived until the 1930s, losing custom to more responsive lending libraries connected to the retail trade such as W.H. Smith, Boots and Harrods – much as today bookshops are losing trade to supermarkets.[8]

The three-volume novel became an albatross for Victorian novelists. Unless an author was extremely talented, its length dictated a formulaic narrative structure which many found dispiriting. G.H. Lewes wrote in the *Fortnightly Review* in 1865:

> ... the combination of powers necessary for the production of three volumes of Circulating Library reminiscences is very common. The intellectual feebleness of readers in general prevents their forming a discriminating estimate of the worth of such works; and most of those who are capable of discrimination have had their standard of expectation so lowered by the profusion of mediocrity, that they languidly acquiesce in the implied assumption that novels are removed from the canons of common-sense criticism. Hence the activity of this commerce of trash.[9]

Mudie's charged one guinea for a year's subscription, undercutting some of its competitors, who were charging twice as much. Subscribers could borrow as many books as they liked. Mudie's was 'modern'. It used advertising. It had a fleet of vans to deliver books from its many branches, and it looked after its rural customers. Originally a lender of non-fiction, the company soon realised that people wanted fiction. In only nine years (1853–62) it bought almost a million volumes, half of them novels.[10] Mudie's also turned into a censor on behalf of middle-class morality, keeping out of its stock anything deemed offensive to Victorian taste – the libertines were a less vociferous lobby than the strait-laced, there were fewer of them, and they knew how to get their 'filth' elsewhere. By advertising a list of new 'books in circulation' Mudie's effectively promoted some authors and condemned others to limbo.[11] Publishers would mutter that if Mudie's was not going to take a book there was no point in publishing it. Mudie's was highly suspicious of foreign stuff: in 1869 its large circulating library in New Oxford Street did not possess any Diderot, Voltaire, Pushkin or Balzac, or even *The Three Musketeers*.[12] Victorians remained provincial – the privilege of those who live in imperial countries.

Lending libraries continued to be a fixture of the cultural panorama of Europe throughout the nineteenth century. They were finished off in the twentieth century by the rise of free public libraries and the significant decrease in the price of books. Enlightened employers, such as the British insurance company the Prudential, in the 1890s a major employer of female clerks, provided them with a library of three hundred volumes.[13]

At the end of the nineteenth century, however, it was still the common practice of even wealthy and powerful people to borrow books rather than buying them (as late as the 1970s, Harrods delivered library books to their account customers' homes). Otto von Bismarck, 'the Iron Chancellor', and Theodor Mommsen, one of the great historians of the century, would regularly send their servants to borrow books at the main Berlin lending libraries such as the Borstell and Reimarus.[14] As Gladstone explained in the House of Commons in 1852:

> The purchase of new publications is scarcely ever attempted by anybody. You go into the houses of your friends, and unless they buy books of which they are in professional want, or happen to be persons of extraordinary wealth, you don't find copies of new publications on their tables purchased by themselves, but you find something from the circulating library, or something from the book-club.[15]

Perhaps Gladstone was forgetting Charles Dickens, whose books were bought, but otherwise he was right: owning books was rare, particularly among the newly enriched manufacturing classes. Owning books, especially the classics, as opposed to new publications, was a habit of the intellectual classes and the clergy. In Elizabeth Gaskell's novel *North and South* (1855), the only visible book in the household of John Thornton, a well-to-do Manchester manufacturer, is the *Bible Commentaries* by Matthew Henry (1662–1714), a non-conformist text in six volumes, a typical 'identity' book, symbol of one's belief, rather than an item of everyday reading. John's sister, the shallow Fanny Thornton, reads Washington Irving's *Legends of the Alhambra* (1832), very popular tales of Medieval Moorish Spain mixed with anecdotes of contemporary life. Margaret Hale, the intellectually snobbish daughter of a Hampshire vicar and the noble heroine of the novel, regards such books as a low genre which she has no desire to read, preferring Dante's *Purgatorio* – in the original, of course.

What was required was for some bold publisher to take on the powerful lending libraries and develop a cheap book policy, using the new technologies available. At a dinner in May 1825 Walter Scott's publisher, Archibald Constable, dreamt of an unparalleled expansion of the book trade as an instrument for 'enlightening and entertaining mankind, and, of course, for making money'.[16] Constable never realised his dream, because a year later he was bankrupt. But the cheap non-fiction imprint he had created, Miscellany, was rescued, and a series of cheap non-fiction books priced at three and a half shillings each started to come out every three weeks. Not surprisingly, with titles such as *American Ornithology* and *Evidences of Christianity*, it was not as popular as had been hoped. The mass market for books remained elusive. The real reason was that five shillings – the usual price of a reprinted 'cheap' novel – was still a considerable sum for many: the average London skilled worker made thirty shillings a week in the 1830s, a Scottish carpenter only half that. Thus the 'cheap' book was in fact the equivalent of a £60 volume today, which was a lot to pay, even for *American Ornithology*. For a handloom weaver trying to live on five shillings a week, a book was an unthinkable luxury: for five shillings one could buy ten pounds of meat. Cheap books did increase the size of the market, but the main beneficiaries were the middle classes. And even for many of them, cheap books were not cheap enough. In 1841 Anthony Trollope was earning £140 a year when he went to work in Ireland for the Post Office.[17] A clergyman might make £300 a year, an army officer two hundred.[18]

But the movement for cheaper books was unstoppable. In 1838 in Paris, Gervais Charpentier started to republish successful novels in a standard one-volume format (the 'Charpentier format'), and at the fixed price of 3.50 francs. Charpentier realised that to lower the price of books it was necessary to achieve a higher print run, and to squeeze more words onto a page to reduce paper costs. It worked, but as in England it worked in favour of the middle classes, not the skilled proletariat. The Charpentier books, mainly good contemporary novels, were instantly recognisable by their yellow board covers – leather had been discarded – and were purchased by students, schoolteachers and, more generally, the urban lower middle classes.[19] Other publishers followed suit and began to publish books in series of similar format and price. They did not try to estimate in advance the return per book. What mattered was the overall profitability. Some titles could be regarded as loss leaders advertising the entire series.

Charpentier's first best-seller was not a novel, but a non-fiction book of general interest: Jean Brillat-Savarin's *Physiologie du goût ou méditations sur la gastronomie transcendante* (originally published in 1825), a treatise on cookery and the pleasures of food. This was regularly reprinted in batches of 2,000–3,000 copies until the 1850s. Charpentier also signed a contract with Balzac to publish fifteen volumes of his works, containing thirty-four titles, for a total of 60,000 copies.[20] In 1841 he signed up Alfred de Vigny, undertaking to publish his collected works. What he really wanted was to get hold of the rights to de Vigny's famous historical novel *Cinq-Mars*, which in Charpentier's cheap yellow covers was reprinted four times in fourteen years – a total of 17,700 copies, a huge sale. Charpentier also published de Musset, Silvio Pellico's best-selling *Mes Prisons*, famous foreign authors such as Goethe, Schiller and Byron, and classics such as Dante, Milton, Virgil, Homer and Thucydides.[21]

Following Charpentier's lead, Arthème Fayard, in 1857, tried to entice the lower middle classes with scientific and historical vulgarisations such as *Les Mémoires authentiques de Garibaldi* in 1860. The timing could not be bettered. 1860 was the year Garibaldi liberated southern Italy. At the same time Fayard published a stream of 'popular novels' with plenty of illustrations – essentially sexual and anti-clerical horror stories with titles such as *Le Curé Mingrat, l'égorgeur de femmes* (The Curate Mingrat, the Woman-Ripper) and the (presumably) very similar *Le Curé Dellacollonge, découpeur de femmes*, sold in weekly or monthly parts.[22] Fayard still used the old peddlers' circuit, but also built up an alternative network using people in 'key' occupations, such as policemen and barbers, who would moonlight as salesmen. Eclecticism pays.

To make money on established classics was much easier than finding new authors. With a classic, much of the required promotion had already been done. Intellectuals and journalists had decreed that this was what a person of taste should read, or at least own. The authors were usually dead – a great advantage for publishers, especially if they have been dead long enough. And there is a permanent and ever-growing educational market.

The working class and the poor were deprived of books not only because they were restricted in their access to education, but because cheap books were still too expensive for them. Even as late as 1900 the typical novel sold in French bookshops cost 3.5 francs. This was half the daily wage of a Parisian worker, and three times that of a woman working in the provinces in a small enterprise.[23] It took decades to achieve the transformation of books from luxury and expensive items, a preserve of the middle classes, into objects of mass consumption. The new cheap books brought into the market the less prosperous sections of the educated classes. Overlapping with this market were the category of the truly popular novels of the time, the so-called 'penny dreadful' novels – the ancestors of the airport novel and the supermarket best-seller. These books were sold by peddlers, as in the past. Unlike the past peddlers were no longer selling mainly religious books and practical manuals, but also books which had been successful in the lending libraries in a new simplified format. Occasionally they were plagiarised forms of famous books with barely a change of title, such as the *Life and Adventures of Albert of Montechristo* (sic) in 1847.[24]

The penny dreadful (each country had its genre, frequently plagiarised from other countries) was usually serialised or sold in parts. *The Monster of Scotland* (No. 11, *The Terrific Register*, 1825) told in 104 penny parts the story of Sawney Beane and his wife who lived in a cave and murdered every person they robbed in order to escape detection. As they were unable to get food by any other means, they ate their victims having 'quartered them, salted and pickled the members, and dried them . . . In this manner they lived, carrying on their depredations and murder, until they had eight sons and six daughters, eighteen grandsons and fourteen granddaughters, all the offspring of incest.' When they were finally captured, 'The men had their privy-members thrown into the fire, their hands and legs were severed from their bodies, and they were permitted to bleed to death. The wretched mother of the whole crew, the daughters and grandchildren, after being spectators of the death of the men, were cast into three separate fires, and consumed to ashes.'[25]

Exciting narratives like this continued to dominate the lower reaches of the market, uncelebrated by the élites, despised by the respectable classes, and devoured with relish by hundreds of thousands of readers for whom such cheap entertainment constituted an escape to a world of dream and fantasy. This was the achievement of the literary sweatshops of the period, and of writers like Thomas Peckett Prest, who wrote for the penny market not only the stories of Sweeney Todd, the serial-killer barber of Fleet Street, but an endless series of Dickensian imitations with titles such as *Nickelas Nicklebery*, *David Copperful* and *Oliver Twiss*, and Hannah Maria Jones, one of the most popular writers of penny novels, each of whose *The Gipsy Girl*, *The Gipsy Mother* and *Emily Moreland* sold 20,000 copies. Her publishers made considerable profits, but not Hannah Maria Jones herself. On 27 January 1854 *The Times* announced that 'Anna Maria Jones, authoress of the *Gipsy* and other popular novels of the day, died on Tuesday . . . in the most abject poverty.'[26]

One of the great entrepreneurs of the penny dreadful genre was the publisher Edward Lloyd (1815–90), who created in 1836 the series 'Lives of the Most Notorious Highwaymen'. Though crime remained the staple of his ever-expanding publishing empire, he quickly diversified into romance with the series *The Gem of Romance*, and even branched into paper-making to keep costs down.

The penny dreadful market existed throughout Europe, but was particularly thriving in the more literate larger countries: Britain, France and Germany. Such 'trash' was openly despised by anyone with some pretension to good taste and refinement. In fact every language developed a pejorative expression for books read and enjoyed by the lower classes, and often read with some embarrassment by the other classes. In most cases they were negatively characterised by their cheapness: penny dreadful, dime novel, *romans de quatre sous*, *romanzo dozzinale*, etc.

Yet the obvious effect of cheap books was to extend book-reading habits to the lower classes, classes which in other countries read nothing at all. Sayyid Ahmad Khan, a northern Indian judge travelling in England in 1869, was astonished to see cabmen reading: 'They keep a paper or a book under their seat.'[27] An Italian, Spanish or Russian judge would have been equally astonished. The 'book under the cabby's seat' was in all probability an eight-page penny pamphlet with an illustrated cover. The text was squeezed into two columns; continuity of story was given scant attention. Occasionally the text ended at the end of the eighth page and then continued, even in mid-sentence, the following week – a novel conception of the 'cliffhanger'. It is told that one author, having managed to get his hero bound to a stake, encircled by wild animals, an avalanche about to bury him, got himself and the hero out of this predicament simply by writing in the following instalment 'and with one bound Jack was free'.[28] The British penny dreadfuls were neither exported to the rest of Europe (though the colonies offered a market for some) nor translated, though they were often plagiarised. They were 'genuine' local popular culture, written by the British for the British, and regarded as unmitigated trash by refined people. Old stories were developed and embellished. Thus Dick Turpin became established as the highwayman *par excellence* only in the nineteenth century, thanks to writers such as Harrison Ainsworth, who in his novel *Rookwood* (1834) supplied Turpin's horse with a name and a distinct identity: the swift Black Bess.[29] This led to a long cult of both Turpin and Black Bess, and to what perhaps was the longest of all penny dreadfuls: Edward Viles's 1861–65 *Black Bess, or the Night of the Road*, in 254 weekly parts of eight pages – over 2,000 pages in all. An unverified claim set its total sales at one million.[30]

The most popular of the 'popular' novelists was probably G.W.M. Reynolds, whose *The Mysteries of London* (1845) was a passable imitation of Eugène Sue's landmark *Les Mystères de Paris* (about which more later). It certainly did not make the impact in upstream British culture which Sue's novel made in France. Reynolds received no accolades from the literary establishment, and after he died his books were not reprinted or ever read again. Like his upmarket rivals he tested his work on a reader, but in Reynolds' case this was not the refined, educated reader employed by a publisher, but a servant or a printer's apprentice – a wise choice, in the circumstances.[31] *The Mysteries of London* was issued over a period of four years, selling at a rate of nearly 40,000 a week before it was issued in one volume.[32]

Reynolds was in fact a writing machine who in the fifteen years between 1841 and 1856 produced some thirty full-length novels, totalling millions of words, making him, were he the single author of the lot, the most prolific writer of the Victorian era. His books refute at a stroke the widely held view of the Victorians as a prudish crowd. This might have been true of the middle class, but Reynolds' working-class readers delighted in the depiction of errant clergymen, thieves, grave-robbers, hunchbacks, dwarfs, working girls driven to prostitution, and adultery.[33]

'Good' Books

Not surprisingly this flood of gory popular literature caused considerable concern. Banning it would be impossible, because of the opposition it would cause – at least in England. In France, particularly under Napoleon III, it was severely controlled. An alternative to repression was to provide the lower classes with good and wholesome books, something they would want to read and which would be decorous and uplifting. Associations seeking to promote 'good' books sprang up all over Europe. In Cologne there was the Borromäus

Verein (named in honour of the saint Carlo Borromeo), founded in 1845 with the aim of establishing a network of Catholic libraries. By 1900 it possessed 1,180,000 volumes and lent 2,500,000 books a year.[34] In France the Catholic Société des Bons Livres (1824) produced a list of 5,000 'good books' by 1875.[35] Even Tsarist Russia had, after 1861, its Society for the Dissemination of Useful Books.

In Britain the impetus towards good literature was even stronger. Victorian pioneers of cheap literature such as Charles Knight lambasted the condescension of aristocratic and intellectual élites, and were seriously determined to educate the 'common people'. Such concern was not entirely devoid of political calculation. The common people, in the years after the Napoleonic Wars, were coming increasingly under the influence of radical thought, radical newspapers and radical journalists who were peddling their own alternative to the penny dreadfuls. Thus, on both moral and political counts, it was felt indispensable to provide the lower orders with good literature.

It had to be, however, *their* literature, something the downtrodden would actually want to read, and not what the learned wanted them to read. It could no longer be what right-thinking people liked, people like the writer and philanthropist of a previous generation Hannah More (1745–1833), a 'bishop in a pettycoat', as William Cobbett called her, 'that most disagreeable of all monsters, a blue-stocking' according to George Eliot, who wrote 'books for the common people', and homilies in which she declared that:

> Beautiful is the order of Society when each, according to his place, pays willing honour to his superiors, when servants are prompt to obey their masters, and masters deal kindly with their servants; when high, low, rich, poor, when landlord and tenant, master and workman . . . sit down each satisfied with his own place.[36]

She believed that 'To teach the poor to read, without providing them with sage books has always appeared to me a dangerous measure.'[37] This was not a view Charles Knight would have disagreed with, except that by the 1820s the option of not teaching people to read was less and less available. His first weapon in the struggle for good cheap literature was the weekly *Penny Magazine*, backed by the Society for the Diffusion of Useful Knowledge (SDUK), set up in 1826 by Lord (Henry) Brougham and other Liberal reformers for the production of cheap publications of good quality. The *Penny Magazine* thus had several advantages: it was linked to a pre-existing organisation, the SDUK (though it ended up subsidising it), and it enjoyed the tacit support of the government, being an active propagandist for Whig ideas. The key problem was distribution, which involved spending considerable amounts of money up front. Charles Knight thought he had solved the problem by organising a network of twenty-nine wholesalers and retail outlets able to sell 200,000 copies per week. He used every means to get his magazine to the booksellers: steamboat, railway, and stage-coach.[38] The contents of the *Penny Magazine*, however, were too educational for the lower classes, and the magazine did better among the middle classes than among its intended readership.[39] Apart from the *Penny Magazine* SDUK also produced the non-fiction Library of Useful Knowledge and, for fiction, the Entertainment Library; then there were the *Penny Cyclopedia* and the *Biographical Dictionary*, both sold in parts, and finally the *Quarterly Journal of Education*, an upmarket version of the *Penny Magazine*.

The *Penny Magazine* first came out in 1832, and was, initially a great success, selling an astonishing 200,000 copies a week. Sales then declined until they bottomed out at 40,000 in 1845, barely covering production costs.[40] The magazine had to close. One reason was the entry into the field of other, less high-minded, publications. The main problem, however, was that a cheap magazine has a very small profit margin, and consequently it has to achieve very high sales. Each copy of the *Penny Magazine* brought in a profit of only 7 per cent, while that of its more expensive competitor *Chambers' Edinburgh Journal* (selling at three and a half pennies) averaged 40 per cent, and that of the upmarket *Blackwood's Magazine* (two and half shillings) 58 per cent.[41]

A further cause for its collapse was that, by all accounts, the *Penny Magazine* was dreadfully boring. The table of contents of the issue of 31 October 1835 gives an idea of what the editors thought would appeal to a working-class audience: 'An Examination of the Fertilising Value of Volcanic Lava' (the magazine admitted that there was 'no recorded volcanic activity in British isles'); 'An Appreciation of the Interior of the Grand Mosque of Sultan Achmet in Constantinople'; 'England as Described by an Eastern Traveller Seventy Years Ago'; and, last but not least, a paper 'capable of interesting the philosopher and the historian as well as the mere practitioner'. This, the magazine explained, had been read by Sir Henry Halford at a 'soirée' at the College of Physicians attended by 'the most distinguished luminaries of the church and the law'. The topic was the causes of death of some 'eminent persons' of modern times, beginning with Henry VIII. Readers were informed that 'Dryden appears to have died of senile gangrene, – a mortification occurring in the extremities of aged persons from ossification of the arteries.'[42]

The problem with Charles Knight, as with many Victorian reformers, was that he regarded workers as abstractions rather than real people – at least, this is what appears from Knight's own account of the making of the *Penny Magazine*, serialised in monthly supplements in 1833, in which machines and processes are discussed, but not the men and women who printed the magazine.[43]

Weeklies like the *Penny Magazine* and *Chambers' Edinburgh Journal* were full of articles on gardening, agriculture, sheep farming, the uses of machines, and a few articles on art and literature. All of this suggests that, despite protestations to the contrary, the target audience was middle class. From a commercial point of view this made perfect sense, since members of this class were also the most likely customers. Why did the *Penny Magazine* fold and *Chambers'* (publishers also of the encyclopaedia) go on for another hundred years? Possibly because *Chambers'*, though more expensive, always included a short story and other light fiction. The middle classes could afford *Chambers'* just as much as its cheaper rival, but they enjoyed *Chambers'* more. Besides, the *Penny Magazine* was, religiously speaking, far too closely associated with non-conformity. This alienated middle-class Tory readers without attracting the non-conformist working classes.[44] Success, in this trade, consists in getting right the price, the target audience and the contents.

Socialist publications had similar problems as the *Penny Magazine*. Socialist activists tried to acquire a mass working-class readership by promoting what they thought was 'good' literature – i.e. what they themselves enjoyed – at lower prices, as if price was the main obstacle. Robert Owen's periodical the *New Moral World* contained advertisements for popular editions of Shelley's *Queen Mab* and Rousseau's *Social Contract*, but we are not sure how widely these were read. Claims made by middle-class activists on the literary competence of workers were often inflated by wishful thinking. Friedrich Engels, possibly generalising from the class-conscious workers he met, claimed that 'it is . . . the workers who are most familiar with the poetry of Shelley and Byron'.[45] It is true that Byron and Shelley were regarded as deeply immoral by the respectable British bourgeoisie, but it does not necessarily follow that many workers read them in 1844. A mass socialist press failed to materialise. When working-class papers emerged – *Reynolds'* and *Lloyd's Weekly* – they were not socialist.

One way of getting ordinary people to read was to provide them with cheap books to borrow. In Britain, the rapidly developing mechanics' institute libraries were developed by philanthropists specifically for the working classes, to wean them away from pornography, socialism and drink. By 1850 there were 610 mechanics' institutes, and they owned 700,000 volumes.[46] The problem was that much of this stock consisted of the books discarded by the philanthropic classes – tons of religious magazines and annual registers, barely read by their original owners and destined never to be read by anyone else. The rest of the libraries' stock was avidly read by the middle classes who could not afford Mudie's annual guinea but could pay the shilling demanded by the mechanics' libraries.

Ever since 1826 the SDUK and Lord Brougham had lobbied Parliament to institute free, publicly funded libraries. The culmination of such efforts was the adoption of the Public Libraries Act of 1850.[47] It was necessary, or so it was held as early as the 1840s, to build up what is now called 'human capital'. In 1841 Robert Peel, then Prime Minister, declared that 'Society is now in the position that increased intelligence and increased knowledge are absolutely essential.'[48] The SDUK lobby explained to the Parliamentary Select Committee on Public Libraries that the key problem was one of access. Britain had a greater literature than any other country, but very few people could get hold of it. Just as in France it was felt that the country lagged behind Britain, the SDUK pointed out that matters were better abroad – the time-honoured ploy of reformers to convince the unconvinced. Another ploy, used by William Ewart MP to pull in the vote of the timorous philistine, was to declare when he introduced the Public Library Bill in the Commons that every penny spent on public libraries would save more on expenditure on criminals and poor relief.[49] The French contrasted the poor network of French libraries (in the 1850s–70s) to that of the British: Leeds had a central library with fourteen branches open all day, while Lyon had just six, open only in the evening.[50] In Britain the SDUK claimed that the British Museum Reading Room was only for the few, while in Paris ordinary people could read in the Bibliothèque Nationale – both national libraries were funded by the equivalent of a tax on books, since publishers had to demonstrate their legal ownership of the copyright by depositing a copy.

In France, François Guizot had established civic libraries in 1833 under the banner of '*la lutte pour les bons livres*' (the struggle for good books), but the system was less developed than in Britain. These debates more or less coincided with the discovery of the problems of industrial society and the conditions of the working class, and with books such as *Les Mystères de*

Paris, which the philanthropic bourgeoisie feared might subvert the working classes.[51] Further support came in 1860 when the French government decided that a proportion of the sums earmarked for school-building should be set aside for the establishment of libraries.[52]

Opponents claimed that people went to libraries not to read books but to keep warm. Yet the people's libraries were not a success, even as warm places. Bordeaux in 1851 had 130,000 inhabitants, but its public library was attended by just seventy readers a day. Toulouse, with 95,000 inhabitants, did better: 140 visitors daily.[53] The range of books may have been a factor, but so were opening hours and, indeed, how warm they were. There was a working-class élite who wanted improving books, but not necessarily those selected by librarians and local notables.[54] Be that as it may, the number of public libraries in France increased consistently, as did the number of books borrowed: 179,000 in 1865, and 955,000 in 1869.[55] The Société Franklin – a French equivalent of the SDUK – had in 1864 a catalogue of recommended books that working people might want to read, but excluded controversial material as well as 'cheap literature'. In the words of its main promoter, Jules Simon, one had to provide '*le grand enfant qu'on appelle le peuple*' (this great child we call the people) with wholesome reading – and that meant Corneille, Molière, Racine, Shakespeare and Schiller. Some twenty years later, in 1883, the Société had compromised a little by including 'light' novels such as those by the patriotic and popular collaboration Erckmann-Chatrian, as well as modern classics: Fenimore Cooper, Walter Scott and Dickens. Most of Balzac's novels remained out of bounds.

In 1882 a new commission on popular libraries was established in what was now republican France. It censored Herodotus, banned Machiavelli, allowed Darwin, and turned down Victor Hugo's *Notre-Dame de Paris* and Tolstoy's *Anna Karenina* (because it was about adultery). Thomas Hardy was banned, of course, and there were plenty of problems with Ibsen (adultery, syphilis, rebellious wives, etc.). Gradually, banned authors were unbanned. Hardy was all right by 1905, as was even Sue's *Le Juif errant* (by then anti-clericalism was in full swing), although Oscar Wilde and Zola were still excluded. It seems that public libraries were ten to twenty years behind prevailing morality.

Unavoidably, libraries, especially publicly funded ones, had to have a policy on which books to stock. A distinction had to be made between good books and wicked ones. This was often less difficult than it may seem: librarians, local politicians and notables used their prejudices to tell the difference. After all, no one could argue that a penny dreadful about a serial killer should be purchased at taxpayers' expense to be handed out to the first comer for free as a public service. Matters were made more complicated by the obvious desire to attract readers, and to wean them away from bad books. But how to entice them without providing them with what they liked, in the hope that they would eventually try reading the more demanding stuff? The journal *Library World* argued in 1904 that 'The ratepayer pays for the library, and they will have the books that please them ... It is no use lining the shelves of a free library with the recondite works of scientists, educationalists and philosophers, or the classical treasures of the past, if people prefer the last brand-new flimsy tale that comes hot from the press.'[56] Even free public-service libraries had to think in market terms, maximising their customers by a mixture of judicious entertainment and diversity of choice – a problem faced by public-service television a century later.

Throughout the nineteenth and twentieth centuries the cry would rise against the expansion of cultural markets and the inevitable lowering of standards. The wars between 'commercialism' and 'quality' may not cause many deaths, but they arouse great passions. In their diary, the Goncourt brothers (arguably the most jaundiced diarists in literature; this genre attracts the irascible) expressed their spleen against publishers such as Michel Lévy, 'the benefactors of any beggar who ventures "to dirty a piece of paper in order to make a living"'. Lévy's crime was to produce books priced at one franc. The brothers fumed: there were no longer *oeuvres*, 'only mere volumes and lower even than volumes, there are but reprints of anything by anybody! ... A levelling out, an infamy – a nothing!' And they continued lamenting the sums earned by writers of vaudeville.[57]

The great French literary critic Sainte-Beuve had percipiently identified a new trend, 'industrial literature', where monetary gain was the only goal, and denounced it in the pages of the *Revue des deux mondes*.[58] He complained that 'what is bad is gaining ground', that the 'demon of literary property' led writers to estimate their importance in terms of how much money they made (thus making critics like himself redundant), that paid notices by publishers swayed the judgement of readers, that newspapers had become the servants of advertisers. And he lamented that the newly formed Société des Gens de Lettres (President: Balzac) welcomed into its ranks anyone who wrote, making no distinction between men of letters and ordinary commercial writers.[59] Sainte-Beuve was echoing what Thomas Carlyle had written ten years previously: 'Philosophy, Science, Art, Literature, all depend on machinery . . . Literature too has its Paternoster-row mechanism, its Trade-dinners, its Editorial conclaves, and huge subterranean puffing bellows; so that books are not only printed, but in a great measure, written and sold by machinery.'[60]

On the stage it was much the same, lamented Théophile Gautier in *La Presse* on 1 January 1838: 'The situation is far from brilliant: it is a total decadence; manufacturing has invaded everything; they make a play the way they make cloth.'[61] Yet some remarkable stuff could be written 'industrially': Stendhal wrote *La Chartreuse de Parme* in fifty-two days, starting on 4 November 1838 and ending on 26 December, dictating it to a typist.

The young Karl Marx, more modern than most, had no hesitation in praising the industrial division of labour in the arts and its organisation: 'In Paris, the great demand for vaudeville and novels brought about the organisation of work for their production, organisation which at any rate yields something better than its "unique" competitors in Germany.'[62] For some writers 'industrial literature' was a golden opportunity to become rich and famous. Balzac relished 'industrial literature': 'Véron has bought *Le Constitutionnel*, knocked down the annual price to 48 francs, and is threatening to steal from *Le Siècle* 45,000 subscribers with *Le Juif errant*, bought for 100,000 francs . . . It's a money tournament. I'm free and shall try to exploit the situation.'[63]

A new chapter had opened in the long history of moral panic and cultural wars.

18

Newspapers, Magazines and Pictures

The Flood

IN THE MID-NINETEENTH CENTURY the development of a mass press was still in its infancy, as were all other aspects of a mass leisure society. Nevertheless, the road to the consumer society of the twentieth century was being opened by the middle classes. The contours of this new world were not yet distinct, but the direction was set – at least in the economically more advanced countries.

Though the middle classes were constantly trying to ape the aristocracy, they were also creating their own standards. In any case, the aristocracy the bourgeoisie thought they were imitating was an idealised aristocracy, that described by middle-class intellectuals in books and newspapers, and represented in plays and operas. The world of class and status is one of images and shadows, of impressions and symbols. In modern society, precisely because it is dynamic, one is never sure where one stands. The widespread anxiety about one's place in the social scale was manifested in the frequency of satires about social climbers, i.e. people who did not know how to behave in their new class. Nineteenth-century literature is replete with this theme, more new aristocrats having been created in the course of that quintessentially bourgeois century than ever before. The genre, however, was much older. Molière, in his celebrated play *Le Bourgeois gentilhomme* (1660), made fun of a *nouveau riche* who was unsuccessfully taught to behave like a gentleman. This image was of comfort to aristocrats in need of reassurance: gentlemen were born, not made. In reality, the making of a gentleman is a rapid process which can take as little as a few months and never more than a generation. Middle-class intellectuals themselves usually define the rules. Once those are set, a modicum of intelligence and a considerable amount of money are all that is required. Who was Molière, after all, but a bourgeois social climber? Becky Sharp, the heroine of Thackeray's *Vanity Fair* (1848), is a real *arriviste*, and is lampooned as such. While the aristocrats described are no better than she is, they don't have to try as hard – but then, Becky is cleverer than any of them. And Dickens in *Our Mutual Friend* (1865) writes wittily of the Veneerings, although many of his readers were similar to them; the difference being that they read Dickens:

> Mr. and Mrs. Veneering were bran-new people in a bran-new house in a bran-new quarter of London. Everything about the Veneerings was spick and span new. All their furniture was new, all their friends were new, their plate was new, their carriage was new, their harness was new, their horses were new, they themselves were new, they were as newly married as was lawfully compatible with their having a bran-new baby.[1]

In reality the taste and behaviour of the 'real' aristocracy – should such a beast exist – were not so different from those of the new classes banging at the door. The aristocracy, as a class, could have taste as coarse as anyone else. While the females of the species were compelled to appear refined, the males enjoyed salacious and violent stories as well as sentimental ones, and relished fairy tales or novels or farces repeating the same old themes. They liked hunting and fishing and fighting and gambling and whoring and drinking. They collected paintings and art, built themselves palatial homes, and dressed extravagantly to show off their wealth, just like the despised *nouveaux riches*. They were as quick to take offence and fight for their 'honour' as any modern street thug demanding 'respect'. Matthew Arnold's jaundiced view was not entirely without substance: 'One has often wondered whether upon the whole earth there is anything so unintelligent, so unapt to perceive how the world is really going, as an ordinary young Englishman of our upper class.'[2]

The serious defenders of 'high' taste were the upper echelons of the cultural establishment, the major producers of culture, the leading intellectuals – and for good reason, since the expansion of cultural markets affected them. This expansion brought into the cultural world a mass of minor intellectuals, scribblers and literary hacks, some of whom made considerable amounts of money. Prestigious intellectuals, inevitably the main gatekeepers of established culture, tried to keep them out. In defending 'aristocratic' culture, they were defending *their* culture. As they had made it to the top of the intellectual tree, they had shaped and interiorised traditional culture. It is always in the interests of those who have made it to the top of the greasy pole to remain among the few. New rules, new products and new cultural operators were a direct challenge to their power. Younger and not yet established intellectuals, for exactly the same reasons, were eager to storm the bastions of culture. The most satisfying way of doing so was to challenge the old rules, innovate, be modern, desecrate the past and glorify the present. Culture wars – the oldest form of warfare – are always fought by the cultural producers themselves.

This process accelerated during the nineteenth century, a reflection of the unremitting expansion of markets. A mass market innovates not just because there is a conscious desire for novelty, but because its sheer weight increases the competition for new consumers, and allows new entrants to experiment. A press which can sell 100,000 copies a day cannot be the same as one that sells 10,000. And numbers made themselves felt in all aspects of cultural consumption. The massive Great Exhibition at London's Crystal Palace in 1851 attracted crowds never seen before, but it also did wonders for other shows and exhibitions in the city. In 1850 the British Museum attracted 750,000 visitors; the following year it was visited by 2.2 million people (a hundred years later the Louvre would be visited by 'only' one million a year), Hampton Court by 325,000 (over 100,000 more than the previous year), the Crown Jewels at the Tower of London by 209,000 (from 32,800 in 1850).[3]

The printed matter which flooded Europe in the decades preceding the appearance of radio and the cinema took the form of newsprint, not books. In 1889 in France alone there were 23,000 printed texts registered as books for the purpose of copyright. Of these, only 5,500 were books in any meaningful sense of the word. Alongside them were hundreds of thousands of daily papers, journals and magazines.[4] These figures were dwarfed by the thirty million copies of newspapers published annually in Britain. This was not just a London trend: by the 1850s most Scottish boroughs had their own daily paper.[5] Mitchell's *Newspaper Press Directory* for 1864 lists more than seventy daily papers and 1,200 non-daily (mainly weekly) ones.[6]

In Britain and the United States it had been clear for some time that the real money, if any, was in newspapers rather than books. The technology had improved further since *The Times* adopted a steam-powered press, the invention of a German, Friedrich König, who, unable to find anyone interested in his country, brought it to London. As *The Times* proudly announced on 29 November 1814, König's new press had produced the entire circulation of the paper at the unprecedented rate of 1,100 sheets per hour:

That the magnitude of the invention may be justly appreciated by its effects ... after the letters are placed by the compositors, and enclosed in what is called the form, little more remains for man to do, than to attend upon, and watch this unconscious agent in its operations. The machine is then merely supplied with paper: itself places the form, inks it, adjusts the paper to the form newly inked, stamps the sheet, and gives it forth to the hands of the attendant, at the same time withdrawing the form for a fresh coat of ink, which itself again distributes, to meet the ensuing sheet now advancing for impression; and the whole of these complicated acts is performed with such a velocity and simultaneousness of movement, that no less than eleven hundred sheets are impressed in one hour.[7]

The adoption of rotary presses in the mid-1850s further increased productivity, as did the web-fed newspaper press, using rolls instead of sheets, invented in 1863 by the American William A. Bullock. This was further improved in 1871 with the introduction of the continuous roll press, enabling the production of as many as 18,000 copies in an hour.

Cheap journalism had come to stay. In this field the British led the way, and probably continue to do so to this day. The philanthropic efforts of the *Penny Magazine* (see pages 304–6) may have been too high-minded, but these pioneers had correctly identified a major gap in the market: the respectable, literate working classes who wanted some form of cheap entertainment. These strata, contrary to some socialist or aristocratic beliefs, far from being an undifferentiated lump, had only their social condition in common. Otherwise, they were divided by a plethora of identities. The new periodical press, by trial and error, tried to plug the holes in the market as they appeared: the *Christian's Penny Magazine* was for the religiously minded, the *Penny Comic Magazine* for the hedonist, the *Penny Novelist* for those in search of fantasies, the *Girl's and Boy's Penny Magazine* for children, and the *Mirror*, a twopenny illustrated magazine, 'for all'.

In Britain the main obstacle to a cheap press was the 1819 stamp duty on all publications. As the duty was fixed at fourpence, it effectively quintupled the price of a penny magazine. Publishers had to pay the tax even on unsold publications. In 1831 a radical printer, Henry Hetherington, refused to pay it, producing the first number of his penny *Poor Man's Guardian*. He was joined by other radical publications. There were protests, arrests, and convictions. Thousands of unstamped papers appeared on the streets of London. The government had to relent, and in 1833 reduced the duty to one penny. In order to keep the paper affordable for working men, the *Poor Man's Guardian* remained proudly unstamped. Hetherington continued to fight for the freedom of the press and against the 'tax on knowledge'. He was in and out of court, and became one of the principal Chartist agitators. Like many left-wing activists who fought for basic liberties, he paved the way for a prosperous, anti-radical tabloid press. Finally, in 1855, Hetherington and his comrades won: the hated stamp duty was abolished. It now became possible to sell a penny newspaper for one penny, thus halving its price. The *Daily Telegraph* dropped its price to one penny immediately, and became the most successful mid-century paper, selling some 160,000 copies. By 1888 it was selling 300,000 copies.[8]

In the 1840s there was already a thriving weekly market which included the *Illustrated London News* (1842), *Lloyd's Illustrated London Newspaper* (1842) and the *News of the World* (1843). The decline in the number of dailies between 1800 and 1830, despite an expanding population, stopped. In 1836, London, with a population of almost one and a half million, had eleven dailies, and twenty in 1864 (more than now). New York, with 250,000 inhabitants, had fifteen dailies. If between 1800 and 1850 circulation was almost at a standstill, in the following fifty years it jumped from less than 5,000 to 200,000 for the leading dailies.[9] There was a parallel development in the United States. In 1833 Benjamin Day founded the New York *Sun*, competitively priced at two cents, while the other dailies cost six cents. Gordon Bennett followed suit with the *Morning Herald*.

Press Freedom

The penny press enlarged the market because it had been realised that it was not possible to expand sales simply by lowering price; nor was it possible to gain new customers by giving them a product designed for an élite interested in political and business news and establishment gossip. One had to appeal to a broader readership by providing a broader range of articles. The New York *Sun*, along with the penny press on both sides of the Atlantic, considerably expanded coverage of crime, violence and human-interest stories.

In France the situation was still unfavourable to the formation of a popular press. Even under the more liberal Press Law of 1822 the government could prevent publication in special circumstances. Severe penalties were levied for 'press crimes' such as slander towards the dignity of the crown or its ministers. You could publish what you wanted, but at your own risk. The impression was of liberalism, but in reality the political press lived in a climate of uncertainty. It fought back courageously, even defiantly, to no avail. In 1832 pre-censorship was reintroduced against caricaturists, fines were increased and prison sentences lengthened.[10]

Émile Girardin, who founded the daily *La Presse* in 1836, was aware that in order to expand the market it was necessary to reassure politicians: why should they not exploit the press for their own ends, he suggested, instead of suppressing it? Restrictions such as taxes and censorship would inevitably drive the press towards the opposition. He suggested, in vain, that the government should facilitate the creation of an official paper, edited, it was implied, by Girardin himself, which would genuinely compete with the opposition press. By increasing competition, not only would the government remove a source of conflict, it would also provide a rallying point for the majority of potential readers, who were more likely to side with the government and law and order than with 'subversion'.[11] The government, however, regarded the bribery of journalists and editors as a more efficient way of controlling the press than having an 'official' organ.

The dictatorial régime of Napoleon III further restricted press freedoms by adopting legislation in 1852 empowering the authorities to refuse, on political grounds, permission to publish any newspapers whose owners had Republican, or Orléanist (pro-Orléans dynasty), or Legitimist (pro-Bourbon monarchy) inclinations. The law explicitly stated that only those enjoying civil and political rights could own or edit a paper. This barred women and foreigners, which is why Adèle Barré's application to be allowed to edit a political journal in Nice was turned down in 1863 even though the regime had supposedly entered its 'liberal' phase.[12]

In Britain, political censorship was minimal. Politicians were as willing to bribe newspapers as their Continental counterparts, but this proved more difficult, because the papers, being on a sounder commercial footing, did not need to take so many bribes. Politicians soon discovered that it was more effective to give the papers what they wanted – news, rumours, gossip – and in so doing, get them to publish certain things while flooding them with misinformation. Contemporary 'spin doctors' have a glorious ancestry. There are always newspapers willing to publish anything. Former journalists turned writers, such as Dickens, knew exactly how the system worked. In his *Dombey and Son* (1848) everyone in the City is curious to obtain information about what is happening to the respected merchant Paul Dombey. Mr Perch, one of his clerks, obliges: 'In ... the King's Arms ... I happened, last week, to let a little observation fall there, and next morning, which was Sunday, I see it worked up in print, in a most surprising manner.'[13]

However, what gave the British press its decisive lead over the French or the German was not better gossip, but advertising and distribution. Literacy was no higher than in France, and the differences in wealth not enormous, but Britain was an industrial capitalist country before France. Its railway network had a fifteen-year lead over the French, and continued to be faster and better for a long time. Even in the eighteenth century the British press was a commercial undertaking, a proper business venture, not a tool for intellectuals with political ambitions or politicians with intellectual pretensions.

Advertising was of paramount importance. In the first quarter of the nineteenth century Parisian dailies published very few personal advertisements, though the French provincial press had no such inhibitions. By contrast, from the end of the eighteenth century the British press was thriving with advertising, mainly personal inserts and announcements. The French started to take advantage of advertising only in the 1830s. By 1850 there were three kinds of press advertisements: the *annonce-anglaise*, or English announcement (small print, short lines, personal announcements); the *annonce-affiche* (a box advertising a particular product in large format, sometimes with an illustration); and the *réclame*, an advertisement pretending to be a feature. Most book and theatre reviews fell into this category.

The French press, compared to the British, was always grossly underfunded by advertising.[14] As there were virtually no nationally branded consumer goods anywhere in Europe, most newspaper advertising was for new books, plays, property, the sale of personal goods, jobs, and above all quack medical remedies, such as lotions for reversing or stopping hair loss (*plus ça change . . .*) or miracle cures for 'secret', i.e. sexually transmitted, diseases.[15]

Funded by a combination of advertising and sales, the Victorians published over 25,000 journals of all kinds, including several hundred reviews and weeklies dealing with literature and addressed to the 'common reader' as well as the 'articulate classes'. In the 1840s the leading papers were not the dailies, which together did not reach 60,000 copies, but Sunday papers like the *Dispatch*, the *Chronicle*, *Lloyd's Weekly*, the *News of the World* and *Bell's Penny Dispatch* (subtitled *Sporting and Police Gazette*). Taken together these sold, every week, some 275,000 copies. There was a whiff of radicalism about them, but on the whole people bought them because they carried the kind of stories that had already proved popular in the chapbooks of the past.[16] Most of them were far from respectable. Right-thinking Victorians were as outraged about them as their contemporary counterparts are about the tabloid dailies. Alexander Andrews's *History of British Journalism* (1859) opened with the remarks that the origins of the British press lay in a 'miserable sheet of flimsy paper, bloated with coarse letter-press, describing some fabulous event, or retailing some more than doubtful story', or a 'mass of slavish panegyric, now of violent and discriminating abuse, issued stealthily, read under the breath, circulated from hand to hand unseen'. Yet the power of the press grew inexorably, continued Andrews: 'suppressed by a king, persecuted by a parliament, harassed by a licenser, burnt by a hangman, and trampled by a mob, the newspaper has been slow in climbing to its present height'. The press was a 'giant which now awes potentates, and it may scarcely be too much to say, rules the destinies of the world'.[17]

Respectable Periodicals

The 'lower orders' were well catered for. But there was something for everyone, including quality material to satisfy the voracious demand of the Victorian middle classes to be kept informed of developments in science and the arts, and the great political and cultural novelties of the age: socialism, Darwinism, modernity and reform. Similar stuff had been published in the eighteenth century for the self-education of a relatively narrow élite. It was now necessary to distil knowledge in short essay form to a wider middle-class public. The new periodical magazines found their market niche between the book, which came out with too great a delay to comment on current developments, and the daily press, which could not reflect extensively on them.

In the new bourgeois world, time was money. It was uneconomic to spend time reading long books. The new bourgeoisie needed not just to be told how to behave, but also what to think. That was what intellectuals were for. As Walter Bagehot explained: 'The modern man must be told what to think – shortly, no doubt, but he must be told it.' Many of the periodicals which had the word 'review' in their title were supposed to have reviews as well as serialisation, but in fact journals like the *National Review*, the *London Review* and Bagehot's *National Review* used the summaries of books as stepping stones for a commentary.[18] The purpose of book reviews was, as Trollope put it, twofold: to tell the public what was worth reading, and to tell them what was in a book so that they could talk about it without having read it. The knowledge acquired would not be very great, but it added to the 'pleasure of life to be able to talk on subjects of which others are speaking'.[19]

By 1860, the circulation figures of the many reviews were remarkable by any standards:

1860: CIRCULATION OF LEADING MAGAZINES. GREAT BRITAIN	
Edinburgh Review	7,000
Quarterly Review	8,000
Westminster Review	4,000
Blackwood's Magazine	10,000
Fraser's Magazine	8,000
National Review	1,000

SOURCE: Walter E. Houghton, 'Periodical Literature and the Articulate Classes' p.7

Readership was actually higher than these figures suggest, because many magazines were read in clubs or borrowed from libraries.

Alongside these reviews were others whose primary task was to carry short stories, poetry and, above all, serialised novels. Of these, the most successful were Dickens's *Household Words* (1850) and its successor *All the Year Round* (1859). Each segment of the upper end of the market was as keenly contested as the lower end. The fashionable world, meaning those living in London's most elegant district and those who wished they did, read about art and exhibitions in *Belgravia*.[20] Tories read *Fraser's Magazine*. Scottish Tories, more intellectual than their English counterparts, opted for *Blackwood's Edinburgh Magazine* (1817). Whigs read the *Edinburgh Review*. The Victorian magazine industry was in constant movement. New entrants constantly challenged established journals. In the 1860s the quarterly reviews faced stiff competition from the new monthlies and weeklies such as *Macmillan's Magazine*, the *Cornhill* (with Thackeray as its first editor), the *Fortnightly Review* (a monthly in spite of its name), and the *Contemporary Review*. The *Westminster Review* changed hands frequently. In 1840 John Stuart Mill sold it to W.E. Hickson, who sold it to the publisher John Chapman, who in 1851 entrusted the *de facto* editorship to Marian Evans (George Eliot).

Literary magazines could be quite profitable. *Blackwood's* made £45,000 annual profit in the 1860s, though only £31,000 by 1900–10. Even when they were not profitable, they could still be regarded as a cheap way of publicising books and authors. The publisher William Tinsley, on finding his *Tinsley's*

Magazine (launched in 1867) losing £25 a month, thought, on reflection, that £25 was a cheap way of advertising his name, his books and his authors.[21]

In France too in the late 1820s there was an explosion of periodical magazines: *La Revue française, La Revue de Paris,* and the enduring *Revue des deux mondes* – after 1840 the pre-eminent French review, indeed the only French review that could rival internationally the British journals. By 1852 it had 6–7,000 subscribers, over 10,000 by 1859 (half exported), while most French magazines did not reach 1,000.[22]

A typical learned journal for the educated upper- and upper-middle-class reader was the monthly *Revue encyclopédique,* or to give it its full name, the *Revue encyclopédique ou analyse raisonnée des productions les plus remarquables dans les sciences, les arts industriels, la littérature et les beaux-arts.* An analysis of a random issue, that of January 1828, gives an idea of its formidable spread. Its 318 pages contain a general feature on the literature of the previous year, an essay by Jean-Baptiste Say on the relevance of economics, an account of the department of the Hérault, various lengthy reviews including one of *L'Histoire naturelle des poissons,* a collection of medieval texts, a chronicle of events concerning the rebellion of the Vendéens and the Chouans against the Republic, a speech by General Foy, and a review of Edward Bulwer-Lytton's youthful epic poem *O'Neill, or the Rebel.* This is followed by 130 pages of bibliographical information, consisting of 134 brief notices on books published in France and elsewhere. Sixty-six of these notices, half the space available, are of foreign books – something no French paper would do today. The coverage of foreign literature and publications – including government reports – is truly comprehensive. There is a feature on Chile (in 1828!), describing the country's new constitution as well as its magazines, bulletins and government gazettes. The magazine then proceeds to list new British books intended for the Christmas market (a title costing one guinea is deemed to be so expensive that it must obviously be addressed to the aristocracy). A section on Russia includes a two-page review of a book on Russian weapon manufacturing with the praise: '*Nous connaissons peu d'ouvrages scientifiques modernes dont l'exécution soit aussi satisfaisante*' (There are few modern scientific works as well written as this). This is followed by a list of tariffs to be paid to Russian customs, reviews of a volume of Russian poetry and books from Poland, Italy, Switzerland, Denmark and Germany, Dante's poetry in German, and various catalogues. Most of the novels reviewed are by women, perhaps an indication that the journal wished to appeal to a wider readership. The reviewer of *La Femme ou les six amours* by Élise Voïart (Paris, 1827) is enchanted by the story, centred on a noble and virtuous heroine, though he is a little upset by the gore in one episode.

In March 1828 the *Revue encyclopédique* itself provided a statistical analysis of the global development of the magazine boom:[23]

NUMBER OF JOURNALS AND REVIEWS IN 1828	
USA	840
France	490
British Isles	483
Other German states	305
Prussia	288
Low Countries	150?
Russia (and Poland)	84
Austria	80?
Denmark	80
Switzerland	30
Italian states	29?
Spain	16?

SOURCE: *Revue encyclopédique*, March 1828

Though the data and the methodology must be questioned (there is no definition of a journal, and no indication of where the figures come from), and some of the figures seem to be inflated, they suggest a boom in periodicals which showed no sign of abating in the course of the nineteenth century.

Another survey appeared in 1847 in the *Revue des deux mondes*. Its author, Charles Louandre, noted the growth over the previous twenty-five years of the *petits journaux*, an eminently French genre which stood in relation to the daily press as the vaudeville did to comedy. Such papers, he complained, did not deal with serious political questions, but merely poured ridicule and sarcasm on well-known personalities. This genre, pioneered by *Le Figaro*, was now represented by *La Caricature*, *Le Charivari* and *Le Corsaire*. But there were also serious reviews, modelled on their British counterparts, as were the new illustrated journals. The market for such reviews, Louandre pointed out, had become increasingly fragmented: periodicals were increasingly cater-ing to specific interests. If you were a bachelor looking for a wife, you would read *Le Messager des mariages*; if a music-lover, you would buy *La Mélomanie*;

if a priest, you would turn to the *Journal des prédicateurs*; and if a gourmet you would follow *Le Gastronome*.[24]

In the whole of Europe the middle classes exhibited a considerable desire to keep up to date with new developments and to improve themselves. Germany, of course, had a vast array of regional daily and weekly newspapers. In Berlin alone, in 1862 there were thirty-two dailies and fifty-eight weeklies. The whole country by the end of the 1870s could boast 2,400 papers.[25] The German middle classes could read literary journals such as the *Literarisches Wochenblatt* (Literary Weekly, 1820–98), weekly illustrated magazines such as the *Leipziger Illustrierte, Über Land und Meer, Daheim* and, above all, *Gartenlaube*. This thirst for knowledge contributed also to the success of Joseph Mayer's 'Penny Library' and to popularisers of science such as Hermann Helmholtz, Ludwig Büchner and Ernst Haeckel (who helped popularise Darwin).[26] Even small countries such as Bohemia (part of the Austrian Empire) had a thriving press, including, from the 1860s, a host of daily newspapers in Czech such as *Čas* (Time), *Národní listy* (The National) and *Pokrok* (Progress). By 1875 there were 195 periodicals in Bohemia, ninety-nine of which were in Czech, and by 1890, 418 (253 in Czech). A woman's magazine, *Ženské listy* (The Women's Paper) was started by the feminist and nationalist Eliška Krásnohorská in 1875. In 1885, a year after its launch, the literary magazine *Zlatá Praha* (Golden Prague), mainly devoted to encouraging literature in Czech, had a circulation of over 8,500. Its owner, Jan Otto, was also the owner of the largest Czech-language publishing press before 1914. With his 'Affordable National Library' he intended to popularise Czech authors and translated famous foreign writers into Czech. The replacement of German as the language of the élite meant that a wider public, whose vernacular was Czech, could obtain access to world (i.e. French and English as well as German) culture.[27]

A secondary market for news was created in France in 1830 when Émile Girardin launched what amounted to the first press agency, distributing news to over a hundred provincial papers.[28] The real breakthrough, however, occurred in 1835, when Charles Havas translated items from the foreign press and sold them to French papers. Soon he had established an agency, the Agence Havas, which would become Agence France-Presse in 1944. Rivals soon sprang up, such as Bernhard Wolff's news agency in Prussia in 1849. In 1851 Paul Julius Reuter – he was born (in Germany) Israel Beer Josaphat and died Baron Paul Julius von Reuter – established the famous London-based news agency. He had started in Aachen using a pigeon-post service, but in

England by 1865, thanks to the new overland and undersea cables, the Reuters Telegrams Company was delivering news from various parts of the world in minutes and hours instead of days and weeks.[29]

News-gathering remained in the hands of the leading press nations: Britain, Germany, France and the USA, where Associated Press (now the largest news service in the world) was formed in 1848 by six New York dailies. The penny dailies, including the *Daily Telegraph*, relied heavily on Reuters for much of their foreign coverage.[30] Until the middle of the century few papers had regular writers. 'Real' journalists at the time did not deign to gather news; they wrote commentaries. Many regarded themselves as men of letters. Real men of letters, like Edward Bulwer-Lytton, thought journalists were 'broken-down sharpers, gamblers, and uneducated blackguards' – a fair assessment, at least in England (in France they had a higher status).[31]

Journalism became a distinct profession only in the second half of the nineteenth century.[32] Until then, dailies addressed themselves to a fairly narrow élite which was, roughly speaking, more or less coterminous with the political establishment. In Paris by 1840 there were twenty dailies, with a total circulation of 108,701, but the four largest had 60 per cent of the market. By 1870 there were thirty-eight dailies, selling a total of over a million copies a day, half of that by only four papers.[33] In Italy in 1872, the highest-circulation daily was the Milanese *Il Secolo* (1866), which sold only 30,000 copies, even though it was as innovative as its foreign equivalents. Italian dailies, like many in France, depended more on ministerial favour, government handouts and banking and business interests than on market demand.[34] *La Nazione* (Florence, 1859) was backed by the steel industry; *La Stampa* (Turin, 1867) was close to the Liberal Party and was eventually bought by the car manufacturer Fiat; *Il Corriere della sera* (Milan, 1876) was funded by textile industrialists and later by Pirelli (rubber); *Il Resto del Carlino* (Bologna, 1885) was backed by the sugar industry; *La Tribuna* (Rome, 1883) was owned by the Banca Commerciale.

As the suffrage spread, the daily press became an important instrument of political propaganda. Its task was not necessarily to change people's political allegiance – most readers were indifferent or already converted – but to provide interested readers with a filter through which to decipher events, arguments with which to defend or criticise politicians, facts which would strengthen and deepen one's political belief. Politics alone could not sell newspapers, but political influence was a commodity which could be sold in high places. Socialist and radical newspapers always had an unbridgeable handicap: they had too pronounced a political profile to appeal to the non-converted, too narrow an interest to appeal to the indifferent, too subversive a position to attract the patronage of the wealthy, and too poor a readership to entice advertisers. In Great Britain, while *Reynolds' Weekly* had a circulation of 300,000 in the 1860s, not one of the main five working-class weeklies, such as the *Bee-Hive* and the *Commonwealth*, managed to sell more than 10,000 copies.[35] Most popular newspapers which appeared in Britain and France in the second half of the nineteenth century were hostile to socialism, while selling to the social groups the socialists hoped to attract.

Periodicals for women were far more profitable than those for socialists. In 1852 Samuel Beeton, then only twenty-one, brought out the monthly *Englishwoman's Domestic Magazine*. Revolutionary in conception, it was ideologically classically 'Victorian': committed to the values of tradition, thrift and industry. Samuel's wife Isabella, the famous Mrs Beeton, contributed notes on cookery and fashion, went to Paris twice a year to report on the spring and autumn collections, and explained how to deal with servants and children. Her advice was then distilled into her best-selling *Book of Household Management*, one of the great publishing successes of the 1860s. The magazine also devised 'the practical dress instructor', the forerunner of the paper dress-making pattern, one of the most heavily patronised services offered by the later women's press. It also pioneered what is now referred to as the agony aunt column: its 'Cupid's Letter Bag' provided an appropriately moralistic and stern advisory section answering queries from readers.

Within two years of its first publication, Beeton's *Englishwoman's Domestic Magazine* was selling 25,000 copies. By 1856 it had reached 37,000, and by 1860, illustrated with colour engravings, 50,000. It kept ahead of its competitors by innovating continuously: no sooner had the 1860 Anglo–French Commercial Treaty been signed than Mrs Beeton had acquired the exclusive British rights to use the fashion plates Adolphe Goubaud had introduced in his *Le Moniteur de la mode*, an expensive glossy magazine which had been published in France since 1843.[36] Even though the 'Woman Question' – as feminism was then called – had become a widely debated issue, the *Englishwoman's Domestic Magazine* kept well away from it. Commercially this was a sound decision. The *Lady's Review* (1860), which tried to debate the conditions of women, ceased publication within a year. The mildly feminist *Woman's Gazette* (1875), which helped needy women to find jobs, was forced to widen its scope and change its name to *Work and Leisure* (1879).

Samuel Beeton, in launching another middle-class magazine called simply the *Queen* (1861), announced his policy: 'When we write for women we write for the home. We shall offend very few when we say that women have neither the heart nor head for abstract political speculation . . . our own liberties, or our political principles . . . may be safely left to men . . . therefore our survey of foreign affairs and of politics generally will be recorded in a few notes.'[37] Women's magazines remained for decades a bastion of traditional values. Occasionally, by the end of the century, mild subversion emerged in unexpected places like the magazine *Housewife*, which in 1890 published articles entitled: 'Strategy with Husbands', 'The Kingdom of the Home and How to Rule it', and 'Are Men Inferior?'[38] The *Englishwoman's Review* (1866–1910) felt that women should not confine themselves only to feminine topics, but should also read science, anti-slavery tracts, ethnology tomes, etc.[39]

In France no fewer than ninety-two women's periodicals were launched in the 1830s and 1840s, including the *Gazette des ménages* and the *Conseiller des femmes*, founded by Eugénie Niboyet in October 1833, a weekly with articles on economics, grammar, literature, fashion and how to raise children.[40] Fashionable women enjoyed *Mode illustrée* during the Second Empire, and then, from 1879, *Petit écho de la mode*. Everywhere illustrated newspapers, such as the German 'family' weekly *Illustrierte Zeitung*, devoted several pages to 'women's matters'.

But the middle classes liked reading about sex just as much as the lower classes. The trick consisted in packaging the material so that it allowed respectable readers to purchase it openly. Exposés of prostitution, child abuse, squalor, homosexuality and moral turpitude enabled the middle classes to feel virtuous and thrilled at the same time. Journalistic slumming became a sub-genre – and a successful one at that, since it is still thriving today. Prompted by his brother, the editor of the 'gentlemen's newspaper' the *Pall Mall Gazette*, the journalist James Greenwood spent a night in January 1866 in a workhouse, disguised as a homeless tramp, and published his findings. His account may have been influenced by Charles Dickens's latest novel, *Our Mutual Friend*, another case of art following life following art.[41] The resulting articles were widely reprinted, and also circulated as shilling pamphlets and even in penny editions ('Startling Particulars. A Night in the Workhouse. How the Poor Are Treated in Lambeth') for the benefit of the respectable poor, who knew little, or so it was thought, of the conditions of their more indigent brethren. Their success revived the flagging financial fortunes of the *Pall Mall Gazette*, turned James Greenwood into a celebrity, and inaugurated the genre of undercover journalism. The subsequent lead article in the *Gazette* suggested that the poor were not just filthy and revolting, but also that they were sexually depraved: 'What was done was worse than what was said and what was said was abominable beyond description or decent imagination.' The suggestion, somewhat coded, was that at night the workhouse turned into a homosexual bordello 'for the hideous enjoyment of those who are already bad, and the utter corruption of those who are obliged to hear what they cannot prevent'.[42]

Workhouses had existed for quite a while, and everyone knew about them, but until they were written about by people like Greenwood and his numerous imitators (workhouses were almost overwhelmed by writers in search of a good copy), there was no scandal. The press had created a moral panic. Politicians had to respond, launch investigations, and show themselves to be concerned about the London poor.

Dailies

When a docile popular press emerged, politicians, realising the political advantages, became more tolerant – even Napoleon III. The most important of the new Paris popular dailies was *Le Petit journal*, launched by Moïse Millaud in 1863 for only five centimes per copy, thanks to huge advertising support. This was a real bargain: a book then cost 3.5 francs – seventy times more – while a kilo of bread in Paris would cost the equivalent of eight newspapers, a litre of milk almost six. In 2004 *Le Monde* cost €1.20, a litre of milk €1.03 and a baguette €0.75.

At the time even dailies were sold exclusively by subscription, and the price took distance into account. Millaud had two great marketing ideas: his daily would cost the same throughout the country, and payment could be made at the point of sale. Neither of these could have occurred without the railways. Such plans had been tried before, but unsuccessfully, in 1832 by Émile Girardin, who lost a third of his readers. The situation was now quite different. It was possible to print in Paris and have the paper reach any city or town with a railway station the following day. Peddlers had to adapt by becoming more regional, picking up their goods at stations and taking them to the surrounding villages. Eventually newsagents reached into the remotest part of every country, and offered printed material to anyone reluctant to walk into a bookshop or unable to reach one. Thus, very gradually, the peddlers who had carried much of Europe's popular culture on their backs largely disappeared. A few of them survived by collecting used books and reselling them on market stalls, but this was a minor circuit.

The old dailies such as *La Presse* or *Le Constitutionnel* were expensive because to receive them it was necessary to subscribe by paying at least three months in advance. In 1852 a year's subscription outside Paris for what was then the largest-circulation daily in France, *Le Constitutionnel*, cost fifty-two francs, or just under 10 per cent of the yearly income of an agricultural worker (1.61 francs a day). Unsurprisingly, the subscribers of *Le Constitutionnel* were solidly middle and upper class.[43] There were, of course, readers who sat in the cafés or in the *cabinets de lecture* and did not pay the full subscription, but few workers were to be found among these.

Le Petit journal owed its vastly enhanced sales to the fact that it was little more than a vehicle for the daily serialisation of novels and crime reports. A typical headline (1863) screamed: 'Horrible crime!!! A Sixty-Year-Old Man Cut in Pieces, Boiled in a Pot and Thrown to the Pigs by his Brother and his Sister-in-Law. Horrible Details!!!'[44] By 1865 the daily was selling some 260,000 copies, and by 1880, over 580,000. Its readership was even larger than this, because more than one person read each copy of the paper. Over the ensuing twenty years *Le Petit journal* had to face new rivals: *Le Petit Parisien* in 1876, *Le Matin* in 1884, and *Le Journal* in 1892. By 1914 these four dailies dominated the Parisian press (75 per cent of sales) and accounted for 40 per cent of national sales.[45]

Le Petit Parisien, which eventually supplanted *Le Petit journal*, was born out of the ashes of Napoleon III's defeat. It aligned itself with the new Republican régime, developing the required mild anti-clericalism. It knew, however, that politics alone could not satisfy its heterogeneous readership. What sold the paper was the usual mixture of crime reports, news about celebrities, serialised novels and short stories.[46] In fact, the range of themes covered by the new popular daily press was similar to that covered by the old peddlers' literature: 'how-to-live' advice, minor erotica, jokes and funny stories, lives of bandits, suggestions on how to get your man or woman, potted summaries of history books, especially of a biographical nature, travel features, mildly coarse and lewd anecdotes, digests of classics.

British papers too reported crime punctiliously, though they still refrained from screaming headlines. Popular Sunday papers (the working classes could not yet afford to buy a paper every day) such as *Lloyd's Weekly* (founded in 1842), the *Weekly Times* (1847) and *Reynolds' Newspaper* (1850) devoted almost a third of their space to crime.[47] They became mass-circulation papers before the advent of the mass daily press. Indeed, they paved the way for it. By the 1880s *Reynolds'* and *Lloyd's* were selling 300,000 a week. Ten years later *Lloyd's* had reached 600,000. In 1896 it was selling one million copies.[48] The dailies had realised early on that there was money to be made and sales to be gained by increasing the fears and anxieties of their readers. Press coverage of the Franz Müller case (1864) transformed a mundane crime (a bludgeoning probably not intended to kill) into a sensational event. *The Times* declared it 'one of the most atrocious crimes that probably ever disgraced this country'. The *Daily Telegraph* went further: 'It would almost seem as if human depravity were an increasing epidemic – a canker eating its way in every walk and rank of life.'[49] Readership expanded, but this did not dent that of the Sunday papers.

In England a respectable cheap daily press had to wait for Alfred Harmsworth (later Lord Northcliffe), a self-educated Irishman who, having successfully relaunched the almost bankrupt *Evening News* in 1894, founded in 1896 the *Daily Mail*, the first major popular British daily. The reason a cheap mass-circulation daily had not emerged before was not lack of readers, for the British read more newspapers than the French. The problem was that the market for popular papers had already been colonised by a succession of competing dailies sold directly in the street rather than by subscription. This was a phenomenon noticed as early as 1828 by the American writer James Fenimore Cooper, author of *The Last of the Mohicans*. Walking back to his lodgings in London one evening, he wrote,

> a fellow near me raised open one of the most appalling street cries it was ever the misfortune of human ears to endure. The words were 'Eve-ning Cou-ri-er – great news – Duke of Wellington – Evening Courier,' screeched without intermission, in a tremendous cracked voice, and with lungs that defied exhaustion. Such a cry, bursting suddenly on one, had the effect to make him believe that some portentous event had just broke upon an astounded world.

Cooper was about to purchase the *Courier* when another cry from the opposite side of the street denounced the *Evening Courier* and peddled a rival rag. 'In this manner,' concluded Cooper a little pompously, 'did these raven-roasted venders of lies roam the streets . . . worthy agents of falsehoods and follies of the hour.'[50]

So keen were the British on reading a daily paper that by the 1830s British tourists visiting Paris could read what was one of the first 'European' papers: *Galignani's Messenger*. This was an English daily edited in Paris since 1830 by a printer of Italian origins, Giovanni Antonio Galignani (1814–95), and soon available in all major European cities. Galignani's bookshop was in fact an elegant literary salon. The English tourist, upon arrival in Paris, would proceed to the rue Vivienne, where he would find a series of rooms, open from eight in the morning to eleven at night, which gave onto internal gardens, two hundred magazines, a lending library with 20,000 volumes, a register where he could put down his name and address (a way of signalling his presence in Paris to other travellers), and learn where to find accommodation, servants, and where to go shopping.[51]

The *Messenger* had a network of correspondents in Germany, Italy, Switzerland and Spain. Using special couriers, it got news faster than the French competition. By 1848 it could get news from London in forty-eight hours, and it was the first to use the new telegraphy system, the cable connecting Dover to Calais laid in 1851.[52] It shamelessly republished any material from British journals it could get hold of. Thackeray, tongue in cheek, declared, 'May the blessings of all Englishmen who have ever been abroad rest on the founder and proprietors of that piratical print!'[53]

The removal of the duty on paper and the expansion of the rail network made British dailies even cheaper. The *Daily Telegraph* rapidly gained a lower-middle-class audience, while the regional press expanded decisively by providing local news. Readers liked the new popular newspapers, dailies and weeklies, addressed specifically to them. As none of the articles were long, they were easy to absorb. This suited people who worked all day and did not have much time to read. The trend towards short, synthetic items – what we now call 'soundbites' – originated then. The simple style meant they could be easily understood by those with little education. Critics who mocked the poverty of the language did not get the point: the new magazines and dailies would not have been successful unless they had been written simply. Scanning a paper empowered the readers. They could make choices, zoom in on something interesting, scan other items, and skip the rest. Editors became aware of this, and were forced to provide a wider reading experience than the relatively narrow one of élite magazines.

In the wealthier countries a new working-class reading public was emerging. This was not, at first, the factory proletariat, the focus of so much attention and research, but domestic servants, the largest single occupational group in Victorian Britain. The social location of these workers was unique. Unlike the factory proletariat, and by virtue of their place of work, they were not unfamiliar with the habits and language of the middle classes, their taste and aspirations. Unlike factory workers, servants could aspire, with some justification, to move up the social ladder. Their level of literacy was reasonably high. They were encouraged to be literate by their employers (literacy was a useful skill). They were in contact with books and newspapers, and often would have been required to borrow books from the lending library on behalf of their employers. Their masters often encouraged them to read 'improving' books, hoping it would make them better servants, more loyal, more docile, more God-fearing, less susceptible to the wrong ideas, or at least less likely to pilfer the contents of the drinks cabinet. Among the publications aimed at this market was the *Servant's Magazine*, a monthly periodical published by the Committee of the London Female Mission which sold some 4,000 copies per month in mid-century.[54] Almost certainly many servant girls preferred the kind of novels Edward Lloyd serialised in his *Sunday Times* in the 1840s, novels with enticing titles like *The Gipsy Boy*, *The Maniac Father*, *Ela the Outcast*, each containing the usual mild dose of Victorian sex and violence.[55] Others showed more refined taste. An enthusiastic lecturer at the Conference of the Church of England Bookhawking Union (held in Derby on 21 September 1859) declared that only twenty years before reading had been the privilege of the middle and upper classes, but now there was a new literate generation; consequently it was one's 'truly Christian' duty to provide them with good books in order to prevent them from reading bad ones. He then told his audience of a book hawker who had not been able to sell any of his wares to a young lady of a grand house who wanted fortune-telling books; the maid who had opened the door, however, bought three, having failed to persuade her mistress to buy any.[56]

Journalists

Political power was only one aspect of press power, although it was the one which received the most attention. Politicians feared it and tried to control it by bribing or cajoling journalists and manipulating them. Both politicians and journalists developed an exaggerated sense of the political influence of the press. Nevertheless, the press was a powerful tool for the self-promotion of those writing in it. A good review, a puff, a mention, a quote was something regarded as so important that those writing in newspapers assumed, gradually, the role and function previously reserved for aristocratic patronage.[57] In the eighteenth century, in most countries, to be a successful writer it was often necessary to have a powerful patron. In the nineteenth century it was better to have a newspaper on your side – better still to write in one.

The journalistic career was open to the young, and made it possible to become well-known as a writer in a short period of time and without having to write a long book. Once established as a journalist it was easier to make it as a playwright or a novelist. One could also make more money. Between 1828 and 1830 Balzac made 2,500 francs from his books, but twice as much from writing for the newspapers. Literary journalists, as opposed to newsgatherers, could command reasonable sums.

It is difficult to quantify the number of journalists, because most figures do not distinguish between various kind of professional writers. Nigel Cross estimates, on the basis of census figures, that there were in Britain during the nineteenth century some 20,000 writers.[58] On the basis of the *Catalogue général de la librairie française* Marc Angenot estimated that in 1886–90 there were 13,500 'writers' in France. The discrepancy between the French and the English figures can be explained by the fact that the French catalogue simply reports all those who had written a book in that period, not all those who were professional writers.[59]

For the average writer, the press probably represented the most regular source of income. *Punch* regulars earned good salaries: £1,500 a year in the mid-1860s.[60] The future politician Adolphe Thiers arrived in Paris in 1821 without money. As a journalist he earned 75,000 francs over the following seven years, the same as a Conseiller d'État, and he also earned – in those happy days – another 50,000 francs as a historian.[61] The newspapers could afford to be relatively generous because the normal way of buying them was by subscription. Though this tended to limit sales, it was paid in advance, and meant that they could plan ahead. Cash flow was not a daily problem.[62]

Zola advised aspiring writers to train as journalists (as he had done himself).[63] Young writers, he wrote later, should throw themselves into the press 'as one throws oneself into the water to learn how to swim'.[64] Aspiring writers could acquire useful skills and tips from journalism. As Millaud's *Petit journal* was substantially a crime-reporting sheet, its journalists acquired an intimate knowledge of policemen, criminals and court procedure. It is not surprising that one of them, Émile Gaboriau, became one of its main house authors, producing detective stories first serialised in the paper itself.[65]

Reviewing books was an important sideline. One could use a review to score points against enemies, **ingratiate** oneself with powerful writers, and earn a living. The habit of sending review copies started in earnest. A review copy of an English book dated 1831 has inscribed on the flyleaf 'With the Author's Compliments to the Editor of *Tait's Magazine*', and inside the front cover is a printed label which gives the publisher's name, the price, a date before which the book should not be noticed, and a request for a copy of the periodical containing the review.[66] The advantages of being a reviewer, for the more celebrated journalists, were considerable: networking with the political and social establishment, being feared by writers, and having access to a circle of well-disposed friends. There were frequent and varied perks. Theatre critics, for instance, could use their reviews to entice young actresses into sexual relations – also a common practice among playwrights, the casting couch having been invented well before Hollywood. The powers of self-promotion of journalists, though still modest by comparison with today's television journalism, were already so self-evident that many realist novelists of the time (Dickens, Zola, etc.), familiar with the *milieu* because they were part of it, often described the louche figure of the unscrupulous hack and, more rarely, the pressman of integrity with a cause to defend. Of course, to be known, it was preferable to be allowed to sign articles, a practice which guaranteed French journalists higher prestige than in England, where anonymity prevailed.

Illustrations

In the twentieth century, radio, the gramophone, then the cinema and finally television ensured that though literacy reached almost the entire population of the Western world, the consumption of images and sound dominated the cultural industry. This was not so in the nineteenth century, but even then the visual element was important, for few novels were published without some kind of 'illustrations'– a neologism that became widely used in England only after 1830. Book decoration had of course existed for centuries, but technological improvements enabled a remarkable expansion in the use of illustration.

In the 1830s there were three basic techniques available: wood engraving, which allowed images to be included in the typography, and was more accurate than the older woodcut technique ; steel engraving, more resistant and cheaper than copper engraving, thus making bigger print runs more accessible; and lithography, a technique based on the water-repellent property of grease or wax (see page 206), which made it possible to obtain an exact copy from an original (though it had to be printed separately from the text).[67]

Wood engraving had come back into fashion thanks to a Newcastle printer, Thomas Bewick (1753–1828), who had used it to illustrate nature books. By the 1820s he had become the leading wood engraver in Britain, and had trained a number of apprentices, many of whom moved to London and provided the expertise for the further development of book illustrations and the new kind of illustrated magazines.[68] Wood engraving permitted illustrations to be printed in large quantities, and was successfully used by Charles Knight in his *Penny Magazine* (see pages 304–6). The new media immediately obtained the support of artists, who had finally found a genuinely commercial outlet for their products.[69] A British engraver, Charles Thomson, went to France to work for the publishers Ambroise Firmin-Didot, and trained others in the use of the new wood-engraving technique. Steel engraving was an American invention whose high degree of precision made it an unrivalled technique for the printing of banknotes. It was immediately adopted by the British, and then spread to the Continent.[70]

What is remarkable is how rapidly technological innovations spread throughout the West, and how here too the lead was firmly in the hands of the British and the French. The British were also quick to develop a magazine in which the visual element prevailed over the text – the *Illustrated London News* (1842), whose circulation reached 45,000 by 1845. It was deliberately marketed as a family paper and was warmly supported by the clergy, influenced perhaps by the distribution of 11,000 free copies among them. It pioneered the use of images in social reporting. Readers could see and not just read about major court events, follow the changes in fashion, participate vicariously in civic processions, banquets, political and religious meetings, theatrical novelties, horse races, ship launches – anything that was attended by crowds.[71] And they could do so without feeling entirely excluded, while harbouring the wish to participate directly in events of whose existence they had previously been only dimly aware.

Curiosity about what celebrities looked like had, of course, preceded illustrated magazines. In 1780 the Summer Exhibition of the Royal Academy at Somerset House in London attracted 61,000 paying visitors in the six weeks it was open. They were there mainly to look at portraits. Gainsborough was perfectly aware that this was the main attraction when he wrote that an artist 'may do great things, and starve in a Garret, if he does not conquer his passions and conform to the common Eye in chusing that branch [portraits] which they will encourage, & pay for'.[72] Now, thanks to illustrations, and soon thanks to photography, the image of the famous became widely available.

But images could also be powerful instruments for denouncing social ills. The *Illustrated London News* capitalised on the desire to be nearer to those who are famous, but it also used its illustrations for social analysis, though it made sure to keep its social conscience within the bounds of decency. It fully publicised the various reports on poverty which were produced in the 1840s, including the inquiry into the conditions of children in coalmines, and it did print one of the illustrations the commissioners had included in the report, showing a naked child dragging a small wagon of coal on all fours – just like a beast. There was an outcry, but mainly because the nudity was regarded as offensive. The less scrupulous *Bell's Penny Dispatch*, a sensationalist penny Sunday, had fewer qualms. *Punch* went as far as publishing a cartoon called 'Capital and Labour', which juxtaposed images of the labouring poor by a coalmine with those of the rich revelling in luxury.[73] The power of the image had been realised at the outset. MPs who wished to defend the mine-owners disputed the reliability of the pictures, while complaining that public opinion had been swayed disproportionately by the strength of the images. Though the outcry led to the 1843 Mines and Collieries Act, which offered some protection to children, successive government reports were not illustrated; but soon illustrations were regularly used to promote whatever vision of society a particular paper wished to uphold.[74]

A mixture of articles and more sophisticated illustrations caught the popular imagination, and the *Illustrated London News* was quickly imitated in France by *L'Illustration* (1843). It was followed later the same year in Leipzig by the *Illustrierte Zeitung*, in 1845 in Lisbon by *A Illustração*, in Stuttgart in 1853 by *Illustrierte Welt*, in Madrid in 1857 by *El Museo Universal* and in 1858 the *Illustraciòn española*, in 1864 the *Illustrated Sydney News* in Australia, and in 1873 the *Illustrazione Italiana* in Italy.[75] Of course, as is always the case, these new magazines were building on an earlier popular culture: the chapbooks of previous centuries always contained illustrations; the penny dreadfuls whose front covers were decorated with lurid woodcut engravings; and the vogue for '*vignettes*' and other pictorial material which arose, especially in France, in the 1830s.[76] In the 1880s, when the cost of reproduction further decreased, the ratio of images to text in illustrated magazines further increased.[77]

The formula could be applied globally: a mix of news, reviews, a *feuilleton*, some poetry, some financial news and plenty of advertising was addressed to a public which was generically conservative but not particularly interested in politics. One kind of illustration, however, was predominantly political: cartoons. These had appeared in Great Britain since the 1730s. They were popular and, by later standards, rather daring. An entire market for political caricatures had sprung up. These often satirised members of the royal family, particularly George IV, his estranged wife Queen Caroline, and his stout mistresses.

Until the early nineteenth century cartoons were expensive. They were sold individually, and were often used to decorate inns and coffee houses. In the 1830s, thanks to new techniques they became cheaper, and started to be used in magazines. This made artists like Charles Williams, George Cruikshank, William Heath and Robert Seymour famous when their work appeared in magazines such as the radical London *Figaro*. Parallel developments occurred in Paris with *La Caricature* and *Charivari*, founded in 1832 by Charles Philipon, which carried the works of Gavarni (1804–66) and Honoré Daumier (1808–79). *Charivari* in turn inspired the Berlin *Kladderadatsch* (1848). *Punch* entered the fray on 17 July 1841, and survived until 2002. The second half of the nineteenth century was the heyday of the political cartoon, above all in England.[78] Many of these cartoons poked fun not at the establishment but at the weak and helpless: *Punch* pilloried Irish immigrants; its American counterpart *Puck* made fun of Jewish immigrants.[79]

The rise of illustrations engendered the rise to fame of illustrators, a profession hitherto almost unknown to the general public – 'almost' because some exceptionally talented print-makers, such as William Hogarth, were already well known in their own right, and accepted as 'great' (partly thanks to Charles Lamb's 1811 essay 'On the Genius and Character of Hogarth'). The cultural legitimisation of Hogarth and the spread of illustrated magazines provided the new Victorian middle classes with another opportunity to ape the upper classes and spend their money in a thriving yet affordable art market by buying prints (alongside knick-knacks, *objets d'art*, etc.) Artists could enjoy a new form of patronage by the new middle classes. Even Turner deigned to illustrate Walter Scott. The constraints were modest. The prints had to be of small format, since the middle classes did not live in palaces, and one had to use popular themes: landscapes and domestic genre scenes. Historic and religious subjects were more difficult to shift. None of this involved any change in the ideological make-up of artists. They were in the habit of obeying. For centuries they had complied with the whims of the aristocracy; now they had to comply with those of the bourgeoisie. Inevitably there were complaints that 'pictures are now but a portion of domestic furniture' (*Saturday Review*, 1857) while as early as 1830 art critics lamented that art had become commercial.[80] As if Titian or Michelangelo had painted for nothing.

In France, illustrators such as Antoine (Tony) Johannot (1803–52), Jean-Jacques Grandville (1803–47) and Gustave Doré (1832–83) became famous. They also became rich. Grandville, for instance, was paid 10,000 francs for the illustrations to the second volume of *Scènes de la vie privée et publique des animaux* (1841). This was considerably more than what was that paid to major authors. Balzac, for instance, received 30,000 francs for twenty volumes of the *Comédie humaine*.[81]

The illustrated press and the illustrated book did for painters what journalism was doing for writers: it provided an alternative source of livelihood. Artists often lived in close proximity to printers and frequented the same circles as writers. New techniques, such as lithography, multiplied the possibilities for artists by enabling cheaper magazines and books to be produced. Artists such as Géricault, Bonington, Vernet, Ingres and Delacroix became involved, while specialist journals such as *L'Artiste*, founded in 1831 by Arsène Houssaye, provided an outlet for the work of artists excluded from the Academy.[82] Popular books, such as *Gil Blas* by Lesage – published in 1835 with six hundred vignettes engraved in wood by Jean Gigoux – and Charles Nodier's *Histoire du Roi de Bohême et de ses sept châteaux* (1830) further enhanced the popularity of engravers.[83]

In 1770 the *Lady's Magazine* had already started carrying embroidery patterns, inset sheet music and even fashion plates. Its pioneering example was followed by many others, including the *Journal des demoiselles* (1833), *Le Moniteur de la mode* (1843) and, in the USA, Godey's *Lady's Book and Magazine* (1830). Most fiction contained illustrations depicting the main characters and even the main scenes. Such pictures, inevitably more powerful than a textual description, invaded the territory of the writer who had used words to represent an image. Flaubert was very conscious of this – he had been upset when *Madame Bovary* was published with an illustration of the heroine on the cover. He instructed his agent not to allow any further illustrations of his books: 'Never, while I am alive, will I be illustrated because even the finest literary description is destroyed by even a mediocre drawing. The drawing of a woman is just the drawing of a woman. The conception is closed, complete, and all words are useless, while a woman described in words alone makes one dream about a thousand women.'[84]

The periodical press provided artists with the kind of opportunities which the Academy could no longer offer. In Britain, for instance, the number of painters had grown far in excess of the capacity of the Royal Academy to absorb them. In 1852 *Fraser's Magazine* declared that although there were nine hundred painters in the country, only forty were members of the Academy.[85] A single periodical could publish anything between five hundred and a thousand images per year (ten to twenty per week), as many as all the pictures exhibited at the Royal Academy Summer Exhibition.[86]

Art became available to a mass market. The German illustrated journal *Die Gartenlaube* praised in 1874 the techniques which had made art cheaper: 'The woodcut, copper and steel engraving, the typography of painting in the form of chromolithograph and photography have taken an ever higher rank, because they have made accessible to large masses the rarest and most expensive treasures of all times and all climes.'[87]

One could now become a professional artist outside the Academy. The periodical press provided work for artists and advertised them, lionising some while disparaging others, thus influencing their market values. The growing commercialisation of Victorian life meant that people were beginning to regard art not as a hallowed object out of their reach, but as a commodity to be bought and sold.[88]

The British Academy in London and the Salon in Paris defended the aristocratic concept of high art until it became indefensible, either because the aristocrats had become too poor or because the bourgeoisie had become too diversified. Ranged against the strongholds of high culture were new institutions such as the Society of British Artists, which specialised in middle-class art. In 1847 the Free Exhibition, later called the National Institution of the Fine Arts, was established with a deliberately mercantile approach, renting wall space to artists.[89]

Illustrators, however, knew their craft lacked prestige, because their illustrated books were not unique, and because they obviously worked for money and not for Art. Some celebrated illustrators, such as Antoine Johannot, managed to show their works at the Salon, but most were excluded. Towards 1860 the illustrated market grew more diversified. Some books were published in two distinct editions: a cheap one, not illustrated or illustrated cheaply, and a limited luxury edition, the *livre d'artiste*, often addressed to collectors of fine books. This provided the illustrators excluded from the British Academy or the Salon with some degree of cultural recognition.[90]

In France the most famous of nineteenth-century illustrators, Gustave Doré (1832–83), provides an interesting case study of the conflict of prestige and money besetting the profession. Doré had set out to acquire some of the prestige of high culture (without giving up on the cash) by illustrating the classics of high literature – Dante's *La Divina Commedia*, Shakespeare, Ariosto, Milton, Corneille, Goethe, Schiller, Virgil, Homer, etc. – and by selling them at the considerable price of a hundred francs per volume, the kind of price commanded by *objets d'art*, he could share in their aura. His strategy was to develop for himself the image of a major cultural figure, adding and retouching his biography, cultivating journalists, exploiting his social skills and his youthful good looks. He was, of course, regularly lampooned by caricaturists and fellow illustrators, who accused him of being too productive, too industrial, too bourgeois, and above all too successful. In 1866 Philip G. Hamerton, an English artist, thought that while Doré was 'the most popular and famous living illustrator in the world', contemporary artists were 'offended by his want of serious study, by his audacity, by his careless fecundity. Perhaps, too, they may in some instances be somewhat jealous of his fame.'[91] Before proceeding to damn Doré ('his chiaroscuro, for instance, is as false as a chiaroscuro can be'), he added: 'And the very popularity of Doré is in itself a circumstance to be noted against his chances of recognition by the highest class.'[92]

In a letter to a friend, Doré admitted that he had been successful with the man in the street, 'someone who, at the bottom of my heart, I totally despise'. This obviously depended on which street the man was walking on. The real 'man in the street' – in the sense of the ordinary person on an average wage – could never afford to buy the magazines illustrated by Doré. The annual subscription of a 'popular' 'arty' illustrated magazine such as *Le Monde illustré* was twenty-four francs, 2 per cent of the salary of a prosperous artisan. It is as if someone with a yearly salary of £24,000 in 2006 was asked to pay £480 for a yearly subscription to a magazine. The annual subscription of *FMR*, a rather beautiful if pretentious monthly Italian art magazine produced by Franco Maria Ricci and deliberately targeted at the upper end of the market, was in 2004 just over £80. Even so, *Le Monde illustré* did rather well, selling 33,000 in 1866 – that is, one copy per thousand people in France, the equivalent of 56,000 copies today.[93]

Doré's reach was global. In 1865 he illustrated the English Bible, and in 1867 he had a major exhibition of his work in London, which led to the creation of the Doré Gallery in New Bond Street. In 1869 he illustrated an art book called *London: A Pilgrimage* for which he was paid £10,000, far more than any novelist would receive. Doré, finally, had been able to gain entrance at the 1857 Salon for a painting celebrating the colonialist policies of the Emperor Napoleon III. However, he failed to make it in the world of 'high' art. While his illustrations of Dante's *Divine Comedy* received thunderous praise (and are still being reprinted), his enormous painting (311cm by 418cm) *Dante et Virgile dans le neuvième cercle de l'enfer* secured only an indifferent critical response. Doré is now regarded as one of the greatest illustrators of the nineteenth century, but as a painter he is hardly ever mentioned in standard histories of art – not at all in Arnold Hauser's *The Social History of Art* (1951) or Ernst Gombrich's *The Story of Art* (1950).[94]

As soon as they had established a tangible presence in the world of books and magazines, illustrators were challenged by a momentous technological revolution: photography (the term replaced 'daguerreotype' in the 1850s). Louis Daguerre, one of the reputed inventors of the new technology, found the 'democratic' possibility of photography appealing – and well he might, as the French government bought the rights of the daguerreotype, put them in the public domain and awarded the inventor a pension. Daguerre believed that now ordinary citizens would be able to produce, and at low cost, their own portraits or landscapes. The average professional painter would become extinct, surpassed by the new technology. The idea that new technology will replace older art forms (the cinema will supplant the theatre, television will destroy the cinema, computers will eliminate traditional books, etc.) crops up constantly in history, and is repeated regardless of the massive evidence to the contrary. Thus the idea that photography would eliminate painting emerged just as painting was becoming more commercial and popular than ever, with the spread of museums throughout Europe and North America and the development, first in France and later in Britain, of a powerful art market that wiped out state patronage and sponsorship by the Academy and transferred power to an élite of self-appointed experts. By the 1860s there were sometimes up to three auctions a day in Paris alone.[95]

Painters turned more bourgeois. To secure new customers they gave the public what it wanted, like the successful painter Rosa Bonheur, who serially produced paintings of pets and other animals.[96] The bourgeoisie did not want their walls decorated with photographic portraits and landscapes. They wanted the Unique. They wanted Art, just like the upper classes they were almost desperately aping. Photography – unlike the fine arts – never became the object of a major autonomous cultural market, even though professional photographers made their works more artistic, using composition and complex lighting techniques that were out of the reach of amateurs. By the 1890s an important art photography movement had started, but it never replaced 'unique' pictures. Photography, however, became a major contributor to the press, to the illustration of books, to postcards. On special occasions (such as weddings) a photographer would be hired to provide the 'artistic' tone which the poor equipment and rough skills of the amateur could not. People went to photographers to have themselves and their families recorded – a cheap form of portraiture for those who could not afford the real thing.

Photography also considerably expanded the market for visual porn-ography. Obscene drawings and engravings had been around for some time. But in pornography, the semblance of realism has a massive advantage over artistic interpretation. Coloured photographs of nude women began to circu-late almost as soon as photography was invented. Particularly exciting was the idea of surprising the subject in an intimate act – the precursor of 'reality' TV. She could be 'caught' by the camera in the act of undressing before going to bed, or about to take a bath.[97] Such pictures, and the magazines that carried them, circulated clandestinely. Only in the second half of the twentieth century were so-called 'girlie' magazines allowed to be sold openly to the general public, and only then did the popular press begin to carry pictures of naked women. In the nineteenth century, however, female nudity remained largely confined to high art and Renaissance masters, while the male nude virtually disappeared from nineteenth- and twentieth-century art.

Overwhelmingly, photography became and has remained a private, family affair, a way of illustrating stories printed in newspapers and magazines, or a way for the police and the authorities to record what suspects or convicted villains look like. Ordinary people started taking pictures of their children, of themselves and of their homes and holidays in an increasingly obsessive way, until by the end of the twentieth century a camera had become the indispensable accompaniment of any celebration or trip. By the end of the twentieth century, every year amateur photographers took some sixty billion photographs – fifteen times the world's population.[98] The real market here was in selling the equipment and the films, and developing the prints. Despite the popularity of the medium, museums, even museums of modern art, while welcoming the strangest artefacts of the avant-garde, remained closed to all but a few of the products of photographers.

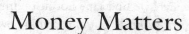

19

Money Matters

Finding Winners

WRITERS WRITE. Some do it for money, some for glory, most for both. Then they hawk around the precious manuscript, expecting someone else to read it, believe in it, invest money in it, find printers to print it, booksellers to stock it, reviewers to review it, and, above all, readers to buy it. This 'someone else', this *deus ex machina*, sometimes loved, frequently despised, is the publisher. Publishers have to guess market preferences and cajole writers into adapting their products to it. They have to read and evaluate a manuscript, devise a budget for its publication, forecast production costs, the initial print run, the size and design, decide whether or not to have illustrations, and liaise with printers. Finally they have to produce a catalogue and promote the book. And much of this has to be done for every single title: four hundred titles, four hundred decisions.

Even in the past, a successful book had to be exploited as much as possible. It could be sold abroad. It could be turned into a play. A cheaper edition could follow an expensive one, or the other way round, to widen sales. It could be adapted for children or simplified for a broader market. The success of *Vie de Jésus* by Ernest Renan in France in 1863 led to a smaller and simplified *Jésus*, without notes, sold for 1.25 francs instead of 7.50.[1] This was remarkable for a text which purported to be a biography of Jesus as a real historical human being who lived at a particular time, not as the son of God.

In cultural production, success is seldom cumulative. One book flops, another succeeds. There are successes in unpopular genres and failures in popular ones. But in most businesses, including publishing, the general rule is that what has worked in the past will work in the future. In the book trade the least risky products appear to be those that have been tested and tried in the past: the classics and their adaptations, well-established reference books and anything that pleases educators, parents, teachers and other writers. Nineteenth-century novels are full of endorsements of the kind of books the authors liked to read. Many of these are the classics. At the beginning of Charlotte Brontë's *Jane Eyre* we find Jane not just – implausibly – engrossed in Bewick's *History of British Birds*, but also reading Swift's *Gulliver's Travels* and Thomas Moore's *Lalla Rookh*, while her friend Bessie reads Samuel Johnson's fable *Rasselas Prince of Abyssinia*. David Copperfield reads Goldsmith, Defoe, Smollett, Cervantes and Lesage's *Gil Blas*.[2] The famous books of the eighteenth and earlier centuries continued to be popular in the nineteenth and beyond: an 1866 report by the French Ministry of Education reveals that the favourite foreign books in schools were, presumably in simplified format, *Robinson Crusoe*, *Don Quixote*, *The Swiss Family Robinson* and *The Thousand and One Nights*.[3]

The assumption that the public will like tomorrow what it liked yesterday is often true . . . except when it is false, as publishers discover – literally – to their cost. George Eliot received her largest advance for *Romola* (1863) because of the huge success of her previous novel, *The Mill on the Floss*. *Romola* lost money. Chappell, the music publishers, paid £100 for the rights to *Faust* (1859), Gounod's masterpiece. He was able to place it with the two rival opera impresarios of the day, Gye and Henry Mapleson. Encouraged, Boosey & Co. paid £1,000 for Gounod's next opera, *Mireille* – which was a total failure.[4] One might almost say that producing a flop after a success is an author's unwitting revenge.

Successful writers became brand names. Readers who had enjoyed one of Dickens's or Dumas's novel were the most obvious customers for the next one. Readers' loyalty could be sought by using the old model of the saga and the simple technique of having the same group of characters pursuing some elusive goal. If one of these was particularly successful it could be assigned to the main character, while accidents, death or other events could eliminate those less popular. Serialised sagas continuously market-tested characters who would be dropped if or when they proved unsatisfactory. Similar principles were later used in television serialisation.

Having the same characters cropping up in a series of novels spared the writer the problem of having to invent new personalities for each book. The affection lavished by readers on a cast of protagonists could be repeated for each successive novel, 'crying at their grief ' – as Trollope put it – 'laughing at their absurdities' and 'enjoying their joy'.[5] This device had further advantages: as each novel could be read independently of all the others, new readers were not deterred by the fact that they had missed the story so far. Furthermore, this created added incentives to purchase the yet unread novels, in which the reader would have the pleasure of finding some of the old characters. Eventually a pattern would be established, with a fixed hero (Sherlock Holmes, James Bond, etc.) and a cast of helpers and villains, as in the saga. In the nineteenth century, however, a series of novels could be grouped together in which characters would play slightly different roles in each: now the main hero, now a secondary one, now just a minor role. Here Balzac was the great pioneer, and Zola his great successor. Balzac used the device of interlinking characters for the ninety or so novels grouped together under the general title of *La Comédie humaine*. Most of these novels were not in sequence, and hence could be read separately, in almost any order. Balzac's decision to depict his work as a representation of contemporary society could be seen as a 'marketing ploy': he hoped that readers would buy the entire work and/or subscribe to future novels, thus ensuring for himself a regular income.[6] Readers found that the more they read, the more they became part of the 'world' created by the writer and at home within it. Balzac realised such possibilities only after having started writing his work, so he went back to some of the novels already written and changed the names of various characters to ensure continuity.

Élite writers (real or potential) affected to despise success, which was seen as coterminous with vulgar popularisation. George Gissing, in a letter in 1885, thought that being read by a small group of highly educated people was 'perhaps . . . better than being popular, a hateful word', while Robert Louis Stevenson – definitely more successful than Gissing – in his essay 'On the Choice of a Profession' (1887–88), implied that nothing could be worse for a writer than to be regarded by conventional middle-class opinion as being 'one of us'.[7] But even élite writers, quite rightly, expected to be paid handsomely once they obtained some recognition. At first Paul Verlaine (1844–96), the French poet and founder of the Symbolist movement, had to pay to get published. As he became established the deal became extremely advantageous for his publishers, who found themselves in the unusual situation of getting paid by their supplier (Verlaine) as well as by their customers. Verlaine discovered that while success could be enjoyable, it was even more so if one was paid for it. He successfully renegotiated his contract, though he kept on moaning that he was not getting enough money. Flaubert too had started out with the common authorial view that publishers were philistine bandits from whom not much, in terms of cash, could ever be extracted. Michel Lévy, his publishers, started instead with the not unreasonable assumption that a writer who had published little represented a high risk, and consequently should be paid as little as possible. As Flaubert became famous he extracted increasing amounts of cash from Lévy.

Great caution, however, was required with new novelists. One should not pay them too little and offend them, in case their first book turned out to be a success and they then went elsewhere. Michel Lévy had given Flaubert eight hundred francs – a miserly sum – for *Madame Bovary* (1856), quite a normal sum for a first novel by an unknown writer.[8] When *Madame Bovary* turned out to be a great success and a *cause célèbre*, Flaubert became more demanding. He explained to Ernest Duplan, a lawyer acting on his behalf, that Lévy was not really buying his next work, but the commercial value the first book had given it. He may have been happy to get eight hundred francs for *Bovary*, but now he wanted 25,000 francs for the next work, *Salammbô*, adding further conditions: there were to be no illustrations, and the publisher would have to buy it without reading it first. Lévy demurred. The sum requested was very large, more than what he paid well established authors like George Sand. It is true that he had not read *Madame Bovary* prior to publication, but then, he had invested only a small amount in it. Now that he was asked to pay a lot more for Flaubert's second work, he felt, not unreasonably, that he should be allowed to read the manuscript first. As for illustrations, these were indispensable if one wanted the book to have a wide readership.[9]

Eventually, Flaubert settled for 10,000 francs, Lévy agreed not to read *Salammbô* before publication, and no illustrations were used. The compromise reached, Lévy wrote a very warm letter to Flaubert (24 August 1862) saying how happy he was that they were 'married again' and no divorce was imminent; he was looking forward to the finished manuscript which he would publish as fast as possible; everyone was thrilled, etc. Publishers had learned early on that, once the financial side was out of the way, it was still necessary to cajole authors and boost their fragile egos. Flattery worked, unfailingly. *Salammbô* did reasonably well (though not as well as *Bovary*). The 2,000 copies of the first impression sold out quickly, three further impressions sold out in 1863, and a further one in 1864.

Flaubert was a special case. With lesser authors, publishers were more proactive, suggesting themes and plots and pretending to know what would sell. Occasionally their role was usurped by newspaper publishers, constantly on the lookout for new novels to be serialised to increase sales. And some authors needed no lessons in the arcane art of self-promotion. Thus, when the serialisation of Eugène Sue's *Les Mystères de Paris* became a sensational success in 1843, Anténor Joly, the enterprising literary editor of *Courier français*, commissioned the young Paul Féval, who had never been to London, to write *Les Mystères de Londres*. This would be peddled as a 'translation' of a novel by a 'Sir Francis Trolopp' (a reference to Frances Trollope, best-selling author and mother of Anthony) and would narrate the revenge of a young Irishman, Fergus O'Breane, on an English aristocrat who has wronged his sister. Féval was just as enterprising as his editor. Having regained his real name, he took an active interest in marketing his own books, requesting that they should be advertised on billboards and in newspapers and reminding his publisher, in a letter of November 1845, that a novel not promoted cannot be successful.[10]

Authors understood that it paid to distinguish themselves from their competitors. One should try to become a literary 'case'. Balzac organised the critical reception of some of his works, realising that a fake bad review lambasting a book with words such as 'This is only for people in search of strong emotions' could boost sales.[11] Such apparently negative verdicts could increase sales even in Victorian Britain. George Sand was widely read in England, often in French, in the 1830s and 1840s, when she was more popular and more admired than Balzac or Hugo. A notice in the *Quarterly Review* of April 1836 did her no damage: Sand's *Lélia* was a 'revolting romance', the writer thundered, 'the heroines . . . are not merely prostitutes but monsters – the men, convicts, maniacs, and murderers', and the book would have been burned in any country but France.[12]

Authors deliberately constructed an image, a personality, a role. Balzac adopted a 'writing costume', the long dressing-gown in which he was regularly portrayed – famously by Rodin – suggesting a man who, overwhelmed by creativity, has no time to get dressed. He also used, as a kind of prop, a walking stick specially designed for him. This delighted caricaturists and facilitated their task.[13] Balzac's strategy worked. He became one of the most famous writers in Europe, and his novels were available all over the world, from India to the USA. A new type of dahlia was named after him, a whaling ship was called *The Balzac*, and in Russia Balzac busts went on sale.[14]

With the rise of mass literature, writers whose readership was relatively restricted devised strategies to distinguish themselves from their more popular colleagues by acquiring an image – such as that of the 'mad genius' (madness, then as now, had a high market value). Writers occasionally became prisoners of their first image. On 25 February 1830, at the first night of Hugo's *Hernani*, a stormy occasion, Théophile Gautier became famous not only for being in the forefront of the Romantic take-over of 'high' art but for wearing an outrageous pink *gilet*. Writing with some nostalgia forty years later, he complained that whenever a philistine who had never read two lines by him heard the name of Gautier mentioned, he would exclaim with the self-satisfied air of someone who is well informed: 'Ah, yes, the young man with the long hair and the red *gilet!*' 'This is how I shall be remembered,' thought Gautier. 'They will forget my poetry, my books, my essays, but they will always remember my red *gilet*.'[15] And indeed a French television documentary film about the famous night (broadcast 6 May 2002) could not fail to produce a handsome Gautier sporting long hair and a red *gilet*.

In order to be noticed, some authors deliberately cultivated a 'bohemian' (i.e. non-conventional) image.[16] Writers having, by definition, a monopoly of writing, made the image popular, aligning themselves with artists, as Henri Murger did in his novel *Scènes de la vie de bohème* (1848), which in turn was adapted by Puccini for his *La Bohème* in 1897.

Publishers too developed a brand image appropriate to their market. Some became distinguished figures, producing high-class editions of consecrated authors and, more or less consciously, projecting an image of themselves as aristocratic patrons. Because they were selling books and not soap, because they discussed literary trends with authors and not fertilisers with farmers, they imagined they were not just another money-grubbing entrepreneur, but a Renaissance prince – or almost. At the other end of the market – the gradations were numerous – we find the stereotypical seedy publisher, lampooned in many novels of the time, who treats books like any other commodity, authors as hacks churning out novels, and readers as an uncultured mass hooked on depraving and corrupting books.

Authors realised that it was important to be published by some publishers rather than others. Prestigious publishers and their writers contributed to define high culture, just as the Academy had defined 'high art'. The history of Cotta, the Stuttgart publishing house, is a case in point. In 1793 Johann Friedrich Cotta (1764–1832) and his partner Christian Jakob Zahn became Schiller's publisher. Thanks to Schiller, Goethe, Kleist, Fichte, Humbolt and other luminaries of the German literary world were added to their stable – all part of a powerful literary network. Then Cotta branched out into press publishing, founding the daily paper *Augsburger Allgemeine Zeitung* (1798), which quickly became one of the most prestigious German newspapers along with *Der Hamburgische Unparteiische Correspondent* (Hamburg's Impartial Correspondent).[17] By the mid-nineteenth century the *Augsburger Allgemeine Zeitung* was required reading for anyone in Germany who wanted to appear well informed.[18] Goethe did well out of Cotta (450,000 marks), and so did Schiller (250,000 marks). But Cotta did better than both. By the time he died in 1832 he was the possessor of a hereditary title, a publishing empire and a fortune estimated at three million marks.

The story of Ernst Keil (1816–78) some fifty years later is equally illuminating. In 1845 he owned an élite liberal monthly. In 1851 he moved a little downmarket with the monthly *Der Illustrierte Dorfbarbier* (The Illustrated Barber of the Village), a paper with plenty of pictures and a print run of 22,000. In 1853 came his real breakthrough: the magazine *Die Gartenlaube* (The Grove of the Garden). This was inspired by the *Pfennig Magazin* created in Leipzig in 1833 by the Parisian bookseller Martin Bossange, inspired in turn by the London *Penny Magazine*.[19] Some ideas floated 'globally' even then.

While the *Penny Magazine* was supposed to appeal to the self-improving working classes (see pages 305–6), *Die Gartenlaube* was explicitly aimed at the core of German society, the *Mittelstand* or middle strata of shopkeepers, self-employed craftsmen, minor bureaucrats and professionals. The magazine advertised itself as informative, apolitical and ideally suited for 'the long winter evenings', to be read within the bosom of one's family.[20] It always included a serialised novel, some popular science, travel writing, and articles on literature. Its contents and relatively low price (one and a half marks) made it very successful: 5,000 subscribers in 1853, 60,000 in 1856, 100,000 in 1861, 157,000 in 1863, 210,000 in 1867 and 378,000 in 1881.[21]

A large readership always attracts potential writers. In July 1868 Friedrich Engels, prompted by his friend Ludwig Kugelmann, optimistically submitted a short piece on Karl Marx's works to the editors of *Gartenlaube*. *Das Kapital*, Engels wrote, trying to appear moderate, might well be of 'great interest' to industrialists. As he informed Marx, he had drafted the piece to suit the 'philistine' magazine. Marx, reluctantly, made further suggestions, in the spirit of pleasing the 'philistines'. The editors knew better, and rejected the piece. Infuriated, Marx decided that there was nothing to gain in dealing with types like Keil.[22] Eventually Engels's piece found a more favourable home in *Die Zukunft* in August 1869.[23]

Even without (or especially without) Marx and Engels's contribution, *Die Gartenlaube* provided Keil with a solid financial basis for expansion into book-publishing proper, and with a means of promoting unknown authors such as Eugenie John (1825–87), a singer who had lost her hearing. Under the pen name of E. Marlitt (thus disguising her sex) she produced a steady flow of female romances. She had an uncanny feel for German middle-class taste. Her heroines were beautiful yet efficient, and unselfishly committed to their families and parents. Even when penniless they always had impeccable genteel taste – almost exactly like the standard Victorian heroine. Their reward was to marry above their station.[24] Marlitt made a fortune, and helped Ernst Keil to increase his. Her best-known work, *Goldelse* (Golden-Haired Elsa), was first serialised in *Die Gartenlaube*, then, in 1867, published as a four-hundred-page volume, and later in a luxury edition. By 1885 *Goldelse* had been reprinted eighteen times, and by 1891 twenty-three times. Marlitt's works were translated into French by the publishers Firmin-Didot and included in the Bibliothèque des Mères de Famille. When she died in 1887 Keil published her collected works in ten volumes at three marks each, and more cheaply in seventy instalments to be bound later. Today she is not even mentioned in most non-German encyclopaedias and reference works, but some of her books are still making money for German publishers.[25]

A published book was an investment to be promoted. Planting or obtaining favourable reviews – as well as the practice of 'puffing' a writer – had been customary for decades. The spread of magazines increased the importance of reviews. In the 1840s it had become commonplace to use billboards to announce the next 'best-seller'. It had been apparent for some time that people were more likely to buy a book if they believed that everyone they knew or were likely to meet was already reading it. In France the publication of *Monsieur Mayeux* (1831), a daring novel by Auguste Ricard (1799–1841), was preceded by a massive publicity campaign of posters and caricatures.[26] Even in Italy, still a modest book-buying market, 'modern' marketing techniques were widely used.[27]

For publishers, especially small publishers, new authors were a necessary gamble. The economic advantage of discovering a new successful writer could be considerable. Hitherto, unpublished authors had been cheap and grateful. 'Greed' (i.e. demanding their rightful recompense) developed only after the first success. The problem for publishers was how to identify the successful books from the sludge of unsolicited manuscripts. A new profession emerged: the publisher's reader – the author's worst enemy or best friend, depending on one's point of view. The reader's task was to decide, if not what should be published, at least what should certainly never be printed. Publishers' readers were also editors, deciding what to excise, what to rewrite and what to expand – in other words responsible for the transformation of manuscripts into publishable texts.

The thriving Victorian publishing world was considerably shaped by the opinions of publishers' readers like Geraldine Jewsbury. In the 1860s and 1870s she was the most trusted adviser at Richard Bentley's, and her reports (she wrote 609 reports on 808 manuscripts) were used as a model for other readers.[28] Jewsbury evaluated both the quality of a manuscript and its commercial potential.[29] She knew the literary scene well, was a friend of the Carlyles, especially Jane Carlyle, with whom she had a passionate correspondence, and wrote 2,300 reviews for the periodical the *Athenaeum* (some, of course, were just a few lines long), as well as six novels, one of which, *The Half Sisters* (1848), was reprinted in 1994.

In her capacity as a reader, however, the main issue she faced was whether a book would sell. By the 1860s she had moved away from the proto-feminist positions of her early novels and had turned 'guardian of the hearth', embracing stereotypical Victorian values.[30] However, the formal ground upon which she made her pronouncements was always commercial. If she was offended, everyone would be offended, and the book would not sell. Or it might sell, but would lower the tone of the house and affect the sales of other books. Thus she turned down Flaubert's *Salammbô* as 'a detestable French novel . . . too confused and tumultuous to interest English readers'. She immediately realised, on the other hand, that *Under Two Flags* (1867) by Ouida (pseudonym of the English novelist Marie Louise de la Ramée) would sell. She was right: it was one of the most popular books of 1867. But her advice to Bentley was: 'I think you would lower the character of your house if you accept it.'[31] And Bentley didn't. Eventually Jewsbury became out of touch with a significant section of the public, particularly the feminine public, many of whom, stuck in the stultifying boredom of the Victorian home, had fantasies of elopement and a new life. Unable and unwilling to do anything about it, they wanted, at the very least, to read about them.

Edward Garnett (1868–1937), another reader operating thirty years later, seems to have had regard only for quality. Working on behalf of a literary ideal, he wanted to publish excellent books and to discover the next great writer. This he seemed to do with surprising regularity: Joseph Conrad, Stephen Crane, Ford Madox Ford, John Galsworthy and D.H. Lawrence were among those he championed. Conrad regarded him as the ideal reader, the one he could trust. In a letter to Garnett (13 April 1896) he asked about 'the thing', his next book:

> Is the thing tolerable? Is the thing readable? Is the damn thing altogether unsupportable? Am I mindful enough of your teaching . . . ? Do tell the truth. I do not mind telling you that I have become such a scoundrel that all your remarks shall be accepted by me without a kick, without a moan, without the most abject of timid whispers! I am ready to cut, slash, erase, destroy, spit, trample, jump, wipe my feet on the MS, at a word from you.[32]

The ego of authors, publishers knew, was like a tender plant, to be nourished and sustained with great care. Some publishers and editors knew exactly how to do this. They prodded, encouraged, discouraged and, if failure was inevitable, mercilessly performed literary euthanasia. Ruffling the feathers of major writers could be dangerous. Dickens, as thin-skinned as any ordinary author, lashed out at his publishers, Richard Bentley: 'If you presume to address me again in the style of offensive impertinence which marks your last communication, I will . . . abandon at once and for ever all conditions and agreements that may exist between us . . .'[33]

Retaining a famous novelist was not easy. Nor was discovering an unknown one and making him famous. Such risks could be left to adventurous publishers. Others – like the great Paris publisher Louis Hachette – started out in safer markets such as educational and reference books. Then, from a position of strength, they could pursue the pleasure of novel-publishing. Yet publishing reference books and manuals required considerable acumen. It was necessary to flood this market with a large number of books so as to establish a brand name, because in selling reference books, the name of the publisher is all-important. It made readers loyal to a firm, not to an individual.

Hachette, Schools and Trains

Louis Hachette, the child of an army pharmacist and a laundrywoman, started his professional life in 1826, at the age of twenty-six, with a bookshop and a stock of six hundred books.[34] When he died in 1864 he was one of the richest men in the country, and perhaps the largest publisher in the world, certainly in France, and he left a fortune estimated at three million francs.[35]

Hachette's first important publication was the unpromising-sounding *Dictionnaire grec-français* by Charles Alexandre, a thousand-page work for which he paid an advance of 6,185 francs in monthly instalments. The work was delivered in 1841, twelve years after the deadline. Priced at 13.50 francs, it was expensive. But it was an excellent investment, constantly reprinted and still in use in schools seventy-five years later.[36] To sell a novel one had to convince thousands of individual buyers. To sell educational books, Hachette needed only to cultivate academic and intellectual élites and, as so many of his publications were for schools, ingratiate himself with the Ministry of Education. He did so with remarkable intelligence and constancy – not an easy trick, since France was in constant political turmoil. He published journals and reviews addressed to schoolteachers, headmasters and academics.[37] *Le Lycée*, 'a journal of education written by a society of professors, former pupils of the École Normale, scholars and men of letters', published by Hachette, mentioned and quoted only his books. His opponents, justifiably, denounced its servile attitude towards those in power.[38] Hachette was unperturbed. He was simply pandering to his real customer, the government. He contracted authors who might be asked by the Education Ministry to provide textbooks, and then lobbied on their behalf. He loudly supported any increase in the education budget. He was a great believer in expanding education. Seldom had the noble cause of popular learning found such an energetic promoter – a further proof that, given the right circumstances, it is perfectly possible both to be high-minded and to look after one's business. Hachette did very well. His primers *Géométrie élémentaire*, *Petite arithmétique raisonnée* and *Petite géographie*, all priced at forty centimes, sold to schools, via the Ministry, in formidable quantities: 500,000 copies of *L'Alphabet et premier livre de lecture* in 1831, and a further 200,000 in 1832. Each impression of the primary-school reading book Ambroise Rendu's adaptation of Defoe's masterpiece, *Robinson dans son île* (1832), was never less than 10,000 copies.[39]

By branching into primary-school texts, not only was Hachette spreading risks, he was also insuring himself against political vicissitudes. Regardless of the complexion of the government (conservative, liberal, monarchist, republican, etc.) elementary school books were all going to be prudently conservative and Catholic. In the provinces, schoolteachers were the backbone of moderation, and parents did not want 'funny' ideas, that is new ones, to be inculcated into their progeny.

Hachette's big break came in 1835, when the Ministry of Education ordered 500,000 copies of *Alphabet des écoles*, 100,000 of *Livret élémentaire de lecture*, and 40,000 of Vernier's *Arithmétique*.[40] The Guizot Laws of 1833 and 1836, encouraging the spread of primary education in France, transformed his business, enabling him to achieve huge print runs, unthinkable in the 'free' market, and to acquire an unassailable position, a near-monopoly, in the educational trade. This provided Hachette with an edge over his competitors in the publishing business: long-term security and a steady cash flow. Not for him the risky search for the next best-seller, second-guessing market preferences and popular taste. The 471 new titles he published in the 1840s, when the volume of sales increased threefold, and the 527 titles published in the 1850s, were still mainly textbooks or great reference books such as the *Dictionnaire de la langue française* of Paul-Émile Littré (1801–81). Between 1863 and 1872 the *Dictionnaire* sold only 11,000 copies, but it sold steadily, generating a steady income not only for Hachette but also for Littré.[41]

Hachette decided to break into the fiction market only when he had identified a new distribution network – and one which insulated him, as far as possible, from competition. He borrowed the idea from the British, who had been the first to realise that the railways offered a great opportunity for selling printed matter. Before the development of the railways, reading while travelling was very difficult. The constant jerking movements of even the most comfortable horse-drawn carriages made the task possible only for the most determined reader. Lighting was almost non-existent. Blankets and heavy coats were often required to fend off the cold. Travelling by train was different. The ride was relatively smooth, gas lighting was available. Trains became very popular very quickly, and understandably so. In 1825 it took six hours to reach Brighton from London by horse-drawn carriage. In 1841, by train, it took only two hours (since then progress has not been quite as spectacular). A London bookseller, William Henry Smith, had used horse carriages to get newspapers such as *The Times* to various cities well before the Post Office. He then used the railways for the same purpose. In 1848 his son, W.H. Smith II, negotiated a concession with North-Western Railways to sell books and newspapers at London's Euston station for £1,500 a year. W.H. Smith's business expanded with the railways. By 1851 he had thirty-five station stalls, and had made deals with other railway companies. By 1855 the strategy had been further refined: everything would be sold at London prices, and Smith issued his own 'railway novels' under the Chapman & Hall imprint.[42] One hundred and fifty years later W.H. Smith still dominates the book and newspaper trade at British railway stations.

Hachette met W.H. Smith at the 1851 Great Exhibition in London. It struck him that the new distribution system could be imported to France. Back in Paris, he reached an agreement with the Compagnie du Nord, obtaining exclusive rights for five years. The company would get a cut of 30 per cent, have a veto on what could be sold, and have its own employees selling the books. A couple of years later newspapers were included in the deal, and Hachette made similar agreements with other rail companies.[43]

The idea spread. In Britain the publishers Longman promoted an imprint of books for travellers at one shilling each. George Routledge introduced the Railway Library of quality novels and non-fiction, publishing 1,300 titles in the ensuing fifty years. When, in 1853, Routledge needed a successful author to attract attention, he offered Edward Bulwer-Lytton £20,000 for the right to publish cheap editions of all his novels for the next ten years. This was unprecedented, but Routledge had made a good business move, and lost no money.[44] In Leipzig, Christian Bernhard Tauchnitz (1816–95) launched in 1841 a series of English-language titles, the Collection of British Authors, aimed at the European tourist trade, beginning with Bulwer-Lytton's *Pelham* and following it with Dickens's *Pickwick Papers*. By 1842 he had issued thirty-two volumes, and by 1937 the firm had published 5,290 volumes of English and American authors (the equivalent of more than one a week over a hundred years).[45] In the 1860s and 1870s Tolstoy read George Eliot in English in the Tauchnitz editions.[46]

The 'train' novel, the forerunner of the 'airport' novel, was born. It was accompanied with the inevitable comments about the End of Civilisation. Thus *The Times* in 1851: 'Persons of the better class who constitute the larger portion of railway readers lose their accustomed taste the moment they enter the station.' And here is Matthew Arnold: 'a cheap literature, hideous and ignoble of aspect, like the tawdry novels which flare in the bookshelves of our railway stations, and which seem designed, as so much else that is produced for the use of our middle-class seems designed, for people with a low standard of life'.[47]

By 1853 Hachette had set up forty-three bookstalls at various railway stations throughout France. By 1896 the number of Hachette stalls had grown to 1,179. In 1853 turnover had been 82,000 francs; ten years later it had reached one million.[48] Hachette's specially designed imprint, La Bibliothèque des Chemins de Fer – another idea 'stolen' from W.H. Smith – sold only 'good classics', respected authors such as Balzac, George Sand, Jules Michelet, Charles Dickens and Madame de Staël. Even the supercilious Flaubert was ready to offer him *Salammbô* if Michel Lévy had turned him down, in spite of the cover picture of a locomotive.[49]

By 1855 Hachette was a general publisher with an amazingly diversified list. He standardised his products and colour-coded them: guide books would be in red covers, travel books green, French literature would have beige, translations would be yellow, and children's books pink (La Bibliothèque Rose). Anything remotely subversive or immoral, he assured the railway companies and the government, would be banned or expurgated. In a country such as France, he explained, bad books were already sold by the thousand by peddlers around train stations, and were bought by young people and even by women who travelled only in order to devour books which they would blush to read at home.[50] Hachette took no risks. He even toned down the children's stories by the prudish Comtesse de Ségur, one of the most popular French writers of the nineteenth and twentieth centuries, and did not hesitate to blacklist important authors such as Maupassant.[51] Authors were not the only ones to be worried by Hachette. Through his exclusive contracts with railway companies he had in fact established a monopoly, since he sold only his own books from his station stalls. Other publishers reacted angrily, especially Napoléon Chaix, the printer and publisher of railway timetables (and the inventor of a machine for printing rail tickets). With Gervais Charpentier he rallied the other publishers, and together they lobbied the government. Eventually Hachette had to backtrack and sell books published by his competitors.[52]

To feed his new railway imprint, Hachette bought the backlists of publishers who were retiring, such as Victor Lecou, thus obtaining, at a stroke, the works of George Sand, Victor Hugo and Théophile Gautier.[53] In 1851 he launched a popular literary magazine, the *Journal pour tous*, to carry serialised foreign fiction (Thackeray, Hawthorne, Beecher Stowe) In 1857 this was followed by a periodical for children, *La Semaine des enfants*, containing both trusted classics such as *The Thousand and One Nights*, illustrated by Gustave Doré, and the tales of the Comtesse de Ségur.[54]

Hachette was producing for a wide public – from those who read only illustrated magazines to intellectuals who wanted to read Michelet or Taine. Writing about Hachette, Edmond About remarked: 'Twenty journals are produced, one of which has, all by itself, a circulation that exceeds 100,000' – this was *Le Journal pour tous* – and added: 'The firm ... covers 10,000 square metres. Seeing the crowd that tumbles out after work, one might take it to be the ministry of the book trade.'[55]

Authors Unite

The book trade – particularly in Germany, Great Britain and France, had become seriously competitive. In England some publishers began to offer discounts through their own outlets, bypassing bookshops. The booksellers reacted by setting up the Booksellers' Committee (1828). In May 1852 Dickens organised a campaign supported by Thomas Carlyle, John Stuart Mill, Richard Cobden, Wilkie Collins and Herbert Spencer against the Booksellers' Association, a grouping of large booksellers which prevented smaller businesses from offering discounts over 10 per cent. Various agreements were signed to protect booksellers' profits. Eventually a long-lasting Net Book Agreement was signed in 1899 between booksellers and publishers, which forbade discounting.[56]

Authors found it difficult, if not impossible, to organise in a similar manner. The isolated nature of the job and the constant flow of new recruits willing to accept modest advances left them – with the exception of a few big names – at the mercy of publishers. Successful authors increasingly found that publishers were prepared to grovel, but the others, the overwhelming majority, found themselves more often among the grovellers than the 'grovelled at'. Matters, however, were beginning to change for them too. Tauchnitz, whose English-language books turned out to be a lasting success, was the first to ask authors for permission to republish their works, and to be prepared to pay them for this privilege. The authors gratefully accepted, and Tauchnitz printed their works with the label 'sanctioned'. Authors began to send him manuscripts at the same time as to their English publishers. When Germany and Great Britain signed a copyright agreement in 1846, Tauchnitz had already secured the good will of most of Britain's major authors.[57]

At first sight it may appear that professional writers stood in relation to their publishers as workers to capitalists. The grudges they bore were fairly similar. It was said by Sir William Fraser that Thackeray's resentment towards publishers was such that, noticing the carpet of a publisher being a gaudy design of red and white, he told him, 'We have been admiring your carpet: it is most appropriate! You wade in the blood and brains of authors!' And later, to someone who said that it must be a fine thing to be a successful author, Thackeray replied: 'You had better break stones on a road.'[58]

Authors and publishers, however, were not like workers and capitalists. Though they were in conflict over the division of the spoils, it was in the interests of both to sell as many of their products as possible. Besides, being an author carried some prestige. Even little-known 'hack' writers, though despised by the intellectual élites, enjoyed a certain status. Trollope, though obsessed with money, admitted that it was 'in the consideration which he enjoys that the successful author finds his richest reward. He is, if not of equal rank, yet of equal standing with the highest, and, if he be open to the amenities of society, may choose his own circles.'[59]

Novelists themselves celebrated their status in a succession of stories showing ambitious young men – and, less frequently, young women – going up to the capital with no capital but ambition and talent, and after a lengthy period of apprenticeship in the art of survival, becoming accepted by the public and the fraternity of writers. One might be able to write books in the pleasant solitude of the countryside, yet most writers congregated in the larger cities. Proximity to the publishers was one reason. Another was that many professional writers needed to be near the press, which provided them with further work. It was also felt necessary to be in a literary network, 'a literary atmosphere'. Trollope thought that 'a man who could write books ought not to live in Ireland, ought to live within the reach of the publishers, the clubs, and the dinner-parties of the metropolis'.[60] Some, of course, succumbed and 'prostituted' themselves by remaining journalists. The idea that novelists were superior to journalists was an article of faith among the former – and some journalists agreed. A hack novelist churning out almost identical novels by the ton was still considered a writer. A journalist writing ephemeral but intelligent articles was a hack. Failed writers could claim to be geniuses ahead of their time. Bad journalists were just failures.

The Romantics had provided the standard narrative: writers, like artists and composers (and, of course, saints), had to endure a period of suffering before obtaining the fame they deserved. This was not just a good storyline (with obvious antecedents: the hero, before finding the magic ring, reaching the Holy Grail, obtaining the hand of the beloved, etc., must go through tribulations meant to test his mettle). It was also a warning to those intending to embrace the profession. They would have to bear the entire cost – economic as well as emotional – of producing the manuscript. It was thus prudent to have an alternative, if less glamorous, source of income such as journalism or teaching. Best of all was to inherit or acquire private wealth.

Once the manuscript was ready and accepted by a publisher, what financial arrangements would govern their relationship? Today, authors' earnings take the form of 'royalty' payments, a percentage of the selling price. Usually the publisher provides the author with an advance against royalties. The basis of any agreement is that the author is the owner of his or her work – a principle enshrined in British law in 1709. This limited copyright to a finite number of years, arguing that a literary work was akin to a patented invention.[61] Such ownership could be sold for a flat fee to a publisher in exchange for the right to publish. This was a kind of bet. If the book did much better than expected, the author had lost, since he could not hope to get any more money. If the book was a failure, the publisher had paid too much.

A possible solution was for the author to assign the copyright to the publisher for a certain period of time, five or ten years. This started an era of haggling that is far from over. Details of such matters can often be found in the correspondence between authors and publishers, a fascinating source for anyone interested in the monetary side of literary history. Take, for instance, George Sand's letter of 31 January 1846 to the publishers Giroux and Vialat, on the subject of her novella *La Mare au diable* (1846) – a favourite in schools ever since, because it is short, the language is direct and relatively simple, it contains suggestions of horror yet it is suitable for almost anyone, and like Sand's other 'rural' stories it enjoyed the praise of the academic élites. In her letter Sand agrees to sell the rights to the novel after its serialisation in the *Courier français*. This agreement would last for eighteen months. After that she would be entitled to sell it to other publishers, though for a cheap edition (like those published by Charpentier) she would have to wait a further year. The novella, however, was too short. Sand agreed to lengthen it by adding a couple of chapters, and to throw in for good measure four articles on socialism (*La Politique et le socialisme*) which could be published as an appendix, though the novel had nothing to do with socialism. She told her publishers that she could add more padding, if necessary. For this the publishers were prepared to pay 2,500 francs, and agreed to print 1,000 copies. 2,500 francs was a good offer – after all, Sand had written the novel in four days. In addition, she had also been paid for the serialisation.

As a final gesture, Sand, by then evidently quite adept in the pleasing art of worrying publishers, added that another publisher had told her she was selling herself too cheaply, and was ready to offer more; of course she had turned him down, preferring good business relations for the longer term.[62] Giroux and Vialat took the hint and immediately offered a long-term agreement for all her future works, but she turned them down: 'Who knows what can happen,' she explained. 'An illness might deprive me of the little talent I have; or I might become more popular and hence more expensive. It's better to make a deal in the short term,' she added shrewdly.[63] She was right. Sand milked *La Mare au diable* for all it was worth, getting money from no fewer than four other publishers: Lecou (1850), Hetzel (1851, 1852, 1857), Hachette (1855, 1860) and Michel Lévy (1858, 1866, 1869).

Publishers and authors – especially those in France and Great Britain, the main book-exporting countries – faced a common peril: piracy. American publishers reproduced English texts without paying royalties, encouraged, to the outrage of the *Westminster Review*, by the protective tariff of the US government.[64] The French, particularly in the 1830s and 1840s, suffered damage from what was called *la contrefaçon Belge*, or Belgian counterfeit – the printing in Belgium of French books without tax or payments. François Buloz thundered from the columns of his *Revue des deux mondes*: 'The real tax which weighs upon all of us is levied by foreigners; Belgium is the true pirate at our doors. The plague which saps us, which saps French literature, are Belgian counterfeits.'[65] He was right to be sore: his journal was regularly copied in Belgium and re-exported to the rest of the world. To counter this, Buloz had to deal directly with Belgian bookshops and offer the real *Revue des deux mondes* at huge discounts.

There were further problems. Some Belgian publishers prepared the plates for a novel as it was serialised in French periodicals, in order to bring out the finished product before the French. In the absence of international copyright agreements they could do so quite legally – as could Bavarian and Austrian publishers with German books – since to produce a book in a different format with a different typeface was regarded as producing an entirely new product. The Belgians would then flood the French market with their pirated editions. During the 1830s, roughly one book in three produced in Belgium was sold abroad, mainly in France. There was a silver lining, at least for some French authors: books censored in France were often printed in Belgium. Thus Pierre Béranger's songs, prohibited in France under the Restoration, were printed in 30,000 copies and sold by Belgian publishers.[66] After 1852 the Belgians published books by French opponents of Napoleon III, including Victor Hugo's *Les Misérables* (published by Lacroix-Verboeckhoven in 1862). Later, left-wing publishers such as Kistemaeckers brought out books by writers exiled after the fall of the Paris Commune.[67]

French publishers reacted by trying to undercut the Belgians. A price war resulted. Eventually, in 1852, a Franco–Belgian agreement recognised the concept of authors' rights. Similar conventions had already been signed by France with the Kingdom of Savoy (1850) and Great Britain (1851), and shortly afterwards with Portugal, various German states, Austria, Prussia and

Switzerland. On 9 October 1886 the International Copyright Convention was signed in Bern. This was the first international convention on artistic and literary property, and it was opposed by many, notably the United States. Yet some kind of international regulation was unavoidable, since it was almost impossible for a single publisher to be able to sell books throughout the world without some kind of agreement with publishers in other countries.

If French authors were exercised by the Belgian piracy, the British were upset by the Americans. In 1880 Wilkie Collins estimated that 120,000 pirated copies of *The Woman in White* had been sold in the USA.[68] Anthony Trollope complained that he had not seen a penny from the publication of his books in the United States. The pirating of English books by American publishers, Trollope thought, self-interestedly but correctly, was to the detriment of American writers, because the publishers could import books already tested for their popularity in Britain, not paying for them and taking fewer risks.[69] American legislation at the time, and for decades to come, established that only US citizens were protected by copyright, a situation which struck James Fenimore Cooper as unjust. He had discussed the matter with Walter Scott, who had been heavily pirated in America and who was then working largely to pay his creditors:

> ... it appeared to me that Sir Walter Scott, in his peculiar circumstances, certainly ought, and possibly might reap some considerable emolument from his works, in America. The sheets were sold, I had understood, to the American publisher, but as an illiberal and unhandsome practice prevailed of reprinting on the American edition, the moment it appeared, and of selling it at a reduced price, it was not in the power of the publishers to pay any such thing as approaching what he otherwise would.[70]

And then, in words which would be later echoed by Trollope, he added: 'We shall never have a manly, frank literature, if indeed we have a literature at all, so long as our own people have to contend with the unpaid contributions of the most affluent school of writers the world has ever seen.'[71]

Charles Dickens was particularly indignant about American piracy. During his trip to the United States in 1842 he had broached the subject, and was promptly rebuked. Such concern with mercenary matters did not become a gentleman, some American papers declared, but a 'haberdasher'. Besides, argued his American critics, the absence of copyright protection meant that Dickens's works could circulate more widely throughout the country. He should be grateful, instead of whingeing.[72]

Throughout the nineteenth century, authors attempted to organise themselves to obtain what they regarded as fair compensation for their work. Their major difficulty was not only the greed of publishers and booksellers, and foreign literary piracy, but new entrants who, mesmerised by the non-monetary appeal of the literary profession, were prepared to accept disadvantageous conditions, thus undermining existing writers, particularly those positioned halfway up the ladder. George Sand's account of her first meeting with the publisher Delatouche reveals how modest were her expectations. 'Don't be under any illusions,' she was told. 'Literature is a meagre resource. And I can tell you that, in spite of the superiority of being a bearded gentleman, I can't make out of it more than 1,500 francs a year, all in all.' She replied that this seemed to her an enormous sum; if she could make that much 'she would feel so rich that she would demand nothing more from either gods or men, not even a beard!' The shrewd publisher laughed and said, 'If your ambitions are that modest, you will make things simple.'[73] As we have seen from her negotiation over *La Mare au diable*, Sand was a quick learner in the art of squeezing blood out of publishers.

The weak position of new writers meant that the defence of the wider interests of the profession would rest on the shoulders of well-established ones: in France Balzac, Eugène Scribe and Hugo, and in England Dickens, Wilkie Collins and Trollope. Balzac's open letter, *Lettre adressée aux écrivains français du XIXe siècle*, encouraged the moves towards copyright legislation and the creation of the Société des Gens de Lettres (1838), with the support of Dumas and Hugo. Balzac himself became its first President. He was not only defending the interests of his fellow writers, but also his own, since his works were massively pirated in Belgium. Plays were also adapted from his books – in a single year (1835), two plays based on *Le Colonel Chabert* were simultaneously performed in Paris, without the author getting anything.[74]

In the theatre, too, established authors took the lead. Eugène Scribe, the best-paid and most prolific playwright in Europe, was behind the Société des Auteurs et Compositeurs Dramatiques (SACD) set up to defend the intellectual property of playwrights and composers. Of course, Scribe had a personal stake in the matter, because only a nationwide network would enable him to control the performances of plays outside Paris.

Publishers could of course adapt and even rewrite old books. Dead authors could not protest or negotiate. Dead foreign authors were even better: publishers could be freer with translations. Thus the French publisher Pierre-Jules Hetzel, having discovered that *The Swiss Family Robinson* had not been successful in France when it first came out, had no hesitation in bringing out in 1864 *Le Nouveau Robinson Suisse*. The educationally sound but boring passages on natural history were eliminated, the wickedness of the children wantonly killing animals toned down, and the preaching tone of the original German edition softened. The name of the original author, Johann Rudolf Wyss, was removed from the title page and demoted to a footnote. Wyss, having died in 1830, was in no position to protest.[75] As the market expanded, publishers increasingly behaved like literary Frankensteins, periodically patrolling literary graveyards to unearth novels long dead.

20

Reading by Instalments

Cutting up Books

BORROWING BOOKS was cheaper than buying them. But one had to be near a library; and walk into it; and pay a yearly subscription; and then go back and forth, withdrawing books and returning them. And all in a hallowed space, under the eyes of supercilious middle-class librarians, and reveal to them one's literary taste or lack of it. Such obstacles, invisible to those at ease in the *milieu*, were real for the majority of potential readers who did not even dare to walk into a bookshop, intimidating establishments that allowed only trusted customers to browse.

Newspapers and periodicals, as we have seen, were of a different order: more available, more approachable, and unquestionably cheaper. Nothing could be simpler for a publisher than to cut up a book and sell it chapter by chapter – or even page by page – to those who could not afford to buy it in one go.

There were three main ways in which a book could be serialised. One was to sell chapters of sixteen or eight pages separately, as weekly or monthly numbers. Readers could eventually collect the parts and have them bound in a volume. The advantage was that one paid a little at a time, and if the story turned out to be boring, one could simply stop buying the instalments. This method was particularly useful to sell large reference works, such as the *Grand Dictionnaire universel du XIXe siècle* by Pierre Larousse. In the end the price paid would be greater than the original, but paying more is the price one pays for being poor. The second way was to insert the chapters in a periodical or a daily, as an addition to the normal fare of news and features. The third way was to have a periodical entirely dedicated to the serialisation of several books. In this way one could hope to minimise the fall in sales after the conclusion of a much-loved novel. With four or five books going on at the same time, there was always a chance that subscribers could be hooked on more than one.

In the nineteenth century, serialisation was one of the most effective ways of selling books, especially novels. The idea of an illustrated popular magazine for the whole family, consisting mainly or entirely of serialised novels, was one of the many British innovations Continentals imitated. This was the explicit aim of Hachette's *Journal pour tous*, which began publication in 1855. In the first issue it was pointed out that the aim was to produce in France the kind of popular periodical which had been circulating for some years in England – where, the readers were told, a penny paper could sell 500,000 copies. The 'moral aim' of the *Journal pour tous* was to make available to both the 'man of the world' and the workman 'the best-known novels of contemporary literature'. The *Journal pour tous* never reached anything approaching half a million copies, but it did contribute to diffusing even more widely the already popular works of Paul Féval and Eugène Sue.[1]

The serialised novel imposed on the author certain characteristics, as well as constraints: the speed of writing typical of journalists obsessed with deadlines, and thus the impossibility of revising and rewriting. The product had to be plot-driven in order to be consumed by a large public one could not afford to bore. It was necessary to bear in mind that new readers had to be informed of past events. It encouraged dialogue and discouraged lengthy descriptions. Publication of a novel by instalments in newspapers, especially dailies, allowed the almost indefinite continuation of the narrative, should it be successful, and its rapid closure when necessary (the connection with television serials is obvious). Of course, serious novels too were serialised. And not just those by the popular Dickens, but also many by the highbrow Henry James, who in 1880–81 published *The Portrait of a Lady* in monthly instalments in the *Atlantic Monthly* (Boston) and *Macmillan's Magazine* in London.

By and large, however, serialisation forced writers to provide regular intermediate climaxes to keep their readers hungry for more. Often the general architecture of the novel was sacrificed for regular sensations, though equally often the novel had no particular architecture: Sue did not know what was going to happen next. Writers like Dickens were able to produce intermediate climaxes regularly – in a nine-hundred-page novel it would be excessive to demand that readers should wait so long before the cathartic climax. Readers required a cliffhanger, if not quite at the end of every episode, at least – where subscriptions were to be renewed quarterly – before the date of renewal. Trollope thought that the production of novels in serial form forced upon the author 'the conviction that he should not allow himself to be tedious in any single part'.[2] The 'cliffhanging' device was widely used in nineteenth-century novels – literally so in the case of Thomas Hardy's first serialised novel *A Pair of Blue Eyes* (1873), in which at the end of Chapter 21 Henry Knight, while walking by the sea with the vicar's daughter Elfride Swancourt, slips and is left hanging on a cliff: 'Knight was now literally suspended by his arms.' Elfride runs off to find help: 'She vanished over the bank from his sight. Knight felt himself in the presence of a personalised loneliness.' The chapter closes here, the readers presumably hanging with Henry, until the next instalment in which he is eventually rescued.

Authors learned the tricks of the trade: how to 'whiten' the text by having plenty of short paragraphs and short chapters to fill up pages, and how to lengthen conversations. In the 1840s Alexandre Dumas undertook to write for the *Siècle* 100,000 lines a year at 1.5 francs a line – which meant that he could have been earning more than 150,000 francs a year, a fortune. Some of his lines were remarkably short. Dumas's dialogue could be parodied, as it was by a contemporary:

> – Have you seen him?
> – Who?
> – Him.
> – Who, him?
> – Dumas.
> – Dumas senior?
> – Yes.
> – What a man!
> – Quite!
> – And what fire!
> – Absolutely!
> – And how prolific. . .[3]

The ruse could not last long, and didn't. Publishers moved on to payment by words. The formulaic nature of the serialised novel, routinely decried by its critics, was unlikely to escape readers. Many learned to recognise a variant on a well-worn theme, and to obtain pleasure and excitement by second-guessing the author. Total passivity is only one possible posture of cultural consumption – and not always the most common. Sometimes, however, serialisation forced a writer to compress the ending, for many journals contracted the number of parts in advance, and could not delay the beginning of subsequent books. Thus Elizabeth Gaskell, under pressure from Dickens, in whose *Household Words* her great 'condition-of-England' novel *North and South* was being serialised, rushed through the end, quickly killing off Mr Bell to ensure that Margaret Hale's self-sacrificing behaviour can be handsomely repaid by inheriting his estate, enabling her to patch things up equally rapidly with a reformed John Thornton so that they can marry and provide readers with a happy ending.

At times, however, popular success demanded that a book be continued. Jean Rousseau, an intelligent critic of Ponson du Terrail, the creator of the pulp character the master criminal Rocambole, remarked in 1858 that even when a novelist had killed off all his characters and could no longer resuscitate them, he could simply continue by having their servants or relatives turn up in 'The Return of . . .', The Revenge of . . .', 'The Son of . . .' – one of the many nineteenth-century ideas borrowed by Hollywood.[4] Sequels were not a peculiarly nineteenth-century idea, or one confined to 'low' genres. In 1795 Mozart's *The Magic Flute* had been a box-office success at the Weimar court theatre. Goethe, behaving like a practical man who wished to cash in on a success, wrote *The Magic Flute Part Two* (*Der Zauberflöte Zweiter Theil*) with the same cast, props and sets of the original, and similar tunes: the now happily married protagonists, Tamino and Pamina, Papageno and Papagena, continue their adventures trying to find their real parents.[5]

Sometimes, but more rarely than is commonly believed, serialisation allowed the writer to respond to readers' requests, much in the way television serials respond to ratings. Even in the eighteenth century what we would now call interactivity existed in a somewhat rudimentary form. Early readers of Richardson's *Clarissa*, including Fielding, begged Richardson, before he published the last volumes, not to kill off Clarissa – to no avail.[6] Trollope claimed to be more responsive. He tells the story, certainly much embellished, that while at his club, the Athenaeum, he overheard two gentlemen complaining that they were sick and tired of the once again reappearing Mrs Proudie (a character in the Barsetshire Chronicles). Trollope rose from his divan, introduced himself and assured them that he would 'kill her before the week is over'. Despite their protestations, that is what he did.[7] Conan Doyle was forced to resuscitate Sherlock Holmes after having 'killed' him in the short story 'The Final Problem' (1893) by having him precipitated, clasped in a mortal embrace with the arch-villain Professor Moriarty, over the Reichenbach Falls. Such refusal to accept that fictional characters are imaginary has continued to this day: when Agatha Christie's Hercule Poirot 'died' in the summer of 1975 the *New York Times* ran a front-page 'obituary'. Ed McBain said that women would write to him that Steve Carella (the detective protagonist of his 87th Precinct series) 'better never cheat on Terry' (Terry being Carella's deaf mute wife).

Market forces, rather than reader pressure, could make writers find an escape route from the most hopeless situation for their characters. The villain may have been burnt to a crisp when the mansion went up in smoke, or drowned in the icy and dark waters of the North Sea, but it turns out there was an underground passage leading out of the mansion, or a fishing vessel happened to be passing by and picked him up, enabling him to set off again on new and extraordinary adventures.

The beginning of a novel had to capture readers, the end had to leave them satisfied. Some striking beginnings were exploited, to the point of parody, such as Edward Bulwer-Lytton's now notorious (thanks to Charles Schulz's *Peanuts* comic strip) opening line of his 1830 novel *Paul Clifford*: 'It was a dark and stormy night . . .'. Endings are equally problematic, as Dickens discovered when, under pressure from his closest friends, he made the ending of *Great Expectations* more optimistic. As George Eliot pointed out, responding to critical remarks about her own endings, 'Conclusions are the weak points of most authors, but some of the fault lies in the very nature of a conclusion,' for inevitably there must be either a reward or a punishment for the protagonists.[8] After all, in real life the only end is death.

The connection between serialisation and publication in book format was not automatic – at least not in France, where dailies increasingly carried serialised novels which were never republished in book form.[9] In England, on the other hand, serialised authors were usually fairly well established, and serialisation was only the first step in the life of a novel. There were always exceptions. In 1836 the almost unknown Charles Dickens, then only twenty-four, started publishing *The Pickwick Papers* in monthly shilling numbers. The original plan of the publishers (Chapman & Hall) was simply to have a text to accompany the distinguished caricaturist Robert Seymour's illustrations. Seymour, however, was in the midst of a massive depression, and killed himself just as the second number was being published. Dickens found himself transformed from a junior partner in a design-led enterprise into the senior partner, able to have a decisive say over the future of the project. He argued successfully that the monthly text should increase from twenty-four to thirty-two pages, that the illustrations should decrease from four to two, that he, now the real author, should judge the illustrations, and that his fee should be raised.[10] He even managed to impose his own illustrator. The success of *Pickwick* was enormous. By the end of the series it was selling 40,000 a month.[11] *The Pickwick Papers*, in the words of Dickens's biographer Peter Ackroyd, 'heralded a revolution in the circulation and appeal of narrative fiction'.[12] There had been serialisations in England before, but this was the first time a new story was being serialised. And it was genuinely popular. There is a contemporary report of a public reading of *Pickwick* by a locksmith to an audience of illiterates who could not afford the shilling for the monthly number, but could pay the twopence borrowing fee from the library.[13] Dickens had started his voyage towards celebrity, and to becoming the most famous of all Victorian writers.

Pickwick began a vogue for serialisation which lasted well into the twentieth century. The publisher Richard Bentley launched *Miscellany*, one of the many monthlies that carried in serialised form the most loved novels of Victorian England. The editor was Dickens, who then launched his own periodicals, *Household Words* and, later, *All the Year Round*. That major novelists (Bulwer-Lytton, Thackeray, Mary Braddon and many more) should edit their own literary magazines was not unusual in Great Britain; it was virtually unheard of in France.

Dickens has remained one of the best-known British writers all over the world. The same cannot be said for his near contemporary David Pae (1828–84). Yet in his day his fifty or so melodramatic and Gothic novels, with titles such as *Flora the Orphan*, *The Lost Child*, *Very Hard Times*, *The Gypsy's Prophecy* and *The Haunted Castle*, were widely read in serialised form in a range of cheap provincial weeklies such as the *People's Journal* of Dundee, the *North Briton* in Edinburgh, and the *Bolton Weekly Journal*.[14] One of the leading entrepreneurs of serialisation was William Tillotson, who, not content with running a string of newspapers in Bolton, also from 1873 had a 'fiction bureau', a newspaper syndication agency which specialised in serial novels.[15] This enabled British writers (novelist-journalists) to make a living in the provinces without undertaking the risk and expense and possible frustration of trying to enter the London publishing networks.[16]

Romans Feuilletons

The discovery of the 'novel by instalments' spread rapidly throughout Europe. In France the upmarket *Revue de Paris* and *Revue des deux mondes* had already been publishing serialised serious literature since their inception. The real revolution, however, was the use of the serialisation in *daily* papers – the *roman feuilleton*. In England such serialisation in dailies (other than Sunday supplements) was unusual. In France it became commonplace thanks to the enterprising editor Émile Girardin.

Girardin's first paper was called, appropriately, *Le Voleur* (The Thief). Using a high-speed steam-powered press, called *la presse anglaise* because it came from England, he produced a digest of articles which had appeared elsewhere. Building on its success, he started other literary periodicals such as *La Mode*, where he published Eugène Sue's *Plick et Plock* (1831) and short stories by Balzac and George Sand.[17]

In 1836 Girardin turned his attention to the daily press. At the time it had a limited market of politically interested readers. The most widely sold was the anti-clerical *Le Constitutionnel*, with a print run of only 9,000 copies. The total circulation of dailies in Paris amounted to fewer than 50,000 copies.[18] The only way of expanding the market was to lower prices below cost, and make up the difference with advertising. This Girardin attempted with *La Presse*, launched in July 1836 and packed with the words of star writers: Théophile Gautier writing on the arts, Victor Hugo on social questions, and Balzac's *Scènes de vie privée*.

Almost at the same time Armand Dutacq started the rival *Le Siècle*.[19] Competition may have been fine in principle, but unless the pool of subscribers could be increased, there would not be enough room for two commercially viable newspapers. The matter was all the more urgent in that *La Presse* faced a serious crisis: only 2,760 subscribers instead of the 10,000 Girardin had hoped for and counted on. He decided to serialise novels in his daily paper, publishing each instalment on the bottom third of the front page, the *feuille*, known as the *rez-de-chaussée* or basement. This space was traditionally reserved for frivolous news (and it still is in some newspapers). It was now the space for the *roman feuilleton* – and since then, in French, the term *feuilleton* has been used for any popular novel with the melodramatic qualities and length of the serialised novel. Novels had been serialised before in periodicals, but the distinct advantage of having a daily instalment meant that it was possible to follow the story each day, as part of one's everyday world. From the point of view of the publisher, daily serialisation would constitute a further incentive for potential subscribers, and might keep them loyal.

Girardin started with *La Vida de Lazarillo de Tormes*, the sixteenth-century Spanish picaresque novel, but it immediately became apparent that what was required was modern novels.[20] Girardin contacted Balzac, a writer who was both prestigious and popular, and bought the rights to his next novel, *La Vieille fille*, which came out in twelve daily episodes starting on 23 October 1836. A huge new market opened up. This is how Balzac, Hugo, Sand and Sue were able to reach a new readership.

Predictably, serialisation came under fire as soon as it developed. It caused the usual outcry: the novels were immoral, unbelievable, in bad taste, badly written. It was the kind of democratic literature Tocqueville disparaged: 'The ever-increasing crowd of readers, and their continual craving for something new, ensures the sale of books which nobody much esteems ... Democratic literature is always infested with a tribe of writers who look upon letters as a mere trade; and for some few great authors who adorn it, you may reckon thousands of idea-mongers.'[21] Théodore Muret, the critic of *La Quotidienne*, suggested that one should not allow one's wife or one's daughter or even one's cook to read it.[22] Almost exactly the same remarks were made almost 130 years later, in October 1960, by Mervyn Griffith-Jones, the prosecuting counsel in the case against Penguin Books' publication of D.H. Lawrence's *Lady Chatterley's Lover*: 'Would you approve of your young sons, young daughters ... reading this book? ... Is it a book you would even wish your wife or your servants to read?' In the mid-nineteenth century magazines such as the *Saturday Review* might still refer to novels as 'the medium through which moral poison is frequently administered'; the real question was how to steer people, especially those thought to be easily influenced such as women, children and the lower classes, towards improving books.[23]

Louis Reybaud, a follower of Saint-Simon before turning reactionary, has left us, in his hugely successful satirical novel *Jérôme Paturot à la recherche d'une situation sociale* (1842), an account of the making of a *roman feuilleton*. The eponymous hero, on the constant lookout for a proper job (thus providing the author with an opportunity to satirise most existing professions) brings his novel to a publisher. The publisher explains to Paturot, and to the readers, the facts of life: the point is to maximise the number of subscribers. Forget eminent writers of the past:

We live, dear sir, in a bourgeois century in the midst of a nation that only likes *la camelote* [rubbish]. What do you want to do? Resist? One must be young to have such notions. I am sure you'll get over them. Today what we need is a family serial. The first bite goes to the parents. Then it's the kids' turn. That's a family newspaper. Thus, if, as an economy measure, the father tries not to renew the subscription, he has to face a rebellion from his entire household. He may have to think again to re-establish marital and domestic peace. Thus our *roman feuilleton* has a social role. And it's so easy to write. Once you've written one, you can write twenty, thirty. The crucial thing is to master the art of the 'cut', that is, when to suspend the story until the next issue. This is the real trick.

Jérôme, ever the apprentice, is told to read the last paragraph of the current *roman feuilleton*. The heroine, Ethelgide, is alone in her room. The silence of the night is interrupted by a mysterious noise. Unexpectedly, from the walls before her she sees a naked arm and a hand holding by the hair a bloody and disfigured face . . . And here, explains the publisher, is where the professional *feuilletoniste* interrupts his story. Not a single reader will fail to renew his subscription. It is possible to write a few dozen like this. Always have a few villains and make sure to punish them in due course to establish your moral standing.[24]

Scandal and outrage are great marketing tools. Balzac was pleased by the controversy he caused. Offers came from all and sundry. He sold his *Le Curé du village* to *La Presse*, then several novellas to *Le Siècle*. The *Journal des débats* got *Modeste Mignon*. Even *Le Constitutionnel* joined the scramble and obtained Balzac's future classics *La Cousine Bette* and *Le Cousin Pons*.[25]

Did serialisation actually increase the circulation of dailies? The figures appear to confirm that it did. When *Le Constitutionnel* started to publish Eugène Sue's *Le Juif errant* it had a print run of less than 10,000 copies. A year later it was selling 25,000 a day. But the paper had undergone other changes too. It had been typographically renewed to look more attractive, and more importantly, it had cut its subscription price from eighty to forty francs a year. There was a general growth in circulation across the board, regardless of serialisation. However, in other instances the impact was unmistakable. In 1865–66 *La Résurrection de Rocambole* by Ponson du Terrail appears to have catapulted *Le Petit journal* from 220,000 to 288,250. Allowing for the upward trend of dailies in general, this is a probable real contribution of 46,500 copies a day, a calculation made credible by the fact that when the serialisation stopped, sales crumbled by 33,000 – the most severe drop of the 1860s.[26]

The problem with easy-to-copy innovations is that if they do not work, the innovator is left to bear all the costs, while if they do work, the market is flooded with entrants who quickly lower the innovator's short-term profits. And so it was with *La Presse*. A year after he had published Balzac's *La Vieille fille* Girardin was still making a loss, even though he had doubled the number of his subscribers.[27] The solution would have been not so much to increase sales as to increase the main source of earning, namely advertising. Although there is a strong connection between sales revenue and advertising, the latter does not expand simply because the former grows. And the competition for advertising – largely personal announcements – was stiff.[28] A demoralised Girardin was eventually forced to sell *La Presse* to Moïse Millaud in 1855.

The serialisation format was successful throughout Europe, but there were significant differences in its standing and prestige in various countries. In Russia much popular literature still circulated via the chapbook or *lubok* circuits. Serialisation was largely reserved to serious literature in the so-called 'thick' élite journals. The liberal *Vestnik Evropy* (The Messenger of Europe) had started out as a quarterly journal of historical scholarship in 1866. It did well, and two years later the editor decided to include literature and politics, and to transform it into a monthly. It became the main Russian 'thick' journal of the second half of the nineteenth century. Though it began to lose prestige in the 1890s, it survived until 1918.[29]

The growth of Russia's political and literary journals was impressive. In 1825, at the beginning of the rule of Tsar Nicholas I, there were fewer than twenty. By its end, in 1855, about fifty, by 1875 about seventy, and by 1885 some 140.[30] Many of these journals could pay writers well, and could charge readers high rates for their annual subscriptions. Thus Ivan Goncharov obtained the princely sum of 10,000 roubles for his novel *The Precipice* (1869) for publication in *Vestnik Evropy*. Its success enabled the journal to increase the number of subscribers and recoup the high fee it had paid. In the absence of a thriving popular literature the high earners were mainly now-consecrated novelists – writers of the stature of Goncharov, Dostoevsky, Tolstoy and Turgenev.[31]

Wealth was out of the reach of most writers in Russia, where in the second half of the nineteenth century a senior high school teacher could earn 1,000 roubles a year, a doctor employed by local authorities 1,000–1,200 roubles a year. Dostoevsky, at the height of his fame, made 3,000 roubles a year, Turgenev 4,500, and Chekhov (in the 1880s and 1890s) 3,500–4,000. However, lesser-known writers would seldom earn more than 1,000–1,500 –

in other words, roughly the same as a high school teacher. Some writers, of course, were independently wealthy, such as Turgenev and Tolstoy (both landlords), others had sinecures as civil servants, Goncharov – not unusually for a writer – was a censor.

The first 'best-selling' novel in Russian literature, Faddei Bulgarin's *Ivan Vyzhigin* (1830), an adventure novel which sold 2,000 copies, was originally published in serialised form in a daily paper of the right allowed to publish political news, *Severnaia pchela* (The Northern Bee, 1825–64) – and Bulgarin was a fervent supporter of absolutist rule. Printing political news meant a subscription of about 3,000, while purely literary journals were officially limited to three hundred subscriptions.[32] The conservative *Russkii vestnik* (Russian Messenger) boosted its sales by serialising many of the works of Dostoevsky, Tolstoy and Turgenev. *Biblioteka dlia chteniia* (Library for Reading, 1834–65) was bought each month by 7,000 people, who thanks to the journal could read in translation Dumas, Fenimore Cooper, Balzac, Dickens, George Sand and many others.[33] Money could be made out of 'thick' journals, which is one of the reasons Dostoevsky started his *Diary of a Writer*, which he published on and off between 1873 and 1881, writing what he wanted, choosing topics freely.[34] Its popularity was such that it became a model for journal-diaries written by novelists to cash in on their fame.

In Spain and Italy, serialisation in newspapers became the norm only after the *feuilletons* had become widespread in France in the 1830s. But it could only appeal to the fairly literate middle-class public which read newspapers. In Spain the first great serialised successful author was Dumas, whose works began to appear in 1837. The first Spanish novel to appear as a *folletin* was Pablo Piferrer's *El Castillo de Monsoliú* in 1840 in the *Diarios de Avisos*.[35] More successful than the *folletines*, however, were the *novelas por entregas*. Helped by the scarcity of lending libraries and reading clubs, the *gabinetes de lecturas*, these were delivered by students or ex-soldiers directly to people's homes, chapter by chapter. During its golden age in the middle of the nineteenth century, a *novela por entregas* could reach a high circulation by the standards of the time, up to 10,000.[36] Spain may have been regarded as backward elsewhere in Europe, but its middle class made huge efforts to behave like its inspirational models in France and England. Thus the mode of the *novelas'* production was as 'modern' as in the more advanced nations: crudely industrial. The subject was often chosen by the publishers; illustrations were bought in bulk from France, with no direct connection to the novel in which they were inserted; and the writer or *entregista* produced at an agreed rate. The more a writer produced, the richer he became. Manuel Fernández y González (1821–88) was said to have kept several secretaries busy transcribing various novels that he worked on simultaneously. He could earn in a single day what a manual worker earned in a year.

Between 1840 and 1900 some 2,000–3,000 *novelas por entregas* by 130–140 authors were published, but fewer in the last quarter of the century, when readers weaned on these novels began to develop a taste for a more serious genre, such as Pérez Galdós's landmark *Doña Perfecta* (1876), which appeared first as a *folletin*.[37]

The Eugène Sue Model

The serialisation of novels brought about a major change in the popular consumption of culture. While the chapbook told a story in a few pages with plenty of illustrations, the serialised novel was usually an overlong, sprawling narrative made up of a large number of sub-plots. The *romans feuilletons* could be fashioned out of any genre. Some explored the recently emerging urban underworld, using vivid fairy-tale characters representing moral absolutes: the fearless hero, the pure heroine, the fallen woman who redeems herself, and the arch-villain. The notion of the self-sacrificing woman who is prepared to die for the sake of the man she loves, for instance, was a central notion in modern culture. In medieval courtly stories it was the man who had the nobility of spirit to give up his life for love. But in Goethe's *Faust*, it is Gretchen, the Eternal Feminine (*Das Ewig-Weibliche*), who intervenes at the end to save the soul of Faust.[38]

The vivid description of the urban landscape and the sociology of the inhabitants of cities such as London and Paris was largely a nineteenth-century novelty, abundantly used, *inter alia*, by Dickens and Balzac, and a natural reflection of the growing importance of the urban classes. Parallel to the encounter with the city in popular narratives was a nostalgic rediscovery of rustic simplicity, epitomised by some of George Sand's novels, such as *La Mare au diable* (1846), *François le champi* (1847) and *La Petite Fadette* (1848), in which rural folk are presented as representatives of a different world.[39] Such books were not intended for rural readers, as Sand herself explained to an imaginary (and civilised) friend in the *avant-propos* to *François le champi*: 'If I let the men of the fields speak as they really speak, the civilised reader would require a translation.'

The same themes were recycled over and over again as the production of novels intensified. Mérimée, in his play *Don Juan de Marana ou la chute d'un ange* (1836), not only recycled his own story *Ames du Purgatoire* (1834), but also Lewis's *The Monk*, some Shakespeare and Goethe as well as the well-established Don Juan theme.[40] The same rhetorical tricks were also used repeatedly. Whenever the situation became tense and a threat loomed on the horizon, the weather deteriorated, with plenty of rain, thunder and lightning: in Sue's *Le Juif errant* (1844–45), at every dramatic turn there is a storm.[41]

The 'classic' Gothic, still popular, was firmly in British hands, occasionally imitated by the French. Between 1857 and 1863 various French publishers (Havard, Lécrivain, Toubon and Michel Lévy) published new translations of Radcliffe and Lewis, who remained fashionable until the end of the century throughout most of Europe.[42] In 1852 Radcliffe's *Udolpho* was turned into an opera by Louis Clapisson with a libretto by Scribe. Fake translations of her novels continued to circulate, and allegedly finished manuscripts kept on being 'found' in her papers years after her death. Many of the early-nineteenth-century Gothic writers, such as Ducray-Duminil and Soulié, were forgotten by the beginning of the twenty-first century, while the generation of the 1830s and 1840s (Dumas and Sue) were still popular under the Second Empire and still in print at the beginning of the twenty-first century. But the new Gothic was not just for uncelebrated hack writers. Writers, now regarded as literary monuments, did not miss the opportunity to make a name and some money for themselves by using this successful genre: from Balzac (*Melmoth réconcilié*, 1835–36) to Maupassant (*Horla*, 1887), from Théophile Gautier's *Récits fantastiques* (1831–56) to Edgar Allan Poe, who, imported into France and then 'legitimised' by no less a talent than Baudelaire, was established – belatedly – as one of the masters of the genre. The generation of mid-nineteenth-century French novelists had all read the Gothic novel. This constituted almost one of their common points of reference – just as some American movies of the 1930s and 1940s formed an entire generation of post-war European and Latin American writers. In England it was routinely assumed that readers would be familiar with its main themes, which could be gently parodied: 'Those darling bygone times, Mr. Carker . . . with their delicious fortresses, and their dear old dungeons, and their delightful places of torture, and their romantic vengeances, and their picturesque assaults and sieges, and everything that makes life truly charming! How dreadfully we have degenerated' – says, without irony, the awful Mrs Skewton to the awful Mr Carker in Dickens's *Dombey and Son* (1848).[43]

Balzac, in his systematic search for the more remunerative genres, took the Gothic novel seriously. His *El Verdugo* (1830) – the story of a heroic son forced to decapitate his old father to save the honour of the family – shows how far he was prepared to go in the use of the gruesome.[44] In his more celebrated *La Peau de chagrin* (1831), Raphaël, the protagonist, finds that whenever he expresses a wish, any wish, the wild ass's skin he has bought shrinks. Realising that his life will not outlast the skin, he tries, in vain, to live without desire. The subject was obviously appealing: in January 1831 Balzac received 1,125 francs in advance, a reasonable but not an enormous sum. In Paris at the time a good bourgeois lifestyle required 6,000 francs a year.[45] When the publishers received it, at the end of July they printed it in two days, and immediately sold out. It was quickly pirated by a Belgian publisher, while a parody of it – with a happy ending – entertained the crowds at the Théâtre de la Gaieté.[46]

Balzac classed under the general name of *Scènes de vie parisienne* most of his urban novels, ably mixing characters from the underworld – most notably Vautrin, the superhuman ex-convict – with others representing various city dwellers: the innocent who arrives from the provinces (Rastignac, Lucien de Rubempré), haughty aristocrats, nasty foreign financiers (Baron Nucingen), grasping landladies (Madame Vauquer) and a crowd of wily journalists, servant girls, prostitutes, students, etc. Far less consecrated than Balzac but more successful were Paul Féval (*Les Mystères de Londres*, 1844) and Frédéric Soulié, whose novels *Les Deux cadavres* (1832) and *Les Mémoires du Diable* (1837–38) were full of bloody and horrible scenes. The hero of the latter, Luizzi, visits a variety of social circles to find vices, crimes, murders, incest and patricide.[47]

The authors of these novels exploited the possibilities offered by the new metropolitan setting, realising that the horror and the bizarre would be even more disturbing if the plot were to unravel in an environment familiar to the readers. Horror is more horrific if it happens nearby, a basic concept well understood by late-twentieth-century Hollywood producers, who began to set horror movies in the heart of suburbia rather than in Transylvania (though even in the original novel, Dracula comes to England). This feeling of estrangement contributed to the extraordinary success of Eugène Sue's *Les Mystères de Paris* – a title derived from *The Mysteries of Udolpho* by Ann Radcliffe, whom he was reading avidly at the time.[48]

Twice a week Sue narrated his *Mystères*, fascinating his readers with his portrayal of life in the back streets of Paris – and also fascinating himself, for before the serialisation began he had no grand plan and no particular structure. Parisian readers knew that the action took place around the corner, but not a corner they knew. Sue's Paris has 'no Latin Quarter, no trade, no theatre, no *demi-monde*, no finance . . .'[49] Since then the theme of the back streets of Paris has proved to be almost inexhaustible. Numerous songs, such as Aristide Bruant's 'Les Bas-fonds de Paris', one of the best-sellers of the Belle Époque, and later those of Edith Piaf and Juliette Greco, celebrated and romanticised the Parisian underworld. The only alternative to Paris would have been London – once glamorised by John Gay's *The Beggar's Opera* (1728), then depicted somewhat sentimentally by Dickens, and finally brought to enduring attention after the Jack the Ripper murders of 1888, and endless films set in 'foggy' London. The back streets of Berlin entered the cultural scene much later, in Weimar days, thanks to the cabaret and the early cinema. Berlin was followed, thanks to the cinema and television, by the criminal underworld of American cities: Chicago, New York, Los Angeles and, of course, *The Streets of San Francisco* and *Miami Vice*.

Sue was not the first to transpose Gothic elements into the urban jungle, but in his day he was the most successful – a success enhanced by the existence of industrial-style publishing, massive print runs and a large-circulation press. To be successful it was necessary to avoid a conspicuous break with past forms (as avant-garde writers, to their economic cost, discovered). Thus Sue's novels preserved many aspects of traditional tales of the past. His hero, Rodolphe, Grand Duke of Gerolstein, the righter of wrongs of *Les Mystères de Paris*, disguised as a worker in the Parisian *bas-fonds*, belongs to a long line of aristocrats or men of noble spirit driven to the underworld by injustice: Robin Hood, Walter Scott's Rob Roy, Goethe's Götz. The gold-hearted prostitute Fleur-de-Marie can invoke Mary Magdalene in the New Testament as her antecedent – or Moses, since her real mother, an aristocrat, had put her in a cot to float away on a stream (she turns out to be Rodolphe's long-lost daughter). Fleur-de-Marie, saint and whore, paves the way for Nancy, the prostitute-martyr in Dickens's *Oliver Twist*, Marguerite Gautier, the heroine of Dumas *fils's La Dame aux camélias* (Violetta in Verdi's adaptation *La Traviata*), and hundreds of other women who make the transition from good-time girl to the nobility of self-sacrifice with surprising ease – including the James Bond girls, who like their predecessors die, thus saving the hero from bourgeois family life. In his *Le Juif errant* Sue had borrowed from traditional popular literature the legend of the Jew who, having refused to let Jesus Christ rest at his door as he carried the cross towards Calvary, is cursed to wander forever, overcome by remorse. This had been a favourite subject of chapbooks as well as 'high' literature since the Middle Ages.[50] Sue re-interpreted it for the newspaper-reading classes. His target was not the 'deicidal' Jews but the arch-enemies of progress and democracy, the Jesuits.

Sue included in his sagas the violence and sadism typical of well-tested narratives such as the Bible and fairy tales. In *Les Mystères* Rodolphe has no hesitation in ordering the blinding of a thief, just as, in a version of *Cinderella*, birds peck out the eyes of the wicked stepsisters, while in the Old Testament God indulges in systematic genocide, and in the marginally less violent New Testament – which opens with a massacre of children – He allows His own child to be nailed to a wooden cross.

The solitary Romantic hero who repairs wrongs has remained a major protagonist of popular narrative. In the 'western' film, a recent setting for stories about the Righter of Wrongs, the lonely gunman approaches on horseback, like a medieval knight. From a hilltop he surveys, like a biblical prophet, the valley below. In the distance, a frontier town is torn by internal dissent and lawless savagery, the poor and the meek are oppressed and humiliated by the cruel rule of rich and powerful cattle barons and their local bullies. We do not know where the gunman comes from. His past is shrouded in mystery; perhaps some terrible loss, a woman he has loved, a wrong suffered or committed, a curse. We shall never know. What we do know is that he will fight on the side of the oppressed and cleanse the town of the terror afflicting it. His methods are, unavoidably and justifiably, as harsh and cunning as those used by his enemies. War, after all, is hell. Then, his work done, he turns his back on the peaceful and honourable bourgeois life he is offered by the grateful inhabitants. He rides away into the sunset, towards new wrongs to put right. He may have extirpated a particular evil, but Evil in general lives on, providing new material for the old story of the eternal struggle. Eugène Sue's Rodolphe scans the urban landscape to find workers deserving his help. He is a messiah, for he is not like those he saves, but an aristocrat, a Prince. He could live in luxury, in safety, but disdaining such comforts, he prefers to dedicate himself to the salvation of humanity, like Jesus Christ and the comic strip millionaire Bruce Wayne, better known as Batman.

Sue, a ship's surgeon by training, had first tried his hand with 'sea' novels: *Kernok the Pirate* (1830), *El Gitano* (1830). Then he experimented with historical biographies. Finally he obtained true fame with *Les Mystères de*

Paris. The first of its 148 parts was launched in *Le Journal des débats* on 19 June 1842, and it ran until 15 October 1843 – nearly sixteen months. It was said, perhaps by a publicity-conscious advertising machine, that the French Cabinet interrupted its meetings because Ministers could not wait to read the next instalment. An English traveller, unable to purchase an episode of *Les Mystères*, was told at the lending library that it was being rented out for ten sous for thirty minutes, and that he would probably be able to have his turn in three or four hours.[51] The critic Sainte-Beuve, who had sympathy for Sue and his works, wrote to a friend that if Sue skipped an issue because he was ill, the paper was forced to reassure 'the ladies who read it as well as their chambermaids that he'll be back in a couple of days', adding: 'If Chateaubriand has gout no one cares, but if Sue has a cold, it's a national disaster.'[52] Gautier was equally rueful (5 October 1842): the key question for the nineteenth century was no longer 'Hamlet's *To be or not to be?*' but 'How will Rodolphe get out of this? Will the Princess de Hansfeld be able to give her pin to Iris, the horrible mulatto?'[53]

For reactionaries such as the young Joseph Gobineau, the attitude to the *roman feuilleton* turned towards the apoplectic: its contents were trivial, *and* subversive, *and* easily available. Contemporary critics lamented that it developed everything to excess at the expense of reason, that it exaggerated feelings, caused daydreaming and excitement, and that it might lead to debauchery and pleasure-seeking mindlessness.[54] There was enough material to launch a thousand moral panics. High-status intellectuals derived part of their status from the fact that their sales were restricted to the discerning few, since popularity was incompatible with élite status. Yet they fumed against the money gained by the *feuilletonistes* (forgetting that for every millionaire writer there are hundreds in poverty). Thus Søren Kierkegaard reflected: 'In Danish literature today the fees even for authors of repute are very small, whereas the tips being dropped in the hats of literary hacks are very considerable. The more contemptible a man of letters is today, the more money he earns.'[55] The laments were echoed in Italy, where Carlo Tenca in his essay *Delle Condizioni dell'odierna letteratura in Italia* complained that literature had become a commerce, and the profession of the author as mechanical as that of the printer, while booksellers and publishers – speaking on behalf of their customers – required and demanded books from authors as one would demand a particular kind of dinner in a restaurant.[56]

Eugène Sue's *roman feuilleton* was the object of three speeches to the National Assembly, in 1843, 1845 and 1847, by the Baron Chapuys de Montlaville. He attributed the revolutionary nature of the French people to an excess of imagination, which made them particularly prone to the seductive appeals of the *roman feuilleton*. Such tastes and temperament were the negative side of democracy. Cultural entrepreneurs were making money by taking advantage of the weak moral fibre of society, *la mollesse des temps*. Like all the critics the Baron had read the *roman feuilleton* out of duty and with great repugnance, but recognised that it was absorbing and fascinating.[57]

Sue's second great serialised novel, *Le Juif errant* (1844–45), confirmed the success of *Les Mystères de Paris*. It also confirmed how profitable writing could be. Sue had received 26,500 francs from *Le Journal des débats* for the *Mystères*. The *Constitutionnel* bought the new novel for 100,000 francs (a skilled worker in Paris would be unlikely then to earn more than 1,000 francs a year). It was a bargain. The number of subscribers increased, while a single page was sold to an advertising broker for 300,000 francs for a year.[58] The two novels were quickly translated into a dozen languages, and serialised in newspapers and periodicals across Europe and the United States. Sue became ever more popular – though he never repeated his success – and continued to be published everywhere. In Victorian Britain, servant girls could read his *The Seven Cardinal Sins* (1848) in the *London Journal* (one penny, weekly print run: 500,000) translated week by week from *Le Constitutionnel*.[59]

Other writers reacted, predictably enough, either by denouncing Sue or by borrowing from him, often by doing both. Balzac, clearly upset at the success of Sue, exclaimed: 'I have neither jealousy nor bitterness towards him or towards the public! Thank God for that! My rivals are Molière and Walter Scott, Lesage and Voltaire and not this Paul de Kock in silks and paillettes.'[60] Yet when he had reviewed Sue's early work *La Salamandre* in the *Revue des deux mondes* (1 March 1832) he had been enthusiastic about Sue's ability to create real, living characters – perhaps the praise was part of a deal, since the review had been arranged by Sue himself.[61]

Victor Hugo wrote *Les Misérables* (1862) as an upmarket version of Sue's *feuilleton*, using the lengthy digression on the sewers of Paris as an extended metaphor of *Les Mystères* and, like Sue, placing himself as an authorial voice guiding his reader in this familiar/unfamiliar world, deciphering its language, using *argot*. Hugo's great innovation, however, was that Jean Valjean, his righter of wrongs, is not a *déclassé* aristocrat as in Sue, but an escaped convict whose last criminal action, before his Christlike redemption, was stealing pennies from a helpless child.

Sue's success generated a spate of books using the words 'Les Mystères de. . .' in the title, including a parody, *Les Mystères de Passy* (1844: Passy was then a bourgeois suburb of Paris; it is now part of the even more bourgeois sixteenth *arrondissement*). Then there were the anonymous *Les Nouveaux mystères de Paris*, *Les Petits mystères de Paris* and, by the ex-policeman Eugène Vidocq, *Les Vrais mystères de Paris* – all published in the same year as the original. The following year the *Mystères* had reached the provinces, with Octave Féré's *Les Mystères de Rouen* (1845), then went abroad with Félix Deriège's *Les Mystères de Rome* (1847). In 1867 Zola, then an up-and-coming author, wrote *Les Mystères de Marseille* at the rate of eight pages an hour for ten centimes a line, earning two hundred francs a month.[62] In Germany there were mysteries of Berlin, Munich, etc. – a grand total of thirty-six 'Mysteries of . . .' in the 1840s alone.[63]

In Spain the *Mystères* had a phenomenal success, with fourteen editions in two years and the inevitable *Misterios de Madrid* (1846).[64] In England George William MacArthur Reynolds' spectacularly successful *Mysteries of London* (1845–47) did not just borrow the title from Sue, but used the device of making the heroines considerably less helpless than those of middle-class romance. In Italy Sue was constantly reprinted by various publishing houses, engendering a proliferation of stories called '*I Misteri di*. . .', such as *I Misteri di Firenze* (1857) by Carlo Lorenzini – who under the name Carlo Collodi would write *Pinocchio* (1880) – *I Misteri di Napoli* (1869–70) by Francesco Mastriani, and '*I Misteri*' of Venice, Turin and Milan, and wherever there was a reading public who might be induced to read a local version of the famous novel.[65] Théophile Gautier, travelling in Italy in 1850, wrote that in Milan (then under Austrian rule) one could easily find even 'the socialist novels of Eugène Sue' and watch a public performance of an episode from *Le Juif errant*.[66]

How many copies did Sue's two most famous novels actually sell? How many readers did it have? The evidence that they were huge successes is overwhelming, but we have no reliable figures to be able to quantify this success. Extrapolating from available figures of print runs, 80,000 copies in two years (including serialisation) for the *Mystères* sounds a reasonable figure.[67] But were they all sold? We have no way of knowing.

The *Mystères* was published in *Le Journal des débats*, a conservative daily which enjoyed a subsidy from the government. Yet the story which unravelled at the bottom of the front page, day in day out, was full of working-class or criminal characters, often seen in a positive light, and *déclassé* aristocrats. The readership was overwhelmingly middle-class, but it also included working-class activists. The *Mystères* was hailed as a socialist novel – something neither *Le Journal des débats* nor its author had expected. Had it been published in the more liberal *La Presse*, it is likely that it would not have sparked such commotion.[68]

Sue had written the text serialised between June and December 1842 prior to publication. Then he wrote less than a month in advance of the serialised text. Eventually he was only a few days ahead, and thus was able, at least in theory, to respond to suggestions contained in the numerous letters he received from his readers. Sue always maintained that he listened to his readers' suggestions, but this is doubtful.[69] The letters, 347 of which have been preserved at the Bibliothèque Historique de la Ville de Paris, give us a glimpse of the most enthusiastic readers of Sue.[70] Half of the identifiable letter-writers were women. A majority were members of the bourgeoisie and the aristocracy. Many letters came from abroad – one from a Mrs Matthews of Gravesend, Kent, another from a Dutch lawyer. There were also working men detailing their social grievances, an ex-convict, an uneducated eighteen-year-old woman who sent Sue her own novel, a laundress who sent a play she wrote, a printer and a concierge.[71] Much of this is the standard fare of the popular novelist. In Sue's case, however, the image of the novelist appears to have been shaped by the book he was writing, a rare (or perhaps not so rare) instance of the author being converted by his work, or rather by the reception of it. Sue was born rich, and needed to write not to acquire a new lifestyle, but to maintain the one he was used to. He was a dandy, an assiduous frequenter of salons and a charmer of women. They must have enjoyed the *frisson* which accompanied him: here was a socialist in designers' clothing, a pioneer of radical chic and champagne socialism or, as the French put it, of *la gauche caviar*, promoting the cause of the wretched of the urban world, sympathising with prostitutes and despising the Church (which was about to become the main support of the régime of Napoleon III).

Much ink has been spent on the subject of Sue's ideology. Was he really a socialist, or merely the kind of bleeding-heart liberal only the grand bourgeois can afford to be?[72] Such distinctions were lost on the supporters of the conservative backlash which was overwhelming France after 1848. They regarded *Les Mystères* – and, by extension, all serialised novels – as a literary poison taken on a daily basis. However, to ban something so popular would have outraged too many people, while to tax it might have looked like just another way of raising revenue while defending 'proper' culture against those who sought to let it be overrun by the new Barbarians. So in July 1850, with

Louis Napoleon as President of the Republic, the Assemblée Nationale passed the Riancey Law, taxing any newspaper carrying a *roman feuilleton*, partly, it claimed, to protect booksellers.[73] The conservative backlash worked. Frightened, *Le Constitutionnel* turned down Sue's new novels. Sue was loyal to his books, and suffered the consequences. In 1847 he was banned from the Jockey Club. This is not quite like being sent to Siberia, but for a Parisian dandy of the time it must have felt like it. Sue was elected as a socialist in a by-election in 1850, and was briefly arrested when Louis Napoleon staged his *coup d'état*. He died in 1857 in exile in Annecy in Piedmont.

The press learned the lesson. Popular literature, though profitable, could be dangerous. It was necessary to eliminate from the serialised novel the faintest whiff of subversion. In any case, much of the fear amounted to a moral panic with very little foundation. Most of the *romans-feuilletons* published in newspapers were quite moralistic in tone, and rather strait-laced. Editors realised that their readers wanted some sex and violence, but little politics. Daily serialisation had almost been taxed out of existence because it had been feared that the 'socialist' Eugène Sue would corrupt the masses – even though his readers seem to have been overwhelmingly middle class. By the time serialisation expanded again, thanks to the massive sales of a new really popular press, a workers' readership had emerged.

In Britain serialisation was rare in the daily press, and in any case there was not yet much of a mass daily press. But Britain was spared the moral panic over Sue. There were a number of reasons for this. The threat of Chartism had been very real, but the régime in Britain rested on solid foundations, and was not regularly overturned as in France. Nothing like *Les Mystères de Paris* had emerged, and while purists and reactionaries always complained, the mainstream serialised novels (Dickens, Wilkie Collins, Thackeray and Trollope) were usually quite inoffensive. They were, of course, quite inoffensive in France too. Sue's main competitors of the time were hardly dangerous: Dumas's *The Three Musketeers* and *The Count of Monte-Cristo*, Balzac's *Splendeurs et misères des courtisanes*, and George Sand's *Consuelo*. It took some time for the French régime to realise that such strict censorship could be counterproductive. Popular culture could easily be quite conservative, once it was allowed to prosper.

Le Petit journal, launched by Moïse Millaud in 1863, understood this perfectly well. It began to publish, day in day out, the massive output of Ponson du Terrail: the equivalent of thirty volumes under the general name of *Les Drames de Paris*, with as its chief character Rocambole, the master criminal. Ponson detested socialists, but he used all the tricks of the trade he had learned from Sue. Critics, of course, ridiculed his style, his plots, his spelling and his shaky grammar.[74] The object of such contempt is not really the writer, who may be doing financially well, but his tasteless and uneducated readers. Ponson got his revenge. He was honoured in his lifetime by being granted, in 1866, the *légion d'honneur* at the same time as Flaubert. Fake follow-ups of the adventures of Rocambole were published well into the twentieth century, although few of Ponson's works are available today, even in French. But he left us the word *rocambolesque*, used in the French language towards the end of the nineteenth century and making it into printed English in 1949.[75]

Nowadays not many people read Sue either. Yet his influence was remarkable. The two aspects, not being read today and being influential, are related. Some writers are influential and inimitable. Each generation rediscovers them. Others – and this is the case with Sue – are influential and eminently imitable. Their influence consists in being imitated, and imitated successfully. The prototype can be discarded in favour of more recent updating and refinements. Who needs to read Sue when we can choose every year from television serials and assorted printed blockbusters?

21

Repressing Culture

Censorship

THE MOST VISIBLE CENSOR is the holder of political power; the most effective is public opinion. Traditionally, censorship consisted of examining previously submitted works and giving them a permit. As the market for culture expanded this became increasingly problematic. It was particularly difficult to pre-censor daily papers and the serialised novels they contained. Gradually, throughout the nineteenth century, governments moved on to a more effective system of censorship whereby the producers – writers, publishers, theatre·managers – would bear the main risk. If they offended public morals or the authorities, they would be prosecuted after the event. The economic costs of being forced to withdraw a book or suspend a play could be great. Thus censorship turned into a deterrent, forcing the cultural producers to second-guess the authorities. Since the demarcation between the acceptable and the unacceptable was constantly shifting, some producers were often tempted to probe it. The pay-off could be rewarding for the path-breakers, but the risks could be equally daunting.

This was particularly true in the case of frequent régime change, since what had been regarded as flattery in one decade could be regarded as subversion in the next. In France during the *ancien régime*, kings could not be represented as ugly or stupid or ridiculous. This was encouraged during the Revolution and the Napoleonic era (1789–1815). Under the Orléans King Louis Philippe (1830–48), one could make fun of the Bourbon kings (1815–30). Louis Philippe, as is frequently the case, started out as a liberal and turned authoritarian, but even in his first year as King he brought 520 suits against the press. During its five-year existence *La Caricature* and its editor Charles Philipon had to endure constant harassment. Honoré Daumier ended up in jail for always representing Louis Philippe as pear-shaped – the image had become so well known that it was sufficient to draw a pear to conjure up the contours of Louis Philippe.[1] In nineteenth-century France the only periods of almost total publishing freedom were the revolutionary or near-revolutionary: 1830–35, 1848–50 and 1870–71. Under Napoleon III one could, of course, make fun of both the Bourbon and the Orléans dynasties, but as Catholicism had become the backbone of the new régime, religion was best left alone – and this included the more sexually embarrassing biblical stories, such as Lot's apparent sexual abuse of his daughters, King David's murder of his mistress Bathsheba's husband, and King Solomon's urge to fornicate with hundreds of women. All these were toned down or ruled out.

In Britain one could make fun of the monarchy at the beginning of the nineteenth century, when the monarchy was rather unpopular and the press freer than in France. Under Queen Victoria, one could criticise and even mock her unpopular German husband Albert, and the Queen herself during her long, gloomy seclusion as a widow. Then, largely thanks to Disraeli, she was reconstructed as the Mother of the Nation and its living embodiment, and remained above criticism and mockery. Repressive legislation was not necessary. Respect for the monarchy was more a matter of public mood than any formal censorship – as is largely the case today.

Censorship worked best if it was regarded as legitimate. To deprive the constantly expanding educated and articulate sections of the population, not all of them subversive, of what they enjoyed could be misunderstood, and would cause enormous resentment. Thus censors too were in the business of acquiring and maintaining legitimacy and popularity. This gave popular and successful authors considerable power *vis-à-vis* the censors, who did not wish to antagonise the public. Censors hesitated before interfering with a genuinely popular writer such as Alexandre Dumas. Verdi did have to bend to the censor, but in the Austrian territories, and especially in Milan, he was able to stand his ground, and the authorities treated him with caution because he had a considerable section of the Milanese establishment on his side.[2]

Public opinion acted as a kind of informal censor. Powerful lobbies, influential groups and personages, the views and susceptibilities of consumers, could determine the contents and form of cultural products quite effectively. Thus, even though Victorian Britain was a beacon of cultural freedom in Europe, in practice its general climate of prudery restricted what censors allowed. The 1857 Obscene Publications Act empowered magistrates to order the destruction of books and prints. Prudent British translators expurgated even mainstream French novels such as Dumas's *Three Musketeers*, which publishers regarded as too sexually blunt for British readers (it treated adultery lightly). As the Victorian bourgeoisie grew in strength and size, so did prudery. British puritanism was such that some periodicals and publishers prided themselves on totally excluding Victor Hugo and George Sand. Hugo had left France in 1851 when Napoleon III had established his dictatorship, but he had trouble with censors outside France too. His play *Le Roi s'amuse* – a box-office disaster – was eventually banned in Britain too.

When *Le Roi s'amuse* was banned in France in 1832, Hugo did not complain to the government that had banned it (in 1830 Louis Philippe, the new King, had devolved the power of censorship to the government), but took to court the director of the Théâtre-Français. Dumas did the same when his play *Antony* was banned, and to avoid a trial the Théâtre-Français paid him damages of 6,000 francs. The government tried to resolve the impasse with a new law on theatre censorship in 1835. A board was established with four 'ordinary bourgeois' who were required, when reading the text of a play or watching its rehearsal, to ask themselves whether they would take their wives and daughters to see it. Bourgeois respectability rather than royal offence became the chief reason for banning a play.[3]

The travails of *Le Roi s'amuse* were not finished. Adapted into the opera *Rigoletto* by Verdi, it opened in Venice in 1851, but the Venetian censors had forced the librettist to turn Francis I (King of France) into the Grand Duke of Mantua, in order to avoid offending a monarch – albeit a foreign one who had been dead for over three hundred years. Victor Hugo sued the librettist for having stolen his plot. He lost; it was considered that the shift from novel to opera made the two products sufficiently different.[4] But why was the original *Le Roi s'amuse* banned? The reason was not Hugo's description of the immoral nature of political power (a King enjoys having a dalliance with the daughter of his clown). This, in 1832, was not regarded as being disrespectful, for it simply confirmed the view that the powerful can act with impunity. What was offensive was the coarseness of the low-life characters. *Le Roi* was not performed again until 1882, when it still offended the public, who were shocked by the sight of paternal love represented in a horrible and deformed buffoon.[5] Hugo's plays, written during a period of great freedom in France (relative to the authoritarian 1850s and 1860s), were all the object of massive controversy and debate, even though he never set out to make them anti-clerical or anti-monarchist. His fault was he did not follow the conventions of the bourgeois plays of Scribe, the romantic melodramas of Dumas *fils* or conventional historical tragedy. He was breaking the bourgeois aesthetic code: his plays contained excesses, vulgarity, profane language, and a soft spot for the underworld.

The publisher Hetzel was constantly 'censoring' one of his most successful writers, Jules Verne, and it must be said that Verne almost unreservedly accepted Hetzel's suggestions with astonishing good grace – even though the publisher did not show the slightest consideration towards an author who was a real money-making machine. Verne was probably intimidated by Hetzel, fourteen years his senior, a legendary editor who had known and published literary monuments like Stendhal, Balzac, George Sand and Victor Hugo.[6] He insisted that events that were attributed to luck and chance in Verne's original manuscripts should be re-assigned to divine intervention. 'Daring' expressions involving the mere suggestion of sexual attraction were routinely removed.[7] Hetzel censored Verne to make him conform to his respectable and God-fearing readership. In so doing he was driven almost exclusively by commercial consideration, and not by his own ideas and prejudices. He was far from being an old-fashioned Catholic monarchist – indeed, he had taken part in the 1848 Revolution and had fled to Belgium when Louis Napoleon (Napoleon III) staged his *coup d'état* in 1851. But he was, above all, a commercial publisher, and Verne's books were destined to be read by young people. It was better not to run any risk.

Authors facing a narrow market, censorship and critical disparagement had an uphill task. Italians trying to write popular novels were particularly disadvantaged, especially if they had the misfortune to live in one of the less enlightened states of the peninsula, such as the Kingdom of Naples, or worse, the Pontifical States. The serialisation of Antonio Ranieri's novel *Ginevra o l'orfana della Nunziata* (1836) was interrupted by the Neapolitan censor, though it was allowed to come out in book format in 1839. Regarded by some as the first Italian social novel, it told the story of the unhappy orphan Ginevra, who lives in a foundling home in Naples until the age of nineteen. Then she suffers a great deal, and eventually she dies.[8] *Ginevra* could not compete with Dickens's *Oliver Twist* – another 'social novel' appearing at the same time. The latter combined a racy narrative, a social dimension, some humour, and an upbeat ending, thus maximising the potential readership. It was serialised in Italy soon after its appearance in England, and was untouched by the censor. The conditions it described were those of England, not of the Kingdom of Naples. Ranieri's novel found no defenders even among the progressive élite, because it was too 'popular'. The great critic de Sanctis, in his lectures at the University of Naples in the mid-1840s, thought that all Ranieri did was to imitate foreigners (i.e. Dickens and Sue): 'He will be soon forgotten,' he predicted, accurately.[9]

Censorship was always aimed at the cheap and popular. The people, it was believed, were a child which must be protected from bad books.[10] Books specifically addressed to children demanded a great deal of self-censorship by authors and publishers, not just in Victorian England but also, and perhaps more, in France under Napoleon III. One example will suffice to illustrate the prudence exercised by publishers. In March 1863 the Comtesse de Ségur, author of the most popular French children's books of her day, wrote to Hachette, her publishers, to complain about the cuts demanded by the periodical *La Semaine des enfants*, where her next book was to be serialised before publication in Hachette's Bibliothèque Rose. The cuts demanded were meant to avoid any reference to feelings or actions which could suggest the possibility of marriage. The editors wished to remove any 'sign of tenderness', such as hugs, between little boys and little girls. The Comtesse, far from being a freethinking libertarian, was a deeply religious woman, some would even say a prig. Yet she was astonished that what she regarded as descriptions of innocent feelings could be read in such a dark light. *La Semaine des enfants* was bound by its agreement with Hachette and had to publish with no cuts, but its editor, dismayed, wrote to Hachette that the Comtesse de Ségur's next book would have to be examined with much greater care to ensure that it was appropriate for young ladies.[11]

There are universal rules in the history of censorship: if only the mature, the rich and the powerful have access to a book, it is less dangerous, and less corrupting. And however depraving and corrupting a book, it cannot deprave and corrupt the censor. There was no point in alienating intellectual élites by censoring what they read and enjoyed, or what could be understood only by those who already had a critical attitude towards the establishment. Marx's *Capital*, unlike the *Communist Manifesto*, was not censored in Tsarist Russia. To be effective, censorship had to be vague, so as to deter cultural producers more effectively. Almost by definition any cultural product, however hackneyed, must contain some novel elements, even if simply a new form of words. Vagueness has the edge over clear rules that can be exploited in a legalistic way, for it is impossible to have foreknowledge of all the possible variants of offensive material. Vagueness encourages not just the self-censorship of publishers, but also that of the author, for it is inextricably mixed with the desire to please a potential readership, as well as publishers and critics.

The boundary between self-censorship and creativity is blurred. Occasionally it is possible to examine the preparatory work for a novel and contrast certain phrases with the finished version, but even so it is difficult to establish the extent to which fear of the censor is the cause of changes. Flaubert's preparatory notebooks for *Madame Bovary* (the electronic age has put an end to such goldmines) reveal an abundant use of coarse language and slang expressions, but we have no way of knowing whether this was abandoned for stylistic reasons, or because of a fear of censorship. Would Flaubert have used some of the language used by D.H. Lawrence in the 1920s in *Lady Chatterley's Lover* if he had thought there was a remote chance of it being published?[12] Here is an example of Flaubert writing for Flaubert: Emma and Rodolphe go riding – they are not lovers yet – and the master of French prose notes: '*montrer nettement le geste de Rodolphe qui lui prend le cul d'une main, et la taille de l'autre – et elle s'abandonne*' (show clearly Rodolphe's gesture: he holds her arse with one hand and her waist with the other – and she gives herself up).[13] In the final version Rodolphe's gesture is left to the imagination as Emma 'gives herself up'.[14] Later Emma is on to Léon, her second lover, and Flaubert now writes: '*L'habitude de baiser la rend sensuelle*' (Frequent fucking had made her more sensual).[15]

Madame Bovary had already been 'censored' by the editor of the *Revue de Paris*, the periodical in which it was first serialised. He imposed on Flaubert seventy-one excisions, some quite mystifying, others to do with excessive realism (Emma's enquiring about her child's colic), politics, religion and, of course, sex, including the famous scene where Emma and Léon make love for the first time, in a carriage speeding on the *pavé* – the least realistic description of the great realist writer.[16] Even this intervention was not sufficient to protect *Madame Bovary* from legal proceedings. When the serialisation in the *Revue de Paris* (1 October to 15 December 1856) was finished, the authorities tried to prevent the novel's publication in book form. The ensuing prosecution shows the difficulty of banning a work which much of the cultural establishment regarded as high art, and which many had read. Flaubert was acquitted, and dedicated the novel to his lawyer.

When it came to high culture, even in Second Empire France, the censors were on the run. Most of the prosecuted writers of prestige were acquitted: Zola, the Goncourts, Maupassant. The main exceptions were Verlaine's poems *Les Amies* (1867), regarded as too daring (as were six of Baudelaire's *Les Fleurs du mal*, regarded in 1857 as too crude and realistic).[17] In fact, throughout Europe, whenever a censorship case was brought before a jury, the chance of the prosecution being defeated was very high. It has been calculated that over 70 per cent of all prosecutions against the press in Piedmont in the 1850s ended up in acquittals.[18] In most cases the defence accepted the premise of the legislation, but argued that the particular work being prosecuted, far from being obscene, was highly moral. The adultery of Madame Bovary was described, pleaded Flaubert's defence lawyer, Marie-Antoine-Jules Sénard (top barrister, former President of the National Assembly and former Minister of the Interior), as a source of torment, regret and remorse, and its outcome was a frightening, 'excessive' punishment.[19]

More complex literary work, almost by definition, is always open to different interpretations. To suggest that there is only one possible reading seems to negate its complexity. Some readers of *Madame Bovary* were surprised that it should appear before a court, since they regarded it, not unreasonably, as a warning to women against both fornication and excessive shopping, and wrote to Flaubert in solidarity.[20] One can only imagine his dismay. As is often the case, an unsuccessful prosecution is an excellent way of increasing sales. Flaubert's publisher Michel Lévy easily sold 30,000 copies, and Flaubert himself was elated by the outrage caused by *Madame Bovary*. In a letter to his friend Jules Duplan he tells of his pleasure and vanity ('*une grande joie de vanité*') when he learned that a priest forbade his parishioners to read the book: 'This flattered me more than any praise.'[21]

Scandals, however, did not always work in favour of writers and their publishers, particularly when it came to poetry. Baudelaire and his publisher, Auguste Poulet-Malassis, lost out from the scandal and trial following the publication of *Les Fleurs du mal* in 1857. The expurgated edition, though, sold reasonably well, for poetry: 1,500 copies. To recoup expenses, however, it was necessary to have a second edition. The publisher came up with the idea of presenting a luxury edition of *Les Fleurs du mal* at the 1862 Universal Exhibition. Baudelaire was sceptical: what parent would give this book as a present to her children?[22] Finally a second edition came out in 1862 with a print run of 1,500 to meet the growing demand.

Prevailing morality was a serious obstacle to free (i.e. authorial) expression of views, and it included, of course, the private morality of the publishers themselves. A conscience backed by effective financial power can be fearsome, as George Lewes found out when the publisher John Blackwood (a religious man) defaulted on his agreement to publish Lewes's *Problems of*

Life and Mind (1874) because of its scorn for religion, though Lewes was so well known that he found another publisher immediately.[23] As the century advanced and the cultural markets expanded, the boundaries of what was regarded as offensive grew and the writer's freedom diminished. Dickens, intent on not losing a single reader, kept on revising *Oliver Twist*, eliminating oaths and cleaning the language of even his most depraved characters. As his biographer explains: 'He was now, after all, a celebrated and important novelist. He had to create the appropriate conditions for his own developing reputation.'[24] In 1841, in the preface to the third edition of *Oliver Twist*, Dickens explicitly described Nancy as a prostitute. By 1867 he had deleted this characterisation.[25] He described her rape and murder by Bill Sykes in such a vague way that children reading it would not realise what had happened.

Most authors, however, did not feel constrained by the moral climate, for the simple reason that they themselves accepted it as just and natural, and worked hard to reinforce it. Trollope quite consciously exhibited what he called a 'sense of responsibility' by ensuring that the wicked always got punished, and claimed that this was the duty of all great novelists from Maria Edgeworth to Jane Austen, Walter Scott to Thackeray, Dickens and George Eliot. 'When men ... have been described as dishonest and women as immodest, have they not ever been punished?'[26]

Bourgeois morality narrowed the range of narrative devices writers could use to resolve a tricky situation, hence the abuse of the unexpected legacy to resolve a character's financial problems, the usefulness of having people thought long dead returning from the colonies, or of sending them there when they had to be removed from action.[27] Once the heroine had married the wrong and unsuitable man, authors had problems in freeing her again, at least in Britain. Murder was out of the question (heroines don't kill), divorce was frowned upon. So the couple (and the reader, vicariously) had to undergo a period of reciprocal suffering until a providential death through accident or illness could release one of them – though not always unscathed, as was the case for Mr Rochester in *Jane Eyre*. The better class of writers had the inventiveness to imply and suggest events, or the ability to suggest some flaws in their positive characters, so as to make their subsequent dubious behaviour acceptable. Thus Gwendolen Harleth probably did let her husband Henleigh Grandcourt drown in George Eliot's *Daniel Deronda*, but then she was not a Nice Girl, and he was quite horrible, and anyway she felt very sorry afterwards. Edith Granger did run away from her husband Mr Dombey, and not a moment too soon, but she was no saint, having married him for his money, albeit pushed by her mother. And Mr Casaubon dies of natural causes in *Middlemarch*, when surely he deserved to be killed by his wife Dorothea Brooke by slow-acting poison – but Dorothea has to remain a saint from beginning to end.

Though the histories of literature regularly report the trials and persecution of writers we celebrate and study today – Flaubert, D.H. Lawrence, James Joyce and many others – state censorship was specifically addressed to cheap and popular novels and large-circulation papers. Cheap texts, sold outside the respectable circuits to readers who probably did not possess the intellect to resist their corrupting influence, were especially dangerous. In Napoleon III's France a book legally obtainable in a respectable bookshop required a permit from the Commission de Colportage in order to be sold by peddlers. A French police report in 1849 noted that peddlers' literature presented a picture of society as divided into two classes, the rich and the poor, with the rich as tyrants and the poor as victims, and that consequently the latter should envy and hate the former. In this way it was justifying civil war instead of a peaceful and contented society.[28] Readers, of course, did not have to read novels in order to find out that the world was divided between the rich and the poor, and that, on balance, being rich was better. In reality the Commission de Colportage, like most censors, behaved in an erratic manner. As was to be expected, it banned obvious republican and anti-clerical tracts, such as *Crimes, délits et scandales au sein du clergé* (Crimes, Misdemeanours and Scandals of the Clergy), but in 1854 it also banned a history of Italy because it advocated the unification of the country and was written from 'a revolutionary point of view'. The same fate befell a technical book on fertilisers, *Les Engrais* (1855), because its preface provided 'wrong information' on the situation in the countryside; the *Traité discret de la vertu évangelique* (1860) because it was regarded as too ascetic; and *Histoire de France* (1868) because it was deemed to be unfair towards Napoleon.[29] The Commission did its job with inordinate zeal, eliminating eight million copies of books, out of nine million printed.[30] Such carnage suggests that the real intention was the actual elimination of all but the most innocuous texts. This provided Belgian printers and publishers with an unexpected opportunity: they printed editions of banned works which were then smuggled to France.

With the fall of Napoleon III in 1870, this repressive system was first substantially modified, and then abolished in July 1881. In 1906 censorship for all books was discontinued. This was done on the quiet, by the device of deleting the section earmarking the funding of the censors' office in the

French budget.[31] The rest of Europe followed this trend: initial liberalisation in the 1860s or 1870s, and eventual abolition of censorship at the beginning of the twentieth century. Thus in the Austrian Empire there was considerable liberalisation in 1862, and major press freedoms conceded in 1903. Even Tsarist Russia conformed to the trend: censorship was eased in 1865, when pre-publication censorship of newspapers of good standing was ended, and abolished for all in 1905. Authority over the press gradually shifted from the censors to the courts.[32] Pornographic *lubki* (chapbooks), shared across Russian classes at the end of the eighteenth century, had become less prevalent by the middle of the nineteenth. Some of the obscene poetry of Ivan Barkov that circulated in the 1770s was still around in the first decades of the nineteenth century, but this was written in imitation of the high classicist genre, with titles such as *Oda k pizde* (Ode to the Cunt) and *Epistol ot khuia k pizde* (Letter from the Prick to the Cunt). Barkov's name is still associated with pornographic material: *barkovshchina*.[33] The model that inspired him was, of course, eighteenth-century French pornographic verse.

In the various German states censorship had been far more oppressive before 1848 than in Great Britain or France. The revolutions of 1848 led to considerable liberalisation, and many of the new rights acquired did not disappear after the inevitable backlash.[34] After German unification there was a more consistent bout of liberalisation, particularly with the Reich Press Laws of 1874, though the law banning 'pornography', 'class hatred' (code for socialism) and insulting the Emperor (*Majestätsbeleidigung*) was applied more severely than elsewhere. Many German restrictions were the result not so much of government riding roughshod over the people as of political campaigns in defence of public morality – the so-called *Sittlichkeitsbewegung*, or morality movements.[35] These were a manifestation of the development of a new kind of mass society, where old values were in danger and could only be defended in a new way.

Traditionally the Roman Catholic Church would have been able to drive undesirable material underground, but by the nineteenth century it had lost much power. In 1832 Pope Gregory XVI had decreed in his encyclical letter *Mirari Vos* that freedom of the press was a 'detestable and execrable moral scourge', but all the Church could actually do was to lobby governments and draft lists of immoral books which Catholics should not read, and should try to prevent others from reading.[36] The *Index of Forbidden Books*, first compiled in 1559, was vastly expanded after the 1870s – just as state liberalisation set in. After 1948 no new titles were added, and after 1966 the penalty of excommunication for reading listed books was lifted. Catholics could read what they wanted without fear of burning in hell for ever and ever.

Where the Church was strong and carried weight with the authorities, matters could be taken to their appropriate conclusion. Thus in June 1864 copies of Victor Hugo's *Les Misérables* were publicly burned in Spain, having been listed by Pope Pius IX in the *Index of Forbidden Books*, along with *Madame Bovary* and all of Balzac's and Stendhal's novels.[37] This was a kind of consecration, one might suggest, with the Church spotting and banning with uncanny accuracy the four most revered French writers of the entire nineteenth century before the century itself had unfolded completely. In Italy between 1870 and 1929 over 4,000 titles and more than 2,400 authors were added to the *Index*, encompassing almost all that was important in modern culture. This could have a devastating commercial effect; as the publisher Carlo Treves declared: 'If mothers and priests declare war on a book, the impact on sales is disastrous.'[38]

Paradoxically, and contrary to the general trend, political censorship in Italy was strengthened after the unification of the country in 1861, when the basic freedoms enshrined in the Piedmontese Constitution of 1848 were eroded. This was in part due to the fact that the new state was facing the unremitting hostility of the Roman Catholic Church. Consequently, as many Catholic newspapers as republican and socialist ones were shut down in the repressive climate of the 1890s.[39] At the same time, the government was trying to avoid offending the Church unnecessarily; thus in 1872 the Prime Minister, Giovanni Lanza, reassured Pope Pius IX, who had protested against anti-clericalism on the stage: 'I do not believe that there is any other civilised country in Europe that enforces censorship of the theatre with greater severity than we do.'[40]

Repressing the Theatre

Throughout Europe, censoring the theatre (and later the cinema) outlasted by decades the lifting of book censorship. A book is read in isolation. A play is watched by a collectivity, almost a crowd. Crowds often behave in a synchronic mode. One laugh sparks general laughter. One person's applause is, in effect, a call for others to join in. It is rare when this does not happen. Even powerful novels and poems cannot match the strength and force of the spectacle. Thus Dante, writing in the Middle Ages, can allow Francesca da

Rimini to sleep with her lover before ending up with him in the *Inferno*, while Silvio Pellico, in the more strait-laced nineteenth century, has his Francesca in *Francesca da Rimini* (1815), a triumph in Milan, only *desire* to sin.

Control of the stage was more difficult than control of the written word, but it had to be done, if we are to believe the words of the Milan censors, whose sentiments were widely shared by conservative élites throughout post-Napoleonic Europe:

> ... theatrical performances can exercise the strongest impressions on those who watch them, are frequented by every sort of person and are organised by individuals who are eager to win applause and therefore inclined to bow to the tastes and opinion of the multitude without being scrupulous about how they may achieve this.[41]

The French Revolution had lifted censorship for books, but not for plays. In 1791 the Mayor of Paris, Jean Silvain Bailly, banned performance of the historical drama *Charles IX* by Marie-Joseph Chénier (author of the lyrics of the hauntingly beautiful Revolutionary hymn 'Le Chant du départ'). He explained that press freedom was the pillar of public freedom, but that was not the case for the theatre, where crowds assemble and '*s'électrisent mutuellement*'.[42]

By 1830 the theatre in Paris was relatively free of major censorship problems. Plays could still be excluded for political reasons, but most plays deal with private relationships or crime, in other words with sex and violence, and not politics. In fact the contents of so many of the new plays led to the main theatre street, the boulevard Saint-Martin, becoming known as the boulevard du Crime. There might have been a desire, on the part of the political authorities, to break the connection between political censorship and the defence of morality. Better to concede what most people wanted – sex and violence – and come down hard on political subversion, about which few really cared.

The censors themselves were subject to a variety of pressures. They did their best to eliminate all political or religious references. In 1835 there was a clampdown. A new breed of censors, delicately called theatre inspectors or examiners, was sought: good pay, tenure, power, some obvious perks such as free theatre tickets, possible favours from actresses, perhaps a few bribes. They had to read the material rapidly – usually two weeks before opening – and decide quickly. Censors were not equipped to consider the overall political significance of plays. They were too close to politics, and censored any-thing which might have been construed as a criticism of current affairs. They were also under severe pressure from all and sundry, including politicians who wanted to favour this or that playwright.[43]

Between 1835 and 1841, out of 3,825 plays submitted to the censors (includ-ing short cabaret sketches), only 123 were turned down.[44] These interdictions were mainly of plays destined for the 'inferior' stages, i.e. the theatres of the Délassements Comiques, Porte Saint-Antoine, Luxembourg and the Pan-théon.[45] The Imperial decree of January 1864 liberalised the French theatre from a complex web of regulations. Censorship was maintained, but the theatre management was free to decide how much to charge for admission, or to establish a new subscription system, while anyone could build new theatres.[46] Though French theatre-going audiences were less strait-laced than those in Britain, official puritanism led to more drastic interventions in matters of morality. Thus the Théâtre-Français changed Molière's *Le Cocu imaginaire* (The Imaginary Cuckold, 1660) into *Le Mari qui se croit trompé* (The Husband who Believes Himself Betrayed), the word *'cocu'* having become taboo.

In pre-unification Italy censorship of the theatre was particularly harsh, especially in the Kingdom of Naples. The authorities had theatres patrolled to ensure that the audience did not make a political point by applauding at the 'wrong' moment – this was not difficult to do, since the repertory was full of stories about tyrants and heroes fighting against them.[47] Matters barely improved after unification.

In Spain the 1849 Organic Decree for the Theatres of the Realm declared that censorship of the stage was particularly important because of the effects that the theatre had on morality and behaviour. Matters improved in the following years, but censorship in the 1860s and 1870s was particularly harsh: out of the 3,608 plays submitted in the years 1851–66, 224 were rejected, and changes demanded to 311.[48]

In Britain in the first half of the nineteenth century the system of patent or authorised theatres meant that only Covent Garden and Drury Lane were allowed to stage performances of 'legitimate' drama. The others could only stage 'entertainments' in which dancing, singing and low comedy prevailed over acting. Playwrights seeking a popular audience were forced to write pantomimes and farces. The situation changed when, in 1843, the Licensing Act was repealed and the new Theatre Regulation Act abolished the monopoly of Drury Lane and Covent Garden. However, official approval and licensing of all stage works performed was required until 1968, when the office of the Lord Chamberlain – Britain's quaint title for censor – was abolished.

British repression may not have been as heavy-handed as on the Continent, but it was pervasive. Gilbert and Sullivan found it difficult to lampoon politicians such as Gladstone because there was a prohibition against portraying living figures on the stage.[49] They had to resort to indirect satire. In Victorian Britain even Verdi's operas were censored, although they were often performed in Italian, the words were not clear, and the public was better educated and richer than that attending prose theatre.[50] Most of the excisions were to do with religion: anything resembling an oath (such as 'Oh God!') was eliminated, as were allusions to the Bible ('too sacred for the stage', mused the Lord Chamberlain). *Nabucco* was 'rechristened' *Nino* (1846) and *Anato* (1850). Even Rossini's *Mosè in Egitto* was converted into *Pietro l'eremita*.[51] Dumas *fils*'s *La Dame aux camélias* had been banned in Paris in 1849 but was allowed two years later by the Interior Minister, a friend of Dumas's.[52] The outcome was that a play performed in France under the yoke of Napoleon III was repeatedly banned in Victorian London (1853, 1859). Not until 1885 was the British public allowed to be moved by the death of the noble-hearted courtesan.[53] Verdi's operatic version, *La Traviata*, however, was given the green light, perhaps because, as the *Morning Chronicle* put it on 26 May 1856, 'all that was repulsive in the French play has been softened down or expunged'.[54] Rome, then under the sovereignty of the Pope, was equally worried by the title of Verdi's *La Traviata* (The Fallen Woman), and it was changed into the inoffensive *Violetta*.[55]

Censoring the theatre by censoring the text is, strictly speaking, of limited effect. All the censors can do is to examine what the playwright has written, assuming that it is the final work. But the play is what appears on the stage, not what is written on the page. Playwrights and censors were quite aware of how the meaning of a sentence could be changed by gestures, emphasis, by the scenario, even by the costume designer, and by the public itself, which might applaud some passages at too great a length, giving them greater weight. Frédérick Lemaître, the great French actor of the mid-nineteenth century, sported two enormous sideburns which reminded everyone of the King when he played the arch-villain Vautrin in Balzac's play of the same name. An actor explained how he was able to introduce an anti-monarchist note by a strategic pause: what should have been 'as generous as the King of Spain' became 'as generous as the King of . . . Spain' – implying: not that of France. Censors were perfectly well aware of such ruses, and some attended rehearsals.[56] All this was time-consuming; it would have been more effective to abolish preventive censorship and get the police to close a theatre in breach of the criminal code, or in cases of riotous behaviour or immorality. But censorship kept authors and producers on their toes. And, as usual, censorship fell far more heavily on the popular theatres, in many cases openly so. A ministerial decree in Piedmont in 1852 declared that control over the theatre should be guided by moral rather than political aims, but added that special attention would be given to the 'popular theatre and its repertory from which we should seek to remove anything that might incite sympathy for crime and hatred for the punitive activities of the state'.[57]

Songs, because they could easily be learned and repeated, and because they appealed to the lower classes, were under strict surveillance. In France between 1815 and 1830 political songs were forbidden. Pierre Béranger (1780–1857), the famous *chansonnier* (a lyricist and composer of songs), was tried and jailed twice.[58] By the middle of the nineteenth century all Paris *cafés-concerts* (see pages 588–90) were strictly controlled by the police to ensure that there were no songs making fun of the army or religion, and that no one sang 'La Marseillaise'. By 1863 singers had to submit their repertoire to the authorities and obtain a licence.[59]

The market too forced upon authors a kind of self-censorship. Clearly, if one wrote for the public, one allowed the public to shape what one wrote. This rule applied with greater force to the theatre than to literature. Publishing a book requires far less investment than producing a play, and involves fewer people. A failed book can be stored to await better times, unlike a failed production of a play (as opposed to the text of the play). Each copy of a book sold reduces the loss from the original investment; each further performance of a play can add to the losses if the number of seats sold falls below a certain level. This forces playwrights to be far more sensitive to public opinion than book writers. Of course, the nature of the theatre also means that it is actually possible to respond quickly to public opinion: Zoe, the mulatto heroine of Dion Boucicault's anti-slavery melodrama *The Octoroon* (1859), commits suicide rather than surrender to the villain. Three years later Boucicault rewrote the ending for the London stage, with Zoe surviving and marrying the white hero – an ending which by celebrating 'miscegenation' would have shocked the original American public. Matters such as these could still shock US audiences a hundred years later: the 1930 Hollywood Production Code (the Hays Code) specifically banned inter-racial sexual relations from being shown in films, while in 1959, the Alabama Public

Library Service Division kept *The Rabbit's Wedding* – a book for children – on its reserve shelf because the state legislature interpreted the marriage between a black and a white rabbit as a plea for integration.[60]

22

Beloved Writers

Hugo as a 'National' Writer

SOME NINETEENTH-CENTURY WRITERS bridged the chasm between high and low genres and achieved the best of both worlds: commercial success as well as recognition in intellectual circles in their own time and for decades after their death. Such success is relatively rare, and when it occurs it must be most enjoyable should there be life after death.

In the summer of 1832 Balzac found himself in Angoulême, where he discovered that he had finally become a celebrity. Ladies, having been made aware of his presence in the town by an article in the local paper, the *Charentais* (the importance of the media in the making of celebrity was as paramount then as now) tried in vain to catch sight of him. Hearing that he had had his hair cut, they besieged the barber's shop, and fought over his locks. The story may not be true (the media made things up then as now), but it is indicative of a fad which is far from contemporary.[1]

The great Russian writers of the nineteenth century, Tolstoy and Dostoevsky, Gogol and Turgenev, were famous in their day, but only among an élite, and reached a popular and international readership only in the twentieth century. Goethe was popular in his lifetime because of *Werther*, and for posterity because of *Faust*. Herman Melville sold little when alive, and though *Moby-Dick* was acclaimed as a masterpiece during his lifetime, only in the twentieth century did it sell in relatively large quantities.

Victor Hugo and Charles Dickens, however, were loved in their time by their readers *and* were consecrated by the academy. Popularity did not disenfranchise them from the pantheon of the Great Writers. They were the lucky ones. They sold well, died rich and are today revered more than ever. To achieve such a feat it is exceedingly helpful to be born in the right country, one with a large book-reading public proud of its culture, and to write in an international language which is widely taught and whose literature is an object of study in other countries. In other words, for a nineteenth-century writer, being French or English was an excellent career move. Geography matters. It was, after all, objectively difficult to become, in the nineteenth century, a great Bulgarian writer, and not that easy to do so even later on. Only towards the end of the nineteenth century, if one adopted the right medium or the right language or the right genre, could the obstacle of confinement in a sparsely populated and linguistically peripheral nation be overcome – as the Norwegian Henrik Ibsen and the Danish Hans Christian Andersen demonstrated.

Hugo and Dickens spoke to their fellow countrymen and countrywomen as if they were national poets, holding up a mirror in which they could recognise themselves. They were not alone. The competition was keen. One can conjure up other names: George Sand, George Eliot, Jane Austen, Thackeray, Flaubert. But, it seems to me, Hugo and Dickens fit better than most the category of 'national writers' enjoying a genuine popular following. Their subsequent canonisation in the restricted group of 'great writers' seems, in fact, to have been granted somehow reluctantly, as if they could not be ignored. It is almost as if they had been elected into the canon by popular demand.

Victor Hugo deployed considerable skills in learning rapidly the difficult technique of acquiring popularity and exploiting the commercial potential of Romanticism. He was more intellectual and political than Dickens, as becomes a French writer. He dropped monarchism when he realised that the new generation of readers, his readers, were overwhelmingly bourgeois liberals. He appreciated the importance of being promoted by an influential literary critic like Sainte-Beuve (who, equally, realised that being associated with a famous writer was the key to success in his chosen genre).[2] Both Dickens and Hugo were 'social' writers, alert to the predicament of the oppressed classes. But Hugo, unlike Dickens, represented more than his works. He incarnated a certain idea of France and of politics: he came to represent social progress, the Republic, the People, Democracy. He was against the powerful, against political repression and capital punishment, against clericalism and, above all, against Napoleon III's dictatorship, preferring an exile of nineteen years in the Channel Islands to a life of ease by compromising his attitude to the man he called, with unmistakable contempt, *Napoléon le petit*. To read Hugo, and to love his poetry and novels, was not only a matter of personal literary preference. It was a declaration of political partisanship. Hugo was one of the first public intellectuals. He demonstrated that fame in one area could be used effectively in another, using the cultural capital he had accumulated to lend support to political and social causes. In so doing he was the precursor of Zola, Jean-Paul Sartre, Bertrand Russell and Noam Chomsky. Of course, he had antecedents: Voltaire, Diderot, perhaps Goethe. But they appealed to much narrower élites. Hugo, who lived in a more democratic age, appealed to 'the people'. His *Le Dernier jour d'un condamné* (1829), by implication a tract against capital punishment, was widely praised far beyond France, quoted everywhere, translated into English.[3] It was the first of his narrative works to be published in Russia.[4]

Hugo lived in exciting times for Europe, but particularly for France. Born in 1802, he was thirteen when Napoleon was defeated at Waterloo, twenty-eight when the Bourbons were ousted, and forty-six when the Republic was proclaimed. He was thus a mature man when Napoleon III established the first modern dictatorship. He lived long enough to outlast Napoleon, returning triumphantly to Paris to witness the re-establishment of the Republic and be worshipped as the authentic representative of France, at a time when the new politicians of the Third Republic had neither the stature nor the opportunity to shine like the great French personages of the past. Hugo gave France a hero who was also a great man of letters. Enough to make everyone happy: the intellectuals, the bourgeois, and even the common people who knew or were told that he was on their side. Some had even read his books.

In his earlier phase Hugo worked on two registers, one for the élite (*Le Roi s'amuse*, written in verses in 1833 for the Théâtre-Français), the other (*Lucrèce Borgia*, also 1833) for the lower (middle) classes who went to the popular Théâtre Saint-Martin. In *Le Roi s'amuse*, the protagonist is a lower-class monster (Triboulet, Rigoletto in Verdi's version) who becomes human when he discovers fatherly love. The people are classic *lumpenproletariat* types: Saltabadil, a contract killer, and Maguelonne, a prostitute. In *Lucrèce* it is the turn of the aristocracy to be despised. The heroine, Lucretia, is an aristocratic monster who becomes a human being only when she discovers maternal love.[5] Later Hugo managed to merge the two markets, and with *Les Misérables* (1862) reach both an élite and a middle-class audience. However, an earlier work, *Marion Delorme* (1829), on the well-trodden theme of the fallen woman redeemed by love, was regarded as pornographic – and consequently the urban lower classes as well as the respectable bourgeoisie flocked to see it. The first production of the play was banned by the censors because of its negative portrayal of a seventeenth-century monarch (Louis XIII). Hugo appealed to the King, but all he obtained was a hefty increase in his poet's pension (from 2,000 to 6,000 francs).

Lucrèce Borgia (1833) was a triumph: it was in prose and not in verse, had poisoning, incest and adultery, and a great actor, Frédérick Lemaître.[6] The first thirty performances brought in 84,769 francs.[7] Hugo's share was 12 per cent, hence 10,172 francs.

Ruy Blas (1838) was a financial success too. In this instance the theatre management had worked particularly hard: ladies were given free programmes/albums during the intervals, while a waxwork dummy modelled fashionable dresses in the foyer. When the play was over there was a ball with an enormous orchestra. The evening was concluded with a raffle. All Paris talked about the event. By 1840 'Hugomania' had spread to the provinces. The domestic market was flooded with pirated editions of his works.[8]

Hugo was already famous at the age of twenty-eight when he became the acknowledged head of the Romantic revolution, an event symbolically launched at the first night of his *Hernani* (25 February 1830) – 'the battle of *Hernani*' – which turned into a generational confrontation, with young writers and aspiring writers celebrating the play (before seeing it) as a rallying point against the older classics and the establishment. On Hugo's side were writers destined to become famous, such as Théophile Gautier and Alexandre Dumas, but he was also supported by the already established, such as Chateaubriand and Balzac. As Gautier reminisced in 1872, it was not an ordinary performance but a clash between two systems, two parties, two armies, two civilisations 'who hated each other heartily as one does in literary wars'.[9] *Hernani* is a play in verse with a conventional plot: a Spanish bandit loves a young woman, who is also courted by her elderly guardian. Today it is hardly performed outside France (except in the operatic version by Verdi), but the first night transformed Hugo into a national celebrity. It was one of the first 'media' events, constantly referred to, embroidered upon and celebrated even years later, as in Albert Besnard's painting *La Première d'Hernani* (1903).

In the year following *Hernani*, 1831, Hugo published his first major novel, *Notre-Dame de Paris*, inspired by Walter Scott's historical novels. Thanks to its ludicrous plot, it became a great popular classic almost at once, making Hugo the most famous living writer in Europe. The historian Jules Michelet was obviously still reeling under the impact of *Notre-Dame de Paris* when he drafted the second volume of his massive *Histoire de la France* (1831–33). When, in the section on medieval art, he describes the cathedral of Notre-Dame, he explains how difficult it is to do this, as 'someone' (his readers could not fail to identify this someone) had marked the monument with his 'lion's claw' (*griffe de lion*). No one else could touch it: 'It is his thing, now and forever; it is his possession; it is Quasimodo's domain. Alongside the old cathedral, a cathedral of poetry has been erected, with foundations as solid and towers as high.'[10]

Thousands of tourists went to see Notre-Dame, described in travel guides six centuries after its completion as 'the cathedral of the book'. Their heads were full of Hugo's personages: Quasimodo, the hunchback in love; the dastardly sex-crazed priest Claude Frollo; and the beautiful and proud Gypsy Esméralda. Like others before, like hundreds of thousands since, the English writer Frances Trollope (Anthony's mother) climbed to the top of the cathedral's tower in 1835 because she had read the description in Hugo.[11] Quasimodo and Esméralda have been kept alive by endless stage adaptations, abridgements, illustrations and lithographs (such as that by Nicolas Maurin of Esméralda), and in the twentieth century by numerous films and animations: a silent movie in 1923, a talking one with a happy ending in 1939 by William Dieterle starring Charles Laughton and Maureen O'Hara, one in colour in 1956 by Jean Delannoy with Gina Lollobrigida and Anthony Quinn, a TV film in 1982, a Disney animation in 1996 (*The Hunchback of Notre Dame*) and even an animated sequel to it (yes: *The Hunchback of Notre Dame II*), where the main characters, Esmeralda and Phoebus, are happily married and the hunchback, 'Quasi', is a family friend. With *Notre-Dame de Paris* Hugo became even more of a European celebrity. The book achieved great prominence in Russia in the early 1830s, and has remained a Russian favourite.[12] In 1841, at the age of thirty-nine, Hugo was elected to the Académie Française. When he made his acceptance speech, the audience was full of young women who had been queuing for hours.[13]

Victor Hugo was, at all times, a professional writer, conscious of his worth and determined to maximise his income. In 1845 he valued his fortune at 300,000 francs.[14] His sales reflected his standing as a public intellectual. *Napoléon-le-Petit* – a vitriolic attack in verse on Napoleon III – appeared two days after Hugo's arrival on Jersey in exile in 1851. In two weeks it sold 8,500 copies. It was printed in Belgium and smuggled into France by visitors who 'stuffed their pockets with it', according to the publisher Pierre-Jules Hetzel.[15] By 1853 it had sold almost 40,000 copies. It was read aloud in secret meetings all over France, and was immediately translated into German (*Napoleon der Kleine*) and Italian (*Napoleone il piccolo*), then into Spanish for Mexican editions (*Napoleon el chiquito* and *Napoleon el pequeño*). *Napoleon the Little* was advertised in London on sandwich boards and on the sides of railway carriages, and sold in various editions including a 'People's Shilling Edition'.[16]

When Hugo was away from Guernsey (where he had moved in 1854), hundreds of visitors were taken on tours of his house, which had been arranged like a sort of museum. They would sign the visitors' book and pick up pebbles by the seashore where Hugo had walked as mementoes. After his return from exile, Hugo's Paris apartment became an object of pilgrimage; once a large party of American tourists even tried to gain entry. On Hugo's seventy-ninth birthday in 1881, 500,000 people passed in front of his window saluting him. Later the section of the avenue d'Eylau where he lived was renamed avenue Victor Hugo (as it is today), and a nearby crossroads became place Victor Hugo. His funeral was attended by two million people, more than the population of Paris. His face was seen on plates, table-mats, pens, paperweights, pipe-racks, braces, cigarette papers, tobacco boxes, walking sticks and wallpaper. A cartoon in *La Comédie politique* when he turned eighty-three showed him entering heaven, and God respectfully giving up his throne to him.[17] The two-volume *Larousse Universel* of 1922 was compelled to have entries for 'hugolâtrie' and 'hugophile'.

Eventually Hugo's face appeared on banknotes. Most cities in France have a street named after him.[18] In 2002, the bicentenary of his birth, he was celebrated throughout the French-speaking world, as a writer, poet, politician, early advocate of the abolition of capital punishment, pioneer of European integration and, thanks to a suitable quotation, even an early supporter of the single European currency. Some two hundred composers, including Berlioz, Donizetti, Verdi, Georges Brassens and Serge Gainsbourg had set his plays and poems as operas and songs.[19]

Everything Hugo wrote sold well. The two volumes of his collection of poems *Les Contemplations* appeared in Brussels and Paris on the same day, in a print run of 5,500 copies – a remarkable feat for an 11,000-verse-long work. These poems generated sufficient income to enable Hugo to purchase, in May 1856, a large mansion (Hauteville House) on Guernsey. When he died in 1885 he left a fortune of seven million francs.[20]

In keeping with the national role he had chosen, Hugo affected not to care about either money or attacks from critics. He wrote to his publisher Pierre-Jules Hetzel on 9 February 1857:

> . . . I attach very little importance to the immediate impact, as I think you
> know. A book always gets what it deserves in the end – glory or oblivion.
> The success of the moment is primarily the publisher's concern and to

some extent depends on him. As for attacks, they are my lifeblood; dia-tribes are my daily bread![21]

In reality Hugo always demanded large sums for his work. In part this was because he liked money, but above all it was because he knew the money was the recognition of his professionalism. He also realised that the larger the advance, the harder the publishers would toil to disseminate his works. Hetzel offered him 150,000 francs for Les Misérables, and wanted the rights for ten years. Hugo eventually sold all rights (i.e. including translation) for twelve years to the Belgian publishers Lacroix and Verboeckhoven for 300,000 francs.[22] The Goncourt brothers, livid with envy, wrote in April 1862 (when they could only just have started reading the book):

> Une grande déception pour nous, Les Misérables d'Hugo ... D'ailleurs, à y bien réfléchir, je trouve assez amusant de gagner deux cents mille francs – qui est la vrai chiffre de vente – à s'apitoyer sur les misères du peuple. (A great disappointment, Hugo's Misérables ... To think about it, it is rather amusing to make 200,000 francs – this is the true figure – by being full of pity for the suffering of the people.)[23]

On 3 April 1862, one of the biggest global marketing operations in the history of publishing took place. The first part of Les Misérables was launched in Paris (Napoleon III did not dare ban it), as well as London, Brussels, Leipzig, Rotterdam, Madrid, Milan, Turin, Naples, Warsaw, Pest, St Petersburg and Rio de Janeiro. On the morning of 15 May 1862, publication day of the second and third parts, a long queue of people waited for the bookshop Pagnerre in the rue de Seine to open. The shop, which had announced that on that day it would sell only Les Misérables, and nothing but Les Misérables, was crammed with copies of the book. It sold out in a few hours.[24] From his exile in Guernsey, Hugo participated actively in the marketing strategy, providing quotable quotes ('Dante made a hell with poetry; I have tried to make one with reality'), suggesting extracts from the Waterloo episode, and telling his publishers to emphasise the novel's patriotic aspect.[25]

Twenty-one pirated editions of Les Misérables came out in the same year. Without the help of serialisation, a work of serious fiction had become a popular best-seller – above all in France, a country where the author had refused to set foot as long as Napoleon remained on his throne (he kept his promise, turning down an amnesty and returning to Paris only in 1870, to endure the Prussian siege while Napoleon died in exile three years later in Chislehurst, Kent). By 1880 Hugo had probably outsold almost every other novelist in France, not just Zola but even the far less cerebral Paul de Kock.

Only Jules Verne may have outdistanced him in the number of copies sold. But then, comparing Hugo with others is difficult. He excelled not only in narrative, but also in essay-writing, poetry and drama, dividing his output (in number of pages) in a surprisingly balanced way: 29 per cent fiction, 10 per cent theatre, 33 per cent poetry, and 27 per cent essays and non-fiction.[26]

The reprinting of his works has been fairly consistent, except for a dip in 1910–33 which coincided with a decrease in the reprinting of many French classics. The sheer size of *Les Misérables* has made it less popular than other French classics. Besides, the academic establishment never ranked Hugo as high as Flaubert. The consequence is that by 1939 *Les Misérables* (1862) had had 'only' twenty-eight editions, while *Madame Bovary* (1857) trumped it with fifty-three.[27] Yet the lasting popular success of *Les Misérables* is unquestionable: it has generated twenty-six cinema and television adaptations, including an American film as early as 1909, another in Japan in 1950, and the musical *Les Misérables* by Claude-Michel Schönberg (London première 1985, still running in 2005), which by 2000 had been performed in twenty-seven countries and translated into sixteen languages.

The success of *Les Misérables* provided George Lewes, acting as George Eliot's *de facto* manager, with a way of meeting Eliot's desire to write a longer novel than that possible under the three-volume requirement of the circulating libraries. The only way to make people buy a very long novel without paying the entire cost in one go was to market it along the lines of the sales campaign of *Les Misérables*, bringing it out in eight parts at two-month intervals, each part costing five shillings, with Eliot to be paid two shillings for each copy sold – a staggering royalty of 40 per cent. Blackwood's accepted, and *Middlemarch* became a remarkable publishing success.[28]

But *Middlemarch*, one of the grand Victorian novels, one of the great novels of all time, never reached the stature and renown of *Les Misérables*, whose main characters became household names: the redeemed, Christlike convict Jean Valjean; the good-hearted prostitute Cosette; her daughter, the stunningly beautiful and pure Fantine; Marius, the romantic hero bursting with kindness and integrity; the Thénardiers, the unspeakably evil couple from hell; Gavroche, the heroic, streetwise Parisian kid; the saintly Bishop Myriel (to show that even an anti-clerical can have a good priest in his novel); and Javert, the obsessive policeman. Yet *Les Misérables* breaks many of the rules of the traditional page-turner. Above all, it employs digressions to an extraordinary extent – they amount to one-third of the novel.[29] It opens with a sixty-page portrait of Bishop Myriel, a character one never encounters again. The battle of Waterloo, which takes up fifty pages, has no narrative function other than to establish that Marius's father thinks he has been rescued by Tenardier, not realising that Tenardier was trying to rob him – something which could have been established in a couple of pages. Jean Valjean's rescue of Marius via the sewers of Paris could also have been dealt with in a few pages, but instead Hugo provides the reader with a detailed twenty-page account of the history of the Parisian sewerage system. This prolixity does delay the action, adding to the suspense, but its length is such that it would not have worked in a serialisation.

Clearly, there is no recipe for literary success. Trollope thought that digressions had to be avoided at all cost, and criticised Dickens's use of them: 'Every sentence, every word through all those pages, should tend towards the telling of the story.'[30] Yet he admitted that Dickens was the most popular writer of his time.[31]

Dickens as a 'Social' Writer

It is difficult to ascertain whether Charles Dickens was the best-selling English author of his age. There is no doubt that he was one of the most popular. Eventually he outdistanced his competitors, and by the twentieth century he was far more internationally well known than the otherwise weightier and deeper George Eliot. Wilkie Collins was never adopted by the academy. Trollope was high in the popularity stakes, but low in the academic ones, and is barely known outside the English-speaking world. Trollope affected to equate literary success with earnings: when his publishers Longman tried to pay him less because of the prestige of their house he commented: 'I did think much of Messrs Longman's name, but I like it best at the bottom of a cheque.'[32] He tailored his works according to his market. In 1848, at the start of his career, his publishers had told him that his early novels lost money because they were set in Ireland, so he expunged Ireland altogether from his works – though keeping some Irish characters.[33] Later the publishers told him they wanted 'an English tale, on English life, with clerical flavour ... On these orders I went to work and framed what I suppose I must call the plot of *Framley Parsonage*.' The story was 'thoroughly English. There was a little fox-hunting and a little tuft-hunting; some Christian virtues and some Christian cant. There was no heroism and no villainy.'[34]

Trollope was, in England, almost as well-known as Dumas and Verne in

France. But the very English qualities which endeared him to the British left the rest of the world cool. He was, quite simply, too 'national': the characters he created did not possess the universality of Dickens's. The kind of politician he described did not exist anywhere else, nor did the parson nor, of course, the parson's wife. The nearest he came to an official consecration was when his ashes were placed in Poets' Corner in Westminster Abbey – a decision which was taken neither by the literary establishment nor the government but, at least formally, by the Dean of Westminster. Trollope received this honour in 1993, 111 years after his death, at a time when such decisions had become increasingly responsive to popular feelings. Some passages from his novels were read by the then Prime Minister, John Major, who like many British Prime Ministers declared Trollope to be his favourite writer, presumably because this could not possibly offend anyone.

Dickens was quite different. His story-telling skills, and his novels teeming with characters, ensured his enduring popularity well after his death. He was often popularised and adapted for children, especially abroad, a task made simpler by his frequent use of children as characters who find themselves suffering in educational institutions, or in difficult family situations, or in fear of authority. Unlike Hugo, Dickens never faced a régime or political institution he wished to eliminate. Constitutional monarchy and the British party system as it existed then suited him fine. However, he depicted his characters as oppressed by institutions (courts, prisons, orphanages, schools), entangled in an impersonal 'system' they could not control and from which they were never able to escape. In *Bleak House* (1853), Gridley, 'the man from Shropshire', is unable to obtain justice in a court of law:

> 'The system! I am told, on all hands, it's the system. I mustn't look to individuals. It's the system. I mustn't go into Court, and say "My Lord, I beg to know this from you – is it right or wrong? Have you the face to tell me I have received justice and therefore am dismissed?" My Lord knows nothing of it. He sits there, to administer the system.'[35]

Dickens's settings were almost exclusively urban, as were the majority of his readers, but within the city no class was left entirely untouched by his story-telling. Unlike Hugo, who was never able to use comic characters or convey a sense of humour, Dickens could move from the comic to the dramatic in a few pages. Much of what he wrote was sentimental, and some was outright crude melodrama – part of his appeal to a wide reading public. His popularity provoked the annoyance of the literary establishment. Thus reads Leslie Stephen's entry for him in the *Dictionary of National Biography*: 'If literary fame could safely be measured by popularity with the half-educated, Dickens must claim the highest position among English novelists.'[36]

Like Hugo, Dickens was in favour of progressive reforms, particularly of the criminal system. Both were early opponents of capital punishment, though never consistently so. The persistence of the death penalty in France and Great Britain may well be seen as proof, if proof were needed, of how ineffectual even popular writers are in advancing the cause of reform. The denunciation of poverty and inequality in Hugo and Dickens did not challenge any of the received opinions of the respectable bourgeoisie of their time. The middle classes were committed to philanthropy, especially in England, and social novels simply confirmed the prevailing views. If Dickens's skill had been simply that of raising social issues in an effective way, he would have been forgotten as soon as the problems he highlighted had been resolved or attenuated. Social denunciation often encourages readers to think better of themselves, even, or especially, when it is expressed with unmistakable passion – as when Dickens, having contrived the death of the crossing-sweeper little Jo in *Bleak House* (1852–53), exclaims, addressing himself directly to his readers and, beyond them, accusingly, to those in power:

> Dead, your Majesty. Dead, my lords and gentlemen. Dead, Right Reverends and Wrong Reverends of every order. Dead, men and women, born with heavenly compassion in your hearts. And dying thus around us every day.[37]

Because his concerns reflected those of his age, social outrage did Charles Dickens no harm financially. Though the idea that he invented the British Christmas is an exaggeration, the huge success of *A Christmas Carol* (1843) made him a popular spokesman for the respectable poor.[38] While Hugo had to flee a dictatorship, Dickens could take advantage of British freedoms. His two principal English publishers, Bradbury & Evans and Chapman & Hall, provided him with six-monthly accounts between 1846 and 1870. They are, in the words of Robert Patten, 'the most detailed and complete record of a major author's publications' available.[39] The records do not, however, include Dickens's income from foreign rights, nor from his journals *Household Words* and *All the Year Round*, nor his income before 1846. Besides, Patten himself warns that the ways books were sold in the nineteenth century, and the various forms of payment, make it impossible to provide accurate figures. It is also difficult to establish the ranking of Dickens's various novels, since they were eventually published in cheap editions which included various books. *Bleak*

House, for instance, was published in serial form (nineteen parts, including the final double one) in 1852–53. It sold a total of 714,250 parts, the equivalent of 34,000 complete runs, much more than *David Copperfield* in 1849–50, or *Dombey and Son* in 1846–48.[40] Why did *Bleak House* do better than *David Copperfield*? It was certainly better promoted: the publishers had spent over £300 on the serialisation, a large sum, though not unusually so. The simple answer is that it is not at all clear why Dickens should have done so well, nor is it clear why he should have outsold so amazingly his competitors, such as Trollope and Thackeray. By 1870 Dickens had made almost £11,000 out of *Bleak House* just from its various serialisations. This is six or seven times more than Thackeray's *Vanity Fair* – a great critical success.[41] When Dickens died in 1870 he left an estate amounting to £93,000, half of which had been earned in the last decade of his life by reading his own works in public.[42]

Dickens's sales continued well after his death. Just in the USA, in 1968 alone, over a million copies of his novels were sold, half of this accounted for by only two novels: *A Tale of Two Cities* and *Great Expectations*.[43] In Dickens's lifetime his works were translated in France, Russia, Italy and Germany. He was successful in France fairly early. The serialisation of *The Pickwick Papers* was concluded on 17 November 1837. It was available (in English) in Paris in book form on 9 December.[44] The following year the French translation, by Eugénie Niboyet, an eighty-year-old feminist who had also translated Maria Edgeworth, was published as *Le Club des Pickwickistes*. By 1864 *Oliver Twist* had been translated three times. In 1851 two translations of *David Copperfield* were published. They were altered 'for the French taste'. Almost the whole of Dickens's output was published in French by Hachette between 1857 and 1874.[45]

Once he was recognised in Germany and France, Dickens became famous in more peripheral countries, such as Romania, where he was probably first read in French – his first full-scale novel translated into Romanian was *Hard Times* in 1894–96; *David Copperfield* was translated only in the late 1920s, *Oliver Twist* in 1944.[46] However, in Italy, virtually the whole of Dickens was translated during the nineteenth century – unlike George Eliot, who had only two books translated: *Daniel Deronda* (by 'Giorgio Eliot') in 1882–83 and *Il Fratello Giacobbe* in 1880. Of course, much of Dickens was severely pruned: *Bleak House* (960 pages in a tightly-packed current Penguin edition) was transformed into a slim volume of 216 pages by the Italian publishers Sonzogno in 1885.[47]

Dickens was a worldwide phenomenon almost from the outset, which caused some jealousy among his contemporaries. In Germany he became a household name almost as promptly as in England. *The Pickwick Papers* obtained high sales and enthusiastic reviews, and was widely imitated.[48] His fiction was attractive to men and women alike, and to people in different classes. It always included something for everyone, from angelic heroines to silly women, henpecked husbands to noble working-class figures, hypocrites, eccentrics, wealthy benefactors, generous convicts and many more.

Like Hugo, Dickens was a great self-promoter. As an editor of periodicals himself he was familiar with the art of advertising and promotion. He was the first English novelist to read his work on the stage. Driven in part by his craving for money, and in part by his craving for the love of the public, he started, in 1866, a reading tour of the country, making an agreement with his publishers, Chappell, according to which they would pay him £1,500 in exchange for thirty readings from his novels, and would also take care of all the expenses incurred. The tour was a great success. Dickens was a born histrionic actor, possessing, according to a contemporary writing in the *Manchester Guardian*, 'an almost equal genius for rendering and for producing lifelike creations of human character'.[49] He extracted from his novels material for a one- or two-hour reading, selecting, on the whole, the more sentimental themes, for instance the story of little Dombey's death from *Dombey and Son*, concluding with a heart-tugging: 'And look upon us, Angels of young children, with regards not quite estranged, when the swift river bears us to the ocean!'[50] He might have been slightly over the top when he impersonated *Oliver Twist*'s Nancy as she begged Sykes to spare her, but according to the *Bath Chronicle* (4 February 1869), 'the acting of Mr. Dickens is much beyond his writing, which strikes us as fantastic and unreal'.[51]

The cinema and television have ransacked Dickens almost continuously. Between 1909 and 1912 alone *Oliver Twist* was adapted for the screen eight times.[52] His works were adapted by film-makers the world over. This added to the unstoppable impetus towards his globalisation.

Dumas and Verne as Popular Writers

Hugo and Dickens are often mentioned in the same breath as Flaubert and George Eliot, as pillars of their national literature. Not so more popular writers like Alexandre Dumas and Jules Verne. Their sales in the twentieth century, considerable as they were, were never boosted by their being included in the academic syllabus. Their literary longevity – only in recent years has their fame been on the wane – was due almost entirely to the best advertising there is: the opinions of their readers. Parallel to the academic canon there is a kind of social canon that ensures that a small band of favourite writers continues to be read across generations. Dumas and Verne are outstanding instances of this social canon, but by no means the only ones. Included in it are some of the celebrated popular classics of the nineteenth century such as the American novels *Uncle Tom's Cabin* (1852) by Harriet Beecher Stowe and *The Adventures of Huckleberry Finn* (1884) by Mark Twain (which also holds a high place in the academic canon). Out of the thousands of detective-story writers, a few, such as Agatha Christie and Arthur Conan Doyle, are still regularly read many years after their deaths; out of the many children's book writers, some are still popular, such as Carlo Collodi, the creator of *Pinocchio*, and Hans Christian Andersen.

What was impressive about Verne and Dumas was not the ability to deliver a one-off success, but their skill in producing a continuing flow of successful books. They are, and by a long margin, the most translated *French* authors (excluding, that is, the Belgian Georges Simenon).[53] The books of Jules Verne (1828–1905) had sold, by the mid-1980s, twenty-six million copies worldwide.[54] In his lifetime, however, his sales amounted to 'only' 1.6 million. Most of the twenty-four million Verne books sold after his death were restricted to a few masterpieces, which, as it turns out, were also those which sold best during his lifetime. He wrote almost sixty novels, plays, short stories and essays, but the ones which made him famous were, at most, ten books, all about travel, adventure and exploration:

JULES VERNE: TOP TEN BEST-SELLING BOOKS DURING THE AUTHOR'S LIFETIME.	COPIES PRINTED
1 Le Tour du monde en quatre-vingts jours	108,000
2 Cinq semaines en ballon	76,000
3 Vingt mille lieues sous les mers	50,000
4 Michel Strogoff	49,000
5 Voyage au centre de la terre	48,000
6 L'Île mystérieuse	44,000
7 Les Enfants du Capitaine Grant	38,000
8 De la Terre à la lune	37,000
9 Voyages et aventures du Capitaine Hatteras	37,000
10 Aventures de trois Russes et de trois Anglais	36,000

SOURCE: Publishers' statement cited in Martin, *La Vie et l'oeuvre de Jules Verne*, pp.280–1

Verne also wrote novels dealing with historical and political topics as varied as the Greek insurrection of 1826, the Boer War, the American Civil War and the Irish question. These, however, sold relatively little, and were hardly ever read after his death, sinking into oblivion well before encountering disapproval for their excessive nationalism (*César Cascabel*), misogyny (*Clovis Dardentor*) or anti-Semitism (*Hector Servadac*). Verne's contemporary image is that generated by his successful books. But why were these so successful? Intuitively, one assumes that some novels are better than others – reflecting our common experience as readers. However, one should not discount the mechanism of reinforcement which makes publishers reprint only the 'good' novels, thereby condemning the 'bad' ones to everlasting oblivion; the 'good' are eventually turned into films, which are major plugs for the books, thus establishing a virtuous circle whereby success breeds success. *Around the World in Eighty Days* has been filmed several times, as has *20,000 Leagues Under the Sea*, about a mysterious submarine, the *Nautilus*. Walt Disney's 1954 film of the latter was so successful that, as if to confirm the belief that life imitates art, the following year the US government decided to call the world's first nuclear-powered submarine USS *Nautilus*. Verne was as popular in the Soviet Union as in the United States: not only was he translated into most of the languages of the USSR, but one of the volcanoes on the far side of the moon was named after him by the Soviets.

The Verne canon relied on a well-established exotic strand, at a time when the newspapers regularly featured stories of exploration, mountain-climbing, scientific experiments, travelling by balloon, and colonialism. He became one of the most translated French authors of all time – the most translated author in nineteenth-century Romania, where he was regarded as the main model for fiction-writing.[55] Verne's popularity in his own lifetime can be gauged by the extent to which features of his most successful works became part of the common discourse beyond his immediate readership. One did not have to have read *Le Tour du monde en quatre-vingts jours* to know the rough outline of the plot or the name of its chief characters – just as today one does not need to have read the Harry Potter books or seen the films to know about the Hogwarts School of Witchcraft and Wizardry. When *Le Tour du monde* was serialised in *Le Temps* in 1872, bets were made on whether Phileas Fogg was going to make it back within the eighty days allotted, while travel companies tried to get the author to include them in the narrative.[56] The assumption that characters are, in a sense, alive (an assumption made by reasonable people who know perfectly well that the characters are fictional), and that one can share their destiny, or at least empathise with it, is the true hallmark of popularity. Narratives have now, thanks to television, been able to reach every home, enabling conversations to take place about the fate of protagonists of popular serials: Will Samantha keep her child? Will Jason find out about Fifi's affair with Antonio? Success is achieved when the fictional world of the writer and his readers becomes part of the imagined world of a wider community.

Verne, like Sue or Dickens, created characters about whom people cared, and put them in interesting situations following a specific formula. Many of his plots have the structure of the traditional epic: a character has a mission which requires him to go from A to B. In the course of the journey he encounters dangers which he overcomes. Often the 'hero' is in fact a group of selected companions, usually three.[57] The head of the group is a reassuring father figure, perhaps a scientist, normally calm and unexcitable. Then there is his young assistant, with whom the young readership is expected to identify. The third character, whose few defects are compensated for by his possession of practical skills, is the classic 'helper' analysed by Propp in his examination of the structures of folk tales.[58] This three-character structure ensures that no single central character is required to bear the burden of readers' identification. It also simplifies the problem of narrative, as the characters constantly interact and inform each other of what has happened, is happening and is likely to happen, examining together various strategies to overcome whatever obstacles the narrator has invented for them. The formula can easily be modified. The team can be made larger, thus multiplying the possibilities of identification. It can include a traitor, thus providing an element of suspense, or a woman, thus facilitating the possibility of a romantic angle with an eye to expanding the female readership – always reluctant to be drawn into 'boys' stories'. But women are very much a minority in Verne: out of 410 characters in his sixty novels, only fifty-four are women, most of them American, which is code for 'emancipated' i.e. adventurous (obviously not in the sense of sexually liberated). The idea of the 'hero as a group', which is of course far older than Verne, was later exploited in adventure and war films, where a mission is devised for a selected team – representing in embryonic form the potential audience – to accomplish.

Verne has often been described as the 'father' (one of the many) of the modern science fiction story because of his space travel novels *De la Terre à la lune* (1864) and its 1869 sequel *Autour de la lune*. In fact only three of his novels are set in the future, and *De la Terre à la lune* is not one of them.

What is more remarkable is his use of science and scientific information in many of his stories, and not only in *Voyage au centre de la terre*, *Vingt mille lieus sous les mers* and *De la Terre à la lune*. In so doing he was building on the thriving demand for popularised science which was growing in Europe and North America, and which had been pioneered in France by writers like Louis Figuier (1819–94), whose books such as *La Terre avant le déluge* (The World Before the Deluge, 1863) were widely translated throughout Europe. This love of scientific and technological innovation provided Verne with a distinctive edge over his competitors for the youth market. His merit was not so much to have predicted the future, as is often claimed, but to have understood the present. While reading Verne one could be learning various snippets of scientific knowledge, just as the generation of Walter Scott could learn history without reading history books. Closely connected to science, at least in the popular imagination, was another popular passion of the reading classes: exploration. Colonialism had produced a new, modern nineteenth-century hero with roots in the sixteenth century, the fearless explorer: Stanley, Livingstone, Speke and Burton, and less-well-known French explorers like René-Auguste Caillié (1799–1838), the first European to reach Timbuktu, and Pierre Brazza (1852–1905, the Congo).

Adolescents were Verne's biggest market. At that time parental guidance was the dominant voice in the selection of reading material for this age group, a dominance reinforced by the high price of books and the lack of real purchasing power enjoyed by nineteenth-century teenagers. Parents could be nudged towards 'useful' reading material, something uplifting and educational yet not too boring. Verne suited this market ideally. He was unmistakably modern (science, travel, etc.). He was not clerical or overtly pious, so would not annoy his main market, the secular bourgeoisie. Yet thanks to the watchful pen of his shrewd publisher, Pierre-Jules Hetzel, Verne's novels were systematically expurgated of anything which could remotely offend religious feelings. Thus teachers and priests used their not insignificant influence to encourage parents to buy Verne.

Verne allowed his publishers enormous powers of interference and editing, as one can see in a letter of 25 April 1865: 'My dear Hetzel ... I will always be ready to accept changes for the general good.'[59] He was also happy to let Hetzel dictate the financial terms. Even when he had become an internationally best-selling author, Verne seemed to be grateful to Hetzel for publishing him. He tied himself to Hetzel by undertaking to write a set number of books a year in exchange for a salary as an advance (plus a small royalty on past sales and serialisation). Thus in 1865 a new contract established that Verne would write three books a year, and be paid 750 francs per month (9,000 francs a year). In 1868 the terms improved a little, to 10,000 francs a year. In 1871 he was allowed to hand in only two books a year and his income was increased to 12,000 francs. Under the terms of the last contract (the sixth) Hetzel granted himself the concession in perpetuity of all the rights to Verne's work. Verne had earned one million francs from his books in forty years, and Hetzel made three times as much.[60] The financial vicissitudes of Verne's relationship with his publishers are the best advertisement for literary agents.

Verne's international reputation was enhanced by his use of characters of various nationalities, often representing national stereotypes. The nationality breakdown of characters of some importance is as follows:

NATIONALITY OF CHARACTERS IN VERNE'S NOVELS

Number of characters	National origins	Number of novels
89	England	25
85	USA	26
82	France	36
27	Scotland	10
20	Russia	7
17	Ireland	6
12	Germany	6
12	Canada	4

SOURCE: Huet, *L'Histoire des voyages extraordinaires. Essai sur l'oeuvre de Jules Verne*, p.191

Strikingly, the French are under-represented. This is exceptional: the overwhelming majority of characters in British novels are British, Russians in Russian novels and so on. The comparative scarcity of French characters in Verne's novels, and his readiness to make an Englishman the hero of a novel like *Around the World in Eighty Days* (and one who falls in love and becomes engaged to an Indian woman), while the Englishman's servant is French, is remarkable. Stereotypes dominate: the Irish are usually lower-class, the Scots are in the army, the English are mainly aristocrats or professionals, most Germans are scientists, the Americans are a little uncouth but practical and generally likeable, and among the Russians there are quite a few aristocrats and political exiles. Most of the nine Romanians are servants. One of the two Jews is an unpleasant money-lender, the other a sympathetic Romanian innkeeper. Of the two Greeks, one is a pirate, the other is the pirate's wife. Of the three Italians, one is a bandit, another an opera singer.[61]

Many such national stereotypes have survived, but it is important to remember how they have been reinforced by literature, and equally how they can be changed by events. Verne's English characters were phlegmatic and eccentric and somewhat loveable until the Fashoda incident of 1898, which sparked a confrontation between British and French imperialism in Africa, whereupon they become hateful. Germans worked hard and were usually inoffensive, but turn insolent and arrogant after the Franco–Prussian war of 1870. As Isaiah Berlin wrote, in 1840 the French were swashbuckling, gallant, immoral, militarised; the Germans were beer-drinking, ludicrously provincial, musical, full of misty metaphysics, harmless but absurd. By 1871 they had turned into obsessed militarists filled with national pride storming through France. The Russians in the nineteenth century were crushed serfs, or darkly brooding semi-religious Slav mystics who wrote philosophical novels, or Cossacks loyal to the Tsar who sang beautifully. Later they turned into godless materialists (or were crushed by them) enamoured of technology and tanks, crusading against capitalism. The English oscillated between ruthless imperialists arrogantly lording it over the 'fuzzy wuzzies' and looking down at the rest of the world, and decent liberals with a sense of humour who invent the welfare state and stand in line in a civilised way.[62]

The success of Alexandre Dumas was based on an even more 'industrial' approach to literature than that of Verne. Dumas's method consisted of a rapid and superficial reading of a magazine article, a history text or an autobiography such as the *Mémoires de Monsieur d'Artagnan, Capitaine Lieutenant de la première Compagnie des Mousquetaires du Roi* – in reality written by Courtils de Sandraz (1644–1712), a specialist in ghosted autobiographies – or a story strikingly similar to the one he used in *Le Comte de Monte-Cristo* which he had found in a memoir of Jacques Peuchet. He then proceeded to focus on the *milieu*, jot down a possible plot, sketch the main characters, making sure that the hero should not be too well-known while ensuring the presence of some famous historical characters. Then he instructed his researchers to find out more about the place, the castle, the furniture and food of the period selected.[63] Dumas had what the French later called a '*nègre*', a virtual co-writer whose name did not appear on the cover (probably a racist reference to Dumas's grandmother, a black woman from Santo Domingo). The 'nègre' was Auguste Maquet, a history teacher whom Dumas met in 1840. Apparently Maquet gave or sold Dumas the plot of a novel. Dumas wrote it up, called it *Le Chevalier d'Harmental*, added his name to that of Maquet and took it to Girardin, hoping he would serialise it in *La Presse*. Girardin told him that 'a *roman feuilleton* signed Dumas is worth three francs per line, one signed Dumas *and* Maquet would not sell for more than 1.5 francs'.[64] Dumas and Maquet found this a compelling argument, though as it turned out it was not *La Presse* but *Le Siècle* which published *Le Chevalier d'Harmental* in 1841.

From 1841 to 1851, Maquet cooperated openly with Dumas, who acknowledged that Maquet's suggestions had been decisive in shaping major novels like *Le Comte de Monte-Cristo*. To use such help, in Dumas's eyes, was nothing to be ashamed of: Renaissance masters like Raphael had used talented assistants, so why should he not do the same? Dumas himself had assisted a Swedish aristocrat, Adolphe de Leuven, in the writing of comedies. It had been a form of apprenticeship.[65] Maquet's tasks were research, to bring to Dumas's attention lost memoirs such as those of d'Artagnan, and occasionally to provide a plot outline. However, Maquet was no Dumas. After they separated in 1851 he wrote several novels – none successful, all forgotten. Nevertheless, Dumas's best-known novels were all written in the ten years of co-operation with Maquet: *Le Comte de Monte-Cristo* (1844), *Les Trois mousquetaires* (1844), *Vingt ans après* (1845), *La Reine Margot* (1845), *Le Chevalier de Maison-Rouge* (1846) and *Le Collier de la reine* (1849).

The production line was impressive. Dumas is reputed to have written 650 novels, with 4,056 main characters and 8,872 minor ones.[66] This is probably an exaggeration: the 1935 *Bibliographie des auteurs modernes (1801–1934)* by Hector Talvart and Joseph Place lists 212 works, and this includes theatrical adaptations.[67] Since then, several Dumas novels have been discovered. Whatever the exact figure, it is evident that his output was enormous. He claimed to write almost 5,000 words a day, every day. In March 1844 *Les Trois mousquetaires* began serialisation in the *Le Siècle*, while *Une Fille du régent* kicked off in *Le Commerce*. In June of the same year the first of the 139 instalments of *Le Comte de Monte-Cristo* appeared in the *Journal des débats*. By the end of the year *La Presse* began the serialisation of *La Reine Margot*. And there were more, including a collection of short stories.[68] This massive production caused envy. In 1845 Eugène de Mirecourt wrote a pamphlet significantly entitled *Fabrique de Roman: Maison A. Dumas et compagnie*, which accused Dumas of being little more than a brand name, a signature for books written by others. The pamphleteer was condemned for slander in the courts, while the literary world rallied round Dumas. The practice of using assistants and co-writers was widespread, though it is most unlikely that Dumas used seventy-three collaborators, as Charles Louandre alleged in 1847.[69]

Dumas continued to make money, but failed – like Balzac – to be accepted as a member of the Académie Française. Delphine Girardin explained why in *La Presse* of 24 February 1845: had he written only one book – small, mediocre and unread – he might have had a chance. Too much luggage is an obstacle to entering the Academy.[70] Dumas would have been somewhat relieved that in 2002, even though the celebrations for the bicentenary of his birth were overshadowed by those for his exact contemporary Victor Hugo, his mortal remains were laid to rest in the Panthéon near those of Rousseau, Voltaire, Hugo and the other representatives of French high culture. In his speech the President of the Republic, Jacques Chirac, paid tribute to Dumas's contribution to the creation of a collective historical memory, and disparaged those (historians and similar pedants, presumably) who wasted time trying to find mistakes in his works: 'Throughout the world the Comte de Monte Cristo symbolises revenge and redemption. Dumas's heroes are like those of Rabelais, Cervantes and Shakespeare.'[71]

Le Comte de Monte-Cristo came out in book form in 1845. Then, with the loyal Maquet, Dumas turned the book into a play in four lengthy parts, the first two of which were first performed in 1848 in Paris (the Revolution impeded a longer run) and then in London. Dumas must have earned at least 150,000 francs from the serialisation alone. Had he been able to benefit from the subsequent sales he would have been far, far richer. *Monte-Cristo* turned out to be one of the most translated novels ever, and one of the most widely adapted to the stage and the cinema. It generated eighty-four pastiches and adaptations, mainly in the twentieth century, as well as forty-five sequels, including *The New Monte-Cristo* by G. W. M. Reynolds (1871), *Mathias Sandorf* by Jules Verne (1885), *An American Monte Cristo* by Julian Hawthorne (1893) and, last but not least, *The Stars' Tennis Balls* by Stephen Fry (2000), in which the hero, after years in a mental asylum, returns at the head of a powerful dot.com company under the pseudonym of Simon Cotter (an anagram of 'Monte-Cristo') to wreak revenge on those who have wronged him.[72]

The construction of the story, however rambling, was a real *tour de force*. Its dominating theme is that of the wronged man who returns, rich and prosperous, to revenge himself: everyone's secret dream. In the first part, Edmond Dantés, a simple sailor, a man of the people, is unjustly accused by evil people who use cunning and trickery to have him thrown into jail. There he meets the Abbot Faria, a surrogate father who gives him an education, and (by dying) provides him with the means of escape and the secret of a buried treasure on the island of Montecristo, off the coast of Italy, not far from Elba, where Napoleon had been exiled before Waterloo. Now Dantés can be born again. He assumes a new identity (another cherished dream of many) and becomes the Count of Monte-Cristo.[73] Much of the rest of the book is an informed account of the vices and follies in financial and military circles during the post-Napoleonic Restoration. *Le Comte de Monte-Cristo* immediately became a cult book. Dumas claimed that tourists asked to visit the Château d'If, where Faria and Dantés were held prisoner, to be shown the spot from where Dantés was thrown into the waters, and bought memorabilia from guides, including pens allegedly made by the Faria.[74] The novel even found its way in 'high' culture: the heroine Mercedes – so loved by the Count – is an obsession of Stephen Dedalus in James Joyce's *Portrait of the Artist as a Young Man* (1914–15), as is the Count himself: 'The figure of that dark avenger stood forth in his mind for whatever he had heard or divined in childhood of the strange and terrible.'[75]

Other books by Dumas were far less successful. *Les Mohicans de Paris*, a title suggesting both Sue and Fenimore Cooper, the longest of his novels (nearly 3,000 pages), was serialised for five years (1854–59) but was almost unread when published in book form, and was not reprinted between 1907 and 1976. The historical novel *La San Felice* (1,640 pages) was not even published in book form after its serialisation in *La Presse* (1863–65). Not until 130 years later did Gallimard achieve a success of a sort by republishing it for Christmas 1996. Nevertheless *La San Felice* made 30,000 francs for Dumas – which may explain its length, since the longer the serialisation the more he was paid. Never one to waste work, Dumas had also published the research for *La San Felice* as a book under the title *Histoire des Bourbons de Naples*.

Like all true professional writers, Dumas was proud of his money-making capacity. His open letter to the electorate when he stood as a parliamentary candidate in the Seine and Oise in 1848 could have been written by an industrialist. He informed the voters that in the course of the preceding twenty years he had written four hundred books, each of which sold for five francs, generating an income of 11,853,600 francs for printers and publishers. To that should be added the 4,580,000 francs earned by lending libraries and the 2,400,000 francs earned by the booksellers. He had also written thirty-five plays, each of which was performed at least a hundred times – a claim which he had certainly vastly inflated. Though the figures don't add up, the point Dumas was making was valid: without exploiting anyone, he had made money for others and entertained many more.[76] Be that as it may, he was trounced; he obtained only 261 votes, the winners had more than 70,000. Even Eugène Labiche, the author of many theatrical farces, beat him handsomely by 12,000 votes.

Like Victor Hugo, Dumas was politically committed: anti-clerical, anti-monarchist and generically pro-democrat. He concluded *La San Felice*, set in Naples during the tumultuous events of the Napoleonic invasion and the popular revolution against the Bourbon monarchy thus: 'For eighteen months I worked hard and conscientiously to erect this monument to the glory of Neapolitan patriotism and the shame of Bourbonic tyranny. Impartial like justice, be it as long lasting as bronze!' However, in general his novels wore their politics rather lightly, and while they would please those who thought like him, would have been unlikely to offend anyone except the staunchest of his political opponents. His causes were chosen with care, such as his support for Garibaldi and the liberation of Sicily. Virtually the whole of enlightened European public opinion (and even those not so enlightened) was strongly behind Garibaldi, undoubtedly the most popular hero of the nineteenth century. It was thus with considerable personal pleasure and the assurance of a lucrative market that Dumas travelled to Sicily in 1860 to meet up with Garibaldi's famous expedition as a reporter. Garibaldi, who knew a thing or two about public relations, welcomed him like a comrade in arms and gave him a luxurious suite in Palermo's royal palace. There Dumas wrote *Les Garibaldiens* – the story of the landing – then continued towards Naples alongside Garibaldi while filing his reports.

Dumas, while disappointed not to have been elected to the Académie Française, remained a modest man, conscious of his precise location in the literary hierarchy. He explained:

> Lamartine is a dreamer. Hugo is a thinker. I am a vulgariser . . . I give substance to the dreams of the first; I give clarity to the thoughts of the second. And I serve this double nourishment to the public who, if served only by the first would have been left hungry for more after such a light meal, and if served by the second would have suffered from indigestion after such a heavy one. But one such meal, spiced up by me goes down well with all the stomachs, from the weakest to the most robust.[77]

Dumas went down well with all stomachs, and not just those of the French. *The Three Musketeers* and *The Count of Monte-Cristo* travelled throughout the world in dozens of translations and adaptations, including Chinese, Vietnamese and Japanese. While he was still alive many of his books were translated into English, Spanish and Italian, and fifty of them into Swedish.[78] In Greece – a country with a high level of illiteracy – during the second half of the nineteenth century some *two hundred* novels by Dumas were translated, which means that a Greek reader born in, say, 1826, could read a new Dumas novel every few months or so until he reached old age.[79] In Spain (but not only in Spain) Dumas was regarded by the critics as being on a par with Hugo, Balzac and George Sand. *Los Tres mosqueteros* was published, within a year of its French edition, by four different publishers in Madrid, Barcelona, Málaga and Cádiz.[80] A flood of imitations followed.

Popular nineteenth-century authors enhanced novel-reading to an unprecedented extent. They also provided plots and themes for the theatre, the opera and, above all, films. The cinema had barely begun to develop the ability to tell a story when Dumas was adapted: in 1903 Georges Méliès produced a version of *The Three Musketeers* which lasted five minutes. He was preceded by the British film-maker George Albert Smith, who adapted Dumas's lesser-known *Les Frères Corses* (The Corsican Brothers) in 1898. Dickens and Hugo, Verne and Dumas also provided the literary education of many of the novelists who came after them, and instilled a love of books and story-telling in generations of readers.

23

Great Genres

The Victory of the Novel

BY THE MIDDLE OF THE NINETEENTH CENTURY the novel was no longer an inferior genre. There were, of course, many novels, perhaps the majority, that were regarded by the educated as little better than sensational trash, but the novel as such was perfectly acceptable. In fact it had become the most successful cultural product of the nineteenth century. Some of the causes of why this should be so have been mentioned: the spread of literacy, the expansion of leisure time, the greater availability of cheap books. But in reality the victory of the novel was almost inevitable. Is it necessary to explain at length why more people may want to read Wilkie Collins's *The Moonstone* rather than Kant's *Critique of Pure Reason*? Over the long term, however, the prize may go to Kant, should the *Critique* remain on university philosophy departments' syllabuses. His fate is in the hands of academic philosophers, and rests, ultimately, on the popularity of philosophy courses. The popularity of Wilkie Collins's works, on the other hand, will be largely determined by decisions made in film and television studios and publishing houses.

Comparing Kant to Collins is hardly a valid exercise. Their products, though similar in format (a bound sheaf of printed paper), are very different, and do not operate in the same markets. Kant does not compete with Collins, but with other philosophers and theorists for space on academic courses and for the attention of contemporary philosophers. A more effective joust is between Kant and Plato, whose *Republic* almost certainly 'beats' the *Critique* because it is shorter and easier to read, and because Plato is better known. Wilkie Collins also competes against other writers in his genre. And while it is true that some people may read Kant for fun, and others may read Collins because he is taught in courses on the popular Victorian novel, Collins is in competition not with Kant, but with other leisure activities. For most people, the alternative to reading Collins on a particular evening would be reading another entertaining book, or watching television or going to the cinema. The popular novel, when it works well, is a piece of entertainment which transports people into another world, making them forget their surroundings – as happens, in fact, to twenty-year-old Jessie in Collins's *The Queen of Hearts* (1859): 'What I want is something that seizes hold of my interest, and makes me forget when it is time to dress for dinner; something that keeps me reading, reading, reading, in a breathless state to find out the end.'[1]

While some novels are difficult and/or lengthy (and some of the most popular were lengthy), access to them is easy. They can be carried. They can be sent through the post. They can be borrowed. And one reads them whenever one wants, and almost anywhere, and one can pause whenever one chooses. Plays are never as available as books. Of all the cultural products of the nineteenth century the novel was the one which had the largest inter-class appeal, even though it was necessary to be literate – which is not the case for the theatre. Its market could increase, at least in theory, immensely. And, again in theory, everyone might eventually be able to read a novel a week. For everyone to go to the theatre once a week was impossible. Only the cinema and, later, television could offer the novel adequate competition.

But there are so many novels. How can one choose? Yes, there are favourite writers. But that's not enough. One develops a liking for a certain kind of novel, for a genre. Genre is a marketing tool, a shorthand description of the product offered for sale. It is not an analytical tool, and does not provide an adequate taxonomy. Besides, genres are constantly overlapping – as the list below illustrates. An erotic novel promises sexual descriptions, but it can also be an adventure novel, an exotic novel, a colonial novel, a detective story.

DEFINING FEATURE	GENRES (EXAMPLES)
Setting	Colonial novel, exotic novel, frontier novel (US), *Heimatroman*, rural novel, *roman champêtre*, historical novel, science fiction, *roman revanchard* (about Alsace-Lorraine), post-revolutionary Soviet novel, novel of reconstruction (Russia), *Ritterroman* (chivalry novel), *roman de cape et d'épée*, swashbuckling novel, Victorian novel, war novel

DEFINING FEATURE	GENRES (EXAMPLES)
Politics	Anti-military novel, anti-colonialist novel, anti-Semitic novel, feminist novel, novel of protest
Social	High-life novel, silver-fork novel (London upper classes), *roman mondain*, working-class novel, proletarian novel, *Räuberroman* (bandit novel), novel of merchant life (Russia)
Age appeal	Adult novel, children's book, novel of initiation (young hero learns the ways of the world)
Gender appeal	Bodice-ripper, erotic novel, libertine novel, pornographic novel, *roman pour concierge*, *roman pour midinette*, *romanzo per sartine*, *roman rose*, *romanzo rosa*
Where it is sold or read	Airport novel, railway station novel, beach novel
Novel of 'mass' appeal	Cheap novel, dime novel, penny dreaful, pulp fiction, *romanzo spazzatura*, *Trivialliteratür*, trash novel
Novel of intellectual appeal	Experimental novel, avant-garde novel, intelligentsia novel (Russia), post-modern novel, *roman à thèse*, *roman à cléf*, *roman engagé*, committed novel
Form	Epistolary novel, diary novel, first-person narrative, autobiographical novel
Contents	*Geisterroman* (ghost story), *Schauerroman*, Gothic novel, horror novel, hard-boiled novel, experimental novel, detective novel, *roman judiciaire*, invasion novel, mystery novel, *roman noir*, fairy story, fantasy novel, revenge novel, adventure novel, magic realist novel, modernist novel, satirical novel, techno-novel, naturalist novel, realist novel
Length	Novella, short story, blockbuster novel, *roman fleuve*

A mere glance at these classifications shows glaring inconsistencies. A ghost story can be erotic, or for children, and/or set in exotic surroundings, and may possess some of the traits of the detective story, and be epistolary and satirical and very long. The *romanzo per sartine* (Italian: seamstress novel) is a female genre, hence romantic and sentimental, likely to be read by working girls such as a seamstress, or concierge, or *midinette*, but a Jane Austen novel, though romantic and sentimental, is also ironic and set in rural England (without being a 'rural' novel), and, because Jane Austen is a canonical author, definitively not for *midinettes* or concierges, though of course some concierges are bound to enjoy them. The novels listed under 'where it is sold or read' need not be sold in airports or railway stations, nor do they require to be read on the beach: the term suggests easy-to-read, uncomplicated novels, suitable for holidays or whiling away the hours. It can be used to denote the kind of story being told (e.g. family saga), or the kind of audience it seeks (children's books), or the period it is set in (the past, the present, the future). Yet, though strong analytical distinctions cannot be made, the terminology used is often readily understood. This is so because a genre comes into being only *post facto*, that is, after a series of novels sharing similar characteristics are published. Franco Moretti, having consulted over a hundred studies on genres, provides a list of forty-four genres over 160 years in Britain alone (1740–1900).[2] A genre, as Edward James has explained, requires a consciousness of certain conventions, readers who have particular expectations, a kind of bond between readers and writers.[3]

Some genuine talent is required to fire on several cylinders at once. Elizabeth Gaskell's *North and South*, first serialised in weekly parts between September 1854 and January 1855 in Dickens's *Household Words*, then published in two volumes in 1855, is a significant attempt at such pluralism. In a recent Penguin edition it is described as a 'condition-of-England' novel: it deals with the differences in views, habits and beliefs between the industrial North and the South, and, unusually, it also deals with the class struggle between workers and employers.[4] But it is also a typical 'woman's romance', a genre in which the intellectually superior heroine meets the object of her desire, a richer but slightly flawed man, and changes him for the better. In *North and South* Mr Right (John Thornton) is a successful entrepreneur but a little uncouth, as Northern manufacturers are supposed to be, and a little heartless with his workers. The central task of the heroine, Margaret Hale, is to teach him how to be a real human being. This she achieves only when he loses some of his power by facing bankruptcy – in other words, when he is somewhat demasculinised. Contemporaneously Margaret, now an orphan and hence freed from family obligations, miraculously inherits a fortune from a family friend. Her wealth and Thornton's ruin enable the two to meet again on a footing of greater equality, and to be able to express their love for each other. In less skilful hands, we would be in classic Mills & Boon territory.

The establishment of a genre can be seen as part of a learning process, whereby readers and writers teach each other the conventions of what will later be formalised as a specific genre. One murder and the presence of a detective who finds the murderer do not make a detective novel. A series of novels built on the process of resolving a murder does create the genre. A single explicitly sexual episode in a novel may not make it into a pornographic novel, though it may offend the unsuspecting reader while disappointing those looking for a wider range of satisfactory masturbatory experiences. A 'proper' pornographic novel must follow the conventions of the genre as it has become gradually established: a strong sexual scene towards the beginning, to establish credibility with the impatient reader, before proceeding to a series of crescendos, with the most libidinous acts being performed towards the end. It should also have a plot, however flimsy, because even sex, on its own, can become rather boring. In the end a genre is defined, within limits, by the readers themselves. Some genres, of course, are more strongly identifiable than others. One could debate forever where the actual boundaries of the 'adventure' novel may be located, since the genre is vague and broad, and might include Jules Verne as well as Homer. But children's books and detective stories – both great nineteenth-century developments – have clearer distinguishing marks.

The Birth of the Detective

The detective novel is a genre that, since its creation towards the middle of the nineteenth century, has prospered constantly and continuously throughout the twentieth, while other genres, such as the 'western', so popular in the nineteenth century, have fallen by the wayside. A further treatment of the detective story will be developed in Part Four (1920–60), the so-called 'Golden Age' of the detective novel. Here I shall limit myself to a few remarks.

Strictly speaking, stories which have at their centre the search for the perpetrator of some crime have existed for centuries. Seen from a wider perspective, the detective is nothing but the classic 'righter of wrongs' of fairy tales. By some definitions Sophocles' *Oedipus* could be classified as a detective story, one where Oedipus, the investigator, hoping to find who killed his predecessor King Laius, finds out that he did it himself (and that Laius was his father, and that he, Oedipus, has married his mother). The imaginative twist – that of the detective-as-the murderer – was later used by crime writers such as Agatha Christie in *The Murder of Roger Ackroyd* (1926). With some imagination, many stories can be recast as detective fiction. The humorist James Thurber, in his short story 'The Macbeth Murder Mystery', sent up the genre by imagining a reader reared exclusively on detective stories, reacting to her first reading of *Macbeth*. Halfway through, she exclaims: 'I don't think for a moment that he killed the King ... I don't think the Macbeth woman was mixed up in it, either. You suspect them the most, of course, but those are the ones that are never guilty – or shouldn't be, anyway.' The real culprit, she confidently asserts, is Macduff.

Fairy tales in which clues are interpreted by uncannily observant characters provided further elements for the development of the genre. A fairy tale of Persian origin written down in Italian by Cristofero Armeno, a Venetian of Armenian origin, printed in 1557 and translated into French in 1719 by the Chevalier de Mailly – *Le Voyage et les aventures des trois princes de Sarendip* – has the three eponymous princes deduce that a certain camel, which they have not seen, is one-eyed, lame, and deprived of a tooth. The camel's blindness in one eye is evident because he eats grass from only one side of a track, although better grass is available on the other. The lameness is shown by the unevenness of its footprints, and the missing tooth from lumps of partly chewed food found. In Voltaire's *Zadig* (1747) the hero provides similar descriptions of animals he has not seen from the clues they leave behind. Pioneering investigators started to appear in narrative, for instance in *The Adventures of Caleb Williams* (1794) by William Godwin, while Eugène Vidocq, an ex-con who became the first chief of the Sûreté, the Parisian police, described his investigating methods in his semi-fictionalised *Mémoires* (1828), ghosted by Émile Morice and Louis-François l'Héritier. A spate of ex-policemen's memoirs followed: from William Russell's *Recollections of a Detective Police-Officer* (serialised in 1849 and 1853) to Thomas Delf (under the pen name of Charles Martel), who wrote *The Diary of an Ex-Detective* (1860), and Andrew Forrester Jr, author of *The Female Detective* in 1864. The French pioneer of the detective story, Émile Gaboriau, invented the detective Monsieur Lecoq (1868), whose name is an obvious allusion to Vidocq.

The idea of resolving mysteries by using clues was being used at the time in novels not normally regarded as 'detective stories'. Dickens in *Bleak House* produced a particularly determined policeman, Inspector Bucket. In Dumas's *Le Comte de Monte-Cristo* the abbot Faria reveals to Edmond Dantés the plot which had caused Dantés to be imprisoned by using clues supplied by Dantés himself. The detective story genre came into being only when a community of readers, writers and publishers began to want to read, write and publish stories which have at their centre the investigation of a crime, usually a murder. Edgar Allan Poe, often described as the father of the genre, did not, when he started writing 'The Murders in the rue Morgue' in 1841, realise that he was writing a 'detective' story. In fact he called such stories 'tales of ratiocination'. Nor did he respect what later became a convention, namely that there should be a murderer. His assassinated characters, Madame l'Espanaye and her daughter, were not killed by a criminal but by an orangutan escaped from a zoo. What was striking was not their spectacular death – quite normal in horror literature – but the omniscient investigator Auguste Dupin, who resolves the case by piecing together clues which had escaped less perspicacious people. The story was seen as a purely intellectual exercise, admirably fitting the spirit of an age in love with science and the scientific method. Poe's subsequent 'The Mystery of Marie Rogêt' is solved by Dupin entirely on the basis of deductions from press cuttings and police reports. Not once does he leave his home. 'The Murders in the rue Morgue' first appeared in April 1841 in the *Graham's Lady's and Gentleman's Magazine* (Philadelphia). It was translated into French in 1846. It certainly helped its success and diffusion in France that Poe should have set his mystery stories in Paris, with French characters, but there was no immediate spate of imitations.

What came to be known as the first modern English detective story, Wilkie Collins's *The Moonstone*, appeared only in 1868, twenty-seven years after Poe's rue Morgue murder. The novel starts like a fairy tale, the story of the curse of a large diamond (the Moonstone). It then develops, rather originally, as a story told by various characters who take it in turn to tell the tale, with the narrative continuing when one leaves off (a technique Collins also used in *The Woman in White*).[6] Thus we have several first-person narrators, all of whom are unable to solve the mystery, or even fully to understand what is going on. *The Moonstone* contains literary references to Dante and to the famous Klopstock ode used by Goethe in *Werther*, perhaps intended to amuse and flatter an educated public. The butler, Gabriel Betteredge, is constantly rereading *Robinson Crusoe*. Fun is made of various eighteenth-century classics, including Richardson's *Pamela* – all, Collins writes, '(of course) immeasurably superior to anything produced in later times; and . . . possessing the one great merit of enchaining nobody's interest, and exciting nobody's brain'.[7] We also have two naïve, baffled narrators who are objects of fun: the butler and Miss Drusilla Clack, a single-minded evangelist. Then there is what would become a classic character: the inefficient policeman (Superintendent Seegrave, a local Yorkshire man). Finally we have the proper detective, 'ordinary' yet highly professional: Sergeant Cuff – almost but not quite as all-knowing as his successor Sherlock Holmes. To add colour to a character who might otherwise appear little more than a detecting machine, Cuff is provided with a hobby, a passion for growing roses – a harbinger of Sherlock Holmes's violin-playing and Nero Wolf's orchids. Geraldine Jewsbury, reviewing the book in the *Athenaeum* (25 July 1868), thought it somewhat unsophisticated, but that its readers would 'devour it without rest or pause'. The epilogue 'redeems the somewhat sordid detective element, by a strain of solemn and pathetic human interest'. The reviewer in the *Spectator* did not like the 'detective' aspect either: '*The Moonstone* is not worthy of Mr. Wilkie Collins's reputation as a novelist . . . The making and guessing of conundrums are both harmless exercises of ingenuity, but when men of intellect engage in them they ought at least to succeed.'[8]

The interest in crimes and their detection was kept alive by the inexhaustible supply of real, or almost real, crimes regularly depicted in the growing popular press. The reporting of crime and the identification of culprits helped to popularise the characters of murderer and investigator. Thus Balzac based his *Une Ténébreuse affaire* (1841) on the mysterious kidnapping of a politician, Senator Clément de Ris, which had occurred in 1800, and used newspaper reports of the murder of Paul-Louis Courier, allegedly by his wife's lover, in 1825, for his novel *Les Paysans* (1845).[9] Wilkie Collins, in *The Moonstone*, used an 1860 murder case involving a sixteen-year-old girl, Constance Kent, who cut the throat of her half-brother and stuffed his body down an outhouse on the family's property.[10]

Studies of Victorian newspapers, mainly in 1840–60, have noted their obsession with the sensational reporting of sexual crimes and violent deaths. This included respectable papers such as *The Times* and the *Daily Telegraph*. The law columns of *The Times* were full of stories of sexual violence. In spite of its pretensions as a respectable journal of record, *The Times* was second to none in reporting rapes, especially if carried out by men 'of good reputation'.[11] Fenimore Cooper, as early as 1828, compared *The Times* unfavourably to the *Morning Chronicle* and to several French papers – 'its reputation strikes me as singularly unmerited' – and attributed this to the fact that 'this paper is treated as property, and that it looks to circulation more than to principles, humouring prejudices with a view to popularity'.[12] To achieve such popularity, the French and British press mimicked novels (just as novelists took their inspiration from newspaper reports), fitting real people into the character roles made popular in fiction. The opportunity to transform a thief or a murderer into a master criminal, thus effectively glamorising him, was seldom missed, and criminals such as the murderer Pierre-François Lacenaire, executed in Paris in 1836, were made into celebrities. What is now regarded as a distinct genre – the detective novel – was thus generically commingled with hundreds of so-called sensational novels, loosely defined as those dependent on rapes, suicides, murders and other mysterious happenings, often set in long corridors and dark stairways. The Gothic antecedents – minus the supernatural – are only too obvious.[13]

Though the respectable middle classes pretended to be alarmed by the popularity of the 'sensational' novel, they read it themselves. In any case, the boundaries of the genre were porous. It could easily include the penny dreadfuls, but also the sensational novels of Wilkie Collins and Charles Dickens. Collins was perfectly aware of the enormous potential this new market presented. In an article written in 1858 ('The Unknown Public') he praised this new literature: 'To the penny journals of the present time belongs the credit of having discovered a new public . . . An immense public has been discovered; the next thing to be done is, in a literal sense, to teach that public how to read . . . the future of English fiction may rest with this Unknown Public, which is now waiting to be taught the difference between a good book and a bad. It is probably a question of time only.'[14]

A major factor in the ascendancy of the detective story was the participation of readers, which was invoked at the outset of the story by providing ways, including the dissemination of clues, in which they could join in the investigation and find the culprit.[15] Though some regard this genre as pure escapism (a rather subjective category, as it is perfectly possible to 'escape' into War and Peace, or to read Proust on the beach), the reader is compelled to be as attentive as a literary critic. There can be no skipping. Every detail counts, however ordinary, since it may be a vital clue. This goes a long way towards explaining why the crime novel, of all the so-called popular genres, is the most celebrated among the educated élites – unlike women's romance or the adventure story. Wilkie Collins's The Woman in White (a mystery rather than a detective novel) was hailed by Thackeray, Dickens, Henry James, and even T.S. Eliot. It was celebrated in France and Germany, where it was immediately translated, though it elicited little academic interest until recently. In Russia and subsequently in the Soviet Union it was a constant best-seller, second only to The Moonstone (Lunnyi kamen'), which had thirty-five editions between 1868 and 1992 and sold well over two million copies. Soviet critics, perhaps seeking some popularity themselves, had decided that Collins, in spite of his 'flat characters' and his books' purely entertaining nature (the view of the Soviet Encyclopaedia), was socially concerned and progressive.[16] By the 1860s The Woman in White had acquired cult status, as demonstrated by the merchandising: 'Woman in White' bonnets, cloaks, perfumes and even waltzes and quadrilles. Cartoons showed people staying up all night to read it.[17]

Edgar Allan Poe too was regarded an 'enormously talented' by highbrow writers such as Dostoevsky. Baudelaire championed him in France, providing a major impetus for his fame in Europe. Poe, who died in 1849, was available in French in 1857, and in Russian (translated from the French translation) in 1858 and Hungarian in 1862.[18] George Bernard Shaw thought that Poe's 'Ligea' (not a detective story) was 'one of the wonders of literature . . . unparalleled and unapproached'.[19] T.S. Eliot, in a lecture delivered in 1948, said: 'So far as detective fiction is concerned, nearly everything can be traced to two authors: Poe and Wilkie Collins. The efficient professional policeman originates with Collins, the brilliant and eccentric amateur with Poe.'[20] Even the Goncourt brothers, so reluctant to praise anyone, hailed Poe as belonging to a new literary world, a precursor of the literature of the twentieth century.[21]

A further important element in the growth of the detective story was that it provided future authors with a formula which aided the vast production of substantially similar works. This framework is more clearly established than those of most other genres. A murder has to be committed in the first chapter or so. Then an investigator has to examine the clues left, and interrogate witnesses, each a distinct character. The narrative is constructed around this frame. Writing a successful detective story, however, required remarkable skills, since the competition could be formidable.

One of the peculiarities of the genre is that it broke with chronological linearity. The detective novel starts with an event – the murder. Much of what follows is the historical reconstruction of what has happened before. The end provides an explanation that gives sense to the entire novel. Detective novels are often described as needing to be read 'at one sitting'; hence they are, conventionally, rather short. In order to construct the story and plant the clues the author must know, at least approximately, the 'right' sequence, that which leads to the murder. This is quite unlike the normal narrative flashback, where the apparently mysterious behaviour of characters is resolved when some event from their past is revealed. In other words, Poe could only have written a story like the rue Morgue mystery in reverse order because he knew beforehand that the murderer was an escaped orangutan.[22] Of course, it is theoretically possible that Poe, having got himself into a corner, had to resort to the orangutan because nothing else 'worked', but this is unlikely.

During the pioneering age of the detective novel, many of the elements of what became the genre were devised. The investigator's main quality is intelligence. Heroism and bravery are subsidiary. The truth is uncovered by the sheer power of detection – another reason why it is the intelligentsia's favoured popular genre. There is a world of difference between the kind of hero who catches the villain by physically overwhelming him – as did Old Captain Collier, the protagonist of some seven hundred dime novels published in the USA in the 1880s and 1890s – and the detective who does so by piecing clues together.[23]

For Children

Many books 'for' children were originally not so conceived, as if to underline the verity of Jacqueline Rose's affirmation that 'There is, in one sense, no body of literature which rests so openly on an acknowledged difference, a rupture almost, between writers and addressee.'[24] In the nineteenth century (as well as later) they were often simplified versions of books written for an adult audience: *Gulliver's Travels*, especially the first section, an obvious childhood fantasy about being a giant in a world of tiny people, has remained popular, as have *Robinson Crusoe* and *Oliver Twist*. Children's books were adaptations of classics, such as Charles and Mary Lamb's *Tales from Shakespeare* (1807), stories from the Bible, and fairy tales. The development, among the wealthier classes, of children's celebrations such as birthdays, name days, first communion, Christmas, school prize-givings, etc., provided an opportunity for morally improving presents, such as books, which doubled up as evident luxury items.

Of all the fictional genres children's books constituted, then as now, a formidable resource for publishers. In France in the 1850s the publisher Pierre-Jules Hetzel (who wrote for children under the pen name of Pierre-Jules Stahl) and his competitor Hachette launched imprints specifically designed for children and young adults. They had realised that successful children's books could easily outsell many texts for adults.

Here, unlike in so many other genres, French and British domination was not completely unchallenged. Not only were many children's fables adaptations from German and Italian folk tales, but one of the earliest examples of an illustrated children's book was *The Visible World in Pictures* by Comenius, a pedagogue from Moravia (now in the Czech Republic), issued in Latin as

Orbis Sensualium Pictus (1658). In Italy Carlo Lorenzini (1826–90), under the pen name Carlo Collodi, wrote *Pinocchio* in 1883 – the best-known book in nineteenth-century Italian literature. Similarly, in Denmark, Hans Christian Andersen (1805–75) became the best-known literary Dane. Selma Lagerlöf (1858–1940), who wrote *The Wonderful Adventures of Nils Holgersson*, the story of a boy who rides on the back of a goose, was the first woman (and the first Swede) to win the Nobel Prize for literature (in 1909). She was more widely read than August Strindberg. One of the few German writers of the period who was popular abroad was Christoph Schmidt (1768–1854), author of 'moral tales' for children. In fact, in the early nineteenth century he was, after Walter Scott, the most translated author into French.[25] Louisa May Alcott, thanks to *Little Women* (1868), became, along with Harriet Beecher Stowe of *Uncle Tom's Cabin* fame, America's best-known writer internationally. The Swiss Rodolphe Töppfer produced picture stories such as *Les Aventures de M. Dubois* (1837) which, by displaying a series of images with captions, was in effect an early form of comic strip, pioneering a revolution in children's literature. We owe *Heidi* (1880) to another Swiss writer, Johanna Spyri.

Children's books were obviously a rewarding market, since many major authors deigned to write them, including Charles Dickens, Rudyard Kipling, Mark Twain, Oscar Wilde and Robert Louis Stevenson. George Sand's *Histoire du véritable Gribouille* (1851) did as well as her most successful 'grown-up' books. In the nineteenth century Balzac was probably outsold by his friend Zulma Carraud (1796–1889), with whom he corresponded for twenty years (1829–50) and who, after Balzac's death, wrote a series of highly successful books for children in primary education such as *La Petite Jeanne ou le devoir* (1852).[26] Thomas Hughes's *Tom Brown's Schooldays*, a sentimentalised portrait of his school, Rugby, was from its first appearance in 1857 a great British, American and Continental success.[27] This celebration of the English public school system was enjoyed even by those who had the advantage of not having endured it. It reversed the negative images of schools as miserable torture chambers propagandised by Dickens, Charlotte Brontë and others. The tear-jerker remained a major sub-genre of children's literature, with the prize, at least in France, going to Hector Malot's *Sans Famille* (1878), about the vicissitudes of an orphan – a book that made children cry for generations. The top best-sellers, however, were fairy tales. In France the three great collections of Grimm, Perrault and la Fontaine sold huge quantities throughout the nineteenth century – Martin Lyons has calculated that la Fontaine's fables sold between 500,000 and 750,000 copies in the first half of the century in France alone.[28]

In France, in the official classification of genres used by the Bibliothèque Nationale between 1812 and 1829–30, there was no category for children's literature.[29] By 1840 children's books were listed separately from 'educational books' in the *Bibliographie de la France*. Between 1840 and 1875 there were 2,800 titles. But the real take-off occurred in the years 1872–90, with 2,050 titles.[30] This correlates with the expansion of primary education, which increased from 51.6 per cent of the age group in 1850 to 73.6 per cent in 1877, five years before it was made compulsory. By then the five million children in schools constituted a formidable market. In Germany too the most rapidly expanding sector was literature for children, including school books: 534 tiles in 1835 (5 per cent of total production) became 5,429 by 1914 (15.5 per cent of total production).[31] Thanks to the support of parents and educational authorities, books such as *Le Tour de France par deux enfants* (1877) and the novels of the Comtesse de Ségur sold in massive numbers. The effect of compulsory schooling, however, remains significant: it concentrates the market around a few 'winners' which become standard classics, read and reread by generations of children, who will buy them for their own children in turn. Middle-class French children before 1870 would read or be read to at home. Under the Third Republic they read mainly in a classroom, surrounded by other pupils, under the supervision of a schoolteacher. School books gained some of the market share previously occupied by novels for children. The Ferry Laws of 1882, establishing compulsory primary education, accelerated rather than initiated the shift towards literacy.[32] It has been calculated that by 1870 virtually all children in France were at school for an average of seven years.[33] This was part of a wider structural change, in which the social control of children was shifting away from the family towards the educational system. Schools and the family would dominate infancy until the advent of television considerably weakened the force of parental and school choice in the selection of culture for the young and the very young. However, well before such changes, children's books had become a major factor in publishing.

In France, as in England at the beginning of the twentieth century, one of the great best-selling authors wrote almost exclusively for children: Sophie Rostopchin (1799–1874). It is worth focusing on her story. She was born in Russia of wealthy aristocratic parentage. Her father, Count Rostopchin, had been the Governor of Moscow who burnt the city before Napoleon's advance.

After the fall of Napoleon he moved to Paris with his family, and in 1819 Sophie married Comte Eugène de Ségur and led the life of an 'ordinary' French aristocrat, producing eight children, of whom seven survived. However, she also frequented literary salons and men of letters – such as Eugène Sue. Sophie found him fascinating and his novels entrancing (her twin daughters appear in Sue's *Le Juif errant* as 'Blanche' and 'Rose'), though she thought she ought to disapprove of him. Eventually, perhaps encouraged by Sue, she sent her stories to the publisher Hachette, who was developing a fiction list alongside his well-established educational books. For five hundred francs Hachette bought her *Les Petites filles modèles* (1855), and had it illustrated lavishly. Her next work was included in Hachette's Bibliothèque des Chemins de Fer. This was the beginning of a series of great publishing successes, first in their serialised version, then in bound volumes.[34] Carrying the same characters from story to story, the Comtesse de Ségur created a world of her own in stories such as *La Santé des enfants* (1855), *Les Petites filles modèles* (1858), *Les Malheurs de Sophie* (1859) and *Mémoire d'un âne* (1860) – all extolling a model of social integration where children compromise and adapt to the world of adults.[35] In so doing she fulfilled the two central conditions for literary success in this genre until the middle of the twentieth century: children would have to enjoy the books, and their parents would have to approve of them.

It did not matter to Rostopchin's middle-class readership that most of the protagonists were little aristocrats with servants and large homes, and that the stories were deeply imbued with aristocratic and religious values. As far as the literary universe of the Countess was concerned, the French Revolution had never taken place.[36] Her world was one where there were only two classes: aristocrats, and their servants and retainers such as guards, priests and gamekeepers. The function of the latter was to look after the former, and to do so proudly and gladly. Though not all the children were good, all the aristocratic adults were. When they were not, it was soon discovered that they were fake aristocrats. Goodness is an aristocratic trait. Rostopchin departed from this world of children rarely, the most significant exception being *La Fortune de Gaspard* (1865). Gaspard, the son of a brutal peasant, wants to improve himself and become rich. He goes to work for Féréor, a factory-owner, and serves him with extraordinary devotion, his tasks including spying on his workmates, denouncing their mistakes and stealing their good ideas. His boundless servility pays off when Féréor (a capitalist who is as paternalistically benevolent yet severe as any feudal lord), who has no children, decides to adopt him. But there is a dark cloud in the shape of Frölichein (a grasping man who speaks with a strong German accent), a competitor who threatens to ruin Féréor. The only way out is for Gaspard – egged on by Féréor – to marry Frölichein's daughter Mina, who he assumes will be as ugly and despicable as her father. To make this possible Féréor gives Gaspard a sweetener of five million francs – half his fortune. Gaspard is finally rich, but at what cost! As it turns out, Mina is tall, blonde, beautiful, charming and, above all, deeply religious. Like a magic fairy she transforms her husband – hitherto servile, selfish and ambitious – into a Christian gentleman and a tender husband. Thanks to her, the entire village becomes an oasis of peace and Christian love. Mina (the only character of whom the Countess fully approves) shows that charity is better than the capitalist pursuit of profit. The factories now close for the Lord's Day of Rest when the villagers fill the church, instead of the cafés – which are driven out of business (there are always losers ...). Charity has tempered some of the soul-destroying features of the new industrial society.[37] The ethic thus revealed is that which dominated most children's books in the nineteenth century (and much of the twentieth): children are inculcated with a respect for traditional values of charity and probity, and a disdain for industrial culture, that is for capitalism.

The Countess had, understandably enough, a soft spot for the servant classes, and would get her publisher to send books for her own servants. But, realising that one should not spoil them too much, she returned those which were 'much too beautiful' for simple servants.[38] She reserved her deepest contempt for the bourgeoisie, whose political and economic rise irritated her. In her books, bourgeois families are regularly pilloried for trying to ape the aristocracy. As in many children's books, violence and sadism abound. Naughty children are regularly beaten: 'My arms, neck and back were all red from the caning,' says little Sophie in Les Malheurs de Sophie. The culprit is her stepmother, Madame Fichini, who far from being an aristocrat, is just a coarse Italian. Sophie complains to her father, who promptly grabs his wife, throws her to the ground and beats her till she screams.[39] Canes and whips, in the enchanted world of the Comtesse de Ségur, seem to be as readily available as ashtrays in the home of a chain smoker.[40] But whips were the usual instruments of chastisement for children in the advanced countries of Europe (Germany, France and Britain) throughout the nineteenth century and most of the twentieth. Children, familiar with the violence, cruelty and sadism of fairy tales and the Bible, were hardly surprised.

Almost everything in the stories of the deeply religious Comtesse seems to have been designed to offend the sensibilities of the progressive, democratic and secular French bourgeoisie – the loyal purchasers of her books until the 1950s. There can be hardly any middle-class person who grew up in France before 1960 who was not given one of Ségur's books to read. Many remember fondly the hours of leisure and fun spent with such books in the pre-television age. Could the secret of the success of the Comtesse de Ségur be that her books were the nearest approximation to a horror story for children? Simone de Beauvoir, in her memoirs, tells how as a child she had been forbidden to read one of Ségur's books in case it gave her nightmares.[41] A more likely reason is that the protagonists of these books were themselves children, and that the world they lived in, though ostensibly aristocratic, was closer to that of the middle-class readership than the world of fairy tales or adventure stories. Ségur offered something different: simple stories of children getting into trouble with adults, being naughty and being punished but always, eventually, forgiven. In spite of her deeply reactionary outlook and upbringing, Sophie Comtesse de Ségur was an authentically modern writer who did not write *tales* for children, but real *novels*. Therein lies her great originality. Her only true rival was Louisa May Alcott with her *Little Women* (1868). Alcott preferred to write real horror stories and stories of aggressive sexual passion, but these never sold as much.

The Comtesse de Ségur's major competitors – many published, like her, in Hachette's Bibliothèque Rose – may have been better writers, but when they turned to children they wrote fairy tales: Hans Christian Andersen, Perrault, the Grimm brothers, Maria Edgeworth (*Popular, Moral* and *Fashionable Tales*), John Ruskin (*The King of the Golden River*, 1841, a tale à la the brothers Grimm and a children's classic at least until the First World War), Thackeray (*The Rose and the Ring*, 1855) and Nathaniel Hawthorne (*Tanglewood Tales for Girls and Boys*, 1853, a reworking of Greek myths).[42] Ségur's originality made her stories difficult to imitate, which is why she survived and was constantly reprinted, unlike many of her fellow writers in the Bibliothèque Rose, such as the prolific Zénaïde Fleuriot (1829–90), who produced, between 1864 and 1890, ninety books in a new genre, the 'novel for young ladies'[43] – the ancestor of the 'chick-lit' of today.

The Comtesse was also a professional writer. Though too aristocratic to appear to care about money, she did. She accepted outright payment for her books, an immensely damaging financial arrangement, because she needed the money fast. In 1855 she got five hundred francs from Hachette for her first book, and eventually was paid 5,000 francs in 1859 for a trilogy. Perhaps someone like her, who had been given 100,000 francs for her twenty-first birthday, regarded all such sums as equally insignificant. Perhaps, unlike George Sand, she was just not a good businesswoman. In a letter to Hachette on 5 February 1858 she asked for five hundred francs that had been promised to be sent to her as soon as possible; she justified her request – which she described as 'strange and bizarre' – by saying that she usually gave her earnings to the poor, and that she had run out of cash adding, 'Vous savez, Monsieur, que dans une communauté conjugale, la bourse du mari ne s'ouvre pas toujours devant les exigences de la femme. . .' (You know, dear sir, that in a marriage the husband's wallet is not always ready to meet the wife's needs). Perhaps an avaricious husband and the desire to achieve a measure of financial independence were contributing factors in Sophie de Ségur's decision to enter the literary profession.[44] Even to obtain such independence she needed her husband's permission. He was reluctant to let her control her own income. She fought him for four years. He finally gave in, and wrote grudgingly to Hachette on 29 May 1859 letting him know he had authorised his wife to do as she pleased with her income from her works, and that the publisher could send the money directly to her. The Comtesse, who had just turned sixty and was one of the best-selling authors in the world, had finally come of age, financially speaking.

Hachette did very well out of the Comtesse de Ségur. Her twenty books (written over eighteen years) were published in two distinct editions, a 'deluxe' leather-bound edition with gold lettering, retailing at 2.75 francs, and a simpler one at two francs. Her books had a yearly print run of between 7,000 and 10,800 copies.[45] Over the next hundred years (from the mid-1860s to the early 1960s) Ségur sold thirty million copies.[46] No cult has ever been established around her work, at least nothing comparable to that devoted to Lewis Carroll, whose Alice's Adventures in Wonderland (1865) delighted grown-ups by its use of nonsense poetry (a genre pioneered by the limericks of Edward Lear in A Book of Nonsense, 1846), fantasy, satire, absurdity and layered complexity.

Children's books had to carry a considerable burden, since unlike books for adults, they were supposed to form the new generations, inculcating in their heads the principles of obedience, conformity and religious morality – in other words, they were supposed to entertain them while systematically brainwashing them. The general assumption was that children started life as little savages who had to be beaten or cajoled into shape. Children's books were subjected to controls which, if applied to other books, would be regarded as pertaining to a totalitarian society: they were controlled by the authorities, by the churches, by the schools, by the parents, and by an endless array of para-religious associations in the grip of a sanctimonious fervour. Children's books were often part of nation-building: in addition to absorbing morals and deference to parental authority, children were also supposed to turn themselves into little citizens, mini-patriots, proud of their country and its achievements.

The idea of educational books for children was an old Enlightenment concern which spread with accelerating impetus in the nineteenth century on the back of a rising tide of nationalism. Thus in Italy in 1833 a group of intellectuals connected to the Gabinetto Vieusseux (a major lending library and the focus of Florentine intellectual life) launched a prize for the best work to be used both as a reading exercise for children and for their moral education as Italians. The 1836 winner, Luigi Alessandro Parravicini's *Giannetto*, turned out to be one of the best-selling school books of the century in Italy. It was almost a mini-encyclopaedia. The high level of factual information, in a book aimed at children between the ages of six and twelve, suggests that it was addressed to adults too – indeed, the author himself, in a later introduction, suggested that the parents should read the book first. *Giannetto* was constantly revised by Parravicini until his death in 1880 – after which the task was continued by others.[47]

Far less educational but more successful internationally was Denmark's best-known author, Hans Christian Andersen (1805–75), whose tales are still widely read and turned into animated films. Andersen's infancy was inauspicious: his grandfather had died insane, his mother was alcoholic and his aunt kept a brothel; his grandmother, though, delighted him with her story-telling. The land Andersen was born into in 1805 was not the rich country it is now. During the Napoleonic Wars, Denmark had sided with the losers. The price paid was heavy: the British navy destroyed the Danish fleet before almost wiping out Copenhagen. Norway had to be ceded to Sweden, and Denmark's overseas market collapsed. The majority of the rural population was in poverty, and the educated classes turned inwards into a provincial 'vicarage culture'. At first Andersen tried his hand at 'higher' genres: drama, a few novels, many poems, and travel books.[48] In 1835, at the age of thirty, he settled down to writing his new fairy tales, producing a collection almost every year, and finally reaching a total of 156 tales.[49] Andersen did not want to write for children. He wanted to obtain the prestige of a serious writer for adults. Northern Romanticism had been his main literary influence and he wanted to be regarded as a Danish E.T.A. Hoffmann or Heine. Very attentive to anything that could make him famous or successful, and give him a glory he craved almost desperately, he travelled throughout Europe meeting aristocrats and men of letters, and spending a considerable amount of time entertaining them in public readings whose success could be compared to that of Dickens.

Though Andersen realised that children were the most likely market for his 'fairy tales', the actual title he gave his first collection was 'Tales Told for Children' (*Eventyr fortalte til børn*), with the implication, at least in Danish, that these tales would exist anyway, with or without a juvenile audience.[50] This, the first of many, contained only four tales. But they were enough to bring great fame to Andersen, and have become among the best-known works in the whole world, adapted in all sorts of ways. Initially the critics were against him: his tales were not real stories for children, they did not have an obvious moralising message, and some had an unhappy ending. But he was widely translated. The first Andersen stories in English were published in 1846, and included still-famous tales such as 'Thumbelina', 'The Little Match-Girl', 'The Princess and the Pea' and the tale of wish-fulfilment 'The Ugly Duckling'.[51] As the genre was regarded as inferior, translators continuously sought to 'improve' Andersen's tales, and many foreign editions bore remarks such as 'adapted', 'based on', or 'rewritten for the very young'. This, of course, may be a cause of their continuing popularity. In Denmark Andersen was not, at first, taken seriously. His tales were not written in what was regarded as 'good Danish', and he continued to write inferior plays and novels for adults.[52] Only towards the end of his life did his international fame make him famous in Denmark too.

Andersen's hankering after prestige by writing poor adult books instead of being content with the enormous success of his tales is illustrative of a wider problem in the hierarchy established in cultural commodities. When all is said and done, it is not the content of books (or films or plays) which defines their standing, but their audience. It is the social status of the reader rather than the quality of the writer that defines cultural status. Writing in a well-established genre, or writing for children or for the lower orders of society, may bring considerable wealth to the few who succeed in such a competitive market, but less prestige. Hence the impressive achievement of writers such as Dickens and Hugo, who won on all counts.

——— ❦ ———

24

Women and Novels

A Woman's Profession

THE WRITERS WHO, in the nineteenth century, produced books for the new reading public came overwhelmingly from the middle classes and the *déclassé* ranks of the aristocracy. There were exceptions, notably the Comtesse de Ségur (see pages 436–40), who probably sold more books than any other novelist in nineteenth-century France. Richard Altick has calculated that around 10 per cent of British authors of some standing had aristocratic titles, and 86 per cent were middle class.[1] In England these middle-class authors were frequently the children of vicars, doctors, lawyers and other writers. This was so also for many of the 213 women writers born after 1800 listed by Elaine Showalter.[2] Many of the male writers (but none of the nineteenth-century women writers) went to Oxford or Cambridge. Many of the more celebrated European writers were subsidised by their family (Flaubert) or their mistress (Balzac), or had inherited money (Baudelaire) or had some kind of sinecure. Some, of course, earned a good living (Zola, George Eliot, Dickens). Some obtained a small pension from the state. The highly popular writers who churned out dozens of books (hundreds in the case of Paul de Kock and Alexandre Dumas) at top speed did so because they needed the money.

How many women writers were there? This is not easy to establish. Marc Angenot has estimated that in France in the 1880s only 4 per cent of those who had written books were women, three-quarters of them novelists.[3] Probably this is a slight underestimate, because some used male pseudonyms. The percentage of British women writers appears to be much higher. Altick calculated that women constituted just over 16 per cent of professional authors (defined as those mentioned in the reference books he consulted) in the period 1835–70, and 21.4 per cent of those active in 1870–1900.[4] However, Nigel Cross, taking the *Cambridge Bibliography of English Literature* as an index of writers in good standing, has calculated that 30 per cent were women.[5] Using other figures, he estimated that women probably formed less than 20 per cent of the literary corps, and 14 per cent of contributors to monthly and quarterly magazines.[6]

Among popular writers there were ladies who had fallen on hard times, and for whom writing was easier and less humiliating than starting a business. In Germany, Johanna Schopenhauer, the widow of a prosperous Danzig merchant and mother of the famous philosopher of pessimism Arthur, went bankrupt in 1819. Luckily for her, her novel *Gabriele* had been published, and became a best-seller. From then on she produced one novel after another. Sophie Cottin had taken the precaution of marrying a rich man, but he died bankrupt in 1793 when she was only twenty. And so she wrote.[7] Fanny Trollope starting writing books because she had become the sole breadwinner of a rather large family. For *The Domestic Manners of the Americans* (1832) she was paid £800 – at the time a good deal of money. Over the next twenty years she supported herself, her ailing husband and her children by writing novels and books on the strange customs of Europeans, including 'portraits' of the Belgians, the Austrians and the French. She seems to have bequeathed her professional attitude to her son Anthony, who spent most of his life working for the Post Office, but also became an author of enormous renown. His autobiography, written in 1875 and published posthumously, as he had wished, debunked the pretensions of élite writers. Rather than lamenting the fact that he was not a writer of genius, or pretending to be one, he chose to glory in his 'industrial' writing habits. Inspiration, he explained, is not something one waits for, because writing books is much like making shoes; sitting at one's desk is no different from being a lawyer's clerk. As soon as he had finished a book, he would start another one.[8] His working pattern consisted of writing three hours a day, starting at 5.30 in the morning, before going off to the Post Office. He wrote with his watch before him at the speed of 250 words every fifteen minutes (the same speed as Dumas). He could thus write ten pages a day. In ten months he could produce three novels.[9]

In his autobiography Trollope never talks about his feelings, his loved ones or his personal life, but he regularly tots up how much money each books has made.[10] He reckoned to have earned between 1847 and 1879 the sum £68,939.17s.5d., an annual average of £2,154 – but in the peak years (1862–74) he averaged £4,500 a year.[11] To put such earnings in perspective, when Trollope went to work for the Post Office in Ireland in 1841 he made £140 a year.[12] Thus, as a writer, Trollope, working only three hours a day, was clearly doing much better than a successful full-time non-fiction writer and literary journalist like George Lewes, whose total literary earnings in 1855 amounted to £430, largely due to his *Life of Goethe*, which brought in £250. His partner Marian Evans (George Eliot), not yet famous, earned £119 from her own journalism; two years later she was making the same as Lewes. In 1858 Lewes was still earning £450 (a reasonable return for a reasonably well-established writer), but Eliot had gone up to £800 thanks to *Adam Bede*.[13]

Trollope was by no means the top earner among English authors. He was eventually outdistanced by George Eliot, who unlike him has remained almost constantly in the top league of the literary canon, regarded as one of the greatest English writers. As if to prove that it is not necessary to be dead to be great, Eliot's income went on rising during her lifetime, and made her publishers prosperous – though it must be said that the profits went up at an escalating rate after her death in 1880. Between 1860 and 1900 she was 'the engine that drove the Blackwood firm to profitability'.[14] The commercial success of *Adam Bede* (almost 10,000 copies were sold in the first six months) further improved Eliot's rating.[15] In 1859 she was offered £3,000 for *The Mill on the Floss* by Blackwood on the same terms as *Adam Bede*, but Bradbury & Evans offered her £4,500.[16] Blackwood successfully counterattacked with £2,000 for the first 4,000 copies, i.e. ten shillings per copy, plus the same for the next 4,000, plus £150 per thousand sold of any edition sold at twelve shillings, plus £60 for any cheap six-shilling edition.[17] Eliot's star went on rising. On the back of the success of *The Mill on the Floss* a new publisher, George Smith, offered her an unprecedented £10,000 for her next novel, *Romola*, to be serialised in his *Cornhill Magazine*. Eliot promptly dropped Blackwood and began to negotiate with Smith. The final deal was somewhat less than anticipated, and worked out as £7,000 – still the highest sum paid for a novel at that time.[18] As it turned out *Romola* was Eliot's least successful novel, and George Smith lost money on it – as he did with Wilkie Collins's *Armadale* (1866). Smith could bear the brunt easily because he had other far more lucrative businesses than publishing, supplying medical products to the government for the Crimean War and telegraphic equipment to India, and he made more than £1 million in 1872 on bottled mineral water.[19] When *Romola* failed to boost the sales of the *Cornhill Magazine* Eliot returned to Blackwood, who offered £5,000 for her next novel, *Felix Holt*. Blackwood was demonstrating a solid publishing principle: the utter futility of bearing grudges against authors who leave for higher advances.[20] *Felix Holt* did not do that well either, selling fewer than 5,000 copies in 1866, and Eliot had to settle for sums in the region of £4,000 for her two masterpieces, *Middlemarch* (1871–72) and *Daniel Deronda* (1874–76). Though her average annual income from writing was then less than Trollope's, Eliot had become a wealthy woman. When, after George Lewes's death, she married John Cross, they bought for £5,000 – the money she had made on one book – an imposing house set in several acres with a sweeping view over a wooded valley in Witley, near Haslemere in Surrey. Few writers today would be able to afford a house of that size on the basis of one's year income from one book.[21]

Money was not just made from new novels. More successful authors could benefit from the republication of their 'Collected Works'. The practice of selling rights for a limited number of years meant that a successful writer, who might have sold his early works cheaply, could eventually recover them and dispose of them at a higher price. The pattern for the top writers – at least in England – was as follows: first, serialisation; then the sale of a bound volume in an expensive edition (mainly bought by lending libraries); then the sale of a cheaper edition; finally the collected works.

Let's take a female author who represented the Victorian middle ground. Margaret Oliphant was a prolific writer (125 novels), much admired in her day and still in print today, though she has neither been consecrated by the literary establishment, like George Eliot or Dickens, nor acquired a cult following in the twentieth century. Like Fanny Trollope she started writing to support her family, her husband having died leaving debts and three children. She flooded the market with travel books, essays and a cycle of provincial novels, though not even her masterpiece, *Miss Marjoribanks* (1866), turned out to be a best-seller. By the end of the century it had sold 1,000 copies in the expensive three-volume one-and-a-half guinea edition, and 785 in the cheap six-shilling edition.[22] Yet Oliphant made a good living from her pen over many decades of hard work.[23] Her first successful book, *Salem Chapel* (1863), did sufficiently well to convince John Blackwood to offer her £1,500 for her next one, *The Perpetual Curate* (1864). This, however, did not do so well: the London Subscription Library took only five hundred copies, probably because the serialisation had not been a success. Blackwood then offered her only £1,200 for *Miss Marjoribanks*, explaining that the reduced sum was due to the disappointing sales of *The Perpetual Curate*. Oliphant complained that other, lesser authors (in her view), such as Wilkie Collins(!)

were getting much more 'for his present rubbish' (presumably *Armadale*, for which he had received £5,000).[24] The sensationalist works of writers like Collins, Oliphant declared disapprovingly, were 'novels in which women marry their grooms in fits of sensual passion; women who pray their lovers to carry them off from husbands and homes they hate; women, at the very least, who give and receive burning kisses and frantic embraces, and live in a voluptuous dream'.[25] No wonder Collins was earning more than she did.

Miss Marjoribanks was published in three volumes in April 1866, just as its serialisation in *Blackwood's Magazine* was almost completed. Blackwood printed just over a thousand copies at a cost of £667, and had sold them for 22s.6d each by June, nearly all of them to the largest lending library, Mudie's – further proof of the market power of the lending libraries. All in all Blackwood had made a profit of £333, not including any revenue from serialisation. Blackwood then printed a further 785 copies in a cheap (six-shilling) edition in August 1866, and sold 667 copies to Mudie's.[26] Blackwood's total profits on *Miss Marjoribanks* amounted to £666.[27]

Did successful writers such as Trollope and George Eliot earn more than a famous barrister or surgeon? It is difficult to tell. The almost £2,500 a year Trollope made on average does not include his journalism, nor of course what he earned from his job at the Post Office. It is clear that even at this level of success (Trollope was one of the richest authors of his day), money alone is not a sufficient incentive. Prestige and fame do matter. How did writers stand *vis-à-vis* other professionals? A study of French writers at the end of the nineteenth century examined how many writers had servants – the employment of domestics being a fairly good indication of bourgeois standing at the time. In 1876, 61.5 per cent of those listed in the census category of 'scientist, scholar, *homme de lettres, publiciste*' employed at least one servant. By 1891 only 44.3 per cent of them had servants, not because servants had become more expensive, but because the number of writers had increased, and hence the number of not very successful writers. They did better than teachers – only 17 per cent of whom had servants – but far worse than doctors and lawyers – almost all of whom had servants.[28]

A top *feuilletoniste* such as Ponson du Terrail earned 100,000 francs in 1866, a good year, and a still considerable 50,000 francs a year for most of the 1860s.[29] Much more money could be made in the theatre: Sardou, Labiche, Émile Augier and others earned more than Zola and Maupassant. Poets were the poorest among the literati, though Hugo obtained 3,000 francs for his *Odes et ballades*, almost as much as Balzac for *Le Père Goriot* (3,500 francs), and much more than the historian Michelet obtained for his 1831 *Introduction à l'histoire universelle*.[30] Balzac wrote to his future wife Madame Hanska in 1835: 'To become solvent, my huge production of books . . . is not enough. I must get into the theatre where revenues are far greater than anything one makes in books.' He was unsuccessful. In 1849–50 George Sand had far better luck: there were over a hundred performances of *François le champi*, an adaptation of her rural novel.[31] In France a promising author could receive between eight hundred and 1,300 francs for a first novel. One of France's top-earning writers, George Sand, could make 10,000 francs for one of her shorter novels.[32] But Sand was an exception. Flaubert got only eight hundred francs for *Madame Bovary*, while the top playwright of the day, Eugène Scribe, could get up to 4,000 francs for a new three-act play, one of several he would write in any one year.[33]

What emerges with great clarity is that writing, and particularly novel-writing, was one of the few ways a woman could make money. To become a painter one needed to go to the Academy, take lessons, draw nudes. In other words, enter an institution where one learned a craft. In the nineteenth century, of all the fields of cultural production, the literary field was the only one where a considerable number of women could make an impact and earn a living. In the visual arts they were relegated, on the whole, to the more modest and less remunerative role of copyists and illustrators. Women were barred from the professions: they could not become doctors, or lawyers, or judges, or bankers, or politicians, or senior civil servants, or officers in the armed services. There were no legal impediments to becoming an entrepreneur, and some made it in the world of business, but the possibility that a woman could be able to negotiate loans and make deals was slim.

While most middle-class women were taught the piano, they were barred from joining an orchestra, and were expected to perform only in the intimacy of their homes and for friends. Being on the stage, any stage, was frowned upon. Women singers and actresses came from a particular 'artistic' fringe, often the daughters of actors and singers themselves. This was the most remunerative career for a woman, and the luckier performers could acquire real wealth; but such occupations were deemed quite unsuitable for middle-class ladies.

There are always exceptions, and there are always reasons for the exceptions: good networking, or a favourable background, or an influential family. One of the few female opera composers, Louise Bertin (1805–77), was very widely introduced in literary circles because her father was the editor of the influential *Journal des débats*. She was a close friend of Victor Hugo and cooperated with him in writing an opera based on *Notre-Dame de Paris – La Esmeralda*, her fourth – which was accepted by the Opéra in 1830, having its first performance in 1836. However, being part of a network can be a disadvantage. The audience – packed with enemies of the Romantic movement and of Bertin's father in particular – booed her opera off the stage.[34] The music critic Hans Werner (pseudonym of François Castil-Blaze), in the *Revue des deux mondes*, thought she should have followed the feminine temperament and opted for Italian melodies *à la* Cimarosa, instead of trying to sound like a German composer.[35] Berlioz, who liked the 'Germanic' school, was cautiously favourable: 'Her musical talent, in my opinion, is based more on reason than feelings . . . but *Esmeralda* has some very beautiful and interesting parts.'[36]

What else could a woman do? A man, even a man without talent, even – as George Eliot put it – a man with 'moderate intellect, a moral standard not higher than the average, some rhetorical affluence and great glibness of speech . . . without the aid or birth or money', could 'most easily attain power and reputation in English society' by becoming an evangelical preacher: 'he will then find it possible to reconcile small ability with great ambition, superficial knowledge with the prestige of erudition, a middling morale with a high reputation for sanctity'.[37] But women could not become vicars. Unlike the Catholic Church there was no formal role for women in the Church of England or any of the Protestant Churches.

Having failed to find a husband, or having lost one, a woman could of course become a governess or a 'ladies' companion' thus maintaining the semblance of gentility without the full humiliation of servitude. There were plenty of those in Victorian Britain: 21,373, according to mid-nineteenth-century census returns. Finally, if they were desperate, they could always become schoolteachers (41,888 in mid-century Great Britain).

Writing was different. No particular training was required, no membership of a conservatory or an academy. But what kind of writing was 'appropriate' for a woman? As they were denied access to universities, women were unlikely to make a great impact in historical and philosophical writings. In fact, a considerable proportion of the range of non-fiction writing was out of their reach. Almost all that was left to them was novels. And write novels they did.

Some women writers were only too conscious of the risks they were taking in exposing themselves to public criticism – an experience for which no middle-class or aristocratic lady was psychologically prepared. Sophie Cottin, in a passage she deleted from the second edition of her *Malvina* (1800), has her character, an English writer, 'Mistriss' Clare, lament:

> In reality it matters little if a woman writes a novel as long as she labours in obscurity. It is not the occupation but its usage that is disapproved. If she entertains her friends with a little tale she has penned herself, no one minds; but in having it published she acknowledges that she thinks highly of it. And thereafter the critics can be severe with a work friends would have treated with some indulgence. By offering her book to the wider public, the author offers herself too. If she writes of women's weaknesses, such weaknesses are attributed to herself; if she writes of their virtues, she is taxed for pride; it will always be assumed that the passions she narrates are in her own heart and the situations she describes in her own life. Women run great risks in such a career and they need courage to undertake it.[38]

Women were well suited to provide a distinctive angle to the central theme of most narratives: the domain of intimacy or sexual and what one might call 'family' politics. By and large women wrote for other women, about problems that afflicted them and their class. This had been clear to women writers for some time. Sophie Cottin's Clare, in the passage cited above (also missing from the second edition), explained:

> I believe novels are women's domain. At fifteen they start reading them, at twenty they live them, and at thirty they have nothing better to do than to write them; besides, I suggest that, excepting some great writers, women are better adapted than men in understanding all the nuances of sentiments for they constitute the history of their life, while they are but an episodes in that of men.[39]

Cottin's concept of feminine difference had a distinctive pre-modern position: novel-writing was a feminine genre *because* 'Women have no depth in their vision, nor logic, and hence no genius.' It was really an occupation for single women.[40] Not surprisingly, many male critics agreed, some unknowingly countering Cottin's argument that women were more familiar than men with the world of feelings by pointing out – as did William Rathbone Greg in 1859 – that the 'lady novelist' knew little about sex: 'Many of the saddest and deepest truths in the strange science of sexual affection are to her mysteriously and mercifully veiled and can only be purchased at such a fearful cost that we cannot wish it otherwise.'[41]

Many women of talent will remember having received advice to desist from becoming a writer, as an occupation most unsuited to women. Those who proffered such advice included the then very famous Robert Southey (Poet Laureate since 1813, and whom hardly anyone reads today), who in March 1837 replied to Charlotte Brontë, who had sent him some of her poems. Though he liked the poems, he discouraged her from attempting to make literature her career:

> Literature cannot be the business of a woman's life, and it ought not to be. The more she is engaged in her proper duties, the less leisure will she have for it, even as an accomplishment and a recreation. To those duties you have not yet been called, and when you are you will be less eager for celebrity.[42]

Brontë replied, grateful for the advice ('I trust I shall never more feel ambitious to see my name in print'). Fortunately for readers of *Jane Eyre*, though, she did not listen to Southey.

With some exceptions, women writers were regarded as practitioners in a minor genre: women's writings. The polemic against the literary pretensions of women was revived by, among others, the painter and caricaturist Honoré Daumier in his satirical series on literary women, *Les Bas-bleus* (The Blue-stockings). Disparagement of women writers was not a prerogative of males, though women critics targeted their prey with greater precision. Willa Cather, a great American novelist, wrote in 1895: 'Sometimes I wonder why God ever trusts [literary] talent in the hands of women, they usually make such an infernal mess of it. I think He must do it as a sort of ghastly joke.' She added, in an unsisterly manner: 'If I see the announcement of a new book by a woman, I – well, I take one by a man instead.'[43] George Eliot, in her essay 'Silly Novels by Lady Novelists' (1856), lambasted a genre characterised by 'the frothy, the prosy, the pious, or the pedantic', and went on: 'the heroine is usually an heiress, probably a peeress in her own right, with perhaps a vicious baronet, an amiable duke, and an irresistible younger son of a marquis as lovers in the foreground, a clergyman and a poet sighing for her in the middle distance, and a crowd of undefined adorers dimly indicated beyond'. The heroine's eyes and wit are dazzling, pitilessly continued Eliot (who had a bad toothache at the time of writing this essay), her nose and her morals have no irregularity, her contralto voice is superb, as is her intellect, and she 'has the triumph of refusing many matches and securing the best'. Eliot's 'silly novels by lady novelists' had all been published in 1856: *Compensation* by Lady Chatterton, *Laura Gay* (anonymous), *Rank and Beauty* (anonymous), *The Enigma: A Leaf from the Chronicles of Wolchorley House*, *The Old*

Grey Church by Lady Scott, and other soon-to-be-forgotten novels much read at the time.[44]

Women writers could aspire to the recognition of their skills by the literary establishment. George Eliot may have offended Victorian morality by living openly with a married man, but she was widely recognised as a literary genius. Her fame spread abroad, but far more slowly than in Britain. Her private life was no impediment; her Englishness might have been. George Sand's behaviour was far more scandalous than George Eliot's: she was a feminist, perhaps a socialist, she occasionally wore men's clothes, she smoked a pipe, she had been the mistress not of one but of several men. Yet her genius was recognised by Heine, Balzac, Whitman, Dostoevsky, Thomas Hardy and Flaubert. Robert Prutz, the German playwright and literary critic, thought Sand was the greatest of all authors, not just the greatest female author.[45] Sand's influence throughout Europe was formidable. She inspired countless women (and not a few men), from Sweden's Fredrika Bremerto to Spain's Fernán Caballero (Cecilia de Arrom).

In 1831, when still little-known, Sand had gone to see a then fashionable writer, Auguste de Kératry – author of, among others, a novel in which a priest rapes a dying woman. She listened patiently to Kératry's theories about the inferiority of women and the impossibility of even the most intelligent among them writing a good book. 'Believe me,' he urged her, 'produce children rather than books.'[46] But Kératry's position, at least among men of letters, was not a typical one, as Sand herself made clear.

Many novels written by women belong to a somewhat 'proto-feminist' genre. The female heroines were always delightful and virtuous, but the men were dastardly scoundrels, and they provided the necessary spice. *L'Ermite des Alpes* (1832), by Anne Bignan, is not untypical. This is the story of an unfortunate young woman forced to flee her incestuous father. She allows herself to be seduced by the wrong man. When he refuses to marry her, she runs away and is rescued from an avalanche in the Alps by her father (who meanwhile has repented and entered holy orders). But she is too ill and cold, and she dies. Her father then tells her story to an officer of the Napoleonic army who is busy building a road through the St Bernard pass. The officer is, of course, the seducer himself. He repents, and asks the father of the woman he has wronged to shoot him. But they forgive each other.[47]

Some of the criticisms of 'lady novelists' were the product of envy at the allegedly large financial rewards available to those writing for the lower end of the market – women writing for women. In 1855 Nathaniel Hawthorne wrote that 'America is now wholly given over to a d—d mob of scribbling women, and I should have no chance of success while the public taste is occupied with their trash.' He believed that these women were selling over 100,000 copies of their novels. This was an overestimate, but some did very well indeed: Maria Cummin's *The Lamplighter* (1854) sold 40,000 in the first eight weeks, while Hawthorne's *The Scarlet Letter* (1850) after six months had sold only 5,000 – and he had been quite pleased with that.[48] But, of course, Hawthorne could only see the successful writers, and not the many hundreds (men and women) who sold very little, deservedly or not. Nor could he see the many who did sell handsomely but did not make much money, a fate that presumably befell male writers as often as female ones.

Take, for instance, the publishing history of Ouida's successful novel *Under Two Flags* (1867).[49] Ouida was the pen name of the British writer Louise Ramée (1839–1908). The novel – set among French troops in Algeria – started being serialised in the *British Army and Navy Review* in August 1865. Unfortunately for Ouida, who was twenty-six at the time, and for her devoted readers, the magazine went out of business in June 1866, before the story was finished. It was taken over by Richard Bentley, but his main reader, the novelist Geraldine Jewsbury, deemed *Under Two Flags* immoral, and advised him to discontinue serialisation (see page 349). Desperate for cash, Ouida turned to Frederick Chapman, to whom she assigned the copyright for £150 in 1870. She was luckier with an American publisher, Lippincott, who gave her £300 and reprinted *Under Two Flags* eight times prior to 1903, but the novel also came out in no fewer than fourteen pirated editions without either the author or her publishers being able to prevent it. Meanwhile, in 1876 Chapman had sold the novel as part of a package to Chatto & Windus for £400–£500, without informing the author (as a publisher was entitled to do), who had to remain content with her original £150. Chatto, in turn, printed and sold in less than three years 35,000 copies of *Under Two Flags* at two shillings each (making a total of £3,500). Twenty years later, in 1896, they brought out a cheap edition at sixpence a copy, which sold 100,000 copies in two years. By 1900 Ouida's popular novel had sold 700,000 copies. In 1871 she had sold the rights for the Continent to Tauchnitz for a few pounds. It was read all over Europe, and was published in a French version by Plon in 1883. Ouida did not get a further penny from any of this, nor from the frequent stage adaptations – twenty, it seems, in the USA alone. The playbill for the first English stage production concentrated on advertising the lead actress, Edith Standford, and did not mention the author. The success of the story continued long after Ouida's death. Its best-known imitation, *Beau Geste* by P.C. Wren (set, unlike the original, in the French Foreign Legion) has been extremely successful since its first publication in 1924, and has been filmed three times. *Under Two Flags* itself has been filmed four times, not counting its many imitations. The second silent version prompted a new edition of the novel in 1923, illustrated with stills from the film. In 1936 Fox made a spectacular film version costing over $2 million and starring Claudette Colbert and Ronald Colman. Everyone seems to have made money out of Ouida except Ouida herself, who died in extreme poverty in Viareggio, on the Tuscan coast.

Denied access to education and the professions, women were virtually excluded from all non-fiction genres except those nearest to fiction: biography, autobiography and travel writing. Most – unless they chose the daring road of reinventing themselves as an emancipated woman – were also excluded from the literary circuits which had replaced the older literary salons (where women, at least in France, had held a leading organisational role): cafés and clubs such as, in London, the Garrick, founded in 1831 and still excluding women at the time of writing. However, even in countries where they were less emancipated than in Britain or France, such as Russia, women made considerable inroads in the field of literary production, even in non-fiction, indeed even in the unlikely field of military memoirs, as was the case with *The Cavalry Maiden: Journal of a Russian Officer in the Napoleonic Wars* (1836), written by Nadezhda Durova (1783–1866), who had spent nine years in military service disguised as a man.[50] Aleksandra Kobiakova's (1823–92) novels and tales about provincial merchant life were popular in the 1860s, while her first important novel, *The Podoshvin Family*, was meant to reveal the despotism and misogyny in a merchant family to the gentry, her presumed readership.[51]

Women of the Russian middle classes, and particularly those of the aristocracy, did not lead lives so remarkably different from the foreign women they regarded as their models: usually French, occasionally British, sometimes German. Praskov'ia Tatlina (1808–99), whose husband belonged to the lower echelons of the state bureaucracy (hence 'middle class' in the Russian sense, unlike the merchant classes who, though richer, were of lower rank), manifested her Westernising ambitions in her autobiography. She read Ann Radcliffe and the other Gothic novelists, and Théophile Gautier. She made her daughter Natasha read (in French) George Sand, Balzac, Sue and Hugo, took her to the opera, made her listen to 'famous pianists, Liszt and many others', bought a Wirth piano, engaged a music teacher and had her taught not only French but also Italian, and made sure 'she knew the history of France inside out'.[52] Such an education might have been a good basis for novel-writing.

The Presence of Women

Women writers, at least in France and Britain, were regarded as almost a 'normal' part of the literary scene. Elsewhere they were rarer, but not absent. In France, as early as 1769 a five-volume *Histoire littéraire des femmes françaises* was published in Paris by the publishers Lacombe. Literary women were sufficiently important to warrant a leading role even in popular novels such as Eugène Sue's *Clémence Hervé*, part of the unifinished cycle *Le Diable Médecin* (1856) the story of three women writers. One is Clémence Hervé, the heroine (Sue's alter ego), a socialist and feminist who writes a popular social novel called *Misères sociales*, is loved by her servants, looks after her home and her adored son admirably, and, being a widow, is unencumbered by a husband (who had been a distinguished historian); then there is Virginie, who writes audacious novels with titles such as *L'Amour au galop* and *Les Cinq baisers de Cydalise*, and who wants to seduce Clémence's son; and finally the young poetess Héloïse, who enables Virginie to redeem herself (also to write good books).[53]

It was accepted that the size of the female reading public was considerable, and that they read mostly novels. Many literary references seem to suggest that this is the case, though it could simply be the expression of a collective prejudice. An investigation of the iconography of reading – cartoons, prints and paintings showing people reading – seems to confirm the strong presence of women as readers. They are shown reading not only 'women's' fiction such as George Sand's stories or Goethe's *Werther*, but also manly stuff like the novels of Paul de Kock, Fenimore Cooper and Defoe.[54]

Much of the nineteenth century in Europe was dominated by the so-called woman question as much as it was by the social question – the two really being part of the same process of modernisation. While the literati celebrated the birth of the *femme fatale*, the Roman Catholic Church spent much of the second half of the century cultivating women as the strongest redoubt against modernity: it recast the cult of the Virgin Mary, promulgated the dogma of the Immaculate Conception in 1854, and developed the cults of Lourdes, where in 1858 a fourteen-year-old girl named Bernadette Soubirous (later St

Bernadette) had visions of the Virgin, and of the village of Marpingen in the Saarland, where in 1876 three eight-year-old girls also 'saw' the Virgin. The nationalists too embraced womanhood, reinventing the nation as the 'mother country' and facilitating the cult of Joan of Arc in France and the rise in Britain of Boadicea, who having led a revolt against the Romans in the first century AD was celebrated by Tennyson in 1859. The iconography of Mother Russia is a creation of the nineteenth century. In Greece the cult of Panagia (one of the names of the Virgin Mary in Greek, meaning the All-Holy) on the Island of Tinos in the Cyclades was officially recognised by the government in 1836, and was closely connected to the struggle for independence. It is still the most important place of pilgrimage in Greece. Socialist leaders (Bebel, Engels) wrote more about the liberation of women than did their counterparts in the twentieth century. In France the opening-up of state secondary education to women was seen as part of the battle against the Church for their souls and minds. Jules Ferry (then Mayor of Paris, later Prime Minister), speaking at the Sorbonne in 1870, declared: 'The Church intends to possess woman and for that reason democracy must force it to loosen its grip. Democracy must decide . . . whether woman will belong to Science or to the Church.'[55]

The frequent habit of women writers adopting either a male pseudonym or anonymity may suggest that the obstacles to being published, or at least to being read, were considerable. Of course, anonymity and pseudonyms had been used also by male writers from Walter Scott to Mark Twain, from Charles Dickens (Boz) to Novalis (Friedrich Leopold von Hardenberg), and many others, but only very rarely did a man adopt a woman's name – though transvestism and sex changes are far more frequent in men's fiction. There is actually little evidence that a change of name was necessary. By the middle of the nineteenth century the reading public was used to the idea of women writers. Perhaps what the women feared was the verdict of critics, often prejudiced against literary women. Marian Evans used the pseudonym of George Eliot in 1856 for her first book, Scenes of Clerical Life, and kept her true identity secret for two years, not because she feared that as a woman she would not get good reviews, but because she felt that a woman in her situation (living with a married man) would not be treated fairly by reviewers.[56] Dickens, percipient as always, guessed that Scenes of Clerical Life was written by a woman: 'all the women in the book are more alive than the men, and more informed from within'.[57] All the nineteenth-century reviewers of George Sand (and their readers) were perfectly aware that she was a woman.[58] Eliot had reason to fear not only male reviewers but also fellow novelists such as Margaret Oliphant (who did not use a masculine pseudonym), who, reviewing regularly in *Blackwood's Magazine* and the *Edinburgh Review*, had established herself as one of the foremost upholders of conventional middle-class values.[59]

Prejudice against women would not necessarily decrease the sales of their novels, since they were probably read more by women than by men, and anyway, 'ladies' novels' were often regarded as a low genre. In the eighteenth century novels were often published anonymously, the writer only admitting to authorship if the work had been successful. For instance, Fanny Burney's *Evelina* was originally written secretly and published anonymously in 1778. When it became a best-seller, Burney revealed herself to be the author and took her place as a leading novelist of the day, even to the extent of being welcomed by Samuel Johnson and his Literary Club.

The adoption of a masculine pen name, however, was common enough to suggest that various forms of prejudice, whether among critics, publishers or readers, did exist. Famous women writers who used pseudonyms included, apart from the two Georges (Sand and Eliot), for some of their books Anne, Charlotte and Emily Brontë (respectively as Acton, Currer and Ellis Bell). Delphine Gay (1804–55) wrote in *La Presse* under the pseudonym of Vicomte Charles de Launay, but fashionable Paris knew perfectly well that she was in fact the beautiful and clever wife of its owner-editor, Émile de Girardin. Daniel Stern was the pseudonym of the Comtesse Marie d'Agoult, whose novel *Nélida* (1846) has a character, Guermann Regnier, an impotent painter, who is widely held to be a representation of Liszt, whose mistress Marie d'Agoult was and who was the father of her three children. The best-selling German writer E. Marlitt was in real life Eugenie John. Ouida – as we have seen – was the pen name of the British writer Louise de la Ramée; in Russia Sofia Khvoshchinskaia wrote in the early 1860s under the pen name of Ivan Vesenev; in Spain Cecilia Francisca Josefa de Arrom (1796–1877), the author of *La Gaviota* (The Seagull, 1849), one of the first modern Spanish novels, wrote under the pseudonym of Fernán Caballero.[60] Women with literary ambition, as distinct to women who needed to maximise sales, needed a good critical reception. Readers were probably less sexist than critics; publishers, for whom what mattered was the market, were the least sexist of all. Still, clearly a feminine name was not an advantage except in strictly women-only genres.

In her autobiography, *Histoire de ma vie* (1854–55), George Sand explained that her first work, *Rose et Blanche* (1831), had been entirely rewritten by Jules

Sandeau, then her lover, so the publisher (Delatouche) decided to attribute it to 'Jules Sand'. 'I had decided to remain anonymous.', explained Sand, who subsequently decided to use the pseudonym for her next novel, *Indiana* (1832). 'The name mattered for sales ... Jules Sandeau out of modesty did not want to accept the paternity of a book he had not contributed to. Delatouche decided that we should keep Sand and that I could choose a first name. I chose George (with no "s") which was a typical name of the Berry.'[61]

Does the gender of the author make any difference to how they represent women? While it is impossible to generalise, it may be true that the depiction of women as either wonderful saints or scheming whores was more frequent among male writers, but the types emerge also in women writers. Charlotte Brontë's Jane Eyre is rather virtuous, for she manages to be quite religious, yet she is against bigotry and is potentially passionate. Dickens's saintly women pale into insignificance before his exciting and complex warped females – but then his 'good' characters of either sex are often just tedious totems erected for the genuflection of the Victorians. In *Dombey and Son* Florence Dombey is not interesting, the flawed Edith Granger is; in *Bleak House*, Esther Summerson's goodness is nauseating while Lady Dedlock is endlessly fascinating. As for Little Nell in *The Old Curiosity Shop* (1841), the last word on her is Oscar Wilde's famous remark: 'One must have a heart of stone to read the death of Little Nell without laughing.'[62] Dickens, however, knew his readers. The pathos of a child's death moved even a public not unused, given the infant mortality rate at the time, to children dying. Little Nell was soon joined by other pathetic Dickensian deaths, such as little Paul in *Dombey and Son* and little Jo in *Bleak House*.

Strong female characters were not unusual in novels written by men – but such women often belonged to the lower class, or were foreign, especially Oriental or Mediterranean, as if to mark their distance from the norm, i.e. from their readers. Alexander Pushkin's narrative poem *The Gypsies* (written in 1824–25 and published in 1827) has a familiar theme – similar to Prosper Mérimée's *Carmen* (1844) – a strong-willed and independent Gypsy has a relation with a man from a different class (an aristocrat in Pushkin, an officer in Mérimée) who kills her in a fit of jealousy.[63] The 'tough' woman, the *femme fatale*, the man-eating woman, acquired importance in literature as the nineteenth century developed: Ayesha in *She* (1887) by Sir Henry Rider Haggard (author of the better-known *King Solomon's Mines*), and Conchita in Pierre Louÿs's *La Femme et le pantin* (1898). In Romantic literature, the *femme fatale*, if spurned, often turned into a castrating female, the reincarnation of a mythological or biblical figure.[64]

The new *femme fatale*, unlike the wicked female monsters of the past – gorgons like the Medusa, harpies and the sirens – was not an ugly demon, or one sent by the devil to bring discord, to destroy cities and brew deadly poisons, as in the Middle Ages.[65] The *femme fatale* was beautiful, and perfidiously used her beauty to ensnare hapless men. These unfortunates, once in love, were enticed towards inescapable perdition, folly and ruin.

That love could make men mad had long been known. Ludovico Ariosto had celebrated in *Orlando Furioso* (1516–32) the folly of men in love. He had done so somewhat ironically – an indication that the genre was well established. But the women loved by Ariosto's heroes were innocent. Men's madness was due to misplaced jealousy; his Angelica is as blameless as Othello's Desdemona. In literature the obstacles to a happy union are usually other men: jealous husbands, stern fathers, cruel kings, selfish guardians, or the dastardly plots of evil rivals. Once the obstacles are overcome, and love has conquered all, a happy ending is assured. The beautiful lady inflicts no pain on the man she loves. She waits, more or less meekly, to be rescued.

Most fictional women were either whores or saints. But there were women of power and influence, wise women, educated women, sexy women, religious women, practical *châtelaines* who looked after the affairs of the domain while her husband was away on the crusade, heroines (Joan of Arc, etc.), voracious sexual beings, choleric and melancholic women, temptresses.[66]

The theme of adulterous women and their punishment offered a highly flexible appeal. The theme of the temptation facing women is, of course, quite ancient and well rehearsed in biblical accounts as well as in mythology. In the nineteenth century it offered an occasion to discuss sexual relations in a way which could be of interest to male and female readers: one could identify with the betrayed husband, the wronged wife, the lover and the seduced and fallen woman. As even the most upright and respectable person encounters, at least occasionally, sexual temptation, and is curious about it, it is not surprising that the genre should have been not only the staple of much popular literature, but also a main theme in the most revered classics of the nineteenth century. Major Victorian writers who sought the approval of the establishment touched on the theme indirectly. On the Continent it was possible to be more daring. Nevertheless, most of the renowned writers of the novel of adultery were men. The heroines, unlike their lovers, usually die: Flaubert's Emma Bovary and Tolstoy's Anna Karenina take their own lives, as does Zola's Thérèse Raquin, while Fontane's Effi Briest dies of heartbreak. Sue in Hardy's *Jude the Obscure* regards the death of her children as a punishment for having left her husband, while Tess in *Tess of the d'Urbervilles*, having been seduced – virtually raped – turns herself into a murderess, and dies on the gallows. Only in the twentieth century did the prospects for adulterers improve. Lady Chatterley in D.H. Lawrence's famous novel, far from committing suicide, continued to have, so far as we know, great sex with her gamekeeper even after leaving Sir Clifford.

Leaving aside the more cerebral women writers, such as George Eliot and George Sand, most of them, like most men writers, followed the established conventions. The easiest way to succeed in literature was not to offend or upset the readership. The female characters of women novelists longed to get married to someone handsome and rich who would cherish and love them – hardly a surprising wish. These heroines were never stupid, but however talented, were always ready to give up their future for a good husband and a family. An American best-seller of 1850, Susan B. Warner's *The Wide, Wide World*, which had sold over 500,000 by 1900, reveals the fairy-tale origin of many books by women: a much-abused heroine, orphaned and beautiful, thanks to her religious values and her innate goodness survives her nasty relatives and marries happily. Someone like Hawthorne, who did not seek popular success (or, if he did, went about it the wrong way) could have as a heroine (in *The Scarlet Letter*) a strong woman ready to defy convention, commit adultery and survive (almost unheard of in nineteenth-century novels).

In Germany, Fanny Lewald, having refused to marry her parents' chosen suitor, obtained from her father permission to write novels provided they were published anonymously. Her first major effort, *Clementine*, published in 1843, was critical of arranged marriages. She often touched on 'difficult' subjects including feminism, and yet was widely read. Some were less lucky: the German poet Maria Janitschek (1859–1927) published in 1889 (to widespread disapproval) *Ein modernes Weib* (A Modern Woman), about a woman who, having challenged her seducer to a duel, is mocked by him ('real women' do not fight duels); as a consequence he is shot (one can almost feel the wave of feminine cheers).[67] The eponymous heroine of Elizabeth Barrett Browning's novel in verse *Aurora Leigh* (1856) manages with some difficulty to resolve the conflict between her professional calling as a writer and the man she loves. Many of the heroines of female novelists are energetic and spirited, not necessarily because the writers were feminists – most were not

– but because they were energetic and spirited, having to tell women's stories in what was largely a men's world; yet in so doing they reaped greater rewards than if they had tried to write plays, fill a canvas or compose music.

25

Challenging the Trailblazers

Facing the French and British Competition

LONDON AND PARIS DOMINATED the production of nineteenth-century European novels. Half the total output was published in these two cities.[1] The French, when they did not read French novels, read British ones – and the British reciprocated. The lion's share of Hachette's foreign list was dominated by the likes of Charlotte Brontë, Dickens, Thackeray, Disraeli and Bulwer-Lytton. There were some Americans, including the great best-seller Harriet Beecher Stowe's *Uncle Tom's Cabin* (1852), which sold 300,000 in its first year and two million copies by the beginning of the Civil War.[2] There were also a few Russians such as Pushkin and Turgenev, but the fame of the other great Russian novelists did not fully materialise until the end of the nineteenth century.

In 1855, during a stay in Paris, by then lionised in France, Dickens sold Hachette the translation rights of the eleven novels he had published so far for 1,000 francs each, and future rights for 1,000 francs per novel. *Little Dorrit* was being published in London in instalments which were translated as they came out, so the French translation was published more or less at the same time as the original came out in volume form.[3] Between 1863 and 1963 Hachette sold 780,000 copies of Dickens's novels. Those that did best in France were the same as in England: *A Christmas Carol*, *David Copperfield*, *Oliver Twist* and *Pickwick Papers*.

The overall dominance of French and British cultural production in the nineteenth century depended on a multiplicity of factors: France and Britain's ability to produce cultural goods of prestige and popularity, their strong home markets, the wide influence of their language, the strength of their states, and, last but not least, the fact that many exiles from Italy, Poland,

Russia and Germany made Paris and London their cities of adoption. Giuseppe Rovani in his *Cento anni* (1857) wrote that '*Parigi è la capitale del mondo; anche senza essere francesi bisogna confessarlo*' (Paris is the capital of the world, one doesn't need to be French to admit it), adding that what gave Paris this role was not its size (London was larger) but its openness to outsiders of intellect.[4]

The subculture of the world of exiles was a powerful bridge between modern artistic and cultural developments and their country of origin. Books would be printed in Paris and London and then smuggled to eastern and central Europe. Thus, for instance, there was considerable printing of Polish books in Paris in the nineteenth century. Between 1864 and 1889 Wladyslaw Mickiewicz (the poet's son) published, from his print works near the Jardin du Luxembourg, dozens of Polish works under the imprint of Biblioteka Ludowa Polska (The Polish People's Library), in small format to be smuggled into Poland.[5]

As the century progressed the export of French books (in French) continued unabated, but their overall share began to decrease.[6] In part this was the inevitable consequence of the expansion of the international book market and of translations, and in part it reflected the decline of French as an international language and the rise of English. The number of English-speakers in British colonies increased at a faster rate than their counterparts in French colonies or areas of influence. English could rely on the systematic expansion of the English-speaking population of the USA, where immigration was turning speakers of Italian, German, Swedish, Russian, Yiddish and Polish into speakers of English. The French could still export to Europe's francophone areas – such as parts of Switzerland and Belgium – and to Spain, Russia, Italy and Latin America, where exports relied on the survival of French as a language of the educated élites. In 1868 there was still much truth in the critic Sylvestre de Sacy's boast that French literature was no longer just aimed at pleasing literary and philosophical salons, 'fine ladies' and the aristocracy, but 'also the masses, a population of forty million. French literature serves universal democracy. Our novels and plays shape the taste of ladies in Bucharest and Moscow. Soon they will reach China and Japan.'[7]

In the century of nationalism, readers did not seem to have problems responding positively to novels written by foreigners, set in distant countries, dealing with different cultures. Dickens's books set in foggy London were read in Lahore, Dumas's historical novels set in seventeenth-century France were enjoyed in Russia, Fenimore Cooper's *Last of the Mohicans* was popular in Berlin. Of course, there was no reason why nationalists should object: neither France nor Britain nor the USA could be seen as the oppressor of national minorities in Europe, that role being held by German-speaking Austrians in places such as Bohemia or the Veneto, by Russians in Poland and by Turkey in Greece. Thus the new cultural nationalism was open to the import of French and British culture. Besides, the various empires were relatively tolerant of local cultures – multi-culturalism is not a recent invention. Venetians under Austrian rule had their own press, and published books in Italian regardless of nationalist agitation. In Bohemia, after 1848, it was accepted that the language of instruction could be the mother tongue, whether German or Czech. By the end of the century, cultural nationalism had created a whole range of institutions there: the Czech National Theatre was opened in 1881 and rebuilt only two years after its destruction by fire in August that year, entirely financed by public subscription, which justifies the proud motto still displayed above the stage: *Národ Sobě* (The Nation to Itself). In 1891 the Czech Academy of Sciences and Arts was founded, and in 1894 the Czech Philharmonic.[8]

Hungary, a constituent part of the Austrian Empire, was a highly literate country with a thriving book production and as open to French and British influence as it was to that of the German-speaking world. The greatest prose writer of Hungarian romanticism, Mór Jókai (1825–1904), a professional novelist able to live grandly relying only on his income as a writer, was influenced by Dickens's *Pickwick Papers* for anecdotal novels such as *Egy magyar nábob* (A Hungarian Nawab, 1853), by Hugo and Scott for epics such as *Köszívü ember fiai* (The Sons of the Man with a Heart of Stone, 1869) and *Fekete gyémántok* (The Black Diamonds, 1870), and by Dumas, Sue and Verne for his adventure novels.[9]

In 1861 Romania was recognised by Turkey as an autonomous principality. In 1866 Carol I (a Hohenzollern German-speaker) was invested as hereditary Prince by the Sultan. The Congress of Berlin recognised Romanian independence in 1878, and in 1881 Carol was proclaimed King. The country's literary classes read all that the rest of Europe was reading, including Scott, Dumas, Bulwer-Lytton, Harriet Beecher Stowe and Dickens.[10] Bulwer-Lytton's *Last Days of Pompeii* (1834) was translated and published in Romanian periodicals in 1853–56, but extracts had been published in magazines as early as 1836.[11] Beecher Stowe's *Uncle Tom's Cabin* was published in Romania only one year after its publication in volume form in the USA, as part of the Romanian progressive *literates'* campaign for the emancipation of Gypsies from serfdom.

The translations were usually retranslations from the French. The popularity of these novels started a native genre, the *banditti*'s novel, such as those of N.D. Popescu, who recognised Scott and Dumas among his masters.[12] In so doing he was simply in tune with Romanian literary taste: a study of the main six lending libraries in Iaşi and Bucharest in the middle of the century revealed that out of 4,779 titles, 4,048 were in French, 481 in English, with German trailing in third with eighty-eight. The vast majority of the books (3,712) were novels. The best-represented authors were, in order of titles, Balzac, Dumas and Walter Scott.[13] Yet, as in much of eastern Europe, the notion of the novel remained hazy in Romania and its literary market narrow. Its most important literary journal, *România literară*, sold only five hundred copies per issue in the 1850s. The readers of novels read, overwhelmingly, French novels of 'high' and 'low' quality, often in the original.[14]

The difficulties in producing a Romanian literature were formidable. Until the nineteenth century there was not even a spoken secular theatre – as was common in south-eastern Europe.[15] What was performed was in French or even in Greek, since there was an influential Greek minority. Real Romanian theatre began in the 1840s with the plays of Vasile Alexandri, designed for an élite familiar with French literature. By the 1880s Alexandri tried to acquire a more popular following by producing progressive 'social' plays – often anti-Semitic ones in which Jews were represented as exploiters of the people and agents of the Alliance Israélite of Paris, intending to colonise the country on behalf of the Great Powers.[16]

In Greece the impetus for novel-writing originated in the popularity of foreign novelists such as Walter Scott.[17] In 1888 Yannis Psicharis (1854–1929) wrote a famous novel, *To Taxidhi Mou* (My Journey), in the vernacular, often regarded as the first literary prose work to be published in *dhimotiki* (demotic Greek, or the vernacular), and extremely influential. This late start was not surprising, since Greece had been part of the Turkish Empire for four centuries. The Greek bourgeoisie were mainly merchants who lived outside Greece in places such as Alexandria. Ancient Greek, unlike Latin, had not given rise to diverse languages such as Italian, French, Castilian and Romanian. There was only *dhimotiki*, spoken by the people and regarded as an inferior language. An attempt was made by the Paris-based Adamantios Korais (1743–1833), greatly influenced by French culture, to take the vernacular and 'purify' it by eliminating Turkish and regional expressions. The result was *katharevousa*, but it was never codified. After that *katharevousa* and *dhimotiki* alternated as the official language in schools according to the politics of the day. Only since 1976 has *dhimotiki* been used throughout the educational system.[18] Even the borders of the country were not clear, since 'Greece' had never had an independent existence as a state prior to 1830.

Sweden had been an independent kingdom since 1523, but by the middle of the nineteenth century 90 per cent of the population lived on the land. Sweden was one of the poorest countries in Europe, though one with a very high rate of literacy. Its language, in spite of affinities with the other Scandinavian languages, had a narrow base: in 1850 the country had only 3.4 million inhabitants, and Stockholm only 93,000 people (London had 2.6 million). This might appear to be a difficult launching pad for a thriving national literature. Once again the dominant influences in novel-writing were French and British rather than German. A large number of literary journals kept intellectual circles in touch with what was going on in France. The local intelligentsia discussed Hugo, translated Balzac, and avidly read Eugène Sue. George Sand was readily translated, but her feminism was regarded as too daring, almost pornographic. Yet Sand's lessons were easily digested: among the early fiction writers in Swedish were realist and feminist novelists such as Fredrika Bremer (1801–65), who was even read outside Sweden with translations into English, French and Spanish.[19] Bremer's *Presidentens döttrar* (The President's Daughter, 1834) was translated into English in 1843, as was *Hemmet* (The Home, 1839), which was well reviewed in the *Westminster Review*.[20] Another Swedish woman novelist, Victoria Benediktsson (under the pseudonym of Ernst Ahlgrén, 1850–88) wrote *Fru Marianne* (Madame Marianne, 1887), a kind of Emma Bovary who is happy with her husband (not so the author, however, who committed suicide).[21]

George Sand also had considerable influence in Germany, becoming a model for other socially committed women writers like Countess Ida Hahn-Hahn (1803–79) and Fanny Lewald (1811–89).[22] But Germany had too its share of urban narratives with their exciting mix of social concerns spiced up with crime and violence *à la* Eugène Sue. In the same year as Sue's *Les Mystères de Paris* was serialised in France (1842–43), Julius Eduard Hitzig and Willibald Alexis began publishing the highly successful *Der neue Pitaval* (*The New Pitaval*, trial stories inspired by a similar compilation of François Gayot de Pitaval, a Parisian lawyer). However, while Sue was read all over Europe, Willibald Alexis remained strictly confined to the German-speaking world.

The same can be said for one of the major German 'nation-building' novels, Gustav Freytag's *Soll und Haben* – translated into English as *Debit and Credit* in 1857. This is a saga involving the young son of a civil servant who becomes an apprentice to a refined and cultured merchant, his ambitious Jewish friend, an impecunious baron and a lawyer who initiates one of the characters in the arcane art of financial speculation. The bourgeoisie here is seen as the fount of culture and refined manners. The aristocracy is degenerate. The novel takes such a poor view of its Jewish characters that it is generally considered to be anti-Semitic, though the author regarded himself as a philo-Semite and took a strong stand against Wagner's attacks on Jews (*Das Judentum in der Musik*, 1869).[23] *Soll und Haben* is one of the few authentically pro-bourgeois books of the nineteenth century, a real defence of the *Mittelstand* (the middle classes). Slav Europe is described as a place that can only be saved by German colonisation. Poland is made to look like the Wild West, full of savages and bandits, a primitive and chaotic wilderness – the consequence, according to Freytag, of the absence of a national bourgeoisie. The model of modernisation proposed to the Slavs is the German, one that avoids a devastating revolution. When *Soll und Haben* was first published German nationalists like Freytag hoped the German bourgeoisie would be self-confident enough to establish its own political agenda (as had that of Britain and France) instead of aping the customs of the aristocracy.[24] The book had sold 100,000 copies by 1900, and 500,000 by 1925, the year the rights expired. It went on selling until the 1950s, then sales dropped, probably because of its anti-Semitic and nationalist reputation, though it was reissued in paperback in 1970.

Countries where the national language was also the national language of a major exporter of culture faced particular problems. In Belgium, French was the language of the cultural and political establishment, which used its connection with French culture to enhance its own prestige, to the detriment of Flemish-speakers, whose external cultural reference point, the Netherlands, was not a major exporter of literature. Consequently Flemish literature (books and plays) could not be used as an adequate countervailing force. The Belgian Walloon (French-speaking) élites, however, found it difficult to produce their own 'national' literature. Though their press was thriving, the publishing world had been traditionally devoted to reprinting, often illegally, French *romans feuilletons*. The major consequence of Belgian 'piracy', however, was to spur the French on to develop cheap publications, thus expanding their own production even further.[25]

The painter Antoine Wiertz (1806–65), in his 'Appel aux écrivains belges', drafted shortly before his death, complained that everything coming out of Paris was received with uncritical admiration, while without the sanction of

Paris, Belgian novelists or playwrights had no hope of achieving critical or commercial success.[26] Only in the second half of the nineteenth century did writers who could genuinely define themselves as Belgian begin to appear. In 1867 Charles de Coster (1827–79) produced an epic novel, *La Légende et les aventures héroïques joyeuses et glorieuses d'Ulenspiegel et de Lamme Goedzack au pays de Flandre et ailleurs*, which, though in French and written by a Walloon, had a Flemish hero; consequently it could be marketed as a Belgian national epic, though the highly popular tales on which it was based had originally been written in Low German in the fifteenth century. The hero, originally a picaresque, fun-loving character, was turned into a fearless fighter for Dutch freedom against Spanish tyranny. As it turned out, the book did better in France than in Belgium. *Ulenspiegel* seemed to provide a unifying theme because it was in French and based on German themes. But this bypassed the Flemish community and their national aspirations. Histories of Belgian literature were forced to start in 1830 with a series of chapters with soul-searching titles centred on the question of whether there was a Belgian literary identity – questions which are seldom asked by their French, German, English or Italian counterparts.[27]

Switzerland's problems were of a similar nature, with the important difference that all the main Swiss languages had important external literatures (German, French and Italian). Switzerland's most famous intellectuals, from Jean-Jacques Rousseau to Madame de Staël and Benjamin Constant, were commonly regarded as French. The best-known Swiss national hero, William Tell, was known mainly thanks to works produced outside Switzerland, such as Rossini's opera.

And the Germans? By any measurement Germany should have been a formidable competitor for the British and the French. By 1890 it had become the largest market for books in the world, its population having expanded since the mid-1850s at a rate of well over 5 per cent a year, catching up and overtaking France. The key determinants of market size had all been in place since the 1840s. Germans constituted the largest linguistic group in non-Russian Europe. By the end of the nineteenth century almost half of Germany's inhabitants were in urban centres, which is where most of the production, sale and consumption of books took place. Berlin had become a metropolis of two million people, Hamburg a city of almost one million, Leipzig of almost 700,000. At the time of its political unification in 1871 Germany had nineteen universities, against England's four, as well as numerous technical high schools.[28] In 1840 in Germany there was one bookshop per 32,981 inhabitants; by 1875 the ratio had halved to one per 15,850 inhabitants; and by 1910 there was one per 8,743.[29]

By the beginning of the twentieth century German book production employed over 100,000 people. In Prussia schooling had been compulsory since 1763. Literacy was almost universal. By the time of unification household incomes were higher than in most European countries. There was a considerable expansion of the *Mittelstand*.[30] In the nineteenth century, in terms of genres, Germany was no different from the other main countries of Europe. The best-selling sector was non-fiction, but fiction did well, and as the market expanded the popular novel – known in Germany with characteristic condescension as *Trivialliteratur* – came into its own. Within fiction, the sector which expanded the most, again in rough parallel with the rest of Europe, was children's and educational literature.[31]

Among German publishers there were an unusual number of high-minded people for whom publishing was a kind of educational mission. Inevitably this meant importing quality, a risky business, but less risky than trying to generate one's own. Thus in the field of popular novels it was safer to import the usual French and British best-sellers rather than publish unknown German ones (though later Karl May, author of German 'westerns' was very popular). The efficiency of German publishers, their broad and well-oiled distribution network, and the German public's appetite for books worked in favour of importing the fictional literature of the hegemonic countries. Thus one of the first major publications of Anton Philipp Reclam (1806–96), a Leipzig bookseller who wanted to publish the classics at low price, was the complete works of Shakespeare in twelve volumes at 1.5 talers each. Only in 1867, when he started publishing his monumental Universal-bibliothek of 'classics for the people', did Reclam dare to publish an economic edition of Goethe's *Faustus* in two volumes, for forty pfennigs the set. National consciousness among the *Mittelstand* had reached such a level that many felt duty-bound to have *Faustus* on their shelves (much as their British counterparts had Shakespeare on theirs). This turned out to be a successful enterprise. In four weeks Reclam sold 5,000 copies of *Faustus*. A year later it was enjoying its third reprint.[32] Reclam was shrewd enough not to produce only canonical texts (those the educated felt they should read) but also entertaining ones which, by being sold alongside the nobler specimens, acquired respectability.[33]

But German popular novels sold well only in Germany. The French and British markets were too saturated with their own production to make it worthwhile to spend money translating German books. As for 'middlebrow' books, the fact is that Germany did not have anyone able to compete with Balzac and Dickens, George Eliot or George Sand, Trollope or Dumas. Here Germany was a net importer. Anselm Schlösser in his *Die englische Literatur in Deutschland von 1895–1934* (1937) provides us with a statistical analysis of the popularity and distribution of English literature in Germany. Of the British authors born before 1825 and who died before 1890 Dickens was first in Germany, as one might expect, but the second was Captain Frederick Marryat (1792–1848), who after a naval career wrote successful sea adventure stories such as *Mr. Midshipman Easy* (1836). The other British writers who did very well in Germany were more mainstream literary names: Scott, Defoe, Swift, Bulwer-Lytton, Carlyle, Byron, Ruskin, Tennyson and Thackeray.[34]

The German novel was no match for the French and British, at least not in the nineteenth century. What of non-fiction? German historians, philosophers and scientists were second to none. One might expect that the country would successfully export these genres to France and Britain, and thence penetrate the rest of Europe. In fact this did not happen. In spite of the efforts of Carlyle and George Eliot and George Lewes, the British were not particularly open to German culture. Nor were the French. It is a characteristic of *hegemons* to see the world through their own eyes and not to trust anyone else. The French and the British knew other countries through their own travellers, historians and philosophers. In the ten years between 1866 and 1875, 80,000 books were published in France, of which only 665 were translations, that is 1 per cent. For the French, the only country which might have anything to teach them was Britain, and vice-versa. In France the most translated philosophers were British: Herbert Spencer and John Stuart Mill. Hegel was translated, but not until fifty years after his original publication in Germany; Darwin's *On the Origin of Species*, by contrast, within two years.[35] German theology was ignored while Cardinal Newman had six of his works translated into French. Comparative philology, a great German speciality, found a way into France's bookshops and libraries mainly through the works of Max Müller, who was German but had the redeeming qualities of teaching at Oxford and writing in English. When German ideas reached the French or British public it was usually via French or British writers. Ernest Renan in his best-selling *Vie de Jésus* cited more German theologians than British ones in his 1867 preface, but few of these were ever translated.[36] At least they were cited. Neglect was the more common pattern. Eighty-five per cent of the reviews in the *Revue des questions historiques* were of books written by French historians, the remainder being mainly British. If one wanted to know about Germany one needed to turn to specialist 'Germanist' journals such as the *Revue historique*.[37]

Russians and Americans

Russia offered a different story. The national market for printed matter exhibited sharply contrasting characteristics. An élite literature of remarkable quality developed in the second half of the nineteenth century, building on the achievements of Pushkin, Gogol and Lermontov in the first half. Alongside this high literature Russia absorbed foreign 'popular' literature in the nineteenth-century meaning of the term: works that were both entertaining and commercial, as they satisfied the taste of the new middle class as well as the existing élite. Here, as elsewhere, the French and the British dominated, but they did not prevent the growth of a Russian literature. There was also a third market, quite separate from the other two. This built on the *lubok* tradition (see pages 56–8): cheap books, folk tales, lives of saints, pastiches of high culture, simplified and adapted foreign novels, imitations. The huge gap between an advanced literature which was admired in the rest of Europe and a popular literature which remained unknown everywhere else was a reflection of the peculiarities of Russian society: advanced and backward at the same time. By the end of the century Russia was one of the most rapidly industrialising societies in the world, while remaining extremely backward in the countryside and devoid of a truly independent middle class. In other words, Russian cultural production appeared as the reflection of its general social stratification.

Not that the countryside was static, far from it. The emancipation of the serfs in 1861 may have disappointed the reformers, but it was not purely cosmetic. The new responsibilities devolved to the village (the *mir*) included matters of personal concern to all its inhabitants. Official decisions taken by their representatives had to be written down, while documents coming from the local authorities had to be interpreted. Literacy was becoming an important resource. The proclamation of emancipation was communicated orally, but everyone knew that it was a written text, signed by the Tsar himself, and that this text had to be read and interpreted. A simplified and abbreviated version of the proclamation was widely distributed in hundreds of thousands of copies. Peasants were encouraged to face change, and many were willing to do so. The prospect of a better future was no longer unrealistic. As a result they organised private schools for their children and sometimes for themselves, the so-called literacy schools (*shkoly gramoty*).

By the late nineteenth and early twentieth centuries primary education had become widely available to a majority of Russian children. Of course they only stayed long enough to acquire some rudiments of literacy; consequently the effect of schooling was more limited than in the west.[38] In 1897, the year of the first census in the Russian Empire, literacy was still very low among the peasantry, although it was relatively high among skilled workers and even day labourers (50–60 per cent), and even higher among urban coachmen, sausage-makers, bakers and waiters in restaurants, and highest of all among domestic servants (over 80 per cent). The literacy of the servant classes was noted as early as the 1830s by Gogol in his *Dead Souls*, where Chichikov's servant Petrushka, he of the 'big nose and thick lips',

> had a noble urge for enlightenment, that is to say, for reading books, without bothering too much about their contents: it made no difference to him whether it was a tale about the adventures of a lovelorn swain or simply a primer or a prayer book – he read everything with equal attention . . . He liked not so much what he read as the reading itself, or, to put it more precisely, the process of reading. . .[39]

It is true that overall only one Russian in five could read – a rate comparable to Bulgaria, Portugal, Romania and Serbia – but there were far more Russians than Romanians. The consequence was an upsurge in publishing for the common people by the common people, because commercial publishing was often in the hands of those of peasant or lower class origin who were familiar with their market. At first these publishers chose the same material previously diffused in the *lubki* literature: established religious texts, folklore and so on. Particularly successful were those authors who met the cultural needs of the peasant readership, such as Ivan Semenovich Ivin (1858–1918 or 1922), who under the name of Kassirov wrote and rewrote stories with titles such as *The Enchanted Castle or the Unhappy Princess* (1889) and *The Witch or a Terrible Night on the Other Side of the Dnieper* (1894).[40]

By the beginning of the twentieth century the material became increasingly secular. In 1912, religious texts constituted only 11 per cent of the total number of copies – roughly the same as in the West. *Lubki* subjects – chivalrous or instructive works and tales – declined from 60 per cent of secular works in 1860 to 20 per cent in 1910, while banditry, crime, science and romance increased. Print runs of 6–12,000 copies became common in the late 1880s.[41] In other words, Russia was converging with the rest of Europe. Distribution was still in the hands of itinerant peddlers, but the centres of publishing were, as in the West, the main cities: St Petersburg, Moscow and, to a lesser extent, Kiev.[42]

This popular literature was, as one would expect, largely for domestic consumption. Less predictable was the wider Continental appeal of Russian élite literature. Had Russia followed the pattern of, say, Italy, one would have expected a limited production of original fiction, since this could be imported from the West, and, at best, domestic specialisation in some élite 'protected' genres, such as poetry. In music one would have expected Russian production to be divided between folk music for the masses and sophisticated Western imports for the élites. The reality turned out to be completely different. Between 1830 and 1870 there was an impressive explosion of narrative and theatre. Beginning with Pushkin's *Eugene Onegin*, Russia delivered, on an almost annual basis, a series of literary masterpieces which not only satisfied the taste of its own middle and upper classes but also those of the West, and not only in the late nineteenth century (when the West began to discover Russian novels) but also throughout the twentieth century down to our own time. The roll-call of such production makes this point manifest:

YEAR	WORK	AUTHOR
1831	*Eugene Onegin*	Pushkin
1831	*Boris Godunov*	Pushkin
1834	*The Queen of Spades*	Pushkin
1836	*The Government Inspector*	Gogol
1840	*A Hero of Our Time*	Lermontov
1842	*Dead Souls*	Gogol
1847	*A Common Story*	Goncharov
1847	*Sportsman's Sketches*	Turgenev
1850	*A Month in the Country*	Turgenev
1855	*My Past and Thoughts*	Herzen
1859	*Oblomov*	Goncharov
1860	*On the Eve*	Turgenev
1860	*The House of the Dead*	Dostoevsky
1862	*Fathers and Sons*	Turgenev
1863	*What is to be Done?*	Chernyshevsky

YEAR	WORK	AUTHOR
1864	*Notes from Underground*	Dostoevsky
1866	*Lady Macbeth of the Mtsensk District*	Leskov
1866	*Crime and Punishment*	Dostoevsky
1869	*The Idiot*	Dostoevsky
1869	*War and Peace*	Tolstoy
1877	*Anna Karenina*	Tolstoy
1880	*The Brothers Karamazov*	Dostoevsky

The question of the backward nature of Russia had dominated its intellectual life throughout the nineteenth and twentieth centuries. Taking the West – i.e. France, Great Britain and Germany – as its model, the Russian intelligentsia constantly lamented, with considerable justification, the primitive state of its polity: an absolute order wedded to obscurantism while liberalism and democracy were emerging in the West; a largely retrograde agriculture with a barely nascent industry while technology advanced rapidly in the West; a primitive religious peasantry co-existing with a state-dependent bureaucratic middle class while the West exhibited a thrusting entrepreneurial and independent bourgeoisie and an increasingly educated and literate working class. The contrast could not be starker. 'Catching up with the West' became the obsession of all the élites.

Yet in the field of so-called 'high' culture, Russia could begin to look to the West without inferiority in at least two areas: narrative and music. Art and architecture would have to wait a few more decades. Two fundamental processes, one from below, the other from above, partly explain Russia's success in bridging the gap and achieving more than countries – such as Poland and Italy – potentially better positioned to join the leading Western nations. In the first place Russian popular culture, substantially insulated from that of the West not least because of its quite different religious basis (neither Catholic nor Protestant), provided rich 'new' material for its transformation into a nationally acceptable literature and music, unlike in either Poland or Italy, where the strength of aristocratic cultural models had kept popular culture at a distance. Italy and Poland had had their Renaissance, and this had created a chasm between the culture of the élites and that of the people. Not so in Russia, where there was no indigenous élite culture to act as a barrier between the people and the higher classes. In the field of music, Russian tradition, both folk and religious (the Orthodox liturgy) had little in common with that of the West. Russian separateness from the West acted in its favour: it provided a different and alternative soil from which a new culture could be forged.

The other great 'advantage' of Russian backwardness was an inferiority complex that forced its intellectual élites to become familiar with the most 'advanced' products of the West. Provincialism, the characteristic of the British and French élites, was not an option. Had Russia simply been 'backward' without knowing itself to be backward, it would have remained so: outsiders unaware of their status never get to see what is inside. But the Russian intelligentsia was profoundly aware of what they were: outsiders looking in on the unparalleled cultural development that was taking place in the West. The Russian intelligentsia was intimately familiar with 'the Other', the Westerner, and knew, painfully, that they did not belong to it. Russian intellectuals were classic insiders/outsiders. And there can be no better position for assaulting the fortresses of the dominant culture and mastering the game – as the entire history of post-colonial culture demonstrates.

As a national group the Russian intelligentsia was the equivalent of the Scots and Irish who transformed British culture (Hume and Adam Smith and Walter Scott and Swift – to go no further than the early nineteenth century), of the southern Italians who renewed that of Italy (from Campanella, via Vico, to Verga and Pirandello and Croce and Gramsci), and the Jews who, once they had shut behind them the doors of the ghetto, propelled themselves to the very centre of European and American culture.

The Russian intelligentsia possessed numerous other advantages. Though in a state of barely contained hostility towards its political establishment, it shared a common goal with the Tsar: to make Russia and Russians great. The political and cultural worlds may have been in conflict, but they fought for the allegiance of the common people – each trying to use it against the other. The Tsar relied on the religiosity and deference of the village to keep the city at bay. The urbanised and Westernised intellectuals, the petty nobility and the bureaucracy worshipped 'the people', hoping that it would emerge from its century-old slumber to reshape the nation. Nothing like this occurred in either Poland or Hungary, or above all in Italy, where the upper classes and the intelligentsia held the people and its culture in total contempt. The Russians embraced the most populist aspect of Herderian Romantic populism, reading and enjoying their own folktales, unlike the Italians, who were ignorant of their rich heritage and preferred importing the aristocratic tales of Perrault or the bourgeois fables of Grimm.

Russian populist nationalism pervaded not just literature but also music. Verdi may have been an Italian nationalist, but in his music he did not use folk tunes. Neither he nor the other Italian opera composers used themes from the rich tradition of Italian folk tales or privileged Italian history over that of other countries. The Russians were different. All of them, even the 'Westernisers', were always more open to folkloric influences than were their Western counterparts. If they could not discover authentically Russian-sounding tunes, they made them up. Of course, in a sense all Russian composers were 'Westernisers' because they were using the institutions of Western music, such as the symphony orchestra.[43]

The Italian intelligentsia did not have a language in common with the mass of Italians, who until well into the twentieth century remained confined in their dialects. The Russian educated classes, on the other hand, though often using French, spoke Russian, the language of the people. The ill-defined Western model which had been imposed upon them since the days of Peter the Great remained just that: a foreign model that reminded them of their own 'backwardness', their 'non-Europeanness'. This made the Russian intelligentsia ill at ease on the path to modernity. Even though they urged the rest of the country to follow them towards an innovative future, they affected to long for the old Russian ways. What these ways were was not clear to anyone, which is why everyone could fantasise about them. Yet such intense cultural conflicts produced over the next century or so remarkable literature, music, ballet, opera, theatre and cinema.

Russian intellectual populists were also staunch upholders of the indivisibility of Russia. The linguistic fragmentation of this multinational empire was not allowed to stand in the way of the cult of Great Russia in which both the Tsar and the dissident intelligentsia participated. Local nationalism had few supporters. Ukrainian was spoken far more widely than either Gaelic or Breton, but in the nineteenth century the notion of reviving Ukrainian and developing Ukrainian literature had no champions of note. And rightly so. Famous Ukrainian-born writers such as Nikolai Gogol, Mikhail Bulgakov and Isaac Babel all wrote in Russian, and consequently acquired an international readership. Those who used only or prevalently the Ukrainian language, such as Taras Shevchenko (1814–61, regarded as the national poet), Ivan Franko (1856–1916) and, in the twentieth century, Mykola Khvylevoy and Oles' Honchar, were barely translated or discussed, let alone known. The eventual promotion of non-Russian languages and non-Russian literature had to wait until the twentieth century, and came from an unlikely source: the Soviet state.

The United States provided a quite different progression. It did produce, in the nineteenth century, some major best-sellers: the tales of Washington Irving, *The Last of the Mohicans*, *Uncle Tom's Cabin* and *Little Women* – all of which achieved wider renown in nineteenth-century Europe than anything the Russians had achieved (Russian literature became known in the West only towards the end of the nineteenth century). The Americans also established a significant presence in 'high' literature thanks to Hawthorne, Melville, Dickinson and Whitman, but made as yet no impact in the theatre or music. American culture was then almost exclusively Anglo-Saxon, that is, produced by writers and artists of British descent; it felt itself subordinate to British culture, of which it was in awe. Culturally speaking, the USA was still a colony. It had not yet acquired the great advantage which would launch its cultural production to the conquest of the world, namely its diversity. The massive influx of European immigrants started only in the 1880s, and at least a generation would have to pass before this massive change would be reflected in the kind of variegated mass market which would reshape American culture. In music the Irish and Scottish influences were already making themselves felt, but not that of the former slaves, still too recently emancipated.

What the USA had, and Russia did not, was an exceptionally thriving popular culture, a huge, highly localised press, and a conveyor-like publishing industry devoted to the production of pulp fiction, largely 'westerns' – America's main indigenous literary genre. After the end of the Civil War in 1865 a distinctive national book trade system emerged. By 1916 the population had tripled, and the annual number of titles grew fivefold, to 13,470, between 1865 and 1915. An army of door-to-door salesmen canvassed people to buy books directly from the publishers, thus reaching buyers who did not normally go to bookshops.[44]

It is neither possible nor particularly useful to provide a firm definition of the popular novel and its alleged polar opposite, the 'literary' novel. Sales and market size are no indication, since many novels regarded by all as 'literary' easily outsell many popular novels. To say that popular novels are those with no literary value would grant literary élites, whose business is to define 'literary value', the power to transform their subjective views into objective categories. In any case, taste changes, the status of novels is regularly contested, literary élites themselves are constantly shifting, and the border between the high and the low can never be established with any degree of reliability. It is probably safer to proceed somewhat empirically, and to regard popular novels as those which target a particular section of the reading public. The fact that such groups are targeted does not mean that such books are read only by them. It is a feature of so-called 'low' culture that many of its products are found attractive by consumers of high culture. We noted in preceding chapters the wide appeal that serialised novels, such as Eugène Sue's *Les Mystères de Paris*, could have, cutting across classes in a way not dissimilar to that of successful television serials at the end of the twentieth century.

Consumers of high culture have the privilege, thanks to their education and status, of being able to choose between different segments of the market, reading detective stories on the beach and avant-garde literature during the cold winter nights. Others, unless uncommonly motivated, having been deprived of an adequate educational environment are also deprived of access. Here cultural capital is not unlike economic capital. To have much of the latter enables you to choose whether to purchase a cheap car or a Porsche. If you have little money, the Porsche is out of reach.

As we have seen, there were a few literary Porsches in the USA, but what was outstanding was the massive production of so-called dime novels. They advertised themselves as a low genre by their cheap binding, their brevity, the simplicity of their prose, the length of their sentences, the frequency of dialogue, the minimal use of descriptions and the rapid identification of characters by a few simple traits. But the main reason behind the success of the genre was the uniform low price – ten cents, hence 'dime' novels – at a time when many books cost $1 and most lower-middle-class households had an income of $20 a week. The ancestors of such books were the chapbooks and broadsheets distributed by peddlers, the fairy tales told and retold in a profusion of versions, and the adaptations of stories which had proved popular in 'higher' versions. A constant lowering of printing costs, a growth in literacy, an increase in leisure time, and ease of transportation, above all the railways, further contributed to the expansion of the popular novel.

By 1850 the American publishing industry, previously widely scattered, was concentrated in a few centres, above all New York, Boston and Philadelphia. Powerful publishers emerged, such as Harper's, which offered series of uniformly bound cheap volumes under diverse imprints, including Harper's Family Library (which ran up to 187 volumes) and Harper's Library of Select Novels – twenty-five-cent paperbacks launched in 1842. The dime novel started to proliferate around 1860, thanks to its most popular genre, the western. This appealed prevalently to East Coast urban-dwellers who knew little about the frontier.

The most successful of the early publishers of dime novels was Irwin P. Beadle & Co., which started in New York in 1860 (it became Beadle & Adams in 1862), and went on printing books until 1898. What was remarkable about the Beadle dime novels was that their production was 'industrial', from the writing the text and the selection of illustrations to the distribution and advertising.[45] This, of course, had been true of many penny dreadfuls, but with Beadle the author almost disappeared, since the publishers suggested plots, revised texts and had more say in the shape of the end product than the authors themselves. Indeed, as Gramsci noted, one of the most characteristic features of popular literature was that the consumers cared relatively little about the identity of the author.[46] One did not buy a novel by X or Y, but a Beadle novel. The publisher was the brand name. This process had started in June 1860 with the first Beadle novel, *Maleska: The Indian Wife of the White Hunter* by Ann S. Stephens. In 128 pages she told the story of a woman destroyed by the racial prejudice of both Indians and whites. Neither the author nor the novel was new. Ann Stephens had written it in 1830, when it was first published. Most of the firm's subsequent novels (631 between 1860 and 1885) were specially commissioned. The novelty was the format – a distinctive orange cover – and the price. Beadle's first best-seller was probably Edward S. Ellis's *Seth Jones or the Captives of the Frontier* (June 1860). Here a 'literary' novel provided the template: the plot and the characters are lifted from Fenimore Cooper's *Leatherstocking Tales*.[47] Dozens followed, with titles such as *Indian Jim: A Tale of the Minnesota Massacre*, *The Lost Trail: A Legend of the Far West*, *The Quaker Scout of Wyoming: A Tale of the Massacre of 1778*. Occasionally the redskins – as the Indians were invariably called – were the heroes, as in *Oonomoo, the Huron*.

Most of the 321 dime novels in Beadle's first series (1860–74) were set in America: colonial times, the Revolution, the War of 1812, the conquest of the west, the wars with the French, with the Mexicans, with the Indians, the Gold Rush, the Civil War, the building of the railways. The firm paid no royalties. The author delivered a 35,000-word manuscript, received between $75 and $150, gave up all subsequent rights and went on to write more. Prolific writers, able to write 5,000 words a day, could produce a novel a week, and at $150 a go could make $7,500 a year, way above the salary of a university professor ($1,500), and even more than the average lawyer ($4,000). But it was very hard work.

This was formula writing at its best, or worst. Take the case of Edward L. Wheeler, one of the leading Beadle authors. Wheeler wrote thirty-three stories featuring Deadwood Dick. Their success increased rapidly once the hero was joined by Calamity Jane in *Deadwood Dick on Deck: or, Calamity Jane, the Heroine of Whoop-Up* (1878) and the subsequent novels in the series. Jane was a tough, cigar-smoking girl, seduced when young and now leading a man's life, regularly rescuing her buddy Deadwood Dick from difficult situations.[48] Unfortunately for Beadle (and for the author himself) Edward Wheeler died in 1885, at the height of his fame, his name having become a brand, like Beadle and Deadwood Dick – all the novels had the words 'Deadwood Dick' in the title. Aware that other writers could write such stories, the publishers kept his death secret and trained others to continue the series with a further ninety-seven instalments, all signed 'Edward Wheeler'. The same fate befell Ned Buntline (pen name of Edward Zane Carroll Judson), the creator of Buffalo Bill. When he died Prentiss Ingraham was appointed to succeed him as 'Ned Buntline', and wrote hundreds of novels using the well-established byline. This particular take on the concept of 'the death of the author' was not restricted to the lowest level of cultural production. Sixty years after the death of the celebrated crime-writer Dorothy L. Sayers the manuscript of her 1936 *Thrones, Dominations* was discovered in a safe at her literary agency. The fact that it consisted of only five chapters did not stop the publishers Hodder & Stoughton from asking another talented writer, Jill Paton Walsh, to 'finish' it. It was published in 1998 as co-authored by both Walsh and Sayers. From the completed chapters it was impossible to guess who the author intended to be the murderer, so it was left to Paton Walsh to decide.

The success of Beadle encouraged other firms almost immediately. Publishers themselves explained the formula to new writers. Here is Ormond Smith to Gilbert Patten, one of his authors: 'It is important that the main character in the series should have a catchy name . . . When the hero is once projected on his travels there is an infinite variety of incidents to choose from . . . A little love element would also not be amiss though this is not particularly important.'[49] In 1863 Elliott, Thomes & Talbot's Ten Cent Novelettes series was launched with Sylvanus Cobb Jr's *The Golden Eagle, or, The Privateer of 1776*. One of its writers was A.M. Barnard, author of *V.V.; or, Plots and Counterplots*, a bloody thriller. Barnard went down in history under her real name, Louisa May Alcott. Tutored by eminent thinkers like Ralph Waldo Emerson and Henry David Thoreau, and therefore quite at home in high culture, she had to support her poverty-stricken family. She tried her hand at short stories, including crime stories, almost three hundred of them, which were published pseudonymously in various magazines. Her writing skills must have been well tested because she eventually achieved literary fame with the largely autobiographical *Little Women* (1868–69) and its sequels *Little Men* (1871) and *Jo's Boys* (1886). She was one of the best-selling American authors of the nineteenth century. In 1886 alone she earned $20,000.[50] It is claimed that in all she sold a million copies of her novels in her lifetime, earning some $200,000.[51] In a letter (1 April 1887) she wrote: 'I am contented with a hundred thousand . . . also a naughty satisfaction in proving that it was better *not* to "stick to teaching" as advised, but write.'[52] By then, however, she had become dependent on narcotics and was a regular user of hashish.[53]

Real-life characters were occasionally used, drastically transformed. *Davy Crockett's Revenge*, a fictionalised account of the famous scout (who was born in 1786 and died defending the Alamo in 1836), saw the light of day in 1853 – by then the Alamo had become a legend. The cowboy Deadwood Dick (1854–1921) really existed, though unlike his literary persona he was black. He was born Nat Love, and acquired his nickname when, after a cattle drive to Deadwood, South Dakota, he won various shooting and rodeo contests. In 1890, the great era of cowboys over, he became a Pullman porter and tried to cash in on his name by writing his autobiography, *The Life and Adventures of Nat Love: Better Known in the Cattle Country as 'Deadwood Dick'*.

Kit Carson (1809–68) was mythologised in the 1870s and 1880s, as was Daniel Boone (1734–1820). Bat Masterson (1853–1921), the hero of novels and later of films and television programmes, really had been the sheriff of Dodge City, Kansas, and really did assist Federal Marshal Wyatt Earp to tame unruly Tombstone, Arizona. In 1869 Ned Buntline discovered William Cody (1846–1917) in Nebraska, and used him as the hero of the novel *Buffalo Bill, the King of Border Men*, which was serialised in Street and Smith's *New York Weekly* between December 1869 and March 1870. Cody, who had done nothing remarkable except kill a vast number of buffaloes (4,000 in less than eighteen months, he claimed) for the Kansas Pacific Railroad, was turned into a star. He exploited his fame, acting in Buntline's play *The Scouts of the Plains* (1872) before going into show business in 1883 with his Wild West Show (signing up the Sioux chief Sitting Bull and the female sharpshooter Annie Oakley). 'Real' Indians appeared in the novels as well: the Ottawa leader Pontiac (c.1720–69); Black Hawk (real name Ma-ka-tae-mish-kia-kiak, 1767–1838), chief of the Sauk; and Sitting Bull (c.1834–90). Westerns left a rich inheritance to the cinema. Famous cinematic characters first saw the light of day in the nineteenth century in humble dime novels, read by clerks and farmers and disposed of without inhibition or exchanged for other similar novels.

These westerns were the tip of an iceberg. By the 1870s an avalanche of publishers swamped the American market with novels serialised in magazines, or sold in parts as reading material for the new lower-middle classes. One day they would be offered an expurgated and simplified version of the *Arabian Nights* tales, another day a rewritten novel by Dickens or Radcliffe. Every week the hundreds of thousands of subscribers to the *New York Ledger* (its owner Robert Bonner claimed over 370,000 in the 1870s) who had paid $3 for their year's subscription (or six cents a week) received enough reading material to keep them going for a week. The largely female audience would be offered serialised novels, poems, childcare advice, fashion news, current events and reviews such as one of Walt Whitman's *Leaves of Grass* on 10 May 1856.

Thanks to the *Ledger* and to outstanding popular writers such as Sylvanus Cobb (1823–87), readers acquired a knowledge, of sorts, of the life and customs of the Gypsies, the red Indians, the Roman emperors, the heroes of the American Revolution, European royalty and life in Oriental courts, and how to detect criminals. The titles promised breathless excitement: *The Gunmaker of Moscow, Karmel the Scout, The Mystic Bride, The Scourge of Sefton Dale, The Wild Knight, Orion the Goldbeater, The Smuggler of King's Cave, The Painter of Parma, The Brigands of Como, The Scourge of Damascus* and *Alaric, or the Tyrant's Vault*. All these stories were highly moral: the villains were always punished, the heroes always victorious, never swore and were never drunk. Women were never raped, not even by the Indians, though they might be killed or scalped. But once a novel was started it was almost impossible to stop reading. Page-turning became addictive. This literature was the true antecedent of the popular cinema and mass television. Most of this made-in-the-USA fiction was not exported, but the foundation stones of a formidable cultural industry were being laid. The American century was about to begin.

Italy and Spain

Alessandro Manzoni had had the ambition of writing *the* great Italian popular novel. *I Promessi sposi* was celebrated by the élites and force-fed to generations of schoolchildren, made into plays, films and eventually television serials, but it never became popular. Italian readers in the nineteenth century were weaned on novels by Dumas, Sue and Verne and their local imitators, as they had been by Scott and his local imitators.[54] And when they went to the theatre they enjoyed French melodramas by Scribe and farces by Labiche. A play based on Balzac's *Père Goriot* was performed seventy times between 1838 and 1850.[55] Contemporary sources mention how 'everyone' was reading Balzac either in the original or in one of the many competing translations. Italian critics, while recognising Balzac's ability to involve the reader in a way no one in Italy was able to do, had a high-minded view of what a great author should be. He should be someone like Manzoni, and the opposite of Balzac: he should be someone with 'values', a certain air of other-worldliness, committed to the educationally uplifting, having a suitable lifestyle, and not overtly concerned with monetary matters. Balzac was regarded as too popular, too entertaining, and hence a corrupting model for Italian writers.[56] The result was that many Italians read Balzac for pleasure, and Manzoni out of duty.

All the genres popular in France and Britain were also popular in Italy. Gothic novels were often imitated, and in some cases even pioneered. One of the Italian Gothic writers, Igino Ugo Tarchetti, set his novel *I Fatali* (1869) in Bohemia before Bram Stoker had set his *Dracula* (1897) in Transylvania or Stoker's fellow Irishman Sheridan le Fanu had written his vampiresque 'Carmilla' (1872), one of the short stories in the collection *In a Glass Darkly*. Tarchetti's hero, Baron Saternez, was a Byronic character: handsome, fair, thin, melancholic, feminine, elegant in his black clothes, very pale – in a word, a vampire (though he is never referred to as such), who dies with a knife in his heart thanks to the intervention of a mysterious dispenser of justice.[57] In Camillo Boito's *Un Corpo* (A Body, 1870) a woman is painted by her lover, who falls in love with the portrait – a well-established theme dear to Edgar Allan Poe and Théophile Gautier. The novel also features a mad scientist who lives in the midst of corpses he has dissected for his experiments (*à la* Frankenstein).[58]

The one cultural form in which Italy held a dominant position in nineteenth-century Europe, the one which it exported massively, was opera, but the more successful instances of this genre, as we shall see, were increasingly written with an eye to the export market. A considerable number of operatic plots were set outside Italy or were borrowed from foreign authors. This *esterofilia*, the love of all that is foreign, has remained a characteristic of Italian cultural consumption to the present day, and was regularly remarked upon by Italian critics themselves. In *L'Anglomania e l'influsso inglese in Italia nel secolo XVIII*, written in 1911 and dedicated to 'the English Nation', 'worthy of its destiny' (*'degna dei suoi destini'*), Arturo Graf commented: 'At first the Italians followed the example of the Spaniards, the conquerors of their land; then they chose the French to be their teachers; then they became infatuated with the English and, recently even with the Germans.' Even anglomania came from France: 'From France we import everything that can possibly be imported: ideas, habits, fashion, games, clothes, ornaments, sweets; and rightly so, because it is commonly accepted that they are superior to us in everything apart from music.'[59]

The linguistic and political fragmentation of Italy (and to a lesser extent of Spain, where Castilian was spoken by a minority of the inhabitants) made the development of a national Italian theatre difficult. The upper classes understood Italian and could follow operas (all in Italian) by buying the libretto and reading it as the action was taking place. There was a thriving regional theatre in dialect aimed at the local bourgeoisie; some of these plays were still produced or remembered in the twentieth century – for instance Giovanni Toselli's *Miserie d'monssú Travet* (1863), about the miseries of the life of a public employee, which was written in Piedmontese dialect, or Carlo Bertolazzi's *El Nost Milan*, written in Milanese and revived as late as the 1960s at the Piccolo Teatro in Milan.[60] But these are exceptions. Being written in dialect, even a powerful dialect such as Venetian or Neapolitan, prevented a work's diffusion in the rest of the peninsula, let alone outside it, or its survival.

A middle class bent on reading foreign novels or their local imitations, or pre-modern classic texts, makes nation-building a complex enterprise. Such cosmopolitan taste accentuated the distance between Italy's élites and 'the people'. Where the people appear in Italian literature they are seen and treated as outsiders, or as if they were foreigners, or primitives, with a colonial condescension. This – as Gramsci noted – is apparent in Manzoni's *I Promessi sposi*, where the lower-class characters are patronised from beginning to end.[61] To some extent this is common to much middle-class literature, but in Italy the condescension was far more pronounced. Dickens's working class can be cruel or kind, but it is never alien, it is never 'un-English'. Zola often regards the people as bestial, but he attributes this to their conditions, not to their essence. But the 'Italian Zola', Giovanni Verga (1840–1922), viewed the people, or at any rate his fellow Sicilians, as mysterious and alien beings who, if unleashed, could bring about the most unexpected and irrational violence, as he described them in his short story 'Libertà', about a popular uprising in the village of Bronte, where the behaviour of a totally senseless mob ('Now that their hands were red with blood, the rest had to be spilled') is contrasted with that of the reasonable middle class.[62]

For well over a century, through films, comedies and popular literature, Italian writers would characterise the lower classes as weak, amusing, unpatriotic, unintelligent, mindlessly devoted to a cause, cowardly, and not truly Italian. In Italian narrative film or novels there is hardly ever a Jean Valjean, the hero of Hugo's *Les Misérables*, or a Jude, the protagonist of Hardy's *Jude the Obscure*. The French and the British were already in the nineteenth century mapping out a modern 'democratic' narrative, dealing with 'fellow' countrymen and countrywomen towards whom they had a feeling of community, albeit one mixed with feelings of class differences, fear and alienation. Not so Italian writers.

The question of the lack of popularity of Italian writers among the Italians themselves was famously examined by Antonio Gramsci in his prison writings.[63] But Gramsci himself, as he made clear, was building on the works of Ruggero Bonghi (1826–95), the author of the significantly titled *Perché la letteratura italiana non sia popolare in Italia* (Why Italian Literature is not Popular in Italy, 1855–56). Bonghi, a journalist and university teacher and later Minister of Education for the moderate right, blamed the prolix and unreadable style of Italian writers, which had forced readers to turn to French and English novels.[64] He also pointed out that Italian writers did not appeal to women – in his view the 'typical' reader, the one who reads for pleasure. If a modern literature could not speak to women, he claimed, it could not speak about life, because women were more sensitive and perceptive than men. Italian books were read only by men of letters, those 'who read to write in order to be read in turn'. Obviously in no mood to curry favour with his fellow literati, Bonghi provided a list of Italian writers who sounded better in French than in Italian, or who were unable to write lucidly, or who wrote in a boring manner – the list included grand men of Italian literature such as Ugo Foscolo (1778–1827), whose pompous adulation of Napoleon he excoriated. Bonghi also deplored the influence of German philosophy among

Italian intellectuals, because once the German had been translated into Italian, it had lost any meaning it might have had.[65]

Some of this criticism was unfair. Francesco Guerrazzi's *La Battaglia di Benevento* and Cesare Cantù's *Margherita Pusterla* were historical novels that presented little difficulty to the average middle-class reader. But they were less exciting than Walter Scott or Dumas. Guerrazzi could not refrain from trying to instil patriotism in his readers, a temptation Scott and Dumas always avoided. Many Italian writers who tried to write for 'the people' (i.e. the lower middle classes) did so with a cause in mind. Thus a Jesuit priest, Father Antonio Bresciani, having read Eugène Sue, had become convinced that the way to halt the growing tide of anti-clericalism was to tackle it head-on by providing countervailing popular narratives. His journal, *La Civiltà Cattolica*, sought to include, among various fare, 'good' serialised novels. He wrote some of them himself, notably *L'Ebreo di Verona*. As was only to be expected, this was trounced by Francesco de Sanctis, Italy's leading literary critic: Padre Bresciani's religiosity was provincial and bigoted, silly and coarse: '*Il padre Bresciani è uomo di poco ingegno e di volgare carattere . . .*'[66] Though Bresciani never became as popular as his French models, he had found a niche market among provincial Catholics. More successful was Francesco Mastriani, a socialist and an overt follower of Sue, author of *I Misteri di Napoli* (1869–70) and the melodramatic *La Cieca di Sorrento* (1852). The Italian *romans feuilletons* which appeared in the nineteenth century were inferior to their French models, not because the genre was so difficult but because not enough Italian writers attempted to write them. There were Italian readers of *romans feuilletons*, and there were journals carrying serialised novels (*Romanzo mensile, Domenica del corriere, Tribuna illustrata, Il Mattino illustrato*), but what they published was French authors who had emerged victorious from keen competition, leaving behind them a large number of forgotten novels and failed authors. Thus Italian writers were competing not against average foreign writers, but against the very best. They often lost: their attempts at horror writing were ridiculed, their *scena madre* or climax arrived too early or too late, their heroes and heroines were too homely.[67]

Spain was to some extent a replica of Italy. Though the country could claim, if not the first novel, at least the one which is most often claimed to be the first, Cervantes's *Don Quixote* (1605–15), and though it had produced outstanding theatrical works in the sixteenth and seventeenth centuries, it was in the nineteenth century essentially an importer of books, and particularly of novels. As in Italy this 'flood' of foreign translations was routinely used to explain the obstacles facing potential Spanish authors in their search for literary and economic success. But, as José Montesinos put it succinctly: '*La novela es un género destinado a un público, y cuando ese público no esiste, no hay novela*' (Novels are a genre aimed at a public; when this public does not exist, there are no novels).[68] The low level of literacy or education in Spain might explain the low level of reading and the narrowness of the market, but not the disproportionate presence of foreign literature, since the spread of such translations implied the existence of a market, of readers and of a distribution network. I have already noted (see page 59) that when it came to peddlers' literature, Spain had as good a network as any country in Europe. But in the mid-nineteenth century Spanish readers wanted to read French serialised novels. To meet this demand (and perhaps to create it) a number of periodicals emerged in the 1840s specialising in the *folletín* (Spanish for *roman feuilleton*), with names such as *La Risa*, *El Fandango*, *El Dómine Lucas* and *La Lanterna mágica*, in which Ayguals de Izco, a journalist, translated Eugène Sue and wrote in 1845–46 his own *Maria o la hija de un jornalero* (Maria, or the Labourer's Daughter). Manuel Angelón's *Crimines célebres españoles* (Barcelona, 1852) was an imitation of Alexandre Dumas's *Crimes célèbres*, which had been published in Barcelona in 1840.[69]

Books by the leading French novelists could be obtained easily at any of the forty-five bookshops which existed in Madrid in the middle of the nineteenth century, three of which were actually owned by Frenchmen. Knowledge of French was virtually mandatory among the Spanish élites if they wanted to keep up with what was going on in Europe, i.e. in France.[70]

French translations, however, provided an impetus for the production of Spanish novels, though some domestic production was also inspired by the tradition of romances and the numerous plays produced during the Spanish Renaissance. The choice for aspiring writers was therefore either simply to imitate the French, or to write for sections of the market not catered for by foreign literature. The first strategy appears the easiest, but was in fact the more difficult, since the competition was stiffer and readers were inclined to go for the original. As translation costs were low and copyright legislation virtually non-existent, Spanish or Italian writers had few economic advantages over their foreign rivals.

The second strategy involved borrowing from abroad while remaining clearly anchored to Spanish life and reality. In fact one of the most successful of mid-nineteenth-century Spanish novels was written by someone with a cosmopolitan upbringing. Francisca Josefa de Arrom (1796–1877), author under the name Fernán Caballero of *La Gaviota* (The Seagull, 1849), had English and Irish ancestry, was born in Switzerland to a German father and a Basque mother, and educated in Hamburg. She was often compared to George Sand, but that was probably because she was a woman writer using a male pseudonym. Unlike Sand she was deeply Catholic and traditionalist, distant from the anti-clerical, modernising writers who were the fashion in France. Because of this she was more in tune with her audience than was someone like Garibaldi, whose priest-bashing historical novels were aimed at celebrating those who, like him, had fought for Italian unity.[71]

26

Improving Oneself

A School for the Middle Classes

THE EXPANSION OF THE MIDDLE CLASSES further enhanced the market
for self-improvement books. The bourgeois inferiority complex towards the
aristocracy – just as extant in 'republican' countries such as France as elsewhere – led to the formulation, and often the invention, of hundreds of rules
on how to speak and write correctly, how to behave towards one's peers and
one's inferiors, and how to carry on a conversation. It was also necessary to
add to one's cultural capital (occasionally almost as important as economic
capital) by acquiring a modicum of knowledge of science, history, politics,
literature and geography – knowledge which the educational system, with its
obsession with the classics, religion and antiquity, was totally unequipped to
provide. In Victorian Britain a book with the significant title *Enquire Within
Upon Everything* (1856), a compendium of advice on social skills, sold 592,000
copies by 1877.[1] Earlier, in 1816, a political pamphlet such as William Cobbett's
Address to the Journeymen and Labourers sold 200,000 in two months.[2] In
France *Paroles d'un croyant* by the Catholic priest Félicité Robert de Lamennais was one of the best-sellers of the 1830s, but none of its first eight
impressions was of more than 1,500 copies. Its dissemination was considerably
enhanced by Pope Gregory XVI's decision, a few weeks after its publication
in 1834, to promulgate against Lamennais the encyclical letter *Singulari Nos*
(On the Errors of Lamennais). His main error was advocating freedom of
conscience: 'We condemn the book because it contains false, calumnious,
and rash propositions which lead to anarchy; which are contrary to the word
of God; which are impious, scandalous and erroneous.' This encouraged the
publisher Daubrée to bring out in 1835 a cheap edition (sixty centimes) with
a print run of 10,000, soon followed by another reprint of the same size. In

1837 Delloye and Bethune produced an even cheaper edition, printing 15,000 copies. By 1849 Lamennais's unlikely best-seller had probably sold 70–80,000 copies.[3]

Books also signalled status. The prestige of a middle-class professional home would be enhanced by the presence on its shelves of major and recognised authors, such as Shakespeare in Britain, Voltaire in France, Goethe in Germany and Dante in Italy. To own Voltaire's entire opus (seventy-five volumes) was a symbol of intellectual standing (reading them was superfluous) and political modernity (as they represented secular enlightenment). By 1825 there existed six competing editions of the complete works of Voltaire. In 1879, the centenary of his death, 89,000 copies were sold.[4] The great Stuttgart publisher Cotta had print runs of 10–20,000 for its *Volksausgaben* or popular editions, but in 1840 it printed 100,000 copies of its prestigious twelve-volume *Sämtliche Werke* (Collected Works) of Schiller.[5]

Popularisations of non-fiction subjects could sell well, if clearly written. George Lewes (George Eliot's companion) published the *Biographical History of Philosophy* in 1845–46 – an overview of philosophy from the Greeks to Comte. By 1857 it had sold 40,000 copies. In June 1855 Lewes sold his *Life of Goethe* to the publisher David Nutt; he was paid £250 on publication and promised another £100 when 1,000 copies had been sold. Lewes was lucky, his *Goethe* sold 1,000 in three months. A second edition was called for in 1864 and a third in 1875, followed by many reprints in America and Britain. It made Lewes's reputation.[6]

Biography was an ancient genre (Plutarch, Vasari and Boswell's eighteenth-century *Life of Johnson* spring to mind), but in the nineteenth century, especially in Great Britain, it became a regular money-maker for authors and publishers (as it is now, at least for some). The main reason for writing (and reading) a biography, it was felt, was to learn from the life of an admirable person, which is why the genre was often hagiographic and almost always respectful. John Forster's *Life of Dickens* (1872–74), now regarded as typical of the Victorian worship of great men, kept quiet about Dickens's extra-marital love affair with Ellen Tennant, as would be expected, but mildly reproved him for his excessive concern about money and fame. Even this was regarded as criticism beyond the bounds of decency by George Eliot: 'Is it not odious that as soon as a man is dead his desk is raked, and every insignificant memorandum which he never meant for the public, is printed for the gossiping amusement of people too idle to re-read his books?'[7] *The Life of Madame de Staël, her Friends, and her Influence in Politics and Literature* by Lady

Charlotte Blennerhassett (1889) managed to ignore the subject's exciting and varied sexual life (her distinguished lovers included Talleyrand and Benjamin Constant).[8]

The market for the 'Lives of Great Men', and occasionally of Great Women, expanded constantly. In 1877 John Morley, the biographer of Burke, Diderot, Voltaire and Rousseau, launched the 'English Men of Letters' series with the publisher Macmillan. Its success convinced the Boston publisher Houghton Mifflin to launch their 'American Statesmen' series. One of its best-selling titles was Henry Cabot Lodge's *Alexander Hamilton* (1882): fifteen impressions in five years. Classic biographical works were translated for the first time: Vasari's *Lives of the Artists* (1550) came out in French in 1839, in English in 1850. In the 1880s Methuen started its 'English Leaders of Religion' series. Very long biographies were no deterrent to sales. The seven-volume *Life of Sir Walter Scott* (1837–38) by John Gibson Lockhart was a great success, as was John G. Nicolai and John Hay's ten-volume life of Lincoln. In Britain John Morley's three-volume *Life of William Ewart Gladstone*, published in 1903, sold 30,000 copies in that year alone. With cheaper editions its sales totalled 130,000 copies in just ten years. The biographical reference book *Who's Who?* was started in 1849, and was soon widely imitated. Between 1885 and 1900 Leslie Stephen edited the massive sixty-three-volume *Dictionary of National Biography* with the aid of 653 contributors, covering 29,120 'lives' in 30,000 pages.[9]

Autobiographies and memoirs too did well. This was an ancient genre, pioneered by St Augustine and made famous by Jean-Jacques Rousseau. Originally these works tended to be contrite accounts of one's life. They soon became less penitent, more self-satisfied and occasionally triumphalist: Goethe's *Aus meinem Leben. Dichtung und Wahrheit* (1809–14, 1830), Thomas de Quincey's *Confessions of an English Opium-Eater* (1821), Silvio Pellico's *Le mie prigioni* (1832), Stendhal's *Vie de Henry Brulard* (1836), George Sand's *Histoire de ma vie* (1854), John Stuart Mill's *Autobiography* (1873), and many others. Various angles could be explored: how I redeemed myself; how I overcame obstacles in spite of a bad start in life; how right I have always been; how I became a recognised genius; how can I say thank you to all the people I have ever met; how can I take revenge on all those who have slighted me; how can I keep myself in the public eye before everyone forgets about me, etc.[10] The dawn of the democratic age was approaching, when almost everyone could write their own autobiography.

Memoirs of those who had played a part, even a small one, in a great event became fashionable in the 1820s and 1830s. Those who had taken part in the Napoleonic wars or the French Revolution put pen to paper and wrote at length, copying here and there and inventing a little. The French literary critic Edmond Biré, writing in 1895, wrote that the public, delighted by the various memoirs of the Revolution, wanted to read the sequel. This prompted publishers to get some 'poor devil' to forge a few memoirs of the Restoration.[11]

Travelogues and journals of exploration were highly popular too, but one of the problems with this genre was that explorers were not necessarily good writers. When the publishers Blackwood started reading John Hanning Speke's draft of his *Journal of the Discovery of the Source of the Nile* (1863) they were dismayed. Speke may have been able to discover the source of the Nile, or so he claimed, but had clearly failed to discover the most elementary principles of grammar and syntax. It was necessary to rewrite the entire work with the co-operation of the 'author', who had to be repeatedly quizzed as to what he really meant. A real writer – John Hill Burton, author of a well-received history of Scotland – was hired for £250, and ghosted what turned out to be one of Blackwood's best-sellers.[12]

The majority of books were non-fiction, but did they outsell the best-selling novels? Most novels did not have a very high print run, partly because most people read them in serialised form in newspapers, or borrowed them from a lending library or from friends. Over a very long time span, a hundred years or so, it is likely that the works of some much-loved writers, or those celebrated by the élites, outsell most other books. Such books are constantly reprinted, taught in schools and universities, and new generations are encouraged to read them. In the shorter run – twenty to fifty years or so – textbooks will have the edge, and so will encyclopaedias or dictionaries, but these, being constantly updated, are strictly speaking not mere reprints.

Religious books, including books with a religious theme (a category not easy to establish) were still popular throughout the nineteenth century. The middle classes were becoming more secular, but new entrants in the ranks of the reading classes often came from the countryside, and were closer to traditional values. The pressure on publishers to produce 'improving' books was considerable, and most were quite happy to provide popular literature which was profitable, harmless and approved by the powers that be. In a highly literate country such as Germany over 14 per cent of all titles published in 1835, and 10 per cent in 1900, were of a religious nature.[13] In 1846 in Italy 23 per cent of books published fell in the religious category, more in the

Kingdom of Sardinia (34 per cent) than even in the Papal States (28 per cent), presumably because there were more educated people, and because other states could import them.[14] In France in the 1880s religious books made up 15–16 per cent of all titles.[15] Various investigations have found that between 1857 and 1908 two-thirds of French working-class homes had at least one religious book other than the Bible.[16] This is hardly surprising, since most Catholic families would have had a catechism, the manual of questions and answers aimed at the religious instruction of the young, widely used in schools, where children were expected to learn it by heart. The same technique was used for the teaching of history, and the Minister of Education François Guizot (a former historian) had 250,000 copies of Claude Fleury's *Petit catéchisme historique* distributed free to schoolteachers in the 1830s.[17]

The best-selling French book of the nineteenth century was not Hugo's *Les Misérables*, nor any of Dumas's or Verne's novels, nor any of George Sand's, but probably the now barely remembered *Notre-Dame de Lourdes* (1869) by Henri Lasserre (1828–1900), a journalist who recovered his eyesight when he rubbed his eyes with water from Lourdes in 1862.[18] He subsequently visited the town and met Bernadette Soubirous (1844–78), the young woman who in February 1858 claimed to have seen and heard the Virgin. At first Lasserre, a devout Catholic, published accounts of these events in the *Revue du monde Catholique*, beginning in December 1867; he then turned these articles into a book, prefaced by Pope Pius IX, which is said to have sold a million copies, with 142 editions in seven years, and translations into eighty languages.[19] It was Lasserre's *Notre-Dame de Lourdes* that established in France and abroad the importance of Lourdes as a place of pilgrimage. By the mid-1860s a large basilica had been erected, and sufferers came from all over Europe. They still do, in spite of the evidence that the vast majority do not recover. A few do, however, and this gives hope to the others for the same reason that lotteries are always in business in spite of the odds. Even Zola was moved to set a novel there.

Lasserre's book followed a precise narrative style whose pattern would be closely reproduced in future books telling the story of the struggle between a humble proponent of an alternative to established science and the scientific establishment itself. It was the story of simple Bernadette and 'the people' against officialdom, including clerical officialdom.[20] But it was also an account of a current event, an 'identity' book the presence of which in one's home signalled a commitment to Catholic values, and also a 'practical' book: you too can be healthy if you follow a certain procedure. How-to manuals had a popular appeal in previous centuries, and still do in our own time. Those who think that vegetarian cookery is a recent fad may do well to reflect that one of the early vegetarian texts – *Makrobiotik* by Christoph Wilhelm Hufeland – was published in Germany in 1796, that the British Vegetarian Society was founded in 1847 and published many tracts on vegetarianism, and that the German treatise *Die natürliche Lebensweise* (The Natural Way of Life, 1867–72) by the Reverend Eduard Baltzer (1814–87), the founding father of German vegetarianism, achieved high sales, as did his cookbook *Kochbuch fuer Freunde der natürlichen Lebensweise*, reprinted fourteen times with sales in excess of 50,000 copies

The expansion of the audience for music during the nineteenth century coincided with an explosion in writing about music. There were guidebooks to the repertoire, self-help treatises about listening, music appreciation and playing instruments, popular histories of music, and programme notes. There was also a substantial growth of periodicals for the concert-going public, such as the *Neue musikalische Presse* (Vienna, 1891) and the Stuttgart-based *Neue Musik Zeitung* (1879).[21]

The new bourgeoisie and petty bourgeoisie, unsure of themselves, were keen to learn how to behave and to converse intelligently. In 1808 Friedrich Arnold Brockhaus (1772–1823) published his *Konversationslexicon* (Manual of Conversation), an encyclopaedic dictionary for the 'educated classes'.[22] In time this became an industry in itself as the number of volumes and of sales (on a subscription basis) increased. In 1833–39 eight volumes had been published, and by 1845–49 there were fifteen available, with ten impressions by 1853. It became the basis of a substantial publishing empire and the development of one of the first modern encyclopaedias, the *Brockhaus Enzyklopaedie*, still going strong. Nor was this the only monumental German encyclopaedia : the *Allgemeine Encyclopädie der Wissenschaften und Künste, in alphabetischer Folge* (Universal Encyclopaedia of Sciences and Arts, in Alphabetical Order), edited by Johann Samuel Ersch and Johann Gottfried Gruber, begun in 1818, was only completed almost a century later, in 1914, when the 168th and final volume was published.

The first great modern encyclopaedia, however, was Ephraim Chambers's *Cyclopaedia; or, an Universal Dictionary of Arts and Sciences, Containing an Explanation of the Terms and an Account of the Things signified thereby in the several Arts and Sciences Compiled from the Best Authors*, published in two volumes in Edinburgh in 1728. An early French translation was one of the main sources of inspiration for Diderot's famous *Encyclopédie ou dictionnaire raisonné des sciences, des arts et des métiers.* The *Encyclopaedia Britannica*, which was first published in Edinburgh between 1768 and 1771 (in one hundred parts), increased in size constantly, reaching twenty-nine volumes in its eleventh (and first truly scholarly) edition in 1911. By then it was more 'Americana' than 'Britannica', since it had been bought in 1901 by American publishers. Every nation seemed to need an encyclopaedia. In Bohemia the Czech nationalist publisher Jan Otto produced a twenty-eight-volume national encyclopaedia that was surpassed in its number of entries and illustrations only by the *Encyclopaedia Britannica*. In Italy Giuseppe Pomba published in 1838–46 a *Storia universale* by Cesare Cantù in thirty-five volumes and an *Enciclopedia popolare* in twelve volumes (1842–49).[23] The encyclopaedia was a great nineteenth-century genre, filling the homes of the upwardly mobile middle classes with an instrument for knowledge which contained, as the publicity put it, all that was needed to know. It filled shelves with large works, giving the homes a genteel touch of intellect.

The increase in travelling and tourism consolidated another literary genre. While their aristocratic predecessors read the travelogues of their peers, the new bourgeois needed something more authoritative. Publishers began to provide guidebooks: John Murray's guides, starting in 1836, covered most of Europe. Three years later they were successfully challenged in Germany by Karl Baedeker, who started translating his German guidebooks into English.[24] England had in fact been the main market for guidebooks for quite a while, simply because most tourists were English. As Heinrich Heine wittily noted in 1828:

> Dear Reader, do not accuse me of anglomania if I often write about the English; today there are just too many English in Italy and one cannot avoid seeing them. They swarm through the country, occupy every inn, run everywhere in order to see everything; there is no lemon tree without an English lady nearby sniffing its perfume, nor a picture gallery without at least sixty or so Englishmen, a guidebook in their hands checking that everything is where it should be.[25]

Books of advice kept doing well, as they had done since the sixteenth century. The genre was so well established that irony crept in. Gustave Droz's phenomenally successful *Monsieur, madame et bébé* (1866) was in reality a string of humorous sketches rather than a practical compendium. By 1882 it had notched up 116 editions, by 1924 a phenomenal 266. As Peter Gay has suggested, the nineteenth century could be called the Age of Advice: it left behind a vast prescriptive literature on how to improve oneself and one's life: 'Anyone who surveys this vast and crowded field must be daunted by its riches and impressed by its astonishing uniformity.'[26]

The most successful of all such books was Samuel Smiles's *Self-Help*, whose translations into fifty-three languages, including Urdu and Hindi as well as Armenian and Siamese, exemplifies how English attitudes came to be exported all over the world. Published in 1859, it sold 20,000 copies in the first year and 150,000 in the following thirty years. Most of the book consists of anecdotes about great men, intended to demonstrate that success comes through one's own efforts.[27] This message seemed to appeal even in Japan, where by 1912 it had sold a million copies.

In Italy the great success of the translation by Gustavo Strafforello with the title *Chi si aiuta Dio l'aiuta* (God Helps those who Help Themselves, 1865) convinced publishers that what was really needed was an adaptation aimed at younger readers. Leading authorities, including the then Foreign Minister Federico Menabrea, clamoured for an Italian 'self-help' with examples from the lives of illustrious Italians. The Associazione per l'Educazione del Popolo (Association for the Education of the People) started a competition, and in 1868 Gaspero Barbèra, a Florentine publisher, commissioned Michele Lessona (a naturalist who translated Darwin) to write *Volere è potere* (To Want to is to be Able to). Lessona was critical of Italians. As he explained in the opening pages, now that the country was united it had to face enemies far more powerful than the Austrians: ignorance, superstition, laziness, envy and provincialism.[28] How to counteract all this? By following the example of worthy Italians, particularly entrepreneurs such as Prince Carlo Cottone di Castelnuovo, who transformed his estate in Palermo into an agricultural school, and Giuseppe Fonsoli, who introduced the textile industry to Umbria.[29] The aim of *Volere è potere* was 'to make the Italians' by forging a common identity. The potted biographies of exemplary Italians – scientists, writers and artists as well as industrialists and businessmen – were organised on the basis of the region in which they were born.[30] Each region of the new country was thus shown to have made a contribution. In its first eight years the book sold some 20,000 copies, and reprinting continued until the 1920s.[31] This was the launching pad of what came to be known as the '*letteratura del* self help' – the term has remained untranslatable into Italian. The titles of some of these works are self-explanatory: *I Discorsi di un maestro di villaggio col popolo* (Speeches of a Village Teacher to the Common People) by Cesare Rosa (1870), *L'Operaia esemplare o una buona madre di famiglia proposta in esempio alle donne italiane* (A Model Working

Woman or Good Family Mother Proposed as an example to Italian Women) by Francesco Manfroni (1873).

Once a manual was established the name of its author would become a brand name, enabling the publishers to have other writers regularly update and even rewrite it. Thus Isabella Beeton's *Book of Household Management* sold 468,000 copies between 1861 and 1888 (price 7s.6d.), having already appeared in monthly parts in the *Englishwoman's Domestic Magazine* produced by her husband Samuel Beeton (see pages 324–5). This meant it had reached almost its entire potential market, since it was deliberately aimed at families earning at least £300 a year. Unfortunately Isabella had died in childbirth of puerperal fever in 1865, at the age of twenty-eight. Her husband discovered that the rights to her name now belonged to the publishers Ward, Lock & Tyler. In 1888 they proceeded to rewrite the entire book, filling it with the stereotypical Victorian household tips and prudish suggestions for which it was later remembered.[32] It contained well over 1,300 recipes, advice on diet, the planning of menus and the management of servants, from the nurse to the butler, instructions on social customs, etiquette and household accounting, as well as general information on the natural sciences and a few historical anecdotes.

History

The success of the historical novel had demonstrated that there was a demand for popular history. The discipline as such was barely established on a scholarly footing in the academy. To be popular, history had to be written by a recognised historian, in order to provide something like a certificate of authenticity for the autodidact. But history is not like science. Its impartiality is always in doubt. It is often, after all, based on a selection of facts arranged in such a way as to reproduce aspects of fictional narratives: heroes on one side, villains on the other. The Romantic revolution had re-centred history as the master narrative where the people, the nation, would find its own biography. Heroes could still be kings and queens, but only because they represented the 'genius' of one's nation. Historians, for centuries the lackeys of sovereigns, now acquired a 'democratic' role, and with this an important market. Nowhere more than in France was history used as the pre-eminent terrain on which national identity could be forged. A people who did not know its history, it was believed, would always be at the mercy of despots by whom they would be hoodwinked and cheated. The people had to be told the truth about themselves. This was the task of historians, the new priests of the secular order. Jules Michelet (1798–1874) epitomised this new creed. For such liberals and lovers of freedom the dictatorship of Napoleon III represented a particularly poignant tragedy, because he had been confirmed in power through a popular plebiscite – the first 'democratic' dictator.

Michelet had understood that the people needed educating before the advent of Napoleon III. On 18 May 1846, reflecting on the kind of books the people should be offered, he wrote in his diary: 'What is needed for the masses? Novels? No. They will always wonder whether it is true.' The popular book *par excellence*, he concluded, unsurprisingly for a historian, was the history book, the book that tells the history of France, and above all the history of the Revolution. Two years later, in 1848, in the midst of the Revolution which re-established the Republic, albeit temporarily, Michelet wrote to his friend the songwriter Pierre Béranger that as the masses did not read, it was imperative that the Republic organised public readings of its bulletins and produced posters with easy-to-read characters and illustrations, and that patriotic songs should be sold by peddlers.[33] With the defeat of the 1848 Revolution Michelet had to forfeit his history chair at the Collège de France. In his valedictory lecture he declared that the only way historians could speak to the people was by telling them their history, what they had achieved and what they could achieve.[34] As he was writing his massive multi-volume *History of the French Revolution* (1847–53) he was, understandably enough, overwhelmed by doubts. He was the presiding genius of the Romantic school of history, and had obtained the chair of history at the Sorbonne (1834) when he was only thirty-six, and then at the Collège de France (1838); but how could he ensure that his history would reach ordinary people – and women in particular? He decided to go beyond political history and to deal with nature and society. In 1856 he wrote *L'Oiseau*, then, in quick succession *L'Insecte* (1858), *L'Amour* (1859), *La Femme* (1860) and, in 1862, a history of women called *La Sorcière* in which he defended witches as unjustly persecuted by the Church for attempting to penetrate the secrets of nature. But these were less successful than his *History of France*, which when completed in 1867 reached seventeen volumes.

What Michelet did not understand, or did not want to understand, was that historians seldom influence 'the people' directly. They write for élites, some members of which will simplify and popularise. To the academic historian the glory of scholarship, to the populariser the cash. Occasionally the two are combined. And always, poised between the two, stands the publisher who knows the differences between the two markets and is ready to exploit them both. Pierre-Jules Hetzel fulfilled Michelet's dream. The first edition of Michelet's seven-volume *Histoire de la Révolution* had been published by Chamerot in 1868 at forty-two francs for the set – a large sum at a time when many members of the middle classes would earn four hundred francs a month. The next edition, published by Lacroix in 1873 (after the fall of Napoleon III), sold for thirty francs. In 1881 Hetzel came up with a much cheaper edition, removed the generic illustrations which had burdened the previous ones and, using the services of a skilled illustrator, Théophile Schuler, introduced pictures which referred specifically to what was narrated in the text. Michelet's history had become illustrated history. Schuler's illustrations built on the wave of patriotism and anti-German feeling arising from the French defeat of 1870 by the Prussians. They showed not only the heroes of French history, the great generals and the famous kings, but also ordinary people at war; and the great heroes themselves were portrayed as, if not good democrats, at least genuinely concerned with the fate of the common people.[35]

Like Hugo, Michelet had spent the 1850s and 1860s in exile; like Hugo he was lionised by the Third Republic, and lived long enough to enjoy his late triumph. Michelet was not read by the common people, but he was read by most schoolteachers. After the fall of Napoleon his books became required reading in schools, and an army of teachers dutifully relayed his interpretation of the past to new generations. As anti-clericalism developed, Michelet's secular themes were echoed with increasing fervour. But more needed to be done, and Hetzel, his publisher, did it. He got the successful duo of patriotic novelists who wrote as Erckmann-Chatrian to produce a best-seller: *Histoire d'un paysan* (1869). In its preface the narrator, a peasant called Michel Bastien, addresses his readership: 'Dear friends' – he writes – 'I am a man of the people and I write for the people. I tell you what I have seen . . . This is the history of our grandfathers, and it is to all of you, bourgeois, workers, peasants and soldiers that I tell it.' This history is, of course, the history of the events between 1788 and 1804, the history of the French Revolution that was told by Michelet in seven volumes.[36]

Rescuing and reconstructing a particular past entailed highlighting certain significant ruptures and emphasising the continuity of the nation. The French celebrated the caesura of the French Revolution while establishing the cult of the ancient people of Gaul and of leaders such as Vercingetorix, and their own continuity with them – with generations of schoolchildren reciting 'Our ancestors, the Gauls . . .'. The Greeks sought to rescue an old heritage which had been taken over by other countries. Constantin Paparrigopoulos (1815–91), author of the influential five-volume *History of the Greek Nation* (1860–72) and supporter of the *Megalidea* ('Great Idea'), developed a view of Greece and of the Greek people as a seamless continuity from ancient times through to Byzantium and the modern age. The British developed what came to be known as 'the Whig Interpretation of History'. This was chiefly due to Macaulay's celebrated yet never completed *History of England*, that presented the course of British history as a gradual and non-conflictual development of parliamentary power. This view was repeatedly challenged by later historians, in a prose which seldom matched Macaulay's own. Their efforts never completely removed from popular sentiment this self-satisfied view of British evolution. And Macaulay's *History of England* did very well commercially: in the twenty-five years after publication in 1848–55 it sold some 300,000 copies (and probably 60,000 in the USA in pirated editions).[37] In Germany the putative 'father' of modern history, Leopold von Ranke (1795–1886), was very successful, very celebrated and very popular. His *Die römischen Päpste* (History of the Popes, 1834–36) went into eight editions by 1885 and was widely translated.

If one wrote well, and did not run too far ahead of the tastes of one's time, it was perfectly possible to make real money writing history books even before the age of television. But one had to know how to write for a wider public. Novelists had a head start over academics. Alexander Kinglake, the successful author of an 'Orientalist' Gothic novel, *Eothen* (1844), had taken part in the Crimean War, and began to accumulate material for a detailed history of the war. At first sight this seemed an inauspicious business proposition, and it was seen as such by the publisher John Murray who made a relatively modest offer of £1,000 for the outright purchase of the copyright. John Blackwood – after some haggling – was slightly more generous: £1,000 for the first edition, the copyright to remain with the author. In 1863 the first two volumes of Kinglake's *History of the Crimean War* came out. They were controversial and profitable, went through four editions and sold 15,000 copies. By July 1873 the work had raked in profits to the tune of £6,454. The third and fourth volumes sold 6,000 copies, generating further profits (£4,107). Kinglake's *History* turned out to be the most lucrative work published by Blackwood in the 1860s.[38] Here are Blackwood's most profitable publishing ventures of that decade:

Kinglake's *History of the Crimea*, Vols 1 and 2	£6,454
Ancient Classics for English Readers	£5,242
George Eliot's *Mill on the Floss*	£4,442
Kinglake's *History of the Crimea*, Vols 3 and 4	£4,107

In the long run the outright winner would be George Eliot, but publishers, like most people, live in the short run, and here non-fiction, and history in particular, won easily. The total eight-volume set of Kinglake remained in the top twelve best-sellers in Blackwood's list for over thirty years, generating £20,000 by the end of the century.[39]

That non-fiction could be more profitable than novels was also demonstrated by the case of Margaret Oliphant, whose most lucrative novels made for Blackwood £850 at most, while her biography of her cousin *The Life of Laurence Oliphant* (1891) made £2,049. In the 1860s only three 'literary' (as opposed to non-fiction) writers generated for Blackwood more than £1,000 profit: George Eliot and the now quite forgotten Samuel Warren and Theodore Martin.[40] Warren's best-seller, the novel *Ten Thousand a Year*, the story of Tittlebat Titmouse, a draper's assistant who inherits a fortune thanks to a forgery, had been serialised in 1839–40 in *Blackwood's Magazine*, and published as a book the following year. In the 1860s it was still in print as part of his eight-volume collected works, and still very profitable. Dante Gabriel Rossetti thought Warren to be as good as Dickens; admittedly Rossetti was only fifteen at the time, but fifteen-year-olds constitute a market too.[41] As for Theodore Martin (1816–1909), his 1860s success *Bon Gaultier Ballads* was a collection of parodies and light poems written in 1845. Nowadays neither Martin nor Warren is mentioned in any mainstream encyclopaedia, and none of their works was reprinted in the twentieth century.

Eliot, Warren and Martin aside, Blackwood made money thanks to non-fiction: not just Kinglake but also Speke's account of his travels in Africa, a book of Scottish hymns, Henry Stephens's *The Book of the Farm* (1844) and Charles McIntosh's *Book of the Garden* (1853). E.B. Hamley's *Operations of War* (1866), another best-seller, may not sound riveting, but many people were and are interested in military matters, and the book, a set text for the entrance examination to the Military Staff College in Camberley, influenced a generation of army officers.[42]

Science and Education

In the nineteenth century it was still possible for the well-educated person to follow scientific developments by reading the works of the scientists themselves, for they often wrote in non-specialist language. Encyclopaedias and dictionaries about animals, often lavishly illustrated, were prized items for scientists and non-scientists alike. Reading science books had an ideological significance: it granted the reader a patent of modernity and, on the Continent, of anti-clericalism. Reading Darwin was not only a matter of simple curiosity about or interest in a much-discussed theory, it was often also a question of identity. To be a supporter of Darwin meant to be against religious obscurantism and in favour of modernity. Thus the French translation of *On the Origin of Species* (1862) had an outspokenly atheistic and republican introduction. The great 'monkeys' debate led to a profusion of books by anti-clerical militants who were not professional scientists but who were committed to the idea that the diffusion of science was a Good Thing because it kept religion down. Some religious publishers sought to counter this influence by publishing tracts seeking to disprove Darwinism; others, realising that the scientific tide could not be reversed, sought to show that religion and science were not contradictory.

By the end of the century, a new kind of science book emerged, with clearly pedagogic aims. Some were sold in monthly parts, often in illustrated magazines, others in cheap paperbacks, others as luxury books and potential gifts. Even Karl Marx, in a letter to the publisher Maurice LaChâtre, welcomed the idea of publishing the French translation of *Das Kapital* in '*livraison périodique*', a serialisation, so as to make it more accessible to the working class, though he was afraid that the rather arduous beginning might discourage the French public.[43]

The favourite scientific topics were not different from those in vogue in the eighteenth (or the twentieth) century: hygiene, botany, astronomy (*Astronomie populaire*, in France, sold 125,000 copies).[44] The educational revolution of the nineteenth century provided the publishing industry with a remarkable business opportunity. Not only did the increase in literacy expand the market of potential readers but, far more importantly, it actually provided a market for textbooks, the true best-sellers of the nineteenth and twentieth centuries. In France, a geography textbook, *Les pays de France* by Pierre Foncin (1841–1916) sold over ten million copies since its publication in 1898.[45] Foncin was outdone by Larive and Fleury's *Première année de grammaire*, first published by Colin in 1871, which was still being reprinted in 1959, when the 231st impression came out.[46] It was in the nineteenth century that a uniform spelling and grammar came to be established.

The basis for such extraordinary sales was centralised public education. In England, where matters were left, by and large, to individual schools, there were in the nineteenth century some nine hundred *new* grammars – they were easy to write, since authors (often schoolteachers) simply redrafted the contents of their predecessors and pocketed the money.[47] In France, matters proceeded from the top: first the Guizot Law (1833) authorised every commune in the country to raise a local tax to set up a primary school. The result was that by 1848 the number of primary schools had almost doubled. Then in 1850 the *loi Falloux* obliged all communes with more than eight hundred inhabitants to set up schools for girls too. Finally in 1881 and 1882 the Ferry Laws made primary school compulsory, though by then the majority of children were already going to elementary schools. By the time this had taken place, a network of publishers had entered the market. Two houses in particular became the pillars of French publishing: Hachette and Larousse, largely thanks to their close relationships with the world of education. The Greek–French dictionary Hachette had published in 1826 continued to sell incrementally throughout the century. Pierre Larousse's fifteen-volume *Grand dictionnaire universel du XIXe siècle*, which started in 1865, turned Larousse (himself a former schoolteacher) into a leading educational publisher. When he died he left a fortune of 850,000 francs.[48] Publishers had to be particularly circumspect with schoolbooks. In France they would be vetted by a commission whose caution was such that it rejected 'religious' books which appeared to dwell excessively on the more sexually embarrassing biblical stories such as the incest of Lot with his daughters, the adultery of King David with Bathsheba (and his murder of her husband), and Solomon's sexual appetites.[49]

Publishers could use the profits from textbooks to expand further, because the demand for books continued to rise rapidly. In Spain such demand remained confined to the urban middle classes well into the twentieth century. Its 1857 *ley Morano* – the Spanish counterpart of the *loi Falloux* – was a pragmatic compromise between Church and state (with the Church having the better of the bargain). All municipalities with more than five hundred inhabitants were required to provide schooling for all children until the age of nine, free of charge for the less well-off. In the state sector textbooks would have their moral content reviewed by the Church, while the Church was allowed to set up its own schools with its own texts. But unlike France, in Spain, a far less urbanised country, education was not yet seen as an instrument of social mobility or economic improvement, and consequently it stagnated and the market for books remained far narrower than in France. In 1895 over 68 per cent of Spanish children were still not at school, and adult illiteracy was estimated at 55–60 per cent – though with pronounced regional differences.[50]

Spanish publishers, like the French and the British, also had at their disposal a potentially enormous market in the Spanish-speakers of Latin America, but this was still a narrow élite market, with publishers directly translating French and English texts or importing them in the original language. Publishers, however, did benefit from the expansion in education in Spain. In 1850 there were 782,000 regular pupils attending 17,434 schools. Thirty years later the numbers had almost doubled. The fortunes of publishers such as Victoriano Hernando, a largely self-taught schoolteacher, were substantially the result of close networking with the educational establishment (which also facilitated export to Latin America). By 1883 Casa Hernando had become a major Madrid publishing house, specialising in education.[51]

The British and the French had a much more captive market in their colonies. British authors, however, were often pirated in the USA (as the French were in Belgium). All countries with a developed educational system saw massive sales of textbooks. In most cases this was an indirect state subsidy: the private library of most French children between the ages of six and thirteen was made up of the five or six books which the state compelled parents to buy. If parents were poor, in many *départements* the local authorities would purchase the books themselves, as had been the practice in some parts of France as early as the beginning of the century.[52] Publishers realised that their key customers were those in charge of education: local administrators, public officials, school and university teachers. The state established a list of textbooks from which the schools would choose. In 1831 an '*abécédé*', a primer designed to introduce children to reading, was printed in 500,000 copies, a catechism had a print run of 100,000, and an adaptation such as *Robinson dans son île* outsold most novels.[53] A good maths book – such as that of Kühn and Kuznik, published by Korn in Germany – sold in a couple of years (1874–75) over 100,000 copies.[54] In France Armand Colin sold some five million books to schoolchildren in the course of the 1880s – almost one per schoolchild. Nathan and Louis Hachette were not far behind. Enterprising publishers had understood as early as 1865 (Delagrave), 1870 (Armand Colin),

1876 (Vuibert) and 1881 (Fernand Nathan) – the dates when they established themselves in Paris – that a new era was dawning, the era of mass education and mass literacy. It was the triumph of the textbook over the serialised novel.[55]

Writers of grammar and scientific books did not have to worry excessively over the ideology of their texts. But historians could not avoid it. Not for nothing was the leading best-seller in the 1830s Laure de Saint Ouen's *Histoire de France*, which not only subscribed closely to the official version of French history, but also provided various devices to help readers remember the succession of French kings and historical dates. As a result it was widely used in French schools.

Poetry

Poetry remained highly popular throughout the nineteenth century, at least in terms of titles published. Even when the number of titles began to decline in the 1890s, the actual number of poems published increased. What changed was where they were printed. Instead of publishing their collected poems in a bound volume, authors were increasingly published in literary magazines. These functioned as an advertisement for the poet's work, because those who had been published in a range of magazines would have a better chance of getting a publisher to print an entire volume. A French study worked out that between 1815 and 1870, 24,029 poetic works were printed, but only 14,530 novels – though it is certain that the novels sold more.[56] Outside the small circle of established poets, most poetry was of the popular genre, a majority of which (53 per cent) was published in the provinces, while very little fiction (5 per cent) was published outside Paris in the 1870s. Undoubtedly, then as now, poets were less financially demanding than novelists. They often paid to be published. Writing a poem has always been easier (and faster) than writing a novel, even a bad novel. Besides, even collections of poetry were usually barely longer than a pamphlet.[57] Thus, while poetry remained in principle a high genre, it was in practice the unpaid activity of provincial amateurs encouraged by the enormous success of poets like Victor Hugo. His poetry sold in large numbers, and everyone could understand it, unlike the 'difficult' symbolist poets who succeeded him in the 1890s. Hugo's poems had a powerful rhythm, sounded even better when declaimed aloud, and were full of passion and solemnity.[58] In England Tennyson and later Rudyard

Kipling fulfilled almost the same function. But most poets, like most writers, were soon forgotten even if they did enjoy a moment of glory.

In Britain one of the best-selling poets was the Reverend Richard Harris Barham. He sold his collection *The Ingoldsby Legends or Mirth and Marvels* (1840) to Bentley for £100. This was a very good deal for the publishers, for by 1856 the *Legends* had sold 20,000 copies, and a further 425,000 copies by 1895.[59] Barham's verse had the virtue of not being complicated, and Victorian audiences enjoyed the narrative and sentimentality of lines such as:

> Odille was a maid of a dignified race;
> Her father, Count Otto, was lord of Alsace;
> Such an air, such a grace, such a form, such a face,
> All agreed, 'twere a fruitless endeavour to trace
> In the Court, or within fifty miles of the place.
> Many ladies in Strasburg were beautiful, still
> They were all beat to sticks by the lovely Odille.[60]

Over the long run poets consecrated by the academy continue to sell steadily thanks to the educational market, which both provided a direct outlet and formed a taste for good poetry. Popular poetry, however, though disdained by high culture, continued to sell. Thus, such was the fashion for Orientalism in mid- to late-nineteenth century Germany that a collection of pseudo-Oriental poems, *Lieder des Mirza Schaffy* (The Songs of Mīrzā Schafī, 1851) by Friedrich Bodenstedt, was reprinted 264 times by 1922, even though it had only sold a thousand copies in its first ten years.[61]

Poetry was always, and still is, a strong seller in the gift market, though this was increasingly dominated, at least in England, by the literary annual, whose popularity was due as much to its steel engravings of famous paintings and fashionable people as to the poetry used to comment on the paintings.[62] Even poets of the standing of Tennyson and Browning deigned to write for annuals, so as to reach the underbelly of the Victorian middle classes.

Another way of becoming a popular poet was to have one's poems set to music. Here the British had to take a back seat to the French and, above all, the Germans. Haydn and Beethoven had set verse to music, but it was Schubert who excelled in the genre, setting the poetry of Goethe, Rückert and Heine, among others, in over six hundred *lieder*. Later in the century the genre was dominated by Robert Schumann, who composed over 250 *lieder*, Wagner, Liszt, Brahms and Hugo Wolf. This relatively novel use of poetry made the genre ever more popular.

In England the great era of poetry seemed to have come to a close with the beginning of the Victorian period. By then the first generation of major British Romantic poets were all dead: Keats in 1821, Shelley in 1822, Byron in 1824, and Blake who died in 1827; Coleridge died in 1834, three years before Victoria became queen. Wordsworth survived to 1850, but had written little of importance since 1835. The same development seems to have occurred in Russia, where the major poets died before the mid-century: Pushkin (1837) and Lermontov (1841). No major Russian poet appeared until the symbolist revolution at the turn of the century. The greatest nineteenth-century Italian poet, Giacomo Leopardi, died in 1837. In France Romantic poetry lasted longer: de Musset died in 1857, Vigny in 1863, Victor Hugo survived until 1885.

Beneath these giants a galaxy of lesser poets did thrive, and beneath them a firmament of amateurs entertained (or bored) their friends and relatives. Anyone who was somewhat literate could try poetry, be it a simple hymn to God or one's beloved, a mere rhyme, or a witty ditty. The proliferation of literary journals, especially in Britain, France, Germany and Russia, provided ample opportunities for finding one's name in print and a few minutes of fame. Until the advent of radio and television and a truly mass daily press there would not be many other such opportunities.

27

Music, Composers and Virtuosi

The Triumph of Dead Composers

UNTIL THE TWENTIETH CENTURY it was not easy to make money out of music. In the eighteenth century composers needed to be subsidised by private, royal or religious patronage, in the nineteenth largely by a combination of political and civic authorities. In the twentieth century music became big business thanks to the recording industry and, later, the broadcasting media, though for composers of so-called 'serious' music subsidies remained a necessity. In previous times, as no system of payment had been devised for each performance of a musical composition, composers preferred to be paid a regular stipend by a patron, to sell their music outright to a publisher or to perform it themselves. Before the middle of the nineteenth century musical copyright was either non-existent or else fragile and precarious, even though there were rights-collection agencies such as the Société des Auteurs et Compositeurs Dramatiques (founded by the playwright Beaumarchais, author of *Le Barbier de Seville* and *Le Mariage de Figaro*, in 1777).

In 1847 three composers of popular songs, Ernest Bourget, Victor Parizot and Paul Henrion, went to the Café des Ambassadeurs, a famous venue in Paris. Having placed their orders they watched the show, which featured many of their own songs. As they were about to leave, they openly refused to pay, accusing the owner of profiting from their works without paying them: 'You consume my music. I consume your wares.' They were taken to court, where a sympathetic judge ordered the café-owner to pay them for the use of the songs.[1] He based his verdict on the 1793 law on the 'right of the author' championed by Beaumarchais. Out of such initiatives was born in 1851 the SACEM (Société des Auteurs, Compositeurs et Éditeurs de Musique). This was almost a trade union, and as such was more effective than its British counterpart, the Society of British Authors (1843) – then more a literary and social circle than a champion of authors' rights.

In Britain the Dramatic Copyright Act of 1833, also known as the Bulwer-Lytton Act, introduced the concept of performance copyright, giving the author of a play the exclusive rights of representation. Previously, once a play had been printed, the author received nothing when it was performed. The Dramatic Authors' Society was constituted to protect the interests of play-wrights, and collect their fees. In 1842 these rights were extended to the composers of music.

This was the beginning of the music business. In the eighteenth century music publishers were in the business of selling music sheets. In the nine-teenth they sought to promote performances for the music they published.[2] Some publishers of musical scores became so powerful that, as was the case with the Ricordi publishing house in Italy, they were able to determine the course of musical history. In 1814 – the year Rossini arrived in Milan – Giovanni Ricordi (1785–1853) was a mere prompter and copyist at La Scala. Then he set up a shop next to the opera house to sell music sheets. By 1825 he had acquired La Scala's entire musical archives. By the end of 1837 he had acquired the exclusive rights to operas written for the Milan and Naples opera houses. In 1842 he began to publish *La Gazzetta musicale* (1842), Italy's leading music magazine. The firm, run by Giovanni's son Tito from 1853 to 1888, and afterwards by Tito's son Giulio, concluded a series of successful take-overs by acquiring its main rival, Francesco Lucca, thus becoming one of the largest music publishers in the world, with 100,000 compositions in its catalogue.[3] And just as his grandfather Giovanni had started out the family fortune by signing up Rossini, Giulio Ricordi continued by signing up Verdi and then Puccini.

Life was more difficult for composers of instrumental music. Brahms was one of the first able to make a good living simply from the sale of his published works without relying on patronage or a salaried appointment like Mozart, Beethoven, Schumann or Mendelssohn.[4] The development of an audience for 'dead composers' made the competition difficult for those still alive, while separating the role of the conductor from that of the composer. Until then the tradition was that composers were also the conductors of their work, as well as being among the players. At most the conductor was just a time-beater. Instead of remaining in the shadows (or in the afterlife), the composer could enjoy the pleasure of being almost like a *prima donna*. Beethoven, until deafness prevented it, was a 'spectacular' conductor. According to the composer Louis Spohr, 'as a *sforzando* occurred, he tore his arms which he had previously crossed upon his breast with great vehemence asunder. At a *piano*, he bent himself down, and the lower, the softer he wished to have it ... To increase the *forte* yet more, he would sometimes, also, join in with a shout to the orchestra, without being aware of it.'[5] Spohr (1784–1859), who in his lifetime was regarded as being in the same league as Beethoven, was one of the first to use the baton, precisely in order to avoid such acrobatics. Major nineteenth-century composers were also active conductors: Mendelssohn, Berlioz, Wagner and Mahler. By the twentieth century most famous conductors – such as Arturo Toscanini, Herbert von Karajan and Claudio Abbado – were not major composers (Pierre Boulez and Leonard Bernstein being the most notable exceptions).

It was composers, however, who made the most important innovation in the art of conducting. Berlioz began to codify the rules of conducting with his *Grand Traité d'instrumentation et d'orchestration moderne* (1843). Wagner revolutionised the writing and staging, as well as the conducting, of opera, as did Mahler, when they moved the conductor's podium to the front of the orchestra so that the conductor would have total control over every element of the performance. By then the rule, strictly enforced for decades in Vienna, that no one should turn their back to the Emperor, not even the conductor, let alone the musicians or the chorus, had been discontinued. This was not just a question of royal caprice: it was the norm for much of the nineteenth century in most opera houses for the conductor to have the orchestra behind him.[6]

Composers conducting their own works were in a position similar to a playwright having to perform in his own plays. Writers and playwrights can remain at home working, letting their works travel. Composers who were also conductors had to travel to propagate their work. Carl Maria von Weber (1786–1826), a virtuoso pianist and a conductor as well as a major composer, intended to write a helpful travelogue – *A Musical Vademecum* – in which he would describe for fellow-musicians the conditions they could expect in cities they toured, whom they should approach for permission to give concerts, what was the prevailing local musical taste, where the best piano could be found, which were the most remunerative days in which to perform, the dates of the season, the prices to be charged, and the likely size of one's earnings.[7]

The pre-eminence of the conductor as the intermediary between the composer and the audience came about as the classical repertoire of instrumental music was being established. Conductors of opera still had to take second place to the singers, who were the main attraction; nevertheless, some conductor-interpreters of great standing emerged, such as Angelo Mariani (1821–73), who realised, as he explained to Verdi in 1869, that he needed to rehearse not only the music but the entire production, welding music and drama together.[8]

In concerts, the professional conductor had already gained the upper hand by the end of the 1830s, partly by favouring the performance of the works of dead composers (who cannot interfere). His name was frequently mentioned on billboards advertising concerts and in press reviews.[9] In the twentieth century, of course, some conductors' names would rank as high as that of the composer – as in the Deutsche Grammophon announcement of a new recording of 'Karajan's Beethoven Symphonies'. The pre-eminence of the conductor was further helped by the increased complexity that some composers, such as Beethoven, had brought to the symphony. Much of this music was too difficult to be performed by amateurs, or in some cases even by professional musicians. This facilitated the task of François-Antoine Habeneck, the conductor who played a leading role in constructing the hegemony of Beethoven.

Conductors acquired a major role in determining the course of musical policy, particularly in Paris. The conductor of the Société des Concerts du Conservatoire in Paris in the nineteenth century would also conduct at the Opéra, and could make or unmake musical careers.[10] Their powers increased exponentially because, by promoting the work of dead composers, they presented themselves as the living embodiment of a departed genius. Living composers were less admiring. Berlioz, splenetic as usual, wrote in his *Mémoires*: 'Poor composers! Behave yourselves . . . because, and do not forget it, the most dangerous of your interpreters is the conductor.'[11] He even wrote, in 1844, a utopian novel in which there is no conductor.[12] *Euphonia ou la ville musicale* – 'a perfectly detestable work', commented *La Grande encyclopédie* (1885–1902) – is set in 2344. It is about a city entirely dedicated to music, where everyone is a musician or a singer and rehearses constantly until his or her audition before the Author, who is also the conductor, and in fact the master of the city. Musical education includes 'concerts of bad music' where pupils listen in disbelief to 'the monstrosities admired for centuries in Europe' such as the cavatinas and finales of the Italian school at the beginning of the century – a dig at Rossini.[13]

Most musicians willingly accepted the supremacy of the conductor. The members of the London Philharmonic Society, who had given themselves a democratic constitution in 1813, elected Michael Costa as conductor in 1846. He had asked for, and was granted, the right to be sole conductor-in-chief, with overall responsibility for the entire orchestra. In 1828 in France, Habeneck had ensured that he retained full powers over the Société des Concerts du Conservatoire. In Italy Angelo Mariani, the star conductor at the Carlo Felice of Genoa, was so powerful that he could use his position to advance the cause of Wagner in Italy after quarrelling with Verdi, whose works he had previously championed.

Conductors and orchestras were only two elements in the development of concerts. Appropriate venues were needed. In the 1830s in many European cities concerts were held in dance halls during the winter, and in parks and other open spaces during the summer (hence promenades). After 1850 formal orchestral concerts with classical programmes replaced the promenades. Larger halls were built, seating more than 1,000 people. Seats became cheaper, and concerts became more professional.[14] The growth was rapid:

NUMBER OF PUBLIC CONCERTS IN LONDON, VIENNA AND PARIS		
SEASON	1826–27	1845–46
London	125	381
Vienna	111	163
Paris	78	383

SOURCE: William Weber, *Music and the Middle Class. The Social Structure of Concert Life in London, Paris and Vienna*, p.16

Vienna remained behind its main rivals in the development of public concerts because it had a rich tradition of private and semi-private music-making, or *Hausmusik*.[15] In 1828 the Paris Odéon was opened as a massive concert hall: it could sit 3,000 people. This was the signal for the orchestra to emancipate itself from its dependency on the opera house where it had performed previously.[16] In London the commercialisation of concerts had started in the eighteenth century, partly because concert-going spread to the suburbs. By the 1850s regular cheap concerts were organised in Manchester, Leeds, Sheffield, Oldham, Bradford and Halifax.[17]

The concert constituted, for the composer, an indirect source of earning. By becoming known as a concert conductor, or by having his music performed, he ensured that he could sell his compositions at a good price to music publishers, and that he would get good sponsors for further concerts. Because Schubert, for example, was unable to make it as either a conductor or a soloist, he remained in his lifetime virtually unknown outside the circle of his admirers.[18]

A typical concert was the 'benefit concert', not on behalf of a charity but of an individual musician, or of the composer himself. The audience would be made up of people who had been taught by the musician, their relatives or people in whose homes he had performed.[19]

The institution of concerts was predominantly middle-class, since the aristocracy had patronised concerts at home – which is why most eighteenth-century music, including symphonies, could be performed by a small chamber orchestra. The rise of the concert place was thus paralleled by the development of the large-scale orchestra and its concomitant, the symphony. Where the middle class appeared earlier, as in England, so did the concert. In the middle of the nineteenth century a middle-class London family earning £1,000 a year could easily afford a top seat at a concert. In relative terms this was cheaper than it was for their Parisian equivalent.[20]

In 1831 François-Joseph Fétis, aware of the financial difficulties facing musicians in France, suggested that an association should be created to protect music. Wealthy benefactors would create a fund to be used to create some regularity in concert life, and at the same time provide for pensions and other benefits for musicians. Isidore Justin Séverin Baron Taylor (1789–1879), a Christian philanthropist, became the first President of the Association des Artistes Musiciens in 1843, and provided the decisive support. By 1844 the association had 1,100 members; ten years later there were 4,482.[21] Clearly, much music-making could not be based on purely commercial criteria.

One of the remarkable features of concert life in London and Paris was that the music performed was overwhelmingly 'foreign', prevalently German – as, in the eighteenth century, it had been predominantly Italian. In London, of course, foreign music dominated in opera as well, which seems to confirm that in so far as 'serious' music was concerned, the nationality of the composer did not matter even in culturally hegemonic countries. The subsequent twentieth-century globalisation of American and – since the Beatles – English popular music thus had a precedent in the non-national character of the musical experience. Of course, the terrain had been long prepared by the European hegemony of Italian music in all its aspects until the seventeenth and eighteenth century. Itinerant performers and composers developed a kind of internationalism. Though the new nationalism took over the musical world and constituted a major impetus for the development of 'national' music in countries such as Bohemia, all composers hoped to gain an international audience. The romantic myth of the 'national' composer (and/or the national poet), however, continued to be peddled for decades. Thus Chopin, who left Poland in 1831 at the age of twenty to settle in Paris, where he spent the rest of his life, has always been described as a true Polish patriot who never renounced his Polishness, the musical equivalent of Adam Mickiewicz. The story was further embellished in the twentieth century when over twenty films were made about him. One of those made in Communist Poland – *The Youth of Chopin*, by Aleksander Ford (1952) – portrayed him as an integral part of the Polish exiles' movement in Paris, joining the Parisian crowds with them during the 1830 uprising.[22] In fact Chopin was not very interested in politics, and though sympathetic to the Polish national struggle, he was never committed to it.[23] And it was not the exiled Polish aristocracy or intelligentsia that helped him in the salons, but the new moneyed aristocracy, mostly Jewish and cosmopolitan, like Maurice Schlesinger, the leading music publisher in Paris and founder of the influential *Revue et gazette musicale*, with whom Chopin signed a contract in 1832, or James and Betty de Rothschild, for whose daughter Charlotte he dedicated his Valse op. 64, no. 2 in C sharp minor (1847).[24]

By the 1820s English music, such as it was, had been buried by the popularity of foreign composers. Specifically English forms, such as the 'glee', were kept out of concert halls and remained the prerogative of amateurs. The glee was a piece of unaccompanied vocal music for at least three voices, usually male. It was very popular in England between 1760 and 1830, when an estimated 10,000 glees were written, but it was totally unknown outside the Anglo-Saxon world. England's dependence on foreign music, foreign conductors and foreign soloists remained remarkable. Foreign musicians, Italians in particular, flocked to London as they had since the eighteenth century, because they were paid far more than in Paris or in Italy, where instrumental performances were scarce. The absence of local production of exportable quality remained a constant of British music, while consumption remained high. In other words, the very considerable domestic demand for music sucked in imports rather than encouraging home-grown talents. Concerts were so popular that increasingly large halls were used – such as the Crystal Palace, where concerts were held in the 1880s, and the Royal Albert Hall, built in 1867–71. The wealthy, by themselves, were no longer able to fund a thriving musical life. One needed to attract the middle classes and to provide adequate space for large audiences.

The growing number of performances available in London required a small army of performers. At the chamber music concerts of 1877 organised by the violinist John Ella, music critic of the *Morning Post* and founder of the Musical Union, the performers included seventy-four pianists, 102 string players and twenty-seven wind players. Of these 203 musicians only forty-eight were English; the French numbered thirty-one, the Germans sixty-four, the Italians fifteen and the Belgians fourteen. Though music was heavily concentrated in London, it was widely appreciated elsewhere in Britain. Liverpool built a Philharmonic Hall (1849) which could accommodate an audience of 2,100 and an orchestra and choir of 250. The businessmen who funded it (though they were not a profit-making organisation) insisted on dress codes reflecting their genteel aspirations. Evening dress was compulsory in the stalls and boxes. Rules were established to ensure that the subscribers could not pass their boxes or stalls to the undesirable. In 1849 Karl Hallé, a German who had first settled in Paris, became the conductor of the Gentlemen's Concerts in Manchester and created, virtually from scratch, an entirely new audience which must have been well heeled, because a reserved seat in 1858 was priced at 2s.6d, the same amount that a cinema seat cost in England one hundred years later.[25]

Paris too, at least in so far as the composers performed, was dominated by foreigners, especially Germans, who wrote over 80 per cent of all works performed in the forty-two years after 1828:

PERFORMANCES OF INSTRUMENTAL WORKS
AT THE SOCIÉTÉ DES CONCERTS DU CONSERVATOIRE,
PARIS, 1828–70

Beethoven	43 per cent
Haydn	11 per cent
Weber	9 per cent
Mozart	6 per cent
Mendelssohn	6 per cent

SOURCE: Jeffrey Cooper, *The Rise of Instrumental Music and Concert Series in Paris 1828–1871*, p.31

No other composer obtained more than 1 per cent. Similar analyses carried out at the Société Sainte Cécile and the Société des Jeunes-Artistes and its successors the Concerts Populaires confirmed the above ranking, including the extraordinary dominance of Beethoven.[26] The third concert of the 1828 season at the Société des Concerts was opened with the Fifth Symphony in a version that was lengthened by repeating the third and fourth movements. After that, Beethoven's works figured in virtually every concert for the next twenty years. Occasionally three Beethoven symphonies were performed consecutively in a single evening.[27]

Beethoven owed his unassailable position to the fact that he was championed by the conductor François Antoine Habeneck (1781–1849), the founder the Société des Concerts du Conservatoire and the foremost representative of 'modern' music. But Habeneck was not his only supporter. Berlioz's unstinting lionisation of Beethoven in the pages of La Revue et gazette musicale de Paris, the most important and influential music journal in nineteenth-century France, also played a major role in establishing him at the centre of the repertory for the concert hall.[28] Wagner was another champion, believing that Beethoven's symphonies were a necessity for anyone who wanted to master modern orchestral techniques.[29]

Beethoven has held his position of unquestionable musical genius without interruption (unlike, say, Mozart) until the present, with only minor challenges in the earlier part of the twentieth century. In the 1930s American and Canadian radio listeners were asked to list their favourite composers, excluding the living. Mozart did not make the top ten. Beethoven was by far the most popular, with twice the votes of the runner-up. These were the top four:

MOST POPULAR DEAD COMPOSERS IN 1930S NORTH AMERICA	
Beethoven	1,878 votes
Brahms	904
Wagner	788
Tchaikovsky	648

SOURCE: Arno Huth, La Radio diffusion puissance mondiale, p.80

Beethoven's prestige was built on a multiplicity of factors: his position as inheritor of the (Viennese) mantle of Mozart and Haydn; his mastery of almost all the musical forms – symphony, concerto, sonata, string quartet, opera; his deafness, which helped the construction of a Romantic myth of the artist as aloof from the rest of society; his being championed by a succession of great musical innovators, above all Wagner; the combination of difficult aspects of his work (the late quartets) which would appeal to the expert, with others that are more easily apprehended such as the 'Spring' sonata, the opening of the Fifth Symphony and, above all, the 'Ode to Joy' choral tune from the Ninth Symphony, which was to become the anthem of the European Union, and was played to celebrate the fall of the Berlin Wall in 1989.

A further contingent factor in determining the prestige of Beethoven and other German composers was the fact that, at the time, the French had produced no important instrumental music. Louis Spohr, writing in the *Allgemeine musikalische Zeitung* in 1821 on the state of music in France – where he had been conducting the previous year – was categorically negative: 'It requires no longer residence to adopt the opinion that the French are not a musical nation.'[30] Even when – thanks to Berlioz, Gounod, Massenet and Saint-Saëns – France developed a major repertoire of instrumental music, the Germans dominated – even in France. In opera it was a different story. The French 'grand opera' ruled over the Parisian stage, and had the edge even on Verdi.

By the middle of the nineteenth century, in so far as instrumental music was concerned, the triumph of dead composers was complete. Their advance had been relentless. Between 1815 and 1825, 77 per cent of works played at the Leipzig Gesellschaft der Musikfreunde were by living composers. Between 1838 and 1848 living composers were down to 53 per cent. By the 1849–59 season only 18 per cent of the programme was made up of the works of living composers. The trend in London, Vienna and Paris was similar.[31]

Dead composers have dominated ever since the genre which is now known as 'classical music', while, in more popular forms the living have the edge. By the second half of the twentieth century very few living composers of 'classical' or 'serious' music would be able to fill a concert hall, and none would be able to dominate a season. Yet as late as the 1840s most Viennese and Parisian concert-goers 'scoffed at the idea that the greatest music might be the music of the past'.[32]

While more and more listeners flocked to the concert hall, most concerts were still performed in private. Some salons, patronised by the very rich, could entice the great piano virtuosi of the age such as Sigismond Thalberg (1812–71), Chopin (who shunned the concert circuit) and, above all, Liszt. But most salon performances were middle-class affairs, the music performed by amateurs, usually young women of marriageable age being shown off. There were plenty of opportunities to do so, as there were in 1846 some 850 salons in Paris.[33] The most important force behind the organisation and patronage of such concerts was provided by businessmen, and above all by their wives. This did not require anyone to be daring or speculative in taste, as the repertory changed very little and was increasingly made up of dead composers. It provided a rare opportunity for wealthy middle-class women – excluded from so much of public life – to do something which required organisational skills, provided the excitement of meeting artists, made them feel like munificent aristocrats, and was much more interesting than charity work.

There were few female role models. One was Alice Mary Smith, a British composer of chamber music, elected Female Professional Associate of the Philharmonic Society in 1867 and honorary member of the Royal Academy of Music in 1884. But women had no access to tuition in orchestration. Oxford and Cambridge did not award degrees in music to women until the 1920s – though Manchester University (then Victoria University) awarded the first music degree to a woman in 1894.[34] What women were taught in the home – piano and singing – had no role in an orchestra, so their skills could not have been transferred even if orchestras had been open to women.

On average, women were far more knowledgeable about music than men. Since childhood they would have spent years singing and at the piano, performing the same sort of exercises which they now imposed on their daughters, for this kind of music was central to the middle-class family. Many must have hated the compulsion of such musical training, which, it was felt, instilled a discipline in young girls who could not be expected, like the boys, to practise sport and the military arts. Some, however, had acquired a love of music that could only be satisfied by becoming unpaid musical impresarios. A few, with great determination, became virtuosi. One was Clara Wieck (1819–96), the daughter of Friedrich Wieck, a piano teacher and music dealer. As a young prodigy she toured Europe with her father (who was completely dedicated to her musical training). At the age of nineteen she was named Königliche Kaiserliche Kammervirtuosin (Royal and Imperial Chamber Virtuosi) – the greatest honour Austria could bestow on a musician – in spite of the triple handicap of being a woman, a Protestant and not an Austrian. Her marriage to Robert Schumann in 1840 brought an end to her brilliant career. Schumann wanted her to be a *Hausfrau*, not an international star. Yet she continued to tour, giving fifteen concerts between 1 January and 25 April 1842 as Clara Schumann. But in those years it was difficult for a woman to travel alone. Robert had to accompany her (as her father had done before), and while travelling he could not compose nor work as a music critic (his only remunerative activity). Clara, though, always performed his music, thus providing him with greater renown than he would otherwise have received. Occasionally she did travel alone, to Robert's dismay. His declining health and her constant pregnancies (she had eight children) put further obstacles in the way of Clara's career. She knew she had married a musical genius, and gradually identified herself completely with him, taking personally any criticism of his work. The deterioration of Schumann's mental state added further complications. After his death in 1856 she consoled herself with the company of Brahms – fourteen years her junior. She continued touring and never remarried.[35] Fanny Mendelssohn was even less fortunate, since her father never allowed her to perform in public, and some of her compositions were made popular by her brother Felix. A concert aria she wrote in 1835 was first performed in 2005.

Music for Free, Music for Fun

The free, or almost free, availability of music in the present day is remarkable: radio and television provide a wide choice of music twenty-four hours a day, not including the music which is imposed 'for free' on indifferent audiences in restaurants, bars, airport lounges, lifts, shops and trains.

Relatively speaking, a wide availability of 'free' music was also part of nineteenth-century life. Listening to the church choir and singing as a member of the congregation was a common experience. People enjoyed taking part, they enjoyed the familiarity with tunes and words. The circulation of hymn books with agreed tunes made it possible for more people to take part, and to practise at home around the piano. Over 1,200 hymn books were published in Britain during the reign of Queen Victoria. Almost every respectable working-class household had a copy of *Hymns Ancient and Modern* (1860) – a phenomenal publishing success, selling at a rate of 3,000 copies a week for thirty-five years, a total of over five million copies by the end of the century.[36] It is still widely used in the twentieth century. And yesterday's favourites are so even today: 'Good King Wenceslas' by J.M. Neale; 'Once in Royal David's City' and 'All Things Bright and Beautiful' by Cecil Frances Alexander (wife of the Bishop of Derry); 'In the Bleak Mid-Winter' by Christina Rossetti; 'Away in a Manger' and 'O Little Town of Bethlehem' by the American Phillips Brooks.

The singing was free but choral societies and church hymns had generated a formidable business. The collection of Scottish hymns *Scottish Hymnals*, published by Blackwood, was one of the firm's most profitable books between 1860 and 1900

Blackwood's *Scottish Hymnals*. Sales 1860–1900	
YEARS	COPIES SOLD
1860–69	181,976
1870–79	704,956
1880–89	841,473
1890–99	727,539
TOTAL	2,455,944

SOURCE: Finkelstein, *The House of Black-wood*, pp.159–64

Many 'English' hymns were in fact imported from Germany, which had a major choral tradition. The German publisher Bertelsmann, today the largest in the world, owes its origins in 1835 to the publication of Protestant hymn books. Many of these were translated and imported into Britain by Jane Montgomery Campbell and Catherine Winkworth (1827–78). The latter was a Christian feminist who became passionate about German hymns when, at the age of eighteen, she spent a year in Dresden. Her *Lyra Germanica* (1854) went into twenty-three editions, while *The Chorale Book for England* (1863) and *Christian Singers of Germany* (1869) introduced British church audiences to seventeenth-century German hymns such as Paulus Gerhardt's still famous 'All my Heart this Night Rejoices' and Martin Schalling's 'Lord, Thee I Love with All my Heart'.

Choral societies and church singing broke down many of the barriers between high music and the lower classes. Handel's *Messiah* (1742), a favourite of the British aristocracy in the eighteenth century, became in the course of the nineteenth a favourite of the church-going lower classes, especially Methodists.[37] Some choirs may have become bored with it, as performers often are with popular hits, but *The Messiah* never failed to please audiences.[38]

The boundaries between amateur and professional musicians were less strongly demarcated than in other genres. There were more opportunities for amateur participation in music-making than were available to the budding writer or actor. All that was required to be a member of a choral society was – apart from enthusiasm – a reasonably good voice and enough time. Here was a collective form of participation in a cultural activity which was open, at least potentially, to large groups of people. Initially the middle and lower-middle classes were over-represented, but the connection with the Church (especially in Protestant countries), local community groups such as mountain choral societies (notably in northern Italy and Switzerland), and patriotic organisations or the military ensured that choral societies – such as the Hungarian choral societies in the second half of the nineteenth century: the Budai Zeneakadémia (Buda Music Academy, 1867) and the Zenekedvelök Egylete (Pest Music Lovers' Society, 1867) – were far less élitist than virtually any other cultural pursuit. Indeed, socialist and trade union organisations, especially in Britain and northern Europe, did not eschew the opportunity to provide their members with ample opportunities to participate in some form of musical activity. The most successful choral societies were to be found in Germany, where they were associated with rising nationalism and civic pride. By the 1830s the Rhine choral festivals had become mass events, but they were based on traditional religious music seen as uniting all Germans: Bach's St Matthew Passion and Handel's oratorios, above all *The Messiah* (probably the all-time favourite in England, where people still stand up for the Hallelujah Chorus as if it were the national anthem). One of the most important new choral works of the nineteenth century was Mendelssohn's oratorio St Paul (*Paulus*), and no one, until Wagner launched his anti-Semitic attack *Das Judentum in der Musik* (Judaism in Music, 1850), thought it strange that such a celebration of German unity and of Christianity should have been composed by a Jew.[39]

In the German states choral societies were perhaps one of the few democratic institutions. At the beginning of the nineteenth century each individual member, man or woman, voted on the decisions of the chorus.[40] Music in Liverpool grew almost entirely out of the impetus provided by amateur choral societies such as the Liverpool Musical Society, backed by a semi-professional orchestra. Choral music in London, however, depended on the professional choirs of the theatres and operas. The middle-class choirs in Manchester, Liverpool and London were not typical of the large choral societies of other industrial towns which provided probably the vast majority of the English people with their own real contact with music. English choral music in the nineteenth century was largely the result of the musical preferences of the nonconformist Churches, and Methodism in particular. Its success was partly due to John Wesley's desire that hymns should be simple and direct, so that the least musical people would understand them, and could sing them and be moved by them. The Methodists always insisted that the entire congregation should sing.[41]

By the mid-nineteenth century choruses had acquired a central position in the musical life of Paris and London. The Sacred Harmonic Society, a choral society created in London in 1832, held, by 1840, twenty concerts a year before audiences of up to 2,000 people. It acquired aristocratic and royal patronage, and performed at the inauguration of the Great Exhibition in 1851. In Paris the Orphéon selected 6,000 singers from 204 choruses to perform before 40,000 people at the Palais de l'Industrie. This was a musical circuit parallel to the still relatively expensive concert halls where professional musicians performed, and which until the middle of the nineteenth century were still barely within the reach of the middle class. In England mechanical institutes and local cultural societies organised concerts and other cultural activities regularly. In 1855 August Manns started weekly symphonic concerts in the Crystal Palace at a shilling a seat. In Paris in 1861 Jules Pasdeloup followed suit with his seventy-five-centime concerts at the Cirque d'Hiver. The condescension with which these events were treated in the bourgeois press suggested that they were attended prevalently by the lower middle classes and artisans.[42]

In Vienna the choral societies – at first dominated by amateurs – became increasingly taken over by professionals, yet the Wiener Männergesangverein (Vienna Men's Choral Society) was overwhelmingly middle-class: in 1891–93 40 per cent of its members were civil servants, 18 per cent were merchants and 13 per cent artisans.[43] Another Viennese choral society, the Schubertbund, was entirely made up of schoolteachers.[44]

Parallel to the development of choral groups was that of brass bands, often military or civic – another illustration of the presence of a 'public sector' element in the diffusion of music and musical skills. In Britain the brass band movement was not military but church-related, and in the same areas where the choral societies were popular. But there were also factory bands funded by employers to keep their workers off the bottle. By the middle of the 1830s a band had become a source of pride, prestige and advertisement for the workplace which sponsored or had created it. The best players were often enticed away to play for other bands and work for other employers.[45]

The other main setting in which people could participate in music was by dancing to it. Before the modern period, dancing – except for special occasions such as the Carnival – was rigidly segregated along class lines. For the upper classes it was a private activity to be performed in a private place. There is evidence in the eighteenth century of semi-public venues, dancing halls charging an entrance fee, such as Carlisle House in London, under the direction of Teresa Cornelys, a singer turned impresario who became known as 'the Empress of Soho' – soon to face competition from William Almack and his assembly rooms (1765), and the Pantheon (1772).[46] These venues were patronised almost exclusively by the aristocracy and the rich. Public balls became an institution in Paris and London in the 1830s, with summer balls in gardens and squares, but also in winter in theatres and places such as the Closerie de Lilas and Le Bal Vivienne in Paris, Vauxhall Gardens in London (already in the eighteenth century), the 'Vauxhall' near St Petersburg, and the 'Tivoli' in Copenhagen. In Vienna, large dance halls such as the Sperl and the Apollosaal, which could host 6,000 dancers, were opened as early as 1808.[47]

For the lower classes, dancing was entirely a public matter, a ritual of special occasion. In the nineteenth century in both Paris and London dancing venues frequented mainly by the respectable working classes and clerical workers became increasingly popular. The Parisian police estimated that there were in the capital 367 'guinguettes' (establishments where people could dance) in 1830.[48]

In the Paris of the 1830s the 'bals publics' took place on Sundays, Mondays and Thursdays. Some were open-air and hence were held only during the warmer months. But there were also indoor venues such as the Tivoli d'Hiver, and charity balls.[49] The 'cabaret dansant' was a smaller affair. In 1833 the Gazette des tribunaux described one such venue in the rue du Paradis as a square room, with benches against the wall, and a lone blind fiddler instead of an orchestra. The favourite dance was still the quadrille. This is almost a show, as four couples use steps and positions similar to ballet. By 1844, though, the polka was all the rage. Here a couple dance without touching, but looking at each other with care so as keep time. The success of the polka brought the waltz back into favour, along with other novelties: the mazurka, la varsoviana, la Schottische – all to the delight of a new profession, the dance teacher.[50]

While Italian opera was appreciated by the élites and was regarded by foreigners as quintessentially Italian, far more popular lower down the social scale was the kind of music performed by military bands (especially Austrians, at least in the north). Peasants embraced and adapted various polkas and mazurkas (in turn adapted into a waltz by Verdi in the aria 'Il tempo giammai non s'arresti' in *I Due Foscari*). Popular tunes were also diffused by itinerant local bands such as those of the village of Viggiano in Basilicata, where three hundred of the 7,000 inhabitants were musicians (all harpists). While travelling – as they had done for generations – they exported their local folk tunes, adaptations of southern composers such as Pergolesi and Cimarosa, and learned various tunes elsewhere.[51] By 1872 there were in Italy some 1,500 military and civic bands giving some form of employment and occupation to 46,422 mainly part-time or amateur musicians.[52]

While the high bourgeoisie set the tone with great balls in élite places such as, in Paris, the Grand Bal de l'Opéra or the Tuileries, the petty and middle bourgeoisie started public balls in theatres and in modest neighbourhood cafés.[53] In great urban centres such as Paris and London the cultural movement between the various social groups encountered fewer obstacles.

The popularity of dance music and its expansion are associated with the waltz. This expansion was due principally to its Parisian success and the Napoleonic wars, which took the waltz to the rest of Europe.[54] Waltzing was daring, revolutionary, and almost indecent. It permitted couples to dance in a close hold, separately from others (and thus able to talk and to flirt). Yet in Vienna it took the court by storm, without any significant religious opposition. Why this should be so is not clear. Perhaps it was because of the kind of musical culture Vienna had enjoyed since the eighteenth century, as epitomised by some of the compositions of Mozart and Haydn, perhaps because of the relative tolerance of the Roman Catholic Church in matters of entertainment.[55] A thriving musical culture provides plenty of opportunities for musicians, but it can also generate an oversupply of trained players who, to make a living and find an audience, must experiment in non-conventional settings. This is how four violinists, led by Joseph Lanner, started performing in taverns and what would later be called cabarets. Some of these attracted a better class of customers such as army officers who had a taste for good music. The setting, the orchestra and the mixed clientèle favoured some lowering of social barriers and of the boundaries between high and low genres. The waltz was at the interface between the two.

Joseph Lanner's use of the waltz proved so successful that he split his musical ensemble into two distinct orchestras in 1825, continuing to compose tunes for both.[56] The leader of the second orchestra, a member of the original quartet, was Johann Strauss (1804–49). By 1825 Strauss (the elder, as he is now known) had toured Europe and made the waltz popular, and composed a large number of them (including the well known 'Lorelei') as well as polkas, quadrilles and galops. He was in London for the coronation of Queen Victoria, and gave seventy-two concerts in 120 days.[57]

Poised between the high Viennese school (Haydn, Mozart and Beethoven) and the popular, Strauss appeared to conquer all. His waltzes prevailed in high-society settings: official balls, embassy balls and wherever the high bourgeoisie and the aristocracy met *en masse*. But they reached beyond. In 1833 the German journalist Heinrich Laube described an evening of dancing to Strauss at the Sperl dancehall:

> To hold the unrestrained crowds in check a long rope is taken, and all who remain in the middle are separated from those actually occupied in dancing ... The couples waltz intoxicated through all the accidental or intentional obstructions, wild delight is let loose ... The start of each dance is characteristic. Strauss begins his quivering preludes ... the Viennese takes his girl low on his arm, they ease themselves in the most wonderful way into the beat ... the real dance begins with all its raging velocity, and the couple plunge into the whirlpool.[58]

Much dancing and music was still performed at home, as it would be for the next hundred years. The spread of home music generated two secondary markets, one for sheet music and one for musical instruments, of which by far the preferred one was the piano, whose prominence in the middle-class home was also a sign of refinement and distinction. It was in the nineteenth century that music moved away from being an entertaining background noise or something to do in church and became regarded as a deep expression of human feelings and emotions. This fetishisation was concomitant with the invention of the Great Composer, and above all, of the cult of Beethoven. While it was believed that most contemporary novels were bad for people and led them to adultery and perdition, music – of a certain kind – was seen as elevating; it was not a simple entertainment, it was almost the voice of God. Tolstoy was not being eccentric when in his story 'The Kreutzer Sonata' (1890, named after Beethoven's violin sonata of the same title) he has the jealous husband, Vasia Pozdnyshev, musing on the powerful effect of music: 'Take the Kreutzer Sonata, for example: is it right to play that first *presto* in a drawing room to ladies in low dresses? To play that *presto*, then to applaud it, and immediately afterwards to eat ice creams and discuss the latest scandal? Such pieces as this are only to be executed in rare and solemn circumstances of life.'[59] Almost fifty years later, the great Viennese architect Adolf Loos was similarly outraged: 'Whoever goes to the Ninth Symphony and then sits down to design a wallpaper pattern,' he declared, 'is either a rogue or a degenerate.'[60]

Instruments

Whether music was the voice of God or of human beings, it required instruments, craftsmen to make them, businessmen to sell them, customers to buy them. The fashion for home music meant that the piano was regarded as being as indispensable to the middle-class home as a CD player is in most households today. Between 1850 and 1900 world production of pianos increased tenfold, to 50,000 a year.[61] In England, pianos could be bought on hire-purchase plans, enabling even the more prosperous working-class homes to acquire a piano by going to the Bethnal Green firm of Moore & Moore or to Archibald Ramsden in Leeds.[62]

An expansion in the sales of anything previously in the exclusive possession of élites inevitably causes social critics to lament a lowering of standards. One journalist writing in the London magazine *Connoisseur* in January 1846 complained: 'In families the piano has extinguished conversation and the love of books.'[63] But love of novelties, which some people call progress, could not be stopped. In 1851 at the Great Exhibition in London, 102 manufacturers exhibited 178 pianos. The predominantly British judges gave the prize for the best piano to Pierre Érard, whose London factory employed 425 men (a very high number for the time) in 1855, and produced 1,500 pianos a year. The situation became more competitive with the entry, in 1853, of the firms of Bechstein (Berlin) and Bluthner (Leipzig). In 1850 a German piano-maker, Heinrich Steinweg, emigrated to New York, hoping to find a market less constrained by guild rules and a multiplicity of states divided by customs duties. New York offered considerable opportunities for German music entrepreneurs. Twenty-five per cent of its population were Germans, making New York the largest German city in the world after Berlin and Vienna. Germans dominated the music business, and made up most of the audiences and the orchestras. In 1854, the New York Philharmonic performed only German music.[64] As we have noted, even in Paris, German instrumental music had a near monopoly.

In New York Steinweg changed the firm's name to the more English-sounding Steinway & Sons (1853). The market may have been less regulated than in Germany, but the competition was stiff. Whereas in 1858 there were only one hundred piano makers, and total production was 712 pianos, by 1863 there were four hundred firms producing 1,623 pianos.[65] Steinway kept in touch with new technological developments through his brother, who had remained in Germany. A strategic decision was taken: Steinway would aim at the top end of the market by making what would be regarded, thanks to advertising, as the best piano in the world. It was a shrewd move, since at the time the top end of the US market was expanding even more rapidly than the economy as a whole. The market went on expanding until in 1928 more than half of urban American homes had a piano, and one in four children above third grade were taking piano lessons.[66]

In the nineteenth century, in order to dominate the quality end of the classical music market it was necessary to obtain European legitimisation. This Steinway achieved by obtaining endorsements from famous pianists to whom the firm had sent a free piano, and by winning prizes at various exhibitions, including the 1867 Exposition Universelle in Paris. They also built Steinway Hall, the second largest concert hall in New York (2,000 seats in 1866), in imitation of what their European competitors had already done or were about to do: Streichler in Vienna, Pleyel in Paris and Bechstein in London (Bechstein Hall became the Wigmore Hall when the First World War made German names unpopular).[67] The French firm of Érard, which had a factory in England to take advantage of the large British market, made sure it was advertised that on Liszt's English tour the great virtuoso would be playing 'Erard's New Patent Grand Piano-forte of Seven Octaves'.[68]

In the first half of the nineteenth century, however, the largest manufacturer of pianos in the world was neither German nor French, but the British firm of Broadwood. It was also one of the pioneers of the arcane art of getting endorsements from leading pianists. In early 1818, as we have seen, Broadwood shipped a mahogany-cased grand piano to Beethoven and received a letter of thanks and gratitude (see page 225). When Beethoven's estate was put up for sale, the Vienna music publisher Carl Anton Spina bought his Broadwood piano and gave it to Liszt as a gift in 1846. Its presence at Weimar was noted by George Eliot in September 1854.[69]

In 1848 Broadwood provided Chopin with three grand pianos for his British tour: one for his lodgings in London, one for his London concerts and one for his tour of Scotland. By 1842, 2,500 pianos a year were being made in the great Broadwood factory in Horseferry Road by its 575 craftsmen, while the largest Viennese manufacturer could only produce two hundred pianos a year. Broadwood had become one of the twelve largest employers in London. At the same time it had six hundred pianos almost permanently rented out, for monthly fees ranging between twelve shillings and £2. 12s. 6d.[70] However, Broadwood failed to anticipate market trends, and continued to produce square pianos instead of the new and lighter upright ones, better adapted for domestic use, which enabled Érard to overtake it in production.

Piano manufacturing was becoming a global enterprise whose centre until the mid-1850s was London, even though London produced neither great music nor great pianists. What London did have was a wealthy piano-playing middle class. Later, in terms of volume, the centre of gravity moved to the USA, thanks to Kimball in Chicago, while Steinway held on to the top end of the market. However, the enormous transport costs associated with pianos meant that American manufacturers were essentially selling to their home market.[71] This enabled the Germans to achieve command of the European market. Soon the Japanese entered the fray: in 1887 Torakusu Yamaha began to make pianos. One century later, Japan and Yamaha had become the world's leading manufacturers of pianos.

The development of the market for musical instruments led not only to an increase in the sales of existing instruments such as the piano and the violin, but also to the invention of new ones. One is particularly worthy of note: the saxophone. Its subsequent fame was linked to the history of jazz, but its origins lay in European band music. It was invented by a Belgian Jew, Adolphe Sax (1814–94), whose father Charles-Joseph was a manufacturer of musical instruments specialising in wind instruments, particularly clarinets and bassoons. Adolphe's brother Alphonse had even set up, in 1863, an all-woman wind ensemble, and made the dubious claim that playing wind instruments helped prevent pulmonary diseases.[72] By the mid-1830s the Sax firm was one of the largest in Europe, and was constantly expanding. In 1841 Adolphe perfected a new wind instrument which he called the saxophone (the patent was registered in 1846), and gave a public performance at the International Exhibition in Brussels. He realised the technical possibilities of the instrument, and extended its range by developing an entire family of saxophones (soprano, tenor, alto, etc.).

By 1848 Adolphe, who had moved to Paris in 1842, was employing two hundred workers. His business, however, was quite different from that of piano manufacturers. The latter were selling and renting mainly to private customers, but the market for wind instruments was predominantly made up of military bands, and hence dependent on the whim of the political establishment. So the decision in 1848 by the new republican government in France not to use wind instruments in regimental bands – probably due to strong lobbying by some other instrument manufacturer – was a major blow for Adolphe Sax.[73]. His fortunes changed again with a change of régime. In 1858 Napoleon III appointed Sax Imperial Instrument Maker, and the saxophone was used in military bands throughout France. Many Sax instruments were used in large symphonic orchestras by innovators like Berlioz, who introduced Sax's clarinet-bass – played by Sax himself – in his Symphonie Funèbre et Triomphale.[74] Appointed director of the Fanfare de l'Opéra de Paris, Sax also developed special trumpets for the famous march in Verdi's Paris première of *Aida* at the Opéra in March 1880.[75] But some of his worldwide renown was also due to the activities of humbler musicians such as the Distin family (a father and his four sons), an English wind quintet. In Paris in 1844, having embraced the new instrument, they performed at a number of venues including at the Opéra-Comique in a concert conducted by Berlioz. They then exported the sound of the saxophone throughout Britain (1845), Germany (1846) and, in 1849, America.[76]

Sax had presented his new instruments in London at the Great Exhibition of 1851. His most important champion, Berlioz, was elated at the success of the French instrument-makers there among whom he included, of course, the Belgian Adolphe Sax, who won the much-coveted Council Medal for his concert of eighty-five instruments. Berlioz sang his praises:

> Mr. Sax has created the saxophone, a charming brass instrument with a clarinet mouthpiece. Its novel timbre permits the most delicate nuances and misty half-tones similar to the majestic tones of religious music. Mr. Sax has provided us with an entire family of saxophones. Composers may not yet appreciate the value of this new addition which they owe to the genius of its creator; the cause is to be traced to the lack of experienced players. This is a difficult instrument; to master it, it is necessary to practise it with dedication and at great length, but so far it has been played too little and not well.[77]

The Invention of the Virtuoso

The evolution of the performer as an interpreter of the work of dead composers, the growing commercialisation of concerts and of the ease of travel, enabled some performers to acquire great renown, as had the Italian castrati in the eighteenth century. Virtuosi toured Europe and the Americas, performing on public stages to fee-paying audiences, while at the same time or as a second career performing in private salons for large sums, as regularly did Adelina Patti (1843–1919), the great soprano of the 1860s and 1870s of whom Verdi said she was '*grandissima, meravigliosa*'.[78] In Milan she asked for, and was given, 10,000 lire per performance, more than any other soprano in Italy, and at a time when a well-paid civil servant was earning 2,380 lire a year. Patti could earn much more elsewhere.[79] In Paris she could command a fee of up to 20,000 francs for one evening, as at the *soirée* of Baron Moritz de Hirsch.[80] Yet, as Edmond About worked out in his *L'ABC du travailleur* (1879), she was 'worth it' economically speaking: 'When Mademoiselle Patti sings for 2,000 francs in the salon of a banker, she produces by opening her mouth a rapidly evaporating utility that is nevertheless regarded as being worth 2,000 francs by the master of the house, who, after all, can count. The young and brilliant singer produces, in forty-five minutes, the equivalent of forty tons of cast iron priced at fifty francs per thousand kilos.'[81] In the 1880s Patti made more money by endorsing Pears' Soap thus: 'I have found Pears' Soap matchless for the Hands and Complexion'.[82]

The salons which in the 1860s and 1870s hosted musicians and singers were a less aristocratic replica of those of the eighteenth century, but because they were patronised by the high bourgeoisie, performers got more money and more respect. They were no longer mere entertainers just a notch above the servants, but rich professionals now deemed to be artists of genius.

The new virtuosi travelling from city to city needed to be talked about by the press, because before arriving in a city even famous singers would not have been previously heard by most opera-goers. It was necessary to get the local papers, often prompted or bribed by concert organisers, to inform their readership of the fame, triumphs and, occasionally, love life of the star about to arrive. Virtuosi were aware of the importance of acquiring a persona, an image. Opera singers, and the *prime donne* in particular, were the obvious beneficiaries of this trend. As it was clear that some people went to the opera in order to hear, and to be able to say that they had heard and seen, a particular singer, it made sense to skip the whole expensive production of an opera, and to have instead the lone singer with a few accompanists. This trend was accelerated by the spreading practice in private homes of people singing arias, separate from operas and songs. Similarly instrumentalists, almost exclusively pianists or violinists, benefited from the popularity of these instruments among a wide number of amateur practitioners.

Great virtuosi were in a league of their own. In the absence of a mass popular culture (sportsmen, pop singers, cinema and television personalities) the field was clear for exponents of 'serious' music. In March–April 1831 the most celebrated violinist of his day, Nicolò Paganini, performed eleven concerts at the Opéra Académie Royale de Musique. It was his Parisian debut, but his fame had preceded him. The contract he had agreed with Louis Véron, the director, stipulated that Paganini would play twice a week, on Wednesday or Friday, for which he would receive two-thirds of the box office receipts, and on Sunday, for which he would get 100 per cent of the box office.[83] One concert would be for charity – a common ploy among artists to avoid accusations of financial greed. Paganini's gross earnings for the concerts came to just over 133,107 francs – an enormous sum, much in excess of what was then the estimated value of Leonardo's *Mona Lisa* (90,000 francs in 1849).

PAGANINI'S EARNINGS AT HIS PARIS DEBUT, MARCH–APRIL 1831

	Box office receipts (in francs)	Paganini's share	Paganini's gross earnings
Wednesday, 9 March	19,069	⅔	12,712
Sunday, 13 March	16,531	100%	16,531
Sunday, 20 March	21,895	100%	21,895
Wednesday, 23 March	20,869	⅔	13,912
Sunday, 27 March	16,014	100%	16,014
Friday, 1 April	14,436	⅔	9,624
Sunday, 3 April	14,113	100%	14,113
Friday, 8 April	16,063	⅔	10,708
Friday, 15 April	9,144	⅔	6,096
Sunday, 17 April	6,105	Charity	0
Sunday, 24 April	11,502	100%	11,502
TOTAL	165,741		133,107

SOURCE: My calculation on the basis of data in François Lesure et al., *La Musique à Paris en 1830–1831*, Bibliothèque Nationale, Paris 1983, p.53

The high earning power of this international virtuoso can be assessed by comparing his income for eleven performances over less than eight weeks with that of other musicians. Luigi Cherubini, hardly an ordinary composer, held the position of the King's Chief Superintendent of Music, yet in the first six months of 1830 his stipend amounted to 6,000 francs. The first violin of his orchestra got only 2,400 francs, the leading cellist 2,000.[84]

After his Parisian successes Paganini performed in May 1831 at the King's Theatre in London, later Her Majesty's. This was the start of a long British tour. For the occasion the theatre announced that it was doubling its usual prices. The Times thundered at an 'extravagance which could only have entered the head of a foreigner, who had beforehand arrived at the happy conviction, moreover, of the infinite gullibility of the English nation'. What particularly irked the paper was that the show was going to be a mere concert: 'there is no chorus, no corps dramatique, nor corps de ballet, to be engaged. Nothing is wanted but an orchestra, the whole attention centring in fact in the single talent of Paganini.'[85]

It is only from the enthusiastic descriptions of his performances, and the fiendish difficulty of his compositions, that we can assume that Paganini was an exceptional violinist. 'It would be impossible to describe the enthusiasm with which the public was seized hearing this extraordinary man; it was delirium, frenzy,' wrote the Revue musicale.[86] His opening night in Paris was attended by – among others – George Sand, Delacroix, Rossini, Cherubini, Halévy, Meyerbeer and Théophile Gautier.[87] He was unquestionably helped by the cult surrounding him, aspects of which had little to do with his performances. He may have had an uncanny talent in marketing his own celebrity, or perhaps he was just lucky, but the legends and stories which accompanied him, and which he made no great effort to deny, seem to have come straight out of a Gothic novel set in Italy. It was said that ordinary people feared dying before having heard him, and that mothers took their children to his concerts so that they would have the experience of their lives.[88] People were told that he had been imprisoned for murdering his wife, or perhaps his mistress (The Genius as a Dangerous Man), that he had learned the violin in prison because he could neither read nor write (The Artist as Single-Minded), that he used the intestines of his wife (or mistress) as strings for his violin (The Artist Makes a Pact with the Devil). Like modern celebrities, Paganini attracted his share of sordid stories, including an action for abduction brought by a young woman widely suspected of being a prostitute trying to make money out of him.

Paganini's talent and fame enabled him to be paid vastly in excess of other violinists. But he worked hard, travelling incessantly like all virtuosi. In the late 1820s he had realised that giving salon recitals meant performing for a distracted and restricted audience. More money and fame could be obtained by forcing the aristocracy to go and listen to him in concert halls, along with the bourgeoisie. Liszt and Sigismond Thalberg, though they both attended salons, followed Paganini's example.[89] In just over two years (January 1829 to February 1831), Paganini visited forty-eight cities and towns in Germany and Poland.[90] Over the following two years he performed everywhere in the British Isles: seventy-five concerts, including London, Brighton, Bath, Bristol, Exeter, Plymouth, Liverpool, Manchester, Leeds, Chester, Birmingham, York, Halifax, Sheffield, Hull, Dublin, Glasgow and Edinburgh.[91] And all reached by horse-drawn coaches.

Liszt (1811–86) too worked hard. He was, by all accounts, the greatest pianist of the nineteenth century. He could play, from memory, almost the entire piano repertoire, including Beethoven's 'Hammerklavier' sonata, hitherto regarded as incomprehensible. Moreover, he expanded that repertoire considerably, transcribing and adapting pieces written for other instruments, including passages from symphonies and operas, thus popularising in easily digestible and reproducible fragments entire works by Beethoven, such as the Ninth Symphony. In Italy, where instrumental music had virtually disappeared since the days of Vivaldi, Liszt was faced with an audience ignorant of non-operatic music, and was reduced to pleasing them by improvising on operatic themes.[92]

Between 1839 and 1847 he was engaged in a formidable Europe-wide tour, performing 1,000 'recitals', a word which started then to be used to describe a concert in which only one musician would perform. He visited Spain, Portugal, France, Germany, Austria, Great Britain, Turkey, Romania, Moldavia and the Ukraine. During his four visits to Britain between May 1840 and July 1841, organised by the impresario Louis Lavenu, he visited scores of towns and cities throughout England, Scotland and Ireland, travelling by carriage, ship and train. He spent six weeks (August–September 1840) as a member of a troupe of itinerant entertainers, and returned two months later for another ten-week tour.[93] Outside the main circuit – the tour included many small market towns – he attracted only small crowds, and was forced to perform on poor-quality pianos.

In the less peripheral cities Liszt performed to packed houses of 3,000 or more, and became the object of a craze comparable to that surrounding international performers in the twentieth century. The frenzy of adulation led Heine to coin the term 'Lisztomania'. Typical of this cult was the painting *Lizst at the Grand Piano* (*Liszt am Flügel*, 1840, now at the National Gallery in Berlin) by Josef Danhauser, showing him playing the piano while observing a bust of Beethoven; at his feet his mistress, Marie Contesse d'Agoult, on a chair George Sand looking almost orgasmic, her hand in Dumas's. Behind them, contemplating the scene, were Rossini, hugging Paganini's shoulders, and Victor Hugo.

Female admirers – Liszt was unusually handsome – sought clippings of his hair and cups he had drunk from to keep as mementos. For a price, high society ladies could have the honour of sitting around the piano during some of his concerts. There were reports that his arrival at a salon in Vienna would stimulate loud cries from the ladies present.[94] Anecdotes about him abounded, probably amplified by his biographers, such as that of the aristocratic lady who retrieved one of his discarded cigars and is said to have carried it in her corsage until the day she died – without, in that pre-Freudian age any awareness of the phallic implications of her gesture. After giving his last performance at Elizavetgrad in Russia Liszt moved to Weimar, where in February 1848 he took up a conducting post offered him by the Grand Duke. In 1854 he was visited by George Eliot, who was struck by his looks and charm: 'In him Nature has not sacrificed the man to the artist . . . See him for a few hours and you will be charmed by the originality of his conversation and the brilliancy of his wits.'[95] Herr Klesmer, the pianist in her novel *Daniel Deronda*, perhaps based on Liszt, was described by Eliot as 'not yet a Liszt, understood to be adored by ladies of all European countries with the exception of Lapland'.[96]

After 1848 Liszt rarely played in public again, and never for a fee. To the music-loving public it was an incomprehensible decision. But his itinerant lifestyle, before the age of the railway, would have been exhausting. The pressure of giving 150 concerts a year as well as composing new works and arrangements for his adoring public must have been – in the long term – unbearable. In retrospect, from the point of view of his later fame, he had taken the right decision. His spell as *Kapelmeister* at Weimar ended in disappointment and he was forced to leave in 1859, having lost the support of both his patron and his public, but the 1850s were his most productive decade as a composer. In this way he achieved the immortality which escaped his great contemporary and rival Thalberg, a Swiss-born virtuoso with whom Liszt fought a pianistic 'duel' in the spring of 1837.

Virtuosi like Paganini and Liszt would now appear to belong to a 'high' genre, but until the nineteenth century the idea that 'light' music was essentially different from serious music was meaningless. All the great composers of the eighteenth and early nineteenth centuries provided entertainment as well as 'serious' music. Beethoven composed minuets, Schubert waltzes.[97] Paganini and Liszt were in the entertainment business, just like the 'Three Tenors' (Pavarotti, Domingo and Carreras) who in the 1990s became as idolised as pop stars.

The affinity between the virtuoso and the circus freak had not escaped Phineas.T. Barnum (1810–91), the great American circus impresario. Already in 1842 he had included in his acts at Scudder's American Museum in New York the midget 'General' Tom Thumb, the Siamese twins Chang and Eng, and other oddly shaped people, as well as celebrities like Bill Cody, the legendary Buffalo Bill. As a shrewd businessman Barnum was quick to realise that people would be just as interested in paying to see and hear a famous soprano as an acrobatic dwarf. In 1850 he enticed the famous soprano Jenny Lind (1820–87), the so-called 'Swedish nightingale', to undertake a major tour of the USA, performing in ninety-three concerts between September 1850 and May 1851. Lind, who had quit the operatic stage in 1849 when she was only twenty-nine, continued to sing in concerts until 1883. In a sense her brief stage career (less than five years outside Sweden) was a preparation for her solo singing. In all the sixty operas in which she performed at the Royal Opera House in Stockholm between 1830 and 1841 she never sang in any of the internationally famous Italian operas except Bellini's *Norma* (in the title role) in 1841.

Lind, entirely aware of her worth, demanded huge fees: $1,000 per evening (or £200 at the rate of exchange of the time), and lavish expenses (in order to allay public envy she announced that she would give the earnings of her first night to charity). Barnum accepted the terms, and confounded his critics, who thought he would lose money in the tour: Lind was reputed to have earned $200,000, while he took home $500,000.[98] Some of the tickets were sold at auction. In Boston the first was sold for $650, an astonished Lind reported in a letter to her parents.[99] America had been made aware of her reputation by an enormous publicity campaign: Barnum had employed twenty-six agents for the purpose. Soon Lind's portrait appeared on water carafes, songs and poems were dedicated to her, and bonnets and shawls, pianos and sausages were called after her. The *New York Herald* declared she was the most popular woman that ever lived.[100] Barnum was a master at press management, and at what we would now call 'hype' and was then called 'ballyhoo': an incessant barrage of publicity handouts and bogus claims.[101] Berlioz even suggested, outrageously, that in New York Barnum had persuaded some poor parents to throw themselves from the rooftops under the wheels of Lind's carriage, shouting 'Viva la Lind' in exchange for a large sum of money destined for their children, but that the police foiled the plan.[102] The audience was made to feel that by going to a concert by Lind, they were taking part in a unique event.

The invention of sound recording has not eliminated such appeal; on the contrary, it has enhanced it. Just as the multiplication of the image of famous paintings generates more visits to museums where such paintings are held, so a famous singer, far from losing his or her aura by being heard frequently in a recorded form, gains even more fame. One did not even have to perform, only to be already famous. In 1876 the creator of the most popular operettas in Europe, Jacques Offenbach, was offered a considerable sum to visit the United States. Amused by his transformation into a circus exhibit, he recounted with delight the vast crowd that assembled outside his hotel in New York, and the 'Welcome Offenbach' banner hanging by the terrace from which he was forced to address the crowd, while in Philadelphia it was decided to name a garden after him (the Offenbach Garden).[103]

Celebrities and virtuosi did not have to be singers or musicians or composers. They could be mimes, like the great Bohemian-born Jean-Gaspard Deburau, star of the Théâtre des Funambules in Paris, which he joined in 1811 (he is the main character in Marcel Carné's cinematic masterpiece *Les Enfants du paradis*). Celebrities could be painters like Delacroix, policemen like Vidocq, chefs like Marie Antoine Carême (1783–1833).[104]

What was indispensable to the creation of celebrities was the press. Before the advent of the mass media, it was difficult to be famous while alive, for it took time for stories and myths to propagate themselves. Thus celebrity is substantially a modern invention; its modernity can be seen by the fact that a fairly 'normal' person involved in a relatively normal occupation (such as singing, playing the piano, etc.) could become famous only if someone wrote about him or her. In the eighteenth century a simple frontier guide like Kit Carson would have been known only within a limited, small territory. But Carson lived in the nineteenth century, and in 1845 Colonel John C. Frémont, the great explorer of the Far West, published an account of his early overland trips through the Rocky Mountains to California with Carson as a guide, *Report of the Exploring Expedition to the Rocky Mountains in the Year 1842, and to Oregon and North California in the Years 1843–1844*. A spate of dime novels followed, making Carson (who died in 1868) famous in his own lifetime even outside the United States, along with other American-Indian-fighting 'heroes' and colonisers such as Daniel Boone, Davy Crockett and

'Buffalo' Bill. Singers and musicians became popular heroes in the nineteenth century. The basis for the star system of the twentieth century was being established.

28

The Triumph of the Opera

The Dominance of the Italians

ROSSINI'S DOMINATION of the operatic field in the first quarter of the nineteenth century was unassailable. And, as in some Olympic relay race, the torch he carried was handed on, in uninterrupted succession, to Bellini, Donizetti, Verdi and, finally, to Puccini. The modern operatic repertoire owes much to these great Italian composers. Rossini had demonstrated that musical inventiveness could please both the public and singers, for the kind of virtuoso singing his works required made celebrities of them. They knew that certain show-stopping arias could become favourites in lucrative drawing-room recitals: arias such as 'Largo al factotum' from *Il Barbiere di Siviglia*, 'Pensa alla patria' from *L'Italiana in Algeri* and 'Bel raggio lusinghiero' from *Semiramide*. Without great singers, there cannot be good opera. Rossini, Donizetti and Bellini had the good luck to write for some of the greatest singers of the nineteenth century: Maria Malibran, Giuditta Pasta, Giulia Grisi, Isabella Colbran and Henriette Sontag.

The success of Italian opera convinced everyone connected with the theatre in Paris and London that even if opera was increasingly dominated by foreigners, it was worth promoting because there was growing evidence that the *nouveaux riches* were willing to spend money on what was the most popular and prestigious genre. Opera dominated Parisian theatrical life until the beginning of the twentieth century. Together with the new light opera or operetta, which made its appearance around 1850, opera accounted, by 1912, for half of the box office receipts of all Paris theatres.[1] Louis Véron, who had taken up the running of the Opéra in 1831, decided that it should no longer be regarded as a salon for the entertainment of narrow élites. He renovated the theatre, improving its acoustics and sight lines and reducing the size of the boxes to maximise audiences. The clientèle, of course, remained an élite, but it was broadened to include the newly enriched classes. It was symbolic of the social changes taking place at the Opéra that the most sought-after box, that next to the king, belonged to the Rothschilds, and not to some old aristocratic family.[2] In the nineteenth century, as indeed later, the association between opera and social privilege remained unchanged as the new economically powerful social groups found cultural legitimisation in patronising what, because of its aristocratic origins, remained 'high' art *par excellence*.

The director has today a leading role in determining the presentation of an opera. The fact that the repertory is limited to a hundred or so works favours introducing some kind of experimentation and innovation in production – such as setting *Carmen* in a junkyard or *Rigoletto* in New York's Lower East Side. In the nineteenth century and for much of the twentieth century, however, the producer had a perfunctory role. The real power remained in the hands of the still-living composers and librettists, the theatre management and the singers. Even in the theatre there was relatively little 'directing', and conventions about how to stage plays – and hence operas – were firmly entrenched. Since audiences were often not familiar with the works they saw, there was little incentive to try to appeal to them by showing new ways of performing well-known works.[3] Besides, operatic plots were no different from the melodramas the bourgeoisie enjoyed so much; indeed the librettos were often written by the same playwrights or derived from the same stage plays. In other words, opera, then as now, was a rather 'middle-brow' form of high art – as most classics are, including Shakespeare and Molière – and costume dramas were favoured. The suspension of disbelief required to watch a play in which people sing to each other instead of speaking worked better in a historical setting.

Verdi's *La Traviata* was innovatory because it was set in the present. When it was first performed at La Fenice in Venice on 6 March 1853 it was not a success, though the play (*La Dame aux camélias* by Alexandre Dumas *fils*, 1852) had been a triumph on the Parisian stage. The plot (a whore who is really a saint, a sinner who repents) had been familiar to Western audiences since the biblical Mary Magdalene, but perhaps the public was not used to operas being performed in modern dress. Indeed, when *La Traviata* was performed again in Venice a year later in seventeenth-century costume (a ploy adopted for much of the nineteenth century), it was received far more warmly. However, this success may have been due to the casting. At the original première, the soprano Fanny Salvini-Donatelli, who played Violetta, was inordinately stout, and the idea of her wasting away of consumption was found to be hilarious. There are limits to the suspension of disbelief. As if to make amends for this poor start, 150 years later in November 2004, when La Fenice reopened after the fire that had destroyed it in 1996, *La Traviata* was chosen for the gala night.

The popularity of some operas led, over the years, to a general acceptance of the mood to be attributed to certain musical phrases, providing the cinema in the twentieth century with a repertory of meaningful sounds. This is achieved by a process whereby the public learns to distinguish sentimental or 'romantic' from threatening music, an invigorating, uplifting, even patriotic sound from a moody one. The dying Violetta in *La Traviata* sings her aria in descending notes, suggesting her impending death. The repeated use of certain sounds, even when separated from their original context, achieves the same effect. Verdi's trumpets in *Aida* are now irretrievably linked with the sound of victory. The overture of Rossini's *Guillaume Tell*, where the hero is riding to the rescue on horseback, having been used throughout the 1950s in the successful American television serial *The Lone Ranger*, is now forever associated with the sound of incoming cavalry (and sparked a humorous definition of an intellectual as someone who can listen to it without thinking of *The Lone Ranger*). Location is equally identifiable, with some music associated with particular regions. The French seem to have been particularly good at popularising 'national' music: Bizet established what Spanish music should sound like (*Carmen*), and was followed by Ravel and Debussy (Manuel de Falla is supposed to have learned how make 'Spanish' music from Debussy); Saint-Saëns, who had toured North Africa, created the Egyptian 'sound' with his piano concerto, and Édouard Lalo did the same for Norway with his Norwegian Fantasy and, being of Spanish descent, furthered the sound of Spanish music with his Symphonie Espagnole (1875).[4] The Russians too joined in the production of 'Spanish' music, largely thanks to Mikhail Glinka, who lived for two years in Spain collecting folk songs. Schubert and Brahms (neither of whom was Hungarian) familiarised people with 'Hungarian' music, while Tchaikovsky used Italian tunes in his Capriccio Italien (1880). Such musical culture would become of inestimable value to film-makers and piano accompanists, particularly in silent movies. It was sufficient to strike up the 'Toreador' aria from *Carmen* for even people who had never heard of Bizet to immediately know that either the setting was in Spain or that something challenging was coming up.

Radio, films and television made such sounds universal. In the nineteenth century, however, opera remained an élite genre. The frequency of the stories that Italian peasants could be heard singing entire acts from well-known operas by Verdi or Puccini while toiling in the fields is a testimony to how the bourgeoisie romanticise the labouring classes. The only way, before the spread of the mass media, that an Italian peasant or even an artisan could have heard an operatic aria was by visiting a village fair where a version of it might have been sung by a travelling entertainer or used in a puppet theatre. It could happen, but it was not common.

Even for the ordinary middle classes, at least in the nineteenth century, access to opera was not easy. One way in was to frequent the 'right' circles and perhaps be drafted as a supporting member of the *claque* (*claquer*: to applaud for money). It was quite normal for supporters of this or that composer to turn up to cheer him or boo his rivals (as has been noted, the first night of Rossini's *Barbiere di Siviglia* was disrupted by Paisiello's supporters). The *claque* system was institutionalised in Paris by the enterprising Véron, the supervising genius of the *embourgeoisement* of the Paris theatre. To attract customers to the theatre, and to one's own theatre in particular, it was necessary to summon up an entire system of advertisement: billboards, press reviews, events highlighting the importance of the show, including disputes between rival playwrights and actors. Word of mouth was a key factor in the success of a play – as it still is. Members of the audience, friends of the author or the theatre-owner, or people paid by them, would cheer enthusiastically, having, it was felt, a psychological effect on the rest of the audience. The principle of the *claque* is still at work when television studio audiences, who usually attend without paying, are instructed by signs telling them to laugh and cheer, or when recorded (canned) laughter is used in comedies. Sometimes the *claque* was bribed by enemies of the authors or actors and, or so it was said, was able to prevent a success.

Under the July Monarchy (1830–48) *claques* became a major theatrical institution. Auguste Levasseur, a professional *claqueur* at the Opéra, was paid in free seats (some of which he sold), attended rehearsals, discussed technical problems with the directors – agreeing, for instance, to arrange a burst of loud applause to cover a tenor's wobbly high C – gave advice and even assessed projected performances.[5] The first night of Victor Hugo's *Hernani* on 25 February 1830 was stormy not only because it was a declaration of cultural war by the new Romantic generation against the defenders of the classical tradition, but also because Hugo had refused to pay the *claque*, preferring to count on the support of his friends and the literary group Jeune France. It certainly paid off. Hugo may have been a Romantic, but he knew the value of money, and it was with some satisfaction that on 7 March, ten days after the first night, he noted in his diary that 'every time it's performed, it's another 5,000 francs of box office receipts'.[6]

In Paris the Théâtre des Italiens performed almost exclusively Italian operas. The season for 1830–31 included Mozart's *Don Giovanni*, but this was regarded as 'Italian', as was the one French opera, Fromental Halévy's *Clari*, because the libretto was in Italian and the action was set in Milan – and probably also because it had been a success when it had been first performed in 1828 with the great Maria Malibran in the title role. The lion's share that season, however, went to Rossini, with *Otello, Tancredi, Il Barbiere di Siviglia, Matilde Shabran, Semiramide, La Gazza ladra, Riccardo e Zoraide, La Cenerentola* and *L'Italiana in Algeri*. The other composers were Giovanni Pacini (*L'Ultimo giorno di Pompei*), Cimarosa (*Il Matrimonio segreto*), Francesco Gnecco (*La Prova di un opera seria*, a very successful opera performed all over Europe for the following thirty years and then forgotten), Bellini (*La Sonnambula*) and Donizetti (*Anna Bolena*). Not content with dominating the Théâtre des Italiens, Rossini – who by then had stopped writing operas – saw also, in the same year, both his *Moïse* and *Guillaume Tell* performed at the Opéra.[7]

One of the few operas by a non-Italian at the Théâtre des Italiens in 1830 was one of the very few female opera composers, Louise Bertin, with her *Fausto* (in Italian), based on Goethe. In fact the Théâtre-Italien seems to have been particularly open to talented women: Angelica Catalani (1780–1849), the great singer, was its first director after the return of the monarchy. She was so often away, however, that the theatre suffered. Matters did not improve when Rossini took over. Running a theatre was more complex than writing operas. This he could do easily and quickly: it had taken him only twenty days to compose *Il Barbiere* and five weeks for *Semiramide*.

From 1801 to 1881 (when it closed) the Théâtre-Italien was the most celebrated opera theatre in Paris, a state within a state, the invincible bastion of Italian culture's most prestigious products: *opera buffa* and *opera seria*. It enjoyed an exceptional repertoire, a peerless troupe of singers, a fanatical public, and a favourable press. Yet it never received the kind of state subsidies granted to other French theatres. During the July Monarchy its annual subsidy amounted to 71,000 francs, a paltry sum compared to the Opéra-Comique

(186,000 francs), the Théâtre-Français (206,000 francs) and, above all, the Opéra, which received a lavish 790,500 francs.[8]

In London Covent Garden decided to follow the Continental fashion and surrender to 'made in Italy' works. It discontinued its policy of producing English operas or foreign operas in English. It had become impossible to ignore Rossini, the darling of operatic circles throughout Europe, and his *Barbiere di Siviglia*, destined to become the most popular opera in nine-teenth-century Italy (and the first to be broadcast on Italian television, in 1954).[9] Covent Garden imported great stars like Maria Malibran, and staged not only Rossini's *Guillaume Tell*, but German masterpieces such as Mozart's *Die Zauberflöte*, Beethoven's *Fidelio* and Carl Maria von Weber's *Der Frei-schütz*, and the new French grand opera of Meyerbeer (*Les Huguenots*) and Daniel Auber (*La Muette de Portici*). Financially, the innovation did not pay off. Those who wanted to hear Italian opera still went to the King's Theatre, London's leading opera house since the days of Handel.

Rather than give up and return to English adaptations and imitations, Covent Garden hired an Italian manager, Giuseppe Persiani, the husband of the *prima donna* Fanny Tacchinardi. It was he who in 1847 rebranded the theatre 'the Royal Italian Opera at Covent Garden' (the word 'Italian' was dropped only in 1892) to challenge Her Majesty's. The opening night, in April 1847, was a triumph, with Rossini's *Semiramide* with the great soprano Giulia Grisi in the leading role. She had been the star of the London stage since 1837, thanks to Bellini's *Norma*, which she sang in almost every season at Covent Garden until her retirement in 1861.

Until the end of the nineteenth century Italian was regarded as the international language of music. Indeed, in 1855 Queen Victoria suggested to Wagner that *Tannhäuser* should be translated into Italian so that it could be performed in London.[10] One can imagine Wagner's dismay, but in fact it was not unusual to perform his works in Italian outside Germany. Even German audiences expected opera to be in Italian.

One of the fundamental reasons for Italy's domination of the opera was the formidable size of its operatic market. Civic pride ensured that every Italian town wanted its own opera theatre, the bigger the better. When Verdi started working as a composer (c.1830) there was a real opera boom which has never been repeated since. The origin of this boom could be attributed to the radical transformation that the Napoleonic conquest had brought about: the power of the old courts had been diminished or wiped out, and with them went the chapels which used to be the centre of musical activity. A new commercial class of merchants and small and medium-size entrepreneurs (enriched by the sale of Church property by Napoleon) emerged. The organisation of music was now in the hands of the bourgeoisie.[11]

Most of the new opera houses were built by local authorities backed by generous patrons. The possession of a theatre allowed a small town, and its local bourgeoisie, to share some of the glamour, gaiety and luxury of larger cities. Besides, theatres were not only for staging plays and operas. They were also gambling places, where men could meet 'women of the theatre' whose less than strict morals were a further inducement to the craze for theatre-building in nineteenth-century Italy. This encouraged composers to turn to opera. Why bother with symphonies and concert music when more money and fame could be achieved with operas? Already in 1799 there were in Italy over a hundred theatres dedicated to the performance of operas.[12] By 1839, when Verdi made his debut with *Oberto conte di San Bonifacio*, the number had gone up to 150. The *Allgemeine musikalische Zeitung*, using a more restricted definition of what constituted a theatre, calculated that during the 1839–40 season operas were performed in eighty Italian theatres.[13] The statistics are debatable, since some of the higher figures may have been inflated by the inclusion of tiny venues sometimes simply carved out of existing *palazzi*. What is certain is that by the time it was unified, Italy had more opera performances than any other country in Europe. The table below offers a comparison of the number of theatres in some European countries. Many of these theatres would stage an opera only occasionally – Paris had forty theatres but only four for operas: the Opéra, Théâtre-Italien, Opéra-Comique and Théâtre-Lyrique – whereas in Italy most theatres were exclusively dedicated to opera.

NUMBER OF THEATRES IN SELECTED
EUROPEAN COUNTRIES 1865

Italy	350
France	340
Austria-Hungary	150
German states	115
Prussia	75

SOURCE: *Le Monde musical*,
St Petersburg, cited in Conati, 'Teatri e
orchestre al tempo di Verdi', p.55

An Italian government survey of 1868, using a different definition of a theatre, found that there were 942 theatres in the whole of Italy, distributed in 650 municipalities, with some 198 having been built between 1861 and 1868.[14] In 1893 there were, according to yet another survey, 1,055 theatres (both prose and opera), 80 per cent of which were in central and northern Italy.[15] By contrast, in 1870 in Germany there were only two hundred theatres, though by 1896, after the lifting of restrictions on theatrical life, the number had trebled.[16] Italian theatres were spread throughout the peninsula, though there continued to be far more in the north and the centre than in the south. Milan, the nearest city to a cultural capital, had fifteen theatres, including four for operas (like Paris, which had six times the population); the remainder were dedicated to plays, vaudeville, puppet shows, variety shows including equine acts, with almost 19,000 seats available. Milan also had an open-air stadium (the Arena) with 30,000 seats. Livorno, a relatively small harbour on the Tuscan coast, had eight theatres with a total of 10,000 seats, for a population of less than 100,000. A tiny town, hardly bigger than a village, Camaiore in the province of Lucca (Tuscany), had in the mid-nineteenth century a theatre (the Teatro dell'Olivo) with five hundred seats. At the end of the twentieth century Camaiore did not even possess a cinema (only in 2003 was the Olivo restored). In 1834 a world-famous soprano like Maria Malibran could sing in Lucca, or even Senigallia on the Adriatic coast, without feeling diminished for not being at La Pergola of Florence, because these theatres had high prestige and could pay the large fees she required.[17]

By 1868, when the main theatrical census was conducted, the new Italian state classified nine theatres as being of 'first importance' (*prim'ordine*), and targeted them for higher subsidies. These were the main opera houses of Milan (La Scala), Venice (La Fenice), Naples (San Carlo), Bologna (Teatro Comunale), Florence (La Pergola), Genoa (Carlo Felice), Turin (Regio), Palermo and Reggio Emilia. Rome, still under the Pope, was excluded. A further fifty theatres were ranked as secondary, and the remainder had to be content with being relegated to the '*terz'ordine*' – third rate.

Each theatre had a primary and a secondary season. In the primary season only 'heroic' operas (*opera seria*) were performed, usually with a ballet. The most popular operas were often performed thirty or forty times in the same season, and audiences would return to hear the same work over and over again. Usually the operas staged were new, and in the case of the more important theatres, composed especially for them. There were often also some 'repeats' of successful operas; or if a new opera flopped, an old one would be performed in its place. The secondary season had *opera buffa* (not necessarily a comic opera, just a general name for any work with a happy ending). In spite of Rossini, *opera buffa* was long regarded as an inferior genre in Italy. As late as 1838 at La Scala seats for this genre were cheaper than for *opera seria*.[18]

Opera was an expensive business. There were not enough paying customers to fill a theatre for the same opera for weeks on end. Thus it was in the interests of the management not to stage the same opera more often than than necessary. Composers had different interests. Though they could write operas with the same rapidity with which popular novelists could dash off novels – Donizetti was particularly prolific, though even he could not compete with Dumas's four hundred books – they could not expect them to be performed with similar frequency. It was possible to write a novel in a month and to see it published almost immediately. It was impossible, even in the nineteenth century, to write an opera *and* to see it performed within a month. So it was necessary for composers to make sure that their works could be performed in as many cities as possible; and if they really wanted to make it big, they needed to aim for an international market. The national market was far too narrow.

The popularity of opera in Italy meant that instrumental music was hardly ever performed there. Even in the 1880s the Italian public remained indifferent to chamber music and symphonic music, even to Beethoven's symphonies – the rage everywhere else. As late as 1929 a contemporary account remarked: 'Beethoven, Schubert, quartets, symphonies: these names seemed mysterious and arcane to us, young people. We knew only operas and we ignored symphonic music including even the great Italian masterpieces of the seventeenth and eighteenth centuries.'[19] Only after the rebirth of Rome's Accademia di Santa Cecilia in 1895 did Italy acquire an important centre of instrumental music.

Italians wanted new operas and new singers. So, even though Rossini's popularity remained high – in the course of the 1832 season his work was performed in thirty theatres – he had to cede terrain to new composers, as the following table shows:

ITALIAN OPERA COMPOSERS.
NUMBER OF ITALIAN THEATRES PERFORMING THEIR WORK

	1832	1839	1841	1843	1844	1845
Gioacchino Rossini	30	15	15	13	8	18
Luigi Ricci	18	9	18	15	9	8
Vincenzo Bellini	17	17	22	19	13	23
Gaetano Donizetti	16	62	59	56	37	58
Saverio Mercadante	14	13	12	14	10	12
Giovanni Pacini	8		9	10		
Federico Ricci		8				
Giuseppe Verdi			3	10	16	37

SOURCE: Conati, 'Teatri e orchestre al tempo di Verdi', p.57

The popularity of opera in Italy was further enhanced by the fact that its appreciation was shared by all Italian élites (though not, of course, by the vast majority of the population, who did not speak Italian). The commercial requirements of performance led to the systematic transfer of productions across the peninsula, thus turning the genre into one of the main manifestations of cultural unity among the élites of the not-yet-unified country, and in this way playing a nation-building role. The language used in the librettos was a rather grandiloquent Italian, partly invented, partly based on eighteenth-century melodrama, epic narratives, celebrations and commemorations (and often used even in the mid-twentieth century for memorial plaques). It was not the language audiences spoke at home (many favoured the local dialect), but a literary Italian they had been forced to learn at school. It was not only the language that these élites shared, but also a mild patriotism. Donizetti, Verdi and the other major composers occasionally used patriotic themes not just because they were patriots themselves, but because they knew that they would be popular.[20]

The print media contributed to the spread of information about new operas. Librettos became best-sellers. Magazines and reviews specialising in music competed fiercely. When, in December 1832, Giacinto Battaglia started a new periodical in Milan entirely dedicated to music, theatre and variety shows and called, appropriately, Il Barbiere di Siviglia there were already several such periodicals in the city.[21] The impetus for new musical press came, as usual, from Paris, where the major dailies carried regular reviews and announcements of the day's performances, and where there was an ever growing musical and theatrical press, from the *Courier des spectacles* to the *Journal des théâtres*. Newspapers would report on operatic evenings, including details of what the women were wearing, the reactions of the audience, who was there. In other words, they reviewed the audience as much as the show.

The expansion of the Italian opera market proceeded until well after the middle of the century. In 1825, 388 operas were performed in Italy; by 1846 the number had more than doubled to 798.[22] In the 1860s, however, there was a crisis in the theatre. The new Italian state (via the municipalities) had taken over the main theatres, including La Scala and the San Carlo, as well as many subsidised provincial theatres. In 1867 most of these were handed over to the municipalities, with no compulsion to keep them open. As a result many were forced to close. Verdi lamented: 'When Italy was divided into many small states, their finances were blossoming. Now that we are united, we are ruined. But where is the wealth of yesteryear?'[23] Verdi may have contributed to such financial problems: many of his operas were as expensive to produce as those of Wagner and Meyerbeer, and difficult to stage in small venues. Of course, such large-scale operas were meeting market demand: to entice the box-owners to pay extra, it was necessary to provide a big spectacle with a long ballet sequence. This led many theatres, including Bologna's Teatro Comunale, to suffer heavy losses throughout the 1860s, 1870s and 1880s.[24] Some of the more prestigious theatres had to 'skip' a season. The San Carlo of Naples closed in 1875–76, the Carlo Felice of Genoa remained closed from 1879 to 1883 following a financial dispute between the *palchettisti*, or box-owners, and the municipality, and in 1898 it was the turn of La Scala. Because the Milan municipality did not think it right to spend public money to subsidise the entertainment of the rich, some of the boxes were eliminated to make room for rows of seats.[25] Thus La Scala began to court a new public of middle and lower bourgeoisie, to the outrage of those who resented the presence of women of the petty bourgeoisie ('cooks and groceries sellers') pretending to be grand ladies.[26]

Faced with this crisis, lobbies were formed to defend the more prestigious theatres. In 1885 Giulio Ricordi, the most powerful music publisher in Italy and a member of Milan's governing council, pointed out that La Scala had to be championed because it was an industrial enterprise which gave work to nearly 2,000 people, of whom almost eight hundred were directly employed by the opera house. The turnover was almost ten million lire for a season which lasted only four or five months.[27] Some of the larger cities – Milan,

Turin, and Naples – were rich enough to continue to weather the storm in spite of the occasional closure, but Italian provincial theatres began to decay.

Italian opera had been dominated by great stars, particularly great *prime donne*. These needed to be paid handsomely, which added to the costs. The opera impresario Maurice Strakosch wrote in his memoirs that by the 1870s the problem was becoming serious. The public 'has acquired a taste for stars', and stars were expensive.[28] The price of the cheapest seats at La Scala in the 1870s was roughly the daily wage of a skilled worker.[29] Today a plumber could easily afford them with his hourly rate.

The Globalisation of the Italians

The crisis of the domestic market did not unduly disturb the most successful Italian composers and singers. They were operating in an international environment. Better communication and transport enabled their work to be performed everywhere. Italian companies travelled as far as Buenos Aires, Rio de Janeiro, Lima, Santiago, Mexico, Cuba, New York and San Francisco. Ultimately the strength of Italian opera composers was that they had been forced to think in global terms because, though Italy provided a large market-place for opera, it was not necessarily the most prestigious or the most remunerative. The country was fragmented until 1860, and even after unity its political standing remained inferior to that of other countries. Its royal court originated from a minor European provincial city, Turin, and its most famous city, Rome, had been reduced, after centuries under the domination of the Roman Catholic Church, to a cultural backwater. Italy's composers had to seek prestige abroad, and following in Rossini's footsteps, this meant Europe's main capitals: first of all Paris, then London, Berlin, Vienna and St Petersburg. Their fame then spread to well-established extra-European cultural enclaves, such as New York – where music-loving Germans provided the backbone of a discerning public – and Latin America. Six of Verdi's operas, including *I Lombardi*, *Nabucco* and *Macbeth*, received their first American performance in Cuba.[30] Italian opera reached New York only in November 1825, when Rossini's *Il Barbiere* was performed; Havana had had an opera house since 1815.

Opera had become a symbol of the sophisticated West, and all those who sought to align themselves with it used opera as one the markers of civilis-ation. In 1843 Tsar Nicholas I invited Giovanni Battista Rubini to assemble a company to take over St Petersburg's largest theatre and make it a centre of Italian opera. In 1869 Ismail Pasha, the modernising *khedive* (viceroy) of Egypt, decided that a new opera house would be a fitting way of celebrating the opening of the Suez Canal. The theatre was designed by Italian architects in imitation of Italian opera houses (a capacity of 850 in three tiers of boxes, stalls and a top gallery). The world's best-known composer, Giuseppe Verdi, was commissioned to produce a new work with an Egyptian setting. After some hesitation, and prompted by the promise of a considerable fee, Verdi proceeded to write *Aida*. The new Cairo opera house did open with Verdi, but *Rigoletto* had the honour, not *Aida*, because the costumes and scenery for the new opera were blocked in Paris during the Franco–Prussian War. *Aida* was eventually performed in Cairo in 1871. When it was staged again in Paris in March 1880 it was a huge success, to Verdi's delight, for he had been pursuing greater Parisian recognition for years. His wife, Giuseppina Strepponi, wrote to her sister that she no longer recognised the Parisian audience, usually so cold, now so enthusiastic. The *Figaro* report confirms that such repeated applause had never been heard before.[31]

The vogue for historical settings enabled Italian composers to use images of the past which, thanks to literature, had already become part of European consciousness – as was noted by French visitors such as Auguste Louis Blondeau, winner of the French Academy's Grand Prix de Rome.[32] Donizetti had exploited to the full English and Scottish history by producing, among others, *Emilia di Liverpool*, set in mountains(!) near Liverpool, *Anna Bolena*, set at the court of Henry VIII, *Elizabetta al castello di Kenilworth* on Elizabeth I, *Rosmonda d'Inghilterra* about the 'Fair Rosamund', mistress of Henry II, *Maria Stuarda* and *Roberto Devereux*, about the Earl of Essex and Queen Elizabeth.

This foreign-oriented strategy had been pioneered by Rossini, and was thoroughly exploited by all other major Italian composers. Rossini had conquered Paris, and so had Donizetti, whose last operas (*Les Martyrs*, *La Fille du régiment*, *La Favorite*, *Don Pasquale* and *Don Sébastien*) were all premièred there. The tables below examine the sources, settings and origins of the plots of the best-known operas (all still in the repertory) of the four great Italian nineteenth-century composers. What clearly emerges is the systematic plundering of a non-Italian repertory for narratives and the overall preference for a foreign setting. Supremacy in the production of opera was not matched by a corresponding hegemony in the production of stories.

ROSSINI

OPERA	SETTING	SOURCE	COUNTRY OF ORIGIN
Tancredi (1813)	Syracuse, 11th century	Tancrède by Voltaire (inspired by Tasso's Gerusalemme liberata)	France
L'Italiana in Algeri (1813)	Algiers, c.1805	L'Italiana in Algeri by Luigi Mosca	Italy
Il Turco in Italia (1814)	Naples	Il Turco in Italia by Caterino Mazzolà	Italy
Il Barbiere di Siviglia (1816)	Seville, Spain	Le Barbier de Séville by Beaumarchais	France
Cenerentola (1817)	Fairy tale	Perrault's Cendrillon	France
La Gazza ladra (1817)	Italy	La Pie voleuse by J.M.T. Badouin d'Aubigny and Louis-Charles Caigniez	France
Mosè in Egitto (1818)	Ancient Egypt	Old Testament and Sara in Egitto by Francesco Ringhieri	The Bible and Italy
La Donna del lago (1819)	Scotland	The Lady of the Lake by Walter Scott	Scotland
Semiramide (1823)	Babylon, 8th century BC	Sémiramis by Voltaire	France
Il Viaggio a Reims (1825)	France	Corinne by Madame de Staël	France
Le Comte d'Ory (1828)	France, 14th century	Le Comte d'Ory by E. Scribe and Charles-Gaspard Delestre-Poiron	France
Guillaume Tell (1829)	Switzerland, 13th century	Wilhelm Tell by Schiller	Germany

BELLINI			
OPERA	SETTING	SOURCE	COUNTRY OF ORIGIN
Il Pirata (1827)	Sicily, 13th century	Bertram, ou Le pirate, by Raimond (Isidore J.S. Taylor) based on Charles Maturin's Bertram or the Castle of St Aldobrand	France and Ireland
La Straniera (1829)	Brittany, c.1300	L'Étrangère by Victor-Charles Prévot d'Arlincourt	France
Zaira (1829)	Jerusalem under the Turks, n.d.	Zaire by Voltaire	France
I Capuleti e i Montecchi (1830)	Verona, Italy, 13th century	Giulietta e Romeo by Luigi Scevola based on Luigi da Porto's Giulietta e Romeo	Italy
Norma (1830)	Gaul under Roman occupation, 50 BC	Norma, ou l'infanticide by Alexandre Soumet	France
La Sonnambula (1831)	Switzerland, early 19th century	La Sonnambule by Scribe and Aumer	France
Beatrice di Tenda (1833)	Near Milan, 1418	Beatrice di Tenda by Carlo Tedaldi-Fores	Italy
I Puritani (1835)	Plymouth, England, during the Civil War (1640s)	Têtes Rondes et Cavaliers by Jacques Ancelor and J.-X.-B. Saintine	France

DONIZETTI (MAIN OPERAS ONLY)			
OPERA	SETTING	SOURCE	COUNTRY OF ORIGIN
Chiara e Serafina, ossia I Pirati (1822)	The Orient (island of Majorica), 18th century	La cisterne by Pixérécourt	France
Emilia di Liverpool (1824)	England, 18th century (?)	Emilia by August Kotzebue	Germany

DONIZETTI (MAIN OPERAS ONLY)

OPERA	SETTING	SOURCE	COUNTRY OF ORIGIN
Otto mesi in due ore ossia gli esiliati in Siberia (1827)	Russia, c.1800	*Elisabeth, ou les exilés de Sibérie* by Sophie Cottin	France
Elisabetta al Castello di Kenilworth (1829)	England, late 16th century	*Kenilworth* by Walter Scott (via Scribe's *Leicester*)	Scotland
Anna Bolena (1830)	England, 16th century	*Henri VIII* by Marie-Joseph de Chenier	France
Ugo Conte di Parigi (1832)	France, end of the 9th century	*Blanche d'Aquitaine* by H.-L.-F. Bis	France
L'Elisir d'amore (1832)	Generic rustic setting	*Le Philtre* by Scribe	France
Lucrezia Borgia (1833)	Italy, c.1500	*Lucrèce Borgia* by Victor Hugo	France
Maria Stuarda (1835)	England, 1580s	*Maria Stuart* by Schiller	Germany
Marin Faliero (1835)	Venice, 1355	*Marino Faliero* by Casimir Delavigne, inspired by Byron's *Marino Faliero*	France
Lucia di Lammermoor (1835)	Scotland, late 17th century	*The Bride of Lammermoor* by Walter Scott	Scotland
Belisario (1836)	Byzantium, 6th century	*Belisarius* by Eduard von Schenk	Germany
Roberto Devereux, ossia il Conte di Essex (1837)	England, c.1600	*Elisabeth d'Angleterre* by François Ancelot	France
Poliuto (1838, banned in Naples, then performed in Paris as *Les Martyrs*)	Armenia, 3rd century	After Corneille's *Polyeucte*, expanded by Scribe and renamed *Les Martyrs*	France

DONIZETTI (MAIN OPERAS ONLY)

OPERA	SETTING	SOURCE	COUNTRY OF ORIGIN
La Fille du régiment (1840)	Tyrol, early 19th century	*La Fille du régiment* by Vernoy de Saint-Georges and Bayard	France
La Favorite (1841)	Spain, 14th century	*Le Comte de Comminges* by Baculard d'Arnaud	France
Dòn Pasquale (1843)	Generic Italian	*Ser Marcantonio* opera by Stefano Pavesi, libretto by Angelo Anelli	Italy

VERDI (POST-1842 WORKS ONLY)

OPERA	SETTING	SOURCE	COUNTRY OF ORIGIN
Nabucco (1842)	Babylon and Jerusalem, 587 BC	*Nabuchodonosor* by Auguste Anicet-Bourgeois and Francis Cornu	France
I Lombardi alla prima crociata (1843)	Milan, Antioch and Jerusalem, 1096–97	*I Lombardi alla prima crociata* by Tommaso Grossi	Italy
I Due Foscari (1844)	Venice, 1457	*The Two Foscari* by Byron	England
Ernani (1844)	Spain, 1519	*Hernani* by Victor Hugo	France
Giovanna d'Arco (1845)	France, 1429	*Die Jungfrau von Orleans* by Schiller	Germany
Alzira (1845)	America during the Spanish Conquest in the mid-16th century	*Alzire ou Les Américains* by Voltaire	France
Attila (1846)	Adriatic lagoons and Rome, 5th century	*Attila, König der Hunnen* by Zacharias Werner	Germany

VERDI (POST-1842 WORKS ONLY)			
OPERA	SETTING	SOURCE	COUNTRY OF ORIGIN
Macbeth (1847)	Scotland, n.d.	Shakespeare	England
I Masnadieri (1847)	Germany, early 18th century	Die Räuber by Schiller	Germany
Il Corsaro (1848)	Greece under the Turks, early 19th century	The Corsair by Byron	England
La Battaglia di Legnano (1849)	Milan and Como, 1176	La Bataille de Toulouse by Joseph Méry	France
Luisa Miller (1849)	Tyrol, 17th century	Kabale und Liebe by Schiller	Germany
Rigoletto (1851)	Mantua, 16th century	Le roi s'amuse by Victor Hugo	France
Stiffelio (1850)	Austria, early 19th century	Le Pasteur ou l'évangile et le foyer by Émile Souvestre and Eugène Bourgeois	France
La Traviata (1853)	Paris and near Paris, mid-19th century	La Dame aux camélias by Alexandre Dumas fils	France
Il Trovatore (1853)	Spain, 1409	El Trovator by Antonio García Gutiérrez	Spain
Les Vêpres Siciliennes (1855)	Palermo, 1282	Le Duc d'Albe by Eugène Scribe	France
Simon Boccanegra (1857)	Genoa, 14th century	Simón Boccanegra by Antonio García Gutiérrez	Spain
Un Ballo in maschera (1859)	Massachussets, USA, late 17th century	Gustave II ou le bal masqué by Eugène Scribe	France
La Forza del destino (1862)	Spain and Italy, mid-18th century	Don Alvaro, o la fuerza del sino by Angelo de Saavedra, Duke of Rivas; with a scene from Schiller's Wallensteins Lager	Spain and Germany

VERDI (POST-1842 WORKS ONLY)			
OPERA	SETTING	SOURCE	COUNTRY OF ORIGIN
Don Carlos (1867)	France and Spain, c.1560	Don Carlos by Schiller	Germany
Aida (1871)	Ancient Egypt	Original scenario by Auguste Mariette	France
Otello (1887)	Venice and Cyprus, late 15th century	Othello by Shakespeare	England
Falstaff (1893)	England, 14th century	The Merry Wives of Windsor and Henry IV by Shakespeare	England

One should note that the choice of the subject-matter was not always made by the composer alone. Considerable market research was undertaken. Potential librettists were consulted, as well as impresarios, publishers and theatre managers. The plots were considerably romanticised, so that the result, regardless of its origins, resembled the popular melodrama of the nineteenth century. The source of the plots shows, once again, the domination of France, followed by Britain and then Germany (almost exclusively Schiller). It is as if three-quarters of Hollywood films were based on original stories by European writers and not set in the United States. Such 'foreignness' in the setting has no equivalent in nineteenth-century novels. In spite of the appeal of exoticism, the development of empire and exploration, and the popularity of adventure books à la Verne, the works of the most celebrated French, British and Russian novelists of the period between 1830 and 1890 were overwhelmingly set in their own countries. Nor did the 'foreignness' of Italian opera change after national unification. Puccini, who in some ways represented the last of the great Italian popular opera composers, remained as committed to a global market as did his illustrious predecessors, as the following table shows.

	PUCCINI		
OPERA	SETTING	SOURCE	COUNTRY OF ORIGIN
Manon Lescaut (1893)	France and America, 18th century	*Manon Lescaut* by Abbé Prevost	France
La Bohème (1896)	Paris, 1830	*Scènes de la vie de bohème* by Henri Murger	France
Edgar (1889)	Flanders, 1302	*La Coupe et les lèvres* by Alfred de Musset	France
Tosca (1900)	Rome, 1800	*La Tosca* by Victorien Sardou	France
Madama Butterfly (1904)	Nagasaki, Japan, c.1900	*Madame Butterfly* by David Belasco, on a short story by John Luther Long adapted from *Madame Chrysanthème* by Pierre Loti	USA and France
La Fanciulla del west (1910)	California, 1849–50	*The Girl of the Golden West* by David Belasco	USA
La Rondine (1917)	Paris, Côte d'Azur, 1850s	A.M. Willner and Heinz Reichert	Germany
Il Tabarro (1918)	Paris, 1910	*La Houppelande* by Didier Gold	France
Suor Angelica (1918)	Italy, late 17th century	Original libretto by Giovacchino Forzano	Italy
Gianni Schicchi (1918)	Florence, 1299	*Inferno* (Canto 30) by Dante Alighieri	Italy
Turandot (1926)	Beijing, ancient times	Modern fairy tale by Carlo Gozzi	Italy

In other countries, opera remained far more 'national'. Almost all of Wagner's operas are set in a mythical Germanic world, and virtually all Russian operas take place in Russia. Bedřich Smetana set his major operas, *The Bartered Bride* and *Dalibor*, in Bohemia, often using Bohemian folk tunes. The French were more diversified: the two best-known operas by Daniel Auber, who had studied under the Italian composer Luigi Cherubini, *La Muette de Portici*

(1822) and *Fra Diavolo* (1830), were set in Naples (although the character of Fenella in *La Muette* was based on Walter Scott's *Peveril of the Peak*). Another pupil of Cherubini's, Jacques Fromental Halévy, set his grand opera *La Juive* (The Jewess, 1835) in fifteenth-century Switzerland. Meyerbeer's *Les Huguenots* was set in France, but his *Le Prophète* was about religious strife in sixteenth-century Holland, *Robert le Diable* was a Gothic fable set in Sicily, and the action of *L'Africaine* takes place in Lisbon and India, and on a ship in between. None of these, however, suggests any conscious attempt to curry favour with non-French audiences.

With Verdi this is not the case. His 'strategy' was first Italy, then the world. A fashionable composer like him was virtually assured of having his new work performed throughout Italy almost immediately. *Nabucco* had its first night at La Scala in 1842; by the end of 1844 it had been performed in thirty-two Italian cities, and then went on to conquer Amsterdam, Barcelona, Berlin, Cadiz, Corfu, Lisbon, London, Malta, Madrid, Oporto, Stuttgart, Vienna, Constantinople, Caracas, Melbourne, Montevideo, and in Havana at the enormous Teatro Tacón (3,000 places, including seven hundred standing) in December 1847. New York followed in April 1848, but the opera had unfavourable reviews there.[33] *I Lombardi alla prima crociata*, Verdi's most 'national' opera and one of the few set in Italy, was premièred in 1843, and by 1846 had been performed even in small towns such as Voghera and Cesena, which had just acquired a new theatre. *Rigoletto* reached provincial Ascoli Piceno a few months after its first night in Venice. *Ernani* (premièred Venice, 1844) was performed in some sixty opera houses in 1846 alone.[34] By 1848 Verdi was recognised in New York as the successor to Rossini, Bellini and Donizetti.[35] By the 1850s he had become a colossus on the global scene, with several operas premièred abroad: *Les Vêpres Siciliennes* (1855) and *Don Carlos* (1867) at the Opéra in Paris, and *La Forza del destino* (1862) in St Petersburg.[36] *I Masnadieri* was first performed at Her Majesty's Theatre in London in July 1847; *Jérusalem*, a revision of *I Lombardi* (1847) and a French version of *Macbeth* (1865) were adapted for French audiences. Even Verdi's style became less Italian. In *Il Trovatore* (1853), particularly in the aria 'Abbietta zingara', he blended the French ballad style with Italian conventions. The result was still culturally Italian, but his subsequent works were less musically national.[37]

Verdi's initial rise to fame occurred in a period of exceptionally intense musical competition. Rossini, and later Bellini and Donizetti, had created a situation in which operatic music had become the dominant form of Italian cultural production. No major native theatre had been built on the heritage of the Commedia dell'arte. There was no important contemporary popular literature, in spite of Manzoni's efforts: Italy's cultural élites read foreign novels, harked back to Italian classics (Dante and Petrarca), and were hostile to innovation. Opera became, almost unavoidably, the national genre. Verdi's early works appeared in the shadows of Donizetti, who died in 1848, allowing Verdi to become his natural successor. From then on, Verdi's star never stopped rising. Of his first fourteen Italian operas (written when Donizetti was still alive), only *Nabucco* and *Macbeth* are still frequently performed, but of the subsequent eight operas, written between 1849 and 1859, seven are still regularly performed today: *Luisa Miller, Rigoletto, Il Trovatore, La Traviata, Les Vêpres Siciliennes, Simon Boccanegra* and *Un Ballo in maschera*. These turned Verdi into a European celebrity. As for his mature operas, *La Forza del destino, Don Carlos, Aida, Otello* and *Falstaff*, they are all regarded as masterpieces.

There was also an important political element in the subsequent fortune of Verdi, for he came to be regarded as the cultural representative of Italian nationalism. A biography published in 1913 called him the 'maestro' of the Italian revolution.[38] Elsewhere in Europe the 'national poet' revered by nationalists was usually a writer. Italy, though, had Verdi. There were few real alternatives: the actual period of the Risorgimento (1848–61) had produced no major Italian poets, no major novelists (Manzoni was still alive but his best works were behind him), and no playwright of note.[39] Yet Verdi's fame as a 'nationalist' was due essentially to the works he had composed between 1842 and 1849, such as *La Battaglia di Legnano*, which led the Roman audience on 27 January 1847 to shout '*Viva Verdi! Viva l'Italia!*', while the aria 'O Signor, che dal tetto natio' (Oh Lord, our native land) in *I Lombardi alla prima crociata* had moved everyone.[40] But many of the political references these works are said to contain (sympathy for oppressed people yearning for liberation, as in 'Va Pensiero', the chorus of the Hebrew slaves in *Nabucco*, and the Scottish exiles' chorus in *Macbeth*) are not easily detectable.

This is not to say that Verdi was not an Italian nationalist; his patriotism coincided with that of the majority of his audience, and added to his renown. That was certainly true in Milan, but less so in Bologna, where the local aristocracy, not as enamoured of Risorgimento rhetoric as others, resisted Verdi's appeal.[41] After *La Battaglia di Legnano* the nationalist element was far less prominent, partly because Verdi had moved onto a wider European scene, where national references would have been lost, partly because of the obstacles erected by censorship in various Italian states.[42]

Historical drama is bound to contain allusions to touchy political events. Rossini (who was rather conservative) wrote *Guillaume Tell* because it was a good story, but one could read into it a celebration of brave little Switzerland fighting for its political liberty. Auber's *La Muette de Portici* is about the Neapolitan insurrection of 1647, caused by poverty and taxation and led by the charismatic fisherman Masaniello. Meyerbeer's *Les Huguenots* blames the Catholic king, religion and monarchy for the massacre of St Bartholomew's Day 1572 – which, as it was written in 1836, could give rise to suspicions.

The international nature of Verdi's market, and the familiarity which Italian audiences themselves had with the subject-matter of his operas, offer a better explanation for his use of foreign historical plots than does the fear of censorship. The rising tide of Italian nationalism did not deter him from pursuing an active search for global renown. In any case, even his most overtly patriotic opera, *La Battaglia di Legnano*, still managed to circulate in Austrian-controlled territories in a mildly censored form, and with the title changed to suggest that it was about the Dutch revolt against Spain – all with Verdi's permission.[43]

There is little doubt that the global strategy paid off. Verdi became not only the best-known representative of Italian culture in the nineteenth century, but probably also the best-known Italian. Perhaps only Garibaldi, a dashing national hero, outdistanced him. His operas were performed abroad almost immediately after their first performances in Italy. London was particularly receptive:

VERDI'S OPERAS IN LONDON			
OPERA	DATE OF COMPOSITION	LONDON PREMIÈRE	THEATRE
Nabucco	1842	1846	Her Majesty's
I Lombardi alla prima crociata	1843	1846	Her Majesty's
I Due Foscari	1844	1847	Her Majesty's
Ernani	1844	1845	Her Majesty's
Attila	1846	1848	Her Majesty's
I Masnadieri	1847	1847	Her Majesty's
Luisa Miller	1849	1858	Her Majesty's
Rigoletto	1851	1853	Covent Garden
La Traviata	1853	1856	Her Majesty's

Il Trovatore	1853	1855	Covent Garden
Les Vêpres Siciliennes	1855	1859	Drury Lane
Un Ballo in maschera	1859	1861	Royal Lyceum
La Forza del destino	1862	1867	Her Majesty's
Don Carlos	1867	1867	Covent Garden
Aida	1871	1876	Covent Garden
Otello	1887	1889	Royal Lyceum
Falstaff	1893	1894	Covent Garden

Though *Otello* and *Falstaff* were performed in London shortly after their Italian premières, the British had to wait far longer for Verdi's other Shakespearean opera, *Macbeth* (1847). It was performed in New York in 1850 and in Dublin in 1859, but did not have its first British performance until 1928, at Glyndebourne. *La Battaglia di Legnano* (1849) was not performed in Britain until 1960, by the Welsh National Opera. *Simon Boccanegra* too had to wait until the twentieth century.

Nevertheless, Italian operas, all written in 'Italian' (i.e. the vernacular spoken in Tuscany), constituted the main 'national' cultural form, a unifying element, albeit only among an élite.

Italy Challenged

In Verdi's view, neither the Germans nor the French offered much competition to Italian opera composers. He thought highly of the productions at the Paris Opéra, but little of their singers. Berlin was 'deplorable', its large orchestras just made a lot of noise, the productions were tasteless, the singers terrible. Vienna was a little better, but not much, and the audiences regularly fell asleep. The Italian system of itinerant companies, he felt, was preferable to the German system of stable local companies, where mediocrity prevailed. The Italian public wanted international divas, real *prime donne*, and to keep them and an entire company employed the whole year would be prohibitively expensive.[44] Verdi wrote this in 1876. By then Italian opera faced a multiplicity of competitors who had been gathering over the previous twenty years. Wagner had written all his major operas except *Parsifal*; Bizet had composed *The Pearl Fishers*; Meyerbeer had come and gone, leaving six French grand operas which had dominated Paris; Berlioz had produced his monumental *Les Troyens* (1856–58). Glinka had composed what could be regarded the first Russian opera, *A Life for the Tsar* (1836), and continued with the more famous *Ruslan and Ludmila* (1842). Czech (Bohemian) opera entered the repertoire thanks to Bedřich Smetana with *The Bartered Bride* (1866). The Czech National Theatre was inaugurated on 11 June 1881, with Smetana's fourth opera *Libuše*. This was, admittedly, in German, but it dealt almost entirely with an invented and glorious Czech past.[45] Hungary produced its first important native-born composer, Ferenc Erkel, who composed the Hungarian national anthem and the first Hungarian opera, *Hunyadi László* (1844). Poland had the oldest operatic tradition in central Europe, but its great 'national' opera, Stanislaw Moniuszko's *Halka* (1848, final version 1858), has remained unknown elsewhere. The same can be said for the first opera in Croatian, *Love and Malice* by Vatroslav Lisinski (1846), composed as part of the nationalist project, and Finland's first opera, *King Charles's Hunt* (in Swedish, 1852), by Fredrik Pacius.[46] In any case, Russia, Hungary, Poland and Bohemia were – operatically speaking – heavily indebted to foreign influences, above all that of Italy.[47] There was virtually no opera in Holland, or in the Scandinavian countries, where German opera often prevailed over Italian. The British were importers (save for Gilbert and Sullivan's light operas, exported mainly to English-speaking countries).

Until Wagner, however, the only substantial challenge to the supremacy of the Italians came from Paris, and was represented by the French grand opera. The French did not immediately adopt those who later became their best-known nineteenth-century composers. Bizet's *Carmen* was a flop when it was first performed in 1875, and Berlioz's work was found unacceptable by an audience used to the Italian genre.[48] Indeed, *Benvenuto Cellini* was booed throughout 'with admirable energy' – wrote Berlioz – when it opened in 1838 at the Opéra.[49] The leading tenor, Duprez, walked out after three performances. And it took time for Wagner to become established outside Germany. It also took time for Verdi to be accepted by Paris critics. The *Revue et gazette musicale de Paris* did not last long enough to revisit its 1853 judgement on *Rigoletto*: 'This opera has precious little chance of staying in the repertoire.'[50] The *Gazette* folded in 1880, and *Rigoletto* lives on.

Paris remained, however, at least in the nineteenth century, the great operatic centre of Europe. But its great exports (above all Giacomo Meyerbeer, 1791–1864) never really challenged the Italians. Meyerbeer, however, did create an operatic genre which approximated later Hollywood 'blockbusters':

the grand opera, with a large cast, a profusion of special effects and plenty of violence. Meyerbeer and the other great grand opera composer, Fromental Halévy, were regarded by some as 'foreign', since both were Jewish, and Meyerbeer was a Berliner whose real name was Jakob Liebmann Beer. Regardless of his origins, in 1815 Meyerbeer, after studying in Venice, adopted the style of Rossini, wrote six Italian-style operas, dropped Jakob to become Giacomo, and succeeded Rossini as the favourite of the Parisian opera-going public. His *Robert le Diable* staggered its first-night audience in November 1831. The first act has a gambling scene, the torture of the heroine, a ballet of debauched nuns, an entire court thrown into deep sleep, and ends with a cathedral wedding. *Les Huguenots* begins with the revelries of Catholic noblemen and continues with a ballet of bathing beauties, followed by a duel, a wedding and a massacre. Another grand opera, *La Juive* (1835), Halévy's first major international triumph, ends with the heroine, Rachel, thrown into a cauldron of boiling oil after she has refused to abjure her Jewish faith. By 1893 – when, unsurprisingly, the original scenery was finally consumed by a real fire – *La Juive* had been performed at the Opéra 550 times, and had become a success throughout Europe and North America, though originally it was poorly received by the critics.[51] Italian composers who accepted commissions from the Opéra were expected to follow Halévy's and Meyerbeer's lead. Verdi did his best, using a libretto by Scribe (the hegemonic playwright in France at the time) for *Les Vêpres Siciliennes*.[52]

Meyerbeer's fame extended to Italy, where Verdi, though the local hero, was not always received uncritically. The *Gazzetta musicale* of Florence (22 February 1855) thought Meyerbeer had no rivals, and was certainly better than Verdi.[53] By the end of the 1860s Meyerbeer had become a favourite of the Italians. Of course his operas were expensive to produce – and hence were regularly shortened – and required large theatres like the new Pagliano of Florence, built in 1853, which could sit 4,000 people, unlike the traditional La Pergola.[54] By the early 1880s Meyerbeer's main operas outsold everyone else's in Rome, thanks to *Robert le Diable* and *Les Huguenots*, both composed in the 1830s. Meyerbeer could not be there to enjoy his continuing triumphs: he had been dead for twenty years.

The other main challenge to Italian supremacy – in the longer run far more decisive than that represented by French grand opera – came from Germany. The German Romantic opera, whose leading representative had been Carl Maria von Weber (1786–1826), had entered by the 1830s a period of decline. Richard Wagner's mission was to rescue it, though even he, at least at the beginning, was influenced by and admired Italian sound, as he explained in his essay *Die Deutsche Oper* (1834). But he also absorbed the theatrical lessons of the French grand opera with its spectacular stage effects.[55] The results were evident in *Der Fliegende Holländer* (The Flying Dutchman, 1841) *Tannhäuser* (1845) and *Lohengrin* (1850). Wagner, however, was, for a composer, an unusually political animal. His reading of the social and economic revolution which was overtaking Europe in the middle of the nineteenth century was that the domination of money and profit-making was negative for the arts. Unlike the Italian composers, who since the days of Rossini were perfectly at home in the entrepreneurial *milieu* which constituted the backbone of the new opera world, Wagner, so innovative in musical terms, was deeply reactionary in social terms. His anti-Semitism, openly expressed in *Das Judenthum in der Musik* (Judaism in Music, 1850), was connected not only to the slights he had received or imagined he had received from Jews such as Meyerbeer (who in reality had lobbied on his behalf) and the music publisher Maurice Schlesinger (without whose support he would not have survived in Paris), or envy of the prestige of Jews like Felix Mendelssohn (who had died in 1847), who had been adored by audiences and worshipped by royalty, but also to his anti-capitalism. He conflated his hatred of Jews with the commercialisation of music; the 'public taste in art' had come 'under the mercantile fingers of the Jews', and Wagner expressed his disgust at 'the banker-music whoring'.[56] The ferocity of his attack shocked even his closest supporters:

> The purely physical aspect of Jewish speech repels us. The first thing that strikes our ear as outlandish and unpleasant in the Jew's production of voice sounds is a creaking, squeaking, buzzing snuffle ... an intolerably jumbled blabber ... the qualities of his dialect make the Jew altogether incapable of giving artistic enunciation to his feelings and expressions through speech ... Music is the speech of passion.[57]

In Wagner's view, each aspect of an operatic work (theatre, costumes, scenario, libretto, music) should be totally integrated by the composer himself, resulting in a 'total work', or *Gesamtkunstwerk*, as he explained in *Oper und Drama* (1850–51). The themes treated in this experimentation over twenty years were not from the modern world but from the mythical world of German antiquity, the world of *The Ring*, and the classical structure of Greek drama.

To fund his work, Wagner could not rely on the market. Experimentation required the support of representatives of the pre-market era: patrons and protectors. These Wagner found at the court in Dresden, in Franz Liszt, who conducted *Lohengrin* and whose daughter Cosima he married, and above all in Ludwig II, King of Bavaria, under whose auspices was built the Festspielhaus, a theatre in Bayreuth designed and constructed especially for the presentation of Wagnerian music dramas, where *The Ring* was first performed. Wagner exploited for nineteen years the patronage of the King, though Ludwig was such a spendthrift that the money he spent on Wagner was a mere fraction of that spent on his lavish decorating and building works.[58]

Audiences were, at first, not so indulgent towards Wagner's innovations. Formidable critics such as Eduard Hanslick of the *Neue Freie Presse*, arbiter of Viennese taste and the leading music writer in the German-speaking world, became virulent opponents of Wagner's works, though Hanslick had liked *Tannhäuser*.[59] It took some time for Wagner's operas to be accepted. Paris always rejected him, increasing his contempt for Jews: what else could one expect of a city in thrall to Meyerbeer, Halévy and Offenbach? 'Offenbach possesses the warmth of a dungheap. All Europe is wallowing in it.'[60] He was more successful elsewhere, but it took time:

WAGNER'S OPERAS: FIRST PERFORMANCES

OPERA	FIRST PERFORMANCE	FIRST ENGLISH PERFORMANCE
Rienzi	1842	1879
Der Fliegende Holländer	1843	1870
Tannhäuser	1845	1876
Lohengrin	1850	1875
Tristan und Isolde	1865	1882
Die Meistersinger von Nürnberg	1868	1882
Der Ring des Nibelungen	1876	1882

The delay became increasingly shorter, but only in the twentieth century did Wagner achieve full recognition and his operas become part of the operatic repertory. Operatic tastes before the second half of the twentieth century were more fickle than is generally appreciated. In his lifetime Bellini, perhaps the most representative exponent of the *bel canto*, was universally loved. Then he fell out of favour. Then, in the 1950s, he was revived by the great sopranos of the second half of the twentieth century: Maria Callas above all, Joan

Sutherland and Montserrat Caballé.[61] At the beginning of the twentieth century Wagner, unlikely as it may seem, had become for some Italian socialists the composer 'of the proletariat' – far preferable to Verdi, by then labelled a mere progressive bourgeois.[62] By the First World War Wagner had become regarded as the purest expression of German militarism, and along with many other German composers was banned in France for the duration of the conflict, with the full support of all the leading French composers from Saint-Saëns to Debussy.[63]

By the 1950s a relatively small repertory of some 120 operas dominated the season of the most important opera houses in the world. Very few composers could hope to enter what had become a closed genre.

29

Theatricals

The Theatre

IN THE COURSE OF THE NINETEENTH CENTURY there was a substantial expansion in the number of theatres throughout Europe, above all in Paris and London. In 1817 there were 16,924 theatre seats available in the French capital. By 1848 this had more than doubled to 34,000; by 1872 there were 44,000. In 1813 there were only thirteen theatres in Paris, twenty-seven in 1847, and thirty-six in 1861. By the 1830s London had two dozen theatres. Madrid in 1842 had forty different places of entertainment, including circuses, museums and private home theatres.[1] In 1903 Paris had forty theatres; New York thirty. By 1920 New York had overtaken Paris: fifty-nine theatres to Paris's forty-seven (average number of seats: one thousand). By the end of the 1920s New York was well ahead: eighty theatres to Paris's sixty-seven. The new competition from the cinema had not yet dented the progression of the stage.[2] This, of course, paralleled economic development in general, and the 2,000 per cent increase in expenditure on entertainment in the nineteenth century, with the occasional drop during revolutions.[3] The larger new theatres in Paris, such as the Ambigu, the Théâtre de la Gaieté and the Porte St-Martin, specialising in 'light' plays, i.e. vaudevilles and melodramas, had around 1,800 seats each and were almost as large as the Opéra, while the next four rivalled in size (c.1,250 seats) the Opéra-Comique and the Théâtre-Italien.[4] Clearly the theatre was reaching an entirely new audience for the first time. By 1847 Parisian theatres catered for 15,000 people a day. It was thus the most popular commercial form of public entertainment.

The provincial theatres provided mainly plays, usually performed by itinerant companies, often interspersed with songs, and very few operas and concerts. Most provincial music took place privately for the 'genteel' classes or as an adjunct to public drinking for the others.[5]

Gas lighting was improved, and soon the more versatile and stronger electrical lighting revolutionised the art of staging plays. One of the first theatres to experiment with this new technology was the Paris Opéra in 1849.[6] Electricity arrived in American theatres in 1879, when it was used at the California in San Francisco. The first English theatre was the Savoy in 1881. La Scala had to wait until 1883. Still the audience remained fully lit for a long time. Only towards the end of the nineteenth century were the house lights dimmed, and even then it often caused surprise.[7]

The expansion of the theatre required a tremendous increase in the supply of new plays. The increase in demand was due not just to more people going to the theatre, but to the same people going more frequently. Before the railways the population which could potentially attend the theatre was relatively small. Consequently theatre managers changed plays very frequently. At the Edinburgh Adelphi in 1842, during the summer season of 150 nights, 132 different plays were produced. Once inside the theatre the people wanted to see not just a single play but also shorter numbers, songs and dances.[8] In Paris between 1831 and 1850 there was an average of four hundred new plays produced every year. In 1852 at the Théâtre du Luxembourg alone ninety-six plays were produced, of which twenty-six were new.[9] The theatre of the time was the equivalent of the cinema in the years before television.

Inevitably, critics complained that quality was not what it was – which is what they always say when quantity increases. Such views are understandable, but they are expressed by those who, precisely because of their work, are forced to see most new productions. Ordinary theatre-goers only go to see plays they think they might like, and they are often right. In the long run there is no obvious reason why an increase in production should not result in better works. Still, the dyspeptics were probably correct. Very little of what was produced in theatres in the first half of the nineteenth century still has an audience today, while we still enjoy the operas, the music, the poetry and the novels of the time. This failure to survive is true not just of the more popular genres, such as Scribe's melodramas and vaudevilles, but also of the works then celebrated by the critics. Very little of the repertory of the Romantic theatre still survives – Alfred de Musset's *Les Caprices de Marianne* (1833) and *On ne Badine pas avec l'amour* (No Trifling with Love, 1834) are hardly ever performed outside the francophone world. Even Victor Hugo's plays are rarely performed outside France, unlike his novels, which have been endlessly adapted into films, animations and musicals. The theatre of the rest of Europe was even less distinguished. The days of Ibsen, Wilde, Shaw, Chekhov and Strindberg were still to come.

Special effects were regularly deployed to please the new audiences, often saving a bad play. In 1868 Victor Séjour's *La Madonne des roses*, performed at the Gaieté in Paris, provided a final scene to remember: suddenly smoke filtered through the scene (the interior of an Italian palazzo), the wood cracked and burst into flames, the ceiling fell, the central beam smouldering on stage. As this was happening the hero descended from a spiral staircase holding a woman in his arms while the flames seemed about to engulf them. The audience was delighted.[10]

Italy's theatres, largely devoted to opera, were, in the words of an informed French visitor, 'grander, more beautiful, better decorated and, above all, better built, than ours'.[11] The problem Italy faced, however, was that its lower level of economic development and its political segmentation had protected aristocratic élites against the emerging middle classes – the backbone of the new theatre audiences elsewhere. Theatre managers were therefore in constant economic difficulties. Practices typical of the *ancien régime* co-existed with those pertaining to modern market relations. The audience was effectively divided into various categories. The *palchettisti* were those who had bought or inherited their permanent boxes, usually as a result of having funded the original construction of the theatre. They did not pay anything, save in some instances a yearly rent. Then there were the *esentati*, who had free access thanks to patronage, the *abbonati*, who had bought a subscription, and finally the *paganti*, or paying customers. Only the last two categories corresponded to 'normal' market conditions. The box-owners, however, often let their boxes out, though the rules prohibited it, to people who in turn occasionally sub-let them. Thus there was something like a secondary market even in the section reserved to the *palchettisti*, but this did not profit the theatre.

Actual control of the theatres was in the hands of three distinct groups. First there was the court, or in some cases the civic authorities, which formally controlled the entire theatrical life of the town. Secondly there were the *palchettisti*, who were *de facto* the part-owners of the theatre.[12] Many of these *palchettisti* were aristocratic ladies who effectively exercised considerable informal control, especially in 'progressive' cities like Parma. It was not uncommon to see women in Italy going to the theatre on their own, and even sitting – never standing – in the stalls.[13] This could not happen in most Paris theatres, where women were not admitted to the orchestra stalls.[14]

The third group were those to whom the effective management of the operatic season had been delegated: the *impresari*, who organised the actual productions, hired composers and decided the programme.[15] They were the true theatrical entrepreneurs. They were usually paid by the court or the civic authorities, which in turn partly depended on the paying customers. They could raise further money from the gambling tables normally allowed in the foyers. The impresario was supposed to deliver a season according to certain specifications. In Bologna he was expected to stage at least one large-scale show (*spettacolo grandioso*) and two or three smaller works (*opera buffa*). He hired and paid the orchestra, the choir and the singers, made sure the theatre was lit, heated, cleaned, etc. It was thus in the interests of the impresario to be attentive to market demands, while at the time deciding how far he could allow himself to be lobbied by local interests and patronage.[16]

It is evident that under such a system, variants of which operated elsewhere in Europe, the box-owners were an impediment to the commercial development of the theatre. But there were other obstacles to an expansion: costs. Operas and large-scale spectacles with special effects were expensive. The demands of the leading stars compounded the problem. It is thus not entirely fortuitous that the increase in demand for theatre was met by a resort to genres which were not only popular but also cheap, like the melodrama and vaudeville. Actors were easier to recruit than singers, their period of training was shorter, and a bad actor was more tolerable than a poor singer. Actors, though, made little money. Their status was much lower than that of singers. The French Auguste Louis Blondeau, travelling in Italy, remarked that the Roman aristocracy would welcome an opera singer as a guest in their homes, but never a theatre actor.[17]

The working conditions of actors were appalling, especially in the 'low' theatres. The situation at the Théâtre du Petit-Lazary in Paris in 1842, as described by Théophile Gautier, was not atypical. The demand for seats was such that the theatre was always full. Actors had to perform the same play twice a day, three times on Sundays. As the audience was crammed into a relatively small place, the temperature would easily rise to thirty-five degrees, while the actors had to dress and undress rapidly to play their various roles.[18]

Acting was a strenuous business. Actors were under heavy pressure; it was not uncommon for them to suffer some kind of physical breakdown at an early age, and to resort to stimulants. Those who could cultivated social success as a way of enhancing their prestige and their fees. Charles Kean, the son of the famous Shakespearean actor Edmund Kean, achieved his goal of obtaining recognition in London by a five-year stint in the provincial theatre, cultivating fashionable society, dining with duchesses and thus being noticed by the press, drafting the help of his Eton schoolmates. His prestige and popularity increased proportionately with his social success. In 1834–35 he earned £1,200 in the provinces; the following season he received £1,111 for 193 performances (£5.15s. per night). But the real money was in London. When he was finally back in the capital he played 225 times in one year, receiving £7,242 – £32.19s. per night.[19]

The idea of directing a play, in the sense of deciding on its interpretation and how it should be performed, was still to come. All the actors needed to know were their lines. Traditional stage direction consisted of getting the entrances and exits of the actors right, and above all their correct placement on stage (Beaumarchais included these in his directions in the printed text).[20] Acting was made simpler by the development of a stock of standardised characters: leading man, leading woman, lead juvenile man/woman, old man/woman, chambermaid, manservant, villains. Actors could specialise and spend their acting life playing much the same character over and over again, just as some Hollywood actors do today. Because of the demand for new plays, the short-term nature of each production and the risk involved, it was common practice to adapt a play from a book. This 'piracy', as Thackeray called it in *On Theatrical Emancipation, and the Rights of Dramatic Authors* (1831), was facilitated by the lack of adequate performance copyright legislation for much of the nineteenth century.[21]

Virtually all successful nineteenth-century novels were adapted for the theatre. Novelists realised that the theatre was by far the most profitable medium of the day (another parallel with the cinema today). Eugène Scribe, the leading playwright of his age, became extremely rich. Edward Bulwer-Lytton could get £500 per play even in the depressed London theatre of the 1830s.[22] The prospect of this kind of money led Eugène Sue to adapt some twenty plays from his novels. Virtually all Dickens's novels were adapted for the stage, with a simpler plot and fewer characters, after they were published. Zola, who regarded himself, quite justifiably, as a professional writer whose duty it was to maximise his gains, explained in 1880 that one hundred performances of a play earning 4,000 francs of box office receipts per performance, with 10 per cent going to the writer, was like selling 80,000 copies of a book, a far more difficult achievement.[23]

Successful writers and their publishers would first publish their novels in serialised form, then in expensive book form, then as a cheap book, while also adapting it into a play. Occasionally a play or a novel would be turned into an opera. Thus the book functioned as an advertisement for its theatrical adaptation: you've read the book, now see the play. A novel, even with illustrations, as was often the case, allowed readers to use their imagination to visualise the setting and the characters, but sufficient curiosity was often aroused for them to go and see how these would actually be represented on stage. A successful play would enhance book sales. It was usual for major playwrights to have their plays published in collected editions. This had been the case for Goldoni and Kotzebue in their own lifetimes.[24] The theatre generated a subsidiary market for publishers, who would bring out the text of the play. This would be sold as part of a programme which also gave details of the actors, and it enabled provincial theatres to produce new plays. After seeing a play it was not unusual for members of the audience to buy the text in a bookshop nearby.[25] As theatres were still brightly lit, it was perfectly possible to follow a play with the text on one's lap, as many students of classics did.[26]

Authors were aware how difficult it was to obtain payment from distant provincial theatres, so they were willing to grant the rights in the text to clever publishers, such as Jean-Nicolas Barba, the leading publisher of plays in France under the Restoration. Even famous playwrights such as Scribe, Delavigne and Pixérécourt would give Barba the property of a play in exchange for half the authors' rights for all theatres outside Paris.[27]

The general organising principle of the cultural industry was that if a product 'worked' in one media, then it would probably work in others. As the theatre was a risky business, it was prudent to minimise the risk by giving the public the kind of things which had already succeeded in another market. New playwrights were under tremendous pressure: their first play had to be a success, for unlike established writers, they would not be given a second chance. For this reason, their first play was seldom innovatory; and the incentive to experiment dwindled with each success. The process of cultural renewal requires risk-taking and courage on the part of the creators and the producers. The more competitive the market, the greater this tendency towards conservatism. In protected markets such as the subsidised theatre, experimentation may work as long as it pleases an influential élite; in the commercial theatre failure is paid for very dearly. This was the situation in the first half of the nineteenth century in all the major capital cities of Europe, and above all in London and Paris, where the growing liberalisation of the theatre and the development of new social classes had vastly increased the supply of plays without producing any works of lasting value.

In Paris in 1830 the theatres faced a gradual cut in subsidies, leading to the growth of managerial control over the leading public theatres such as the Opéra, the Opéra-Comique and the Théâtre-Italien. This provided further impetus for the growth of a highly commercial theatre which excelled in vaudevilles, melodrama and light comedies. This led to a distinction between high and low genres within élite culture. The high genre was regarded as part of the national heritage, while the low 'popular' genre was part of the entertainment of the new bourgeoisie. The higher the genre, the higher the ticket price and the higher the subsidy: in 1854, for thirty centimes it was possible to have an evening of uncomplicated fun at the Funamboles; for one franc one could go to the Comédie-Française for Molière or Racine; but the Opéra required at least 2.50 francs.[28] Outside Paris, in the provinces, civic pride decreed that one had to do as in the capital and maintain theatres which, unless subsidised, would close down.

The views of the critics mattered little in determining the success of the favourite playwrights of the day. In the 1830s the majority of French critics lambasted anything Scribe wrote, and praised de Vigny and Hugo, but to no avail. Scribe went from success to success. The critics were outraged when the Académie Française, in one of its periodic searches for popularity, elected Scribe to join the august body in 1836, and even more so when twenty-four of his plays came to be performed at the Comédie-Française – a record in the nineteenth century for a contemporary playwright.[29] But Scribe had passed the crucial test, that of the market, a test critics seldom have to sit. Their performances must satisfy an editor, but cannot easily be measured against readers' opinions. At the end of the twentieth century a director of the National Theatre in London voiced the common complaint of actors and artists throughout the ages: 'Critics do not pay a penalty for failing. Nobody chastises them if they do a bad job, nobody notices if they do a good job.'[30]

The expansion of the theatre in Paris in the 1830s had attracted not only the middle classes but also people from the suburbs, and even illiterates. A seat in the 'gods' or standing in the stalls was cheap. The same theatre could show adaptations of 'high' classical plays, simple vaudeville, well-made bourgeois plays, or farces with songs. The theatre had become a place where different social classes mixed – while excluding, as it still does, the working and the poorer rural classes. The pressures towards expansion of the market were such that theatre directors, playwrights and actors, in fact all the main economic beneficiaries of such an expansion, would constantly examine ways of producing plays and entertainment that would attract a wider public. A lowering of prices was a contributing factor to this expansion. More important was the increase of supply. In the twentieth century the rise of the cinema and other ways of spending leisure hours (car trips, picnics, holidays, sport, cycling and, eventually, radio and television) repositioned the theatre as a middle- and upper-class enclave, though the impact was cushioned by the expansion of the middle classes and the expansion of free time.[31]

The Light Opera: Paris and Vienna

Grand opera was too expensive and not entertaining enough for the emerging middle classes. They wanted something less demanding than opera which still possessed some of its cultural prestige. The 'light' opera was born.

It is pointless to attempt to establish a distinction between the different forms of musical theatre: opera, operetta, musical, light opera etc. No definition is likely to prove satisfactory. In both opera and operetta the musical element dominates: the composer prevails over the librettist – though, at least in the early part of the nineteenth century, the libretto and its plot were uppermost in the minds of theatre managers.[32] Some might think that opera contains more 'complex' music, but this is too subjective a concept. It is true that operettas do not end tragically, but not all operas do so either. The distinction is largely a matter of social conventions. Opera is what musicians, audiences and critics call opera, what is performed in opera houses, and for which prices are higher and performers are better paid. Successful light opera composers did not contest this social definition. Having gained money and prestige with their light opera, few sought to gain a place next to Verdi or Wagner with an opera. Some, however, did, and at least one succeeded: Jacques Offenbach, whose *Tales of Hoffmann* is regularly performed in leading opera houses (though poor Offenbach died in 1881, before the première). Arthur Sullivan (of Gilbert and Sullivan fame) tried and failed: his grand opera *Ivanhoe* (1891) was seldom performed. The lure of establishing high culture credentials continued to manifest itself with famous practitioners of more popular genres. Gilbert Bécaud, one of the most popular French singers of the 1950s, tried his hand in 1962 with an opera, *L'Opéra d'Aran*, premièred at the Théâtre des Champs-Élysées in Paris. Paul McCartney's *Liverpool Oratorio* (1991), commissioned by the Royal Liverpool Philharmonic Society and co-written with the composer Carl Davis, who conducted the première, made the top of the *Billboard* classical chart but was panned by the critics.

Light opera or operetta is now associated with Vienna, but its origins are more than the simple expression of Viennese gaiety. In 1776 Joseph II, Emperor of Austria, had made the Burgtheater (built in 1741) the centre of serious theatre in Vienna. The light-hearted Altwiener Volkstheater (Folk Theatre of Old Vienna) was dispatched to the suburbs, where it flourished under the name of Theater an der Wien (1801) under the management of Emanuel Schikaneder (the librettist of *The Magic Flute*). The Viennese bourgeoisie as well as the aristocracy clearly preferred this easier fare. This was the basis for the subsequent development of a distinctive genre, the Vienna operetta.

Operetta was a bourgeois genre that hid its lower origins in the *Singspiel*, the French vaudeville, the Viennese *Volksstück*, the *opera buffa*. It was a middlebrow cultural genre – the equivalent of the popular novels of Verne and Dumas in the nineteenth century and the Broadway musical of the twentieth, the true successor to the nineteenth-century operetta. It was also the only artistic genre – along with the waltz – associated specifically with the Austrian Empire.

One of the distinctively Austrian components of the genre was the parody, so fashionable in Vienna at the beginning of the nineteenth century. Latin verses would be transposed into a modern setting with modern language – the incongruity and anachronism providing the parodic element. It was almost a society game. One of the masters of ironic adaptation was Johann Nepomuk Nestroy (1801–62), an Austrian actor, opera singer and playwright. Hermann Herzenskron (1792–1863) adapted French farces and melodramas. Joachim Perinet turned Hamlet into the 'prince' of a flea market in *Der Prinz von Tandelmarkt* (1807). Aloys Gleich's *Fiesko, der Salamikrämer* (1813) transposed Schiller's *Fiesque* among the Italian salami-sellers of the Prater near Vienna. Nestroy, in *Le Brasseur de Preston*, transposed Stuart England to modern Austria and made fun of Flotow's *Martha*.[33] Nestroy was essentially an actor who had been forced into writing by the lack of scripts and the need to increase his earnings. To please the censors he also tried his hand at an older genre, the so-called *Besserungsstück*, a moralising play aimed at improving the audience. The pattern – pioneered by Molière – was to take a protagonist with some character defect, such as being a miser or a misanthrope, with whom the audience was supposed to identify. In Nestroy's hands the moralising element was kept to a minimum.[34] By the 1850s his works had become so well-known that on 19 November 1859 the Viennese audience laughed at a serious passage in Wagner's *Tannhäuser* because they had all previously seen Nestroy's parody of it.[35] Hegel, impressed though he was by music in Vienna, felt let down by the drama on offer.[36]

It is evident that a playwright-actor like Nestroy was parasitic on other people's texts. These usually came from France. Vienna, at the time, had virtually no significant literary tradition (though this was amply compensated for by music and opera). There were few literary salons, mainly because women were kept out of them (most literary discussions were held in cafés, as in Italy). The few exceptions were those kept by cultured women of the Jewish bourgeoisie, such as the talented daughters of Daniel Itzig (the Emperor's banker), Fanny von Arnstein (1758–1816) and Caecilia von Eskeles (1760–1836), and his granddaughter Henriette von Pereira. These salons closely followed Berlin's ideas and fashions, and were visited by German luminaries such as August Schlegel.[37]

The Viennese could not do texts, but they could do music. Their own *Singspiel* tradition made them particularly receptive to the operetta with its mix of parody, witty dialogue and songs. The genre, however, was born outside Vienna, in France and its paramount practitioner was a German-born composer, Jacques Offenbach (1819–80), born Jakob Eberst, the son of a Jewish cantor, who is supposed to have coined the term 'operetta', which he regarded as the inheritor of the French opéra-comique.[38] His career took off after a period as a conductor at the Théâtre-Français (1849), then he started his own theatre, the Bouffes-Parisiens (1855–61), and finally the Théâtre de la Gaieté (1873–75). By 1875 he had composed ninety operettas, many of them to librettos by a fellow Jew, Ludovic Halévy.

Offenbach's success in Paris was unrivalled, and his works were sought in all leading European capitals. He had seen off his critics, including Jean Janin, the chief musical critic of the *Débats*, who found Offenbach's *Orphée aux enfers* (1858), with its mockery of ancient Greece, deeply upsetting. *Orphée* nevertheless helped put Offenbach's Bouffes-Parisiens on a sound financial footing.[39]

The new light operas represented a business opportunity Nestroy did not let pass. He secured on behalf of his Carltheater the rights to perform Offenbach's works.[40] This choice proved successful: in a few years (1856–62) sixty Offenbach operettas were produced in Vienna.[41] The reviews and reports of the time confirm the enthusiasm of the audiences crowding Nestroy's Carltheater. The admiration for all things French played a part in this, and though for some Paris meant revolution (the days of 1848 were still very vivid), for most it meant elegance, frivolity, and the now fashionable champagne.[42] It must have been a cause of immense pride for Nestroy when one of his own plays (*Zu ebener Erde und erster Stock*) was adapted for the Paris Théâtre du Palais-Royal by Mélesville and Carmouche in 1842, with the title *Du Haut en bas ou banquiers et fripiers*.[43] Had he lived until the second half of the twentieth century he would have had the pleasure of seeing the American musical *Hello, Dolly!* (1964), Thornton Wilder's play *The Matchmaker* (1954) and Tom Stoppard's *On the Razzle* (1981) – all based on his *Einen Jux will er sich machen* (1842). He would also have been pleased to see that he was the sixth most-performed author on the German stage in 1973–74, just after Schiller.[44]

The success of the new genre led others to enter the fray. Franz von Suppé (1819–95) was a composer and conductor of Belgian and Italian origins, born Francesco Suppe in what was then Spalato and is now Split in Croatia. In 1865 he became conductor at the Leopoldstädt Theatre in Vienna. Much of his work consisted of composing music for the stage: overtures, dance music, and choral music. This had acquainted him with a whole range of works, from popular dance music, such as the popular waltz, to songs from melodrama and *Singspiel*. He also wrote his own operas, several a year – all sounding the same. The public wanted original works, something like the grand operas performed in Paris. Suppé and the other local composers could not match Meyerbeer's grand operas, let alone Verdi and Wagner. They could, however, presume to match Offenbach. Suppé and his fellow composers switched to the new genre.[45]

However, they lacked good new librettos. Nearly all the texts they had were old French ones, usually by Scribe. Austrian writers did not like writing librettos; it was a poorly paid, low genre. Besides, they were not protected by copyright, unlike in France, where there was a law compelling theatres to pay a percentage to librettists. The birth of the Vienna operetta coincided with the establishment of authors' rights.[46] In the meantime Suppé and his Austrian contemporaries had continued to borrow heavily from French texts. Suppé's *Fatinitza* (1879) was based on *La Circassienne* by Scribe; Johann Strauss Jr's *Der Karneval in Rom* (1873) on *Piccolino* by Victorien Sardou, and his *Die Fledermaus* (1872) was an adaptation of *Réveillon* by Meilhac and Halévy; Karl Millöcker's *Der Bettelstudent* (1882) was based on *Fernande* by Victorien Sardou, in turn 'borrowed' from Bulwer-Lytton's *The Lady of Lyons*.[47]

Suppé, however, was not simply an imitator of Offenbach; he also used the local tradition of the *Singspiel* as well as Italian tunes. There are also traces of Austrian military music in his generous use of brass instruments. And unlike Offenbach, Suppé avoided political satire.[48] He used the sonority and complexity of the high genre (Meyerbeer, Verdi and Wagner), and applied it to the operetta – thus raising a low genre. Offenbach, in Paris, had done the opposite: he had brought the grand opera 'down', and was consequently often reviled by establishment critics and even by modern writers such as Zola. Zola's famous novel *Nana* (1880) opens with an extremely negative description of the first night of a fictitious operetta, *La Blonde Vénus*, at the Théâtre des Variétés. The actresses cannot act, and are accepted only because they are willing to show their bodies and can move their hips, the audience is odious, and the producer is only interested in money.[49] Zola's target was obvious to all: the opening night in 1864 of Offenbach's *La Belle Hélène* at the Bouffes-Parisiens and its star, the famous Hortense Schneider, who had been promised the then unheard-of sum of 2,000 francs a month.[50] Yet *La Belle Hélène* enjoyed a very long run, and Schneider became the 'uncontested queen of the Paris musical stage'.[51] By 1867 she was paid 4,500 francs a month to perform in Offenbach's *La Grande-Duchesse*.[52] A few years later she was enthusiastically received in London with ovations of eight to ten minutes.[53]

By the 1860s Vienna had become a major cultural capital, not simply the repository of a glorious musical past. In 1860 the Vienna Philharmonic Orchestra started to conduct regular concerts, introducing the then radical music of Liszt, Wagner and Brahms. Wagner conducted a concert of extracts from his operas in 1872. The Theater an der Wien had a very large stage and was able to mount exceptionally complex special effects shows with various contraptions and animals – almost as in Paris. And, of course, there was the operetta, but this remained a local genre until the rise of Johann Strauss Jr's star in the 1870s, which coincided with the waning of Offenbach's fame a few years before his death in 1880. Strauss Jr used all the standard tropes of the French operetta and vaudeville, such as the cuckolded husband as figure of fun (*Die Fledermaus*), as well as the classical comedy situation in which a couple with high social rank is contrasted to one with low status (for instance the Contessa and Conte versus Susanna and Figaro in *Le Nozze di Figaro*).[54]

Suppé's light opera was exported to France only in the first decade of the twentieth century. The new genre created stars with international appeal. One of them, Marie Geistinger (1833–1903), having become famous in Vienna, went on to sing the title role in Offenbach's great operetta *La Belle Hélène*, and was subsequently invited by Gustav Amberg, the director of the Deutsche Oper in New York, to undertake a two-year tour of the United States starting in 1879. She was to be paid, on average, $200 per performance, even though she was past her prime. She ended up touring for four years, performing 826 times; hence, if she did get her $200, she would have earned the enormous sum of $165,200.[55]

Operetta turned out to be an international genre. Though originating in France, it was now quintessentially Viennese. The British too developed their own kind of operetta with Gilbert and Sullivan. Though their works were performed in Paris, they remained firmly anchored in the English-speaking world. Their success in the USA and the 'white' colonies made them very rich: Gilbert earned £20,000 a year throughout the 1880s, his period of greatest success with Sullivan.[56] They, and their brilliant impresario Richard d'Oyly Carte (who eventually built the Savoy Theatre in London for the express purpose of performing their works), had realised that operetta could be even more successful in Victorian Britain if it were purged of any association with lower-class music halls and of 'French vulgarity'. In 1906 Gilbert explained that he and Sullivan had resolved, early on, that their plots should not give offence and that no lady of the company should be required to wear a dress she would not wear with absolute propriety offstage.[57]

Russia, to the dismay of the populist movement in the theatre perennially seeking Russian roots, never developed its own genre. Offenbach's operettas, appropriately Russified, remained the most popular shows throughout the reign of Alexander II.[58] A Spanish development of the French operetta, the zarzuela, remained even more obscure in Europe than Gilbert and Sullivan, but was much appreciated in Latin America. The zarzuela was originally a burlesque musical play, originating in the seventeenth century (La Zarzuela was a royal residence) before becoming overshadowed by the tonadilla, a comic opera of French or Italian derivation. By the early nineteenth century they had all been forgotten. Their revival was due to Offenbach's fame and the desire to create a national operatic genre. It was immediately successful. Rafael Hernando's El Duende had over one hundred performances after its first night at the Teatro de Variedades in Madrid in 1849. In 1856 a large theatre was built in Madrid with the express purpose of staging zarzuelas (called, inevitably, the Teatro de la Zarzuela). Another zarzuela, Francisco Barbieri's masterpiece Pan y toros (1864), dominated the stage for twenty years. How 'Spanish' the new zarzuela was is debatable, because much of the music was of Italian derivation, and the plots were based on French plays and operas. Joaquín Gaztambide's El Valle de Andorra (1852) was based on Halévy's opera Le Val d'Andorre, his Catalina (1854) on Meyerbeer's L'Étoile *du Nord*; Francisco Barbieri's *Los Diamantes de la corona* (1854) was based on Daniel Auber's opera *Les Diamants de la couronne*. The first part of Jules Verne's novel *Les Enfants du Capitaine Grant* (1867) was turned into the zarzuela *Los Sobrinos del Capitán Grant* (1877). The inspiration of Offenbach was so marked that even the name of his theatre, the Bouffes-Parisiens, was adapted in 1866 by the Catalan singer Francisco Arderius for his theatrical troupe, the Compañía de los Bufos Madrileños.[59]

But a more national genre also emerged, thanks in part to Luis Mariano de Larra (1830–1901), son of the great romantic poet Mariano José de Larra. He left a legacy of mainly co-authored librettos for the Teatro de la Zarzuela, including *Las Hijas de Eva* (1862), *La Guerra Santa*, based on Jules Verne (1879), and *La Insula Barataria* (1864), inspired, like Gilbert and Sullivan's later *The Gondoliers* (1889), on a passage in Cervantes's *Don Quixote* where the knight promises an island to Sancho Panza. Larra's major claim to fame was the three-act *El Barberillo de Lavapiés* (1874), one of the defining works in the history of *zarzuela*, in which he mixed a conventional aristocratic verse drama with the popular language and characters of Madrid.

By the 1890s there were eleven theatres in Madrid, mainly performing *zarzuelas*. Then a long decline started, and by the 1960s it had become a protected and subsidised genre.

The Melodrama

In the eighteenth century the (Italian) term *melodramma* denoted a play with music. Later the kind of plots used in such a genre came to be used in any work in which the author exploited events to act on the emotions of the audience. The plots were variations on the moral dilemmas that were central to classical drama: honour versus money, power versus love, love of family versus the love of a woman/man, private love versus public duty. What was different was the simpler and more clear-cut way in which the story was told. The melodrama affected to be a 'popular' genre. It was usually performed in theatres reserved for non-élite culture. In fact the upper classes flocked to see the melodrama. They went to see the classics as a kind of social duty and to mark their status, and then went to the melodrama to have fun. The classical drama remained the staple of élite theatres, but the melodrama came into its own as the favourite genre. It was a quintessential bourgeois genre, not because it defended the values of this class, but because it offered a prism through which the bourgeoisie could gaze at itself and see its problems depicted – in a relaxed manner and in greater comfort than their aristocratic predecessors. Théophile Gautier, the most influential theatre critic of his day, understood it: 'The common people do not like popular vaudeville. They prefer illusion to reality. It is the European aristocrats who love the vaudeville and the dramas performed at the *variétés* and the Palais-Royal.'[60]

The Paris melodrama was, unquestionably, dominated by Eugène Scribe. He was the best-known playwright not just in France but in the whole of Europe. He was admired by the bourgeoisie, who recognised in him 'one of them': bourgeois in origin, in style and in taste. He was not so admired by the critics. Gautier, in his column of 31 July 1837, declared himself relieved that there were no new plays that particular week: 'The unstoppable flood of vaudevilles and melodramas' had subsided – 'all in all, a good week'. Most new plays, he complained, seemed to have been written by Eugène Scribe; all of them were the same, with the same characters doing the same things. Gautier was annoyed with the 'realism' of much current melodrama: so much of the dialogue resembled ordinary conversation. What was the point of going to the theatre? At least at the opera one got kings and emperors, knights and noblewomen. The crowds flock to the opera in order to escape from everyday life, he added, and though the librettos are very second-rate, the music, such as Meyerbeer's, 'gives wings to the lame'.[61] Gautier died in 1874, just as the number of new plays began to fall considerably. In 1875 the Comédie-Française had only four new plays (four more than now, one might add), while the popular Théâtre Porte Saint-Martin simply showed 360 times the adaptation of Jules Verne's *Le Tour du monde en quatre-vingts jours*.[62]

To be successful at the time, a novelist or playwright had to mass produce, but while at least a few of the hundreds of novels written by Dumas or the sixty or so written by Verne have made it to posterity, little remains of the 425 plays Scribe wrote between 1810, when he was nineteen, and 1861, when he died.[63] What has remained are some of his thirty opera librettos, notably Meyerbeer's *L'Africaine*, *Le Prophète* and *Les Huguenots*, and the operas based on his plays, such as Rossini's *Le Comte d'Ory*, Bellini's *La Sonnambula*, Donizetti's *L'Elisir d'amore* and Verdi's *Les Vêpres Siciliennes* and *Un Ballo in maschera*.

Though now almost forgotten, Scribe was, in his lifetime, inescapable. His production of plays had an industrial character, with a theatre workshop in which numerous collaborators, 'assistants' or co-authors were busy producing plays cooperatively under the supervision of Master Scribe, who thus provided work for older and younger writers.[64] The enterprise also churned out dozens of librettos, often for composers who were less well-known than Scribe. Between 1816 and 1820 Scribe averaged ten to twelve plays a year; in 1820 alone he wrote sixteen plays, earning more than 20,000 francs. And that was only the beginning: his highest earnings were achieved over the following thirty years:

EUGÈNE SCRIBE: YEARLY EARNINGS FROM PLAYS

1820	20,760 francs
1821	43,759 francs
1824	66,339 francs
1825	76,248 francs
1828	115,998 francs
1830	130,899 francs
1833	148,378 francs
1840	170,227 francs
1851	200,362 francs
1854	211,018 francs
1855	232,070 francs

SOURCE: Jean-Claude Yon, *Eugène Scribe, la fortune et la liberté*, pp.103–4

Scribe amassed a vast fortune writing plays that would soon be forgotten. He was able to live a life of luxury.[65] Very few successful novelists could match his earnings. Scribe was perfectly aware of it. In 1840, as he totted up his earnings for the year, he wrote in his account book: 'This is enormous. I shall not mention it to anyone: the hatred of my colleagues and the insults of the newspapers grow in proportion to my income.'[66]

Scribe's early production was mainly of vaudevilles, a generic term encompassing the farce, the satire and the parody. As his prestige increased he shifted to the sentimental comedy, using a new theatre, the Gymnase (1820), which was modern, with proper lighting, elegant and welcoming. It was soon patronised by Marie Caroline, Duchesse de Berry, the cultural trendsetter of the day – someone who, quick to notice a trend about to surface, made sure to set it first. The Gymnase was adept at public relations. Journalists were given the best places for the first few nights, while the management pretended to others that all performances were sold out, thus creating a buying panic. All this helped, but little would have come of it if Scribe had not supplied a steady stream of plays. In the 1820s he delivered 107, and a further sixty-eight between 1830 and 1848.[67] As Théophile Gautier reluctantly admitted, it was quite an achievement to be able to remain at the top of the theatrical scene in a city like Paris for twenty-five years with plays of 'no special value'.[68]

Scribe's characters reflected the composition of his audience, which was made up of a sprinkling of the recently ennobled (mainly bankers), the remnants of the old aristocracy, and then merchants, clerks, students, artists, magistrates, and a few prosperous farmers in Paris for business who preferred to go to the theatre rather than the brothel. His plays were always set in the contemporary world, making references to current events, habits and fashion. They dealt with the problems facing their audiences: money, arranged marriages versus love unions, respect for rules rather than principles. The bourgeoisie is often satirised, but never cruelly. Politics is kept at some distance, except for a few patriotic references that pleased everyone.

The plots were usually borrowed from novels summarised by Scribe's assistant – Scribe himself had little time to read books. His co-authors would also write the short songs which were interspersed with the dialogue, find a musical accompaniment, and attend the rehearsals, in the course of which dialogue was often altered. But Scribe always remained in charge of the main architecture of the play. His role resembled that of a film director, and he was the main 'author' of a collective work, though, generously, he always ensured that the names of his principal assistants appeared alongside his own as co-authors. He was perfectly aware of the kind of literature he was producing. In his *Le Charlatanisme* (1825), the main character, a writer of vaudevilles, presumably Scribe's *alter ego*, declares, 'One loses money in high literature. One gets rich in the low one. You are welcome to spend ten years on a masterpiece! In three days we produce a play – and, often, there are three of us!'[69]

However, once established as the unchallenged king of the theatres of the boulevard, even Scribe could not resist the lure of 'high art'. He succeeded in having some of his plays performed in the temple of drama, the Comédie-Française. For this he dispensed with co-authors. High art is a solitary endeavour: 'For the Théâtre-Français one must work alone and arrive alone,' he explained. Scribe knew when and how to bend: to be performed at the Comédie-Française he deliberately modified his style, eliminating traces of the vaudeville such as the frequent use of couplets. In his *Discours de réception* à *l'Académie Française* (18 January 1836) he thanked the august body which 'by allowing me to enter its precincts elevates and ennobles the humble abode where I . . . reside. This would inspire in me much pride if an author of vaudevilles could have any.'

Having conquered Paris, it was relatively simple to conquer the provinces and the rest of Europe. Scribe was the theatrical equivalent of Walter Scott, in the sense that neither writer had deliberately set out to write for a European public.[70] Both appealed to different social groups, and to men as well as to women. Scribe's style, like that of Scott decried by the critics as unexciting, was easy to translate. Moreover, so widespread was the use of the French language that plays were performed in it in many foreign cities, including London (in Tottenham Court Road), New Orleans, Rio de Janeiro and Odessa.[71] In Naples, between 1830 and 1860 nearly a third of all plays performed were Scribe's.[72] Between 1825 and 1889 seventy-two of his plays were performed in Denmark. In 1868 in Turin a new French theatre, Il Teatro Scribe, was inaugurated by the King.[73] In England he was the most successful foreign playwright, and was lionised during his visit in 1850 on the occasion of the world première of Halévy's opera *La Tempesta* (text by Scribe from Shakespeare's play) at Her Majesty's Theatre. He retired in 1855, and died in 1861. His star began to wane almost immediately. His plays could not last more than a season or two, which was why he had to mass produce them. By 1870 he was seldom performed. His centenary in 1891 passed unnoticed.[74]

Outside France only the Irish playwright Dion Boucicault (1820–90) could rival Scribe, and he came almost a generation later. But Boucicault's fame was largely restricted to Britain and America; he divided his time between London and New York, where he lived between 1853 and 1876. He too was prolific: 150 plays (he claimed 250), most of which he 'borrowed' from novels and other plays. His first play, *London Assurance* (1841), has remained his best-known, along with his adaptation of *Rip van Winkle* (1865) and *The Shaughraun* (1874). In 1857 Boucicault had a great success in New York with the play *The Poor of New York*, which he had plagiarised from a French play. The play changed its name and was slightly adapted according to where it was performed. Thus, as it travelled, it turned into *The Poor of* Liverpool, Manchester, Leeds, London, Dublin and even *The Streets of Islington*. He declared: 'I am making a hundred pounds a week on the damned thing.'[75] In 1860 he persuaded the London theatre manager Benjamin Webster to pay him a royalty on box office receipts. This enabled him to earn £10,000 for a single play, *The Colleen Bawn*. Until then playwrights earned perhaps as little as £2 per night, and £300 per play.[76] Even so, this was far from Scribe's spectacular earnings.

Music, Songs and Drinks

Of all the various theatrical experiences available in the nineteenth century, the most popular was the music hall. This was not only a place where one could hear music, but also where couples could be together, yet sufficiently in view not to give rise to the idea that their relationship was sexual (though, of course, it could give rise to gossip).

The British music hall was born in the 1830s and 1840s, and dominated commercialised popular culture throughout the second half of the nineteenth century. The 1843 Theatres Act had given many suburban and East End theatres the right to perform dramatic works without inserting songs and playing continuous music in the background. Places selling drinks and food while providing variety turns and music were classed separately. These were the earliest music halls. They were, in the main, small buildings, the audiences were local, and the entertainers largely working-class. Many pub-owners set aside in their establishment a so-called 'music saloon' that provided entertainment as well as alcohol. Some grew to become very large. The three largest venues in Manchester – the Casino, the Victoria Saloon and the Polytechnic Hall – had audiences of several thousand a week, mainly young workers of both sexes, though with a clear majority of men. These large music halls developed rapidly in the provinces and especially in the north. The Surrey Music Hall in Sheffield (1852) could squeeze in 4,000 people. Unsurprisingly, it was the largest building in the city. But London was not left behind: Charles Morton was the owner of a pub, the Old Canterbury Arms in Upper Marsh, Lambeth, where concert performances were held three nights a week. These became so popular that in May 1852 Morton opened a concert hall, the Canterbury Hall, next to it. By 1866 there were thirty music halls in London, with an average capacity of 1,500. To these should be added nearly three hundred singing saloons in pubs, etc.[77] This was the most highly organised sector of the entertainment industry. As David Russell has noted, it prefigured the mass entertainment business of the twentieth century. In London it was certainly the principal source of musical entertainment for most working-class and lower-middle-class people. In the 1890s some fourteen million music hall tickets were sold annually.[78]

This was not an attentive audience. It treated the venue as late-eighteenth-century aristocrats treated the opera. Singers and actors had to provide a somewhat 'over the top' performance in the hope of catching the attention of a crowd eating, drinking, talking and flirting. Many of the customers were young clerks and shop assistants who, reluctant to resort to prostitutes, 'salvaged their masculine pride by identifying with the assertive sexuality' of music hall stars, whose acts were full of risqué jokes and sexual innuendoes.[79] But music hall promoters also wanted the respectable middle-class public – an aim almost reached in the late 1890s when they flocked in from the suburbs, though middle- and upper-class males had long frequented the music halls as voyeurs of low life. By then the music halls had become more like theatres: tables were replaced by rows of seats facing the stage; there were fixed starting times, with audiences being replaced at each performance. Drinking was confined to the bars, talking was frowned upon; though occasionally the audience could still be boisterous, with young people throwing eggs, heckling performers and being described as hooligans.[80] The barriers between 'high' and 'low' genres were breached by programmes mixing them in an uninterrupted flow, almost a harbinger of television programming before the spread of multi-channel broadcasting. For instance, the programme for an evening in October 1866 at Day's Music Hall in Birmingham included circus numbers, music, theatre, performing dogs, birds, seals and baboons, as well as a ballet ('grand garland divertissement'), a selection of arias from Bellini's Norma, a comic singer, an orchestra waltz and a pantomime ballet.[81] The programme at the Surrey in Sheffield in the late 1850s mixed snatches from Mendelssohn, Rossini and Verdi with comic songs, dance numbers and acrobats. There was something for everyone.[82] When it came to the songs, however, the tendency was towards the humorous, in the 'cheeky working class' mode, often sung with a Cockney or regional accent – as in the song 'Oh! 'Ampstead' (1914):

> Now if yer want a 'igh old time,
> Just take a tip from me.
> Why 'Ampstead, 'appy 'Ampstead
> Is the place to have a spree.

Or the mock-sentimental, as in 'He.Jay.Hann' (1895):

> I must be as soft as butter
> For my heart gets in a flutter
> When 'er pretty name I utter . . .
> Elizabeth Jane Hann.

When them pretty eyes starts winkin'
I comes over faint an' sinkin'
Blowed if I can sleep for thinkin'
Of my He.Jay.Hann.[83]

Music publishers stood to gain the most from the spread of publicly performed music, since they could then sell the lyrics and the scores. Boosey,
Chappell and Novello dominated the London music publishing world. Chappell was the largest shareholder of St James's Hall, the main venue for
chamber music in the 1870s and 1880s. Chamber music was one of Chappell's
main interests. Boosey hired the hall on Wednesday for their British ballads
concerts. This was a genre much favoured by the Victorian middle classes
and one in which Boosey had a virtual monopoly.[84]

By the end of the nineteenth century there was a trend towards larger
venues for 'family' entertainment, such as the Coliseum in London's
St Martin's Lane, opened in 1904. It was huge, had a triple revolving stage,
contained a multitude of confectionery stalls, and presented four shows a
day.[85] It was a modern venue: all seats could be booked in advance and by
post. Its owner, the Australian Oswald Stoll, was also the chairman of a chain
of music halls scattered throughout the country. This enabled a circuit system
to be established. Stars had to sign up with Stoll (or with his rival, the
entertainment mogul Edward Moss). This guaranteed them a steady income,
but also put them at the mercy of an increasingly powerful distribution
system.[86]

Nothing of the sort happened in France. The cafés-concerts, similar in
many respects to the British pub's singing rooms, spread wide, but each was
an independent business. By 1885 there were, in Paris alone, 360 of these
establishments. Though several were upmarket, the typical café-concert
catered for artisans, clerks and skilled workers. Entry was usually free, but
customers were expected to order a drink (not necessarily alcoholic) every
hour or even half-hour. A glass of wine would cost half a franc (as long as it
was not Burgundy or Bordeaux, which would cost three times as much), so
a two-hour show and four glasses would cost two francs – what a seamstress
would earn in a day.

Nevertheless, cafés-concerts were among the cheapest forms of public
entertainment available in Paris. They would open at seven in the evening,
and could go on until one in the morning. Many were also opened on Sunday
afternoons as family entertainment – something unheard of in Great Britain,
let alone Scandinavia, where Sundays were devoted to religion, not to fun.

The typical show would start with some circus acts, such as acrobats or talking dogs. Then for nearly an hour the orchestra would play dance music, mostly favourite tunes including operatic arias. The customers would join in and practise the new steps, many of which had been introduced from abroad, such as the waltz from Austria (where it was originally known as the *Ländler*), the mazurka from Poland and, above all, the polka (which under the name *pülka* originated from Bohemia, and not from Poland), which had become the craze in France in the mid-1840s. The second part of the show would be opened by female singers selected – unlike their male counterparts – for their good looks, and who deliberately flaunted their attractiveness, much as they do today. They would be followed by the main attraction, a known singer, usually male, who would sing up to forty songs. Finally, during the third and final part of the evening, a duo would sing various snatches from operettas or vaudevilles.

It was possible, though rare, for stars to emerge even in this environment and earn considerable sums, more than many opera singers – as was the case with the celebrated French singer Thérésa (1837–1913), whose real name was Emma Valadon. By 1864 she was earning around 100,000 francs a year, while most of her less fortunate colleagues had to be content with five hundred francs a month or less.[87]

The most glamorous of these *cafés-concerts* adopted names suggesting exotic connections, such as the Alhambra in London and the Alcazar in Paris. The décor often consisted of adopting what was regarded as the luxurious environment of the upper classes, often in an undiscriminating way; hence the lavish use, in the larger and more expensive places such as the Paris Folies Bergère (1869), built in imitation of London's Alhambra, of marble, velvet carpets, chandeliers, gold-plated ornaments, caryatids, etc. Later this opulent style, pejoratively called *kitsch*, would routinely be used in hotels, cinemas and casinos.

The shows at the Alhambra were remarkably daring, and put into question the conventional view of Victorian respectability: 'At the Alhambra . . . old and young, prostitutes and innocents, all intermingle to watch Finette do in the heart of London's West End what was in Paris banished to the Madille, the Château Rouge, and the Closerie de Lilas, in Montmartre.'[88] And what did Finette do? She used her legs to flip up her skirts, revealing leggings and plenty of undergarments, in a version of the cancan. It was suggestive and, given the bordello-like setting, set the pulses racing in 1868.

Such style encouraged the vogue, among the middle and upper-middle classes, of visiting the better class of *café-concert* under the delusion that they were 'roughing it'.[89] In fact they were the real customers, not intruders from another class. The 'authentic' dives were really rough, unsanitary and dangerous, and frequented only by the low-life. The middle classes were offered shows which also suited the respectable working classes (artisans, mechanics, etc.); most of the material was recycled from the entire cultural spectrum: circus, operetta, opera, plays, magic tricks, drawing room songs. Thus the *cafés-concerts* became a public space where various classes intermingled – each thinking (and hoping) that they were intruding into the territory of the other. The result was that class divisions were less pronounced than in the theatre or the opera, where people would either be segregated by pricing policy or excluded by differences in taste. From the point of view of class as well as décor, the *cafés-concerts* were the harbinger of the cinema, which became, and long remained, one of the least class-ridden sections of the entertainment industry.

The expansion of *cafés-concerts* reached its peak around 1900, but statistics here are even less reliable than usual. Any place which provided some form of entertainment while the clientèle consumed drink and food would fall within the definition, including cabarets, clubs and pubs. However, the term '*café-concert*' remained identified with a particular French experience – no pub with a band in Dublin, or bar with musicians in New York, would call itself a '*café-concert*'.

Urban music was not a prerogative of industrialised societies. During the second half of the nineteenth century a distinctive form of Greek urban popular music emerged in the seaports of western Asia Minor. These oriental *cafés-chantants* displayed entertainers of Greek, Armenian, Jewish or Gypsy origins. Often dancing men would perform. By 1870 women were permitted to sing and dance. The repertory would often be Turkish or *ala Turka* rather than *ala franka*, the term used to denote European music. Where the public was prevalently Greek, Greek lyrics would be introduced in the Turkish songs. The principles of composition and performance were based on the Turkish–Persian *makam* system – essentially a set of improvisations within a distinctive framework consisting of a prescribed starting note, an ascending and descending scale and a melodic contour. The musicians would draw from the large stock of tavern songs, folk melodies and even Turkish classical music. There was no notation, no established author.[90] As in the Western *cafés-concerts*, the performance was everything.

Music halls and *cafés-concerts* led to songs specifically written for these venues – not folk songs, not courtly songs, not drawing-room songs and not yet pop songs. They gave rise to singers whose features, thanks to developments in printing, could be seen in magazines, and on postcards and posters.[91] The words were as important as the music, especially in genres like the Victorian ballad, which grew out of popular poetry.[92] The songs would deal with a wide range of topics: love and romance, of course, but also current affairs, including famous murders and political scandals.[93] Some remained in the repertory for decades, well beyond the particular political or social conjuncture which produced them. Thus the French anti-German 'revanchard' songs of the 1870s and 1880s such as 'Le Clairon', 'Le Fils de l'allemand' and 'Le Maître d'école alsacien' gained a major lease of life in the anti-German wars of the twentieth century; British jingoistic songs such as 'Rule Britannia', composed by James Thomson in 1740, were still being sung more than 250 years later. 'L'Internationale' (1888), written by the former communard Eugène Pottier with the music by the Flemish Pierre de Geyter and first performed in the estaminet 'La Liberté', was adopted by the Bolsheviks in Russia, ensuring its global renown.

In most British music halls and French cabarets, the new 'urban' songs used the well-trodden themes of old – love, sex and marriage – in an urban and working-class situation.[94] But some of the more lasting songs of the British repertory originated in nineteenth-century operatic culture. 'Home Sweet Home' was an original tune by Sir Henry Rowley Bishop (who got a knighthood for tunes such as this), who wrote incidental music for the prose theatre, adapting composers such as Mozart and Rossini. 'Home Sweet Home' (the words were by John Howard Payne) had been an aria in Bishop's *Clari, or the Maid of Milan* (Covent Garden, 1823), which became universally popular when adopted by the soprano Adelina Patti, who included it regularly in her Royalty ballad concerts.

The spread of the music hall, the *cafés-concerts* and similar venues throughout the main European cities contributed to the development of the popular song. Each country produced distinctive genres. In Germany the main source of inspiration was the popular *Singspiel*; in France it was a new kind of poetic *chanson* pioneered by Béranger and based on eighteenth-century love and wine songs. In Italy some 'full-throated' songs, to be sung in the style of operatic aria, acquired great renown. They were a blend of popular tradition, operatic arias and drawing-room songs. The lyrics were written by poets. From the middle of the nineteenth century certain songs – including some written in the Neapolitan dialect and translated into Italian

– came to represent *the* Italian song *par excellence*, as was the case with Teodoro Cottrau's 'L'addio a Napoli':

> Sul mare luccicca
> l'astro d'argento
> placida è l'onda
> prospero è il vento
> Venite all'agile
> barchetta mia
> Santa Lucia
> Santa Lucia.[95]

(Upon the sea twinkles/the silver star/The sea is calm/The wind is good/Come in my swift boat/Santa Lucia/Santa Lucia)

What became the most famous of all Neapolitan songs was 'O sole mio' (1898). Written first as a poem by Giovanni Capurro, it was set to music by Edoardo Di Capua.

> O sole mio
> Che bella cosa 'na jurnata 'e sole,
> n'aria serena doppo 'na tempesta!
> Pe' ll'aria fresca pare già 'na festa . . .
> Che bella cosa 'na iurnata 'e sole.

(How beautiful, after the storm/when the day is sunny and the air is tranquil!/ There's already a feel of joy in the fresh air . . .)

It became famous almost at once, at least among Italian emigrants. Subsequently it became metonymic for the Italian song in general, crossing various cultural boundaries and sung by virtually every tenor – from Caruso to Beniamino Gigli, Fritz Wunderlich, Luciano Pavarotti and Plácido Domingo, as well as by popular singers, notably Frank Sinatra and Elvis Presley ('It's Now or Never', 1960, which reputedly sold twenty million records). The group Pearl Jam played the initial bars at a concert in Verona in 2000, and Paul McCartney used it to test the sound system for his concert in Rome in June 2003.

Once, towards the end the eighteenth century, Italy – thanks to Gothic novels – had been a sombre country, full of castles in ruin and conspiratorial Jesuits. A century later, thanks to music and tourists, it had turned into 'sunny Italy', land of love and of the joy of living.

III

1880–1920

THE REVOLUTION

30

The Revolution in Communications

Technological Breakthroughs and Nation States

IN 1880, IF ONE WANTED to see a story being enacted or hear a piece of music, it was necessary to go to the place of performance – just like in 1780. Then, in a few years the tyranny of live performance came to an end. People were able to see recordings of people in motion, hear the sounds of singers and musicians imprisoned, as if by magic, in a cylinder or disc and, a little later, coming from a box situated in their own homes. They were even able to hear voices at a distance.

These innovations (cinema, gramophone recording and radio), all in the last years of the nineteenth century, signalled the dawn of a new century, and of a new, technology-led, cultural industry. Throughout the eighteenth century and until the first half of the nineteenth, few scientific innovations were directly applicable to the cultural industry – photography being the most noteworthy. The most significant improvements in printing – Ottmar Mergenthaler's linotype (1886) and Tolbert Lanston's monotype (1889) – permitting large print runs and a high-circulation press, also occurred at the end of the nineteenth century. Photo-engraving enabled a much faster reproduction of printed replicas. But these were simply improvements of existing technology, not the kind of breakthroughs which made possible the recording of images (photography), motion (the cinema) and sound (the gramophone), and the transmission of sound first by cable and then via air waves. Every novelty has a past. The patent for electric telegraphy, the first instrument of instantaneous transmission of information, was deposited in England by C. Cook and D. Wheatstone in 1837. Thirteen years later, in 1850, it was possible to transmit seventeen words a minute across 2,200 miles; more, if one used the system invented by the Americans Samuel Morse and the Vail brothers in 1838. Underwater and land cables under the Channel (1851) and under the Atlantic (1866) linking the west coast of Ireland to Newfoundland, further extended the range. Up to the 1830s a letter posted in London would take five to eight months to reach India. On 14 April 1865 President Lincoln was assassinated, but the readers of *The Times* did not know about it until 27 April. In 1870 a telegraph linking Britain with India via Constantinople, Persia, the Gulf and thence to Karachi made it possible to send a cable to India in five hours.[1] By 1889 one could make a telephone call by dialling the number oneself. In 1890 wireless telegraphy was born, an innovation disputed by Heinrich Hertz (Germany), Édouard Branly (France), Oliver Lodge (UK), Aleksandr Stepanovich Popov (Russia) and Guglielmo Marconi (Italy). The various disputes over who was 'the first' is the surest indication that all the necessary technological and scientific work required for such a development had already been done. The lucky inventor was at the end of a long technological chain.

Though the USA had considerable production capacity in the manufacturing and laying of cables for telephones and telegraphy, British domination of the new cable technology, not least because of its geographical propinquity to the rest of Europe, lasted until the 1890s. In effect all international communication had to go through London. Britain's primacy in this field was further enhanced when Heinrich Hertz's experiment with electromagnetic waves led to the development of wireless telegraphy. This hegemony attracted foreign inventors such as Marconi, who went to Britain in 1896 hoping to interest others in his own application of Hertz's experiment: a working wireless system. By the end of 1897 the British Post Office and various investors were showing an interest in the invention.[2] Speaking at a distance without wires soon became a reality.

Speaking via telephone wires was already becoming relatively common. Already in 1888 the Germans made 155 million phone calls, escalating to one billion in 1904 and 2.5 billion in 1913.[3] These figures were dwarfed by those of the USA, by that time the largest industrial country in the world: Americans exchanged three times more telephone calls than the whole of Europe.[4] In 1878 the first telephone network in the world – in New Haven, Connecticut, established one year before that of London and two years before that of Paris – had only twenty-one subscribers. By 1880 there were 30,000 American subscribers. By 1885 there were 260,000 telephone owners in the world; 60 per cent of these were in the USA. The gap persisted: on the eve of the First World War there were 14.5 million operational telephones in the world – 9.5

million in the USA.[5] By the 1920s, at least in the USA, members of the middle classes could already aspire to their own private line. Europe lagged behind: in 1922 in Sweden only 8 per cent of the population had a line, 6 per cent in Denmark, 3 in Germany, 2 in Britain, 1 in France, and 0.5 in Italy and Spain.[6] The long technological gap between Europe and the USA was opened. It would take a hundred years to narrow it.

The telephone never became an instrument for the distribution of culture. For a few years there was a 'concert-phone', a service whereby an employee of a concert hall would hold a telephone receiver up during a performance, allowing a subscriber at home to hear live music on their own receiver. Thus in 1878 at Bellinzona in Switzerland one could hear, at a distance, Donizetti's *Don Pasquale*. In 1881, in a special hall equipped with headphones, one could hear a performance taking place at the nearby Opéra. In 1889 in Philadelphia one could listen to a concert being held in New York.[7] The system was still going strong in 1911, enabling Marcel Proust to listen, at home on 20 February, to the third act of Wagner's *Die Meistersinger*.[8]

The phone was the first interactive system of communication at a distance. Before its invention, the only way one could communicate with an absent person was to resort to a messenger. The telephone's impact has been enormous. It has reduced the isolation of individuals, created a business communication network, enabled news to be conveyed to newspapers much faster than ever before. It has changed, sometimes imperceptibly, human relations.[9]

Telegraphy had opened the path to a new, more 'democratic' informality in style by dropping, for reasons of convenience, the elaborate courtesy of letter-writing (electronic mail – email – would go even further in this direction). The telephone further enhanced this modern informality, users beginning all conversations with a single conventional (and often international) form of reply, such as 'Hello' – one of the first English expressions to be adopted by the French (transformed into '*Allo*') – and the almost military '*Pronto*' (ready) of the Italians.

The telephone could not become a mass instrument for the diffusion of cultural commodities because all it did was to offer the possibility of communicating between two points. What was required was a system that enabled concurrent communication with a multiplicity of receiving points – such as radio and television. The rule is: at least one sender, many receivers. Culture has been, and is still, not only an interactive system, but a relay mechanism of messages which proceed from producers to consumers. Consumers respond by market or quasi-market signals – that is, by consuming cultural messages. The internet will probably expand the number of producers, as all previous technological developments have done, but it is unlikely to affect the substance of cultural communications, which is likely to remain predominantly hierarchical.

The obvious antecedent of the telephone and telegraphy was letter-writing. This is why it seemed natural that telecommunication would be subject to a regulation similar to that of the postal system, which in the nineteenth century was already one of the most extensive services provided by the state, along with policing and the defence of the country. Even in Britain and the USA, then as now bastions of liberal economics, the Post Office was the first major nationalised industry. The British Post Office was a government department from 1840, headed by a Minister, the Postmaster General. The Telegraph Acts of 1868 and 1869 gave the state a monopoly (under the Post Office) over any apparatus for 'transmitting messages and other communications by means of electric signals'.[10]

It is thus not entirely surprising that, though started as a private enterprise, the telephone network ended up being controlled by the state not only in Great Britain but also in most European countries. In many instances the private sector was not sufficiently entrepreneurial, and was too short-termist to provide the massive investment required for long-term returns. Thus in Great Britain a private company enjoying a concession from the state, the National Telephone Company, though it had a virtual monopoly over its 88,000 subscribers, was reluctant or unable to expand rapidly. This led to the re-acquisition by the Post Office of the telephone system, establishing in 1912 a public monopoly that lasted until the 1980s, when British Telecom was privatised. In Germany the state took over the telephone network from the outset because of its strategic-military importance. In France the government had established its monopoly on telecommunications even before the telephone was invented: a law of May 1837 prevented anyone from transmitting signals by telegraphic machine or *any other means* without state authorisation. This took care of any subsequent invention.[11] In Italy private companies had concessions, but when these expired in 1907 the government took over the two largest companies. The Russian telephone system was set up by the US International Bell Company around 1881, but by 1901 the Russian government acquired control and gave concessions to small private companies and some municipalities.[12]

In the USA, contrary to the European pattern, the telephone system was in private hands, and there was plenty of investment. But even here the outcome was a monopolistic provider – the American Telegraph and Telephone Company, a private monopoly regulated by the federal government. At first there was a highly competitive period and the network actually expanded, though AT&T's profits decreased. After Theodore Newton Vail became the president of the company in April 1907 he set out to eliminate competitors by lobbying politicians under the banner of 'One Policy, One System, One Universal Service'. An agreement was eventually reached with Congress, the so-called Kingsbury Commitment. This resulted in regional companies, each with a *de facto* local monopoly, while long-distance operations remained in the hands of a sole provider. When America entered the First World War in 1917, existing telegraphic equipment was confiscated and control transferred from the Department of Commerce to the navy, which became, as everywhere else, the key player in the development of radio. This led to its further centralisation. When it was returned into private hands in 1919, AT&T found itself effectively in charge of a heavily regulated yet extremely lucrative industry.

Such an outcome seemed inevitable. The railway and electricity industries converged inexorably towards a monopoly. Competition seemed to involve unnecessary duplications in telephony and telegraphy too. Principles other than competition emerged, and were soon applied to radio: there should be a universal entitlement to the service, and to fulfil that objective there should be cross-subsidisation, a principle already at work in the postal service.[13]

This aspiration – a single universal service – could never have been applied to any of the previous ways of transmitting culture. On the contrary, all the nineteenth-century cultural industries, the press, publishing, even the theatre, were in the throes of intense national competition. The new technology-led industries, however, were soon either publicly owned or dominated by a few oligopolies. Telegraphy had, from the start, an international structure and international regulation. In 1865 the first international telegraphic convention, establishing the International Telegraphic Union, was signed in Paris. A Universal Postal Convention was adopted in 1874, followed by the General (later Universal) Postal Union in 1875.

From 1876, thanks to the telephone – patents for which were deposited at the US Patent Office on the same day by Alexander Graham Bell and Elisha Gray (the courts recognised Bell as the original inventor) – it was possible to hear the human voice at a great distance. The following year, on 19 December, Thomas Edison shouted 'Mary had a Little Lamb' into a hand recorder that scratched soundwaves on to a cylinder covered with foil. It worked, and the great inventor was able to patent his system for recording sound and founded the Edison Speaking Phonograph Co. to manufacture the instrument.

Between 1875 and 1914 a large number of technological innovations came about. Many had the distinctive characteristic of being directly consumable, instead of being aids to production, as so often in the past. In 1885 the American George Eastman developed a simple-to-use portable camera. Ten years later, the French brothers Lumière 'invented' the cinema, in other words perfected a procedure which had preceded them. In 1893 the first petrol-powered 'horseless carriages' appeared. In 1906 an experimental cathodic tube – harbinger of television – was devised by the American Lee De Forest. Electricity was of course applied to manufacturing as well as to the 'cultural industry': among its first users in 1875 were the French chocolate-manufacturer Meunier and Milan's famous opera house La Scala. The first electric power station was opened in 1882 in New York. Electric lightbulbs (the carbon-filament lamp) started being produced in 1878–79, an electric toothbrush was advertised in *Harper's Weekly* in 1886, and the first battery-operated vibrator (designed by the British physician Joseph Mortimer Granville) in the 1880s: in 1900, $200 plus postage would secure the top-of-the-range Chattanooga vibrator.[14] Orville and Wilbur Wright made the first successful aeroplane flight in 1903 at Kitty Hawk, North Carolina. World brands appeared, mainly British or American: Philadelphia cream cheese (1880), Maxwell House coffee (1892), Del Monte canned fruit (1892), Cadbury's chocolate (1897). Campbell's soup had been canned since 1869. Heinz's first bottle of ketchup appeared in 1876.[15]

Innovations in older forms of communication, such as shipping and the railway, proceeded apace throughout the world. The *Mayflower* had taken almost ten weeks to cross the Atlantic in 1620. In 1819 the *Savannah* became the first steamship to make the crossing, taking only twenty-one days, though it used steam power for a mere eight hours (it could not carry all the coal that would have been necessary). In 1857 a fast steam-liner could make the crossing in nine days, though new fast oceanic clippers such as the *Cutty Sark* went on carrying most inter-oceanic freight until the end of the century (tea and tobacco, the standard goods carried by clippers, did not need to be moved as fast as mail). Railway-building became a global enterprise. By the end of the century the American, Canadian, Russian and Indian rail networks were the most extensive in the world. The international capital flow required to sustain such investment was the largest of the nineteenth century.[16]

The context for these developments was the Western colonisation of the rest of the planet. This first modern globalisation – to use a word that has now become popular – was inseparable from the consolidation of nation states. Italy came into being in 1861, Germany in 1870, Austria made a compromise with Hungarian nationalism, turning itself into the Austro-Hungarian Empire in 1867. Russia, previously tolerant of non-Russian cultures, launched, under Alexander III, a policy of Russification, while the USA, having eliminated the threat of Southern secession during the Civil War (1861–65), completed its westward thrust in the 1890s. Japan became a major actor on the international stage thanks to successful wars with China (1894–95) and Russia (1904–05). Nation states became the fundamental units of the new world order.

National states encouraged the growth of virtually all new or improved communications systems. In most cases they underwrote the initial costs. Steamships, for instance, were quite unprofitable in the 1820s and 1830s. Only governments used them, and only when necessary. Ordinary freight and passengers used sailing ships. The P&O company, founded in 1840, survived thanks to government contracts; underwater and overland cables were laid to meet the requirements of colonial policy.[17] The cable networks were privately owned but were dependent on government contracts, policies and subsidies. The era of the triumph of capitalism was in reality an era of state interventions, of state subsidies, of state contracts.

The state, however, kept out of most cultural industries. It kept out of publishing, as it had always done. It kept out of newspapers, though the press was only as independent as its owners. It kept out of the new media: the cinema and the recording of music. Of course, it regulated and even censored them, but on the whole, less than it had done previously. Not so for the first forms of broadcasting. These were kept out of the reach of the private sector, at least in Europe.

The Birth of the Radio

To consume texts, that is, to read them, it is necessary to have a particular skill: literacy. No support or apparatus other than the text itself is required. The new technologies developed towards the end of the nineteenth century required no reading skills, only the acquisition of a piece of equipment in order to consume the cultural goods on offer: a gramophone to play the disc or a radio to hear the programme. The cinema, like theatre, opera and all performances, could be appreciated by the illiterate.

However, new infrastructures were required, the most important of which was access to electricity. Until the 1920s gramophones were driven by spring motors, so not only could they be moved around easily, but they did not require electrification. There was no return to such portable music players until the 1960s (for the 45 rpm disc) and the development of easy-to-use recorded cassettes – all requiring stored energy, in the shape of batteries. Such exceptions notwithstanding, access to the new cultural goods required electricity. At a time when it is assumed that sooner rather than later everyone in Europe and North America will have a computer, it may be useful to remind ourselves that the full electrification of Europe – an obvious precondition not only for using computers, but also radios and televisions – is relatively recent. In the 1937 in the East End of London many families still had gas lighting, though some had a radio whose glass battery would be taken to the local cycle shop twice a week to be recharged.[18] Even in one of the richest European countries, France, as late as 1954, when television broadcasts started, 7 per cent of households were without electricity. In poorer regions such as Brittany the figure rose to 23 per cent.[19] The completion of France's electrification was achieved only at the beginning of the 1960s.[20] Even in 1945 almost half the farms in the USA had no electricity, while almost all urban homes had it. By 1950, largely thanks to the Rural Electrification Administration (a New Deal agency established in 1935), almost all farms had electricity – and in that year radio too achieved 100 per cent penetration.

Thus electrification was achieved almost everywhere, including the USA, under the direction, the help or the pressure of the central government. Much the same occurred for the development of radio. Marconi had approached private cable companies to provide investment for his attempt to send signals across the Atlantic, but they turned him down. It was with the help of the Post Office, the Admiralty and the War Office that he created, in 1897, the British Marconi Company. On 12 December 1902 signals crossed the Atlantic between Poldhu in Cornwall and St John's in Newfoundland. Soon Marconi had established an American subsidiary and expanded in Belgium, Russia, Argentina, France and Australia. By 1914 it had become the world leader in communications.

The German company Telefunken was one of Marconi's main rivals.

Created in 1903 as a result of an alliance between AEG and Siemens, the company, soundly financed, extended its activities to central Europe, Sweden and Russia. It was also present in the USA, Japan and South America. During the war it transferred its reserves to neutral Holland, thus saving its assets. The French were not in that league. The economic structure of the country, its conservative banking system and the strength of its small enterprises did not facilitate large-scale developments. At the beginning of the century no French firm could match Marconi or Telefunken. The war of 1914–18, however, proved beneficial to national enterprises, and by 1920 the two European giants Marconi and Telefunken were joined by the Compagnie Générale de Télégraphie sans Fils.[21]

The history of the radio as a broadcasting medium belongs to the era after the First World War. In its prehistory various industrial groups, or states, acquired communication networks, mainly telegraphy, which would pave the way to radio broadcasting. The war turned out to be an excellent testing ground for wireless transmission. For military and security reasons it was firmly put under government control.

Some enterprises took the long view, as was the case of that founded in 1886 by George Westinghouse. The company installed the first commercial alternating-current power line, having bought the patents from its inventor, the Serbian-born Nikola Tesla (1856–1943). It became the leading manufacturer of electrical power plants, and in 1920 in Pittsburgh, where it had its headquarters, it started the legendary KDKA, the first commercial radio station in the USA, financed by Westinghouse to encourage people to buy radios. Its main competitors understood the importance of knowledge to commercial expansion. They launched a policy of 'Research and Development' (it was not yet called R&D) and of patents acquisition. Many of these patents, especially those connected to communications, were temporarily taken over by the government during the war. This further consolidated the closeness between big business and the government.

By 1918 most, but not all, of the firms operating in the field were American, though the largest was the British Marconi, which had grown immensely during the war. To expand further it needed to acquire a network of high-frequency alternators, but these were controlled by General Electric, the technology leader in this field. Under pressure from the US government (furiously lobbied by the navy), General Electric was forced to refuse the sale. The politics behind this was clear. There was no future in the USA for a company which was not completely American-owned. The military, particularly the navy (for whom communication was regarded as an absolute priority), wanted a state monopoly over communication. Congress, bending to private interests, resisted. President Woodrow Wilson reached a compromise: private American firms would enter an alliance (its opponents called it a cartel or a trust) aimed at keeping foreigners out of the country. It went like this: in 1919 General Electric bought US Marconi, then, with Westinghouse and AT&T, set up RCA. RCA was required to buy 40 per cent of its materials from Westinghouse and 60 per cent from GE.

Marconi suffered an enormous setback when it had to give up its branch in the USA, where its enormous lead in R&D could have ensured it a technological lead between the wars. The blow was cushioned, however, by the fact that it developed inside a protected market, that of the British Empire, whose size compensated British-based firms for the narrowness of their domestic markets.

The Advance of the USA

The presence of the USA in this book has been so far rather slight. The revolution in communication would transform it in the course of the twentieth century into the hegemonic power of all major cultural forms. The British and the French gradually lost ground – as did, of course, the laggard countries, which never caught up. The Europeans should not have been surprised. In market size and wealth, the USA had caught up with everyone. Its economic development between 1860 and 1910 had been astonishing, well outstripping that of the Russians. By 1900 the USA had the largest rail network in the world, and was the first producer of steel. By 1910 its population was the largest in the industrial world: ninety-two million people, thanks to a high birthrate and massive immigration. To some extent Europe's labour was chasing after Europe's capital, for the USA was also the recipient of a constant and massive flow of European investment. In 1913 British long-term investment in the USA (£754.6 million) was greater than that in any of the existing colonies and dominions: Canada (£514 million), Australia (£416 million) and India (£378 million). The USA also topped Germany's table of outward investment.[22]

The result of this economic expansion was that while in 1860 the USA was mainly an exporter of food, by 1900 it had also become a manufacturing power, exporting to Europe a huge array of branded consumer goods including innovations such as Singer sewing machines, Kodak cameras, Gillette razors, Vaseline hair tonic, Arrow shirts, Maxwell House instant coffee, Waterman pens and Edison lightbulbs. Some of these items were status symbols, ownership of which denoted various degrees of prosperity at a time when such distinctions were becoming ever more important. Others, such as the sewing machine, led to the democratisation of dressmaking, as it became easier to make clothes both at home and industrially.

America was now projecting an image of modernity, but in 1900 this had not yet found its cultural forms. This came later with the cinema, music and television. Before 1920 Americans were still minor players in the global cultural industry: no major singers or songwriters, no operas to speak of, no important composers of serious music, no popular playwrights, only a few popular writers (Washington Irving, Fenimore Cooper, Alcott, Stowe). In the visual arts, which they largely dominated in the second half of the twentieth century, Americans were still importers, even though in the nineteenth century more than a thousand American artists had exhibited some 5,000 works at the annual Salons in Paris, the overwhelming majority between 1870 and 1899.[23] American intellectuals went to Europe to learn or to live. European intellectuals toured the USA to lecture and get paid.

The role of the USA as an importer of culture was underlined by its disregard for international agreements protecting intellectual property (while having its own copyright legislation since 1790). These agreements were, and are, devised to favour the culturally rich, not the deprived. When the Berne Convention was established in 1886 it was ratified only by fourteen European countries – the non-signers included China, the Ottoman Empire and the USA. By the end of the twentieth century the situation had changed. Culturally rich America, dominant in films, television programmes and music, decided in 1989 to join the Convention, and turned into a zealous upholder of intellectual property rights. In reality the Americans were not totally oblivious of the need to show willingness to join the Europeans in the international regulation of intellectual property. In 1891 the US Congress had passed the Chace Act, which provided for payments to authors, but only for works published after that date. Whatever had been published before was excluded from its provisions. Jerome K. Jerome, author of the best-selling *Three Men in a Boat* (1889), mused that if only he had waited a few years he would have made a fortune, because the book had 'an enormous sale in America – from first to last well over a million'.[24] But it was not so simple. To obtain protection in America a book had to be published on the same day both abroad and in the United States, and at least two copies of the American edition had to be set up, printed and produced entirely in the USA. In 1891 this was a tall order. These regulations caused serious financial damage to many famous writers, but also ensured that they would be far better known than would otherwise have been the case. Piracy enabled Americans to print books more cheaply than in England, thus attracting a wider market.[25]

The expansion of the American reading public proceeded relentlessly. This can be gauged by the rapid growth of its press. The diversification of the fare offered by newspapers – news, gossip, features, comic strips, sensational stories, the use of photography after 1897 – increased readership. By the beginning of the twentieth century there were in the USA more than 2,300 dailies. Many of the new readers were immigrants, whose literacy, as we have noted, was higher than the European average. At first their presence encouraged the development of foreign-language papers, bringing into their homes a habit of newspaper-reading which did not exist in the 'old' countries such as Russia, Poland and Italy. By 1914 the USA had 160 foreign-language dailies. The children of the immigrants, however, read English-language papers. They knew the Old World, that of their fathers and mothers, and had started building the new one. They provided the terrain for the formidable rise of the USA as the foremost producer, consumer and exporter of culture in the twentieth century.

31

Workers, Jews, Women

Workers and Socialists

INCREASED PROSPERITY was far from being a purely American phenomenon. In 1913 industrial wages as a whole were higher – in real terms – in Great Britain than anywhere else in Europe, but far below those of the USA.[1] While long working hours in sweatshops still prevailed, and agriculture employed more people than industry almost everywhere in Europe, the darkest days of capitalism seemed to be over. The wages of unskilled workers in Germany, France and Great Britain increased regularly in the period from 1880 to the First World War, while the cost of their main staple, bread, declined.[2] But while a French unskilled worker earning 3.40 francs a day would have had no problem purchasing his daily bread (twenty-three centimes per kilo), he would have had some difficulty buying the Comtesse de Ségur's *Les Malheurs de Sophie* for his children – had he been inclined to do so – for this was priced at 2.25 francs (and an extra 1.25 for a red leather-bound copy, which would have wiped out his earnings for that day). Today an unskilled worker on the UK minimum wage of £5.05 per hour (as from 1 October 2005) would be perfectly able to buy *Harry Potter and the Goblet of Fire* by J.K. Rowling at £6.99 (getting over 600 pages of text), and even more so *Alice's Adventures in Wonderland* at £1.50. Nineteenth-century books were still expensive, but as they were manufactured they were far cheaper than a craft object like a simple lady's fan, which would retail at the Magasin du Louvre for anything between twenty and 150 francs, out of the reach of even skilled workers.[3]

In 1880, an unskilled worker in Great Britain would earn just over 3s.6d. a day, while a kilo of bread would cost 2½d. This meant that he could buy 16.5 kilos of bread, more than his French and German counterparts (respectively 14.7 kilos and 11 kilos). Inequalities were very high. Assuming he worked six days a week, the British worker would have an annual income of £56.3s. a year, while the 90,000 households which made up the British middle classes had an income of between £300 and £1,000.[4] By 1908, those earning above £700 a year (3.1 per cent of the population) could be deemed rich, while those earning between £160 and £700 were merely 'comfortable'.[5] In practice, between the truly rich (the landlords, major bankers and industrialists) and the really poor (those with no jobs, the so-called dangerous classes) there was a variety of social groups, each separated from the next by minor differences in income and status (semi-skilled workers, skilled workers, shopkeepers, clerks, etc.) so that there was no stark separation between the classes. Only the truly poor could be said to have quite different lifestyles from the groups socially adjacent to them. In Germany an unskilled worker at the end of the nineteenth century was earning 2.65 marks a day, or 826 marks a year; an elementary schoolteacher would earn twice that, as would the lowest ranks of the academic profession; but higher-ranking schoolteachers would earn 5,000 marks. Senior university professors earned on average 12,000 marks, but as their salary would be increased from student fees paid when enrolling in their courses, they could earn as much as 40,000 marks, eight times the salary of a senior schoolteacher.[6] Today such a differential would be unthinkable: a senior schoolteacher could earn £30,000, but no academic anywhere in Europe – and certainly not in the United Kingdom – earns eight times that.

Countries where the distribution of income approximated the ones described above, i.e. all the main industrial countries, were ideally positioned for developing a consumer society, since even a modest reduction in the price of a commodity would considerably increase the size of the consumer market. Working-class culture may have been distinctive and even inward-looking, but as incomes increased, it was more than willing to taste whatever cultural goods were on offer. The professional classes, who produced many cultural goods, were well positioned to act as mediators between the various layers of society, since most of them did not originate from the landowning and aristocratic classes, but were often born into middle-income families. They used their higher education, rather than their wealth, to distinguish themselves from those lower down the social scale, but the very act of distinguishing signified that they were familiar with 'inferior' tastes and attitudes.

Among the working classes, at least in the richer countries, the worst years were behind. Though this may seem paradoxical, their growing confidence in the beneficial effects of industrial capitalism was partly due to the increasingly powerful socialist parties and trade unions that sought to represent their interests. The fear of revolution gave impetus to the trend towards social regulation. Workers not only had more money, but also more leisure than before. By the time of the First World War, working hours in mining and industry in Germany were one third lower than they had been in the middle of the nineteenth century.[7] The idea of leisure as a universal was emerging. As early as 1892 a conference on the question of leisure time (*Freizeitkonferenz*) was held in Germany. Needless to say, socialist activists as well as the more enlightened factions of the upper classes were united in the belief that the new task of organising leisure should be under their direction.[8]

That reading could be a normal leisure activity for workers was recognised not only by the Churches and the socialist organisations, as one might expect, but also by some entrepreneurs. As cinema-going was about to become one of the workers' chief recreational activities, and as they could now afford to go to variety shows, cabarets and *cafés-concerts*, it was discovered that the book, until recently regarded as a possible cause of subversion and distraction, was, after all, a Good Thing. Thus towards the end of the nineteenth century philanthropic entrepreneurs created libraries in their own factories, with some degree of success. Forty-seven per cent of the workers of the Rheinische Stahlwerke (Rhine Steelworks) in Duisburg joined the factory library. In the Düsseldorf area in 1911 there were thirty-six factory libraries, the largest being those of the Bayer chemical works (the firm that discovered aspirin) at Leverkusen, with over 13,500 volumes, and of the Krupp steelworks in Essen, whose 60,000-volume library was regularly used by half the workforce in 1909.[9]

As one would expect, socialists denounced factory libraries as a form of narcotic used by the bosses to dupe the workers. But then, socialists – especially the Germans of the Sozialdemokratische Partei Deutschlands (SPD) – had long encouraged workers to read books. 'Culture makes you free' had been a socialist slogan since the 1830s. On 5 February 1872 the SPD leader Wilhelm Liebknecht had declared that 'Knowledge is power, and power is knowledge,' and that social democracy was the party of culture.[10] But where would this culture for the working class originate? In theory, socialists were committed to the development of an autonomous workers' culture, whatever that meant. In practice they ended up promoting what was best in bourgeois culture. Enlightenment would come from above. Marx and Engels disagreed. In a letter sent in September 1879 to August Bebel, Wilhelm Liebknecht, and other social democratic leaders, they insisted that the emancipation of the working class had to be undertaken by the workers themselves, not by 'enlightened' and philanthropic people who openly declared that workers were culturally incapable (*ungebildet*).[11]

However, most socialist intellectuals – almost all of whom were of middle-class origin (like Marx and Engels themselves) – shared with bourgeois intellectuals and institutions the goal of the cultural improvement of the workers on the basis of what they thought was the 'right' culture. Unlike romantic intellectuals, they despised traditional popular culture as manifested in fairs and carnival celebrations, which they regarded as plebeian, or the cultural expression of simple rural folk, with its superstitions and infantilisms. They equally despised the culture of the old régime, which they condemned as reactionary. They viewed the workers as the heirs of a national culture, and accordingly accelerated the integration of workers into bourgeois culture. Just as socialist reforms improved capitalism and strengthened it, so the socialist cultural movement became an instrument of the *embourgeoisement* of labour.[12] In the meantime the real bourgeois, i.e. the capitalists, or at least those involved in the cultural industry, were busy giving the workers what they wanted – cheap books and entertainment – not what they ought to want.

German social democrats, being thorough, set up in 1906 a Central Commission for Culture which drew up a list of 'good' books to be stocked by the huge network of socialist lending libraries (*Arbeiterbibliotheken*) – before 1914 there were 1,147 *Arbeiterbibliotheken*, with a total stock of 833,857 volumes.[13] The SPD's publishing imprint, the Buchhandlung Vorwärts (Forward Library), had already been printing socialist classics at low price: one of the best-sellers was August Bebel's *Die Frau und der Sozialismus* (Women and Socialism, 1879).[14] But the SPD, or rather its leadership, was equally committed to what it called *Schöne Kultur* (fine culture) – especially if German and with some social content. Consequently it promoted theatrical performances for the workers which included Lessing's *Emilia Galotti* (1772), Schiller's plays, Goethe's *Faust*, Hebbel's *Maria Magdalena,* Kleist's anti-authoritarian comedy *Der Zerbrochene Krug* (The Broken Jug, 1806), Ibsen's *An Enemy of the People* and *A Doll's House*, Molière's *The Miser*, Gerhart Hauptmann's *Die Weber* (about Silesian weavers) and Shakespeare's *Hamlet*, as well as operas from Beethoven's *Fidelio* and Carl Maria von Weber's *Der Freischütz* to Wagner's *Tannhäuser*. In 1913–14 alone socialist and workers' theatres staged some 675 performances, attracting 302,306 people.[15]

Yet, as is often the case, the working class was a great disappointment to the socialists. The bulk of books borrowed by the workers from socialist libraries were neither social science tomes nor philosophical treatises but novels, reflecting perhaps the fact that the majority of borrowers were women – and that the long working hours which still prevailed in industry were not an incentive for serious reading. The works of Marx and Engels were hardly ever borrowed. The figures speak for themselves: in 1912, according to a survey of sixteen large socialist libraries, out of 310,123 books loaned, 228,419 (73 per cent) were novels, including children's fiction. The social science (*Sozialwissenschaften*, which included socialist literature) borrowings amounted to 11,802 – roughly 3 per cent of the total.[16]

The socialists' commitment to educating the workers was a Europe-wide phenomenon, although it was somewhat less conspicuous in Great Britain, where there was no significant socialist party until the start of the twentieth century, and where socialist intellectuals were few, though there were plenty of Victorian philanthropists and radicals desiring to educate the workers. Elsewhere activists selected, from the established 'bourgeois' canon, a 'socialist' canon of their own. In Italy, the socialist Turin publisher Nerbini not only published the still popular *Mystères de Paris* by Eugène Sue and sold it to the tune of 200,000 copies, but also Tolstoy, Dostoevsky and Henryk Sienkiewicz's popular *Quo Vadis?* (1896).[17] Thanks to the socialists and their publishers, Tolstoy was widely regarded in Italy as a socialist – unlike, say, in France: further proof, if proof is necessary, that marketing influences reception. Tolstoy's complex thought was a suitable case for differing interpretations. Socialists stressed his pacifism, his dislike of clerical hierarchies, his opposition to Tsardom, his 'primitive' Christianity, his populism and his distaste for wealth. But his commitment to religious values appealed also to conservatives like his French champion Eugène-Melchior de Vogüé, who hoped Tolstoy could be used to fight against the 'sordid positivism' of the likes of Zola – whose books were in all socialist libraries.[18]

Tolstoy's success in Italy was considerable: 133 translations between 1886 and 1920, and half of these between 1900 and 1906 – the period of an unparalleled Tolstoy boom in Italy, coinciding with the remarkable growth of socialist organisations.[19] The socialist paper *Avanti* serialised *Resurrection* (Tolstoy's most socially concerned novel) in 1899–1900. A year later, in December 1901, its supplement for the young *Sempre avanti* included it along with *Anna Karenina*(!) in its listing of suitable books for young socialists. The list also included books by Victor Hugo and Zola, Hauptmann's *Die*

Weber, Beecher Stowe's *Uncle Tom's Cabin*, *Looking Backward* by the American journalist Edward Bellamy (1888, translated in 1890 as *L'Anno 2000. Un racconto americano*), and William Morris's *News from Nowhere* (1890, translated in 1895 as *La Terra promessa*). The only Italian book was *Primo Maggio* (1901) by the totally unknown and never-heard-of again Giovanni Battista Bianchi.

In Belgium the Parti Ouvrier Belge, following the lead of the SPD, organised popular education with pamphlets, excursions, choral societies, lectures and books.[20] *Le Peuple*, the party daily, to attract readers and entertain existing ones, had started publishing serialised novels from its inception in 1885. Its favourite author was Zola, with nine novels, followed by other naturalist writers such as the Goncourt brothers and Alphonse Daudet. But it also regularly serialised generally popular books such as Erckmann-Chatrian's patriotic novels and Émile Gaboriau's new 'detective' stories. The list was mainly French, but also included Tolstoy, Gorky and Upton Sinclair.[21] Cultural policy in socialist parties was in the hands of middle-class intellectuals who wanted proletarian novels 'of quality', but these were hard to find, and when found, were not always popular. Sue's *Mystères* did not always pass the quality test, but because he was both popular and a socialist, he had to be included. His leading follower in Italy, Francesco Mastriani, was a committed socialist too, but his socialism was barely perceptible underneath the complex layers of his plots. His most famous novel, *La Cieca di Sorrento* (The Blind Girl of Sorrento, 1852), is typical: Beatrice witnesses the murder of her mother, the Countess of Rionero. The shock makes her blind. The murderer is found and executed. Years later, the murderer's son, now a world-famous English surgeon, rich but deformed, falls in love with Beatrice and gives her back her sight. When his true identity is revealed she dies of heartache. A great read, perhaps, but not a call to revolution. It was republished constantly throughout the twentieth century and turned into a film in 1934 (the debut of Anna Magnani) and again in 1952.[22]

Even socialists had to compromise before the imperative of the markets. New readers needed to be enticed. A struggling radical newspaper would find it cheaper to buy serialisation rights from agencies, which in turn had bought the rights for a fixed sum from the authors. Often these were popular writers with no pretence of ideological correctness; yet some of these novels revealed the miserable conditions in which many lived. Quite clearly an author aspiring to a working-class market could not afford to be 'anti-popular' by depicting workers as feckless, and strikers as subversives who deserved to be shot. While the pleasures of being rich were undeniable, wealthy characters had to be given other attributes (generosity, etc.) in order to make them attractive, for just being rich and heartless guaranteed general antipathy. What was difficult to produce was anything resembling a 'proletarian' novel. The success of the canonical texts of 'proletarian' literature – Zola's *Germinal* (1885), Hauptmann's *Die Weber* (1892), Upton Sinclair's *The Jungle* (1906) and Gorky's *The Mother* (1907) – was due not just to their intrinsic merit but also to their being among the rare instances of novels almost entirely set in a recognisable proletarian milieu. Their gritty representations of the life and struggle of the working classes made them relatively popular among socialists of all classes, but the working classes were equally enchanted by stories in which the heroes temporarily found themselves among the lower orders until a lucky break promoted them to the ranks of the class to which most people would rather belong: the rich. Thus a typical *roman feuilleton* such as Charles Mérouvel's *La Veuve aux cent millions*, serialised in the socialist *Petite République Française* in October 1883, starts by telling the story of a shop assistant who loses her job when she resists her employer's unwanted advances. Thus far we are firmly in Zola's territory. However, as it turns out, she is the former Marquise Séraphine de Varannes, and though she lives in squalor for a while she is soon rescued by Georges de Candeilles, a childhood friend who marries her so that she can get her castle back.[23]

Peasants fared a little better in novels. There was a well-established tradition of rural novels – particularly in France, thanks to Balzac (*Les Paysans*) and George Sand (*La Petite Fadette* and *La Mare au diable*). They were the path-breakers for Zola's *La Terre* (1887), Eugène le Roy's *Jacquou le croquant* (1899), about oppressed peasants in the Périgord, and René Bazin's books set in the Vendée such as *La Terre qui meurt* (1899) and *Le Blé qui lève* (1907). Their success, at least in France, was due not only to the country's large peasantry but also to the general conservative mood which prevailed at the end of the century.[24] Rural novels often idealised the peasantry, and seldom discussed their specific problems. The problem with peasants is that they read even less than the workers. Catholic activists in the countryside, particularly in Wilhelmine Germany, were painfully aware of the ignorance of the rural communities, and like the socialists they championed the development of a popular culture (in the sense of championing *their* idea of what culture the people should have), but with about as much success. Catholics too had to make do with their own pulp novelists, like the Swiss-born Joseph Spillmann, author of many sentimental best-selling novels.[25] *Volkisch* ruralism and the popular *Heimatroman* (from *Heimat*, a concept often translated as 'home' but which carries a suggestion of nostalgia and longing) were promoted by periodicals such as *Deutsche Heimat* (German Homeland, 1900–04) which worshipped the German farmer. One of the most successful novels of this genre was *Der Büttnerbauer* (Farmer Büttner, 1895) by Wilhelm von Polenz (1861–1903), in which an old farmer falls into the clutches of unscrupulous Jewish businessmen (as in Fontane's posthumously published *Der Stechlin*). Another typical *Heimatroman* was *Jörn Uhl* (1901) by Gustav Frenssen (1863–1945), which had sold 463,000 copies by 1940.[26] This was bettered by Hermann Löns's *Der Wehrwolf* (The Wolf Fights Back, 1910), the history of the Wulf family from prehistory to the present: 565,000 copies sold by 1940.[27] The reading public liked them; the critics did not, nor did foreigners.

As for the British – who had a particularly idealised view of the country-side – their rural novels were set among the farming bourgeoisie and the petty aristocracy rather than the agricultural workers. More often than not they used the countryside as the background for a larger tale – as was the case for Thomas Hardy's *Far from the Madding Crowd* (1874) and *The Mayor of Casterbridge* (1886). Only when the farming community had almost disappeared did Britain produce its most loved and popular representation of the rural world and its problems in the long-running radio series *The Archers*, which started in 1951 (and is still running as I write).

Did the new prosperity brought about by capitalist growth transform workers into avid readers? It is difficult to say, though there is some connection between better living standards and book-reading. The Germans at the turn of the twentieth century (as at the turn of the twenty-first) read far more books than, say, the Italians. In fact they probably read more books than anyone else in Europe, and certainly published more.[28] But was this due to the greater prosperity of German workers, or to the larger size of its middle class? In poor countries, such as Italy in 1900, the life of the working classes was still very grim, and in the countryside matters were even worse. Illiteracy was still very high: one-third of Italians could not even sign their names on the marriage register, while in Germany everyone could and did. Nevertheless, not many people read books regularly, even in Germany.[29] What determined the size of the book and newspaper market was not the prosperity or literacy of the working classes, but that of the middle class and its expansion.

Here Italy was not particularly laggard. In 1901 it had – in proportion to population – more doctors than Germany, and six times more lawyers.

In 1881 the Italian professional classes – teachers, civil servants, notaries, apothecaries, lawyers and doctors – constituted 1.5 per cent of the population. This provided a high-quality reading public.[30] Yet fewer books and newspapers were sold in Italy than in Germany (or France, or Great Britain). This was because it was no longer just the professional middle classes that mattered, but the growing army of shopkeepers, skilled workers, tradesmen and office workers who, as they became longer-established, were acquiring the habit of buying a newspaper and borrowing books – as was the case in Great Britain and Germany, but not in France and Italy.

Book-buying went on expanding (and has been expanding ever since) despite the fact that prosperity also led to a greater amount of leisure time and hence to the expansion of leisure activities competing with books. An examination of the records of the Portsmouth Public Library in 1887–88 reveals that out of 1,734 new borrowers who stated their occupation (952 did not) there were 124 'scholars and students', eighty-seven schoolteachers, five waiters, twelve secretaries, six pastry cooks, fifty-four dressmakers and milliners, forty-five labourers, eighteen journalists, forty-five drapers, thirty-three carpenters, fifteen shoe-makers and thirty-six domestic servants, as well as twenty-two 'ladies' and nine 'gentlemen'. At the Leyton Public Library in east London the largest group was 'scholars and students' (720 out of 2,027 who stated their occupation), followed by clerks (342) and 192 'married women'. Their borrowing was probably in line with that at the Leicester Central Public Library (1889–90): out of over 134,000 borrowings, two-thirds were novels and a further 38,236 were 'juvenile'.[31] As the latter were, presumably, largely narrative works, it would seem that the overall percentage of fiction borrowed was 94 per cent.

The Middle-Class Intelligentsia

As the number of consumers of cultural goods expanded, so did that of cultural producers. Already by the early twentieth century some 100,000 Germans supported themselves from writing and performing music, plays, books and newspaper articles – more if we include related occupations ranging from printing to administrative staff.[32] In England and Wales the 1881 census registers 6,893 authors, editors and journalists. By 1911 their number had doubled. Comparable rates of growth occurred in France and Germany. To these one should add academics: 1,468 in Germany in 1864 growing to 3,807 by 1909, while there were, by the first decade of the nine-teenth century 2,355 in Britain, 2,200 in France, 1,618 in Austria, 1,141 in Italy, 589 in Hungary and 480 in Spain.[33] In Hungary alone at the beginning of the century there were 5,614 people professionally involved in literature and the arts, of whom almost half lived in Budapest.[34] Merit rather than birth or patronage played a major role in the acquisition of membership of such professions. 'Merit', however, is defined by those who are already established; consequently, membership of the intellectual classes was in the hands of the intellectuals themselves. They played an increasingly preponderant role in determining the ranking of what was on offer by decreeing what was 'good' and what was 'bad' – at least that is what they thought they were doing. While this was essentially an aesthetic task, it had the function of creating distinct cultural markets. The problem is that the intelligentsia was constantly expanding. This led to attempts by those already in the club to limit and restrict access. There is, after all, no point in being a member of an élite if it is easy to join.[35]

As many among the new cohorts of graduates found it difficult to find jobs in the established professions, they tried to enter new ones, such as journalism, where access was less restricted. The intellectuals found them-selves facing an insoluble contradiction. On the one hand they tried to restrict access to their ranks, because in so doing they maintained their own 'rarity' value; on the other they profited from the expansion of education and cultural markets, and were often the main force behind such expansion. This inevitably created a class of déclassé intellectuals. Some of these turned out to be quite dangerous – as the birth of terrorist activities by the educated shows. In some instances, particularly in central Europe, restrictions on university entrance and the nationalist defence of language were used by the old order to defend their positions from new classes and from ethnic groups such as the Jews.[36]

The old order, however, was on the losing side of history – as is inevitably the case, almost by definition. The cleverest among its representatives negoti-ate the necessary changes and remain on top. But the growth of the society of money, the bourgeois order, meant that money-making played an increas-ingly important role in the definition of the successful man of letters. For decades the literary classes themselves had glamorised and romanticised the vicissitudes of those who tried to make a living by writing. The trope of the artist or writer living in a garret who eventually obtains recognition by dint of hard work, genius and luck has served as an encouragement to an endless stream of writers. A few were actually successful. The majority remained in their garret, or more likely in their middle-class home, and eventually found a decent if less glamorous job. The reality of literary life was described more soberly by George Gissing in his masterpiece *New Grub Street* (1891). As Raymond Williams wrote, 'The book is not likely to be read by any kind of writer, now, without a number of wry recognitions.'[37] The *fin-de-siècle* literary London described by Gissing is one in which copyrights are sold to the highest bidder and circulating libraries exercise such a stranglehold that novelists are almost compelled to write an annual three-volume novel. One of the main characters of the book, Jasper Milvain, explains the facts of literary life to his sisters, hack writers of 'ladies' romances':

> Literature nowadays is a trade. Putting aside men of genius, who may succeed by mere cosmic force, your successful man of letters is your skilful tradesman. He thinks first and foremost of the markets; when one kind of goods begins to go off slackly, he is ready with something new and appetising.[38]

The literary scene of their day, Milvain continues, 'is supplied with telegraphic communication, it knows what literary fare is in demand in every part of the world, its inhabitants are men of business, however seedy'. He advises them accordingly:

> Get together half a dozen fair specimens of the Sunday school prize; study them; discover the essential point of such composition . . . then go to work methodically, so many pages a day. There is no question of the divine afflatus . . . We talk of literature as trade not of Homer, Dante and Shakespeare . . . I don't advocate the propagation of vicious literature; I speak only of good, coarse, marketable stuff for the world's vulgar . . . I maintain that we people of brains are justified in supplying the mob with the food it likes . . . If only I had the skill, I would produce novels out-trashing the trashiest that ever sold fifty thousand copies. But it needs skill, mind you; and to deny it is a gross error of the literary pedants. To please the vulgar you must, one way or another, incarnate the genius of vulgarity.

Gissing contrasts Milvain's cynicism to the high-mindedness of his *alter ego*, the struggling writer Edwin Reardon, whose wife Amy is angered by what she calls Reardon's 'morbid conscientiousness'. She says: 'There was no need to destroy what you had written. It was all good enough for the market.' 'Don't use that word, Amy, I hate it!' replies Reardon. 'You can't afford to hate it,' is her rejoinder, adding, 'However it was before, you *must* write for the market now ... Art must be practiced as a trade ... This is the age of trade.'[39] Gissing knew all this to his cost: he only got £150 for *New Grub Street*, and spent much of his life in poverty.

As we have seen, the lament that 'good' literature was contaminated by the 'bad' literature of mere scribblers who wrote for money was hardly new. What was new was that now a distinction was being made between good, serious and respectable novels, and those that were not. Novels could belong to a noble genre. As the reward and renown for writing 'for the market' increased, it was easier to accept literary *déclassement* – a way of saying that it was better to be a wealthy *déclassé* than a poor one.

Who were the popular authors who wrote the novels serialised in large-circulation newspapers and magazines? A French study examining the career of ninety-eight popular writers (including seventeen women) active in 1900–14 provides, along with a wealth of data, some interesting portraits. Take Joséphine Maldague, a tailor's daughter who went to Paris seeking her literary fortune just like one of Balzac's heroes. Under the pseudonym of George Maldague (an allusion to George Sand) she published her first novel, *La Parigote*, in 1884 at the age of twenty-seven. This serious novel on the social condition of women was ignored by the literary establishment. Not discomfited, Maldague made a good living anyway by giving up literary feminism and writing numerous sentimental novels which were serialised in the Parisian popular press and republished in the provincial one.[40] But why did *La Parigote* fail? Why do some novels fail and other succeed? This is almost impossible to explain. Some publishers, under the illusion that it is they who can 'make' a novel, will say that it is to do with the marketing, the price and the format. Critics will say that, eventually, merit prevails and bad novels sink without trace. Writers blame publishers (the marketing was wrong or non-existent, the price was too high, the cover horrible), the bookshops (they don't stock it) or the public (immature philistines). While some or a number of these explanations may have been valid in the case of *La Parigote*, there could be others. Perhaps it failed because it did not contain enough sex.

Or take Maurice Leblanc, born in Rouen, like Flaubert, of a wealthy father, like Flaubert's, and committed to 'naturalism', just like Flaubert. And here the parallels stop. He was unsuccessful, ignored, discouraged and depressed. Then a publisher, Maurice Lafitte, suggested he should write a short story for a new magazine, *Je Sais tout*. The resulting detective story, *L'Arrestation d'Arsène Lupin*, was so successful that Leblanc was persuaded to start a series of books based on the Lupin character. Their success was enormous, the public delighted, and the critics ecstatic. Leblanc – and Arsène Lupin – became famous, and many of the books are still available. Money and fame, however, exact a price. Leblanc was now in the hands of his readers, of his market, and was dismayed that what he regarded as his 'real' books never received any attention.[41] The fate of Sir Arthur Conan Doyle, the creator of Sherlock Holmes, is remarkably similar. He would have preferred to be known as the author of historical romances such as *Micah Clarke* (1889) and *The White Company* (1891), but these have remained obscure, while *The Hound of the Baskervilles* (1902) gained him literary immortality. Writers are usually chosen by their readers, the reverse is more rarely the case.

Radical writers and artists rejected such subjection to the laws of the market, yet the avant-garde, despite its apparently 'anti-bourgeois' ethos, was clearly bourgeois in economic terms, because its conflict with officially approved public art forced it to seek private help. It levelled objections against state regulation, censorship, anything which would interfere with market forces. At the same time it almost desperately tried to situate itself outside the bourgeois world and nearer to the 'common people'. A typical position was epitomised in 1898 in an editorial in *Ver Sacrum*, the house journal of the radical artists' group the Viennese Secession, which declared that it rejected the difference between art for the rich and art for the poor: 'Art is a common treasure, a necessary manifestation of the life of intelligent people.'[42] The market itself, however, was bridging this gap, since the growth of popular literature extended the reach of 'bourgeois' culture. Socialists believed then (and some still do) that the working classes wanted to read about their own struggles. Reality is more complex. Escaping from the working classes is probably a more exciting theme. In Gissing's *New Grub Street* Mr Sykes, a failed popular writer, says of another:

> . . . when I first made his acquaintance, [he] had an idea of writing for the working classes; and what do you think he was going to offer them? Stories about the working classes! Nay, never hang your head for it, old boy; it was excusable in the days of your youth. Why . . . nothing can induce working men or women to read stories that treat of their own world. They are the most consumed idealists in creation, especially the women.[43]

Jews

An expanding market always attracts new entrants. It offers an opportunity to those hitherto excluded. As new businesses can flourish and new networks are established, outsiders are welcomed, or encounter less hostile opposition. The new bourgeois world provided chances to hitherto excluded minorities, and the European Jews took their chance in cultural markets with remarkable success.

Jews had been a successful minority well before the nineteenth century, but not in Christian Europe. Around the tenth century, when the mercantile and urban communities of the Arab Mediterranean were far more advanced than those of Christian Europe, and European Jews were poor and persecuted, those Jews lucky enough to be in the Muslim world (especially in Cordoba and Granada) became major figures in public life, in commerce, in manufacturing, in scholarship, in the liberal professions, in poetry and the sciences.[44] Their fortunes declined with the loss of power of the Islamic world (Jews were expelled from Spain in 1492); those of their European counterparts improved much later, in the nineteenth century, with the rise of the modern secular West and the political decline of Christianity.

East European Jews emerged from their medieval past with some distinct cultural advantages. These derived in part from their strange status as an oppressed minority enjoying special privileges. They were periodically persecuted, but were often under the protection of local rulers. This put them in a better position than the overwhelming majority of the population, mainly impoverished peasants and rural workers with no rights at all. Assimilated Jews, equipped with the requisite skills, had a new world of opportunities before them. The more they were able to integrate, the higher was the rate of conversion to Christianity. By the First World War in Austria-Hungary, most of the major Jewish editors had already converted.

As business expanded, so did the Jewish presence in trade. The professions were particularly attractive, since they provided status as well as income. Jews did especially well in Germany when, after the unification of 1870, the new German state abolished all restrictions on their civil and political rights. In France such restrictions had been abolished, at least formally, after the Revolution. In England the process was slow but constant.

Jewish over-representation in the central European intelligentsia dates from the closing decades of the nineteenth century, though the immigration of poor Jews from Poland and Russia, the *Ostjuden*, meant that they were also disproportionately represented among the indigent. In many instances, of course, the large number of Jews in the literary profession was simply a reflection of their great concentration in key areas. At the beginning of the twentieth century, for instance, the cultural life of Budapest appeared to be dominated by Jews, but by 1910 they already made up 20 per cent of the city's population.[45] In Hungary as a whole, Jews were 'only' 4.5 per cent of the population. But Budapest, culturally speaking, was what mattered. Given the Jewish presence in commerce, it is not surprising that there should have been a relatively high proportion of Jews (often from Germany) operating in the publishing industry – the terrain where business and culture meet. In 1881, 30 per cent of Budapest's printers were Jewish, as were 43 per cent of book-sellers and art dealers. According to the statistician Alajos Kovàcs, in 1910, 76 per cent of those involved in printing and publishing were Jewish. These figures should be taken with some caution, for Kovàcs had an agenda: to 'show' that Jews were taking over Hungary, but he was also an eminent statistician nevertheless.[46] The perception of a high Jewish presence in the cultural world was very widespread. Stefan Zweig claimed that in Vienna, Jews were the real public: they filled the theatres and concert halls, bought the books and paintings.[47] In France Jewish playwrights such as Georges de Porto-Riche (1849–1930), Gaston Caillavet (1869–1915), Tristan Bernard (1866–1947) and Henri Bernstein (1876–1953), the author of *Israel* (1908) – in which an anti-Semite discovers that his real father is Jewish – belonged to the mainstream of Parisian theatrical life.

The Jewish presence in European publishing was, by the turn of the century, equally considerable. In 1842 the brothers Michel, Alexandre-Nathan and Calmann Lévy (the sons of a book-peddler) founded a publishing enterprise which became one of the most important in France, publishing Balzac, Dumas, George Sand and Flaubert. By the 1880s Calmann-Lévy (as it became in 1875) was one of the largest firms in the country. In 1881 another Jew, Fernand Nathan, became a leading educational publisher. Paul Ollendorff, son of a Polish immigrant, launched one of the leading reviews of the pre-World War I era, *Gil Blas*. Arthur Meyer founded the newspaper *Le Gaulois*, while the brothers Natanson launched the cultural journal *La Revue blanche*. In Italy Jewish publishers, mainly of German origin, included Leo S. Olschki, Emilio Treves (the largest in Italy at the end of the nineteenth century and the publisher of Samuel Smiles's *Self-Help* and *David Copperfield*), Donath (originally from Berlin) and Bemporad (the publishers of *Pinocchio* when the firm was still called Felice Paggi, the name of Enrico Bemporad's father-in-law).

Jewish involvement in publishing was quite ancient, particularly where tolerance prevailed, as in Islamic Spain and parts of Italy in the fifteenth and sixteenth centuries. Jews also played an active part in the book trade during and after the invention of printing. It was, however, only in the nineteenth century that they achieved prominence, above all in Germany thanks to major publishers such as Karl Loewenthal (later Lönig when he converted). By the middle of the century almost every German city had a major Jewish publisher such as Levi in Stuttgart in 1840, J. Guttentag in Berlin in 1842, and Moritz Perles in Prague in 1844.[48] Ullstein became one of the country's largest newspaper publishers, dominating Berlin's thriving press with the *Berliner Morgenpost* and the tabloid *BZ am Mittag*. S. Fischer Verlag (1886) rapidly became a centre of avant-garde literary life. Erich Reiss in Berlin (1908) published luxury books. Jews were also publishers of great liberal papers such as the *Frankfurter Zeitung* and the *Berliner Tageblatt* (one of the many papers in Rudolf Mosse's press empire). The largest publishing house in Scandinavia, Albert Bonnier Förlag, was also established by a Jew.

In Britain the Jewish presence in publishing grew in importance only in the twentieth century, with William Swan Sonnenschein (1855–1931) who became a director of Routledge, Leonard Woolf (founder with his wife Virginia Woolf of the Hogarth Press, 1917), Victor Gollancz (1928) and Secker & Warburg (1936). The trend continued after the Second World War with a further influx of Jewish refugees from central Europe such as George Weidenfeld, an Austrian who co-founded Weidenfeld & Nicolson, André Deutsch, Robert Maxwell (a Czech, born Jan Ludvick Hoch), who started Pergamon Press in 1948, and Paul Hamlyn.

A similar process occurred in the USA, where some immigrants did fulfil the rosiest expectations of the American dream. Joseph Pulitzer was a German-speaking Jew, born in Hungary in 1847. He emigrated to the USA at the age of seventeen, fought in the Civil War and in 1867, at the age of twenty, became a reporter for the German-language daily *Westliche Post* in St Louis. Ten years later he was the leading newspaper publisher in that city. In 1883, now a rich man, he went to New York and bought the daily the *World* and later, in 1887, launched the *Evening World*. He endowed the famous Pulitzer School of Journalism at Columbia University and the Pulitzer Prizes for journalism. However, as in England, the great boom in Jewish-American publishing occurred later: Alfred A. Knopf (1892–1984) began publishing in 1915 (the firm is now part of Random House), Richard L. Simon and Max Schuster founded Simon & Schuster in 1924 (it is now part of the media giant Viacom), Roger W. Straus started Farrar, Straus & Giroux in 1946, and Arthur Rosenthal started Basic Books in 1952.

Anyone could set up a business and become a publisher, particularly if they had converted to Christianity – a small price to pay for many who remembered the earlier part of the nineteenth century, when most German Jews were paupers, and 70 per cent of Prussian Jews led insecure lives as wandering peddlers and beggars. By 1867 almost 15 per cent of high school students in Berlin were Jewish, three or four times the total percentage of Jews in the city population. As Jews went up the social ladder, the anti-Semitism which had been the prerogative of a few crackpots, or a remnant of the older religious intolerance of medieval times, became part of the fears and anxieties of the new middle classes.[49] The entry of Jews into some professions was seen by their non-Jewish competitors as a threat. In 1910 Jews accounted for 10–12 per cent of junior instructors in German universities, but were kept out of the higher grades by the nationalist anti-Semitism of their senior colleagues. At the University of Berlin in that year there was not a single Jewish senior professor.[50] One of the consequences of being kept out of the academy was that many intellectual Jews were forced into other professions. Thus in Berlin in 1907, 18 per cent of journalists were Jewish, as were most of the newspapers owners and editors of the liberal press in Vienna: the members of Concordia, the Viennese association of journalists and writers, were nearly all Jewish.[51] In 1910 in Hungary, Jews constituted 49 per cent of the medical and legal professions, and 42 per cent of journalists. There were, however, very few Jews employed in the civil service, which was under aristocratic patronage, and only 5 per cent of schoolteachers were Jewish.[52] As a consequence of this, many intellectual Jews emigrated to western Europe, particularly France. But at the end of the nineteenth century there were in France only 70–80,000 Jews out of thirty-nine million inhabitants, 60 per cent of them in Paris.[53] Anti-Semitism was a Paris phenomenon, used and exploited by the Catholic monarchist right in search of nationalist and patriotic credentials. This further solidified the commitment of Jews, particularly the intelligentsia, to French republican values. For exactly the same reasons, the rapid growth of anti-Semitism in Vienna, epitomised by the election of the Christian Social demagogue Karl Lueger as Mayor in 1895, linked the Jews further to the Emperor Franz Joseph, who with the support of the Catholic hierarchy had initially refused to sanction Lueger's election.

Women

By the turn of the twentieth century, in much of Europe, Jews, provided they were prepared to tone down their Jewishness, could be accepted in most professions and occupations. This was not so for women. The barriers to their entry into the professions, including the cultural industries, whether erected by convention or by law, were still formidable. However, some of these had begun to falter. In the 1880s Russian women were accepted into universities, though the French were only beginning to discuss the possibility.[54] In London, University College had opened its doors to women some decades before. Cambridge already had colleges for women, such as Newnham Hall (1871) and Girton (created in 1869, it became Girton College in 1873), but they achieved full status as members of the university only in 1948. At the end of the nineteenth century there were only sixty professional women in Italy (excluding teachers): two lawyers, two doctors and fifty-six pharmacists.[55] Only in one field were women significant players: novel-writing. This was true not only in Britain and France, but also in the rest of Europe. Italy had Grazia Deledda (Nobel Prize 1926) and Matilde Serao. Spain, having produced earlier in the century the pioneer of the new Spanish novel in the person of Fernán Caballero (Cecilia Josefa de Arrom), had a major novelist in Emilia de Pardo Bazán de Quiroga (1852–1921). Angela Grassi became the editor of the magazine *El Correo de la moda* (1867–83), and María del Pilar Sinués de Marco founded the journal *El Ángel del hogar* (named after her novel) and edited it from 1864 to 1869.[56] In Finland Minna Canth wrote novels and plays on female emancipation, while Maria Jotuni's play on the break-up of a marriage, *Man's Rib*, was a major success when it was first performed in 1914.

Over one hundred women's autobiographies were published in Russia in the nineteenth century.[57] Sofia Khvoshchinskaia wrote provincial 'novels of merchant life' under the name Ivan Vesenev. Anastasia Verbitskaia (1861–1928), a regular contributor to the so-called 'thick' journals, wrote feminist 'sensational' racy novels, such as the six-volume *The Keys to Happiness* (1909–13), which sold 35,000 each, at a time when a 10,000 edition was unusual.[58] Such sales were achieved regardless of Verbitskaia's politics, her feminism, her commitment to social democracy and her distaste for anti-Semitism, then particularly virulent in Russia. Her books were part of a new wave of women's literature in which female characters were not always trying to preserve their virginity while searching for Mr Right, or losing it in the arms of Mr Wrong. Mania, the heroine of *The Keys to Happiness*, hesitates between her two lovers, Nelidov, the anti-Semitic Russian *Übermensch*, and Steinbach, the sensitive and cultivated Jew. Understandably now, but less so then, she chooses the cultured Jew, who becomes her patron, takes her to Paris, teaches her (and the book's readers, mainly women who had recently moved up from the working classes) about Dante, Homer, the Louvre, Italy, etc.[59] Clearly the move away from the sentimental 'woman-as-victim' mode towards the increasingly fashionable 'New Woman' variety was underway even in Russia. It was now possible for women to have sex, even sex with more than one man, without a trace of bourgeois guilt, and this kept *The Keys of Happiness* in print long after the Revolution.

Neither in Russia nor elsewhere were significant inroads made by women in other cultural domains (leaving aside, of course, acting and singing): there were few female painters, playwrights or composers. Hardly any women were musicians, as they were kept out of orchestras – except for the occasional harpist. Some great European orchestras such as the Vienna and the Berlin Philharmonics managed to maintain such discrimination until the end of the twentieth century.

Women's presence in literature worried many. The French writer Jules Bertaut produced, in 1909, a three-hundred-page tract about what he regarded as a worrying trend: 'the success of feminine literature has been like lightning. It has taken us by surprise. We were caught unprepared. We have been mortified. We have been a little humiliated.'[60] Bertaut's polemic was aimed at women writers who tried to tackle 'modern' themes. 'Women,' he declared, 'are sensitive, vibrant, highly strung, very instinctive, near to nature . . . far from the kind of virile energies which modern life requires.'[61] Feminism was a sign of female egoism, of a lack of interest in family and children.[62]

Bertaut was mistaken in his belief that women had, all of a sudden, picked up their pens. The phenomenon was much older. Nor was he the first (or the last) to claim that women writers inevitably neglect their children. One of the most overtly misogynist cartoons of Honoré Daumier depicts a woman writing at her desk; the floor is dirty, chairs are overturned and her child is drowning. The caption reads: 'The mother is in the heat of composition, the baby is in the bathwater.'[63] Bertaud was right, however, in detecting some new developments. While the female romance showed no sign of abating – it is now, one hundred years later, stronger than ever – a new generation of women writers, particularly in France, was ready to talk about sexuality in a far less inhibited way than before. They reflected the 'New Woman' emerging at the turn of the century, a mannish and overly sexualised woman much feared by the popular press such as the *Daily Telegraph* and *Punch*. But the New Woman was also a feminist icon demanding a 'share in the struggles, the responsibilities and the honour of the world' – so declared the *Woman's Herald* in August 1893.[64]

The genre of 'daring' novels by women was not entirely new. As we have seen (page 453), Ouida's novels had scandalised some. A *Punch* cartoon of 1867 has a man inspecting a book in a store and complaining: 'I see it is written by a lady, and I want a book that my daughters may read. Give me something else.'[65] Mary Elizabeth Braddon in *Lady Audley's Secret* (1862) introduced a new type of heroine: pretty and innocent-looking, yet a bigamist, a liar, an arsonist and a would-be murderer.[66]

In France, a new generation of women writers discarded sentimentality in favour of the sordid, the disturbing and the sensual – writers such as Gyp (pseudonym of Sibylle-Gabrielle de Martel de Janville, 1849–1932), Rachilde (Marguerite Eymery, 1860–1953) and Colette (Sidonie Gabrielle Claudine Colette, 1873–1954). Gyp's *Bijou* (1896) had several strong women characters in control of events throughout the novel; the eponymous heroine is intelligent and beautiful, and by the end of the novel has discarded several lovers, ruined several marriages, destroyed several friendships and caused a suicide. Rachilde's *Monsieur Vénus* (1884) has a young working-class male, Jacques Silvert, seduced and driven to death by the heroine Raoule de Vénérande, who is beautiful, proud and rich.[67] In the same author's *L'Animale* (1893) Laure Lordès, the heroine, a seductress from a young age, has an affair with an ugly one-eyed clerk, Lucien Séchard, who eventually kills himself, while she turns to seducing a priest. After various sad affairs, she kills herself too.[68] In *La Jongleuse* (1900) the heroine, Éliante, reaches orgasm ('*un spasme*') by embracing an alabaster vase in the presence of her suitor, who gasps: '*C'est scandaleux! Là ... dévant moi ... sans moi? Non, c'est abominable!*' ('It's disgusting! Here ... before me ... without me? It is abominable!').[69]

Colette's four 'Claudine' novels (1900–03) were sexually frank, semi-autobiographical stories (originally she had used her husband Henri Gauthier-Villars's pen name, Willy). The first, *Claudine à l'école* (1899), was a *succès de scandale* and sold 40,000 copies in two months.[70] It was followed by *Claudine à Paris* in 1901, *Claudine en ménage* in 1902, and *Claudine s'en va* in 1903. By then 'Claudine' had become a type – a sexually free, bisexual *garçonne*. The books were turned into successful plays with a lead actress, Polaire, who looked like Colette herself. Cabarets regularly featured Claudine impersonators. Colette's husband used his skills as an impresario to exploit her fame. Claudine became a brand name: the ice-cream maker Latinville created the Claudine ice-cream, a pastrycook invented the gâteau Claudine (still sold after the Second World War). Then there was the perfume Claudine, the perfume Colette, the Claudine hat, the cigarette Claudine, and the Claudine stockings.[71] Colette almost turned herself into her character, leading a scandalous life, exposing her breasts in the musical melodrama *La Chair* (1907, six hundred performances in five years). She dressed like a man well before the post-World War I design revolution, spearheaded by Coco Chanel, launched the classic suit with straight, collarless jacket and short skirt, to be worn with a hat over short hair.[72]

Colette is now well-remembered, not only in France, and her works are still available in translation. Not so Gyp, who wrote over a hundred novels, twenty plays, hundreds of articles, and four volumes of memoirs. Her works were favourably commented on by the likes of Anatole France and Friedrich Nietzsche (and unfavourably by Octave Mirbeau and Ezra Pound). Most of her novels – such as *Hors du monde* (signed Jack Frank) were written in dialogue form (*roman dialogué*). Her mother, Marie de Mirabeau (1827–1914), a Countess, had been a literary figure in her own right. She had started off with pious religious literature – there was a strong market for this genre – writing *Prières et pensées chrétiennes*.[73] But fashion paid more than Christianity, and Marie moved on to *La Vie Parisienne*, a popular illustrated weekly advising readers on what to wear and how to distinguish real from fake chic.[74] She then turned to light and slightly risqué short stories,[75] and then to novels, such as *L'Impératrice Wanda*, in which a few descriptive passages frame pages and pages of dialogue, and, in 1889, a detective story, *Le Crime de la rue Marignan* (under the pen name of Flagy), where it is the *femme de chambre*, and not the police, who discovers the identity of the murderer.[76]

Gyp followed her mother's lead, and started writing in *La Vie Parisienne*. Aristocrats still regarded writing for such journals as rather undignified, so they sent their articles anonymously, with various pseudonyms. To get paid they had to go the offices of the magazines, where they would be shown to an individual waiting room (which Marcelin Planat, the editor, called an *isoloir*) so as to avoid been seen by other contributors. Then they would produce a specimen of their handwriting and would be paid. It is thus clear that Gyp wrote not because she wanted prestige or fame, but in order to support her expensive lifestyle. Her first character was 'Bob' (1881), a slang-speaking eight-year-old boy who delighted in mocking the pretensions of bourgeois aristocratic society. So every week the readers of *La Vie Parisienne* would read about 'Bob au Salon', 'Bob au Jardin d'Acclimatation', 'Bob à l'Hippique'. This led to the book-length *Petit Bob*, the first of over sixty works Calmann-Lévy published, usually after serialisation in *La Vie Parisienne*. A contract drawn up in 1884 gave Calmann-Lévy, then the most prestigious publisher in France, the exclusive rights over Gyp's production for the next six years. They were in effect buying a string of best-sellers, while Gyp received the assurance of a steady income. The terms, by today's standards, were favourable to the author: a 15 per cent royalty on the first printing of 1,500 copies.[77]

Gyp's readers were members of the so-called *nouvelles couches*, the new social strata (essentially middle-class) that had emerged in the first few years of the Third Republic, people without much leisure time who wanted to read a novel between train stations. They needed books which could be read in a fragmentary way, without excessive concentration and without excessive details. Gyp's massive use of short, crossfire dialogue, similar to a comic strip, was ideally suited to these new readers.[78] Her slightly anti-bourgeois-establishment streak may have appealed to her readers, as did her growing anti-Semitism, though this created problems for her publisher, particularly when it became increasingly strident in the years leading to the Dreyfus affair. Calmann-Lévy tried to convince her to tone down her prejudices, but he was reluctant to offend one of his most successful and profitable writers, nor did he want to provide ammunition to those who claimed that the Jews controlled publishing by intervening in too high-handed a manner in a writer's freedom of expression.[79] Gyp too did not want to lose the publisher's outstanding marketing network. By publishing with Calmann-Lévy she was assured of pre-publication in his prestigious *Revue de Paris*, then she could be certain that the novel would be reviewed (positively) in several of Calmann-Lévy's publications, would be advertised in them, and prominently displayed in his bookshops.[80]

By 1897, however, the exasperated publisher broke all relations with the author, declaring Gyp *persona non grata*. Now she could unleash her anti-Jewish spleen without inhibitions, declaring herself a 'ferocious anti-Semite' and putting forward her solution to 'the Jewish Question': 'Let's frighten them! I'm not personally asking that they be killed . . . But let's chase them out.'[81] It was not her anti-Semitism that led to Gyp's high sales, but her easy style of writing, and above all her uninhibited heroines. The female reading public enjoyed seeing women in control of their lives, and finally treating men the way men had treated women in novels (and in life). This was not unique to French readers. The impact of this kind of raw feminism (like the raw socialism of the naïve anti-Semite) was felt throughout Europe.

32

The Internationalisation of the Novel

New Commercialism

THE HISTORIES OF the nineteenth-century literature of minor countries are peppered with comments such as, Zsigmond Kemény was the Hungarian Balzac, Eugen Kumičić the Croatian Zola, France Prešern the Byron of Slovenia, while Mihai Eminescu, the Romanian national poet, followed in the footsteps of Hölderlin. Éduard Vilde was the Estonian Balzac. Reinis and Matiss Kaudzite, authors of *Mernieku laiki* (The Age of Surveyors, 1879), were, jointly, the Latvian Gogol (who was Ukrainian but wrote in Russian). Women were not spared: the Czech Karolina Světlá, being a woman, got to be the Czech George Sand. The leading nineteenth-century Czech poet Jaroslav Vrchlický (Emil Frida, who came from a family of rabbis) was the Czech Hugo. Hendrik Conscience, author of *De Leeuw van Vlaanderen* (The Lion of Flanders, 1838) and dozens of other historical novels, was the Flemish Walter Scott. In Norway, Ibsen was Ibsen, but even an acclaimed Nobel Prize-winner like Knut Hamsun had to put up with being the Norwegian Dostoevsky (or Tolstoy).

All this was a sign that the growth of the cultural industry coincided with the diversification of its centres of production. When the reading public was relatively small, novels had to aspire to attract a considerable proportion of it. When there are many consumers it is often better to think in terms of market segments. It is thus not fortuitous that a proliferation of genres – such as the crime novel and the science fiction story – occurred in the period 1880–1920.

French and English novels continued to dominate European literary life, but their hegemony began to falter. Italian, German, Russian and American novels were still catering mainly for their home markets, but some (particularly the Russians and the Americans) did well abroad. Even difficult writers like Henry James, someone who 'wanted to sell without selling out', did reasonably: 20,000 copies of *Daisy Miller* (1878) were sold on publication, 13,000 of *The Princess Casamassima* (1886), but most of his other books sold only about 5,000 copies. The mature and difficult novels on which much of his posthumous fame rests, *The Wings of the Dove* (1902), *The Ambassadors* (1903) and *The Golden Bowl* (1904), were liked by neither the critics nor the public.

Publishing houses changed too. Earlier in the nineteenth century they were associated with a single entrepreneur. By the end of the century many became corporate entities, often as a result of mergers. Competition among publishers for well-known authors increased. There were rich prizes for discovering new authors, but once they were discovered it was difficult to hold on to them. One also needed to know the markets. The trend was towards cheaper books, but Albert Quantin, a French printer turned publisher, realised that there was also a demand for '*de luxe*' editions of modern classics – the new bourgeoisie liked to show off beautifully bound editions lining their shelves. At a considerable cost Quantin snatched Victor Hugo from Calmann Lévy, and between 1880 and 1885 managed to sell some 300,000 volumes of Hugo's works at 7.5 francs each. When Hugo died in 1885 Quantin was quick to publish also an economic edition for only two francs per volume.[1]

The contract between Hugo and Quantin had been negotiated by an agent, Paul Meurice, one of a new breed of literary entrepreneurs who charged an exorbitant commission for his efforts: 27.71 per cent of a writer's total earnings. The rise of the literary agent, at least in Great Britain and the USA, coincided with an expansion of the novel-reading public. Since agents act on behalf of a number of writers, they have a wider and better view of what constitutes the typical contract between a publisher and an author. They are thus the nearest thing to trade union representatives in a profession characterised by profound segmentation and individualism. Agents have other useful functions: they dissuade new authors from sending unpublishable manuscripts to publishers; they haggle with publishers and make their life difficult, thus enabling authors to adopt the lofty pretence of being above mercenary matters; they act as first readers, making suggestions; and finally they provide moral support for writers during their regular depressions ('I can't write! I have writer's block! No one likes me any more!'). Needless to say, agents were regarded as parasites by publishers and by some authors, yet while in 1894 only six agencies were registered in the London Post Office Directory, by 1914 there were more than thirty, including C.F. Cazenove's Literary Agency and Curtis Brown, an American firm which opened a branch in London in 1899.[2]

The way authors were paid changed. Previously they would be paid a lump sum for selling a manuscript outright to a publisher or for granting them all rights in it for a set number of years. If the work was successful, the publishers had an incentive to republish it. Even successful authors seemed to like this system, because it provided them with ready cash. However, as print runs increased, authors wished to receive a percentage of the income from sales, which led to the birth of the royalty system, by which they acquired a direct financial interest in the number of copies sold. Inequalities between publishers, booksellers and authors remained. The publisher Basil Blackwell put it aptly in his 1932 Dent Memorial Lecture when he said that 'The publisher takes a relatively small number of big risks, and the bookseller a large number of small risks.'[3] He could have added: and authors take one very big risk, since each book is the fruit of months or years of work. A publisher or a bookseller can afford to have the occasional failure on their list. Few authors can survive more than one or two. Every author wants his or her books to be promoted as widely as possible; publishers have to make choices: advertising, posters, interviews, fancy cover illustrations, window displays in bookshops. Some authors became adept at marketing themselves. Dickens became a virtual entrepreneur. Gabriele D'Annunzio and Oscar Wilde understood that developing an image, especially an outrageous one, could help sales. Of course some authors had behaved outrageously before, but in the age of Byron this may have been spontaneous. Now the environment was more competitive, and one had to distinguish oneself from one's rivals. Wilde realised this before his 1881–82 lecture tour in the USA: he agreed with his sponsors that he would present himself to the Americans as an Oxonian aesthete, and would dress, speak and act accordingly.[4] Having acquired a public persona, authors could use it to endorse commercial products, for a fee. Oscar Wilde endorsed 'Madame Fontaine's Bosom Beautifier', the publicity for which assured potential purchasers that 'Just as sure as the sun will rise tomorrow, just so sure it will enlarge and beautify the bosom.'[5] Rudyard Kipling plugged the beef extract Bovril as a tonic for troops fighting in the Boer War: '. . . an Invigorating and Nourishing Food, preparing the soldier for battle and aiding him to recovery when wounded by wounds and disease'.[6]

There was a growing homogenisation of the reading public. Writers themselves, even across countries and continents, had a relatively similar cultural background, since they read the same books, lived in cities, had a similar education, bought similar consumer goods, followed the same fashions, went to see the same plays and enjoyed the same entertainments. In the Middle Ages too there was a global community (in Europe), speaking the same language (Latin), believing in the same things (Christianity) and reading the same books, but the new late-nineteenth-century global community of readers and writers was far larger.

The enormous expansion of literature led to fears about quality. Such cultural alarms have become a characteristic of modern society. John Yule, a character in Gissing's *New Grub Street*, once successful but now a loser in the new, brash literary world, laments: 'Who is it that reads most of the stuff that's poured out daily by the ton from the printing press? . . . Your Board schools, your popular press, your spread of education! Machinery for ruining the country, that's what I call it.'[7]

The proliferation of literary prizes at the turn of the century was an indication that it had become necessary to find ways of distinguishing books 'of quality' from those appealing to a mass market. The French in particular pioneered this new marketing tool. The first, and still the most prestigious, French literary prize was the Prix Goncourt, which started in 1903 thanks to a legacy from Jules Goncourt. Others followed: the Grand Prix du Roman de l'Académie Française, the Prix Fémina (the jury being entirely made up of women), the Prix Renaudot, the Prix Interallié and the Prix Médicis. Quality was not always identified, however. Detractors of prizes always take considerable pleasure in contrasting the winners who have since been utterly forgotten with the losers we now revere. They point out that the Goncourt 'missed out' Céline, Camus, Sartre and Yourcenar, while the Nobel ignored James Joyce, Italo Svevo and Tolstoy.

Poetry, an 'elevated' genre at the end of the eighteenth century, expanded even more than fiction. In France the annual production of novels increased by some 25 per cent between 1876 and 1905, but collections of poetry increased by 74 per cent.[8] The production of single poems was always greater than other publications, since an optimistic amateur can write a poem in less than an hour, but not a novel. They are also easier to place in short-lived publications that carry poems and brief essays, but nothing more substantial. Poetry is seldom produced for the market. Publishers discovered that young poets did not expect to be paid; indeed, many were willing to pay for the pleasure of seeing their work in print. Poetry, like academic writing, occasionally brings prestige, rarely money. To distinguish themselves, some poets try experimentalism; this is less likely to fail in a poem than in a novel, for a short eccentric text may amuse, while a three-hundred-page avant-garde novel can easily become a bore. The majority of poets, however, like the majority of painters, shun novelty and imitate the kind of works they themselves like.

This spread of poetry, particularly in the provinces, facilitates the creation and expansion of literary clubs and networks where one can read one's short poems to one's friends.[9] The outbreak of the First World War led to an unprecedented outbreak of published poetry. In Britain alone during the war some 2,225 poets were published, in 3,104 volumes of verse. We still remember and celebrate some of the anti-war poetry of the time, that of Siegfried Sassoon and Wilfred Owen (whose poetry was recognised only after his death), but most of the rest was fervently patriotic and written in an archaic language, echoing the verse that the poets had read at school and the King James Bible.[10]

Two profitable avenues, however, opened up to poets later in the twentieth century. The first was writing lyrics for popular songs. The craft was ancient, but the rewards could be considerable. The second was provided by the rapidly expanding advertising industry, which needed memorable ditties and slogans to tie to products. 'Beanz Meanz Heinz' may not sound like Shakespeare, but it was memorable, and perhaps effective in the marketing of canned baked beans.

Publishers

A book published in France in 1904 called *La Crise du livre*, by Henri Baillère (himself a publisher), sounded an alarm which had been sounded many times before: there were too many publishers and too many booksellers undercutting each other; and too many unsold books quickly remaindered or sold by peddlers for pennies. There were also too many books: in 1898 the Germans published 23,908, the French 14,781, the British 14,498, the Americans 10,630 and the Italians 9,567.[11] Once there were four of five Latin grammars, now there were thirty, Baillère claimed – wrongly, because between 1828 and 1848 hundreds of manuals of Latin and Greek were published, it was just that only three of four were adopted.[12] France was exporting fewer books: 'Even foreigners don't want our books any more.'[13] So 'tricks' had to be devised, Baillère claimed, to sell more books: pretty covers, illustrations, gift vouchers in sealed envelopes inserted in the book, exaggerated claims about sales.[14] There was no Balzac, Dumas, Sue or Sand – and Zola and Daudet had just gone. Instead there was a 'barbaric invasion' from Poland, Russia and Scandinavia.[15] People were turning to practical reference books – books 'no one reads but everyone consults', such as Larousse's dictionaries, which had sold 150,000 copies.[16]

Baillère, like all his successors decrying the crisis of the book and lamenting that no one read them any more, was wrong. The statistics at our disposal may not be very good, but they are better than Baillère's: at his time there were more readers than ever. Publishers, responding to market demand, provided them with what they wanted: cheap books. Of course, many of these would have been described by Baillère and those like him as unadulterated trash, and indeed many were. The point is that along with the 'trash', the new cheap books being produced also included the entire literary canon of the nineteenth century, almost all the great classics as well as a considerable number of new authors.

Earlier in the century, cheap books had meant cheap literature, *Triviallit-eratur* to be bought and discarded. By the 1880s the Germans started to exploit their considerable market for books by developing the idea of the cheap classic that had been pioneered by the British and the French. At first publishers, because they were cautious, offered the new readerships books which had been popular with previous generations at low prices. Only after that did they dare to offer something new. Thus the publisher Anton Philipp Reclam brought out, under the imprint Universal Bibliothek (UB), hundreds of cheap German and foreign 'classics', loosely defined as 'good literature' and 'of national interest'. UB was so successful that by 1896, when Reclam died, he had published 3,740 titles. His operating principle was similar to that of the French publisher Charpentier in the 1830s and 1840s (see pages 299–300): the books all had the same format and the same price, and the imprint as a whole had to pay for itself, with some titles subsidising others, each title advertising the rest of the collection. Readers were thus educated in expecting to be able to find any modern or older classic in the Universal Bibliothek. UB became an institution. When in 1910 it reached its 5,000th title, the company published a volume of 1,200 pages consisting of all the letters of congratulation it had received from readers, politicians, crowned heads of state and intellectuals praising it for having had faith in the intelligence of the German people.[17] Reclam innovated on the bookselling front too: he offered booksellers specially designed shelves to exhibit his books; in 1912 in Erfurt he introduced the first coin-operated automatic distributors of books, designed by the great architect Peter Behrens. They were positioned in public buildings, railway stations and hospitals, and during the war in military hospitals and at the front line. By 1914 there were thousands of machines in operation, selling 1.5 million volumes each year.

Publishing classics facilitated the expansion of the market. Further expansion requires conceiving of the book as part of the 'entertainment culture', to be marketed as a commodity, using ingenious new tricks of the trade, such as labelling an imprint 'Herren-Bibliothek' and subtitling it 'Only for Gentlemen or for Really Curious Ladies', as did the publisher Michael Stern in Vienna in 1887.[18] But the single most important cause behind the expansion was the fall in the price of books. Mass markets require cheap goods.

The magazine trade proceeded along similar lines. By 1909 Leopold Ullstein, already one of Germany's largest publishers, decided that the yearly subscriptions most magazines required their readers to pay in advance were a deterrent to an increase in sales. Ullstein decided to have his weekly *Berliner Illustrierte Zeitung* delivered to readers' homes by booksellers who would receive a weekly payment, something no one had attempted in Germany before. Thirty years later the magazine was selling some two million copies every week.[19]

In France the main publisher of cheap books was Fayard, who in the 1880s and 1890s published older popular books in instalments at only five centimes. In 1904 Fayard was publishing books by contemporary writers at ninety-five centimes, at a time when similar books cost over three francs. Often Fayard simply bought other publishers' backlists and merely reprinted previous bestsellers. Authors of books which had formerly sold only in their thousands were attracted by the prospect of very large print runs, which could be as high as 100,000. The authors (or their heirs) who benefited were writers of sentimental stories dealing with adultery and the traditional popular genre of victims' stories (battered orphans, women seduced and abandoned, people unjustly accused), which attracted a largely female readership. Their titles were emblematic: *Deux orphelines* by d'Ennery, *Sans famille* by Hector Malot, *Chaste et flétrie* by Charles Mérouvel and *La Porteuse de pain* by Xavier de Montépin. Popular also was the risqué genre, where the daring tone was mollified by a comic vein, such as *Aimé de son concierge* and *La Conquête d'une cuisinière* by Eugène Chavette (1827–1902). The new reading public, weaned onto reading by publication in instalments, took to the new format with relish. De Montépin's *Porteuse de pain* sold over a million copies, the stories of Fantômas the master-criminal by Souvestre and Allain over five million. By publishing for ten centimes the classics taught in French schools, Fayard secured an important market throughout the first half of the twentieth century.[20]

The losers were the lending libraries and the booksellers, whose profit margin on each title was now smaller, while the cost of stocking them remained the same. But turnover was faster thanks to greater sales, which profited the more efficient booksellers. Profits were more easily achieved in bookshops owned by the publishers themselves. Thus began a long trend towards the vertical integration and the concentration of the industry. In France, for instance, between 1880 and 1910 the number of bookshops fell from 7,000 to 5,000.[21] The serialisation of books too began its long decline. Originally it had been a way of circumventing the high price of books, of getting the customers to pay in instalments by delivering in instalments. In practice there was a limited number of outlets for serialisation, and each newspaper could only carry four or five novels a year.[22]

The Laggards Strike Back

In *La Crise du livre* Henri Baillère had been worried not just about new 'low' genres or an excess of books, but also about the fact that not enough of them were French. He had a point. A mass market for printed text had come into being. It was no longer necessary for authors to be French or British to be read outside their own country. The international market was becoming more diversified. Conversely, popularity in the hegemonic countries no longer automatically translated into success abroad. The Alsatian writers Émile Erckmann (1822–99) and Alexandre Chatrian (1826–90), writing under the pseudonym of Erckmann-Chatrian, were extremely successful in France with a series of patriotic novels, but they did not replicate the international success of Dumas or Verne – though one of their stories, *L'Ami Fritz* (1864), was adapted for the operatic stage by Mascagni (*L'Amico Fritz*, 1891). Such patriotic and nationalist literature was not meant to be exported. It was part of a cultural war between national intellectual élites. Erckmann-Chatrian's books lamented the loss of Alsace to the Germans, while the German occupants invented a 'true Alsatian' culture replete with stories of 'fresh-faced farm boys, smiling women in native costume and grandfatherly village mayors'.[23] Unusually, these books were popular in the countryside, among farmers as well as among the young. They were easy to read, and short. They were marketed with great skill by Hetzel, one of the most formidable French publishers of the time. Above all, the writers knew their market, having done considerable fieldwork among the peasantry.[24]

Anything popular with the French peasantry is unlikely to be popular among the élites or abroad. Thibaudet's *Histoire de la littérature française de 1789 à nos jours* (1936) regarded Erckmann-Chatrian as mere regional authors writing for children. Flaubert described them to George Sand in 1859 as 'two guys with a rather plebeian soul'.[25] In Britain, where eighteen of their works were published by Ward, Lock & Tyler at one shilling a volume, they were often read in French as an aid to learning the language.[26] In Romania they were known mainly as playwrights, but at least they were known.[27]

The emergence of a provincial literature was paralleled by the appearance of international best-sellers which were no longer French or British. Some Italian novelists made an impact in France (Gabriele D'Annunzio, for instance), Norwegian plays (i.e. Ibsen) were performed in London, while Europe discovered the importance of Russian novels. Lermontov's *A Hero of our Time* and Gogol's *Dead Souls* had been translated into English in the 1850s, respectively fourteen and twelve years after their Russian publication, but Turgenev's *Fathers and Sons* (1862) had to wait only five years for its British debut. Pushkin's *Eugene Onegin* (1831) and Gogol's *The Inspector General* (1836) were not translated into English until over fifty years after their original publication. Dostoevsky's *Crime and Punishment* (1866) waited 'only' twenty years, but *The Brothers Karamazov* (1879) was not available in English until 1912. After the Revolution of 1917 there was a spate of translations from Russian throughout Europe, probably because the USSR had left the copyright convention, and foreign publishers no longer had to pay any royalties to Russian authors.

The Germans, almost absent since Goethe, returned to the centre of the European stage with dramatists such as Arthur Schnitzler (Austria), Gerhart Hauptmann and Frank Wedekind. But they still lagged behind in novel-writing. As Heinrich Mann's nationalist anti-hero Diederich Hessling in *Der Untertan* (1914–18) explains to his wife, the novel, *der Roman*, was 'not an art form at all! At least, thank God!, not a German one. You can tell by the name.'[28] On the wider global scene nineteenth-century German culture meant philosophy, history, poetry and above all music, but not the novel. One of the most successful mid-century German novelists, Gustav Freytag, author of *Soll und Haben* (1855), remained known mainly within the German-speaking world, as did Friedrich Spielhagen, 'one of the most successful writers of the last four decades of the nineteenth century'.[29] *Der Grüne Heinrich* (Green

Henry, 1854–55), by the Swiss novelist Gottfried Keller (1819–90), a *Bildungs-roman* regarded as 'one of the outstanding works of the nineteenth century' by *The Columbia Encyclopedia* (sixth edition, 2001), was translated into French (by the Swiss) only in 1933, and into English only in 1960. Even *Effi Briest* (1895) by Theodor Fontane, the main novel of the leading German novelist of his day, regarded by Thomas Mann as one of the six most signifi-cant novels ever written, did not see a French translation until 1957 and an English one until 1967 – though there was one in Italian in 1944.[30]

What did travel, eventually, were books like Thomas Mann's first impor-tant novel, *Buddenbrooks*, published in 1901 and translated into English in 1904. This was part of the kind of 'élite literature' which benefited from the fact that élites were now much larger than in the past. But what really took off were 'international best-sellers' – some from countries hitherto excluded from the mainstream. The case of the Polish writer Henryk Sienkiewicz, the author of *Quo Vadis?*, the success of which has remained unparalleled in Polish literature – is emblematic. Sienkiewicz did not emerge from a vacuum. The eighteenth-century dismemberment of Poland between Austria, Ger-many and Russia meant that the Polish intelligentsia was unusually aware of cultures other than its own. Many writers had known exile, usually in Paris, and their works reflected this: from Boleslaw Prus's *Lalka* (The Doll, 1890) to Wladyslaw Sabowski's *Niepodobni* (The Different Ones, 1873).[31] Eliza Orzeszkowa wrote *Meir Ezofowicz* (1878) and the epic *Nad Niemnem* (On the Banks of the Niemen, 1888), while Józef Ignacy Kraszewski wrote between 1873 and 1883 some ninety novels in which the characters were types representing elements of the Polish nation. The values of these novels were still those of the gentry, to whom all social problems were in reality moral ones.[32]

Then came Henryk Sienkiewicz's *Ogniem i mieczem* (With Fire and Sword, 1884), the first volume of a historical trilogy set in seventeenth-century Poland. Until then Polish culture and literature were virtually unknown outside Poland. International sympathy for Poland's plight may have played a role in Sienkiewicz's fame, but the key factor was the stalwart efforts of his translator Jeremiah Curtin, a linguist who knew not only Russian and Polish but also Hindi and many African languages – it was claimed that he spoke seventy languages – and collected folk tales and myths.[33] Curtin's English translation of *With Fire and Sword* was published in 1890. Further translations followed. Aware of the possibility of foreign fame, Sienkiewicz wrote a new novel with a non-Polish theme: it was set in ancient Rome, at the time of the persecution of the Christians by the Emperor Nero. Entitled *Quo Vadis?*

(Where are you Going?), it was first serialised in *Gazeta Polska* in 1895, and was promptly translated by Curtin into English. In 1897 it was translated into Czech and Russian, in 1898 into German and Italian, in 1899 into Bulgarian, Armenian, Danish and Portuguese. A Latin translation was presented to Pope Leo XIII. By 1900 *Quo Vadis?* had sold 400,000 copies in the US, 40,000 in Italy, and 150,000 in Germany. It was adapted into a play in 1901, into an opera by Jean Nougués in 1909, and was satirised in French cabarets: *Rococo vadis* and *Ou qu'on va, dis?*. Sienkiewicz received the Nobel Prize in 1905.[34] A big-budget film version (the first of several) was made in Italy in 1913 for what was then the huge sum of $9,000.

Significantly, *Quo Vadis?* had begun its journey towards global fame in the USA, and reached Paris only five years later: it was not until 1900 that it was finally translated into French. Despite the initial hostility of the critics, it was an unprecedented success with the French public.[35] Its publication coincided with a revival of the vogue for historical novels and plays, including Edmond Rostand's verse play *Cyrano de Bergerac* (1897), Anatole France's *Thaïs* (1890), Pierre Louys's *Aphrodite* (1896) and Jean Bertheroy's *Cléopâtre* (1891). Renewed interest in the link between the ancient world and the erotic was manifest in Prosper Castanier's plays *La Courtisane de Memphis* (1900), *L'Orgie Romaine* (1897) and *Les Amants de Lesbos*. With *Quo Vadis?* French publishers had been slow off the mark, probably because they thought a Polish novelist would not sell in France.[36] Its international success convinced them to take the plunge. Inevitably, French nationalists complained that only foreigners could now be successful in Paris.

Sienkiewicz himself, though a Polish patriot, was far from being an inward-looking nationalist. He was steeped in French and British literature, had learned much from Walter Scott and Alexandre Dumas, had travelled widely across the USA in 1876, and lived in Paris while writing *Quo Vadis?*. The novel, by being set in ancient Rome and not in Poland, could be read by an international public as what it seemed to be: a narrative concerning a period of history that most readers had been made familiar with in their school days: the Rome of Nero and the Christian martyrs. The historical background was enlivened by a traditional love story between the patrician Roman Vinicius and the Christian convert Lygia (also an aristocrat). In Poland the novel was usually interpreted as a metaphor for the struggle of the Poles against tyranny. Elsewhere it was just an exciting story.

Polish cultural pride received a huge boost from the renown of Sienkiewicz. The writer gained financially and had honours heaped upon him. Well before he received the Nobel Prize, a national subscription was successfully launched to buy back for him his ancestral castle at Oblegorek, near Kielce. Polish literary critics, however, were embarrassed: few of them could bring themselves to declare – as they were expected to – that *Quo Vadis?* was on a par with *War and Peace* or *The Brothers Karamazov*. Modernist writers, including Polish ones such as Stanislaw Brzozowski (1878–1911), fiercely attacked Sienkiewicz for his conventionality and lack of depth.[37] But notwithstanding his Catholicism, Sienkiewicz was still celebrated decades later by the communist régime, which ensured the publication of his complete works in sixty volumes.

The Swedish Academy whose task it was from 1901 onwards to award the Nobel Prize for Literature was favourably inclined towards writers from countries which, like Sweden, were not culturally dominant. All the better if they were also popular, particularly as the recently established prize needed to become better known. As the Secretary of the Academy explained in his presentation speech in 1905, the year in which Sienkiewicz received the award, 'in every nation there are some rare geniuses who concentrate in themselves the spirit of the nation and represent its national character to the world'.[38] Indeed the Swedish Academy awarded its prizes with the clear intention of bringing to wider attention writers from relatively 'peripheral' countries (and not always novelists) – as is still the case:

NOBEL PRIZE FOR LITERATURE 1901–13

1901	Sully-Prudhomme	France	Poet
1902	Theodor Mommsen	Germany	Historian
1903	Bjørnstjerne Bjørnson	Norway	Playwright
1904	José Echegaray	Spain	Playwright
	Frédéric Mistral	France	Poet
1905	Henryk Sienkiewicz	Poland	Novelist
1906	Giosué Carducci	Italy	Poet
1907	Rudyard Kipling	Britain	Novelist and poet
1908	Rudolf Eucken	Germany	Philosopher
1909	Selma Lagerlöf	Sweden	Novelist
1910	Paul Heyse	Germany	Novelist
1911	Maurice Maeterlinck	Belgium	Playwright
1912	Gerhart Hauptmann	Germany	Playwright
1913	Rabindranath Tagore	India	Poet

There were only two French and one British writers in the list, yet the Academy was not being eccentric. Major playwrights were coming to the fore, many from outside Great Britain and France. Novelists from southern and central Europe, from Russia, from Scandinavia and from the USA were acquiring international fame. Some, it is true, required and/or sought French and to a lesser extent British seals of approval, but many did without. Paris was no longer the centre of the cultural world. Thus, though at the turn of the century any Hungarian intellectual or artist worth his salt had go on an intellectual pilgrimage to Paris, they were increasingly under the influence of German culture, and finding out about Dostoevsky, Gorky, Ibsen and others from countries other than France.[39]

The nationally-conscious intellectual élites of the 'culturally peripheral' countries found themselves afflicted by a curious ambivalence. They sought, above all else, the emergence of an 'authentic national literature', thus following in the footsteps of the Romantic intelligentsia of the beginning of the nineteenth century (see page 79). At the same time they were aware that just as a nation required international recognition, so did an 'authentic national literature'. So pride in one's own writers grew with their status abroad. For many writers, external recognition was a necessary condition for becoming lionised at home. To be famous abroad, however, it was necessary to give foreigners what they wanted, to deal with themes which had wider resonance: in other words it was necessary not to be too national-specific. Thus a world literature (largely European) continued to develop, using similar themes and similar characters, borrowing them from the past, gaining sustenance and ideas from other writers in other countries in other times. Such a dilemma, in the late twentieth century, became part of the predicament of African and to a lesser extent Asian writers, some of whom realised that their readership would be larger and their renown greater if they wrote in English (or French), and not in the local language.

Inevitably, novels from culturally peripheral countries were, overwhelmingly, novels (and plays) aimed at the new middle-class reading public. They were seldom penny dreadfuls or low-level *romans-feuilletons*, but what we would now call, with barely suppressed condescension, 'middlebrow' novels, different not only from weighty classics but also from the new, complex, modernist novels championed by the intelligentsia. Few of these 'middlebrow' novels would ever become classics or would be read a century later, but in the meantime they made their authors rich. Thus Pierre Loti's *Pêcheur d'islande* sold 110,000 copies in 1906, and 500,000 by 1919.[40] In England

Arnold Bennett (1867–1931), author of *Anna of the Five Towns* (1902), and John Galsworthy (1867–1933), author of a series of novels about the wealthy Forsyte family, were equally popular.

The Periphery

This spread of translations and of domestically-produced literature was part of the new wave of nation-building taking place in central Europe even before the final collapse of the Austro-Hungarian Empire at the end of the First World War. Some of the most popular writers in peripheral countries were even translated into English or French, as was the case with the prolific Bulgarian novelist Ivan Vazov, whose *Under the Yoke* (1893) appeared in English in 1912. But the obstacles were formidable.

What happened in a culturally peripheral area of Europe, with a relatively small linguistic base, with no significant written literature and no important indigenous aristocracy? What happened in nineteenth-century Transylvania? At the time it was a part of the Austro-Hungarian Empire (it became a part of Romania in December 1918). The linguistic fragmentation of the region was significant: even as late as 1930 Romanian was the language of only one-third of the urban population, which in turn was only 17.4 per cent of the Transylvanian population.[41] A minority spoke Hungarian. Most of the population spoke their local dialect. The majority subscribed to the Orthodox Church, whose language was Slavic while Romanian is a Latin language. And while the region was clearly in the German cultural area, many local intellectuals were more influenced by French culture.

By the end of the nineteenth century, along with Dumas, Dickens and Scott, the writer most translated into Romanian was the Swiss novelist Heinrich Zschokke.[42] Zschokke was not a contemporary: he was born in 1771 and died in 1842. Most histories of German literature devote one paragraph to him, if that. He wrote historical novels *à la* Walter Scott, banditry novels – such as his best-known work, *Aballino, der grosse Bandit* (1794) – and Gothic-style novels such as the posthumously published *Das Abenteuer einer Neujahrsnacht* (The Adventure of New Year's Eve, 1856–59). Their translation and serialisation in the Romanian press was not aimed at the Transylvanian intellectual élites who could read mainstream European literature in the original, but at a new expanding reading public who knew only Romanian. These had been weaned onto books not by foreign classics (Rousseau's *La*

Nouvelle Héloïse, translated in 1837, and *Don Quixote*, in 1840) but by French 'sensational' novels, like those of Xavier de Montépin, Alexandre Dumas, Paul Féval, Ponson du Terrail and Eugène Sue.[43]

In the 1870s only twelve novels were serialised in the Transylvanian press, eighteen in the 1880s, and thirty in the 1890s. Of the 107 novels serialised between 1839 and 1918, forty were French; Britain, Germany and Russia followed with fourteen or fifteen each. The most translated author was Jules Verne (five), followed by Conan Doyle (four) and Karl May.[44] In the same period forty-nine Romanian novels (three by women) were also serialised, all but one by Transylvanian writers such as Ioan Slavici (1848–1925), Ioan C. Drăgescu (1844–1915), the author of *Nopţile carpatine* (Nights on the Carpathians, 1867), and Iosif Vulcan (1841–1907), who wrote *Ranele Naţiunii* (The Plagues of the Nation, 1876). Thus the growth of foreign translations did not appear to harm domestic expansion, both trends being a response to the growth of a reading public. The role played by the press was determinant. Dailies such as *Tribuna*, published in Sibiu and edited from 1884 by novelist Ioan Slavici, with a circulation of 3,000 copies a day (the highest in the region), promoted Hugo, Dumas, Anatole France, Bulwer-Lytton, Conan Doyle and many others, including Italians such as Fogazzaro, D'Annunzio, Silvio Pellico and Manzoni, and Americans such as Lew Wallace (the author of *Ben Hur: A Tale of the Christ*, 1880).[45]

Hungary too, more prosperous than Transylvania, and after 1867 a co-partner in the Austro-Hungarian Empire, did not possess a major literary language. Native Hungarians were barely a majority within their own kingdom, which also included large minorities of Slovaks, Romanians and Serbs. Budapest, the result of the union of Buda, Pest and Obuda in 1873, was mainly German-speaking. The drive to Magyarisation occurred in a nation whose many cultural producers, whether composers or writers, did not speak Hungarian. The Jews (prevalently German- and Yiddish-speakers), as we have seen, a strong cultural presence, were keen on integration and responded with some enthusiasm to Magyarisation, which included the modernising of Hungarian – a language not yet codified.[46] Jews who wanted to resist integration maintained or created their own literature and newspapers in German or Yiddish – some Jewish newspapers had existed since 1837, such as the weekly *Allgemeine Zeitung des Judenthums*, founded by Rabbi Ludwig Philippson of Magdeburg. Others followed, but like other 'community' or 'ideological' journals (Christian, socialist, etc.) they needed to attract a wider readership than those already committed. So they serialised fiction to entice new readers. They would have liked to publish 'Jewish' novels, but ended up imitating successful German family journals like *Gartenlaube* and rewriting novels such as those of E. Marlitt, the leading author of female romances in Germany in the 1870s and 1880s (see page 348). They kept the plots while changing the stereotypes: the villains were usually anti-Semitic aristocrats or Catholic priests and religious fanatics who kidnapped Jewish children to turn them into Christians.[47]

In much of central and southern Europe nationalists were often middle-class intellectuals who regarded the absence of a national literature as a handicap to the formation of a national identity. In Bohemia, for instance, there was a thriving theatrical life, with some five hundred amateur theatrical companies operating in Prague.[48] Much of their production, however, was in German – reflecting also the size of the German-speaking community in Prague. In such circumstances the building of a National Czech Theatre, where plays would be performed in Czech, was regarded as an important political question. In 1868 the foundation stone for the new theatre was laid in a ceremony attended by 80,000 people. The theatre was inaugurated in 1881, with a dedication aimed not at a ruler or a divinity, but 'To Ourselves'. Destroyed by fire almost at once, it had been entirely rebuilt by 1883. Finally the German theatre faced competition. By then, of course, the German population of Prague, Catholic, Protestant and Jewish, was declining, while Czech nationalists gloated at the prospect of a 'Slavic sea' engulfing the German presence.[49]

Such processes of imitation and cross-fertilisation were taking place throughout Europe, leading towards a more uniform culture. Nationalism in literature went hand in hand with the absorption of foreign products. In Hungary, for instance, the period 1905–19, regarded as a literary golden age, was also one of continuing penetration by foreign writers. The literary modernist monthly *Nyugat* (West) – one of fifty-nine Hungarian literary magazines – published, before 1919, fifty-six translations from the French and 137 articles on French literature, and thirty-one translations from English as well as eleven translations from German and fifty-four articles on German literature.[50]

The development of local talents in the face of cultural imports occurred also in other laggard countries such as Italy and Spain. Spain's backwardness was reflected by its low levels of urbanisation and of literacy (in 1900 just over half the men and 22 per cent of women were literate). Yet in the second half of the nineteenth century, reading serialised novels or *folletíns.*

had become a popular pastime. By 1868 perhaps as many as a million people were reading them. Urbanisation must have helped: in 1840 Madrid was a town of 160,000 inhabitants – about the same size as Rome. By 1885 it had reached 400,000 inhabitants. But a provincial city like Valladolid, a former capital of Spain, did not have a bookshop in 1900, though the newsagent in Plaza Mayor, the 'Centro de periódicos', also sold cheap novels.[51] The magazine *El Cuento semanal*, almost entirely dedicated to fiction, reached in 1907– 12 a print run of 60,000.[52] An analysis of books published in 1915–34 showed, however, that the authors most frequently published were foreign. Local best-sellers emerged strongly only after the First World War.[53]

When, at the beginning of the century, the publishers Sopena launched their low-priced Biblioteca de Grandes Novelas with a list consisting of the 250 'best' novels, there were hardly any Spanish names on it. It was a roll call of the usual names: Sue (still the most widely read author in Spain until the 1920s), Dumas, Ponson du Terrail, Hugo, Sienkiewicz, Bulwer-Lytton, Dickens, Manzoni, Scott, Tolstoy, Poe, Defoe, Balzac, etc.[54] But reading foreign novels encouraged the Spaniards to write their own. The prolific Benito Pérez Galdós (1843–1920), one of Spain's major authors and the leading exponent of naturalism, could sell as many as 150,000 copies of his books, an extraordinary achievement given the limitations of the Spanish market.[55] A reason for his success is that even his most literary novels owed a considerable debt to the downmarket '*novela por entregas*'.[56] Another was the existence of the Latin American market, which helped Spanish writers to maintain their market share even in the 1920s, when they faced a new flood of translations.[57] Elsewhere, most Spanish writers remained barely known.

Spain, of course, like Italy, was a popular setting for novels, operas and music throughout the nineteenth century and much of the twentieth. A certain (foreign) idea of Spain emerged: seductive Gypsies, hot-blooded males, haughty noblemen, bullfighting, an over-sensitive concept of honour, and a particular kind of music (the Andalusian *flamenco*). These images were largely the work of non-Spaniards: Prosper Mérimée's *Carmen* (1846) and Bizet's opera (1875), Ravel's Rhapsodie Espagnole (1908), the writings of Théophile Gautier, Victor Hugo and, much later, Ernest Hemingway (*Death in the Afternoon*, 1932). The Spaniards themselves cooperated by developing a native genre, the bullfighting novel, popular in Spain in the decades between 1870 and 1920. Some – like *Sangre y arena* (Blood and Sand, 1908) by Vicente Blasco Inbañez – became known abroad probably because they conformed .to the received view.[58]

Some countries underwent in a few years the kind of literary development which had taken others much longer – the typical fate of the laggard catching up. Portugal had a relatively important literature in the sixteenth century, including Luís Vaz Camões (c.1524–80), author of the great epic *Os Lusíadas* (1572), but it had little influence in the rest of Europe. Romantic populism almost bypassed the country, though by the end of the nineteenth century folk literature was revisited in literary-historical magazines like *Revista Lusitana* (1887).[59] The popularity of foreign novels, especially Zola's, encouraged the development of Portuguese naturalism, notably in the works of José Maria de Eça de Queirós, who lived abroad for most of his adult life, and in Paris from 1888 to his death in 1900, whose principal works, *O Crime do Padre Amaro* (The Sin of Father Amaro, 1875) and *Os Maias* (1888), were inspired by the principles of the realist novel then triumphant throughout Europe. And beyond: Western literature reached Korea via China and Japan towards the end of the nineteenth century, and the first Korean novels – a low genre written in demotic or spoken language – were produced shortly afterwards.[60]

The age of nationalism produced a cosmopolitanism among the middle classes, who showed a growing interest in other countries, an interest constantly nurtured by the proliferation of magazines and journals that kept them informed about what was going on abroad, and by political events, such as the scramble over colonies, which captured the imaginations of Europeans. Nor should one ignore the role of influential critics. In France, for instance, the Vicomte Eugène-Melchior de Vogüé contributed more than anyone to the renown of Russian novels. In a series of articles in the *Revue des deux mondes* published between 1883 and 1886 (collected in 1886 in the volume *Le Roman Russe*) he extolled Tolstoy, Dostoevsky and Turgenev, discovering in them a European spirit. In 1883 there were two or three French translations from Russian, eight in 1884, and twenty-five in 1888.[61] Vogüé was by no means uncritical: he dismissed Dostoevsky's *The Idiot* and *The Brothers Karamazov* ('intolerably dull', 'few Russians have had the courage to read to the end this interminable tale'[62]). Yet he did have an impact. *War and Peace* had come out in French in 1879. Five years later it had sold only five hundred copies. At the beginning of 1886, de Vogüé's *Le Roman Russe* came out. By the end of the year *War and Peace* was being reprinted, and thereafter new impressions came out almost every year. Its success led to further translations of Tolstoy's works: seven in 1887, and eight in 1890. Publishers started chasing the other Russian authors mentioned by Vogüé.[63]

By making the Russians known in France, de Vogüé made them known elsewhere, for France still acted as an exploratory agent on behalf of European literary culture. Thus Tolstoy's *Anna Karenina* appeared in Italian in 1886, the same year as in France, but translated from French and with the same Frenchified title: *Anna Karenine*; *War and Peace* was also translated into Italian from French, with the French introduction by de Vogüé.[64]

Inevitably there was a backlash. In 1894 Jules Lemaître, writing, like de Vogüé, in the *Revue des deux mondes*, warned his readers that in philosophy and literature 'our competitors' were advancing slowly but surely, while 'we follow behind, at times successfully, but to follow is not to lead'. 'Twelve years ago', he continued, 'there emerged the cult of the 'now forgotten' George Eliot, 'regarded as superior to the French realist school'. Yet, he exclaimed, anything one can find in George Eliot can be found in George Sand, and anything Dostoevsky expresses was expressed by Zola and Flaubert. And now, he added, one had to brace oneself for Ibsen and Bjørnson from Norway, Gerhart Hauptmann from Germany, and Strindberg from Sweden. Lemaître's conclusion was disconsolate: '*Les idées générales qui transforment l'Europe ne sortent plus de l'âme française*' (The general ideas that change Europe no longer emerge from the spirit of France).[65]

He was not entirely wrong. The real beginnings of modern Scandinavian literature occurred in the last twenty years of the nineteenth century.[66] One hundred years later extra-European literature, often written in one of the main European languages, would make the same inroads into the literary canon. The laggards were striking back.

De Vogüé had also championed Scandinavian writers in 1890, but it is reasonable to assume that Ibsen (like Tolstoy) would have become famous anyway – not least because he had champions elsewhere, notably a remarkable publicist like George Bernard Shaw. Nor was Ibsen a solitary case. Until the 1880s Hans Christian Andersen was the only Scandinavian writer who had managed to achieve popularity outside his linguistic area. Then, in 1888, a long extract from the novel *Hunger* by the Norwegian Knut Hamsun was published in the journal *Ny Jord* (New Earth). It caused a sensation, first in Norway and Denmark, then elsewhere in Europe, and in 1920 he obtained the Nobel Prize, the second Norwegian to do so (the first was the playwright Bjørnstjerne Bjørnson in 1903).

And Italy?

Russia was regarded by advanced European opinion as the seat of Oriental despotism and absolutist rule. This did not stop anyone from admiring Russian writers, many of whom became revered classics. What of Italy? Its history and culture were well known. Its struggle for independence and unification had elicited the sympathies of progressive people everywhere. Yet Italy exported few novels or plays. The more popular end of the Italian market was dominated by foreign popular narrative. Italians read Nick Carter and Nat Pinkerton, Gaston Leroux (the author of *The Phantom of the Opera*) and the stories of Arsène Lupin. The Milan publisher Edoardo Sonzogno continued to publish all the standard French popular novels.[67] In the important middle market, however, the other major Milan publisher, Treves, was signing up many Italian writers: Giovanni Verga, Grazia Deledda, Edmondo De Amicis, Luciano Zuccoli, Luigi Capuana, Gabriele D'Annunzio, Matilde Serao, Arturo Graf, Arrigo Boito, Paolo Mantegazza, etc.[68] Sales were still fairly low, but reasonably successful Italian writers were able to sell 20,000 copies or so.[69]

In the last decade of the century Italian critics were obsessed by what they called 'the crisis of the book' (this is a current *leitmotif* everywhere). The word 'crisis' recurred constantly in a book of interviews with leading literary figures, *Alla Scoperta dei letterati* (1895), edited by Ugo Ojetti (who eventually became a fascist). There was, they said, a crisis of culture, a literary crisis; there were no readers of average culture, no structures for a proper publishing industry, and men of letters felt isolated. Yet the production of novels in Italy was increasing. There were 251 novels published in 1894, 308 in 1898, 362 in 1905, and 411 in 1909.[70]

The preponderance of foreign novelists, however, remained a constant in Italian publishing. Treves's 1903 catalogue lists 657 novels, of which only ninety or so were by Italians. Of these, half were by a single writer, Anton Giulio Barrili (1836–1908).[71] Needless to say, not one of Barrili's books was translated into French or English, nor are any of his novels in print in Italy now. Nevertheless, at the time he was one of Italy's best-loved novelists, especially by women readers, who liked his gentle love stories and his easy-going style.

The Italian market was becoming increasingly segmented, a sign of expansion. Italian women read foreign popular literature and its Italian imitators such as Carolina Invernizio, the men nearly exclusively Italian middlebrow *feuilletons* (De Amicis, Serao, Fogazzaro). Socialists read Zola, Hugo and Tolstoy. Domestic servants – according to a 1906 source – read 'pornography', presumably romances of adultery and novels whose cover illustration and title suggested more sexual content than was actually delivered: for instance *Infedeltà* (1884) by the highly respectable Enrico Panzacchi (1840–1904), or D'Annunzio's *Le vergini delle rocce*.[72] Italian writers themselves, whether popular or 'literary', had in turn been raised on a diet of foreign novels. Carolina Invernizio, for example, mentioned Dumas, Ponson du Terrail and Walter Scott as having constituted her early reading experiences.[73]

British and French novelists never discussed which foreign models to imitate or avoid, but any debate on the state of Italian literature turned on the question of which foreign model was more appropriate to Italy. Should it be Scott and Dickens, or Zola? Should Italians be alarmed by the success of French popular novels? Was Luigi Capuana (1839–1915) the Italian Zola, or was it Verga?[74] Above all, why were Italian writers not known abroad?

Antonio Fogazzaro (1842–1911), for instance, was one of the best-known Italian novelists of his day, author of novels in which a great passion is usually resolved by painful renunciation (usually by the woman). His masterpiece, *Piccolo mondo antico* (1895), sold 60,000 copies between 1896 and 1918, and another 80,000 between 1918 and 1943.[75] It was translated into several languages, but outside Italy it quickly sank without a trace. It narrates the story of Franco and Luisa in the years leading to Italian unification. They marry against the will of Franco's rich (and pro-Austrian) grandmother. Their daughter drowns. Luisa reacts by becoming an embittered woman, while Franco turns to Christianity and patriotism. The grandmother regrets her intransigence on her deathbed.[76]

Matilde Serao (1857–1927), born in Greece but raised in Naples, published her first novel very young, in 1881. In 1885 she married Edoardo Scarfoglio, a right-wing journalist. The couple started a newspaper, the precursor of *Il Mattino*, still Naples's leading daily paper. Serao eventually parted ideological company with her husband – she was closer to the socialism of Naples's famous popular writer Mastriani (see pages 380, 486, 612). Her anti-fascist novel *Mors tua . . .* (1926) probably cost her the Nobel Prize (it went, unexpectedly, to Grazia Deledda). Between 1905 and 1927 she was a fashionable writer, read by aristocratic ladies as well as by their maids.[77]

Matilde Serao's female characters live according to the subordinate conception of women prevailing at the time. They come in two sorts: those with passions who sacrifice all for love, and the humiliated ones who accept their martyrdom.[78] Either way, it's grim for them. In some cases Serao's women are simply not brave enough – greater failures than Madame Bovary. For instance, the eponymous heroine of *La Virtù di Checchina*, serialised in *La Domenica del corriere* (1883) and published in 1884, would like to give herself to an aristocrat who desires her. Her husband is a rather one-dimensional character, a miser who snores in bed, and evidently deserves to be cuckolded. But Checchina never gets up her courage. Something goes wrong every time: she forgets her umbrella, is afraid to be seen by the concierge, etc. Her virtue is not really a question of high principles: she is a failed adulteress. What makes the novel distinctly Italian is the author's effort to reproduce dialect, but Italianising it (as Verga had been doing for Sicilian), thus creating a language no one speaks – something for which she was lambasted by critics such as her ex-husband, which compelled her to abandon dialect altogether in later editions.

There was, of course, the enduring problem of the Italian language then not being commonly used even by the middle classes. Realism dictated that 'proper' Italian should not be used in what was marketed as a regional novel; but had dialect been used, few readers would be able to understand it. If a novelist had everyone in Naples speak in proper Italian, it would not be credible, as few people spoke Italian then. So some kind of hybrid had to be devised, a problem the Italian cinema industry resolved after the Second World War by having characters speak in Italian but with a heavy regional accent (usually Roman or Neapolitan).[79]

Though relatively unknown abroad, Matilde Serao was widely read in Italy, particularly by women conscious, as was the author, of their condition of subjection. As Serao herself wrote: 'I know, as many women know, that under our present laws women cannot find happiness, not in marriage, not in free love, not in illicit love.'[80] Mr Right does not exist. Women's sentimental hearts are the cause of their ruin. Those who let themselves be seduced do so not out of sexual need but because they desire to be loved, and are then plagued by remorse to their dying day.[81]

Far more stereotypical were the female characters of another successful Italian writer of the time, Carolina Invernizio (1858–1916), author of some 130 novels, mostly serialised in *La Gazzetta di Torino* and *L'Opinione nazionale*. The target readership was overtly feminine – in the introduction to her best-known novel, *Il Bacio di una morta* (1889), she addresses herself to '*le mie lettrici*' (my women readers). Invernizio knew the trade. In interviews granted in 1904 and 1912 she explained that a good title was half the reason behind the success of a popular novel. She culled her plots from crime reports, and could write a novel in a week once the crucial opening chapter was out of the way.[82] Bad and good characters were immediately identified by their names: the bad ones are called Nara (Nera), Sultana or Nigra and are usually brunettes, while the good ones are blonde, aristocratic, and called Chiara, Lilina or Aurora.[83] The male characters are ordinary men entangled in a world they can barely understand. Then the women come to the rescue, re-establish things as they were or should have been, and save the family.[84] Women learn how to carve a space for themselves in a man's world. Their solidarity cuts across classes – hence the supportive relationship between ladies and their maids.[85] *Il Bacio di una morta* is typical: Nara (who is black), a ballerina from Java, seduces Guido away from his bride-to-be Clara (who is very white – her skin is ivory, etc. – and unlike Nara she is always good to her servants). Nara convinces Guido that Clara has a lover, and persuades him to try to kill her. When the truth is revealed, Nara goes mad, and eventually kills herself in the lunatic asylum to which she is sent. Evil has been vanquished, and Guido and Clara can now marry. Guido, who after all had attempted to kill Clara, is forgiven by all and sundry. The fault was entirely that of Nara, the seductress. Men can hardly be expected to resist lust and jealousy.[86] Invernizio never made the literary canon. And though her name is regularly used in Italy as a pejorative designation for cheap literature, many of her novels are still in print there. Her fame, such as it was, remained almost completely limited to Italy and Italian-speakers. *Il Bacio di una morta* was translated into Portuguese (*O Beijo da morta*), and there is a Maltese translation of *La Figlia della portinaia* (*It Tifla tal purtinara*, 1982), but there is nothing of her works in French or English.

Three Italian authors did make it to the wider international scene. One was Carlo Collodi, author of the still-famous *Pinocchio* (see pages 702–3). Another was Edmondo De Amicis (1846–1908), author of *Cuore* (see pages 852–3). The third was Gabriele D'Annunzio (1863–1938), who by the turn of the century had become the contemporary Italian writer with the widest international renown – mainly thanks to novels such as *Il Piacere* and *L'Innocente*, both immediately translated into French, rather than to his poetry.[87] Unlike the authors of *Pinocchio* and *Cuore*, D'Annunzio aimed at the higher reaches of the cultural world. To some extent he succeeded. In 1895 an enthusiastic essay in the *Revue des deux mondes* by Eugène-Melchior de Vogüé, the champion of Russian writers, hailed him as one of the pioneers of a new Latin Renaissance.[88] In 1893 Hugo von Hofmannsthal called him one of the most original writers in Italy,[89] D'Annunzio had thus obtained the all-important foreign acclaim, a necessary condition of his pre-eminence in Italy.

To enhance his popularity this poet, dramatist, novelist and essayist used all the available techniques of image-making – even as a teenager he had faked his own death to attract attention to his first verses.[90] D'Annunzio played the role he was assigned, by adopting a grand 'Renaissance' lifestyle.[91] His Renaissance, it must be said, owed more to Ruskin and Pater than to the stodgy output of the Italian academy. He ensured that his life, his habits and the home he had decorated were constantly photographed, and became part of the presentation of the author to his public.[92] He deliberately created a new style of writing, borrowing outside the Italian tradition from Baudelaire, Swinburne and Gautier, with their love of androgyny, sado-masochism, decay, lust, blood, the Orient, antiquity. His philosophy was part Nietzsche, part Oscar Wilde. Yet the form of his poetry, with its uncommon effervescence, its baroque opulence of words, its extraordinary musicality, its astonishing command of the language, was utterly original. In 1895 Giovanni Pascoli, now regarded as the leading Italian poet of his day but then still up-and-coming, hailed D'Annunzio as 'il primo poeta d'Italia', adding 'few abroad are as good as he is'.[93]

D'Annunzio's technical virtuosity turned out to be highly marketable in a country desperate for a modern writer to counterpoise the French and the British, the Germans and the Russians. In his ambition to produce a language for a linguistically fragmented country, he followed in the footsteps of every major Italian writer, from Dante to Manzoni.[94] This could be done, he claimed, by creating a new style, but Italian prose was still in its infancy. It was necessary to study it, and above all to master it, eschewing everyday Italian and the realism of Zola and his followers.[95]

It may appear that D'Annunzio's use of a 'high' style was simply a further example of the élitism of Italian men of letters, typical of a country with a pronounced tendency towards a sharp distinction between the languages of the élite and of the masses. In reality D'Annunzio's novels and plays, once stripped of their linguistic devices, were fairly ordinary melodramas which could appeal to the emerging middle-class audiences. One of his themes, that rules and laws are for inferior beings, while the superior person rises above them, was a standard *topos* of the *fin-de-siècle*, and could be found equally in Carolina Invernizio.[96] But D'Annunzio's stylistic complications had the function of embellishing the contents of his work, reassuring consumers that they were being provided with high culture. D'Annunzio himself, noting the growth of mass literature, recognised that 'the subtle and perverse novel of passion that a lady savours voluptuously and slowly in the melancholy of her salon' had something in common with 'the bloody adventure novel that the plebeian woman devours sitting in her shop' – both fulfilled the same desire to dream and to transcend the narrowness of common life.[97]

Other Italian writers followed D'Annunzio's lead, and learned from him the art of creating an aura of excitement around themselves. Guido da Verona (1881–1939), a writer of Jewish origins who added the 'da' to his surname for aristocratic effect, ensured that his fast living, his cars, horses and women, would get him talked about in fashionable magazines. He became a fascist early on, but the frequent accusation of being a 'pornographer' led the regime to distance itself from him well before his Jewishness came to be regarded as a handicap. His great success, *Mimí Bluette, fiore del mio giardino* (1916), sold 300,000 copies between 1916 and the early 1920s.[98] What was appealing in works such as these was the aura of subversiveness. Many God-fearing bourgeois probably felt that reading Guido da Verona made them less boring and more a 'man of the world' like the author. Thus, in *Mimí Bluette*, Cecilia's loss of virginity is described not in shocked tones but as something which, eventually, is bound to happen to most virgins.[99]

The best craftsmen were amply repaid with appropriate contemporary fame, though unlike D'Annunzio, they never made the canon. Their protagonists are usually aristocrats who have the (literary) advantage of not having to work, and are thus available for great passions. The descriptions of luxurious homes, elegant clothes, travel in *wagons lits* (then regarded as the height of luxury) and other upper-class habits appealed to middle- and lower-middle-class readers.

Another great specialist in this genre was Luciano Zuccoli (born Luciano von Ingenheim, 1868–1929), author of best-sellers such as *I Lussuriosi* (1893), *Il Designato* (1894), *Roberta* (1897) and *La Divina fanciulla*. In 1923 an eminent critic like Luigi Russo held him in high regard. Today he is virtually unknown. Here is a taste of *La Divina fanciulla*, published in 1920. The protagonist is Manoela, an amoral woman of the lower classes (like Zola's *Nana*), After being raped at the age of fifteen by Michele Barra, the cousin of Duke Dani di Bagnasco, she is forced into a whorehouse. The Duke, unaware of her past, becomes her lover. When the jealous Duke finds out about Manoela's past, he decides to avenge his honour (not hers). He persuades Manoela to try to seduce Michele without sleeping with him. Unfortunately she cannot resist Michele, and ends up running away to London, where she becomes the mistress of a Lord before being killed by a casual lover she has picked up – like Wedekind's Lulu (*Pandora's Box*, 1902), who is killed by Jack the Ripper. The Duke, unable to find her, turns to drugs, loses his mind and dies insane in an asylum.[100] Death remains the usual fate of 'subversive' (i.e. unconventional and immoral) women. As Gramsci noted, only in the comic sketch can a woman be a liberated *cocotte* and get away with it.[101]

French Fears

It is around this period that the fear of losing cultural hegemony began to haunt the French intelligentsia. Surveys of writers in literary magazines such as the *Revue blanche* (in 1897) and the *Mercure de France* (in 1902) seem to confirm this. Few writers take an overtly nationalist position, but most manifest anti-German feelings for obvious political reasons, rather than aesthetic ones. French novelists had no doubt that 'their' novels were superior, but they were ready to recognise the greater importance of recent German contributions to philosophy and social theory.[102] Such literary anxieties did not perturb the British, for whom hegemony was much more bound up with the fact of Empire and worldwide military supremacy than with culture. For the British the closing decades of the nineteenth century were years of unparalleled national confidence which could hardly be threatened by the appearance of a few foreign novels.

Everywhere, even in France, those responsible for the spread of foreign novels were the publishers themselves. They were, after all, in the business of selling books. From a business point of view, the main problem with a foreign book is that it has to be translated and therefore has a higher cost. For most of the nineteenth century Hachette, which had opened a bookshop in London's King William Street near Charing Cross Road as early as 1859, translated mainly English novels and continued to do so into the 1890s, because these were, by and large, the kind of foreign novels the French seemed to prefer, and because it was easy to find translators. But Hachette was quick to realise that publishing was changing, and started translating novels from other countries such as Fogazzaro's *Piccolo mondo antico* and the Hungarian Mór Jókai's *Az új földesúr* (1862) – as *Le Nouveau seigneur* (The New Landlord) in 1910; it was never translated into English. Hachette was also the first to publish Tolstoy in France.[103]

The French were also beginning to learn from abroad, particularly from their great enemies the Germans. Louis Hachette, grandson of the founder of what was still the largest publisher in France, speaking to the French Publishers' Association in 1917, analysed the growing German influence in French publishing.[104] Though a ferocious real war was going on, Hachette's speech showed no bellicose feelings. He was a businessman speaking to colleagues, not an ideologue rousing a mob. The central part of his speech analysed the nerve centre of the German book trade, the Leipzig book association or *Börsenverein*. 'For us publishers', explained Hachette, Leipzig, the capital of the book, had become a real obsession. An efficient railway system and an ideal geographical position 'at the heart of Germany like a spider in the middle of its web' had enabled Leipzig to dethrone Frankfurt. Every book in Germany had to go through the Leipzig distribution system. Its influence extended into Scandinavia, Russia (where one and half million people spoke German) and German Switzerland. Germany had also the advantage of the growing number of German-speakers in the USA (two million in 1870, and nine million in 1910), Argentina, Brazil and elsewhere.[105]

The French did not possess a distribution system on a par with that of Leipzig. Almost all the publishers were in Paris, whereas in Germany they were scattered throughout the main cities. This is why the Germans have always had to rely on distributors, who act like bankers, settling the accounts once a year at Easter during the Leipzig Book Fair. Bookshops were encouraged to hold stocks of books by being able to return them if unsold (the system known as *a conditione*). A bookseller in Hamburg (one of the 12,394 members of the booksellers' federation) did not have to send the various orders from his customers to dozens of different publishers. He sent a single order to Leipzig, and a single consignment was sent to him at great speed by rail. Years later Stanley Unwin, President of the British Publishers' Association (1933–35), was still extolling the Leipzig system as 'the greatest achievement in book distribution there has ever been . . . the whole mechanism moved with the precision of a well-oiled clock'.[106]

The Leipzig book trade did not survive Nazism and the subsequent destruction of the city during the war, not to speak of the fifty years under communism. This turned out to be Frankfurt's gain – the new host of the *Börsenverein* and, eventually, of the international book fair. But before the First World War, at the time Hachette was speaking, the large Leipzig distributors like Volckmar held enormous stocks: its warehouses stored some thirty million volumes; its catalogue, sent for free to 30,000 bookshops throughout Germany, had 1,500 pages.[107]

French influence, however, remained strong. The ability of some French novelists to shape the taste of new generations of readers continued to make itself manifest throughout the nineteenth century, until its close. The torch that had been held by Balzac, Dumas, Hugo and Verne was passed to Zola – perhaps the last of the great French popular writers. He epitomised the new generation of professional writers, aware of the market and unashamed of their role in it while at the same time pursuing critical prestige. His influence outside France was greater than that of other writers of his time. He also carved out a new role, in which French writers excelled, that of the public intellectual who uses the cultural capital accumulated in the pursuit of a particular cause not as part of a movement or a party, but as an autonomous force in the new field of democratic politics. So it is to Zola that we now turn.

33

Zola: Money, Fame and Conscience

Modernity

ZOLA WAS self-consciously modern:

> Je crois à mon siècle, de toute ma tendresse moderne. Seuls, les croyants
> sont forts. Quiconque, en politique et en littérature, ne croit pas à son
> temps, tombe dans l'erreur et l'impuissance. (I believe in my century,
> with all my modern affection. Only those who believe have strength.
> Those who have no faith in their age, be it in literature or in politics, will
> lose their way and their capability).[1]

He produced novels which relied on a formula of high enough quality to
obtain great literary prestige, while being eminently marketable. By insisting
that he was merely the exponent of a school, and not a lone operator, he
gave a feeling of identity and community to a generation of writers with few
traits in common. Their task, he explained, was to create a new kind of novel
which he called 'experimental' or realist or naturalist.

At Hachette, where he worked for four years, Zola had learned much
about publishing. From childhood he had immersed himself in popular
literature, and above all in Balzac, from whom he borrowed the idea of a
cycle of novels with reappearing characters. The public liked these long sagas,
and they assured the publisher a loyal market and the author a regular
remuneration. But first one needed to become established. Zola's first success,
Thérèse Raquin (1867), a lurid story of sexual passion and murder, made him
famous. As early as 1868 he had planned to depict the four modern 'worlds'
of society: the lower classes, the world of business and commerce, the world
of the bourgeoisie and the grand world of the ruling classes. Then there was
also '*un monde à part*', the underworld of whores, murderers and artists.[2] All
these worlds were to be explored over more than two decades in the twenty

novels, exploring the changing fortunes over several generations of two branches of a family, that eventually made up Zola's Rougon-Macquart series.

Inseparable from Zola's plan was his conception of the modern writer as a well-paid professional. Of course, as we have seen, many writers, such as Dickens and Trollope, were perfectly aware that they were operating in a market, and that social prestige and financial reward were closely connected. But neither made grand claims for himself. They thought that payment was the just reward for a job well done. Zola, however, regarded the rise of the novelist as a professional as part of a new stage in literary history. In an article first published in March 1880 in the St Petersburg-based *Vestnik Evropy* (The Messenger of Europe) he criticised those who accused writers of debasing themselves by becoming merchants of their works. Times had changed, he claimed; the world that the critics of the past (Sainte-Beuve) had defended with passion was no more. The old world was one in which the man of letters was supposed to be an erudite figure bound to his desk, where literature was the leisure activity of a small section of society, where money did not seem to matter, and where books were expensive and read only by the few. Sainte-Beuve's world was one in which writers were a luxury for aristocrats, who granted them pensions and patronage. But now, Zola continued, the aristocracy was no more, and the writer wrote for a public, a market.[3] He underlined the financial success of Victor Hugo and George Sand, hailed Balzac as a '*véritable industriel*', and had words of praise for popular writers like Ponson du Terrail, who had no great literary merit, but who worked hard and kept an entire network of publishers, printers and booksellers afloat.[4]

The status of Zola as a professional writer was confirmed by the contract the publisher Lacroix offered him in 1869. As an employee at Hachette he had earned one hundred francs a month in 1862, and two hundred in 1866. As a writer Zola was to be paid a 'salary' of five hundred francs a month, in exchange for two novels a year.[5] At the time the salary of a teacher was fifty francs a month.

Zola was an indefatigable propagandist for the 'naturalist' school of fiction (a term he never adequately defined), discussing it with the same passion and the same sectarianism normally associated with political causes. He distinguished between two literary traditions, both revolutionary: the Romantic, in which he included Rousseau, Chateaubriand, Madame de Staël, Hugo and Sand; and the 'naturalist', which he traced back to Diderot, Stendhal, Balzac, Flaubert, the Goncourts and, by implication, himself.[6] Naturalism was 'the literature of the Republic'. Zola thus claimed an enormously inflated role for the writer. Not only was he to be a money-making professional, but he also incarnated the progress of society:

> A man is in his study, still, seated, for hours. Before him only pen, paper, and ink. There is complete silence. Nothing happens. But this man is Rabelais; this man is Molière; this man is Balzac. And beyond this apparent repose of the senses, a formidable activity takes place; one that changes the world, speeds up the centuries, makes humanity progress . . .[7]

Such a role, understandably enough, appealed to writers, particularly in countries still engaged in nation-building, which at the time included almost all European countries. Naturalism or realism spread in literary circles throughout the Continent. It suited the love affair with the 'scientific method' and the sway of positivism. The writer would describe the world as it really was, without prettifying it or sentimentalising it.

Money-Making

What made Zola famous, however, was not narrative methodology but his two 'scandalous' novels, *L'Assommoir* (1877) and its sequel *Nana* (1880). The first told the story of the degradation of Gervaise, in spite of her efforts to redeem herself through hard work as a laundress. Though Zola was committed to theories of dubious value emphasising the burden of inherited traits, the downfall of Gervaise was largely caused by bad luck, the brutality of her lover Étienne Làntier and the alcoholism of her husband Coupeau (itself the result not of some genetic mark, but of his despair at having become unemployable after a work accident). Particularly shocking to respectable opinion was the sordid *ménage à trois* which seems to arise almost naturally from the complex situation. Eventually Coupeau dies of alcoholism, Gervaise's daughter Anna (the later Nana) turns to prostitution and Gervaise, having taken to drink, dies of hunger. The sequel, *Nana*, takes up the story of Anna's rise as a high-class courtesan who corrupts the great and the good of the Second Empire before dying horrifically of smallpox as the Franco–Prussian war is breaking out – the end of an era.

L'Assommoir sold 40,000 copies in the year it was published, *Nana* 80,000, but *La Débâcle*, one of the last in the Rougon-Macquart cycle, outsold them all in Zola's lifetime: 100,000 copies were sold in four weeks, another 50,000 in the next four months, and a total of 176,000 in its first year of publication.[8] The setting was the Franco–Prussian War of 1870 and the Paris Commune of 1871. The protagonists are Jean and Maurice, two French soldiers, friends during the war but on opposing sides during the Commune. These events constituted, for the reading public of 1892, their most important common memory; the clever balancing act performed by the author ensured that *La Débâcle* could be read as a novel of national reconciliation rather than a partisan one. It closes with Jean, the survivor of the two, '*marchant à l'avenir, à la grande et rude besogne de toute une France à refaire*' (walking towards the future, towards a great and daunting task: rebuilding France).

Here are the publishing fortunes of Zola's Rougon-Macquart books:

TITLE	YEAR OF PUBLICATION	COPIES PRINTED BY 1893	COPIES PRINTED BY 1902
La Fortune des Rougon	1871	26,000	35,000
La Curée	1871	36,000	47,000
Le Ventre de Paris	1873	33,000	43,000
La Conquête de Plassans	1874	25,000	33,000
La Faute de l'Abbé Mouret	1875	44,000	52,000
Son Excellence Eugène Rougon	1876	26,000	32,000
L'Assomoir	1877	127,000	142,000
Une Page d'amour	1878	80,000	94,000
Nana	1880	166,000	193,000
Pot-Bouille	1882	82,000	92,000
Au Bonheur des dames	1883	62,000	72,000
La Joie de vivre	1884	48,000	54,000
Germinal	1885	88,000	110,000
L'Oeuvre	1886	55,000	60,000
La Terre	1887	100,000	129,000
Le Rêve	1888	88,000	110,000
La Bête humaine	1890	88,000	99,000
L'Argent	1891	83,000	86,000
La Débâcle	1892	176,000	202,000
Le Docteur Pascal	1893	66,000	90,000
TOTAL		1,499,000	1,775,000

SOURCE: Alain Pagés, 'L'expérience du livre. Zola et le commerce de la librairie', in Jean-Yves Mollier (ed.), *Le commerce de la librairie en France au XIXe siècle 1789–1914*, IMEC/Maison de l'Homme, Paris 1998, pp.427–35, p.434

But fashions change, and by 1927 *Nana* had moved into first place. By the end of 1972, in the paperback imprint Livre de Poche, *Germinal* came first with 1.1 million, followed by *L'Assommoir* (805,000), *Thérèse Raquin* (729,000), *La Bête humaine* (668,000) and *Le Rêve* (607,000). *Nana* was sixth, with almost 600,000.[9] As with other classics, sales are primarily influenced by the educational authorities who determine the adoption of books in schools and universities.

The sales figures of Zola's books have to be put in perspective. According to a contemporary source, 90 per cent of French novels at this period sold about five hundred copies, barely enough to cover costs. Selling 1,500 copies constituted a reasonable success. Pierre Louÿs's *Aphrodite* (1896), which was regarded as a best-seller and the publication of which had been preceded by a serialisation, was printed in no more than 3–4,000 copies.[10]

More money could be made from plays than from novels. Accordingly almost all of Zola's books were turned into plays. Most of these, however, were unsuccessful. There were exceptions, such as *L'Assommoir*, which had three hundred performances after it opened at the Théâtre de l'Ambigu in 1879. Its success was due not only to the scandal surrounding the novel, but also to the ability of the playwright, William Busnach, a talented hack highly skilled in turning popular novels into plays.[11] The play *L'Assommoir* inspired all kinds of satires. The characters were mimed by clowns at the Cirque d'Hiver, and there was a nightclub where patrons were supposed to turn up dressed like its characters.[12] Almost as successful was the English version, renamed *Drink* and adapted for the London stage by Charles Reade. *L'Assommoir* was also adapted in 1909 by Pathé as a single-reel 'art film'.

Turning a book into a play is not easy, and to be successful an adaptation must 'betray' its source, as subsequent cinematic adaptations of literary masterpieces have confirmed. *Nana* was not a critical success on the stage. It opened on 29 January 1881 at 7.30 p.m. Because its nine scenes required complex and lengthy changes it did not end until two in the morning. The audience was sleepy and disappointed: they had been given an expurgated version, without any of the violent sexuality of the book. *Nana* the play made 400,000 francs, 200,000 less than *L'Assommoir*.[13]

Plays were not only more remunerative than novels, they also attracted more attention, not always welcome. *Germinal*, which had sold 88,000 copies in its first eight years, far fewer than *Nana*, provoked no political reaction until Zola adapted it for the stage. William Busnach, his co-writer, urged him to delete a scene in which gendarmes attack the strikers: 'They would never allow such a raw portrayal of civil war,' he wrote. Zola ignored him. Yet Busnach was right. In October 1885 the government forced the Théâtre du Châtelet to drop *Germinal* even though, at the last minute, Zola had agreed to remove the notorious gendarmes.[14] What was on the stage always encountered more obstacles than what was on the page. In France it was usually politics which offended the censorious. In England it tended to be sex; thus when the Independent Theatre Company of J.T. Grein staged Zola's adaptation of *Thérèse Raquin* at the Royalty Theatre in London in 1891, the play dismayed most of the critics, who were alarmed at the coarse depiction of human deprivation – roughly what the French press had said eighteen years previously when the play was first staged in France.[15]

Zola became internationally well-known. In the same year as *La Débâcle* came out in France, 1892, it was also published in translation in Germany, Great Britain, the USA, Spain, Portugal, Italy, Bohemia, Holland, Denmark, Norway, Sweden and Russia.[16] Zola, who had not yet shown much concern about foreign rights, now took charge of his sales abroad. This was a frustrating matter, since the 1886 Berne Convention had just come into operation in a few countries, but not in the USA, where a Philadelphia publisher (Peterson & Brothers) produced bad translations of nine of Zola's novels (1878–82), and even sold thousands of copies to Britain without giving Zola a penny. He had better luck later, selling *Au Bonheur des dames* (1883) to Tinsley Brothers in London. In Austria the *Neue Freie Presse* had translated and serialised *Pot-Bouille* (1882) – for which Zola received 10,000 francs – but its readers did not like it, and the paper did not take *Au Bonheur des dames*. Zola soon learned that waiting too long to obtain a good deal from a publisher simply provided more time for the publication of a pirate edition – which is what happened with *Au Bonheur*, which was published in German by a Hungarian 'pirate'.[17]

Nana

Zola's next work after *L'Assomoir*, *Une Page d'amour* (1877–78), appeared to be so tranquil after the excitement of its predecessor that the paper in which it was serialised told its readers that it could be left 'unguarded' on the family table.[18] But Zola was preparing a much more riveting story, the sequel to *L'Assomoir*, the tale of the prostitute Nana. The republican *Le Voltaire* fought hard to obtain the serialisation rights, outbidding ten other dailies. The marketing campaign was unprecedented: on the eve of publication in October 1879 billboards advertising *Nana* were plastered all over Paris, while a hundred 'sandwich men' paraded the streets with posters reading '*Lisez Nana! Lisez Nana!! Lisez Nana!!!*'[19] And this was not just in Paris, but also in the provinces. France seemed to be inundated with posters about *Nana*.[20] *Le Voltaire* went one step further, and offered all subscribers a free copy of *L'Assommoir*.[21] The serialisation of *L'Assommoir* had earned Zola 8,000 francs; *Nana* made him 20,000.[22] Rumours that the government might seize the book helped the sales. Fifty-five thousand copies, at 3.50 francs each, were sold overnight at a time when selling 4,000 copies of a novel was regarded as remarkable. Charpentier, the publishers, immediately reprinted a further 11,000. By the end of the year *Nana* had been reprinted ninety-one times.[23] This led to a revival of sales for Zola's previous works. By 1885, 440,000 copies of the novels making up the Rougon-Macquart cycle so far were circulating in France. *L'Assomoir* and *Nana* alone accounted for more than half.[24]

Zola was perfectly aware that the story of a prostitute, albeit a *de luxe* one, could not fail to please the public. In the eighteenth century the prostitute enjoyed her work (in novels), had a good time and eventually repented – like Moll Flanders. There were exceptions: Manon, in the Abbé Prevost's *Manon Lescaut* (1731), sends her lover back to his father, just as Marguerite did almost a century later in Dumas *fils*'s *La Dame aux camélias* (1852). By then prostitution was regarded as a social evil, inevitable perhaps, but an evil nevertheless. Fictional prostitutes with a golden heart were tolerated and even fashionable, provided they die in the end. Mimi Pinson in Henri Murger's *Scènes de la vie de bohème* (1848) and its famous operatic version, *La Bohème* by Puccini, becomes the mistress of a wealthy man, but comes home to die in the arms of Rodolphe, the poor artist she loves. Hugo's *Marion Delorme* and Fantine in his *Les Misérables* suffer the same fate. The golden-hearted woman of easy virtue, whether courtesan, kept woman or prostitute, is still standard Hollywood fare – as, for instance, in Billy Wilder's film *Irma la Douce* (1963), with Shirley MacLaine, and *Pretty Woman* (1990), with Julia Roberts in the role of the prostitute Vivian Ward. And not just Hollywood: Fellini's *Le Notti di Cabiria* (1957) has just such a loveable prostitute who in the end finds Mr Right; and Melina Mercouri in *Never on Sunday* (1960) is a hard-working prostitute – except, of course, on Sunday, when she watches classical Greek plays (enough to make an intellectual's heart melt with joy). At least today they do not always die.

Hugo and Dumas *fils* had idealised the courtesan and the prostitute, transforming her into a saintly figure in spite of her environment and up-bringing. Zola's whores – Nana above all – were represented as the inevitable product of inherited and environmental factors.[25] Nana neither has a golden heart nor does she redeem herself. On the contrary, she contaminates every-thing she touches, and is almost autistic in her utter lack of concern for those who surround her. Zola's contempt for his anti-heroine is expressed even in his attribution of her literary tastes; she likes the kind of novels Zola hates, and hates the kinds of novels Zola writes:

> She had read that day a novel that had made much noise, the story of one of those girls; she was revolted . . . offended by that hideous literature that pretended to depict nature; as if one could show everything! As if novels were not written to while away the hours pleasantly. In matters of books and drama, Nana had firm views: she wanted tender and noble works to make her dream and ennoble her soul.[26]

Zola's polemic against the 'romantic' conception of the prostitute is visible from the start of the novel. The setting is the Théâtre des Variétés, where an operetta, *La Blonde Vénus*, is being performed – an unmistakable reference to Offenbach's *La Belle Hélène*, which represented for Zola the coarse and philistine bourgeois society he despised so much.[27] Nana sings the leading role, having slept her way into it, for she can neither sing nor act. No matter, she has sex-appeal, and the male public forgives her.

In reality Zola too was building on a stereotype: the *femme fatale* whose immediate origins were in the Romantic literature of the earlier nineteenth century, the castrating female who drives men to perdition. The stereotype of women as the source of primordial sexual energy – and hence 'superior' to conventional men – proved as enduring as that of the golden-hearted whore: Wedekind's Lulu (in *Die Büchse der Pandora* – Pandora's Box, 1904, the source for Pabst's film of 1928), Hofmannsthal's *Elektra* (1904, also Richard Strauss's opera of 1909) and Hauptmann's Pippa in *Und Pippa tanzt!* (And Pippa Dances!, 1906).[28]

Nana, by the standards of the nineteenth century, was scandalous. It was banned in Denmark and Germany. It shocked even the French. To Zola's indignation, *Le Voltaire* deleted from its serialised version some of the more scandalous passages – the hints of lesbianism and some indecent words and expressions which later appeared in the book. Jules Laffitte, the editor of *Le Voltaire*, did not have Zola's freedom. He was close to Léon Gambetta, then the most powerful politician in France, and needed his support and that of his party for favours and subsidies.[29] The market within which newspapers operated was quite different from that facing writers. Writers had only their public to please. Newspapers had also to please advertisers and politicians.

Zola had not hesitated to offend writers and critics. *Nana* gave his opponents an opportunity to answer back. Louis Ulbach in *Gil Blas* (24 February 1880) declared that this was a novel with no psychology, no ideas, no feelings, no style and no shame. Others called it 'a thuggish novel', 'an accumulation of trash'. Zola was depicted as a greedy writer in pursuit of money at all costs: 'If the public wants shit, Monsieur Zola will give it to them,' wrote Albert Millaud in *Le Figaro*.[30]

Zola was now rich. In a letter of 8 November 1885 replying to Lorédan Larchey, who was writing an article on the earnings of writers, he declared that *Nana* had been his most profitable novel so far: 20,000 francs from the newspaper serialisation, 75,000 from sales of the book, and a further 20,000 from the illustrated edition. His yearly income varied considerably, but he estimated that a new novel would bring him, on average, 60,000 francs while the previous ones brought him 20,000 francs plus 15,000 in foreign rights. He did not mention what he earned from his journalism or from the adaptation of his novels for the stage. He concluded: 'I earn my living handsomely, but we are far from the millions people talk about.'[31] In the mid-1880s Zola was probably earning approximately 100,000 francs a year – far more than the director of the coalmining company he described in *Germinal*.[32] One hundred thousand francs might be regarded as comparable to £200,000 today. This is considerably more than most people earn, but less than a successful barrister or consultant surgeon can achieve today, and far less than even the least successful chief executive of one of the top hundred British or American companies. In relative terms, however, 100,000 francs was an enormous sum, since an unskilled worker in 1885 would earn only 1,000 francs a year. Today, someone earning a hundred times more than an unskilled worker (say £15,000) would be in the £1½-million-a-year income bracket.

The Public Intellectual

By the time *La Débâcle* was published Zola was a national monument, but in April 1876, before the serialisation of *L'Assommoir* had begun in *Le Bien public*, he was still just another well-known writer. *Le Bien public*, a republican daily, launched a vigorous campaign on behalf of *L'Assommoir*, with sellers hawking the paper at street corners and cabbies distributing it among passengers. Zola was attacked from the left for depicting the working class in unflattering terms, and from the right for his use of slang and his depiction of a *ménage à trois*. *Le Bien public*, scared, dropped the serialisation after only one month. A literary journal, *La République des lettres*, picked it up.[33] Controversy, helpful to sales, continued, with *Le Figaro* denouncing *L'Assommoir* as pornographic and the republican government forbidding the sale of the magazine at railway stations.[34] Such denunciations from all sides enhanced the attractiveness of the novel and strengthened Zola's claim that the writer was above mere politicians, and a servant of the truth.

Zola's independence was highlighted by his decision to switch his column from *Le Voltaire*, politically close to him, to the right-wing and monarchist *Le Figaro*, which was also going to pay him considerably more. In a letter to his friend Henry Céard on 12 September 1880, he said he would be paid 18,000 francs a year – three times what *Le Voltaire* paid him. In addition *Le Figaro* had 100,000 readers, ten times as many *Le Voltaire*.[35]

Le Figaro had come to recognise that it could no longer defend the past. The monarchy had gone for good. With Zola as one of its columnists, it could recast its image. By acquiring Zola the paper was purchasing a symbol. It was now a newspaper in tune with changing times. The move was shrewd, since the editor knew perfectly well that Zola would continue to attack fearlessly the politicians of the Third Republic which *Le Figaro* despised.

Zola now had access to a new, larger public, and greater freedom to write what he wanted, since *Le Figaro* did expect him to write a conservative column. Zola's appeal was that he was not *engagé* on behalf of a party, but was above the squalid debates of the party politician. This position was helped by an absence of clear ideology. As we have seen (pages 612–13), many of his books – *Germinal* above all – were part of the standard library of socialist activists, but his 'socialism' amounted to little more than pity for the oppressed. Zola could equally have been recruited into the ranks of those supporting *laissez-faire* capitalism, of which he was a proponent. The main male protagonist of *Au Bonheur des dames* (1883), Octave Mouret, is a shrewd entrepreneur, the owner of a department store (the model was Le Bon-Marché). His enterprise and sense of business are repeatedly praised – almost glorified – by Zola. But Mouret has a major character defect: he thinks that money can buy him happiness, and above all the heart of the woman he loves, who, being a woman, prefers the world of feelings to that of money. Meanwhile Mouret ruins small shopkeepers, for whom Zola sheds a hurried tear. After all, they belong to the past; Mouret is the future. This is as near as one gets to that rare thing, a frankly pro-capitalist novel which openly declares that capitalism may be heartless, but is unavoidable.

Au Bonheur des dames pleased the respectable press, but mainly because it was sentimental. *Le Radical* of 14 March 1883 wrote with evident satisfaction that after the alcoholism of *L'Assommoir* and the debaucheries of *Nana*, one could finally read the romantic story of Denise, a humble and honest girl, in a book in which virtue is recompensed and vice punished.[36]

Zola may not have been pro-capitalist, but he certainly was in favour of *laissez-faire*, at least where culture was concerned. He deplored all state subsidies to the arts and literature, '*la laide maladie que nous avons en France d'être protégés et encouragés par l'État*' (the ugly disease we have in France: the need to be protected and encouraged by the state). He thundered against the tax on books sold at railway stations on the grounds that this was a political attempt to distinguish between 'improving literature' and that for the people.[37]

His columns in *Le Figaro* – he wrote a weekly article for fifty-two weeks from September 1880 to September 1881 – not only helped the sales of his novels, but also provided him with a regular audience at a time when two of his more famous novels (*L'Assommoir* and *Nana*) were fresh in people's minds. His hatred of politicians pleased the public:

> Take someone with scrofula, or a cretin or with brain-damage, and we might still be able to find in such person the stuff of the politician ... Neither intelligence nor strength nor originality are necessary, only allies and a certain personal flatness. If you have failed in everything and everywhere, and have been a second-rate lawyer, a second-rate journalist, and a second-rate person from head to toe, politics can take you and change you into a minister as good as the next one...[38]

The hatred was reciprocal. Conservative politicians regarded Zola as a dangerous and immoral man who was against God and tradition – a fair assessment. Radical politicians – the mainstream of the time – did not like his superior tone of moral integrity; they much preferred ordinary anti-clerical popular literature which clearly identified and demarcated the good guys from the bad ones.[39] Zola's politics went on offending well after his death in 1902. He had the 'honour' – an honour he would have relished – of having his works burnt by the Nazis in their huge bonfire of books in Berlin's Orpenplatz in May 1933 – unsurprisingly for someone they regarded as both a socialist and a 'Jew-lover'.

The *Affaire Dreyfus* of the 1890s, in which Zola played a famously prominent role, vastly enhanced his image as a public intellectual, someone who was ready to use the cultural capital he had accumulated in order to uphold political and social causes. The importance of Zola's open letter in support of Dreyfus, *J'Accuse* (1898), was not so much that a writer was taking sides – it had occurred before – but that he changed the terms of the debate. It was no longer just a question of the innocence of an unjustly accused person. Zola widened the attack to include those more widely responsible for the injustice done: the armed forces and those politicians harking back to the bygone days of Catholic-monarchist supremacy.

In the long run, Zola's campaign probably confirmed the view that he was a socialist, but the politics of a novel, where they exist, are often obvious only to those who are already politically minded. *Germinal* – set in a coalmine – was regarded as a distinctly socialist novel by those who were already predisposed to regard it as one. The Belgian socialist daily *Le Peuple* started serialising it in its first issue in 1885, not surprisingly, as coalminers were a key component of the Parti Ouvrier Belge (Belgian Workers' Party). Zola knew how to be generous. He wrote a letter to *Le Peuple* which was published in its first issue: 'Take *Germinal* and publish it. As your paper is poor and you defend the poor I will charge you nothing.'[40] It was hardly surprising that *Germinal* was regarded as a socialist novel: the plight of the miners and the justice of their cause are powerfully illustrated, but so is the violence they deploy (an unsympathetic shopkeeper is lynched and his corpse castrated by a frenzied crowd of miners' wives). Zola described without sentimentality the situation facing the miners, and also showed the link between their miserable conditions and capitalist exploitation. The miners acquire a consciousness of class antagonism at the workplace during a strike that is essentially to do with economic conditions (a dispute over payment in kind and other forms of wage cuts). The story celebrated the importance of mass action, while allowing individual characters their flaws.[41] Its realism made it successful among the workers, unlike later Soviet 'social realist' novels which idealised workers in the manner of pietistic popular Christian literature.

When a writer takes an overt political stance he automatically offends a section of his audience. And so it was with Zola. He may be remembered and admired now for his forthright defence of Captain Dreyfus, but at the time at least half of France was on 'the other side' – and more than half among the middle-class book-buying public. Anti-Semitic publications, such as Édouard Drumont's famous *La France juive. Essai d'histoire contemporaine*

(1886), were best-sellers too. Drumont's tract sold out in its first forty-eight hours, and went on being almost continuously reprinted until the early 1940s, spawning the publication of other anti-Semitic books, pamphlets and articles.[42]

Zola's stance may have cost him in terms of sales. His novel *Rome* did well when it came out in 1896–97, selling 100,000 copies, but between 1898 and 1902, at the height of the Dreyfus affair, few copies were sold. Zola's English publisher Henry Vizetelly calculated that in 1898 Zola earned only a third of what he had earned the year before – not nearly enough to cover the expenses of his various households and his brief exile in England to escape arrest.[43] The sale of his recent books had much diminished, at least in part because provincial booksellers were afraid of offending their customers by stocking them.[44] Vizetelly himself had to suffer the brunt of conservative attacks. In 1888 he was committed to trial for publishing Zola's *La Terre*, *Nana* and *Pot-Bouille*. Herbert Asquith, later Liberal Prime Minister, working for the prosecution as a junior counsel, had spent two weeks identifying twenty-one objectionable passages in *La Terre*. The jury, on being read the first few, declined to hear the rest of what the prosecuting counsel called 'bestial obscenity'. Realising he would lose, Vizetelly changed his plea to guilty, was fined, and promised to withdraw Zola's works from circulation. The press voiced its approval, *The Times* in particular.[45]

Zola remained controversial long after his death. He was on the Index of Forbidden Books of the Roman Catholic Church until the Index itself was abolished in 1966. In 1958 the regional government of Quebec in Canada banned a film about Zola (*J'Accuse*) precisely because his books were still on the Vatican's Index. As for *Nana*, it was banned in Hastings Banda's Malawi until the 1990s.

Zola Abroad

As the definition of the naturalist school is somewhat vague, anyone who writes about the lower classes and eschews sentimentality or irony becomes, almost automatically, a 'naturalist' writer. The label could be useful, since it provided readers with an indication of the genre. It also encouraged local talents, since many readers were ready to tackle realistic novels set in their own country.

Under this banner it was possible to package a considerable amount of sex and violence, while proudly celebrating the mission of the writer to tell the truth. Zola and his great contemporaries, such as Guy de Maupassant, thus gave, directly or indirectly, legitimisation and succour to a variety of writers who adopted or were accorded the brand name of realism. There would have been a 'naturalist' school even without Zola: Ibsen would still have written his dramas, as would have Strindberg and Hauptmann. But plays need to be staged and performed. A novel can rapidly be translated and printed, and can be read at the same time in the four corners of the world. Zola internationalised the genre. He was widely translated, and became the best-known living French writer of his time. He was one of the few foreign writers to contribute regularly to a Russian 'thick' journal (*Vestnik Evropy*, in 1875–80).[46] He became famous in Italy, then in Germany, and eventually in the rest of Europe and North America.

Zola's influence was strongly felt in the United States, where a new generation of writers was trying to find a distinctive modern style. Stephen Crane (1871–1900) was one of the first Zola-esque American writers. His first novel, *Maggie, a Girl of the Streets* (1893), which he published at his own expense, was the story of a New York prostitute who commits suicide. Crane was followed by a solid phalanx of writers who launched the new American literature of the twentieth century, including Jack London (1876–1916), Frank Norris (1870–1902) and Theodore Dreiser (1871–1945).

In Italy the Sicilians Giovanni Verga (1840–1922) and Luigi Capuana (1839–1915) were Zola's recognised followers, but the now almost-forgotten Paolo Valera (1850–1926) elaborated upon the more shocking themes of the French master with the aptly named *Amori bestiali* (1884) and *La Folla* (1901), a vivid portrayal of the miseries of the sub-proletariat.[47] In what turned out to be a profitable marketing move, *Amori bestiali* – a series of sketches on sexual passion – was regularly reissued with changes. The 1923 edition, the fourth, consisted of seventeen stories, almost all of which had not been published before. Later editions became increasingly crude and cruel. The 1920 edition had a female nude on the cover; the 1923 had a smirking man-satyr. One of the stories, 'Lionessa', is about a woman devoured by stormy passions: 'Better the coffin,' says the heroine, 'better prey of the feasting joy of worms than being abandoned by you.' Women say things like 'He slapped me, he hurt my breasts, he bit my cheeks, he walked all over my body ...'[48] The banner of 'naturalism' gave this kind of writing a patent of legitimacy. Its readers could pretend that they were absorbed in high culture.

Giovanni Verga, by contrast, was eventually canonised and is rightly regarded as one of the major nineteenth-century Italian novelists. Initially, however, far from being a Zola-esque realist, he had tried his hand at various other genres: the patriotic Risorgimento novel (*I Carbonari della montagna*, 1861) and the sentimental genre with his successful *Storia di una capinera* (1871). By the 1870s Italian literary circles were debating the merits of the 'naturalist' novel and of Zola. The great progressive critic Federico de Sanctis, in a public lecture in Naples on 10 June 1879, praised *L'Assommoir* for not being just the story of the unfortunate Gervaise, but also social history. It could have been set in Naples, he wrote, but 'None of us has had the courage to go there and investigate its misery. Disgust keeps us distant. Well, Zola in Paris had the courage.'[49] Verga thought he might have the courage too, and began to experiment with the documentary style. Thanks to the success of his first realist short story, 'Nedda', set in Sicily, he left behind his early tales and became the champion of the *verismo* literary movement (from the Italian word for 'true': *vero*), producing masterpieces such as *I Malavoglia* (1881) and *Mastro Don Gesualdo* (1889), depicting the Sicilian peasantry in a clinical and stark light.

Local Zolas multiplied. George Moore (1852–1933) was hailed as the Irish Zola, as he had hoped.[50] Nagai Kafū (1879–1959), thanks to his short stories, turned out to be the Japanese Zola. The Norwegian Christian Krohg (1852–1925), a painter, had become familiar with Zola's works when he was in Paris in the 1880s. He wrote a Zola-esque novel, *Albertine* (1886), inevitably about a poor prostitute. It became a favourite theme for his paintings. In Denmark Zola's realism inspired Henrik Pontoppidan (1857–1943, co-winner of the 1917 Nobel Prize) and Martin Andersen Nexø (1869–1954), the author of the saga on migration *Pelle the Conqueror* (1906–10, turned into a successful film in 1988). In Greece the publication of *Nana* had a powerful influence on the new generation of writers active in the 1880s.[51] In Germany Thomas Mann claimed that his *Buddenbrooks* was a *naturalistischer Roman*.[52] In Brazil Aluísio Azevedo (1857–1913) produced in 1881 an influential 'social' novel, *O Mulato*, said to have been inspired by Zola's school. In fact Zola's influence on Latin American literature remained considerable. Even in the 1960s he was still the model for the continent's literature of protest, such as the Ecuadorian Jorge Icaza's first novel *Huasipungo* (1934) and the Peruvian Ciro Alegría's *El Mundo es ancho y ajeno* (Wide and Alien is the World, 1941), both concerned with the plight of the Indians.

In Spain Zola inspired radical intellectuals, who called one of their journals *Germinal* and another *Revista blanca* after the Paris magazine *Revue blanche*.[53] Emilia Pardo Bazán in the prologue to her novel *Un Viaje de novios* (1881) praised the naturalist novel, though she distanced herself from what she regarded as its French excesses, its indecency and its emphasis on despair and sadness.[54] Benito Pérez Galdós, having read *Nana*, wrote *La Desheredada* – the story of Isadora, who lives in the hope of an inheritance and, when the hope is shattered, sinks into prostitution.[55] In Portugal Eça de Queirós (1845– 1900), regarded now as the country's leading nineteenth-century novelist, rewrote, under the impact of his reading of Zola, his first novel *The Sin of Father Amaro* (first version 1875, second version 1876), about clerical hypocrisy.[56]

Even some of those who were Zola's direct contemporaries came to be regarded as followers instead of being part of the same movement. This was the case with Camille Lemonnier (1844–1913), one of the major Belgian writers, whose best-known novel, *Un Mâle* (1881), a tale of rural seduction, was written shortly after the successes of *L'Assomoir* and *Nana*. When the book started to appear in the Brussels daily *L'Europe*, it was criticised for immorality and the paper was banned from railway stations. The book was nevertheless reprinted ten times in one year.[57]

One could multiply the examples, but none 'proves' that without Zola there would have been no 'realist' novels. The genre, one might say, was in the air. In Finland, in 1870, there appeared Alexis Kivi's 'realist' four-volume *Seitsemän Veljestä* (Seven Brothers), an unsentimental rural novel. It could not owe anything to Zola, since Kivi, while writing his fourth volume, would have been able to read, at most, *Thérèse Raquin*, which had come out in 1867. *Seven Brothers* was the first important novel written in Finnish, and it changed the course of Finnish literature. However, being written in Finnish, and not in French or English, or even Russian, German or Italian, it was guaranteed not to have the slightest impact abroad. It was finally translated into French in 1926 and into English in 1952, but has remained unknown in non-specialist literary circles outside Scandinavia. In Finland itself, Alexis Kivi is much celebrated. His birthday, 10 October, is a school holiday throughout the country – small consolation for a writer who died in abject poverty at the age of thirty-eight.

Realism developed in Germany too, sometimes on the back of Zola, sometimes independently of him. Gerhart Hauptmann's (1862–1946, Nobel Prize 1912) *Bahnwärter Thiel* (1888) tells the story of an inarticulate working man who kills his brutal second wife, who is responsible for the death of his son from a previous marriage. Hauptmann's next drama, *Die Weber* (The

Weavers, 1892), about the struggle of the weavers, was widely believed to be socialist propaganda. The socialists themselves adopted it enthusiastically, as they adopted Zola's *Germinal*. At first the police banned the play, then the court authorised its performance when it realised that workers would not be able to afford to see it.[48] German realism was never as successful, even in Germany, as the French or the British variety.

That Zola should have had no followers in Britain is easier to explain: realism was already a well-established British literary trend. It needed no advice from foreigners. Dickens's realism, of course, was much too tempered by sentimentality to warrant the patent, but Thomas Hardy could not be accused of it. He was part of the same movement as Zola, and was influenced by the same scientific determinism. Hardy took his theories from Darwin, Zola from Claude Bernard. Hardy's late novels – *The Mayor of Casterbridge* (1886), *Tess of the d'Urbervilles* (1891) and *Jude the Obscure* (1895) – were as controversial and bleak as any of Zola's (which occasionally, almost grudgingly, had a happy ending). France could cope with Zola as long as he kept out of politics. Hardy, however, was regarded as a godless blasphemer, particularly in his pessimistic *Jude the Obscure*. Daunted by criticism, he eventually desisted from writing novels, dedicating the last thirty years of his life to poetry.

Realism remained a major force in literature, drama and films throughout the twentieth century, in spite of modernism, surrealism, magical realism, and the everlasting appeal of romance and the compulsion of the happy ending. To see the world as it is, without the embellishment of sentimental optimism, has maintained all its charms. The depressing picture which often emerges can be a consolation for those who share the conditions described: they are not forgotten, their plight has been made visible. The luckier ones have their consciences gently massaged and are reminded of their good fortune: they do not work in appalling conditions, are not beaten by violent men, and are not forced into prostitution.

Realism was seen as a clinical and dispassionate look into human affairs. It was about outrage at the conditions of the poor and the oppressed. Before the Dreyfus affair, Zola had only been a famous writer. The affair turned him into a celebrity, a brand name. He joined Victor Hugo in the Pantheon of the public intellectual. This is ironic, since Zola had always looked down on Hugo's sentimental view of the downtrodden. It was, he felt, a negative model, a way of sentimentalising poverty. Yet he was at one with Hugo in speaking up, as an intellectual and a writer, in defence of those who had no voice.

At Zola's funeral (he died at the age of sixty-two in 1902 in mysterious circumstances in his own home of carbon monoxide poisoning) thousands of mourners lined the streets of Paris. The intelligentsia of France headed the procession; they were led, among others, by Alfred Dreyfus, freed but not yet rehabilitated. His wreath, 'À Émile Zola – Alfred Dreyfus', was visible to all as it was carried alongside the coffin. A miners' delegation followed, wearing their work clothes and chanting, 'Germinal! Germinal!' At Montmartre cemetery, the novelist and friend of Zola Anatole France pronounced his eulogy at the graveside: 'He was the conscience of humanity.' And, if not the whole of humanity, at least the people of Paris seemed to agree; thousands passed the open grave to deposit the flowers they were carrying.[59]

34

Stories of Crime and Science Fiction

Crime Stories

As the market for novels expanded, new genres came to be established. The detective novel, 'invented' in the middle of the nineteenth century, took off to become one of the most successful genres of the twentieth, providing formulas for endless plays, films and television serials. Edgar Allan Poe had started the genre, without knowing it was one, but soon a number of novels in what became eventually a recognisable trend were published. In 1867 *L'Affaire Lerouge* by Émile Gaboriau had borrowed two crucial aspects of the Poe stories: the rational investigator (Poe's Auguste Dupin) – Gaboriau's was called Monsieur Lecoq, a reference to Vidocq, the chief of the Paris Sûreté – and his befuddled friend/narrator – Gaboriau's was called Father Absinthe. Further crime writers appeared, notably in the USA, with the first major woman writer of detective stories (the first of many), Anna Katharine Green, whose Inspector Ebenezer Gryce made his debut in *The Leavenworth Case* (1878).

The genre remained dominated by Americans, French and British, though various European countries produced their own 'local' detective stories. This confirmed the international appeal of the genre, and how easy it was to adopt. Thus, in 1893 the 'first' Swedish crime novel appeared when Prins Pierre (pen name of Fredrik Lindholm) published *Stockholmsdetektiven* (The Stockholm Detective). Soon the genre was thriving in Sweden, including in 1913 even an anti-Semitic detective, Leo Carring, who in the novel *Antisemiten* (1921) by Samuel August Duse allows, with some glee, the murder of seven Jewish Bolsheviks.[1] Detective stories were not quite as successful elsewhere. In Italy, for instance, Arthur Conan Doyle was translated as early as 1895, but the publishers chose his historical novels. *The Sign of Four* (1890), featuring

Sherlock Holmes, appeared in Italian only in 1908, published by a Florentine firm, Salani. They must have felt that the genre could sell in Italy, because that year they also published Gaston Leroux's 'Yellow Chamber' story, which had just come out in France.[2] Then the Milan publishers Sonzogno began publishing a series of books under the label 'I Romanzi Polizieschi', presented as 'not the usual adventure stories' but as mysteries with a 'rational' solution. Nearly all the first books published were centred around the 'famous British detective' William Tharps. The author was 'G. Meirs' an Italian imitator of Conan Doyle using an English-sounding pseudonym.[3] Detective stories seemed to demand a British, or American, or French location (in fact Tharps operated in France), even though there were Italian novels that could pass as detective stories: Emilio de Marchi's *Il Cappello del prete* (The Priest's Hat, 1887) and Salvatore Farina's *Il Segreto del nevaio* (The Secret of the Glacier, 1909), defined by the author as a *romanzo giudiziario* (a legal novel), citing as his models Poe's 'The Tell-Tale Heart', Dostoevsky's *Crime and Punishment* and Zola's *Thérèse Raquin*. These are not quite detective stories, but there is a crime and a trial, and a mystery which is resolved.[4]

By the 1880s a vast stock of characters and plots had been created in France, Great Britain and the USA. In 1884, the detective Nick Carter appeared in New York, invented by John Russell Coryell. Carter was a non-drinking, non-smoking detective, courteous to women, gathering clues and arresting villains. By 1891 an entire magazine, the *Nick Carter Detective Library*, was dedicated to this hero. In its 282 weekly issues there appeared 240 original stories of between 20,000 and 33,000 words. As John Russell Coryell was required for another series, the publishers simply assigned the Nick Carter stories to other writers. When the magazine was discontinued the hero reappeared in other imprints, including *Nick Carter Magazine*, which lasted until 1936.[5]

1887 saw the birth of Sherlock Holmes in Conan Doyle's *A Study in Scarlet*, which eventually appeared in *Beeton's Christmas Annual*. Its successor, *The Sign of Four*, was published in 1890. In 1899 Raffles, a gentleman-thief, was created by E.W. Hornung. In 1905 Maurice Leblanc gave birth to another 'gentleman-thief', Arsène Lupin, an obvious allusion to Poe's Auguste Dupin. In 1907 Gaston Leroux, author of *Phantom of the Opera*, wrote *Le Mystère de la chambre jaune*, in which his hero, the journalist-detective Rouletabille, resolves a locked room mystery – one of the first. Since then there have been hundreds of such stories.[6] Rouletabille's 'Dr Watson' is a young lawyer who is also the narrator, and there is a master-criminal, Ballmeyer. Leroux's characters have august predecessors in the stories of Poe and Conan Doyle.[7] The dominance of the Anglo-Saxon model had already been accepted. This domination was inexorably confirmed. In 1910 Father Brown entered the scene thanks to G.K. Chesterton (*The Blue Cross*). In 1912 it was the turn of Fu Manchu by Sax Rohmer, and in 1915 John Buchan wrote *The Thirty-Nine Steps*. In 1920 in England, the Belgian Hercule Poirot resolved *The Mysterious Affair at Styles* thanks to Agatha Christie, while in the same year in the USA the magazine *Black Mask* was launched.

This list includes only a fraction of the best-loved practitioners of the genre; many readers will have their own chart; but there are hundreds who failed, or had a fleeting success before sinking away without trace. Robert Escarpit claimed that every year 80 per cent of literary production sinks into oblivion, and 99 per cent in twenty years.[8] What really matters, however, is not which books should be included in the canon of detective stories, but the historical fact that no discussion of the specific genre of 'detective' story could have occurred in the decades prior to the 1880s. So the real question should be: what were the conditions that favoured the rise of the genre?

As I have suggested, the crucial factor was the massive enlargement of the general market for books. Such expansion requires diversification in order to cater for the various sections of the market. The public, authors and publishers 'learn' to recognise different genres. The public learn that they like a particular kind of story, something that can occur only when there is an abundant supply and one must choose. Then the wheels are in motion. Publishers look out for more crime stories, since they sell. Authors, themselves avid readers of the growing number of such novels, try their hand at it. The detective story met the expectations of readers who wanted a clear narrative plot driven towards the solution of a single mystery. It is almost as if the sprawling urban social novels of Sue, Hugo and Dickens had been pruned of all digressions, and tightened up into a pithy and short narrative. Indeed, the early detective stories were short stories. While the length was curtailed, the pace of the action slowed down, in complete contradiction to the rule of the serialised novels. These build up suspense by digression while speeding up the action. In the detective story the action is deliberately slowed down, thus building up suspense. Poe, the pioneer, had known it instinctively: in 'The Purloined Letter', Auguste Dupin has guessed the solution but delays the dénouement, teasing the official investigators and hence the readers. He won't tell, not yet, but he knows.

The detective redresses wrongs out of some sense of mission or justice, like the hero of Sue's *Les Mystères de Paris*. But finding the murderer is also a kind of intellectual exercise. The detective is detached. He does not share the pain of the main characters, their hatred, their envy, or their passion. Like the readers, he uses his brains, and not his courage or his strength, to resolve problems. Like the readers, he is not part of the drama, and like them he is often generically middle class (Dorothy L. Sayers's Lord Peter Wimsey is an exception), lording it paternalistically over the lower orders while apprehending erring aristocrats. He (occasionally she) is never encumbered by a romantic attachment. The other characters kill and are killed, love and suffer, are envious and miserable, covet and conspire. Not so the detective, who is an outsider. Once the murderer is found, the story is over. We are not interested in the drama that follows the discovery of the culprit.[9]

Readers know exactly how detective stories end. They know the mystery will be solved and the criminal apprehended. They do not yet know who did it and how he or she is going to be found out, but they know they will. Detective stories are not about moral justice – maybe the victim 'deserved' to be killed, maybe the murderer had his reasons. The detective story is about the Truth. The social dilemmas present in Dickens, Sue and Hugo are replaced by the cold necessity of applying the law. If one were to choose a genre which symbolises bourgeois culture (but, alas, life is more complex than this), then it is the detective story. No wonder that, of all the nineteenth-century innovations in narrative, it has proved the most successful and enduring, loved by all classes and easily adaptable to theatre, film and television. Within this broad genre, subsidiary themes emerged. Ever more ingenious crimes were committed in ever more ingenious ways. Humdrum causes of crime, such as poverty, were disregarded.[10]

Heroes and Anti-Heroes

The most significant selling point in establishing readers' loyalty is the principal character, the detective, around whom a series of books is built. He or she (there were lady detectives as early as 1864 – for instance the anonymously published *The Revelations of a Lady Detective*), is almost never a conventional policeman following routine practices. The detectives develop endearing foibles and eccentricities: Sherlock Holmes injects himself with cocaine, plays the violin and likes early music (the motets of the sixteenth-century Flemish composer Orlando di Lasso); Nero Wolfe collects orchids; Lord Peter Wimsey plays the piano; Hercule Poirot is a funny Belgian; and Miss Marple is a classic spinster. P.D. James's Adam Dalgliesh writes poetry and Colin Dexter's Inspector Morse likes opera – thus demonstrating that, being cultured, they are not ordinary cops. The genre gives the appearance of realism, since everything is plausible. In real life, however, murder cases are solved either by the police or not at all, but never by an outsider, whether a private detective, a journalist, a lawyer, a doctor or a village spinster. In detective stories the amateur triumphs, the police fumble in the dark. When the policeman is able and intelligent, it's because he is unconventional, and likes to break police rules. While the reader is supposed to identify with the investigator, his true persona is the naïve dumb cop or the puzzled friend (Dr Watson), to whom things must be patiently explained. Alongside the infallible detective there also emerged the figure of the villain-as-hero, the super-villain – this, of course, is a staple of fairy stories and religious myth (Satan, Beelzebub, etc.). The modern super-villain, first immortalised in the Balzac character Vautrin, is the natural counterpart of the hero, since an incompetent baddy would not represent much of a challenge.

The production of crime stories became almost industrial, like the Beadle dime novels (see pages 479–80). Let us take, as an example, one of the most successful of the Fayard production line in cheap novels, the Fantômas series created by Marcel Allain and Pierre Souvestre. Between 1911 and 1913 the thirty-two volumes of Fantômas sold some five million copies at the very low price of sixty-five centimes. The authors used the new technology available: the novels were dictated into a recording machine and then typed up by a secretary. From start to finish a novel took the two authors four weeks. Each new volume was timed to appear at exactly the right interval: not too soon, to give slow readers time to finish reading the previous one; and not too late, lest the reader's appetite be distracted by a rival. The cover illustrations were particularly perturbing: nuns with guns, opened graves, thieves on rooftops.[11] The victims, mostly women, were killed horribly, though the stories contained no eroticism, in keeping with one of the unwritten rules of the genre. Political and religious controversies were similarly ignored. All were translated into Italian and most of them into Spanish and Portuguese, a few into English, Flemish, German, Czech and Serbo-Croat. As recently as the 1960s the publishers Mondadori (Milan) and Aguilar (Madrid) were still reprinting them. Films were made from Fantômas books almost as soon as they appeared. In 1987 Robert Laffont republished the entire *opus* in three volumes in its series Bouquin.

The plots were centred on five permanent characters: Fantômas, the arch-villain; Lady Beltham, his mistress, a British aristocrat; the policeman Juve; a journalist, Fandor; and Fantômas's daughter Hélène. Though Fantômas is a brutal murderer and has virtually no redeeming features, the reader is invited to identify with him and to share his derision for the policeman.[12] In 1958, over forty years after the appearance of the books, the surviving co-author, Marcel Allain, provided a profile of the characters for the designers of a comic strip adaptation: Fantômas is an elegant gentleman who is at home in high society; Juve, the policeman, is lower-middle class, badly dressed, and chain-smokes cheap cigarettes (Gauloises); Fandor, the journalist, is young and handsome, neither a snob like Fantômas nor boring like Juve, but a touch arrogant.[13] Readers who have seen films like *The French Connection* or television serials such as *Colombo* will readily identify the type of the grubby and badly dressed detective pursuing upper-class or wealthy villains. But Fantômas itself was not innovative. Almost every aspect of the novels could be found in previous texts.[14] Marcel Allain, trying to explain the success of the series, attributed more importance to the way it was marketed than the way it was written. The authors had given up the royalties on the first volume to ensure that it would be sold cheaply and that Fayard would spend lavishly on promotion and advertising, buying up entire pages in newspapers.[15] Sales took off from the fourth or fifth volume of the series, and reached a plateau at the tenth. By the thirty-second volume sales had plummeted to the level of 'normal' books, and the publishers decided to discontinue the series.[16]

The Fantômas stories arose at a time when it was no longer necessary to play the moralistic card that had been mandatory a few decades previously. The villain could be somewhat appealing, even though his crimes are out of the ordinary: Fantômas mutilates people, disfigures women with acid, causes railway crashes with hundreds of victims, makes floors collapse in crowded department stores, spreads the plague on a ship and observes, unperturbed, the death of five hundred passengers. This is probably why the stories won the approval of a significant intellectual group in France: the modernist avant-garde of Apollinaire, Cocteau, Blaise Cendrars (who called the Fantômas books 'the modern *Aeneid*'), Antonin Artaud and Max Jacob.[17] Their hostility towards respectable bourgeois culture attracted them to 'trashy' popular novels like those of Fantômas, where the villain remained unpunished and, unlike in other crime stories, bourgeois order was not re-established. Instead of disparaging popular taste, the avant-garde sought to provoke the bourgeoisie (which, as a class, easily resists intellectual provocations) by praising what they were not supposed to praise. In reality, not much had changed. The avant-garde was not as revolutionary as it believed. It was simply reasserting anew the traditional role of intellectuals as the arbiters of taste. If they decided that Fantômas was good, then it was good. One year it might be Proust, another year James Bond, sometimes both, thus always taking the hapless bourgeois by surprise. It was the beginning of the kind of literary criticism which, instead of ghettoising popular literature, decided to treat its practitioners as on a par with Shakespeare.

As the plots of the Fantômas stories were banal, the style pedestrian and the characters conventional, the 'discovery' in them of literary merits entailed declaring that they, as intellectuals, could see what others – blindly anchored to a surface reading – could not see. Popular authors so unexpectedly celebrated were often the first to be surprised. Jean Cocteau recalled that the authors of Fantômas were amazed by his and Apollinaire's enthusiasm.[18] Marcel Allain lived long enough, unlike Souvestre, to be interviewed in September 1967 before an audience of scholars and specialists at one of the prestigious intellectual gathering known as the Colloques at Cerisy ('Une Journée Marcel Allain', as part of 'Entretiens sur la Paralittérature'). Asked what he thought of the fact that, fifty years after its creation, distinguished academics were seriously scrutinising his Fantômas, Allain replied that he was very flattered, but also very surprised, since he had always regarded writing Fantômas as just an enjoyable way of making money. He was astonished that anyone could attach any importance to it. He also refused to admit that he had read his 'predecessors' such as Sue or Ponson du Terrail, and insisted, so very conventionally, that Flaubert was one of his favourite authors.[19]

A longing for recognition by high culture is not uncommon among crime-story writers. Arthur Conan Doyle famously tried to 'kill' Sherlock Holmes, in the hope that his other contributions to literature would be recognised. His historical novels were then almost as popular as his detective stories, particularly *Micah Clarke* (1888), *The White Company* (1890) and *Rodney Stone* (1896). But such was the demand for Sherlock Holmes, and the sums publishers were prepared to pay, that Conan Doyle resuscitated him. The result, *The Hound of the Baskervilles* (1892) – probably still the most widely read of his works, partly as a result of countless film and television adaptations – further increased his popularity, while his historical novels have sunk without trace.

The intellectual celebration of crime literature was by no means universal. It upset the traditional left, including those like Paul Nizan who left the avant-garde to join the French Communist Party. Reviewing a new thirty-two-volume edition of Fantômas in the communist *L'Humanité* (24 March 1933), he fulminated:

> This is the kind of 'proletarian' literature that the bourgeoisie manufactures by the metre. The unfortunate thing is that the proletarians actually read it, thus enriching the distasteful businessmen who publish it. Workers must no longer read these books which the bourgeoisie fill with the worst of poisons to corrupt the proletariat.[20]

Yet even Nizan, in articles published in 1939, distinguished between 'trash' and the better class of detective stories. He liked Poe, Sherlock Holmes, Father Brown and, above all, Dashiell Hammett, whom he ranked on a par with William Faulkner and Erskine Caldwell, the author of *Tobacco Road* (1932).[21] Novels of detection in which an investigator uses his wits to piece together clues could not fail to appeal to the highly educated. But crime stories also appealed to the uneducated, and as we know, had done so since the days when peddlers roamed the countryside carrying cheap pamphlets with stories of murders. The genre also seemed remarkably free of gender bias: men and women liked it, as they had liked Gothic novels. In an era of an abundance of books, it is no wonder that publishers printed them in their hundreds in the hope of finding a winner amidst the inevitable crowd of losers.

The appeal of crime stories was not confined to fictional narrative. Court cases involving murder were covered in detail by the press, both popular and élite. In Britain the amateur criminologist and lawyer William Roughead attended every trial of significance held in the High Court in Edinburgh between 1889 and 1949, and wrote them up for legal journals. Then they became best-selling books, with titles like *Malice Domestic, The Evil that Men do, What is Your Verdict?, In Queer Street, Rogues Walk Here, Mainly Murder.*[22] In France a similar multi-volume collection with all the interesting police stories since the days of Louis XIV was published in 1864.[23]

Today Conan Doyle, Gaston Leroux and Chesterton still delight readers. And Fantômas has been updated and turned into a musical, called appropriately *Fantômas revient.*[24] Others, such as the early American detective stories featuring Nick Carter and Nat Pinkerton, are now almost forgotten. Yet these were extremely popular, and not just in the USA. In Russia before the

Revolution there was a Pinkerton craze or *Pinkertonovshchina* when the books started being published in 1907 in 5–10,000 print runs for the relatively high price of fifteen to twenty kopecks. The following year the price had fallen to five or even two kopeks. During 1908 some ten million volumes of detective stories were published in Russia.[25] In the USA the Pinkerton books were part of a stream of detective stories launched by the fictionalised memoirs of Allan Pinkerton, the founder of Pinkerton's National Detective Agency and author of anti-labour novels like *The Molly Maguires and the Detectives* (1877). In Russia they were often totally rewritten. Sherlock Holmes and Watson were made to tour Russia to resolve cases such as that of a Gypsy kidnapper in Odessa and pirates on the Black Sea.[26]

Nick Carter made his Paris debut in the magazine *Nick Carter le grand détective Américain* on 22 March 1907, and was an immediate runaway success. For seven years, every Wednesday readers paid thirty-five centimes to find out how Carter thwarted crooks and gangsters thanks to his intuition and his charm, which allowed him to win over policemen and 'stupid craven niggers'. The young Sartre was a keen fan, dragging his mother through the second-hand booksellers along the quai des Grands Augustins where old issues could be bought at reduced prices. Soon he had amassed a complete collection.[27]

Science Fiction

The detective story had a distinguished ancestry. So had what we call – since the 1920s – 'science fiction'. As is often the case, the precise boundaries of the genre are vague. Critics who attempt to establish rigid rules are regularly discomfited by the evolution of plots. To establish its high culture credentials the origins of science fiction are often traced back to the utopian literature about how a better society (or a worse one, in the case of dystopia) might be structured, starting with Thomas More's *Utopia* in 1516 (one could, of course, invoke Plato's *The Republic*), Francis Bacon's *The New Atlantis* (1627) and Tommaso Campanella's *Civitas Solis* (City of the Sun, 1623), written during his twenty-seven years in prison in Naples for heresy. The idea of utopias also inspired nineteenth-century radical writers such as Étienne Cabet (*Voyage en Icarie*, 1840), Samuel Butler in his satirical *Erewhon* ('nowhere' – almost – spelt backwards, 1872), the story of an imaginary land, William Morris's *A Dream of John Ball* (1888) and *News from Nowhere* (1891) – where 'socialism' looks like the Middle Ages plus machines which do all the work, plus beautiful women who pour drinks for men who discuss the meaning of life – and Edward Bellamy's best-selling *Looking Backward, 2000–1887* (1888), about a socialist society in the year 2000: its popularity in the USA was such that that soon after it came out some 165 Bellamy Clubs were founded.[28] Another socialist utopia was *Freeland* (1890) by the Austrian economist Theodor Hertzka (1845–1929). Other antecedents included fantastic travels such as Cyrano de Bergerac's *L'Histoire comique des états et empires de la lune* (1656) and *L'Histoire comique des états et empires du soleil* (1662) and Swift's *Gulliver's Travels* (1726) – the best-known of hundreds of examples of imaginary travel literature. Some might include in the canon Mary Shelley's *Frankenstein* (1818), since it deals with the theme of the negative effects of scientific advances which might come in the future.[29]

Stricter definitions of the genre require that a science fiction should be set not in a present-day fictional world but in a time to come. In this case the most obvious candidate for the first science fiction novel is Louis-Sébastien Mercier's *L'An deux mille quatre cents quarante* (The Year 2440, 1771), which was widely translated before 1800. Later in the nineteenth century there were numerous stories in which the protagonist wakes up in the future or is transported there. In *Le Monde tel qu'il sera* (1845–46) by Émile Souvestre, a young couple who are followers of the social philosophers Saint-Simon and Fourier are put to sleep by Mr John Progress, who has travelled from the future. When they wake up in the year 3000 they discover that the world has not improved; everyone is conditioned and technology is at the service of petty utilitarianism. This is not a novel but a utopia in the classic mode, as is the optimistic *Paris dans l'an 2000* by Tony Moilin (1879), who described Paris after a socialist takeover. Direct income tax ensures that no one earns more than 12,000 francs a year (a substantial sum in 1869), while the poorest earn 2,400 a year.[30] There is full employment, no servants and full equality between men and women.[31] Some things never change: marriage is still the foundation of society, men expect their future wives to be young, beautiful and elegant, while the young ladies, though they would prefer their men to be handsome, are prepared to put up with those who are bald or grey if they have some standing in society.[32] A distinctive Parisian trait of this socialist society of the future is that all women dress according to the very latest fashion: 'Elles sont toujours rigouresement mises à la dernière mode.'[33] Almost equally didactic but with a greater element of narrative was *L'An 5865* (1865) by Dr H. Mettais, the story of Daghestan, a journalist working for the *Gazette de Caucasie* who travels the world before arriving in what was formerly France.[34] The country had collapsed in the year 2000, weakened by squabbling journalists and generals until it was sacked by marauding Cossacks.[35]

Particularly successful was the lavishly illustrated *Le Vingtième siècle* (1883), by Albert Robida. Though a somewhat pedagogical intent was still lingering there, the book was supposed to be entertaining, describing Paris in 1952 with floating buses, fast trains shortening the trip from Paris to Bordeaux to one hour, and a kind of television called the '*téléphonoscope*'.[36] All professions were 'now open to women: commerce, finance, civil service, the law, medicine . . . women have obtained equal rights, opened all doors'.[37] But obviously they are never content, because in 1953 a violent feminist revolution takes place. It is successful, and establishes its own countervailing feminine institutions, such as a Women's Stock Exchange where all the brokers are elegant women and the secretaries are young men.[38] The President of the Republic is now a mechanical robot . . . and so on in this vein.

None of this would pass any of the 'science fiction' tests of a devotee of the genre. As we have often suggested, genres do not appear when the 'first' work is published, but when a number of works with similar plot characteristics appear and constitute a new market. It is thus not entirely accidental that modern science fiction should emerge when the market for novels comes of age. Once again the French and the British are the pioneers. If Mercier is the best-known grandfather of science fiction, Jules Verne and H.G. Wells are among the recognised fathers. Such paternity can be disputed, but not the renown due to those who have the luck to write in a major literary language. Even writing in German would not guarantee worldwide diffusion. In 1879–80 Kurd Lasswitz published *Bilder aus der Zukunft* (Pictures from the Future) and *Seifenbläsen* (Soap Bubbles); in 1898, when Wells's *The War of the Worlds* was first published, Kurd Lasswitz published *Auf zwei Planeten* (On Two Planets), also about a benign alien invasion. *The War of the Worlds* became a worldwide success, while Lasswitz's book was soon forgotten. A talented Polish sci-fi author, Jerzy Żulawski, wrote a 'lunar' trilogy at the beginning of the twentieth century – *The Silver Globe* (1903), *The Victor* (1910) and *The Old Earth* (1911). He was successful at the time not only in Poland but also in Germany, but like so many others, he never made it onto the wider international literary scene.

This was far from being the case with Jules Verne, who did not consciously write science fiction, but adventure stories. Some of his books, however, are often included in the canon, notably *Journey to the Centre of the Earth* (1864),

From the Earth to the Moon (1865) and *20,000 Leagues Under the Sea* (1870). He wrote many other books, but these turned out to be his best-known ones. Wells, who called 'his' genre 'scientific romance', started out at the age of twenty-seven with *The Time Machine* (1895) about travels in the future. It made him financially independent. His next books were about 'experiments gone wrong' *à la* Frankenstein in *The Island of Dr Moreau* (1896) and *The Invisible Man* (1897); he then moved on to the sub-genre of alien invasion with *The War of the Worlds* (1898) and space exploration with *The First Men in the Moon* (1901) – almost immediately adapted for the cinema by Georges Méliès with *Le Voyage dans la lune* (1902) – *not* an adaptation of Jules Verne, as is often thought.

We tend to classify novels such as *The War of the Worlds* as science fiction, but we could equally well classify it as one of the many 'invasion novels' which were popular at the turn of the century, wherein England is invaded by the French or the Germans. The paranoia seems to have started as soon as a Member of Parliament, Sir Edward Watkins, proposed a Bill in 1882 calling for the construction of a tunnel between Dover and Calais (in 1876 a pre-emptive pamphlet had appeared: *The Channel Tunnel, or, England's Ruin* by 'Cassandra'). A spate of novels followed: *The Surprise of the Channel Tunnel. A sensational novel of the future* (1883) by C. Forth, *How John Bull Lost London, or, the capture of the Channel Tunnel* (fourth edition by 1882) by 'Grip', and *Under the Deep, Deep Sea, the Story of the Channel Tunnel* (1887) by Robert Jones Griffiths. Invasion novels were equally popular in France – the stories of Erckmann-Chatrian for instance – but at least France had really been invaded by Germany as recently as 1870 and was still partly occupied, hence the pessimistic *La Guerre franco–allemande de 1878*, published in 1877, and *La Guerre prochaine entre la France et l'Allemagne* (1881).[39]

At the back of much science fiction are immortal elements from fairy tales. Wells's *The Invisible Man* reminds us of tales where the wearer of a magic hat can make himself invisible, his *The Time Machine* reminds us of the magic carpet, his monsters from outer space are the dragons of old. Science fiction often seems to be fairy tales for the modern age.[40]

In so far as most other countries were concerned, when it came to science fiction or detective stories, the real invasion was that of British and American writers, who once again defined the genre for years to come. Other countries were reduced to the role of importers, with the occasional domestic foray into the genre. The Italians, for instance, had started writing their own Gothic stories before the genre was revived. Igino Ugo Tarchetti's *I Fatali* came out in 1869. The protagonist is Baron Saternez, who hails from Bohemia. He is described as a sort of Byronesque character, handsome, fair, too thin, melancholic, slightly feminine, elegant in his black clothes, very pale – in a word, a vampire (though he is never called this). He dies with a knife in his heart.[41] Vampires in literature, of course, had been around for a while. Théophile Gautier had written in 1836 *La Morte amoureuse*, in which a female vampire, Clarimonde, seduces a young priest but reverts to dust when some holy water is cast upon her. Far greater success, however, was enjoyed by Robert Louis Stevenson's *The Strange Case of Dr Jekyll and Mr Hyde* (1886) and Bram Stoker's *Dracula* (1897). With the far earlier *Frankenstein* (1818), these three novels provided plots for a formidable array of other novels, films and television adaptations.

35

Popular Novels, for Young and Old

British Novels

THE *FIN-DE-SIÈCLE* was a period of great expansion in the international appeal of the British novel. Previously Britain had produced relatively few international best-selling writers of the stature of Dumas and Verne. Of course Dickens, Trollope and Wilkie Collins had considerable popularity in English-speaking countries, but were not as widely translated as French writers. Then, between 1880 and 1920, the British unleashed a series of best-sellers which appealed not only to their own home market and the wider English-speaking world, but also triumphed in the rest of Europe. The crucial market now was no longer that constituted by 'sophisticated' élites, which was far too small to act as a catalyst. Nor was it the popular end of the market, for here the ease of imitation and the formulaic framework made major inroads difficult.

The key market was the so-called middlebrow. This included adaptations of classics, as long as they were simplified and shortened. American publishers were particularly good at this (probably helped by the fact that their own cultural élites were too weak to object). The ten-cent Lakeside Library launched by Donnelly, Lloyd & Co. in 1875 made famous British and French authors hitherto available only in expensive $1.50 editions. A cultural democratisation of a sort was thus taking place.

Many of the books in this new 'middlebrow' genre were discussed in the previous chapter: detective stories, or the new genre of 'spy' fiction such as Erskine Childers's *The Riddle of the Sands* (1903), warning the British public about the threat posed by German re-armament. Or, in a similar vein John Buchan's *The Thirty-Nine Steps* (1915). Or the adventure novels of the Hungarian-born Baroness Emmulska Orczy, author of the immensely popular

Scarlet Pimpernel (1905). This described the adventures of a dashing British aristocrat, Sir Percy Blakeney, who rescues members of the French nobility from the clutches of horrible revolutionaries – almost designed to ensure the hostility of Republican France. Then there was the revival of the Gothic story, with successes such as Robert Louis Stevenson's *The Strange Case of Dr Jekyll and Mr Hyde* (1886) and Bram Stoker's *Dracula* (1897), and the birth of science fiction epitomised by H.G. Wells's novels. All of these have at least one traditional element in common: the plot must be satisfactorily resolved – ambiguity in the ending is the prerogative of serious 'modernist' literature. These genres turned out to be among the most cross-culturally successful. They carried on from where the cheap popular literature of the previous centuries had left off: the great epic stories, the quest, fairy tales and the utopian imagining of a different world. Thus, even though the modern detective novel arose in France and in the Anglo-Saxon world, it soon caught the imagination of other cultural milieus. The Russian common people, used to the cheap *lubok* literature, moved on rapidly to the serialised novels (*vypuski*) published in cheap newspapers in the 1880s, most of which were detective stories and westerns.[1]

Literature provided a steady income for very few writers. In an interview in the magazine *Je Sais tout* in 1906, Marcel Prévost, President of the Société des Gens de Lettres, said that most of the 1,360 members of the society earned with their work (including journalism) something like 15–20,000 francs a year: better, but not that much better, than an average doctor or a senior teacher in a leading *lycée* in Paris. Only a small group of professional writers, ten at the most, probably earned over 50,000 francs; only four or five earned 100,000 francs.[2] Hardly any of these writers are remembered, let alone read, today. In their day they had a certain fame and made a good living. They had devoted readers. They were sought after by publishers. Then – like ageing film stars – they disappeared, never to be reprinted, unmentioned in the annals of literature or in encyclopaedias.

One of these professionals was Maurice Jogand (1850–1917). His first successful novel, *L'Enfant de la folle* (1879), was regularly reprinted until 1898. In the 1880s he churned out extremely lengthy serialised novels such as *Les Forçats de l'amour* (eight hundred pages) *L'Amant de la Juive*, *Les Aventures de Dumollard* (1,200 pages) and (under the pen name of Maxime Valoris) *La Breban ou l'affaire du Courrier de Lyon* (2,414 pages). Under the pseudonym of Marc Mario he became in the 1890s one of the pillars of Éditions Rouff, publishing twelve novels in five years. As he also wrote under other pseudonyms, it is not easy to trace his entire *oeuvre* – which he obviously never regarded as an *oeuvre*, but just as what he did to earn a living. He happily allowed his publisher complete control over his work. They could change it, cut it, and publish it in any format. Jogand also ghosted other people's books. For instance, Xavier de Montépin, a great name of the *roman feuilleton*, was getting too old and lazy to write any more novels, so Rouff got Jogand to write two: *La Voleuse de l'amour* (1893) and *La Demoiselle de l'usine* (1895). Montépin simply signed them. The deal was enshrined in a proper contract dated 9 March 1895.[3] By the time he died, Maurice Jogand had written tens of thousands of pages. In the 1890s, when he was at his most prolific, he may have earned anything between 12,525 and 29,000 francs a year – the actual amount is almost impossible to estimate, and for all we know he may have been writing or ghosting for other publishers. So he was doing well, better than a university professor, far better than a carpenter in Paris (2,250 francs). Nowadays a London carpenter charging £150 a day and working five days a week for forty-eight weeks a year would be earning £34,000 a year (the average academic salary). In proportion, to be in line with Jogand's earnings, a modern hack writer would have to make something between £180,000 and £340,000 a year – which is wildly improbable.

The success of middlebrow books did not depend on favourable reviews, or even on being reviewed at all. They relied, of course, on some marketing and advertising by the publishers, but above all on readers whose enthusiasm would spill over among their circle of friends and family: the idea of 'word of mouth', still the most important force behind a best-seller. This mechanism can only work either in a highly élitist society where all the literati know each other, or in a truly modern society where the barriers between groups, classes, genders and nations are more permeable than in the past; one in which people interact with each other, converse, exchange views. This requires a strong element of sociability, of friends visiting friends, of places where men and women work together, of clubs and circles and bars and cafés where views can be exchanged. Such networking requires an urban setting – ideally an intellectual capital where the main publishing houses can concentrate, along with authors and journalists.

In France and Britain, Paris and London dominated the publishing scene. In newer countries the situation was more complex. Italy's real publishing capital, before unification, was Milan. It remained so at the turn of the twentieth century, and still is. In Germany before unification there was competition between various cities. The Prussian-led unification of the country transformed Berlin into the intellectual capital of the new state. Its population had increased between 1848 and 1905 from 400,000 to two million, 3.5 million if one included the city's huge suburbs. In 1835 Leipzig published four times more books than Berlin, but by 1913 it had been overtaken by the new capital. More and more writers and journalists moved to Berlin: 23–24 per cent of the total in 1883–1907, according to the handbook *Kurschners Gelehrtenkalendar*, while Munich, Leipzig and Dresden had only 5 or 6 per cent.[4] St Petersburg and Moscow accounted in 1897 for 46 per cent of Russia's scholars and writers, and 31 per cent of its 18,000 musicians, artists and actors.[5]

Good networking was the foundation of the success of Marie Corelli (1855–1924).[6] Through her father, Charles Mackay, a professional journalist, she was acquainted with the publisher George Bentley, to whom she sent her first works. His readers' reports were negative, but Bentley, undeterred, published her *A Romance of Two Worlds* in 1886. The reviewers too were, on balance, negative, yet the book was a popular success. Over the next five years Marie Corelli published five more novels, each for a £500 advance plus royalties. Convinced that Bentley was not marketing her properly – she thought he may have been cheating her – she then switched to a new publisher, Methuen, and insisted that no review copies of her books should be sent to the press.[7] Methuen advertised her next two novels, *Barabbas* (1893) and *The Sorrows of Satan* (1895) as best-sellers – a way of starting a 'word of mouth' effect. Both sold massively. *Barabbas*, an occult romance set in the time of the crucifixion which makes Judas innocent of betrayal, went into fourteen editions in just over a year, and was translated into forty languages.[8] *The Sorrows of Satan* sold 50,000 copies in its first seven weeks, and 70,000 in less than a year. Arnold Bennett, writing in 1901, said that 'in the popular mind' *The Sorrows* was one of the two 'most striking novels of the last decade'.[9]

Critics kept making scathing comments, but Corelli kept on making money with a string of books with titles like *The Murder of Delicia* (1896), *Ziska* (1896), *Jane* (1900) and *The Master-Christian* (1900), about a time-travelling Jesus making a grand tour of Europe. Bennett, reviewing it in the *Academy*, wrote that the book revealed an 'egotistic, theatrical, vindictive, obtuse, and perhaps vain' personality (though not mean, he hastened to add). Yet Marie Corelli believed in what she was doing, just as much as her readers believed in her books. What upset those who cared about art was that she sold so well. 'Try as you may to ignore the multitude,' commented the ever-realist Bennett, 'you cannot. Numbers will tell, and it is right that they should. There is not a writer living today who does not envy Miss Corelli her circulation; and it is just that circulation which the artists of literature cannot understand.'[10] Marie Corelli was not just appreciated by the 'masses', but was also supposed to have been read, and liked, by Tennyson, Oscar Wilde, Queen Victoria and Gladstone.[11] Until her death in 1924 she was Britain's best-known best-seller. Some of her books are still in print, but success in one's lifetime does not always translate into literary immortality. Seventeen years after her death the annual revenue to her estate from royalty cheques had dwindled to less than £29.[12]

Another of the great publishing successes of the 1890s was *Trilby* (1894) by George du Maurier. It was set in mid-century Paris – in the 'arty' milieu the author knew well, since he was born and grew up in Paris and had been an art student there (his other career was as an illustrator for, among others, *Punch*). Du Maurier established the authenticity of his story by a lavish description of streets, cafés and theatres. The setting was the stereotypical 'Bohemian' Paris made famous by Henri Murger in his *Scènes de la vie de bohème* (1848). This had been almost forgotten, but now 'Bohemian' society underwent a revival, partly thanks to *Trilby*. Puccini, with a nose for cultural fashion, jumped on the bandwagon with *La Bohème* (1897), an adaptation of Murger's book.

Trilby O'Ferrall, du Maurier's protagonist, is under the influence of her mysterious mentor, Svengali. Her friends are three English art students (clearly suggestive of *The Three Musketeers*). As the critic of the *Pall Mall Gazette* put it, the three were 'British prigs cut in pasteboard', thus making them perfectly recognisable to their English audience.[13] But Trilby is Irish, and hence freer and more emotional. The first description of Svengali identifies him at once as the villain, a kind of Bluebeard, possibly Jewish or anyway central European, with a heavy foreign accent which the author transliterates phonetically for a few pages.[14] Trilby is an artists' model and hence 'naturally' uninhibited, but thanks to Svengali she can also sing beautifully – in reality she is 'mesmerised' by Svengali, who has the power to sing *through* her. The main subplot of *Trilby* is the story of how, having fallen in love with one of the students – and he with her – Trilby gives him up when asked to do so by his respectable mother, Mrs Bagot, 'a philistine of the philistine', who turns up with an equally stiff and conventional uncle.[15] This is an exact replica of the subplot of *La Dame aux camélias* by Dumas *fils* (1848), taken up as the central plot by Verdi for *La Traviata*. The audience naturally sympathises with the young woman – an attitude that makes them feel enlightened and modern. Even those who feel that it would be a dishonour for the scion of utterly ordinary upper-middle-class parents to marry a model admire Trilby's integrity and altruism. Eventually everyone realises that she is a modern saint, and far better than any of them. Luckily it is too late: Trilby, like Violetta and Marguerite, dies, thus following to the letter the Law of the Golden-Hearted Whore (see page 664). Once it is established that her heart is golden she must perish, to avoid embarrassing her loved one into marrying a wanton siren.

The success of *Trilby* was remarkable. It became an American best-seller despite its relatively high price of $1.75. By February 1895 it had sold 200,000 copies. In Britain it sold 80,000 in the first three months, though this may not have been a record, since it appears that in 1897 Hall Caine's *The Christian* sold 50,000 in a single month.[16] The novel was immediately adapted to the stage, with Herbert Beerbohm Tree playing Svengali. The painter James Whistler managed to attract further attention to it (and to himself) by complaining that a character in the novel (the painter Joe Sibley) was based on himself. There was an increase in the sales of the songs mentioned in the book. There were Trilby shoes (the novel repeatedly mentioned her beautiful feet), Trilby sausages, and, of course, the Trilby hat – worn in the play but not in the book by Trilby. George du Maurier added some spice by stating that Trilby had not slept with Svengali with the tantalising *caveat* 'when free from mesmeric influence'.[17] The word 'Svengali' entered the English language, with the sanction of the OED, to be used of any sinister person who controls another in a mysterious way.

Budding authors always wonder what is the secret of the success of a book such as *Trilby*. The answer is that if there is a secret, it does not lie with the author alone. Much depends on what I would call the 'literary situation'. This is constituted by other novels, plays and fictional accounts, newspaper reports, current preoccupations, political events. Some conjunctures favour some books more than others. Writers know this perfectly well. One successful novel can launch a thousand clones, some better than the original. Of course, to be able to guess ahead what a future literary conjuncture might be like requires remarkable skills – which publishers and agents claim to possess. The talent of authors is not insignificant, since they face considerable competition. *Trilby* may not be highly ranked in the annals of literature, but it was presumably regarded as a better read than most of its rivals.

The Popular Russian Novel

In spite of very high rates of illiteracy (still 75 per cent in 1913), the Russian book market increased constantly in the provinces throughout the nineteenth century.[18] Between 1895 and 1912 the number of copies published more than trebled, from 42,987,000 to 130,167,102. The number of titles grew at a parallel rate.[19]

TITLES PUBLISHED IN THE RUSSIAN EMPIRE, 1825–1914	
1825	583
1845	864
1850	696
1855	1,239
1860	2,085
1887	7,366
1895	11,548
1908	23,852
1912	34,630
1914	32,338

SOURCE: Brooks, *When Russia Learned to Read*, p.60

By 1905 there were also 1,100 dailies.[20]

One of the most popular genres was the bandit story, such as the enormously long serial novel *The Bandit Churkin* by Nikolai Ivanovich Pastukhov (1822–1911), which ran in *Moskovskii listok* (he was the editor) from January 1882 to the spring of 1885.[21] Bandit or outcast stories, of course, are plentiful in the West too, but in the West the hero is an outcast because he has suffered a personal injustice (Robin Hood, etc.), and serves the community against the powers that be or redeems himself by the good deeds he has performed. In Russia, bandits can only redeem themselves by being re-integrated by the religious and political establishment. The sanction as well as the forgiveness comes from above; in other words, they submit.[22] They attain redemption in the form of a state pardon granted because they have performed some patriotic act, seeking pardon through state service when they see the error of their ways. This plotline ensured some degree of official tolerance towards popular literature, which was amply repaid by publishers such as Sytin, which in 1913 prudently issued almost four million copies of books and pamphlets celebrating the three hundredth anniversary of the Romanov dynasty.[23]

It should be clear, however, that as elsewhere, 'popular' literature was not something read by the poor peasantry, the vast majority of the Russian population, but by the lower middle classes. These read literary magazines such as *Moskovskii listok*, which was widely imitated by others. The so-called kopek press, such as the *Gazeta kopeika* (1908–17) of St Petersburg, was probably read by the more educated workers, who might also have sympathised with its social goals. Its peak circulation, in 1910, was 250,000. The more expensive *Russkoe slovo*, however, sold twice as much – an indication of how narrow the truly popular market still was in *fin-de-siècle* Russia.[24]

Russia may have had a high rate of illiteracy, but it had a vast population. Its potential reading public was therefore one of the largest in Europe. The size of the country, however, was such that its distribution system had to rely on the kind of peddlers' networks that had almost disappeared in France and Great Britain. They distributed the usual mix of self-help titles, from handbooks on medical cures to books containing advice for newly married women, to the truculent tales loved by everyone, like *Novel from the Lives of the Moscow Thieves and Thugs* by I.A. Chmyrev.[25] Such books were very profitable: peddlers could sell them at twice the price they had paid for them, at times even three or four times as much. Their profits were enhanced by government restrictions on their numbers: peddlers needed a permit, and the number of these issued remained static from 1870 to 1912. Then the distribution network expanded rapidly. By 1913 the conservative newspaper publisher A.S. Suvorin had six hundred news stalls at railway stations and over a thousand in the rest of the country. In 1864 there were only sixty-three bookshops in Russia, but this increased to 611 in 1874, 1,725 in 1893 and 3,000 in 1903. Of these 205 were in Moscow, 142 in St Petersburg and 137 in Warsaw.

The supine condition of the population contrasted with the populism of the Russian intelligentsia. This was all-pervasive, and was common to traditionalists as well as to the Westernised modernisers. In no other European country did young aristocrats set out in significant numbers 'to learn from the people' by going to the villages, as they did in Russia in 1874 (only to be quickly disillusioned). In no other European country did so many students (a tiny élite in the late nineteenth century) join subversive organisations dreaming of remaking Russia. Writers seldom saw themselves as purely professional producers of cultural commodities. Though the Russians loved and still love Dumas, Verne and Walter Scott, authors whose mission in life was to entertain and educate their readers, they themselves did not produce any similar writers of such renown.

Russian writers were able to develop a mystique of suffering, and in so doing, feeling they were part of the people. Many did indeed suffer and end tragically.[26] Lermontov and Pushkin died in duels. Dostoevsky and many others endured periods of exile in Siberia. Tolstoy renounced fame and honours and took refuge on his estate in full mysticism. Later it got worse: Sergei Yesenin, Vladimir Mayakovsky and Marina Tsvetaeva committed suicide (respectively in 1925, 1930 and 1941); Osip Mandelstam and many others died in labour camps. While the great French and English writers were revered in their lifetime, were financially successful, and were consecrated soon after their death, the Russians suffered. For all their populism, however, the great Russian writers never wrote for the people, but for the members of their own class: *déclassé* aristocrats, state functionaries, enlightened landlords, officers, professionals. As a result, they used the idiom of an international urban class. Their political distaste for commerce and the market often extended to a distaste for the literature produced by the market. The more liberal critics, from Vissarion Belinsky (1811–48) to Kornei Chukovsky (1882–1969), however, regarded commercial literature as unavoidable, and even useful in breaking down peasant culture.[27] The gap in Russia between popular literature and serious novels and poetry remained constant throughout the communist era.

Westerns and Adventures

Cheap novels, it was suggested above, did not always travel well, even when successful in their own countries. But some genres did, as was the case with detective stories such as the Nick Carter novels. In other instances, local replications or adaptations worked equally well. The American author Owen Wister (1860–1938), for instance, wrote a famous western novel, *The Virginian* (1902), which sold for years, was made into a successful play, then into several films, and, decades later, into a television series (1962–71), but the original book was never particularly successful in Continental Europe. Zane Grey (1875–1939) was another American novelist who wrote mainly westerns. He was one of the most popular authors of the first quarter of the century thanks to *Riders of the Purple Sage* (1912), *The Thundering Herd* (1925) and *Code of the West* (1934), yet he remained unknown in Europe. Unlike the western films which eventually captured the imagination of Europeans, the cheap American novel was not a major export. The great publisher of dime novels, the Beadle Co., had even opened an office in London in 1861, where they reprinted many of their dime novels specifically for the British market, but it closed after five years. Yet the western genre was very successful in Europe, and nowhere more than in Germany, thanks to Karl May (1842–1912), the most widely read novelist in nineteenth-century Germany.

Karl May was the beneficiary of a favourable literary 'conjuncture'. The home-grown western novel had long been popular in Continental Europe. Gustave Aimard (pen name of Olivier Gloux, 1818–83), 'the French Fenimore Cooper', wrote some eighty novels, including the popular *Les Trappeurs de l'Arkansas* (1858). The Irish Captain Mayne Reid, who had served in the US Army, wrote sixty 'chase' novels for Beadle. Ferenc Belányi's westerns delighted the Hungarian reading public. Rudolph Muus wrote over five hundred novels, making him one of the most popular Norwegian novelists ever. The European vogue continued well into the 1950s and 1960s thanks to writers such as the Frenchman George Fronval, who between 1925 and his death in 1975 wrote six hundred westerns.[28]

Germany turned out to be more receptive to the western than any other European country, perhaps because by the middle of the nineteenth century Germans constituted the largest immigrant group in the United States. Some of these immigrants became writers and journalists, creating a sub-genre of westerns (as 'spaghetti' westerns became a cinematic sub-genre in the 1960s and 1970s). Writers like Charles Sealsfield (the pseudonym of the Moravian monk Karl Postl), Friedrich Armand Strubberg, Friedrich Gerstäcker, Balduin Möllhausen and Karl May used their first-hand experience or their imagination to produce hundreds of western novels. This is a genre which demands prolific production. Strubberg (1806–89), having lived in Texas for twenty-five years, wrote fifty-seven novels. Gerstäcker (1816–92) is credited with 150 volumes of travel accounts and adventure novels, nearly all of which deal with the American west, praising rough frontier justice, organised chases and mass lynchings. Balduin Möllhausen's 178 volumes of travel accounts, narratives and novels made him, according to Richard Cracroft, the most popular German writer in Europe in the 1860s and 1870s.[29] The most famous of all European western writers, however, was without doubt Karl May. By the time he died he had sold two million copies of his books. By 1953 his German-language book sales had reached twenty-five million copies.[30] His collected works, reprinted by the publisher Fehsenfeld of Freiburg between 1892 and 1910, spanned thirty-three volumes.[31]

May had served a long apprenticeship writing lengthy serialised novels – one a year between 1882 and 1887, including several with his Arab hero Kara ben Nemsi. However, he owed his popularity to his westerns – and above all to *Winnetou, der rote Gentleman* (Winnetou, the Red Gentleman, 1893), narrated in the first person by 'Old Shatterhand', *der Westmann* (the man of the west), a fair-haired German Catholic named Karl who had migrated to the USA as a teacher and eventually got involved in the business of righting wrongs and fighting Indians in barefisted combat – hence his nickname. With his friend Winnetou, an Apache chief, they right wrongs in the classic mode, rescuing helpless females captured by the 'savages', avenging crimes, helping deserving Indians and fighting nasty Yankees. Karl May had never been in the west, or even in the United States, but then neither had his numerous readers, though they had all read western novels, and hence were familiar with the conventions of the genre. These May followed almost instinctively. His heroes respect women and do not drink or swear. The world of his novels is almost exclusively masculine; male bonding and friendship are important values.[32]

Though Karl May's attitude towards the Indians was characteristically paternalistic (they were there, essentially, either to be fought or to be helped by superior whites), it was by no means hostile. The Romantic myth of the noble savage was still lingering in the air. This was so even in the USA. While real Indians were often massacred, and their resistance decried as savagery, Indians in fiction were often celebrated. An early example of this was the play *Metamora: Or the Last of the Wampanoags* (1829) by the American playwright John Augustus Stone. This was a fictionalised account of 'King Philip's War' (1675–76), in which the Indian *sachem* (chief) Metacomet, leader of the Wampanoags, led the last resistance to European colonisation in what is now Massachusetts, Connecticut and Rhode Island. Metacomet (nicknamed 'King Philip' by the English) became a popular American hero in the 1830s and 1840s, when the play dominated the Philadelphia theatre almost uninterruptedly.[33]

Karl May claimed that his stories were authentic. Authenticity, however, was not what attracted his readers. The sales remained unaffected even when a Benedictine monk, Ansgar Pöllmann, went to the trouble of writing a book, *Ein Abenteurer und sein Werk* (1910), to 'prove' that May's stories were fictional.[34] He remained almost unread outside Germany, though the patriotic

French school publisher Mame put self-interest before anti-German feelings and had the Winnetou series translated into French. In the 1960s May's novels provided a source for an amusing series of Euro-western films starring Lex Barker in the role of Old Shatterhand – just as Italy was beginning to produce its own 'spaghetti westerns'. In Germany May is still popular today (though he was banned for a time in communist East Germany). In 1970 a Karl-May-Gesellschaft (Karl May Society) was established, with an annual scholarly journal, the *Karl May Jahrbuch*, in which May's life and works are studied. Regular festivals dedicated to May take place in Elspe in North-Rhine-Westphalia and in Bad Segeberg (Schleswig-Holstein), and in 2001 a very successful film parodying May, *Der Schuh des Manitou* (The Shoe of Manitou), became the top-earning German film ever – nearly all its revenue originating from German ticket sales. And Germany long remained a strong market for western novels.[35]

Karl May owed at least part of his success to the fact his books were among the few exciting German novels for young men to receive the express endorsement of the Church. May made sure to wear his Christian faith openly. His character Winnetou, the archetypal Indian chief for generations of Germans, died like a good Christian, the Ave Maria on his lips. May remained on all reading lists for German youth, including those approved by the Nazis – it was said that he was among Hitler's favourite authors.[36] But he also captivated anti-Nazi artists such as Georg Grosz and Rudolf Schlichter.[37]

Karl May did not export well, unlike Italy's *Pinocchio* and Denmark's Hans Christian Andersen. To win the hearts of the popular German reading public it was necessary to play the card of exoticism. While the French and the British plundered their own history and represented their heroes as moral and generous strugglers against fiendish foreigners, the successful Italians and Germans set their stories in foreign territory, almost as if the novels themselves were written by foreigners. This was the path taken by one of the greatest Italian popular writers of the turn of the century, Emilio Salgari (1862–1911). In the 1880s he set his serialised tales of piracy in exotic places, mainly Malaysia and India. He knew little about either, but imaginatively used geographical and scientific magazines available in Italy. Salgari himself never set foot abroad, and the only sea voyage he ever undertook was a trip along the eastern coast of Italy when he was eighteen. What is the point of personal experience when reading other books provides one with so much material?

Like Karl May and most successful popular writers, Salgari did not despise his audience, did not feel they were inferior to him. He wrote adventure stories because he liked adventure stories. Like so many of his readers, he identified with his characters. A devoted family man with a loving wife and four children (who were given exotic names like Omar and Fatima), he maintained that he had been once a sea captain who had lived in exotic places, fought pirates and passionately loved and lost a beautiful young woman. The inhabitants of his native Verona could not possibly have believed any of this, since he had hardly left the place, but once he had settled in Turin he could rewrite his autobiography.

But Salgari was ill-equipped to deal successfully with the buccaneers of the trade, the publishers. He eagerly accepted the offer of a monthly stipend from his publishers (first Donath and later Bemporad). Had he been paid royalties – which the law of 1865 on copyright would have entitled him to – he would have been a rich man. His *Il Corsaro nero* (The Black Corsair) sold more than 100,000 copies at 3.50 lire each.[38] This would have brought in 350,000 lire, entitling him to more than 30,000 lire for just one novel. And Salgari wrote dozens. Instead, in 1906, at the peak of his popularity, he was earning around 8–10,000 lire, a reasonable professional salary (the director of Turin's municipal transport was earning 7,500 and a worker 1,100 lire), but not the large sums his readers imagined.[39] In spite of his enormous popularity he was always in difficult economic circumstances and in poor health. Deeply depressed, he eventually committed suicide in 1911. His publishers Bemporad had taken the precaution of insuring his life in favour of themselves, but his family was left destitute. His death did not stop the flow of a constant stream of books 'by Salgari' written by others.[40]

Salgari was dubbed the Italian Verne, which is not entirely inaccurate. Sometimes he stole even his titles from Verne: *Vingt mille lieues sous les mers* (1869–70) became *Duemila leghe sotto l'America* (1888), and Verne's *Un Drame dans les airs* (1851) was plagiarised into *Un Dramma in aria* (same plot, sometimes even the same words).[41] However, Verne's novels exhibited a typical *fin-de-siècle* positivist commitment to science that is quite absent from Salgari's.[42] Yet his novels were informative. His readers – a new reading public made up of students, artisans and white-collar workers – were given profuse factual information on geography, British and Dutch colonialism, trade, Malaysia, Hinduism and its 'superstitions' (particularly the cult of the blood-thirsty goddess Kali and her devotees the Thugs, a sect of robbers and killers). His novels were almost 'multi-racial', as they depict Arabs, Chinese, Burmese, Indians, Javanese.[43] The hero of his stories is Sandokan, a Malaysian prince who has lost his kingdom and who seeks to regain it, helped by a chain-smoking Portuguese sidekick. The arch-enemy is Britain, the great colonial power, which in spite of the widespread anglophilia of the Italians was also an object of their hostility, since they felt they had missed the colonial boat. In his westerns (such as *Il Re della prateria* in 1896 and *Le Selve ardenti* in 1910) – and he wrote a lot of them – Salgari recognised the genocide of the Indians, but thought, as it was generally believed at the time, that Western colonisation was both inevitable and justifiable.[44]

Salgari's novels occupied the place of the colonial novel in a country devoid of colonies but with colonial ambitions. They exploited a widespread interest in colonial exploration and travels – the stream of news from Africa and Asia, from Speke's exploration of the African lakes to Stanley's exploration of the Congo and his encounter with Livingstone, to the Mahdi's (Muhammad Ahmad) revolt in the Sudan and his famous victory against General Gordon in Khartoum (1885). These, and more besides, had been widely covered in the illustrated press, and had all become grist to Salgari's mill. When the Italian explorer Luigi Amedeo, the Duke of the Abruzzi, led an expedition in 1899 to the North Pole, reaching the northernmost latitude yet, Salgari quickly wrote a novel about it.

During his lifetime Salgari was ignored abroad, save for a brief period of popularity in France (there was a translation in 1899). In Italy, however, he continued to be read and admired well into the 1950s, as he deserved to be, for having been able to make his mark in the difficult terrain of Italian popular literature. By the beginning of the twenty-first century he had become one of the most translated Italian writers.[45]

Pinocchio and the Others

Salgari failed to become internationally famous, but Carlo Collodi, the author of *Pinocchio*, succeeded. It is somewhat puzzling that a book aimed at children, written by the son of a cook and a maid, should turn out to have been Italy's best-known nineteenth-century literary export.

Carlo Lorenzini, Collodi's real name, was born in 1826. After a stint as a bookshop assistant he became a clerical worker and eventually a modest journalist. He wrote a string of unsuccessful books. At the age of fifty he was commissioned by a Florentine publisher to produce a new translation of some of Perrault's fairy tales. This gave him the idea of writing educational books for children in accordance with the prevailing Italian view on how one should write for children: the plot and characterisation should be a thinly veiled excuse for providing the young readers with masses of 'useful' information. Eventually *The Story of Pinocchio* was born. The first version was serialised in the *Giornale dei bambini* (7 July 1881) with the title *Storia di un burattino* (The Story of a Puppet). It was finally completed in 1883. The relatively long serialisation was due to the author, who having led a life of gambling and drinking, often failed to deliver his copy on time. Then the publishers, the Paggi brothers of Florence, asked the artist Enrico Mazzanti to prepare the illustrations for the book version. Mazzanti's visualisation of Pinocchio was adopted with minimal changes by Walt Disney in 1940 – the ridiculous Tyrolean trousers being one of its elements.

The worldwide success of *Pinocchio* was not instantaneous, but the number of editions and translations grew continuously, many countries adapting the name and varying the plot. The 1913 German version by the Catholic publisher Herder was reprinted eighty-four times, selling a total of 300,000 copies in the following decades. Called *Die Geschichte vom hölzernen Bengele* (The Story of a Wooden Kid), it was illustrated by Wolfgang Felten, who imitated the style of Wilhelm Busch, the creator of 'Max und Moritz', one of the first modern comic strips (1865). Pinocchio was dressed like them, and was given a German name. Bengel (kid, or street urchin). Other translations referred to him as Bimbo (child in Italian) or Kasperl (a well-known German puppet). In 1905 there was a very free adaptation by Otto Julius Bierbaum called *Zäpfel Kerns Abenteuer* (The Adventures of Pinenut). Here Pinocchio, instead of turning into a real child as in the original, prefers instead, in what is a blatant piece of German primitivism, to return to his original shape as a piece of wood, and return to the forest with his brother trees.[46] The first Romanian edition (1911) also renamed the characters: Pinocchio became Tăndărică ('wood splinter').[47] In Czechoslovakia, where it was translated in 1929, it was called Little Nut, perhaps because pine nuts (from the Italian word *pinolo*, from which the original took his name) were then unknown in Czechoslovakia.[48] In Russia, after a first translation in 1908, there was a version by Alexis N. Tolstoy (1882–1945), who would be decorated with the Order of Lenin in 1938. Written in the 1920s, it was based on Tolstoy's vague recollection of his reading of the Italian original. It was this second version which was translated into all the languages of the USSR.[49] In the first English version (1891), anything which could upset Victorian children was removed: the mutilation of the ears of the donkey and the leg of the cat, the crushing of the cricket, etc.[50] By 1983 there had been 135 illustrated editions in Italy, besides a large number of derivative publications, including, in 1927–28, 'Pinocchio the Fascist'.[51]

Why this story should be so successful is impossible to establish. Its main elements are present in a number of stories and myths, mostly of a religious nature: Pinocchio – like Jesus, Moses, etc. – is of mysterious birth, his father/creator is called Gepetto (one of the many nicknames for Giuseppe, i.e. Joseph in Italian) and is a carpenter; he has no mother, though the fairy (in Italian the *Fata dai capelli turchini*, or Blue-Haired Fairy – she turns blonde in the Disney film) who protects him may be a stand-in for the Virgin Mary. Pinocchio usually succumbs to temptation instead of listening to the cricket (the *Grillo Parlante* or talking cricket in the original, Jiminy Cricket in Disney), who represents his conscience or the voice of (religious) authority. Pinocchio is even hanged on an oak tree with two thieves (the Crucifixion), and is eaten by a whale like Jonah.[52] The nose which grows, giving him away whenever he lies, provides a further set of fairly obvious Freudian interpretations.

The opening lines of the story announce to its young readers that, though this may sound like a traditional fairy tale, it is not:

> C'era una volta ... Un re – diranno subito i miei piccoli lettori.
> No, ragazzi, avete sbagliato. C'era una volta un pezzo di legno.
> (Once upon a time there was ... 'A King!' my young readers will say.
> No, kids, you're wrong. Once upon a time there was a piece of wood.)

Pinocchio's world is neither orderly nor rule-bound: the police arrest the wrong people, the innocent are punished, Pinocchio squashes his conscience (the talking cricket). It is an irrational world, difficult to comprehend – as the real world is for many children. Pinocchio always gets into trouble, and though he promises to mend his ways, is unable to do so, thus he learns nothing and in this sense remains innocent. While the story is full of warnings and can be used as a moral tale about the dangers of telling lies, thus appealing to parents and teachers, it is also one where a strange and frightening world is depicted – thus appealing to the young.[53] The structure of the book consists of scenes or narrative units, each terminating with a moral citation, following the pattern of the popular theatre. When Collodi wrote Pinocchio he probably had in mind the commedia dell'arte, and perhaps assumed his readers would be familiar with it.[54]

Collodi's great achievement did not spark a run of international success for Italian children's books, though it did give impetus to a considerable domestic production. Equally, Hans Christian Andersen's stories produced no heirs in Denmark, nor did Johanna Spyri's *Heidi* (1880) in Switzerland. Sweden's Selma Lagerlöf, however, was succeeded by Astrid Lindgren (1907–2002), a single mother like J.K. Rowling, whose adventures of the nine-year-old Pippi Longstocking have been translated throughout the world.

Adaptations of successful novels took varied routes. In 1907 the Florence-based *Giornalino della Domenica* announced that it would publish the diary of a boy, Gian Burrasca (Burrasca means storm, so: Johnny Storm). *Gian Burrasca* eventually became a comic strip, but the character, the uncontrollable kid, permanently ready to cause trouble and mischief but good at heart, became one of the mainstays of Italian literature for children along with Pinocchio. *Gian Burrasca* was in reality an adaptation of an American humorous book *A Bad Boy's Diary* (1880), by Metta Victoria Fuller Victor (1831–85).[55] Metta Victor was a leading light of American popular literature. She was the editor of the monthly *The Home: A Fireside Companion and Guide for the Wife, the Mother, the Sister, and the Daughter*, published by Irwin P. Beadle & Co., the foremost publishers of 'dime' novels. She had written a stream of novels, such as the slave story *Maum Guinea*, *The Gold-Hunters* and instructional works such as the enticingly entitled *The Dime Recipe Book: Embodying the latest and best information for the American household : a directory for the parlor, the nursery, the sick-room, the toilet, and the kitchen*.

Metta Victor's *A Bad Boy's Diary* – which led, inevitably and fairly, to the sequel *A Naughty Girl's Diary* (1884) – belongs to a successful American genre: the Good Bad Boy, of which Thomas Aldrich's *Story of a Bad Boy* (1869) is one of the best-known pioneers. There are, of course, European antecedents, but not in books aimed at children.[56] The Italian stories were far less optimistic than their American equivalents. Gian Burrasca (like Pinocchio) hardly ever meets anyone well-disposed towards children, just as Russian adaptations often turned happy American endings into sad ones. And, perhaps inevitably, there was in 1971 *The Erotic Adventures of Pinocchio*, in which every time he is unfaithful to Gepetta it is not his nose that grows . . .

A few other countries were able to produce international classics for children, but not many. One might mention, in Hungary, Ferenc Molnár (The Boys of Pal Street, 1907), and in Austria Felix Salten, who after producing a pornographic novel about the sexual initiation of a child prostitute, *Josefine Mutzenbacher* (1906), wrote *Bambi. Eine Lebensgeschichte aus dem Walde* (1928), immortalised by Walt Disney's 1942 animation film.

French production of children's books continued with a steady stream of successes such as *Poil de carotte* by Jules Renard (1894) and *La Guerre des boutons* by Louis Pergaud (1912), but in this field at least, the 'Anglo-Saxons' prevailed. While the Americans could field Louisa May Alcott, Mark Twain and L. Frank Baum (the *Wizard of Oz* series, 1900), the British – in seeming contradiction to the stereotype that they much preferred pets to children – dominated the genre. And this domination has remained strong to this day. The roll call is impressive: from *Tom Brown's Schooldays* (1857) by Thomas Hughes, in the genre of the public-school story, to *Alice's Adventures in Wonderland* (1865) and *Through the Looking-Glass* (1872) by Lewis Carroll, adventure stories such as *Treasure Island* (1883) by Robert Louis Stevenson, E.M. Nesbit's *The Phoenix and the Carpet* (1904) and *The Railway Children* (1906), to Rudyard Kipling's great *The Jungle Book* (1894), *The Wind in the Willows* (1908) by Kenneth Grahame and J.M. Barrie's *Peter Pan* (1904–06). Even a hundred years later British primacy still seems unassailable, thanks to what might be the best-selling series of all time, J.K. Rowling's Harry Potter saga.

The British had a children's literature already established at the beginning of the nineteenth century. To some extent this compensated for the lack of fairy tales such as those of Perrault and the Grimm brothers. British authors, more commercially-minded than those on the Continent, did not disdain to write for children. As parents were the main purchasers, they often tended to buy for their children books by authors they were reading themselves. Sometimes children's books came first; thus Maria Edgeworth wrote two collections of short stories for children, *The Parent's Assistant* (1796) and *Moral Tales* (1801), before her main literary successes for adults.

The first great wave of children's books in late Victorian Britain, as in France, was firmly middle and upper class. In stories where the heroes were the children themselves (as in the French Comtesse de Ségur, see pages 436–40) the preferred setting tended to be the school, invariably a public school as with *Tom Brown's Schooldays* and the more realistic *Stalky and Co.* (1899) by Rudyard Kipling. Equally middle-class is the Darling family in J.M. Barrie's *Peter Pan*. The Peter Pan character had first appeared in Barrie's novel *The Little White Bird* (written in 1896 and published in 1903), not intended for children, in which the narrator tells the story of Peter Pan to a child.[57] Then Barrie was prompted by the impresario Charles Frohman and the actress Maud Adams to develop the story as a play: *Peter Pan, or the Boy who Would Not Grow Up* (1904, first performed 1905). It was an immediate success, and Barrie himself supervised its annual revivals, which continued until 1928. Since then it has been performed almost continuously in Great Britain and the USA. It has been turned into a musical, and one of Walt Disney's more celebrated animated films is among its many screen adaptations.

The rise of children's books often has such a snowballing effect. Success generates success. Eventually Hollywood, by transforming many of these books into films, considerably extends their lease of life. The success of books for young people has remained a significant feature of fiction publishing. It has been enhanced by the encouragement of reading, which is seen by parents and educators as a preferable activity to the cinema (and, later, listening to music, watching television and playing video games). Books, not videos (so far), are distributed by schools as prizes to the best students. The idea that books could be dangerous did not lose its appeal, but those who had panicked at the threat of cheap novels understood that the only way to ensure that young people read the right things was not by banning 'bad' books but by providing approved material.

The idea of giving a book to children on special occasions – a birthday, first communion, Christmas – proved popular with parents and publishers, and perhaps even with some children. The youth market for books remained solidly in the hands of parents – only after the Second World War was there the rise of a truly mass youth market almost autonomous from parental choice. Their choices, in turn, were directed by élites quite distinct from those which helped form the literary canon. They consisted of the political and religious classes. Successful children's writers were overwhelmingly those who succeeded in appealing to parents. These, regardless of their personal convictions, continued to be inclined to choose 'moral' literature for their children, the idea being that a modicum of religious belief was an essential part of growing up. Even in France, where the Catholic Church, after the fall of Louis Napoleon, had to face the growing anti-clericalism of the political establishment, it remained a force to be reckoned with in deciding which books were suitable for children. By 1867 one French publisher from Tours, Alfred Mame (1811–93), had a virtual monopoly of the school prize-book market thanks to the backing of the Church. In his old age he declared: 'In my entire career I have never printed a single line against religion or morality, whose servant I have always been.'[58] This attitude turned out to be exceedingly remunerative – at least until 1881, when the French state began its protracted struggle against clerical influence in schools. The prize-books, or *livres de prix*, were distributed once a year to the best pupils at an elaborate ceremony attended by parents and local dignitaries. Mame could print 20,000 books a day, since any book chosen as a *livre de prix* was automatically deemed particularly suitable for children, and would be bought by parents whose children were not so meritorious.

In England too, Sunday school prize-books were profitable. The British state did not intervene, unlike the French, but the Religious Tract Society, the Society for the Promotion of Christian Knowledge and the Reward Books promoted edifying moral tales distributed at Sunday schools. Milvain, the cynical character in Gissing's *New Grub Street*, advises his sisters to write children's books: 'They sell like hot cakes.'[59] He was right. A good children's book, one regarded as wholesome and moral, can outsell anything – as J.K. Rowling and her lucky publishers know well.

36

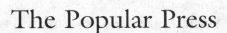

The Popular Press

The Press and Business

THE LAST QUARTER of the nineteenth century saw the beginning of the mass popular press in France, Great Britain, Germany and the USA, where mail-order monthlies such as the *People's Literary Companion, Ladies' World* and *Youth Companion*, addressed to a rural readership, had achieved circulations in the hundreds of thousands. In 1893 *Munsey's, McClure's* and *Cosmopolitan*, modelled on élite magazines such as *Harper's* and the *Atlantic Monthly*, increased their sales by dropping their price to ten cents (the élite magazines cost thirty-five cents). By 1905 there were twenty monthlies in the United States with a circulation of over 100,000, for a total of 5.5 million.[1] They were overwhelmingly addressed to women and financed by substantial advertising. Arnold Bennett, one of the most perceptive observers of the publishing and literary scene of his day, had this to say:

> Another factor is the unique position of and influence of young women in the United States. We are told that it is the women who rule the libraries of England; much more is it the women who rule the libraries in America . . . If you would know what sort of an intellectual creature the American woman is . . . read her especial organ, *The Ladies' Home Journal* of Philadelphia, which is one of the most brilliantly edited papers in the world, and has a circulation of over 800,000 a month. Here, in this glowing and piquant miscellany . . . you will discern . . . the width of her curiosity, the consuming fire of her energy, her strange knowledge and her stranger ignorances, her fineness and crudity, her imperial mien and her simple adorations. It is fitting to remark of the American woman that she has a magnificent future.[2]

Prior to the advent of the cinema, the press constituted the largest cultural market, bigger than publishing and far bigger than the theatre. The use of advertising meant that selling papers to readers was only a part of the business. Equally or more important was selling space to advertisers. According to the editorial of the launch issue of the *Gentlewoman* (a ladies' magazine) in 1898, sales covered only half the costs.[3] By the 1890s in England advertising was an essential part of the newspaper and magazine business, even though by then excise duties on paper and stamp duty on newspapers had been repealed in stages (1853, 1855, 1860 and 1861). Classified advertising (personal announcements), in turn, generated not only revenue but readers' interest.[4]

The last two decades of the nineteenth century saw an explosion in the market for women's magazines, particularly in Great Britain. This, of course, reflected the wider growth of the press, the improvement in women's education – the Education Act of 1870 set up elementary schools by local boards and the Education Act of 1876 made education compulsory until the age of thirteen and, in 1891, free for all. The crucial reason, however, was that magazines, like books, became cheaper. Paper costs decreased thanks to the production of sulphite, extracted from wood pulp (a Swedish breakthrough) – hitherto rags, scarce and expensive, had been the main raw material for paper. Distribution became more efficient, and fast rotary presses were introduced.[5]

By then all women's magazines devoted a massive proportion of their space to advertising and personal classified announcements. The development of this press should be regarded as an integral part of the development of a consumer society at the end of the nineteenth century. Increased prosperity had created a significant market of middle-class women who were in control of a sizeable proportion of the family budget. The tendency of women's magazines to appeal to different segments of the market facilitated the use of advertising. Quality papers like the *Lady* (1885) were designed to appeal to 'women of education', while *Women's World* (1903), packed with sensational fiction, targeted housewives and working women who needed something to read on the way to work or during their lunch break. At the lower end of the market, the unmarried working girl and the lady's maid were provided with new all-fiction weeklies such as *My Lady's Novelette* – lurid stories and serial 'shockers'.[6] Teenagers did not yet exist, but as pocket money had just been invented, they were not far behind. In 1880 the prescient *Girl's Own Paper* appeared. The rise of the housewife led to a plethora of magazines aimed at equipping her with basic skills with respect to nutrition, hygiene, childcare, etc., such as *Housewife* (1886), the *Mother's Companion* (1887) and *Woman at Home* (1893). How to keep up appearances on a limited budget gave rise to the 'problem page' and hence to the rise of the expert. By reading the *Lady's Companion* middle-class women could find out the rules of conduct that would enable them to be socially adroit. An article of 3 March 1900 explained: 'A woman prefers it to be taken for granted that she has always moved in what is known as good society and that she is perfectly *au fait* with all the intricacies of modern etiquette.'[7]

In 1891 the enterprising Alfred Harmsworth formed the Periodical Publishing Company in order to publish exclusively women's magazines such as *Forget-Me-Not*, aimed at the middle classes; by July 1894 its circulation had risen to 141,000 – massive by the standards of most Continental countries. The growth of this press reflected the rapid changes in the condition of women, many of whom discussed political and social matters, engaged in sports, rode bicycles, joined clubs (needlework, camera), ate in fast-food establishments and shopped at the new department stores. The older magazines had carried reports on what was going on at court and in High Society for a readership who were only once or twice removed from such events. Now such reports were written up in a way that would be of interest to women (and men) who had not the slightest opportunity to enter that society. They made the upper classes familiar to them.[8] In a way these magazines were extensions of the eighteenth- and nineteenth-century novels (and twentieth-century television serials) in which the private life of the rich, famous and powerful is presented, somewhat vicariously, for public consumption.

Newspapers were (and still are) a peculiar kind of business, since making a profit may not be the only, or even the main, reason for owning them. A desire for power, influence and prestige is an important motive. Of course, a steel magnate or a railway tycoon may wield power and influence too, but a newspaper can boost or damage politicians, make or unmake actors or writers, contribute sometimes decisively to the success of a novel, a play or a film, talk up or ignore an issue, make something fashionable or declare it *passé*. The press can transform. Given favourable circumstances, it can shape other cultural markets.

The press did not simply report events, it also generated them. Exclusively reporting a major event could be profitable. It increased sales and attracted advertising. The connection between newsworthy events, the press and business was thus established, at least in countries with a thriving press and an eager business community. An example was the sponsorship of polar expeditions. The *Daily Mail* of January 1914 carried a gossip item describing how the explorer Ernest Shackleton operated: 'Any day you may see Sir Ernest . . . taxiing from one newspaper to another. He is trying to arrange the best terms and it is going to be a battle royal both for the news and pictorial rights.' The *Mail* may have been envious of the *Daily Chronicle*, which had bought the rights to Shackleton's next expedition, and have decided to belittle the explorer.[9]

Journalism became a profession. The first international congress of the press took place in London in 1893; the same year, in Paris, a picture gallery exhibited one thousand portraits of writers and journalists. In 1899 France created the first school of journalism. In 1912 the Columbia University School of Journalism was founded with a $1 million donation by Joseph Pulitzer.

A profession awards status and demands a reasonable income and the opportunity to earn even more – a senior editor in Berlin could earn as much as a high civil servant.[10] Berlin had a thriving press, dominated by the publisher Ullstein, which owned the largest-circulation newspaper, the *Berliner Morgenpost*, and the tabloid *BZ am Mittag*. The new capital had the greatest density of newspapers of any city in Europe.[11] Modern marketing techniques were devised to increase the sales of papers. August Scherl and his *Berliner Lokal Anzeiger* had been a path-breaker: the first issue (4 November 1883) was sent free to all households. Scherl stripped the paper of the ponderous leading articles characteristic of the respectable press, and provided a large number of small items of information – a move which would be copied by Hermann Ullstein when he launched the *Berliner Morgenpost* in 1898.[12]

August Scherl's main innovation, though, was in the distribution process. At the end of the nineteenth century the distribution of newspapers in Germany was done through agencies. These delivered papers directly to readers' homes. Scherl decided to use his own distribution network. His paper, the *Lokal Anzeiger*, quickly became Berlin's most widely read journal. It dispensed with long articles and put the news on the front page (another innovation). A competition war ensued. Scherl had asked his readers to pay one month in advance, Ullstein asked only one week 'up front' for his new *Morgenpost*. By 1899 it was outselling Scherl's *Lokal* by 160,000 to 120,000.[13] Later in 1904 Ullstein also brought out the tabloid *BZ am Mittag*, which paid particular attention to sports. Finally in 1913 he took over the old *Vossische*

Zeitung, the oldest Berlin paper (founded in 1705), modernised it and used his own network of correspondents throughout the world, instead of relying exclusively on news agencies.[14]

But Berlin did not have in Germany the pivotal role that Paris had in France or London in Great Britain. It had to face the competition of Munich, Leipzig, Hamburg and Frankfurt. Outside Germany there was Vienna – another German-speaking pole. In the Austro-Hungarian Empire, competing Hungarian and Czech nationalists tried to escape the hegemony of German. In Prague the Czech-language paper *Narodni Listy* (National Paper) printed 4,000 copies a day in 1880 and 22,000 in 1895, while its German rival printed only 5,000. In 1910, of a total of 1,823 newspapers and periodicals published in Hungary, only one was in German.[15]

Many German papers, especially the Berlin press, had solid financial backing because they were part-owned by banks (as was much of German industry). August Scherl's press group became the largest in Germany in 1910 when it took over another publishing group, the Union Deutsche Verlags-gesellschaft (UDV), thanks to a Leipzig bank. The interconnection with industrial and financial capital did not stop there. Scherl was then bought by Alfred Hugenberg (a former Krupp director), who was also one of the founders of the Universum Film AG (UFA, 1917), soon Europe's main film producers. UFA was owned by a consortium comprising Deutsche Bank, Dresden Bank and Allgemeine Elektrizitäts Gesellschaft. Thus, much of the German press was dominated by industrial and banking circles, for whom making money out of the press was secondary to exercising political influence. This insulated the German press from markets, and hence from readers.

In Italy developments were similar, even though the reading public was much smaller. In the 1890s Italy still published only one newspaper per 17,000 inhabitants, a third less than Switzerland, Belgium, Germany and France.[16] The *Secolo* of Milan, a radical paper campaigning against corruption, owned by the publisher Edoardo Sonzogno, one of the first daily papers (it was founded in 1866), was selling more than 100,000 copies in the 1890s. The *Corriere della sera* was created in 1876 by Eugenio Torelli-Viollier as the paper of the Milan financial and commercial establishment. Its initial print run of 3,000 copies was turned into 50,000 in 1887 and 90,000 in 1900.[17]

The low level of sales made the Italian press strongly political and ideological, because it was highly dependent on the political and business classes. Ministerial hostility could spell financial ruin for any newspaper. For example, when the Prime Minister Francesco Crispi instructed the Prefect of Milan to boycott the *Gazzetta Piemontese* in 1894, circulation fell from 25,000 to 7,000.[18] Even when sales expanded the Italian press remained closely connected to big business and/or politicians. The Rome daily *Il Giornale d'Italia* (1901) was partly financed by Sidney Sonnino (Prime Minister Giovanni Giolitti's right-wing opponent) and by the nationalist agrarian bourgeoisie. The Turin-based *La Stampa* was edited between 1900 and 1920 by Alfredo Frassati, a supporter of Giolitti, the dominant politician of the day, who secretly subsidised it out of public funds.[19] Between 1920 and 1925, under Luigi Salvatorelli, *La Stampa* even opposed fascism. But in 1926 it was bought by the automobile group Fiat and turned into a pro-fascist paper, the price paid by Fiat to acquire Mussolini's favour. A parallel development was that of *Il Corriere della sera*. In 1900 its principal shareholder, Luigi Albertini (1871–1941), was also its editor and could oppose Giolitti. When the paper turned against the Duce after the murder by fascist thugs of the socialist leader Giacomo Matteotti in 1924, Albertini was removed.

Spain had lower newspaper readership. Most of it was concentrated in Madrid and Barcelona, but the average print run for a Madrid daily in 1910 was only 6,000 copies (100,000 in London).[20] In 1890 there were in the whole of Spain only forty-seven presses able to produce newsprint, and thirty of these were in the Basque country. By contrast Italy had 153, France 525 and Germany 891.[21] Even in 1915 the consumption of newsprint in Spain was only 14,000 tons, against 185,000 in France. The Spanish press, aware that a small increase in cost might wipe out their tiny market, turned to the government for help in exchange for subservience.[22]

Such close connections with the political or business classes did not exist in Great Britain or the USA. There, press groups were powerful capitalist concerns in their own right. Their owners often interfered in politics for their own ideological reasons or in order to obtain favours for their companies, but they were press barons, dependent above all on the market. They pretended to keep their distance from party politics, stressing the often spurious distinction between facts and comment – spurious because the selection of facts can be far more tendentious than comment.

The French Press

The years between 1870 and 1914 were the golden age of the French press. The costs of newspaper production decreased in real terms, as did the price. In 1871 a yearly subscription for a Paris daily was thirty-six francs. This would have required 164 hours' work for an average worker. In 1910 it was down to twenty-four francs, or seventy-three hours of work.[23] The market expanded constantly. The number of dailies was, by present standards, staggering. In 1870 there were nearly forty dailies in Paris alone, selling a total of a million copies. There was room even for a thriving socialist press: in 1903 the party's paper L'Humanité, edited by the socialist leader Jean Jaurès, printed 75,000 copies a day, more than any party political paper prints today in most European countries.[24] By 1880 there were sixty dailies selling nearly two million copies. Altogether, in 1880 the republican press (which included the three top sellers, led by Le Petit journal) outsold the monarchist press (led by Le Petit moniteur and Le Figaro) by a ratio of three to one, out of a total of 1,984,000 copies printed a day.[25] In 1910 there were seventy dailies, though twenty-four had an insignificant circulation.[26]

By 1914 four Paris dailies dominated the French press, with a combined print run of 4.5 million copies, three quarters of total sales. They were Le Petit journal (1863), Le Petit Parisien (1876), Le Matin (1885) and Le Journal (1892). Of the four, Le Petit journal was the least Paris-based, with 80 per cent of its sales outside the capital, Le Petit Parisien followed with 65 per cent, while the others sold 60 per cent of their print run in the provinces. They were thus national papers.[27]

Le Matin gave itself 'Anglo-Saxon' credentials by declaring that it would give priority to news and reporting rather than to comment. It favoured the rather flat style of press agency reports rather than the more flowery style of traditional French journalism. Its journalists were no longer, as had been traditional in France, men of letters.[28] They were professional journalists, either devoid of literary ambitions or able to keep them under wraps.[29] Le Journal – founded in 1892 by Fernand Xau, once the French agent for Buffalo Bill's circus – was a hybrid, halfway between the traditional literary journalism (it carried regular features and comments by men of letters such as Zola and Maurice Barrès) and the 'new' US-style journalism.[30] By 1895 Le Journal was selling 300,000 copies a day. Its main concern was not politics but profits. It was thus market-driven, and aimed at an obvious market section: urban white-collar workers.[31]

Targeting particular sections of the market (rather than trying to please everyone) proved a successful strategy. Socialist papers like *Le Cri du peuple* (1883) did reasonably well, and *L'Humanité* had a print run of 84,000 in January 1912. The far-right press did well too, with *L'Écho de Paris* selling 135,000 copies a day in 1914, while the Catholic *La Croix* (a daily after 1883) did a little better with 140,000 copies.[32] The rest of the centrist political press did not worry quite so much about its market; it was content to remain in the good books of the government which, openly or secretly, funded it.[33]

The best-selling paper was *Le Petit Parisien*: its 1.4 million copies was almost double the number sold by its nearest rival, *Le Petit journal* (780,000).[34] *Le Petit Parisien* was conceived, from its inception, as a 'popular' paper in the French sense, meaning a working-class paper. An editorial signed 'Jean Frollo' (a pseudonym used by various politicians) on 13 October 1893, dedicated to the theme of 'Le Journal Populaire', noted that a paper which cost only one sou (the smallest coin, five centimes) represented only a few minutes' work, and enabled workers to find out what was going on. Thus, he added with undisguised satisfaction, 'In a great country such as ours, the same thought, at the same hour, enters the minds of the whole population . . . it is the press which produces this sublime community of souls . . . thanks to the newspaper we live a kind of common life.'[35] The global village had been discovered.

Le Petit Parisien's five-centime price was maintained without interruption from 1876 to 1917, the increase in profits substantially the result of an increase in sales. The paper managed not to appear either pro- or anti-Dreyfus simply by producing a great quantity of detailed news, sometimes contradictory. Its readers were on the whole quite apolitical, and did not take a particular interest in the famous *affaire*. They were interested in the diversity offered by the paper: domestic and international news, crime, sport, business news, the stock market, weather forecasts, advertisements, games and prize money and, in 1903, a comic strip.[36] Only after 1928 did advertising become crucial.

Le Petit Parisien became anti-clerical when the government was anti-clerical, and patriotic without being warmongering.[37] In other words it was always vaguely pro-government, without ever taking a strong stand on anything unless public opinion was clearly on its side. Far from forming public opinion, all the paper did was to hedge its bets, always ready to switch its position when necessary. This is one of the two strategies available to popular newspapers. Either they clearly identify themselves with one segment of the population and represent its ideas, or they strike a careful balancing act, remaining somewhere in the middle. Either strategy, if played out intelligently, can be all that is needed to convince all and sundry that the newspaper is a real power in the land and an effective shaper of public opinion, when in reality it is just as much responding to it. Thus the anti-clericalism of *Le Petit Parisien* was always relatively moderate. When its public reacted negatively to some extreme anti-clerical novels it serialised, such as those by Hector France, the paper changed tack.[38]

Le Petit Parisien was right to be careful. The competition was formidable. The threats came not only from its Paris rivals but also from the provincial newspapers. In 1889, even in small towns such as Vervins in the Aisne, which had 3,500 inhabitants, there were three local weeklies. In Ariège, a mountainous department of only 210,000 inhabitants whose largest town had a population of only 9,000, most of whom spoke Occitan, there was not only a daily but fourteen weeklies, all with a readership of five hundred or less.[39] Some were filled with the usual horror stories, often about child murders: '*Ignoble monstruosité. Mort affreuse d'une petite fille de 4 ans coupée en morceaux. Nouveaux details*' (Terrible monstrosity. Horrible death of a four-year-old girl cut into pieces. New details).[40]

Towering over the rest were the great provincial papers like *Le Petit Lyonnais*, *Le Petit Marseillais* and *La Dépêche* of Toulouse. Their success blocked the expansion of the Paris press. *La Dépêche*, founded in October 1870, was at first a small, inconsequential paper, yet by 1880 it was the third largest provincial paper in France after the *Petit Lyonnais* and the *Petit Marseillais*.[41] By 1898 it sold over 125,000 copies a day. Its outlook was secular, somewhat anti-clerical, with a patriotic cult of the Revolution. It was widely respected, partly thanks to the renown of its main leader writers, the anti-clerical Auguste Huc, one of the great journalists of his time, Georges Clemenceau, a future Prime Minister, and Jean Jaurès, leader of the Socialist Party.[42] The real reason why it was popular, however, was that it provided a constant supply of local news.[43]

La Dépêche, like most newspapers, thought it was forming public opinion. Papers may indeed influence public opinion when it is not formed yet. Otherwise they cannot go against the feelings of their readers without paying a price. Take the Dreyfus affair. One would have expected anti-clerical opinion-makers like Auguste Huc and his colleagues to rally immediately to the cause of Dreyfus, since he was obviously under attack from those monarchists and Catholics who had never accepted the Republic. Nevertheless, one should not underestimate the anti-Semitism then prevailing. Huc regarded the Jews as 'an inferior race', and wrote of the need for France to defend itself against 'a people who aspire to domination'. French radicals conceived of the Republic as an entity which could not tolerate any form of ethnic separateness. Those who refused to assimilate or insisted on maintaining their own distinctiveness were a threat. Besides, the Jews were thought to possess undue financial influence, and though the radicals were not against capitalism as such, they were against the very rich. This is why in 1894 and 1895 *La Dépêche* did not pay the slightest attention to the emerging Dreyfusard movement. Its star writer, Georges Clemenceau, had at first believed in the culpability of Dreyfus, but when he became convinced of the contrary in 1897 he launched himself into the campaign, using his columns in *La Dépêche* (as did Jaurès), and wrote nearly a hundred articles on the *affaire*.

La Dépêche could hardly censor a politician on the rise such as Clemenceau, yet Huc and his closest colleagues went on believing in Dreyfus's guilt and attacking Zola. By 1899, public opinion and, above all, the paper's readership had rallied round Dreyfus. *La Dépêche*, not to be left behind, joined them. Huc at first remained silent, then, in 1904, after the victory of the Dreyfusards, he grudgingly admitted that he should have embraced the cause sooner.[44]

The British and American Popular Press

The rapid development of the press in Britain built on the success in the 1840s of the semi-clandestine 'unstamped papers' which created a sizeable popular readership for crime stories and current affairs. Most towns of 20,000 inhabitants had three or four cheap publications. In London the *Weekly Police Gazette* (mainly about crimes) had a circulation of 32,000. Total circulation could have been in the millions.[45] The new popular press of the 1880s and 1890s, however, required considerable capital, since a high volume of sales was indispensable to cover costs, attract advertising, maintain low prices and make a profit. To set up the *Daily Mail* in 1896 Alfred Harmsworth (Lord Northcliffe in 1905) estimated he needed £½ million for start-up costs.[46] Thus the era of press barons necessarily coincided with the rise of the popular press. The initial print run of the *Daily Mail*, priced at half a penny, was 200,000 copies a day, as much as the *Daily Telegraph*. By 1898 the *Mail* had doubled to 400,000. By 1900 it had reached 989,000.

Its presentation and layout, at first, were not particularly innovative: the front page was still made up of advertising and classified announcements.[47] Harmsworth, however, having started his career in popular magazine journalism, applied its principles to the new daily, provided it with an efficient distribution method and pursued a popular, racy version of conservatism, upholding patriotism and imperialism – almost unavoidable during the Boer War.[48] As Colin Seymour-Ure explained: 'The *Daily Mail* reported the news ... But it was also full of chat and gossip, regaling readers with trivia about the great and famous, and thereby creating a spurious sense of knowingness and shared intimacy.'[49] The *Daily Mail* did not leave news out, but demoted it, forcing it to compete for space and attention with other items. News was one of the main selling points of the paper, but 'news' no longer meant just 'politics'. For instance, on 13 October 1908 the paper contained thirty-three news items, including pieces about a woman killed by a motor car while attempting to save her dog, a romance between an Italian Duke and an American woman, and a ballooning accident.[50] News was defined as anything out of the ordinary, not only sex and crime, but also the uncanny, the unexplained and the bizarre – what came to be known as 'man bites dog'. This was the time when newspapers began to launch their own crusades without waiting for others to do so. Even at the beginning of the twentieth century, as is the case now, 'safe', i.e. popular, campaigns were regularly launched against child abuse and child prostitution. At the same time trivialities, such as stunts or a new shape of hat, were promoted.[51]

Harmsworth understood that popular journalism had to be the servant of the people, giving them what they wanted, or perhaps what the owner and the editors thought it wanted. He declared:

> The things people talk about are news – and what do they mostly talk about? Other people, their failures and success, their joys and sorrows, their money and their food and their peccadilloes. Get more names in the paper – the more aristocratic the better, if there is a news story round them. You know the public is more interested in duchesses than servant-girls.[52]

Jingoism met the taste of the *Mail*'s readers, but jingoism is not a tight ideology. It enabled a wide range of positions, including articles on sufferings in India such as the Bombay plague of 1896 and the famine of 1896–97. The idea of the white man's burden encouraged a compassionate attitude towards colonial people and added to the general feeling of British superiority.[53]

Very soon Harmsworth controlled a wider share of the national press than any newspaper baron in the twentieth century. This gave him considerable power: he was ennobled at the age of forty and given ministerial positions during the First World War.

A major consequence of Harmsworth's revolution was the development in Britain of a truly national press at the expense of the provincial press – the opposite of the process occurring in France. While at the beginning of the twentieth century the gap between national sales and provincial sales was not significant, by the end of the Second World War the provincial market was almost entirely reduced to evening papers.[54]

Popular magazines too did well in Great Britain, including *Cassell's* and *Good Words* (family journals), *Pearson's Weekly* (informative and entertaining), *Tit-Bits* (racy), *Cottager* (pious and evangelical), *Artisan* (pious and evangelical) and *Clarion* (secular).

Tit-Bits was exemplary. Launched in 1881, as its full title (*Tit-Bits from all the Most Interesting Books, Periodicals and Newspapers of the World*) suggested, it was replete with short and easily assimilated news. It was informative without requiring the reader to spend more than a few minutes on any one item. Mr Whelpdale, one of the characters in Gissing's *New Grub Street*, explained the theory behind it when coming up with the idea of magazines called *Tittle-Tattle* and *Chit-Chat*:

> Let me explain my principle. I would have the paper address itself to the quarter-educated; that is to say, the great generation that is being turned out by the Board schools, the young men and women who can just read, but are incapable of sustained attention. People of this kind want something to occupy them in trains, and on buses and trams. As a rule they care for no newspapers except the Sunday ones; what they want is the lightest and frothiest of chit-chatty information – bits of stories, bits of description, bits of scandal, bits of jokes, bits of statistics, bits of foolery. Am I not right? Everything must be very short, two inches at the utmost; their attention can't sustain itself beyond two inches. Even chat is too solid for them: they want chit-chat.[55]

The most innovative popular press, however, was not the British but the American. The Americans invented the interview, which had become common journalistic practice in the 1860s.[56] The word, in English, was included in the *Grand dictionnaire universel du XIX siècle* published by Larousse in 1890 (2nd supplement). Americans also invented the 'tabloid' format so that papers such as the *New York Daily News* (1919) could be easily read on public transport. By the first decade of the twentieth century the American daily press was the first in the world in terms of copies sold per inhabitant (one copy per 3.8 inhabitants), followed by France (one per 6.5), Britain (one per eight), Italy and Japan (one per twelve) and Russia (one copy per fifty-eight).[57] By 1900 there were well over 2,000 daily newspapers in the United States.

The American press was able to cater for the wide diversity existing in the country. It has been noted that by 1914 the USA had 160 foreign-language dailies. American religious fervour, particularly pronounced at the turn of the century, provided a market for magazines and books disseminating Pente-costalist ideas – in 1908 at least thirty-four journals were specifically aimed at this market segment – helped by low postal charges, a highly developed rail system, and state subsidies to religious literature.[58] Even socialist news-papers did well, reaching a total circulation of two million in 1913.

Along with diversity there was also a trend towards homogeneity: one group controlling a number of newspapers and providing each with similar features and information. Founded in 1894, the Scripps-McRae League of Newspapers formed a press agency (later United Press International) and a newspaper syndicate, the Newspaper Enterprise Association, to provide their papers with material. By 1914 the League owned twenty-three papers. Its main rival was the group formed by William Randolph Hearst. By 1904 he owned six newspapers; twenty by 1922, as well as various weeklies and two wire services. The large size of the country permitted such operations. By comparison, European press barons faced a far more restricted market. In some European countries, above all in Great Britain, the trend was towards the establishment of national papers, while in the USA it was towards a large number of local papers sharing some features, leading articles, columns and comic strips. The choice was immense. A traveller crossing the United States in, say, 1880, would have been able to pick up the *Mobile Register* in Alabama, the *New Orleans Times-Picayune* in Louisiana, the *Arkansas Gazette* in Ar-kansas, the *Kansas Weekly Herald* in Kansas, the *Nebraska Palladium and Platte Valley Advocate* in Nebraska, and the *Chico Enterprise-Record* in Cali-fornia. In each of these states there were usually several competing dailies. The choice one hundred years later is probably narrower.

Pictures Everywhere

The development of photography had empowered the individual. A simple machine, easy to use, enabled those deprived of any talent for drawing or painting to capture a face or a scene that took their fancy. But at the end of the nineteenth century the camera was still an expensive gadget. The middle classes went to a photographer to have their portrait taken, framed it and then hung it on the wall of their home. Yet another former prerogative of the aristocracy – the conservation of one's image – became part of bourgeois life, albeit in a somewhat demoted form. As usual, some complained. Baudelaire, shocked that photographs had been accepted for exhibition at the Salon of 1859, with typical élitism condemned it on the grounds that it would destroy the art of painting, while hideous crowds would narcissistically rush to look at themselves.[59]

Newspapers, by reproducing photographs of the famous, made their features known to all. At the end of the eighteenth century very few people would have been able to recognise the face of the King whose barely discernible features graced the coins of the realm. By the beginning of the twentieth century a mass daily press, taking its cue from the success of the illustrated weekly, began a process which made even unknown people famous, though perhaps, as Andy Warhol suggested, for fifteen minutes only. A talented designer and painter like the Moravian-born Alphonse Mucha (1860–1939), one of the main exponents of Art Nouveau, whose posters covered so many kiosks and walls of Belle-Époque Paris, having understood the commercial possibilities of the new technique of colour lithography, used it for posters to promote, among others, the actress Sarah Bernhardt, his pre-eminent client and one of the first internationally acclaimed superstars.[60] Mucha also secured commissions from the biscuit-manufacturer Lefèvre-Utile (for Biscuits Champagne as well as their famous cognac), Nestlé and the cycles Perfecta, creating what we now call 'brand awareness'.[61]

Photography gave the illusion of realism in an age that was hungry for it. A painting may lie, but not a photograph, or so it was thought, and so it would later be said about television images. In fact photographs, just like paintings, acquire their meaning from their setting, their title, their headline, their caption; in other words, from their wider context.[62] Hurried readers or viewers take in text and picture at the same time on the basis of what they expect and already know. As Roland Barthes put it, 'No photograph has ever convinced or refuted anyone (but the photograph can "confirm") . . .'[63]

Photography did not even displace prints, which in some form or other were more popular than ever in the nineteenth century. In France the so-called 'Images d'Épinal' were a lucrative business. They originated in the seventeenth century, and their enduring popularity was considerably enhanced by the spread of a huge body of popular religious literature, now lost or yet to be rediscovered, in support of the cult of the Virgin Mary, or *Panagia*, that was springing up all over Europe, from Greece, where it coincided with the struggle for national independence in the 1820s (Mary the Mother of the Nation) to Lourdes and Marpingen in Germany. By 1870 some seventeen million such images had been produced and sold at enormous profit (Jay Winter estimates it at 1,500 per cent). They were not all religious, for the phenomenon was also fed by a romantic reading of the Napoleonic wars and fed into the cult of the Emperor, enabling the most important industrial producer of the *Images*, the firm of Pellerin based in Épinal, to make a fortune. Nor was it simply a French business: Pellerin exported some 30 per cent of its output.[64] These much-reviled artefacts – the term *Image d'Épinal* is now synonymous with lower-class sentimental religiosity – influenced avant-garde artists such as Dufy, Braque, Léger and Picasso, inspired patriotic war posters and internationally successful (and highly profitable) films such as Abel Gance's *J'Accuse* (1919).[65] In Belgium too, Antwerp and other cities produced millions of religious images which were sent throughout the world. In the second half of the nineteenth century Belgium, a country with a population of five or six million, produced five million images.[66]

Photography had to wait for the war of 1914–18 to become equally popular. In Italy, for instance, some 100,000 pictures were taken during the conflict. Many were then used in photographic exhibitions throughout the country, making the war a shared experience in a way which had not been possible previously.[67] Even before the war, however, the market for the *Images d'Épinal* had almost disappeared.

The highly portable Kodak camera, introduced at the beginning of the twentieth century, revolutionised the newspaper world. Artists' renderings were still used, but increasingly the photograph would show the world 'as it really is'. The ease of photography brought about a change in the conception of the illustrated periodical. German newspaper publishers such as August Scherl and, later, Hermann Ullstein, were among the first to recognise that the modern illustrated magazine would no longer use pictures to illustrate a text, but to tell the story.[68] However innovative, the Germans were outdistanced in terms of sales by the long-standing strength of the British illustrated press. This, however, was soon to be overtaken by the Americans, thanks to their larger market and better organisation in news and photo gathering.

In France the first news photo appeared on 31 May 1890 in *L'Illustration*, the first colour photo in 1907. By 1914 the print run of the magazine had climbed to 280,000 copies. Dailies developed a weekly illustrated edition: the *Figaro* introduced the *Figaro illustré* in 1890. The popular *Journal illustré*, which had started in 1864 with engraved illustrations, adopted photographs in 1897, as the supplements of the *Petit journal* and the *Petit Parisien* had done in 1895.[69] By 1912 the *Miroir* was completely illustrated with photographs – drawings by then were considered out of date. The success of these new picture magazines depended largely on presenting old genres in new formats. Photographs told sensational news through illustrations – just like the chapbooks of old with their woodcut prints.[70] Thus the French magazine *Excelsior* on its front page of 14 December 1913, using photographs, told the story of the *Mona Lisa*, stolen in August 1911 and just recovered in Florence. At the centre of the page was an oval-shaped picture of the thief, Vincenzo Perruggia. Set around this were ten pictures retracing, like stills from a film, the various steps taken to remove the painting from the wall of the Salon Carré and get it out of the museum. Quite appropriately, the name given to this construction was a *récit-photo*, i.e. a photographic narrative.

Illustrated magazines spread throughout Europe. Though relatively expensive, they were easier to read than dailies, and were popular across classes. Publishers diversified from books to illustrated magazines with ease, often using the same distribution network. Thus the Italian publishing house Treves, which between 1880 and 1914 had become the leading publisher of foreign contemporary literature, started in 1863 *Illustrazione popolare. Giornale per le famiglia* (ten cents), which was followed by the more upmarket *L'Illustrazione Italiana* (1873) at sixty cents, to which were added the *Corriere illustrato della Domenica, Il Secolo, Rivista popolare illustrata* and, for children, *Mondo piccino*. Treves followed a policy of trying to cater for the entire social spectrum. Thus the women's magazine *Margherita. Giornale delle Signore Italiane di gran lusso di mode e letteratura* (1878) cost one lira (only fifty cents without the sewing patterns). Those of more modest means could buy the fortnightly *L'Eleganza* (1878, thirty cents), while the *Corriere per le signore* (ten cents), which also contained a serialised novel, and *L'Eco della moda* (also ten cents) were aimed at those on a tight budget.[71] But it was in ordinary daily papers, in stories about current affairs, that photos came into their own. They illustrated the stories, adding apparent realism to the written word. Slowly they became common even on the front page of popular papers – only some of the prestige papers avoided them for a long time (*The Times* and *Le Monde*).

The relaxation of censorship in France after 1881 facilitated the spread of satirical magazines. *L'Assiette au beurre* (1901–12) was one of dozens of such publications published in the first years of the new century. Most tended to be left-wing. *L'Assiette*, whose print run fluctuated between 25,000 and 40,000, was staunchly against the various moral leagues which tried to set standards for popular culture. It campaigned on behalf of prostitutes, seen as victims of men, but towards the end of its run it also developed a strong anti-Semitism which conflated 'the rich' with 'the Jews.'[72]

The Comic Strip

Illustrated magazines, invented in the nineteenth century, became a key cultural product of the twentieth. Another form of printed entertainment born in the nineteenth became part of the new mass culture: the comic strip. Though nowadays there is a considerable body of 'arty' graphic stories, the comic strip has remained a humble genre with, in English, a low name. Comic strips were rarely preserved in libraries and have not, until recently, been the object of scholarly criticism.[73] A few authors of comic strips have become famous – for instance Hergé, the creator of Tintin, and Charles Schulz of 'Peanuts' fame – but on the whole readers know the characters not their author, an unmistakable sign that this is not a 'high' genre. Gaining access to 'high' culture is no simple matter. The cinema took a long time to emancipate itself from its humble fairground origin and become accepted as an art, revered by intellectuals, taught in universities and discussed in learned journals. Even today 'going to the cinema' does not have the cultural *cachet* of 'going to the theatre'.

Even in its mode of distribution the comic strip showed its lowly origin: not for it the independence of print, but as a newspaper feature, a mere incentive to purchasers, or in a 'funnies' section specifically aimed at children. Like the cinema, born at the same time, the comic strip was unmistakably aimed at a popular market, something to be quickly produced, quickly consumed, and then discarded.

The definition of the comic strip has exercised specialists in the field. It is generally agreed that more than one cartoon with a caption is required to constitute a comic strip. There must be a story in sequence, where the characters express themselves with a caption below the frame or in a kind of bubble. Those who wish to provide the comic strip with an illustrious ancestry invoke ancient Egyptian tombs; the Parthenon with sculptures on its pediment depicting the birth of Athena; the frieze that winds around Trajan's Column in Rome representing Trajan's conquest of Dacia; the Bayeux Tapestry representing the conquest of England by William the Conqueror, with 1,512 figures in seventy-two scenes. There are also Renaissance paintings where a story is told visually in stages, such as Vittore Carpaccio's *Legend of St Ursula* (1490–95) at the Accademia in Venice, or Fra Angelico's *Annunciation* (1433–34) in Cortona (Tuscany). On a golden strip which seems to come out of his mouth the Archangel Gabriel says: '*Spiritus Sanctus supeveniet in te et virtus Altissimi obumbrabit tibi*' (The Holy Spirit will come upon you, and the power of the Most High will overshadow you). And the Virgin Mary replies: '*Ecce ancilla Domini. Fiat mihi secundum Verbum Tuum*' (Behold, I am the handmaiden of the Lord; let it be to me according to your word).[74] Paolo Uccello's panels *The Profanation of the Host by the Jews* (c.1467) show a Christian woman trying to exchange a stolen sacrament at a Jewish pawnbroker's; the pawnbroker attempting to damage it; the restoration of the sacrament to the altar, the repentance of the woman; the burning of the Jew at the stake; and devils and angels struggling for the soul the woman (one assumes that that of the Jew goes to hell without anyone fighting over it).[75]

The real forerunners, however, were caricaturists such as James Gillray ('Democracy or a Sketch of the Life of Bonaparte' – a sequence on Napoleon's rise to power) and George Cruickshank in his cartoon about the Peterloo massacre of 1819, 'A Strong Proof of the Flourishing State of the Country', where he has captions in bubbles: an upper-class gentleman, sitting on sacks labelled 'The Fat of the Land', is showing a picture of prosperous life in the colonies ('The Cape of Forlorn Hope') to a group of half-starved and unemployed visitors, distracting their attention from a representation of the massacre.[76]

But it is the Swiss Rodolphe Töpffer (1799–1846) who is most often regarded as the 'father' of the comic strip. Inspired by William Hogarth's works such as *The Rake's Progress* (1735), which consisted of separate prints which if seen together made up a story, Töpffer linked his images in a continuous narrative. Continuity is one of the difficulties of the genre, because it is necessary to distinguish each character, yet the reader must recognise the same characters in each image. This Töpffer achieved in his 'histoires en images' (picture-stories), creating various story books such as *Histoire de M. Jabot* (1833), *Monsieur Crépin* (1837) and *Monsieur Pencil* (1840), collected in 1846 in *Histoires en Estampes* (Engraved Stories).[77]

A further step towards the modern comic strip was taken when the German satirical magazine *Fliegende Blätter* asked a caricaturist, Wilhelm Busch (1832–1908), to experiment with stories made up of images with a rhyming text at the bottom of the picture. This was the birth of Busch's famous strip featuring two brothers, 'Max und Moritz' (1865). Here the succession of images was more strictly connected than in Töpffer, the sequence acquiring a faster and faster rhythm towards an inevitably funny, if catastrophic, outcome. It prefigures the movements of the film camera and other cinematic techniques such as the passage from the open plan to the close-up.[78]

For our purposes the identification of the 'first' actual comic strip is an exercise which has little interest – though it clearly fascinates the army of specialists.[79] What matters is the connection between the expansion of comic strips and that of newspapers and magazines. 'Max und Moritz' had paved the way, but the vogue for illustrated stories did not start until the 1880s – their development depended on an improvement in the techniques of reproducing images. In France the magazine *Le Chat noir* (1882) published more and more illustrated stories (with no text): eleven in 1882, thirty-nine in 1885, and fifty-two in 1891.[80]

In Great Britain and the USA, weeklies dedicated mainly to comic strips were already circulating in 1891: *Ally Sloper's Comic Kalender* and *Illustrated Chips*. In 1890 Alfred Harmsworth's Periodical Publishing Company launched *Comic Cuts*, which was selling 300,000 copies after less than a year. It became Harmsworth's biggest earner at a time when his new *Daily Mirror*, the first daily newspaper for women, was losing money. *Comic Cuts* relied on imported American strips, and was not specifically aimed at children, though many read it. Only in 1914 did Harmsworth launch an illustrated journal for children, the *Rainbow*, which quickly sold a million copies a week.[81]

In all European comic strips, including English ones, the captions were at the bottom of the frame, not enclosed in a speech balloon. Balloons were an American speciality that the Europeans refused to adopt for decades, until their superiority – as we shall see – became manifest. Here the palm of 'first' would probably go to 'The Yellow Kid', designed by Richard F. Outcault (1863–1928), which appeared for the first time – as a single cartoon – in May 1895 in Pulitzer's *New York World*.[82] The caption initially appeared on the shirt of the Kid. A year later it had become a strip and the text was enclosed in a balloon. It was actually called 'Hogan's Alley' and represented a somewhat Oriental-looking child, bald, with ears sticking out – hence 'the yellow kid', a name originally given by readers themselves (the press had started using colours for some of its features).

The United States provided the best terrain for the expansion of the comic strip. Because there was no national press, comic strips quickly became established as part of the syndicated press. This system was remarkable, making it possible to start a local paper at low cost. A limited staff could write the local news, the rest would be written up by news agencies and the whole given greater weight by purchasing nationally syndicated columns. Thus one should conceive of the American press not as a myriad of newspapers competing for market shares (this occurred only in the larger cities) but as near-local monopolies carrying almost identical national and international features and commentaries – almost like a single gigantic national newspaper with added local news. Such a system could not possibly develop on a large scale in Europe, and not only because of its linguistic fragmentation. The American market was not simply big, but also highly diversified. This heterogeneous population was not literate enough (in English) to impinge significantly on the market for narrative and non-fiction, but it did consume the less literary aspects of popular culture: music, variety shows, the cinema and the popular press. The comic strip could be read by a public that was, on average, more literate than the European one, yet not so educated as to demand complex reading material.

Though no one could possibly know whether comic strips led to increased sales, competitors felt that they should follow suit. Hearst even enticed Outcault away from the *New York World*, and got him to continue 'The Yellow Kid' in the *New York Journal*. The ensuing legal battle (won by Hearst) convinced every newspaper publisher that comic strips were essential.

Though the comic strip came to be regarded as a quintessential American export – indeed, as the first major specifically American cultural product to be exported – some of the early examples were based on European characters. For instance 'The Katzenjammer Kids', created by Rudolph Dirks in 1897 and drawn by him until his death in 1958, were inspired by Wilhelm Bush's 'Max und Moritz'. The 'Katzenjammer Kids' strip was then adapted by the French in 1911, where the boys were called the 'Petits Chaperché' and, in 1935, 'Pam et Poum'. In the USA the strip's German name, initially an asset in New York with its vast German population, turned into a liability during the First

World War. 'The Katzenjammer Kids' became 'The Shenanigan Kids' in 1918, but reverted only two years later to their original name.

In Europe the comic strip had a slow start. In France, for instance, where it would eventually acquire great popularity, the comic strip, or *bande dessinée* (commonly referred as BD, meaning 'drawn-up strip'), was initially seldom used. The *Petit Français illustré* however began to publish 'La Famille Fenouillard à l'exposition' (of 1889), the story of a provincial petty bourgeois family, rather stupid and unattractive, and in awe of Paris and the Eiffel Tower. Its author, Georges Colomb (later Deputy Director of Botanic Science at the Sorbonne), adopted, for obvious reasons, the pseudonym of Christophe, and drew the strips to supplement his modest academic salary. By the decade leading up to the war the publisher Fayard was using the genre for children, a market which was highly promising, especially since technical progress had made it possible to produce a sixteen-page magazine at a reasonable price.[83] Once established as being for children (though widely read by adults), the comic strip continued to be regarded as an inferior genre, viewed with suspicion by the religious authorities.[84]

'The Yellow Kid' was the first comic strip in Italy, in the weekly *Novellino*. Then the Italians – later great producers and consumers of comic strips – published their own, without balloons but with captions. These first appeared in the *Corriere dei piccoli*, a magazine for children launched in 1908, and discontinued only in 1971, published by the leading Italian press group, the *Corriere della sera*. The first editor of the *Corriere dei piccoli*, Silvio Spaventa Filippi, was an anglophile and an admirer of English literature, especially of Dickens. Like many *esterofili* (as lovers of all things foreign are called in Italy) his distaste for Italian provincialism manifested itself by importing and adapting stories and characters from abroad, especially from the United States: 'Buster Brown' (another of Richard F. Outcault's creations) was turned into 'Mammolo'; 'Happy Hooligan' (created by Frederick Burr Opper, 1857–1937), a character dressed in rags and wearing a tin hat, became 'Fortunello' and was adapted for the cinema by the famous comic actor Ettore Petrolini.[85] Readers were often unaware of the foreign origins of the material.[86]

As in France and other European countries, the Italian comic strip after 1900 became a children's genre. The early strips – eight frames with captions written in eight-syllable rhymed couplets – exhibited the mix of the pathetic and the populist characteristic of recent 'national' children's literature such as De Amicis's *Cuore* (see pages 852–3) and Collodi's *Pinocchio* (see pages 702–3).[87] Soon the comic strip became one of the most popular forms of literature in Italy. Attilio Mussino produced an astonishing range of characters, including a little black child, Bilbolbul, whose almost surrealist adventures took place in a fantastic Africa. In 1917 Sergio Tofano published in the *Corriere dei piccoli* the adventures of Signor Bonaventura, who always ends up by winning one million lire. This strip lasted for decades, and was adapted for the theatre (five plays) and the cinema (1942).

Realising the possible propaganda value of the comic strip in a country with high illiteracy, the Italian authorities commissioned a strip for war veterans called *La Tradotta* (The Convoy, March 1918–July 1919) which, alongside the inevitable patriotic themes, contained some genuine satire and caricature. With the advent of fascism, a movement particularly attentive to popular culture, the comic strip became more political and was used in some of the youth publications of the regime such as the *Giornale dei balilla* (1923) for boys and *La Piccola Italiana* (1927) for girls.[88]

Finding the right market slot was important early on. The French magazine *La Semaine de Suzette* (1904) was aimed at young middle-class girls. The heroine of its comic strip was Bécassine, a clumsy young servant girl from Brittany (the term *une Bécassine* still designates a naïve and silly young woman). The success of *La Semaine de Suzette* (and of 'Bécassine') convinced others to launch weeklies with comic strips for girls. These tended to contain stories of a sentimental nature (orphans, etc.) rather than humorous ones (which, it was assumed, would amuse mainly boys).

Market forces and the realisation that there were many adult readers encouraged some publishers to be more daring. In 1908 the Offenstad brothers launched *L'Épatant*, which deliberately set out to be offensive, using street slang, celebrating bad taste (always an attraction for children), depicting robbers and incompetent gangsters such as the 'Pieds Nickelés' (drawn by Louis Forton) and mocking politicians. For girls, the most popular 'naughty' character was the streetwise girl 'l'Espiègle Lili' (Mischievous Lili) in the magazine *Fillette*. Though the genre was supposed to be ephemeral, some of the most popular strips survived for an extraordinary length of time: 'Bécassine', 'Les Pieds Nickelés' and 'L'Espiègle Lili' all survived into the 1970s. The magazine *Noël*, launched in 1895 with a print run of 100,000, lasted until 1939. Such longevity is a feature of cultural products addressed to children, largely because, before television advertising, parents could influence the reading habits of their children and tended to recommend what they themselves had enjoyed.

But longevity was always exceptional. As for most novels, the first edition of a comic strip is likely to be the last. In France at the beginning of the twentieth century, when the country was not yet hooked to the comic strip, there were hundreds of strip serials which disappeared after a few months. The industry gave work to over two hundred designers who, in the best tradition of industrial literature, worked for several magazines at the same time and disguised their real identities under American-sounding pseudonyms. Even then there was considerable variety: the humorous, the grotesque, and a wide range of themes borrowed from popular literature such as melodrama, fairy tales, legends and myths, folk themes, military tales, adventure stories set – following Jules Verne – in distant and exotic lands, from the Argentinian pampas to the North and South Poles to the American far west, or in settings favoured by nineteenth-century novels including the Italian Renaissance, the French and American Revolutionary Wars, ancient Egypt, the Middle Ages, the occult, and so on. Controversial subjects were eschewed. The comic strip was an escapist genre, just like the *roman feuilleton* which preceded it. It redrafted in a new format whatever had pleased the public in previous decades or even centuries. When there was a clear national consensus – such as during the First World War – the comic strip was patriotic, fearlessly depicting (in France) German soldiers as stupid sausage-eating idiots or heartless brutes.

Though it was not realised at the time, the comic strip, being easy to read, opened the world of printed stories not only to children but also to new groups of readers hitherto excluded from it because of their limited reading skills. The term 'comic strip', with its emphasis on the humorous, is a real misnomer in English (as well as in some other languages such as German or Spanish). The French term *bande dessinée* is more accurate. When speech balloons were introduced, the Italians adopted the term *fumetto* (literally: 'small smoke').

There were multiple connections between the cinema and the comic strips. 'The Yellow Kid' appeared in the same year as the first Lumière film (1895). The first comic film, Lumière's *L'Arroseur arrosée* (1895), was directly inspired by a comic strip published in *La Caricature* in 1887. The strip uses a number of techniques similar to those used by the cinema: a frame to establish the setting with two or more characters, then a 'zoom' narrowing to a close-up of the talking characters.[89] The montage or editing of frames is essential.

European strips started adopting the American balloon more widely only in the 1920s – Alain Saint-Ogan's 'Zig et Puce' was one of the French pioneers in 1925. Until then captions remained firmly at the bottom of the frame. Yet the balloon has considerable advantages over the caption. Not only does it allow more words, but it enables the reader to read the words and look at the picture at the same time. With traditional captions the reader had to decide which to 'see' first.[90] Balloons facilitate dialogue, because it is easier to establish who is speaking. They force the writer to reduce or eliminate the voice of the narrator – as in the theatre and in films. To comment on actions and intentions, dialogue between characters had to be used – as in films or in popular novels: Tintin regularly addresses himself to his dog Snowy, the way Sherlock Holmes explains what is going on to Dr Watson. Because in Western scripts a text is read from left to right, comic strips normally position the character who is going to speak first on the left of the frame – that way their balloon will be read first. Such cultural bias may have slowed down the global expansion of the comic strip into cultures with different reading conventions – such as Arabic, where script is read from right to left, or Chinese and Japanese – but it did not stop it (Chinese and Japanese comics are often drawn from the top to the bottom of the page).

The comic strip became widely adapted thanks to the press – thus confirming its dependence on existing media. In Portugal the first strip, 'Quim e Manecas' by Stuart Carvalhais, started out in 1915 in the *Seculo comico*, the humorous supplement to the *Seculo*.[91] In Barcelona on 3 January 1904 the Catalan review *En Patufet* carried a strip designed by the writer Folch i Torres with the child Patufet, which lasted until 1938. In 1907 the daily *ABC* had a comic strip supplement called *Gente munda*. By 1917 the Spanish comic strip had become well-established thanks to the weekly magazine *TBO*, which systematically adapted American comics – for instance, the 1919 *TBO* strip 'Pipiolin' (the first Spanish strip with speech bubbles) was an adaptation of the American 'The Newlyweds' by George McManus, and 'La Pequeña Annie' an adaptation of 'Little Annie'. By 1935 the print run of *TBO* was 195,000 – enormous by Spanish standards.[92]

Poland had already imported Wilhelm Busch's old 'Max und Moritz' under the name 'Wis and Wacek', as well as the more recent 'Bécassine' from France.[93] The 'invasion' of the American comic strip occurred only in the 1930s, when nearly 75 per cent of Polish home consumption came from the USA. The Dutch too mainly imported comic strips until the 1920s, when the daily *Rotterdamsch Nieuwsblad* produced its own 'Yoebje en Achmed'.[94]

The first Finnish comic strips appeared in 1917 when the designer Fogeli (Ola Fogelberg, 1894–1952) created 'Jann Ankkanen', a duck who commented on current affairs in the weekly *Suomen Kuvalehti*. Fogeli went on to create the most celebrated comic strips in Finland: 'Pekka Puupää' (Peter the Fool), in support of the social democrats, a rare link between comic strips and politics. After Fogeli's death the 'Pekka Puupää' strip was continued by his daughter, Toto Fogelberg-Kaila. Until the end of the 1920s there were virtually no foreign comics in Finland except that of the Swedish Oscar Andersson.[95] Andersson, the first Swedish comic strip designer, had started publishing at the end of the nineteenth century and became famous in the Nordic countries with the somewhat surrealistic series 'Mannen som gör vad som faller honom in' (The Man who Does Everything that Comes into his Mind – such as putting his car into his pocket or throwing away his umbrella when the rain stops). However, after Andersson the majority of Swedish comic strips were imported.[96]

Eventually the comic strip, with its uncanny resemblance to the cinema, provided ideas for the animated cartoon. In America in 1914–15 John Randolph Bray and Earl Hurd used transparent overlays made of sheets of cellulose on which the moving figures were drawn in their sequential poses, whilst the non-moving parts were drawn on a sheet of paper – a process which remained the foundation of animated films until the advent of computer-aided design in the 1980s. Then in December 1916 William Randolph Hearst set up the International Film Studio to exploit the cinematic adaptation of comic strip characters which appeared in his papers.[97] The integration of cinema, design and the press had taken another step forward.

❧

37

Shows

The New Theatre

THE DOMINATION of the French theatre in Europe, boosted in the previous decades by Scribe's melodramas and Eugène Labiche's farces, continued almost unabated throughout the 1880s and 1890s. 'Almost' because, at least in the sphere of the 'serious' theatre, the French contributed relatively little. French farces remained unrivalled thanks to the emergence of a new star writer, Georges Feydeau (1862–1921). The success of his plays was due to their complex, if implausible, plots and situations, rather than to their psychological depth. Feydeau, like Labiche before him, provided the audience with an evening of fun, while its more perceptive members could detect some ferocious social criticism amidst the wisecracks. Such firing on several cylinders has remained the hallmark of long-term success. In the age of mass entertainment the ability to speak to several audiences at the same time is an effective long-term strategy.

Feydeau was not an innovator. He played by the well-established rules of the vaudeville. In the first act, all the principal characters are introduced. In the second they meet in circumstances they wish had not taken place. This is the height of the comic moment. Finally, in the third act, the misunderstandings are resolved.[1] His first great success, *Tailleur pour dames* (1884), opened with a husband returning home just as his wife's lover is encircling her waist with his hands. He is told the man is the tailor, who has come to take her measurements. *Tailleur* was performed seventy-nine times, an unusually long run at the time. This produced a substantial income for the young playwright, who was paid, as established by law, 12 per cent of box office receipts.[2] Feydeau increased his earnings by pioneering the use of covert advertisement in his plays. In *Feu la mère de Madame* (1908) the heroine mentions her favourite perfume (Rose Coty) and how much it costs – part of deal between Feydeau and Coty, who delivered a considerable quantity of the expensive perfume to him every month the play was being performed.[3]

Feydeau's farces are still popular today, but other successful playwrights of his time have fared less well. The historical dramas of Victorien Sardou (1831–1908), popular in his lifetime (note his *Madame Sans-Gêne*, 1893), remained unknown outside France and are now seldom performed even there. A similar fate befell the social satires of Émile Augier (1820–89), while the francophone Belgian Maurice Maeterlinck is remembered, if at all, as the author of *Pelléas et Mélisande* (1892) thanks to Debussy's operatic adaptation.[4]

An unusual play written in verse, however, has continued to delight: Edmond Rostand's *Cyrano de Bergerac*. After its opening night at the Théâtre Porte Saint-Martin on 28 December 1897 it became one of the great triumphs in the history of the French theatre, with four hundred performances by March 1899. The play is 'a heritage park of allusions to all the sources of national pride: *pâtisseries* and sauces, garments and fashion accessories, the evocative commonplaces of French history as transmitted by the French education system and the novels of Alexandre Dumas'.[5]

The French remained unable to export their classical theatre. The works of Racine and Corneille depended too much on the beauty of their language – a beauty lost in translation – and not enough on the drama of the action or the building-up of characters. Molière was different: characters were central to his plays. The German classical theatre relied mainly on Goethe, Schiller, Lessing and Kleist, few of whom encountered lasting international success. Shakespeare, on the other hand, had both good plots and great mastery of language. As a result he became, in the course of the nineteenth century, the global representative of great classic theatre, to the dismay of the French. He was particularly popular in Russia and Germany. In fact Shakespeare was virtually regarded as a German author even by rabid nationalists. In the middle of the First World War, when anti-British feelings were at their highest, the playwright Gerhart Hauptmann wrote: 'There is no nation, not even the British, which is more entitled to call Shakespeare its own than Germany. Shakespeare's characters have become part of our world, his soul has become one with ours . . .'[6] Still, the French might console themselves with the knowledge that in Germany, and particularly in Munich, the most successful plays at the end of the nineteenth century were French farces and salon plays and their German imitations. They all dealt with the upper classes and sex.[7] The same situation prevailed in most European cities.

The French repertory remained influential at the lower end of the market. Quality theatre became international. Here writers from peripheral countries achieved significant renown: from Norway Henrik Ibsen (1828–1906) and his *A Doll's House* (*Et dukkehjem*, 1879), which made him known throughout Europe; and from Sweden August Strindberg (1849–1912), arguably that country's greatest writer, successful in his time in both Germany (1,035 performances of twenty-four of his plays between 1913 and 1915) and France, but far less known in Britain.[8] Some of Strindberg's plays are still regularly performed throughout Europe and North America. His shock value has not abated since *Miss Julie* (1888) was called, in *The Times* (15 May 1912), 'the most unpleasant play ever written'.

Other countries too entered the theatrical fray. In Russia there were five state (Imperial) theatres: three in St Petersburg and two in Moscow (the Bolshoi or Great Theatre for ballet and opera, and the Small Theatre for drama). The abolition in 1882 of the state monopoly on the theatre led to the opening of the privately-run Moscow Arts Theatre in 1897 by the playwright Vladimir Nemirovich-Danchenko and the director Konstantin Stanislavsky. Russia, which had already provided some early world theatre classics, such as Gogol's great satirical play *The Inspector General* (1836), continued to produce home-grown vaudevilles and patriotic drama until the 1860s. It had a lively street and pantomime theatre based on an ever changing mixture of European and Russian folk stories. Then it produced a world theatre of great force thanks to four plays written by Anton Chekhov (1860–1904) between 1896 and 1904: *The Seagull, Uncle Vanya, Three Sisters* and *The Cherry Orchard.*

France, because of its considerable domestic production, past and present, imported relatively little of these foreign works. In the 1880s and 1890s half a million Parisians went to the theatre once a week, more than twice as many once a month. Since a stage success was the surest road to fame and fortune in the world of letters, there was a constant supply of new works to satisfy this large market.[9] Even an innovative theatre director open to outside influence such as André Antoine relied overwhelmingly on French drama for his Théâtre-Libre and subsequently the Théâtre-Antoine (founded in 1897). Of the seventy-three playwrights whose plays he staged between 1886 and 1902, only eight were foreign: Giovanni Verga (Italy), Edgar Allan Poe (USA), Turgenev, Tolstoy, Hauptmann, Bjørnson, Strindberg and Ibsen. Yet these productions of foreign writers were daring, because it was very rare in France at the time to stage foreign plays, particularly ones as controversial as Ibsen's

Ghosts (initially banned in Norway, Germany and England and first performed in 1882 in Chicago before an audience of Scandinavian immigrants) and Strindberg's *Miss Julie,* which had been banned in Denmark.[10] Camille Mauclair, writing in 1899, complained that theatre managers either staged established classics, which carried little risk, or melodrama and suchlike, which met public expectations. When they staged a good modern play, they did it out of a sense of duty, almost hoping that it would fail, proving that new plays were a hopeless enterprise.[11] Foreign authors were so delighted to be performed in Paris that, unlike French playwrights, they made modest economic demands. The French were often novelists who had adapted their novels for the theatre and for whom the Paris stage was the principal source of revenue and where monetary reward was linked to their prestige.[12]

Paris remained the centre of European theatrical life, the pole of attraction, particularly for modern experimentation, thanks, at least in part, to the widespread use of the French language among the intelligentsia, above all in Russia. But while their capital remained in the vanguard, the French themselves did not. Modernity was often in the hands of foreigners. Ballet had long been a Parisian genre. The terminology was French as were the great dancers. As early as the 1840s, special effects had been used in ballet: in 1843 Carlotta Grisi 'fell' – thanks to steel wires – from a 'cloud' into the arms of Lucien Petipa (the brother of the great choreographer Marius).[13] It was at this time that the traditional ballerina costume was adopted.

Then the Russians took over the genre, though admittedly some of the credit was owed to the French-born choreographer of the Imperial Ballet of St Petersburg, Marius Petipa. The roll-call of the great Russian ballet classics of the time includes virtually the whole of the established repertory: first Tchaikovsky's three great ballets (all choreographed by Petipa), *Swan Lake* (1877), *The Sleeping Beauty* (1889) and *The Nutcracker* (1892). Then the genre was revolutionised by a Russian choreographer, Michel Fokine (1880–1942), with *The Dying Swan* (1905, for the legendary Anna Pavlova) and *Les Sylphides* (1909), and then, with Diaghilev's Ballets Russes, *Schéhérazade* (1910), *The Firebird* (1910), *Petrushka* (1911) and *Daphnis and Chloë* (1912). Diaghilev used the talents of great French painters such as Henri Matisse, Georges Braque and Maurice Utrillo for the designs, and commissioned new scores from Igor Stravinsky, including *The Firebird, Petrushka* and the highly controversial *The Rite of Spring* (1913). Diaghilev also choreographed *Daphnis and Chloë* (music by Maurice Ravel) and *The Three-Cornered Hat* (1919, by Manuel de Falla). His torch was then passed on to other Russian-born choreographers who dominated the twentieth century: George Balanchine, Léonide Massine, Bronislava Nijinska and Serge Lifar.

Paris, however, provided the location. The Russian dancer Ida Lvovna Rubinstein (1885–1960), who had settled in Paris with the Ballets Russes, formed a rival company to Diaghilev, then she tried her hand at acting, and in 1913 convinced the director Vsevolod Meyerhold (1874–1940) to stage Gabriele D'Annunzio's play *La Pisanella*.[14] This shocked the Parisian public almost as much as Diaghilev's choreography of Stravinsky's *The Rite of Spring*. Paris was slowly becoming used to being shocked by foreigners and their novelties rather than shocking them. The French actors in *La Pisanella* were reluctant to comply with Meyerhold's modernist views and his insistence that diction should be simple and realistic, and that they should avoid tremolos and 'hamming'. It should be added that, since Meyerhold's French was perfunctory, they did not always understand what he was saying.[15] Some of the critics denounced the play, probably for chauvinistic reasons: a play in Paris written by an Italian, directed by a Russian and with a Russian actress in the lead was too much to take.

With the exception of D'Annunzio (*La Figlia di Iorio, Francesca da Rimini*), now seldom performed even in Italy, and Sem Benelli (1877–1949), whose *La Cena delle beffe* (The Jester's Supper, 1909) was produced in New York in 1919, Italy still failed to produce playwrights of note – even though there were excellent actors such as Eleonora Duse (1858–1924), who was internationally known, Ermete Zacconi (1886–1936) and Emma Gramatica (1875–1965). The problem was that the Italian theatre was in the hands, as it had been for centuries, of the *capocomico*, the leading actor or actress (as was the case with Emma Gramatica), who was also the business and artistic manager. Unable to sustain themselves in a single city, companies were forced to tour, stopping for a few days in towns and minor cities, taking advantage of the enormous number of theatres which dotted the country. It was a risky business, because the theatre owner would demand (and obtain) the takings of an agreed number of seats, whether these were sold or not. What was left would be shared between him and the company. Touring companies were forced to go for tried-and-tested popular fare: variety shows, operettas and vaudeville. As Gramsci complained: 'the theatre has become an industry', and 'Turin has become a fair'.[16] In effect, the Italian theatre was sharply divided along cultural lines. Many towns had two theatres: the one for the middle classes followed Paris, the one for the lower classes produced plays and burlesque in the local dialect.[17]

A similarly dire situation existed in Spain, whose golden age had been in the distant seventeenth century – an extraordinary period dominated by two major playwrights, Lope de Vega (1562–1635) and Pedro Calderón de la Barca (1600–81). Then the grip of Christianity and Spanish intellectual decadence led to a long period of stagnation. By the end of the nineteenth century there was little of note other than so-called 'chico' plays (light comedies) and the simple moral tales of the Madrid playwright Jacinto Benavente y Martínez (1866–1954, Nobel laureate 1922) such as a El Nido ajeno (The Nest of Others, 1894) and La Noche del sabato (1903), about a courtesan torn between worldly success and maternal instinct.

To some extent the state of theatre, from the point of view of the wider cultural industry, mattered little, though it mattered a lot to those dependent on it (who could be a powerful lobby). A considerable proportion of the repertory at the top end of the market, the least profitable, was made up of classics, i.e. dead authors. The classical repertoire tended to expand, because the number of new classics increased at a marginally faster rate than the drop-outs. This was partly to do with the fact that most of the theatrical repertoire of the last five hundred years had been preserved, while almost all the production of Sophocles, Aeschylus and Euripides was lost. Another reason was that the popularity of theatre and the number of theatres increased in Europe (and in North America) throughout the twentieth century – even after the dawning of the age of cinema and television. This greater audience capacity could not be fed by novelties alone. Besides, a classic work has undeniable marketing advantages, and not just because writers long dead demand no royalties. However, classical productions remained expensive and required some form of subsidy. The 'theatre of the people' advocated by socialists such as Maxim Gorky ended up being the classical aristocratic or bourgeois theatre, subsidised by the people for the benefit of the middle classes – as was the case in France, where the subsidised Comédie-Française and the Odéon remained the homes of high-culture drama, while the theatres of the boulevard provided the venues for successful productions: largely comic-sentimental plays.

One of the functions of the theatre was to provide some sorely needed extra cash for novelists (whose books were adapted), employment for actors (and, eventually, a training ground for the cinema), and social prestige for audiences and theatre-owners. In spite of its unquestioned expansion and growing commercialisation, a by-product of the growth of the middle classes, the theatre never became a real industry, and always provided employment for a relatively small number of people. In 1893 the journal *Der Kunstwart* reported that some 4,000 new plays were submitted to German theatres annually, but only 3 per cent were performed.[18] One of the consequences of this state of affairs was that many young playwrights, faced with their lack of success, blamed the philistine and crass taste of the bourgeoisie and developed a strong hostility towards it. Similar feelings were common in other cultural areas (art, novels, music). Those who did make the grade did not transform themselves overnight into paladins of the established order. Having obtained some success in opposition to bourgeois taste, they continued, at least for a while, to bite the hand that was feeding them – in the circumstances quite a sensible strategy.

Urbanisation and the growth of the universities had brought young intellectuals together in major cities. To avoid isolation, and probably to escape from their cheap and depressing lodgings, they gathered in cafés and pooled their resources.[19] Intellectuals need to be close to the centres of intellectual production: publishers, newspapers, theatres, art galleries, and other writers. They must be in London, Paris, Berlin, Hamburg, Munich, Brussels, Edinburgh, Vienna, Barcelona (rather than Madrid), Moscow and St Petersburg, Naples, Florence and Milan (rather than Rome), New York and Boston. It is significant that while in the 1850s and 1860s the literary and artistic outposts – what Baudelaire called, ironically, the avant-garde, thus coining the expression – were concentrated in Paris and, to a lesser extent, in London, the vanguards of the *fin-de-siècle* could be found in almost all major European cities. Oxford and Cambridge, where so many intellectuals worked and studied, never achieved a real intellectual dominance in English cultural life.

Some had been forced to find gainful if temporary employment in the more commercial environment of Bohemian cafés. Frank Wedekind (1864–1918), the great forerunner of the German expressionist theatre, was one of these. In 1886 he found a job in the advertising division of the newly created Maggi soup company, where he was paid by the line for writing advertising jingles in praise of instant soup.[20]

However, the vast majority of plays were neither modernist nor avant-garde. The 'trivial' theatre, which catered for 90 per cent of the theatre-going public, provided a significant lobby which protected the business as a whole – and hence also the avant-garde. Thus when in 1919 the US Congress passed a War Revenue Bill which included a theatre admission tax of 10 per cent, theatre managers as well as leading actors responded with a massive campaign which collected more than eight million signatures in 2,465 cities, from people from all walks of life. The campaign was supported by hotels, newspapers and universities, as the theatre was then still seen as 'the most popular of all the arts'. They won, and the tax was repealed.[21]

The theatre, unlike the increasingly fossilised opera repertory, continued to develop. Many of those who made their mark between 1880 and 1910 are still in the standard international theatrical repertory today, including the six listed below:

PLAYWRIGHT	COUNTRY	WORKS
Henrik Ibsen (1828–1906)	Norway	*A Doll's House* (1879)
		Ghosts (1881)
		Hedda Gabler (1890)
August Strindberg (1849–1912)	Sweden	*Miss Julie* (1888)
		The Dance of Death (1912)
Oscar Wilde (1854–1900)	Great Britain	*Lady Windermere's Fan* (1892)
		The Importance of Being Earnest (1895)
		An Ideal Husband (1895)
George Bernard Shaw (1856–1950)	Great Britain	*Major Barbara* (1905)
		Pygmalion (1913)
Anton Chekhov (1860–1904)	Russia	*The Seagull* (1896)
		Uncle Vanya (1899)
		Three Sisters (1901)
		The Cherry Orchard (1904)
Frank Wedekind (1864–1918)	Germany	*Pandora's Box* (1904)
Maxim Gorky (1868–1936)	Russia	*The Lower Depths* (1902)
		The Mother (1905)

Significantly, there are no French or American playwrights, while the 'periphery' has advanced: Ibsen from Norway and Strindberg from Sweden, the two 'British' writers, Wilde and Shaw, were Irish (and one could add J.M. Synge's *The Playboy of the Western World*, 1907), Gorky was from Nizhnii Novgorod (the city was renamed Gorky between 1932 and 1991) and Chekhov – the grandson of a serf – was born in Taganrog on the Sea of Azov in south-west Russia.

This new generation of playwrights provided material for the growing number of theatres which were springing up throughout Europe. Most of the thirty-five plays produced in Budapest by Sándor Hevesi (1873–1939) at the theatre of the Thália Society in 1904–08 were not by Hungarians.[22] Of course, three of the five Budapest theatres extant in 1900 were entirely dedicated to the vaudeville (with frequent songs almost like an operetta), but George Bernard Shaw too was popular.[23] Shaw's Hungarian success merits a brief account. In 1903 László Beöthy, the founder and manager of the leading vaudeville theatre of Budapest, the Király, had decided to introduce prose plays in his theatre so as to give his singers a rest. As Shaw had been particularly successful in Austria and Germany Beöthy decided to test his audience with *Arms and the Man* (1894), set in Bulgaria. The play opened in February 1904. The critics liked it, but the audience, used to pretty girls and farcical situations, found Shaw stodgy. By 1906 the climate had changed. The local intelligentsia had become aware of Shaw's growing fame in Austria and Germany, and did not wish to be left behind. The public too became interested: the Budapest papers had reported in some detail the scandal caused by the opening of Shaw's play on prostitution *Mrs Warren's Profession* at the Garrick Theatre in New York in October 1905, where it was immediately banned and the actors and the theatre manager arrested. At a subsequent court hearing it was decided that the play, though unpleasant, was not indecent. Though written in 1893, the play was not printed until 1898, and was performed in London in an uncensored form only in 1902 – and then only as a private performance (only in 1925 was it performed for the general public).[24] With such credentials *Mrs Warren's Profession* opened in Budapest in 1907 under the direction of Beöthy, to the delight of its audiences.[25]

Shaw's international success was among the signs that London was becoming one of the great centres of world theatre – a position it has maintained ever since. Paris, of course, remained foremost in terms of output: thousands of scripts were submitted to the censor's office each year – such swamping being a major cause of the abolition of theatre censorship in Paris in 1904.

The evolution of the London stage, then still very anglocentric, was only partly the result of the availability of better-quality drama or of greater output. An important dimension was the domination of famous actors, steeped in Shakespearian roles, such as Sir Henry Irving, the first actor to be knighted (1895), a sign of new respect for the profession, Herbert Beerbohm-Tree (knighted in 1909) and Mrs Patrick Campbell (for whom Shaw wrote the role of Eliza Doolittle in *Pygmalion*). While actors remained the main box office attraction, there was also increasing recognition of directors such as Harley Granville Barker and Gordon Craig. More than ten new theatres opened in London between 1880 and 1900, including the Comedy, the Savoy, the Playhouse, the Lyric, the Garrick, the Duke of York's and Wyndham's. Foreign companies visited from Paris (Antoine's Théâtre-Libre), Germany (the Meininger) and even Japan.[26]

Foreign dramatists of note, including Maeterlinck, Ibsen and Haupt-mann, were staged – though Ibsen's controversial *Ghosts* did not receive a public performance until 1914, when *The Times* referred to 'the lugubrious and malodorous world of Ibsen'.[27] The majority of shows, in London as elsewhere, were musicals, light operas and revues. At the turn of the century the favourite playwright was neither Oscar Wilde nor George Bernard Shaw, but Sir Arthur Wing Pinero (1855–1934), author of popular farces and social melodramas with titles such as *Dandy Dick* (1883), *The Schoolmistress* (1886) and *The Cabinet Minister* (1890). Pinero's serious 'problem' play, *The Second Mrs Tanqueray* (1893), in which the statutory fallen woman commits suicide – is the only one still relatively known.

Real money, however, was made with the ever-popular Viennese operetta, such as the Hungarian Franz Lehár's *Die Lustige Witwe* (The Merry Widow), which opened triumphantly at His Majesty's Theatre in 1906. Even more could be made from a long-running musical such as *Chu Chin Chow* by Frederick Norton, which ran at His Majesty's from 1916 to 1921. A glance at any of the papers of the period, such as a *Sunday Sketch* from July 1917, shows the great popularity of musical comedies. The alleged lowering in taste this revealed was widely attributed to the war. The *World's Pictorial News* of 28 November 1919 complained that at the theatre or a fashionable dance one could see 'as much of a woman as any man has any right to see, and sometimes much more'.[28] In reality musicals had been popular throughout the nineteenth century, and continued to dominate the twentieth – as evidenced by the success of Leonard Bernstein and Stephen Sondheim's *West Side Story* (1958–61) and Andrew Lloyd Webber's *Cats* (1981) and *The Phantom of the Opera* (1987).

Women, particularly in Great Britain, formed a significant part of the audience, particularly those in the afternoon, the so-called matinées, where 60 per cent of plays performed in late Victorian Britain were shown. There women outnumbered men twelve to one.[29] Paradoxically, controversial plays were 'tested' in the afternoon before being allowed to progress to the evening performance. The result was that women were often the first public for famous Ibsen plays such as *Hedda Gabler*.

The Emergence of the Director

As the theatre prospered, so did the director, increasingly seen as a key creator of the modern 'serious' theatre. Most contemporary plays, as well as 'light' plays and vaudevilles, remained for a long time rehearsed by the author, the theatre manager or one of the most experienced actors. There was little if any unified direction about how a play should be interpreted, how it should be acted, or what scenery should be used. In Italy the rule of the *capocomico* or writer-actor continued throughout the twentieth century, delaying the development of an Italian theatre (Pirandello remained a notable exception), since these leading actors, real *prime donne*, structured the play entirely around their own acting skills, the play often dying with them.

The development of naturalism in literature contributed to the rise of the director. Experiment in literature led to experiment in the theatre. In Germany the Meininger Theatre Company, directed by George II, Duke of Saxe-Meiningen and headed by his wife, the actress Ellen Franz, innovated in having historically accurate stagings and costume designs, three-dimensional scenery and an ensemble conception of theatre rather than one based on the leading actors. Between 1874 and 1890 the company performed in Berlin and other German cities as well as European cities including London, St Petersburg and Moscow, Trieste, Stockholm, Copenhagen and Brussels (but never in Paris). It even played Shakespeare in German at the Drury Lane in London. Shakespeare's *Julius Caesar* was its most-performed work (330), followed by *The Winter's Tale* (233) and Schiller's *Wilhelm Tell* (223).[30] In 1890 alone the company toured thirty-eight European cities. The theatre was becoming international.

This pioneering example was followed by the French director André Antoine (1858–1943), whose Théâtre-Libre (for subscribers only) became a major centre of experimentation when it opened in 1887. With the backing of Zola, Antoine produced short one-act plays (the *quart d'heure*) alongside longer works by established writers. The short play allowed a more naturalistic style of acting: actors no longer declaimed, but tried to interpret. The sets too attempted to reproduce reality.[31] The star system gave way to company acting. Antoine used accurate translations rather than loose adaptations, attempted to create realistic detail in all his settings and directed his actors to behave onstage as they would in a real room.

Antoine was open to the new European theatre. He had visited London in 1889 with his company and been struck by the effects obtained with lights by Henry Irving for a production of *Macbeth*, and by Irving's insistence on having accurate texts. Antoine also studied the performance techniques of the Meininger company, in particular the way crowds were integrated into the action instead of being, as at the Comédie-Française, just a group of people looking on.[32] London–Paris–Berlin: the tendency towards a coherent European theatre was unstoppable. The success of Antoine, the visit to Moscow by the Meininger company in 1890 and the translation into Russian of major contemporary authors such as Ibsen (*A Doll's House* in 1883 and, by 1891, *An Enemy of the People* and *The Woman from the Sea*) stimulated the birth, in 1897, of the Moscow Arts Theatre of Danchenko and Stanislavsky.[33] The movement also had an impact in London (the London Independent Theatre), Berlin (the Freie Bühne) and Budapest (the above-mentioned Thália Society theatre), but the most important of this new breed was the Moscow Arts Theatre.

Its director, Konstantin Stanislavsky (1863–1938), came to be widely regarded as the major theatrical innovator of his generation. He established the principles that actors and text should be at the centre of the enterprise, that each production should have its own scenery and costumes, and that the performance should be treated as an artistic and not a social occasion – applause at performers' entrances and exits was forbidden. The project had characteristically Russian populist undertones: Stanislavsky instructed his company that the aim was to improve the cultural condition of the poorer classes and brighten their 'dark existence'.[34] The 'method' used was frankly naturalistic: before staging *Othello*, Stanislavsky went to Venice in his search for authenticity, sketching the costumes depicted in frescos; when he revived Chekhov's *The Seagull* (it had flopped in St Petersburg the first time round) he spent a few weeks in the countryside to imbibe the atmosphere.[35]

By writing detailed instructions on how a play should be staged, Stanislavsky began to usurp the role of the playwright. Take *The Seagull*: at the end of the first act all Chekhov had written was that Dorn says to Masha: 'But what can I do, my child? Tell me, what can I do? What?' Stanislavsky made Masha burst into sobs, kneel, bury her head on Dorn's knees and Dorn stroke her head, while an unseen piano struck up a waltz which grew louder, soon to be replaced by the sound of church bells, as well as a peasant song, the noise of frogs and of a cornfield rustling, the knocking of the nightwatchman and all sorts of other nocturnal sound effects. Unsurprisingly, Chekhov thought this was much too noisy. Stanislavsky took no notice, and continued to provide the actors with detailed instructions on everything, including when and how to smack their lips or smoke a pipe. The first performance in December 1898 was a great success, but Chekhov was somewhat perturbed. He wrote to Gorky: 'On the whole, the play was not bad, and it gripped me. In places, I could hardly believe it was I that had written it.'[36]

Matters did not improve with Stanislavsky's staging of *The Cherry Orchard* (1904), which was soon playing to half-empty houses. Chekhov complained: 'Is it my *Cherry Orchard*? With the exception of two or three parts nothing in it is mine. I am describing life, ordinary life, and not blank despondency.' Stanislavsky was equally upset. He thought that rehearsals had been going well, 'the blossoms had just begun to appear', and then 'the author arrived and messed up everything for us'.[37]

Stanislavsky wanted his actors to forget that they were on the stage and to become the character, finding 'inside themselves' a justification for what their role required. Such principles, consciously or unconsciously, were later widely used in the cinema, the main acting conventions of which were almost entirely based on those of naturalism, partly because the expression of the actors could be seen in greater detail than at the theatre, partly because the lack of direct contact with an audience, the presence of an intrusive camera crew, and the necessity of filming in fragments to be edited later, required the actors to try to extricate themselves from their immediate environment far more than in a theatre.

The new rule of the director did not meet much resistance. Playwrights were either dead or grateful. Directors were, generally speaking, more in tune with the taste of the audience than was the playwright. They could be challenged only by a major actor, and there were few of those; lesser actors were, then as now, reluctant to quarrel with those in charge of giving out parts. The director's supremacy resided in his effective control of the final result. As Gordon Craig explained in *The Art of the Theatre* (1905): 'The Art of the Theatre is neither acting nor the play, it is not scene or dance, but it consists of all the elements of which these things are composed.'[38] Playwrights such as George Bernard Shaw tried to retain as much control as possible, writing detailed instructions to 'help' actors understand their character better, but nothing could stop the growing control of directors even over plays written by living authors.

The role of the director increased in importance throughout the twentieth century. This is partly a reflection of the regular performance of a relatively small number of classic works (small relative to the total output). Directors could interpret the same work differently – much like music conductors.

This could make repeated viewings of, say, *Hamlet*, a rewarding experience. In one version Hamlet could be interpreted as a neurotic, mother-fixated teenager, in another as a noble soul racked by existential doubts. The complexity of the work allows a profusion of readings: but the reading was made by the director.

The emergence of the director in no way diminished the appeal of the star. While some directors such as Gordon Craig were clearly more interested in design and lighting, others such as Max Reinhardt (1873–1943), second to none in championing the supremacy of the director, insisted on the overwhelming importance of the actor. Actresses such as Eleonora Duse and Sarah Bernhardt were authentic diva-celebrities whose private vicissitudes were followed with attention by the growing reading public of magazines and newspapers. The dearth of complex acting roles for women led them to intrude into male parts. *Hamlet* in particular seems to have been a favourite role for actresses, notably Bernhardt herself, who also played Napoleon's son in Rostand's *L'Aiglon* (1900) and Shylock in New York in 1916, by which time she had only one leg, following an amputation. The Bernhardt *Hamlet* was a major event in the performance of Shakespeare in France. Until then the play had always been performed in various adaptations and in bowdlerised forms. Bernhardt had to commission a new translation. The premiere took place on 20 May 1899 at the Théâtre Sarah Bernhardt in the place du Châtelet, the theatre the actress, then fifty-four, had just acquired. Her original interpretation of Hamlet as a decisive avenger (rather than a mad one) impressed the critics.[39]

Theatre for the People

By the end of the nineteenth century there were repeated attempts to create a 'people's theatre'. The intention was not to produce popular plays – the commercial theatre was dedicated to precisely that objective – but to bring plays of 'quality' to people who, because of their education or class background, were intimidated from going to the theatre. It was the equivalent of creating public libraries, publishing 'good books' and other educational initiatives. The motivations behind this phenomenon, which prevailed in Germany, Russia and France, were largely political. In France the movement was launched at the time of the Dreyfus affair, when the intellectuals of the Third Republic thought they should wean the masses away from clericalism and bring them around to the values of the Revolution and the ideals of national fraternity.[40] The leading light was Maurice Pottecher (1867–1960), who founded the People's Theatre of Bussang in the Vosges – an open-air theatre with 2,000 seats in a small town of 3,000 inhabitants. Initially the productions were highly didactic: the first play, by Pottecher himself, was *Le Diable marchand de goutte* (1 September 1895), about the dangers of alcoholism.[41] The popular theatre movement received a further boost when Romain Rolland's play *Le 14 Juillet* opened in Paris in 1902. Though the reviews were favourable, audiences rapidly declined and the play closed after just over a month.[42] Rolland outlined the theory of the concept of the popular theatre in his book *Le Théâtre du peuple* (1903). By early 1904, however, it had become clear that none of the existing popular theatres could continue without public funds. Yet it was difficult for them to obtain state or municipal subsidies because of the perceived connection between the popular theatre and socialism. Subsidising respectable theatre productions for the middle classes was, however, quite in order, and the four leading state-run theatres in Paris continued to receive state handouts.

Romain Rolland's vision of a popular theatre and Maurice Pottecher's experiment in Bussang with his 'theatre for the people' impressed Firmin Gémier (1869–1933), an actor with André Antoine's Théâtre-Libre, to such an extent that in 1911 he created a travelling company in order to take the Parisian theatre to the provinces. The venture was a financial disaster. The problem with the popular theatre was that it was not popular enough.

Better results were achieved in Germany with the Berlin Freie Volksbühne (the Free People's Theatre, 1890), run from 1892 to 1896 by a major SPD intellectual, Franz Mehring. It helped that it had a powerful socialist party backing it. The idea was to apply socialist principles to the theatre by offering the working classes either the culture from which they had been excluded (i.e. the repertory of contemporary bourgeois theatre) or specifically socialist plays. By 1913 the Volksbühne had 70,000 members. By 1914 it had become one of Berlin's leading playhouses. By 1930 there were 305 Volksbühne clubs with a total of 500,000 members.[43] Its lower prices succeeded in attracting many workers to the theatre, but no specifically 'proletarian' theatre as a new art form emerged.[44]

In Russia the populism which pervaded all strata of the establishment ensured that the movement for a popular theatre enjoyed a considerable success. Many theatres were financed by the state. In 1872 a theatre at popular prices devoted to the classics, under the sponsorship of the Interior Ministry, opened at the Polytechnic Exhibition, but it did not become permanent. The movement for an accessible theatre conformed to the literary credo of the Russian intelligentsia: art should advance the progress of society.[45] Aimed at workers and peasants, so-called 'temperance' theatres – the reasoning, or the illusion, was that if the workers were at the theatre they wouldn't be drinking – emerged, organised by intellectuals as touring companies in order to take the theatre to the people. By 1905 there were 361 government-sponsored temperance theatres and 420 in 1909, many performing folk plays. By then the intelligentsia no longer found folk theatre as charming as they had previously. They deemed the folk theatre to be of little value, and felt that culture had to be brought to the people in the same way as scientific know-ledge was brought to the peasantry to help them improve their crops. The people responded. From the 1890s a new, relatively uneducated audience began to flow into the existing theatres. There was a flowering of cultural institutions for the masses in pre-revolutionary Russia: libraries, reading rooms and schools. Enlightened factory-owners added theatres to the facili-ties available to their workforce, hoping perhaps that it would cut down on absenteeism and alcoholism. Thus in Russia, well before the Bolshevik revolution, commercial forces played a minor role in the popular theatre movement.[46] Of course the classic plays favoured by the intellectuals, such as Pushkin's *Boris Godunov* (1825), Gogol's *The Inspector General* (1835), Alex-ander Griboyedov's *Woe from Wit* (1824) and Turgenev's *A Month in the Country* (1850) were not sufficient to constitute a popular theatre. So the intellectuals found employment in producing their own plays, dramatising fairy tales, adapting vaudevilles or translating Western plays.

Stanislavsky's Moscow Arts Theatre could be regarded as belonging to the people's theatre movement, since both he and Nemirovich-Danchenko were committed to the idea of reaching the masses (the original name of the theatre had been 'the Accessible Arts Theatre'), and provided cheap seats for students and the poor alongside expensive stalls seats for the rich.[47]

In 1886 in St Petersburg the Nevsky Society was formed to provide enter-tainment for the workers. It acquired the use of a park for festivals and entertainments, staging plays, concerts, funfairs, *tableaux vivants* and dances. A hundred thousand people visited it in 1892, and the two summer theatres played to audiences of over a thousand (they spilled across the lawn). Questionnaires revealed that many of the respondents found the plays too heavy, though they were grateful they were being performed at all. One of the most frequent suggestions made was that the plays should be explained to them beforehand, with some information on the background of the characters.[48]

In 1903 Countess Panin, who since 1891 had devoted her philanthropic efforts to popular education, established another popular theatre in St Petersburg, the Ligovsky People's House. The plays were not always an unmitigated success – at least from the point of view of the Countess: the audience got drunk and made ribald jokes at the actors. Yet in ten years the Ligovsky Theatre filled 145,605 seats for 260 performances.[49]

The bourgeoisie presumably behaved better than the workers, but their taste was not very different. In Germany the commercial theatres, like their counterparts elsewhere, offered a light diet of operetta and variety, and catered to the tastes of a rather conventional middle-class audience. Thus Munich, a city of 350,000 inhabitants in 1890, had four theatres. Only one of these, the Nationaltheater, showed operas and classical tragedies. The Gärtnerplatz performed musicals and operetta, and the Residenztheater was dedicated to comedies and conversational drama, including highly censored versions of Ibsen. The fourth, and only privately-owned, theatre, the Volkstheater, provide a diet of Bavarian plays and skits. To show more substantial modern plays it had been necessary to form a theatrical society with limited membership – only then was it possible to perform uncensored Ibsen (*Ghosts*), Hauptmann (*Vor Sonnenaufgang*) and Strindberg (*Miss Julie*).[50]

The problem with the theatre 'of quality' is that the disappearance of court or state patronage forced producers (writers, directors, actors and management) to cater for a new audience, either by staging commercial plays, often uncomplicated entertainment, or plays aimed at an educated minority of intellectuals. The 'people' – meaning the vast majority with no effective access to the theatre – were unlikely to be attracted by either strategy. They were deterred from the first by social conventions and the cost of seats, and from the second by their lack of education. This was the audience that would soon be captured by the cinema, and later by television.

Other ways of attracting new audiences, albeit still from the ever-expanding middle classes, could be achieved by using special effects. Of the many spectacular plays staged in Paris at the end of the century none did better than those based on Jules Verne's novels, especially *Around the World in Eighty Days*, launched in 1874 and still going strong in 1898: its staging included the smoking room of the Reform Club in London, moving panoramic views of Suez and India, balloons, burning funeral pyres, a railway train, and a steamer in a storm; it took an army of 1,800 people to stage it.[51]

During the tenure of Augustus Harris at the London Drury Lane (1879–96) shipwrecks, earthquakes and explosions were often shown on stage. In 1879 electricity enabled some New York theatres to use lifts to bring about spectacular scene changes swiftly.[52] The first revolving stage in Europe was installed by Karl Lautenschläger in 1896 at the Residenztheater of Munich, and in 1905 Max Reinhardt used it at the Berlin Deutsche Theatre as an integral part of the staging of *A Midsummer Night's Dream*. Electric lamps had been used at the Paris Opéra for some time, but even in 1878 the auditoriums were all lit by gas.[53] In 1881 Richard d'Oyly Carte's new Savoy Theatre in London became the first to be lit entirely by electricity. This could be dimmed quickly and effectively, unlike gas lighting.[54] The constant risk of fire in theatres – such as the serious loss of life in the 1881 fire at the Théâtre-Italien of Nice – ensured that the adoption of electricity was not resisted.

The Cabaret

The prosperity which the working classes were beginning to enjoy at the end of the nineteenth century did not automatically entail a wider access to entertainment. Much of the traditional 'pleasures' open to the lower classes had been eliminated by legislation or changes in public behaviour. In Great Britain the gin palaces had virtually disappeared, drinking hours had been restricted, and children excluded from 'grown-up' venues such as pubs; cock-fighting and bear-baiting had been proscribed as early as 1835; fox-hunting, however, became popular, even though deer-hunting was regarded as more classy. Boxing was increasingly regulated, with the introduction of gloves and the Queensberry rules in the 1860s and 1870s. Gambling was restricted, tea gardens eliminated, and public executions at Newgate abolished in 1868. Key aspects of respectable bourgeois entertainment were introduced, usually with state funding, such as parks, museums, exhibitions and public libraries.[55] Museums had enormously expanded, though they still catered to a clientele much narrower than today. Tourism began to expand, and included sights not all would regard as desirable in our own time. For instance, a visit to Paris in the nineteenth century could not fail to include the Morgue, to which Thomas Cook's guided visits attracted a million visitors a year. Built in 1864 behind Notre-Dame, the Morgue was open to the public for free from dawn to dusk seven days a week. Fresh, still unidentified bodies were exhibited in a special hall protected by a huge glass pane along which visitors filed by from left to right, their noses pressed against the glass.[56] The better class of dead, of course, could not be viewed, but one could see their wax figures at the Musée Grévin, Paris's answer to London's Madame Tussaud's.

For a more lively diversion one could go to cabarets and *cafés-concerts*, though these were not yet places of working-class entertainment. The cost of visiting a centrally located *café-concert* or music hall such as the Nouveau Cirque, the Olympia or the Ambassadeur, was between two and five francs, in line with the lowest price for bastions of élite culture such as the Opéra and the Théâtre-Français.[57] This was still too expensive for the average working-class salary, which was three francs a day for an unskilled worker, and seven francs for a skilled one. The Moulin Rouge and the Folies Bergère, not normally regarded as high-culture sites, were by the 1890s almost luxury palaces. The workers liked sport, but going to the races (the main spectator sport of the time) was very expensive, though for one franc it was possible to watch standing up, well away from the *beau monde*.[58] In fact the '*petit peuple*' of Paris did not frequent the centre of the city, which was virtually reserved for the bourgeoisie and the tourists. They remained in their neighbourhoods, where they could drink wine or absinthe for very little.

Bourgeois taste and sensitivities did not make much difference to what was on show at places like the Moulin Rouge and the Folies Bergère, except that the higher prices, by keeping away the allegedly impressionable uncultured crowds, allowed the spectacle to be rather coarse. The main shows consisted of parading scantily-clad women – what we would now call striptease. The star of L'Alcazar d'Été, Mademoiselle Cavelli, would remove her hat, then her dress, then her underskirts, then her corset, and finally her shirt – the pause between each passage being an essential ingredient of the act.[59]

The *café-concert* and the cabaret offered, along with pubs and drinking places and some fashionable restaurants, a relaxed form of entertainment. The audience shared with eighteenth-century aristocratic audiences a distinctive feature: the music on offer was not there to be listened to attentively. Spasmodic listening (when, on occasion, a favourite singer was performing the audience would quieten down) was part of a distinctive cultural experience. The show acted as a kind of background, adding atmosphere to a place where drinking, talking, meeting people, seeing and being seen were as much part of the spectacle as the show on offer.

The cabaret offered a collective urban experience that had the peculiarity of enabling the individual to remain isolated if he preferred. Lone drinking surrounded by other lone drinkers is a somewhat different experience to drinking while watching a show which consisted, usually, of songs and dances, some comic routines, the odd illusionist act or some show of dexterity, some dances. As the name suggests, the cabaret was supposed to be quintessentially French – they began to flourish in Paris in the 1880s. In reality, similar places existed all over Continental Europe. The best-known of the Paris cabarets was the painter Rodolphe Salis's Le Chat Noir. It opened in 1881 in Montmartre – then the licentious and criminal area of Paris, and cheaper than the Latin Quarter. In 1897 Le Chat Noir was replaced, on the same site, by Le Mirliton (The Reed-Pipe), run by Aristide Bruant (1851–1925), a *chansonnier* immortalised in Toulouse-Lautrec's paintings and posters.[60] In 1889, again in Montmartre, a new *café-concert* was inaugurated, Le Moulin Rouge, where a daring dance was performed by women in a sexually provocative manner: the can-can. This was a deformation of the traditional *quadrille*, entailing somersaults, violent swings of the hips, high kicking and daring *écarts*. Its origins were in popular balls like the *mabille* in the 1830s. The can-can – the name derives from a slang term for scandalous gossip – had been popular in the music halls of Paris around 1840. Though vulgar, it acquired genteel credentials when Jacques Offenbach wrote a can-can for his operetta *Orphée aux enfers* (1858).

The cabaret was a kind of *café-concert* with intellectual and artistic pretensions. What really made the difference was not the show but the kind of people who went there. Artists, poets, intellectuals and so-called bohemians gave the 'tone' to the place. The rest of the audience, the majority, were ordinary bourgeois who went there to feel they were not ordinary bourgeois. The 'bohemians' would mock the bourgeoisie, to the delight of a 'bourgeois' public who, by being derided, acquired the aura of the powerful, for only the truly powerful are worth being mocked. Being insulted was part of the show. If a guest left in the middle of a song, Aristide Bruant would stop singing and would be joined by the audience in the refrain: '*Tous les clients sont des cochons. . .*' (All customers are swine, especially those who go before time).[61] Latecomers would be greeted with, 'You, big sausage, squeeze your carcass between those two who are laughing like idiots.'[62] The cabaret pretended to be subversive, thus providing the necessary *frisson*, though in reality it was quite inoffensive. Cabarets such as Le Chat Noir and Le Mirliton and venues such as the Moulin Rouge revealed to the wider and innocent public the underworld of the capital, with its girls, its pimps and its thugs. This thrilled the audience and boosted the self-image of the criminals. The public had read about murders and other crimes in novels, and seen them enacted at the theatre. Now they could encounter those who perpetrated them in 'real' life with virtually no risk.

The success of cabarets and other places of evening and night entertainment was astonishing. Around 1885 there were, in Paris alone, 360 *cafés-concerts*. Their owners were a new generation of entrepreneurs who were also in the music business, hiring singers, conductors and musicians. When they took over an establishment they deployed the entire arsenal of advertising then available – postcards, billboards, promotional objects such as ladies' fans, pocket handkerchiefs, etc. – to launch it.[63]

Some of the artists involved acquired the celebrity status once reserved for operatic *prime donne*. The famous cabaret singer Thérésa (real name Emma Valadon, 1837–1913; see page 588) increased her earnings by having her songs sold and printed. Her memoirs, ghosted by three journalists and published by Dentu in 1865, sold 60,000 copies in a few months. Canned soups and bottled alcoholic drinks were named after her (for which she was paid), and she advertised Géraudel throat lozenges. In 1893 she retired to a manor house, but kept her name in the public domain by granting regular interviews to the press, reminiscing about her life and allowing her photograph to be reproduced on postcards.[64]

The *fin-de-siècle* Parisian cabaret met the pretensions of its public by holding on to high-culture credentials, borrowing in playful format from some of the grand names of the *enfants terribles* of fifteenth- and sixteenth-century French literature. From François Villon the *chansonniers* took the themes of villains, losers and ne'er-do-wells. From Rabelais they took obscene word games.[65] From the vaudeville they took a genre of performance which was short and pithy and injected into it some socially critical themes, particularly when it moved from France to Germany, where it thrived.[66]

Cabarets spread into northern Europe, above all Holland and Germany. Once more French, or rather Parisian, cultural hegemony ensured that the country would set the tone for the entertainment of the rest of Europe and beyond. At times the imitation was slavish. Henry B. Harris and Jesse Lasky, opening their Folies Bergère in New York in 1911, explained in their advertising how the word cabaret should be pronounced ('cabaray'), declared that their venue 'was frankly inspired by Parisian éclat', and promised to make it 'more Parisian than Paris'.[67] Paris had succeeded in marketing itself as a city of charm, culture and entertainment to a far greater extent than any other city in the world. Though most Parisians, one must suppose, were as dull bourgeois as one can find anywhere else, the city provided a theme park where a visitor could find much of what had been described in the most successful novels and plays of the nineteenth century: an aura of charming vice, the *frisson* of transgression, a varied and remarkable cuisine, a wide range of hotels. London was Paris's nearest rival, but London's middle classes were too staid, its upper classes isolated themselves in clubs and country houses, and its working classes were sullen and dangerous. New York was too far away. Rome and the other Italian cities were visited for their ancient glories, but they provided no marketable fun. Berlin and Vienna were too provincial, and anything one could obtain there one could get better in Paris.

Foreign artists and entertainers visiting Paris would learn the tricks of the trade and use them profitably when they returned home. Eduard Jacobs, a Dutchman who had trained as a diamond cutter, frequented Aristide Bruant's Mirliton and played the piano at the Moulin Rouge, accompanying, among others, the famous Pétomane, whose act consisted of farting popular tunes. Back in Amsterdam in 1895, Jacobs opened a cabaret in De Pijp, the city's seedy district, the equivalent of Montmartre, and sang translations of French songs about whores insulting his audience *à la* Bruant.[68]

The first German cabaret, Elf Scharfrichter (Eleven Executioners), opened in Munich, then the country's artistic centre, in April 1900. There the young Frank Wedekind performed experimental songs and a vamp-like star, Marya Delvard, thin and pale, sang songs of sex and death in a clinging black dress (fifty years before Juliette Gréco).[69] In 1901 Max Reinhardt founded the Schall und Rauch (Noise and Smoke) in Berlin. The cabaret spread throughout German-speaking territory, including Zurich and Vienna, where in 1903 Marya Delvard and her partner Marc Henry opened the Nachtlicht. By 1905 there were forty-five cabarets in Berlin alone, providing a platform for playwrights and theatre producers.

In Poland cabarets did not start in the 'modern' capital of Warsaw but in ancient Krakow, a crossroads of German and French cultures. The first was Zielony Balonik (The Little Green Balloon), which became far more central to the life of Krakow than Le Chat Noir could ever hope to be in Paris. As Krakow was also a centre of nationalism, French acts were injected with Polish national themes, particularly with the use of *szopka* – nativity puppet-shows as a framework for topical songs and sketches.[70]

In Russia, Nikita Baliev's Chauve-Souris (The Bat, 1908) incorporated traditional Russian folk songs and ballads. Like many other Moscow cabarets it was associated with the avant-garde and the Moscow Arts Theatre. One could almost predict that the further one went from Paris, the more the cabaret would appeal to a narrower intelligentsia; yet the association with avant-garde artistic activity was common throughout Europe. In Moscow a cabaret such as Charles Aumont's Théâtre-Concert was regarded as on a par with a brothel – not entirely unjustifiably. When Aumont, in the summer of 1896, included films in his programme he attracted the educated and respectable sections of the Russian public. They had an excuse to listen to the *chansonettes* and watch the French can-can. The playwright Evgenii Chirikov wrote to his wife that the cinema itself was 'excellent but it is surrounded by the worst debauchery and by a market in women's bodies . . . But, because of the cinematograph, even "respectable" ladies come here with their husbands . . . to see what is going on.'[71]

The 1920s and 1930s were the golden age of the cabaret, largely in France and Germany. The veneer of immorality they seemed to exude, part of their attraction, was further enhanced by their representation in films such as Josef von Sternberg's *Der Blaue Engel* (1930, The Blue Angel, based on Heinrich Mann's 1905 novel *Professor Unrat*), released simultaneously in German and English. It was one of the first 'talkies', and featured the then unknown Marlene Dietrich, who famously sang Udo Lindenberg's 'Ich bin von Kopf bis Fuss auf Liebe eingestellt' (From head to toe I am destined for love):

> Männer umschwirr'n mich
> wie Motten das Licht.
> Und wenn sie verbrennen
> dafür kann ich nichts.
> (Men are attracted to me
> Like moths to a flame;
> And if they burn,
> Do not blame me.)

Ever since, the cabaret has conjured up – for the wider public – images of seductive female singers sitting astride a chair, wearing alluring black silk stockings – a glimpse of which, at the time, was still something shocking.

38

Music

Popular Music

PEOPLE DANCED in taverns and at *cafés-concerts*, embassies, hotels and aristocratic homes. Dancing music was one of the least class-bound forms of entertainment, yet everything else about dancing was redolent of class: the venues, the participants, the clothes, the time of day. Musicians performed for the rich whenever they could, but they were often forced to perform for the middle classes, and occasionally for the working classes. They carried tunes up and down the social ladder well before radio did.

The music used for dancing was what we would now call 'popular' music. Festivities – such as those surrounding great gatherings for the international exhibitions of London (1851, 1862), Vienna (1873), Philadelphia (1876), Paris (1878, 1889, 1900) and Chicago – were opportunities for the popularisation of new snatches of dance music. It was at the Austrian Embassy in Paris that Johann Strauss performed for the first time outside Vienna his *An der schönen, blauen Donau* (The Blue Danube). It was a real hit. British visitors at once invited Strauss to London, where he conducted the promenade concerts at the Royal Italian Opera House. Promenades were low-status concerts attended by the lower middle classes, sometimes in parks or dance halls, where the public was allowed to walk, eat and drink during the performance. They were increasingly profitable and professional, and were ideally suited to Strauss's music.[1]

The Viennese publisher of the music sheet could barely cope. Other successes followed: *Geschichten aus dem Wienerwald* (Tales from the Vienna Woods, 1866), *Wein, Weib und Gesang* (Wine, Women and Song, 1869) and *Kaiserwalzer* (The Emperor's Waltz, 1889). Then Strauss went 'global' by going to Boston in 1872 on the occasion of the World Peace Jubilee and

International Musical Festival. The huge fee he received ($100,000) was commensurate with his fame and the size of the audience: 100,000 people.[2]

Public balls were the most diffuse form of collective entertainment. In Paris alone, the European capital of public balls, there were in 1899 alone 376 ballrooms in all sorts of venues from hotels and cafés to the Casino de Paris, the Moulin Rouge and the Tivoli-Vauxhall.[3]

Private balls had strict rules. Dances such as polkas and waltzes should not last more than five minutes. The gentlemen were expected to ask the lady of the house for a dance. If she did not dance, one should ask her daughter. If there was no daughter, or the daughter was too young, then one should ask one of her relatives. It was impolite to dance too often with the same person. Ladies could not refuse the same gentleman twice. The hosts were expected to provide a small orchestra, not just a piano.[4]

Pianos were used for small and more relaxed private balls in ordinary middle-class homes. For public balls there was no substitute for a full orchestra. Then a new instrument, which could replace an entire orchestra, came to the fore, the accordion. A considerably improved version of the German instrument the Handäoline, developed in the 1820s, the piano-accordion became popular in the 1850s. It was usually played by a lower-class musician, not classically trained, and often Italian – for years Italy was the leading manufacturing centre of the accordion.[5] The instrument required the player to press one or more of its keys while pumping the bellows. This created a very loud sound – ideal for public dancing. Long the preferred instrument of street mendicants, the accordion was far easier to learn than the violin, far more versatile and louder than the guitar, and easily transportable. It rapidly spread throughout Europe, and could be found in beer halls of Germany as well as the village fairs of Italy.

The public of music halls, cabarets and dance venues heard, every week, a good many new songs and pieces of music. If they wanted to listen to them again, there was no alternative to buying the scores and performing them at home on the pianos which by the 1880s had become a feature of even some 'respectable' working-class homes.[6]

The piano provided a thriving market for music scores. In Italy, Ricordi, one of the largest music publishers in Europe, printed 50,000 pages of music in 1880 alone.[7] The issue which perturbed publishers above all others was that piracy had become only too easy. Lithography, which by then had become exceedingly common, enabled operators to provide, at a fraction of the price, the most fashionable songs in a very short time.[8] In Great Britain various Copyright Acts (1882, 1886, 1888, 1906) tried to protect publishers. By the 1880s – when America was poised to become a major exporter of popular culture, especially musical popular culture – the US Congress moved towards enshrining the protection of foreign copyrights into US law, provided that reciprocity could be established. It still refused to sign the 1886 Berne Convention and continued, in the scandalised words of the English *Musical Times*, 'to walk alone in the path of self-interest and dishonesty' (1 March 1886).[9] However, many East Coast publishers entered agreements with British ones for the right to publish English works almost simultaneously, but in the mid-West and more distant regions there was wide disregard of such agreements. The USA acceded to the Berne Convention only in 1989 to defend the interests of its cultural industries.

But Americans were rapidly becoming self-sufficient in music. A thriving music industry based on what were virtually assembly-line production techniques (before the invention of the assembly line) was achieved even before the development of the recording industry and the spread of the radio. This was the famous Tin Pan Alley – the name given to the area (Twenty-Eighth Street between Broadway and Sixth Avenue) where, in the 1880s and 1890s, most of the New York music publishing business was concentrated, and where publishers hired lyricists and composers to mass-produce songs which were then promoted and sold, in those pre-recording days, as music sheets.

When the gramophone appeared in 1889, this industrial organisation of popular music enhanced the already considerable advantages enjoyed by the US. In a still linguistically divided country, where an increased proportion of the population were first-generation immigrants, music could become the most unifying of the arts. The necessity of producing music and songs which appealed to a wide, but still culturally fragmented audience, meant that there was a premium in achieving a constant fusion between various musical idioms, especially from communities which had a thriving tradition of popular music, such as the Irish, the Italians and above all the blacks, whose music started to develop rapidly after the Civil War. Jazz emerged at the turn of the century in New Orleans, a music-rich city with three opera companies and the first black symphony orchestra (formed in the 1830s). However, being based on improvisation, jazz could not be notated and published. Written scores, when they existed, were used purely as a structure around which improvisation could take place. Thus jazz remained outside the commercial music circuits for a long time. It could only be heard in cabarets and black entertainment circuits. The absence of an audience allowed the recording session to become an extension of the process of rehearsal.

While the main input into jazz was West African (the territories that are now between Senegal and Cameroon, where most of the slaves came from), it developed by building on European popular music and European musical instruments such as brass bands, and the saxophone in particular. To some extent jazz is the music of black America adapted to the taste of white Americans.[10] Even this is imprecise. There never was a homogeneous 'black' or 'African' music, but a mosaic of distinctive traditions.[11] Some of the instruments used along the West African coast, such as the one-string fiddle, the lute and the hour-glass drum, were of Arab origin.[12]

In this sense this follows the general rule: the more 'contaminated' – i.e. less 'pure' – is a musical genre, the longer and more widely it will travel. Jazz, now an élite form, started out by breaking class and national barriers. Jelly Roll Morton (1885–1941), the great Creole pianist, reminisced about New Orleans nightspots in 1902, where 'all the girls that could get out of their houses' mixed with brilliant pianists and millionaires:

> We had Spanish, we had colored, we had white, we had Frenchmens, we had Americans, we had them from all parts of the world because there were more jobs for pianists than any other ten places in the world . . . whenever you came to New Orleans, it wouldn't make any difference that you just came from Paris or any part of England, Europe, or any place – whatever your tunes were over there, we played them in New Orleans.[13]

Jazz was not a particular genre of music but a particular genre of performing music. In this sense it simply used any suitable tune and 'arranged' it in jazz style.[14] It was thus performer-driven rather than composer-led, and less culture-bound than some other musical forms. Its success in earlier forms, such as the highly syncopated ragtime and the 'cakewalk' dance in France and Britain, started precisely at the turn of the century, when American entertainment began to be exported to Europe. 'Serious' modernist composers occasionally adopted some of its expressions, notably Debussy in his children's piano solo 'Golliwog's Cakewalk' (1908), while Stravinsky introduced a ragtime in his The Soldier's Tale (1918).

In turn jazz performers 'borrowed' and transformed European music styles such as hymns, marches, dance music and light operatic music. At first the jazz style emerging in the early twentieth century in New Orleans used instruments such as the piano, the cornet, the trumpet, the violin and the

clarinet, along with the guitar or banjo. Drums provided the rhythmic accompaniment. Military touring bands and music hall performers contributed to
the dissemination of brass instruments in the United States such as the
saxophone – though mainly after 1918. The high mobility of people within
the USA (Jelly Roll Morton, Scott Joplin and others eventually brought jazz
and ragtime to Chicago in these years), the constant flow of immigrants
(back and forth), the ease of transatlantic transport, enabled the rapid spread
of entertainment music. The St Louis Universal Exhibition of 1904 contributed to the expansion of ragtime. War, as usual, contributed to international
exchange. The brilliant French foxtrot song 'Je cherche après Titine' (1917,
music by Léo Daniderff) delighted American soldiers dispatched to France.
They took it back to the USA, and the music was used by Charlie Chaplin
in his film *Modern Times* (1936). This made the song famous once again,
enabling its subsequent revival in France thanks to the singer and dancer
Mistinguett. Yves Montand was still singing 'Titine' to great acclaim in the
early fifties.

Jazz shared with other types of music, for instance Indian classical music,
the absence of a fixed musical score. But in Indian classical music the tradition
was for each practitioner to learn his art at the feet of a master. This oral
transmission did not occur with jazz, or at least not to the same extent,
because the birth of jazz coincided with the birth of the gramophone and
radio broadcasting. Many of the great jazzmen, such as Count Basie and
Charlie Parker, learned jazz and fell in love with it listening to the radio or
to records. Had jazz been entirely transmitted from live performances it
would have progressed more slowly. Instead it evolved rapidly because each
performer had before him an enormous range of recorded musical
experience.[15]

The Fate of the Opera

In the nineteenth century the opera had been a middlebrow genre patronised
by the aristocracy and the better-off urban upper middle classes. The twentieth century saw the bifurcation of operatic consumption into two distinct
compartments. The first – what one might call 'opera' proper – was fossilised
into a fairly rigid and almost unchanging repertory made up of a large
selection of nineteenth-century opera to which was added a limited selection
from the eighteenth century, largely Gluck's and Mozart's works. This reper-

tory constituted more than 90 per cent of what was staged in the main opera houses of the West, what was sold by record companies and what provided a platform for the great opera singers of the second half of the twentieth century. There were constant attempts to expand the repertory, either by promoting new work (often unsuccessfully) or by dipping into the rest of the repertory of the seventeenth or eighteenth centuries (Handel, Purcell, Monteverdi, etc.). Until almost the end of the nineteenth century, pre-Mozart composers were rarely performed. Then some became popular, and have remained so: Bach and Handel, and, much later, Vivaldi. Others are known only from some isolated pieces (Albinoni's Adagio, Pachelbel's Canon). Virtually none of the over 120 pre-1750 French operas was ever performed in the nineteenth century.[16]

Instrumental music followed a similar path. The concert hall became a museum where the work of old times was preserved. New composers had to compete with those of the preceding two hundred years, composers who had left accurate notation of how their music was to be performed. Writing the same kind of music would have been self-defeating, since that of the old masters was available. One solution was to use folk idioms in a new way, a strategy adopted by Russian composers such as Mikhail Glinka, Modest Mussorgsky and Nikolai Rimsky-Korsakov, and followed by the Czechs Antonín Dvořák and Bedřich Smetana, the Norwegian Edvard Grieg, the Finnish Jean Sibelius and the Spanish Manuel de Falla.

Musical nationalism considerably helped composers from peripheral countries. Sibelius, as the first great Finnish composer, was supported by enthusiasts in his native land. The same could be said of Smetana and Dvořák. In Germany they might not have had such privileged positions. Being in a small country presents problems, but one can more easily become one of the best-known Finns in the world than one of the best-known French or English.[17] The other strategy was to innovate dramatically: hence Debussy, Stravinsky, Schoenberg, Shostakovich and many others.

To convey the plight of new composers we could envisage a similar situation for a different art form: imagine if cinema-goers were content with revisiting the *oeuvre* of the first sixty years or so of cinematic history, going over and over again to see the films of Pudovkin, Eisenstein, Griffith, Renoir, John Ford, Hitchcock and Fellini instead of demanding new films every week. To be able to enter such a market would be almost impossible for new directors, and the result would be the opposite of the present: big cinema distributors would show Eisenstein and co., while small art cinemas screened the 'new' cinema, which would be deemed incomprehensible by the majority of cinema-goers.

Once, composers had to find patrons. Since the era of modern democracy is also the era of the market, and since new serious instrumental music is not commercially profitable, composers, far from becoming autonomous producers as they would have liked, became ever more dependent on political and social patronage. It was necessary to conduct a major orchestra, establish networks, gain the support of established composers – and this was so even in the most modern and 'democratic' of Europe's republics, France.[18]

Within the opera canon, however, there was some movement. The success of some operas was connected to particular singers or conductors. Some simply fell out of favour but reappeared much later. Luigi Cherubini's *Médée* had its first night in Paris in 1797. Londoners did not see it until 1865. Italians waited even longer: it was finally performed at La Scala in 1909. Then it was quite forgotten until 1953, when Maria Callas, a soprano possessed of uncommon musical genius – no doubt attracted by its splendid title role – revived it at the sixteenth Maggio Musicale Fiorentino and subsequently performed it all over the world. Only then did it make its way back to Paris.

Alongside the 'classical' repertory has grown another which is made up of a selection of works of the twentieth century. With the exception of Puccini and Richard Strauss, none of the operas of the great masters of the twentieth century – Claude Debussy, Igor Stravinsky, Sergei Prokofiev, Dmitri Shostakovich, Benjamin Britten, Alban Berg, Leoš Janáček, Arnold Schoenberg – has become an international popular favourite. Béla Bartók does not pull the operatic crowds attracted routinely by Rossini, Bellini, Donizetti, Verdi, Wagner, Bizet, Berlioz and others. While *La Bohème*, though it was received with little enthusiasm at its opening night in Turin in 1896, went on to become a safe bet for any opera house in the world, Debussy's *Pelléas et Mélisande* remained a 'difficult' opera. Its first night in 1902 was another of those scandals which seems to mark key moments on the French stage, along with Hugo's *Hernani* in 1830 and Stravinsky's *Rite of Spring* in 1913. Debussy was accused of producing 'music which is not music' and of 'a crazy pursuit of novelty'.[19]

Such 'scandals' today are confined to visual art. Today's cultural élites relish the knowledge that what they are offered is truly novel; the belief that something is an authentic innovation is enhanced by the incomprehension of others. At the beginning of the twentieth century, however, these élites were still dominated by the moneyed high bourgeoisie and the conventional intelligentsia – not a crowd in search of novelties. The dismay which greeted *Pelléas* showed that in those days the bourgeoisie could still be shocked. Now it knows better, and sticks to what it really likes. But it learns. Wagner too, when he started flooding the operatic stage with works which eschewed the separation between arias and recitative, encountered much incomprehension. But by the 1900s *Lohengrin*, for instance, was regularly performed in Paris every year. In fact Wagner was a sure box office success in Paris, in spite of prevailing anti-German sentiment.[20] At Covent Garden Hans Richter conducted three cycles of the *Ring* in 1903, in a season in which twenty-nine out of seventy-three performances were of Wagner's works. In 1908 and 1909 the *Ring* was given in English, and in 1909 *Die Meistersinger* was given in English as well. After that, performing opera in English at Covent Garden appeared to be reserved for 'difficult', i.e. unpopular, works such as Janáček's *Jenufa* (1956) and Schoenberg's unfinished *Moses und Aron* (1932).

Puccini, writing in a nineteenth-century musical idiom, has turned out to be the only twentieth-century opera composer whose works are routinely performed – and he is barely into the twentieth century. *La Bohème* is, along with Bizet's *Carmen*, one of the most frequently performed operas ever, while *Tosca* and *Madama Butterfly* are the 'cash cows in every company barn'.[21]

In Germany, Wagner's fatherland, Italian opera dominated the operatic league table in the mid-1970s:

FEDERAL REPUBLIC OF GERMANY. ATTENDANCE FIGURES FOR OPERATIC PERFORMANCES, 1973–74

COMPOSER	TOTAL ATTENDANCE
Mozart	1,033,000
Verdi	1,025,000
Puccini	670,000
Wagner	500,000
Richard Strauss	425,000
Rossini	345,000
Donizetti	199,500

SOURCE: Werner Schulze-Reimpell, *Development and Structure of the Theatre in the Federal Republic of Germany*, Deutscher Bühnenverein, Cologne 1975, p.21

According to a report in the *Chicago Tribune* (1 November 2002), twenty-seven productions of *La Bohème* were planned in North America (including

Canada) for the 2002–03 season alone, boosting the total since 1991–92 to 207. When *La Bohème* was performed in November 2003 at the Metropolitan Opera of New York, it was the 1,444th time it had been staged there. In 1977 it was *La Bohème* that was chosen for the first live television broadcast of a Metropolitan Opera production (with Renata Scotto and Luciano Pavarotti in the leading roles). *La Bohème* was also the first complete opera broadcast in the USA. The historic date was 5 September 1922. The place was neither New York nor Boston, but Salt Lake City, where the radio station KDYL assembled an amateur cast and a tiny orchestra of seven or eight musicians.[22] Yet when *La Bohème* was first performed in Turin in 1896, *La Stampa* declared with confidence: 'It will not leave much impression in the history of our lyric theatre.'[23] Nevertheless, it made enough of an impact to be regularly used in films, from *The Sun Comes Up* (1949), starring the dog Lassie, to Visconti's *Death in Venice* (1971), *Prizzi's Honor* (1985), Woody Allen's *Hannah and Her Sisters* (1986), *Fatal Attraction* (1987) and Oliver Stone's *Natural Born Killers* (1994), in which music from *Madama Butterfly* is played alongside 'Burn' by Nine Inch Nails.

This is the operatic league table from 1991–92 to 2002–03 in the USA and Canada:

OPERA PRODUCTIONS IN THE USA AND CANADA, 1991–92 TO 2002–03		
1	*La Bohème* (Puccini)	207
2	*Madama Butterfly* (Puccini)	193
3	*La Traviata* (Verdi)	175
4	*Carmen* (Bizet)	173
5	*Il Barbiere di Siviglia* (Rossini)	154
6	*Tosca* (Puccini)	151
7	*Le Nozze di Figaro* (Mozart)	144
8	*Die Zauberflöte* (Mozart)	143
9	*Don Giovanni* (Mozart)	133
10	*Rigoletto* (Verdi)	132

SOURCE: Opera America, reported in the *Chicago Tribune*, 1 November 2002

Significantly, neither Wagner nor Richard Strauss, nor Beethoven's *Fidelio*, appears on this list. Nor do any of the French grand operas which dominated the 1860s and 1870s. Only *Carmen* and *The Magic Flute* have a libretto in a language other than Italian.

Puccini's 'victory' confirms the validity of his adoption of the 'global' strategy launched by Verdi (see pages 588–61). His *Manon Lescaut* (1893), set in France, was based on the novel by the Abbé Prevost. *La Bohème* (1896) is set in the Quartier Latin in Paris. *Tosca* (1900), though set in Rome, was based on a play by Victorien Sardou. Here the heroine, as usual, dies for love, but not before stabbing to death the hateful Baron Scarpia – a rare instance of a woman killing someone on the stage. *Madama Butterfly* (1904), set in Japan with an American male protagonist, was based on a one-act play by the American David Belasco that Puccini had seen in London in 1900. The play itself was based on a magazine story by John Luther Long about a real incident. Puccini then tackled a 'western' theme by composing an opera entirely set in the American west. This was *La Fanciulla del west* (The Girl of the Golden West), again based on a play by Belasco, which premiered in New York in 1910. The day before the first night Puccini admitted to the New York press that though he did not know the west, he had read so much about it that he felt as if he had been there.[24] His last, unfinished work, *Turandot* (produced posthumously in 1926), was set in a fairy-tale China. Italy barely figured in Puccini's *oeuvre*.

Puccini's Italian contemporaries or near-contemporaries were no rivals. Amilcare Ponchielli (*La Gioconda* 1876), Arrigo Boito (*Mefistofele*, 1868), Umberto Giordano (*Andrea Chenier*, 1896), Alfredo Catalani (*La Wally*, 1892), Ruggero Leoncavallo (*I Pagliacci*, 1892) and Pietro Mascagni (*Cavalleria Rusticana*, 1890) are known, if at all, for only one or two operas. And no work by an Italian opera composer after Puccini has entered the international repertory.

Puccini's foray to the USA was far from unusual. The increased competition among operatic performers, the brevity of the 'season' in Europe, and the greater ease of transatlantic travel meant that European operas were regularly staged in South and North America with the original casts. The new bourgeoisies of the leading Latin American and US cities wanted to have the same social and cultural life as those of Europe. La Scala was well situated to cash in on this globalisation. Exploiting its prestigious image, it had eleven theatrical agencies abroad to organise the transfer of its productions to places as distant as Buenos Aires, Montevideo, Havana, Chicago and San Francisco. It sent not just singers and conductors but also its dressmakers, jewellers and stage designers. In the 1880s some 1,200 Italian artists travelled to the New World to perform. Impresarios from Montevideo, New York, Caracas, Santiago, etc. went to Milan to stock up on props and sign up artists and musicians. The success of the Italians in the USA was considerable. In New York the 1910–1911 season at the Metropolitan was dominated by Puccini. In addition to the première of *La Fanciulla del west*, there were performances of *Madame Butterfly*, *La Bohème* and *Tosca*.[25] Needless to say, the musical intelligentsia of both Italy and France had nothing but contempt for the kind of melodrama Puccini represented. While the public went wild for *La Fanciulla del west* or *Manon Lescaut*, *Pelléas et Mélisande* failed in Rome in April 1909.[26]

In Europe, moreover, growing nationalism in France, Germany and Russia made life difficult for Italian opera. In Paris the Théâtre-Italien was in decline, and in 1875 the Théâtre National de l'Opéra moved into a new opera house built by Charles Garnier (Opéra-Garnier). Its repertoire was overwhelmingly dominated by French opera. The first season (1875–76) had a new production of Jacques François Halévy's *La Juive* (1835), ballets by Delibes (including *Coppelia*), Ambroise Thomas's *Hamlet*, Meyerbeer's *Les Huguenots* and Charles Gounod's *Faust*. The only two Italian operas performed, Donizetti's *La Favorite* and Rossini's *Guillaume Tell*, had originally been premièred in Paris and were in French.[27] The Opéra-Garnier continued to favour French opera – or at least opera in French – until the beginning of the twentieth century. Between 1875 and 1962 the most-performed opera was Gounod's *Faust* with 2,233 performances; his *Roméo et Juliette* was performed 620 times. Meyerbeer did very well too: *L'Africaine* was performed 259 times, *Les Huguenots* 568 times, *Le Prophète* 252 times, *Robert le Diable* 175. Halévy's *La Juive* was staged 196 times, Auber's *La Muette de Portici* thirty-four times, and Thomas's *Hamlet* 295.[28] Wagner's *Die Walküre* and *Tannhäuser* were great successes too, as were Verdi's *Rigoletto* and *Traviata* and Rossini's *Guillaume Tell*, but while Wagner, Verdi and Rossini are still regularly performed, Meyerbeer, Auber and Thomas are nowadays performed rarely even in France.

Italian opera continued to be popular, particularly in countries with little or no national operatic tradition such as Spain, Portugal and Great Britain. In Vienna between 1869 and 1880, out of 2,466 opera nights (ninety operas performed), 426 were by the four great Italians: Rossini, Bellini, Donizetti and Verdi. Italy still had more theatres than anyone else, but their season was short. The season at La Scala in 1879–80 consisted of only sixty performances, of which fifty-six were of Italian opera:

LA SCALA 1879–80 SEASON: PERFORMANCES	
Aida (Verdi)	23
La Gioconda (Ponchielli)	14
Lucia di Lammermoor (Donizetti)	11
Rigoletto (Verdi)	8
Faust (Gounod)	4
TOTAL	60

SOURCE: *Il Pungolo*, 1–2 April 1880 in *Carteggio Verdi-Ricordi 1880–81*, Istituto di Studi Verdiani, Parma 1988, p.229

The Hoftheater (now the Staatsoper) in Vienna was open ten and a half months a year, La Scala less than four months (from mid-December to mid-April). The Hoftheater produced 260 shows, La Scala sixty. The superiority of the Austrian and German opera houses was due to their lavish public funding and stringent organisation. Each theatre was run by a well-paid manager who decided on the programme and the artists for the season. Each theatre had its own permanent company committed to two rehearsals a day in special rooms, which meant it could work on several productions at the same time (a practice unknown in France and Italy). The performance started early, at 6.30 p.m., and was interrupted only once. In Italy it seldom started before 9 p.m. and was lengthened by frequent intervals (to allow the patrons to mingle and to show off their clothes). Opera houses' personnel was in proportion to the generosity of the funding. Those in Berlin, Vienna and Munich were and probably still are the most subsidised in the world. Italy, however, produced more novelties than Germany or Austria: forty new operas a year between 1870 and 1890 (with a peak of fifty-two in 1890). Most however lasted only for a season, and sank without trace.

In the United States no significant native operatic repertoire materialised. From early 1925 to 1930 NBC broadcast an opera every week (in abridged format), setting a standard for all other broadcasters. The company tried to include a few American works such as Charles Wakefield Cadman's 'Indian' opera *Shanewis* (1918), but to no avail.[29] Cadman (1881–1946) remained better-known for the song 'From the Land of the Sky Blue Water' than for his opera. Having missed – like the British – the nineteenth-century opera era, very few American composers in the twentieth century would make it to the repertory – John Adams's *Nixon in China* (1987) being a possible exception, as would some works that straddle the divide between musicals and operas, such as George Gershwin's *Porgy and Bess*. The powerful classical music culture which came into being in the USA after 1918 was focused on performance and not on composition: great conductors, great orchestras, great singers and great instrumentalists, all performing European music.

The creation of an almost unchangeable classical repertory for opera is an excellent way of minimising risks, since only 'successful' operas are performed (the cutting down of rehearsal time is a further, though not necessarily significant, gain).[30] Variety is necessary to attract the same audience to the same opera, but such variety can be achieved by marketing singers (so that having seen Tebalda's *Traviata*, one is encouraged to see Callas's) or, more recently, by providing a production which changes the setting: hence *Tosca* in fascist Italy, a punk *Così fan tutte*, *Don Giovanni* in Harlem, and *Rigoletto* set among gangsters in New York's Lower East Side.

A further consequence of the stability of the operatic repertory has been the revival, in the second half of the twentieth century, of neglected operas by popular composers. The popularity of many of Verdi's operas had started to decrease shortly after his death in 1901. The cool obituary Verdi received in *The Times* (28 January 1901) mentioned his 'deservedly forgotten operas' (*Giovanna d'Arco* and *Alzira*, both 1845, and *Attila*, 1846), his declining popularity in England (except for *Aida*), and the failure of *Otello* and *Falstaff* to win the popular acclaim they had obtained from the critics. In Italy itself, at La Scala in the last decade of the century, while he was still alive, only *Rigoletto*, *Traviata* and *Don Carlos* were performed (apart from the new operas *Otello* and *Falstaff*). In Parma, Verdi's home town, only two of his operas were performed between 1904 and 1911: *Aida* and *Rigoletto*. In Bologna, by then enamoured of Wagner, only three of Verdi's works were performed between 1887 and 1912: *Rigoletto* (1901), *Traviata* (1901) and *Aida* (1908).[31] Yet in 1951, out of the seventy-five operas staged in the three main Italian theatres (La Scala of Milan, the San Carlo of Naples and the Teatro dell'Opera of Rome), twenty-one were by Verdi, including two which had become completely forgotten: *Oberto Conte di San Bonifacio* and *Giovanna d'Arco* – admittedly the fiftieth anniversary of Verdi's death would have bumped up the total.[32]

What rescued Verdi and, more generally, Italian opera was the invention of the gramophone. This greatly increased the number of listeners. Early discs could carry only individual arias and not the 'total opera' experience – few had the finances or the incentive to buy an entire opera, which would consist of dozens of discs. This worked to the detriment of Wagner and to the advantage of the Italians. Discs gave star singers even greater renown than previously. The sales of records constituted a formidable market incentive for the more famous singers to record their voices and to regard public performance as the most prestigious element of their profession, but not necessarily the most remunerative – contrary to their initial fears. The record-buying public could familiarise themselves with the voice and the music without entering the daunting and expensive palaces where opera was actually performed. At the same time the increase in operatic knowledge (of singers, of arias, even of entire operas) provided an incentive to go, once in a while, to listen to the real thing.

The second development was the role of the conductor. Already well established in the nineteenth century, the conductor developed in the twentieth a new role. As the operatic repertory became stable in its late eighteenth- and nineteenth-century mould, the conductor provided a brand name alongside that of the opera and the composer. One did not go simply to Verdi's *Rigoletto*, but to Toscanini's. The conductor thus became the custodian of the great nineteenth-century tradition, making sure that the intentions of the composer were respected – intentions defined by the conductor himself. Even in Italy, where a cavalier attitude towards operatic rigour had gone hand in hand with its great popularity, a less exuberant mood prevailed. Opera became a serious genre to be revered, not just a reason for an evening of fun. The chief architect of this revolution was Arturo Toscanini – by 1900 already the dominating force in the opera world, though he was only thirty-three years of age. It was Toscanini who introduced to Italy the principles of conducting prevailing in Germany, and above all respect for the score written by the composer. Wagner's operas – long though they were – were to be performed without cuts. Popular arias were not to be repeated during a performance, regardless of how many times the public shouted 'Encore' or 'Bis'. 'Toscanini non ripete' ('No repeats from Toscanini') became a common expression. Singers were reined in: no unnecessary trills or ornamentation, no showing off, no exhibitionism. In 1908 Toscanini went to New York and brought to the Metropolitan the same demanding standards he had exacted from La Scala.[33]

Yet the Italian public continued to remain undisciplined. Critics complained that the audiences talked among themselves and showed no respect for the integrity of the composition, stamping their feet and banging their walking sticks to demand an encore.[34] The orchestras were no better than the public. Even Italy's best orchestra, the Accademia of Santa Cecilia in Rome, failed to satisfy Mahler. Having conducted it in 1910 he wrote to Alfredo Casella: 'This orchestra is *horrible*. It has been impossible to do anything with them and I have cancelled the third evening . . . and I am leaving immediately . . . I have never encountered such a shameless and ignorant lot . . . Santa Cecilia will never see me again.'[35] Perhaps this is why Toscanini conducted mainly operas in Italy, and preferred using foreign orchestras for instrumental music.

In Italy as elsewhere, Toscanini was still worshipped decades after his death, his memory kept alive by the constant reissuing of recorded interpretations. But he did not spring out of nothing. There was a solid nineteenth-century Italian tradition of conducting, represented by Angelo Mariani, who not only conducted Verdi (not always to Verdi's liking), but championed Wagner in Italy.

Conducting was an international profession throughout the nineteenth century (and, of course, even more throughout the twentieth), yet during the period surveyed in this chapter, outside the USA there was always a preponderance of 'native' conductors. There were exceptions: Gaspare Spontini conducted the Berlin opera (1819–41), and was followed by a Frenchman of German birth, Meyerbeer (1842–48). Otherwise the domination of Germans in Germany was virtually uncontested – and most of them were Wagnerians (but then, most late-nineteenth-century European conductors had become Wagnerians). The French relied almost exclusively on French conductors, the Italians on Italians. The British imported many of theirs, usually from Germany (Carl Rosa, born Carl Rose in Hamburg, 1842–89), Austria-Hungary (Hans Richter, 1843–1916) or Italy (Michael Costa, 1833–79) but they also nurtured local talents such as Henry Wood and Thomas Beecham. The Russians also imported foreigners to conduct Russian opera.

In New York, then the capital of music in the USA, most conductors before 1920 were foreigners. Between 1884 and 1908 the orchestra of the Metropolitan Opera was conducted by Walter Damrosch (1884–91) and then by Anton Seidl, Alfred Hertz and Artur Bodanzky – all Germans. In 1908–10 it was conducted by Mahler, and then by Toscanini until 1915. A similar foreign domination characterised the New York Philharmonic Orchestra throughout most of the twentieth century.

The dictatorship of the conductor was somewhat restrained by orchestra members deciding, democratically, who should be their dictator. In 1882 members of the Berlin-based Bilsesche Kapelle, owned and conducted by

Benjamin Bilse since 1867, resigned *en masse* because their wages were too low. They reorganised themselves as the Berlin Philharmonic Orchestra and appointed their own conductor, Franz Wüllner, who was followed by Joseph Joachim in 1884, Hans von Bülow in 1887 and Artur Nikisch in 1895, achieving international fame. In 1922 their new conductor, Wilhelm Furtwängler, managed to obtain funding from the city of Berlin in return for twenty popular concerts per year. This model of organisation was adopted by the Czech Philharmonic in 1896 and the London Symphony in 1902 (in competition with Henry Wood and his Queen's Hall Promenade Concerts).[36]

Thus all the institutions defining 'classical' music were in place before the advent of the gramophone: a repertory, designated venues (such as concert halls), orchestras and conductors, dedicated audiences, and a symbolic importance attached to the genre (refinement, good taste, wealth, education, etc.). The term 'classical' itself, loaded with high-culture meanings, was often used to designate even 'new' music which aimed to be accepted into the 'classical canon'. And it had to be Western. Even in Japan, which has its own tradition of 'classical' music, the term used in music stores to designate Western (not Japanese) serious music is 'classical' (*kurashikku*) music.[37]

Home Music

The enormous diffusion of the piano, and the expansion and streamlining of sheet-music production, proceeded in parallel with the popularity of variety theatres and social dancing. At home one could play songs and tunes one had heard in shows, and practise dancing. Sociability among peer groups – and not just among relatives – long a privilege of the middle classes, was now becoming relatively common among the working classes. While in the 1880s the diffusion of the gramophone was a little way off, the automatic player-piano (or Pianola, originally a registered brand name) became increasingly popular in America and Europe. The pianola provided its owner with more than the illusion of playing an instrument, since some skill was required in deciding what was the suitable tempo. Advertisers appealed to those who had unused pianos, proposing a part-exchange with player-pianos like the 'autopiano': 'No more idle pianos, the Autopiano is the live piano and can be used where the ordinary piano fails.'[38] Great composers were not slow to become interested in the instrument, albeit commercially. The *Illustrated London News* of 4 November 1911 carried an advertisement for a pianola with a picture of Richard Strauss, and his own lengthy endorsement of it. In the 18 November 1911 issue it was the turn of Edvard Grieg to do exactly the same; on 20 April 1912 Edward Elgar gave his endorsement. In 1910 a Broadwood player-piano went with Captain Scott's Antarctic expedition, was taken to the base-camp, and played on the ice.[39]

Private patronage did not disappear from the field of serious music, because the commercial market was never sufficiently developed to sustain it, and state support was limited. Philanthropic interventions continued throughout the first half of the twentieth century, providing direct financial support for composers. The flair of some of these benefactors was remarkable. Winetta Singer (daughter of Isaac Singer, the inventor of the sewing machine) was an exemplary representative of this now virtually extinct breed. She was born in New York in 1865, but moved to Paris with her family in 1867. In 1893 she married Prince Edmond de Polignac (it was her second marriage). He died in 1901, leaving the Princesse de Polignac, now possessor of a grand name as well as a great fortune which she could use to dispense favours to remarkable composers (she lived until 1943). The roll call of her protégés included Gabriel Fauré, Emmanuel Chabrier, Maurice Ravel, Reynaldo Hahn, Isaac Albeniz, Igor Stravinsky (one of her major beneficiaries), Erik Satie, Manuel de Falla, and many others.[40]

If one could not sing or make music at home, or pay someone else to do it, one could still sing in a church choir. Though choral music has been and is the natural accompaniment to religious services throughout most of the world, in Europe this has tended to be particularly significant in Protestant lands, or where the influence of the Germanic tradition is strong (such as the Alpine regions of north-eastern Italy). One of the most popular of all Christmas carols, for instance, 'Stille Nacht, Heilige Nacht' ('Silent Night'), was written by an Austrian village priest, Josef Mohr, to the music of a local organist in 1818. Travelling musicians picked up the tune and its lyrics and took the carol around Europe, reaching the United States in 1839. By the end of the century it had become a standby of Christmas choirs. Choral festivals became popular in working-class communities in Germany, Scandinavia and Great Britain. Nationalists too used choral music, instituting language-based festivals such as the Welsh National Eisteddfod (1860). Working-class organisations followed suit, especially where radical politics and religious life were connected, such as in the Welsh mining valleys – the South Wales Choral Union triumphed in the first national choir contest, held at London's Crystal Palace in 1872.

In Germany, the first choral societies exclusively for the (male) workers appeared as early as the 1860s. The most important workers' cultural organisation in the decades before the First World War was the Deutscher Arbeiter-Sängerbund (DASB – German Workers' Choral Federation), which by 1914 had a membership of 200,000.[41] Only 1 or 2 per cent of SPD members were actually active in politics, but one in five joined the DASB (which ended up being criticised by the party for distracting the workers). By 1912 membership of the working-men's choir had overtaken the thriving 'bourgeois' choir.[42] The music was not particularly revolutionary: most of the songs in the party's official songbook, Max Kegel's *Sozialdemokratisches Liederbuch* (1891) had been toned down, and the names chosen by the choral societies tended to be more along the lines of 'Alpenglühen' (Alpine Glow) and 'Liederlust' (Delight in Songs) than 'Rote Fahne' (Red Flag).[43]

In Britain, choral and brass bands offered opportunities to socialise, meet famous musicians, and even visit the USA.[44] Gilbert and Sullivan became the favourites of operatic societies. By the beginning of the twentieth century, productions of their operettas were largely by enthusiastic amateur societies.[45] The huge expansion of music-making can be measured by the increase in the number of musicians recorded in census returns – from 19,000 in 1871 to 47,000 in 1911. In 1856 there were at most half a dozen brass band contests in England; in 1896 there were 240. In 1913 an audience of 70–80,000 attended the Crystal Palace National Band Championship. Music hall artists toured the country, performing virtually the same repertoire at each venue. Some 500,000 sheet-music copies of Sullivan's 'The Lost Chord' were sold between 1877 and 1902. Henry Round's arrangement of Donizetti's *Lucrezia Borgia* was used in almost 20 per cent of the 240 brass band contests held in 1896. By the end of the nineteenth century a mass musical culture had emerged in England. Though women were barred from brass bands, music provided working-class women with some opportunities, since music hall success was one of the few ways in which a woman could be come nationally famous, as was the case with Marie Lloyd and Vesta Tilley.[46]

There was plenty of singing in the Victorian drawing room. Scottish songs were the rage in the 1850s, Irish songs in the 1860s. Hymns were arranged for home use. Profane music was turned into sacred; thus Mendelssohn's 'Gutemberg der Grosse Mann' became the famous 'Hark, the Herald Angels Sing'. Gounod's 'Chant évangelique' became a hit as 'Nazareth'. In the 1870s American gospel and Civil War songs became fashionable, especially 'The Battle Hymn of the Republic' (also known as 'John Brown's Body') and

'Tramp! Tramp! Tramp!' This interest had been sparked by the British tour in 1871 of the Jubilee Singers, a group of emancipated slaves who had performed in the drawing room of the Duke and Duchess of Argyll, where they received a visit from Queen Victoria, to whom they sang 'Go Down Moses'. They came back in 1875, and in Liverpool 12,000 children turned up to hear them. In 1879, after a successful European tour, they set themselves up as a joint stock company. Some of their songs were arranged for the drawing room and are still very well-known today.[47]

The most performed song in the world, though, was almost certainly 'Happy Birthday to You', written in 1893 by two American schoolteachers, Mildred J. Hill and Patty Smith Hill, and originally used as a classroom greeting: 'Good Morning to All'. Copyrighted in 1963, the rights were sold to Warner Brothers in 1988, bringing in $2 million a year in royalties.

Professional singers were crucial to sales promotion: they made ballads known, and by singing them, endorsed them. But home was still the centre of music-making. In one of the most beautiful short stories ever written in English, 'The Dead' (1907), James Joyce gives us a partially autobiographical snapshot of this domestic world.[48] The occasion is the annual Christmas dance held by the Morkan sisters, Kate and Julia, and their niece Mary Jane in their middle-class home. The guests are 'everybody who knew them': relatives, friends, members of Julia's choir, Kate's older pupils. They dance waltzes and the quadrille. Mary Jane plays some demanding pieces on the piano to the hushed drawing room. Aunt Julia, though no longer young, sings faultlessly, with her soprano voice, 'Arrayed for the Bridal'. They converse about music and opera, lamenting the good old days when famous Italian companies visited Dublin, when one could see Donizetti's *Lucrezia Borgia*, and wishing they could hear Caruso – 'I'd give anything to hear Caruso sing,' says Mary Jane. The guests then toast the three ladies, singing 'For they are jolly gay fellows'. Then one of the guests, the tenor Bartell d'Arcy (modelled on Barton M'Guckin, the leading tenor with the Carl Rosa Opera Company), though hoarse, sings a song, 'The Lass of Aughrim' – and it is this tune, this ballad, though uncertainly sung, that brings to the mind of another guest, Gretta, memories of a young lover who used to sing that song, and who died of love for her long ago. Her mood prompts her husband, Gabriel, to ask for an explanation. She tells him. Gabriel, more envious of her emotions, and of the young man's passion, than jealous of a rival, is overwhelmed by self-pity: 'better pass boldly into that other world, in the full glory of some passion, than fade and wither dismally with age'. So, in a few pages, are laid before us the elements of the power of music, even modest home music played by amateurs on a simple piano: dancing, amusement, celebration, merriment, virtuosity, mood.

Listening to songs in pubs and music halls, singing them with friends and companions in clubs and churches, playing tunes around the home piano with the help of music scores – thus Europeans and North Americans prepared themselves for the great invention which would revolutionise the consumption of music in the twentieth century: sound recording.

39

Recorded Sound

Sound in a Box

THE RECORDING OF SOUND revolutionised the consumption of music. It put music on a par with the printed text. One could take the 'sound' home and hear, for the first time in history, the music of one's own choice, again and again, performed by highly skilled musicians. Recording was thus as momentous an invention for sound as printing was for text. Perhaps more, since a single reading will often relinquish all the pleasures of a particular text, but the joys of music demand repetition. Most people read a novel only once, occasionally twice, though there are exceptions, particularly children's stories which are reread many times. But when it comes to music, repeated listening to the same passage is the norm. The pleasure of a song is enhanced by repetition. The pleasure of a tale, of exactly the same tale, soon decreases.

To read a printed text it is necessary to be literate. To listen to music – like listening to a tale being told – requires no skills. However, no equipment is necessary to read a text apart from the text itself. With recorded music we need a piece of 'hardware', a machine to reproduce the sound, as well as the 'software', i.e. a recording. Thus the expansion of the recording industry relied on consumers making at least two distinct purchases, first the gramophone, and then particular records to play on it. An initial considerable expenditure required a predisposition to make subsequent smaller ones.

Thomas Edison's phonograph saw the light of day in 1877, but once the initial excitement had subsided, it seemed that this recording machine was of little use. It took twelve years before the 'talking machine' could be sold to the public (1889). At first the machine weighed about a hundred pounds, was expensive to make, and the recordings, made on tin foil, could be played only a few times.[1] In 1886 Alexander Graham Bell had come up with a cylinder made of wax-coated cardboard. Then Edison improved on Bell by using solid wax. These early phonographs had a distinctive advantage: one could make one's own recordings using the same cylinder – just like a cassette tape recorder.[2] In 1887 Emile Berliner, a young German who had emigrated to the USA, had begun to use flat discs capable of being mass produced, and dubbed his invention the 'gramophone' ('phonograph' remained the American usage). In 1889 he sold a licence to a German firm of toy-makers, Kammerer & Reinhardt. The earliest contraptions were hand-propelled, and in England were sold for two guineas. This included six 'free' records. At that stage the gramophone was still a toy. For a while cylinders co-existed with discs – in France longer than elsewhere. Eventually the disc prevailed. In terms of the quality of recorded sound, at least initially, cylinders were better, because their speed was more constant, but they were difficult to stack, more fragile, and more expensive to make.[3]

In the 1890s, recorded sound was also sold via publicly operated coin machines in drugstores, but soon the main business became the sale of record players for home use. When Edison invented the phonograph it was not obvious that music would rapidly dominate the field of recorded sound. Edison himself was not sure how his invention could be used, but suggested various possibilities. These included dictating letters, phonographic books for the blind or for children, elocution teaching, family records, educational, keeping records of memorable speeches, the last words of a dying man or the passionate declaration of a lover – the way photographic equipment is used to record salient moments in one's life such as marriage, children and holidays – and, last but not least, the reproduction of music.[4] Indeed, initially some customers were prepared to pay to have their voices recorded so that they could listen to them again and again.

Talking records were produced and sold early on in the history of the industry. The Italian catalogue of the Gramophone Company (later EMI) included passages of Dante's poetry recited by Ernesto Zacconi (1903), a 'Teach Yourself German' (1907, though at three or four minutes per disc not much German could be learned), a sermon (1922) and even a 'Message to the North American People and the Italians of America' (1926).[5] The market for spoken recordings has always remained small, even when, as is the case today, audio books have become widely available. The North American Phonograph Co. tried to market the phonograph as a business machine (in order to save on stenographers). It did not work.[6]

Recording was a very cumbersome process. A brass band recording of the song 'My Country, 'tis of Thee' required ten machines, each with a cylinder inserted. When the band finished playing, the machines were loaded again with new cylinders and the band would strike up again. It took three hours to record three hundred cylinders that were sold for $1 each.[7] This was a luxury product: at the time a skilled steelworker in Pennsylvania earned $13 a week and spent almost half of that on food. Still, a record player was not entirely out of his reach. One introduced by the Columbia Phonograph Company in 1897 cost only $10, while a 'Genuine Edison Phonograph' could be had for $30. In Europe similar machines were selling for twice as much.[8] Prices fell rapidly. Only the previous year Columbia had advertised a record player for $50 in an advertisement depicting a family – grandfather, mother, father and small boy – gathered around the horn of a small gramophone, a machine so simple to use, it said, that 'even a child can make it pour forth the most enchanting selections of the world's greatest Musicians, Singers, Actors, and Speakers'.[9]

Electricity was not required to use the gramophone. The discs were revolved by a mechanism not dissimilar to the system of springs used in clocks. All that was required was the initial winding up of the spring. Sound was reproduced by a sound box, which consisted of a steel needle attached to a vibrating diaphragm. The needle had to be changed very frequently. Nevertheless, the expansion of the record market proceeded rapidly. The leading gramophone companies expanded their range of records to satisfy the demands of their customers and to entice new ones. As the music historian J.B. Steane put it: 'In 1900 the gramophone was a toy, in 1902 a musical experiment, in 1904 an established medium.'[10]

In 1891 the Columbia record company had a ten-page catalogue listing twenty-seven marches, thirteen polkas, ten waltzes (two by Johann Strauss) and an arrangement from *Il Trovatore*. By 1893 the catalogue had grown to thirty-two pages and the marches numbered eighty-two.[11] By 1900 in every important Russian city there was a record shop, even though until 1902 there were no record manufacturers in the country. Of course, records were still for an élite. The record shop of St Petersburg, on Nevsky Prospekt, had Persian carpets on the floor, potted palm trees and antique furniture. The owner, Rappaport, disappointed by the lack of style of the labels on the records (a uniform black, but an improvement on the previous practice of scratching information about the recording into the centre of the disc) commissioned the Gramophone Company to produce a series of recordings featuring Russian opera stars with a red label and gold lettering.[12] It was the beginning of the Red Label series.

Sales increased constantly. In 1900 three million records (cylinders and discs) were sold in the USA, in 1910 thirty million, in 1921 140 million. Phonograph production in the US was 345,000 in 1909, 514,000 in 1914, and 2,230,000 in 1919. In 1915 Russian record sales were twenty million, but Germany had reached a production of eighteen million in 1907 (six million of which were exported).[13] Record sales in Britain in 1913 were thirteen million.[14] In 1920 there were already eighty record companies in the UK and two hundred in the USA. Thus, from its inception, the recording of music acquired all the characteristics of a major capitalist undertaking.

Compared with publishing, the first music companies were large. A publisher could make a profit by selling only a thousand copies of a book, and sustain itself by publishing a hundred books a year. This was impossible in the new recording industry. The national markets were far too narrow. Selling a thousand copies of a record was uneconomic. A large number of recordings had to be made available to potential buyers in order to give them an incentive to buy a gramophone. Thinking globally became mandatory.

Emile Berliner had started making commercial recordings in the 1890s in both Europe and the USA. In 1891 he set up the US Gramophone Company (which held his patents), and in 1895 the Berliner Gramophone Company (to exploit those patents). The Victor Talking Machine Company (later RCA) was formed in 1901 in New Jersey to take over his interests in the USA. The British-based Gramophone Company (later His Master's Voice and then EMI), partly owned by the Victor Company, was meant to exploit the European market, while by 1907 the Victor Company focused on the US, China, Japan and the Philippines. Before the First World War the Gramophone-Victor concern accounted for half the world sales of records.[15] In effect, by 1903 the recording industry was in the hands of an oligopoly, excluding possible entrants and eliminating competitors thanks to their hold on most of the patents.[16]

In Continental Europe the Gramophone Company's main competitors were the Italian Fonotipia Company with its partners in France and Germany. The French brothers Charles and Émile Pathé started manufacturing cylinders in 1894 at their works in Chatou near Paris, which became the centre of the French record industry. By 1910 Pathé had built factories in Vienna, Moscow (making Russian films for a rapidly expanding market) and Belgium, in addition to a new factory near Paris. Their recording studios were in rue Richelieu near the Opéra and the Opéra-Comique. They too experimented with the musical coin machines. These were not in drugstores, as in New York, but in their palatial Salon du Phonographe on the boulevard des Italiens, fitted with plush carpets. Inside, customers could sit by a mahogany cabinet with hearing tubes and a dialling machine and a catalogue. They chose a record, dropped fifteen centimes in a slot, dialled the corresponding number, and an assistant would bring the record up from the basement and put it on the gramophone connected to the tube. The whole dial-a-record process took ten seconds. The takings averaged 1,000 francs per day.[17]

In Germany the dominant firm was Deutsche Grammophon. Its success was due to its ability to break out of the narrow domestic market and export in large quantities, particularly to Russia, where it built a pressing plant in Riga and opened record shops in all the major cities. The First World War further enhanced the development of the music market. In Italy, for instance, the Columbia Gramophone Company – the dominant company – donated gramophones to the 'Case dello soldato' (barracks where soldiers could social-ise near the frontline), expecting, presumably, to sell more records as a result.[18] While most of the soldiers were of peasant stock, the records were mainly operatic. For the first time, key aspects of musical 'high' culture entered the world of the rural classes.

It was the Victor Company which decided that the mass production of discs was preferable to that of cylinders. This was largely due to the availability of a material suitable for discs based on shellac, the secretion of a tropical beetle hitherto used for the manufacture of buttons. It was replaced by vinyl only during the Second World War, when the Allies were cut off from the Far East, where the beetles were found.[19]

The speed of the first discs was fixed at seventy revolutions per minute – the speed eventually stabilised at 78 rpm in 1926. A faster speed would have produced a better sound, but the playing time would have been too short; a slower speed would have produced too poor a sound.[20]

Standardisation of machines and discs became imperative; but would everyone want to buy the same music? The international spread of the novel suggested that different cultures could enjoy the same story, and the worldwide appreciation of opera, particularly Italian opera, was another signal that, at least within similar social groups, there was a convergence of taste. The industry, however, initially assumed that musical tastes were highly culture-bound. Its first strategy was to cater for diversified tastes. This was implemented so thoroughly that by the early 1910s even Icelandic, Estonian, Welsh and Breton record-buyers were supplied with their own music.

In 1902 the Gramophone Company (founded in London in 1898 by a group of English and American businessmen who held Emile Berliner's disc recording patents) sent Fred Gaisberg (1873–1951), one of their senior executives, to India to open new markets, establish agencies and acquire a catalogue of native recordings. They acted in part out of fear of the competition, having been informed that the Victor Talking Machine Company was 'flooding' India with its equipment.[21] Gaisberg had significant experience in Europe and Russia, travelling across the continent recording hundreds of titles as far afield as Nizhnii Novgorod and Kazan, where he made 'a few hundred Tartar records'.[22] In Calcutta, where he stayed for six weeks, he recorded several hundred titles with local singers. Several of these songs remained popular locally for the next two decades, their reputations enhanced thanks to the recordings.[23] After India, Gaisberg went on to Siam, China and Japan, where he recorded six hundred titles.[24] He and his colleagues would set up their recording equipment for a week or so in a hotel room and record artists selected by a local agent, as he had done on his previous tours. In Kazan, he wrote in his diary,

> we stopped at our agents Malacapff . . . He took us around to the Hotel de France where I rigged my outfit, and old Malacapff chased off to get Tartar artists. The first he brought in was a petrified, yellow-skinned accordion player with a musty smell to him. Very likely he did his best but his music haunts me still.[25]

Gaisberg knew almost nothing about the music he recorded. Of some Chinese female singers he wrote 'their voices have the sound of a small wailing cat'. Of the men he wrote: 'As a Chinaman yells at the top of his power when he sings, he can only sing two songs an evening and then his throat becomes hoarse.'[26]

By 1910 the Gramophone Company had made over 14,000 recordings in Asia and North Africa, including 4,410 in India, 1,925 in Turkey, and 1,192 in Egypt. In India the company had catalogues reflecting ethnic subdivisions (Hindi, Bengali, Urdu, Punjabi, etc.).[27] However, since recorded music necessarily appealed more to the prosperous Western-oriented upper classes, the company also sold Western music in these markets, promoted as an essential part of a modern lifestyle. An advertisement for the Gramophone Company in the *Madras Times* of 20 March 1913 makes this clear:

Grand opera at home. You may never live in the musical centres where there are regular seasons of grand opera. You may be far away from any city where concerts are given by the great bands and orchestras. You may never have the opportunity of hearing any of the leading artists on their concert tours. And yet with a 'His Master's Voice' Gramophone and the wonderful repertoire of 'His Master's Voice' records you can in your own home hear the greatest artists and develop a better understanding of the world's best music than if you were privileged to attend such per-formances.[28]

The enterprise – which was about selling gramophones by making recordings of local music available – was not always successful. A study of the Balinese record market found that it was difficult to get many people to buy record players in order to listen to Balinese music when so much of it was available for free all around them, in the thousands of temples and households.[29]

In Japan, however, Western music made a considerable impact. The ground had been prepared by the remarkable openness of the Japanese towards Western culture, and Western music in particular, the diffusion of locally-made pianos (by Yamaha), and a government circular of 1874 which ordered court musicians to learn Western music. In 1909 a Japanese company started producing gramophones and music records. By the end of 1920 there were six manufacturers. By the end of the 1920s there was a flood of Western music.[30] As Gaisberg admitted, writing in 1942: 'To this day I have not been able to account for the Japanese gluttony for Western classics.'[31]

Recording Singers

The most sought-after singers had gained their popularity in some other medium, usually the stage. Thus, at its inception, the industry depended on success gained elsewhere. By the 1910s another strategy was in place: the use of relatively unknown studio singers and orchestras producing assembly-line recordings of new songs.[32]

Initially, operatic arias dominated the market for recorded music. Purists, and occasionally composers, were dismayed at the fragmentation of operas into distinct arias. Yet this had become the norm in recitals in private salons, such as the famous soirée at the home of Baron Hirsch in Paris on 8 April 1880 which caused such grief to Verdi for its cavalier use of his *Aida*.[33] In the early years of the twentieth century, famous singers such as Adelina Patti (1905, though by then she was sixty-two, had retired from the stage and was past her peak), Enrico Caruso (1902), Lilli Lehmann (the leading Wagnerian soprano of her age), Nellie Melba, Francesca Tamagno, Medea Mei-Figner (an Italo-Russian soprano who made more than twenty recordings between 1901 and the late 1920s) and others recorded the most popular items from their repertory. A new source of prestige and income had been discovered. As the discs and cylinders could only carry a few minutes of music, this determined the kind of music that was recorded: songs and short tunes. Most arias had to be cut to fit. Not until the development of the long-playing record after the Second World War would it be possible to make a recording of an entire concert or an opera with significant commercial prospects, though as early as 1906, in Berlin, Bizet's *Carmen* was recorded on eighteen discs (both sides) and Berlioz's *La Damnation de Faust* on seventeen. 1913 saw the first recording of a full symphony, Beethoven's Fifth (without double-basses and timpani). But these were exceptions; such products were simply too expensive for the market. Thus, for the first decades in the development of the gramophone, the field was left to songs and operatic arias. The rise of popular music only enhanced the triumph, financial and otherwise, of singers over instrumentalists as the central figures in the world of music – as they had been throughout the eighteenth and nineteenth centuries.

At first operatic singers viewed the new invention with suspicion. Once their voices were recorded, they felt, their services would no longer be necessary. They soon realised that recording would in fact profit them both directly and indirectly, by increasing their fame and attracting new audiences. The original reaction was understandable. Great voices could earn formidable sums without the help of the recording industry. In 1890 the great Italian coloratura soprano Luisa Tetrazzini (1871–1940) could earn £3,500 in a month in Buenos Aires, at the age of eighteen. By the time she was twenty, still in Argentina, which was in the midst of an unprecedented economic boom, she was earning £5,500 a month.[34] Latin America had to compensate for its lack of international prestige by paying famous singers more than they would get elsewhere. In 1907 Tetrazzini was offered and accepted £1,200 for ten performances of *Traviata* at Covent Garden. The offer was not attractive, she wrote in her memoirs, but London was. There her voice 'would be heard and described to the world by some who had heard and described and helped to make famous that constellation of divine songstresses of a dying age' – singers such as Adelina Patti and Jenny Lind.[35] As it happened, after a cool start she was acclaimed as 'the new Patti'. Realising that new audiences had to be cultivated, but denied the usual big hall for her first concert in San

Francisco, she gave an open-air concert on Christmas Eve 1910 which was attended by 250,000 people and reported throughout the USA.[36] Between 1908 and 1914 she recorded extensively. The large sums earned should be viewed in the context of what is often a relatively short career. Tetrazzini's operatic life lasted twenty-four years (1890–1914), and though she went on giving recitals for another twenty, she spent or lost all she had earned ($5 million in a thirty-two-year career) in the following twenty-six, and died penniless.[37]

There were technical reasons why recording the human voice was preferred to recording instrumental music: in the pre-electric days (until 1925 recordings were made entirely by mechanical means) the narrower range and timbre of the human voice could be recorded with greater ease and realism. Fred Gaisberg, who recorded most of the famous artists of his day, gave an account of the state of the business at the beginning of the twentieth century, when he recorded English artists in the smoking room of the Coburn Hotel in London, which had been turned into a studio:

> There stood the recording machine on a high stand; from this projected a long thin trumpet into which the artist sang. Close by, on a movable platform, was an upright piano. If there was an orchestral accompaniment, then half-a-dozen wind instrumentalists, also on high stands, would be crowded in close to the singer. . .
>
> Our diaphragm was not very sensitive and we still required robust, even voices to make good records. Fat, jolly Bert Sheppard, with his powerful tenor voice and clear diction, gave us our most successful results. We used him under many names and as an old minstrel man he was very versatile. His repertoire comprised negro airs, Irish and English ballads, comic and patter songs, parodies and yodels . . . Bert Sheppard's 'Whistling Coon' and 'The Laughing Song' were world-famous. In India alone over half a million records of the latter were sold.[33]

The master copies of the recordings made in London were sent to Berliner's Telephon Fabrik in Hanover, where they were reproduced as seven-inch, single-side 'Berliner's Gramophone discs'.[34] These were sold worldwide. Soon the Gramophone Company established agencies in a number of countries, including, in Germany, Deutsche Grammophon.

In 1905 the company's largest market, in terms of turnover, was Germany, with a share of 35 per cent. Russia followed, with 22 per cent (Russia was the source of 40 per cent of its profits), then Great Britain with 15 per cent. France – where Pathé, whose machines were incompatible with others, had a strong position – provided 12 per cent. Italy, with 4.4 per cent, was a smaller market than India, which had 5 per cent.[40] The Italian market remained small for years to come, as Ricordi, with the help of the courts, managed to keep foreign interests out.

It was obvious that expansion could proceed in two ways, first by lowering the cost of gramophones, and secondly by increasing the number of records available. The *Daily Mail* of 16 October 1903 advertised two differently priced gramophones, 'Style No. 4' at £4.4s., and for an extra pound 'Style No. 5'. The fact that they were advertised in a mass-circulation paper gives an indication of the kind of market the company was targeting. In the same paper on 16 November 1903 Pathé (London) advertised records by Caruso for 3s.6d. ('salon size'). Edison, which called itself 'a purely British company', advertised 'the cheapest record in town' – only one shilling (*Daily Mail*, 10 October 1903). The sound, Edison claimed, was 'loud, clear and distinct', and the performances were by 'really British artists' and British bands, manu-factured by British experts, with British capital and British labour. The singers, customers were reassured, exhibited 'no nasality or Disagreeable Foreign Accents' – hence, presumably, no Caruso.[41] Bringing prices down must have worked. By 1914 'talking machines' could be found in the homes of the industrial working classes. Though no pre-1914 data have survived, estimates suggest that there were by then three million gramophones in Britain – one for every three households.[42]

Increasing the number of available records was important too, since every new record enhanced the attractiveness of purchasing a gramophone. But records were very expensive too. In 1907 a single disc could cost as much as a pair of shoes. From the point of view of the consumer it was not worth buying a machine if all it could do was play ten records. It became worthwhile only if there was plenty of choice.

What Did They Sell?

In 1905 the orchestra of La Scala recorded a number of overtures. In 1909 Odeon issued Tchaikovsky's *Nutcracker* on four double-sided discs – the first recording of an extended work. The 1915 Victor catalogue listed thousands of records, including 1,200 selections from a hundred operas. These were usually only relatively short passages, since not much more than four minutes could be recorded on one side. A further limitation was imposed by the narrow range of sounds that could be captured: very high or very low notes were particularly distorted. Brass instruments were better than strings. In fact the lower strings were often replaced by a violin whose soundbox had been replaced by a diaphragm – the so called Stroh violin, after its inventor, the London instrument-maker Charles Stroh.[43]

The listing of the Milan production of the Gramophone Company shows that the overwhelming majority of records issued for solo male and female voices consisted of operatic arias, followed by Italian songs, often performed by operatic singers. It was around this time that the Neapolitan song emerged as the 'typical' Italian song not only in Italy, but abroad as well. Older songs could now be sold in recorded format everywhere in the world. This contributed to the national and international success of the great Neapolitan successes of the previous decades, songs such as 'E spingole frangese' (1888), 'O sole mio' (1898), 'I te vurria vasà' (1901), which had accompanied the Italian cafés-concerts and the rise of stars such as Carolina Otero ('la Bella Otero'), Lina Cavalieri and Anna Fougez.[44]

Thus Naples had already been a leading production centre of songs when, at the beginning of the twentieth century, recording companies began to be formed. In 1908 the Società Fonografica Napoletana, soon to become the Phonotype Record Company, started to record thousands of songs, arias and comic sketches in dialect – but very little instrumental music.[45] Among the earliest solo voice recordings were Neapolitan romances such as Di Capua's *Maria Marí* (1903), though the lion's share were arias from famous operas: Verdi's *Rigoletto* ('La donna è mobile' was recorded in 1903), *Otello* ('Era la notte') and *Traviata*, and Puccini's *Manon Lescaut* ('In quelle trine morbide', recorded in 1901, sung by Bice Adami).[46]

The main beneficiary of the vogue for recorded arias and Italian songs was Enrico Caruso, generally regarded as the first singer to become internationally known through his records. In 1902 Caruso was already La Scala's main star and well known on the world operatic circuit, but it was his recording of ten arias exclusively for the Gramophone and Typewriter Co.'s Red Seal Records on 11 April 1902 that turned him into a true international star. Fred Gaisberg had enticed him into a room turned into a recording studio at the Grand Hotel in Milan, a few minutes from La Scala. Caruso had demanded £100 plus a percentage of sales. The Gramophone Company thought this exorbitant – it was – and cabled Gaisberg not to record. Gaisberg ignored these orders and went ahead. The arias recorded were all famous at the time, though only a few have remained so, including 'Questa o quella' from Verdi's *Rigoletto* and 'Una furtiva lagrima' from Donizetti's *L'Elisir d'amore*. This was the beginning of Caruso's worldwide fame among a new public who had never been inside an opera house. The Gramophone Company recouped its initial £100 outlay many times over.[47]

The price of records varied according to the fame of the singer: Caruso's were the most expensive, at $3 per record. It was said that he made $2 million from his royalties. Gaisberg thinks it was more like $5 million.[48] The total revenue accruing to the Victor Talking Machine Co. of New Jersey, which eventually 'owned' Caruso's voice, is unknown, though it is still growing. In 1951 RCA Victor re-released the collection and have sold nearly a million records.[49] Far from making live appearances a thing of the past, as Caruso feared, recording increased his earning powers. In 1907–08 – his highest single year of earnings – he was paid $140,000 by the Metropolitan for sixty-eight opera performances and two concerts.[50]

Famous stars became even more famous, and recording also made more modest singers famous, at least for a time and in specific areas. Take, for instance, Greek urban songs, often Greek lyrics sung to a Turkish or Oriental tune. These had evolved as a distinct genre in taverns and cafés, and under the name of *rebetika* acquired ever more 'Greek' characteristics. Once the performance had been everything, but when the songs started being recorded they became associated with particular singers. By the 1930s *rebetika* music, often recorded on EMI labels, had its own stars, towering over the humble café performers – artists like Markos Vamvakaris, who accompanied himself on his bouzouki, and Rosa Eskenazi, a female singer of Jewish Sephardi extraction.[51]

In Britain, hundreds of music hall records were issued, featuring the better-known performers of the day, such as the archetypal cockney Albert Chevalier and the Scottish comedian Harry Lauder. Similar genres prevailed in other European countries: in Russia record buyers laughed at the comic duo Bim and Bom, while the Swedes enjoyed the dialect songs of *bonde-komiker* (country comedians). Thanks to recording, music travelled even faster than before, and lax copyright legislation ensured that it could be happily pirated.[52]

Celebrity (i.e. opera) performers were paid royalties, but popular singers were paid a one-off fee (five to ten guineas a record), and regarded record-making as publicity for their live performances.[53] A popular singer and entertainer like Harry Lauder would record a song for £1, or six for a 'fiver'. The famous Irish tenor John McCormack, in 1904, had a contract with the Gramophone Company for twenty-five songs at one guinea each.[54]

Everywhere the operatic repertory was soon overtaken in terms of sales by 'popular' songs. These were essentially urban songs, quite distinct from the folk songs of the past, in that they were produced specifically for a market. The distinction is roughly similar to that between the fairy tale and the popular novel. The popular song, of course, preceded the invention of the gramophone, but its performance in *cafés-concerts*, music halls and cabaret, not to speak of what came to be called the Victorian drawing-room song, had a limited compass. The recording industry transformed it into a genuine mass item of consumption. It was the first music to depend on recorded forms for its success.[55] The legal framework which was established favoured the spread of songs when the US Copyright Act of 1909 decreed that no one could have the exclusive rights to a song, but authors would be paid a royalty by the performers (the way it is with plays, operas and indeed all music, but not with books). Performers thus competed over the interpretation of songs.[56] Recording made it possible to compare the different ways of interpreting music across decades, something which is even now difficult to do as extensively with theatrical performances.

The record industry created an entirely new market for music, but it also became a tremendous force for preservation. Since the development of notation, Western music had been able to preserve, by recording the notes, much of its repertory, unlike, say, Chinese or Indian classical music, which relied mainly on oral transmission. With the invention of recording it became possible not just to preserve the notes, but the actual performance. This had a remarkable effect on what came to be known as 'serious' music. The nineteenth century had seen the triumph of dead composers (Beethoven, Haydn, Mozart, etc.) as their music, preserved in scores as well as in endless repetition by instrumentalists and conductors, now found a new outlet. In literature the weight of dead generations of writers was manifest in the creation of a body of classics, but because readers need to be supplied with novelties, there was always a market for new fiction. In music, where repetition rules, any aspiring entrant in the market of classical music had to fight it out with generations of predecessors whose deaths had not impeded the ever-growing popularity of their music. In literature the imitation of a successful genre pays off, because readers seek to recreate the pleasure of reading similar but not identical stories. It pays to write detective stories after the fashion of Conan Doyle, or horror stories inspired by Bram Stoker's *Dracula*. In 'serious' music this avenue is not as profitable. What is the point of writing music 'almost' like Brahms when music lovers can have access to the real thing by buying a record and listening to it again and again?

Two important consequences follow from this. The first is that composers of serious music were forced to innovate radically in order to distinguish themselves from their predecessors. This led to a rapid distancing from the established parameters of harmony and constant experimentation, such as atonal music, which ensured that new 'serious' music remained the prerogative of relatively narrow élites. The second consequence was the further strengthening of the role of performers, musicians, singers and above all conductors, for they could provide the market with the necessary element of novelty even before the next improvement in recording technology. Brahms's or Mozart's works could be recorded again and again, and sold again and again, because the interpretation was different. In the autumn of 1915 British magazines began to carry advertisements showing portraits of Thomas Beecham and Henry Wood with details of their latest recording. This was the first time that the conductor was used as the selling point. The new force behind this came from the English branch of Columbia which also hit on the idea of recording the songs of the successful wartime revue.[57] The rise of the conductor, as we have seen (page 243), had started before the middle of the nineteenth century. By 1880, particularly in Italy, they had become stars, interrupting the performance to turn to the public and accept their applause – 'worse than prima donnas', according to an outraged critic of the time. Verdi complained of their arrogance, and was dismayed to be told that a conductor at the San Carlo in Naples had written in the margin of the score of one of Meyerbeer's operas: 'This aria is to be skipped because it's very bad.'[58]

Nothing could stop the advance of recorded sound. By the mid-1920s all of Beethoven's symphonies were available in full. Wanda Landowska had started her legendary harpsichord recordings. Louis Armstrong had made his first record. This did not, in any way, damage live performance. Records acted as formidable advertisements for all forms of live music. As the recording industry expanded there were more venues for music, more operas were performed, more concerts. Popular music became genuinely popular, but so-called 'serious' music, while remaining a minority taste, developed a huge public compared to that of the nineteenth century. Nor did records kill the sale of musical instruments or sheet music. On the contrary, the greater availability of recorded music may well have acted as an incentive for people to learn to play the piano or the guitar. New genres in the printed media were enhanced by the growth of the recording industry: books and magazines appeared to advise music lovers on which recordings to buy. The first issue of the *Gramophone* magazine came out in April 1923 (it is now the oldest such magazine in the world), and in 1924 Oxford University Press published *The First Book of the Gramophone Record*, in which the music critic Percy Scholes introduced his favourite recordings.[59]

The days when music lovers would carry recorded music around with them, able to immerse themselves in it at a push of a button, had not yet arrived. But the preconditions were all in place. For many years the pleasures of reading had been firmly in place for all those who sought them. The pleasures of music were about to become equally democratised. As is often the case, great writers perceived the new world, however dimly. In 1912 Thomas Mann started writing *The Magic Mountain*. This literary monument would be completed and published only twelve years later. Its protagonist, Hans Castorp, obsessively plays his favourite records over and over on a gramophone – his way of escaping time, making it stand still, just as his famous literary predecessor, Goethe's Faust, wished, even if for a moment, that the marvellous instant of accomplishment would persist for eternity: 'Then to the moment could I say: Linger you now, you are so fair.'[60] But Castorp is in the throes of modernist despair, Faust still in those of bourgeois optimism.

40

The Moving Image

The 'Birth'

THE INVENTION AND SPREAD of the cinema constituted, along with recorded sound, a major revolution in culture. Motion could be recorded and shown to a paying public. Recorded sound and recorded moving images, and their reproducibility, were the first new cultural industries to arise within capitalism.

The cinema, as the term is used here, was not simply a technological adaptation of previous breakthroughs, but a new form of collective consumption. What defined it was the collective viewing of recorded images in motion. Different audiences congregate in designated places to experience identical recorded performances, not – as in the theatre – to watch a live spectacle which is the dramatic interpretation of a previously written text. The darkened auditorium became one of the distinguishing features of cinema consumption: an individual relationship with what is going on on the screen, since one's fellow audience members are barely seen, while undergoing the sensation of a collective experience. Magic lantern shows also featured a darkened auditorium, as did Wagner's operas at Bayreuth, but the common experience of collectively viewing a live show was one in which the audience was in full light.[1] Darkness also provided a sense of danger and foreboding, and provided a perfect setting for the kind of inappropriate sexual behaviour favoured by generations of teenagers. In 1916, in a poem which must rank as one of the earliest celebrations of petting at the movies, the Russian Tatiana Vechorka wrote:

> . . . I recall it like a dream . . .
> And in the dark I feel his lips
> Caressing my scented hair.

So secret and so urgent, the touch of silky furs.
So wicked and so wilful, my smiling, sinful gaze.
Shadows flicker on the screen. . .[2]

The degree of involvement of cinematic audiences was, and has remained, unprecedented. Theatrical and operatic audiences were easily distracted, partly because until the second half of the nineteenth century, few stable conventions of listening had evolved, and partly, as we have seen, because theatre-going and opera-going were activities which were also part of social habit, ways of asserting one's identity, one's class, one's taste. One did not necessarily go to the theatre or the opera to listen. Book-reading, like music-making, is an activity largely under the control of the reader or the player. It can usually be interrupted at any time and often is by external events: an unexpected visit, a phone call, a craving for food or drink, a corporal need.

The invention of the cinema was made possible not just by the invention of the camera, but by a host of apparently unrelated products, such as celluloid, which made films possible.[4] It is thus quite appropriate that most histories of the cinema do not designate as 'the birth of the cinema' the invention of the camera or of film, but the first public performance. The search for a singular birth could have celebrated February 1870, when Louis Ducos du Hauron's Phasmatrope projected images of a moving acrobat; or 1881, when Eadweard Muybridge (1830–1904) invented the zoopraxiscope, a device by which he reproduced a running horse on a screen; or 1891, when W.K.L. Dickson developed a camera, the Kinetograph; or 1893, when Edison's kinetoscope appeared – this showed motion, but the viewer had to peer through a coin-operated box.

In fact the birth of the cinema is conventionally, though perhaps not accurately, assumed to be 28 December 1895, when films made by the brothers Auguste and Louis Lumière were shown to a paying audience at the Grand Café on the boulevard des Capucines in Paris. On that day what was born was not an invention but a new cultural industry. In fact one of the films had been presented before 28 December, notably on 10 November at the Congress of the Society of Photography in Brussels. The event received no press coverage.[3] Had the Lumières been a little slower, they would have been beaten by another half-dozen inventors well before the end of 1896.[5] Perhaps they had been beaten: Max and Emil Skladanowsky showed their 'Bioscop' to the public at the Berlin Wintergarten on 1 November 1895 – more than a month before the Lumière show (and to a paying audience).

The Lumière brothers had conceived of their cinematograph not as a new art-form, a new aesthetics, a new technological development, but as a new business enterprise.[6] Indeed, most early film-makers regarded themselves as businessmen and not as the pioneers in a new art.[7] It is also appropriate that one of the first images shown to the first audience was of workers – and *female* workers at that – coming out of the photo equipment factory of the Lumière brothers in Lyons, and that in a sense the first film was both an advertisement for its manufacturer and an unwitting celebration of the working classes, the principal patrons of the new art.

As it turned out, the Lumière brothers withdrew from film-making early on, though they had done well out of it, making 2.4 million francs between 1895 and 1900. They were afraid of spreading themselves too thinly, for they regarded themselves as manufacturers of the equipment, and not as film-makers. 'We did not even consider becoming impresarios,' Louis Lumière declared in 1913.[8] They had seen the cinema as a technical-scientific as well as commercial proposition, and not as a new phase in the development of the entertainment industry.[9]

The early 'films' lasted a minute or so, because the length of the reels was only twenty to twenty-five metres. They consisted of a single shot. The new 'art' had to be absorbed in a short burst, like other 'new' cultural commodities such as the newspaper article and the brief pieces of music available on the new flat discs. The limited span of attention required for cultural consumption is not a recent invention, as some of today's alarmist voices claim.

The initial appeal of films, in any case, was not the story depicted in the early 'movies', but the trick of it: to see people and objects in motion. *L'Arrivée d'un train à la gare de Ciotat*, projected on that fateful day in December 1895, astonished the audience by its novelty. The often-repeated story that the audience 'panicked' at the sight of the approaching train is much exaggerated. A more typical reaction may well have been that of a spectator in Le Havre in June 1896:

> The arrival of the train takes place before your eyes. It approaches rapidly, stops, the doors are opened and the passengers come out and make for the station exit. Then the doors are closed and the train starts up again. It all seems absolutely real.[10]

What was being contemplated was not a cultural artefact in the conventional sense, certainly not a work of art, but something strange and clever, not so different from the conjuror's tricks in a circus. Some scientists (1898) hoped that the invention of the cinema would not be vulgarised as mere entertainment but would remain the preserve of science: it recorded movement and enabled the observation of fast movements, or slow movements (the gallop of a horse and the blossoming of a flower). Such hopes did not seem unfounded. The X-ray, another scientific invention of the time, was also initially marketed as a show. At first people flocked to see the mysterious rays that could go through flesh and reveal bones. But once you had seen this a few times, there was little more to do, and X-rays never became part of the cultural industry.[11]

Among the audience present at the famous first Lumière show was Georges Feydeau, the most successful playwright of his day, and his friend the actor Marcel Simon. Curiosity had attracted them. From their recollections of the event it is clear that they did not have the slightest inkling of the potential of the new medium. In fact Feydeau was not even aware that it was a new medium.[12] By 1908 such innocence had been replaced by anxiety. Feydeau was asked by a film production company to write scripts – they had already signed up leading writers such as Edmond Rostand and Anatole France. He refused, fearing that the cinema would kill the theatre. By 1912 his opposition had subsided, and he sold one by one the film rights of most of his plays for cinema adaptation.[13]

In 1912 no one could doubt the vitality of the cinema; in 1895 its future was uncertain. *The Times* – 'the paper of record' – covered the first exhibition of the Lumières' show in London at the Regent Street Polytechnic on 20 February 1896 (and on the same day at Finsbury Technical College), and then systematically ignored the cinema for eight years.[14] This was not entirely surprising: the Lumières' famous first show received scant coverage. Yet a few months later, after more public performances, the press reports multiplied.[15] Nor did the Lumières themselves expect much from their invention. It is said that when they hired their first projectionist they explained that it would not be a long-term position but a six-month job, perhaps one year, a matter of going round fairs.[16]

The first films may look extremely simple today, yet some of them had a narrative structure. *Le Jardinier* (later known as *L'Arroseur arrosé*), also shown on 28 December 1895, had a simple storyline, effectively and economically shot in a single take with a stationary camera: without being noticed by the gardener, a boy steps on the hose to stop the flow of water. When the surprised gardener looks into the hose, the boy releases the water, drenching the gardener, who chases the boy and chastises him.[17] The antecedents are obvious: the acts of circus clowns, the *pochade* of cabarets and vaudevilles.

Everything needs to be short, so a 'film' might simply be the spectacle of a gentleman courting a lady, raising his hat to her, only to discover that his wig has come off. Such single-gag films constituted a high proportion of the early cinema – unsurprisingly, since in one or two minutes one can hardly film *War and Peace*. Ten years later a typical Pathé comic film, such as *La Chaussette* (The Sock, 1905), though cinematically far more complex than *Le Jardinier*, consists of a simple joke: a man who has stuffed a troublesome sock in his pocket inadvertently wipes his brow with it while dancing with a lady who, horrified, faints.[18] In 1896 the typical film lasted sixty to ninety-six seconds. A year later, the length of a reel was still no more than twenty-five metres, that is two minutes.[19]

This constant flow of comic films was largely due to the time constraints imposed on the medium by the technology. A comic situation can be expressed in a short period of time. Jokes, after all, are shorter than fairy tales, and fairy tales shorter than novels. The universality of the comic sketch in the early cinema, however, was also a response to other factors, such as the popularity of the kind of slapstick comedy which dominated variety shows.[20] It is thus not entirely by accident that one of the first cinematic spectacles was the chase – something which could never be shown adequately on the stage. And the chase has remained a standby of the cinema, though it progressed, if that is the word, from the comic chase to the pursuit of the criminals by foot, car, motorcycle, speedboat.

New cultural forms rest on their antecedents. In Victorian London there were peep shows such as the Cosmorama in St James's Street: peepholes fitted with convex lenses to magnify pictures of scenes such as Mount Etna in Sicily (in eruption), or the Bosphorus.[21] The film pioneers, as they experimented with new technologies, sought to imitate live performance. The camera captured what an audience could have seen, and reproduced it for other audiences. What was being sold to them was not an object (like a book or a record), but the experience of the performance – like a live show. Yet it was not live. The film itself remained the property of the production company: it was hired, not sold to the exhibitors.

As the length of films increased, longer and more complex plots were required. The new medium did not need to make them up *ab novo*. It had at its disposal centuries of story-making, tested by time, refined by endless adaptations and retellings. Almost from the outset the cinema embarked upon the systematic pillaging of popular narrative, especially that of the nineteenth century. To some extent this should not be surprising. Much of the theatre and almost all operas had been adaptations of previous narratives. Any new medium will seek to use that which has been successfully tested in previous formats, as was especially the case for serialised novels. Film was no exception. Many narrative techniques commonly used in celebrated novels had formerly been used in 'low' genres, and were adopted later in film narrative: the flashback, the interior monologue, the concurrent event (just as Fabrice in Stendhal's *La Chartreuse de Parme* is kissing Gina, her husband is heard arriving[22]). The narrative structure of a novel like Zola's *Germinal* (about a coalminers' strike) is similar to that of a western. Étienne Lantier walks slowly towards the mining village of Montsou, where he gets to know the local inhabitants, leads them in a strike against a more powerful enemy, defeats his rival in love and takes his woman. He then leaves.

The cinema systematically plundered not just the narrative repertory of the nineteenth century – in turn the adaptation of stories of the past, myth, folklore and fairy tales – but the great genres of the past: the melodrama, the farce, the penny dreadful, the high-minded moral tale, the psychological drama, the crime story, the Gothic, the horror story, the costume drama, the romance, the western (such as the French *Indiens et cowboys*, 1904), science fiction, and even the erotic (the French *Peeping Tom*, 1901, and *L'Amour à tous les étages*, 1903) – all could be turned around and re-adapted directly and indirectly. Nineteenth-century novels and plays had been an excellent testing ground for the cinematic narrative of the twentieth.[23] Most of the narrative clichés of the cinema had been pioneered in the previous century – even the archetypal rescue of the woman tied to a railway track, pioneered in plays such as Augustin Daly's *Under the Gaslight* (1867).[24]

For the cinema to be properly invented it was necessary for it to move beyond merely offering the public the novelty of moving photography or even recorded theatre, though it seems that, at least until the first few years of the new century, audiences were probably satisfied with just marvelling at moving images. What was required was progress towards an ever more complex narrative structure. This was largely brought about by the competition among individual film-makers.[25] This stimulated audiences' interest, and created the subsequent film boom. Such competition was enormously facilitated by the rapid globalisation of the new medium. Had it remained anchored in a few countries, as the novel had been in the eighteenth century, it would have taken much longer to move from the 'cinema of attraction' – as Tom Gunning has felicitously called the early cinema – to a cinema of narrative.[26]

The early cinema may appear cumbersome to us. Nowadays we can watch a film almost anywhere. All one needs is a television, or a videocassette player, or an internet link. Yet in 1896, compared to what else was available, the cinema could be regarded as a relatively simple affair, like the transmission of recorded music: all that was required was a projector, a projectionist, a film and a white wall. Globalisation was almost immediate. Within a year of its first presentation, the historic show of 28 December 1895 was seen throughout the world: in Naples in April 1896, at the Watson's Hotel in Bombay in July, in Mexico City in August, and in Japan and Shanghai later that year (Beijing, however, had to wait until 1902). The dissemination of techniques and equipment was remarkably rapid within the relatively small international network of operators, impresarios, inventors and film-makers.[27]

The cultural establishment kept its distance. The cinema was not regarded as a new art, or indeed an art at all. It was a low genre, irremediably contaminated by its circus-like setting, its low content and its ephemeral nature. Film was not worth storing, and indeed it was difficult to do so. As a result many of the early films have disappeared or deteriorated beyond hope. It is estimated that only 25 per cent of pre-1918 German film production has survived.[28] The beginnings of a new cultural form leave behind few traces. Films did not have the aura of books and paintings, and no culturally powerful institution lobbied for their archival preservation. The tendency towards the ephemeral has proceeded at the same pace as our obsession with preservation. Books have a longer shelf life than films, films a longer shelf life than most television programmes. It is easier for each new generation to read Balzac or Dickens than to see Eisenstein's or Bergman's films.

Of the 150,000 films shot during the silent era, very few have survived – not surprisingly, since there were very few copies of each to begin with (unlike books, which would have had a print run of at least 1,000 copies). Prints were routinely destroyed after a film had finished its run. In some instances, as when a remake was being made, the 'original' would have to be destroyed as part of the contract. No system for the preservation of films existed until the 1930s, and in any case storage costs were too high.[29]

Those that survived inevitably did so without their unrecorded musical accompaniment. Such music, far from being incidental, helped the narrative, for each dramatic situation required a motif, a rhythm; it could bind the audience together. And, last but not least, music also covered the noise of the projector.[30] Even on the occasion of the first Lumière show there was a piano accompaniment – as occurred frequently at the theatre during a play.

It was this live component which made each representation of a film unique. This, however, should not be over-stressed. An initial period when the accompanying music bore no connection to the actions represented in the film was followed by one in which standardised snatches of music were performed at predictable moments. The distributors of *L'Assassinat du Duc de Guise* (1908) included a score of Saint-Saëns together with each print delivered.[31] By 1910 films were usually distributed with helpful cues for accompanists: a jolly Irishman would be accompanied by a 'typical' Irish jig, a gloomy Russian by an equivalent mournful tune adapted from Mussorgsky. By the 1920s there were manuals for the film accompanists: religious music meant Handel's Largo or 'Onward, Christian Soldiers', 'sadness' would send them straight to Chopin, Beethoven and others.[32] A set of conventions was soon established linking certain musical phrases and events: whenever the pianist started 'Fingal's Cave' from Mendelssohn's 'Hebrides' Overture (1832), the audience knew the villain was about to turn up – as Jean-Paul Sartre recalled from his infancy.[33] There were, of course, always dim-witted (or subversive) accompanists who would produce a funny little polka for a funeral.

Expansion

A year after its birth, the new medium had barely progressed. The list of films shown in Rome at the beginning of 1897 included a baby being made to 'dance', King Umberto and Queen Margherita of Italy walking in their park in Monza, Niagara Falls, and Sudanese natives dancing.[34] And all at the standard length of 15–17 metres, lasting just over one minute. There was no storyline, just moving photography. The 1902 Pathé catalogues listed the following genres: open-air scenes, comic scenes, *scènes à trucs* (i.e. with special effects), sport and acrobats, historic and political scenes (news), piquant stories, dances, drama and realistic scenes, fairy tales, and religious subjects.[35] One of the first problems that faced the cinema was that it was difficult to conceive of a long film. A dozen films would last twenty to thirty minutes in all. This was too short for a proper show, so one gave paying customers further material, such as live performances by magicians, clowns, singers, etc. Often the films were not even the main attraction. The programme for the Palace Theatre in London for a show in 1910, fifteen years after the first Lumière showing, is a typical music hall mishmash: a juggler, a comedienne, an Italian violinist, Miss Margaret Cooper and her piano, the first appearance in England of the great Russian ballerina Anna Pavlova and, finally, a series of short films including 'Paris the Gay City' and 'Arrival of Lord Kitchener at Southampton'.[36] Even Georges Méliès's longer films, such as the eighteen-minute *Les Quatre cents farces du diable* (1906), got no more than an end-of-programme screening at the Folies Bergère.

Even when films became longer they continued to compete not just with traditional public entertainments, but also with short films. Groups of films would be shown together in new purpose-built cinemas such as the nickelodeons in America – so called because entrance cost five cents (a nickel) – the first of which opened in Pittsburgh in 1905. This signalled the beginning of the US film industry, though at first the nickelodeons were fuelled by imported films, mainly from the largest producer in the world, the French Pathé.[37] Later full-length films were shown in 'proper' cinemas. Thus, while one could see short comic films at the local nickelodeon for five cents, one had to pay as much as $2 to see D.W. Griffith's *The Birth of a Nation* (1915), though cheaper films were available for twenty-five cents. Attempts were made to bridge the gap between the two. In October 1914 in Pittsburgh, the East Liberty Regent opened its doors on an impressive, luxurious auditorium with nine hundred seats, murals in Italian tiles, a cream-coloured terracotta façade and, in the entrance lobby, a marble fountain topped with the bronze figure of a naked cherub. It charged only ten or twenty cents a show, but it could not sustain such prices by showing the traditional simple fare, and one month after opening it was forced, notwithstanding its Italian tiles and cherub, to return to five cents per seat.[38]

Originally it was thought that the audiences crowding the Manhattan nickelodeons were lower-class immigrants. Then it was thought that perhaps they were middle-class. In 1995 Ben Singer's thorough research established that a significant proportion of the 220 nickelodeons in Manhattan in 1908, were in the most high-density areas, such as the Lower East Side, where immigrants, Jews in particular (300,000 at the turn of the century), lived.[39] In all likelihood the early exhibitors had decided to locate their viewing theatres where their customers lived (and also, possibly, where rents were cheaper). The New York exhibitors themselves were often immigrants, with a strong Jewish presence – William Fox, Marcus Loew and Adolph Zukor each owned several theatres – unsurprisingly, since Jews constituted 25 per cent of the population of Manhattan. Italians were present in rough proportion to their share of the population, but Germans stayed clear of the business.[40] The Jewish entry into the world of the cinema was preceded by their wholehearted adoption of 'low' genre entertainment such as the music hall and the vaudeville – to the unmitigated alarm of rabbis and Jewish socialist intellectuals alike. By 1905 most major streets in the Lower East Side had electric signs advertising 'Jewish Vaudeville House', or 'Music Hall'.[41]

The cohabitation with 'lower' genres such as the circus, and with lower-class people, gave the cinema the stamp of being a popular form of entertainment as well as a business, a characteristic which has dominated its entire history, regardless of the number of 'artistic' films made and the spread of the *cinéma d'auteur*. Whether or not the cinema can be regarded as an art may still be disputed in some quarters. That it is also a business has never been in dispute. Histories of literature which make no reference to the publishing industry are commonplace, while a history of the cinema that left out the industry would be eccentric. It is usual in literary history to concentrate on authors at the expense of readers, but the sociology of the cinema audience attracted the attention of scholars almost from the beginning. Emilie Altenloh's pioneering 1914 study of cinema audiences in the city of Mannheim, *Zur Soziologie des Kino: Die Kino-Unternehmung und die sozialen Schichten ihrer Besucher* (Towards a Sociology of Cinema: The Cinema Business and the Social Strata of its Audiences), noted the particularly wide social spectrum of cinema audiences compared to all previous forms of cultural entertainment: the press, the book, the theatre, live music.[42] Different social strata, however, had different preferences. A fifteen-year-old machine-fitter, the son of a Mannheim boilermaker, responded to the question 'Which kind of films do you like best?' with 'Love dramas, stories about trappers and Red Indians, current news from around the world and films about aviation and airship travel' (perhaps he was an unusual young machine-fitter, since to the question 'What do you like best?' he answered Mozart, Wagner and Schiller).[43] The 'lowest' group, the young unskilled workers, liked westerns and crime stories ('The majority take in everything indiscriminately ... the sole unifying tendency seems to be an extraordinarily keen interest in anything erotic or sensual'[44]). Altenloh concluded, percipiently, that 'Cinema is a phenomenon to which most people feel some connection if they are at all caught in the mood of our modern times.'[45] In this sense the cinema was a new 'democratic' medium suited to the twentieth century, the century of mass suffrage, of populist dictatorships, of mass consumption.

Commentators frequently noted that at the cinema one could see, shoulder to shoulder, officers and soldiers, prostitutes and ladies, doctors and working men, children and their nannies. This somewhat idealised picture left out the vast masses still inhabiting the cinema-less countryside, but in contrast to previous forms of entertainment it was clear that the cinema audience was more socially mixed than those for previous 'low' entertainment. The social composition was determined more by the venue than by what was shown. In 1905 there were virtually no specially dedicated cinemas. Films were screened at fairs or in cafés. When they were shown in fairground tents and music halls, as they were in Great Britain, the audience tended to be more working-class. If vaudeville houses were used, as in the USA at the turn of the century, films attracted a reasonably prosperous audience willing to pay twenty-five cents.[46] The attitude of cinema patrons sharply contrasted to those of the theatre, let alone the opera. They treated the cinema as if it were a cabaret or a café, something to be visited impulsively. One could walk in at any time during the performance, a tradition which in some countries, such as Italy, lasted until well into the 1970s. There was no formality, no need to dress up or to impress anyone. Yet audiences were relatively well-behaved, especially in comparison with the aristocratic opera audiences of the late eighteenth century. They sat fairly quietly, and the voices heard would usually be comments on the action (a sign of an attentive audience) or murmurs of disappointment at an excessively flickering or damaged picture, together with the overpowering noise of the projector, and the all-too frequent interruptions caused by a rupture in the celluloid film.

The cinema industry created professions and occupations which did not exist before: projectionists, distributors, technicians who made copies and so on. And it recast old professions in novel ways. Writing for the silent cinema was hardly comparable to writing a play or an opera libretto. It consisted of writing a plot to be enacted without dialogue. Directing a film was unlike directing a play, since the director could frame whichever sequence he wanted, in order to suggest a point of view. At the theatre the audience watched the whole of the action presented. In films one could make it focus on what the characters could see. Film acting, particularly in the silent days, was quite different from acting on stage.

The key business question was not that of producing films, but of distributing them. No one seriously made a film without thinking how to distribute it. The early pioneers of the cinema were entrepreneurs, people like the Italian Filoteo Albertini (1869–1937), who understood that it was necessary to open up as many projection rooms as possible (characteristically, the genre and the place of consumption have the same name – cinema – in most languages), and to be both producer and distributor. Vertical integration was the name of the game.[47]

The cinema shared with other performing arts (the concert, the opera, the theatre) the peculiarity that its product was just as expensive if the audience was small or large, so ideally one wanted theatres able to accommodate as large an audience as possible, and to change the programme as frequently as possible in order to keep attracting large crowds. If the cinema was to survive it was necessary both to build more and larger theatres *and* to make more and more films. Expansion was built into the new medium. This was understood by all concerned. In 1906 there were only ten cinemas in Paris. Two years later there were eighty-seven.[48] In 1911 the largest cinema in Europe was built in Paris: the Gaumont-Palace, with 3,400 seats.[49] By the end of the First World War there were thousands of screens in every major country. In the main Russian cities, cinemas, at first simple converted shops, were by the mid-1910s luxury places inspired by the French versions. In St Petersburg one of the first luxury cinemas was called Kak v Parizhe (Just like Paris, 1907). It was followed by the Kak v Nitse (Just like Nice). These were exact copies of the most elegant French cinemas, with cafés, foyers, pretty barmaids, usherettes and deep-pile carpets.[50] The expansion of the cinema in the USA was even more impressive. In 1905 there were only a few nickelodeons in any one city; in 1906 there were a few dozen in major centres such as Chicago. By 1910 there were 10,000 cinemas in the United States.[51]

Impressive movie houses were built, guarded by heavily decorated uniformed ushers – perhaps in imitation of the soldiers who often guarded the opera houses of the nineteenth century (usually out of fear of rioting). Cinema-owners, like Balaban & Katz in Chicago, wanted to discourage the rowdy crowds associated with fairgrounds in favour of a better class of people – mothers, children and families. They transformed the cinematic landscape of Chicago. By 1924 the city could boast one of the largest cinemas in the world, with 5,000 seats. Here patrons could be treated like royalty – or rather, as they thought royalty was treated. The cinema provided smoking rooms, childcare, art galleries and ushers recruited from local colleges, sporting plush red uniforms, white gloves and golden epaulettes, and trained to be extremely polite to all patrons.[52] Such a model of the regimentation of crowds by intimidating them with an extravagant and lavish (and highly scripted) welcome would be used much later in other mass-entertainment reception centres, such as those of Disneyland.

Narrative and Non-Fiction

Nevertheless, it was France, the culturally hegemonic country of the nineteenth century, that dominated the early years of the cinema (1895–1907). Between 60 and 70 per cent of all imported films worldwide were French. Pathé-Frères (founded by Charles Pathé) became the largest film company in the world, forced into an aggressive worldwide expansion by the relatively small size of the French market and enjoying the advantage of a large colonial market. Virtually from the start Pathé became an international company, with production offices in Moscow, New York, Vienna, Milan, London, Barcelona, Amsterdam and Odessa, and thence to India, Singapore and Beijing – all between 1904 and 1908.[53] Its main international rival, the Gaumont company (founded in 1895), was also French. Pathé became the first film company to move into mass production. It developed better cameras and projectors. It established regional subsidiaries and top-to-bottom control over distribution by renting rather than selling its films, a model which was followed by Gaumont.[54] Pathé produced seventy films in 1901, 350 in 1902, over 500 in 1903, or ten a week.[55] Soon its logo, a very Gallic cockerel (adopted in 1903), appeared on screens throughout the world.

In 1906 Pathé created a luxury cinema in Paris (Omnia-Pathé). This was followed by a chain of cinemas throughout the country, shifting film exhibition away from fairgrounds – though these retained for a while a considerable importance.[56] By 1909 Pathé had the largest circuit in Europe, including some two hundred cinemas in France and Belgium. By 1905 it had become the leading supplier of 'moving pictures' for the US market.[57] By 1908 it was distributing twice as many films in the USA as all American producers combined, and between 30 and 50 per cent of films shown in the nickelodeons were from Pathé.[58]

Also French was the first great master of the cinema, Georges Méliès (1861–1938), one of the pioneers who contributed to propel film from its prehistory to its real birth by beginning to construct a cinematic language. Méliès, the first great world producer of fiction films, was a former conjuror and magic lantern specialist. Between 1896 and 1912 his Star-Film Company produced hundreds of films – only a few longer than ten minutes – for a transnational market: Méliès had a studio in Montreuil near Paris and distribution offices in Barcelona, London, Berlin and New York (1902–03).[59] Nevertheless, the pattern of work was fairly primitive. Méliès wrote most of the scripts, designed the sets and costumes, and often acted. A stationary camera would be set up at a distance so the shot would frame the entire bodies of the actors. There was little editing.

Méliès, a great artist but a poor businessman, was never able to compete with Pathé's industrial approach to the cinema.[60] By the 1920s he was reduced to selling toys and sweets at the Gare Montparnasse with his second wife, a former actress.[61] However, Méliès was a true film narrator. His technique consisted of finding images to sustain a narrative, something that the theatre, or the pantomime, or the music hall, had never done.[62] He used and invented cinematic tricks and special effects such as the exploding head (in *L'Homme à la tête de caoutchouc*, 1901). His famous *Le Voyage dans la lune* (1902), one of the longest and most complex films he made (thirteen minutes), used special effects obtained by using 'stop-motion' techniques, that is by stopping the camera, removing or inserting an object or person, and starting the camera again. *Le Raid Paris–Monte-Carlo* (1906) was in 'colour', the result of painstakingly colouring each frame by hand.

Considerable progress towards a narrative structure occurred between 1902 and 1907, when film-makers began to use different shots. What would be the connection between a succession of shots? Today, most conventional films use chronology within each fragment of a narrative: each shot is a piece of action taking place after the preceding one. This was not the case in the very early cinema, where the film-maker often repeated the same shot from a different angle or from a closer position. The problem of linking each shot arose because by 1908 the introduction of a three-hundred-metre reel made it possible to shoot longer films. Each reel lasted fifteen minutes, and by changing reels it was possible to have films which lasted an hour – the public could put up with four interruptions an hour, but not with twenty. Here the pioneers were the Australians – the first film to last more than an hour was *The Story of the Kelly Gang* (1906).[63] Length permitted the development of more complex story-telling and less one-dimensional characters. Still, before 1910 most fictional films were shot as if they were a filmed play: the actors stand in a row, their entire bodies visible, and act against a background almost identical to that of a theatre. Yet even then the cinema was quite distinctive, since the choice of frame compelled the viewer to focus attention on a part of reality selected by the film-maker.

The absence of spoken dialogue and the brevity of the early films influenced editing techniques: the adoption of closer shots, changes in framing through camera movement, cut-in close shots, point-of-view shots, tracking shots, dissolves, split screens, reverse-angle cutting. Thanks to the close-up spectators could see the actors' faces – which few could do in the theatre – and the actors could use their faces to show emotions.[64] A new kind of acting developed, enhanced by the absence of dialogue, which forced actors to rely almost exclusively on body movements and facial expressions. Like theatre actors before them, film actors were often inspired by portraiture, which had established the basic stereotypical expressions available.[65] Only with the advent of the talkie would it be possible to use the inflection of the voice to signal feelings, but in the silent movie the expression of the face and the deportment of the body were all-important. It also became possible to 'show' what a character was thinking in the same frame, and to use flashback – which the theatre could never use as effectively.[66] Even well after sound had been introduced it remained perfectly possible to have lengthy sections of a film with no dialogue at all, only action – something else which was impossible to achieve in a play. Action movies in the late twentieth century made possible the rise of cinema stars with almost no speaking role, as was the case with Arnold Schwarzenegger, who in *Terminator* (1984), has a seventy-four-word part. Until 1910 inter-titles were used mainly to explain the action, afterwards they were used for some rudimentary dialogue. A clearer division of labour emerged as the distinctive roles of the director, producer, screenwriter and cameraman took shape.

By the time the First World War had ended, most of the basic elements of film aesthetics had been discovered: how to achieve depth, multiple points of view, how to use close-ups, landscape shots and camera movements.[67] The technique of montage was developed in the 1910s and 1920s, but even early film-makers had realised that by putting together different images it was possible to achieve great economy of narrative and speed in the development of the action. A man walks from left to right, a woman from right to left, they meet, shake hands, the man points at something, the woman appears to look in the direction indicated, an imposing house – the White House – is seen. Viewers have the impression of an uninterrupted sequence. Those who can identify the White House assume the couple are in Washington – yet Lev Kuleshov, in the 1920 experiment now known as the Kuleshov effect, had simply filmed a photograph of the White House from a magazine, while the actors had never left the studio. The essence of the cinema, he explained, is montage.[68] An action – such as someone walking across a room – can take, thanks to editing, only a few seconds, the viewers imagining the 'missing' frames.

Almost from the beginning, the filmic experience was based on speed.

Modernity had found its medium. In the words of Vsevolod Pudovkin (1893–1953), the great Russian film-maker and theorist, editing or montage was the 'basic creative force by power of which the soulless photographs are engineered into living, cinematographic form'. Nature and actors, he claimed, provided only the raw material for the eventual composition of the film, arranged by editing.[69] 'What matters most,' wrote Kuleshov, 'is not what each piece represents but how the pieces are arranged. The essence of film art should be sought not within a single shot but in the succession of shots.'[70]

Controlling the actual film was not the same as controlling its projection. Here there were problems. The projection of films was manually operated, and the speed of the action was often increased by projectionists who were in the habit of driving the picture faster than it had been shot. To circumvent this, some directors – especially in Russia, where the problem was more pronounced than elsewhere – introduced lengthy pauses to counteract the tendencies of frenetic projectionists. The director Ivan Mosjoukin lamented in 1915: 'I cannot convey the feeling you experience when you watch your own scene transformed . . . into a wild dance.'[71] When films portraying the Imperial family were projected, the theatre manager would often be standing next to the projectionist to ensure that no speeding of the action would give rise to undignified amusement (for the same reason, the Russian censor in the 1910s prohibited musical accompaniment when showing the Imperial family on film).

This problem may have been particularly strong in Russia, but it occurred everywhere. In the early days of the cinema, films were often only part of a longer programme, and projectionists were under pressure to make sure that everything fitted into the evening's entertainment. Film buffs avoided the last performance of the day, in which projectionists, anxious to get home, speeded up the action even more. Sometimes, however, the speed was too slow: Eisenstein complained in 1929 that a London performance of his *Battleship Potemkin* was so leisurely that it destroyed 'all the dynamics of the rhythmic relationship'.[72]

Speeded-up movement went against the descriptive realism which was the basis of much of cinema, particularly at a time when a considerable proportion of its output consisted of 'non-fiction' such as news and documentaries purporting to show real people doing what they would have done anyway. But such a distinction between fiction and non-fiction is often arbitrary.[73] The selection of images, their editing, the need to construct a narrative, gives many documentaries the same structure as a fictional story, while some fictional stories are constructed almost like a documentary. Politicians were quick to see the potential of the new medium and exploit it. Pancho Villa, one of the great heroes of the Mexican revolution, fascinated by the thought of being on screen, gave repeated interviews to the press, and sold his image exclusively, earning $25,000 from the Mutual Film Corporation. He even changed his military timetables to enable better film shots, and allowed the use of simulated or reconstructed events. It is said that he delayed the assault on Ojinaga because he was waiting for the cameramen.[74]

Unspoken conventions between viewers and producers lead to some images, facts and descriptions being accepted as 'real' while others are not – just as in novels. The train arriving at the station of Ciotat in the Lumières' film was a 'real' train which would have arrived at Ciotat even if the camera had not been there. The train in a Méliès film was not a 'real' train, but a toy filmed in close-up. Yet a documentary on the construction of the railways which used a toy train would not necessarily be regarded as fiction, while an adventure film using images of real trains in motion would. What matters is the overall narrative context, but as this is not always clear, making the distinction between non-fiction and fiction has remained problematical.

The distinction came to be made only when 'narrative' films became well-established. Thus the term 'documentary' was adopted in English only in the 1920s, to indicate a non-fiction representation of reality. But even a documentary had a narrative structure, it always told a story, even in fragments, highlighting its radical distinction from a printed scientific text, with its scholarly apparatus of proof, its doubts and its footnotes. Documentaries were always ways of popularising a view. They refracted research conducted elsewhere. The need for them to entertain was constantly evident in the selection of words and pictures. In popular natural science films the urge toward anthropomorphism in the descriptions of animal behaviour was seldom resisted even at the dawn of the genre. Thus a Pathé documentary of May 1912 on the antlion (the larva of an insect with large, powerful jaws that digs a hole in the sand and lies there waiting for its prey) anthropomorphised even the title: *Un Bandit des grands chemins, la larve de fourmilion* (A Highway Robber, the Larva of the Antlion).[75]

The origin of the documentary film lies in a mid-nineteenth-century genre of popular science: the illustrated lecture, essentially a live narration, often given by explorers, scientists and archaeologists. Indeed most of the basic genres of documentary – travel, ethnography, social issues – were already in place before the invention of the cinema. Films gradually replaced slides, while the spoken narrative was replaced by inter-titles. By 1910 major expeditions routinely included a film cameraman. The First World War provided further scope for an expansion of the genre.[76]

It was quite normal for early newsreels and documentaries to use the technique of 're-enactment'. What you saw purported to be historically true: 'it really happened', but what had happened had been re-enacted using actors and special effects. This, like so much of the early cinema, had been borrowed from some live performances and circus acts such as Buffalo Bill's Wild West Show. Occasionally even battles were re-enacted, and the audience was asked to believe (and many presumably did) that what they saw was an accurate representation of a historical event. Early documentary films would restage a public execution, with an actor doing a credible impersonation of someone being hanged.[77]

Documentaries as well as newsreels were soon reduced to programme fillers as the cinema programme acquired what for much of the twentieth century would be its classical shape: a lengthy main feature backed by a secondary one which could be either a shorter movie or a programme of short films and news. The total length approximated two to three hours.

Adapting Literature

Almost all of the 286 surviving early (i.e. pre-1919) Russian films were literary adaptations, reflecting the facts that most of the directors originated in the theatre and that most of the audience were middle-class. Only eighteen were adaptations of foreign works, including three by Maupassant, some French farces, Strindberg's *Miss Julie*, Zola's *Thérèse Raquin* and a film called *The Russian Sherlock Holmes* (1915). The greatest successes, however, were cinematic adaptations of Russian popular fiction such as Yakov Protazanov's ten-reel 1913 film of Anastasia Verbitskaia's 'sensational' novel *The Keys to Happiness* (see pages 624–5), screenings of which sold out days in advance.[78] Unsurprisingly, such parochialism in literary adaptations was just as strong in France. The difference is that most of the French texts were widely known throughout Europe, and in many instances had already been adapted for the opera: *Eugénie Grandet* (1910), *Carmen* (1910), *André Chénier* (1910), *Notre-Dame de Paris* (1911), *La Dame aux camélias* (1912). The theatre, of course, long remained the source for many films. It has been estimated that, between 1913 and 1915 alone, around half of Paramount's output was theatrical adaptations.[79]

The adaptation of existing narratives was not only due to an almost desperate search for plots. There were financial considerations. Even a short film represented some kind of investment, and it paid to minimise the risks by using what had been successful in the past. Some of the audience had already encountered the plots in the course of their education, and would have been intrigued to see how the stories of the Bible or historical events or novels would be reproduced on the screen.

Alexandre Dumas would have been delighted (or dismayed) to know that some of his lengthy novels, originally serialised in hundreds of episodes, were adapted into short films at the very dawn of the cinematic age. Méliès's 1903 version of *The Three Musketeers* lasted only five minutes. It must have been successful, because Dumas novels were regularly filmed over the following years. The British film-maker George Albert Smith adapted Dumas's lesser-known *Les Frères Corses* (The Corsican Brothers) in 1898, in which he conjured up a ghost by draping part of the set in black, filming a shot, then rewinding the film to include a ghost which seemed to appear through the original set.[80] In the USA, Francis Boggs shot the first *Count of Montecristo* in 1907. Louis Feuillade, Gaumont's most important director, adapted *Le Collier de la reine* in several episodes in 1909. He then turned his skills to turning into films the best-selling novels based on the character of Fantômas, then all the rage (see pages 680–2), enabling Gaumont to overtake Pathé on the eve of the the the First World War.[81] Jules Verne was equally cinematic: *Around the World in Eighty Days* was adapted in 1913, 1919, 1922–23, 1931 (with Douglas Fairbanks), 1956 (with David Niven) and 2004 (with Steve Coogan). *Vingt mille lieues sous les mers* was adapted in 1907 by Georges Méliès as an eighteen-minute film, and then again in 1910, 1915, 1916, 1920, 1931, 1936, 1954, 1961 and many more.[82] Films followed popular novels in developing a continuing series in which one film after another could be organised around a central character.

The cinema lost no time in adapting whatever happened to be successful in print. As the Nick Carter detective novels were being translated into French, Victorin Jasset was turning them into films (1908–10).[83] The French Nick Carter was, of course, heavily Frenchified: he was more cerebral and bourgeois and less adventurous than his American original. Indeed, many of the early crime films were British- or American-made: *Daring Daylight Burglary* (UK, 1903), *Automobile Thieves* (USA, 1906) and the serial *What*

Happened to Mary? (USA, 1912).[84] In Denmark, Nordisk started a Sherlock Holmes series, while in France Pathé produced the Nick Winter films and Eclipse those based on the Nat Pinkerton stories. During the war many French and English films were banned in Germany, but this did not prevent the production of German detective films with heroes called Joe Deebs, Harry Higgs, Joe Jenkins and Miss Nobody, the famous female detective, not to speak of Stuart Webbs (modelled on Sherlock Holmes), the hero of fifty films between 1914 and 1926.[85] Evidently the detective had to be English or American, but there were always exceptions: one of the rare early German detective films, *Wo ist Coletti?* (1913), has as its hero the master-detective Jean Coletti, who sports a French first name, an Italian surname and a beard generally regarded as English, thus simultaneously appealing to the main film markets of the world while satisfying a domestic audience in awe of everything foreign.[86]

The success of the Gothic genre in literature was quickly transferred to films. Louis Feuillade's *Les Vampires* was a seven-hour film shot between 1915 and 1916 and originally shown as a serial. The camera was fairly static, barely moving; most scenes were little staged, with a single long shot as in a theatre. What made the difference was the use of special effects: severed heads turning up in hat boxes, people thrown out of windows, explosions, car chases. The villainous heroine, Irma Vep, is a chanteuse in the Howling Cat Café, the power of the camera and the imagination of the audience conjuring up the demonic effects of her singing even though the film is silent.

The cinematic adaptation of novels had to proceed in a way not too dissimilar from theatrical or operatic adaptations: a simplification of the plot, a reduction of dialogue, the suppression of much of the historical background, the highlighting of certain characters, the representation in human form of ideological concepts, a starker definition of the villain, a clearer demarcation between good and evil, a much more rigid chronology.[87]

A symbiotic relationship evolved: the cinema used the best-known novels, thus hoping to attract an audience already familiar with the book, or perhaps only its plot or themes, or wishing to be made aware of its contents without having to read it. In so doing the cinema made the novel even better known, and assured it a longer life than it would otherwise have had. Until the cinema it was difficult for a novel to survive, in the sense of being regularly reprinted and read by successive generations, without being part of a literary canon decided by a relatively restricted élite – though Dumas and Verne managed it. With the cinema, many of the masterpieces of popular literature completely bypassed the élites and acquired a new lease of life. The two markets, the literary and the cinematic, thus reinforced each other. Literary adaptations also contributed to legitimise the cinema. In France, between 1906 and 1908, a string of legal opinions agreed with the industry that films could be regarded as literary and artistic creations, thus making them subject to the principles then in operation concerning intellectual property.[88]

The cinema did not only adapt popular literature. It adapted everything: Dickens, Shakespeare, dime novels, the Bible, penny dreadfuls, Homer – every author, great or small, famous or forgotten, was susceptible of being adapted to the cinema. It even adapted paintings, since, as the theatre had done, historical characters were regularly represented in the clothes worn in their famous portraits: for instance Henry VIII in the portrait by Hans Holbein, and Charles I in hunting clothes as depicted by Anthony Van Dyck.

The predilection for adapting classics helped the new medium to disengage further from the circus and the funfair. It had to attract the new middle classes, families, everyone. It had to become respectable. It had to stem the flow of vituperation from the cultural élites, which had only recently accepted that the novel, or at least some novels, had artistic merits comparable to poetry or the epic theatre. Inevitably, the cinema was producing the kind of moral panic other popular forms had generated. Children were perceived as being particularly vulnerable. Studies began to 'prove' that the cinema could have deleterious effects on the young. The industry responded by producing 'good' films, in Germany with *Kulturfilm*, in France by the Société du Film d'Art, created by Paul Lafitte in 1908 to lure the middle classes into the cinema with scripts written by members of the Académie Française – such as *L'Assassinat du Duc de Guise* (May 1908), with actors from the Comédie-Française and music by Camille Saint-Saëns. This was one of the first films to show actors turning their backs to the camera, marking the end of the frontal theatrical cinema.[89] Then there was the drafting in of the great stage diva Sarah Bernhardt to act in the film of *La Dame aux camélias* (1912) – playing, at the age of sixty-eight, the role of the young consumptive courtesan. Bernhardt remained an exception, the art of make-up never quite keeping pace with the development of close-up techniques.

The close-up allowed a far greater intimacy with the leading actress than did either the theatre or the opera. This cult of the cinema diva – the direct descendant of the operatic *prima donna* – captivated audiences and was enhanced by the rapid development of the illustrated press, which provided information about the private lives of celebrities. There was, as yet, no male counterpart. The famous male actors were comics or the soon-forgotten muscular heroes of Italian films set in antiquity, the forerunners of more recent Rambos, Robocops and Terminators. The divas were quite different. The great Italian star of *Cabiria* (1914), Lyda Borelli, the diva *par excellence*, expressed her sensuality, melancholia and anxiety in mannered poses. The diva, like the soprano in the nineteenth century, was often the main box office attraction – as film stars are even today. Not until the 1920s, with stars like the Italian-born Rudolf Valentino – born Rodolfo Guglielmi – did male actors become objects of sexual attraction and fantasies.[90]

Many early film stars came from the theatre, but many had no training at all, being chosen for their particular expressive quality or their looks. This relative disregard for training became part of the legend of the cinema. Everybody knew that not anyone could be an opera singer, and that even those with the gift required lengthy training. But anyone could become a film star. There is a material basis for this belief. The kind of acting required by the cinema, especially in silent films, was quite different from that required by the theatre. As a perceptive witness to the development of the early cinema, Antonio Gramsci, wrote in 1916, the superiority of the cinema over the theatre consisted of reducing 'the role of actors to movement alone as it is silent'.[91] Many stage actors could never make the transition to the screen. In the theatre, an actor must project his or her voice, and dominate the stage. In film the actor's domination of the screen is achieved by cinematic means, such as the close-up. Feelings can be shown by a tiny movement of the face, while far more exertion is required in the theatre. Cinema actors found that their performance was constantly interrupted, consequently they had to re-enter their role almost continuously. As the final cut is decided by others, the actor was often required to try out several alternative styles, and had little control over the final choice. They were often, as Alfred Hitchcock is supposed to have said, 'treated like cattle', a condition somewhat buttressed by the enormous fees the more famous among them were able to command.

Max Linder, hired by Pathé in 1905 for a fee of twenty-five francs per film, earned by 1909 150,000 a year.[92] High salaries rapidly became the norm for those in non-starring roles too. The Russian director Evgenii Bauer (1865–1917) had been a theatre stage designer until 1912, then he turned to directing films, and by the end of 1913 he was paid by the Khanzhonkov production company the enormous sum of 40,000 roubles and had become one of company's main shareholders.[93] The sums earned as well as those spent added to the glamour of the cinema. What the Bolsheviks regarded as the new proletarian art – Lenin proclaimed it to be 'the most important of all the arts' – made more millionaires than all the other arts combined. Pleasing the masses turned out to be more profitable than pleasing noble patrons.

——— ❦ ———

41

Cinema: Europeans and Americans

The Rise of the American Cinema

UNTIL THE FIRST WORLD WAR, Europeans dominated world cinema. Of the 1,200 films released in 1907 in the USA, only four hundred were American. The USA was relatively late in entering the international film industry, probably because it had a large home market, which provided the oligopoly that controlled US production with a reasonable profit. Earnings from exports were welcome, but not vital. Their main preoccupations were to keep potential entrants out, and to restrict foreign access to its own market. They were fairly successful in this latter endeavour: 'after 1908 it became increasingly difficult for foreign companies to gain access to the American exhibition field'.[1] Initially, access to the American market mattered more to the Europeans than access to the European market mattered to the Americans. Pathé, the world's leading firm, had tried to delay its inevitable exclusion from the USA by entering into agreements with American companies, but the emergence of independent companies and Eastman Kodak's monopoly on film stock eroded Pathé's position.[2] In such conditions all agreements made were inevitably more favourable to the US interests.

In 1910 a cartel of ten companies, the US Motion Picture Patents Company (MPPC), was formed to restrict access to the American market and to keep out independent companies, especially those run by Jews.[3] At first it succeeded in taking over many of the independent companies which had emerged in the previous years. In 1918, anti-trust laws ensured the dissolution of the cartel, but by then many small competitors had been eliminated. By 1919 most of the films shown in the USA were American. As a result, a new wave of independent firms emerged – Fox, Zukor, Laemmle, Sam Goldwyn and Lasky. These did not stay small for long, and would dominate the American film industry for decades. The small independent companies of the early years of the cinema could survive simply because it was not necessary to be very large in order to make short films. Little capital was required. It was more difficult to raise the large sums required for major features. As the cinema moved out of an era where a show was made up of many small films, and into one centred on a feature film, the death knell started to ring for all but the largest companies.[4]

This is the economic context in which the USA became the world's greatest exporter of films and one of its chief producers. Numbers alone cannot give an idea of the extent of its domination, because it is impossible to quantify the overall impact of such an unprecedented concentration of cultural power. In the production of books or the staging of plays, the British and the French had prevailed in the nineteenth century, as the Italians had in the field of opera, but their preponderance pales into insignificance when compared with the lead acquired by the USA.

The First World War facilitated a process of Americanisation of world cinema which had already started. The war put an end to the free movement of films. Foreign technicians had to return to serve in their countries' armed forces. General mobilisation emptied the studios. Cinemas closed. Newsreels were restricted. Cinema moved rapidly from cosmopolitanism to nationalism.[5] Charles Pathé had to resupply his business by becoming increasingly a distributor rather than a producer. French cinema production plummeted, while American production expanded in both quantity and quality. By 1919 Paramount alone could supply the US and world markets with 351 films made in the previous two years. An exhibitor could show a different film every day, and never close. Wave upon wave of new stars were launched: Mary Pickford, Douglas Fairbanks, John Barrymore, Charles Ray, Fatty Arbuckle.[6]

By the end of 1913 US films were already invading the European markets. First came the wave of Keystone comedies, and by the summer and autumn of 1915 the films of Charlie Chaplin (Frenchified in France as Charlot). By the end of the war the American cinematic invasion of Europe had become an established fact: for every 5,000 metres of French films presented weekly in France there were 25,000 metres of imported films, mainly American.[7] In Great Britain the situation was even more dramatic: US share of the British market was 60 per cent in 1914, and in London it was 75 per cent. Even as early as 1909–10, British production accounted for only about 15 per cent of programmes, while the US had 30 per cent, the French 40 per cent and the

Italians 10 per cent.[8] Far more American than German films were shown in Germany.

The war simply accelerated a process which had started around 1910, when the main American film studios had moved to Hollywood, whose population, 5,000 in 1910, had jumped to 36,000 by 1920. The Americans began to take a greater interest in the foreign market. Before the war most US companies were content to sell European rights to British companies, which then re-exported the films to the Continent. Now films like D.W. Griffith's *Birth of a Nation* (1915) and Thomas Ince's *Civilization* (1916) were instead marketed on a country-by-country basis by their American producers. The USA, as Walter Uricchio explains, 'came out of the war with a massive and relatively healthy domestic market, and an aggressive and well-oiled studio system'.[9] It completely conquered the relatively small Australian and New Zealand markets – a 95 per cent market share in what were, after all, members of the British Empire.[10] The Europeans reacted as best they could, forging alliances, using protective tariffs and centralising production. Nevertheless, by the time sound came in the late 1920s, the USA had gained a considerable lead in virtually all world markets.

Were there 'ideological' reasons which helped this process? There is little doubt that even before the war, and even more after it, Europeans hated each other more than they disliked Americans. Or, to put it more strongly: there was no special reason for most Europeans to dislike the USA, and plenty of good reasons to hate the French or the Germans or the Italians or the British. This was true for the world as a whole – with the possible exception of Latin America. Everyone hated colonialists, even when they tried to imitate them. And the colonialists were invariably Europeans – British, French, Dutch and Belgians. The idea of America, on the other hand, was quite appealing. Here was a country which welcomed immigrants and enabled them to make a fortune, a country which was modern without being colonialist. Compared to old Europe, the USA appeared more democratic, more expansive, more popular, more available to all.[11] On their own, such ideas would have made little difference to ticket sales. Yet they were enhanced by the films themselves: the wealth exhibited, the speed of the action, and above all the divas.

The American cinema created stars with a systematic self-consciousness never reached by the European cinema. In Europe the stars were the by-product of the spread of the cinema. In the USA the stars were brand names. In the cultural industry the consumer, faced with so many individual works, needs to be told whether what is on sale is similar to something previously enjoyed. In literary fiction this works essentially through the creation of genres and the fame of individual authors. In film it is achieved above all thanks to the identification of the actors. The star system, borrowed in part from the opera, gave the cinema a kind of stability.[12] The stars' private lives became public, a phenomenon fuelled by the proliferation of magazines and specialised journalists or gossip columnists. Film stars became the object of worship. Theatre actresses and opera singers had been worshipped too, but from afar by those who had only heard of them, or by the small group of privileged people who did see them. The film star could be seen by everyone.

In 1926 two biographies came out in Italy. The first was *Dux*, about Benito Mussolini, the saviour of Italy, written by his Jewish mistress, the talented Margherita Sarfatti. The second was the Italian translation of *La Vita amorosa di Rodolfo Valentino*, the local boy who had become a star in America and throughout the world, and who had died that year. Rudolf Valentino sold 40,000 copies, far more than the Duce.[13]

The importance of stars was further enhanced by the nature of the American distribution system, which was far more decentralised than the European one. The vertical integration system pioneered by Pathé meant that the production company took all the decisions – from what films were made to what was shown in which cinemas. Distributors did not have a choice. They simply received instructions about which films they had to show. The American system was more like a real market, with distributors having to make choices, having to ask themselves what the public would prefer. The presence of a popular star could often be the element which made a difference between a profit and a loss. Besides, the public wanted a rapid succession of new films, but they also wanted an element of continuity. They wanted to know what they could expect. Actors provided this necessary element. People knew what to expect if a film starred Lillian Gish, or Charlie Chaplin, or Buster Keaton.

The Europeans too had excellent actors, but relatively few stars. What was it that made an actor a star? One element was continuous presence. This was far more difficult to achieve in Europe, whereas in America the star system meant that actors were tied, albeit for a limited amount of time, to a particular studio. The studio would then 'market' them, developing the system of public relations – now commonplace, but then at its dawn – with magazine articles, interviews, books, pictures, fan clubs. The films themselves were marketing instruments for future films. Actors became typecast: the glamour girl, the beefy man, the ruggedly handsome stud, the comic turn, the old and wise, the romantic girl, the tough bitch, the man of principles, the sadistic gangster, the debonair gentleman, the vacuous blonde, the strong streetwise woman, and many others. Thus the cinema-going public rapidly acquired the shared knowledge and the cinematic culture which enabled it to establish references across films. It had taken more than a hundred years of novel-writing to reach such a stage in literature. It took less than twenty years to do the same in films. The star system entailed the systematic organisation of the private life of the stars. They belonged both to the studio and to their audience. The glamour girl must also be glamorous in her private life, however much she would like to be a dutiful wife baking cakes and potty-training her children.[14] Europe too, of course, had stars, but they were not the product of a conscious 'industrial' project. European stars were just very well-known film actors. Their stardom was often simply a variant of that enjoyed by theatre or operatic stars.

The difference between the vast number of American stars and the paucity of Europeans has persisted to this day. The French, for instance, appear to be able to launch only one star at a time, so that it looks – from abroad – as if their films are all made, at any given moment, by one actor, with, if a man, Jean Gabin making way for Gérard Philippe, then Jean Paul Belmondo and Alain Delon, then Gérard Depardieu and Philippe Noiret, and then Daniel Auteuil; or actresses such as Michèle Morgan, Martine Carol, Jeanne Moreau, Brigitte Bardot, Catherine Deneuve and Juliette Binoche. The Italians proceed along similar lines: between 1960 and 1980 most of their films seemed to star Alberto Sordi or Ugo Tognazzi or Marcello Mastroianni or Gian Maria Volontè for the men, or Silvana Mangano, Gina Lollobrigida, Sophia Loren, Monica Vitti and Claudia Cardinale for the women. The star system in Europe may also have been slow to start, to the extent that it started at all, because for the first ten years or so few of those who appeared in a film would have boasted of being a film actor. It was almost like admitting to being a failed theatre actor. With the diffusion of series (Fantômas, Nick Carter) it was not the actor but his character who was remembered. Only around 1912, in France, did billboards start advertising actors' names.[15]

American hegemony should be put into perspective. Better conditions, higher pay, and persecution in Europe attracted film-makers, technicians and actors from the old Continent, depleting the European film industry to the advantage of Hollywood. Between 1908 and 1911 most of the films produced by Méliès ('the father of the French cinema') were westerns shot in Texas.

An important aspect of the global success of the Americans was their ability to recycle and recast European culture in a new popular idiom. Much of what Americans made was based on stories which had originated in Europe. To this should be added a factor which is difficult to establish: American films were simply 'better' than European ones. They were faster, more gripping and more entertaining, because they were better edited and better scripted. A film like Griffith's deeply racist *Birth of a Nation* had an average shot length (or ASL – length of the film in feet divided by the number of shots) of seven, while a German film like *Zweimal Gelebt* (1912) has an average shot length of twenty-seven – in other words, it appeared to be almost four times as slow. In the German film it takes someone the better part of a minute to drag a corpse twenty metres, while a proper use of cross-cutting would have reduced the time to a few seconds.[16] The film historian Barry Salt found no film in Europe with an ASL shorter than eleven before 1917, while he found no American films with an ASL longer than ten.[17] Americans also moved on to narrative far more quickly than the Europeans. By the end of 1903 they were producing and distributing more feet of fictional film than newsreel, and by 1907 more fiction than 'factual' films.[18] It is, of course, perfectly possible to make an exciting film with very long shots, but one needs to be extremely talented: Hitchcock's *Rope* (1948) contained only eleven shots, an average length of ten minutes.[19]

When the average film was fairly short, economy of action was an important factor. Americans, constantly worried about entertaining the public, hurried their actors along and warned against 'stagey' acting. The actress Florence Lawrence recalled that D.W. Griffith's response to actors' complaints about excessive speed was, 'The exhibitors don't want illustrated song slides.' She added: 'So we made our work quick and snappy, crowding as much story in a thousand-foot picture as is now portrayed in five thousand feet of film . . . There was no chance for slow or "stage" acting.'[20] As the technique of editing improved, and multi-reel films became more common, actors could relax a little.

The most decisive explanation for the success of American popular culture, however, rests in the peculiarity of its market. The enormous immigration of the 1880s and 1890s had led to a population which was a microcosm of that of Europe: not only the Irish and the English, but also the Italians and the Poles, the Germans and the Russians, the Jews and the Scandinavians as well as the recently emancipated former slaves. To succeed in this market it was necessary to produce a commodity which would satisfy all these groups, or as many of them as possible, something which could not be national-specific. It could not be specifically Irish or German, or Swedish or Italian. Once tested in such a formidably diversified market, the film, or the song, or the comic strip, was ready to cross the Atlantic and conquer the world. No European city at the end of the nineteenth century could match in ethnic diversity a major and rapidly growing city such as Pittsburgh. Between 1880 and 1920 its population had trebled. Even in 1894, 30 per cent of its 344,000 inhabitants were first-generation immigrants. Even in the early 1930s those born of foreign parents made up 30 per cent of the population, and two-thirds were either first or second generation Americans. Not only was this population diversified, but it was getting richer by the day – unsurprisingly, since Pittsburgh had become the steel capital of the world.[21]

The Americans were not the first to make lengthy feature films, but while in Europe these were usually literary or historical adaptations, and hence somewhat ponderous in tone, the USA pioneered the use of original contemporary topics – as was the case with *Traffic in Souls* (1913), about the white slave trade.[22]

Finally, the Americans surpassed the Europeans – both qualitatively and quantitatively – in the production of serials, the 'natural' filmic adaptation of the newspaper serialisation of fiction which had been such a success in the nineteenth century. Unlike the series, which had the same characters but in which each story stood on its own, the serial was a story told in connected episodes. It was a way of making a feature film in segments. The advantages were obvious: the audience would be hooked on the story and would come back for more. All the tricks of press serialisation – such as frequent cliffhangers – could be deployed in films. It was cheap to make, as each episode could use the props, costumes and sets of the previous one – a principle later widely adopted for television serials. The genre pleased both exhibitors and audiences, who wanted new films every week. Often the film adaptation followed almost immediately, or was even concurrent with, the serialisation of a story in newspapers – the press thus being used as advertisement for the motion picture.

The American serials were targeted at a working-class, immigrant audience, and promised strong emotions, explosions, torture, fights, chases, last-minute rescues and escapes. *The Hazards of Helen*, a railway adventure yarn, ran for 113 weekly episodes between 1914 and 1917. Another of the most successful was *What Happened to Mary* (released in 1912), which also appeared in print in *Ladies' World*. It turned the actress Mary Fuller, who played the leading character Mary Dangerfield, into a popular star. Those were the years of the serial 'queen': the main protagonist was almost always a woman, perhaps reflecting the gender bias of the audience (just as the radio and television 'soap' operas had a female audience in mind). The heroines were gutsy and tough, and were spies, detectives or reporters, never passive housewives – though they were often rescued by Mr Right.

The plots were fairly standardised. A villain would seek to possess the heroine, or to steal a special object (the key to a treasure hidden in an ebony idol, the blueprint of a secret weapon, etc.), or would kidnap the heroine's father, a powerful man, a scientist, politician or tycoon. The heroine would usually be Daddy's girl – one who had adopted his 'manly' qualities. As in many women's novels (of the later Mills & Boon or Harlequin type), the mother would seldom appear – if she did she would be a minor, weeping character, a 'typical' female.[23] The detective and crime element was designed to appeal to a mixed audience, particularly since the crime genre, in its literary form, was achieving great popularity in those years.

This was far from being an American speciality, since in France too, in the 1910s, there was an outpouring of the genre, starting with *Zigomar* (1911), its sequel *Zigomar contre Nick Carter* (1912), *Le Cercueil de verre* (1912) and many others produced by the studios of Éclair, the only French company, along with Pathé and Gaumont, with resources that enabled it to produce its own films in the lucrative American market.[24] The trend, however, was towards longer films, with the Italians specialising in antiquity while the French ransacked the nineteenth century repertory of popular fiction, including Victor Hugo, Zola and the then inevitable Sue's *Les Mystères de Paris*.[25] The First World War relaunched the patriotic melodrama – a genre which had almost been created in the previous war against the Germans, the Franco–Prussian war of 1870. Female stars such as Mistinguett and Gabrielle Robine, acquired a new prominence in France even in patriotic cinema films such as *Alsace* (1915) and *Mères françaises* (1916).[26]

Of course, Europe remained for long the centre of cultural creativity. The main trends in what one might still call 'high culture' (cubism, surrealism, Dadaism, art deco, etc.) came from Europe. An American invented the sewing machine, but high fashion was European and has remained so ever since: in the winter of 1857–58, Charles-Frédéric Worth – an Englishman(!) – set up his fashion house in Paris in the rue de la Paix, the first of a line of houses which produced what came to be known as *haute couture* (a legally protected label awarded every year since 1945 by a special body of the French Department of Industry, the Chambre Syndicale de la Couture Parisienne). And it was Worth who thought of using young women, or *sosies*, to show the clothes (the first fashion models). Lanvin was founded in 1909, Chanel and Patou in 1919.[27] Levi Strauss & Co. patented denim jeans in 1873, but it would be another three-quarters of a century before jeans became international. Americanism eventually triumphed, but it took some time.

National Genres

Modern Russian history has been haunted by the elusive prospect of catching up with the West. Tsars and commissars had in common more than an authoritarian frame of mind. Both were obsessed with Russian backwardness. If they did not catch up, declared Stalin in a famous speech in February 1931, they would fall behind: 'We are fifty or a hundred years behind the advanced countries. We must make good this distance in ten years. Either we do it, or they crush us.' Yet in high culture – music, ballet, poetry and novel-writing – Russia was as 'advanced' as any of its rivals. And when it came to the new art, film-making, it did not lag behind the West. It has been estimated that between 1907 and 1919, 1,716 films were made in Russia, of which 286 have survived.[28] This formed the basis of the subsequent Soviet cinema.[29] Initially, as with so much of Russian industry, foreign capital, particularly French capital, was a determinant factor. Pathé's offices in Moscow and St Petersburg created their own market by selling projectors, establishing a system of distribution, selling their own French films and making Russian ones. Russian enthusiasm for the new art was very pronounced. By early 1908 Pathé's profits in Russia were greater than those in any other country in the world except the USA.[30]

Russian films exhibited a marked preference for tragic endings (with a 'happy' ending specially made, from time to time, for export) and a relatively static *mise-en-scène*.[31] Tragic endings derived from the melodramatic *lubok* literature of the nineteenth century (see pages 56–8 and 471), static direction from the acting style of the Moscow Arts Theatre (the 'Chekhov' style). A not untypical early Russian film was *Drama in a Gypsy Camp near Moscow* (1908), by Vladimir Siversen, in which an inveterate gambler is driven to wager his bride-to-be. Having lost, he tries unsuccessfully to convince his fiancée to run away with him (not unreasonably, she is upset at being gambled away in a game of cards). So he murders her and then kills himself. The whole film lasts just five minutes, long enough to confirm the gloomy image of Russian culture (which has also produced plenty of clownish characters).

The export of Russian films was made more difficult by the persistent use of Russian subjects then barely known in the West: the bandit Stenka Razin, the Boyars, Peter the Great (1910), Ivan the Terrible (1909), stories culled from Russian folk songs, including Jewish folk songs (in the film *Lekhain*, 1911, one of several with a Jewish theme and a sympathetic portrayal of Jews), Gogol's *Dead Souls* and *Taras Bulba*, Dostoevsky's *The Idiot* (1910), Pushkin's *Boris Godunov* (with actors speaking the parts behind the screen, an example of a talkie during the silent period), and many other classics of Russian literature. The unexportability of Russian films, in spite of their considerable production, has remained a feature of the country's cinema. A large domestic market (as with the Indian cinema for much of the twentieth century) makes exports less important. Besides, a national-bound art form enables domestic production to compete more effectively with imports in the home market.

Italy proceeded quite differently. Its cinema production could be divided into two distinct sectors. The first consisted of mass-produced short, comic slapstick sketches which were both unexported and unexportable – as was the case in most other countries. The numbers are impressive: in 1912 alone some 1,127 films were released.[32] The second sector was lengthy feature films. The dominant genre was the comic short, where the French were supreme. The Italians responded to French supremacy by importing the French actor André Deed, Italianising his character ('Boireau' in France) into Cretinetti or 'Little Cretin' (1909–11), and getting him to star in two hundred films. Other companies followed this example, using home-grown clowns.[33] Between 1909 and 1914 Italy produced more than 1,100 comic films and created some forty stars, such as Leopoldo Fregoli and Ettore Petrolini, showing them in the network of *cafés-concerts* which had sprung up in the larger Italian cities in the 1890s.[34]

The humour and farcical situations of these early comic films were of a kind that could easily be exported to many countries. Thus Cretinetti was turned into Foolshead in English-speaking countries (was 'Cretinetti' too opaque, or too Italian?), Müller in Germany, Lehman in Hungary, Toribio in Spanish-speaking countries, and Glupyshkin in Russia.[35] The brevity of the comic films led film companies to use the same character repeatedly. Here too the technology shaped the genre. In a very short film, building up a character is far more difficult than in a long one. It is thus preferable to use the same character again and again, in the process turning him into a brand.

The character could assume any profession (boxer, policeman, etc.) while remaining, in essence, the same. A wide range of settings and situations could be used, and Cretinetti or Foolshead or whoever could have any occupation required, yet the audience knew that they could expect the type of comic situations they had come to love and appreciate.[36]

Having lost André Deed to the Italians, Pathé replaced him with Max Linder, whose success in the 'Max' series turned him into the world's most popular comedian. A few years later the European comic series almost disappeared, partly because of the war but also because the public became more demanding. In any case, the public taste for short comic films was more than catered for by imports from the US. This was the beginning of the European dependence on American popular culture. The Keystone Comedy Studio (the comedy arm of the New York Motion Picture Company), established by Mack Sennett in 1912, dominated the field, using the new editing techniques developed by Griffith, with whom Sennett had worked. Keystone actors such as Roscoe 'Fatty' Arbuckle and Charlie Chaplin became the best-known international stars of comedy. The rival studio of Hal Roach countered with Harold Lloyd, Stan Laurel and Oliver Hardy. Attempts were made to make multi-reel comedies, an early example being *Tillie's Punctured Romance* (1914) with Marie Dressler – the film that made Charlie Chaplin famous – but feature-length comedies caught on only a few years later when Chaplin directed himself in *A Dog's Life* in 1918. Only then did his competitors Buster Keaton, Harold Lloyd and Harry Langdon enter the fray.[37]

The Italians played a key role from 1909–10 onwards in the development of a lengthy narrative cinema (up to two hours), broken up in segments edited together to form a coherent story. The success of Italian spectaculars was largely due to the production companies based in Turin, then Italy's cinema capital (and home to more than fifty companies). It was there that the Italians developed an industrial model of cinema production, with a proper division of labour between producers, cameramen, scriptwriters and directors. A new genre, the cast-of-thousands spectacular costume epic, impressed everyone: *Giulio Cesare* (1909), *Il Conte Ugolino* (1909, from Dante's *Inferno*), *The Fall of Troy* (1910), the 1,000-metre long *La Gerusalemme liberata* (Jerusalem Delivered, 1911, from Torquato Tasso's great classic), *Gli Ultimi giorni di Pompeii* (1913), and especially the two-hour, 2,250-metre *Quo Vadis?* (1913) from the best-selling novel by Henryk Sienkiewicz, with 5,000 extras, a chariot race, real lions. The 1914 *Cabiria* made by Giovanni Pastrone was even longer (2,250 metres – well over three hours), and showed the burning of the Roman fleet and Hannibal crossing the Alps – the most lavish film of the pre-war period. Pastrone used new techniques, including a complex system of rails which allowed for camera movements – the tracking shot. Pathé's special-effects specialist, Segundo de Chomón, was hired for the occasion, and Italy's most famous writer, Gabriele D'Annunzio, was involved in the writing of the inter-titles.[38] Ildebrando Pizzetti (1880–1968) – later director of the Milan conservatory – composed a symphonic score for the film, which was accompanied by a large symphony orchestra in the major Italian cities. Such systematic use of high culture turned the film into an international success.[39]

Italian films were exported not only to Italy's European neighbours and the USA, but also to Latin America. The Americans were impressed. The *New York Times* wrote of *Quo Vadis?*: 'This is the most ambitious film in the history of the cinema.' The reviewer of *Cabiria* in the *New York Dramatic Mirror* extolled the 'perfect succession of big scenes vying with each other in beauty, immensity or excitement'.[40] The film was shown at the Keith Hippodrome in Cleveland before thousands of people.[41] George Kleine, the American distributor, had invested over $200,000 before he received any money from the box office. He was abundantly repaid, and sought to import more Italian films; he even built a production studio in Italy.[42] The Italian 'spectacular' was an attempt to diversify the market, which was then dominated by the comic short. Spectaculars set in Roman times became a distinctive cinematic trend, outdoing the use of ancient Rome in nineteenth-century literature. Cleopatra, who had become a standardised nineteenth-century *femme fatale*, was particularly cinematic. The Italian *Marcantonio e Cleopatra* (1910) was succeeded by – among others – the American *Cleopatra* (Fox Film, 1917), Cecil B. DeMille's *Cleopatra* (1934), Gabriel Pascal's *Caesar and Cleopatra* (1945, based on the play by George Bernard Shaw) with Vivien Leigh, which ran way over budget as did the famous Joseph Mankiewicz *Cleopatra* of 1963 with Richard Burton and Elizabeth Taylor.

These Italian successes showed that countries at a relatively low level of economic development (in European terms) could compete successfully in the new medium. Italy had its own resources: an artistic and cultural past which it could exploit, a theatrical and operatic tradition, and an important home market. In the era of the silent cinema, language was not the obstacle it was in literature and drama – hence the more pertinent parallel is with opera.

Spurred by the success of *Quo Vadis?* and *Cabiria*, D.W. Griffith, unable to convince Biograph – for whom he had previously made some 450 films, mainly one-reelers – to experiment with the new big productions, joined another company, Reliance-Majestic, for whom he made *The Birth of a Nation* (1915). This was the first American film to be released with its own musical score played by a large orchestra and the same admission price as a Broadway play ($2). It made use of the most sophisticated editing techniques available at the time, including the shot/reverse shot, the 'point-of-view' shot, cross-cutting, the close-up, the flashback, the fade-out, soft-focus photography and parallel action (cutting between pursuer, pursued and rescuer) which heightened tension. This film, along with *Intolerance* (1916), was of enormous importance in the development of cinematic techniques, and both were very influential in Europe, and above all in Russia. Vsevolod Pudovkin acknowledged that 'The *Americans* were the first to discover in the film-play the presence of peculiar possibilities of its own . . . The camera, until now a motionless spectator, at last received, as it were, a charge of *life*. It acquired the faculty of movement on its own, and transformed itself from a *spectator* to an active *observer* . . . It was at this moment that the concept of *close-up*, *mid-shot*, and *long-shot* first appeared in cinematography.'[43] Lev Kuleshov too argued vigorously in favour of a hefty dose of 'Americanitis' to revive the Russian cinema, and mentioned a survey taken in Russia in 1916 which revealed that audiences preferred foreign films to Russian ones, and American ones to any others. They liked wild chases and fearless fights: 'American films are successful because they focus on the cinematic: maximum movement and heroic romantic adventure.'[44] With the Americans, narrative cinema had come into its own.

In these pioneering days a small country such as Denmark, armed with little more than a few alert and enterprising business talents, was able to corner an important sector of the international market. Since its home market was small, it could not count on it as an adequate springboard; it had to sell abroad. Initially it specialised in what was then known as the Danish erotic melodrama. Soon it developed quality films. One production company dominated all others: Nordisk. Created in 1906 by Ole Olsen, surrounded by a team of intelligent film-makers and photogenic actors including Asta Nielsen, who became one of the first international film stars, by 1913 Nordisk was one of the major companies in the world in terms of sales. Copenhagen became a centre of world cinema, and its giant 3,000-seat Paladsteatret cinema was the largest in northern Europe.[45] This position did not last long. The outbreak of the First World War had put paid to Pathé's ambitions in the German market, and Nordisk took advantage, expanding its German subsidiary. In a few years it had become the country's largest distributor, under the management of a German citizen, David Oliver. To finance its expansion the company was registered in Germany and the link with Denmark was almost rescinded.[46] Asta Nielsen – whose performance in Urban Gad's *Afgrunden* (The Abyss, 1910) had made her internationally well-known (perhaps thanks to the first long-drawn-out kiss in cinematic history) – moved to Germany with her husband Urban Gad, and together they made twenty-four films in three years, including comedies which exploited cross-dressing, ambiguous sexual identities and her impersonation of *Proletariermädchen* – unladylike, 'vulgar' characters. Germany lacked a substantial industry then, and was the second most profitable market for American films. Only in the five years leading up to the outbreak of World War I did the German film industry acquire many of the characteristics of a capitalist enterprise: standardisation of products, a distribution system, and even a star system modelled after that of the theatre and the opera.[47]

Before that, the German cinema had been a modest affair, dominated by a single director-producer, Oskar Messter – though his pre-eminence may have owed much to his sense of public relations and history (and the advantage of living a long life).[48] As in other countries, a multiplicity of firms, many operating in the 'magic lantern' business, were competing as vehemently as in Paris or London. Messter was the great survivor, thanks to his technical ingenuity and business flair.[49]

In what appeared to be an international division of genres, the most successful feature-length films of the early German cinema fell squarely into the Gothic/horror genre, beloved of Romantic German literature. Paul Wegener's *Der Student von Prag* (1913) tells the story of a student whose image is 'stolen' – a trope whose literary ancestry can be found in – among others – *Peter Schlemihls Wundersame Geschichte* by Adelbert von Chamisso (1781–1838). Max Mack's *Der Andere* (1913) is somewhat borrowed from *Dr Jekyll and Mr Hyde*. Wegener's *Der Golem* (1915) is based on a medieval Jewish tale in the genre of *Frankenstein* (the story of Rabbi Jehuda Löw of Prague, who made a living creature out of clay). The story was popularised by Gustav Meyrink in a novel written in 1915. *Homunculus* (1916), a film in six parts, also falls squarely in the typology of the monster seeking revenge upon his creator, a scientist *à la* Frankenstein. *Der Rattenfänger von Hameln* (The Pied Piper of Hamelin, 1916) is a revisiting of the famous folk tale. *Das Kabinett des Dr Caligari* (1919) is about a criminal doctor who runs a psychiatric asylum, *Orlacs Hände* (Orlac's Hands) about a pianist who, having lost his hands in an accident, is given the hands of an executed criminal, with predictably murderous consequences. The German 'Impressionist' cinema would continue and develop this genre. The Germans also produced many films about fallen women and assorted *femmes fatales*: *Hilde Warren und der Tod* (Hilde Warren and Death, 1917), *Das Tagebuch einer Verlorenen* (Diary of a Lost Woman, 1918), *Die Herrin der Welt* (The Mistress of the World, 1919–20). There were also Orientalist fantasies such as Ernst Lubitsch's *Die Augen der Mumie* (The Eyes of the Mummy, 1918), and Wegener's *Das Weib des Pharao* (The Pharaoh's Wife, 1921) and *Sumurum* (1920), about a woman of the harem who loves the carpet salesman Nur-al-Din.

Britain was in a peculiar position. In the silent days of the cinema the fact that it had a common language with the USA should not have made any difference to its standing in the film industry. Yet there was a systematic drain of talent away from Britain to the United States – Charlie Chaplin and Alfred Hitchcock being the best-known instances. 'British stars,' a critic has written, 'were made in Hollywood and Hollywood stars made British films.'[50] The country concentrated on distribution – until 1916 it was the world's main distributor – rather than production, almost conceding US dominance before it had even started. Half the films shown in the UK were made in the USA; Italian and French films made up most of the rest. The British film industry never had a golden age, unlike the French, the German and the Italians (or, for that matter, the Danes). Britain has imported more than it produced throughout its history. Up to 1907–08 it mainly produced newsreels and short comic films.

In 1905 the major British film-maker of the day, Cecil Hepworth (1874–1953), was producing his shorts in his back garden in Walton-on-Thames. His most important film, *Rescued by Rover* (1905), had a cast which included himself, his wife, his baby and his dog (the eponymous Rover). The total cost of production was £7.13s. 9d., and the film lasted seven minutes. Nevertheless it was extremely profitable, as each copy was sold for £10.12s.6d. and Hepworth sold 395 copies, though the film had to be remade twice because the constant reprinting had worn out the negatives.[51] Despite everything, it was technically innovative as well as a major commercial success.[52] British film companies were slow to make multi-reel films, while many British exhibitors entered into exclusive contracts with American companies.[53]

George A. Smith, another British pioneer of the cinema, was equally innovative. Between 1897 and 1903, in Hove (near Brighton), he produced films in which early techniques of editing, and the use of close-ups, led the way in the creation of filmic sequences, notably in *Grandma's Reading Glass* (1900).[54] In spite of the existence of a thriving theatre life, a strong literary tradition and a popular press, the British seemed unable to develop an exportable popular cinema. British producers 'were painfully slow to learn what films were about and showed a deplorable provincialism of outlook compared with Europe and Hollywood'.[55] At first (i.e. 1896–1906) the British could still compete, but then decline and stagnation became so evident that they have been the focus of much British film history scholarship.[56] Investment went into cinema-building and renovation and distribution, rather than production. Why risk money on British films when it was so much easier to import foreign ones? The innovative British film-makers such as Smith did not adapt to new developments, and fell behind.[57]

Elsewhere, film production was slow to start. In Hungary, for instance it began only in 1912, with film-makers mainly trained in France. By 1918, of the forty-five film-makers who had produced films in Hungary, twelve were foreigners and only fifteen were professional Hungarian film-makers (the others had worked only occasionally in the cinema).[58] The communist revolution of 1919–20 lasted only 133 days before being crushed by the counter-revolutionary White Terror. Yet in that short period some thirty-one films (both features and documentaries) were produced by the newly nationalised Hungarian film industry. The nationalisation was welcomed by the producers, who felt they were exploited by the powerful distributors who owned the actual cinemas.[59] After the defeat of the revolution, Miháli Kertész, Sándor Korda and László (Ladislaus) Vajda, who had been appointed to senior positions in the film industry by Béla Balázs – the film-maker in charge of the film section of the Ministry of Culture – went into exile.[60] This was a talented group: Vajda went to Germany where he wrote the screenplays of G.W. Pabst's most important films: *Pandora's Box* (1929), *The Western Front 1918* (1930) and *The Threepenny Opera* (1931). Mihály Kertész turned up in Hollywood as Michael Curtiz, making dozens of films including classics such as *Yankee Doodle Dandy* (1942) with James Cagney, *Mildred Pierce* (1945) with Joan Crawford, and *Casablanca* (1942) with Humphrey Bogart and Ingrid Bergman. Sándor Korda (born Sándor László Kellner) had made nineteen films in Hungary by 1918, and eventually settled in Britain, where as Alexander Korda he became more British than the British (and, in due course, Sir Alexander Korda). There he made dozens of films including *The Private Life of Henry VIII* (1933), *The Scarlet Pimpernel* (1934) and *The Four Feathers*

(1939), built Denham Studios and imported technicians from Europe to train British ones.

The Hungarian brain drain included Béla Blasko (1882–1956), an actor noted for his interpretation of Hamlet in Budapest, who was forced to leave the country because of his support for the communist revolution. He reached America in 1921. Six years later, under the name of Béla Lugosi (from Lugos, his native town), he impersonated the vampire in a Broadway adaptation of Bram Stoker's famous novel *Dracula*. When Universal bought the film rights he was the obvious choice for the title role. Thereafter he was one of Hollywood's most successful impersonators of monsters, murderers and mad scientists.

Had such talented film-makers been able to remain in Hungary they might have transformed the history of the nation's cinema. Yet in all probability, outside the boundaries of Hungary's tiny cinematic market they would have remained unknown to all except for a few cognoscenti. The advent of sound would have made it even more difficult for their films to cross linguistic boundaries. Had Mihály Kertész remained in Hungary (and not become Michael Curtiz), he would never have made *Casablanca*, never have directed stars like Humphrey Bogart and Ingrid Bergman (and if she had remained in Sweden . . .).

Other countries could not hope even to produce for the domestic market. They were laggards in every sense. In Bulgaria, for instance, the first cinema opened in Sofia only in 1908. It was called, appropriately, 'The Modern'. In 1910 a second was opened, the Odeon. The films shown were all international successes. Even the first 'Bulgarian' newsreel, featuring the wedding of King Ferdinand in 1908, was shot by a foreign company. The first Bulgarian feature film was produced only in 1915: Vassil Gendov's *Balgaran e gallant* (The Bulgarian is Gallant). Production remained low throughout the interwar years.[61] China joined the cinema world at about the same time as Bulgaria. Its first short feature film, *The Difficult Couple* (1913) by Zhang Shichuan was critical of arranged marriages. China, unlike Bulgaria, had a huge market and by the mid-thirties it was making four hundred films a year, many based on its operatic tradition.

The cinema was the first medium really open to outsiders. Internationally-known novelists had first to succeed in their own domestic market, as did composers. Not so for the cinema, the new 'democratic' art form of the twentieth century. The springboard, however, had to be American.

42

Cultural Panics

Defending Civilisation

WHAT DID CHILDREN DO in the late nineteenth century? If they were lucky enough to be born in a rich country such as Great Britain, but unlucky enough to be born among the working classes, they (especially if girls) probably helped their parents around the house. At the age of ten they would start working (the school leaving age was increased to fourteen in 1918). The games available to them included hopscotch, skipping rope, shuttlecock and paddle – games they could play in the street and which did not require expensive equipment. Some were too busy even to do that.[1]

Notwithstanding those who long for the community spirit of old, working-class life was in fact both too isolated and not private enough. Several families might live in the same house, yet there would be little time or desire for social intercourse, and not much time to visit places of entertainment.[2] Yet compared to the preceding decades, more leisure was available to a greater number of people than ever before. As we have seen in the preceding chapters, more people read books, played a musical instrument, attended concerts and music halls, and frequented the recently introduced cinemas. Some bought the new gramophones and listened to discs.

The growth in popular leisure and entertainment was a formidable egalitarian instrument. Once, only gentlemen and ladies read novels, newspapers and magazines, went to the theatre and the opera, and listened to music. Now, as the age of the masses approached, such pursuits had become almost commonplace among the middle classes and among some groups within the working classes. But they were not the same pursuits, not the same novels, the same theatres, the same music, the same newspapers. The more socially concerned men of culture, for whom the education of the working classes was a desirable goal, sought, in the manner advocated by Matthew Arnold, not 'to teach down to the level of inferior classes', but 'to do away with classes; to make the best that has been known and thought in the world current everywhere . . . This is the *social idea*; and the men of culture are the true apostles of equality.'[3] Others panicked. The huge quantity of popular culture unleashed upon the once-innocent masses, no longer under their control, destabilised civilisation as they had defined it, and might bring about the end of respect and deference. As we now know, they were right to express such fears, though they might not have been right to have had them.

Two assumptions, one psychological and one sociological, were made by the originators of cultural moral panics. The first was that culture had consequences. We do not remain unaffected by what we read and what we see. The cultural environment shapes behaviour at least as much as, possibly more than, our genes. Panic-mongers of a religious disposition assumed that evil was lurking inside all of us, and could be unclenched by the wrong cultural inputs. Not all of us have strong moral fibre. Resistance to noxious influence is not equally distributed. But one did not have to have religion in order to panic. A scientific frame of mind would do the job just as well. Positivists already thought they could predict human behaviour from what was put into people's heads: reading degenerate books, they opined, would make one degenerate. Erotic literature was not just immoral, it was like a germ: bad for you. The report presented by Alexandre Coote to the anti-pornography Paris Congress of 1908 was full of medical references.[4]

The sociological assumption introduced a class element. The working classes were more liable than the middle classes to be affected by what they read and saw. They had weaker moral fibre; they were less intelligent, more gullible – just like women and children. This view was all-pervasive: culture could subvert the workers. When Hauptmann's *The Weavers* (1892) was banned in Berlin, the courts, much to the Emperor's displeasure, overturned the decision. There was further opposition. Eventually a compromise was reached: the tickets were made more expensive, thus keeping out the lower orders and permitting entry only to those who had never met a Silesian weaver in their life.[5] The double standard was the norm. In Russia, hundreds of plays approved for the 'expensive' theatre were banned in cheap popular theatres.[6]

The expansion of the cultural market, of education, of literacy, of leisure time, of science and technology, the increase in wealth and prosperity, the proclamation of social and political equality, in a word 'the new order', was the target of the new panic-mongers such as the Comte d'Haussonville (1843–1924): 'A new class, hitherto subjected to rules, has come to share power with the old ruling class ... the France of this *fin-de-siècle* with its steam engines, electricity, universal suffrage and the republic was more different from the France of the First Empire and the restoration than was the France of Louis XVI from that of Louis XIV.' Yet 'This same France has more murderers, thieves, debauched people, beggars and vagabonds than half a century ago.'[7] 'The taste for the theatre,' explained Haussonville, 'is very wide-spread among the common people and it is assuredly to be much regretted,' because it disclosed new horizons. When 'we' (i.e. the readers of the *Revue des deux mondes*) go to the theatre we observe passions we have felt, and things we have seen. But for the workers this was all new. A superior and unknown world was revealed to them. They had the illusion of being, albeit for a few hours, in the company of great lords and beautiful ladies. They got ideas.[8]

The suppliers – publishers, newspaper editors, film producers – were squeezed in the middle. Should they satisfy their readers, regardless of what the élites said? The temptation was great, and was seldom resisted. Having gained considerable freedom from the kind of censorship which prevailed in the nineteenth century, they realised that their freedom was now limited by the market, that is by the taste of their customers. Nowhere was this more obvious than for the press. Politically speaking, the victory of the free press amounted to a victory of the middle and lower classes – the majority of readers – against aristocratic privileges and political interference. But readers' power could be galvanised by politicians and pressure groups, who could thus regain through the back door what direct control the old élites had lost.[9] Thus most Victorian pressure groups cultivated the press by developing a large following, which they knew the papers could not ignore. Public relations had come into being. A shrewd operator like the suffragette leader Christabel Pankhurst quickly established that her 'major rule of political life' should be never to lose her temper with the press. A volunteer recalled the daily routine at the Women's Social and Political Union (WSPU): obtain all the press cuttings relating to the women's movement from the Durrant's Press Cuttings Agency, index them, and send a daily report to the leaders for their use in campaigns and speeches.[10] It was also necessary to attract the attention of the press by playing their game. Once it was understood what kind of stories they (and their readers) wanted, the trick was to provide them, and if possible to control the coverage – what today is called 'spin'. Hence the stunts, what today is called a 'photo-opportunity'. Christabel Pankhurst explained: 'Much depended, in militancy ... upon timing and placing, upon the dramatic arrangement and sequence of acts and events.'[11]

Panic-mongers were somewhat in a quandary, particularly when it came to books. Would books bring about the collapse of the moral order? Did they really cause crimes? The evidence for this was almost non-existent. Most criminals came from the lower orders – the strata of society least prone to reading books or going to the theatre. Yet lack of evidence was never an obstacle to moral hysteria. Eugène de Budé, the secretary of the Geneva-based Bureau International Contre la Littérature Immorale and the author of *Du Danger des mauvaise lectures et des moyens d'y remédier* (1883), was perfectly aware that 80 per cent of convicts could not read, hence his admission that ignorance was 'as much' a cause of crime as bad books.[12] If you educate the poor they will read bad books. If you don't, they won't know right from wrong. Budé's discouragement can be felt throughout his book, particularly as he noted that his own country, France, had an excess of bad books. The situation, luckily, was better in the USA, thanks to its thriving religious press, and in England, at least among the upper classes, where the emphasis on sport and physical exercise had a beneficial effect on the morality of the young. Still spared the worst effects of French literature were the Netherlands and the Scandinavian countries, and the non-French-speaking regions of Belgium and Switzerland.[13] But France was a bad influence on Italy and Spain.[14] Many Italians, explained Budé, knew French and had access to the novels of writers such as Xavier de Montépin – which suggests that even the highly literate classes, at any rate those who knew French, were in danger of moral degeneration.[15] In Germany the situation was as bad as in France: the *Gartenlaube* with its 380,000 subscribers was a pernicious influence. Besides, the country had a 'subversive' socialist press – though Budé was pleased that some socialists were actively against serialised novels.[16]

Budé's examples could have been better chosen. The Italians who read Xavier de Montépin were law-abiding clerks, the German subscribers to *Gartenlaube* were respectable middle-class women. But the alarmist genre is in no need of empirical verification. The pleasure of panicking lies in making converts rapidly. Anecdotes aimed at disseminating moral panics were retold with gusto by Budé and his supporters. There is the story of an honest worker, living comfortably with his wife and children until, unfortunately, he acquired a taste for reading. Devoured by his new-found passion for exciting serialised novels, he spent an increasing proportion of the night reading books. This made him too tired for work. He then spent the morning in bed, reading. As he was frequently late, he was sacked. His marriage broke down. His wife, broken-hearted, died. He sank into alcoholism. His children ended up in an orphanage. If only he had not read such gripping novels! Then there was the story of a young, God-fearing chambermaid of irreproachable demeanour, fresh from the countryside. One day, seized by an epileptic fit, she collapsed. She was taken to her room by her employers who discovered, to their horror, an erotic novel hidden among her belongings. No doubt the excitement produced by such books caused the poor girl to have a fit.

Maids were not the only ones negatively affected by improper books. In 1913 a Catholic magazine declared that serialised novels caused more harm to women's brains than alcohol. A curate explained that many young girls, having bought for only sixty-five centimes a novel with an appealing title, would spend the whole of Sunday in bed reading it, instead of going on a healthy walk or to church. They compounded the problem by retelling the story to their workmates. Thus the disease spread.[17] The nefarious influence afflicted not only working-class girls, but some upper-class ones as well, with dismal consequences. It even affected George Sand. Her obituary in the *Manchester Guardian* (9 June 1876) asserted with confidence that 'that laxity of moral principle and many of those wild and erroneous theories which became developed in her character . . . resulted from the unrestricted course of reading . . . in girlhood'.

The books Budé singled out as pernicious were not banned pornographic novels or sadomasochistic underground literature, but the standard serialised fare of the penny press and the classics of nineteenth-century French litera-ture: books by Sue, Gautier, Musset, Balzac, even the lachrymose Hector Malot, and above all the novels of George Sand with their justification of adultery.[18] In the list of books considered immoral by the Association Suisse Contre la Littérature Immorale and its allies throughout Europe there co-existed, alongside now forgotten erotic novels, Maupassant's *Bel Ami* and *La Maison Tellier*, Hardy's *Jude the Obscure*, Zola's *Nana*, Homer's *Odyssey* and even the popular children's book *Poil de carotte* by Jules Renard (1894).[19]

The Catholic author Paul Bureau (1865–1923), in *La Crise morale des temps nouveaux* (1908), lamented that every institution was in crisis: the family, primary education, liberalism, capitalism and religion. Even anti-clericalism was in crisis. Symptoms of this moral decay were alcoholism, late marriages, a low birthrate, adultery, homosexuality, divorce, the failure to distinguish between legitimate and illegitimate children, abortion, contraception, greed, vanity, socialism, trade unions, high wages, anti-militarism and anti-clericalism. The main cause was the excessively high number of schools built over the previous twenty-five years. Schoolteachers, having taught the children to read and write, abdicated their responsibilities and allowed them to become easy prey of cheap novels and corrupting news-sheets costing a few pennies. Later these children would read contemporary novels – full of rape, fraud, murder, infanticide, duels, betrayals, mysteries, insanity, incest and, above all, adultery. The increase in the number of readers, explained Bureau, profited pornographers whose books and magazines poisoned every day the minds of ordinary people.[20] And he included in his outcry the numerous *cafés-concerts* and *bals-musette* of Paris, which offered an unprecedentedly humiliating spectacle 'for our fellow human beings, who so often speak of human dignity'.[21]

In much of the moral panic about literature there was a political subtext. The enemy was not just sex, but anti-patriotism, socialism, liberalism – everything which could be connected to what was eventually labelled 'the permissive society'. The books approved by Budé and co. were the patriotic novels of Erckmann-Châtrian, the moralising Smiles's *Self-Help*, and the English writer 'Ed Jenkins' – he meant the now entirely forgotten John Edward Jenkins (1838–1910), a social reformer and imperialist, for his wholesome treatment of working-class deprivation – presumably *The Devil's Chain* in particular, a polemic against alcoholism (much more wholesome than that of Zola, added Budé).[22] What should people read? Budé suggested practical scientific books on subjects such as how to improve wheat cultivation, or Rendu's *Les Moeurs pittoresques des insectes*.[23] Perhaps realising that not everyone had his high-minded tastes, he also praised Verne, Walter Scott, Dickens and Elizabeth Gaskell's *North and South* (because it is against strikes). But even scientific books were suspect. Some explained methods of contraception to women, thus helping them surrender to lust.[24] Even Shakespeare was dangerous: Budé held the then not entirely bizarre view that the Bard's plays had caused an increase in suicides in sixteenth-century England, and that eighteenth-century literature had been directly responsible for the crimes of the French Revolution.[25]

These views may well appear eccentric today, as indeed they are, yet the denunciation of greed and consumerism, of the hedonism of the young, of the decay of the family, is unmistakably modern. Nor are the assumptions underlining such views out-of-date, namely that images and words have considerable force. Paradoxically, some of the liberals who opposed Budé and his like found themselves forced to hold the opposite view, namely that culture has no negative effect. Yet both sides would probably have agreed that the diffusion of literature, the theatre and the cinema enlarged the horizons of those who had access to it. The expansion of cultural markets created a community of people with the shared experience of reading and watching the same things. What is now called the 'global village' is thus a not entirely misleading expression. Purchasing cultural goods and having access to them has an effect quite different from purchasing other goods. The globalisation of Coca-Cola may internationalise the experience of drinking it, but it does not add to our knowledge of other peoples. The globalisation of books and plays does. As in all processes there are losers: those who are no longer able to control the shared experience of their 'community'. In the new world of cultural markets, the losers are the 'elders of the village', the religious authorities, the parents and the teachers. No wonder the opposition to popular culture came substantially from the spokesmen for the old order of things.

A common assumption was that there was something untoward about 'escapist' literature. The idea that one might use stories in order to escape, albeit ephemerally, from the daily worries of work, family, etc. seemed to be regarded as something negative, almost like alcoholism or drug abuse. The Puritan argument is that there should be a purpose to cultural consumption, and that this should be self-improvement. Yet many of those propounding such views did not regard the absorption of large doses of Shakespeare, Dante or Goethe as escapism, even though it is not self-evident why reading them might 'improve' us any more than reading Agatha Christie. Even 'high culture', however, could be regarded as a threat, particularly when it was new and not yet canonised. Richard Strauss's opera *Salome*, based on Oscar Wilde's play, was widely regarded as obscene in most countries except Germany, where it received its premiere in Dresden in 1905. When it reached New York in 1906 it caused a scandal. A doctor wrote to the *New York Times*: '*Salome* is a detailed and explicit exposition of the most horrible, disgusting, revolting and unmentionable features of degeneracy that I have ever heard, read of, or imagined.' The doctor was not a lone voice. After a single performance the Metropolitan decided that the opera was 'objectionable and detrimental to the best interests of the Opera House', and removed it.[26] *Salome* did not reach London until 1910 – in a revised version without the severed head of John the Baptist. Vienna had to wait until 1918.

The problem with *Salome* was that it was on the stage, and the stage remained, after the cinema and until the advent of television broadcasting, the most censored of all arts. Juries had become more tolerant of books since the days when Flaubert and Baudelaire were reprieved and their sales improved. The word 'bloody' could be printed, but it was first heard on the London stage only in 1914, when Eliza Doolittle exclaimed, quite forcefully, 'Not bloody likely!' in George Bernard Shaw's *Pygmalion*.[27] *The God of Vengeance* by the Yiddish playwright Sholom Asch was banned (by a jury) for indecency in New York in 1922 because it showed a lesbian kiss. This was still shocking in 1992 when the play was revived at the Jewish Repertory Theatre.

Banning political and anti-clerical plays provoked relatively little scandal, because what the theatre-going public really liked were boudoir farces and suggestive vaudeville. While these offended the Church, the authorities, socialists and the intelligentsia – groups which were otherwise at each other's throats – they also made money. Bourgeois society was prepared to ban the unpopular and the unprofitable, but was reluctant to do away with what it liked. It is thus not surprising that these genres were not more regulated than they were. In any case, the theatre was not really dangerous. Bedroom farces annoyed only the high-minded, because they deluded themselves that if they did not exist, the theatre-going public would turn to the Greeks, or Racine or Shakespeare.

Much of the success of the various vaudevilles, farces and comedies which were so popular in Paris, Berlin and London was due to their being able to provide a vague frisson of the forbidden. The risqué genre relied on the ability of its producers (the writer, the actors and the director) to stop just short of immorality. This transformed the utter conventionality of most of these plays into daring and modern works. The theatre-goer could feel flattered: he (or she) got a little bit of smut cleverly packaged as social criticism. In fact, the endings usually supported conventional morality: adultery might be fun, but it was bad if it was committed by married women. Plays that truly challenged prevailing bourgeois attitudes, such as most of Ibsen's, encountered greater obstacles. Good Christians disliked what they regarded as the blasphemy and obscenity of Ibsen and Strindberg, not to speak of Wedekind, while they were prepared to put up with the sexual innuendoes of bedroom farces. Audiences were often equally alarmed. Gramsci, reviewing a performance of *A Doll's House* in Turin in 1917, noted that the audience applauded the first two acts but were bewildered by the ending, when Nora famously slams the door on her husband and chooses freedom outside marriage. Things were soon put right. A play with a similar plot, Arnaldo Fraccaroli's *Non amarmi così!*, was performed the same year. Gramsci ridiculed it: this was Ibsen's Nora 'improved' by Fraccaroli; Margherita, the heroine, slams no door but stays with her husband as a good wife should, and all's well that ends well.[28]

Censorship kept theatres on their toes. Since no one seriously advocated total theatrical freedom, which would have opened the way to truly pornographic shows offensive to the majority, some threats backed by legislation were inevitable; if vague enough, they would allow the more daring to push the boundaries of what was permissible as mentalities changed. In practice, censorship served as a deterrent. Effective pre-censorship would have been impossible. In France in a single year (1900) the four 'theatre inspectors' (i.e. the censors) would have had to read 9,000 plays – an impossible and tedious task. A series of bad and unpopular judgements made the system even more ridiculous. And so in 1906 censorship of the theatre was effectively terminated in France, not by the passing of a law abolishing it, but by the simple expedient of cutting the budget of the 'inspectorate'.[29]

A Freer Society

The panic about mass culture followed almost naturally from the less repressive attitude to censorship which some European governments adopted towards the end of the nineteenth century. Once, one could rely on religion and the fear of eternal damnation to stop people reading 'bad' books. If that failed, there was a strict censorship machine. When the fear of hell or prison subsided, there was a real cause for panic. In those parts of eastern Europe under the rule of the Tsar, censorship continued unabated. Indeed political censorship increased to meet the challenge of a new breed of revolutionaries and subversives: the Russian censorship laws of 1882 were a step back from 1855, when it was possible for the press to criticise the government, though not the Tsar.[30]

But if the Tsarist Empire still wallowed in darkness, elsewhere matters improved. In Austria-Hungary, after the 'Compromise' of 1867 (which created Austria-Hungary) a relatively free press was ushered in, though such freedom tended to be limited to the Hungarians and the Austrians, and not to the Romanian ethnic minority of Transylvania. Freedom of the press in Hungary in 1900 was more extensive than after 1918, when Admiral Horthy staged his

counter-revolutionary coup, or under the post-Second World War communist government. The liberalisation of the press proceeded even in Spain,
especially after the 'Glorious Revolution' of 1868 and Isabella II's forced
abdication, when the new government lifted press restrictions and declared
that the role of the press was to educate the people, and that newspapers
were the books of the labouring classes.[31] Further restrictions were lifted in
1883, paving the way for a revival of Spanish literature.

In France the Third Republic had emerged out of the ruin of a fairly
restrictive regime, that of Napoleon III, which it must be said had entered a
liberal phase in its second and final decade of existence. The new republican
regime could hardly fail to improve matters further. Its first decree, on
4 September 1870, extended an amnesty to all press crimes. Yet a few years
later, in 1875, tribunals were as busy as ever enforcing press crimes such as
injuries against the authorities and morality. Then in 1881 a new law abolished
censorship and established freedom of the press. The limits to this freedom
were more clearly stated than previously: it was forbidden to insult judges or
the President of the Republic, or even foreign heads of state; it was forbidden
to incite people to avoid military service; and it was illegal to publish material
contrary to public morality and religion (*outrage à la morale publique et
religieuse et aux bonnes moeurs*).[32] The most important difference with
previous practice was that pre-publication censorship was abolished. This
somewhat increased the risk to authors and publishers, since one could
not be sure if what one wrote or published would be deemed offensive.
Louis Desprez found to his cost that his 1884 novel *Autour d'un clocher*
(Round a Bell Tower) was condemned because of its account of peasant
sexuality. He had to pay a fine and to spend a month in prison.[33] Anarchist
publications such as *Le Père Peinard* and *La Révolte* were suspended in
February 1894.

The British laws were drafted in such a way that the prosecution had to
establish that a text or picture had the tendency to 'deprave or corrupt' –
merely offending or shocking people was not enough. Such was Chief Justice
Cockburn's famous 1868 interpretation of the 1857 Obscenity Act: to 'deprave
and corrupt those whose minds are open to such immoral influences, and
into whose hands a publication of this sort may fall'.[34] Cockburn's judgement
held sway for a hundred years. The British also used a battery of parliamentary Acts. The Vagrancy Laws were used to arrest door-to-door salesmen who
sold erotic literature. The Post Office Protection Act of 1884 prohibited the
sending of obscene material by post. Morality was, of course, a grey area, but

here Budé, the Victorians and standard stereotypes were quite right: when it came to sex in print or on the stage the French were more relaxed than other countries.

Humour came in for severe restrictions, particularly in Germany, where it tended to be subversive of the existing social order (in Britain, *Punch* was by comparison quite tame). While in Great Britain the operettas of Gilbert and Sullivan had become, by the 1880s, an institution in spite (or because) of their mild anti-establishment humour, in Germany the magazine *Simplicissimus* (founded 1896) aroused the wrath of the authorities, who often confiscated it, banned it, fined it and imprisoned its editors.[35] The other great German liberal satirical magazine, *Kladderadatsch* (1848), with a circulation of 50,000 by 1890, was also frequently in trouble with the authorities. The playwright Frank Wedekind, who wrote under the pen name of 'Hieronymus' in *Simplicissimus*, was prosecuted in 1898 for a poem on King David whose obvious target was the Emperor Wilhelm II. He was forced into temporary exile, but the circulation of the magazine grew rapidly from a few thousand copies to 85,000.[36] The Italian satirical magazine *L'Asino* (founded in 1892) was frequently suspended. Its crude attacks on the Church, on political and private corruption, on Prime Ministers (including Giolitti and Crispi), offended the world of the *bien-pensants*. Its coarse caricature of priests as venal and scheming, however, proved popular. By 1904 it had reached a circulation of 60,000, and before 1912 it reached 100,000, an amazing print run in a country where most newspapers were selling only a few thousand copies.[37]

By the beginning of the twentieth century, in democratic countries, it was rare for a book to get into trouble with the authorities simply because of its political contents. Depictions of immorality and immoral behaviour seemed far more subversive. Maxim Gorky, for instance, after the Bloody Sunday demonstration (9 January 1905) and a subsequent short spell in prison, went to New York on a lecture tour in April 1906 to raise funds for Russian revolutionaries. This the American authorities tolerated. But when it was discovered (after a leak from the Russian Embassy) that he was not married to the woman he was living with, he was ostracised and turned out of his lodgings. He responded with a vitriolic attack on America (*The City of the Yellow Devil*) before embarking on the first part of his great proletarian novel *Mother*, which he completed in the not entirely proletarian surroundings of Capri. The publication of the novel in New York and London met with no hindrance of any kind, though what was later regarded as a masterpiece of

Socialist Realism went unnoticed. Clearly, living in sin was regarded as far worse than inciting a revolution (especially one in another country).[38]

Erotic books had to enable potential readers to identify them. An examination of the erotic literature of 1881–1914 published in France – the main producer of the stuff – showed the widespread use by authors either of aristocratic pseudonyms ('Lord X', 'le Comte de Y') or an explicit *nom-de-plume* such as 'Un amateur flagellant', 'Erosmane' and the not very subtle 'Fuckwell' (though this would require some knowledge of non-literary English).[39] Many such novels were set in convents, monasteries or boarding schools for girls where randy priests and oversexed nuns perverted the young – all tropes well established in the eighteenth century, which found renewed favour in the anti-clerical *fin-de-siècle*.[40] Often stories were set in exotic countries – Russia being particularly popular, with titles such as *Souvenir d'une princesse russe d'après son journal particulier et secret* (1899) and *Les Mémoires d'une danseuse russe par E.D. auteur du Défilé de fesses nues* (1893).[41] Following an Orientalist tradition (another return to the eighteenth century), the Middle East also provided ample opportunity for pornography: harems, refined and somewhat cruel erotic practices, spicy food inviting luscious and luxurious sex – a view enhanced by the (usually clandestine) publication of Indian sex manuals such as Nefzawi's *The Perfumed Garden* and Vātsyāyana's *Kamasutra*. Great Britain, perhaps because of the cold weather, was a favourite setting for novels with a flagellation theme, often involving aristocratic ladies enjoying being brutalised by their servants.[42]

It is a hallmark of this kind of literature that things are not what they appear: refined women enjoy rough games, priests prefer crude sex to devotion to a godly life. Sinful women are often punished in the end, but only after a considerable amount of sinning, so as to justify the expense of buying the book in the first place. The customary way in which the writers and publishers of erotic literature protected themselves was by engineering a moral ending. This often worked. Take the novel *Les Invertis* (1906), by Armand Dubarry, the story of the Baroness of Morangais. Her father is a cocaine-user, her mother dies insane of narcotics abuse, and her sister safeguards herself from her husband's excessive lust by subduing him with morphine. Meanwhile the Baroness tries to seduce her sister-in-law. In spite of this promising plot, the book was spared by the magistrate who investigated it because the author was manifestly in favour of 'normal' sex and had ensured that all the 'perverts' died in the end.[43] Charles Mérouvel (1832?–1920?), hardly a pornographic author but regarded as such by his puritanical critics, was another expert in finding a moral and edifying conclusion to a risqué story. His female protagonists were regularly subjected to terrible humiliations and thorough degradation. Then, towards the end, matters improved remarkably, the villains were punished and the women ended up happily married to warm and sensitive men.[44]

A way of getting the law off one's back was to invoke some pseudoscientific reason for publishing the book: to warn people against incest, or against excessive sex, etc., while providing plenty of detailed evidence. The intention of the author was always regarded as highly relevant. Middle-class juries were reluctant to convict. Indeed, so difficult was it to obtain a conviction that, at least in France, there were very few obscenity trials between 1881 and 1910. Pubic hair, however, was out, even in France. In 1917 the Paris police closed down a Modigliani exhibition because of the pubic hair on his female nudes.

If the author was certain that the book would only circulate underground, there was no point in repentance. Josefine Mutzenbacher, the ten-year-old heroine of *Die Lebensgeschichte einer Wienerischen Dirne, von ihr selbst Erzählt* (The Life of a Viennese Prostitute Told by Herself), which circulated in Vienna in 1906, is initiated into sex by her brothers, her father, various priests and other inhabitants of a working-class district of Vienna. She thoroughly enjoys sex, and when she finds out that people are prepared to pay for it she has both fun and money. But morals change. What was once regarded simply as a dirty book, still published in the late 1960s and early 1970s by publishers such as Brandon House in North Hollywood and King's Road Publishing and the Venus Press in London, was republished in 1998 by the eminent French publisher Gallimard in its prestigious paperback collection Folio, in spite of moral panics about child pornography.[45] The true author was not the fictional Josefine but Siegmund Salzmann, born in Budapest, the son of a rabbi and later the President of Austrian PEN. Under the pseudonym of Felix Salten he also wrote the famous *Bambi* (1923), to the delight of children, of whom he was obviously rather fond. Disney's 1942 film made Salten's deer far more internationally well-known than his child prostitute.

The erotic literature of the eighteenth century provided a rich source for imitations, inspirations and outright plagiarism. Some erotic classics such as John Cleland's 1749 *Fanny Hill: Memoirs of a Woman of Pleasure* resurfaced. In 1887 a new French translation (*Les Mémoires de Fanny Hill*) was immediately followed, in 1888, by an English-language edition printed in France with a notice explaining that this edition was specifically for British readers who could not get the book in England.[46] As recently as 1963 a paperback edition of the novel was seized by the British authorities for contravening the Obscene Publications Act. This ensured thriving sales after the trial.

It is difficult to estimate how significant was the market for erotic literature. An examination of the 'forbidden' books kept in the Bibliothèque Nationale in Paris (in the section known as 'L'Enfer') reveals 1,730 works since the sixteenth century. This is a tiny fraction of all books published.[47] Even in the years 1890–1912, when there was a major expansion of erotic literature (or of literature regarded as such by the librarians of the Bibliothèque Nationale), the proportion was only one book in 1,300.[48] In Spain, where the book market was relatively small, erotic novels like *Del Frio al fuego* and *Las Posadas del amor* sold, respectively, 16,000 and 13,320 copies in 1919, a remarkable achievement.[49]

The importance of such books would be slight were it not for the ripple effect they have on the rest of literature. It is a commonplace observation that, at least since the nineteenth century, explicit descriptions of sexual activity in visual and written media have gained growing acceptance in Western societies. By the end of the twentieth century moral panics have centred mainly on the availability of pornography to children (the term includes post-puberty adolescents) and the use of children in pornography – an indirect way of acknowledging that the depiction or description of sex between consenting adults should be freely available. The contemporary debate is exacerbated by the ease of reproduction: videotape, internet, photocopying. Material can be manufactured in one country with tolerant legislation or a weak state, and exported elsewhere. But the international trade in pornography is far from new. Associations formed to fight pornography in a variety of countries met in Paris in May 1908 to coordinate activities. They all blamed France for its leniency towards erotic literature. But in the middle of the nineteenth century the centre of the pornographic and erotic book trade was Belgium, from whence pirated editions of French books (of all genres) found their way back into France, to the alarm of French publishers and booksellers. These Belgian publishers were not all the stereotypical grubby purveyors of dirty books. The leading Belgian publisher of erotic literature of his day, Henri Kistemaeckers (1851–1935), had also been since 1875 an important publisher of socialist tracts and of books banned in France for political reasons. In the 1880s, presumably to fund his political business, he started trading in eroticism – a genre which then included books that are now regarded as classics, such as Maupassant's short story 'Mademoiselle Fifi' (1882).[50]

The popular press had identified a flagrant contradiction in people's outlook. Many of their readers, perhaps even a majority, enjoyed stories about sex and crime, but did not like to think of themselves as belonging to the class of people who liked to read about sex and crime. The obvious solution was to denounce sex and crime by writing at length about them. The problem of how to carry lewd and risqué stories in late Victorian times was resolved in the traditional British hypocritical manner: by denouncing the phenomenon, and in so doing bringing it to the attention of readers. William Stead, editor of the *Pall Mall Gazette* in the 1880s and regarded by some as the father of British sensationalism, regularly launched moral crusades against juvenile prostitution in the course of which he interviewed brothel-keepers and young prostitutes. Headlines like 'The Violations of Virgins', 'The London Slave Market', 'The Child Prostitute' and 'The Confessions of a Brothel-Keeper' gained the *Gazette* 80,000 new readers.[51]

Similarly in France, the Paris-based *Le Journal* always took the high moral ground, from where it would scrape the bottom of the social barrel with endless tales of immorality and adultery, lamenting the fall in moral standards with plenty of examples of moral decay, including, in 1894–95, a long debate on whether women who rode bicycles were shameless. Readers could thus delight themselves with salacious stories while adopting a holier-than-thou attitude.[52]

New Panics: The Cinema

The diffusion of the cinema helped books to acquire greater respectability. Reading now appeared to be a nobler activity – much as the cinema itself later acquired greater prestige with the advent of television. The moral panic concerning printed texts in the years 1880–1920 was the sign of the end of an era. Those advocating censorship turned against the cinema, the new popular art. While many objected to censorship of the press, books and the stage, few did so about the cinema – just as today people are more censorious about television. Having arisen entirely outside the circuit of élite culture, the cinema, this coarse entertainment of the plebeian masses, appeared to represent all that was lurid in European popular culture. Its rapidly increasingly popularity was the surest sign of its morally damaging nature. An article in the Milan *Corriere della sera* in 1910 admirably summarised the new moral panic:

Since the time of the Huns there has been no invasion more formidable than that of the cinematograph. The theatre, which is already under assault from the *café-concert*, now languishes under the blows of the cinematograph. Our great tradition of history, legend, poetry and the glories of our art are now all prey to the manipulators of the moving film and fifth-rate actors who celebrate on dim screens in darkened rooms this new triumph of vulgarity and the growing tyranny of bad taste.[53]

As usual, the established Church behaved with greater foresight than many of its followers. It embraced the cinema from the outset. In 1897 Pope Leo XIII gave his blessing while facing a camera, and by implication – today we would say 'virtually' – blessed all those watching the film. Those who regarded the new cinema as immoral were groups of well-thinking people such as the Italian Unione per la Moralitá (1906). Their opposition increased during the vogue, around 1910, of German and Scandinavian films, especially those starring Asta Nielsen (see page 828). The Church was more circumspect. Nevertheless, in 1909 priests were instructed not to go to the cinema, and in 1912 churches were banned from showing films – which suggests that they had been doing so. This ban did not extend to cinemas attached to churches, where 'decent' films could be shown freely.[54] These parish cinemas provided Italy with a formidable distribution infrastructure – one of the most extended cinematic networks in Europe. In Spain both the intelligentsia and the Church were more backward than their Italian counterparts, even in Catalonia, the most modern region in Spain and the centre of Spanish cinema. Catholic pressure groups such as the Association of Catholic Fathers ensured that 'dangerous' literature was removed from station bookstalls. As late as 1924 the Spanish Church (by then the intellectuals had given up the fight) was still suggesting that going to the cinema was a sin, as argued the priest Ramon M. de Bolós in his pamphlet *Es Pecat anar al cine?* (Is Going to the Cinema a Sin?), but also on the grounds that that it made people depressed, atrophied the brain, caused suicides among impressionable people, was bad for the eyesight, and was dangerous (fires were frequent in cinemas).[55]

About the risk of fire, the priest was right. The lamps required for the projection turned out to be extremely dangerous, particularly when used in conjunction with gas lighting. Celluloid was highly flammable. Less than a year and a half after the birth of the cinema, on 4 May 1897, some 120 people were burnt alive at a cinema in Paris.[56] For a while the city's authorities closed all the cinemas.

Some people did not wait for earthly fires, but shut down cinemas for fear of those of the afterlife. In 1908 the Mayor of New York, George B. McClellan, decided that all cinemas should close for Christmas on moral grounds. He was probably responding to pressures from Church groups which had declared the film industry 'a Jewish syndicate furnishing indecencies for the city'.[57] The industry – via the *Moving Picture World* of 4 July 1908, defended itself by pointing out that 'moving picture shows are doing temperance work quietly . . . Men who formerly were rarely seen on the streets in company with their wives and children have come to the practice of taking their family for an hour almost nightly to the five cent shows.'[58]

New moral quandaries emerged. Should one represent Jesus in films? The British Board of Film Classification, set up in 1912 by the industry, included a ban on depicting Jesus in 1929 among forty-three rules covering sex, religion, politics, violence, the armed forces, the Empire, etc. The Holy Synod of the Russian Orthodox Church (which had the power of censorship) had done the same earlier in the century when it decided that while Jesus could be represented in paintings, he could not appear on screen or on the stage.[59] Since the modernist and avant-garde theatre seldom dealt with religious subjects, the sophisticated audience of the Moscow Arts Theatre could thus have access to the best of the European theatre as well as intelligent and witty Russian contemporary plays.[60]

A similar outcome followed the decision of the Holy Synod to remove all religious themes from films: as long as there were no priests, no Jesus, no rites and sacraments, and the word God did not appear in the inter-titles, they were content to let the rest go by. As a result much of the Russian cinema of the time was more daring than in the West. Some of the results were ludicrous: in Wiaczeslaw Wiskowski's film of Turgenev's *Fathers and Sons* a shot of the nihilist Bazarov's mother making the sign of the cross at her son's grave was cut, thus making her appear as nihilistic as her son. But then, after the Revolution, a shot of a woman crossing herself when the news of Lenin's death was announced in 1924 was cut because it was felt it would have offended the atheist Lenin.[61]

The ban on Jesus did not extend to Moses, at least in the West. An advertising poster for the five-reel Vitagraph film *Life of Moses* (USA, 1910) intoned: 'The sublime story of the young Hebrew, who put aside the diadem of mighty Egypt, and became an outcast with a price on his head that he might deliver his people, told in Five Thrilling Scenes.'[62]

Religious films, some felt, might diminish clerical antagonism. After all, if good books could be used against bad ones, why not have good films? Thus in Belgium, where in 1910 there were 650 cinemas for a population of 7.5 million, in response to complaints that people consumed beer in places showing films (many were variety theatres transformed into cinemas) and to numerous moral crusades launched by religious authorities, film distributors included morally acceptable films and invited local dignitaries to see them. This would be used in advertising: 'The Bishop came to see this film and liked it, and so did the Mayor.'[63] If people complained that too much alcohol was imbibed in cinemas, distributors would include films such as Ferdinand Zecca's *Les Victimes de l'alcoolisme*.[64] In New York the newly established Board of Censorship (1909) was delighted to watch *A Drunkard's Reformation*, which contained both a 'moral lesson' and a 'happy ending'.[65] None of this, of course, stopped the proliferation of associations such as the Ligue du Cinéma Moral pour la Belgique – Association Contre la Licence et l'Immoralité des Spectacles en Belgique (1913).

Though such movements may seem retrograde in our permissive times, one should not forget that the debate over what constitutes 'offensive' material has not died down, and is unlikely to do so. There is now a wide consensus, at least in the West, that racist material, for instance, should be censored, and there is no consensus that there should be no censorship at all. The moralists of the *fin-de-siècle* were very aware that should they tolerate toleration, there would be no limit to the spread of anti-religious material. The evidence was all around them. In Munich in 1895, the playwright Oskar Panizza, having celebrated the virtues of 'carnivalesque' popular theatres, wrote *Das Liebeskonzil*, a play set in the Borgia papal court and in which God is an old fool, Jesus stupid and impotent, and the Virgin Mary an oversexed young woman, while papal orgies are enacted to the singing of the *De profundis*. Unsurprisingly, this did not go down well with Bavarian Catholics. A largely lower-middle-class jury condemned Panizza to a year in jail – a peasant one would have lynched him. He was eventually committed to an asylum in 1904, and died in 1921.[66]

Religion and Politics

Controlling culture, the business of religion since time immemorial, had become the business of the state, occasionally in conflict with religion. The Churches became, in effect, pressure groups seeking to eliminate whatever they regarded as immoral from the reach of the lower classes. In France, when the Education Minister Jules Ferry introduced compulsory primary education in 1882, he removed religion from the curriculum, ensuring state control, direct or indirect, over the largest market for books. This now included all teaching books, at all levels of education, from elementary classes to university, down to school prize books – accounting for two-thirds of the paper used by French publishers by 1914. Publishers did not object to publishing what the state wanted, as long as they and not the state printed it.[67] Nothing was published in this enormous educational domain without the sanction, overt or implicit, of public authorities. These authorities were not just the powerful civil servants in the Ministry of Education, but the body of schoolteachers who were the backbone of the new régime of the Third Republic. The Ferry Law prohibited priests to enter state schools, let alone teach in them.[68] Catholic schools were allowed, but they were private and styled themselves *écoles libres*, as they had since 1831. The manuals used in these schools were subject to dual control, from the Church as well as from the state. Yet the Church maintained some influence on state manuals, because by putting them on the Index of banned books, it encouraged believers to send their children to Catholic schools.[69]

By the 1880s the principle of compulsory education had been enshrined, at least for elementary schools, in most countries. This became one of the nation-building tasks of governments – particularly in the new united Germany; in France, where the Third Republic needed to defeat monarchic Catholicism; and in Italy, which having achieved political unification in 1861 wished to promote linguistic unification. Yet, particularly in Germany and Italy, the weight of the past and of educational conservatism manifested themselves in the continuation of the classical education which for generations had trained the teachers whose task it now was to educate the young. Thus, in spite of political requirements, German history and German literature were given low priority in German schools in the 1870s and 1880s. In 1856 pupils in the German gymnasiums devoted twice as much time to Greek as to German, and four times as much to Latin. The situation had barely changed in 1882. In 1877 Berlin University appointed the first Professor of

Modern German Literature in the country. Pupils received a Catholic or Protestant interpretation of Germany's past according to whether they were in Bavaria or in Prussia.[70] Germany, it should be noted, unlike most European states (but like the USA), had no uniform national system of censorship. In Italy, however, state-building required far more centralisation. Already in the Kingdom of Piedmont before unification the Ministry of Education controlled everything that was to be taught in schools, and approved textbooks – a common pattern in the rest of Europe.

In France it was not just a question of building up the Third Republic, but also of uniting the country in a common feeling of revulsion against Germany and of sorrow for the loss of the provinces of Alsace-Lorraine, annexed by the new German Empire in 1870. The educational reforms of the Third Republic created a captive market for school textbooks. The most important of these was an educational reading book, probably the most important best-seller of its day, *Le Tour de France par deux enfants* (1877), with a significant subtitle: '*Devoir et patrie*'. The author was Augustine Thuillerie (1833–1923), wife of Alfred Fouillée, a positivist philosopher, but she used a non-gendered pseudonym: 'G. Bruno'. Set in 1871, after France's defeat by the Prussians, it is the story of two children, fourteen-year-old André and seven-year-old Julien, from Phalsbourg in Lorraine, now under German occupation, who leave their home town and criss-cross France in an attempt to find their lost uncle. This was the dying wish of their father, an ardent patriot. Their extended travels are a thinly veiled excuse for a systematically didactic series of chapters on France. It is a deliberately educational book, earmarked for secondary school, masquerading as a novel. As a textbook it is quite lively, as a novel it is dull. If the protagonists happen to be in Lorraine, the young readers are offered a thorough description of the crystal works in Baccarat; if they are in Mirecourt they get several paragraphs on musical instruments. The book also provided a wealth of information on the flora and fauna of each region, the characteristics of its inhabitants and the great local men and women: scientists, soldiers, writers and national heroes. The first edition contained many maps and over two hundred pictures, including a set representing the 'four human races': the White, '*la plus parfaite des races humaines*' (the most perfect of the human races), the Reds (i.e. the American Indians), the Yellow and the Black.[71]

In its first ten years *Le Tour de France* sold three million copies, and six million by 1900.[72] It was still in print in 1976, by which time it had sold a total of 8.35 million copies.[73] It was regularly revised, becoming, in the years leading up to the First World War, increasingly anti-German and anti-clerical. It reflected, in fact, the ideology contained in the textbooks of the time. It decried 'class envy' – i.e. socialism – and praised the '*bon français*' who loves his country, is useful to society, and is a good and honest worker. A list of Great Men was provided, mainly kings and leaders such as the Gallic chieftain Vercingétorix and Jeanne d'Arc (Napoleon was conspicuously left out), some revolutionaries (but neither Robespierre nor Saint-Just) and women (not only Joan of Arc – a saint for both Catholics and secular nationalists – but also the revolutionary Madame Roland).

This was the time when great historical clichés and anecdotes were manufactured or revived everywhere in the West: Caesar crossing the Rubicon, Louis IX under the oak tree dispensing justice, St Francis talking to animals, King Canute ordering the tide to recede, George Washington telling his father he cannot tell a lie, Newton discovering gravity after noticing an apple falling, and so on. The formula contained in *Le Tour de France par deux enfants* proved so successful that it was later adapted to the benefit of French colonies, or rather, to the benefit of the French who had settled there – for instance in Algeria, where in 1888 *Les Étapes d'un petit Algérien dans la Province d'Oran* told the story of the transformation of North Africa into French Algeria.[74]

The Italians too produced a major 'national novel', though it was never regarded as such by the literary élites. Its mawkishness, sentimentality, naïve patriotism and elementary style set it well below Manzoni's *I Promessi sposi*, whose own sentimentality towards the people had the kind of condescension which appealed to the educated. Nevertheless its success, national and international, was undeniable. *Cuore* (Heart) is the fictional diary of a boy, Enrico Bottini, in the third year of primary school. Published in 1886, it was in effect the joint project of the author, Edmondo De Amicis, and his publisher (Treves).[75] The protagonist describes his schoolmates, their parents and his teachers, as well as the events in which they play a role, in the course of the school year from October to July. They represent a cross-section of Italian society: members of the merchant classes rubbing shoulders with aristocrats, clerks and workers. This was supplemented by the 'story of the month' – usually dealing with 'social' problems such as the emigration of the southern poor – told by the teacher.

Much like *Le Tour de France par deux enfants*, *Cuore* was an expression of secular, modernising, nationalist culture – inevitably that of northern Italy, where such values had a stronger and wider basis than in the south.[76] The success of the book was enormous. By 1913 it had sold a million copies. It was immediately translated into several languages, including Spanish (1887), Polish and Japanese.[77] De Amicis was a socialist of that high-minded brand fashionable in respectable bourgeois circles at the turn to the century: a kind of secular faith on the side of the oppressed, stressing community and unity rather than class struggle and calling upon the bourgeoisie to redeem itself and become truly modern by helping the less fortunate classes.[78] As the book was entirely about boys, in 1922 Ida Finzi, under the pseudonym of Haydée, wrote a version for girls called *Allieve di Quarta. Il Cuore delle bambine* (published in Florence by Bemporad), but it was nowhere near as successful.[79]

Cuore achieved such enormous success not just because it appealed to children, but because it succeeded in accomplishing the feat of pleasing everyone: children, parents, teachers and the authorities. The absence of a single linear plot was a further advantage: it could be read in the classroom in easy segments, much like a collection of short stories.

The genre – it could be called 'discovering your country and how to love it' – travelled well, and was particularly successful in Sweden, where the authorities asked Selma Lagerlöf (1858–1940) to write a book to help school-children to learn the geography of the country. She complied enthusiastically, writing in 1907 *Nils Holgerssons underbara resa genom Sverige* (The Marvellous Travels of Nils Holgersson through Sweden) – the story of a boy and a goose – for which she won, in 1909, the Nobel Prize – the first woman to do so.

Nation-building patriotism partially replaced religious morality in schools, though only in France did it take a strong anti-clerical tinge, when in the wake of the Dreyfus affair all references to prayers and God were deleted from school textbooks, including Bruno's *Le Tour de France*.[80] Nevertheless, even patriotism held on to many aspects of traditional religious morality: the cult of family, hard work, the fatherland and the values of a traditional society.[81] This was so everywhere in Europe, where primary and secondary education remained deeply conservative in both content and form. Education emphasised the continuity of the nation and its manifest destiny. In the absence of alternative sources of knowledge, such as the yet-to-come mass media, these world views remained unchallenged. Whether all this indoctrination had any effect is an open question. All we know is that the generation which slaughtered each other on the battlefields of Flanders had been thoroughly imbued with traditional values.

Even in Great Britain, where nation-building might not have seemed a particularly urgent task, the building-up of pride in the Empire entailed a similar process of educational proselytism. Textbooks and the study of the nation's history in schools were not the only, and perhaps not even the principal, means of educating the new generations in patriotism. Children's literature, and in particular boys' magazines, had a major part to play. There was not necessarily a conscious will to indoctrinate, only the knowledge on the part of the producers that as their market was constituted essentially by middle-class children, it was necessary to pander to the prejudice of their parents while entertaining their offspring. Thus between 1892 and 1914 there was a shift in boys' magazines towards turning the readers into good patriots and citizens, and not just good Christians. Magazines such as the *Boy's Own Paper* (1879, a weekly sponsored by the Religious Text Society), *Young England* (1880, a monthly sponsored by the Sunday School Union), *Chums* (1892, weekly) and the *Captain* (1899, monthly) all subscribed to the prevailing middle-class ethic, used the same writers, and celebrated public schools and athleticism.[82]

The most successful of these, the *Boy's Own Paper*, kept its political commitment rather low-key, and announced itself to be dedicated to 'pure and entertaining reading'. The stress was on unselfish manliness and the 'muscular Christianity' made popular by the Christian socialist Thomas Hughes (a founder of the Working Men's College in London) in his famous 1857 *Tom Brown's Schooldays* – a fictional account of Rugby public school. Yet, by 1900 the *Boy's Own Paper* was regarded as stuffy, and was in no position to compete against new magazines such as *Chums*, which though sponsored by evangelical organisations quickly became a commercial success by developing exciting adventure stories set in the colonies.[83] Thus even in the field of children's literature the imperative of pleasing the audience, following the market, prevailed over political and moral considerations. In the fact the real loser in this battle for hearts and minds was the religious message, because the Empire provided plenty of opportunities for the kind of stories British boys were likely to like anyway. By 1900 virtually all the boys' magazines were pro-imperialist. This forced even the *Boy's Own Paper*, whose original evangelical commitment was hostile to militarism, to promote the new patriotism.[84]

When the war did come, however, the moralists were discomfited. Traditional values received a severe knock – as they always do in times of war. The lowering of morals in London was attributed to the presence of so many soldiers in the streets. Huntley Carter, who investigated the effects of the war on the theatre, noted not only an increase in venereal diseases, but also, citing an abundance of newspaper sources, the birth of a new depravity, including open orgies on Hampstead Heath. This new climate, he claimed, affected the stage because many theatres sought to attract soldiers on leave. He cited the *Observer* of 2 January 1916 : 'The forty theatres and music halls now offering attractions in the West End and round about could show figures of a nature quite exceptional in the records of theatrical earnings in holiday time. For this condition of rich prosperity various reasons might be advanced ... To be considered are two important facts – the presence of the military in great numbers, and the improved financial condition of the working classes.'[85]

Carter could console himself with the thought that in wartime Paris it was even worse, particularly when American soldiers arrived. Faced with the less inhibited attitude towards pleasure that distinguished the French capital, these soldiers helped diffuse in America the image of Paris as the Sin City of Europe. Clearly, in this case, the soldiers were the victims of temptation rather than the cause. Nor was any of this new. The 1911 Baedeker guide to *Paris et ses environs* noted with characteristically fake prudery that at the Théâtre du Palais Royal: '*On joue des vaudevilles et des farces d'une moralité souvent peu rigoureuse; mais on y rie beaucoup*' (They perform farces somewhat lacking in moral rigour; but one laughs a lot).

IV

1920–1960

THE INTERVENTIONIST
STATE

43

States and Markets

After the War

THE FIRST WORLD WAR had brought unparalleled devastation upon
Europe. The countries which 'won' (France, Great Britain, Italy, Belgium,
the USA and others, including Russia, which dropped out in 1917) lost over
five million soldiers, double the total casualties of those which lost (Germany,
Austro-Hungary, Bulgaria and Turkey). France lost 31 per cent of its men
between the ages of twenty and thirty-five, Germany 24 per cent, Great
Britain 17 per cent, Italy 12 per cent and the USA 1 per cent.[1] These were the
combatants. Then there were the civilian casualties, not as numerous as in
the Second World War, but millions who died of famine and massacres
(notably the Ottoman Armenians – as many as 1.2 million out of a pre-war
population of 1.8 million). And then there was the Russian Revolution and
Civil War, in which the Bolsheviks pitted the Red Army against various
counter-revolutionary White armies and the Western Allies. How many died?
Probably between seven and ten million, of whom 800,000 were soldiers
who were killed in action or died from disease; the rest were executed
(100,000?) or died of hunger, typhus and influenza. Such figures do not
include the lowered life expectancy of the survivors.[2] To these one should
add another five million victims of the famine on the Volga in 1921–22.
Included in the casualties were tens – perhaps hundreds – of thousands of
Jews murdered by the Whites, a number in excess of those killed in the
Tsarist pogroms of the previous hundred years. And then there was the
worldwide influenza pandemic of 1918–19 which killed twenty to twenty-five
million people. The death toll in Europe alone – leaving aside the influenza
– was far in excess of the previous greatest carnage in European history, the
Thirty Years' War of 1618–48.

What followed was worse. In Italy, Germany and the Soviet Union new forms of authoritarian regimes emerged. Germany, by 1940, had embarked on a war which would engulf almost the whole of Europe and much of the Middle East and bring about the death of millions. The war in the Pacific was almost as gruesome in its human cost, particularly for the Japanese. The anti-Jewish policies promulgated by the Nazi regime in the 1930s were unprecedented in their intensity and thoroughness in the lengthy history of European anti-Semitism. What followed during the dark years of the war turned out to be the most widespread and extensive intentional massacre of human beings ever undertaken in the entire history of the world: Jews, Gypsies, homosexuals, the mentally ill, Jehovah's Witnesses, political dissidents, Russian prisoners of war and many other groups were herded into labour and extermination camps.

In communist Russia savage political repression, famines, forced deportation, labour camps, economic incompetence and last but not least the German invasion of 1941 led to a death toll which may well have surpassed that of the Nazi concentration camps. Individual rights and freedoms as they had been defined in the nineteenth century were restricted in the majority of countries. By 1940 most of Europe was under some kind of dictatorship.

The interwar years were marked everywhere by the growth of the power of the state. An obvious if rough index was the expansion of military spending as Europeans approached the war. In 1933, when Hitler came to power, it was 3.2 per cent in Germany, 5.5 in Italy, 4 per cent in France and the USSR, and 2.1 in Great Britain. By 1938 it had shot up to over 28 per cent in Germany, 9.2 in Italy, 7.2 in France, 12.8 in Great Britain and 19.7 in the USSR. The USA remained aloof in the security of its isolation: it spent 1 per cent of GNP in 1933 and 1.3 per cent in 1938.[4] But military spending offers only a vague indication of the growth in state power. The real extent is difficult to quantify, because the state – for better or for worse – became stronger in all its facets in every single country in Europe. Governments intervened more, partly because they wanted to, partly because their own citizens wanted them to. The workers wanted legal protection against employers and more regulation of labour markets. Employers wanted to be protected against imports and against their workforces (who were rapidly organising in trade unions). Farmers wanted duties imposed on imported foodstuffs. As the car spread, everyone wanted more roads. As more immigrants arrived, 'natives' wanted them to be kept out. When unemployment grew, the unemployed demanded that governments should do something about it. When firms went bankrupt, both owners and workers asked the government to rescue them. The Great Depression accelerated the trend towards state power, as did the two wars that flanked it. As the state intervened more everywhere, it also intervened in cultural markets.

In the nineteenth century the idea of a national culture had been part of a movement of emancipation of oppressed peoples within large multinational empires, or the recovery of pride in local traditions, or a wider policy of nation-building and development. In the interwar years the defence of national culture became an essential element of the new economic nationalism. The rapid globalisation which had been a dominant feature of the years between 1880 and 1914 came to a halt, and by some criteria was even reversed. The 1920s, and even more so the 1930s, were years of widespread protectionism as well as of economic depression. Yet cultural markets became at the same time more international and more state-controlled – the latter often a response to the former.

New states had emerged out of the break-up of the Russian and Austro-Hungarian Empires: Poland, Finland, Lithuania, Estonia, Latvia, Hungary, Austria, Yugoslavia (subsuming Serbia and Montenegro) and Czechoslovakia. In 1922 the Irish Free State was promulgated. Each of these states developed its own brand of national pride, wrote or rewrote its own history, re-exhumed its 'great' literary men, and set out to define and defend its own culture – or rather, what it called its own culture, in reality a local amalgam of selected adaptations originating from everywhere, filtered in a variety of ways, and just as 'impure' as anyone else's culture. On the eve of the Second World War almost all of these states were in the hands of various forms of authoritarian rule and dictatorship – Czechoslovakia, the only exception on Continental Europe, had already been destabilised by German intervention. Some of the older states had also gone the same way: Italy, Germany, Spain, Portugal, Albania, Greece. The lights had been turned off in much of 'enlightened' Europe. The USA was spared much of this agony. Growing rapidly before the First World War, it emerged from it with its industrial infrastructure intact. Already the first industrial power in the world before the conflict, it was now also the leading financial power. Its gross national product, 60 per cent of that of the whole of Europe, was by 1925, when Europe had recovered, 80 per cent.[5] Much of this growth was due to the constant expansion of its domestic market and its workforce, thanks to immigration. After the 1914–18 war the shutters came down on mass immigration – Canada and Australia were not far behind.

State Constraints

Throughout the interwar years the power of the state, already boosted by the First World War, increased enormously throughout Europe, including the surviving redoubts of democratic Europe: the Scandinavian countries, Great Britain, France, Belgium and Holland.

The nineteenth-century search for a national literary culture was continued with even greater force, because the collapse of the Russian and Austro-Hungarian Empires had produced new states in need of a national epic, national poets and a contemporary literature in the vernacular. Independence may resolve a few problems, but it creates many new ones which can no longer be blamed on the old ruling class. Thus Hungary may have been finally 'free' of Austrian domination, but the costs were considerable. Instead of being one of the centres of a large multinational empire, Budapest, like Vienna, was reduced to being the capital of a small state with little cultural influence. In fact, through the Treaty of Trianon Hungary had lost two-thirds of its territory and its population. Hungarian nationalism, in the nineteenth century essentially a middle-class credo, now acquired a distinct populist and rural tinge, depicting the dangers (i.e. the Jews) threatening the purity of the Magyar race.[6]

Unlike Hungary, Romania had emerged from the war, thanks to the treaties of St Germain (with Austria) and Trianon (with Hungary), as a much bigger country. It had acquired most of Bukovina, all of Transylvania, a strip of Hungary, and Bessarabia. As in other east European countries, growing populism, often anti-Semitic, caused the rise of a rural 'national' literature. There was nothing spontaneous about this. The Society of Romanian Writers (1911), three hundred strong in 1925, was funded by the state; its members obtaining numerous benefits in cash and in kind – as they would decades later when Romania became a communist state.[7] One of its most active members was the novelist Liviu Rebreanu Liviu, whose work was in tune with official cultural policies because he dealt with rural themes – notably in *Ràscoala* (1932), about the peasant uprising of 1907. This is almost a celebration of peasant violence, seen as an ineluctable force of nature, tied to the land, confirming the nostalgic views of the new bourgeoisie, both proud and ashamed of its peasant origin. Much as fascist Italy regarded itself – thanks to Mussolini – as a 'proletarian' nation, Romanians were regarded as *the* peasant nation in the traditional representation of the two nations of historical Transylvania (the 'aristocratic' nation being the Hungarian).[8]

When states promote some cultural products, they inevitably prevent others from emerging, just as taxation modifies the competitive environment. The Greater Romania that emerged out of the war was ethnically quite diverse: its non-Romanian population was close to 30 per cent – including almost 8 per cent Hungarians, 4 per cent Germans and 4 per cent Jews.[9] The linguistic unification of the country proceeded largely through educational reforms, the aim of which was the 'nationalisation' of the recently acquired provinces, absorbing their élites and excluding the non-Romanian population.[10]

But no state can limit itself to mere 'promotion'. The habit of moral and political censorship, already well enshrined in the preceding period, was reinforced between the wars and survived well into the post-1945 years. Cultural repression was, of course, the hallmark of the communist bloc and of the right-wing dictatorships of Spain and Portugal. But various forms of censorship, though mild in comparison, survived even in the democratic states. Allegedly risqué books such as The Well of Loneliness (1928) by Radclyffe (Marguerite) Hall (1883–1943), with its lesbian theme (in reality more a plea for tolerance), were regularly banned in Britain. It had been published by Jonathan Cape, arousing the rage of the Sunday Express. Threatened by the Home Secretary, Cape stopped publication, had the book printed in Paris and smuggled back into Britain, only to be tried and ordered to destroy all the remaining copies (the book had, of course, become a best-seller). It was published legally again in Britain only in 1949.[11] The French were supposedly more tolerant, particularly if it could be argued that a book had literary merit: James Joyce's Ulysses was allowed to circulate in Paris in 1922 but not in London or New York, while Vladimir Nabokov's Lolita was published in the original English in Paris in 1956 by the Olympia Press, and was only later allowed in Great Britain and the USA. There were limits, however, even for the French. As recently as 1958 a Paris tribunal fined Jean-Jacques Pauvert for publishing the works of the Marquis de Sade, including Les 120 Journées de Sodome and La Philosophie dans le boudoir, and ordered the books' destruction.[12] Yet in 1990 the complete works of Sade were published by Gallimard in the prestigious Bibliothèque de la Pléiade, and they are currently available in cheap editions.

In 1959 in Great Britain the Obscene Publications Act was passed. The intention was to modernise the legislation, insisting that a text had to be judged as a whole, and not on the basis of particular passages. Yet the Act was immediately used against Penguin Books – a widely respected house, often praised for its democratic attitude to popular learning – for publishing a cheap paperback edition of D.H. Lawrence's *Lady Chatterley's Lover*. The novel had been available for some time, but not in paperback. The book and its publisher, Allen Lane, were acquitted. The view of the prosecutor was that Penguin's 'sin' had been to make the book available to anyone who could afford a few shillings. Similar motivations were given by the French prosecutor in the 1950 in the case against Boris Vian's *J'Irai cracher sur vos tombes*, who argued that no great harm would have been done had the book been published in a luxury edition for sophisticated bibliophiles. But a *roman noir*, printed in 50,000 copies, costing 165 francs, the price of a pack of American cigarettes, available everywhere, 'even in the countryside', and to all, including perverted adolescents, was quite a different matter.[13] Needless to say, during the trial the book sold extremely well. Vian was sentenced to a fortnight in jail, but was promptly amnestied. Still in France (where Article 11 of the 1789 Declaration of the Rights of Man and Citizens guaranteed 'free circulation of ideas and opinions'), in 1958 Stanley Kubrick's film *Paths of Glory* (on the mutiny of French soldiers in 1919) was banned by the authorities and remained so until 1976, while a law forbidding insulting a foreign head of state (lest it endangered the country's international relations) was used in 1968 to ban Armand Gatti's play *La Passion du Général Franco*. For similarly political reasons the play by Roger Vailland *Le Colonel Foster plaidera coupable* (1951), against US intervention in the Korean War, was also banned.[14]

Such examples, recalled nowadays with a feeling of self-righteous satisfaction at living in more enlightened times, were typical of 'democratic' censorship: they may have been annoying, disturbing, bigoted, stupid and ineffectual, but they wrecked relatively few lives. Elsewhere the penalties were far more severe and extensive: broken careers, lengthy terms of imprisonment, sometimes execution. But censorship also highlighted the difficulties of establishing clear criteria for state intervention. In many democratic countries violence, obscenity and sexual descriptions could be redeemed if the book that contained them exhibited some literary qualities. The French publisher Pauvert, frequently in the dock for publishing immoral books, managed with relative ease to reissue in 1956 Georges Bataille's pornographic *L'Histoire de l'oeil* (1928) and to publish *L'Histoire d'O*, an admirably well-written sado-masochistic tale by Pauline Réage (Dominique Aury, 1908–98), ennobled by a preface from a member of the Académie Française and winner of a literary prize in 1955.

Yet if one believes that reading about violence and sexual perversions leads one to commit them, literary quality should be irrelevant. Indeed, well-written pornography might be more convincing and enticing than inferior versions. Besides, there is no reason to assume that the skill involved in writing an 'ordinary' pornographic novel – including the all-important building-up to the erotic scene – is in any way inferior to that involved in writing a good moral tale on why one should love Jesus. Why should a well-written pornographic book be less corrupting or depraving than a badly-written one? The debate barely conceals the surviving élitist view that sophisticated porn (relabelled 'erotic writing') should be allowed because it will appeal only to educated readers (who can cope with anything), while what needs to be banned is low-level pornographic 'trash' which appeals to the uneducated who prefer their porn untrammelled by style. But are the educated less dangerous to others or themselves if corrupted by their reading? Or is it the case that they are less likely to become corrupt? Is education an insurance against depravity? Such questions highlight the importance of market segments in all operations of the control of culture. In some cases it is possible to restrict consumption to those above a certain age – censorship for children's books was re-introduced in France in 1949 – but otherwise it is the format of the cultural commodity, its packaging, its title, its aura, which selects its market.

Even in authoritarian countries market considerations often entered into the calculations of the regulators. Even the most 'totalitarian' dictatorship cannot force everyone to read certain books or watch certain films – at least most of the time. If it wants to promote specific books or spectacles widely, it must seek to make them interesting or amusing. Markets do this by advertising or by price promotion. Repressive regimes of the left often negotiate an informal compromise to keep some books out of the reach of some people, while letting others read them. In the USSR, at least in the 1970s and 1980s, many banned books were always available to some categories of readers: the line between legal and clandestine literature (or *samizdat)* was increasingly flexible. An intellectual or a 'respectable' party functionary could always get hold of a copy of Alexander Solzhenitsyn's books. Besides, banning some books does not necessarily restrict the supply of books in general. In the 1930s, the decade of purges, deportations and executions, the USSR gave the utmost priority to literacy, reforming the Cyrillic alphabet and eradicating dialects, thus making the literary language available to a greater number of people.

Censorship should not be seen as a remnant of traditional authoritarianism but as the state's response to the massive expansion of the cultural industry in the twentieth century, when more newspapers and books were sold than ever before, when the cinema became an entertainment for the mass of the working class, when music became available to all thanks to the radio and the gramophone.

Authoritarian regimes such as Soviet Russia, Mussolini's Italy and Franco's Spain facilitated the spread of the cinema and the radio as much as, or even more than, would have been the case had it been left to the vagaries of the market. The fear of the masses, so forcefully expressed by much of the *fin-de-siècle* establishment, neither abated nor disappeared. On the contrary it remained, quite literally, a distinguishing feature of the intelligentsia: an intellectual being defined, increasingly, simply as someone who did not have the same taste as the masses (or who had 'better taste', as some of them would like to think). The political classes too, and rightly so, feared the masses, either because they had the power of the ballot or because they needed to be appeased or cajoled. Markets, however, were 'naturally' democratic, since mass production required mass consumption. Markets, particularly cultural markets, 'tested' the people systematically, offering them the products they appeared to want. They tried to shape popular taste largely by economic means, by providing not what the people ought to consume, but by suggesting that this or that product would be found enjoyable. The contemporary victory of the market cannot be divorced from its seeming ability to embrace the pleasure principle and to be on the side of the gratification of desire. The market panders to the Freudian 'id', the state to the 'super-ego'; no wonder the 'id' wins so frequently.

Cultural markets and cultural politics (in the hands of cultural élites) found themselves in a conflictual yet symbiotic relationship. From an economic point of view the task of cultural markets would have been to satisfy whatever cultural needs appeared in the marketplace – needs which were largely determined by a number of factors such as past consumption, financial power, education, leisure time available, access and social stratification. What was desirable from a political point of view, however, depended on one's politics. In practice various compromises had to be negotiated, however informally. Markets had to take account of existing power relations, while élites had to take account of popular wishes. Even in the freest of markets, social rules, laws, conventions, sentiments and feelings could not be ignored. Neither democracies nor authoritarian regimes permitted the sale of pornographic goods, or subversive material, or material deemed to be offensive to some section of the population. Religious lobbies successfully restricted access to cultural consumption. In Great Britain, for instance, no cinema was allowed to open on Sundays (the day of leisure *par excellence*) until 1932 thanks to the efforts of the Lord's Day Observance Society, an organisation with minority support.[15] In England theatres, but not supermarkets, are still closed on Sundays – unlike Catholic Italy. Markets were always constrained or shaped by subsidies, tariffs, and by the constant interference of the state in their operation.

In a direct continuation of Victorian attitudes, new patriotic associations, by no means all of them with a clear right-wing image, told people what to read. Between the wars the Masaryk Institute in Czechoslovakia provided libraries with books, created a people's university (the Huss School for the Development of General Culture and National Education), organised concerts, radio broadcasts, film and puppet shows 'for the people'. In the USA a host of religious and high-minded groups circulated reading lists, such as that called 'Reading with a Purpose' from the Library Association. In interwar Hungary the Ministry of Education had its own list of 'Books for the Hungarian People', while in pre-communist Romania the Ministry of Labour promoted the 'Library of Labour' which recommended good books to the workers.[16]

The belief in the market mechanism, still growing in the 1920s, somewhat toned down by the Great Depression and given considerable impetus during the great economic boom of the Western economies between 1945 and 1975, appeared well entrenched for most consumer goods. Hardly any political party, however, was willing to support the strict application of the market mechanism in the field of culture. Traditionalist and religious parties sought to preserve the 'good' culture of yesterday. The new proto-fascist right (Robert Brasillach and Pierre Drieu la Rochelle in France) excoriated bourgeois culture. Left-wing parties worried that if left to their own devices, the workers to whom they regularly appealed would read trash and watch mindless comedies. Conservatives thought that paid holidays would simply lead to more working-class alcoholism. The idea of removing all forms of restriction was advanced only by small groups of avant-garde intellectuals, who were thus unwittingly confirming their *de facto* adherence to ultra-liberal principles of capitalist economics. Thus ideological difficulties pervaded the reception of products of modernist culture.

This was apparent above all in the visual arts, where success consisted of being bought by the rich while being ignored or reviled by the masses who preferred traditional art. But such contradictions existed even in literature. James Joyce's *Ulysses* may tell the story of a day in the life of an ordinary man, but when it was first published in 1922 by Sylvia Beach's Shakespeare & Co., the famous Paris bookshop, it was in a luxury edition of one thousand copies sold at three different prices (according to the quality of the paper) not to readers of novels but to collectors of rare books and to dealers who kept them unsold for a while to boost the price.[17]

The idea of cultural or artistic freedom, so dear to the liberal world, was in the early twentieth century an essentially normative concept, to be invoked when opportune but otherwise devoid of clear meaning. Yet markets themselves are far from being oases of cultural freedom. Economic necessity shapes their development. Regardless of its artistic value, a film whose costs are likely to exceed its revenue will not be made, unless it is part of a wider project of cross-subsidisation of products or of a political project to curry favour with certain audiences. A book whose sales have fallen beneath a certain level will be pulped, regardless of its merit. Cultural markets, moreover, constantly respond to state decisions. A political decision to suspend the compulsory learning of Latin in middle school (as happened in Italy in the 1960s) will shrink the market for Latin grammars. The decision to adapt for television or the cinema some of Jane Austen's novels will expand the market for her work.

Telling people what to read works sometimes and fails sometimes, an infuriating situation for cultural entrepreneurs. If the bourgeoisie spoke with one voice and if the proletariat was a monolith, then something approximating a marketing strategy might be developed. But life is complex and often unpredictable, as Siegfried Kracauer, writing in 1931, explained:

> What is the social standing of the audience that is the vehicle for successful books? Such successes are by no means attributable to proletarian consumers. The proletariat primarily reaches for books whose contents have been given a stamp of approval, or else it reads what the bourgeoisie has already read. It is still the bourgeoisie that accords certain authors dubious fame and indubitable wealth. But the bourgeoisie is no longer the relatively self-contained class it was before; it has become a multiplicity of strata that extends from the high bourgeoisie down to the proletariat. These strata are a new development that has emerged over the last fifty years and is still undergoing radical transformation. What do we know about them? The fact that we know nothing or next to nothing about them easily explains why it is impossible to ascertain the chances of a book's success in advance. We do have a sort of class instinct, but even

that is faulty. As a result, every literary creation that becomes marketable is like a winning number in a lottery.[18]

The single most important determinant of the expansion of cultural markets was the expansion of the markets themselves. 'Appetite comes with eating' (*L'appetit vient en mangeant*), François Rabelais famously wrote in *Gargantua*. That may not be true of food, but it is certainly true of culture. Unlike food, one may be able to live without culture, though it might be a grim life. As prosperity expanded, social groups with hitherto limited access to culture made good in a few decades the cultural hunger of past centuries. First, however, hunger for food must be assuaged. In prosperous France, even as recently as 1930, a typical working-class family would spend 60 per cent of its income on food, while a middle-class family would need to spend (on better-quality food) only 21 per cent, a little less than in the period 1873–1913.[19]

The Cultural Public Sector

In the nineteenth century, even in the most centralised or authoritarian state, there was virtually no cultural public sector. The state did not own newspapers, or publishing houses of any significance. Where theatres were state-owned (as was the case after 1702 in the Russia of Peter the Great), it was largely in order to protect and sustain the survival of an élite culture for the relatively privileged or to build up that of a new nation. The new cultural industries, cinema and the gramophone industry, were privately owned. Of course state policies determined markets, but control was indirect. Even during the First World War, when censorship was established with vigour, the state refrained from acquiring either newspapers or publishing houses. It limited itself to dictating what could not be published, as it had often done in the past.

As Europe emerged from the war such 'liberal' attitudes continued to prevail in much of the continent. There was one exception: the new broadcasting medium – radio – became part and parcel of the state apparatus, even in Great Britain, still the main 'liberal' country in Europe (in the *laissez-faire* sense).

Leisure was becoming a political matter, indeed a matter of international agreement. Part XIV of the Versailles Treaty of 1919 established the principle of the limitation of the length of the working day, which was reaffirmed in the same year at the Conference of Washington. Until then relatively few categories of workers enjoyed paid holidays. Trade unions organising printers, miners and railway workers demanded and occasionally obtained paid leave. The few days of rest usually coincided with religious festivities.[20] In France in 1936 a Bill instituted, among other things, the *congé payé*, or the right to a paid holiday – the product of workers' militancy and of Catholics, for whom this measure signified more family leisure.[21] Legislation providing for paid holidays had existed before the mid-1920s in Germany, Austria, Denmark, Norway, Finland, Italy, Czechoslovakia and Poland. Between 1926 and 1934 similar legislation was enacted in Luxemburg, Greece, Romania, Chile, Mexico, Spain, Peru, Brazil and Portugal, and after 1936 in Ireland, Iraq, Belgium and Bulgaria.[22] In Great Britain the Trades Union Congress obtained representation on a government-appointed committee of inquiry into the claim for an annual holiday with pay, and as a direct result in 1938 a law was passed extending paid holidays from three million workers to eleven million – though the trade unions failed to obtain the eight-hour working day. This, however, swept its way throughout Europe: proclaimed in Russia after 1917, it was promulgated in 1918–19 in Finland, Norway, Germany, Italy, Poland, France, Spain, Czechoslovakia, Austria, Holland, Portugal and Sweden.[23]

A number of international conferences were held at which it was decided to encourage various forms of popular entertainment and education. Much of this consisted of political patronage: encouraging the formation and development of amateur societies, spreading opportunities to hear music, making museums and libraries more accessible and building new ones, ensuring that films could be circulated more freely (for instance by reducing import duties), and solemnly declaring that radio – state-controlled almost everywhere in Europe – should, according to the Brussels Congress of June 1935, sponsored by the International Labour Organisation, 'respond to the higher taste of listeners, meeting their needs and their wishes in a more authentically democratic way than that which would result from the heretical conception which pretends to give the public what they want'.[24]

There were of course significant differences in cultural intervention in the 1930s, not only between authoritarian and liberal countries, but within the liberal camp itself. In the US and the UK post-school popular education was left to non-government organisations. In the Scandinavian countries political parties (both social democrat and rural-based) intervened decisively and with considerable success.[25] European states developed a 'cultural' policy, assigning greater value to particular cultural forms. In spite of the great political diversity of interwar states (communism, fascism, democracy, traditional authoritarianism), they shared a certain reverence for the literary and artistic canon which had emerged in the nineteenth century. This was so because, regardless of the regime in power, élites whose tastes were formed in a previous educational environment retained an important say in the formation of cultural policies. Most exhibited a 'natural' hostility towards novelty. A defence of the past seems to be an automatic reflex of even the most revolutionary governments. It may seem paradoxical, but it is nevertheless true that seventy years of Soviet communism were more successful than were Western 'bourgeois' governments in the defence and preservation of traditional 'high' culture. Even Albania, the home of the most obscurantist communist regime in Europe (and the poorest), proceeded with alacrity to translate into Albanian the great European classics of the nineteenth century: from Victor Hugo to Anton Chekhov, from Pushkin to Balzac, and not just the more predictable socialist realist works such as Maxim Gorky's *The Mother* or Nikolai Ostrovsky's *How the Steel was Tempered*.[26]

Fascist Italy – though it presented itself as a revolutionary movement – consolidated the compulsory teaching of Latin in schools, the cult of Dante, Boccaccio and Petrarca, and the consecration of Manzoni as Italy's greatest novelist. Fascism did not innovate the cult of the Roman past, which had flourished in the late nineteenth century and which had been used (and went on being used) to legitimate colonialism.[27] Nor was it unique in selecting 'bits' of the past for political purpose. In social-democratic Sweden, carefully chosen aspects of the past were privileged, such as the Viking era and the rural Sweden of the 1880s.[28]

The new media, radio and the cinema, because of their popularity, were the focus of undisguised state control. No country refrained from intervention. Some was aimed at preserving the country's heritage and keeping foreign influence at bay. As 'heritage' is always a contested term, eternally disputed, reinvented and redefined, it was usually the state which had the last word. The new mass ways of diffusing culture provided an excellent opportunity for the state to persuade those social strata which did not read newspapers and books, or go to the theatre – the overwhelming majority. Here too there was considerable continuity with the past. In Spain the myth of *Hispanidad* – almost a necessity after the Civil War – was further developed under Franco's dictatorship, but it had its origins when Spain ceased to be a colonial empire, 'lost' Cuba to the USA in 1898, and came closer to Latin

America in a reaction against US expansionism in the area. In mass cultural terms such a national mythology required personalisation through the celebration of key figures in Spain's past: Charles V, Philip II and Isabella of Castille (part of a celebration of women characteristic of the end of the nineteenth century).[29] In the construction of *Hispanidad* a key role was played by newsreels, which in 1943 became totally under the aegis of a state agency: the Noticiario Cinematográfico Español NO-DO (Noticiario-Documental), which remained in force until 1975.[30] In 1938 a press law established rigid censorship. In 1941 the Law for the Defence of Language banned the use of non-Castilian languages and of foreign words.[31] Some of these measures, such as press censorship, were the prerogatives of authoritarian dictatorships, yet others, such as a defence of the language, were commonplace everywhere. The state had always been involved in the business of culture. In the twentieth century it came to occupy a central space.

Many state policies towards culture were a kind of cultural welfare. The already educated élites sought to spread some of the cultural capital which had been in their almost exclusive possession. Fascist Italy instituted the *dopolavoro*, or after-work, programme, whereby factory workers would be provided with a location where, once the working day was over, they could educate or simply enjoy themselves. This may be seen as a typical top-to-bottom organisation of leisure time – as indeed it was. But not so dissimilar activities were conducted by democratic states. In Belgium, for instance, there was already, before the 1930s, an intense community life, and a large number of non-state organisations (but including socialist and Catholic parties) had been committed, in some instances since the nineteenth century, to the objective of improving the intellectual and spiritual life of their community. Then, after the First World War and the institution of the eight-hour day, the government created the Conseil Supérieur de l'Éducation Populaire, and appointed a board with members from the existing associations, thus transforming them into public officials. The Conseil, through its funding powers and the subsidies it was empowered to grant, published magazines, established libraries and printing firms, and dispensed advice on home improvement, allotment farming, physical education, artistic education, music, etc.[32] Few corners of the ever-expanding cultural markets were left out of the reach of the modern state.

Culture and Communism

Controlling Minds – Some Problems

MODERN STATES try to shape culture and what their people think. The instruments at their disposal may appear formidable: the entire education system, the broadcasting system, a considerable power of patronage inherited from an older regime, and, if all else fails, an apparatus of repression. Controlling hearts and minds has never been simple, even for authoritarian states, because hearts and minds are determined by much more than what one reads, hears and watches. The real problem is that only a small proportion of cultural output is obviously political. Most of it is made up of narrative and sounds whose politics is recondite for most of those who consume it – if it exists at all.

It may appear a simple matter to produce a pro-communist or pro-fascist play or novel: just make the hero a communist or fascist and the villain an anti-communist or anti-fascist. But this can be done successfully only with a limited number of novels, plays or films. Besides, most fiction deals with the private world of emotions: growing up, falling in love, private sorrows. Do communists fall in love in a special way? An endless stream of propagandistic artefacts is, ultimately, counter-productive. A hero is not a hero unless it is possible for the reader or the spectator to have some sort of identification with him or her, and unless one is political to begin with (and few people are), one will fail to identify with a heroic political activist. Good drama requires a genuine conflict of emotions. Take the novel *Quiet Flows the Don* (1928–40) by the Russian Mikhail Sholokhov (1905–84), a Nobel Prize-winner. This was celebrated as a great achievement of socialist realism, and the author became an intransigent defender of orthodoxy. Yet the hero of the book, Grigory Melekhov, is constantly unsure whether to fight on behalf of the Bolsheviks or the Cossacks, and ends up choosing the 'wrong' side.

The most communist character, Misha Koshevoi, becomes a bloodthirsty killer. In the film *Chapaev* (1934) by Serge and Georgii Vasilev, the hero, far from being an obedient communist, is an authentic individual, unlike the grey Commissar. He occasionally disobeys instructions, imposes discipline using unorthodox methods and cannot tell the difference between the Second and Third International. Yet *Chapaev* was one of the most popular Soviet films of the 1930s, the decade of the great Stalinist purges. Or again, take the film *Tsirk* (The Circus, 1936), by Grigory Alexandrov. This is set in the USA, and is ostensibly about American racism and the outrage this provokes in the hero, a Russian trapeze artist. However, the circus acts – not politics – are the real focus of the film, whose main aesthetic influence was Busby Berkeley's musicals with their innovative, fast-moving camerawork. Even the sentimental subtext owes much to Hollywood.[1] Such American influences were also at work in Alexandrov's jazz-flavoured musical *The Happy Guys* (1934), *Volga-Volga* (1938), and Ivan Pyriev's *kolkhoz* musical *The Tractor Drivers* (1939).[2]

One can go a surprisingly long way in producing a good yarn within ideological constraints, as is demonstrated by Sergei Malashkin's novel *Luna s pravoi storony* (The Moon on the Right Side), a popular success when it was serialised in 1926. It is the tale of Tanya Aristarkhova, a good Komsomol (communist youth) girl of impeccable peasant origin who is corrupted by Trotskyist degenerates when at university. Soon she has slept with no fewer than twenty-two men, taken part in orgies and experimented with drink and drugs. Finally she recovers her self-respect through work and returns to the Party as a pure woman.[3] This sounds almost like a communist adaptation of eighteenth-century novels *à la Moll Flanders*, where the heroine, after having had considerable fun and entertained the readers with tales of sex and depravity, finds Jesus (or the Communist Party) and truly repents.

The politicisation of novels was a phenomenon of the post-World War I era. There are, of course, various examples of political novels before that, but these either denounced a specific evil (such as Harriet Beecher Stowe's *Uncle Tom's Cabin*, 1852), or portrayed the dismal conditions of the poor (Dickens) or the workers (Zola's *Germinal*, 1885, Upton Sinclair's *The Jungle*, 1906), or preached class reconciliation (George Eliot's *Felix Holt the Radical*, 1866, Disraeli's *Sybil or the Two Nations*, 1845), or were set in a highly political *milieu* (such as Anthony Trollope's Pallisers novels). A novel which overtly set out to advocate a political cause was relatively rare. For obvious reasons the genre proliferated in the USSR, with few significant international successes in spite of the marketing done on its behalf by the communist parties.

Im Westen nichts Neues (All Quiet on the Western Front) by Erich Maria Remarque (original name Erich Paul Remark) represented a rare case of an international best-seller with a strong political orientation. It had first been submitted to the publishers Fischers, who felt it would not sell, since no one wanted to hear any more about the war.[4] Eventually it was bought by Ullstein, which first serialised it in its magazine *Vossische Zeitung* (10 November– 9 December 1928). Thus the novel was much talked about in the weeks leading up to Christmas, and the publishers received many orders from individual readers and bookshops – all the more remarkable as the author was an unknown journalist.[5] The book itself came out in January 1929, its publication preceded by an advertising campaign never seen before in Germany. Full-page advertisements for the book appeared at weekly intervals in the four weeks preceding publication. The initial print run was 50,000 copies; by the end of the year it had sold almost a million copies in Germany. The foreign rights had been sold well before publication in Germany to ensure that translations would affect its reception in Germany. First out was the English version in March 1929, which sold 275,000 copies in just over six weeks, to the astonishment of *The Times Literary Supplement*.[6] By November 1929 – less than a year after its publication – the book had sold over a million copies outside Germany:

ERICH MARIA REMARQUE, *ALL QUIET ON THE WESTERN FRONT* (TRANSLATIONS): SALES BY NOVEMBER 1929

Country	Copies sold
Denmark and Norway	60,000
USA	215,000
France	300,000
Great Britain	300,000
Holland	50,000
Sweden	50,000
Spain	25,000
Czechoslovakia	20,000
Romania	6,000
Finland	5,000
TOTAL	1,031,000

SOURCE: Claude R. Owen, *Erich Maria Remarque: A Critical Bio-Bibliography*, Rodopi, Amsterdam 1984, p.73

By the end of 1929 it had been translated into twenty languages, including Chinese and Esperanto. In 1966 Remarque claimed that the book had sold twenty to thirty million copies in forty-five to fifty languages.

A high political profile can have consequences for a book. Some passages of *All Quiet on the Western Front* were regarded as too anti-militaristic for the French and the Americans, and were excised (only in 1979 would the unexpurgated version, based on the original Putnam translation, become available in the USA[7]). In Italy it was at first banned, then the government relented and allowed an Italian edition to come out in 1931.[8] A year after its publication the (American) film of the book, now regarded as a classic, directed by Lewis Milestone (who won the Oscar for best director) and produced by Universal Pictures (Oscar for best production), came out amidst acclaim and outrage (the protagonist, a soldier, is made to say lines such as 'When it comes to dying for your country, it's better not to die at all'). When it was first screened in Berlin, Nazi activists led by Joseph Goebbels, then Gauleiter of the Berlin section of the party, disrupted the show by throwing stink bombs and releasing white mice, causing panic and forcing the projection to be suspended.[9] The Nazi campaign succeeded in getting the film banned in Germany, and drove Remarque into exile. As he told *Die Welt* in 1962: 'In 1931 I had to leave Germany, because my life was threatened. I was neither a Jew nor oriented towards the left politically. I was the same then as I am today: a militant pacifist.'[10] The book figured prominently (along with the works of Joyce, Thomas and Heinrich Mann, Brecht, Hemingway, Freud and Gorky) in the book-burning ceremony held in the Opernplatz in Berlin on 10 May 1933. It did not reappear in German bookshops until 1952.[11] For years to come, *All Quiet on the Western Front*, a novel not particularly valued by literary critics and barely mentioned in conventional histories of German literature, remained the anti-war novel *par excellence* – in the way that *Uncle Tom's Cabin* (also not regarded by the critics as a great American novel) was *the* anti-slavery novel. Yet the case against war, except for true pacifists, usually depends on the kind of war being fought. Though few people have ever claimed that wars are good things, and even fewer would say that trench warfare can be fun, no anti-war novel written against the background of the subsequent world war against Nazi Germany would have had much chance of becoming popular worldwide. Anti-militarism too faces ideological difficulties, as was reflected in the Soviet vicissitudes of *All Quiet on the Western Front*. When it came out in 1929 it was immediately published in the USSR – after all, the First World War had been a capitalist war decried by Lenin. It was banned in 1949, when pacifism became unfashionable. It was reinstated in 1962, when *détente* became the prevailing view and the USSR was preaching world peace. By 1964, claimed the *Frankfurter Allgemeine Zeitung*, it had sold 3.65 million copies in the USSR.

Political novels appeared here and there according to the political climate – another way of saying that market conditions were favourable to the politics. In France, in the years of the Popular Front, André Malraux's successful *L'Espoir* (1937) was one of the many books which recycled the old theme of the aristocrat who puts himself at the service of the poor – except that in this case it was a bourgeois intellectual (with whom readers could identify) joining the ranks of the working class. On a similar note, Édith Thomas's *Le Refus* (December 1936) depicted the daughter of the boss joining the workers in the socialist struggle.[12] The Americans too produced a spate of highly political novels, including John Dos Passos's (1896–1970) communist-inspired denunciation of American capitalism and materialism (the trilogy *USA*, published in the 1930s), written using modernist 'collage' techniques (mixing popular songs, newspaper headlines, etc.).

Throughout Europe the left became the leading proponents of culture for the people. Their motivations were shared with traditionalists and fascists alike. The interventionism of the French Popular Front governments of the 1930s was continued by the right-wing Vichy regime during the war. Catholics, communists, traditionalists, fascists, Christians of various hues all shared the view that the market, if left to its own devices, would flood society with mindless and cheap, perhaps dangerous, products. The left's engagement with culture was particularly marked in France. In the mid-thirties the Popular Front parties seriously examined the idea of a state publishing house whose objective would be the republication of all the masterpieces of French literature.[13] As it turned out, this was something the so-disliked market was doing anyway – the advantage of masterpieces is that one does not pay copyright and there is always a ready market for them, thanks to the influence of the same intellectual élites. But the left also pushed for the expansion of public libraries, public art (murals), public concerts. They advocated, for the first time, the idea that a fixed percentage of the state budget should be spent on culture. Partly as a result of such endeavours a large number of composers and musicians rallied to the left, including prestigious names such as Darius Milhaud and Arthur Honneger. Politics had started to occupy the place left vacant by the aristocratic patrons of yesteryear. No 'unpopular' music (i.e. music with a relatively narrow market) could function without the subsidies and encouragement of those committed to culture for the people.[14]

On the whole, politically committed culture meant left-wing culture and, at least in the 1930s, it often meant pro-communist culture. There were, of course, plenty of writers who were conservative or pro-fascist, but most novelists kept politics out of their works. In fact political novels are rare, and few are very successful. Among the exceptions are anti-communist novels such as George Orwell's *Animal Farm* (1946) – published, with some difficulty, in the immediate aftermath of a war in which the USSR had been an ally, and Arthur Koestler's *Darkness at Noon* (1941), which became a best-seller later, particularly in France, where with the title *Le Zéro et l'infini* it sold 200,000 copies in a few months in 1945.[15] Books by Russian dissidents, exiles as well as ex-communists, also did well – for instance Viktor Kravchenko's *J'ai Choisi la liberté* (1947) – throughout the Cold War. Later, being banned in the USSR would guarantee an increase in sales in the West even when the political content of the novel was not unduly prominent. Boris Pasternak's *Dr Zhivago* (1957) might have been regarded by readers more as a love story than a particularly anti-communist novel, had it not been politicised by Soviet intervention. Similarly, some might argue that the vast majority of spy novels and films made in the West before the collapse of the USSR were anti-communist, for they sought an identification of readers and viewers with the Western spy while depicting his antagonists as the Other: mysterious, unknowable, sinister, the enemy to defeat. But such plot-driven books at most reinforced existing views. In all probability they were simply enjoyed for what they were: new ways of telling the old story of the eternal struggle between good and evil. Far more questioning of prevailing political views were the spy stories which emerged as a reaction to the Cold War, such as John Le Carré's novels, which gave the enemy humane characteristics, while the Western hero, George Smiley, was racked by doubts about the means used by his side.

In communist states, intellectuals and cultural producers had to pay obeisance to the party for reasons of political opportunity and personal freedom. No such compulsion existed in democratic states. Intellectuals flocked to the parties of the left voluntarily. Communist parties did not and could not impose their view of the world on the intelligentsia. In the 1920s communist parties in the West had no clear idea of what they could expect from the intelligentsia, other than using them for propaganda purpose. As the French Communist Party (PCF) was beginning to work out the implications of advocating a proletarian culture it found itself courted by writers and artists connected to the surrealist movement. Nothing about surrealism – its modernism, its irreverence, its nihilism and its obsession with the unconscious and the free flow of thought – would have suggested any proximity with the communist goals of the messianic emancipation of the proletariat or the centrally planned economy. Yet the surrealists, who regarded themselves as anti-bourgeois revolutionaries, were in fact asking to be recognised as such by the one organisation in society, the Communist Party, which then seemed to represent the Revolution, and hence the Future. The *imprimatur* of the PCF would imply that it accepted that the surrealists themselves could speak about culture in the name of the Revolution. Not by accident, the debate between the PCF and the surrealists paralleled that which was occurring in the USSR between the avant-garde and the government. The French communists were faced with a dilemma. Their ideology, which by 1928 had taken an extremely sectarian form, suggested that they should not delegate to anyone the definition of revolutionary culture. But communist leaders also realised that political capital could be made out of intellectual recognition, and in spite or because of their working-class origins, understood perfectly well that intellectual respectability is something which can only be granted by the intellectual establishment.

Working-class communists had a kind of inferiority complex towards the intelligentsia which the surrealists, almost all middle-class, did not possess. What happened was that a two-tier system was created, at first in an unplanned way: some, André Breton, Louis Aragon, Paul Éluard, Pierre Unil and Paul Nizan for instance, joined the Party individually and gave up surrealism. Others were not required to recant, but could at most only seek individual membership in one of the front organisations created by the PCF such as the AEAR (Association des Écrivains et des Artistes Révolutionnaires).[16] The newly committed communist writers like Aragon and Nizan had gained considerable literary prestige before joining the party. Inside the PCF they assumed a great authority. They had done what the Party had asked of them: accepted its leadership. Now they enjoyed a dominant position within the Party and were able to assert their own authority.

In Great Britain the Labour Party had no tradition of cultural intervention, and developed none. Some left-wing intellectuals did join the Communist Party of Great Britain, *faute de mieux*, but the CPGB was too small to matter in British culture. The rest of the left intelligentsia hovered around the Labour Party, but since this had no conception of what cultural politics

would entail, they were free to do as they wished. They organised auton-
omously around journals and publishing houses. The most successful was
Victor Gollancz's Left Book Club, set up in 1936. Members would receive a
book each month (selected by Harold Laski, John Strachey and Gollancz
himself), as well as *Left Book News*, a literary bulletin which included a
regular survey of Soviet matters. The response was remarkable. By the end
of 1936 the club had 40,000 members, and at its peak in 1939, 57,000. The
books they received each month were overwhelmingly political non-fiction,
with a few novels thrown in.[17] The 'proletarian' novel remained as elusive as
ever.

Political novels, however successful, were read and in some instances
continued to be read, by the better-educated readers, but save the usual
exceptions, never became a genre able to challenge the supremacy of the
detective and adventure stories, westerns, horrors and romances. The trouble
with culture is that, in the final analysis, it is supposed to entertain and
educate, and no one can be forced to find entertaining or interesting something that is deeply boring. Once established, authoritarian regimes ignored
or persecuted the avant-garde writers who had once been among their supporters. Just as the Russian surrealists learned the hard way that they were
unpopular with both the Party and the masses, the German modernists of the
far right were discomfited when they realised that Goebbels' newly-created
Reichkulturkammer (Reich Chamber of Culture, 1933) had little time for
modernism, and busied itself purging 'decadent art' from German galleries
and burning books.

In Italy there was a contradiction between fascism's desire to have an
innovative theatre and the kind of theatre which pro-fascist conservatives
wanted. There were many reasons to become a fascist in Italy in the 1920s:
hatred of socialists and trade unionists, patriotism, a desire for law and order,
admiration of Mussolini, fear of the masses and democracy, a yearning for
economic stability. To promote modernism in literature, music and the
visual arts was not a good reason for anyone, except for the few who produced
or enjoyed them. Traditional plays continued to be written, traditional books
with traditional plots to be published, romantic comedies continued to
appear on the flickering screens of Italy's numerous cinemas. But even those
writers and theatre people who were close to fascism made hardly any attempt
to promote fascist myth and ideology through their work.[18] Hopeful budding
writers thought that their chances of seeing their plays and books accepted
would increase if they wore their fascist belief openly, and thousands of them

sent scripts of fascist plays to the censors, but most were too didactic or dreadful or both – as is the case with the vast majority of scripts sent to publishers.

To be politically effective it is necessary to be far more subtle; and subtlety requires some kind of ambiguity and allowing consumers to decode the 'real' message for themselves. But how can one trust them to decode it the right way? One reading of *Anna Karenina* is that the wretched woman gets what she deserves. Adultery does not pay. She should have stuck with her husband and not let herself be seduced by a dashing officer. Yet this may not be how women married to boring and pompous men and longing for dashing officers may see it. Anna may just have been unlucky in her choice of men. After all, many women are. Instead of killing herself, she should have tried someone else. Sooner or later Mr Almost-Right might have turned up. Writing moral novels is not that easy.

Communism and the Regulation of Culture

The revolutionaries who took over the Tsarist empire wanted to overturn capitalism, abolish exploitation and help the proletariat to become a new ruling class. Many of them had received a thoroughly 'bourgeois' education and been brought up with the masterpieces of Russian and European literature. Those of working-class origins had distinguished themselves by their autodidactic mentality and their commitment to a high literary culture. They all assumed that the people had, potentially or in actuality, a progressive leaning, and that their present commitment to religious dogma or passive acceptance of their condition of life was temporary. The populism of the Bolsheviks was, after all, not so different from the reactionary populism of the slavophiles: the people, in their innocence, had remained unsullied by capitalism and progress. Such people-worship did not extend to respect for their literary and cultural heritage, save for aspects of folklore deemed by the intelligentsia, following the Romantics, to contain some sparkle of the true soul of the people. The new revolutionaries, like the old intelligentsia, were in no mood to let market preferences determine cultural consumption. The purpose of culture was not frivolous entertainment, or to provide a means of whiling away the hours, but self-improvement. The distance between paternalistic Victorian moralists (and their Russian counterparts) and truculent Bolshevik revolutionaries was not as great as either thought.

The Bolsheviks could thus build on a pre-existing tradition of populism, on Tolstoy's ideas that the old *lubok* could be the springboard for a renewal of popular culture, and on the Soldiers' Libraries which had provided those fighting in the First World War with hundreds of books about heroic soldiers dying for their country.[19] The Soviet authorities were committed to censorship, but their idea of what they were supposed to censor varied. This is hardly surprising. The censor is committed to the questionable notion that the effects of literature and culture in general are predictable. To be an effective censor it is therefore necessary to have a good idea of what the consequences of what is forbidden would be were it not forbidden (to deprave and corrupt, to undermine society, etc.). Censorship, moreover, has a multiplicity of purposes. One of these is to regiment cultural workers, forcing them to consider for themselves the possible repercussions of their work, or at least, to second-guess the censors. The Soviet authorities knew that they were supposed to create a new proletarian culture, but they did not know what that was supposed to be. They knew that it could not be the culture consumed by the working class and the peasantry in the pre-Revolution period, for this was reactionary and religious. Initially they relied on what appeared to be the most obviously anti-bourgeois art, that of the avant-garde. Yet in the past that had been supported mainly by bourgeois patronage, since that of the Tsarist state was obviously denied to it and market forces were against it. After the Revolution this private patronage was replaced by that of the state. As a consequence, radical artists were regarded as revolutionaries and the pioneers of the new order. They were appointed to important positions in state art schools and the cultural bureaucracy.[20] Though the Bolsheviks did not really know what these artists should do, they put them in charge of Narkompros, the People's Commissariat for Enlightenment. At its head they placed Anatolii Vasilevich Lunacharsky (1875–1933), a supporter of the avant-garde but a poor administrator.[21] The ranks of futurists, 'supremacists' and cubists was further swelled by the return of exiled artists such as the abstract painter Vasilii Kandinsky and the sculptor Naum Gabo, one of the founders of the Constructivist movement, who advocated the use of industrial materials rather than traditional carving in stone or casting in bronze.

The members of the avant-garde, like the Bolsheviks, were not quite clear what their politics should be, as long as they were anti-bourgeois. In Russia they initially sided with the Bolsheviks, but in Italy many allied themselves with the fascists, for similar 'revolutionary' reasons. Gramsci recalls that at the

Second Congress of the Communist International (Comintern) in Moscow in 1921, Lunacharsky, 'in excellent Italian', told the Italian delegates that Filippo Tommaso Marinetti, a supporter of fascism, was a revolutionary intellectual.[22] And he was not entirely wrong. Indeed, a year later the Turin section of the communist cultural organisation Proletkult (proletarskaya kultura) invited Marinetti – whose anti-bourgeois credentials were then obvious to all – to an exhibition of Futurist paintings to explain what they meant.[23]

The enthusiasm of the Russian avant-garde, who dominated the Prolet-kult, led them to claim that all bourgeois culture was irrelevant and should be destroyed. But the politicians – deeply imbued with bourgeois culture and educated in the respect for bourgeois forms – could not understand slogans such as 'Let's burn down Raphael', or acts such as disfiguring the Mona Lisa by adding a moustache and a goatee, as Marcel Duchamp had done. By 1920 the Bolsheviks, and Lenin in particular, had turned against the avant-garde – though Lunacharsky remained in office until 1929. Lenin condemned non-realism and claimed in 1920 that the new proletarian culture had to be based on 'the best artistic tradition of the old order'. He was being consistent here, since as early as 1909, in Materialism and Empiriocriticism, he had crossed swords with the most important theorist of proletarian culture, Alexander A. Bogdanov, whom he described in 1920 as a puerile leftist avant-gardist.[24] This hostility towards the avant-garde, of course, corresponded to the feelings of the majority of consumers of culture, not only in the USSR but in the rest of Europe. In the USA the avant-garde had been almost entirely restricted to the visual arts, a market then confined to a rich élite. Artists, be they cubists or surrealists, influenced the cinema. Montage could be deemed the equivalent of collage. But their markets were entirely different: on the one hand the sale of unique works to a moneyed élite, on the other the sale of reproducible spectacles to large groups of people. In film and television, industries directed towards a large audience, avant-garde experimentations have always been completely defeated: the vast majority of fiction has employed fundamentally similar conventional temporal and spatial narratives.

In Russia the avant-garde achieved, at first, a better deal than in capitalist countries. The avant-garde artists responded to the alleged philistinism of the bourgeoisie by insisting on the social usefulness of the new art. Instead of painting pretty pictures to hang on bourgeois walls or, even worse, on those of museums, they turned everyday objects into works of art, whether in fashion design (Alexandra Exter, 1884–1949), theatre design and stamps (Nathan Altman 1889–1970), porcelain (Kandinsky), book covers and photography (El Lissitzky, 1890–1941, and Alexander Rodchenko, 1891–1956) or furniture (Nikolai Suetin, 1897–1954).[25] Such trends were also taking place in the West, where they appealed to those who sought to distinguish their acquisitions from the machine-made products of the new industrial society. In the new Russia too the main consumers of such new productions were the *nouveaux riches* of Soviet society, the 'Nepmen' – those who had made money out of the partial re-establishment of market relations after the end of the Civil War in the period when Lenin promulgated the New Economic Policy (NEP). The avant-garde, however, was too revolutionary for the Bolsheviks, who realised that it was important to keep on their side both ordinary people and the bulk of the intellectuals of the old regime, many of whom sympathised with the new order but not with the avant-gardists.

In 1922 the Cultural Commission set up by the Politburo was in effect a coalition of contrasting tendencies, ranging from the new literary establishment (i.e. Gorky), to the so-called 'proletarian' writers from St Petersburg and Moscow (the Proletcult movement), to futurists like Mayakovsky, 'imagists' (a poetic movement that developed in the United States and Great Britain between 1909 and 1917) like Sergei Yesenin, to the relatively conservative group known as the Serapion Brothers, and many others. As a further symbolic return to the past, Lenin ordered the re-establishment of the 'thick' journals of the past, now fully integrated into the new regime.[26]

In film-making, as in publishing, private companies were allowed to operate and compete with public ones. They were responsive to the market, and had to be self-supporting. In 1927 the Soviet film industry encompassed some thirteen organisations, one of which, Sovkino, accounted for half the total capitalisation. It faced the competition of a private production company, Mezhrabpom, which though much smaller, was the third largest Soviet company. Mezhrabpom produced highly profitable popular films.[27]

Capitalism of a sort, including cultural capitalism, was back under the Bolsheviks. The stabilisation of Soviet cultural policies took some time. As the regime tried to develop a model of how culture should be organised under the new order, there was a reaction from young communist militants and many of the revolutionary groups which had emerged in 1922–23, who wanted to assert the values of a 'real' proletarian art. Organisations such as the Association of Artists of Revolutionary Russia, the All-Union Association of Proletarian Writers (RAPP), the Russian Association of Proletarian

Musicians (RAPM) and the militant group of proletarian writers, October, wanted to eliminate 'bourgeois' hegemony in culture, which instead of disappearing, was growing under communism. By the late 1920s a 'cultural revolution' had developed which, because it was not initiated by the Party, was eventually crushed. Lunacharsky was removed in September 1929, and the Party established control (as it was doing throughout the economy).[28] RAPP was dissolved, and in its place the respectable and less ideological Union of Soviet Writers was established. 'Proletarian' art – like modernism in the West – could have had an important niche in the new society, but not to the exclusion of the rest. The Stalinist restoration of order was further sanctioned by the considerable reduction (in the mid-thirties) in the social discrimination in educational enrolment which had been practised in the 1920s: the children of the bourgeoisie flocked to the universities, since the regime needed all the help it could get. To the delight of the bourgeois intelligentsia, the communists under Stalin provided many of the old cultural institutions (such as the Academy of Sciences, the Bolshoi Theatre and its opera and ballet companies, the Moscow Arts Theatre) with political protection and patronage – just like in the good old days before the Revolution.[29] They were of course subject to censorship, and had to express their loyalty towards the regime (as in the old days) but they were allowed to cater for the taste of an exclusive and privileged caste.[30]

Artists and writers who knew how to behave with the authorities were offered a privileged life in Stalin's Russia, in excess of what was granted to many of their counterparts in the West, for whom the market could be an implacable master. They were granted larger flats, holiday homes, better salaries. They were not required to adopt Marxism, though they had to pretend they did. Gorky himself, who defined socialist realism and promulgated the idea of non-class heritage in the arts, was never a member of the Communist Party. Stanislavsky had no interest in politics, but got the authorities to endorse the Moscow Arts Theatre against the RAPP communists, thus securing the disgrace of his rival, the overtly pro-communist Vsevolod Meyerhold. Meyerhold, who had staged innovative productions of classics and new works in the 1920s, was eventually arrested in 1939 and shot in prison in 1940.

From a communist point of view, Stanislavsky's 'naturalist' conception of the theatre was far more traditional than Meyerhold's. The latter insisted that the audience should never forget that they were watching actors (a principle which later became almost a dogma for Brecht, whose communism was eventually regarded as above suspicion). In a state where materialism was assumed to be the dominant ideology, one might have expected that Meyerhold would have been favoured, since his theatre was more didactic and 'objective'.[31] But artists and writers in the new Russia, after the first years of elation, were not supposed to produce for the future, but for the people. The way to do so was to follow the particular artistic models the communists – for a variety of reasons – had decided to legitimise.[32] In the theatre they had to emulate Stanislavsky, in literature Gorky, they had to paint like good nineteenth-century bourgeois painters and write music respecting the traditional laws of harmony. It was as if the communists had given up trying to work out what Marxist-Leninist music or literature or cinema might be. They turned to a politically inoffensive mainstream culture and declared that to be the standard, as long as it did not overtly contradict the Party. The result was – at best – a notch or two above the proliferating mass popular culture of the West.

Some of the ideological difficulties facing the communist authorities can be easily explained. If they resorted to 'class belonging' in order to select the 'right' kind of writers, they would have had to eliminate virtually the whole of the nineteenth-century Russian canon, from Tolstoy, Turgenev and Push-kin to Chekhov and Dostoevsky.[33] If they resorted to ideology they would have faced a similar problem, since nineteenth-century Russian literature had not produced the equivalent of Zola and Dickens (who, with some effort, could be transformed into proto-socialists). In the twentieth century matters improved somewhat thanks to Gorky's *The Mother*, Dmitrii Furmanov's *Chapaev*, Nikolai Ostrovsky's *How the Steel was Tempered* and Mikhail Sholo-khov's *Virgin Soil Upturned*.[34] But one could not build a new literature on such a narrow basis.

The transition to a proletarian culture proved to be rather problematical. In schools and universities the old Tsarist textbooks were still widely used in the 1920s and even the 1930s. It was impossible to rewrite them rapidly to make them conform to the new politics, particularly when the new politics changed so rapidly. University students themselves were still overwhelmingly middle-class. A quota for the sons and daughters of peasants and workers was established in the 1930s but it was difficult to fill, because some minimum qualifications were indispensable, so the quota was filled with ideologically sound applicants. As a result one-third of places were taken up by 'commu-nist' students – including, presumably, some for whom communism was an avenue of social advancement.[35]

As for a 'proletarian culture', that was as elusive as ever. It was easier to try to centralise, bureaucratise and institutionalise everything. So, if writers or film-makers were unruly or unreliable, the problem could be assuaged through the formation of a single Writers' Union or a single film cartel (Soyuzkino) in the early 1930s. Shortly afterwards all writers were required to conform to the principles of socialist realism, a term first used in 1932. What this meant was not clear, except that it was supposed to be a 'truthful' account of social reality. In practice it expected writers and artists to be 'Party-minded', in the sense of being on the side of communism. It was actually a rather elusive concept, for it was not possible to know beforehand if something was for or against communism, and in any case, few literary works can be easily read merely as one or the other. The authorities indicated which works the writers had to follow as models. But these models provided few indications. The plots may have been formulaic, but then, most popular literature is based on formulae. Making all the baddies rich and all the heroes poor is hardly a hallmark of communist novels, since it is a common theme.[36] There is no point in applying highbrow criteria to 'socialist realist' novels, since they were intended to be literature for the masses, or at most middlebrow literature. As Katerina Clark puts it, there is no point berating Nikolai Ostrovsky, the author of the Soviet model classic *How the Steel was Tempered* (1932), for not being Henry James.[37] The 'democratic' goal of the Stalinist system was not to satisfy the taste of the élites, but to transform readers into 'model Soviet readers'. To some extent this goal was achieved. Surveys show that by the late 1940s, the high tide of socialist realism, Soviet readers genuinely liked Gorky's works, and enjoyed *How the Steel was Tempered* and Aleksandr Fadeyev's *The Young Guard* (1945), all of which were taught in Soviet schools.[38] This is hardly surprising. School can work. Flaubert and Jane Austen are more popular, respectively, in France and Great Britain than either is in Italy or Germany. The institutional shaping of taste does have effects.

Socialist realism overtly harked back to the bourgeois realist novels of the nineteenth century: Dickens and Balzac, not to speak of Zola, were the great models, the kind of literature which, in a simplified form, is in the best-seller lists throughout the West even in 2005. In the figurative arts socialist realism went even further back, to the celebratory (and popular) representations of Christianity. The themes, of course, had to be altered, something the abstract painter Pavel Filonov understood when he complied to pressure and produced in 1931 his *Tractor Workshop at the Putilov Factory*.

In effect all acceptable writers and artists were regarded as practising 'socialist realism', including wildly different people from Sholokov to Mayakovsky and, later, communist non-Russian writers including Pablo Neruda, Bertolt Brecht and Louis Aragon.[39]

'Socialist' Films

The cinema represented a particular problem for the Soviet authorities. Formally they had realised that film was going to be the mass art of the twentieth century. Lenin himself had declared it to be the most important of all the arts – or so it was said. The industry was nationalised in 1919, but what the state had acquired had been seriously damaged by the war, and suffered from a lack of equipment and spare parts. Distribution was essentially an urban affair in what was largely a rural country. Cinemas were forced to show old films repeatedly. The NEP U-turn led to the revival and development of private enterprise in the film industry, which by 1923 was largely in private hands. To raise money the authorities allowed the importation of foreign films, to be screened throughout the country so that the revenue could be ploughed back into making Soviet films. For this to be successful it was necessary to show films that would attract a large audience – and these were largely American.[40] By 1924 approximately 95 per cent of films distributed in the Soviet Union were foreign.[41] The Douglas Fairbanks picture *The Thief of Baghdad* (1924) was shown at Moscow's largest cinema for three and a half months, and the same actor's *The Mark of Zorro* (1920) was another great favourite. These films were not just appreciated by audiences, but also by critics.[42] American films were heavily promoted in the Soviet press. The American film industry had in fact taken over the cinema market of the first communist country in the world.[43]

In the 1930s, for political reasons, the import of foreign films decreased, but Soviet production did not increase, while audiences grew in size. Clearly, choice had been drastically reduced by the development of Stalinist policies. With literature there was already an imposing body of classical works that were widely accepted. But in films there was no repertoire, no classics. The great 'montage' Soviet film-makers, Pudovkin and Eisenstein, were revered among an élite – though some Soviet films were banned in the West: for instance, Pudovkin's *The Mother* was banned in France, Italy, the USA and Great Britain in the 1920s (West Ham Borough Council, a Labour local authority in east London, circumvented the ban in 1930).[44] Pudovkin's internationally successful *Storm over Asia* (1928), depicting a nationalist revolt in Mongolia, was suppressed in Australia after pressure from the British Colonial Office.

The problem was to produce a mass cinema, a cinema which would entertain the masses and at the same time please the communists. The works of Eisenstein and Pudovkin have remained established classics among film-lovers, but the most popular Soviet director in the 1920s was Yakov Protazanov (1881–1945). He had left Russia during the Civil War, having made some eighty films since 1911, but he returned in 1923 and became the major director of the Soviet screen between 1924 and 1930.[45] Part of his success was due to his practice of introducing suitable political elements into what were popular melodramas, thus pleasing the audience and keeping the communists happy. His science fiction film *Aelita* (1924) has as its hero an engineer who visits Mars in a spaceship of his construction, and falls in love with a Martian princess. The film, which included the depiction of a Bolshevik revolution on Mars, was launched in 'capitalist' style, with thousands of advertising leaflets dropped from the air.[46] In spite of the care taken to introduce 'Soviet' elements, *Aelita* was regularly attacked by film critics and political activists from 1924 to 1928.[47]

A further step towards developing the film industry was taken with the creation in 1930 of Soyuzkino, which centralised administration with a view of overseeing the transition from silent film to sound.[48] What was required was an efficient and rational system for imposing on film-makers a communist view of what films should be like. Since it was unclear what was the correct ideological position – and mistakes could be a matter of life and death – only forty-five films were released in 1934 – a considerable drop since 1928, when 109 films were released. Meanwhile a massive building programme of cinema outlets was successfully implemented, because here the Party's call was clear: the more the better. In 1927 there were just over 7,300 exhibition outlets, by 1933 the total had reached 27,500, half permanent and half with portable projectors.[49] There were fewer films, but a far greater number of Soviet citizens had access to them. Soviet film-makers had realised that the public liked American films more than Soviet films and European films. American films were funnier, more cheerful and life-affirming, and had happy endings and glamorous stars. Learning from the Americans became a motto just as film-makers were being urged to produce Soviet films for the Soviet masses.[50]

Soviet film-makers, most of whom had been trained in the pre-Revolutionary era, responded as best they could. Their main problem was a lack of clear guidelines. The censors were responsible to higher authorities. If they were too restrictive they would be criticised for not providing consumers with enjoyable yet politically correct stories. If they were too lax, they risked being associated with 'anti-Party' activities and with being 'objectively' 'enemies of the people'. Moreover, since censorship was ultimately a political question, the censors could not always be aware of an impending change of political line. In making a historical film it was easy to select the appropriate background – a revolutionary situation – and make sure that the good guys were peasants or workers or anti-Tsarists. It was more difficult to figure out what a Soviet melodrama or a Soviet comedy should be like. Still, film-makers tried, and not always unsuccessfully, as was the case with Sergei Komarov's 1927 *Mary Pickford's Kiss*, which satirised popular movie madness. The 'hero' of the film is a bumbling cinema usher whose moment of glory occurs when Mary Pickford and Douglas Fairbanks visit a Moscow film studio (a real event attended by 300,000 fans). He is kissed on the cheeks by Pickford, and finds himself lionised by female admirers of the American film stars. Needless to say, critics found the film 'decadent'.[51]

Such a film could not have been made ten years later. But greater repression did not make matters clearer. When Leonid Lukov made the second part of *Bol'shaia zhizn'* (A Great Life; the first part had been completed in 1939), he must have thought he would receive the blessing of the authorities. The film was after all about the reconstruction of the Donbass coalmines towards the end of the Second World War, and a celebration of the patriotism and courage of Soviet workers. Lukov may have suspected that a new phase of cultural repression was in the offing. In 1945 *Ordinary People* by Grigorii Kozintsev and Leonid Trauberg had been condemned, and Pudovkin had been forced to remake his *Admiral Nakhimov* (1946), criticised because it concentrated on court balls instead of the strategic aspects of the Crimean War. Eisenstein was too ill to redo *Ivan the Terrible Part Two* (1946), and the film was withdrawn. Eisenstein's Ivan was seen as a possible representation of Stalin, and not a flattering one: he was depicted as a brooding and isolated autocrat, no longer the man of the people of *Ivan the Terrible Part One* (1942). With the Donbass coalminers Lukov should have been on safer grounds. But he wasn't. At its meeting of 25 July 1946 the Arts Committee of the Ministry of the Cinema, i.e. the censors, had given the film its blessing. But on 9 August the Orgburo of the Central Committee of the Communist

Party of the Soviet Union denounced the film. The chairman Zhdanov, in the presence of Stalin, remorselessly enumerated its defects:

> The reconstruction of the Donbass coalmines is treated as if it were just a question of physical effort and not of the intelligent use of machinery and technology. The heroic workers are seen as acting almost independently of the state and of Party organisation – which are often represented as obstacles to surmount, or indifferent. The miners never seem to discuss the war (which is still going on).

During the discussion Stalin frequently intervened to support Zhdanov. Various members of the Arts Committee immediately 'understood' that they had made a mistake, and now demanded that the film be banned. Lukov too 'understood' and admitted that the film was flawed, explained how guilty he now felt and begged to be allowed to re-edit it, inserting new scenes so that 'Soviet money' not be wasted (the film was quite expensive). In spite of subsequent efforts by the Arts Committee, authorisation to re-edit the film was not granted. Nothing dramatic happened to Lukov. He was not arrested or deported, but for four years he made no films. Finally, in 1950, he was allowed to make a new version called *The Coalminers of the Donbass*, in which he demonstrated that he had 'understood' what was required of him.[52]

This illustrates the climate of fear which the Stalinist purges had brought about. It might be thought that the existence of state control over the publication and distribution of books and other cultural commodities would have been sufficient to ensure that nothing which was disapproved of by the regime could circulate. In such circumstances the large-scale deportation and murder of so many writers and intellectuals would have been unnecessary. Writers who cannot publish their works are not much of a threat. Part of the explanation for the purges no doubt resides with their unstoppable mechanism, so extensive as to appear to defy logic or necessity. Nevertheless, they also fulfilled a task which censorship on its own could not achieve: they enforced an unprecedented degree of self-censorship. The greater the degree of fear and uncertainty, the more effective they became. In a market economy the cultural entrepreneur risks his investments, the writer his or her time, and the possibility of commercial failure will deter some, perhaps many. But the fear of losing one's liberty or one's life is bound to constitute an even more formidable deterrent.

Even composers, few of whom were deported, and who on the whole fared far better than writers and musical administrators, were afraid – as was the case with Shostakovich.[53] His second opera, *Lady Macbeth of Mtsensk*

(1934), might have been criticised in some quarters in the West for its daring storyline. One can imagine a traditional Western critic condemning it using the same words as *Pravda*'s critic in 1936: 'coarse and vulgar'. But adverse reviews in the USSR at the time could mean losing one's life. The effects on Shostakovich and his music are still being debated. Was he in fact a loyal communist and a Soviet patriot? Or should one read into his music a constant denunciation of communism and Stalinism? His Fourth Symphony was withdrawn in the autumn of 1936 while it was being rehearsed. But was this because the music did not fit the new anti-formalist line, or because Shostakovich's patron Marshal Tukhachevsky was out of favour (he was arrested and executed in 1937)?[54] Was his rehabilitation following the Fifth Symphony (1937) due to its popular success (it remained the most popular of all his symphonies in the West too), or because he had subtitled it 'A Soviet Artist's Response to Just Criticism'?

In reality most music has no overt political meaning, save perhaps in the title which the composer may choose to give to his work. Shostakovich's Seventh Symphony ('Leningrad', 1942) was dedicated to 'our struggle with fascism, to our coming victory over the enemy, and to my native city, Leningrad', but if his memoirs (*Testimony*, published posthumously in 1979) are not a fake, he had planned most of the symphony before the siege of Leningrad, indeed before the war.[55] His Symphony No. 11 in G Minor (1957) is held to refer to the 1905 Revolution because of its subtitle, 'The Year 1905', but without such a clue few would have connected the musical sounds to 1905. As Igor Stravinsky wrote in his *Autobiography* (1935): 'Music is, by its very nature . . . powerless to express anything at all' – which is probably why Stravinsky's anti-communism and anti-Semitism are not apparent in his own works.[56]

Politics can be far more easily decoded in films than in music, yet Eisenstein's difficulties were not entirely due to his refusal to bend with the prevailing politics. In fact he often did bend. His *Staroe i novoe* (The General Line, 1929) was ostensibly made to celebrate Stalin's collectivisation of agriculture, but its technique was firmly based in Eisenstein's own artistic views. The problem with Eisenstein and others like him was that his market appeal, in the short term, was relatively narrow (though, of course, if one takes the long view, it is now evident that a film like *Ivan the Terrible* has been and will be watched when his more commercial rivals have been forgotten). Eisenstein did not fare any better when he went to Hollywood in 1930. One of the reasons he and other Soviet film-makers went to the USA was to learn about sound. But Eisenstein's experience was not a happy one. He had intended to film Theodore Dreiser's novel *An American Tragedy*, highlighting the social side and trying to develop new techniques such as interior monologue. But Paramount wanted a crime and love story, not a denunciation of American society, and they handed the film to Joseph von Sternberg. Eisenstein's *Que viva Mexico!* (1932) was drastically re-edited by the distributors. The Soviet authorities were asked to help financially, but refused. In fact Boris Shumyatsky, the great boss of Soyuzkino, the centralised Soviet film organisation, regarded Eisenstein in the same manner as did Hollywood: as an undisciplined genius who had no idea how to plan a budget or appeal to a wide audience. And well he might, since Russian audiences preferred Douglas Fairbanks's *Robin Hood* to *Battleship Potemkin*.[57] Even Lunacharsky had been aware that films had to please audiences, and could not systematically avoid depicting 'romantic experience of an intimate and psychological character'.[58] Eisenstein's *October* (1927), it was reported by a visitor, had been a failure in Russia.[59]

In Chapter 41 (page 820) we noted that before the First World War American-made films had many more shots than European ones.[60] This was still true in the 1920s: the average American film consisted of seven hundred shots, while a German one used 430. Eisenstein, in *Potemkin*, used (some would say over-used) montage to an unparalleled extent: 1,300 shots, with an average duration of three seconds.[61] In the 1930s Boris Shumyatsky turned against the obsession with montage which characterised the great Soviet directors such as Eisenstein and Lev Kuleshov. This was formalism, he declared, using the key term of abuse adopted by the new Soviet aesthetics. There should be a proper script, conventional narrative, a plot, real actors instead of non-professionals representing types (*typage*). Shumyatsky would have been far more acceptable in Hollywood than Eisenstein. Indeed, eager to learn from the West, he led a delegation in 1935 to Paris, London and Hollywood. Alarmed to discover that the USSR was producing fewer films than one Hollywood studio, he launched the idea of a Soviet Hollywood in the south-western corner of the Crimea: Kinogorod (Cine-City). But this never progressed beyond the planning stage. Stalin did not spare him: Shumyatsky was arrested in 1937 and executed in 1938.[62]

The Soviet cinema, however, enjoyed an advantage that its counterparts in western Europe did not: it was protected from American competition (to the detriment, it could be argued with much justification, of Soviet audiences). In the 1930s very few American films were shown. During the war there was a general reappraisal of the American cinema and its contribution to that of the USSR. Friendly delegations were exchanged, and expressed their mutual approval.[63] Such trends could not be allowed to proceed, since it was clear to all except the most naïve observer that, in a situation of free trade, the USSR would be swamped by American films, while few Russian films would be seen outside a handful of New York art houses.

The New Socialist Camp

The aftermath of the Second World War resulted in almost all of central and eastern Europe coming under the control of the Soviet Union. The centralisation in the production and distribution of culture was accelerated. It would probably have occurred in any case, though less oppressively or drastically. The war had heightened nationalist feelings and had provided a new set of narrative possibilities connected to the description of heroic resistance against Nazi oppressors. Communist reconstruction and nationalism could proceed concurrently. In most countries of eastern and central Europe the passage from interwar nation-building to post-war communist reconstruction proceeded fairly smoothly. Education, as in most of the rest of Europe, was centralised by the various Ministries of Education. They decided on school curricula, programmes and textbooks. The advent of communism meant that all that needed to be revised was the content of the history and literature textbooks, not the way in which education was administered. Pre-war nation-building policies had simply shifted to the new regimes.

In pre-war Yugoslavia, for instance, approved textbooks included selections from Serbian, Croatian and Slovenian literature, as well as a large number of folk songs, riddles and poems.[64] A supra-national epic representing 'Yugoslav' culture was required, and in 1947, as the country was preparing to celebrate the hundredth anniversary of the publication of Petar Petrović Njegoš's *The Mountain Wreath*, it was thought that this could serve the purpose, even though the author was a prince and a bishop. The problem was that it was a Serb work, and Njegoš had been favoured by the previous regime. This did not stop the celebrations. New editions were printed in Serbia, Croatia and Bosnia, and a new translation appeared in Slovenia, as well as the first ever Macedonian translation (25,000 copies were published in Montenegro, Njegoš's birthplace). Njegoš's heroes were described as the antecedents of those of World War II, and the fact that these heroes were fighting against the Muslims was glossed over (Muslims represented 12 per cent of the population of the new Yugoslavia).[65] National modern literature was represented by the partisan epic, notably by Vladimir Nazor's *With the Partisans* (written in 1943–44), a memoir of the author's experience with Tito's resistance forces, and Dobrica Ćosić's *Far Away is the Sun* (1951), about a group of Serbian partisans and the conflict between two conceptions of the resistance: a regional one, connected to the liberation of the various nations (Croats, Serbs, etc.) which make up Yugoslavia, and the 'truly' national one (from the point of view of the new regime), where the war is one for the liberation of the whole Yugoslav nation.[66]

Partisan novels sprouted all over Europe, regardless, once again, of the growing Cold War divide. Their function was obvious: on the one hand they offered readers an exciting war narrative, action-packed, with clearly defined villains (the Nazis, the fascists and their various stooges) and heroes (the partisans, representing the entire people and, by implication, the reader). The occasional departure from the prescribed interpretation, for instance the Italian Italo Calvino's *Il Sentiero dei nidi di ragno* (The Path to the Nest of Spiders, 1947), would not fail to arouse anger and distress.

In Poland one of the most successful television heroes was Kapitan Kloss, an officer of the Polish secret services during the war who, disguised as a German officer, is able to neutralise many operations of the German HQ. The case of East Germany is particularly interesting. The newly formed DDR had, after all, the same cultural traditions as the Federal Republic: the same language, literacy rates, educational system, etc. The fundamental reason the eastern part of the country became a communist state is because the Red Army stopped where it did, rather than because of any greater strength of socialism there (though as a matter of fact it contained large areas where the left had been strong before the advent of Hitler). Like all regimes the new government had no particular problems with the preceding high bourgeois and pre-bourgeois culture. It annexed *in toto* all the great glories of the past: Goethe, Schiller, Heine, classical German philosophy. It looked as if the DDR was poised to oversee a great renaissance of German culture. It did not start with a clean slate, but it offered a favourable terrain to all those who wished to contribute to a revival of 'good' culture. The war and Nazism provided an excellent framework for an endless stream of films and novels. Left-wing writers and artists who had left Germany in the 1930s were more attracted to the DDR than to the Federal Republic, which, led by the elderly, authoritarian and conservative Konrad Adenauer, seemed to incarnate the least pleasant aspects of Wilhelmine culture. Many talented exiled writers opted to return to the DDR: the playwright Bertolt Brecht, the poet Johannes R. Becher (one of whose poems provided the lyrics for the new East German national anthem), the composer Hanns Eisler (who set it to music) and the novelist Anna Seghers. Alfred Döblin's novel *Hamlet oder die lange Nacht hat ein Ende* (Hamlet, or The End of the Long Night) was first published in the DDR.[67]

The East German communist establishment favoured imitations of politically correct Russian novels: stories set against the background of the great achievements of the construction of socialism, such as building power stations. But the writers who had returned were not young innocents trying to make their way in a politically new environment. The very fact of their exile meant that they valued their intellectual independence. Those who had accepted communism had done so not in order to prosper, but often because they regarded communism as Nazism's worst foe. Writers like Anna Seghers returned well acquainted with the new American novel (i.e. Hemingway and Faulkner), James Joyce, French existentialism and Kafka. Bertolt Brecht was already a prestigious writer when he returned. His opting for the DDR was not entirely ideological. He had much greater freedom to produce his plays in communist Germany than he would have had in the USA, where market considerations (and also anti-communism) would have considerably restricted productions that were not in any case regarded as very commercial.

Paradoxically, some left-leaning intellectuals, at least in the years immediately following the war, developed a form of pro-Americanism which was the mirror image of the anti-Americanism of traditional intellectuals. They saw in American culture the fresh breath of modernity, a potential ally in the struggle against conventional forms of music, the rigid rules of the Academy, the stuffy upholding of élitist values. Eventually, particularly in the 1960s and afterwards, to affect to like US culture could be seen as an expression of political dissidence, but in the first decade after the war this was not so. This progressive intelligentsia was perfectly able to differentiate between the policies of the American political establishment and American music, American films and American comic strips. The traditional intellectuals of western Europe did exactly the opposite. They regarded US foreign policy as their chief protection against the expansion of totalitarian communism, and supported it with ambiguity. But they also despised the manifestations of American popular culture: from the food and drink (Coca-Cola and chewing gum were the main targets) to the music ('barbaric African rhythm', it was said, with barely disguised racism).

A further complication was introduced into the equation by the adoption, on the part of the various communist regimes, of a form of nationalism required for their own nation-building. The intellectual allies of these regimes turned out to be the more traditional intelligentsia, who had relatively few problems with the new communist establishment. It glorified national culture, and so did they. It kept US popular culture out, thus protecting their own captive market. It refused to commercialise culture, thus ensuring a ready audience for their own work. It decried experimentation, thus upholding their own values. It stood steadfastly against 'immoral' behaviour, just as the traditionalists had hoped. The unwritten contract between the regimes and the traditionalists was not always a smooth one, and the latter had to be careful, pay lip-service and be more politically aware than they would have liked – but they had little choice.

The most interesting site of this complex conflict was the DDR. Here any cultural policy would have to face constant problems connected to the newly divided country's recent past. Consider jazz. This could be regarded as an innovative and exciting rhythm, the expression of the 'struggle of the Negro people' against US racism. Yet it was despised by much of the traditional music establishment. The communists were invited to join in the condemnation. Was not this music clear evidence of American degenerate culture, characteristic of imperialism in its decaying phase? Yet matters were not quite so simple. When jazz had arrived in Germany in the 1920s it had been regarded by the right-wing nationalists as music created by 'niggers', linked to primitive sexuality and marketed by Jews.[68] Yet even the Nazis never banned jazz completely from the airwaves.[69] And in the 1960s a Marxist musicologist of high calibre, the Hungarian János Maróthy, defended jazz, pointing to its 'proletarian' antecedents, 'the common meeting point when the former Negro slave and the former white smallholder, petty bourgeois, etc. had met in the common proletarian fate, at the time of the first great boom of American capitalist development'.[70]

The DDR had to compromise. Keeping American culture out had proved to be impossible. In early 1958 the East German Ministry of Culture imposed a quota on broadcast music programmes: 'only' 40 per cent of the output could consist of imports from the West, but some youth clubs run by the communist youth organisation continued to use music from Western radio stations (see pages 1272–5 for a wider analysis).[71] Such compromises were dictated by necessity. Unlike the citizens of other communist states, East Germans, and East Berliners in particular, were free to come and go from West Berlin until the erection of the Wall in 1961. Thus for the first fifteen years of the post-war era, crucial years for the penetration of American culture into Europe, East Berliners went shopping in West Berlin, had access to US films, tuned in to US music on their radios, and were perfectly aware of the sexual icons of the West from Marilyn Monroe to Brigitte Bardot, and of Elvis Presley.[72]

In Hungary, as elsewhere in eastern and central Europe, the establishment of a communist regime in March 1948 led to the nationalisation of the film industry. This provided both economic protection, since foreign films were rationed, and funding for domestic production – as long as the films were politically acceptable or inoffensive. Socialist realism was defined somewhat loosely, meaning a realistic film which could be understood by a wider audience. In this sense most Hollywood films were 'socialist realist'. Socialist 'feel-good' optimism required a happy ending – as did Hollywood conventions. The war and the communist-led resistance against the fascists and the Nazis offered abundant material for celebratory and exciting narratives, a further parallel with the production of war films in the USA and Great Britain, and indeed everywhere. Domestic production remained, of course, for domestic consumption. The only section of the international film market which Hungary could exploit was that of quality films, particularly when some gradual liberalisation occurred in the years after the events of 1956. State subsidies, protection from the excessive American competition, openness to the influences of the French *nouvelle vague*, Italian neo-realism and the new Polish cinema, and the growth of television, which provided a new outlet for the production of cartoons and shorts, led to a significant 'quality' development of the Hungarian cinema and the international fame of Hungarian new wave directors such as Miklós Jancsó in the 1960s, above all with *Szegénylegények* (The Hopeless, 1965, shown in the West under the title *The Round-Up*).

Meanwhile in the Soviet Union the purges of the 1930s had cleared the ground of numerous pre-revolutionary writers. A new generation of writers committed to communism had occupied much of the literary space, supported by the powerful cultural machine of the regime. The Great Patriotic War against fascism had created a political consensus, a shared memory, and had provided writers and film-makers with an endless stream of narrative possibilities. This, of course, is hardly surprising. In the USA the flood of Second World War films and novels has lasted some sixty years (as the commercial success of Steven Spielberg's 1998 film *Saving Private Ryan* shows), and – apart from Pearl Harbor – no American territory was bombed at any time during the war. The USSR, on the other hand, was invaded and occupied, much of its industrial capacity was destroyed, the inhabitants of Leningrad starved to death, and total casualties reached, it is claimed, twenty million victims. The subsequent 'obsession' with the war is hardly surprising. It provided unifying cultural themes which the construction of communism, the Five-Year Plans and the collectivisation of the countryside could not offer. The new writers, as Isaiah Berlin reported from Russia to the British Foreign Office at the end of 1945, were 'facile, naïve, and copious, varying from crude and wooden orthodoxy to considerable technical skill, capable at times of moving, at others of genuinely gay, and often vivid, journalistic reportage'. The most successful and most representative of these, according to Berlin, was Konstantin Simonov, a journalist, playwright and poet whose work, like that of other authors in the same mould, was of 'impeccably orthodox sentiment' with the right kind of Soviet hero, 'brave, puritanical, simple, noble, altruistic, entirely devoted to the service of his country . . . tough, hearty, capable, resolute, single-minded young engineers or political commissars ("engineers of human souls"), or army commanders, shy and manly lovers, etc . . .'[73] It is not difficult to see behind this characterisation the standardised hero of folk tales, of boys' adventure stories, of Jules Verne and some Dumas, of the American western (one immediately thinks of the characters played by John Wayne).

The proliferation of such narratives in the USSR was facilitated by a vast increase in literacy, one of the great achievements of Soviet communism. Accounts of Western eyewitnesses such as Isaiah Berlin vouch for the book hunger manifested after the war, as evidenced by 'the crowded bookshops with their understocked shelves, the eager interest displayed by the government employees who run them, the fact that even such newspapers as *Pravda* and *Izvestia* are sold out within minutes of their rare appearance in the kiosks'.[74] Such popular respect for the book preceded communism and was symbolised by the traditional Russian habit of cutting a newly born baby boy's umbilical cord on a book, in the hope that he would become an educated person and climb the social ladder.[75] Book hunger was also enhanced by the political decision to keep the price of books at an artificially very low level – something that the transition to market democracy in the 1990s brought to an end.

The Soviet Union was also committed to a strong form of cultural autonomy, as long as it was quite separate from politics. It encouraged folk culture, but repressed any real or imagined threat of separatism. Minority languages were protected. Literary works, old and new, foreign and national, were rapidly translated into the various languages of the 'nationalities' of the USSR – and from them, especially from Ukrainian, Georgian, Armenian, Uzbek and Tajik. Between 1798 (when Ukrainian was first used for printing) and 1917, only 3,214 Ukrainian-language titles had been published. This was of course partly due to the low level of literacy of the peasantry, but also because of Tsarist language policies. The situation deteriorated in 1863 – after the Polish uprising – when the Tsarist government allowed 'good literature' in Ukrainian but banned religious and popular books in the language.[76] After 1905 the ban was lifted. Ukraine flourished in the 1920s. In 1926 the Soviet regime sought to expand literacy there, at a time when less than half the population was literate. It was decided to use Ukrainian, since it would be easier if people were taught to read their native language – which in any case is closely related to Russian. By 1932, 89 per cent of children were taught in Ukrainian schools.[77] These policies led to a steady decrease in the publication of books in Russian in Ukraine. In 1923, Russian books made up 80 per cent of all titles; by 1926 less than half were, and by 1928 two-thirds of all titles were in Ukrainian.[78]

What had happened was a total reverse of policies. The Tsarists had allowed learned books in Ukrainian, and only allowed Russian for popular books. Now scholarly works were mainly in Russian, but popular literature and schoolbooks were mainly in Ukrainian.[79] While encouraging the development of the cultures of the various nationalities within its domain, the USSR harshly repressed all attempts to use cultural pride for political, i.e. nationalist, ends. Kazakh folk-dancing was promoted; Kazakh nationalism was banned. The policies remained highly contradictory: Stalin's Russification proceeded at the same time as the promotion of regional national cultures.[80] Communist policies towards culture, in spite of the rhetoric which occasionally accompanied it, were characterised from start to finish by uncertainty. Some have seen this uncertainty as the result of trying to steer a path between the necessity of pleasing both the political masters and the audience. This view is too simple, since it assumes that the politicians knew what was required, and that the audience was undifferentiated. In reality cultural production had to proceed as it always had: by trial and error, by exploring boundaries without racing too far ahead and losing touch with its market. Herein lies the common trait shared by culture under capitalism and culture under communism.

45

Fascism

Nationalism in Culture

IN THE NINETEENTH CENTURY, nationalist culture was about patriotism and nation-building. In the twentieth century, with the end of multi-national empires such as the Russian and the Austro-Hungarian, and new nations emerging, economic protectionism was added to the package. It was not sufficient to produce one's 'own' culture; it was necessary to keep that of foreigners out. This received the enthusiastic backing of the vast majority of domestic producers. Reducing the competition for patriotic reasons seemed to be the best of both worlds. Consumers were less keen. In Italy in the 1920s the nationalist and fascist Lydia Dosio De Liguoro tried to persuade upper-class Italian women to shun Parisian cloth and fashion, but her success was limited.[1] The *Zeitgeist* was not yet ready for the made-in-Italy.

Cultural nationalism was not the prerogative only of the right. In the 1930s communists and socialists – who until then did not really have a policy on culture – embraced it, seeking to consolidate their national credentials. In France, on 14 July 1935, when the Popular Front against fascism was launched, Jean Perrin, the 1926 Nobel Prize-winner for physics and a socialist, called on the left to rescue all the symbols of the Motherland from the clutches of the right:

> They have taken Jeanne d'Arc, a daughter of the people, abandoned by
> the King, whose victory was achieved thanks to the people's struggles.
> She was burnt at the stake by the same people who then turned her into
> a saint. They have tried to take away from you the flag of '89, this noble
> tricolour, banner of the victories of the Republic, Valmy, Jemmapes,
> Hohenlinden and Verdun . . . symbol of the freedoms you have achieved.
> It will be hoisted next to the red flag, now the banner of the Soviet Union

– symbol of the hopes of the wretched. Finally they have even tried to steal from you the heroic 'Marseillaise', the revolutionary and fierce hymn whose sound made the thrones of Europe shake.[2]

Yet, apart from a few celebrations, no patriotic mass culture emerged in France or anywhere else. Much of this cultural nation-building was a variation of nineteenth-century Romanticism; but 'popular' arts and crafts were too weak a foundation for the anti-modernist desire to reinvent traditional folk culture.

Attempts were made in almost all European countries, whether fascist, communist or liberal democratic, to develop or rescue a national art. In drama, for instance, there was the Italian Società di Arte Filodrammatica, in Britain the Village Drama Society, in Poland the Association of People's Theatres and its equivalents, while Russia sought to give the people an amateur theatre which included 'the best' of what was modern and national. There were similar developments in music and literature. But such rearguard action could hardly withstand the increased professionalism of mass culture.

In Spain the Franco regime – which, after all, lasted longer than its authoritarian counterparts in Nazi Germany and fascist Italy – also failed to create a national popular culture. Spanish historical film epics never managed to match those of Hollywood. The dictatorship, unable to produce a distinctive culture of its own, simply manipulated existing forms and suppressed the alternatives.[3] Part of the problem was that until the 1950s there was little modern mass culture in Spain. Few people went to the cinema, even fewer read books or newspapers. Popular culture was essentially Catholic culture. This, of course, was for years supportive of the regime, but there was nothing distinctively Francoist about it, except for the particularly bellicose brand of 'national-Catholicism' which the Church had deployed during and after the Civil War, when its crusading zeal led to the terrifying massacres of those regarded as belonging to the 'Judeo-Masonic-Soviet front'.[4]

And when it came to morality, censorship in democratic countries could be just as fierce as in clerical-authoritarian ones. In the new Irish Free State, for instance, strict censorship was established against 'filthy' literature, with the strong backing of various Catholic associations such as the Irish Vigilance Association, the Catholic Truth Society and its Evil Literature Committee. Protestants were hardly more libertarian.[5]

The idea that countries devoid of democratic institutions are able to establish total control over culture and education is unwarranted. The concept of totalitarianism often deployed in such instances is largely a propagandistic notion promulgated by the opponents of the dictatorship – and occasionally, as was the case with Mussolini and some of his supporters, by their proponents. Dictatorships can repress their obvious enemies, but this leaves the field open for what the dictatorships themselves are forced to regard as 'legitimate' positions. The spectrum may be narrower, but ideological conflicts continue within the interstices of what is permissible; they can never be eliminated. Thus in post-war Franco's Spain, when the last vestiges of the Civil War had been eliminated in a bloodbath, the communists and socialists banned, the press and publishers brought under control, there was still considerable competition between the Falange Party (a near-fascist party forced by Franco to merge into a broader National Movement) and the Roman Catholic Church. As always, control of education was the real objective of this struggle, with the predictable triumph of the Catholics, who enjoyed wider popular support. But the Catholics had to concede something to the regime as well. In exchange for the *de facto* privatisation of schools, which resulted in well over half the education system coming under clerical control, the ideology promulgated conformed to that of Franco's nationalism: the elementary primer *Yo soy Español* by Agustín Serrano de Haro began the history of Spain with Adam and Eve, and ended with the benevolent regime of Franco, via a triumphalist description of how Spain had civilised Latin America.[6] Recent history, including the Civil War, was hardly touched upon. Throughout the school system, teachers – like their counterparts in most European countries – were expected to cover the entire history of civilisation, beginning with its 'cradle', i.e. the Greeks and the Romans, rather than for instance the Sumerians or the ancient Egyptians.

Schools, however, have little effect on popular culture, and this had become a major preoccupation of all political forces. Throughout the fascist period, Italians continued to discuss the problems first aired by Ruggero Bonghi in the middle of the nineteenth century in his *Why Italian Literature is not Popular in Italy* (see page 485). Increased nationalism brought about a new dimension: why is Italian literature not popular in the rest of Europe? This was the core of Ercole Reggio's lament in an article in *Nuova antologia* on 1 October 1930.[7] How could it be otherwise, asked Gramsci, when Italian literature was not popular even in Italy? It was no use, he added later, to complain – as the journal *Critica fascista* had done (1 August 1930) – of the serialisation in two major daily newspapers of novels by the ever-popular Alexandre Dumas. This complaint would have been stronger, added Gramsci, if Italians produced popular novels.[8]

Fascist autarchy, or self-sufficiency (and the Depression), had reduced the import of foreign goods, but not the number of translations, which increased remarkably:[9]

TRANSLATIONS INTO ITALIAN, 1925 AND 1935			
Year	From French	From English	From German
1925	109	27	24
1935	393	327	185

The success of foreign writers worried the regime, but it also alarmed – for obvious reasons – young Italian writers. Vitaliano Brancati, then a fascist, later an anti-fascist and author of fine novels like *Don Giovanni in Sicilia* and *Il Bel Antonio*, did not hesitate to ask his fascist friends to stop the publisher Arnaldo Mondadori printing all this foreign 'pornography'.[10] Umberto Fracchia, in the review *L'Italia letteraria*, demanded legislation to limit the number of translations. Some writers, of course, did not need any protection; they were popular and, usually, pro-fascist: Mario Appelius (1894–1946, known as the Duce's megaphone and author of the soundbite 'May God extra-damn the English' – which sounds better in Italian: *Dio stramaledica gli inglesi*), Antonio Beltramelli (1879–1930), Arnaldo Cipolla (1879–1938, 'The Italian Kipling', who volunteered to fight in Ethiopia) and Yvon De Begnac (1913–83), who wrote a biography of Mussolini. These are now regarded as minor writers, if they are not forgotten altogether. But most well-remembered figures had joined fascism with some enthusiasm, often well before it became prudent to do so: Puccini, never a radical either politically or musically, Pirandello, Italy's greatest playwright, and Giovanni Gentile, one of the leading philosophers, eventually Minister of Education.

Finally, in 1938, with economic protectionism in full swing, the regime decreed that booksellers' shop windows should not give more than 25 per cent of their space to foreign authors, and that publishers needed a permit to translate their works.[11] Previously it had forbidden dailies to serialise foreign novels on their third page, which had great status in Italian newspapers as *the* cultural page – though this injunction was not always respected.[12] None of these restrictions meant that foreign authors were banned. The timidity of such moves shows how hampered were the authorities: real cultural protectionism, such as a ban on imports, was impossible.

Complaints about a literary foreign invasion were frequent in Italian literary circles. Yet literary periodicals played a considerable role in bringing prestigious foreign writers to the attention of the élites. The Rome journal *La Ronda* published Thomas Mann, G.K. Chesterton and George Bernard Shaw. *Novecento*, also in Rome, was initially written in French and published James Joyce, Ilya Ehrenburg, André Malraux and Virginia Woolf. In Florence *Solaria* published Marcel Proust, Ernest Hemingway, André Gide and a chapter from Joyce's *Ulysses*.[13] In Milan, Enzo Ferrieri and his journal *Il Convegno* (1920) called for 'reconnecting' with contemporary European high culture (meaning Kafka, Thomas Mann, Joyce and D.H. Lawrence), implying that Italy was little more than a provincial backwater.[14] Paradoxically it was the Ministry of Culture itself, with an ordinance of August 1929, that reined in the cultural nationalism of the police, guilty of making life difficult for the Italian publishers of Gorky, Dostoevsky, Tolstoy and Jack London.[15]

The more modern sectors of the Italian fascist literary establishment were frankly pro-American. Indeed, when it was decided in the early 1930s to create Italy's first school of journalism, its director, Ermanno Amicucci, thought it should take as a model the Columbia School of Journalism.[16] The 'pro-US' modernisers acted as a powerful lobby inside Italy's publishing establishment. Of course the more nationalist were alarmed at the American invasion, but this did not stop the publisher Valentino Bompiani from translating Erskine Caldwell, John Steinbeck and James M. Cain (whose 1934 novel *The Postman Always Rings Twice* was turned – in 1943 – into the film *Ossessione* by Luchino Visconti, set in Italy and scripted by Paolo Alatri, who in the 1950s was in charge of the Italian Communist Party's cultural policy). Nor did fascism stop the publication, in the middle of the war, of an anthology of American writing, unambiguously called *Americana* and edited by the pro-communist Elio Vittorini (translator of Edgar Allan Poe). Throughout the 1930s the Turin publishing houses Carlo Frassinelli and Giulio Einaudi published a steady stream of translations from the USA, from classics such as Melville to Sherwood Anderson's influential short stories, Gertrude Stein's experimental novels and Edgar Lee Masters's poetry. Mondadori published Sinclair Lewis, John Dos Passos, William Faulkner, William Saroyan, Poe, Nathaniel Hawthorne, Henry James, Edith Wharton, Frank Norris, Theodore Dreiser and so on.[17]

Those who complained about the foreign invasion often did not understand the economics of publishing. It was always far less risky to translate authors who had been successful abroad (and who had a good chance of being successful in Italy too) than to risk promoting unknown Italian writers, particularly given their poor track record in terms of popular fiction. Foreign authors were cheap: the royalties demanded were only 5 per cent or so. Italian writers exacted between 15 and 25 per cent, and did not sell as many books. Consequently Italian books were comparatively more expensive than foreign ones, and anyway, publishers assumed that they would not sell many, making an inexpensive edition unprofitable. Better print a few copies, sell them as luxuries to connoisseurs, and make real money with foreign books. These, of course, had to be translated, but Italy was full of unemployed intellectuals more than willing to translate a novel for little money. Some of them even knew foreign languages. So publishing foreign books was a way of subsidising Italian writers. With a few exceptions, even successful Italian writers could not possibly earn a reasonable sum unless they wrote a book nearly every year, because their works were hardly ever reprinted. So they were forced to dabble in journalism, review books, publish short stories in newspapers . . . and translate foreign authors.

Italian writers, like writers everywhere, were never able to present a united front to 'protect' themselves from foreign imports, the way steel magnates were able to lobby in favour of tariffs. Those already established did not mind so much, because the flood of foreign books made life difficult for local talents who might have moved into their niche. Those who were not famous, having published little or nothing, were in no position to demand anything. How could they compete with Simenon: the rights to his novels were not expensive, and the books themselves were short and could be translated easily. One did not even need to design original covers, but simply buy the French ones. Rights, translation and design costs would come to less than 1,500 lire. Even adding printing and distribution costs and the book-sellers' cut, publishers did not need to sell too many of them at three lire each to make a profit. And Simenon's books actually sold between 10,000 and 16,000 copies each.[18]

But even when conditions changed, the love of Italian readers for foreign novels – or, to put it differently, the chronic inability or unwillingness of Italian writers to write popular novels – seemed to be an enduring feature of the Italian literary landscape. As late as 1998 an article by Donata Righetti in the *Corriere della sera* bore a headline which could have been written at any time in the previous hundred years: '*Bestseller, ma dove sono finiti gli scrittori italiani?*' (But where are all the Italian writers?).[19]

Fascist Books

The regime did its best to promote Italian books, fascist books in particular. In 1934 the journal *Nuova antologia* launched a new prize for a 'novel for the fascist era'. The results were disheartening. Most of the forty-four novels submitted were unreadable and a little 'too fascist' even for a jury which was chaired by Luigi Federzoni, then President of the Senate, and included, along with some of the best-known critics of the time, Giuseppe Bottai (Minister of Education 1936–43). When the jury reconvened on 16 December 1936 it found that most of the authors had taken the 'fascist' injunction a little too literally, and had been preoccupied with not missing out any of the significant dates of the fascist era. They felt unable to award the first prize to anyone, but gave the second to *Questi ragazzi* by Romolo Moizo and the third to Mario Massa's *Scatena*. The most remarkable aspect of the jury's report is that it never explained how either book was particularly fascistic.[20] Thus the eponymous hero of *Scatena*, poor and disabled, does not behave in a particularly fascist way until the very end, when he finds happiness in Rome's Piazza Venezia mixing with the crowd listening to the Duce. To modify the novel's ideological angle would have required little more than substituting – say – Stalin and Red Square in Moscow, or the Pope in Piazza San Pietro, for Mussolini.

The regime then tried to manufacture a best-seller: *La Marcia su Gondar* (1937) by Achille Starace, then National Secretary of the Partito Nazionale Fascista. This was an account and celebration of Italian victories in the 1935–36 Ethiopian campaign by one of its participants. It was published by the compliant Arnaldo Mondadori and printed in 100,000 copies, an absurdly high print run. The entire Fascist Party was mobilised in the marketing campaign. In each province a Mondadori sales representative would turn up with an official letter of introduction to the local fascist boss, who in turn put pressure on the local bookshops. In spite of this the take-up was poor, particularly in central Italy. Booksellers did not mind fascism, but they did mind cluttering their shops with unwanted stock. Mondadori complained to the authorities, providing a list of defaulting cities.[21] It was possible to force bookshops to stock a book, but it was more difficult to get people to buy it, let alone read it. There are limits to the 'totalitarian' state. As it turned out, Starace's book probably did better than Mondadori's other 'fascist' books. No doubt Mondadori would have liked to make money out of these as well, but he regarded them as costs incurred as part of his long-term strategy to become the Duce's favourite publisher.[22]

The problem was that the 100 per cent 'politically correct' book – to use a modern expression for a concept which has been around for centuries – is very difficult to achieve, since most books worth reading are open to more than one interpretation. For instance, Emil Ludwig's *Conversations with Mussolini* (1932), which consisted of a lengthy interview with the Duce, might have been expected to please the regime. The author was sympathetic to Mussolini – 'I recognise that fascism has achieved great things for Italy,' he wrote in the introduction[23] – and Mussolini was sympathetic to the interviewer. The book, first published abroad, was widely regarded as presenting a positive image of fascism. The German text had been submitted beforehand to Mussolini, who had warmly approved it. But there was uncertainty among his advisers. Mussolini, aware that the book was aimed at a foreign public, had presented himself as a benevolent, tolerant, almost liberal politician, willing to enter into debate, allowing others to disagree with him, claiming that 'I make twenty mistakes and I admit it.'[24] This did not match his Italian image, as a superman who was always right.[25] Moreover, Mussolini had made some statements which, in his own interests, should have been left out, particularly those in which he showed his contempt for Italians ('The masses, until they are organised, are nothing but a flock of sheep') and his antediluvian views of women: 'Women must obey . . . I am against feminism of all kinds. In our state women must not count . . . Do you know how the Anglo-Saxons will end up? As a matriarchy!'[26] Mondadori – who had sold the foreign rights to publishers in thirteen countries – had prudently sent the proofs to Mussolini, and was already advertising the forthcoming book as *the* authorised text.[27] Mussolini, by now better briefed, was unwilling to prevent publication of the first edition, which had sold 20,000 copies, but insisted that Mondadori should let him have a look at the second edition. Various changes were made, designed to bring the text into line with conventional morality and not offend the Church, but this edition sold only a few copies. After 1938 Mondadori was expressly forbidden from reissuing the book, which could have caused the Duce embarrassment. As the anti-Semitic campaign was then in full swing, readers would have found odd those passages in which he claimed: 'There is no anti-Semitism in Italy. Italian Jews are good citizens, and fought bravely during the war. They have high positions in the universities, the army and the banks.'[28] Besides, Ludwig was

Jewish – as was Margherita Sarfatti, Mussolini's ex-mistress and author of *Dux*, a very successful biography of her former lover.

The conflict between politics and the market was reproduced in the public libraries. Librarians stocked everything the authorities wanted them to, but they also had to attract readers. And the almost exclusively middle-class readers wanted the usual stuff: the canonical literature of the nineteenth century and early twentieth century. They wanted Dostoevsky, Tolstoy and Gogol; they wanted the great French classics (Hugo, Dumas, Flaubert and Zola); they wanted Kipling and Jack London. And they also wanted the traditional Italian fare: Salvatore Gotta's fiction, made popular by numerous film adaptations, and *Pinocchio*, Salgari and De Amicis.[29] This presented problems. Teachers and priests were not keen on *Pinocchio*. It was clearly not high culture; it contained a subversive streak and strange allusions to religion, such as the crucifixion of Pinocchio. Salgari was anti-British, which was fine, but he was clearly 'low' culture, and none of his heroes were Italian or had even set foot in Italy. Salgari might as well have been a foreign novelist, which no doubt was part of his appeal. De Amicis's *Cuore* too was problematical. The book (see pages 852–3) was an eternal favourite; it was patriotic; it was a celebration of Italian unity. But, alas, De Amicis had been a staunch socialist (as had Mussolini, once).

The Italian books that were most popular during fascism were those that had been popular before, such as the slightly daring novels of Pitigrilli and Guido Da Verona, whose *Mimì Bluette, fiore del mio giardino* (see page 645) sold, it is thought, some three hundred thousand copies after its publication in 1916, as did Pitigrilli's *Mammiferi di Lusso* (1920).[30] Pitigrilli (1893–1975) was a popular author throughout the fascist period, though there is little that could be regarded as 'fascist' in his novels. Born Dino Segre, a bourgeois and assimilated Turinese Jew, Pitigrilli was a cynical purveyor of aphorisms making fun of ideals, feelings, literary society and everything which was hallowed and sacred, thus providing a comforting read for those to whom nothing is sacred – or who pretended to be part of a cool, cynical upper-class bourgeoisie instead of members of the frightened petty bourgeoisie which constituted the real core of Pitigrilli's readership. In *Cocaina* (1921) the 'hero' is an uninhibited journalist, Tito Arnaudi, down and out in Paris, whose mistress is Kalantan Ter-Gregorianz, an eccentric Armenian *femme fatale*. In a low dive where cocaine is snorted he meets a pimp who tells him how he turned Cristina, an honest working girl, into a prostitute:

'Cristina and I worked in a factory where five hundred women were working. They all had tuberculosis or, at the very least, were anaemic. The boss exploited them. I couldn't get them all out. So I got Cristina out. Now I exploit her. I don't see why I am any more despicable than the boss who has five hundred girls on the go. And anyway, her new job is less tiring, more hygienic and better paid. They say it dirties the mind. Who cares, as long as the hands are clean.'[31]

Pitigrilli's apparent immorality was a way to *épater les bourgeois*, a marketing ploy exploited before him by the Dadaists, the futurists and previously by Oscar Wilde, D'Annunzio and many others. The ploy worked also because he knew what his audience really was: a new reading public emerging out of the First World War, scoffing at the conventions of yesterday, wishing to embrace a new lifestyle, mistrusting their elders and authority. Above all they wanted to be modern, or to appear to be so. Pitigrilli's novels were built like film scripts: a series of scenes or tableaux and almost uninterrupted dialogue.[32] His leading female characters recycle a theme well developed abroad before the war: women are *femmes fatales*, obscure objects of desire who drive men mad, man-eating females.[33] They are Mildred in Somerset Maugham's *Of Human Bondage* (1915), Zola's Nana, Concha Perez in Pierre Louÿs's *La Femme et le pantin* (1898, adapted for the cinema by Josef von Sternberg in 1935 as *The Devil is a Woman*, with Marlene Dietrich in the leading role), Rosa Fröhlich, the heroine of *Professor Unrat* (1905) by Heinrich Mann (the film adaptation, *The Blue Angel*, 1930, also had Dietrich in the lead) and Frank Wedekind's *Lulu*. This could please both genders. Men could find in these fictional women, so unlike their wives and mothers, the fulfilment of some of their less complicated fantasies. Women could take vicarious pleasure in heroines who, instead of being seduced and abandoned, pregnant and poor, got their own back by doing some of the seduction themselves before abandoning 'the bastard' to his well-deserved fate.

Pitigrilli, unusually for an Italian novelist of his generation, was translated into several languages, including Spanish, French, English and Russian. His most successful novel, *Dolicocefala bionda* (1936), sold 250,000–300,000 copies by 1943.[34] As in some of Wilde's work, the plot of *Dolicocefala bionda* is but a pretext for aphorisms and clever quotes: 'Like all those who are in a position of power or, more simply, like all those sitting behind a government desk, he thought he understood what Teodoro Zweifel thought before he had finished explaining it.' The Grand Duchess Giselda, ruler of the mini-state of Glottenburg, was bound to remind readers of Mussolini: 'When there was some threat of social unrest she had a few rebels arrested, gave jobs to some of them, an important one to the most dangerous, then bribed a couple of opposition papers, lowered the price of wine and everything was back in order.'[35]

These books never became classics, but they were part of a middlebrow literary fashion far less provincial than the Italian novelettes of the past. They responded to the growing internationalisation of genres and the growing homogenisation of the European reading public. The same kind of literature, for instance, was being produced in France by writers like Maurice Dekobra (better known in Europe than Pittigrilli), whose real name was Ernest-Maurice Tessier. His books – like those of Pitigrilli – appealed for their depiction of a far more uninhibited world than that inhabited by their readers: a world of cruises, casinos, nightclubs and people drinking champagne. Such books, though plot-driven, provide readers with lifestyle information about how the swinging rich really live, feed their fantasies and give them the illusion of being one of them. All that is necessary is the acquisition of minor posturing, much as some in the 1960s, having read a couple of James Bond thrillers, or seen the films, thought themselves deliciously cool by ordering their dry martini 'shaken, not stirred'. Some writers became quite aware that they were writing manuals of behaviour. The Italian romance novelist Liala openly boasted that she had taught her female readers how to behave in social circles where they would not normally be accepted.[36]

Dekobra's *La Madone des Sleepings* (1925), which sold over 500,000 copies by 1931, was typical of this style of writing – ideally suited for cinematic adaptation. Its heroine, Lady Diana Wyndham (the British aristocracy had retained its charm), is sexually uninhibited, dances naked at 'the Garrick's' (sic) for charity, and boasts of her numerous lovers. The novel is full of contemporary literary references which flatter the reader: a German Professor of Sexology charges large sums for consultations at which he has explanations for everything, all equally wrong. There is a Bolshevik woman, Irina Mouravieff, who is characterised as the Marquise de Sade of Red Russia. Some of the characters are Bolsheviks, but like the writer are all rather cynical about politics and ideals – for it is not fashionable to take anything too seriously. One of them warns Lady Wyndham that her servants will not always tolerate class differences, and will eventually refuse to clean up after her or supinely accept to travel third class while she travels in first.[37] The luxury train on which much of the action takes place provides an ideal and simple narrative structure (like the cruise ship or the luxury hotel). Dekobra was read and enjoyed by readers in different social groups and from different political positions, the way detective stories are. Sartre, reminiscing about what he read in a PoW camp, mentioned his pleasure at reading a 'totally ridiculous' book about India by 'a certain' Dekobra (presumably *Au Pays des tigres parfumés*).[38] Had Dekobra become, by 1941, quite so forgotten, or was Sartre reluctant to admit that he knew who he was?

Yet it was writers like Pitigrilli and Dekobra who contributed decisively to the expansion of the book-reading public. Some of those who started by reading Dekobra went on to read writers like Sartre. Great fame would fall upon publishers who recognised that the reading public is not as sharply divided as the literary élites like to think it is. In fascist Italy, one publisher above all others understood this perfectly: Arnaldo Mondadori.

The Great Mondadori

Mondadori became (as the firm he founded still is) Italy's biggest publisher largely because of his single-minded commitment to the diffusion of the book. Italy's backwardness, in terms of readership, was turned to its advantage. In other countries, such as France, where Hachette had been established for decades, it would have been difficult for a new publisher to expand into the mass market. In Italy this market had to be created from scratch, and a new publisher was as likely to make it as an old one. In fact Mondadori probably brought to the business a populist attitude absent among well-established publishers such as Sonzogno and Treves, who had hitherto dominated the market. Unlike them he was not born into the bourgeoisie, but was the son of a socialist shoemaker. Unlike them (but like Mussolini) he had been a socialist in search of modernity, was radicalised by the First World War, in tune with the aspirations of the new generation, sympathetic to the anger and frustration of the petty bourgeoisie and disdainful of the rather stodgy socialist intelligentsia of *fin-de-siècle* Italy.

The crucial factor behind the rise of Mondadori was the same which was behind the rise of Mussolini: World War I. Far from recoiling in pacifist horror, they embraced it with enthusiasm. It was Italy's chance to gain its rightful place in the sun, to be a great power and not simply dream of being one. Mussolini denounced the socialists' policy of non-interventionism and, once expelled, founded a new party and took off on his own peculiar itinerary.

Mondadori's war was less dramatic but more commercially profitable. It provided him with an excellent business opportunity, and the platform from which to become Italy's largest publisher and to revolutionise the industry. Before the war he had already progressed from being a humble printer's apprentice to acquiring his own print works. Then he began publishing schoolbooks, children's books, and some propaganda. When the war started he obtained commissions to produce books for the soldiers' schools the army had set up, as well as a trench magazine, *La Tradotta*.[39] The army was a new captive reading public. As all soldiers know, wars consist of relatively long periods of inactivity interrupted by sporadic fighting. One waits, nervously, for action. Those who could read, read more than they had ever done before. The literate would read to the illiterate. Officers and journalists often commented about how much reading was done in the barracks and the trenches. The authorities were aware that disaffection could spread through literature. They could try to flood the trenches with pro-war propaganda, but they knew that few soldiers would read it. The best strategy was to provide safe 'entertainment' books and newspapers which kept well away from politics. This is what Mondadori supplied. By the end of the war he was a rich man, and his print works in Verona were in a favourable geographical position to take advantage of the new territories annexed to Italy: Trento and Trieste.

His great advantage was that, unlike publishers in other countries, but like other Italian entrepreneurs (one thinks of Fiat), the mass market he was aiming for was not already occupied by other entrepreneurs. But he had to move fast. Treves and Sonzogno – who already had the main Italian authors on their lists – were sizing up this wider market. Mondadori moved to Milan, the centre of the Italian book trade, and expanded by buying existing firms and poaching prestigious names from other publishers – such as Gabriele D'Annunzio, 'stolen' from Treves. His print works became the backbone of an ever-expanding, vertically integrated business. Mondadori would print a book in Verona and then, using his distribution company, stock and restock his own bookshops.

Mondadori's cultural empire survived Mussolini's. In the 1950s, with fascism long gone, Mondadori's Verona printing plant had become the largest and most efficient in Europe. By 1968 Mondadori had become the twenty-third largest industrial group in Italy. This would have seemed impossible in the 1920s, when the largest groups were all in steel, chemicals, electricity or railways, and the future seemed to be in cars and machine goods. But at a time when most Italian editors still thought in terms of a restricted readership and niche markets, and were still at the stage of craft production, Mondadori, along with Rizzoli and Bompiani, realised that it was necessary to think in industrial terms and to develop a strategy of maximum expansion into a future mass book market. Mondadori aimed at a comprehensive range: educational books, reference books, non-fiction books, high culture, low culture, middlebrow, comic strips (importing Disney), newspapers, and magazines for women (*Grazia*), for the lower middle classes (*Tempo*), and for children. He published Goethe and D.H. Lawrence as well as cheap thrillers. He was, by far, the most dynamic publisher in Italy. To the public Mondadori was the firm with the best authors; to the authors it was the firm with the largest public.[40]

Mondadori then bought a daily newspaper, *Il Secolo*, which overtly supported Mussolini during the Matteotti affair, unlike its rival the *Corriere della sera*, then Italy's leading paper. In 1922, as Mussolini 'marched' on Rome, Mondadori had leaflets and posters printed announcing the 'Revolution'.[41]

He adapted foreign encyclopaedias from Great Britain and the USA, and kept up with technological changes in printing and graphics.[42] He fed the thirst for self-improvement of the Italian petty bourgeoisie with initiatives such as the Biblioteca Mondadori (February 1926), a series of two hundred small volumes covering all the knowledge necessary for 'the man of average culture' or 'a civilised family'. By the late 1920s an Italian child could learn to read from Mondadori's primers, then use Mondadori textbooks at school and entertain himself with Mondadori comic strips and children's books while his parents read Mondadori magazines, crime novels, sentimental stories, classics, new Italian novels, recently translated US best-sellers, art books and encyclopaedias.

In his desire to cajole the authorities Mondadori had published relatively few foreign books in the 1920s, but once he had established his credentials with Mussolini, he launched a series of successful foreign narrative imprints between 1929 and 1933. The Biblioteca Romantica Mondadori (May 1930) was particularly significant in combining political opportunity with commercial objectives. The project involved publishing fifty major *foreign* writers, but translated by fifty major *Italian* writers. The ultimate demonstration that it is quite possible to have one's cake and eat it too, the initiative would make the public happy, for they would feel that they had new and better translations of great classics (all of them out of copyright); it would also make Italian writers happy, because they would obtain recognition of their status and make some money. This was a prestige collection, expensively priced.

French authors made up the lion's share of the list, and some critics pointed out that this was a waste of resources, since 'everyone in Italy could read French'. This was partly true. French was the second language of the Italian élites. But it also shows how narrow the book-buying public was. Effective expansion required translation. Mondadori defended his programme of translating from French, arguing that in this way Italy would need to import fewer books from France, thus saving foreign currency. He never hesitated to make a political case, in which somehow the wider interests of the nation coincided with the commercial interests of his firm. Another argument in defence of the high number of French translations was that it would provide more work for Italian writers, since most of them could only translate from French.[43]

Mondadori's decision, taken in 1929, to import foreign writers, just as the international economy was about to collapse (following the Wall Street Crash) and the fascist regime, along with everyone else, was about to embrace protectionism, may seem somehow counter-intuitive. But by then Mondadori had a huge backlist, some 30,000 works, a very large print works and a highly efficient distribution system. He had to keep on growing, and one way of doing so was to import titles. But translating books – though a kind of 'import' – is completely different from importing steel or cars. Translating books provided jobs to printers, translators and booksellers. In a recession people may cut back on 'superfluous' expenditure, such as cultural goods, but the Great Depression did not bring about a fall in cultural consumption (though without it, cultural consumption might have risen even more). More people than ever bought books, records and radio sets, and went to the cinema. Mondadori did not hesitate to go to what was regarded as the bottom of the market: the detective story. His rival Sonzogno had preceded him, starting the imprint Romanziere Poliziesco, in weekly parts (134 in all), all by foreign authors, of whom the best-known were French pioneers of the genre such as Émile Gaboriau and Maurice Leblanc (of Arsène Lupin fame).[44] But Mondadori's main source of inspiration came from France, where the weekly collection Le Masque, created in 1927, averaged a print run of 25,000, and which would sell, over fifty years, some 130 million volumes.[45] The public was ready for book-buying and page-turning rather than waiting for the next weekly instalment.

The new crime imprint was I Gialli Mondadori, so called because of the books' yellow (*giallo*) glossy covers (first seen in Switzerland), bearing sensational images by the British designer Abbey. The first four *gialli* were launched in 1929. At 5.50 lire each they were not cheap, but soon the price dropped to two lire.[46] The innovation, which led to considerable sales, was the distribution system: the *gialli* were sold at newsagents' kiosks rather than in the forbidding bookshops. Italian bookshops were not consumer-friendly – or rather, were not friendly to the unsophisticated reader. Until the early 1950s they were laid out with the books behind a counter, from where the bookseller would ask customers which books they wanted to see. The assumption was that they knew. Mondadori was one of the first who understood that there was a difference between selling books and selling soap (while trying to sell books like soap). In his bookshops books would be laid out so that they seemed to be expecting the customers. The idea of browsing had finally reached Italy.[47]

The new distribution system worked. The books had to be sold in a very short period of time to make room for the new ones. Stocks were kept to a minimum. Successful books were rapidly reprinted and distributed. The first *gialli* sold some 20,000 copies in their first edition, then sales stabilised between 10,000 and 15,000, with Edgar Wallace and S.S. Van Dine managing 20,000.[48] Some reached sales of 30,000. By 1985 the average weekly Mondadori *giallo* sold 50,000 copies.[49] Almost all the detective stories were translations. Mondadori's editorial director Lorenzo Montaldo (a Jew, whose real name was Danilo Lebrecht) tried to find Italian writers willing to write detective stories. The results were not dazzling. The no longer young Alessandro Varaldo was one of the few who indulged Mondadori with some reasonable success. Fascist politicians would occasionally send Mondadori detective stories written by friends and relatives (or themselves), with letters endorsing them. Patiently, Mondadori and Montaldo wrote back pointing out that detective stories were a serious business, and that there was no room for amateurish endeavour. Longanesi, Mondadori's main competitor in this genre, who would later become the main Italian publishers of American 'hard-boiled' crime stories (Raymond Chandler, Dashiell Hammett, Chester Himes and James Hadley Chase), did no better in encouraging home-grown talent. The genre was stubbornly 'Anglo-Saxon', at least in so far as Italy was concerned.

Cultural history is full of ironies and unintended consequences. Many Bauhaus architects were originally socialists, but some of them became successful in the USA, where their clear modern lines came to define the look of corporate capitalism. The fascist authorities in Italy wanted to develop national writers and local talent. They were annoyed that the most popular crime writers in the 1930s were foreign and not Italian. At the same time they wanted to present a view of Italy as crime-free, and pressured newspapers to cut down on reporting crime. An allegedly crimeless society, as Italy was supposed to be, was a further obstacle to the rise of the Italian detective story. By contrast Agatha Christie's home counties, the setting for Miss Marples's investigations, with their alarmingly high murder rate, must have seemed an exceedingly dangerous place.

Mondadori's great successes in the genre were writers like Edgar Wallace, whose entire output he had purchased. The plan was to publish one Wallace a month to attract new readers to the *gialli* imprint. Though Wallace died in 1932, he had left behind not only the script for the film *King Kong* but also 173 novels. Thus, between 1929 and 1941 Mondadori published fifty-three Wallace books.[50] There were some minor translation problems, such as the criminal jargon Wallace used, for which there was no Italian equivalent (Italian criminals at the time would be unlikely to speak anything but their local dialect). The translators invented an Italian criminal jargon which eventually, in accordance with the principle that life follows art, was adopted by the more literate members of the criminal classes.[51] More serious was the question of political correctness. In 1933 Lorenzo Montaldo noticed with some alarm that all the criminals in Wallace's *The Fourth Plague* (1913) were Italian. The nationality of the criminal band was duly changed. This problem was not uncommon. National sensibilities throughout Europe were higher in the 1930s than they are now – and not only in fascist Italy but also in Britain, where members of the British Board of Film Censors objected to the portrayal of English people as villains in American films.[52] In the USA the Hays Office was protecting the best interests of the industry abroad by inserting a clause in its code requiring films to bear in mind the 'national feelings' of foreigners. Yet as it was difficult to ignore the national origins of famous gangsters like Al Capone, films like Howard Hawks's *Scarface* (1932) were banned in Italy. Since the Soviet market was virtually closed to film imports and they were communists anyway, only the Russians could be safely insulted.[53] As for Edgar Wallace – the most filmed author of the 1930s, with thirty-nine American and British films – there were troubles for him even in Britain, where the censors turned down scripts of his play *On the Spot* (1930) six times ('a sordid tale of crime and lust from start to finish'[54]).

The Austrian novelist Vicki Baum's *Bubenreise*, set in Italy, could not be published there in spite of the author's great popularity, because it made an unfavourable judgement of Italians. This was the view not of the censor but of one of Mondadori's editorial directors, Livia Mazzucchetti, who was a great admirer of Baum.[55] Her prudence was remarkable. Here is her opinion on Bernhard Kellerman's *Die Brüder Schellenberg* (1925), written in the 1930s: the book 'contains many cars, villas, cheques, plane trips, luxury hotels and other similar knick knacks which will please our petty bourgeois readers. The author lives in Germany and is not Jewish.' She also suggested that the German Paul Ernst's *Das Glück von Lautenthal* (The Luck of the Lautenthals, 1933) should be published for political reasons, to please the fascists, and advised the acceptance of Theodor Kröger's *Kleine Madonna*, published in 1938 by Propyläen Verlag (the newly 'Aryanised' Ullstein), pointing out that one of Kröger's books had been turned down some years previously because it was too right-wing, but now the Party (i.e. the fascists) thought highly of the author. Yet even Mazzucchetti had standards. She had once been an admirer of Hans Fallada, but was upset by his trick of making himself popular with the Nazis by adding a pro-regime conclusion to his new novels. One should not publish, she wrote, such 'false, bitter, artificial, rotten books'.[56] In fact some of Fallada's books were forbidden by the Italian authorities not for political reasons but because they were about young prostitutes (the author's intention was to show how decadent Germany had been before Hitler's advent).

The distribution strategy of popular Mondadori books was based on the principle of their regular publication (usually at fortnightly intervals), a practice common in other countries. The idea was to create brand loyalty, not to authors (something impossible except for a few very successful writers), but to the imprint. The customers would know what they were getting. Thus the Romanzi della Palma (a palm tree was used as the logo), published fortnightly (monthly between 1936 and 1942), were addressed to a largely female public, though the frequency of illustrations of semi-naked women on the covers suggests attempts to draw a male readership. The readers' reports for this imprint were examined by a committee made up of the woman director of a Mondadori women's weekly magazine, a lawyer, a female student at the music academy, a graduate and a representative of the company which had the concession of all newsagents and bookshops in train stations. Here too, in spite of fascist preferences, foreign authors prevailed, especially German, American and English. The first book was Ursula Parrott's *The Ex-Wife* (1929). This was a daring choice. The novel had been published anonymously in the USA, with the identity of the author revealed only after buoyant sales. The book was so racy that it had been banned in Boston and other strait-laced cities. Its success was such, however, that in 1930 it was adapted into a film, *The Divorcee*, with Norma Shearer, who won the Oscar for best actress.

The collection was directed at 'housewives and seamstresses' – at least this was the editorial directors' view of the Palma market. Seamstresses and housewives must have had good taste since the Palma books included not only F. Scott Fitzgerald's *The Great Gatsby* but also Saint-Exupéry, George Bernard Shaw, Gerhart Hauptmann, André Maurois, François Mauriac and Joseph Kessel. For three lire the housewives had access to a foreign world. Inside each illustrated cover, 'for the convenience of our readers and booksellers', a coloured mark indicated whether the novel was slightly audacious (red) or for everyone (blue).[57] The average print run was 12–15,000.

The Medusa series was Mondadori's upmarket 'quality' imprint. It was equally dominated by foreign authors – even Joyce's *Ulysses* was seriously considered for publication in 1933. The covers were more sober and the books were more expensive (between ten and fifteen lire) – and, presumably, were not aimed at seamstresses and uneducated housewives. Like the Palma books, those of the Medusa came out every other week.

One of Mondadori's best-selling authors was Vicki Baum. Her novel *Grand Hotel* had been serialised in Ullstein's *Berliner Illustrierte Zeitung* in 1928, and rivalled in sales Remarque's famous war novel. The Italian publishers Bemporad, whose list was replete with foreign writers (and whose owners were Jewish, as was Baum), had published it in 1932. They had hoped to publish her other novels, but Mondadori, thanks to its close connection with Baum's German publishers Ullstein, thwarted Bemporad and obtained the rights for them.[58] By then Baum had left her native Vienna and moved to California (she died in Hollywood in 1960). When Hitler took over in Germany Ullstein was 'Aryanised' and Baum's books were banned. In 1938, after Mussolini had joined Hitler's camp and had passed anti-Semitic legislation, they were banned in Italy too, as was another German-Jewish Mondadori writer, Irmgard Keun. Mondadori had managed to publish her *Gilgi; eine von uns* (Gilgi, One of Us, 1931) under the Palma imprint, and had then bought the rights to her entire *oeuvre* but was forced to desist.

Mondadori continued selling and publishing Jewish authors even after 1938, out of commercial sense. The fascist censorship was quite inconsistent. For instance, Lavinia Mazzucchetti, Mondadori's chief adviser on German books, wanted to publish Felix Salten's sequel to *Bambi* (*Bambis Kinder*, 1939), but refrained because Salten was Jewish. Yet *Bambi's Children* was published without any problem by Baldini and Castoldi in 1941.[59] Mondadori was often puzzled why certain books were banned. He asked, with no success, why *Un Incontro a Parigi* (A Meeting in Paris), by the Hungarian writer Gabor Vaszary, sold in German in Germany and available in German in Italy, was forbidden in Italian. The story was banal, but hardly anti-fascist: young Hungarian aristocrat lives a bohemian life in Paris, meets girl, falls in love, she loves him, she then dies in a traffic accident. Daniel-Rops's novel *Mort, où est ta victoire?* (1934) was turned down in 1942 by the Ministry of Culture for reasons which had little to do with politics and much to do with Vatican pressure. The author, Daniel-Rops (pen name of Henry Petiot, 1901–65), was a much-respected French Catholic writer who could write slightly titillating books with a moral purpose. *Mort, où est ta victoire?* tells the story of a beautiful orphan who provokes lustful thoughts in all the men she meets. Having become a governess, she is loved by the husband of the lady of the house. He poisons his wife. The girl finds this out only later, but is forced to become the mistress of the family lawyer, who suspects the husband and forces her to accept his advances. Eventually she marries the lawyer, but is of course miserable. Only in old age does she find happiness, in the solitude of a convent.[60]

Yet Mondadori went with the flow, cajoling the Duce, doing favours, producing at enormous expense the collected works of Gabriele D'Annunzio (in 1926–27) to show his willingness to publish great Italian writers (especially if favoured by the regime). Mondadori never hesitated in cutting or censoring novels. Sometimes plots were drastically altered. For instance, in Irmgard Keun's *Gilgi; eine von uns* an entire family decide to kill themselves because they have fallen into misery. Suicide was frowned upon by both Mussolini and the Church (even the double suicide in Shakespeare's *Romeo and Juliet* upset the authorities). So the Italian version is deliberately ambiguous: did the family really intend to die, or was it an accident? *Ten Little Niggers* by Agatha Christie (1939) – now known under the less offensive title of *And Then There Were None* or *Ten Little Indians* – was rejected by Mondadori because it contained two suicides which could not be removed without altering the plot completely.[61]

Though Mondadori himself was ideologically close to fascism, he did not hesitate to publish Trotsky's autobiography in 1930. He got away with it probably because Trotsky was Stalin's enemy. However, he needed Mussolini's support, because in a country with a relatively low readership the most important market for books was not that which was left to the mercy of the free market and the decisions of thousands of individual readers, but the educational market – and this had only one customer: the Ministry of Education. Novels could sell in their thousands, but the single textbook which the regime decided all primary school pupils should use had a print run of millions, and Mondadori printed it. Even before this, however, he was already producing one-third of all Italian schoolbooks.[62] The decision, in 1930, to have a single state textbook and to award the contract to Mondadori was, of course, a shock to the other publishers who had just modified their texts to make them more acceptable to the regime.

Textbooks could resolve many problems for Italian publishers, since the book market remained small. Even popular books could not be sold easily. An international blockbuster like *Gone with the Wind*, which had sold a million copies in a few months in English sold in Italy 'only' 100,000 copies in five years. With the war against 'the Anglo-Saxon plutocracies' in full swing, Somerset Maugham's *Of Human Bondage*, published originally in 1915 and translated in 1940 with the enticing title of *Schiavo d'amore* (The Slave of Love), sold just as much as Mitchell, and so did Daphne du Maurier's *Rebecca*.[63] But the regime interfered increasingly. In 1941, as America was about to enter the war, Mondadori began to publish Erle Stanley Gardner's Perry Mason stories – though the instruction given to the translator of *The Case of the Haunted Husband* was clear: 'De-Americanise as much as possible.'[64]

Still, *Gone with the Wind* made it to the top of the best-seller list published by the monthly *Il Meridiano* in Rome in January 1938. How reliable this list was is a different story: in second place after Margaret Mitchell's international best-seller was Luigi Pirandello's *Novelle per un anno*. Pirandello was then the grand old man of Italian literature, much revered by fascism. But could his book of short stories really become a best-seller? The following month Pirandello ousted Mitchell and made it to the top. Even more strangely, Mitchell was the only foreigner in the top ten. Perhaps the authorities had the list doctored. Foreign writers were allowed, but evidently it was not necessary to feature them quite so prominently.[65]

There were, of course, genuinely popular Italian authors. The best-known and most celebrated was a writer of women's romance, Liala (pseudonym of Amalia Liana Cambiasi Negretti, 1896–1995). How successful she really was in the 1930s is not clear. Widely differing claims are made. Some have claimed that her first novel, *Signorsi* (1931, Mondadori) sold a million copies in its first few months.[66] This is a wild claim. Pietro Albonetti, on the basis of archival evidence, suggests an initial print run of less than a thousand. It would have taken a thousand reprints to reach a million copies.[67] Sales of *Signorsi*, however, continued steadily after the war, and the book made it to the top of a best-seller list prepared by the marketing research organisation Doxa in 1949.[68] Between 1931 and 1946 Liala wrote two novels a month, and a further thirty novels between 1946 and 1955. In fact it was probably only after the war that she became a real best-seller: *Il Pianoro delle ginestre* was reprinted four times between 1944 and 1947, and sold 50,000 copies.[69]

Liala's stories are fairly standard (like those of her main competitor, Milly Dandolo): the leading female character can be happy only if she is self-sacrificing; if she follows her passions she ends up marrying the wrong man, or following the wrong sort of lover, or getting the wrong job.[70] Most of the novels are variations on this theme. But then, in such stories standardisation is mandatory, and the author cannot allow herself to betray readers' expectations. It is just not possible in such books to get away with having a subversive plot, in which Fifí, the heroine, dumps her honest, sensitive, rich and handsome husband and her delightful young children to follow a professional knife-thrower and gambler, seldom sober and always stoned, with whom she lives happily ever after having found personal fulfilment as a lap-dancer in a nightclub. Such plots belong to another, perhaps more exciting, genre.

Films

Throughout the 1920s the Italian film industry – like the rest of the economy – was left in private hands. Indeed, in 1923 Mussolini had declared: 'Far from me is the idea of encouraging official art. Art belongs to the individual. The state has only one task: to protect the arts, provide a good environment to artists and encourage them for national and artistic reasons.'[71] In films, the fascist regime intervened in one area only, the one it cared about most: newsreels and documentaries. In 1924 it created the Institute Nazionale LUCE (L'Unione Cinematografica Italiana), with the specific purpose of education and propaganda. At the time, cinema programmes consisted of feature films and a newsreel. One of the reasons why the regime did not bother with the contents of films was that their popularity attracted a vast audience, who would then inevitably have to watch the newsreels produced by LUCE. In a country devoid of a mass press, newsreels were powerful instruments of political propaganda. On their own they would have attracted only a small audience. Attached to a brilliant comedy or love story or American film, they could be seen by millions.

Of course, even newsreels had to be constructed as narratives, and due weight had to be given to the need to entertain the audience. Nevertheless, the regime had little choice: the vast mass of Italians did not read newspapers and did not have access to a radio. The radio in any case, at least until 1929, was not a major instrument of fascist propaganda. The cinema was the only available mass medium. Even in the 1930s, when radio had come into its own, the LUCE newsreel was the most widely diffused fascist instrument of propaganda, since all cinemas were obliged to show a newsreel.[72]

The post-war period saw a decline in the Italian film industry. Fewer films were made; technicians and directors emigrated; audiences grew, but so did the penetration of foreign films; exports stagnated. Film-makers hoped that restrictions on imports would protect them, but distributors and cinema-owners – not tied to production companies – opposed them. Foreign films were profitable, and if the Italian film industry was in the doldrums, it should seek foreign investment or government subsidies and tax concessions.[73]

The unstable situation favoured the rise of audacious entrepreneurs. Stefano Pittaluga, in particular, began a systematic policy of acquisition of cinemas. By 1926 he controlled one-eighth of all Italian cinemas, and 80 per cent of film distribution. Of the 140 films he distributed in 1929, only six were Italian, eighty-nine American, and the rest from other European countries.[74] At the same time he began to produce popular films, such as light-hearted comedies (one was called *Voglio tradire mio marito* – I Want to Betray my Husband) and an endless series set in antiquity featuring the popular mythical muscular hero Maciste.[75] Having become the overall master of the industry, Pittaluga lobbied the fascist regime not to restrict foreign films, but at the same time to reduce the tax on Italian-made films. One of the baits he used was the making of films supporting the fascist view of history by depicting ancient Rome and the Risorgimento in a way which would obtain the approval of the authorities – by making analogies, for instance, between Garibaldi and Mussolini, and between the red shirts of the former and the black shirts of the latter. Pittaluga died in

1931, just as the industry was beginning to suffer the consequences of the Depression.

Like the Soviet communists, pro-fascist Italian film-makers realised that propaganda needed to be hidden and not overt. The fascists, unlike the communists, wanted Italian films to be sold abroad, and this increased the difficulties since non-Italian audiences would be hostile to fascist films.[76] Like the Soviet communists the Italians admired the professionalism of American films. Though the critics disdained the alleged naïvety and unsubstantial nature of US melodramas and comedies, they realised that films needed to please and attract audiences. Committed fascist film-makers, such as Alessandro Blasetti in films like *Terra Madre* (1931), aimed at celebrating the draining of marshland and the duty of absentee landlords to return to their estates and to a sense of public responsibilities, used a profusion of American (and Soviet) editing techniques.[77] Blasetti also used fairly standard melodrama themes and clichés. The city lady is blonde, sleeps late, dolls herself up and struts around the estate wearing fashionable clothes. The country girl is a brunette (who will get the young landlord in the end), has strong beliefs in the redeeming possibilities of the land, and is just as beautiful as the city girl. The upper classes are card-playing, bored and effete, the peasants sturdy and sincere.[78]

The fascists had a multiplicity of incompatible goals – hardly a unique position. They wanted a thriving cinema industry. They also wanted fascist films, but they were split over what that meant. One movement, '*strapaese*', preached a return to traditional provincial and rural values. Another sought the rediscovery of ancient Italian glories (Rome, the Renaissance and the Risorgimento). Another wanted modernity and avant-gardism. The bulk of the public wanted what audiences wanted everywhere in Europe and North America: films that moved the emotions, that amused them and made them laugh, that excited and entertained. Nevertheless, in the 1920s few fascists took any interest in the cinema. Nor was there a single view about what a fascist cultural policy should be. This was not surprising, since the fascists were never strong enough to take on the whole Italian intellectual class. Their task was confined to holding the fort, letting the various cultural and commercial lobbies fight it out. As long as no anti-fascist movement emerged, this was all that was required of them.

Such a *laissez-faire* attitude could not survive the Great Depression. Faced with economic collapse, the state took over much of the banking system and created a public holding company, the Istituto per la Ricostruzione Industriale. The state had become the largest entrepreneur in Italy. The problems faced by the cinema industry were even more serious than those facing the rest of the economy. The fall in investment and the lower demand for tickets due to the rise in unemployment affected the industry, but the introduction of sound meant re-equipping hundreds of cinemas, which entailed further long-term investment. To cap it all, in September 1935 two of the four studios belonging to the country's leading production company, Cines, representing almost 25 per cent of Italian studio capacity, were devastated by a fire.

Disasters can offer new opportunities. Mussolini realised that it was important to rebuild these facilities if Italy wanted to compete with foreigners, above all with the Americans. It was felt that the Italian film industry needed the kind of concentration achieved in Hollywood to enable studios to achieve economies of scale. In 1937, on 21 April (the day, allegedly, on which Rome was founded), Mussolini in full uniform (black shirt, black fez-like hat based on an Egyptian model, military trousers and boots), followed by the similarly attired Luigi Freddi, a former Blackshirt now in charge of the film section at the Ministry of Popular Culture, inaugurated Cine-città – as it was then spelt – the Roman Hollywood. A choir accompanied the proceedings, singing the soundtrack of the great new production of the Italian cinema: *Scipione l'Africano*, about the Carthaginian invasion of Italy, with a cast of thousands, elephants and spectacular sets, but marred by a lack of attention to detail, including a notorious shot of extras wearing wristwatches – something no one had noticed at the time.[79]

The film – almost entirely funded by the government – represented what the regime wanted the new studios to produce: large-scale films which would inspire Italians, impress foreigners, hark back to the glories of the Italian cinema of the 1910s before the Americans had invented Hollywood. The African and Roman themes were particularly suitable, as Italy had just concluded its conquest of Ethiopia. The failure of the pro-fascist epic *Camicia nera* by Giovacchino Forzano (1933), expensively funded by LUCE, had convinced the fascists that it was better to celebrate fascism indirectly through spectacular films which would be liked by the public, set during the great turning points of Italian history: the age of the great city-states of the Middle Ages, the Renaissance, the Risorgimento, the Great War, and culminating with the fascist revolution.

That lessons had to be learned from the Americans was not an uncommon position among fascists. Luigi Freddi regarded US films as 'honest, optimistic, enjoyable, generally of a high moral value and most often of a noble meaning'. Nor was he alone in regarding the American cinema as the foreign product most suitable for fascist Italy. Vittorio Mussolini, the Duce's son, wrote in 1936 that it would be dangerous to follow European models rather than the American one: 'From a moral point of view our youthful spirit finds a chorus line of a hundred beautiful girls less vulgar than the trite farce typical of the French,' with its 'double meanings, poorly concealed nudity and sterile intellectuality'.[80] As a result, until the war few American films were banned or cut in Italy. When they were, it was usually out of national pride of moral bigotry. As has been noted, *Scarface* (1932) was banned because the gangsters were Italian; the film version of Hemingway's *A Farewell to Arms* (1932) because it mentioned the disastrous Italian defeat at Caporetto in 1917; *Dead End* (nominated for the 1937 Academy Award for best picture) because it was about juvenile delinquency; and *The Adventures of Marco Polo* (1938) because the Italian traveller was not treated respectfully.[81]

Cinecittà was 'a European moviemaker's dream': it used advanced technology under the supervision of Hollywood-trained Italian engineers.[82] Most of the films produced there, however, were not in the epic genre. These were laborious to make, very costly, and did not sell well abroad. Italians preferred comedies and melodramas, which were much cheaper, set in upper-class homes and known as 'white telephone' films because the actors used white telephones, regarded then as the height of sophistication and luxury. Even critics failed to conform to the regime's preference for large-scale movies. The 1937 Venice Film Festival did not give the top prize to *Scipione l'Africano* but to Jean Renoir's pacifist *La Grande illusion*. Thereafter the authorities made sure that the jury gave prizes to the 'right' films, though in reality very few 'right', i.e. fascist, films were made during the fascist era.

Nazi Culture

Much has been written on Nazi cultural policies, on what the Nazis repressed and what they favoured. Yet the regime was not in power long enough – six years of relative peace (1933–39) followed by six years of total war – to develop a fully-worked-out cultural policy. In spite of the rhetoric of ruralism, anti-modernity, *Heimat*, blood and soil and the primeval forest, mainstream culture *under* Nazism (as opposed to Nazi culture) was not so different from that of other countries. The fall in unemployment enabled many Germans to enjoy items of popular consumption: cars and the new

Autobahn system, holidays abroad, radios, films, clothes, Americanisation and modernity.[83] Turning to nature (camping, canoeing) was promoted as providing relaxation, health and privacy rather than as a political duty. *Kraft durch Freude* (Strength through Joy) quickly became a cheap travel agency.[84]

The mass rituals and political choreography which are given so much prominence in documentary films about the period petered out soon after the early years.[85] The four-hour military parades to celebrate the Führer's birthday were watched by people from the sidelines. Then they went home and read their usual newspapers and listened to their usual music or went to watch their usual films. National festivals were easier to arrange than overhauling the entire theatrical and cinematic production of the country. Even Hitler, once the ceremony or the parade was over, returned to his rather conventional artistic tastes.[86] Some right-wing and pro-Nazi writers became best-sellers: Karl Heinrich Waggerl's *Schweres Blut* (Thick Blood, 1931), Hans Grimm's *Volk ohne Raum* (Nation Without Space, 1926), which sold almost half a million copies, Artur Dinter's deeply anti-Semitic *Die Sünde wider das Blut* (The Sin Against Blood, 1917) and Ernst Jünger's anti-bourgeois and modernist novel *Der Arbeiter* (The Worker, 1932).[87] But non-German books were as popular as German ones: the novels of the Scottish A.J. Cronin (such as *The Citadel*, 1938), the Norwegians Trygve Gulbranssen and Knut Hamsun, and the Americans William Faulkner, Sinclair Lewis, Ernest Hemingway and, above all, Margaret Mitchell's *Gone with the Wind*, which sold nearly as much as the Nazi best-seller *Glaube an Deutschland* by Hans Zöberlein. Even during the war it was perfectly possible for Germans to read Dorothy L. Sayers and Agatha Christie. Few of the women responding to a Nazi questionnaire on leisure time were interested in officially organised leisure.[88] What the Nazis did was to eliminate undesirable books or books written by 'undesirables': Jews, socialists, avant-garde writers, moral degenerates, etc.[89]

Racist novels were not particularly popular, except among that section of the intelligentsia committed to then-fashionable racial theories. Rural literature, medieval and *Völkisch*-historical novels were of course popular and much favoured by the Nazis, but such literature had been popular before. Writers who had been popular favourites in Wilhelmine Germany, such as Karl May (see pages 698–700), continued to sell well in the 1930s, as they had in the 1920s.[90] A novel generally regarded as 'Nazi', such as *Der Femhof* (1934) by Josefa Behrens-Totenohl, one of the best-sellers of the 1930s (160,000 copies sold in eight years), was more typical of the *Völkisch*, rural historical novel than of Nazi culture – save for the appearance of a hideous Jew, nasty but clever, inserted perhaps to pander to the new regime but perfectly in keeping with past literary representations of the Jews.[91] This is not to say that there had not been a spate of anti-Semitic novels in the years leading to the Nazis' capture of power, but the evidence suggests that the German book-buying public (the largest in Europe) actually *preferred* the kind of books which the Nazis banned or disapproved of, or whose authors turned against Nazism. At the top of the best-seller list of German novels published between 1899 and 1940 we find Thomas Mann's *Buddenbrooks* (1901) with 1.3 million, followed by Alfred Hein's *Kurts Maler* (1922) and Erich Maria Remarque's *All Quiet on the Western Front*, which sold more than 900,000.[92] Many of those in the top hundred were Jewish or left-leaning or both – and though this should not be taken to mean that Germans preferred novels by Jews or socialists, it can be taken to mean that ideology and ethnic origin did not matter much when it came to selecting a novel. In fact the Nazis had to refrain from banning on racial grounds some revered German writers who had Jewish blood, such as the playwright Hugo von Hofmannsthal (whose great-grandfather was a rabbi), Heinrich Heine and Arthur Schnitzler.

Music, it appears, was different. Gustav Mahler's Jewish blood could not be passed over in silence. Nor could Mendelssohn's, even though he was a practising Lutheran. The great statue of Mendelssohn that stood in front of the Gewandhaus in Leipzig where he had been a conductor between 1835 and 1847 was pulled down in 1936. His works were not performed under the Nazis. Nor were those of Mahler, who had been the second-most performed composer (after Richard Strauss) in 1919–33. Strauss, who cooperated with the Nazis, remained at the top throughout the 1933–1945 period, way ahead of Hans Pfitzner, an outspokenly nationalist and anti-Semitic composer. The Nazis favoured Bruckner over Brahms, but Brahms was always more popular: his works outperformed those of Bruckner by two to one in the period 1919–33, and even more in 1933–45.[93]

The Nazis, like the Italian fascists, needed to be legitimised by the musical establishment. Since both disapproved of modern music, especially the atonal music of Arnold Schoenberg (another Jew), it might seem that they would simply rally together under Wagner's conception of *Volksgemeinschaft* held together by ritualistic music drama. As it turned out there were problems, since a cardinal tenet of the traditionalist, as represented by the great German conductor Wilhelm Furtwängler, was that music should remain autonomous from politics.[94] Indeed, Furtwängler had written to Goebbels in April 1933 asking him not to exclude Jewish musicians, yet when threatened with exclusion he reluctantly signed an oath of loyalty in 1934. Foreign musicians and conductors such as Arturo Toscanini, Arthur Schnabel and Pablo Casals refused to perform in Germany.

It was never clear what 'Nazi' music could possibly be, other than that it should not be composed by Jews – which ruled out Mendelssohn, Meyerbeer, Offenbach, Mahler and Schoenberg. Beethoven was a little doubtful, because his physical characteristics suggested 'racial miscegenation' (he was dark). Bach was saved. Schubert was suspected of effeminacy. Handel was reluctantly accepted in spite of his preference for the Old Testament, but his oratorio *Judas Maccabeus* (about Jewish resistance against the Romans) was performed with a different text and name. Chopin was a Pole, but at least he was not Jewish.[95]

A bigger problem was the enormously popular Johann Strauss Jr, whose distant Jewish origins were traced by some over-zealous scholars in 1938, just as Hitler was preparing to take over Austria. Goebbels, of course, liked Strauss's waltzes, as did many Germans. Realising that even committed Nazis were unlikely to be convinced that 'The Blue Danube' was an instrument of the international Jewish conspiracy to destroy the moral fibre of the German race, Goebbels had all trace of the Jewishness of the Strauss family removed from the records.[96] Franz Lehár's wife Sophie was Jewish, but as *The Merry Widow* was Hitler's favourite operetta, she was made an honorary Aryan and allowed to live in peace. Not so lucky was Lehár's longstanding librettist Fritz Löhner, who died at Auschwitz.[97] It was equally embarrassing for the Nazis that eleven of the forty German Nobel Prize-winners prior to 1933 were Jewish.

Of course, Hitler's *Mein Kampf* was a best-seller, though the ten million copies which were sold, as was claimed, probably reflected the print run and the numbers of copies distributed.[98] Like the Bible, *Mein Kampf* in Hitler's Germany is a typical 'symbolic' book – that is, a text the possession of which is a sign of formal acceptance of authority. It is scarcely believable that many people would have read more than a few pages of a book which, regardless of its ideology, is exceedingly dull and much too long. *Mein Kampf*'s iconic status seems to have pre-empted the marketing of a slim propagandistic text which, by denouncing the international Jewish-Bolshevik-communist conspiracy and promising ordinary Germans a world to conquer, might have achieved high sales in its own right.

The theatre, though an élite institution, also came under direct Nazi control within a year of the seizure of power. Goebbels's Ministry of Culture ensured the submission of theatre directors, managers and playwrights by the sacking of potential dissidents. Yet very few plays were banned. Directors knew what was acceptable.[99] Once all the undesirable plays had been removed for the usual reasons, only half of the pre-1933 plays were left in the repertoire. The thriving German theatre of the 1920s reeled under the impact. It had accounted for 30 per cent of productions in 1929–33. After the Nazi advent this sank to 5 per cent. The consequence was a revival of historical plays. As many of these had plots with a charismatic figure facing treachery and difficulties, all that was required was a modest tinkering with the text to ensure that those who wished to imagine Hitler being reincarnated in the heroes of the past could do so. Shakespeare's *The Merchant of Venice* and Marlowe's *The Jew of Malta* became tools of Nazi anti-Semitism. The meaning of great plays can rely on the production and the acting more than on the text. After the Second World War *The Merchant of Venice*, when it was produced at all in Germany, always portrayed Shylock as the noble representative of suffering Jewry, and his opponents as morally tainted.[100]

The cabaret, the quintessential Weimar spectacle, was almost destroyed. Those in Berlin, a city regarded by Goebbels as a cesspool of decadent Jewish-Bolshevik culture, were often physically attacked, many of the performers and writers (almost all Jewish) fled into exile, and some committed suicide. The Depression had already forced many cabarets to fold. An art form which did not take itself too seriously, which was sexually uninhibited, only too keen to send up the powers-that-be, essentially urban and modern, and dominated by Jews and leftists, was unlikely to thrive under the Nazis.[101] Until the Depression, the most 'subversive' Weimar cabaret was Berlin's Kabarett der Komiker (shortened as 'Kadeko'), founded by the Viennese Jew Kurt Robitschek in 1924. Already in 1930, before the Nazi seizure, Robitschek had to tone down his act for fear that its radicalism would damage receipts. When the Jews were removed from Kadeko, the show went on, but its critical edge was increasingly dulled.[102] In Munich mild criticism of the regime could still be encountered: the cabaret comedian Weiss Ferdl joked that though 98 per cent of the inhabitants were on Hitler's side, it was his constant bad luck that he kept on meeting those who belonged to the other 2 per cent.[103]

In so far as the Nazis had a cultural outlook at all, it was anti-modernist. They regarded modernism, with some justification, as the kind of art that Jews and left-wing subversives had promoted. Modernism was closely associated with the Weimar Republic – though many of its cultural tendencies were in existence in Imperial Germany. Nazi anti-modernism was perfectly in tune with the conventional outlook of the German middle classes – indeed of the middle classes throughout Europe. In 1937 the regime staged an exhibition in Munich of 'degenerate' modern art, or *Entartete Kunst*. As it was visited by two million people, it must have occurred to the organisers that some of the visitors may not have shared their feelings of hostility, and might have actually liked the works of Max Beckmann, Otto Dix, Oskar Kokoschka and Ernest Kirchner. But many also went to see the parallel exhibition of approved art. This 'Nazi' art turned out to be conventional figurative art, with pastoral landscapes, portraits and pictures of animals accounting for 85 per cent of the total.[104] The taste of the average Nazi activist was no different from that of the average person.

A similar conclusion can be drawn for the vast majority of films shot and distributed under Nazism. Like their counterparts in Italy, they represented the usual range of cinematic experience available to Europeans in the 1930s, the same mix of genres, the same wholesale adoption of Hollywood techniques. Most of them had nothing to do with politics.[105] The Nazis found themselves promoting commercially successful films in order to alleviate the losses made by the industry in 1936 because of rising costs associated with sound production and the high salaries paid to German stars to prevent them from going to Hollywood.[106]

About 50 per cent of the films made in Nazi Germany were love stories and comedies, and 25 per cent were crime stories and musicals.[107] The Nazis regarded the main purpose of films to be *Wirklichkeitsflucht* – escapism. During the war the desire for escapist movies increased, and even more 'apolitical' films were made. This was actually encouraged by Goebbels's Ministry of Culture, which had a propensity for promoting 'light' and harmless entertainment to distract people from the hardships of war.[108] For similar reasons Goebbels encouraged all manner of cultural events – at least until the escalation of the war, with the opening of the Soviet front and the eventual Allied bombing, made it impossible. Concert life, cinema-going and Berlin nightclubs featuring American jazz continued.[109]

The German occupation of most of Europe during the Second World War provided an opportunity for an expansion of the market for German films as an alternative to US domination, attracting to Berlin directors, actors and technicians from central Europe.[110] Occupation, however, presented the Nazis with further ideological problems, since those who collaborated with them – if they had an ideology other than their own survival – had national feelings which needed to be pandered to. The local anti-Semites they often recruited were nationalist themselves, and used the opportunity to 'cleanse' the cultural industries of what they regarded as ethnic stains. Thus in France the prestigious publishing house Calmann-Lévy was taken over and its name changed to the more 'authentically' French Maison de Balzac. German occupation simply meant that a pre-existing right-wing French literary tradition was able to assert itself now that the field had been almost cleared of its more powerful leftist rivals. To define what this tradition might be is even more difficult that to define a left-wing book. Catholicism, on its own, is insufficiently precise as a definer. François Mauriac is unquestionably a Catholic writer, and that is apparent from his books, but his politics are less evident, and in any case, Mauriac became anti-fascist. In fact he was the only member of the Académie Française who joined the Resistance.[111] Anti-British sentiments were guaranteed to please both the occupiers and their friends. Indeed the Renaudot Prize for 1941 was given to Paul Mousset for his somewhat Anglophobic war novel *Quand le temps travaillait pour nous*. But anti-English feelings can be found in French literature well before the war, and can hardly be deemed to reflect a left–right divide. The Germans had decided that France should have a rural destiny. General Pétain and his Vichy regime were also committed to the values of rural France, the France of the regions against the modernising and anti-clerical influence of Paris: the Goncourt Prize for 1941 was given to the regionalist writer Henri Pourrat for *Vents de Mars*.[112]

By and large, states under right-wing dictatorial regimes, far from being 'totalitarian', were forced to respond, in culture as in other fields, to pressures from various commercial and artistic lobbies. As we have seen in the previous chapter, even a state like the USSR, which had taken over the economy and abolished private capitalism, found it difficult to determine the actual content of its artistic production. One might be able to prevent some cultural expressions, suppress criticism and frighten writers, artists and film-makers, yet in the end some market elements prevail: consumers exercise some choice. They will not flock to watch what they do not like, they will not read what they find boring or obscure, they will not listen to music they find tedious or incomprehensible. The Italian fascists and the Nazis, unlike the communists, did not abolish capitalism; markets were regulated, controlled and subsidised, but not extinguished. Newspapers, all in private hands, needed readers. Film-makers wanted a public, as did producers and distributors.

They had to remain within the bounds of what fascism and prevailing morality allowed, but these bounds were not so narrow as to prevent Italian culture, and the cinema in particular, from developing in the way it probably would have even if Mussolini had never 'marched' on Rome in October 1922.

46

Mass Culture:
The American Challenge

THE CHALLENGE OF THE US consisted of the fact that after the First World War America exported far more of its culture to Europe than it imported, reversing the previous trend. Of course, much of what it exported was not wildly dissimilar from European culture.

The beginning of this challenge can be dated with some precision to the immediate post-World War I years. Over the following twenty years American films, American music, American comic books, American thrillers and a generally American style of popular culture were bought by Europeans, and widely imitated and adapted. The countries that were particularly receptive to American culture were those with a strong culture of their own, such as France. The reason is plain – culturally advanced countries already possess the industrial structures which permit the rapid circulation of foreign cultural goods: a market for books and films, concert halls, nightclubs, a record industry, bookshops, an advanced educational system which provides readers and translators, and so on.

Technology also helped: the spread of jazz to Europe in the 1920s was the first great trend in music history to occur mainly through recording. Recording was particularly important for the spread of jazz, since much of it had no notation and the tours of jazz performers in Europe were fairly short. Yet tours mattered: the Original Dixieland Jazz Band arrived in Liverpool in 1919, and went on to perform at the London Hippodrome.[1] Emigration 'in reverse' mattered too: the American dancer and singer Josephine Baker left the Cotton Club in Harlem in 1925 to settle in Paris, and became in the 1930s the star of the Folies Bergère and the Casino de Paris.

The 'American question' in European cultural industries did not reside only in the very high level of US exports to Europe, but also in the very low level of European export to the USA. A rough description of the two-way traffic would go like this. In the nineteenth century Europe exported its culture to the USA. This culture originated mainly from Great Britain (including Ireland) and France, with in addition the culture of immigrants from all over Europe and of the former African slaves. This was absorbed by 'local', i.e. settlers', culture – largely British, with some Creole input (from the early French or Spanish settlers). This amalgam was recast radically to fit the increasingly diversified US mass market. American cultural operators were perfectly conscious of this. Will Hays, the head of the Motion Picture Producers and Distributors of America, speaking in London in 1923, said that 'America in a very literal sense is truly the world state. All races, all creeds, all men are to be found here.'[2]

The lack of a pre-existing aristocratic culture and the strength of its middle class contributed to the 'popular' characteristics of America's cultural markets. By the twentieth century, taking advantage of new technologies (film and recorded sound) and the large domestic market, the US was able to re-export much of its cultural output to the developing mass societies of Europe and Latin America. By the last quarter of the twentieth century, thanks to even more powerful means of diffusion, such as television, it flooded the rest of the world with its cultural artefacts.

The export of American popular culture to Europe was paralleled by a massive one-way trade of European high-culture artefacts to the USA. The European aristocracy was becoming less and less wealthy. Challenged by the *nouveaux riches* of industry, collapsing agricultural prices (cheap American wheat was partly responsible) and the increasing costs of maintaining their ancestral homes, Europe's aristocrats began to shed – between the mid-1880s and the end of the 1920s – the artistic treasures which they had accumulated in the previous centuries. At first Europe's own new millionaire class – such as the Rothschilds – acquired these treasures. But soon the unparalleled economic strength of the new American millionaire class dominated the art market.[3] A great art dealer like Joseph Duveen played four American millionaires against each other: John Pierpont Morgan, P.A.B. Widener, Benjamin Altman and Henry Clay Frick.[4] Just as Hollywood was about to invade and conquer Europe, an endless stream of paintings by old and new masters, eighteenth-century furniture, ceramics and porcelain, rare books, tapestries, sculptures, portraits of other people's ancestors, mistresses and loved ones, faïence bowls, clocks, snuffboxes, Limoges enamels, Augsburg silver, *chinoiserie* and *japonaiserie* was heading in the opposite direction. Since it did not require a great fortune to acquire rapidly a good collection of Queen Anne silver or rare porcelain figures, even those who were not tycoons could play the game.[5] In Europe, places like Blenheim Palace were emptied of their treasures to the benefit of people like Cornelius Vanderbilt, William Randolph Hearst and Isabella Stewart – a symbolic mark of the passage of power, wealth and patronage from the old continent to the new.

Along with its treasures Europe exported its workforce, but in exchange it was preparing itself to receive Americanism. And since America was the first society to exhibit the traits and characteristics of mass culture, the first truly capitalist society unburdened by the weight of an aristocratic past, the first consumer society (that is, a society whose mass production of commodities was actually purchased by the producers themselves), it was also consequently the first truly modern society.[6] Thus much of the Europeans' debates about and criticisms of Americanism were in fact criticisms of modernity under another name.

In the period we are examining here (1920–60), America's larger share of the global cultural market relied mainly on films and music. By the end of World War II, the cinema was by far the most formidable cultural industry. The USA produced more films than anyone else, had the largest domestic market in the world, and the largest and most luxurious cinemas: the Roxy in New York had over 6,000 seats. The size of this market enabled Hollywood producers to sell their films more cheaply in Europe. It would be naïve, however, to assume that this was purely the result of market forces and the superiority of American products.

The major Hollywood companies successfully lobbied the federal government to do everything it could to restrict the import of foreign pictures, while keeping foreign markets open to them. The combination of economic and political power and the commercial superiority of American films ensured their dominance in all English-language markets and in most of Europe as early as the mid-1920s. The fiercest resistance came from Japan and the USSR.

The main obstacle to the diffusion of US films was the rudimentary cinema infrastructure that still prevailed in most of the world in the 1920s. By improving this infrastructure, the Europeans further facilitated US penetration. Just as the expansion of the market for books depends on education, literacy and bookshops, that of films depends on the existence of cinema circuits. Europeans were worried. Depriving audiences of American films was an option, but this was resisted by distributors. What was the point of building cinemas if one was not allowed to show popular films? As we have seen in the two preceding chapters, fascist and communist regimes attempted to keep American films out, with varying degrees of success – a consequence of the nationalist or anti-capitalist politics which inspired them. But the fact is that everyone tried to restrict the import of American films.

How could Europeans hope to flood the US market with films, for instance, when the USA produced some 15,000 feature films between 1915 and 1960?[7] In 1935 alone, in the middle of the Depression, the USA produced 525 films. In terms of volume, this supremacy did not last long. Already in 1952, while the USA produced 384 films, Japan made 258 and India 233 (the same as in 1935), and the gap was narrowing. But the significant difference was that a large number of US films were exported, whereas only a few art films from Japan or India ever made it abroad. The point about the USA's 15,000 films is that they were, culturally speaking, in tune with the mass European market precisely because they were familiar.

But why could not the Europeans compete? Why could they not produce a popular culture sufficiently enticing for Americans – many of whom had been Europeans until recently? Partly this was to do with the fact that most European countries (some of more recent birth than the USA) would have found it difficult to appeal to the highly protected American market without introducing into their cultural wares aspects which would speak specifically to Americans – to which cultural nationalists would have complained vociferously. One way of doing so was to stress their own national stereotypes in a way which would intrigue or amuse American audiences. The success of British films in the USA was in part due to the UK's unique selling points: class, aristocracy, heritage, history, kings and queens. All this went down well in the New World. The French tried to market their own alleged charms and distinctions. The enduring popularity of Maurice Chevalier in the USA as the debonair Frenchman with a twinkle in his eye and an ability to charm women was the kind of self-image which pleased the French and entertained the Americans. Stereotypes are immeasurably strengthened when the objects of the stereotype themselves participate in their diffusion. These, however, were niche markets barely able to compete with the mass appeal of popular American genres.

In culturally strong countries such as France, the arguments deployed by the élites were the same as those used against other products of mass culture. What was objectionable about American imports was not just that they were

American, but that they were 'low culture'. Since it is difficult, in the era of populist democracy, to argue against what is popular, the élitist position often ended up propounding a nationalist argument.

In France, those who wished to defend the French cinema often pointed out that the success of American films was due to the considerable support Hollywood obtained from the federal government. René Jeanne, writing in 1930, deplored the neglect of the cinema by the French state, which had backed it during the war for propaganda reasons.[8] He also lambasted the American film industry for its catering to the lowest common denominator, its ability to dump cheap films onto the European market, its systematic pillaging of European directors and actors, and its take-over of French companies such as Gaumont. The result was that in 1928 France imported four hundred US films, Germany 221, Great Britain 512, Finland 364 and Norway 204. In the same year Germany imported only twenty-three French films and fifteen British ones. 'This is not simply a colonisation of France,' wrote Jeanne, 'it is a colonisation of Europe.'[9] The French press, while denouncing this state of affairs in its cultural pages, simultaneously promoted what it denounced by devoting endless column inches to American actors and films. American film companies compounded the problem by their superior public relations.[10]

This litany barely changed over the successive decades: American films – it is said – carry a distorted Americano-centric vision of the world. An American Second World War film showing the victory parade under the Arc de Triomphe in Paris gives the impression that the USA won the war on its own. The American film *Beau-Geste* (1924) depicts French officers in the Foreign Legion as cruel and brutal. Paris is typically represented as a den of vice where innocent Americans fall prey to women of easy virtue.[11]

The various attempts to resist Americanism, whether from politically hostile forces (communism, fascism) or from the exponents of élite culture, at best contained the phenomenon. They never blocked it. Indeed, as we have seen, even communists and fascists found much to praise in America. For every statement by a European lamenting the inexorable tide of American trash, the infectious germs of brash modernity, the coarse and low taste of American people, one can find a countervailing one praising America's politics, its culture, its technology, its lifestyle. Soviet film-makers went to Hollywood in droves, hoping to discover the secret of popular cinema. Jazz was imported into Stalin's Russia. President Roosevelt's book *Looking Forward* was translated into Italian and favourably reviewed by Mussolini in *Popolo d'Italia* (7 July 1933). Mussolini's son Vittorio was a great admirer of American films; his other son, Romano, became a fine jazz pianist. Mussolini was probably aware that he had a good press in the USA – he received a favourable profile in 1928 in the *Saturday Evening Post* (three million copies sold). Strongly ideological fascists (both nationalist and provincial) remained staunchly anti-American – as was the case with Leo Longanesi's *L'Italiano* and Bottai's *Critica fascista* – but the more official periodical *Gerarchia* exhibited few traces of extreme anti-Americanism.

Thoughtful European intellectuals reacted by pointing out that Europeans should blame themselves if they produced no popular alternative to American culture. In many areas they were able to do so. The first mass-consumption society may well have been American, but when Europeans caught up they made and bought their own goods. Americans may have pioneered mass private transport, the automobile, but there never was a mass penetration of American cars into Europe. The Germans, the French, the Italians and the British all developed their own small-size cars, such as the Volkswagen and the Fiat 500 (the 'Topolino'). While mass motoring was already in existence in the United States in the 1920s, when 90 per cent of world vehicle production was carried out in the USA, Europeans kept them out partly by tariff barriers and partly by investing heavily in their own manufacturing. Other American products were kept out simply because Europeans could not afford them. The numerous gadgets which filled American kitchens became available to Europeans only in the 1950s. European furniture manufacturers were protected by the high cost of transportation. And while a French intellectual of the right (and a devout supporter of American foreign policy) such as Raymond Aron lamented the 'the tin can' replacing home cooking, Coca-Cola replacing wine and 'the taste-destroying refrigerator' replacing the earthen cellar, much of the fast food available (flattened grilled minced-meat, chips, fried fish, pizza, kebabs, etc.) has unimpeachable European or Mediterranean origins.[12] American mass-produced clothes could not yet compete against cheap European tailor-made clothes for the middle classes and home-made products for everyone else (made, it must be said, on American sewing-machines).

Cultural products, even novels, were in a different league. The penetration of US novels could not be stopped easily. They were, after all, translated and printed in Europe. What was being imported was the idea, the 'software', not the physical object. European intellectuals mocked the mediocrity of these ideas; yet Europe produced its own share of mindless 'trashy' books, while the most-loved American imports included novels such as Sinclair Lewis's *Babbitt* (1922), which criticised the small-mindedness and monotony of small-town American middle-class life. Antonio Gramsci, a communist writing in a prison cell, surveying the provincialism of Italian culture under fascism, hailed *Babbitt* as a demonstration that the USA was building a society critical of itself, aware of its strengths and its weaknesses. European intellectuals may laugh at the mediocrity of the novel's eponymous central character, he wrote, but Europe was full of Babbitts.[13] Some fascist critics too admired *Babbitt* for its modern and unadorned prose, while rejecting its allegedly non-spiritual views.[14] By the end of the twentieth century, middle-class suburban bliss would be celebrated by American Gothic films in which privileged and contented people are suddenly terrified by 'The Thing' – which Fredric Jameson sees as manifesting the anxiety of a privileged situation, a kind of collective guilt.[15]

Italian intellectuals had gone through various phases of *esterofilia* (love of all things foreign): love of the French and English for their novels, poetry and political institutions, love of German social theory. Under fascism the long love affair with American modernity was about to start. Young critics and writers such as Cesare Pavese and Elio Vittorini (neither of whom had ever visited the USA) and Emilio Cecchi (who had) admired a mythical America they had, in part, constructed themselves, just as many Italian immigrants had gone to the USA with a mirage embellished by the tales told by those who had returned.[16] They discovered 'good' American literature: Edgar Allan Poe ('discovered' by Baudelaire fifty years previously), Melville and Edith Wharton. They discovered Hawthorne, even if the first Italian translation of his stories was called *Storie del far west* (though they were all set on the East Coast).[17]

Travel books written by European intellectuals offering their impressions of America and Americans became a distinct genre in the 1920s and 1930s, particularly in France: André Siegfried's *Les États-Unis d'aujourd'hui* (1927), Lucien Romier's *Qui sera le maître, Europe ou Amérique?* (1927), André Tardieu's *Devant l'obstacle, l'Amérique et nous* (1927), Henri Bérenger's *Paroles d'Amérique* (1926).[18] Some are lucid. Others abound in clichés. In Emilio Cecchi's *America Amara* (Bitter America), published in 1940 from notes taken during visits in 1930–31 and 1937–38, the picture of America is more complex, though he found the Americans, 'as a social mass', to be like sheep (while Italy in 1940 . . .), while American students were coarse swots with no critical spirit (Cecchi, a literary and art critic, spent some time at Berkeley).

Clemenceau's judgement on Americans – that their coffee was terrible and they lacked a broad view of things – was still valid, thought Cecchi. Deeply shocked by the widespread practice of lynching, he noted the hypocrisy of America condemning Italy and Germany for their anti-Semitic laws while itself practising extensive social discrimination against Jews.[19] Georges Duhamel's *Scènes de la vie future* (1930), whose title in the English translation is the harsher *America the Menace*, depicts the USA as a technological nightmare, paralysed by a morbid fear of microbes, dirt and foreign contagion, where people eat what calory-counting experts tell them to.[20] American cinemas are luxurious in the way a 'bourgeois bordello' is, 'an industrial luxury made by soulless machines for a crowd devoid of soul' – 'Any people subjected for fifty years to the American cinema is destined to decadence', music is tinned, and the country is in the grips of an absurd Puritanism.[21] And what is particularly frightening about the US? That they are a mass unaware of where they are heading – like ants.[22] Three years after Duhamel, it was the turn of André Maurois to report. The America he visited was in the grip of the Depression, with millions of unemployed. Yet Maurois's tone was non-judgemental. The New Deal is explained with care and sympathy. This is not the America that frightens, but one that is providing the example of a regulated capitalism where a conscious will can shape society without the consequences of fascism or communism.[23]

Most Europeans knew very little about the United States. Some had information from the letters they received from their relatives who had emigrated there. Then there were the stories told by those who had returned. In the 1920s very few books on America were published in Italy.[24] The situation elsewhere was not much better. Newspapers barely covered the USA since it was not the major focus of international news (US isolationism made its foreign policy irrelevant). What the vast majority of people knew about America came from films and from opinion-makers whose own knowledge was perfunctory. All over Europe the staple clichés of anti-Americanism were not based on politics but on a contrast between quality (Europe) and quantity (America), spirit (Europe) and matter (America), man (Europe) and machine (America), tradition (Europe) and modernity (America).

In the 1920s and 1930s 'modernity' was a recent novelty even in the USA. The country was as rural as France and Germany, and far more religious than either, though this was seldom manifested in films, which were addressed to urban dwellers. In 1917 electricity was available to only 25 per cent of the American population, though by the end of the 1920s it reached 75 per cent.[25]

The country was clearly marching rapidly towards 'progress', and Europeans did not have to wait for the post-1945 era to discover American modernity. Ever since the end of the nineteenth century it had been obvious that the USA was the centre of consumers' innovation.

When it came to cultural trends and fashions, many Europeans still looked to Paris and its artistic circles, but these, especially in the 1920s, were relatively pro-American. This was due to the pluralistic nature of American cultural exports. There was something for everyone. American films and novels could be populist and anti-rich, or could celebrate the glamour of the rich; they could criticise big business, or tell the story of how an ordinary person becomes a millionaire. They could even be read as anti-American, and be critical of their nation, something which at the time no Russian or Italian could be, and which very few British or French were. And, of course, the vast majority of US cultural exports were not political in any meaningful sense of the word.[26]

The only potential rivals facing the USA were the two hitherto culturally dominant countries, France and Great Britain. In practice they were no threat. Their élite culture could not be popular, and their popular culture was provincial and regional. Germany had recently lost the war, and had little experience in exporting its own popular culture. It kept its lead (i.e. its market share) in certain fields – classical music above all – but otherwise, instead of exporting its products it exported its producers: inflation, unemployment and the racist policies of the Nazis led a steady stream of exiles to make their way to France and Britain and, above all, to the USA. Russia was in a similar position: its popular culture was strictly for home consumption. Its high culture gave it prestige, but little else. Small countries – whether Greece or Portugal, Hungary or Czechoslovakia, Denmark or Sweden – could produce the odd success story to assuage national pride, but little else. Even without the threat of persecution in Europe by authoritarian regimes the USA would have been a pole of attraction for leading artists. Politics added its weight. By the end of the 1930s many of Europe's most revered musicians and composers had gone to the USA: Arturo Toscanini, Bruno Walter, Fritz Busch, Fritz Reiner, Eugene Ormandy. It looked as if the USA exported popular culture and imported not just high culture but its practitioners.

A further explanation for the success of US cultural artefacts was that, quite simply, the country was sociologically and economically more advanced than Europe: it had a much bigger middle class, its working class was more prosperous, it was far more advanced in the development of a consumer society: it had more radio sets, more gramophones, more telephones, more cars, more of everything. In the mid-1920s US real wages were 60 per cent higher than in Great Britain and 2.5 times higher than in France. Even during the Depression Americans did not cut down on cultural items such as cheap novels, women's magazines and going to the cinema.[27] The new American social groups were also unencumbered by constraints inflicted upon them by an older bourgeoisie or aristocracy. The consumption of commercial 'vulgarity', inhibited in Europe by the condescension visited by each class on the one below it, was left free to romp, to find its market and then to find its way to the rest of the world.

This is why best-selling US books of the 1930s which explained how to get on in life were translated into other languages only after the war. That was the case with Dale Carnegie's famous *How to Win Friends and Influence People* (1936) and Napoleon Hill's *The Law of Success* (1928) and *Think and Grow Rich* (1937), which claimed to be 'teaching, for the first time, the famous Andrew Carnegie formula for money-making, based upon the Thirteen Proven Steps to Riches' – eventually it was translated even into Urdu. Books like these had a simple message: success depends on our own will and desires, our faith in ourselves. The first principle of Hill's self-confidence formula stated:

> I know that I have the ability to achieve the object of my Definite Purpose in life, therefore, I DEMAND of myself persistent, continuous action towards its attainment, and here and now promise to render such action.[28]

Napoleon Hill (1883–1970), having found a goldmine, never stopped digging. After *Think Your Way to Wealth . . . Presents the Entire 17 Principles of Personal Achievement, Condensed for Quick Reading, Based on the Lifetime Experiences of More than 500 of America's Top-Ranking Successes* (1937) he drafted his wife, Rosa Lee Hill, into producing the enticing *How to Attract Men and Money: An Intimate Revelation for Women Past Eighteen. With Some Facts Men Ought to Know – Especially Those Who Wish to Stage a Come-Back After Experiencing Defeat . . . (With Special Contributions by her Husband – Napoleon Hill)* (1940). Years later even blacks could become rich, and Hill, though dead, co-authored with Dennis Kimbro *Think and Grow Rich: A Black Choice* (1991).

Hill was far from ploughing a lonely furrow. Dorothea Brande (1893–1948) taught people how to be a successful author in *Becoming a Writer* (1934) and how to make the most of life in *Wake up and Live!* (1936), full of helpful hints such as 'Act as if it were impossible to fail,' while an entire chapter dedicated to 'On Saving Breath' includes the admonition not to ask for unnecessary advice.[29] Walter B. Pitkin, Professor of Journalism at Columbia University, promoted the view that *Life Begins at Forty* (1932), which must have comforted those reaching that age with the thought that 'fools die young', research having shown that 'the feeble-minded and the insane, even when protected within the walls of institutions, die considerably younger than the average man',[30] and also wrote *More Power to You* (1933).

While Samuel Smiles's *Self Help* (see page 496) asked its readers to adopt exemplary characters as role models, the new books adopted as their founding myth of modern America the story of the small guy who makes it big. The commercialisation of such a widely spread myth (originating in the epic story) could only have taken place in a society on the move, one in which there were considerable possibilities of social advancement. In a rapidly moving society in which decisions, including the decision to hire and fire, must be taken swiftly, on the spur of the moment, making a good impression is of decisive importance. Hence the importance of self-presentation and image-making: having the right look, giving the right impression, wearing the right clothes in the right manner. In a relatively static society, much of this would be unnecessary. People know each other; perhaps they see each other every day. What matters is not so much to look right, but to know the right people. What is the point of 'making a good impression' if you cannot hope to improve your station in life, if the social scale is relatively fixed? Improving one's image is now the staple of magazines all over Europe, but these took some time to develop, taking their first timid steps in the interwar years, when the genre was already blossoming in the USA. Nowadays such instructional manuals are also promoted via the internet. The learningannex.com website sells courses on 'How to Turn $40,000 Into $22 Million While You Sleep', 'How to Build Your Real Estate Fortune', 'How to Shoot Nudes Using a Live Model' and 'Talking to Heaven: How to Receive Messages from the Beyond'.

Though never the original inventors of various genres of non-fiction (the real identity of such inventors is a constant source of amusing but seldom accurate debate – spurious claims are often made for untraceable origins: the *first* cookery book, the *first* self-help book, etc.), Americans pioneered their popularisation. In a society of immigrants and high social and geographical mobility, each generation must learn again, or learn for the first time, what members of more sedate societies learn from their parents and grandparents. Cookery books may have existed for centuries, but the need for them, and for recipes in magazines, escalated when young brides were separated from their mothers. Similarly the raising of children, long transmitted by intergenerational advice, was put, in the US before other countries, on a 'scientific' footing. The Italian Maria Montessori (1870–1952) may have pioneered a method of bringing up children, but the real globalisation of the idea of a text about parenting started in the USA, reaching its climax with Dr Benjamin Spock's *The Common Sense Book of Baby and Child Care* (1946). Europeans first scoffed, but eventually bought Spock and his numerous imitators with the same relish as Americans.

Americans also pioneered the popularisation of social-science surveys, creating a market for the desire to know what other people do and think. This too is a hallmark of modernity. In rural societies, what people think and do is either a matter of little interest or of public knowledge transmitted via word of mouth (gossip). In larger societies this information was originally carried by newspapers on the basis of limited sources, in fact a nobler form of gossip. In the 1930s George Horace Gallup (1901–84) developed scientific surveys and opinion polls based on random sampling to replace or complement informed gossip. First he measured the interest of readers in the features and advertisements of newspapers, and later measured the reactions of radio audiences. Because of its anonymity this technique could be used for the kind of things Europeans would admit to almost no one except, in some circumstances, their confessor: particularly politics and sex. In 1948 an eight-hundred-page book almost entirely based on scientifically based random sampling turned out to be one of great publishing successes since *Gone with the Wind*. It was *Sexual Behavior of the Human Male*, better known as The Kinsey Report. It sold 100,000 copies on the first printing. Its title, one must surmise, was part of the appeal. As is often the case, the sequel, *Sexual Behavior of the Human Female* (1953), did not do as well.

American modernity did have its ideological contradictions. On the one hand it promulgated the idea of endless opportunity for the individual, on the other it also promoted the view that the individual was trapped in a predestined trajectory. This deterministic view could take a religious form – hence the large sales of Bibles and religious books, and the proliferation of organisations distributing them, and of a pseudo-scientific genre which facilitated the spread of popular forms of psychoanalysis and genetics. European countries were far from immune; however, they were protected from the more virulent forms of religiosity or pseudo-science by their attachment to old-fashioned religion and tradition. Eugenics, however, was also widespread in Europe, and in the case of Nazism with far more terrifying consequences than the 20,000 people reputedly sterilised in California before 1960; but it did not give rise to popular best-sellers like the pro-sterilisation and racist *The Rising Tide of Color* (1920) by Lothrop Stoddard – alluded to by Scott Fitzgerald in *The Great Gatsby* (as *The Rise of the Coloured Empire* by 'this man Goddard'). Stoddard envisaged a clash of civilisations between an increasingly outnumbered white race and the rest, and advocated restricting immigration into the USA to Nordic Europeans (superior, in his view, to the 'Alpines' and the 'Mediterraneans'). This was not the first such diatribe, and as we know it would not be the last. Enforced sterilisation had been adopted in a number of American states before the First World War, and in the 1920s in Switzerland and all the Scandinavian countries (often by social-democratic governments). *The Passing of the Great Race* (1916) by the American eugenicist Madison Grant was translated by the Nazis in 1925.[31] Ideas, including those now regarded as loathsome, floated freely across the Atlantic.

The Spectre of Mass Culture

Mass culture was the new spectre haunting Europe – made even more terrifying by the surge of mass political movements such as communism and fascism. Yet it was their enemy, bourgeois society, which had created mass culture.

Gustave le Bon (1841–1931), following Hippolyte Taine's work on collective behaviour (the volume on the Revolution in his *The Origins of Contemporary France*, 1875–94), had popularised a pseudo-scientific approach to crowd psychology, arguing in *La Psychologie des foules* (1895) that the crowd would always be swayed by sentimental and irrational thought. This 'cultural Cassandra' (the felicitous expression is Susanna Barrows') thought that educational progress was utopian, since free schooling created an army of discontented youth, unwilling to return to peaceable rural life. Luckily crowds, being submissive, are ready to follow a superior leader. The real leader needed to seduce the masses, pretend to have sympathy for their plight, and make exaggerated promises.[32] In Germany Adolf Halfeld, a right-wing cultural critic, wrote in *Amerika und der Amerikanismus* (1927) that 'the culture of Europe, in particular of Germany, is threatened by America with its concentration on materialism and the mechanisation of life'.[33] Oswald Spengler, in his famous *The Decline of the West* (1918–22), offered another dyspeptic view of mass culture, and above all of the popular press:

> The liberal bourgeois mind is proud of the abolition of censorship, the last restraint, while the dictator of the press – Northcliffe! – keeps the slave-gang of his readers under the whip of his leading articles, telegrams and pictures. Democracy has by its newspaper completely expelled the book from the *mental* life of the people ... The people reads the one paper, 'its' paper, which forces itself through the front doors by millions daily, spellbinds the intellect from morning to night ... Unleash the people as a reader-mass and it storms through the streets, hurls itself upon the target indicated, terrifying and breaking windows ... The press today is an army with carefully organised arms and branches, with journalists as officers, and readers as soldiers. But here, as in every army, the soldier obeys blindly, and war aims and operation plans change without his knowledge. The reader neither knows, nor is allowed to know, the purposes for which he is used, nor even the role that he is to play.[34]

Some intellectuals of the left – such as Theodor Adorno, Herbert Marcuse, Walter Benjamin and Max Horkheimer, all based at the Institut für Sozialforschung (Institute for Social Research) founded in 1923 within Frankfurt University – lambasted popular culture in all its forms with the same gusto with which nineteenth-century critics such as Sainte-Beuve, Thomas Carlyle and Matthew Arnold had denounced the industrialisation of culture. They defended the high culture of European society against the mass societies of fascism and capitalist America. In 'On the Fetish Character in Music and the Regression of Listening' (1938) Adorno attacked the *Kulturindustrie* as leading to the impoverishment of the original forms of culture, music in particular, because of the development of recording and broadcasting. High art had become part of mass culture, marketed in the same ways and with the same negative consequences, which converted the listener 'along his line of least resistance, into the acquiescent purchaser'; the street ballad 'and all the swarming forms of the banal' had once attacked the cultural privilege of the ruling class, but now that the 'power of the banal extends over the entire society' their function had changed and was no threat. Success had become 'the mere reflection of what one pays in the market for the product. The consumer is really worshipping the money that he himself has paid for the ticket to the Toscanini concert.'[35] In an essay written with Horkheimer, 'Dialectic of Enlightenment', Adorno asserted that the cinema and radio do not even have to pretend to be art: 'The truth that they are just business is made into an ideology in order to justify the rubbish they deliberately produce'; and 'The whole world is made to pass through the filter of the culture industry.'[36] This was done with the full cooperation of the people:

> Capitalist production so confines them, body and soul, that they fall helpless victims to what is offered them. As naturally as the ruled always took the morality imposed upon them more seriously than did the rulers themselves, the deceived masses are today captivated by the myth of success even more than the successful are. Immovably, they insist on the very ideology which enslaves them ... The industry submits to the vote which it has itself inspired. What is a loss for the firm which cannot fully exploit a contract with a declining star is a legitimate expense for the system as a whole.[37]

The French communist intellectual Paul Nizan attacked the 'mechanical means of culture, cinema, radio, record player' (1937).[38] Walter Benjamin, in his essay 'The Author as a Producer' (1934), which foreshadows his famous and much-cited 'Das Kunstwerk im Zeitalter seiner technischen Reproduzierbarkeit' (The Work of Art in the Epoch of its Technical Reproducibility, first version 1935), maintained that the more a work of art is reproduced, the more it loses its aura of uniqueness; whereas in reality its diffusion by reproduction adds aura to the original, which is why millions go to the Louvre to see the *Mona Lisa* or to a live concert to hear Michael Jackson, even though they can buy the reproduced image or the recorded sound for a fraction of the price.[39]

George Orwell in *The Road to Wigan Pier* (1937) regarded mass culture more conventionally: 'It is quite likely that fish and chips, art-silk stockings, tinned salmon, cut-price chocolate ... the movies, the radio, strong tea and the Football Pools have between them averted revolution.' The 'thing has happened' not by an 'astute manoeuvre by the governing class ... but by an unconscious process – the quite natural interaction between the manufacturers' need for a market and the need of half-starved people for cheap palliatives'.[40]

For every intellectual or organisation which expressed its fear or distaste for mass culture, one can cite another which welcomed it, either by finding in it elements of yesterday's high culture or by discerning an aspect of a modernity much to be welcomed. For every Adorno (a forceful critic of communist authoritarianism) who expressed distaste for jazz, there was a Louis Aragon (a regular apologist for Stalin's Russia) who welcomed – in 1961 – the transformation of a poem into a song, part of the democratisation of life in the last two centuries, coinciding as it did with new forms of listening, above all the transistor radio which, Aragon wrote, established the habit of private listening.[41] In July 1931 Jean-Paul Sartre, then twenty-six, delivered the inaugural address to new students, at the *lycée* in Le Havre where he taught, urging them to go to the cinema: 'Your parents,' he declared, 'may rest assured; the motion picture is not a bad school. It is an art . . . which reflects civilisation in our time.'[42] In January 1961 the French communist literary weekly *Les Lettres Françaises*, edited by Aragon, celebrated the crime novels of Dashiell Hammett.[43]

There is a sense of *déjà vu* in this debate, almost as if it were yet another revival of the old dispute between the early-nineteenth-century Romantics, eager to discover in popular folklore the basis for a renewed culture, and the upholders of traditional classical standards. The new dividing line had traditional intellectuals (of both left and right) lining up solidly in defence of high cultural standards, which had kept the masses at bay for centuries, facing various brands of right and left populists (including many communists and fascists) and modernising capitalists keen to develop a broad popular culture. Barbarism can be perceived behind every innovation, but equally, each novelty can be seen as a liberation. Fast food, washing machines and the Pill liberate women. Alternatively, fast food makes us fat and may eventually kill us. Cheap travel facilitates tourism and brings peace, harmony and mutual understanding. Alternatively, it causes havoc in settled and peaceful traditional societies, and destroys the environment. Television brings culture to every home and holds the family together. Alternatively, it transforms people into passive receptacles of cultural garbage.

The novelty was that 'the masses' in the years after the First World War appeared to be far wider than 'the people' of the Romantics. The latter were really the rural people, remote from the intellectuals themselves. The masses of the modern ages were urban, often citizens in their own right, and far from passive. Nor were they exclusively rural or urban, peasants or workers. When intellectuals thought of 'the masses' they usually included the new lower middle classes: the white-collar workers who were increasingly numerous and constituted a sizeable proportion of those who went to the cinema, listened to the radio and read magazines and novels. The class distance narrowed. Intellectuals rubbed shoulders with 'the masses' whenever they went to the cinema. Both read detective stories. Both listened to the radio. In some instances they even liked the same music. Siegfried Kracauer, in his 1926 essay 'Cult of Distraction', noted that the film audience in a large city like Berlin, with four million inhabitants, was becoming homogeneous and cosmopolitan. All of its members, 'from the bank director to the sales clerk, from the diva to the stenographer', had the same responses.[44] While the idea of similar responses is questionable and difficult to test, Kracauer was right to point to a mass cosmopolitanism. The growing international film market meant that the 'new' masses consumed the culture of other countries (usually that of the USA, itself an amalgam of various cultures). This was particularly true in small countries – for instance Sweden or Hungary – where consumers ended up being more cosmopolitan than those in Britain or the United States. In the nineteenth century people who had access to culture listened to German music, watched Italian opera, and read French and British novels. This kind of upper-middle-class cosmopolitanism became far more inclusive in the twentieth century.

Such cosmopolitanism reveals a paradox: the economic and cultural protectionism and nationalism of the 1920s and 1930s clashed with a growing globalisation of culture. National states and national intelligentsias, of course, attempted to oppose this flow, and though they may have been successful in stemming it, they failed to stop it. As we have seen in the previous chapters, it became possible to listen to jazz even in communist Russia, to watch Hollywood films in autarchic Italy, and in Paris in the 1920s, the *années folles* which produced the image of 'Gay Paree', much of the dance music fashionable at the time came – then as now – from the USA.[45]

47

Interwar Cinema

An International Community

THE YEARS BETWEEN 1920 AND 1960 were the great era of the cinema, the time of peak consumption before television sent so many spectators back home. The peak years almost coincided with the advent of television: 1943 for the USA, when 4,400 million visits were paid to the cinema; 1946 for the UK with 1,600 million; 1955 for Italy with 819 million; 1956 for West Germany with 818 million; and seventy million in Holland in 1956. The French peak was reached in 1957, and Japan's in 1958.[1] Then cinema audiences started to decrease until the mid-1980s, when they increased gradually.[2] The British figures show an almost doubling of attendances from the mid-1930s to the mid-1940s, and a subsequent dramatic collapse.

CINEMA ATTENDANCE: UK

Year	Figure in millions
1935	912
1939	990
1943	1,541
1946	1,635
1950	1,395
1955	1,181
1960	500
1965	326
1970	193
1975	116

Year	Figure in millions
1980	101
1985	72
1990	97
1995	114
2000	142
2002	176

SOURCE: British Film Institute *www.bfi.org.uk*

In the interwar years Europe as a whole made more films than the United States, but only the Americans had a really global industry. In 1937, for instance, America produced 567 films, but Japan made five hundred, more than any other country outside the USA, and India 350 – but this production was directed exclusively at the domestic market.[3] The Chinese too, though they started late, made some one hundred films a year by the late 1920s. India was producing two hundred films a year in the early 1930s, when thanks to sound it could use the central feature of its traditional theatre: song and dance. Thousands of films were made, but the overwhelming majority were strictly for the domestic market.

The Europeans never quite conceived of the cinema as an industry. The Americans always did. This is reflected in the cinema's literature. A history of the European cinema is often the story of its great directors – just as a history of literature is often the story of great writers. But a history of the American cinema is first of all a history of the industry, of Hollywood, of producers, technicians, studios, genres and stars, as well as famous directors.[4]

The popularity and diffusion of the cinema as a cultural genre had no historical precedent. In the nineteenth century millions read books and newspapers, and thousands went to cabarets, variety shows and theatres, but the average person hardly ever read a book or even a newspaper. In the 1930s in France the *average* person age went to the cinema more than five times a year – nine times a year between 1945 and 1955. In the nineteenth century there were hundreds of theatres in France and Italy, but in 1918, when the cinema was just over twenty years old, there were 1,444 cinemas in France alone, 4,200 in 1929, and 5,834 in 1959. And France was far from being the most cinematic country in Europe. In Great Britain there were 5,000 cinemas as early as 1914 (though 28 per cent of these had fewer than five hundred seats). In 1919 there were 2,836 cinemas in Germany, and by 1929, 5,300, making Germany the largest European film market.[5] But towering over every other country for the sheer size of its market was the USA.

NUMBER OF CINEMAS IN 1937	
USA	17,000
Germany	5,395
Great Britain	5,000
Italy	4,900
France	4,500
Spain	3,500
Czechoslovakia	1,847
Sweden	1,783
Japan	1,717
Australia	1,541
Brazil	1,246
Mexico	1,115
Canada	1,089
Argentina	1,021
Belgium	1,000

SOURCE: Ramsaye (ed.), *The 1938–39 Motion Picture Almanac*, p.932

The USSR claimed to have 26,000 outlets, though it must be assumed that included in the total was almost any room or shed where screenings could take place.

The huge American market (eighty-eight million people going to the cinema every week in 1938) should be put in perspective. The bulk of the revenue in the late 1930s came from the theatres located in the larger cities (those with over 50,000 inhabitants), of which there were just under 5,000.[6]

In terms of population, British attendances were in line with those of the USA. Though attendances decreased between the mid-1920s and the mid-1930s because of high prices (made higher by the Entertainment Duty, a tax also levied in other countries), the cinema in Great Britain had become the main form of working-class entertainment as early as 1918. Weekly attendance averaged fifteen million, reaching twenty million in the 1930s.[7] Children were involved too: in 1931, 30 per cent of children *under five* regularly attended, often dragged by their parents.[8] In 1943, 20 per cent of British teenagers went to the pictures more than twice a week.[9] In the nineteenth century bourgeois audiences went to the theatre for the melodramas of playwrights like Pixérécourt and Scribe (see pages 286–9 and 581–5), where they would see a fantastic depiction of their world. The new cinema audiences, prevalently lower-middle-class and working-class, seldom saw themselves on the screen, but they enjoyed the discovery of a world which seemed to them one of fantasy: expensive cars, luxury restaurants, grand hotels, dashing rich men and beautiful women. It was the modernisation of the fairy tale.

Reliable evidence on cinema attendances before the Second World War is scarce. One of the few sources available for British audiences in the 1930s is the ledger of the Regent cinema in Portsmouth, the most luxurious and largest (1,992 seats) of the twenty-nine cinemas in a town of approximately 258,000 inhabitants in 1939. The overall average annual attendance figure in the 1930s was 787,000.[10] The patrons of the Regent went to see American films far more than British films: 311 American first features against 142 British. There were nine American films in the top thirteen hits of the decade – the top box office success was *Snow White*.[11]

Entertainment for children and young adults, hitherto a largely private affair, rapidly became a formidable cultural market in its own right. Already in 1914 the pioneering sociologist of the cinema Emilie Altenloh had noted the high frequency of attendance by children, who rarely went to a concert, a variety show, a circus or a theatre.[12]

By the end of the First World War only in America was this enormous thirst for movies quenched by domestic production alone. Not only did the USA produce several times more films than Germany, Europe's largest producer, but it had almost as many cinema seats as all other countries combined. European countries had to import films from the USA, while America could do without European films. Full protectionism was never a serious option in Europe; it always was in the USA. Besides, Hollywood's foreign operations benefited from the efficient assistance of the US Department of Commerce, and American Embassies gathered a wealth of information on the motion picture trade in foreign countries and the likes and dislikes of their audiences. The industry successfully lobbied Congress to establish a Motion Picture Department within the Department of Commerce 'on the grounds that movies acted as the silent salesmen of American goods to audiences worldwide'. No European film industry was similarly spurred towards export by its own government – defending the home market was the main aspiration.[13] The Motion Picture Producers and Distributors of America (MPPDA), headed by Will Hays (famous for the code, see pages 964–5) and established in the early 1920s, was a well-organised lobby representing the might of all the major Hollywood studios, aligned and united to do everything it could not to give an inch of the domestic market to foreign films. Speaking in London in 1923, Will Hays declared: 'We are going to sell America to the world with American motion pictures.'[14] The American film industry also intended to keep as large a share of the inter-national market as possible. In April 1930 the *Harvard Business Review* pointed out that there were few American industries so dependent on foreign markets as the film industry.[15]

. Europeans, on the other hand, went on importing American films right up to the war, even in Hitler's Germany and Mussolini's Italy, not because they were in any way committed to the principles of free trade – far from it – but because they could not make enough films themselves to satisfy their own markets, nor could they risk depriving their public of its main form of entertainment. Americanism seemed unstoppable except by war or commu-nism. The introduction of sound in the late 1920s did affect American exports, but far less than anticipated. Eventually dubbing and subtitles ensured the globalisation of Fred Astaire and Ginger Rogers.

By the mid-1920s the sway of America's cultural industries was so great that Europeans talked incessantly of their fear of Americanisation. The French cinema – once the first in the world – was reduced to defending its own home market from the American 'invasion'. The Germans were equally alarmed at being saturated with *Amerikanismus* as the country watched American pictures, received American finance and listened to American jazz, while reading books denouncing American popular culture written by conservatives and socialists alike. In Britain, the *Daily Express* commented in 1927: 'The bulk of picture-goers are Americanised to an extent that makes them regard the British film as a foreign film . . . they talk America, think America, dream America; we have several million people, mostly women, who, to all intents and purposes, are temporary American citizens.'[16] Ten years later the alarm bells were still ringing, even though Europe had turned much more protectionist. Britain's *World Film News* of November 1937 lamented: 'The American drive to obliterate every vestige of a native British film industry is succeeding admirably. Cynics are comparing the situation with the Italian conquest of Abyssinia, and there are indeed certain resem-blances.'[17]

There was little reciprocity, even though the British 1938 Films Act successfully encouraged American distributors to import British films. European films could not invade the USA. They could not even invade each other's markets. They could not even prevail within their own colonial empires: in 1926 only 5 per cent of films shown within the British Empire were of British origin. Perhaps British films deserved such poor attendance: many of them were slow and ponderous, with a poorly constructed narrative.[18] In the 1930s, however, British films gained in popularity, in comparison with the 1920s, in spite of the release of many more US films.[19]

The situation in France was a little better: domestic production amounted to 12 per cent of films shown, against nearly two-thirds of American imports.[20] Everyone began to introduce quotas. The Germans were the first in 1925 with the so-called *Kontingent*, the Italians followed in 1927, the French in 1928, by which time Europe was intersected by a complex quota system. The British reacted to the American 'invasion' with the Cinematograph Act 1927 (also known as the Quota Act), aimed at curbing foreign films (in practice American ones) for economic as well as cultural reasons. Films promoted trade, it was argued in the House of Commons, and it was also necessary to defend one's national identity: the British should not 'be compelled to imbibe the ideas of foreigners'. Exhibitors complained, pointing out that one could not force people to watch British films. In spite of the rhetoric the legislation was ineffectual, and was probably intended to be so.[21] It required that 5 per cent of films shown had to be British, hardly a demanding requirement, and far inferior to the quotas imposed by the French and the Germans. The requirement was gradually increased: by 1936 it was 20 per cent. British 'quota quickies' fillers (cheap films made almost exclusively to achieve the quota) were manufactured rapidly, and it showed, making the reputation of British films sink even lower. Nevertheless, the Act signalled a new direction for the British government. Previously its only involvement in films was in taxing them or censoring them. Now films were seen as something valuable in themselves, an element of national identity, to be protected.[22] Besides, even the 'quota quickies' provided a training ground for British film personnel.[23]

Protectionism worked, in the sense that there was a revival of domestic production, facilitated by the introduction of sound and the additional costs required for dubbing US films. In the 1920s some 80 per cent of films shown in France were made in the USA. By 1931, quotas, various restrictions and the introduction of sound cut the figure by half,[24] and by 1937 most European countries had introduced protectionism for their films. Those that had not – such as Belgium and Holland – had little to protect. By the late 1930s American films shown in Continental Europe earned only $3 million annually, while revenues from the British market were between $35 and $50 million.[25] A film like *Stagecoach* (loosely adapted from Guy de Maupassant's *Boule de Suif* and starring John Wayne and Monument Valley) made, between 1939 and 1943, over $214,000 in the British Commonwealth, but only $53,500 in Europe ($19,000 in Italy alone).[26] Such figures are, of course, skewed by the fact that with the advent of the war many foreign markets were abruptly closed to the USA, including those of Spain, France, Japan, Poland, Italy and Germany.

Taking advantage of the relatively poor quality of British films (and importing the best British technicians and directors, such as Alfred Hitchcock, who moved to Hollywood in 1939), the Americans made their own 'British' films (150 of them between 1930 and 1945), i.e. either films set in Britain or adapted from British literary sources. MGM in particular made many of the most popular 'British' films: *David Copperfield* (1934), *Mutiny on the Bounty* (1935), *Goodbye Mr Chips* (1939), *The Barretts of Wimpole Street* (1934), *Mrs Miniver* (1942) and *The White Cliffs of Dover* (1944), shot partly at Malibu because 'Our cliffs were better – whiter and cliffier,' according to its director, George Cukor.[27] The same logic was used by Vincente Minelli, who did not shoot *Brigadoon* (1958) in Scotland because Scotland did not look Scottish enough.[28]

Only English-speaking countries could be so penetrated. The US never bothered to make French films for the French, or German films for the Germans. Thus the British film industry was faced with the kind of competition no other country ever had to face. Sound protected, partially, the French, who could at least export their films to their own colonies, Belgium and the French-speaking areas of Switzerland and Canada. The Germans had Austria and German Switzerland. The Indians had a vast market, as did the Japanese and Chinese. The British, however, saw themselves at the cinema as Hollywood saw them. Mark Glancy's pioneering study *When Hollywood Loved Britain: The Hollywood 'British' Film 1939–45* (1999) uncovered how profitable this state of affairs was for Hollywood. Real British films did not do so well in the USA – at least not until World War II. American 'British' films did well in the USA, but much better in Britain – with people flocking to see the white cliffs of Malibu. Conversely, the few really British films that did well in the USA had been produced with the American market in mind.

Here foreigners were often more in tune with international taste. It was not by accident that the greatest interwar success of the British in the USA, *The Private Life of Henry VIII* (1933), was made by an expatriate Hungarian, Alexander Korda, whose cameraman was French and whose scriptwriter was another Hungarian.[29] Birmingham-born Michael Balcon, one of the leading film producers of the interwar period, did not need marketing lessons. Recognising that Hitchcock's projected adaptation of John Buchan's *The Thirty-Nine Steps* was a winner, he made sure that the dialogue avoided phrases 'purely of importance to a British audience', and that Robert Donat, who was known in the USA, headed the cast.[30]

Some, the French and the Germans in particular, defended themselves by making films reflecting what they thought was their own national identity. This pleased the critics as well as home audiences, but was of little interest to foreigners. French serial films harked back to the great successes of its nineteenth-century serialised novels – a stream of stories of detectives pursuing criminal gangs, costume dramas such as *Les Trois mousquetaires* (1921), adapted from the ever-popular Dumas, and melodramas.[31] The Europeans tried to counter the American invasion by starting a kind of cinematic German-dominated Common Market – 'Film Europe' – with joint productions and reciprocal distribution. Four hundred and thirty-six films were made under this initiative, more than half of them German; then the advent of the sound movie thwarted this European effort.[32]

The cinema continued to be heavily dependent on written texts. Novels and plays provided the plot for two-thirds of the 1,300 films made in France in the 1930s.[33] Avant-garde attempts to subvert traditional narrative failed in the cinema as they did in the novel: little followed canonical works such Luis Buñuel's *Un Chien Andalou* (1929) and *L'Age d'or* (1930), just as James Joyce's *Finnegans Wake* has remained an isolated case in literature. The avant-garde, instead, selected 'cult' films, i.e. conventional narrative films (such as *Casablanca*) which could be read in an unconventional way.

Many of the new and old penny dreadful and dime stories translated into film very easily.[34] Other films were adaptations of the nineteenth-century 'well-made play', proceeding in a standardised fashion from the exposition of the situation and the characters, to conflict, crisis and resolution. Historical films treated history with the same cavalier attitude exhibited by the historical novel since the days of Walter Scott. Once a genre was well under way, it was difficult to subvert its rules, however ahistorical they were. Western films devised the idea of the gun challenge, whereby the duellists would face each other in a contest with the same kind of rules of chivalry, honour and loyalty that had been celebrated in literature since the middle ages. The western hero would claim, like a noble knight, that he would 'never shoot a man in the back' – though common sense would suggest that shooting someone in the back was far safer than a gunfight. The cinema systematically traduced, 'betrayed', adapted and modified older narratives, delighting the many (who had never encountered these works before) and scandalising a few. Among the scandalised were Theodor Adorno and Max Horkheimer, who declared in 1944: 'What is new about the phase of mass culture compared with the late liberal stage is the exclusion of the new. The machine rotates on the same spot. While determining consumption it excludes the untried as a risk. The movie-makers distrust any manuscript which is not reassuringly backed by a best-seller.'[35]

The legendary Hollywood producer David O. Selznick would not have disagreed with Adorno. Writing to Hitchcock on 12 June 1939 about his 'disappointing' first draft of the script for *Rebecca*, the adaptation of Daphne du Maurier's novel, he explained that 'No one, not even the author of an original work, can say with any degree of accuracy why a book has caught the fancy of the public; if it were this easy, the author of the original could duplicate these elements and duplicate the success, which we know very few authors of successful works are able to do.' It follows, he continued, that it is necessary 'to try as far as possible to retain the original'. 'This is not a theory,' he added. 'I have too long and too successfully resisted attempts to movie-ise successful works not to be sure that my process of adaptation is sound. While others monkeyed around distorting original works, I insisted upon faithfulness in a long list of transcriptions.'[36] Hitchcock, of course, held the diametrically contrary view: 'I owe much of the success I have been lucky enough to achieve,' he had said in 1936, 'to my "ruthlessness" in adapting stories for the screen.'[37] Yet he had no wish to antagonise the powerful Selznick (nor to return to England, as war was about to break out): the treatment was rewritten in accordance with Selznick's wishes.[38] But Selznick had to agree to a major change in the plot. In the book Rebecca had been killed by her husband. The Hays Code would not have allowed a murderer to get away with it, so in the film Rebecca dies in an accident.[39]

The systematic ransacking of literature for plots and characters is not unique to the cinema. The theatre had been using other people's works uninhibitedly, and continued to do so. Hugo von Hofmannsthal adapted *Elektra* (1903) from Sophocles and *Der Turm* (The Tower, 1925) from Calderón de la Barca. Bertolt Brecht's *Mutter Courage* (1941) – one of his best plays – was grounded in a literary tradition that included Grimmelshausen's *Courasche*, Schiller's *Wallensteins Lager* and Alfred Döblin's *Wallenstein* (1920).[40] The cinema pillaged literature, but it also gave something back. Having seen the film, many people wanted to read the book. The stories of Pinocchio and Bambi were given a new lease of life thanks to Walt Disney.

What the cinema was doing was to create an extensive community of film-goers united by the common experience of watching similar films – though the context of their viewing and their existing values and tastes were different. The printed text had facilitated the creation of nations, now celluloid created an international community – though national hostility and rivalries continued unabated. A generation of Italians and Germans reared on American films did little to oppose their countries' entry into a war against America.

Adapting for the cinema encompassed far more than the narratives of the past, its history and its myths. It involved reframing as a narrative not only documentaries – the main genre of the very early cinema – but also news and current affairs, as the press had done. To compete with fictional films these genres had to acquire some of their characteristics. The popular genre of the lecture by travellers, illustrated with photographs, paved the way for the silent-era documentary in which the 'lecturer' had to be eliminated: the images had to speak for themselves. Robert Flaherty's famous 1922 film *Nanook of the North* (shot in northern Canada) was centred on a member of the Inuit people (an Eskimo, as was then said) and his family. Nanook was made to perform the role of the romanticised primitive.[41] The novelty was that the life of the Inuit appeared from the point of view of one of them. Indeed, the Inuit were involved in various stages of the production, and even fished Flaherty's camera out of the water, took it apart, cleaned it and put it together again.[42] Yet much of the film was staged, and some details were arranged to fit in with the Western idea of how primitive people lived. Thus Nanook was seen hunting with a spear and building an igloo, whereas in real life he hunted with a rifle, used cash and wore Western clothes. Flaherty thought that his staging made the film more 'authentic', since his aim was to show how the Inuit might have lived had they not been colonised.[43] The unwritten rules of the documentary remained similar to those of non-fiction: everything represented purported to be true, while in fiction it was left to the reader to disentangle fiction from reality.

Before their virtual demise as a mainstream genre following the arrival of television, documentaries were often part of the programme offered to viewers alongside the main feature and the newsreel. As such they did not have an independent market, but were acquired by distributors to make the fare on offer more substantial. This provided the documentary with a wider public than it would have had, and offered the audience an educational experience which they would have been unwilling to undergo otherwise (as was later the case with television, the eventual home of the overwhelming majority of documentaries). In the 1930s and 1940s synchronised sound introduced into documentaries and newsreels a booming and aggressive male voice-over commentary that took the audience from the first shot to the last in an authoritatively authorial way. This 'Voice of God', unthinkable in human form, suggested absolute mastery over the story.[44] It brooked no dissent.

Documentaries remained a subsidiary genre in spite of the acknowledged brilliance of specialist film-makers such as Flaherty, Leni Riefenstahl (the Nazi director of *Triumph of the Will*, 1935 and *Olympia*, 1938), Pare Lorentz, who made films dealing with the American Depression and environmental issues (*The Plough that Broke the Plains*, 1936), the Dutch Joris Ivens, a socialist whose films denounced the working conditions of miners and celebrated revolutionaries all over the world (in Spain, Indonesia, Cuba, Vietnam, China, etc.), and the British producer John Grierson, who coined the term 'documentary' and who directed films on behalf of government agencies such as the Empire Marketing Board, the Post Office and the National Film Board of Canada. The private sector seldom took any deep interest in documentaries until the late 1990s and early 2000s, with commercial successes such as the British *Touching the Void* (2003) and the American Michael Moore's highly political documentaries *Bowling for Columbine* (2002) and *Fahrenheit 9/11* (2003).

Controlling Films

The attraction of the cinema to a 'mass' audience caused even greater alarm than had the despised popular genres of the nineteenth century. Since – as everyone knows – people are malleable and can be easily swayed, it was unthinkable that the modern state, now so much more powerful and 'democratic' (in the sense that it had to rest on some form of popular mobilisation), could remain indifferent to what they went to see in droves. The risks for producers were far greater than those facing nineteenth-century publishers. Printing a book only to see it banned was bad business, but to have an expensive film, with a large cast and famous stars, removed from circulation was disastrous. Film producers had to tread a careful path: they had to avoid offending articulate and politically powerful minorities, while pleasing their audiences, who on the whole liked sex and violence.

A complex machinery of control, formal and informal, came to be erected throughout Europe and North America. Countries which had just abolished stage censorship, such as France, Sweden and Denmark, now introduced film censorship.[45] The French set up their Commission de Contrôle des Films (1916) and the Swedes the Board of Film Censors (1911). In Great Britain the Cinematograph Act 1909 gave power to local authorities to exclude a film from local cinemas – the Act, ostensibly, was aimed at fire safety. The industry responded, as did its American counterpart, by establishing in 1912 its own internal 'police', hoping to avoid excessive state interference. This was the British Board of Film Censors (BBFC). At first it was regarded as too liberal, even though in its first year it made cuts to 144 films and banned twenty-two others. Form seemed to matter more than content. Alexander Butler's *Damaged Goods*, a morality film about the dangers of contracting sexually transmitted diseases by consorting with prostitutes, was allowed to proceed with so many cuts that it was difficult to follow the plot. It could be screened in Belfast only if men and women sat on different sides of the cinema.[46]

By the 1920s the BBFC had adopted a stricter attitude, which led to its powers being given almost official status by most local authorities.[47] Its function was to decide whether a film could be seen by 'adults only' (an A certificate) or by everyone (U), or whether it could be seen at all. To gain a certificate, cuts were often suggested in accordance with a helpful list of forty-three rules devised by the BBFC President T.P. O'Connor in 1917 ('O'Connor's 43'). Thirty-three of these rules concerned questions of morality, such as depictions of prostitution, premarital or extra-marital sex, perversions and venereal disease.[48] Some political themes, such as references to the struggle 'between Capital and Labour' were also to be avoided. Between 1913 and the 1970s more than five hundred films were rejected.[49] Twelve films were banned in 1930 because they mentioned or dealt with blackmail associated with immorality, cruelty to animals, abortion, birth control, showed the Salvation Army unfavourably, showed a man and a woman in bed together, or were just sordid.[50] The BBFC became more liberal in the 1950s, in response to a drop in audiences.[51] This may have been an attempt by the Board to stop them falling, or simply an indication that as the medium was becoming less popular it could afford to risk more. Or that times were changing.

The BBFC intervened in politics too, though of course far less than its equivalents did in fascist Italy or communist Russia. When appeasing Hitler was official government policy, the Board followed suit. In some cases it even led the way. A string of scripts dealing with the persecution of Jews in Nazi Germany were turned down throughout the 1930s as 'unsuitable at least in the present juncture', or because they were 'pure anti-Hitler propaganda and as such unsuitable for production as a film'. It turned down a proposal for a film called *A German Tragedy* about a Jewish doctor who loses his job as a result of anti-Semitism because it 'might provoke a disturbance' – a reference to fights between anti-fascist activists and fascist supporters.[52]

A similar self-policing outlook pervaded the American film industry, which in 1909 had set up the National Board of Censorship. By the early 1920s a spate of scandals had created a negative image of Hollywood: drugs, drinks (in the era of Prohibition), sex and, in 1921, the rape and subsequent death of a young actress involving the obese and popular comedian Roscoe 'Fatty' Arbuckle (he was subsequently acquitted). As a result the industry asked William H. Hays (1879–1954), the US Postmaster-General, to create an office in 1924 ('the Hays Office') within the MPPDA, with the specific task of suggesting cuts to films and scripts. The Hays Code became the self-regulatory doctrine of the American cinema industry (it was finally abolished in the 1960s, when film classification was introduced). In practice Hays dictated what Hollywood's moral framework should be, and in so doing what the cinema-going public in the rest of the world could watch (though in theory 'expunged' scenes could be re-introduced for export).

The Code, strengthened in 1930, established that adultery should not be made to look attractive; kisses and embraces should not be too lascivious; passion could be shown only moderately and should not stimulate basic instincts; sexual 'perversions' (i.e. homosexuality) should not even be alluded to; sexually transmitted diseases were never to be mentioned; sexual relations between whites and blacks were taboo (and remained so for decades); there was to be no nudity, or mention of white slavery or drug trafficking; childbirth scenes, direct or indirect, were to be avoided; no fun should be made of religion or of clergymen and priests; dancing could be shown only if obscene and suggestive movements were avoided; profanities were to be cut, including 'son-of-a-bitch', 'God', 'hell' and 'damn'; the word 'nuts' should only be used when it meant 'crazy'; rape 'should never be more than suggested, and only when essential for the plot'; double beds should be avoided even in a married couple's bedroom (a ban imported from Britain). A further injunction in 1939 refined the list while making it more ambiguous and hence more open to debate. Thus, in 1930, 'scenes of passion should not be introduced except when definitively essential to the plot'. By 1939 such scenes were to be 'treated with an honest acknowledgement of human nature and its normal reactions', however, 'many scenes cannot be presented without arousing dangerous emotions on the part of the immature, the young or the criminal classes'.[53]

Anything that might be regarded as an insult to the American flag was prohibited. The prohibition of 'damn' worried David O. Selznick, the producer and mastermind of *Gone with the Wind*, since the film he had just finished included Clark Gable's often-quoted 'Frankly my dear, I don't give a damn.' On 17 October 1939 Selznick wrote to Will Hays: 'Naturally I am most desirous of keeping this line and, to judge from the reactions of two preview audiences, this line is remembered, loved and looked forward to by the millions who have read this new American classic.' He reminded Hays of some of his previous moral pictures such as *David Copperfield* and *Little Lord Fauntleroy*, that he had always respected the Code, that the offensive word was perhaps a 'vulgarism' – as described in the *Oxford English Dictionary* – but not a curse or an oath; besides, it had been used in the *Atlantic Monthly* and *Woman's Home Companion*; and that the sentence was in Margaret Mitchell's book. Hays granted permission to use 'damn', and a *frisson* of delight pervaded audiences thereafter.[54]

The Code's prudishness inhibited the production of scenes which had been acceptable in earlier times, such as the allegedly first 'nude' in *A Daughter of the Gods*, a 1916 Fox Corporation film directed by Herbert Brenon in which the Australian swimming star Annette Kellerman's breasts are barely visible beneath her long, flowing hair.[55] The Code considerably helped American films in Catholic countries, partially countering the Vatican's constant worry that the Americanisation of the masses would bring about the dethroning of religion by the consumer society, the destruction of the family by emancipated women, and the poisoning of the minds of the young and the lower classes. In 1935 the Papal Encyclical *Vigilanti Cura* defined the guidelines for the Catholic position on the cinema, but of course since the 1920s bishops had had to advise their priests on what could be watched and what should be avoided. Catholics eventually realised that most American films were relatively harmless products for the entire family. The 'dangerous' ones were overwhelmingly European. Yet in some instances Europeans were more alarmist than Americans. *Frankenstein* (1931), one of the four horror movies the British director James Whale made in Hollywood, was banned in Italy, Czechoslovakia, Sweden, both parts of Ireland, and Australia.[56]

In Weimar Germany censorship was rather liberal, considering that prevailing opinion among right-thinking people was as prudish as everywhere else. During the 1920s very few films were banned outright, though one-third of the total was classified as for adults only.[57] In the 1930s, of course, matters changed remarkably, and not just because the Nazi regime was as oppressive as the Weimar Republic had been liberal, but because, like everywhere else, the 1920s were less restrictive than the 1930s. This was true even in the USA, which was more politically liberal in the 1930s under Roosevelt than in the 1920s, when Prohibition prevailed.

Between 1915 and 1921 the sex farce was second only to the musical comedy in the preferences of the American theatre-going public. Inspired by the tradition of the French farce, these works had suggestive titles such as *The Girl in the Limousine, Up in Mabel's Room, Getting Gertie's Garter* and *The Demi-Virgin*. On 26 April 1926 Mae West could even star in a play she had written herself (under the pseudonym of 'Jane Mast') called, provocatively, *Sex*. Though (or because) the critics regarded it as a 'crude and inept play, cheaply produced and poorly acted' (*New York Times*) and 'nasty, infantile, amateurish with vicious dialog' (*Variety*), it was the only play in Broadway to attract full houses through the summer and the autumn.[58] *Sex* ran for 375 performances and was seen by more than 325,000 people. Orchestra seats cost $10 at a time when $2.80 was normally the top price.[59] It was set in a bordello, where the heroine, Margy, played by West, uses her sexual allure to get ahead. She is neither punished nor does she repent – a flagrant breach of the unwritten morality code. The content was only part of the problem, the underlying one being that West was bringing burlesque to Broadway, thus crossing the line that divided the 'low' genre from the 'legitimate' theatre.

The authorities reacted by demanding that the play be closed. The great comic actress and writer refused; consequently she was arrested, tried and convicted for writing an indecent play.[60] She was fined and spent ten days in jail, to the delight of the other female inmates. After further stage works such as her 'homosexual plays' *The Drag* and *The Pleasure Man*, and further arrests, Mae West went on to Hollywood where she adapted one of her plays,

Diamond Lil (for which she had been arrested), for a Paramount production with the title *She Done Him Wrong* (1930). The Hays Office, unsurprisingly, rejected the script. Paramount, then in some financial trouble and in need of a commercial success, declared itself willing to defy the industry's censor and defend itself in court. A compromise was found. The film, though banned in some states, was a success. It made the line 'Come up and see me some time' famous. Paramount was encouraged to try another Mae West film, *I'm No Angel*, which contained no sex scenes but further immortal lines such as 'When I'm good, I'm very good. But when I'm bad, I'm better,' and 'It's better to be looked over than overlooked.' By 1935 West was making almost half a million dollars a year.[61] The Hays Office exacted its revenge. A campaign was launched against Mae West for the crime of showing that the role of the uninhibited female sexual aggressor could be used in comic films. By 1938 she found herself on the Hays blacklist. Paramount, scared, did not renew her contract.[62] The way was opened for the more subdued Doris Day films of the 1950s, in which women could have jobs and be assertive, but remained virgins.

Hollywood and Europe

After the First World War the USA had successfully insisted that the Europeans open their markets to American films. The Hollywood studios created a formidable networking system, unique in the world. Production was rationalised – inspired by the new assembly-line system – and concentrated in a few giant companies. Each company was vertically integrated, from production to distribution to exhibition. Most borrowed money from the New York financial system, yet production, the 'artistic' side, kept well away – 3,000 miles – from the money men. The system was probably inefficient, but somehow it worked. As the urban geographer and historian Peter Hall put it:

> Los Angeles was a place where people came to leave behind their old ideas about cities, industries and culture. This is what allowed it to welcome new industries and make them its own. That is the essence of the innovative milieu.[63]

Concentration in urban centres had been essential for the development of the various branches of the nineteenth-century European cultural industry, giving a disproportionate role to key cities such as Paris, London, Berlin,

Frankfurt, Munich, Milan, St Petersburg and Vienna. By the time Hollywood had been created, the narrative-based large-scale feature film had become the standard, though documentaries and newsreels were also regularly made. A system had been formed which had few competitors in Europe. It consisted of a restricted number of studios, each headed by a tycoon, able to attract consistent investment from banks.[64]

Adolph Zukor, head of the Famous Players Film Co. – eventually absorbed by its distribution company Paramount founded by Jesse Lasky in 1916 – was financed by Kuhn, Loeb & Co. Samuel Goldwyn founded Goldwyn Pictures Corporation (1916), which became Metro-Goldwyn-Mayer in 1924 when it was taken over by Louis B. Mayer (who ruled the company in a famously autocratic way until he was ousted in 1951) – though until 1936 production was in the hands of the 'boy wonder' Irving Thalberg. MGM was funded by the New York bank Loew's Inc., which also controlled the Loew chain of cinemas. William Fox, who founded Twentieth Century-Fox with the financial backing of Halsey, Stuart & Co. and Loew's Inc., was in turn backed by W.C. Durant of General Motors and Harvey Gibson, Chairman of Liberty National Bank. United Artists was created in 1919 by a group of exceedingly well-paid actors (Charles Chaplin, Mary Pickford and Douglas Fairbanks) and the director D.W. Griffith to distribute their own independently produced films. 'So the lunatics have taken charge of the asylum,' said Richard Rowland, the MGM President, expressing a widely shared scepticism.[65] Harry, Albert and Samuel Warner – all born in Poland – and Canadian-born Jack created Warner Brothers. In 1903 they had opened a nickelodeon in a small town in Pennsylvania. By 1918 they had their own studio in Hollywood. In 1923 they formed Warner Bros Pictures, Inc., and in 1927 they produced the first picture using incorporated sound effects: *The Jazz Singer*. In 1920 the brothers Jack and Harry Cohn founded Columbia (originally CBC), heading it from 1924 to the mid-1950s. This was the smallest of the major Hollywood studios, and the only one not to be vertically integrated. Carl Laemmle, who had started his career in Chicago with a nickelodeon in 1906, moved to Hollywood in 1915, buying a large site in the Hollywood Hills and renaming it Universal City, seat of Universal.

Many of the pioneering film producers were Jewish immigrants who had started their careers in the nickelodeon business. Louis B. Mayer came from Minsk, Samuel Goldwyn from Poland, Adolph Zukor and William Fox from Hungary, and Carl Laemmle from Germany. Jack and Harry Cohn were American-born Jews. The strong presence of Jews in the US film industry –

as producers, directors, scriptwriters, technicians and actors – would be further strengthened by the arrival in the 1930s of those escaping the Nazis. Unaffected by any great nostalgia for the 'Old Country' – often a land of persecution – already urbanised and literate, Jews were more predisposed towards integration into American society than many other immigrants.[66] The new industry provided an ideal platform for ambitious young Jews – there were fewer obstacles to their advancement than elsewhere, no ancient prejudices, no pre-existing closed networks. Of course they faced anti-Semitism, as they did elsewhere, but discrimination existed against other minorities too, such as Italians and, above all, blacks. There were familiar anti-Semitic outbursts, like that in Henry Ford's *Dearborn Independent* (the company paper of a company town) which dedicated its 1 January 1921 issue to the question of the 'Jewish control' of Hollywood (republished the following year in Henry Ford's *The International Jew*):

> ... the motion picture industry is ... entirely Jew-controlled; with the natural consequence that the civilised world is increasingly antagonistic to the trivialising and demoralising influence of that form of entertainment as at present managed. Every ... day literally millions of people give up from 30 minutes to 8 hours to the 'Movies'; and this simply means that millions of Americans every day place themselves voluntarily within range of Jewish ideas of life, love and labor; within close range of Jewish propaganda, sometimes cleverly, sometimes clumsily concealed. This gives the Jewish masseur of the public mind all the opportunity he desires; and his only protest now is that exposure may make his game a trifle difficult.[67]

The established Hollywood majors never successfully managed to bar entry to new competitors. When sound was introduced, RCA (Radio Corporation of America) decided to enter the industry, and created RKO. Another studio emerged that would corner the market in animated films: Walt Disney (it did not produce live motion pictures until after the war). But the most glamorous of the majors was MGM. Its roaring lion announced a galaxy of stars without peer ('More stars than there are in heaven' was its slogan): Lillian Gish, Greta Garbo, Clark Gable, Buster Keaton, the Marx Brothers, Jean Harlow, Norma Shearer, Joan Crawford, Katharine Hepburn, Walter Pidgeon, Greer Garson, James Stewart, Mickey Rooney, John and Lionel Barrymore, Spencer Tracy, Fred Astaire, Mary Astor and, eventually, Elizabeth Taylor, Paul Newman and Elvis Presley. MGM produced a string of successes: *Ben Hur* (1925), *The Crowd* (1928), *Grand Hotel* (1932), *Mutiny on* the Bounty (1935), The Wizard of Oz (1939), Ninotchka (1939), The Philadelphia Story (1940) and Mrs Miniver (1942). It also distributed the most successful film of the 1930s, probably the most successful film of all time: Gone with the Wind (1939).

Gone with the Wind's box office revenues in North America amounted to a staggering $31 million, far outstripping the next biggest hit of the 1930s, Walt Disney's first full-length animation, Snow White and the Seven Dwarfs ($8 million), while in third place San Francisco (also MGM, 1936) was trailing behind.[68] The reasons behind Gone with the Wind's success are not immediately apparent. It was a historical melodrama, but hardly the first. Its setting, the Civil War, was still very divisive in America (it provided an idealised, almost idyllic, view of the South as a 'lost civilisation', gone with the wind), and was relatively unfamiliar to Europeans. The central character, Scarlett O'Hara, far from being likeable, is a spoilt and self-centred woman who eventually gets her comeuppance by losing her child and the man she loves – though the closing line ('Tomorrow is another day') conforms to the central tenet of American optimism. Yet Scarlett is a formidable, free-spirited woman, a proto-feminist icon and a powerful symbol of self-identification for the women who watched the film.[69] Not for nothing was the real enterprising spirit behind the film – the de facto director – the extremely hands-on producer David O. Selznick, known as a 'women's producer', particularly attuned to female sensibilities – a commercial advantage at a time when it was widely assumed that a couple's film-going decisions rested with the woman.[70] Scarlett uses all the weapons available to her, her sexuality above all (and even a gun to shoot a plundering soldier), and reveals an unsuspected business acumen, driven by her determination 'never to be hungry again'.

A crucial element in the success of the film – apart from its lavish production and its astonishing camerawork – was the fact that it was an adaptation of the great international runaway best-seller of 1937 (published in 1936) by Margaret Mitchell, an Atlanta reporter who never wrote another book – although it is not clear why the novel was such a success in the first place. The film was directed by the unknown Victor Fleming, after two other directors, including the great George Cukor, had been fired. Fleming himself collapsed with exhaustion, and had to let others finish the film. He remained relatively unknown in spite of making another great popular success, The Wizard of Oz (1939). Up to twelve writers worked on the script of Gone with the Wind, including Ben Hecht and F. Scott Fitzgerald. The leading male role was taken by the most popular star Hollywood could field at the time, Clark

Gable, but the leading lady was the then unknown British actress Vivien Leigh, sporting a believable Southern drawl and whose presence dominated the entire three-and-half-hour film. The unpredictable nature of cultural products could not be better illustrated than by the extraordinary success of this film. Coming as it did just before the start of the Second World War, *Gone with the Wind* symbolised the complete and unrivalled mastery acquired by the Americans in film production.

But well before the international success of the story of Scarlett's fall from grace, the powerful and self-confident Hollywood studios, backed by Wall Street, the world's leading financial system, presented Old Europe with a formidable challenge. Germans spoke to Germans, French to French, Italians to Italians – but the Americans spoke to all. Only one European national cinema, that of Germany, might have been able to challenge the USA in the 1920s. Not only did it lose the fight, but Nazism and the Second World War, the dismantlement of UFA (see below) and the post-war division of Germany contributed to keep the German cinema down and out until the present. It never became a rallying point for the European cinema. It never had a golden period, like the Italians (Vittorio De Sica, Roberto Rossellini and Luchino Visconti, and later Federico Fellini and Michelangelo Antonioni, and even later Bernardo Bertolucci). The German cinema produced a few internationally-known 'art' directors in the 1970s (Werner Herzog, Rainer Werner Fassbinder, Volker Schlöndorff and Wim Wenders), but it never had great spectacular world successes like the British (for instance David Lean's films), and it did not have a long cinematic tradition from the 1930s to the 1960s as did the French.

Yet, in the early 1920s, the prospects for Germany were not unfavourable. The country had considerably progressed from the pre-1914 period, when it was a major importer of films: between 1905 and 1910, 90 per cent of the films shown in Germany were foreign – 30 per cent from France, 25 per cent from the USA, 20 from Italy, and 15 from Scandinavia.[71] Then, under the Weimar Republic, Germany became the leading European producer in quantitative as well as qualitative terms. This was due to a combination of direct protectionist measures – import of pictures was forbidden until 1921 – and economic vicissitudes: the great inflation of 1923–24 made import prohibitively expensive.[72] Because Germany had been, technically speaking, a laggard country before 1914, it was readier to learn from the Americans once the First World War had ended. Other, better established countries did not yet realise the cinematic gap which was being created between themselves and the

USA. Germany (and the USSR) did. This learning curve was accompanied by a massive expansion of cinemas: 1,000 in 1910, 1,500 in 1912 and, after a huge construction programme, 3,731 in 1920.[73] Such expansion was dominated by a giant production company, UFA (Universum Film-Aktiengesellschaft), which controlled 25 per cent of distribution. Thus the main conditions for a thriving domestic cinema industry had been established: a large protected market and a massive distribution system.

Protectionism has many deleterious effects, particularly for consumers, whose choice is thereby considerably restricted. It may, however, have advantages. In some circumstances it can promote innovation and encourage experimentation. This is what occurred in Germany. Confident of their domination of the domestic market, and not unduly worried about market share, German producers could even indulge in the luxury of quality cinema which yet succeeded in being reasonably popular. Films such as Robert Wiene's *Das Kabinett des Dr Caligari* (1919) – a major influence on Hollywood films such as James Whale's *Frankenstein* and many of Hitchcock's films – and *Orlacs Hände* (1925) obtained commercial as well as critical success.

Weimar films have often been regarded as coterminous with 'expressionist cinema', though only a few could actually be so labelled. Originally the term – derived from the Expressionist art movement of the day and artists such as Otto Dix and George Grosz – was meant to indicate that the reality depicted on screen was the world as seen by the subject, and not the world 'as it really was'. This 'point of view' situation – difficult, perhaps impossible, to show on stage – was facilitated by *chiaroscuro* effects showing odd-shaped staircases, twisted streetlamps, and plenty of elongated and dark shadows. The Gothic genre lent itself particularly to this technique, hence films like *The Cabinet of Dr Caligari* and *The Golem* (1920). Expressionist cinema turned out to be good for export in a world still highly prejudiced against Germany, since the genre was suggestive of anti-militarism and of a willingness to be critical of Germany's imperial past.[74] *The Cabinet of Dr Caligari* was a commercial and critical success in the rest of Europe, above all in France, where anti-German feelings were particularly high. The film was a Decla production (an independent production company headed by Erich Pommer), but UFA too made art films which had some success even in the USA, for instance Ernst Lubitsch's *Madame Dubarry* (1919), the first German film to be released in the United States after World War I, whose success led Mary Pickford to invite Lubitsch to the United States to direct *Rosita* (1923) for her.

UFA further rationalised the fragmented German industry by taking over many independent groups, including Decla, thereby acquiring Pommer's expertise and flair in foreign markets. Following the new American management model, UFA became a producers' company. The director was displaced from his previous position as the controller of a film throughout the various stages of production. The producer was now supreme. Pommer, as Head of Production at UFA, developed a dual strategy: consolidate one's presence in the domestic market by producing many commercial films (thus weaning the Germans away from too large a diet of American films), and produce prestige films for the European market (art films being an area where American competition was less severe). Hyper-inflation helped this strategy along, since export earnings, however small, were magnified by the constant depreciation of the German currency. Thus the earnings from the export of a single film to a small market like German-speaking Switzerland could finance the production of a new film in Germany.[75]

A golden season of outstanding films ensued. One of UFA's greatest artistic *coups* was the production of G.W. Pabst's masterpiece *Pandora's Box* (1928). This was adapted from the controversial play by Frank Wedekind – a wordy drama transformed into a silent film. The lead actress, Louise Brooks, came from Hollywood (a rare case of brain drain in reverse), having just been released by Paramount. Her interpretation of Lulu, the high-class prostitute, is quite extraordinary – though at the time, according to the actress's own recollections, her acting was regarded as appalling.[76] Indeed, a Berlin daily wrote: 'Louise Brooks cannot act. She does not suffer. She does nothing.'[77] Yet as Lulu, Brooks is exactly as she should be: selfishly passive while all around her founder in an emotional storm. Since this was one of the last silent films, her highly seductive mixture of innocent vulnerability and sexuality is achieved mainly through her smile and other facial expressions. Henri Langlois, the legendary head of the Paris Cinémathèque, said of her: 'She is the intelligence of the cinematographic process . . . she embodies in herself all that the cinema rediscovered in its last years of silence: complete naturalness and complete simplicity.'[78] The film was shocking: there is an incestuous son, the screen's 'first' unambiguous lesbian, the Countess Geschwitz (played by the Belgian actress Alice Roberts), and Lulu's complete lack of 'shame' – and though she dies, she dies unrepentant. In fact none of the characters was likeable, yet they were all acting 'naturally'. Louise Brooks wrote of Pabst's direction: 'And perhaps that was his most brilliant directorial achievement – getting a group of actors to play characters without "sympathy", whose only motivation was sexual gratification.'[79] In spite of its dramatic plot (*femme fatale* who gets her 'just deserts' by being killed in the last reel by Jack the Ripper), the film was not a commercial success.

As German films, thanks to the depreciation of the currency, were cheap to make, they could also hope to sell abroad. Yet the dominance which the German industry had achieved in its home market in the early 1920s was seriously eroded by the mid-1920s. In 1923 the US exported 102 films to Germany, against a domestic production of 253; by 1929 the Americans had almost caught up: 142 US films were imported, while domestic production had fallen to 183. If one includes shorts, which unlike full-length films did not receive protection, the situation was even more dramatic: US dominance was clear even in 1923 – 149 US shorts against ninety-four German ones. In 1929 Germany produced only five shorts, while it imported 316 from the US.[80] German distributors themselves cooperated actively in the demise of their own industry. The fundamental reason behind this is that in a market economy 'nationalist' considerations play an insignificant role. The German public was eager to see American films, and German distributors were in the business of pleasing their customers, not of defending a 'national' industry. UFA may have been created to establish a dominant position in the domestic market, and to use its influence on governments to obtain special favours, but it also pursued US contracts with zeal. At the same time its smaller rivals were far more afraid of UFA than of Hollywood.[81]

Founded in 1917 with the active support of the military authorities, UFA (the result of a merger combining various companies) remained the largest film company in Germany until the end of the Second World War, when, having been nationalised by the Nazis in 1936, it was dismantled by the Allies in 1945 as part of the de-Nazification programme. The only possible European rival to any of the Hollywood majors died along with the Third Reich. UFA was in fact organised vertically, like a Hollywood major, from producing films to distribution. Its studios in Neubabelsberg near Berlin were enormous. With awe Siegfried Kracauer described them in 1926 as '350,000 square meters' that housed 'a world made of papier-mâché. Everything guaranteed unnatural and everything exactly like nature.'[82]

Yet the German film industry needed US money, because German funding was inadequate. This was also true of the economy at large. Germany in the mid-1920s had become dependent on the USA thanks to major loans and the constant flow of American capital into the country. This, of course, would be the undoing of Weimar. When Wall Street crashed, US banks called their loans in, or did not renew them. The subsequent collapse of the German economy, and the massive unemployment that followed, was one of the main contributing factors to the demise of the Weimar Republic and the rise of Hitler.

The German cinema did produce complex and lengthy films which proved successful in the home market, but few of these crossed national boundaries. Take Fritz Lang's *Metropolis*, still a film buff's favourite. This opened in January 1927 in Berlin amidst great excitement. It was the most expensive film ever made in Europe, employing 36,000 extras and going three times over budget, which virtually bankrupted UFA. A variety of gimmicks were used for the launch, including coating the cinema exterior with a silvery substance to convey a futuristic feel. The poster advertising the film was illustrated by the great designer Heinz Schultz-Neudamm. The story resembled a classic fairly tale, with an upper-class hero having to win over a simple girl, Maria. It included a Jewish-looking villain, the magician/inventor Rotwang who builds a robot resembling Maria but with a charged sexuality. The robot Maria acts like an *agent provocateur*, seducing the workers into rebellion. Thus there was magic, industrial relations and politics, romance, science fiction – all ingredients which, in the belief of the producers, should have guaranteed a large audience. But the film lasted three hours. The complexity of the narrative and the multiplicity of themes disoriented the audience. It had to be re-edited for the US market, where it did not achieve the success hoped for.[83]

It was increasingly felt, and not just in Germany, that to be successful in meeting the American challenge it was not just necessary to adopt American business methods, but also to imitate American products. European films became faster with higher cutting rates and thus shorter average shot lengths (see page 820).[84] Critics in Europe continued to be scornful of American films, which they regarded with characteristic condescension. These films consisted, they claimed, of endless chase scenes and mindless violence, and pandered to the lowest common denominator, to the taste of 'hillbillies in Arizona'.[85] The reader will perhaps have a sense of *déjà vu*, such has been the frequency of such remarks over the last century. The point is not that the critics were wrong, but that they were simply reflecting the nature of the cultural industry. Much of the mass literature of the nineteenth century also 'pandered to the lowest common denominator'. The bulk of the German or the Italian or the French cinema would not pass a quality test either. What the European cinema produced, unlike Hollywood, was the kind of quality film which satisfied more sophisticated audiences, whilst Hollywood never set the standard for the 'art film'. The conventional explanation is that much of the USA was – allegedly – deprived of high culture. With the exception of a few isolated East Coast outposts there was little theatrical tradition, and indeed few theatres and concert halls, whilst every small town in Germany had both. Thus the market-size argument worked only for the masses, the American population being much larger than the German (or the French, the Italian, etc). But, so the argument went, when it came to more refined culture the European market, although divided by nationality, was bigger than that of the USA. This argument may well have some validity, though it also reflects conventional European stereotypes. Few film critics would dare to suggest that American films such as Erich von Stroheim's *Greed* (1923–25) or King Vidor's *The Crowd* (1928) could not compete with Europe's best artistic films, and Orson Welles's *Citizen Kane* (1941) regularly tops the 'best film' leagues.

Germany, even in the late 1920s, when it was a massive importer of US films, was doing better than the other major European countries. As we noted above, domestic production of feature films in 1929 was actually higher than imports from the USA (183 against 142) – a possible sign that Germans actually liked German films. Surveys conducted by the industry suggest that while US films – not necessarily the same films – did better among the upper and working classes, they did not do so well among the lower-middle classes (so much for the 'lowest common denominator' argument).[86]

The financial difficulties of UFA in 1926 (partly because of *Metropolis*) forced it to seek the financial help of MGM and Paramount. UFA was accused of betraying Germany. In reality it always acted as a business concern, which is what it was. When it was convenient to use the nationalist card to obtain government protection, it did so. When it became necessary – for commercial reasons – to cooperate with the USA, it did so without a second thought. The idea that business has no national feelings may be a cliché, but it is nonetheless true. American companies behaved in exactly the same way. Impressed with the talents of the German industry, they sought its best actors, producers and directors. They 'imported' Pola Negri, the Polish-born actress, as well as Ernst Lubitsch – then the best-known German director – who obtained a contract with Warner Brothers and produced endless adaptations of European comedies and melodramas. *Der Blaue Engel* (The Blue Angel, 1930) by Josef von Sternberg, whose origins were Austrian (though he was raised in New York and invented, as many Germans do, the 'von' to seem aristocratic) was produced in a German as well as an English version. On the back of her success as Lola in that film Marlene Dietrich went to the United States, where she became internationally known as a film star and a singer.

UFA's financial difficulties must have appeared insignificant to the Italian film industry. Once one of the strongest of the world, by the 1920s it had virtually collapsed: in 1920 it produced 130 films, in 1929 fewer than ten. Distributors imported, at a fraction of the cost, American films, which made up over 70 per cent of those shown in Italy during the 1930s.[87] Since the cinema was the most popular form of entertainment, one can only conclude that under Mussolini's totalitarian rule, in spite of the undoubted popularity of Italian films, the most widespread cultural consumption available to the mass of Italians was made in the USA.

The supremacy of the American cinema was recognised by all Europeans. Exporting European films to the USA in significant numbers was never seriously attempted. Niche markets and the odd success were all that could be expected. So the Europeans retrenched, and fought a rearguard action aimed at containing US imports. In some lucrative fields, such as animation, there was no challenge at all to Hollywood – and in particular to Walt Disney and Warner Brothers (whose 'Bugs Bunny' was successfully launched in 1936). Adventure films were overwhelmingly American. There were few star-driven films. However, foreign markets were far from unimportant to Hollywood. Foreign stars working in Hollywood, such as Charles Laughton, Maurice Chevalier, Marlene Dietrich, Charles Boyer and Greta Garbo attracted foreign audiences. Many ended up impersonating certain types vaguely connected to an American image of Europe: Garbo and Dietrich were experienced *femmes fatales*, Chevalier had to exude French *joi de vivre*, Charles Boyer Gallic charm and sophistication. Rudolf Valentino, great star of the silent era, was inevitably a Latin lover. The price to pay was accepting that only Hollywood could transform an actor into a real international star. Of course, many failed, including some who continued to be great stars at home – for instance Danielle Darrieux in the late 1930s and Michèle Morgan in the 1940s.[88]

The greatest of star of them all, at least in the 1920s, was an Englishman of Irish, French and Gypsy antecedents who emigrated to the USA at the age of twenty-one, but always refused naturalisation: Charlie Chaplin (1889–1977). He first appeared on the screen in 1913 with the Keystone Film Company of Mack Sennett. 1914 saw the birth of the 'little tramp' character that

Chaplin used in some seventy films (most of them shorts). The antecedents of the 'tramp' can be traced to the vaudeville and the variety show. He is one of the downtrodden who defies authority while remaining content with his station in life – a characteristic of the mawkish sentimentality of the Victorian age. It helped that Chaplin's own real-life story was quite remote from that of the tramp: a rags-to-riches life (already in 1916 he was earning $10,000 *a week*), marriage to a succession of beautiful and talented women, and radical left-wing politics that made him challenge authority more seriously than the tramp ever did (and be chastised for it).

The shorts featuring the tramp, and the full-length features *The Tramp* (1915) and *The Kid* (1921) made Chaplin famous worldwide. Eisenstein called him 'the incomparable Charlie Chaplin', adding, 'The craze everywhere is for Chaplin – Charlie! The newspapers enthuse, "Charlie goes for a walk . . . Charlie on his bike . . . Charlie on skates . . ."'[89] This encomium was written in 1922, before Chaplin had produced his greatest films, *The Gold Rush* (1925), *City Lights* (1931), *Modern Times* (1936) and *The Great Dictator* (1940). Perhaps his most formidable achievement was that he was able both to please the supporters of high culture and to delight a mass audience. His one great competitor, Buster Keaton, was not a big box office success in the 1920s – in spite of the unquestionable excellence of *The General* (1927). Keaton became a 'rival' to Chaplin only in the 1950s, as more movies from the silent era were rediscovered and analysed. By the 1970s he obtained the final accolade when critics began to write lines such as: 'With Keaton silence and expressiveness of image do seem part of a single ontological condition.'[90]

It has often been said that Chaplin was a genius, but unlike the standard nineteenth-century artistic genius he was also a formidable businessman, shrewd enough to escape the tyranny of the Hollywood majors by creating, with other equally businesslike actors (above all Mary Pickford, probably the highest-paid woman in the world with earnings of $350,000 a year), the powerful United Artists studio. Not even Verdi, Rossini, Dickens or Hugo (all of whom were keen to make money) had ever envisaged acquiring control of the production of their own works. Besides, Chaplin was in complete charge of his films, doing exactly what he wanted without any producer or accountant interfering – as was Buster Keaton, who was his own producer, director and editor in the 1920s.

The success of Chaplin was symbolic of the attractiveness of Hollywood. Had he remained in London, it is extremely unlikely that he would have become the 'universal' Chaplin. Yet what he initially contributed to Hollywood was quintessentially English: a working-class entertainment based on slapstick comedy and the music hall (both his parents had walked the stage).

One of the many reasons why American films were so successful was – as we have seen – that many of their producers and some of their stars were immigrants themselves. To them Europe was not an unknown entity, whilst America remained a mystery to Europeans. The brain drain continued throughout the 1920s and 1930s. It is true that many German film 'exiles' did not go directly to the USA. Some went to Austria (before 1938), Hungary, France, England or Holland, producing between 1933 and 1950 some two hundred films.[91] But most eventually ended up in the USA, while, under-standably, hardly any US directors 'emigrated' to Europe. Hollywood attracted a growing number of European actors, turning them into stars. We have mentioned Marlene Dietrich and Pola Negri. Others preceded and followed them, including Hedy Kiesler (born in Vienna), who having starred, swimming bare-breasted, in the Czech film *Extase* (1933) by Gustav Machatý, became Hedy Lamarr in Hollywood, and Emil Jannings, who has remained better known as the unfortunate high school teacher in *The Blue Angel*. Many went to the USA as political refugees. Bela Lugosi (1882–1956), the greatest of Hollywood's Draculas, a participant in the communist revolution of 1918–19 in Hungary, went into exile after its defeat, first to Germany and then to the USA in 1921. Fritz Lang, an anti-Nazi, left shortly after Hitler's advent to power. Peter Lorre, who had starred in Lang's famous film *M* (1931), went to Hollywood in 1935 (via Paris). The Russian-born Anatole Litvak arrived in California – also via Paris – in 1936. But most went to Hollywood simply because it had become the centre of the international film world.[92] Greta Garbo (1905–90), who was born in Stockholm, went to the USA originally because the Swedish film director Mauritz Stiller had gone there to work for by Metro-Goldwyn-Mayer. In silent movies accents were immaterial, but Garbo made the transition to sound and to English with great ease, becoming the star *par excellence* thanks to *Grand Hotel* (1932), based on the German writer Vicki Baum's famous best-seller, *Mata Hari* (1932), *Queen Christina* (1933), *Anna Karenina* (1935) and *Ninotchka* (1939), one of the most successful of Lubitsch's comedies. With a few exceptions, such as Dietrich and Garbo, most foreign actors did not do well in the USA when sound was introduced. They were reduced to small roles as German officers or *femmes fatales*. Some, like Pola Negri, who made many silent pictures in the US between 1923 and 1928, found themselves virtually out of work afterwards.

The Americanisation of the world had many roots in Europe. Hollywood was more 'European' than it seemed either to those working in it – keen to appear as American as possible – or to Europeans, who saw distinctive American features in everything that came from the other side of the Atlantic. Indeed, many Americans followed the Protestant and Catholic Churches in viewing Hollywood as anti-American (some still do), almost a conspiracy by Jews and pagans and, more recently, liberals, to debauch the country.[93]

The European exodus to Hollywood continued even after the war started. Thus the Nazis not only destroyed the German film industry, but reinvigorated that of the Americans (and, to a lesser extent, the British) thanks to an influx of notable film personalities: in addition to actors and directors such as Max Ophüls, Billy Wilder and Robert Siodmak, there were producers such as Erich Pommer and Arnold Pressburger, and composers such as Hanns Eisler. A 'typical' American film like *Casablanca* (1942), a cult film regarded by many as one of the best *American* films ever, was directed by Michael Curtiz, who was born in Hungary as Mihaly Kertész. Apart from Humphrey Bogart (originally Ronald Reagan had been envisaged for the role of Rick) there are virtually no credited American-born actors: Ingrid Bergman was a Swede, Peter Lorre was born in Slovakia as Lászlo Loewenstein; Claude Rains and Sidney Greenstreet were English; Conrad Veidt – Strasser, the Gestapo officer – was a German who had escaped from the Gestapo (he was an anti-Nazi with a Jewish wife); Paul Henreid, the Czech anti-Nazi, was born in Trieste when it was part of Austria-Hungary; Madeleine LeBeau was, of course, French; while S.Z. Sakall was from Budapest. Most of the actors playing Nazis were German Jews. The art director, Carl Jules Weyl, was born in Stuttgart; the costumes were designed by an Australian; Perc Westmore, the head of make-up, was a native of Canterbury, England; the composer was the Viennese Max Steiner (who provided the music for over a hundred films including *Gone with the Wind*); the editor, Owen Marks, was English. Dooley Wilson, the black pianist 'Sam' who plays 'As Time Goes By' ('You must remember this, a kiss is still a kiss . . .') was completely American, since he was born in Texas – though he faked his piano-playing: in real life he was a drummer.

The point is that the American cinema was only partially American. Many of its stories originated from Europe (or had been recycled in Europe from the Orient), as did many of the technical personnel, the stars, the producers and the scriptwriters. The American genius consisted precisely of this: it recast European culture for the new modern mass society, and re-exported it to Europe and the rest of the world. The strength of Hollywood was in its capacity to attract so many talents, organise them, and provide them with the largest market in the world.

'Quality' European directors did not always do well in America. They had acquired their reputation and fame by making films for an international élite. Enticed by Hollywood, they often discovered that the place had its own rules. Jean Renoir wrote in his autobiography that when he went to California in 1941, Twentieth Century-Fox welcomed him 'with open arms', but:

> Soon I realised that Fox expected me to adopt Hollywood methods and was not interested in my own methods. I repeatedly explained to Zanuck, the great boss, that if all he wanted from me were the kind of films they usually made, then why ask me? Hollywood was already full of talents . . . In their field I could only be a pale imitator. In mine I might contribute something new.[94]

What irked Renoir was the diminished role of the director. He wanted to use location scenes; the Americans wanted everything to be shot in studios. He wanted to be the author of the film; the Americans believed in an industrial division of labour: the director was supposed to direct, and that was it. But often, Renoir complained, this consisted of doing little more than saying 'Action' and 'Stop.' The dramatic coach rehearsed the actors, the cameraman positioned the lights, the stage designer designed the stage. The director was not even in charge of the final cut, which was the prerogative of the producer. Renoir said of Darryl Zanuck's editing that it was excellent, 'perhaps better than if I had done it myself. But it was not my cut. Yet editing was one of the most efficacious tools at the disposal of the author to make his mark.'[95]

One genre even dispensed with actors: animation. Here the American lead was even more impressive than in other fields. From 1928, when *Steamboat Willie* had Mickey Mouse singing and other sound effects synchronised with the motion, Americans had no competition. While the Europeans (or at least the Belgians and the French) were able to counterattack in the related field of the comic strip, in animation films US hegemony was so great that those who sought to make animation had to carve out for themselves a niche market. In eastern Europe in particular, especially after 1945, there was remarkable production of 'high culture' animation building on an older tradition of silhouette and puppets.[96] Popular cartoons, however, were an American preserve, and exclusively so until the worldwide impact of Japanese made-for-TV cartoons.

The genre was firmly aimed at children. But as the most popular stories for children came from Europe, Walt Disney's first full-length animated films gave life to *Snow White and the Seven Dwarfs* (1937, based on one of the most famous tales of the brothers Grimm), *Pinocchio* (1939, based on the story by the Italian Collodi), *Bambi* (1942, originally by the Austrian Felix Salten) and *Peter Pan* (1953, from the play by the Scot J.M. Barrie). *Snow White* became one of the highest-earning films ever. Unlike other films, these animated pictures spawned a new commercial trend: the merchandising of toys, gadgets and clothes related to the film. Shortly after *Steamboat Willie* was released, for instance, Macy's, the New York department store, sold a thousand Mickey Mouse watches in a single day.[97] Since these films were directed at children but also appealed to parents, and since Disney had a virtual monopoly, they could be re-released at intervals, usually every seven years or so, ensuring that an entire new generation of children, accompanied by their parents, would provide a new audience. By using stories which, regardless of their national origins (if any) had become universal (albeit 'universal' in the Western sense), animated films appealed to the mass of parents and children to whom the stories were already familiar. Those who wanted to see in the successes of Walt Disney the triumph of their particular national culture could do so. Thus Leni Riefenstahl, the Nazi film-maker whose *Olympia* had beaten Disney's *Snow White* for the Coppa Mussolini at the 1938 Venice Film Festival, praised Disney for having 'the German feeling', and for using German fables and fairy tales for inspiration. This is probably why *Snow White* was excluded from the Nazi ban on the import of American movies. But Disney was also praised by Eisenstein, who marvelled at his 1938 short *Merbabies*: 'What purity and clarity of soul is needed to make such a thing.'[98]

Disney's experimentation with high culture was always mass-directed. *Fantasia* (1940), an attempt to express musical passages in animation, used composers ranging from Bach and Beethoven to Stravinsky. This use of European high culture added to the wider legitimacy of Disney. But then, Old Europe was deeply intertwined in almost everything Hollywood created. The western might be regarded as an entirely American genre were it not for the fact that one of its main strands, that of the stranger riding into town and setting things right, is obviously reminiscent of the legendary righter of wrongs of chivalric medieval stories. The novels from which the successful Tarzan films originated were written by an American, Edgar Rice Burroughs, but Burroughs felt the need to give Tarzan English aristocratic ancestry, and the best-known interpreter of the role, Johnny Weissmuller, was an Austrian born near Timisoara (Romania).

The Advent of Sound

Of all the technological innovations in the cinema, the introduction of sound has been the most outstanding, along with the possibility of showing films of a sufficient length to create a proper narrative. Since then there have been further technological improvements, such as colour, and quite a few failures or dead ends, such as cinerama and 3-D films (for which the audience had to wear special spectacles), at one time hailed as a revolution but in fact of limited commercial success. But the step forward in sound entailed a step back in colour, or rather in tinting. Tinting, a colouring process widely used in silent films, could not be used in sound films because the tinting dyes covered the soundtrack area as well as the picture area.[99]

The first sound film, *The Jazz Singer*, was released in 1927. By the end of that year only a few others had been made in the US, and none in Europe. In 1929 the majority of films produced in Hollywood used sound. This forced a rapid conversion to sound on Europe, which unlike the USSR and Japan was a major importer of US films.

The Jazz Singer was actually a silent movie with synchronised sound attached to it for a few lines of dialogue and musical sequences – a total of ten minutes or so. Even Hitchcock's *Blackmail* (1929), widely advertised as the first full-length all-talkie film made in Britain, was mostly silent: the dialogue extended to no more than thirteen minutes.[100] At the end of 1927, just after the release of *The Jazz Singer*, only 157 of the 21,700 movie theatres in the US could play sound. By late 1928 this number had increased to 1,046, and by April 1929 to about 2,500. By 1930 the evolution towards sound was clearly unstoppable. The speed at which this came about in the USA demonstrates the priority it gave to the domestic market and the highly competitive atmosphere in which the Hollywood majors operated. No studio could afford to be left behind, since it was evident that the public would flock to the talkies and leave the silent era behind. MGM did not make another silent movie after *The Kiss* (with Greta Garbo) in 1929. Chaplin resisted the use of dialogue though he did use synchronised sound effects and music in *City Lights* (1931) and *Modern Times* (1936). With *The Great Dictator* (1940) he too abandoned the silent film.

But the advent of sound coincided with an era of nationalism and protectionism, and the export of US films faltered. The various domestic markets in Europe and elsewhere thought that their time had come. The changes in Germany were emblematic. In 1929 it imported 142 US films (ten of which were sound), but in 1931 only eighty-four (fifty-eight with sound), while it released 144 home-made films (of which only two were silent).[101] The coming of sound seemed heaven-sent to film-makers outside the English-speaking world. The advance of the Americans had been slowed down, albeit temporarily. But the Europeans, unlike the Japanese, were quick to adapt to sound reception. By 1935 seven out of thirteen distribution chains were American or, though French, were distributing almost exclusively US films.[102]

The new problem of linguistic barriers in the consumption of film was initially 'resolved' by reshooting scenes with other actors speaking German or French or Italian, using the same sets and the same costumes. Later, subtitles and dubbing were introduced. Subtitles, however, were never a satisfactory solution. They remained the norm in Britain, mainly because the 'foreign' (i.e. not in English) imports were watched by a relatively small audience. Dubbing turned out to be the winning solution everywhere else (in some countries – including Italy, Spain, France and Germany – films had to be dubbed by law). Actors, having just acquired the means to make their voices heard, lost it in foreign markets, where local actors spoke their lines in synchronisation with their lip movements. This is a further indication of the relatively low importance of dialogue in films. The development of dubbing in the mid-1930s undid many of the gains of nationalists, though it meant that dubbing costs had to be added to the cost of the picture, and out-of-work local actors could get work as the voice of Greta Garbo, Clark Gable, Errol Flynn, Olivia de Havilland, etc.

From a long-term perspective, the decision by US distributors to convert their cinemas to sound rapidly was, of course, correct. Old formats (e.g. bound books) can survive indefinitely, but not old technology. Books will survive as long as the advantages they have over computers endure: you can't curl into bed, yet, with a computer; you can't flick through it; and if you can take it to the beach or on a train, it is still easier and cheaper to take a book instead – and books don't need to be recharged. But long-term considerations are not sufficient to explain the speed of the conversion to sound in the middle of the Depression. The immediate reason was that once conversion had taken place, cinemas could do without the services of musical accompanists, not just solo pianists but often, in the larger towns, a full-size orchestra. All at once hundreds of musicians lost their jobs, sacrificed to recorded sound, as so many similar jobs were also being lost (and gained) thanks to the diffusion of recorded music. Movies became even more standardised, since now the same music accompanied a film throughout the world. With the elimination of the accompanist, film-makers had acquired much greater control over the commodity. Now they could choose the music and the kind of noise accompanying the film, rather than leaving it to unknown pianists in myriad cinemas.

Just as technology wipes out jobs, so it creates them. New technical roles began to appear. Sound engineers, latecomers to the world of cinema, were never regarded as being as important as cameramen, nor were they paid as much – to their regret. Malcolm Stewart, a sound engineer who worked on major British films such as *The Bridge on the River Kwai* (1957), recollected the 'battles' between the sound people (who were treated as 'mere technicians') and the camera department (who regarded themselves as 'artists' and had ambitions to become directors).[103] The whole set revolved around the camera, yet sound had to be picked up by microphones. These were originally rather large and heavy (to make a microphone more sensitive it was necessary to increase the power of the magnet inside it, therefore increasing its size and weight). They were fitted on a long crane (a boom) manipulated by an operator who moved from actor to actor as they spoke. This required a great deal of cooperation from the cameramen, who had to make sure that the pole (and its shadow) remained out of shot.[104]

Sound movies needed far more sophisticated dialogue than the old intertitles, and therefore they needed writers. They needed more complex music than traditional accompanists could provide, to the joy of composers. Writers and composers, having come to the fore in the nineteenth century as independent professionals were given a powerful new lease of life in the twentieth – at the cost of becoming dependent on the requirements of film-making. Writing for the cinema turned out to be highly lucrative – much more than writing novels or plays. The price to pay was in one's diminished fame. Screenwriters, unless they were already famous, were never recognised as the 'authors' of the film. In the popular mind films were either *by* a director or, more commonly, *with* a star. The name of the screenwriter, appropriately, came well after that of the producer, director and main actors in the credits. A composer could gain further acclaim if a film's music was marketed separately, but there was never an important market for the screenplay. Some famous writers involved in screenwriting, such as William Faulkner, used their earnings to subsidise their 'difficult' novels, just as nineteenth-century writers had used journalism.

Sound modified the behaviour of the whole team on the set. In the silent era the set was a beehive of noise, with instructions conveyed loudly during shooting. Now silence was imperative; only the actors could speak. And at first all music had to be recorded on the set, as the scene was being shot.[105] If necessary an entire orchestra would have to be located near the set while a romantic moonlit scene was filmed. After 1933 a technique was established whereby a poor-quality soundtrack was recorded (the 'guide track') on the set. Then dialogue was re-recorded in the controlled environment of the sound studio, where actors watched the replayed action on a screen, listened to the guide track and tried to repeat their performances, synchronising their delivery to their lip movements on the screen.

Sound required actors with good voices. Visual expressiveness was no longer sufficient. Theatre actors, hitherto shunned by the cinema, came back with a vengeance. In France stage stars who had been almost ignored by the French cinema in the 1920s (Arletty, Jean Gabin, Louis Jouvet, Edwige Feuil-lère, Marguerite Moreno) dominated screens throughout the 1930s.[106] Some great silent stars fell by the wayside, making way for newcomers like Joan Crawford, Myrna Loy, William Powell, Clark Gable and Jean Harlow. Ronald Colman and Norma Shearer, established silent stars, made the transition to sound successfully.

The silent era, however, had taught film-makers an important lesson which would not be forgotten with the advent of sound: how to dispense with dialogue, using images and expressions instead. They had learned how to use editing as a substitute for dialogue, conveying considerable information without using the spoken word. The glances, facial expressions and body language of the silent film had gradually distanced themselves from the unavoidable theatricality of the stage, where a glance could barely be perceived by most of the audience. Film acting – even with sound – remained a subdued genre, the word dominated by the image.

Take Howard Hawks's *To Have and Have Not*, scripted by William Faulkner, loosely adapted from a story by Hemingway and released in 1944, fifteen years after the introduction of sound. In a key scene Harry Morgan (Humphrey Bogart) is in his room in a rundown Martinique hotel, talking to his friend Gerard. The voice of Marie (Lauren Bacall, then nineteen years old), is heard off-screen: 'Has anybody got a match?' Then she appears, slouching insolently and sexily against the frame of the door in a long shot which includes Bogart. Bogart nonchalantly throws a box of matches. Bacall, cat-like, catches it with one hand, barely moving (the scene was shot many times because Bacall, nervous, kept missing). A series of rapid shots in quick succession tells the rest of the story: medium shot of Bogart, medium shot of Bacall, close-up of Bogart, close-up of Bacall, then a close-up of Gerard looking at one and then at the other, and finally the cathartic close-up of Bacall who leaves the room saying 'Thanks,' the only word uttered since her initial off-screen request for matches. But we understand (trained by other films) that Harry and Marie are weighing each other up, exchanging sexual sparks and taking pleasure in the delicious feeling of the possibility of passion. We understand, as does Gerard, that something is beginning between the two – the pleasure of this discovery was heightened for later audiences by the knowledge that a year after the release of the film, Bogart and Bacall did marry in real life.[107]

Television fiction hardly ever uses images and silence like the cinema. Most of its fiction, above all serials and series (from *Bonanza* to *Friends*, from *Dallas* to *Sex and the City*), has been dialogue-led, with the camera at the mercy of the words. Situation comedies rely on even more limited visual information. They are in fact almost like radio plays, since the entire action often takes place, by definition, in a single room – though few would deny that great situation comedies such as *I Love Lucy* (1951–57) worked far better on TV than on radio.

In films, dialogue – even in the era of sound – continued to rank low. Clark Gable smiles, James Stewart looks vacant (*Mr Smith Goes to Washington*, 1939), John Wayne grunts and Marlon Brando mumbles. Women smile invitingly (Marlene Dietrich in von Sternberg's *The Devil is a Woman*, 1935), or sadly (Norma Shearer in *The Barretts of Wimpole Street*, 1934), or longingly (Claudette Colbert in *Cleopatra*, 1934), or haughtily (Bette Davis in *Dangerous*, 1935), or broadly (Katharine Hepburn in *Mary of Scotland*, 1936). Frankenstein's creature, in the original novel by Mary Shelley, is a rather articulate monster, but in James Whale's film version (1931) he barely speaks.[108] The musical score adds to the non-verbal information given to viewers.

Films use visual and geographical markers to let us know where the action is taking place, making them even more internationally well-known. A shot of the Eiffel Tower means 'We are in Paris'; the Great Wall means China; the Pyramids, Egypt; Big Ben or Tower Bridge, London; the Colosseum, Rome. Monument Valley, which lies between southern Utah and northern Arizona, was used by John Ford to stand in for 'the west' in general, even if the action was supposed to take place in flat Texas or Kansas, and he used it profligately: in *Stagecoach* (1939), *My Darling Clementine* (1946), *Fort Apache* (1948), *She Wore a Yellow Ribbon* (1949), *Rio Grande* (1950), *The Searchers* (1956) and *Cheyenne Autumn* (1964). Unsurprisingly it was also widely used by advertisers, including in the famous 'Marlboro man' commercials .[109]

Old Europe Towards War

As Europe was advancing towards war, each country's cinema became ever more inward-looking. The USSR, just re-emerging from ghoulish purges which decimated its intelligentsia, was making films only for itself, as did Nazi Germany. Italy had no world-class directors – though some outstanding ones were waiting in the wings. Britain was, more than ever, an American dependency.

And France? In the nineteenth century it had been a culturally hegemonic country. It had invented and popularised the cinema. At the end of the First World War, Pathé was a powerful, vertically integrated production group. Then everything began to change. While American film tycoons were investing heavily, Charles Pathé, Europe largest film entrepreneur, had started disinvesting, selling the various parts of his huge empire. In 1921 he announced that he was withdrawing from film production; the French cinema no longer paid, he explained.[110] Recording and phonograph manufacturing were split from the group's film production – Pathé-Cinéma. In 1923 Pathé sold its US film company, Pathé-Exchange. In 1927 it ceded the manufacturing of celluloid film to Kodak, its main competitor.[111] Pathé's main French rival, Gaumont, followed the same policy of retrenchment. Thus, as the sound revolution was about to take place and Hollywood was about to reshape world cinema industry, the only European production firm other than UFA which could play a major role in it opted for consolidating its capital and withdrawing inside the nation state.

Pathé was eventually bought by Bernard Natan in 1930, and reconstituted as a thoroughly French company. It made sixty films in 1930–35, relaunched the Pathé-Journal newsreels, and invested in radio (Radio-Natan-Vitus) and the new medium of television (Télévision-Baird-Natan). Pathé and Gaumont invested heavily in sound, and above all in an expanded cinema circuit catering for a rapidly expanding audience. In 1931 the French made 139 films.[112] Then the company found itself in serious financial difficulties, and in 1938 Natan was declared bankrupt amidst considerable anti-Semitic and nationalist outcry (Natan was a Romanian Jew who had changed his name from Natan Tenenzapf). Convicted of fraud in 1939 and then again in 1941, he was freed in 1942, only to be immediately handed over to the German authorities, who promptly despatched him to Auschwitz, where he died.[113]

However, throughout the 1930s protectionism offered the French film industry plenty of opportunities for experimentation and for feats of technical prowess equal or even superior to those in Hollywood. Even in the 1920s, when the French cinema was barely able to defend itself, producing fewer and fewer films (only fifty-five in 1926), some of those that were made have remained milestones: Abel Gance in *La Roue* (1923) used techniques later studied and copied by Pudovkin and Eisenstein in Russia, and Akira Kurosawa in Japan.[114] His *Napoleon* (1927) was even more revolutionary. Its most famous, but scarcely imitated, innovation was to film some sequences with three cameras pointing in different directions, in effect filming three contiguous sections of the action. When projected together, a vast panorama unfolded.[115] The coming of sound appeared to signal a further defeat for the French cinema. When *The Jazz Singer* opened in Paris on 30 January 1929 it was shown to more than half a million spectators in forty-eight weeks. But relatively few French cities had cinemas equipped for sound, even as late as 1931.[116] Gaumont had experimented with sound before, trying to solve the problem of synchronisation – to no avail. All the registered patents for sound projection were American. The nation that had given the cinema to the world had failed to provide the next major breakthrough – nor would it provide any of the successive ones.

Yet the introduction of sound and quotas provided the French cinema with a new opportunity. It never could aspire to become an international force, but it could survive handsomely by providing French films for the French, and an alternative to Hollywood in some other markets. The surveys of cinemas conducted by the fortnightly *La Cinématographie Française* showed that in the 1930s the French preferred French films and French actors to American ones. In 1936 the top twenty films were all French, except for Chaplin's *Modern Times*, in sixth place. In 1937 too there was only one US film in the top twenty: *Camille* with Greta Garbo, based on a French subject and set in France (it is an adaptation of Dumas's *La Dame aux camélias*) in eleventh place; in 1938 the number one place was reached by a US film, *Snow White and the Seven Dwarfs*, as well as number six (*Robin Hood*, with Errol Flynn) and number nineteen (*Marie Walewska*, with Greta Garbo and the French actor Charles Boyer). Of the top ten actresses in 1936, six were French and four 'American' (Greta Garbo, Marlene Dietrich, Shirley Temple and Jeanette MacDonald, who had starred in several comedies with Maurice

Chevalier). The charts for the successive two years were fairly similar. French actors were also the favourites of the French: Fernandel, Jean Gabin, Charles Boyer and Louis Jouvet regularly upstaged the few Americans who made it to the top ten (Chaplin, Gable, Robert Taylor).[117] Though such statistics are not to be taken literally, as they almost certainly overstate the popularity of the French cinema, they do confirm that in so far as the French were concerned, the successful foreign films were all American. They also reveal that there was not yet a strong divide between popular and 'art' films. At the top we find Marcel Pagnol, Jean Renoir and Marcel Carné alongside now almost-forgotten films. Even though the mid-1930s were the years of the Popular Front and the anti-fascist mobilisation of France (as if almost half of the country had not voted for the other side), the preferred genre was the military-patriotic: French submarines, French ships, the French Foreign Legion, French colonial wars.[118] One of the most successful of these was Jean Grémillon's *Geule d'amour* (1938), about Lucien (Jean Gabin), a dashing soldier garrisoned in the south of France who cannot keep the heart of Madeleine, the heartless woman he loves, once he is back in civilian clothes and is riding a bicycle rather than a horse. Asked to choose between love and money, Madeleine unhesitatingly prefers the money. Naturally Lucien strangles her.[119]

The celebrated 'social cinema' of the era of the Popular Front contributed some innovative masterpieces: Renoir's *Le Crime de Monsieur Lange* (1936) about a worker's cooperative, his pacifist *La Grande illusion* (1937) and his famed *La Règle du jeu* (1939); René Clair's *Le Million* (1931), *À Nous la liberté* (1932) and *Le Quatorze Juillet* (1933); and Marcel Carné's *Quai des Brumes* (1938), *Hôtel du Nord* (1938) and *Le Jour se lève* (1939). These influenced directors the world over, including in Hollywood. Initially the term 'social cinema' referred to documentaries such as Jean Vigo's *À Propos de Nice* (1930), where the hidden poverty of Nice was contrasted with the wealth of its tourists and the coarseness of its carnival – thus taking a swipe at the uncouth élites as well as the uncouth populace.[120] Vigo's subsequent films, *Zéro de conduite* (1932) and *L'Atalante* (1934), remained among the main reference points of the French cinema but failed to achieve popularity.

But it was the failure of capitalism rather than its greed that damaged the French cinema of the 1930s. During the Depression, investment in film-making fell from seventy million francs in 1933 to 17.3 million in 1935. There were numerous bankruptcies. The two largest production companies withdrew from making films. By 1935, 115 films were produced by eighty-three different companies.[121] This probably influenced positively the quality of

French films. It is true that French films (and many European ones) had very distinctive features, some obvious (language and setting), some less so. At the technical level the differences were not always apparent. Films made in Hollywood and films made in Europe had a very different 'feel', but shared many stylistic elements not always apparent to the ordinary cinema-goer, who is often wrapped up in the plot.

The truth of the matter is that in the film world the learning process among practitioners was far faster than in literature. It was, after all, perfectly possible for a single person to view a large part of the world output of films – watching, say, two hundred films in four hundred hours. The same could not be said of literary output. As for drama, that would require frequent and expensive travels. Novelists could be aware of only a small part of the production of their contemporaries. Theatre directors knew little of what others were doing. In films, however, one could learn quickly. Orson Welles's *Citizen Kane* and John Ford's *Stagecoach* may seem to be very different films, but Welles, impressed by its 'deep staging' technique, watched *Stagecoach* forty times. The technique had also been used by Eisenstein, in a film which has little in common with either *Citizen Kane* or *Stagecoach*: *The General Line* (1929, a celebration of the collectivisation of agriculture) introduced visual depth, or deep space, and Renoir used similar techniques in a number of films.[124] The development of directing skills, how to direct actors, how to achieve desired effects, how to use narrative, meant that film directors were seldom the equivalent of novelists. Novelists specialised in a genre. There are, of course, exceptions, but generally speaking they stuck with the genre they thought they were best at – detective stories, romantic fiction, science fiction, historical novels, etc. Film-makers could make wildly different films. This is not true of all directors. Hitchcock's films, on the whole, have enough common traits to define a territory. So do Woody Allen's (his forays into non-comic films were not successful). John Ford made mainly, but not exclusively, westerns. But archetypical Hollywood directors such as Howard Hawks made gangster films (*Scarface*, 1932), screwball comedies (*His Girl Friday*, 1940), hard drama (*To Have and Have Not*, 1944), hard-boiled detective films (*The Big Sleep*, 1946), westerns (*Red River*, 1948, and *Rio Bravo*, 1949), epics (*Land of the Pharaohs*, 1955), science fiction (*The Thing*, 1951) and musicals (*Gentlemen Prefer Blondes*, 1953) – an astonishing range achieved in the course of a career in which Hawks directed almost a film a year. Few European directors could match such a range – or Hawks's 'genius' in being able to combine tragic and comic elements.[123]

48

The Cinema After World War II

War and Films

WARS ARE GOOD FOR BUSINESS, but peace is even better. Pent-up demand is unleashed. And though this is not always true, it was true for the entertainment industry, which prospered both during and after the Second World War. In 1946 in Great Britain, 1,635 million tickets were sold – thirty-five tickets per person.[1] Even in 1953 the British spent three times as much on going to films as the Germans or the French, and two and a half times as much as the Italians (who constituted the second-largest market in Europe).[2] Great Britain also had one of the greatest densities of seats (the ratio of seats to population) in Europe – only low-population countries such as Belgium and Sweden did better. In terms of the number of cinemas, however, Great Britain was not particularly high in the league:

RATIO OF SEATS TO POPULATION AND NUMBER
OF CINEMAS IN 1949

	Persons per seat	*Cinemas*
USA	12.4	18,351
USSR	36.4	12,614
Italy	14.7	8,138
Germany	28.6	5,832
France	15.8	5,163
Great Britain	10.9	5,000
Spain	15.8	3,674
Sweden	9.6	2,462
India	262	1,948

	Persons per seat	Cinemas
Czechoslovakia	20.9	1,928
Belgium	13.9	1,289
Holland	39.5	440
Egypt	101	194
(World)		(90,000)

SOURCE: *Foreign Commerce Weekly* (US Dept of Commerce) Vol. 35, No.3–4 pp.40–1, 1949

By 1960 British audiences had fallen by two-thirds, and the average age of the spectators had dropped.[3] Older people stayed at home to watch television. The British public, the most captivated in Europe by the cinema in 1951, had been overtaken, by 1959, by both Italy and Germany. France still lagged behind:

CINEMA SEATS SOLD IN 1951 AND IN 1959 (MILLIONS)

	1951	1959
Sweden	50	70
Great Britain	1,365	581
Belgium	116	90
Italy	706	748
France	373	352
Spain	200	360
Germany	555	659
Holland	64	55
USA	2,700	2,184
Egypt	45	120
India	700	800

SOURCE: Lo spettacolo, Vol.10, No 2, April–June 1960, p.111 and BFI Film
and Television Handbook (2003–04 bfi screenonline)

Films, of course, continued to be made throughout the war, and not only in countries which did not suffer from bombing (like the USA) or from foreign occupation (like Great Britain). One of the most famous of all French films, Marcel Carné's *Les Enfants du paradis*, was shot largely in occupied Paris, though it was not released until March 1945, well after the liberation of the city.[4] The Nazi occupation had found the French film industry prostrate, deprived of investment and dependent on foreign technology. The Nazis and the collaborationist Vichy government banned pre-war 'militaristic films' (i.e. anti-German), as well as British films. Then, in 1942, they also banned American films. In 1937, 48 per cent of all films shown in France were American. After 1941 there were none. German films were hardly a substitute for the likes of *Gone with the Wind*. In 1937 only 6 per cent of films shown in France were German; in 1941 the figure shot up to 56 per cent, taking up the slack from the US. By 1944 German films had collapsed to only 15 per cent.[5] Why the drop? Almost certainly because German films were not commercially viable, and exhibitors reduced the supply. This rejection owed little to anti-fascist feelings, it was just that German historical films and light operettas were not to French taste.[6]

The result of all this, according to the director Claude Autant-Lara, was that the new French cinema, deprived of competitors, 'was king'. Now that many of France's most talented film-makers had left the country or, in the case of Jews and anti-fascists, been expelled or deported, the war provided opportunities for those left behind, like Henri-Georges Clouzot, Robert Bresson and, of course, Autant-Lara.[7] Fewer French films, however, were produced during the war (a total of 220 between 1940 and 1944, or forty-four a year, compared to pre-war production of about 120 a year).[8]

The French films which benefited from the Second World War kept well away from politics. A film like *Les Enfants du paradis*, which had no obvious political message, was praised from all sides of the political spectrum, since it could be interpreted as a celebration of the distinctiveness of French culture against the Nazis, or just as a celebration. Above all it could be seen as a story of love in adversity against the seductive background of theatrical life in nineteenth-century Paris. Since it was a spectacular film with a large cast, it felt as if it could take on Hollywood at its own game.[9]

In Italy, a similar fate befell Roberto Rossellini's *Roma città aperta* (1945). Though this – unlike *Les Enfants du paradis* – was an obviously political film, since its subject was the resistance to Nazi occupation, it sought to represent a national consensus of all Italians, including communists and Catholics (each with its own heroic representative), against the common enemy, the Nazis (Italian fascists are shown in limited and subservient roles). The film was conceived shortly after the liberation of Rome, and shot in late 1944, when northern Italy was still under Nazi and fascist rule.[10] It was later claimed that the film's gritty realism was a counter to Hollywood. Yet it was not so (Hollywood had made plenty of gritty realist films too), nor did it signal the development of a new kind of Italian cinema. Nor were the neo-realist films particularly popular in Italy at the time, though they were highly influential with a generation of directors, from Egypt to India and Japan. Commercial success went to the kind of films which had been successful before the war: melodramas, comedies and adaptations of operas.

The war also offered an opportunity for Great Britain. In spite of threats of bombing – 160 cinemas were bombed during the war – attendances at cinemas increased even in the south.

UK CINEMA ADMISSIONS

Year	Figure in millions
1938	987
1939	990
1940	1,027
1941	1,309
1942	1,494
1943	1,541
1944	1,575
1945	1,585

SOURCE: *BFI Film and Television Handbook* (2003–04 bfi screenonline)

Statistically speaking, it looks as if almost everyone under the age of forty went to the cinema almost every week. Cinema audiences, like eighteenth-century opera audiences, tended to be regular. They did not pick and choose what to see. They went to the pictures almost irrespective of the film, much as many, in the era of single-channel television, watched whatever programme was on offer, since there was not much else to do. A reader's letter in the *Picturegoer* of July 1947 noted that there was virtually the same audience every Saturday night, often in exactly the same seats.[11] Some people went to the cinema almost every day, many went three times a week; but a survey conducted in 1943 (at a time when audiences were near their peak) revealed that 30 per cent of the population never went at all. Women went to the cinema more than men, the lower classes more than the managerial and professional, the young more than the old, and the urban more than the rural.[12] Many people simply went to the local cinema and watched whatever was being shown. It would have been rather difficult to find out what was on elsewhere. To a large extent people's cinema choices were determined far more by the distributors than by their own preferences.

Yet in every sense of the term the Second World War and its immediate aftermath was the Golden Age of British cinema.[13] Quantity was accompanied by quality. Audiences preferred the costume melodramas produced by Gainsborough studios such as *The Man in Grey* (1943), critics preferred David Lean's *Brief Encounter* (1945); but many others are now regarded as among the best British films of any period, particularly in comparison with those produced in the 1920s and 1930s. These include *49th Parallel* (1941), *The Life and Death of Colonel Blimp* (1943), *A Matter of Life and Death* (1946), *Black Narcissus* (1947) and *The Red Shoes* (1948), all produced and directed by Michael Powell and Emeric Pressburger – a Hungarian-born refugee from Germany who had worked for UFA. Yet the US market remained as elusive as ever. Even a cheaply made Hollywood B-movie was expected to make at least half a million dollars, yet in the 1940s that sum was never reached even by Oscar-winning British films such as *49th Parallel*, which has been seen by 9.3 million people in the UK. *Blithe Spirit* (1945), directed by Noël Coward (a writer and performer popular on both sides of the Atlantic) and based on his play, made just $450,000, while *The Life and Death of Colonel Blimp* made only $300,000.[14] More successful was the outstanding British film of the immediate post-war period, *The Third Man* (1949), directed by Carol Reed with a script by Graham Greene (Grand Prize at the Cannes Film Festival and an Academy Award for Robert Krasker's camerawork). The film was not wholly British, not just because it was set in Vienna, but because the hero was an American actor, Joseph Cotten, the 'romantic interest' was the Italian actress Alida Valli, and the actor who stole the film with his virtuoso twenty-minute performance was Orson Welles. Had the director been Italian, the film would have been immediately regarded as 'neo-realist'.

Facing the Americans

Even if these quality British films had been more successful in the USA they would hardly have dented Hollywood's dominance of its own domestic market. British film production was simply too limited. J. Arthur Rank, the great British producer who dreamt of acquiring a presence in the USA, realised full well that the chief weakness of the British cinema was that it was unable to export, and that to do so it was necessary to acquire some kind of political power in the USA.[15] His failure was – at least in part – due to the fact that he always remained an interloper, unable to counteract the considerable help Hollywood received from the US government. The other problem was that while the Rank Organisation accounted at one stage for more than 50 per cent of British film production, it was also a major stockholder in a number of US conglomerates. Exporting British films to the USA would often mean displacing other American films – to no obvious benefit to Rank, whose much-vaunted 'patriotism' was always subservient to his business interests. Besides, the British were always behind Hollywood in film technology, in animation and newsreel and the kind of material that could be used a part of the necessary filler for an afternoon or evening at the cinema.[16] J. Arthur Rank's ambition to head a British film conglomerate collapsed in 1948. The company faced bankruptcy, and Rank was forced to make way for his deputy, John Davis, who turned towards producing low-budget comedies for the domestic market such as the *Doctor in the House* series (1954–70) and the 'Carry On' films. Eventually the Rank company, though still in the entertainment business, made most of its real money from the Rank Xerox photocopying franchise.

Rank had thought he could make a dent in the US market with prestige productions, yet the Ealing comedies produced by Michael Balcon were far more successful: *Hue and Cry* (1947), *Passport to Pimlico* (1949), *Whisky Galore* (1949), *The Man in the White Suit* (1951), *The Maggie* (1954), *Kind Hearts and Coronets* (1949), *The Lavender Hill Mob* (1951), *The Titfield Thunderbolt* (1953) and *The Ladykillers* (1955). Though none of them can be found in the list of the top hundred most popular films in Great Britain, they were mildly successful not just at home but also overseas, perhaps because their self-deprecating sense of humour met foreign expectations of what constituted 'the British'.

The achievement of the Ealing comedies was all the more remarkable because comic films are the most difficult to export. George Formby's numerous comedies of the 1930s had no success in the USA. Norman Wisdom was a top box office draw in Britain in the 1950s and 1960s, but not in the USA.[17] American comic films, however, did well abroad – and not just Chaplin, Keaton and Laurel and Hardy, but also Bob Hope and Jerry Lewis. All of them, even Jerry Lewis, though perhaps not Bob Hope, were regarded as

geniuses by the Parisian cinematic establishment grouped around the celebrated journal *Les Cahiers du cinéma*. Some of the great American comics
were in fact British (Chaplin, Stan Laurel and Hope). Had they remained at
home, it is very unlikely that they would have gained international fame.
French comic films, such as those with the actor Fernandel, were occasionally
appreciated as far away as Italy and the Mediterranean basin, but no further.
The Italian popular comedies of the 1950s were great successes in Italy, and
did reasonably well in Latin America and parts of the Middle East, but
remained unknown everywhere else; the comic actor Totò became increasingly celebrated by Italian intellectuals in search of street credibility, and had
some success in the eastern Mediterranean, but not in the rest of Europe.
His successor, Alberto Sordi, a remarkable actor, was deeply appreciated by
his fellow countrymen, who recognised part of themselves in his impersonation of the 'average Italian' (in a somewhat derogatory way). Foreigners did
not. The British *Doctor in the House* (1954) and its sequels, like the later
'Carry On' comedies with their core team of actors and excruciating smutty
humour, did extremely well in the UK, but *Carry On Sergeant* (1958), *Carry
On Nurse* (1959), *Carry On Cabby* (1963), *Carry On Cleo* (1964), *Carry On
Cowboy* (1965), *Carry On up the Khyber* (1968) and the other twenty-five
films in the series never really crossed the Channel, let alone the Atlantic. As
for German comedies, the rest of the world remained unaware of their
existence.

In Continental Europe the expansion of cinema audiences had first
favoured the Americans. Deprived of American films during the war, post-
war European audiences seemed determined to catch up with the movies
they had missed in the previous five years. As there were plenty of them
available, and at low cost, exhibitors were keen to meet the pent-up demand.
Besides, American prestige was at its height throughout western Europe. A
love of all things American prevailed everywhere, particularly in Italy, where
it was gently parodied in songs such as 'Tu vuoi fare l'Americano' (You
Want to Pass for an American) and films such as *Un Americano a Roma*
(1954), with Alberto Sordi in the part of a young Roman infatuated with
anything American.[18]

The backlog of American films amounted to two thousand features waiting to be unloaded in European theatres. The so-called Blum–Byrnes agreement of May 1946 allowed American films access to the French market.
There were some limitations to free trade, however. French exhibitors were
compelled to show French films for at least four weeks out of every thirteen.

Nevertheless, soon the Americans had acquired a 70 per cent share of films shown in France.[19] This led to outbursts such as: 'The American films . . . which are invading our screens do not merely deprive our artists, musicians, workers and technicians of their daily bread. They literally poison the souls of our children, young people, young girls who are to be turned into the docile slaves of the American multi-millionaires, and not into French men and women attached to the moral and intellectual values which have been the grandeur and glory of our fatherland.'[20] The speaker was Maurice Thorez, leader of the French Communist Party, but the words could have come out of the mouth of a supporter of de Gaulle.

Faced with a new American invasion, European producers, and the French and Italians in particular, successfully pressed for further quotas. The French cinema picked up market share. Indeed, in 1947–48 it even obtained a better share than that envisaged by the quota system, leading some to suspect that the pessimists had been wrong, and that the French public, on balance, rather liked French films.[21] On average, French films had almost twice the attendance of American films, and about half the top ten were French.[22]

In the meantime, Italy was invaded by US films: 668 in 1948, while only fifty-four Italian films had been made in that year. Elsewhere the situation was even more disastrous for domestic production. In Hungary, for instance, only four films were produced in 1945–46, while in the country's 280 cinemas some hundred American films were exhibited.[23] Only a further four films were made by 1948.[24] Then the communists nationalised film production, thus laying the basis for a successful Hungarian cinema industry. After the fall of communism, widespread privatisation virtually wiped it out.

As has been seen, by the 1950s animation was a well-established American monopoly. Warner Brothers shorts were equally popular. The only market segment left free for Europeans to fill was that of the 'quality' animated film. Here the east and central European tradition of puppet theatre supplied the cultural backdrop, while the protectionist policies of successive communist governments provided adequate financial support. The Czechs in particular proved to be particularly adept at the 'art' animated film. The career of Jiří Trnka (1912–69), the most esteemed Czech animator, provides an illustration. Trnka learned the art of puppet-making from a master puppeteer, Josef Skupa, and in 1936 founded his own puppet theatre. After the Second World War he became the artistic manager of the famous Prague animation studio Studio Bratři v triku, where he produced a steady stream of animations by filming either a series of drawings or puppets in action. Some were aimed at children, but many tried to make complex points about artistic freedom and the dangers of technology, such as *Kybernetická babička* (The Cybernetic Grandmother, 1962), where a child's grandmother is replaced by a robot.

European films were increasingly shown in the USA in the 1950s because there was a diminution in the American audience as well as in US film production (the rise of television is regarded as the main culprit). Faced with empty seats, a few American exhibitors turned, somewhat unenthusiastically, to European films. They were right to be unenthusiastic, since these made very little money, whether they were Italian neo-realist masterpieces or highly rated French *films noirs* such as *Les Diaboliques* (1955) by Henri-Georges Clouzot.[25] Occasionally a European film such as Roger Vadim's *Et Dieu créa la femme* (1956) did well, probably because of the sex cult surrounding its leading actress, Brigitte Bardot; but few European stars acting mainly in European films – Bardot, Marcello Mastroianni and Sophia Loren being the main exceptions – ever established the box office pulling power of American stars.

In 1948, 96 per cent of American exhibitors told the *Showman's Trade Review* that they never showed British films.[26] Assumptions about taste, the long-held habit of recasting European culture rather than importing it unchanged, and various hidden forms of protectionism kept European films out of the US market, or reduced them to 'quality' or 'prestige' status, the kiss of death in commercial terms. Those British films that were imported to America were often quality films for an élite, with relatively limited commercial appeal. However, such a bleak picture should be tempered. America, being a large country, has a correspondingly large élite. *In Which we Serve* (1942), *Henry V* (1944), *Caesar and Cleopatra* (1945) and *Brief Encounter* (1945) did well at the box office.[27] Clever marketing helped: *In Which we Serve* was sold as a film showing how class conflict had been superseded by a harmonious community of equals fighting the common enemy – just like America.[28] Laurence Olivier's *Henry V* could have been more difficult to sell, but United Artists (who distributed it) targeted educated audiences, schools, college towns. In Boston it played to full houses for several weeks, but it did well even in some parts of Texas (though it never reached much of Florida, Alabama or Wyoming).[29] *Henry V*'s success helped Olivier's *Hamlet* (1948), in spite of its absence of horses and major battles – and it won the Oscar for best film.

Usually non-American films were shown almost exclusively in 'art houses', cultural ghettoes where one could go and see Japanese, Indian, Italian and French productions. In 1951, according to the *International Motion Picture Almanac*, there were 16,880 cinemas in the USA, with 11.3 million seats. There were also ninety art-houses, with roughly 50,000 seats. It follows that foreign films could be seen by only 0.5 per cent of the American film market.[30] British B-movies were too culture-bound for American audiences. Some of the Italian neo-realist films of the 1940s – such as *Paisà* (1946), *Rome Open City* (1945) and *Bicycle Thieves* (1948) did reach substantial audiences in the USA, but US distributors attributed their success to the sexual advertising used to promote them.[31]

From 1927 to 1940 more films were imported by the USA from Germany than from any other country. Britain was always second, except in 1930, the only year in which it topped the league. After 1940 Britain prevailed in most years until the end of the 1950s.[32] British films did better in America than French or Italian films, but they too had problems. While on the Continent British films, like American ones, were always dubbed, they were not in the USA, where a British accent was not always understood – or so the distributors complained, perhaps unaware that few people in Britain ever understood what John Wayne said (not that it mattered). British producers, J. Arthur Rank above all, were ready to meet the expectations of American audiences, using American stars, but had limited success. Only David Lean's Hollywood-type spectaculars like *The Bridge on the River Kwai* (1957), based on a French novel by Pierre Boulle, and *Lawrence of Arabia* (1962) – for each of which Lean won the Academy Award for best director – reached a global audience, as did his *Dr Zhivago* (1965) and *A Passage to India* (1984).

Only one British production company was able to address itself largely to an international market rather than a domestic one: Hammer Films. They specialised in a genre had been a successful British export since the eighteenth century: the horrific. *The Quatermass Experiment* (1955) – derived, significantly, from one of the earliest television series – was followed by the equally profitable *The Curse of Frankenstein* (1957). Then the systematic and imaginative ransacking of Gothic literature produced a stream of films about Egyptian mummies returning to life, ordinary people becoming dangerous werewolves at the first sign of a full moon, housewives turning into devil-worshipping witches, monsters being created *à la* Mary Shelley, and a long stream of Transylvanian aristocrats with strangely prolonged teeth. Most of these bloody events were filmed in tranquil Cookham in Berkshire, where Hammer's small studio was located.

In the home market the real British successes of the war years were Gainsborough bodice-rippers such as *The Wicked Lady* (Leslie Arliss, 1945), with James Mason and Margaret Lockwood. Enormously popular in the late 1940s were films such as *I Live in Grosvenor Square* (1945), *Piccadilly Incident* (1946), *The Courtneys of Curzon Street* (1947), *Spring in Park Lane* (1948) and *Maytime in Mayfair* (1949, the colour version of *Spring in Park Lane*), all starring the most popular British actress of the 1940s, Anna Neagle. These were classic escapist middlebrow movies, all set in London in upper-class circles. In the league of the top hundred British films (ranked by total attendance in the UK) they rank very high. *Spring in Park Lane* – the kind of film in which the footman is really an aristocrat in disguise – was still in fifth position in 2004, having been seen by 20.5 million people, more than *Titanic* (1998, 18.91 million), while *The Courtneys of Curzon Street* had been seen by 15.9 million (more – so far – than *The Lord of the Rings: The Return of the King*, 2003).[33]

Far more important in terms of numbers were British war movies, of which there was a steady production during the war and throughout the 1950s. This however was a difficult genre to sell abroad, particularly in markets where the perception of who won the war and who fought the hardest differed dramatically. *In Which we Serve* was one of the few British war films to make an impact in the USA.[34]

For most European countries, the war constituted a narrative problem. Few could offer an unproblematic history of resistance to foreign invaders, since for most of them cooperation with the occupying powers had been almost inevitable. Thus the kind of war films which prevailed in France and Italy tended to describe either the suffering of those who were caught up in terrible events they could not control, or provided an account of the heroism of the few who did resist. Such treatments could hardly become popular, as they reminded audiences of their past suffering, or induced a vague feeling of guilt among the majority either for not having suffered as much as others or for not having behaved with the requisite degree of courage. Besides, how the French or the Italian or the Yugoslav people resisted was of limited interest to others. The more such films tried to make a political or moral point, the less likely they were to succeed outside their domestic market.

To a large extent each country behaved as if it had been the centre of the war. The Russians, who lost more lives than any other nation, concentrated on their heroic retreat, their dogged defence and their eventual advance until the final victory in what was known as 'the Great Patriotic War'. The British concentrated on their 'finest hour', when they stood, alone but united, against a terrible foe. War films, war novels, war memoirs and war comic books dominated the British market throughout the 1950s. These included great successes such as *The Dam Busters* (1955), seen by 8.4 million people so far, and *The Bridge on the River Kwai*, seen by 12.6 million.[35] A 1955 survey of the most popular British actors almost coincided with the names most familiar to war-movie audiences: John Mills, Jack Hawkins and Trevor Howard.[36] The continuing existence of rationing until the early 1950s, and of National Service throughout the 1950s, may well have been helped the genre – John Ramsden has identified some one hundred British war films made between 1946 and 1965 – while there were few 'home front' films celebrating the courage of the men and women who endured the German bombing.[37] War was a sequence of battles, an adventure story in which boys turned into men – while actresses remained in the background to provide the odd brief 'romantic interest'.

The vast majority of American war films were about American forces in Europe and the Pacific, but they did not try to make any particular political point. They celebrated courage in adversity. Their international success was partly due to their successful 'de-ideologisation' of the war, which was seen essentially not as a clash of civilisations but as a struggle between Good and Evil. Apart from an inevitable homily in the middle of the film reminding the audience of what the war was 'all about', the conflict was little more than a setting for action-packed adventure. By contrast, in France and Italy war films were heavily political. Then, in the 1950s, war films decreased in number and turned into the semi-pacifist 'war is hell' variety, or comic renditions on the theme of 'war can be funny'.

For obvious reasons, not many war films were made in Germany; those that were concentrated on stories of survival amidst the ruins (the so-called 'rubble films' or *Trummerfilme*). The most popular post-war genre (20 per cent of total production) was the nostalgic *Heimatfilm*, with titles such as *Grün ist die Heide* (Green is the Heather, 1951), set mainly in the Bavarian countryside, with heroines in regional costume, German folk music on the soundtrack, green forests and pristine villages.[38] It is no wonder that these barely made it across the Swiss border.

Everywhere in Europe the main problem was lack of capital. To remedy this, France and Italy entered various co-production agreements in the 1940s. By 1957, 230 Franco-Italian films had been produced.[39] Another way of facing the competition of the Americans was to open up film-making facilities to them. The Americans could spend some of the money they made with their films in Italy and which they could not invest in the USA, while Italian producers would obtain access to the global distribution system of the Americans.[40]

Language was not a problem for the Franco-Italian co-productions, since by then dubbing had become a normal practice in both countries. One of the effects, apart from the obvious one of enabling more capital to be raised, was the creation of a wider market, since such films usually had a mix of popular actors from both countries. French stars such as Fernandel, Martine Carol, Michèle Morgan and others became well known in Italy, while Gina Lollobrigida, Silvana Mangano and Sophia Loren (then not internationally well-known) became household names in France.[41]

These co-production films may have been successful in slowing down the import of US films, but of course many of them were attempts to make Hollywood-type films with local colour. Some, however, were genuinely Franco-Italian, though a shade more Italian than French. The best examples were the highly successful films of *Don Camillo e l'onorevole Peppone*, a comic rendition of the unending struggle in an Italian town between the communist Mayor, Peppone, played by the Italian actor Gino Cervi, and the parish priest Don Camillo, played by the famed French comic actor Fernandel. The director, Julien Duvivier, was French, as were the cameraman Nicolas Hayer and the scriptwriter René Barjavel. The original best-selling novels had been written by the satirical Italian author Giovanni Guareschi. His *Le Petit monde de Don Camillo* had topped the 1955 best-seller list in France, a very unusual achievement for a foreign novel.[42] The films enhanced its success. By 1961 the French translation of *Don Camillo* had sold 800,000 copies.[43]

What united politically France and Italy at the time was the presence in both countries of significant communist and Catholic subcultures. The debate between the Mayor and the priest mirrored the kind of dispute familiar in many small towns in both France and Italy. The films, judiciously, gently mocked both sides, and never demonised the main characters, both of whom were granted human failings as well as merits. The director himself declared: 'What I liked in the protagonists was their human quality. My constant worry was to avoid that anyone could claim that this was party political . . . If something bends towards one side, there was at once a detail or a retort to rebalance the whole.'[44] Needless to say, this ensured a wider audience than an anti-communist or a priest-bashing film would have achieved. It would have been unthinkable in the USA, at the height of the

Cold War, to make a commercial film depicting communists as sincere human beings. The utter failure of these films in the USA and Great Britain is further proof of how culture-bound they were.

Italian Films

Nevertheless, even culture-bound films could have a positive effect on the cultural balance of payments if they were successful: they may not have sold elsewhere, but they kept down imports. The boom of American films in Italy occurred when the Italian cinema was still recovering from the destruction of the war. It began to subside once Italians started making their own movies in massive numbers: imports from the USA acted as a substitute, fuelled by the desire on the part of the Italian public to catch up with films they had not been able to see during the war. When recovery was under way, fewer American films were imported.

IMPORT OF FOREIGN FILMS IN ITALY 1948–1954

	1948	1949	1950	1951	1952	1953	1954
USA	668	502	394	230	246	222	209
UK	91	110	49	18	31	31	41
France	1	37	31	42	59	42	28
USSR	8	7	9	3	9	9	0
Others	76	13	56	49	49	55	29
Total imports	**844**	**669**	**539**	**342**	**394**	**359**	**307**
Italian films	54	71	92	104	132	146	190

SOURCE FOR IMPORTED FILMS: Presidenza delle Consiglio dei Ministri. Direzione dello spettacolo in *Lo spettacolo*, Vol.5 No. 3, July–September 1955, p.207
FOR ITALIAN FILMS: Quaglietti, *Storia economico-politica del cinema italiano 1945–1980*, p.245

Italian films were exported mainly to Mediterranean and Latin American countries – the majority were either sentimental light comedies, such as *Pane amore e fantasia* (1953), the so-called *commedia all'italiana*, whose origins lie in the comic music hall tradition, or Hollywood-type blockbusters, some-times with an American actor in order to increase sales abroad, as was clearly the case with *Ulisse* (1954) with Kirk Douglas, directed by Mario Camerini, one of the leading figures of the Italian cinema in the fascist period.[45] This enabled Italian cinema to hold its own against the competition from the rest of Europe (although the USA was unassailable). For instance, in Argentina, in 1959, half of the 452 films shown were from the USA, but Italy was second with forty-five, just ahead of Great Britain (forty-four), France and Germany (each with thirty-seven), Argentina (twenty-three) and Spain (twenty-one).[46]

A distinctive feature of the Italian film industry is that it had a large domestic market – thanks to a very high number of cinemas (8,000 in 1949 – the highest in Europe) and the fact that television did not become widely established until the early 1960s. Italy's 'normal' complement of cinemas was increased by the numerous 'parish' cinemas built as extensions to churches – part of a Catholic policy of providing the young with entertainment. Consequently, in the 1950s attendances were high: the average Italian bought sixteen tickets per year, more than in the USA (fifteen), Germany (thirteen), Spain (eleven) and France (nine), though much fewer than Great Britain, which towered over all other countries with twenty-five tickets per person per year.[47] Even when television became the dominant medium, the Italian cinema succeeded in maintaining a considerable, though decreasing, audience. The number of seats bought between 1955 and 1960 went down from 819 million to 748 million; in France the decline was from 395 million to 352 million, and in the UK from 1,182 million to 601 million.[48]

The product the Italian cinema offered was distinctive. Italian state television, afraid to offend the Church and the leading political party, the Christian Democrats, offered fiction which tended to be of reasonably high quality, often adaptations of Italian or foreign classics, which avoided even the limited nudity and violence of the cinema of the time. The main attractions on television were popular quiz shows and imported programmes. The cinema offered robust competition, not excessively inhibited by moral codes. Film-makers, including prestigious ones, knew this perfectly well, and played the sex card quite openly. The most successful neo-realist film of the post-war period was Giuseppe De Santis's melodrama *Riso amaro* (1949), which sported a ravishing Silvana Mangano in the role of an exploited rice-picker in the Po Valley, whose beautiful thighs (highlighted in all the posters) showed none of the ravages normally resulting from strenuous rice-picking knee-deep in water. Large audiences flocked to see Federico Fellini's *La Dolce vita* (1960), the top Italian earner in the first six months of 1960, making twice as much as the second-most successful film, *David and Goliath*.[49] Its success should not be attributed exclusively to widespread admiration for the work of the great director (though this was a factor), but also to the controversy surrounding a scene in which the actress Anouk Aimée performs a striptease (very demure by later standards) during an 'orgy' among the Roman aristocracy and their hangers-on. However, the main 'come-on' was the poster depicting Anita Ekberg, a voluptuous Swedish actress, immersing herself, sexily dressed, in the Trevi Fountain. Fellini himself, twenty-five years later, admitted that even for him *La Dolce vita* was inseparable from Anita Ekberg and his own childish fantasies.[50]

Much of the annual production of the Italian film industry remained firmly in the home market and eventually being shown as B-movies in South America. Nevertheless it provided popular cinema in a country which had never been able to produce a national popular culture. The inferiority complex Italians had had since the nineteenth century towards contemporary European culture, particularly that of France, lost its rationale in the cinematic field. Quantitavely, in 1950 the two countries were producing roughly the same number of films – 104 in Italy and 106 in France[51] – but then the Italian cinema rapidly outdistanced the French. Qualitatively – a matter of critical taste – Italian production held its own easily, with Rossellini, Visconti, De Sica and Fellini a fair match for Robert Bresson, Clouzot and Jacques Tati.

The existence of a popular audience in Italy for high-culture films suggests that, as in Britain, people simply opted for a night out without actively selecting a particular film – hence the surprisingly high ratings obtained by famous art directors. So considerable was the proportion of the film-going public that went to see Fellini's or Visconti's films that cinematic parodies making fun of the 'nobler' Italian films became almost a matter of routine; thus *Totò, Peppino e la dolce vita* came out a few months after Fellini's film, and *Rocco e le sorelle* (1961) made fun of Visconti's *Rocco and his Brothers* (1960).[52]

Italians went on spending more on the cinema than on any other form of entertainment even at a time when many were acquiring their first television sets. Sport was well behind, and the theatre lost ground.

ITALY: PERCENTAGE SPENDING ON ENTERTAINMENT

Year	Theatre	Cinema	Sporting events	Others	Radio and TV
1954	6.3	71.0	5.3	7.9	9.3
1955	5.4	69.2	5.3	7.5	12.4

Year	Theatre	Cinema	Sporting events	Others	Radio and TV
1956	5.1	67.9	5.3	8.0	13.5
1957	4.8	64.4	5.7	8.7	16.1
1958	4.6	61.3	5.5	10.2	18.2
1959	3.8	59.6	5.7	10.1	20.5
1960	3.8	56.8	6.7	9.7	22.8
1961	3.7	56.0	6.8	11.5	21.7
1962	3.4	55.1	6.4	11.6	23.3
1963	3.6	51.9	6.3	13.3	24.7
1964	3.8	50.3	6.4	12.9	26.3

SOURCE: Mariagrazia Fanchi and Elena Mosconi (eds), *Spettatori. Forme di consumo e pubblici del cinema in Italia 1930–60*, Biblioteca di Bianco e Nero Marsilio, Venice 2002, p.258

The success of the cinema in Italy kept down the number of foreign films with greater success than Mussolini's policy of self-sufficiency had in the 1930s. In the years 1931 to 1938 the percentage of foreign films out of all those distributed always hovered above the 80 per cent mark. In the years 1952 to 1959, when Italy was ruled by a pro-American coalition, foreign films made up around 70 per cent of the total.[53]

The German cinema was never as successful as the Italian, and never regained the importance it had had in the Weimar era. As we have seen (pages 979–80), the change-over to sound and the brain drain to Hollywood hit the German industry hard. Under Nazism, protectionism had kept many American films out, enabling a recovery of the industry, though it lost many of its increasingly shrinking foreign markets. In 1944 the UFA studios, the largest in Europe, were destroyed by Allied bombing. In nearly thirty years of existence UFA had produced three thousand films. After the war cinemas were built and, thanks to economic recovery, the public rapidly returned to the movies. In 1956, 122 German films were produced, but by 1965 the number was down to thirty-five, partly because of the impact of television, and partly because foreign films flooded the market, mainly but not exclusively from the USA. In the 1950s much of the cinema production was for the local market: lots of peasants and ladies in castles.[54] Few films were exported except for the relatively successful trilogy about the Habsburg Princess 'Sissi', which made the Austrian actress Romy Schneider internationally famous. Otherwise, when it came to films, Germany was an American province to a far larger extent than were the other large European countries.

The Cold War kept most American production out of the communist camp, but the American government itself tried to damage the prospects of some of their films. In Turkey, for instance, distributors of American films were not able to pay the Hollywood studios in dollars. Since Turkey was a vital player in the Cold War confrontation with the USSR, the US government, aware that American films were good for the international image of the United States, helped the distributors through agencies such as the US Information Service. However, not all American films fulfilled the prerequisite of providing a sufficiently positive image of the US. In the years 1956–62 the films not favoured by the American government included *The Blackboard Jungle* (1955), *Baby Doll* (1956), *Rebel Without a Cause* (1955) and *Elmer Gantry* (1960, winner of three Oscars).[55]

Nevertheless, the wide appeal of US films, manifest before the war, became unstoppable. Europeans increasingly made popular films for local audiences and 'artistic' films for international ones. The Americans made popular films for everyone. A study carried out in Longwy (in Lorraine, in the north-east of France) on film audiences between 1945 and 1960 revealed that while French films did very well in the bourgeois neighbourhoods, American films triumphed in working-class areas, particularly those where Italian immigrants predominated.[56]

In Italy the top-earning films in 1957 were mostly American and Italian:

TOP-GROSSING FILMS IN ITALY IN 1957

Ranking	Title	Country	Genre
1	The Ten Commandments	USA	Cecil B. DeMille Biblical epic
2	Poveri ma belli	Italy-France	Romantic comedy
3	Anastasia	USA	Historical film set in Russia, with Ingrid Bergman
4	Giant	USA	Modern drama with Elizabeth Taylor and James Dean
5	Belle ma povere	Italy-France	Romantic comedy
6	Gunfight at the OK Corral	USA	Western with Burt Lancaster and Kirk Douglas
7	Arrivederci Roma	Italy	Romantic comedy
8	Lazzarella	Italy-France	Romantic comedy
9	Du Rififi chez les hommes	France	Film noir

Ranking	Title	Country	Genre
10	*The Sun Also Rises*	USA	Adaptation of Hemingway's novel set in WWI with Tyrone Power, Eva Gardner and Errol Flynn

SOURCE: *Lo spettacolo*, Vol.10, No. 2, April–June 1960, p.117

In the next ten titles there were six romantic comedies, all either Italian or Franco-Italian co-productions. A Totò comic film directed by Vittorio De Sica, *Totò, Vittorio e la dottoressa*, was twenty-third. One of Fellini's masterpieces, *Le Notti di Cabiria*, was thirtieth. Chaplin's *A King in New York* ranked forty-second. From the rankings, it would be tempting to conclude that Italians preferred American dramas and Italian comedies, but one should not generalise. In the following year there were no Italian romantic comedies at all in the top ten, while the domination of the USA continued.

TOP-GROSSING FILMS IN ITALY IN 1958

Ranking	Title	Country	Genre
1	*La Tempesta*	Franco-Italian	Historical drama with Silvana Mangano
2	*Peyton Place*	USA	Modern drama
3	*The Bridge on the River Kwai*	UK	WWII film
4	*La Maja desnuda*	Franco-Italian	Historical drama
5	*Sayonara*	USA	Sentimental war movie set during the Korean War
6	*A Farewell to Arms*	USA	WWI film set in Italy (adaptation of Hemingway's novel)
7	*The Young Lions*	USA	WWII film with Montgomery Clift and Marlon Brando
8	*The Vikings*	USA	Historical epic
9	*Cat on a Hot Tin Roof*	USA	Modern drama with Paul Newman and Elizabeth Taylor (adaptation of Tennessee Williams's play)
10	*Vertigo*	USA	Hitchcock thriller

SOURCE: *Lo spettacolo*, Vol.10, No. 2, April–June 1960

The mass production of Italian comic films continued steadily, with four Totò films in the top hundred: *Totò, Peppino e le fanatiche* (thirty-seventh), *Totò a Parigi* (fortieth), *Totò nella luna* (sixty-sixth) and *Totò e Marcellino* (seventy-seventh).

While the French and the Italians managed to export some of their popular production to the rest of southern Europe, Latin America and the Middle East, only prestige European films succeeded in making it in the international market, thanks to art houses and the growing number of film connoisseurs. Here even small countries, cinematically speaking, could hold their own, sometimes on the back of a single director of great talent, such as the Swede Ingmar Bergman, who, building on the work of Victor Sjöström, received critical acclaim with *Det Sjunde Inseglet* (The Seventh Seal, 1957) and *Smultronstället* (Wild Strawberries, 1957); or the Pole Andrej Wajda, whose *Kanal* (1957), about the uprising of the Warsaw ghetto, and *Popiól i Diamenti* (Ashes and Diamonds, 1958) inaugurated a rebirth of the Polish cinema; or the Japanese Akira Kurosawa (*Rashomon*, 1950) and Yasujiro Ozu (*Tokyo Story*, 1953); or the Indian Satyajit Ray (*Pather Panchali*, 1955). For countries such as Japan and India, producing hundreds of films a year, these renowned directors were the internationally visible tip of a massive iceberg.

It is at this stage that a firmer distinction between art films and popular films arose. The art film movement was almost as old as the cinema itself, but in the aftermath of the war, new institutions were created and older ones revived to separate quality products from those destined for mass consumption. Their natural home was Europe, since the only segment of the international market in which European (and Asian) films could compete with the Americans was that of the art film. Specialised journals came into being – not glossy magazines dedicated to the celebration of famous stars, but intellectual journals which regarded the *auteur* of the film (usually the director) as on a par with literary authors. Film festivals such as Cannes, established in 1946, and Venice, created by the fascist regime in the 1930s and revived in the post-war period, gave prizes to films they regarded as outstanding, demarcating themselves from the US-centred Academy Awards (the Oscars). The British Film Institute (BFI) had been established in 1933, but it received a major impetus only in the post-war era, as did the Paris Cinémathèque. Film critics aspired to gain equality with art and literary critics, though it would take years for film criticism to gain admittance to the academy, and even now it is often regarded as lacking the prestige of the study of literature and art history.

Americans were never left behind in the production of major art films. Orson Welles's *Citizen Kane* (1941), shot by the great innovative cameraman Gregg Toland (he received an Oscar nomination, but not the prize), has remained at the top of the critics' 'best film ever' lists, along with his *The Magnificent Ambersons* (1942). Alfred Hitchcock, though never fully Americanised, became the quintessential *auteur*, not only because of the excellence of many of his films, but also because he marketed himself as a brand name (unusual in the USA for a director), inspired a successful television series in the late 1950s (*Alfred Hitchcock Presents*), and achieved popular success as well as critical acclaim, particularly among French critics and film-makers (such as Claude Chabrol and Eric Rohmer, whose book *Hitchcock* was published in 1957).[57] Commercially speaking, Hitchcock's profitability was in serious decline in America throughout the second half of the 1940s. *Spellbound* (1945) and *Notorious* (1946) made large profits (in excess of $2 million), but *Rope* (1948), *Under Capricorn* (1949), *Stage Fright* (1950), *Strangers on a Train* (1951) and *I Confess* (1952) made losses or small profits. Then the situation changed, and failures alternated with spectacular successes such *Rear Window* (1954, cost $2.1 million to make, earned $5.3 million revenue in North America) and *North by Northwest* (1959, $4.3 million cost, $6 million profit), while *Vertigo* (1958), arguably his masterpiece, made a tiny profit. *Psycho* (1960) was made on a shoestring (less than $1 million), and made $9 million in North America.[58] Hitchcock may be one of the best-known directors in the history of the cinema, perhaps the best-known, but at the time his commercial success was limited, though the chances are that people will still be watching some of his films in the future, when his more profitable contemporaries will have been forgotten.

As the 1950s came to a close, so did the Golden Age of Hollywood. While it is true that the competition of television inflicted the most important blow, Hollywood had to fight on several fronts. The most significant was the drop in audiences which had started with the move of the population away from urban centres to the suburbs, and which was soon compounded by television. Cinemas in shopping centres, and drive-ins (which increased from only three hundred in 1946, to 4,500 in the mid-1950s), partially remedied the situation, but the signs clearly pointed to a massive shift towards home entertainment and the rebirth of the family as the principal centre of consumption.[59]

Equally important was the loss of political influence. This was partly due to the activities of the House Committee on Un-American Activities (HUAC), which in 1947, under the chairmanship of an East Coast Democrat,

J. Parnell Thomas (later sentenced to prison for embezzlement), held hearings on supposed communist influence in the film industry. This resulted in the imprisonment and subsequent blacklisting of a group of directors and writers (the 'Hollywood Ten'), and the sacking of others (some of whom went to Europe). More decisive was the Consent Decree of 1946, an anti-trust move by the US government, upheld by the Supreme Court (United States v. Paramount Pictures, 1948), which forced the Hollywood majors to divest themselves of their theatres – they owned 70 per cent of first-run cinemas in the largest cities (25 per cent of the total).[60] One of the by-products of this was an opening-up of American cinemas to European art films, since independent American exhibitors no longer had to show fourth-run studio products, but could choose whatever they wanted. In a college town or a big city, a first-run European film was more likely to draw a crowd than a fourth-run American film.

The era of the vertically integrated studio with actors, directors and technicians on its permanent payroll was drawing to a close. The studio system had considerable advantages, particularly in formula production. The same directors could shoot similar scenes on similar sets with the same actors and technicians they knew well – the kind of mass production which would be adopted in television serials and soap operas. The contraction in audiences and the competition from television forced Hollywood to rely increasingly on independent production companies and to produce something distinctive: spectacular films using special effects; or films where the depth of field was essential (westerns); or, above all, musicals. In fact the years 1945–60 were the heyday of the great Hollywood musical, a genre quite unmatched in Europe until the rise of Andrew Lloyd Webber's productions in the 1970s and 1980s. A musical could be tested on the Broadway stage, while the recording of its music provided a significant market. The outstanding American musical tradition of the 1930s and 1940s had established a world market. MGM in particular dominated the genre, with *Meet Me in St Louis* (1944, Vincente Minnelli), *Easter Parade* (1948, Charles Walters), *On the Town* (1949, Gene Kelly and Stanley Donen, based on the musical by Leonard Bernstein), *An American in Paris* (1951, Minnelli), *Singin' in the Rain* (1952, Kelly and Donen), *Brigadoon* (1954, Minnelli) and *Gigi* (1958, Minnelli).

What of the Audience?

Compared to the opera-going audience of the end of the eighteenth century, the cinema audience was a model of behaviour, yet audiences in the Golden Age of the cinema (1920–1960) were noisy compared to those in the decades after the 1960s, whose attention was almost religious. One should be circumspect when one is presented with reminiscences or descriptions of a noisy audience. It could well be that the noise was noted precisely because there was an expectation of silence. After all, no one would remark on a noisy public at a football match or a pop concert, where quiet attention would be a matter of headlines. Nevertheless, the evidence should not be dismissed lightly. An account in the British magazine *Picturegoer* of February 1947 tells of the writer's attempt to watch a movie in peace: here commercial travellers snoring, there a group of women talking, the back row the monopoly of couples for whom the film was far less exciting than their embraces.[61] Towering above all else was the noise of children energetically chewing their toffees, mouths open like so many small hippopotamuses by a tranquil pond along the upper Nile. Meanwhile the film was accompanied by the witty comments of local clowns, egged on by a chorale of loud guffaws. It all sounds like a restrained version of the behaviour of aristocratic audiences of eighteenth-century opera houses. Behaving badly at the cinema was nothing new: a French cinema critic, writing in 1922, noted that most of those reading aloud and commenting on the inter-titles were women (not realising, perhaps, that reading the inter-titles was some people's only experience of using their literacy skills). Another complained, as early as 1921, that people were eating noisily in cinemas: they ate oranges, spitting out the pips, or crushed *des bonbons anglais*.[62] At least in those days they did not have giant buckets of popcorn.

Audiences in distant places were rather similar. In the 1950s in Ozieri, a small town of fewer than 10,000 inhabitants some forty kilometres from Sassari in Sardinia, there were two cinemas, the Dessena, owned by the Church, and the Diana, whose owners also owned the only bookshop in town. At the Cinema Dessena, the priest would put his hand across the projector to hide 'sexy' scenes (i.e. kisses, etc.) from the audience – the kind of practical censorship made internationally famous by the film *Cinema Paradiso* (1988) by Giuseppe Tornatore, set in a Sicilian village in the 1950s, and which went on in China as late as 1977, with a local party functionary standing in for the priest.[63] The most popular show of the week in Ozieri was at three o'clock on Sunday, mainly attended by children. The noise they made was so fierce that the cinema employed an elderly man who, armed with very long cane (two–three metres) would patrol the aisles, hitting those who laughed too loudly or threw projectiles at each other.[64]

Throughout the 1950s, as 'youth culture' emerged, the cinema became a space for inter-generational conflicts. The young used certain films as occasions for rowdiness, interjections and catcalls, much to the chagrin of the older audience, for whom the cinema was a private or family space. As television became commonplace in people's living rooms, cinema audiences became younger, more homogeneous and less rowdy. By the 1970s they were relatively quiet. The disagreeable smell of enormous containers of popcorn, the vulgar licking of ice creams and the irritating unwrapping of sweets remained the only occasions for disturbance. Hooliganism was transferred to football terraces.

In 1960, outside the worlds of politics and royalty, and until the world-wide surge of the television market, international celebrities were still mainly film celebrities. There were a few well-known sport celebrities, who owed their fame (chiefly among males) to some special record-breaking feat, or to boxing or football, but their private lives were not followed with the passion of today, except perhaps in their own country. Singers shared some of this privilege, if we can call it so, but it was more the skill of their performances than their lives which mattered. Film stars, however, were the true celebrities. A British survey in 1958 asked children which they would rather be: a film star, a television star, an author or a 'wireless' star. They chose to be a film star. An author, incredibly, was second. The least desirable was the TV star.[65] In 1958 television had not yet come of age.

49

More Books

The Numbers

BETWEEN 1920 AND 1960 the cinema was the main focus of mass entertainment throughout Europe. Its nearest rival was radio broadcasting. Its
future rival, television, was rapidly advancing but had not yet become ubiquitous. Yet the cinema did not abolish previously established cultural media.
More theatres were built, more plays were written, more books were published, and more newspapers were read than ever before. Throughout the
1920s the output of books, fiction as well as non-fiction, reached record
levels. In Britain the largest increase in radio licences in a single year was in
1930 (at a rate of more than a thousand a day), which was also the best year
for books in the history of British publishing up to then.[1] The idea that new
cultural media inevitably replace old ones has little foundation in reality. Yet
many of those who are supposed to form popular opinion, including superficial futurologists, shallow journalists and other assorted charlatans, hold
that view with touching credulity. The highest sales of novels and newspapers
were achieved in countries with the highest levels of cinema attendance –
the cinema feeding the book, the book feeding the cinema. Books adapted
for the cinema increased their sales. Best-selling books were rapidly adapted
for the cinema. In Britain, the book of the animated Walt Disney film *The
Three Little Pigs* sold 188,000 copies in three months in 1935. The press also
thrived on the back of films. Women's weeklies devoted an increasing
number of features to films and stars. *Mickey Mouse Weekly* began publication
in 1936 as a follow-up to the successful Disney films. Mass-Observation
surveys noted that the most frequently bought books among the British
lower classes were those which had been filmed, such as *The Grapes of
Wrath*, *Gone with the Wind* and *Rebecca*.[2] The book held its own against the

competition; and the competition was not just the cinema and broadcasting, but the new entertainment possibilities offered by an increasingly prosperous society.

Comparing figures is far from easy. Figures about book publishing are especially unreliable. For a long time there was not even an international agreement about what constituted a book. In 1955, UNESCO decided to define a book as a non-periodical publication containing forty-nine or more pages not including covers. Pamphlets were between five and forty-eight pages. Any printed material shorter than five pages was to be regarded as a 'leaflet'. In fact, even after 1955, many national statistics have continued to go their own way. The Italians and the Irish, among others, called a pamphlet anything up to one hundred pages provided it did not have a spine, while in Hungary and the USA pamphlets are a maximum of sixty-three pages long, and in Iceland they are less than seventeen pages.[3] A change in definition can make a huge difference. The decrease in book production which occurred in a number of countries between 1937–39 and 1954 was due to the fact that pamphlets, included in 1937, were excluded in 1954. This led to a 'collapse' of book production in Germany of 15 per cent, in Hungary of 12 per cent, in Italy of 13 per cent, in Czechoslovakia of 32 per cent, and in Japan a worrying 35 per cent.[4] As definitions change, any historical run of statistics can give us, at best, only a general idea of trends.

Most available figures indicate the number of titles published, not the number of copies printed. A larger number of titles may be an indication of increased creativity, but not necessarily literacy.[5] To complicate matters, 'titles' may include reprints, subsequent impressions or slightly modified versions of the same book (e.g. with a different introduction – technically a 'new' book). Should one use the figures for the number of copies printed, or the number of copies sold (leaving aside the greatest mystery of them all: actual number of copies read)? How about library books with multiple readers? What about countries where there is a thriving trade in second-hand books?

The unreliability of statistics on book production does not preclude us from determining general trends and making cautious comparisons. Laws, such as those existing in Great Britain, France and Italy, compelling publishers to deposit at least one copy of each book printed in a state library, give us an idea of the number of titles published, assuming that publishers comply with the law. Even so, there are further problems. Soviet statistics put the USSR as the first country in Europe in 1956 for the number of titles published (59,550). But that figure includes all official publications, half the total amount, and many of these were distributed free.[6]

Sometimes the official statistics conflict with the number of copies sent to the national library. Thus, for Italy, those who use figures from ISTAT (the national statistics institute) will find that they differ slightly from those arrived at by using the entries into the national library in Florence. If we take, arbitrarily, the year 1931, we see that ISTAT claims that 11,181 books were published, while if we take the Biblioteca Nazionale returns we have 12,196 titles. The difference is around 10 per cent.[7]

UNESCO statistics offer this comparative picture of pre-war and post-war book production:

BOOK PRODUCTION IN SELECTED COUNTRIES (NUMBER OF TITLES). RANKED IN TERMS OF 1954 FIGURES

1920	1937–39 annual average	1954	1977
USSR	43,348	50,109	83,395
Germany	25,400	21,650	48,736
Japan	30,732	19,837	40,955
UK	16,087	19,188	36,196
USA	10,873	11,901	84,542
France	8,124	10,622	31,673
Spain	.		24,896
Brazil			20,025
Korea (South)			13,081
India			12,885
Poland			11,552
Italy	10,509	9,158	10,116
Czechoslovakia	10,994	7,518	

SOURCE: UNESCO, *An International Survey of Book Production During the Last Decades*, Statistical Reports and Studies No. 26, Paris 1982, pp.4, 9
Germany: figures for 1954 combine the Federal Republic and the DDR; for 1977 FRG only.

China is excluded from these statistics. Had it been included it would have boosted the non-European presence in the 1977 league table, though with 46.3 per cent of the estimated total world number of titles published, Europe as a whole (but not including the USSR), still appeared to maintain its cultural hegemony. In reality such a high figure reflects not just the wealth and literacy levels of Europe, but above all its linguistic fragmentation. Within Europe, according to 1975 figures, the top four countries were, in ranking order of number of titles: the Federal Republic of Germany, the UK, France and Spain. These were followed by the Netherlands, Yugoslavia, Czechoslovakia, Poland and Switzerland. At the bottom of the top twelve were Italy, Sweden and Hungary.[8] Taking the percentage of books produced per 100,000 inhabitants gives us a better indication of which countries are major consumers of books in relative terms. Here Iceland clearly led the field, at least in 1954, possibly a result of high literacy, tiny population, and long winter nights. And there are some surprises: Italians produce fewer books than Thais, the Greeks more than the French, and the Bulgarians more than the British.

PRODUCTION OF BOOKS PER 100,000 INHABITANTS
IN 1954

Iceland	255
Luxembourg	106
Norway	81
Switzerland	75
Holland	66
Sweden	62
Czechoslovakia	58
Portugal	55
Austria	52
Denmark	52
Finland	49
Bulgaria	43
Belgium	41
Great Britain	38
Germany, East	33
Germany, West	33
Greece	31
Yugoslavia	28
Hungary	28

PRODUCTION OF BOOKS PER 100,000 INHABITANTS
IN 1954 – *continued*

USSR	26
France	25
Poland	25
Japan	23
Thailand	21
Italy	19
Argentina	17

SOURCE: UNESCO, *An International Survey of Book Production During the Last Decades*, Statistical Reports and Studies No.26, Paris 1982, p.6

Top-selling books are an important part of total sales. They are a publisher's best protection against the inevitable losses incurred by the books that do not make the grade. In what was a relatively small market for books, that of Italy between the wars, fewer than fifty books – not counting detective stories sold by Mondadori at news stalls – had a print run of over 50,000 copies, and only seventeen sold more than 200,000 copies.[9] Most books sold a thousand copies or less. Thus a single best-seller would do far better than fifty less successful books added together, since each additional copy printed and distributed would cost marginally less than any of the first thousand.

Most best-sellers are novels, but only if sales are calculated over a relatively short span of time. A book will sell well when it comes out, then sales will stabilise, then the 'word of mouth' system will swing into action and sales will become high again for a while, then slowly decline. If the book becomes a classic, it will go on selling reasonably well for years to come. But fiction represents a small percentage of book production – often around 10 per cent of the total. Various sources indicate that in the 1930s novels constituted 12 per cent of Italian book production, 15 per cent of French, 20 to 22 per cent of German and American, and 30 per cent of British.[10]

Over the long term, most successful fiction is outsold by reference books, manuals and school books. It has been calculated, for instance, that in France alone school books, in 1959, made up 31 per cent of total production (fifty-six million copies out of 178 million books).[11] Highly successful cookery books, 'indispensable' travelling guides, gardening manuals, popular textbooks, dictionaries and lifestyle manuals are among the great best-sellers of the twentieth century. *80 Years of Best Sellers*, produced by the publishers of the American magazine *Publishers' Weekly*, puts five non-fiction books in the top five American best-sellers for 1895–1975: Benjamin Spock's *Pocket Book of Baby and Child Care* (1946), with 23,285,000 copies sold, followed by *Better Homes and Gardens Cook Book* (1930) with 18,684,976, Webster's *New World Dictionary of the American Language* with 18.5 million, *The Guinness Book of Records* (16.4 million) and *Betty Crocker's Cookbook* (thirteen million). In sixth place was a novel, Mario Puzo's *The Godfather* (1969), with 12.1 million copies sold.[12] Such figures are today dwarfed by the international sales of the Harry Potter books and *The Da Vinci Code*.

The Cheap Book

The modern paperback appeared in the 1930s. In Britain, Allen Lane's Penguin Press (1935) sold its first 'paperback' books, all of them reprints of successful novels and biographies, for sixpence, the price of a packet of cigarettes. What were these books? Agatha Christie's *The Mysterious Affair at Styles*, Dorothy L. Sayers's *The Unpleasantness at the Bellona Club*, six other novels including Hemingway's *A Farewell to Arms*, the popular writer Beverley Nichols' autobiography and André Maurois's life of Shelley (*Ariel*). Most of these are still in print. This was an unprecedented success. By the end of 1938 nearly two hundred Penguins had been published along with forty Pelicans (non-fiction), a dozen Penguin specials (on issues of the day) and half the Penguin Shakespeare. The Penguin format was widely copied. A marketing principle, still valid today, was thus established: if a publisher wants to sell more books, it must drop its prices and find new outlets.[13] The first Penguins were sold in newsagents, chain stores such as Marks & Spencer and Woolworth's, and even from a Penguin vending machine installed in Charing Cross Road in London.[14]

In the USA the first paperbacks were issued by Simon & Schuster in 1939 under the imprint of 'Pocket Books'. Publishers kept costs to a minimum by paying lower royalties to authors and selling paperback rights, and above all by publishing books in large quantities, lowering per-unit costs. A book could be had now for only twenty-five cents. The war, as usual, was good for culture. In Britain during the Second World War people spent more on books, newspapers and magazines than they had before, in spite of severe paper rationing. More bookshops were opened. More books were borrowed from libraries. People read more, and in 1941 the publishers Hutchinson sold over ten million books.[15] Bored soldiers made a captive readership. In the USA many of the books soldiers read were obtained thanks to philanthropic donations, the libraries of the armed forces and the Council on Books in Wartime, which distributed free copies to the troops. Reading habits thus acquired were not forgotten upon returning to civilian life.

In the post-war period most countries expanded their publication of cheap paperbacks. In Italy in 1949 Rizzoli launched its Biblioteca Universale Rizzoli, dedicated to the publication of cheap, out-of-copyright classics. In France Hachette launched the Livre-de Poche in 1953. Its publication of classics reached sales levels not matched before: *Les Liaisons dangereuses* sold 225,000 in a single year, Stendhal's *Le Rouge et le Noir* 181,000. Even Pascal's *Pensées* sold 60,000. By 1963, twenty-four million Livres de Poche had been sold.[16] By 1961 *The Diary of Anne Frank* had sold 500,000 copies, Camus's *La Peste* 330,000 and Malraux's *La Condition humaine* 330,000.[17] In 1965 Mondadori launched its Oscar paperbacks with Hemingway's *A Farewell to Arms*. In a week it had sold 75,000 copies, a month later 200,000 copies. The cheap book policy demonstrated that there was a considerable popular demand for so-called high culture, and that given the right pricing policy, high culture could be as profitable as, or more profitable than, so-called popular culture.

Such success did not just involve fiction. Books offering succinct histories of countries, religions and political movements did well too, as did series in which each volume was, in practice, the equivalent of an entry in a large encyclopaedia. This was the approach pioneered by Penguin and developed in France in 1941 with Que sais-je? (What do I know?), an imprint of the Presses Universitaires de France (PUF). The assumption behind such ventures was that there was a relatively large public, mainly but not exclusively made up of students (an ever-growing sector of the population), who required substantial information on ideas and events but had little time for ploughing through large volumes. They wanted to know about existentialism without going through the massive tomes of Jean-Paul Sartre, about Marxism without trying to master *Das Kapital*, and about the main religions without spending a long time reading treatises on Christianity, Islam or Buddhism. The volumes in the Que sais-je? collection would supply this need for cheap information for those in a hurry to learn. Thus Henri Lefèbvre's *Le Marxisme* sold 50,000 copies. *L'Existentialisme* by Paul Foulquié sold, between 1947 when it first came out and 1958, some 110,000 copies. Like all the volumes in the collection, *L'Existentialisme* was just over a hundred pages long and gave a non-polemical, fairly balanced account of the evolution of the main concepts associated with the philosophical approach popularised by Sartre and the different 'souls' of existentialism (atheistic, Christian, etc.). The same was done in the 1950s for the most varied topics, from monkeys, the calendar, Greek literature and ancient Egypt, to the subconscious, choral singing, and the history of the Boy Scouts (*Histoire du scoutisme* by H. Van Effenterre). In the course of the 1950s, the Que sais-je? imprint sold some fifteen million copies.[18] The works of Freud and Marx – or works about them – were now available to almost all those who wanted them. But who were those who wanted to know about Freud, Marx and ancient Egypt? Price had been an obstacle to reading until the mid-1930s. Most books were simply too expensive for most people. Cheap books, and in some countries a network of publicly supported libraries, had brought to an end the most obvious market obstacle. But the real obstacle remained education. Not the simple ability of knowing how to read, but the desire and the capacity to read page after page of print. As education expanded – not just school education but the wider education obtainable with more accessible cultural goods such as cinema, radio and magazines – readership expanded too.

In Britain there was a remarkable growth of lending libraries, both public and subscription. In 1924 British libraries had a stock of fifteen million books. By 1949 that had increased to forty-two million, and some twelve million readers borrowed three hundred million books a year. Such was the thirst for reading that shops started lending books purely in order to attract customers – as Boots the chemist had done as early as 1899, when it started the Boots Booklovers' Library.[19] Far from damaging publishers, the growth in library lending was matched by the explosion of cheap paperbacks.

Of course, cheap books had been available for decades, but they were usually penny dreadfuls and other lowbrow genres. Now reputable authors and classics were within reach of almost everyone. Cheap books have continued to sell rapidly even in our day, in spite or because of the proliferation of new media and the publication of more books discussing the death of the book. In Italy in 1992 the publisher Marcello Baraghini launched the *libro a mille lire* – the 1,000-lire book, the price of an espresso coffee, based on a low profit and a minimum print run of 50,000. In 1992 two million copies were sold. This was quickly imitated elsewhere, with the French trying out the *livre à 10 francs* and in Great Britain the £1 book (usually well-established, out-of-copyright). In 1995 Penguin produced a series of tiny books priced at sixty pence for its sixtieth anniversary. These books, often a single short story, sold in their thousands.

It may seem strange that price should have such a strong effect on sales, that the demand for books should be, in the language of economists, so elastic, so responsive to price variations. In a letter published on 22 March 1927 in the *Nation & Athenaeum* , the economist John Maynard Keynes wrote that an article in *La Bibliographie de la France* noted that the price of books (as compared to before the war) had practically halved, and this was due to the great expansion in the book-buying public; an 'enviable' state of affairs, commented Keynes.[20] The calculations on pricing depend largely on the size of the print run publishers hope to sell. Keynes, in a previous letter (12 March 1927), calculated that the initial fixed cost (i.e. the cost regardless of how many copies are printed) was in the region of £150 per title. As the average cost of production decreases rapidly as production expands, publishers had to guess how many copies a book would sell at which price, and hence how many to print. Prudence suggested a high price: 'Thus, from the purely business point of view, there is no case for reducing the price of books, unless and until the potential book-buying public is very greatly increased.'[21] This, of course, returns us to the original question: how elastic is the demand for books? As the term 'books' covers many quite different commodities, the calculation involves discovering a large range of demand curves, that is the preference schedules of millions of potential buyers. This is what often makes publishing an interesting way in which to go bankrupt.

As many more people started to buy books, the books themselves began to change. Gone were the days of the interminable serialised novel, or the three-volume Victorian book. Novels grew shorter: the standard length shrank from 220,000 to 120,000 words.[22] Women's magazines still carried serialised novels, but these were now much shorter. Books are not just bought to be read. They are symbols of what we are and what we like, as are furniture and decorative objects. At the same time, again like clothes and furniture, they reveal something of what we are, what we think we are, and what we want other people to think we are. One may buy *War and Peace* because eventually, in the fullness of time, when older and wiser, we shall read it. Or our children will read it. And *War and Peace* looks good on our shelves.

Arthème Fayard, whose publishing house had been one of the pioneers of the French popular book (see page 300), understood that if one could print many copies, it was possible to produce cheap books that looked good and that would be bought by the ever-increasing ranks of the aspiring middle classes. In the 1920s Le Livre de Demain supplied them with books written by major authors on important subjects (*Histoire de France*, etc.), printed on good paper, all bound in yellow covers to stand out on one's shelves, and adorned with modern illustrations.

How to create a demand for books through marketing became a routine problem. Even an experimental French novel such as Raymond Radiguet's *Le Diable au corps* (1923, when the author, who died in that year, was only twenty-one) was widely advertised on billboards, to the astonishment of Italian publishers.[23] There were even manuals on how to launch books, such as Édouard Théodore-Aubanel's *Comment on lance un nouveau livre* (1937), which insisted – unoriginally – that the best way of marketing a book was by advertising in the press.[24] But it also suggested that publishers put pressure on governments and schools, libraries and other book-buying institutions (or institutions that induced others to buy books); court, cajole, even bribe reviewers and literary editors; create what is now called a 'buzz' around certain books by suggesting that everyone else will be buying it; and use an enticing title and an alluring cover. Finally they could facilitate the creation of literary prizes, of which in the interwar period there was an enormous development: France had at least eighty-six literary prizes in 1937.[25] Some of these had a rather narrow remit: there was even a 'Prix en l'Honneur de la Vierge' for the best work celebrating the Virgin Mary; this was created by the Académie des Sciences et Belles-Lettres de Clermont-Ferrand, and offered the winner eight hundred francs – the modesty of such a sum would certainly have met with the approval of the Virgin. The press could not resist newsworthy items such as a yearly fight among literary figures for the most prestigious prizes. Authors and publishers could not ignore them, but winning did not necessarily ensure high sales.

Even Marcel Proust – who sought all possible honours and distinctions – lobbied hard to ensure that his *À l'Ombre des jeunes filles en fleurs* (Within a Budding Grove) won the Goncourt in 1919. Proust had mobilised all his influential friends, taking many to have lunch at the Près Catalan and dinner at the Ritz.[26] At first the press had been cold towards Proust's novel, the second volume of *À la Recherche du temps perdu*.[27] Yet the lunches and dinners may have helped, because in December 1919 it won the prize by six votes to four. The runner-up was Roland Dorgelès's *Les Croix de bois*, a masterpiece about life in the trenches during the war. The prize now became the centre of a major literary debate: in the month following its award, more than a hundred press articles about it appeared. Some praised Proust, others preferred Dorgelès's war novel. Proust vented his annoyance with Gallimard, his publishers, for not doing enough for the book, as authors often do. They had not reprinted it fast enough; they had not treated the press with due courtesy and caution.[28]

Before winning the prize *À l'Ombre des jeunes filles en fleurs* had sold 3,000 copies. The prize did boost sales, but, by the end of 1920 it had sold as much as the first book of *À la Recherche*, *Du Coté de chez Swann* –15,000 copies. Meanwhile, *Les Croix de bois* – which had already sold 17,000 copies before the prize – had sold by May 1920 a total of 45,000 copies, three times as many as Proust's book.[29] Dorgelès's publishers were quick to reprint the book with bands announcing 'Prix Goncourt', and in small print 'four votes out of ten' (three months later they were fined for misleading the public, but three months can be a long time in publishing).[30] *Les Croix de bois* (it won another important literary prize) sold more, but this was only to be expected for a war novel published a year after the end of the First World War. Proust's long novel, part of an even longer series, was never likely to do better than Dorgelès, Goncourt or no Goncourt. In the long run, prizes may not matter much. In the short run, however, they do, because they focus attention on a few books jostling for attention among an ever larger number of publications.

In the short run publishers are often wrong, and so are some writers. André Gide, on behalf of Gallimard, famously turned down *Du Coté de chez Swann* ('Too many duchesses. Not for us'). Proust paid Grasset to publish it (1913), and it was received with critical acclaim. Gide repented and wrote to Proust: 'This rejection will remain our most serious error and (since I am ashamed to be responsible) one of the most burning regrets of my life . . .' Gallimard bought *Du Côté* from Grasset and became Proust's publisher.[31] Publishing is not a science. Mistakes are inevitable. In the end publishers must trust their instinct. Gallimard's Comité de Lecture, made up of men of letters, never asked themselves whether something would sell. But Gallimard himself did, and published some popular detective novels such as Gaston Leroux's Rouletabille stories. When his editors complained, Gallimard explained the facts of publishing life: if they wanted to publish writers like Valéry and Claudel, they would have to lump Gaston Leroux.[32] The Comité had not liked *Gone with the Wind*, but Gallimard did. And so did his finance editor's wife, who commented that it would sell 'like a Delly' (the most successful writer of women's romance in France). She was right: the French translation sold 800,000 copies.[33]

Foreign Books

Throughout the decades from the 1920s to the 1950s, the domination of France and Great Britain in the international book markets continued, but the USA emerged as a major rival poised to overtake them both in the years after 1960, while the French lead over English-language novels and non-fiction, especially in southern Europe, was eroded in this period. British writers were continuing to produce a steady stream of popular novels, crime stories (Edgar Wallace, Agatha Christie), and children's books, of which they became great specialists.

The diversification of the world market for narrative, which we noticed emerging in the 1880s (see Chapter 32), continued with the expansion of the book market and is still continuing, though American literature has become ever more dominant. By 2004 a visitor to any large bookshop in Paris, Rome, London or New York would be able to purchase books written by Egyptian, Chinese, Japanese, Indian, Nigerian, Albanian and Latin American novelists. This was far from being the situation in the 1920s, but the market, especially outside Great Britain and France, had become open to authors from 'difficult' languages. Hungarian authors such as Ferenc Körmendi and Lajos Zilahy, barely available in English and French before the war (and not much afterwards), were fashionable in Italy throughout the 1930s.

Germany, a minor player in the nineteenth century, became a major exporter of narrative. Before the First World War, British Germanists complained, with some justification, that the British ignored German culture and literature; by the late 1920s *The Times Literary Supplement* was alerting its readers to an invasion of German books. The editor of the *London Mercury*, J.C. Squire, complained that 'The present tendency is to think that anything that comes out of Germany must be good.' Lion Feuchtwanger's books (especially *Jew Süss*, 1925) were mentioned by reviewers in the same breath as the works of Tolstoy and Balzac. The *Spectator* pronounced Jacob Wassermann (whose *Christian Wahnschaffe*, 1919, became an American success with the title *The World's Illusion*) and Vicki Baum, author of the international best-seller *Grand Hotel* (1929), the greatest writers alive.[34]

German books were also fashionable in Italy from the 1920s. This had little to do with Nazism and fascism. Before the advent of Hitler and for some years after that, a pro-German position would not necessarily have curried favour with the fascist regime. The promotion of German books responded to commercial criteria of diversification. The German writers translated into Italian were those who were becoming known throughout Europe, such as Stefan Zweig, one of the most popular German authors in Italy between the wars.[35] Mondadori's leading German specialist, Lavinia Mazzucchetti, had a great flair for identifying German books that would do well in Italy, and thanks to her a quarter of the books in Mondadori's quality imprint, the Medusa collection, were by German writers, as well as almost half of those in the more commercial Romanzi della Palma.[36]

Equally popular, in Italy as elsewhere, was the relatively new genre of the fictionalised biography, of which the acknowledged master at the time was Emil Ludwig, author of *Napoleon* (1927), *Bismarck* (1927), *Lincoln* (1930), *Goethe* (1928) and many others. Siegfried Kracauer complained of the new vogue: 'If prior to the World War I the biography was a rare work of erudition, today it is a widespread literary product . . . soon there will be scarcely any major politician, general, or diplomat who has not been commemorated by a more or less ephemeral monument.'[37] What would Kracauer have said of one of the literary successes of 2003, the autobiography (co-authored) of a young footballer, then twenty-eight: David Beckham, *My Side: The Autobiography* – which had been preceded five years earlier by *David Beckham: My Story*?

Dependency on translated narrative continued to prevail in countries such as Spain. Pioneer entrepreneurs like Nicolás María de Urgoiti, owner of the great progressive daily *El Sol* and the magazine *Dédalo* (1922), launched in 1919 his Colección Universal, an imprint of paperbacks at unbeatably low prices aimed at the enlightened middle classes, who were at the time and for decades afterwards a fairly rare commodity in Spain. This published almost exclusively foreign books (94 per cent of the total), on which the publishers did not bother to pay royalties. Spanish authors would have wanted a 12 per cent royalty, which would have required a print run of 8,000 to be profitable, while 4,000 was the most Colección Universal could hope for. Thus the Spanish middle classes were fed a steady stream of foreign novels, while Spanish novelists remained few in numbers.[38] Throughout the 1920s the majority of translations into Spanish were from French – as they had been throughout the nineteenth century. In fact, in 1931 the Librairie Hachette had obtained the monopoly of bookselling in Spanish railway stations (which they kept throughout the Franco era), but the days of French cultural hegemony in Spain were now numbered. After 1930 English translations prevailed also in Spain.[39] In 1933 even the Libreria Francesa (French Bookshop) of Barcelona was full of books in English.[40]

Unlike Italy, Germany (except under Nazism) or even France, Great Britain translated few foreign books. But this was not new. In 1890 only 3.1 per cent of new titles were translations. In 1930 it was still 3.1 per cent, and in 1960 it was 3.9 per cent – with ups and downs in between (2.2 per cent in 1950) – half of these from French and only 10 per cent from Italy and Russia. The market, however, had expanded. In 1890 Britain published just over 8,000 new titles. By 1935 this had more than doubled.[41] The popularity of German books in the 1930s would have seemed strange only a few years before when, amidst the carnage of the war, there was in France, Great Britain and even the US a virulent hatred for all things German. In fact, the war sparked a fascination with the enemy. Popular books included the war memoirs of the Kaiser and most of his generals, including Margarete Ludendorff's *My Married Life with Ludendorff* (1930) and Eugen Ketterl's *The Emperor Francis Joseph: An Intimate Study by his Valet de Chambre* (1929), a precursor of books by the servants of prominent figures such as Mao's bodyguard and his personal doctor, and Princess Diana's butler. Other successful German authors included Vicki Baum (*Grand Hotel*, 1930, *Result of an Accident*, 1931, *Helene*, 1932), Gina Kaus (*Luxury Liner*, 1932), Heinrich Mann (*Mother Marie*, 1927), Anna Seghers (*The Revolt of the Fishermen*, 1929), Hans Fallada (*Little Man What Now?*, 1932) and Erich Maria Remarque (his great best-seller *All Quiet on the Western Front*, 1929, discussed on pages 875–7). Nor should one forget that, in the 1930s, the most important works of Nazi leaders were promptly translated into English, including, of course, *Mein Kampf* in 1933, and also books by Goebbels and Hermann Goering.

In terms of consumption, however, the USSR became the world's most important market for books – as well as one of the most regulated. At the end of 1921 there was a great publishing boom which coincided with the end of 'war communism' and the return to a market economy. Many publishing houses had been taken over by the state, but others were owned by the Party, the cooperatives and other organisations, and some private publishing was allowed. By 1927–28 the USSR was publishing 35–36,000 titles a year, and the print runs for the works of Tolstoy, Gorky and Pushkin ran into millions of copies.[42]

Translations enabled 'high' culture authors to be adopted by literary élites in culturally dominant countries, thus assuring their intellectual longevity. Nevertheless it remained very difficult for novelists from small countries to remain popular abroad long after their death. It was easier for playwrights (such as Ibsen and Strindberg) and children's authors (Hans Christian Andersen and the authors of *Pippi Longstocking* and *Pinocchio*).

Polish popular literature remained ignored. The great success of Henryk Sienkiewicz's *Quo Vadis?* at the beginning of the century (see pages 639–41) was not repeated. Though united and independent, Poland between the wars did not offer a substantial market for books; literacy was very low, 20 per cent of the inhabitants were German-speakers, books were expensive, and there were only a thousand bookshops in the entire country. Polish literary élites, overwhelmingly concentrated in Krakow and Warsaw, were well catered for: in 1935 there were about five hundred publishers in Poland, producing over 6,000 titles and almost 9,000 in 1938, while a literary weekly sold 10,000 copies a week.[43] Compared to Italy, Poland was not doing too badly.

Novelists from the rest of Europe, not to speak of Asia, Africa and Latin America, are almost absent. The majority of new entrants came from the larger countries (Japan) or from countries where a major world language was used: the Latin Americans who wrote in Spanish and Portuguese, and the Indians and Africans who wrote in English.

After the Second World War literary international exchange developed apace. According to the *Index Translationum* – a publication connected to the League of Nations and later to UNESCO – 10,014 translations appeared in thirty-two countries in 1949. By 1954 there were more than twice that number (21,676).[44] Those countries which are low down in the translation league are either poor, such as recently decolonised countries with low literacy levels, or those whose own production is so vast that a translated book would have to face stiff competition as well as incurring translation costs (for instance Great Britain and the USA).

The figures for the communist countries should be handled with caution. Czechoslovakia and Poland undoubtedly translated considerable material from the Russian for political and not for market reasons. The enormous number of translations for the USSR (both into and from Russian) hides the fact that much of this is internal to the USSR, the top translating country in the world. Many Russian books were immediately translated into the hundreds of languages of the USSR. This was one of the cultural achievements of the communist system: had it been left to market forces, most Russian cultural production (including nineteenth-century classics, scientific manuals and textbooks) would never have been made available to non-Russian-speakers throughout the vast and multi-ethnic territory of what was then the

Soviet Union. Translation may give some idea of cultural influence, but it does not give the full picture. If an economy is flooded with foreign imports, a possible strategy is what economists call import substitution. In culture, this consists of imitating or adapting foreign genres which are successful. Some genres, however, come with a particular national flavour. The popularity of the English detective story led the German Edmund Finke to set his *Der Mörder verliert den Robber* (1935) in smog-filled London. In 1941, under the pseudonym Frank Harding, the French Léo Malet wrote *Johnny Metal*, a hard-boiled story set in New York with a statutory blonde who turns up unexpectedly to ask for help. In 1946 Boris Vian wrote, under the pseudonym of Vernon Sullivan, a hard-boiled thriller in the American style, *J'Irai cracher sur vos tombes* (1946), whose sexual content was so explicit that he was taken to court. Vian himself said that the idea of writing *J'Irai cracher* came during a conversation with the publisher Halluin, the editor at Scorpion, who was in financial difficulties and wanted something erotic, something like James Hadley Chase's *No Orchids for Miss Blandish* (1939).[45]

Writers

The expansion of the readership led to its increased fragmentation. Niche markets and genres, which had developed rapidly in the decades after 1880, had become clearly recognisable. Chapter 23 listed, in no particular order, a large number of genres. The years 1920–60 saw a veritable explosion. Some could be classified in terms of their social setting: working-class, military, rural, colonial, public school; others by the kind of event which brings together the protagonists: war, disaster, earthquake, etc.; others by the kind of readership they sought (experimental, children's books); others yet by their form (first-person narrative, diary). Such lists, and the subdivisions they create, are often quite arbitrary, and they can be expanded *ad infinitum*. And one can add more, *ad infinitum*, since each category spawns subcategories. Thus the thriller (in reality an adventure story with an element of mystery and suspense) was further subdivided into the mafia thriller (Mario Puzo), the legal thriller (John Grisham), even the trashy gangster thriller (James Hadley Chase's *No Orchids for Miss Blandish* and Mickey Spillane's books), the techno-military thriller (Michael Crichton's *The Andromeda Strain*), the Cold War techno-military thriller (Tom Clancy), and so on and on and on.

Yet the real genres, those which warranted special imprints by publishers or distinctive shelves in bookshops, were those which had become popular in the second half of the nineteenth century: detective stories, science fiction, and women's romance.

Some sub-genres are attributed according to the colour of their cover, as was the case with the Italian 'giallo' (yellow), which stands for crime story (see page 917). In Chinese a yellow book, however, is an erotic novel. Some categories are really just different ways of suggesting what the contents might be: novels intended to be marketed for their sexual content can be called 'adult', 'sexy', 'pornographic', 'libertine', 'erotic'. Low-culture novels for women have a series of depreciative names.

The distinction between high and low genres can also be seen as a marketing mechanism, the distinction being emphasised by the covers, the ways of selling of the book and the advertising which accompanies publication. They are occasionally produced in different ways. The high novel is written slowly, with care, with an insistence on stylistic composition. The low novel is written fast, as it is supposed to be read. Some authors have been able to alternate between the two genres, occupying two cultural spaces which are usually thought of as incompatible.[46] This was the case with the French writer Jacques Laurent (1919–2000). In the 1940s he started writing, under a variety of pseudonyms (Gilles Bargy, Laurent Labattu, etc.), crime stories and women's romances. For each of these, which he wrote in a couple of afternoons (or so he claimed), he was paid, in 1947, 20,000 francs. Such speed depended on a successful formula. Thus love stories were based on a well-trodden routine: the protagonists love each other, but there are obstacles, so he goes to the colonies or to America, he returns wealthy, a changed and much improved man, is now able to overcome the obstacles, and they marry. This, if a happy ending is required. Alternatively, he goes off, she marries another, he returns, he sacrifices himself nobly.[47]

One could make a living with such books, but Jacques Laurent needed a success. The best way of writing one is to take inspiration from an existing best-seller. This is how Laurent tells the story of his rise to fame (but one must always be suspicious of the genre 'How I Became Successful', particularly when told by a novelist): an old friend of his, Charles Frémanger, who had started a publishing house (Froissart), was in need of a blockbuster. He pointed out that the great recent successes were *Gone with the Wind* and *Forever Amber*. The majority of their readers were women, who liked history. Laurent examined both books and settled for *Amber* as a model.[48] *Forever*

Amber (1944) by Kathleen Winsor was the story of an English adventuress who becomes the mistress of Charles II. The book had sold three million copies in the USA, particularly after it had been banned in Boston as obscene. The Massachusetts Attorney-General had listed seventy references to sexual intercourse, thirty-nine illegitimate pregnancies and ten descriptions of women undressing in front of men.[49] With such endorsement it was difficult to fail. Laurent worked out that the *Forever Amber* formula was a mixture of history, sex, psychology, adventure and sentiment. He decided to have a woman as the leading character (like *Amber* and *Gone with the Wind*), since women would be the book's main purchasers. It would be set at the time of the French Revolution, an obvious French counterpart to Restoration Britain and the American Civil War. He chose as a pseudonym Cecil Saint-Laurent because 'Cecil' in French (albeit with a final 'e') could also be a woman's name, while Saint-Laurent was suggestive of French Canada (the St Lawrence is a major river), thus adding a touch of transatlanticism.

Jacques Laurent worked on *Caroline Chérie* from 15 April to 1 August 1947, dictating to a secretary in a hotel room between three and seven in the afternoon. His main moral support was the interest of the secretary, who wanted to know what was going to happen next. The *Caroline* book was expected to fund the completion of his great novel *Les Corps tranquilles*. The former had taken him three and a half months to write, while *Corps tranquilles* – a sprawling 1,070 pages – had taken seven years (1941–48). It was a complete flop, ignored, as the author admitted, by critics and public alike.[50] *Caroline*, however, sold 225,000 copies immediately. Its sequels (*Le Fils de Caroline Chérie*, 1950; *Un Caprice de Caroline Chérie*, 1952) enabled Cecil Saint-Laurent to subsidise Jacques Laurent. The literary split personality reached its high point when Laurent, writing on literature for the cultural journal *Arts* in 1955, explained that real writers should keep themselves independent from the market, and not be obsessed with how many copies they sell.[51]

Eventually, however, Laurent obtained the high-culture recognition he craved. His novel *Les Bêtises* (1971) won the prestigious Goncourt Prize, and in 1986 he was elected to the Académie Française to succeed the eminent and revered historian Fernand Braudel. Neither Laurent's speech of acceptance nor the encomium by Michel Déon, delivered on 5 March 1987, made the slightest mention of Caroline Chérie.[52] By then some of the 'low' novels were published by the prestigious publisher Gallimard.

Laurent, who had acquired further political prestige by aligning himself with the right (further signalling his non-conformity in a country where the majority of intellectuals position themselves on the left), wrote his high-culture books for the high-culture reader – a gender-neutral category. His Caroline Chérie books were aimed at women, thus confirming the common view that popular books have a clearer gender bias (romance for women and adventure for men). If so, his choice was, from a marketing point of view, a shrewd one.

That women constituted the majority of readers of novels had been suspected for some time, but it was only from the 1920s onward that women writers made serious inroads into the ranks of best-selling authors. Books written by women, though strictly speaking not a genre, began to make a significant impact on sales. In the previous century, as we have seen, writing was one of the few professions open to women. Now women had far greater opportunities, but their contribution to literature continued to grow. This was partly a reflection of the still massive difficulties facing them in other cultural fields: radio, television, the cinema (other than acting) and music (other than singing) were still (and still are) dominated by men. Writing was different. Women's romance 'had' to be written by women, almost as science fiction 'had' to be written by British or Americans. In France and elsewhere publishers associated with women's pulp placed the photographs of young and attractive women novelists on the back covers of their books. The French publisher René Julliard used the actual persona of his women writers in his massive advertising campaigns. Some of his successes are still remembered, such as the marketing of Françoise Sagan as a new kind of unsentimental realist woman writer. Her *Bonjour tristesse* (1954) sold 840,000 copies in France and 4.5 million copies in translation by 1962.[53]

According to *The Guinness Book of Records 2001*, the top three best-selling novels of all time are all by American women writers – selling approximately thirty million copies each. They are *Gone with the Wind* (1936) by Margaret Mitchell (her only novel), about a woman trying to make it during the American Civil War; *To Kill a Mockingbird* (1960) by Harper Lee (her only novel), about a woman remembering her father (a white lawyer in Alabama) defending a black man accused of rape; and *Valley of the Dolls* (1966) by Jacqueline Susann, about the struggles of three women trying to make it in show business. These records seem to have been pulverised by another woman, J.K. Rowling, whose Harry Potter books by November 2003 had sold (according to the Encyclopaedia *Encarta*) 250 million copies in sixty languages.[54] But these are the success stories, the tip of the iceberg. In the real world most authors are not published, and most of those who are sell very little. Writing in the 1920s, Keynes thought that authors earned too little: 'Very few authors can earn £500 a year' (which is more, I should add, than a university lecturer earned at the time). Keynes, like many authors, blamed the customers: 'The fault lies, first and foremost, with the public – with their wrong psychology towards book buying, their small expenditure, their mean and tricky ways where a book, the noblest of man's work, is concerned.'[55]

Noble or not, all writers are concerned with earnings, even those who are rich to start with, because earnings are the best index of popularity and recognition – though not the only one. Cultural recognition is sought after too, but in a market economy, cash is an important barometer. When Jean Paul Sartre met Ernest Hemingway in 1949 in Cuba, where Hemingway had a house, they did not talk about literary theory or existentialism, but about foreign rights and sales – to the despair of Mary Welsh, Hemingway's wife, who thought they sounded like two businessmen.[56] Sartre and Hemingway had a point: they were both formidable best-sellers. By 1978 Sartre was one of the most profitable writers in the stable of Gallimard.[57] Sometimes 'high' culture pays handsomely.

Many writers hope that one best-seller will carry them into a prosperous old age, but the more common strategy is to write a large number of books which sell reasonably well. That way one develops a rapport with one's readership, and gains new readers who might buy one's previous works. Few writers are likely to reach immortality and to be read decades after their death. But in the meantime there is a mirage of wealth gained without requiring one to climb the ladder in a company or to set up a new one. Living a long life, in such circumstances, may be useful. Catherine Cookson, for instance, whose reading public was essentially British in spite of translations into twenty-three languages, died just before turning ninety-two in 1998 as one of the richest women in Great Britain. By then she had published ninety-seven novels mainly about working-class women in Victorian Tyneside, their misery, and the sexual harassment and violence they faced. By the time she died she had sold 123 million copies of her novels. Thirty-five of her books were in the top hundred books borrowed from public libraries. As she wrote faster than she could be published, her publishers, Heinemann, had a stockpile of novels which they continued to bring out at the rate of two a year when the author was too old and frail to write.[58] Cookson's success was, at least in part, due to her ability to be in touch with her readers, aware of their feelings, resentments and aspirations – all the more so since she had shared with them a difficult and deprived childhood in poverty-stricken north-east England.

Many of the professional novelists of the interwar years were supremely conscious of the importance of the readers in shaping their work. Pitigrilli, in his autobiographical *Pitigrilli parla di Pitigrilli* (1949), explained that though the novel was written by the novelist, the real authors were the readers. The writer simply puts down on paper and gives shape to what readers want. He creates characters who think and speak like his readers. Thus readers are seldom told anything they do not already know, but find in the novels the thoughts they had given form and shape. It is as if the writer drafts a text already in the mind of the reader.[59]

This characterisation of writers as the echo chamber of their readers explains why they are often not themselves aware of the strategies they use to create certain effects. The book is written, and it is then read. It speaks, not always in the same way, to different people. Then, if the book is deemed to belong to a higher genre, literary critics gather to 'explain' what it is really about. They know its secret, a secret neither readers nor author knows – or so they claim, as did, in an honest if brazen way, the famous German literary critic Marcel Reich-Ranicki, who declared that the distinguished German novelist Anne Seghers understood absolutely nothing of her novel *Seventh Cross* (1942): 'She had no inkling of the sophistication of the artistic devices used in her novel, or of the virtuosity of the composition.' Most writers, Reich-Ranicki continued, understand very little of literature. 'They are the last people to judge their own work.' This is the task of the critic. Though one cannot ignore what authors have to say about their work (!), one should not take it too seriously.[60] This is not a new idea. The great Sephardic philosopher Moses Maimonides (1135–1204), in *Guide to the Perplexed*, written in Arabic, mused that 'A great disparity subsists between the knowledge an artificer has of the thing he has made and the knowledge someone else has of the artefact in question.' Critics are the writer's enemy – always, even when they praise. Fortunately for most writers, the majority of the reading public is unaware of the existence of critics.

The key personage from the writer's point of view is the publisher. The publisher is the author's first real reader (wives and husbands, lovers and friends cannot be trusted). At first, author and publisher are like a couple in love. They have seduced each other. Now they are going to have a baby, a book. The publisher hopes that this new relationship will bring back the excitement of past love affairs (the successful books and authors). Perhaps he will find that most elusive of commodities – true love. Perhaps this time it will be the real thing: a book that sells and sells, *and* obtains critical approval; the delicious combination of prestige and money. The author, rejected by others who did not recognise true genius, or at the very least talent, hopes that the publisher will turn out to be Mr Right.

The day of publication marks the high point of this sentimental journey. Then the troubles start. The baby is out into the world, subjected to the examination of critics and the verdict of readers. Its fate is now in the hands of shopkeepers who may like books in general, but not necessarily that particular book. Perhaps the baby was not quite as beautiful as its parents imagined. The author's friends, unable to find the book in booksellers or reviews in newspapers, say – Iago-like – 'Perhaps your publishers could have done more.' Maybe they did not work hard enough, did not wine and dine potential reviewers, did not send out enough review copies, did not spend enough money on marketing. The author discovers now what he or she had known all along. Publishers are polygamous. They have many affairs, many writers, many books, many babies, all demanding attention. Writers are entirely different: they are serially monogamous; they have only one baby at a time, and all their love and hopes are with that one creature.[61]

50

Popular Genres:
Crimes and the Future

Science Fiction

THE DEFINITION OF GENRES is often regarded as an academic occupation, but readers and sellers have their own effective if unclear taxonomy. Categorisation has a marketing purpose. One enters a large, modern bookshop as one enters a well-mapped world. Cookery books at the front, thick and glossy, hold promises of gastronomic delights. Not far from such paradise there is the inevitable purgatory: diet books to make us slim and desirable. At the back we can find travel books, not far from art books. History books have their own domain, divided by wars, centuries and places. Biographies are at the front where the voyeurs can intrude, their conscience clear, into the privacy of the great or the temporarily famous. Then, along the shelves on the right are the crime books, usually slim, promising a few hours of relaxation. Not far away is science fiction, destined, one assumes, for a more masculine readership, as is perhaps the contiguous genre of 'Horror'. Somewhere else, exclusively for women but surreptitiously purchased by some men (as if it were pornography), one can find romances, where women continue their fruitless search for the perfect man who will give them passion and companionship. 'Real' novels are firmly at a distance, untainted by 'crime' and 'sci fi'.

'Classics' are novels whose fame outlasts the lives of their authors. They can be found in all genres. Most authors are never famous, or are famous for a year. Some die famous, and in less than a generation, more commonly in less than ten years, are utterly forgotten. The only way out of literary mortality is either to be canonised by the intellectual élites or to acquire 'cult' status, as Dumas and Verne achieved until recently. Agatha Christie and Georges Simenon are twentieth-century exemplars. At first ignored by the literary élites, they entered a 'social canon' by remaining popular with successive generations of readers. Only then did they attract the interest of literary élites, who need to explain such longevity. They are then examined, analysed and deconstructed in an attempt to explain why they succeeded while hundreds of imitators failed to dislodge them in the literary fray.

How a genre is defined is never clear, except in one sense: even the best crime story cannot aspire to the highest echelons of 'high culture' – though some are appreciated by sophisticated critics. Dostoevsky's *Crime and Punishment* is not a 'crime novel', though there is a crime, a criminal and an investigator. André Gide's *Les Caves du Vatican* (1914) has a totally amoral villain who is a master of disguise, and a hero, Lafcadio, who has committed a crime just to test his mettle, and Carola, the statutory golden-hearted prostitute, who is killed as convention demands. One will find all of these in a hard-boiled thriller, yet *Les Caves du Vatican* will never be next to Mickey Spillane.

The enduring genres – the crime stories, the futuristic novels, the bodice-rippers – existed before the First World War, but after the war the production of such well-established genres expanded massively. It moved into 'industrial' production, as the American western novels had done in the nineteenth century. Detective stories may have started with Edgar Alan Poe or Wilkie Collins, but their enormous expansion was accompanied by the rise of crime magazines in the USA and by cinema adaptations. The science fiction story had a similar itinerary. The modern forebears were – as in other genres – French (Jules Verne) and British (H.G. Wells), though there were many early German science fiction writers such as Hans Dominik (1872–1945) and Kurd Lasswitz (1848–1910), the author of *Auf zwei Planeten* (1897) – a book translated into English only in 1971 (and then in an abridged version).[1] Nevertheless, in the first half of the twentieth century, SF stories were dominated by Americans and British.

The rule that a genre spreads more rapidly through new outlets is valid here as well. Originally, science fiction stories were not sold in bookshops but were serialised in magazines, as many novels were in the nineteenth century. They found their real home, not accidentally, in the USA, where as far as Europeans were concerned the future was the present. A key protagonist was Hugo Gernsback (1884–1967), who migrated to the United States from Luxembourg and who founded, in April 1926, the pulp fiction periodical *Amazing Stories*, the first magazine entirely devoted to science fiction, or as he called it then, 'scientifiction' (it became 'science fiction' in 1929, when

Gernsback founded another magazine called *Science Wonder Stories*). This enterprising publisher had launched, earlier, a magazine called *Science and Invention* with the intention of popularising science. The success of an entire issue devoted to 'scientifiction' led him to change the name to *Amazing Stories* – the initial step towards great success.

Among the distinguishing features of *Amazing Stories* – apart from the traditional cheap paper used (hence 'pulp' fiction) – were the garish illustrations used for the front and back covers, the work of the imaginative designer Frank R. Paul. Though initially Gernsback simply reprinted the classics of SF (Poe, Wells, etc.) the ludicrous covers ensured that no one could possibly think that *Amazing Stories* was a respectable magazine – though, like the crime story, the genre has its canon of respected masters: Arthur C. Clarke (*Childhood's End*, 1953 and the short story *The Sentinel*, also 1953, which inspired Stanley Kubrick's film *2001: A Space Odyssey*, 1968); Isaac Asimov (*I, Robot*, 1950) and, more recently, Ursula Le Guin, Brian Aldiss, J.G. Ballard and the 'cult' cyberpunk author William Gibson. Like the crime story, the genre has been used by major writers such as the Czech Karel Čapek, whose play *R.U.R.* or *Rossum Universal Robots* (1921) introduced the word 'robot', Aldous Huxley (*Brave New World*, 1932), George Orwell (*Nineteen Eighty-Four*, 1949), the Polish writer Stanislaw Lem (*Solaris*, 1961), and Doris Lessing (*The Marriages Between Zones Three, Four and Five*, 1980, and *The Sirian Experiments*, 1981). But such authors were exceptions. The vast majority of SF writers wrote in the invasion paranoia mode pioneered by H.G. Wells, with in addition a touch of older explorers' novels to celebrate the superiority of the human race, usually the white race and often just the American one.[2]

Amazing Stories defined the major tropes for the genre: spaceships, interplanetary or intergalactic travel, aliens, robots, genetic engineering, computers, time travel, alternative history and utopias.[3] There was considerable reader involvement: the magazine published letters and established fan clubs, often a springboard for future SF writers.[4] *Amazing Stories* had a flood of imitators, including *Astounding Science Fiction* (1937, later rechristened *Analog*), which under the editorship of John W. Campbell (who became obsessed with Dianetics and Scientology) produced what many regarded as the best SF pulp.[5] Later magazines included *Fantasy and Science Fiction* (1949) and *Galaxy Science Fiction* (1950), edited by H.L. Gold.

The spread of such magazines explains why Americans have dominated the field so much. The huge output constituted the basis for a formidable selection process, permitting European publishers to wean out the best. They were thus able to publish sure winners, and disregard what they and their readers regarded as pathetic domestic attempts to imitate Americans of the calibre of Asimov, Theodore Sturgeon, A.E. van Vogt and Ray Bradbury. European SF magazines developed all over the Continent, publishing mainly translations before producing the finished stories as books in a separate imprint, as Mondadori did in Italy with the series Urania. The USSR established a strong tradition of science fiction in the 1920s. Some of it was published in the state-owned magazine *World Pathfinder* (1925), but much of the rest found its way in the still existing private sector.[6] The American magazines lifted European science fiction from the intellectually demanding realm of social criticism, where Karel Čapek and the Russian Yevgeny Zamyatin (1884–1937, who died in exile in France), and later Orwell, would have kept it. Zamyatin's *We* (1920, banned in the USSR in 1923) is a classic dystopia, similar in many respects to the later Huxley's *Brave New World* (1932) and Orwell's *1984* (1949): people are brainwashed into being happy, but are not free; sex does not exist, or is freely available to anyone who asks for it, making it asexual.[7] In most SF there is no romantic interest and no sexual love.

Such philosophical underpinnings were relatively rare in American science fiction, which was produced by a cohort of underpaid hacks who turned out stories by the dozens for a wide readership. They concentrated, as Edward James put it, 'on action not thought'.[8] It was a formula machine integrated in the wider cultural industry, feeding the comic strip and the B-movie. The genre was eminently adaptable for television. The first TV SF series was the American *Captain Video* (1949–52). In 1929 Phil Nowlan started to write the comic strip *Buck Rogers*. *Flash Gordon* started in 1933. In 1938 the Marvel Comics group started to publish their successful series of ten-cent comics which included the Human Torch, a man who could turn his body into flame, and Prince Namor, 'the Sub-Mariner', an undersea hero.[9]

In spite of the novels' downmarket reputation and garish covers, the typical SF readers were students and young people with a better than average education, genuinely interested in science and technology, as were some of the masters of the genre. Asimov, author of some 150 books, had a Ph.D. from Columbia University (1948), and taught biochemistry for ten years at the Boston University School of Medicine. Before publishing his famous *Foundation Trilogy* (1951–53), which includes *I, Robot* (where the three laws of robotics were introduced), he had published extensively in the pulp magazines of the 1940s. Arthur C. Clarke had a first-class degree in physics and mathematics from King's College, London (1948). William Olaf Stapledon (1886–1950), author of *Last and First Men* (1930), *Odd John* (1936), *Star Maker* (1937) and *Sirius* (1944), was a philosophy lecturer at the University of Liverpool. Robert A. Heinlein was a student at the University of California, Los Angeles, in the 1930s. Ursula K. Le Guin went to Radcliffe College and Columbia University and was a Fulbright Fellow.

SF borrowed heavily from the epic story and the colonial novel, from the fairy tale and the medieval story. It recycled themes from popular and high culture by reinterpreting them in a SF mode, as in the American Alfred Bester's update of Dumas's *Count of Monte Cristo* (and other revenge stories) in *The Stars my Destination* (1956), with its allusions to William Blake (the original title was *Tiger! Tiger!*). The classic SF film *Forbidden Planet* (1956) was directly inspired by Shakespeare's *The Tempest*, with Robby the Robot as a kind of Ariel. The film's plot was spiced up with pop Freud, since it has an 'education machine' that materialises any object desired, including 'Monsters! Monsters from the Id!'

Some SF did not hesitate to add a touch of mysticism to the techno-scientific framework within which so much of it was set. Some novels which could be classified as SF were harking back to a very traditional Christianity, such as those of C.S. Lewis (Professor of Medieval and Renaissance English literature at the University of Cambridge), *Out of the Silent Planet* (1938) and the popular children's novels *Chronicles of Narnia*, which included *The Lion, the Witch and the Wardrobe* (1950). A mystical revisitation of Germanic and Norse mythology by an Oxford professor, J.R.R. Tolkien, was the cycle *The Lord of the Rings*, whose primitive plot and non-existent characterisation were blended with the creation of a highly inventive universe that readers could discover. These became enormously popular in the 1960s and, as films, in the first years of the twenty-first century.

One standard theme of traditional SF, deployed *ad nauseam* in B-movies, was the alien invasion. At first the aliens are impervious to the earthlings' sophisticated weaponry and to the resources of conventional science. They are eventually defeated because of the initiative of brave and lonely individuals, whether an 'alternative' scientist who defies convention and his stuffy colleagues, or a hero who uses his common sense, or by an act of faith, thus upholding the traditional values of American populism ('the individual versus the institutions'). Edgar Rice Burroughs (1875–1950), the creator of Tarzan, was one of the many who wrote formula science fiction too, with an undertone of sex and violence. His scantily-dressed women are regularly threatened with rape, but are always saved by muscular heroes who also repel alien invasions from Mars.[10] Another popular theme, taking a leaf from Mary Shelley's *Frankenstein* and Robert Louis Stevenson's *Dr Jekyll and Mr. Hyde*, was that of the scientific discovery that goes wrong. Much SF writing was suspicious of science and technology, celebrating instead a humanist or religious conception of the human essence. By the 1950s the era of SF magazines appeared to come to a close. The balance began to shift towards books. SF short stories gave way to longer and more complex plots.[11] Symbolism came to prevail.

In spite of its popularity, and the enormous success of later SF films such as George Lucas's *Star Wars* (1977) and Steven Spielberg's *Close Encounters of the Third Kind* (1977) and *E.T. – The Extra Terrestrial* (1982), science fiction remained a niche genre. Some of this fascination may be related to the fact that a considerable number of people do believe in the supernatural. Such a belief is not just a standby of almost all religions but also reflects the fact that more people are drawn to strange beliefs than rationalists like to think. This may be true even for a majority if we are to believe in a CNN poll taken in 1997, according to which 64 per cent of Americans believe that aliens from another planet have contacted human beings, and half think that these aliens have abducted human beings – even though over 90 per cent admit that they have never been abducted themselves, and do not know anyone who has.[12] Whether belief in opinion polls remains unaffected by such staggering findings is another matter, though rationalists need to be reminded that people have believed in witches and monsters for centuries.

Crime Cults

Simple stories of folks being murdered and investigators finding out who did it have long engrossed book-readers, film-goers and television-watchers. This genre has a special status. It is far more easily identifiable than any other. Other equally 'strong' genres, such as its main nineteenth-century competitor the western novel, became almost extinct, killed perhaps by the western film – and this too in recent times has declined rapidly. But the crime story lives on in books, films, plays and television serials.

Scholars, who love classification and distinction, warn against the lumping together of spy thrillers, crime stories, detective stories, etc. Readers are less choosy. Those who like one sub-genre often like the others. Booksellers, closer to readers than to scholars, know this, and often lump them together. The Mystery Writers of America's Edgar Award for the best novel of the year, named after Edgar Allan Poe and first given in 1946, does not take sides, having been awarded to exciting spy stories like Ken Follett's *The Eye of the Needle* (1979) and John Le Carré's *The Spy who Came in from the Cold* (1965), as well as to classic novels of detection such as Barbara Vine's *A Dark-Adapted Eye* (1987). This is not only due to questions of format and length. Spy stories and criminal ones have much in common. The spy fights on behalf of a recognisable and usually uncontested cause, as does the detective. The spy must solve a mystery, and often this mystery requires the uncovering of a traitor. A traitor appears to be 'one of us', but in reality he is 'one of them', like most of Agatha Christie's murderers.

Another sub-genre of the mystery novel was that of the 'hard-boiled', of which the most celebrated practitioners were Raymond Chandler, Dashiel Hammett, James M. Cain, and Mickey Spillane (whose hero is Mike Hammer) – but the genre should also include the English writer James Hadley Chase's *No Orchids for Miss Blandish* (1939), one of the most popular books in Great Britain during the war – the story of the abduction of an heiress by a gang who rape and torture her repeatedly, driving her to suicide. Hammett's writing, especially his dialogue, was influenced by some of the films of the period when the wisecrack and the vaudeville one-liner were particularly valued.[13] The hard-boiled had an overwhelmingly American image, though some of its best-known practitioners have been British (Peter Cheyney, James Hadley Chase and Raymond Chandler) and the genre was enthusiastically adopted by the French, who produced an endless string of *romans noirs* which emphasise the crime, such as Auguste le Breton's *Du Rififi chez les hommes*, a complex story of a jewel heist, or Boileau-Narcejac's *Les Diaboliques*, where it appears that a man kills his wife aided by his mistress, when in fact the wife and the mistress plot together to get rid of him. In this sub-genre the temporal structure of the classic novel of detection (first the crime, then the investigation which reconstructs the sequence of events which led to the crime) is subverted. The narrative occurs in real time. The investigator is contacted not to resolve a mystery, but for other reasons. Then a crime is committed. Or a crime is planned, and the suspense consists in finding out how it will take place and how it will be discovered. Curiosity drives the reader forward, turning page after page, unable to stop, until the conclusion.[14]

The readers of mystery novels span the social classes and cut across the gender barrier. Crime novels are read by men and women, and written by men and women. At the end of the nineteenth century (see page 678) Anna Katherine Green was writing novels with a legal background such as *The Leavenworth Case* (1878), where Inspector Ebenezer Gryce made his debut. Then there was Mary Roberts Rinehart (1876–1958), author of *The Circular Staircase* (1908), the story of a young woman in danger in an old house. Since then the roll-call of women writers from the early 1920s to the present is impressive: Agatha Christie, Dorothy L. Sayers, Frances Noyes Hart, Josephine Bell, Margery Allingham (creator of sleuth Albert Campion), Patricia Wentworth (creator of Miss Maud Silver), Josephine Tey (creator of Inspector Grant) and, later, Ngaio Marsh, Margaret Millar (author of *Beast in View*, 1955), Patricia Highsmith, Ruth Rendell (aka Barbara Vine), P.D. James, Sara Paretsky (creator of V.I. Warshawski), Patricia Cornwell (creator of the pathologist Kay Scarpetta), Sue Grafton (creator of Kinsey Millhone), Caroline Graham, Gillian Slovo and many others. While almost all of the internationally well-known women crime writers have been British or American, women have been active in other countries too. In France, according to *Le Monde*, there have been some two hundred women crime writers, authoring 1,750 titles. In Japan the best-selling domestic writer in the genre is Shizuko Natsuki, author of over eighty novels, including *Murder at Mount Fuji* (1984).[15]

Some books are read furtively. The reader is aware that books say something about those who read them. Reading a woman's romance published by Harlequin or Mills & Boon in public, for instance on a train, may attract condescension or even contempt; the intelligence and culture of the reader are in doubt. Similarly, a young man leafing through a 'girlie' magazine, even one with some intellectual pretensions such as *Playboy*, and pausing to examine the pictures, smiling contentedly, might suffer embarrassment and censure. Those reading crime stories cause no reaction. Such stories are read by people who read nothing else, by people who only read occasionally, and by intellectuals. It is not a matter of astonishment to be told that one of Wittgenstein's favourite novels was the hard-boiled thriller *Rendezvous with Fear* by Norbert Davis.[16] It would have been rather strange, however, had he confessed to be an avid reader of Mills & Boon and Harlequin romances.

Yet the largest-selling genre is women's romance. None of the romance novelists, however, not even the British doyenne of the genre, Barbara Cartland, seems to have mustered the personal success of the great crime writers. It is often claimed, for instance, that the most translated English author in the world after Shakespeare is Agatha Christie. The publishers HarperCollins in their July–December 2001 catalogue introduce their 'Agatha Christie Collection' on page 50 with the statement that she outsells 'even Shakespeare with over two billion books in print in more than 100 languages'. This is supported by UNESCO's *Index Translationum* (1996), whose 1994 data rank Christie at the top of the ten most-translated authors, with 218 translations (no doubt helped by being translated into all the languages of the former Soviet Union), easily outdistancing the number two, another writer of women's romances, Danielle Steele (131). *The Guinness Book of Records* gives the same sales figure as HarperCollins (two billion), but in 'only' forty-four languages. Boileau-Narcejac, who offer no source, provide a lesser but still awesome figure, one billion books, and rank Christie as the third-most translated writer (after Lenin and Tolstoy, and presumably not including the Bible). In France alone her *The Murder of Roger Ackroyd* (1926) appears to have sold 1.5 million copies by the early 1990s.[17] Others have claimed, and not only in Britain, that Enid Blyton (1899–1968) ranks third, which seems unlikely, as her series such as The Secret Seven (from 1949) and The Famous Five (1942) were never as popular in the USA, though in France alone, where Hachette had translated, by the mid-1970s, 170 of her six hundred books, she sold twenty-six million copies.[18]

These three best-selling writers appear to have little in common except their nationality: Shakespeare is the statutory canonical high-culture author. Agatha Christie, certainly the most widely read detective-story writer, has remained unrecognised by the academy. The third, Enid Blyton, was a writer of children's books, a genre not highly regarded by the literary élites, though her Famous Five stories have the same structure as a police story. Perhaps the top three authors of all time really are all English (leaving aside the Bible and the Victorian assumption that God must have been an Englishman): Shakespeare, Agatha Christie and Enid Blyton, whose sales must now have fallen behind the new rising star J.K. Rowling, also English.

Be that as it may, crime may not pay, but writing about it can pay handsomely, and increasingly so, since Agatha Christie sold her first novel, *The Mysterious Affair at Styles* (1920), for £25 with no further royalties. The interwar years launched into orbit a vast galaxy of crime writers. Those of the 1920s built on their *fin-de-siècle* predecessors, but while the early detective stories (by writers like Wilkie Collins, Emile Gaboriau and Conan Doyle) always contained an element of adventure, the novel of detection of the 1920s and 1930s – the classic British *whodunnit* – is 'a puzzle that presents crime exclusively as a riddle to be solved through ... a chain of questions the detective poses'.[19]

There were a few unwritten rules (which some, such as the Revd Ronald Knox and the American crime writer S.S. Van Dine attempted to write down – the latter in a much-quoted article in 1928 in the *American Magazine*). The murder had to occur at the beginning of the book. The entire story had to be aimed at the resolution of the crime, and hence projected backwards towards the 'historical' antecedent: what happened before the beginning of the novel. The solution should not be due to chance or supernatural events, but should be arrived at on the basis of known facts, immediately revealed to the reader, so that readers can have the illusion that they can play the same game as the investigator and find the solution. The murderer should not be obvious, and should come from a finite number of suspects who have all been introduced in the first few chapters. Neither the detective nor the butler should be the murderer. There should not be long digressions. The culprit should not be a professional criminal. In reality most of these rules are regularly broken – except one, implied but unmentioned, that the mystery *must* be resolved. To leave the reader wondering would be a real crime.

That the murderer should be given an important narrative role is a rule that holds true even in crime stories which do not entirely fit the genre of the novel of detection, such as some of the 'hard-boiled' genre immortalised by Raymond Chandler and Dashiell Hammett, where even though the action takes place in a complex and sprawling urban world, with gangland murders, rackets and whores, as well as expensive homes and fine ladies, the murderer is always part of a circumscribed set of suspects. In the hard-boiled novels of James M. Cain, such as *The Postman Always Rings Twice* (1934) and *Double Indemnity* (1943), however, the mystery is not who the murderer is, but how he is going to be found out.

Of course, in genres there are no strict rules, and in an effort to offer the reader a product which is different, it is necessary to innovate, though the constraints are severe. For instance, the motives for killing someone remain unavoidably limited: it's either passion (love, revenge, etc.) or interest (money). Keen readers quickly learned the rules, forcing authors to become ever more ingenious, and hence less and less realistic. They had to keep ahead of readers, who quickly realised that the body had not necessarily been killed where it was found, that the most likely suspect did not do it and was likely to be the second victim, and that those with no alibi were innocent.[20] Thus the genre had to develop, characters had to be given more depth, settings become more interesting (the Middle Ages, ancient Egypt) and detection more refined (the police procedural).

The typical detective was not a physically active person, skilled in the art of fighting, but a rationalist with idiosyncratic traits. The model was Sherlock Holmes, whose cocaine habit, sexless lifestyle and violin-playing marked him out sharply from the typical hero of adventure stories. Those who are now regarded as the 'classic' authors of the interwar years emerged in the face of fierce competition, creating their own world with, at its centre, an investigator with memorable characteristics, since few readers remembered the novels' plots for long after they had finished reading them:

AUTHOR	DETECTIVE	YEAR	CHARACTERISTIC TRAIT
Agatha Christie	Hercule Poirot	1920	Belgian
Dorothy L. Sayers	Lord Peter Wimsey	1923	Aristocratic collector of Ming vases
Earl Derr Biggers	Charlie Chan	1925	Chinese Detective Sergeant and later Superintendent
S.S. Van Dine	Philo Vance	1926	Art connoisseur, gentleman of leisure
Ellery Queen	Ellery Queen	1929	Intellectual
Margery Allingham	Albert Campion	1929	Ageing aristocrat
Agatha Christie	Miss Jane Marple	1930	Middle-aged spinster
Georges Simenon	Maigret	1931	Ordinary policeman
Dorothy L. Sayers	Montague Egg	1933	Commercial traveller
John Dickson Carr	Dr Gideon Fell	1933	Historian and lexicographer
Erle Stanley Gardner	Perry Mason	1933	Lawyer
Ngaio Marsh	Inspector Roderick Alleyn	1934	Cultured policeman
Rex Stout	Nero Wolf	1934	Recluse, gourmet, orchid-lover

Most of the investigators in the interwar crime novels were not policemen but amateurs, possibly a reflection of attitudes towards the police in Anglo-Saxon cultures. In Great Britain the policeman is often depicted as a working-class incompetent, out of his depth in the upper-middle-class *milieu* where the crime takes place. In the USA the police were widely regarded, with some justification, as corrupt. The investigator was often an incorruptible amateur or a private detective. In the post-war period, and especially since the 1960s, technological developments made it increasingly unrealistic that the mystery could be solved by a clever amateur. In the era of forensic science, computers and DNA analysis, the policeman, backed by labs and specialists, has come to prevail over the enthusiastic amateur. The real solution will still depend on a hunch, or on human intelligence, since a mystery solved by computers is not worth reading about.

If we were to compare the era of the pioneers (say, pre-1914) and the Golden Age (the 1920s and 1930s), we would see significant similarities. This is unsurprising, since the pioneer's job is to establish the market and the fundamental parameters for the genre. Thus the detectives are usually unmarried, whether forerunners (Auguste Dupin, Sherlock Holmes, Rouletabille, Father Brown) or from the Golden Age (Poirot, Ellery Queen, Miss Marple, Philip Marlowe, Sam Spade, Nero Wolf, Perry Mason, Mike Hammer). Lord Peter Wimsey is in love with Harriet Vane (a crime writer), and marries her only in *Busman's Honeymoon* (1937), virtually the last novel in which he appears. Albert Campion is in love with Amanda, but they do not marry. Maigret is a rare exception: he is married. The unmarried rule seems to continue even in the more recent period. No permanent relationship troubles the life of Lieutenant Adam Dalgleish, P.D. James's poetry-writing hero; Henning Mankell's Inspector Wallander has been abandoned by his wife Mona. Lieutenant Columbo's wife remains unseen throughout the popular television series, even though she is mentioned in every episode.

A possible reason for such matrimonial absences is that the genre requires that everything be functional to the plot. There is no room for digression. If in the first chapter someone scratches himself on a nail on a wall, that nail will become relevant to the solution. Such sober narrative lines make the detective story eminently adaptable to the cinema. Wives, husbands, children, etc. serve no purpose whatsoever in the solving of the crime, though in sub-genres such as the hard-boiled and the spy story, the unmarried status of the protagonist (Marlowe, James Bond, Sam Spade) makes it possible to sustain a certain sexual tension between him and the female characters. Sidekicks are often used (following the invention of Dr Watson): they add to readers' identification, and provide opportunities for conversations in which the hero can sum up the story so far and ponder the clues. Simenon's Maigret, once again, is an exception to the rule: he has no Dr Watson.

But there are, of course, other reasons for the prevalence of the unmarried. The detective story is a modern form of the saga of the righter of wrongs, who because he has no family is free to move on with a clear conscience in order to put the rest of the world in order. A state of matrimony does not suit traditional male heroes. Ulysses may hark for his wife, but he is away from her for twenty years. And this continues: Tintin is not married, nor is Indiana Jones.

None of this, on its own, explains the popularity of the detective story. Boileau-Narcejac, the pseudonym of two famous French crime-story writers, Pierre Boileau and Thomas Narcejac – authors of *D'Entre les deux morts* (1954), which inspired Hitchcock's famous film *Vertigo*, and *Celle qui n'était plus* (1953), adapted as *Les Diaboliques* in 1954 by Henri-Georges Clouzot – point to further elements. One is that detective books are short. They can be bought and read in a few hours.[21] Thus the pleasure is concentrated, ideally suited for the situations in which modern readers read: late at night after a hard day's work, or during a journey. Not by accident the long novel, the so-called blockbuster, is regarded as being particularly suited to the summer vacation, when many people have two weeks or more to laze around. In such circumstances a novel which can be read in a few hours is not suitable. The saga is suitable for the beach.

The brevity of the detective story is also functional to the narrative. Five hundred pages, or even three times that much, on the history of modern culture is entirely acceptable. Five hundred pages of piecing together clues and interviewing witnesses would be very boring. Brevity, and the importance of plots and characters, make the excellence of the writing less important than in other genres. A detective or science fiction novel can be badly written and still be interesting.[22] A badly-written *War and Peace* would not survive. Authors with high-culture credentials – such as André Gide (*Les Caves du Vatican*, 1914), Umberto Eco (*The Name of the Rose*, 1980), Jorge Luis Borges, Graham Greene, Friedrich Dürrenmatt (*Der Richter und sein Henker* – The Judge and his Hangman, 1952 – and *Das Versprechen* – The Pledge, 1958), Michel Butor (*L'Emploi du temps*, 1956), Carlo Emilio Gadda (*Quer brutto pasticciaccio de Via Merulana*, 1946), and Leonardo Sciascia (*Il Giorno della civetta* – The Day of the Owl, 1961) are not usually defined as detective-story writers.

The murder must be very complex, and usually premeditated, so that finding the solution requires special skills. The general pattern is of clever murderers pitted against clever detectives.[23] There is therefore always a lack of realism in what are, on the whole, otherwise supremely realistic novels: in real life, murderers are not particularly intelligent, and either kill their nearest and dearest in anger or madness, or total strangers to rob them. Relatively few murderers are upper-middle-class. Murders are normally solved by the police using normal police methods – not by lawyers, private investigators, journalists or Home Counties spinsters.

Georges Simenon and the Others

Lorenzo Montano, Mondadori's shrewd detective-stories specialist, had seen it at once: Georges Simenon represented something new in the genre of crime writing. From a publishing point of view, this was an ideal situation. A singularly distinctive style within a well-established genre might attract new readers, as well as creating a loyal readership among those already addicted to the genre. They would not simply ask for a detective novel, but one by Simenon. To underline this, Mondadori decided to publish Simenon outside the normal *gialli*. His books, shorter and more sexually daring than the others, would be instantly recognisable. A correspondence started between the Milanese publisher and the Belgian-born 'French' writer. The intention was to buy his works as they came out in French. Their brevity would keep down translation costs, always a major factor. There were only a few conditions, which Simenon was only too pleased to meet: chief among them was to bear in mind the sensitivity of the fascist censors and refrain from making the slightest disparaging remark about Italians. A significant proportion of immigration into France was then Italian, and it was an easy temptation, particularly for a writer as insensitive about race as Simenon (he had been active in a right-wing Catholic anti-Semitic group in his native Belgium), to have pimps and gangsters of Italian extraction.[24]

Small countries which share a language with more culturally powerful countries find it difficult to establish their own contribution to culture. Hergé's internationally successful comic strip 'Tintin' was seldom recognised as Belgian – even though the author had started out as a supporter of a clerico-fascist nationalist group. Simenon, also originally a right-wing extremist, was regarded as a Frenchman by many of his readers. Both authors, in order to obtain wider renown, deliberately either left the national origins of their heroes and the setting of their stories vague (as in Tintin) or made them clearly French (as in the case of Simenon's Inspector Maigret).[25]

Simenon's strength was that he was able to offer variations within the limits of the genre. For instance, in *L'Affaire Saint-Fiacre* (1932) he imagined an Agatha Christie-like situation (though at that time the genre was not firmly set): dinner in the dining room of the castle of Saint-Fiacre, with all the suspects present ready for the discovery of the culprit. The difference is that it is not the detective but one of the suspects who leads the proceedings. Maigret is a slightly baffled witness: 'Perhaps it was the first time that he had the very precise sensation of feeling inadequate.'[26] Simenon broke many of the rules of the classical crime story (so much so that his books are often not classified as detective stories). Inspector Jules Maigret's 'quirk' is that he is an 'ordinary' policeman, happily married, though childless, with no particular quirks. He is quite distant from Sherlock Holmes or Auguste Dupin. He makes mistakes, and his criminals are not particularly clever.[27] He uses his intuition even more than his intelligence. Maigret does his detection by entering into the world of those he pursues, trying to understand not the psychology of the villains so much as their logic.[28]

Simenon's original ambition was to be a 'literary' writer, not a mere hack. He wanted to be a Conrad, or at the very least a Jack London.[29] But the money he made from his Maigret stories was good. His sober prose was ideal for cinematic adaptation. His little black book, in which he kept an account of his earnings, reveals that in 1931 he made over 295,000 francs, of which 188,000 was from the Maigret books published by Fayard and 75,000 from film adaptations – a quarter of his total income.[30] In 1935 he abandoned Fayard for the far more prestigious publisher Gallimard, with whom he drove a hard bargain, undertaking to write six novels a year, for which he would receive 10 per cent royalties for the first 10,000 copies sold, and a 50–50 split on foreign and film rights (unless he himself negotiated them, in which case the split was 75–25). He tried his hand with a 'real' novel, *Le Testament Donadieu*, in 1937. It is long, at least by Simenon's standards. There is no Maigret. There is a death in strange circumstances, but the focus of the plot is a family in dispute over an inheritance. André Gide gave Simenon the *imprimatur* he sought so much: 'I hold Simenon to be a great novelist: the greatest perhaps and the most authentic novelist that we have today in French literature.'[32]

But there was a problem. The novels written by Simenon in the second half of the 1930s were 'literary', and Gaston Gallimard was a prestigious publisher, but the fact was, as Gallimard told Simenon, that 'literary' novels sold less than the Maigret stories he used to write for Fayard.[33] That, for the publisher, was tolerable. What was not tolerable was that Simenon be paid the large advances he requested when his books sold only 8,000 copies or so. It was difficult to sell a large number of 'literary' titles. Bookshops did not want to stock dozens of books by the same author, unless they could be classified as 'crime novels'. Simenon went back to Maigret though he continued to write non-mystery novels – over two hundred in all by some accounts, with Maigret selling two or three times more than the others.[34] More than twenty-five years after his death, Simenon obtained a consecration he would have particularly savoured: Gallimard launched a collection of his works in the famous series La Pléiade, bound in the same format as the other greats of French literature.

It is far from clear why Simenon and Agatha Christie, of all 'classical' crime writers, have turned out to be so globally successful, probably doing better than cult hard-boiled American writers such as Dashiel Hammett and Raymond Chandler, in whose books the emphasis is on the crime and the investigator. There is obviously a self-generating marketing mechanism: in a field where so much depends on word of mouth and availability, success breeds success. Publishers, aware of the initial popularity of some authors, constantly reprint them. Booksellers stock them and display them prominently. Readers, searching for more of the same, get the same. Nevertheless, there must be some intrinsic merit behind all this. A good formula, an agile form of writing, an economy of development, authorial loyalty to the formula, readers' growing affection for a protagonist who reappears regularly, are all ingredients of the successful package. In addition to such features we should consider the conventional cross-cultural morality embraced by both authors. In neither Simenon nor Christie is there any glamorisation of violence, and there is little (Simenon) or no (Christie) overt sex. Christie's traditional setting is often a genteel country house or its overseas extensions (a cruise ship, a luxury train); the detective is an affable amateur; there is no real violence; everyone, especially the murderer, behaves in a highly civilised manner throughout; the clever criminal is worthy of the talent of the investigator; and there is a gradual, rational reconstruction of the events leading to the murder or murders. Christie's Miss Marple novels pay enormous attention to the suspects, who are genuinely interesting people in their own right. Miss Marple chats with them, in a vicarage, over a cup of tea, and we get to know them.[35] Though the plot appears to dominate the story, it is the characters who hold our attention. Could such a nice lady, who appears to be very much like our favourite aunt, be the determined killer who poisoned the pharmacist? Is the debonair young man, so charmingly in love with the young debutante, really the same person who strangled in his sleep the elderly heiress? Ordinary people doing extraordinary things always have considerable appeal.

While it is true that sex and violence sell, it is equally true that they offend. Their absence is seldom an obstacle to sales. Christie and Simenon have sold in Muslim countries, Asian countries, deeply Catholic countries and communist countries. Simenon has even sold in Israel, in spite of the enduring traces of anti-Semitism which occasionally appear even in some of his post-World War II novels.[36] On the whole these books are devoid of a particularly religious or political agenda. That criminals should be caught, regardless of the nefariousness of the victim, is not a point of view which is culturally determined. This in part explains why a Soviet Professor of French Literature at the University of Leningrad, Eleonora Schraiber, published in the USSR a biography of Georges Simenon of over three hundred pages, of which 30,000 copies were printed for the numerous followers of Simenon in the USSR, and why she also published editions of Simenon in French for schools and colleges, with footnotes.[37]

Simenon and the numerous British and American crime writers had many imitators and followers in other countries, including some of remarkable talent. None of these, however, was ever able to establish a global following, until recently. In Sweden, for instance, where the crime story had many enthusiastic readers, the writers of the interwar period occasionally had to masquerade under Anglo-Saxon pseudonyms, as did Gunnar Serner, who adopted the pen name of Frank Heller and whose main detective was Filip Collin, an exile academic and gentleman thief (à la Arsène Lupin) who operated in London. Another Swedish interwar crime writer, Kjerstin Göransson-Ljungman, wrote Agatha Christie-type murder stories.[38] The genre remained so British in the eyes of foreigners that in the 1950s Italian radio not only broadcast Sherlock Holmes stories on the radio, but also invented British stories such as those of the baronet policeman Sir Alex Dean and his Scotland Yard rival Inspector Popp.[39] Exceptions always existed, such as the highly talented Giorgio Scerbanenco, an Italian of Ukrainian origin who produced in the 1960s a string of 'hard-boiled'-type detective stories set in Milan.[40] Aware that he was writing in a low genre read by educated people, Scerbanenco, like many Italian crime writers, sprinkled his books with high-culture references for the delectation of some of his readers: for instance, in I Ragazzi del massacro (1968) he included references to Bertrand Russell, Immanuel Kant and the mathematician Alfred North Whitehead.[41]

Only in the last twenty years or so have other European countries produced widely acclaimed crime writers: from Sweden's Henning Mankell, an international best-seller, to Spain's Manuel Vázquez Montalbán (1939–2003) and his gourmet Barcelona detective Pepe Carvalho, and Italy's Andrea Camilleri, who paid homage to Montalban by naming his own gourmet Sicilian policeman Montalbano, and whose *L'Odore della notte* (2001) contains references to Kafka and the philosopher Norberto Bobbio.

51

The Press

The Mass Press

BORN IN THE NINETEENTH CENTURY, the real development of the press
as a mass medium occurred in the twentieth century. Newspaper readership
in Great Britain increased remarkably between the wars. That its centre
should be London is hardly surprising, since this was the largest capital city
in Europe. Almost six million national dailies were sold in Britain in the
1920s. It seemed as if there could be no further growth. To increase readership
it was necessary to steal it from one's competitors. By the mid-1930s the
British daily press was in the middle of one of its regular circulation wars.
In 1933, for instance, the *Daily Herald* offered cameras, fountain pens, tea
kettles and even the complete works of Dickens for eleven shillings to those
who subscribed for ten weeks.[1] The *Daily Mail*, *Daily Express* and *News
Chronicle* immediately responded by offering the complete Dickens for ten
shillings. The result of such competition, however, was an increase in total
readership by the end of the 1930s. The further rise of a working-class
readership during the Second World War resulted in over fifteen million
dailies being sold by the late 1940s.[2] In addition to this huge national daily
press there was also a thriving regional press. A considerable segment of both
was under the control of press empires such as that of the Harmsworth
brothers (Lord Northcliffe and Lord Rothermere). As early as 1908 one man,
Alfred Harmsworth (Lord Northcliffe), owned the *Daily Mail*, the *Daily
Mirror*, *The Times*, the *Observer* and the *Evening News*, as well as a string of
periodicals and regional papers. Such concentration remained for a long time
a British exception, as was the large sale of newspapers.

    In other countries, such as France and Germany, the working class was
less committed to the daily habit of purchasing a newspaper. And where no

mass daily press existed at the beginning of the twentieth century, as was the case in Italy or Spain, none arose. The new mass media, such as the radio and, later, television, did not seriously damage existing newspapers, but they prevented the development of new ones.

No major innovations occurred in the collection of news either. The agencies established at the end of the nineteenth century still dominated the scene in the post-war period. Reuters, founded in 1851, was still the largest European press agency a hundred years later. Though it had started as a private enterprise, it eventually became collectively owned by the British press. Its nearest rival, Agence France-Presse, founded in 1944, was in everything but name the successor to the Havas Agency, founded in 1835. The Associated Press (AP), formed in the USA in 1848, was still the largest worldwide news service in the world one hundred years later. United Press International (UPI) was formed in 1958, but it was the result of a merger between older agencies: United Press (1907) and International News Service (1909). Other countries had news agencies – such as TASS for the USSR, Deutsche Presse Agentur for Germany, ANSA (Agenzia Nazionale Stampa Associata) for Italy – but none had the global reach of the big four.

Illustrated magazines, though a nineteenth-century invention, developed only in the twentieth, the century of the visual. The introduction in the 1930s of new lightweight cameras such as the Leica enabled photojournalism to flourish. The new cameras allowed photographers to develop real news reporting. The greater versatility of roll film enabled them to discard the cumbersome plate camera. They could catch the fleeting moment, and fix it forever and quickly. The new technology enabled photographers to think in terms of a spontaneous picture sequence, a kind of picture story that was to become a familiar feature of popular illustrated magazines. Now a single image could stand in for a complex situation, as painters had done before, from Goya's *Third of May* (1814), showing civilians being shot by Napoleon's soldiers, to Picasso's almost immediate response to the bombing of Guernica in 1937. The new cameras were immediately tested in the first widely photographed war, the Spanish Civil War (which broke out in the same year *Life* magazine was born). Robert Capa, one of the first photographers to arrive at the front, shot a picture which became famous: a Republican soldier, arms spread wide, falling backwards at the moment of being shot. It was published in *Life*, and turned Capa into a celebrity despite rumours that it had been faked.[3] Eventually, in 1947 in New York, a group of photographers set up their own agency to give themselves more control over their work. The now legendary Magnum photo agency was founded by Capa, a Hungarian Jew (real name André Friedmann) and the main driving force behind it, Henri Cartier-Bresson, a radical Frenchman, David Seymour, a Polish Jew (real name David Szymin) and George Rodger, an English public-school boy.[4] Until then magazine editors assumed that when they paid a fee to a photographer, they bought all rights to the photograph. Magnum virtually invented the concept of copyright for photography.[5]

Though there was a thriving photojournalistic dimension to the German press at the end of the 1920s, the original models for the new kind of generalist illustrated magazines were American, and their most important European imitators were French. The Americans started *Time* (1923), *Newsweek* (1933), *Life* (1936) and *Look* (1937). The French responded with *Match* (note the English-sounding title) in 1938 and *Marie-Claire* (addressed to women) in 1937, while the Winckler Press introduced a whole range of US publications to France.[6] *Match* was revived in March 1949 with the name *Paris-Match*, overtly modelled on the American *Life*.[7] Later the French *Le Nouvel observateur* and *L'Express* and the German *Der Spiegel* were modelled on the American *Time* and *Newsweek*.

In Britain. a thriving tabloid press specifically targeted at the working classes (the *Daily Mirror*) and the lower-middle classes (the *Daily Express*), and the huge sales of Sunday papers (the *News of the World* above all) made it virtually impossible for a generalist illustrated press to develop. Britain never had a successful version of the generalist weekly.

The Italians, who had no mass press, developed a thriving market for illustrated weeklies. Treves's *L'Illustrazione Italiana* (started in 1873) was aimed at an upper-class public. It advertised fashionable drinks, all good for one's health, such as Liquore Strega and Amaro Tonico Fernet-Branca, both good 'digestives', '*gran turismo*' cars, the famous Borsalino hats, home machines to make espresso coffee and the usual remedies for falling hair (for men), dry skin (for ladies) and laxatives (for everyone).[8] It contained caricatures, pictures and political information. The pictures were usually of politicians, generals, foreign dignitaries, men in beards and hats. Issue No. 3, 1922, was typical: it included pictures of the main participants at the international conference held in Cannes (Lord Curzon, Lloyd George, etc.), as well as the Croisette in Cannes and the conference hall. Leafing through the magazine one would find a striking picture ('never published before') of Petrograd in July 1917, a picture of Lenin, emaciated and undernourished children in Russia, various Soviet leaders accompanied by articles on humanitarian aid to Russia. There was room for a few pictures of the actor Ermete Zacconi in some of his best-known roles, but politicians, aristocrats and generals dominated the pages of *L'Illustrazione Italiana*. These were the celebrities of the time.

Photojournalism, of course, was older than the new glossy weeklies. The idea of pursuing celebrities, convicted criminals and royalty, invading their privacy, catching them unawares, was born as soon as the camera had emancipated itself from the photographic studio. In London in 1910, within an hour of the return to their offices of the 'paparazzi' (to use the expression coined in Fellini's 1960 film *La Dolce vita* after one of the characters, a photographer), the pictures were printed and run off the newspaper presses. Readers became vicarious onlookers.[9]

In weeklies such as *Life* and *Paris-Match* images had the leading role. The text was minimal. Photography had come into its own, not as an 'art form' (though it came to be accepted as such) but as the centrepiece of a 'text' where words were subservient. The twentieth century redefined modernity as a commitment to transient images and sounds, as opposed to the more permanent nature of the written word. But the written word survived easily. As we have seen, when broadcasting started, the printed media first feared the new competition, then embraced it. A successful radio press rapidly developed (often owned by the broadcasting organisations themselves). In Germany alone in the 1930s there were seventy publications addressed to radio listeners, selling a total of 5.5 million copies, one million for the *Deutsche Radio Illustrierte*.[10] In the same period in Britain, just one publication, the *Radio Times*, was already selling over two million copies each week.[11]

In post-war Italy, the newly recovered freedom had been welcomed by a huge number of newly created dailies – most of which were highly political, aimed at the top end of the market, and utterly unprofitable. Publishers such as Mondadori revived the illustrated magazines and launched new ones. These provided the kind of information which in Great Britain (and to a lesser extent in France and Germany) would be provided by so-called tabloids: gossip about film stars and foreign royalty, and massive coverage of sport. The social groups who read tabloids in other countries did not read anything in Italy, or read the numerous weekly magazines. Some of these tried, not unsuccessfully to strike a middle path, providing a mix of political news, gossip and crime stories. Magazines such as *L'Espresso* (1955) offered investigative journalism, sensational crime reporting, scantily-dressed 'starlets', sport commentary, as well as solid political news. Mondadori's new illustrated magazine *Epoca*, inspired by the French *Paris-Match* and the American *Life*, offered an uncomplicated pro-Americanism and, more importantly, looked American – Mondadori, once a pro-fascist publisher, knew which way the wind was blowing before the wind itself. The main reason for the success of *Epoca* in the 1950s, as well as other heavily illustrated weekly magazines such as *Settimo giorno*, *Il Mondo* (both relatively upmarket news magazines) and the best-selling *Oggi* (crime and gossip) was a simple unadorned style that, unlike the baroque and old-fashioned prose of dailies like the *Corriere della sera*, could be understood by a person of average education. Imitation of foreign periodicals was the name of the game. In 1967 *Panorama*, graphically based on the US *Time* and *Newsweek*, the German *Der Spiegel* and the French *L'Express*, was launched and its success forced the older *L'Espresso* to adopt the same design.

The old *Domenica del corriere*, with its elaborate hand-drawn front and back pages, eschewing politics in favour of unusual *faits divers* – the kind of story which would be ridiculed as 'Newly married couple eaten alive in church by stray mountain wolf' – now looked like a cheap nineteenth-century peddlers' magazine. It remained popular for a while before sinking into a prolonged oblivion before its overdue closure in 1989.

Buying Influence

In some countries, notably Great Britain, the press was a commercial enterprise in its own right, in the sense that the purpose of printing newspapers was profit. But power and influence are commodities too. A powerful manufacturing or financial group could absorb losses from newspapers as long as it felt that the political advantages gained were worthwhile. This was the case for, among others, the press in Italy. While some newspapers really made money, others belonged to powerful groups. In 1920, for instance, *Il Secolo* (Milan) was owned by a conglomerate of banks, real estate and insurance companies, as was *Il Giornale d'Italia*. In Genoa both the *Secolo XIX* and the *Corriere mercantile* were owned by the steel tycoon Perrone, who also controlled *Il Messaggero* (Rome), *Il Popolo Romano* (Rome) and *Il Mattino* (Naples).[12] In France in the 1930s *Le Figaro* turned to Coty (perfumes), *Les Débats* to Wendel the steel baron, and *Paris-soir* to Prouvost the textiles magnate. The ownership of such papers gave their owners influence and access to a Minister's office, whilst the editors in their pay helped to arrange, as Paul Jankowski puts it, 'some of the countless little compromises that bound together the élites of this Republic'.[13]

As a result of the strength of business interests involved in it, the Italian press remained solidly anti-left, making it almost mandatory for the Communist Party, after 1945, to devote large resources to having its own newspapers. Yet the lack of influence of the Italian press, which was addressed to an elite, was reflected by the fact that even though it supported the electoral law of 1953 (called the 'Legge Truffa', or Swindle Law, by its left-wing and liberal detractors), the coalition of parties that supported it did not obtain a majority at the 1953 general elections, despite the fact that none of the three main dailies, the Corriere della sera, La Stampa and Il Messaggero, published even a single photograph of the leader of the opposition (compared to eighteen of Christian Democrat leaders).[14]

All in all, the press in the 'free' world was dependent on the private sector: first of all because its owners could impose, within limits, their political preferences, and secondly because they depended on advertising. As we shall see, there were exceptions. A press baron such as Alfred Hugenberg (1865–1951) in Germany influenced his own papers but also the smaller independent ones through his press agency services and the provision of news items. His fortune was made in manufacturing (he was chairman of Krupp Armaments Company in 1909), and he used it to build up a considerable stake in the cultural industry, from the large film production company UFA to several provincial newspapers. He was a right-wing nationalist, a founder of the DNVP (German National People's Party) and from 1929 a backer of Hitler, who appointed him a Minister in 1933. However, Hugenberg resigned after the Nazis suppressed the DNVP. By 1943 his newspaper empire had been confiscated. Political influence matters in a democracy far more than under a dictatorship.

In France, major politicians had learned how to use and control the press not by legal means but by establishing alliances and support. The simplest way was to favour the owners financially, obtaining political support. The attitude of politicians towards newspapers, however, was always vitiated by an overestimation of their political effects. It was mistakenly assumed that the readership was as interested in political matters as were the politicians and the journalists. In fact the political content of most newspapers decreased as their readership increased. By the 1920s only 14 per cent of The Times was devoted to news on politics, economics and social affairs. For the more downmarket *Daily Mail* and *Daily Mirror* the figure was only 10 per cent.[15]

The same was true in France, where anti-clerical papers such as *La Dépêche*, published in Toulouse, on the Garonne in the south of the country, sold simply because they appealed to a wide regional public. Yet it was regularly courted by local politicians, not so much because it could deliver votes, but because of the influence it had on those already in power.[16] Its great editor Arthur Huc held on to an intransigent anti-clericalism throughout his tenure, from the beginning of the century to the 1920s. He fought against take-over bids by magnates, such as that by Maurice de Rothschild in 1922, but could only do so by appealing to other magnates. This and other commercial imperatives often contradicted Huc's commitment to comment over news, ideas and doctrines against what he regarded as the 'Americanisation' of the press (i.e. its depoliticisation).[17] In fact *La Dépêche*, in order to maintain its readership – which is what attracted advertisers and impressed politicians – and to contain the advance of its rivals, provided the normal fare of a popular paper: serialised romances, a woman's page with recipes, advice on childcare and beauty products (while never discussing the issue of woman's suffrage), and widespread sport and crime coverage.[18] It watered down its radicalism *à la* Third Republic (a very mild and bourgeois radicalism) until it became almost indistinguishable from most of its competitors. In fact it was a normal conservative paper, like the majority of the press throughout Europe. This depoliticised politics served everyone fairly well, since by remaining solidly in the middle *La Dépêche* offended few people and pleased investors, politicians and advertisers. By pandering to the prejudices of the majority of the population, it reflected public opinion rather than shaping it – while pretending to itself and others that the opposite was the case.

Occasionally the peculiar ideology of press barons stood in the way of commercial common sense. Lord Rothermere, who owned the *Daily Mail* was an outspoken anti-Semite and supporter of Adolf Hitler, and of Oswald Mosley's British Union of Fascists, a movement which had only minority support. Rothermere's editorial in the *Mail* on 8 January 1934, 'Hurrah for the Blackshirts', praised them for their 'sound, commonsense, Conservative doctrine', while his paper conducted a campaign against the number of German Jews entering Britain as refugees: 'The way that stateless Jews from Germany are pouring in from every port of this country is becoming an outrage' (*Daily Mail*, 30 August 1938).[19] Such campaigns against asylum seekers continue to this day in the same paper. After the violence of a June 1934 Olympia meeting (endorsed by the *Mail*), involving clashes between the

BUF and anti-fascists, the *Mail*'s sympathies for the far right were toned down as its main competitors, the *Daily Express* and the *Daily Telegraph* (but not *The Times*), took their distance from fascism.[20] Lord Rothermere, however, remained an ardent supporter of Hitler up to and including the Munich crisis. Throughout such momentous times, the readers of the *Mail* were not substantially perturbed by its politics.

The relatively low level of political commitment, unless pandering to whatever party is in power counts as commitment, was one of the chief characteristics of the popular press. The best-selling daily of the Third Republic, *Le Petit Parisien*, was a case in point. Since it was generally supportive of centrist governments, it was at first hostile to the Popular Front government elected in 1936. It then accepted it in order – so it said – to 'defend' the Republic. When France fell to the Germans it rallied, like the majority of public opinion, around the Vichy Republic and those who collaborated with the conquerors. That turned out to be a wrong move, since *Le Petit Parisien* did not survive the fall of Vichy either.[21] However, its fortunes had very little to do with its politics. Surveys conducted in the late 1930s for both *Le Petit Parisien* and its main rival *Paris-soir* found that readers of both dailies had little interest in political news.[22]

Far more important was the changed social composition of their readership, the kind of advertising they could attract, the price they charged, the costs they faced, and the successes and failures of their competitors. In 1932 *Le Petit Parisien* was selling 1.62 million copies a day. By 1940 sales had fallen to 912,000. Since the price had increased consistently in the 1930s, the paper assumed that cost was a major factor in its declining sales.[23] To uncover further causes, it undertook a number of investigations. One, produced in 1938, examined the huge drop in sales in Lyons (40 per cent). The main reason, it appeared, was the competition from cheaper local evening papers, such as *Le Progrès* and *Lyon républicain*, which did not face the cost of distribution across the entire country.[24] In Paris the paper also faced the competition of an evening paper, *Paris-soir* (one million copies sold per day in 1938), since both targeted the same working-class readership. Moreover, new weeklies such as *Gringoire* and *Candide* (which sold some 500,000 copies each), and *Paris-dimanche*, the Sunday edition of *Paris-soir* (over 1.8 million) attracted a huge advertising revenue at the direct expense of *Le Petit Parisien*.[25] The paper tried to resolve its problems by making itself more attractive to women (who were deserting it) by reducing its political coverage even more, and introducing more features and interviews.

Few dailies were overtly party political in Europe, whether before or after the Second World War. The main exceptions were dailies which actually belonged to political parties. Here the only relatively successful ones were those of the larger communist parties of western Europe, namely *L'Humanité* in France and *L'Unità* in Italy. These could rely on a network of activists who not only bought the paper but also sold it and subsidised it. Otherwise the only real exception was the British *Daily Herald*, whose support for the Labour Party was part of its marketing position. It closed in 1964, and was resurrected, if that is the word, as the *Sun* owned by the press baron Rupert Murdoch. When the *Herald* closed, its circulation was still one million copies. It could be argued that its fall was due to its inability to attract advertisers, rather than its record in attracting readers. The implication is that advertisers shunned the paper because it was anti-capitalist. But perhaps the failure of the *Daily Herald* was due to the success of another working-class Labour-leaning paper, the *Daily Mirror*. It was not the generic politics of the *Herald* which was the problem, but its excessive interest in the minutiae of Labour Party politics (the inner workings of the party, the annual conference, and matters of little interest to anyone other than deeply committed Labour activists). This did not stop it reaching a million working-class readers, but the *Daily Mirror*, also pro-Labour but never regarded as an in-house party journal, at its peak reached three million readers, and scooped up the advertising aimed at the working class.[26] One could contrast this with the success of more 'up-market' dailies with a marked political and social identity: the pro-Tory *Daily Telegraph* (dubbed the 'Torygraph' by its critics), whose readership was overwhelmingly conservative, and the left-of-centre *Guardian*, which appealed to public-sector professionals, a rising market in the 1970s and 1980s. The *Telegraph*, which in the nineteenth century supported the Liberal Party and the reform of the House of Lords, and opposed capital punishment, changed its politics to suit its owners, becoming pro-imperialist and remaining right-wing ever since – as, indeed, have been its owners. The *Guardian*, once a regional paper (it was called the *Manchester Guardian* until 1959), was funded by nonconformist textile merchants and was eventually bought, in 1905, by its editor C.P. Scott. When Scott's son died in 1932, ownership was passed on to a board of trustees, making the paper almost impregnable to take-over bids.

Another European paper which managed to escape both the domination of business and political patronage was the Parisian *Le Monde*. It was born, however, as a Gaullist paper, when in December 1944 Charles de Gaulle, leader of France after its liberation from German occupation, wanted a new daily of some prestige, that would be above parties and would back him (since he too was above parties, or so he thought). A state loan provided the funding and the ownership was entrusted to an editorial board led by Hubert Beuve-Méry (editor of the paper 1944–69). In practice the paper was controlled by its journalists, members of the Société des Rédacteurs du Monde. The departure of de Gaulle from office in 1953, and the disappearance of the left-of-centre Catholic party MRP, which was the closest to the editor, freed the paper from political patronage. *Le Monde* eventually acquired a distinctive political identity (non-aligned, pro-European, critical of the USA, disenchanted with the Fourth Republic, yet supporting the anti-Gaullist Pierre Mendès-France). It saw itself as a public service, almost like a printed version of the BBC. Its austere presentation, lack of photographs, and exceedingly long background articles with bibliographies and statistics accompanying a compilation of reports from news agencies, seemed ideally suited to its sophisticated, mainly Parisian readership, and its circulation in the 1960s was just under 500,000 (around 300,000 in the 1990s, in line with the collapse of the readership for national papers). Surveys conducted in the 1950s showed that two-thirds of *Le Monde*'s readers belonged to the wealthiest 20 per cent of the population. Another conducted in 1973 showed that over half of its readers had received higher education (against 31 per cent for *Le Figaro*, its right-wing rival).[27] Its high price compensated for its low advertising revenue. Only an élite paper could afford not to be in hock to newspaper magnates and advertisers, but it would still need to respond to the commercial environment, keeping its readers, acquiring new ones, and attracting advertisers.

Political independence is not a prerequisite for success, unless a paper's readership regards it to be of major importance. The *Corriere della sera*, the best-selling Italian paper, tried at first to preserve its independence from Mussolini. By 1925 its owners, the Crespi family, decided that they could not afford to offend a regime which now seemed to be well-entrenched. Its respected editor, Luigi Albertini, was sacked and a more compliant one found. This did not lead to a fall in readership. The car manufacturer Fiat did the same with its daily, *La Stampa*, by getting rid of the former owner and editor Alfredo Frassati. Since all Italian newspapers were regional, the *Corriere* was a virtual monopoly in and around Milan, just as *La Stampa* was in and around Turin. In fact the *Corriere* did better under fascism than afterwards. In 1924 it sold 800,000 copies a day (one million on Sundays). In 1944, by then a fascist mouthpiece, it still sold 900,000 copies.[28] After the war a new non-fascist editorial team was put in charge. By 1949 sales had dropped to 300,000. They then started climbing steadily, and the *Corriere* remained the best-selling Italian daily (occasionally overtaken after 1980 by *La Repubblica*).[29] The rationing of paper had given the new authorities considerable powers, but a black market in paper gave an undue advantage to those able to obtain proper funding.[30]

A government decree of 31 May 1946 liberalised the press and limited the rights of the authorities to confiscate newspapers. The author of the decree was Palmiro Togliatti, the communist leader and Deputy Prime Minister, who regarded a free press as an indissoluble aspect of Italian democracy (though not of the Soviet Union). Pope Pius XII, less liberal than Togliatti, explained to British and American journalists who had gathered around him on 11 July 1946 that freedom of the press should be restricted in order not to undermine the moral and religious fibre of the individual or the peace and harmony between nations.[31]

What that meant could be seen in the aftermath of the clear stand in favour of the Republic in the 1946 referendum taken by the new anti-fascist editor of the *Corriere della sera*, Mario Borsa. The move was seen as 'left-wing', since the Christian Democrats did not take a stance on the referendum and Fiat's *La Stampa* supported the monarchy. As a direct consequence the Crespi family, owners of the *Corriere*, removed Borsa and appointed a more compliant editor. Throughout the 1950s and early 1960s the *Corriere*, though occasionally critical of the Christian Democratic Party (particularly when it oscillated towards the left), remained solidly conservative, and virtually uncritical of American foreign policy – like most other dailies in Italy. Though it regarded itself as the paper of the Milan bourgeoisie, it never seriously discussed either economics or industrial relations, leaving such matters to academics committed to a distinctly old-fashioned (then) economic liberalism (thus appearing to distinguish the paper from government interventionism) or to the *Sole–24 Ore*, a daily financial paper printed on pink paper like the London *Financial Times* and owned by the employers' association, the Confindustria.

Newspapers were given plenty of protection to further consolidate their dependence on political power. The liberal Minister of Finance, Luigi Einaudi (later President of the Republic), opposed any compulsion for newspapers to publish their accounts, as did the rising star of the Christian Democratic Party, the then young Giulio Andreotti. There would be no transparency in finding out who financed the newspapers.[32] The government further helped newspapers with subsidies through a state-run paper agency (which discriminated against opposition papers), and journalists on private pension schemes received further contributions from the state, were able obtain cheap mortgages, and were given huge discounts on train and air travel (both nationalised industries).[33] Readership, however, remained low, and though the actual figures were secret, estimates suggest that in 1949 the *Corriere* sold 300,000 copies, *La Stampa* (Turin) 180,000, *Il Messaggero* (Rome) 140,000, *La Nazione* (Florence) 120,000, and the communist *L'Unità* 130,000. All other papers sold less than 100,000 copies.[34] By 1952 there were in Italy 111 dailies – sixty-one in the north. Of the 111, thirteen belonged to political parties, six to Church organisations, and four were entirely dedicated to sport – one of these, *La Gazzetta dello sport*, outsold almost all the other papers.[35]

All the main Italian dailies shared roughly the same ideology, supporting the general direction of Italian politics. There were few if any right-wing populist newspapers, or any that were overtly pro-clerical, pro-socialist or pro-communist (except those owned by socialist and communist parties). Yet in the 1950s and 1960s, 80 per cent of the electorate supported either the Church-aligned DC, the socialists or the communists. The Italian press spoke to the few and, unsurprisingly, sold to the few.

A large readership, however, is not always necessary. Quality papers aimed at a rich readership attract quality advertising. In Weimar Germany the *Frankfurter Zeitung* was a prestige paper with a small circulation (50–70,000), but its financial pages were regarded as compulsory reading in financial circles.[36] Thirteen per cent of the readership were professionals. Hitler, in *Mein Kampf*, regarded it, along with the *Berliner Tageblatt*, as organs of the Jewish intelligentsia: written for an intellectual 'demi-monde . . . for them their tone is chosen, and on them they exercise their influence', using 'the freedom of the press . . . – their term for poisoning and lying to the people'.[37] But the *Frankfurter Zeitung*'s left-of-centre line lost it advertising. It borrowed money, and by 1927 it was deeply in debt. It was rescued by the chemical conglomerate Interessengemeinschaft Farbenindustrie (IG Farben), Germany's (and Europe's) largest corporation, which the paper had previously criticised. As the Nazis advanced, the paper adopted an increasingly conciliatory line, moving steadily to the right, removing critical journalists and becoming committed to what one of its leader writers called 'the lesser evil'. In 1934 the heirs of Leopold Sonnemann, who had founded the paper in 1856, sold their remaining holdings to an investment company acting for Farben. Having achieved its political aims – the evisceration of a critical paper – Farben had no interest in keeping it, and gave it away to the Nazi Party as 'a birthday present' to Adolf Hitler.[38] Farben turned out to be one of the main beneficiaries of the use of slave labour in German-occupied Europe, and the producer of the Zyklon-B gas used for the mass extermination of Jews and other 'inferior' peoples.

The European map of the press did not change substantially from the interwar era to the post-war, at least in western Europe. Most of the main Italian, French and British papers survived into the post-war era. There were some new entrants, such as the already-mentioned *Le Monde* and the Milan *Il Giorno* (1956), owned by the state oil company ENI (the ownership would be kept secret until 1959), and whose graphic model was the London *Daily Express*.[39] In France and Great Britain no brand-new daily of any significance emerged in the 1950s or 1960s. In the 1970s and 1980s new entrants appeared such as, in Italy, the conservative *Il Giornale nuovo* (1974) and the left-of-centre *La Repubblica* (1976), in France the left-wing *Libération* (1973), and in 1986 the *Independent* in Great Britain. What was peculiar to Italy was the existence of no fewer than three far-left dailies emerging out of the student movement of the late 1960s: *Il Manifesto* (1971), *Lotta Continua* (1972) and *Il Quotidiano dei lavoratori* (1974). All three together never reached more than 70,000 copies.

Courting Women

The stereotypical reader of the mass-circulation daily paper was a working man who, after a day's hard work, returned home, put his slippers on and read the newspaper while his wife prepared dinner – the kind of image celebrated from the 1950s in the 'Andy Capp' comic strip by Reg Smythe in the *Daily Mirror*. Surveys conducted in the interwar period somewhat belie this image. Newspapers tried to attract a female readership by including features which would appeal to women, alongside the coverage of sport which was overwhelmingly aimed at men.

This is not to say that women's periodicals were not read by men too. Readership is subject to an opportunity factor. Thus a newspaper or magazine could be bought by the primary reader and then read by other members of the family simply because it is around the house (not to speak of those read by people waiting in doctors' and dentists' surgeries). In 1967, 10 per cent of the readership of the weekly *Petticoat*, for instance, in spite (or because) of its title, were men, as were 11 per cent of the readers of *Mother* and 20 per cent of those of *Woman's Own*.[40]

A specifically feminine press, however, had existed since the nineteenth century, when it addressed itself to middle- and upper-middle-class women, dealing largely with fashion and household management (see pages 324–6). The expansion of the lower-middle-class and working-class readership, and the growth in the number of housewives in the first half of the twentieth century, provided an opportunity for a further development of the feminine press. The mix on offer varied according to the readership targeted, but it included features on celebrities, love stories, family matters (how to bring up one's children, take care of one's husband's ego, and cope with one's mother). Of increasing importance was the presentation of oneself in everyday life: how to look attractive and desirable. The more successful exemplars of the feminine press were those able to mirror the preoccupations and anxieties of their readership without ever sounding patronising. Thus the shrewd editor of the relatively upmarket *The Lady* sent, on 24 June 1920, an indirect message to its old genteel readership while appealing to a new one, by assuming a common status between those who had been used to domestic servants and now did not have any, and those who had never had them but thought they should:

> In these days of increasing expenditure and diminishing income, it behoves us – the New Poor – to adapt ourselves to altered circumstances, and to learn how comparatively simple it is to do many things for ourselves that formerly necessitated sending for a workman.[41]

A host of new magazines appeared in Britain throughout the 1920s. Many were British editions of American magazines, such as *Vogue* (1916), *Good Housekeeping* (1922) and *Harper's Bazaar* (1929). *Modern Woman* (1925) and *Woman and Home* (1926) were aimed at the middle and lower-middle classes; *Woman's Own* (1932) and *Woman's Illustrated* (1936) were among the first mass-circulation periodicals.[42] New technology, such as photogravure, was used in *Woman* (1936), the first to adopt this process. It was expensive, but it paid off because the print run was very large.[43]

A similar explosion in the women's magazine market was taking place in other European countries, with magazines such as *Femmes d'aujourd'hui* in Belgium (1933) and *Marie-Claire* (1937) in France, which by 1938 was already selling 730,000 copies.[44] Japan did not wait for Europe: the Seiji publishing empire launched nine magazines, all of which had six-figure circulations including *Shufu-no-Tomo* (The Housewife's Friend, 1917) and *Le-no-Hikari* (Light of Home, 1925). Nor was China left behind: the first issue of *Ling Lung* (meaning 'elegant and fine') came out in March 1931.

In this kind of periodical the cover was of decisive importance.[45] The style of the drawing or photo was a powerful signal of the expected readership. The contents reflected the new preoccupations of its readership: the film craze of the 1930s had sparked a still-enduring interest in the private lives of stars, fuelled by the studios' propaganda machines; the increasing failure of marriages led to agony columns proffering, even in the relatively demure 1930s, sexual advice. During the Second World War in Great Britain, women's magazines became one of the main instruments used by the government to propagandise how women should ration consumption.[46] Like much of the press, women's magazines were rather good at keeping up with changes without ever daring to initiate them. They were quick to adapt and reinforce change, but prudence dictated their action. How to gauge the desires of the readers became important, hence the panoply of surveys, readers' questionnaires, letters from readers and reports on drops or increases in sales in particular areas.

※

52

Comic Strips

The Triumph of the Comic Strip

COMICS WERE a quintessential American genre. The USA had established a global supremacy in the cinema, but the cinema was born and acquired its initial impetus in Europe. In literature, at least in the interwar years, US penetration was confined to genres such as crime, although American literary novels were beginning to be discovered. Europe's broadcasting remained solidly national, and its press remained distinctive, though as we have seen, imitations of US weekly photo-based periodicals were making inroads. American songs were the most popular internationally, but there were strong local and international competitors, such as Latin American rhythm. In comics, the most American of all new cultural fields, the US lead established at the beginning of the twentieth century (see pages 725–33) was never lost. Even after the Second World War, when the European comic strip revived, international dominance was largely American, dented only by a few francophone exceptions such as 'Tintin' and 'Astérix'.

Until the late 1920s the Europeans refused to innovate. They stuck to their traditional graphic style and bottom-of-the-frame captions (instead of the bubbles which permitted the concurrent reading of the text and looking at the picture). In the 1930s, American comics were imported in large quantities. One of the first countries to open its doors to them was France, when the 'Mickey Mouse' strip appeared in the *Petit Parisien* in 1930. On 24 October 1934 the *Journal de Mickey* was distributed by Paul Winkler's Opera Mundi, a press agency representing the largest US syndicate of comic strips (King Features Syndicate). This was two years earlier than the deal struck with Disney by the British-based Oldham Press which led to *Mickey Mouse Weekly*. The sales of the *Journal de Mickey* quickly reached 400,000 copies, and

Winkler launched further US products. Soon American comics were translated and adapted throughout Europe, and eventually much of the rest of the world. Mickey landed in Finland in 1931, and was quickly followed by Bonzo, Felix the Cat, Flash Gordon, etc. The Portuguese read 'O Mickey' and the Italians 'Topolino'. This enhanced the growing globalisation of culture, well before the term had become common currency in the 1990s. The Irish novelist John Banville, reviewing J.M. Coetzee's autobiography *Boyhood: Scenes from Provincial Life* (1997), noted that comparing Coetzee's childhood in South Africa with his own in a small Irish town in the 1940s and 1950s, he experienced a shock of recognition: not only did they both own the same brand of bicycle and a Meccano set, but they both read 'Superman' and 'Mandrake'.[1]

The USA had the advantage of having pioneered almost all comics genres during the 1920s and 1930s (the European golden age arrived twenty years later). Many of the early American comics – such as Martin Branner's 'Winnie Winkle' (1920) and Harold Gray's 'Little Orphan Annie' (1924) – favoured a family setting. Then followed adventure, crime and, above all, science fiction: from the detective Dick Tracy by Chester Gould (1931) to Dick Calkins' Buck Rogers, a science-fiction hero in the twenty-fifth century (1929, based on Philip Nowland's novel *Armageddon 2419*), and Tarzan, adapted from Edgar Rice Burroughs' novels. Other characters, some of them endowed with superhuman powers, followed: the Human Torch, the Sub-Mariner, Captain Marvel, Captain America, and Alex Raymond's Flash Gordon (1934). Each of the heroes faced a super-villain: Lex Luthor (Superman), the Joker (Batman), Cobra (Mandrake) and the Emperor Ming the Merciless (Flash Gordon). A fusion of science fiction with the Arthurian Middle Ages proved particularly successful in comics such as Harold Foster's 'Prince Valiant' (1937) – perhaps one of Tolkien's inspirations.

The heroes were almost always white, young and male – Dalia Messick's intrepid reporter Brenda Starr (1940) is the best-known exception. The villains are usually unattractive, foreign and older. The heroes are awkward with women. Sex is absent, while desire is present. There were some 'daring' comic strips such as the *Daily Mirror's* celebrated 'Jane's Journal' (1932) which as the years went by displayed increasing nudity, until in the middle of the war Jane removed all her clothes to get into her bath, to the delight of many and the outrage of some. Occasionally the hero's female friend longs for marriage, but that is unthinkable. Superman married to Lois Lane, settling in suburbia and raising kids would horrify the readership. Married life was represented in an ironic manner in the *ménage* of Blondie and Dagwood Bumstead (created by Chic Young in 1930).

The longevity of some strips was remarkable: 'Superman', 'Mandrake', 'Peanuts' and 'Dick Tracy' lasted more than fifty years. Characters never grow old (though Blondie kept up with the times, turning from a stylish housewife into a chic businesswoman). The authorial role consisted of devising and designing the characters. The storylines remained formulaic, and could be continued by others. Thus when the eyesight of Mary Tourtel, the creator of 'Rupert Bear' (1920), began to fail in 1935, the *Daily Express* turned to Alfred Bestall, who went on drawing Rupert for another thirty years.[2]

Europeans shamelessly imitated and adapted American strips. Translations could be achieved very quickly. Imitation was easy. The pictures could also be edited or censored to fit in with local requirements. The Belgian publisher Jean Meeuwissen, who started a Flemish weekly for children in May 1936, packed it with US imports such as 'Flash Gordon', 'Felix the Cat' and 'The Katzenjammer Kids', and gave his own local product American pseudonyms.[3] In Spain the magazine *Pinocho* (from the Italian Pinocchio) had started to publish some US strips as early as 1925 but this turned into a flood in the mid-1930s thanks to 'Betty Boop', 'Flash Gordon', 'Tarzan', 'Popeye' and 'Buck Rogers'. During the Civil War, comic-strip nationalism prevailed, and *Chicos* (1938) published mainly Spanish designers, with a characteristically streetwise Spanish central character in the kid Cuto.[4]

The prestigious *Frankfurter Allgemeine Zeitung* published 'Mickey Maus' in the 1930s, while M.M. Branner's 'Winnie Winkle' (created in 1920) became 'Kalle, der Lausbubenkönig' when it was published in the 1930s by the weekly youth magazine *Neue Jugend*, with Branner's name deleted to disguise the strip's American origins. Most readers were unaware of such cultural transfers. A Spanish child could hardly know (or care) that his hero Juan Centella was Dick Fulmine in Italy and Alain la Foudre in France; nor did Italian children reading the journal *Topolino* in 1937 realise that the stories of 'Saturno contro la Terra' were based on Flash Gordon (an idea of Cesare Zavattini, an editor at Mondadori, later the leading scriptwriter of Italian neo-realist films). The Belgians' Buck Danny (1947 – still going strong in the 1990s) was based on Buck Rogers. The Belgians also made up their own western hero, Jerry Spring (1954), who with his Mexican sidekicks regularly routed the Ku Klux Klan. The British detective Buck Ryan (*Daily Mirror*, 1937) was based on Dick Tracy.[5] There was further cross-fertilisation. Brick

Bradford, a British science fiction hero *à la* Buck Rogers devised in 1933 by William Ritt and Clarence Gay, became in fascist Italy Guido Ventura. Walter Booth's travelling boy Rob the Rover (1920 in *Puck* magazine), one of the first British comic heroes, was turned in Italy into Lucio l'avanguardista, a young fascist aviator.[6]

On the whole, comics were not political. Even under fascism Italian designers preferred generic adventure stories, adapted Dumas, Kipling and Jules Verne, and used standard characters such as the mad scientist (*Virus, il mago della foresta Morta*, 1939). Even when a strip glorified fascism, such as *Romano il legionario* (1938) by Kurt Caesar, the setting followed the American conception of exoticism: the frozen Arctic, Mayan ruins, or underwater.[7] Comic strips actually set in Italy depicted not American-type supermen but lower-middle-class Italians mocked for their aspirations towards self-improvement, such as 'Mortadella' (1928), Carlo Bisi's 'Sor Pampurio' (1929) and the scientist Pier Cloruro De'Lambicchi (1930).[8]

During the war, rampant anti-Americanism in France and Italy (not to speak, obviously of Germany) compelled editors to eliminate references to the US origins of their comic strips. Superman became, in France, 'François l'Imbattable'. French anti-Semitism produced the character of Professor Vorax (dark hair, black beard, protruding eyes, large ears, crooked nose). But, as with the cinema, without US competition French designers thrived during the war.[9] The same occurred in several other countries, notably Holland.[10] In Italy too, one of the few positive effects of fascist autarchy was the development of an Italian school of designers. After the war Americanism returned to fashion. Italian-drawn strips were made to appear American (Americans were popular, and adaptation saved on copyrights). In 1946 'Amok' made its appearance. This was a giant Superman designed by 'Tony Chan' and 'Phil Anderson' – pseudonyms for Antonio Canale and Cesare Solini. In 1950 the *Corriere dei piccoli* (which had adapted American comics since its inception in 1908) devised a Tarzan lookalike, Akim.

Italian-made western characters, such as Pecos Bill and Tex Willer (created by Giovanni Luigi Bonelli in September 1948) – the antecedent of the famed 'spaghetti' westerns – started to entertain several generations of children. In the mid-1970s, 18 per cent of Italian comics were westerns.[11] Adaptation of westerns was not exclusively Italian: the British had Matt Dillon, and the Argentinians Sergeant Kirk. The Belgian designer Morris (Maurice de Bévère), joined by René Goscinny in 1957 (who later, with Albert Uderzo, created Astérix), invented Lucky Luke in 1946; but while 'Lucky

Luke' was a parody of a western, the Italian Tex Willer and Pecos Bill were deadly serious. One peculiarity of the European western heroes, however, was their pronounced sympathy for the Indians.

Styles and Conventions

The modern American comic strip had two striking features. The first was that the words were written in a bubble that appeared to come out of the mouth of the character. The second was the frequent use of stark colours with no shadows, each colour enclosed within clear continuous black lines demarcating characters and objects.

Bubbles were introduced on Continental Europe much later than in the USA, though the largely wordless 'Adamson' strip in Sweden's *Söndag-Nisse*, designed by Oscar Andersson (1920), occasionally used them, and bubbles appeared in pre-World War I British comic strips such as 'Ally Sloper' (1888). Mickey Mouse, when he first appeared in the *Petit Parisien* in 1930, had no bubbles. When 'Tintin' was first imported into France from Belgium, the publishers eliminated the bubbles.[12] In 1925 Saint-Ogan used bubbles in his famous 'Zig et Puce' comic strip, but French prejudice against them was such that in other series he reverted to the traditional caption. Eventually European designers, above all the Belgians, adopted the bubble and used its graphic flexibility: a discontinuous line indicated that the character was thinking rather than speaking; the size of the text suggested the volume at which the words were spoken. Onomatopoeic conventions were devised for non-verbal utterances: a dog's bark was 'oua-oua' in France, 'bao-bao' in Italy, and 'woof-woof' in Great Britain. Conventions also included the possibility of showing a sequence within a single frame, such as that in the Tintin story *Le Crabe aux pinces d'or* (1940), where five Bedouin fighters respond differently because each is depicted at a slightly deferred moment in time.[13]

Cinema

There was a constant interchange of characters and situations with the cinema. As early as 1920 there were comic strips featuring Charlie Chaplin and Harold Lloyd. This synergy was hardly accidental. Films routinely use storyboards resembling comic strips, and the two genres use similar techniques, from the establishing shot to the close-up. The principles of montage were at work in the comic strip too.

The closeness of the comic strip and the movies led to a stream of referential parodies. Each opening frame of the Belgian 'western' 'Lucky Luke' resembles a classic western film: a wide panoramic shot of a lonely rider in a valley, with mountains in the background. A close-up follows. In the final frame Lucky Luke is seen from the back riding off towards the horizon, singing (in English) 'I am a poor lonesome cow-boy and a long way from home.'

The success of the comic book and comic magazines coincided with the development of animated films, and the two genres proceeded side by side, feeding each other. In the 1930s Universal Pictures bought the rights to many comic strips and made serial films out of them, occasionally as animated pictures but more often as fillers to keep the children amused.[14] Alongside nineteenth-century American heroes such as Deadwood Dick, immortalised in the 1860s in the Beadle books (see pages 479–80), one could find, suitably Americanised, 'British' heroes such as Tarzan. In the original *Tarzan of the Apes* (1914), the first of over twenty books by the American Edgar Rice Burroughs (1875–1950), Tarzan is British, the son of Lord Greystoke, 'the type of Englishman that one likes best to associate with the noblest monuments of historic achievement upon one thousand victorious battlefields – a strong, virile man – mentally, morally, and physically'.[15] Lost in the jungle and raised by animals, Tarzan cannot fit back into 'civilised' society and renounces his title and matrimonial bliss with Jane Porter to return to the jungle for further adventures – proudly announcing that his mother was an ape (a typical New World rejection of the values of ancestry). The famous opening lines of his first encounter with Jane, 'Me Tarzan, you Jane,' are apocryphal. In the original book Tarzan's declaration of love is contained in a letter: 'I am Tarzan of the Apes. I want you. I am yours. You are mine,' before concluding, irresistibly, with 'I am the mightiest of the jungle fighters. You are Jane Porter.'[16] In the comic strip version which started in January 1929, and in the films of the 1930s (with the champion swimmer Johnny Weissmuller), Tarzan's British aristocratic origins are quietly forgotten and he turns into a standard-issue all-American righter of wrongs.

Both cinema and comic strips used every conceivable plot, and feature stories from the classic fairy tales to the Gothic genre, from medieval sagas to westerns, from science fiction to celebrated children's stories. Italian designers in particular would seek establishment approval by adapting classics, from *The Thousand and One Nights* (1941) to *Don Quixote* (1950). Adaptations of classics were also produced in Spain and Yugoslavia (above all by Andrija Maurović, who turned Shakespeare, Dumas, Sienkiewicz and Robert Louis Stevenson into comics). The vast anthropomorphic menagerie of fairy tales was expanded to include ducks, mice, dogs, cats, elephants and deer.

A successful comic strip would almost inevitably lead to a cinema adaptation. The famous strip featuring the ineffectual husband Dagwood Bumstead and his cool wife Blondie spawned twenty-eight 'Blondie' movies with Penny Singleton in the title role (a true professional, Singleton became in later life the Vice-President of the American Guild of Variety Artists, the union representing touring performers, chorus girls and other entertainers). In the pre-television era, these films were the equivalent of TV serials: *Blondie Meets the Boss, Blondie on a Budget, Blondie has Servant Trouble, Blondie Plays Cupid, Blondie Goes to College,* and so on and on. Each lasted seventy minutes, was cheap to make and was largely addressed to the US market.

American comic strips reworked, with a remarkable lack of inhibition, traditional myths. *Superman,* first published in 1938, written by Jerry Siegel and drawn by Joe Shuster, follows in the footsteps of other righters of wrongs from Moses to Jesus Christ by not being of 'normal' birth. A native of the doomed planet Krypton, he is placed in a spaceship (like Moses in his papyrus basket) by his parents, in order to save him. His earthly parents (who are farmers) are not his real ones – a common fantasy. Like Achilles, Superman has a weak spot: his special powers are diminished if he is exposed to the debris from his native planet (one's origins are frequently an obstacle). The storyline is made more interesting by Superman's double identity. He leads a normal life as Clark Kent, a reporter for the *Daily Planet,* changing when necessary into Superman's costume, which is both futuristic (the Lycra-like tights) and projected towards the past (a non-functional cape reminiscent of a knight's). The *Doppelgänger* status of Clark Kent/Superman is enhanced by the fact that in his 'normal' mode he wears spectacles, the conventional hallmark of the feeble intellectual, the reverse of the action man. Thus another common fantasy, prevalent among boys, is fulfilled: weak men and small boys can escape their dismal present and become powerful and admired. This is all the more evident in the romantic connection between Clark Kent and his colleague Lois Lane. Lois is 'best friends' with Clark but is attracted by Superman: short-sighted journalists in crumpled suits – unlike supermen – don't get the girls. The context is specifically American: a modern city of skyscrapers, Metropolis, which resembles the New York or Chicago of the 1930s.

Imitations follow success. A year after Superman's appearance Bob Kane and Bill Finger's Batman and his boy sidekick Robin began their fight against evil, wearing strange and exciting costumes and sporting dual identities (in 'normal' life Batman is a rich recluse, Robin his ward). Their lack of superhuman powers is more than compensated for by the possession of an extraordinary car, the Batmobile. In 1942 Wonder Woman was created, presumably in order to entice a young female audience, though her sexually alluring costume was just as likely to excite boys' fantasies. More recently, in 1962 Marvel Comics introduced Spiderman, whose special powers were acquired after he was bitten by a radioactive spider (nuclear radiation supplies a 'rationalist' explanation more credible than old-fashioned magic).

Comic Strip Values

The American comic strip was often accused of exporting American values, or even of upholding American imperialism (see the classic text *How to Read Donald Duck* by Ariel Dorfman and Armand Mattelart, originally published in Chile in 1971 as *Para Leer al Pato Donald* and banned in 1973 by the military dictator Augusto Pinochet). Yet comic strips, like most popular literature, at most reinforce existing values while trying to remain aloof from politics. After all, Superman, instead of rescuing cats from trees, could have simply got rid of communism, particularly during the Cold War. But in comics, as in popular films and fiction, the real conflict is not with communism but with Satanic evil men who want to rule the world.

Comic strips, just like novels and films, do not present a uniform moral universe. 'Peanuts' and 'Superman' have little in common. Some of the more successful strips have elements of irony and parody. Al Capp's 'Li'l Abner' (1934) was a satire on American society and culture, mocking business tycoons, politicians and gangsters. The 'Popeye' strip created in 1929 by E.C. Segar (a former projectionist) has odd protagonists: a thin, one-eyed, pipe-smoking sailor with overdeveloped muscles, and his jealous and irritable fiancée Olive Oyl, who unlike conventional comic-strip beauties is completely flat-chested. The other characters (Ham Gravy, Castor Oil, Brutus) are obese, or very short, or stupid. One is a glutton constantly devouring hamburgers. No one behaves as they should: Popeye slurps his soup loudly, beats up everyone (including Olive), and eats an absurdly large quantity of spinach (which gives him uncommon strength).

European cultural élites regarded comic strips with distaste, not because they brought American values, but because they represented low culture. Intellectuals in communist countries, whose main reference point was high-bourgeois culture, felt the same way, yet the genre was never banned. US comic strips were kept out of circulation, but local products, often imitative, were available in post-war communist countries.

As had been the case for virtually all forms of culture, especially those connected to children, there was a moral panic. Educators and parents worried that comic strips would sap the minds of the young; that children would no longer read 'real' books or develop the attention span required for ordinary printed stories. In Germany, Manfred Welke's study of comic strips, *Die Sprache der Comics* (1958), pointed to their allegedly deleterious consequences for children – though there was already a law forbidding comics dealing with crime and horror. The panic was enhanced by the realisation that by the early 1950s, between three and five million strips were sold in Germany each month. German publishers, alarmed, created in 1955 their own regulatory agency, to the detriment of home-grown strips in favour of the much safer US brands.

But the Americans too were worried. In his popular book *Seduction of the Innocent: The Influence of Comic Books on Today's Youth* (1954), extracts from which were published in widely read magazines such as *Reader's Digest*, the psychiatrist Fredric Wertham frightened Americans into believing that there was clinical evidence that children who read comics were more likely to become juvenile delinquents. Senator Estes Kefauver led a Senate committee investigating the industry, which frightened the publishers into forming their own self-regulatory body, the CCA (Comics Code Authority), with draconian powers.[17] In Sweden, the psychiatrist Nils Bejerot's book *Barn Serier Samhälle* (Children Comics Society, 1954) was used in order to add severe restrictions to the distribution of comics.[18] In France the new censorship law of July 1949, on behalf of which the Catholic Church had lobbied hard, banned comic strips which presented in a favourable light 'banditry, lying, theft, laziness, disloyalty, hatred, debauchery, and any criminal or unnatural act liable to demoralise children and young people or cause them to hold ethnic prejudices'.[19] Goscinny, who eventually created Astérix, explained that publishers insisted that comic-strip artists should not draw 'sexy' women. To keep out of trouble he avoided women completely.[20]

In many churches, priests provided parents with lists of 'bad' comic strips. In 1950 a French teachers' group, the Ligue de l'Enseignement, attacked comics; the Catholic *L'Éducateur* launched a campaign against Tarzan. In Spain, the Church – though grateful to the USA for keeping communism at bay – complained of the scantily-dressed women in American comic books. Violence seemed more permissible, particularly if perpetrated against distant galaxies – after all, the Crusades had not been invented by comic-strip designers. The left too was unhappy. In 1955 Jean-Paul Sartre's *Les Temps modernes* published a lengthy extract from Wertham's *Seduction of the Innocent*, the book which had tried to galvanise American public opinion against comics.[21] In Great Britain the Churches (as well as the Communist Party) lobbied in favour of the Children and Young Persons (Harmful Publications) Act of 1955 (renewed in 1965), brought in to prosecute comic books which escaped the established definitions of obscenity. The legislation was, of course, quite useless, a case of panic law enacted to calm public opinion, which had been alarmed by the politicians themselves supported by the press: there was only one prosecution, in 1970, when an East End firm was fined £25 for importing comic books with titles such as *Tales from the Tomb*.[22]

Those who panicked remained a minority. The expansion of the comic strip for children had become unstoppable ever since popular dailies began publishing full pages of comic strips. This removed one of the strongest obstacles to their diffusion: parental opposition. Having brought newspapers into the home, it was not easy to stop children reading something which was so clearly aimed at them. Thus the serialisation of comics created a wider demand among children for further comic-strip products. The growth was dramatic. By 1980 comic-strip books and magazines were selling in France to the tune of 170 million a year.[23]

France had become, after the war, the largest European market for comics. These, however, were regarded by the communists as too American, by the Catholic Church as too violent, and by nationalists as not sufficiently French. But they all recognised that comics could not be ignored, and often developed their own. The French Communist Party, as early as 1944, published its own comics magazine, *Vaillant* (not to be confused with the Belgian Catholic *Coeurs Vaillants* – 220,000 subscribers in 1940 – equally inspired by the principle of taking a leaf from the Devil's book).[24] *Vaillant* exalted the Resistance, but above all it provided the usual fare of adventure and humour. It was never as ideological as its Catholic counterparts, and provided a platform for some of the finest designers and writers of comic strips in

France including René Goscinny, later of 'Lucky Luke' and 'Astérix' fame, who having spent five years in the USA (1945–50) was familiar with the American scene. By 1952 even the dour Party daily *L'Humanité* carried comic strips.

By the 1960s intellectuals discovered comic strips (they had probably read them when young). The 'high culture' antecedents of comic strips, such as the Bayeux Tapestry or some early Renaissance paintings, were rediscovered. Designers acquired status. Old editions of 'Tintin' were sought and reprinted, learned societies were formed, and university courses on the comic strip were set up.[25] In 1962 Umberto Eco wrote 'The Myth of Superman', in which Aristotle, Sartre's *Being and Nothingness* and Edmund Husserl's phenomenology are invoked.[26] In the USA Roy Lichtenstein promoted his comic-strip paintings, such as *Good Morning, Darling* (1964), an enlargement of an original panel from a strip, reproduced by painting on a huge scale the dots, lines and colours used in printing. In 1966 Joseph Losey turned 'Modesty Blaise' into a film starring Monica Vitti, while in 1968 the comic strip 'Barbarella' was adapted by Roger Vadim, a director with *nouvelle vague* pretensions, with Jane Fonda in the title role. In 1990 comic strips scored another high-culture victory when the Louvre held an exhibition on 'Peanuts' and the French government awarded its designer, Charles Schulz, the title of Commandeur des Arts et des Lettres.

The European Counter-Offensive

Until the 1950s European-made strips sold mainly to their own local readership. The international market was a virtual US monopoly. But what American comics had achieved was the creation of a wider market in Europe, and this provided opportunities for European designers as well. Some of them achieved fame outside their own linguistic boundaries, but only in the 1950s and 1960s, when the great francophone comics 'Tintin' and 'Astérix' became internationally successful. In the USA, however, 'Tintin' remained a minority taste – though this might change, as Steven Spielberg acquired the film rights in 2002.[27]

In spite of its ironic nationalism (a corner of Gaul holding out against the might of the Roman Empire), Astérix was successful throughout Europe, translated into forty languages, adapted for radio, films and plays.[28] And in 1989, in direct imitation of and challenge to Disneyland (not yet established in France) an Astérix theme park was erected near Paris. *Astérix chez les Bretons* – which sold 600,000 copies in two weeks when it was published in 1966 – did well in Britain too, even though (or because) it made fun of the British, using, tongue in cheek, all the standard clichés (the British smother all food with mint sauce, and constantly drink cups of hot water because the French have not yet taught them to make tea).[29]

In 1958 the Belgian Peyo created an imaginary community of endearing creatures called the Schtroumphs, threatened by Gargamel the magician and his cat Azrael. The Schtroumphs gained international recognition in the 1980s, as well as considerable merchandising, a theme park near Metz in northern France and an American cartoon series, suitably re-baptised into the more pronounceable Smurfs ('I Puffi' in Italy, the 'Smuref' in Brazil, 'Schumple' in Germany, 'Los Pitufos' in Portugal and 'Hupikek Torpikek' in Hungary).

But even the most successful European strips have been no match for the Americans in the global market. Charles Schulz's 'Peanuts' sold, by 1987, three hundred million books worldwide, against ninety million for 'Tintin' and 180 million for 'Astérix'. Nothing beats a large domestic market. In the USA, a major designer would be syndicated from coast to coast. The syndication system provided them also with a mechanism whereby they could be sold across the world. The English, for the same reason, benefited too. Thus Reg Smythe's 'Andy Capp' in spite of its markedly 'national' setting (although its working-class loafer and his long-suffering wife are obviously a universal issue), became syndicated in thirty countries – including the USSR and the USA – after it was first published in the *Daily Mirror* in 1957.

In the 1950s the US comic strip began to lose ground not just in Europe but also at home, as American children started their long-term affair with television (until the advent of video games).

In Italy the appearance of US domination remained, but in reality the strips were mainly designed by Italians like Romano Scarpa, some of whose Mickey Mouse stories were even re-exported.[30] The characters had been Italianised since the 1930s: Mickey became Topolino ('little mouse'), Donald Duck became Paperino ('little duck'), Scrooge McDuck became Paperone ('big duck'). The French, who had kept the names of Donald and Mickey, eliminated Dickensian references, turning Scrooge McDuck into Oncle Pic-sou (Uncle Pickpenny). Donald's three nephews, Huey, Dewey and Louie, who had first appeared in 1937, had names alluding in a recondite way to American politics: Thomas Dewey was in 1937 the District Attorney of New

York County (later he became Governor of New York and Republican nominee for the presidential elections); Huey Long was Governor of Louisiana (1928–31) and a US Senator from 1932 to 1935, when he was assassinated; while Louie was named after the animator Louie Schmitt. In Italy the nephews became Qui, Quo and Qua; in France, Riti, Fifi and Loulou; in Czechoslovakia, Bubík, Dulík and Kulík; in Finland, Tupu, Hupu and Lupu; in Portugal, Huguinho, Zezinho and Luisinho; in Spain, Hugo, Paco and Luis, and so on. Changes of name were common. Donald Duck turned into Anders And in Denmark, Kalle Anka in Sweden, Aku Ankka in Finland, Pato Donald in Portugal. The stories offered European children a view of typically American suburban bungalows with the mailbox at the garden gate. Thus, in a thousand different ways, from westerns to crime films, from comics to detective stories, Europeans learned how Americans lived (in narrative) well before television. There was no reciprocity. Americans, outside a small circle of cosmopolitans, knew little of Europe, except what their relatives told them about the 'old country' they had left behind.

Politics constantly interfered in the learning process of Europeans. When, in 1938, fascist Italy became overtly anti-American (and pro-Nazi), pressure was put on the publisher Mondadori to stop publishing its version of 'Mickey Mouse'. Mondadori managed to stall by pointing out that 140,000 Italian children would be told that fascism had deprived them of their beloved Topolino. It was eventually agreed – once Italy had declared war on the USA – that all references to Walt Disney would be excised for the duration of the war. Once democracy was restored, Topolino could go on being freely published into the new millennium.

Few Italian comic strips were actually set in Italy. Italian consumers regarded the comic strip, like sci-fi, westerns and crime stories, as quintessentially American, and their adaptations and imitations remained broadly faithful to the spirit of the originals. In so doing they prevented the emergence of a genuinely Italian children's strip. Good designers preferred to dedicate themselves to the adult comic strip, for which, however, there was no substantial market until the 1960s. Its most celebrated exponent, Hugo Pratt, left Italy in the late 1940s and settled in Argentina for several years, returning to Italy in the late 1960s with his 'Corto Maltese' strip.

In France cultural pride and resistance to American culture played a role in providing opportunities for original 'French' work. As we have seen, many of these 'French' designers were in reality Belgian, including the greatest of them, Georges Rémi, the creator of Tintin – whose initials in reverse (RG) form his pseudonym, Hergé. 'Tintin' was born on 21 April 1929 and was originally published in the *Petit vingtième*, the weekly supplement to the right-wing daily *Vingtième siècle*. Only in 1946 was there a separate weekly 'Tintin'.

Tintin is a classic righter of wrongs, unencumbered by family. Though clearly on the side of the forces of Good, he has none of the superhuman qualities of US heroes such as Superman. The great conflict between Good and Evil, common in the American strip, is less pronounced in Europe. Tintin's enemies are dastardly, but they don't want to destroy the world. They traffic in drugs, deal in slaves, counterfeit money and deal in arms. Tintin is himself almost humourless but is surrounded by comic characters such as Captain Haddock, an alcoholic sea captain with an astonishingly wide range of verbal abuse; a dog, Milou (Snowy in the English version), who has human failings; an absent-minded scientist (whose deafness is found irritating); and two totally incompetent policemen, Dupont and Dupond (who look like twins, although the slight difference in the spelling of their surnames – perfectly translated into English as Thompson and Thomson – suggests otherwise). There is, in other words, a tendency not to take oneself too seriously, perhaps a sign of the profound European ambivalence about the status of the genre. Even in the supremely 'nationalist' French strip, 'Astérix', where a corner of Gaul-France is defended against Roman imperialism, the Romans are funny and inefficient, and while Astérix himself, rather like Tintin, is straight and humourless, his sidekick Obélix is there to attract the laughter. The protagonists of the popular European comic strip totally lack in sex appeal. Captain Haddock is an object of desire only for the formidable opera singer Bianca Castafiore, and is frightened by her.

The 'Tintin' strip originally appeared in the weekly children's supplement of the Brussels daily *Vingtième siècle* – a far-right Catholic publication run by Norbert Wallez, a fascistic, anti-Semitic priest who supported Mussolini and Hitler. This may not have been the ideal *milieu* for the birth of a comic strip which would delight people in diverse cultures over the next fifty years or so, but the history of culture often proceeds in mysterious ways. In 1928 Wallez asked Hergé to edit a new supplement for children, *Le Petit vingtième*.[31] The first Tintin strip, *Tintin au pays des Soviets* (1929), was strongly anti-communist, poorly designed and had no discernible plot. However, it systematically used the bubbles so common in American comic strips. Gradually 'Tintin' emancipated itself from its ideological origins, though *Vingtième siècle* remained staunchly right-wing. Tintin's emancipation was also financial.

In 1933 Hergé received an offer he could not refuse from the publisher Casterman – an old Belgian publishing house (founded in 1780), cash rich because it was the sole printer of telephone directories. Casterman undertook to publish Tintin in book format once the serialisation in *Le Petit vingtième* was terminated. Hergé thus acquired another source of income from *Les Cigares du Pharaon*, the first substantial 'Tintin', in which our hero investigates the mysteries of the tomb of the Pharaoh Kih-Oskh. The story introduced a villain who reappeared in later stories, a Levantine businessman with an Italian first name (Roberto) and a Greek surname (Rastapopoulos) . . . and not Jewish at all.

As the years went by the ideological contents of 'Tintin' underwent further changes. The early *Tintin en Amérique* (1931) had a humanitarian attitude towards the Indians – but this would fit in with right-wing populist views. *Le Lotus Bleu* (1934) clearly sided with the Chinese against the Japanese occupation of Manchuria. The villain in *Tintin en Syldavie* (1938 – it became *Le Sceptre d'Ottokar*) is called Müssler, a combination of Hitler and Mussolini (a reference which escaped the notice of the censor during the war). However, in *L'Étoile mystérieuse*, written under German occupation, the villains are Americans and the nefarious capitalist is called Blumenstein (after the war he turned into the less Jewish-sounding Bohlwinkel). But Hergé moved with the times. In the original *Tintin au pays de l'or noir* (1948) there were references to the Jewish terrorists of the Irgun (Finkelstein in the first version, Goldstein in the second) and to the British occupation of Palestine (British officers arrest Tintin). Both allusions were deleted after pressures from 'Tintin's' British publishers Methuen. *Le Temple du Soleil* (1943) shows respect for ancient Inca culture and casts as villains those who treat natives with contempt. *Coke en stock* (1956) includes a denunciation of the modern slave trade, and in the 1976 *Tintin et les picaros* there are allusions to Che Guevara.[32]

Such allusions were lost on most young readers of 'Tintin'. Nevertheless they show a writer who remained actively interested in politics as his original outlook gradually evolved from clerical-fascist to liberal-humanitarian, veering towards pacifist. Had Hergé remained committed to the extreme right his books would not have sold in the millions and been translated into so many languages. In one respect, however, Hergé remained faithful to the ideology of the boys' adventure story: gender. The 'Tintin' stories contain no female characters other than a few minor and outlandish figures of fun such as Bianca Castafiore, a stereotypical Italian *prima donna*, and Peggy

Bazarov, a bossy American matron whose appalling taste in clothes matches her harpy-like behaviour (*Tintin et les picaros*).

As in all best-selling products, much depended on the regularity of the supply, since each new strip advertised all previous ones. 'Tintin' kept going with impressive regularity throughout the 1930s, 1940s and 1950s.

'TINTIN': DATES OF FIRST SERIALISATION	
1929	*Tintin au pays des Soviets*
1930	*Tintin au Congo*
1931	*Tintin en Amérique*
1932	*Les Cigares du Pharaon*
1934	*Le Lotus Bleu*
1935	*L'Oreille cassée*
1937	*L'Ile noire*
1938	*Le Sceptre d'Ottokar*
1939	*Au Pays de l'or noir*
1940	*Le Crabe aux pinces d'or*
1941	*L'Étoile mystérieuse*
1942	*Le Secret de la Licorne* and *Le Trésor de Rackam le Rouge*
1943	*Les Sept boules de cristal* and *Le Temple du Soleil*
1950	*Objectif lune* and *On a Marché sur la lune*
1954	*L'Affaire tournesol*
1956	*Coke en stock*
1958	*Tintin au Tibet*
1961	*Les Bijoux de la Castafiore*
1966	*Vol 714 pour Sydney*
1975	*Tintin et les picaros*

NOTE: Original titles occasionally different

'Tintin' along with its main rival, 'Spirou' (1938, suspended during the hostilities until the liberation of Belgium in 1944) dominated the French-speaking world throughout the 1950s though Spirou, a streetwise kid (there was a Flemish equivalent, 'Robbedoes') never acquired the global renown of Tintin. Spirou was not just a character. It was a magazine created as part of a strategy by the printer-editor Jean Dupuis to extend the appeal of his publications. At first the magazine contained mainly US imports, but after 1947 *Spirou* became increasingly francophone.[33] In fact the success of the Belgian and French in this field is quite outstanding. The *Dictionnaire mondial de la bande dessinée* – admittedly a French publication, with an inevitable bias – discusses 218 French strips and two hundred Belgian ones. The USA ranks third with 174, followed at a distance by Italy (fifty-two) and Great Britain (twenty-eight).[34]

The 'Photonovel'

The Italians invented a new genre: picture stories laid out like comic strips, with bubbles coming out of the mouths of characters, but using photography instead of drawn images. It was called the *fotoromanzo* or photonovel. The analogy between the comic strip and film was carried to its logical conclusion. While an animated film was the animation of a drawn comic strip, thus dispensing with actors, the *fotoromanzo* was a motionless film entirely consti- tuted of 'stills', dispensing with designers and introducing 'actors' who stood motionless. The *fotoromanzi* were almost exclusively devoted to serialised sentimental novels aimed at a female readership. The passage to the *foto- romanzi* was gradual. In June 1946 the Del Duca brothers launched in Milan (Italy's main cultural centre) a magazine called *Grand Hotel* (named after the popular novel by Vicki Baum) which carried sentimental stories for adults in drawn strip format. Its success was such that competitors quickly entered the field: *Bolero Film* by Mondadori and *Sogno* by Rizzoli.[35] A year later it was decided to use photography, which meant that the context of the stories had to be scaled down to 'ordinary' bourgeois homes.[36] One can draw the Taj Mahal, but to build a photo story around it was more expensive.[37] The plots could be lifted from the wide romance literature available: a young woman, about twenty years of age, is in love with a slightly more mature and sexually experienced man. There are the usual obstacles: wars, separ- ations, hostile parents, unfounded suspicions of disloyalty, and rivals. The couple, who remain chaste throughout the story, finally marry. Sometimes famous novels were adapted, such as Thomas Hardy's *Tess of the d'Urbervilles* (in the magazine *Sogno* in 1951) and Tolstoy's *Anna Karenina* in *Grand Hotel* (1957). The actors posing for the pictures were made up to resemble glamor- ous Hollywood stars – the Rita Hayworth look was particularly popular.[38]

Grand Hotel sold almost a million copies a week for some thirty years, making it by far the best-selling purveyor of fiction in Italy. *Sogno* and *Bolero* together sold 600,000 copies.[39] Some of the 'actors' they employed eventually became famous as real actors: Vittorio Gassman, Sophia Loren and Sandra Milo. The genre was exported to Scandinavia, Latin America, Turkey and France – one of the very few genres of popular culture that Italy exported. To call it a genre is, of course, a misnomer. The plots were those already developed in women's romances. What was new was the format. The photographs eliminated the need for description. The pictures spoke for themselves. All that was left to insert was the dialogue. It was like bringing home the stories and images popularised by the cinema and having a private view. The level of literacy required was similar to that required for comic strips. The *fotoromanzo* popularised a simplified form of reading for a public – prevalently working women but also many men, between 25 and 35 per cent of the total readership, according to some estimates – who had recently joined the ranks of the literate.[40] In more literate France too, however, the genre was enormously popular with both men and women. Eventually the growth of literacy, of television and of the cheap paperback reduced the diffusion of the *fotoromanzo*.

Conclusion

Television dealt a major blow to the market for children's comics, not just because children could watch television instead of reading comics, but because the market for animated films expanded tremendously. Comic books were transformed into animated shorts made for television. As children deserted comics, adults discovered them. The comic strip evolved artistically and socially, appealing to the literate. Once again the Americans were the pioneers. Jules Feiffer used his eponymous strip (1956) to comment on current affairs, as did Garry Trudeau in his 'Doonesbury' strip (1970–). While Marvel Comics 'invented' new righters of wrongs with superhuman powers (the Human Torch, Spiderman) or *Doppelgänger* characters such as the Incredible Hulk (1962), about a scientist accidentally exposed to radiation who turns into a green monster when he gets angry, 'underground' cartoonists such as Robert Crumb subverted the genre by using characters such as Fritz the Cat and scatological and obscene humour. The more 'artistic' comic books used the term 'graphic novel' (the pioneers date back to the 1920s, with the Belgian-born Frans Masereel's *Passionate Journey*), targeting the more prestigious end of the market: the artwork was produced with great care, as was the text. These were not meant to be read in a hurry, but to be absorbed slowly. Some graphic books dealt with major issues, such as the Holocaust: *Maus: A Survivor's Tale* (1986) by Art Spiegelman (winner of the Pulitzer Prize).

The comic strip became global. In the Arab world it expanded substantially only in the 1970s, modelled on American comics and the more sophisticated European ones such as the Italian and, especially in Algeria, the French.[41] As children switched to television cartoons, sex became a feature of an increasing number of comics. By the early 1960s they occupied centre stage, with the British 'Modesty Blaise' (1962), designed by Jim Holdaway, 'Tiffany Jones' (designed by two women, Pat Tourret and Jenny Butterworth), 'Varoomshka', mixing sex and politics in the left-of-centre *Guardian* (1969), and the tongue-in-cheek feminist women of the French Claire Brétécher. The Italians went one step further, encouraged by the fact that by the 1960s adults had probably become the main consumers of the genre. They developed erotic comic-strip characters such as the 'Valentina' stories by Guido Crepax (beginning in 1966), who also adapted famous erotic novels such as *Histoire d'O* and *Justine* in the 1970s, while Milo Manara experimented with the clearly pornographic in the 1980s. The Italians also produced a steady stream of horror and crime comics – which would have caused a scandal only ten years previously – with characters such as Kriminal, Demoniak, Fantax, Mister X, Tetrus, Spettrus (the living brain of a mad scientist), Sadik (an evil spirit that enters the bodies of the living) and Diabolik (1962), the most successful of them all, designed by two sisters, Angela and Luciana Giussani. Diabolik, clearly inspired by Fantômas (see pages 680–3), is a superior criminal and a master of disguise who lives in luxury, and is always faithful to his girlfriend, the very beautiful Eva Kant (an obvious high-culture reference to the philosopher Immanuel Kant).

For the first time in colour comics openly sold, there was plenty of blood. The Italians went further, developing the erotic-sadistic sub-genre with 'Messalina', 'Jungla' and 'Auranella'. In a notorious strip in *Action* (14 February 1976), the British agent Dredger introduces a hand grenade into the mouth of an Arab to force him to speak. By the 1970s Dan Dare was no longer a courteous gentleman but a violent thug.[42]

Soft-porn comics such Crepax's 'Valentina' were aimed at the relatively educated, the high standard of the graphics providing an artistic justification for the purchase. Characters in Crepax stories are occasionally shown reading books by recognisable authors: Adorno, Bellow, Moravia and Faulkner.[43]

Hugo Pratt's cult *La Ballata del mare salato* (1967) has characters reading Melville, Coleridge, Rilke, Euripides and Shelley.[44]

The largest producer of comics in the world now is Japan. *Manga* – as it is called in Japan – emerged as a major literary form in the 1990s. In 1998 the number of copies sold was estimated as over 4.6 million per day, 25 per cent of all publication in Japan.[45] As in Japanese animated films, most of the characters have Caucasian features and most of the female characters look like Barbie dolls.[46] The globalisation of the American comic strip had reached its pinnacle. As in other cultural forms, the periphery strikes back. It absorbs the original form and regurgitates it, somewhat transformed, into the wider world. No position of supremacy is ever held for long.

❦

53

Live Spectacles

A Running Show: The Crisis of the Theatre

ACTING – PRETENDING TO BE SOMEONE ELSE, in the flesh, on a stage, facing 'real' people, declaiming lines – is, along with singing, the oldest profession in the cultural industry. The English theatre director Peter Brook, in 1968, wrote that all that is needed for an act of theatre is a man walking across an empty space while someone else watches him.[1] From the point of view of this book, what is needed is for the person who does the watching to pay the person who does the walking.

How could this economic relationship possibly survive the arrival of the cinema? How could it defy the broadcasting of words and sound? Yet live spectacles, whether theatrical performances, concerts, public singing or modest shows with 'girls' and stand-up comedians, continued to thrive well after the arrival of television. Contrary to pessimistic forecasts, the theatre lived on. Demand continued to expand as prosperity and leisure time increased. Since saturation had not yet been achieved, the cinema or radio, and later television, did not subtract audiences from the theatre.

In the interwar years the British were the keenest cinema-goers in Europe. Yet London's sixty-one theatres put on, during the 1930s, some 4,256 productions. A diminution in the 1950s in the number of people going to the cinema coincided with a diminution in the number of London theatres (down to fifty-two) and the number of productions (down to 3,117).[2]

Of course there was alarm. Élites lamented that 'people' no longer went to the theatre; or, if they went, that the theatre attracted the 'wrong' sort of people (i.e. the lower-middle classes), and consequently, was itself becoming increasingly coarse and vulgar; or that, conversely, the theatre was still the preserve of moneyed élites and had failed to attract less prosperous groups.

The remedies advocated were always the same: if the theatre appealed only to the bourgeoisie, then it should provide working-class stories with which ordinary people could identify. But perhaps people were attracted to the theatre, but it was far from home, started late and ended even later, and ordinary working people had to get up early to go to work. Or it was just too expensive. So it was suggested that the theatre should start earlier and finish in time for the audience to catch a train home. Subsidies could be introduced, but for which plays? Obviously not cheap farces, bedroom melo-dramas, coarse comic acts. These were commercial enough. What should be subsidised was the great theatre of the past: Shakespeare, Racine, Molière and Schiller – the kind of theatre the intellectuals debating the crisis of the theatre favoured.

No solution could ever be found as long as the 'crisis' was entirely seen as one 'of the theatre', rather than the much wider question of access to culture. The enjoyment of high culture was not 'natural' among the classes deprived of it. They had to be taught. Formal education played a role, but was this enough? Here a key role was played by the new broadcasting media. This was understood by modern organisers of the new media such as John Reith at the BBC and the Popular Front government in France in 1936, when plays performed at the Comédie-Française and concerts by subsidised Paris orchestras began to be regularly broadcast on the radio at weekends.[3]

Whether the working class constituted the main audience for broadcast plays is another question, but then workers began to be able to enjoy them-selves only in the 1920s and 1930s, and only in the richer countries. In Britain, for instance, they went dancing to big bands, or to gramophone music in youth clubs; they went cycling and hiking; they read cheap paperbacks (seven million copies a year sold); they borrowed more from the expanded public library system; they listened to the radio (by 1939 there were nine million radio receivers); they went to chapel bible classes (especially in Wales); they played in and listened to brass bands; they joined choral societies and garden-ing clubs; and they played football, cricket, darts, dominoes and lawn bowls.[4] There were, of course, popular spectacles where stand-up comedians and orchestras would entertain an audience attracted by feature films as part of the show. The function of the orchestra was also to provide the musical accompaniment to the films, which were increasingly regarded as the main attraction. The arrival of sound eliminated many of these orchestras and their modest shows (though in Italy they survived until the 1950s).

Puppet shows remained popular, particularly for children. In eastern

Europe and the Balkans they were a serious art form, and in cities such as Zagreb, Belgrade and Ljubljana there were state theatres for puppets. In Paris, at the Jardin d'Acclimatation in the Bois de Boulogne, there were regular puppet shows which delighted children throughout the 1950s and beyond.

The theatre, however, remained a bastion of middle-class taste. In Great Britain the interwar years produced well-made plays by masters of the craft such as Terence Rattigan and Noël Coward, both more subversive than their critics at the time realised, but nonetheless loved by the middle classes who were at the centre of their work. This was theatre of the middle classes, by the middle classes, about the middle classes, for the middle classes. A more audacious British theatre developed after the 1950s, above all with the works of John Osborne and Harold Pinter (Nobel Prize 2005), one of the central figures of world theatre in the twentieth century. France contributed not only the traditional commercial 'boulevard theatre', usually set in Parisian drawing rooms and obsessed with the theme of adultery, but also Jean Cocteau, Marcel Pagnol and, after the war, Jean Anouilh. The USA made its mark with Eugene O'Neill and, after the war with Tennessee Williams and Arthur Miller. More disturbing drama appeared in other countries, from Pirandello's modernist plays in Italy to Bertolt Brecht's epic theatre.

A not inconsiderable part of the serious theatre of the twentieth century presented itself as a revisitation of that of the Greeks: Hugo von Hofmannsthal's *Elektra* (1903), O'Neill's *Mourning Becomes Electra* (1931), Cocteau's *La Machine infernale* (1934, based on *Oedipus*), Jean Giraudoux's *La Guerre de Troie n'aura pas lieu* (1935), T.S. Eliot's *Family Reunion* (1939) and Sartre's *Les Mouches* (1943) – both based on the *Oresteia* – and Anouilh's *Antigone* (1942).[5]

The seeming impossibility of turning the theatre into a mass business, as was being done with more reproducible cultural artefacts such as records, films and books, was increasingly deplored by progressives and populists, communists and fascists. They tried to break down the barriers between the theatre and the people, and occasionally they succeeded. Much of this chapter will be devoted to a survey of such efforts.

Down with Bourgeois Theatre!

The problem can be put simply: the 'bourgeois' theatre consisted of 'well-made plays' (the *pièce bien faite* – a positive attribution in the nineteenth century). Their purpose was to provide relaxation and amusement; they put style before innovation.[6] They were plot-driven and followed a formula as rigid as the ancient Aristotelian unities: the play would open with an exposition of the situation, would then focus on the problem, or knot (*nœud*), of the plot, and conclude with the *dénouement* – the untying of the knot. A series of climaxes would provide suspense, thus avoiding any risk of tedium.

The reaction to the well-made bourgeois play consisted of devising theatrical forms which subverted it by by attempting to produce a 'working-class' theatre centred around the preoccupations of socialist activists; or introducing ever stronger elements of naturalism, *à la* Zola; or doing away with the linear plot. Since theatre revolutionaries and reformists all loved the theatre, the main issue on which they could all agree was the necessity of expanding audiences.

Why attracting the lower classes to the theatre was a Good Thing was never clearly established, though the answer can easily be guessed. Theatre-lovers, like other culture-lovers, thought the theatre could be an instrument of human redemption, that those coming out of the theatre after watching a play by Shakespeare or listening to one of Beethoven's symphonies would find themselves improved in some unfathomable way; that culture and the arts could be tools for the solution of social problems. Clearly the issue was not how to attract 'new' social groups to the theatre in general, but to the kind of theatre approved of by the élites. Once in touch with the culture of the élites, the lower classes would be more genteel, and more like the élites. To maintain their distinctive position, these, presumably, would need to move on towards new cultural redoubts still untouched by the lower orders.

There was a self-serving element in all this. Culturally prestigious theatre was uneconomic, and subsidies, in the age of the triumph of democracy and capitalism, could only be justified by appealing to the interests of the whole of society – which was difficult to do if audiences were tiny and unrepresentative. The strategy of expanding the audience was complicated by the fact that much innovative theatre was even less approachable than conventional bourgeois theatre. The 'revolutionaries' often concentrated on form rather than content, insisting on the importance of scenery, or staging, or music, or acting, or reasserting the importance of the text, as Jacques Copeau (founder in 1913 of the Théâtre du Vieux-Colombier in Paris) did with his poetic and stylised productions.

The real innovators were not in France or Great Britain (where theatre, as a commercial enterprise, did thrive), but in Germany – above all Max Reinhardt (see page 747), already influential before the First World War, who continued to dominate in both Germany and Austria until he was forced to leave Vienna in 1938. The 1920s, of course, were far from the most propitious time for the German theatre, since the inflationary crisis of the early part of the decade had in effect wiped out both state subsidies to the old *Hoftheater* and audiences. But unemployment among the acting profession meant that it was easier to stage crowd scenes. Reinhardt took full advantage of this ample supply of labour, staging plays requiring large casts. His *Massenregie* (mass production) reached its pinnacle in a staging of Schiller's *Die Räuber* in 1921, when eight hundred actors were used. In Romain Rolland's *Danton*, Reinhardt, who staged it in 1919, had actors sit in the audience and shout lines of the play, thus inviting the audience to identify with the revolutionary crowds. Scenery remained expensive, but the abstract sets favoured by the expressionist theatre (inspired by the cinema) were cheaper than conventional ones. The film industry indirectly subsidised the theatre because it provided a source of income for actors (as television would do later), who could spend part of the day filming, and then perform at the theatre in the evening.[7]

Expressionism reduced the importance of traditional acting with its nineteenth-century declamatory style, and celebrated the importance of staging – one of the reasons it was popular with directors. Erwin Piscator, the director of the Proletarisches Theater in Berlin in the 1920s, exploited the cinema by using, alongside his expensive multiple stage levels, projected filmed scenes during plays. Brecht's Munich production of his version of *Edward II* (after Marlowe's play) had titles preceding scenes, and his Berlin production of *The Threepenny Opera* (1928) had the titles of the songs projected on a screen while they were being sung.

The problem with the anti-bourgeois theatre was that there were not many good anti-bourgeois plays, hence the constant resort to new stagings of classics or frequent productions of major contemporary plays such as those by Wilde, Maeterlink, Hofmannsthal and Pirandello. Between 1913 and 1915 there were, in Germany alone, 1,035 performances of twenty-four of Strindberg's plays – championed by Max Reinhardt.[8] The more serious problem with the working-class theatre was that it failed to attract the working classes. Piscator's Proletarisches Theater was kept afloat by rich benefactors. The first-night audience at the Theater am Nollendorfplatz for his production of Ernst Toller's expressionist *Hoppla, wir leben!* (Hoppla, Such is Life!, 1927) was socially very mixed thanks to exceptionally low ticket prices and good marketing. It was also very theatrical, using music, dance and film, and it borrowed heavily from working-class genres such as the music hall and the cabaret. But it was not popular.[9]

Piscator had a point when he wrote in *Das Politische Theater* (The Political Theatre, 1929) that, apart from the revolving stage and electricity, the theatre had changed little since Shakespeare: 'a rectangular opening, an optical box through which the spectator might cast a "forbidden glance" into a strange world . . . For three centuries a glass wall divided the stage from the audience.'[10] The theatre depended on the false idea that there was no audience present. The cinema had contributed to jolting the theatre from its complacency. Brecht learned Piscator's lessons. There was no point asking the audience to lose themselves in the play, as if they were part of it. This might occur in the darkness of the dream palaces, where one could gaze directly into the eyes of the stars, but it could not take place in the theatre. Brecht, who understood this, developed a style of theatre whose influence could still be felt at the end of the twentieth century.

Brecht was a communist, as was Piscator, but communist parties remained suspicious of the 'proletarian theatre' after the heady years immediately following the October Revolution. The communist paper *Rote Fahne* (Red Flag) took a high-minded stance on 17 October 1920, saying that the proletariat needed not propaganda but art, whether it was bourgeois or not.[11] Of course, initially the Soviet theatre was far more innovative than that in most European countries, with the exception of Germany. It was also far more open than elsewhere. While in 1920 only 10 per cent of plays performed in Paris were foreign, in Moscow the Kamerny Theatre offered a wide range of foreign authors, from Synge to Goldoni, Labiche, Hoffman, Claudel, Shaw and O'Neill.[12]

But the Kamerny was a small theatre (*kamerny* means 'chamber'). The solution to the problem of popular access could be solved, or so it was felt, by staging monumental open-air spectacles with thousands of performers and spectators, breaking the distinction between audience and actors – like some of the medieval mystery plays. The subjects chosen were events connected to the Revolution (as the mystery plays were all connected to the life and death of Jesus). Thus Meyerhold's staging of Mayakovsky's *Mystery Buff* in

1918 took place on the first anniversary of the Revolution, with the square of the Winter Palace as its stage. On 1 May 1920 *The Mystery of Freed Labour*, directed by Yuri Annenkov and Alexander Kugel, staged next to the former stock exchange in St Petersburg with a cast of a thousand and 35,000 spectators, showed the unfolding of the popular struggles leading to the Bolshevik seizure of power.[13] Among the influences behind this kind of theatre were Romain Rolland's *The People's Theatre* (translated into Russian in 1910) and the revival of the pageant theatre in Great Britain and the USA (such as the St Louis Pageant of 1914). Though Russian mass spectacles were discontinued after the civil war, mass scenes remained popular throughout the 1920s, and influenced films such as Eisenstein's *Strike* and *Potemkin*.[14]

There is nothing necessarily anti-bourgeois in mass staging (though the content usually was), or in staging works in historically relevant contexts. After all, T.S. Eliot wrote *Murder in the Cathedral* (1935) specifically for a pageant at Canterbury Cathedral, and Hofmannsthal based his *Jedermann* (1911) on the English morality play *Everyman*, for ritual performance before the cathedral doors in Salzburg – where it is performed every year.[15] The most famous integration between audiences and actors in western Europe has taken place every ten years since 1680 in the Bavarian village of Oberammergau, where a passion play with anti-Semitic undertones is performed by the villagers in gratitude for deliverance from the plague. Almost half of the 5,000 inhabitants are involved, and it has been a major tourist attraction since the nineteenth century, when Thomas Cook organised visits by English and American travellers.[16]

By the end of the 1930s virtually all Soviet experimentation was dead, though directors such as Nikolai Okhlopkov developed innovations such as 'theatre in the round' (where the audience surrounds the stage). Theatrical life improved a little during the war, but by 1953 the censorship was such that the Soviet theatre was in deep crisis, and people, especially young people, stayed away in droves, while many dramatists were afraid to write for it, though there was never a return to the particularly harsh repression of the Stalin period.[17]

By the 1950s there was no single censor but a somewhat nebulous network of review committees and advisers whose individual decisions constituted a powerful web of constraints. In each theatre there was a Literary Director, responsible for finding suitable scripts. An artistic committee comprised of actors, technical staff, directors and outside advisers would give the final approval, within guidelines: some productions had to deal with contemporary Soviet life, others had to be non-Russian (giving preference to plays from other socialist countries), others had to be classic, and so on. On the positive side, since commercial considerations did not rank high, there was little pressure to keep rehearsal time short.[18] By then, of course, the anti-bourgeois theatre had become the prerogative of relatively small groups of élite intellectuals – just as in the West.

The Fascist Theatre

Prose theatre, unlike opera, was not highly regarded in twentieth-century Italy. The lack of major nineteenth-century Italian playwrights and of great classics to rank alongside Shakespeare, Molière, Racine, Goethe and Schiller led many intellectuals, from Giacomo Leopardi to Benedetto Croce, to regard the theatre as an inferior form of art. Pietro Gobetti, Gramsci's liberal contemporary, made equally disparaging comments about the theatre – its importance, he said, was vastly overestimated.[19]

Mussolini, however, like the communists in the USSR and most educators everywhere, wanted to promote a popular theatre, a 'theatre for the masses'. The fascists devised, after 1929, institutions such as I Carri di Tespi, a circus-like itinerant troupe whose task it was to perform plays in remote or small cities excluded from the circuit of the major theatrical companies. Then they invented the so-called Sabato Teatrale (Saturday Theatre), with subsidised amateur companies, as well as a national drama competition (the 'Littoriali'). But all this represented only a small proportion of the theatrical activity of the country. In most theatres frequented by the bourgeoisie, the kind of plays performed were those which would have been performed even if Mussolini had never taken power. Respectable bourgeois families enjoyed the usual romantic comedies and farces, just like their counterparts elsewhere; plays like the famous comedy by Aldo De Benedetti, *Due Dozzine di rose scarlatte* (1936), translated into thirty languages, and others like it such as Guido Cantini's *Passeggiata col diavolo* (1937), Cesare Giulio Viola's *L'Inferno* (1937) and Gherardo Gherardi's *Questi ragazzi* (1934).[20]

Few plays were fascist just as in the USSR few plays were communist.[21] One of the few instances of fascist theatre, *Redenzione* (Redemption) by Roberto Farinacci (first performed in Milan on 12 December 1927, it was adapted for the cinema in 1943 by Marcello Albani), was as didactic as any Soviet realist play. The hero is a socialist who 'repents'. Mortally injured after a heroic deed, his last words express his desire to join the Fascist Party.[22] Some, like Alessandro Blasetti, a distinguished film-maker, tried to do a little better than this. Inspired by the Soviet re-enactment of the storming of the Winter Palace, he decided to re-enact the Battle of the Piave in Florence's Le Cascine (a park) with a play called *18BL*, after a military truck which appears at three crucial moments in Italian history: the First World War, the march on Rome (which brought Mussolini to power) and the draining of the Pontine Marshes. The fiasco was palpable, since the audience did not understand what was going on, the critics were critical, and the authorities abandoned further plans for a theatre for the masses.[23] A similar genre of open-air theatre with thousands of participants was attempted in Franco's Spain shortly after the end of the Civil War, with similarly disappointing results.[24]

The Italian Ministry of Popular Culture tried to obtain good scripts of 'fascist' plays. Thousands of hopefuls sent them in. Almost all were too bad to be performed, and even fewer could be deemed 'fascist', since it was rare to find in any of them an overt endorsement of the Duce or the Blackshirts, or a celebration of the domestic role of women.[25]

The main predicament of the Italian theatre during fascism was not connected to the authoritarianism of the regime. Other countries faced similar crises, and some, for national and nationalistic reasons, tried to promote the theatre through public subsidy and the constitution of a 'national theatre' along the pattern of institutions such as the Comédie-Française – as was the case in Greece, Czechoslovakia, Poland and Yugoslavia.[26] Even in the USA the free-market approach was tempered by Roosevelt's Federal Theatre Project, which pumped money into the performing arts. The Italian crisis was compounded by falling audiences, the lack of funding for the numerous unprofitable theatres and, above all, the slow death of the figure of the *capocomico*, the actor heading the touring company on which the Italian theatre was based (see page 744).[27] The kind of director's theatre which was emerging in other European countries could not co-exist easily with the *capocomico*, often the head of a family business who had inherited the job from his father. To be an actor one had to join a company and then hope that one's talents would be recognised, since until 1935, when the Accademia d'Arte Drammatica was set up, there was not even a major drama school in Italy.

It was not in the interests of itinerant companies to spend any money on sets or production. The trick of the game consisted of maximising the audiences for a few nights by giving them the same old fare, and then moving on. All the innovations of the European theatre, from Antoine to Copeau, from Reinhardt to Piscator, from Stanislavsky to Meyerhold completely bypassed the Italian theatre until Giorgio Strehler (1921–97) founded, with Paolo Grassi, the Piccolo Teatro in Milan in 1947. The foreign influences were manifest: it was publicly funded, was modelled after Jean Vilar's Théâtre National Populaire, and introduced Brecht to the Italian theatre.[28] Playwrights popular at the turn of the century, for instance Paolo Ferrari and Giuseppe Giacosa (who adapted for Puccini *La Bohème* from Murger's novel and *Tosca* from Sardou's play), still popular in the 1920s, had taken as a model the French theatre of Sardou, Alexandre Dumas *fils* and Augier.[29]

In the 1920s the traditional touring companies were being throttled by an increasingly competitive environment: there were seventy-eight companies, of which eleven performed in dialect and thirty-nine specialised in light opera. There was still a vast number of theatres, most of them unprofitable: official statistics established that in 1923 there were twenty-three major theatres, 213 'second category' and 1,244 'third' (mainly small theatres for amateur productions, increasingly converted into cinemas), and almost all in the centre and the north of the country:

	IN LOMBARDY, PIEDMONT, VENETO, TUSCANY AND EMILIA	IN THE WHOLE OF ITALY
Opera houses	8	14
Theatres	273	403
Theatres/cinemas	263	363
Cinemas (mainly)	670	1,055
Not in use	49	96

SOURCE: ISTAT *Annuario Statistico Italiano 1939*, Vol. VI, p.85

While audiences for the cinema grew exponentially, those for live performances decreased:

LIVE PERFORMANCES AND CINEMA
(REVENUE IN MILLIONS OF LIRE)

	1924	1935
Prose theatre	58	31
Operetta	22	6
Opera	50	23
Cinema	150	329

SOURCE: Pedullà, 'Il Teatro italiano tra le due
guerre mondiali', in Soldani and Turi (eds), Fare
gli italiani, p.330, on the basis of SIAE figures

Opera, as a high genre, could still rely on public subsidies. Operetta, being a middle genre, was doomed, and resurfaced only as part of variety shows. As for the prose theatre, the crisis was evident. The touring companies were faced with constantly rising costs: salaries, copyrights, transport and the high percentage (usually 35–40 per cent) they had to give the owners of the theatres.[30] The difficulties faced by the *capocomico* since the end of the nineteenth century had opened up a space for theatrical managers or impresarios. In Milan the impresario Luigi Zerboni modernised the Teatro Olympia and transformed it into one of the most lucrative theatres of the city. With his partner Emilio Suvini he also developed the Kursaal Diana, also in Milan, as a large complex which offered variety shows, light opera, plays, restaurants, a swimming pool, a dancing ring, and even a bowling alley. At the same time they bought theatres in many other cities of the north and centre of the country, and diversified into cinema exhibition and sport, buying shares in the San Remo casino and setting up a recording company.[31] Producing plays had become a small part of the business of the company.

A major playwright had actually emerged in fascist Italy: Luigi Pirandello (1867–1936). The regime liked him – though no overt political message was present in his texts, certainly nothing pro-fascist – and he liked the honours showered upon him. Though respected, he was not particularly popular. The Italian public much preferred the well-made plays imported from France (such as those of Sacha Guitry), or even from Hungary (Ferenc Molnár), and vaudevilles and farces. Audiences, largely aristocratic and bourgeois, treated the theatre as they had treated the opera in the eighteenth century. There was loud heckling, coarse comments, long applause when the *capocomico* entered the stage (a habit still extant in the 1970s, particularly in the provinces).

Such behaviour was regarded with contempt by the intellectual elites, who lamented, as they always did, the provincialism of Italians. The leading theatre critic of the fascist period, Silvio D'Amico, complained that audiences went to see actors rather than plays, and would see a classic only if their favourite actress was in it. The futurist writer Filippo Marinetti showed similar contempt for the taste of Italian audiences: theatre-going was an excuse for parading in fine clothes and enjoying the vanity of being in an expensive place.[32]

What everyone realised, including the more intelligent fascists such as Giuseppe Bottai (Minister of Education 1936–43), was that plays of some cultural prestige, unlike the commercial theatre, required a subsidy; since these were precisely the plays which might contain some criticism of the regime, it followed that the authorities were required to fund (and hence have considerable influence over) what could, at least potentially, be of some threat. Subsidies came with strings attached: companies had to stage far more Italian plays than foreign ones, provide performances of 'high' cultural value, and use young actors who were professionally registered (a way of controlling the influx into the profession).[33] Which all goes to show that the best form of control is not necessarily through direct censorship of texts.

Eventually the authorities suggested which plays were more likely to receive subsidies, which designers and actors should be employed and how much they should be paid, where plays should be performed and even which costumes should be worn.[34] The consequence of all this was a systematic lobbying by everyone involved in the theatre to obtain favours and jobs. Of course the Italian theatre had to contend with censorship, but compared with Nazi Germany and Soviet Russia in the 1930s, fascist censorship was a mild affair. Most drama had little to do with politics, and fascism was only worried about overt anti-fascism. Otherwise censorship dealt with public order and morality. The censorship principles fascism added to those inherited from the previous regime included many which existed in democratic countries too: crime must not be seen to pay; class hatred must not be preached; there should be no offence to the King, the Pope, the Duce, his Ministers or the sovereigns and rulers of foreign countries; nothing should hurt national feelings, or attack institutions such as the army or the family. In theory almost everything could be censored. In practice much depended on the mood of the moment, the popularity of the play, the intransigence or otherwise of the local authorities (in 1929 performance anywhere in Italy was allowed if permission had been obtained in any one place). This cumbersome system was difficult to police.[35] Often the authorities intervened only after private complaints. Thus Catholic groups complained that the dancers in the variety shows of a Viennese touring company performing in Milan wore skimpy costumes. Josephine Baker was not allowed to tour in 1930, but countervailing pressure enabled her to triumph in 1932. This triumph was too great, because the authorities informed the Prefect of Milan that 'Giuseppina' Baker would not be allowed to perform again.[36]

Censorship became much more severe after the invasion of Ethiopia in 1935 and the declaration of sanctions against Italy by the League of Nations. In November of that year a decree ordered the elimination from the repertoire of theatre companies of the works of authors from countries that supported sanctions, with the exception of Shakespeare and George Bernard Shaw. Shakespeare could not be eliminated because of his universalism (and the fact that so many of his works were set in Italy), and Shaw because he had expressed his support for Mussolini. French works were to be examined separately (and more leniently), 'as a homage of the attitude shown by the great majority of French intellectuals towards Italy'.[37] Respect for the Church following the pact with the Vatican (1929) meant that Machiavelli's play *La Mandragola* was banned and the staging of suicide prohibited, which meant that many famous tragedies had their endings rewritten.

The fascists had no clear strategy regarding culture and artistic production, partly because they cared little for it, assuming – rightly – that the real mass entertainment was the cinema. Then they promoted funding institutions which soon became vehicles for patronage and corruption. In 1928 the Minister of Education tried to promote performances of works (prose and music) by Italians rather than foreigners, establishing a 50 per cent quota. This attempt to favour Italian writers and composers had started before fascism and was, as the figures below suggest, decreasingly successful as fascism became more entrenched:

	PERFORMANCES OF ITALIAN WORKS	PERFORMANCES OF FOREIGN WORKS
1927	4,778	5,439
1928	3,758	5,190
1929	4,555	5,770
1930	3,569	5,459
1931	2,859	4,068

SOURCE: Scarpellini, *Organizzazione teatrale e politica del teatro nell'Italia fascista*, p.70

Almost half of the foreign performances in 1931 were by French authors; the British followed with 825, then Germany with 590, Hungary with 391, the USA with 267, and Russia with 181.[38]

One of the main problems was that there were not enough Italian plays, in spite of various inducements and prizes. When it came to opera, however, there was a vast repertoire, and fascist interventionism was muted, though there was a revival of the works of Donizetti and Bellini, and of Rossini's serious operas. The league of the most-performed works by dead composers would not have been any different had fascism never ruled Italy:

MOST-PERFORMED OPERATIC COMPOSERS, 1935–36 TO 1942–43	
Verdi	105
Puccini	87
Donizetti	34
Rossini	27
Bellini	12
Boito	9
Catalani	7
Leoncavallo	6
Monteverdi	6
Ponchielli	6

SOURCE: Nicolodi, *Musica e musicisti nel ventennio fascista*, p.25

Nor was fascism xenophobic when it came to opera, since presumably there was no point in offending the opera-going public, whose 'natural' preferences were for Italian composers. Still, there were productions of operas by Richard Strauss and Igor Stravinsky, as well as Wagner of course, Mozart, Massenet and Bizet. However, when the League of Nations approved sanctions against Italy following its invasion of Ethiopia, a ministerial circular imposed similar restrictions to those operating in the theatre. Borodin and Rimsky Korsakov paid the price. The British had nothing to fear, since there were no British operas. The French were a problem, since everyone liked Bizet, so it was decided that performances of French opera should be decreased. Luckily for music-lovers (though for hardly anyone else), Nazi Germany and fascist Italy were friendly, which meant that Richard Strauss and Wagner could be heard.

Even what the Nazis regarded as 'degenerate' music, such as Berg's *Wozzeck*, was still performed, but not, after 1938, works by Jewish composers such as Meyerbeer and Offenbach.[39]

The defeat of fascism did not signal a renewal of the Italian theatre. The commercial theatre never recovered from the post-war boom of the cinema. In the 1950s, on Sundays, Italian cinemas were full; in many instances there was standing room only. In Milan alone there were 130 cinemas, plus another hundred screens in churches. Many of the top box-office successes were low-level Italian films such as *Tormento*, *Totò sceicco*, *Il Caimano del Piave* and *47 Morto che parla*. Ten years later the quality had much improved, thanks to *Il Sorpasso*, *Il Gattopardo* and Fellini's *8½*, which was ranked eleventh.[40]

The Italian theatre, however, remained a tiny preserve of largely foreign plays, with the exception of works by Dario Fò (1926–, Nobel Prize-winner 1997) and Edoardo De Filippo (1900–84), who, being actor-writers, were in the tradition of the *capocomico*. Both were ostracised for much of their careers by the political establishment.

MOST SUCCESSFUL THEATRE PRODUCTIONS IN ITALY IN 1959, IN TERMS OF SEATS SOLD

		Days	Seats sold
Requiem for a Nun	William Faulkner (Albert Camus adaptation)	77	58,898
La Pappa reale (La Bonne soupe)	Félicien Marceau	104	58,740
Ghosts	Henrik Ibsen	81	58,550
Gli Arcangeli non giocano a flipper (Archangels Don't Play Pinball)	Dario Fò	119	52,124
A View from the Bridge	Arthur Miller	68	51,067
La Locandiera	Carlo Goldoni	51	50,338
D'Amore si muore	Giuseppe Patroni Griffi	77	48,508
The Merry Wives of Windsor	Shakespeare	86	48,101
Saturday, Sunday, Monday	Edoardo De Filippo	65	32,258
Madame Sans-Gêne	Victorien Sardou	78	30,592

SOURCE: *Lo Spettacolo*, Vol 10, No. 3, July–September 1960, p.185

These box-office successes would be included in most critics' lists of 'serious theatre' (with the exception of Patroni Griffi's light comedy *D'Amore si muore*). The next forty works in the list would pass a similar test, as they include Pirandello, Balzac, Brecht, *A Midsummer Night's Dream*, Chekhov and Eugene O'Neill. But the list also reveals how tiny the market was: the top ten works played to an average audience of six hundred people in 1959, the year in which Italy was at the peak of the most sustained period of economic growth in its history.

54

The Triumph of the Song

Popular Music

BY THE LATE 1920S three distinct yet related innovations had each contributed to the transformation of music. The radio, available in an increasing number of homes, was most of the time little more than a system for relaying music, above all songs. The development of the recording industry, the mass acquisition of electric record-playing equipment (with enhanced sound quality) and of records, ensured that the possibility of playing one's favourite music again and again in the comfort of one's home was now available to the middle classes and an increased proportion of the working classes. The chief characteristic of the record – only relatively short musical passages could be recorded on the standard discs of the time – meant that most of the music people bought was songs. Finally the advent of the 'talkies' transformed films. From now on not only the human voice and the musical accompaniment, sound effects, etc. could be heard, but also the songs of films. Such songs benefited from unparalleled advance publicity.

As some forty million or so Americans went to the cinema at least once a week in the 1930s, any song inserted in a film would be heard by a vast number of potential music-buyers. Famous singers could have their songs relayed in films, broadcast by hundreds of radio stations, and sold as records. They could still perform live, their fame, and hence their fees, vastly enhanced by the new media. The spread of dance halls, nightclubs and other venues further accelerated the enormous popularity of what, only now, could legitimately be called 'popular music'. This was a genre, in true American style, which was not identified with a particular class, except perhaps a generic 'middle class'. A similar development was taking place in Europe.

The overwhelming majority of songs had a romantic theme. Political songs were seldom popular, except in exceptional circumstances, such as the First World War, the songs from which remained famous for decades, or connected to a particular patriotic event – for instance, in Italy, the conquest of Ethiopia, which made 'Faccetta nera' (Little Black Face) popular until the downfall of fascism. Italian songs of the Resistance were often based on old tunes or previous revolutionary songs ('Sbarcarà gli inglesi' was originally 'Stornelli dell'esilio', and the famous 'Fischia il vento' is from a Russian folk song, 'Katiusha'[1]). The most popular song of the Second World War, 'Lili Marlene', is about a soldier who goes back to the front remembering the embrace of a prostitute. It was composed by the classically trained Norbert Schultze (1911–2002) in 1938, to the words of a poem by Hans Leip, written in 1915 when Leip was serving in the German army on the western front. Lale Andersen recorded it in 1939. The song became a success only after it was broadcast on German radio from Belgrade. In Italy it was recorded by Gianna Pederzini. It was translated into French by Henri Lemarchand and recorded in 1942 by the most glamorous Parisian cabaret singer of the time, Suzy Solidor. Then the song moved to Britain, where it was recorded by Anne Shelton. Marlene Dietrich recorded it in 1944 and used it in her concerts for Allied troops. It appealed to soldiers on both sides, and had nothing to do with patriotic fervour.

Composers no longer needed to depend on the sale of sheet music. They could now write directly for the cinema, for the radio and for the recording industry. They could find out how near they were to fame by checking their progress on the charts which began to appear in trade magazines such as the US *Variety*. The 'Music Popularity Chart' was published for the first time in *Billboard* in July 1940. Great Britain followed the trend only twelve years later, in 1952, when the first UK singles chart was compiled and published in the *New Musical Express*.

Such intimate and open connection with commercial success had existed in the nineteenth century, when book publishers boasted of sales (often inflating the figures), but writers were seldom confronted with a monthly or weekly public account of who was up and who was down. The charts fulfilled the role of what was previously the proverbial word of mouth, something one heard from friends and relatives. Now, in the era of mass society, of democracy, there was an assumption of similar taste. The intellectual élites and the influence of their aesthetic decisions had to take a step back. Their alarm is manifest in almost the entire literature on mass society: horror, shock, and disconsolate musings about the fate of civilisation.

The dance fever of the 1920s launched the production of thousands of dance records (foxtrots, tangos, waltzes).[2] One could finally dance at home, among friends, without the need of a bulky piano or the skill to play it. Europe was 'invaded' by new dances from North and South America: two-steps, one-steps, the foxtrot, black bottom, Charleston and the tango. They were broadcast on the radio, played in *brasseries*, nightclubs and dance halls.

But songs too became big business. Their industrialisation had started in the USA at the end of the nineteenth century when Tin Pan Alley publishers in New York were mass-producing music sheets. By the 1920s Hollywood studios, such as Warner, had taken over from Tin Pan Alley. The unification of various media proceeded apace in the USA. The case of RCA (Radio Corporation of America) is exemplary. It was created in 1919 by General Electric to acquire the American assets of the British-owned Marconi. In 1921 it started radio broadcasting. In 1926 it formed the National Broadcasting Company (NBC), the first radio network. Then it entered the motion-picture industry and acquired a chain of cinemas. In 1929 it bought the Victor Talking Machine Company, a manufacturer of gramophones which became the RCA-Victor Company and whose trademark, a dog looking for the source of 'his master's voice' in an old-fashioned phonograph speaker, became world-famous.

In Britain, EMI took over the leading British music publishers, Chappell, one of many mergers that by 1940 resulted in two companies, EMI and Decca, controlling music production in the UK; in the US the dominant firms were RCA-Victor and Decca; in France it was Pathé-Marconi; and in northern and central Europe it was the Dutch company Philips. In Italy Ricordi, the most important sheet-music publisher in the nineteenth century, became the most important record manufacturer in the twentieth. Mainstream capitalism was now firmly ensconced in the cultural industry. Independent companies survived to take risks and experiment. If they succeeded they were taken over and their management co-opted into the world of corporation. If they failed, they failed – just like in any other business. It was through music that a new synergy was achieved in the cultural industry. Previously book publishing was quite distinct from music publishing, press barons did not meddle in book publishing, and live spectacles were a small-scale operation. In the twentieth century, in the USA but also in the UK and Germany (and to a lesser extent in France), global entertainment conglomerates emerged.

The American domination of the cinema was partially replicated in the popular song industry. Though people preferred songs in their own language, when they ventured onto foreign territory this was usually American, then Latin American and Italian, with a few French and Spanish hits. Afro-Cuban music in its various rhythms (the rumba, the conga, the mambo and later the cha-cha-cha) had a powerful effect on Western popular music and dancing.

Most of the songs of this period had the familiar thirty-two-bar structure and rhythmic repetition of the parlour songs of the nineteenth century and even of the late eighteenth century, including Mozart's aria 'Non più andrai' (*Le Nozze di Figaro*), Verdi's 'La donna è mobile' (*Rigoletto*) and Schumann's 'Träumerei'.[3]

In the 1930s the third floor of the Paris department store Le Printemps sold a wide range of records. Most were French, but those which were not were American popular successes such as 'Tiger Rag', 'St Louis Blues', Duke Ellington's 'Mood Indigo' and Gershwin's 'I Got Rhythm', 'The Man I Love' and 'Lady, be Good'. Though lyrics were of great importance to the famous American songs of the 1930s and 1940s, many of these songs became popular even in non-English-speaking countries, particularly those written by a prestigious sextet, all of whom, except for Cole Porter, were Jewish and born or raised in New York:

1. Jerome Kern (1885–1945), author of 'Old Man River', 'Look for the Silver Lining', 'Why do I Love You?' and 'Smoke Gets in Your Eyes', as well as major Broadway musicals such as *Show Boat* (1927).

2. Irving Berlin (1888–1989), the son of a Jewish cantor, wrote songs celebrating the cultural industry ('There's no Business Like Show Business'), patriotism ('God Bless America') and the Christian calendar ('White Christmas' and 'Easter Parade') – quite a feat for someone born in Mogilyov (now in Belarus) and whose real name was Israel Baline.

3. Cole Porter (1891–1964), who studied music at Yale and Harvard, wrote both the words and the music for 'Night and Day', 'Begin the Beguine', 'What is this Thing Called Love' and 'I've Got You Under My Skin'.

4. George Gershwin (1898–1937), a former Tin Pan Alley composer whose brother Ira wrote the lyrics for some of the best-known

songs of the 1930s: 'The Man I Love', 'I Got Rhythm' and 'Someone to Watch Over Me'.

5. Richard Rodgers (1902–79), who studied at Columbia and the Institute of Musical Art, composed the music for the most famous American musicals of his day, from *Pal Joey* (1940) and *Oklahoma!* (1943) to *Carousel* (1945), *South Pacific* (1949), *The King and I* (1951) and *The Sound of Music* (1959), and classic songs such as 'The Lady is a Tramp' and 'Bewitched, Bothered and Bewildered'.

6. Harold Arlen (1905–86), born Hyman Arluck, wrote music for the Cotton Club in Harlem, the musical scores of many films including *The Wizard of Oz* (1939), and the remarkable song 'Stormy Weather' (1932).

Many of these songs were originally show songs, often part of Broadway musicals. Such 'musical theatre' or 'musicals', whose antecedents can be found in the French and Viennese operetta and, above all, in the works of Gilbert and Sullivan (see page 579), came to be regarded, in the minds of Europeans, as an intrinsic part of American culture. Americans too felt this way, and musicals became 'an enacted demonstration of Americanism', often taking 'a defining role in the construction of a collective sense of "America"'.[4] The worldwide success of the songs launched by the musical enshrined the general vision of America as the most formidable producer of global popular culture.

By the 1950s the United States had become the world's leading producer of music, and the major source of musicals. Today we remember the hits, but we should equally remember the far more numerous 'misses', for it is a characteristic of success that it should prove itself the survivor of a truly competitive race. Rodgers and Hammerstein produced five musicals in the 1950s. Of these only two, *The King and I* and *The Sound of Music*, with which they opened and closed the decade, were successful, while few today remember *Me and Juliet*, *Pipe Dream* or *Flower Drum Song*.[5] The three misses all had American settings, the two successes were 'European' – one based on the memoirs of Anna Leonowens, a Victorian governess at the court of the King of Siam, the other on the memoirs of Maria Augusta, nanny to the von Trapp children in the Austria of the 1930s. Lerner and Lowe's great hit *My Fair Lady* (1956) was set in London and required some vague notion of the British obsession with class and accents, and their *Camelot* (1960) was set in Arthurian England, *Fiddler on the Roof* (1965) was inspired by Sholom

Aleichem's stories set in a Jewish *shtetl* in Tsarist Russia. Cole Porter's *Kiss me, Kate* (1948) and Leonard Bernstein and Stephen Sondheim's *West Side Story* (1957) were set in a very recognisable America but their subject-matter was very recognisably Shakespearian. *Hello Dolly!* (1964) was an American rewrite of Johann Nestroy's classic Austrian operetta, *Einen Jux will er sich machen* (see page 577). *Sweet Charity* (1966) by Neil Simon was based on the screenplay of Federico Fellini's film *Le Notti di Cabiria*. *Sweeney Todd* (1979) by Stephen Sondheim was set in Fleet Street. *Cabaret* (1966) was set in Nazi Germany and based on the stories of Christopher Isherwood. The heroine Sally Bowles, originally English, became American in the film. There were, of course, plenty of all-American successes, but the real American achievement with the musical was to have created a genre that was both 'national' and could easily be sold across the world stage.

Irving Berlin's 'White Christmas' – a theme which might appear culture-bound – is reputed to have sold 125 million records and has been recorded in Dutch, Swahili, Japanese and Yiddish.[6] The tunes of this and other songs, piped through airport lounges and wedding reception dances, lived on, though their longevity decreased as the market for popular music expanded. In the end the relatively static nature of 'serious' music protected Mozart more efficiently than it protected Cole Porter.

American domination, particularly in the interwar years, was not untrammelled. There was also a craze for Latin American and Italian music, often in translation: 'Le Tango des fauvettes' was the French version of the Italian 'Il Tango delle capinere' (1928), whose author, Cesare Bixio, wrote a series of international hits in the 1920s and 1930s. One of the most popular French singers, Tino Rossi, was a Corsican who sang like an Italian.[7] The Argentinian tango 'La Cumparsita', first performed in Buenos Aires in 1917, arrived in Paris in 1924, and then became global and one of the most famous tangos. Radio and films were major vehicles for the spread of Latin American music. The tango was a combination of the Argentinian *milonga*, the Spanish-Cuban *habanera*, the Spanish *contradanza* and black African music played by ex-slaves in the outskirts (*orillas*) of Buenos Aires. It became known abroad in its softer and urbanised version.[8]

The triumph of the song as the leading music form after the First World War owes much to the limitation of recording – the few minutes which could be recorded on a disc – but the chief determinant for its wider popularity is that music in its popular manifestation has always required the human voice, the cheapest and most widely available musical instrument.

The radio, the main way of diffusing songs in the 1930s, was still beyond the reach of the majority. Gramophones were relatively common in middle-class homes, but rarer in those of the working class. Nevertheless, even small countries such as Finland, Norway and Ireland sold about a million records each in 1920. Sweden sold three million, Germany thirty million, Great Britain fifty million and France probably twenty million. So records must have been within range of the average person.[9]

In France in particular, influences from jazz (which in France, though not in Britain, was regarded as a 'high' or avant-garde genre) were strong, though American songs became very popular only in the 1950s. The francophone world even produced notable jazz musicians such as the violinist Stephane Grappelli, the tenor saxophonist Alix Combelle and the Belgian guitarist of Roma origin Django Reinhardt (co-founder with Grappelli of the Quintet of the Hot Club of France in 1934). The impact of jazz in France was enhanced by the frequency of visits by black musicians. It was possible to hear in France after the First World War Sidney Bechet, Louis Armstrong, Duke Ellington and Fats Waller.[10]

Many French singers were deeply influenced by the new transatlantic rhythm. Charles Trenet (1913–2001) is a case in point. His 1930s hits, such as 'Y'a d'la joie' and 'Boum!', were genuine popular successes and, at least in France, kept on being performed for the succeeding fifty years. 'Y'a d'la joie' (There is Joy) had a jazzy refrain and a hammered cadenza. Originally it had been written by Trenet in 1937 for Maurice Chevalier, but when Trenet sang it himself a year later, he deliberately turned it into a less polished version. With devastating novelty he jumped around, mistreating the mike as if overcome by the vitality and dynamism of the song. The song has a few phrases, a series of juxtaposed visions and a syncopated rhythm, and changes of register are signalled by changes in accent. Though it was unmistakably French, it could not have come into being without an understanding of the 'scat' style of jazz improvisation in which wordless syllables are used, made widely popular by black American singers such as Louis Armstrong and Ella Fitzgerald. As French, compared to English, has fewer onomatopoeic sounds, Trenet resorted to alliteration, pun-making and tongue-in-cheek exaggeration – a procedure favoured by surrealist poets such as Max Jacob and Robert Desnos.[11] Even these songs, however, relied on a conventional melodic structure. The great conductor Wilhelm Furtwängler took comfort in his notebook in 1939: 'It is said that the age of melody is past. The ever-changing popular song reveals the opposite.'[12]

One of Trenet's later songs, 'La Mer' (1945), was broadcast throughout the world, and frequently used as a signature tune as an indication of Frenchness. Intellectuals, far from disdaining them, welcomed songwriters.[13] Interwar cabarets where such songs were performed were habitually frequented by intellectuals. In Parisian dives such as Le Boeuf sur le Toit, Le Coq and L'Arlequin one could see Pablo Picasso, the composers Darius Milhaud, Francis Poulenc, Arthur Honegger and Erik Satie, and the surrealist writers André Breton and Louis Aragon.[14] The show *Paris qui jazz* was the great success of 1925, when Josephine Baker and her Revue Nègre arrived in France, straight from New York's Cotton Club. The popularity of Argentinian tangos and Cuban rumbas enhanced the connection between the song and the dance (it had been unusual, previously, to dance to a song). The text became almost incidental. The love of the Dadaist Tristan Tzara for 'Negro music' and the passion of the poet Robert Desnos for Cuban and Latin American music followed the enthusiasm that cubist painters had shown for African masks. Jazz arrived in London too in the 1920s, with a white band, the Original Dixieland Jazz Band. Soon Europe became a pole of attraction for black American musicians. Yet until the 1950s US imports were of significance only in Britain, though Duke Ellington and Louis Armstrong had long been successful in France, and some American hits were adapted into French and made successful by French singers, such as 'Jezebel', written by William Shanklin, sung by Frankie Lane in 1951 and later translated by Charles Aznavour for Edith Piaf. To be successful in France in the late 1950s and 1960s, singers like the Greek Nana Mouskouri and the British Petula Clark had to sing in French.

In France writers found they could achieve renown outside their normal markets if their poems were set as songs. In the late forties, existentialist philosophy became associated with some of the cabarets of the Latin Quarter in Paris, such as Le Boeuf sur le Toit, and with young singers such as Juliette Gréco. Such an association between a modern philosophical school and cabaret songs was, of course, completely spurious. The connection was sociological and geographical: the cabarets were mainly in the Latin Quarter, and a substantial part of the audience was made up of students and assorted intellectuals. Others were attracted by the intellectual aura of such places. Listening to the songs and watching singers dressed in black slacks and jumpers may have conferred on the listeners some cultural capital, and perhaps saved them from the effort of reading the hundreds of pages of Jean-Paul Sartre's *L'Être et le néant* (Being and Nothingness). Nevertheless,

Sartre provided the words for the Gréco song 'La Rue des Blancs-Manteaux'; Raymond Queneaux, who tried to capture the rhythm of the spoken language in some of his poetry (for instance 'L'Instant fatal', 1948), provided the words for the famous 'Si tu t'imagine'. These songs alternate highly literary forms with argot, sarcasm and a rapid change of register, particularly developed by the leading songwriter of the day, Joseph Kosma, a classically trained composer of Jewish-Hungarian origins.[15]

The origins of the distinctive literary French song can be traced to revolutionary songs, folk songs and some of the *chansons* (often settings of poems) by nineteenth-century composers of serious music. There was also an influence from the political cabarets of the interwar period imported from Weimar Germany, thanks in part to singers and composers forced into exile by the advent of Nazism such as Kurt Weill (a student of Ferruccio Busoni and Engelbert Humperdinck) and Hans Eisler (a student of Arnold Schoenberg and Anton Webern), both of whom popularised the lyrics of Bertolt Brecht. The key figure here was the politically committed singer Marianne Oswald (Marianne Colin), who in 1934 introduced in France the genres of the Berlin cabarets where she had worked for ten years. As the German cabaret had originally been an adaptation of the *fin-de-siècle* Parisian cabaret (see pages 753–5), it was like a return. Agnès Capri (*née* Sophie Rose Friedmann), a communist activist, used some of the poems of Jacques Prévert, such as 'La Pêche à la baleine', with music by the then unknown Joseph Kosma. She later asked for lyrics from established writers such as Louis Aragon and Max Jacob, and music from major composers such as Poulenc. Agnès Capri was to become recognised as the great populariser of the distinctive style of French song.[16] A trend had begun: poems by major literary figures such as Verlaine, La Fontaine ('La Cigale et la fourmi'), Eluard, Villon (F. Leclerc, 'Le Testament') and Rimbaud ('Les Corbeaux') were set to music. Georges Brassens used François Villon ('Ballade des dames du temps jadis'), Corneille ('Marquise'), Lamartine ('Pensées des morts') and Hugo ('La Légende de la Nonne' and 'Gastibelza'). Singers such as Leo Ferré made poets like Louis Aragon popular among a very wide audience.[17]

Few French literary songs, so popular in the francophone world, became major successes abroad. The exceptions can be rapidly enumerated: Edith Piaf's 'Je ne regrette rien' (which she also recorded in English), some of Jacques Brel's songs in translation, and Trenet's 'La Mer'. Kosma and Prévert's 'Les Feuilles mortes' (1946), first heard in Marcel Carné's film *Les Portes de la nuit*, where it was sung by Yves Montand, was made famous in the USA when it was sung by Nat King Cole in Robert Aldrich's film *Autumn Leaves* (1956), starring Joan Crawford, and later in a jazz version by Miles Davis (1963). The rest, outside francophile and intellectual circles, have remained almost unknown. The overwhelming importance of the text may account for this failure. As Georges Brassens, one of the most celebrated composers and interpreters of songs, explained: 'I love words. I choose them. I seek them . . . I do this from morning to evening: I look for words.'[18] Yet Italian opera travels, and so do Schubert's *lieder*, even though few understand the words. But in Schubert and Verdi the music is far more significant than the words. Clearly French songs (unlike Italian or American songs and, later, British pop songs) could not be successful outside their national reference points. Exceptional voices, such as that of Edith Piaf, could have a more universal appeal. Piaf, the eternal victim, incarnated human and social misery, unable to find love and peace. Her songs were straight out of the nineteenth-century melodrama *à la* Victor Hugo and Eugène Sue: she is '*une ombre de la rue*', a shadow of the street, a prostitute consoling a Lord rejected by his lover ('Milord', 1959); she is a humble café worker in 'Les Amants d'un jour' (1956) :

> Moi j'essuie les verres au fond du café
> J'ai bien trop à fair' pour pouvoir rêver
> (I wash glasses at the back of the café, and have no time for dreams)

The connection between popular songs and the intelligentsia was unique to France. Elsewhere intellectual support was not required for musical success. The New York bohemian intelligentsia may have liked Louis Armstrong or Cole Porter, but that did not influence their popularity. In Italy, intellectuals were far too concerned with maintaining their separateness from the masses to enthuse about common songs. They just about tolerated Rossini. But then, in no other country did intellectuals matter as much as in France. Few provided literary figures ready and willing to write words for songs, and to find interpreters and an audience for them. It is difficult to imagine T.S. Eliot, or even W.H. Auden – some of whose poetry could have perfectly well been used in ballads – writing popular cabaret songs, though Auden wrote opera librettos for Benjamin Britten and Igor Stravinsky. It was only when T.S. Eliot was dead and gone that some of his comic lyrics for children (*Old Possum's Book of Practical Cats*, 1939) were used in one of the most successful musicals ever, Andrew Lloyd Webber's *Cats* (1981).

A different kind of song emerged in Italy, where the influence of opera was such that the most popular singers of the interwar period were those with beautiful and mellifluous high voices. The cabaret was almost non-existent, though some of the popular Italian songs which told a story were inspired by the melodrama, songs like 'Balocchi e profumi' – a lachrymose complaint by a child whose mother buys perfume for herself and never toys for her child – or 'Vipera' – a man's lament at his rejection by the *femme fatale* (a 'viper') he craves.

An international division of labour quickly emerged in the field of music. Germany sold band music, instrumental recordings, the classical repertoire and operetta. Its biggest recording artist in the 1920s was the tenor Richard Tauber. Little of its 'pop' production made it abroad. The Americans dominated international trade in popular songs. In the interwar years it was rare to hear records played on the radio. The main radio stations had their own musicians and dance bands who would play live.[19] The great popular successes of the late 1930s – selling a million records each – were all American: 'One O'Clock Jump', sung by Harry James, 'Boogie-Woogie', sung by Tommy Dorsey, Ella Fitzgerald's 'A-Tisket, a-Tasket', and three hits by Artie Shaw (born Arthur Arshawsky): 'Begin the Beguine', 'Nightmare' and 'Back Bay Shuffle'.[20]

'Serious' Music

And what of 'serious' music, the kind of music performed in élite venues such as concert halls and opera houses? The arrival of popular music did not dent this market. The new media, the radio (later television) and recorded music (records and, after 1960, cassettes and CDs), made this genre of music available to many more people than could have been imagined in the nineteenth century. New ways of diffusing music were constantly invented. In the USA, the Muzak Corporation, set up in 1934, provided music over telephone lines for distribution by loudspeakers. The music was bought by companies in the belief that it would stimulate their workforce. Soon Muzak's music was heard in lifts, waiting rooms, restaurants and airport lounges. Later in the century it was used in shops, planes taking off, planes landing, hotel foyers and bars. Later still, snatches of 'serious' and not so serious music were used as ringtones on mobile phones, on answering machines to keep one waiting on busy phone lines, as an accompaniment to computer games, and when switching computer software on or off. Vivaldi, in his wildest dreams, could not have hoped for the unparalleled diffusion of snatches from 'The Four Seasons' – though it is well to be reminded that the first American recording of it was made only in 1948 (by the Concert Hall Chamber Orchestra under the direction of Henry Swoboda). Nearly sixty years later, it has now been recorded more than a hundred times. Composers such as Haydn, whose music was used as background entertainment at the Esterházy estate in the eighteenth century, were now 'democratised', entertaining the masses. Music turned up everywhere. The angel of silence was banished forever. Perhaps Schoenberg's hostility towards the 'boundless surfeit of music' caused by radio, gramophone and sound-film was based on a premonition that the sheer volume of noise would make people less sensitive to it.[21]

In Europe the live performance of serious music continued to be largely subsidised by the state, in the USA by a mixture of public subsidy, commercial sponsorship and charitable endeavours by the same élites which consumed it. The market alone was never able to fund the live performance of this kind of music – just as had been the case in previous centuries. The training of performers in schools and conservatories was also largely at public expense. What was commercially viable was the sale of such music in its recorded format. The consequence is that the profitable end of the market, the recorded end, was in practice subsidised too, since it is unlikely that it could exist without live performances. Public broadcasting services allowed greater musical experimentation than the commercial sector. Thus the BBC, when it took over the Henry Wood Promenade Concerts in 1927, developed a far more adventurous repertoire in classical music than had hitherto been the case, it subsidised orchestras in the provinces, and in 1930 established its own orchestra under Adrian Boult.[22]

There was also a considerable feedback effect. Recorded music acted as an incentive for the growth of a public keen to listen directly to the music they had heard on their radios and gramophones. By the mid-1920s most of the orchestral repertoire had been recorded, even though the standard speed of discs was still 78 rpm, which meant that each side lasted only five minutes or so. By the late 1940s the new lower-speed 33 rpm microgroove long-playing record (LP), with narrower grooves and made of more resistant material (vinyl), meant that it was possible to record up to twenty minutes for 33 rpm. Records could be piled up on a metal·pole on the gramophone, and an automatic mechanism dropped each record when the previous one was finished. A smaller disc requiring a speed of 45 rpm could be used for shorter works, such as songs. There were now three speeds and two hole sizes (a narrow one for 33 and 78, and a large one for 45), which led to the development of gramophones which could play all of them. It was obvious that 33 rpm was going to be used for classical music while the short 45 was destined to carry popular music.[23]

Since the repertoire of serious music was fairly static, the market relied for its expansion on different performances of the same piece, or on the 'rediscovery' of forgotten pieces or overlooked composers. The scope was considerable: the three-volume *Penguin Lives of Great Composers* published in the 1930s did not mention Mahler or Vivaldi, something that would be regarded as absurd today. Of all the pre-Bach composers, only Palestrina, Byrd and Purcell were mentioned.[24] Then one could re-record the same music in slightly different ways. Thus by 1974 there were twenty-seven different recordings of Beethoven's Fifth Symphony available. Music originally composed for a particular instrument – such as Bach's organ music – was performed on another (such as the piano). 'Early' music (i.e. earlier than Vivaldi), often played on period instruments, further expanded the classical repertoire.

What of the atonal music of Berg, Schoenberg and Webern? This was and is, of course, performed relatively frequently, but not remotely as often as that of the great masters of the past. Yet this kind of music and its derivatives are used in films as background or accompanying music to car chases, science fiction wars between rival intergalactic systems, and battles.[25] Similarly, avant-garde film techniques and effects are more frequently used in commercials than in feature films. Avant-garde art and sound turned out to be particularly suited to advanced consumer capitalism.

Technology helped the market by making previous recordings obsolete. Thus the development of stereophonic recording in the late 1950s made, at a stroke, all previous recordings old-fashioned. A huge re-recording process gave recording companies a new lease of life. Unlike books, the price of records remained fairly uniform, at least until the 1970s. Companies avoided price competition, thus providing a future incentive for individual pirating (including home recording).

Much of the serious music composed in the classical mode in the twentieth century failed to attract the mass of consumers of serious music (though, of course, this mass was increasing rapidly). Recent music failed to please. In some instances it took decades for some music to reach a wider audience. By the end of the twentieth century the most popular 'contemporary' music was that composed in the first half of the century by Claude Debussy (1862–1918), Richard Strauss (1864–1946), Maurice Ravel (1875–1937), Béla Bartók (1881–1945), Igor Stravinsky (1882–1971), Sergei Prokofiev (1891–1953), Francis Poulenc (1899–1963), Aaron Copland (1900–90) and Dmitri Shostakovich (1906–75).

The limited nature of the repertoire is more marked in opera, largely because opera is far more expensive to produce. The twentieth-century additions to the operatic repertoire are few and far between: they are those by Richard Strauss (1864–1946), whose most successful operas were all composed between 1905 and 1919, Benjamin Britten (1913–76), Leoš Janáček (1854–1928) and a few others.

In ballet, both repertoire and attendance are even narrower. Thanks largely to the British choreographer Ninette de Valois (pseudonym of Edris Stannus, 1898–2001), founder of the Royal Ballet, who dominated British ballet from the 1920s to the 1970s, the nineteenth-century Russian repertoire became the cornerstone of international ballet. Few were added to the four all-time great classics – *Giselle* (1841), *Swan Lake* (1877), *Sleeping Beauty* (1890), and *The Nutcracker* (1892): *Les Sylphides* (1832), *Don Quixote* (1869), *Coppélia* (1870) and *La Bayadère* (1877). The twentieth century provided *The Firebird* (1910), *Petrushka* (1911), *L'Après-midi d'un faune* (1912), *The Rite of Spring* (1913) and *Romeo and Juliet* (1938). The field was dominated by few choreographers: Marius Petipa (1818–1910), Michel Fokine (1880–1942), Vaslav Nijinsky (1890–1950), George Balanchine (1904–83), Ninette de Valois (1898–2001), Frederick Ashton (1904–88), Roland Petit (1924–), Martha Graham (1894–1991) and, more recently Pina Bausch (1940–), while the avant-garde was presided over by Merce Cunningham (1919–).

For much of this period (1920–60) the recording market for serious music was dominated by American companies – above all RCA-Victor and CBS – and the British EMI (which included HMV). Philips, a Dutch company, entered the business only in the 1950s, creating in 1962, with Siemens (Germany), the PolyGram Group, which became one of the world's most powerful entertainment companies. The Japanese, in the shape of Sony, created in 1946 (with a more Japanese name), entered the recording scene only in the 1970s. Its push towards a global presence, however, had been made manifest in 1960 when the Sony Corporation of America was established, the first Japan-based company listed on Wall Street. The rise of Sony would not have been possible without a large domestic market for Western classical music, larger in fact than that of any individual European country other than the USSR. There were no French or Italian companies of comparable size.

The USSR presents, as usual, a special case. In the late twentieth century there were joint ventures with Western companies, notably with EMI in 1931. But in practice the market remained closed to the West. All recording was in state hands, and not until the 1950s were Soviet artists allowed to sign recording contracts with Western companies. In the West recording companies had succeeded in keeping a tight control over artists by getting them to sign an exclusive contract binding them to the company (like the Hollywood studio system). Thus Maria Callas was tied to EMI, Joan Sutherland to Decca and the violinist Jascha Heifetz to RCA. The system started breaking down in the 1950s – just like Hollywood. The cost of entry into the recording business, however, was relatively low. As a result the structure of the industry was like that of an iceberg, with a very large number of independent companies and a sprinkling of giants.[26]

In spite of the competition from broadcasting and the fall in living standards during the Depression, the market for records expanded almost uninterruptedly throughout the interwar period, except for a few years in the early 1930s in the USA.[27] The Depression, however, affected black music disproportionately, as 'race' labels, bars and cabarets closed down.[28] Black music that white people enjoyed, such as Benny Goodman's, however, did very well. The Depression also affected classical music recording in the United States, where recording companies did not sell enough to justify the expense of producing it, so they resorted to imports from Europe. But in Europe too the profitability of classical music declined even before the full impact of the Depression, forcing the two largest British manufacturers (HMV and Columbia) to merge and form Electrical and Musical Industries (EMI). Some record companies devised an advance subscription system which turned out to be profitable. This system, promoted by in the UK by Walter Legge at HMV, was soon adopted in France, where important recordings were made by the Polish-born Wanda Landowska (Bach's 'Goldberg Variations' on the harpsichord), the Catalan Pablo Casals playing Bach's cello suites, and the Austrian Fritz Kreisler playing Beethoven's violin sonatas.[29]

The considerable financial rewards and the prestige it offered convinced most artists and conductors to record music. The use of microphones instead of recording horns considerably improved the quality of recorded orchestral sound. This was to the benefit of conductors, like Leopold Stokowski, who made the Philadelphia Orchestra internationally famous after he became its music director in 1931, and Serge Koussevitzky, who did the same for the

Boston Symphony Orchestra between 1924 and 1949. Koussevitzky was born in Russia, Stokowski in London to a Polish father. The foreign origins of such famous conductors confirmed the general American view (and the European, if it needed confirming) that high culture was something that emanated from Europe. This was further corroborated by the rise to prominence of Arturo Toscanini, whose antagonism towards the fascist regime in his native Italy was such that he decided to settle in the USA, even though La Scala had given him enormous powers: he could choose the repertoire, the singers, and even impose on the public his own rules of behaviour.[30] At first hostile to recording, Toscanini eventually made, with the New York Philharmonic Orchestra and the National Broadcasting Symphony Orchestra, 262 recordings of 186 different works, and broadcast hundreds of hours of performances on the radio.[31] The quality of American orchestras, in spite of the lack of public subsidy, was remarkable. Furtwängler, who visited New York in 1929 and conducted the New York Philharmonic, noted that it had assembled the best forces in the world, from Austrian and Bohemian violinists to French woodwind players: 'The technical virtuosity, lightness, elegance and natural beauty of tone of such an orchestra are extraordinary.'[32] The cult of conductors, already extant at the beginning of the century, came into its own, sometimes so extravagantly that even Furtwängler wrote: 'The conductor is given a crucial importance which he does not, in fact, generally have.'[33] Later conductors, like Herbert von Karajan, took a keen interest in how his records could be advertised. By then, of course, the conductor had become a Supreme Being.

International trade in recording could proceed more speedily than for traditional goods. Instead of shipping bulky records, the recording company could simply send a metal stamp to plants in the various countries where it could be used to manufacture records. Smaller countries would import from their neighbours. In 1929, when German domestic sales amounted to twenty-seven million records, as many as fourteen million were exported.[34] Thus a Louis Armstrong record would be recorded in New York, made in Germany and sold in Finland.

The USSR was insulated to an extent from European popular music. This was partly a question of ideology, partly a question of finance, but more Western music entered Stalin's Russia than is often believed. In the 1930s – but even more during the Second World War – there were various Russian channels for the distribution of American music, particularly jazz: personal contacts, records brought in by diplomats, but also the broadcasting of foreign records. Duke Ellington was particularly popular. As mentioned before (see page 897), Soviet élites were divided between two contrasting views of jazz: it was either degenerate music, or the musical expression of the 'Negro' people. The jazz musician and film star Leonid Utesov (1895–1982) thought that Soviet jazz should base itself on the best American and European models, while Maxim Gorky in his 1928 article 'On the Music of the Gross' denounced jazz influences.[35] A jaundiced view of jazz was also voiced by some Western intellectuals. Theodor Adorno, for instance, regarded jazz as formulaic, its famous improvisations mere frills, its popularity constructed by the recording industry and its most striking traits 'all independently produced, developed and surpassed by serious music since Brahms'.[36] The Nazis, of course, regarded jazz as 'Negro' music subject to pernicious Jewish influences. But in Moscow jazz arrived in the same years as it arrived in Paris and London, the first jazz concert being held on 1 October 1922 at the State Theatre Institute in Moscow. Black artists such as Louis Mitchell's Jazz Kings, who had been performing at the Casino de Paris since 1920, toured the USSR.[37] The foxtrot (an American couple dance based on fast, jazzy quickstep, possibly invented by Harry Fox in 1913 as part of the Ziegfeld Follies routines) was regularly performed in the 1920s in fashionable nightclubs and restaurants in Moscow and Petrograd.[38] Jazz was also used, along with the Charleston (a black dance originating from the eponymous town in South Carolina) and the foxtrot, in what was one of the first Soviet ballets, Red Poppy, by Reinhold Glière (1875–1956), later an exponent of socialist realism. Red Poppy was first performed at the Bolshoi in 1927. The plot was simple and politically appropriate: a Soviet ship arrives in a Chinese port. The captain and his sailors help the exploited Chinese dockers unload the ship, to the rage of the local port authority. A Chinese woman dancer, Tao Hua, seized by admiration for this gesture of solidarity, offers the captain a bouquet of flowers. The captain selects a red poppy and gives it to one of the exploited Chinese dockers as a symbol of freedom. Tao Hua is eventually shot by the baddies while the ship leaves the harbour.[39]

The avant-garde RAPM (Russian Association of Proletarian Musicians) – for whom far too many Russian songs lacked the necessary revolutionary zeal – tried to stop the spread of jazz and 'decadent' bourgeois or Western influences throughout the 1920s. They objected in particular to the foxtrot, and denounced the 'native' foxtrot ('Tahiti Trot') adapted for orchestra by Shostakovich (1928), which was really a transcription of Vincent Youmans's 'Tea for Two' (from his 1925 musical No, No, Nanette).[40] The dissolution of

RAPM in 1932 led to a more liberal climate even during the worst years of Stalinist purges. The Composers' Union and all the official music organs were almost universally critical of developments in contemporary Western music (as were their Western counterparts), yet some Western music was performed in the 1930s, and the works of Schoenberg, Berg and Hindemith were discussed. Even in 1936 (during the anti-formalist campaign) the Arts Committee Music Board resolved to include the most interesting works by western European modernist composers in the forthcoming concert programme of the Moscow Philharmonic.[41] Indeed, some composers, such as Prokofiev, returned to the USSR, where it was easier to be performed than in the more commercially minded USA, where the Depression had made life difficult for some modernist composers.[42]

American music made its mark also in Sweden, where the foxtrot was soon adapted to sound like the *shottis*, a popular type of Swedish dance music, thanks to the leading Swedish singer of his day, Ernst Rolf. In the 1920s American dance music was known in Sweden as *jazz*, and the word *jazza* meant to go out dancing, yet it was not associated with black music. Most Swedes were vaguely aware that the foxtrot had some American connection, but because they danced it to local bands and heard the songs in Swedish (adapted to make them sound more Swedish), they did not regard it as 'American' music. Even in the 1950s most European teenagers did not realise the black origin of Elvis Presley's sound or Bill Haley's music.[43] Overtly or in disguise, Americanism had become one of the foundations of European culture.

55

Radio

National Boundaries

THE REGULATION OF broadcasting was strictly national, but sound waves did not stop at national borders. The 'global village' did not start with the internet or even with television. It started on 15 June 1920 when Nellie Melba, the great Australian coloratura soprano, then sixty-one, held a recital at Chelmsford (Essex, England) which was broadcast. The event, organised by the *Daily Mail*, was picked up in Paris by receivers placed on top of the Eiffel Tower, and also in Norway, Italy and even Persia.[1] Melba's brief performance included 'Home Sweet Home', Mimi's 'Farewell' aria from Puccini's *Bohème* and a few bars of 'God Save the King'. Six months later, on 3 December, in New York, from a studio set up in the Hotel McAlpin, Luisa Tetrazzini, another great coloratura soprano, broadcast arias from Ambroise Thomas's *Mignon* and Bellini's *La Sonnambula* to naval ships four hundred miles away.[2]

Regular broadcasting began, appropriately, in the USA, when on 2 November 1920 KDKA, a Pittsburgh radio station installed in a garage owned by Westinghouse, broadcast the results of the presidential elections. The company had realised that if it wanted people to buy its radios it would have to give them something to listen to. By March 1922, some sixty broadcasting licences had been granted. By November of that year there were 564; by 1924 there were 1,105.[3]

We are not far from modern broadcasting. In May 1922 in Great Britain the boxing match between the French world light heavyweight champion Georges Carpentier and his challenger Ted 'Kid' Lewis (an East End Jew whose real name was Gershon Mendeloff) was broadcast live on radio. A concert followed, and then a speech by the Prince of Wales to the Boy Scouts. The British Broadcasting Company (precursor of the British Broadcasting

Corporation) was formed on 18 October of that year. In the same year radio broadcasting was also launched in Denmark, Argentina and Russia. Germany, Belgium, Finland, Switzerland and Czechoslovakia followed in 1923; Austria, Italy, Spain, Holland and Sweden in 1924; in 1925 it was the turn of Hungary, Lithuania, Poland and Japan. In the nineteenth century, catching up took decades. In the twentieth it could take just a few months.

By 1927 there was a radio in 25 per cent of American homes. In Russia too, though the statistics are unreliable, there was a massive expansion, for the Bolsheviks, whose advent to power coincided with that of broadcasting, were not slow to realise the educational and propaganda advantages of broadcasting in a huge country with a high rate of illiteracy. Huntley Carter, the correspondent in Russia of the new English radio journal *The Broadcaster*, remarked in the late 1920s that, 'Today every village has a wireless apparatus – one at least in its central hall where mass listening takes place. Every toiler family in Moscow and Leningrad is in possession of an installation.'[4]

In 1925 the International Broadcasting Union was created in Geneva in an effort to establish international regulation of radio broadcasting. By 1934 international broadcasting bands were allocated (the Lucerne agreement). In the 1930s in parts of Europe a trans-national community of listeners came into being: they listened to music from Vienna, operas from Radio-Toulouse and Rome, *cafés-concerts* from Hamburg and dance music from Madrid. Programmes were increasingly exchanged.[5]

In the early 1920s in Europe, the radio was still a status symbol. Matters improved rapidly even though the sets remained expensive. By the late 1930s in France, a cheap radio could cost as little as 250 francs, at a time when a Parisian worker would earn, on average, fifty francs a day, while a good set would cost eight hundred francs (some luxury ones could reach 4,000 francs). In addition one would need a noise-suppressing device for better reception, an aerial and, after 1933, the licence fee.[6] Still, five days' wages for a radio set compares well with a television set in the 1960s.

By the 1930s radio – once a hobby dominated by well-to-do amateurs – had become a mass phenomenon. In France, in the ten years between 1930 and 1940 the number of receivers increased tenfold, from 500,000 to five million, and in Britain from 3.4 million to nine million.[7] By 1937 there were twenty-six million receivers in the USA, reaching 70 per cent of the population. France had three million subscribers, much fewer than Great Britain (8.5 million) and Germany (7.5 million). Italy had only 610,000, fewer than Denmark (641,000), Belgium (850,000), Holland (950,000), Sweden

(914,000) and Czechoslovakia (874,000). In Japan there were three million radio sets, in Australia one million.[8] The distribution of radio listeners was skewed towards the richer areas and the better-off. In the late 1930s there were only 20,000 radios in the whole of Bulgaria and 10,000 in the whole of Greece.[9] Only 20 per cent of Italian subscribers before 1940 were in the south, and only 22 per cent were salaried workers.[10] By 1950 near-saturation had been reached in all the most advanced countries, even though radios were still expensive. In Italy a radio set cost, in 1950, 30,000 lire, a month's wages for an unskilled worker. This did not stop the number of radio subscribers (paying the annual licence fee) increasing from 1.5 million in 1944 to 5.5 million in 1954.[11] The expansion in the number of receivers was accelerated not only by increased prosperity but also by technological innovations: transistor radios, smaller radios, portable radios, car radios, and eventually a radio in every room.

Radio reached homes even before electricity. In the late 1930s, as Malcolm Stewart remembers, his parents' modest home in the East End of London only had gas lighting, but though they had no books, they owned a wireless (as it was then called in England) which required his father to take the glass battery to the local cycle shop twice a week to be recharged so that they could listen to their favourite programme – a radio 'show' called *Band Waggon*.[12] *Band Waggon* – the original idea came from an American show of the same name – was launched in January 1938 with considerable pre-publicity. It was to be a serial built around the comedian Arthur Askey, who adapted music hall slapstick and surreal fantasy to radio. After some initial difficulties the show rapidly overtook most other variety programmes in audience appreciation, becoming the big hit programme of the winter before the war.[13] It made Arthur Askey a household name and one of the first authentic radio stars in Great Britain – with his life story serialised in *Tit-Bits*. It parodied other programmes and made fun of establishment figures such as radio announcers. It became a cult. Wednesday-evening cinema audiences were at their lowest as people stayed at home to listen to *Band Waggon* – a harbinger of things to come.[14]

In France one of the most successful radio shows was *La Famille Duraton*, in which an allegedly 'ordinary' family commented on news events every day – the show carried on until 1966.[15] The success of Radio-Paris was due in no small measure to the popularity of its main anchorman, Marcel Laporte, who under the name of 'Radiolo' became one of the first radio personalities in the country.

In the decade before the outbreak of war the professionals of the new medium were on a steep learning curve. In ten years, in France and in Britain they invented or imported from the USA the main radio genres: quiz shows, games, serialised stories, radio plays, reporting (including sports reporting), variety shows with songs and chat, political satire. Much of this material was recycled later for television.

At first radio programmes were limited to a few hours a day, usually during lunch and dinner. Sunday was the peak listening day (though John Reith's Calvinism ensured that there would be no broadcasts on the BBC before 12.30, so that people could go to church). The evening was prime listening time. People planned to listen to specific programmes, a habit which gradually almost disappeared. The fare was made up of a few news bulletins – usually reports of events already covered in the newspapers – some theatre and comedy sketches, a conversation or lecture. Music, then as now, dominated the airwaves. The radio was, substantially, a music box to which news and other items were added. Broadcasters had quickly realised that the audience did not so much choose a programme as a listening time, and often scheduled popular programmes just before cultural ones. Gradually the gaps were filled, and individuals, such as housewives, rather than families, became a prime target for morning broadcasts. Broadcasting continuity became one of the main incentives for the expansion of radio. The number of programmes it was possible to broadcast in the course of a single week was so extensive that the different preferences of many types of listeners could be satisfied. For the first time, culture was on tap.

Who Pays?

How should broadcasting be funded and regulated? The traditional market mechanism, where buyers and sellers exchanged cash for goods, did not apply in this field, since given the available technology, it was impossible to devise a way whereby the public paid for each programme it listened to. The nearest model was the subscription format used for newspapers and magazines, whereby consumers bought in advance the production of the next month or year. Since consumers were required to spend a considerable sum on the purchase of the equipment (the receiver), and it was impossible for each broadcaster to levy its own subscriptions the way newspapers were able to do, the only way out was either to provide the broadcasts for free and find another source of income, or to impose a yearly levy on owners of receivers, and use that to fund the programmes. The simplest way was to have a central tax, levied by the state, which would pass it on to a public utility company. In Europe, but not in the USA and Latin America, this model prevailed, and public (state) broadcasting maintained a near-monopoly until the last quarter of the twentieth century.

Public intervention in broadcasting worked to the advantage of the manufacturers of the receivers, since it provided the necessary incentive for consumers to purchase radio sets. The ease with which the state was allowed to assume charge of broadcasting was due to the absence of vested private interest in producing programmes. Making programmes was a risky commercial undertaking which would need to rely on the ability to recoup the cost by selling advertising. This required a large market for homogeneous goods, hence a fairly advanced consumer society. Such a society existed, in the 1920s, only in the USA. Since radio advertising had to be targeted at an expanding and constantly changing audience, it had to be based on general non-class-specific commodities, such as food, soap, shaving cream and household products. To keep people 'hooked' to specific radio programmes, American broadcasters resorted to the great standby of the nineteenth-century press: serialisation. The 1930s saw a massive development of what came to be known as 'soap operas' in the USA. A 1938 study estimated that some housewives listened to as many as ten radio 'soaps' a day. Companies paid $18,000 a week to advertise their wares on a soap which cost $3,000 to make. Clever entrepreneurs like Frank Hummert and Anne Ashenhurst (a husband-and-wife team) started an agency for the production of serials, commissioning texts on the basis of a very detailed framework, just like the mass-produced serialised novels of the nineteenth century.[16]

Funding by advertising was more difficult in fragmented European markets, where the interests of manufacturers of sets would be better served if free programmes could be made by the state (or by companies licensed by the state). The use of advertising to fund broadcasting also encountered the unremitting hostility of powerful press groups, who feared they would face a shrinking market – an ironic development since the first British broadcast (the Nellie Melba concert) had been sponsored by the *Daily Mail*.

It would have been possible, in Europe, to allow the formation of private monopolies in the electricity, telephone and communication business, and give them the opportunity to branch out into broadcasting. But this would have given them enormous powers. Had anti-trust legislation been used to break up such conglomerates, the resulting smaller firms would have been easy prey for foreign corporations – as had been the case with the railways in the nineteenth century. Besides, a multitude of small firms would have led to an escalation of costs, and would have made the expansion of the market far more difficult, perhaps impossible. So the European model of a clear separation between private conglomerates in the main utilities, and a publicly controlled broadcasting system, seemed the best option.

The US model – funding exclusively by advertising – had considerable appeal. It kept the medium out of the hands of politicians, and did not require an enforcement agency to levy the tax. Above all it meant that the only cost facing the consumer was the once-and-for-all cost of buying the set. This made radio the cheapest form of entertainment available. The disadvantage was that the market thus created was one in which the broadcasters had to deliver an audience to advertisers. The educational use of radio was therefore limited. US radio remained heavily dependent on private sponsors who wished to avoid offending or disturbing even a small section of their potential market. The consequence was a bias in favour of the prevailing consensus – but then, that was also the case in Europe, where broadcasters avoided offending politicians. Advertisers became dependent on the radio. By the 1940s Procter & Gamble spent more than half of its advertising expenditure on radio.

The upshot was that, in the vast majority of 'market' economies, the new cultural medium, potentially far more powerful than anything created so far, was largely in public hands, usually through the Minister of Post. Though some European countries had started out with a highly regulated private system, by the 1930s public control and/or ownership had become the norm. In Ireland the system was in state hands from the very beginning, and from the very beginning it was seen as a way of promoting the diffusion of Irish, norms of hygiene, modern agricultural techniques and the overall education of listeners. Entertainment was not thought to be particularly important.[17] By 1933 Radio Eireann had the most important symphony orchestra in the country.[18] It broadcast ballad series under the title *Ireland is Singing*, and ran competitions for new verses.[19] Many of the programmes were given first in English and then in Irish, but few listened to those in Irish – a language most Irish people found hard to follow. Broadcasting was seen, in Ireland as elsewhere, as a major cultural institution and not a commercial enterprise.[20]

Unlike publishing, the press, the record industry and the cinema, radio was a not-for-profit industry – except for the actual manufacturing and sale of receivers. The European country most committed to 'the market' – Great

Britain – became the home of the most revered public broadcasting corporation, the BBC, a highly centralised organisation whose first Director General, John Reith, constructed the concept of 'public service broadcasting' whose fundamental task was to educate as well as entertain the listeners. Such principles were not peculiarly British: they were commonly accepted in the rest of Europe. Reith's mission statement, 'To entertain, to educate and to inform,' was present in the charter of other national broadcasting organisations, notably that of the French.

Reith's principles and outlook were not that different from those operating in a well-run public library. To attract customers it was necessary to provide a judicious mix of good-taste entertainment and intelligent talk, relevant and balanced comment, good music and uplifting information. But one had to strike a balance. Too high-minded an approach would act as a disincentive to expansion. Yet if the fare supplied was too populist, the aim of public service would be traduced. The BBC had to ensure not to appear to be the voice of a particular political party, thus reflecting the values and cultural preferences of the British establishment. Since the first listeners were overwhelmingly middle-class, there was very little conflict. The BBC was initially run by the middle classes for the middle classes. The assumption was that there was a 'great audience' out there – one whose tastes and interests could be developed over time. Reith was convinced, and he may well have been right, that radio helped to bring into existence a new audience for serious music.[21]

Radio faced the hostility of the press, which regarded it as a dangerous commercial threat, since it sought the same market. The BBC, at first on the defensive, agreed not to use newspaper material for broadcast news, to obtain news exclusively from the news agencies, and not to broadcast it at all before 7 p.m., so as to protect the evening press.[22] Such restrictions were barely tolerated by John Reith, who succeeded in gradually widening the scope of broadcast news. Yet an informal compromise was reached, facilitated by the fact that the popular dailies gave the people what they thought it wanted – crime stories, divorces, scandals, etc. – while the BBC gave its listeners what they ought to want: balanced news coverage. In any case, between the wars there was an expansion of both newspapers and radio listening. The real competitor of the BBC was the serious national press, but its middle-class readers never regarded broadcasting as an alternative to buying newspapers such as the *Manchester Guardian*, *The Times* and the *Daily Telegraph*.

The kind of market the BBC addressed itself to in the late 1920s was exemplified by its ability to turn a music critic, Percy Scholes, into a household name (at least in households with a radio), while T.S. Eliot and W.H. Auden gave talks on poetry and music programmes included even the works of Schoenberg and Webern.[23] The putative audience was a schoolteacher interested in the theatre, new music and philosophical issues, and who wanted to improve himself or herself – all the members of the middle and lower-middle classes who wanted access to high culture but could not afford it, and who lived in areas where it was difficult to go to a concert or the opera. In fact the assumed radio audience was strikingly similar to the general reading public. The schedule on French radio for 18 August 1927 had a concert of classical music in the morning, a lecture on legal matters at eight in the evening, followed by a fifteen-minute talk on astronomy, then one on animal diseases which can be passed on to humans, then one on developments in chemistry. The listening day concluded with another concert of classical music.[24]

By the 1940s – as Malcom Stewart, a sound engineer working for the Home Service of the BBC, recollects – programmes were recorded on seventeen-inch acetate discs, at a speed of 33.3 revolutions per second. As the maximum time on each disc was ten minutes, they used to record with an overlap of about fifteen seconds. When replaying the recorded discs, great skill was required in changing from one record to the next without anyone noticing the changeover.[25]

French radio, like its British counterpart, sought respectability. Radio-Paris did not hesitate to try to co-opt the cultural establishment, by including among its trustees Maurice Ravel and Paul Valéry. With the spread of multi-channels the imagined schoolteacher audience was catered for by specially designated cultural programmes such as the Third Programme of the BBC.[26] Other countries followed suit, such as Italy with Il Terzo Programma in October 1950. The gradual ghettoisation of audiences had begun.

Radio was a cautious medium. The BBC was more sensitive to minorities' views than was the press, which could print harrowing accounts of crimes, while even a mild coarseness in a radio programme caused a scandal – a scandal quickly given ample resonance by popular newspapers using images of naked women for sales promotion and image-building.[27] The BBC was careful, leaving little to chance. Unscripted discussions were not broadcast until the 1950s. In 1948, for instance, a debate on the existence of God (a taboo subject before the war) between Bertrand Russell and Father Frederick Copleston, the Jesuit philosopher, was produced by having the two participants first freely talk without a script. A transcript of the discussion was then edited, and the script was read out by the two participants and recorded for broadcast.[28] As a result their delivery was stilted and the programme lacked spontaneity, but a decorous and inoffensive debate was guaranteed:

> Russell: Then I can only say that you're looking for something which can't be got, and which one ought not to expect to get.
> Copleston: To say that one has not found it is one thing; to say that one should not look for it seems to me rather dogmatic.[29]

Such a high-minded attitude also prevailed in France, where every Thursday a play performed by the Comédie-Française was broadcast, and intellectuals and writers such as Jean Cocteau, Jacques Prévert and Raymond Queneau debated cultural matters.

Radio created celebrities, and transformed writers and unknown academics into famous people. Regular members of *The Brains Trust* (1942–49), one of the great successes of the wartime BBC, such as the scientist Julian Huxley and the philosopher C.E.M. Joad, became household names. Media 'dons' have been around longer than people think. Isaiah Berlin gave four talks on famous thinkers in 1952, making him far better known than he ever had been before. He recollected with glee: 'I talked and talked – which I do anyway – and that was the basis of my being thought to be a possible candidate for the Chair of Social and Political Theory at Oxford. Because, what had I written before that? Only a book on Karl Marx. Nothing else at all that counted. And the broadcasts made my career in Oxford.'[30]

It was not only intellectuals who had been recruited on behalf of the war effort. Singers such as Vera Lynn, promptly characterised as 'the Forces' Sweetheart', were identified with a particular kind of patriotism. Public interest in personalities, thus far a matter of press reporting, found in the radio an ideal means of diffusion. A profusion of innovative programmes characterised the BBC during the war. War radio also provided advice on health (the first of many radio doctors) and gardening. J.B. Priestley commented in his controversial *Postscripts* at the end of the main evening news. A serial – *The Archers* – devised to impart advice on how to cope with rationing in an entertainment format, and first broadcast in 1950, became the longest-running radio soap in the world – still popular as I write (2006), and broadcast five days a week with an omnibus edition on weekends. Another BBC favourite, *Desert Island Discs* started in 1942. It consisted of asking a weekly guest to select favourite snatches of music should he or she be marooned on a desert island. The musical excerpts were interspersed with a deliberately non-hostile and non-controversial interview. The programme is still going as I write, though the tone has somewhat modified, from Roy Plomley's excessively polite 'And what was your greatest achievement?' to Sue Lawley's 'And how did you feel when your husband left you?' 1947 saw the birth of *Round Britain Quiz* and 1948 of *Any Questions?* and the first Reith Lecture (with Bertrand Russell). Radio production may have been ephemeral, but good programmes outlasted their original creators.

The term 'public system' covered a variety of possible forms of state-controlled broadcasting. In Weimar Germany, radio was at first mainly in private hands, though almost immediately (1922) the state, through the Reichpost (Ministry of Post), regulated broadcasts, which were largely local. By 1932 the proliferation of regional radio stations had reached such a level that the Chancellor, Franz von Papen, established a national broadcasting company, the Reichs Rundfunk Gesellschaft, funded like the BBC by a tax levied on listeners.[31] A few months later the Nazis had taken power, and found themselves in charge of state broadcasting. After the war the Allies (and in the East the Russians) controlled German broadcasting, which by 1948 was decentralised in the West under the control of the various *Länder*. A common service was ensured in 1953 with the creation of Deutsche Welle (The German Wave), and in 1962 the Deutschlandfunk, which broadcast throughout West Germany (and which could be heard in the East).

In Italy the state created in 1924 the Unione Radiofonica Italiana, a 'private' company in which the government was the majority shareholder. This soon became the Ente Italiano Audizioni Radiofoniche (EIAR), with a monopoly of broadcasting, funded by a tax on receivers as well as limited advertising. After the war EIAR became RAI (Radio Italiana), and remained a state monopoly under the direct patronage of the leading government parties.

In France the law had established that radio was a public service and that it should belong to the state. However, the state granted a concession to broadcast to a number of private stations, and regulated broadcasting strictly. In Great Britain the BBC was, legally speaking, not owned by anyone, but was almost entirely financed by the state, and its board was appointed by the government. Other countries in Europe followed a similar pattern. Romanian broadcasting, for instance, was run by the Societatea de Difuzuine Radiotelefonica. Private capital was entitled to own up to 40 per cent of the shares, but the state held the rest and appointed the board. The board of the

Danish Statsradiofonien was appointed by the government, as were those of the Hungarian Magyar Telefon Hirmondo, the Norwegian Norsk Rikskring-kasting and the Swedish Radiotjänst. The pattern was clear: radio was – directly or indirectly – in the hands of the state everywhere in Europe. Only two countries followed neither the US market model nor the main European model: Belgium and Holland. In Belgium the Institut National Belge de Radiodiffusion was appointed by the government and appeared similar to the BBC. Yet it provided considerable broadcasting space to what one might call the organisational pillars of civil society: the different ideological families into which the country was divided: Catholic, liberal and socialist (each in turn subdivided along linguistic lines: Flemish and French-speaking socialists, French liberals, etc.). Each organisation was then free to dispose – within limits – of its broadcasting space. The rest of non-political broadcasting and an 'objective' news programme continued to be produced by the central organisation. In Holland too broadcasting was funded by associations of listeners (Catholic, Protestant, socialist, liberal) as well as by a tax levied by the Post Office. Advertising was forbidden. By 1936 Holland had one of the highest densities of sets in the world.

In Europe there were few exceptions to public broadcasting. One was in Luxembourg, where in 1924 radio-set owners created a broadcasting associ-ation backed by French capital. By 1933 it was broadcasting late into the evening programmes aimed at an international audience, drawn from all the neighbouring countries. The funding came entirely from advertising, much of which originated from British firms (since there was no advertising on the BBC). As the list of programmes for 10 November 1935 reveals there was a preponderance of 'popular' classical music, largely drawn from the nineteenth-century repertoire, and news in French and in German.[32]

In the USA the state only kept for itself control of over technical aspects of broadcasting, such as bands and ownership. This was administered after 1934 by the Federal Communications Commission (FCC), an independent federal agency. At first dozens of independent radio stations managed to survive thanks to local advertising. By the end of the 1930s, however, radio was dominated by three powerful networks: the National Broadcasting Company (NBC), with a hundred stations, Columbia Broadcasting System (CBS), with seventy-five, and the Mutual Broadcasting Corporation (MBC), which had in Cincinnati the most powerful transmitter in the USA prior to the Second World War.

Radio had taken off throughout the world. The laggard countries soon caught on.

NUMBER OF RADIO STATIONS			
	1926	*1930*	*1936*
USA	750	695	917
Europe	170	238	381
Latin America	40	85	298
Australia and New Zealand	20	51	123
Asia	10	26	189
Africa	5	10	21
TOTAL	995	1,105	1,929

SOURCE: Huth, *La Radiodiffusion, Puissance mondiale*, pp.39, 57

The number of radio receivers, though still far from the saturation levels reached in the post-war period, became very high compared to any alternative way of consuming culture. The figures in the table below underestimate audience size, since in many countries, notably the USSR, Italy and Germany, collective listening was common.

NUMBER OF RADIO-SET RECEIVERS PER THOUSAND PEOPLE		
	1936	*1951*
USA	178	566
Denmark	164	285
Great Britain	161	227
Sweden	134	298
Holland	113	185
Germany	108	144
Switzerland	103	214
Belgium	92	161
Canada	83	244
Austria	83	180
France	63	178
Czechoslovakia	58	166
Chile	47	93

	1936	1951
Finland	39	164
Ireland	26	93
Japan	24	100
Italy	12	56

These figures starkly reveal the backwardness of France in radio ownership and diffusion. In spite of the surge in subscribers (1.3 million sets in 1933, five million in 1939), France was not among the top countries in the world.[33] This contrasts with the hegemonic cultural role France had played in the nineteenth century. In the development of previous media, such as publishing and the theatre, industrialisation had played a secondary role. But the new technologies required a complex industrial system, and the inescapable fact was that France was industrially far less developed than its main competitors. France began to lose its cultural lead. The period 1919–39 was one of missed opportunities insofar as French radio was concerned. French society was inadequate at adapting itself to modernity. Even after the war, the Monnet Plan was all about steel and coal and iron. It neglected new technologies such as the telephone network, a key element for the competitiveness of the economy.[34] Even the electricity network was less extensive in France than in many other west European countries. The figures for electricity consumption correlate not only with the climate, but also with radio density:

CONSUMPTION OF KILOWATTS PER PERSON 1937

Norway	2,820
Canada	2,747
Switzerland	1,633
Sweden	1,261
USA	1,118
Germany	696
Belgium	629
Great Britain	500
France	433

SOURCE: Patrice Carré, 'La Transformation de l'espace privé ou la magie électrique' in Lévy-Leboyer and Morsel (eds), L'Interconnexion et le Marché 1919–1946, p.1332

Radio and Politics

Though radio was part of the state system, the limited nature of the medium and the underestimation by politicians of its power meant that, at least until the mid-1930s there was relatively little overtly political propaganda on the radio. Nevertheless radio strengthened and consolidated the existing state of affairs. It did not and could not challenge conventional beliefs. Inevitably, it buttressed and upheld them. The BBC may have refrained from pro-Conservative propaganda in the 1930s, but there was no question that it stood on the side of conservatism with a small 'c'. It unquestioningly upheld the Empire, the monarchy and established religion. Broadcasting House, headquarters of the BBC, bore in its atrium the Latin inscription 'This Temple of the Arts and Muses is dedicated to Almighty God'; the Governors prayed that listeners, 'inclining their ears to whatsoever things are beautiful and honest and of good report, may tread the path of wisdom and upright-ness'. 'Religious broadcasting in a Christian country,' explained the BBC Handbook in 1940 'is the aim of the Church – to proclaim, in worship and preaching, the gospel of God in Jesus Christ.'[35] No jazz or light music was broadcast on Sundays. Christian monarchies were not so very different from present-day Islamic republics.

In France broadcasting was subject to the kind of political patronage which had enabled the Third Republic's politicians to exercise some influence over the press, but the object was to keep political broadcasting weak and servile.[36] Inevitably, given the fractious and changing state of French politics, politicians decided that politics was too sensitive an issue to be left to broadcasters. Having acquired power in 1936, the Popular Front tried to purge radio of right-wing journalists. When the tide turned, in December 1938, the Prime Minister acquired the final authority over political broadcast-ing.[37] Centralisation was further accelerated by the Vichy government during the war. This was not altered when France was liberated. Indeed, in Novem-ber 1944 the few remaining private stations were placed under the control of Radiodiffusion Française (RDF). A wide purge of those who had worked in radio under Vichy and under Nazi occupation took place.[38] Political patron-age remained operative even after the creation in 1964 (under de Gaulle) of the ORTF (Office de la Radiodiffusion-Télévision Française), a public corporation.

While in Denmark the political parties carved political broadcasting up among themselves, in Norway, Sweden, Switzerland and Czechoslovakia political propaganda was forbidden (1931). Some governments used the radio for political propaganda, as was the case in the USSR and the states under right-wing dictatorship, but even in Italy the fascist regime broadcast little propaganda, preferring posters, speeches and banners. Nor did the regime have plans for using broadcasting as part of its cultural policies, though it had aspirations to establish 'a radio in every village'.[39] Mussolini used the radio for some important announcements, but did not systematically broadcast his thoughts. As the number of sets increased, the politicians became more interested. Even so, tuning in to Italian radio in the late 1930s one was more likely to hear a serialisation of one of Dumas's novels than the words of il Duce.[40] The best-known radio personality of the 1930s was not Mussolini but the sports broadcaster Nicolò Carosio, whose football broadcasts continued to entertain listeners into the 1960s.

None of the great dictators of the interwar period regularly addressed radio audiences. The first time Russians heard Stalin was after the German invasion in 1941 (they were surprised by his thick Georgian accent). The war changed all this. And democratically elected leaders were as quick as, or quicker than, the dictators to take advantage of the new media. Some of Churchill's House of Commons speeches were later rebroadcast on the radio. Matters were different in the USA, where the extent of broadcasting was such that politicians like Roosevelt understood its import earlier than in Europe. FDR's radio 'fireside chats' were an opportunity to explain policies in a tone which suited the new medium far better than the inspirational rhetoric characteristic of the public platform. A genre developed which could be called 'addressing the nation', in which the Prime Minister or President would hold forth portentously on the grave situation facing the country, with which, by the mere act of speaking, he could identify himself. As the Second World War approached, such appeals multiplied. King George VI's broadcast on 3 September 1939 highlighted the intimate nature of radio broadcasting. It opened with words addressing the mass of the British people as individuals separate from each other, in the privacy of their own homes:

> In this grave hour, perhaps the most fateful in our history, I send to every household of my peoples, both at home and overseas, this message, spoken with the same depth of feeling for each one of you as if I were able to cross your threshold and speak to you myself.[41]

The potential of political broadcasting was discovered only in the 1930s. Not until 1932 did French politicians use the radio for electioneering purposes.

They were not very good at it. They were used to speaking at length to crowds in public squares, crowds made up of party supporters to be galvanised. Such rhetoric for the already converted was not easily transferable to the unconverted listening to the radio. One of the few politicians who made an impact was the communist leader Maurice Thorez.[42] Unlike his political opponents, he used simple and clear language, addressing himself to the listener with the familiar '*tu*'. His famous radio speech on the *main tendue* ('the hand proffered', 7 February 1936) was far more effective than the more subtle one by his socialist rival Léon Blum:

> We stretch out our hand to you, Catholic, worker, employee, artisan, farmer. We stretch our hand to you, national volunteer, veteran who has become a Croix-de-Feu because you are a son of the people, because you suffer, like us, the consequences of the disorder and corruption, because, like us, you want to ensure that the country does not descend into ruin and catastrophe ... We communists who have reconciled the tricolours of our forefathers to the red flag of our hopes, we call on all of you, workers, farmers, intellectuals, young and old, men and women, all of you, you people of France, to struggle with us and to take a stand on 26 April for prosperity against misery, for freedom against slavery, for peace against war.[43]

In the interwar years politics remained marginal to radio. Government intervention was more directed towards keeping people out than to shaping programmes. Thus, during the General Strike in Britain (1926), no trade unionists were interviewed by the BBC. Ramsay MacDonald, the leader of the opposition, was banned. In 1935 the BBC was forced to cancel a debate between a communist leader, Harry Pollitt, and Oswald Mosley, the leader of the British Union of Fascists – and was not allowed to reveal that it had been the government's decision.[44]

Paradoxically, the power of broadcasting increased during the war, when broadcasts were most heavily censored. But the paradox is only apparent: censorship becomes a reality not only when the situation demands it, but when the medium being censored has acquired real power. Just as wireless communication had been boosted by the First World War, so public service broadcasting came into its own during the Second. This was particularly the case with the BBC. It grew in size and prestige. Its own sense of priorities was close to that of the government.[45] Yet it was trusted more. Besides, if one wanted the most up-to-date news – and during a war this need is felt particularly keenly – one would turn to the BBC. As one of the few broadcasting organisations operating in a democracy, it also became very influential abroad. Because it was important that everyone should understand the news, the language was simplified, made more 'audience-friendly'.

The war also brought about greater competition, since each of the belligerent countries broadcast its own news into enemy territory. The Germans broadcast to Britain the speeches of 'Lord Haw-Haw' (William Joyce), an Irishman with an upper-class accent and a good radio voice. The British broadcast to Italy as Radio Londra with the voice of 'il Colonello Stevens'. Radio Moscow broadcast to Italy the voice of the leader of the Italian Communist Party, Palmiro Togliatti, under the pseudonym Mario Correnti.

Broadcasting Music

In principle the radio enables individuals to appropriate cultural production outside collective consumption (concerts, theatres etc.). In reality consumption becomes systematically individualised only when radio sets become cheap and portable, and this is true only after the 1960s. Until then the consumption of radio programmes occurred essentially in a family setting, though in some countries there was a degree of collective consumption, with radio programmes listened to in public places such as bars, recreational or political circles or public squares. However, the radio was fundamentally a household good. The listeners were a family unit sitting around the set, harbinger of television. It was the first form of cultural entertainment tailored to the family unit, and was reminiscent of the habit in some nineteenth-century middle-class households of reading aloud around the fireplace. Broadcasters were thus faced with the question of trying to satisfy different age and gender groups – a situation mass-circulation newspapers had started facing at the end of the nineteenth century. The prevalence of listening to the radio at lunchtime and dinnertime, when the family was gathered together, determined the selection of programmes. But it was above all the available technology and the prevailing ideology of the broadcasters which shaped the content, and determined the domination of music.

Broadcasting music had considerable advantages. Its vast repertoire had been tested over decades, sometimes centuries. Novelties could be introduced alongside old favourites. Being one of the least overtly political or ideological art forms made music particularly acceptable. It offered an ample gradation from the avant-garde to the classical to the popular.

The statistics are often vague and do not permit a precise comparison, but today even the most perfunctory survey of what is available across the band waves almost anywhere in the world would have no difficulty in establishing that music has – by far – the lion's share. Most local radio stations consists of a wisecracking anchorman or woman who changes records and reads a few items of news. But the domination of music was well entrenched even in the mid-1930s. According to various estimates, music broadcasts amounted then to 69 per cent of the BBC's total output. Almost half was 'light music', 15 per cent 'serious music' and almost 10 per cent 'dance music'. 'Lectures' amounted to 7 per cent, religion to 4.7 per cent, news 8.8 per cent and educational subjects 6 per cent. In Germany music broadcasts amounted to 34.8 per cent, 'lectures' 13.3 per cent, 'information' 33.1 per cent, and 'news' 4.3 per cent. In Italy music broadcasting was 44.3 per cent of the total, news and information 25.8 per cent and religion 2 per cent (less than half the figure for the BBC). In the USSR music amounted to 52.8 per cent of the total (including 'the music of the Tartars of Crimea', Ukrainian songs, Jewish popular songs, Georgian music, Gypsy music). 'Communist education' took up only 4.9 per cent of total broadcast time, but the more generic 'political information' amounted to 9.7 per cent. Music also dominated Austrian broadcasting (58.2 per cent), as it did in almost all the other European countries. In the USA it amounted to 63 per cent. Japan was a special case: music constituted only 10 per cent of its radio output.[46]

Broadcasting in the USA was commercial from the outset; however, since those owning radio sets were still disproportionately in the higher income brackets, there was considerable 'serious music'. CBS made Toscanini a household name by broadcasting Sunday-afternoon concerts by the New York Philharmonic. Nevertheless, Toscanini never had as much air space for new music as Sir Adrian Boult had as conductor-in-chief of the new BBC Symphony Orchestra.[47] In 1928 the fascist authorities passed a law which empowered EIAR to broadcast any concert it liked. During the lengthy period in which the opera theatres remained closed, EIAR offered a full operatic season. Thus in 1931 thirty-five operas were broadcast.[48] The mission to 'educate' as well as 'to entertain' was not confined to the BBC.

Musicians and performers were initially hostile to broadcasting. They feared that people would no longer pay to hear them perform when they could do the same while staying at home. Nellie Melba may have launched the era of music broadcasting in 1920, but she refused to allow her 1923 performance in La Bohème at Covent Garden to be broadcast; her agent had advised her against it, because 'to enable 100,000 people to hear her for nothing might lessen her value in the concert-room'.[49] As we know, such panic was unwarranted. Fifty years later singers would go to considerable lengths to be on the radio, which was the most important stepping stone towards fame and money. In fact soon the broadcasting of music (as well as the sale of records) started to constitute a significant supplementary source of income for musicians. Composers of 'serious music' realised that a new work by one of them was probably heard by a greater number of people than would have heard a piece by Beethoven in that composer's entire lifetime. Whether it would endure as long was a different question.[50] But there were losers too. The army of musicians playing background music in restaurants, hotels, cafés and, of course, accompanying films were replaced by broadcast music, recordings and jukeboxes. Famous singers (i.e. singers made famous by broadcasting) did better, but their earnings remained a small proportion of total earnings from music (as is the case for writers). The Beatles kept 8 per cent of the total amount when they were recording with EMI (which kept 40 per cent of the total, while the retailers took a further 26 per cent). Frank Sinatra received only 6.6 per cent of the $11 million spent on his songs between 1941 and 1946. Billie Holiday said that that she never made a penny from the 270 songs she recorded between 1933 and 1944.[51]

One of the main effects of national public service broadcasting was to stem the flow of American music. To some extent this corresponded to perceived popular taste. Local talents were preferred. But there was clearly a protectionist agenda at work. It is quite likely that under conditions of free competition there would have been more American jazz and swing. As it turned out, broadcasting was a way to keep 'the Yanks' if not out, at least down, and if not forever, at least for a while. In France and Italy the most popular music programmes of the 1930s were those on which home-grown talents performed. This policy continued well after the war. The Italian state broadcasting company, RAI, took it as given that it should defend Italian songs against American jazz and 'Afro-Cuban' music. The Festival of San Remo was broadcast from 1951. Only Italian songs could compete, and listeners were asked to vote. The winner of the first two festivals was Nilla Pizzi, who was then one of the most characteristic representatives of the Italian way of singing.

When broadcasting appeared it seemed that it would break national boundaries. After all, sound waves did not recognise the borders between states. Today's futurologists predict the end of the nation state now, just as others predicted it then. Yet broadcasting, in its twentieth-century form, strengthened the nation state far more than book publishing or the cinema. While great books and famous films went around the world, broadcasting was essentially a home-grown affair. It was directly controlled by national governments. Its agenda was national-patriotic. It hardened the sway of the national language over dialects. It broadcast 'national' news, creating a sense of community among listeners. It promoted national music, national intellectuals and national views. It could not be penetrated by foreign broadcasting organisations (except by promoting a different political agenda, particularly in time of war or enmity). One could acquire foreign books and watch foreign films in even the most controlled society, but the vast majority of the population would find itself assembled around a receiving machine whose controlling source was, ultimately, entirely national.

V

AFTER 1960

THE ERA OF THE
MASS MEDIA

56

Television:
The Universal Medium

Real Life

WE ARE IN THE EARLY 1960S, somewhere in western Europe. A stereo-typical nuclear family sits on the couch, the lights dimmed. Opposite them, in pride of place, is a large box. Someone switches it on. The box warms up and black-and-white images begin to flicker, formed by the transmission of a succession of small tonal elements on a screen. These moving images, accompanied by synchronised sound, are watched at the same time by other households thanks to a network of transmitters. Listening to the radio, which only offered sound, was similar, but with the advent of television, radio lost its primacy in the household – though it retained a large share of the morning audience, and became an instrument for the solitary listener. The other harbinger of television, the cinema, had at first only images. Television, from its inception, had both sound *and* images. The broadcasting of the images alone would have been commercially unthinkable.

Television gave us what was provided by the press, the cinema, the radio, the theatre and the gramophone, but effortlessly and directly in our own homes. Once upon a time, only the very rich, the princes and the potentates, could be entertained in the privacy of their salons. With television, culture, in the era of capitalism, completed its democratisation – hence the enthusiasm it causes and the dismay and moral panics it generates.

In 1939 there were only 20,000 sets in Great Britain. In 1963 there were 12.5 million in Britain, eight million in Germany, three million in France, and about a million in Italy. In Greece there was no television at all; it was introduced in 1969, well after Venezuela, where it started in the early 1950s. In Spain in 1960, only 1 per cent of the population had a television; fifteen years later 87 per cent had one. Inequalities of access remained high: in 1981 in North America there were 618 TV sets per thousand inhabitants, while in Europe (including the USSR) there were only 309. The world average was then 152 sets per thousand people, but the figure was only ten in sub-Saharan Africa. By 1990 there were seventeen million sets in Italy, nineteen million in France, twenty-two million in the UK, and twenty-three million in Germany. Television had conquered the West; at first a luxury, it had become a necessity. It is not so everywhere, however:

RADIOS AND TELEVISIONS
PER THOUSAND INHABITANTS
IN SELECTED COUNTRIES: 1995 FIGURES

	Radio	Television
USA	2,093	805
UK	1,433	448
Australia	1,304	495
Finland	1,008	519
Germany	944	554
Japan	916	684
France	895	587
Switzerland	851	419
Italy	822	446
Poland	454	311
Greece	430	220
Romania	211	220
Nigeria	197	55
Burkina Faso	28	5.7

SOURCE: UNESCO, *World Culture Report*, 1998

Already in 1970 television was taken for granted in the richer countries. People came home after work and switched on the set automatically. It remained there, blaring in the background, waiting for someone to watch it. It was calculated in Germany in 1993 that the average household kept the TV switched on for 286 minutes a day, but watched it for only 168 minutes.[1] By then multi-channel television had become the norm. This considerable choice provided quarrelsome families with new opportunities for conflict. Non-dysfunctional families harmoniously and tacitly established the rules of television-viewing. They needed to do so, since in the era of the remote control, furious zapping could only be the prerogative of the solitary viewer, or at most the couple; zapping decreases as the number of viewers expands, because it requires instantaneous decisions. The protracted negotiations (lasting one or two minutes) demanded by a large audience (say three or four) make fast zapping impossible. As everyone knows, democracy slows down decision-making. Both the remote control and videocassette recording altered the relationship between viewers and television. Thanks to the VCR, it was possible to become independent from the tyranny of the television schedule, to watch what one wanted when one wanted, and not have to choose between two conflicting programmes – as long as someone in the household knew how to programme it. It was also possible to destabilise the source of funding of commercial television by recording programmes and fast-forwarding through the advertisements.

New power relations emerged in the household. A more or less spontaneous agreement was reached as to where each member should sit: the floor, the 'comfy' chair, the sofa. It was agreed when interruptions were acceptable, and who was to hold the supreme instrument of power: the remote control. Before the arrival of 'the remote', it was the weakest and most malleable member of the family who had to be cajoled into getting up and walking all the way to the set, changing channel and then walking all the way back to their seat. And fewer women than men set the video recorders.[2]

Watching television may be a way of feeling close to one's partner or one's children. One watches the programme they like in order to share in the experience. Conversely, switching on the television as soon as one is home may be a way of declaring that one does not wish to talk to anyone – just as reading a book may also signify, 'This is my time, this is my space. I do not wish to communicate.' Some members of the family have 'their' programmes, the ones they like above all others, programmes for which they have acquired a right of pre-emption – and here gender stereotyping is unavoidable: the football match is reserved for the men, the soaps for the women.[3]

Some programmes acquired a kind of multifunctionality. Throughout the 1950s and 1960s advertising was allowed on Italian television, but it was subject to stringent rules. Each spot had to last two minutes and fifteen seconds, and within this period the actual advertising of the product could not last more than thirty-five seconds. This forced advertisers to produce a short story or sketch, told with great economy of images and directed towards a final punchline.[4] All advertising had to be shown together in a ten-minute slot, known as *Carosello*, squeezed between the end of the television news (8.50 p.m.) and the beginning of the main evening programme (9 p.m.). Since this corresponded to peak viewing time, it satisfied the advertisers; since the slots were very good, everyone watched and remembered the advertising slogans and jingles; and since the end of *Carosello* coincided with children's bedtime, being sent to bed after *Carosello* became a common experience of children throughout the country.

How much do people watch TV? It is difficult to know, and difficult to compare. Most statistics rely on surveys, but the different methodologies used make international comparisons difficult. Besides, not all surveys distinguish between time spent watching and time the TV is switched on. What is beyond doubt is that watching television is most people's main cultural pursuit. Viewing figures vary remarkably among age and income groups. It is obvious that an elderly person with a modest income or a couple with young children will spend far more time watching television than a young middle-class executive without children. There is no homogeneity nor connection between wealth and audience size (though in the West, those who watch little television tend to be urban middle-upper classes with no children). According to 1997 figures, the Indonesians watch for three and half hours per day, people in the neighbouring Philippines only two, like prosperous Singapore. Chileans watch for about two hours a day and Mexicans for four, as do Americans, but Canadians watch for three. Italian-speaking Swiss spend thirty minutes more a day glued to the sets than do their German-speaking fellow-countrymen.

1997: DAILY CONSUMPTION OF TELEVISION IN MINUTES IN SELECTED COUNTRIES.	
Japan	240
Mexico	239
USA	238
Russia	224
Turkey	222
Hungary	221
Indonesia	216
UK	215
Greece	212

1997: DAILY CONSUMPTION OF TELEVISION IN MINUTES
IN SELECTED COUNTRIES. – *continued*

Spain	209
Italy	207
Czech Republic	203
Puerto Rico	203
Poland	202
Belgium (Wallonia)	193
Australia	193
Canada	188
Argentina	187
Germany	183
Peru	183
Ireland	182
France	180
Venezuela	176
Columbia	175
Hong Kong	174
Brazil (Sao Paulo)	169
Portugal	165
South Korea	165
Belgium (Flanders)	161
New Zealand	160
United Arab Emirates	159
Switzerland (Italian-speaking)	157
Denmark	155
Holland	151
Finland	150
Brazil (Rio de Janeiro)	149
Norway	144
Malaya	144
Switzerland (French-speaking)	143
Sweden	141
South Africa	141

1997: DAILY CONSUMPTION OF TELEVISION IN MINUTES IN SELECTED COUNTRIES. – *continued*	
Taiwan	132
Switzerland (German-speaking)	127
Chile	127
Philippines	126
Singapore	126
Thailand	126

SOURCE: *Eurodata* and partners in various countries in Delphine Martin, '1997, une année de télévision dans le monde' in *Audience: Le Journal de médiametrie*, No. 19, June 1998

Family Viewing

Television has altered interpersonal relations far more thoroughly than the book, the record or the cinema. What was there, previously, for the family to do together? There was the radio, of course. There was the cinema; but the cinema became prevalently a genre for peer groups (friends and couples). In the nineteenth century there was some reading aloud in some families, but most reading was done in solitude. So what else was there to do together, other than sitting round the dinner table or going to church? Indeed, historically speaking, television could be seen as the successor of the two previous institutional forms of family togetherness: the communal meal and going to church. Nowadays few pray, and many of those who do, pray on their own, or with strangers. As for the communal meal, this is often taken in front of the television. By not going to church individuals have cut themselves off from a community experience, one many regarded as a tedious imposition. By eating in front of the television others avoid talking with their spouses and their children. Television has become the most common leisure activity.

The television-viewing family is now confronted with images and sounds from everywhere. There are precedents. Pictures and paintings, coins and engravings familiarised those confined within a restricted territory with how other people and other landscapes looked. Songs and speech carried tales and music from distant places or times. But television carries 'real life', as it unfolds. It is, of course, the illusion of real life, as always. The camera selects images, edits out, chooses an angle, a focus, holds an image and then moves on. But we do the same in 'real life'. We glance, pause, and move on. We avert our gaze, or look distractedly, or see without absorbing or understanding, or absorb intensely, oblivious to everything else. Though we can watch TV in isolation, it is not an isolating experience, as can be curling up on a sofa with a book. Television may be restricted to our immediate circle, but we are aware that whenever we watch and whatever we watch, we are part of a wide community of millions of watchers. We do not know them, but we may feel closer to them because we watch the same images. As Rudolph Arnheim noted as early as 1935, the television viewer 'is the final product of a century-long development, which has led from the campfire, the market-place, and the arena to the lonesome consumer of spectacles today'.[5]

There are exceptions to household viewing. When sets were expensive (as they still are in some countries), communal viewing occurred in bars, cafés and other public places. Günter Grass in the chapter '1952' of his autobiographical *My Century*, has Gundel (his fiancée) buying a TV for his father's inn, with the consequence that 'People came from far and wide, because the number of those who could afford TV sets was, and long remained, minimal.'[6] Later, television sets would be found in airport lounges and even in laundrettes. In the US too, at first, TV was watched more in bars than in the home.[7] In the late 1950s, on Thursday evenings in Italy, cafés and bars equipped with a television were full of people watching the popular show *Lascia o raddoppia?*, a quiz game adapted from the American *The $64,000 Question* (1955). In the USA this was a half-hour show; in Italy, it was more popular and lasted considerably longer. Some cinemas even interrupted the film to show it.[8] In Comasina, a working-class suburb of Milan with a considerable number of immigrants from the south, communal viewing was the norm in the 1950s. By 1962, however, 90 per cent of families there had a set (far more than the Italian average), and the era of television viewing in bars was almost over – at least in Comasina.[9]

The velocity of change can be epitomised by the history of the develop-ment of television in a tiny rural community in Italy, Torre Noverana, a village a few kilometres from Ferentino (a small town of 16,000 inhabitants in 1960), and only seventy kilometres from Rome.[10] In the 1950s Torre Noverana was a poor farming community of seventy-five households. Communal life was thriving: the church was full every Sunday, and weather permitting, in the evening most people would sit outside to chat. In 1950 electricity had reached the village, and with it radio.[11] The first TV set was acquired by the most prosperous household in 1960, six years after the beginning of television broadcasting in Italy, spurred on by the prospect of being able to watch the Rome Olympics. The acquisition was in part a response to pressures from the younger family members and the women. The old grandfather objected, and refused to watch to his dying day. Ten other families, related to the lucky TV-owning family, regularly watched with them. The family accepted that the privilege of being 'the first' entailed the moral and social obligation to let other villagers visit them to watch television. On Saturday evening, if the weather was good, the set was wheeled into the street to enable a wider section of the community to watch.[12] Ten years later, one-third of the households owned a television, and virtually everyone had a radio.[13]

The arrival of television coincided with other major changes for the citizens of Torre Noverana: public works programmes and the real estate boom in Rome had enticed local workers to go to the big city.[14] The years 1958–62 were, particularly in Italy, a period of unprecedented economic growth and considerable social change. It is thus difficult to isolate the specific effects of television. In the development of a common language, however, the importance of television was paramount. In 1960 the inhabitants of Torre Noverana spoke only their local dialect. Italian was the language the younger generation had been taught at school, and was used, with some difficulty, with officialdom. Since dialect was never used on television, the inhabitants became exposed almost every evening to an uninterrupted flow of Italian. Italy may have been united since 1861, but linguistically speaking this unification was completed only in the 1960s, largely thanks to television. In 1951, 5.4 million Italians (almost all illiterate) were not able to speak Italian, twenty-six million spoke dialect with their friends and relatives, and only 7.8 million spoke Italian habitually.[15]

In spite of their relative isolation, the television preferences of the villagers were similar to those of the rest of the country. In 1970 they hardly ever watched programmes aimed at farmers, probably because they were not concerned with the kind of farming typical of the area (small-scale tobacco cultivation), but assumed a far more sophisticated agriculture. One programme even showed how to use a helicopter to sow fields – this was regarded by one of the locals as 'making fun of us'. Hardly anyone watched cultural programmes, but they all watched the news, *Il Telegiornale*. Since the level of literacy was low and the newspapers were all written in Italian, the inhabitants of Torre Noverana had previously known what was going on in the wider world only through the radio and the newsreel at the cinema in

Ferentino. The *Telegiornale* opened wider horizons and it was watched by everyone, and indeed has remained one of the most popular programmes of RAI. As there was no popular press in Italy, the advent of the *Telegiornale* constituted the birth of the only 'popular newspaper' the country has ever had.[16] This addiction to the news in what was a politically controlled state television system, far from inspiring widespread acquiescence, exacerbated a diffuse cynicism about information received (thus the whole village watched the Apollo 11 moon landing in July 1969, but many thought it was all a trick).[17]

Even when TV ownership has become almost universal, some programmes, such as sporting events, are watched collectively. These demand some emotional participation by the audience – with many men preferring to watch their favourite team with their male friends or in a bar than in the calmer and more sober bosom of their family.

A cultural medium centred on the family presents both opportunities and dangers. Of this Pope Pius XII was fully aware (unsurprisingly, since the Vatican had embraced radio since the 1920s). In his 'Letter on Television' of 1 January 1954 he welcomed the new medium, but warned:

> We have before us the painful results of the evil and perturbing power of the cinema. How could we not be horrified at the possibility that television might carry inside the domestic walls the same poisoned atmosphere of materialism, mindlessness and hedonism that surrounds people in so many cinemas?[18]

In the short term his fears were misplaced, since, at least in Italy, much of the television personnel were Catholics who supported the main government party, the Christian Democrats. Conventional morality ruled. The family was safe, or indeed safer, since throughout Europe television kept men in the home and away from taverns, pubs, bars and cafés.

The Audience

Television audiences are a serious object of study. From the wide variety of surveys conducted it seems that people in culturally different countries exhibit similar patterns of behaviour, even though they may not watch the same things or interpret them in the same way. In urban India, for instance, in the 1980s (before television ownership had become a mass phenomenon) the television was placed in the middle of the drawing room, children watched from the floor (along with servants), and the grown-ups were arranged hierarchically on more comfortable chairs and sofas. Though the head of the family may have had final authority on programme selection, mothers often had a decisive say, and children's sulking power influenced, sometimes decisively, the choice of programmes. Just as in the West. There is something true behind the cliché of 'the global village'.[19]

Television audiences did not marvel at the new medium. There are no reports of anyone being astounded by the magic box. When television arrived in remote parts of Europe, old people who could barely read and had hardly ever been to the cinema did not think it was an invention of the devil. They sat down and watched it as if they had done so all their lives. To some extent the cinema, and above all the radio, the great anticipator of television, had prepared the way. But while the generation of the 1930s recollect cinema-going as pleasurable and sometimes daring – such memories tinged with feelings of loss – the generation of the 1950s does not recollect the arrival of television with the same romantic feelings.[20]

We watch calmly, and then, equally calmly, we switch off. No particular ritual accompanies the experience. There are no crowds with which to commune, as in the theatre, the cinema or the concert hall. Watching television we are completely safe, in our home, between our own walls, alone or with our nearest and dearest. We watch television with no awe or respect. We voice our feelings aloud. We make ourselves a hot drink. We go to the toilet. Some people have sex. Others eat. Children do their homework; others do the ironing, glancing occasionally. Our attention is sporadic. Research conducted in the USA in 2002 over a ten-day period showed that people spend 46 per cent of the time with the TV switched on doing things other than watching it. In Germany the percentage of attentive viewers was even smaller: 33 per cent. The most attentive were the old.[21] Impatient viewing is a hallmark of television. Probably because it is free, we are less willing to wait. A few minutes spent watching an expressionless face on television would lead most people to switch channels, while in a different context – such as the cinema – we would give boredom some chance, since we cannot switch off, but would have to walk out and go home, acknowledging the loss of money and time.[22]

Television offered us what we already had, albeit in a different format. It gave us news, but we had that on the radio, in newspapers and photojournalism reportage. It gave us fiction, but we already read the same stories in novels, and saw them at the theatre and the cinema. Television did not invent detective stories, or westerns, or costume drama. It gave us sitcoms, but we already had the vaudeville. It gave us soap operas and serials, but we had serialised novels. It gave us games and quiz shows, but contests and jousts are even older than the book. It showed us sporting events, but the Greeks had them. It gave us talk shows, but we had conversations and debates. It gave us documentaries, but printed essays, illustrated lectures and film documentaries had preceded them. It gave us 'live' events, but these could be watched . . . live. All of these, however, were radically changed by television. Besides, before television, access to many cultural products required skills, such as reading, or ease of travel, or substantial sums, and in all cases, some effort. With television, all these things became available instantly, at the touch of a button, in the privacy of our home. We could see 'real life' without experiencing it. And the beauty of it all is that, in the era of the triumph of capitalism and of market forces, everything we watch is completely free. Once a TV set is purchased and the tax or the cable subscription is paid, we make no further economic calculations in deciding what to watch or how much. When we speak on the telephone – at least in Europe – the more we talk, the more we pay. When we watch television, all that matters is whether we like the programme and whether we have the time to watch it. It is like a public library, an open museum, a personal cinema, a free newspaper.

Inventing TV

Like the cinema, television has no authentic inventor. Unlike the cinema, there is no canonical date of birth. There is no epic photograph of the first broadcast. As is often the case with many technological breakthroughs, parentage is multiple. Thus, though most people have heard of Gutenberg, the first *European* to use movable type, fewer have heard of John Logie Baird, often referred as *the* inventor of television. Yet he did devise a thirty-line system which was publicly demonstrated in London on 27 January 1926. A 240-line system was used on further experimental broadcasts on 30 September 1929 in Long Acre in London. To reach this stage a range of discoveries and inventions had been necessary, from the discovery of selenium in 1817 by Jöns Jakob Berzelius, a Swedish chemist, to the work on electromagnetism by the British scientist Michael Faraday (1791–1867) and on optics (1877) by the Scottish physicist John Kerr. In 1884 Paul Nipkow, a German engineer, produced 'the master television patent', which showed how to scan mechanically an image into elemental points through a perforated disc.[23] The cathode ray tube, a vacuum tube inside which a beam of high-energy electrons focuses on a fluorescent screen to give light, had also been developed in the late nineteenth century, and was improved by a Russian scientist, Boris Rosing, in 1907.[24] Further progress was made by Vladimir Kosma Zworykin, a student of Rosing who had emigrated to the USA, where in 1927 Philo Farnsworth patented an electronic camera tube and worked on how to synchronise cameras and receivers electronically.

As with the cinema, what matters is not the invention, but its use and its audience. To speak of television existing makes sense only when there a mass audience, and this did not come about until the 1950s. The first regular television service was launched by the BBC in November 1936, using a 405-line electronic system invented by EMI and Marconi (rather than Baird's 240-line system). *The Times* of 3 November 1936 praised this new public service victory with appropriate national pride: 'The foresight which secured to this country a national system of broadcasting promised to secure for it also a flying start on the practice of television. At this moment the British Television Service was undoubtedly ahead of the rest in the world. Long might that lead be held.' The lead was not held for long: in 1939 the service was discontinued due to the war – just as, in the words of the *BBC Handbook*, 'the ordinary man was beginning to realise that he could have it in his own home for a few shillings a week'.[25] In reality the tiny audience, only 20,000, was hardly 'ordinary'.

The United States had started television broadcasting in 1939, but it too suspended it when the country entered the war. Only after the war did American television really start its spectacular ascent. The three dominant companies, NBC, CBS and ABC (created in 1943 when the government forced RCA to give up one of its two national radio networks), were already the largest conglomerates in radio broadcasting, and were well equipped to dominate the television industry. In 1948, only 3 per cent of Americans owned a TV set (185,000 receivers at the beginning of the year; over a million by the end). In 1953 France had only 60,000 sets.[26] In 1954, when European television began in earnest, the USA had already 30.5 million sets. By 1955, 67 per cent of American households had a set, that is about forty-five million, and colour transmissions had started. In the same year Italy had fewer than 100,000 subscribers, and even in 1973 only 6 per cent of French viewers had colour TV.[27] An American consumption lead of such magnitude remained unparalleled; it did not occur with subsequent technological developments: portable (transistor) radios, hi fi, cassette recorders, CD players, video recorders, mobile telephones and computers – all of which Europeans acquired soon after the Americans.

But in TV, Europe lagged behind. The main problem was, as always, wealth and linguistic fragmentation. Even some small countries were divided by language. Until 1953 Belgian owners of TV sets watched Dutch or French stations. In Holland the Nederlandse Televisie Stichting managed, in 1953, to broadcast only three hours per week to the 10,000 receivers in the country. Denmark broadcast its first programmes only in 1953, with the BBC supplying most of the material. Sweden and Norway had only experimental broadcasts until 1953. These were large countries with small populations, and could not afford regular television until 1956. Almost everywhere, most of the material was imported from the USA.[28] The model, however, was firmly based on the public service ethos on which all European radio broadcasting systems (except that of Luxembourg) were based. It was usually funded by a broadcasting fee, supplemented by advertising as was the Italian RAI from its inception and the French state network after 1968, or almost entirely by advertising as was TVE, the Spanish public broadcaster. The West German system was a direct result of the reorganisation of the country as a federal state. TV broadcasting was, after 1952, under the authority of the *Länder* (the states). By 1955 there were nine regionally based broadcasting companies, for instance WDR (Westdeutscher Rundfunk) in Cologne, NDR (Norddeutscher Rundfunk) in Hamburg, BR (Bayerischer Rundfunk) in Munich, and so on. Coordination of programmes was assured through the ARD (Arbeitsgemeinschaft der Öffentlich-Rechtlichen Rundfunkanstalten der Bundesrepublik Deutschlands, Working Association of the Public Radio-TV Organisations of Germany). In 1959 the Chancellor, Konrad Adenauer, tried to set up a second commercial channel, financed by state loan and under the control of the central government. The Constitutional Court deemed the proposal unconstitutional, but agreed that a second television channel (ZDF – Zweites Deutsches Fernsehen) could be set up under the supervision of the *Länder*, and in practice 'colonised' by the political parties. In the ARD companies, the political connection is even more flagrant.[29]

The other obstacle to the spread of TV was the low purchasing power of Europeans after the war. Many countries with no electronic industry or a weak one (such as France) were forced to import cathode ray tubes and other parts, at great cost. Since few people could afford to buy a set outright, a system of delayed payment (hire purchase) was adopted almost universally. In some countries, notably Great Britain, televisions were regularly hired – a system which lasted well into the 1980s.

For technological reasons live television, like live radio, preceded recording. This forced television to develop techniques which had no parallel in the cinema, not just in the broadcasting of plays but in the highly popular coverage of live events, including sports. To achieve this, a number of technical problems had to be resolved. And resolved they were: in July 1952 a whole week of programmes was relayed from Paris to London as part of an 'Anglo-French week' whose aim was to familiarise the British with the French and vice-versa. This consisted of transmitting live programmes taking place in seventeen different places.[30]

Sport was crucial to television from the beginning, and has continued to dominate global television (especially football, tennis, golf and boxing). All the main sporting events were televised from the earliest years: cricket, football, cycling, tennis. Some minority sports, thanks to television, acquired a much wider public (wrestling in France, darts in Britain). In France in 1957 there was more time dedicated to sport (two hundred hours) than to fiction (126 hours), and as early as the second half of the 1950s, sport constituted over half of the total broadcasts on Eurovision.[31]

Live broadcasts sold sets. Without television, people were not just missing out on programmes, they were missing out on history. In October 1952 a thousand sets were sold in the days before a France–Germany football match. In June 1953, 5,000 sets were sold *in France* in the week preceding the broadcast of the coronation of Queen Elizabeth II.[32] This should have caused no surprise. The first radio broadcast by King George V, in April 1924, was believed to have been a major early influence on the sale of wireless sets, as was the coronation of George VI in May 1937.[33]

In 1946 there was no alternative to the broadcasting of live events, since there was virtually no way of recording images. German audio recording was exceptionally advanced, but it was only after the war that this technology became available to the Americans and the British.[34] Malcolm Stewart, then a young sound engineer attached to the Broadcasting Unit of the British Army, recalls his amazement at what he saw in post-war Hamburg:

> When I arrived and was put in charge of the recording department, the equipment I found had all been confiscated from the German Army. The disc recorders . . . were similar to those at the BBC, but the magnetic

tape recording I discovered was technologically so much in advance of ours. It was incredible. Our field magnetic recorders were so primitive, while they had developed ¼-inch magnetic tape ... the quality was so superior.[35]

By the end of 1948 the three main US networks were making television recordings of many of their programmes. In 1950 the Oxford–Cambridge boat race was broadcast live and also 'tele-recorded' and shown later that evening.[36]

The coronation of Queen Elizabeth II was one of the first events to be broadcast live in a number of European countries. Inside Westminster Abbey there were two British commentators and (with a French Canadian audience in mind) one French. Permission was refused for an American commentator.[37] A million people saw the coronation in France. It was filmed by thirty-two broadcasting organisations (sixteen European, others from countries including Japan and the USA).[38] A tele-recording was flown to Canada and shown, via a special television link between Montreal and Buffalo, by both NBC and ABC. The event was not solemn enough for the Americans to broadcast it without advertising, which is why the inauguration of one of the longest reigns in British history was marked, in the USA, by commercial breaks for deodorants and other products. In the middle of the communion service there was an 'interview' on NBC's *Today* with 'J. Fred Muggs', a banana-eating chimpanzee.[39] The British establishment's suspicions of commercial television were further heightened.

The crowds outside were drenched by intermittent heavy showers, but those who were within reach of television watched it all safely and in comfort. As *The Times* of 3 June 1953 put it: 'They were denied the glory of colour which blazed within the Confessor's great church, but they shared with the 7,000 privileged members of that glittering congregation the enormous significance of all that was done. Much of it indeed was more apparent in its detail and fullness to the viewers in their homes than to the guests of high dignity in state and Empire and from foreign lands who thronged the azure galleries of the Abbey.'

The extraordinary pageantry, from the shots of the procession moving slowly towards the centre of the Abbey to the majestic moment when the Archbishop of Canterbury lifted the huge St Edward's Crown and deposited it on the head of the young sovereign (whose gender, attractiveness and apparent frailty ensured her popularity with the wider public), marked a turning point in the history of both the monarchy and the media. Born with television, the British monarch and her family were to live in the constant glare of the cameras.

Events were not yet tailored to accommodate television, but they soon would be, when it was realised that viewers were not interlopers who happened to have gatecrashed the event thanks to television cameras, but the 'real' audience for whom the event had been devised.

Politicians were not slow to discover this. In 1959 Charles de Gaulle appeared only twice on television, and on both instances the occasion was a press conference – the TV audience listening in on an event from which they had hitherto been excluded. A year later he was addressing the French people directly on television.[40] And he was quick to learn. During his first broadcast de Gaulle, wearing spectacles, read carefully from his notes, holding his head down. Alerted by the more intelligent of his cronies that this was a disaster, he decided to memorise his next speech, discard his glasses, hold his head high and look into the camera.[41] The old-fashioned General, groomed for the new media, became a television success. In his memoirs he explained unselfconsciously that 'in order to remain true to my image' he had to address the viewers looking at them 'eye to eye, without papers and without spectacles' Aware that everything he said would be analysed and commented on, it was required of 'this seventy-year old man, sitting alone behind a desk, under implacable lights, that he should appear lively and spontaneous to seize and retain the attention'.[42]

Aspiring politicians must be 'good on television' They must adopt a role ('the true leader', 'one of us', 'the wise old man', 'the guy you can trust', 'the iron lady', 'the youthful innovator', 'the experienced helmsman', etc.). As Neil Postman has remarked, it was extremely unlikely that someone like the twenty-seventh President of the USA (1909–13), the 'multi-chinned, three-hundred-pound' William Howard Taft, a poor public speaker, would even have contemplated running for the presidency in the 1980s.[43]

Politicians have had to learn to exploit the particular filtering system that sifts through the range of possible news, and 'pick out the material most likely to capture the public's attention'.[44] Looking good on the box is not simple. It means being articulate without appearing to pontificate, engaging without being cloying, radiating a positive image while remaining believable, being able to simplify matters without talking down, and above all, appearing trustworthy while making promises. In the television age such qualities soon became crucial in the selection of political leaders. Previously, party leaders were able to convey complex messages to their activists, who in turn, suitably galvanised, transmitted these messages in a simplified form among their friends, colleagues and relatives. With television, communication became more direct, and also lost the elements of complexity.

The mere fact of appearing regularly on television added to the dimension and appeal of the more powerful politicians. Each became the embodiment of his party (less frequently, her party), his features known to an extent unimaginable in pre-television days. There were precedents, of course, namely the photojournalism and the cinema newsreels of the 1930s. Soon everyone realised that regular appearances on television could transform almost anyone into a celebrity. Newsreaders became household names. Even programme announcers, usually attractive females in elegant evening dress, who introduced the next programme with a few words and a smile, became institutions. Their life stories, loves and preferences became a regular feature of the popular press. At the origins of television this was the most significant role open to women.

Fear and Loathing of TV

The effects of television have been endlessly debated. Would it cause even more damage than literature, the press and the cinema? Does it really shorten the attention spans of children, making them incapable of thoughtful reception? Does it transform people into passive recipients? An early British study on the effects of television on children concluded that there were few negative effects. The study was undertaken in 1958, when only a minority had a television and when the medium was still young, but anxiety was already in the air, as it always is when children are involved.[45]

Since television reports anything unpleasant that happens in a society (crimes but not the lack of crime, the behaviour of hooligans but not the tranquil attitude of most football fans, drunkenness but not sobriety), anything unpleasant can be attributed to the corrupting influence of television. An enormous panic literature developed.[46] In vain did many researchers point out that the 'television audience' is an artificial construct, that in reality audiences are highly variegated, that each segment responds differently (or not at all) to different messages, that the messages sent by television are equally differentiated.

A considerable amount of violence is portrayed in television fiction (as in all fiction). Much of it is not 'rewarded'. That crime does not pay is still the operating principle. Since an increase of violence can be attributed to many factors, and it is not possible to isolate the specific effects of television viewing from other factors, holding the media responsible seems to be just one option one can choose to adopt, rather than anything supported by strong evidence. The idea that television makes violence more acceptable as a way of resolving disputes is equally debatable.

Moral panics are a normal part of social and political debates. Television, being universal, unlike all previous means of cultural diffusion, is highly responsive to moral panics and social pressures. The injunction that viewers who risk being offended or upset by television can always watch something else or switch off can never be taken seriously. Television is inside the home, free and available, impossible or difficult to avoid, unlike newspapers, films and books.

One of the most significant effects of television coverage is that it solicits the creation of media events by politicians, activists and pressure groups. Everyone knows that to attract attention to one's cause it may be necessary to engage in some 'spectacular', i.e. televisual, form of action. Signing a petition and delivering it to 10 Downing Street is unlikely to bring it to the attention of the evening news. Having it delivered by twenty naked people might. A further effect of a reported activity is that it is a speedy way of conveying information. An anti-tax riot in one neighbourhood, if reported, may entice others of a similar disposition to realise that they are not alone in thinking the way they do, and that by rioting they join a wider movement. This clearly has some bearing in the arena of terrorism. Yet it is difficult for the media in a democratic society to ignore such acts, even on the grounds that ignoring them will reduce the chances of further terrorist activities.

Such considerations are far from being the only motivation for examining the effects of television on audiences. Studying the audience is a normal part of the business of television. Television's peculiar connection with the market (programmes, unlike books, are not sold directly to consumers, and audiences are 'sold' to advertisers) has led to a new field of study: the analysis of audiences and the estimation of their size. Who watches what, when they watch it, which social class or gender they belong to, are matters of great importance. Such a preoccupation is understandable. Only some people read books, and even fewer go to the opera, but everyone watches television. Knowing the audience is important, since the choice of future programmes depends on it, as do careers, and the prestige and jobs of many people.

Attempts to measure the audiences were begun in the 1940s in the USA by companies such as Nielsen in order to establish the rankings of radio programmes. After the war the methodology was further developed for television viewing. One way to test the public was to phone a random sample of viewers and ask them what they were listening to or watching. This required, of course, a large number of calls taking place at the same time. Another system was to ask a sample to keep a viewing diary, updated every fifteen minutes for three weeks. A more impersonal system, and hence allegedly more objective, was developed, which involved placing a detector inside the television to establish when the set was switched on, for how long and on which channel (but it was difficult to know whether anyone was watching). Later, randomly selected viewers were induced to respond to questions asked via computers. Since then ever more formidable systems have been developed, including cameras fixed on the television, able to detect not just whether anyone is actually watching but whether they show any interest at all.

Programmers can generate a higher rating for some programmes by a clever and imaginative use of schedules. It is obvious that a programme shown late at night will have, all things being equal, a lower rating than one shown at prime time. It is equally obvious that setting a programme against a popular programme on another channel may decrease its potential audience. RAI, the Italian state broadcasting company, having invested considerable money and effort in the serialisation of Manzoni's novel *I Promessi sposi* in 1967, made sure that it was set against programmes of low appeal such as folk music or instrumental music. Thus the large audience reached (eighteen million viewers) was not simply attracted by a story known to all Italian schoolchildren.[47]

But these matters are complex, since many popular programmes are ostracised by significant minorities who would welcome more adventurous fare. The art of scheduling is arcane and sophisticated, and those in charge of such matters are seen by insiders as the real power in television. Where advertising is important, scheduling a cheap programme in non-prime time may be economically rational because the ratio of audience to cost may be better than that reached by an expensive programme shown at prime time (when the competition is fierce).

Advertisers, of course, can never be sure whether the audience is actually watching the commercials, since good programmes are precisely those in which the advertising break is the signal for making a drink or going to the toilet. But advertisers are not interested in audiences, they are interested in convincing companies that advertising is necessary, that it keeps the competition on its toes and stops other firms from entering the market by raising the cost of entry. The remote control added to advertisers' problems, since zapping is far more frequent during breaks than during the programme. Finally, the use of video recording gave the audience the possibility of skipping through the commercial breaks in recorded programmes. Digital (personal) video recorders can do this even better. How advertising 'works' remains one of the many mysteries of modern life.

In spite of all the studies, all we know is what kind of genres people like. What we do not know is why a particular specimen of a genre will be liked so much more than others. As in everything else about cultural markets, no one really knows. Todd Gitlin, author of *Prime Time* (1983), was told by a Vice-President at CBS that:

> Because it's a mass audience . . . the audience's tastes are so diffused and so general that you've got to be guessing. You can work off precedents about what's worked on television before. You can work off whatever smattering of sociological information you gleaned from whatever sources . . . But you never really know.[48]

Another Vice-President of CBS, Arnold Becker, did not really care: 'I'm not interested in culture. I'm not interested in pro-social values. I have only one interest. That's whether people watch the program. That's my definition of good. That's my definition of bad.'[49]

Some of the fears about television were an expression of a long-standing fear of the Americanisation of Europe. Generations of young minds, it was feared, would grow up imbued with American values and culture, and would lose their identity. No one would deny the ubiquitous nature of American youth culture, but the most popular television programmes are not American, American programmes do not dominate prime time, and on the whole they are more respectful of conventional morality.

By the late 1990s 'reality TV' had become the butt of criticisms by those who complained about the deterioration in the quality of television.[50] Yet the genre now dominates our screens. In May 2003 Tessa Jowell, the British Secretary of State for Culture, hoped that viewers would show their dismay at the constant debasing of television by reality shows, yet a year later she accepted that programmes like *Big Brother* were within the public service's 'broader remit'.[51]

People who watch an excessive amount of television are often denigrated, while those who read many books are praised, and those who go regularly to the theatre or the cinema are considered intellectuals or cinephiles. Those who like television are 'couch potatoes', while in Germany TV is disparaged as the *Glotze*, or 'goggle box'. People who watch television are accused of having a short attention span – an assumption which is the result of calculating the amount of channel switching in a given segment of time. The assumption is often unwarranted, since if a viewer is watching a programme which is interrupted every fifteen minutes by a commercial break during which she zaps fifteen times, it will seem as if she has spent only one minute on each programme.

The disparaging of television has often been the automatic response of intellectual élites – after all, this has been their response to all developments in mass culture. Yet there can be little doubt that public sector television (the dominant European model) has been the most significant factor in the expansion of knowledge. All over Europe those in charge of radio and television knew that they had to meet the expectations of several groups. They had to please the politicians by providing a more balanced perspective than that of newspapers. They had to please the intelligentsia and those seeking to improve themselves (a consistent tendency, as we have seen – for instance in Chapter 26) by providing programmes with educational content. Finally, they had to please everyone by providing entertainment. Except for a small minority, most of the people in charge of television were closer to the world of education and public service than to the world of business, and were committed to an ideal of cultural television against its commercialisation.

The result was the relatively high educational standard of programmes on European state television. For instance, in France between 1953 and 1978, 119,163 hours of programmes were broadcast. Out of these, 4 per cent had historical content (fiction and non-fiction), not much less than those of the much-disparaged variety shows (6.4 per cent in 1974 and 4.2 per cent in 1977). After 1975, the fragmentation of ORTF and the multiplication of channels led to a diminution of historical programmes, many of which were shunted away from prime time broadcasting.[52]

As television density increased, the percentage of the uneducated watching it increased (inevitably), so programmes had to adapt themselves to a lower level. Far from 'lowering' standards, television was part of the progressive increase in the educational level of the population. A survey conducted by RAI established that in 1964, 45 per cent of the Italian population were not sure what '*assemblea parlamentare*' (parliamentary assembly) meant, 21 per cent did not know what was meant by '*nazionalizzazione dell'energia elettrica*' (the top issue at the time of the survey), 29 per cent did not know what 'currency' meant, and 74 per cent did not know what was meant by the term '*aggiornamento*', then widely used to denote the modernisation agenda set by the Vatican Council for the Roman Catholic Church. In April 1969, 65 per cent did not know what was meant by inflation.[53] Of course, a few years later, they understood it only too well.

An understanding of the low level of general education in the pre-television age might have tempered the critics' litany of complaints. In fact this had begun as soon as television started: 'Télévision: la qualité diminue' was the telling headline of an article by the cinema critic André Bazin in *France-Observateur* in 1956.[54] It never subsided.

The general respect which surrounds British television (it has won by far the greatest number of awards such as the Prix Italia) is due largely to a unique combination of circumstances: the pioneering public service ethic of radio and television personnel, which was derived substantially from the same ethical spirit which was (and is) characteristic of the Civil Service, including a world view based on empire-building; the autonomy of the BBC from the political system, which insulated it from the need to kowtow to politicians (unlike most of its counterparts in Europe); its lack of dependency on commercial pressures, which meant it never needed to satisfy commercial sponsors (as in the USA). The early start of commercial television in Britain (1955, almost at the beginning of the spread of the medium), and the controversies and hostilities surrounding it, meant that commercial television always had the BBC as a model, and felt the need to produce high-quality popular programmes while providing the BBC with strong competition (elsewhere, commercial television arose as a reaction to a public service system which had failed to satisfy its public). Some of these conditions existed elsewhere; for instance the Dutch socialist broadcasting TV network VARA had much in common with the BBC's 'Reithian' philosophy.[55] But the BBC had an additional advantage: a large linguistic market which enabled it to sell its products to the four corners of the world. In 2004, 26 per cent of its funding originated from the sales of its programmes abroad – a far, far higher percentage than any other broadcasting organisation in Europe.[56]

In April 1999 a report carried out on behalf of the British government accused British broadcasters of making 'the wrong type' of programmes for overseas buyers. The programmes were too British, 'too dark', 'too slow', and perhaps of too high a quality. However, another report, also commissioned by the government, pointed out that not only did British broadcasters export six times more than their nearest competitors (France and Australia), but that their share of the global broadcasting market was, at 9 per cent, better than the country's overall share of world trade (4 per cent).[57] In 2005 a report called *Rights of Passage: British Television in the Global Market*, commissioned by the television industry, challenged the 1999 report: Britain was still the second-biggest player in the global television market, with 10 per cent of the total, after the USA (a staggering 70 per cent) and ahead of Canada (3.9 per cent), Germany (3.5 per cent), France (2.1 per cent), Australia (2.1 per cent) and Japan (1.4 per cent).[58]

The role of the BBC was central to the positioning of the UK in this global market. This constituted a remarkable commercial feat for a public organisation. Though, constitutionally speaking, it was no different from most other public service broadcasting organisations in Europe – its Board of Governors were appointed by the government, and its income was in the gift of the government – the BBC often succeeded in being seen as beholden neither to private interests nor to the state. Over the decades it had acquired a special aura: that of being at one with the nation. Criticisms from government, notably in 2003, in the months preceding and following the war in Iraq, only served to reinforce its aura of independence. The fact that it attracts criticism from all sides is used to demonstrate that the BBC remains loftily above parties. It is oppositional, yet it represents the establishment. It is often complacently middle-class, while it ruffles the feathers of the middle classes by the judicious deployment of populist 'dumbing down' programmes. Such acrobatics have, so far, paid off and allowed it to remain the pre-eminent British cultural organisation.

57

The Flow of Genres on Television

Television Genres

TELEVISION PRESENTS ITSELF as a constant flow punctuated by conventional interruptions. The credits signal the end of one programme, a tune or a presenter announces the beginning of another. In multi-channel systems, now the norm, we make up our own private patchwork of programmes. Unlike books and plays, what is offered on television is a sequence 'available in a single dimension and in a single operation'.[1] Watching television absorbs a considerable part of our time, yet each image offers an ephemeral experience, quintessentially modern. To paraphrase Baudelaire, it is transitory, fleeting, contingent.[2] Forgetfulness is an intrinsic part of television. Politicians are aware of this, and like advertisers, repeat the same things constantly. With the usual rare exceptions, programmes are erased from our memory almost instantly, or remembered only subliminally. Not for nothing has Marshall McLuhan's 'The medium is the message' become one of the best-known aphorisms about television.

The medium has virtually no history. Histories of television deal with institutions, policies, relationship with government, but seldom contain a history of programmes, though successful programmes and genres are mentioned. It is as if histories of literature or cinema barely mentioned books and films. A study of the history of the contents of radio and television would face serious problems. The quantity is staggering: one year of broadcasts on five terrestrial channels, at a modest fifteen hours per channel per day, produces over 27,000 hours a year. One thousand Bollywood films a year at three hours each makes only 3,000 hours. In literature there is a canon to be remembered while the rest is forgotten. On television, instead of a canon there are cult programmes. Poor preservation techniques in the early days of broadcasting, lack of interest, and the high number of unrecorded live broadcasts mean that radio and television archives are undeveloped compared to the vast array of nineteenth-century newspapers carefully preserved in libraries. Historical amnesia pervades even the practitioners themselves. In the mid-1990s at the BBC, no one involved in a new TV adaptation of Dickens's *Martin Chuzzlewit* remembered at first that there had been a previous adaptation in 1964, and no one could see it because it had not been preserved.[3] Television never had a 'high' culture history, though like literature and the cinema it has generated laments for a golden age that never was.

When there were only one or two TV channels it was possible to experiment – the benefit of a lack of competition. With competition the rewards for successful innovation (the discovery of something both new and popular) are very great, but they do not last very long, for imitation saps the initial advantage. So it pays to play safe. One can leave experimentation to others, and steal their ideas.

All cultural artefacts can be adapted to television. Plays become television plays; farces become situation comedies (sitcoms); melodramas become soaps; serialised novels become TV serials; comic strips become TV cartoons; journalism becomes news; cookery books become cookery programmes. Genres can be mixed even more easily than in a magazine. A show can start with dancers, then a singer sings, then the singer is interviewed, then she is introduced to a writer who promotes his latest book. Thus a variety show becomes a song programme and turns into a literary fair. Television genres are never entirely separated. Some networks, such as Italy's state broadcasting corporation, RAI, developed what was called '*programma-contenitore*' lasting several hours on a Sunday afternoon. Held together by its presenter Renzo Arbore, the programme *L'Altra domenica* (1976) introduced guests, promoted music, had comedy acts and sport. It was like an old-fashioned variety show where there was a bit of everything. Viewers could watch a little now and then, or spend the entire afternoon being entertained by Arbore and his friends. The *programma-contenitore* became a genre in itself. Later versions, such as *Domenica in*, would start out at 12.30 p.m. with an audience of over seven million, and fluctuate from a low of 4.8 million to peak at 10.9 million between 8 p.m. and 9 p.m.[4]

By creating a large community of viewers, television creates its own self-referential world. This world is full of newsreaders, presenters, chat show hosts, comedians and actors. In the early days of the medium, actors regarded television as a stepping stone on the way to the cinema or the theatre, where real fame or prestige could be obtained. But soon it became apparent that the sheer volume of those who watched television soaps gave celebrity status even to minor talents. Andy Warhol's famous prediction, 'In the future, everyone will be famous for fifteen minutes,' would have no basis without television. In game shows even those who knew the Bible by heart could become famous. The apotheosis was reached with reality TV, where fame could be obtained without any skill, training or preparation.[5]

With the mixing of genres, the distinction between made-up images and reality fades, since all images are 'made up' by virtue of being selected and edited. Viewers care for fictional characters as much as (or more than) for real ones – as did the nineteenth-century readers of serialised novels. Such fiction can have a direct impact on reality. In 2003, when it became obvious that Fernanda, the ex-high-class prostitute heroine of Brazil's top-rated Globo TV *telenovela*, *Mulheres apaixonadas* (Women in Love) – widely exported and watched regularly by thirty-five million Brazilians – was going to be killed, the representative of the Rio de Janeiro tourist industry begged the producers not to make her die in case it added to the negative image of the city as a dangerous place.[6] In the event Fernanda was killed by a stray bullet, as happens not infrequently in Rio. This serial, as others, raised social and personal questions that are not always taken seriously: the husband who beats up his wife; the teacher who is an alcoholic; the rich boy who gets the maid's daughter pregnant; the wife who has sexual problems with her husband and starts going out with the maid's boyfriend.[7] Such things are normal in soaps, and could come straight out of a nineteenth-century melodrama. There is, however, a significant difference between the television serial and the serialised novel. The serialised novel can be published in its entirety and read as a 'regular' novel – and indeed, most were. The fifty hours of a serial such as *Dallas* could not be absorbed by most normal lovers of the genre in one go. Repetitions, which are functional in a serial, would become irritating.[8] The serialised novel was a necessity dictated by the expense and difficulty of circulating novels. The TV serial is a genre in itself.

Live Broadcasting

Television took over from radio the function of being the foremost instrument of national identity. It enhanced it, redefined it, and confirmed it. The community of viewers it created was essentially a national community. This was, of course, far stronger during the first decades of television, when there were few channels. Distinct 'global villages' without national borders may appear in the future as channels multiply, though this is likely to be limited to social groups with common transnational interests (such as academic or business networks) and for occasional viewing. Some events – such as the Olympic Games – induce global broadcasting. But most people cheer for their country's team. The most watched sporting event of 1998 was the World Cup football tournament, but in each country the most viewed event was a match their team was involved in (except Poland, Portugal and Greece, where it was, quite rightly, the France–Brazil final). The top 1998 event in the USA was the Superbowl, in Melbourne, Australia, it was cricket, and in Sydney, Australia, it was rugby league.[9] Some programmes, mainly American fiction, have an exceptionally wide international audience; others, such as game shows and reality TV, are often national adaptations of an original prototype. But it seems premature to imagine the formation of a global village in the sense of a generic homogenisation of the world.

Italy is a heavy importer of American television fiction, beginning with *Perry Mason* and *Bonanza* in the early years, but in the forty years after 1960 the largest audiences were achieved with local live programmes, such as the *Canzonissima* final (where the public is invited to choose their favourite song) or the Festival of San Remo (where the 'best' song of the year is selected). These entertainment programmes, featuring almost exclusively Italian pop songs, reached an audience of thirteen to fourteen million in 1963 and 1964, climbing to over twenty million in 1969. Even higher figures were reached by football matches: Italy–Brazil in the 1970 World Cup reached 28.2 million, only to be dwarfed by Italy–Germany in the 1982 tournament with 36.7 million. In the forty years since 1960 the top audience for Italian television was usually for an Italian variety show or a football match. Even Italy–Bulgaria (1994) was watched by a staggering 25.8 million.[10] By contrast the most popular series in 1982, the US *Colombo*, reached 9.5 million, twice as many as the 'best' Italian series, an adaptation of the Nero Wolfe detective stories (4.4 million). Both were well behind mainstream films shown on TV, whether the reputable *Cat on a Hot Tin Roof* (adapted from Tennessee Williams's play, with Elizabeth Taylor and Paul Newman), which had an audience of 15.7 million, or the forgettable and forgotten *Penelope la magnifica ladra* – a dubbed version of Arthur Hiller's 1966 *Penelope*, with Natalie Wood in the role of the kleptomaniac banker's wife (10.7 million).[11]

Live broadcasts do not constitute a genre. Many are not 'live' at all, in the strict sense of the word, but are pre-recorded beforehand. For most talk shows this is routine. Viewers have the impression that what they watch is live. This, for our purpose, is what matters. When the newsreader turns to 'our man' in Beirut, who immediately provides an account of the events he has just witnessed and the impressions he has just gathered, it matters little that the broadcast was recorded shortly before. It fulfils the unwritten convention between programme-makers and viewers, namely that what is being seen should be 'as it is happening in reality'. Thus the assassination of John F. Kennedy was seen live by relatively few people, but millions saw the images replayed soon afterwards, and had the impression of watching history unfold.

Broadcasting live events is what made television 'special', quite different from watching films at home. Once upon a time, live events were events which would have occurred anyway. They just happened to be caught by the cameras. Soon events became made-for-television. The speed of change was remarkable. At the funeral of King George VI in February 1952, the television cameras stopped, respectfully, at the doors of Westminster Hall. A year later, at the coronation of Elizabeth II, the cameras were *inside* the Abbey. This enabled 56 per cent of the British population to see the service; 7.8 million people at home, 10.4 million in the homes of friends, and 1.5 million in public places.[12]

The coronation (see pages 1161–2) was the first of a number of rituals built round the royal family that created shared memories among the British public thanks to television. Others followed: the regular ceremony of the State Opening of Parliament by the Queen, the Jubilee of 1976, the marriage of Prince Charles and Diana in 1981, and the funeral of the Princess of Wales in 1997. Whether these televised events helped to increase affection for the royal family is far less certain. It certainly made them more 'popular', in the sense of being better known; but as we are all aware, familiarity inevitably breeds if not contempt, at least a critical perspective. The hallowed respect generated by distance was rapidly sapped by having Queens, Presidents and other celebrities in one's living room on a daily basis. The 'royal' version of the popular TV game *It's a Knockout* (the British version of the French *Jeux sans frontières*) in 1987, with Princess Anne, Prince Edward and the Duke and Duchess of York (known simply as 'Fergie') was a peak (or a low, depending on one's point of view) of royal populism.

'Ceremonial' television, as Daniel Dayan and Elihu Katz have called it, has particular features.[13] It demands an out-of-the-ordinary level of attention;

it follows a much more leisurely rhythm than news programmes, since it is often in real time (the broadcast of the coronation lasted eight hours); normal programmes are suspended, further highlighting the importance of the event; they are largely foreseen (the opening ceremony of the Olympic Games, the visit of the Egyptian President Anwar Sadat to Israel in 1977, the funeral of Pope John Paul II in 2005); above all, they are consensual, that is to say, it is assumed that everyone shares the same feelings about them. The requirements of the genre do not permit a balanced view.[14] The funeral of Diana was a moment of national, and indeed international, sadness; Sadat's visit was about peace in the Middle East; the funeral of John Paul II was about an admirable and much-loved man, etc.

Those who did not share these feelings may have felt at variance with the general will, and were in effect silenced. Feminists wearing a button bearing the warning 'Don't do it, Di!' prior to the Charles and Diana wedding (with hindsight, remarkably prescient advice) were mentioned, if at all, as harmless eccentrics. Television commentators act out the mood. Their words are respectful, carefully crafted, and measured. The commentators, often unseen, act out the 'general' feeling (joyful for a wedding, sombre for a funeral, respectful for anything religious). They are part of the comment. There is no distancing. Those 'allowed' to speak are experts, friends, supporters and members of the crowd (each representing a segment of the community). All have been preselected to go along with the general consensual message. If critics are interviewed, they are introduced as a dissenting voice, out of tune with the overwhelming majority. Those who hold dissenting opinions do not express them unless they feel that others will agree with them. If the media does not air them, the dissenters will still hold their views, but will not voice them – what Elisabeth Noelle-Neumann has called 'the spiral of silence'.[15] An ideological event is thus shown as if it were devoid of ideology. The partisan nature of such staged ceremonies can be determined by reflecting on the unlikelihood of a live broadcast (in the West) of the funeral of Chairman Mao in China in 1976, or of the Red Army parading on Moscow's Red Square on the anniversary of the October Revolution. Exceptionally, international pre-eminence is given to a national event. The French cancelled all TV programmes in 1965 when Churchill died, replacing them with classical music and the soundtrack of the film *The Bridge on the River Kwai*(!).[16] Needless to say, the British did not reciprocate when de Gaulle died in 1970.

Extravagant claims are often made on behalf of ceremonial live broadcasts. 'The entire world is watching' was a common perception in the West of Princess Diana's funeral. The claim is understandable, though false – the overwhelming majority of Chinese did not even know who she was when she died. Yet even if scaled down to, say, a 'mere' five hundred million, it would have been one of the largest audiences in history.

Gradually television networks learned to mix live broadcasts with archive films. The tedium of the length of a ceremony could be interrupted by providing a helpful background 'documentary' lasting a few minutes in which it was put in its historical context (e.g. previous funerals or weddings). Pre-recorded interviews could be inserted. Where there is competition, as when the wedding of Charles and Diana was broadcast by both the BBC and ITV, there was some differentiation: the BBC would almost automatically veer towards the traditionalist and almost pompous, while the commercial ITV would produce a faint whiff of modernity.[17] Needless to say, when it comes to the live televising of national occasions, the BBC wins every time.

The 'miracle' of large-scale televised events is that they address an extremely large public as if it were relatively homogeneous. This can only be achieved by simplifying the story and expressing a simple meaning. How else can one 'sell' the funeral of a Pope to an audience which includes members of different religions, as well as agnostics and dissident Catholics? It cannot be done by underlining the conservative position of John Paul II on specific theological matters, or his condemnation of the war in Iraq, or his prohibition on the use of contraceptives, or his dislike of the consumer society. It can be done by reminding everyone of his charisma, his travels, his generic religiosity, his strength of character. Not everyone can get this treatment. Imagine a television programme on Adolf Hitler focusing on his charisma, his kindness to children and animals, and his vegetarianism.

Reality

In its early days, television, like cinema newsreels and photo-journalism, showed people doing special things. Then a new genre came about: 'reality TV', where ordinary people were shown doing 'ordinary' things – if being filmed twenty-four hours a day living with perfect strangers counts as 'ordinary'. Not all of this is new. Earlier incarnations showed 'ordinary' people as contestants in panel games, or subjected to practical jokes (*Candid Camera*, a much-imitated American programme, started in 1948), or as a participant member of a live audience, or being interviewed in the street to comment about current affairs, or being the subject of a 'fly-on-the-wall' documentary such as *An American Family*, a twelve-part series first broadcast on public television in 1973. This was constructed just like a narrative film, down to the appropriate musical background, combining 'the shooting style of observational cinema with particular features of television as a storytelling medium'.[18] It turned Pat and Bill Loud of Santa Barbara, California, and their five children into household names. Pat and Bill's marriage deteriorated on screen, as Bill's frequent affairs were made manifest and their eldest son's homosexuality was revealed – just like a 'real' soap opera. In 1974 the Wilkins household in Reading (England) was subjected to similar treatment. Then Americans were regaled by Fox's *Cops* (starting in 1989), where police officers are followed chasing villains and arresting them. There were programmes involving judges and counsellors (such as *Divorce Court*, widely imitated in Europe) trying to mediate between real couples in difficulty who were willing to describe their personal miseries to millions. People would admit past mistakes, or discuss their problems, often of a sexual nature, or reveal a childhood of abuse to Oprah Winfrey in her famous 'confessional' talk show (1984–), or – as in *The Jerry Springer Show* – would be confronted with people they had harmed or offended, to the delight of an audience who would incite them to manifest their anger. When asked whether she minded everyone knowing her intimate affairs, one participant replied that she came from a small community where everyone knew them anyway.[19] A mixture of sadistic enjoyment of the misery of others and genuine concern are the hallmark of these shows. *The Jerry Springer Show* offers a modern version of a gladiatorial sport. We watch ('live', though the show is pre-recorded) how people confront others and urge our sympathy in a private argument now made public. Claims that such shows enlarge 'the public sphere' seem to be rather weak.[20] Everyone plays a role: the audience is indignant, the participants pretend to undergo a therapeutic experience.

The development of reality TV owes much to the apparent narcissistic desire that many people have to know how different they are from other people, and to an unlimited supply of exhibitionists ready to oblige. In April 1996 Jennifer Kaye Ringley, an American student, connected a video camera situated in her home to the internet so that the whole world could watch her twenty-four hours a day. She lived 'on line' until she disconnected herself almost eight years later, on 1 January 2004. She received emails from all over the world, some of them including helpful advice such as 'If you sleep that way you are going to have a back problem.'

Once one needed to observe one's neighbours and to gossip with others. Now one can switch on the TV. The popularity and cheapness of these programmes has led to their multiplication. In 2005 *The Times* announced that there were 176 reality programmes due for broadcast in Britain, including *Extreme Health Farm* and *So You Think You Can Teach?*[21] Contestants are auditioned to become part of a pop group (*Popstars*), or have to convince a successful entrepreneur that they are worth hiring (*The Apprentice*), or are taught how to cook by an irascible famous chef who screams at them, or are marooned on a desert island together (*Survivor*). Sometimes barely-known celebrities are 'left' in the 'jungle' (*I'm a Celebrity, Get Me out of Here*), or 'ordinary' people co-exist in a sealed-off house (*Big Brother*). In many of these shows the contestants are gradually eliminated by a jury or by the audience, or by the other contestants. In others, overweight contestants who undertake to lose weight are inspected every week and reprimanded or congratulated; people with no dress sense (and little sense) are 'made over' by 'specialists' (*What Not to Wear*); others who can't keep their house tidy (*How Clean is Your House?*), or look after their children (*Supernanny*), or get to grips with life, are shown how to do so by handsome and well groomed 'experts'; homes are redecorated, faces made up, problems sorted. In one show, tantalisingly called *Wife Swap*, the wives from two families change places for a fortnight (the programme contains, so far, no sex). In another show a woman must choose from a range of hopeful suitors the one she thinks (or pretends to think) is very rich (*Marjolaine et les millionaires*, in France in 2003 and 2004); in another seductively dressed young women vie for the favours of a single man (*Le Bachelor*, 2002). An older version of such shows was *Blind Date* (1985), where after putting various questions to unseen suitors (but visible to viewers) the contestant had to choose one and go with him or her (and a television crew) on a date in an exotic place – and report back.

In Europe the most popular reality programme was *Big Brother*, based on the 'constant surveillance' model. It was started in Holland in 1999 by Endemol, a TV company owned by John de Mol, and based on a Swedish idea. By 2004 *Big Brother* had been adapted in forty countries, trading under various names, but it did not do particularly well in the USA. In the fifth UK series (2004) fourteen million people took part in voting contestants out

– not many fewer than those who voted in the European elections of that year (seventeen million).

The success of these programmes depends substantially on the selection of the participants (people who can stay away from work and family for three months or so, who are young and healthy, and who do not have boring traits such as strong political or religious opinions, or being likely to spend all day reading books). Also crucial are the positioning of the cameras (mercifully, so far, participants can defecate in peace and unseen), the choice of zooms and the editing, which is quite considerable, since the broadcast version is only thirty minutes out of twenty-four hours (in some instances there is an unedited live version available on cable or satellite). Reality TV may be seen as a soap using amateur actors left free to impersonate whoever they want. They become 'characters' according to the narrative conventions of dramas and documentaries.[22] The main innovation is the direct participation of the public (already indirectly involved in television through the measurements of ratings and on the radio through phone-ins). Amidst cries of joy and despair, the viewers eliminate them one by one, as in *Ten Little Indians* (1939) by Agatha Christie, though now the audience is the murderer.[23] *Big Brother* associated the public with a show to a greater extent than ever before. The public, in fact, determined the vicissitudes of the story itself, becoming, if not the author, at least one of the co-participants.[24]

The international success of the programme owes something to chance as well as to an understanding of local conditions. The French channel M6, for instance, had tried to obtain the American reality show *Survivor*. They lost, and bought *Big Brother*, intending to use it to spoil the chances of *Survivor*. They had not realised at first that they had a winner. *Survivor*, a success in the USA, flopped in most European countries, including France. To avoid what they regarded as the negative connotations of the title, the French turned *Big Brother* into *Loft Story*. They also toned down the potential for conflict among the participants because they feared the reaction of intellectual élites (who had already condemned the foreign version, and whose judgement might negatively affect the renewal of M6's licence). In other countries the views of the intelligentsia matter very little, but in France they still function as a kind of secular clergy.[25]

In 1998 the film *The Truman Show* by the (Australian) director Peter Weir imagined a television show where the hero, Truman Burbank, has his entire life filmed by hidden cameras and watched by millions of people without his knowledge. Life follows art, and in 2005 a British company (Shed

Production) announced that it had acquired ten houses in which ten families would live and be filmed. They will go to work and come back in the evening, perhaps to watch themselves being filmed watching themselves on television. Collective narcissism will have reached its zenith. Viewers will be able to play God by voting off families they do not like. Selection is a form of casting: families who shout at each other make better television than those who simply sit and read morosely. The advertisement for contestants reads: 'Does your family have more ups and downs than *EastEnders*? We are looking for colourful families and households.'

The Talk Show

A well-established variant of 'reality' TV is the talk show. A presenter entertains and converses with famous guests. This format has considerable advantages. It is cheap, since guests are present for free or for very little money, hoping that they will come out 'looking good' and able to peddle their cause or their products and/or themselves. It is also extremely flexible, since one can have such shows on virtually any topic at any time of the day or night and tailor it for a specific audience (youth, women, people interested in politics, etc.). The presenter is the central character, the *vox populi*, the voice of the public. The show is often named after him or her. The guests play the role assigned to them, prodded by the presenter with a mixture of flattery and leading questions. The flattery ensures that other distinguished guests will agree to take part in subsequent shows. Conversations tend to be cloying: 'Did you enjoy working with XY, the film director?' 'XY is a wonderful director, a real genius.' Yet there always lurks the possibility of reducing the guest to tears, or getting them to say something embarrassing, thus ensuring further publicity for the show. This genre too was pioneered in the USA, home of its most successful exemplar: *The Tonight Show*, which has been going since 1954, and associated with Johnny Carson who hosted it for thirty years (1962–92).

The popularity of this genre with television companies is unquestionable. In Italy there is a talk show every night, often at prime time or close to it. An endless stream of politicians, gurus, writers and alleged experts parade and talk, often surrounded, for unfathomable reasons, by half-naked girls. Such shows are even more frequent on British television, but are seldom during prime time. On Monday, 6 March 2000, on various British terrestrial channels one could watch *Kilroy*, *Trisha*, *Esther* and the American imports *The Roseanne Show*, *The Oprah Winfrey Show* and *Montel Williams* – but all of them before 5 p.m.[26] Most of these are constructed as social occasions where the private and the public can mix. Paradoxically, members of the audience and many of the guests are readier to tell their private stories on such obviously public platforms than to tell them to their friends and relatives in their private life.[27]

Many of these shows require considerable audience participation, with the presenter normally taking the side of the audience against 'experts', advocates or politicians. Much of the enmity between politicians and broadcasters – each dependent on the other – lies precisely in their competing claim that they 'represent' the people. Many talk shows have an adversarial element. They pit guests selected for their strong partisan views against each other. This enables the gladiatorial element to be played to the full, and makes the more high-minded subjects, such as politics and high culture, more entertaining. At the same time, television is perceived as an impartial medium providing a public space for discussion.

Interviews with celebrities share many elements of the talk show (indeed, some shows consist of a series of interviews). Television interviews with film stars, such as those conducted in the pioneering British cinema programmes of the 1950s *Film Fanfare* and *Picture Parade*, stressed the informality of the context, the friendliness between the interviewer and the star, while working hard to maintain the star's aura.[28] What is particular about the television interview is that it consists not only of getting the guest to discuss the area they are an expert in (the star discusses cinema, the footballer sport, etc.), but also of trying to find the 'real' person under the politician, the actor or the athlete, getting them to reveal something about their private life. The popular interview involves narrowing the space of the private.[29] Experts use the capital and goodwill accumulated in their field in order to obtain an audience for their views in other fields. The public intellectual, a figure invented at the end of the nineteenth century (see pages 666–70), has now become a public celebrity. Actors and pop stars are asked their views about politics, and TV personalities are regularly used by charities, on the assumption that if one likes their programme then one will also like their ideas. Regardless of their intentions and motives, public personalities are constrained by the need to offend as few people as possible. Thus pop stars campaign against world hunger and global warming, and not for unpopular causes such as an increase in progressive income taxes.

Fun and Games

Like most TV genres, TV game shows were pioneered in the USA. *The $64,000 Question* became *Double Your Money* (1955–68) in Britain, *Quitte ou double?* in France and *Lascia e raddoppia?* in Italy. *Name that Tune* (1954) became *Il Musichiere* in Italy (1957).

The popularity of these cheap-to-make shows led to their mass production from the 1960s onwards: *The Generation Game* (1972–81, 1990–2002), in which family members attempted various tasks for points in front of a studio audience; *The Price is Right* (1984–88), where contestants had to guess the value of certain items; straightforward general knowledge competitions such as *Mastermind* (1972–99, 2003–), and *Who Wants to be a Millionaire?* (1998–), adapted in forty countries, which offers contestants the chance to win up to £1 million by answering fifteen general knowledge questions correctly, with the limited help of audience and friends. The German version was broadcast three times a week, with eleven of the shows ending up in the top twenty programmes for 2001.[30] A general knowledge knockout quiz, *The Weakest Link*, launched in 2000, turned out by 2005 to be one of the most successful exports of the BBC, adapted in almost a hundred countries. Contestants answered questions and eliminated their 'weakest' opponent, until only one was left. Here viewers' sadism was given a further boost by the icy stare and sarcastic tone with which the presenter, Anne Robinson, despatched the losers by saying, 'You are the weakest link,' adding, for good measure, well-thought-out putdowns such as 'You make a dim room look positively brilliant.' The presenter's lack of warmth and empathy was part of the design of the product. Robinson was so successful (and Americans so reluctant to impersonate someone who does not want to be loved) that she was asked to present the American adaptation in 2001. By then the flow of ideas went both ways across the Atlantic. The tricks of 'trash TV' were easily learned, and Europeans proved as deft with 'trash' as the Americans. *Big Brother* originated in Europe, as did *The Weakest Link*. The British *Pop Idol* (2001) became *American Idol* when it was remade by Fox, the patriotic US network owned by Australian-born Rupert Murdoch.

The original nationality of such programmes is rather irrelevant, since they require adaptation to local conditions. Questions regarded as very easy in France (Who wrote *À la Recherche du temps perdu?*) are a little harder in Idaho. The success of these shows depends not just on the formula but also on the personality of the presenter and of the carefully selected contestants.

Fiction and the American Supremacy

Fiction, on television, consisted at first of televised plays and films. It was soon discovered that the medium was ideally suited for reviving two popular literary genres: the serialised novel (the TV serial or soap opera) and the succession of novels with the same leading characters (the TV series). Here a sub-genre emerged: the sitcom, or situation comedy, in which the same characters would gather in the same location (often a living room) to enact a comedy. British sitcoms such as *Steptoe and Son* (1962), *The Likely Lads* (1964), *Till Death Us Do Part* (1965), *Last of the Summer Wine* (1973), the enormously successful *Only Fools and Horses* (1981, which with twenty-one million viewers for one of its episodes was top programme in 2001) and the apparently 'politically incorrect' *Men Behaving Badly* (1992) respected the classical Aristotelian unities as reinvented in the sixteenth century: unity of place, action and time (the plot unfolding in a single day in a single location). While these were quintessentially British, and built on the BBC experience of radio sitcoms (hence the superiority of the BBC in this field), Americans had developed such an expertise in the genre – from *The Jack Benny Show* (1950–64) to the *Cosby Show* (1984–92) – that they exported sitcoms throughout western Europe, virtually pre-empting the rise of a Continental form of the genre.

Sitcoms have a slim narrative basis: a rudimentary plot serves to create a situation which can generate comic effects. The sitcom is the only fictional genre in which there is an unseen audience whose 'presence' is made manifest by roars of usually pre-recorded laughter. This 'fourth wall' adds to the theatricality of the experience. With sitcoms, the line between fiction and a variety show with stand-up comedians is thin.[31] Sitcoms are short, usually thirty minutes long, and produced in batches of six to twelve episodes. They always end well. They are first shown at prime time, and then repeated for years to come.[32] The proliferation of satellite channels has created a market for even the oldest and least successful sitcoms.

Sitcoms are the natural home of stereotypes: in Great Britain the male working class are often 'cheeky chappies' or prejudiced fools, housewives are frustrated, the upper classes are effete snobs, pretty girls are silly, country folks are bumbling, crusty old colonels are crusty and old, and so on. British sitcoms (like serials) have often been set in a working-class environment: *On the Buses* (1969–73), *Steptoe and Son* (1962–74), *The Likely Lads* (1964–66) and *Till Death Us Do Part* (1965–75). Sitcoms featuring the upper classes usually show them as *nouveaux pauvres*. In *The Upper Crust* they are shown trying to cope in a council flat. In *To the Manor Born* (1979) Audrey fforbes-Hamilton, an upper-class widow, demoted to genteel discomfort, lives in the lodge of her former estate in close proximity to the wealthy (and uncouth) businessman who bought her ancestral home. On the Continent the lower classes are given regional rather than class characteristics. In the USA only two classes seem to exist in most sitcoms: the well-to-do middle class and the rich.

Taken together, television fiction accounts for much of the international trade in programmes, and in each country fiction constitutes an important proportion of programmes, particularly during prime time; but it does not dominate, unlike in the cinema and the theatre, which are almost exclusively fiction-producing machines. In the 1980s on French TV, fiction occupied less than a quarter of total output, though more than news and current affairs (c.20 per cent).[33] In Italy, where television fiction is overwhelmingly imported from America, only two made-for-television fiction programmes appeared in the annual top ten in the forty years after 1960: *Sandokan* in 1976 (an adaptation of novels by Emilio Salgari, 'Italy's Jules Verne' – see pages 700–2), with an audience of 27.3 million, and Franco Zeffirelli's *Gesù di Nazaret* (written by Anthony Burgess), with 26.7 million.[34] In its first ten years Italian television showed 5,486 hours of fiction, including literary adaptations, films, serials, soaps, TV films, etc. Many of these (but far from a majority) came from the US, which could sell an hour's worth of fiction for anything between $500 and $1,500, far less than it cost to make. The number of hours devoted to news, current affairs, sport and documentaries, however, was greater: 8,577.[35]

Virtually everywhere in Europe, the initial forays of television into the world of fiction deliberately sought to popularise high culture. These were mainly filmed plays, usually adapted. In France, one of the first television adaptations was of the celebrated children's book *Le Tour de France par deux enfants* by G. Bruno (see page 851). As it was a French Canadian production, the kids leave Canada and not Alsace to try to find the uncle they have never met.[36]

In Italy in 1954, when broadcasting began, there was a play every Friday, starting with one of Carlo Goldoni's; the first opera, broadcast on 23 April, was Rossini's *Barber of Seville*.

Britain, the only country in Europe with a pre-war television system, had used its three-year lead to good purpose. Between 1936 and 1939 BBC television broadcast over three hundred plays, mainly from the stage. The first television serial, *Ann and Harold*, about the growing love between a London couple, was broadcast in 1938. By the time the service was forced to close for the duration of the war, the 20,000 viewers were getting almost a play a day, a massive volume of home fiction.[37] After the war the BBC started to commission writers, such as J.B. Priestley, the most popular playwright of the day, to provide plays. Inevitably these 'television plays' began to look like films, since they started using the conventions and techniques of film-making, including close-ups, zooms, jump cutting and crane shots. There was little real editing until the early 1960s, but the director edited while the action was taking place by selecting which of two or three cameras constantly in action should be used.

ITV's *Armchair Theatre* (1956–74) and the BBC production of a regular *Wednesday Play* (1964–70), followed by *Play for Today* (1970–84), nurtured and employed a whole new generation of actors and writers, thus contributing to the survival and development of the live theatre. Writers like Harold Pinter (*A Night Out*, 1960), Alun Owen (*Lena, O My Lena*, 1960), David Mercer (*And Did Those Feet?*, 1965), Nell Dunn (*Up the Junction*, 1965), and Dennis Potter (*Vote, Vote, Vote for Nigel Barton*, 1965) produced a modern theatre for television that was far more transgressive and daring than most of the commercial productions of the West End theatre. When Pinter's *The Birthday Party* (1958) was virtually hounded off the West End stage by conservative theatre critics, it was soon revived by ITV.[38] Pinter himself calculated that to match the audience of 6,380,000 viewers who saw his television play *A Night Out*, his stage play *The Caretaker* would have had to run for thirty years.[39] Ken Loach's docu-drama (as fictionalised treatments in narrative form of contemporary events came to be called) *Cathy Come Home* (1965), about a homeless young mother and her children, showed how much more potent television could be in bringing social issues to public attention than the press or the stage.

The French lagged behind, but after a period of broadcasting stage plays, they too began to write and produce them. Compared to films, the quantity of fiction produced for television was enormous. The reason is obvious. Given the huge demand for stories and the reluctance of film studios to let television have their films, television was obliged to make its own 'narratives'. One of the first French producers, Marcel Bluwal, explained in the mid-1950s that the cast would rehearse the entire play in one go, as they would for the theatre. But for the actual performance, instead of an audience there were four cameras playing a sort of ballet with the actors, behaving as if they were shooting a film – except that the film was transmitted 'live'.[40] There were no separate 'takes' as in film, and an eventual editing process provided the continuity required. It was thus not uncommon for a television producer to produce four or five plays a year, an average no mainstream film-maker could possibly aspire to. These pioneers made legal dramas such as *En Votre âme et conscience* and detective serials such as *Les Cinq dernières minutes*. Television turned into a formidable machine for the production of stories – unsurprisingly, given the role of narrative in popular culture. Many of the favourite serials turned out to be solidly based on the serialised literature of the nineteenth and early twentieth centuries: *Rocambole* (1964), *Belphégor* (1965), *Vidocq* (1967) and *Jacquou le Croquant* (1969), as well as adaptations of successful classics for children (also from the nineteenth century): Dickens, Hector Malot, Jules Verne and the Comtesse de Ségur. Everything could be recycled, either as adaptation or as inspiration.

While Hollywood at its peak could churn out some three hundred films a year, corresponding to five hundred hours of fiction, television's appetite turned out to be much vaster than this. And since it was cheaper to import than to produce, each European country was virtually compelled to buy the products of the more advanced country, the United States, just as in the nineteenth century everyone was translating French and British novels. Few, however, missed the opportunity to adapt their own national literary texts. Thus even the Italians, whose scarcity of popular nineteenth-century narrative has already been noted, took advantage of television to popularise not only international classics such as Dostoevsky's *The Idiot* (broadcast in 1959), but also their own national novels, many of which were not widely known even at home, such Antonio Fogazzaro's *Piccolo mondo antico* (1896, broadcast in 1957), Ippolito Nievo's *Confessioni di un Italiano* (1857–58, broadcast as *La Pisana*, 1960), Emilio De Marchi's *Demetrio Pianelli* (1888–90, broadcast in 1963), Giovanni Verga's *Mastro don Gesualdo* (1889, broadcast in 1964) and Manzoni's *I Promessi sposi* (broadcast in 1967). When it came to popular genre fiction, such as detective stories, RAI either adapted well-known foreign titles such as *Padre Brown* (G.K. Chesterton's Father Brown) or Simenon's *Inspettore Maigret*, or made up its own detectives while maintaining the imperative that the setting should be abroad, preferably in the USA, as in *Il Tenente Sheridan* (where the audience had to guess the identity of the murderer).

Adapting canonical texts had its advantages. It contributed to legitimise television in the eyes of the literary establishment; it helped local actors and writers; it helped fulfil the mission of public service broadcasting: to educate and entertain. Adaptations, however, were expensive, could not easily be sold abroad, and could not fill the large space available in the new media. Hence the need to import fiction from the USA, home of popular cinema, and a massive producer of fiction for the forty million American households with television already existing in 1958 – more than the whole of Europe put together. Thus an avalanche of American serials and series made their way onto European screens: *Maverick, Gunsmoke, Have Gun, Will Travel, Bonanza* (1962, initially directed by Robert Altman), *Lassie, I Love Lucy, Perry Mason, Dr Kildare, The Untouchables* and *Wanted: Dead or Alive* (with the then unknown Steve McQueen). This led the French to devise their own products, such as *Jannick aimée* (1963), a soap with contemporary characters, and the historical serials *Thierry la Fronde* (1963–66) and *Le Chevalier de Maison Rouge* (1961–63).[41]

For a European series to make it in other countries, it had to find a niche market as a 'cult' series: a popular series loved by intellectuals and in which some aspects of the show, such as mannerisms, dialogue and props, are regarded as more important than the plot. They often have a slightly surreal or magical element.[42] The British were particularly good at 'cult'. *The Avengers* (1961) turned up in the USA, but also in France as *Chapeau melon et bottes de cuirs*, in Italy as *Agenti speciali*, and in Argentina as *Los Vengadores*. *The Prisoner* (1967) and *The Saint* (1962, with Roger Moore) became cult series in Continental Europe and North America. Occasionally an animated series – such as the American *The Flintstones* in the 1960s and even more so the satirical *The Simpsons*, created by Matt Groening in the late 1980s – became an object of cult and made it to prime time. Some American series and serials, such as the relatively recent *ER, Sex and the City, Frasier, The West Wing, The Sopranos* and the internationally popular *Friends*, appealed to a wide European public that included the better-educated. In 'action' television serials the USA remained supreme, as they have in the cinema, with *The A-Team* (1983–87), *Mission Impossible* (1966–73, 1988–89) and many more. Some achieved 'cult' status, the achievement of fans rather than critics. *Star Trek*, for instance, received no critical acclaim when it was first broadcast in 1966, though sci-fi addicts enjoyed it. The series was about to be ditched, but was saved by several letter-writing campaigns – one totalling 400,000 letters. A convention of fans held in New York in 1972 attracted 3,000 people, including, unusually for a sci-fi event, many women. The seventy-eight episodes broadcast were syndicated across the USA and sold in most west

European countries. Washington agreed to name one of the first Space Shuttles after *Star Trek*'s USS *Enterprise*. Then there was a TV cartoon series; then a film, made in 1987 (*Star Trek: The Next Generation*), launched new characters, which generated further TV series, totalling well over five hundred episodes. *Star Trek* represented the new kind of American liberalism: Spock, the alien Vulcan with pointed ears, became everyone's favourite character, along with Captain Kirk, the clean and honest American; the crew was multi-ethnic (black Americans, Russians, even a Scot), and included several women (though all attractive and none with a leading role – there are limits to liberalism); Kirk and Spock might have been gay, but neither ever 'came out'. The crew was bound by a Prime Directive prohibiting any interference in other cultures.[43]

That American fiction was supreme has never been contested – though sometimes lamented – in the substantial literature on the subject.[44] The facts are clear. Every country in the world imports more fiction from the USA than it does from any other country in the world.

ORIGINS OF FICTION IMPORTED BY TV IN THE EUROPEAN UNION
(IN BROADCAST HOURS), 1994

	German	*French*	*British*	*Italian*	*US*
Germany		1,167	1,706	966	28,059
France	814		1,649	548	13,643
Great Britain	85	246		98	26,691
Italy	544	538	1,045		18,515

SOURCE: *Statistical Yearbook 1996*, European Audiovisual Observatory, p.162

Even taking all programmes, American supremacy is not in doubt:

WESTERN EUROPE: COUNTRY OF ORIGIN OF IMPORTED
PROGRAMMES AS A PERCENTAGE, 1983

US	44
British	16
German	7
French	5
Other west European countries	8
Eastern Europe and the USSR	3
Eurovision	7

WESTERN EUROPE: COUNTRY OF ORIGIN OF IMPORTED
PROGRAMMES AS A PERCENTAGE, 1983 – *continued*

Co-productions	·	4
Others		6
		100

SOURCE: *La Circulation internationale des émissions de télévision*, UNESCO
No. 100, 1986 (ed. Tapio Varis)

Even Arab countries import more from the USA than from any other part
of the world, including each other: in 1983, 32 per cent of their broadcasting
came from the USA, 13 per cent from France, 7 per cent from the UK, while
the total from all other Arab and Middle Eastern countries was a creditable
30 per cent.[45]

American political and economic power ensures that American issues are
covered by the international media more than those of other nations. As a
result, Europeans who watch the news regularly know far more about American politics than about those of any country other than their own, whereas
Americans know very little about other countries unless US interests are
involved – yet another instance in which cultural superiority has cultural
costs. The figures are startling: the USA is almost cut off from the rest of the
world's television. Nothing of what is produced elsewhere is shown at prime
time, and very little is shown at any time.

PERCENTAGE OF TV PROGRAMMES IMPORTED, 1983

	% of all broadcasts	% of prime time broadcasts
Canada	38	31
USA	2	0
India (Delhi)	11	10
Argentina	49	53
Cuba	24	9
Austria	43	61
Belgium	28.5	c.30
Denmark	46	32
Spain	33	32
France	17	17

PERCENTAGE OF TV PROGRAMMES IMPORTED, 1983 – *continued*

	% of all broadcasts	% of prime time broadcasts
Italy	18	19
Holland	25	24
Germany (ZDF)	23	23
Great Britain (BBC)	15	21
Great Britain (ITV)	14	20
Great Britain (C4)	26	15
Egypt	35	41

SOURCE *La Circulation internationale des émissions de télévision*,
UNESCO No. 100, 1986 (ed. Tapio Varis)

The high figures for imported programmes in countries such as Argentina, Austria, Denmark, Canada and Egypt are explained by the fact that they are located within a wider linguistic and cultural area. Even the 2 per cent imported by the USA outside prime time comes, overwhelmingly, from areas linguistically close to its population: 25 per cent from Great Britain, and 54 per cent from Latin America. The balance of trade of programmes between the EU and the USA has always been massively favourable to the USA. In 1995 American TV companies sold $5,300 million-worth of audiovisual programmes to EU countries. EU countries sold only $518 million-worth to the US. In 2000 the USA exported $9 billion-worth and imported only $827 million-worth (mainly from the UK).[46] Great Britain has had some successes in exporting television programmes to the USA, but many of these tend to be destined for the more sophisticated section of the audience. For instance, the twenty-six-episode serial *The Forsyte Saga* (1967) was extremely popular in Great Britain, and was shown in fifty countries, including the USSR, Romania and Czechoslovakia, but in the USA the only outlet interested in it was National Education Television.[47] The cultural gap can be bridged by adapting cultural products. Thus, the British *Till Death Us Do Part* became, in 1971, *All in the Family*. The comic conflict between Alf Garnett, the working-class east London racist forever regretting the end of the Empire, and the rest of his family was toned down. Archie Bunker, the American Alf Garnett character, was middle-class and not working-class; class and political issues were turned into ethnic issues by making the family white Anglo-Saxon

Protestant and the son-in-law a Polish Catholic (while his British counterpart was a Labour supporter from Liverpool).[48] *All in the Family* was a hit in America, with fifty million viewers watching it every week.

The west European television system least penetrated by the USA – the British – was also the one which had started earliest, and which had developed competition earlier than its European counterparts. Though half of the fiction shown on British television is imported from the USA, it is overwhelmingly 'banished' to the off-prime time slots. The ratings for Christmas 2004 show the dominance of home-made products:

UK: TOP-RATED PROGRAMMES, CHRISTMAS 2004
(AUDIENCE FIGURES IN MILLIONS)

	Genre	Audience	Network/channel
EastEnders	Soap	12.3	BBC1
The Vicar of Dibley	Sitcom	11.8	BBC1
Coronation Street	Soap	11.3	ITV1
News	News	10.3	BBC
Harry Potter and the Philosopher's Stone	Film	7.9	BBC1
Emmerdale	Soap	7.5	ITV1
News	News	7.1	ITV
Absolutely Fabulous	Sitcom	6.6	BBC1
Midsomer Murders	Series (crime)	6.3	BBC1
Who Wants to be a Millionaire?	Game show	6.2	ITV1

SOURCE: *Guardian*, 27 December 2004

In 2001, in the top twenty-five programmes for the year (in terms of ratings) in Britain, there was not a single US made-for-TV programme (though there were three US feature films: *The Mummy* and two 'Indiana Jones', ranked sixteenth, nineteenth and twentieth).[49] None of the critically acclaimed US fiction series and serials such as *The X-Files*, *The West Wing*, *The Sopranos* or *Sex and the City* made it to the top twenty-five original drama productions – partly because they were not shown in prime time.

British television did a better job at protecting itself from American products than other west European nations, including the French, though the French too have succeeded in maintaining their prime time largely in 'national' hands. But France has imported more serials from the USA than it has produced itself. By the early 1990s the country had produced 354 serials, series and sitcoms, but in the same period it imported 396 from the USA. Imports from Britain followed, with eighty-nine (including 'Allo 'Allo and *Fawlty Towers*), and from Germany with thirty.[50]

In spite of the legal requirement in many countries to carry a certain percentage of domestic fiction, American fiction has dominated west European screens from the beginning. The reasons are not hard to discern. American films had created a popular taste for American products throughout Europe. Hollywood production was massive. Much of this consisted of B-movies in well-established genres (such as westerns, science fiction, gangster movies or melodramas). Television became an ideal receptacle for them. They were cheap to acquire, and satisfied the average viewer's taste. Even in made-for-TV fiction the USA had a considerable advantage. It was cheaper to acquire American series than to make new ones. Europeans concentrated on producing fiction for prime time, and often treated American products as 'fillers'. Here too there are variants. In Flemish-speaking Belgium (Flanders), local production was dwarfed by American imports even in prime time, but in the French-speaking provinces (Wallonia), prime time was dominated by French or Belgian–French co-productions. In Great Britain, Germany and France, viewers watch their own fiction during prime time. Italy, however, produces hardly any of its own series (around 10 per cent, less than Flanders). Not surprisingly, a survey of Italian children conducted as early as 1971 revealed that their five favourite programmes were all imported: the French *Thierry la Fronde* and the American *Rin Tin Tin, Laurel and Hardy* (in Italy *Stanlio e Olio*), *Lassie* and *The Abbott and Costello Show* (*Gianni e Pinotto*).[51] Yet Italy had in those years a thriving cinema industry, making far more films than most European countries. Its very limited and modest production of home serials left a space for US imports even on prime time television. Thus, while *Desperate Housewives* in the UK is shown at 10 p.m. or later, in Italy it occupies the crucial 9 p.m. slot on the second channel of RAI (September 2005).

The share of US fiction has increased substantially with the growth of private channels, since new entrants need to fill their screen time rapidly, and American imports are one of the most efficient ways of doing so. The percentage of broadcasting time devoted to fiction was substantially higher in the commercial sector than in the public sector in Belgium, Holland, Great Britain, Germany, France and Italy. Fiction occupied, on average,

37.4 per cent of TV time, with the public sector average well below this (22 per cent) and the commercial well above (48.9 per cent).[52] The first German private network, SAT1 (1985), showed *Star Trek*, *The Avengers* and *Bonanza*, as well as adaptations of game shows pioneered abroad.

How do European countries fare on the import of other European fiction? No European country is able to export a sizeable percentage of its product outside its own linguistic area. There are some significant single exceptions. The German detective series *Inspector Derrick* (which lasted twenty-five years) and *Kommissar Rex* are widely sold, as is the French soap *Sous le soleil*. Indeed Germany, the largest producer of television fiction in Europe, does well in the French market, perhaps helped by the scarcity of French production and anti-American quotas and prejudices.[53] In the UK hardly any European fiction is imported (2.2 per cent on BBC and 7.2 per cent on the commercial networks).[54] This is often attributed to British hostility towards dubbing. Subtitles are not a realistic alternative: they are an automatic signifier of 'art' and 'cultural' products – the kiss of death in terms of audience size.

Clearly, Europeans prefer their own fiction. In 1997 in France the top eight serials were all French (the top was *Julie Lescaut*, with nine million viewers). *ER* (USA) was ninth with 5.6 million, the British *Mr Bean* was fourteenth with 5.1 million, and the German *Inspector Derrick* was twentieth, with 4.7 million.[55] On Danish public television in 1998 there were 564 hours of US fiction, but Danish fiction came second with 313 hours, and British third with 174 hours (comprising 80 per cent of European fiction on Danish screens).[56] In Germany, German fiction (or German-speaking fiction from Austria and Switzerland) such as the serials *Tatort* (detective) and *Traumschiff* (Dream Boat, an adaptation of the USA soap *Love Boat*), easily outdistances American fiction on all networks, whether private or public.[57] Even in Italy, where American fiction dominates, there were nine Italian-made fictional programmes in the top ten television fiction slots for the year 2002, the number one spot going to a film on the life of Pope John XXIII.[58] And in the 1980s Swedish children watched many more of the television adaptations of Astrid Lindgren's *Pippi Långstrump* (Pippi Longstocking) stories (over forty) than US programmes.[59] In Germany in 1999, nine of the top ten audience figures for films shown on TV were achieved by German films.[60] So to say that Europe is united by American narratives is an exaggeration.

Moral panics over Americanisation have been a common feature of the European cultural landscape since the 1920s. This panic escalated with the international popularity of the soap *Dallas* in the early 1980s. It is difficult to find a coherent explanation for the international success of this US serial – save for the fact that unlike most of the soaps which preceded it, *Dallas* had a considerable male following. The story was obviously enticing, the acting reasonably good, the plot easy to follow, for it was a traditional family saga, that of the oil-rich Ewings who live together on a luxurious ranch near Dallas. But other US serials have had good actors, dialogue and plots. The narrative device used by *Dallas* is typical of nineteenth-century *feuilletons*. It is an interminable story, with sub-stories each with a beginning, a middle and an end, enabling new viewers to come in at any time and quickly catch up. It had two recognisable villains, one male and one female, 'J.R.' Ewing and Alexis Carrington, and a long-suffering alcoholic wife. Its cost, $700,000 per episode, was normal for the USA, but enormous for countries with a small market. Purchasing it (in some instances for a few thousand dollars per episode) enabled them to acquire an expensive product they could not make themselves. In Britain *Dallas*, though highly popular, never reached the exceptionally high ratings of home-grown soaps like *Coronation Street* and later *EastEnders* (both far too embedded in British working-class life to appeal to a foreign audience). In Brazil too *Dallas* never succeeding in displacing home-grown soaps (which, unlike *Coronation Street*, are widely exported) – Globo, the largest Brazilian network, is one of the largest producers of television fiction in the world.

Dallas's international audience was already familiar with the conventions of American film and television fiction. As Ien Ang explained, 'In Hollywood since the beginning of this century certain iron rules of cinematography have been developed (such as continuity editing, classic montage, etc.) to create this suggestion of narrative spontaneity. But we no longer experience these rules as rules, because we have become so used to this dominant American film language that we no longer even recognise it as a language.'[61] *Dallas* contained no complex irony or distancing devices, no unusual camera movements, and no experimentation. Everything that happened was part of the narrative. There were a limited number of locations (mainly in the ranch, South Fork), and nearly all the scenes consisted of conversation. And, of course, it was made by Americans for Americans, and set in America. Greek TV soap operas were also full of magnates, corrupt politicians and incestuous love affairs, but the chances of foreign TV companies acquiring a Greek soap opera and dubbing it were always rather slim.

A further reason for the success of *Dallas* was that in most countries it was broadcast at prime time, on the self-fulfilling assumption that it would attract a large audience. In Holland half of the audience watched it every week in the spring of 1982.[62] In Israel, *Dallas* was as popular with Palestinians as with Jewish settlers from eastern Europe and Morocco. In Japan, however, *Dallas* was removed after six months because it was unable to compete with Japan's own soaps, whose characters were less one-dimensional. In any case, the Japanese preferred good US 'home drama', or *hômu dorama*, like *Little House on the Prairie*, to *Dallas*.[63] 'Home dramas' sharply demarcate themselves from community-based British soap operas such as *Coronation Street* and wealthy-family-centred American ones such as *Dallas* and *Dynasty*.[64] Japan's popular culture is not as Westernised as it might seem from some of the animated films Japan exports: soap-opera plots for teenagers and cyberpunk films such as *Akira* draw on Japanese folklore.[65] As for the popularity of *Dallas* in many Third World countries, this is assumed rather than established.[66]

There were some feeble attempts to respond to what was regarded as the 'threat' of *Dallas* by imitating it, notably by the French with *Châteauvallon*, which simply turned the Texan city into a French provincial town and the oil family into a stylish publishing dynasty. The Germans reacted to the advance of *Dallas* by trying out stories in which the painfully rich strut about in grand homes with *Das Erbe der Guldenburgs* (The Inheritance of the Guldenburgs) and *Rivalen der Rennbahn* (Rivals of the Racecourse). They were more successful at imitating the British: *Lindenstrasse* (Linden Street, 1985) began as a German adaptation of *Coronation Street*, spiced up with sex and violence.[67] Far less working-class than its British model, it also refrains from suggesting an all-German nostalgic *Heimat* by including characters from various backgrounds: Greek restaurateurs, a Vietnamese refugee, a French woman, an Italian Jew, a disabled teenager, two homosexuals, Polish immigrants and an adopted Mexican boy.[68] *Schwarzwaldklinik* (1985) used the well-trodden setting of the hospital (like the older British *General Hospital* and *Emergency Ward Ten*).

The best weapon against American penetration – if a weapon was needed – was to have one's own serials, and to make them unassailable by having them deeply rooted in the national psyche. This is what the British achieved with *Coronation Street* (which began in 1960 and is still going strong in 2006) and its BBC rival *EastEnders* (1985–), aimed at a more southern and perhaps younger audience than *Coronation Street*. These reached an unparalleled share of the audience.

EUROPEAN SOAPS: 1997 AUDIENCES

		Audience share %	Audience size in millions
Germany	*Lindenstrasse*	11.8	8.2
Germany	*Gute Zeiten, Schlechte Zeiten*	5.5	3.9
Holland	*Goede Tijden, Slechte Tijden*	12.3	1.7
Great Britain	*Coronation Street*	31	16.5
Great Britain	*EastEnders*	32	17.0

SOURCE: Tamar Liebes and Sonia Livingstone, 'European Soap Operas: The Diversification of a Genre', in *European Journal of Communication*, Vol. 13, No. 2, June 1998, p.158

Coronation Street – the product of British commercial television and arguably the most important television series ever to be broadcast in the United Kingdom[69] – is the quintessential social realist soap opera, a feat the USSR had never been able to replicate. Like all real soap operas and serialised novels, *Coronation Street* relies on its working-class characters rather than its plot. Characters provide continuity (and provide long-term employment to actors, who grow old with their characters and with their audiences). New viewers may not be immediately caught up in the serial, because a few viewings may not be sufficient to become interested in the characters; but once caught, they are likely to remain caught for a very long time. The setting is an unidentified northern city (but obviously Manchester, where the production company, Granada, is located). From the start the series eschewed traditional melodrama, preferring the social realist tendency then prevailing in the theatre.[70] Its scripts were produced by some of the ablest writers in British television, such as Jack Rosenthal. First shown twice a week, it quickly established itself as a three-times-a-week soap; the characters speak with a local accent, wear the modest, even shabby, clothes of the northern working class, and display such class-conscious behaviour as reading tabloid newspapers, going to the pub (The Rover's Return, run by Jack Walker from 1960 to 1984), playing bingo and watching football. They are, however, seldom part of the factory proletariat, since this would take them too far from the *Street*. 'Being working class' has little to do with occupation, and everything to do with a cultural attitude. One of the main characters, Ken Barlow, once a scholarship boy, eventually became a university graduate (and an anti-Vietnam War activist) and a teacher, but his father Frank was a postman and his mother Ida worked in the kitchen of a large hotel; Mike Baldwin is a boss, owner of a denim factory, but has a Cockney accent; Reg Holdsworth managed a supermarket (1989–94); others have service sector jobs such as being dustmen. Bert Tilsley did work at the local steelworks, but only during the night shift, so that he could be around during the day.[71] One of the key characters in the early years was Ena Sharples, the upholder of conventional morality and caretaker of the Mission of Glad Tidings. Its quintessential working-class Englishness was one the major factors behind *Coronation Street*'s success (well over 5,000 episodes so far, and thirty books written about it); it was also the greatest impediment to its success abroad.

An entirely different soap, *Sous le soleil* (marketed abroad, for obvious reasons, as *Saint-Tropez*), shown since 1999 in France on TF1, has a wider international appeal, due perhaps to its less culturally-specific theme. It is, to quote the description of the producing company Marathon:

> . . . a psychological drama and romantic comedy, portraying the touching destinies of three women, Laure, Caroline and Jessica, who fight against every obstacle to live out their professional and romantic passions. Now with 360 one-hour episodes, *Saint-Tropez* has created a family of characters that viewers can identify with. We experience the emotional dramas of modern life (sterility, adoption, divorce, raising children, medical and psychological issues, the loss of a loved one), and share in the moral and professional dilemmas of our heroines. The series is shot on film and on location in Saint-Tropez, a sunny and glamorous place where our characters mix laughter with tears and combine the joys of love and friendship with the fears of uncertain destinies.

Shown on Saturday afternoons, *Sous le soleil* gets on average over a quarter of the audience, with over a third of the female audience under thirty-five watching it.[72] Unusually for a French soap it has been widely sold, though not to a major American company, while in Britain it has been acquired only by BBC Knowledge as part of their language-learning programmes.

The main global challenge to US hegemony in fiction does not come from Europe but from Latin America. Mexican and Brazilian *telenovelas* are the foreign genre most favoured in the USA (largely because of the size of the Hispanic population). They are also exported to much of southern Europe, particularly Spain and Portugal. In Portugal the private network Sociedade Independente de Televisão (SIC) dedicates much of its prime time to soap operas bought from the Brazilian TV giant Globo. The Spanish too position US imported fiction outside prime time, which is reserved for both domestic fiction and the *telenovelas*. Like *Dallas* and *Dynasty* (and unlike most of the British genre), Latin American soaps are about the 'problems' in the lives of very wealthy people. Indeed, one of the first Mexican *telenovelas* was called *Los Ricos también lloran* (The Rich Also Cry).[73] When it was broadcast on Russian state television it became so popular that it had to be shown twice a day to please all shift workers.[74] The lesson was digested, and Russified *telenovelas* began to be mass-produced. Even in Poland, where US fiction rules the broadcasting waves, the favourite soaps are mostly domestic (on public television) or Latin American (on the private networks).[75] Mexican and Brazilian soaps have been very successful even in China, but so have local Chinese soaps such as *Yearnings*, first broadcast in Nanjing in November 1990.[76]

What a series needs above all is a good setting, like a police station, a hospital, a street, a school (but why never a university?), a pub or bar where friends meet, a shared flat (for peer group), a newspaper, a family. In other words, what is necessary is what some authors call a power structure, a social locus for gender relations.[77] People in *Coronation Street* meet in the pub, the garage, the shops – all public spaces. Thanks to such soaps, it is often claimed, viewers obtain some kind of emotional release, relieve their boredom and loneliness, obtain advice (what to do with men), have the illusion of having a surrogate family life and a network of friends, and can participate vicariously in other people's lives.[78] In other words, people get from soaps everything they obtained from nineteenth-century melodramas, but much more vividly and with less effort.

The most adaptable genre of fiction is the crime story, above all in its modern television form as the police series. The Italians deployed gentle *carabinieri* such as *Il Maresciallo Rocca*, and honest anti-Mafia investigators such the *carabinieri* in *La Piovra*, who usually die in the final episode of each series, killed by the Mafia, something which would not happen in an American serial. The French, whose affection for the *film noir* and the *roman policier* is well established, have produced a steady stream of what they call 'polars'. The British more than equalled the French with series celebrating the 'bobby on the beat': the neo-realist *Dixon of Dock Green* (1955–76), where the police are loveable, the gritty *Z Cars* (1962–78) and the violent *The Sweeney* (1975–78), where the police use tough methods, but then 'it's a jungle out there', and various detectives such as *Inspector Morse* (1987–2000), based in Oxford and *Midsomer Murders* (1997–), set in the kind of high-crime village made famous by Agatha Christie's novels.

In recent years European countries – with the exception of France – have increased remarkably their production of domestic fiction:

HOURS OF DOMESTIC FICTION BROADCAST

	1996	2001
Germany	1,690	1,800
Great Britain	1,059	1,463
France	691	553
Spain	459	1,306
Italy	221	761

SOURCE: Eurofiction, cited in Milly Buonanno (ed.), *Eurofiction 2002. Sesto Rapporto sulla fiction televisiva in Europa*, VQPT-RAI No. 191, Rome 2003, p.37

Spain and Italy increased their production enormously, helped probably by the realisation that their audiences preferred domestic fiction. In 1996 Italy produced only 5 per cent of the fiction of the top five countries. By 2001 it was producing 13 per cent, against France's 9 per cent. The main factor behind this increase is the development of local soaps – one of the presumed side effects of the success of *Dallas*. In 2001 France did not produce any serials of its own, and paid the consequences. The development and success of *Sous le soleil* was the French riposte to its previous laggardness. Italy started producing its own soaps in 1996, and the results were remarkable – even though in 2001, taking RAI and the commercial network Mediaset together, 71 per cent of fiction shown in Italy originated from the USA and Latin America (with Mediaset being the main importer).[79]

Serious Television: News, Documentaries and Current Affairs

Television and radio are the primary source for news in every European country, even in those, such as the UK, with high newspaper readership.[80]

The antecedent of the TV newsreader is not the cinema newsreel but radio journalism – indeed, until the end of the fifties most news bulletins were simply read out with the help of a few photographs obtained from agencies. People sometimes say about television news: it's all about images, it's all about pictures. If the truth be told, it is *never* about images or pictures. It is always about words, the friendly words that accompany the images.

Equally it is about the unseen hands that have selected the images and sewn them together into the patchwork quilt we call 'the news'. At the cinema, the booming newsreel voice had a god-like authority. It exhorted us to marvel. On television the newsreader or the reporter tells us how things are, in a matter-of-fact way. The pictures are there to underline what he or she says, often, but not always, almost as illustrations.

Media specialists are fond of citing examples of documentaries about the same events making completely different points (one made by a Czech exile on the Soviet invasion of his country in 1968 and another, Soviet-made, supporting the intervention) using virtually the same pictures.[81] Media archives enable the standardised use of images to go with the written story: good stories from Africa show everyone dancing happily, bad ones show everyone starving.

Television news, like newspapers, does not need to send a team to cover every distant story (it can use agency pictures), but major wars (those deemed important in the West) require correspondents to go to the conflict area. Their exposure to real or apparent danger seems to be designed mainly to give the impression that a genuine effort has been made to bring original and exclusive news to the viewers. Most of the analysis is done at head-quarters, where journalists have access to a wider range of information than does the correspondent. Most of the hundreds of correspondents sent to cover the occupation of Iraq in 2003 came up with roughly the same pictures and provided a similar analysis to that which could have been manufactured at home on the basis of the pictures received from a handful of journalists working for the main television agencies. Nothing beats, however, the spec-tacle of a familiar face being filmed in a conflict zone speaking a familiar language above the roar of the cannons. Little novel information is conveyed, since to make sense of what is going on, they are forced to rely on official statements and anecdotes that are difficult to check. Where the dangers are high, as in Iraq after the American intervention in 2003, many Western journalists stay in their safe hotels and use footage filmed by Iraqi stringers, then just do the voice-over.

TV newsreaders and reporters have a dual role. They provide infor-mation, but they are mediators. They pretend to be 'us' rather than 'them'. The world out there, they seem to say, is an inferno of unspeakable horrors – wars, starvation, tragedy and brutality – which must be spoken about; yet you who are watching us are safe. Do not let our tales frighten you; by watching our pictures you have shared in the suffering of mankind and shown your concern. Now you can relax, enjoy the rest of the programme, and have a good evening.

Some current affairs programmes become authoritative. The BBC's *Panorama*, presented by Richard Dimbleby in the 1960s and 1970s, conveyed the sense of speaking on behalf of a socially concerned establishment for an equally concerned audience. In France this function was performed by Pierre Lazareff's equally authoritative *Cinq colonnes à la une* (1959). Lazareff had realised that the prestige of British and American current affairs programmes was due to their ability to attract many journalists from the printed press. However, a television programme, unlike an élite newspaper, must try to speak to the widest possible audience. On television there is no real 'high culture' – only different kinds of mass culture. *Cinq colonnes* and *Panorama* were high-minded with audiences in the millions, while newspapers like *Le Monde* and the *Guardian* sell fewer than 400,000 copies. By the early 1960s, 40 per cent of semi-skilled workers in western Europe had their own television set.[82] They were highly likely to watch current affairs programes, and equally unlikely to read the *Guardian* or *Le Monde*. American television never successfully developed programmes like *Cinq colonnes* or *Panorama* in which social or political or historical issues are analysed at length – programmes which are, in any case, less and less present on European television.

The person reading the news was a solitary man, fatherly for some, even grandfatherly (notably, in America in the 1970s, Walter Cronkite of CBS), sexy for others, serious and intellectual or debonair and relaxed. Newsreaders look directly and frankly towards us (though in reality they are reading words which appear in front of them). Those they interview speak to them, not to us. This 'friend in the living-room' who tells us what is going on in the world used to be, exclusively, a man. A woman, eventually, was allowed to replace him, though she had to be, invariably, attractive, neither motherly nor bossy, and not too intellectual. In time, she was even allowed to grow older. Increasingly, following an American practice, a man and a woman shared a desk, occasionally pretending to flirt with each other, and concluding with a smile and a mild joke. Some rudimentary acting skills are necessary (as they are in real life): a sad expression for sad items, a smile for happy ones, and strict neutrality for anything for which there is no consensus among the viewers. Newsreaders are smartly dressed: dark suits for men (flashy ties are allowed), casual chic for women. Morning news, a relatively recent development, allows a more relaxed attitude: some networks have men in sweaters reading the news. In some countries, particularly the USA and Britain, those interviewed call the presenter by his or her first name: 'John' or 'Sue'. Far from showing condescension, this practice highlights the special status of the presenter: he is everyone's friend, unlike the politician who is being interviewed. Here strict formality is maintained, even when the questioning is harsh: 'Secretary of State, some people have accused you of wilful deceit. What do you say to that?' 'Well, Jeremy, I am glad you asked me this question. It allows me to clear up a misunderstanding...' At the heart of this, there is often a real conflict. The politician must convey his or her message and promote his or her image. But the interviewer too can try to convey an identity, let the people know he is their champion and experiment with an abrasive tone. This, however, is only too rare, and when it occurs it is often on the BBC, either early in the morning on radio or late at night on television.

The news is told in clean, clear and unpretentious sentences, even in Italy, Spain and France, where the journalists of the printed press often use complex prose, as if they were aspiring academics (sometimes they are). On television, as on radio, the rule is simple: any piece of news, however complex the background, can be told in one or two minutes, sometimes a few seconds. Everyone accepts this rule. Experts who have spent a lifetime of research decoding the intricacies of Middle Eastern politics or Japanese elections happily condense it all for the sake of being on television, seen today as the fountain of intellectual consecration. Those who cannot, or will not, are not asked again. Intellectuals may be people who believe that not everything in the world can be explained in two minutes, but by appearing on television they accept that, on the contrary, everything can. Advocates of conflicting causes play the role assigned to them: by clashing in public they confirm the balanced nature of television news and the mediating role of the news presenter. Experts do not say anything the newsreaders could not have said themselves (perhaps after consulting an expert). But it looks better and sounds better coming from someone who is labelled an 'expert'. It shows the effort made to arrive at the truth or to present a range of opinions. A confrontation between experts also has the purpose of legitimising their two positions: both are valid, both can be expressed, neither is beyond the pale – one is unlikely to witness a televised confrontation between pro-Nazi and anti-Nazi 'historians'. What the expert will say, and how he/she will say it, is known in advance. Interviews break the monotony of having, as used to be the case at the beginning of TV broadcasting, the uninterrupted sound of a single voice. News may be about real life, but like all accounts of real life, narrative rules must be established, and roles distributed.

What kind of news makes the news? By and large it reports the views of the powerful since what they say is of more import than the views of the powerless. Then it reports bad news, since good news is either the norm or boring, unless it comes as the happy *dénouement* of bad news ('Lost Children Rescued', 'Serial Killer Caught'). The selection of 'bad news' is crucial because it determines a political agenda: the frequent reporting of violent crimes, which occur regularly in all societies, may generate a demand for more police or more severe sentences; the frequent reporting of hospital mishaps, which also happen regularly, may provoke demands for better training or higher spending. Both are interesting, but both are 'normal' bad news. All politicians, lobbies, firms, trade unions and other organisations are aware of this, and try to produce events which will be covered by television.

Technology has shortened the time between the occurrence of an event and the broadcasting of the event. In the mid-1970s nearly everything was first shot using 16mm film. It then had to be transported to a laboratory, developed and then edited. Shooting the film required a cameraman, a sound recording engineer and sometimes a lighting specialist. Then video, at first called Electronic News Gathering or ENG, came to dominate the news. Developing was no longer necessary. Thanks to satellites the material could easily be beamed back to the studio from anywhere in the world. Cameras grew so light that they could be carried by rapidly moving journalists. Eventually phone-cameras enabled an even faster response. If the Berlin Wall comes down, it is imperative that all leading politicians provide a statement of their position, and that that statement should be encapsulated in a short sentence. Since the mind's capacity for analysis has not developed at the same pace as technology, responses are increasingly made with little reflection. Policies are often made on the spur of the moment, with an eye to the emotions they will generate among the public.

Television news is what matters most to politicians, for obvious reasons. Since state television has maintained a commanding presence throughout Europe, one would have expected television news to be politically controlled or biased. The development of public sector TV news occurred, almost everywhere in western Europe, in the 1950s under the aegis of conservative governments (Germany, Italy, Great Britain and France). Control, however, has been indirect, and bias never as obvious as in the written press. News has reflected generic conservative values, but seldom a party position. Bias manifested itself by excluding the opposition, as was the case in Italy and France, where until the 1960s communist politicians hardly ever appeared on TV.

What kept news and current affairs programmes relatively balanced was the realisation that, in a democratic system, TV needed to consolidate itself as the 'people's medium', reflecting the broad values of its viewers. This could be better achieved by creating the image of the newsreader as above parties and politics, locating him or her alongside the audience, fearlessly pursuing truth. In authoritarian regimes this was impossible, since the entire media were generally seen as an emanation of the state, and often viewed with suspicion. In democracies too, however, there was a widespread belief that television news refrained from offending powerful government politicians.

Those in charge of television news have in fact fairly limited room for manoeuvre. They are unlikely to experiment. They have budget constraints (their correspondents are already in places which are likely to generate news). They have to take into account establishment pressures. They would not have reached the position they occupy if they were not regarded as 'safe'.[83]

The fact that public sector television was ultimately controlled by a democratically elected government remained a veiled justification for the prevalence of political bias in many west European countries, notably France, particularly under de Gaulle, Italy under the Christian Democrats and the socialist Bettino Craxi and even more so under the premiership of Silvio Berlusconi, and Greece under PASOK. In other countries, such as Britain, the alternation of political parties in power and a diffuse sense of public service ethic reinforced the autonomy of television. Bias is often difficult to detect because it consists of editing out news that does not fit into the preselected agenda. Those who do not know the 'full story' (or the fuller story) are not, by definition, in possession of the information required to detect a lack of balance. Selection is normally based on the values prevailing in the political system and on what is regarded as important and significant by powerful agents such as governments and the main political parties.

The universal nature of television somehow kept its news programmes more balanced and objective than the printed press, which could air its views with open partiality. This has remained true even in the age of privatisation and deregulation. In Britain ITV News was modelled on the BBC News, and had no discernibly greater political bias. Sky News, part of Rupert Murdoch's global media empire, is far more balanced than the newspapers that belongs to the same group (or his US-based Fox News). In France the news on Canal Plus, the largest encrypted channel, is often regarded as less partisan than that shown on public channels. There are some exceptions, however, such as the outrageous and perhaps self-defeating pro-Berlusconi bias on Rete Quattro in Italy (while the news on his Canale Cinque is biased mainly in its obsession with traffic accidents and murders).

Of course, from a strictly commercial point of view, until the further segmentation of television it pays not to be partisan. That way the risks of offending viewers and advertisers are kept to the minimum. If television has a bias, it lies in its avoidance of controversy. Television is reluctant to cause offence. Controversial intellectuals were kept out of TV. Bertrand Russell, often on radio in the 1940s, was hardly ever on British television after his anti-war and anti-American activism became manifest. Jean-Paul Sartre was almost excluded from French television in the 1960s and 1970s, unlike the admittedly more photogenic (but also more in tune with dominant views) Bernard-Henri Lévy, who twenty years later seemed hardly ever to be off the screen. Noam Chomsky, a controversial best-selling author, is seldom granted the access to mainstream US networks which lesser gurus enjoy.

The long-lasting and ever-lasting issue of the effect of television news tends to hide the more interesting question of the effect of television on politicians. Since television has become their main conduit to the electorate, much time and expertise has been spent devising ways of appearing good on television, expressing oneself in a convincing manner and creating a positive image. All of this must be achieved under severe time constraints. Unable to speak at length, or at any rate at the length they would wish, politicians have been forced to adopt the pithy, concise style of newsreaders and advertisers. Obfuscations are still used, but they have to be short. Politicians have to appear human, men and women of the people, yet at the same time they have to resonate with an air of intelligence, leadership and decisiveness. The monarchs of old used symbolic gestures and special costumes to obtain deference and signal power. Today such signs must be broadcast to a much wider audiences. Thus American Presidents such as Jimmy Carter and Bill Clinton are seen jogging; George W. Bush interrupts his game of golf to exchange pleasantries with journalists and announces 'victory in Iraq' wearing a combative leather jacket; Vladimir Putin chaired his first cabinet, partly shown on TV, wearing a V-necked sweater – unlike his ministers, all in statutory baggy grey trousers.

Documentaries

Sex, death and violence predominate in the three main documentary sub-genres: natural history, with its propensity for animals preying on others and their mating habits; ethnological documentaries privileging dark-skinned natives and their 'strange' rituals; historical documentaries overwhelmingly about the First and Second World Wars and Nazi Germany and the Holocaust, though art history has a strong presence, unsurprisingly given the visual nature of the medium.

Such preferences are not surprising. Contemporary history has the lion's share not just because it is closer to the experience and knowledge of most viewers, but because there are good images. This circumscribes the range of topics. Thus Italy is interesting because of Mussolini and the Mafia, Spain because of Franco and the Civil War, Russia because of communism. France – in the twentieth century – is relatively uninteresting, except to the French, since it has no dictators, civil wars or large-scale massacres; on the other hand its losses in the trenches of the First World War and, during the Second World War, its collaboration and resistance, have provided topics of interest, unlike the usually neutral and peaceful Nordic countries. Germany is a constant source of good historical documentaries, with the result that its entire post-Second World War history is often regarded (outside Germany) purely in terms of its past. The questions constantly asked are: Have the Germans learned from the past? Are they truly sorry?[84]

Everywhere historical programmes emphasise national history and national preoccupations, reinforcing a bias already largely present in books and the history taught in schools.[85] Controversial aspects of national history, however, are often passed over in silence. In France Marcel Ophüls's celebrated documentary Le Chagrin et la pitié (The Sorrow and the Pity, 1971), which revealed the extent of French collaboration with the Nazi occupiers, was for long kept off TV, for which it had originally been intended. Nor did the Algerian war receive the kind of regular treatment that the French resistance did. In Great Britain, British repression of anti-colonial struggles was barely mentioned, unlike Britain's 'finest hour' during the Second World War. And most Italians are still convinced that they were 'good' colonisers in Ethiopia.

Some aspects of the past are far more popular than others. Ancient Egypt is a constant favourite, unlike ancient China (or indeed any aspect of China before the twentieth century). Dinosaurs are a constant source of interest, presumably because they were very large.

The BBC has been in the forefront of high-calibre documentary series. These were a remarkable success at home, and were diffused worldwide. The first blockbuster was *Civilisation* (1969), fronted by the art historian Kenneth Clark, who described the evolution of Western society through art. This was followed by *The Ascent of Man* (1973), where another academic, Jacob Bronowski, provided a science-oriented perspective. Perhaps even more successful was David Attenborough's *Life on Earth* (1979), a thirteen-part series that became a worldwide success and a model for documentaries on nature. The British commercial sector was almost equally active, above all with Thames Television's twenty-six-part series *The World at War* (1974) on the Second World War, ranked by British media professionals as the nineteenth-'best' programme ever (in a 2000 poll organised by the British Film Institute). No other television network in any other country even remotely matched such achievements – all of which are unlikely to be repeated in the era of the fragmentation of television.

Television also dealt with serious matters in a 'light' way, provided it could claim to popularise a difficult subject. Thus the Holocaust became a kind of soap opera, bringing to the attention of millions what professional historians were unable to do. In 1979 West German television showed over four consecutive evenings the US-made serial *Holocaust*. Millions of viewers were deeply moved. Subsequently a string of films on the Nazi period were made in Germany, including Edgar Reitz's justly celebrated *Heimat* (1984).

The ground for the reception of *Holocaust* had been well prepared. Schools were provided with information packs. Panels of specialists were made available after the programmes to discuss the issues raised. There were phone-ins and an ample debate in the press. Any criticism that the film trivialised the genocide, or that it distorted the past by not mentioning the many non-Jews who had been exterminated, could easily be rebuffed by pointing out that the overall effect had been positive. For the first time ordinary Germans were made to identify with the suffering of the Jews.[86]

Serious programmes become popular when there is relatively little competition. A one- or two-channel television system ensured massive viewing figures for programmes which would seem esoteric in a situation where twenty or more channels are available. The dream of using the new media technology to provide an entire population with a basic understanding and appreciation of what the élites regarded as 'culture' seemed to have come true. It had in fact come true, at least until the multiplication of channels. Once again the élites lost out to market forces.

58

The Break-Up of Television

Multi-Channels

ONCE UPON A TIME there were only a few television channels, and they broadcast for only a few hours a day. Now there are, potentially, no limits to the number of channels, and many broadcast twenty-four hours a day.

Once upon a time television embraced a national community more effectively than the printed texts of old. In most European countries these channels were all publicly owned. It was 'national' television in the strong sense. Funding was relatively generous, thanks to a compulsory tax, and there was plenty of advertising available to supplement it.

Then the channels multiplied and the state sector began to recede. The process of commercialisation was lengthy. The private sector was at first reluctant to risk money in what was a new venture; now that the market existed, it demanded to be allowed in. In the USA the private sector had ruled from the beginning, but in Europe the first breach in the fortress of state monopoly was accomplished in Great Britain in 1955 with the creation of Independent Television (ITV), a network of regionally based independent companies. The companies had to undertake to provide high-quality television with an appropriate mix of entertainment and education. A public watchdog, the Independent Television Authority (later the Independent Broadcasting Authority or IBA), would periodically review their performance and decide whether to renew their licences. In effect, ITV was required to take public service television as its model. And that is what happened. British commercial television produced its share of variety shows, soaps and other programmes which pleased the majority of viewers, but it also produced serious current affairs programmes, plays written by major authors, intelligent documentaries praised by critics and audiences. It soon obtained an overwhelming share of the audience.

In principle, the BBC needed only to retain the good will of the political classes, since its funding was not linked to audience share (unlike that of ITV, which depended on advertising). In reality audience shares mattered to everyone; partly because even the most cynical producers would want as many people as possible to watch their works, but above all because the legitimacy of the licence fee (the broadcasting tax) which funded the BBC could be sustained only by having a large audience. The BBC was forced to react to the new competitive environment by being populist and popular. In the era of universal television, with a limited number of channels, all providers had to abide by some market rules, namely the provision of a mix of programmes to maximise overall audiences.

In the course of the 1960s new channels were introduced by the public sector in many European countries. BBC2, the third British channel, was launched in 1964, as was Germany's third; the second French channel also started in 1964, the third in 1972. BBC2 did what, in retrospect, the BBC was good at: popularising high culture, notably with the thirteen-part *The Ascent of Man*. The surreal comedy show *Monty Python's Flying Circus* (1969–74), also on BBC, became internationally famous, advertising a particularly 'British' zany sense of humour. Thought out 'wholly in terms of television ... It took as the material for many of its jokes not just the culture and content of television ... but its very "grammar": the forms, codes and conventions of the medium.'[1] Since it was mocking television genres (game shows, talk shows, etc.) it could be understood by audiences familiar with them.[2]

European television was changing. Until the 1980s only Great Britain, Luxembourg, Holland and Finland had a private television network. The high-minded Dutch system was shattered by the introduction in the late 1960s of a new broadcasting organisation, TROS, a former 'pirate' broadcaster whose unashamed populism was very successful, and quickly gained one-third of the audience. Soon commercial Dutch-language TV stations operating from Luxembourg beamed their entertainment packages via satellite.[3] Twenty years later the Dutch system, once a public monopoly, had been transformed into one of the most competitive in Europe. By the end of the 1990s there were three public and six commercial channels. Ten years before, there were only three in total.[4]

The pioneer of extreme deregulation, however, was Italy. In 1976 the supreme court ruled that the state monopoly of broadcasting was not legal for regional broadcasts. The result was an explosion of private local radio and television stations. By the early 1980s it was possible, in major cities like Rome, to watch nearly thirty channels. The evasion rate of the broadcasting tax increased to 19.4 per cent of the owners of television sets, the highest in Europe (Finland, the lowest, was estimated to be 4 per cent; in Great Britain it was 7.7 per cent).[5] Protected by powerful politicians, a single operator, the network Fininvest (now Mediaset), owned by Silvio Berlusconi, was able to acquire almost complete control of the three main private channels, as well as the main advertising agency in the country, the largest publishing house, Mondadori, and several newspapers.

Such overwhelming, near-monopolistic control, straddling various media, would have been illegal in other market economies such as the USA or Great Britain. Berlusconi's successful move into politics (he was Prime Minister in 1994 and 2001–06) enabled him to add to his control of private broadcasting the enormous influence that a Prime Minister can exercise on public service television – a situation legally impossible in the majority of Western countries, including the USA. Berlusconi was never a press baron like Murdoch, or like Robert Hersant in France or Axel Springer in Germany. His rise to media power required the favours of the political establishment. When this establishment fell, and in particular when his 'godfather' the socialist leader Bettino Craxi, was overwhelmed by the *tangentopoli* ('kickback city') corruption scandal, he had no choice but to enter politics directly to defend his media empire.[6] In this he was successful: in April 2002 his Mediaset network's share of the audience was 45.3 per cent, against RAI's 43.9.[7]

Changes were taking place elsewhere too, though at a less bracing pace. In France in the 1970s everything remained in state hands, but programmes could be commissioned from outsiders. Public television, the ORTF, was split in 1974 into seven companies (while remaining in the public sector). Matters would change rapidly in the 1980s. The right – that is the Gaullists and their allies – had defended the public sector out of commitment to the idea of 'the French nation'. Besides, the ORTF was 'theirs', and subject to their political control, unlike the press. This explains the paradox that the socialists, after they gained power in 1981, started the process of liberalising broadcasting.[8] They allowed the creation of Canal Plus (a subscription channel) in 1984, then Cinq and TV6 in 1985. When Jacques Chirac became Prime Minister in 1986, with François Mitterrand still President, he had little choice but to continue the development of private TV.[9]

In Greece too, a latecomer to the world of television, state monopoly was abolished by the socialist PASOK, though the initial push had been made by the (conservative) mayors of Athens and two other major towns in 1987 when they launched a 'free' radio.[10] After the defeat of PASOK in the 1989 general elections, a fairly chaotic growth of television and radio stations ensued, producing dozens of television stations. The share of advertising revenue accruing to the Hellenic Broadcasting Corporation (ERT) dropped dramatically, and its ratings shrank to less than 10 per cent.[11]

In Spain the liberalisation process was started with radio broadcasting in the newly established autonomous regions, such as Catalunya Radio in Catalonia, but it was the socialist government of Felipe González which opened up television to the market in 1989.

In West Germany the development of private broadcasting was due to initiatives by the *Länder*, first by Lower Saxony in 1985. The constitutional court, in judgements in 1986 and 1987, allowed private broadcasters to meet lower standards, provided public broadcasters achieved higher ones[12] – an odd way of imposing higher regulation on the public than the private media. After unification each of the new *Länder* of the former DDR set up its own TV station.[13] In 1987 RTL, a private station which had started in Luxembourg in 1984, transferred to Cologne. It went where others did not yet dare to go, showing mildly erotic films such as *Emmanuelle*, and the *Playboy Late Night Show*, as well as a sex game show borrowed from the Italian *Colpo grosso*, where contestants (a man and a woman) must remove items of clothes (stopping before they became completely naked). Thanks to the development of private television Italian broadcasting had moved from being one of the most strait-laced in Europe to one of the most permissive. In 1977–78, for instance, TeleTorino International showed housewives indulging in amateur striptease, encouraged by their husbands and fathers, all in search of their fifteen minutes of fame.[14]

The discovery of sex occurred with the first explosion of private television, but it turned out to be a far less interesting commercial proposition than was at first hoped or feared. Since it was out of the question to show sex during prime time, erotic shows were banished to the midnight hours, and once the novelty wore off, viewers returned to their old favourites: game shows, romantic comedies, sitcoms and violent action movies. Television proved more profitable if it remained a family entertainment.

The multiplicity of channels, however, has so far had the same effect as the multiplicity of radio stations. Their expansion did not fragment the audience unduly, because most of it was concentrated around five or six channels. For instance, by the end of 1993 two-thirds of Germans were able to get sixteen channels, but five of those had three-quarters of the audience.[15] In 1998, 96.6 per cent of the French listened to the radio at least once a week, but 13 per cent tuned in to one station only.[16] In 2002 in Holland the top ten television channels were holding 86 per cent of the audience.[17] The fact that it is technically possible to receive a hundred channels does not mean that the audience will fragment across all of them.

Multiplicity of channels went hand in hand with the commercialisation of television. But the alternative of public versus private did not exhaust all the available options. One of the most original developments came, once again, from Britain. In the 1970s the ITV companies wanted a second channel, to achieve parity with the BBC which by then had two. The establishment reacted. Anthony Smith, once a *Panorama* producer, later President of Magdalen College (Oxford), suggested in 1972 that a fourth television channel should be conceived as a not-for-profit electronic publishing house. In 1977 a committee chaired by Lord Annan (once Master of King's College, Cambridge, and Provost of University College London) included this idea in a proposal for a new television authority.[18] The Independent Broadcasting Authority added the proviso that the new channel should not duplicate the kind of programmes broadcast on ITV, but should commission material from independent companies. It would be financed by the ITV companies, which in return would be allowed to sell the channel's advertising airtime. This led to the creation of Channel Four in 1982. The new channel was widely regarded as 'left-wing' – not necessarily an epithet which would endear it to the government, then led by Mrs Thatcher. In fact Channel Four provided a model for a public–private partnership – at a time when the expression had not yet been coined. The example, however, was not followed in the rest of Europe, where the 1980s witnessed massive deregulation and commercialisation.

Nowhere in Europe had there been strong popular pressure for the deregulation or privatisation of TV, though once it was done, it is unlikely that it could be reversed. No mechanism existed for consulting the public (even though watching television for twenty-four hours a week meant that it took up more time than any activity except working and sleeping). Others acted on behalf of the viewing public: politicians, producers and trade unionists. Cultural and religious élites resisted commercialisation, while the world of business and commerce supported it. Even this generalisation needs to be contextualised. Commercial television could damage newspapers by attracting advertising, so press groups were ambivalent. They opposed commercial television unless they were allowed to own networks themselves. Once they were, they became enthusiastic supporters. All the main European publishing groups acquired a stake in private television. 'Alternative' and 'counter-culture' groups were equally ambivalent. They tended to oppose big business and state television on principle, but they also wanted jobs and new outlets. The spread of private radio stations was initially welcomed by such groups, particularly in Italy, where they were seen as an alternative to RAI and its system of political patronage. In reality 'private' radio, with some exceptions, quickly became largely purveyors of pop music and low-level provincial coverage, while RAI remained the main source for radio news, particularly in what became, all over Europe, peak listening time: early morning.[19]

It might have been thought that political patronage would protect state television from competition. The Italian RAI, by 1972, employed 12,000 people and was paying fees and retainers to some 20,000 external 'consultants', including almost all the most prestigious intellectuals of the country.[20] So the network had considerable protectors who, once the supreme court had ruled against a state monopoly over broadcasting, might have rallied around the objective of a new, highly regulated broadcasting system open to the private sector. But the Italian establishment was not a monolithic bloc. It was divided by incessant political infighting. The resulting institutional paralysis played into the hands of entrepreneurs such as Silvio Berlusconi.[21] Regulation occurred only when he had established his near-complete control over the private sector. The result was a strengthening of his empire.

Deregulation and Fragmentation

The process of deregulation was somewhat tortuous. In Germany in 1976 the Federal Commission on Communication (KTK) suggested experimentation with cable transmission. The leaders (Prime Ministers) of the eleven *Länder* backed the idea, as did the new coalition CDU/CSU, elected in October 1982. The cable network was massively expanded thanks to the new CDU Minister for Posts and Telecommunications, a leading advocate of commercial broadcasting.[22] CDU *Länder* took advantage of the initiative and the Social Democrats were forced to accept 'the new realities' in 1984.[23] In 1986 the constitutional court ruled in favour of a 'dual broadcasting system': a national public sector alongside regional commercial systems.

The public was unenthusiastic, as was, at first, the private sector. Eventually the first network, SAT1, was established in 1985 by an association of ten press groups.[24] Since the *Länder* remained in charge of regulation, no common system evolved throughout the Federal Republic. During 1989 the public sector's share of the audience fell dramatically.[25] By 1991–93 the big press groups, such as Springer and Bertelsmann, had acquired major stakes in broadcasting.[26]

By the mid-1990s public service broadcasting had dropped to less than 50 per cent of prime-time television almost everywhere in western Europe:

TERRESTRIAL PUBLIC SERVICE TELEVISION: SHARE OF PRIME-TIME AUDIENCE

Country	Channels	Percentage share
Austria	ORF1, ORF2	58.5
Belgium (Wallonia)	RTBF	21.7
Belgium (Flanders)	TV-1, Canvas	37.7
Denmark	DR, TV-2	78.5
Finland	TV-1, TV-2	44.7
France	France 2, 3, 5	40.7
Germany	ZDF, ARD, Third Channels	46.0
Greece	ET-1, NET	11.2
Ireland	RTE	46.9
Italy	RAI	45.6
Netherlands	Nederland 1, 2, 3	37.6
Portugal	RTP	24.7
Spain	TVE, plus regional stations	51.7
Sweden	SVT	50.0
Great Britain	BBC	38.9

SOURCE: Adapted from Iosifidis, Steemers and Wheeler, *European Television Industries*, p.20

By 1997 audiences were further fragmented, with few channels achieving more than a 30 per cent share of the audience: TF1 in France, MTV 3 in Finland, and Nova TV in the Czech Republic (and Globo in Brazil). The future pattern is likely to replicate the situation in the USA or Canada, where no network has more than 20 per cent of the audience.[27]

Had television gone the way of radio, where simply purchasing a receiver enables one to obtain, for free, any programme, advertising would have remained the only source of revenue. It was necessary to find ways of charging for sending signals 'direct to home' (DTH). One option was DBS ('direct broadcasting by satellite'), which required the purchase of a special dish and a special decoder. This enabled the new networks to charge their customers for a package of programmes. Previously this could be done via cable – a system which had existed in the US since the 1960s, initially as a means of enabling long-distance broadcasting. The first European countries to use cable were those whose markets were small and who shared common languages with neighbouring countries (Switzerland and Belgium). By January 1990 a quarter of German households were connected to cable.[28] Satellites and cables were the two technological weapons which enabled commercial television to stop relying entirely on advertising. Subscribers were now charged a monthly fee, usually in excess of what the state taxed them. But now viewers had a choice. This choice would not be exercised unless the new DBS and DTH channels were able to provide irresistible fare – a problem which also faced the new commercial 'free' channels (since without an audience they would not obtain any advertising). But how could they compete with the stock of talents available to the state sector? How could they invest in new, exciting and original fiction, and run the risk of failure? Since they were neither able nor willing to make successful programmes, only three avenues were open. One was to buy the exclusive rights of the most popular broadcasts – and this meant, in Europe, football, making football stars even richer than they were before. Thus the German conglomerate Kirch acquired broadcasting rights to the football World Cups of 2002 and 2006 for $2.36 billion. In Britain BSkyB paid £1.1 billion for live coverage of the domestic Premier League for the years 2001–04 (one-third of its total programme budget).[29] Another strategy was the systematic purchase of American fiction, in direct competition with the state sector. The third was the purchase of the stock of films and old television fiction owned by the main Hollywood studios. All of these were attempted, with excellent results. By and large most of the programmes broadcast by the new commercial sector were not 'in-house'.

The digitalisation of cable systems, feasible since the late 1990s, made possible the reception of hundreds of channels, as well as pay-per-view services (where a fee is paid for each programme, including past programmes on video). Before that, the main technological breakthrough, reception via satellite (which eventually eliminated the obstacle of a limited range of frequencies), had been made possible by the launch in July 1962 of the first communications satellite, Telstar, a joint venture between NASA and AT&T. For the first time television images could be transmitted across the Atlantic. It was immediately predicted that there would be a global TV system within a few years, even though many areas of the globe did not yet have radio broadcasting or electricity. Needless to say, broadcasting remained staunchly national. It takes more than technology to change the world. At first only 'important' events were internationally broadcast, such as the 1968 Mexico Olympics and, in July 1969, the landing of Apollo Eleven on the moon and the first steps of Neil Armstrong and Edwin 'Buzz' Aldrin. Soon a network of satellites enabled the transmission of sound and images from anywhere in the world to anywhere in the world, and overcame the limitations of free-to-air transmission.

Technological developments were crucial in saving radio from possible extinction. The replacement in the 1950s of the wireless valve by a solid-state device, the transistor, made up of a tiny piece of semiconductor, usually silicon, enabled the development of portable radio receivers. It became possible for each member of the household to have his or her own portable radio, and for every room, including the bathroom, and cars, to have a radio. Such ubiquity meant that radio broadcasts were listened to while doing something else. Programmes had to be adjusted for the shorter and less intensive attention span: rolling news, endlessly repeated, chat shows and plenty of music. Thus the proliferation of radio stations was not reflected in the supply of programmes. In any case, most people listened regularly to only one or two stations. Only state broadcasting, and particularly the BBC, succeeded in providing a really varied fare: not only music and news, but also current affairs, soaps, plays, book reading, game shows, satire and comedy, debates and chat shows. The result was that in 2001 half the audience still stuck with the BBC, but only at the national level, followed at a distance by Classic FM, entirely dedicated to classical music, with 4 per cent of the audience. The rest was fragmented among the remainder of local commercial radio.[30]

Dropping Standards?

Did an increase in the number of television channels lead to a deterioration in the average cultural level of programmes? That it should obviously be so – regardless of one's definition of 'quality' – is easily explainable. New entrants need to acquire market share quickly in order to attract advertising, so they buy cheap programmes, because what matters is the ratio of advertising to audience. Since the pool of advertising revenue is not unlimited and the competition is keen, there is less money available for making 'quality' programmes which would attract a large audience. Since advertising funds not only radio and television but also the press and the cinema, the repercussions would be felt throughout the cultural industry. This, for instance, is what happened in Italy:

ITALY: PERCENTAGE SHARE
OF TOTAL ADVERTISING
EXPENDITURE

	1970	1990
Television	12.4	50.4
Cinema	6.4	0.3
Daily press	30	23.3

SOURCE: Antonio Pilati, 'La Pubblicità dei mezzi di comunicazione' in Valerio Castronovo and Nicola Tranfaglia (eds), *La Stampa italiana nell'età della TV*, Laterza 1994

Of course, one could imagine a scenario of ever-expanding advertising income, or the possibility of obtaining large-scale investment 'up front' for many new programmes, but these are unlikely to occur. Or the regulatory authorities could compel new entrants to produce a certain percentage of good quality programmes – but if the percentage were set too high, it would deter entry. Or channels, instead of being generalists, could specialise. The American CNN had shown that a 'rolling news' channel could be a winning idea. However, since its is unlikely that there is room and advertising revenue for many CNNs, in the end there would be only one or two news channels with the resources to cover the globe with a network of correspondents – fewer than is the case now. What is more likely is the segmentation of audiences according to the same 'high culture'/'low culture' criteria at work in other sectors of the cultural industry. Such differentiations have, of course, operated within generalist channels, and even within the old public sector system there were and are channels which promise, and occasionally deliver, more demanding fare, such as RAI Tre in Italy, the ultra-intellectual ARTE in France and Germany, and BBC2 in Great Britain. But segmentation by genre and standards does not by itself ensure higher standards; it simply provides viewers with a not-too-demanding way of accessing genres they like. Besides, changing the flow of programmes on each channel from generalist to specialist might constitute a psychological obstacle to dipping into new genres. Paradoxically, the fabled laziness of the pre-remote 'couch potato' viewers, too inert to get up and change channels, was a powerful educational tool: having watched the 213th episode of *Nurses and Doctors*, they might become absorbed in the following programme, say a documentary on *Rembrandt's Lesser-Known Early Drawings*. Such fare might not turn them into better human beings, but it might open up some new horizons and give them more leisure choices in life.

Multi-channel television also shifted programming from 'in-house' production to outside independent producers. These live in a very different environment from that of producers operating in the relatively cosseted and trade-union-protected public sector environment of the previous era. 'Independent' producers are 'independent' the way freelance workers are: at the mercy of everything. They work around stringent budgets, hire fewer technicians, work to tight schedules. The business is very risky, as is all small-scale production (most production companies employ fewer than ten people). There may be thousands of companies (as there are thousands of artists and actors), but few are active. In France there are some 1,100 production companies, but only sixty or so are really active, and sixteen of them produce 50 per cent of total production. Most of the programmes produced are one-offs, with no repeats and very little chance of export.[31] Besides, programme-makers are at the mercy of those in charge of schedules and what is on offer on other channels. Since most non-prime-time fiction is easily filled with American products which can be bought cheaply (at below their cost of production in the USA), the small independents are torn between being content with a share of the late-night audience or competing for a share of prime time, a crowded and highly competitive market.

When there was little competition, programmes which would be regarded as intellectually demanding obtained a fair share of the audience. Thus in Italy in 1969, when there were only two channels, the top programmes of the year (with just over twenty million viewers) were variety shows where viewers could choose their favourite song, such as *Canzonissima* and the San Remo Festival, followed by the 'moon landing; but a television adaptation of Shakespeare's *Othello* obtained just over ten million viewers, and Puccini's *Turandot* entranced five million.[32] Even in January 1982 a documentary on the restoration of Leonardo's *Last Supper* shown at 10 p.m. managed to get an audience of 4.3 million viewers. RAI's popular serial *Marco Polo* obtained an audience of 26.1 million, but Ibsen's *Doll's House* was seen by 6.8 million viewers, and *The Taming of the Shrew*, shown at prime time, a highly creditable 6.1 million.[33]

This era seems to have come to a close. For twenty years or so, television broadcasting had created a national community. On most evenings 'the country' would sit in front of their screens and watch the same programmes, building up a stock of shared knowledge and memories. This is no longer the case. As Elihu Katz eloquently put it: 'We have all but lost television as the medium of national political integration.'[34] Television is no longer a shared public space where a nation gathers together. The return of cultural fragmentation may well reposition audiences along a high culture/low culture divide. High-level programmes will still be made, but with less cash and aimed at smaller, ghettoised audiences. Governments such as that of Great Britain will still declare that their aim is 'to ensure that the BBC continues to play a central role in the nation's life as its most important cultural institution'.[35] Whether they will be able and willing to do so is uncertain.

59

Going Out: Cinema and Theatre

Introduction

TELEVISION BROUGHT US BACK to the home after the heady temptations of the cinema. In reality, we had not been outside the domestic walls for long. The lure of gramophone records and radio and cheap books had been with us for decades. To be amused and entertained and, if one wished, educated, one could simply stay at home and read and listen, well before television (and the computer and the internet) had become familiar. The private sphere may have seemed to be as private as ever, yet it was wide open to outside influences. Once only churches and schools challenged parental control; now many wondered whether parents had any control at all.

In spite of the attractions of domesticity, out-of-home entertainment accelerated rapidly. Eating out was no longer the privilege of the rich or the resort of the lonely. Bars and restaurants multiplied. Holidays abroad were available to the working class. The expansion of car ownership made a day in the country or a weekend away a possibility for a significant proportion of the population. The growing expansion of telephone ownership after 1960 gave almost everyone the possibility of keeping in touch with friends and relatives and organising entertainment with them. A majority of Westerners acquired privileges which were once the prerogative of the upper classes. Older forms of out-of-the-home entertainment survived. Some, such as going to concerts, prospered. Others, such as variety shows, stagnated or decreased in popularity. The theatre, as we shall see, became more popular in the age of television than it was before. The great loser was cinema-going.

The Fate of the Cinema

In 1960 few people had a television. By 2000 almost everyone had one. A majority had a video recorder. Some had a DVD player. A few could download films on their computers. The number of films available to the average person had thus grown exponentially since 1960. In the home one could access, thanks to television, many of the films made in the past, including those originally made as fillers or B-movies. The stock of film turned out to be a goldmine in the age of the multiplication of television channels. Buying a Hollywood studio, such as Twentieth Century-Fox, bought by Murdoch in 1985, or Columbia, purchased by the Japanese Sony in 1991, enabled the new owners to gain access to thousands of films and show them on their television networks. In Germany the networks ARD and ZDF bought massive film stocks from the US, as did the media tycoons Silvio Berlusconi in Italy, Robert Hersant in France, and Axel Springer and Leo Kirch in Germany (between 1973 and 1975 almost half of the films shown by ZDF were bought from Kirch, who held 10,000 to 15,000 titles).[1] Hollywood was still making films, but by the early 1990s the largest Hollywood companies (Paramount, Twentieth Century-Fox, Warner, Universal, Disney, Columbia and MGM/ United Artists) produced half the prime-time television fiction.[2]

Television viewers could watch films released only a year or two before, sometimes even six months before, films released in other countries but not in one's own, films not intended for cinema release but made for television, films that failed to be released and, more recently, films made for the videocassette and DVD market. In 1996 the average viewer in the European Union watched fifty films a year at home, but only two in the cinema. On television alone the supply of films was overwhelming compared to cinema distribution: just in Italy, in 1999, 6,757 films were shown on television – 2,344 by the state network RAI, 2,848 by the Berlusconi network Mediaset, and 1,565 by the small network TMC.

In France in 2000, according to government figures, the average person watched an impressive 250 films on television or on a video recorder, and only three in a cinema.[3] The main source of classic film culture had become television and videocassettes:

FRANCE, 2000: PERCENTAGE OF PEOPLE WHO HAD SEEN
SELECTED CLASSIC FILMS IN A CINEMA AND ON TELEVISION

Title	Cinema	TV or video	Total
Gone with the Wind	19	59	78
West Side Story	16	39	55
La Grande Illusion	11	36	47
Les Enfants du Paradis	10	32	42
Some Like it Hot	7	26	33
Casablanca	8	24	32
Battleship Potemkin	9	24	33
La Dolce Vita	9	18	27
Citizen Kane	6	18	24

SOURCE: Ministry of Culture, *Développement culturel* No. 135, September 2000, 'La Culture cinématographique des Français'

The trend of watching films on a box at home rather than on a large screen in public will become even more widely spread thanks to downloading films and renting DVDs via the internet. The pioneer, of course, was the USA, where subscription cable networks such as HBO (Home Box Office) started delivering, in the 1980s, current films as well as their own films and serials, such as the prize-winning *The Sopranos*, produced by the company itself. Between 1972 and 1982 the number of US households subscribing to cable jumped from 6.5 million to 29 million, while the revenue from videocassette distribution exceeded that from the box office before the end of the 1980s.[4]

There may be a crisis of the cinema, but there is no crisis of films. Instead of going to the cinema, we watch movies at home. A film such as Mike Leigh's *Naked* (1993), modestly successful in the cinema, reached twenty times as many people when shown on television.[5] There is nothing new about that. Cinema audiences are not in the same league as those for television. It took more than fifty years for *Gone with the Wind* to sell thirty million tickets in Great Britain, while just the opening episode of the fourth series of *I'm a Celebrity, Get Me Out of Here* (a reality television show competing with many others) in November 2004 was seen by nine million people.

The product shown in theatres or at home may be the same, but the experience of viewing it is vastly different. Seeing a film in the dark, with total strangers, on a large screen with a powerful sound system, provides a sensation which cannot be reproduced even by a large flat-screen high-definition television; but it is expensive and time-consuming. It was expensive for the cinema industry, which required a formidable distribution network for the diffusion of its products, namely large edifices in prime locations. With television the consumer bears the main distribution cost by buying the receiver.

Going out is expensive for the consumer too. In London, a modest evening out in 2005 for a couple with young children could turn out to be a costly event: £17 for two tickets at the local cinema, £20 for the babysitter (four hours), £30 for two pizzas, salads and two (small) beers adds up to £67. Unsurprisingly, attendances at cinemas dropped rapidly between 1955 and 1977, and continued to drop, at slower and varying rates, in the 1990s. A modest revival was registered at the time of writing.

AVERAGE ANNUAL CINEMA ATTENDANCE PER PERSON
IN SELECTED COUNTRIES, 1955–95

	1955	1977	1990–95
USA	15	7.2	3.9
Brazil	5	1.9	n/a
Argentina	4	2.6	0.5
Japan	10	1.5	1.1
France	10	3.2	2.2
Italy	17	6.6	1.6
Norway	10	4.2	2.7
Netherlands	6	1.9	1.0
UK	23	1.9	2.0
Bulgaria	7	12.9	0.6
Poland	8	4	0.4
USSR	13	15.8	n/a

SOURCES: UNESCO, *Statistics on Film And Cinema 1955–1977*, Statistical Reports and Studies No. 25, Paris 1981
1990–95: UNESCO, *World Culture Report*, 1998

The decrease was particularly marked in Great Britain in 1955–77 and in the former communist countries in the 1990s. American audiences had started to decrease in the 1950s. In West Germany in 1984 the average citizen went to the cinema 1.8 times a year, more or less in line with the European average, but two-thirds of Germans had not been to the cinema for a year. Ninety per cent of married couples declared that they had stopped going to the cinema. Those who did go were young: 66 per cent were in the fourteen-to-twenty-four age group.[6] In France too there was an almost exact correlation between age and going out in the evening.[7] By the 1970s, 75 per cent of US cinema audiences were under twenty-nine years of age. Soon the fate of the international film industry was in the hands of popcorn-munching American teenagers.[8] No wonder the 'oldies' – those over forty – stayed at home watching television.

The subsequent relative stabilisation of film audiences in western Europe in the 1990s – in some countries one can speak of a revival – was due to an increase in the number of screens as large cinemas were transformed into multi-screen venues, offering a wider choice to a smaller, younger and more affluent audience. Screen density (the number of screens per inhabitant) is even more important than their number in determining the success of a film industry. And here the USA is supreme, with one hundred screens per million people in the mid-1990s (against eighty in France and thirty-four in Great Britain).[9] By 1994 there were 4,414 screens in France, 3,763 in Germany and 1,969 in Great Britain.[10] In 1997 Italy had 4,206 screens, almost the same as in 1938 (4,013), having peaked at over 10,000 in the late 1950s. In 1938, however, cinemas were much larger. The 4,013 screens of 1938 attracted 343,851,000 spectators in the course of the year (85,684 each); the 4,206 screens of 1997 only attracted 102,782,000 (24,436 each).[11].

In Europe (east and west) 1,026 films were produced in 1986, but only 630 in 1994 – still more than in the USA.[12] Much of this drop was due to the collapse of the eastern European cinema. In 1975 eastern Europe had greater seating capacity per thousand inhabitants than any other group of countries (65.6 per thousand people, against 50.8 in the USA and 40 in western Europe) as well as the highest attendance (14.3 per inhabitant, against 5.7 in North America and 4.3 in western Europe).[13] Such cultural advantages disappeared along with communism, and attendance dropped dramatically to below the EU average.

AVERAGE ANNUAL CINEMA ADMISSIONS PER
INHABITANT IN EASTERN AND CENTRAL EUROPE, 1986–94

	1986	1994
Lithuania	13.26	0.38
Russia	12.28	2.62
Estonia	11.88	0.91
Bulgaria	10.55	1.44
Romania	6.97	1.10
Hungary	6.45	1.55
Czechoslovakia	4.92	1.25 (Czech Rep.)
DDR	4.26	1.63 (all Germany)
Slovenia	3.97	1.41
Slovakia	3.60	n/a
EU average	2.01	1.83

SOURCE: *Statistical Yearbook 1996*,
European Audiovisual Observatory

The immediate beneficiary was the US film industry:

US FILMS RELEASED IN EASTERN AND CENTRAL EUROPE, 1986–94

	1986 Total films released	Of which US films	1994 Total films released	Of which US films
Bulgaria	170	7	147	123
Czech Republic	180	26	151	113
Hungary	195	25	176	106
Poland	152	15	160	98
Slovenia	231	65	151	114
Slovakia	241	10	162	112

SOURCE: *Statistical Yearbook 1996*, European Audiovisual Observatory

Who Makes Films?

The inevitable consequence of the rise of television was a drop in the production of films for the cinema, but television also saved films by financing them. Some of the most significant and critically acclaimed European films were financed by television networks such as the BBC and Channel Four (Great Britain), RAI (Italy) and Canal Plus (France). In Germany, ARD and ZDF contributed to the development of the so-called new German cinema, funding, among others, films by Volker Schlöndorff, Alexander Kluge, Rainer Werner Fassbinder, Werner Herzog and Wim Wenders. The majority of the German public continued to prefer American films or spectacular German ones like Wolfgang Petersen's *Das Boot* (1981), but German cinema rediscovered an audience, at least for a while, though it never regained the prestige or the style of Weimar days.[14]

The domination of American films accelerated in the years after 1960. In the early 1960s, though the USA was the main source of imported films, European home production was still considerable, as was the importation of films from some of the main European producers such as France, Italy and Great Britain.

FILM PRODUCTION AND FILM IMPORTATION IN SELECTED COUNTRIES, 1962–63

Country	Home films	Country of origin of imported films			
		USA	France	Great Britain	Italy
Sweden	19	109	32	54	40
Great Britain	71	117	46		33
Belgium	4	124	106	34	31
Italy	245	166	35	34	
France	139	91		20	53
Spain	119	103	24	22	28
Czechoslovakia	28	36	16	12	12
Germany	58	120	80	n/a	38
USSR	90	80	18	16	18
Holland	5	118	72	73	64
Egypt	50	172	41	26	35
USA	145		55	53	70
India	310	135	0	35	22
Japan	357	146	46	18	38

SOURCE: Data collected by *Lo Spettacolo*, Vol. 14, No. 2, April–June 1964, using *Bulletin d'Information Centre National de la Cinématographie*, *Le Film français* and *Variety*.

In the early 1970s Europe still provided a considerable proportion of foreign earnings to the US film industry, over 30 per cent of which originated from just four countries: Great Britain (10.4 per cent), Italy (9.3 per cent), France (6.9 per cent) and Germany (5.2 per cent). By 1994 the USA was even more dominant, at least in Europe. In France, the European country with the strongest film industry, 60.4 per cent of tickets sold were for US films. Elsewhere, American market share was higher: 61.1 per cent in Italy, 72.3 per cent in Spain, 81.6 in Germany and 90 per cent in Great Britain.[15] The consequence was that the American film industry's dependence on exports increased further. Jack Valenti, head of the Motion Picture Association, told US Senators in 1991 that 40 per cent of the revenues of the US film industry were earned abroad (half of that from Europe). Entertainment had become America's second largest export after aircraft manufacturing.[16] This was achieved not by flooding the market with a large number of films, but by making films that appealed to a world market. The rest of the world had long made more films than the USA, but these were aimed mostly at their own local markets:

ESTIMATED WORLD FILM PRODUCTION BY GROUPS OF COUNTRIES

	1955	1977
North America	310	180
Latin America	170	220
Asia (excluding Arab states)	1,430	1,940
Western Europe	680	820
USSR and eastern Europe	170	320
Oceania	negligible	40
Arab states (mainly Egypt)	60	70
Africa (excluding Arab States)	negligible	negligible
Estimated world total	2,800	3,600

SOURCE: UNESCO, *Statistics on Film and Cinema 1955–1977*, Statistical Reports and Studies No. 25, 1981

Greece alone made, in the 1960s, an average of a hundred films a year.[17] This is approximately the Hollywood average for the 1990s, while India in 2005 was producing eight hundred films (one hundred or so in Mumbai – 'Bollywood'). Every day ten million people went to the cinema in India – about half the world's cinema visits.[18] This is a substantial change from 1962, when 'only' 1,400 million seats were sold in India.[19]

By the early years of the twenty-first century some Indian films (such as Mira Nair's *Monsoon Wedding*, 2001) made it into the international circuit – part of a deliberate strategy adopted by the Indian film industry to make films for Western markets. The Chinese did the same, and produced a number of internationally successful films, such as *Wo Hu Zang Long* (*Crouching Tiger, Hidden Dragon*, 2000), made by the Taiwanese director Ang Lee, and those made by Zhang Yimou (notably the astonishing *Dahong Denglong Gaogao Gua – Raise the Red Lantern*, 1991) and Chen Kaige (*Bawang Bieji – Farewell, My Concubine*, 1993).[20] None of this dented – at least for the time being – the global supremacy of the USA. Asia was counterattacking, but it was also a growth area for American corporations such as Walt Disney, which derived 20 per cent of its income from Asia in 2003.[21]

US films were supreme in Latin America, with nine out of the ten top-grossing films in Brazil, five out of ten in Mexico, seven out ten in Venezuela and ten out of ten in Colombia (1986 figures).[22] The top international hits of the decade 1986–95 were mainly from Hollywood. There were a few exceptions, such as *Four Weddings and a Funeral* (1994, UK), *A Fish Called Wanda* (1988, UK), *Crocodile Dundee* (1986, Australia) and *The Last Emperor* (1987, Italy).[23] But the first three of these all had American actors in leading roles and played with the well-trodden theme of the contrast between America and Old Europe (or Australian outback primitiveness). In fact *Four Weddings*, a British film with an overwhelmingly British cast, was advertised in Britain as 'America's No. 1 Smash Hit Comedy!'.[24] *The Last Emperor* was in style a Hollywood film, and in fact obtained nine Academy Awards – though its director, Bernardo Bertolucci, was Italian, its producer British and its funding international. Even one of the most internationally commercially successful films in the entire history of British cinema, *Mr Bean* (1997) – derived from a series of half-hour TV comedy shows – was set in Los Angeles and had at its centre one of the best-known American paintings: *Arrangement in Black and Grey No. 1: The Artist's Mother* by James McNeill Whistler.[25]

The USA may make fewer films than previously, but they are more expensive and are deliberately aimed at a global market. European films – not to speak of Indian or Egyptian – found it almost impossible to break into the American market as had been the case in the previous decades. Such difficulty was also experienced by 'independent' or 'art' American films (such as those of Woody Allen, arguably more popular in Europe than in the USA). European art films were able to find a niche in places such as New York, but the obstacles were considerable. Advertising films in New York is not cheap. An unfavourable review in New York would make it even more difficult for a film to be distributed elsewhere, and in any case, outside New York or major university towns, a film without a recognised star would have little chance of finding a distributor. Art European films, since they tended to be more sexually explicit than American ones, often end up with an X-rating (seldom given to violent films). Such a rating, previously regarded as an indication that a film was for adults, was increasingly seen as the sign of a 'foreign' film and regarded by distributors as an unprofitable proposition – besides, it would be ostracised by the growing morality lobby.[26]

As we saw in Chapter 48, this is not a new situation. America's favourite films are American. A survey published in 1972, based on earnings per film (rather than the more meaningful number of seats sold), confirms it:

TOP TEN EARNING FILMS IN THE USA BY 1972

		Millions of dollars
Gone with the Wind	1939	74.2
The Sound of Music	1965	72
Love Story	1970	50
Airport	1970	44.5
The Graduate	1968	43.1
Dr Zhivago	1965	43.0
Ben Hur	1959	40.7
The Ten Commandments	1957	40.0
My Fair Lady	1964	32.0
Mary Poppins	1964	31.0

SOURCE: *Variety*, 5 January 1972

All of these are, strictly speaking, American films, but we should bear in mind a point previously made (see page 980) on the difficulty of defining the nationality of a film. The director of *Dr Zhivago*, David Lean, was British, as was Robert Bolt, the screenwriter. The film was based on a Russian novel by Boris Pasternak. Its leading stars were British (Julie Christie) and Egyptian

(Omar Sharif). It paraded an array of distinguished British stage actors, from Alec Guinness and Ralph Richardson to Tom Courtenay and Rita Tushingham. The Oscar-winning score (which included 'Lara's Theme') was by the French composer Maurice Jarre. Geraldine Chaplin and Rod Steiger (both rather 'European' American actors) were left to carry the US banner. Finally, the film followed the old American rule that actors in historical films set in Europe should adopt British accents. *Gone with the Wind*, the only pre-war film on the list, is also the only one with a clearly historically based American story. Only three of the rest are set in the USA – *Love Story*, *Airport* and *The Graduate*. *Ben Hur* (by the German-born director William Wyler) and *The Ten Commandments* were set in the ancient world. *My Fair Lady* and *Mary Poppins* were set in England – exploiting a quaint view of English-ness. *Mary Poppins* has an English singer-actress (Julie Andrews) in the leading role of the miraculous nanny, and was based on a book written in 1934 by the Australian-born P.L. Travers. *My Fair Lady* had an English actor (Rex Harrison) in the lead (and a Dutch-born female star, Audrey Hepburn – but she was widely regarded as American) and was based on the musical adaptation of *Pygmalion*, the play by an Irish-born British author, George Bernard Shaw. *The Sound of Music*, an adaptation of Maria von Trapp's autobiography, was set in Nazi-controlled Austria in the 1930s and had a British star in the lead (Julie Andrews again).

Some European films, funded by Americans, managed to attract trans-atlantic attention by using American stars – for instance Bertolucci's *Last Tango in Paris* with Marlon Brando, and Visconti's *The Leopard* with Burt Lancaster in the role of Prince Fabrizio Salina, but American films continued to be more international than those of other countries. Take *Cold Mountain* (2003), produced by Miramax, an American company. The film was set in the USA during the Civil War. It is an adaptation of a best-selling American novel – vaguely inspired by Homer's *The Odyssey* – which traces the adven-tures of a soldier returning home to his wife after a long and brutal war. The director was Anthony Minghella, the child of Italian immigrants to Great Britain (he was born on the Isle of Wight) and hence British. The actor playing the lead part of Inman was Jude Law, born in Lewisham in south London. The lead female role (Ada) was played by Nicole Kidman, who though born in Honolulu (USA) was brought up in Australia by her Austra-lian parents. Maddy, the witch-like creature who rescues Inman, was Eileen Atkins, an esteemed English actress born in Clapton, east London. The sultry Sara, nearly raped by soldiers and rescued by Inman, was the Israeli actress

Natalie Portman. Renée Zellweger (Ruby) is Texan, but the actor playing her father is the Irish Brendan Gleeson. The music was composed by Gabriel Yared, naturalised French and born in Beirut. The extras impersonating the Civil War soldiers were conscripts of the Romanian army (and all the war scenes were shot in Romania).

The universality of American films could not be matched by their European rivals (whose main line of defence was to protect their domestic market share by making highly 'national' films). The Americans were able to recast 'typically' European themes, such as that of class, represented by Shaw's *Pygmalion*, test them in various forms (musicals or comic strips), and send them back to Europe suitably packaged for a mass market. As competition from television increased, the most successful films became those that gained considerably from being shown on a large cinema screen, providing the kind of experience impossible to achieve on television. The more intimate (and cheaper) stories preferred by Europeans could never hope to compete with biblical blockbusters with casts of thousands, expensive chariot races and special effects able to show the ten plagues of Egypt and the parting of the Red Sea. The tradition of popular religiosity epitomised by the chapbooks of the eighteenth century and the religious images of the nineteenth found their natural heirs in the Hollywood biblical and ancient Rome films. These, of course, built on European foundation stones such as the Italian *Cabiria*, made in 1914, which showed the burning of the Roman fleet and Hannibal crossing the Alps (see pages 825–6). And while Great Britain had become a unique talent base for special effects, particularly after Stanley Kubrick made *2001: A Space Odyssey* (1968) in Britain,[27] the funding and the use of special effects remained a prerogative of the American cinema.

By the 1970s and 1980s the Americans were using their own tradition of comic strips, science fiction and adventure stories (these too, as we have seen, often had European origins) to launch global successes such as the *Star Wars* films, the *Superman* series, the *Jaws* films, *Titanic* and, more recently, such adaptations of British books as *The Lord of the Rings* and the Harry Potter films. The supreme and unrivalled master of this new American cinema was Steven Spielberg, whose formidable versatility ranged wide across genres:

STEVEN SPIELBERG: SELECTED FILMOGRAPHY

Film	Year	Genre/description
Duel	1971	TV film, thriller, one actor and a truck
Sugarland Express	1974	Road movie
Jaws	1975	Thriller, special effects
Close Encounters of the Third Kind	1977	Science fiction, nice aliens
Raiders of the Lost Ark	1981	Comic-book-style adventures
Indiana Jones and the Temple of Doom	1984	
Indiana Jones and the Last Crusade	1989	
E.T.: The Extra-Terrestrial	1982	Science fiction, nice alien
The Color Purple	1985	Race drama
Empire of the Sun	1987	Boy surviving in Shanghai during Japan's Second World War occupation
Hook	1991	Adaptation of *Peter Pan*
Jurassic Park	1993	Science fiction – special effects, dinosaurs
Schindler's List	1993	Holocaust film, in black and white
Amistad	1997	Celebrating 1839 slave rebellion
Saving Private Ryan	1999	Second World War
Artificial Intelligence: AI	2001	Science fiction
Minority Report	2002	Science fiction
The Terminal	2004	Immigrant stranded at airport
War of the Worlds	2005	Science fiction, bad aliens

Most of these films were spectacular commercial successes which no European director could aspire to unless he went to Hollywood. Directors or actors did not have to be American. What was American was the way of telling the story and the style of the film – though it should be added that Spielberg and his fellow 'movie brats' (such as Martin Scorsese, Francis Ford Coppola and Brian de Palma) always acknowledged their indebtedness to European masters, old and new.

Expensive American films were advertised expensively in the expectation of success. In some instances – *Jurassic Park* is often cited as an example –

the promotion budget was as significant as the cost of making the film. And success often, but not always, followed. The commercial fortunes of a film depend more than ever on the assumptions of distributors and the way in which the distribution system operates. In Great Britain, the oligopoly structure of film distribution ensures that only the films which are expected to succeed, actually succeed. British distributors assumed in 2002 that *Harry Potter and the Chamber of Secrets* would do very well, and indeed it did, but also because it opened in 524 venues. Such predictions do not always work: the film *Ali G in da House* (2002), a spin-off from a TV comedy, opened on 396 screens, with limited success. But the critically acclaimed *The Magdalene Sisters* (2003), shown on only thirty-one screens, could not possibly hope to match the receipts of the low-cost (£5 million) and crudely funny *Ali G in da House*.[28]

There was a strong American component in half of the top ten most popular European films in Europe.

TOP TEN EUROPEAN FILMS DISTRIBUTED IN THE EU IN 2002, BY NUMBER OF SEATS SOLD

Title	Country of origin	Seats sold (million)
Harry Potter and the Chamber of Secrets	UK/US	39.7
Asterix and Obelix: Mission Cleopatra	France/Germany	19.7
Die Another Day (James Bond)	UK/US	18.6
About a Boy	UK/US/Germany/France	8.7
Harry Potter and the Philosopher's Stone	UK/US	8.1
Huit femmes	France/Italy	5.8
Hable con ella (*Talk to Her*)	Spain	4.9
Gosford Park	UK/US/Germany/Italy	5.8
Pinocchio	Italy/France/Germany	4.5
Resident Evil	UK/Germany/France	3.5

SOURCE: *BFI Film & Television Handbook 2004*

And the USA dominated the rankings for the most popular films in Europe, though the top three were culturally British.

TOP TEN FILMS RANKED BY SEATS SOLD IN THE EU, 2001		
	Seats sold	*Country of origin*
Harry Potter and the Philosopher's Stone	42,942,206	US/GB
Bridget Jones's Diary	26,439,136	US/GB
The Lord of the Rings: The Fellowship of the Ring	21,104,825	US/NZ
Shrek	20,971,755	US
What Women Want	20,685,021	US
Hannibal	18,060,768	US
American Pie	17,549,403	US
The Mummy Returns	17,366,868	US
Pearl Harbor	16,967,801	US
Castaway	16,879,650	US

SOURCE: *Observatoire Européen de l'audiovisuel 2002*

Real profits accrued to highly expensive films with plenty of special effects which could appeal to a global audience – the kind of films Hollywood had long specialised in. The budget for *Lord of the Rings: The Fellowship of the Ring*, a film that employed 3,000 people, was over $90 million, but in its opening weekend in the USA (Christmas 2001) it grossed $66 million from 3,359 screens.[29] Such films also have a long life after their theatre exhibitions. They are bought and rented on VHS and DVD, shown on cable and terrestrial television, and generate vast sums thanks to their spin-offs in toys, records, soundtracks, books, computer games, posters, T-shirts and colouring books. Pepsico paid $2 billion for the right to use *Star Wars* images until the year 2005.The six *Star Wars* films, from the release of *Star Wars Episode IV* (as it was subsequently called) in 1977 to 2005, had an estimated revenue of $20 billion, more than the GDP of Bulgaria, Lebanon or oil-rich Libya.[30]

The principal source of inspiration for the first *Star Wars* was adventure comics such as Buck Rogers and Flash Gordon – typical boys' adventure stories; there was only one female character, Princess Leia (played by Carrie Fisher, who had little to do), and the central dynamics of the plot were based on the friendship between two men, Hans Solo (Harrison Ford) and Luke Skywalker (Mark Hamill), the master–pupil relationship between Obi-Wan

Kenobi (Alec Guinness) and Luke Skywalker, and the antics of the robots C-3Po and R2-D2 – all ancient and well-tested tropes in literature and films. Films like these do not need positive reviews, since a significant proportion of their viewers are children who enjoy watching the same film over and over again (as their children will, one day). As Louis Menand put it, the *Star Wars* director and producer George Lucas, 'like a true reactionary . . . did not need to invent more than he absolutely had to. He just raided the past.'[31] Yet as we have seen, raiding the past is part of the culture game, and Lucas knew how to do it, alluding to and parodying old movies with relish.

Special-effects-based blockbuster movies continued to attract a considerable proportion of the audience, but so did various genres of American films. Thus, in West Germany between 1981 and mid-1985, only 127 (out of 1,800) films were seen by more than a million people. Of such fortunate films, seventy-two were American and only nineteen German. In 1985, seven films took 25 per cent of the takings. Of these, five were American (*Amadeus*, by a Czech director, Milos Forman, *Rambo*, *Beverly Hills Cops*, *Ghostbusters* and *Police Academy II*), one was British (a James Bond) and only one German (*Otto. Der Film*, the first of a series with the popular comedian Otto Waalkes).[32]

In Italy, with a stronger cinema than Germany, some of the most popular films were Italian, but the best-loved foreign films were Anglo-American. Here is the ranking for the seven top-earning films of 2002:

TOP-EARNING FILMS IN ITALY, 2002

Natale sul Nilo	Italian comic
Pinocchio	Italian comic
La Leggenda di Al, John e Jack	Italian comic
Harry Potter e la camera dei segreti	*Harry Potter and the Chamber of Secrets*
Il Signore degli anelli: Le due torri	*Lord of the Rings: The Two Towers*
Matrix Reloaded	US science fiction
Il Mio grosso grasso matrimonio greco	*My Big Fat Greek Wedding* (US comedy)

SOURCE: *La Repubblica*, 5 August 2003

Things had changed since the 1960s, when television had not yet become ubiquitous and the Italian film industry was not yet in crisis. In 1962–64 the ten most popular films included Luchino Visconti's *The Leopard*, Francesco Rosi's *Salvatore Giuliano* and *Boccaccio 70* – a compilation of short films by

Federico Fellini, Visconti and Vittorio De Sica. In the late 1960s, though comic and adventure genres did well, so did art films, such as those of Luis Buñuel and Michelangelo Antonioni:

ITALY: TEN MOST POPULAR FILMS, 1967–69

	Genre	Seats sold
Da Uomo a uomo	Italian western	3,645,000
Belle de jour	France (Buñuel)	3,549,000
Il Bello, il brutto e il cretino	Italian comedy	3,180,000
Vado l'ammazzo e torno	Italian western	3,057,000
El Dorado	US western (Howard Hawks)	2,692,000
Odio per odio	Italian western	2,432,000
The War Wagon	US western (John Wayne)	2,378,000
Blow-Up	(Antonioni)	2,085,000
4 Bassotti per un danese	(The Ugly Dachshund) US comedy (Disney)	2,024,000
Padre di famiglia	Italian comedy	1,924,000

SOURCE: Lo Spettacolo, Vol. 20, No. 1 January–March 1970

In the years between 1959 and 1975, outstanding Italian directors produced a large number of high-quality films. These ranged from 'difficult' movies dealing with the alienation of modern life (Antonioni's L'Avventura, 1960 and La Notte, 1961) to post-neo-realist films such as Roberto Rossellini's Il Generale della Rovere and Mario Monicelli's La Grande guerra – both 1959 Venice Festival prize-winners – to the political films of Elio Petri and Francesco Rosi. These years also witnessed the establishment of the comic genre known as the 'commedia all'italiana', spaghetti westerns (some 150 of them), some well-made Italian horror films (Dario Argento's L'Uccello dalle piume di cristallo, 1970) and the rise of major new talents (Bernardo Bertolucci, the Taviani brothers, Ettore Scola and Marco Ferreri). Older, well-established directors – Fellini, Bolognini, Visconti and De Sica – were still producing some of their best films.[33]

This output, quite outstanding in comparison to that of most other countries, achieved great popular success. In the 1970s it looked as if, at least in Italy, quality could go hand in hand with popularity. The second-biggest box office success of 1969–70 was Visconti's *La Caduta degli dei*, the fifth was Fellini's *Satyricon*; Pasolini's *Decameron* was second in 1971–72, Bertolucci's *Last Tango in Paris* was second in 1972–73 (when *The Godfather* was first).[34] Up to 1975, Italians flocked to the movie houses in droves. The lion's share of this thriving market was captured by Italian films. A country which had failed to generate a popular literature or a popular press had succeeded in creating a situation intellectuals dream about: an art which combined high quality with commercial success. Films which in England or the USA could be seen only in select art houses patronised by cinema buffs were enjoyed in Italy's local cinemas by 'ordinary' people, barmaids and barristers, prostitutes and professors. A less edifying hypothesis is that in the early 1970s the surest way to show sex in films was to package it as high art; even this did not save *Last Tango* from being banned in Italy, though only after everyone had seen it. True, there were also comic sexy films, often parodies of high culture with extravagant and almost untranslatable titles (e.g. *Quel gran pezzo dell'Ubalda tutta nuda e tutta calda*, 1972, which might be rendered as 'Ubalda, a Great Piece of Ass so Hot and so Naked'), but they lacked any erotic charge (probably because they were comically vulgar). By the late seventies the situation had radically changed. One could see soft-porn films at local cinemas and on TV, without having to put up with Pasolini and co.

In the late 1970s American films and cheap Italian comedies were winning the popularity stakes, but Italian audiences fell by 50 per cent during that decade.[35] The liberalisation of television and the multiplication of channels following the 1976 decision of the Italian supreme court, making the state monopoly of television unconstitutional, was the *coup de grâce*. The enormous Italian thirst for films could be satisfied at home. The industry made fewer ambitious films, and by 2000 Italy was earning less than 1 per cent of box office receipts in European markets.[36]

Only the USA could make large-budget films, but these were risky. A studio could go bust by relying on a single film – as happened to United Artists, virtually bankrupted by Michael Cimino's *Heaven's Gate* (1980), a long western (well over three hours) whose budget grew out of all proportion. To avoid excessive risk-taking, successes often generated sequels, usually but not always less successful than the original, and sequels of sequels, with cheaper directors and unknown actors, until the final pennies had been squeezed out of the series. Thus Jason Voorhees started his killing spree in the horror series *Friday the 13th* in 1980, and went on to do so in various reincarnations for at least a further nine movies until 2002:

THE FRIDAY THE 13TH SERIES	
Friday the 13th	1980
Friday the 13th Part II	1981
Friday the 13th Part III: 3D	1982
Friday the 13th: The Final Chapter	1984
Friday the 13th: A New Beginning	1985
Friday the 13th Part VI: Jason Lives	1986
Friday the 13th Part VII: The New Blood	1988
Friday the 13th Part VIII: Jason Takes Manhattan	1989
Jason Goes to Hell: The Final Friday	1993
Jason X	2002

Actors, directors and genres, especially the former, were still the main selling points for a film. Superstars, paid super salaries, were able to determine the direction of the industry. In the 1930s they were paid vast sums, but had to do what the studio told them. Now the stars were in charge.[37] And world stars have remained, with a few exceptions, American, and overwhelmingly male: Robert De Niro, Al Pacino, Jack Nicholson, Tom Hanks, Michael Douglas, Warren Beatty, Harrison Ford and Tom Cruise, though Julia Roberts (ranked third most powerful person in the American entertainment industry in 2000)[38] and Nicole Kidman too currently belong to this super-league, as did, for a while, Jane Fonda, Meryl Streep and Diane Keaton. Other participants in film-making remain unknown to the general public, and though some, like scriptwriters, are highly paid, at least in the USA, they remain as obscure as the librettists of famous operas. The lament of Bruce Robinson, the Oscar-nominated screenwriter of *The Killing Fields* (1984), and author and director of the cult film *Withnail and I* (1987), is exemplary:

> They have no idea how awful it is to be a screenwriter. Somehow they think it's glamorous, but it isn't. It can be a soul-destroying prospect, writing for the cinema. You talk to any screenwriter, they tell you the same thing ... Writers are dirt in this business ... the writer ... is still treated like shit. No one would dream of taking a painter, not even a third-rate Picasso, and saying 'Oh, I see you've got blue trees in the background here. I think we'll make those green'. With a writer they take unbelievable licence.[39]

Sex in Films

By 1968 the censorious Hays Production Code had been abandoned by Hollywood in favour of age-based classification. Censorship remained extant everywhere in the West, aimed mainly at the depiction of sex. Nevertheless, the preponderance of sex in films constituted, for several decades, one of the advantages of the cinema over television. Television had to be restrained, and often nudity was edited out of films shown on the small screen. If one wanted to see the simulation of the sexual act on screen, one had to go to the cinema. From the 1960s there grew, alongside the respectable end of the industry, where sex scenes had to be either functional to the story or interludes to it, a genre dubbed 'sexploitation' which inhabited the grey area between illegal 'hard-core' pornography and mainstream movies with an erotic theme. Clear-cut classifications are here impossible because of the constantly and rapidly changing view of what constituted conventional morality. In the late 1950s it was quite possible to see entirely naked women on British cinemas screens – unlike Italy and even France – provided they were shown in 'nudist' documentaries which never mentioned sex. By the late 1970s matters had moved on, and up to one-fifth of British production was classified as 'sex' films. Many were comedies with titles such as *Confessions of a Window Cleaner* and *Can You Keep It Up, Jack?* that de-dramatised sex by treating it as a comic activity in the manner of music-hall jokes and 'funny' seaside postcards where men are wimps and women have very large breasts.[40] Yet this was hardly an exclusively British genre: Italy made dozens of erotic comedies in the 1970s with titles such as *La Liceale* (The Schoolgirl), *L'Insegnante* (The Schoolmistress) and *La Poliziotta* (The Policewoman).

The USA is the home of the most important Christian revivalist movement in the West, but it is also the home of the largest sex industry in the world. In no other country does there exist a 14,000-square-foot store such as the Fairvilla Megastore near Orlando in Florida, selling (also online) thousands of erotic videos and DVDs, vibrators, sex toys, sexual enhancers, 'kama sutra products', massage lotions, 'games for couples', 'bachelorette party supplies' and lubricants.

Pornographic films are cheap to make: the set is a bedroom where the furniture is constantly rearranged; most of the performers are paid very little; the director is less important than the cameraman; the cast is narrowed down to three or four characters; there are hardly any extras; the films are often made in five or six days. An expert in the field, the French director Éric de

Winter, explained that these films have a watertight budget, the studio is rented for a precise length of time, and improvements in the quality of the picture beyond a strict minimum are a waste of money and time because they will not increase the size of the audience.[41]

The difficulty, cinematically speaking, consists of finding a narrative to fill in the spaces between the sex scenes, since a film made up only of sex scenes would bore most viewers. Each film costs little, but most make little money. There are exceptions. *Deep Throat* cost only $25,000 when it was made in 1972, but grossed $33,000 in its first week. By January 1973 it had played in seventy cities across the USA and grossed $3.2 million.[42] A French porno film like *Bourgeoise et . . . pute!* by Gérard Kikoïne was only seen by 143,000 spectators when it was released in France in 1982, but that was significantly more than *Halloween II* (61,000) or *Grease II* (54,000), and not much less than *One From the Heart* (Francis Ford Coppola, USA, 1982, photography by the great Vittorio Storaro) with 163,366.[43] A soft-core film photographed with considerable skill, Just Jaeckin's *Emmanuelle* (1974), became, commercially speaking, one of the most successful French films ever. *Quel gran pezzo dell'Ubalda tutta nuda e tutta calda*, mentioned above, cost sixty million lire ($100,000) in 1972, and earned ten times as much.[44]

It has been estimated that the overall revenues of the porn-film industry compare favourably with Hollywood revenue at the box office, and exceed the revenue of NBC, CBS and ABC put together.[45] But statistics here are particularly unreliable. While it is true that sex sells, it must often be sex packaged in a wider story. The most popular films of the last twenty years have hardly any sex scenes – a few kisses at most. Besides, going to the cinema is a relatively public activity. Many men do not wish to be seen going into a sex film. The image of the consumer of pornography is negative. Far from suggesting a free-thinking, seductive stud with numerous girlfriends, being part of the audience of a pornographic movie conjures up the image of a lonely masturbator. And though many people have, at one time or another, masturbated in solitude, they do not wish to suggest that this is their chief source of sexual satisfaction. The availability of pornographic material on cable television, in recorded formats and on the internet dented the profitability of sex films aimed at cinemas. The commerce in nudity has increased, in step with the increase in all forms of cultural commerce, but the much-feared flood of pornography has not taken place.

And in the end, what saved the cinema were not 'dirty' movies but films for the young and the young at heart that spoke of sweet love, magic, the future, dinosaurs, sinking ships, disasters, good-looking heroes and gentle aliens.

Theatre

Watching a film at home, we have noted, is not the same as going to a cinema. Yet the difference between the two pales into insignificance if we compare going to the theatre with watching a filmed play on a television screen (with no close-ups). Films, whether for cinemas or television, are edited and recorded. Theatre is a live performance. It is, with music-making, the oldest surviving cultural form.

Neither the cinema nor television eliminated the theatre. On the contrary, in many countries there were more theatres at the end of the twentieth century than at its beginning. The theatre, however, is seldom profitable. Throughout Europe prestige theatres were regarded as educational and social institutions, aimed at preserving the theatre of the past, its special aura of distinction, and at promoting the best new works. In the nineteenth century the patronage of the aristocracy gave way to that of the rich. By the twentieth century local and central authorities had become the main source of extra-commercial funding. Without public subsidies (or charitable donations) very few Continental theatres would have survived. The West End of London, home to some forty theatres, has remained a largely commercial operation, but it has few counterparts in the rest of Europe. In (West) Germany, though, in 1972–73 over a thousand plays, operas and operettas and ballets were performed to twenty-two million spectators.[46] In 1996–97 there were still 809 registered theatres in Germany, with a total seating capacity of 276,000.[47] This is a direct consequence of the massive subsidies enjoyed by the German theatre – in 1973 ticket sales covered only 18.5 per cent of the total theatre budget[48] – the low price of tickets and popular subscription schemes. Yet all forms of performance still thrive in Germany, including the cabaret, with groups such as the Cologne-based travelling all-woman company 'Mamma Grappa', who have been performing all over Germany since 1981 to adoring audiences, and the internationally well-known singer Ute Lemper, the greatest living interpreter of the songs composed by Kurt Weill to Brecht's texts.

Subsidies were required to preserve what were regarded as the best works of the past. These, if left to the private market, might not have survived – at least not everywhere. The case of Spain is emblematic. As Franco consolidated his victory during the Civil War, he returned to private ownership the theatres which had been nationalised by the Republicans. However, the preference of the majority of audiences for sentimental comedies contrasted with the regime's desire to uphold high cultural standards. This led to the decision in 1940 to set up two national theatres (Teatro Español and Teatro María Guerrero) under state control.[49]

And so it was in most of Europe. Commercial plays were performed in the private sector, while the glories of the past and some of the new avant-garde plays became the preserve of the subsidised theatre. A main 'national' theatre had long existed in various parts of Europe, such as France, where the Comédie-Française had been established in 1680 (six more were added in the course of the following centuries), Denmark (the Royal Theatre, 1772), Hungary (1840), Romania (1854), Serbia (1869), Austria (the Burgtheater, 1776), Sweden (the Royal Dramatic Theatre, 1788), Holland (1870), Bulgaria (1907), Greece (1930) and Belgium (1945). Britain was for long an exception, until in 1963 the National Theatre was finally established.

The repertoire of the theatre is neither as static at that of the opera nor continually renewed like that of the cinema. The present repertoire consists of most of what has survived from Greek drama, a selection of the theatre of the sixteenth and seventeenth centuries (Shakespeare, Lope de Vega, Calderon de la Barca, Molière, Racine), a sprinkling of eighteenth-century works (such as those of Goldoni), some of the writers of the romantic period (Goethe, Musset, Schiller, Hugo) and, finally, the major late-nineteenth-century and twentieth-century playwrights (such as Ibsen, Chekhov, Wilde, Shaw, O'Neill, Strindberg, Pirandello, Brecht). To these one could add the more recent Jean Anouilh, Arthur Miller, Tennessee Williams, Samuel Beckett, Eugène Ionesco, Max Frisch, Friedrich Dürrenmatt and Edoardo De Filippo and the even more recent Peter Weiss, Dario Fò, Harold Pinter, John Osborne, Alan Ayckbourn, Michael Frayn and Tom Stoppard.

These vie and compete with contemporary popular works and musicals. In West Germany, for instance, in the 1973–74 season the most performed authors were, in order, Brecht, Shakespeare and Molière, but a modern comedy forced Schiller into fifth place.[50] In the middle-to-longer run the classics win out: the most frequently produced playwrights in Germany in the period 1964–74 were – in order – Shakespeare, Brecht, Molière and Schiller.[51]

Whenever a near-static repertoire emerges in live performance, innovation becomes the prerogative of those in charge of the performance.

Musicians and conductors innovate in classical instrumental and operatic music, and in the theatre the directors have become the fundamental innovators. The élite European theatre after 1960 – like that of the end of the nineteenth century – was characterised by a surge of charismatic directors who staged old plays in entirely new ways and used their power to introduce new plays into the old repertoire.

Some eventually almost created their own plays, either by reworking established classics or by using plotlines borrowed from an assortment of disparate texts. The career of Jerzy Grotowski, a native of Rzeszow in Poland, is exemplary. In 1957 he staged the first Polish production of Eugène Ionesco's avant-garde *The Chairs*, and then, in the course of a distinguished career, directed Chekhov plays at the Stary Teatr in Krakow, Byron's *Cain*, the classic Indian story *Sakuntala*, Goethe's *Faust*, Adam Mickiewicz's *Forever Eve*, Marlowe's *The Tragedy of Faust* and *A Study of Hamlet* 'after' Shakespeare – developing new forms of actor training. In his experimental Laboratory Theatre in Wroclaw he introduced a concept of the theatre devoid of inessentials such as lighting and scenery ('the poor theatre'), emphasising the centrality of actors, whose mission was to forge 'an encounter with the spectator – intimately, visibly, not hiding behind a cameraman, wardrobe mistress, stage designer or make-up girl'.[52] . Yet the actor 'can only be guided by someone who is wholehearted in his creative activity'.[53] The idea of 'recreating' a work was adopted, with understandable enthusiasm, by directors such as Peter Brook in Great Britain and subsequently in France, Giorgio Strehler in Italy, Ingmar Bergman in Sweden, Yuri Lyubimov in Russia, Peter Stein in West Germany and Ruth Berghaus in the DDR. They often became the real authors of staged plays,

Even without major changes, the staging of any play can completely alter its received meaning. Take, for example, Shakespeare's *The Merchant of Venice*, which was regarded before the Second World War and the Holocaust as offering a negative portrayal of Jews, or at the very least of a particular Jew, Shylock. This created a problem for the iconic 'genius' status of Shakespeare. Such status was traditionally justified by pointing to the eternal truths contained in his plays. Obviously anti-Semitism is not an 'eternal truth' but a historically determined prejudice. Shakespeare's other 'problem' play, *The Taming of the Shrew*, presents similar difficulties in the age of feminism.

The 'solution', after 1945, was to make Shylock a hero by highlighting particular aspects of the play, and in particular the famous lines:

Hath not a Jew eyes? Hath not a Jew hands, organs, dimensions, senses, affections, passions? Fed with the same food, hurt with the same weapons, subject to the same diseases, healed by the same means, warmed and cooled by the same winter and summer, as a Christian is? If you prick us, do we not bleed? If you tickle us, do we not laugh? If you poison us, do we not die? And if you wrong us, shall we not revenge?

Emphasising such lines alerts the spectator not only to the common humanity shared by Jews and non-Jews alike, but also to Shylock's expectation that he is entitled to formal legal equality – an absurdity for those who do not believe in it, a minimal demand for those who accept a modern view of justice. The effect could be further heightened by getting a 'heroic' actor – such as Laurence Olivier – to perform Shylock. Without the Holocaust it is unlikely that the character would have had such a rewrite. When the play was performed in Israel in the 1950s, the part was given to Aharon Meskin, the most heroic-looking among local actors, and everyone identified with him. Every orthodoxy, however recent, calls forth a revision, but not everyone is authorised to carry this out. Thus in 1970 in Israel a young director, Yosef Yezraeli, turned Shylock back into a money-grasping usurer, but one who, though not being either heroic or noble, has certain rights which ought to be respected – a commendable notion, but one which is somewhat removed from the Elizabethan period.[54]

In the years since 1960, in spite (or because?) of television, the theatre is thriving more than ever before. The proliferation of acting jobs on television and in advertising has expanded the prospects for actors, making it possible for some to subsidise their stage work with more profitable jobs elsewhere. A majority of actors are unemployed at any one time. Their pay – when working on stage – is poor. The minimum trade union rate in the West End of London (the prime theatrical space in Europe) was, in 2005, £358 a week for eight shows. This, for someone working all year round with no holiday, means less than £20,000 a year – less than half what a plumber could earn. But then, there are few amateur plumbers (outside their own homes), while in Great Britain alone there are over 5,000 amateur dramatic and operatic societies. Besides these there were, in 2003, 541 theatres.[55] Theatre actors in other countries are less fortunate than those in Britain. The London stage is based on stars more than, say, that of Germany, and British actors speak, of course, English, which means they can aspire to work in American films, making some of them, such as Anthony Hopkins, Emma Thompson, Peter O'Toole, Richard Burton and Laurence Olivier international stars.

One of the consequences is that London has remained a great centre for the theatre. Just in the month of January 2003, thirty-eight new productions opened in London (only one of which was a translation (almost): David Farr's adaptation of Dostoevsky's *Crime and Punishment*, performed at the Arcola Theatre, a disused factory-turned-theatre in Dalston, east London).[56] In the two weeks between 23 April and 9 May 2003 twenty-five new productions opened.[57] In Germany in the early 1970s there were regular theatre productions in hundreds of theatres, providing nearly 50,000 performances.[58] Italy in 1963 claimed 456 theatres, though this represents the figure for venues 'officially' registered as theatres.[59]

Given the cost of going to the theatre, far greater than any other non-performance-based entertainment, the theatre is still an élite genre. Audiences in Europe and North America are far more likely to hold professional jobs and to earn more than the average.[60] But these élites are far larger than previously. The London National Theatre, a complex of three theatres, held a total of a thousand performances in 2003–04, selling 731,000 seats (in 1999 tickets sold amounted to 593,000) of which 100,000 were to first-time visitors.[61]

It was because of the restricted numbers having access to it that the theatre progressed from being the most censored of cultural forms – as it was in the nineteenth century – to one of the most permissive. In communist Yugoslavia, for instance, in the 1950s one could see on the stage Arthur Miller's *Death of a Salesman*, *The Crucible*, *A View from the Bridge*, Tennessee Williams's *The Glass Menagerie* and *Cat on a Hot Tin Roof*, and John Osborne's *Look Back in Anger*. Samuel Beckett's *Waiting for Godot* was banned in 1955, but the outcry ensured that it was performed the following year, albeit in a small experimental theatre (Atelier 212, in Belgrade).[62] But Beckett had had problems in 'liberal' Britain too. *Waiting for Godot* was first performed at a private London theatre club, the Arts Theatre, in August 1955. It was directed by Peter Hall, then twenty-four years old, and had been turned down by the most famous British actors, including John Gielgud and Alec Guinness. *The Times* was unimpressed: the characters, it felt, were 'figments in whom we cannot ultimately believe since they lack universality'. The play was transferred to the Criterion Theatre the following year with some changes imposed by the Lord Chamberlain (the censor), such as the removal of the word 'erection'.[63] Beckett continued to have problems with the British censor throughout the 1950s. He had to remove from his second play, *Endgame*, words such as 'balls', 'arse' and 'pee', as well as an alleged obscenity, before it could be performed in 1958.[64]

Alongside prestige productions there continues to exist a thriving commercial theatre. Since the 1960s the dominant genre has no longer been the melodramas and farces which prevailed in the nineteenth century – television serials and half-hour comedies have proved to be fierce competition. The theatre had to provide a quite different experience, such as the musical. Here the domination of the Americans had long been overwhelming (see page 1111). After 1960, however, this dominance began to falter. In 1956 a French musical opened in Paris: *Irma la Douce*. It used the conventional view of Paris since Murger's *Scènes de la vie de Bohème* (1848), the inspiration for Puccini's *La Bohème* (1897). Irma's Paris, like that of Mimì and Musetta (the women in *La Bohème*), was a world of failed artists, sexually predatory rich old men, prostitutes with hearts of gold (notably Irma herself) and lovable pimps. The music was by Marguerite Monnot, Edith Piaf's main songwriter. The dialogue, of course, was in French. *Irma la Douce* became internationally popular only when it was turned into English and had a resounding success on Broadway and in London's West End.[65] Its success opened the way for British and French musicals to challenge the Americans.

Such a challenge was made easier because the generation of American composers and lyricists that had dominated the Broadway stage since the 1930s had died or stopped being productive after 1960. Oscar Hammerstein died in 1960 and Cole Porter in 1964. Frank Loesser died in 1969, but had produced little after *How to Succeed in Business Without Really Trying* (1961) – his last great hit had been *Guys and Dolls* (1950). Frederick Loewe died in 1988, but had produced little of note since *Camelot* (1960) and the film musical *Gigi* (1958).

Americans still produced hits, above all the innovative *Hair* (1967), a rock musical with a score by Galt MacDermot and lyrics by Gerome Ragni and James Rado, but their hegemony was no longer assured. Lionel Bart and David Heneker with *Lock up Your Daughters* (1959) and *Oliver!* (1960) paved the way for the emergence of a 'British' musical. This could not have happened had London not been one of the most important theatre centres in the world, had the language not been English, and had the West End not been an almost obligatory stopover for thousands of American tourists on their way to visit the rest of 'old Europe.' This is the context for the emergence of a string of successful British musicals composed by Andrew Lloyd Webber. He started with a kind of cantata, *Joseph and the Amazing Technicolor Dreamcoat* (1968), and followed with *Jesus Christ Superstar* (1971), inspired, musically speaking by *Hair*; then *Evita* (1976), based on the life of Eva Peron,

Cats (1981), based on poems by T.S. Eliot, an extraordinary success in spite, or because, of the absence of any recognisable plot, then the *Starlight Express* (1984, with 7,406 performances in eighteen years), then the phenomenally successful *The Phantom of the Opera* (1987), based on Gaston Leroux's 1911 novel. It was a sign of the 'global' nature of this market that few of these were particularly 'British', just as so many of Verdi's or Puccini's operas did not have a specifically Italian theme.

The genre had become international, or rather British and French. One of the great hits of the 1980s and 1990s was *Les Misérables*. This was a 'French' musical in the sense that its authors, the composer Claude-Michel Schönberg, a popular songwriter, and the writers Alain Bloubil and Jean-Marc Natel were French, and that it was an adaptation of Victor Hugo's famous master-piece (see pages 406–7). The musical version was first performed, to no great acclaim, on the Paris stage in 1980, and would probably have been forgotten had it not been noticed by the London producer Cameron Mackintosh (the producer of *Cats*). It was translated into English for the London stage in 1985, having been further adapted to non-French tastes by the addition of new numbers and doing away with the character of the street kid Gavroche, familiar to every French schoolchild but totally unknown everywhere else. In fact the plot of Hugo's great novel was almost unknown outside France. Musically speaking *Les Misérables* was written in the rock-opera style follow-ing the model of *Hair* and *Jesus Christ Superstar*, but the part of Cosette suited an almost operatic soprano voice.[66] By 2000 it had been performed in twenty-seven countries and translated into sixteen languages. The French team tried their luck a second time with a story with no connection with France: *Miss Saigon* (1989), an adaptation of Puccini's *Madame Butterfly* set in Saigon during the last stages of the Vietnam War. It became one of the most successful musicals in the history of the British stage, and went on to conquer Broadway and to be performed in eighteen other countries.

Thus the theatre, as did the cinema, survived the onslaught on television, renewing itself, specialising, offering the audience something they could not get from the screen in the box at home.

60

Culture in the 'Other' Europe: Communism

The Contrast

ON THE CAPITALIST SIDE of Europe there was consumption. There was fashion. There was fun. The cars came in different styles, sizes and colours. The music celebrated love and sex. There were cheap paperbacks filled with romance or violence. There was plenty of American culture: films, television programmes, music and books – all celebrating, by their very existence, modernity. There were scandal-mongering newspapers and brash magazines and also informative daily papers – mostly on the side of big business, unsurprisingly, since they were themselves big business, but there were also some that were critical.

In the East, everything was drab and boring. The clothes were dowdy; the concept of fashion non-existent; cars were unavailable or of poor quality. Everything was rationed, including books, records, gramophones and radios. Broadcast and printed news reflected the wishes of the governments. Books were censored, as were films and plays. The most exciting culture in the world, that of the Americans, was unavailable.

The West was in Technicolor. The East was grey. The Berlin Wall was the most vivid illustration of this contrast. On its eastern side it was policed by sombre-looking guards in ashen uniforms, and remained pristine and stark. Its western side was multicoloured, decorated by graffiti artists in all hues. This may appear a caricature of reality, and it is, but only a little.

We should refrain from assuming that communism in eastern and central Europe (the 'socialist camp', as the communists called it) exhibited the same features everywhere. What was forbidden in the USSR was not necessarily forbidden in the other communist countries. The American television children's programme *Sesame Street*, for example, was regarded in the USSR as an instance of cultural imperialism, but it was regularly shown on Hungarian and East German television. In 1957 a Polish magazine even ran excerpts from George Orwell's *Nineteen Eighty-Four* – a taboo text in the USSR.[1]

No censorship system can be easily imposed without a considerable amount of support or a formidable amount of terror. Even the latter does not always work. For instance, in the 1980s in Romania, when Nicolae Ceauşescu imposed a regime of austerity to repay the country's debt to the West, most entertainments, including cinemas, were compelled to close after 9 p.m. People, of course, could stay at home and watch TV, but this too was restricted; one of the two channels was suspended and the other reduced to fifteen hours a week. The country had common borders with the USSR, Yugoslavia, Hungary and Bulgaria, from where it was possible to receive broadcasts with special aerials. Soon there was a black market in aerials and a thriving network of people willing, at a price, to erect them on the roofs of buildings. These could easily have been detected by the feared Securitate, but the authorities tolerated their proliferation, perhaps because they regarded the hostility they would encounter not worth the price of allowing people to watch the news from other communist states. In the capital Bucharest one could only tune in to Bulgarian TV, broadcast in a Slavic language quite different from Romanian (a Latin language). But people watched anyway, and there was a noticeable increase in the demand for Bulgarian-language courses.[2]

Censorship was often supported by ordinary people who felt that dissident writers were attacking some of their dearly held beliefs. A study of readers' letters sent to newspapers during the campaign against Boris Pasternak in 1958–59 (after *Dr Zhivago* had been first published abroad) shows that the majority had not been inspired from above but had been sent by those genuinely offended by the book's alleged attack on the Revolution.[3]

Censorship 'functions' well when it is widely supported. It does not even have to depend on the political authorities. In the USA the supermarket giant Wal-Mart – the largest seller of books, DVDs and CDs – refuses to stock anything that offends its version of family values. To avoid being banned from the stores, some publishers have taken to showing Wal-Mart the contents of their material before publication. Obscenities in some pop songs are bleeped out of existence.[4] But in the USA one can legally obtain these books and records from other sources. In the communist countries the only alternative was the black market.

An Abundance of Culture

Censorship restricted the range but not the quantity. The citizens of eastern and central Europe, when communism prevailed, did not have as many consumer goods as those in the West, but they had plenty of culture. Take, for instance, the attendance at live events in a group of countries on either side of the East–West divide:

PERFORMING ARTS COMPANIES. ANNUAL ATTENDANCE PER THOUSAND PEOPLE IN SELECTED COUNTRIES, 1980–85	
Hungary	664
Romania	649
Poland	609
Denmark	547
Finland	545
Germany	503
Canada	385
Albania	321
Holland	235
Italy	229
Greece	205
Belgium	144
Portugal	61

SOURCE: UNESCO, *World Culture Report*, 1998 (no data available for the UK, the USA and France)

The East does not emerge badly. A poor country like Albania does better than Holland or Italy. Of course, the focus here is on quantitative data (and the data is provided by the countries themselves). The fare on offer may have been an endless stream of folk dancing and plays celebrating the Albanian resistance during the Second World War and praising the wise leadership of Enver Hoxha, who led the country from the 1940s until his death in 1985. But not all those celebrating the resistance were party hacks.

Among the dross there was some gold (as in the West). Ismail Kadare, now discovered and praised in the English-speaking world, the author of novels including *The General of the Dead Army* (1964) and *The Big Winter* (1977), was celebrated in his own country in the 1960s and 1970s.[5] He was not translated into English until the 1990s (except for some retranslations from the French and some Albanian-sponsored translations). As he had not been regarded as a dissident before the fall of communism, he was not regarded as marketable in Great Britain and the USA (though his books were widely available in France and Germany).

The absence of a market mechanism does not entail a lack of competition. Most film-makers want to make successful films, films that will attract a sizeable audience. They also want to make the films they choose. Matching their desires to those of the audience is, for the majority, the main issue. One of the chief problems for film-makers in all countries in the 1970s and 1980s was not so much political censorship as the fact that television was keeping such a high proportion of their potential audience at home. Many of the 'difficult' Soviet film-makers would have found it even more difficult to find funding in Hollywood – as they discovered to their cost when communism came tumbling down. The evidence is strong: in the late 1980s the USSR was turning out about 150 films a year (roughly the same number as Hollywood). In 1996, when the worst of the transition seemed to be over, production was down to twenty films.[6] Censorship had been abolished, but as the film-maker Karen Shakhnazarov declared in 1991, 'We do not have any films to censor.'[7] The problem had started even earlier, since it was possible during Mikhail Gorbachev's *perestroika* (rebuilding) in the late 1980s for producers to make critical films which concentrated on the seamier side of Soviet life and still get public funds. Audiences, however, did not like them. Western critics did, because the films were in accordance with what they thought films should be about: honest and realistic depictions of drug addiction, prostitution, juvenile delinquency and other social ills – in other words the exact opposite of the image so often peddled by the conventions of socialist realism.[8]

The press in the USSR was muzzled, but there were thousands of newspapers in the dozens of languages spoken in the country. *Pravda* in the late 1960s had a circulation of nine million, *Izvestiia* 8.5 million. There were 5,000 magazines.[9] The élite monthly periodical *Novy Mir* (New World) – in which the most daring literary material was published, including the serialisation of Alexander Solzhenitsyn's novel about his prison experiences, *One Day in the Life of Ivan Denisovich* (1962) – was printing 150,000 copies a month in the early 1960s, and 430,000 copies in 1985. Many of these, of course, remained unsold, but many were bought and presumably enjoyed by their readers. The magazine's print run collapsed to 14,215 in 1999.

Books were cheap in the USSR, and there were also 350,000 libraries. Politics did not dominate broadcasting. On 4 February 1970 on Moscow One (the main radio station of the capital), of the twenty hours of continuous broadcast only one hour and five minutes could be classified as straightforward political propaganda (a programme on the teachings of Lenin). In addition there were 140 minutes of news, political commentary and press reviews. The remainder was worthy, high-minded stuff: folk songs, a talk on the balalaika, a dramatisation of a story by Kipling for children, a programme for schoolchildren learning French, and plenty of classical music (2,000 concerts a month).[10]

In the study of history, if one wanted to do real scholarly work it was better to concentrate on the Middle Ages or the distant past, or on foreign countries, and to exercise caution. Paradoxically, one was freer if one worked at some distance from Moscow and Leningrad. In other communist countries there were significant variations. In Poland matters were more relaxed in the 1970s and 1980s, while in Romania the authorities' unfortunate interest in history made life difficult for scholars committed to the discipline. Since Romania's boundaries have been unstable throughout the twentieth century, and the country was in dispute with Hungary and the USSR over them, what was mentioned or left out could be politically controversial (as it would have been under a right-wing nationalist regime). If they were prepared to conform there was, unusually for Romania (or anywhere else), plenty of public funding for historians.[11]

News on Soviet television was strictly controlled, but there was no sense of news priority or understanding of what made a good story. Subservience to politicians meant showing party leaders making speeches regardless of their significance, inaugurating collective farms regardless of their marginal importance. When a foreign delegation visited the country its arrival would be shown on all channels as if it were a major event, with the plane landing, the guard of honour being reviewed, a little girl offering flowers, the anthems being performed and the limousines driving off to the Kremlin.[12] Some of this sort of thing occurred occasionally on Western networks, such as Italy's RAI in the 1960s (and Berlusconi's media since the 1990s), but never with the single-mindedness of Soviet television. Soviet TV was there to serve the state, or, rather those who controlled it.

In the 1970s and 1980s foreign television programmes were regularly shown on Soviet television, more than half of them originating in the West. In the early 1970s Soviet audiences could watch the twenty-six episodes of the BBC's landmark 1967 serial *The Forsyte Saga*. A commentary at the beginning of the programmes explained that the subject matter was the decline of sections of the ruling British bourgeoisie – a fair, if perhaps unexciting, description. It was very successful even though it was not dubbed: instead the original soundtrack was faded down as an announcer read a Russian translation.[13] Being broadcast in the USSR legitimised the acquisition of Western programmes everywhere in central and eastern Europe. In Poland *The Forsyte Saga* was broadcast twice, once with Polish voice-over over the English soundtrack, and the second time in the original version.

But the countries of the eastern bloc were not clones of the USSR. In Poland the communists, aware of their lack of popularity, tried to placate the public's demand for exciting television programmes. Polish television did not just import series from the USA such as *Dr Kildare*, *Bonanza* and *Perry Mason*, but, inspired by *Dr Kildare*, produced a serial about a woman doctor who leaves the city in order to work in a village.[14]

In the West, eastern and central European television was commonly regarded as propaganda. This was only partly true. The main focus of the broadcasting authorities was a paternalistic use of the media as an instrument for the improvement of the cultural level of the population. This view was so widespread that publishers did not think it odd to declare that their job was to produce books people 'really needed, and not the books they wanted'.[15] Yet readers were constantly urged to give their opinions, to write explaining what was good and what was bad in the books they had read in order to 'help' writers correct their 'shortcomings' and write better books.[16]

In the absence of competition there was no drive for television stations to maximise ratings. These were high anyway, because there was no competition – as was still the case in much of the West. A high-minded view of culture was the prevailing ethos. Thus in 1965, to celebrate the seven hundredth anniversary of the birth of Dante Alighieri, Hungarian radio produced a three-part adaptation of *The Divine Comedy*. A six-episode adaptation of Homer's *Iliad* followed in 1969. But there were also soaps such as *The Matysiak Family* in Poland and *The Szabó Family* in Hungary – the story of

Uncle Szabó the self-taught communist, Mrs Szabó who is religious and good-hearted, and their children, one of whom wants to get rich, the other a pampered university student. Such series were extremely successful and attracted thousand of letters from viewers.[17]

The authorities' mission to 'improve' the people's cultural habits were constantly undermined by the need to please consumers. Authoritarian regimes can stop people from reading certain books, but they cannot force them to read what they do not want to. Moreover, technology can also increase the power of consumers (as the internet has shown): acquiring a gramophone means one can listen to what one likes. The Soviet authorities vigorously promoted the cause of classical music. Cheap concerts and plenty of classical music on the radio produced large audiences. But as more workers acquired gramophones, they listened less to classical music. Eventually Melodia, the state recording company, needing to achieve some kind of commercial success, started to produce more and more popular music at the expense of classical music.[18] Some market elements, at least in the 1970s, had begun to surface.

The main problem facing cultural diffusion, almost as important as the repression of culture, was its chronic disorganisation, which particularly in the USSR replicated the dysfunction of the wider economy. The central authorities established targets. Each segment of the production process had its own performance indicators. Publishers had to publish so many books, printers had to print them, and bookshops had to stock them. Each had to worry only about fulfilling their targets. The size of print runs was decided by the All-Russia Union for the Diffusion of the Book. Publishers and printers were not free to print what they wanted, although they could refuse to print certain kinds of books (since everyone was aware of the failings of the central plan, considerable haggling was regarded as inevitable). Printers, required to meet quantitative targets, often refused to take on books with numerous illustrations or of an awkward size, because they would take longer to print. Bookshops could refuse to hold books which they did not think they would sell (since it would prevent stock turnover). Publishers, however, could publish such books regardless of whether they would sell or not. The lack of coordination between publishers, printers and booksellers – in the West through a price mechanism of a sort and some guesswork (which does not prevent the regular destruction of unsold stock) – made the system anarchic.[19] The three hundred publishing houses in the USSR, all belonging to the state or to central organisations such as the trade unions, the Union of Communist

Youth or the Academy of Sciences, did not have to worry about profit, because their budgets were guaranteed. There was no point trying to modernise or be more efficient, or sell more books or acquire new authors.

The problem with communism was not that everything was planned, but that there was no possibility of planning. Publishers, for instance, found it advantageous to republish the classics. There was no risk of displeasing the authorities, there were no conflicts with long-dead authors, and the costs of production were cheaper since there was no need to edit a manuscript. As a result Pushkin was reprinted 1,999 times between 1948 and 1988, with a total print run of 339,700,000 copies (probably in excess of the turnover of the literate population during those forty years); Gorky was reprinted over 2,000 times (a total of 197,600,000 copies), Chekhov 1,120 times (176,400,000, copies) and Tolstoy 2,191 times, with a staggering 408,800,000 copies.[20] Were these books read? We do not know, but then we do not know how many people in the West actually read Stephen Hawking's *A Brief History of Time* (1988), which sold million of copies.

In the West the real money is made with best-sellers, so there is an incentive to publish new works in the hope of striking gold. In the USSR there was no such incentive, which is why the all-powerful chief editors would sit on a manuscript for three or four years.[21] And when a publisher had a success with a new book, snapped up immediately by keen readers, especially if a foreign translation, it would not necessarily be reprinted, because the size of the print run had already been decided and could not be altered easily.

Being a member of a book club entailed having priority for the purchase of certain books. When such subscriptions became available, a queue would form overnight. Knowing the right people helped. Salaries appeared inferior to those in the West, but the problem was not the lack of money, but the lack of goods. Since communism had decreed that books should be available to all, they had to be cheap. The country had the largest book market in the world, and its bookshops were full of books, but those the public really wanted were in scarce supply.

This was one of the consequences of the most important achievement of communism: the high educational standards it achieved. This is manifest if one compares the levels of literacy achieved in former Soviet republics with those of neighbouring countries:

ADULT (OVER FIFTEEN) LITERACY RATES AS A PERCENTAGE, 1995		
Former Soviet Republics	Armenia	100
	Turkmenistan	100
	Uzbekistan	100
	Tajikistan	100
	Azerbaijan	98
	Kazakhstan	98
	Georgia	98
	Kyrgyz Republic	97
Others	Turkey	82
	Iran	69
	India	52
	Iraq	51
	Bangladesh	38
	Pakistan	38

SOURCE: UNESCO, *World Culture Report*, 1998

Of course, not all communist countries had such dysfunctional planning rules. It helped to be small and to have an excellent educational system. It helped even more to have some form of market mechanism under socialism. The result was that in Slovenia, for instance, people owned more books per capita than in any other nation in Europe.[22]

For Soviet readers the problem was that there were too many books they did not want to read (or had already read), and not enough of those they wanted to read. And what did they want? Best-seller lists were either non-existent or unreliable. The number of copies printed was no indication of popularity – unless one is willing to believe that Brezhnev's collected works were best-sellers. These usually made it to the top of the list of number of copies printed (not sold). Few, however, expected people to buy them. The first four volumes, issued in 1974, were in an attractive boxed edition with type so small that it was obviously meant as a gift item, suitable for presentation at party ceremonies.[23]

An idea of what was popular, however, can be guessed at by investigating the preferences expressed in the late 1970s by the participants in a particular voucher scheme. In 1974, following the increase in the price of petrol, it was decided to encourage Soviet citizens to recycle newsprint. Since they were assumed to lack the social collectivist spirit of citizens in the West who did it for free, Soviet citizens were induced to recycle by being given vouchers which could be exchanged for books from an approved list for every twenty kilos of paper recycled. For this incentive to work, the books on the list had to be popular.[24] The scheme (known as *makulatura* – the word for pulp fiction as well as recycled paper products) was at first run in ten cities, and later extended to fifty. Soon 25 per cent of the paper recycled in the USSR was collected under the scheme by 14 per cent of the population, involving ten million families.[25]

The books on the list included children's books, mainly Russian but also classics such as Kipling's *The Jungle Book*, and the Russian favourites: Jules Verne, H.G. Wells, Conan Doyle, Wilkie Collins, Dickens, Dumas, Balzac, Stendhal, Maurice Druon's saga *Les Rois maudits*, as well as Russian classics and biographies such as A.K. Vinogradov's enormously popular life of Paganini.[26] Russian readers, like those who ruled them, had solid, conventional taste. They had no choice. They were free to buy foreign crime stories and science fiction, but only 'quality' writers were translated: Georges Simenon, Isaac Asimov, Arthur C. Clarke, Ray Bradbury, Agatha Christie and classics such as Edgar Allan Poe and G.K. Chesterton. Mickey Spillane and James Hadley Chase were, of course, unavailable, while the very right-wing Simenon was available because – it had been decreed – he placed humanity at the centre of his work – as the socialist realist tradition required.[27]

Crime stories had long been popular among Russians. The genre could easily be co-opted on behalf of the regime. Criminals were, after all, selfish individuals who put their private interests above those of the collectivity, stealing and killing. Policemen were doing an honest job on behalf of society. They deserved to be admired and helped. Television endlessly adapted such stories (as it did in the West). The longest-running series on Soviet television, *The Investigation is Conducted by Experts* (1971–89), was based on real cases and was immensely popular.[28]

One of the most celebrated Soviet television series was *Semnadtsat' mgnovenii vesny* (Seventeen Snapshots of Spring), made in 1972–73 by Tatiana Lioznova, broadcast twice a day and constantly repeated. It is the story of Stirlitz, a Soviet spy who has succeeded in infiltrating the SS during the Second World War. His mission is to find out who inside the German high command is conducting secret negotiations with the Americans. But there is also a human 'private' element: he wants to rescue his wife Katia, who is a prisoner of the Gestapo.[29] The differences from the James Bond films, with which the Stirlitz series has been compared, are not insignificant: Stirlitz is a good married man, Bond is a womaniser; Bond regularly kills people, Stirlitz hardly ever; Bond's hobbies are 'manly', while Stirlitz is seen cooking and gardening. But there are some similarities. In the Bond films the enemy is only occasionally the USSR, more often than not he is a rogue element or an arch-villain; Stirlitz's main enemy is pre-Cold War. Bond has unashamedly 'bourgeois' taste (he knows about fine wine, the best tobacco, etc.), and so does Stirlitz, who likes French cognac and prepares Western-style coffee.[30]

Series such as these were successful on all fronts. They were liked by the general public and they pleased the authorities. Television authorities as well as publishers knew what was expected of them. It paid to be prudent. There were a few *causes célèbres*, but after 1960 censorship had become a humdrum affair and the system was more tolerant. The boundaries of dissent were clear to all. Thus by the mid-1960s it was imprudent to mention Stalin's purges, even though they had been denounced by Khrushchev in 1956. This is what led Andrey Sinyavsky to publish his 'heretical' writings abroad under the pseudonym of Abram Tertz. For such 'slanders' against the Soviet mother-land Sinyavsky and his fellow dissident writer Yulii Daniel were sentenced to hard labour in 1966.

Some books were available only to trusted members of some professional organisations and trade unions. They did not make it to general bookshops, but would be bought by Party organisations for those who 'needed to know' – people who might be incensed and make a fuss if they were deprived of particular texts. Then there was the *samizdat* of the 1970s, much of it tolerated and occasionally made available to trusted people.[31] Even in Czechoslovakia after the repression following the Prague Spring of 1968 there was an abund-ance of dissident literature: 'illegal' magazines such as *Kritický sborník*, *Obsah*, *Historické studie*, *Revolver Revue* and *Vokno*, some seventy 'underground' publishing houses such as Edice Petlice, Kvart and Edice Expedice, and publishing houses in exile in Zurich (Konfrontace), Cologne (Index) London (Rozmluvy) and Munich (Poezie mimo domov).[32]

Censorship was not just political but also moral and aesthetic: 'trash' literature was discouraged or even banned outright. Mass literature existed, but it had to have some redeeming features: no sex and violence for the sake of it, slang had to be avoided, humanitarianism, patriotism and communism (defined as the future society without exploited and exploiters and without classes) had to be promoted.

Some right-wing authoritarian regimes, such as that of Franco in Spain, underwent a similar relaxation of censorship in the 1960s. In the case of Spain, of course, the pressures were greater because the regular influx of tourists made it difficult to keep foreign influences at bay, because Spanish migrant workers became aware of what was available elsewhere, and because the expansion of television ownership made it difficult to produce the entire television output domestically. America was Spain's main international ally, but American culture, with its emphasis on rock music, sex, advertising and youth culture, had a destabilising effect on the rigorous Catholicism on which the authorities relied. As a result new press laws were introduced in 1966, removing pre-censorship.[33]

In the communist bloc, the intellectual establishment acquired a determinant power in deciding who was acceptable and who was not. The reason Joyce and Kafka were suppressed in the USSR in the 1960s and 1970s was not that they could be regarded as 'anti-Soviet', but that they offended the notions of realism cherished by a politically powerful section of the intellectual establishment.

Decently veiled, even satire was acceptable: One of the most popular Soviet films of the 1970s was Eldar Ryazanov's *Ironiia sudby* (Irony of Fate, 1975), in which the hero, drunk after a party, takes the night train to Leningrad by mistake. Having arrived, still drunk, he lets himself into the flat of a woman he has never met but whose apartment has the same number as his, looks similar to his and is in a street and a building that look like the ones in Moscow. The two, of course, fall in love, and there is a happy ending. To many this was a brave social criticism of the drab uniformity of Russian life disguised as an upbeat romantic comedy.[34] A similar romantic comedy could easily have been made in the West by setting it in a suburban landscape where people's 'natural' individualism has been suppressed by the heartless, alienating conformity of late capitalism – or some such formulaic expression.

Critical films could be made at public expense, and critical books published by state-owned publishing houses. Sometimes it paid to be critical. Some boring books became popular because they were critical. Some authors obtained prestige in intellectual circles because they were critical. Some were even published in the West, where, by the late 1970s, Soviet writers could not be effectively marketed without being labelled 'dissident'. An elaborate set of informal rules separated 'critical' products from anti-Soviet and anti-communist ones. Yevgeny Yevtushenko, for instance, was never regarded as a dissident, though some of his work was criticised by the authorities. He was regularly published, gave readings of his poetry to large audiences, was frequently allowed to travel abroad and was almost regarded as a national resource (and as evidence of official tolerance). His poem 'Babi Yar' (1961), about the massacre by the Nazis of over 30,000 Ukrainian Jews, was frowned upon – the official Party line was that those murdered were first of all Ukrainian, their Jewishness being irrelevant. Yevtushenko's obvious target was not Nazism but Russian anti-Semitism, against which, in his view, all 'true Russians' should struggle. The poem contained lines which became famous:

> No Jewish blood runs among my blood,
> but I am as bitterly and harshly hated
> by every anti-Semite
> as if I were a Jew. By this
> I am a Russian.

A less celebrated example of dissent 'within the system' is Chingiz Aitmatov's novel *I dol'she veka dlitsia den'* (The Day Longer Than a Century Does Last), published in *Novy Mir* in 1980. Aitmatov, a Kirghiz from Muslim central Asia, constructed the novel in keeping with the canons of socialist realism: the hero, a manual worker, must complete a task – such as building a dam, fulfilling the plan or driving out the enemy – and in the process matures politically. In Aitmatov's novel the hero, Burannyi Yedigei, is a railway worker, but in this case his task is to bury an old friend and fellow worker, the village patriarch Kazangap, according to the old Muslim rituals of the Kazakhs.[35] The novel, which uses science fiction elements (the burial occurs near the launching site of a Soviet space mission while a joint Soviet– American space mission makes contact with a doomed cosmic civilisation), was widely acclaimed and translated into the numerous languages of the Soviet Union, as well as into English (as *The Day Lasts More than a Hundred Years*, 1983). Aitmatov's earlier novel *Jamila* (1958) was equally 'subversive', since it dealt with a woman who falls in love with another man while her husband is away as a combatant soldier. In the end the lovers abandon their village in defiance of traditional morality. Since Aitmatov was not a 'real' dissident he was ignored almost everywhere except in France, where *Jamila* was translated by the renowned communist poet Louis Aragon in 1959. A Soviet-sponsored translation into English was ignored in the USA and Britain.

Russians had their own favourites. And as Russian readers were not different from Western readers, what they read in large quantity was neither the great classics of the past, nor dissident or critical literature. Their favourites, according to a Russian survey in 1983, were the novels of Mikhail Alekseev, Alexei Cherkasov, Fyodor Abramov, Ivan Stadniuk, Petr Proskurin, Semion Babaevsky – all virtually unknown in the West. The most successful Soviet writer of the post-war era was Anatolii Ivanov, thanks to his family novel *Vechnyi zov* (Eternal Call, 1970), which a 1998 poll (readers were asked to send in the names of their favourite books) ranked second only to Sholokov's *And Quiet Flows the Don* among twentieth-century works.[36]

There was, as there always is, a grey area which provided a contested ground where those who dared fought it out with the retrogrades. The daring, those labelled 'dissidents' in the West, were regarded by the authorities as dangerous. They kept going because they hoped that sooner or later the climate would change – hopes fortified by the knowledge that many authors banned in the past had been 'reprieved'. Their enemies were not just inept bureaucrats but, in most cases, fellow writers who, having supported the original ban, were reluctant to agree to the lifting of it. In many instances the reprieve had to wait until the process of *glasnost* (openness) of the late 1980s. Thus Anna Akhmatova's great poem 'Requiem', written in the late 1930s, was only published officially in 1987, along with Boris Pasternak's Nobel-winning *Dr Zhivago* and the works of Solzhenitsyn, Osip Mandelstam (though the memoirs of his widow, Nadezhda Mandelstam, were published in 1970) and Joseph Brodsky (who had been exiled in 1972).

The distinction, much beloved by the Western media, between a small band of brave dissidents and a cowed or opportunistic majority fails to identify the complex strands that made up the world of cultural producers in the USSR. The terror of the Stalin era was projected across the following forty years in spite of the glaring differences between Stalin's regime and that of Brezhnev. Before the war, according to the Smolensk archives (captured by the Germans in 1941 and sent to the USA at the end of the war), censorship was deployed against anything deemed 'propaganda against the Soviet system' – this included arousing nationalism, being pro-religion, pornography, mysticism, and classified information on epidemics, crime figures, disorder, etc. After the death of Stalin this kind of top-to-bottom comprehensive censorship became less important. It was realised that appointing the right people and establishing the conditions for self-censorship would be more effective and more tolerable.[37]

The more relaxed years since the 1960s enabled Russian readers to revisit some of the popular writers of the 1920s such as Alexander Grin (born Grinevsky). Grin was neither a dissident communist nor an avant-garde *littérateur*, nor was he a 'Soviet' writer, though he had taken part in revolutionary activities in Tsarist Russia.[38] He was born in 1880, one year after Stalin, and spent much of his lifetime writing 'westerns' in the mode of Fenimore Cooper, 'disturbing' stories *à la* Edgar Allan Poe and adventure and fantastic stories in the mould of Verne – stories which, according to Grin's main champion in the West, Nicholas Luker, contained some philosophical depth.[39] Virtually unknown in the West, and not mentioned in most histories of Russian literature, he was outside the canon, like Verne in France, Karl May in Germany and Emilio Salgari in Italy – and like them he was loved by his numerous readers. The Russian Revolution did not affect his style. He simply continued to write his books, and his affectionate readers continued to read them, until the growth in influence of the militant Russian Association of Proletarian Writers restricted his output to only one novel a year and prohibited any reprinting of work published previously.[40] Grin died in 1932, just after the RAPP had been disbanded. In the late 1940s and 1950s, at the height of the Stalinist repression of culture, his works were proscribed. The press ceased to mention him. His novels were removed from libraries. Yet he was not forgotten, and in the mid-1970s he became once again one of the most popular writers in the USSR.[41]

By the 1970s and 1980s popular literature (science fiction or *nauchnaia fantastika*, romantic stories, detective and spy novels and assorted epic blockbusters) was increasingly tolerated and increasingly popular. Writers had understood that they had to deploy a double strategy: write an engaging and exciting story which would keep the readers turning the pages, while at the same time ensuring the support of the authorities by using acceptable themes (for instance, the hero had to be a hard-working, patriotic Soviet worker, the setting an agricultural collective, etc.). These themes were typical of the 'tractor novels' of the Stalinist 1940s, whose standard plot was satirised in 1951 (when Stalin was still alive) in an article by Aleksandr Tvardovsky: there is a principled *kolkhoz* president who is modern and there is one who is out of touch, there is a girl called Galya and a tractor driver called Vanya.[42] Most of the novel is about how Vanya gets Galya and how the modernisers win out, thus satisfying the political authorities and the majority of the readership.

Those who understood this were recompensed by large sales and the gratitude of the authorities. Take Vladimir Menshov's successful film *Moscow*

Does Not Believe in Tears (1980), winner of the Oscar for the best foreign film. This is the story of Katya, a young woman from provincial Russia who arrives in Moscow in the 1950s and is seduced and abandoned by the usual unreliable man (an intellectual who works in television). She does not let this experience shatter her: she works her way up to become a factory manager, and twenty years later she finds true love in the arms of Mr Right, a lathe operator. The film had great popular success: the characters were attractive, the plot easy to follow, the description of the hard days of the past (the early 1950s) caused nostalgia, and the better days that followed brought about hope in the future. The film was optimistic – just like a Hollywood melodrama. It is said that Brezhnev was moved to tears by it.[43] Only the literary circles of Moscow and Leningrad disparaged it, just as their counterparts in the USA disparage Hollywood successes. Menshov, the critics thought, had prostituted himself. To pander to mass taste (and even making Katya's seducer an intellectual) was political servility.

Literature and films proceeded along the same tracks. The optimism and structure of some of the Russian blockbuster novels had American counterparts. The novel *Airport* by Arthur Hailey was a great success in the USSR in 1971 when it appeared in translation in *Inostrannaia Literatura*. But an earlier Russian novel, Galina Nikolaeva's *Battle en Route* (1957), had a similar plot. In both novels the heroes fight powerful superiors who refuse to adopt their modernising ideas to reform the organisation they work in. Both are helped by women who are not their wives and with whom they fall in love.[44] They both succeed, and while the readers are hooked by the plot, they are also given plenty of information on how organisations work. In fact optimism and the pedagogical attitude of 'learning can be fun' pervade not just Soviet popular novels but also those of the West, as was the case with Hailey's other novels such as *Wheels* and *Hotel*.[45]

The Fall

The fall of communism in 1989–90 led to an economic crisis and a collapse of consumption throughout the former communist bloc. Yet pent-up demand meant that books which had not been previously available could now be sold openly. In Russia there was a considerable expansion of publishing houses, from 6,000 in 1993 to 11,000 in 1998. Many of these new ones, probably half, existed only on paper, since it had become easy to obtain a permit to set up a publishing house, and many of the new entrepreneurs simply obtained them in case they decided to exploit that particular market. The works of dissidents were now made available, but they did not sell significantly. The best-selling genres were still detective stories and women's romance. The large and unrealistic print runs of the communist era disappeared. More titles were available, but there were fewer books. While 1.8 billion books were printed in 1988, there were only 422 million in 1996.[46]

It was the same elsewhere in the former communist bloc. In 1990 the number of books available to readers in the German Democratic Republic (DDR) doubled. There were fewer public libraries, but more bookshops. Some people, during the first traumatic years of post-communism, read less, even though there were more books around. In the new *Länder*, the number of those who never read a book jumped up, from 8 per cent to 21 per cent. However, those who were still reading books read more than ever before.[47] One can surmise that a considerable percentage of readers in the old DDR read books because they had nothing better to do. Now they could travel more, and buy more things. For them reading was second best. In Romania there were, in 1988, 4,097 different periodicals, magazines and newspapers, with a total print run of nearly fifty-nine million. Ten years later there were more titles (6,231) but a much smaller total print run (fourteen million).[48] During the communist era the magazines were printed, but few people actually bought them. In Hungary, for instance, the prestigious 'high culture' literary weekly *Élet és Irodalom* (Life and Literature, nicknamed 'and' by those who claimed that it was about neither life nor literature) was published in almost 60,000 copies, but it is impossible to ascertain how many readers it had: in the 1990s millions of back copies of journals and books were found in remote storage places.[49] Books, heavily subsidised under communism, became far more expensive in real terms. In Hungary the average price of a book went up two and a half times in real terms between the mid-1980s and 2001.[50] Under communism, of course, books were very cheap in Hungary, and were 'sold' directly by publishers to state distribution agencies. Writers' royalties were paid according to the number of copies printed (after negotiations between publishers and distributors), not the number of copies sold, and the state made good any publishers' losses.[51] This world is no more.

In the new post-communist world in Russia, 'difficult' works were now published in a few thousand copies – as in the West. In 2001 a third of all titles appeared in editions of five hundred or less, and only 0.7 per cent of all books published in that year had a print run of over 100,000 copies.[52]

Foreign fiction did well. At first there was a great deal of catching up to do: in 1992, 78 per cent of fiction was foreign, and the figure was still 47 per cent in 1996. The readership of *Novy Mir*, the leading intellectual 'thick journal', crumbled, while the new *Barbie Doll Magazine* sold a million per issue in 1996.[53] Many thick journals disappeared, while the Russian editions of *Playboy*, *Elle* and *Cosmopolitan* prospered – partly because they could pay high fees to Russian writers. The print run of the major newspapers collapsed, and the price of newsprint skyrocketed. *Pravda*, with 10.5 million subscribers in 1985, dropped to 337,000 in 1993 (in spite of becoming far more readable, not a major feat); the weekly *Argumenty i Fakty* moved from thirty-three million subscribers in 1990 to 5.5 million in 1994; the daily *Izvestiia*, at 10.4 million in 1988, was down to 435,000 in 1994; and the liberal *Komsomolskaia Pravda* dropped from twenty-two million in 1990 to 871,000 in 1994.[54] The ownership of the press remained largely in Russian hands, as did the new private television stations. The owners were either the new multi-millionaires who had seized control of the country's vast natural resources with the complicity of Boris Yeltsin.[55] Their downfall is likely to benefit mainly the political class. In the rest of the former Soviet bloc (especially in the Czech Republic, Poland and Hungary) a significant proportion of the press and publishing came under the control of foreign capital from Germany.[56]

In Bulgaria too there was a sharp decrease in circulations in 1999 and 2000 (largely due to the increase in the price of paper), and an equally sharp increase in translations from English (from 8 per cent of books published in 1985 to 66 per cent in 1995). Translations from Russian, of course, collapsed.[57] Hungary was invaded by what Hungarian intellectuals (and not just Hungarian) regarded as American 'trash' novels. In Poland, Harlequin, the Canada-based international publishers of women's romance, became, in 1997, the largest publishing house, with sales of just under ten million books. In the Czech Republic too Danielle Steele's novels and Harlequin books acquired new, hitherto deprived readers. Publishers like Ivan Beránek, the chief editor of a newly established press (Havran), admitted in 2001 that he did not plan to publish original Czech literature 'at present': 'I realise what a praiseworthy enterprise it would be, but it is far too risky. Especially in the case of a newly established publishing house, which can't be expected to have unlimited capital. And even more so because, to be honest, I find it highly improbable that a new successful author is soon to be discovered.'

The alarm cry about the commercialisation of culture was raised everywhere. During *perestroika* Russian readers had been able to acquire the works of authors who previously could not be obtained, or only with great difficulty, including Vladimir Nabokov, Nietzsche, Schopenhauer, Kierkegaard and Freud.[58] With the definitive fall of communism, along with freedom came the freedom to buy 'trash literature'. It was finally possible to buy *Andrei*, a Russian version of *Playboy*, and *seks-katalogs*, go to *seks-klubs*, wear one's hair spiky, cover one's body in tattoos or read *Ptiuch*, a trendy magazine for youth.[59]

Women in Soviet society were often depicted as sanctified mothers, ready to sacrifice themselves for their sons. Now 'Mother Russia' (as the Virgin had to do in the West) had to compete with the large-scale production of pornography. Russians had discovered sex.[60] It may not have been *kul'tura* by the standards of cultural élites or the Communist Party, but it was Russia's introduction to a brave new world of culture in which pornography could co-exist with sophisticated introspection.

The fall of communism was not an unmitigated blessing for writers and cultural producers. Some writers who had been genuinely popular before, such as Petr Proskurin, became even more popular. Under communism police fiction heroes were KGB agents bravely solving crimes committed by nasty Western capitalists and their agents. Now their counterparts battled against the Russian *mafya*. A *detektiv* writer such as Aleksandra Marinina – now the leading best-seller – far from challenging Russia's past, expresses an understandable degree of nostalgia for a lost era of security and certainties. Anastasia Kamenskaia, Marinina's protagonist, is a police lieutenant colonel (as Marinina herself had been) who is honest and in pursuit of justice, just like the characters of many Soviet novels. She does not try to build communism, but is profoundly disturbed by the insecurity and perils of contemporary Russian society – much as Philip Marlowe (the hero of Raymond Chandler's books of the 1940s and 1950s) is interested in truth and justice, unlike his wealthy and seamy patrons. She solves complex crimes with machine-like logic, while being incompetent at traditional female pursuits and caring little for fashion.[61] She is above all else a policewoman, for in the new Russian crime stories, just as in the old Soviet ones, there are virtually no private detectives.[62] The protagonists are agents of the state, imbued with a collective spirit, as sturdy as the heroes of the past, as solid as John Wayne.

The introduction of market principles and the elimination of censorship were celebrated with genuine pleasure. In some fields foreign competition obliterated, at least for a while, native imitations. East European and Russian rock music seemed to be quickly relegated to history.[63] Under communism the Hungarian state recording company Hungaroton had thrived on producing rock music. After the fall it tried to survive somehow. It was privatised in 1995, lost 90 per cent of its market share and went bankrupt, while its former staff were hired by foreign companies such as EMI. Local forms of rock such as 'lakodalmas rock' (wedding rock), a combination of entertainment music played on occasions such as weddings with electronic synthesised disco music, did not last long either.[64] Yugoslav rock, the most developed in eastern Europe, was torn asunder not so much by the rapid introduction of market forces but because the rise of ethno-nationalism broke up what had been a multi-ethnic genre.[65] Under communism the greatest obstacle to the expansion of rock had been economic rather than political. Its development had been helped by communist economic protectionism, but equipment was expensive, it had to be imported or was of poor quality, the purchasing power of teenagers was low, and revenues from weekend dance concerts were insufficient to support a major rock scene.[66]

In the transition to post-communism everything changed – and not just because of the massive economic crisis. Mentalities had to change. Publishers had to become responsive to the market. Authors used to having their works printed and reprinted found themselves unemployed. Foreign films and foreign books flooded the cultural market. Intellectuals, including those who had been critical of communism, were aghast. They had moved from the dictatorship of the party to the true 'dictatorship of the proletariat': consumer capitalism.

Local genres did thrive too. In Poland the initial flowering of periodical literature in the post-communist years gave way, in 1995–96, to the closure of some of the leading magazines – Tygodnik Literacki, Nowy Nurt and Wiadomości Kulturalne. New magazines emerged. Some were successful, such as the science fiction magazine Nowa Fantastyka, which quickly reached a high circulation – not surprisingly, since the genre had long been popular in Poland, both before and during communism. The most successful, however, were women's magazines such as Twój Styl (with a circulation of 430,000), Elle (185,000) and Cosmopolitan (137,000).[67]

Under communism, intellectuals had enjoyed considerable privileges. They had better housing and better holidays than most of their fellow citizens; many could go abroad; many had a dacha in the countryside and a car. Books forbidden to others were available to them. Even in deeply impoverished Romania intellectuals had privileges. They had a salary, as well as royalties from their books, access to sanatoria, nurseries and kindergartens for their children, special restaurants, extra pensions, holidays at 'creative resorts' and loans.[68] In Bulgaria the Union of Writers owned considerable real estate including restaurants, cafés, offices and holiday homes.[69] Intellectuals in the West were never pampered in this way, except for the few who acquired ease of access to the media.

In most of the communist bloc generous literary prizes were regularly dangled to ensure, if not obedience (as in Stalinist days), at least some form of passive consent. If they were 'awkward' intellectuals would lose their jobs and sinecures, or their works would not be published or would be given a low print run and poor distribution. Only in exceptional cases were writers imprisoned because of their writings. Even in Poland, where the majority of writers were hostile to the regime, they had salaries regardless of how many copies their books sold. Once a writer had a contract with a publisher such as Czytelnik or PIW, he or she would received a salary calculated by the Ministry of Culture on the basis of the number of pages written.[70]

When communism collapsed the social status of writers, particularly but not exclusively those involved with the former regimes, diminished. Respect (and fear) now coincided with personal wealth – just as in the West. There was a significant rise in the prestige of television celebrities. Television acquired an aura of Americanism; i.e. it became less inhibited. It was soon less inhibited than terrestrial television in the USA (which was turning more puritanical). In 2003 the top pop act on Russian television was TaTu, a teenage duet, Lena Katina and Yulia Volkova, who sang while adopting provocative sexual poses, sometimes in scanty school uniforms, and flirted with lesbianism – their song 'All the Things She Said' shot to number one in the British charts, a first for a Russian act. On television the news was now read by the very attractive Maria Kiseleva. The same woman, but now black-leather-clad, hosted *Slaboye Zveno* (2002), the Russian version of *The Weakest Link*. The US game show *Wheel of Fortune*, adapted as *Pole Chudes* (Fields of Miracles), became, in 1997 the show with the highest ratings in Russia. Russians could also enjoy *Kto Khochet Stat' Millionerom* (Who Wants to be a Millionaire) – the main cultural difference was that the Russian questions were far more 'highbrow' than in the West, and that Russian players were willing to take more risks. There was also *Russian Extreme*, an adaptation of *Survivor*, and a Russian adaptation of *The Oprah Winfrey Show*. Old and new Western programmes such as the ancient *I Love Lucy*, the smutty *Benny Hill Show*, *The Simpsons*, *The X-Files* and *Murder, She Wrote* were also imported.[71] State television managed to retain a good audience, though much reduced, partly because the government was now covering only a fraction of its operating costs, and partly because of the proliferation of private stations, particularly in the larger cities.[72]

The losers of the post-communist era were, paradoxically, the dissidents and the more high-minded intellectuals. They had been unable to thrive under communism, which tried to impose a stultifying conformity on them. But neither could they thrive under market conditions. They did not write or speak to a mass audience, and often their works were difficult and complex. Under communism their books were not published and their films not made because they did not fit with the prevailing aesthetics of the system. Under capitalism they still did not fit. Before, when they were dissident, they had a role and a function and were lionised in the West. But now the West no longer cared.

The DDR

After the fall of communism, in what was once East Germany the situation for intellectuals was particularly acute. Elsewhere in eastern Europe the loss of privileges was partly compensated for by the gain of new freedoms, new jobs, new perspectives. Since intellectuals were often more in touch with political circles than ordinary people are, they also knew when and how to distance themselves from the losing side and recycle themselves (as many communists did). In the DDR this was not possible. In the first place the intelligentsia (as a whole) was more pro-communist (or less dissident) than that of, say, Hungary, not to speak of the Polish intelligentsia, whose contempt for the regime had been manifest for years. Many had denounced each other to the Stasi, the secret police, thus making their integration into a post-communist world more difficult. Moreover, the fall of the DDR did not mean a limited turnover of personnel at the top, as was the case elsewhere; it meant being taken over by the Federal Republic, the FRG, from where, once the Berlin Wall was down, television and radio operators, university teachers, journalists and theatre managers descended. Their mission was to integrate the old DDR into the FRG and set it back on the road to democracy. For Poland or Czechoslovakia or Hungary, post-communism could be seen as an evolution and a liberation. Their people were now free to do what they wanted. For many East Germans it seemed more like having to catch up with a long-lost relative who in the meantime had become prosperous and who was willing, more or less patiently, to explain what life as a grown-up entailed.

The regime of the DDR had a deserved reputation for upholding a particularly unimaginative brand of Marxism. The sparks of originality which could occasionally be seen in Hungary or Poland were absent. The country was, after all, an entirely artificial construct, its future dependent on the goodwill of the USSR, without which it would not exist. It was always negatively compared with the Federal Republic, for decades western Europe's strongest economy. Of course East Germans too had household goods like refrigerators and washing machines. In the ownership of televisions East Germany lagged behind West Germany but not exceedingly so: in 1964, 42 per cent against 50 per cent and in 1986, 94 to the FRG's 97.[73] One is, of course, always more aware of what is missing: in the West virtually everyone had a telephone; in East Germany only 9 per cent of households had one. In the West every household seemed to own a car; in the East this was true for just over half.[74] Since 1961 the Berlin Wall had constantly reminded East Germans that had they been liberated by the Americans instead of the Russians they would all be citizens of the Bundesrepublik, and driving a Mercedes (or so they thought) instead of a Trabant.[75]

However, behind the aura of drab austerity, the political repression and generalised *angst*, an interesting cultural life developed in the DDR. In the 1950s political control was so strict that Hanns Eisler's opera libretto *Johann Faustus* was rejected even though Eisler was a committed communist who had chosen to settle in East Germany, and even though he had composed 'Auferstanden aus Ruinen', the national anthem of the DDR. Eisler was far too avant-garde and too reminiscent of 'late bourgeois decadence'.[76] Things began to change in the 1960s – paradoxically after the wall had been built.

As in the USSR, the DDR had annexed to the cause of socialism the classical realist writers of the bourgeois tradition (Dickens, Zola, Balzac, etc.), all the leading German writers (Schiller, Goethe, Heine, etc.) and major twentieth-century writers such as Thomas Mann (whose collected works were first published in the DDR). The DDR could also pride itself on its own major writers. The best-known of them all, Bertolt Brecht, had been given his own theatrical company, the Berliner Ensemble, but he had died in 1956, with few people aware of his increasing doubts about the communist system. Anna Seghers (pseudonym of Netty Reiling) died much later (1983), but had remained steadfastly loyal to the Communist Party throughout her tenure as President of the Union of Writers (1952–78). She was widely admired in the West, but critics always pointed out that her best novels had been written before she had turned into a pillar of the DDR. Though she occasionally interceded privately on behalf on fellow writers, in public she was a fully-fledged believer.[77]

Political restrictions, however, did not prevent the production of important novels such as Christa Wolf's *Nachdenken über Christa T.* (The Quest for Christa T), published first in the West (1970) and then in the DDR (1973). Her later works, such as *Cassandra* (1982), were all published in the DDR as well as abroad, as were those of Stefan Heym and Ulrich Plenzdorf. Those who clearly stepped out of line, such as the singer and poet Wolf Biermann, were stripped of their citizenship and expelled. Others left the country of their own volition. The regime was unable to innovate and was fearful of change. It was secretive and starkly authoritarian, but it was not cruel: writers and artists were not killed, and relatively few, by the standards of communist repression, were arbitrarily arrested and imprisoned. Censorship was exercised by the heads of publishing houses within parameters set by the authorities. This generated a climate of uncertainty. Open-minded publishers ran risks and tried to widen the boundaries of what was acceptable – and some, such as Walter Janka, paid the price. As head of Aufbau-Verlag he had launched an ambitious literary programme, publishing not only the complete works of Thomas Mann but, circumventing currency restrictions and paying Western authors in kind (including Russian mink coats), he tried to publish a vast array of high-quality books. A critical supporter of the regime, Janka was accused of treason in a show trial in 1957 and not released until 1960. Prudent publishers employed *Lektoren* (readers) familiar with the canons of Marxism-Leninism, a generic term for government policies. But matters never worked the way they were supposed to. Some *Lektoren* were reliable, others weren't, and others still were simply obtuse (or pretended to be).[78]

By the late 1960s there was room in the DDR for Christoph Hein's candid chronicles of life in the DDR (his post-1990 work displeased Western critics because it was too anti-capitalist), the caustically feminist novels of Irmtraud Morgner and Ingeborg Bachmann, and Plenzdorf's ironic *The New Sorrows of Young Werther* (1972), written in 'youth-speak'. Some novels were never published, others suffered long delays while the bureaucratic machine ruminated away; but many were published – making the wait and the compromises seem worthwhile. Those unwilling to compromise or hostile to the communist regime often managed to leave the country. Others, such as

Stefan Heym and Christa Wolf (a Party member throughout), remained loyal to the ideals of socialism and constantly urged democratic reform, but had a difficult relationship with the regime. Heym was criticised by the Party in 1956, decorated in 1959, and criticised again in 1965. He was translated into Russian, Polish, Hungarian and Czech and, in the 1970s, in the West. The price he and Wolf paid for their loyalty and the inevitable compromises they made resulted, after 1990, in their being accused of opportunism by younger critics who never had to face similar dilemmas.

Critical writers are often difficult writers. They can be more easily tolerated because, almost by definition, they address themselves to a relatively narrow segment of the population. East Germans wishing to have something less demanding after a hard day's work could read the works of Erwin Strittmatter (1912–94), such as *Der Laden* (The Shop), published in three volumes between 1983 and 1993, a kind of family saga set around a shop, or Hermann Kant's *Die Aula* (1965), a humorous description of university life in the DDR.

The repression of culture in the communist world is often seen, sometime almost exclusively so, in terms of high culture and famous writers. In reality changes in the cultural and political climate are reflected more readily in popular culture, and music in particular. In the West to enjoy rock and roll meant, among other things, to distinguish oneself from one's parents and assert one's youth and cultural independence. This was true in the DDR too, but in the DDR rock music also meant 'the West', America and modern capitalism.

Initially the regime was optimistic: it thought it could outdo the West in everything and that eventually it would be able to produce a wholesome communist popular culture. In 1959 Walter Ulbricht, the Party leader, declared that there was no point in criticising Elvis Presley until the country was not able to offer something better.[79]

Nothing 'better' than Elvis materialised. The history of *Rock in der DDR* was one of surrender before the superiority of the West. Hostility had to be mollified by an endless series of compromises. On 21 September 1961, a few weeks after the Wall went up, the Politbüro of the Central Committee of the SED (i.e. the Communist Party) instructed Party members to show toleration and understanding towards beat music since it was loved by so many young East Germans.[80] Taking this as sign of acceptance, the young formed pop bands and began learning the new sound from foreign radio stations such as Radio Luxembourg. A thriving market in smuggled records developed.

The regime was cautious. A harsh response might be counter-productive. To denounce Elvis Presley and the Beatles as agents of capitalism would have made capitalism appear more exciting than it already was; meanwhile in London the BBC had banned the Beatles' 'A Day in the Life' and 'Lucy in the Sky with Diamonds' because of their supposed references to drug-taking.

Presumably the regime hoped that beat music would remain circumscribed. But it did not. Beatlemania arrived in the DDR too. Some of the group's songs could even be heard on the radio of the DDR – the risks of many youngsters tuning routinely to foreign radio stations was best avoided. There was a flowering of local bands such as the Franke-Echo-Quintett, the Sputnik and the Music Stromers. These pioneers of DDR rock were followed by the Showrocks, the Strangers, the Greenhorns, the Black Devils, the Five Stones, the Fellows and the Gringos – the English names openly avowing the origin of their inspiration.[81]

Mick Jagger and co. had previously been denounced as 'decadent', but in 1965 the band Theo-Schumann-Combo was allowed to perform two classic Rolling Stones songs in German: 'Das kann doch nicht wahr sein' ('The Last Time') and 'Satisfaction'. But this was too daring; the authorities had second thoughts. The two songs were withdrawn and remained banned until the fall of the Wall.[82]

1965 signalled a return to the past. The policy of toleration had not paid off. The authorities were frightened by police reports of pop concerts: there were fist-fights, drunkenness, sexual excesses and other modes of behaviour 'typical of the West'. The security organs drew a link between beat music and juvenile delinquency. Beat music was 'the poison of the class enemy'; the behaviour of fans was compared to that of Nazi thugs in the 1920s and 1930s.[83] Ulbricht was aghast (as were some in the West): 'My view, comrades, is that the time has come to stop the monotony of this "Yeah, Yeah, Yeah", or whatever it is they call it ... Is it really necessary for us to copy any Western rubbish?'[84]

The new, less tolerant climate forced many bands to change their names: the Bell-Boys became the Sextett Leipzig, the Black Stones became the Schwarze Steine, the Swinging Guitars turned, of course, into the Schwingenden Gitarren – though the music did not change. As some bands were dissolved, others were formed. The semi-illegal capitalism of recording studios continued. In 1967 the Party had second thoughts again. A softer tone emerged, helped by the success of some of the DDR's social and economic policies. People worked less, earned more and had longer holidays, and thus had more money to spend and more time for leisure. Then the accelerating crisis in Czechoslovakia convinced the authorities of the danger of the 'slippery slope'. They felt that further concessions would inevitably degenerate into a major challenging of the whole system. Had not Czechoslovakia been invaded by beat music before being invaded by Soviet (and East German) tanks?[85] Alexander Dubček's 'communism with a human face' was dealt a death blow. Soon after the Czech crisis, however, the climate improved thanks to Willy Brandt, the West German Chancellor, and his *Ostpolitik*. The line of reciprocal *détente* and openness between the two Germanies was supported by the USSR and was popular among most Germans. A period of relaxation had started.

In 1971 Walter Ulbricht gave way to Erich Honecker. Honecker had been hard when it was necessary to be hard. Now it was time to be soft, and he softened accordingly. Policies might change, but continuity of personnel was the hallmark of the regime – after all, the same Politburo member, Kurt Hager, had been in charge of cultural policy (as ZK-Sekretär für Kultur, Volksbildung und Wissenschaft) uninterruptedly from 1957 to 1989. With *détente* there developed a new emphasis on 'consumer socialism'. Rock became more acceptable. The regime decided that since it could not ban the bands, it should try to co-opt them. It organised rock festivals and competitions, provided subsidies and searched for new talents. In 1985 the Culture Ministry even sponsored an Association for Rock Music, which by 1989 had 570 members.[86] There were also private networks of fans, tolerated by the regime, not quite legal but not in opposition either. The authorities also tolerated a kind of 'rock capitalism' with venues, concerts, studios, one hundred professional bands and 2,000 non-professional ones – often playing with musical instruments illegally imported from the West – anything to avoid a confrontation with an already alienated youth.[87]

A disregard for legal norms was inevitable in the DDR. The country was run by a plethora of rules and regulations which could not possibly be obeyed or enforced in their entirety. For instance, to be recognised as a singer it was necessary to possess a diploma from an accredited music school (a document Elvis or Jimi Hendrix never possessed). Amateur groups needed a permit. Bands had to make sure that no more than 60 per cent of the music they played originated from the 'non-socialist camp'.[88] In the 1980s the authorities – faced with the widespread disregard for the law – decided to regularise the twenty or thirty private recording studios which, by the end of the decade, were in fact producing most of the rock music of the DDR. Since the 1970s rock and pop music had been regularly commented on and debated in the press, including periodicals such as *Melodie und Rhytmus* and *Unterhaltungskunst*. Radio and television had their own dedicated programmes about music and their *Hitparade*. By 1980 the DDR state radio, not foreign stations, had become the main source for the diffusion of rock and pop music. Its youth station, DT64, constantly expanded its broadcasting time (twenty hours a day in 1987).[89] The intention was to lure listeners away from foreign pop stations. Whether it liked it or not, the regime could not avoid competition. The market reared its head from everywhere. DT64 was so successful that when, after the collapse of the country, its frequencies were about to be re-allocated to an American-run Berlin radio station, there were so many protests from young listeners that the plan was dropped.[90] A somewhat similar parallel development had taken place in the West. In 1960s Britain, for instance, offshore 'pirate' radio stations shaped the musical taste of the young. The (Labour) government tried to shut them down, but the carrot was used there too, with the BBC developing its own pop music stations.

Most young East Germans, like their counterparts in the Federal Republic, were profoundly pacifist. They liked the ideals of hippy culture, love and peace and the spirit of Woodstock.[91] The DDR too was all for peace, not least because war would have meant its utter annihilation. On this point there was full agreement between the communist authorities and German youth. A more open culture was promoted. The World Youth Games of 1973, held in East Berlin, had shows and rock concerts with over two hundred local bands. East German rock stars emerged, and their records, more easily available than those from the West, began to sell in substantial quantity. The golden era of rock in the DDR had begun.[92] By the time the Wall was brought down in November 1989, East German youth was quite familiar with the cultural delights of advanced capitalism.

Some loosening of controls had occurred in virtually all other forms of entertainment. Cabarets, for instance, remained a distinctive outlet for entertainment even in communist Germany, but in the 1950s the cabarets of the DDR were so moralising and educational that they were losing audiences. The relaxation of the 1970s corresponded to a revival of the genre, and audiences grew from 215,000 in 1971 to 585,000 in 1979.[93] The satirical magazine *Eulenspiegel*, which was selling 350,000 copies in 1973, saw its sales rise to 500,000 in 1985. Of course it had to avoid making fun of politicians, but the magazine received and published a vast number of letters from its readers complaining – in a non-political manner – about various aspect of life in the DDR; this was the key to its success.[94] A similar evolution occurred in comic strips. In the 1950s the two main comic-strip magazines, *Mosaik* and *Atze*, had strong political and educational aims. By 1964 the strips had become pure entertainment, with some being imported from Italy (*Atomino*).

The DDR had glorified itself as 'the land of reading' (*Leseland*).[95] The reading was, of course, wholesome. Officially there was no *Schmutz und Schundliteratur* (smut and trash literature). What this meant was that there were no horror or erotic books in the DDR, and not even the kind of sentimental women's romances published by Harlequin in the West. But there were plenty of crime stories and science fiction – an approved and popular genre with well over 4,000 titles published, including, alongside Germans, Russians and Poles as well as all the Western classics.[96]

The authorities of the DDR wanted to uphold orthodox Marxism. Many of the leaders were hardened men who had survived Nazi persecution and the deprivation of the war. Many had been in exile in the USSR, and had survived Stalinism by displaying the most intransigent loyalty to the system. In the early years of the DDR, the regime was weak; the USSR was ready to let Germany be reunited as long as the country remained non-aligned; in 1953 rationing and food shortages led to workers' unrest which had to be suppressed; and a continuous stream of people was leaving the country.

Unlike other countries in the communist bloc, the DDR could not be easily insulated. By contrast with, say, Bulgarians and Romanians, East Germans were well acquainted with how things worked in the West. Until 1961 anyone could easily obtain books or newspapers from the West, and leave the country freely. Even when the Wall was built, people could listen to West German radio and television: West German television channels could be received in up to 85 per cent of the territory of the DDR.[97] Shared roof aerials enabled the reception of the ARD and ZDF channels beamed from the Federal Republic. The communist leaders soon realised that if they wanted people to tune in to DFF (Deutscher Fernsehfunk, the state network) they would have to provide game and variety shows.[98] In Hungary or Bulgaria or the USSR, if people did not like what was on television they could only switch it off. In East Berlin they could switch to West Berlin stations. The DFF (which became Fernsehen der DDR, Television of the DDR, in 1969 when a second channel was introduced) found itself in a competitive situation, unlike Italian or French television – as a result it became the best television network in Eastern Europe. In the DDR, direct competition with West Germany meant that heavily politicised current affairs programmes had to be balanced with light entertainment and serials. It was acknowledged that there should not be too many boring programmes. In 1981–82, under the slogan '*Alternative Programmgestaltung*' (alternative programme production), prime-time television was further enlivened by importing escapist programmes from abroad and from West Germany – this was a direct result of a drop in ratings of the DDR network.[99]

This did not mean that East German television was going to renounce its educational mission, only that education had to be sweetened with fun and games. The process was helped by the fact that its West German counterpart, ARD, was not into cheap populism either (it transmitted lengthy passages from Goethe's *Faust* during its test phase in 1951). Throughout Europe television was used to familiarise audiences with the masterpieces of the theatre and literature. In the DDR too plays from the theatrical canon or celebrated novels turned into plays were regularly broadcast, provided they followed what we would now call 'political correctness': members of the oppressed classes (such as servants) were to be shown as better people than their masters, with more natural feelings, and able to improve their conditions without damaging fellow class members.[100] This occasionally restricted the range.

In 1971–72 Honecker himself had launched a campaign for 'good entertainment'.[101] There was a clearer shift towards mass appeal and *Volksverbundenheit* ('closeness to the people').[102] Much of this was genuinely popular. The television of the DDR was not devoted to an endless stream of stereotyped propaganda. This outdated image fails to take account of the significance of the competition it faced from the Federal Republic. Viewers in the DDR were like those in the Bundesrepublik (or indeed anywhere else): they wanted relaxation and entertainment, and watched the channel which offered the programmes they wanted to see. By 1969 East Germans close enough to West Germany's transmitters were spoilt for choice. While British or Italian viewers had only three channels, they had five, three from West Germany and two from the DDR.[103] By the early 1980s the two channels of the DDR had a fairly adequate 35-to-40 per cent share of the potential audience. That does not mean that 60 per cent watched 'the other side'. Some people worked shifts, others went to bed early or did not watch television at all. It was assumed that 20 to 25 per cent watched Western programmes.[104] Of course loyal Party members such as those working at the Institut für Marxismus-Leninismus were asked to refrain from watching programmes from the other side, but everyone knew that ordinary people did not take such injunctions seriously.[105]

Scheduling became a weapon in the struggle. If the FRG showed something attractive, the DDR responded with a variety show or a thriller. If the FRG was broadcasting a programme of no interest to Eastern audiences, the DDR took advantage by showing a documentary or a current affairs programme.[106] The minutes of the meetings of those in charge of schedules in the DDR reveal how attentive they were to what their competitors were up to. Thus in West Germany the competition between ARD and ZDF had led to a mutual understanding that Wednesday evening prime time would be devoted to current affairs programmes on both channels. This enabled DDR television to use that slot for the same kind of programme too.[107] Wednesday must have been movie night for Germans on both sides of the Wall.

East German news was reassuring: instead of a constant stream of disasters, hold-ups and other crimes, viewers were offered a vision of a society at peace with itself, becoming increasingly prosperous (which was true), while in the West there were drugs and violence (the image was confirmed by Western films seen in the East). The problem was that most viewers did not believe the news.[108] Had the political authorities been a little more secure or intelligent, they would have allowed the odd criticism and complaint, thus allowing the rest of the programme to be taken more seriously.

Yet there were high-quality documentaries in the DDR. The topics, of course, had to be chosen with care: the advent of democracy in Portugal and Spain in the mid-1970s, the anti-colonial struggle in Namibia, racism in the USA, the remnants of Nazism in West Germany, US air bombing in Vietnam, the *coup d'état* against Salvador Allende in Chile – in other words, left-wing subjects. The documentary-makers Walter Heynowski and Gerhard Scheumann produced over seventy films in twenty-five years, gaining an international reputation. They were soon in complete charge of their films, and were even allowed to set up their own autonomous company, Studio H&S, in 1969, and to trade the international rights of their productions.[109] They could travel abroad whenever they wanted, and their documentaries were shown at prime time. But in 1982 the two film-makers (both convinced communists), thinking that their success had made them unassailable, made the mistake of criticising the media policy of the DDR. This was fatal. They lost their privileges and Studio H&S was closed, though they continued to make films inside the ordinary state network.[110] Gradually they recovered their standing, though not the autonomy they had enjoyed before 1982. They prepared a film about the fortieth anniversary of the formation of the DDR, celebrating the achievement of socialism in East Germany. The timing could not have been more catastrophic. It was broadcast in three parts in October 1989, just as thousands of DDR citizens were fleeing socialism via Hungary, just as the wall was about to come down.[111]

Another unusual team of documentary-makers was that set up by a West German communist living in the FRG, Franz Dötterl, and a DDR journalist, Sabine Katins. Their films became a fixture of DDR TV.[112] Sabine Katins's *What do the West Germans Think About the DDR?* (1974) was shown in both Germanies. The magazine *Der Spiegel* praised the work of Group Katins as 'one of the few journalistic rays of hope' in the East. The team was careful never to deal with subjects from the DDR. Their programme *Everyday in the West* produced between 1972 and 1987 almost three hundred films, over half of them about West Germany, far in excess of what the West Germans produced on the DDR. They were showered with prizes at international festivals.[113]

The DDR was good at quality production, and was even better when the subject matter was quite detached from touchy subjects such as socialism or the USSR. The theatre could even be experimental. Intellectuals were placated by being provided with some of what they liked. Since economic efficiency was not pursued there was in some areas a lavishness unknown in the West. All sixty-odd theatres belonged to the state, and each was over-staffed. Actors and producers had abundant time for rehearsal. As there was no star system, the stress was on ensemble production (just as in the most innovative companies in the West).[114] The authorities encouraged the classics from the canon, contemporary plays from the 'socialist camp', the 'critical realist' theatre (i.e. the established bourgeois theatre such as Ibsen and Shaw), anti-imperialist and socialist plays from the West and the Third World. In practice what was banned were the kind of romantic comedies and melodramas which attracted the majority of audiences in the West. Thus there was some overlap between East and West Germany: for in the West too the classical canon enjoyed considerable public patronage and public funding, as did the modern bourgeois canon and the best of socialist theatre (especially Bertolt Brecht in Italy, thanks to Giorgio Strehler's famous Piccolo Teatro in Milan).

As in Great Britain, everyone was safe with Shakespeare. According to the ideology of the socialist camp, great art foreshadowed the ultimate victory of socialism and 'humanism'. Since the two terms were used almost interchangeably in the DDR, Shakespeare was OK; he was universal, and being universal, was almost a proto-socialist. Intellectuals who wanted their Shakespeare did not bother to question this rather strange view of culture. Some even sought to please communist officials by explaining that Hamlet's 'bold notion of Man remained an ideal, whose translation into life was reserved into a later epoch ... in our time the contradiction between the spirit and power has been resolved. What was once a yearning in Shakespeare ... reaches our audiences today as a modern aim in life.'[115] Anyone – including critics of the regime – could use Shakespeare. In 1983 at the Hans-Otto-Theater in Potsdam, Piet Drescher's production of *Hamlet* was unashamedly and overtly political. Denmark was represented as a kind of Orwellian nightmare, and when Polonius asked Hamlet what he was reading he angrily declaimed the famous line 'Words words words,' throwing a copy of the official Party newspaper to the floor.[116] The production played to packed houses.

East German theatre-goers missed out on modernism and the avant-garde. They did not see Samuel Beckett's *Waiting for Godot* until 1987.[117] More approachable were some of the films made by the state company DEFA. These included 'westerns', or as they were called in the DDR *Indianerfilme* ('Indian films'), such as the hugely successful *Die Söhne der Grossen Bärin* (The Sons of Great Mother Bear, 1965–66), partly shot on location in Yugoslavia, like some US westerns and Italian 'spaghetti' westerns. The love for westerns in German popular culture – as evidenced by the nineteenth-century success of Karl May's novels and their television versions in West Germany during the 1960s – helped the film and the series of DDR westerns which followed. These contained the standard ingredients of Hollywood westerns: the ambush of a stagecoach, an attack on a railroad, people walking into saloon bars through swinging doors, good guys and bad guys. The good guys, however, were almost always the Indians struggling against corrupt whites.[118]

When it was all over for the DDR and the 'good guys' from the West came to its rescue, a strangely nostalgic attitude ('*ostalgia*', as it was ironically called) pervaded a significant section of the older generations. Reruns of old films and television programmes were watched with sentimental feelings. No one seemed to regret Ulbricht and Honecker, but many were reluctant to declare the previous fifty years to have been just a waste of time and a cultural disaster.

61

A World of Readers

Books are Good

IN A WORLD OF READERS, being unable to read is a major handicap. To be literate, however, does not necessarily mean reading books. Once there were literacy campaigns to teach people how to read; now there are campaigns urging people to read books. Parents lament that their children never read books, but not that they rarely watch television, play video games or listen to pop music. Surveys quantifying the percentage of non-readers are noted with dismay by the reading classes.

Reading a book, almost any book, is regarded as 'better' than any other cultural activity. Two hundred years of technological revolution in culture has not substantially modified this basic belief. Illiteracy was a good reason for not reading. In the era of compulsory schooling, the non-reader still lurking among us is regarded as a collective failure.

Surveys indicating the percentage of non-readers give conflicting results – unsurprisingly, since different methodologies and definitions are used. An Italian survey in the 1980s revealed that 22 per cent of the population never read anything, not even newspapers.[1] Perhaps this was an improvement, since in 1962 the proportion of Italian non-readers was 40 per cent – the same as in Hungary and Holland, countries with a huge production of books. In France, home of the intellectual, the percentage of non-readers was even higher: 53 per cent.[2] This suggests a massive deterioration, since according to another survey in 1955 'only' 38 per cent of the French had not read a book in the past year.[3] Between 1989 and 1997 matters improved, at least in France: non-readers were now 25 per cent.[4] There was, however, further bad news from Italy: in 1986 half of the adult population had not read a book in the preceding six months.[5] The ISTAT (Italian state statistical office) figures for 1988 suggest that in reality the situation was even worse: 62 per cent had not read a book in the previous year, perhaps because nineteen million Italians live in towns without a bookshop.[6] The problem is not confined to Italy. In 1980, the market analysis agency Euromonitor surveyed the European Community and found that 55 per cent 'were not reading a book at the moment'.[7] In July 2005 yet another Italian survey, this time commissioned by publishers, revealed that 54 per cent never read books, and that only 35 per cent had bought a book during the previous year. This represented an improvement since 2003.[8]

The precise percentages are of limited interest. Those who read books are horrified to live in a country where 20, or 30, or 40 per cent of the population never read anything. Non-readers are themselves mortified. They know that to have books in the home is a mark of social status. When asked to explain themselves, they adopt a tone of contrition: they do not have time, they are too tired after a day's work, they promise to catch up during the holidays. They regard books as a leisure activity.[9] They are not wrong. If one, along with Roland Barthes, thinks that books can be entertaining, not reading them is a pity not because one fails to ennoble one's soul or widen one's horizons, but because one is missing out on pleasure.[10] In an ideal world everyone should read books. Yet there is no obvious reason why reading a book (any book?) is better than watching television (any television programme?). What is wrong with never reading books? The much-touted contrast between watching television and reading is true only at the extreme of the spectrum: heavy television watchers do not read much, and those who read a lot do not watch much television.[11] Perhaps those who read are depriving themselves of the pleasures of television.

The people who read the most are, unsurprisingly, the better educated. The wealthiest 20 per cent of the population read plenty of books, yet they also have the latest television gadgetry, DVDs, computers and internet access; they go to the cinema, the theatre and the opera more than the rest. Most of those who never read belong to the class of those who, throughout history, have never read anything: the poor. It is true that today books are cheap, and that there are plenty of public libraries. Being poor, however, is not just about not having enough cash: it can also lead to a lack of the predisposition, the will and the curiosity to widen one's horizons. Not reading is to do with inequality and poverty. However, women, not the most privileged sector of society, read more than men. In France, government statistics for 2003 show that 38 per cent of men and 'only' 28 per cent of women had not read a book in the preceding twelve months (which, of course, does not tally with other sets of statistics from the same source – see above), while women also listened to classical music more frequently and went to the theatre, ballet, art galleries and museums more often. Among the young, that is those aged between fifteen and twenty-four, the gender gap was particularly impressive: 33 per cent of men were non-readers, but only 13 per cent of women. Compared to 1973, men read less and women read more, more than compensating for the drop in male readers. The percentage of 'strong' readers – those reading at least twenty-five books a year – had decreased since 1973, though far more among men than among women.[12]

Among the university-educated there is a surprisingly high number who never read books. In Italy, among the non-readers, along with 91 per cent of farmers and 71 per cent of workers, are 23 per cent of university-educated people.[13] Of course there is an increasing number of graduates, so it is not surprising that many of them do not read.

One could look on the bright side and note the progress that has been made. Today reading is normal, and not reading abnormal. In the nineteenth century – or even the mid-twentieth – it was the reverse, as is still the case in many parts of the world. In the 'advanced' countries, more books are printed each year than there are people.

NUMBER OF COPIES OF BOOKS PRODUCED PER YEAR PER HUNDRED INHABITANTS IN SELECTED COUNTRIES, 1991–94	
Belarus	775
Bulgaria	509
Italy	507
China	489
Latvia	433
South Korea	360
Portugal	272
Spain	261
Poland	256
Japan	253
Romania	221
United Arab Emirates	213
Israel	178

SOURCE: UNESCO, *World Culture Report*, 1998

France, Germany, Great Britain and the USA did not return data, but everything indicates that they would be comfortably in the top league, though perhaps behind Belarus.

We do, however, have a fuller listing for book titles:

NUMBER OF BOOK TITLES PUBLISHED PER 100,000 INHABITANTS IN SELECTED COUNTRIES, 1991–94	
Finland	246
Holland	221
Norway	159
Sweden	158
UK	148
Belgium	138
Spain	113
Hungary	98
Germany	86
France	78
Bulgaria	71
Portugal	68
Italy	58
Poland	28
Romania	16
Albania	12
Ukraine	10

SOURCE: UNESCO, *World Culture Report*, 1998

And elsewhere? As one would expect, small, poor countries don't do well at all. And it is not just about books, it is about everything. Books are a sign of prosperity. Bookless countries have fewer televisions, radios and cinemas. The gap between Ghana (not one of the poorest countries in Africa) and Greece (not one of the richest countries in Europe) is stark: in 1995 Ghana had five telephone lines per thousand people (494 in Greece), published 0.1 book titles per 100,000 people (thirty-nine in Greece), sold eighteen copies of daily papers per thousand people (183 in Greece), had 231 radios and ninety-two televisions per thousand people (430 radios and 220 TVs in Greece).

African writers, in order to be read globally, have to write in the language of former colonial powers. Their own market is too small, and their books are unlikely to be translated. Besides, it is not easy to obtain literary success in Nigeria, with its four hundred dialects, or in Ghana, with a hundred dialects, or in Sierra Leone, which has, with a population of 5.7 million, about twenty languages and a literacy index of only 36 per cent. In global terms, the world of books is the world of the rich.

Best-Sellers

The obsession with best-sellers – a literary genre in itself – is particular to the world of culture. Few, outside the business, care to know which is the best-selling type of wine, or cut of beef, or brand of shampoo. It is not so with records, films and books.

It is only recently that we have had (almost) reliable figures for best-sellers, yet even today there are occasionally glaring discrepancies between lists. The British magazine the *Bookseller* publishes BookTrack lists of the best-selling books sold the previous week. BookTrack, in turn, obtains these figures from 1,500 outlets. A rival company, Bookwatch, does the same with data collected from 628 booksellers. In the week ending 16 August 1997 BookTrack claimed that Jonathan Dimbleby's *The Last Governor: Chris Patten and the Handover of Hong Kong* had sold a total of 1,500 copies, while Bookwatch stated that 5,478 copies of the book were sold in the same week. Bookwatch claimed that the paperback edition of Helen Fielding's *Bridget Jones's Diary* sold 17,589 copies, while BookTrack put the sales at 6,926. In the last week of October 1997, Daisy Goodwin's anthology *The Nation's Favourite Love Poems* sold 4,943 copies according to the *Observer* ('from data supplied by 658 bookshops'), but according to the *Sunday Times* (which uses Bookwatch figures) only 1,483. The variations for *Bridget Jones's Diary* are even more pronounced: BookTrack set its sales at 5,783, Bookwatch estimated 11,611, and the *Observer* went for a figure of 20,434.[14]

To be strictly comparable, figures for books' sales would need to be tracked across the same period. This is seldom done. Some textbooks, even some scientific books, achieve a better sales record over the years than ephemeral best-sellers. Paul Samuelson's *Economics: An Introductory Analysis*, first published in 1948, translated into over forty languages and regularly updated (now by other authors), has sold millions of copies, as has – and still does – the famous *Gray's Anatomy* (first published in 1858), the name of the original author having been incorporated in the title.[15]

Books are not big business, but big best-sellers are. Between August 2004 and August 2005, books by Dan Brown of *Da Vinci Code* fame and J.K. Rowling accounted for 6 per cent of all books sold in the UK.[16] Big sellers include some that pass the 'quality' test as defined by literary critics The Gold Book Awards (launched in 2001), given to any title that sells more than 500,000 copies over a period of five consecutive years (Platinum awards are given for those selling over one million) included among their winners literary novels such as Monica Ali's *Brick Lane*, Paulo Coelho's *The Alchemist*, Ian McEwan's *Atonement*, Philip Pullman's *His Dark Materials* trilogy, Zadie Smith's *White Teeth* and Lynne Truss's clever book on punctuation, *Eats, Shoots & Leaves*.[17]

Just as it is difficult to spot a winner among novels, so it is with some academic books. When Michel Foucault's *Les Mots et les choses* (*The Order of Things*) was published in 1966, Pierre Nora, the publisher at Gallimard, thought it would sell at most 10,000 copies. Within a year it was reprinted six times and topped the non-fiction best-seller list. By 1969, as Nora recalls, it had sold 40,000 copies.[18] Translated into English, the book achieved an enormous international success. It turned Foucault into a late-twentieth-century guru, and became a long-lasting international best-seller.

Foucault's book straddled several categories of serious non-fiction:[19]

— Expensive monographs bought by a few specialists and academic libraries. These are unlikely to sell more than 1,000 copies, at most 2,000, in the larger European countries. Little marketing takes place and sales rely mainly on reviews in the specialist press. The books will be stocked for a relatively long time, but will not be reprinted.

— Books for non-specialist intellectuals. These might sell 5,000 copies. They need to be reviewed in prestigious dailies and weeklies. If successful, they become classic texts.

— The 'guru' book. Here marketing is essential, and requires the support of prestigious dailies and weeklies, and media exposure. It should be short and low-priced. It should make a simple point forcefully, enabling journalists to understand it quickly. It must convey the impression that by reading it one gains an understanding of a major contemporary issue (terrorism, poverty, the future, what kind of society we live in). It should aim to sell more than 10,000 copies.

— Academic textbooks. These should be in paperback, and require academic recommendation since their main market is university students. The successful ones sell between 10,000 and 30,000 copies; some sell a million over twenty years – such as Terry Eagleton's *Literary Theory* (1983) or the *Cours d'orthographe* by Édouard and Odette Bled, which sold 246,000 in its first year (1946), and 18 million by 1982.[20] Most fail.

— Some books, those we call 'classics', continue to sell long after the death of their author. In countries where the school curriculum is centrally decided, such as France, they can make any best-seller tremble. In 1964–66 dead authors achieving huge sales included – in order of popularity – Molière, Racine, Balzac, Corneille, Zola, Verne and Hugo:[21]

This ranking reflects the French national education curriculum. People do not choose to read Racine or Corneille. They have to. Some of the works of Balzac, Hugo and Zola would have been bought anyway and read for pleasure. In his lifetime Zola sold 1,775,000 copies of his works (see page 661). Sixty years after his death in 1902 he sold as many in only two years. Many of the best-sellers of the nineteenth century, such as Émile Gaboriau, Eugène Sue and Rétif de la Bretonne, have fallen by the wayside. Anne-Marie Thiesse, who conducted numerous interviews in the late 1970s with French people born at the end of the nineteenth century, noted that no one remembered having read two novels still regarded as universally popular in early-twentieth-century France, Adolphe d'Ennery's *Les Deux orphelines* (1887–89) and Xavier de Montépin's *La Porteuse de pain* (1884).[22]

Only Dumas and Verne, with no help from the educational authorities, hold sway in France and elsewhere.[23] The Marquis de Sade did well too, even though he was not taught in the *lycée*. But he was regarded as a good writer, and was studied in many universities. This enabled copies of works such as *Justine* (1791) to proliferate in cheap editions to be carried around with no shame even by those for whom Sade was classic masturbation material.

The lower price of books and the paperback revolution turned to the advantage of high culture, both past and modern classics. Between 1950 and 1980 Sartre (twice rejected by Gallimard) sold 2,470,000 books, more than Voltaire (2,276,949) but less than Hugo (4,166,213). In the same period Proust, who had to pay to get *Du Côté de chez Swann* published in 1913, sold 865,000 copies.[24]

In 1961 the *Bulletin du livre* published data on '*Les best sellers du siècle*' in France.[25] The journal admitted that the data were unreliable; it did not even have figures for some well-loved writers such as Marcel Pagnol. Nevertheless, the listing provided some rough parameters. Since a book published in 1900 would have had a sixty-year advantage over one published in 1960, it is not surprising to find reference works such as the dictionary/encyclopaedia *Petit Larousse illustré* at the top of the league, with twenty-five million sold. What is more significant is that, over sixty years, the best-selling novels had sold just over a million copies, a target now routinely reached in a single year by some best-sellers. The books which were above the million mark in 1960 include Saint-Exupéry's *Vol de nuit*, the humorous *Les Carnets du Major Thompson* (Pierre Daninos, 1954), and each of the nineteen 'Tintins' thus far published. Just below the million mark there were only two translations: Margaret Mitchell's *Gone with the Wind* (*Autant emporte le vent*) and the Italian *Don Camillo* by Giovanni Guareschi, which topped the list in 1955.[26] American sales were always higher, even in proportional terms. In 1967, according to *Publishers Weekly*, the paperback edition of Jacqueline Susann's *The Valley of the Dolls* sold 7.2 million. Since then book sales have expanded.

Former hegemonic countries often behave as if they were culturally self-sufficient. The 1989–90 list of the top twenty best-sellers in France consists exclusively of French books; in the six years between 1975 and 1980 we find few exceptions – one being Erica Jong's *Fear of Flying*.[27]

Great Britain appears to be even more linguistically insular. Little is translated and it is rare for a translation to reach the top hundred, though non-British writing in English encounters no such difficulties. The British best-seller list for 1994 (paperbacks only) was topped by *The Client* by John Grisham with 1,165,700 copies.[28] It was followed by the Australian Thomas Keneally's *Schindler's Ark* – a book originally published in 1982, when it won the Booker Prize. Its revival in 1994 was due to Steven Spielberg's award-winning film *Schindler's List*. The two dead authors in the top hundred also benefited from films: Mary Shelley's *Frankenstein*, thanks to Francis Ford Coppola's *Mary Shelley's Frankenstein*, and W.H. Auden's 'Tell Me the Truth About Love', a poem which, because it featured in the film *Four Weddings and a Funeral*, sold over 120,000 copies. In fifth place, just after Jilly Cooper's *The Man Who Made Husbands Jealous*, we find *Wild Swans* by Jung Chang (a Chinese writer who writes in English) and, lower down, Vikram Seth's *A Suitable Boy*. The top hundred list, though dominated by novels, also included some practical and self-help books such as *The Flowering Shrub Expert*, *The Greenhouse Expert* and *The Flower Arranging Expert* by D.G. Hessayon, as well as Anneka Rice's *100 Recipes in No Time at All* and Rosemary Conley's *Flat Stomach Plan*. Only one translation appeared in the list: Peter Hoeg's *Miss Smilla's Feeling for Snow*, a translation from Danish.

The situation had not changed significantly in 2004.[29] In the top hundred there was only one non-English book, a translation of the Brazilian Paulo Coelho's novel *Eleven Minutes*. Eighty-nine of the hundred paperback best-sellers were novels, half of them written by women. The top-selling book was, this time too, by an American: Dan Brown's *The Da Vinci Code*, which sold twice as many as Grisham (the 1994 winner). J.K. Rowling's Harry Potter books sell so many in hardback that they seldom make the top of the paperback list. There were eleven non-fiction books, including Bill Bryson's *Short History of Nearly Everything* (in third place), *You Are What You Eat*, Michael Moore's *Dude, Where's My Country?* and seven biographies or memoirs.

Non-fiction books do better in the long term. A listing of the American best-sellers for 1895–1975 published in 1977 shows the strength of books like Dr Spock's *The Common Sense Book of Baby and Child Care* (1946), erotic pseudo-confessions such as *The Happy Hooker* by Xaviera Hollander (1972) which, with a sale of 7.1 million, beat *Lady Chatterley's Lover* (1932) with 6.3 million. The Kinsey reports – both *Sexual Behavior in the Human Male* (1948) and *Sexual Behavior in the Human Female* (1953) did better, unsurprisingly, than the same author's previous effort, *Edible Wild Plants of Eastern North America* (1943). Kinsey's reports opened an era of less inhibited sex manuals such as *The Sensuous Woman* by 'J' (1969, 8.8 million) and *Everything You Always Wanted to Know About Sex, But Were Afraid to Ask* (1969, eight million). Some of these successes were ephemeral. As the field became crowded, it was more difficult for such books to make it to the top. *The Sensuous Woman* did not become a classic. Shelf life is longer for easy-to-read college classics such as George Orwell's *Nineteen-Eighty-Four*, which sold 8.1 million. Some serious novels were helped by films – a major factor in turning Boris Pasternak's *Dr Zhivago* (1958) into the only non-English-language book in the top hundred (ranked sixty-second).[30]

Lists like these provide pointers to the complexity of the mass market in books. They contain little else that is useful. There is not much that one can deduce from knowing that by 1975 Barry Goldwater's *The Conscience of a Conservative* (1960) had sold three million copies, as many as Ian Fleming's *Casino Royale* (1953). We know that people want advice books, political books, acceptable sex books, thrillers and adventure novels, and that if they have seen the film they may want to read the book. Yet one does not need a list to figure those things out. The list does not tell publishers which particular erotic novel or self-help book or spy story will triumph, and which will go straight from the printers to the pulping machines. In publishing the successes are known, the failures hidden. In Essex, England, there is a firm that handles almost 10 per cent of all books published – and shreds them. Every day trucks arrive carrying doomed titles – a 'literary death row' with little hope of a reprieve.[31]

The failures change from country to country. In 2003 the great diet best-seller in Britain and the USA was *The Atkins Diet*. Millions were sold. In France the book, duly translated, sold fewer than 20,000.[32] Diet books are not as popular in France as in the USA, and presumably the French follow the Atkins diet anyway: they eat, quite spontaneously, cheese, beef, butter and cream. The thriller writer Ken Follett, an international best-seller whose books are translated into many languages, has modest sales in France compared to his huge success in neighbouring Italy and Germany, where his masterpiece, *Pillars of the Earth* is one of the Germans' all-time favourites.

One does not have to buy books. In the nineteenth century, as we have seen (Chapter 17), people borrowed them. By the end of the twentieth century subscription libraries had almost disappeared, but a thriving network of public libraries existed almost everywhere in Europe.

NUMBER OF BOOKS IN
PUBLIC LIBRARIES PER THOUSAND
INHABITANTS IN SELECTED
COUNTRIES, 1991–94

Ukraine	772
Finland	712
Bulgaria	680
Sweden	513
Hungary	489
Norway	462
Poland	353
Ireland	309
Belgium	294
Holland	271
UK	223
Romania	204
Germany	158
France	154

NUMBER OF BOOKS IN
PUBLIC LIBRARIES PER THOUSAND
INHABITANTS IN SELECTED
COUNTRIES, 1991–94 – *continued*

Albania	127
Spain	76
Italy	48
Portugal	39

SOURCE: UNESCO, *World Culture Report*, 1998

We do not have reliable comparative statistics on borrowing, but the introduction of the Public Lending Right (whereby authors are paid a fee when their works are borrowed) has provided accurate statistics for Great Britain. These reveal that the most-borrowed books are books for children (thirty-two of the top hundred), thrillers and books read by women. In 2000–01 the list was topped by Catherine Cookson, and the top ten included the omnipresent Danielle Steel and Agatha Christie, Jack Higgins of Second World War thrillers' fame, Jacqueline Wilson who writes for young girls, and the crime writers Dick Francis and Ruth Rendell. The only non-Anglo-Saxon writer in the top hundred is Goscinny, the creator of Astérix (number sixty-three). Not a single author in the top hundred was part of the academic canon or could be regarded as a literary writer (such as a winner of a major literary prize).

In 2003 the BBC launched a competition called 'The Big Read', designed to find Britain's favourite book (or at least the favourite of some radio listeners). The German TV station ZDF followed suit with '*Das Grosse Lesen*'. The results were, as usual, influenced by the cinema, at least partially explaining the success of Tolkien's *Lord of the Rings* in both countries. Otherwise there is little in common, save the scarcity of books in the literary canon:

GREAT BRITAIN AND GERMANY, FAVOURITE BOOKS ACCORDING TO PREFERENCES
SUBMITTED TO THE BBC AND ZDF

BBC: '*The Big Read*'		ZDF: '*Das Grosse Lesen*'	
The Lord of the Rings (J.R.R. Tolkien)	UK	*The Lord of the Rings* (J.R.R. Tolkien)	UK

BBC: 'The Big Read'		ZDF: 'Das Grosse Lesen'	
Pride and Prejudice (Jane Austen)	UK	The Bible	n/a
His Dark Materials (Philip Pullman)	UK	The Pillars of the Earth (Ken Follett)	UK
The Hitchhiker's Guide to the Galaxy (Douglas Adams)	UK	Perfume (Patrick Süskind)	Germany
Harry Potter and the Goblet of Fire (J.K. Rowling)	UK	The Little Prince (Antoine de Saint-Exupéry)	France
To Kill a Mockingbird (Harper Lee)	US	Buddenbrooks (Thomas Mann)	Germany
Winnie the Pooh (A.A. Milne)	UK	The Physician (Noah Gordon)	USA
Nineteen-Eighty-Four (George Orwell)	UK	The Alchemist (Paulo Coelho)	Brazil
The Lion, the Witch and the Wardrobe (C.S. Lewis)	UK	Harry Potter and the Philosopher's Stone (J.K. Rowling)	UK
Jane Eyre (Charlotte Brontë)	UK	Pope Joan (Donna Cross)	US

The BBC list has nine British books and one American, while that of the ZDF contains only two German books. Topped by a British book set in an imaginary 'Middle Earth', the German list has, after the Bible (excluded from the BBC list), a massive novel centred around the building of cathedrals in the Middle Ages by the British Ken Follett. In fifth position is a French book aimed at children, in eighth a Brazilian best-seller, and then there is Harry Potter, yet another success which enabled Great Britain to maintain unchallenged its century-old global dominance in the genre of children's books.

J.K. Rowling's Harry Potter series turned out to be the biggest-selling books ever. According to Nielsen Bookscan figures, the fifth book of the series (Harry Potter and the Order of the Phoenix) sold in the UK 1.8 million copies on the day it came out (21 June 2003). By 2005, before the publication of the sixth novel, Harry Potter and the Half-Blood Prince (16 July 2005), the five books had sold 270 million copies in sixty-two languages. The films helped, but the huge sales pre-existed the films. As is always the case, we have absolutely no idea how many people, and in particular how many children, actually read them, particularly since some, such as The Order of the Phoenix, are very long.

The books' detractors point to the conventionality of the setting: the series tells the story of a boy in an English public school – a favoured genre since Thomas Hughes's *Tom Brown's Schooldays* (1857) – though Harry's school is for wizards. Harry is a hero, but seems to be weak and shy (he wears glasses); his guardians (Harry's real, dead parents were 'superior' – a standard fairy tale trope) and their son, the awful Dudley, treat our hero as the Ugly Sisters treated Cinderella. Harry launches into quests, undergoes trials, makes friends, successfully challenges baddies, and so on. The books' success rests on centuries of fairy tales. 'For anything to become a phenomenon in Western society, it must become conventional,' argued Jack Zipes, a scholar of the fairy tale.[33] But since all the elements of the conventional novel are at the disposal of all writers, and not just of Rowling, it remains to be discovered why she managed to triumph where so many others failed. For most writers for children fail. A survey of children's authors undertaken on behalf of the British booksellers Waterstone's found that 7 per cent (all women) earned nothing at all from their writing in 2004, 49 per cent earned less than £15,000, 26 per cent earned between £15,000 and £30,000, and 17 per cent earned over £30,000.[34] As for J.K. Rowling, she is reputed to be the richest woman in the United Kingdom.

Jack Zipes has suggested that the Harry Potter 'phenomenon' must be seen in a wider context, namely that surrounding the author and her work. Harry's adventure is also the adventure of the author, J.K. Rowling, who was a single mother on welfare, working hard writing books, who struck it rich (the 'rags to riches' story) and of the book, which was rejected by several publishers before finding the 'right' publishers. Provoking the fury of Christian fundamentalists who denounced the books as pagan added further impetus to sales.[35] Less obtuse Christians would have applauded Harry Potter, whose integrity and personal code of honour resemble those of a medieval knight in shining armour, and who receives the admiration and plaudits of so many of the girls in the novels – most of whom are mere accessories to his exploits, in the same way as the ladies in traditional fairy tales.

The defenders of the Harry Potter books remain convinced that they inspire children to read. Many teachers regard them as a valuable educational resource: 84 per cent of them say that they have improved children's reading skills.[36] None of this establishes how many Harry Potter books children actually read, but it certainly suggests that the view that children do not read books any more needs some more empirical backing.

Translations

Hegemonic countries are provincial, inward-looking and narcissistic. In 2004–05, domestic authors wrote 61 per cent of all books sold in the UK. In the USA the figure was 91 per cent; in Germany 24 per cent. To be in possession of an inward-looking mentality is a common accusation levelled at the USA. It is, nonetheless, quite true. This has nothing to do with the American 'character', and much to do with its domestic production. No one needs to import what it can do without. Besides, in this case importing often means translating, and translation is an added cost in an uncertain business.

The USA is not alone. While the Spanish publishing industry spends 1.1 per cent of its total expenditure on translations, and Italy 1 per cent, France spends 0.5 per cent, Germany 0.3 per cent, and Britain only 0.2 per cent.[37] British and American publishers do not need to commission translations; they just buy books from each other. Britain is at the bottom of the various league tables of translations because of the large number of books available in the English language. The British do not read only 'British' books, but they read almost exclusively books originally written in English. Most of the importations come from the United States, others from Australia and Canada, and many are written in English by Indians or Africans. The result is the very low British position in the translation league:

TRANSLATIONS IN SELECTED EUROPEAN COUNTRIES, 1991

	France	Great Britain	Italy	Spain	Germany	Total
Total titles published	24,909	63,867	33,893	42,207	61,015	225,891
Translations	4,406	1,625	8,602	10,977	8,321	33,931
Translations as a percentage of the total	17.6	2.5	25	26	14	15

SOURCE: Ganne and Minon, 'Géographies de la traduction', using data from BIPE, Whitakers, ISTAT and Spain's Ministry of Culture

Britain is not particularly culturally deprived. In 1990–91 it published more new titles than any country in Europe, 49,900, just above Germany (48,879) and much more than Spain (33,183), Italy (22,654) and France (16,578). In percentage terms, small, wealthy countries translate more books than large ones. As they are small, they cannot produce a wide range; as they are rich, they can afford to translate. Thus Holland translated, in 1989, 24 per cent of its production, Denmark 18.9 per cent and Sweden 60 per cent.[38] Italy, in spite of having as many people as France, has a smaller book market, but those who buy books are better off than the average, and foreign authors are often more appreciated than local ones. The consequence is that foreign books sell proportionately more than Italian ones.[39]

Being a communist country, in this instance, can be of some help: in 1965 Albania (at the time regarded, quite justifiably, as the most isolated country in Europe), with 23.3 per cent translations, did better than Belgium with 22.3 per cent. However, at the bottom of the pile with the USA and Great Britain we find the USSR (provided we include only translations from non-Soviet languages).[40]

The leading 'target' languages, that is, the languages 'importing' foreign literature, are, in order of importance, German, Spanish, French, English and Japanese, followed by Dutch, Portuguese, Russian, Danish and Polish. English is by far the most translated language in the world.

TOP TEN LANGUAGES TRANSLATED

	Number of works in translation
English	813,739
French	154,506
German	136,597
Russian	88,637
Italian	45,921
Spanish	35,241
Swedish	26,522
Latin	14,111
Danish	13,650
Greek (ancient)	12,586

SOURCE: UNESCO, *Index Translationum*, cumulative online, accessed May 2005
http://databases.unesco.org/

Hegemonic languages export popular novelists and a few of their top classics. Thus, in English-language literature Agatha Christie, Barbara Cartland and Enid Blyton trump Shakespeare, and the French and Belgian comic-strip writers Goscinny and Uderzo (Astérix) and Hergé (Tintin) co-exist with

Balzac. The top ten German exports, however, contain only a single 'pulp' writer (Konsalik); the others are children's writers, theorists, a great name (Goethe), a guru novelist (Hesse) and a plain guru (Rudolf Steiner). The Italians have three modern novelists, two children's writers (Rodari, and Collodi of *Pinocchio* fame), one pulp writer (Salgari – see pages 700–2), three classics and one modern theologian (Cardinal Carlo Maria Martini). The Spanish list is far more 'high culture' than any of the others, as befits an international language which has contributed relatively little to world popular culture. It contains a successful writer of teaching books on drawing and painting (Parramon), a high-quality crime-story writer (Montalbán), and a string of highly regarded literary figures, including two Nobel Prize-winners (Neruda and García Márquez) and a great classic (Cervantes). The Spanish list is also the most international: three Spanish writers, two Chilean, one Peruvian, two Argentinians and one Colombian.

TEN MOST TRANSLATED AUTHORS FROM FOUR SELECTED LANGUAGES

French	English	German	Spanish	Italian
Jules Verne	Agatha Christie	Jacob Grimm	Gabriel García Márquez	Umberto Eco
Alexandre Dumas	Enid Blyton	Wilhelm Grimm	Isabel Allende	Italo Calvino
Georges Simenon	Barbara Cartland	Karl Marx	Jorge Luis Borges	Emilio Salgari
René Goscinny	William Shakespeare	Rudolf Steiner	Mario Vargas Llosa	Alberto Moravia
Balzac	Danielle Steel	Friedrich Engels	Jose Maria Parramon	Gianni Rodari
Charles Perrault	Stephen King	Hermann Hesse	Cervantes	Carlo Collodi
Albert Camus	Isaac Asimov	Franz Kafka	Federico García Lorca	Dante
Hergé	Mark Twain	Friedrich Nietzsche	Pablo Neruda	Carlo Maria Martini
Antoine de Saint-Exupéry	Jack London	Goethe	Julio Cortazar	Boccaccio
Uderzo	Arthur Conan Doyle	Heinz G. Konsalik	Manuel Vázquez Montalbán	Machiavelli

SOURCE: UNESCO, *Index Translationum*, cumulative online, accessed May 2005

Such lists must be interpreted with great care. Since the ranking depends on the number of works translated, it is easier to make it to the top of the list by writing a hundred books, each each of which is translated into ten languages, than one book which is translated into a hundred languages. Thus Enid Blyton 'beats' Shakespeare, but Shakespeare may be more widely read. The numerous languages of the former USSR also contribute to distorting the figures, since many books were almost automatically translated into a variety of languages regardless of market demand. This explains why the 'works' of the Communist Party of the USSR would rank fiftieth among the most translated ever. It also explains why in 1969 Lenin was the most translated author in the world with 309 works, followed by Verne with 135, Simenon with 131, Shakespeare with 111, Enid Blyton with 103, Dostoevsky with 101, Karl Marx with ninety-one, Tolstoy with seventy-nine, Engels with seventy-eight, and Agatha Christie with seventy-seven.[41]

This makes the cumulative list of the ten most translated Russian authors a mixture of the political and the classics: Lenin is first, followed by Dostoevsky, Tolstoy and Chekhov followed by 'the USSR', 'the Communist Party' and Mikhail Gorbachev, then Pushkin and Gorky, who pip to the post the tenth 'author', the unlamented Leonid Brezhnev. This also explains why Lenin makes it to the list of top ten authors worldwide, and why Sigmund Freud is not in the top fifty. The most translated 'author' in the world, according to UNESCO, is the Walt Disney Company, but since this is a brand name rather than a single author, I have removed it from the list of worldwide most translated authors of all time, though I have left the Bible, beaten into second place by Agatha Christie. Here is the amended list of five men, four women and God.

TOP TEN MOST TRANSLATED AUTHORS

	Number of translations
Agatha Christie	5,649
The Bible	4,930
Jules Verne	3,688
Lenin	3,478
Barbara Cartland	3,222
Enid Blyton	3,221
Shakespeare	2,971
Hans Christian Andersen	2,335

TOP TEN MOST TRANSLATED AUTHORS – *continued*

	Number of translations
Danielle Steel	2,314
Jacob Grimm	2,197

SOURCE: UNESCO, *Index Translationum*, cumulative online, accessed May 2005
http://databases.unesco.org/xtrans.stat/xTransStat.a?VL1=A&top=50&lg=0

Nothing illustrates the expansion of the reading public more than the comparison between this cumulative list and that of the most translated authors in the period 1948–54. In 2005 there is only one high-culture name: Shakespeare. In 1948–54 the top ten were Tolstoy, Dickens, Balzac, Shakespeare, Verne, Dostoevsky, Hans Christian Andersen, Jack London, Pearl Buck and Robert Louis Stevenson.[42] The presence of so many illustrious names is an indication that the earlier reading public was still relatively restricted. If we go back to 1932–34 we find Edgar Wallace, P.G. Wodehouse, Galsworthy, Goethe, Jack London, Dumas, Tolstoy, Stefan Zweig, Virgil and Homer – that is, only one 'pulp' writer and a strong mix of middlebrow and high classics.[43] Some might infer that there has been a deterioration of standards, when in reality, given the huge expansion of the book market, regularly mapped out in UNESCO figures, what we face is the presence of new readers, people who, before, did not read anything at all or very little. Whether reading Agatha Christie is better than reading nothing, and taking a walk instead, is a matter of personal judgement.

The lists here highlight the domination of fiction. Self-help and non-fiction are of major importance, but do not have the staying power of novels. Poetry, as we all know, is what is 'lost in translation' and does not travel well, but poetry books, with a few exceptions, hardly ever make the top-selling lists even in their own country of origin.

Classics cannot withstand the onslaught of the prolific writers. Homer, after all, 'wrote' only two books, Barbara Cartland wrote hundreds. If we had accurate lists for the most translated works, it is unlikely that a single Cartland novel would make it to near the top. Shakespeare's presence in virtually all lists must be of some comfort to his numerous supporters. The reasons for his advantages over rivals such as Dante and Goethe can be quickly enumerated: he wrote thirty-seven plays, straddling various genres (comedy, tragedy and history); he wrote them in English; they are short to read; since they are plays they can be seen as well as read; his works are easily adaptable into films, musicals and other plays; the conflicts he describes are fairly universal (envy, jealousy, ambition, lust, etc.).

Such lists cannot highlight the renown acquired by academic writers whose works are translated into relatively few languages but which are widely regarded as influential, such as those of the numerous French thinkers who have become established in the English-speaking world, from Jacques Derrida to Michel Foucault, from Gilles Deleuze to Claude Lévi-Strauss, from Pierre Bourdieu to Jean Baudrillard, Paul Ricoeur and Emanuel Levinas.[44] This 'market', largely controlled by academic élites, is subject to fashion just like less prestigious literature. An examination of the frequency of the occurrence of certain words in the titles of philosophical books reveals the popularity of anything with 'existence', 'existential' and 'existentialism' in its title in the years between the end of the war and 1958.[45] Then 'structure' and 'structural' became fashionable. Algirdas Julien Greimas was told by his publishers that he would sell an extra thousand copies of his forthcoming *Sémantique* if he added the word *structurale*. He did, and *Sémantique structurale* became a key text.[46] After 1968 *le structuralisme* began to wane, while 'discourse' became fashionable, along with 'post-modern' and 'identity'.

Great philosophers stay great, but some are greater than others at different times. Between 1966 and 1975, at least in France, Marx, Engels and Freud were at the top. In 1976–85 there was a revival of Hegel and Heidegger (and of St Thomas Aquinas). In 1986–94, while Freud stayed on top, Marx and Engels dropped out in favour of 'newcomers' such as Schopenauer, Aristotle, Plato, Kant and Spinoza. The sales of Gramsci, Marx and Lenin dropped in Italy along with the popularity of communism.

Marketing

Writers write books, but publishers sell them. This gives them some rights. They choose how to market the book so as to maximise sales. They suggest cuts and alterations. Sometimes they come up with a title. Sometimes it is a good one. Jean-Paul Sartre wanted to call his first novel *Mélancolie*. Gaston Gallimard proposed *La Nausée* (1938) and Sartre agreed.[47]

How are books sold? Unlike soap powder or banks or drinks or computers or even some films, few books receive massive advertising. Publishers rely on word of mouth, on reviews, debates, and mentions or extracts in newspapers. Nothing is better than a television or cinematic adaptation.

Before 1967 the sales of John Galsworthy's *The Forsyte Saga* (1922) were in the region of 2,000–2,500 a year; then, between January 1967 and November 1970, the nine novels sold, in total, 1.9 million copies. The reason is that between January and July 1967 the entire saga was shown on TV in twenty-six parts – and then again between September 1968 and March 1969. It was shown in France in 1970, resulting in Calmann-Lévy selling 400,000 copies.[48]

Anyone famous in one field can achieve literary success by explaining how he or she 'did it' – a real rags to riches story. If they can't write, someone else will write it for them. Hence the proliferation of books – often autobiographies – by singers, television personalities, journalists, singers, sportsmen and film stars. Authors line up to be in touch with their potential readership. They give interviews, take part in shows, and sit in bookshops to sign their books, trying not to look embarrassed.

The makers of a distinctive drink, such as Coca-Cola, invest huge resources in promotion, but they make a single commodity. Those who like it want exactly the same beverage – again and again. Books are different. A reader, having liked a book by Ken Follett, will want to replicate the pleasure by purchasing a similar book, either by the same author or in the same genre. The author's challenge lies in constructing a new book containing the old magic.

Publishers know that what has sold before will probably sell again, and what did not probably will not, but they cannot be sure. Some publish a thousand books a year, knowing that a few will lose money, some will make some, and lurking somewhere are best-sellers that will save the rest. Since most of the products will not survive long, it is necessary to replenish the stock, not only by getting reasonably successful authors to write more books, but by finding new ones. Publishers are torn between different strategies: to seek the best-seller at all costs, to average a 'reasonable' profit (10–15 per cent) per title, or to look to the long term. Prestigious houses go for the last option. Unable to pay large advances and take the risk that entails, they look for the quality which will sell over the long term. This was the message Gaston Gallimard (1881–1975), the great French publisher, handed on to his successors: to search for new talents and publish manuscripts whose success is uncertain. The mission of the enterprise, he said, consisted of establishing and augmenting a literary fund of quality, and not of obtaining quick profits from commercial successes without a long-term future. This, of course, required enlightened publishers or patient shareholders.[49] There are not many of either left.

A proliferation of literary prizes seeks out readers. The most prestigious, like the Goncourt in France, the Man Booker in Great Britain, the Viareggio in Italy, add considerably to sales of the winning or shortlisted titles. Others simply draw the attention of specialised readers. The list of prizes catalogued in the French *Guide des Prix Littéraires* (1972) runs to two hundred pages, from the famous to the highly specialised, such as the Prix Littéraire des Vins de St-Émilion for any book about wine, and in particular about St-Émilion. The winner gets a barrel of this sumptuous Bordeaux.

Today there are more readers than ever, but there are also more writers. At first they seek glory. Once published they seek money, dimly aware that few writers can live off their royalties – just as most actors are unemployed, dispiritedly waiting for a call that never comes. The new technologies and the greater leisure time have made life easier for aspiring writers. They write on a computer, and can thus easily improve the original draft without endlessly retyping it. They can make copies more easily. As a result, publishers are flooded by manuscripts. Some use readers to sort out this 'slush pile'. A tiny percentage is published. In Great Britain and the USA, literary agents are expected to play a major role in the selection process. Some publishing houses, notably in France, use a two-tier system of readers. The more humble ones are there to eliminate the absolute no-hopers. This can often be done in a few minutes.[50] Most bad books, they claim, are bad from the first sentence. There is no point hoping for a miracle.

Some highly successful books, particularly children's books, can generate sales in other markets. So-called merchandising, barely known in the nineteenth century, is now an important part of publishing. 'Thomas the Tank Engine', an engine with a human face, was created in 1942 by the Reverend W.H. Awdry, who lived long enough to die a rich vicar in 1997. The books were made more successful after 1984 by the animated television series *Thomas the Tank Engine and Friends*, narrated by, among others, Ringo Starr, and broadcast in 121 countries. In 1982 the television producer Britt Allcroft, a shrewd businesswoman, acquired the world rights for a specified period of time. Soon there were Thomas the Tank Engine cups, lunchboxes, pencils, pencil cases, train sets and videos. By 1998 twenty tons of cheese triangles depicting Thomas the Tank Engine were consumed in Britain each week, a stream of toys was on the market, and a Thomas the Tank Engine theme park opened in Japan. In 1996 the Britt Allcroft Company was floated on the stock exchange.[51]

Not all books are sold to be read. Some, such as reference books, manuals and encyclopaedias, are sold to be consulted. They also decorate the home and may eventually be read by the children and help them (or did until the advent of Google), with their homework. Famous classics published in multi-volume editions, beautifully bound in leather or pretend leather, are sold for obviously decorative purposes, particularly in countries where there are many non-readers, such as Italy, Greece and Spain. In Italy these *Grandi opere*, sometimes sold as separate magazines to be bought every week at a newsagent and then bound (thus resulting in a huge outlay), have been particularly successful.[52]

Since the 1980s various agreements fixing the price of books have been abolished all over Europe. As a result large bookshop chains were able to offer discounts, and many small bookshops disappeared. Selling books has never been easy. The stock is varied, and sales are unpredictable. Then came the supermarkets, now the largest sellers of books. They concentrated on the most popular books and could offer even greater discounts than bookshops. Many buyers are intimidated by 'normal' bookshops, but in a supermarket, as one is spending vast sums on groceries, a few pounds or euros or dollars on a book do not seem very significant. And the best-seller or the romantic novel is carted away along with the frozen fish and the fresh fruit. The more technologically minded can order books from one of the many websites such as Amazon, which sell them at a discount and deliver them to one's home.

Concentration in retail is paralleled by the increasing concentration of publishers. A few large houses dominate the trade, leaving risky experimentation to smaller firms. The German publisher Bertelsmann, which began in business by selling hymn books in the nineteenth century, bought the American Random House in 1998, thereby scooping up in its net such prestigious publishing names as Knopf, Pantheon, Ballantine, Jonathan Cape and Chatto & Windus, and famous ones such as Fodor's Travel Guides. It is now the largest 'American' publisher. In Italy Mondadori, owned by Silvio Berlusconi, increased its domination of Italian publishing by buying a plethora of publishers including the prestigious (and left-wing) Einaudi. In Great Britain publishing is dominated by three firms: Random House (owned by Bertelsmann), Pearson (owner, *inter alia*, of Longman and Penguin) and HarperCollins (owned by Rupert Murdoch's News Corporation, and publishers of this book). These conglomerates also have stakes in private television networks, newspapers and magazines. And since, according to the British Council, there will be two billion people studying English by 2015, any English-language publisher has, with a potential market of one-third of the world's population, an enormous advantage over its competitors.[53]

Mergers and acquisitions have led to an unprecedented concentration of the media. Nationality has decreasing importance. In Great Britain this has been true for over a century, for the country has a long history of providing a fertile terrain for newspaper magnates from other parts of the English-speaking world. Alfred Harmsworth, later Lord Northcliffe, who acquired or founded the *Evening News* (1894), the *Daily Mail* (1896), the *Daily Mirror* (1903), the *Observer* (1905) and *The Times* (1908), was an Irishman born near Dublin. William Beaverbrook, a Canadian, became owner of the *Daily Express* (1916) and founder of the *Sunday Express* (1918) and the *Evening Standard* (1923). Another Canadian, Roy Thomson, took over the *Sunday Times* (1959) and *The Times* (1967). These press barons, however, always regarded Great Britain as the centre of their operation (Beaverbrook also became a politician of some importance). The following generation of magnates were true root-less global players. Their leading representative, the Australian-born Rupert Murdoch, unlike Harmsworth, Beaverbrook and Thomson, had no ambition to become a British Lord. Britain was a trampoline from where Murdoch, having expanded the family newspaper business in Australia, launched his global conquests. He began to penetrate the UK market in the late 1960s, buying the *Sun*, which he transformed into an uninhibited downmarket daily, and the Sunday *News of the World* – which could not be brought further downmarket. He then acquired the prestigious *Times* and *Sunday Times* (1981). From Britain Murdoch moved on to establish a media empire in the USA, becoming a US citizen to avoid American discrimination against foreigners owning major sections of their media. His News Corporation, created in 1980, acquired dailies such as the Chicago *Sun-Times*, various television stations (which eventually became part of his Fox Television network in 1986), and the Twentieth Century-Fox studios. He then expanded into Hong Kong, buying the *South China Morning Post* (1987, since sold) and acquiring, in 1993, a majority stake in the Hong Kong-based satellite broadcaster Star TV, and established the main British satellite broadcaster Sky TV (1983, now BskyB). He consolidated his publishing empire by acquiring and merging the American Harper & Row with the British William Collins, forming HarperCollins (1989).

The Mass Paperback

What sells?

Everyone knows that sex sells, but it is necessary is to package the sex scenes in a good narrative so that the main element of appeal of the book is the story, not the sex. Many people are reluctant to admit to themselves and others that they seek material for masturbatory fantasies. They want their sex packaged in sophistication, eroticism with undemanding elements of high culture. The book needs to be well-written and possibly French, like *Histoire d'O, Emmanuelle* and the more recent *La Vie sexuelle de Catherine B* (2001). *Emmanuelle* contains descriptions of sophisticated settings – the first-class cabin of an intercontinental aircraft, wealthy expat society in Thailand, lovely homes and quotations from authors such as Mallarmé, Goethe, Tennyson, Baudelaire, Homer and Dante.[54]

'True' stories of abused childhood, such as Dave Peltzer's *A Child Called 'It'* (2000) and Jane Elliot's *The Little Prisoner* (2005) sell well, just as they did in the days of Dickens's *Oliver Twist*, *Poil de Carotte* by Jules Renard and Hector Malot's lachrymose *Sans famille*. *Sans famille* (1878) tells the story of Remi, a foundling sold to a circus traveller with a troupe of animals, who is arrested while Remi falls in love with Lise, a dumb girl etc. Eventually his real parents are found; they are, of course, British aristocrats, and young Lise is cured of her infirmity.

Crime too sells more than ever. The setting need no longer be the English vicarage, foggy London or the streets of New York or Los Angeles. Crime novels can join forces with history and be set in seventh-century China with Robert van Gulik's Judge Dee, or in a twelfth-century monastery with Brother Cadfael, the monk created by Ellis Peters, or in ancient Egypt with the Egyptian scribe Huy (Anton Gill), or medieval Italy with the erudite Brother William of Baskerville in Umberto Eco's best-selling *The Name of the Rose*.

Self-help books have been a favourite genre since Baldissare Castiglione's *Il Cortigiano* (1528, on how to be a proper courtier). In June 2005 the new titles on offer from the USA included *The PMZ Way: Strategies of Highly Successful Real Estate Agents* by Michael P. Zagaris, who is, he claims, a highly successful estate agent; *Land of the Free, Home of the Brave* by Frankie Simons, who instructs us 'how to break free of fear' (i.e. drugs) and 'find true happiness'; and the highly practical *Take the Fear out of Intermediate Algebra* by Kimberly Neuberger. And as people get fat and 'thin is beautiful' rules, diet books sell more than ever. Spring 2005 saw the launch of *My Big Fat*

Greek Diet, The Body Clock Diet, The No Carbs After 5 p.m. Diet, Reprogramming the Overweight Mind, The Ultimate Weight Solution, The No-Grain Diet, The Traffic Light Diet, Eat Fat Lose Fat and, inevitably, *Beyond Atkins.*

In the last decades of the twentieth century the flood of women's romances – the much-vilified genre where women find the right man and make their dream come true – was as strong as ever. The profits of Mills & Boon, the British market leader, escalated by between 20 and 30 per cent throughout the 1960s.[55] In Italy, a country where, if we are to believe the statistics, few people read, the twenty-six titles a month of the publishing house Curcio's imprint Bluemoon sold nine million books a year, and the imprint Harmony produced thirty-two titles a month, also selling almost nine million copies a year. Harmony and Bluemoon do not have the prestige of Einaudi or Laterza, but in 1985 their share was 90 per cent of the Italian market in novels – or so it is claimed, statistics being unreliable in the murky business of publishing.[56] The Italian readers of these novels used to read the '*fotoromanzo*' or 'photo-novel' (see pages 1087–8). Education and wider literacy led many to tackle the more difficult genre of the non-illustrated novel.

Harmony is an imprint of Mondadori-Harlequin, a firm set up in 1981 by the Italian publishers and the Canadian Harlequin.[57] In France Hachette made a similar deal with Harlequin in 1985, thus granting Hachette a virtual monopoly in this genre. In Britain the great publishers of women's romance were Mills & Boon, founded in 1908 and taken over by Harlequin in 1971. Thus the romances Italian, French and British women (and those of much of the rest of Europe) read with such avidity are part of a global empire dominated by a Canadian firm founded in 1949 and now part of the Canadian Torstar Corporation. Harlequin claims to have sold 144 million books in 2003, publishing 110 titles a month in twenty-seven languages.[58] Twelve of these titles appeared on the *New York Times* best-selling list in 2004 for a combined total of forty-six weeks. Since its creation Harlequin has printed just under five billion books. In 1989, to mark the company's fortieth anniversary, every one of Harlequin's hundred foreign markets published the same book, *A Reason for Being* by Penny Jordan, on the same day.[59]

In France the market share of the modern sentimental novel is said to be 10 per cent of all books sold in the country. The genre, in France as elsewhere, is treated with complete contempt not just by most feminists, academics and critics, but even by women's periodicals such as *Elle* and *Cosmopolitan.* Yet such novels are read, in France alone, by three million women, half of whom are under the age of thirty-five. Each reader buys some ten novels a year, and would therefore qualify, by most definitions, as a middle-to-heavy reader.[60] While they read, their husbands and boyfriends, one surmises, watch sport on television.

With the Harlequin series one should also include the wider genre of women's romances, such as the best-selling novels of Barbara Cartland (who is often sold under an entirely separate imprint) and the more modern Danielle Steel. In France there is still a thriving market for the older pre-World War I French romances of Delly (a brother-and-sister team whose real surname is Petitjean de la Rosière, who wrote over a hundred novels). In Italy, Liala, who dominated the genre in the 1940s and 1950s (see pages 922–3), is still reprinted and read. The Harlequin genre, however, sells the brand, not the author. The author remains a shadowy figure with a woman's name or pseudonym, almost always Anglo-Saxon. The books are rarely reprinted.[61]

This is a highly dynamic genre which follows carefully the radical changes in morality and outlook of the last decades and the revolution in women's attitudes and perceptions brought about – at least in part – by the feminist revolution of the 1970s. In the late 1970s the ruling 'ideology' of the women's romance still decreed that the heroine should be a sexually inexperienced young woman. She had to be younger than the hero, was often an orphan or living with a sole parent, often her father. There was no sex between the hero and the heroine except for a few passionate kisses, harbinger of future delights.[62] There were exceptions, however. In *Price of Love* (1967) Paula, an older woman and a doctor, is pursued by a playboy. They eventually marry, and in his villa in the south of France she discovers the joys of sex:

> The dress fell around her feet and his hands came up to her breasts, his body close against hers, then he swung her into his arms and carried her to bed . . . Drying herself with a large fleecy towel, she inspected her body in the mirror, marvelling that it looked no different since last night. Memories coloured her cheeks and she savoured the joy of them. With what sensuous delight Jason had made love to her; awakening her to such tumultuous passion that everything had been forgotten except her overwhelming desire to become part of him.[63]

By the 1980s the heroine could be a young widow or a divorcee. Virginity was no longer central. The age difference decreased, physical relations increased, there was some nudity and even the occasional sexual intercourse.

Marriage was still the final aim. Adultery was still ruled out, as was homo-sexuality, or violence by men.[64]

The original framework remained intact. The narrative proceeds by having an omniscient narrator telling the story largely from the point of view of the heroine. She is beautiful, relatively well-educated, blonde, lower-middle-class or living in genteel poverty – in other words an idealised version of the readers. The hero is handsome and dark, lean and tall, hard-muscled and rich, with a strong jaw, a full head of hair, possibly a dash of French, Italian or Greek blood, a little cynicism and a glamorous inapproachability. He is capable of passion and tenderness. He is a professional, preferably an architect, though airline pilots, doctors, entrepreneurs, lawyers, journalists and composers are equally acceptable. Academics, unless they are scientists destined to save the world, are quite unacceptable. The men have higher social status than the women, who are nurses, secretaries, etc. However, they have some mild character defects, and are often initially attracted by the 'wrong' woman, often a brunette who is sexually more experienced than the heroine. The heroine's task is to get rid of her rival by the sheer strength of her goodness, and to get her man. In the process he is reformed and transformed from the flawed man he is – for all men have flaws – into a civilised human being, worthy of her love and dedication. Inevitably, she is successful.[65] Such novels are obviously different from the 'bodice-ripper' historical novels, which are longer, have more characters and are more explicit, and where the heroine is often raped or nearly raped.[66]

The Harlequin novels map out the various stages of the development of a relationship: the first meeting, the misunderstandings, the surge of desire, the rejection, the lack of trust, the jealousy, the reconciliation, and the cathartic recognition of requited love. Each step follows logically from the previous one.[67] The narrative is simple and linear, with one major plotline and few secondary characters.[68]

This classic format is no longer dominant. In keeping with the expansion of the readership, the consequent fragmentation of the cultural world, and the popularity among women of books such as Jacqueline Susann's *Valley of the Dolls* (1966), eroticism became part of the genre. Women's romances proceeded cautiously. *Song in My Heart* by Rachel Lindsay, published by Mills & Boon in 1961, was regarded as a departure for the firm because the heroine is in love with a married man. She desires him ('If you want me, I'm yours. What's the use of pretending any more?'), but he remains 'decent' because it would not be fair on his wife. Luckily for both the wife is murdered by her lover and they can marry and have sex.[69]

The world – and romance – has moved on. Harlequin books are now divided into separate sub-genres, each keeping a connection with the original plot outline. One of the series, Blaze, is sexually explicit and aimed at the younger market. It contains scenes of masturbation, bondage and oral sex, and has titles such as *A Wicked Seduction*, *Body Contact* and *A Man for the Night*, in the last of which the heroine, Josie, hires a gigolo for her class reunion and gets him to work through a magazine list of the top ten 'women's fantasies'. Blaze is in competition with Black Lace, the erotic imprint launched by Virgin Publishing in 1993.[70] Major publishers, aware of the success of Harlequin, have produced their own competing series.

The most innovative aspect of Harlequin lies in its strategy of transforming readers into writers. Writers have almost always started out as avid readers of the kind of books they write. Since romantic novels are a 'low' genre, their readers are likely to lack the self-confidence to become writers themselves. Yet a genre can be successful only if its writers do not despise the readers, but share their hopes and dreams. Harlequin actively solicits and encourages readers to become writers. Its website has 'learn to write' pages describing the different kind of imprints – Blaze is for those who regard themselves as a '*Cosmo* girl at heart' and enjoy the television programme *Sex and the City*: 'The Blaze line of red-hot reads ... features sensuous, highly romantic, innovative stories that are sexy in premise and execution ... writers can push the boundaries in terms of characterisation, plot and explicitness.'

Yet the traditional romance is not dead. The website informs potential writers that it should be seen as a celebration 'of women's experiences in life, and especially in love set against a variety of international settings', that it should be written in the third person, from the heroine's viewpoint, and that 'a strong, charismatic hero is essential'. The key feature of the traditional romance, however, is that

> readers must be able to identify intimately with a believable, engaging heroine. Stories should capture the rush of excitement as the couple strives to overcome the emotional barriers keeping them apart. These conflicts should be contemporary and relevant to today's women. Whilst sexual description won't be explicit, there should be an edge of sensual tension.

This will not please everyone. Self-assertive women can opt for the imprint Silhouette Bombshell, which

features an emotionally complex heroine whom female readers can identify and empathise with. In addition, the Silhouette Bombshell heroine
has some special skill or talent. That skill can be physical, like weaponry
or martial arts, or it can be intellectual . . . She can be an ordinary woman
called into an extraordinary situation, like a flight attendant who must
suddenly rely on her survival training to keep her fellow plane crash
survivors alive. The main thing is that your heroine be smart and capable,
with the kind of confidence that every woman dreams of carrying into
her own life.

Aspiring writers are encouraged to send a letter with some biographical
details and a two-page synopsis. Alternatively they can send a manuscript
which will be submitted to the company's 'romance writing experts', i.e.
editors, who will assess it, at a price ($1 a page), and return it within six to
eight weeks with a two- or three-page critique.[71] This had long been a Mills
& Boon policy, whose guidelines had been available for years (in cassette
form in 1986).[72] Thus the democratic dream, every reader a writer, becomes
the goal of the largest purveyor of romance in the world. There are ironies
so ironic that they need no labouring.

Women's romances were among the genres virtually banned in the
former communist world by an informal alliance between communist ideology and high-culture intellectual prejudice. The West decried, and justly so,
the persecution of writers and the restrictions imposed on their freedom of
expression, but the repression of mass 'pulp' literature was seldom lamented.
In the German Democratic Republic people could watch West German
television, but they were not able to find what was easily available on the
other side: the *Heftromane* – a '*Trivialliteratur*' demarcated from 'nobler'
genres not only by its content but by its format: the *Heftroman* is, in effect,
a short booklet (usually sixty-four pages) in A5 format, bound in soft covers,
devoid of a spine (like a pamphlet – *Heft* means booklet) and sold at newsagents every week. These 'pulp' novels were, in effect, the modern heirs to
the 'penny dreadful' literature of the nineteenth century. Since the early
1950s, 162 different series had become available in West Germany, including
the main popular fictional genres: romantic, '*Heimat*', aristocratic, wild west,
science fiction, Gothic, mystery, medical or military. The series were known
mainly by the name of the leading character rather than that of the author
(often a team of writers).[73] This was big business published by specialised
houses such as Bastei Verlag, Kelter-Verlag, Pabel-Moewig and CORA-Verlag
of Hamburg in a joint venture with Harlequin.

In the DDR some concessions towards pulp literature were made in the

1980s, before the fall of the Wall, when Karl May's western novels were republished, but it was only after unification that one could finally read all the *Heftromane*, whether sentimental novels, erotic stories, historical romances for men (*Männerromane*) or the kind of women's romances published by Harlequin (*Frauenromane*). The DDR had, traditionally, had a higher percentage of readers than the Federal Republic, in keeping with the strong communist commitment towards transforming the country into a *Leseland*, a 'land of reading'.[74] Many of the older readers remembered pre-war popular literature: the booklets depicting the adventures of Buffalo Bill, John Kling, Frank Allen and, during the Nazi era, Sun Koh – all aimed at teenagers. The women had read *Trotzköpchen*, *Nesthäkchen*, *Pucki* and Johanna Spyri's *Heidi*, and the novels of E. Marlitt (see page 348) and the ever-popular Hedwig Courths-Mahler (1867–1950), author of love stories such as the best-selling *Ich lasse Dich nicht* (I Will Not Leave You, 1912) one of over 208 novels, mainly about marrying the right man and climbing up the social ladder.

For those born and bred in the DDR, the *Heftroman* was a novelty. In their previous incarnation as citizens of the German Democratic Republic they had become familiar with the works of Maupassant, Zola, Hans Fallada, Dumas and Dostoevsky. When reunited with the Federal Republic, as a survey carried out by Cordula Günther suggested, they discovered the Gothic stories featuring 'John Sinclair' (all written by Helmut Rellergerd, who signs himself 'Jason Dark'), an English *Geisterjäger* or ghostbuster who pursues demons relentlessly. The publishers print and sell some 62,000 a week, and since there have been more than 1,200 booklets so far, one can estimate a total sale of more than seventy-four million. Those who do not like stories about demons and witches can read about dashing doctors like 'Dr Norden', or the hard-boiled crime series about the FBI agent 'Jerry Cotton', set in the USA, or the science fiction stories of 'Perry Rhodan' and, above all, the romantic novelist of yesteryear, Hedwig Courths-Mahler – still a favourite of older women. Even many of those who in the days of the DDR had read serious West German authors such as Heinrich Böll and Günter Grass now admitted to reading 'light' novels as relaxation after a hard day at work.

The DDR had, of course, made available the more intellectually acceptable detective stories and science fiction (Edgar Allan Poe, Conan Doyle, Georges Simenon, Isaac Asimov, etc.), but not the *Heftromane* of 'John Sinclair', 'Perry Rhodan' and 'Dr Norden'. East Germans had been spared or deprived of novels featuring 'Jerry Cotton', whose more recent books have titles such as *Der Kokain-Baron* (The Cocaine Baron), *Die Prinzessin aus der Bronx* (The Princess of the Bronx), *Der Rattenfänger von Brooklyn* (The Rat-Catcher of Brooklyn) and – updating the currency – *Eine Milliarde Euro* (One Billion Euros). They could not read the various *Serie Romantik*, or the more explicit novels from CORA-Verlag (publishers of the Harlequin series Blaze), or the historical romances often set among nineteenth-century British aristocrats.

The stories of 'Perry Rhodan', written by a team of writers since 1961 and published every week, describe the adventures of the immortal American commander of a spaceship who combats cosmic evil. It is claimed to be the sci-fi series with the largest print run worldwide, has more than a hundred fan clubs around the world and is published in France, the Netherlands, the Czech Republic, Brazil and Japan, but is no longer available in the English-speaking world. When one has Star Trek, one does not need 'Perry Rhodan'.

Those who read these books, Cordula Günther's survey suggests, did not necessarily stop reading the 'good' literature they had grown up with. A proportion of modern readers are truly representative of the culturally fragmented world: they encounter culture not as a totality to be embraced, but occupy several cultural niches. Just as traditional intellectuals use to read the occasional detective story between Robert Musil and James Joyce, so many 'ordinary' readers exhibit a similar omnivorous approach, alternating serious literary fiction with the kind of *Heimat* novels in which, as the yodelling reverberates around snowy Alpine peaks, Gretchen professes her undying love for Helmut.

The readers of 'pulp' literature, as Harlequin realised and Cordula Günther's survey confirms, are perfectly adept at decoding the books they read. They are aware of the repetitive nature of the various genres, as well as of the variations constantly introduced within each sub-genre. What attracts them is not suspense about the happy ending – there is never any doubt that, as with Shakespeare's comedies, all's well that ends well, but how the plot will proceed towards the expected *dénouement*. The readers of mass-produced paperback books are not exploited or manipulated. They buy a product perfectly aware of what it contains. The unwritten contract between writers and readers is always fully respected.

Formulaic genres must meet readers' expectations. Thus in Italy in the 1950s, readers of detective stories expected authors to be Anglo-Saxons, since they were regarded as the masters of the genre. Mainstream publishers such as Mondadori, Garzanti and Longanesi had signed up the best of these writers, and small publishers could not compete. The obvious solution, adopted by EPI, a small publishing house in Rome, was to use pseudonyms. On 1 July 1955 they launched a series, I Narratori Americani del Brivido (American Writers of Suspense), whose first book was *Avventura a San Diego* by 'Larry Madison' (Giovanni Ugo Simonelli). By 1956, with six publishers in this market, seventy-six titles had been published – all written by Italians using pen names. By 1960 1,176 'spaghetti' detective stories had been published. By 1970 these small Roman publishers had published 3,000 titles. A single writer, Renato Carocci, wrote 126 novels in seven years. The sales of these books are not huge, and the profits are modest. The authors are often paid a flat fee – just like penny dreadful writers in the nineteenth century. Sometimes they are credited as 'translator'. The covers, almost unfailingly, show sex and violence (a semi-naked woman, guns, knives). The settings are always American or London/Scotland as seen on TV or at the cinema, in other words foggy, threatening, mysterious.[75]

These pulp Italian writers were following in the tradition of some distinguished French writers of the 1940s, when Boris Vian turned himself into 'Vernon Sullivan' and Léo Malet into 'Frank Harding' and 'Leo Latimer'. On the whole, however, few French writers disguised their national origins. This holds true even of one of the most popular series in French literature: the novels of 'San Antonio', known by the name of the leading character, *Commissaire* Antoine San Antonio of the French police. The author, Frédéric Dard, kept his name off the covers of the 174 novels he published between 1949 and 1999 (he died in 2000). The novels are the French equivalent of the hard-boiled genre. The hero is sexy, unattached and attractive to women. The style is unique, since it consists of an exasperated street slang almost all invented by the author. One of his characters, in the novel *Maman, les petits bateaux* (1975), explains: '*Me fais pas toujours chier comme quoi c'est pas français. Si t'es puriste, relis ta feuille d'impôts, elle, elle est en pur français, garanti académique, pauvre melon!*' Which could be loosely translated as: 'Don't piss me off, always telling me that's not French. If you're a purist, read your Inland Revenue form, that's in pure French, and guaranteed by the Academy, you sad old fruit!'

The 'total impression produced by the density of verbal invention, mixing of registers, amassing of references' and the 'deliberate linguistic embellishment' cannot fail to please some intellectuals.[76] Some 'pulp' novelists can have their high-culture cake and eat it too.

The Circulation of Dailies

The young do not read newspapers any more. 'The strongest determinant of daily reading is age,' according to Eurobarometer data.[77] And everyone else says so too. Income also has an effect. The higher one's income, the more likely one is to read a daily paper. Europe still has the highest newspaper readership and circulation in the world, but it might follow the fate of the American press, and decline gradually.

Yet the sales of newspapers throughout the world increased by 2 per cent in 2004, reaching a total of 395 million readers, according to figures from the World Association of Newspapers. Much of this increase, however, is concentrated in Asia, particularly in China. The largest European market, that of Great Britain, declined by 4.5 per cent in 2004 and by more than 11 per cent since 2000. The markets in expansion included those of Poland (up 15 per cent) and Portugal (6 per cent). Free newspapers expanded considerably. There were now, in the world, 112 funded exclusively by advertising, representing 40 per cent of the market in Spain, 29 per cent in Italy and 27 per cent in Denmark.[78]

The bigger markets have reached saturation. In November 1975 in Great Britain, the sales of dailies reached 14,230,000 copies (15,170,000 on Sundays). In November 1998 dailies sold 13,550,000 copies, the Sunday papers 14,424,190. In May 2005 the figures had dropped further: 11,653,000 dailies and 12,670,000 on Sundays. Old readers die, and are not replaced at the same rate. Television news and, more recently, internet news contribute to the overall stagnation. Advertisers have increasingly switched to the net, as have people (the *Guardian* online version, *Guardian Unlimited*, has between 700,000 and a million visitors a day).[79] To increase sales it is necessary to attract readers from one's competitors. As a result newspapers, particularly but not exclusively in Great Britain, are thicker than ever. On Sunday, following the US example, a huge amount of newsprint is purchased, with inserts and specialised supplements.[80]

Some newspapers catering to a potential worldwide readership have gone global, enormously helped by the development of English as a world language. The automatic typesetting machines and fast rotary presses that were the launchpad for the mass press of the late nineteenth century have been replaced by electronic typesetting systems. Journalists type their copy directly onto computers, making typesetters redundant. Data transmission made it possible to decentralise printing facilities. The *Financial Times* started an international edition in Frankfurt on 1 January 1979, made possible by the development of these new technologies. In 1998 the *FT* was printed simultaneously in Frankfurt, New York, Paris, Tokyo, Stockholm, Madrid, Los Angeles, Hong Kong, Milan and Chicago. By then it was selling more copies outside the UK than inside it. By 2004 the *FT* had become the world's most international newspaper (ahead of rivals such as the *Wall Street Journal*). It was printed in twenty-four cities, had correspondents in fifty-three countries and readers in 110. Its website, FT.com, had three million users each month – but only 76,000 paying subscribers.[81] The trend continued, with falling sales in the UK and rising sales abroad:

FINANCIAL TIMES CIRCULATION		
	November 1998	April 2005
Great Britain and Ireland	171,998	136,000
Europe (excl. UK), Middle East/Africa	112,585	133,000
North America	56,162	123,000
Asia and Australasia	13,899	35,000
TOTAL	**354,644**	**427,000**

SOURCE: *The Global FT* (insert) in *Financial Times*, 6 November 1998, and the *Observer*, 5 June 2005

Only Great Britain has a truly national popular press. Germany has only one true tabloid, *Bild-Zeitung*, while Britain has the *Sun*, the *Daily Mail*, the *Daily Mirror*, the *Daily Express* and the *Daily Star*, selling in 1997 a total of eleven million, against 4.4 million for *Bild*. The same goes for the Sunday tabloids: in 1997 the *News of the World*, the *Sunday Mirror*, the *People*, the *Mail on Sunday*, the *Sunday Express* and the *Sunday Sport* sold twelve million, while *Bild am Sonntag* sold 2.5 million. This 'tabloid' press (the name is increasingly a misnomer: serious dailies such as *The Times* and the *Independent* are now published in tabloid format; their success induced others – such as the *Guardian* – to change to a smaller format as well) uses a telegraphic style, plenty of pictures, a distinctively 'messy' front page. It highlights crime stories, the love affairs of celebrities, scandal and sport. Its mission is to amuse rather than to inform. It is thus not selling the same commodity as the serious press.

Attempts to start popular papers in other countries have met with mixed successes. In Italy, while the serious *La Repubblica* (candidate for the title of daily of the 'enlightened bourgeoisie') and *Il Giornale* (created by Indro Montanelli as a reaction to the alleged leftward shift of the *Corriere della sera* under the editorship of Piero Ottone) succeeded, the downmarket *L'Occhio* (1979) failed. In Spain the sensationalist *El Claro*, owned by the Springer Press (Germany), failed, while the upmarket pro-socialist *El País*, launched in 1976 shortly after Franco's death, quickly became the country's leading paper. In Switzerland *Blick*, launched in 1959 and modelled after the German tabloid *Bild-Zeitung*, reached, in 1967, the respectable circulation of 200,000 copies, but it sold predominantly in the countryside, and attempts to launch a second German-language tabloid failed.[82] What are successful, at least in Italy and Spain, are sports dailies such as the Spanish *Marca* (the largest-selling sports newspaper in Europe) and the Italian *Gazzetta dello sport* and *Corriere dello sport*.

Thanks to the success of the popular press, the circulation of dailies in Great Britain is much higher than in Italy:

GREAT BRITAIN: NEWSPAPER CIRCULATION, MAY 2005

Dailies	Circulation	Sundays	Circulation
Sun	3,230,000	News of the World	3,653,000
Daily Mail	2,259,000	Mail on Sunday	2,172,000
Daily Mirror	1,780,000	Sunday Mirror	1,545,000
Daily Telegraph	865,000	Sunday Times	1,335,000
Daily Star	862,000	People	932,000
Daily Express	837,000	Sunday Express	847,000
The Times	643,000	Sunday Telegraph	629,000
Daily Record	467,000	Sunday Mail	556,000
Guardian	346,000	Daily Star Sunday	420,000
Independent	228,000	Observer	412,000
Financial Times (UK only)	136,000	Independent on Sunday	169,000
TOTAL	**11,653,000**	TOTAL	**12,670,000**

SOURCE: Audit Bureau of Circulation (ABC)

The contrast with the circulation of newspapers in Italy is striking:

ITALY: NEWSPAPER CIRCULATION, OCTOBER 2002	
Corriere della sera	690,000
La Repubblica	624,000
Gazzetta dello sport (Mondays)	584,000
Il Sole 24 ore	415,000
La Stampa	398,000
Corriere dello sport (Mondays)	322,000
Il Messaggero	262,000
Il Giornale	217,000
Il Resto del Carlino	178,000
La Nazione	143,000
TOTAL	**3,833,000**

SOURCE: Mediaforum, Vol. 34, No. 2, 4 February 2003: Data ADS

Italian readers of daily papers are the equivalent of the British readers of the 'broadsheet' press. Without the popular press, British circulation figures for dailies would be down to 2,218,000 copies; without the sport dailies, the Italian figure would be 2,927,000 copies. The difference is not substantial. What this means is that the Italian counterparts of the British readers of tabloids do not read daily papers at all. In terms of their awareness of 'news' they may not be worse off if they watch the news on television regularly. A word count of the British press (all London-based dailies and Sundays as well as the *Scotsman* (Edinburgh) and the Glasgow *Herald*) showed that in the week 15–21 June 2003, 176,772 words were devoted to the transfer of the footballer David Beckham from Manchester United to Real Madrid, while the European Union constitution debate warranted only 38,039 words, the continuing fighting in Iraq 30,720 words, and Iran's nuclear ambitions 23,462 words.[83]

In theory the Italian press, unlike the British, should have room for expansion, but it faces the obstacle of a shrinking share of revenue because of the enormous spread of advertising-funded terrestrial private television stations. Much of the Italian press, however, is owned by industrial and commercial groups able to make good the inevitable deficits. Since some of these groups, such as Fiat, are in financial difficulties, the prospects are not rosy. To try to increase sales the two leading Italian dailies, the *Corriere della sera* and *La Repubblica*, have competed by offering readers a gift, either a videocassette, a CD (more recently a DVD, as elsewhere), a book or a game, sometimes by increasing the price of the paper, but by an amount inferior to the value of the 'gift'. This ploy was started by the communist daily *L'Unità*, which in 1985 succeeded in doubling its sales by offering, at a discount, a paperback of Gramsci's letters from prison.

Do dailies matter? The consensus is that they do. Since, in this field, perception is all-important, one should say that newspapers matter because people who matter think that they do. In politics, newspapers are important because they set the agenda for television. The explanation is that television news must maintain a greater degree of balance and objectivity than the daily press – an inheritance of television's monopolistic or semi-monopolistic origins. Newspapers provide television with the necessary 'cover': the morning newspaper headlines often become those of television, opinionated comments can be reported and attributed to their source, controversies first aired in newspapers can become matters of debate.

Newspapers are important also because politicians regard them as important. They are courted and feared. They are attributed great powers of persuasion. Leading journalists are regarded as 'opinion-makers', on the basis of a somewhat primitive notion of how opinions are arrived at. But politicians and their advisers, who seldom watch television, devour newspapers and take them seriously. Everyone does. Advertisers pay vast sums in the belief that newspapers matter. Actors and directors fear theatre and film critics. Restaurants hope to be noticed, writers to be mentioned.

Political columnists are the reviewers and critics of politicians. They provide arguments for television interviewers. They raise issues that might otherwise be forgotten. They are lobbied by supporters of good causes and the PR personnel of the rich and powerful. Their opinions reverberate around dinner tables and pubs. The newspaper columnist provides a one-way conversation of the kind that occurs in a bar room or a restaurant – with all the possible gradations of the genre – providing ammunition for its readers to sustain similar conversations. One thousand well-chosen words can reach hundreds of thousands of people (in Britain millions). Few books can match such a readership.

The evidence that newspapers make a huge difference to political life is not very strong, and is difficult to establish, allowing the debate about the power of the press to endure. The Italian left (socialists and communists) managed to be at least as strong, electorally, as the left in other countries without ever having the press on its side. The absence of Catholic dailies of any significance in Italy did not stop the Christian Democratic Party from ruling uninterruptedly from 1945 to 1992. The new parties that emerged in Europe since 1980 enjoyed very little press support. In Italy the separatist Northern League, ostracised by almost the entire press and boycotted by television, managed to obtain one-third of the northern vote in the 1990s. Silvio Berlusconi, thanks to money and television, started a political party that enabled him to win elections and become Prime Minister with little help from the press (other than his *Il Giornale* which is not one of the best-selling papers). The various xenophobic parties that have arisen in Austria, Holland and France had no or little press support. The 2005 referendum on the European constitution was lost in France and Holland even though the overwhelming majority of the press was in favour. Such evidence matters little, since it can always be argued that xenophobia or anti-Europeanism would be even more pronounced if the press took a different stand, or that the press is powerful in countries where there are strong popular dailies, such as Great Britain, and weak where there are none, as in Italy.

More generally, it might be argued that what really influences people is the agenda set by the press, the slant of the headlines, and the insistence on covering particular news. If criminal acts committed by immigrants are given undue prominence, then xenophobia might be encouraged even without a call to arms.

Magazines

The obituary of consumer magazines – a thriving genre – has often been written, as it has for books, the theatre, films and newspapers. The combination of television and the internet, it has been opined, will relegate magazines to the doctor's waiting room. Yet they continue to thrive, increasing in numbers and sales. In Great Britain alone, in 2004 over 8,000 titles were published, selling a total of 1.3 billion copies, 25 per cent more than in 1994.[84]

Magazines are big business, and an integral part of many European and international publishing groups. Germany, home of what may well be the world largest book publishers, Bertelsmann, is also the home of one of Europe's largest newspaper groups, the Springer Press, created by Axel Springer in 1946. In the 1950s Springer launched Germany's tabloid *Bild-Zeitung* and bought the more respectable *Die Welt*. By the late 1960s Springer controlled 40 per cent of West German newspapers, 80 per cent of regional newspapers, 90 per cent of Sunday newspapers, 50 per cent of periodicals including car magazines such as *Auto Bild*, the best-selling computer magazine in Germany, *Computer Bild*, women's periodicals such as *Bild der Frau* and *Allegra*, and music magazines such as *Musikexpress*. Like all other major groups it had sought to be become 'multimedia', acquiring television and radio stations and record companies. Since the fall of communism Springer has entered the eastern European market with alacrity, buying and revamping old newspapers and creating new ones. It bought, in 1997, seven out of the nineteen Hungarian provincial dailies; it launched in Poland women's magazines such as *Olivia* in 1998 and dailies such as *Fakt*, and took over publishers such as Automedia in the Czech Republic, Budapest Lapkiado in Hungary, and the Romanian magazine publisher LvB Invest International.[85] This foreign-oriented strategy has also been pursued by the other German multimedia conglomerate, Bertelsmann, which started its assault on the American and British publishing industries in the 1980s (see page 1302). The French Hachette has also entered the British market by buying Orion, which had formerly taken over Weidenfeld & Nicolson.

The various companies publishing magazines followed in the footsteps of these global organisations. The home market alone was not sufficient to sustain expensively produced glossies. It was necessary to seek transnational markets. The operating principle was that the various niche markets existing in each country were fairly homologous across the world. Middle-class teenagers, housewives, upwardly mobile young women, or young executives in Manila, Berlin, Rome, Buenos Aires, San Francisco and Tokyo had enough in common to read the same magazines. This is not new. In the nineteenth century some of the best-known French and British literary journals had an international clientele. There was enough in common among a particular segment of the upper-middle classes in Russia, the United States, France, Italy, Germany and Great Britain to constitute a large market. This principle applied with greater vigour at the end of the twentieth century, when the process of Westernisation had created wider cultural communities across traditional national boundaries.

Magazines were better suited than daily papers to tackle such transnational markets. Daily papers are still far too connected to national politics and culture to be global – indeed, in many instances the region is their focus. The exception to this, as we noted above, are business papers such as the *Financial Times* and the *Wall Street Journal*, or papers designated for an international readership such as the *International Herald Tribune*. Magazines are in a different category. They are often tailored to specific interests or lifestyles and, particularly the monthlies, have longer deadlines. Since advertising is their main source of revenue, the development of global brands has facilitated the worldwide spread of magazines.

The term 'magazines', of course, covers an enormous range of products. There are specialised weeklies dealing with hobbies from music to angling, from computers to hi fi. There are generic political weeklies printed on glossy paper, such as *L'Express* and *Le Nouvel observateur* in France, *Der Spiegel* in Germany and *L'Espresso* and *Panorama* in Italy – these last two, in a desperate attempt to increase sales and show that they are uninhibited and modern, regularly use photographs of naked women on their covers and in feature articles. 'Glossy' political weeklies do not exist in Great Britain, but the British non-glossy *Economist* has an international reputation and remarkable sales – though not in the league of glossy American weeklies such as *Time* and *Newsweek*.

There is, above all, an ever-proliferating mountain of women's magazines. Alongside the old well-established monthlies such as the French *Elle* and *Marie-Claire*, now global brands published in several languages (including, for instance, Greek), and distinctly old-fashioned periodicals such as *Woman's Own* in Great Britain, there is a plethora of magazines, many of which have an ephemeral life. Some of the British ones have been long-lasting: *Home and Chat*, born in 1895, survived until 1958; *Queen*, born in 1861, went on until 1970; *Modern Woman*, born in 1925, lasted until 1965; *Sincerely*, which started in 1858, merged with *True* (born in 1944) and died in 1984; *Weldon's Ladies' Journal* (1879) made it to 1954; and *Woman's World* (1903) disappeared in 1963. Most, however, lasted a decade or two. Some which did disappear, such as the *Tatler* (1709–1966), were soon resurrected (1968).[86]

The changing condition of women in Europe over the last forty or fifty years has led the large publishing groups that publish women's magazines to target niche markets. Before 1960, the world of female readers was less fragmented. There were three basic groups: the 'single girl', the middle-class married woman (catered for by magazines such as *Elle* in France or *The Lady* in Britain, where nannies advertised their services and whose circulation in 1968 was just over 70,000) and, thirdly, the working-class married woman with magazines such as *Woman's Own* (1937) – still selling one million copies in 1987. Then age and lifestyle became important. *Annabel* (1966) was addressed to the middle-class married market aged twenty-five to thirty-five, while the weekly *Petticoat* was for the young single girl (fourteen to nineteen years old). This last market was far from insignificant. Prospective advertisers in *Petticoat* were told in the mid-1960s that working teenage girls had more than £250 million a year of uncommitted spending money, including £8.5 million to spend on cosmetics, £33 million on clothes, £13 million on underwear, £22 million on stockings and £26 million on footwear.[87] A considerable sum, if accurate, since the *World's Press News* (a press trade magazine) of 4 March 1960 estimated the *entire* teenage market to be worth £1,000 million a year (including cinema, beer and tobacco).[88] Price was the clearest indicator of class. In 1968, among 'fashion' magazines, *Petticoat* (circulation 182,000) cost one shilling while *Fashion* (circulation 63,000) was four times as expensive. But price was also a function of frequency: *Petticoat* was a weekly, *Fashion* a monthly. In the end, the outlay was the same.[89]

As the number of women in higher education increased and their job prospects improved, new magazines, such as the graphically innovative *Nova* (1965), began to carry features specially designed to appeal to educated, intelligent and, above all, 'trendy' women.[90] *Nova* was marketed as 'The New Magazine for the New Woman' – at a time when the second wave of feminism had not yet erupted. It was edited by a man, Dennis Hackett (who previously edited another woman's magazine, *Queen*). Its peak circulation was 160,000 in 1966 – a reasonable figure for a publication aimed at the quality advertising market, like *Queen*, *Vogue* and *Harper's* – all of which were selling less than *Nova*.[91] As *Nova* became successful, others imitated it, and *Nova* did not look so attractively outrageous any more. By 1975 the success of *Cosmopolitan*, a new magazine for the sexually emancipated girl (launched in 1972), forced *Nova* to close down. The *Cosmo* girl was born, and with her a multiplicity of siblings, including the feminist *Spare Rib* (1972).

The trend towards the global publishing of women's magazines started around 1980. By 2003 Hachette (bought in 1981 by the French aerospace conglomerate Lagardère – a missile manufacturer) was producing its flagship magazine *Elle* in Brazil, Canada, China, the Czech Republic, Germany, India, Italy, Japan, Korea, Spain, Sweden and Taiwan. BEAP (British European Associated Publishers) launched the magazine *Caroline*, devoted to knitting, simultaneously in Belgium, France, Germany and Austria and Switzerland. The German publishers Gruhner & Jahr launched in Britain the magazine *Best*, backed by a £1.5 million advertising campaign and modelled on their French magazine *Femme actuelle*.[92] Later Spanish publishers went global with the celebrity-based *Hello!*, based on their *Hola!*.

By 2004 the panorama of women's magazines had changed considerably. British weeklies such as *Woman* and *Woman's Own*, which sold in the 1960s, respectively, 2.5 million and two million copies, were down to 524,000 and 435,000. Customers' loyalty was no longer as reliable as it once had been. Women's magazines fought fiercely for every niche in the market, and the national markets were still very strong, particularly for weeklies.

The strength of the feminine press in Great Britain was in stark contrast to that in countries such as France and Italy, probably because British working-class women read magazines, unlike their French and Italian counterparts. Any of the British women's weeklies would be in the top ten best-selling weeklies in Italy.

ITALIAN WEEKLIES, 2002		BRITISH WOMEN'S WEEKLY MAGAZINES, 2004	
Sorrisi e canzoni TV	1,438,000	*Take a Break*	1,200,000
Famiglia Cristiana	808,000	*Chat*	597,000
Oggi	714,000	*That's Life*	571,000
Gente	658,000	*Now*	565,000
Telesette	557,000	*Heat*	530,000
Panorama	556,000	*Woman*	524,000
Chi	513,000	*Closer*	477,000
Guida TV nuova	406,000	*OK!*	459,000
Espresso	394,000	*Woman's Own*	435,000
Telepiù	394,000	*Bella*	412,000

SOURCE: Italy: *Mediaforum*, Vol. 34, No. 24, February 2003: Data ADS for October 2002
Great Britain: ABC figures to June 2004

Heat and *Now* are celebrity magazines. *Closer* is a hybrid between the traditional weekly and the celebrity magazine and lists television programmes for the week. It reached a circulation of 477,000 a week a year after its launch. The main appeal of Italian magazines such as *Sorrisi e canzoni*, *Telesette*, *Guida TV nuova* and *Telepiù* is the extensive television listings, essential in a country with a proliferation of terrestrial television stations. *Espresso* and *Panorama* are glossy political weeklies. *Gente* and *Oggi* are mainly dedicated to celebrities and gossip and are read prevalently by women. *Famiglia Cristiana* is also read by women (probably middle-aged married women), but perhaps not bought by them, since it can be obtained free in many parish churches. Published by the Pia Società di San Paolo, an organisation created at the beginning of the twentieth century to preach the message of the Roman Catholic Church using mass communications, it has tried, rather successfully, to keep up with the times.[93]

In France too, the best-selling weeklies are those containing listings of television programmes. Even in the early 1980s, when there were only three channels, *Télé sept jours* sold 2.7 million copies and *Télé poche* 1.8 million. *Paris-Match* was still selling almost a million copies. The Catholic monthly *Messager du secour Catholique*, with almost a million a month, sold as much as *Marie Claire* and *Marie-France* combined.[94]

Women's magazines have been in existence for well over a hundred years. Men's magazines, at least in Europe, tended to be political and literary weeklies (the American *Esquire* and the *New Yorker* had few if any counterparts in Europe). Then in 1953 Hugh Hefner's *Playboy* started a vogue for soft-core prurient glossy magazines for men. This magazine became increasingly popular in the 1960s, as readers associated it with a hedonistic, uninhibited 'bachelor' lifestyle. Bare breasts – *Playboy*'s main selling point, in spite of its pretensions – were seldom seen in the daily press until the late 1960s. This helped *Playboy*'s circulation to reach almost seven million copies in 1973. The magazine made buying pictures of naked women acceptable because they were interlaced by well-written articles of genuine general interest, often written by literary heavyweights. *Playboy* would not hesitate to carry interviews with Miles Davis, Jean-Paul Sartre, Orson Welles, Fidel Castro, Bertrand Russell and Yasser Arafat, and articles by Gore Vidal, amidst incongruous depictions of scantily dressed 'playmates'. Then the competition closed in, an easy enough matter, since the formula could be easily imitated, and the escalation from the depiction of breasts to pubic hair was almost inevitable, while Sartre and Bertrand Russell could be dispensed with. However, being first had an advantage for *Playboy*: the cash generated could be invested in new media such as videocassettes and 'adult' television channels – though ventures such as 'The Playboy Club', with its waitresses dressed up like rabbits and its attendant merchandising (ties, cufflinks, cigarette lighters, etc.), would now look embarrassingly archaic. *Playboy*'s sales have slipped considerably since the 1970s, though it is available in local editions in a large number of countries, including Bulgaria, Slovenia, Croatia, Poland, Romania, Russia and Serbia, while it closed in Argentina (1995), Italy (2003), Norway (1999) and Turkey (1995).

The concept of 'men's' magazines evolved. Naked women remained *de rigueur*, but the focus – following the example of *Playboy* – shifted towards a lifestyle concept, which was essential, since a thriving advertising base was paramount to profitability. So was the globalisation of magazines. Lifestyle had become relatively homogeneous among an international class of young readers in executive posts, earning a good salary. Such homogenisation also cut across the gender gap, as an interest in clothes, scents and toiletries became part of the young executive lifestyle too. 'Lads' too began to worry about looking good, smelling good, and being good in bed. The ease of divorce, the growing number of those who remained or became single, and the need for a successful social life helped the spread of periodicals such as *Maxim*, *Loaded* and *FHM*. The older and more serious American men's magazines, such as *Esquire* and the more recent *GQ*, selling class rather than sex, found it increasingly difficult to compete.

In fact, the new breed of men's magazines is almost classless in outlook, as is the young executive market to which it is addressed. The imagined reader has no great intellectual pretensions, and probably feels far more comfortable in the company of other men than of women, in the belief that all men are the same at heart.[95]

This, however, is a highly unstable market, as is that of women's magazines. The cover is of the essence, since a considerable number of copies are bought on impulse at the newsagent. There is relatively little readers' loyalty – as compared with the daily press. The instability of the market can be ascertained by comparing the top-selling magazines of 1996 with those of 2004.

CIRCULATION OF MEN'S MAGAZINES IN GREAT BRITAIN

January–June 1996		July–December 2004	
Loaded (IPC)	238,000	FHM (Emap)	580,000
FHM (Emap)	181,000	Nuts (IPC)	275,000
GQ (Condé Nast)	131,000	Zoo (Emap)	240,000
The Face (Emap)	112,000	Maxim (Dennis)	234,000
Esquire (National Magazines)	107,000	Men's Health (National Magazines)	229,000
Arena (Emap)	93,000	Loaded (IPC)	220,000
		GQ (Condé Nast)	125,000

SOURCE: ABC, cited in www.magforum.com/mens2.htmfhm

SOURCE: *Guardian*, 21 February 2005

Loaded's lead in 1996 was due to its innovative outlook. It took some of the features of tabloid journalism – the idea of irreverent, streetwise, oversexed, beer-swilling, back-slapping, burping and farting 'lads' enjoying life – and packaged them into a glossy magazine. While *Esquire* and *GQ* taught men how to smell nice, dress well and have a conversation, *Loaded* asserted the aesthetic of smut, drink and football. Once someone else has thought of it, anyone can do it. An inevitable flood of 'lads'' magazines eroded *Loaded*'s advantage. Success is rapidly imitated and market shares are quickly gained and lost, which is why the solution is not to try to defend one's position, but to introduce new magazines. *Loaded* never went global, assuming that its Englishness would not travel. But Dennis Publishing, under the guidance of its owner, Felix Dennis, assumed that there were some universal traits to laddishness and took *Maxim* to the USA (obtaining a phenomenal success), France, Italy, Spain, Holland, Belgium, Greece and a host of other countries including, in 2004, China, with an edition in Mandarin and one in Cantonese.

For every success story there is a failure. *Jack* started in 2002 and closed in 2004; *Mondo* (2000), *Nine* (2002), *Escape* (1996), *Ego* (1999) and countless others folded after a few years.

The avowed strategy of one of the main British magazine conglomerates, Emap, has been to launch fewer, but bigger magazines each year. By 2005 it had achieved one major launch a year, but its aim is to 'establish a capability that will support two'. Twenty-one per cent of Emap's growth between 2000 and 2005 has come from new titles such as *Sneak, Closer* and *Zoo*.[96] Publication in English favoured British monthly magazines, since it gave them access to a worldwide market. Translations follow. The sector has a high degree of concentration: by 2005 most of the British magazines were in the hands of British and American companies such as Emap, IPC (part of Warner), National Magazines, Condé Nast and Dennis Publishing.

Emap plc, whose turnover is almost £1 billion (according to its annual report and accounts for 2005), also owns radio stations and online services and is in the conferences and exhibitions business. Consumer magazines (excluding, that is, trade magazines), however, are its core business, generating, worldwide, 52 per cent of its profits (of which 22 per cent are in France alone). Forty-three per cent of the group's revenue comes from advertising. Its staff is rather young – only 14 per cent are over forty-five. It claims to sell more magazines to men than any other publisher. It sells *Max, Classicars* and *Car*, which are all about cars, *Q*, which is about rock music, *Golf World* (about golf, unsurprisingly) and many others. There are in fact in Britain

3,500 magazines on offer. But it's the top two hundred that matter, for these account for 80 per cent of the market. Emap has thirty of these crucial two hundred titles. These are the ones stocked by the larger supermarkets – hence the difficulty for a small-circulation magazine to enter this fiercely competitive market. Supermarkets such as Tesco, Sainsbury, Asda and Morrison's sell 23 per cent of consumer magazines, with a further 15 per cent sold by the newspaper retailer W.H. Smith.[97]

The jewel in the crown of Emap is the men's magazine *FHM* (*For Him Magazine*), which was relaunched in 2004, becoming the top-selling men's monthly in the UK. The August 2005 issue contains advertising for watches, mobile phones, moisturisers, cars, fragrances, razors, Diet Coke, beer (but not champagne or cognac), deodorants, an advertisement from the National Health Service warning that smoking restricts the flow of blood to the penis, expensive crisps, gadgets, anti-dandruff shampoo, and brand-name clothes and shoes such as Levi's, Adidas, Ben Sherman and Ralph Lauren – but not truly expensive brands such as Louis Vuitton or Giorgio Armani – except for a single page where an £11,500 Rolex and a £587 pair of sunglasses are advertised, possibly as an indication of hoped-for future status. The readers are reasonably well-off bachelors, unencumbered with families, but are not seriously rich. Compare this to *Vanity Fair* of the same month, with its advertisements for Chanel, Veuve Cliquot, Bollinger, Rolex, Graff jewellery, Harrods, Gucci and Peroni beer (an ordinary beer in Italy, but a sign of connoisseurship in the USA and Great Britain).

In *FHM*, as in all its competitors, advertising dwarfs the contents which is mainly about sex, as its headlines suggest: 'Ask Tera. The Porno Star Supremo Answers the Questions Other Agony Aunts Just Can't'; 'Ladies' Confessions'; 'Girls on a Sofa'; 'Pamela Anderson. The Blonde Bombshell Supreme Allows us into her World'; 'Shameless'.

To sustain itself the magazine had to sell worldwide, in various languages, adapting its basic formula to different cultures. *FHM* by 2005 had become a global brand:

FHM CIRCULATION, 2005	
Australia	110,000
Denmark	29,000
France	179,000
Germany	216,000

FHM CIRCULATION, 2005 – *continued*

Hungary	39,000
Indonesia	50,000
Latvia	19,000
Malaysia	20,000
Mexico	55,000
Netherlands	51,000
Philippines	130,000
Romania	29,000
Russia	100,000
Singapore	32,000
Slovenia	15,000
South Africa	116,000
Spain	300,000
Taiwan	10,000
Turkey	22,000
UK	580,000
USA	1,235,000
TOTAL	3,337,000

SOURCE: http://www.fhm-international.com/contact.asp?num=31

Adaptation is the name of global culture. The Indonesian edition of *FHM*, aimed at the largest Muslim population in the world, is less sexual than its Western editions. There are no bare breasts, but the text differs little from the Western versions. *Cosmopolitan* does the same, instructing Indonesian ladies on 101 ways of reaching orgasm.[98] Thus such magazines help spread Western civilisation throughout the globe.

62

Exploding Pop

Sounds, Discs and Radio

THERE IS MUSIC EVERYWHERE. We wake up to radio tuned to a music station. We go to work listening to music in our car or commute with our Walkmans, Discmans or iPods plugged into our ears. We go to bars, pubs and restaurants, and there is music. We make a phone call and are put on hold to music. Our mobile phone rings with our favourite tune. We wait in a lounge, in an airport, in a hotel lobby, and there is music. We take a lift and there is music. Our planes take off and land to the sound of music. We visit shops or shopping malls, and there is music. We go to keep-fit classes and lift weights to the beat of music. We listen to music while we are doing household chores, eating, reading and making love. This music, freely available to everyone, belongs to someone. This music, so public, is private property. It is copyrighted. Singers, composers and, above all, companies make money out of the sound of music.[1]

Music has been around since the dawn of time. Yet before the Second World War the music industry was, financially speaking, relatively unimportant. Between 1950 and 1978 the sales of records in the West increased twenty-three times.[2] By 1994 the sales value of recordings amounted to almost $40 billion.[3] This was almost the size of the GNP of Bulgaria, Slovakia and the Czech Republic rolled together. In the European Union in the same year, some 857 million records, cassettes and CDs were bought, of which 239.9 million were bought in Great Britain, 213 million in Germany and 128 million in France, making the European Union close to being the largest music market in the world.[4]

WORLD RECORD SALES, MILLIONS OF UNITS

	1986	1995
USA	618	1,100
UK	198	267
Germany	176	252
Japan	177	416
Italy	42	44
Spain	38	53
Netherlands	33	44
USSR/Russia	136	83
Czechoslovakia	14	8
Brazil	71	75
India	n/a	303
China	110	123
WORLD TOTAL	2,290	3,349

SOURCE: Gronow and Saunio, *An International History of the Recording Industry*, using IFPI figures

The boom in popular music coincided with a new music genre, 'rock and roll' – a term whose sexual connotations were familiar to those acquainted with black American slang ('rock' and 'roll' being expressions for having sex). Its birthplace was the USA around 1955, and it displaced a jazz-based musical aesthetic which had made the fame and fortune of the likes of Frank Sinatra, Perry Como, Doris Day, Nat King Cole, Eddie Fisher, Frankie Lane and Johnnie Ray. The new names were Elvis Presley, Chuck Berry, the Platters, Bill Haley, Little Richard and Buddy Holly.[5] These made it to the top, and some have remained there years after their death, but none of them impeded the continuing existence of other musical expressions. 1964 may have been the year of the Beatles, but it was also the year of Petula Clark's great international success 'Downtown'.

The rock and roll revolution quickly arrived in Britain. In November 1954, Vera Lynn's 'My Son, My Son' occupied the number one spot in the *New Musical Express* singles charts. A year later, it was 'Rock Around the Clock' by Bill Haley and the Comets. Disseminated by radio and television stations and on cheap vinyl records, the new music had an audience that was younger, wealthier and less inhibited than its predecessors.

Radio found a new function as a purveyor of recorded music. Hours of broadcasting could be filled by acquiring records and having someone (the 'disc jockey', or DJ) introduce them and read the odd news bulletin and sponsorship announcement. The promotional powers of some DJs should not be underestimated. If a DJ was well-entrenched in a successful radio show, he could nudge a song towards the top of the charts.[6]

The pressures for the licensing of private radio stations proved irresistible. Even countries with a heavily regulated mass media, such as Holland in the 1950s, were allowed from 1959 to have programmes dedicated exclusively to pop music.[7] The role of radio in promoting music turned out to be crucial. Radio announcers and producers were courted and occasionally bribed to broadcast particular songs. Before radio, songs often became known because they were part of a musical (or, previously, an operetta or opera). Then they could be launched by a film, as was the case with Bill Haley's 'Rock Around the Clock' (1956), popularised by the film *Blackboard Jungle* (1955), which because it dealt with juvenile delinquency contributed to the 'dangerous' image of rock and roll. After that songs increasingly required radio broadcasting as well as the support of the huge specialised musical press, which wrote about the singers and produced charts. A huge number of periodical magazines came onto the market, mainly directed at budding musicians and music lovers and dealing with instruments (such as *Guitar Player*, 1967, *Modern Drummer*, 1977, and *Electronic Musician*, 1986) and all contributing to the formation of a cultural bond throughout the industry.[8] There was also a specialised musical press (but not aimed at the trade) which has been particularly thriving in Great Britain, ranging from the *New Musical Express* to the now defunct *Melody Maker* to Q. In addition a plethora of weeklies and monthlies as well as the daily press keep their readers informed with who is up and who is down (and who is up to what) in the world of popular music.

The increased prosperity of western Europe, North America and Japan fuelled the development of this massive music industry. It was helped by a succession of technological developments which made obsolescent a far wider range of products than in other cultural sectors. In the late 1940s people were still buying 78 rpm records, but they soon moved on to the 45 rpm format and, later, to the twelve-inch LP (33 rpm). All of such developments could be accommodated by gramophones bought in the late 1940s. A significant breakthrough occurred in the 1960s with the development of cassettes. This was achieved by Philips when it decided to make the innovation available to all – an intelligent strategic decision which blocked parallel non-compatible systems from emerging in the USA. As it was free, the Philips cassette became the standard, and Philips enjoyed its lead rather than the dubious advantage of a temporary monopoly. In 1978 Sony introduced a further refinement: the Walkman, a portable headset stereo system which played cassettes. Now one could isolate oneself and carry one's music around. One could be in a crowd and yet on one's own – almost the definition of modern individualism. The usual closed-minded critics rang the usual alarmist bells: 'But as long as they have the Walkman on, they cannot hear what the great tradition has to say. And, after its prolonged use, when they take it off, they find they are deaf.'[9] And those who wished the world to share their music walked around carrying a so-called 'ghetto blaster'.

In the 1980s compact discs (CD), developed by Philips, were introduced. This required the further purchase of a CD player, as well as the repurchase of one's music collection in the new format. Archival sounds could be remastered and sold once again. By 1992 vinyl album sales had plummeted to a fraction of what they were in 1981, and cassette sales had tripled. But between 1987 and 1992, CD sales increased almost five times. By 1995 CD sales accounted for 60 per cent of world units of album and singles, and 70 per cent of market value.[10] Recording companies had been able to sell most of their old stock several times over, at virtually no extra cost. The CD had given the industry a new lease of life.[11] An ICM poll commissioned in Britain by *Observer Music Monthly* in 2005 revealed that CDs formed the largest proportion of the music collection of 76 per cent of those interviewed. The newer digital MP3 players were the main format for only 5 per cent.[12]

Each of these innovations had further effects. In the 1950s people had a radio in their car, then they had a radio-cassette, then a CD with radio. To this one should add the improvements in home listening thanks to amplifiers, stereophony and speakers. By the end of the century a gainfully employed family in the West could easily purchase a modern sound system incorporating a CD player, an AM/FM radio, a turntable, one or two tape decks, three-way speakers, a digital clock and an assortment of adjusters and equalisers to modify the sound to one's taste. The entire thing could be regulated at a distance thanks to a remote control. By 1996 there was more than one CD player *per household* in Great Britain (which tops the league), Denmark, France, Norway, Sweden and Switzerland, though not yet in the USA, Canada or Japan.[13] Dissemination of music was further enhanced in the 1960s and 1970s by the multiplication of radio stations mainly devoted to music (including many that were illegal), and in the 1980s by dedicated satellite television channels such as MTV (Music Television) – arguably the world's biggest TV channel. Until the development of video promos and MTV, rock and roll musicians and singers were less comfortable on television than the crooners of the past, who were in their element – the television studio being too constraining for live rock and roll exuberance.[14] Video promos – soon one of the most important ways of promoting music – changed all this, since the fast editing and shooting speed originally devised for advertising were now available for a new genre. The new technologies (cable in particular) facilitated its spread.

Technology, however, has also brought about the most dangerous threat to the industry: the digital revolution and the development of the internet. The advent of computer downloading and CD 'burning' led to a considerable drop in the sales of home components such as stand-alone compact disc players and stereo amplifiers – down by almost 30 per cent in the USA in the first half of 2003.[15] Music can be made freely available on the internet and downloaded at home onto one's computer using a file compression software such as MP3 (short for Motion Picture Experts Group 1, Audio Layer 3), and thence to portable MP3 playback devices such as an iPod or by burning directly on to CDs. Home 'pirating', of course, had been available since the introduction of cheap cassette recorders in the 1960s, when the enormous sales of blank tapes revealed the scale of pirated recording – by the late 1970s this was the third most common way of listening to music (after buying legal copies and listening to the radio).[16] In 1993, well before the development of internet downloading, one hundred million illegal CDs and cassettes were sold in Europe, with Germany, Italy and Poland accounting for more than half of the pirate market.[17] It is estimated that in 1996 £3.1 billion-worth of recorded music was pirated, and that one in three CDs manufactured was sold illegally.[18] This was still the situation in June 2005, according to the International Federation of the Phonographic Industry (IFPI).[19]

The ease with which this 'piracy' can be achieved is due not just to technology but also to a psychological predisposition: though recording companies point out that copying a piece of music illegally is 'theft' (it is, in reality, a breach of copyright, and not theft), the vast majority of those who do so for their personal use do not feel the slightest guilt (only 33 per cent of the respondents to a 2005 survey in Britain regarded illegal downloading as 'wrong').[20] This is not a minor point: a 'crime' difficult to detect, easy to perpetrate and not regarded as immoral by a large group of people cannot be stopped. Such 'criminal' conduct (it is, in reality, a civil not a criminal offence) by so many people is further assisted by the knowledge that the music industry is dominated by a few large corporations. Few, in the age of the victory of capitalism, actually like them. 'Ripping them off' is regarded as fair game. This is not just victimless crime (as tax dodging may appear), but better (or worse), since one knows who the 'victims' are – large corporations and highly paid superstars – and the 'criminals' do not care (and some might even feel pleased). The industry is in a constant state of alarm. In 1999 *Wired* magazine reported that seventeen million MP3 files were downloaded from the net every day.[21] And that was in 1999. A typical editorial in *Music Business International* (February 2000) reads: 'Lest we forget: beating piracy is still priority number one.' Companies that have always promoted the ideology of technological progress and used it to move capital around the world complained that the same technology was being used against them. The downloading of music files thanks to Napster, a file sharing site, was an extension of the old principle of word of mouth. Just as one would exchange books with friends, music originally bought legally could be exchanged on the principle of P2P (peer-to-peer) with like-minded strangers.

The second factor behind 'piracy' is the very high price of CDs. A new disc costs almost $20 in the United States, yet it cost, in the mid-1990s, $1 to produce, $1 for the distribution, $1 or $2 to the artist, and $5 to the retailers.[22] The main reason behind the high prices is that virtually the entire cost of a recording (records, pre-recorded cassettes, CDs) occurs in making the original master tape (securing the artist, hiring producers, engineers, etc.). The more intelligent among the leaders of the industry, such Thomas Middelhoff, Chairman of Bertelsmann, broke rank with other music conglomerates and attempted to keep Napster going until a legal version of the file sharing service could be launched. His view was that Napster had created a new potential market, and that the only issue was to find a way for consumers to pay for it. Record labels, Middelhoff believed, should focus primarily on signing and developing talent and marketing their music.[23] Manufacturing records would become a thing of the past. Yet there is no hard evidence that downloading causes a fall in sales. The American rapper 50 Cent's *In Da Club* was much downloaded when it came out in 2003, yet it sold nine million albums.[24] Of course, it can always be argued that it would have sold more . . .

There was a legal crackdown on websites which gave away music. A deal was made with Napster which some saw as revolutionary and others as one of the 'follies of the interactive era'.[25] Napster went 'legal'. At the time of writing, legal downloading is available, but though it cuts out the cost of distribution and retailing, it still seems to be far too expensive, whether one pays per unit downloaded or buys a monthly subscription – downloading from iTunes (an Apple company) cost, in September 2004, £0.79 per track, from Napster between £0.88 and £1.09, or one could buy unlimited down-loads from Wippit (with very limited choice) for £50 a year.[26] Some, of course, argue that if you can get something for free no price is cheap enough. In 2005 P2P file sharing was still thriving, though this is likely to be curtailed by a US Supreme Court ruling which entitled recording companies to sue software companies encouraging their users to swap tracks. Time will tell.

Buying one track at a time completely subverts the idea of an album containing a number of tracks, since one needs to buy only the tracks one likes. It is as if one could buy from a newspaper site only the articles one might read.

Such problems confirm a particular feature of the music trade, that of being a software industry before the term was coined. Exporting and import-ing music seldom entailed the actual physical movement of goods. The real trade was always the licence agreement. What actually crosses a border is a master tape. This is used to manufacture records or tapes in the importing country, while the exporting company receives a royalty on sales. Manufac-turing can take place in a country where the records are not sold.

Studio Technology and Live Performance

Technology has not only had an effect on reproduction, but also on the production of music. Making music is now unthinkable without electro-acoustic manipulation. For centuries music was produced first of all for live performance; since the 1960s the production of recorded music became the main purpose of commercial music-making.[27]

Until the 1960s music performance was essentially in the hands of the singers and musicians themselves. They performed music written by composers. Then all three activities (composing, singing and musical accom-paniment) converged into one. Bands such as the Beatles and the Rolling Stones wrote their own songs, sang them, and accompanied themselves playing their own instruments. The music was not then known as 'rock' –

the term that came to be used generically in the late 1960s and early 1970s –
but as 'beat' music. The band, typically consisting of four or five members,
achieved a great sound intensity with an economy of means: two or three
electric guitars (one of the loudest instruments in existence, unlike its antecedent, the acoustic guitar, which is one of the softest), drums and occasionally an electric keyboard. Everything, voice and instrumentation, is highly
amplified, so that in a sense the sound system is an instrument too.[28]

The spread of music education in schools, the ease with which some
proficiency could be achieved in playing the instruments, and the widespread
peer-group prestige acquired by the performers led to the appearance of
such bands throughout Europe and North America. Formal education was
perfunctory. The music was learned by ear from records and the radio. The
manufacturers of equipment such as guitars, amplifiers, filters, loudspeakers
and other electronic acoustic apparatus expanded production. Melodic treatment was reduced, since compared to classical, folk and even jazz music,
most of the new live rock and pop music was very loud, typically ninety
decibels (120 is the pain threshold, a jet engine is 100 decibels and a vacuum
cleaner is eighty). The simple and highly repetitive rhythmic base provided
one of the music's essential appeals: the possibility of dancing to it. The lyrics
became less important – at least in comparison to the American songs of the
1930s and 1940s, and to singers with the diction of Bing Crosby, Frank Sinatra
and Ella Fitzgerald, or the 'text-poems' loved in France, so suggestive of an
underclass and a *demi-monde* of pimps and prostitutes. The distortion of
words, of course, is nothing new in international music – it is sufficient to
think of traditional opera.

Compared to the cost of writing a novel, the cost of forming a band was
high. One needed the instruments, a van to carry them, a place to practise –
which, given the volume, had to be either in the middle of nowhere or in a
well-insulated studio, or amongst tolerant neighbours.[29] However, some
modest income could accrue from performing in the proliferating dance
clubs. From the point of view of the industry this was an advantageous
situation, since considerable testing and selection took place outside the
industry, and at no cost at all to it.[30] Live performances were both a form of
advertisement and a source of income for bands, pending their hoped-for
entry into the 'real' music business and the sale of records.

Though pop music seemed to provide working-class youth with a possibility of financial and social advancement (like sport), pop bands were often
of a more middle-class background than their images suggest. This was

certainly so in France, where an investigation conducted among bands of the Nantes region showed that only 12 per cent were from working-class families.[31] The spread of such bands occurred even in small countries whose language and relative marginalisation in the global music industry made the prospect of international fame somewhat remote. Take Hungary in the late 1960s. The country appeared insulated from western Europe by its communist regime. Consumer goods were scarce. Rock music did not conform to the aesthetic principles upheld by the regime (which were almost indistinguishable from conventional 'bourgeois' taste). Yet in 1968 there were in Budapest alone over 1,200 bands, each with equipment of the value of 40,000 florins – the annual salary of a skilled worker.[32] Data made available in 1973–77 shows that the share of 'entertainment' music sold in Hungary was just over 70 per cent, that of serious music 20 per cent, while folk and 'labour' songs languished behind with only 7 per cent.[33] By the mid-1970s rock music was doing well in Hungary and was increasingly tolerated – even the rock opera *István, a király* (Stephen the King), contrary to the fears of its promoters, received official recognition.[34] Matters had been the same in Czechoslovakia in the 1960s. Czech rock groups looked to the West for inspiration, like those in the rest of Europe. They even adopted English names (Hell's Devils, Crazy Boys) just as Czech musicians in the eighteenth century had adopted Italian pseudonyms (Josef Myslivecek had turned himself into Venatorini).[35] The post-1968 repression slowed matters down, but in 1986 the first national rock festival was organised in Prague, and by 1989 – just as the entire system was about to collapse – there were 1,500 rock groups in Bohemia.[36]

The communist authorities did not like the new sound, but they did not wish to further alienate the young generation. In the West too there was much dislike, but then there was also money to be made. Western reactionaries joined forces, at least in spirit, with the communists in the east. Paul Johnson, eventually a fervent supporter of Thatcherism but in 1964 editor of the left-wing *New Statesman*, expressed what many thought after having watched a televised pop music concert:

> While the music is performed, the cameras linger savagely over the faces of the audience. What a bottomless chasm of vacuity they reveal! The huge faces, bloated with cheap confectionery and smeared with chain-store makeup, the open sagging mouths and glazed eyes, the hands mindlessly drumming in time to the music, the broken stiletto heels, the shoddy, stereotyped, 'with-it' clothes: here, apparently, is a collective portrait of a generation enslaved by a commercial machine ... Those

who flock around the Beatles, who scream themselves into hysteria, whose vacant faces flicker over the TV screen, are the least fortunate of their generation, the dull, the idle, the failures: their existence . . . is a fearful indictment of our education system.[37]

The views of the chief television critic of the *New York Times* on Elvis Presley's first television appearance in 1956 sound equally reluctant to come to terms with the *Zeitgeist*:

> Mr Presley has no discernible singing ability. His specialty is rhythm songs, which he renders in an undistinguished whine; his phrasing, if it can be called that, consists of the stereotyped variations that go with a beginner's aria in a bathtub.[38]

The crooners of the 1940s and 1950s had endeared themselves to their audiences by being smartly dressed and smiling enticingly. Their audiences behaved adoringly, as those of Liszt and Paganini had done over a hundred years before. In some instances, however, like Sinatra's in New York in 1957, they almost rioted. In the 1960s singers like Petula Clark exhibited restraint and modesty, allowing the sexual ambiguity of her songs to be revealed with circumspection.[39] The new sound and the performing of it, and the behaviour of the audiences, were quite different. It was often suggestive of sex and violence, with jerky movements by performers and public, sometimes to the accompaniment of intermittent stroboscopic lights. Accompanying a performance with gestures is far from unusual in music, including classical music and jazz. But the somewhat distracted and noisy operatic audience of the late eighteenth century (see pages 232–7) ignored the music. Pop and rock audiences, on the contrary, take an active part in the proceedings, accompanying the musicians by moving and dancing to their rhythm.

The avant-garde is, occasionally, prescient. The conductor Joseph Eger, keen on crossover between rock and classical music, suggested that John Cage's 'composition' *4′33* (1952), where the performers are silent and the music consists of whatever sounds there happen to be – including those generated by the restlessness of the audience – almost prefigured some pop concerts, such as those of the Beatles, where the fans scream so loudly that they cannot hear the music itself.[40]

The spread of American music was accompanied by changes on the dance floor. Hitherto dancing had been strictly for couples. With the advent of the 'twist', and the gyration of the hips and torso it involved, there was no need for any contact with one's partner. New ways had to be devised for exchanging sexual signals. Each dancer was isolated and yet part of an ensemble.

The suggestive movements, the outrageous clothes, the hints at violence, drugs and sex, and the shock expressed by the older generations and 'right-thinking' people, were powerful marketing tools in enticing the young generations to express their alleged alienation from modern society and their parents by the simple and harmless expedient of growing their hair (if male), wearing short skirts (if female) and liking the 'wrong' sort of music. And it got worse or better, according to one's point of view. The short-lived but still influential punk rock (1975–78) launched an aggressive style of music designed to shock and disgust, as the avant-garde had been trying to do for over fifty years. The most energetic exponents, the UK band the Sex Pistols, thrived on feeding the popular press with sensational stories, another case of the so-called underground society providing solid cash to the 'upper ground'. When the cover of their single 'God Save the Queen' portrayed the sovereign with a safety pin through her lip, it shot – in 1977, the Queen's Jubilee year – to the top of the charts.

The tremulous parents of the 1960s were spared the inevitable escalation which occurred when their own children became parents. They were spared a trail of fornication, drug addiction and various 'shocking' performances: Madonna simulating orgasm in a wedding dress while performing 'Like a Virgin' at a live show in 1984; or her video of 'Like a Prayer' (1989) which featured burning crosses, statues weeping blood and a black Jesus Christ (Vatican condemnation simply increased Madonna's already vast earnings). Then there was a rock star sending excrement in gift boxes to journalists who had annoyed him, and another welcoming visitors to his website with a feature showing himself masturbating.[41] Ozzy Osbourne, lead singer of the heavy metal group Black Sabbath, would pelt his audience with pigs' intestines and calves' livers, and once bit off the head of a bat thrown on stage by a fan. The band Frankie Goes to Hollywood had their song 'Relax' banned from the BBC in 1984 when it was realised that the lyrics were suggestive of oral sex ('When you want to suck to it/Relax don't do it/When you want to come/Come-oh oh oh/But shoot it in the right direction'). Needless to say, this contributed to propelling the song to the top of the UK singles charts.

Other singers, such as Christina Aguilera, tried to shock right-thinking people by wearing sexually provocative clothes – or hardly any, as when singing the song 'Dirrty' (2003). More disturbing was the appearance of 'rap music', occasionally homophobic and misogynist, frequently celebrating violence and drugs, by rap singers such as Eminem (Marshall Bruce Mathers III) and groups like 2 Live Crew, Public Enemy and NWA (Niggaz With

Attitude), whose notorious 'Fuck tha Police' provoked, understandably enough, the ire of the FBI. The reputation of rap singer 50 Cent was enhanced by the knowledge that he had been a crack dealer and had been shot nine times. There was always plenty of money to be made from any kind of modern youthful revolution. Even in the 1960s groups such as the Rolling Stones exploited this mood ably and intelligently, distinguishing themselves from the softer tunes of the Beatles. As Charlie Gillett put it: 'The Stones carved their own niche, and sat tight in it.'[42]

· The revolution, however, was not musically as deep as it seemed. The typical pop song is usually tonal, almost classical in its principal harmonies. The refrain sets the form and the couplets determine a progression. The words are less important than the arrangement and orchestration. Texts are usually banal, almost entirely borrowed from traditional poetic conventions: the key words, the meter, the rhymes and the repetition.[43] Though every generation remains convinced that 'their' music is original, there was a great deal of continuity from the 1980s through to the beginning of the twenty-first century. The Beatles were more innovatory, though. Many of their most successful songs had no introduction or build-up (as in a typical nineteenth-century aria), the opening musical phrases plunging directly into the movement.

Live performances, far from having been made obsolete by recording technology, continued to play a major role. In 1999, four million fans spending some £92 million, attended just fifteen pop concert venues in Great Britain.[44] During her three-year 'Living Proof Farewell Tour', which ended in 2005 (325 shows across North America, Europe and Australia), Cher sang to 2,880,000 fans and grossed $194 million.[45]

Live performances have a multiplicity of functions. Since music listening is prevalently in isolation (whether directly from radio or from recordings), a public space where fans and supporters get together is still required. It has symbolic functions as well as that of publicising the band's new output. As a result, in the era of reproducible sound there are more concerts than ever before. In 1994–95 there were in the (then) fifteen member states of the European Union some 305,000 pop concerts as well as 11,720 music venues. These were attended by millions of people (5.5 million in Italy and 9.9 million in Great Britain). Classical music was loved more than ever, with 85,000 concerts being performed by the 46,500 classical musicians operating in the EU.[46] Pop music was harnessed to the cause of 'making poverty history' in July 2005 when the Live8 concerts, an initiative by the rock star Bob Geldof, took place in a number of venues across the world (Tokyo, Johannesburg, London, Rome, Berlin, Moscow, Paris, Philadelphia and Barrie in Canada), drawing enormous live and television audiences. Twenty years previously, in June 1985, Geldof's Live Aid, a sixteen-hour concert held at Wembley Stadium, London, and JFK Stadium, Philadelphia, was broadcast around the world, raising vast sums for famine relief.

Every aspect of music production was geared to the production of records able to position themselves in the best-selling charts. Radio broadcasts were the main launching pad for new songs. If successful they would be played again and again. The business of making music became increasingly technical and studio-based. Technological improvement means that a single note can be re-recorded, not just a longer sequence. So a modern record is made up of tiny fragments with every passage played 'perfectly', something which can rarely be achieved live. The role of engineers in shaping sound had been pioneered in the recording of classical music in the early 1950s by Walter Legge, the artistic director of EMI records. Producers like George Martin (of Beatles fame) and Phil Spector (whose company released thirty-seven singles between 1961 and 1966, of which twenty-nine made the charts) 'created' songs by deciding where to position the microphones, and how to mix and blend the sounds.[47]

Such studio-centred production was further enhanced by the development of combining already existing recorded tracks ('sampling' and 'remixing') in new patterns, creating longer versions, often for use in dance clubs, and raising interesting issues for copyright legislation.[48] Early 'sampling' was used in hip hop, then, in 1987, sampling techniques were used by M/A/R/R/S – a group which also included mixers and DJs such as Chris MacIntosh and Dave Dorrell – to produce what became a mega-hit, 'Pump Up the Volume', a milestone in the development of dance music, the dominant form of music in the 1980s.

Much of this development was due to DJs. In some dance clubs they began to emancipate themselves from the modest role of choosing a piece of music to play to an audience. Some became stars in their own right, with thousands of people turning up at a venue because of the presence of a particular DJ. Originally the DJ had two turntable decks, so music could be played on one deck while the record was changed on the other one. The idea was to save time, but it also made it possible to merge two recordings seamlessly together (by manually coordinating the rhythm). Eventually, beginning in the 1970s, the sounds from the two decks began to be mixed, the vinyl records could be slowed down by hand, or 'scratched' by moving the portion of the groove containing a sharp sound, such as a drum snap, to and fro past the stylus by hand.[49] This use of the two decks, or 'turntablism', gave way to patterns of 'scratching' with names such as Flare, Orbit and the Crab. Such use of pre-recorded sounds offered the possibility of making new music without musical instruments, or rather, using the equipment itself as an instrument. It also transformed the DJ into a composer at a live performance. A high degree of spontaneity could be achieved, making each performance unique.

The new digital equipment, such as mixing desks, synthesisers and samplers, provided people with new ways of creating music at very little cost. Thus, along with the further concentration of the industry at the top end, small-scale producers were free to experiment without being too worried about copyright laws. As in other cultural fields, homogenised styles co-existed with avant-garde experimentation. The idea that techno music is little more than organised noise could be levelled, and has been, at contemporary 'serious' music.

Popular music was building, probably unknowingly, on the back of the kind of 'serious' music experimentation associated with the avant-garde studios of the 1940s and 1950s, and specifically with the French composer Pierre Schaeffer, who created music by manipulating tapes recorded with 'real sounds'. This he called *musique concrète*. Similar experiments were conducted in the early 1950s in Cologne, where Karlheinz Stockhausen and others constructed 'music' entirely from electronic sounds, and in Italy where Luciano Berio composed using electronically modified sounds. Some of these *musique concrète* techniques, such as the use of tapes played backwards and splicing, were later used by George Martin in the making of the Beatles's *Revolver* album (1966), which contained 'Eleanor Rigby' and 'Yellow Submarine'. The album, like the Rolling Stones' *Aftermath* (released in the same year), was more than a compendium of singles, it was, probably unconsciously, 'a self-contained work . . . its tracks working interdependently like movements in a classical concerto'.[50] The now legendary *Sergeant Pepper's Lonely Hearts Club Band* album, released in 1967, would not have been possible without the four-track tape recorder. The role of the music producer, such as Martin for the Beatles, became central because of the new possibilities for moulding the sound. Martin was even prepared (and able) to put in another drummer's sound if Ringo Starr's sound did not satisfy him when he recorded the Beatles's 'Love Me Do' in 1962.[51]

The upshot of this process, and of the drop in price of sequencers and synthesisers, was the popularity of the 'remix' – which can be a major revisitation of an original track, leaving little of the original recording (just like arrangements in classical music and jazz improvisation on an established theme). By the late 1990s a majority of singles released in the UK, in genres from rock to jazz, came with at least one remix. This also led to a proliferation of genres, not all musically distinguishable from each other, but useful marketing tools in an industry which is always on the lookout for novelties. In what seems a reproduction of the old contrast between high and low culture in other genres, 'pop' has become a generic term for generally acceptable, unproblematic popular music loved by pre-teenagers and young teenagers, such as the Spice Girls, while the more demanding genres, usually dance music, almost all originating in black communities of the USA, trade under names such as techno (fast, computerised repetitive sounds originating in black west Detroit, but since appropriated by whites), jungle (even faster, broken – off/up – beat, aimed at a dance audience), garage (a moderate jungle, allegedly named after a New York club, the Paradise Garage, a popular remix style, especially for R&B tunes), house (simple rhythm with some occasional jazz influence, 120 beats per minute), hard house (a cross-breed of house and techno, but faster – 140 beats per minute) and hip hop (originating in the south Bronx, using electronic snippets of funk records, at first a black American genre, in which a DJ plays snatches of a record in brief bursts, rhythmically scratching the needle on the record, while a 'rapper' recites, at top speed, a rhymed rhythmic speech or rap). Thanks to these developments, record producers such as Dr Dre (Andre Young), the author of studio-produced sound on albums such as *No Diggity*, a 1996 number one hit, *Chronic* (1997), and *2001* (2000), came to be regarded as the real creator – as the likes of Phil Spector had been for years.

New developments never entirely wiped out previous successes, since, as we have noted, each generation carries with it a selection of the music it liked when young (adding a few recruits along the way). The survivors from the selection, whether soul singers such as Nina Simone, rhythm and blues, rock and roll (Elvis, Chuck Berry), reggae (Bob Marley), the Beatles, Jimi Hendrix, the Doors and the various stars of each decade, came to constitute a popular music canon.

Industry and Singers

By the mid-1990s in Great Britain, the main world player in the music business after the USA, the music sector employed some 115,000 people, and generated private consumer spending of £2.9 billion. This meant that the music industry was much larger than the chemical industry or shipbuilding, and that the musicians' union was bigger than the miners' union, something regarded as impossible twenty years previously. At the time, in the Merseyside region, home of the Beatles, there were a thousand bands competing for the attention of a population of 1.5 million people. In London alone there were 377 separate venues for the live performance of popular music.[52]

Pop stars sell millions of records, but they also perform before the largest imaginable live audiences. The stars make the industry and the industry makes the stars. Marketing, promotion and 'hype' contribute to success, but as in most cultural matters, there is no way to be sure of picking winners, so companies concentrate on already-well-established artists with whom they have a contract and in whom they have already invested large sums. The general strategy is to promote a number of possible winners, in the hope that some will really win. This is an inescapable necessity: new talents must be continuously discovered, because very few stars remain on top for long.[53] They surge out of nowhere and rapidly become established. In 1992 the group Oasis gave only eight performances in Great Britain, seven of which were on 'home territory' (the north-west of England – the group's home town is Manchester). Their success was rapid. Between January 1994 and August 1996 Oasis gave eighty-seven concert performances in Britain and 144 overseas. Manchester saw them only twice.[54]

Superstars, of course, are a microscopic proportion of the profession, almost by definition. But they operate on a global scale, and even though they command huge royalties, they also offer the prospect of huge returns. Michael Jackson's *Thriller* album sold forty million copies and almost single-handedly revived lagging sales across the music industry in the mid-eighties.

No one knows how a particular performer becomes a superstar, just as no one knows what will be the next hit (all companies call their newest product 'the next hit', but in reality this is a hope based on past performance). Since only one in five record releases covers its costs (the advance, recording, manufacturing and distribution, advertising and promotion), superstars are nurtured and cherished. It has been estimated that the British record industry assumes that only one in eight of the artists who are signed and recorded will recoup the initial investment.[55] The other seven, presumably, are losers who will lose money – though of course they are necessary to find the eighth.

Companies remind everyone of their successes, but, understandably not of their failures. In any case, one can always have second thoughts. At first the US company Capitol Records, which had first rights to any British EMI releases, turned down the Beatles' records. As the group's popularity in the USA expanded, Capitol decided to release them, and spent what was then the large sum of $50,000 on the promotion campaign.[56] 'Love Me Do', the Beatles' debut single, number seventeen in Great Britain when first released, shot to the top of the US charts in April 1964, helping the Beatles accomplish the feat of occupying the top five positions in the *Billboard* singles chart.

Though everyone agrees that the key factor is that uncertain concept called 'word of mouth', this became quantified in the charts, the stock exchange of the music business. If everyone is buying it and if I can hear it everywhere, I should buy it too. But here previous success can pay. There is a bandwagon effect: since superstars sell more records, they also have more listeners, and these listeners can discuss their music with more people. In the mid-1990s shrewd superstars with good advisers, aware that they were the keystones to the global success of their record companies, obtained huge contracts: $65 million for Michael Jackson (Sony), $60 million for Madonna (Time Warner), $44 million for the Rolling Stones (EMI).[57] In 2002 the British rock star Robbie Williams signed a recording deal with EMI worth an estimated £80 million.

Big hits make a lot of money, but old favourites may bring in more than ephemeral successes. In France the song 'Pour un flirt' by Michel Delpech was all the rage in January 1973, and brought in performance rights of 63,400 francs (then a tidy sum), but by July 1973 its earnings had dropped to 21,700 francs, while in the same month 'La Cumparsita', an Argentinian tango written by Matéo Rodriguez in 1933, was still earning, thanks to its use in ballrooms, an average of 45–47,000 francs a month. Georges Brassens never made it to the top of the charts, but he sold 600,000 LPs year in year out.[58]

To be successful it is preferable to be already successful, and to hope that decline will be delayed for as long as possible. Decline is normal, but not inevitable. Footballers can't play much after their mid-thirties, but singers can go on and on even when their voice has been ruined by old age, as long as they have a loyal public, as Frank Sinatra demonstrated. One factor helps ageing superstars: their fans age too. As they get older they keep a nostalgic memory of the music of their youth, and resist new music (as their parents did before them). They now have more money to spend. They keep on playing the old music, and try some of the new albums of their old favourites. They discuss it with their friends. Occasionally they even succeed in influencing the younger generations, some of whom may even like it. As a result, groups like the Rolling Stones, though no longer in the charts as often as they once were, have a firm fan base, enjoy steady sales and frequently go on nostalgia tours. Some dead singers live on. 'Elvis Lives' may be a comforting slogan for his numerous admirers, but it rings true to record companies: in 1992 alone Elvis Presley sold 1,500,000 records, Jimi Hendrix 900,000 and Bob Marley 550,000.[59]

The career of Paul McCartney is emblematic. As a member of the Beatles, and as a co-author of nearly all of their 186 songs, he obtained unparalleled global success in the 1960s. But the Beatles lasted, in practice, only eight years. Then they became a legend. After the break-up of the band McCartney succeeded in scoring a number of hits with his band Wings (disbanded in 1981). His 1977 ballad 'Mull of Kintyre' sold 2.5 million copies in Britain alone. His world tour, 'Back to the World', staged in 2003 when he was just over sixty, attracted enormous audiences, including many young people who were not even born when the Beatles disbanded. In 2001 a collection of twenty-seven of their number one hit songs, called simply *The Beatles 1*, topped the charts in Britain and the USA.[60]

But how did the Beatles become famous in the first place? There were favourable circumstances. They were shaped by a world in which English had become an international language. After 1960 it became almost impossible for a song to become a global success in a language other than English. The Beatles were operating in a country where teenagers had become a highly distinctive identity group in advance of their peers in any other European nation (and thus closer to the USA). Britain was the home of EMI, one of the largest recording companies in the world. The country had no well-established tradition of pop songs and hence no well-entrenched set of interests. In a sense Britain had no distinctive musical voice. The French had their own special sound, as did the Italians. That of the Germans, in its popular form, was unexportable. What Britain did was to import American music. In culture the rule is that every massive import leads, sooner or later, to adaptation, and this is what happened in Britain. American music was sold in all British record stores; it could be heard on the radio, mainly Radio

Luxembourg, the various 'pirate' radio stations of the late 1950s and early 1960s, and even on the BBC. Then there were the Beatles' films.[61] And above all there was a language in common.

Liverpool, home of the Beatles, was traditionally closer to the USA than the rest of the country. The town was frequented by sailors who went back and forth across the Atlantic, returning with the latest hits. These 'Cunard Yanks', as they had been called even before the Second World War, may have been the carriers of the black American sound which turned into the 'Mersey Beat'. When the Beatles became successful, every northern city claimed to have its own distinctive 'sound': the Manchester sound, the Birmingham sound, and even Tottenham in north London claimed to have its 'sound' (the Dave Clark Five). British commercial culture had long been London-centred. Now the periphery was striking back. Regional accents and regional singers were 'in' (Cilla Black and crooners Tom Jones and Engelbert Humperdinck – born Arnold Dorsey).

Britain acted as a 'musicological hothouse' for the various innovations of black American musicians: minstrelsy, ragtime, Dixieland, Charleston, swing, boogie-woogie, rock and roll, twist, blues, Motown and funk. Between 1955 and 1959 more than half the records in the British top ten were by Americans.[62] This was not the case in Germany, Italy or France, where locally made songs were favoured. The 'black' music that reached British shores had already been heavily adapted by black vocal groups to make it attractive to the white American record-buying public. Then it was further revisited by white singers, even more acceptable to the public at large. Though purists will regret this, there is no doubt that the strategy of meeting the expectations of the market, common in cultural production, paid off, though it dispro-portionately favoured white performers such as Elvis Presley, Jerry Lee Lewis, Bill Haley and Buddy Holly.

The popularity of Elvis Presley with European teenagers sparked numer-ous local imitations: Cliff Richard in Britain, Johnny Hallyday in France and Adriano Celentano in Italy. Not only did they fill a need, but they have remained popular for over forty years (Celentano had two albums, *Esco di rado* and *Io non so parlare d'amore*, in the top ten in 2000). Elvis's sources of inspiration were ignored. In 1952 the black blues singer Willie Mae 'Big Mama' Thorton recorded 'Hound Dog' (a song written by two whites). In 1956 Elvis recorded a more violent and harsher version of the song, more suitable for dancing. Between 1958 and 1965 there were five Swedish record-ings of 'Hound Dog' – all based on the Elvis version. These were followed –

still in Sweden – by a further *fourteen*, and again, not one went back to Big Mama's version.[63]

Elvis was, musically speaking, at home in Britain in a way he could never be in Italy or France. On the Continent people wanted a local version of Elvis, in their own language – though these often used English-sounding pseudonyms (particularly in Italy, where there were plenty of Freds and Tonys) and affected American pronunciation. Tony Dallara, an Italian crooner of the early 1960s (though he was called an *urlatore*, a screamer), occasionally doubled up vowels (in 'Come Prima'), an affectation he copied from the Platters' successful 'Only You'. The French could surrender to rock only by 'Frenchifying' it. And it worked. In 1959 the newly legalised radio station Europe No. 1 started a radio programme specifically for the young, *Salut les copains* (Hey, Mates!). Soon a magazine of the same name appeared which became of central importance for French rock. At concerts a singer called Jean-Philippe Smet, with an Elvis hairstyle and Elvis-like clothes, would throw himself to the ground clutching his guitar to his stomach, using the pseudonym of Johnny Hallyday. A young Egyptian-born Jewish singer, Richard Antony, imitated Paul Anka (a Canadian of Lebanese origins). The song 'Let's Twist Again', made famous by the black American singer Chubby Checker, was turned into 'Viens danser le twist' (1961). Even Maurice Chevalier jumped on the bandwagon with 'Le Twist du canotier'. By 1961 all French rock and roll singers followed the US charts, and record companies bought up the rights to successful American songs. In 1965 rock became acceptable even at the Communist Party fund-raising cultural festival Fête de l'humanité.[64]

In Britain among the first adapters of Elvis Presley were Billy Fury, Marty Wilde and Cliff Richard – only the latter lasted, and for decades. Cliff Richard had songs custom-written for him, often by members of his backing band, the Shadows. He was popular beyond Britain, but in the early 1960s was almost unheard of in the USA.[65] The challenge to his reign came from Liverpool, where warehouses, jazz clubs, dance halls, ballrooms, even ice rinks, became venues for the new 'beat' music.[66] The Beatles were one of the 350 groups competing for attention in the Mersey area at the end of 1962. They played American songs, like all the others, but they also wrote their own – an amalgam of the range of largely black styles (soul, Motown, ballads, rock and roll, and country and western) now world famous.[67] What became known as 'the Mersey sound' (barely distinguishable from the sound of other non-Liverpool-based bands) was, in the words of an American critic in 1964,

'1956 American rock bouncing back at us'.[68] It certainly bounced back. When the Beatles toured the USA in 1964 three of their singles went straight to the top six in the charts, their albums were at number one and two, and 100,000 Beatles dolls and thousands of Beatles wigs were produced, as well as various Beatles clothes. Beatles-licensed products grossed $5 million.[69] On the back of the Beatles, American radio programmes were swamped with British hits, and riding on the back of its American success, the British sound swept across Europe, Australia and New Zealand, and parts of Asia. Some American groups, such as the Byrds, even began to imitate the Beatles and to affect an English accent. Bob Dylan told one of his biographers of his first encounter with the sound of the Beatles: 'They were doing things nobody was doing. Their chords were outrageous, and their harmonies made it all valid . . . It was obvious to me that they had staying power. I knew they were pointing the direction of where music had to go . . . in my head the Beatles were *it*.'[70] The influences from Great Britain were manifold and reciprocal. In 1962 Dylan recorded 'The House of the Rising Sun', a folk song probably originating in seventeenth-century England, first recorded by the black bluesman Texas Alexander in 1928. Then, in 1964, the song was recorded in Britain by the group the Animals, using electric guitars. After hearing it in England Dylan told a friend in New York: 'My God, ya oughtta hear what's going on there. Eric Burdon, the Animals, ya know? Well, he is doing "House of the Rising Sun" in rock. *Rock!* It's fuckin' wild! Blew my mind.'[71] Thus culture travels.

The Beatles were not alone. Other British groups followed, either imitating them or demarcating themselves sharply: the Dave Clark Five, the Rolling Stones, the Animals, the Kinks, the Undertakers and the Pretty Things. Their music was directly and openly inspired by black American music, but it had become necessary to be distinctive in other ways. It was important to dress in a special way, as Elvis Presley had done and as the Beatles – the trend-setters throughout the 1960s – continued to do with their strange lapel-less jackets and haircuts. It was also necessary to create an image, possibly one of non-conformity. It was indispensable to affect to despise the money-making music industry which was transforming some of them into millionaires and the rest into hopeful aspirants to that state.

All culture contains symbolic elements that bind people together. Music, more than other forms, except perhaps dress codes, has long provided an identity, a sign of belonging: church music, opera, national anthems, regimental music, regional bands, etc. The rapid changes in musical fashion have helped music to enable the young to distinguish themselves from their parents and from the generations immediately preceding them. The gap between each 'generation' (once about twenty years) became considerably abbreviated, since each cohort needed to demarcate itself from those even a few years older. Thus when the short-lived British pop group the Spice Girls became famous in 1996–98 with hits such as 'Wannabe' and '2 Become 1', and was worshipped by pre-pubescent girls in Britain and North America, they were immediately looked upon with contempt not just by rusty old accountants but by girls in their late teens who regarded them as a phenomenon manufactured just for the 'teeniebopper' market.

Imitating les Anglo-Saxons

For the French, Anglo-American popular music is part of the culture of *les Anglo-Saxons,* a particularly inappropriate appellation, since much of this music is of African origin, or was written by Jews (Berlin, Gershwin, Bob Dylan) or sung by Italo-Americans (Frank Sinatra, Connie Francis, Perry Como, Dean Martin, Madonna). Nevertheless, there is no doubt that global music since the end of the Second World War has been American, and since 1960 Anglo-American. Though local singers have continued to be popular in their own countries, they seldom succeeded in making it onto the global scene. Exceptions to Anglo-American dominations were rare. Domenico Modugno's 'Nel blu dipinto di blu', internationally known as 'Volare', was one of them. The song was number one in the USA singles chart list for five weeks in 1958 – the first foreign language single to reach that position. Dean Martin and Bobby Rydell later sang it in English with success. But Modugno never succeeded in repeating this initial American triumph, nor did 'Volare' produce a new breed of Italian songs for the world market.[72] Edith Piaf had a good following in the USA, but this tended to belong to the 'arty' niche occupied by people who smoked Gauloises. The Neapolitan song, being a static repertory, remained a niche genre which pleased tourists in search of the 'genuine Italy' and the more nostalgic among the older generation of Italo-Americans.

Of course, not all American music was genuinely American. Frank Sinatra's 1968 hit 'My Way' was originally the French 'Comme d'habitude', sung in 1968 by the then highly popular Claude François (born in Ismailia, in north-eastern Egypt) to music by Jacques Revaux. It was then reworked by

Paul Anka for Frank Sinatra, who made it internationally famous – though it was also recorded by Nina Simone, Elvis Presley, Shirley Bassey and, eventually, Sid Vicious of the Sex Pistols. Hardly anyone in the US knew it was originally French.

Almost forty years later, the domination of American music is less obvious. What has happened is that the influence of American music has been so massive that it has contributed to various genres of 'world music' (as Western critics have decided to call music from outside the West, while 'music' *tout court* designates Western music). World music is indebted to American music but, blended with other influences, has produced new forms.

The advance of other countries in the global music market has somewhat coincided with the retrenchment of the global reach of British popular music, particularly in its traditional leading foreign market, the USA. *Billboard*'s cumulative index of the top hundred artists in 1955–2003, constructed on the basis of their success in the charts, shows that in the top ten there are four British names. Here is the full listing:

TOP TEN ARTISTS IN THE USA, 1955–2003	
	Points
Elvis Presley	8,067
The Beatles	4,696
Elton John	4,473
Madonna	4,333
Stevie Wonder	3,707
Michael Jackson	3,455
Janet Jackson	3,448
Mariah Carey	3,349
The Rolling Stones	3,138
Paul McCartney/Wings	2,983

SOURCE: *The Billboard Book of Top Hits*, Billboard Books, New York 2004

In the 1960s it was not just the Beatles and the Rolling Stones who were successful in the USA but also other British groups including the Dave Clark Five, Gerry and the Pacemakers, Herman's Hermits, the Searchers, Tom Jones, the Animals and the Kinks. In the 1970s British successes included Elton John, Led Zeppelin, David Bowie, Genesis, ELO (Electric Light Orchestra), Jethro Tull and Pink Floyd. In the mid-1980s Dire Straits, Phil Collins, the Police and others still captured 28 per cent of the USA's best-selling albums market. By 1999 it was down to 0.2 per cent.

In April 2002, for the first time since October 1963, there was not a single British artist in the top 100 singles chart in the USA. The best-selling album and singles in 2000 in the USA were the Beatles (thirty years after they disbanded, thanks to *The Beatles 1*), Tom Jones was still popular in France and Italy, while the Spice Girls conquered Russia.[73]

People like their own music, sung in their own language, by their own singers. Domestic production in all the main markets increased, on average, from 58.3 per cent in 1991 to 68.2 per cent in 2001 – contrary to the trend towards globalisation.[74] The international stars, however, are largely American, as can be seen from the scorecard in *Billboard* of 12 July 2003, which lists albums simultaneously attaining top ten chart status in three or more of the leading music market countries.

INTERNATIONAL STARS, JULY 2003

	Nationality	Ranked in the top ten in the following countries
Beyoncé	USA (Texas)	USA, Canada, Japan, UK, Australia, Netherlands
Michelle Branch	USA (Arizona)	USA, Canada, Japan
Evanescence	USA (Arkansas)	USA, Australia, Canada, Japan, UK, Italy, Germany, France
50 Cent (Curtis Jackson)	USA (New York)	USA, Canada, UK
Norah Jones	USA (New York, daughter of Ravi Shankar)	USA, Canada, Australia, France, Netherlands
Annie Lennox	UK (Scotland)	USA, UK, Germany, Italy
Metallica	USA	USA, Canada, Australia, Netherlands, Spain, Italy
Radiohead	UK (England)	UK, Canada, Australia, Italy
Eros Ramazzotti	Italy	Italy, Spain, Netherlands

SOURCE: *Billboard*, 12 July 2003

The only non-Anglo-American on the list, Eros Ramazotti, is third in the 'Eurochart' by virtue of his success in Holland, Italy, Spain, Belgium, Austria and Switzerland. He is not in the top ten in any English-speaking country, or in Japan or France. The rap singer 50 Cent, who in July 2003 was in the top ten in English-speaking countries only, was by April 2005 in the top ten in all the countries surveyed except Italy and Japan.[75]

Of course such listings reflect not 'taste' in general, but the taste of the purchasers of albums, particularly those in the top music markets (USA, Great Britain, Japan and Germany). In 1978 the USA bought 726 million units (LPs, singles and cassettes), followed by Germany, Japan and the UK with around two hundred million each.[76] The situation had not changed significantly twenty years later, when the USA, Japan, Germany and the UK accounted for almost 70 per cent of total global music sales. The USA on its own accounted for a third of the market, while the European Union had about a quarter.[77] In 2000 music consumption per capita in Britain was higher than that of Germany, the USA or Japan.[78]

The shift away from the USA has been impressive. In 1950, 80 per cent of all records sold worldwide were sold in the USA and only 10 per cent in Europe. In 1978 the share of the USA was down to 40 per cent, with Europe close to 35 per cent.[79] And within Europe there are only three big players, with almost three-quarters of the market:

TOP TEN EUROPEAN MUSIC
MARKETS, 2002 (IN MILLIONS
OF DOLLARS)

UK	2,859
France	1,989
Germany	1,988
Italy	554
Spain	542
Holland	397
Sweden	282
Russia	257
Norway	254
Switzerland	253
TOTAL	9,375

SOURCE: International Federation of the Phonographic Industry (IFPI) in *Billboard*, 12 July 2003

Over the past few years the trend has been towards an increased market share for domestic repertoire in most European markets. Since the local repertoire accounts for a sizeable proportion of the market, each music conglomerate, though global, cannot subsist on the basis of global superstars alone. They must find local winners, though these are less profitable than international stars.[80] The USA still maintains the leading role, and not only because it is the leading market and the main supplier of megastars. It also has the role in popular music which France and Britain had in literature in the nineteenth century: it provides music with the all-important stamp of approval. Making it in the USA may open up the doors of the Japanese and Australian market. This is why English is truly the language of pop. To make it in the global market it is necessary to sing in English. This is evident as soon as we look at the singers who over the years have become internationally well-known, in spite of coming from a 'peripheral country'. The recent phenomenon of world stars such as the Colombia-born Shakira, who sings in Spanish (in Latin America) and English (to the rest of the world) is a case in point. Her album *Laundry Service* sold thirteen million worldwide in 2001, but 'only' 3.3 million in the USA.[81] The musical style is 'Latin pop', a hybrid devoid of clear stylistic or ethnic influences and quite different from traditional Latin American international successes. The Colombian Shakira has famous precedents such as ABBA (Sweden), one of the most successful groups in the world in the 1970s, and Björk (Iceland), famous since the late 1980s. Irish singers and bands such as Bob Geldof and U2 would not have achieved worldwide popularity had they been singing in Gaelic.

ABBA gained its renown at the Eurovision song contest of 1974, singing the winning entry 'Waterloo'. Their hits were grounded in American and British pop music, but were enriched by an Italianate approach to melodic treatment, as well as *Schlager* (literally: hit) music, popular in Germany and the Nordic countries, especially Finland, but regarded elsewhere as just schmaltzy ballads. Outsiders may not have been aware of it, but the Nordic countries had (and have) a thriving pop scene. Even in the 1960s in Finland and Sweden half the records sold were of domestic music.[82]

ABBA's accessible tunes turned the quartet into the number one band in Europe until they disbanded (the two romantically linked couples who made up the band separated) in 1982. They had imitators and followers everywhere, including the Pakistani sisters Salma and Sabina (*Salma and Sabina Agha Sing ABBA Hits in Hindi*). The success of a Swedish band surprised many. If anyone was going to break the Anglo-American duopoly in Europe, why not the French, Spaniards or Italians – all of whom had a powerful international musical tradition? Yet such traditions and the large internal market constituted an obstacle. Italian and French bands were concerned with their own internal markets. The French, at best, sought to hold on to the wider francophone market. The Spaniards hoped to penetrate Latin America. Sweden had a tiny market, though by 2002 it was a bigger export earner than the whole of the Russian market. This was an insufficient springboard for global musical success, but Swedish music education programmes in the 1970s and 1980s had provided generations of schoolchildren with proficiency in playing a musical instrument. Young Swedes were familiar with Anglo-American pop, and were provided with adequate rehearsal venues by local authorities. There was also widespread technological expertise and affordable musical instruments. As a result of ABBA, Swedish music export earnings per capita were considerably higher than those of Britain.[83] In a country of 8.4 million inhabitants, 100,000 played in bands.[84]

The Eurovision Song Contest provided a trampoline towards lasting international success for very few singers other than ABBA. One was Julio Iglesias, who represented Spain in 1970 with 'Gwendolyne', and though he did not win, went on to sing the song all over the world, breaking into the charts in the USA in 1981 with the old Cole Porter song 'Begin the Beguine' and selling millions of records for over twenty years. Another was Celine Dion, a native French-Canadian who won for Switzerland in 1988. Having learned to sing in English (as had Iglesias), she had a considerable number of global successes, including the theme song of the movie *Titanic* (1997), and was in the number one position in the US charts for eighteen weeks.[85] One could also mention the British success of 1967, Sandie Shaw's 'Puppet on a String'. Otherwise, most famous singers shun the contest (losing would be damaging, winning would not increase their fame). The contest is despised by popular music purists (for these exist), yet it generates massive television coverage throughout Europe (some eighty million viewers) and provides a nationally based competition in a world seemingly dominated by one or two countries. The contest was started in 1956 by the European Broadcasting Union. It was designed as a popular way of exploiting the possibility of linking television broadcasts across Europe with live transmissions. Each country was to present what was regarded as native popular music – in reality it was a pastiche of tunes not yet revisited by American music. The main influence was not European but Latin American. Eventually a new dominating style emerged: an indistinct 'Europop'. English became the dominant language (the winning entry in 1989 was the Yugoslav song 'Rock Me').[86]

Though global music continued to be dominated by American music, the business became less US-centred. Of the main players today only Warner is entirely American-owned. Sony (which bought CBS in 1987 and Columbia Pictures in 1988) is Japanese; EMI is British; BMG (Bertelsmann Music Group) is German. MCA (Universal) was originally American, but was bought by Matsushita Electric Industrial, then (in 1995) by Seagram, a large Canadian distillers conglomerate, which was in turn bought in 2000 by the French company Vivendi, making Vivendi Universal one of the world's largest communication companies. But not for long, this industry being in constant flux. In October 2003 Vivendi Universal was merged with NBC. By the end of 2004, NBC Universal was 80 per cent owned by General Electric. In 2004 Sony Music merged with BMG, creating the largest music group in the world with 25.1 per cent of the international market, followed by NBC Universal with 23.5 per cent, EMI with 13.4 per cent and Time-Warner (US) with 12.7 per cent. The so-called 'independent' companies shared the remaining 25.3 per cent.[87]

To attribute nationality to some global companies, however, is less and less enlightening. In the culture industry, global players borrow capital in all markets and invest wherever they can. The products they sell are not determined by company choices but by market needs. Their strategy is to try to connect the disparate aspects of their business around a particular product or a particular performer – hence the search for a 'total star' whose songs will top the charts in most countries, be played on the most important radio stations, be promoted on music-only video channels such as MTV, and generate merchandising and advertising for other products. The star will also, eventually, write a best-selling 'autobiography'.

This total star need not be American, since the marketing strategy aims at trying to transform any local star singing in a recognisably international style into a global asset. Meanwhile local stars occupy a section of their local markets which could have been colonised by others. France, for instance, is the main consumer and producer of hip hop and rap music after the USA, the genre having been widely adopted among the second-generation North Africans who see themselves as the French counterpart of American blacks and the peripheries of French cities as the equivalent of American urban ghettos.[88] Some French rappers acquired international fame, such as the Senegal-born MC Solaar, even in the USA after his 'La Belle et le bad boy' was featured in the final episode of *Sex and the City*. The use of lyrics in

French hip hop has some antecedents in the linguistic slang and play on words used decades previously by Charles Trenet and Yves Montand.[89] Clearly the genre could travel, and travel it did. Since 1996 there has been an annual government-sponsored hip hop conference in Cuba; there is 'Islamic' rap in Great Britain (one of the most prominent figures is Aki Nawaz of the group Fun-Da-Mental), as well as Bulgaria.[90] In Italy there are far-left groups of rappers with names such as Assalti Frontali and AK47, and there are lively hip hop scenes in India, Korea and Japan. In Turkey hip hop, which still circulates prevalently outside the commercial circuit, is strongly influenced by German-Turkish rappers.[91]

Favourite songs are often domestic products, even though the foreign favourites tend to be Anglo-American songs. Thus in Italy among the best-selling albums of 2002 there were four Italian artists (Vasco Rossi, Ligabue, Celentano and Giorgia), followed by Queen, U2 (*The Best of 1990–2000*) and the Red Hot Chilli Peppers (*By the Way*).[92] In April 2005 the best-selling single in Finland was 'Taivas Iyo Tulta' by Terasbetoni, in Hungary 'Elment az en Rozsam' by Balkan Fanatik, in Italy 'I Bambini fanno oh' by Povia, in Japan 'Sakura Sake' by Arashi, and in France 'Un Monde parfait' by Ilona Metrecey.[93] Everyone seems to like home-grown singers.

Local rhythms and tunes are often blended with American ones, creating a hybrid. Migration and communication favour such constant diffusion. The formation of a global music market may appear obvious now, but its rise can be found in the peculiar nature of the music business, for music travels much more thoroughly, much more rapidly and can be re-interpreted far more quickly and efficiently than literature or films. Take the west Nigerian market town of Kafanchan. In the mid-1970s the town's 25,000 inhabitants had no electricity; there were only two television sets in places with private power supplies, there was only one cinema, an open-air movie theatre showing mainly Hong Kong and Indian films, literacy was in English (most of the books available in the small local bookshop were educational or religious texts in English). But radios and record players, using batteries, were common, and pirated cassettes were easily available, West Indian reggae could be easily adapted on instruments produced in Nigeria, and there were popular Nigerian music stars such as Fela Kuti, Sunny Ade and Ebenezer Obey.[94]

Music may be global, but tastes are sufficiently different to produce distinctions even between closely connected cultures: a comparison of the album charts in June 1998 reveals that there were only two albums in common between Continental Europe and Great Britain, and none between the US and the UK.[95]

The Classical World

'Pop' and 'rock' dominate music consumption, but there is life beyond them. The genre, after all, absorbs not much more than 50 per cent of sales revenue. In the USA, for instance, rock and pop music, taken together, accounted in 1980 for 55 per cent of sales, with 'country', 'soul' and 'jazz' holding on to over 23 per cent.[96]

Folk music was in the nineteenth and for much of the twentieth century the favourite music of traditionalists and nationalists. In the 1930s (in the USA) and the 1960s (in Europe too) it acquired a left-wing and radical flavour thanks to the influence of the American protest and civil rights movements. Newly composed or re-adapted protest songs, such as those of Pete Seeger ('If I had a Hammer', 'We Shall Overcome') and Bob Dylan ('Blowin' in the Wind'), written in a distinctive folk style, became vastly popular.

French songs retained their distinctiveness, whether sung by Edith Piaf, Yves Montand, Gilbert Bécaud, Jacques Brel or Charles Aznavour. They had a following abroad, but it was a niche market. In Italy they sparked imitators (but often more political than the French), the so-called *cantautori* (singers who wrote their own songs), such as Gino Paoli, Enzo Jannacci, Giorgio Gaber, Luigi Tenco, Fabrizio De André and Lucio Dalla.

Many European regions also remained loyal to genres of music strictly for domestic consumption. In the Alpine arc in German-speaking Switzerland, Bavaria and western Austria, people delight in yodelling, brass bands, accordion groups, an 'oompah-pah' style of delivery, and a deeply Catholic message, all in the local dialects. This kind of *Volksmusik* is the counterpart of American country and western but lacks its wider appeal.[97]

In the USA, Christian fervour has assured regular sales of religious music. *Billboard* magazine routinely provides separate charts for 'Top Christian' and 'Top Gospel' albums – with the ubiquitous Elvis's 'Ultimate Gospel' at number twenty-seven in the latter chart on 9 April 2005. In such repertoires there is, compared to the dynamic world of rock and pop, little new music. The distinction between 'classical' or 'serious' music on the one hand and 'popular' on the other is a matter of dispute. But we must use a common language. 'Popular' music includes music which has never been popular. 'Classical' music includes the 'serious' music of the past – some of which is popular – and, by some social definition (venues and marketing techniques), some recent music which aspires to become 'classical'.

The repertoire for classical music has remained static, as has the operatic one. Large, prestigious and heavily subsidised opera houses are even less adventurous: under Rudolf Bing's twenty-two years as director of the New York Metropolitan Opera only three world premières were staged. One of his successors, Joseph Volpe (1990–2006), did little better.[98] Bing was quite open about his aims: 'We are similar to a museum: my function is to present old masterpieces in modern frames' (8 October 1965, *Time* magazine). Since there are virtually no American composers in the traditional repertoire, but quite a few among post-1960 operatic composers, the reluctance to try anything contemporary *de facto* works against American composers. When asked to calculate what kind of subsidy a new opera required, Rudolf Bing investigated the Met's box office receipts when Benjamin Britten's *Peter Grimes* was performed. 'The results,' he explained, 'were discouraging'. After two performances at 93 per cent of seat occupancy in the first year, *Grimes* dropped to 70 per cent in the following year.[99] Bing remarked:

> Some day a new operatic genius will arise whose works draw the public . . . Failing such a genius I am not wildly interested in presenting contemporary opera at the Metropolitan. My colleague in Hamburg does contemporary opera after contemporary opera, and the press loves him and he plays to empty houses, and the state pays. But in America the state does not pay.

Performing operas from the traditional repertoire is financially sound. It is not just that the public likes them. Successful productions can be kept going for years with the same costumes and scenery. The costumes for the Met's *Rigoletto* of 1951 were still being worn in 1972.[100] Even new productions of old operas can be cost-effective since they cut down on rehearsal time, as the highly paid superstars would want to be paid even more if they had to learn a new part. Having sung Violetta many times, a soprano can rapidly fit into a new production, even though she may be required to sing the part wearing a spacesuit.

New 'serious' music is not popular even though, given the size of the market, there are always amateurs for even difficult pieces of contemporary music. The great hits of the past, suitably rebranded and remarketed, constitute a not insignificant market – at least in Europe.

SALES OF CLASSICAL MUSIC AS A PERCENTAGE OF
TOTAL RECORD SALES IN SELECTED COUNTRIES, 1994

Holland	14.0
Belgium	10.9
Switzerland	10.7
Mexico	10.0
Czech Republic	10.0*
France	9.2
Germany	9.0
Austria	8.9
South Korea	8.8
Great Britain	8.7
Italy	7.9*
Hungary	6.6
Finland	6.2
Norway	5.6
Sweden	5.0
Denmark	4.5
Poland	4.0
USA	3.7

* % of total monetary value

SOURCE: IFPI, *The Recording Industry in Numbers*, 1995

Classical music generates some occasional major hits, almost always caused by bringing an old favourite to the attention of a public unfamiliar with classical music. Thus when 'Nessun Dorma', an aria from Puccini's *Turandot* and sung by Luciano Pavarotti, was selected as the theme tune for the BBC's coverage of the 1990 Football World Cup, it was in the British singles charts for eleven weeks – for three weeks even in second position, after Elton John.[101] In the USA, where football (soccer) is a minority sport, 'Nessun Dorma' did not make it into the top hundred.

'Nessun Dorma's' success helped that of the 'Three Tenors' album later that year – featuring Pavarotti, Plácido Domingo and José Carreras – which sold more than ten million copies worldwide.[102] Even without the help of television some fabled performers can outsell, thanks to their longer shelf-life, many pop stars. Thus Dietrich Fischer-Dieskau, specialising in a niche market, that of nineteenth-century German *lieder* (of which he was regarded as the greatest interpreter), sold millions of records. Some conductors entirely dominated the market. Herbert von Karajan, for instance, as director of the Berlin Philharmonic Orchestra (1955–89) and artistic director of the Vienna State Opera (1955–64) and the Salzburg Music Festival (1957–59), as well as conducting the Orchestre de Paris and that of La Scala, was also in control of central European musical life on record. In the course of his career he recorded all of Beethoven's symphonies four times. At one stage one-third of Deutsche Grammophon records sold in England were Karajan's.[103]

Such fame is totally out of the reach of the composers of new music, though significant sums can be made composing film scores and music for commercials. Very few can afford to be full-time professional composers. Most make a living by teaching, or playing in an orchestra or conducting it.[104] Modern music is regarded as 'difficult'. Contemporary art is 'difficult' too, but the advantage with it is that it is not necessary to spend more than a minute (or even a few seconds) before a contemporary painting one does not like. Sitting through a concert is a different matter.[105] The unpopularity of contemporary music is reflected in the much lower prices asked for live performances. In order to obtain the most expensive seats at the Royal Opera House at Covent Garden for Wagner's *Die Meistersinger* and Verdi's *La Traviata* in 2002–03 one needed to spend £160 (Wagner) and £140 (Verdi). For a modern classic such as Alban Berg's *Wozzeck* or the world première of Nicholas Maw's *Sophie's Choice*, £50 was sufficient. This discrimination is at work even for the cheapest seats (standing at the back, at the top): £2 secured Alban Berg, £4 Verdi and £5 Wagner. New music finds an audience with difficulty partly because it seeks to emancipate itself from any contamination with what is popular. This was not what Mozart or Haydn did: they deliberately used rural folk music and new urban songs. They sought to please a wider and more bourgeois public.[106] Later, nineteenth-century composers abandoned such populist concessions. By the end of the twentieth century, ostentatious dissonance had reached its apotheosis.[107]

Huge audiences for classical music can be achieved by using the music in advertising (Bach's 'Adagio in G' advertising Hamlet cigars) or in films (snatches from Beethoven's Ninth Symphony in Stanley Kubrick's *A Clockwork Orange*) or as the default Nokia ring tone (Francisco Tárrega's 'Gran Vals'). Some of those who had never heard Bach or Beethoven developed a liking for them. Of course, the size of the audience is not a measure of the popularity of the music. Kiri te Kanawa sang 'Let the Bright Seraphim' from Handel's oratorio *Samson* at the royal wedding of Charles and Diana. It was heard by hundreds of millions of people, but this is no indication of the popularity of Handel.[108] It would, of course, be very unlikely for Schoenberg to have been chosen for the wedding.

Pop songs too benefit from their use in a new television context. The song chosen for Diana's funeral in 1997 was Elton John's 'Candle in the Wind' (an adapted version of his 1974 hit). It entered the charts immediately, and quickly sold thirty-three million worldwide, the biggest-selling single to date.[109] One wonders whether Handel, eventually, will have sold more than Elton John. Time will tell. In terms of audience size (which we cannot measure) Handel might not be as popular as Elton John. But in the long term Handel may catch up. The great advantage he has is that he has few competitors for his particular 'niche' market, unlike Elton John.

In the eighteenth century performers and composers were often the same. In the late twentieth and early twenty-first centuries this is truer of pop music than of 'serious' music. The typical classical music professional is not an original creator but a skilled interpreter – a singer, a conductor or an instrumentalist. They ensure novelty in a genre stuck in the past. Verdi is constantly renewed because singers like Luciano Pavarotti or conductors like Georg Solti make sure that *Simone Boccanegra* is seen as new. The rock era may have started in 1955, but 1955 was also the year of Bach's 'Goldberg Variations' played by the twenty-three-year-old Glenn Gould at quickfire speed and with sudden switches of tempo and mood – one of the most influential classical music recordings ever.

The live performances of the genre are heavily subsidised – in Europe by the state, in the USA by private corporations and benefactors who enjoy tax rebates (and thus, here too, there is a public subsidy). The lion's share goes to ballet and opera – 70 per cent of spending on music by the Arts Council in 1978–79 (55.6 per cent just to the two main London theatres). In Norway 39 per cent of government spending on music went to the Oslo Opera and 22 per cent to the top four symphony orchestras. The Paris Opéra, in the same year, obtained one-third of all state music spending (and this has been going on for the past hundred years).[110] In instrumental music the 'classics' obtain far more subsidies than contemporary 'serious' music.

More classical music was performed in Great Britain in the 1990s than in the 1890s, thanks to the 211 symphony and chamber orchestras operating in 1990s. In 1960 there were only three permanent opera companies (the Royal Opera House, Sadler's Wells and, if we deign to include Gilbert and Sullivan, the D'Oyly Carte Opera Co.). The three following decades added the Glyndebourne Touring Opera, the Welsh National Opera, the Scottish National Opera, Opera North, Opera 80 (later English Touring Opera) and Opera Factory.[111] And while there were in the fifteen states of the European Union of 1994–95 over 300,000 pop concerts, there were also 85,000 classical music concerts.[112] There are many who think that high culture is on the way out. But there is no strong evidence. A Policy Studies Report for 1988 in Britain noted a rising trend over the previous decade for audiences at theatres (up, in London's West End, by 28 per cent since 1981), symphony concerts (28 per cent since 1974) and museums (6 per cent between 1976 and 1985).[113]

The explosion of pop music, far from causing the crash of the classics, was in reality part of a boom of music in general.

CONCLUSION

The World Wide Web

Seeking the Unique

A LONG LINE OF PEOPLE shuffles round a building in the spring of 1972. The building is a shrine dedicated to high culture, the British Museum, where the canonical works of the past are exhibited and whose colonnaded façade imitates a Greek temple. The remains and 'treasures' from the tomb of an almost unknown ancient ruler of Egypt are being shown to a reverential and curious crowd. In the course of a several months, some 1.7 million people undergo the experience (one could say the ritual, so close is it to a procession of pilgrims) of witnessing the irreproducible, the authentic, the unique. The crowd know exactly what they are going to admire, for they have seen the treasures of the Pharaoh Tutankhamen before, in numerous photographs and illustrations, in television documentaries and cinematic reconstructions. Many have heard the enticing story of the curse that befell the members of the desecrating expedition that broke into his tomb. Ancient Egypt – like the dinosaurs – is a well-established crowd-puller. The experience is to be repeated in 2007.

Tutankhamen was lucky. Not in his lifetime, of course, because he lived only to the age of eighteen, but in his afterlife, not – as he might have hoped – as a star journeying across the firmament, but as a modern celebrity.

The legend of the Curse of Tutankhamen had little that was substantial. The tomb was discovered in November 1922 by an expedition led by Howard Carter and Lord Carnarvon. In February 1923 the archeologists opened the tomb. Less than two months later Carnarvon, aged fifty-seven, died of pneumonia, which before the invention of antibiotics was the most common cause of death in adults. There was also a power failure in Cairo – not a miraculous portent, then or now, but it was seen as such. Carnarvon's dog, Susie, was reported to have died at the same time as her master (though this has proved impossible to establish). Howard Carter, however, lived on a further seventeen years, dying at the age of sixty-six, the average age for someone born in 1873; and nothing untoward happened to the rest of those involved in the expedition. But a narrative context added the necessary spice to a genuine story of archeological discovery: one of the most popular novelists of the day, Marie Corelli (see pages 692–3), claimed to own an early Arabic text detailing the curse that would follow the desecration of Tutankhamen's tomb. Press interest, enhanced by Arthur Conan Doyle's belief in the legend and by Arthur Weigall's popular Egyptological book *Tutankhamen and Other Essays* (1923), amplified the good story and further diffused it. Popular culture provided a solid backing to the fame of these artefacts of high culture.

So-called 'blockbuster' exhibitions have continued ever since – not in antagonism towards modern commercial culture, but in unperturbed partnership. The 'Genius of China' exhibition in London in 1973–74 drew 771,000 visitors. 'Monet in the Twentieth Century', held first in Boston (1998) and then in London (1999), drew over 800,000. An earlier exhibition of a single painting – the *Mona Lisa* – held in 1963 in New York and Washington, attracted 1.6 million visitors, each spending slightly less than a minute gaping at the famous portrait.[1]

The public exhibition of artistic treasures in museums and art galleries is hardly new. In 1683 Oxford University established the Ashmolean Museum. In 1734 the Capitoline Museum was opened in the Vatican. In 1743 it was the turn of the Uffizi in Florence, and a year later Dresden acquired its public picture gallery. The British Museum started in 1753. The Louvre, planned before the Revolution, was inaugurated in 1793. In the course of the nineteenth century the trend accelerated: in 1808 the Koninklijk Museum opened in Amsterdam (it became the Rijksmuseum in 1815), the Prado in Madrid in 1819, and the National Gallery in London in 1824. In Berlin in 1830, what became known as the Alte Nationalgalerie provided the core for an entire set of museums. St Petersburg saw the opening of the Imperial Museum of the New Hermitage in 1852 – the same year as the South Kensington Museum (later renamed the Victoria and Albert Museum). In the USA the Metropolitan Museum of New York and the Museum of Fine Arts in Boston were started in 1870 and the Art Institute of Chicago in 1879.

It is not just high culture that is exhibited, but anything that attracts a crowd. London's Great Exhibition of 1851, prompted by the success of the French Industrial Exposition of 1844, was visited by six million people who viewed exhibits ranging from fine prints and statues to brass and iron-works, agricultural machines, leather, rope-making and hydraulic presses. Madame Tussaud's waxworks, which started in Paris in 1780, reached London in 1835. It is still, in the age of the internet, one of the main crowd-pullers in London. In the 1850s at the Brighton Aquarium one could gape at midgets, giants, Zulu chiefs and Javanese dancers – all more popular attractions, apparently, than aquatic creatures.[2] Around 1900 in London one could see at the Portobello Gardens 'bush savages from the Wilds of South Africa' exhibiting 'the Habits and Customs of their Native Country'; at the Royal Agricultural Hall in Islington spectators could admire Singalese and Tamil dancers, while at the exhibition grounds at Earl's Court a 'real' native village was recreated, 'inhabited by the savages of the Dark Continent . . . pursuing their ordinary vocations, one of their most interesting being the manufacture of the lucky Kaffir bangle'.[3]

Far from disappearing under the impact of film, radio and television, the internet and all the apparatus of reproducible culture, the desire to see the unique has increased. It is almost as if the entire technological machinery for the diffusion of culture mobilised itself to promote the importance of seeing the real rather than the merely virtual. In Britain, while the most visited attraction in 2004 was Blackpool Pleasure Beach (over six million people), the second in the league was the National Gallery with 4.9 million, closely followed by the British Museum (4.8 million) and Tate Modern (4.4 million). The Science Museum had more visitors than the Tower of London, and the National Portrait Gallery more than Legoland Windsor.[4] Big culture, particularly when free, can be big business.

More museums were built in the era of television and the internet than ever before. In 1977 a large new museum and exhibition centre was erected in the centre of Paris, the Beaubourg. The Musée d'Orsay opened on the Left Bank of the Seine in 1986, carved out of what had been a railway station. The Louvre was expanded in 1993. In 1997 the Getty Center in Los Angeles acquired a new, larger site on a dramatic hilltop. A former power station on the banks of the Thames in London was resurrected as Tate Modern in 2000. The New York Museum of Modern Art was reopened with twice its former capacity at the end of 2004. Cities outside the great art circuit, such as Bilbao, put themselves on the cultural map by hosting one of the Guggenheim European centres in a new, excitingly modern building. In the USA between 1950 and 1980, 123 art museums were built from scratch or considerably expanded.[5]

The enormous expansion of tourism and travel turned out to be a major force behind the ever-growing popularity of exhibitions. In 1997, in the space of four months, more than 770,000 people queued at the Technical and Industrial Museum in Mannheim to admire 'Bodyworlds' (*Körperwelten*), a collection of some two hundred human anatomical specimens, pieces of diseased and healthy tissue, organs in glass cases and eighteen 'plastinated' corpses. In Japan the exhibition was visited by three million people, in Seoul (Korea) by two million, in Los Angeles (2004) by 920,000, in Chicago by 930,000 and in London by almost 800,000. The number of visitors for all the 'Bodyworlds' exhibitions totalled seventeen million.[6] The fascination with the dead stretches from ancient Egyptians to more recent, less illustrious, cadavers.

Originally, museums such as the Amsterdam Rijksmuseum were seen as monuments to national identity, but they needed authentic artefacts. Now the 'unique' can be manufactured from scratch. And there is no end to it. Thus, in the early 1980s in Catalfaro, a Sicilian town of 10,000 inhabitants, some local administrators and intellectuals sought to promote the image of their town as a 'city of art' by creating a museum, producing a magazine containing articles on local history and inventing two local celebrations: the Week of the Baroque (La Settimana del Barocco) on the seventeenth century, and the Festival of the Indian Fig (La Sagra del Fico d'India) – both with loose connections to the history of the town.[7]

Museums have generated their own sub-markets. Their shops, selling reproductions of the exhibits or even just art books and fancy objects, are major money-makers. The exhibition 'Renoir's Portraits: Impressions of an Age', held in 1997 at the National Gallery of Canada, was treated as a business by its sponsors, the National Gallery of Canada, the Canadian Tourism Commission and the Department of Canadian Heritage. A study they commissioned concluded that $31.5 million in consumer spending occurred in Ontario and Quebec solely because of the exhibition.[8] To exit, the visitors had to go through a shopping space with posters, reproductions, handbags, ceramic tiles, mugs, calendars, T-shirts, picture puzzles, postcards, notecards, umbrellas, aprons, refrigerator magnets, shopping bags, dolls, toy dogs, baby bonnets – all with a Renoir theme – and racks of Provençal wines specially commissioned with a 'Renoir' label.[9] It is now almost unthinkable for a museum not to have its shop, and the catalogues of blockbuster exhibitions often become best-sellers. Since not many can buy the unique, a thriving market in posters has expanded since the 1960s. To own an Old Master is a rare privilege, but everyone can have a *Mona Lisa* poster in the bedroom.

The museums fulfilled the 'democratic' task of making public works of art which once belonged to private owners. By opening their doors to all comers they multiplied the availability of the artworks exhibited while preserving their unique status. Visiting country houses, once the exclusive domain of the aristocracy and the rich, now provides a popular leisure activity for millions of people. What used to be – literally – a private heritage became in the 1970s part of the national heritage.

Fashion has gone the same way. Once, '*haute couture*' was for the exclusive benefit of wealthy women. It ensured that what they wore was unique – and thus that they would never face the indignity of wearing the same dress as another woman. The dress would be, literally, tailored to the body. In 1985 the top twenty-one houses classified in France as *haute couture* employed only 2,000 workers in the *ateliers* where their made-to-order clothes were made, and had no more than 3,000 women customers in the whole world. These houses no longer made a profit on *haute couture* – on selling the unique. The money was made by selling standardised products – ready-to-wear clothes, accessories and perfumes – to the many. In the mid-1980s perfumes accounted for 50 per cent of Lanvin's profits. Since the 1960s, licensing agreements by *haute couture* houses have also involved glasses, leather goods, tableware, pens and lighters. In the mid-1980s Yves Saint-Laurent derived two-thirds of its profits from royalties. Pierre Cardin was relying on more than six hundred foreign licences. *Haute couture* had become a marketing tool to sell to a mass market.[10]

The Screen at Home

Only a minority go to exhibitions and museums. In the Europe of 2004 those who never visited a gallery or an exhibition ranged from 64 per cent in Denmark to over 90 per cent in Greece.[11] Cultural practices are often like a package. If you read *Le Monde*, the *Frankfurter Allgemeine Zeitung* or the *Guardian* you are less likely to watch TV for four hours a day (the average in most countries), and more likely to go to the theatre, exhibitions and classical music concerts.

The cinema is visited by more than half the population at least once a year, but only a minority go at least once a month. The majority stays at home reading books and newspapers, listening to the radio and music (which can also be done while on the move) and, above all, watching television. The young, various surveys suggest, read less in 1990 than in 1970.[12] Yet more books than ever are published and sold. In 1990, 65,000 titles were published in the United Kingdom. Ten years later, when a sizeable proportion of the population had broadband access, the total of books published, including reprints, stood at 161,000.[13] Of course, we know how many books are bought, but not how many are read. When books were expensive they were chosen with care, either to be read and reread or, if well-bound, to be displayed in the home as a demonstration of the taste of the owner. Now that they are cheap they can be bought as presents by keen parents and friends, and left unread by the recipients.

Surveys conducted in France confirm what is regarded as a general trend in the West: the increasingly home-centred nature of cultural consumption.[14] In reality the home was always the centre of cultural consumption. Of all the cultural forms surveyed in this book, only the cinema succeeded, for a historically brief period, in getting a majority of people to consume culture outside the home. Otherwise entertainment outside the home is largely of a social nature: meeting friends in cafés, pubs, restaurants and bars, attending sporting events and, for the young, dancing.

Since the 1980s home entertainment has further expanded thanks to the development of computer games. At first, in the 1970s, to play such games it was necessary to go to an entertainment arcade and use coin-operated consoles provided with joysticks. Soon it became possible to purchase handheld devices designed for specific video-game systems and to play at home. Then computer games played on personal computers became widely available. The ancestors of most of these games were the various card solitaires, puzzles, problem-solving and games of dexterity which entertained the solitary in the nineteenth century. The themes developed in the late 1970s borrowed heavily from popular culture and sport. In 1972 the Japan-based Atari Company introduced a game called 'Pong', based on table tennis. Players of 'Space Invaders' learned to exterminate ranks of aliens as they appeared on the screen. In the mid-1980s Nintendo, another Japanese company, introduced 'Super Mario Bros', whose advanced graphics enabled the industry to revive after a temporary slump. Throughout the 1990s three Japanese companies, Nintendo, Sega and Sony, battled for dominance of the international home video-game market. The software is dominated by the USA and Japan, but among Europeans the British have a significant foothold, having given the world 'Tomb Raider' (which had sold more than twenty-eight million units worldwide by 2003) and a game in which, among other diversions, players can pay to have sex with a prostitute and then murder her to get their money back: 'Grand Theft Auto' (the 'Vice City' version was the best-selling game in the USA in 2002).[15] The UK is the largest market for games in Europe and the third largest in the world after the USA and Japan. Korea and China are not far behind. The industry provides employment to 21,500 people in Britain (1999), and exports worth £503 million against only £284 million imported. But the passion for games knows no boundaries. In Europe between 1995 and 2003, some nine hundred million games were sold.[16]

Games and the graphics they use display increasing sophistication. As personal computers became widely available and their operating power expanded, so did the complexity of the games. Their distinctiveness was that they were authentically interactive. The action is linked to a fixed narrative structure, usually borrowed from traditional genres developed in the cinema and comic strips: detective stories, cops and robbers battling it out in an urban landscape, lost kingdoms in semi-mythological times. In films and comic strips, however, the consumer was in the role of the traditional reader, identifying vicariously, perhaps, with the protagonists. Now the player could become the actor, repel the invaders and kill the villains.[17] As the player proceeds and fails there is a learning process, a gradual adaptation to the world which is being conquered. This addictive process takes place within well-established narrative conventions such as those of the epic quest: one has to reach a goal, encounter enemies and monsters to be destroyed, obtain the support of helpful friends. With the spread of broadband internet it was possible to play against unknown opponents throughout the world.

This new cultural form is as disparaged as the genres which inspired it – yet the skills that can be developed in terms of logical reasoning and reflex-ivity are remarkable, at least compared with the passive accumulation of factual knowledge or with reading *Harry Potter* (an activity near-unanimously endorsed by parents). In the game 'Pokemon', for instance, players need to learn to read 'complex combinations of print and icons, and to find ways to insert these and themselves into the narrative and trading structure of the game. They need to recognise and make use of the skills, strengths and attributes of some 150 different characters.'[18]

While adolescent girls use computers as much as boys, games are played more, though not much more, by boys.[19] A combination of feminist pressures and good business sense led the industry to produce games that appeal to girls. Surviving gender stereotypes ensure that girls play the more abstract or intelligent forms – such as 'Tetra', or 'Sims', where players create families and determine the course of their lives – while boys prefer exterminating galaxies. The result of such efforts is that computer games are now bigger business than films. In 2004 the release in the UK of the new *Harry Potter* and *Lord of the Rings* films grossed some £10–12 million, but the latest version of 'Grand Theft Auto (San Andreas)' grossed £24 million.[20]

The spread of video games was accompanied by the spread of personal computers. Video games made Japanese firms rich, but computers were, and, have so far remained, an American affair. While manufacturing, essentially a simple assembly job, could be located anywhere in the world where labour is cheap and unions weak, the ideas are American: the main prototypes for the desktop personal computer came from IBM, while the victor in the software battle was a new company, Microsoft, which eventually dominated the industry. Apple computers, also American, provided the only significant breach in what would have been a remarkable monopoly. Amazon, Netscape, Napster, Google, eBay, etc., all the pillars of the dot.com revolution, have come from the USA.

But not the world wide web or internet – without which computers would not have become the revolutionary consumer goods they now are. The web originated in Switzerland at the CERN laboratory, the world's largest particle physics centre, founded in 1954 and one of Old Europe's first joint ventures. It was Tim Berners-Lee, a British scientist at CERN, who conceived of a system – later called the world wide web – to meet the demand for automatic information sharing between scientists working in different universities and research centres throughout the world. Universities found the web an ideal system for exchanging information on a peer-to-peer basis, while the military were attracted to a system which, because it had no strategic centre, would be impervious to a single attack.

The structure of the web replicates the structure of the expansion of culture. Each distinct item originates from a particular sender, just as Dickens was the 'original' author of *Oliver Twist*; but once an item is launched it is accessible to all those equipped to receive it. The original author has little control over its final destination, what will be done with it, how it will be interpreted, changed and passed on. And this is as it ought to be in the great universe of cultural exchanges, for Dickens himself, after all, is only the author of a particular text embodying a story which pre-existed him, with characters well-tested in other stories.

Culture is the original world wide web: a vast communication network in which each carrier throws its seed into a cultural pond. The web is as good as the communication technology which supports it. In the 'olden days', human legs, horses, ships and railways transported beliefs, sounds, stories, fashions and ideas. Now rapid, instantaneous electronic impulses do the job.

Access, of course, is far from complete. As of 2005 more than one-third of Europeans and nearly 70 per cent of North Americans are internet users, but only 2.7 per cent of Africans. Nevertheless, nearly a billion people have access to the internet:

WORLD INTERNET USERS

Region	Population (2005 est.)	Percentage of world population	Internet usage	Percentage population penetration	Percentage of world users
Africa	896,721,874	14.0	23,867,500	2.7	2.5
Asia	3,622,994,130	56.4	327,066,713	9.0	34.2
Europe	731,018,523	11.4	273,262,955	37.4	28.5
Middle East	260,814,179	4.1	21,422,500	8.2	2.2
North America	328,387,059	5.1	223,779,183	68.1	23.4
Latin America/ Caribbean	546,723,509	8.5	70,699,084	12.9	7.4
Oceania/ Australia	33,443,448	0.5	17,655,737	52.8	1.8
WORLD TOTAL	6,420,102,722		957,753,672	14.9	

SOURCE: www.internetworldstats.com, updated on 30 September 2005.

In the wealthy West and much of Asia the speed of growth is such (165 per cent between 2000 and 2005 worldwide) that it is reasonable to assume that saturation – on a par with television – will be reached within the next generation. In Great Britain, according to government statistics, 55 per cent of households could access the internet from home in May 2005, and 60 per cent of adults in Great Britain had used the internet in the first months of that year, ordering goods, travel tickets, accommodation or holidays, videos or DVDs, music or CDs, and tickets for cultural and sporting events. A core group, representing 17 per cent of all adults, declared that they had never really considered using the internet and were not likely to do so in the future.[21]

The possession of home-located receivers such as radios and televisions revolutionised domestic cultural consumption in the twentieth century. The computer, once it became linked to the outside world, extended the receiving capacities of the individual household, adding a new component: homes did not now have to remain passive recipients, but could send messages. Hitherto this could be done exclusively on a one-to-one basis, by sending letters or making phone calls. Now interactivity has become a major trend. Of course, nothing comes out of nothing, it only changes forms. Interactivity was pioneered in the letters pages of newspapers, and more recently radio phone-in programmes. These taught the non-professional public to express their views to a wider audience. The first timid steps were taken towards the construction of a new public space.

Radio and television were and still are organised hierarchically, from one centre to a network of receivers, unlike the telephone, which is a two-way peer-to-peer instrument. The organisation of culture (its distribution) always works from a production centre (one) to many consumers (like all capitalist processes), but when production is cheap and easy, as it is thanks to computers, distribution centres will multiply. The consequences of this are unpredictable – a possible reason why there are so many books and programmes telling us what these consequences will be.

In the 1960s few people seriously thought that computers would become so easily available and so ubiquitous. Even in the early 1980s they were still used mainly for work, for handling vast amounts of data or as word processors – in other words they were used for the production of culture, not for its consumption. Quickly computers developed in the direction of multi-tasking. One could listen to CDs, watch DVDs and, if connected to the web, order goods, book tickets, play games and communicate via email. Information held anywhere on the net could be accessed almost immediately thanks to search engines such as Google.

The repercussions of the world wide web are widely debated. A popular trend consists of forecasting the end of various traditional cultural forms, from books to the cinema and the theatre. Such views, as we have seen, have a long history. Socrates (as reported by Plato in *Phaedrus*) warned that the introduction of the written text 'will create forgetfulness in the learners' souls, because they will not use their memories; they will trust to the external written characters and not remember of themselves', and that the innovation 'is an aid not to memory, but to reminiscence', that it would give its practitioners 'not truth, but only the semblance of truth' and that they would be 'hearers of many things and will have learned nothing'.[22] In 1859 Baudelaire blamed photography for the impoverishment of the *'génie artistique français, déjà si rare*.[23] Discussing in 1937 the advent of radio and sound recording, Paul Valéry, in 'Notre destin et les lettres', wondered whether 'very soon oral and sound culture will not replace the written text'.[24] Walter Benjamin, in a famous essay originally published in 1936, suggested that 'in the era of mechanical reproduction' the days of the museum objects, with their aura of uniqueness and authenticity, were numbered. 'Painting,' he wrote, 'simply is in no position to present an object for simultaneous collective experience,' adding: 'That which withers in the age of mechanical reproduction is the aura of the work of art.'[25]

Yet as we have seen, museums thrive more than ever. Nor did the cinema kill the theatre or the gramophone do away with live performances. Predictions, such as those expressed in *Le Bulletin du livre* in 1969, that 'soon', according to 'experts', textbooks and schoolteachers would be replaced by computers, turned out to be, to say the least, somewhat premature.[26] In 1979 Christopher Evans, a psychologist and computer scientist at Britain's National Physical Laboratory, wrote a book on the oncoming microcomputer revolution: *The Mighty Micro: The Impact of the Computer Revolution*, after which the BBC produced a six-part documentary on the subject. Struck by the infinitely higher storage capacity of computers compared to the printed text, and the minimal costs of storage, Evans predicted that 'The Death of the Printed Word' would come about in the 1980s.[27] Yet Jeff Bezos's Amazon, the first major online commercial operation in the world, was in the business of selling conventional books. The company, having started in 1995 and survived the dot.com crisis of 2000, remained unprofitable until 2002. By 2005 Amazon was selling $8 billion-worth of products to its fifty million active online shoppers, some of whom not only buy books but review and recommend them to other customers.[28] Word of mouth had invaded the world wide web.

The operating principle behind Amazon is suggestive of the authentic breakthrough constituted by the internet: it reduces the main obstacles to a further diffusion of culture. Such obstacles could be roughly divided into two categories: those associated with access, and those associated with supply.

Access has to do with education, predisposition, personal preferences, class, income and gender. People may avoid the opera because they do not like it, or because it is too expensive, or too far away, or because it does not address their concerns, or because it has inappropriate symbolic elements, or because they have never seen one. Others have never read Proust because they can't read, or because they have not received the education required for appreciating him, or because they read a few pages and found them boring, or because they never read novels – not even *The Da Vinci Code*.

Supply is a different matter. Since it may be uneconomic to carry huge stocks, booksellers have to take decisions on which books to display; in so doing, they inevitably narrow the range of what is potentially on offer. Publishers do the same. They assume that a particular book may sell only a thousand copies, and decide on the print run accordingly. Once this stock is sold they will reprint only if they have reasonable expectations that another thousand will be sold. If they do not reprint there may be five hundred disappointed readers, readers willing to pay, but not worth supplying. The same principle operates with video and DVD rental shops, as well as plays and films. A cinema able to accommodate an audience of a thousand might show the current blockbuster for a week only, because it would play to decreasing audiences afterwards. The economically rewarding strategy is to replace it quickly with an equally popular film, thus potentially disappointing hundreds of spectators who missed the first film.

Films, if shown for a longer period, and books, if regularly reprinted and stocked, might in the long run continue to find many customers. What makes this uneconomic is not the lack of demand but the cost of holding stocks. Storage requires space, and space costs money. Inventories tie up capital which could be used for more profitable purposes, and take the space of faster-selling products. The trend of publishing books 'on demand', printing them one at a time on request after the first print run has been exhausted, is an attempt to avoid holding stocks. It is the application of 'just-in-time' production – pioneered by Toyota – to the world of books.

Online retailers such as Amazon resolved part of the problem. They still need to hold stocks, and very large ones at that, but not in an expensive high street bookshop. The stocks are held in distant warehouses, thus reducing the cost of holding them, and Amazon can offer customers a price reduction, which often more than compensates for the cost of transportation. The development of the internet exploited and expanded such possibilities because the downloading of music, films and books completely removes the cost of stocking goods. It allows non-mainstream products to be held for a long time. As Chris Anderson, the editor-in-chief of *Wired*, pointed out in 'The Long Tail' (2004), a pathbreaking essay, 'The future of entertainment is in the millions of niche markets at the shallow end of the bitstream.'[29]

In the pre-internet era, the producers of cultural goods were constantly under pressure to recoup their initial costs in the short term. The motto was

'Sell as much as you can as soon as you can, and then get rid of the unsold stuff'. Lending libraries were an early attempt to circumvent such problems. In the days when books were expensive only two hundred copies might be sold, too small a print run to be profitable, but if held in libraries, a thousand copies might be read by 10,000 consumers prepared to pay for renting what they could not afford to buy.

Selling old films to television networks is a way of lengthening their life. DVDs and videos too prolong the life cycles of films, bypassing the physical limitations of cinemas. Holding 'virtual' stocks in the ether is even better because there are – in practice – almost no stocks to hold. Digitalised cultural commodities can 'live forever'. Some will sell little every year, but in the long term it adds up, and there are no costs.

This does not mean that traditional books – the 'codex' form (sheets of paper bound in hard or soft covers) – or traditional films (shown in a large dark room and watched by perfect strangers) will disappear. On the contrary, they will acquire a new lease of life because there will be more formats available. Markets which are too small or too poor to be supplied in the traditional manner may thrive. It is certainly easier to read a book than a screen, but if a book is difficult to get, a screen will do.

New technologies may eliminate old formats, but they often expand possibilities. For instance, Nigeria produces some thousand films a year (cheaply-made products manufactured in a few weeks), and 300,000 people are employed in what is now called 'Nollywood'. But there are hardly any cinemas in a country of 120 million inhabitants. If cinemas were the only outlets for film production, none would be made and no one would be employed. However, two-thirds of the population has access to VCRs, and this is how they watch films. Nigerian films are not made for cinemas but directly for videocassettes and DVDs.[30]

As we have seen, changing the way cultural products are distributed is bound to affect what is produced. The downloading of songs, if this becomes the dominant format, will not eliminate songs, but it might eliminate albums. Why buy the entire package if one wants only one or two tracks which can be downloaded from iTunes? Even downloading could soon become outdated if everything was not just available all of the time, but was also easily accessible. Imagine: a huge stock of cultural products available from one's home or from portable wireless receivers, all based on the system of pay-on-demand, tiny sums which would obviate the situation of paying the same price for a record one would listen to only three or four times and one to be listened to repeatedly for years. Consumers would no longer need to 'own' a cultural product, just as library users do not need to own books.

Broadcasting too will be affected. When there was only one television channel, the physical constraint of time created a problem similar to that of holding stock. Viewers were at the mercy of a schedule imposed by the network. Multi-channel television increased the power of the viewer. Video recording further enhanced consumer power, since one could watch selected programmes at a time of one's choosing. The arrival of digital television transforms the scenario even further. Television companies can produce a stock of programmes to be accessed at any time, months and perhaps years after they have been produced.

Instead of buying a physical product, people might increasingly buy subscriptions, as many already do: a monthly subscription to Napster or Real Networks' Rhapsody, a cable subscription for television, a DVD service, a mobile phone; and then there is broadband connection. *Billboard* has calculated that in 2005 a fully-paid-up member of the digital society spends $3,000 a year in subscriptions.[31]

Mainstream films, books and television programmes would still be made, but what Chris Anderson called 'the tyranny of the lowest common denominator' might be considerably reduced. He points out that an animated film such as the French-made *Les Triplettes de Belleville* (2003, released in Britain as *Belleville Rendezvous*), nominated for the best animated feature Oscar, opened on just six screens in the USA, thus preventing many American viewers from watching it. In the UK – whose population is one-fifth that of the USA – the film opened on sixty screens, enabling many more people to see it. 'In the tyranny of physical space,' explained Anderson, 'an audience too thinly spread is the same as no audience at all.'

Only a relatively small percentage of cultural products – books, films, tunes – end up being profitable. Some of the remainder would be profitable too if they had a longer 'shelf life'. And many which are not produced, because they are deemed to be of interest to too small a market, might see the 'digital' light of day.

It is unlikely that popular books, like the Harry Potter series or *The Da Vinci Code*, would ever be widely read in digital form – though there are reports that in Japan, where there are eighty-five million mobile phones, young people read full-length novels on their mobiles on subscription websites such as that of Bandai Networks.[32] Reading a conventional book is simpler and more pleasurable than staring at a screen. But what of expensive academic monographs? A two-hundred-page book such as *Catholicism and Austrian Culture*, edited by Ritchie Robertson and Judith Beniston, published in 1999 and sold for £70 by Edinburgh University Press, required a subsidy and is likely to be purchased only by university libraries. Its electronic version, however, would be much cheaper and would appeal to scholars in distant places whose libraries cannot afford them. Online encyclopaedias or those published only on CD-Rom and regularly updated, such as Microsoft's *Encarta*, are easier to consult in electronic format. Academic journals, written and edited for free by academics and sold by publishing houses back to the universities for exorbitant sums, could free themselves of a useless middle-man and put their texts online to reach a wider and more global audience. The result would be to empower an ever increasing number of consumers, expanding their choice, thus following the general trend of the evolution of cultural markets and of capitalism.

Online access enables consumers to choose from within a hitherto fixed package: a single essay inside a book, a single article inside a journal, a comment or an editorial inside a newspaper, a track on an album. Consumers, and not just products, can be targeted too: advertising, instead of taking a potshot at millions of consumers, can be delivered, as Google and Amazon have demonstrated, to those who indicate some interest in the products. Interactivity empowers 'weak' producers too. Those wishing to promote their skills and services globally, nationally or locally can do so without having to face huge advertising costs. All they need is to have their own website.

The scarcity of newspapers and the disproportionate influence of columnists can be circumvented by anyone desirous of sharing their thoughts with others by setting up a 'web-log' or 'blog', an online column or diary which any of the billion people with internet access can read. In some situations, such as wars and natural disasters, bloggers contribute to the global flood of information, as was the case with the so-called Baghdad blogger 'Salam Pax'. Salam obtained wide notoriety when the *Guardian* started publishing his entries during the invasion of Iraq in 2003 (eventually published in book format as *Salam Pax: The Baghdad Blog*) and when his filmed reports were broadcast by the BBC, thus showing that conventional outlets can use blogs too. Even relatively powerful people whose thoughts and works are seldom reported by the conventional media have become bloggers, as is the case with Margot Wallström, the Swedish Vice-President of the European Commission (since 2004), whose task is to improve how the Commission communicates

'Europe' to its citizens, and whose blog contains musings about her family life and her son's birthday.[33]

Online 'newspapers' such as the BBC's http://news.bbc.co.uk/, perhaps the largest in the world, helped by the spread of English and the reputation of the BBC as a brand name, will not kill the cheap and portable sheets of newsprint which can be read anywhere and disposed of so easily, but they might alter their content and format. Paradoxically the web may lengthen the life of some newspaper articles, since these can often be accessed well after the hard copy has been disposed of and recycled.

There may, of course, be a price to pay for such expanded multiplication of producers. A world of few books read by the literate, few films seen by many, and a few television and radio channels seen and heard by all, is a world of shared cultural experiences. The main effect of creating such a shared memory and democratisation of information is that it gives the community of readers, viewers and listeners something to talk about. When strangers meet, if they are interested in each other, they have, in their initial conversation, a feeling of exploration. They exchange tentative views on the music they like, the radio station they tune in to, the television programmes they watch, the books they read, the culture they absorb. Travel and the technology of communication created what some prematurely called a 'global village'. In fact the global village is ancient. Once upon a time there was a common international aristocratic culture: everyone belonging to it was expected to be acquainted with a (limited) range of texts and music. Then, in the nineteenth century, there was bourgeois culture. In the twentieth century the cinema, recorded music, the popular press and the cheap paperback created a mass culture. The apotheosis was radio and television broadcasting. These created national communities, listening to and watching similar programmes in the private comfort of their living rooms.

Of course, the global village was dominated by a limited number of cultural centres. The novels were predominantly British and French, then Russian and American; music was Italian, German and French, later American, British and Latin American; the cinema was soon overwhelmingly American, as was the international trade in television programmes. American supremacy is likely to diminish as its lessons, techniques and forms are absorbed into new products.

The world wide web has enhanced the common elements of international culture, but because the producers have multiplied and will go on multiplying, what is produced is likely to have even less coherence than the cultures of the past. There will be more fragmentation and more diversity. Greater freedom and consumer choice may mean that each group will focus on what it prefers and will experiment less. The global village can be balkanised.

There is no more reason to lament such diversification than to lament the so-called cultural imperialism of the very recent past. The termination of some cultural experiences or themes or forms may be a matter for regret, but it has happened before (for instance, the virtually non-renewable nature of the operatic repertoire), and the world moved on. Some protectionist measures and the preservation of public service broadcasting may help maintain diversity, but diversity and change are, in any case, 'genetic' components of the cultural process.

Over the last two hundred years the West has provided cultural products to the rest of the world out of all proportion to its population. I leave the verdict of whether this was all to the good to single-minded moralists – as I will let them ponder whether today's culture is worse than that which preceded it. The business of historians is more complex: it consists of mapping out the past, thus putting the present into perspective. To decide which culture is good and which is bad is a matter for all human beings, a category that includes historians but excludes no-one. All I know is that a world without culture, whether high or low, whether Tolstoy or 'Grand Theft Auto', would be a world even more savage than that facing us now.

ACKNOWLEDGEMENTS

I would not have been able to write a book of this length and scope in less than ten years had this project not been backed by the Leverhulme Trust, which awarded me a three-year Major Research Fellowship (2000–03), and by the Nuffield Foundation with a Social Science Research Fellowship (1997–98). Further support was received from Queen Mary with a year's sabbatical leave in 2003–04 and various grants, and from the British Academy with a travelling grant to Italy in 1998.

I wish to thank Maurice Aymard of l'École des Hautes Études en Sciences Sociales and Administrateur of la Maison des Sciences de l'Homme for the help given me over the years, including a fellowship in 2002 and providing me with the facilities of the Maison Suger where I have stayed many times. I also thank the staff of Maison Suger, in particular its director M. Jean-Luc Lory, Madame Françoise Girou and Madame Nadia Cheniour.

Most of the French part of the research was carried out at the Bibliothèque Nationale, whose excellent and efficient staff I thank warmly.

In New York I was a Visiting Fellow at the Remarque Institute of New York University (January–March 2001). I am grateful to the Director of the Remarque Institute, Tony Judt, and its Administrator, Ms Jair Kessler, for their kindness.

I thank the staff of the Biblioteca Nazionale Braidense (Brera) of Milan; of the Biblioteca dell'Istituto della Enciclopedia Italiana in Rome, in particular its Director, Elsa Adducci; of the Biblioteca della Scuola del Cinema, Cinecittà, Rome; of the Biblioteca di Storia Moderna e Contemporanea, Rome, in particular its Director, Rosanna de Longis; of the Biblioteca Nazionale Centrale in Rome; and of the University of Trento library.

I thank the University of London Library at Senate House, the library of Queen Mary, University of London, and its Arts Librarian Eilis Rafferty.

I thank the British Library and its staff and the staff of the New York Public Library.

I thank François Poirier and the Université de Paris XIII where I spent April 2005 as a Professeur Invité.

I thank the makers of the French TV serial *Sous le soleil*, the film production company Marathon and its director and producer Pascal Breton, for providing me with information on their activities and accounts.

I am also particularly grateful to the Biblioteca Fondazione Feltrinelli and its *eccellente* and kind Director David Bidussa. I am also grateful to the Biblioteca Nazionale in Florence – above all to the determined librarian who found a book I needed even though she was not supposed to enter the stacks where it was stored because an architect had left the safety certificate unsigned (for ten months).

I also thank the Biblioteca di Comunicazioni di Massa of the RAI (the Italian state broadcasting company), and in particular its helpful Director Anna Maria Tucci and her colleague Giovanna Lipari.

I thank Judith Summers, who read with patience, a sense of humour and sensitive intelligence vast sections of this book.

I also thank friends, colleagues, and acquaintances who have given me advice or bibliographical help: Alberto Abruzzese (La Sapienza, Rome); Barbara Garvin (University College London, for advice on Gioacchino Belli); Charles Rearick (University of Massachusetts at Amherst); Enrica Villari (University of Ca' Foscari, Venice, for advice on Walter Scott), Dora Giannaki (for advice on Greek TV); Edward Wright (popular music genres); Eric Hobsbawm; Joel Findler (for advice on the cinema); Gabriella Turnaturi (Bologna University, for illuminating conversations); Giovanna Zucconi (Effe Feltrinelli); Giulio Sapelli (State University of Milan); the late Professor Giuseppe Petronio (University of Trieste); Hans-Joerg Stiehler (University of Leipzig, Institut für Kommunikations und Medienwissenschaft); Jad Adams; Jane Schneider (CUNY) and Peter Schneider (Fordham University); John Jungclaussen (of *Die Zeit*); Jonathan Smele and Virginia Davis, both of Queen Mary, University of London; Judith Goldstein (of Vassar College, for convincing me, rightly, that I should start in 1800 rather than in 1850 as I had originally intended, thereby adding to the length of the book); Loredana Cornero, Director of the Ufficio Studi of the RAI; Benedetta Bini, former Director of the Italian Cultural Institute of London and professor at the University of Viterbo; Lucio Sponza (Westminster University); Luisa Finocchi (Director of the Mondadori Foundation); Isabelle Veyrat-Masson (Sciences Po, Paris); Marina Paladini Musitelli (University of Trieste); Marta Petrusewicz (Hunter College, New York), Massimo Loche for details of cinema-going in Sardinia in the 1950s; Ombretta Ingrascì; Ruediger Steinmetz (University of Leipzig); Ruth Ben-Ghiat (New York University); Cordula

Günther (Halle University, Institut für Medien-und Kommunikationswissen-schaften); and Vassilis Fouskas (University of Stirling).

I thank Philip Norman for giving me the benefit of his advice and expertise on British popular music. I thank Ilaria Favretto (Kingston University) for her helpful suggestions on several chapters. I also thank Imogen Tilden of the *Guardian* for contributing her advice and editing skills to the chapter on popular music. I thank my colleague Mark Glancy who read some of the chapters on the cinema and gave me invaluable advice.

I thank my publisher Richard Johnson for remaining calm as the length of the book increased beyond what had been originally planned, and my editor Robert Lacey for editing well over 600,000 words without complaining.

I thank my daughter Tanya Sassoon for providing me with information on the British periodical press, for her editing skills, and above all for putting me right where I was wrong in the chapter 'Exploding Pop'.

Last but not least, particularly heartfelt thanks must go to Beatrice de Gerloni of Trento for her considerable help with a variety of sources and queries, for providing German texts, often with helpful notes and translations, and for getting in touch with German academics on my behalf.

Donald Sassoon
London, January 2006

NOTES

Introduction

1 *Creative Industries Mapping Document 2001*, pp.00–05
2 Tylor, *Primitive Culture*, p.1
3 Braudel, *Écrits sur l'histoire*, pp.258–9
4 Cited by Braudel in *Écrits sur l'histoire*, p.259
5 Arnold, *Culture and Anarchy and other Writings*, p.59
6 Beletski, 'Étudier l'histoire du lecteur' pp.49–51
7 Sismondi, *De la littérature du midi de l'Europe*, pp.5–6
8 See remarks by Lévi-Strauss, *Entretiens avec Claude Lévi-Strauss*, p.97
9 Propp, *Morphology of the Folktale*
10 Lodge, *The Art of Fiction*, pp.7, 9, 75
11 Barthes, *Image Music Text*, pp.142–8
12 Jauss, 'Literary History as a Challenge to Literary Theory', in *New Directions in Literary History*, pp.11–41 – originally 'Literaturgeschichte als Provokation der Literaturwissenschaft', in Hans Robert Jauss, *Literaturgeschichte als Provokation*
13 Iser, 'The Reading Process: a phenomenological approach', p.220
14 Schaeffer, 'Du texte au genre', pp.187–8
15 Viëtor, 'L'histoire des genres littéraires', p.29
16 Jauss, 'Littérature médiévale et théorie des genres', p.49
17 See Bourdieu, *Distinction* and his *The Field of Cultural Production*
18 Bourdieu, 'Vous avez dit "populaire"', p.98
19 Certeau *La Culture au pluriel*, pp.72–4
20 Scholes, *Structuralism in Literature*, pp.129–38
21 *www.uis.unesco.org/ev-en.php?ID=2867201&ID2=DOTOPIC*
22 Latouche, *L'occidentalisation du monde*, p.29
23 *Creative Industries Mapping Document 2001*, p.3–01
24 Anderson, *The Origins of Postmodernity*, p.94
25 Lallement, 'Essai d'une définition économique du livre', p.107
26 Moulin, *De la valeur de l'art*, p.188

PART I

1800–1830 : THE PRE-CONDITIONS

1 : Sources of Cultural Expansion

1 'India's advertising luminaries take a bow', *Financial Times*, 30 October 2003
2 Livi-Bacci, *La popolazione nella storia d'Europa*, pp.14–15. Slightly different data can be found in Armengaud, 'Population in Europe', p.29
3 Anderson, 'Western Nationalism and Eastern Nationalism', p.32
4 For the statistics on immigration see Bairoch, *Histoire économique et sociale du monde du XVIᵉ siècle à nos jours*, Vol. 2, *Victoires et déboires*, pp.176–9
5 Gallaway and Vedder, 'Emigration from the United Kingdom to the United States: 1860–1913', pp.885–97
6 Higgs, 'Race, Skills, and Earnings: American Immigrants in 1909', p.424
7 Stearns, 'The Effort at Continuity in Working-Class Culture', p.638
8 Lopez, *The Birth of Europe*, pp.260–1
9 Porter, *London. A Social History*, p.98
10 Burke, 'The Invention of Leisure in Early Modern Europe', p.137, where he warns, however, against an excessively monolithic image of pre-industrial culture

11 Headrick, *The Tools of Empire*, p.130

12 Barbier, 'Le commerce international de la librairie française au XIXᵉ siècle', pp.100–3

13 Aveni, *Empires of Time*, p.96

14 Klancher, *The Making of English Reading Audiences 1790–1832*, p.27

15 Berend, *The Crisis Zone of Europe*, p.4

16 Cipolla, *Literacy and Development in the West*, pp.18, 77–8

17 Graff, *The Legacies of Literacy*, pp.301–2

18 Johansson, 'The History of Literacy in Sweden', pp.153, 156

19 Gough, 'Implications of Literacy in Traditional China and India', p.70

20 Harris, *Ancient Literacy*, p.7

21 Goody, *Capitalism and Modernity*, p.74 citing J. M. Bloom, *Paper Before Print: the History and Impact of Paper in the Islamic World*, Yale University Press 2001

22 Gregory of Nyssa's sermon *De deitate filii et spiritus sancti*, in *Patrologiae Graecae*, Vol. 46, column 557. I thank Beatrice de Gerloni for helping me to track this down

23 See Amanda Vickery's *The Gentleman's Daughter*, especially the chapter called 'Prudent Economy'

24 Germaine de Staël, *De l'Allemagne*, Vol. I, p.134

25 White, *Women's Magazines 1693–1968*, pp.23–40

26 Stearns, 'Stages of Consumerism: Recent Work on the Issues of Periodization', p.105

27 Ibid., pp.109, 113

28 Jardine, *Worldy Goods*, p.421

29 Haskell, 'The Market for Italian Art in the seventeenth Century', p.50

30 Cited in Wilson, *Bohemians*, p.16

31 Cited in Brewer, *The Pleasures of the Imagination*, p.146

32 Ibid., pp.146–7, also pp.148–9 on Goldsmith's ambivalence towards the literary world

33 Germaine de Staël, *De l'Allemagne*, Vol. I, p.149

34 See Weil, *L'Interdiction du roman et la librairie 1728–1750*

35 Gersmann, 'Le monde des colporteurs parisiens de livres prohibés 1750–1789', p.39

36 Darnton, *The Forbidden Best-Sellers of Pre-Revolutionary France*, p.88

37 Association Hôtel Mame Centre Culturelle, *Mame. Angers-Paris-Tours. Deux siècles du livre*, p.10

38 Chandler, *England in 1819*, p.350

39 Stone, 'Literacy and Education in England 1640–1900', p.96

40 Williams, *The Long Revolution*, p.136

41 Grew and Harrigan, 'The Availability of Schooling in Nineteenth-Century France' esp. p.34

42 Stone, 'Literacy and Education in England 1640–1900', p.89

43 Einhard, *The Life of Charlemagne*, section 25 available at *www.fordham.edu/halsall/basis/einhard.htmlStudies*

44 Burke, 'The Uses of Literacy in Early Modern Italy', p.22

45 Botrel, 'Les recherches sur le livre et la lecture en Espagne aux XVIIIe–XXe siècles', p.53

46 Cipolla, *Literacy and Development in the West*, pp.71–2

47 Albertini, *L'École en France XIX–XX siècle de la maternelle à l'université*, p.7

48 Graff, *The Legacies of Literacy*, p.302

49 Van Horn Melton, 'From Image to Word: Cultural Reform and the Rise of Literate Culture in Eighteenth-Century Austria', pp.95–6

50 Davis, 'Italy', p.84

51 Lopez, 'Notes sur le fonds ancien des petits récits en prose dans la *Literatura de Cordel*', p.13

52 Cipolla, *Literacy and Development in the West*, p.11

53 Hammond, *The Town Labourer*, pp.48–9

54 Lyons, *Le Triomphe du livre*, p.72

55 Charle, *Les intellectuels en Europe au XIXe siècle*, p.59

56 Johansson, 'The History of Literacy in Sweden' p.152

57 Graff, *The Legacies of Literacy*, p.13

58 Fox, *Oral Literate Culture in England, 1500–1700*, pp.13–14

59 Baron, 'Will Anyone Accept the Good News on Literacy?' p.B10

60 See Stephens, *Education, Literacy and Society 1830–70*, and Thomas, 'The Meaning of Literacy in Early Modern England' p.102

61 Cipolla, *Literacy and Development in the West*, p.71

62 On Italy see Sallmann, 'Les niveaux d'alphabétisation en Italie au XIXe siècle', p.186

63 Burke, 'The Uses of Literacy in Early Modern Italy', p.22

64 Saul, 'Aesthetic humanism (1790–1830)', p.209

65 See Ridders-Simoens. 'Mobility', pp.416–48, especially pp.441–2

2 : Triumphant Languages

1 D'hulst, 'Traduire l'Europe en France entre 1810 et 1840', p.143

2 See Asor Rosa (ed.), *Letteratura italiana. Storia e geografia*, Vol. 3, p.11 and De Mauro, *Storia linguistica dell'Italia unita*, Vol. 1, p.43

3 Fernández-Armesto, *Civilizations*, p.185

4 Western ideas of what constitutes religion may be quite different from the African, see Goody, *The Logic of Writing and the Organization of Society*, p.4, and his *The Interface Between The Written And The Oral*, pp.125–6

5 The term diglossia, modelled on the French *diglossie*, was coined by Charles A. Fergusson in 1959; see his 'Diglossia', pp.325–40

6 Ibid., p.336

7 Ong, 'Writing is a Technology that Restructures Thought', p.42

8 Houston, *Literacy in Early Modern Europe*, p.204

9 Carmichael, 'Coming to terms with the Past: Language and Nationalism in Russia and its Neighbours', pp.268, 272

10 Lyttelton, 'Origins of a National Monarchy: the House of Savoy', p.327

11 De Mauro, *Storia linguistica dell'Italia unita*, Vol. 1, p.32

12 Foster, *Modern Ireland 1600–1972*, pp.121, 311, 340

13 Phillips, *Printing and Bookselling in Dublin, 1670–1800*, pp.100ff

14 Schlegel, *Lectures on the History of Literature, Ancient and Modern*, p.159

15 Bernard, 'J. Kopitar, lien vivant entre la slavistique et la germanistique', pp.191–209

16 Deme, 'Writers and Essayists and the Rise of Magyar Nationalism in the 1820s and 1830s', p.626

17 Törnquist-Plewa, 'Contrasting Ethnic Nationalisms: Eastern Central Europe', p.188

18 Wachtel, *Making a Nation, Breaking a Nation*, pp.25–7

19 Kostallari, 'La langue littéraire nationale albanaise et notre époque', pp.10, 27

20 Berend, *The Crisis Zone of Europe*, p.14

21 Lloshi, 'Modern Albanian in different culture contexts', p.171

22 Sokolova, 'L'Intelligentsia Albanaise à l'époque de la renaissance et la nouvelle culture albanaise', pp.57, 62, 69–70

23 Törnquist-Plewa, 'Contrasting Ethnic Nationalisms: Eastern Central Europe', pp.193–7

24 Todorova, 'Dialogue de la littérature macédonienne avec la tradition nationale et les littératures étrangères', p.844

25 Lehtonen, 'La littérature finlandaise au carrefour des cultures', pp.691–2

26 Vikør, 'Northern Europe: Languages as Prime Markers of Ethnic and National Identity', pp.113–14. The intricacies of the Norwegian linguistic conflicts are dealt with in E. Haugen, *Language Conflict and Language Planning: the Case of Modern Norwegian*, Harvard University Press 1966

27 Morton and Morris, 'Civil Society, Governance and Nation, 1852–1914', p.361

28 Cited in Habermas, *The Postnational Constellation*, pp.6–8

29 Balibar and Laporte, *Le Français national*, p.31, citing *Histoire de la Langue française*, a multi-volume work started in 1906 by Ferdinand Brunot

30 Weber, *France Fin de Siècle*, p.44

31 The full text can be found in Balibar and Laporte, *Le Français national*, pp.198–215

32 Certeau, Julia and Revel, *Une politique de la langue*, pp.11, 47

33 Balibar and Laporte, *Le Français national*, p.59

34 Chartier, 'Frenchness in the History of the Book: from the History of Publishing to the History of Reading', pp.304–5

35 Quaghebeur, 'L'identité ne se réduit pas à la langue', p.68

36 See Frickx, 'Littérature belge de langue française ou littérature française de Belgique?', pp.24–5

37 See Grassi, 'Introduction'

38 Asor Rosa, 'Centralismo e policentrismo nella letteratura italiana unitaria', p.8

39 Lanza, *Porta e Belli*, pp.12–13

40 Belli, *Sonetti*, p.8, cited in Gibellini, *Il coltello e la corona*, p.15

41 Gibellini, '"Peuple" et "Nation": Notes sur la littérature dialectale italienne', 1982, p.4

42 Gramsci, *Selections from the Cultural Writings*, p.268

43 Yates and McKenzie (eds), *Viennese Popular Theatre*, preface

44 Duțu, 'La circulation de l'imprimé dans le Sud-Est européen entre le XVIIIe et le XIXe siècle', p.165

45 Staël, *De l'Allemagne*, Vol. I, p.96

46 Lüsebrink and Reichardt, 'La traduction, indicateur de diffusion: imprimés français traduits en allemand', p.409. This is an

analysis of 6,500 texts translated into German between 1770 and 1815. On the German Romantics' commitment to translations see Berman, *L'épreuve de l'étranger. Culture et traduction dans l'Allemagne romantique*

47 Alfieri, 'La lingua di consumo', p.210
48 Calvet, *La guerre des langues et les politiques linguistiques*, pp.249–50
49 Staël, *De l'Allemagne*, pp.119–20
50 Rietbergen, *Europe. A Cultural History*, p.296
51 Jonard, *La France et l'Italie au siècle des lumières. Essai sur les échanges intellectuels*, p.37
52 Calvet, *La guerre des langues et les politiques linguistiques*, pp.73–4
53 Cited in Graf, *L'anglomania e l'influsso inglese in Italia nel secolo XVIII*, p.2
54 McMahon, *Enemies of the Enlightenment*, pp.6–7
55 Staël, *De l'Allemagne*, Vol. I, p.93
56 As described by Graf in *L'anglomania e l'influsso inglese in Italia nel secolo XVIII*, p.57
57 Lai (ed.), *Adam Smith Across Nations*, p.xvi
58 Robb, *Balzac*, p.85
59 Cited in Mollier, 'Un siècle de transition vers une culture de masse', p.187
60 Arnould, *Essais de théorie et d'histoire littéraire*, p.321
61 Crystal, *The Cambridge Encyclopedia of the English Language*, p.54
62 Fox, *Oral Literate Culture in England*, p.51
63 Joyce, 'The People's English: Language and Class in England c.1840–1920', pp.156–8, and p.163
64 Brontë, *Jane Eyre*, Chapter 31
65 Joyce, 'The People's English', p.165
66 Ibid., p.157
67 Cited in Crystal, *English as a Global Language*, p.66
68 Goethe, *Conversations of Goethe with Eckermann*, p.255, entry for 12 March 1828
69 Rousseau, *Émile, ou de l'éducation*, p.316
70 Soriano, *Guide de littérature pour la jeunesse*, p.25
71 Heiderich, *The German Novel of 1800*, p.168n, where he cites Peter Michelsen's study *Laurence Sterne und der deutsche Roman des achtzehnten Jahrhunderts*, Göttingen 1962
72 Both *Les Sauvages de l'Europe* and *Les Amants François* were published anonymously
73 Cooper-Richet, 'Les imprimés en langue anglaise en France au XIXe siècle: rayonnement intellectuel, circulation et modes de pénétration', pp.123–5
74 On Robinson Crusoe in Russia see Cross, *Anglo-Russica*, p.76
75 Vainchtein, 'Les bardes anglais et la critique russe', pp.147–56
76 Eliot, '*Patterns and Trends* and the *NSTC*: Some initial observations. Part Two', p.103
77 Anderson, 'Western Nationalism and Eastern Nationalism', p.40
78 Orton, 'Did the Slavs Speak German at Their First Congress?', p.517

3 : Publishing

1 Rubinstein, *Wealth and Inequality in Britain*, especially p.33
2 See more details in Hodgkin, 'New Technologies in Printing and Publishing: the Present of the Written Word', p.153
3 Sadleir, 'Aspects of the Victorian Novel', p.7. This is the text of a lecture delivered in November 1937
4 Pollard 'The English Market for Printed Books', p.35; this is the unrevised text of Pollard's 1959 Sandars Lectures at Cambridge University
5 Barrell, 'Divided we Grow', p.10
6 Lyons, *Le Triomphe du livre*, pp.56–7
7 Bellos, 'La conjuncture de la production', p.731
8 Erickson, *The Economy of Literary Form*, p.4
9 Chartier, 'Lecteurs dans la longue durée: du *codex* à l'écran', p.272
10 Ibid., pp.276–7
11 Ibid., p.273
12 Chartier, 'Du livre au livre', p.70
13 Eisenstein, 'The Advent of Printing and the Problem of the Renaissance', pp.19–89
14 Williams, *The Long Revolution*, p.159
15 Schlegel, *Charakteristiken und Kritiken II*, p.53
16 Carlyle, *Sartor Resartus*, p.31. Originally an unsigned article in the monthly *Fraser's Magazine*, published in book form in 1836
17 Febvre and Martin, *The Coming of the Book*, p.30
18 Goody, *Capitalism and Modernity*, p.133
19 Hobson, *The Eastern Origins of Western Civilisation*, pp.184–5
20 Houston, *Literacy in Early Modern Europe*, p.157
21 Pollard, 'The English Market for Printed Books', p.12

22 Houston, *Literacy in Early Modern Europe*. p.156, see also Febvre and Martin, *The Coming of the Book*, pp.181–6

23 Febvre and Martin, *The Coming of the Book*, p.209. On Russia see Gary Marker, 'Russian and the "Printing Revolution": Notes and Observations' in *Slavic Review*, No. 2, Summer 1982, p.269

24 Febvre and Martin, *The Coming of the Book*, p.218

25 Fox, *Oral Literate Culture in England*, cit., pp.13–14

26 Jardine, *Worldly Goods. A New History of the Renaissance*, p.147

27 Houston, *Literacy in Early Modern Europe*, p.185

28 Thomson, *The Making of the English Working Class*, p.261

29 Warner, *Licensing Entertainment*, p.133n

30 Hobbes, *Leviathan*, p.100

31 Angenot, 'La littérature populaire française au dix-neuvième siècle', p.314

32 Crubellier, 'L'élargissement du public', p.31

33 Chartier, 'Frenchness in the History of the Book', p.302

34 Barbier and Bertho Lavenir, *Histoire des médias, de Diderot à Internet*, p.22

35 Mollier, 'Un siècle de transition vers une culture de masse', p.188

36 Santoro, *Storia del libro italiano*, p.289

37 Berengo, *Intellettuali e librai nella Milano della restaurazione*, pp.3–5

38 Lyons, 'Les best-sellers', pp.410, 419

39 'The Popular Novel in the Nineteenth Century', special issue of *Canadian Review of Comparative Literature*, Vol. 9, No.3, September 1982

40 Bellos, 'Le Marché du livre à l'époque romantique: recherches et problèmes', p.647–9

41 Eliot, '*Patterns and Trends* and the *NSTC*: Some initial observations. Part One', p.80

42 Barker, 'The Rise of the provincial book trade in England and the growth of a national transport system', p.141. This author uses the ESTC, the catalogues of books printed in the British Isles

43 Cross, *Anglo-Russica*, p.76

44 Marker, 'Russian and the "Printing Revolution": Notes and Observations', pp.276–7

45 Karamzin, 'The Book Trade and the Love of Reading in Russia', p.113

46 Botrel, 'Les recherches sur le livre et la lecture en Espagne aux XVIIIe–XXe siècles', pp.52, 55

47 Kortländer, 'Traduire. "La plus noble des activités" ou "la plus abjecte des pratiques" ', p.126

48 Blackbourn, *The Fontana History of Germany 1780–1918*, pp.39–40, citing data from Rolf Engelsing, *Analphabetentum und Lektüre*, Stuttgart 1973, pp.119–20, 128

49 Angenot, 'Ceci tuera cela, ou: la chose imprimée contre le livre', p.87

50 Barbier and Lavenir, *Histoire des médias, de Diderot à Internet*, pp.41, 46

51 Ibid., pp.43–4

52 Bienkowska and Chamerska, *Books in Poland*, p.26

53 Saul, 'Aesthetic humanism (1790–1830)', p.210

54 Schuster, 'Popular Literature in Germany: 1800–1850', pp.334, 341–2

55 Saul, 'Aesthetic humanism (1790–1830)', p.217

56 Staël (Madame de), *De l'Allemagne*, Vol. I, p.42

4 : Peddling Stories

1 Cooper, 'Surviving the Reformation', p.21

2 Fontaine, 'Colporteurs de livres dans l'Europe du XVIIIe siècle', pp.27–8

3 Chartier, *The Cultural Uses of Print in Early Modern France*, p.240

4 Houston, *Literacy in Early Modern Europe*, pp.182–3

5 Andries. 'Les livres de savoir pratique dans la France des XVIIe et XVIIIe', p.173

6 Bollème, *La Bibliothèque Bleue*, pp.8–13

7 Chartier, *The Cultural Uses of Print in Early Modern France*, pp.241–6

8 Coleridge, *Biographia Literaria*, Vol. 2, pp.1–2

9 Fontaine, *Histoire du colportage en Europe (XVe–XIXe siècle)*, p.189

10 Chartier, *The Cultural Uses of Print in Early Modern France*, p.268

11 Houston, *Literacy in Early Modern Europe*, p.183

12 Angenot, 'La littérature populaire française au dix-neuvième siècle', pp.308–9; Darmon, *Le Colportage de Librairie en France sous le Second Empire*, p.142

13 Eisenstein, 'The Impact of Printing on Western Society and Thought: A preliminary report', p.31

14 Ó Ciosáin, *Print and Popular Culture in Ireland, 1750–1850*

15 Brooks, *When Russia Learned to read*, p.xvii

16 Cox, 'Fairy-Tale Plots and Contemporary Heroes in Early Russian Prose Fiction', pp.86, 89–90

17 Behrman, 'Le Lecteur des vies des saints', p.65

18 Warrilow, 'Some Recent German Periodicals on Book and Book-Trade History, a Summary', p.87

19 See Capp, *Astrology and the Popular Press*

20 Darmon, *Le Colportage de Librairie en France sous le Second Empire*, pp.294–5

21 Mills Todd III, 'Periodicals in literary life of the early nineteenth century', pp.47, 45

22 Beaven, 'Russian Literary Almanacs of the 1820s and their Legacy', see especially pp.65–6 and 76–7

23 See illustration in Chartier, *The Cultural Uses of Print in Early Modern France*, p.177. *The Colporteur* can be found at the Musée des Arts et Traditions Populaires in Paris

24 Chartier, 'Introduction', p.13; see also Fontaine, 'Colporteurs de livres dans l'Europe du XVIIIe siècle', p.24

25 Alexandu Duțu, 'La circulation de l'imprimé dans le Sud-Est européen entre le XVIIIe et le XIXe siècle' p.166

26 Braida, 'Quelques considérations sur l'histoire de la lecture en Italie . . .', p.30

27 Fontaine, *Histoire du colportage en Europe (XVe–XIXe siècle)*, p.189 and Berengo, *Intellettuali e librai nella Milano della restaurazione*, p.75

28 Botrel, *La diffusion du livre en Espagne (1868–1914)*, pp.11, 28

29 Chartier, 'Introduction', p.14

30 Botrel, 'La littérature *de cordel* en Espagne. Essai de synthèse', pp.271, 275; Ouimette, ' "Monstrous Fecundity": The Popular Novel in Nineteenth-Century Spain', p.383

31 Fontaine, *Histoire du colportage en Europe*, p.190

32 Botrel, *La diffusion du livre en Espagne (1868–1914)*, p.19

33 Sauvy, 'Noël Gille dit La Pistole, "marchand forain libraire rouland par la France" ', pp.183, 185, 190

34 Fox, *Oral Literate Culture in England*, p.15

35 Chartier, *The Cultural Uses of Print in Early Modern France*, p.168

36 Bollème, *La Bibliothèque Bleue*, pp.18, 21, 29ff, 53, 64, 115

37 Seguin, *L'Information en France avant le périodique*, p.74; the appendix contains the long titles of 517 canards printed between 1529 and 1631

38 The figure comes from Williams, *The Long Revolution*, p.165 but he provides no source for such a large sale

39 See text in *http://gaslight.mtroyal.ab.ca/ gaslight/martbald.htm*

40 See collection first published in 1882 by Chatto and Windus: *Chapbooks of the Eighteenth Century*, edited by John Ashton

41 Rowe and Schelling, *Memory and Modernity*, pp.86–7

42 Reprinted in Pecchio, *Della produzione letteraria*, p.14

43 Ibid., p.161

44 Ibid., pp.153–6

45 See Chapter Eight

46 Cross, *The Common Writer*, pp.169–70

47 Ibid., p.172

48 Bellos, 'Le Marché du livre à l'époque romantique', p.654

49 Villot, *Notice des Tableaux exposés dans les galeries du Musée National du Louvre*, p.108

50 Bellos, 'Le Marché du livre à l'époque romantique', p.655

51 Ibid., p.652

52 Vachon, 'Balzac en feuilletons et en livres . . .', p.276

53 Ibid., pp.260–2

54 On Barberino see Allaire, *Andrea da Barberino and the language of chivalry*, pp.6–7

55 Manzoni, *I Promessi sposi*, pp.328–9 and 329n

56 Chartier, *Cultural History*, pp.152–4

57 Ibid., p.157

58 Ibid., p.163

59 Farci, 'Le temps libre au village', p.260

60 Chartier, *Cultural History*, p.167. Chartier is less sceptical in his *The Cultural Uses of Print in Early Modern France*, p.155

61 Chartier, *The Cultural Uses of Print in Early Modern France*, p.146; the study cited is Albert Labarre's *Le Livre dans la vie amiénoise du seizième siècle. L'Enseignement des inventaires après décès 1503–1576* (1971)

62 See Daumard, *Les Bourgeois de Paris au XIXe siècle*

63 Hunter, 'The Novel and Social/Cultural History', p.25

64 Carson, 'Enlightenment, popular culture, and Gothic fiction', p.262

65 Chartier, *The Cultural Uses of Print in Early Modern France*, p.204

66 Hunter, 'The novel and social/cultural history', p.25

67 Brewer, *The Pleasures of the Imagination*, p.177
68 Houston, *Literacy in Early Modern Europe*, p.174
69 Cross, *The Common Writer*, p.168
70 Houston, *Literacy in Early Modern Europe*, p.175. Other sources suggest higher figures, see for instance Erickson, *The Economy of Literary Form*, p.127
71 Botrel, *La diffusion du livre en Espagne (1868–1914)*, p.26
72 Saul, 'Aesthetic humanism (1790–1830)', p.210
73 Bödeker, 'D'une "histoire littéraire du lecteur" à l'histoire du lecteur. Bilan et perspectives de l'histoire de la lecture en Allemagne', p.107
74 Berengo, *Intellettuali e librai nella Milano della restaurazione*, pp.133–4
75 Ibid., pp.185, 192
76 Ibid., p.200
77 Mollier, 'Un siècle de transition vers une culture de masse', p.191
78 Bellos, 'Le Marché du livre à l'époque romantique', p.658
79 Parent-Lardeur, *Lire à Paris au temps de Balzac*, p.200
80 Bellos, 'Le Marché du livre à l'époque romantique', p.656
81 Pichois, 'Les Cabinets de Lectures à Paris, durant la première moitié du XIXe siècle', p.526
82 Parent-Lardeur, *Lire à Paris au temps de Balzac*, p.200
83 Boscq, 'L'implantation des librairies à Paris (1815–1848)', pp.36–7
84 Lyons, *Le Triomphe du livre*, p.127
85 Pichois, 'Les Cabinets de Lectures à Paris . . .' p.528
86 Fantham, *Roman Literary Culture. From Cicero to Apuleius*, p.38
87 Rutherford, 'Introduction' to Cervantes, *Don Quixote*, p.xix
88 Ashton, *George Eliot*, p.144
89 Waugh, *Brideshead Revisited*, pp.150–1
90 Price, *The Anthology and the Rise of the Novel: From Richardson to George Eliot*, p.84
91 Letter of 23 October 1814 in Hayden (ed.), *Walter Scott. The Critical Heritage*, p.75
92 Cited in Ashton, *George Eliot*, p.313
93 Cited in Chandler, *England in 1819*, p.309
94 Erickson, *The Economy of Literary Form*, p.158
95 Alfieri, 'La lingua di consumo', p.189
96 Ashton, *George Eliot*, p.286
97 See his remarks during an interview for BBC2 in 1968 reprinted in *The Listener*, 10 October 1968
98 Price, *The Anthology and the Rise of the Novel*, p.105
99 Ibid., p.87
100 Ibid., pp.13, 17
101 Adburgham, *Silver Fork Society*, pp.23–5
102 Price, *The Anthology and the Rise of the Novel*, p.106

5 : Foundation Stories

1 Figgis, 'Artistes et amateurs des îles britanniques à Rome', p.121
2 Raspi Serra, 'Fouilles et découvertes, personnages et débats', p.116
3 Schlegel, *Lectures on the History of Literature, Ancient and Modern*, p.21
4 Close, *The Romantic Approach to 'Don Quixote'*, p.29
5 Schlegel, 'Letter about a Novel', p.77
6 Schlegel, *Lectures on the History of Literature, Ancient and Modern*, p.3
7 See Houston, *Literacy in Early Modern Europe*, p.221 – which mentions only the Boccaccio connection
8 On the Ossian cult in Italy see Graf, *L'anglomania e l'influsso inglese in Italia nel secolo XVIII*, pp.294–5
9 Price, *English Literature in Germany*, p.123
10 Boswell, *Life of Johnson*, p.614, entry for 7 April 1775
11 On the English reaction see Shiach, *Discourse on Popular Culture*, p.112
12 See Fabrizi, *Studi inediti di Vittorio Alfieri sull'Ossian del Cesarotti*, and Alfieri, *Estratti d'Ossian e da Stazio per la Tragica*
13 Darnton, 'Extraordinary Commonplaces', p.83
14 Cottin, *Malvina*, Vol. 1, p.67
15 Scott, *The Singing Bourgeois*, p.28
16 Goethe, *The Sorrows of Young Werther*, p.95
17 See MacDonald, *In Defence of Ossian*, 1906, probably Edinburgh but reprinted from the *Oban Times*
18 Thiesse, 'Littérature et folklore, l'invention érudite de la culture populaire', p.244
19 Herder, 'Extract from a Correspondence on Ossian and the Songs of the Ancient Peoples', pp.154–61. This quote is on p.154
20 Ibid., p.155
21 Ibid.; see also Bruckner, 'Histoire de la Volkskunde', p.226
22 Boyle, *Goethe. The Poet and the Age*, Vol. 1, pp.97–100. *Goetz* in turn inspired

Jean-Paul Sartre's play *Le Diable et le Bon Dieu*

23 Francillon, 'La quête d'une identité helvétique dans la Suisse romande du XVIIIe siècle', pp.54–5

24 Staël, *De l'Allemagne*, Vol. I, p.70

25 Staël, *Corinne ou l'Italie*, pp.172, 160. Elizabeth Barrett Browning's citation is in Caplan's Introduction to *Aurora and other poems*, p.17

26 See Giuli, 'Tracing Sisterhood: Corilla Olimpica as Corinne's unacknowledged Alter Ego'

27 De Staël, *Corinne*, p.136

28 Weinmann, 'Étranger, étrangeté: de l'allemand au français au début du XIXe siècle', p.53

29 Macherey, *À quoi pense la littérature?*, pp.30–1

30 Thiesse 'Littérature et folklore, l'invention érudite de la culture populaire', p.248–9

31 Besançon, 'Comment la Russie a pensé au peuple' p.110. On the Voltaire connection, see Dmitrieva, 'Vers l'âge d'or de la culture russe', p.127. On Richardson see Cross, *Anglo-Russica*, p.81

32 Cited on the first page of Wachtel's significantly titled *An Obsession with History*

33 Besançon, 'Comment la Russie a pené au peuple', p.110–11

34 Marquis de Custine, *Letters from Russia*, p.20

35 See Haxthausen, *Studies on the Interior of Russia*, originally published in 1843–44

36 Florovsky, 'The Problem of Old Russian Culture', pp.5–7

37 Plakans, 'Peasants, Intellectuals, and Nationalism in the Russian Baltic Provinces, 1820–90', pp.468–9; see also Vâikis-Friebergs (ed.), *Linguistics and poetics of Latvian folk songs*

38 Boyer, *Histoire des littératures scandinaves*, pp.106, 131

39 Wachtel, *An Obsession with History*, p.32

40 Thiesse, 'Littérature et folklore, l'invention érudite de la culture populaire', p.245

41 Ibid., p.242

42 Šilbajoris, 'Kristijonas Donelaitis, A Lithuanian Classic', pp.252, 261–2

43 Lehtonen, 'La littérature finlandaise au carrefour des cultures', pp.691–3

44 There is now a full English edition: *The Complete Sagas of Icelanders* edited by Vidar Hreinsson, Leifur Eiriksson, Reykjavik in five volumes and a selection: *The Sagas of Icelanders: A Selection* with a preface by Jane Smiley and an introduction by Robert Kellogg, Penguin, Harmondsworth 2000

45 For the historical record see Cardini, *Europe and Islam*, pp.45–8

46 See opinions and comments reported in 'Jugements', the appendix to the Classiques Larousse edition of *La Chanson de Roland*, edited and trans. by André Cordier, Larousse, Paris 1935, pp.104–5

47 Werner 'La place relative du champ littéraire dans les cultures nationales . . .', p.29

48 Belmont, 'L'Académie celtique et George Sand', pp.29–31; Agulhon, 'Le problème de la culture populaire en France autour de 1848', p.55

49 Acocella, 'The Neapolitan Finger', p.48

50 Mar-Molinero, 'The Iberian Peninsula: Conflicting Linguistic Nationalisms', pp.88, 92, 101

51 Kiberd, *Inventing Ireland*, pp.286–7

52 Bruckner, 'Histoire de la *Volkskunde*. Tentative d'une approche à l'usage des français', p.242

53 Mouralis, *Les contres-littératures*, pp.123–4. On the making of Great Britain see Colley's *Britons. Forging the Nation 1707–1837*

54 Lefebvre, 'L'introduction de la philosophie allemande en France au XIXe siècle. La question des traductions', pp.467, 473

6 : Fairy Tales

1 Lévi-Strauss, *Anthropologie structurale*, p.249

2 Lévi-Strauss, *Tristes tropiques*, p.205

3 Carter, *The Virago Book of Fairy Tales*, p.x

4 Propp, *Morphology of the Folktale*, especially pp.19–65

5 See àlso Pentikäinen, 'Structural Patterns of an Oral Repertoire', especially pp.827–8, 839 and Larivaille, *Le Réalisme du merveilleux*, 1982

6 This is suggested in an educational game for children devised by Rodari in his *Grammatica della fantasia. Introduzione all'arte di inventare storie*

7 Thurber, 'The Little Girl and the Wolf', pp.16–17

8 *Roal Dahl's Revolting Rhymes* in Tatar (ed.), *The Classic Fairy Tales*, p.22

9 See Canepa, ' "Quando 'nc'è da ccà a lo

luoco dove aggio da ire?": Giambattista
Basile's Quest for the Literary Fairy Tale',
pp.37–80. For a wider treatment of the
significance of Basile see also Canepa,
From Court to Forest

10 Tatar, *The Classic Fairy Tales*, p.x and
Warner, *From the Beast to the Blonde: On
Fairy tales and Their Tellers*, pp.16–36

11 Larivaille, *Le Réalisme du merveilleux*,
p.118

12 Figes, *Natasha's Dance*, p.112

13 Cardini, *Europe and Islam*, p.168

14 Zipes, *When Dreams Come True*, p.75

15 Wyss, 'Jacob Grimm et la France', p.62

16 François, 'Les échanges culturels entre la
France et les pays germaniques au XVIIIe
siècle', p.46

17 Zipes, *When Dreams Come True*,
pp.69–70

18 See Shklovsky, *Theory of Prose*, p.18. The
study he used was Vsevolod F. Miller's
'The Universal Legend in the Light of
Culture and History' published in
Russkaya mysl (Russian Thought) in
November 1894

19 Zipes, *Happily Ever After*, pp.42–51

20 Velay-Vallantin, 'Little Red Riding Hood
as Fairy Tale. . . .', p.311

21 Cited in Kinnell, 'Childhood and
Children's Literature: the Case of M.J.
Godwin and Co., 1805–25', p.83

22 Zipes 'Of Cats and Men; Framing the
Civilizing Discourse of the Fairy Tale',
p.191

23 On the modern invention of the concept
of childhood see Ariès, *L'Enfant et la vie
familiale sous l'Ancien Régime*

24 Caradec, *Histoire de la Littérature
enfantine en France*, p.90

25 Crubellier, 'L'élargissement du public',
p.36

26 Cardigos, *In and Out of Enchantment*,
pp.43–4

27 Shklovsky, *Theory of Prose*, pp.27–9, 42

28 Coleridge, *Biographia Literaria*, Vol. 2,
pp.1–2 (Chapter XIV)

29 Shklovsky, *Theory of Prose*, p.11

30 Doody, 'Samuel Richardson: fiction and
knowledge', p.117

31 Watt, *Myths of Modern Individualism*,
pp.190–3

32 MacKay, *The Double Invitation in the
Legend of Don Juan*. The eighty-one
versions are printed in the appendix,
pp.118–235

33 See Hoffmann's short tale 'Don Giovanni'
in *Six German Romantic Tales*, p.114

7 : Novels

1 Levitt, *Russian Literary Politics and the
Pushkin Celebration of 1880*, pp.96–7, 108,
128–30

2 This is what Doody does in her *The True
Story of the Novel*

3 Barber, *Daphnis and Chloe, the markets
and metamorphoses of an unknown
bestseller*

4 *Byron's Letters and Journals* Vol. 10, p.161.
See also Erickson, *The Economy of
Literary Form*, pp.22–3

5 Robb, *Victor Hugo*, p.100

6 Lyons, *Le Triomphe du livre*, p.130

7 Erickson, *The Economy of Literary Form*,
p.22

8 Aristotle, *Poetics*, p.59

9 Robb, *Balzac*, p.122

10 Trollope, *An Autobiography*, pp.139, 140,
141

11 Robb, *Balzac*, p.422

12 Boyd, *Vladimir Nabokov. The American
Years*, pp.122, 478, 494

13 Karamzin, 'The Book Trade and the Love
of Reading in Russia', p.114

14 Gasperetti, *The Rise of the Russian Novel*,
p.59

15 Meynieux, 'Les traducteurs en Russie
avant Poushkine'

16 Gasperetti, *The Rise of the Russian Novel*,
p.55

17 Cited in Toschi, 'Alle origini della
narrativa di romanzo in Italia', p.16

18 Moretti, 'Conjectures on World
Literature', p.55, but see also his 'The
Slaughterhouse of Literature', pp.207–27

19 Sutherland, *Longman Guide to Victorian
Fiction*, p.1

20 Schulte-Sasse, 'High/Low and Other
Dichotomies', p.3

21 Davis, *Factual Fictions*, p.125

22 Louandre, 'Statistique littéraire de la
production intellectuelle en France depuis
quinze ans', p.681

23 Woolf, 'A Feminine Past? Gender, Genre,
and Historical Knowledge in England,
1500–1800', pp.650–5

24 Wollstonecraft, 'A Vindication of the
Rights of Woman', p.330

25 Douchin, 'L'influence des publications
populaires sur l'oeuvre de Flaubert',
pp.27–38

26 Tieck, 'Eckbert the Fair', p.25

27 Pushkin, *Eugene Onegin*, p.69

28 Burney, *Evelina*, p.7; see also Harman,
Fanny Burney. A Biography, p.91

29 *The Lounger*, No.20, 18 June 1785
30 Gasperetti, *The Rise of the Russian Novel*, pp.64–5
31 Boetcher Joeres, 'The German Enlightenment (1720–1790)', p.165
32 Schlegel, *Lectures on the History of Literature, Ancient and Modern*
33 Miltchina, ' "Sacrée leur apparaît toute feuille imprimée . . ." ', p.131
34 Darnton, *The Forbidden Best-Sellers of Pre-Revolutionary France*, cit., p.133
35 Reeve, *The Progress of Romance*, Vol. 1, pp.13–14, 112, 115, 117, 118, 126, 133, 135, and in Vol. 2, pp.13–14, 30. This edition is a facsimile of the original
36 Sauvy, 'Une littérature pour les femmes', p.501
37 In de Vigny, *Poèmes antiques et modernes. Les Destinées*, p.207
38 Cited in Davis, *Factual Fictions*, p.123
39 Tomkins, *The Popular Novel in England 1770–1800*, pp.70–1, first published in 1932
40 For an analysis of the connection between libertinism and libertarianism in eighteenth-century France see Darnton, *The Forbidden Best-Sellers of Pre-Revolutionary France*
41 Schuster, 'Popular Literature in Germany: 1800–1850', p.342
42 Unwin, 'On the Novel and the Writing of Literary History', p.10
43 Davis, *Factual Fictions*, p.108
44 Ibid., pp.180–1
45 Miltchina, ' "Sacrée leur apparaît toute feuille imprimée . . ." ', pp.134–5
46 McMahon, *Enemies of the Enlightenment*, pp.3–5
47 Watt, *Myths of Modern Individualism*, p.147
48 Price, *English Literature in Germany*, pp.41–2. On Campe's influence see Shavit, 'Literary Interference between German and Jewish-Hebrew Children's Literature during the Enlightenment: the Case of Campe', pp.41–61
49 Watt, *Myths of Modern Individualism*, pp.280–1
50 Ibid., p.255
51 Note the objections against a Western definition of the novel in the introduction to Lynch and Warner (eds), *Cultural Institutions of the Novel*, p.4
52 Bloom, *Cervantes's 'Don Quixote'*, p.145, reprinted from Harold Bloom's *The Western Canon*, 1994, and his introduction to Cervantes, *Don Quixote*, trans. by Edith Grossman, Random

House, London 2003 extracted in the *Guardian*, 13 December 2003
53 Defoe, *Essay upon Literature* (1726), p.308
54 Warner, *Licensing Entertainment*, especially pp.46–7
55 Pope, *The Dunciad*, p.120 (lines 154–5); the derogatory remarks are in note 149 on p.119
56 Cited by Edward Garnett in his introduction to the Ebook 6422 version of Defoe's *The Life, Adventures and Piracies of the Famous Captain Singleton*, The Project Gutenberg, file first posted on 10 December 2002 *www.gutenberg.net/etext04/cpsng10.txt*
57 Davis, *Resisting Novels*, pp.114, 122, 165ff. See also Oakley's 'A Taxonomy of the Emotions of Literary Response and a Theory of Identification in Fictional Narrative', pp.53–74, see esp. pp.67–8
58 I have deliberately taken as examples the novels discussed in Watt, *Myths of Modern Individualism*
59 Adorno, *Notes to Literature*, Vol. 1, p.30
60 Stone, *The Family, Sex and Marriage in England 1500–1800*, pp.282–4
61 Brunel, *Vincenzo Bellini*, pp.125–6
62 Angenot, 'La littérature populaire française au dix-neuvième siècle', pp.317–18
63 Hunter, 'The Novel and Social/Cultural History', p.28
64 Lyons, *Le Triomphe du livre*, pp.115–16, 129, 140, and Lyons 'Les best-sellers'; p.428
65 Rousseau, *Émile, ou de l'éducation*, pp.166–70

8 : Trailblazers

1 Escarpit, *La révolution du livre*, p.22
2 Rutherford, 'Introduction', pp.xii–xiii, see also Chapters 59–60 of the main text
3 Moretti, *Atlas of the European Novel 1800–1900*, pp.171–3
4 Paulson, *Don Quixote in England*, p.ix
5 Watt, *Myths of Modern Individualism*, pp.219–25
6 Close, *The Romantic Approach to 'Don Quixote'*, pp.1, 43–4
7 Nietzsche, *On the Genealogy of Morals*, p.48
8 Hartmann, 'La réception de Paméla en France: Les anti-Paméla de Villaret et Mauvillon', pp.45–56, p.46
9 Carlo Goldoni, *Memoirs of Goldoni*, pp.380–1

10 Graf, *L'anglomania e l'influsso inglese in Italia nel secolo XVIII*, pp.281–2

11 Brewer, *The Pleasures of the Imagination*, p.129

12 Hill, 'Clarissa Harlowe and her Times', pp.102–23

13 Doody, 'Samuel Richardson: fiction and knowledge', pp.106–8

14 See Beebee's brilliant study *Clarissa on the Continent: Translation and Seduction*, see in particular pp.3, 9 and 199

15 Ibid., p.9; see also Sgard, *Prévost romancier*, pp.539–43

16 Pigoreau, *Petite Bibliographie biographico-romancière ou dictionnnaire des romanciers*, p.352

17 Kahn, *Narrative transvestism: rhetoric and gender in the eighteenth-century English novel*

18 Novak, 'Defoe as an innovator of fictional form', p.58

19 See Park and Daston, 'Unnatural Conceptions: the Study of Monsters in Sixteenth- and Seventeenth-Century France and England', pp.20–54

20 Altick, *The Shows of London*, p.39

21 Ibid., pp.252–6

22 Cardini, *Europe and Islam*, p.105

23 Moretti, *Atlas of the European Novel 1800–1900*, pp.16–17

24 Peck, *A Life of Matthew G. Lewis*, p.20

25 Thackeray, *Vanity Fair*, p.112

26 Austen, *Northanger Abbey*, pp.60–1

27 See Clery, 'Introduction', pp.xii–xiii

28 Montesinos, *Introducción a una historia de la novela en España en el siglo XIX*, p.73

29 Clery, 'Introduction', p.viii

30 Scott, *Waverley, or, 'Tis Sixty Years Since*, pp.3–4

31 Heiderich, *The German Novel of 1800*, pp.32–8

32 Frank, *The First Gothics*, p.ix. This goldmine of a book contains the plots and other useful information on five hundred Gothic novels

33 In fact there were, in the same year, two editions, one by Oxford University Press edited by Kim I. Michasiw, and the other by the Canadian Broadview Press edited by Adriana Craciun

34 Roper, *Reviewing before the 'Edinburgh' 1788–1802*, p.125

35 Ibid.

36 Ibid., pp.135–6, 142

37 Killen, *Le Roman terrifiant ou Roman Noir de Walpole à Ann Radcliffe*, p.95

38 Angenot, 'La littérature populaire française au dix-neuvième siècle', p.313 and Killen, *Le Roman terrifiant*, p.102

39 The claim is made by Angenot in his *Le roman populaire. Recherches en paralittérature*, p.19

40 Angenot, 'La littérature populaire française au dix-neuvième siècle', pp.311–15

41 Sand, *Histoire de ma vie* in *Oeuvres autobiographiques*, Vol. 1, Gallimard/Pléiade, p.887, see also editorial note p.1416

42 Gautier, *Voyage en Italie*, p.69

43 Killen, *Le Roman terrifiant*, pp.83–4

44 July 1804, in Stendhal, *Correspondance Générale*, Vol. 1, 1800–1809, pp.184–5

45 Brooks, *When Russia Learned to read*, p.248

46 Honoré de Balzac, *La muse du département*, pp.716–18

47 Robb, *Balzac*, p.89

48 Peck, *A Life of Matthew G. Lewis*, p.29

49 Killen, *Le Roman terrifiant*, p.116

50 Bellos, 'Le Marché du livre à l'époque romantique', p.656

51 Killen, *Le Roman terrifiant*, p.128

52 Ibid., pp.97–8

53 Korwin-Piotrowska, *Balzac et le monde slave*, pp.90–1; see also Sinko, 'La mode "Gothique" en Pologne dans le contexte européen', pp.399–404

54 Lundin, *The Swedish Crime Story*, p.11

55 Staël (Madame), *De l'Allemagne*, Vol. I, p.237

56 Heiderich, *The German Novel of 1800*, pp.15–17

57 Coward, 'Popular fiction in the nineteenth century', p.75

58 Coward, *The Philosophy of Restif de La Bretonne*, pp.5–6

59 Cellard, *Un génie dévergondé. Nicolas-Edme Rétif, dit 'de La Bretonne' (1734–1806)*, pp.420, 546

60 Cellard, *Un génie dévergondé*, p.387–8

61 Parent, 'Des nouvelles pratiques de lecture', pp.810–16

62 Lyons, *Le Triomphe du livre*, p.117

9 : Walter Scott 'in Unclouded Splendour'

1 'Morning arose in unclouded splendour' is the opening line of Chapter 12 of Walter Scott's *Ivanhoe*

2 Haskell, 'The Manufacture of the Past in Nineteenth-Century Painting', pp.110, 116

3 Clayton, *The English Print: 1688–1802*, p.215

4 Anderson, 'The Political Uses of History in Mid-Nineteenth Century England', pp.90–4

5 Erickson, *The Economy of Literary Form*, p.148

6 Edgeworth, *Letters from England 1813–1844*, p.341, letter of 4 February 1822

7 Gramsci, *Selections from the Cultural Writings*, pp.215–16

8 Jameson, *Postmodernism or the Cultural Logic of Late Capitalism*, p.23

9 Trollope, *An Autobiography*, p.141

10 Anderson, *The Journal of Sir Walter Scott*, p.319

11 Edgeworth, *Letters from England 1813–1844*, p.323

12 Cited in Anderson, *The Journal of Sir Walter Scott*, p.319

13 Cited by Lamont, in her Introduction to Walter Scott, *Waverley*, p.ix

14 Scott, *Rob Roy*, p.5

15 Lukács, *The Historical Novel*, p.31

16 Daiches, 'Sir Walter Scott and History', pp.459–64

17 Lukács, *The Historical Novel*, p.37

18 Moretti, *Atlas of the European Novel 1800–1900*, pp.38–40

19 Shaw, *The Forms of Historical Fiction*, p.22

20 Wachtel, *An Obsession with History*, p.50

21 Carlyle's review of Scott's memoirs originally in *London and Westminster Review*, No.12, 1837, now in *Critical and Miscellaneous Essays*, Vol. 2, pp.148, 156, 176–7

22 Price, *English Literature in Germany*, p.329

23 Hazlitt, 'Sir Walter Scott' in *The Spirit of the Age* in *The Selected Writings*, Vol. 7, p.130, originally in the *New Monthly Magazine*, April 1824

24 Chandler, *England in 1819*, pp.11, 350

25 Ibid., p.12

26 Ibid., p.311

27 Anderson, 'Introduction' in *The Journal of Sir Walter Scott*, p.xxix

28 Ibid., p.xxxiii

29 Erickson, *The Economy of Literary Form*, p.81

30 Gasperetti, *The Rise of the Russian Novel*, p.44

31 The sixteen cases not identified were probably translations from French too; see Cross, *Anglo-Russica*, pp.82–3

32 Montesinos, *Introducción a una historia de la novela en España en el siglo XIX*, pp.60–1

33 Maigron, *Le roman historique à l'époque romantique*, pp.99–100

34 Lyons, *Le Triomphe du livre*, pp.137–9

35 Legouis, 'La fortune littéraire de Walter Scott en France', pp.493–4; this is a lecture given at the Sorbonne on 21 January 1933

36 Bellos, 'Le Marché du livre à l'époque romantique', p.655

37 Maigron, *Le roman historique à l'époque romantique*, p.105

38 Ibid., p.107

39 Ibid., p.108

40 Mitchell, *The Walter Scott Operas*, p.57

41 Lyons, *Le Triomphe du livre*, cit., p.135

42 See Wright and Joannides, 'Les Romans historiques de Sir Walter Scott et la peinture française, 1822–1863'

43 Lyons, *Le Triomphe du livre*, p.134 and Robb, *Balzac*, p.62

44 Robertson, 'Scott', p.429

45 Benedetti, *Le traduzioni italiane di Walter Scott e i loro anglicismi*, p.16

46 See the two studies by Mitchell, *The Walter Scott Operas. An analysis of operas based on the works of Walter Scott* and *More Scott Operas*

47 Charlton, 'The Nineteenth Century: France', p.136

48 On Balzac's resentment see Robb, *Balzac*, p.135

49 Ashton, *George Eliot*, p.21

50 Ibid., p.313

51 Hayden (ed.), *Walter Scott. The Critical Heritage*, p.373

52 Balzac, *Le Curé de village*, p.58

53 Balzac, *Illusions perdues*, p.161

54 Ibid., p.227

55 Flaubert, *L'éducation sentimentale*, p.48

56 Anfray, 'La lectrice ou la révélation du désir: étude de la scène de lecture dans les romans du XIXe siècle', pp.113–14

57 Cited in Smith III, 'Honoré de Balzac and the "Genius" of Walter Scott: Debt and Denial', p.214

58 Hayden (ed.), *Walter Scott*, p.305

59 Legouis, 'La fortune littéraire de Walter Scott en France', p.497

60 Hayden (ed.), *Walter Scott*, pp.326–8

61 Boyle, *Goethe*, Vol. 1, p.168

62 Ibid., p.546

63 Louandre, 'Statistique littéraire de la production intellectuelle en France depuis quinze ans', pp.682–3

64 Goethe, *Conversations with Eckermann*, pp.263, 268, conversations of 3 and 9 October 1828

65 *Ibid.*, p.394, conversation of 8 March 1831
66 Ouimette, ' "Monstrous Fecundity": The Popular Novel in Nineteenth-Century Spain', pp.385–6
67 Bettencourt Pires, *Walter Scott e o romantismo português*, pp.26, 40, 121–8, 137–43
68 Klaniczay, *Histoire de la littérature hongroise des origines à nos jours*, p.198, see also Tezla, *Hungarian Authors. A Biographical Handbook*, pp.260–1
69 Verzea, 'The Historical Novel as Popular Literature. Notes on the Success of the English and American Novel in Nineteenth Century Romanian Literature', p.266
70 Wachtel, *An Obsession with History*, p.80
71 Cited in Clyman and Vowles (eds), *Russia Through Women's Eyes*, pp.60, 85
72 Boyer, *Histoire des littératures scandinaves*, p.118
73 Berengo, *Intellettuali e librai nella Milano della restaurazione*, p.122
74 Benedetti, *Le traduzioni italiane di Walter Scott e I loro anglicismi*, p.11
75 Rovani, *Cento anni*, Vol. 2, p.259
76 Ruggieri Punzo, *Walter Scott in Italia 1821–1971*, pp.20, 24, 30, 36, 43
77 Ceserani and Salibra, 'Popular Literature in Nineteenth-Century Italy: *Letteratura amena*', pp.363–4
78 See Baynard Quincy Morgan, *A Critical Bibliography of German Literature in English Translation 1481–1927*, p.34
79 The story is told in Lindop, *The Opium-Eater. A Life of Thomas De Quincey*, pp.272–5. De Quincey's review as well as his 'translation' are in Vol. 4 of *The Works of Thomas De Quincey*
80 Gasperetti, *The Rise of the Russian Novel*, p.23
81 Price, *English Literature in Germany*, pp.331–43
82 See Del Litto, 'Stendhal et Walter Scott'. Stendhal's article 'Walter Scott et la Princesse de Clèves' appeared in *Le National*, 19 February 1830
83 Stendhal, *Souvenirs d'égotisme*, p.1472
84 Flaubert, *Bouvard et Pécuchet*, pp.200–2
85 Balzac, *Illusions perdues*, p.228
86 Rubinstein (ed.), *Sir Walter Scott: An Annotated Bibliography of Scholarship and Criticism 1975–1990*
87 Shaw, *The Forms of Historical Fiction*, p.10
88 Maigron, *Le roman historique à l'époque romantique*, p.iv

89 See Punzo, *Walter Scott in Italia 1821–1971*, pp.5–6, 207–8, 229
90 Arslan, 'Romanzo popolare e romanzo di consumo tra Ottocento e Novecento', p.23
91 Costa, 'Storia e "fictio" nelle pagine delle "Biblioteche Italiane" ', pp.44–5
92 Turchi, 'K.X.Y.: Una sigla per recensire', pp.24, 30
93 See key passage in text reprinted in Manzoni, *Tutte le Opere*, Vol. 2, pp.1762–3
94 De Sanctis, *Teoria e storia della letteratura*, pp.259–60
95 Maigron, *Le roman historique à l'époque romantique*, p.109, citing his letter from Berlin of 16 March 1822 to the *Rhine-Westphalia Chronicle*
96 Maigron, *Le roman historique à l'époque romantique*, p.99
97 Lukács, *The Historical Novel*, p.33
98 Lyons, *Le Triomphe du livre*, pp.137–8
99 Cited in Lukács, *The Historical Novel*, p.66

10 : Cultural Hegemony

1 Marx and Engels, *The Communist Manifesto*, pp.223–4. For Goethe's view see, *inter alia*, *Conversations with Eckermann*, p.165, 31 January 1827
2 Moretti, *Atlas of the European Novel 1800–1900*, pp.174–85
3 *Conversations with Eckermann*, p.202, 3 May 1827
4 Staël, *De l'Allemagne*, Vol. I, pp.213–14
5 Grimmelshausen, *Mother Courage*, p.34
6 Adorno, *Notes to Literature*, Vol. 1, p.80
7 D'hulst, 'Traduire l'Europe en France entre 1810 et 1840', p.144
8 Cited in Boyle, *Goethe*, Vol. 1, pp.170, 193
9 *Ibid.*, p.187
10 *Ibid.*, pp.175, 262
11 Hulse, 'Introduction' to Goethe's *The Sorrows of Young Werther*, p.14
12 Boetcher Joeres, 'The German Enlightenment (1720–1790)', p.188. The passage can be found in Goethe, *The Sorrows of Young Werther*, p.43
13 Goethe, *Sorrows of Young Werther*, p.134
14 Schuster, 'Popular Literature in Germany: 1800–1850', p.335
15 Louandre, 'Statistique littéraire de la production intellectuelle en France depuis quinze ans' pp.674–5, 682
16 Berengo, *Intellettuali e librai nella Milano della restaurazione*, p.211

17 Ibid., p.205

18 Petronio, *L'attività letteraria in Italia*, p.519; the article mentioned is 'Sulle maniera e l'utilità delle traduzioni'

19 Carpi, 'Egemonia moderata e intellettuali nel Risorgimento', pp.436–9, 442

20 Ricuperati, 'I giornalisti italiani dalle origini all'Unità', pp.1113–14

21 Ibid., pp.1120, 1123

22 Derla, *Letteratura e politica tra la Restaurazione e l'Unità*, p.219

23 Gautier, *Voyage en Italie*, p.53

24 Santoro, *Storia del libro italiano*, pp.291–3

25 Figures in Berengo, *Intellettuali e librai nella Milano della restaurazione*, pp.344, 375

26 Ibid., pp.265–8, p.289

27 Ibid., pp.300–1

28 Ibid., p.275

29 Raven, 'Le commerce de librairie "en gros" à Londres au XVIIIe siècle', p.157

30 Camerino, 'Un topos critico: il riassunto dei romanzi nelle recensioni ottocentesche', p.32

31 Vecchiotti, 'Poetica e ideologia nei romanzi di Pietro Chiari', pp.123–5

32 Alfieri, 'La lingua di consumo', p.181

33 De Sanctis, *Storia della letteratura italiana*, Vol. 2, pp.386–7

34 Jonard, *La France et l'Italie au siècle des lumières*, p.81

35 Alfieri, *Vita scritta da esso*, Vol. 1, p.93; see also Natali, *Storia letteraria d'Italia. Il Settecento* Vol. II, p.409

36 Jonard, *La France et l'Italie au siècle des lumières*, p.84

37 Camerino, 'Il romanzo nella prima metà dell'Ottocento' in *Problemi*, p.207

38 Jonard, *La France et l'Italie au siècle des lumières*, p.93

39 Strazzuso, 'F. D. Guerrazzi e l'"Assedio di Firenze": aspetti politici di un mito repubblicano', p.101

40 Petronio, *Viaggio nel paese della poesia*, p.60

41 Berengo, *Intellettuali e librai nella Milano della restaurazione*, pp.311–12

42 Vegliante, 'Perception française de l'Italie et traduction de l'italien. Histoire d'un malentendu', pp.73–5

43 Ouimette, ' "Monstrous Fecundity": The Popular Novel in Nineteenth-Century Spain', pp.383–4

44 Bretz, *Voices, Silences, and Echoes*, p.3

45 Bianchini, *Cent'anni di romanzo spagnolo 1868–1962*, p.54

46 Ouimette, ' "Monstrous Fecundity": The Popular Novel in Nineteenth-Century Spain', pp.385–6

47 Beletski, 'Étudier l'histoire du lecteur: un problème actuel de l'histoire littéraire', p.41

48 Ibid., p.46

49 Zorine and Nemzer, 'Les paradoxes de la sentimentalité' (1989), p.91

50 Freeborn, *The Rise of the Russian Novel. Studies in the Russian Novel from Eugene Onegin to War and Peace*, p.5

51 Gasperetti, *The Rise of the Russian novel*, p.5

52 Cross, *Anglo-Russica*, p.180

53 Ibid., p.197

54 Garrard, 'Narrative Technique in Chulkov's *Prigozhaia povarikha*', pp.554–6

55 Schaarschmidt, 'The Lubok Novels: Russia's Immortal Best Sellers', pp.435, 430

56 Berend, *The Crisis Zone of Europe*, pp.15–17

57 Andreeva-Popova, 'Le siècle des Lumières et la renaissance bulgare', p.440

58 Najder, 'The Development of the Polish Novel: Functions and Structure', p.651–3

59 On the pathology of martyrdom and Mickiewicz see Zamoyski, *Holy Madness. Romantics, Patriots and Revolutionaries 1776–1871*, pp.291, 286

60 Boyer, *Histoire des littératures scandinaves*, pp.126–7

61 D'hulst, 'Traduire l'Europe en France entre 1810 et 1840', p.143

62 Wachtel, *Making a Nation, Breaking a Nation*, p.1

63 Martinenche, *L'Espagne et le romantisme français*, p.18

64 Ibid., p.154

65 Ádám, 'Les traductions hongroises de l'oeuvre de Chateaubriand', pp.171–80

66 Dekker and Williams (eds), *Fenimore Cooper. The Critical Heritage*, pp.83–5

67 Originally in *Autour de ma table*, Paris 1856, pp.261–72, here in Dekker and Williams (eds), *Fenimore Cooper. The Critical Heritage*, p.261

68 Boyle, *Goethe*, Vol. 2, p.451

69 Battestin (ed.), *Dictionary of Literary Bibliography*, Vol. 39: *British Novelists 1660–1800*

70 Pigoreau, *Petite Bibliographie biographico-romancière ou dictionnnaire des romanciers*, 1821, see list of authors pp.141–347

71 See citations in editorial note to Madame Riccoboni, 'Suite de Marianne' in

appendix to Marivaux's *La vie de Marianne*, p.627

72 Crosby, *Une romancière oubliée: Mme Riccoboni*, pp.7, 63, 162

73 Austen, *Letters*, p.54, see letter of 9 November 1800

74 Sand, *Histoire de ma vie*, pp.210–11

75 Cohen, *The Sentimental Education of the Novel*, p.27

76 See Kobak, 'Malvina Recovered', p.21

77 Balayé, Preface to de Staël, *Corinne ou l'Italie*, p.xvii

78 Heiderich, *The German Novel of 1800*, p.23

11 : This is Not a Fiction

1 Data in the *Guardian*, 27 December 2003

2 Bellos, 'La conjuncture de la production', p.739

3 Maurice Crubellier, 'L'élargissement du public', p.31

4 Chartier, 'Frenchness in the History of the Book', p.302

5 Lyons, *Le Triomphe du livre*, p.13

6 Brewer, *The Pleasures of the Imagination*, p.171

7 Simon Eliot, 'Patterns and Trends and the NSTC: Some initial observations. Part Two', pp.100, 106

8 Webb, 'The Victorian Reading Public', p.199

9 Davis, *Factual Fictions*, p.201

10 See Macaulay's 'Review of Henry Neale's *The Romance of History*' in *The Edinburgh Review*, May 1828, pp.364–5, cited in Chandler, *England in 1819*, p.158

11 Barber, 'The English-language guide book to Europe up to 1870', p.98

12 Brewer, *The Pleasures of the Imagination*, p.181, citing the work of Paul Kaufman, *Borrowing from the Bristol Library, 1773–1784: A Unique Record of Reading Vogues*

13 Barber, 'The English-language guide book to Europe up to 1870', p.101

14 For an examination of the construction of 'Eastern Europe' see Wolff, *Inventing Eastern Europe*

15 Mattlock, 'Novels of Testimony and the "invention" of the modern French novel', pp.24–5

16 Neville-Sington, *Fanny Trollope*, pp.148–67

17 Trollope, *Domestic Manners of the Americans*, p.20

18 Ibid., p.38

19 Ibid., p.40

20 Ibid., p.314

21 Trollope, *Paris et les Parisiens en 1835*, pp.12, 301–4

22 Neville-Sington, *Fanny Trollope*, pp.301, 302

23 Ibid., p.352

24 Cardini, *Europe and Islam*, p.142

25 Said, *Orientalism*, p.81

26 Taymanova, 'Alexandre Dumas in Egypt: Mystification or Truth?', pp.182–3

27 Aubin's novel is reprinted with a commentary in Backschneider and Richetti (eds), *Popular Fiction by Women 1660–1730*, pp.114–51

28 Gasperetti, *The Rise of the Russian Novel*, pp.199–202, 206

29 Ackroyd, *Dickens*, pp.40–7

30 Thackeray, *Vanity Fair*, p.79; Dickens, *David Copperfield*, pp.59–60

31 See Conant, *The Oriental Tale in England in the Eighteenth Century*, where ninety-three Orientalist tales are listed, and Pierre Martino, *L'Orient dans la littérature française au XVIIe Siècle* (1908)

32 Colley, *Captives. Britain, Empire and the World 1650–1850*, pp.43–6, 59

33 Collini and Vannoni, 'Un'impresa editoriale del primo Ottocento . . .', pp.218–22

34 See the texts collected in Hellegouarc'h (ed.), *L'art de la conversation*; see also Burke, *The Art of Conversation*

35 Chartier, 'Des "Secrétaires" pour le peuple?', pp.159–207

36 One of the earliest version was published in Troyes by Baudot. See also Darmon, *Le Colportage de Librairie en France sous le Second Empire*, pp.138ff

37 Cross, *Anglo-Russica*, p.86

38 Andries. 'Les livres de savoir pratique dans la France des XVIIe et XVIIIe siècles', p.173

39 Lyons, 'Les best-sellers', p.433

40 Ibid.

41 Vigarello, 'De la "médecine du peuple" aux magazines de santé', p.227

42 Spang, *The Invention of the Restaurant*, p.27

43 See Adburgham, *Silver Fork Society*

44 Porter, *London*, p.99

45 Woolf, 'A Feminine Past? Gender, Genre, and Historical Knowledge in England, 1500–1800', p.645

46 Lyons, 'Les best-sellers', p.426

47 Gay, *The Naked Heart*, p.332

48 Ibid., pp.102–49, especially pp.107–8

49 Doody, 'I am an Irregular Verb', p.22–3

50 There is now a scholarly edition of *The Memoirs of Laetitia Pilkington* edited by A.C. Elias Jr, University of Georgia Press, Athens 1997

12 : News and Pictures

1 Pinkard, *Hegel. A Biography*, p.242

2 Carlyle, 'The Hero as Man of Letters' in *On Heroes, Hero-Worship, and the Heroic in History*, p.141

3 Carlyle, *The French Revolution. A History*, Vol. I *The Bastille*, Book VI, p.223

4 O'Boyle, 'The Image of the Journalist in France, Germany and England, 1815–1848', p.300

5 Ibid., p.300

6 Letter of 13 October 1837, in Stendhal, *Correspondance Générale*, pp.76–7. Stendhal had found this in the *Gazette des Tribunaux* of 4 October 1837

7 See *Thomas Hardy's 'Facts' Notebook*, edited by William Greenslade, Ashgate, Aldershot 2004, pp.51, 113, 172–3

8 Robb, *Balzac*, p.171

9 Reîtblat, 'Les honoraires littéraires, médiation entre les écrivains et le public', pp.146–8

10 Houston, *Literacy in Early Modern Europe*, p.213

11 Wachtel, *Making a Nation*, p.27

12 Albert, *Histoire de la Presse*, p.10; Houston, *Literacy in Early Modern Europe*, p.177–8

13 Porter, *London*, p.171

14 Harris, *London Newspapers in the Age of Walpole*, pp.192–3

15 Porter, *London*, p.170

16 *The History of the Times. 'The Thunderer' in the making 1785–1841* (Vol. 1), Times Publishing Company, London 1935, p.27, my emphasis

17 Ibid., p.47

18 Scott, 'Victorian Newspaper Advertising: Counting What Counts', p.12

19 Curran and Seaton, *Power without Responsibility*, pp.7–8

20 Lyons, *Le Triomphe du livre*, p.49

21 Scott, 'Victorian Newspaper Advertising: Counting What Counts', p.12

22 Fox Bourne, *English Newspapers. Chapters in the History of British Journalism*, 1887 reprinted by Routledge and Thoemmes Press in the series *Chapters in the History of British Journalism*, 1998, Vol. 1, pp.354, 358

23 Klancher, *The Making of English Reading Audiences 1790–1832*, p.21

24 Porter, *Flesh in the Age of Reason*, pp.113, 116

25 Cited in Klein, 'Politeness and the Interpretation of the British Eighteenth Century', p.875

26 Jonard, *La France et l'Italie au siècle des lumières*, p.65

27 Gasperetti, *The Rise of the Russian Novel*, p.21

28 Klancher, *The Making of English Reading Audiences*, p.ix

29 Boetcher Joeres, 'The German Enlightenment (1720–1790)', pp.197–9

30 Quin, *A Steam Voyage Down the Danube*, Vol. I, pp 167–171, text in *www.fordham.edu/halsall/mod/1836mikequin.html*

31 Brewer, *The Pleasures of the Imagination*, p.139

32 Roper, *Reviewing before the "Edinburgh" 1788–1802*, p.20

33 Ibid., pp.24–6

34 Erickson, *The Economy of Literary Form*, p.28

35 Ibid., pp.72, 80

36 Ibid., p.75

37 Ibid., pp.77–9, see also Klancher, *The Making of English Reading Audiences*, p.69

38 Erickson, *The Economy of Literary Form*, pp.88–90

39 Haskell, 'The Market for Italian Art in the 17th Century', pp.48–9

40 Ibid., p.55

41 Gray, 'Early Victorian scandalous journalism . . .', pp.318–20

42 Ibid., p.330

43 Darnton, *The Forbidden Best-Sellers of Pre-Revolutionary France*, p.138

44 Gray, 'Early Victorian scandalous journalism . . .', pp.337–45

45 Clayton, *The English Print: 1688–1802*, p.155

46 Ibid., p.209

47 Taylor, '1790', p.94

48 Twyman, *Lithography 1800–1850*, pp.4–5, 13, 18

49 Ibid., p.243

50 Ibid., pp.41–55

51 Solomon-Godeau, 'The Other Side of Venus', pp.147–8 quoting Jeffrey Howard Rosen's unpublished 1988 doctoral dissertation (Northwestern University) on the Lemercier firm

52 Goldstein, 'Realism without a Human face', p.82; see also the catalogue of the

exhibition *Putting Pen to Paper: Honoré Daumier and the Literary World* at the UCLA Hammer Museum

53 Summers, *Empress of Pleasure*, illustration 23

54 Goldstein, 'Realism without a Human face', pp.68, 75

55 Brooks, *When Russia Learned to read*, p.65

56 Barbier and Lavenir, *Histoire des médias, de Diderot à Internet*, pp.77–8

57 Watt, *Myths of Modern Individualism*, p.282

58 Graff, *The Legacies of Literacy*, p.335

13 : The Music Market

1 See the painting by Louis Watteau, *Le Violoneux* (1785) at the Musée des Beaux-Arts at Lille, described also in Chartier, *The Cultural uses of Print*, p.229

2 Kramer, *Music as Cultural Practice, 1800–1900*, pp.9–10

3 Vignal, *Joseph Haydn*, p.i196; Johnson, *Listening in Paris*, pp.210–11

4 Rice, *Antonio Salieri and Viennese Opera*, pp.525–6

5 Staël, *De l'Allemagne*, Vol. I, p.95

6 See 'Notation' in *New Grove Dictionary of Music and Musicians* edited by Stanley Sadie, Macmillan 1980

7 Shankar 'Interview' (August 1972), p.157

8 Mathiesen, 'Harmonia and Ethos in Ancient Greek Music', pp.264–79, especially pp.269–78

9 Weber, 'Learned and General Music Taste in Eighteenth Century France', pp.60–1

10 Mahling, 'The Origin and Social Status of the Court Orchestral Musician in the Eighteenth and Early Nineteenth Century in Germany', p.226

11 Robinson, 'Music', p.243

12 Weber, 'Learned and General Music Taste . . .', p.68

13 Mahling, 'The Origin and Social Status of the Court Orchestral Musician . . .', pp.224–5

14 Berlioz, *Mémoires*, pp.106–7

15 John, *The Magic Flute*, p.47; see also Barbier, *Opera in Paris, 1800–1850*, p.67

16 Rosen, 'The Future of Music', p.64

17 Raynor, *A Social History of Music*, p.337

18 Vignal, *Joseph Haydn*, p.219

19 Rosen, 'The Great Inventor', p.52

20 Ong, 'Writing is a Technology That Restructures Thought', p.32

21 See Geerz, *The Religion of Java*, pp.262–3, cited by Inglis in his *Clifford Geertz*, p.79

22 Chanan, *Musica Pratica*, p.77

23 Lesure, et al., *La Musique à Paris en 1830–1831*, p.10

24 Hopkinson, *A Dictionary of Parisian Music Publishers 1700–1950*, pp.ix, 6

25 Staël, *De l'Allemagne*, Vol. I, p.58

26 Hortschansky, 'The Musician as Music Dealer', pp.207–15

27 Weber, 'Mass Culture and the Reshaping of European Musical Taste, 1770–1870', p.9

28 Lawford-Hunrichsen, *Music Publishing and Patronage*, p.3

29 Ibid., pp.5–6

30 Beethoven, *The Letters of Beethoven*, pp.47–8

31 Chanan, *Musica Pratica*, p.121

32 Weber, 'Mass Culture and the Reshaping of European Musical Taste, 1770–1870', p.11

33 Nenadic, 'Middle-Rank Consumers and Domestic Culture in Edinburgh and Glasgow 1720–1840', p.153

34 Harding, *The Piano-Forte*, p.76

35 Ibid., p.158

36 Ibid., p.160

37 Russell, *Popular Music in England, 1840–1914*, p.1

38 Loesser, *Men, Women and Pianos*, p.56

39 Ibid., p.155. For a detailed chronology of the technological improvements in piano-making see the essays by Barrie Heaton and David S. Grover, *http://www.uk-piano.org/*

40 Loesser, *Men, Women and Pianos*, pp.59–60

41 Ibid., pp.64–5; see also Chanan, *Musica Pratica*, p.202

42 Casanova, *Histoire de ma vie*, Vol. 3 (Chapter 4), p.511. I thank Judith Summers for this and the following note

43 The portrait, attributed to the studio of Jean-Marc Nattier, is held at the Château de Versailles et de Trianon

44 Castiglione, *The Book of the Courtier*, p.215

45 *The Poems of Schiller*, trans. by E.P. Arnold-Forster, Heinemann, London 1901, where the German 'Clavier' is wrongly translated as 'spinet'. The word for spinet in German is *Spinet*

46 Loesser, *Men, Women and Pianos*, p.143

47 Leroy, *Histoire des arts du Spectacle en France*, p.211

48 Loesser, *Men, Women and Pianos*, p.147

49 Chanan, *Musica Pratica*, p.201

50 www.uk-piano.org/broadwood/ lvb_wood.html (accessed 2001)

51 Dillaz, 'Diffusion et propagation chansonnières au XIXe siècle', p.57

52 See Bércy, 'Chanson et révolution', pp.404–8

53 Biget, 'Long terme et court terme des acquis musicaux de la Révolution française', p.35

54 Brochon (ed.), Béranger et son temps, pp.25, 35–6, 41

55 Figes, Natasha's Dance, pp.114–15

56 Klein, Florilège de la Chanson Française, p.55

57 Ibid., p.60

58 Ibid., p.35

59 Summers, Empress of Pleasure, see in particular pp.108, 111, 125–6

60 Hess, La Valse, p.92

61 Goethe, The Sorrows of Young Werther, p.41

62 Austen, Emma, p.229

63 Hess, La Valse, p.168

64 Ibid., p.139

65 Cited in Lotman, 'Conversations on Russian Culture . . .', p.24

14 : Audiences and Performers

1 Johnson, Listening in Paris, pp.28–31

2 Christiansen, Prima Donna, p.12

3 Johnson, Listening in Paris, pp.10–11

4 Fischler, 'Guano and Poetry: Payment for Playwriting in Victorian England', p.45

5 Johnson, 'Musical Experience and the Formation of a French Musical Public', p.196

6 Balzac, La Peau de Chagrin, pp.184–5

7 Johnson, 'Musical Experience and the Formation of a French Musical Public', p.202

8 Johnson, Listening in Paris, pp.99–100

9 Leroy, Histoire des arts du Spectacle en France, pp.126–7

10 Giuliani, 'Le public de l'Opéra de Paris de 1750 à 1760', pp.174–6

11 Johnson, Listening in Paris, p.55

12 Cited in Weber, Music and the Middle Class, pp.3–4

13 Rosselli, 'Opera as a Social Occasion', pp.451, 466

14 Johnson, Listening in Paris, p.192

15 Johnson, 'Musical Experience and the Formation of a French Musical Public', p.208

16 Carlo Goldoni, Memoirs, Vol. 1, p.238

17 Johnson, Listening in Paris, pp.59, 60

18 Ibid., p.60

19 Gay, The Naked Heart, p.16

20 Cited in Tutti I libretti di Rossini, edited by Beghelli and Gallino, p.74

21 Stendhal, Vie de Rossini, p.229

22 Blondeau, Voyage d'un musicien en Italie (1810–1812), p.153. See also Venturini, 'Il rapporto segnale-rumore: note sull'ascolto contemporaneo', p.85; Barbieri, Vite Ardenti nel teatro, Milan 1931

23 Berlioz, Mémoires, p.248

24 Barbier, Opera in Paris, 1800–1850, pp.32–3

25 Johnson, Listening in Paris, p.23

26 Sorba, Teatri, pp.96–7

27 Johnson, Listening in Paris, pp.17–18, 27

28 Rosselli, 'Opera as a Social Occasion', pp.471–2

29 Mozart to his father, 12 November 1778, in The Letters of Mozart and his Family, p.630

30 Johnson, Listening in Paris, p.240

31 Cited in Robb, Victor Hugo, p.142

32 Landon, Haydn in England 1791–1795, p.151

33 See Bakhtin, Rabelais and His World, and Mitzman, 'Roads, Vulgarity, and Pure Art: The Inner Space in Flaubert and French Culture', p.516

34 See the story in Allin, Zarafa: A Giraffe's True Story

35 Porter, London, p.289

36 Ibid., p.178

37 Ibid., pp.175–6, 289

38 Kerman, 'Beethoven and the Big Change', p.27

39 The later image of Beethoven has been carefully surveyed by Comini, The Changing Image of Beethoven. A Study in Mythmaking

40 DeNora, Beethoven and the Construction of Genius, pp.61, 69, 145

41 Ibid., pp.61–67, 78 and passim. For a critique of DeNora see Menger, 'Le génie et sa sociologie. Controverses interprétatives sur le cas de Beethoven', pp.967–99, especially pp.977–85

42 Raynor, A Social History of Music, p.314

43 Weber, Music and the Middle Class, pp.5–6

44 Raynor, A Social History of Music, pp.317–18

45 Ibid., p.351

46 Johnson, Listening in Paris, p.71, and, by the same author, 'Musical Experience and the Formation of a French Musical Public', p.196

47 Durant, *Conditions of Music*, pp.36–40
48 Weber, *Music and the Middle Class*, p.59
49 Buch, 'Le chef d'orchestre: pratiques de l'autorité et métaphores politiques', p.1004
50 Ibid., p.1006
51 Raynor, *A Social History of Music*, p.319
52 Loesser, *Men, Women and Pianos*, p.205
53 Summers, *Empress of Pleasure*, p.171
54 Raynor, *A Social History of Music*, p.320
55 Porter, *London*, p.177
56 Landon, *Haydn in England 1791–1795*, p.30
57 On Haydn, see advertisement from *The Times* reported in Larsen, *Haydn*, p.62; on Mrs Cornelys, see Summers, *The Empress of Pleasure*, p.171
58 Raynor, *A Social History of Music*, p.326
59 Johnson, *Listening in Paris*, p.201
60 See his letters to his father of 3 March and 20 March 1784, in *The Letters of Mozart and his Family*, pp.869–72
61 Raynor, *A Social History of Music*, p.323
62 Letter to Leopold Mozart, 3 July 1778, in *The Letters of Mozart and his Family*, p.558
63 Parakilas, 'Classical Music as Popular Music', pp.1–3
64 Weber, 'Artisans in Concert Life of Mid-Nineteenth-Century London and Paris', p.254
65 Gumplowicz, *Les travaux d'Orphée*, pp.40–2
66 Weber, 'Artisans in Concert Life of Mid-Nineteenth-Century London and Paris', pp.257–60
67 Johnson, *Listening in Paris*, pp.197–8
68 Ibid., p.200
69 De Van, *L'opéra italien*, p.31
70 Johnson, *Listening in Paris*, p.20
71 Ibid., p.67
72 Barbier, *Opera in Paris, 1800–1850*, p.213
73 Ibid., p.49
74 Ibid., pp.53–4
75 Ibid., pp.41–3
76 Barbier, *Histoire des Castrats*, pp.120–3
77 Wierzbicki, 'Dethroning the Divas. Satire Directed at Cuzzoni and Faustina', pp.176, 183–4
78 Leroy, *Histoire des arts du Spectacle en France*, p.307
79 Barbier, *Opera in Paris, 1800–1850*, p.177
80 Christiansen, *Prima Donna*, pp.14, 45, 82
81 Hazlitt, 'Madame Pasta and Mademoiselle Mars' in *The Selected Writings of William Hazlitt*, Vol. 8, p.303, originally in the *New Monthly Magazine* in January 1825
82 Barbier, *Opera in Paris, 1800–1850*, p.211

83 Robb, *Victor Hugo*, pp.94–5, 113
84 Villot, *Notice des Tableaux exposés dans les galeries du Musée National du Louvre*, p.108
85 Barbier, *Opera in Paris*, p.155
86 Leroy, *Histoire des arts du Spectacle en France*, p.262
87 Christiansen, *Prima Donna*, p.20
88 Delécluze, *Journal de Delécluze*, pp.488–9
89 Segalini, *Divas*, p.36
90 Strakosch, *Souvenirs d'un impresario*, pp.32–4
91 De Van, *L'opéra italien*, p.13
92 Durante, 'The Opera Singer', p.395
93 Raynor, *Music and Society since 1815*, p.29
94 This is the gist of Sherwin Rosen's classic paper 'The Economics of Superstars', pp.845–58; see also the further refinement, here taken into account, by Adler, 'Stardom and Talent', pp.208–12
95 Rosselli, 'Opera as a Social Occasion', p.450
96 Information in *Dizionario Biografico degli Italiani*, pp.266–7
97 Barbier, *Opera in Paris, 1800–1850*, p.149
98 Osborne, *Rossini*, p.26
99 Boyle, *Goethe*, Vol. 2, p.701

15 : Opera

1 De Van, *L'opéra italien*, pp.8–9
2 Carter, 'The Seventeenth Century', pp.28–9
3 Caruzzi, 'Il libretto d'opera e la società romantica', p.1161
4 Summers, *Empress of Pleasure*, p.41
5 Murata, 'Why the first opera given in Paris wasn't Roman', pp.87–105
6 Cannone, *Musique et littérature au XVIIIᵉ siècle*, pp.26–7, 32–3
7 Abraham, *The Concise Oxford History of Music*, pp.366–7
8 Bauman, 'The Eighteenth Century: Serious Opera', p.57
9 See musical analysis in Abraham, *The Concise Oxford History of Music*, pp.467–8
10 Raguenet, *Parallèle des Italiens et des Français en ce qui regarde la musique et les opéras*, pp.28–9, 30–41, 76–7, 82–3, 68
11 The name is occasionally spelt Barbaja
12 Osborne, *Rossini*, pp.25, 51
13 Ibid., pp.23–4
14 Abraham, *The Concise Oxford History of Music*, p.372
15 Moynet, *L'envers du Théâtre*, pp.279–84
16 Christiansen, *Prima Donna*, p.81

17 Mangini, 'Tramonti di un antico teatro veneziano', pp.94–6

18 De Van, *L'opéra italien*, pp.18–19

19 Sorba, 'Teatro d'opera e società nell'Italia ottocentesca', pp.37–8

20 Bauman, 'The Eighteenth Century: Serious Opera', p.48

21 Johnson, *Listening in Paris*, pp.186–8

22 Bauman, 'The Eighteenth Century: Serious Opera', p.49

23 Johnson, *Listening in Paris*, p.57

24 Körner, 'The Theatre of Social Change: nobility, opera industry and the politics of culture in Bologna . . .', p.352

25 Cited in John, *The Magic Flute*, p.7

26 John, *The Magic Flute*, p.47; see also Barbier, *Opera in Paris, 1800–1850*, p.67

27 Information in *http://m1.300.telia.com/ ~u30006326/opera5.html*, accessed February 2004

28 On Lortzing see Millington, 'The Nineteenth Century: Germany', p.214

29 Barbier, *Opera in Paris*, pp.147–8

30 Strakosch, *Souvenirs d'un impresario*, p.130

31 Charlton, 'The Nineteenth Century: France', p.130

32 Barbier, *Opera in Paris, 1800–1850*, pp.162–3

33 Osborne, *Rossini*, pp.61–5

34 See *Byron's Letters and Journals*, p.132 and Rose, *Letters from the North of Italy, 1819*, II, p.123, both cited by Osborne in his *Rossini*, p.47

35 See Pinkard, *Hegel*, pp.519–20

36 Johnson, *Listening in Paris*, pp.182–4

37 Stendhal, *Vie de Rossini*, p.35

38 See Balzac, *Illusions perdues*, in *La Comédie humaine*, Vol. 5, p.198 and *La duchesse de Langeais*, in Vol. 5, p.909

39 Balzac, *Massimila Doni*, in *La Comédie humaine*, Vol. 10, p.589

40 Cited in Barbier, *Opera in Paris, 1800–1850*, p.211

41 *The Times* obituary for Gioacchino Rossini appeared on 16 November 1868 *www.the-times.co.uk/*

42 Berlioz, *Mémoires*, p.92

43 Bordas, 'Bel ou mal canto? Le chant romantique selon Hector Berlioz', p.57

44 Tyrrell, 'Russian, Czech, Polish, and Hungarian Opera to 1900', pp.237–9

45 Ibid., p.245

46 Zórawska-Witkowska, 'La stampa polacca degli anni 1825–1830 su "Il Barbiere di Siviglia" di Gioacchino Rossini', pp.163–76

16 : Theatre

1 So says Eyre in *National Service. Diary of a Decade*, p.340

2 Mendelsohn, 'When not in Greece', p.35

3 Grégoire de Nysse, *Lettres*, p.179

4 Gili, *La Comédie italienne*, p.13

5 Information in *http://m1.300.telia.com/ ~u30006326/opera5.html* accessed in February 2004

6 Taylor, '1790', pp.88–9

7 Larson, 'Wieland's Shakespeare: A Reappraisal', pp.229–52

8 Larson, 'Shakespeare between Aufklärung and Sturm und Drang' *http:// aurora.wells.edu/~klarson/papers/ mmla88wells.htm*; update of 17 February 2000

9 Voltaire, *Lettres philosophiques*, p.149; see also Price, *English Literature in Germany*, p.221

10 Boyle, *Goethe*, Vol. 1, p.250

11 Bradshaw, 'Shakespeare's Peculiarity', *Proceedings of the British Academy*, pp.121–2 (citing Eleanor Rowe, *Hamlet: A Window on Russia*, New York 1976)

12 Price, *English Literature in Germany*, p.276; for Charles Kean's influence on the German theatre see Braun, *The Director and the Stage*, p.11

13 Information in *http://m1.300.telia.com/ ~u30006326/opera5.html*, accessed February 2004

14 Kupzova, 'La gestuelle théâtrale en Russie', pp.159–60

15 Descotes, *Les Grands rôles du théâtre de Molière*, pp.3–5

16 Branscombe, 'Reflections on Raimund's Artistic Relationships with his Contemporaries', p.34

17 Moynet, *L'envers du Théâtre*, p.59, see also p.91

18 Stendhal, *Souvenirs d'égotisme*, p.1443

19 Heine, *Italian Travel Sketches*, p.231, this volume includes letters on the French stage addressed to August Lewald

20 Vlock, *Dickens, Reading, and the Victorian Popular Theatre*, pp.24–5 and Peters, *Theatre of the Book 1480–1880*, p.285

21 *The Selected Writings of William Hazlitt*, Vol. 3, *A View of the English Stage*, pp.9, 20; originally in the *Morning Chronicle* of 26 January and 9 May 1814

22 Heine, *Italian Travel Sketches*, p.231

23 Delécluze, *Journal de Delécluze*, p.492

24 Brewer, *The Pleasures of the Imagination*, p.327

25 Place, 'Le théâtre de l'Opéra sous la Révolution: les rapports entre l'administration du théâtre et le gouvernement', pp.72–3, 78, 79, 83

26 Barbier, *Opera in Paris, 1800–1850*, pp.8–10; Le Hir, *Le romantisme aux enchères*, pp.7–8

27 Barbier, *Opera in Paris, 1800–1850*, p.60

28 Leroy, *Histoire des arts du Spectacle en France*, pp.142

29 Porter, *London*, pp.177–8

30 Ibid., p.292

31 Taylor, '1790', p.89

32 Williams, *The Long Revolution*, p.263

33 Candiani, ' "Quegli eterni *Promessi sposi*". La fortuna musicale del romanzo manzoniano', pp.676–83

34 *Jane Austen's Letters*, pp.43, 53, 103, 181

35 Information from Citizen Association Milislav, Litomyšl, accessed 6 February 2004, *http://web.quick.cz/sdruzeni.milislav/ Pages/aRepertoar.htm*

36 Austen, *Mansfield Park*, p.93 (Chapter 13)

37 Boyle, *Goethe*, Vol. 2, pp.716, 729

38 Biré, *Nouvelles causeries littéraires*, p.97, essay originally written in 1894

39 Descotes, *Le public de théâtre et son histoire*, pp.220–2

40 For data on Coelina, see Le Hir, *Le romantisme aux enchères*, p.155

41 Krakovitch, *Hugo censuré. La liberté au théâtre au XIXe siècle*, p.34

42 Louandre, 'Statistique littéraire de la production intellectuelle en France depuis quinze ans', pp.693–4

43 Goethe, *Conversations with Eckermann*, p.143

44 Le Hir, *Le romantisme aux enchères*, p.45

45 Ibid., p.15

46 Ibid., p.5

47 Descotes, *Le public de théâtre*, pp.225–6, 229

48 Ibid., pp.281–8

49 Mounin, *Linguistique et traduction*, pp.162–3

50 See French theatre statistics in *www.quid.fr/2000/Q010320.htm*, accessed 25 February 2004

PART II

1830–1880 : THE TRIUMPH OF BOURGEOIS CULTURE

17 : Books for the People

1 Marx and Engels, *The Communist Manifesto*, p.221

2 Erickson, *The Economy of Literary Form*, p.6

3 Mollier, 'Les mutations de l'espace éditorial français du XVIIIe au XXe siècle', p.30

4 Barbier, *L'empire du livre*, p.47

5 Barbier, 'Une production multipliée', p.109; original source: *Bibliographie de la France*

6 Charle, 'Le champ de la production littéraire', p.139

7 Griest, *Mudie's Circulating Library*, pp.64–6

8 Ibid., p.6

9 Lewes 'Criticism in Relation to Novels', p.353

10 Altick, *The English Common Reader*, pp.295–6

11 Griest, *Mudie's Circulating Library*, pp.20, 64–5

12 Moretti, *Atlas of the European Novel 1800–1900*, p.148

13 Pennybacker, 'Les moeurs, les aspirations et la culture politique des employés de bureau londonien des deux sexes, 1889–1914', p.85

14 Barbier, *L'Empire du livre*, p.503

15 Cited by Altick, *The English Common Reader*, p.294

16 Altick, *The English Common Reader*, p.268

17 Trollope, *An Autobiography*, p.37

18 Altick, *The English Common Reader*, p.276

19 Mollier 'Histoire de la lecture, histoire de l'édition', pp.260–1

20 Vachon, 'Balzac en feuilletons et en livres. Quantification d'une production romanesque', p.271

21 Lyons, *Le Triomphe du livre*, pp.73–4

22 Grandjean, 'Les éditions Fayard et l'édition populaire', p.229

23 Thiesse, *Imprimés du pauvre, livres de fortune*, p.92

24 Ibid., pp.93–4

25 This story was chosen by Peter Haining at the start of his anthology *The Penny Dreadful*, pp.25–9

26 Cross, *The Common Writer*, pp.174–9

27 Harbgmeier, 'European media in the Eyes of Muslim Observers', p.25

28 Haining (ed.), *The Penny Dreadful*, pp.15–6

29 Spraggs, *Outlaws and Highwaymen*, pp.256–7

30 Haining, *The Penny Dreadful*, p.15

31 Altick, *The English Common Reader*, p.292

32 Rosenman, 'Spectacular Women: *The Mysteries of London* and the Female Body', p.31

33 Neuburg, *Popular Literature*, pp.157–8

34 Barbier, *L'Empire du Livre*, p.509

35 Coward, 'Popular fiction in the nineteenth century', p.86

36 Cited in Altick, *The English Common Reader*, p.105. The citation from George Eliot is in Shaw's Introduction to Hannah More, p.xxv. For a spirited defence of Hannah More see Stott, *Hannah More*

37 Cited by Shaw in Introduction to Hannah More, p.xvi

38 Fox, *Graphic Journalism in England*, pp.138, 143, 144–5

39 Bennett, 'Revolutions in thought: serial publication and the mass market for reading', pp.226–7

40 Neuburg, *Popular Literature*, cit., p.196

41 Bennett, 'Revolutions in thought: serial publication and the mass market for reading', pp.236, 239

42 The issue can be read online by visiting *http://www.history.rochester.edu/pennymag/*

43 Wadsworth, 'Charles Knight and Sir Francis Bond Head . . .', pp.375–6

44 Altick, *The English Common Reader*, p.334

45 Engels, *The Condition of the Working Class in England*, pp.272–3

46 Altick, *The English Common Reader*, p.198

47 Black, *A New History of the English Public Library*, p.26

48 Cited in Black, *A New History of the English Public Library*, p.68

49 Ibid., pp.69, 70–1

50 Lyons, *Le Triomphe du livre*, p.170

51 Richter, *Les bibliothèques populaires*, p.4

52 Lyons, *Le Triomphe du livre*, pp.177–8

53 Barnett, *Histoire des bibliothèques publiques en France de la Révolution à 1939*, p.135

54 Richter, *Les bibliothèques populaires*, p.146

55 Darmon, *Le Colportage de Librairie en France sous le Second Empire*, p.229

56 Cited in Black, *A New History of the English Public Library*, p.191

57 Entry of 10 May 1856, in Goncourt, *Journal*, Vol. 1, 1851–65, pp.169–70

58 The original text of *De la littérature industrielle* appeared in the *Revue des Deux Mondes*, 1 September 1839, the text used here is in Sainte-Beuve, *Pour la critique*, pp.197–222

59 Sainte-Beuve, *Pour la critique*, pp.198, 201, 202–3, 208, 209, 217

60 Carlyle, 'Sign of the Times', originally in *Edinburgh Review* of June 1829 now in *A Carlyle Reader*, p.36

61 Gautier, *Histoire de l'art dramatique en France*, Vol. 1, pp.82–3

62 Marx, *The German Ideology*, p.206

63 Brown, *Zola. A Life*, p.143

18 : Newspapers, Magazines and Pictures

1 Dickens, *Our Mutual Friend*, p.6

2 Arnold, *Culture and Anarchy*, p.91

3 Altick, *The Shows of London*, p.467

4 Angenot, 'Ceci tuera cela, ou: la chose imprimée contre le livre', p.86

5 Morton and Morris, 'Civil Society, Governance and Nation, 1852–1914', p.410

6 Fox, 'Murder in Daily Instalments . . .', p.272

7 *The Times*, 29 November 1814, *http://www.the-times.co.uk/*

8 Fox 'Murder in Daily Instalments . . .', p.273

9 Chalaby, *The Invention of Journalism*, pp.12–13, 35, 38–9

10 Bellanger et al. *Histoire Générale de la Presse française*, Vol. 2, pp.103, 111–13

11 Pellissier, *Émile de Girardin*, pp.64–6

12 See the document reprinted in Archives nationales, *Contrôle de la presse, de la librairie et du colportage sous le Second Empire 1852–1879*, Paris 1995, p.29

13 Dickens, *Dombey and Son*, p.836

14 Martin, 'Presse et publicité dans la France du XIXe siècle', pp.201–2, 209

15 Ibid., pp.206–9

16 Williams, *The Long Revolution*, pp.54, 176

17 Andrews, *The History of British Journalism*, p.1

18 Houghton, 'Periodical literature and the articulate classes', pp.3–7

19 Trollope, *An Autobiography*, pp.167–8, 173

20 Roberts, 'Exhibition and Review: the periodical press and the Victorian art exhibition system', pp.79–80

21 Finkelstein, *The House of Blackwood*, pp.96–7

22 Régnier, 'Littérature nationale, Littératures étrangères au XIXe siècle. La fonction de la *Revue des Deux Mondes* entre 1829 et 1870', p.291 and Loué, 'La *Revue des Deux Mondes* et ses libraires étrangers dans la lutte contre la contrefaçon belge (1848–1852)', p.327

23 Balbi, 'Essai statistique sur la presse périodique du globe', pp.593–603

24 Louandre, 'Statistique littéraire de la production intellectuelle en France . . .', pp.444–5

25 Blackbourn, *The Fontana History of Germany 1780–1918*, p.276

26 Ibid., p.277

27 Sayer, 'The Language of Nationality and the Nationality of Language: Prague 1780–1920', pp.198–9

28 Pellissier, *Émile de Girardin*, p.51

29 Read, 'The Relationship of Reuters and other News agencies with the British Press 1858–1984 . . .', p.150

30 Palmer, 'The British Press and international news, 1851–99: of agencies and newspapers', p.207

31 Cited in Elliott, 'Professional Ideology and organisational change: the journalist since 1800', p.176

32 Martin, 'Journalistes et gens de lettres (1820–1890)', p.107

33 Allen, *In the Public Eye*, appendix Table A.3

34 Santoro, *Storia del libro italiano*, pp.281–5

35 Coltham, 'English Working Class Newspapers in 1867', pp.166–7

36 White, *Women's Magazines 1693–1968*, pp.44–6, 80

37 Cited in White, *Women's Magazines 1693–1968*, pp.47–51

38 Bourke, 'Housewifery in Working-Class England 1860–1914', p.189

39 Flint, *The Woman Reader 1837–1914*, p.151

40 Adler, *À l'aube du feminisme: Les premières journalistes (1830–1850)*, pp.79, 91

41 The following account is taken from Koven, *Slumming. Sexual and Social Politics in Victorian London*, pp.26ff

42 Ibid., p.47

43 Walter, 'Littérature de colportage et roman-feuilleton . . .', p.153

44 Hébrard, 'Les canards', p.521

45 For Parisian sales see Allen, *In the Public Eye*, appendix Table A.3

46 Amaury, *Histoire du plus grand quotidien de la IIIe République: Le Petit Parisien, 1876–1944*, Vol. 1, pp.108–16, 122, 273

47 See table in Berridge, 'Popular Sunday Papers and mid-Victorian society', p.256

48 Ibid., p.249

49 Fox, 'Murder in Daily Instalments . . .', pp.275–7

50 Cooper, *Gleanings in Europe. England*, p.199

51 Cooper-Richet, 'La librairie étrangère à Paris au XIXe siècle . . .', p.63

52 Cooper-Richet, 'Les imprimés en langue anglaise en France au XIXe siècle . . .', p.129

53 Thackeray, *Vanity Fair*, p.718

54 James, 'The Trouble with Betsy . . .', pp.352–3

55 Ibid., p.356

56 The text has been republished: De Bunsen, 'The Hawker: His Work and His Day', pp.89, 92

57 Brewer, *The Pleasures of the Imagination*, p.164

58 Cross, *The Common Writer*, p.3

59 Angenot, *1889. Un état du discours social*, p.53

60 Cross, *The Common Writer*, p.106

61 Daumard, 'L'argent et le rang dans la société française du XIXe siècle.', p.21

62 Martin, 'Journalistes et gens de lettres (1820–1890)', p.114

63 Zola, 'L'argent dans la littérature' in *L'encre et le sang*, pp.60–1, originally published in *Vestnik Evropy* (St Petersburg) in March 1880 and *Le Voltaire* (23–30 July 1880)

64 Zola, 'Adieu' in *Le Figaro*, 22 September 1881 in *L'encre et le sang*, cit., p.323

65 Dubois, 'Naissance du recit policier', p.49

66 Pollard, 'The English Market for Printed Books', p.39

67 Le Men, 'Book Illustration', p.95

68 Houfe, *The Dictionary of Nineteenth Century British Book Illustrators and Caricaturists*, p.33

69 Fox, 'The Development of Social Reportage . . .', p.91

70 Le Men, 'Book Illustration', p.96

71 Fox, 'The Development of Social Reportage . . .', pp.91–3

72 Cited in Dorment, 'The Great Room of Art', p.33

73 Fox, 'The Development of Social Reportage . . .', pp.98–9

74 Ibid., p.106
75 Watelet, 'La presse illustrée', p.374
76 Le Men, 'Book Illustration', p.94 and Haining (ed.),*The Penny Dreadful*, p.15
77 Gretton, 'Difference and Competition: the Imitation and Reproduction of Fine Art . . .', p.147
78 Douglas, 'At the Cutting Edge', pp.30–1
79 Gay, *The Cultivation of Hatred*, p.389
80 Roberts, 'Exhibition and review: the periodical press and the Victorian art exhibition system', pp.88–9, 94
81 Kaenel, 'Autour de J.-J. Grandville . . .', pp.51–2
82 Boime, 'Entrepreneurial Patronage in Nineteenth-Century France', p.161
83 Le Men, 'Book Illustration', p.102
84 Letter to Ernest Duplan, 12 June 1862 in Flaubert, *Correspondance*, p.221
85 Roberts, 'Exhibition and review . . .', p.91
86 Gretton, 'Difference and Competition . . .', p.148
87 Gay, *The Naked Heart*, p.289
88 Roberts, 'Exhibition and review . . .', pp.80–1
89 Ibid., p.93
90 Kaenel, ' "Le plus illustre des illustrateurs" . . .', p.36
91 Hamerton, 'Gustave Doré's Bible', p.669
92 Ibid, p.671
93 Gretton, 'Difference and Competition . . .', p.155n
94 Kaenel, ' "Le plus illustre des illustrateurs" . . .', pp.42–5
95 Moriarty, 'Structures of cultural production in nineteenth-century France', p.18
96 Homberger, 'The model's unwashed feet: French photography in the 1850s', p.132
97 Ibid., p.137
98 Stallabrass, *Gargantua. Manufactured Mass Culture*, p.13

19 : Money Matters

1 Mollier, 'Histoire de la lecture, histoire de l'édition', pp.207–8; see also Thiesse, *Imprimés du pauvre, livres de fortune*, p.92
2 Dickens, *David Copperfield*, pp.59–60
3 Lyons, *Le Triomphe du livre*, pp.160–3
4 Boosey, *Fifty Years of Music*, pp.23–4
5 Trollope, *An Autobiography*, p.115
6 Robb, 'Where to begin the feast?', p.3
7 Cited by Skilton in his introduction to Trollope, *An Autobiography*, p.xix
8 Wall, *Flaubert. A Life*, p.229
9 See the criss-crossing of letters in Flaubert, *Correspondance*, Volume III, pp.221–2, 225–6, 227–8, 1175 and the Flaubert-Lévy correspondence in *Lettres inédites de Gustave Flaubert à son éditeur Michel Lévy*, pp.67–73
10 Galvan, *Paul Féval. Parcours d'une oeuvre*, pp.16–17
11 Robb, *Balzac*, p.89
12 Thomson, *George Sand and the Victorians*, pp.11–15
13 Robb, *Balzac*, pp.209, 262
14 Ibid., p.351
15 Gautier, *Histoire du Romantisme*, p.77; see his reference to a red gilet in his short story *Onuphrius* in Gautier, *Récits Fantastiques*, p.93
16 Doubine, 'Culture classique, culture d'élite, culture de masse . . .', p.99
17 Barbier, *L'empire du livre*, pp.83–5
18 Kaschuba, 'German *Bürgerlichkeit* after 1800: Culture as Symbolic Practice', p.392
19 Koszyk, *Deutsche Presse im 19. Jahrhundert*, p.267
20 Gay, *The Cultivation of Hatred*, p.337
21 Barbier, *L'empire du livre*, p.89
22 See the three-way correspondence in Marx and Engels, *Werke*, vol. 32, Dietz Verlag, Berlin 1973, pp.126, 127–9, 555, 573; letters of 26 July, 29 July, 31 July, and 26 October 1868; I thank Beatrice de Gerloni for tracking down this material
23 See Engels, 'Karl Marx' in *Marx Engels Werke*, cit., vol. 16, Berlin 1975, pp.361–6
24 Gay, *The Cultivation of Hatred*, pp.338–9
25 Barbier, *L'Empire du livre*, pp.87–91
26 Coward, 'Popular fiction in the nineteenth century', p.77
27 Camerino, 'Il romanzo nella prima metà dell'Ottocento', p.215 citing Carlo Tenca's 1844 article 'Del commercio librario in Italia e dei mezzi di riordinarlo'
28 Fryckstedt, *Geraldine Jewsbury's 'Athenaeum' Reviews*, p.12
29 Fritschner, 'Publishers' Readers, Publishers, and Their Authors', p.48
30 Showalter, *A Literature of Their Own*, p.177
31 Fritschner, 'Publishers' Readers, Publishers, and Their Authors', pp.66–7
32 Ibid., p.59
33 Ackroyd, *Dickens*, p.294
34 Mistler, *La Librairie Hachette de 1826 à nos jours*, pp.31–4
35 Mollier, *Louis Hachette*, pp.444–5
36 Mistler, *La Librairie Hachette*, p.40
37 Mollier, *Louis Hachette*, pp.140–1

38 Ibid., pp.143ff, 151
39 Ibid., pp.163, 167
40 Mistler, *La Librairie Hachette*, p.49
41 Ibid., p.179
42 James, 'An Insight into the Management of Railway Bookstalls in the Eighteen Fifties', pp.64–6
43 Mistler, *La Librairie Hachette*, p.125
44 James, 'The Publication of Collected Editions of Bulwer Lytton's Novels', pp.46, 51; Henry Curwen, *A History of Booksellers*, p.438
45 Todd, 'Firma Tauchnitz: A Further Investigation', p.17
46 Blumberg, 'Tolstoy and the English Novel . . .', pp.562
47 Cited in Williams, *The Long Revolution*, pp.54–5, 169
48 Mistler, *La Librairie Hachette*, p.298
49 Letter to Jules Duplan, 10 June 1862 in Flaubert, *Correspondance*, Vol. 3, p.221
50 Mistler, *La Librairie Hachette*, pp.123–4
51 Dufour, *Comtesse de Ségur née Rostopchine*, p.473; Parinet, 'Les bibliothèques de gare . . .', pp.95–6, 104
52 Mollier, *Louis Hachette*, pp.301–19
53 Mistler, *La Librairie Hachette*, p.141; Mollier, *Louis Hachette*, pp.339–40
54 Mistler, *La Librairie Hachette*, pp.116–22
55 Brown, *Zola. A Life*, p.101
56 Pollard, 'The English Market for Printed Books', p.43
57 Pressler, 'The Tauchnitz Edition . . .', pp.63–78 and Todd and Bowden (eds), *Tauchnitz International Editions in English 1841–1955. A Bibliographical History*, pp.4–6
58 Originally in Fraser, *Hic et Ubique* (1983), now as an essay ('The Jester with a Melancholy Face') in *Thackeray. Interviews and Recollections*, Vol. 1, pp.140–1
59 Trollope, *An Autobiography*, p.136
60 Ibid., p.88
61 Brewer, *The Pleasures of the Imagination*, p.152
62 Sand, *Correspondance*, Vol. VII (July 1845–June 1847), pp.259–60
63 Letter of 8 February 1846 in George Sand, *Correspondance*, Vol. VII, cit., p.269. Giroux and Vialat, who were mainly printers, immediately sold the rights to *La Mare au diable* to Desessart, a common practice at the time
64 Unsigned (John Chapman?), 'The Commerce of Literature', *Westminster Review*, Vol. 1, April 1852, p.526
65 Unsigned editorial 'À nos lecteurs' in *Revue des Deux Mondes*, 15 March 1848, p.1098 cited in Loué, 'La *Revue des Deux Mondes* . . .', p.317
66 Lyons, *Le Triomphe du livre*, p.69
67 Baudet, *Grandeur et misères d'un éditeur belge: Henry Kistemaeckers*, p.8
68 Hüttner, '*The Woman in White*': Analysis, Reception and Literary Criticism of a Victorian Bestseller', p.155
69 Trollope, *An Autobiography*, pp.196–7
70 Cooper, *Gleanings in Europe. England*, p.119
71 Ibid., p.120
72 Ackroyd, *Dickens*, pp.364, 369, 372
73 Sand, *Histoire de ma vie* in *Oeuvres autobiographiques*, Vol. 2, p.151
74 Perrod, 'Balzac "avocat" de la propriété littéraire', p.270
75 Compère, 'Le *Robinson Suisse* relu et récrit par Hetzel', pp.223–32

20 : Reading by Instalments

1 Polette, 'Le concept "populaire/peuple" . . .', pp.41–2
2 Trollope, *An Autobiography*, p.93
3 Cited in Maurois, *Les Trois Dumas*, pp.175–6
4 See *Le Rocambole*, special issue of the *Bulletin des Amis du Roman populaire*, No. 2, Fall 1997, pp.31–3 which reproduces the article by Jean Rousseau originally in the *Figaro* of 11 November 1858
5 Boyle, *Goethe. The Poet and the Age*, Vol. 2, pp.304–5
6 Doody, 'Samuel Richardson: fiction and knowledge', p.109
7 Trollope, *An Autobiography*, p.177
8 Ashton, *George Eliot. A Life*, p.177
9 Goimard, 'Quelques structures formelles du roman populaire', p.20
10 Patten, *Charles Dickens and his Publishers*, pp.64–5, 68. See also Feltes, *Modes of Production of Victorian Novels*, p.13; Ackroyd thinks these suggestions could have come from the publishers, see his *Dickens*, p.193
11 Vann, 'The Early Success of *Pickwick*', p.51
12 Ackroyd, *Dickens*, p.190
13 Ibid., p.208
14 Law, *Serializing Fiction in the Victorian Press*, pp.xi, 216
15 Ibid., p.64
16 Ibid., pp.153–4
17 Pellissier, *Émile de Girardin*, pp.41–2

18 Allen, *In the Public Eye*, appendix Table A3

19 Pellissier, *Émile de Girardin*, pp.97–9

20 Walter, 'Littérature de colportage et roman-feuilleton . . .', p.155

21 Tocqueville, *Democracy in America*, p.332

22 Tournier, 'Les livres de comptes du feuilleton (1836–1846)', p.127

23 Flint, *The Woman Reader 1837–1914*, p.73

24 Reybaud, *Jérôme Paturot à la recherche d'une situation sociale* (1842), the passages I have cited or paraphrased are on pp.61–9

25 Albert, *Histoire de la Presse*, p.121

26 Walter, 'Roman-feuilleton et hausse du tirage des journaux . . .', pp.78–83

27 Pellissier, *Émile de Girardin*, p.224

28 Albert, *Histoire de la presse*, p.122

29 Pogorelskin, 'The Messenger of Europe', pp.129, 144

30 Pipes, *Russia under the Old Regime*, p.264

31 Reitblat, 'Les honoraires littéraires, médiation entre les écrivains et le public', pp.149–52

32 Schaarschmidt, 'The Lubok Novels: Russia's Immortal Best Sellers', p.426

33 Belknap, 'Survey of Russian journals, 1840–80', p.98

34 Martinsen, 'Dostoevsky's "Diary of a Writer"', pp.152–3

35 Ouimette, '"Monstrous Fecundity": The Popular Novel in Nineteenth-Century Spain', p.388

36 Ibid., p.389

37 Ibid., pp.394–8

38 Watt, *Myths of Modern Individualism*, p.203

39 Belmont, 'L'Académie celtique et George Sand. . . .', p.35

40 Killen, *Le Roman terrifiant ou roman noir*, p.196

41 Atkinson, *Eugène Sue et le Roman-Feuilleton*, p.18

42 Killen, *Le Roman terrifiant ou roman noir*, p.207

43 Dickens, *Dombey and Son*, p.465

44 Robb, *Balzac*, p.162

45 This is what was the income of P-H Azaïs who left us a diary of his daily routine, see Michel Baude, 'Le journal de P-H Azaïs, père de famille et philosophe', pp.56–68

46 Robb, *Balzac*, pp.176–81

47 Angenot, 'La littérature populaire française au dix-neuvième siècle', p.320

48 Atkinson, *Eugène Sue et le Roman-Feuilleton*, p.18

49 Moretti, *Atlas of the European Novel 1800–1900*, p.101

50 See Knecht, 'Le Juif errant. Éléments d'un mythe populaire', pp.84–96, who also provided an exhaustive bibliography in his 'Le mythe du Juif errant', pp.101–15

51 Atkinson, *Eugène Sue et le Roman-Feuilleton*, p.68

52 Cited in Galvan, *Les Mystères de Paris. Eugène Sue et ses lecteurs*, Vol. 1, p.9

53 Gautier, *Histoire de l'art dramatique en France depuis ving-cinq ans*, Vol. 2, p.277

54 Quéffelec, 'Peuple et roman à l'époque romantique . . .', pp.51–4

55 *The Diary of Søren Kierkegaard*, p.67

56 Cadioli, 'Un'indagine sull'editoria', p.87

57 Quéffelec, 'Peuple et roman à l'époque romantique . . .', pp.58–61

58 Thiesse, *Le Roman du quotidien*, p.84

59 James, 'The trouble with Betsy . . .', p.360

60 Letter to Madame Hanska cited in Vachon, 'Balzac en feuilletons et en livres . . .', p.277

61 Bory, *Eugène Sue*, p.207

62 Brown, *Zola. A Life*, p.149

63 Lanoux, 'Introduction' to Eugène Sue, *Les mystères de Paris*, p.3

64 Michael, 'From Scarlet Study to *Novela Negra*', pp.23–4

65 Ceserani and Salibra, 'Popular Literature in Nineteenth-Century Italy: *Letteratura amena*', pp.362–5

66 Gautier, *Voyage en Italie*, p.53

67 Orecchioni, 'Eugène Sue: mesure d'un succès', p.165

68 Galvan, *Les Mystères de Paris. Eugène Sue et ses lecteurs*, p.23

69 See the analysis by Svane, *Les Lecteurs d'Eugène Sue*, p.10

70 They are now published and edited in two volumes by Galvan, *Les Mystères de Paris. Eugène Sue et ses lecteurs*

71 Thiesse, 'L'éducation sociale d'un romancier. Le cas d'Eugène Sue', pp.57–8

72 For a version of the second see Tannenbaum's clever 'The Beginnings of Bleeding-Heart Liberalism: Eugene Sue's *Les Mystères de Paris*', pp.491–507

73 Leclerc, *Crime écrits. La littérature en procès au 19e siècle*, pp.73–4

74 Angenot, 'La littérature populaire, française au dix-neuvième siècle', pp.323–4

75 See *Le Rocambole*, special issue of the *Bulletin des Amis du Roman populaire*, No. 2, Fall 1997 for more details on the fortune of Rocambole

21 : Repressing Culture

1   Gay, *The Cultivation of Hatred*, p.398
2   Davis, 'Italy', p.95
3   Krakovitch, 'Les romantiques et la censure au théâtre', pp.35–6
4   Mollier, 'Le siècle d'or du plagiat littéraire', p.75
5   Krakovitch, *Hugo censuré*, pp.19, 24
6   Soriano, *Jules Verne*, pp.110–12
7   Dumas, 'Hetzel, censeur de Verne', pp.127–36, especially pp.128–9
8   Brancaleoni, 'La Ginevra di Antonio Ranieri ed il Twist di Charles Dickens . . .', pp.163, 186
9   De Sanctis, *Teoria e storia della letteratura*, Vol. 1, p.266
10 de Certeau, *La culture au pluriel*, p.52
11 See the exchange of letters in Comtesse de Ségur, 'Lettres à son Éditeur' in Comtesse de Ségur. *Oeuvres*, pp.lxxxvi–lxxxvii
12 This is what Leclerc thinks, but he has no evidence, see his *Crimes écrits*, p.140
13 Flaubert, *Madame Bovary*, nouvelle version précédée des scénarios inédits, p.77
14 Flaubert, *Madame Bovary*, Flammarion, p.228
15 Flaubert, *Madame Bovary*, nouvelle version précédée des scénarios inédits, p.30
16 Leclerc, *Crimes écrits*, see pp.325ff for the list of the cuts demanded
17 See list in Leclerc, *Crimes écrits*, pp.435–8
18 John Davis, 'Italy', p.104
19 See the text in appendix to Gustave Flaubert, *Madame Bovary*, the passage cited is on p.467
20 Leclerc, *Crimes écrits*, p.32
21 Letter to Jules Duplan, 3 or 4 October 1857 in Flaubert, *Correspondance*, Vol. 2, pp.766–7
22 Pichois, *Auguste Poulet-Malassis. L'éditeur de Baudelaire*, p.130
23 Ashton, *G. H. Lewes*, pp.259–60; see also her *George Eliot. A Life*, p.336
24 Ackroyd, *Dickens*, pp.290–1
25 Gay, *The Naked Heart*, p.157
26 Trollope, *An Autobiography*, p.143
27 See Williams, *The Long Revolution*, pp.65–6
28 Certeau, *La culture au pluriel*, p.51
29 Darmon, *Le Colportage de Librairie en France sous le Second Empire*, pp.81, 296–7
30 See the lengthy analysis in Darmon, *Le Colportage de Librairie en France sous le Second Empire*, pp.83–90
31 Mollier, 'Un siècle de transition vers une culture de masse', pp.188–90
32 Brooks, *When Russia Learned to read*, p.110
33 Farrell, 'The Bawdy Lubok: sexual and scatological content in eighteenth-century Russian Popular Prints', pp.16–17 and, in the same collection, Levitt, 'Barkoviana and Russian Classicism', p.219
34 Lenman, 'Germany', pp.49–50
35 Dickinson, 'The Men's Christian Morality Movement in Germany, 1880–1914 . . .', pp.59–100
36 The citation from the Pope is in Goldstein (ed.), *The War for the Public Mind*, p.5
37 Robb, *Victor Hugo*, p.401
38 Davis, 'Italy', p.119
39 Ibid., p.108
40 Ibid., p.115
41 Cited in ibid., p.93
42 Cited by Bartlet, 'On the Freedom of the Theatre and Censorship . . .', p.25
43 Krakovitch, *Hugo censuré*, pp.75, 99
44 Krakovitch, 'Les romantiques et la censure au théâtre', p.37
45 Vivien, 'Études administratives. III. Les théâtres', p.400
46 Leroy, *Histoire des arts du Spectacle en France*, pp.91–3
47 Sanguanini, *Il pubblico all'italiana*, p.158
48 Shubert, 'Spain', pp.189, 193
49 Gay, *The Cultivation of Hatred*, p.403
50 Marvin, 'The Censorship of Verdi's Operas in Victorian London', p.586
51 Ibid., pp.590–2
52 Goldstein, 'France', p.133
53 Marvin, 'The Censorship of Verdi's Operas in Victorian London', p.599
54 Cited in ibid., pp.599–602
55 Caruzzi, 'Il libretto d'opera e la società romantica', p.1164
56 Krakovitch, *Hugo censuré*, p.87
57 Cited in Davis, 'Italy', p.105
58 Condemi, *Les cafés-concerts*, p.23
59 Ibid., pp.28, 32–3
60 Yearwood, 'United States: African American Culture', p.2523

22 : Beloved Writers

1   The episode is told in Second, *Le tiroir aux souvenirs*, p.7
2   Robb, *Victor Hugo*, pp.119–21, 126–7, 133, 142–3
3   Gay, *The Cultivation of Hatred*, pp.178–9
4   Busch, 'Victor Hugo's Narrative Prose Debut in Russia', p.20

5 Krakovitch, *Hugo censuré*, p.16

6 Robb, *Victor Hugo*, p.177

7 Boussel and Duboit, *De Quoi Vivait Victor Hugo?*, p.88

8 See Robb's masterly biography: *Victor Hugo*, pp.215, 218, 219

9 Gautier, *Histoire du Romantisme*, p.96

10 Michelet, *Oeuvres complètes*, Vol. IV, p.606

11 Trollope, *Paris et les Parisiens en 1835*, pp.110–12

12 Busch, 'Victor Hugo's Narrative Prose Debut in Russia', pp.18–20

13 Robb, *Victor Hugo*, p.225

14 Ibid., p.258

15 Hugo, Pierre-Jules Hetzel, *Correspondance*, Vol. 1 (1852–1853), p.219

16 Robb, *Victor Hugo*, pp.321–2

17 See the catalogue of the 1985 Paris exhibition at the Grand Palais, *La Gloire de Victor Hugo*, Édition de la Réunion des musées nationaux, Paris 1985, p.95

18 Robb, *Victor Hugo*, pp.386, 404–5, 493, 513–14, 529

19 See list in Laster, 'La Musique', pp.649–57

20 Boussel and Duboit, *De Quoi Vivait Victor Hugo?*, p.164

21 Robb, *Victor Hugo*, p.366

22 Boussel and Duboit, *De Quoi Vivait Victor Hugo?*, p.139; see exchange of letters in Leuillot, *Victor Hugo publie les Misérables*, pp.28–31

23 Goncourt, *Journal. Mémoires de la vie littéraire*, Vol. 1, entry for April 1862 (no day), p.808; reading the book was finished on 28 September, p.862

24 Robb, *Victor Hugo*, p.378

25 Ibid., p.377

26 Rosa, ' "Quot libras in duce?" . . .', p.234

27 Devars, Petitier, Rosa and Vaillant, 'Si Victor Hugo était compté. Essais de bibliométrie hugolienne comparée', pp.339, 359

28 Ashton, *George Eliot. A Life*, p.312

29 Robb, *Victor Hugo*, pp.380, 383

30 Trollope, *Autobiography*, p.153

31 Ibid., p.158

32 Ibid., pp.71, 74

33 Ibid., pp.54–5

34 Ibid., pp.94–5

35 Dickens, *Bleak House*, p.268

36 Cited in Churchill, 'The Genius of Charles Dickens', p.137

37 Dickens, *Bleak House*, p.705

38 Ackroyd, *Dickens*, p.440

39 Patten, *Charles Dickens and his Publishers*, p.345

40 Ibid., pp.349–416

41 Ibid., pp.220–34

42 Ibid., p.325

43 Ibid., p.332

44 Cooper-Richet, Diana, 'Les imprimés en langue anglaise en France au XIXe siècle . . .', p.133

45 Monod, 'Les premiers traducteurs français de Dickens', pp.120, 123, 126

46 Vereş 'Dickens Criticism in Romania Before World War II', p.270

47 *Catalogo generale della libreria italiana dall'anno 1847 a tutto il 1899*, Kraus Reprint, Vaduz 1964

48 Price, *English Literature in Germany*, p.347

49 Collins, *Charles Dickens, The Public Readings*, p.xviii

50 Ibid., p.153

51 Ibid., p.469

52 Cousins, *The Story of Film*, p.44

53 See study based on UNESCO's *Index Translationum* for 1969 printed in 1971: 'Étude sur l'*Index Translationum*', in *Bibliographie de France*, 22 September 1971, Vol. 160, No. 38, pp.561–2

54 Lyons, *Le Triomphe du livre*, p.145

55 Popa, 'Jules Verne dans une perspective Roumaine', p.305

56 Unwin, 'On the Novel and the Writing of Literary History', p.6

57 Lyons, *Le Triomphe du livre*, p.164

58 Propp, *Morphology of the Folktale*

59 Martin, *La vie et l'oeuvre de Jules Verne*, p.138

60 Ibid., pp.140–1, 154, 176, 188, 212–13

61 I calculate this on the basis of Huet's *L'Histoire des Voyages extraordinaires. Essai sur l'oeuvre de Jules Verne*, see appendix, pp.191–9

62 This is a paraphrase of Berlin, 'Notes on Prejudice', a hitherto unpublished note which appeared in the *New York Review of Books*, 18 October 2001, p.12

63 Bouvier-Ajam, *Alexandre Dumas ou cent ans après*, p.133

64 Cited in Maurois, *Les Trois Dumas*, p.174, but no source given

65 Dumas, *Causeries*, pp.43–4

66 Coward, 'Popular fiction in the nineteenth century', pp.78–9

67 Talvart and Place (eds), *Bibliographie des Auteurs Modernes (1801 – 1934)*, Volume 5

68 Zimmerman, *Alexandre Dumas le Grand*, p.408

69 Louandre, 'Statistique littéraire de la production intellectuelle en France depuis quinze ans', p.687

70 Zimmerman, *Alexandre Dumas le Grand*, pp.420–1

71 Jacques Chirac, speech of 30 November 2002, full text at *http://www.elysee.fr/cgi-bin/auracom/aurweb/search/file?aur~file=discours/2002/021130DU.htm*

72 Full list of pastiches, adaptations and sequels at *http://www.pastichesdumas.com/pages/livres.html*

73 See the analysis by Klotz, 'Apoteosi, passione e azione nel "Conte di Montecristo" di Dumas'

74 Dumas, *Causeries*, p.30

75 Joyce, *Portrait of the Artist as a Young Man*, p.62, see also pp.65, 66

76 See the text of the electoral leaflet reprinted in *Cahiers Alexandre Dumas*, No.12, 1983, p.61

77 Dumas, *Causeries*, p.2

78 Baeckvall, 'Dumas dans un récit suédois du XIXᵉ siècle', pp.30–4

79 This – admittedly scarcely believable – claim was made by Dimaras, in 'Réalisme et naturalisme en Grèce. L'offre et la demande', p.260

80 Montesinos, *Introducción a una historia de la novela en España en el siglo XIX*, p.92

23 : Great Genres

1 Cited in Flint, *The Woman Reader 1837–1914*, p.274

2 Moretti, 'Graphs, Maps', pp.67–93, especially pp.80–1

3 James, *Science Fiction in the 20th century*, p.51

4 Gaskell, *North and South*

5 Lacassin, *Mythologie du roman policier*, pp.66, 69

6 See remarks in Ousby, *The Crime and Mystery Book*, p.31

7 Collins, *The Moonstone*, pp.488–9

8 See text of reviews in appendix to Collins, *The Moonstone*, pp.543–5

9 Bodin, 'Les Paysans et Paul-Louis'

10 Farmer, 'Introduction' to Collins, *The Moonstone*, p.26

11 Gay, *The Cultivation of Hatred*, p.205

12 Cooper, *Gleanings in Europe. England*, p.202

13 Boyle, *Black Swine in the Sewers of Hampstead*, pp.119–20

14 Hüttner, 'The Woman in White': Analysis, *Reception and Literary Criticism of a Victorian Bestseller*, p.25

15 Moretti, 'The Slaughterhouse of literature', p.214

16 Hüttner, 'The Woman in White', pp.1, 19, 257–8, 264–5

17 Ibid., pp.144–5

18 Györgyev, 'The Influence of Whitman and Poe on Hungarian Literature', pp.856–9

19 Clarke, 'Poe and his Critics', pp.575–8

20 Eliot, *From Poe to Valéry*, p.4

21 Entry of 16 July 1856 in Goncourt, *Journal. Mémoires de la vie littéraire*, Vol. 1, p.189

22 Boileau-Narcejac, *Le roman policier*, p.26

23 Cook, *Mystery, Detective, and Espionage Magazines*, p.xx

24 Rose, *The Case of Peter Pan*, p.2

25 D'hulst, 'Traduire l'Europe en France entre 1810 et 1840', p.144

26 Carraud was a shrewd reader of Balzac's works; see Balzac, *Correspondance avec Zulma Carraud*

27 Gay, *The Cultivation of Hatred*, p.104

28 Lyons, 'Les best-sellers', p.428

29 Rosa, 'Comptes pour enfants . . .', p.350

30 Limousin, 'Essais statistiques sur l'évolution de l'édition du livre pour enfants . . .', p.704; Guy Rosa has similar though not identical data, see her 'Comptes pour enfants', pp.351–2

31 Barbier, *L'Empire du livre*, p.56

32 Rosa, 'Comptes pour enfants', p.355

33 Grew and Harrigan, 'The Availability of Schooling in Nineteenth-Century France', and Grew, Harrigan and Whitney, 'La scolarisation en France 1829–1906'

34 Guérande, *Le Petit monde de la Comtesse de Ségur*, p.29

35 Cohen, 'Women and fiction in the nineteenth century', p.66

36 Soriano, *Guide de littérature pour la jeunesse*, p.480

37 Comtesse de Ségur, *La Fortune de Gaspard*, with a penetrating introduction by Marc Soriano

38 Comtesse de Ségur, *Lettres à son Éditeur*, p.lxxxix, letter of 23 May 1863

39 Dufour, *Comtesse de Ségur née Rostopchine*, p.287

40 Laurent, 'Préface' to *Comtesse de Ségur. Oeuvres*, pp.vii, xiii

41 De Beauvoir, *Mémoires d'une jeune fille rangée*, p.23

42 For an intelligent development of this

view see Marconi, *La Comtesse de Ségur
ou le bonheur immobile*, especially
pp.55–64 and pp.71–84. On Ruskin's *The
King of the Golden River* see Tim Hilton,
John Ruskin. The Later Years, pp.87–8

43 Caradec, *Histoire de la Littérature
enfantine en France*, pp.143–53

44 Comtesse de Ségur, *Lettres à son Éditeur*,
p.lxv

45 Rosa, 'Comptes pour enfants', p.358

46 Mistler, *La Librairie Hachette de 1826 à
nos jours*, pp.150–1

47 Rambelli, 'La letteratura educativa per i
giovani e per il popolo', pp.169–71

48 Boyer, *Histoire des littératures scandinaves*,
p.118

49 Ibid., pp.120–1

50 Boyer, 'Introduction' in Hans-Christian
Andersen, *Oeuvres*, Vol. I, pp.xxxii,
xxxiv–v, xlix

51 Ibid., p.li

52 Ibid., pp.liii, lxix

24 : Women and Novels

1 Altick, 'The sociology of authorship . . .',
pp.393–4

2 Showalter, *A Literature of Their Own*,
pp.320–50; this list includes writers up to
1939

3 Angenot, *1889. Un état du discours social*,
p.70

4 Altick, 'The sociology of authorship',
p.392

5 Cross, *The Common Writer*, p.167

6 Ibid., pp.165–6

7 Gay, *The Cultivation of Hatred*, pp.341,
343, 344

8 Trollope, *An Autobiography*, pp.81–2

9 Ibid., pp.174–5; on Dumas's speed see
Zimmermann, *Alexandre Dumas le
Grand*, p.408

10 Trollope, *An Autobiography*, pp.84–5, 87,
106, 110, 182, and 230–1

11 Ibid., pp.230–1

12 Ibid., p.37

13 Ashton, *George Eliot*, p.152, 195, 250

14 Finkelstein, *The House of Blackwood*,
p.34

15 Ashton, *George Eliot*, p.212

16 Ibid., p.227

17 Ibid., p.231

18 Ibid., p.257

19 Ibid.

20 Anderson, ' "Things Wisely Ordered":
John Blackwood, George Eliot, and the
Publication of *Romola*', pp.34, 36

21 Ashton, *George Eliot*, pp.283, 352, 353,
356

22 Finkelstein, *The House of Blackwood*,
p.167

23 Haythornthwaite, 'The Wages of Success:
"Miss Marjoribanks". . . ', p.91

24 Ibid., pp.92–4

25 Cited in Flint, *The Woman Reader
1837–1914*, p.275

26 Haythornthwaite, 'The Wages of Success:
"Miss Marjoribanks". . . ', p.102

27 Finkelstein, *The House of Blackwood*,
p.167

28 Charle, 'Le champ de la production
littéraire', p.157

29 Martin, 'Journalistes et gens de lettres
(1820–1890)', p.114

30 Charle, 'Le champ de la production
littéraire', pp.160–3

31 Lough, *Writer and Public in France*, p.347

32 See letter of 21 July 1845 from Louis Véron,
editor of the *Constitutionnel*, to Sand
accepting her terms for her next novel, in
Sand, *Correspondance*, Vol. VII, p.17

33 Charle, 'Le champ de la production
littéraire', p.162

34 Letzter and Adelson, *Women Writing
Opera*, p.76

35 H.W. (Hans Werner), 'La musique des
femmes: Louise Bertin', pp.616–17

36 Berlioz, *Mémoires*, p.285

37 Ashton, *George Eliot*, pp.144–5

38 Cottin, *Malvina*, Vol. 2, pp.84–5

39 Ibid., pp.86–7

40 Ibid., pp.88, 90

41 Greg, 'The False Morality of Lady
Novelists', p.149 cited in Showalter, *A
Literature of Their Own*, pp.26–7

42 The letter (and Brontë's reply) can be
found in *The Oxford Book of Letters*,
edited by Kermode and Kermode,
pp.276–8

43 Cited in Acocella, *Willa Cather and the
Politics of Criticism*, pp.39–40

44 Eliot, 'Silly Novels by Lady Novelists',
pp.140–63. The essay was originally
published in the *Westminster Review*,
October 1856

45 Gay, *The Cultivation of Hatred*, pp.331,
349–50

46 Sand, *Histoire de ma vie* in *Oeuvres
autobiographiques*, Vol. 2, p.150

47 Bignan, *L'Ermite des Alpes* in Bignan,
Romans et nouvelles, pp.425–79

48 Gay, *The Cultivation of Hatred*, p.335
where Hawthorne's citation can be found

49 Most of my information on Ouida is

based on Phillips, 'Under Two Flags: the Publishing History of a Best-Seller 1867–1967', especially pp.67–71; and Sutherland, 'Introduction' to Ouida, Under Two Flags, especially p.xvi

50 Clyman and Vowles (eds), Russia Through Women's Eyes, p.20. See a recent English translation by Mary Fleming Zirin for Indiana University Press, Bloomington 1989

51 Clyman and Vowles (eds), Russia Through Women's Eyes, p.74

52 Ibid., pp.261–2

53 Sauvy, 'Une littérature pour les femmes', p.504

54 Nies, ' "Où peut conduire la lecture du Constitutionnel" . . . :, p.139

55 Mayeur, L'Éducation des filles en France, pp.139–40

56 Ashton, George Eliot, p.164

57 Ibid., p.164, pp.188–9

58 See the reviews cited in Thomson, George Sand and the Victorians, pp.11–28

59 Haythornthwaite, 'Friendly Encounters . . .', p.80

60 Showalter provides a lengthy list of women writers' male pseudonyms in her A Literature of Their Own, p.58

61 Sand, Histoire de ma vie, p.138; the editor claims that her part in selecting the name was much more important than Sand suggested in her account, see p.1335

62 Ellmann, Oscar Wilde, p.441

63 Lowe, 'Pushkin and Carmen', pp.72–6, who points out that Mérimée translated Pushkin's poem in 1852

64 Praz, La carne, la morte e il diavolo nella letteratura romantica, pp.171–86

65 Blamires (ed.), Woman Defamed and Woman Defended, pp.100–2

66 Larrington, Women and Writing in Medieval Europe, p.227

67 Gay, The Cultivation of Hatred, pp.345–7

25 : Challenging the Trailblazers

1 Moretti, Atlas of the European Novel 1800–1900, p.186

2 Gay, The Cultivation of Hatred, p.347

3 Mistler, La Librairie Hachette, pp.155–6, 159. On Dickens's renown in France see Ackroyd, Dickens, p.788

4 Rovani, Cento Anni, Vol. 2, p.616

5 Bienkowska and Chamerska, Books in Poland, p.29

6 Barbier, 'Le commerce international de la librairie française . . .', p.109

7 de Sacy, Rapport sur le progrès des lettres, p.26

8 Sayer, 'The Language of Nationality and the Nationality of Language: Prague 1780–1920', pp.200–2

9 Klaniczay, Histoire de la littérature hongroise des origines à nos jours, pp.249–54

10 Verzea, 'The Historical Novel as Popular Literature . . .', pp.264–5

11 Ibid., p.267

12 Ibid., pp.266–8

13 Popa, 'Les conditions sociologiques de la naissance du roman roumain', p.24

14 Cornea, 'La sociologie du roman roumain au XIXe siècle', pp.7, 14

15 Iorga, La société roumaine du XIXe siècle dans le théâtre roumain, pp.12–14

16 Ibid., pp.27, 48

17 Dimaras, Histoire de la littérature néo-hellénique, p.352

18 Trudgill, 'Greece and European Turkey: From Religious to Linguistic Identity', pp.247–8

19 Wingård, 'Le dix-neuvième siècle suédois . . .', pp.104–5

20 Forsås-Scott, Swedish Women's Writing 1850–1995, pp.31–4

21 Boyer, Histoire des littératures scandinaves, p.170

22 Schuster, 'Popular Literature in Germany: 1800–1850', pp.345–6

23 Le Rider, 'Soll und Haben de Gustav Freytag . . .', pp.164–74

24 Ibid., pp.179–81; see also Ureña, 'Mobilizing German Women Against "Cultural Drunkenness" . . .'

25 Bellos, 'Le Marché du livre à l'époque romantique: recherches et problèmes', p.658

26 See text in Aron (ed.), La Belgique artistique et littéraire, p.374

27 See Quaghebeur, Balises pour l'histoire des lettres belges, Labor, Brussels 1998, pp.19–20

28 Blackbourn, The Fontana History of Germany 1780–1918, pp.200, 275

29 Barbier, L'empire du livre, p.161

30 Ibid., pp.32–7

31 Ibid., p.55

32 Ibid., pp.93–4

33 Hohendahl, Building a National Literature, p.330

34 Hüttner, 'The Woman in White', p.232

35 Carbonell, 'La réception de l'historiographie allemande en France (1866–1885) . . .', pp.329–30

36 Ibid., p.343
37 Ibid., p.337
38 Brooks, *When Russia Learned to read*, pp.xiv–xv, 4–6, 36
39 Gogol, *Dead Souls*, pp.29–30; this is a consideration made by Brooks, *When Russia Learned to read*, p.13
40 Brooks, *When Russia Learned to read*, p.82
41 Ibid., pp.66–8
42 Ibid., p.92
43 Taruskin, 'Some Thoughts on the History and Historiography of Russian Music', pp.331–3
44 Winship, 'The Rise of a National Book Trade System in the United States, 1865–1916', pp.297, 300
45 Bold, *Selling the Wild West*, p.1
46 Gramsci, *Selections from the Cultural Writings*, p.350
47 Bold, *Selling the Wild West*, p.10
48 Ibid., p.13
49 Ibid., p.5
50 Stern, *Louisa May Alcott. A Biography*, p.315, first published 1950
51 Ibid., p.330
52 *The Selected Letters of Louisa May Alcott*, p.308
53 *The Louisa May Alcott Encyclopedia*, p.86
54 Ragone, 'La letteratura e il consumo . . .', p.704
55 De Cesare, *Balzac e Manzoni e altri studi su Balzac e l'Italia*, pp.315–16
56 Giachino, ' "Il famoso, forse troppo famoso Balzac" . . .' pp.119–20 and pp.126–7
57 Desideri, 'Il fantastico', p.970
58 Ibid., p.976
59 Graf, *L'anglomania e l'influsso inglese in Italia nel secolo XVIII*, pp.ix, 16–17, 32
60 Paccagnella, 'Uso letterario dei dialetti', pp.531–2
61 Gramsci, *Selections from the Cultural Writings*, pp.210, 213
62 Verga, *Le novelle*; the citation is on p.357
63 Gramsci, *Selections from the Cultural Writings*, p.200
64 Bonghi, *Lettere critiche*, p.66. This text was originally published in the journal *Lo Spettatore* (Florence) in 1855 with the title 'Lettere critiche' and the subtitle 'Perché la letteratura italiana non sia popolare in Italia 1855–56'. The actual letters are addressed to Celestino Bianchi, the editor of *Lo Spettatore*
65 Bonghi, *Lettere critiche*, pp.67–8, 78, 83–4, 121–2

66 De Sanctis, ' "L'Ebreo di Verona" del Padre Bresciani', pp.873, 891
67 Arslan, 'Romanzo popolare e romanzo di consumo tra Ottocento e Novecento', p.41
68 Montesinos, *Introducción a una historia de la novela en España en el siglo XIX*, p.xii
69 Michael, 'From Scarlet Study to Novela Negra', pp.23–4
70 Botrel, 'Les libraires français en Espagne 1840–1920', pp.61, 70
71 On Garibaldi see Piromalli, 'Giuseppe Garibaldi e i suoi scritti', p.259

26 : Improving Oneself

1 Joyce, 'The People's English: Language and Class in England c.1840–1920', p.159
2 Williams, *The Long Revolution*, p.164
3 Lyons, *Le Triomphe du livre*, p.130
4 Rosa, ' "Quot libras in duce?". . . ', p.228
5 Barbier *L'empire du livre*, p.70
6 Ashton, *G. H. Lewes*, pp.161–2
7 Ashton, *George Eliot*, p.340
8 Gay, *The Naked Heart*, p.174
9 Ibid., pp.153–6
10 A similar typology was first attempted by the Danish literary critic Brandes (1842–1927), see Gay, *The Naked Heart*, p.112
11 Biré, *Mémoires et souvenirs (1789–1830)*, Vol. 1, p.v
12 Finkelstein, *The House of Blackwood*, pp.49–69
13 Barbier, *L'Empire du livre*, p.52
14 Ragone, 'La letteratura e il consumo: un profilo dei generi e dei modelli nell'editoria italiana (1845–1925)', pp.688–9
15 Angenot, *1889*, p.70
16 Mollier, 'Le manuel scolaire et la bibliothèque du peuple', p.79
17 Albertini, *L'École en France XIX–XX siècle*, pp.23–4
18 Lasserre, *Notre-Dame de Lourdes*, pp.422–3
19 Harris, *Lourdes: Body and Spirit in the Secular Age*, p.180
20 Ibid., pp.19, 183
21 Botstein, 'Listening through Reading: Musical Literacy and the Concert Audience', p.131
22 Barbier, *L'Empire du livre*, pp.77ff
23 Ferretti, ' "Grandi opere" per il "popolo" ', p.866, see also Perini, 'Editori e potere dalla fine del secolo XV all'Unità', pp.841–4

24 Barber, 'The English-language guide book to Europe up to 1870', pp.103–4
25 Heine, *Tableaux de Voyages*, p.171
26 Gay, *The Cultivation of Hatred*, pp.491, 493
27 Gay, *The Naked Heart*, p.163
28 Chemello, *La biblioteca del buon operaio*, p.59
29 Lanaro, 'Il Plutarco italiano: l'istruzione del "popolo" dopo l'Unità', pp.560–2
30 Rambelli, 'La letteratura educativa per i giovani e per il popolo', p.174
31 Perini, 'Editori e potere dalla fine del secolo XV all'Unità', p.851
32 Mason, 'A Little Pickle for her Husband', p.33
33 Maurice Agulhon, 'Le problème de la culture populaire en France autour de 1848', p.60
34 Roussier-Puig, 'Michelet, Hetzel, et les véroniques du peuple', pp.8–9
35 Ibid., pp.10, 13
36 Ibid., p.8
37 Gay, *The Naked Heart*, p.186
38 This is told in admirable detail by Finkelstein in his *The House of Blackwood*, pp.29–31
39 Ibid., p.32
40 Ibid., pp.33–6
41 Steig, 'Subversive Grotesque in Samuel Warren's *Ten Thousand a-Year*', p.154
42 Finkelstein, *The House of Blackwood*, pp.36–7
43 Marx, letter to Maurice LaChâtre, 18 March 1872, in *Marx-Engels Werke*, vol. 33, p.434
44 Tesnière, 'Le livre de science en France au XIXe siècle', pp.71–3
45 Mollier, 'Un siècle de transition vers une culture de masse', p.197
46 Choppin, *Les manuels scolaires*, p.80
47 On the production of grammars see Michael, 'The Hyperactive Production of English Grammars in the Nineteenth Century: A Speculative Bibliography', pp.23–61
48 Barbier, 'Une production multipliée', p.119
49 Choppin, *Les manuels scolaires. Histoire et actualité*, p.35
50 Boyd, *Historia Patria. Politics, History, and National Identity in Spain, 1875–1975*, pp.4–9
51 Botrel, 'Naissance et essor d'une maison d'édition scolaire . . .', pp.116, 123, 130
52 Marchand, 'Le commerce du livre classique dans le département du Nord fin XVIIIᵉ–1914', pp.258–9
53 Choppin, *Les manuels scolaires. Histoire et actualité*, p.31
54 Barbier, *L'empire du livre*, p.71
55 Mollier, 'Le manuel scolaire et la bibliothèque du peuple', pp.79–82
56 Rosa, Trzepizur and Vaillant, 'Le peuple des poètes – Étude bibliométrique de la poésie populaire de 1870 à 1880', p.22
57 Ibid., pp.27–8
58 Ibid., p.33
59 Gettmann, *A Victorian Publisher: A Study of the Bentley Papers*, pp.125–7
60 'The Lay of St. Odille' in *The Ingoldsby Legends* by Ingoldsby, p.162
61 Warrilow, 'Some Recent German Periodicals on Book and Book-Trade History, a Summary', p.88, see also Sidorko, 'Nineteenth century German travelogues as sources on the history of Daghestan and Chechnya', p.286
62 Erickson, *The Economy of Literary Form*, pp.40–1

27 : Music, Composers and Virtuosi

1 Kretschmer, 'The Failure of Property Rules in Collective Administration . . .', p.127
2 Ibid., p.128
3 *Enciclopedia Italiana*, Treccani, Roma 1949, entry for Ricordi; also 'Ricordi' in *The New Grove Dictionary of Music Online*
4 Rosen, 'Aimez-vous Brahms?', p.64
5 Spohr, *Autobiography*, p.186
6 Raynor, *Music and Society since 1815*, p.42
7 The project was outlined in a letter sent by Weber to his friend Johann Gänsbacher and now in Carl Maria von Weber, *La vie d'un musicien et autres écrits*, pp.23–4
8 Guccini, 'Directing Opera', p.152
9 Streletski, *Aspects de la direction d'orchestre en France de 1830 à 1880*, p.8
10 Ibid., p.16
11 Berlioz, *Mémoires*, p.288
12 Buch, 'Le chef d'orchestre: pratiques de l'autorité et métaphores politiques', pp.1006–7. Berlioz's text was originally published in *Revue et Gazette musicale de Paris*, 28 April 1844. See entry on Berlioz in *La Grande Encyclopédie*
13 Berlioz, *Euphonia ou la ville musicale*, pp.57–8

14 Weber, 'Mass Culture and the Reshaping of European Musical taste, 1770–1870', pp.13–14

15 Rosen, 'Steak and Potatoes', p.19

16 Raynor, A Social History of Music, p.319

17 Russell, Popular Music in England, 1840–1914, p.32

18 Raynor, Music and Society since 1815, p.17

19 Weber, Music and the Middle Class, p.18

20 Ibid., p.24

21 Fauquet, 'L'association des artistes musiciens et l'organisation du travail de 1843 à 1853', pp.105, 111

22 Mazierska, 'Multifunctional Chopin: the representation of Fryderyk Chopin in Polish films', p.260

23 Pekacz, 'Deconstructing a "National Composer" . . .', p.171

24 On Chopin and Schlesinger see Ellis, Music Criticism in Nineteenth-Century France, p.146

25 Raynor, Music and Society since 1815, pp.106–8

26 Cooper, The Rise of Instrumental Music and Concert Series in Paris 1828–1871, p.44–5, 51

27 Johnson, Listening in Paris, pp.257–9

28 Ellis, Music Criticism in Nineteenth-Century France, pp.104–12

29 Raynor, Music and Society since 1815, p.118

30 Entry on Spohr, The New Grove Dictionary of Music Online ed. L. Macy (accessed July 2003), www.grovemusic.com

31 Weber, 'Mass Culture and the Reshaping of European Musical taste, 1770–1870', p.18

32 Ibid., p.5

33 Weber, Music and the Middle Class, p.30

34 Scott, The Singing Bourgeois, pp.60–3

35 Reich, Clara Schumann, pp.25, 98, 111, 126–7, 136

36 Bradley, Abide with me. The world of Victorian hymns, pp.54–5

37 Russell, Popular Music in England, 1840–1914, pp.154–5 and 210–15

38 Ibid., p.263

39 Taruskin, 'Nationalism'

40 Raynor, Music and Society since 1815, p.90

41 Ibid., pp.93–4

42 Weber, 'Artisans in Concert Life of Mid-Nineteenth-Century London and Paris', pp.261–4

43 Botstein, 'Listening through Reading: Musical Literacy and the Concert Audience', p.134

44 Ibid., p.135

45 Raynor, Music and Society since 1815, pp.154–5

46 Summers, The Empress of Pleasure, especially Chapter Thirteen

47 Lamb, 'Waltz' in The New Grove Dictionary of Music Online

48 Gasnault, 'Les salles de bal du Paris romantique: décors et jeux des corps', p.7

49 Lesure, et al., La Musique à Paris en 1830–1831, p.8

50 Gasnault, 'Les salles de bal du Paris romantique . . .', pp.9–12, 16

51 Morelli, 'L'Opera', pp.92–3

52 Carlini, 'Le bande musicali nell'Italia dell'ottocento . . .', p.85

53 Condemi, Les cafés-concerts, p.19

54 Hess, La Valse, p.119

55 This is the view of Hess, ibid., p.125

56 Ibid., p.135

57 Ibid., p.171

58 Cited in Lamb, 'Waltz'

59 Comini, The Changing Image of Beethoven, p.19

60 Ibid., p.417

61 Chanan, Musica Pratica, p.208

62 Russell, Popular Music in England, 1840–1914, p.177

63 Cited by Weber, Music and the Middle Class, p.17

64 Lieberman, Steinway and Sons, p.15

65 Ibid., p.23

66 Ibid., p.133

67 Ibid., pp.48, 53

68 Allsobrook, Liszt: My Travelling Circus Life, p.20

69 Comini, The Changing Image of Beethoven, p.210

70 Raynor, Music and Society since 1815, p.61; see also www.uk-piano.org, accessed September 2000

71 Chanan, Musica Pratica, p.206

72 Haine, Adolphe Sax, p.40

73 Ibid., pp.52, 71, 123–5

74 Ibid., p.91

75 See report in Il Secolo, 3–4 April 1880 in Carteggio Verdi-Ricordi 1880–81, p.241

76 Carse, 'Adolphe Sax and the Distin Family', pp.193–201

77 Berlioz, 'Rapport Fait à la Commission Française du Jury International de l'Exposition Universelle de Londres', http://www.hberlioz.com/London/Berlioz1851.html

78 Segalini, Divas. Parcours d'un mythe, p.71. For Verdi's view see his letter of

22 October 1877 in *Verdi intimo*, pp.205–6

79 Nicolodi, 'Il teatro lirico e il suo pubblico', p.290

80 *Les soirées parisiennes de 1880* by 'Un Monsieur de l'Orchestre' (Arnold Mortier), Dentu, Paris 1881, pp.163–5

81 About, *A B C du Travailleur*, pp.53–4

82 Scott, *The Singing Bourgeois*, p.133

83 Lesure, et al., *La Musique à Paris en 1830–1831*, p.53

84 Ibid., pp.18–19

85 Cited in Kendall, *Paganini. A Biography*, p.84

86 Cited in Metzner, *Crescendo of the Virtuoso*, p.131

87 Neill, *Nicolò Paganini*, p.248

88 Johnson, *Listening in Paris*, p.265

89 Weber, *Music and the Middle Class*, p.40

90 Neill, *Nicolò Paganini*, pp.242–4

91 Ibid., p.264

92 Sorba, *Teatri: L'Italia del melodramma nell'età del Risorgimento*, p.89

93 On his British tour see Allsobrook, *Liszt: My Travelling Circus Life*, 1991

94 Weber, *Music and the Middle Class*, p.36

95 Eliot, 'Liszt, Wagner, and Weimar' originally in *Fraser's Magazine*, July 1855, now in her *Selected Critical Writings*, p.82

96 Eliot, *Daniel Deronda*, p.280

97 Raynor, *Music and Society since 1815*, p.147

98 Segalini, *Divas. Parcours d'un mythe*, p.54

99 Letter of 27 September 1850 in Lind-Goldschmidt, *Memoir*, Vol. 2, p.418

100 Bulman, *Jenny Lind. A biography*, pp.242–4

101 Chanan, *Musica Pratica*, pp.155–6

102 Berlioz, *Les soirées de l'orchestre*, p.130

103 Offenbach, *Notes d'un musicien en voyage*, pp.23, 173

104 Metzner, *Crescendo of the Virtuoso*, p.9

28 : The Triumph of the Opera

1 Leroy, *Histoire des arts du Spectacle en France*, L'Harmattan, Paris 1990, p.161

2 Johnson *Listening in Paris*, pp.242–5

3 Miller, 'Doing Opera', p.12

4 Rosen, 'Within a Budding Grove', pp.29–32

5 Barbier, *Opera in Paris, 1800–1850*, p.126 and Johnson, *Listening in Paris*, p.246

6 Hugo, *Choses vues 1830–1846*, p.103

7 Lesure et al., *La Musique à Paris en 1830–1831*, pp.54–60

8 Barbier, *Opera in Paris, 1800–1850*, pp.173–8

9 Sorba, *Teatri: L'Italia del melodramma nell'età del Risorgimento*, p.176

10 Raynor, *Music and Society since 1815*, p.125

11 Piperno, 'Opera Production to 1780', pp.33ff; Conati, 'Teatri e orchestre al tempo di Verdi', pp.49–55

12 Sorba, *Teatri: L'Italia del melodramma nell'età del Risorgimento*, p.25

13 Conati, 'Teatri e orchestre al tempo di Verdi', p.51

14 Sorba, *Teatri: L'Italia del melodramma nell'età del Risorgimento*, pp.26, 31

15 Nicolodi, 'Il teatro lirico e il suo pubblico', p.270

16 Jelavich, *Munich and Theatrical Modernism*, p.102

17 Nicolodi, *Orizzonti musicali Italo-Europei 1860–1980*, p.27

18 Rosselli, 'Opera Production, 1780–1880', pp.82–3

19 Decio Cortesi, in the *Corriere d'Italia* of 18 May 1929 cited in Meloncelli, 'Sul rinnovamento della vita musicale romana', p.220

20 Sorba, 'Teatro d'opera e società nell'Italia ottocentesca', p.40

21 Berengo, *Intellettuali e librai nella Milano della restaurazione*, p.214

22 Conati, 'Periodici teatrali e musicali italiani a metà dell'800', pp.13–21

23 Letter of 16 June 1867 in *Verdi intimo*, pp.78–9

24 Körner, 'The Theatre of Social Change . . .', p.354

25 Nicolodi, 'Il teatro lirico e il suo pubblico', p.268

26 Ibid., p.279

27 Nicolodi, *Orizzonti musicali Italo-Europei 1860–1980*, p.16

28 Strakosch, *Souvenirs d'un impresario*, p.147

29 Nicolodi, 'Il teatro lirico e il suo pubblico', p.277

30 Martin, 'Verdi Onstage in the United States: Nabucodonosor', p.244n

31 See editorial notes in *Verdi intimo*, pp.244–5

32 Blondeau, *Observations sur les théâtres italiens*, originally published in 1839, now in his *Voyage d'un musicien en Italie (1810–1812)*, pp.50–1

33 Martin, 'Verdi Onstage in the United States: Nabucodonosor', pp.230, 232

34 Sorba, *Teatri: L'Italia del melodramma nell'età del Risorgimento*, pp.91, 177, 179

35 Martin, 'Verdi Onstage in the United States. *Oberto, conte di San Bonifacio*', p.469

36 Chusid, 'Toward an Understanding of Verdi's Middle Period', pp.1–3

37 Hepokoski, 'Ottocento Opera as Cultural Drama: Generic Mixtures in *Il trovatore*', pp.173–5

38 Montaldi, *Il Maestro della rivoluzione italiana*, Società editoriale italiana, Milan 1913, cited in della Peruta, 'Verdi e il Risorgimento', p.3

39 Simionato, 'Risorgimento e il melodramma', p.577

40 Nicolodi, 'Il teatro lirico e il suo pubblico', p.257

41 Körner, 'The Theatre of Social Change . . .', p.343

42 See Luez and Mironneau, 'La Révolution dans l'opéra français au XIXe siècle 1828–1880', pp.117–32

43 Rosselli, 'Music and Nationalism in Italy', p.186

44 Letter of 5 February 1876 in *Verdi intimo*, pp.186–7

45 Tyrrell, 'Russian, Czech, Polish, and Hungarian Opera to 1900', p.246

46 Everett, 'National Opera in Croatia and Finland 1846–1899', pp.183–200, especially p.185

47 Tyrrell, 'Russian, Czech, Polish, and Hungarian Opera to 1900', p.258

48 Barbier, *Opera in Paris, 1800–1850*, p.84

49 Berlioz, *Mémoires*, p.288

50 Ellis, *Music Criticism in Nineteenth-Century France*, p.197

51 Jordan, *Fromental Halevy*, pp.62ff

52 Raynor, *Music and Society since 1815*, pp.77–9

53 Nicolodi, *Orizzonti musicali Italo-Europei 1860–1980*, p.43

54 Ibid., pp.58–9

55 Millington, 'The Nineteenth Century: Germany', pp.219–20

56 Weiner, *Richard Wagner and the Anti-Semitic Imagination*, p.53

57 Cited in Lebrecht, *Discord*, p.43

58 See the calculations in Eger, 'The Patronage of King Luwig II' in *Wagner Handbook*, p.325

59 Lebrecht, *Discord*, pp.28–31

60 Cited in ibid., p.87

61 Letellier, 'Bellini and Meyerbeer', p.361

62 Gervasoni, 'Musique et socialisme en Italie (1880–1922)', p.32

63 Buch, ' "Les Allemands et les Boches". . . ', p.59

29 : Theatricals

1 Peters, *Theatre of the Book 1480–1880*, p.66

2 Leroy, *Histoire des arts du Spectacle en France*, p.156

3 See graph in Leroy, *Histoire des arts du Spectacle en France*, p.366

4 Lesure et al., *La Musique à Paris en 1830–1831*, p.4

5 Ibid., pp.150–1

6 Ibid., p.58

7 Descotes, *Le public de théâtre et son histoire*, p.11

8 Mullin (ed.), *Victorian Actors and Actresses in Review*, p.xvii

9 Leroy, *Histoire des arts du Spectacle en France*, pp.242–3

10 Moynet, *L'envers du Théâtre*, p.153

11 Blondeau, *Voyage d'un musicien en Italie 1810–1812*, p.63

12 Sorba, *Teatri: L'Italia del melodramma*, pp.67–8

13 Blondeau, *Observations sur les théâtres italiens*, p.71

14 Baedeker, *Paris and its environs*, p.51

15 Sorba, 'Teatro d'opera e società nell'Italia ottocentesca', pp.39–40

16 Körner, 'The Theatre of Social Change', pp.353–4

17 Blondeau, *Voyage d'un musicien en Italie 1810–1812*, p.61

18 Article in *La Presse* of 18 August 1842 reprinted in Gautier, *Histoire de l'art dramatique en France*, Vol. 2, p.269

19 Wilson, 'Charles Kean in the Provinces 1833 to 1838', pp.41, 42, 44–5. See also Davis, *The Economics of the British Stage 1800–1914*, p.214

20 Peters, *Theatre of the Book 1480–1880*, p.257

21 Ibid., pp.76, 78

22 Ibid., p.81

23 Brown, *Zola. A Life*, pp.155–6. See also Zola, 'L'argent dans la littérature' in *L'encre et le sang*, pp.58–61

24 Peters, *Theatre of the Book 1480–1880*, p.73

25 Krakovitch, 'Le théâtre sous la Restauration et la monarchie de Juillet: lecture et spectacle', p.148

26 Hemmings, *The Theatre Industry in Nineteenth-Century France*, p.43

27 Krakovitch, 'Le théâtre sous la Restauration et la monarchie de Juillet: lecture et spectacle', p.156

28 Leroy, *Histoire des arts du Spectacle en France*, pp.145–7

29 Yon, *Eugène Scribe*, p.13

30 Eyre, *National Service*, p.215

31 Leroy, *Histoire des arts du Spectacle en France*, pp.176, 188

32 Barbier, *Opera in Paris, 1800–1850*, pp.50–1

33 Bauer, 'La parodie dans les lettres autrichiennes: d'Aloys Blumauer à Johann Nepomuk Nestroy', pp.25, 33

34 Charue-Ferrucci, 'Du mélodrame à la comédie féerique . . .', pp.49, 50

35 Gregor-Dellin, *Richard Wagner*, p.466

36 Pinkard, *Hegel. A Biography*, p.521

37 Bauer, *La Réalité, royaume de Dieu*, pp.42–3

38 Yon, *Jacques Offenbach*, p.179

39 Ibid., pp.211–13

40 Hüttner, 'Die Vereitelte Offenbachpflege im Theater', pp.25–39

41 Branscombe, 'Die Frühe Offenbach-Rezeption in Wien und Nestroys Anteil Daran', pp.41–51

42 Marschall, 'Champagne, depolitisation, gemütlichkeit . . .', p.87

43 Valentin, 'Nestroy sur la scène française', pp.177–92

44 Schulze-Reimpell, *Development and Structure of the Theatre in the Federal Republic of Germany*, p.20

45 Spohr, 'L'Opérette viennoise de Franz von Suppé', pp.53, 55

46 Ibid., p.55

47 Pistone, 'L'opérette Viennoise a Paris 1875–1904', pp.155

48 Marschall, 'Champagne, depolitisation, gemütlichkeit . . . .' pp.87–98

49 Descotes, 'Les Comédiens dans les Rougon-Macquart', pp.137

50 On Schneider's honorarium see Traubner, *Operetta*, p.45

51 Traubner, *Operetta*, p.48

52 Ibid., p.55

53 Davis, *The Economics of the British Stage*, p.131

54 Marschall, 'Champagne, depolitisation, gemütlichkeit . . .', p.93

55 Walle, 'Marie Geistinger. La reine de l'operette', p.126

56 Fischler, 'Guano and Poetry: Payment for Playwriting in Victorian England', p.51

57 Traubner, *Operetta*, p.155

58 Selenick, 'Theatre', p.269

59 Sentaurens, 'Les neveux du capitaine Grant: Jules Verne sur les treteaux de la Zarzuela', pp.170–2, 168

60 Article in *La Presse* of 18 August 1842 reprinted in Gautier, *Histoire de l'art drammatique en France depuis*, Vol. 2, p.265

61 Ibid., Vol. 1, pp.15, 17

62 Leroy, *Histoire des arts du Spectacle en France*, p.246

63 Yon, *Eugène Scribe*, pp.8–9

64 Ibid., p.51

65 Daumard, 'L'argent et le rang dans la société française du XIXe siècle', p.21

66 Yon, *Eugène Scribe*, p.103–4

67 Ibid., pp.69–72

68 In *La Presse*, 18 August 1842, reprinted in Gautier, *Histoire de l'art drammatique en France*, Vol. 2, p.269

69 Cited in Yon, *Eugène Scribe*, pp.85–6

70 Ibid., pp.237–8

71 Ibid., p.241

72 Mezzacappa, 'The performance of Scribe's plays in Naples', pp.191–241

73 Yon, *Eugène Scribe*, p.242

74 Ibid., p.307

75 Fischler, 'Guano and Poetry: Payment for Playwriting in Victorian England', pp.43, 47–8

76 Cross, *The Common Writer*, p.104

77 Kift, *The Victorian Music Hall*, pp.1, 17–18, 21, 24ff; see also Bratton, *The Victorian Popular Ballad*, pp.29–30

78 Russell, *Popular Music in England, 1840–1914*, pp.83–4

79 Bailey, 'Conspiracies of Meaning: Music-Hall and the Knowingness of Popular Culture', p.164

80 Ibid., pp.142, 163–6, 68, 70

81 Russell, *Popular Music in England, 1840–1914*, pp.105–6

82 Kift, *The Victorian Music Hall*, p.28

83 See text of songs in Gammond (ed.), *Best Music Hall and Variety Songs*, pp.268, 52–3

84 Boosey, *Fifty Years of Music*, p.15

85 Pearsall, *Edwardian Life and Leisure*, p.231

86 Ibid., pp.231–3

87 Condemi, *Les cafés-concerts*, pp.83–5, 157

88 Davis, *The Economics of the British Stage*, p.130

89 Condemi, *Les cafés-concerts*, p.87

90 Conway Morris, 'Greek Café Music', especially pp.79–82

91 Dillaz, 'Diffusion et propagation chansonnières au XIXe siècle', p.61

92 Bratton, *The Victorian Popular Ballad*, pp.12, 18

93 Dillaz, 'Diffusion et propagation chansonnières au XIXe siècle', p.63

94 On the British urban song see Kift, *The Victorian Music Hall*, p.37

95 Franzina, 'Inni e Canzoni', p.122

PART III

1880–1920 : THE REVOLUTION

30 : The Revolution in Communications

1 Headrick, *The Tools of Empire*, pp.130, 160
2 Weightman, *Signor Marconi's Magic Box*, pp.19–24
3 Blackbourn, *The Fontana History of Germany 1780–1918*, p.354
4 Griset, *Les révolutions de la communication XIXe–XXe siècle*, p.18
5 Bairoch, *Victoires et déboires*, pp.127, 128
6 Barbier and Bertho Lavenir, *Histoire des médias*, p.137
7 Huth, *La Radiodiffusion*, p.33
8 Tadié, *Marcel Proust*, p.659
9 See the essays in de Sola Pool (ed.), *The Social Impact of the Telephone*, especially Sidney H. Aronson, 'Bell's Electrical Toy: What's the Use? The Sociology of Early Telephone Usage'
10 Thatcher, *The Politics of Telecommunication*, p.32
11 Griset, 'Les communications en France', p.1256
12 Griset, *Les révolutions de la communication XIXe–XXe siècle*, pp.30–4
13 Thierer, 'Unnatural Monopoly: Critical Moments in the Development of the Bell System'
14 On the electric toothbrush see picture in Malvin E. Ring, *Dentistry. An Illustrated History*, p.188; on the vibrator see Maines, *The Technology of Orgasm: 'Hysteria', the Vibrator, and Women's Sexual Satisfaction*, p.15
15 Sweet, *Inventing the Victorians*, p.48
16 Headrick, *The Tools of Empire*, p.181
17 Ibid., pp.142, 158–9
18 Stewart, *My Other Life*, July 2004
19 Beltran and Carré, *La fée et la servante*, p.296
20 Dubois, 'La société de consommation électrique', p.613
21 Griset, *Les révolutions de la communication XIXe–XXe siècle*, pp.37–9
22 See tables in Porter, *European Imperialism, 1860–1914*, pp.41–2
23 Fink, *American Art at the Nineteenth-Century Paris Salons*, pp.130, list of artists on pp.313–409
24 Jerome, *My Life and Times*, p.61
25 Maidment, 'John Ruskin, George Allen and American Pirated Books', pp.11, 15

31 : Workers, Jews, Women

1 See calculation based on purchasing power parity in Zamagni, 'An International comparison of Real Industrial Wages, 1890–1913 . . .', p.119
2 See figures in Bairoch, 'Wages as an Indicator of Gross National product', p.58
3 Prices from Cardot, 'L'électricité, merveille du siècle', p.240
4 Perkin, *The Rise of Professional Society*, p.29
5 Rubinstein, 'Educations and the Social Origins of British Élites', p.170
6 Ringer, 'Higher Education in Germany in the Nineteenth Century', p.126
7 Blackbourn, *The Fontana History of Germany 1780–1918*, p.355
8 Thiesse, 'Organisation des loisirs des travailleurs et temps dérobés (1880–1930)', pp.307–10
9 Barbier, *L'Empire du Livre*, p.511
10 Ritter, 'Workers' Culture in Imperial Germany . . .', p.166
11 Letter of 17–18 September 1879 in Marx and Engels, *Werke*, pp.394–408
12 Langewiesche, 'The Impact of the German Labor Movement on Workers' Culture', pp.516–17
13 Fricke, *Die Deutsche Arbeiterbewegung 1869–1914*, p.496
14 On the popularity of this text see Hobsbawm, *The Age of Empire 1875–1914*, p.209 and Barrington Moore, Jr, *Injustice*, p.210
15 Fricke, *Die Deutsche Arbeiterbewegung*, pp.495–6
16 Ibid., pp.496–7
17 Tortorelli, 'Una casa editrice socialista nell'età giolittiana: la Nerini', pp.231–3
18 On this see Charle, 'Champ littéraire français et importations étrangères . . .', p.251
19 Mazzoni, 'La fortuna di Tolstoj nel movimento operaio italiano', p.175–9

20 Aron, *Les écrivains belges et le socialisme (1880–1913)*, p.23

21 Ibid., pp.251–2

22 On the publishing history of *La Cieca di Sorrento* see Arslan, 'Storia e destinazioni della *Cieca di Sorrento*', especially pp.56–61

23 Neuschafer, 'Naturalismo e feuilleton. Il "romanzo sociale" nei giornali parigini del 1884', p.193

24 Ponton, 'Les images de la paysannerie dans le roman rural à la fin du 19e siècle', pp.62–3

25 Blackbourn, *The Fontana History of Germany 1780–1918*, p.392

26 Richards, *The German Bestseller in the 20th Century. A complete Bibliography and Analysis 1915–1940*, p.56

27 Ibid., p.55; Richtie Robertson, 'From Naturalism to National Socialism (1890–1945)', pp.333–4

28 Barbier, *L'empire du livre*, p.47

29 Ibid., p.477

30 Meriggi, 'The Italian *Borghesia*', pp.430–1

31 Black, *A New History of the English Public Library*, pp.269–71

32 Blackbourn, *The Fontana History of Germany 1780–1918*, p.390

33 Charle, *Les intellectuels en Europe au XIXe siècle*, pp.174, 179

34 Fenyo, 'Writers in Politics: The role of *Nyugat* in Hungary, 1908–19', p.197

35 Barbagli, *Disoccupazione intellettuale e sistema scolastico in Italia (1859–1973)*, p.22

36 Charle, *Les intellectuels en Europe au XIXe siècle*, pp.201–3

37 Williams, *Culture and Society*, p.174

38 Gissing, *New Grub Street*, pp.6–7

39 Ibid., pp.44–6

40 Thiesse, 'Les infortunes littéraires. Carrières des romanciers populaires à la Belle-Époque', p.35

41 Ibid., p.36

42 Hanák, 'Why fin de siècle?', p.104

43 Gissing, *New Grub Street*, p.354

44 Goody, *Capitalism and Modernity*, p.62, citing H. Zafrani's *Juifs d'Andalousie et du Maghreb*

45 Sármány-Parsons, 'Jewish Art Patronage in Budapest at the Turn of the Century', pp.115–24

46 Karady, 'Les Juifs dans l'édition hongroise avant 1945', p.66

47 Charle, *Les intellectuels en Europe au XIXe siècle*, p.276

48 Information from *Encyclopaedia Judaica*, Vol. 13, entry 'Publishing'

49 Elon, *The Pity of It All: A Portrait of German Jews 1743–1933*, pp.206–8

50 Craig, *Germany, 1866–1945*, p.204

51 Charle, *Les intellectuels en Europe au XIXe siècle*, pp.204–5

52 Karady and Kemény, 'Les juifs dans la structure des classes en Hongrie . . .', p.56

53 Weber, *France Fin de Siècle*, p.131

54 The parliamentary report of the proposed law on women's access to higher education is examined by Janet in 1883 in 'L'Éducation des femmes'

55 Cammelli and di Francia, 'Studenti, università, professioni', p.63

56 Sieburth, *Inventing High and Low. Literature, Mass Culture, and Uneven Modernity in Spain*, p.7

57 See list in Clyman and Vowles (eds), *Russia through Women's Eyes. Autobiographies from Tsarist Russia*

58 Brooks, *When Russia Learned to read*, pp.153–4

59 Ibid., pp.156, 159; Kelly, *A History of Russian Women's Writing 1820–1992*, pp.149–51

60 Bertaut, *La littérature féminine d'aujourd'hui*, p.1

61 Ibid., p.70

62 Ibid., p.224

63 See illustration in Cohen, *The Sentimental Education of the Novel*, p.170

64 Tusan, 'Inventing the New Woman . . .', p.169

65 Cited in Griest, *Mudie's Circulating Library*, p.151

66 Fryckstedt, *Geraldine Jewsbury's 'Athenaeum' Reviews: A Mirror of Mid-Victorian Attitudes to Fiction*, p.43

67 Rachilde, *Monsieur Vénus*

68 Rachilde, *L'animale*

69 Rachilde, *La jongleuse*, p.51. On Gyp and Rachilde see Cohen, 'Women and fiction in the nineteenth century' and Porter, 'Decadence and the *fin-de-siècle* novel'

70 Francis and Gontier, *Colette*, p.148

71 Ibid., p.172

72 Ibid., pp.174, 205, 220ff

73 Silverman, *The Notorious Life of Gyp*, p.30

74 Ibid., pp.46–7

75 Some of these were included in the collection *Shocking!*, Paris 1879

76 Flagy (Marie de Mirabeau), *Le crime de la Rue Marignan*

77 Silverman, *The Notorious Life of Gyp*, pp.59, 238

78 Ibid., pp.61–2

79 Ibid., pp.112, 165

80 Ibid., pp.111–15
81 Ibid., p.138

32 : The Internationalisation of the Novel

1 Mollier, *L'argent et les lettres,* pp.156–8
2 Finkelstein, *The House of Blackwood,* pp.129–32
3 Cited in Feltes, *Literary Capital and the Late Victorian Novel*, p.11
4 Gagnier, *Idylls of the Marketplace. Oscar Wilde and the Victorian Public*, p.56
5 Sweet, *Inventing the Victorians*, p.43
6 Ibid., p.52
7 Gissing, *New Grub Street*, p.20
8 Charle, 'Le champ de la production littéraire', p.139
9 Thiesse, 'Revues et maisons d'édition provinciales à la Belle Époque', pp.218–20
10 Bogacz, ' "A Tyranny of Words": Language, Poetry, and Anti-modernism in England in the First World War', p.647
11 Baillère, *La crise du livre*, pp.11–12; such statistics are not to be taken literally
12 On manuals see Choppin, *Les manuels scolaires. Histoire et actualité*, p.64
13 Baillère, *La crise du livre*, pp.13–14, 19
14 Ibid., p.20
15 Ibid., p.34
16 Ibid., p.82
17 Barbier, *L'empire du livre*, pp.95–6
18 Ibid., p.102
19 Ullstein, *The Rise and Fall of the House of Ullstein*, p.62
20 Grandjean, 'Les éditions Fayard et l'édition populaire', pp.230ff
21 Parinet, 'Le prix du livre: un vieux sujet de débat', p.203
22 Mauclair, 'La condition matérielle et morale de l'écrivain à Paris', p.32
23 Wilkinson, 'The uses of popular culture by rival élites: the case of Alsace, 1890–1914', pp.604–7
24 Rioux, *Erckmann et Chatrian ou le traité d'union*, pp.52, 99, 101, 118
25 Ibid., p.15
26 Roth, 'Erckmann-Chatrian en Angleterre et aux États-Unis', pp.123–5
27 Braescu, 'Erckmann-Chatrian en Roumanie', p.127
28 Cited in Craig, *Germany, 1866–1945,* p.222. The English translation is entitled *Man of Straw*; the citation is at the end of Chapter Five
29 The description is by Swales, 'The Development of German prose-fiction', p.178
30 See Thomas Mann's claim in 'Anzeige eines Fontane-Buches' in Thomas Mann, *Das essayistische Werk*, Frankfurt 1968, pp.106ff and cited by Chambers; 'Afterword' to the English translation of *Effi Briest*, p.233
31 Kulczycka-Saloni, 'Les personnages du roman polonais du XIXe siècle', p.60
32 Najder, 'The Development of the Polish Novel: Functions and Structure', p.655
33 Segel, 'Sienkiewicz's First Translator, Jeremiah Curtin', pp.189–92
34 Kosko, *Un 'best-seller', 1900: Quo Vadis?*, pp.14, 15, 33. Other sources, such as *http:// www.nobel.se/literature/laureates/1905/ press.html,* give even higher selling figures
35 Kosko, *Un 'best-seller', 1900: Quo Vadis?,* p.31
36 Ibid., pp.95–6
37 *http://www.kirjasto.sci.fi/sienkiew.htm*
38 *http://www.nobel.se/literature/laureates/ 1905/press.html*
39 Nagy, 'La révolution littéraire hongroise du début du XXe siècle et son contexte européen', p.621
40 Mollier, 'Histoire de la lecture, histoire de l'édition', p.197
41 Data cited in Livezeanu, *Cultural Politics in Greater Romania*, p.10
42 Popa, 'Analyse quantitative du roman publié dans la presse de Transylvanie de 1838 à 1918', p.182
43 Ibid., p.183 on the basis of Dinu Pillat's essay 'Romanul de senzaţie in literatura română din a doua jumătate a secolului al XIXlea' (1978) – 'The Novel of Sensation in Romanian Literature in the second half of the twentieth century'
44 Ibid., pp.184–6
45 Ibid., pp.190–8
46 Sármány-Parsons, 'Jewish Art Patronage in Budapest at the Turn of the Century', p.114
47 Shedletzky, 'Some Observations on the Popular *Zeitroman* in the Jewish Weeklies in Germany from 1870 to 1900', especially pp.349–59
48 Michel, 'Sociabilité urbaine et nationalité à Prague à la fin du XIXe siècle', pp.75–6
49 Cohen, *The Politics of Ethnic Survival: Germans in Prague 1861–1914*, p.86
50 Fenyo, 'Writers in Politics: The role of *Nyugat* in Hungary, 1908–19', p.195
51 Botrel, *La diffusion du livre en Espagne (1868–1914)*, p.23

52 Bouche, Magnien, and Salaun, 'Les collections populaires de contes et nouvelles au début du XXᵉ siècle . . .', pp.259–61

53 Barrère, 'La crise du roman en Espagne 1915–1936 . . .', pp.259–64

54 Ibid., pp.269–70

55 Botrel, 'L'aptitude à communiquer: Alphabétisation et scolarisation en Espagne de 1860 à 1920', pp.105–40

56 Caudet, 'En folletin en *Fortunata y Jacinta*', pp.195–220

57 Barrère, 'La crise du roman en Espagne 1915–1936 . . .', p.266

58 Barrère, 'Le roman de tauromachie de 1870 à 1921, ou l'échec d'un genre populaire', p.226

59 Curto, 'Littérature de large circulation au Portugal (XVIe–XVIIIe siècles)', p.299

60 Ogg, 'Littérature coréenne', p.1273

61 Charle, 'Champ littéraire français et importations étrangères . . .', pp.253–5; See also Bonamour, '*Le Roman Russe* et les slavophiles', pp.37–51

62 de Vogüé, *Le Roman Russe*, pp.243, 250

63 Pascal, introduction to de Vogüé, *Le Roman Russe*, p.27

64 *Catalogo generale della libreria italiana dall'anno 1847 a tutto il 1899*

65 Lemaître, 'De l'influence récente de la littérature du Nord', pp.848–51

66 Wingard, 'Le dix-neuvième siècle suédois: courants littéraires et traditions de recherche', pp.107, 110

67 Ragone, 'La letteratura e il consumo: un profilo dei generi e dei modelli nell'editoria italiana (1845–1925)', p.731

68 Ibid., p.732

69 Ibid., p.751 and Candeloro, *Storia dell'Italia moderna*, Vol. 6, p.288

70 Ragone, 'La letteratura e il consumo', p.750

71 My computation on the *Catalogo generale*, Fratelli Treves Editori, pp.58–60

72 Ragone, 'La letteratura e il consumo' cit., pp.757, 738. Ragone's source is *I libri più letti dal popolo italiano*, Società Bibliografica Italiana presso la Biblioteca di Brera, Milan 1906, pp.11–12. The reliability of this source is not clear

73 Zambon, 'I protagonisti', pp.91–2

74 Madrignani, *Ideologia e narrativa dopo l'Unificazione*, pp.27–8, 32–3, 36

75 Giocondi, *Lettori in camicia nera*, pp.24–5

76 Piromalli, 'Antonio Fogazzaro e il pubblico', p.147

77 Pezzini, 'Matilde Serao', p.82

78 Madrignani, *Ideologia e narrativa dopo l'Unificazione*, p.146

79 Ibid., pp.158–9

80 Cited in Pezzini, 'Matilde Serao', p.64

81 Ibid., pp.69–72

82 Zambon, 'I protagonisti', pp.91–2

83 Federzoni, 'Carolina Invernizio', pp.35–6

84 Eco, 'Tre donne sulle donne per le donne', pp.23–5

85 Federzoni, 'Carolina Invernizio', pp.46–7

86 Sola, '*Il bacio di una morta*: un romanzo giallo' and Zambon, 'I protagonisti', pp.69, 74–5, 96–9

87 Alatri, *D'Annunzio*, p.74

88 de Vogüé, 'La Renaissance latine. Gabriele D'Annunzio: poèmes et romans', p.186

89 Lorenzini, *D'Annunzio*, p.204

90 Ibid., p.11

91 Casini, 'Il rinascimento immaginario di D'Annunzio', p.160

92 Abruzzese and Grassi, 'La fotografia', p.1195

93 Ojetti, *Alla scoperta dei letterati*, p.147

94 Asor Rosa, 'Centralismo e policentrismo nella letteratura italiana unitaria', p.36

95 Ojetti, *Alla scoperta dei letterati*, pp.310–13

96 Arslan, 'Romanzo popolare e romanzo di consumo tra Ottocento e Novecento', p.47

97 Interview in Ojetti, *Alla scoperta dei letterati*, pp.317–18

98 Arslan, 'Storia e destinazioni della *Cieca di Sorrento*', p.56. See also De Donato and Gazzola Stacchini (eds), *I best seller del ventennio*, p.680

99 Conforti, 'Scomposizione di un personaggio: Cecilia Malespano, Mimi Bluette, Maria Maddalena', p.61

100 Giannetto, 'La "costruzione" del romanzo e il livello tematico', pp.203–4

101 Gramsci, *Selections from the Cultural Writings*, p.71

102 Charle, 'Champ littéraire français et importations étrangères . . .', pp.256–9

103 Mistler, *La Librairie Hachette de 1826 à nos jours*, pp.277–8

104 The text of the speech can be found in the *Revue des deux mondes* of 1 May 1917, Vol. 87 as Louis Hachette, 'L'avenir du livre français'

105 Ibid., p.152

106 Unwin, *The Truth about Publishing*

107 Hachette, 'L'avenir du livre français', pp.156–8

33 : Zola: Money, Fame and Conscience

1 Zola, 'La Démocratie' in *Le Figaro*, 5 September 1881, now in Zola, *L'encre et le sang*, p.310

2 Mitterand, *Zola*, Vol. 1, p.711

3 Zola, 'L'argent dans la littérature' originally published in *Vestnik Evropy* (St Petersburg) in March 1880 and then in *Le Voltaire* (23–30 July 1880), now in Zola, *L'encre et le sang*, pp.34–6, 38–9, 46–7, 56

4 Ibid., pp.63, 72–3

5 Mitterand, *Zola*, Vol. 1, p.733

6 Zola, 'Le naturalisme' in *Le Figaro*, 17 January 1881 in Zola, *L'encre et le sang*, pp.186ff

7 Zola, in *Le Figaro*, 11 October 1880, now in *L'encre et le sang*, p.179

8 Pagés, 'L'expérience du livre. Zola et le commerce de la librairie', pp.428; Brown, *Zola. A Life*, p.641

9 Becker, Introduction to Emile Zola, *Nana*, p.lxvii

10 Mauclair, 'La condition matérielle et morale de l'écrivain à Paris', pp.29–31

11 Braun, *The Director and the Stage*, p.25

12 Brown, *Zola. A Life*, p.489

13 Zola, *L'encre et le sang*, pp.50–3

14 Zola, *Correspondance*, Vol. 5, 1884–1886, pp.292n, 316

15 Schumacher, '*Thérèse Raquin* en Grande Bretagne' in Dezalay (ed.), *Zola sans frontières*, p.105

16 Pagés, 'L'expérience du livre. Zola et le commerce de la librairie', p.430

17 Brown, *Zola. A Life*, pp.50–1

18 Ibid., p.394

19 Bakker (ed.), '*Naturalisme pas mort*'. *Lettres inédites de Paul Alexis à Émile Zola 1871–1900*, p.144–5

20 Auriant, *La véritable histoire de 'Nana'*, p.88–9

21 Becker, Introduction to *Nana*, p.lxvii

22 Brown, *Zola. A Life*, p.431

23 Walker, 'Introduction biographique' to Zola, *Correspondance*, Vol. IV, p.19

24 Brown, *Zola. A Life*, pp.434–5

25 Zola 'Comme elles poussent' in *Le Figaro*, 21 February 1881 and 'La Fille au Théâtre' *Le Figaro*, 12 January 1881, both in Zola, *L'encre et le sang*, pp.209, 197ff

26 Zola, *Nana*, p.272

27 Becker, Introduction to *Nana*, p.xii

28 Ritchie Robertson, 'From Naturalism to National Socialism (1890–1945)', p.329

29 Mitterand, 'Présentation' to Zola, *L'encre et le sang*, p.15

30 Becker, Introduction to *Nana*, p.lxxv

31 Letter of 8 November 1885 in Zola, *Correspondance*, Vol. 5, pp.328–9

32 Brown, *Zola. A Life*, pp.482–3

33 Ibid., p.364

34 Mitterand, 'Présentation' to Zola, *L'encre et le sang*, p.14

35 Zola, *Correspondance*, Vol. IV, p.104

36 Walker, 'Introduction biographique' to Zola, *Correspondance*, Vol. V, pp.44–6

37 Zola, 'Un prix de Rome littéraire' now in Zola, *L'encre et le sang*, p.87; see also, in the same collection, 'La République et la littérature' originally in *Vestnik Evropy* of April 1879, pp.150, 153

38 'La Haine de la Littérature' originally in *Le Voltaire*, 17 August 1880, now in Zola, *L'encre et le sang*, p.99

39 Brown, *Zola. A Life*, p.62

40 Aron, *Les écrivains belges et le socialisme (1880–1913)*, p.45

41 Mitterand, *Le Discours du roman*, pp.134–6

42 Silverman, *The Notorious Life of Gyp*, p.78

43 Brown, *Zola. A Life*, p.753

44 Mitterand, *Zola*, Vol. III, *L'honneur 1893–1902*, p.662

45 Manchester, 'Henry Vizetelly', p.2584

46 Pogorelskin, 'The Messenger of Europe', pp.142–3

47 See Botta, 'Paolo Valera e gli "abissi plebei" di Milano fin de siècle: immagine letteraria e realtà sociale', pp.3–36

48 Madrignani, *Ideologia e narrativa dopo l'Unificazione*, pp.116–19

49 De Sanctis, 'Zola e "L'assommoir"' in *Opere*, p.1070

50 Thorel-Cailleteau, 'George Moore et le Naturalisme. "Un cas d'intoxication littéraire"', p.153

51 Oktapoda, 'La traduction de Nana en Grèce et son retentissement sur le naturalisme néohellénique', pp.185–206; Dimaras, *Histoire de la littérature néo-hellénique*, p.398

52 Chevrel, 'Vers une histoire du Naturalisme dans les littératures de langues européennes?', p.126

53 Charle, *Les intellectuels en Europe au XIXe siècle*, p.330

54 Bretz, *Voices, Silences, and Echoes*, p.82

55 Santa, 'L'influence du Naturalisme français et de Zola dans *La Desheredada* et *Tormento* de Benito Pérez Galdós', pp.177–84

56 Basilio, 'Zola et son impact: naissance d'un romancier, Eça de Queirós', p.169
57 See Gorceix, 'Introduction' to Camille Lemonnier, p.218
58 Ritchie Robertson, 'From Naturalism to National Socialism (1890–1945)', p.330
59 Mitterand, *Zola*, Vol. III, pp.804–6

34 : Stories of Crime and Science Fiction

1 Lundin, *The Swedish Crime Story*, pp.13, 14, 19
2 Raffaelli, 'Il genere poliziesco in Italia prima del 1929. Le collane a carattere poliziesco', p.230
3 Ibid., pp.235–6
4 Petronio, 'Quel pasticciaccio brutto del romanzo poliziesco', p.18
5 Cook, *Mystery, Detective, and Espionage Magazines*, p.377
6 See Ashley's short survey in his anthology *Locked Rooms Mysteries and Impossible Crimes*, pp.520–9
7 Leroux, *Le Mystère de la chambre jaune*, pp.67, 171
8 Escarpit, 'Le problème de l'âge dans la productivité littéraire', pp.105–11
9 See the perceptive analysis by Dubois in 'Naissance du récit policier'
10 Moretti, *Atlas of the European Novel 1800–1900*, p.137
11 Albonetti (ed.), *Non c'è tutto nei romanzi*, p.28 and Stragliati, 'Fantômas? oui, mais', p.73. More Fantômas facts than anyone could possibly require are contained in Alfu (pseudonym), *L'encyclopédie de Fantômas. Étude sur un classique*. See also 'Bibliographie de Fantômas' in *Europe*, Vol.56, No. 590–1, June–July 1978, pp. 150–61
12 Juin, 'Pour éveiller nos joies un beau crime est bien fort', p.8
13 The text was published in 1978: Allain, 'Fantômas et les autres vus du premier rang de l'orchestre', pp.34–40
14 Olivier-Martin, 'Héroïnes et cruauté', p.107
15 See Souvestre's letter of 14 January 1911 to Fayard republished in *Europe*, Vol.56, No.590–1, June–July 1978, p.51
16 See the memo by Allain to Fayard and published in 1978 as 'Du Roman Populaire et de ces possibilités commerciales', in *Europe*, Vol. 56, No.590–1, June–July 1978, p.23
17 Lacassin, 'Préface', p.9
18 Cocteau, preface to Leroux, *Le Mystère de la chambre jaune*, p.8
19 Thiesse, 'Les infortunes littéraires . . .', p.37
20 Nizan, *Pour une nouvelle culture*, p.68
21 Ibid., pp.260, 261, 311
22 See *William Roughead's Chronicles of Murder* by Whittington-Egan; see also Joyce Carol Oates, 'The Mystery of Jon Benét Ramsey', p.31
23 *Les mystères de la police*, Librairie centrale, Paris 1864
24 *Le Monde*, colour supplement, 2 April 2005
25 Brooks, *When Russia Learned to read. Literacy and Popular Culture 1861–1917*, p.142
26 Ibid., pp.145–6
27 Cohen-Solal, *Sartre. A Life*, p.35
28 Scholes and Rabin, *Science Fiction History Science Vision*, p.10
29 Ibid., p.6
30 Moilin, *Paris dans l'ans 2000*, pp.135, 63
31 Ibid., pp.79, 71
32 Ibid., pp.84–5
33 Ibid., p.183
34 Mettais, *L'An 5865*
35 Ibid., p.329
36 Robida, *Le Vingtième siècle*, pp.70, 174
37 Ibid., p.19
38 Ibid., p.286
39 Clarke, 'Forecasts of Warfare in Fiction', p.11
40 See Evgéni Zamiatine (Yevgeny Zamiatyn), *Le Métier Littéraire*, p.68
41 Desideri, 'Il fantastico', p.970

35 : Popular Novels, for Young and Old

1 Brooks, *When Russia Learned to Read*, p.xvii
2 Thiesse, 'Les infortunes littéraires . . .', p.40
3 Dubourg, Diebolt and Caillot, 'De Leo Taxil à Maurice Mario. Marc Mario', pp.401–4
4 Charle, *Les intellectuels en Europe au XIXe siècle*, p.187
5 Rogger, *Russia in the Age of Modernisation and Revolution 1881–1917*, p.126
6 Information on Marie Corelli in Feltes, *Literary Capital and the Late Victorian Novel*, pp.118–29
7 Ransom, *The Mysterious Miss Marie Corelli*, p.81
8 Ibid., p.75

9 Bennett, *Fame and Fiction. An Enquiry into Certain Popularities*, p.17

10 Ibid., p.90

11 Ransom, *The Mysterious Miss Marie Corelli*, p.7, quoting the obituary in the *Manchester Guardian*, 22 April 1924, see also p.64

12 Ibid., p.213

13 Citation in Gilder and Gilder (eds), *Trilbyana*, p.28

14 du Maurier, *Trilby*, p.10

15 Ibid., pp.114, 249

16 Pick, Introduction to George du Maurier, *Trilby*, p.xxvii

17 Gilder and Gilder (eds), *Trilbyana*, pp.16–17, 19, 26

18 Beaven, 'Readership in Early Nineteenth-century Russia: Recent Soviet Research' in *Slavic Review*, p.277

19 Data in Brooks, *When Russia Learned to Read*, pp.61–4

20 Barbier and Bertho Lavenir, *Histoire des médias*, p.162

21 Brooks, *When Russia Learned to Read*, p.123

22 Ibid., pp.169–71

23 Ibid., pp.190, 314

24 Ibid., pp.128–32

25 Ibid., p.93

26 Stroev, 'Lire en Russie', p.16

27 Brooks, *When Russia Learned to Read*, pp.296, 325, 333

28 Lamar (ed.), *The New Encyclopedia of the American West*, p.1200

29 Much of the material on German western writers can be found in Cracroft, 'World Westerns: The European Writer and the American West', pp.159–79. It can be accessed on *www.tcu.edu/depts/prs/amwest/pdf/wlo159.pdf*

30 Ashliman, 'The American West in Twentieth-Century Germany', p.83

31 Barbier, *L'empire du livre*, p.71

32 Schumacher, 'Le triomphe d'un menteur honnête: Les romans de Karl May', pp.147–8

33 Wood, 'The Bloodiest War', p.44

34 Schumacher, 'Le triomphe d'un menteur honnête: Les romans de Karl May', p.143

35 Ashliman, 'The American West in Twentieth-Century Germany', p.84

36 Schumacher, 'Le triomphe d'un menteur honnête: Les romans de Karl May', p.145

37 Blackbourn, *The Fontana History of Germany 1780–1918*, p.393

38 Ceserani and Salibra, 'Popular Literature in Nineteenth-Century Italy: *Letteratura amena*', p.367

39 Arpino and Antonetto, *Vita, tempeste, sciagure di Salgari il padre degli eroi*, pp.56, 63, 94

40 Sarti, *Bibliografia Salgariana*, pp.9–13

41 Arpino and Antonetto, *Vita, tempeste, sciagure di Salgari il padre degli eroi*, p.111

42 Guagnini, 'Alcuni aspetti dell'influenza di Verne sulla cultura italiana e il caso Yambo' in *Problemi*, p.243

43 Piromalli, 'Motivo di narrativa popolare nel ciclo dei "Pirati della Malesia"', p.34

44 Carloni, 'Nazionalismo, eurocentrismo, razzismo e misogenia nel "Ciclo del Far-West" di Emilio Salgari', p.179

45 UNESCO *Index Translationum*. Cumulative online accessed May 2005

46 Cusatelli, 'Pinocchio in Germania', pp.142–7

47 Lucian, 'Collodi in Romania', p.344

48 Zanotto, 'Pinocchio all'estero', p.78

49 Risaliti, 'Pinocchio in Russia', p.513

50 Zanotto, 'Pinocchio all'estero', pp.84–5

51 Lucas, 'Introduction' to Carlo Collodi, *The Adventures of Pinocchio*, p.viii

52 Faeti, 'Le figure del mito', p.29

53 Squarotti, 'Gli schemi narrativi di Collodi', pp.90–105

54 Tempesti, 'Pinocchio', pp.119–21

55 Tempesti, 'Gian Burrasca', pp.141–2

56 Lurie, 'The Good Bad Boy', pp.15–16

57 Rose, *The Case of Peter Pan or The Impossibility of Children's Fiction*, p.5

58 Glénisson, 'Le livre pour la jeunesse', p.465 ; the author is citing from the catalogue of the exhibition *Mame. Angers-Paris-Tours. Deux siècles du livre*, p.31

59 Gissing, *New Grub Street*, p.10

36 : The Popular Press

1 Garvey, *The Adman in the Parlor: Magazines and the Gendering of Consumer Culture, 1880s to 1910s*, p.9

2 Bennett, *Fame and Fiction*, pp.166–7

3 White, *Women's Magazines 1693–1968*, p.63

4 Cocks, 'Peril in the personals: the dangers and pleasures of classified advertising in early twentieth-century Britain', p.5

5 White, *Women's Magazines 1693–1968*, pp.58–60

6 Ibid., pp.70–1

7 Ibid., p.79

8 Ibid., pp.74–8

9 Raban, 'Journey to the End of the Night', p.14

10 Charle, *Les intellectuels en Europe au XIXe siècle*, p.192
11 Fritzsche, *Reading Berlin 1900*, p.16
12 Ibid., pp.72–4
13 Ullstein, *The Rise and Fall of the House of Ullstein*, pp.69–72
14 Ibid., p.124
15 Fenyo, 'Writers in Politics: The role of *Nyugat* in Hungary, 1908–19', p.194 and Charle, *Les intellectuels en Europe au XIXe siècle*, p.189
16 Davis, 'Italy', p.109
17 Candeloro, *Storia dell'Italia moderna* Vol. 6, p.280
18 Davis, 'Italy', p.110
19 Ibid., p.112
20 Charle, *Les intellectuels en Europe au XIXe siècle*, p.186
21 Desvois, 'L'industrie papetière et le prix du papier journal en Espagne de 1898 à 1936', p.266
22 Ibid., p.275
23 Albert, 'La presse française de 1871 à 1940', p.141
24 Figures for *L'Humanité* in Albert, Feyel and Picard, *Documents pour l'histoire de la presse nationale aux XIXe et XXe siècles*, p.50
25 Ibid., p.38
26 Albert, 'La presse française de 1871 à 1940', p.137
27 Ibid., p.297
28 Angenot, *1889*, cit., p.115, Martin, 'Journalistes et gens de lettres (1820–1890)', p.116
29 Ferenczi, *L'Invention du journalisme en France*, p.14
30 Ibid., p.16
31 Dumont, *Études de mentalité*, pp.5–7
32 Albert, Feyel, Picard, *Documents pour l'histoire de la presse nationale*, p.57
33 Angenot, *1889*, p.529
34 Albert, 'La presse française de 1871 à 1940', p.137
35 Cited in Amaury, *Histoire du plus grand quotidien de la IIIe République: Le Petit Parisien, 1876–1944*, Vol. I, pp.271–2
36 Ibid., p.274
37 Ibid., Vol. II, pp.665–7
38 Ibid., p.923
39 Angenot, *1889*, pp.982–3
40 Ibid., p.989
41 Lerner, *La Dépêche*, Vol. I, p.84
42 Ibid., pp.96, 106
43 Ibid., p.113
44 Ibid., pp.561–8
45 Hollis, *The Pauper Press*, pp.123–4
46 Curran and Seaton, *Power without Responsibility*, p.27
47 Seymour-Ure, 'Northcliffe's Legacy', p.10
48 Williams, *The Long Revolution*, p.203
49 Seymour-Ure, 'Northcliffe's Legacy', p.12
50 Chalaby, 'Northcliffe: Proprietor as Journalist', pp.29–33
51 Ibid., pp.33–6
52 Ibid., p.40
53 Kaul, 'Popular Press and Empire: Northcliffe, India and the *Daily Mail*, 1896–1922', p.46
54 Seymour-Ure, 'Northcliffe's Legacy', p.15
55 Gissing, *New Grub Street*, p.428
56 Chalaby, *The Invention of Journalism*, p.127
57 Barbier and Bertho Lavenir, *Histoire des médias*, p.150
58 Taylor, 'Pentecostal Faith Publishing, 1906–1926', pp.65–7
59 Baudelaire, 'Salon de 1859' in *Écrits sur l'art*, p.254
60 See the posters reproduced in *Alphonse Mucha*, catalogue of the exhibition, Lund Humphries Publishers in association with Barbican Art Gallery, London 1993, pp.15–16
61 Rennert 'Would Mucha Have Made It on Madison Avenue?', pp.55–7
62 Barthes, *Image Music Text*, pp.15, 26
63 Ibid., p.30
64 Winter, 'Nationalism, the Visual Arts, and the Myth of War Enthusiasm in 1914', p.360
65 Winter, *Sites of Memory, Sites of Mourning*, pp.119–38
66 Convents, 'Les catholiques et le cinéma en Belgique (1895–1914)', p.23
67 Gibelli, *L'officina della guerra*, p.11
68 Ullstein, *The Rise and Fall of the House of Ullstein*, p.85
69 Albert, 'La presse française de 1871 à 1940', p.303
70 Watelet, 'La presse illustrée', pp.375–7
71 See Fratelli Treves Editori, *Catalogo generale*, December 1903, pp.2–3
72 See Paul Jobling's entry 'L'assiette au beurre' in *Censorship. A World Encyclopedia*, pp.118–20
73 Boltanski, 'La constitution du champ de la bande dessinée', p.38
74 The words are in *The Gospel According to Luke*, 1.35, 36; see also the analysis by Arasse, in *Le Détail*, pp.18–22
75 Kunzle, *History of the Comic Strip*, Vol. I, p.4

76 See cartoon in Chandler, *England in 1819*, p.229. The original is now at the Huntington Library, California
77 Netz, 'Suisse', pp.16–17
78 Bunk, 'Allemagne', pp.12–13
79 There is a 150-page bibliography of books and articles on the comic strips as an appendix to Massart, Nicks and Tilleuil, *La Bande dessinée à l'université . . . et ailleurs. Études sémiotiques et bibliographiques*, pp.267–415
80 Couperie, Filippini and Moliterni, 'France', p.21
81 Gifford, 'Grande Bretagne', pp.82, 93–5
82 One must bear in mind, however, Kunzle's strongly argued objection to the view that the US invented the comic strip in his *History of the Comic Strip*, Vol. I, p.xix
83 Couperie, Filippini and Moliterni, 'France', p.22
84 Filippini, Glenat, Martens, and Sadoul, *Histoire de la bande dessinée en France et en Belgique*, p.9
85 Lorenzi, *I segreti del varietà*, p.16
86 Faeti, 'Il *Corriere dei piccoli*', pp.154–5
87 Bertieri, 'Italie', p.60
88 Ibid., pp.60–2
89 See Tilleuil's analysis in *Pour analyser la Bande Dessinée. Propositions théoriques et pratiques*
90 Caradec, *Histoire de la Littérature enfantine en France*, p.209
91 Mesquita, 'Portugal', p.138
92 Gasca, 'Espagne', p.124
93 Skarzynski, 'Pologne', p.152
94 van Gool, 'Pays-Bas', p.122
95 Kaukoranta, 'Finlande', p.148
96 Hegerfors, 'Suède', p.147
97 Crafton, 'Tricks and Animation' in Nowell-Smith (ed.), *The Oxford History of World Cinema*, p.74

37 : Shows

1 Gidel, *Georges Feydeau*, p.70
2 Ibid., p.81
3 Ibid., p.215
4 Braun, *The Director and the Stage*, p.37
5 Robb reviewing Edmond Rostand's *Cyrano de Bergerac* performed at the Swan Theatre, Stratford in *Times Literary Supplement*, 19 September 1997, p.20
6 Hortmann, *Shakespeare on the German Stage*, p.3
7 Jelavich, *Munich and Theatrical Modernism*, p.103
8 Patterson and Huxley, 'German drama, Theatre and dance', p.219
9 Weber, *France Fin de Siècle*, p.158
10 Knapp, *The Reign of the Theatrical Director*, p.63
11 Mauclair, 'La condition matérielle et morale de l'écrivain à Paris', p.29
12 Charle, 'Champ littéraire français et importations étrangères . . .', p.254
13 Christout, 'La Féerie romantique au théâtre . . .', p.83
14 Abendour, 'Meyerhold à Paris', p.8
15 Ibid., p.17
16 Gramsci, *Selections from the Cultural Writings*, p.56
17 Ceserani and Salibra, 'Popular Literature in Nineteenth-Century Italy: *Letteratura amena*', p.368
18 Jelavich, *Munich and Theatrical Modernism*, p.102
19 Charle, 'Situation spatiale et position sociale . . .', p.58
20 Jelavich, *Munich and Theatrical Modernism*, pp.104–6
21 Wainscott, *The Emergence of the Modern American Theatre 1914–1929*, pp.37–52
22 Szafkó, 'Sándor Hevesi and the Thália Society in Hungary', p.115
23 Pálffy, 'George Bernard Shaw's reception in Hungary: The early years, 1903–1914', p.101
24 Stephens, 'Bernard Shaw' in *Censorship. A World Encyclopedia*, p.2220
25 Pálffy, 'George Bernard Shaw's reception in Hungary . . .', pp.103–6
26 Braun, *The Director and the Stage*, p.77
27 Ibid., pp.26–32
28 Cited in Huntley Carter, *The New Spirit in The European Theatre 1914–1924*, p.52
29 Barstow, ' "Hedda is all of us": Late Victorian Women at the Matinée', pp.387–8
30 Osborne, *The Meiningen Court Theatre 1866–1890*, p.178
31 Knapp, *The Reign of the Theatrical Director*, p.8
32 Ibid., pp.17, 19
33 On Ibsen in Russian see Kalbouss, 'The Birth of Modern Russia Drama', p.180
34 Braun, *The Director and the Stage*, pp.60–1
35 Ibid., p.62
36 Ibid., pp.63–6
37 Gilman, *Chekhov's Plays: An Opening into Eternity*, p.203; see also Figes, *Natasha's Dance*, p.210
38 Craig, *On the Art of the Theatre*, p.138

39 Taranow, *The Bernhardt Hamlet. Culture and Context*, pp.3, 13, 139–43
40 Fisher, 'The Origins of the French Popular Theatre', p.461
41 Ibid., p.463
42 Ibid., p.471
43 Patterson, *The Revolution in German Theatre 1900–1933*, pp.27–8
44 Ritter, 'Workers' Culture in Imperial Germany . . .', pp.175–6
45 Senelick, 'Theatre', p.268
46 Thurston, 'The Impact of Russian Popular Theatre, 1886–1915', pp.238–42
47 Figes, *Natasha's Dance*, p.205
48 Thurston, 'The Impact of Russian Popular Theatre . . .', p.258
49 Ibid., pp.262–4
50 Jelavich, *Munich and Theatrical Modernism*, pp.44–5
51 Weber, *France Fin de Siècle*, p.164
52 Leroy, *Histoire des arts du Spectacle en France*, p.50
53 Baedeker, *Paris and its environs. Handbook for travellers*, p.50
54 Patterson, *The Revolution in German Theatre 1900–1933*, p.23
55 Stedman Jones, *Languages of class*, pp.194–5
56 Schwartz, 'Le goût du public pour la réalité: le spectateur de cinéma, avant la lettre', p.135
57 Baedeker, *Paris and its environs. Handbook for travellers*, pp.52–3
58 Csergo, 'Extension et mutation du loisir citadin', pp.150–1
59 Ibid., p.161
60 Appignanesi, *Cabaret: The First Hundred Years*, p.26
61 Ibid., p.28
62 Senelick (ed.), *Cabaret Performance. Europe 1890–1920*, p.42
63 Condemi, *Les cafés-concerts*, pp.72, 112
64 Dillaz, 'Diffusion et propagation chansonnières au XIXe siècle', pp.61, 65
65 Dull, 'From Rabelais to the Avant-Garde: Wordplays and parody in the Wall-Journal *Le Mur*', pp.200–1
66 Jelavich, *Munich and Theatrical Modernism*, pp.138–9
67 Erenberg, *Steppin' Out: New York Nightlife and the Transformation of American Culture, 1890–1930*, p.115
68 Senelick (ed.), *Cabaret Performance. Europe 1890–1920*, p.50
69 Appignanesi, *Cabaret*, p.42
70 Senelick (ed.), *Cabaret Performance. Europe 1890–1920*, p.134
71 Cited in Yuri Tsivian, et al. (eds), *Silent Witnesses: Russian Films, 1909–1919*, p.544

38 : Music

1 Weber, *Music and the Middle Class*, cit., pp.86–7
2 Hess, *La Valse*, cit., p.224
3 Ibid., p.232
4 Eugène Giraudet, *La dance, la tenue, le maintien, l'hygiène et l'éducation* cited in Hess, *La valse*, p.233
5 Billard and Roussin, *Histoires de l'Accordéon*, pp.22, 171
6 Russell, *Popular Music in England, 1840–1914*, p.5
7 See *Musical Opinion and Music Trade Review* of September 1881, in *Music Publishing, Copyright and Piracy in Victorian England*, p.12
8 Coover, 'Introduction' to ibid., p.viii
9 Ibid., p.27
10 Raynor, *Music and Society since 1815*, p.157
11 van der Merwe, *Origins of the Popular Style. The Antecedents of Twentieth-Century Popular Music*, p.27
12 Ibid., p.29
13 Extract from Alan Lomax's *Mister Jelly Roll* (1950) in Gottlieb (ed.), *Reading Jazz*, p.4
14 van de Merwe, *Roots of the Classical*, p.461
15 Hennion, *La passion musicale*, p.313
16 Ibid., p.40
17 Burkholder, 'Museum Pieces: The Historicist mainstream in Music of the Last Hundred Years', p.124
18 Chimènes, 'La "Nomenklatura" Musicale en France sous la IIIe République', pp.111–45
19 Lebrecht, *Discord*, p.89
20 Pasler, 'Opéra et pouvoir: forces à l'oeuvre derrière le scandale du *Pelléas* de Debussy', see table on p.173
21 Fodor, 'Not Entirely Nice', p.32
22 McPherson, 'Before the Met: The Pioneer Days of Radio Opera. Part 1, An Overview', p.7
23 Peter Aspen interview with Joseph Volpe, director of the New York Met in *Financial Times Magazine*, 10 January 2004
24 Franzina, 'L'America', p.353
25 Rich, 'Puccini in America', p.41
26 Nicolodi (ed.), *Musica italiana del primo Novecento*, p.vii
27 Wolff, *L'Opéra au Palais Garnier (1875–1962)*

28 Ibid., pp.545–50
29 McPherson, 'Before the Met: The Pioneer Days of Radio Opera. Part 2 . . .', p.210
30 Greffe and Dupuis, 'Quand l'opéra découvre la gestion', p.65
31 Conati, 'L'arte di Verdi fra "le ingiurie del tempo" e gl'infortuni della critica', p.71
32 Gualerzi, 'Appunti per una storia recente degl'interpreti verdiani'
33 Steane, *The Grand Tradition*, p.42
34 Nicolodi, introduction to *Musica italiana del primo Novecento*, p.v where she cites the outraged Arnaldo Bonaventura, 'Il nostro buon pubblico' in *La Nuova Musica*, No.145, January 1908, pp.1–2
35 Ibid., p.6
36 Chanan, *Musica Pratica*, pp.160–1
37 Parakilas, 'Classical Music as Popular Music', p.2
38 Advertisements in the *London Magazine*, January 1907, reproduced in Ord-Hume, *Clockwork Music*, p.267
39 Heaton, *The U.K. Piano Pages* http://www.uk-piano.org – update of 15 September 2000
40 Chimènes, 'La princesse Edmond de Polignac et la création musicale', pp.125–45
41 Dowe, 'The Working Men's Choral Movement in Germany before the First World War', p.269
42 Ibid., p.277
43 Ibid., pp.282, 285
44 Russell, *Popular Music in England, 1840–1914*, pp.272–4
45 Ibid., p.266
46 Ibid., pp.5–7, 11–12
47 Scott, *The Singing Bourgeois*, pp.93, 101, 106, 110, 112, 116
48 For the background to the story see Ellmann, *James Joyce*, pp.245–51

39 : Recorded Sound

1 Martland, *A Business History of The Gramophone Company Ltd 1897–1918*, p.22
2 Gronow and Saunio, *An International History of the Recording Industry*, p.5
3 Welch, Brodbeck and Stenzel, *Tinfoil to Stereo*, p.110
4 Gronow and Saunio, *An International History of the Recording Industry*, p.1
5 *His Master's Voice/La voce del padrone, The Italian Catalogue*, p.26
6 Gelatt, *The Fabulous Phonograph 1877–1977*, pp.42–3
7 Ibid., p.47
8 Ibid., pp.70, 100
9 Ibid., p.69
10 Steane, *The Grand Tradition*, p.14
11 Gelatt, *The Fabulous Phonograph 1877–1977*, pp.48, 52
12 Wiernicki, *Dal divertimento dei nobili alla propaganda. Storia del Jazz in Russia*, p.33
13 Gronow, 'The record industry: the growth of a mass medium', p.59
14 Martland, *A Business History of The Gramophone Company Ltd 1897–1918*, p.363
15 Gronow, 'The Record Industry Comes to the Orient', p.260
16 Martland, *A Business History of The Gramophone Company Ltd 1897–1918*, p.56
17 Gelatt, *The Fabulous Phonograph 1877–1977*, pp.103–4
18 Gibelli, *L'officina della guerra*, p.177–9
19 Chanan, *Repeated Takes*, p.28
20 Gelatt, *The Fabulous Phonograph 1877–1977*, p.66
21 Kinnear, *The Gramophone Company's First Indian Recordings 1899–1908*, p.10
22 Gaisberg, *The Music goes Round*, p.33
23 Kinnear, *The Gramophone Company's First Indian Recordings*, p.12
24 Gaisberg, *The Music goes Round*, p.59
25 Cited in Gronow, 'The Record Industry Comes to the Orient', pp.273–4
26 Gaisberg, *The Music goes Round*, pp.62–3
27 Gronow, 'The Record Industry Comes to the Orient', pp.251–7
28 Hughes, ' "The Music Boom" in Tamil South India: gramophone, radio and the making of mass culture', p.447
29 Cited in Gronow, 'The Record Industry Comes to the Orient', p.273–4
30 Galliano, 'I compositori giapponesi del primo novecento . . .', p.185
31 Gaisberg, *The Music goes Round*, p.61
32 Gronow, 'The record industry: the growth of a mass medium', pp.60–2
33 *Carteggio Verdi-Ricordi 1880–81*, p.35
34 Tetrazzini, *My Life of Song*, p.104
35 Ibid., p.173
36 Ibid., pp.251–3
37 Limansky, 'Luisa Tetrazzini. Coloratura secrets', p.541
38 Gaisberg, *The Music goes Round*, p.41
39 Martland, *A Business History of the Gramophone Company Ltd 1897–1918*, p.89
40 Figures in ibid., p.114
41 Ibid., pp.199, 249, 279, 288
42 Ibid., pp.261–3

43 Gronow and Saunio, *An International History of the Recording Industry*, pp.22–3
44 Franzina, 'Inni e Canzoni', pp.135, 144
45 A list of recordings is provided in Pesce, *Napoli a 78 giri*
46 *His Master's Voice/La voce del padrone, The Italian Catalogue*, pp.27, 112
47 Gaisberg, *The Music goes Round*, p.47. Information on Caruso recording from William R. Moran, 'Discography of Original Recordings' in appendix to Enrico Caruso Jr, *Enrico Caruso. My father and my family*, pp.403–35
48 Gaisberg, *The Music goes Round*, p.48
49 Gelatt, *The Fabulous Phonograph 1877–1977*, pp.114, 145, 148
50 Enrico Caruso Jr, *Enrico Caruso. My father and my family*, p.353, citing Irving Kolodin, *The Metropolitan Opera: 1883–1939*
51 Conway Morris, 'Greek Café Music', pp.80–2
52 Gronow and Saunio, *An International History of the Recording Industry*, p.26
53 Martland, *A Business History of the Gramophone Company Ltd 1897–1918*, p.372
54 Ibid., p.373
55 Raynor, *Music and Society since 1815*, p.160
56 Chanan, *Repeated Takes*, pp.34–5
57 Gelatt, *The Fabulous Phonograph 1877–1977*, p.196
58 Nicolodi, *Orizzonti*, pp.65–6
59 Gronow and Saunio, *An International History of the Recording Industry*, p.33
60 Goethe, *Faust Part Two*, p.270

40 : The Moving Image

1 Tsivian, *Early Cinema in Russia and its Cultural Reception*, p.18
2 Ibid., p.25
3 Rossell, *Living Pictures*, pp.57ff
4 Onclincx, 'Les débuts du cinématographe des frères Lumière à Bruxelles d'après les journaux du temps', pp.219–20
5 Aumont, 'Lumière revisited', pp.416–30
6 The business steps are delineated in Fihman, 'La stratégie Lumière: l'invention du cinéma comme marché', pp.35–46
7 Brown, ' "England is not big enough . . ." American rivalry in the early English film business . . .', p.22
8 Meusy and Straus, 'L'argent du Cinématographe Lumière', pp.57, 55
9 Aumont, 'Lumière revisited', p.423
10 Cited in Bottomore, 'The Panicking audience?: early cinema and the "train effect" ', p.180
11 Deslandes and Richard, *Histoire comparée du cinéma*, Vol. 2, pp.13–14
12 Gidel, *Georges Feydeau*, pp.146–7
13 Ibid., pp.217, 235
14 Chanan, *The Dream That Kicks*, p.25
15 Onclincx, 'Les débuts du cinématographe des frères Lumière à Bruxelles . . .', pp.221–2
16 Jeancolas, *Histoire du cinéma français*, p.12
17 Pearson, 'Early Cinema', pp.17–19
18 Abel, *The Ciné Goes to Town: French Cinema, 1896–1914*, p.137
19 Deslandes and Richard, *Histoire comparée du cinéma*, Vol. 2, p.217
20 Robinson, 'Comedy', p.78
21 Porter, *London. A Social History*, p.290
22 Point made by Finch, in her 'Reality and its representation in the nineteenth-century novel', p.48
23 This argument is developed by Fell, in his *Film and the Narrative Tradition*
24 Ibid., p.22
25 Salt, *Film Style and Technology*, p.40
26 Gunning, 'The Cinema of Attractions . . .', pp.56–62
27 Rossell, *Living Pictures*, p.143
28 Witte, 'The Spectator as Accomplice in Ernst Lubitsch's *Schuhpalast Pinkus*', p.114
29 Pierce, 'The legion of the condemned – why American silent films perished', pp.5–22
30 Gorbman, *Unheard Melodies: Narrative Film Music*, p.53; Cherchi Usai, 'The Early Years', pp.11–12; Abruzzese, *Metafore della pubblicità*, p.51
31 Tsivian, *Early Cinema in Russia and its Cultural Reception*, p.78
32 Chanan, *The Dream That Kicks*, pp.259–63
33 Sartre, *Les Mots*, p.98
34 Brunetta, *Storia del cinema italiano 1895–1945*, p.23
35 Deslandes and Richard, *Histoire comparée du cinéma*, Vol. 2, pp.312–13
36 Chanan, *The Dream That Kicks*, p.26
37 Abel, ' "Pathé Goes to Town": French Films Create a Market for the Nickelodeon', pp.13ff
38 Aronson, 'The Wrong Kind of Nickel Madness: Pricing Problems for Pittsburgh Nickelodeons', pp.72–5
39 Singer, 'Manhattan Nickelodeons: New Data on Audiences and Exhibitors', p.22

40 Ibid., p.26
41 Warnke, 'Immigrant Popular Culture as Contested Sphere . . .', p.330
42 Altenloh, 'A Sociology of the Cinema', pp.249–93
43 Ibid., p.267
44 Ibid., p.266
45 Ibid., p.287
46 Pearson, 'Early Cinema', p.22, and Pearson, 'Transitional Cinema', p.36
47 Brunetta, *Storia del cinema italiano 1895–1945*, p.34
48 Pearson, 'Transitional Cinema', p.27
49 Abel, 'French Silent Cinema', p.112
50 Tsivian, *Early Cinema in Russia*, p.24
51 Gomery, 'The Movie Palace Comes to America's Cities', p.137
52 Ibid., p.143
53 Jeancolas, *Histoire du cinéma français*, p.18
54 Abel, *The Ciné Goes to Town*, pp.9, 34
55 Jeancolas, *Histoire du cinéma français*, p.15
56 Ibid., p.19
57 Abel, ' "Pathé Goes to Town" . . .', p.3
58 Abel, 'French Silent Cinema', p.112
59 Pearson, 'Early Cinema', p.15
60 Abel, *The Ciné Goes to Town*, p.36
61 Ezra, *Georges Méliès*, p.19
62 Cherchi Usai, *Georges Méliès*, p.16; Ezra, *Georges Méliès*, p.6
63 Vasey, 'The World-Wide Spread of the Cinema', p.53
64 Salt, *Film Style and Technology: History and Analysis*, pp.47–59; Pearson, 'Transitional Cinema', pp.23, 29
65 See the discussion on the pictorial acting in the theatre and the cinema in Brewster and Jacobs, *Theatre to Cinema*, pp.99–110
66 Pearson, 'Transitional Cinema', p.31
67 See Bordwell, *On the History of Film Style*
68 The famous experiment was described by Pudovkin in *Film Technique and Film Acting*, p.88
69 Ibid., pp.25–6
70 Kuleshov, 'The Banner of Cinematography', p.41
71 Tsivian, 'Some Preparatory Remarks on Russian Cinema', p.30
72 Tsivian, *Early Cinema in Russia*, pp.53–4, 127
73 The point is frequently made; for a treatment of it see Oksiloff, *Picturing the Primitive*, p.23ff
74 Zaïd, 'La guérilla comme spectacle', pp.96–7, citing Magarita de Orellana's *La Mirada circular. El cine norteamericano de la Revolución mexicana 1911–1917*, Artes de México, México 1999, pp.73–5

75 Gaycken, ' "A Drama Unites Them in a Fight to the Death" . . .', pp.358–9
76 Musser, 'Documentary', pp.87–9
77 Whissel, 'Placing the spectator on the Scene of History . . .', pp.225–6
78 Youngblood, 'The return of the native: Yakov Protazanov and Soviet Cinema', p.107
79 Brewster and Jacobs, *Theatre to Cinema*, p.vi
80 Cousins, *The Story of Film*, p.25
81 Pearson, 'Transitional Cinema', p.28
82 Renzi, *Jules Verne on Film*
83 Abel, 'French Silent Cinema', p.113
84 O'Brien, 'Silent Screams', p.8
85 Hesse, 'Ernst Reichler alias Stuart Webbs: King of the German Film Detectives', p.142
86 Knops, 'Cinema from the Writing Desk: Detective Films in Imperial Germany', pp.133–4
87 Baldelli, 'Bilancio dei rapporti Letteratura-Cinema', p.524
88 Abel, *The Ciné Goes to Town*, p.181
89 Cousins, *The Story of Film*, pp.38–9
90 Cherchi Usai, 'Italy: Spectacle and Melodrama', p.129
91 Gramsci, *Selections from the Cultural Writings*, p.54
92 Morin, *Les Stars*, p.17
93 Tsivian et al. (eds), *Silent Witnesses: Russian Films, 1909–1919*, p.548

41 : Cinema: Europeans and Americans

1 Vasey, 'The World-Wide Spread of the Cinema', p.55
2 Abel, *The Ciné Goes to Town*, pp.44–5
3 Cousins, *The Story of Film*, p.42
4 Bachlin, *Histoire économique du cinéma*, p.34. See also Quinn, 'Distribution, the Transient Audience, and the Transition to the Feature Film', p.44
5 Musser, 'L'industrie du cinéma en France et aux États Unis entre 1900 et 1920 . . .', pp.63–4
6 Ibid., pp.65–6
7 Abel, 'French Silent Cinema', p.116
8 Chanan, *The Dream That Kicks*, pp.198–9
9 Uricchio, 'The First World War and the Crisis in Europe', pp.63, 65, 67
10 Thompson, *Exporting Entertainment*, p.42
11 Uricchio, 'The First World War and the Crisis in Europe', p.70
12 Musser, 'L'industrie du cinéma en France et aux États Unis entre 1900 et 1920', p.76

13 Decleva, *Arnoldo Mondadori*, p.91
14 Morin, *Les Stars*, p.55
15 Aimone, 'Un statut pour les acteurs: 1910–1920', p.85
16 See the examination of the average shot lengths of European and American films in Salt, 'Early German Film: The Stylistics in Comparative Context', pp.225–36 and especially his discussion of *Zweimal Gelebt* on p.229
17 Salt, *Film Style and Technology*, pp.146–7
18 Grieveson and Krämer (eds), *The Silent Cinema Reader*, p.77, using figures from Robert C. Allen's *Vaudeville and Film*, Arno Press, New York 1980, p.181
19 Cousins, *The Story of Film*, p.194
20 Cited in Brewster and Jacobs, *Theatre to Cinema*, p.108
21 Data in Michael Aronson, 'The Wrong Kind of Nickel Madness: Pricing Problems for Pittsburgh Nickelodeons', p.75
22 Brewster, '*Traffic in Souls* (1913), An experience in feature-length narrative construction', pp.226–41
23 Singer, 'Serials', pp.105–10
24 Abel, *The Ciné Goes to Town*, p.51
25 Jeancolas, *Histoire du cinéma français*, p.32
26 Abel, 'French Silent Cinema', pp.115–16
27 Lipovetsky, *The Empire of Fashion*, pp.56–9
28 Tsivian, et al. (eds), *Silent Witnesses: Russian Films, 1909–1919*, p.16
29 Tsivian, *Early Cinema in Russia and its Cultural Reception*
30 Abel, *The Ciné Goes to Town*, p.43
31 Tsivian, 'Some Preparatory Remarks on Russian Cinema' in Tsivian et al. (eds), *Silent Witnesses*, pp.26–8
32 Cherchi Usai, 'Italy: Spectacle and Melodrama', p.123
33 Ibid., p.124
34 Gili, *La Comédie italienne*, pp.14–17
35 Robinson, 'Comedy', p.79
36 Ibid.
37 Ibid., pp.81–2
38 Cherchi Usai, 'Italy: Spectacle and Melodrama', pp.125–7
39 Brunetta, *Storia del Cinema Italiano 1895–1945*, p.156
40 Finler, *Silent Cinema*, p.61
41 Brunetta, *Storia del Cinema Italiano 1895–1945*, p.56
42 Horwitz and Harrison (eds), *The George Kleine Collection of Early Motion Pictures*, p.xvii

43 Pudovkin, *Film Technique and Film Acting*, pp.81–3, emphasis in the original
44 Kuleshov, 'The Banner of Cinematography' (1920), p.40
45 Elsaesser (ed.), *The BFI Companion to German Cinema*, pp.182–3
46 Hampicke, 'The Danish Influence: David Oliver and Nordisk in Germany', pp.72–8
47 Pearson, 'Transitional Cinema', pp.23–4
48 The revisionist thesis is advanced by Rossell, 'Beyond Messter: Aspects of early cinema in Berlin', pp.53–69
49 Ibid., pp.54, 63
50 Betts, *The Film Business*, p.46
51 Chanan, *The Dream That Kicks*, pp.201–2
52 Finler, *Silent Cinema*, p.21
53 Hawkridge, 'British Cinema from Hepworth to Hitchcock', pp.132–4
54 Gray, 'Smith the showman: The early years of George A. Smith', p.8
55 Betts, *The Film Business*, p.34
56 For instance Rachel Low's monumental seven-volume *The History of the British Film*, see review of the 1997 reprint by Ian Christie in *Journal of Popular British Cinema*, No. 2, 1999, pp.136–8
57 Finler, *Silent Cinema*, p.37
58 Nemeskürty: 'Le Cinéma hongrois avant 1945', p.17
59 Ibid., p.19, see also Micheli, *Cinema Ungherese*, p.49
60 Tegel, 'Bela Balazs: fairytales, film, and *The Blue Light*', p.498
61 Micheli, *Il cinema bulgaro degli anni settanta*, pp.7–9

42 : Cultural Panics

1 Bourke, *Working Class Cultures in Britain 1890–1960*, p.136
2 Ibid., p.143
3 Arnold, *Culture and Anarchy*, p.79
4 Stora-Lamarre, *L'Enfer de la IIIe République. Censeurs et Pornographes (1881–1914)*, p.145
5 Stark, 'Gerhart Hauptmann' in *Censorship. A World Encyclopedia*, p.1036
6 Goldstein, *The War for the Public Mind*, p.11
7 Comte d'Haussonville, 'Le Combat contre le vice. Part II', pp.573–4
8 Comte d'Haussonville, 'Le Combat contre le vice. Part I', pp.131–3
9 Harrison, 'Press and pressure group in modern Britain', pp.261–3
10 Ibid., p.267
11 Ibid., p.271

12 de Budé, *Du danger des mauvaises lectures et des moyens d'y remédier*, p.12

13 Ibid., p.38

14 Ibid., p.33

15 Ibid., p.31

16 Ibid., p.33

17 Thiesse, 'Organisation des loisirs des travailleurs et temps dérobés (1880–1930)', p.303

18 de Budé, *Du danger des mauvaises lectures . . .*, pp.42, 50, 59

19 See appendix to Stora-Lamarre, *L'Enfer de la IIIe République*, pp.243–6

20 Bureau, *La crise morale des temps nouveaux*, pp.8, 170–2

21 Ibid., p.30

22 de Budé, *Du danger des mauvaises lectures . . .*, pp.84, 88

23 Ibid., pp.197–8

24 Stora-Lamarre, *L'Enfer de la IIIe République*, p.59

25 de Budé, *Du danger des mauvaises lectures . . .*, pp.18, 90

26 Lebrecht, *Discord*, p.91

27 Stephens, 'Bernard Shaw', p.2221

28 Gramsci, *Selections from the Cultural Writings*, pp.70, 73

29 Krakovitch, *Hugo censuré*, pp.260–1

30 Westwood, *Endurance and Endeavour*, p.102

31 Sieburth, *Inventing High and Low. Literature, Mass Culture, and Uneven Modernity in Spain*, p.35

32 Casselle, 'Le régime législatif', p.47

33 See account in *Censorship. A World Encyclopedia*, p.854

34 Ibid., p.313

35 Allen, *Satire and Society in Wilhelmine Germany*, p.3; see also Gay, *The Cultivation of Hatred*, Vol. 3, p.405

36 Allen, *Satire and Society in Wilhelmine Germany*, p.407

37 Davis, 'Italy', p.113

38 Freeborn, *The Russian Revolutionary Novel: Turgenev to Pasternak*, pp.44–5

39 Stora-Lamarre, *L'Enfer de la IIIe République*, p.24

40 Ibid., p.25

41 Ibid., pp.25–6

42 Ibid., pp.28–9

43 Ibid., p.159

44 Angenot, 'Pornographies Fin-de-siècle', pp.48–9

45 Mutzenbacher, *Histoire d'une fille de Vienne racontée par elle-même*. In the same year an Italian version appeared: *Josefine Mutzenbacher, ovvero la storia di una prostituta viennese da lei stesso narrata*, ES edition, Milan 1998

46 Stora-Lamarre, *L'Enfer de la IIIe République*, p.32

47 See the two volumes listing *Les Livres de l'Enfer. Bibliographie critique des ouvrages érotiques dans leurs différentes éditions du XVIe siècle à nos jours*, by Pascal Pia, C. Coulet et A. Faure, Paris 1978

48 Stora-Lamarre, *L'Enfer de la IIIe République*, p.204

49 Garcia Lara, 'Exito y difusion de la novela erotica española'

50 Stora-Lamarre, *L'Enfer de la IIIe République*, pp.170–1

51 Chalaby, *The Invention of Journalism*, p.159

52 Dumont, *Études de mentalité*, pp.20–3

53 Cited in Davis, 'Italy', pp.115–16

54 Bernardini, 'Les catholiques et l'avènement du cinéma en Italie: promotion et contrôle', pp.4–6

55 Minguet Batllori, 'L'Église et les intellectuels espagnols contre le cinéma', pp.12–18

56 The precise figure is difficult to determine: see Grosser, 'The Bazaar de la Charité fire: The reality, the aftermath, the telling', p.74

57 Singer, 'Manhattan Nickelodeons: New Data on Audiences and Exhibitors', p.35

58 Cited in Grieveson, ' "A kind of recreative school for the whole family" . . .', p.67

59 Tsivian, 'Censure Bans on Religious Subjects in Russian Films', p.74

60 Thurston, 'The Impact of Russian Popular Theatre, 1886–1915', p.237

61 Tsivian, 'Censure Bans on Religious Subjects in Russian Films', p.76

62 Uricchio and Pearson, ' "You Can Make the *Life of Moses* Your Life Saver" . . .', p.197

63 Convents, 'Les catholiques et le cinéma en Belgique (1895–1914)', pp.24–7

64 Jeancolas, *Histoire du cinéma français*, p.16

65 Grieveson, ' "A kind of recreative school for the whole family" . . .', pp.64–5

66 Jelavich, *Munich and Theatrical Modernism*, pp.70–4 and, by the same author, the entry 'Oskar Panizza' in *Censorship. A World Encyclopedia*, pp.1807–8

67 Choppin, *Les manuels scolaires*, p.57

68 Freyssinet-Dominjon, *Les Manuels d'histoire de l'école libre 1882–1959*, p.19

69 Ibid., p.36

70 Albisetti, *Secondary School Reform in Imperial Germany*, pp.141–2
71 Bruno, *Le Tour de France par deux enfants. Devoir et patrie*, p.184
72 Mollier, 'Le manuel scolaire et la bibliothèque du peuple', pp.82–3
73 Soriano, *Guide de littérature pour la jeunesse*, p.105
74 Lüsebrink, ' "Littérature nationale" et "Espace national". . . ', pp.272–6
75 Ragone, 'La letteratura e il consumo . . .', p.733
76 Asor Rosa, *Storia d'Italia*, Vol. 4, Tome 2, p.927

77 Gigli, *Edmondo de Amicis*, p.307
78 Bertone, ' "Parlare ai borghesi": De Amicis, Il "Primo maggio" e la propaganda socialista', p.169
79 Faeti, '*Cuore*', p.108
80 Fourment, *Histoire de la Presse*, pp.148–9
81 Mollier, 'Le manuel scolaire et la bibliothèque du peuple', pp.85–8
82 MacDonald, 'Reproducing the Middle-class Boy . . .', pp.518–21
83 Ibid., p.523
84 Ibid., p.527
85 Huntley Carter, *The New Spirit in the European Theatre 1914–1924*, pp.37–9

PART IV

1920–1960 : THE INTERVENTIONIST STATE

43 : States and Markets

1 Bairoch, *Histoire économique et sociale du monde du XVIᵉ siècle à nos jours*. Vol. III, pp.17–18
2 Mawdsley, *The Russian Civil War*, pp.285–7
3 Hobsbawm, *The Age of Extremes*, pp.120–1
4 Bairoch, *Histoire économique et sociale du monde du XVIe à nos jours*, Vol. III, p.88
5 Ibid., p.22
6 Martonyi, 'La littérature populaire en Hongrie', p.240
7 Gheorghiu, 'La construction littéraire d'une identité nationale . . .', p.41
8 Ibid., pp.34–5
9 Livezeanu, *Cultural Politics in Greater Romania*, pp.9–10
10 Ibid., p.192
11 Ojala, 'Radclyffe Hall', pp.1019–21
12 See the transcript of the trial in appendix to Pauvert, *Nouveaux (et moins nouveaux) visages de la censure*
13 Kuhlmann, Kuntzmann, and Bellour, *Censure et bibliothèques au XXe siècle*, pp.9–10
14 Balmand, 'Les best-sellers de la guerre froide', p.75
15 Cross, *Time and Money*, p.46
16 Bloch-Lainé, *L'emploi des loisirs ouvriers et l'éducation populaire*, pp.132–7
17 Arnold, *The Scandal of Ulysses*, p.17

18 Kracauer, 'On bestsellers and their audience', p.92
19 Auffret, *La France de l'entre-deux-guerres 1919/1939*, p.105
20 Cross, 'Vacations for All: The Leisure Question in the Era of the Popular Front', p.600
21 Cross, *A Quest for Time*, p.226
22 Horden, 'Genèse et vote de la loi du 20 juin 1936 sur les congés payés', p.20
23 Cross, *A Quest for Time*, pp.131–5. See also Van Voss, 'The International Federation of Trade Unions and the Attempt to Maintain the Eight-hour Working Day (1919–1929)', p.519
24 Bloch-Lainé, *L'emploi des loisirs ouvriers et l'éducation populaire*, pp.30–2
25 Ibid., p.56
26 Kambo, 'Certains aspects de la lutte du PCA pour la création et la propagation de la culture spirituelle socialiste . . .', pp.25–50
27 Visser, 'Fascist Doctrine and the Cult of the Romanità', p.6
28 Holmlund, 'Pippi and Her Pals', p.5
29 Barrachina, *Propagande et culture dans l'Espagne franquiste: 1936–1945*, p.169
30 Ibid., pp.210–12
31 Grugel and Rees, *Franco's Spain*, p.139
32 Bloch-Lainé, *L'emploi des loisirs ouvriers et l'éducation populaire*, p.93

44 : Culture and Communism

1 Argentieri, *Il cinema sovietico negli anni trenta*, pp.160, 237
2 Ibid., p.194
3 Fitzpatrick, 'Sex and Revolution: An Examination of Literary and Statistical Data on the Mores of Soviet Students in the 1920s', p.257
4 Baker and Last, *Erich Maria Remarque*, p.34
5 Owen, *Erich Maria Remarque: a critical bio-bibliography*, p.69
6 Baker and Last, *Erich Maria Remarque*, p.35
7 Owen, *Erich Maria Remarque*, p.78
8 Albonetti (ed.), *Non c'è tutto nei romanzi*, pp.61–3
9 Baker and Last, *Erich Maria Remarque*, p.41
10 Ibid., p.18
11 Taylor Jr, *Erich Maria Remarque. A Literary and Film Biography*, p.80
12 Ory, *La Belle Illusion*, p.211
13 Ibid., pp.220–1
14 Ibid., pp.276, 292
15 Balmand, 'Les best-sellers de la guerre froide', p.74
16 For this analysis and the following paragraph see Péru, 'Une crise du champ littéraire français. Le débat sur la "littérature prolétarienne" ', pp.56–8. See also Short, 'The Politics of Surrealism, 1920–36', pp.3–25, especially pp.10–13
17 Samuels, 'The Left Book Club', pp.66–8
18 Cavallo, 'Theatre Politics of the Mussolini Régime and Their Influence on Fascist Drama', pp.114–15
19 Brooks, *When Russia Learned to Read*, pp.315, 326
20 Bowlt, 'The Failed Utopia: Russian Art, 1917–32', p.40
21 Holter, 'The Legacy of Lunacharsky and Artistic Freedom in the USSR', pp.262–82; also Bailes, 'Sur la "Théorie des Valeurs" de A. V. Lunacarsky', pp.223–5
22 Gramsci, *Selections from the Cultural Writings*, p.49
23 Ibid., p.53
24 McClelland, 'Utopianism versus Revolutionary Heroism in Bolshevik Policy: The Proletarian Culture Debate', p.407
25 Bowlt, 'The Failed Utopia: Russian Art, 1917–32', p.46
26. Kemp-Welch, 'New Economic Policy in Culture and Its Enemies', pp.451–2
27 Kepley, Jr, 'The First *Perestroika*: Soviet Cinema under the first Five-Year Plan', p.37
28 See Fitzpatrick, 'Cultural Revolution in Russia 1928–32'
29 Fitzpatrick, 'Culture and Politics Under Stalin: a Reappraisal', pp.214–19
30 Ibid., pp.220–1
31 This was the view of the Russian writer Yevgeny Zamiatyn, the author of the dystopian novel *We*: see Zamiatine, 'Le Théâtre Russe', p.494
32 Fitzpatrick, 'Culture and Politics Under Stalin: a Reappraisal', pp.223–4
33 Shneidman, 'The Russian Classical Literary Heritage and the Basic Concepts of Soviet Literary Education', pp.626–8
34 Ibid., p.637
35 Fitzpatrick, 'Sex and Revolution . . .', p.252
36 Clark and Holquist, *Mikhail Bakhtin*, p.270
37 Clark, *The Soviet Novel. History as Ritual*, pp.x–xi
38 Dobrenko, *The Making of the State Reader*, pp.284–6, 294–5
39 Hingley, *Russian Writers and Soviet Society 1917–1978*, p.198
40 Kepley, 'The origins of Soviet cinema: a study in industry development', pp.60–72
41 Youngblood, *Movie for the Masses*, p.15
42 Ibid., pp.51–2
43 Ibid., p.43
44 Robertson, *The Hidden Cinema*, pp.34–5
45 Youngblood, 'The return of the native: Yakov Protazanov and Soviet Cinema', pp.103–4
46 Ibid., p.111
47 Ibid., p.110
48 Kepley, 'The First *Perestroika*: Soviet Cinema under the first Five-Year Plan', pp.43–4
49 Ibid., p.48
50 Youngblood, *Movie for the Masses*, p.55
51 Ibid., p.76
52 Natacha, 'L'interdiction du film *Une Grande Vie*: la reprise en main du cinéma soviétique en août 1946', pp.137–54, which contains lengthy extracts from the minutes of the meeting
53 On the relative leniency of the Soviet regime towards composers see Brooke, 'Soviet Musicians and the Great Terror', pp.397–413
54 Ibid., p.407
55 On the unreliability of *Testimony: The Memoirs of Dmitri Shostakovich* subtitled

'as Related and Edited by Solomon
Volkov' see Fay, 'Shostakovich versus
Volkov: Whose Testimony?', pp.484–93

56 On Stravinsky's self-confessed anti-
Semitism see citation in Brooke, 'Soviet
Music in the International Arena
1932–41', p.246

57 Argentieri, *Il cinema sovietico negli anni
trenta*, p.194

58 Ibid., p.198

59 Carter, *The New Spirit in the Russian
Theatre 1917–28*, p.291

60 Salt, *Film Style and Technology: History
and Analysis*, pp.146–7

61 Cousins, *The Story of Film*, p.105

62 Argentieri, *Il cinema sovietico negli anni
trenta*, pp.213–14

63 Davies, 'Soviet Cinema and the Early
Cold War: Pudovkin's *Admiral Nakhimov*
in Context', pp.51–2

64 Wachtel, *Making a Nation, Breaking a
Nation*, p.98

65 Ibid., pp.142–4

66 Ibid., pp.150–2

67 Batt, 'Tradition et renouveau. Réflexions
sur la création littéraire en RDA', p.69

68 Poiger, 'Rock 'n' Roll, Female Sexuality,
and the Cold War Battle over German
Identities', p.581 and Kater, *Different
Drummers: Jazz Culture of Nazi Germany*,
pp.33–43

69 Kater, *Different Drummers*, p.47

70 Maróthy, *Music and the Bourgeois. Music
and the Proletarian*, p.491, the Hungarian
edition was published in 1966

71 Poiger, 'Rock 'n' Roll, Female
Sexuality . . .', p.602

72 Ibid., pp.582, 587–8

73 Isaiah Berlin's Report was called 'A Note
on Literature and the Arts in the Russian
Federated Social Republic in the Closing
Months of 1945' and has been republished
with the title 'The Arts in Russia under
Stalin' in Berlin, *The Soviet Mind*,
pp.16–17

74 Ibid., p.21

75 Stroev, 'Lecture en Russie', p.189

76 Liber, 'Language, Literacy and Book
Publishing . . .', pp.674–5

77 Carmichael, 'Coming to terms with the
Past . . .', p.277

78 Liber, 'Language, Literacy and Book
Publishing . . .', pp.677–9

79 Ibid., p.682

80 Carmichael, 'Coming to terms with the
Past . . .', p.270

45 : Fascism

1 Aspesi, *Il lusso e l'autarchia*, pp.20–21 and
Paulicelli, *Fashion under Fascism*,
pp.39–50

2 Cited in Ory, *La Belle Illusion*, p.82

3 Grugel and Rees, *Franco's Spain*, p.140

4 See Casanova, *La Iglesia de Franco*, pp.48,
214ff

5 Pašeta, 'Censorship and its Critics in the
Irish Free State 1922–1932', pp.196–8

6 Boyd, *Historia Patria. Politics, History,
and National Identity in Spain, 1875–1975*,
p.267

7 Gramsci, *Selections from the Cultural
Writings*, p.362

8 Ibid., p.206

9 1925 data from Di Luzio, *L'appropriazione
imperfetta*, p.257. 1935 data from Decleva,
'Présence germanique et influences
françaises dans l'édition italienne aux
XIXe et XXe siècles', p.201 using the
database of the Italian National Library,
Florence. The editors of Gramsci,
Selections from the Cultural Writings,
p.252, provide different statistics but
confirm the increase in translations

10 Albonetti (ed.), *Non c'è tutto nei romanzi*,
pp.82–3 (much of this useful book
consists of letters and documents from
the Mondadori archives); see also
Decleva, *Arnoldo Mondadori*, p.153

11 Albonetti (ed.), *Non c'è tutto nei romanzi*,
p.556; Decleva, *Mondadori*, p.227

12 Ibid., p.36

13 Raboni, 'La narrativa straniera negli anni
'20–'40', p.51

14 Corti, *Ombre dal Fondo*, pp.84–5

15 Gramsci, *Selections from the Cultural
Writings*, p.252

16 See Gallavotti, *La scuola fascista di
giornalismo (1930–1933)*

17 Fernandez, *Il mito dell'America negli
intellettuali italiani*, p.14–15

18 Albonetti (ed.), *Non c'è tutto nei romanzi*.
pp.98–100

19 Righetti, 'Bestseller, ma dove sono finiti
gli scrittori italiani?', p.31

20 See the report in De Donato and
Stacchini (eds), *I best seller del ventennio.
Il regime e il libro di massa*, Riuniti, Rome
1991, pp.616–18

21 Di Luzio, *L'appropriazione imperfetta*,
pp.22–3

22 Decleva, *Arnoldo Mondadori*, p.211

23 Ludwig, *Colloqui con Mussolini*, p.5

24 Ibid., p.127

25 Decleva, *Arnoldo Mondadori*, pp.168–70
26 Ludwig, *Colloqui con Mussolini*, pp.92, 131
27 See the account by Arnoldo Mondadori himself in 1946 –'Breve cronistoria della genesi della prima e della seconda edizione dei *Colloqui con Mussolini*' reprinted in the most recent Italian edition of the book, Ludwig, *Colloqui con Mussolini*, pp.xiii–xxix
28 Ludwig, *Colloqui con Mussolini*, p.54
29 Di Luzio, *L'appropriazione imperfetta*, p.82
30 Giocondi, *Lettori in camicia nera*, p.16; this author does not provide a source for his figures
31 Pitigrilli, *Cocaina*, p.66
32 Achilli, 'Le maschere dell'eros', pp.12–13
33 Ibid., p.18
34 Renai, 'Il caso Pitigrilli: analisi di *Dolicocefala bionda*', p.273
35 Ibid., pp.279–83
36 Bordoni, *Il romanzo di consumo*, pp.88–9
37 Dekobra, *La Madone des Sleepings*, in particular pp.88–9 and 56
38 Cohen-Solal, *Sartre. A Life*, p.158
39 Decleva, *Arnoldo Mondadori*, pp, 16, 33
40 Ibid., pp.55, 58, 60
41 Guerri, 'La Mondadori e la politica del ventennio', p.38
42 Decleva, *Arnoldo Mondadori*, pp.76–9, 82–5
43 Calvino, 'La "Romantica"', pp.173–6
44 Raffaelli, 'Il genere poliziesco in Italia prima del 1929. Le collane a carattere poliziesco', pp.237–8
45 Boileau-Narcejac, *Le roman policier*, p.118
46 Albonetti (ed.), *Non c'è tutto nei romanzi*, p.50
47 Decleva, *Arnoldo Mondadori*, p.450
48 Albonetti (ed.), *Non c'è tutto nei romanzi*, p.100
49 Bordoni, *Il romanzo di consumo*, p.36
50 Albonetti (ed.), *Non c'è tutto nei romanzi*, pp.122–3
51 Ibid., pp.52–3
52 Richards, 'The British Board of Film Censors and Content Control in the 1930s: images of Britain', p.103
53 Glancy, *When Hollywood loved Britain*, p.41
54 Richards, 'The British Board of Film Censors . . .', p.105
55 Albonetti (ed.), *Non c'è tutto nei romanzi*, p.152
56 Ibid., pp.245–7, 343, 263
57 Ibid., pp.70–2
58 Ibid., pp.74–5
59 Ibid., p.343
60 Ibid., p.512
61 Ibid., p.443
62 Guerri, 'La Mondadori e la politica del ventennio', pp.90–1
63 Decleva, *Mondadori*, pp.230–1, 251
64 Albonetti (ed.), *Non c'è tutto nei romanzi*, p.560
65 Beynet, 'L'image fasciste de l'Amérique', p.62
66 De Donato and Stacchini (eds), *I best seller del ventennio*, pp.616–18
67 Albonetti, *Non c'è tutto nei romanzi*, p.37
68 Bordoni, *Il romanzo di consumo*, p.87
69 Ibid., p.73
70 Ibid., pp.88–9
71 Article in *Popolo d'Italia*, 27 March 1923 cited in Silva, *Ideologia e Arte del fascismo*, p.105
72 Argentieri, *L'occhio del regime*, pp.24, 49
73 Brunetta, *Storia del cinema italiano 1895–1945*, pp.221–4
74 Forgacs, *Italian Culture in the Industrial Era 1880–1980*, p.70
75 Brunetta, *Storia del cinema italiano 1895–1945*, p.227
76 Ben-Ghiat, *Fascist Modernities. Italy, 1922–1945*, p.75
77 Ibid., pp.80–4
78 On the urban–rural conflict see Hay, *Popular Film Culture in Fascist Italy*, pp.139–49
79 Details from Mariotti and Siniscalchi, *Il mito di Cinecittà*, pp.18–19
80 Hay, *Popular Film Culture in Fascist Italy*, pp.71–2
81 Ibid., p.87
82 Victoria De Grazia, 'Mass Culture and Sovereignty: The American Challenge to European Cinemas, 1920–1960', p.75
83 Rabinbach, 'La lecture, le roman populaire et le besoin impérieux de participer . . .', p.110
84 Peukert, *Inside Nazi Germany*, p.195
85 Ibid., p.188
86 Mosse, *The Nationalization of the Masses*, pp.116–17
87 Robertson, 'From Naturalism to National Socialism (1890–1945)', pp.383–5; see also Stark, *Entrepreneurs of ideology*, p.241
88 Rabinbach, 'La lecture, le roman populaire . . .', pp.116–17
89 Ibid., pp.116–18
90 Ibid., pp.123–4. Even better according to Richards, *The German Bestseller in the 20th Century. A complete Bibliography and Analysis 1915–1940*, figures on p.184

91 Rabinbach, 'La lecture, le roman populaire . . .', pp.124–6
92 Richards, *The German Bestseller in the 20th Century*, p.55
93 See the figures in Levi, *Music in the Third Reich*, pp.216–17
94 Meyer, 'The Nazi Musicologist as Myth Maker in the Third Reich', p.649–50
95 Ibid., p.661
96 The story is told by Fantel in his *Johann Strauss. Father and Son*, pp.219–20; the authentic documents were found in 1945
97 Gronow and Saunio, *An International History of the Recording Industry*, p.83
98 Stark, *Entrepreneurs of ideology*, p.241. *Mein Kampf* is not listed at all, perhaps for political reasons, in Richards, *The German Bestseller in the 20th Century*
99 Panse, 'Censorship in Nazi Germany . . .', pp.141–2
100 Verch, '*The Merchant of Venice* on the German Stage since 1945', pp.85–7
101 Jelavich, *Berlin Cabaret*, pp.230–31, 244–5
102 Kater, *Different Drummers: Jazz in the Culture of Nazi Germany*, pp.94–5
103 Kershaw, *Popular Opinion and Political Dissent in the Third Reich: Bavaria 1933–1945*, pp.148–9
104 Hermand, 'Art for the People: the Nazi Concept of a Truly Popular Painting', pp.38, 44, 46
105 Rentschler, 'The testament of Dr. Goebbels', p.317
106 De Grazia, 'Mass Culture and Sovereignty . . .', p.77
107 von Papen, 'Keeping the home fires burning? Women and the German homefront film 1940–43', p.48
108 Peukert, *Inside Nazi Germany*, p.191
109 Kater, *Different Drummers*, p.112
110 De Grazia, 'Mass Culture and Sovereignty . . .', p.79
111 Sapiro, 'Salut littéraire et littérature du salut', p.36
112 Sapiro, 'La raison littéraire . . .', p.6

46 : Mass Culture: The American Challenge

1 Gronow and Saunio, *An International History of the Recording Industry*, pp.72–3
2 Trumpbour, *Selling Hollywood to the World*, p.19
3 Reitlinger, *The Economics of Taste*, Vol. 1, pp.176–7
4 Ibid., p.181
5 Ibid., Vol. 2, pp.225–7
6 Claeys, 'Mass Culture and World Culture on "Americanization" . . .', pp.76–7
7 This figure is cited in Bordwell, Staiger and Thompson, *The Classical Hollywood Cinema. Film Style and Mode of Production to 1960*, Routledge, London 1985, p.10
8 Jeanne, 'L'invasion cinématographique américaine', pp.857–8
9 Ibid., pp.866–7
10 Ibid., p.869
11 Ibid., pp.879–82
12 Aron's words can be found on p.81 of Claeys, 'Mass Culture and World Culture on "Americanization" . . .'
13 Gramsci, *Selections from the Cultural Writings*, pp.278–9
14 Ben-Ghiat, 'Italian Fascism and the Aesthetics of the "Third Way"', p.302
15 Jameson, *Postmodernism or the Cultural Logic of Late Capitalism*, p.289
16 Fernandez, *Il mito dell'America negli intellettuali italiani*, pp.19–20
17 Ibid., p.67
18 See the excellent survey by Galloux-Fournier, 'Un regard sur l'Amérique: voyageurs français aux États-Unis (1919–1939)', pp.308–23
19 Cecchi, *America Amara*, pp.41, 49, 82, 255
20 Duhamel, *Scènes de la vie future*, p.38
21 Ibid., pp.49, 53, 59, 203–6
22 Ibid., pp.244–5
23 Maurois, *Chantiers Américains*, pp.174, 180
24 Gentile, 'Impending Modernity: Fascism and the Ambivalent Image of the United States', p.7
25 Carré, 'La transformation de l'espace privé ou la magie électrique', p.1330
26 Beynet, 'L'image fasciste de l'Amérique', pp.48–60
27 Cross, *Time and Money*, pp.134, 145
28 Hill, *Think and Grow Rich*, p.71
29 Brande, *Wake Up and Live!*, pp.72, 107
30 Pitkin, *Life begins at Forty*, p.31
31 Traverso, *The Origins of Nazi Violence*, p.122
32 Barrows, *Distorting Mirrors*, pp.162, 170–3, see also her chapter on Taine, pp.73–92
33 Kaes, 'Cinema and Modernity: On Fritz Lang's *Metropolis*', p.29
34 Spengler, *The Decline of the West*, Vol. 2, pp.462–3
35 This essay has been reprinted in Adorno, *The Culture Industry*, see pp.32, 34; 38
36 Adorno and Horkheimer, *Dialectic of Enlightenment*, pp.121, 126

37 Ibid., pp.133–4
38 See Paul Nizan's review of Jean-Richard
    Bloch's *Naissance d'une culture* in the
    February 1937 issue of the magazine
    Commune, now in Nizan, *Pour une
    nouvelle culture*, p.252; see also Gramsci's
    critique in his *Selections from the Cultural
    Writings*, p.101
39 See the discussion in Caygill, *Walter
    Benjamin*, pp.97–106
40 Orwell, *The Road to Wigan Pier*, p.117
41 Aragon, 'Léo Ferré et la mise en chanson'
42 Cohen-Solal, *Sartre*, p.79
43 Monod, 'Dashiell Hammett, L'Amérique
    et le Stylo-Camera'
44 Kracauer, originally written in 1926, now
    in *The Mass Ornament*, p.325; see also
    Mülder-Bach, 'Cinematic Ethnology:
    Siegfried Kracauer's The White Collar
    Masses', p.52
45 Auffret, *La France de l'entre-deux-guerres
    1919/1939*, p.110

47 : Interwar Cinema

1   See figures on Japan, the USA, Great
    Britain, West Germany, Italy, France and
    Spain in Docherty, Morrison and Tracey,
    *The Last Picture Show? Britain's changing
    film audiences*, p.3
2   Further data in Forest, 'L'évolution de
    l'exploitation en France dans les années
    cinquante', pp.191–2; see also, for Britain,
    Hiley, ' "Let's go to the pictures". The
    British Cinema Audience in the 1920s and
    1930s', p.46
3   Ramsaye (ed.), *The 1938–39 Motion
    Picture Almanac*, pp.7, 1015
4   I have extended a point made by Richard
    Taylor in his 'Ideology as mass
    entertainment: Boris Shumyatsky and
    Soviet cinema in the 1930s', p.193
5   Saunders, *Hollywood in Berlin*, p.20
6   Ramsaye (ed.), *The 1938–39 Motion
    Picture Almanac*, p.927
7   Hiley, ' "Let's go to the pictures". . . '
    pp.40–1
8   Ibid., p.47
9   Ibid., p.48
10 Harper, 'A Lower Middle-Class Taste-
    Community in the 1930s: admissions
    figures at the Regent Cinema,
    Portsmouth, UK', pp.565–7
11 Ibid., p.570
12 Altenloh, 'A Sociology of the Cinema',
    p.260
13 Vasey, 'The World Wide Spread of the
    Cinema', p.57 and De Grazia, 'Mass
    Culture and Sovereignty . . .', p.59
14 Trumpbour, *Selling Hollywood to the
    World*, p.17
15 Ibid., p.62
16 Cited in De Grazia, 'Mass Culture and
    Sovereignty . . .', p.53
17 Trumpbour, *Selling Hollywood to the
    World*, p.2
18 Hawkridge, 'British Cinema from
    Hepworth to Hitchcock', pp.134–5
19 According to the index of popularity or
    'popstat' constructed by Sedgwick in his
    *Popular Filmgoing in 1930s Britain. A
    Choice of Pleasures*, Chapter Four,
    especially pp.92–6
20 Vasey, 'The World-Wide Spread of the
    Cinema', pp.57–8
21 Stead, 'Hollywood's Message for the
    World: the British Response in the
    Nineteenth Thirties', pp.20–1
22 Jaikumar, 'An Act of transition: empire
    and the making of a national British film
    industry, 1927', p.122
23 Glancy, *When Hollywood Loved Britain*,
    p.21
24 Ibid., p.11
25 Ibid., p.10
26 Ibid., pp.32–3
27 Ibid., pp.67, 75, 77
28 Nowell-Smith, 'The beautiful and the bad:
    notes on some actorial stereotypes', p.138
29 Glancy, *When Hollywood Loved Britain*,
    p.73
30 Glancy, *The 39 Steps*, pp.27–9
31 Abel, 'French Silent Cinema', pp.119–22
32 Vasey, 'The World Wide Spread of the
    Cinema', p.59
33 Ropars-Wuilleumier, 'Entre Films et
    Textes: L'intervalle de l'imaginaire', p.69
34 Fell, *Film and the Narrative Tradition*,
    pp.44–5
35 Adorno and Horkheimer, *Dialectic of
    Enlightenment*, p.134
36 Selznick, *Memo from: David O. Selznick*,
    pp.258
37 Cited in Leff, *Hitchcock and Selznick*, p.39
38 Ibid., p.47
39 Ibid., p.70
40 Robertson, 'From Naturalism to National
    Socialism (1890–1945)', p.372
41 Musser, 'Documentary', p.90
42 Cranston, 'In Fact: Nanook of the North'
43 Burton and Thomson, 'Nanook and the
    Kirwinians . . .', p.79
44 Charles Wolfe, 'Historicising the "Voice
    of God". . . .', p.149

45 Goldstein, *The War for the Public Mind*, p.9

46 See Greg Garrett's entry on 'Film' in *Censorship. A World Encyclopedia*, p.802

47 Kuhn, *Cinema, Censorship and Sexuality, 1909–1925*, p.25

48 Richards, 'The British Board of Film Censors and Content Control in the 1930s: images of Britain', p.96

49 Robertson, *The Hidden Cinema. British Film Censorship in Action 1913–1975*, p.2

50 Stead, 'Hollywood's Message for the World: the British response in the nineteen thirties', p.24

51 Robertson, *The Hidden Cinema*, p.159

52 Richards, 'The British Board of Film Censors and Content Control in the 1930s: foreign affairs', pp.41–2

53 Ramsaye (ed.),*The 1946–47 Motion Picture Almanac*, pp.765, 771

54 Selznick, *Memo from: David O. Selznick*, pp.221–2

55 See picture in Robertson, *The Hidden Cinema*, p.9

56 Trumpbour, *Selling Hollywood to the World*, cit., p.39

57 Saunders, *Hollywood in Berlin*, p.30

58 Lillian Schlissel, 'Introduction' to Mae West, *Three Plays*, pp.10, 15. This is the first published edition of the plays

59 West, *Goodness Had Nothing to Do with It*, p.93

60 Wainscott, *The Emergence of the Modern American Theatre 1914–1929*, p.54

61 West, *Goodness Had Nothing to Do with It*, p.190

62 Entry on 'Mae West' by Kattelman in *Censorship. A World Encyclopedia*, pp.2618–19

63 Hall, *Cities in Civilization*, p.552

64 What follows has been culled from Finler's useful compendium, *The Hollywood Story*

65 Ibid., p.322

66 Desser, ' "Consumerist realism": American Jewish life and the classical Hollywood cinema', p.261

67 Ford, *The International Jew*, Chapter Ten, available online at a number of anti-Semitic sites, such as *www.biblebelievers.org.au/intern_jew.htm*

68 Finler, *The Hollywood Story*, p.472

69 See Taylor, *Scarlett's Women. Gone with the Wind and its Female Fans*, in particular, pp.95–101

70 Leff, *Hitchcock and Selznick*, p.37

71 Saunders, *Hollywood in Berlin*, p.21

72 Ibid., pp.4–5

73 Ibid., p.23

74 Elsaesser, *Weimar Cinema and After*, p.63

75 Ibid., pp.117–19

76 Brooks, 'Pabst and Lulu', p.124

77 Cited in Elsaesser, *Weimar Cinema and After*, p.260

78 Cited in ibid., p.259

79 Brooks, 'Pabst and Lulu', p.125

80 Saunders, *Hollywood in Berlin*, p.55

81 Ibid., p.57

82 Siegfried Kracauer, 'Calico-World' in his *The Mass Ornament*, p.281

83 Kaes, 'Cinema and Modernity: On Fritz Lang's *Metropolis*', pp.19–22

84 Salt, *Film Style and Technology*, pp.190–1

85 Saunders, *Hollywood in Berlin*, pp.103, 130

86 Ibid., pp.150ff

87 See graphs in appendices B and C in Hay, *Popular Film Culture in Fascist Italy*

88 Sellier, 'Danielle Darrieux, Michèle Morgan and Micheline Presle in Hollywood: the threat to French identity', pp.201–14

89 Eisenstein, *Selected Works*, Volume I, *Writings, 1922–34*, pp.31–2

90 Rubinstein, 'Observation on Keaton's *Steamboat Bill, Jr*', p.245

91 Horak, 'German exile cinema, 1933–1950', p.374

92 See John Russell Taylor, *Strangers in Paradise. The Hollywood Émigrés 1933–1950*

93 Maltby, 'The Production Code and the Hays Office', pp.53–4

94 Renoir, *Ma vie et mes films*, p.177

95 Ibid., p.185

96 Crafton, 'Tricks and Animation', pp.75–7

97 Cousins, *The Story of Film*, p.165

98 Leslie, *Hollywood Flatlands*, pp.219–22, 230

99 Salt, *Film Style and Technology*, p.181

100 Belton, 'Awkward transitions: Hitchcock's *Blackmail* and the dynamics of early film sound', p.235

101 Saunders, *Hollywood in Berlin*, p.223

102 De Grazia, 'Mass Culture and Sovereignty . . .', p.72

103 Malcolm Stewart, *My Other Life*, unpublished manuscript, July 2004

104 Cousins, *The Story of Film*, p.118

105 Stewart, *My Other Life*

106 Billard, *L'Âge classique du cinéma français*, p.27

107 I am indebted for aspects of this description to Michael Wood's review of Todd McCarthy's *Howard Hawks: the*

Grey Fox of Hollywood (1997), entitled 'Looking Good' in New York Review of Books, 20 November 1997, p.27. In McCarthy's book the scene is mentioned on p.371, Chapter 26, but not in detail

108 Cousins, The Story of Film, p.137

109 McMurtry, 'The West without Chili', pp.38–9

110 Rossel-Kirschen, Pathé-Natan. La véritable histoire, pp.21ff

111 Willems, 'Aux origines du groupe Pathé-Natan', p.95

112 Choukroun, 'Contrôler les studios, un atout pour les grandes compagnies françaises des années trente?', p.113

113 Willems, 'Aux origines du groupe Pathé-Natan', pp.109–10

114 Cousins, The Story of Film, pp.90–2

115 Ibid., p.94

116 Billard, L'Âge classique du cinéma français, pp.23, 29

117 Ibid., pp.660–5

118 Ibid., pp.211–15

119 Slavin, Colonial Cinema and Imperial France, 1919–1939, pp.184–5

120 Grottle Strebel, 'French Social Cinema and the Popular Front', p.499

121 Ibid., p.501

122 Cousins, The Story of Film, pp.175–6

123 Rivette, 'Génie de Howard Hawks', p.16

48 : The Cinema After World War II

1 BFI Film and Television Handbook 2003–4 (bfi screenonline)

2 Ciampi, 'Limiti per la spesa per spettacoli in Italia', p.101

3 Harper and Porter, 'Cinema Audience Tastes in 1950s Britain', pp.66–8

4 Forbes, Les Enfants du Paradis, p.9

5 Garçon, 'Ce curieux âge d'or des cinéastes français', p.198

6 Ibid., p.199

7 Forbes, Les Enfants du Paradis, p.13

8 Garçon, 'Ce curieux age d'or des cinéastes français', p.194

9 Forbes, Les Enfants du Paradis, pp.18–19

10 Forgacs, Rome Open City, pp.10, 65–70

11 Geraghty, 'Cinema As a Social Space: Understanding Cinema-Going in Britain, 1947–63' in online version: http://www.frameworkonline.com/42cg.htm

12 Hill, 'British Cinema as National Cinema: Production, Audience and Representation', p.248

13 Macnab, J. Arthur Rank and the British Film Industry, pp.36–7

14 Ibid., pp.163–4

15 Ibid., pp.40, 48

16 Ibid., p.121

17 Ibid., p.61

18 Ellwood, 'Un Americano a Roma: a 1950s Satire of Americanization', p.94

19 Le Forestier, 'L'accueil en France des films américains de réalisateurs français à l'époque des accords Blum-Byrnes', p.80

20 Cited in Jeancolas, 'From the Blum-Byrnes Agreement to the GATT affair', p.51

21 Le Forestier, 'L'accueil en France des films américains . . .', p.92

22 Hubert-Lacombe, Le cinéma français dans la guerre froide 1946–1956, pp.154–9

23 Micheli, Cinema Ungherese, p.79

24 Haudiquet: 'Le cinéma hongrois (1945–1963)', pp.29–30

25 Balio, 'Les films français et le marché du cinéma d'art et essai aux États-Unis 1948–1995', pp.196–7

26 Swann, 'The British Culture Industries and the Mythology of the American Market . . .', p.42

27 Street, Transatlantic Crossings. British Feature Films in the USA, p.94

28 Ibid., p.95

29 Ibid., pp.99–104

30 Statistics reported in Mage, 'L'exploitation des films européens aux États-Unis', p.43

31 Ibid., p.36

32 See figures in Street, Transatlantic Crossings, pp.250–9

33 Figures on audience: BFI http://www.bfi.org.uk/features/ultimatefilm/chart/complete.php

34 Macnab, J. Arthur Rank and the British Film Industry, p.84

35 Figures on audience: BFI http://www.bfi.org.uk/features/ultimatefilm/chart/complete.php

36 Ramsden, 'Refocusing "The People's War": British War Films of the 1950s', p.42

37 Ibid., pp.36, 45

38 Rentschler, 'Germany: Nazism and After', p.381

39 Jäckel, 'Dual Nationality Film Productions in Europe after 1945', pp.232–3

40 Nowell-Smith, 'Introduction' in Nowell-Smith and Ricci (eds), Hollywood and Europe, p.9

41 Jäckel, 'Dual Nationality Film Productions in Europe after 1945', p.234

42 Balmand, 'Les best-sellers de la guerre froide', p.74, who cites as his source *L'Express* of 16 April 1955
43 'Le livre d'humour' in *Bulletin du livre*, 1 July 1961, pp.13–19
44 Cited in Codelli, 'La Commedia Italo-Francese', p.26
45 De Pirro, 'Espansione all'estero del film italiano nel dopoguerra', pp.209, 215
46 Data in *Lo spettacolo*, Vol. 10, No. 2, April–June 1960, p.121
47 Ciampi, 'Aspetti delle diffusione del cinematografo nelle zone depresse dell'Italia', pp.3–4
48 Data in *Lo spettacolo*, Vol. 10, No. 2, April–June 1960, p.104
49 Data in *Lo spettacolo*, Vol. 10, No. 4, October–December 1960, p.281
50 Fellini, *Intervista sul cinema*, p.107
51 'Qualche confronto internazionale sullo sviluppo del cinematografo dall'anteguerra ad oggi' in *Lo spettacolo* No. 2, April–June 1951, p.183
52 Menarini and Pescatore, 'Il cinema popolare e i processi di definizione dello spettatore', pp.177–81
53 See tables in Fanchi and Mosconi (eds), *Spettatori. Forme di consumo e pubblici del cinema in Italia 1930–60*, p.261
54 Huber, *La RFA et sa Télévision*, pp.30–1
55 Erdoğ and Kaya, 'Institutional Intervention in the Distribution and Exhibition of Hollywood Films in Turkey', pp.49–53
56 Montebello, 'Les intellectuels, le peuple et le cinéma', p.171
57 O'Neil, 'Alfred Hitchcock', pp.310–11
58 Figures in Finler, *Alfred Hitchcock*, pp.166–7. This book is a goldmine of information on the profitability of Hitchcock's films
59 Gomery, 'Transformation of the Hollywood System', p.443
60 Finler, *The Hollywood Story*, pp.15–22
61 See Geraghty, 'Cinema as a Social Space: Understanding Cinema-Going in Britain, 1947–63'
62 Lefcourt, 'Aller au cinéma, aller au peuple', pp.109–10
63 Zha, *China Pop*, p.141
64 Source: Massimo Loche, native of Ozieri, 5 September 2003, verbal communication
65 Himmelweit, Oppenheim, and Vince, *Television and the Child*, p.492

49 : More Books

1 McAleer, *Popular Reading and Publishing in Britain 1914–1950*, p.57
2 Ibid., pp.65, 87
3 UNESCO, *An international survey of book production during the last decades*, p.1
4 Ibid., p.4
5 Dumazedier and Hassenforder, *Éléments pour une sociologie comparée de la production, de la diffusion et de l'utilisation du livre*, p.15
6 Ibid., p.17
7 These figures were used in two different papers at the same conference on publishing: ISTAT: *Sommario di statistiche storiche dell'Italia 1861–1965* was cited by Livolsi in his 'Lettura e altri consumi culturali negli anni '20–'40', p.76, while those reported in the *Bollettino delle pubblicazioni italiane ricevuto per diritto di stampa*, Florence 1942 (i.e. the Biblioteca Nazionale Centrale of Florence) were used by Borruso, 'Aspetti della nascita dell'industria editoriale', p.87
8 UNESCO, *An international survey of book production during the last decades*, p.15
9 Livolsi, 'Lettura e altri consumi culturali negli anni '20–'40', p.66
10 Ibid., p.63
11 Escarpit, *La révolution du livre*, p.39
12 Payne and Burke (eds), *80 Years of Best Sellers 1895–1975*, p.10. The Bowker company are the publishers of *Publishers' Weekly*
13 Schmoller, 'The Paperback Revolution', pp.298–301
14 McAleer, *Popular Reading and Publishing in Britain*, p.59
15 Ibid., pp.45–6, 62–3, 74
16 Mistler, *La Librairie Hachette de 1826 à nos jours*, p.384
17 Dumazedier and Hassenforder, *Éléments pour une sociologie comparée . . .*, p.30
18 Ibid., p.29
19 McAleer, *Popular Reading and Publishing in Britain*, p.49
20 Keynes, *Collected Writings*, Vol. XIX, p.670
21 Ibid., pp.664–70, originally in *The Nation and Athenaeum*, 12 March 1927, pp.666–8
22 McAleer, *Popular Reading and Publishing in Britain*, p.55
23 Albonetti (ed.), *Non c'è tutto nei romanzi*, p.28
24 Théodore-Aubanel, *Comment on lance un*

nouveau livre, pp.13, 17 (pseudonym of D.B. Drucker and W.R. Borg)

25 Ibid., see list
26 Assouline, *Gaston Gallimard*, p.116
27 Tadié, *Marcel Proust*, p.822
28 Ibid., p.830; and Carter, *Marcel Proust. A Life*, pp.710–11
29 Tadié, *Marcel Proust*, p.831
30 Carter, *Marcel Proust*, p.211
31 Assouline, *Gaston Gallimard*, p.62
32 Ibid., pp.121–4
33 Ibid., pp.279–80
34 Halkin, *The Enemy Reviewed*, pp.2–3, 97
35 Albonetti (ed.), *Non c'è tutto nei romanzi*, p.42
36 Ibid., p.84
37 Kracauer, 'The Biography as an Art Form of the New Bourgeoisie' (1930), now in *The Mass Ornament*, p.101
38 Barrère, '*Dédalo*, 1922: un fil d'Arianne dans le labyrinthe de la concentration industrielle (Domaine du livre espagnol)', pp.157–60
39 Botrel, 'Les recherches sur le livre et la lecture en Espagne aux XVIIIe et XXe siècles', p.57
40 Botrel, 'Les libraires français en Espagne 1840–1920', p.78
41 Halkin, *The Enemy Reviewed*, pp.9, 11–13
42 Goudkov and Doubine, 'La culture littéraire' (1988), pp.251–3
43 Bienkowska and Chamerska, *Books in Poland. Past and Present*, pp.30–1
44 Mounin, *Linguistique et traduction*, p.24
45 Ganne, *Interviews impubliables* (1952), p.105
46 De Singly, 'Un cas de dédoublement littéraire', pp.77–8
47 Ganne, *Interviews impubliables*, pp.122–30
48 Laurent, *Histoire égoïste*, p.252
49 Showalter, 'Emeralds on the home front'
50 Laurent, *Histoire égoïste*, pp.251–3
51 De Singly, 'Un cas de dédoublement littéraire', p.79
52 See both texts in Laurent, *Discours de réception de Jacques Laurent à l'Académie Française*
53 Winston, 'Gender and sexual identity in the modern French novel', p.225
54 *Microsoft Encarta Premium Suite 2005*. 1993–2004
55 Keynes, *Collected Writings*, Vol. XIX, pp.664–5
56 Cohen-Solal, *Sartre. A Life*, p.323
57 Ibid., p.113
58 Jones, *Catherine Cookson. The Biography*, pp.292, 294, 300, 320

59 Renai, 'Il caso Pitigrilli: analisi di *Dolicocefala bionda*', p.275–6
60 Reich-Ranicki, *The Author of Himself. The Life of Marcel Reich-Ranicki*, pp.240–1
61 Reflections inspired by a passage in the publisher Robert Laffont's memoirs: Robert Laffont, *Éditeur*, p.196

50 : Popular Genres: Crimes and the Future

1 For an overview see Fischer, *The Empire Strikes Out: Kurt Lasswitz, Hans Dominik, and the Development of German Science Fiction*
2 Roberts, *Science Fiction*, pp.69–70
3 Ibid., p.15
4 Scholes and Rabin, *Science Fiction History Science Vision*, p.39
5 Fischer, *The Empire Strikes Out*, pp.6–7
6 James, *Science Fiction in the 20th century*, p.39
7 Scholes and Rabin, *Science Fiction History Science Vision*, pp.28, 204
8 James, *Science Fiction in the 20th century*, p.48
9 Scholes and Rabin, *Science Fiction History Science Vision*, pp.105–9
10 Ibid., p.12
11 Roberts, *Science Fiction*, p.81
12 http://www.cnn.com/US/9706/15/ufo.poll/index.html
13 Atwood, 'Mystery Man', p.21
14 Todorov, 'Typologie du roman policier' in *Poétique de la prose*, pp.14–15
15 Abescat 'Depuis le commencement, le polar s'écrit aussi au féminin', p.26
16 Monk, *Ludwig Wittgenstein. The Duty of Genius*, pp.528–9
17 Boileau-Narcejac, *Le roman policier*, p.118
18 Soriano *Guide de la littérature pour la jeunesse*, p.97
19 Pyrhönen, *Murder from an Academic Angle: An Introduction to the Study of the Detective Narrative*, p.10
20 Ousby, *The Crime and Mystery Book*, p.84
21 Boileau-Narcejac, *Le roman policier*, pp.35–6
22 Ibid., p.35
23 Ibid., p.38
24 See Lorenzo Montano's report in Albonetti (ed.), *Non c'è tutto nei romanzi*, pp.129–31
25 Gorceix, 'En manière d'introduction . . .' in Gorceix (ed.), *L'identité culturelle de la Belgique et de la Suisse francophones*, p.15
26 Simenon, *L'Affaire Saint-Fiacre*, p.159
27 Grella, 'Simenon and Maigret', pp.54–61

28 Petronio, 'Quel pasticciaccio brutto del romanzo poliziesco', p.16
29 Assouline, *Simenon. Biographie*, pp.99, 107, 149 and passim
30 Ibid., p.179
31 Ibid., pp.218–19
32 Ibid., p.240
33 Ibid., p.260
34 Ibid., p.486
35 Boileau-Narcejac, *Le roman policier*, pp.65–6
36 Assouline, *Simenon*, p.55
37 See notes in *Désiré*, Vol. 14, No.20, 1978, pp.485–90
38 Lundin, *The Swedish Crime Story*, pp.17–19
39 Isola, *Cari amici vicini e lontani*, p.279
40 Petronio, 'Sulle tracce del giallo' p.59; Canova, 'Scerbanenco e il delitto alla milanese'; Canova, 'Giorgio Scerbanenco'
41 Scerbanenco, *I ragazzi del massacro*, pp.15, 25, 65

51 : The Press

1 Chalaby, *The Invention of Journalism*, p.39
2 Williams, *The Long Revolution*, p.204
3 Miller, *Magnum. Fifty years at the front line of history*, p.27
4 Ibid., p.19
5 Ibid., p.51
6 Ory, *La Belle Illusion*, p.28
7 Sauvage and Maréchal, 'Les racines d'un succès', pp.32–3
8 See the issue of *L'Illustrazione italiana*, No. 2, 1922
9 Thwaites, 'Circles of Confusion and Sharp Vision: British News Photography 1919–39', p.100
10 Huth, *La Radiodiffusion, Puissance mondiale*, p.82
11 McAleer, *Popular Reading and Publishing in Britain 1914–1950*, p.47
12 Capecchi and Livolsi, *La stampa quotidiana in Italia*, p.102
13 Jankowski, *Stavisky: A Confidence Man in the Republic of Virtue*, p.133
14 Murialdi, *La Stampa italiana*, p.111
15 Chalaby, *The Invention of Journalism*, p.77
16 Lerner, *La Dépêche, Journal de la Démocratie*, p.472
17 Ibid., pp.205–9, 230
18 Ibid., pp.260–1
19 Cited in Curran and Seaton, *Power without Responsibility*, p.49
20 Lawrence, 'Fascist violence and the politics of public order in inter-war Britain: the Olympia debate revisited', pp.246–7
21 Amaury, *Histoire du plus grand quotidien de la IIIe République: Le Petit Parisien, 1876–1944*, Volume Two, p.1227
22 Ibid., Volume One, p.290
23 Ibid., pp.284, 353
24 Ibid., pp.285, 288
25 Ibid., pp.289–91
26 Smith, 'The Fall and Fall of the Third *Daily Herald*, 1930–64', pp.179–82
27 Jeanneney and Julliard, '*Le Monde*' de Beuve-Méry ou le métier d'Alceste, pp.8, 47, 57, 62, 74, 257; Padioleau, '*Le Monde*' et le '*Washington Post*', pp.18, 19, 23, 32, 57, 64
28 Asor Rosa, 'Il giornalista: un mestiere difficile', pp.1234–5
29 Murialdi, *La Stampa italiana. Dalla Liberazione alla crisi di fine secolo*, pp.26–7
30 Ibid., p.38
31 Ibid., p.61
32 Ibid., pp.52, 55, 57, 60, 64–5
33 Ibid., p.135
34 Ibid., p.90
35 Ibid., p.109
36 Ekstein, 'The Frankfurter Zeitung: Mirror of Weimar Democracy', p.5
37 Hitler, *Mein Kampf*, pp.222–3
38 Ekstein, 'The Frankfurter Zeitung: Mirror of Weimar Democracy', pp.6, 15, 18, 27, 28
39 Murialdi, *La Stampa italiana*, p.144; the author was *Il Giorno*'s first deputy editor
40 White, *Women's Magazines 1693–1968*, p.214
41 Ibid., pp.94–5
42 Ibid., p.95
43 Barrell and Braithwaite, *The Business of Women's Magazines*, p.18
44 Figures in Amaury, *Histoire du plus grand quotidien de la IIIe République*, Vol. One, p.396
45 Giet, '20 ans d'amour en couverture', p.18
46 White, *Women's Magazines 1693–1968*, pp.96, 99, 108, 123

52 : Comic Strips

1 Banville, 'A Life Elsewhere', p.24
2 Bott, *The Life and Works of Alfred Bestall: illustrator of Rupert Bear*, pp.66–8
3 Filippini, Glenat, Martens and Sadoul, *Histoire de la bande dessinée en France et en Belgique. Des origines à nos jours*, p.37
4 Gasca, 'Espagne', pp.126–7
5 Gifford, 'Grande Bretagne', p.99
6 Becciu, *Il fumetto in Italia*, pp.72, 95
7 Bertieri, 'Italie', p.64
8 Ibid., pp.63–4

9 Filippini, Glenat, Martens and Sadoul, *Histoire de la bande dessinée en France et en Belgique,* p.20

10 Van Gool, 'Pays-Bas', p.123

11 Schizzerotto, 'I fumetti: consumi e contenuti', p.228

12 Caradec, *Histoire de la Littérature enfantine en France,* p.210

13 Masson, *Lire la bande dessinée,* p.79; the frame can be found on p.38 of the album

14 Singer, 'Serials', p.110

15 Burroughs, *Tarzan of the Apes,* p.6

16 Ibid., p.157

17 Springhall, *Youth, Popular Culture and Moral Panics,* pp.125–41

18 Lent, 'Comic Books', pp.556–7

19 Couperie, Filippini and Moliterni, 'France', pp.41, 43

20 Pilloy, *Les compagnes des héros de BD. Des femmes et des bulles,* p.11

21 Wertham, 'Les "crimes comic-books" et la jeunesse américaine', pp.468–536 ; see also Boltanski, 'La constitution du champ de la bande dessinée', p.56

22 Springhall, *Youth, Popular Culture and Moral Panics,* pp.141–6

23 Masson, *Lire la bande dessinée,* p.129

24 Ibid., p.130

25 Boltanski, 'La constitution du champ de la bande dessinée', pp.40–51

26 Originally 'Il mito di Superman e la dissoluzione del tempo', now in English in Eco, *The Role of the Reader,* pp.107–24

27 'Tintin goes to Hollywood', *Observer,* 2 March 2003

28 Gaumier and Moliterni (eds), *Dictionnaire mondial de la Bande Dessinée,* pp.30–1

29 'Les Best sellers 1958–68', *Le Bulletin du Livre,* 15 Décembre 1968, pp.20–6

30 Becciu, *Il fumetto in Italia,* p.133

31 Assouline, *Hergé,* pp.41, 46, 52, 59

32 A full account of such references can be found in Farr, *Tintin: The Complete Companion,* the indispensable text for Tintin addicts

33 Filippini, Glenat, Martens and Sadoul, *Histoire de la bande dessinée en France et en Belgique,* pp.32–7, 63

34 Gaumier and Moliterni (eds), *Dictionnaire mondial de la bande dessinée*

35 Ventrone, 'Tra propaganda e passione. *Grand Hotel* e l'Italia degli anni '50', p.603

36 Bravo, *Il fotoromanzo,* p.15

37 Ventrone, 'Tra propaganda e passione. *Grand Hotel* e l'Italia degli anni '50', p.606

38 Giet, '20 ans d'amour en couverture', p.21

39 Bravo, *Il fotoromanzo,* p.16

40 On the readership see ibid., pp.77, 79

41 Douglas and Malti-Douglas, *Arab Comic Strips,* pp.3–6

42 Gifford, 'Grande Bretagne', p.104

43 Cavalone, 'Il bibliofilo a fumetti', pp.147–9

44 Eco, *Tra menzogna e ironia,* pp.99–100

45 Ito, 'The World of Japanese Ladies' Comics: From Romantic Fantasy to Lustful Perversion', p.68

46 Ibid., p.71

53 : Live Spectacles

1 Huxley and Witts (eds), *The Twentieth-Century Performance Reader,* p.112

2 Figures from the introductions to *The London Stage 1930–1939* and *The London Stage 1950–1959,* both edited by J.P. Wearing

3 Ory, *La Belle Illusion,* pp.379, 304

4 Perkin, *The Rise of Professional Society in England since 1880,* pp.281–3

5 Steiner, *The Death of Tragedy,* p.324

6 Braun, *The Director and the Stage,* p.23

7 Patterson, *The Revolution in German Theatre 1900–1933,* pp.29–38ff

8 Ibid., p.43

9 Ibid., pp.120–4

10 Piscator, *Le Théâtre politique,* pp.130–1

11 Cited in ibid., p.43

12 Mounin, *Linguistique et traduction,* p.153 and Carter, *The New Spirit in the Russian Theatre 1917–28,* p.311

13 Deák, 'Russian Mass Spectacles', pp.7–8

14 Ibid., pp.20–2

15 Steiner, *The Death of Tragedy,* p.311

16 Shapiro, *Oberammergau,* especially pp.119–20

17 Zaitsev, 'Soviet Theatre Censorship', p.120

18 Ibid., pp.126–7

19 Gobetti, *La Frusta teatrale,* p.151

20 Girolami, 'Il carro di Tespi: teatro e fascismo', p.267

21 Verdone, 'Mussolini's "Theatre of the Masses"', pp.134–5

22 Girolami, 'Il carro di Tespi: teatro e fascismo', pp.279–80

23 Verdone, 'Mussolini's "Theatre of the Masses"', p.276

24 Linares, 'Theatre and Falangism at the Beginning of the Franco Régime', p.224

25 Cavallo, *Immaginario e rappresentazione,* pp.7–8, 36

26 Pedullà, 'Il teatro italiano tra le due guerre mondiali', p.332

27 Ibid., p.321

28 Sanguanini, *Il pubblico all'italiana*, p.275
29 Pedullà, 'Il teatro italiano tra le due guerre mondiali', p.322
30 Scarpellini, *Organizzazione teatrale e politica del teatro nell'Italia fascista*, pp.1–2
31 Ibid., pp.3–6
32 Ibid., pp.11–16
33 Ibid., p.143
34 Ibid., pp.196–7
35 Ibid., pp.79–80
36 Ibid., p.85
37 Ibid., pp.187–8
38 Ibid., p.188
39 Nicolodi, *Musica e musicisti nel ventennio fascista*, pp.28–30
40 Petrillo 'La Santificazione a consumo. La domenica della Milano operaia negli anni cinquanta', p.197

54 : The Triumph of the Song

1 Franzina, 'Inni e Canzoni', pp.156–7
2 Gronow and Saunio, *An International History of the Recording Industry*, p.40
3 Van der Merwe, *Origins of the Popular Style*, p.271
4 Knapp, *The American Musical and the Formation of National Identity*, p.103
5 Gänzl, *The Musical. A Concise History*, p.285
6 Rosen, *White Christmas: the Story of an American Song*, p.6
7 Saka, *Histoire de la chanson française de 1938 à nos jours*, pp.16–17, 20
8 Rowe and Schelling, *Memory and Modernity. Popular Culture in Latin America*, pp.35–6
9 Gronow, 'The record industry: the growth of a mass medium', p.64
10 Panassié, *Histoire du vrai jazz*, p.201
11 Cantaloube-Ferrieu, *Chanson et poésie des années 30 aux années 60*, pp.73–5
12 Furtwängler, *Notebooks 1924–54*, p.101
13 Cantaloube-Ferrieu, *Chanson et poésie des années 30 aux années 60*, p.72
14 Ibid., pp.16–17
15 Ibid., p.213
16 Ory, *La Belle Illusion*, p.334
17 Cantaloube-Ferrieu, *Chanson et poésie des années 30 aux années 60*, pp.268–9, 278
18 Interview with Brassens in *Marie-France*, No.127, September 1966, p.46
19 Gronow and Saunio, *An International History of the Recording Industry*, p.67
20 Ibid., p.69
21 For Schoenberg's citation see Chanan, *Repeated Takes*, p.117

22 Chanan, *Repeated Takes*, p.63
23 Bicknell and Philip, 'Gramophone'
24 Chanan, *Repeated Takes*, pp.13–15
25 Schiff, 'Fit only for the filmgoer', p.18
26 Chanan, *Repeated Takes*, p.54
27 Gronow, *Statistics in the Field of Sound Recordings*, p.2, and Gronow and Saunio, *An International History of the Recording Industry*, pp.86, 89
28 Chanan, *Repeated Takes*, p.79
29 Ibid., pp.80–1
30 Buch, 'Le chef d'orchestre: pratiques de l'autorité et métaphores politiques', p.1023
31 Gronow and Saunio, *An International History of the Recording Industry*, p.89
32 Furtwängler, *Notebooks 1924–54*, p.33
33 Ibid., p.36
34 Gronow and Saunio, *An International History of the Recording Industry*, p.53
35 Brooke, 'Soviet Music in the International Arena 1932–41', pp.241–2
36 Adorno, *Prisms*, pp.121–4
37 Wiernicki, *Dal divertimento dei nobili alla propaganda. Storia del Jazz in Russia*, pp.54, 79
38 Ibid., pp.60ff
39 Ibid., p.123
40 Rothstein, 'The Quiet Rehabilitation of the Brick Factory: Early Soviet Popular Music and its Critics', p.374
41 Brooke, 'Soviet Music in the International Arena 1932–41', pp.237–8
42 Ibid., p.241
43 Edström, 'How schottis became "bonnjazz", how Swedish foxtrot defeated jazz, or has Afro-American music ever existed in Sweden?', pp.679–80

55 : Radio

1 Huth, *La Radiodiffusion*, p.34
2 McPherson, 'Before the Met: The Pioneer Days of Radio Opera. Part I, An Overview', p.7
3 Huth, *La Radiodiffusion*, p.34
4 Carter, *The New Spirit in the Russian Theatre 1917–28*, p.292
5 Miquel, *Histoire de la Radio et de la Télévision*, pp.41–2
6 Méadel, 'Programmes en masse, programmes de masse? La diffusion de la radio en France pendant les années trente', p.55
7 Ibid., pp.51–2, and Pegg, *Broadcasting and Society 1919–1939*, p.7
8 Figures in Huth, *La Radiodiffusion*

(section on country by country statistics);
see also Miquel, *Histoire de la Radio et de
la Télévision*, p.8, and, for Britain, Pegg,
Broadcasting and Society, p.7

9 Huth, *La Radiodiffusion*, pp.168, 183
10 Isola, 'Dalla scatola della musica al
radiocane . . .', p.131
11 Isola, *Cari amici vicini e lontani*, pp.264,
348
12 Stewart, *My Other Life*
13 Briggs, *The History of Broadcasting in the
United Kingdom*, Vol. II, p.606
14 Scannell and Cardiff, *A Social History of
British Broadcasting*, Vol. 1, *1923–39*,
pp.269–73
15 Griset, 'Les communications en France',
p.1267
16 Frédéric Barbier and Catherine Bertho
Lavenir, *Histoire des médias, de Diderot à
Internet*, Armand Colin, Paris 1996,
pp.210–11
17 Gorham, *Forty Years of Irish Broadcasting*,
p.14
18 Ibid., p.169
19 Ibid., p.137
20 McLoone, 'Music Hall Dope and British
Propaganda? Cultural Identity and early
broadcasting in Ireland', p.304
21 Briggs, *The History of Broadcasting*, Vol.
II, p.37
22 Nicholas 'All the News that's Fit to
Broadcast: the Popular Press *versus* the
BBC, 1922–45', p.124
23 Carpenter, *The Envy of the World: Fifty
Years of the BBC Third Programme and
Radio 3: 1946–1996*, p.4
24 Duval, *Histoire de la radio en France*, p.85
25 Stewart, *My Other Life*
26 Carpenter, *The Envy of the World*, p.14
27 Nicholas 'All the News that's Fit to
Broadcast . . .', p.126

28 Carpenter, *The Envy of the World*, p.74
29 The full text can be accessed on *http://
www.bringyou.to/apologetics/p20.htm*
30 Carpenter, *The Envy of the World*,
p.127
31 Miquel, *Histoire de la Radio et de la
Télévision*, p.30
32 Maréchal, *Radio Luxembourg 1933–1993*,
pp.22, 70, 77, 81
33 Ory, *La Belle Illusion*, p.29
34 Griset, 'Les communications en France',
p.1270
35 *BBC Handbook*, 1940, p.63
36 Griset, 'Les communications en France',
pp.1257–8
37 Miquel, *Histoire de la Radio et de la
Télévision*, p.53
38 Cowans, 'Political Culture and Cultural
Politics: The Reconstruction of French
Radio after the Second World War',
pp.150–2
39 Isola, *Cari amici vicini e lontani*, pp.126–8
40 Isola, 'Dalla scatola della musica al
radiocane . . .', pp.130–1
41 *BBC Handbook*, 1940, p.35
42 Griset, 'Les communications en France',
p.1266
43 Miquel, *Histoire de la Radio et de la
Télévision*, p.76
44 Curran and Seaton, *Power without
Responsibility*, p.119
45 Ibid., p.139
46 Huth, *La Radiodiffusion*, pp.118, 132, 140,
148–9
47 Chanan, *Repeated Takes*, p.62
48 Morelli, 'L'Opéra', pp.82–3
49 McPherson, 'Before the Met: The Pioneer
Days of Radio Opera. Part I, An
Overview', p.10
50 Chanan, *Repeated Takes*, pp.60–1
51 Ibid., p.84

PART V

After 1960 : THE ERA OF THE MASS MEDIA

56 : Television: The Universal
Medium

1 Bourgeois, *Radios et télévisions privées en
Allemagne entre la loi et le marché*, p.82

2 Morley, *Television, Audiences and Cultural
Studies*, pp.152–3
3 The classic text on family viewing is
David Morley's *Family Television.
Cultural Power and Domestic*

Leisure,–originally written in 1986; see pp.23–5 and the family interviews described in chapter five

4 Cepak, 'Pubblicità e fiaba in "Carosello"', p.1092

5 Arnheim, 'A Forecast of Television', p.9

6 Grass, *My Century*, p.134

7 McCarthy, '"The Front Row Is Reserved for Scotch Drinkers": Early Television's Tavern Audience', p.32

8 Grasso, *Storia della Televisione Italiana*, p.71

9 Foot, 'Il boom dal basso . . .', p.633

10 Principali, *La TV in una piccola comunità rurale del Lazio*, typewritten document. The author of this interesting study, then a student, belonged himself to this community

11 Ibid., p.2

12 Ibid., p.54

13 Ibid., p.63

14 Ibid., p.48.

15 De Mauro, 'Lingua parlata e TV', p.253

16 Abruzzese and Pinto, 'La radiotelevisione', p.847

17 Principali, *La TV in una piccola comunità rurale del Lazio*, pp.66–76

18 Pius XII, 'Lettera sulla televisione', p.73

19 Yadava and Reddi, 'In the Midst of Diversity: Television in Urban Indian Homes', pp.127–9

20 See Kuhn, 'Heterotopia, heterochronia: place and time in cinema history', p.107

21 Schmitt, Woolf and Anderson, 'Viewing the Viewers . . .', pp.265–81; Bourgeois, *Radios et télévisions privées en Allemagne*, pp.83–4

22 See Jameson, *Postmodernism or the Cultural Logic of Late Capitalism*, p.72

23 Abramson, *The History of Television, 1880–1941*, pp.7–15

24 Ibid., p.26

25 *BBC Handbook*, 1940, p.53

26 Miquel, *Histoire de la Radio et de la Télévision*, p.197

27 Grasso, *Storia della Televisione Italiana*, p.52; Barbier and Lavenir, *Histoire des médias, de Diderot à Internet*, p.240

28 Miquel, *Histoire de la Radio et de la Télévision*, pp.198–9

29 Huber, *La RFA et sa Télévision*, pp.16–24

30 Brochand, *Histoire générale de la radio et de la télévision en France*, Vol. II, p.389; Missika and Wolton, *La Folle du logis*, p.25; Briggs, *The History of Broadcasting in the United Kingdom*, Vol. IV, p.454

31 Brochand, *Histoire générale de la radio et de la télévision en France*, Vol. II, pp.425–6

32 Miquel, *Histoire de la Radio et de la télévision*, p.195

33 Pegg, *Broadcasting and Society 1919–1939*, p.192

34 Abramson, *The History of Television*, pp.19–20

35 Stewart, *My Other Life*

36 Abramson, The History of Television, pp.32, 38

37 Briggs, *The History of Broadcasting*, Vol. IV, p.424

38 Ibid., p.431

39 Ibid., p.433

40 Missika and Wolton, *La Folle du logis*, p.41

41 Mousseau and Brochand, *Histoire de la télévision en France*, p.69

42 Charles de Gaulle, *Mémoires d'espoir. Le renouveau 1958–1962*, p.302

43 Postman, *Amusing Ourselves to Death. Public Discourse in the Age of Show Business*, p.16

44 Meyer with Hunchman, *Media Democracy. How the Media Colonize Politics*, p.29

45 See Himmelweit, Oppenheim, and Vince, *Television and the Child*.

46 The positions of some of the protagonists of this ancient debate can be found in Elihu Katz and Paul Lazarfeld, *Personal Influence*, 1955; W. Shramm, J. Lyle and E. Parker, *Television in the Lives of Our Children*, 1961; Todd Gitlin's 'Media Sociology: the Dominant Paradigm' in *Theory and Society*, No. 2, 1978; and Justin Lewis's *The Ideological Octopus*, 1991

47 Servizio Opinioni, *L'accoglienza del pubblico alla riduzione televisiva de 'I Promessi sposi'*

48 Gitlin, *Prime Time*, p.23

49 Ibid., p.31

50 For a survey of French negative reaction in the press see Antona, 'Reality Show: critique télévisuelle et "lieux du genre"', pp.133–43

51 See the website of the BBC (*BBC.co.uk*) last updated 13 May 2003 and the *Guardian* of 29 May 2004.

52 Isabelle Veyrat-Masson, *Quand la télévision explore le temps*, pp.19, 35

53 RAI Servizio Opinioni, *Dati sulla comprensione di alcune parole da parte di varie categorie di persone 1964–69*

54 Cited by Bourdon, 'L'archaïque et la postmoderne . . .', p.16

55 Ang, *Desperately Seeking the Audience*, p.31

56 Data in Iosifidis, Steemers and Wheeler, *European Television Industries*, pp.12, 30–1,

57 Ibid., p.137

58 *Rights of Passage. British Television in the Global Market*, February 2005, commissioned by the British Television Distributors' Association and available at *www.pact.co.uk*

57 : The Flow of Genres on Television

1 Williams, *Television. Technology and Cultural Form*, p.87

2 'La Modernité, c'est le transitoire, le fugitif, le contingent' wrote Charles Baudelaire in an 1863 essay on the painter Constantine Guys, 'Le Peintre de la vie moderne', p.1163

3 Lodge, *The Practice of Writing*, p.232

4 Servizio Opinioni, *Ascolto e gradimento per le trasmissioni televisive del 1982*, RAI

5 Levi, *Le Trasmissioni TV che hanno fatto (o no) l'Italia*, p.258

6 Front page of report in *Le Monde*, 9 July 2003

7 Personal communication by Gianni Carta

8 Morin, 'Le présent actif dans le feuilleton télévisé', p.241

9 *Audience: Le journal de médiamétrie*, pp.26–7

10 All these figures are culled from Grasso, *Storia della Televisione Italiana*

11 Servizio Opinioni, *Ascolto e gradimento per le trasmisisoni televisive del 1982*

12 Briggs, *The History of Broadcasting in the United Kingdom, Vol. IV, Sound and Vision*, pp.420, 429

13 The term is used in the French version of the book: Daniel Dayan and Elihu Katz, *La television cérémonielle*, PUF, Paris 1996; the original English version, *Media Events. The Live Broadcasting of History*, Harvard University Press 1992, uses the term 'media events'; I prefer 'ceremonial', but I shall cite henceforth from the English version

14 Dayan and Katz, *Media Events*, pp.4–9

15 See Noelle-Neumann, *The Spiral of Silence: Public Opinion – Our Social Skin*

16 Barbier and Lavenir, *Histoire des médias, de Diderot à Internet*, p.242

17 Dayan and Katz, *Media Events*, pp.111–12

18 Ruoff, *An American Family*, p.53

19 Coles, 'Sleazy does it for Jerry', *Guardian*, 19 February 1998

20 Lunt and Stenner, 'The Jerry Springer Show as an emotional public Sphere', p.62

21 *The Times*, 21 April 2005, p.13

22 Piper, 'Reality TV, *Wife Swap* and the drama of banality', p.276

23 Sanguanini, *Grande fratello: istruzioni per l'uso*, pp.19, 110–11

24 Mehl, 'La télévision relationnelle', pp.68ff

25 Some of this information is based on a seminar on *Loft Story* held at the Institut d'Études Politiques on 5 April 2002 with Thomas Valentin, the producer of *Loft Story* for the French channel M6, and the media specialist Dominique Mehl

26 Tolson (ed.), *Television Talk Shows*, p.9

27 Livingstone and Lunt, *Talk on Television*, p.180

28 Holmes, ' "As they really are, and in close up": film stars on 1950s British television', p.171

29 Charaudeau and Ghiglione, *La Parole confisquée. Un genre télévisuel: le talk-show*, p.63

30 Hallenberger, 'La quiete prima della tempesta. La fiction tv tedesca nel 2001', p.81

31 Schechner, Performance Studies, p.92

32 Wagg, 'At ease, corporal', p.3

33 *Dossier de l'audiovisuel* No. 11, January–February 1987, p.5

34 Figures in Grasso, *Storia della Televisione Italiana*

35 Data from *Dieci anni di TV in Italia*, ERI, Rome 1964

36 Mousseau and Brochand, *Histoire de la Télévision en France*, pp.66–8

37 *BBC Handbook*, 1940, p.57

38 Lawson, 'Many Happy Rover's Returns', *Guardian*, media supplement, 16 May 2005

39 Briggs, *The History of Broadcasting in the United Kingdom*, Vol. V, p.192

40 Bluwal, *Un Aller*, p.129

41 Missika and Wolton, *La Folle du logis*, p.39

42 Pasquier, *Les Scénaristes et la télévision*, p.101

43 James, *Science Fiction in the 20th century*, pp.161–3

44 See the data in De Bens and de Smaele, 'The Inflow of American Television Fiction on European Broadcasting Channels', pp.51–71

45 *La Circulation internationale des émissions de télévision*, UNESCO, No. 100, 1986, edited by Tapio Varis, p.45

46 Iosifidis, Steemers and Wheeler, *European Television Industries*, p.134

47 Paulu, *Radio and Television Broadcasting in Eastern Europe*, p.173

48 Miller, *Something Completely Different*, pp.78, 144–5

49 *BFI Film & Television Handbook 2004*, edited by Eddie Dyja, p.58

50 Calculation based on Jelot-Blanc, *Télé-feuilletons. Le dictionnaire de toutes les séries et de tous les feuilletons télévisés depuis les origines de la télévision*, which lists all serials and series of more than thirteen episodes

51 Santoro 'I giudizi dei ragazzi sui programmi a loro dedicati', p.37

52 De Bens and de Smaele, 'The Inflow of American Television Fiction on European Broadcasting Channels', p.55

53 Data in Chaniac and Jézéquel, 'Julie Lescaut vince su Loana. La fiction tv francese nel 2001', p.67

54 De Bens and de Smaele, 'The Inflow of American Television Fiction on European Broadcasting Channels', p.56

55 *Les Écrits de l'image*, 'Le Top 20 des meilleures series televisés en 1997', p.165

56 Agger and Nielsen, 'Il Buono, il brutto e il banale. La fiction tv danese nel 1998', p.186

57 Hallenberger, 'La quiete prima della tempesta . . .', pp.85, 89, 93

58 *La Repubblica*, 5 August 2003

59 Holmlund, 'Pippi and Her Pals', p.4

60 *European Films on European Televisions*, European Audiovisual Observatory, 2000

61 Ang, *Watching Dallas*, p.39

62 Ibid., pp.1, 3, 4–5, 8–9, 22, 30, 40

63 Liebes and Katz, *The Export of Meaning. Cross-cultural readings of 'Dallas'*, pp.xi, 131–8

64 Harvey, 'Nonchan's Dream. NHK morning serialized television novels', p.135

65 See essays by Gill, 'Transformational Magic. Some Japanese super-heroes and monsters' and Standish, 'Akira, Postmodernism and Resistance', pp.33–55, 56–74

66 Hannerz, in his *Cultural Complexity. Studies in the Social Organization of Meaning*, p.243, doubts that many people actually watched *Dallas* in Third World countries.

67 Liebes and Livingstone, 'European Soap Operas. The Diversification of a Genre', p.14

68 Frey-Vor, *Coronation Street: Infinite Drama and British Reality*, p.42

69 So argues its archivist, Little in *The Coronation Street Story*, p.5

70 Frey-Vor, *Coronation Street: Infinite Drama and British Reality*, p.38

71 Ibid., pp.57–8; details of characters added using Little, *The Coronation Street Story*, pp.301–11

72 I thank the makers of *Sous le soleil*, Marathon and its managing director Pascal Breton, for providing me with this information

73 Rowe and Schelling, *Memory and Modernity. Popular Culture in Latin America*, pp.108–9

74 Borenstein, 'Public Offerings: MMM and the Marketing of Melodrama', p.55

75 Andrzejczyk, 'Lo Specchio della vita quotidiana. La fiction tv polacca nel 2001', pp.159–60

76 Zha, *China Pop*, pp.26–7, 34, 36–9

77 Liebes and Livingstone, 'European Soap Operas . . .', p.159

78 Rosen, 'Soap Operas. Search for Yesterday', p.45

79 Buonanno, 'Un orizzonte nebuloso. La fiction italiana nel 2001', pp.101–2

80 *Creative Industries Mapping Document 2001*, Department of Culture, Media and Sport (UK), p.13–02

81 Jeanneney, 'Quelques réflections sur les films de montage', p.204

82 Bousser-Eck and Sauvage, 'Le règne de *Cinq colonnes* 1959–1965', pp.45, 51–2, 63

83 Schlesinger, *Putting 'reality' together. BBC News*, pp.245ff

84 Manigand and Veyrat-Masson, 'Quelle Allemagne? Pour quels Français?', p.113

85 Veyrat-Masson, *Quand la télévision explore le temps*, p.93

86 Lüdtke, ' "Coming to terms with the Past": Illusions of Remembering, Ways of Forgetting Nazism in West Germany', p.544

58 : The Break-Up of Television

1 Crisell, *An Introductory History of British Broadcasting*, p.125

2 Miller, *Something Completely Different*, p.132

3 Ang, *Living Room Wars*, pp.29, 33

4 van der Wurff, 'Supplying and Viewing Diversity. The Role of Competition and Viewer Choice in Dutch Broadcasting', pp.215, 223

5 *Statistical Yearbook 1996*, European Audiovisual Observatory, p.21

6 I have explained the background in my 'Tangentopoli or the Democratization of Corruption: considerations on the end of Italy's First Republic', pp.124–43

7 RAI, Direzione Marketing Strategico, *Innovazione Offerta e Progetti Speciali. Ascolto della TV Mensile TV*, April 2003 (internal document)

8 Missika and Wolton, *La Folle du logis*, pp.68, 79

9 Dominique Wolton, *Éloge du grand public*, p.27

10 Papatheodorou and Machin, 'The Umbilical Cord That was Never Cut', pp.43, 44

11 Papathanassopoulos, 'Media Commercialization and Journalism in Greece' in *European Journal of Communication*, pp.508–9

12 Iosifidis, Steemers and Wheeler, *European Television Industries*, p.25

13 Bourgeois, *Radios et télévisions privées en Allemagne*, p.14

14 Ortoleva, 'La televisione tra le due crisi 1974–1993', p.99

15 Bourgeois, *Radios et télévisions privées en Allemagne*, pp.82, 86

16 *Audience: Le journal de médiamétrie*, No. 19, June 1998, pp.14–15

17 Iosifidis, Steemers and Wheeler, *European Television Industries*, p.121

18 See Lord Annan's recognition of Smith's role as a progenitor in Catterall (ed.), *The Making of Channel 4*, p.92

19 Monteleone, 'Radio pubblica e emittenti commerciali dal 1975 al 1993', pp.193–4

20 Ortoleva, 'La televisione tra le due crisi 1974–1993', p.110

21 I have described this process in my 'Political and Market Forces in Italian Broadcasting', *West European Politics*

22 Humphreys, *Media and Media Policy in Germany*, p.240

23 Ibid., p.247

24 Huber, *La RFA et sa Télévision*, pp.40–7

25 Humphreys, *Media and Media Policy in Germany*, p.271

26 Ibid., p.281

27 Martin '1997, une année de television dans le monde', pp.12–13

28 Porter and Hasselbach, *Pluralism, Politics and the Marketplace*, p.32

29 Iosifidis, Steemers and Wheeler, *European Television Industries*, p.122

30 *Creative Industries Mapping Document 2001*, Department of Culture, Media and Sport (UK), p.13–03

31 Monique Dagnaud's seminar presentation on her research on television producers, organised by the *Temps, médias et société* group, Paris, 8 April 2005

32 Madeo and Raveggi, *Il Servizio Opinioni cos'è com'è*, RAI

33 Servizio Opinioni, *Ascolto e gradimento per le trasmissioni televisive del 1982*

34 Katz, 'And Deliver Us from Segmentation', p.23

35 The Funding of the BBC. Government Response to the Third Report from the Culture, Media and Sport Committee, session 1999–2000, CM 4674, p.1

59 : Going Out: Cinema and Theatre

1 Huber, *La RFA et sa Télévision*, pp.72–3, 81

2 Barbier and Lavenir, *Histoire des médias*, p.310

3 Ministry of Culture, *Développement culturel*, No. 135, September 2000, 'La culture cinématographique des Français'. The figure seems excessive

4 Hilmes, 'Television and the Film Industry', p.473

5 Murphy, 'Popular British Cinema', p.7

6 Huber, *La RFA et sa Télévision*, pp.97–8

7 Olivier, *Les Pratiques culturelles des Français. Enquête 1997*, p.45

8 Puttnam, *The Undeclared War. The Struggle for Control of the World's Film Industry*, p.288

9 Ibid., p.320

10 *Statistical Yearbook 1996*, European Audiovisual Observatory, p.85

11 Fanchi and Mosconi (eds), *Spettatori. Forme di consumo e pubblici del cinema in Italia 1930–60*, p.260; source: Società italiana autori editori

12 *Statistical Yearbook 1996*, European Audiovisual Observatory, pp.74–5

13 Statistics on film and cinema 1955–1977, UNESCO, No. 25, pp.21, 24

14 Rentschler, 'From New German Cinema to the Post-Wall Cinema of Consensus', p.114

15 *Statistical Yearbook 1996*, European Audiovisual Observatory, p.95

16 Cited in Puttnam, *The Undeclared War*, p.6

17 Soldatos, *Enas Aionas Ellinikos Kinimatografos*, (A Century of Greek Cinema), Vol. 1, Kochlias, Athens, 2001, information supplied by Dora Giannaki

18 *The Times Weekend Review*, 9 April 2005, *www.thetimesonline.com/weekendreview*

19 UN Yearly Statistics, 1962

20 On the global ambitions of the Indian and Chinese film industry see *India Today*, 2 June 2003

21 'Disney's Big Adventure in Asia' in *Financial Times*, 30 October 2003

22 *Variety*, 25 March 1987, pp.92, 94, 96

23 Moretti, 'Planet Hollywood', pp.90–2

24 Puttnam, *The Undeclared War*, p.290

25 On the success of the film see Raphael, 'Fears of a Clown'

26 Balio, 'The art film market in the new Hollywood', pp.9, 65

27 Puttnam, *The Undeclared War*, p.306

28 Figures from *BFI Film & Television Handbook 2004*, p.31

29 See the International Movies Database website: *http://www.imdb.com/title/tto120737/business*

30 Smith 'Star Wars Empire strikes gold', *Observer*, 15 May 2005

31 Menand, 'Billion-dollar baby', p.11

32 Huber, *La RFA et sa télévision*, p.98

33 Miccichè, 'Un decennio di transizione', pp.4–6

34 Rossi, 'Il pubblico del cinema', pp.33–8

35 Torri, 'Industria, mercato, politica', p.19

36 Waterman and Jayakar, 'The Competitive Balance of the Italian and American Film Industries', p.519

37 Puttnam, *The Undeclared War*, pp.281–2

38 *http://news.bbc.co.uk/1/hi/entertainment/1055516.stm*

39 Robinson, *Smoking in Bed. Conversations with Bruce Robinson*, pp.249–50

40 Conrich, 'Forgotten cinema: the British style of sexploitation', pp.89, 90–91

41 'Interview with Éric de Winter' in *La Revue du cinéma*, pp.56–7

42 Simpson, 'Coming Attractions: a comparative history of the Hollywood Studio System and the porn business', pp.644–5

43 Data in *La Revue du cinéma*, special issue 'La saison cinématographique', 1983

44 Repetto, 'Ciao Mamma, ovvero porno soffice ed erotismo da ridere', p.321

45 Simpson, 'Coming Attractions . . .', p.635

46 Schulze-Reimpell, *Development and Structure of the Theatre in the Federal Republic of Germany*

47 Sandford (ed.), *Encyclopedia of Contemporary German Culture*, p.600

48 Schulze-Reimpell, *Development and Structure of the Theatre in the Federal Republic of Germany*, p.36

49 Linares, 'Theatre and Falangism at the Beginning of the Franco Régime', p.211–13

50 Schulze-Reimpell, *Development and Structure of the Theatre in the Federal Republic of Germany*, pp.19–20

51 Ibid., p.114

52 Grotowski, 'Statement of Principles', p.188

53 Ibid., p.109

54 Shaked, 'The Play: gateway to cultural dialogue', pp.21–22

55 Arts Council of England, Economic impact study of UK theatre, p.7

56 *Theatre Record*, Nos 1–2, 18 February 2003

57 *Theatre Record*, No. 9, 27 May 2003

58 Schulze-Reimpell, *Development and Structure of the Theatre in the Federal Republic of Germany*, p.17

59 'Primi risultati del censimento dei locali dello spettacolo esistenti in Italia al 30 giugno 1963' in *Lo spettacolo*, Vol. 14, No. 2, April–June 1964, p.164

60 See the survey in Corning and Levy, 'Demand for Live Theater with Market Segmentation and Seasonality', pp.217–35, especially pp.218–19

61 See Annual Report 2003–4 at *www.nationaltheatre.org.uk*

62 Marjanovic, 'The theatre', *http://www.rastko.org.yu/isk/pmarjanovic-theater.html*

63 Hall, 'Godot Almighty', *Guardian*, 25 August 2005

64 Herrick, 'Samuel Beckett'

65 Gänzl, *The Musical*, p.306

66 Ibid., pp.394–5

60 : Culture in the 'Other' Europe: Communism

1 Paulu, *Radio and Television Broadcasting in Eastern Europe*, pp.143, 274

2 Campeanu, 'Romanian Television: From Image to History', p.114

3 Kozlov, 'Soviet Readers, Historical Consciousness, and the Erosion of the Enemy Paradigm During the Thaw: From Pasternak to Siniavskii and Daniel, 1958–1966', *http://daviscenter.fas.harvard.edu/seminars_conferences/cnsschedule.html*

4 Younge, 'When Wal-Mart comes to town', *Guardian*, 18 August 2003

5 See the praise for Kadare in Albania by Bihiku, 'Le Roman contemporain albanais

et l'actualité', pp.45–65, especially pp.46–8, and Bulo, 'Les Lettres albanaises et la résistance antifasciste', pp.115–17

6 Faraday, *Revolt of the Filmmakers*, p.2

7 Ibid., p.115

8 Ibid., pp.176–7

9 Paulu, *Radio and Television Broadcasting in Eastern Europe*, p.26

10 Ibid., pp.84–6, 154–5

11 Verdery, *National Ideology under Socialism*, pp.218–19, 221

12 Mickiewicz, *Changing Channels*, pp.52, 54

13 Paulu, *Radio and Television Broadcasting in Eastern Europe*, p.173

14 Ibid., p.300

15 Thiesse and Chmatko, 'Les Nouveaux éditeurs russes', p.77

16 Dobrenko, *The Making of the State Reader*, pp.34–5

17 Paulu, *Radio and Television Broadcasting in Eastern Europe*, pp.388, 295

18 Fisher and Volkov, 'The Audience for Classical Music in the USSR; the Government as Mentor', pp.481–3, citing research conducted in the 1970s in industrial centres by Vladimir Samoilovich Tsukerman

19 Goudkov and Doubine, 'La culture littéraire' (1988), pp.254–5

20 Ibid., p.257

21 Ibid., p.264

22 Carmichael, ' "A People exists and that people has its language". . . ', p.227

23 McNeal, 'Brezhnev's Collected Works', p.409

24 Stroev, 'Lire en Russie', p.28

25 Levinson, 'Papier récupéré et livres', pp.197–8

26 Ibid., pp.208–11

27 Salvestroni, 'L'Unione Sovietica e la letteratura di consumo', pp.485–7

28 Prokhorova, *Fragmented Mythologies: Soviet TV Mini-series of the 1970s*, http://etd.library.pitt.edu/ETD/available/etd-06062003–164753/unrestricted/prokhorova_etd2003.pdf

29 Baudin, 'Le phénomène de la *série culte* en contexte soviétique et post-soviétique. L'exemple de Semnadcat' mgnovenij vesny', pp.49–50

30 Ibid., pp.51–7

31 Berg, 'About the Literary Battle', in *Russian Studies in Literature*, p.46.

32 Hamrlíková, 'The Czech Republic'

33 Grugel and Rees, *Franco's Spain*, pp.146–7, 150

34 Faraday, *Revolt of the Filmmakers*, pp.98–9

35 Clark, 'The Mutability of the Canon: Socialist Realism and Chingiz Aitmatov's *I dol'she veka dlitsia den'* in *Slavic Review*, pp.576–7

36 Chvedov, 'Les livres qui avaient nos préférences', pp.222–3

37 Paulu, *Radio and Television Broadcasting in Eastern Europe*, p.47

38 Luker, *Aleksandr Grin: The Forgotten Visionary*, pp.15ff

39 Ibid., pp.52–4

40 Ibid., p.43

41 Luker, 'Alexander Grin's *Grinlandia*', pp.190–1

42 Clark, *The Soviet Novel*, p.208

43 Faraday, *Revolt of the Filmmakers*, p.107

44 Clark, ' "Boy gets tractor" and all that: the parable structure of the Soviet novel', pp.358–9

45 Ibid., p.362

46 Thiesse and Chmatko 'Les nouveaux éditeurs russes', p.78

47 Löffler, 'Normalisierung und Kontinuität. Entwicklung des Leseverhaltens in den neuen Bundesländern', pp.111–25

48 Lazăr and Livezeanu, 'The Romanian Case'

49 Schiller, Reményi and Fodor, 'Hungary'

50 Ibid.

51 Bart, 'Publishing: service and/or commodity?', pp.38–9

52 Shneidman, 'Contemporary Prose in Post-Soviet Russia', accessed at *www.utoronto.ca/tsq/08/shneidman08.shtml*

53 Thiesse and Chmatko 'Les nouveaux éditeurs russes', p.82

54 Mickiewicz, *Changing Channels*, p.219

55 Ibid., p.276

56 Ibid., p.275

57 Ilieva, 'Bulgaria'

58 Sarnov, 'A List of Benefits', p.7

59 Barkler, 'The Culture Factory: Theorizing the Popular in the Old and New Russia', p.13; Goldschmidt, 'Pornography in Russia', p.323; and Condee, 'Body Graphics: Tattooing the Fall of Communism', pp.339–61

60 Goldschmidt, 'Pornography in Russia', p.318

61 Theimer Nepomnyashchy, 'Markets, Mirrors, and Mayhem: Aleksandra Marinina and the Rise of the New Russian *Detektiv*', pp.169–70

62 Menzel, 'Some Reflections on High and Popular Literature in Late and Soviet

Russia', accessed at *www.fask.uni-mainz.de/inst/is/russisch/menzel/pdf/refl_helsinki.pdf*

63 Szemere, *Up from the Underground: the Culture of Rock Music in Postsocialist Hungary*, pp.190–1

64 Ibid., pp.140, 143, 144

65 Ibid., p.223

66 Ambroic-Pai, 'Mass Media and Pop Groups in Yugoslavia', p.119

67 Oklot and Nowak, 'Poland'

68 Lazăr and Livezeanu, 'The Romanian Case'

69 Ilieva, 'Bulgaria'

70 Oklot and Nowak, 'Poland'

71 Heller, 'Russian "Sitkom" Adaptation: The Pushkin Principle', pp.60–72

72 Mickiewicz, *Changing Channels*, pp.220, 229

73 Meyen and Nawratil, 'The Viewers: Television and Everyday Life in East Germany', p.358

74 Fulbrook, *The Fontana History of Germany 1918–1990*, p.227

75 On the symbolic similarities between the two cars see Confino and Koshar, 'Régimes of Consumer Culture: New Narratives in Twentieth-Century German History', p.157

76 Gilbert, ' "Ich habe von einem Esel gelernt": Eisler Pro and Contra Schönberg', p.68

77 Brandes, 'Anna Seghers's Politics of Affirmation', pp.180, 186–7

78 Westgate, *Strategies Under Surveillance. Reading Irmtraud Morgner as a GDR Writer*, p.63

79 Walter Ulbricht, *Fragen der Entwicklung der sozialistischen Literatur und Kunst*, in Ulbricht, *Zur sozialistischen Kulturrevolution*, Bd. 2, Berlin 1960, p.474, cited in Rauhut, *Rock in der DDR*, p.7. This book is my main source for rock music in the DDR. I am grateful to Beatrice de Gerloni who translated ample passages.

80 Rauhut, *Rock in der DDR*, p.25

81 Ibid., pp.21, 23

82 Ibid., p.27

83 Ibid., p.29

84 Walter Ulbricht in *Stenographisches Protokoll*, SAPMO-BArch, DY 30/IV2/1/190, cited in Rauhut, *Rock in der DDR*, p.38

85 Ibid., p.41

86 Ibid., p.8

87 Ibid., p.11

88 Ibid., p.13

89 Ibid., p.15

90 Goodwin, 'After Unification', p.51

91 Rauhut, *Rock in der DDR*, p.45

92 Ibid., p.56

93 Poumet, *La Satire en R.D.A. Cabaret et presse satirique*, pp.11–13

94 Ibid., p.298

95 Löffler, 'Lektüren im "Leseland" vor und nach der Wende', pp.20–1

96 Spittel, *Science Fiction in der DDR, Bibliographie*, also *www.spittel.de/sf/a.htm*. Olaf Spittel is himself a science fiction writer

97 Meyen and Nawratil, 'The Viewers: Television and Everyday Life in East Germany', p.355

98 Breitenborn, 'Memphis Tennessee' in Borstendorf, *Boundaries Set and Transcended in East German Television Entertainment*, p.393

99 Meyen and Nawratil, 'The Viewers . . .', p.360

100 Schültze, 'Television Theater in East Germany, 1965–1989: an interim report', p.458

101 Steinmetz and Viehoff, 'The Program History of Genres of Entertainment on GDR Television', p.320

102 Schültze, 'Television Theater in East Germany, 1965–1989 . . .', p.459

103 Dittmar, 'GDR Television in Competition with West German Programming', pp.327–8

104 Meyen and Nawratil, 'The Viewers . . .', pp.360–1; see also Meyen and Hillman, 'Communication Needs and Media Change. The Introduction of Television in East and West Germany', p.465

105 Personal communication by Beatrice de Gerloni (25 June 2005), who frequently visited the Institute

106 Dittmar, 'GDR Television in Competition . . .', p.336

107 Ibid., p.337

108 Meyen and Nawratil, 'The Viewers: Television and Everyday Life in East Germany', p.359

109 Steinmetz, 'Heymowski & Scheumann: the GDR's leading documentary film team', pp.365–79

110 Ibid., p.375

111 Ibid., p.377

112 Prase, 'The Structure, Coverage and Surprising End of a Conspiratorial Film Team', pp.381–9

113 Ibid., pp.383, 387

114 Hortmann, *Shakespeare on the German Stage*, p.359
115 Ulf Keyn, 'Hamlet unser Zeitgenosse' (1964), cited by Maik Hamburger in Hortmann, *Shakespeare on the German Stage*, p.384
116 Ibid., p.418
117 Ibid., p.364
118 Gemünden, 'Between Karl May and Karl Marx. The DEFA Indianerfilme', p.399

61 : A World of Readers

1 Asor Rosa, 'Centralismo e policentrismo nella letteratura italiana unitaria', p.13
2 Barker and Escarpit, *La Faim de lire*, pp.117–18
3 Horellou-Lafarge and Segré, *Regards sur la lecture en France*, p.32
4 Ministère de la Culture et de la Communication, *Développement culturel*, No.124, June 1998
5 Livolsi (ed.), *Almeno un libro*, p.3
6 Peresson, *Le cifre dell'editoria 1995*, p.283. On the lack of bookshops see Ferretti, *Il Best Seller all'italiana*, p.23
7 Mann, *From Author to Reader*, p.125
8 Retigo, 'Stregati dai libri, in Italia boom di lettori'
9 Abruzzese, *Analfabeti di tutto il mondo uniamoci*, pp.89–90
10 Barthes, *Le Plaisir du texte*, p.62
11 Establet and Felouzis, 'Livre et télévision: deux médias en concurrence', pp.125–37
12 Donnat, 'La féminisation des pratiques culturelles'
13 Buzzi, 'Il pubblico dei lettori: caratteristiche strutturali e specificità culturali', pp.33–49
14 Information collected from the 'N.B.' columns in *The Times Literary Supplement* of 29 August 1997 and the 'J.C.' column of 31 October 1997
15 Mann, *From Author to Reader*, p.51
16 Data in *Guardian*, 10 October 2005
17 *http://www.nielsenbookscan.co.uk/?pid=126*
18 Nora, 'Une Lueur d'espoir pour les sciences humaines', p.15
19 Extrapolated from Godechot, 'Le Marché du livre philosophique', pp.10–28, table on p.19
20 Choppin, *Les manuels scolaires. Histoire et actualité*, pp.81–2
21 Vaillant, 'L'un et le multiple, essai de modélisation bibliométrique', pp.194–6
22 Thiesse, *Le Roman du quotidien*, p.39
23 Devars, Petitier, Rosa and Vaillant, 'Si Victor Hugo était compté. Essais de bibliométrie hugolienne comparée', pp.368–9
24 Ibid., p.384; on Sartre being turned down by Gallimard see Cohen-Solal, *Sàrtre. A Life*, p.113
25 *Le Bulletin du livre* 'Les Best sellers du siècle', 15 October 1961, pp.32–3
26 *Le Bulletin du Livre*, 15 December 1968, 'Les Best sellers 1958–68', pp.20–6
27 Mengin, 'Les Répercussions économiques de la télévision sur le marché du livre', pp.154, 177
28 See Alex Hamilton's compilation in the *Guardian*, 10 January 1995
29 Alex Hamilton, 'The Winners Decoded', *Guardian*, 1 January 2005
30 Payne, Hackett and Burke (eds), *80 Years of Best Sellers 1895–1975*, pp.10–11, 14
31 Stephen Moss, 'Bookends', *Guardian*, 19 March 2002
32 *Financial Times*, 21 February 2004, p.25
33 Zipes, *Sticks and Stones*, Routledge, New York and London 2001, p.175
34 Ezard, 'Harry Potter and the stony broke authors', *Guardian*, 14 July 2005
35 Zipes, *Sticks and Stones*, pp.173–4
36 Smith, 'Potter's magic spell turns boys into bookworms', *Observer*, 10 July 2005 citing a survey carried out by the Federation of Children's Book Groups
37 Ganne and Minon, 'Géographies de la traduction', p.57
38 Ibid., p.66
39 Peresson, *Le Cifre dell'editoria 1995*, p.102; and Grossi, 'Il libro di successo . . .', p.72
40 UNESCO, *Index Translationum 1965*
41 'Étude sur l'*Index Translationum*' in *Bibliographie de France*, 22 September 1971, Vol. 160, No. 38, pp.561–2
42 Milo, 'La Bourse mondiale de la traduction: un baromètre culturel?', p.93
43 Ibid., p.98
44 See UNESCO, *Index translationium 1985*
45 Godechot, 'Le Marché du livre philosophique', pp.10–28
46 Weinberg, 'Une Histoire du structuralisme', p.15
47 Cohen-Solal, *Sartre. A Life*, p.116
48 Fréchet, 'Galsworthy hier et aujourd'hui', pp.178–9
49 Assouline, *Gaston Gallimard*, p.14
50 Simonin and Fouché, 'Comment on a refusé certains de mes livres. Contribution à une histoire sociale de la littérature', p.107

51 Martin, 'Thomas the Tank Engine Stole my Son'

52 Gambaro, 'Approches théoriques de l'industrie du livre', p.99

53 *Pearson Annual Review 2004*, p.17

54 Benelli, 'Il romanzo erotico in Francia: il caso "Emmanuelle" ', p.463

55 McAleer, *Passion's Fortune. The Story of Mills & Boon*, p.115

56 Bordoni, 'Il romanzo di consumo', pp.110–12, who cites no sources

57 Ibid., pp.99, 107

58 For this and other data on the firm see their website: *www.eHarlequin.com*

59 McAleer, *Passion's Fortune*, p.285

60 Pequignot, *La Relation amoureuse*, pp.11–13, 82ff

61 Ibid., pp.28, 35–8

62 Ibid., p.17

63 McAleer, *Passion's Fortune*, p.279

64 Pequignot, *La Relation amoureuse*, pp.18–19

65 Ibid., pp.98–9

66 Dudovitz, *The Myth of Superwoman*, pp.111–12

67 Pequignot, *La Relation amoureuse*, p.40

68 Dudovitz, *The Myth of Superwoman*, pp.108–9

69 McAleer, *Passion's Fortune*, pp.255–6

70 Bedell, 'Mills & Boom Boom', *Observer Magazine*, 15 December 2002

71 *www.eharlequin.com/cms/learntowrite/ltwToc.jhtml*

72 McAleer, *Passion's Fortune*, p.6

73 Much of what follows on the *Heftroman* in post-1990 Germany relies on Cordula Günther's *Heftromanleser in den neuen Bundesländer* (Leipzig 1994) available at *http://www.medienkomm.uni-halle.de/forschung/publikationen/halma11.pdf*. I wish to thank Dr Günther for replying to my queries and to Beatrice de Gerloni for acting as an intermediary and translating sections of Dr Günther's work. The notes on various German heroes of *Heftromane* rely on Ingrid Scheffer's notes available at *http://www.goethe.de/kug/kue/lit/dos/en142247.htm*

74 Köhler, 'Lesekultur in beiden deutschen Staaten. 40 Jahre – ein Vergleich. Geschichte – Theorie – Empirie'

75 Pirani, 'Le collane poliziesche romane dal 1955 al 1970', pp.78–80

76 Words taken from Noreiko, 'From serious to popular fiction', p.189

77 Lauf, 'Research Note: The Vanishing Young Reader. Sociodemographic Determinants of Newspaper Use as a Source of Political Information in Europe, 1980–98', p.238

78 *Guardian*, 1 June 2005

79 Preston, 'The writing's on the wall, or rather the web', *Observer*, 22 May 2005

80 Preston, 'Some Good News Between the Lines', *Observer*, 3 January 1999, using data from Audit Bureau of Circulation

81 *Pearson Annual Review 2004*

82 Bollinger, *La Presse suisse: structure et diversité*, p.35

83 *Guardian*, 21 June 2003

84 O'Sullivan, 'The glossies that shone brightest in a bumper year', *Observer*, 19 December 2004

85 For figures and further information of Springer see *www.ketupa.net*, a site of Caslon Analytics profiling major media groups, accessed version of August 2003

86 See Barrell and Braithwaite, *The Business of Women's Magazines*, p.169

87 White, *Women's Magazines 1693–1968*, pp.182–4, 8

88 Barrell and Braithwaite, *The Business of Women's Magazines*, p.42

89 Figures in White, *Women's Magazines 1693–1968*, Appendix VI

90 Ibid., p.203

91 Barrell and Braithwaite, *The Business of Women's Magazines*, p.37

92 Ibid., p.85

93 Portaccio, 'Buona e bella. I periodici femminili cattolici negli anni '50', p.141

94 Giet, '20 ans d'amour en couverture', p.22

95 O'Hagan, 'Disgrace under Pressure'

96 Emap plc, *Annual Report and Accounts 2005*, p.17

97 All figures come from Emap plc, *Annual Report and Accounts 2005*

98 Donnan, 'Read all about lads' *Financial Times*, 26/27 February 2005, US edition

62 : Exploding Pop

1 Frith, 'Music and the Media', pp.172–4

2 Arming, 'Economic aspects of the Phonographic Industry', p.75

3 See Table 9 in Throsby, 'The Role of Music in International Trade and Economic Development' in *World Culture Report 1998*, UNESCO, p.197

4 Figures in Commission Européenne. Direction générale X, *Statistiques de la culture en Europe. Premiers éléments*, 1996; see also IFPI, *The Recording Industry in Numbers 1995*, p.2

5 Paterson, 'Why 1955? Explaining the Advent of Rock Music', p.273

6 Raynor, *Music and Society since 1815*, p.161

7 Dolfsma, 'Radio and Magazines: valuing pop music in the Netherlands (1955–1965)', p.31

8 Téberge, 'Musicians' Magazines in the 1980s: the creation of a community and a consumer market' pp.254–5, 266

9 Bloom, *The Closing of the American Mind*, p.81

10 Strobl and Tucker, 'The Dynamics of Chart Success in the UK . . .', p.115

11 Burnett, *The Global Jukebox*, p.45

12 *Observer Music Monthly*, July 2005, p.21

13 *World Culture Report 1998*, UNESCO, pp.371–2

14 Fabbri, 'A Theory of Musical Genre', p.25

15 London, 'The sound of the stereo fades into history', *Financial Times*, 18 November 2003, p.14

16 Gronow, *Statistics in the Field of Sound Recordings*, p.4

17 Hardy and Laing, *The European Music Business*, p.27, citing IFPI sources

18 Beavis, 'Piracy steals notes from sound talent', *Guardian*, 10 January 1997, p.26

19 *www.ifpi.org/site-content/press/20050623.html*

20 *Observer Music Monthly*, July 2005, p.38

21 Garofalo, 'I want my MP3: Who owns Internet music?', p.89

22 Burnett, *The Global Jukebox*, p.2

23 Report in the business section of the *Los Angeles Times*, 27 February 2001

24 *Observer*, business supplement, 24 July 2005

25 Champ, 'Keys to success' in *Music Business International*, August 2001, p.13

26 Information from the magazine *Q*, September 2004, p.88

27 Bontinck, 'The Project: Aims and Results', p.3

28 Berio, 'Commentaire au rock', p.60

29 Longhurst, *Popular Music and Society*, pp.64–5

30 Blaukopf, 'Les jeunes musiciens dans la société industrielle . . .', pp.227–9

31 Doublé-Dutheil, 'Pratiques et goûts musicaux de la jeunesse urbaine', pp.329–31

32 Blaukopf, 'Les jeunes musiciens dans la société industrielle', using the findings in Erika Bácskai, Ivan Vitányi and others, *Beat*, Budapest 1969

33 Sági, 'Music on records in Hungary', p.113

34 Szemere, *Up from the Underground: the Culture of Rock Music in Postsocialist Hungary*, pp.11, 35

35 Opekar, 'Two great world influences to the Czech music culture', p.652

36 Dvorak, 'Situation of Rock Music in Changing Czech Society', pp.687–9

37 Johnson, 'The Menace of Beatlism', pp.195–8

38 Cited in Pleasants, 'Elvis Presley' (1974), p.256

39 See Glenn Gould's comments in 1967 on the aesthetics of her songs: 'The Search for Petula Clark', pp.285–92, originally in *High Fidelity*, November 1967

40 Eger, 'La Révolution dans le public: Une profession de foi', p.91

41 Q, April 2003

42 Gillett, *The Sound of the City*, p.270

43 Hennion and Vignolle, *Artisans et industriels du disque*, p.196

44 National Arenas Association figures covering fifteen venues, reported in *Metro*, 18 December 2000

45 *Billboard*, 28 May 2005, p.20

46 European Commission, Staff working paper SEC (98) 837, *Culture, the Cultural Industries and Employment*, http://europa.eu.int/comm/avpolicy/legis/forum/culti_en.htm

47 Gronow and Saunio, *An International History of the Recording Industry*, p.152

48 Schumacher, '"This is a sampling sport". Digital Sampling, Rap Music and the Law in Cultural Production', pp.170–4; originally in *Media, Culture and Society*, No. 2, 1995

49 Steve and Alan Parker, *You Can Make It as a DJ!*, pp.50–2

50 Norman, *Shout! The True Story of the Beatles*, p.293

51 Ibid., p.160

52 National Music Council, *The Value of Music*, a report into the Value of the UK Music industry prepared by the University of Westminster (Cliff Dane, Andy Feist and Dave Laing), London 1996, pp.14–15

53 Strobl and Tucker, 'The Dynamics of Chart Success in the UK . . .', pp.117–18

54 National Music Council, *The Value of Music*, p.91

55 Negus, 'Between Corporation and Consumer: Culture and Conflict in the British Record Industry', p.41

56 Aronowitz, 'The Beatles: Music's Gold Bugs', p.12, originally in *Saturday Evening Post*, March 1964

57 Burnett, *The Global Jukebox*, p.24

58 Hennion and Vignolle, *Artisans et industriels du disque*, pp.138, 140
59 Burnett, *The Global Jukebox*, pp.27–8
60 Norman, *Shout!*, p.xxvi
61 Longhurst, *Popular Music and Society*, pp.104–5
62 Gillett, 'Big Noise from Across the Water: the American Influence on British Popular Music', pp.61–2
63 Lilliestam, 'Musical acculturation: "Hound Dog" from Blues to Swedish Rock'n'Roll', pp.4, 22, 31
65 Gillett, 'Big Noise from Across the Water . . .', pp.67, 74
66 Norman, *Shout!*, p.106
67 Moore, *The Beatles: Sgt Pepper's Lonely Hearts Club Band*, p.13
68 Cited by Aronowitz, 'The Beatles: Music's Gold Bugs', p.12; for a view on the hype surrounding the term 'Mersey Sound' see Gillett, *The Sound of the City*, p.267
69 Norman, *Shout!*, p.227
70 Scaduto, *Bob Dylan*, p.175
71 Ibid., p.176
72 Leydi, 'La musica e lo spettacolo musicale', p.539
73 Frith, 'Does British music still matter?', pp.45, 48–9
74 Ibid., p.46
75 *Billboard*, 9 April 2005, p.47
76 Gronow, *Statistics in the Field of Sound Recordings*, p.10
77 Data from *MBI World Report 1996* in Strobl and Tucker, 'The Dynamics of Chart Success in the UK . . .', p.131n; Frith, 'Does British music still matter?', p.47; Longhurst, *Popular Music and Society*, p.40
78 IPFI figures reported in *Music Business International*, April 2001, p.56
79 Arming, 'Economic aspects of the Phonographic Industry', p.75
80 Masson, 'Labels Bank on Domestic Talents'
81 Cobo, 'Shakira x 2', p.23
82 Gronow and Saunio, *An International History of the Recording Industry*, p.164
83 Kretschmer, Klimis and Wallis, *The Global Music Industry in the Digital Environment: A Study of Strategic Intent and Policy Responses (1996–99)*, accessed at *www.mica.at/pdf/kretschmer_c.pdf*, p.18
84 Fornäs, 'Moving Rock: Youth Culture and popular music', p.320
85 *The Billboard Book of Top Hits*, p.830
86 Björnberg, 'Musical Spectacle as Ritual: the Eurovision song contest', pp.375–6
87 *Le Monde*, 21 July 2004
88 Prévos, 'Hip-Hop, Rap, and Repression in France and in the United States', p.1
89 Prévos, 'Postcolonial Popular Music in France. Rap music and hip-hop culture in the 1980s and 1990s', pp.42–3
90 See Swedenburg, 'Islamic Hip-Hop versus Islamophobia', p.57; and, for Bulgaria, Claire Levy's essay 'Rap in Bulgaria', in the same collection
91 Solomon, ' "Living underground is tough": authenticity and locality in the hip-hop community in Istanbul, Turkey', pp.1–20
92 *La Repubblica*, 5 August 2003
93 'Hits of the World' in *Billboard*, 9 April 2005, p.46
94 Hannerz, *Cultural Complexity*, pp.23–4, 241
95 *Guardian*, 6 June 1998
96 Gronow, *Statistics in the Field of Sound Recordings*, p.10
97 Gronow and Saunio, *An International History of the Recording Industry*, p.165
98 Fenton, 'The librettist's tale', *Guardian*, 27 November 2004
99 Bing, *5000 Nights at the Opera*, p.209
100 Ibid., p.327
101 *Complete UK Hit Singles 1952–2004*, p.588
102 Clark, 'All shook up over classical music'
103 Gronow and Saunio, *An International History of the Recording Industry*, pp.174, 175–6
104 Menger, *Le paradoxe du musicien*, pp.32–3, 43, 65
105 Rosen, 'Who's Afraid of the Avant-Garde', p.22
106 Rosen, *The Classical Style. Haydn, Mozart, Beethoven*, p.333
107 Van der Merwe, *Origins of the Popular Style*, p.19
108 Parakilas, 'Classical Music as Popular Music', p.17
109 *Complete UK Hit Singles 1952–2004*, p.403
110 Menger, *Le Paradoxe du musicien*, p.155
111 National Music Council, *The Value of Music*, pp.20, 22, 28
112 European Commission, working paper SEC (98) 837, *http://europa.eu.int/conm/avpolicy/legis/forum/cult1_en.htm*
113 Myerscough et al., *The Economic Importance of the Arts in Britain*, pp.16–18

Conclusion : The World Wide Web

1 I have described the rise of the *Mona Lisa* to global celebrity in my *Mona Lisa*

2 Barber, *The Heyday of Natural History, 1820–1870*, p.123

3 Schneer, *London 1900: The Imperial Metropolis*, pp.94–5

4 Statistics collected by ALVA, the Association of Leading Visitor Attractions, see *www.alva.org.uk/ visitor_statistics/*

5 Moulin, *De la valeur de l'art*, p.218

6 *www.koerperwelten.com*

7 Palumbo, 'The Social Life of Local Museums', p.20

8 See *Renoir's Portraits: Impressions of an Age Visitor Profile and Economic Impact Study. Final Report*, p.10, accessed on *www.pch.gc.ca/progs/arts/pdf/renoir_e.pdf*. These findings have been contested by Stanley, Rogers, Smeltzer and Perron, in 'Win, Place or Show: Gauging the Economic Success of the Renoir and Barnes Art Exhibits', pp.243–55

9 Herbert, 'Renoir the Radical', p.8

10 Lipovetsky, *The Empire of Fashion. Dressing Modern Democracy*, pp.89–91

11 According to a survey commissioned by the Italian Ministry of Culture reported in *Il Venerdì*, the supplement of *La Repubblica* of 18 February 2005

12 For France, see Donnat and Cogneau, *Les Pratiques culturelles des Français 1973–1989*, p.82; for other data see Chapter 61

13 Data in the *Guardian*, 10 October 2005

14 Donnat and Cogneau, *Les Pratiques culturelles des Français 1973–1989*, p.6

15 *Creative Industries Mapping Document 2001*, p.8–03, and ELSPA (Entertainment and Leisure Software Publishers Association), *Computer and video games*, White Paper, August 2003, pp.8–10, accessed at *www.elspa.com/about/pr/ elspawhitepaper1.pdf*

16 ELSPA, *Computer and video games*, p.9

17 Stallabrass, *Gargantua. Manufactured Mass Culture*, pp.85–9

18 Beavis, 'Reading, Writing and Role-Playing Computer Games', p.48, accessed at *http://cmeskill.tripod.com/beavis.pdf*

19 Becker, 'Who's Wired and Who's Not: Children's Access to and Use of Computer Technology', p.64, accessed at *www.teacherlib.org/articles/becker.pdf*

20 Leading article, 'Time to move on', *Guardian*, 8 November 2004

21 Great Britain *National Statistics Omnibus Survey*, accessed on 6 October 2005, *http://www.statistics.gov.uk/CCI/ nugget.asp?ID=8&Pos=1&ColRank= 1&Rank=192*

22 Plato, *Phaedrus*, translated by Benjamin Jowett, available at *http:// ccat.sas.upenn.edu/jod/texts/phaedrus.html*

23 Baudelaire, *Salon de 1859. Lettres à M. le Directeur de La Revue Française*, *http:// baudelaire.litteratura.com/ressources/pdf/ oeu_4.pdf*, p.10

24 Valéry, *Regards sur le monde actuel et autres essais*, p.214

25 Benjamin, 'The Work of Art in the Age of Mechanical Reproduction', pp.236, 223

26 Saporta, 'Trois voies nouvelles pour l'édition Américaine', p.9

27 Evans, *The Mighty Micro. The Impact of the Computer Revolution*, pp.106–9

28 Klein, 'Amazon gambles on the high street', *Guardian*, 28 March 2005; see also interview with Jeff Bezos, *Guardian*, 24 October 2005.

29 Anderson, 'The Long Tail', *Wired*. His book *The Long Tail: Why the Future Is Selling Less of More* is scheduled to be published in 2006

30 Servant, 'Nollywood Boulevard', *Le Monde*, 30 April 2005

31 Schlager, 'How Many More Monthly Fees Can Consumers Stand?'

32 McCurry, 'Mobiles turn a new page for Japan's youth', *Guardian*, 25 March 2005

33 For Salam Pax see *http:// dear_raed.blogspot.com/* and *http:// justzipit.blogspot.com/*; for Margot Wallström see *http://weblog.jrc.cec.eu.int/ page/wallstrom*

BIBLIOGRAPHY OF WORKS CITED

AA VV *Editoria e cultura a Milano tra le due guerre (1920–1940)*, Atti del Convegno, Milan 19–21 February 1981, Fondazione Arnoldo e Alberto Mondadori, Milan 1983

Abel, Richard ' "Pathé Goes to Town": French Films Create a Market for the Nickelodeon' in *Cinema Journal*, Vol. 35, No. 1, Fall 1995

Abel, Richard 'French Silent Cinema' in Nowell-Smith (ed.) *The Oxford History of World Cinema*

Abel, Richard *The Ciné Goes to Town: French Cinema, 1896–1914*, University of California Press, Los Angeles 1994

Abendour, Gérard 'Meyerhold à Paris'in *Cahiers du Monde Russe et Soviétique*, Vol. 5, No. 1, January-March 1964

Abescat, Michel 'Depuis le commencement, le polar s'écrit aussi au féminin', *Le Monde*, 11 July 1997

About, Edmond *A B C du Travailleur*, Hachette, Paris 1868

Abraham, Gerald *The Concise Oxford History of Music*, Oxford University Press 1979

Abramson, Albert *The History of Television, 1880–1941*, McFarland and Co., Jefferson NC and London 1987

Abruzzese, Alberto *Analfabeti di tutto il mondo uniamoci*, Costa & Nolan, Genoa 1996

Abruzzese, Alberto and Carlo Grassi, 'La fotografia' in Asor Rosa (ed.) *Letteratura italiana. Storia e geografia*, Volume 3: *L'età contemporanea*

Abruzzese, Alberto and Francesco Pinto, 'La radiotelevisione' in Asor Rosa (ed.) *Letteratura italiana*, Vol. 2, *Produzione e consumo*

Abruzzese, Alberto *Metafore della pubblicità*, Costa & Nolan, Genoa 1997

Achilli, Tina 'Le maschere dell'eros' in De Donato and Stacchini (eds) *I best seller del ventennio. Il regime e il libro di massa*

Ackroyd, Peter *Dickens*, Vintage, London 1999

Acocella, Joan 'The Neapolitan Finger' in *New York Review of Books*, 21 December 2000

Acocella, Joan *Willa Cather and the Politics of Criticism*, Nebraska University Press 2000

Ádám, Ánikó 'Les traductions hongroises de l'oeuvre de Chateaubriand' in Ballard (ed.) *Europe et Traduction*

Adburgham, Alison *Silver Fork Society. Fashionable Life and Literature from 1814 to 1840*, Constable, London 1983

Adler, Laure *À l'aube du féminisme: Les premières journalistes (1830–1850)*, Payot, Paris 1979

Adler, Moshe 'Stardom and Talent' in *American Economic Review*, No. 1, March 1985, Vol.75

Adorno, Theodor W. and Max Horkheimer *Dialectic of Enlightenment*, Verso, London 1997

Adorno, Theodor W. *The Culture Industry*, edited by J. M. Bernstein, Routledge, London and New York 1991

Adorno, Theodor W. *Notes to Literature*, Vol. 1 edited by Rolf Tiedemann, trans. From the German by Weber Nicholsen, Shierry Columbia University Press, New York 1991 (originally: *Noten zur Literatur*)

Adorno, Theodor W. *Prisms*, MIT Press, Cambridge, Mass. 1981

Agger, Gunhild and Alexander P. Nielsen 'Il buono, il brutto e il banale. La fiction tv danese nel 1998' in Milly Buonanno, *Eurofiction 1999. Terzo Rapporto sulla fiction televisiva in Europe*, VQPT-RAI No 171, Rome 1999

Agulhon, Maurice 'Le problème de la culture populaire en France autour de 1848' in *Romantisme*, No. 9, 1975

Aimone, Isabella 'Un statut pour les acteurs: 1910–1920' in Benghozi and Delage (eds) *Une histoire économique du cinéma français (1895–1995)*

Alatri, Paolo *D'Annunzio*, UTET, Turin 1983

Albert, Pierre 'La presse française de 1871 à 1940' in Bellanger et al, *Histoire Générale de la Presse Française*, Vol. 3

Albert, Pierre *Histoire de la Presse*, Presses universitaires de France, Paris 1970

Albert, Pierre, Gilles Feyel and Jean-François Picard, *Documents pour l'histoire de la presse nationale aux XIXe et XXe siècle*, Centre de documentation sciences humaines, CNRS, Paris 1980

Albertini, Pierre *L'École en France XIX-XX siècle de la maternelle à l'université*, Hachette 1992

Albisetti, James C. *Secondary School Reform in Imperial Germany*, Princeton UP, Princeton New Jersey 1983

Albonetti, Pietro (ed.) *Non c'è tutto nei romanzi. Leggere romanzi stranieri in una casa editrice negli anni '30*, Fondazione Mondadori, Milan 1994

Alcott, Louisa May *The Selected Letters of Louisa May Alcott*, edited by Joel Myerson and Daniel Shealy, The University of Georgia Press, Athens and London 1995

Alfieri, Gabriella 'La lingua di consumo', in Luca Serianni and Pietro Trifone (eds) *Storia della lingua italiana*, Vol. 2 *Scritto e parlato*, Einaudi, Turin 1994

Alfieri, Vittorio *Estratti d'Ossian e da Stazio per la Tragica*, edited by Piero Camporesi, Casa d'Alfieri, Asti 1969

Alfieri, Vittorio *Vita scritta da esso*, edited by Luigi Fassò, Casa d'Alfieri, Asti 1951

Alfu (pseudonym), *L'encyclopédie de Fantômas. Étude sur un classique*, Alfu (self-published), Paris 1981

Allain, Marcel 'Fantômas et les autres vus du premier rang de l'orchestre' in *Europe*, Vol.56, No.590–591, June-July 1978

Allaire, Gloria *Andrea da Barberino and the language of chivalry*, University Press of Florida 1997

Allen, Ann Taylor *Satire and Society in Wilhelmine Germany. Kladderadatsch and Simplicissimus 1890–1914*, The University Press of Kentucky 1984

Allen, James Smith *In the Public Eye, A History of Reading in Modern France 1800–1940*, Princeton University Press 1991, appendix Table A.3 'Circulation of Parisian Newspapers'

Allin, Michael *Zarafa: A Giraffe's True Story, from Deep in Africa to the Heart of Paris*, Walker and Co., New York 1998

Allsobrook, David Ian *Liszt: My Travelling Circus Life*, Macmillan, London 1991

Alphonse Mucha catalogue of the exhibition, Lund Humphries Publishers in association with Barbican Art Gallery, London 1993

Altenloh, Emilie 'A Sociology of the Cinema', in *Screen*, No. 42–3, Autumn 2001

Altick, Richard D. 'The sociology of authorship. The social origin, education and occupation of 1100 British writers 1800–1935', in *Bulletin of the New York Public Library*, vol.66, June 1962

Altick, Richard D. *The Shows of London*, Harvard University Press, Cambridge Mass.
1978

Amaury, Francine, *Histoire du plus grand quotidien de la IIIe République: Le Petit
Parisien, 1876–1944*, 2 Vols. Presses universitaires de France, Paris, 1972, Tome 1:
La Société du Petit Parisien, Tome 2: *Instrument de propagande au service du régime*

Ambrožic-Paić, Arlette 'Mass Media and Pop Groups in Yugoslavia' in Irmgard
Bontinck (ed.) *New Patterns of Musical Behaviour*, Universal Edition, Vienna 1974

Anderson, Benedict 'Western Nationalism and Eastern Nationalism' in *New Left Review*,
No. 9 May-June 2001

Anderson, Chris 'The Long Tail', *Wired*, Vol. 12, No. 10, October 2004, available on
www.wired.com/wired/archive/12.10/tail.html

Anderson, Olive 'The Political Uses of History in Mid-Nineteenth Century England' in
Past and Present No 36, April 1967

Anderson, Perry *The Origins of Postmodernity*, Verso, London 1998

Anderson, R. F. ' "Things Wisely Ordered": John Blackwood, George Eliot, and the
Publication of *Romola*' in *Publishing History*, No. 11, 1982

Anderson, W.E.K. *The Journal of Sir Walter Scott*, Canongate, Edinburgh 1998

Andreeva-Popova, Nadezda 'Le siècle des Lumières et la renaissance bulgare' in Köpeczi
and Vajda (eds) *Proceedings of the 8th Congress of the International Comparative
Literature Association*

Andrews, Alexander *The History of British Journalism. From the Foundation of the
Newspaper Press in England to the Repeal of the Stamp Act in 1855* in two volumes,
originally Richard Bentley publishers, London 1859 now reprinted by Routledge &
Thoemmes Press in the series *Chapters in the History of British Journalism* 1998
3 vols

Andries. Lise 'Les livres de savoir pratique dans la France des XVIIe et XVIIIe siècles' in
Chartier and Lüsebrink (eds) *Colportage et lecture populaire*

Andrzejczyk, Hanna 'Lo specchio della vita quotidiana. La fiction tv polacca nel 2001' in
Buonanno (ed.) *Eurofiction 2002*

Anfray, Clélia 'La lectrice ou la révélation du désir: Étude de la scène de lecture dans les
romans du XIXe siècle' in *Revue d'histoire littéraire de la France*, Vol. 105, No. 1,
January-March 2005

Ang, Ien *Living Room Wars. Rethinking media audiences for a postmodern world*,
Routledge, London 1996

Ang, Ien *Watching Dallas. Soap opera and the meodramatic imagination*, Methuen,
London 1985

Ang, Ien *Desperately Seeking the Audience*, Routledge, London 1991

Angels, Santa 'L'influence du Naturalisme français et de Zola dans *La Desheredada* et
Tormento de Benito Pérez Galdós' in Dezalay (ed.) *Zola sans frontières*

Angenot, Marc 'Ceci tuera cela, ou: la chose imprimée contre le livre' in *Romantisme*,
Vol. 14, No 44, 1984

Angenot, Marc 'La littérature populaire française au dix-neuvième siècle' in *Canadian
Review of Comparative Literature*, Vol. 9, No.3, September 1982

Angenot, Marc 'Pornographies Fin-de-siècle' in *Cahiers pour la littérature populaire*,
No.7, Autumn-Winter 1986

Angenot, Marc *Le roman populaire. Recherches en paralittérature*, Ed. Presses de
l'Université du Québec, Montréal 1975

Antona, Marie-France '*Reality Show*: critique télévisuelle et "lieux du genre" ' in
Christian Plantin (ed.) *Lieux communs, topoï, stéréotypes, clichés*, Éditions Kimé,
Paris 1993

Appignanesi, Lisa *Cabaret: The First Hundred Years*, Methuen, London 1984

Aragon, Louis 'Léo Férré et la mise en chanson' in *Les Lettres Françaises*, No 859, 19–25 January 1961

Arasse, Daniel *Le Détail. Pour une histoire rapprochée de la peinture*, Champs Flammarion, Paris 1996

Archives nationales, *Contrôle de la presse, de la librairie et du colportage sous le Second Empire 1852–1879*, Paris 1995

Argentieri, Mino *Il cinema sovietico negli anni trenta*, Riuniti, Rome 1979

Argentieri, Mino *L'occhio del regime. Informazione e propaganda nel cinema del fascismo*, Vallecchi, Florence 1979

Aristotle, *Poetics*, Harvard University Press, Cambridge and London 1995

Armengaud, André 'Population in Europe' in Carlo M. Cipolla, *The Industrial Revolution*, Vol. 3 of *The Fontana Economic History of Europe*, Collins, Glasgow 1980

Arming, Wolfgang 'Economic aspects of the Phonographic Industry' in Kurt Blaukopf (ed.) *The Phonogram in Cultural Communication*, Springer-Verlag, Vienna and New York 1982

Arnheim, Rudolph 'A Forecast of Television' reprinted in Richard P. Adler, *Understanding Television. Essays on Television as a Social and Cultural Force*, Praeger, New York 1981

Arnold, Bruce *The Scandal of Ulysses. The Sensational Life of a Twentieth-Century Masterpiece*, St. Martin's Press, New York 1991

Arnold, Matthew *Culture and Anarchy and other Writings*, edited by Stefan Collini, CUP 1993

Arnould, Edmond *Essais de théorie et d'histoire littéraire*, Paris 1858, reprint Slatkine 1971

Aron, Paul (ed.) *La Belgique artistique et littéraire. Une anthologie de langue française (1848–1914)*, Éditions Complexe, Brussels 1997

Aron, Paul *Les écrivains belges et le socialisme (1880–1913)*, Éditions Labor, Brussels 1985

Aronowitz, Al 'The Beatles: Music's Gold Bugs' in Barney Hoskyns, *The Sound and the Fury, 40 Years of Classic Rock Journalism*, Bloomsbury, London 2003

Aronson, Michael 'The Wrong Kind of Nickel Madness: Pricing Problems for Pittsburgh Nickelodeons' in *Cinema Journal*, Vol. 42, No. 1, Fall 2002

Arpino, Giovanni and Roberto Antonetto *Vita, tempeste, sciagure di Salgari il padre degli eroi*, Rizzoli, Milan 1982

Arslan, Antonia (ed.) *Dame, droga e galline. Romanzo popolare e romanzo di consumo tra Ottocento e Novecento*, Unicopli, Milan 1986

Arslan, Antonia, 'Romanzo popolare e romanzo di consumo tra Ottocento e Novecento' in Arslan (ed.) *Dame, droga e galline*

Arts Council England, *Economic impact study of UK theatre* (Dominic Shellard), April 2004

Ashley, Mike (ed.) *Locked Rooms Mysteries and Impossible Crimes*, Robinson, London 2000

Ashliman, D. L. 'The American West in Twentieth-Century Germany' in *Journal of Popular Culture* Vol.2, No. 1, Summer 1968

Ashton (ed.) John *Chapbooks of the Eighteenth Century* (first published in 1882 by Chatto and Windus), Skoob publishing, London no date

Ashton, Rosemary *G. H. Lewes. An Unconventional Victorian*, Pimlico, London 2000

Ashton, Rosemary *George Eliot. A Life*, Penguin Books, Harmondsworth 1997

Asor Rosa, Alberto 'Il giornalista: un mestiere difficile' in Corrado Vivanti (ed.) *Storia d'Italia. Annali 4. Intellettuali e potere*, Einaudi, Turin 1981

Asor Rosa, Alberto *Storia d'Italia*, Vol. 4, Tome 2, *La Cultura*, Einaudi, Turin 1975

Asor Rosa, Alberto (ed.) *Letteratura italiana*, Vol. 2, *Produzione e consumo*, Einaudi, Turin 1983; Vol. 3, *L'età contemporanea* (1989), Einaudi, Turin 1989

Asor Rosa, Alberto, 'Centralismo e policentrismo nella letteratura italiana unitaria' in Asor Rosa (ed.) *Letteratura italiana. Storia e geografia, Vol. 3*

Aspesi, Natalia *Il lusso e l'autarchia. Storia dell'eleganza italiana 1930–1944*, Rizzoli, Milan 1982

Association Hôtel Mame Centre Culturelle, *Mame. Angers-Paris-Tours. Deux siècle du livre*, Catalogue de l'exposition, Tours-Paris 1989

Assouline, Pierre *Gaston Gallimard: un demi-siècle d'édition française*, Balland, Paris 1984

Assouline, Pierre *Hergé*, Folio-Gallimard, Paris 1996

Assouline, Pierre *Simenon. Biographie*, Julliard, Paris 1992

Atkinson, Nora *Eugène Sue et le Roman-Feuilleton*, André Lesot, Nemours 1929

Atwood, Margaret 'Mystery Man', *New York Review of Books* , 14 February 2002

Audience: Le journal de médiamétrie. No 19 June 1998, and No 20, December 1998

Auffret, Marc *La France de l'entre-deux-guerres 1919/1939*, Ed. Culture Art Loisir, Paris 1972

Aumont, Jacques 'Lumière revisited' in *Film History*, Vol. 8, No. 4, 1996, pp.416–30

Auriant, *La véritable histoire de 'Nana'*, Mercure de France, Paris 1943

Austen, Jane *Emma*, Everyman Library, London 1906, facsimile reprint 1991

Austen, Jane *Mansfield Park*, Everyman, J.M. Dent, London 1993

Austen, Jane *Northanger Abbey*, Penguin, Harmondsworth 1985

Austen, Jane, *Jane Austen's Letters*, collected and edited by Deirdre Le Faye, OUP 1995

Aveni, Anthony *Empires of Time. Calendars, Clocks, and Cultures*, Tauris Parke, London 2000

Bachlin, Peter *Histoire économique du cinéma*, La Nouvelle Édition, Paris 1947

Backschneider, Paula R. and John J. Richetti (eds) *Popular Fiction by Women 1660–1730*, Clarendon Press, Oxford 1996

Baeckvall, Hans 'Dumas dans un récit suédois du XIXe siècle' in *Cahiers Alexandre Dumas*, No. 13, 1984

Baedeker, *Paris and its environs. Handbook for travellers*, Leipzig and London 1878

Bailes, Kendall E. 'Sur la "Théorie des Valeurs" de A. V. Lunacarsky' in *Cahiers du monde russe et soviétique*, Vol.8, No.2, April-June 1967

Bailey, Peter 'Conspiracies of Meaning: Music-Hall and the Knowingness of Popular Culture' in *Past and Present*, No.144, August 1994

Bairoch, Paul 'Wages as an Indicator of Gross National product' in Scholliers (ed.) *Real Wages in nineteenth and twentieth Century Europe*

Bairoch, Paul *Histoire économique et sociale du monde du XVIe siècle à nos jours* Vols. 2 & 3: *Victoires et déboires*, Gallimard/Folio, Paris 1977

Baker, Christine R. and R.W. Last, *Erich Maria Remarque*, Oswald Wolff, London 1979

Bakhtin, Michael *Rabelais and His World*, Harvard University Press, Cambridge, Mass 1968

Bakker, B.H. (ed.) *'Naturalisme pas mort'. Lettres inédites de Paul Alexis à Émile Zola 1871–1900*, University of Toronto Press, Toronto 1971

Balayé, Simone. 'Preface' to Madame de Staël, *Corinne ou l'Italie*, Champion, Paris 2000

Balbi, Adrien 'Essai statistique sur la presse périodique du globe' in *Revue encyclopédique* Tome XXXVII, March 1828

Baldelli, Pio 'Bilancio dei rapporti Letteratura-Cinema' in *Problemi*, No.11–12, September-December 1968

Balibar, Renée and Dominique Laporte *Le Français national. Politique et pratiques de la langue nationale sous la Révolution française*, Hachette, Paris 1974

Balio, Tino 'Les films français et le marché du cinéma d'art et essai aux État-Unis 1948–1995' in Benghozi and Delage (eds) in *Une histoire économique du cinéma français (1895–1995)*

Balio, Tino 'The art film market in the new Hollywood' in Nowell-Smith and Ricci (eds) *Hollywood and Europe*

Ballard, Michel (ed.) *Europe et Traduction*, Artois Presses Université, Arras and Les Presses de l'Université d'Ottawa 1998

Balmand, Pascal 'Les best-sellers de la guerre froide' in *L'Histoire*, No.151, January 1992

Balzac, Honoré de, *Massimila Doni*, in *La Comédie humaine*, édition Gallimard/Pléiade, Vol. 10, 1979

Balzac, Honoré de *Illusions perdues*, Folio Gallimard, Paris 1988

Balzac, Honoré de *La muse du département* in *La Comédie humaine*, Vol. IV, Pléiade/Gallimard, Paris 1976

Balzac, Honoré de *Le Curé de village*, Livre de Poche, Paris 1965

Balzac, Honoré de *Illusions perdues*, in *La Comédie humaine*, édition Gallimard/Pléiade, Vol.5, 1977

Balzac, Honoré de *La duchesse de Langeais*, in *La Comédie humaine*, édition Gallimard/Pléiade, Vol.5, 1977

Balzac, Honoré de *La Peau de Chagrin*, Garnier Flammarion, Paris 1971

Banville, John 'A Life Elsewhere' in *New York Review of Books*, 20 November 1997

Barbagli, Marzio *Disoccupazione intellettuale e sistema scolastico in Italia (1859–1973)*, Il Mulino, Bologna 1974

Barber, Giles 'The English-language guide book to Europe up to 1870' in Robin Myers and Michael Harris (eds) *Journeys through the market. Travel, Travellers and the Book Trade*, St. Paul's Bibliographies, Folkestone 1999

Barber, Giles *Daphnis and Chloe, the markets and metamorphoses of an unknown bestseller* (The Panizzi Lectures 1988), The British Library, London 1989

Barber, Lynn *The Heyday of Natural History, 1820–1870*, Jonathan Cape, London 1980

Barbier, Frédéric 'Le commerce international de la librairie française au XIXᵉ siècle (1815–1913)' in *Revue d'Histoire Moderne et Contemporaine*, Vol. XXVIII, January-March 1981

Barbier, Frédéric 'Une production multipliée' in Chartier and Martin (eds) *Histoire de l'édition française*, Vol. 3

Barbier, Frédéric and Catherine Bertho Lavenir, *Histoire des médias, de Diderot à Internet*, Armand Colin, Paris 1996

Barbier, Frédéric *L'empire du livre. Le livre imprimé et la construction de l'Allemagne contemporaine (1815–1914)*, Les Éditions du Cerf, Paris 1995

Barbier, Patrick *Histoire des Castrats*, Bernard Grasset, Paris 1989

Barbier, Patrick *Opera in Paris, 1800–1850. A Lively History*, Amadeus Press, Portland Oregon 1995

Barbieri, R. *Vite Ardenti nel teatro*, Milan 1931

Barbour, Stephen and Cathie Carmichael (eds) *Language and Nationalism in Europe*, Oxford University Press 2000

Barker, Adele Marie (ed.) *Consuming Russia. Popular Culture, Sex, and Society since Gorbachev*, Duke University Press, Durham NC and London 1999

Barker, Nicolas 'The Rise of the provincial book trade in England and the growth of a national transport system' in Frédéric Barabier, Sabine Juratic, and Dominique Varry (eds) *L'Europe et le Livre. Réseau et pratique du négoce de librarie XVIe-XIXe siècles*, Klincksieck, n.p. 1996

Barker, Ronald E. and Robert Escarpit, *La faim de lire*, UNESCO Paris 1973

Barnett, Graham Keith *Histoire des bibliothèques publiques en France de la Révolution à 1939*, Promodis, Paris 1987

Baron, Dennis 'Will Anyone Accept the Good News on Literacy?' in *The Chronicle of Higher Education*, 1 February 2002

Barrachina, Marie-Aline *Propagande et culture dans l'Espagne franquiste: 1936–1945*, ELLUG, Grenoble 1998

Barrell, Joan and Brian Braithwaite, *The Business of Women's Magazines*, Kogan Page, London 1988

Barrell, John 'Divided we Grow' in *London Review of Books*, 5 June 2003

Barrère, Bernard 'Le roman de tauromachie de 1870 à 1921, ou l'échec d'un genre populaire' in *Les productions populaires en Espagne 1850–1920*, Université de Pau, CNRS, Paris 1986

Barrère, Bernard '*Dédalo*, 1922: un fil d'Arianne dans le labyrinthe de la concentration industrielle (Domaine du livre espagnol)' in *Livres et librairies en Espagne et au Portugal (XVIe-XXe siècles)*. Actes du Colloque international de Bordeaux, CNRS Paris 1989

Barrère, Bernard 'La crise du roman en Espagne 1915–1936. Le cas d'un romancier: Alberto Insúa' in *Bulletin Hispanique*, Vol. 85, No 3–4, July-December 1983

Barrows, Susanna *Distorting Mirrors. Visions of the Crowd in Late Nineteenth-Century France*, Yale University Press 1981

Barstow, Susan Torrey '"Hedda is all of us": Late Victorian Women at the Matinée' in *Victorian Studies*, Spring 2001

Bart, István 'Publishing: service and/or commodity?' in *New Hungarian Quarterly*, Vol. 26, No.99, 1985

Barthes, Roland *Image Music Text*, Fontana Press, London 1977

Barthes, Roland *Le plaisir du texte*, Éditions du Seuil, Paris 1973

Bartlet, Elizabeth C. 'On the Freedom of the Theatre and Censorship: the *Adrien* Controversy (1792)' in Hennion (ed.) *1789–1989 Musique, Histoire, Démocratie*, Vol. I

Basilio, Kelly 'Zola et son impact: naissance d'un romancier, Eça de Queirós' in Dezalay (ed.) *Zola sans frontières*

Batt, Kurt 'Tradition et renouveau. Réflexions sur la création littéraire en RDA' in *Europe*, Vol. 51, No.531–532, July-August 1973

Battestin, Martin C. (ed.) *Dictionary of Literary Bibliography*, Vol. 39: *British Novelists 1660–1800*, Gale Research Co., Detroit Michigan 1985

Baude, Michel 'Le journal de P-H Azaïs, père de famille et philosophe' in *Romantisme*, Vol.7, Nos 17–18, 1977

Baudelaire, Charles 'Le Peintre de la vie moderne' in *Oeuvres complètes*, Gallimard La Pléiade, 1961

Baudelaire, Charles *Écrits sur l'art*, Livre de Poche, Paris 1992

Baudelaire, Charles *Salon de 1859. Lettres à M. le Directeur de La Revue Française*, collection Litteratura.com, p.10 *http://baudelaire.litteratura.com/ressources/pdf/oeu_4.pdf*

Baudet, Colette *Grandeur et misères d'un éditeur belge: Henry Kistemaeckers (1851–1934)*, Éditions Labor, Brussels 1986

Baudin, Rodolphe 'Le phénomène de la *série culte* en contexte soviétique et post-soviétique. L'exemple de Semnadcat mgnovenij vesny' in *Cahiers de Monde Russe*, Vol. 42, No. 1, January-March 2001

Bauer, Roger 'La parodie dans les lettres autrichiennes: d'Aloys Blumauer à Johann Nepomuk Nestroy' in Stieg and Valentin (eds) *Johann Nestroy 1801–1862*

Bauer, Roger *La Réalité, royaume de Dieu, études sur l'originalité du théâtre viennois dans la première moitié du XIXe siècle*, Max Hueber Verlag, Munich 1965

Bauman, Thomas 'The Eighteenth Century: Serious Opera' in Parker (ed.) *The Oxford Illustrated History of the Opera*

Baumann, Gerd (ed.) *The Written Word. Literacy in Transition*, The Clarendon Press, Oxford 1986

BBC Handbook 1940

Beauvoir, Simone de *Mémoires d'une jeune fille rangée*, Gallimard, Paris 1958

Beaven, Miranda 'Readership in Early Nineteenth-century Russia: Recent Soviet Research' in *Slavic Review*, No. 2, Summer 1984

Beaven, Miranda 'Russian Literary Almanacs of the 1820s and their Legacy' in *Publishing History*, No. 17, 1985

Beavis, Catherine 'Reading, Writing and Role-Playing Computer Games' in Ilana Snyder (ed.) *Silicon Literacies: Communication, Innovation and Education in the Electronic Age*, Routledge, London 2002, *http://cmeskill.tripod.com/beavis.pdf*

Beavis, Simon 'Piracy steals notes from sound talent', *Guardian*, 10 January 1997

Becciu, Leonardo *Il fumetto in Italia*, Sansoni, Florence 1971

Becker, Corinne 'Introduction' to Émile Zola, *Nana*, Classiques Garnier, Paris 1994

Becker, Henry Jay 'Who's Wired and Who's Not: Children's Access to and Use of Computer Technology' in *The Future of Children And Computer Technology* Vol. 10, No. 2, Fall/Winter 2000, p.64 accessed *www.teacherlib.org/articles/becker.pdf*

Bedell, Geraldine 'Mills & Boom Boom' in *Observer Magazine*, 15 December 2002

Beebee, Thomas O. *Clarissa on the Continent: Translation and Seduction*, Pennsylvania State University Press, University Park Penn. 1990

Beethoven, Ludwig van, *The Letters of Beethoven* edited by Emily Anderson, Vol. I, Macmillan, London 1961

Beghelli, and Nicola Gallino (eds) *Tutti I libretti di Rossini*, Garzanti, no place, 1991

Behrman, Baruch 'Le lecteur des Vies des saints' (1982) in Stroev (ed.) *Livre et lecture en Russie*

Beletski, Alexandre 'Étudier l'histoire du lecteur: un problème actuel de l'histoire littéraire' (1922) in Stroev (ed.) *Livre et lecture en Russie*

Belknap, Robert L. 'Survey of Russian journals, 1840–80' in Martinsen (ed), *Literary Journals in Imperial Russia*

Bellanger, Claude, Jacques Godechot, Pierre Guiral and Fernand Terrou, *Histoire Générale de la Presse française*, Vol.2, PUF, Paris 1969 and Vol.3, 1972

Belli, Giuseppe Gioacchino *Sonetti*, Mondadori, Milan 1978

Bellos, David 'La conjuncture de la production' in Chartier and Martin (eds) *Histoire de l'édition française*, Vol.2, *Le livre triomphant 1660–1830*

Bellos, David 'Le Marché du livre à l'époque romantique: recherches et problèmes' in *Revue Française d'histoire du livre*, Vol. 47, No. 20, July–September 1978

Belmont, Nicole 'L'Académie celtique et George Sand. Les débuts des recherches folkloriques en France' in *Romantisme*, No. 9, 1975

Belton, John 'Awkward transitions: Hitchcock's *Blackmail* and the dynamics of early film sound' in *The Musical Quarterly*, Vol. 83, No. 2, Summer 1999

Beltran, Alain and Patrice A. Carré, *La fée et la servante. La société française face à l'électricité XIXe-XXe siècle*, Belin, Paris 1991

Benedetti, Anna *Le traduzioni italiane di Walter Scott e i loro anglicismi*, Olschki, Florence 1974

Benelli, Graziano 'Il romanzo erotico in Francia: il caso "Emmanuelle"' in Petronio and Schulz-Buschhaus (eds) *'Trivialliteratur?'*

Ben-Ghiat, Ruth 'Italian Fascism and the Aesthetics of the "Third Way"' in *Journal of Contemporary History*, Vol. 31, No. 2, April 1996

Ben-Ghiat, Ruth *Fascist Modernities. Italy, 1922–1945*, California University Press, Berkeley and Los Angeles 2001

Benghozi, Pierre-Jean and Christian Delage (eds) *Une histoire économique du cinéma français (1895–1995)*, L'Harmattan, Paris 1997

Benjamin, Walter 'The Work of Art in the Age of Mechanical Reproduction', in *Illuminations*, edited by Hannah Arendt, Jonathan Cape, London 1970

Bennett, E. A. (Arnold) *Fame and Fiction. An Enquiry into Certain Popularities*, Grant Richards, London 1901

Bennett, Scott 'Victorian Newspaper Advertising: Counting What Counts' in *Publishing History*, No.8, 1980

Bennett, Scott 'Revolutions in thought: serial publication and the mass market for reading' in Shattock and Wolff (eds) *The Victorian periodical press*

Bércy, Robert 'Chanson et révolution' in Hennion (ed.) *1789–1989 Musique, Histoire, Démocratie*, Vol. II

Berend, Ivan T. *The Crisis Zone of Europe*, trans. by Adrienne Makkay-Chanbers, CUP 1986

Berengo, Marino *Intellettuali e librai nella Milano della restaurazione*, Einaudi, Turin 1980

Berg, Mikhail 'About the Literary Battle' in *Russian Studies in Literature*, Vol. 34, no.2, Spring 1998

Berghaus, Günter (ed.) *Fascism and Theatre. Comparative Studies on the Aesthetics and Politics of Performance in Europe, 1925–1945*, Berghahn Books, Providence and Oxford 1996

Berio, Luciano 'Commentaire au rock' in *Musique en jeu*, No.2, March 1971

Berlin, Isaiah 'Notes on Prejudice', *New York Review of Books*, 18 October 2001

Berlin, Isaiah, *The Soviet Mind. Russian Culture under Communism*, Brookings Institution Press, Washington DC 2003

Berlioz, Hector 'Rapport Fait à la Commission Française du Jury International de l'Exposition Universelle de Londres' *http://www.hberlioz.com/London/ Berlioz1851.html*

Berlioz, Hector *Euphonia ou la ville musicale*, Petite Bibliothèque ombres, Toulouse 1992

Berlioz, Hector *Mémoires*, Flammarion, Paris 1991

Berlioz, Hector *Les soirées de l'orchestre*, Éditions Stock, Paris 1980

Berman, Antoine *L'épreuve de l'étranger. Culture et traduction dans l'Allemagne romantique*, Gallimard, Paris 1984

Bernard, Antonia 'J. Kopitar, lien vivant entre la slavistique et la germanistique' in Espagne and Werner (eds) *Philologiques III. Qu'est-ce qu'une littérature nationale?*

Bernardini, Aldo 'Les catholiques et l'avènement du cinéma en Italie: promotion et contrôle' in Cosandrey, Gaudreault and Gunning (eds) *Une invention du diable? Cinéma des premiers temps et religion*

Berridge, Virginia 'Popular Sunday Papers and mid-Victorian society' in Boyce, Curran and Wingate (eds) *Newspaper History*

Bertaut, Jules *La littérature féminine d'aujourd'hui*, Librairie des annales, Paris 1909

Bertieri, Claudio 'Italie' in Moliterni (ed.) *Histoire Mondiale de la Bande Dessinée*

Bertone, Giorgio ' "Parlare ai borghesi": De Amicis, Il "Primo maggio" e la propaganda socialista' in *Movimento operaio e socialista*, Vol. 3, No.2–3 1980

Besançon, Alain 'Comment la Russie a pensé au peuple' in *Romantisme*, No. 9, 1975

Bettencourt Pires, Maria Laura *Walter Scott e o romantismo português*, Universidade Nova de Lisboa, Lisbon 1979

Betts, Ernest *The Film Business. A History of the British Cinema 1896–1972*, Allen and Unwin, London 1973

Beynet, Michel 'L'image fasciste de l'Amérique' in *Aspects de la culture italienne sous le fascisme. Actes du Colloque de Florence 14–15 décembre 1979*, Université de Grenoble, 1982

BFI Film & Television Handbook 2004 edited by Eddie Dyja, bfi publishing, London 2003

BFI Film and Television Handbook 2003–4 (bfi screenonline)

Bianchini, Angela *Cent'anni di romanzo spagnolo 1868–1962*, ERI, Turin 1973

Bianconi, Lorenzo and Giorgio Pestelli (eds) *Opera Production and Its Resources*, University of Chicago Press 1998

Bibliographie de France 'Étude sur l'*Index Translationum*', 22 September 1971, Vol. 160, No. 38

Bicknell, David and Robert Philip, 'Gramophone' in *The New Grove Dictionary of Music and Musicians*

Bienkowska, Barbara and Halina Chamerska, *Books in Poland. Past and Present*, Otto Harrassowitz, Wiesbaden 1990

Biget, Michelle 'Long terme et court terme des acquis musicaux de la Révolution française' in Hennion (ed.) *1789–1989: Musique, Histoire, Démocratie*, Vol. I

Bignan, Anne, *L'Ermite des Alpes* in A. Bignan, *Romans et nouvelles*, Dentu, Paris 1858

Bihiku, Koço 'Le roman contemporain albanais et l'actualité' in *Studia Albanica*, No. 2, Vol. 18, 1981

Billard, François and Didier Roussin, *Histoires de l'Accordéon*, Climats-INA, Paris 1991

Billard, Pierre *L'age classique du cinéma français*, Flammarion, Paris 1995

Billboard Book of Top Hits edited by Joel Whitburn, Billboard Books, New York 2004

Bing, Rudolf *5000 Nights at the Opera*, Doubleday, New York 1972

Biondi, Marino and Alessandro Borsotti (eds) *Cultura e fascismo. Letteratura arti e spettacolo di un Ventennio*, Ponte alle Grazie, Florence 1996

Biré, Edmond *Mémoires et souvenirs (1789–1830): la Révolution, l'Empire et la Restauration*, Victor Retaux et fils, Paris 1895

Biré, Edmond *Nouvelles causeries littéraires*, Vitte, Lyons 1908

Björnberg, Alf 'Musical Spectacle as Ritual: the Eurovision song contest' in Hennion (ed.) *1789–1989 Musique, Histoire, Démocratie*, Vol. II

Black, Alistair *A New History of the English Public Library: Social and Intellectual Contexts, 1850–1914*, Leicester University Press, London 1996

Blackbourn, David *The Fontana History of Germany 1780–1918. The Long Nineteenth Century*, Fontana Press, London 1997

Blamires, Alcuin (ed.) *Woman Defamed and Woman Defended. An Anthology of Medieval Texts*, Clarendon Press, Oxford 1992

Blaukopf, Kurt, 'Les jeunes musiciens dans la société industrielle: essai sur de nouvelles formes de comportement' in *Cultures*, Vol.1, No. 1, 1973

Bloch-Lainé, François *L'emploi des loisirs ouvriers et l'éducation populaire*, Librairie du Recueil Sirey, Paris 1936

Blondeau, Auguste Louis *Voyage d'un musicien en Italie (1810–1812)*, edited by Joël-Marie Fauquet, Mardaga, Liège 1993

Bloom, Harold *Cervantes's 'Don Quixote'*, Chelsea House Publishers, Philadelphia 2001

Blumberg, Edwina Jannie 'Tolstoy and the English Novel: A Note on *Middlemarch* and *Anna Karenina*' in *Slavic Review*, Vol. 30, No. 3, September 1971

Bluwal, Marcel *Un Aller*, Éditions Stock, Paris 1974

Bödeker, Hans Erich 'D'une "histoire littéraire du lecteur" à l'histoire du lecteur. Bilan et perspectives de l'histoire de la lecture en Allemagne' in Roger Chartier (ed.) *Histoire de la lecture*, IMEC/Éditions de la Maison des Sciences de l'Homme, Paris 1995

Bodin, Thierry 'Les Paysans et Paul-Louis' in *Balzac à Saché*, Bulletin de la société Honoré de Balzac de Touraine No. XIV, n.d. but 1978

Boetcher Joeres, Ruth-Ellen 'The German Enlightenment (1720–1790)' in Watanabe-O'Kelly (ed.) *The Cambridge History of German Literature*

Bogacz, Ted '"A Tyranny of Words": Language, Poetry, and Anti-modernism in England in the First World War' in *Journal of Modern History*, Vol. 58, No.3, Sept 1986

Boileau-Narcejac, *Le roman policier*, PUF, Paris 1994

Boime, Albert 'Entrepreneurial Patronage in Nineteenth-Century France' in Edward C. Carter, Robert Foster, and Joseph N. Moody, *Enterprise and entrepreneurs in nineteenth- and twentieth-century France*, Johns Hopkins University Press, Baltimore and London 1976

Bold, Christine *Selling the Wild West: Popular Western Fiction 1860–1960*, Indiana University Press, Bloomington and Indianapolis 1987

Bollème, Geneviève *La Bibliothèque Bleue. La littérature populaire en France du XVIe au XIXe siècle*, Julliard, Paris 1971

Bollinger, Ernst *La presse suisse: structure et diversité*, Lang, Bern and Frankfurt 1976

Boltanski, Luc 'La constitution du champ de la bande dessinée' in *Actes de la recherche en sciences sociales*, Vol. 1, No.1, January 1975

Bonamour, Jean '*Le Roman russe* et les slavophiles' in Michel Cadot (ed.) *Eugène-Melchior de Vogüé le héraut du roman russe*, Institut d'Études Slaves, Paris 1989

Bonghi, Ruggiero *Lettere critiche. Perché la letteratura italiana non sia popolare in Italia*, Marzorati editore, Milan 1971

Bontinck, Irmgard 'The Project: Aims and Results' in Kurt Blaukopf (ed.) *The Phonogram in Cultural Communication*, Springer-Verlag, Vienna and New York 1982

Boosey, William *Fifty Years of Music*, Ernest Benn Ltd., London 1931

Bordas, Éric 'Bel ou mal canto? Le chant romantique selon Hector Berlioz' in *Romantisme*, Vol. 29, No. 103, 1999

Bordoni, Carlo 'Il romanzo di consumo' in Livolsi (ed.) *Almeno un libro*

Bordoni, Carlo *Il romanzo di consumo. Editoria e letteratura di massa*, Liguori, Naples 1993

Bordwell, David *On the History of Film Style*, Harvard University Press, Cambridge, Mass 1997

Bordwell, David, Janet Staiger and Kristin Thompson, *The Classical Hollywood Cinema. Film Style and Mode of Production to 1960*, Routledge, London 1985

Borenstein, Eliot 'Public Offerings: MMM and the Marketing of Melodrama' in Barker (ed.) *Consuming Russia*

Borruso, Edoardo 'Aspetti della nascita dell'industria editoriale' in AA VV *Editoria e cultura a Milano tra le due guerre*

Bory, Jean-Louis *Eugène Sue*, Mémoire du Livre, Paris 2000

Boscq, Marie-Claire 'L'implantation des librairies à Paris (1815–1848)' in Mollier (ed.) *Le commerce de la librairie en France au XIXe siècle*

Boswell, James *Life of Johnson*, edited by R. W. Chapman, OUP 1980

Botrel, Jean-François 'L'aptitude à communiquer: Alphabétisation et scolarisation en Espagne de 1860 à 1920' in *De l'alphabétisation aux circuits du livre en Espagne*, CNRS, Centre régional de publication de Toulouse 1987, pp.105–40

Botrel, Jean-François 'La littérature *de cordel* en Espagne. Essai de synthèse' in Chartier and Lüsebrink (eds) *Colportage et lecture populaire*

Botrel, Jean-François 'Les libraires français en Espagne 1840–1920' in *Histoire du livre et de l'Édition dans les pays ibériques*, Presses Universitaires de Bordeaux, 1986

Botrel, Jean-François 'Les recherches sur le livre et la lecture en Espagne XVIIIe–XXe siècles' in Chartier (ed.) *Histoire de la lecture*

Botrel, Jean-François 'Naissance et essor d'une maison d'édition scolaire: La Casa Hernando de Madrid (I.1828–1883)' in *Livres et libraires en Espagne et au Portugal (XVIe-XXe siècles). Actes du Colloque international de Bordeaux*, CNRS Paris 1989

Botrel, Jean-François *La diffusion du livre en Espagne (1868–1914). Les libraires*, Casa de Velazquez, Madrid 1988

Botstein, Leon 'Listening through Reading: Musical Literacy and the Concert Audience' in *19th-Century Music*, Vol. 16, No. 2, Fall 1992

Bott, Caroline G. *The Life and Works of Alfred Bestall: illustrator of Rupert Bear*, Bloomsbury, London 2003

Botta, Cinzia 'Paolo Valera e gli 'abissi plebei' di Milano fin de siècle: immagine letteraria e realtà sociale' in *Rivista di Storia Contemporanea*, Vol. 17, No 1, January 1988

Bottomore, Stephen 'The Panicking audience?: early cinema and the "train effect"' in *Historical Journal of Film, Radio and Television*, Vol. 19, No. 2, 1999

Bouche, Michel, Brigitte Magnien, and Carmen Salaun 'Les collections populaires de contes et nouvelles au début du XXᵉ siècle: écritures, mythes et mentalités. Méthode d'approche et d'analyse: *El Cuento Semanal* 1907–1912' in *Les productions populaires en Espagne 1850–1920*, Université de Pau, CNRS, Paris 1986

Bourdieu, Pierre 'Vous avez dit "populaire"' in *Actes de la recherche en sciences sociales*, No. 46, March 1983

Bourdieu, Pierre, *Distinction. A Social Critique of the Judgement of Taste*, Routledge, London 1984

Bourdieu, Pierre, *The Field of Cultural Production*, Polity Press, Cambridge 1993

Bourdon, Jérôme 'L'archaïque et la postmoderne. Éléments pour une histoire d'un peu de télévision' in Jérôme Bourdon and François Jost (eds) *Penser la télévision. Actes du Colloque de Cerisy*, Nathan, Paris 1998

Bourgeois, Isabelle *Radios et télévisions privées en Allemagne entre la loi et le marché*, CIRAC, Levallois-Peret 1995

Bourke, Joanna 'Housewifery in Working-Class England 1860–1914' in *Past and Present*, No.143, May 1994

Bourke, Joanna *Working Class Cultures in Britain 1890–1960*, Routledge, London 1994

Boussel, Patrice and Madeleine Duboit *De Quoi Vivait Victor Hugo?*, Deux Rives, Paris 1952

Bousser-Eck, Hélène and Monique Sauvage 'Le règne de *Cinq colonnes* 1959–1965' in Jeanneney and Sauvage (eds) *Télévision, nouvelle mémoire*

Bouvier-Ajam, Maurice *Alexandre Dumas ou cent ans après*, Les éditeurs français réunis, Paris 1972

Bowlt, John E. 'The Failed Utopia: Russian Art, 1917–32' in *Art in America*, Vol.59, No. 4, July-August 1971

Boyce, George, James Curran and Pauline Wingate (eds) *Newspaper History from the seventeenth century to the present day* edited by Constable, London 1978

Boyd, Brian *Vladimir Nabokov. The American Years*, Chatto & Windus, London 1992

Boyd, Carolyn P. *Historia Patria. Politics, History, and National Identity in Spain, 1875–1975*, Princeton UP, Princeton NJ 1997

Boyer, Régis 'Introduction' in Hans-Christian Andersen, *Oeuvres*, Vol. I, Pléiade/Gallimard, Paris 1992

Boyer, Régis *Histoire des littératures scandinaves*, Fayard, Paris 1996

Boyle, Nicholas *Goethe. The Poet and the Age*, Vol. 1, *The Poetry of Desire*, The Clarendon Press, Oxford 1991; Vol..2, *Revolution and Renunciation (1790–1803)*, The Clarendon Press, Oxford 2000

Boyle, Thomas *Black Swine in the Sewers of Hampstead. Beneath of the Surface of Victorian Sensationalism*, Hodder and Stoughton, London 1990

Bradley, Ian *Abide with me. The world of Victorian hymns*, SCM Press, London 1997

Bradshaw, Graham 'Shakespeare's Peculiarity', *Proceedings of the British Academy*, OUP 2001

Braescu, Ion 'Erckmann-Chatrian en Roumanie' in *Europe*, Vol. 53, No. 549–50, January–February 1975

Braida, Lodovica 'Quelques considérations sur l'histoire de la lecture en Italie. Usages et pratiques du livre sous l'Ancien Régime' in Chartier (ed.) *Histoire de la lecture*

Brancaleoni, Francesca 'La *Ginevra* di Antonio Ranieri ed il *Twist* di Charles Dickens. Il Romanzo sociale agli esordi' in *Critica Letteraria*, n.102, Vol. 27, 1999

Brande, Dorothea *Wake Up and Live!*, Arthur Barker Ltd, London 1936

Brandes, Ute 'Anna Seghers's Politics of Affirmation' in Ian Wallace (ed.) *Anna Seghers in Perspective*, Rodopi, Amsterdam and Atlanta 1998

Branscombe, Peter 'Die Frühe Offenbach-Rezeption in Wien und Nestroys Anteil Daran' in *Austriaca*, Cahiers Universitaires d'Information sur l'Autriche, No. 46, June 1998

Branscombe, Peter 'Reflections on Raimund's Artistic Relationships with his Contemporaries' in W. E. Yates and John R. P. McKenzie (eds) *Viennese Popular Theatre: A Symposium*, University of Exeter 1985

Brassens, Georges 'Interview avec Georges Brassens' by Thérèse Hamel in *Marie-France*, No.127, September 1966

Bratton, Jacqueline S. *The Victorian Popular Ballad*, Macmillan, London and Basingstoke 1975

Braudel, Fernand *Écrits sur l'histoire*, Champs Flammarion, Paris 1969

Braun, Edward *The Director and the Stage*, Methuen, London 1982

Bravo, Anna *Il fotoromanzo*, Il Mulino, Bologna 2003

Breitenborn, Uwe ' "Memphis Tennessee" in Borstendorf: Boundaries Set and Transcended in East German Television Entertainment' in *Historical Journal of Film, Radio and Television*, Vol. 24, No. 3, 2004

Bretz, Mary Lee *Voices, Silences, and Echoes. A Theory of the Essay and the Critical reception of Naturalism in Spain*, Tamesis Books, London 1992

Brewer, John *The Pleasures of the Imagination. English Culture in the Eighteenth Century*, HarperCollins, London 1997

Brewster, Ben '*Traffic in Souls* (1913): An experience in feature-length narrative construction' in Grieveson and Krämer (eds) *The Silent Cinema Reader*

Brewster, Ben, and Lea Jacobs *Theatre to Cinema. Stage Pictorialism and the Early Feature Film*, OUP 1997

Briggs, Asa *The History of Broadcasting in the United Kingdom*, Vol. II, IV and V, Oxford University Press 1995

Brochand, Christian *Histoire générale de la radio et de la télévision en France*, Vol. II, *1944–1974*, La documentation française, Paris 1994

Brochon, Pierre (ed.) *Béranger et son temps*, Éditions sociales, Paris 1956

Brooke, Caroline 'Soviet Music in the International Arena 1932–41' in *European History Quarterly*, Vol.31, No. 2, April 2001

Brooke, Caroline 'Soviet Musicians and the Great Terror' in *Europe-Asia Studies*, Vol. 54, No. 3, 2002

Brooks, Jeffrey *When Russia Learned to read. Literacy and Popular Culture 1861–1917*, Princeton UP, Princeton N.J. 1985

Brooks, Louise 'Pabst and Lulu' in *Sight and Sound*, Vol. 34, No 3, Summer 1965

Brown, Frederick *Zola. A Life*, Macmillan, London and Basingstoke 1997

Brown, Richard ' "England is not big enough . . ." American rivalry in the early English film business: the case of Warick v. Urban, 1903' in *Film History*, Vol. 10, No. 1, 1998

Bruckner, Wolfgang 'Histoire de la *Volkskunde*. Tentative d'une approche à l'usage des français' in Isac Chiva and Utz Jeggle (eds) *Ethnologies en miroir*, Éditions de la Maison des sciences de l'homme, Paris 1987

Brunel, Pierre *Vincenzo Bellini*, Fayard, Paris 1981

Brunetta, Gian Piero *Storia del cinema italiano 1895–1945*, Editori Riuniti, 1979

Bruno, G. *Le Tour de France par deux enfants. Devoir et patrie*, Eugène Belin (1877), facsimile edition, Firmin-Didot 1974

Bruscagli, Riccardo and Roberta Turchi (eds) *Teorie del romanzo nel primo ottocento*, Bulzoni, Rome 1991

Buch, Esteban ' "Les Allemands et les Boches": la musique allemande à Paris pendant la Première Guerre mondiale' in *Le Mouvement Social*, No. 208, July–September 2004

Buch, Esteban 'Le chef d'orchestre: pratiques de l'autorité et métaphores politiques' in *Annales*, July-August 2002, No.4

Bulletin du livre (*Le*) 'Les best sellers du siècle', 15 October 1961

Bulletin du livre (*Le*)'Les Best sellers 1958–68', 15 Décembre 1968

Bulman, Joan *Jenny Lind. A biography*, James Barrie, London 1956

Bulo, Jorgo 'Les lettres albanaises et la résistance antifasciste' in *Studia Albanica*, No. 2, Vol. 21, 1984

Bunk, Thomas M. 'Allemagne' in Moliterni (ed.) *Histoire Mondiale de la Bande Dessinée*

Buonanno, Milly (ed.) *Eurofiction 2002. Sesto Rapporto sulla fiction televisiva in Europa*, VQPT-RAI No 191, Rome 2003

Buonanno, Milly 'Un orizzonte nebuloso. La fiction italiana nel 2001' in Buonanno (ed.) *Eurofiction 2002*

Bureau, Paul *La crise morale des temps nouveaux*, Bloud, Paris 1908

Burke Peter and Roy Porter (eds) *Language, Self, and Society. A Social History of Language*, Polity Press, Cambridge 1991

Burke, Peter 'The Invention of Leisure in Early Modern Europe' in *Past and Present*, No.146, February 1995

Burke, Peter 'The Uses of Literacy in Early Modern Italy' in Burke and Porter (eds) *The Social History of Language*

Burke, Peter and Roy Porter (eds) *The Social History of Language*, CUP, Cambridge 1987

Burke, Peter *The Art of Conversation*, Polity Press, Cambridge 1993

Burkholder, J. Peter 'Museum Pieces: The Historicist mainstream in Music of the Last Hundred Years' in *The Journal of Musicology*, Vol. 2, no.2 Spring 1983

Burnett, Robert *The Global Jukebox. The international music industry*, Routledge, London 1996

Burney, Fanny *Evelina*, Oxford University Press, 1982

Burroughs, Edgar Rice *Tarzan of the Apes*, Methuen, London 1920

Burton, John W. and Caitlin W. Thomson, 'Nanook and the Kirwinians: Deception, Authenticity, and the Birth of Modern Ethnographic Representation' in *Film History*, Vol. 14, No 1, 2002

Busch, Robert L. 'Victor Hugo's Narrative Prose Debut in Russia' in Richard Freeborn, R. Milner-Gulland and Charles A. Ward (eds) *Russian and Slavic Literature*, Slavic Publishers Inc., Cambridge, Mass. 1976

Buzzi, Carlo 'Il pubblico dei lettori: caratteristiche strutturali e specificità culturali' in Livolsi (ed.) *Almeno un libro*

Byron, George (Lord) *Byron's Letters and Journals* Vol. 10, 1822–1823, edited by Leslie A. Marchand, Belknap Press and Harvard University Press, Cambridge Mass., 1980

Cadioli, Alberto 'Un'indagine sull'editoria' in *Problemi*, No.96, January–April 1993

Cahiers Alexandre Dumas, No. 12, 1983

Calvet, Louis-Jean *La guerre des langues et les politiques linguistiques*, Hachette, Paris 1999

Calvino, Italo 'La "Romantica"' in AA VV *Editoria e cultura a Milano tra le due guerre (1920–1940)*

Camerino, Marinella Colummi 'Il romanzo nella prima metà dell'Ottocento' in *Problemi*, No. 65, September–December 1982

Camerino, Marinella Colummi 'Un topos critico: il riassunto dei romanzi nelle recensioni ottocentesche' in *Problemi*, No. 78, January–April 1987

Cammelli, Andrea and Angelo di Francia, 'Studenti, università, professioni' in Maria Malatesta (ed.) *Storia d'Italia, Annali 10, I professionisti*, Einaudi, Turin 1996

Campeanu, Pavel 'Romanian Television: From Image to History' in Phillip Drummond, Richard Paterson and Janet Willis (eds) *National Identity in Europe. The Television Revolution*, BFI, London 1993

Candeloro, Giorgio *Storia dell'Italia moderna* Vol. 6: *Lo sviluppo del capitalismo e del movimento operaio 1871–1896*, Feltrinelli, Milan 1978

Candiani, Rosy ' "Quegli eterni *Promessi sposi*". La fortuna musicale del romanzo manzoniano' in *Critica Letteraria*, Vol. 27, No.105, 1999

Canepa, Nancy (ed.) *Out of the Woods: The origins of the Literary Fairy Tale in Italy and France*, Wayne State UP, Detroit 1997

Canepa, Nancy ' "Quando 'nc'è da cà a lo luoco dove aggio da ire?": Giambattista Basile's Quest for the Literary Fairy Tale' in Canepa (ed.) *Out of the Woods*, cit.

Canepa, Nancy *From Court to Forest. Giambattista Basile 'Lo cunto de li cunti' and the Birth of the Literary Fairy Tale* Wayne State UP Detroit 1999

Cannone, Belinda *Musique et littérature au XVIIIᵉ siècle*, PUF, Paris 1998

Canova, Gianni 'Giorgio Scerbanenco' in *Problemi*, No. 88, May–August 1990

Canova, Gianni 'Scerbanenco e il delitto alla milanese' in Vittorio Spinazzola (ed.) *Il successo letterario*, Unicopli, Milan 1985

Cantaloube-Ferrieu, Lucienne *Chanson et poésie des années 30 aux années 60. Trenet, Brassens, Ferré . . . ou les 'enfants naturels' du surréalisme*, A.G. Nizet, Paris 1981

Capecchi, Vittorio and Marino Livolsi *La stampa quotidiana in Italia*, Bompiani, Milan 1971

Caplan, Cora 'Introduction' to Elizabeth Barrett Browning, *Aurora and other poems*, The Women's Press, London 2001

Capp, Bernard *Astrology and the Popular Press: English Almanacks 1500–1800*, Faber, London 1977

Caradec, François *Histoire de la Littérature enfantine en France*, Albin Michel, Paris 1977

Carbonell, Charles-Olivier 'La réception de l'historiographie allemande en France (1866–1885): le mythe du modèle importé' in Espagne and Werner (eds) *Transferts. Les relations interculturelles dans l'espace franco-allemend (XVIIIe-XIX siècle)*

Cardigos, Isabel *In and Out of Enchantment: Blood Symbolism and Gender in Portoguese Fairytales, Folklores Fellows' Communications* No. 260, Suomalainen Tiedeakademia Academia Scientiarium Fennica, Helsinki, 1996

Cardini, Franco *Europe and Islam*, Blackwell, Oxford 2001

Cardot, Fabienne 'L'électricité, merveille du siècle' in François Caron and Fabienne Cardot, *Espoirs et Conquêtes 1881–1918*, Vol. One of *Histoire Générale de l'Électrcité en France*, Fayard, Paris 1991

Carlini, Antonio 'Le bande musicali nell'Italia dell'ottocento: il modello militare, I rapporti con il teatro e la cultura dell'orchestra negli organici strumentali' in *Rivista italiana di musicologia*, Vol. 30, No. 1, 1995

Carloni, Massimo 'Nazionalismo, eurocentrismo, razzismo e misogenia nel "Ciclo del Far-West" di Emilio Salgari' in *Problemi*, No. 97, May–August 1993

Carlyle, Thomas *A Carlyle Reader. Selections from the Writings*, edited by G. B. Tennison, CUP 1984

Carlyle, Thomas *Critical and Miscellaneous Essays*, Vol. 2, Chapman, London 1888

Carlyle, Thomas *On Heroes, Hero-Worship, and the Heroic in History*, University of California Press 1993

Carlyle, Thomas *Sartor Resartus*, OUP 1987

Carlyle, Thomas *The French Revolution. A History*, Volume I *The Bastille* Book VI, The Folio Society, London 1989

Carmichael, Cathie ' "A People exists and that people has its language": Language and Nationalism in the Balkans' in Barbour and Carmichael (eds) *Language and Nationalism in Europe*

Carmichael, Cathie 'Coming to terms with the Past: Language and Nationalism in Russia and its Neighbours' in Barbour and Carmichael (eds) *Language and Nationalism in Europe*

Carpenter, Humphrey *The Envy of the World: Fifty Years of the BBC Third Programme and Radio 3: 1946–1996*, Weidenfeld and Nicolson, London 1996

Carpi, Umberto 'Egemonia moderata e intellettuali nel Risorgimento' in Vivanti (ed.) *Storia d'Italia. Annali 4 Intellettuali e potere*,

Carré, Patrice 'La transformation de l'espace privé ou la magie électrique' in Lévy-Leboyer and Morsel (eds) *L'Interconnexion et le Marché 1919–1946*

Carse, Adam 'Adolphe Sax and the Distin Family' in *The Music Review*, Vol. 6, No. 4, November 1945

Carson, James P. 'Enlightenment, popular culture, and Gothic fiction' in Richetti (ed.) *The Cambridge Companion to the Eighteenth-Century Novel*

Carteggio Verdi-Ricordi 1880–81, Istituto di Studi Verdiani, Parma 1988

Carter, Angela (ed.) *The Virago Book of Fairy Tales*, Virago, London 1990

Carter, Huntley *The New Spirit in The European Theatre 1914–1924. A comparative study of the changes effected by the war and revolution*, Ernest Benn, London 1925

Carter, Tim 'The Seventeenth Century' in Parker (ed.) *The Oxford Illustrated History of the Opera*

Carter, William C. *Marcel Proust. A Life*, Yale University Press, New Haven and London 2000

Caruso Jr, Enrico *Enrico Caruso. My father and my family*, Amadeus Press, Portland, Oregon 1997

Caruzzi, Antonella Licalsi 'Il libretto d'opera e la società romantica' in *Problemi* No.27, May-June 1971

Casanova, Giacomo *Histoire de ma vie*, Robert Laffont, Paris 1993, Vol.3

Casanova, Julián *La Iglesia de Franco*, Temas de Hoy, Madrid 2001

Casini, Paolo 'Il rinascimento immaginario di D'Annunzio' in *Problemi*, No.82, May-August 1988

Casselle, Pierre 'Le régime législatif' in Chartier and Martin (eds) *Histoire de l'édition française*, Vol. 3

Castiglione, Baldissare *The Book of the Courtier*, Penguin, Harmondsworth 1967

Catalogo generale, Fratelli Treves Editori, Decembre 1903

Catalogo generale della libreria italiana dall'anno 1847 a tutto il 1899, Kraus Reprint, Vaduz 1964

Catterall, Peter (ed.) *The Making of Channel 4*, Frank Cass, London 1999

Catterall, Peter, Colin Seymour-Ure and Adrian Smith (eds) *Northcliffe's Legacy. Aspects of the British Popular Press, 1896–1996*, Macmillan, London 2000

Caudet, Francisco 'En folletin en *Fortunata y Jacinta*' in *Les productions populaires en Espagne 1850–1920*, Université de Pau, CNRS, Paris 1986, pp.195–220

Cavallo, Pietro 'Theatre Politics of the Mussolini Régime and Their Influence on Fascist Drama' in Berghaus (ed.) *Fascism and Theatre*

Cavallo, Pietro *Immaginario e rappresentazione. Il teatro fascista di propaganda*, Bonacci, Rome 1990

Cavalone, Franco 'Il bibliofilo a fumetti' in Vittorio Spinazzola (ed.) *Pubblico 1977*, Il Saggiatore, Milan 1977

Caygill, Howard *Walter Benjamin. The Colour of Experience*, Routledge, London and New York 1998

Cecchi, Emilio *America Amara*, Sansoni, Florence

Cellard, Jacques *Un génie dévergondé. Nicolas-Edme Rétif, dit 'de La Bretonne' (1734–1806)*, Plon, Paris 2000

Censorship. A World Encyclopedia edited by Derek Jones, Fitzroy Dearborn, London and Chicago 2001

Cepak, Nivea 'Pubblicità e fiaba in "Carosello"' in *Problemi*, Nos.25–26, January-April 1971

Certeau, Michel de *La culture au pluriel*, Seuil 1993, Paris 1993

Certeau, Michel de, Dominique Julia and Jacques Revel *Une politique de la langue. La Révolution française et les patois*, Gallimard, Paris 1975

Ceserani, R. and E. Salibra 'Popular Literature in Nineteenth-Century Italy: *Letteratura amena*' in *Canadian Review of Comparative Literature*, Vol. 9, September 1982

Chalaby, Jean 'Northcliffe: Proprietor as Journalist' in Catterall, Seymour-Ure and Smith (eds) *Northcliffe's Legacy*

Chalaby, Jean K. *The Invention of Journalism*, Macmillan Press, Basingstoke and London 1998

Chambers, Helen 'Afterword' to the English translation of Theodor Fontane's *Effi Briest*, Angel Books, London 1995

Champ, Hamish 'Keys to success' in *Music Business International*, August 2001

Chanan, Michael *Musica Practica. The Social Practice of Western Music from Gregorian Chant to Postmodernism*, Verso, London 1994

Chanan, Michael *Repeated Takes. A Short History of Recording and Its Effects on Music*, Verso, London 1995

Chandler, James *England in 1819. The Politics of Literary Culture and the Case of Romantic Historicism*, Chicago University Press 1998

Chandrika Kaul 'Popular Press and Empire: Northcliffe, India and the *Daily Mail*, 1896–1922' in Catterall, Seymour-Ure and Smith (eds) *Northcliffe's Legacy*

Chaniac, Régine and Jean-Pierre Jézéquel 'Julie Lescaut vince su Loana. La fiction tv francese nel 2001' in Buonanno (ed.) *Eurofiction 2002*

Chapman, John (? Unsigned article) 'The Commerce of Literature' *Westminster Review*, Vol 1, April 1852

Charaudeau, Patrick and Rodolphe Ghiglione, *La parole confisquée. Un genre télévisuel: le talk show*, Dunod, Paris 1997

Charle, Christophe 'Champ littéraire français et importations étrangères. De la vogue du roman russe à l'emergence d'un nationalisme littéraire (1886–1902)' in Espagne and Werner (eds) *Philologiques III*

Charle, Christophe 'Le champ de la production littéraire' in Chartier and Martin (eds) *Histoire de l'édition française*, Vol. 3, *Le temps des éditeurs*

Charle, Christophe 'Situation spatiale et position sociale. Essai de géographie sociale du champ littéraire à la fin du 19e siècle' in *Actes de la recherche en sciences sociales*, No. 13, February 1977

Charle, Christophe *Les intellectuels en Europe au XIXe siècle. Essai d'histoire comparée*, Seuil, Paris 2001

Charlton, David 'The Nineteenth Century: France' in Parker (ed.) *The Oxford Illustrated History of the Opera*

Chartier, Roger (ed.) *Histoire de la lecture*, IMEC Éditions et Éditions de la Maison des Sciences de l'Homme, Paris 1995

Chartier, Roger 'Des "Secrétaires" pour le peuple?' in Roger Chartier (ed.) *La correspondance. Les usages de la lettre au XIXe siècle*, Fayard, Paris 1991

Chartier, Roger 'Du livre au livre' in Roger Chartier (ed.) *Pratiques de la lecture*, Rivages, Paris 1985

Chartier, Roger 'Frenchness in the History of the Book: from the History of Publishing to the History of Reading' in *Proceedings of the American Antiquarian Society*, 1987 97/2

Chartier, Roger 'Introduction' in Chartier and Lüsebrink (eds) *Colportage et lecture populaire*

Chartier, Roger 'Lecteurs dans la longue durée: du *codex* à l'écran' in Chartier (ed.) *Histoire de la lecture*

Chartier, Roger and Hans-Jürgen Lüsebrink (eds) *Colportage et lecture populaire. Imprimés de large circulation en Europe XVIe-XIXe siècles*, Éditions de la Maison des Sciences de l'Homme, Paris 1996

Chartier, Roger and Henri-Jean Martin (eds) *Histoire de l'édition française*, Vol.2, *Le livre triomphant 1660–1830*; Vol. 3, *Le temps des éditeurs. Du romantisme à la Belle Époque*, Fayard, Paris 1990

Chartier, Roger *Cultural History. Between Practices and Representation*, Polity, Oxford 1988

Chartier, Roger *The Cultural Uses of Print in Early Modern France*, translated from the French by Lydia G. Cochrane, Princeton University Press 1987

Charue-Ferrucci, Jeanine 'Du mélodrame à la comedie féerique. Victor Ducange Trente ans ou la vie d'un joueur et Nestroy: Dreissig Jahre aus dem Leben eines Lumpen' in Stieg and Valentin (eds) *Johann Nestroy 1801–1862*

Chemello, Adriana *La biblioteca del buon operaio. Romanzi e precetti per il popolo nell'Italia unita*, Unicopli, Milan 1991

Cherchi Usai, Paolo 'Italy: Spectacle and Melodrama' in Nowell-Smith (ed.) *The Oxford History Of World Cinema*

Cherchi Usai, Paolo 'The Early Years' in Nowell-Smith (ed.) *The Oxford History Of World Cinema*

Cherchi Usai, Paolo *Georges Méliès*, La Nuova Italia, Florence 1983

Chevrel, Yves 'Vers une histoire du Naturalisme dans les littératures de langues européennes?' in Dezalay (ed.) *Zola sans frontières*

Chimènes, Myriam 'La "Nomenklatura" Musicale en France sous la IIIe République' in Hugues Dufourt and Joël-Marie Fauquet (eds) *Musique et médiations. Le métier, l'instrument, l'oreille*, Klincksieck, Paris 1994

Chimènes, Myriam 'La princesse Edmond de Polignac et la création musicale' in Dufourt and Fauquet (eds) *La musique et le pouvoir*

Chirac, Jacques speech of 30 November 2002, full text at *http://www.elysee.fr/cgi-bin/ auracom/aurweb/search/file?aur_file=discours/2002/021130DU.htm*

Choppin, Alain *Les manuels scolaires. Histoire et actualité*, Hachette, Paris 1992

Choukroun, Jacques 'Controler les studios, un atout pour les grandes compagnies française des années trente?' in Benghozi and Delage (eds) *Une histoire économique du cinéma français (1895–1995)*

Christiansen, Rupert *Prima Donna*, Pimlico, London 1995

Christie, Ian review of Rachel Low's *The History of the British Film*, in *Journal of Popular British Cinema*, No. 2, 1999

Christout, Marie-Françoise 'La Féerie romantique au théâtre: de la Sylphide (1832) à la Biche au bois (1845), choréographie, décors, trucs et machines' in *Romantisme*, No. 38, 1982

Churchill, R. C. 'The Genius of Charles Dickens' in Boris Ford (ed.) *The New Pelican Guide to English Literature*, Vol. 6: *From Dickens to Hardy*, Penguin, London 1990

Chusid, Martin (ed.) *Verdi's Middle Period, 1849–1859: Source studies, analysis and performance practice*, Chicago University Press 1997

Chusid, Martin 'Toward an Understanding of Verdi's Middle Period' in Chusid (ed.) *Verdi's Middle Period, 1849–1859*

Chvedov, Sergueï 'Les livres qui avaient nos préférence' in Stroev (ed.) *Livre et lecture en Russie*

Ciampi, Antonio 'Aspetti delle diffusione del cinematografo nelle zone depresse dell'Italia' in *Lo Spettacolo*, Vol. 5, No. 1, January March 1955

Ciampi, Antonio 'Limiti per la spesa per spettacoli in Italia' in *Lo spettacolo*, Vol 3, no 2, April–June 1953

Cipolla, Carlo *Literacy and Development in the West*, Penguin, Harmondsworth 1969

Claeys, Gregory 'Mass Culture and World Culture on "Americanization" and the Politics of Cultural Protectionism' in *Diogenes*, 1986 No. 136

Clark, Andrew 'All shook up over classical music' *Financial Times*, 22 March 1997

Clark, Katerina ' "Boy gets tractor" and all that: the parable structure of the Soviet novel' in Richard Freeborn, R. R. Milner-Gulland and Charles A. Ward (eds) *Russian and Slavic Literature*, Slavic Publishers, Cambridge, Mass. 1976

Clark, Katerina 'The Mutability of the Canon: Socialist Realism and Chingiz Aitmatov's *I dol'she veka dlitsia den*' in *Slavic Review*, No. 4, Winter 1984

Clark, Katerina and Michael Holquist, *Mikhail Bakhtin*, Harvard University Press 1984

Clark, Katerina *The Soviet Novel. History as Ritual*, Indiana University Press, Bloomington and Indianapolis 2000

Clarke, Graham 'Poe and his Critics' in Edgar Allan Poe, *Tales of Mystery and Imagination*, J. M. Dent Everyman, London 1993

Clarke, I. F. 'Forecasts of Warfare in Fiction' in *Comparative Studies in Society and History*, Vol. 10, No 1, October 1967

Clayton, Timothy *The English Print: 1688–1802*, Yale University Press 1997

Clery, E. J. 'Introduction' to Ann Radcliffe, *The Italian*, OUP 1998

Close, Anthony *The Romantic Approach to 'Don Quixote'. A critical history of the romantic tradition in 'Quixote' criticism.* Cambridge University Press 1977

Clyman, Toby W. and Judith Vowles (eds) *Russia Through Women's Eyes. Autobiographies from Tsarist Russia*, Yale University Press, New Haven and London 1996

Cobo, Leila 'Shakira x 2', *Billboard*, 28 May 2005

Cocks, H.G. 'Peril in the personals: the dangers and pleasures of classified advertising in early twentieth-century Britain' in *Media History* Volume 10 Number 1, April 2004

Cocteau, Jean preface to Gaston Leroux, *Le Mystère de la chambre jaune*, Le Livre de Poche, Paris 1996

Codelli, Lorenzo 'La Commedia Italo-Francese' in Jean A. Gili and Aldo Tassone (eds) *Parigi-Roma 50 anni di coproduzioni italo-francesi (1945–1995)*, Il Castoro, Milan 1995

Cohen, Gary *The Politics of Ethnic Survival: Germans in Prague 1861–1914*, Princeton University Press , Princeton NJ, 1981

Cohen, Margaret 'Women and fiction in the nineteenth century' in Unwin (ed.) *The Cambridge Companion to the French Novel*

Cohen, Margaret *The Sentimental Education of the Novel*, Princeton University Press 1999

Cohen-Solal, Annie *Sartre. A Life*, Heinemann, London 1988

Coleridge, Samuel Taylor *Biographia Literaria*, Volume Two, William Pickering, London 1847

Coles, Joanna 'Sleazy does it for Jerry', *Guardian*, 19 February 1998

Colley, Linda *Captives. Britain, Empire and the World 1650–1850*, Jonathan Cape, London 2002

Collier, Peter and Robert Lethbridge (eds) *Artistic Relations. Literature and the Visual Arts in Nineteenth-Century France*, Yale University Press, New Haven and London 1994

Collini, Silvia and Antonella Vannoni, 'Un'impresa editoriale del primo Ottocento: la collana Sonzogno del "Viaggi più interessanti". I resoconti di viaggio da relazione scientifica a opera letteraria' in *Problemi*, No. 98, September–December 1993

Collins, Philip *Charles Dickens, The Public Readings*, Clarendon Press, Oxford 1975

Collins, Wilkie *The Moonstone*, edited by Steve Farmer, Broadview, Toronto 1999

Coltham, Stephen 'English Working Class Newspapers in 1867' in *Victorian Studies*, Vol. 13, No. 2, December 1969

Comini, Alessandra *The Changing Image of Beethoven. A Study in Mythmaking*, Rizzoli, New York 1987

Commission européenne. Direction générale X, *Statistiques de la culture en Europe. Premiers éléments*, 1996

Compère, Daniel 'Le Robinson Suisse relu et récrit par Hetzel' in Christian Robin (ed.) *Un Éditeur et son siècle. Pierre-Jules Hetzel*, ACL-Crocus édition, Saint-Sébastien 1988

Complete UK Hit Singles 1952–2004, edited by Graham Betts, Collins, London 2004

Conant, Martha Pike *The Oriental tale in England in the Eighteenth Century*, Columbia University Press, New York 1908

Conati, Marcello 'L'arte di Verdi fra "le ingiurie del tempo" e gl'infortuni della critica' in *Rassegna Musicale Italiana*, Vol. 7, No. 22, 2002

Conati, Marcello 'Periodici teatrali e musicali italiani a metà dell'800' in *Periodica Musica*, Vol. 7, 1989

Conati, Marcello 'Teatri e orchestre al tempo di Verdi' in Istituto di Studi Verdiani di Parma, *Giuseppe Verdi, vicende, problemi e mito di un artista e del suo tempo*, catalogue of exhibition 31 August–8 December 1985, Colorno 1985

Condee, Nancy 'Body Graphics: Tattooing the Fall of Communism' in Barker (ed.) *Consuming Russia*

Condemi, Concetta *Les cafés-concerts. Histoire d'un divertissement (1849–1914)*, Quai Voltaire, Paris 1992

Confino, Alon and Rudy Koshar, 'Régimes of Consumer Culture: New Narratives in Twentieth-Century German History' in *German History*, Vol. 19, No. 2, 2001

Conforti, Maria 'Scomposizione di un personaggio: Cecilia Malespano, Mimi Bluette, Maria Maddalena' in Arslan (ed.) *Dame, droga e galline*

Conrich, Ian 'Forgotten cinema: the British style of sexploitation' in *Journal of Popular British Cinema*, No. 1, 1998

Convents, Guido 'Les catholiques et le cinéma en Belgique (1895–1914)' in Cosandrey, Gaudreault and Gunning (eds) *Une invention du diable? Cinéma des premiers temps et religion*

Conway Morris, Roderick 'Greek Café Music' in *Recorded Sound*, No. 80, July 1981

Cook, Michael L. *Mystery, Detective, and Espionage Magazines*, Greenwood Press, Westport Conn. and London 1983

Cooper, Helen 'Surviving the Reformation' in *London Review of Books*, 15 October 1998

Cooper, James Fenimore *Gleanings in Europe. England*, State University of New York Press, Albany 1982

Cooper, Jeffrey *The Rise of Instrumental Music and Concert Series in Paris 1828–1871*, UMI Research Press, Ann Arbor, Michigan 1983

Cooper-Richet, Diana 'La librairie étrangère à Paris au XIXe siècle. Un milieu perméable aux innovations et aux transferts' in *Actes de la recherche en sciences sociales*, No. 126–127 March 1999

Cooper-Richet, Diana 'Les imprimés en langue anglaise en France au XIXe siècle: rayonnement intellectuel, circulation et modes de pénétration' in Michon and Mollier (eds) *Les mutations du livre*

Coover, James 'Introduction' to *Music Publishing, Copyright and Piracy in Victorian England*

Corbin, Alain (ed.) *L'avéement des loisirs 1850–1960*, Aubier, Paris 1995

Cornea, Paul 'La sociologie du roman roumain au XIXe siècle' in *Cahiers Roumains d'Etudes littéraires* (Bucarest) No. 2, 1980

Corning, Jonathan and Armando Levy 'Demand for Live Theater with Market Segmentation and Seasonality' in *Journal of Cultural Economics*, Vol. 26, No. 3, August 2002

Corti, Maria *Ombre dal Fondo*, Einaudi, Turin 1997

Cosandrey, Roland, André Gaudreault and Tom Gunning (eds) *Une invention du diable? Cinéma des premiers temps et religion*, Les Presses de l'Université Laval and Éditions Payot, Sainte-Foy and Lausanne 1992

Costa, Simona 'Storia e "fictio" nelle pagine delle "Biblioteche Italiane"' in Bruscagli and Turchi (eds) *Teorie del romanzo nel primo ottocento*

Cottin, Sophie *Malvina*, Maradan, Paris 1800

Couperie, Pierre Edouard François, Henri Filippini and Claude Moliterni, 'France' in Moliterni (ed.) *Histoire Mondiale de la Bande Dessinée*

Cousins, Mark *The Story of Film*, Pavilion Books, London 2004

Cowans, Jon 'Political Culture and Cultural Politics: The Reconstruction of French Radio after the Second World War' in *Journal of Contemporary History*, Vol. 31, No.1, January 1996

Coward, David 'Popular fiction in the nineteenth century' in Unwin (ed.) *The Cambridge Companion to the French Novel*

Coward, David *The Philosophy of Restif de La Bretonne*, Voltaire Foundation, Oxford 1991

Cox, Gary 'Fairy-Tale Plots and Contemporary Heroes in Early Russian Prose Fiction' in *Slavic Review*, Vol. 39 No. 1, March 1980

Cracroft, Richard H. 'World Westerns: The European Writer and the American West' in *The Literary History of the American West* (1987) edited by J. Golden Taylor and Thomas J. Lyon et al., The Western Literature Association, Texas Christian University 1987 accessed on *www.tcu.edu/depts/prs/amwest/pdf/wlo159.pdf*

Crafton, Donald 'Tricks and Animation' in Nowell Smith (ed.) *The Oxford History of World Cinema*

Craig, Edward Gordon *On the Art of the Theatre*, Heinemann paperback, London 1980

Craig, Gordon R. *Germany, 1866–1945*, OUP 1981

Cranston, Ros 'In Fact: Nanook of the North', NFT leaflet, National Film and Television Archive, no date

Creative Industries Mapping Document 2001, Department of Culture, Media and Sport (UK)

Crisell, Andrew *An Introductory History of British Broadcasting*, Routledge, London 2002

Crosby, Emily A. *Une romancière oubliée: Mme Riccoboni. Sa vie, ses oeuvres, sa place dans la littérature anglaise et française du XVIIIe siècle*, Rieder et Cie, Paris 1924

Cross, Anthony *Anglo-Russica. Aspects of Cultural relations between Great Britain and Russia in the Eighteenth and early Nineteenth Centuries*, Berg, Oxford 1993

Cross, Gary 'Vacations for All: The Leisure Question in the Era of the Popular Front' in *Journal of Contemporary History*, Vol. 24, No. 4, October 1989

Cross, Gary *A Quest for Time. The Reduction of Work in Britain and France, 1840–1940*, University of California Press, Berkeley 1989

Cross, Gary *Time and Money, The Making of Consumer Culture*, Routledge, London 1993

Cross, Nigel *The Common Writer. Life in Nineteenth-Century Grub Street*, CUP, Cambridge 1985

Crubellier, Maurice 'L'élargissement du public' in Chartier and Martin (eds) *Histoire de l'édition française*, Vol. 3, *Le temps des éditeurs. Du romantisme à la Belle Époque*

Crystal, David *The Cambridge Encyclopedia of the English Language*, CUP 1995

Csergo, Julia 'Extension et mutation du loisir citadin' in Corbin, *L'avènement des loisirs*

Curran, James and Jean Seaton *Power without Responsibility. The press, broadcasting, and new media in Britain*, Routledge, London 2003

Curto, Diogo Ramada 'Littérature de large circulation au Portugal (XVIe–XVIIIe siècles)' in Chartier and Lüsebrink (eds) *Colportage et lecture populaire*

Curwen, Henry *A History of Booksellers, The Old and the New*, Chatto and Windus, London 1874

Cusatelli, Giorgio 'Pinocchio in Germania' in *Studi Collodiani*

Custine, Astolphe de (Marquis), *Letters from Russia*, translated by Robin Buss, Penguin, Harmondsworth 1991

d'Haussonville, Comte 'Le Combat contre le vice. Part I' in *La Revue des Deux Mondes*, Vol. 57, 1 January 1887 and 'Le Combat contre le vice. Part II' in *La Revue des Deux Mondes*, Vol. 57, 1 April 1887

D'hulst, Lieven 'Traduire l'Europe en France entre 1810 et 1840' in Ballard (ed.) *Europe et Traduction*

Dagnaud, Monique, seminar presentation on her research on television producers, organised by the Temps, médias et société group, Paris, 8 April 2005

Daiches, David 'Sir Walter Scott and History' in *Études anglaises*, Vol. 24, No. 4, October-December 1971

Darmon, Jean-Jacques *Le Colportage de Librairie en France sous le Second Empire. Grands colporteurs et culture populaire*, Plon, Paris 1972

Darnton, Robert 'Extraordinary Commonplaces' in *New York Review of Books*, 21 December 2000

Darnton, Robert *The Forbidden Best-Sellers of Pre-Revolutionary France*, Fontana, London 1996

Daumard, Adeline 'L'argent et le rang dans la société française du XIXe siècle', in *Romantisme*, No. 40, 1983, Vol. 13

Daumard, Adeline *Les Bourgeois de Paris au XIXe siècle*, Flammarion, Paris 1970

Davies, Sarah 'Soviet Cinema and the Early Cold War: Pudovkin's *Admiral Nakhimov* in Context' in Rana Mitter and Patrick Major (eds) *Across the Blocs*, Frank Cass, London 2004

Davis, John A. 'Italy' in Goldstein (ed.) *The War for the Public Mind*

Davis, Lennard J. *Factual Fictions. The Origins of the English Novel*, Columbia UP, New York 1983

Davis, Lennard J. *Resisting Novels. Ideology and Fiction*, Methuen, London 1987

Davis, Tracy C. *The Economics of the British Stage 1800–1914*, Cambridge University Press 2000

Dayan, Daniel and Elihu Katz *La télévision cérémonielle*, PUF, Paris 1996

Dayan, Daniel and Elihu Katz *Media Events. The Live Broadcasting of History*, Harvard University Press 1992

De Bens, Els and Hedwig de Smaele 'The Inflow of American Television Fiction on European Broadcasting Channels' in *European Journal of Communication*, Vol. 16, No. 1, March 2001, pp.51–71

de Budé, Eugène *Du danger des mauvaises lectures et des moyens d'y remédier*, Sandoz et Thullier, Paris 1883

De Bunsen, Henry George 'The Hawker: His Work and His Day' in *Publishing History*, No. 12, 1982

De Cesare, Raffaele *Balzac e Manzoni e altri studi su Balzac e l'Italia*, Vita e pensiero, Milan 1993

De Donato, Gigliola, and Vanna Gazzola Stacchini (eds) *I best seller del ventennio. Il regime e il libro di massa*, Editori Riuniti, Rome 1991

de Gaulle, Charles *Mémoires d'espoir, Le renouveau 1958–1962*, Plon, Paris 1970 de Grazia, Victoria 'Mass Culture and Sovereignty: The American Challenge to European Cinemas, 1920–1960' in *Journal of Modern History*, Vol. 61, No. 1, March 1989

De Mauro, Tullio 'Lingua parlata e TV' in *Televisione e vita italiana*, ERI, Turin 1968

De Mauro, Tullio *Storia linguistica dell'Italia unita*, Vol. 1, Laterza, Rome-Bari 1979

De Pirro, Nicola 'Espansione all'estero del film italiano nel dopoguerra' in *Lo spettacolo*, Vol. 5 No. 3, July-September 1955

De Quincey, Thomas, *The Works of Thomas De Quincey*. General Editor, Grevel Lindop. Pickering and Chatto, London 2000

De Sanctis, Francesco *Opere* edited by Niccolò Gallo, Ricciardi Editore, Milan-Naples 1961

De Sanctis, Francesco *Storia della letteratura italiana*, Vol. 2, Feltrinelli UE, Milan 1960

De Sanctis, Francesco *Teoria e storia della letteratura* edited by Benedetto Croce, Vol. 1, Laterza, Bari 1926

de Sola Pool, Ithiel (ed.) *The Social Impact of the Telephone*, MIT Press, Cambridge Mass. 1977

De Van, Gilles *L'opéra italien*, PUF, Paris 2000

de Winter, Éric 'Interview with Éric de Winter' in *La Revue du cinéma*, No. 384, June 1983

Deák, František 'Russian Mass Spectacles', *Drama Review*, Vol. 19 No. 2, June 1975

Decleva, Enrico 'Présence germanique et influences françaises dans l'édition italienne aux XIXe et XXe siècles' in Michon and Mollier (eds) *Les mutations du livre et de l'édition*

Decleva, Enrico *Arnoldo Mondadori*, UTET, Turin 1993

Defoe, Daniel *Essay upon Literature* (1726) in Daniel Defoe, *Writings of Travel, Discovery and History*, edited by P. N. Furbank, Pickering and Chatto, London 2001

Dekker, George and John P. Williams (eds) *Fenimore Cooper. The Critical Heritage*, Routledge, London and New York 1997

Dekobra, Maurice *La Madone des Sleepings*, Pocket, Paris 1997

Del Litto, V. 'Stendhal et Walter Scott' in *Études anglaises*, Vol. 24, No. 4, October–December 1971

Delécluze, Étienne-Jean *Journal de Delécluze*, edited by Robert Baschet, Grasset, Paris 1948

Della Peruta, Franco 'Verdi e il Risorgimento' in *Rassegna Storica del Risorgimento*, No. 1, Vol. 88, January-March 2001

Deme, Laszlo 'Writers and Essayists and the Rise of Magyar Nationalism in the 1820s and 1830s' in *Slavic Review* No. 4, Winter 1984

DeNora, Tia *Beethoven and the Construction of Genius: Musical politics in Vienna, 1792–1803*, University of California Press, Berkeley and Los Angeles 1995

Derla, Luigi *Letteratura e politica tra la Restaurazione e l'Unità*, Vita e Pensiero, Milan 1977

Descotes, Maurice 'Les Comédiens dans les Rougon-Macquart' in *Revue de la Société d'Histoire du Théâtre*, Vol. 10, No. 2, 1958

Descotes, Maurice *Le public de théâtre et son histoire*, Presses Universitaires de France, Paris 1964

Descotes, Maurice *Les Grands rôles du théâtre de Molière*, Presses Universitaires de France, Paris 1960

Desideri, Giovanella 'Il fantastico' in Alberto Asor Rosa (ed.) *Letteratura italiana. Storia e geografia*, Volume 3: *L 'età contemporanea*, Einaudi, Turin 1989

Désiré, Vol. 14, No. 20, 1978, pp.485–90

Deslandes, Jacques and Jacques Richard *Histoire comparée du cinéma*, Vol 2: *Du cinématographique au cinéma 1896–1906*, Casterman, Paris 1968

Desser, David ' "Consumerist realism": American Jewish life and the classical Hollywood cinema' in *Film History*, Vol. 8, No. 3, 1996

Desvois, Jean-Michel 'L'industrie papetière et le prix du papier journal en Espagne e de 1898 à 1936', *Bulletin hispanique*, Vol. 95, No. 1, 1993

Devars, Pascal, Edgar Petitier, Guy Rosa and Alain Vaillant, 'Si Victor Hugo était compté. Essais de bibliométrie hugolienne comparée' in *La Gloire de Victor Hugo*

Dezalay, Auguste (ed.) *Zola sans frontières*, Presses Universitaires de Strasbourg 1996

Di Luzio, Adolfo Scotto *L'appropriazione imperfetta. Editori, biblioteche e libri per ragazzi durante il fascismo*, Il Mulino, Bologna 1996

Dickens, Charles *Bleak House*, Penguin, London 1985

Dickens, Charles *David Copperfield*, Penguin, London 1996

Dickens, Charles *Dombey and Son*, Penguin 1970

Dickens, Charles *Our Mutual Friend*, Oxford University Press 1989

Dickinson, Edward Ross 'The Men's Christian Morality Movement in Germany, 1880–1914: Some Reflections on Politics, Sex, and Sexual Politics' in *The Journal of Modern History*, Vol. 75, March 2003

Dieci anni di TV in Italia, ERI, Rome 1964

Dillaz, Serge 'Diffusion et propagation chansonnières au XIXe siècle', in *Romantisme*, Vol. 23, No. 80, 1993

Dimaras, C. Th. *Histoire de la littérature néo-hellénique*, Collection de l'Institut Français d'Athènes, Athens 1965

Dimaras, C. Th. Réalisme et naturalisme en Grèce. L'offre et la demande' in *Synthesis*, Vol. 2, 1975 (Bucharest)

Dittmar, Claudia 'GDR Television in Competition with West German Programming' in *Historical Journal of Film, Radio and Television*, Vol. 24, No. 2, 2004

Dizionario Biografico degli Italiani, Istituto dell' Enciclopedia Italiana, Treccani, Rome 1979

Dmitrieva, Katia 'Vers l'âge d'or de la culture russe. Réflexions sur quellques figures complexes de relations triangulaires' in Dmitrieva and Espagne (eds) *Transfers culturels triangulaires Philologiques IV*

Dmitrieva, Katia and Michel Espagne (eds) *Transfers culturels triangulaires France-Allemagne-Russie. Philologiques IV*, Éditions de la Maison des Sciences de l'Homme, Paris 1996

Dobrenko, Evgeny *The Making of the State Reader. Social and Aesthetic Contexts of the Reception of Soviet Literature*, Stanford University Press, Stanford 1997

Docherty, David, David Morrison and Michael Tracey *The Last Picture Show? Britain's changing film audiences*, BFI Publishing, London 1987

Dolfsma, Wilfred 'Radio and Magazines: valuing pop music in the Netherlands (1955–1965) in *Media History*, No. 1, April 2004

Donnan, Shawn 'Read all about lads' *Financial Times*, 26/27 February 2005, US edition

Donnat, Olivier 'La féminisation des pratiques culturelles' in *Développement culturel*, No. 147, June 2005 (Bulletin of the French Ministry of Culture)

Donnat, Olivier and Denis Cogneau, *Les pratiques culturelles des Français 1973–1989*, La Découverte/La documentation française, Paris 1990

Donnat, Olivier, *Les pratiques culturelles des Français. Enquête 1997*, Ministère de la culture et de la communication, Paris 1998

Doody, Margaret Anne 'I am an irregular verb' in *London Review of Books*, 22 January 1998

Doody, Margaret Anne 'Samuel Richardson: fiction and knowledge' in John Richetti (ed.) *The Cambridge Companion to the Eighteenth-Century Novel*, CUP 1996

Doody, Margaret Anne *The True Story of the Novel*, HarperCollins, London 1997

Dorment, Richard 'The Great Room of Art' in *New York Review of Books*, 13 June 2002

Dossier de l'audiovisuel No. 11, January–February 1987

Doubine, Boris 'Culture classique, culture d'élite, culture de masse. Une mécanique de différenciation' in *Romantisme*, No. 114, 2001

Doublé-Dutheil, Catherine 'Pratiques et goûts musicaux de la jeunesse urbaine' in Hennion (ed.) *1789–1989: Musique, Histoire, Démocratie*, Vol. II

Douchin, Jacques-Louis 'L'influence des publications populaires sur l'oeuvre de Flaubert' in *Flaubert et Maupassant. Écrivains normans*, edited by the Institut de Littérature Française de l'Université de Rouen, Presses Universitaires de France, Paris 1981

Douglas, Allen and Fedwa Malti-Douglas *Arab Comic Strips. Politics of an Emerging Mass Culture*, Indiana UP, Bloomington 1994

Douglas, Roy 'At the Cutting Edge' in *BBC History Magazine*, Vol. 2, No. 3, March 2001

Dowe, Dieter 'The Working Men's Choral Movement in Germany before the First World War' in *Journal of Contemporary History*, Vol. 13, No. 2, April 1978

Dubois, Jacques 'Naissance du recit policier' in *Actes de la recherche en sciences sociales*, No. 60, November 1985

Dubois, Jean 'La société de consommation électrique' in Henri Morsel (ed.) *Une oeuvre nationale; l'équipent, la croissance de la demande, le nucléaire (1946–1987)*, Vol. 3 of *Histoire Générale de l'électricité de France*, Fayard, Paris 1996

Dubourg, Maurice, Evelyne Diebolt and Patrice Caillot 'De Leo Taxil à Maurice Mario. Marc Mario' in *Désiré*, Vol. 14, No. 20, 1978

Dudovitz, Resa L. *The Myth of Superwoman. Women's Bestsellers in France and the United States*, Routledge, London 1990

Dufour, Hortense *Comtesse de Ségur née Rostopchine*, Flammarion, Paris 1990

Dufourt, Hugues and Joël-Marie Fauquet (eds) *La musique et le pouvoir*, Aux Amateurs du livre, Paris 1987

Duhamel, Georges *Scènes de la vie future*, Mercure de France, Paris 1930

Dull, Olga Anna 'From Rabelais to the Avant-Garde: Wordplays and parody in the Wall-Journal *Le Mur*' in Phillip Dennis Cate and Mary Shaw (eds) *The Spirit of Montmartre. Cabarets, Humor, and the Avant-Garde, 1875–1905*, State University of New Jersey, Rutgers 1996

Dumas, Alexandre *Causeries*, 1861 no publisher, no place

Dumas, Olivier 'Hetzel, censeur de Verne' in Christian Robin (ed.) *Un Éditeur et son siècle. Pierre-Jules Hetzel*, ACL-Crocus édition, Saint-Sébastien 1988

Dumazedier, Joffre and Jean Hassenforder *Éléments pour une sociologie comparée de la production, de la diffusion et de l'utilisation du livre*, Bibliographie de la France, Vol. 151, No. 24, 15 June 1962, p.15

Dumont, Patrick *Études de mentalité. La petite bourgeoisie vue à travers les contes quotidiens du Journal (1894–1895)*, Minard, Paris 1973

Durant, Alan *Conditions of Music*, Macmillan, London and Basingstoke 1984

Durante, Sergio 'The Opera Singer' in Bianconi and Pestelli (eds) *Opera Production and its Resources*

Duțu, Alexandu 'La circulation de l'imprimé dans le Sud-Est européen entre le XVIIIe et le XIXe siècle' in Chartier and Lüsebrink (eds) *Colportage et lecture populaire*

Duval, René *Histoire de la radio en France*, Alain Moreau, Paris 1979

Dvorak, Pétr 'Situation of Rock Music in Changing Czech Society' in Hennion (ed.) *1789–1989: Musique, Histoire, Démocratie*, Vol. III

Eco, Umberto et al. *Carolina Invernizio Matilde Serao Liala*, La Nuova Italia, Florence 1979

Eco, Umberto *The Role of the Reader*, Hutchinson, London 1981

Eco, Umberto *Tra menzogna e ironia*, Bompiani, Milan 1998

Edgeworth, Maria *Letters from England 1813–1844*, edited by Christina Colvin, Clarendon Press, Oxford 1971

Edström, Olle 'How schottis became "bonnjazz", how Swedish foxtrot defeated jazz, or has Afro-American music ever existed in Sweden?' in Hennion (ed.) *1789–1989: Musique, Histoire, Démocratie*, Vol. III

Eger, Joseph 'La Révolution dans le public: Une profession de foi' in *Cultures*, Vol. 1, No. 1, 1973

Eger, Manfred 'The Patronage of King Luwig II' in *Wagner Handbook*, edited by Ulrich Müller and Peter Wapnewski, Harvard University Press, Cambridge Mass. and London 1992

Einhard, *The Life of Charlemagne*, translated by Samuel Epes Turner, Harper & Brothers, New York 1880

Eisenstein, Elizabeth L. 'The Advent of Printing and the Problem of the Renaissance' in *Past and Present*, No.45, November 1969

Eisenstein, Elizabeth L. 'The Impact of Printing on western Society and Thought: A preliminary report' in *Journal of Modern History*, Vol. 40, No.1, March 1968

Eisenstein, Sergey M. *Selected Works*, Volume I, *Writings, 1922–34*, edited and translated by Richard Taylor, BFI Publishing and Indiana University Press, London and Bloomington 1988

Ekstein, Modris 'The *Frankfurter Zeitung*: Mirror of Weimar Democracy' in *Journal of Contemporary History*, Vol. 6, no.4, 1971

Eliot, George *Daniel Deronda*, Penguin, Harmondsworth 1987

Eliot, George *Selected Critical Writings* edited by Rosemary Ashton, Oxford University Press

Eliot, George *Selected Essays, Poems and Other Writings*, Penguin, London 1990

Eliot, Simon '*Patterns and Trends* and the *NSTC*: Some initial observations. Part One', in *Publishing History*, No. 42, 1997

Eliot, Simon '*Patterns and Trends* and the *NSTC*: Some initial observations. Part Two' in *Publishing History*, No. 43, 1998

Eliot, T. S. *From Poe to Valéry*, A Lecture Delivered at the Library of Congress, 19 November 1948, Washington 1949

Elliott, Philip 'Professional Ideology and organisational change: the journalist since 1800', in Boyce, Curran and Wingate (eds) *Newspaper History*

Ellis, Katharine *Music Criticism in Nineteenth-Century France: 'La Revue et Gazette Musicale de Paris', 1834–1880*, Cambridge University Press 1995

Ellmann, Richard *James Joyce*, Oxford University Press 1982

Ellmann, Richard *Oscar Wilde*, Hamish Hamilton, London 1987

Ellwood, David '*Un Americano a Roma*: a 1950s Satire of Americanization' in *Modern Italy*, Vol. 1, No. 2, Autumn 1996

Elon, Amos *The Pity of It All: A Portrait of German Jews 1743–1933*, Allen Lane The Penguin Press, London 2003

Elsaesser, Thomas (ed.), *A Second Life. German Cinema's First Decades*, Amsterdam University Press 1996

Elsaesser, Thomas (ed.), *The BFI Companion to German Cinema*, BFI Publishing, London 1999

Elsaesser, Thomas (ed.) *Early Cinema: Space Frame Narrative*, BFI, London 1990

Elsaesser, Thomas *Weimar Cinema and After. Germany's historical imaginary*, Routledge, London and New York 2000

Emap plc, *Annual Report and Accounts 2005*

Enciclopedia Italiana, Treccani, Roma 1949

Encyclopaedia Judaica, Vol. 13, Keter and Macmillan, Jerusalem 1971

Engels, Friedrich 'Karl Marx' in *Marx Engels Werke*, Vol. 16, Berlin 1975

Engels, Friedrich *The Condition of the Working Class in England*, trans. and edited by W. O. Henderson and W. H. Challoner, Blackwell, Oxford 1958

Erdoğ, Nezih and Dilek Kaya 'Institutional Intervention in the Distribution and Exhibition of Hollywood Films in Turkey' in *Historical Journal of Film, Radio and television*, Vol. 22, No. 1, 2002, pp.49–53

Erenberg, Lewis A. *Steppin' Out: New York Nightlife and the Transformation of American Culture, 1890–1930*, University of Chicago Press, Chicago 1984

Erickson, Lee *The Economy of Literary Form. English Literature and the Industrialization of Publishing, 1800–1850*, Johns Hopkins University Press, Baltimore and London 1996

Escarpit, Robert 'Le problème de l'age dans la productivité littéraire' in *Bulletin des bibliothèques de France*, Vol. 5, No. 5, May 1960

Escarpit, Robert *La révolution du livre*, PUF, Paris 1969

Espagne, Michel and Michael Werner (eds) *Philologiques III. Qu'est-ce qu'une littérature nationale? Approches pour une théorie interculturelle du champ littéraire*, Éditions de la Maison des Sciences de l'Homme, Paris 1994

Espagne, Michel and Michael Werner (eds) *Transferts. Les relations interculturelles dans l'espace franco-allemand (XVIIIe-XIXe siècle)*, Éditions Recherche sur les Civilisations, Paris 1988

Espagne, Michel and Michael Werner *Philologiques I. Contribution à l'histoire des disciplines littéraires en France et en Allemagne au XIXe siècle*, Éditions de la Maison des sciences de l'homme, Paris 1990

Establet, Roger and Georges Felouzis 'Livre et télévision: deux médias en concurrence' in *Cahiers de l'économie du livre*, n. 8, December 1997

European Commission, Staff working paper SEC (98) 837, *Culture, the Cultural Industries and Employment*, *http://europa.eu.int/comm/avpolicy/legis/forum/cult1en.htm*

European Films on European Televisions, European Audiovisual Observatory, 2000

Evans, Christopher *The Mighty Micro. The Impact of the Computer Revolution*, Victor Gollancz, London 1979

Everett, William A. 'National Opera in Croatia and Finland 1846–1899', *The Opera Quarterly*, Vol. 18, No. 2, Spring 2002

Eyre, Richard *National Service. Diary of a Decade*, Bloomsbury, London 2003

Ezard, John 'Harry Potter and the stony broke authors' *Guardian*, 14 July 2005

Ezra, Elizabeth *Georges Méliès*, Manchester University Press 2000

Fabbri, Franco 'A Theory of Musical Genre' in Frith (ed.) *Popular Music*, Vol. III, *Popular Music Analysis*

Fabrizi, Angelo *Studi inediti di Vittorio Alfieri sull'Ossian del Cesarotti*, Centro nazionale di studi alfieriani, Asti 1964

Faeti, Antonio '*Cuore*' in Isnenghi (ed.) *I luoghi della memoria*

Faeti, Antonio '*Il Corriere dei piccoli*' in Isnenghi (ed.) *I luoghi della memoria*

Faeti, Antonio 'Le figure del mito' in Zanotto (ed.) *L'immagine nel libro per ragazzi*

Fanchi, Mariagrazia and Elena Mosconi (eds) *Spettatori. Forme di consumo e pubblici del cinema in Italia 1930–60*, Biblioteca di Bianco e Nero Marsilio, Venice 2002

Fantel, Hans *Johann Strauss. Father and Son, and Their Eras*, David & Charles, Newton Abbot 1971

Fantham, Elaine *Roman Literary Culture. From Cicero to Apuleius*, Johns Hopkins UP, Baltimore 1996

Faraday, George *Revolt of the Filmmakers: The Struggle for Artistic Autonomy and the Fall of the Soviet Film Industry*, Penn State University Press, University Park Penn. 2000

Farci, Jean-Claude 'Le temps libre au village' in Corbin (ed.) *L'avènement des loisirs*

Farr, Michael *Tintin. The Complete Companion*, John Murray, London 2001

Farrell, Dianne Ecklund 'The Bawdy *Lubok*: sexual and scatological content in eighteenth-century Russian Popular Prints' in *Eros and Pornography in Russian Culture* edited by M. Levitt and A. Toporkov, Ladomir Publishing House, Moscow 2000

Fauquet, Joël-Marie 'L'association des artistes musiciens et l'organisation du travail de 1843 à 1853' in Dufourt and Fauquet (eds) *La musique et le pouvoir*

Fay, Laurel E. 'Shostakovich versus Volkov: Whose Testimony?' in *The Russian Review* Vol. 39, 1980, pp.484–93

Febvre, Lucien and Henri-Jean Martin *The Coming of the Book. The Impact of Printing 1450–1800*, Verso, London 1984

Federzoni, Marina 'Carolina Invernizio' in Eco et al., *Carolina Invernizio Matilde Serao Liala*

Fell, John L. *Film and the Narrative Tradition*, University of Oklahoma Press 1974

Fellini, Federico *Intervista sul cinema*, Laterza, Rome-Bari 1983

Feltes, Norman N. *Literary Capital and the Late Victorian Novel*, The University of Wisconsin Press, Madison 1993

Feltes, Norman N. *Modes of Production of Victorian Novels*, University of Chicago Press, Chicago and London 1986

Fenton, James 'The librettist's tale' *Guardian*, 27 November 2004

Fenyo, Mario D. 'Writers in Politics: The role of *Nyugat* in Hungary, 1908–19' in *Journal of Contemporary History*, Vol. 11, No. 1, January 1976

Ferenczi, Thomas *L'Invention du journalisme en France. Naissance de la presse moderne à la fin du XIXème siècle*, Plon, Paris 1993

Fergusson, Charles A. 'Diglossia' in *Word*, Vol. 15, 1959

Fernandez, Dominique *Il mito dell'America negli intellettuali italiani*, Sciascia editore, Caltanisseta-Rome 1969

Fernández-Armesto, Felipe *Civilizations*, The Free Press, New York 2001

Ferretti, Giancarlo *Il Best Seller all'italiana. Fortune e formule del romanzo 'di qualità'*, Masson editoriale ESA, Milan 1993

Ferretti, Giancarlo '"Grandi opere" per il "popolo"' in *Problemi*, Nos 19–20, January–April 1970

Figes, Orlando *Natasha's Dance. A Cultural History of Russia*, Penguin, London 2002

Figgis, Nicola 'Artistes et amateurs des îles britanniques à Rome' in de Polignac and Raspi Serra (eds) *La fascination de l'antique 1700–1770*

Fihman, Guy 'La stratégie Lumière: l'invention du cinéma comme marché' in Benghozi and Delage (eds) *Une histoire économique du cinéma français (1895–1995)*

Filippini, Henri, Jacques Glenat, Thierry Martens and Numa Sadoul, *Histoire de la bande dessinée en France et en Belgique. Des origines à nos jours,* Éditions Glénat, Grenoble 1984

Financial Times, 30 October 2003 ('India's advertising luminaries take a bow')

Finch, Alison 'Reality and its representation in the nineteenth-century novel' in Unwin (ed.) *The Cambridge Companion to the French Novel*

Fink, Lois Marie *American Art at the Nineteenth-Century Paris Salons*, CUP 1990

Finkelstein, David *The House of Blackwood: Author-Publisher Relations in the Victorian Era*, Penn State, University Park Pa. 2001

Finler, Joel W. *Alfred Hitchcock. The Hollywood Years*, B. T. Batsford, London 1992

Finler, Joel W. *Silent Cinema. World cinema before the coming of sound*, B. T. Batsford, London 1997

Finler, Joel W. *The Hollywood Story. Everything you ever wanted to know about the American movie business*, Mandarin, London 1992

Fischer, William B. *The Empire Strikes Out: Kurt Lasswitz, Hans Dominik, and the Development of German Science Fiction*, Bowling Green State University Popular Press, Bowling Green Ohio 1984

Fischler, Alan 'Guano and Poetry: Payment for Playwriting in Victorian England' in *Modern Language Quarterly*, Vol. 2, No. 1, March 2001

Fisher, David James 'The Origins of the French Popular Theatre' in *Journal of Contemporary History*, Vol. 12, No. 3, July 1977

Fisher, Wesley A. and Solomon Volkov 'The Audience for Classical Music in the USSR; the Government as Mentor' in *Slavic Review* Vol. 38, No. 3, September 1979

Fitzpatrick, Sheila 'Cultural Revolution in Russia 1928–32' in *Journal of Contemporary History*, Vol. 9, No. 1, January 1974

Fitzpatrick, Sheila 'Sex and Revolution: An Examination of Literary and Statistical Data on the Mores of Soviet Students in the 1920s' in *Journal of Modern History*, Vol. 50, No. 2, June 1978

Flagy (Marie de Mirabeau) *Le crime de la Rue Marignan* Calmann Lévy, Paris 1889

Flaubert, Gustave *Bouvard et Pécuchet*, Gallimard Folio, Paris 1994

Flaubert, Gustave *Correspondance*, Gallimard, Paris 1991, Vols 2 and 3

Flaubert, Gustave *L'éducation sentimentale*, Flammarion, Paris 1969

Flaubert, Gustave *Madame Bovary*, Flammarion, Paris 1986

Flaubert, Gustave *Madame Bovary, nouvelle version précédée des scénarios inédits* edited by Jean Pommier and Gabrielle Leleu, Corti, Paris 1949

Flaubert, Gustave, *Lettres inédites de Gustave Flaubert à son éditeur Michel Lévy* edited by Jacques Suffel, Calman-Lévy, Paris 1965

Flint, Kate *The Woman Reader 1837–1914*, Clarendon Press, Oxford 1993

Florovsky, Georges 'The Problem of Old Russian Culture' in *Slavic Review* Vol. 21, No.1, March 1962

Fodor, Jerry 'Not Entirely Nice' in *London Review of Books*, 2 November 2000

Fontaine, Laurence 'Colporteurs de livres dans l'Europe du XVIIIe siècle' in Chartier and Lüsebrink (eds) *Colportage et lecture populaire*, cit

Fontaine, Laurence *Histoire du colportage en Europe (XVe-XIXe siècle)*, Albin Michel, Paris 1993

Foot, John 'Il *boom* dal basso: famiglia, trasformazione sociale, lavoro, tempo libero e sviluppo alla Bovisa e alla Comasina (Milano), 1950–1970' in Stefano Musso (ed.)

Tra Fabbrica e società. Mondi operai nell'Italia del Novecento, Annali Feltrinelli, Milan 1999

Forbes, Jill *Les Enfants du Paradis*, British Film Institute, London 1997

Ford, Henry *The International Jew*, available online at *www.biblebelievers.org.au/ intern_jew.htm* and various other anti-Semitic sites

Forest, Claude 'L'évolution de l'exploitation en France dans les années cinquante' in Benghozi and Delage (eds) *Une histoire économique du cinéma français (1895–1995)*

Forgacs, David *Italian Culture in the Industrial Era 1880–1980*, Manchester University Press 1990

Forgacs, David *Rome Open City*, BFI, London 2000

Fornäs, Johan 'Moving Rock: Youth Culture and popular music' in Hennion (ed.) *1789–1989: Musique, Histoire, Démocratie*, Vol. II

Forsås-Scott, Helena *Swedish Women's Writing 1850–1995*, Athlone Press, London 1997

Foster, Roy F. *Modern Ireland 1600–1972*, Penguin, Harmondsworth 1989

Fotini, Papatheodorou and David Machin, 'The Umbilical Cord That was Never Cut' in *European Journal of Communication* Vol 18, No 1, March 2003

Fourment, Alain *Histoire de la Presse des jeunes et des journaux d'enfants (1768–1988)*, Éditions École, Paris 1987

Fox, Adam *Oral Literate Culture in England, 1500–1700*, OUP 2000

Fox, Celina 'The Development of Social Reportage in English Periodical Illustration During the 1840s and Early 1850s' in *Past and Present*, No. 74, February 1977

Fox, Celina *Graphic Journalism in England during the 1830s and 1840s*, Garland Publishing, New York and London 1988

Fox, Warren 'Murder in Daily Instalments: The Newspapers and the Case of Franz Müller (1864)' in *Victorian Periodicals Review*, Vol. 31, No.3, Fall 1998

Fox Bourne, Henry Richard *English Newspapers. Chapters in the History of British Journalism*, 1887 reprinted by Routledge & Thoemmes Press in the series *Chapters in the History of British Journalism* 1998 Volume 1

Francillon, Roger 'La quête d'une identité helvétique dans la Suisse romande du XVIIIe siècle' in Gorceix (ed.) *L'identité culturelle de la Belgique et de la Suisse francophones*

Francis, Claude and Fernande Gontier *Colette*, Perrin, Paris 1997

François, Étienne 'Les échanges culturels entre la France et les pays germaniques au XVIIIe siècle' in Espagne and Werner (eds) *Transferts. Les relations interculturelles dans l'espace franco-allemand (XVIIIe-XIXe siècle)*

Frank, Frederick S. *The First Gothics. A Critical Guide to the English Gothic Novel*, Garland Publishing, New York 1987

Franzina, Emilio 'L'America' in Isnenghi (ed.) *I luoghi della memoria*

Franzina, Emilio 'Inni e Canzoni ' in Isnenghi (ed.) *I luoghi della memoria*

Fréchet, Alec 'Galsworthy hier et aujourd'hui' in *Études anglaises*, Vol. 24, No.2, April–June 1971

Freeborn, Richard *The Russian Revolutionary Novel: Turgenev to Pasternak*. CUP, Cambridge 1985

Freeborn, Richard *The Rise of the Russian Novel. Studies in the Russian Novel from Eugene Onegin to War and Peace*, CUP, Cambridge 1973

Freyssinet-Dominjon, Jacqueline *Les Manuels d'histoire de l'école libre 1882–1959. De la loi Ferry à la loi Debré*, Armand Colin, Paris 1969

Frey-Vor, Gerlinde *Coronation Street: Infinite Drama and British Reality*, Wissenschaftlicher Verlag, Trier 1991

Fricke, Dieter *Die Deutsche Arbeiterbewegung 1869- 1914*, Dietz Verlag, Berlin 1976

Frickx, Robert 'Littérature belge de langue française ou littérature française de

Belgique?' in Gorceix (ed.) *L'identité culturelle de la Belgique et de la Suisse francophones*

Frith, Simon (ed.) *Popular Music. Critical Concepts in Media and Cultural Studies*, Vol. I, *Music and Society*, Vol. II, *The Rock Era*, Vol. III, *Popular Music Analysis*, Vol. IV, *Music and Identity*, Routledge, London 2004

Frith, Simon 'Does British music still matter?' in *European Journal of Cultural Studies*, Vol. 7, No 1, February 2004

Frith, Simon 'Music and the Media' in Simon Frith and Lee Marshall, *Music and Copyright*, Edinburgh University Press 2004

Fritschner, Linda Marie 'Publishers' Readers, Publishers, and Their Authors' in *Publishing History*, No.7, 1980

Fritzsche, Peter *Reading Berlin 1900*, Harvard University Press, Cambrdige Mass. 1998

Fryckstedt, Monica Correa *Geraldine Jewsbury's 'Athenaeum' Reviews: A Mirror of , Mid-Victorian Attitudes to Fiction*, Acta Universitatis Uppsala, Stockholm 1986

Fulbrook, Mary *The Fontana History of Germany 1918–1990. The Divided Nation*, Fontana, London 1991

Furtwängler, Wilhelm *Notebooks 1924–54*, translated by Shaun Whiteside, edited by Michael Tanner, Quartet Books, London 1995

Gagnier, Regenia *Idylls of the Marketplace. Oscar Wilde and the Victorian Public*, Scolar Press, Aldershot 1987

Gaisberg, Frederick W. *The Music goes Round*, Arno Press, New York 1977; reprint of 1942 edition

Gallavotti, Eugenio *La scuola fascista di giornalismo (1930–1933)*, SugarCo, Milan 1982.

Gallaway, Lovell E. and Richard K. Vedder, 'Emigration from the United Kingdom to the United States: 1860–1913' in *The Journal of Economic History*, Vol. 31, 1971, pp.885–97

Galliano, Luciana 'I compositori giapponesi del primo novecento e l'apprendimento della musica europea' in *Rivista italiana di musicologia*, Vol. 29, No. 1, 1994

Galloux-Fournier, Bernadette 'Un regard sur l'Amérique: voyageurs francais aux États-Unis (1919–1939)', *Revue d'Histoire moderne et contemporaine*, Vol. 37, April-June 1990, pp. 308- 23

Galvan, Jean-Pierre *Les Mystères de Paris. Eugène Sue et ses lecteurs*, L'Harmattan, Paris 1998

Galvan, Jean-Pierre *Paul Féval. Parcours d'une oeuvre*, Encrage, Paris 2000

Gambaro, Marco 'Approches théoriques de l'industrie du livre' in *Cahiers de l'économie du livre*, n. 8, December 1997

Gammond, Peter (ed.) *Best Music Hall and Variety Songs*, Wolfe Publishing, London 1972

Ganne, Gilbert *Interviews impubliables*, Presses Pocket, Paris 1975 (originally published in 1952)

Ganne, Valérie and Marc Minon 'Géographies de la traduction' in Françoise Barret-Ducrocq (ed.) *Traduire l'Europe*, Payot, Paris 1992

Gänzl, Kurt *The Musical. A Concise History*, Northeastern University Press, Boston 1997

Garcia Lara, Fernando 'Exito y difusion de la novela erotica española' in *Les productions populaires en Espagne 1850–1920*, Université de Pau, CRNS, Paris 1986

Garçon, François 'Ce curieux âge d'or des cinéastes français' in Jean-Pierre Rioux (ed.) *Politiques et pratiques culturelles dans la France de Vichy*, CNRS, Cahier No 8, June 1988

Garnett, Edward in his introduction to the Ebook 6422 version of Defoe's *The Life, Adventures & Piracies of the Famous Captain Singleton*, The Project Gutenberg, file first posted on December 10, 2002 *www.gutenberg.net/etext04/cpsng10.txt*

Garofalo, Reebee 'I want my MP3: Who owns Internet music?' in Frith (ed.) *Popular Music*, Vol. II, *The Rock Era*

Garrard, J. G. 'Narrative Technique in Chulkov's *Prigozhaia povarikha*' in *Slavic Review* Vol. 27, No. 4, December 1968

Garrett, Greg 'Film' in *Censorship. A World Encyclopedia*

Garvey, Ellen Gruber *The Adman in the Parlor: Magazines and the Gendering of Consumer Culture, 1880s to 1910s*, Oxford University Press, New York & Oxford 1996

Gasca, Luis 'Espagne' in Moliterni (ed.) *Histoire Mondiale de la Bande Dessinée*

Gaskell, Elizabeth *North and South*, edited by Patricia Ingham, Penguin, Harmondsworth 1995

Gasnault, François 'Les salles de bal du Paris romantique: décors et jeux des corps' in *Romantisme*, No. 38, 1982

Gasperetti, David *The Rise of the Russian Novel. Carnival, Stylization, and Mockery of the West*, Northern Illinois University Press, DeKalb 1998

Gaumier, Patrick and Claude Moliterni (eds) *Dictionnaire mondial de la Bande Dessinée*, Larousse, Paris 1994

Gautier, Théophile *Histoire de l'art dramatique en France depuis ving-cinq ans*, Slatkine reprint, Geneva 1968 (original edition Leipzig 1858–59) 6 Vols

Gautier, Théophile *Histoire du Romantisme*, L'Harmattan, Paris 1993

Gautier, Théophile *Récits Fantastiques*, GF-Flammarion, Paris 1981

Gautier, Théophile *Voyage en Italie*, Charpentier, Paris 1875

Gay, Peter *The Bourgeois Experience. Victoria to Freud*, Vol. III *The Cultivation of Hatred*, HarperCollins, London 1994; Vol.IV: *The Naked Heart*, 1996

Gaycken, Oliver ' "A Drama Unites Them in a Fight to the Death". Some remarks on the flourishing of a cinema of scientific vernacularization in France 1909–1914', *Historical Journal of Film, Radio and Television*, Vol. 22, No. 3, 2002

Gelatt, Roland *The Fabulous Phonograph 1877–1977*, Cassell, London 1977

Gemünden, Gerd 'Between Karl May and Karl Marx. The DEFA Indianerfilme' in *Film History* Vol. 10, No 3, 1998

Genette, Gérard, et al. *Théorie des genres*, Seuil Points, Paris 1986

Gentile, Emilio 'Impending Modernity: Fascism and the Ambivalent Image of the United States' in *Journal of Contemporary History*, Vol. 28, No.1, January 1993

Geraghty, Christine 'Cinema As a Social Space: Understanding Cinema-Going in Britain, 1947–63' in *Framework* No. 42: Summer 2000, online version: *http://www.frameworkonline.com/42cg.htm*

Gersmann, Gudrun 'Le monde des colporteurs parisiens de livres prohibés 1750–1789' in Chartier and Lüsebrink (eds) *Colportage et lecture populaire*

Gervasoni, Marco 'Musique et socialisme en Italie (1880–1922), in *Le Mouvement Social*, No. 208, July-September 2004

Gettmann, R.A. *A Victorian Publisher: A Study of the Bentley Papers*, Cambridge University Press 1960

Gheorghiu, Mihai D. 'La construction littéraire d'une identité nationale. Le cas de l'écrivain roumain Liviu Rebreanu (1885–1944)' in *Actes de la Recherche en sciences sociales*, No.98, June 1993

Giachino, Monica ' "Il famoso, forse troppo famoso Balzac" e la critica italiana (1830–1850)' in *Problemi*, No.91, May-August 1991

Giannetto, Nella 'La "costruzione" del romanzo e il livello tematico' in Arslan (ed.)
Dame, droga e galline

Gibelli, Antonio *L'officina della guerra. La Grande Guerra e le trasformazioni del mondo
mentale*, Bollati Boringhieri, Turin 1991

Gibellini, Pietro ' "Peuple" et "Nation": Notes sur la littérature dialectale italienne' in
Romantisme, No. 37, 1982

Gibellini, Pietro *Il coltello e la corona*, Bulzoni, Rome 1979

Gidel, Henry *Georges Feydeau*, Flammarion, Paris 1991

Giet, Sylvette '20 ans d'amour en couverture', *Actes de la recherche en sciences sociales*,
No. 60, November 1985

Gifford, Denis 'Grande Bretagne' in Moliterni (ed.) *Histoire Mondiale de la Bande
Dessinée*

Gigli, Lorenzo *Edmondo de Amicis*, UTET, Turin 1962

Gilbert, Michael ' "Ich habe von einem Esel gelernt": Eisler Pro and Contra Schönberg'
in Grimm and Hermand (eds) *High and Low Cultures*

Gilder, Joseph. B. and Jeanette L. Gilder (eds) *Trilbyana. The Rise and Progress of a
Popular Novel*, The Critic Co., New York 1895

Gili, Jean A. *La Comédie italienne*, Henri Vernier, Paris 1983

Gill, Tom 'Transformational Magic. Some Japanese super-heroes and monsters' in
Martinez (ed.) *The Worlds of Japanese Popular Culture*

Gillett, Charlie 'Big Noise from Across the Water: the American Influence on British
Popular Music' in Davis, Allen F. (ed.) *For Better or Worse. The American Influence
in the World*, Greenwood, Westport Connecticut 1981

Gillett, Charlie *The Sound of the City*, Souvenir Press, London 1983

Gilman, Richard *Chekhov's Plays: An Opening into Eternity*, Yale University Press, New
Haven and London 1995

Giocondi, Michele *Lettori in camicia nera. Narrativa di successo nell'Italia fascista*, Casa
editrice G. D'Anna, Florence 1978

Girolami, Patrizia 'Il carro di Tespi: teatro e fascismo' in Biondi and Alessandro
Borsotti (eds) *Cultura e fascismo. Letteratura arti e spettacolo di un Ventennio*,
Ponte alle Grazie, Florence 1996

Gissing, George *New Grub Street*, J.M. Dent (Everyman paperback), London
1997

Gitlin, Todd *Prime Time*, Pantheon Books, New York 1983

Gitlin, Todd 'Media Sociology: the Dominant Paradigm' in *Theory and Society*, No 2,
1978

Giuli, Paola 'Tracing Sisterhood: Corilla Olimpica as Corinne's unacknowledged Alter
Ego' in Karina Szmurlo (ed.) *The Novel's Seduction. Staël's Corinne in Critical
Enquiry*, Bucknell University Press, 1999

Giuliani, Elizabeth 'Le public de l'Opéra de Paris de 1750 à 1760' in *International Review
of the Aesthetics and Sociology of Music*, Vol. 8, No. 2, December 1977

Glancy, Mark *The 39 Steps*, I. B. Tauris, London 2003

Glancy, Mark *When Hollywood loved Britain. The Hollywood 'British' film 1939–45*,
Manchester University Press 1999

Glénisson, Jean 'Le livre pour la jeunesse' in Chartier, and Martin (eds) *Histoire de
l'édition française*, Vol. 3, *Le temps des éditeurs*

Gobetti, Pietro *La Frusta teatrale*, Corbaccio, Turin 1923

Godechot, Olivier 'Le marché du livre philosophique' in *Actes de la recherche en sciences
sociales*, No. 130, December 1999

Goethe, Johann Wolfgang *Faust Part Two*, Penguin, Harmondsworth 1987

Goethe, Johann Wolfgang *Conversations of Goethe with Eckermann*, Da Capo Press, New York 1998

Goethe, Johann Wolfgang, *The Sorrows of Young Werther*, Penguin, London 1989

Gogol, Nikolai *Dead Souls*, Penguin, Harmondsworth 1961

Goimard, Jacques 'Quelques structures formelles du roman populaire' in *Europe*, Vol. 52, June 1974

Goldoni, Carlo *Memoirs*, Henry Colburn, London 1814, Vol. 1

Goldschmidt, Paul W. 'Pornography in Russia' in Barker (ed.) *Consuming Russia*

Goldstein, Judith L. 'Realism without a Human face' in Margaret Cohen and Christopher Prendergast (eds) *Spectacles of Realism: Body, Gender, Genre*, University of Minnesota Press, Minneapolis 1995

Goldstein, Robert Justin (ed.) *The War for the Public Mind. Political Censorship in Nineteenth-Century Europe*, Praeger, Westport Connecticut 2000

Goldstein, Robert Justin 'France' in Goldstein (ed.) *The War for the Public Mind*

Gomery, Douglas 'The Movie Palace Comes to America's Cities' in Richard Butsch (ed.) *For Fun and Profit. The Transformation of Leisusre into Consumption*, Temple University Press, Philadelphia 1990

Gomery, Douglas 'Transformation of the Hollywood System' in Nowell-Smith, *The Oxford History of World Cinema*

Goncourt, Edmond et Jules de *Journal. Mémoires de la vie littéraire.* Vol. 1, *1851–65*, Robert Laffont, Paris 1989

Goodwin, Peter 'After Unification' in Geoffrey Nowell-Smith and Tana Wollen (eds) *After the Wall*, BFI, London 1991

Goody, Jack (ed.) *Literacy in Traditional Society*, Cambridge University Press 1968

Goody, Jack *Capitalism and Modernity. The Great Debate*, Polity, Cambridge 2004

Goody, Jack *The Interface Between The Written And The Oral*, Cambridge University Press 1987

Goody, Jack *The Logic of Writing and the Organization of Society*, Cambridge University Press 1986

Gorbman, Claudia *Unheard Melodies: Narrative Film Music*, BFI, London 1987

Gorceix, Paul (ed.) *L'identité culturelle de la Belgique et de la Suisse francophones. Actes du colloque international de Soleure (juin 1993)*, Honoré Champion, Paris 1997

Gorceix, Paul (ed.) *La Belgique fin-de-siècle*, Éditions Complexe, Brussels 1997

Gorham, Maurice *Forty Years of Irish Broadcasting*, The Talbot Press, Dublin 1967

Goudkov, Lev and Boris Doubine 'La culture littéraire' (1988) in Stroev (ed.) *Livre et lecture en Russie*

Gough, Kathleen 'Implications of Literacy in Traditional China and India' in Goody (ed.) *Literacy in Traditional Society*

Gould, Glenn 'The Search for Petula Clark' in Frith (ed.) *Popular Music*, Vol. IV, *Music and Identity*

Graf, Arturo *L'anglomania e l'influsso inglese in Italia nel secolo XVIII*, Ermanno Loescher, Turin 1911

Graff, Harvey J. (ed.) *Literacy and Social Development in the West: A Reader*, Cambridge University Press 1981

Graff, Harvey J. *The Legacies of literacy. Continuities and Contradictions in Western Culture and Society*, Indiana University Press, Bloomington 1987

Gramsci, Antonio *Selections from the Cultural Writings*, edited by David Forgacs and Geoffrey Nowell-Smith, Lawrence and Wishart, London 1985

Grandjean, Sophie 'Les éditions Fayard et l'édition populaire' in Mollier (ed.) *Le commerce de la librairie en France au XIXe siècle*

Grass, Günter *My century*, Faber and Faber, London 1999

Grassi, Corrado 'Introduction' to Graziadio Isaia Ascoli (1829–1907), *Scritti sulla questione della lingua*, Einaudi, Turin 1975

Grasso, Aldo *Storia della Televisione Italiana*, Garzanti, Milan 1992 and 2000

Gray, Donald J. 'Early Victorian scandalous journalism: Renton Nicholson's *The Town* (1837–42)' in Shattock and Wolff (eds) *The Victorian periodical press*

Gray, Frank 'Smith the showman: The early years of George A. Smith' in *Film History*, Vol. 10, No. 1, 1998

Greenslade, William *Thomas Hardy's 'Facts' Notebook*, Ashgate, Aldershot 2004

Greffe, Xavier and Xavier Dupuis 'Quand l'opéra découvre la gestion' in *Revue Française de Gestion*, No 30, March-April 1981

Gregor-Dellin, Martin *Richard Wagner*, Fayard, Paris 1981

Gregory of Nyssa (Grégoire de Nysse) *Lettres*, edited by Pierre Maraval, Les éditions du Cerf, Paris 1990

Gregory of Nyssa, 'De deitate filii et spiritus sancti', in *Patrologiae Graecae* edited by J. P. Migne, vol. 46 column 557, Paris 1858.

Grella, George 'Simenon and Maigret' in *Adam, International Review*, Simenon Issue, Nos. 328–330, 1969

Gretton, Thomas 'Difference and Competition: the Imitation and Reproduction of Fine Art in a Nineteenth-Century Illustrated Weekly News Magazine' in *Oxford Art Journal*, Volume 23, Number 2, 2000

Grew, Raymond, P.J. Harrigan and J. B. Whitney, 'La scolarisation en France 1829–1906' in *Annales*, Vol. 39, No.1 January-February 1984

Grew, Raymond and Patrick J. Harrigan, 'The Availability of Schooling in Nineteenth-Century France' in *Journal of Interdisciplinary History*, Vol. 14, No.1, Summer 1983

Griest, Guinevere L. *Mudie's Circulating Library and the Victorian Novel*, David and Charles, Newton Abbot 1970

Grieveson, L. Lee ' "A kind of recreative school for the whole family": making cinema respectable, 1907–09', *Screen*, Volume 42, No 1, Spring 2001

Grieveson, Lee and Peter Krämer (eds) *The Silent Cinema Reader*, Routledge, London and New York 2004

Grimm, Reinhold and Jost Hermand (eds) *High and Low Cultures. German Attempts at Mediation*, University of Wisconsin Press, Madison 1994

Grimmelshausen, Johann von *Mother Courage*, trans. Walter Wallich, The Folio Society, London 1965

Griset, Pascal 'Les communications en France' in Lévy-Leboyer and Morsel (eds) *L'Interconnexion et le Marché 1919–1946*

Griset, Pascal *Les révolutions de la communication XIXe-XXe siècle*, Hachette, Paris 1991

Gronow, Pekka 'The Record Industry Comes to the Orient' in *Ethnomusicology*, Vol. 25, No.2, May 1981

Gronow, Pekka 'The record industry: the growth of a mass medium' in *Popular Music 3*, edited by Richard Middleton and David Horn, CUP 1983

Gronow, Pekka and Ilpo Saunio, *An International History of the Recording Industry*, trans. from the Finnish by Christopher Moseley, Cassell, London and New York 1998

Gronow, Pekka *Statistics in the Field of Sound Recordings*, Division of Statistics on Culture and Communication, UNESCO, Paris n.d. but 1980, stencilled text

Grosser, H. Mark 'The Bazaar de la Charité fire: The reality, the aftermath, the telling' in *Film History*, Vol. 10, No. 1, 1998

Grossi, Giorgio 'Il libro di successo. Elementi di analisi del mercato editoriale dei libri più venduti (1982–1984)' in Livolsi (ed.) *Almeno un libro*

Grotowski, Jerzy 'Statement of Principles' in Huxley and Witts (eds) *The Twentieth Century Performance Reader*

Grottle Strebel, Elizabeth 'French Social Cinema and the Popular Front' in *Journal of Contemporary History*, Vol. 12, July 1977

Grugel, Jean and Tim Rees *Franco's Spain*, Arnold, London 1997

Guagnini, Elvio 'Alcuni aspetti dell'influenza di Verne sulla cultura italiana e il caso Yambo' in *Problemi*, No. 89, Sept.-Dec 1990

Gualerzi, Giorgio 'Appunti per una storia recente degl'interpreti verdiani' in *Rassegna Musicale Italiana*, Vol. 7, No. 22, 2002

Guccini, Gerardo 'Directing Opera' in Bianconi and Pestelli (eds) *Opera Production and Its Resources*

Guérande, Paul *Le Petit monde de la Comtesse de Ségur*, Les Seize, Paris 1964

Guerri, Giordano Bruno 'La Mondadori e la politica del ventennio' in AA VV *Editoria e cultura a Milano tra le due guerre (1920–1940)*

Gumplowicz, Philippe *Les travaux d'Orphée. 150 ans de vie musicale amateur en France. Harmonie, Chorales Fanfares*, Aubier, Paris 1987

Gunning, Tom 'The Cinema of Attractions: Early Cinema, its Spectator and the Avant Garde' in Elsaesser (ed.) *Early Cinema: Space Frame Narrative*

Günther, Cordula, *Heftromanleser in den neuen Bundesländer* (Leipzig 1994) available at *www.medienkomm.uni-halle.de/forschung/publikationen/halma11.pd.*

Györgyev, Clara 'The Influence of Whitman and Poe on Hungarian Literature' in Köpeczi and M. Vajda (eds) *Proceedings of the 8th Congress of the International Comparative Literature Association*

Habermas, Jürgen *The Postnational Constellation. Political essays*, Polity, Cambridge 2001

Hachette, Louis 'L'avenir du livre français' in *Revue des Deux Mondes*, 1 May 1917, Vol.87

Haine, Malou *Adolphe Sax, sa vie, son oeuvre, ses instruments de musique*, éditions de l'Université de Bruxelles 1980

Haining, Peter (ed.) *The Penny Dreadful*, Gollancz, London 1975

Halkin, Ariela *The Enemy Reviewed. German Popular Literature through British Eyes between the Two World Wars*, Praeger, Westport Conn. 1995

Hall, Peter 'Godot Almighty', *Guardian*, 25 August 2005

Hall, Peter *Cities in Civilization*, Phoenix, London 1999

Hallenberger, Gerd 'La quiete prima della tempesta. La fiction tv tedesca nel 2001' in Buonanno (ed.) *Eurofiction 2002*

Hamerton, Philip G. 'Gustave Doré's Bible' in *The Fortnightly Review*, No. 24, 1 May 1866

Hamilton, Alex 'The Winners Decoded', *Guardian*, 1 January 2005

Hammond, J. L. and Barbara *The Town Labourer*, Doubleday Anchor Books, Garden City, New York 1968

Hampicke, Evelyn 'The Danish Influence: David Oliver and Nordisk in Germany' in Elsaesser (ed), *A Second Life. German Cinema's First Decades*

Hamrlíková, Lea 'The Czech Republic', paper presented at the conference 'Remaining Relevant After Communism', Dubrovnik, June 2001

Hanák, Péter 'Why fin de siècle?' in *CEU History Department Handbook*, 1994–1995

Hannerz, Ulf *Cultural Complexity. Studies in the Social Organization of Meaning*, Columbia University Press, New York 1992

Harbgmeier, Michael 'European media in the Eyes of Muslim Observers' in *Culture and History* No. 16 (Scandinavian University Press), 1997

Harding, Rosamond E. M. *The Piano-Forte. Its History traced to the Great Exhibition of 1851*, Heckscher, London 1978 (1st ed. 1933)

Hardy, Phil and Dave Laing *The European Music Business*, FT Management Report, London 1995

Harman, Claire *Fanny Burney. A Biography*, HarperCollins, London 2000

Harper, Sue 'A Lower Middle-Class Taste-Community in the 1930s: admissions figures at the Regent Cinema, Portsmouth, UK' in *Historical Journal of Film, Radio and Television*, Vol.24, No.4, 2004

Harper, Sue and Vincent Porter 'Cinema Audience Tastes in 1950s Britain' in *Journal of Popular British Cinema*, No. 2, 1999

Harris, Michael *London Newspapers in the Age of Walpole*, Associate University Press, London and Toronto 1987

Harris, Ruth *Lourdes: Body and Spirit in the Secular Age*, Allen Lane The Penguin Press, Harmondsworth 1999

Harris, William V. *Ancient Literacy*, Harvard University Press 1989

Harrison, Brian 'Press and pressure group in modern Britain' in Shattock and Wolff (eds) *The Victorian periodical press*

Hartmann, Pierre 'La réception de Paméla en France: Les anti-Paméla de Villaret et Mauvillon' in *Revue d'Histoire littéraire de la France*, Vol.102, No. 1, January-February 2002

Haskell, Francis 'The Manufacture of the Past in Nineteenth-Century Painting' in *Past and Present*, No.53, November 1971

Haskell, Francis 'The Market for Italian Art in the seventeenth Century' in *Past and Present*, No.15, April 1959

Haudiquet, Philippe, Jean-Pierre Jeancolas and István Nemeskürty, *Le cinéma hongrois*, Centre Georges Pompidou, Paris 1979

Haudiquet, Philippe 'Le cinéma hongrois (1945–1963) in Haudiquet, Jeancolas, and István Nemeskürty, *Le cinéma hongrois*

Haugen, E. *Language Conflict and Language Planning: the Case of Modern Norwegian*, Harvard University Press 1966

Hawkridge, John 'British Cinema from Hepworth to Hitchcock' in Nowell-Smith (ed.) *The Oxford History of World Cinema*

Haxthausen, Franz *Studies on the Interior of Russia*, edited by F. Starr and trans. by E.L.M. Schmidt, University of Chicago Press 1972

Hay, James *Popular Film Culture in Fascist Italy*, Indiana University Press, Bloomington and Indianapolis 1987

Hayden, John O. (ed.) *Walter Scott. The Critical Heritage*, Routledge, London 1995

Haythornthwaite, J. A. 'Friendly Encounters: A Study of the Relationship between the House of Blackwood and Margaret Oliphant in her Role as Literary Critic' in *Publishing History*, No.28 1990

Haythornthwaite, J. A. 'The Wages of Success: "Miss Marjoribanks", Margaret Oliphant and the House of Blackwood' in *Publishing History*, No.15, 1984

Hazlitt, William *The Selected Writings of William Hazlitt*, edited by Duncan Wu, Pickering and Chatto, London 1998

Headrick, Daniel R. *The Tools of Empire. Technology and Imperialism in the Nineteenth century*, OUP 1981

Heaton, Barrie *The U.K. Piano Pages http://www.uk-piano.org* – update of 15 September 2000

Hébrard, Jean 'Les canards' in Chartier and Martin (eds) *Histoire de l'édition française*, Vol. 3

Hegerfors, Sture 'Suède' in Moliterni (ed.) *Histoire Mondiale de la Bande Dessinée*

Heiderich, Manfred W. *The German Novel of 1800. A Study of Popular Prose Fiction*, Peter Lang, Berne 1982

Heine, Heinrich *Italian Travel Sketches*, Foulis, London 1927

Heine, Heinrich *Tableaux de Voyages*, L'Instant, Paris 1989

Hellegouarc'h, Jacqueline (ed.) *L'art de la conversation*, Classiques Garnier, Paris 1997

Heller, Dana 'Russian "Sitkom" Adaptation: The Pushkin Principle' in *Journal of Popular Film & Television*, Vol. 31, No 2, Summer 2003

Hemmings, F. W. J. *The Theatre Industry in Nineteenth-Century France*, Cambridge University Press 1993

Hennion Antoine and J.P. Vignolle, *Artisans et industriels du disque. Essai sur le mode de production de la musique*, CSI-CORDES, 1978

Hennion, Antoine (ed.) *1789–1989: Musique, Histoire, Démocratie*, 3. Vols, proceedings of the conference organised by Vibrations and IASPM (International Association for the Study of Popular Music), Éditions de la Maison des Sciences de l'homme, Paris 1989

Hennion, Antoine *La passion musicale. Une sociologie de la médiation*, Métailié, Paris 1993

Henri Baillère, *La crise du livre*, Librarie Baillère et fils, Paris 1904

Hepokoski, James 'Ottocento Opera as Cultural Drama: Generic Mixtures in *Il trovatore*' in Chusid (ed.) *Verdi's Middle Period, 1849–1859*

Herbert, Robert L. 'Renoir the Radical' in *New York Review of Books*, 20 November 1997

Herder, Johann Gottfried 'Extract from a Correspondence on Ossian and the Songs of the Ancient Peoples' translated by Joyce Crick, in *German aesthetic and literary criticism: Winckelmann, Lessing, Hamann, Herder, Schiller, Goethe*, edited by H.B. Nisbet, Cambridge University Press, 1985

Hermand, Jost 'Art for the People: the Nazi Concept of a Truly Popular Painting' in Grimm, and Hermand (eds) *High and Low Cultures*

Herrick, Jim 'Samuel Beckett' in *Censorship. A World Encyclopedia*

Hess, Rémi *La Valse. Révolution du couple en Europe*, Métailié, Paris 1989

Hesse, Sebastian 'Ernst Reichler alias Stuart Webbs: King of the German Film Detectives' in Elsaesser (ed), *A Second Life. German Cinema's First Decades*

Higgs, Robert 'Race, Skills, and Earnings: American Immigrants in 1909' in *Journal of Economic History*, Vol. 31, 1971

Hiley, Nicholas ' "Let's go to the pictures". The British Cinema Audience in the 1920s and 1930s' in the *Journal of Popular British Cinema*, No 2, 1999

Hill, Christopher 'Clarissa Harlowe and her Times', originally in *Essays in Criticism*, 1955, reprinted in John Carroll (ed.) *Samuel Richardson. A Collection of Critical Essays*, Prentice Hall, New Jersey 1969

Hill, John 'British Cinema as National Cinema: Production, Audience and Representation' in Robert Murphy (ed) *The British Cinema Book*, BFI, London 1997

Hill, Napoleon *Think and Grow Rich*, The Ralston Society, Meriden Conn. 1938

Hilmes, Michèle 'Television and the Film Industry' in Nowell-Smith (ed.) *The Oxford History of World Cinema*

Hilton, Tim *John Ruskin. The Later Years*, Yale UP, New Haven and London 2000

Himmelweit, Hilde, A. N. Oppenheim, and Pamela Vince *Television and the Child. An empirical study of the effect of television on the young*, Oxford University Press 1958

Hingley, Ronald *Russian Writers and Soviet Society 1917–1978*, Methuen, London 1979

His Master's Voice/La voce del padrone, The Italian Catalogue. A Complete Numerical Catalogue of Italian Gramophone Recordings made from 1898 to 1920 in Italy and elsewhere by The Gramophone Company Ltd., compiled by Alan Kelly, Greenwood Press, New York 1988

History of the Times 'The Thunderer' in the making 1785–1841 (Vol.1), Times Publishing Company, London 1935

Hitler, Adolf *Mein Kampf*, translated by Ralph Mannheim, Hutchinson, London 1969

Hobbes, *Leviathan*, Penguin, Harmondsworth 1968

Hobsbawm, Eric *The Age of Empire 1875–1914*, Weidenfeld and Nicolson, London 1987

Hobsbawm, Eric *The Age of Extremes. The Short Twentieth Century 1914–1991*, Michael Joseph, London 1994

Hobson, John M. *The Eastern Origins of Western Civilisation*, Cambridge University Press 2004

Hodgkin, Adam 'New Technologies in Printing and Publishing: the Present of the Written Word' in Baumann (ed.) *The Written Word*

Hoffmann, E.T.A. 'Don Giovanni' in *Six German Romantic Tales*, trans. by Ronald Taylor, Angel Books, London 1985

Hohendahl, Peter Uwe *Building a National Literature. The Case of Germany, 1830–1870*, Cornell University Press, Ithaca and London 1989

Hollis, Patricia *The Pauper Press. A Study in Working-Class Radicalism of the 1830s*, OUP 1970

Holmes, Susan ' "As they really are, and in close up": film stars on 1950s British television' in *Screen*, Vol. 42, No. 2, Summer 2001

Holmlund, Christine 'Pippi and Her Pals' in *Cinema Journal*, Vol. 42, No. 2, Winter 2003

Holter, Howard R. 'The Legacy of Lunacharsky and Artistic Freedom in the USSR' in *Slavic Review*, Vol. 29, No. 2, June 1970, pp.262–82

Homberger, Eric 'The model's unwashed feet: French photography in the 1850s' in Collier and Lethbridge (eds) *Artistic Relations. Literature and the Visual Arts in Nineteenth-Century France*

Hopkinson, Cecil *A Dictionary of Parisian Music Publishers 1700–1950*, printed for the author, London 1954

Horak, Jan-Christopher 'German exile cinema, 1933–1950' in *Film History*, Vol. 8, No. 4, 1996

Horden, Francis 'Genèse et vote de la loi du 20 juin 1936 sur les congés payés' in *Le Mouvement social*, No 150, January-March 1990

Horellou-Lafarge, Chantal and Monique Segré, *Regards sur la lecture en France. Bilan des recherches sociologiques*, L'Harmattan, Paris 1996

Hortmann, Wilhelm *Shakespeare on the German Stage. The Twentieth Century*, CUP 1998

Hortschansky, Klaus 'The Musician as Music Dealer' in Salmen (ed.) *The Social Status of the Professional Musician*

Horwitz, Rita and Harriet Harrison (eds) *The George Kleine Collection of Early Motion Pictures*, Library of Congress, Washington 1980

Houfe, Simon *The Dictionary of nineteenth Century British Book Illustrators and Caricaturists*, Antique Collectors' Club, Woodbridge Suffolk 1996

Houghton, Walter E. 'Periodical literature and the articulate classes' in Shattock and Wolff (eds) *The Victorian periodical press*

Houston, R. A. *Literacy in early Modern Europe. Culture and Education 1500–1800*, Longman, London and New York 1988

http://dear_raed.blogspot.com/

http://gaslight.mtroyal.ab.ca/gaslight/martbald.htm

http://justzipit.blogspot.com/

http://m1.300.telia.com/~u30006326/opera5.html accessed in February 2004

http://news.bbc.co.uk/1/hi/entertainment/1055516.stm

http://web.quick.cz/sdruzeni.milislav/Pages/aRepertoar.htm

http://weblog.jrc.cec.eu.int/page/wallstrom

Huber, Richard *La RFA et sa Télévision*, INA/Champs Vallon, Paris 1988

Hubert-Lacombe, Patricia *Le cinéma français dans la guerre froide 1946–1956*, l'Harmattan, Paris 1996

Huet, Marie-Hélène *L'Histoire des Voyages extraordinaires. Essai sur l'oeuvre de Jules Verne*, Minard, Paris 1973

Hughes, Stephen P. ' "The Music Boom" in Tamil South India: gramophone, radio and the making of mass culture' in *Historical Journal of Film, Radio and Television*, Vol. 4, 2002

Hugo, Victor and Pierre-Jules Hetzel *Correspondance*, Vol. 1 (1852–1853) edited by Sheila Gaudon, Klincksiek, Paris 1979

Hugo, Victor *Choses vues 1830–1846*, Gallimard-Folio, Parais 1972

Hulse, Michael 'Introduction' to Johann Wolfgang Goethe's *The Sorrows of Young Werther*, Penguin, London 1989

Humphreys, Peter J. *Media and Media Policy in Germany. The Press and Broadcasting since 1945*, Berg, Oxford 1994

Hunter, J. Paul 'The novel and social/cultural history' in Richetti (ed.) *The Cambridge Companion to the Eighteenth-Century Novel*

Huth, Arno *La Radiodiffusion, Puissance mondiale*, Gallimard, Paris 1937

Hüttner, Johann 'Die Vereitelte Offenbachpflege im Theater' in *Austriaca*, Cahiers Universitaires d'Information sur l'Autriche, No. 46, June 1998

Hüttner, Kirsten *'The Woman in White' Analysis, Reception and Literary Criticism of a Victorian Bestseller*, Wisseschaftlicher Verlag, Trier 1996

Huxley, Michael and Noel Witts (eds) *The Twentieth-Century Performance Reader*, Routledge, London 1996

IFPI, *The Recording Industry in Numbers*, 1995

Ilieva, Angelina 'Bulgaria' paper presented at the conference 'Remaining Relevant After Communism', Dubrovnik, June 2001

Illustrazione italiana No 2, 1922

Index Translationum. UNESCO. *http://portal.unesco.org/culture/en/ev.php-URL_ID= 7810&URL_DO=DO_TOPIC&URL_SECTION=201.html*

India Today, 2 June 2003

Inglis, Fred *Clifford Geertz*, Polity, Oxford 2000

Ingoldsby, Thomas (Richard Barnham) *The Ingoldsby Legends*, Frederick Warne and Co. Chandos Classic Collection, London and New York, no date

Iorga, Neculai *La société roumaine du XIXe siècle dans le théâtre roumain*, Gamber, Paris 1926

Iosifidis, Petros, Jeannette Steemers and Mark Wheeler *European Television Industries*, bfi publishing, London 2005

Iser, Wolfgang 'The Reading Process: a phenomenological approach', *New Literary History*, 3, 1972

Isnenghi, Mario (ed.) *I luoghi della memoria. Personaggi e date dell 'Italia unita*, Laterza, Bari-Rome 1997

Isola, Gianni 'Dalla scatola della musica al radiocane. Radiofonia e tempo libero nell'Italia del Novecento' in *Tempo libero e società di massa nell'Italia del Novecento*

Isola, Gianni *Cari amici vicini e lontani. Storia dell'ascolto radiofonico nel primo decennio repubblicano*, La Nuova Italia, Florence 1995

Ito, Kinko 'The World of Japanese Ladies' Comics: From Romantic Fantasy to Lustful Perversion' in *Journal of Popular Culture*, August 2002, Vol. 36, No. 1

Jäckel, Anne 'Dual Nationality Film Productions in Europe after 1945' in *Historical Journal of Film, Radio and Television*, Vol. 23, No. 3, 2003

Jaikumar, Priya 'An Act of transition: empire and the making of a national British film industry, 1927' in *Screen*, Vol. 43, No. 2, 2002

James, Edward *Science Fiction in the 20th century*, Oxford University Press 1994

James, Elizabeth 'An Insight into the Management of Railway Bookstalls in the Eighteen Fifties' in *Publishing History*, No. 10, 1981

James, Elizabeth 'The Publication of Collected Editions of Bulwer Lytton's Novels' in *Publishing History*, No. 3, 1978

James, Louis 'The trouble with Betsy: periodical and the common reader in mid-nineteenth-century England' in Shattock and Wolff (eds) *The Victorian periodical press*

Jameson, Fredric *Postmodernism or the Cultural Logic of Late Capitalism*, Verso, London 1991

Janet, Paul 'L'Éducation des femmes' in *Revue des Deux Mondes*, Vol. 53, 1 November, 1883

Jankowski, Paul F. *Stavisky: A Confidence Man in the Republic of Virtue*, Cornell University Press, Ithaca 2002

Jardine, Lisa *Worldy Goods. A New History of the Renaissance*, Macmillan, London 1996

Jauss, Hans Robert 'Literary History as a Challenge to Literary Theory', in *New Directions in Literary History*, edited by Ralph Cohen, Johns Hopkins University Press, Baltimore 1974

Jauss, Hans Robert 'Littérature médiévale et théorie des genres' in Genette et al. *Théorie des genres*

Jeancolas, Jean-Pierre *Histoire du cinéma français*, Nathan, Paris 1995

Jeancolas, Jean-Pierre 'From the Blum-Byrnes Agreement to the GATT affair' in Nowell-Smith and Ricci (eds) *Hollywood and Europe*

Jeanne, René 'L'invasion cinématographique américaine' in *Revue des Deux Mondes*, Vol.100, 15 February 1930

Jeanneney, Jean-Noël 'Quelques réflections sur les films de montage' in Jean-Noël Jeanneney and Monique Sauvage (eds) *Télévision, nouvelle mémoire. Les magazines de grand reportage 1959–1968*

Jeanneney, Jean-Noël and Jacques Julliard, *'Le Monde' de Beuve-Méry ou le métier d'Alceste*, Seuil, Paris 1979

Jeanneney, Jean-Noël and Monique Sauvage (eds) *Télévision, nouvelle mémoire. Les magazines de grand reportage 1959–1968*, Édition du Seuil, Paris 1982

Jelavich, Peter *Berlin Cabaret*, Harvard University Press, Cambridge Mass. and London 1993

Jelavich, Peter *Munich and Theatrical Modernism. Politics, Playwriting, and Performance 1890–1914*, Harvard UP, Cambridge 1985

Jelavich, Peter, 'Oskar Panizza' in *Censorship. A World Encyclopedia*

Jelot-Blanc, Jean-Jacques *Télé-feuilletons. Le dictionnaire de toutes les séries et de tous les feuilletons télévisés depuis les origines de la télévision*, Ramsay, Paris 1993

Jerome, Jerome K. *My Life and Times*, John Murray, 1983

Jobling, Paul 'L'assiette au beurre' in *Censorship. A World Encyclopedia*

Johansson, Egil 'The History of Literacy in Sweden' in Graff (ed.) *Literacy and Social Development in the West*

John, Nicholas *The Magic Flute*, John Calder, London 1980

Johnson, James H. 'Musical Experience and the Formation of a French Musical Public' in *Journal of Modern History*, Vol. 64, No.2, June 1992

Johnson, James H. *Listening in Paris. A Cultural History*, University of California Press, Berkeley 1995

Johnson, Paul, 'The Menace of Beatlism' in *New Statesman*, 28 February 1964, now in Harif Kureishi and Jon Savage (eds) *The Faber Book of Pop*, Faber and Faber, London 1995

Jonard, Norbert *La France et l'Italie au siècle des lumières. Essai sur les échanges intellectuels*, Honoré Champion, Paris 1994

Jones, Kathleen *Catherine Cookson. The Biography*, Constable, London 1999

Jordan, Ruth *Fromental Halevy. His Life and Music 1799–1862*, Kahn and Averill, London 1994

Joyce, James *Portrait of the Artist as a Young Man*, Viking Press, New York 1969

Joyce, Patrick 'The People's English: Language and Class in England c.1840–1920' in Burke and Porter (eds) *Language, Self, and Society*

Juin, Hubert 'Pour éveiller nos joies un beau crime est bien fort' in *Europe*, Vol. 56, No. 590–591, June-July 1978

Kaenel, Philippe ' "Le plus illustre des illustrateurs . . ." Le cas Gustave Doré 1832/1883' in *Actes de la recherche en sciences sociales*, No.66/67, March 1987

Kaenel, Philippe 'Autour de J.-J. Grandville: les conditions de production socio-professionelles du livre illustré "romantique" ' in *Romantisme*, No. 43, Vol. 14, 1984

Kaes, Anton 'Cinema and Modernity: On Fritz Lang's *Metropolis*' in Grimm and Hermand (eds) *High and Low Cultures*

Kahn, Madeleine *Narrative transvestism: rhetoric and gender in the eighteenth-century English novel*, Cornell University Press, Ithaca, N.Y. 1991

Kalbouss, George 'The Birth of Modern Russia Drama' in Richard Freeborn, R. R. Milner-Gulland and Charles A. Ward (eds) *Russian and Slavic Literature*, Slavic Publishers Inc., Cambridge, Mass. 1976

Kambo, Enriketa 'Certains aspects de la lutte du PCA pour la création et la propagation de la culture spirituelle socialiste au cours des années 1944–48' in *Studia Albanica*, 1981, Vol. 18 No 1 pp.25–50

Karady, Victor 'Les Juifs dans l'édition hongroise avant 1945', in *Actes de la recherche en sciences sociales*, No 130, December 1999

Karady, Victor and Istvan Kemény, 'Les juifs dans la structure des classes en Hongrie: essai sur les antécédents historiques des crises d'antisémitisme du XXe siècle' in *Actes de la recherche en sciences sociales*, No.22, June 1978

Karamzin, Nikolai "The Book Trade and the Love of Reading in Russia' in *Russian Intellectual History. An Anthology* edited by Marc Raeff, Harcourt Brace, New York 1966

Kaschuba, Wolfgang 'German *Bürgerlichkeit* after 1800: Culture as Symbolic Practice' in Kocka and Mitchell (eds) *Bourgeois Society in Nineteenth-century Europe*

Kater, Michael *Different Drummers: Jazz in the Culture of Nazi Germany*, OUP, New York and Oxford 1992

Kattelman, Beth A. 'Mae West' in *Censorship. A World Encyclopedia*

Katz, Elihu 'And Deliver Us from Segmentation' in *Annals of the American Academy of Political and Social Science*, edited by Kathleen Hall Jamieson, July 1996

Kaukoranta, Heikki 'Finlande' in Moliterni (ed.) *Histoire Mondiale de la Bande Dessinée*

Kelly, Catriona *A History of Russian Women's Writing 1820–1992*, Clarendon Press, Oxford 1994

Kemp-Welch, A. 'New Economic Policy in Culture and Its Enemies' in *Journal of Contemporary History*, Vol.13, no.3, July 1978

Kendall, Alan *Paganini. A Biography*, Chappell and Co and Elm Tree Books, London 1982

Kepley, Vance 'The First *Perestroika*: Soviet Cinema under the first Five-Year Plan' in *Cinema Journal*, Vol. 35, No. 4, Summer 1996

Kepley, Vance 'The origins of Soviet cinema: a study in industry development' in Taylor and Christie (eds) *Inside the Film factory*

Kerman, Joseph 'Beethoven and the Big Change' in *New York Review of Books*, 24 June 1999

Kershaw, Ian *Popular Opinion and Political Dissent in the Third Reich: Bavaria 1933–1945*, Clarendon Press, Oxford 2002

Keynes, John Maynard *Collected Writings*, Vol. XIX, Macmillan, London 1981

Kiberd, Declan *Inventing Ireland. The Literature of the Modern Nation*, Vintage, London 1996

Kierkegaard, Søren *The Diary of Søren Kierkegaard*, trans. by Gerda M. Anderson, Peter Owen Ltd., London 1961

Kift, Dagmar *The Victorian Music Hall. Culture, class and conflict*, Cambridge University Press 1996

Killen, Alice M. *Le Roman terrifiant ou Roman Noir de Walpole à Ann Radcliffe*, Édouard Champion, Paris 1923

Kinnear, Michael S. *The Gramophone Company's First Indian Recordings 1899–1908*, Sangam Books, New Delhi 1994

Kinnell, Margaret 'Childhood and Children's Literature: the Case of M. J. Godwin and Co., 1805–25' *Publishing History*, No.24, 1988

Klancher, Jon P. *The Making of English Reading Audiences 1790–1832*, University of Wisconsin Press, Madison 1987

Klaniczay, Tibor *Histoire de la littérature hongroise des origines à nos jours*, Corvina Kiadó, Budapest 1980

Klein, Jean-Claude *Florilège de la Chanson Française*, Bordas, Paris 1990

Klein, Lawrence E. 'Politeness and the Interpretation of the British Eighteenth Century' in *The Historical Journal*, vol. 45, No. 4, December 2002

Klein, Saul 'Amazon gambles on the high street', *Guardian*, 28 March 2005

Klotz, Volker 'Apoteosi, passione e azione nel "Conte di Montecristo" di Dumas' in Petronio and Schulz-Buschhaus (eds) '*Trivialliteratur?*'

Knapp, Bettina L. *The Reign of the Theatrical Director. French Theatre: 1887–1924*, The Whitston Publishing Company, Troy, New York 1988

Knapp, Raymond *The American Musical and the Formation of National Identity*, Princeton University Press 2005

Knecht, Edgar 'Le Juif errant. Eléments d'un mythe populaire' in *Romantisme*, No. 9, 1975, pp.84–96

Knecht, Edgar 'Le mythe du Juif errant' in *Romantisme*, Vol. 7, No.16, 1977, pp.101–15

Knops, Tilo 'Cinema from the Writing Desk: Detective Films in Imperial Germany' in Elsaesser (ed), *A Second Life. German Cinema's First Decades*

Kobak, Anette 'Malvina Recovered' in *Times Literary Supplement*, 4 January 2002

Kocka, Jürgen and Allan Mitchell (eds) *Bourgeois Society in Nineteenth-century Europe*, Berg, Oxford/Providence 1993

Köhler, Ursula E.E. 'Lesekultur in beiden deutschen Staaten. 40 Jahre – ein Vergleich. Geschichte – Theorie – Empirie', Teil 1, in *Archiv für Soziologie und Wirtschaftsfragen des Buchhandels* LXIV. Beilage zum Börsenblatt für den Deutschen Buchhandel, Frankfurter Ausgabe No. 24, 23 March 1990

Köpeczi, Béla and György M. Vajda (eds) *Proceedings of the 8th Congress of the International Comparative Literature Association* (Budapest 1976), Kunst und Wissen & Erich Bieber, Stuttgart 1980

Körner, Axel 'The Theatre of Social Change: nobility, opera industry and the politics of culture in Bologna between papal privileges and liberal principles' in *Journal of Modern Italian Studies*, Vol. 8, No. 3, Fall 2003

Kortländer, Bernd 'Traduire. "La plus noble des activités" ou "la plus abjecte des pratiques"' in Espagne and Werner (eds) *Philologiques III. Qu'est-ce qu'une littérature nationale?*

Korwin-Piotrowska, Sophie de *Balzac et le monde slave. Balzac en Pologne* (first edition 1933), Slatkin reprints, Geneva 1976

Kosko, Marja *Un 'best-seller', 1900: Quo Vadis?*, José Corti, Paris 1960 (1st edition: 1935)

Kostallari, Androkli 'La langue littéraire nationale albanaise et notre époque' in *Studia Albanica*, Vol. 22, No. 1, 1985

Koszyk, Kurt *Deutsche Presse im 19. Jahrhundert*, Colloquium Verlag, Berlin 1966

Koven, Seth *Slumming. Sexual and Social Politics in Victorian London*, Princeton University Press 2004

Kozlov, Denis 'Soviet Readers, Historical Consciousness, and the Erosion of the Enemy Paradigm During the Thaw: From Pasternak to Siniavskii and Daniel, 1958–1966' presented at the Davis Center for Russian and Eurasian Studies, Harvard University, 28 March 2004, accessed from *http://daviscenter.fas.harvard.edu/seminars_conferences/cnsschedule.html*

Kracauer, Siegfried 'On bestsellers and their audience' in his *The Mass Ornament. Weimar Essays,* Harvard University Press Cambridge Mass. and London 1995

Kracauer, Siegfried *The Mass Ornament. Weimar Essays,* Harvard University Press, Cambridge Mass and London 1995

Krakovitch, Odile 'Le théâtre sous la Restauration et la monarchie de Juillet: lecture et spectacle' in Vaillant (ed.) *Mesure(s) du livre*

Krakovitch, Odile 'Les romantiques et la censure au théâtre' in *Romantisme*, No. 38, 1982

Krakovitch, Odile *Hugo censuré. La liberté au théâtre au XIXe siècle*, Calmann-Lévy, Paris 1985

Kramer, Lawrence *Music as Cultural Practice, 1800–1900*, University of California Press, Berkeley 1990

Kretschmer, Martin 'The Failure of Property Rules in Collective Administration: Rethinking Copyright Societies as Regulatory Instruments' in *E.I.P.R.*, No. 3, 2002; *www.cippm.org.uk/pdfs/kretschmer_eipr_032002.pdf*, accessed June 2004

Kretschmer, Martin, George Michael Klimis and Roger Wallis *The Global Music Industry in the Digital Environment: A Study of Strategic Intent and Policy Responses (1996–99)*, paper at conference on Long-Term Developments in the Arts and Cultural Industries, Erasmus University of Rotterdam, 23–25 February 2000, accessed at *www.mica.at/pdf/kretschmer_c.pdf*

Kuhlmann, Marie, Nelly Kuntzmann, and Hélène Bellour *Censure et bibliothèques au XXe siècle*, Cercle de la Librairie, Paris 1989

Kuhn, Anette *Cinema, Censorship and Sexuality, 1909–1925*, Routledge, London and New York 1988

Kuhn, Annette 'Heterotopia, heterochronia: place and time in cinema history' in *Screen*, Vol.45, No.2, Summer 2004

Kulczycka-Saloni, Janina 'Les personnages du roman polonais du XIXe siècle' in *Proceedings of the XIIth Congress of the International Comparative Literature Association*, Vol. 2, Iudicium Verlag, Munich 1990

Kuleshov, Lev 'The Banner of Cinematography' (1920) in his *Fifty Years of Films*, Raduga, Moscow 1987

Kunzle, David *History of the Comic Strip*, Vol.I, *The Early Comic Strip*, University of California Press, Berkeley, LA, London 1973

Kupzova, Olga 'La gestuelle théâtrale en Russie' in Dmitrieva and Espagne (eds) *Transfers culturels triangulaires Philologiques IV*

La Chanson de Roland, edited and translated by André Cordier, Larousse, Paris 1935

La circulation internationale des émissions de télévision, UNESCO No. 100, 1986 edited by Tapio Varis

La Gloire de Victor Hugo, catalogue of the exhibition at the Grand Palais, Édition de la Réunion des musées nationaux, Paris 1985

Lacassin, Francis 'Préface' to *Fantômas* (Collected works), Bouquin/Robert Laffont, Paris 1987

Lacassin, Francis *Mythologie du roman policier*, Christian Bourgois Éditeur, Paris 1993

Laffont, Robert *Éditeur*, Laffont, Paris 1974

Lai, Cheng-chung (ed.) *Adam Smith Across Nations. Translations and Receptions of 'The Wealth of Nations'*, OUP 2000

Lallement, Jérôme 'Essai d'une définition économique du livre' in *Cahiers de l'économie du livre*, no.9, March 1993

Lamar (ed.) Howard R. *The New Encyclopedia of the American West*, Yale University Press, New Haven and London 1998

Lamb, Andrew 'Waltz' in *The New Grove Dictionary of Music Online* ed. L. Macy (Accessed 29 July 2003), *http://www.grovemusic.com*

Lamont, Claire Introduction to Walter Scott, *Waverley, or, 'Tis Sixty Years Since*, Clarendon Press, Oxford 1981

Lanaro, Silvio 'Il Plutarco italiano: l'istruzione del "popolo" dopo l'Unità' in Vivanti (ed.) *Storia d'Italia. Annali 4 Intellettuali e potere*

Landon, H. C. Robbins *Haydn in England 1791–1795*, Thames and Hudson, London 1976

Langewiesche, Dieter 'The Impact of the German Labor Movement on Workers' Culture' in *Journal of Modern History*, Vol.59, No.3, September 1987

Lanoux, Armand 'Introduction' to Eugène Sue, *Les mystères de Paris*, Laffont, Paris 1989

Lanza, Maria Teresa *Porta e Belli*, Letteratura Italiana Laterza, LIL 43, Roma-Bari 1981

Larivaille, Paul *Le Réalisme du merveilleux. Structures et histoire du conte*, Université Paris X-Nanterre, 1982.

Larrington, Carolyne *Women and Writing in Medieval Europe*, Routledge, London 1995

Larsen, Jen Peter *Haydn*, Macmillan, London and Basingstoke 1984

Larson, Kenneth E. 'Shakespeare between Aufklärung and Sturm und Drang' in *http://aurora.wells.edu/~klarson/papers/mmla88wells.htm*; update of February 17, 2000

Larson, Kenneth E. 'Wieland's Shakespeare: A Reappraisal' in *The Lessing Yearbook*, Volume XVI, 1984

Lasserre, Henri *Notre-Dame de Lourdes*, Victor Palme Éditeur, Paris 1869

Laster, Arnaud 'La Musique' in *La gloire de Victor Hugo*

Latouche, Serge *L'occidentalisation du monde*, Éditions La Découverte, Paris 1989, p.29

Lauf, Edmund 'Research Note: The Vanishing Young Reader. Sociodemographic Determinants of Newspaper Use as a Source of Political Information in Europe, 1980–98' in *European Journal of Communication*, Vol. 16, No.2, June 2001

Laurent, Jacques *Discours de réception de Jacques Laurent à l'Académie Française*, Gallimard, Paris 1987

Laurent, Jacques *Histoire égoïste*, La Table Ronde, Paris 1976

Law, Graham *Serializing Fiction in the Victorian Press*, Palgrave, Basingstoke and New York 2000

Lawford-Hunrichsen, Irene *Music Publishing and Patronage. C. F. Peters: 1800 to the Holocaust*, Edition Press, Kenton Middlesex 2000

Lawrence, Jon 'Fascist violence and the politics of public order in inter-war Britain: the Olympia debate revisited' in *Historical Research*, Vol. 76, No. 192, May 2003

Lawson, Mark 'Many Happy Rover's Returns', *Guardian*, media supplement, 16 May 2005

Le Forestier, Laurent 'L'accueil en France des film américains de réalisateurs français à l'époque des accords Blum-Byrnes', *Revue d'histoire moderne et contemporaine*, Vol. 51, October-December 2004 No.4

Le Hir, Marie-Pierre *Le romantisme aux enchères: Ducange, Pixérécourt, Hugo*, John Benjamins Publishing Company, Philadelphia 1992

Le Men, Ségolène 'Book Illustration' in Collier and Lethbridge (eds) *Artistic Relations. Literature and the Visual Arts in Nineteenth-Century France*

Le Monde, colour supplement, 2 April 2005

Le Rider, Jacques '*Soll und Haben* de Gustav Freytag. Un bréviare de l'identité nationale "bourgeoise"' in Espagne and Werner (eds) *Philologiques III*

Le Rocambole, special issue of the *Bulletin des Amis du Roman populaire* No. 2, Fall 1997

Lebrecht, Norman *Discord. Conflict and the Making of Music*, André Deutsch, London 1982

Leclerc, Yvan *Crimes écrits. La littérature en procès au 19e siècle*, Plon, Paris 1991

Lefcourt, Jenny 'Aller au cinéma, aller au peuple' in *Revue d'histoire moderne et contemporaine*, Vol. 51, No.4, October-December 2004

Lefebvre, Jean-Pierre 'L'introduction de la philosophie allemande en France au XIXe siècle. La question des traductions' in Espagne and Werner (eds) *Transferts. Les relations interculturelles dans l'espace franco-allemand (XVIIIe-XIXe siècle)*

Leff, Leonard F. *Hitchcock and Selznick*, University of California Press, Berkeley 1999

Legouis, Émile 'La fortune littéraire de Walter Scott en France' in *Études anglaises*, Vol. 24, No 4, October-December 1971

Lehtonen, Maija 'La littérature finlandaise au carrefour des cultures' in Köpeczi and Vajda (eds) *Proceedings of the 8th Congress of the International Comparative Literature Association*

Lemaître, Jules 'De l'influence récente de la littérature du Nord' in *Revue des Deux Mondes*, Vol. 64, 15 December 1894

Lenman, Robin 'Germany' in Goldstein (ed.) *The War for the Public Mind*

Lent, John A. 'Comic Books' in *Censorship. A World Encyclopedia*

Lerner, Henri *La Dépêche, Journal de la Démocratie. Contribution à l'Histoire du Radicalisme en France sous la Troisième République*, Publications de l'Université de Toulouse Le Mirail, Toulouse 1978

Leroux, Gaston *Le Mystère de la chambre jaune*, Le Livre de Poche, Paris 1996

Leroy, Dominique *Histoire des arts du Spectacle en France*, L'Harmattan, Paris 1990

Les écrits de l'image, 'Le top 20 des meilleures séries télévisés en 1997', No. 18 Spring 1998

Leslie, Esther *Hollywood Flatlands*, Verso, London 2002

Lesure, François et al. *La Musique à Paris en 1830–1831*, Bibliothèque Nationale, Paris 1983

Letellier, Robert Ignatius 'Bellini and Meyerbeer' in *The Opera Quarterly*, Vol. 17, No 3, Summer 2001

Letzter, Jacqueline and Robert Adelson, *Women Writing Opera. Creativity and Controversy in the Age of the French Revolution*, University of California Press, Berkeley 2001

Leuillot, Bernard *Victor Hugo publie les Misérables*, Klincksieck, Paris 1970

Levi, Erik *Music in the Third Reich*, Macmillan, London 1994

Levi, Roberto *Le trasmissioni TV che hanno fatto (o no) l'Italia. Da 'Lascia o raddoppia?' al 'Grande Fratello'*, Rizzoli, Milan 2002

Levinson, Alekseï 'Papier récupéré et livres' (1985) in Stroev (ed.) *Livre et lecture en Russie*

Lévi-Strauss, Claude (with Georges Charbonnier) *Entretiens avec Claude Lévi-Strauss*, Julliard, Paris 1961

Lévi-Strauss, Claude *Anthropologie structurale*, Plon Pocket, Paris 1974

Lévi-Strauss, Claude *Tristes tropiques*, Plon/Presses Pocket, Paris 1984

Levitt, Marcus C. '*Barkoviana* and Russian Classicism' in *Eros and Pornography in Russian Culture* edited by M. Levitt and A. Toporkov, Ladomir Publishing House, Moscow 2000

Levitt, Marcus C. *Russian Literary Politics and the Pushkin Celebration of 1880*, Cornell University Press, Ithaca and London 1989

Levy, Claire, 'Rap in Bulgaria', Mitchell (ed), *Global Noise*

Lévy-Leboyer, Maurice and Henri Morsel (eds) *L'Interconnexion et le Marché 1919–1946*, Vol. Two of *Histoire Générale de l'Électrcité en France*, Fayard, Paris 1994

Lewes, George H. 'Criticism in Relation to Novels' in *The Fortnightly Review*, Vol. 15, 15 December 1865

Leydi, Roberto 'La musica e lo spettacolo musicale' in *Televisione e vita italiana*, ERI, Turin 1968

Liber, George 'Language, Literacy and Book Publishing in the Ukrainian SSR, 1923–1928' in *Slavic Review* No. 4, Winter 1982

Libri Santoro, M.A. 'I giudizi dei ragazzi sui programmi a loro dedicati' in *Lo Spettacolo*, Vol. 21, no 1, January–March 1971

Lieberman, Richard K. *Steinway and Sons*, Yale UP, New Haven 1995

Liebes, Tamar and Elihu Katz *The Export of Meaning. Cross-cultural readings of 'Dallas'*, Polity, Cambridge 1993

Liebes, Tamar and Sonia Livingstone 'European Soap Operas. The Diversification of a Genre' in *European Journal of Communication*, Vol. 13, No. 2, June 1998

Lilliestam, Lars 'Musical acculturation: "Hound Dog" from Blues to Swedish Rock'n'Roll' in Hennion (ed.) *1789–1989: Musique, Histoire, Démocratie*, Vol.III

Limansky, Nicholas E. 'Luisa Tetrazzini. Coloratura secrets' in *The Opera Quarterly*, No. 4, Autumn 2004

Limousin, Odile 'Essais statistiques sur l'évolution de l'édition du livre pour enfants et l'évolution de la scolarisation de 1800 à 1966' in *Bibliographie de la France*, 3 November 1971, No. 44, Vol.160

Linares, Francisco 'Theatre and Falangism at the Beginning of the Franco Régime' in Günter Berghaus (ed.) *Fascism and Theatre*

Lind-Goldschmidt, Jenny *Memoir. Her Early Life and Dramatic Career 1820–1850*, edited by Henry Holland, Scott and W. S. Rockstro, Vol. 2, John Murray, London 1891

Lindop, Grevel *The Opium-Eater. A Life of Thomas De Quincey*, Dent, London 1981

Lipovetsky, Gilles *The Empire of Fashion. Dressing Modern Democracy*, trans. Catherine Porter, Princeton UP 1994

Little, Daran *The Coronation Street Story*, Granada, London 2001

Livezeanu, Irina and Marius Lazăr 'The Romanian Case', paper presented at the conference 'Remaining Relevant After Communism', Dubrovnik, June 2001

Livezeanu, Irina *Cultural Politics in Greater Romania. Regionalism, Nation Building, & Ethnic Struggle, 1918–1930*, Cornell University Press, Ithaca and London 2000

Livi-Bacci, Massimo *La popolazione nella storia d'Europa*, Laterza, Roma-Bari 1998

Livingstone, Sonia and Peter Lunt *Talk on Television. Audience Participation and Public Debate*, Routledge, London 1994

Livolsi, Marino (ed.) *Almeno un libro. Gli italiani che (non) leggono*, La Nuova Italia, Florence 1986

Livolsi, Marino 'Lettura e altri consumi culturali negli anni '20-'40' in AA VV, *Editoria e cultura a Milano tra le due guerre*

Lloshi, Xhevat 'Modern Albanian in different culture contexts' in *Studia Albanica*, Vol. 21, No. 2, 1984

Lo spettacolo 'Primi risultati del censimento dei locali dello spettacolo esistenti in Italia al 30 giugno 1963', Vol 14, No 2, April-June 1964

Lo spettacolo, No 2, April-June 1951, No 2, April-June 1960; No 4, October-December 1960

Lodge, David *The Art of Fiction*, Penguin, Harmondsworth 1992

Lodge, David *The Practice of Writing*, Penguin Books, Harmondsworth 1997

Loesser, Arthur *Men, Women and Pianos*, Dover Publications, New York 1954

Löffler, Dietrich 'Lektüren im "Leseland" vor und nach der Wende' in *Aus Politik und Zeitgeschichte*, B 13/98, 20 March 1998, Supplement to the weekly *Das Parlament*, Berlin-Trier

Löffler, Dietrich 'Normalisierung und Kontinuität. Entwicklung des Leseverhaltens in den neuen Bundesländern', in AA. VV. *Leseverhalten in Deutschland im neuen Jahrtausend. Eine Studie der Stiftung Lesen*, Spiegel Verlag und Stiftung Lesen, Hamburg 2001, pp. 111–125

Lomax, Alan *Mister Jelly Roll* (1950) in *Reading Jazz* edited by Robert Gottlieb, Bloomsbury, London 1997

London, Simon 'The sound of the stereo fades into history', *Financial Times*, 18 November 2003

Longhurst, Brian *Popular Music and Society*, Polity Press, Cambridge 1995

Lopez, F. 'Notes sur le fonds ancien des petits recits en prose dans la *Literatura de Cordel*' in *Les productions populaires en Espagne 1850–1920*, Université de Pau, CNRS, Paris 1986

Lopez, Robert *The Birth of Europe*, Dent and Sons, London 1967

Lorenzi, Alberto *I segreti del varietà*, Edizioni CELIP, Milan 1988

Lorenzini, Niva *D'Annunzio*, Palumbo, Palermo 1993

Los Angeles Times 27 February 2001

Lotman, Iurii 'Conversations on Russian Culture. Russian Noble Traditions and Lifestyle in the Eighteenth and Early Nineteenth Centuries' in *Russian Studies in History*, Vol. 35, No. 4, Spring 1997

Louandre, Charles 'Statistique littéraire de la production intellectuelle en France depuis quinze ans' in *Revue des Deux Mondes*, Vol.20, 15 November 1847

Loué, Thomas 'La *Revue des Deux Mondes* et ses libraires étrangers dans la lutte contre la contrefaçon belge (1848–1852)' in Mollier (ed.) *Le commerce de la librairie en France au XIXe siècle*

Lough, John *Writer and Public in France: From the Middle Ages to the Present Day*, The Clarendon Press, Oxford 1978

Louisa May Alcott Encyclopedia (The) edited by Gregory Eiselein and Anne K. Phillips, Greenwood Press, Westport Connecticut and London 2001

Lounger (The) No.20, 18 June 1785

Lowe, David A. 'Pushkin and *Carmen*' in *Nineteenth-Century Music*, Vol. 20 No. 1, Summer 1996

Lucas, Ann Lawson 'Introduction' to Carlo Collodi, *The Adventures of Pinocchio*, Oxford University Press 1996

Lucian, Ion 'Collodi in Romania' in *Studi Collodiani*

Lüdtke, Alf ' "Coming to terms with the Past": Illusions of Remembering, Ways of Forgetting Nazism in West Germany' in *Journal of Modern History*, Vol.65, September 1993

Ludwig, Emil *Colloqui con Mussolini*, Mondadori, Milan 2000

Luez, Philippe A. and Paul Mironneau 'La Révolution dans l'opéra français au XIXe siècle 1828–1880' in Hennion (ed.) *1789–1989: Musique, Histoire, Démocratie*, Vol. I

Lukács, Georg *The Historical Novel*, Merlin Press, London 1962

Luker, Nicholas J. L. 'Alexander Grin's *Grinlandia*' in Richard Freeborn, R. R. Milner-Gulland and Charles A. Ward (eds) *Russian and Slavic Literature*, Slavic Publishers Inc., Cambridge, Mass. 1976

Luker, Nicholas J. L. *Aleksandr Grin: The Forgotten Visionary*, Oriental Research partner, Newtonville Mass. 1980

Lundin, Bo *The Swedish Crime Story*, Svenska Deckare, Sundbyberg 1981

Lunt, Peter and Paul Stenner 'The Jerry Springer Show as an emotional public Sphere' in *Media, Culture & Society*, Vol. 27, No. 1

Lurie, Alison 'The Good Bad Boy' in *New York Review of Books*, 24 June 2004

Lüsebrink, Hans-Jürgen ' "Littérature nationale" et "Espace national". De la littérature hexagonale aux littératures de la "Plus Grande France" de l'époque coloniale (1789–1960)' in Espagne and Werner (eds) *Philologiques III. Qu'est-ce qu'une littérature nationale?*

Lüsebrink, Hans-Jürgen and Rolf Reichardt, 'La traduction, indicateur de diffusion: imprimés français traduits en allemand' in Frédéric Barbier, Sabine Juratic, and Dominique Varry (eds) *L'Europe et le Livre. Réseau et pratique du négoce de librairie XVIe-XIXe siècles*, Klincksieck, n.p. 1996

Lynch, Deidre and William B. Warner (eds) *Cultural Institutions of the Novel*, Duke University Press, Durham and London 1996

Lyons, Martin 'Les best-sellers' in Chartier and Martin (eds) *Histoire de l'édition française*, Vol. 3, *Le temps des éditeurs*

Lyons, Martin *Le Triomphe du livre. Une histoire sociologique de la lecture dans la France du XIXe siècle*, Promodis, Paris 1987

Lyttelton, Adrian 'Origins of a National Monarchy: the House of Savoy' in *Proceedings of the British Academy: 2001 Lectures*, OUP 2002

MacDonald, Keith Norman *In Defence of Ossian*, 1906, probably Edinburgh but reprinted from the *Oban Times*

MacDonald, Robert H. 'Reproducing the Middle-class Boy: From Purity to Patriotism in the Boys' Magazines, 1892–1914' in *Journal of Contemporary History*, Vol.24, no.3, July 1989

Macherey, Pierre *À quoi pense la littérature?*, PUF, Paris 1990

MacKay, Dorothy Epplen *The Double Invitation in the Legend of Don Juan*, Stanford University Press 1943

Macnab, Geoffrey J. *Arthur Rank and the British Film Industry*, Routledge, London and New York 1993

Madeo, Liliana and Gian Piero Raveggi *Il Servizio Opinioni cos'è com'è*, RAI, Rome 1970 (Appunti del Servizio stampa No 31)

Madrignani, Carlo A. *Ideologia e narrativa dopo l'Unificazione*, Savelli, Rome 1974

Mage, David 'L'exploitation des films européens aux États-Unis' in *Cahiers du Cinéma*, Vol.4, No. 22, April 1953

Mahling, Christoph-Hellmut 'The Origin and Social Status of the Court Orchestral Musician in the eighteenth and early nineteenth Century in Germany' in Salmen (ed.) *The Social Status of the Professional Musician. . .*

Maidment, Brian E. 'John Ruskin, George Allen and American Pirated Books' in *Publishing History*, No.9, 1981

Maigron, Louis *Le roman historique à l'époque romantique. Essai sur l'influence de Walter Scott*, Hachette, Paris 1898

Maines, Rachel P. *The Technology of Orgasm: 'Hysteria,' the Vibrator, and Women's Sexual Satisfaction*, Johns Hopkins University Press, Baltimore 2001

Maltby, Richard 'The Production Code and the Hays Office' in Tino Balio, *Grand Design: Hollywood as Modern Business Enterprise 1930–1939*, Charles Scribner's Sons, New York 1993

Manchester, Colin 'Henry Vizetelly' in *Censorship. A World Encyclopedia*

Manfred W. Heiderich, *The German Novel of 1800. A Study of Popular Prose Fiction*, Peter Lang, Bern 1982

Mangini, Nicola 'Tramonti di un antico teatro veneziano' in *Archivio Veneto*, Serie V, Vol. 137, 1991

Manigand, Christine and Isabelle Veyrat-Masson 'Quelle Allemagne? Pour quels Français?' in Jeanneney and Sauvage (eds) *Télévision, nouvelle mémoire. Les magazines de grand reportage 1959–1968*

Mann, Peter *From Author to Reader. A Social Study of Books*, Routledge and Kegan Paul, London 1982

Manzoni, Alessandro *I Promessi sposi*, with an introduction and notes by Vittorio Spinazzola, Garzanti, Milan 1988

Manzoni, Alessandro *Tutte le Opere*, Vol. 2, Sansoni, Florence 1988

Marchand, Philippe 'Le commerce du livre classique dans le département du Nord fin XVIIIᵉ–1914' in Mollier (ed.) *Le commerce de la librairie en France au XIXe siècle*

Marconi, Francis *La Comtesse de Ségur ou le bonheur immobile*, Artois Presses Université, Arras 1999

Maréchal, Denis *Radio Luxembourg 1933–1993. Un media au Coeur de l'Europe*, Presses Universitaires de Nancy, 1994

Mariotti, Franco and Claudio Siniscalchi, *Il mito di Cinecittà*, Mondadori, Milano 1995

Marjanovic, Petar 'The theatre' in *The history of Serbian Culture*, Porthill Publishers, London 1995, in *www.rastko.org.yu/isk/pmarjanovic-theater.html*

Marker, Gary 'Russian and the "Printing Revolution": Notes and Observation' in *Slavic Review*, No. 2, Summer 1982

Mar-Molinero, Clare 'The Iberian peninsula: Conflicting Linguistic Nationalisms' in
    Barbour and Carmichael (eds) *Language and Nationalism in Europe*
Maróthy, János *Music and the Bourgeois. Music and the Proletarian*, Akadémiai Kiadó,
    Budapest 1974
Marschall, Gottfried 'Champagne, depolitisation, gemütlichkeit – Presence et effacement
    des traces françaises dans l'operette de Franz Suppé et Johann Strauss fils' in
    Austriaca, Cahiers Universitaires d'Information sur l'Autriche, No. 46, June 1998
Martin, Andrew 'Thomas the Tank Engine Stole My Son' *Independent*, 22 August 1998,
    Weekend Review section
Martin, Charles-Noël *La vie et l'oeuvre de Jules Verne*, Michel de l'Ormeraie, Paris 1978
Martin, Delphine '1997, une année de télévision dans le monde' in *Audience: Le journal
    de mediametrie*. No 19 June 1998
Martin, George 'Verdi Onstage in the United States. *Oberto, conte di San Bonifacio*',
    Opera Quarterly, Vol. 18, No. 4, Autumn 2002
Martin, George 'Verdi Onstage in the United States: *Nabucodonosor*' in *The Opera
    Quarterly*, Vol. 19, No.2, Spring 2003
Martin, Marc 'Journalistes et gents de lettres (1820–1890)' in Vaillant (ed.) *Mesure(s) du
    livre*
Martin, Marc 'Presse et publicité dans la France du XIXe siècle' in *Historiens et
    Géographes*, No. 338, December 1992
Martinenche, Ernest *L'Espagne et le romantisme français*, Hachette, Paris 1922
Martinez, D. P. (ed.) *The Worlds of Japanese Popular Culture. Gender, Shifting
    Boundaries and Global Cultures*, Cambridge University Press
Martinsen, Deborah (ed), *Literary Journals in Imperial Russia*, CUP, Cambridge 1997
Martland, Peter *A Business History of The Gramophone Company Ltd 1897–1918*,
    unpublished dissertation, PhD University of Cambridge 1992
Martonyi, Eva 'La littérature populaire en Hongrie' in *Trames. Littérature populaire.
    Peuple, nation, région*, Actes du colloque 18–20 Mars 1986 à Limoges, Université de
    Limoges 1988
Marvin, Roberta Montemorra 'The Censorship of Verdi's Operas in Victorian London'
    in *Music and Letters*, Vol. 82, No. 4, November 2001
Marx, Karl and Friedrich Engels *The Communist Manifesto*, Penguin, London 2002
Marx, Karl and Friedrich Engels *Werke*, vols. 32, 33, and 34, Dietz Verlag, Berlin 1973
Marx, Karl *The German Ideology*, in Karl Marx *Selected Writings* edited by David
    McLellan, OUP 2000
Mason, Michael 'A little pickle for her husband' in *London Review of Books*, 1 April 1999
Massart, Pierre, Jean-Luc Nicks and Jean-Louis Tilleuil, *La Bande dessinée à l'université
    . . . et ailleurs. Études sémiotiques et bibliographiques*, Faculté de Philosophie et
    Lettres, Université de Louvain, Louvain-la-Neuve 1984
Masson, Gordon 'Labels Bank on Domestic Talents', *Billboard*, 12 July 2003
Masson, Pierre *Lire la bande dessinée*, Presses universitaires de Lyon, Lyon 1985
Mathiesen, Thomas J. 'Harmonia and Ethos in Ancient Greek Music' in *The Journal of
    Musicology*, Vol. 3, No. 4, Summer 1984
Mattlock, Jann 'Novels of Testimony and the "invention" of the modern French novel'
    in Timothy Unwin (ed.) *The Cambridge Companion to the French Novel. From 1800
    to the present*, CUP 1997
Mauclair, Camille 'La condition matérielle et morale de l'écrivain à Paris' in *Nouvelle
    revue*, Vol. 21, 1 September 1899
Maurier, George du *Trilby*, Penguin, Harmondsworth 1994
Maurois, André *Chantiers Américains*, Gallimard, Paris 1933

Maurois, André *Les Trois Dumas*, Hachette, Paris 1957

Mawdsley, Evan *The Russian Civil War*, Birlinn, Edinburgh 2000

Mayeur, Françoise *L'Éducation des filles en France*, Hachette, Paris 1979

Mazierska, Ewa 'Multifunctional Chopin: the representation of Fryderyk Chopin in Polish films' in *Historical Journal of Film, Radio and Television*, Vol.24, No.2, 2004

Mazzoni, Dania 'La fortuna di Tolstoj nel movimento operaio italiano' in *Movimento operaio e socialista*, Vol. 3, No.2–3 1980

McAleer, Joseph *Passion's Fortune. The Story of Mills and Boon*, Oxford University Press 1999

McAleer, Joseph *Popular Reading and Publishing in Britain 1914–1950*, Clarendon Press, Oxford 1992

McCarthy, Anna ' "The Front Row Is Reserved for Scotch Drinkers": Early Television's Tavern Audience' in *Cinema Journal*, Vol. 34, No 4, Summer 1995

McCarthy, Todd *Howard Hawks: the Grey Fox of Hollywood*, Grove Press, New York 1997

McClelland, James C. 'Utopianism versus Revolutionary Heroism in Bolshevik Policy: The Proletarian Culture Debate' in *Slavic Review*, Vol. 39 n.3, September 1980

McCurry, Justin 'Mobiles turn a new page for Japan's youth', *Guardian,* 25 March 2005

McLoone, Martin 'Music Hall Dope and British Propaganda? Cultural Identity and early broadcasting in Ireland' in *Historical Journal of Film, Radio and Television*, Vol. 20, No. 3, 2000

McMahon, Darrin *Enemies of the Enlightenment. The French Counter-Enlightenment and the Making of Modernity*, Oxford University Press 2001

McMurtry, Larry 'The West without Chili' in *New York Review of Books*, 22 October 1998

McNeal, Robert H. 'Brezhnev's Collected Works' in *Slavic Review*, Vol. 36, No.3, September 1977

McPherson, Jim 'Before the Met: The Pioneer Days of Radio Opera. Part 1, An Overview' in *The Opera Quarterly*, Vol. 16, No. 1, Winter 2000 and 'Before the Met: The Pioneer Days of Radio Opera. Part 2, the NBC National Grand Opera Company' in *The Opera Quarterly*, Vol. 16, No. 2, Spring 2000

Méadel, Cécile 'Programmes en masse, programmes de masse? La diffusion de la radio en France pendants les années trente', in Robin (ed.) *Masses et culture de masse dans les années 30*

Mehl, Dominique 'La télévision relationnelle' in *Cahiers internationaux de sociologie*, Vol. 112, 2002

Meloncelli, Raoul 'Sul rinnovamento della vita musicale romana' in Nicolodi (ed.) *Musica italiana del primo Novecento. 'La generazione dell'80'*

Menand, Louis 'Billion-dollar baby' in *New York Review of Books*, 24 June 1999

Menarini, Roy and Guglielmo Pescatore 'Il cinema popolare e I processi di definizione dello spettatore' in Fanchi and Mosconi (eds) *Spettatori*

Mendelsohn, Daniel 'When not in Greece' in *New York Review of Books*, 28 Match 2002

Menger, Pierre-Michel 'Le génie et sa sociologie. Controverses interprétatives sur le cas de Beethoven' in *Annales*, July-August 2002, No. 4

Menger, Pierre-Michel *Le paradoxe du musicien; Le compositeur, le mélomane et l'État dans la société contemporaine*, Flammarion, Paris 1983

Mengin, Sabine 'Les répercussions économiques de la télévision sur le marché du livre' in *Cahiers de l'économie du livre*, n. 7, March 1992

Menzel, Birgit 'Some Reflections on High and Popular Literature in Late and Soviet Russia' in *Perelomnye periody v russkoi literature I kul'ture. Studia Russica*

Helsingiensia et Tartuensia VIII, Helsinki 2000, pp.422–434 accessed at *www.fask.uni-mainz.de/inst/is/russisch/menzel/pdf/reflhelsinki.pdf*

Meriggi, Marco 'The Italian *Borghesia*' in Kocka and Mitchell (eds) *Bourgeois Society in Nineteenth-century Europe*

Mesquita, Victor 'Portugal' in Moliterni (ed.) *Histoire Mondiale de la Bande Dessinée*

Mettais, Hippolyte *L'An 5865*, Librairie Centrale, Paris 1865

Metzner, Paul *Crescendo of the Virtuoso. Spectacle, Skill and Self-Promotion in Paris during the Age of Revolution*, University of California Press, Berkeley 1998

Meusy, Jean-Jacques and André Straus, 'L'argent du Cinématographe Lumière' in Benghozi and Delage (eds) *Une histoire économique du cinéma français (1895–1995)*

Meyen, Michael and Ute Nawratil 'The Viewers: Television and Everyday Life in East Germany' in *Historical Journal of Film, Radio and Television*, Vol. 24, No. 3, 2004

Meyen, Michael and William Hillman, 'Communication Needs and Media Change. The Introduction of Television in East and West Germany' in *European Journal of Communication*, Vol. 18, No. 4

Meyer, Michael 'The Nazi Musicologist as Myth Maker in the Third Reich' in *Journal of Contemporary History*, Vol. 10, n.4, October 1975

Meyer, Thomas with Lew Hunchman *Media Democracy. How the Media Colonize Politics*, Polity, Cambridge 2002

Meynieux, André 'Les traducteurs en Russie avant Poushkine' in *Babel. International Journal of Translation*, Vol. 3, No. 2, June 1957

Mezzacappa, Antonio L. 'The performance of Scribe's plays in Naples', in *Annali dell'Istituto Universitario Orientale, sezione romanza*, Vol. 9, No. 2, July 1967

Miccichè, Lino (ed.) *Il cinema del riflusso. Film e cineasti degli anni '70*, Marsilio, Venice 1997

Michael, Ian 'From Scarlet Study to *Novela Negra*' in Rob Rix (ed.) *Thrillers in the Transition. 'Novela negra' and Political Change in Spain*, Leeds Iberian papers series, Trinity and All Saints, Leeds 1992

Michael, Ian 'The Hyperactive Production of English Grammars in the Nineteenth Century: A Speculative Bibliography' in *Publishing History*, No 41, 1997, pp.23–61

Michel, Bernard 'Sociabilité urbaine et nationalité à Prague à la fin du XIXe siècle' in Miklos Molnár and André Reszler (eds) *Vienne, Budapest, Prague, . . . Les hauts-lieux de la culture moderne de l'Europe centrale au tournant du siècle*, PUF, Paris 1988

Michelet, Jules *Oeuvres complètes*, Vol. IV, Flammarion, Paris 1974

Micheli, Sergio *Cinema Ungherese*, Bulzoni, Rome 1982

Micheli, Sergio *Il cinema bulgaro degli anni settanta*, Bulzoni, Rome 1979

Michon, Jacques and Jean-Yves Mollier (eds) *Les mutations du livre et de l'édition dans le monde du XVIIIe siècle à l'an 2000*, L'Harmattan, Paris 2001

Mickiewicz, Ellen *Changing Channels: Television and the Struggle for Power in Russia*, Duke University Press, Durham NC and London 1999

Microsoft Encarta Premium Suite 2005. 1993–2004

Miller, Jeffrey S. *Something Completely Different. British Television and American Culture*, Minnesota University Press, Minneapolis 2000

Miller, Jonathan 'Doing Opera' in *New York Review of Books*, 11 May 2000

Miller, Russell *Magnum. Fifty years at the front line of history*, Pimlico, London 1999

Millington, Barry 'The Nineteenth Century: Germany' in Roger Parker (ed.) *The Oxford Illustrated History of the Opera*, OUP 1994

Mills Todd III, William 'Periodicals in literary life of the early nineteenth century' in Martinsen (ed), *Literary Journals in Imperial Russia*, CUP 1997

Milo, Daniel 'La bourse mondiale de la traduction: un baromètre culturel?' in *Annales*, Vol. 39, No.1, January-February 1984

Miltchina, Vera ' "Sacrée leur apparaît toute feuille imprimée . . ." ' (1982) in Stroev (ed.) *Livre et lecture en Russie*

Minguet Batllori, Joan M. 'L'Église et les intellectuels espagnols contre le cinéma' in Cosandrey, Gaudreault and Gunning (eds) *Une invention du diable? Cinéma des premiers temps et religion*

Ministère de la Culture (France), *Développement culturel*, No.124, June 1998 and No.135, September 2000

Ministry of Culture (UK), *The Funding of the BBC. Government Response to the Third Report from the Culture, Media and Sport Committee*, session 1999–2000, CM 4674

Miquel, Pierre *Histoire de la Radio et de la Télévision*, Perrin, Paris 1984

Missika, Jean-Louis and Dominique Wolton, *La Folle du logis. La télévision dans les sociétés démocratiques*, Gallimard, Paris 1983

Mistler, Jean *La Librairie Hachette de 1826 à nos jours*, Hachette, Paris 1964

Mitchell, Tony (ed) *Global Noise. Rap and Hip-Hop Outside the USA*, Wesleyan University Press, Middletown Connecticut 2001

Mitchell, Jerome *More Scott Operas: Further Analyses of Operas based on the Works of Sir Walter Scott*, The University Press of America, Lanham, Maryland, 1996

Mitterand, Henri *Le Discours du roman*, PUF, Paris 1980

Mitterand, Henri *Zola*. Vol. I, *Sous le regard d'Olympia 1840–1871*, Fayard, Paris 1999, Vol. III, *L'honneur 1893–1902*, Fayard, Paris 2002

Mitzman, Arthur 'Roads, Vulgarity, and Pure Art: The Inner Space in Flaubert and French Culture' in *Journal of Modern History*, Vol. 51, No.3, September 1979

Moilin, Tony *Paris dans l'an 2000*, Librairie de la Renaissance, Paris 1869

Moliterni (ed.) Claude *Histoire Mondiale de la Bande Dessinée*, Pierre Horay Editeur, Paris 1980

Mollier, Jean-Yves (ed.) *Le commerce de la librairie en France au XIXe siècle 1789–1914*, IMEC/Maison de l'Homme, Paris 1998

Mollier, Jean-Yves 'Histoire de la lecture, histoire de l'édition' in Chartier (ed.) *Histoire de la lecture*

Mollier, Jean-Yves 'Le siècle d'or du plagiat littéraire' in *L'Histoire*, No.152, February 1992

Mollier, Jean-Yves 'Les mutations de l'espace éditorial français du XVIIIe au XXe siècle' in *Actes de la recherche en sciences sociales*, No. 126–127, March 1999

Mollier, Jean-Yves 'Un siècle de transition vers une culture de masse' in *Historiens et Géographes*, No. 338, December 1992

Mollier, Jean-Yves 'Le manuel scolaire et la bibliothèque du peuple' in *Romantisme*, Vol. 23, No.80, 1993

Mollier, Jean-Yves *L'argent et les lettres. Histoire du capitalisme d'édition 1880–1920*, Fayard, Paris 1988

Mollier, Jean-Yves *Louis Hachette*, Fayard, Paris 1999

Monk, Ray *Ludwig Wittgenstein. The Duty of Genius*, Jonathan Cape, London 1990

Monod, Martine 'Dashiell Hammett, L'Amérique et le Stylo-Camera' in *Les Lettres Françaises*, No 859, 19–25 January 1961

Monod, Sylvère 'Les premiers traducteurs français de Dickens' in *Romantisme*, Vol. 29, No. 106, 1999

Montebello, Fabrice 'Les intellectuels, le peuple et le cinéma' in Benghozi and Delage (eds) *Une histoire économique du cinéma français (1895–1995)*

Monteleone, Franco 'Radio pubblica e emittenti commerciali dal 1975 al 1993' in Valerio Castronovo and Nicola Tranfaglia (eds) *La stampa italiana nell'età della TV*, Laterza 1994

Montesinos, José F. *Introducción a una historia de la novela en España en el siglo XIX*, Castalia, Madrid 1973

Moore, Allan F. *The Beatles: Sgt Pepper's Lonely Hearts Club Band*, Cambridge University Press 1997

Moore, Jr., Barrington *Injustice. The Social Bases of Obedience and Revolt*, Macmillan, London and Basingstoke 1978

Morelli, Giovanni 'L'Opera' in Isnenghi (ed.) *I luoghi della memoria*

Moretti, Franco 'Conjectures on World Literature' in *New Left Review*, No. 1, Jan-Feb 2000

Moretti, Franco 'Graphs, Maps, Trees' in *New Left Review*, No. 24, November-December 2003

Moretti, Franco 'Planet Hollywood' in *New Left Review*, No. 9, May-June 2001

Moretti, Franco 'The Slaughterhouse of Literature' in *Modern Language Quarterly*, No. 1, March 2000, pp.207–27

Moretti, Franco *Atlas of the European Novel 1800–1900*, Verso, London 1998

Morgan, Baynard Quincy *A Critical Bibliography of German Literature in English Translation 1481–1927*, Stanford UP 1938

Moriarty, Michael 'Structures of cultural production in nineteenth-century France' in Collier and Lethbridge (eds) *Artistic Relations. Literature and the Visual Arts in Nineteenth-Century France*

Morin, Edgar *Les Stars*, Éditions du Seuil, Paris 1972

Morin, Violette 'Le présent actif dans le feuilleton télévisé' in *Communication*, No. 39, 1984

Morley, David *Television, Audiences and Cultural Studies*, Routledge, London and New York 1992

Morley, David *Family Television. Cultural Power and Domestic Leisure*, Routledge, London and New York 1990

Mortier, Arnold *Les soirées parisiennes de 1880* by 'Un Monsieur de l'Orchestre' (Arnold Mortier), Dentu, Paris 1881

Morton, Graeme and R. J. Morris 'Civil Society, Governance and Nation, 1852–1914' in R. A. Houston and W. W. J. Knox (eds) *The New Penguin History of Scotland*, Penguin, London 2001

Moss, Stephen 'Bookends' *Guardian*, 19 March 2002

Mosse, George L. *The Nationalization of the Masses*, Howard Fertig, New York 1975

Moulin, Raymonde *De la valeur de l'art*, Flammarion, Paris 1995

Mounin, Georges *Linguistique et traduction*, Dessart & Mardaga, Brussels 1976

Mouralis, Bernard *Les contres-littératures*, PUF, Paris 1975

Mousseau, Jacques and Christian Brochand *Histoire de la Télévision en France*, Nathan, Paris 1982

Moynet, M. J. *L'envers du Théâtre. Machines et décorations*, Hachette, Paris 1873

Mozart, Wolfgang Amadeus, *The Letters of Mozart and His Family*, edited by Emily Anderson (rev. 1985), Macmillan, London 1989

Mülder-Bach, Inka 'Cinematic Ethnology: Siegfried Kracauer's *The White Collar Masses*' in *New Left Review*, no.226, November-December 1997

Mullin, Donald (ed.) *Victorian Actors and Actresses in Review. A Dictionary of Contemporary Views of Representative British and American Actors and Actresses, 1837–1901*, Greenwood Press, Westport Connecticut and London 1983

Murata, Margaret 'Why the first opera given in Paris wasn't Roman' in *Cambridge Opera Journal*, Vol. 7, No.2, July 1995

Murialdi, Paolo *La Stampa italiana. Dalla Liberazione alla crisi di fine secolo*, Laterza, Rome-Bari 1995

Murphy, Robert 'Popular British Cinema' in *Journal of Popular British Cinema*, No. 1, 1998

Music Publishing, Copyright and Piracy in Victorian England. A Twenty-five year chronicle, 1881–1906, Mansell publishing, London and New York 1985

Musser, Charles 'Documentary' in Nowell-Smith (ed.) *The Oxford History of World Cinema*

Musser, Charles 'L'industrie du cinéma en France et aux États Unis entre 1900 et 1920: l'évolution du mode de production' in Benghozi and Delage (eds) *Une histoire économique du cinéma français (1895–1995)*

Mutzenbacher, Josephine *Histoire d'une fille de Vienne racontée par elle-même*, Folio Gallimard, Paris 1998

Nagy, Peter 'La révolution littéraire hongroise du début du XXe siècle et son contexte européen' in Köpeczi and Vajda (eds) *Proceedings of the 8th Congress of the International Comparative Literature Association*

Najder, Zdzislaw 'The Development of the Polish Novel: Functions and Structure' in *Slavic Review*, Vol. 29, No. 4, December 1970

Natacha, Laurent 'L'interdiction du film *Une Grande Vie*: la reprise en main du cinéma soviétique en août 1946' in *Communisme*, No 42–44, 1995

Natali, Giulio *Storia letteraria d'Italia. Il Settecento* Vol. II, Vallardi, Milan 1973

National Music Council, *The Value of Music,* report into the Value of the UK Music industry prepared by the University of Westminster (Cliff Dane, Andy Feist and Dave Laing), London 1996

National Theatre (UK) *Annual Report 2003–4* in *www.nationaltheatre.org.uk*

Negus, Keith 'Between Corporation and Consumer: Culture and Conflict in the British Record Industry' in Frith (ed.) *Popular Music*. Vol. II, *The Rock Era* cit.

Neill, Edward *Nicolò Paganini*, Fayard, Paris 1991

Nemeskürty, István 'Le Cinéma hongrois avant 1945' in Haudiquet, Jeancolas, and Nemeskürty, *Le cinéma hongrois*

Nenadic, Stana 'Middle-Rank Consumers and Domestic Culture in Edinburgh and Glasgow 1720–1840' in *Past and Present*, No.145, November 1994

Netz, Robert 'Suisse' in Moliterni (ed.) *Histoire Mondiale de la Bande Dessinée*

Neuburg, Victor E. *Popular Literature: a History and Guide. From the beginning of printing to the year 1897*, Penguin, Harmondsworth 1977

Neuschafer, Hans-Jörg 'Naturalismo e feuilleton. Il "romanzo sociale" nei giornali parigini del 1884' in *Problemi*, No. 73, May-August 1985

Neville-Sington, Pamela *Fanny Trollope: The Life and Adventure of a Clever Woman*, Viking, New York 1997

New Grove Dictionary of Music Online ed. L. Macy *www.grovemusic.com*

New Grove Dictionary of Music and Musicians edited by Stanley Sadie, Macmillan 1980, entry 'Notation'

Nicholas, Siân 'All the News that's Fit to Broadcast: the Popular Press *versus* the BBC, 1922–45' in Catterall, Seymour-Ure and Smith (eds) *Northcliffe's Legacy*

Nicolodi, Fiamma (ed.) *Musica italiana del primo Novecento. 'La generazione dell'80'*, Olschki, Florence 1981

Nicolodi, Fiamma 'Il teatro lirico e il suo pubblico' in Soldani and Turi (eds) *Fare gli italiani*

Nicolodi, Fiamma *Musica e musicisti nel ventennio fascista*, Discanto, Fiesole 1984

Nicolodi, Fiamma *Orizzonti musicali Italo-Europei 1860–1980*, Bulzoni, Rome 1990

Nies, Fritz '"Où peut conduire la lecture du *Constitutionnel"*: lecteurs et lectures de textes à grande diffusion – une promenade iconographique au XIXe siècle' in Chartier and Lüsebrink (eds) *Colportage et lecture populaire*

Nietzsche, Friedrich *On the Genealogy of Morals*, Oxford University Press 1996

Nizan, Paul *Pour une nouvelle culture*, Grasset, Paris 1971

Noelle-Neumann, Elisabeth *The Spiral of Silence: Public Opinion – Our Social Skin*, University of Chicago Press 1993

Nora, Pierre 'Une lueur d'espoir pour les sciences humaines' in *Le Bulletin du Livre*, 15 January 1969

Noreiko, Stephen F. 'From serious to popular fiction' in Unwin *The Cambridge Companion to the French Novel*

Norman, Philip *Shout! The True Story of the Beatles*, Pan Books, London 2004

Novak, Max 'Defoe as an innovator of fictional form' in Richetti (ed.) *The Cambridge Companion to the Eighteenth-Century Novel*

Nowell-Smith, Geoffrey (ed.) *The Oxford History of World Cinema*, OUP 1996

Nowell-Smith, Geoffrey 'The beautiful and the bad: notes on some actorial stereotypes' in Nowell-Smith and Ricci (eds) *Hollywood and Europe*

Nowell-Smith, Geoffrey and Steven Ricci (eds) *Hollywood and Europe. Economics, Culture, National identity 1945–95*, British Film Institute, London 1998

Ó Ciosáin, Niall *Print and Popular Culture in Ireland, 1750–1850*, Macmillan, Basingstoke and London 1997

O'Boyle, Leonore 'The Image of the Journalist in France, Germany and England 1815–1848' in *Comparative Studies in Society and History*, Vol. 10, No.3, April 1968

O'Brien, Geoffrey 'Silent Screams' in *New York Review of Books*, 17 December 1998

O'Neil, Edward 'Alfred Hitchcock', in Nowell-Smith, *The Oxford History of World Cinema*

O'Hagan, Andrew 'Disgrace under Pressure', *London Review of Books*, Vol. 26, No. 11, 3 June 2004

O'Sullivan, Sally 'The glossies that shone brightest in a bumper year', *Observer*, 19 December 2004

Oakley, Keith 'A taxonomy of the emotions of literary response and a theory of identification in fictional narrative' in *Poetics*, Vol. 23, 1994, pp.53–74

Oates, Joyce Carol 'The Mystery of Jon Benét Ramsey' in *New York Review of Books*, 24 June 1999

Offenbach, Jacques *Notes d'un musicien en voyage*, La Flute de Pan, Paris 1979

Ogg, Li 'Littérature coréenne' in *Encyclopédie de la Pléiade. Histoire des Littératures*, Vol. 1, Gallimard, Paris 1977

Ojala, Jeanne A. 'Radclyffe Hall' in *Censorship. A World Encyclopedia*

Ojetti, Ugo *Alla scoperta dei letterati*, Dumolard, Milan 1895

Oklot, Michal and Piotr Nowak 'Poland', paper presented at the conference 'Remaining Relevant After Communism', Dubrovnik, June 2001

Oksiloff, Assenka *Picturing the Primitive. Visual Culture, Ethnography, and Early German Cinema*, Palgrave, New York 2001

Oktapoda, Efstratia 'La traduction de *Nana* en Grèce et son retentissement sur le naturalisme néohellénique' in Dezalay (ed.) *Zola sans frontières*

Olivier-Martin, Yves 'Héroines et cruauté' in *Europe*, Vol.56, No.590–591, June-July 1978

Onclincx, Georges 'Les débuts du cinématographe des frères Lumière à Bruxelles d'après les journaux du temps' in *Revue d'Histoire Moderne et Contemporaine*, Vol.2, July-September 1955

Ong, Walter J. 'Writing is a Technology That Restructures Thought' in Gerd Baumann (ed.) *The Written Word. Literacy in Transition*, The Clarendon Press, Oxford 1986

Opekar, Alès 'Two great world influences to the Czech music culture' in Hennion (ed.) *1789–1989: Musique, Histoire, Démocratie*, Vol. III

Ord-Hume, Arthur W.J.G. *Clockwork Music*, Allen and Unwin, London 1973

Orecchioni, Pierre 'Eugène Sue: mesure d'un succès' in *Europe*, Vol. 60, No. 643–644, November-December 1982

Ortoleva, Peppino 'La televisione tra le due crisi 1974–1993' in Valerio Castronovo and Nicola Tranfaglia (eds) *La stampa italiana nell'età della TV*, Laterza 1994

Orton, Lawrence D. 'Did the Slavs Speak German at Their First Congress?' in *Slavic Review*, Vol. 3, No. 3, September 1974

Orwell, George *The Road to Wigan Pier*, in George Orwell *Orwell's England*, Penguin, London 2001

Ory, Pascal *La Belle Illusion. Culture et politique sous le signe du Front populaire 1935–1938*, Plon, Paris 1994

Osborne, John *The Meiningen Court Theatre 1866–1890*, CUP 1988

Osborne, Richard *Rossini*, J.M. Dent, London 1986

Ouimette, Victor ' "Monstrous Fecundity": The Popular Novel in Nineteenth-Century Spain' in *Canadian Review of Comparative Literature*, Vol. 9, September 1982

Ousby, Ian *The Crime and Mystery Book*, Thames and Hudson, London 1997

Owen, Claude R. *Erich Maria Remarque: a critical bio-bibliography*, Rodopi, Amsterdam 1984

Oxford Book of Letters, edited by Frank Kermode and Anita Kermode, Oxford University Press 1995

Paccagnella, Ivano 'Uso letterario dei dialetti' in Luca Serianni and Pietro Trifone (eds) *Storia della lingua italiana*, Vol. 3 *Le altre lingue*, Einaudi, Turin 1994

Padioleau, Jean-G. *'Le Monde' et le 'Washington Post'*, PUF, Paris 1985

Pagés, Alain 'L'expérience du livre. Zola et le commerce de la librairie' in Mollier (ed.) *Le commerce de la librairie en France au XIXe siècle*

Pálffy, István 'George Bernard Shaw's reception in Hungary: The early years, 1903–1914' in *Theatre History Studies*, Vol. 4, 1984

Palmer, Michael 'The British Press and international news, 1851–99: of agencies and newspapers' in Boyce, Curran and Wingate (eds) *Newspaper History*

Palumbo, Bernardino 'The Social Life of Local Museums' in *Journal of Modern Italian Studies*, Vol. 6, No. 1, Spring 2001, pp. 19–37

Panassié, Hugues *Histoire du vrai jazz*, Laffont, Paris 1959, p.201

Panse, Barbara 'Censorship in Nazi Germany. The Influence of the Reich's Ministry of Propaganda on German Theatre and Drama, 1933–1945' in Berghaus (ed.) *Fascism and Theatre*

Papathanassopoulos, Stylianos 'Media Commercialization and Journalism in Greece' in *European Journal of Communication*, Vol. 16, No 4, December 2001

Parakilas, James 'Classical Music as Popular Music' in *The Journal of Musicology*, Vol. 3, No. 1, Winter 1984

Parent, Françoise 'Des nouvelles pratiques de lecture' in Chartier and Martin (eds) *Histoire de l'édition française*, Vol.2, *Le livre triomphant 1660–1830*, cit

Parent-Lardeur, Françoise *Lire à Paris au temps de Balzac. Les cabinets de lecture* à Paris. 1815–1830, Édition de l'école des hautes études en sciences sociales, Paris 1981

Parinet, Élisabeth 'Le prix du livre: un vieux sujet de débat' in Mollier (ed.) Le commerce de la librairie en France au XIXe siècle

Parinet, Elisabeth 'Les bibliothèques de gare, un nouveau réseau pour le livre' in Romantisme, Vol. 23, No.80, 1993

Park, Katharine and Lorraine J. Daston 'Unnatural Conceptions: the Study of Monsters in Sixteenth-and Seventeenth Century France and England' in Past and Present, No.92, August 1981, pp.20–54

Parker, Roger (ed.) The Oxford Illustrated History of the Opera, Oxford University Press 1994

Parker, Steve and Alan You Can Make It as a DJ!, Miles Kelly, Great Bardfield 2003

Pašeta, Senia 'Censorship and its Critics in the Irish Free State 1922–1932' in Past & Present November 2003; Vol. 181, No. 1

Pasler, Jann 'Opéra et pouvoir: forces à l'oeuvre derrière le scandale du Pelléas de Debussy' in Dufourt and Fauquet (eds) La musique et le pouvoir

Pasquier, Dominique Les scénaristes et la télévision, Nathan, Paris 1995

Paterson, Richard A. 'Why 1955? Explaining the Advent of Rock Music' in Simon Frith (ed.) Popular Music. Critical Concepts in Media and Cultural Studies, Vol. II, The Rock Era

Patten, Robert L. Charles Dickens and his Publishers, Clarendon Press, Oxford 1978

Patterson, Michael and Michael Huxley 'German drama, Theatre and dance' in Eva Kolinsky and Wilfried van der Will (eds) The Cambridge Companion to Modern German Culture, CUP 1999

Patterson, Michael The Revolution in German Theatre 1900–1933, Routledge and Kegan Paul, London 1981

Paul, A. S. Harvey 'Nonchan's Dream. NHK morning serialized television novels' in Martinez (ed.) The Worlds of Japanese Popular Culture

Paulicelli, Eugenia Fashion under Fascism. Beyond the Black Shirt, Berg, Oxford 2004

Paulson, Ronald Don Quixote in England. The Aesthetic of Laughter, The Johns Hopkins University Press, Baltimore 1998

Paulu, Burton Radio and Television Broadcasting in Eastern Europe, The University of Minnesota Press, Minneapolis 1974

Pauvert, Jean-Jacques Nouveaux (et moins nouveaux) visages de la censure, Les Belles Lettres, Paris 1994

Payne Hackett, Alice and James Henry Burke (eds) 80 Years of Best Sellers 1895–1975, Bowker Company, New York 1977

Pearsall, Ronald Edwardian Life and Leisure, David and Charles, Newton Abbot 1973

Pearson Annual Review 2004

Pearson, Roberta 'Early Cinema' in Nowell-Smith (ed.) The Oxford History of World Cinema

Pearson, Roberta 'Transitional Cinema' in Nowell-Smith (ed.) The Oxford History of World Cinema

Pecchio, Giuseppe Della produzione letteraria, Edizioni Studio Tesi, Pordenone 1985

Peck, Louis F. A Life of Matthew G. Lewis, Havard University Press, Cambridge Mass. 1961

Pedullà, Gianfranco 'Il teatro italiano tra le due guerre mondiali' in Soldani and Turi (eds) Fare gli italiani

Pegg, Mark Broadcasting and Society 1919–1939, Croom Helm, London 1983

Pekacz, Jolanda T. 'Deconstructing a "National Composer": Chopin and Polish Exiles in Paris, 1831–49' in *Nineteenth-Century Music*, Vol. 24, n.2, Fall 2000

Pellissier, Pierre *Émile de Girardin. Prince de la Presse*, Denoël, Paris 1985

Pennybacker, Susan D. 'Les moeurs, les aspirations et la culture politique des employés de bureau londonien des deux sexes, 1889–1914', in *Genèse*, No. 14, January 1994

Pentikäinen, Juha 'Structural Patterns of an Oral Repertoire' in Köpeczi and Vajda (eds) *Proceedings of the 8th Congress of the International Comparative Literature Association*

Pequignot, Bruno *La Relation amoureuse. Analyse sociologique du Roman Sentimental Moderne*, L'Harmattan, Paris 1991

Peresson, Giovanni *Le cifre dell'editoria 1995*, Editrice Bibliografica, Milan 1995

Perini, Leandro 'Editori e potere dalla fine del secolo XV all'Unità' in Vivanti (ed.) *Storia d'Italia. Annali* Vol.4 *Intellettuali e potere*

Perkin, Harold *The Rise of Professional Society. England since 1880*, Routledge, London and New York 1990

Perrod, Pierre-Antoine 'Balzac "avocat" de la propriété littéraire' in *L'Année balzacienne*, 1963

Péru, Jean-Michel 'Une crise du champ littéraire français. Le débat sur la "littérature prolétarienne"' in *Actes de la Recherche en sciences sociales*, No.89, September 1991

Pesce, Anita *Napoli a 78 giri*, Avagliano editore, Naples 1999

Peters, Julie Stone *Theatre of the Book 1480–1880, Print, Text, and Performance*, Oxford University Press 2000

Petrillo, Gianfranco 'La Santificazione a consumo. La domenica della Milano operaia negli anni cinquanta' in *Tempo libero e società di massa nell'Italia del Novecento*

Petronio, Giuseppe 'Quel pasticciaccio brutto del romanzo poliziesco' in *Problemi*, No. 60, January-April 1981

Petronio, Giuseppe 'Sulle tracce del giallo' in *Delitti di carta*, No. 1, Vol. 1, October 1997

Petronio, Giuseppe and Ulrich Schulz-Buschhaus (eds) *'Trivialliteratur?' Letterature di massa e di consumo*, Lint, Trieste 1979

Petronio, Giuseppe *L'attività letteraria in Italia*, Palumbo, Palermo 1987

Petronio, Giuseppe *Viaggio nel paese della poesia*, Mondadori, Milano 1999

Peukert, Detlev J. K. *Inside Nazi Germany. Conformity, Opposition and Racism in Everyday Life*, Penguin, Harmondsworth 1987

Pezzini, Isabella 'Matilde Serao' in Eco et al. *Carolina Invernizio Matilde Serao Liala*

Phillips, Celia '*Under Two Flags*: the Publishing History of a Best-Seller 1867–1967' in *Publishing History*, Vol.3, 1978

Phillips, James W. *Printing and Bookselling in Dublin, 1670–1800*, Dublin Irish Academic 1998

Pia, Pascal *Les Livres de l'Enfer. Bibliographie critique des ouvrages érotiques dans leurs différentes éditions du XVIe siècle à nos jours*, C. Coulet et A. Faure, Paris 1978

Pichois, Claude 'Les Cabinets de Lectures à Paris, durant la première moitié du XIXe siècle' in *Annales*, Vol. 14, No 3, July-September 1959

Pichois, Claude *Auguste Poulet-Malassis. L'éditeur de Baudelaire*, Fayard, Paris 1996

Pick, Daniel 'Introduction' to George du Maurier, *Trilby*, Penguin, Harmondsworth 1994

Pierce, David 'The legion of the condemned – why American silent films perished' in *Film History*, Vol. 9, No. 1, 1997

Pigoreau, Alexandre *Petite Bibliographie biographico-romancière ou dictionnnaire des romanciers 1821*; reprinted in facsimile by Slatkine, Geneva 1968

Pilloy, Annie *Les compagnes des héros de BD. Des femmes et des bulles*, Harmattan, Paris 1994

Pinkard, Terry *Hegel. A Biography*, CUP 2000

Piper, Helen 'Reality TV, *Wife Swap* and the drama of banality' in *Screen*, Vol. 45, No.4, Winter 2004, p.276

Piperno, Franco 'Opera Production to 1780' in Bianconi and Pestelli (eds) *Opera Production and Its Resources*

Pipes, Richard *Russia under the Old Regime*, Penguin, Harmondsworth 1977

Pirani, Roberto 'Le collane poliziesche romane dal 1955 al 1970' in *Delitti di carta*, Vol.1, No.1, October 1997

Piromalli, Antonio 'Antonio Fogazzaro e il pubblico' in *Problemi*, No.82, May-August 1988

Piromalli, Antonio 'Giuseppe Garibaldi e i suoi scritti' in *Problemi*, No.71, September-December 1984

Piromalli, Antonio 'Motivo di narrativa popolare nel ciclo dei "Pirati della Malesia"' in *Problemi*, No.60, Jan-April 1981

Piscator, Erwin *Le Théâtre politique*, L'Arche éditeur, Paris 1962

Pistone, Danièle 'L'opérette Viennoise a Paris 1875–1904' in *Austriaca, Cahiers Universitaires d'Information sur l'Autriche*, No. 46, June 1998

Pitigrilli, *Cocaina*, Bompiani, Milano 1999

Pitkin, Walter B. *Life begins at Forty*, Whittlesey House, New York 1932

Pius XII 'Lettera sulla televisione' reprinted in *Lo Spettacolo*, Vol. 4, no 1, January-March 1954

Place, Adélaïde de 'Le théâtre de l'Opéra sous la Révolution: les rapports entre l'administration du théâtre et le gouvernement' in Dufourt and Fauquet (eds) *La musique et le pouvoir*

Plakans, Andrejs 'Peasants, Intellectuals, and Nationalism in the Russian Baltic Provinces, 1820–90' in *Journal of Modern History*, Vol. 46, No. 3, September 1974

Plato, *Phaedrus*, translated by Benjamin Jowett, available at *http://ccat.sas.upenn.edu/jod/texts/phaedrus.html*

Pleasants, Henry 'Elvis Presley' (1974) in Frith (ed.) *Popular Music*, Vol. II, *The Rock Era*

Pogorelskin, Alexis 'The Messenger of Europe' in Martinsen (ed), *Literary Journals in Imperial Russia*

Poiger, Uta G. 'Rock 'n' Roll, Female Sexuality, and the Cold War Battle over German Identities' in *Journal of Modern History*, Vol.68, No. 3, September 1996

Polette, René 'Le concept "populaire/peuple" à la lecture des rubriques "À nos lectures" parues dans les livraisons de romans et de journeaux de la deuxième moitié du XIXe siècle' in *Trames. Littérature populaire*

Polignac, François de and Joselita Raspi Serra (eds) *La fascination de l'antique 1700–1770. Rome découverte, Rome inventée*, Somogy édition, Paris 1998

Pollard, Graham 'The English Market for Printed Books' in *Publishing History*, No 4, 1978

Ponton, Rémy 'Les images de la paysannerie dans le roman rural à la fin du 19e siècle' in *Actes de la recherche en sciences sociales*, No. 17–18, Nov 1977

Popa, Mircea 'Analyse quantitative du roman publié dans la presse de Transylvanie de 1838 à 1918' in *Synthesis*, VI, 1979

Popa, Mircea 'Jules Verne dans une perspective Roumaine' in *Synthesis*, Vol. VIII, 1981

Popa, Mircea 'Les conditions sociologiques de la naissance du roman roumain' in *Cahiers Roumains d'Études littéraires*, No. 2, 1980

Pope, Alexander *The Dunciad* edited by James Sutherland, Routledge, London 1993

Portaccio, Stefania 'Buona e bella. I periodici femminili cattolici negli anni '50' in *Memoria*, No. 4, June 1982

Porter, Andrew *European Imperialism, 1860–1914*, Macmillan, London 1994

Porter, Laurence M. 'Decadence and the *fin-de-siècle* novel' in Unwin (ed.) *The Cambridge Companion to the French Novel*

Porter, Roy *Flesh in the Age of Reason*, Allen Lane, London 2003

Porter, Roy *London. A Social History,* Penguin, Harmondsworth 1996

Porter, Vincent and Suzanne Hasselbach *Pluralism, Politics and the Marketplace. The Regulation of German Broadcasting*, Routledge, London 1991

Postman, Neil *Amusing Ourselves to Death. Public Discourse in the Age of Show Business*, Heinemann, London 1986

Poumet, Jacques *La satire en R.D.A. Cabaret et presse satirique*, Presses universitaires de Lyon, Lyons 1990

Prase, Tilo 'The Structure, Coverage and Surprising End of a Conspiratorial Film Team' in *Historical Journal of Film, Radio and Television*, Vol. 24, No. 3, 2004

Praz, Mario *La carne, la morte e il diavolo nella letteratura romantica*, Sansoni, Florence 1966

Pressler, Karl H. 'The Tauchnitz Edition: Beginning and End of a Famous Series' in *Publishing History*, No.6, 1979

Preston, Peter 'Some Good News Between the Lines', *Observer*, 3 January 1999 using data from Audit Bureau of Circulation

Preston, Peter 'The writing's on the wall, or rather the web', *Observer*, 22 May 2005

Prévos, André 'Hip-Hop, Rap, and Repression in France and in the United States', *Popular Music and Society*, Summer 1998

Prévos, André 'Postcolonial Popular Music in France. Rap music and hip-hop culture in the 1980s and 1990s' in Mitchell (ed), *Global Noise*

Price, Laurence M. *English Literature in Germany*, University of California Press, Berkeley 1953

Price, Leah *The Anthology and the Rise of the Novel: From Richardson to George Eliot*, CUP 2000

Principali, Luciano *La TV in una piccola comunità rurale del Lazio*, RAI, Roma 1971, *Appunti del Servizio Opinioni* No 125, typewritten text

Prokhorova, Elena *Fragmented Mythologies: Soviet TV Mini-series of the 1970s*, unpublished PhD dissertation, University of Pittsburgh 2003, accessed at *http:// etd.library.pitt.edu/ETD/available/etd–06062003–164753/unrestricted/ prokhorova_etd2003.pdf*

Propp, Vladimir *Morphology of the Fairy Tale*, University of Texas Press 1968

Pudovkin, Vsevolod I. *Film Technique and Film Acting,* translated and edited by Ivor Montagu, Vision Press and Mayflower, London 1958

Pushkin, Alexander *Eugene Onegin*, trans. by Charles Johnston, Scolar Press, London 1977

Putting Pen to Paper: Honoré Daumier and the Literary World, catalogue of the exhibition 23 January to 15 April 2001, at the UCLA Hammer Museum

Puttnam, David *The Undeclared War. The Struggle for Control of the World's Film Industry*, HarperCollins, London 1997

Pyrhönen, Heta *Murder from an Academic Angle: An Introduction to the Study of the Detective Narrative*, Camden House, Columbia SC 1994

Q – The Ultimate Rock'N'Roll Magazine, April 2003, September 2004

Quaghebeur, Marc 'L'identité ne se réduit pas à la langue' in Gorceix (ed.) *L'identité culturelle de la Belgique et de la Suisse francophones*

Quaghebeur, Marc *Balises pour l'histoire des lettres belges*, Labor, Brussels 1998 (First edition 1982)

Quéffelec, Lise 'Peuple et roman à l'époque romantique: le débat autour du roman-feuilleton sous la Monarchie de Juillet' in *Trames. Littérature populaire*

Quin, Michael J. *A Steam Voyage Down the Danube*, Richard Bentley, London 1836, Vol. I, pp 167–71, text in *www.fordham.edu/halsall/mod/1836mikequin.html*

Quinn, Michael 'Distribution, the Transient Audience, and the Transition to the Feature Film' in *Cinema Journal*, Vol. 40, No 2, Winter 2001

Raban, Jonathan 'Journey to the End of the Night' in *New York Review of Books*, 10 June 1999

Rabinbach, Anson 'La lecture, le roman populaire et le besoin impérieux de participer: réflexions sur l'expérience publique et la vie privé durant le IIIe Reich' in Robin (ed.) *Masses et culture de masse dans les années 30*

Raboni, Giovanni 'La narrativa straniera negli anni '24-'40' in AA. VV. *Editoria e cultura a Milano tra le due guerre (1920–1940)*

Rachilde, *L'animale*, Mercure de France, Paris 1993

Rachilde, *La jongleuse,* Édition Des Femmes, Paris 1982

Rachilde, *Monsieur Vénus*, Flammarion, Paris 1977

Raffaelli, Raffaella 'Il genere poliziesco in Italia prima del 1929. Le collane a carattere poliziesco' in *Problemi*, No. 65, September-December 1982

Ragone, Giovanni 'La letteratura e il consumo: un profilo dei generi e dei modelli nell'editoria italiana (1845–1925)' in Asor Rosa (ed.) *Letteratura italiana*, Vol. 2

Ràguenet, François *Parallèle des Italiens et des Français en ce qui regarde la musique et les opéras*, Minkoff reprint, Geneva 1976

RAI, Direzione Marketing Strategico, *Innovazione Offerta e Progetti Speciali. Ascolto della TV Mensile TV*, April 2003 (internal document)

RAI, Servizio Opinioni, *Ascolto e gradimento per le trasmisisoni televisive del 1982*, RAI, Rome 1984 (Appunti del Servizio Opinioni No 405)

RAI, Servizio Opinioni, *Dati sulla comprensione di alcune parole da parte di varie categorie di persone 1964–69* Rome, RAI 1970, Appunti del Servizio Opinioni N. 112

RAI, Servizio Opinioni, *L'accoglienza del pubblico alla riduzione televisiva de 'I Promessi sposi'*, Rome, RAI 1967 (Series Appunti del servizio opinioni n. 31)

Rambelli, Loris 'La letteratura educativa per i giovani e per il popolo' in *Problemi*, No.91, May-August 1991

Ramsaye, Terry (ed.) *The 1938–39 Motion Picture Almanac*, Quigley Publishing Co., New York 1938

Ramsaye, Terry (ed.) *The 1946–47 Motion Picture Almanac*, Quigley, New York

Ramsden, John 'Refocusing "The People's War": British War Films of the 1950s' in *Journal of Contemporary History*, Vol.33, no. 1 January 1998

Ransom, Teresa *The Mysterious Miss Marie Corelli, Queen of Victorian Bestsellers*, Sutton Publishing, Stroud 1999

Raphael, Amy 'Fears of a clown', *Observer*, 30 March 2003, Review section

Raspi Serra, Joselita 'Fouilles et découvertes, personnages et débats' in Polignac and Raspi Serra (eds) *La fascination de l'antique 1700–1770*

Rauhut, Michael *Rock in der DDR*, Bundeszentrale für politische Bildung, Bonn 2002

Raven, James 'Le commerce de librairie "en gros" à Londres au XVIIIe siècle' in Frédéric Barabier, Sabine Juratic, and Dominique Varry (eds) *L'Europe et le Livre. Réseau et pratique du négoce de librarie XVIe-XIXe siècles*, Klincksieck, no place 1996

Raynor, Henry *A Social History of Music from the Middle Ages to Beethoven*, Schoken Books, New York 1972

Raynor, Henry *Music and Society since 1815*, Schoken Books, New York 1976

Read, Donald 'The Relationship of Reuters and other News agencies with the British Press 1858–1984: revise at Cost or Business for Profit?' in Catterall, Seymour-Ure and Smith (eds) *Northcliffe's Legacy*

Reeve, Clara *The Progress of Romance*, Éditions d'aujourd'hui, Plan de La Tour 1980

Régnier, Philippe 'Littérature nationale, Littératures étrangères au XIXe siècle. La fonction de la *Revue des Deux Mondes* entre 1829 et 1870' in Espagne and Werner (eds) *Philologiques III. Qu'est-ce qu'une littérature nationale?*

Reich, Nancy B. *Clara Schumann. The Artist and the Woman*, Victor Gollancz, London 1985

Reich-Ranicki, Marcel *The Author of Himself. The Life of Marcel Reich-Ranicki*, Weidenfeld & Nicolson, London 2001, translation of *Mein Leben*, Stuttgart 1999

Reîtblat, Abraham 'Les honoraires littéraires, médiation entre les écrivains et le public' (1991) in Stroev (ed.) *Livre et lecture en Russie*

Reitlinger, Gerald *The Economics of Taste*, Vol. 1, *The Rise and Fall of the Picture Prices 1760–1960*, and Vol. 2, *The Rise and Fall of the Objets d'Art Prices Since 1750*, Barrie and Rockliffe, London 1961–1963

Renai, Pier Luigi 'Il caso Pitigrilli: analisi di *Dolicocefala bionda*' in Arslan (ed.) *Dame, droga e galline*

Rennert, Jack 'Would Mucha Have Made It on Madison Avenue?' in Victor Arwas, Jana Brabcová-Orlíková, and Anna Dvořák (eds) *Alphonse Mucha. The Spirit of Art Nouveau*, Yale University Press 1998

Renoir, Jean *Ma vie et mes films*, Flammarion, Paris 1974

Rentschler, Eric 'From New German Cinema to the Post-Wall Cinema of Consensus' in Mette Hjort and Scott MacKenzie (eds) *Cinema and the Nation*, Routledge 2000

Rentschler, Eric 'Germany: Nazism and After' in Nowell-Smith, *The Oxford History of World Cinema*

Rentschler, Eric 'The testament of Dr. Goebbels' in *Film History*, Vol. 8, No.3, 1996

Renzi, Thomas C. *Jules Verne on Film. A Filmography of the Cinematic Adaptations of His Works, 1902 through 1997*, McFarland and Co., Jefferson North Carolina and London 1998

Repetto, Monica 'Ciao Mamma, ovvero porno soffice ed erotismo da ridere' in Miccichè (ed.) *Il cinema del riflusso*

Repubblica (La) 5 August 2003

Retigo, Alessandra 'Stregati dai libri, in Italia boom di lettori' in *La Repubblica*, 8 July 2005

Revue du cinéma, special issue 'La saison cinématographique', 1983

Reybaud, Louis *Jérôme Paturot à la recherche d'une situation sociale* (1842), Club Français du livre, Paris 1965

Riccoboni, Marie-Jeanne (Madame) 'Suite de Marianne' in appendix to Marivaux's *La vie de Marianne* edited by Frédéric Deloffre, Garnier, Paris 1963

Rice, John A. *Antonio Salieri and Viennese Opera*, University of Chicago Press 1998

Rich, Maria F. 'Puccini in America', *Opera Quarterly*, Vol. 2, No. 3, pp.27–45

Richards, Donald Ray *The German Bestseller in the 20th Century. A complete Bibliography and Analysis 1915–1940*, Herbert Lang, Bern 1968

Richards, Jeffrey 'The British Board of Film Censors and Content Control in the 1930s: images of Britain' in *Historical Journal of Film, Radio and Television*, Vol. 1, No. 2, 1981

Richetti, John (ed.) *The Cambridge Companion to the Eighteenth-Century Novel*, CUP 1996

Richter, Noë *Les bibliothèques populaires*, Cercle de la Librairie, Paris 1978

Ricuperati, Giuseppe 'I giornalisti italiani dalle origini all'Unità' in Vivanti (ed.) *Storia d'Italia. Annali 4 Intellettuali e potere*

Ridders-Simoens, H. de 'Mobility' in *A History of the University in Europe* Vol. 2, CUP 1996

Rietbergen, Peter *Europe. A Cultural History*, Routledge, London 1998

Righetti, Donata 'Bestseller, ma dove sono finiti gli scrittori italiani?', in *Corriere della Sera*, 25 April 1998

Rights of Passage. British Television in the Global Market, February 2005, commissioned by the British Television Distributors' Association and available on *www.pact.co.uk*

Ring, Malvin E. *Dentistry. An Illustrated History*, Mosby, St. Louis Missouri 1985

Ringer, Fritz K. 'Higher Education in Germany in the Nineteenth Century' in *Journal of Contemporary History*, Vol. 2, No.3, 1967

Rioux, Jean-Pierre *Erckmann et Chatrian ou le traité d'union*, Gallimard, Paris 1989

Risaliti, Renato 'Pinocchio in Russia' in *Studi Collodiani, Atti del I Convegno Internazionale*

Ritter, Gerhard A. 'Workers' Culture in Imperial Germany: Problems and Points of Departure for Research' in *Journal of Contemporary History* Vol.13, no.2, April 1978

Rivette, Jacques 'Génie de Howard Hawks', *Cahiers du Cinéma*, Vol.4, No. 23, May 1953

Robb, Graham 'Where to begin the feast?', *Times Literary Supplement*, 21 May 1999

Robb, Graham *Balzac*, Macmillan, Basingstoke and London 1994

Robb, Graham theatre review of *Cyrano de Bergerac* in *Times Literary Supplement*, 19 September 1997

Robb, Graham *Victor Hugo*, Picador, London 1997

Roberts, Adam *Science Fiction*, Routledge, London and New York 2000

Roberts, Helene E. 'Exhibition and review: the periodical press and the Victorian art exhibition system' in Shattock and Wolff (eds) *The Victorian periodical press*

Robertson, F. 'Scott' in Annick Benoit-Dusausoy and Guy Fontaine (eds) *History of European Literature*, Routledge, London 2000

Robertson, James C. *The Hidden Cinema. British Film Censorship in Action 1913–1975*, Routledge, London and New York 1989

Robertson, Richie 'From Naturalism to National Socialism (1890–1945)' in Watanabe-O'Kelly (ed.) *The Cambridge History of German Literature*

Robida, Albert *Le Vingtième siècle*, Paris 1883, now in facsimile reprint, Slatkine, Geneva-Paris 1981

Robin, Régine (ed.) *Masses et culture de masse dans les années 30*, Les Éditions ouvrières, Paris 1991

Robinson, Bruce *Smoking in Bed. Conversations with Bruce Robinson*, edited by Alistair Owen, Bloomsbury, London 2001

Robinson, David 'Comedy' in Nowell-Smith (ed.) *The Oxford History Of World Cinema*

Robinson, Harlow 'Music' in Rzhevsky (ed.) *Modern Russian Culture*

Rodari, Gianni *Grammatica della fantasia. Introduzione all'arte di inventare storie*, Einaudi, Turin 1973

Rogger, Hans *Russia in the Age of Modernisation and Revolution 1881–1917*, Longman, London and New York 1983

Ropars-Wuilleumier, Marie-Claire 'Entre Films et Textes: L'intervalle de l'imaginaire' in Robin (ed.) *Masses et culture de masse dans les années 30*

Roper, Derek *Reviewing before the "Edinburgh" 1788–1802*, University of Delaware Press, Newark 1978

Rosa, Guy ' "Quot libras in duce?" L'édition des oeuvres de Hugo, 1870–1885' in Vaillant (ed.) *Mesure(s) du livre*

Rosa, Guy 'Comptes pour enfants. Essai de bibliométrie des livres pour l'enfance et la jeunesse (1812–1908)' in *Histoire et Mesure*, Vol. 5, No.3–4, 1990

Rosa, Guy, Sophie Trzepizur and Alain Vaillant, 'Le peuple des poètes – Études bibliométrique de la poésie populaire de 1870 à 1880' in *Romantisme*, Vol. 23, No.80, 1993

Rose, Jacqueline *The Case of Peter Pan or The Impossibility of Children's Fiction*, Macmillan, London and Basingstoke 1984

Rosen, Charles 'Aimez-vous Brahms?', *New York Review of Books*, 22 October 1998

Rosen, Charles 'Steak and Potatoes', *New York Review of Books*, 14 March 2002

Rosen, Charles 'The Future of Music', *New York Review of Books*, 20 December 2001

Rosen, Charles 'The Great Inventor', *New York Review of Books*, 9 October 1997

Rosen, Charles 'Who's Afraid of the Avant-Garde', *New York Review of Books,* 14 May 1998

Rosen, Charles 'Within a Budding grove' in *New York Review of Books*, 21 June 2001

Rosen, Jody *White Christmas: the Story of an American Song*, Fourth Estate, London 2002

Rosen, Ruth 'Soap Operas. Search for Yesterday' in Todd Gitlin, *Watching Television*, Pantheon Books, New York 1986

Rosen, Sherwin 'The economics of superstars' in *American Economic Review*, No 5, December 1981, Vol. 71, pp.845–58

Rosenman, Ellen Bayuk 'Spectacular Women: *The Mysteries of London* and the Female Body', in *Victorian Studies*, Vol.40, no.1, Autumn 1996

Rossel-Kirschen, André *Pathé-Natan. La véritable histoire*, Pilote 24 édition, Périgeux 2004

Rossell, Deac 'Beyond Messter: Aspects of early cinema in Berlin' in *Film History*, Vol. 10, No. 1, 1998

Rossell, Deac *Living Pictures. The Origins of the Movies*, State University of New York Press, Albany 1998

Rosselli, John 'Music and Nationalism in Italy' in Harry White and Michael Murphy (eds) *Musical Constructions of Nationalism: Essays on the History and Ideology of European Musical Culture 1800–1945*, Cork University Press, 2001

Rosselli, John 'Opera as a Social Occasion' in Parker (ed.) *The Oxford Illustrated History of Opera'*

Rosselli, John 'Opera Production, 1780–1880' in Bianconi and Pestelli (eds) *Opera Production and Its Resources*

Rossi, Umberto 'Il pubblico del cinema' in Miccichè (ed.) *Il cinema del riflusso*

Roth, Arman 'Erckmann-Chatrian en Angleterre et aux États-Unis' in *Europe*, Vol. 53, No 549–550, January-February 1975

Rothstein, Robert A. 'The Quiet Rehabilitation of the Brick Factory: Early Soviet Popular Music and its Critics' in *Slavic Review* Vol 39 n.3, September 1980

Rousseau, Jean-Jacques *Émile, ou de l'éducation*, Werdet et Lequien fils, Paris 1826, tome one (Vol. 8 of *Oeuvres de Rousseau*)

Roussier-Puig, Marianne 'Michelet, Hetzel, et les véroniques du peuple' in *Romantisme*, Vol. 23, No.80, 1993

Rovani, Giuseppe *Cento anni*, Rizzoli, Milan 1935

Rowe, William and Vivian Schelling *Memory and Modernity. Popular Culture in Latin America*, Verso, London 1991

Rubinstein, David 'Educations and the Social Origins of British Élites' in *Past and Present*, No. 112, August 1986

Rubinstein, E. 'Observation on Keaton's *Steamboat Bill, Jr*' in *Sight and Sound*, Vol. 44, No 4, Autumn 1975

Rubinstein, Jill (ed.) *Sir Walter Scott: An Annotated Bibliography of Scholarship and Criticism 1975–1990*, Association for Scottish Literary Studies, Occasional Paper No. 11, Aberdeen n.d.

Rubinstein, W. D. *Wealth and Inequality in Britain*, Faber and Faber, London 1986

Ruggieri Punzo, Franca *Walter Scott in Italia 1821–1971*, Adriatica editrice, Bari 1975

Ruoff, Jeffrey *An American Family. A Televised Life*, University of Minnesota Press 2002

Russell, Dave *Popular Music in England, 1840–1914*, Manchester University Press, Manchester 1997

Rutherford, John 'Introduction' to Cervantes, *Don Quixote*, Penguin, Harmondsworth 2000

Rzhevsky, Nicholas (ed.) *Modern Russian Culture*, Cambridge University Press 1998

Sacy, Sylvestre de *Rapport sur le progrès des lettres*, Hachette, Paris 1868

Sadleir, Michael 'Aspects of the Victorian Novel' in *Publishing History*, No.5, 1979

Sági, Mária 'Music on records in Hungary' in Kurt Blaukopf (ed.) *The Phonogram in Cultural Communication*, Springer-Verlag, Vienna and New York 1982

Said, Edward *Orientalism*, Routledge, London 1980

Sainte-Beuve, Charles-Augustin de *Pour la critique*, Folio Gallimard, Paris 1992

Saka, Pierre *Histoire de la chanson française de 1938 à nos jours*, Nathan, Paris 1989

Saka, Pierre *Les années Twist*, Édition 1, Paris 1996

Sallmann, Jean-Michel 'Les niveaux d'alphabétisation en Italie au XIXe siècle' in *Mélanges de l'École française de Rome. Italie et Méditerranée*, Vol. 101, No.1, 1989

Salmen, Walter (ed.) *The Social Status of the Professional Musician from the Middle Ages to the nineteenth Century*, trans. from the German by H. Kaufman and Barbara Reisner, Pendragon Press, New York 1983

Salt, Barry 'Early German Film: The Stylistics in Comparative Context' in Elsaesser (ed), *A Second Life. German Cinema's First Decades*

Salt, Barry *Film Style and Technology: History and Analysis*, Starword, London 1992 (1st published in 1983)

Salvestroni, Simonetta 'L'Unione Sovietica e la letteratura di consumo' in Giuseppe Petronio and Ulrich Schulz-Buschhaus (eds) *'Trivialliteratur?' Letterature di massa e di consumo*, Lint, Trieste 1979

Samuels, Stuart 'The Left Book Club' in *Journal of Contemporary History*, Vol. 1, No. 2, 1966

Sand, George *Correspondance*, Vol. VII (July 1845-June 1847), Éditions Garnier, Paris 1970

Sand, George *Histoire de ma vie* in *Oeuvres autobiographiques*, Vol.1 Gallimard/Pléiade, Paris 1971

Sand, George *Histoire de ma vie*, Livre de Poche, Paris 2004

Sandford, John (ed.) *Encyclopedia of Contemporary German Culture*, Routledge, London 1999, p.600

Sanguanini, Bruno *Grande fratello: istruzioni per l'uso: Per concorrenti, autori, giornalisti e audience*, CLEUP, Padua 2002

Sanguanini, Bruno *Il pubblico all'italiana. Formazione del pubblico e politiche culturali tra Stato e Teatro*, FrancoAngeli, Milan 1989

Santoro, Marco *Storia del libro italiano*, Editrice Bibliografica, Milan 1994

Sapiro, Gisèle 'La raison littéraire. Le champ littéraire français sous l'Occupation (1940–1944)' in *Actes de la Recherche en sciences sociales,* Nos 111–112, March 1996

Sapiro, Gisèle 'Salut littéraire et littérature du salut' in *Actes de la Rechèrche en sciences sociales,* Nos 111–112, March 1996

Saporta, Marc 'Trois voies nouvelles pour l'édition Américaine' in *Le Bulletin du Livre* 15 January 1969

Sármány-Parsons, Ilona 'Jewish Art Patronage in Budapest at the Turn of the Century' in *CEU History Department Handbook,* 1994–1995

Sarnov, Benedikt 'A List of Benefits' in *Russian Studies in Literature*, Vol. 34, no.2, Spring 1998

Sarti, Vittorio *Bibliografia Salgariana*, Libreria Malavasi, Milan 1990

Sartre, Jean-Paul *Les Mots*, Gallimard, Paris 1964

Sassoon, Donald 'Tangentopoli or the Democratization of Corruption: considerations on the end of Italy's First Republic', *Journal of Modern Italian Studies*, Vol.1, No.1, Fall 1995

Sassoon, Donald, 'Political and Market Forces in Italian Broadcasting', *West European Politics*, vol. 8, No.2, April 1985, reprinted in R. Kuhn (ed.) *Broadcasting in Western Europe,* Frank Cass 1985

Sassoon, Donald, *Mona Lisa*, HarperCollins, London 2001

Saul, Nicholas 'Aesthetic humanism (1790–1830)' in Watanabe-O'Kelly (ed.) *The Cambridge History of German Literature*

Saunders, Thomas J. *Hollywood in Berlin. American Cinema and Weimar Germany*, University of California Press, Berkeley 1994

Sauvage, Monique and Denis Maréchal, 'Les racines d'un succès' in Jeanneney and Sauvage (eds) *Télévision, nouvelle mémoire*

Sauvy, Anne 'Noël Gille dit La Pistole, "marchand forain libraire rouland par la France"' in *Bulletin des bibliothèques de France*, Vol. 12, No. 5, May 1967

Sauvy, Anne 'Une littérature pour les femmes' in Chartier and Martin (eds) *Histoire de l'édition française*, Vol. 3

Sayer, Derek 'The Language of Nationality and the Nationality of Language: Prague 1780–1920' in *Past and Present*, No. 153, November 1996

Scannell, Paddy and David Cardiff, *A Social History of British Broadcasting, Vol 1, 1923–39*, Basil Blackwell, Oxford 1991

Scarpellini, Emanuela *Organizzazione teatrale e politica del teatro nell'Italia fascista*, La Nuova Italia, Florence 1989

Scerbanenco, Giorgio *I ragazzi del massacro*, Garzanti, Milan 1994

Schaarschmidt, Gunter 'The Lubok Novels: Russia's Immortal Best Sellers' in *Canadian Review of Comparative Literature*, Vol. 9, No.3, September 1982

Schaeffer, Jean-Marie 'Du texte au genre' in Genette et al., *Théorie des genres*

Schechner, Richard *Performance Studies*, Routledge, London 2002

Scheffer, Ingrid '. . . lived happily ever after', dossier available at *www.goethe.de/kug/kue/lit/dos/en142247.htm*

Schiff, David 'Fit only for the filmgoer' in *Times Literary Supplement*, 2 July 1999

Schiller, Erzsébet, Andrea Reményi and Éva Fodor, 'Hungary', paper presented to the conference 'Remaining Relevant After Communism', Dubrovnik, June 2001

Schiller, Friedrich von *The Poems of Schiller*, translated by E. P. Arnold-Forster, Heinemann, London 1901

Schizzerotto, Antonio 'I fumetti: consumi e contenuti' in *Problemi dell'Informazione*, Vol.3, April-June 1978

Schlager, Ken 'How Many More Monthly Fees Can Consumers Stand?', *Billboard*, 28 May 2005

Schlegel, Friedrich 'Letter about the Novel' (*Brief über den Roman*) in *German aesthetic and literary criticism the romantic ironists and Goethe* edited by Kathleen M. Wheeler, Cambridge University Press 1984

Schlegel, Friedrich *Charakteristiken und Kritiken II*, Verlag Ferdinand Schöningh, Munich 1975

Schlegel, Friedrich *Lectures on the History of Literature, Ancient and Modern*, H.G. Bohn, London 1859

Schlesinger, Philip *Putting 'reality' together. BBC News*, Constable, London 1978

Schlissel, Lillian 'Introduction' to Mae West, *Three Plays. Sex, The Drag, The Pleasure Man*, Nick Hern Books, London 1997

Schmitt, Kelly L., Kimberley Duyck Woolf and Daniel R. Anderson, 'Viewing the Viewers: Viewing Behaviors by Children and Adults During Television Programs and Commercials' in *Journal of Communication*, June 2003, Vol.53, No 2, pp. 265–81

Schmoller, Hans 'The Paperback Revolution' in Asa Briggs (ed.) *Essays in the History of Publishing*, Longman, London 1974

Schneer, Jonathan *London 1900: The Imperial Metropolis*, Yale University Press 1999

Scholes, Robert and Eric S. Rabin *Science Fiction History Science Vision*, OUP, New York 1977

Scholes, Robert *Structuralism in Literature, an Introduction*, Yale University Press, New Haven 1974

Scholliers, Peter (ed.) *Real wages in nineteenth and twentieth Century Europe. Historical and Comparative Perspectives*, Berg, Oxford 1989

Schulte-Sasse, Jochen 'High/Low and Other Dichotomies' in Grimm and Hermand (eds) *High and Low Cultures*

Schültze, Steffi 'Television Theater in East Germany, 1965–1989: an interim report', in *Historical Journal of Film, Radio and Television*, Vol.24, No. 3, 2004

Schulze-Reimpell, Werner *Development and Structure of the Theatre in the Federal Republic of Germany*, Deutscher Bühnenverein, Cologne 1975

Schumacher, Claude '*Thérèse Raquin* en Grande Bretagne' in Dezalay (ed.) *Zola sans frontières*

Schumacher, Jean-Jacques 'Le triomphe d'un menteur honnête: Les romans de Karl May' in *Recherches en linguistique étrangère XVII*, Annales littéraires de l'université de Besançon, Paris 1994

Schumacher, Thomas '"This is a sampling sport". Digital Sampling, Rap Music and the Law in Cultural Production' in Frith (ed.) *Popular Music*, Vol. II, *The Rock Era*, Routledge 2004

Schuster, Ingrid 'Popular Literature in Germany: 1800–1850' in *Canadian Review of Comparative Literature*, Vol. 9, September 1982

Schwartz, Vanessa R. 'Le goût du public pour la réalité: le spectateur de cinéma, avant la lettre' in Benghozi and Delage (eds) *Une histoire économique du cinéma français (1895–1995)*

Scott, Derek *The Singing Bourgeois. Songs of the Victorian Drawing Room and Parlour*, Open University Press, Milton Keynes 1989

Scott, Walter *Rob Roy*, Oxford University Press 1998

Scott, Walter *Waverley, or, 'Tis Sixty Years Since*, edited by Claire Lamont, Clarendon Press, Oxford 1981

Second, Albéric *Le tiroir aux souvenirs*, Dentu, Paris 1886

Sedgwick, John *Popular Filmgoing in 1930s Britain. A Choice of Pleasures*, University of Exeter Press, Exeter 2000

Segalini, Sergio *Divas. Parcour d'un mythe*, Actes Sud, no place 1986

Segel, H. B. 'Sienkiewicz's First Translator, Jeremiah Curtin' in *Slavic Review*, Vol. 24, No. 2, June 1965

Seguin, Jean-Pierre *L'Information en France avant le périodique*, Maisonneuve et Larose, Paris 1964

Ségur, Comtesse de *La Fortune de Gaspard*, Jean-Jacques Pauvert, Paris 1972

Ségur, Comtesse de *Lettres à son Éditeur'* in *Comtesse de Ségur. Oeuvres*, Robert Laffont, Paris 1990

Sellier, Geneviève 'Danielle Darrieux, Michèle Morgan and Micheline Presle in Hollywood: the threat to French identity' in *Screen*, Vol. 43, No. 2, Summer 2002, pp. 201- 214

Selznick, David O. *Memo from: David O. Selznick. From the confidential files of Hollywood greatest producer*, selected and edited by Rudy Behlmer, Grove Press, New York 1972

Senelick, Laurence 'Theatre' in Rzhevsky (ed.) *Modern Russian Culture*

Senelick, Laurence (ed.) *Cabaret Performance. Europe 1890–1920*, PAJ publications, New York 1989

Sentaurens, Jean 'Les neveux du capitaine Grant: Jules Verne sur les treteaux de la Zarzuela' in *Les productions populaires en Espagne 1850–1920*, Université de Pau, CNRS, Paris 1986

Servant, Jean-Christophe 'Nollywood Boulevard' in *Le Monde*, 30 April 2005

Seymour-Ure, Colin 'Northcliffe's Legacy' in Catterall, Seymour-Ure and Smith (eds) *Northcliffe's Legacy*

Sgard, Jean *Prévost romancier*, Librairie José Corti, Paris 1989

Shaked, Gershon 'The Play: gateway to cultural dialogue' in Hanna Scolnicov and Peter Holland (eds) *The Play Out of Context. Transferring Plays from Culture to Culture*, CUP 1989

Shankar, Ravi 'Interview' (August 1972) in *Cultures*, Vol.1, No.1, 1973

Shapiro, James *Oberammergau. The Troubling Story of the World's Most Famous Passion Play*, Little Brown and Co., London 2000

Shattock, Joanne and Michael Wolff (eds) *The Victorian periodical press: samplings and soundings*, Leicester University Press, 1982

Shavit, Zohar 'Literary Interference between German and Jewish-Hebrew Children's Literature during the Enlightenment: the Case of Campe' in *Poetics*, Vol. 13, No. 1, 1992, pp.41–61

Shaw, Clare MacDonald 'Introduction' to Hannah More, *Tales for the Common People and other Cheap Depository Tracts*, Trent Editions, Nottingham 2002

Shaw, Harry E. *The Forms of Historical Fiction. Sir Walter Scott and His Successors*, Cornell UP, Ithaca 1983

Shedletzky, Itta 'Some Observations on the Popular *Zeitroman* in the Jewish Weeklies in Germany from 1870 to 1900' in *Canadian Review of Comparative Literature*, Vol. 9, September 1982

Shiach, Morag *Discourse on Popular Culture. Class, Gender and History in Cultural Analysis, 1730 to the Present*, Polity Press, Cambridge 1989

Shklovsky, Viktor *Theory of Prose*, Darkley Archive Press 1990

Shneidman, N. N. 'The Russian Classical Literary Heritage and the Basic Concepts of Soviet Literary Education' in *Slavic Review*, No.3, September 1972

Shneidman, N. Norman 'Contemporary Prose in Post-Soviet Russia' in *Toronto Slavic Quarterly*, No. 8, 2004 accessed at *www.utoronto.ca/tsq/08/shneidman08.shtml*

Short, Robert S. 'The Politics of Surrealism, 1920–36' in *Journal of Contemporary History* Vol. 1, No. 2, 1966

Showalter, Elaine 'Emeralds on the home front', *Guardian*, 10 August 2002

Showalter, Elaine *A Literature of Their Own. British Women Novelists from Brontë to Lessing*, Virago, London 1978

Shubert, Adrian 'Spain' in Goldstein (ed.) *The War for the Public Mind*

Sidorko, Clemens P. 'Nineteenth century German travelogues as sources on the history of Daghestan and Chechnya' in *Central Asian Survey*, Volume 21, No 3, September, 2002

Sieburth, Stephanie *Inventing High and Low. Literature, Mass Culture, and Uneven Modernity in Spain*, Duke UP, Durham NC and London 1994

Šilbajoris, Rimvydas 'Kristijonas Donelaitis, A Lithuanian Classic' in *Slavic Review* No2, Summer 1982

Silva, Umberto *Ideologia e Arte del fascismo*, Mazzotta, Milan 1973

Silverman, Willa Z. *The Notorious Life of Gyp. Right-wing Anarchist in Fin-de-Siècle France*, OUP 1995

Simenon, George *L'affaire Saint-Fiacre*, Pocket, Paris 1994

Simionato, Giuliano 'Risorgimento e il melodramma' in *Rassegna Storica del Risorgimento*, No. 1, Vol. 88, January-March 2001

Simonin, Anne and Pascal Fouché, 'Comment on a refusé certains de mes livres. Contribution à une histoire sociale de la littérature' in *Actes de la recherche en sciences sociales*, No. 126–127, March 1999

Simpson, Nicola 'Coming Attractions: a comparative history of the Hollywood Studio System and the porn business' in *Historical Journal of Film, Radio and Television*, Vol.24, No.4, 2004

Singer, Ben 'Manhattan Nickelodeons: New Data on Audiences and Exhibitors' in *Cinema Journal*, Vol. 34, No 3, Spring 1995

Singer, Ben 'Serials' in Nowell-Smith (ed.) *The Oxford History Of World Cinema*

Singly, François de 'Un cas de dédoublement littéraire' in *Actes de la recherche en sciences sociales*, Vol. 2, No 6, December 1976

Sinko, Zofia 'La mode "Gothique" en Pologne dans le contexte européen' in Köpeczi and Vajda (eds) *Proceedings of the 8th Congress of the International Comparative Literature Association*

Sismondi, J. C. L. Simonde de *De la littérature du midi de l'Europe*, third edition, Treuttel and Würtz, Paris 1829

Skarzynski, Jerzy 'Pologne' in Moliterni (ed.) *Histoire Mondiale de la Bande Dessinée*

Slavin, David Henry *Colonial Cinema and Imperial France, 1919–1939*, The Johns Hopkins University Press, Baltimore 2001

Smith, Adrian 'The Fall and Fall of the Third *Daily Herald*, 1930–64' in Catterall, Seymour-Ure and Smith (eds) *Northcliffe's Legacy*

Smith, David 'Potter's magic spell turns boys into bookworms', *Observer*, 10 July 2005

Smith, David 'Star Wars Empire strikes gold' in *Observer* 15 May 2005

Smith III, Edward C. 'Honoré de Balzac and the "Genius" of Walter Scott: Debt and Denial' in *Comparative Literature Studies*, Vol.36, no.3 1999

Sokolova, Bojka, 'L'Intelligentsia Albanaise à l'epoque de la renaissance et la nouvelle culture albanaise' in *Études Balkaniques* (Bulgaria) 1991 Vol. 27 No. 2

Sola, Piero '*Il bacio di una morta*: un romanzo giallo' in Arslan (ed.) *Dame, droga e galline*

Soldani, Simonetta and Gabriele Turi (eds) *Fare gli italiani. Scuola e cultura nell'Italia contemporanea*, Vol. 1, *La nascita dello stato nazionale*, Il Mulino, Bologna 1993

Soldatos, Yannis *Enas Aionas Ellinikos Kinimatografos* (A Century of Greek Cinema), Vol. 1, Kochlias, Athens 2001

Solomon, Thomas ' "Living underground is tough": authenticity and locality in the hip-hop community in Istanbul, Turkey', in *Popular Music*, Vol.24, No. 1, January 2005

Solomon-Godeau, Abigail 'The Other Side of Venus' in Victoria de Grazia (ed.) *The Sex of Things*, University of California Press, Berkeley 1996

Sorba, Carlotta 'Teatro d'opera e società nell'Italia ottocentesca' in *Bollettino del diciannovesimo secolo*, vol. 4, No. 5, 1996

Sorba, Carlotta *Teatri: L'Italia del melodramma nell'età del Risorgimento*, Il Mulino, Bologna 2001

Soriano, Marc *Guide de littérature pour la jeunesse*, Flammarion, Paris 1975

Soriano, Marc *Jules Verne*, Julliard, Paris 1978

Spang, Rebecca *The Invention of the Restaurant: Paris and Modern Gastronomic Culture* Harvard University Press, Cambridge 2000

Spengler, Oswald *The Decline of the West.* Volume 2, *Perspectives of World-History,* Allen and Unwin, London 1980

Spittel, Olaf R. *Science Fiction in der DDR, Bibliographie*, Verlag 28 Eichen, Barnstorf 2003 *www.spittel.de/sf/a.htm*

Spohr, Louis *Autobiography*, Longman Green, London 1865

Spohr, Mathias 'L'Opérette viennoise de Franz von Suppé' in *Austriaca, Cahiers Universitaires d'Information sur l'Autriche*, No. 46, June 1998

Spraggs, Gillian *Outlaws and Highwaymen: the Cult of the Robber in England from the Middle Ages to the nineteenth century*, Pimlico, London 2001

Springhall, John *Youth, Popular Culture and Moral Panics. Penny Gaffs to Gangsta-Rap, 1830–1996*, Macmillan, London 1998

Squarotti, Giorgio Barberi 'Gli schemi narrativi di Collodi' in *Studi Collodiani*

Staël, Germaine de (Madame) *De l'Allemagne*, Flammarion, Paris 1968

Staël, Germaine de (Madame) *Corinne ou l'Italie*, Champion, Paris 2000

Stallabrass, Julian *Gargantua. Manufactured Mass Culture*, Verso, London 1996

Standish, Isolde 'Akira, Postmodernism and Resistance' in Martinez (ed.) *The Worlds of Japanese Popular Culture*

Stanley, Dick, Judy Rogers, Sandra Smeltzer and Luc Perron, 'Win, Place or Show: Gauging the Economic Success of the Renoir and Barnes Art Exhibits' in *Journal of Cultural Economics*, Vol.24, No. 3, August 2000, pp.243–55

Stark, Gary D. 'Gerhart Hauptmann' in *Censorship. A World Encyclopedia*

Stark, Gary D. *Entrepreneurs of ideology. Neoconservative Publishers in Germany 1890–1933*, The University of California Press, Chapel Hill 1981

Statistical Yearbook 1996, European Audiovisual Observatory

Statistics on film and cinema 1955–1977 UNESCO No 25, Statistical reports and Studies, Paris 1981

Stead, Peter 'Hollywood's Message for the World: the British response in the nineteenth thirties' in *Historical Journal of Film, Radio and Television*, Vol. 1, No. 1 1981

Steane, J. B. *The Grand Tradition. Seventy Years of Singing on Record*, Duckworth, London 1974

Stearns, Peter N. 'Stages of Consumerism: Recent Work on the Issues of Periodization' in *Journal of Modern History*, Vol. 69, No.1, March 1997

Stearns, Peter N. 'The Effort at Continuity in Working-Class Culture' in *Journal of Modern History*, Vol. 52, No. 4, December 1980

Stedman Jones, Gareth *Languages of class. Studies in English working class history 1832–1982*, CUP 1983

Steig, Michael 'Subversive Grotesque in Samuel Warren's *Ten Thousand a-Year*' in *Nineteenth-century Fiction*, Vol. 24, No. 2, September 1969

Steiner, George *The Death of Tragedy*, Faber, London 1961

Steinmetz, Rüdiger 'Heymowski & Scheumann: the GDR's leading documentary film team' in *Historical Journal of Film, Radio and Television*, Vol. 24, No. 3, 2004

Steinmetz, Rüdiger and Reinhold Viehoff 'The Program History of Genres of Entertainment on GDR Television' in *Historical Journal of Film, Radio and Television*, Vol. 24, No. 3, 2004

Stendhal *Correspondance Générale*, edited by V. Del Litto, Vol. I, VI, Librairie Honoré Champion, Paris 1997–9

Stendhal *Souvenirs d'égotisme*, in *Oeuvres Intimes*, Bibliothèque de la Pléiade Gallimard, Paris 1966

Stendhal *Vie de Rossini*, Folio Gallimard, Paris 1992

Stephens, John Russell 'Bernard Shaw' in *Censorship. A World Encyclopedia*

Stephens, W. B. *Education, Literacy and Society 1830–70: The Geography of Diversity in Provincial England*, Manchester 1987

Stern, Madeleine B. *Louisa May Alcott. A Biography*, Northeastern University Press, Boston 1999

Stewart, Malcolm *My Other Life*, unpublished manuscript, July 2004

Stieg, Gerald and Jean-Marie Valentin (eds) *Johann Nestroy 1801–1862. Vision du monde et écriture dramatique*, Institut d'Allemand d'Asnières (Paris III), Paris 1991

Stone, Lawrence 'Literacy and Education in England 1640–1900' in *Past and Present*, No. 42, February 1969

Stone, Lawrence *The Family, Sex and Marriage in England 1500–1800*, Weidenfeld and Nicolson, London 1977

Stora, Annie Lamarre *L'Enfer de la IIIe République. Censeurs et Pornographes (1881–1914)*, Éditions Imago, Paris 1990

Stott, Anne *Hannah More. The First Victorian*, Oxford University Press 2003.

Stragliati, Roland 'Fantômas? oui, mais' in *Europe*, Vol.56, No.590–591, June-July 1978

Strakosch, Maurice *Souvenirs d'un impresario*, Paul Ollendorff , Paris 1887

Strazzuso, Marcella 'F. D. Guerrazzi e l' "Assedio di Firenze": aspetti politici di un mito repubblicano' in *Problemi*, No.64, May-August 1982

Street, Sarah *Transatlantic Crossings. British Feature Films in the USA*, Continuum, New York and London 2002

Streletski, Gérard *Aspects de la direction d'orchestre en France de 1830 à 1880*, Mémoire de maitrise, Université de Paris IV UER de Musique, 1987

Strobl, Eric A. and Clive Tucker 'The Dynamics of Chart Success in the UK. Pre-recorded Popular Music Industry' in *Journal of Cultural Economics*, Vol. 24, No. 2, May 2000

Stroev, Alexandre (ed.) *Livre et lecture en Russie*, IMEC Éditions, Paris 1996

Stroev, Alexandre 'Lecture en Russie' in Chartier (ed.) *Histoire de la lecture*

Studi Collodiani, Atti del I Convegno Internazionale, Pescia, 5–7 Ottobre 1974 (Fondazione nazionale Carlo Collodi) Cassa di Risparmio di Pistoia e Brescia 1976

Summers, Judith, *Empress of Pleasure, The Life and Adventures of Teresa Cornelys*, Penguin, London 2003

Sutherland, John 'Introduction' to Ouida, *Under Two Flags*, Oxford University Press 1995

Sutherland, John *Longman Guide to Victorian Fiction*, Harlow 1988

Svane, Brynja *Les Lecteurs d'Eugène Sue*, Akademik Forlag, Copenhagen 1986

Swales, Martin 'The Development of German prose-fiction' in *The Cambridge Companion to Modern German Culture*, CUP 1998

Swann, Paul 'The British Culture Industries and the Mythology of the American Market: Cultural Policy and Cultural Exports in the 1940s and 1990s' in *Cinema Journal*, Vol. 39, No 4, Summer 2000

Swedenburg, Ted, 'Islamic Hip-Hop versus Islamophobia' in Mitchell (ed), *Global Noise*

Sweet, Matthew *Inventing the Victorians*, Faber and Faber, London 2001

Szafkó, Péter 'Sándor Hevesi and the Thália Society in Hungary' in *Theatre History Studies*, Vol. 2, 1982

Szemere, Anna *Up from the Underground: the Culture of Rock Music in Postsocialist Hungary*, Pennsylvania State University Press 2001

Tadié, Jean-Yves *Marcel Proust*, Gallimard, Paris 1996

Talvart, Hector and Joseph Place (eds) *Bibliographie des Auteurs Modernes (1801 – 1934)*, Volume 5, Editions de la Chronique des Lettres Françaises, Aux Horizons de France, Paris 1935

Tannenbaum, Edward R. 'The Beginnings of Bleeding-Heart Liberalism: Eugene Sue's *les Mystères de Paris*' in *Comparative Studies in Society and History*, Vol. 23, No. 3. July 1981, pp.491–507

Taranow, Gerda *The Bernhardt Hamlet. Culture and Context*, Peter Lang, New York 1996

Taruskin, Richard 'Nationalism' in *The New Grove Dictionary of Music Online* ed. L. Macy, accessed May 2002, *http://www.grovemusic.com*

Taruskin, Richard 'Some Thoughts on the History and Historiography of Russian Music' in *The Journal of Musicology*, Vol. 4, No. 4, Summer 1984

Tatar, Maria (ed.) *The Classic Fairy Tales*, W. W. Norton and Co., New York 1999

Taylor, Gary '1790' in *Reception Study* edited by James L. Machor and Philip Goldstein, Routledge, New York and London 2001

Taylor Jr., Harley U. *Erich Maria Remarque. A Literary and Film Biography*, Peter Land, New York and Berne 1989

Taylor, Helen *Scarlett's Women. Gone with the Wind and its Female Fans*, Virago, London 1989

Taylor, John Russell *Strangers in Paradise. The Hollywood Émigrés 1933–1950*, Faber and Faber, London 1983

Taylor, Malcom 'Pentecostal Faith Publishing, 1906–1926' in *Publishing History*, No. 42, 1997

Taylor, Richard 'Ideology as mass entertainment: Boris Shumyatsky and Soviet cinema in the 1930s' in Taylor and Christie (eds) *Inside the Film factory*

Taylor, Richard and Ian Christie (eds) *Inside the Film factory. New Approaches to Russian and Soviet Cinema*, Routledge, London and New York 1991

Taymanova, Marianna 'Alexandre Dumas in Egypt: Mystification or Truth?' in *Travellers in Egypt* edited by Paul and Janet Starkey, Tauris Parke, London 2001

Téberge, Paul 'Musicians' Magazines in the 1980s: the creation of a community and a consumer market' in Frith (ed.) *Popular Music. Critical Concepts in Media and Cultural Studies*, Vol. I, *Music and Society*

Tegel, Susan 'Bela Balazs: fairytales, film, and *The Blue Light*' in *Historical Journal of Film, Radio and Television*, Vol. 24 No 3 August 2004

Tempesti, Fernando 'Pinocchio' in Isnenghi (ed.) *I luoghi della memoria*

Tempesti, Fernando 'Gian Burrasca' in Isnenghi (ed.) *I luoghi della memoria*

Tempo libero e società di massa nell'Italia del Novecento, edited by the Istituto milanese per la storia della resistenza e del Movimento operaio, FrancoAngeli, Milan 1995

Tesnière, Valérie 'Le livre de science en France au XIXe siècle' in *Romantisme*, Vol. 23, No.80, 1993

Tetrazzini, Luisa *My Life of Song*, Cassell, London 1921

Tezla, Albert *Hungarian Authors. A Biographical Handbook*, The Belknap Press/Harvard University, Cambridge Mass. 1970

Thackeray, William *Vanity Fair*, Penguin, Harmondsworth 1968

Thackeray, William *Thackeray. Interviews and Recollections*, Vol. 1, edited by Philip Collins, St. Martin's Press, New York 1983

Thatcher, Mark *The Politics of Telecommunication. National Institutions, Convergences, and Change*, OUP 2000

Theatre Record, No.1–2, 18 February 2003 and No 9, 27 May 2003

Theimer Nepomnyashchy, Catharine 'Markets, Mirrors, and Mayhem: Aleksandra Marinina and the Rise of the New Russian *Detektiv*' in Barker (ed.) *Consuming Russia*

Théodore-Aubanel, Édouard *Comment on lance un nouveau livre*, Intercontinental d'Édition, Paris 1937

Théodore-Aubanel, Édouard *Cueillons des Lauriers. Promenade à travers le Jardin des Prix littéraires*, Intercontinental d'Édition, Paris 1937

Thierer, Adam D. 'Unnatural Monopoly: Critical Moments in the Development of the Bell System', *The Cato Journal*, Volume 14 Number 2, Fall 1994, online edition: *http://www.cato.org/pubs/journal/cjv14n2–6.html*

Thiesse, Anne Marie '*Imprimés du pauvre, livres de fortune*' in *Romantisme*, No.43, Vol. 14, 1984

Thiesse, Anne Marie 'L'éducation sociale d'un romancier. Le cas d'Eugène Sue' in *Actes de la recherche en sciences sociales*, No 32–33, April-June 1980

Thiesse, Anne-Marie 'Les infortunes littéraires. Carrières des romanciers populaires à la Belle-Époque' in *Actes de la recherche en sciences sociales*, No. 60, November 1985

Thiesse, Anne-Marie 'Littérature et folklore, l'invention érudite de la culture populaire' in Alain Vaillant (ed.) *Écrire/Savoir: littérature et connaissances à l'époque moderne*, Éditions Printer, Saint-Étienne 1996

Thiesse, Anne-Marie 'Organisation des loisirs des travailleurs et temps dérobés (1880–1930)' in Corbin (ed.) *L'avènement des loisirs*

Thiesse, Anne-Marie 'Revues et maisons d'édition provinciales à la Belle Époque' in Vaillant (ed.) *Mesure(s) du livre*

Thiesse, Anne-Marie and Natalia Chmatko 'Les nouveaux éditeurs russes' in *Actes de la recherche en sciences sociales*, No. 126–127 March 1999

Thiesse, Anne-Marie *Le Roman du quotidien. Lecteurs et lectures populaires à la Belle Époque*, Le Chemin Vert, Paris 1984

Thomas, Keith 'The Meaning of Literacy in Early Modern England' in Baumann (ed.) *The Written Word. Literacy in Transition*

Thompson, Kristin *Exporting Entertainment. America in the World Film Market 1907–34*, BFI Publishing, London 1985

Thomson, E. P. *The Making of the English Working Class*, Penguin, Harmondsworth 1968

Thomson, Patricia *George Sand and the Victorians. Her Influence and Reputation in Nineteenth-century England*, Macmillan, London and Basingstoke 1977

Thorel-Cailleteau, Sylvie 'George Moore et le Naturalisme. "Un cas d'intoxication littéraire"' in Dezalay (ed.) *Zola sans frontières*

Throsby, David 'The Role of Music in International Trade and Economic Development' in UNESCO, *World Culture Report* 1998

Thurber, James 'The Little Girl and the Wolf' in Tatar (ed.) *The Classic Fairy Tales*

Thurston, Gary 'The Impact of Russian Popular Theatre, 1886–1915' in *Journal of Modern History*, Vol.55, No.2, June 1983

Tieck, Ludwig 'Eckbert the Fair' in *Six German Romantic Tales*, trans. by Ronald Taylor, Angel Books, London 1985

Tilleuil, Jean-Louis *Pour analyser la Bande Dessinée. Propositions théoriques et pratiques*, Academia, Louvain-la-Neuve 1986

Tocqueville, Alexis de *Democracy in America*, translated by Henry Reeve, Oxford University Press, London 1946

Todd, William B. and Ann Bowden (eds) *Tauchnitz International Editions in English 1841–1955. A Bibliographical History*, Bibliographical Society of America, New York 1988

Todd, William B. 'Firma Tauchnitz: A Further Investigation' in *Publishing History*, No. 2, 1977

Todorov, Tzvetan *Poétique de la prose*, Éditions du Seuil, Paris 1971

Todorova, Liljana 'Dialogue de la littérature macédonienne avec la tradition nationale et les littératures étrangères' in Köpeczi and Vajda (eds) *Proceedings of the 8th Congress of the International Comparative Literature Association*

Tolson, Andrew (ed.) *Television Talk Shows: Discourse, Performance, Spectacle*, Lawrence Erlbaum, Mahwah, NJ 2001

Tomkins, J. M. S. *The Popular Novel in England 1770–1800*, Methuen, London 1969, first published in 1932

Törnquist-Plewa, Barbara 'Contrasting Ethnic Nationalisms: Eastern Central Europe' in Barbour and Carmichael (eds) *Language and Nationalism in Europe*

Torri, Bruno 'Industria, mercato, politica' in Miccichè (ed.) *Il cinema del riflusso*

Tortorelli, Gianfranco 'Una càsa editrice socialista nell'età giolittiana: la Nerini' in *Movimento operaio e socialista*, Vol. 3, No.2–3 1980

Toschi, Luca 'Alle origini della narrativa di romanzo in Italia' in Massimo Saltafuso (ed.) *Il viaggio del narrare*, La Giuntina, Florence 1989

Tournier, Isabelle 'Les livres de comptes du feuilleton (1836–1846)' in Vaillant (ed.) *Mesure(s) du livre*

Trames. Littérature populaire. Peuple, nation, région, Actes du colloque 18–20 Mars 1986 à Limoges, Université de Limoges 1988

Traubner, Richard *Operetta. A Theatrical History*, Gollancz, London 1984

Traverso, Enzo *The Origins of Nazi Violence*, The New Press, New York 2003

Treves (Fratelli Treves Editori), *Catalogo generale*, December 1903

Trollope, Anthony *An Autobiography*, Penguin, Harmondsworth 1996

Trollope, Frances *Domestic Manners of the Americans* edited by Pamela Neville-Sington, Penguin, Harmondsworth 1997

Trollope, Frances *Paris et les Parisiens en 1835*, Fournier, Paris 1836

Trudgill, Peter 'Greece and European Turkey: From Religious to Linguistic Identity' in Barbour and Carmichael (eds) *Language and Nationalism in Europe*

Trumpbour, John *Selling Hollywood to the World*, CUP 2002

Tsivian, Yuri 'Censure Bans on Religious Subjects in Russian Films' in Cosandrey, Gaudreault and Gunning (eds) *Une invention du diable? Cinéma des premiers temps et religion*

Tsivian, Yuri *Early Cinema in Russia and its Cultural Reception*, Routledge, London 1994, first Russian edition: 1991

Tsivian, Yuri et al. (eds) *Silent Witnesses: Russian Films, 1909–1919*, British Film Institute and Edizioni Biblioteca dell'immagine, London and Pordenone 1989

Turchi, Roberta 'K.X.Y.: Una sigla per recensire' in Bruscagli and Turchi (eds) *Teorie del romanzo nel primo ottocento*

Tusan, Michelle Elizabeth 'Inventing the New Woman: Print Culture and Identity Politics During the Fin-de-Siècle' in *Victorian Periodicals Review*, Vol. 31, No 2, Summer 1998

Twaites, Peter 'Circles of Confusion and Sharp Vision: British News Photography 1919–39' in Catterall, Seymour-Ure and Smith (eds) *Northcliffe's Legacy*

Twyman, Michael *Lithography 1800–1850*, OUP 1970

Tylor, Edward Burnett *Primitive Culture*, John Murray, London 1873

Tyrrell, John 'Russian, Czech, Polish, and Hungarian Opera to 1900' in Parker (ed.) *The Oxford Illustrated History of the Opera*

Ullstein, Herman *The Rise and Fall of the House of Ullstein*, Simon and Schuster, New York 1943

UN Yearly statistics 1962

UNESCO *Index translationium* 1985

UNESCO *An international survey of book production during the last decades*, Statistical Reports and Studies No.26, Paris 1982

UNESCO *Index Translationum* 1965

UNESCO *World Culture Report* 1998

Unwin, Stanley *The Truth about Publishing*, Allen and Unwin, London 1976

Unwin, Timothy (ed.) *The Cambridge Companion to the French Novel. From 1800 to the present*, CUP 1997

Unwin, Timothy 'On the Novel and the Writing of Literary History' in Unwin (ed.) *The Cambridge Companion to the French Novel*

Ureña, Lenny A. 'Mobilizing German Women Against "Cultural Drunkenness": *Rassenhygiene* and Colonial Discourse in the Prussian-Polish Provinces, 1890–1914', paper presented at 'Gender and Power in the New Europe', the 5th European Feminist Research Conference, August 20–24, 2003 Lund University, Sweden *www.5thfeminist.lu.se/filer/paper635.pdf*

Uricchio, William 'The First World War and the Crisis in Europe' in Nowell-Smith (ed.) *The Oxford History Of World Cinema*

Uricchio, William and Roberta Pearson '"You Can Make the *Life of Moses* Your Life Saver": Vitagraph's Biblical Blockbuster' in Cosandrey, Gaudreault and Gunning (eds) *Une invention du diable? Cinéma des premiers temps et religion*

Vachon, Stéphane 'Balzac en feuilletons et en livres. Quantification d'une production romanesque' in Vaillant (ed.) *Mesure(s) du livre*

Vâikis-Friebergs, Vaira (ed.) *Linguistics and poetics of Latvian folk songs: essays in honour of the birth of Kr. Barons*, McGill-Queen's University Press, Kingston, Ontario 1989

Vaillant, Alain (ed.) *Mesure(s) du livre*, Colloque organisé par la Bibliothèque Nationale et la Société des études romantiques 25–26 Mai 1989, Bibliothèque Nationale, Paris 1992

Vainchtein, Olga 'Les bardes anglais et la critique russe' in Espagne and Werner (eds) *Philologiques III. Qu'est-ce qu'une littérature nationale?*

Valentin, Jean-Marie 'Nestroy sur la scène française' in Stieg and Valentin (eds) *Johann Nestroy 1801–1862*

Valéry, Paul *Regards sur le monde actuel et autres essais*, Gallimard, Paris 1945

van der Merwe, Peter *Origins of the Popular Style. The Antecedents of Twentieth-Century Popular Music*, Clarendon Press, Oxford 1992

van der Wurff, Richard 'Supplying and Viewing Diversity. The Role of Competition and Viewer Choice in Dutch Broadcasting' in *European Journal of Communication*, Vol. 19, No 2, June 2004

Van Gool, C. 'Pays-Bas' in Moliterni (ed.) *Histoire Mondiale de la Bande Dessinée*

Van Horn Melton, James 'From Image to Word: Cultural Reform and the Rise of Literate Culture in Eighteenth-Century Austria' in *Journal of Modern History*, Vol,.58, No.1, March 1986

Van Voss, Lex Heerman 'The International Federation of Trade Unions and the Attempt to Maintain the Eight-hour Working Day (1919–1929)' in Fritz Van Holtoon and Marcel van der Linden (eds) *Internationalism and the Labour Movement 1830–1940*, Vol. II, E.J.Brill, Leiden 1988

Vann, J. Don 'The Early Success of *Pickwick*' in *Publishing History*, No. 2, 1977

Variety, 25 March 1987

Vasey, Ruth 'The World-Wide Spread of the Cinema' in Nowell-Smith (ed.) *The Oxford History Of World Cinema*

Vecchiotti, Anna 'Poetica e ideologia nei romanzi di Pietro Chiari' in *Problemi*, No.82, May-August 1988

Vegliante, Jean-Charles 'Perception française de l'Italie et traduction de l'italien. Histoire d'un malentendu' in *Romantisme*, No 106, 1999

Velay-Vallantin, Catherine 'Little Red Riding Hood as Fairy Tale, *Faits-divers*, and Children's Literature: The Invention of a Traditional Heritage' in Canepa (ed.) *Out of the Woods*

Ventrone, Angelo 'Tra propaganda e passione. *Grand Hotel* e l'Italia degli anni '50' in *Rivista di Storia contemporanea*, Vol 17, No. 4. October 1988

Venturin, Fabio 'Il rapporto segnale-rumore: note sull'ascolto contemporaneo' in *Problemi*, No.72, January-April 1985

Verch, Maria '*The Merchant of Venice* on the German Stage since 1945' in *Theatre History Studies*, Vol. 5, 1985

Verdery, Katherine *National Ideology under Socialism. Identity and Cultural Politics in Ceauşescu's Romania*, University of California Press, Berkeley 1991

Verdi intimo. Carteggio di Giuseppe Verdi con il conte Opprandino Arrivabene (1861–1886) edited by Alberti, Annibale Mondadori, Milan 1931

Verdone, Mario 'Mussolini's "Theatre of the Masses"' in Berghaus (ed.) *Fascism and Theatre*

Vereş, Grigore 'Dickens Criticism in Romania Before World War II' in *Synthesis*, Vol. 8, 1981 (Bucarest)

Verga, Giovanni *Le novelle*, Garzanti, Milan 1980

Verzea, Ileana 'The Historical Novel as Popular Literature. Notes on the Success of the English and American Novel in Nineteenth Century Romanian Literature' in *Synthesis*, Vol. 8, 1981

Veyrat-Masson, Isabelle *Quand la télévision explore le temps. L'histoire au petit écran 1953–2000*, Fayard, Paris 2000

Vickery, Amanda *The Gentleman's Daughter: Women's Lives in Georgian England*, Yale UP, New Haven and London 1998

Viëtor, Karl 'L'histoire des genres littéraires' in Genette et al. *Théorie des genres*,

Vigarello, Georges 'De la "médicine du peuple" aux magazines de santé" in *Esprit*, No 3–4 March-April 2002

Vignal, Marc *Joseph Haydn*, Fayard, Paris 1988

Vigny, Alfred de *Poèmes antiques et modernes. Les Destinées*, Gallimard, Paris 1973

Vikør, Lars S. 'Northern Europe: Languages as Prime Markers of Ethnic and National Identity' in Barbour and Carmichael (eds) *Language and Nationalism in Europe*

Villot, Frédéric (ed.) *Notice des Tableaux exposés dans les galeries du Musée Nationale du Louvre*, 1ère partie, Écoles d'Italie, Musées nationaux, Paris 1849

Visser, Romke 'Fascist Doctrine and the Cult of the *Romanità*' in *Journal of Contemporary History*, Vol. 27, no.1, January 1992

Vivanti, Corrado (ed.) *Storia d'Italia. Annali 4 Intellettuali e potere*, Einaudi, Turin 1981

Vivien, Alexandre-François 'Études administratives. III. Les théâtres' in *Revue des Deux Mondes*, 1 May 1844

Vlock, Deborah *Dickens, Reading, and the Victorian Popular Theatre*, CUP, 1998

Vogüé, Eugène-Melchior de *Le Roman Russe*, Slavica, no place (but Switzerland) 1971 (reprint)

Vogüé, Eugène-Melchior de 'La Renaissance latine. Gabriele D'Annunzio: poèmes et romans' in *Revue des Deux Mondes*, 1 January 1895

Volpe, Joseph, interview by Peter Aspen, *Financial Times Magazine*, 10 January 2004

Voltaire *Lettres philosophiques* in *Oeuvres Complètes*, Vol.22 (Mélanges), Garnier Frères, Paris 1879

von Papen, Manuela 'Keeping the home fires burning? Women and the German homefront film 1940–43', in *Film History*, Vol. 8, No. 1, 1996

Wachtel, Andrew Baruch *An Obsession with History. Russian Writers Confront the Past*, Stanford University Press 1994

Wachtel, Andrew Baruch *Making a Nation, Breaking a Nation. Literature and Cultural Politics in Yugoslavia*, Stanford University Press 1998

Wadsworth, Sarah 'Charles Knight and Sir Francis Bond Head: Two Early Victorian Perspectives on Printing and the Allied Trades' in *Victorian Periodicals Review*, Vol. 31, No. 4, Winter 1998

Wagg, Stephen 'At ease, corporal' in *Because I tell a joke or two. Comedy, Politics and Social Difference*, edited by Stephen Wagg, Routledge, London 1998

Wainscott, Ronald H. *The Emergence of the Modern American Theatre 1914–1929*, Yale University Press, New Haven and London 1997

Wall, Geoffrey *Flaubert. A Life*, Faber and Faber, London 2001

Walle, Marianne 'Marie Geistinger. La reine de l'opérette' in *Austriaca, Cahiers Universitaires d'Information sur l'Autriche*, No. 46, June 1998

Walter, Klaus-Peter 'Littérature de colportage et roman-feuilleton. Quelques remarques sur la transformation du circuit littéraire à grande diffusion en France entre 1840 et 1870' in Chartier and Lüsebrink (eds) *Colportage et lecture populaire*

Walter, Klaus-Peter 'Roman-feuilleton et hausse du tirage des journaux. Une évaluation quantitative de la popularité de quelques romans à succès de Sue à Gaboriau' in *Trames. Littérature populaire*

Warner, Marina *From the Beast to the Blonde: On Fairy tales and Their Tellers*, Chatto & Windus 1994

Warner, William B. *Licensing Entertainment. The Elevation of Novel Reading in Britain 1684–1750*, University of California Press, Berkeley 1998

Warnke, Nina 'Immigrant Popular Culture as Contested Sphere: Yiddish Music Halls, the Yiddish Press, and the Processes of Americanization, 1900–1910' in *Theatre Journal* Vol. 48 No.3 October 1996

Warrilow, Georgina 'Some Recent German Periodicals on Book and Book-Trade History, a Summary' in *Publishing History*, No. 9, 1981

Watanabe-O'Kelly, Helen (ed.) *The Cambridge History of German Literature*, CUP 1997

Watelet, Jean 'La presse illustrée', in Chartier and Martin (eds) *Histoire de l'édition française*, Vol. 3

Waterman, David and Krishna P. Jayakar 'The Competitive Balance of the Italian and American Film Industries' in *European Journal of Communication*, Vol. 15, No. 4, pp.501–28 December 2000

Watt, Ian *Myths of Modern Individualism. Faust, Don Quixote, Don Juan, Robinson Crusoe*, CUP 1996

Waugh, Evelyn *Brideshead Revisited*, Penguin Books, Harmondsworth 1962

Wearing, J. P. (ed.) *The London Stage 1930–1939: A Calendar of Plays and Players*, The Scarecrow Press, Metuchen NJ and London 1990

Wearing, J. P. (ed.) *The London Stage 1950–1959: A Calendar of Plays and Players*, The Scarecrow Press, Metuchen NJ and London 1993

Webb, R. K. 'The Victorian Reading Public' in Boris Ford (ed.) *The New Pelican Guide to English Literature* Vol.VI, *From Dickens to Hardy* (1958, 2nd ed. 1982)

Weber, Carl Maria von *La vie d'un musicien et autres écrits*, trans. from German by Lucienne Gérardin, J.C. Lattès, 1986

Weber, Eugen *France Fin de Siècle*, Belknap Press, Cambridge, Mass. 1986

Weber, William 'Artisans in Concert Life of Mid-Nineteenth-Century London and Paris' in *Journal of Contemporary History*, Vol.13, no.2, April 1978

Weber, William 'Learned and General Music Taste in Eighteenth Century France' in *Past and Present*, No. 89, November 1980

Weber, William 'Mass Culture and the Reshaping of European Musical taste, 1770–1870' in *International Review of the Aesthetics and Sociology of Music*, Vol. 8, No. 1, June 1977

Weber, William *Music and the Middle Class. The Social Structure of Concert Life in London, Paris and Vienna*, Croom Helm, London 1975

Weightman, Gavin *Signor Marconi's Magic Box*, HarperCollins, London 2003

Weil, Françoise *L'Interdiction du roman et la librairie 1728–1750*, Éditions Amateurs du Livre, Paris 1986

Weinberg, Achille 'Une Histoire du structuralisme' in *Sciences Humaines*, No. 10 October 1991, p.15

Weiner, Marc A. *Richard Wagner and the Anti-Semitic Imagination*, University of Nebraska Press, Lincoln and London 1997

Weinmann, Frédéric 'Étranger, étrangeté: de l'allemand au français au début du XIXe siècle' in *Romantisme*, Vol. 29, No. 106, 1999

Welch, Walter L., Leah Brodbeck and Burt Stenzel, *Tinfoil to Stereo. The Acoustic Years of the Recording Industry 1877–1929*, University Press of Florida, Gainesville Fl 1994

Werner, Hans (signed H.W.), 'La musique des femmes: Louise Bertin', *Revue des deux mondes*, Vol. 8, 1836

Werner, Michael 'La place relative du champ littéraire dans les cultures nationales. Quelques remarques à propos de l'exemple franco-allemand' in Espagne and Werner (eds) *Philologiques III. Qu'est-ce qu'une littérature nationale?*

Wertham, Fredric 'Les "crimes comic-books" et la jeunesse américaine', *Les Temps Modernes*, Vol. 11, 1955

West, Mae *Goodness Had Nothing to Do with It*, Virago, London 1996

Westgate, Geoffrey *Strategies Under Surveillance. Reading Irmtraud Morgner as a GDR Writer*, Rodopi, Amsterdam and New York 2002

Westwood, J. N. *Endurance and Endeavour. Russian History 1812–1986*, OUP 1987

Whissel, Kristen 'Placing the spectator on the Scene of History: the battle re-enactment at the turn of the century from Buffalo Bill's Wild West to the Early Cinema', *Historical Journal of Film, Radio, and Television*, Vol. 22, No. 3, 2002

White, Cynthia L. *Women's Magazines 1693–1968*, Michael Joseph, London 1970

Whittington-Egan, Richard (ed.) *William Roughead's Chronicles of Murder* by Moffat, Lochar (Scotland) 1991

Wiernicki, Krzysztof *Dal divertimento dei nobili alla propaganda. Storia del Jazz in Russia*, Ed. Scientifiche italiane, Naples 1991

Wierzbicki, James 'Dethroning the Divas. Satire Directed at Cuzzoni and Faustina' in *Opera Quarterly*, Vol. 17, No 2, Spring 2001

Wilkinson, James 'The uses of popular culture by rival élites: the case of Alsace, 1890–1914' in *History of European Ideas*, Vol. 11, 1989

Willems, Gilles 'Aux origines du groupe Pathé-Natan' in Benghozi and Delage (eds) *Une histoire économique du cinéma français (1895–1995)*

Williams, Raymond *Culture and Society*, The Hogarth Press, London 1987 (1st published 1958)

Williams, Raymond *Television. Technology and Cultural Form*, Fontana/Collins, London 1974

Williams, Raymond *The Long Revolution*, Harper and Row, New York 1966

Wilson, Elizabeth *Bohemians. The Glamorous Outcasts*, Tauris, London 2000

Wilson, M. Glen 'Charles Kean in the Provinces 1833 to 1838' in *Theatre History Studies*, Vol. 1, 1981

Wingard, Kristina 'Le dix-neuvième siècle suédois: courants littéraires et traditions de recherche' in *Romantisme*, No. 37, 1982

Winship, Michael 'The Rise of a National Book Trade System in the United States, 1865–1916' in Michon and Mollier (eds) *Les mutations du livre et de l'édition*

Winston, Jane 'Gender and sexual identity in the modern French novel' in Unwin (ed.) *The Cambridge Companion to the French Novel*

Winter, Jay 'Nationalism, the Visual Arts, and the Myth of War Enthusiasm in 1914' in *History of European Ideas*, Vol.15, No.1–3 1992

Winter, Jay *Sites of Memory, Sites of Mourning. The Great War in European Cultural History*, Cambridge University Press 1995

Witte, Karsten 'The Spectator as Accomplice in Ernst Lubitsch's *Schuhpalast Pinkus*' in Elsaesser (ed) *A Second Life. German Cinema's First Decades*

Wolfe, Charles 'Historicising the "Voice of God": the place of vocal narration in classical documentary' in *Film History*, Vol. 9, No. 2, 1997

Wolff, Larry *Inventing Eastern Europe. The Map of Civilization on the Mind of the Enlightenment*, Stanford University Press 1994

Wolff, Stéphane *L'Opéra au Palais Garnier (1875–1962)*, no publisher, Paris 1962

Wollstonecraft, Mary 'A Vindication of the Rights of Woman' in *The Vindications*, edited by D. L. Macdonald and Kathleen Scherf, Broadview, Toronto 1997

Wolton, Dominique *Éloge du grand public. Une théorie critique de la télévision*, Flammarion, Paris 1990

Wood, Gordon S. 'The Bloodiest War' in *New York Review of Books*, 9 April 1998

Wood, Michael 'Looking Good' in *New York Review of Books*, 20 November 1997

Woolf, D. R. 'A Feminine Past? Gender, Genre, and Historical Knowledge in England, 1500–1800' in *American Historical Review*, Vol. 102, No. 3, June 1997

Wright, Beth S. and Paul Joannides, 'Les Romans historiques de Sir Walter Scott et la peinture française, 1822–1863' in *Bulletin de la Société de l'Histoire de l'art français*, 1982, pp.119–32 and 1983 pp.95–115

www.alva.org.uk/visitor_statistics/

www.bfi.org.uk/features/ultimatefilm/chart/complete.php
www.bringyou.to/apologetics/p2o.htm
www.cnn.com/US/9706/15/ufo.poll/index.html
www.eHarlequin.com
www.eharlequin.com/cms/learntowrite/ltwToc.jhtml
www.elspa.com/about/pr/elspawhitepaper1.pdf
www.history.rochester.edu/pennymag/
www.imdb.com/title/tt0120737/business
www.internetworldstats.com (accessed October 2005)
www.ketupa.net
www.kirjasto.sci.fi/sienkiew.htm
www.koerperwelten.com
www.nobel.se/literature/laureates/1905/press.html
www.pastichesdumas.com/pages/livres.html
www.pch.gc.ca/progs/arts/pdf/renoir_e.pdf
www.quid.fr/2000/Q010320.htm accessed 25 February 2004
www.statistics.gov.uk/CCI/nugget.asp?ID=8&Pos=1&ColRank=1&Rank=192
www.the-times.co.uk/
www.uis.unesco.org/ev_en.php?ID=2867201&ID2=DOTOPIC
www.uk-piano.org/ -update of 15 September 2000
www.uk-piano.org/broadwood/lvb_wood.html (accessed 2001)
Wyss, Ulrich 'Jacob Grimm et la France' in Espagne and Werner, *Philologiques I.*
    Contribution à l'histoire des discipline littéraires en France et en Allemagne . . .

Yadava, J. S. and Usha V. Reddi 'In the Midst of Diversity: Television in Urban Indian
    Homes' in James Jull (ed.) *World Families Watch Television,* Sage, Beverly Hills and
    London 1988
Yates, W.E. and John R. P. McKenzie (eds) *Viennese Popular Theatre: A Symposium,*
    University of Exeter 1985
Yearwood, Susan 'United States: African American Culture' in *Censorship. A World
    Encyclopedia*
Yon, Jean-Claude *Eugène Scribe: la fortune et la liberté,* Nizet, Saint-Genouph 2000
Yon, Jean-Claude *Jacques Offenbach,* Gallimard, Paris 2000
Youngblood, Denise J. 'The return of the native: Yakov Protazanov and Soviet Cinema'
    in Taylor and Christie (eds) *Inside the Film factory*
Youngblood, Denise *Movie for the Masses. Popular cinema and Soviet society in the 1920s,*
    Cambridge University Press 1992
Younge, Gary 'When Wal-Mart comes to town', *Guardian,* 18 August 2003

Zaïd, Gabriel 'La guérilla comme spectacle' in *Esprit,* No. 274, May 2001
Zaitsev, Mark 'Soviet Theatre Censorship' in *Drama Review,* Vol.19, no.2, June 1975
Zamagni, Vera 'An International comparison of Real Industrial Wages, 1890–1913:
    Methodological issues and Results' in Scholliers (ed.) *Real wages in nineteenth and
    twentieth Century Europe*
Zambon, Patricia 'I protagonisti' in Antonia Arslan (ed.) *Dame, droga e galline*
Zamiatine, E. 'Le Théâtre Russe' (originally in *Le Mercure de France,* 15 November 1932)
    reprinted in *Cahiers du Monde Russe et Soviétique,* Vol. 5, No. 4, October-
    December 1964
Zamiatine, Evguéni (Yevgeny Zamiatyn) *Le Métier Littéraire,* Éditions L'Age d'Homme,
    Lausanne 1990

Zamoyski, Adam *Holy Madness. Romantics, Patriots and Revolutionaries 1776–1871*, Weidenfeld and Nicolson, London 1999

Zanotto, Piero (ed.) *L'immagine nel libro per ragazzi. Gli illustratori di Collodi in Italia e nel mondo*, Province of Trento, Trento 1977

Zha, Jianying *China Pop. How Soap Operas, Tabloids, and Bestsellers Are Transforming a Culture*, The New Press, New York 1995

Zimmerman, Daniel *Alexandre Dumas le Grand*, Julliard, Paris 1993

Zipes, Jack 'Of Cats and Men; Framing the Civilizing Discourse of the Fairy Tale' in Canepa (ed.) *Out of the Woods*

Zipes, Jack *Happily Ever After. Fairy Tales, Children and the Culture Industry*, Routledge, London and New York 1997

Zipes, Jack *Sticks and Stones*, Routledge, New York and London 2001

Zipes, Jack *When Dreams Come True. Classical Fairy Tales and Their Tradition*, Routledge, London 1999

Zola, Émile *L'encre et le sang. Littérature et politique*, Édition Complexe, Paris 1989

Zola, Émile *Nana*, Classiques Garnier, Paris 1994

Zola, Émile, *Correspondance*, Vols. 4 and 5 edited by B. H. Bakker, Les Presses de l'Université de Montréal and éditions du CNRS, Montreal and Paris 1985

Zórawska-Witkowska, Alina 'La stampa polacca degli anni 1825–1830 su "Il Barbiere di Siviglia" di Gioacchino Rossini' in *Quadrivium* Vol. 4, 1993, pp.163–76

Zorine, Andreï and Andreï Nemzer, 'Les paradoxes de la sentimentalité' (1989) in Stroev (ed.) *Livre et lecture en Russie*

INDEX

ABBA (Swedish pop group), 1353–4
Abbado, Claudio, 510
ABC (broadcasting company), 1158
Abeille, L' (journal), 152
Abel, Carl Friedrich, 243
About, Edmond, 354, 530
Abraham, Max, 220
Abramov, Fyodor, 1261
Abruzzi, Luigi Amedeo, Duke of, 702
Académie Française: admits Hugo, 404;
    Balzac and Dumas not accepted, 420, 422;
    admits Scribe, 584; Grand Prix du Roman,
    633
Academy of Sciences (Russia), 885, 1225
Accademia d'Arte Drammatica (Italy), 1099
accordion, 758
Ackroyd, Peter, 367
actors, 279–82, 570–1; *see also* films; theatre
Adams, John: *Nixon in China* (opera), 768
Adams, Maud, 706
'Adamson' (comic strip), 1075
Addison, Joseph, 82, 200
Ade, Sunny, 1356
Adenauer, Konrad, 896, 1159
Admiral Nakhimov (film), 890
Adorno, Theodor, 162, 948–9, 960, 1123
Adventures of Marco Polo (film), 927
*Adventures of Priscilla, Queen of the Desert,
    The* (film), 134
advertising: in newspapers and journals,
    198–9, 317, 710, 1058; slogans, 634; on
    radio, 1129–30; on television, 1149–50,
    1169, 1214–15, 1217
Aelita (film), 889
aeroplanes: beginnings, 600
Aeschylus: *Oresteia*, 272–3
Afgrunden (film), 828
Afzelius, Arvid August, 87
Age d'or, L' (film), 959
Agence France-Presse, 1057
Agoult, Comtesse Marie d' *see* Stern, Daniel
Aguilera, Christina, 1338
Ahlgrén, Ernst *see* Benediktsson, Victoria
Aimard, Gustave (i.e. Olivier Gloux), 698
Aimée, Anouk, 1007

Ainsworth, W. Harrison, 303
Airport (film), 1229–30
Aitmatov, Chingiz: *I dol'she veka dlitsia den'*,
    1260
AK47 (rap group), 1356
Akhmatova, Anna: 'Requiem', 1261
Alabama Public Library Division, 398–9
Alarcón, Ruiz de: *Le Verdad sospechosa*, 279
Alatri, Paolo, 906
Albani, Marcello, 1098
Albania: languages, 25–6; translated books
    in, 871, 1295; cultural life in, 1250–1
Albeniz, Isaac, 773
Albert, Prince Consort, 152, 204, 385
Albertini, Filoteo, 802
Albertini, Luigi, 714, 1065
Albonetti, Pietro, 923
Alcott, Louisa May, 180, 435, 439, 480–1, 605,
    706; *Little Women*, 477, 481
Aldiss, Brian, 1040
Aldrich, Robert, 1116
Aldrich, Thomas: *Story of a Bad Boy*, 705
Alecsandri, Vasile: *Doine*, 87
Alegria, Ciro: *El Mundo es ancho y ajeno*, 672
Aleichem, Sholom, 1111–12
Alekseev, Mikhail, 1261
Alexander III, Tsar of Russia, 601
Alexander, Cecil Frances: hymns, 519
Alexander, Texas, 1348
Alexandre, Charles: *Dictionnaire grec-
    français*, 351
Alexandri, Vasile, 465
Alexandria (Egypt), 30
Alexandrov, Grigory, 874
Alexis, Willibald (i.e. Wilhelm Häring):
    Walladmor, 157; *see also* Hitzig, Julius
    Eduard
Alfieri, Vittorio, 81, 169
Algeria, 852
Ali, Monica: *Brick Lane*, 1286
Ali G in da House (film), 1233
All in the Family (TV programme), 1190–1
All the Year Round (periodical), 319, 367, 410
All-Russia Union for the Diffusion of Books,
    1254